BASEBALL PROSPECTUS 2018

The Essential Guide to the 2018 Season

Edited by Aaron Gleeman, Bret Sayre and Geoff Young

Emma Baccellieri, Mark Barry, Demetrius Bell, George Bissell, Mo Bjonski, John Bonnes, J.P. Breen, Grant Brisbee, Russell Carleton, Ben Carsley, Matt Collins, Zack Crizer, Ben Diamond, Patrick Dubuque, Kate Feldman, Ken Funck, Mike Gianella, Steven Goldman, Craig Goldstein, Derrick Goold, Stacey Gotsulias, Bryan Grosnick, Matthew Gwin, Joshua Howsam, Christina Kahrl, Wilson Karaman, Sung Min Kim, Zachary Levine, Rob Mains, Erik Malinowski, Adam McCalvy, Rachael McDaniel, Pedro Moura, Eric Nusbaum, Robert O'Connell, Jeffrey Paternostro, Dan Rathman, Liz Roscher, David Roth, Meg Rowley, Travis Sawchik, Nick Schaefer, Jarrett Seidler, Adam Sobsey, Alex Speier, Nick Stellini, Matt Sussman, Brett Taylor, Matthew Trueblood, Ashley Varela, Levi Weaver, Marc Webster, Collin Whitchurch, Jason Wojciechowski, Jared Wyllys, Kazuto Yamazaki

Dave Pease and Stephen Reichert, Consultant Editors
Harry Pavlidis and Rob McQuown, Statistics Editors

TURNER
PUBLISHING COMPANY

Library of Congress Cataloging-in-Publication Data:
paperback
ISBN-10: 1681626438
ISBN-13: 978-1681626437

Project Credits
Cover Design: Karen Sitras
Interior Design and Production: Jeff Pease, Dave Pease
Layout: Jeff Pease, Dave Pease

Cover Photos
Front Cover: Joey Votto. © Aaron Doster-USA TODAY Sports
Back Cover: Topps ® trading cards used courtesy of The Topps Company, Inc.

Team logos and trademarks used with permission of MLB Advanced Media.

Baseball icon courtesy of Uberux, from https://www.shareicon.net/author/uberux

Manufactured in the United States of America
10 9 8 7 6 5 4 3 2 1

Table of Contents

Foreword

by Jayson Stark

What did we do before there was such a thing as Baseball Prospectus? How did we survive? For people like me—people who love baseball and its special, defining numbers—questions like those are kinda like our version of Bill Gates asking, "What did we do before there were computers?"

And the truth is, it's hard to even remember, isn't it? We've got it so good now. We're so spoiled nowadays that we're used to living in a world where the answers we need are always a click or two away. And I'll be first in line to say it's awesome to be living in that world.

Just this past winter, I was a guest pundit on Brian Kenny's addictive, data-driven MLB Now show on MLB Network. And one of the subjects on that show was a topic guaranteed to get us through any day of the baseball winter—pitch clocks. I wondered what the potential impact might be on the game if MLB settled on, say, a 23-second pitch clock versus the 20-second clock that's been used in the minor leagues. How many pitchers would it affect? How many hitters would it affect?

There was a time when questions like that couldn't possibly have been answered—not by me, anyway. But fortunately for TV viewers everywhere, it was the year 2017, and Baseball Prospectus and other great sites like it exist. So within minutes, we had ourselves two definitive lists—of every pitcher and every hitter in the major leagues whose average time between pitches last season was 23 seconds or greater.

Woohoo!

But of course, nobody in the building actually shouted, "Woohoo," because we all took for granted that, on the planet we're fortunate enough to live on these days, we can ask these things and someone actually knows! Someone actually kept track. And did the math. And uploaded the math to our favorite new-age baseball site. We stumbled in there and scooped up their fantastic info for our own beautiful purposes. And viewers everywhere saw nothing life-altering or mind-blowing about it. They just expect it now, don't they?

But friends, they didn't always. It wasn't so many years ago when we lived on a very different planet, a planet where numbers still existed—but not numbers like this. And there were ways to find those numbers, but you practically had to put on your miner's helmet and start shoveling to find them. So what did we do before there was such a thing as Baseball Prospectus? Since I've now covered baseball for several decades, I can tell you exactly what we did. We roughed it.

And by that, I mean that people like me and Tim Kurkjian—huge fans of quirks and oddities and weirdly illuminating stats as far back as the '80s—would just concede in advance that we had no life. So if we had to go hunting for stuff that we'd have to research by hand and it meant "wasting" hours of our theoretically valuable time, we were prepared to waste however long it took. We kept track of all sorts of stuff by hand, by writing it down in our little notebooks, every single day.

I'm not even embarrassed to say I still do some of that today. And so does Tim. It's no longer technologically necessary. I know that. But it forces me to pay attention to every team in baseball every day of every year. So I still believe it's worth it. If you don't agree, hey, humor me. Okay? But at least I've scaled way back on what I keep track of now. In those days, we had to write down pretty much everything if we ever wanted to go back and look for stats and trends, hot streaks and cold streaks. And it didn't stop there.

For 20 years, Tim cut box scores out of the newspaper every frigging day and pasted them in a big spiral notebook, because there was literally no other way to go back and find out what happened in baseball on, say, May 12, 1991. I did that for a while myself, too. I admit it. But about 10 seconds after box scores started appearing on the Internet, I stopped, while Tim kept pasting for another dozen years. I admire him for that diligence. Really.

To find the goofy numbers that made me happy, I'd gladly comb through my day-by-day books or my box-score books or all the other books I crammed onto my shelves. I'd show up at the World Series with what I called "my work bag," but everyone else referred to as a "suitcase." That, too, was in the name of research, just so I could look back at postseason box scores from yesteryear and be able to tell the world that Joe Whatsisname just became the first pitcher to give up seven runs in an inning in a World Series game since Harry Whosethat did it in 1926.

But I'll admit there were times that the pursuit of epic numbers could get even more ridiculous than that. In 1991, when I covered baseball in Philadelphia, the Phillies had an outfielder named Von Hayes who went to the plate 323 times and hit zero homers. Zero. And just the year before, he'd hit 17. So I'm not sure exactly why I had to know if anyone had ever gone from 17 home runs one year to zero the next in a season of that many plate appearances. But I did. Or at least I convinced myself that I did.

If I needed to know that today, it would take me about 18 seconds to find it on a computer. But back then, I made a few calls, hoping I'd find somebody, anybody who could help. Then I did something crazy. I took a trip—through the entire Baseball Encyclopedia. From 1876 to 1991. I'd sit there in front of the TV, as my wife and kids tried to pretend I hadn't lost my mind, and I'd flip through 20 years one night, 30 the next, 40 the next, until I had my answer.

It. Had. Never. Been. Done.

Hey, you're welcome.

So what did we do before Baseball Prospectus? How did we survive? We suspended all pretenses that there was a single sane brain cell in our heads. Then we figured out ways to unearth the best, most fun, most illuminating numbers that could possibly be unearthed. I can't say I miss any of that. But I'm not embarrassed by it in the least. Not by any of it.

As you flip through the pages of this incredible book, I want you to think about that. I want you to appreciate that we're all so much better, smarter and happier now, just because we're existing in a universe where we can spew out any player's VORP or WARP or BRAA at any given moment, without having to devote an entire week of our lives to digging it up.

I want you to contemplate how far we've traveled, not just as a sport but as a species, in the pursuit of bold new information. I bet people sitting in the upper deck would be shocked by how front offices think in this era—how deeply they delve not merely into numbers but into sport science, and sleep studies, and body clocks, and wearable-technology studies.

You could see the reflection of how that deep thinking has evolved last October. Those four teams in the two League Championship Series—the Astros, Yankees, Dodgers and Cubs—weren't just baseball teams. They were baseball think tanks, processing information you've never even heard of at levels your brains couldn't possibly comprehend, and applying them to every pitch, every inning, every lineup card, every pitching change.

And all of this is spreading so far beyond your local ballpark, it's hard to keep up with. I took a trip to Syracuse University just this past November, and met with students who are enrolled in the first sports-analytics program at any major American university. I was blown away by their smarts, their passion, their excitement over getting to study this stuff in the name of education. Would it shock anyone if we looked up in a decade and 100 schools offered programs like this?

So what did we do before there was such a thing as Baseball Prospectus? Well, we did the best we could. We rounded up the best numbers we could find. We passed them along to whatever segment of the population found them useful, or at least entertaining. We dreamed of a day when we could answer all the questions that popped into our heads, practically instantaneously.

And now—whaddaya know—that day is here. And it's so darned exciting, it even got my buddy Tim Kurkjian to put away his box-score glue sticks. Forever.

Statistical Introduction

Why don't you get your nose out of those numbers and watch a game?

It's a false dilemma, of course. We would wager that Baseball Prospectus readers watch more games than the typical fan. They also probably pay better attention when they watch. The numbers do not replace observation; they supplement it. Having the numbers allows you to learn things not readily seen by mere watching and to keep up on many more players than any one person otherwise could.

This book doesn't ask you to choose between the two. Instead, we combine numerical analysis with the observations of a lot of very bright people. They won't always agree. Just as the eyes don't always see what the numbers do, the reverse can be true. To get the most out of this book, however, it helps to understand the numbers we're presenting and why.

Offense

The core of our offense measurements is True Average, which attempts to quantify everything a player does at the plate—hitting for power, taking walks, striking out and even making "productive" outs—and scale it to batting average. A player with a TAv of .260 is average, .300 exceptional, .200 rather awful.

True Average also accounts for the context a player performs in. That means we adjust it based on the mix of parks a player plays in. Also, rather than use a blanket park adjustment for every player on a team, a player who plays a disproportionate number of his games at home will see that reflected in his numbers. We also adjust based on league quality: The average player in the AL is better than the average player in the NL, and True Average accounts for this.

Because hitting isn't the entirety of scoring runs, we also look at a player's Baserunning Runs. BRR accounts for the value of a player's ability to steal bases, of course, but also accounts for his ability to go first to third on a single or advance on a fly ball.

Defense

Defense is a much thornier issue. The general move in the sabermetric community has been toward stats based on zone data, where human stringers record the type of batted ball (grounder, liner, fly ball) and its presumed landing location. That data is used to compile expected outs for comparing a fielder's actual performance.

The trouble with zone data is twofold. First, unlike the data we use in the calculation of the statistics you see in this book, zone data wasn't made publicly available; it was recorded by commercial providers who kept the raw data private, only disclosing it to a select few who paid for it. Second, as we've seen the field of zone-based defensive analysis open up—more data and more metrics based upon that data coming to light—we see that the conclusions of zone-based defensive metrics don't hold up to outside scrutiny. Different data providers can come to very different conclusions about the same events. Even two metrics based on the same data set can come to radically different conclusions based on their starting assumptions, assumptions that haven't been tested, using methods that can't be duplicated or verified by outside analysts.

The quality of the fielder can bias the data: Zone-based fielding metrics will tend to attribute more expected outs to good fielders than bad fielders, irrespective of the distribution of batted balls. Scorers who work in parks with high press boxes will tend to score more line drives than scorers who work in parks with low press boxes.

Our Fielding Runs Above Average (FRAA) incorporates play-by-play data, allowing us to study the issue of defense at a granular level without resorting to the sorts of subjective data used in some other fielding metrics. We count how many plays a player made, as well as expected plays for the average player at that position based on a pitcher's estimated ground-ball tendencies and the handedness of the batter. There are also adjustments for park and base-out situations.

In addition, catchers have different defensive responsibilities than other defensive players, in particular framing pitches to make umpires more likely to call them strikes and blocking errant pitches. We incorporate PITCHf/x data, where available, and adjust for the pitcher, umpire, batter (including handedness) and home-field advantage using a mixed-model approach to determine how many strikes a catcher is adding to or subtracting from his pitchers' ledgers, and then convert those extra or lost strikes to runs using simple linear weights. We use a similar approach to determine how much better or worse than average a catcher is at letting errant pitches past him (regardless of whether the official scorer labels it a passed ball or a wild pitch)—PITCHf/x is a particularly powerful tool in this regard because we can tell which pitches end up in the dirt (and at what angle and speed) even though basic play-by-play data simply records the pitch as a ball or a swinging strike because the catcher successfully blocked it.

These metrics, as well as the catcher's abilities to prevent steals, are incorporated into catchers' FRAA along with their ball-in-play fielding (e.g., popups and bunts near home plate).

Pitching

Of course, how we measure fielding influences how we measure pitching. Most sabermetric analysis of pitching has been inspired by Voros McCracken, who stated, "There is little if any difference among major-league pitchers in their ability to prevent hits on balls hit in the field of play." When first published, this statement was extremely controversial, but later research has, by and large, validated it. McCracken (and others) went forth from that finding to create a variety of defense-independent pitching measures. One that you'll see in the book is FIP, Fielding Independent Pitching, which accounts for walks, strikeouts, hit-by-pitches and homers accumulated by a pitcher and puts them into one number on an ERA scale. Another is cFIP, which takes those FIP inputs, makes a variety of adjustments (including the batter, catcher, umpire, stadium, home-field advantage and handedness) and puts the whole thing on a "100 minus" scale in which the lower the number the better. The standard deviation of cFIP is forced to 15, so you know that a 56 cFIP is nearly three standard deviations from the mean.

The trouble is that many efforts to separate pitching from fielding have ended up separating pitching from pitching—looking at only a handful of variables in isolation from the situation in which they occurred. What we've done instead is take a pitcher's actual results, event by event, and adjust each event based on the environment in which it occurred, including park factor, batter, catcher, umpire, base-out situation, run differential, inning, defense, home-field advantage, whether the pitcher is a starter or reliever and game-time temperature. We also consider the pitcher's effect on basestealing (both in terms of likelihood of stealing and likelihood of success) and the pitcher's effect on passed balls and wild pitches. Out of all this comes Deserved Run Average (DRA), our core pitching metric. It is the rate stat on which pitcher Wins Above Replacement Player is determined.

One key point to note is that DRA is set on the same scale as runs allowed per nine innings, not ERA. Looking only at earned runs tends to overrate three kinds of pitchers:

1. Pitchers who play in parks where scorers hand out more errors. Looking at error rates between parks tells us scorers differ significantly in how likely they are to score any given play as an error (as opposed to an infield hit);
2. Ground-ball pitchers, because a substantial proportion of errors occur on groundballs; and
3. Pitchers who aren't very good. Good pitchers tend to allow fewer unearned runs than bad pitchers, because good pitchers have more ways to get out of jams than bad pitchers. They're more likely to get a strikeout to end the inning and less likely to give up a home run.

Top-Line Pitching Metrics

While there is no shortage of metrics that purport to describe how "good" or "bad" a pitcher really is, there has been less focus on metrics that describe how a pitcher gets to their results. This, then, is the goal of the metrics introduced here: to provide as comprehensive a picture of a pitcher as possible, to be used as quantitative illustrations with their results. We are happy to introduce three new "top-line" pitching metrics, each on a 0-100 scale.

Power Rating

What is a "power pitcher"? We hear the term a lot, usually in reference to someone like Justin Verlander, but it's never been an exact term, for all that it seems to apply to the same general set of characteristics. As part of developing a new suite of pitching metrics and diving deeper into the ways we break down the art of throwing a ball very hard, we're taking a look at "power pitching" and quantifying exactly what it means to be a "power pitcher."

Luckily for us, the pieces to measure whether someone is quantifiably a "power pitcher" already exist, it's just deciding how best to put them together. Clearly, velocity is a large part of the equation, as the "power" part of the description, and we weight peak fastball velocity the heaviest when constructing these rankings.

Stamina Rating

As with all of these metrics, our measure of stamina, alone, has nothing to do with how "good" or "bad" a pitcher is; it is simply an objective measurement of how much of a workload any pitcher is capable of carrying. Since workload exists beyond Major League Baseball, we also included any of a pitcher's regular-season minor-league efforts in calculating Stamina.

To calculate Stamina Rating, we looked at different ways of valuing days of rest, numbers of pitches and batters faced per game. What we found most effective is a model that combines calculating the daily number of pitches thrown from a six-day moving average, with the straight average of batters faced per game against the square root of the mean of the days of rest between games.

Command Rating

One of the most challenging aspects of pitching to quantify, command indicates that a pitcher can throw the ball where he intends to. Our Command Score builds on Called Strikes Above Average (CSAA), which is the pitcher's component of our framing model. To build on that, we've identified target points in each corner of the zone using the likelihood of a pitch to be called a strike and quantify the pitcher's ability to hit that spot consistently. Pitchers are penalized for missing spots by a significant amount—either getting too much of the plate or missing off of it—to highlight their ability to effectively work the edges of the zone.

Projections

Many of you aren't turning to this book just for a look at what a player has done, but for a look at what a player is going to do: the PECOTA projections.

PECOTA, initially developed by Nate Silver (who has moved on to greater fame as a political analyst), consists of three parts:

1. Major-league equivalencies, to allow us to use minor-league stats to project how a player will perform in the majors;
2. Baseline forecasts, which use weighted averages and regression to the mean to produce an estimate of a player's true talent level; and
3. A career-path adjustment, which incorporates information on how comparable players' stats changed over time.

Now that we've gone over the core stats, let's go over what's in the book.

Team Prospectus

The bulk of this book comprises team chapters, with one for each of the 30 major-league franchises. On the first page of each chapter, you will be greeted by a box laying out some key statistics for each team. You can see Oakland's box on the facing page.

At the top, 2017 W-L is exactly as it sounds, the unadjusted tally of wins and losses. Pythag presents an adjusted 2017 win percentage by taking the runs scored per game (RS/G) and allowed (RA/G) by the team last season and running them through a version of Bill James' Pythagorean formula refined and developed by David Smyth and Brandon Heipp, called "Pythagenpat."

A team's runs scored is accompanied by True Average (TAv) and Baserunning Runs (BRR), both of which were described above, to give a picture of how a team scores its runs. In terms of run-prevention ability, we present a team's TAv allowed (TAv-P), FIP and Defensive Efficiency Rating (DER), which is simply its rate of balls in play turned into outs.

Then we have several measures not directly related to on-field performance. B-Age and P-Age tell us the average age of a team's batters and pitchers, respectively. Salary tells us how much the team cost to put on the field, and Doug Pappas' Marginal Dollars per Marginal Win (M$/MW) tells us how much a team paid above the bare minimum it had to pay and how much production above replacement it received for that money.

Finally, we count up the number of disabled-list days a team had, as well as the amount of salary paid to players while they were on

ATHLETICS PROSPECTUS

2017 W-L: 75-87, 5TH IN AL WEST

Pythag	.447	19th	B-Age	28.7	*21st*
RS/G	4.56	17th	P-Age	27.5	*6th*
RA/G	5.10	26th	Salary	$81.7M	*27th*
TAv	.258	19th	M$/MW	$2.5M	*24th*
TAv-P	.264	19th	DL Days	978	*17th*
FIP	4.54	19th	$ on DL	6%	*3rd*
DER	.705	11th			

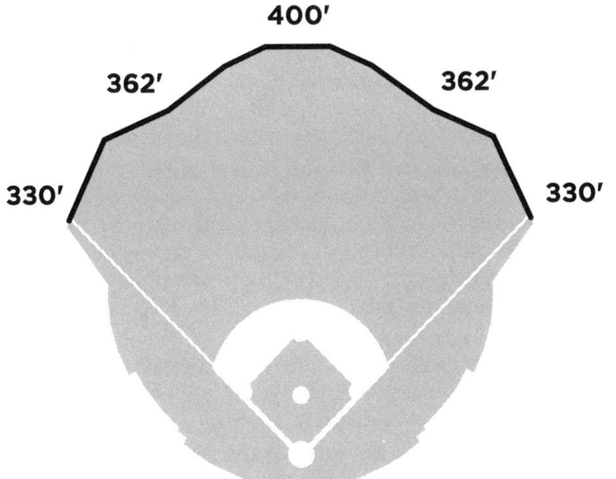

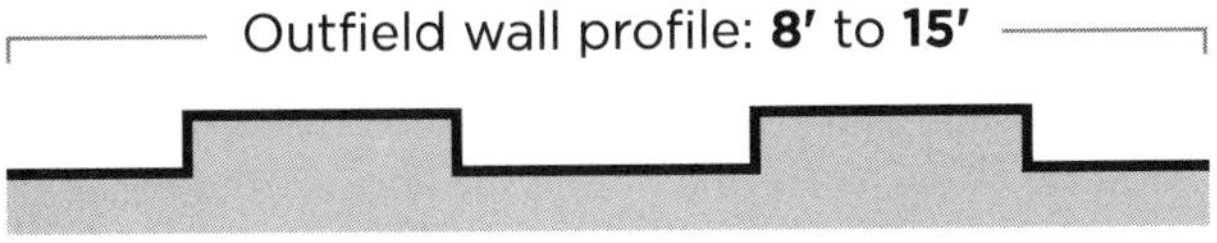

Three-Year Park Factors

Runs	Runs/RH	Runs/LH	HR/RH	HR/LH
99	99	97	93	91

Top Hitter WARP	2.7 Matt Chapman
Top Pitcher WARP	2.3 Sonny Gray
Top Prospect	A.J. Puk

the DL, expressed as a percentage of the total payroll.

Next to each of these stats, you see the team's MLB rank in that category, where 1st signifies a good outcome (e.g., highest TAv, lowest TAv-P) and 30th a bad outcome (highest $ on DL, lowest DER), except for salary, where we make no value judgments—1st is highest.

After the team information comes a variety of data about the home ballpark: a diagram of the park's dimensions showing distances to the outfield wall; a graphic that shows the height of the wall from the left-field pole to the right-field pole, reading left to right; and a table showing the three-year park factors presented in their usual 100-scale fashion, with 100 being average, 110 meaning that the park inflates the stat by 10 percent and 90 meaning the park deflates the stat by 10 percent.

On the second page of each chapter, you will see three graphs. The first graph, titled "2017 Hit List Ranking," shows the Hit List Rank for this team on every day of the 2017 season and is intended to give you an idea of the shape of the season. Hit List Rank is a measure of overall team performance that drives the Prospectus Hit List power ranking at baseballprospectus.com. It is based on team run differential and includes adjustments for park, league and quality of opposition. You can see more about Hit List Ranking at http://bbp.cx/a/4383.

The second graph is entitled "Committed Payroll" and is intended to give you an idea of how this team's player budgets match up with the competition historically and going forward. The payroll figures are current as of January 1, 2018; with several free agents still unsigned as of this writing, keep in mind the final 2017 figure will be significantly different for many teams. You can always find current data at Baseball Prospectus' Cot's Baseball Contracts page. MLB and division averages are also plotted to allow for quick comparison.

The third graph is entitled "Farm System Ranking" and shows the Baseball Prospectus prospect team's ranking of this team's farm system for the last several years.

Following the graphs is the "Personnel" section. Here you'll find some of the important people in the organization and any former Baseball Prospectus staff who are currently part of the team's front office or scouting staff.

Last, but not least, we have special 2017 category leaders cards courtesy of our friends at Topps.

Position Players

After a bylined opening essay about each team, the chapters move to the player comments, which are also bylined, though the vagaries of player movement and the group-project nature of the book mean that the names you see at the head of each chapter are more a rough guide than a precise accounting of the division of labor.

Each player is listed with the major-league team by whom he was employed as of mid-December 2017, meaning that players who changed teams via free agency, trade or otherwise later in the offseason will be listed under their previous employer.

As an example, take a look at Carlos Correa: his stat block is at the top of the next page.

The player-specific sections begin with biographical information (age is as of June 30) before moving onto the column headers and actual data. The column headers begin with standard information like year, team, level (majors or level of minors), and the raw, untranslated tallies found on the back of a baseball card: PA (plate appearances), R (runs), 2B (doubles), 3B (triples), HR (home runs), RBI (runs batted in), BB (walks), K (strikeouts), SB (stolen bases) and CS (caught stealing).

Following those are untranslated "slash" statistics: batting average (AVG), on-base percentage (OBP) and slugging percentage (SLG). The slash line is followed by True Average (TAv), which, as described above, rolls all those things and more into one easy-to-digest number.

BABIP stands for Batting Average on Balls in Play and is what it sounds like: How often did a ball put in play by the hitter fall for a hit? An especially low or high BABIP may mean a hitter was especially lucky or unlucky. However, hitters who hit the ball hard tend to have especially high BABIPs from season to season; so do speedy hitters who are able to beat out more grounders for base hits.

Next is Baserunning Runs (BRR), which, as mentioned earlier, covers all sorts of baserunning accomplishments, not just stolen bases. Then comes Fielding Runs Above Average (FRAA); for historical stats, we have the number of games played at each position in parentheses. For multi-position players, we can only

Carlos Correa SS Born: 09/22/94 Age: 23 Bats: R Throws: R Height: 6'4" Weight: 215 Origin: Round 1, 2012 Draft (#1 overall)

YEAR	TEAM	LVL	AGE	PA	R	2B	3B	HR	RBI	BB	K	SB	CS	AVG/OBP/SLG	TAv	VORP	BABIP	BRR	FRAA	WARP
2015	CCH	AA	20	133	25	15	2	7	32	15	25	15	0	.385/.459/.726	.387	22.2	.447	0.0	SS(28): 4.5	2.9
2015	FRE	AAA	20	113	19	6	1	3	12	12	14	3	1	.276/.345/.449	.281	4.8	.286	-2.3	SS(24): -4.8	0.0
2015	HOU	MLB	20	432	52	22	1	22	68	40	78	14	4	.279/.345/.512	.295	32.1	.296	0.4	SS(99): -7.4	2.6
2016	HOU	MLB	21	660	76	36	3	20	96	75	139	13	3	.274/.361/.451	.297	53.7	.328	1.8	SS(153): -4.5	5.1
2017	HOU	MLB	22	481	82	25	1	24	84	53	92	2	1	.315/.391/.550	.320	47.4	.352	-3.0	SS(108): -1.4	4.6
2018	*HOU*	*MLB*	*23*	*615*	*87*	*33*	*2*	*26*	*91*	*64*	*119*	*11*	*3*	*.285/.362/.496*	*.302*	*54.9*	*.322*	*0.3*	*SS -3*	*4.6*
2019	*HOU*	*MLB*	*24*	*549*	*84*	*30*	*2*	*26*	*86*	*64*	*105*	*10*	*2*	*.292/.378/.527*	*.309*	*46.7*	*.323*	*-0.1*	*SS -2*	*4.8*

Breakout: 4% Improve: 64% Collapse: 0% Attrition: 0% MLB: 99% *Comparables: Miguel Cabrera, Jason Heyward, Ryan Zimmerman*

display the two positions the fielder played most frequently that season.

One of our oldest active metrics, Value Over Replacement Player (VORP), considers offensive production, position and plate appearances. More specifically, it is the number of runs contributed beyond what a replacement-level player at the same position would contribute if given the same percentage of team plate appearances. VORP scores do not consider the quality of a player's defense.

The last column is Wins Above Replacement Player. WARP is our total-value stat that, for a hitter, combines a player's batting runs above average (derived from True Average), BRR, FRAA, an adjustment for positions played and a credit for plate appearances based upon the difference between the "replacement level" (derived by looking at the quality of players added to a team's roster after the start of the season) and the league average.

The final line below the comment is PECOTA data, which is discussed further below.

Catchers

There is a separate box for catchers showing some of the defensive metrics that apply particularly to them. As an example, let's check out Buster Posey.

Buster Posey

YEAR	TEAM	P. COUNT	FRM RUNS	BLK RUNS	THRW RUNS	TOT RUNS
2015	SFN	13948	11.6	2.0	0.9	14.4
2016	SFN	17017	26.5	2.0	2.2	30.7
2017	SFN	13474	1.8	0.1	2.2	4.1
2018	*SFN*	*17228*	*15.3*	*1.8*	*2.0*	*19.1*
2019	*SFN*	*15686*	*13.7*	*1.6*	*1.8*	*17.1*

The YEAR and TEAM columns are what you'd expect. P. COUNT is the number of pitches the catcher "received," though really it's the number of pitches thrown by pitchers when the catcher was in the battery; that is, it includes swinging strikes, fouls and balls in play. FRM RUNS is the total runs the catcher added by getting the umpire to call strikes where the average catcher did not (or vice versa). The calculation of this statistic is described above. BLK RUNS, also described above, expresses in runs above or below average the catcher's ability to prevent wild pitches and passed balls. Finally, THRW RUNS sums the catcher's ability to dissuade runners from stealing and to catch them when they do run. This statistic is calculated similarly to the Framing and Blocking stats, and takes into account various factors, including the pitcher (who may have a quick or slow delivery, or a good or bad pickoff move) and the baserunner (who may be Billy Hamilton or Billy Butler). The final column, TOT RUNS, is the sum of the previous three.

Pitchers

Now let's look at how pitchers are presented, using Luis Severino. His stat block is at the top of the facing page. The first line and the YEAR, TEAM, LVL and AGE columns are the same as in the hitters example above. The next set of columns—W (wins), L (losses), SV (saves), G (games pitched), GS (games started), IP (innings pitched), H (hits), HR (home runs), BB9 (walks per nine innings), K/9 (strikeouts per nine innings) and K (strikeouts)—are the actual, unadjusted stats compiled by the pitcher during each season.

Next is GB%, which is the percentage of all batted balls that were hit on the ground, including both outs and hits. As mentioned above, this is based on observation by human stringers and can be skewed based upon a number of factors. We've included the number as a guide, but please approach it skeptically.

BABIP is the same statistic as for batters, but often tells you more in the case of pitchers, because most major-league pitchers have little control over their batting average on balls in play. A high BABIP is often due to a poor defense or bad luck rather than a pitcher's own abilities and may be a good indicator of a potential rebound. A typical league-average BABIP is around .290–.300.

WHIP and ERA are common to most fans: The former measures the number of walks and hits allowed on a per-inning basis, while the latter prorates earned runs allowed on a nine-innings basis. Neither is translated or adjusted in any way.

FIP was discussed above: It puts onto an ERA scale a measurement of how the pitcher performed on the events that do not involve the fielders behind him.

Deserved Run Average (DRA) was also described above. It is the basis of pitcher WARP and measures how many runs (not earned runs) the pitcher "deserved" to allow per nine innings. One important point about minor leaguers is that because we do not have all the data we would need to fully calculate minor-league DRA, what is listed under "DRA" for minor leaguers is really a runs-allowed-per-nine figure calculated based on cFIP's components.

Because, as has been true of BP's pitching metrics in the past, neither DRA nor the conversion from DRA to WARP contains a "leverage" multiplier, WARP for relief pitchers (especially closers) may seem lower than you might see elsewhere and may conflict with how we feel about relief aces coming in and "saving" the game. This is by design: Saves give extra credit to the closer for what his teammates did to put him in a save spot to begin with; WARP is incapable of feeling excitement over a successful save and judges them dispassionately. Furthermore, DRA controls for players who have the benefit of pitching in short durations and at maximum ability.

cFIP, described above, adjusts FIP for a variety of factors and scales it on the familiar 100 scale; because these are pitchers preventing runs, below 100 is good and above 100 is bad.

MPH is the pitcher's 95th percentile velocity for that season—the goal is to give you a sense of the pitcher's peak fastball velocity, not his average. This comes from PITCHf/x data and thus is not publicly available for minor leaguers.

CMD, PWR and STM, as described above, are our new Command Rating, Power Rating and Stamina Rating on a 0-100 scale.

PECOTA

Both pitchers and hitters have PECOTA projections for next season, as well as a set of biographical details that describe the performance of that player's comparable players according to

Luis Severino RHP Born: 02/20/94 Age: 24 Bats: R Throws: R Height: 6'2" Weight: 215 Origin: International Free Agent, 2011

YEAR	TEAM	LVL	AGE	W	L	SV	G	GS	IP	H	HR	BB/9	K/9	K	GB%	BABIP	WHIP	ERA	DRA	WARP	MPH	CMD	PWR	STM
2015	TRN	AA	21	2	2	0	8	8	38	32	2	2.4	11.4	48	46%	.319	1.11	3.32	1.47	1.7				
2015	SWB	AAA	21	7	0	0	11	11	61[1]	40	0	2.5	7.3	50	42%	.237	0.93	1.91	2.59	1.9				
2015	NYA	MLB	21	5	3	0	11	11	62[1]	53	9	3.2	8.1	56	51%	.265	1.20	2.89	3.16	1.4	97.8	45	59	65
2016	SWB	AAA	22	8	1	0	13	12	77[1]	75	4	2.1	9.1	78	46%	.321	1.20	3.49	2.70	2.3				
2016	NYA	MLB	22	3	8	0	22	11	71	78	11	3.2	8.4	66	45%	.324	1.45	5.83	3.93	1.1	99.0	43	60	65
2017	NYA	MLB	23	14	6	0	31	31	193[1]	150	21	2.4	10.7	230	50%	.272	1.04	2.98	3.05	5.4	99.5	48	65	78
2018	*NYA*	*MLB*	*24*	*13*	*7*	*0*	*29*	*29*	*174*	*151*	*22*	*3.0*	*10.1*	*195*	*47%*	*.291*	*1.19*	*3.45*	*3.62*	*3.6*	*99.0*	*48*	*65*	*73*
2019	*NYA*	*MLB*	*25*	*12*	*9*	*0*	*31*	*31*	*193[2]*	*161*	*25*	*2.6*	*10.8*	*232*	*47%*	*.29*	*1.12*	*3.58*	*3.65*	*4.0*	*98.9*	*48*	*66*	*74*

Breakout: 30% Improve: 65% Collapse: 11% Attrition: 18% MLB: 96%

Comparables: Marcus Stroman, Carlos Martinez, Rich Harden

PECOTA. The book contains two years of PECOTA projections for every player.

The 2018 and 2019 lines are the PECOTA projection for the player at the date we went to press in late December. The player is projected into the league and park context as indicated by his team abbreviation. All PECOTAs represent a player's projected major-league performance. The numbers beneath the player's stats—Breakout, Improve, Collapse, Attrition—are a part of PECOTA. These estimate the likelihood of changes in performance relative to a player's previously established level of production, based upon the performance of the comparable players:

Breakout Rate is the percent chance that a player's production will improve by at least 20 percent relative to the weighted average of his performance over his most recent seasons.

Improve Rate is the percent chance that a player's production will improve at all relative to his baseline performance. A player who is expected to perform just the same as he has in the recent past will have an Improve Rate of 50 percent.

Collapse Rate is the percent chance that a position player's runs produced per plate appearance will decline by at least 25 percent relative to his baseline performance.

Attrition Rate operates on playing time rather than performance. Specifically, it measures the likelihood that a player's playing time will decrease by at least 50 percent relative to his established level.

Breakout Rate and **Collapse Rate** can sometimes be counterintuitive for players who have already experienced a radical change in performance level. It's also worth noting that the projected decline in a player's rate performances might not be indicative of an expected decline in underlying ability or skill, but rather something of an anticipated correction following a breakout season.

MLB% is the percentage of similar players who played in the major leagues in their relevant season.

The final pieces of information are the player's three highest-scoring comparable players as determined by PECOTA. Occasionally, a player's top comparables will not be representative of the larger sample that PECOTA uses. All comparables represent a snapshot of how the listed player was performing at the same age as the current player, so if a 23-year-old pitcher is compared to Barry Zito, he's actually being compared to a 23-year-old Barry Zito, not the version of Zito the Giants couldn't wait to be rid of, nor to Zito's career as a whole.

A few points about pitcher projections. First, we aren't yet projecting peak velocity, so that column will be blank in the PECOTA lines. Second, projecting DRA is trickier than evaluating past performance, because it is unclear how deserving each pitcher will be of his anticipated outcomes. However, we know that cFIP estimates future run scoring very well, and that cFIP and DRA are based on a similar structure and model. Thus, the projected DRA figures you see are based on the past cFIPs generated by the pitcher and comparable players over time, along with the other factors described above.

Lineouts

The stats box in the Lineouts section contains all the same information, but only has the 2017 stats for each player.

PECOTA Leaderboards

As a result of the way it weights previous seasons, PECOTA can tend to appear bullish on players coming off a bad year and bearish on players coming off a great year. And because we list the 50th percentile projections—the middle of the range the system thinks this player is capable of producing—it rarely predicts any player will hit 40 home runs or strike out 250 batters. At the end of this book, though, we've ranked the top players according to their projections. It's often as helpful to know who the system thinks will be the top second baseman as what his actual stats are likely to be.

ARIZONA DIAMONDBACKS

Essay by Patrick Dubuque

Player comments by Nick Stellini and BP staff

Professional sports are modern mythology, and no sport is better suited for the role than baseball. The structure of the game—its pace, its duration, its randomness and its fearlessness in assigning blame and failure—feels designed to wrap around the skeleton of the narrative structure. In an urban age, when participation in sports becomes rarer and more difficult, more and more fans interact with their sport not by playing it but by deciphering it, an active verb even when performed from the couch or the bleachers. Baseball is more art than ever before, something to be taken, deconstructed and understood, whether for the sake of our fantasy teams or our own satisfaction.

Baseball seasons and mythologies share one more thing in common: They're nearly all alike. Joseph Campbell, in his seminal work *The Hero With a Thousand Faces*, scoured the myths of every civilization he could find, and from them he pieced together a system of common facets, a monomyth, out of which he fused an abstract of shared human desires. Campbell bemoaned the state of modern society for having lost touch with this primeval urge in its search for rationality, not out of a religious fear but because of our loss of communal inspiration. Simply put, shared mythology is the balm against isolation and alienation, a force that bonds us and inspires us to cooperate and thrive. Heroes, to Campbell, are an essential element of society. At this point, athletes are basically what we've got.

Fortunately, the model translates fairly well. Campbell's examination of heroes unearthed a system he called The Hero's Journey, a series of stages that every hero undergoes for the sake of their people. Through it we can find the plot structure of all the great stories: Jesus, Luke Skywalker, Gandhi, Frodo Baggins and the Arizona Diamondbacks. Join us, for a moment, on the quest of a baseball team, and the phases of the journey they find themselves, like Jason and his Argonauts, traveling:

1. The Call to Adventure

Get a team, basically, and try to win the World Series. Look, they're not all going to be amazing metaphors.

2. Refusal of the Call

The protagonists, having been called to quest, must decide whether to accept the mission. Those who opt out are doomed to the dreariness of the non-heroic existence, sentenced to wonder what might have been. You don't read many stories about heroes who get tripped up on Stage 2, because they aren't really stories; you do see a lot of lives lived this way, however. Every quest requires labor, a willingness to venture beyond the comfortable and the known. Moreover, for our purposes, going on the journey requires taking risks, abandoning the easy and the unquestionable, the reliance on the accepted truisms of the past.

No story boils down the call more directly to a single binary choice than *The Matrix* does with its red and blue pills, the choice to live in comforting falsehood or face the truths of life as they really

DIAMONDBACKS PROSPECTUS

2017 W-L: 93-69, 2nd in NL West

Pythag	.597	5th	B-Age	28.2	*13th*
RS/G	5.01	8th	P-Age	28.0	*12th*
RA/G	4.07	3rd	Salary	$93.1M	*26th*
TAv	.270	9th	M$/MW	$1.8M	*28th*
TAv-P	.250	7th	DL Days	923	*15th*
FIP	3.81	4th	$ on DL	17%	*18th*
DER	.705	10th			

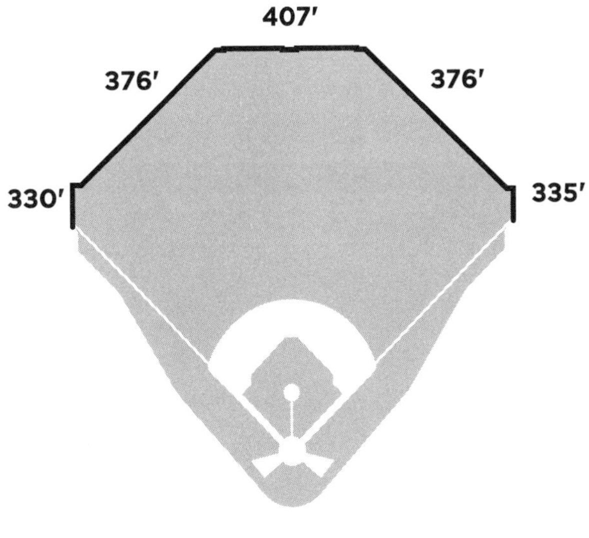

Outfield wall profile: **7'6" to 25'**

Three-Year Park Factors

Runs	Runs/RH	Runs/LH	HR/RH	HR/LH
108	109	106	106	103

Top Hitter WARP	6.4 Paul Goldschmidt
Top Pitcher WARP	5.8 Zack Greinke
Top Prospect	Jon Duplantier

2017 Hit List Ranking

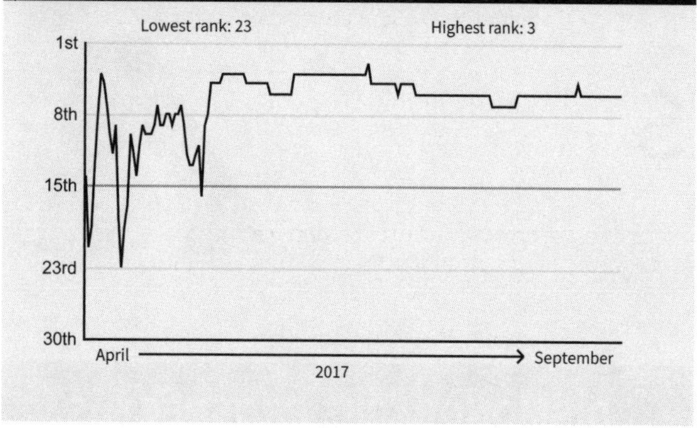

Committed Payroll (in millions)

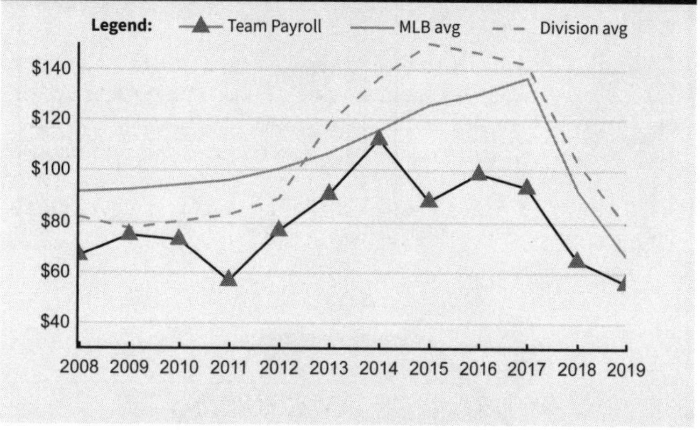

Farm System Ranking

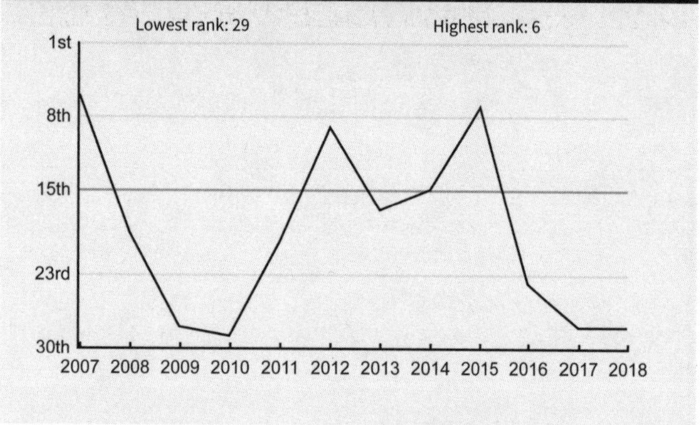

Personnel

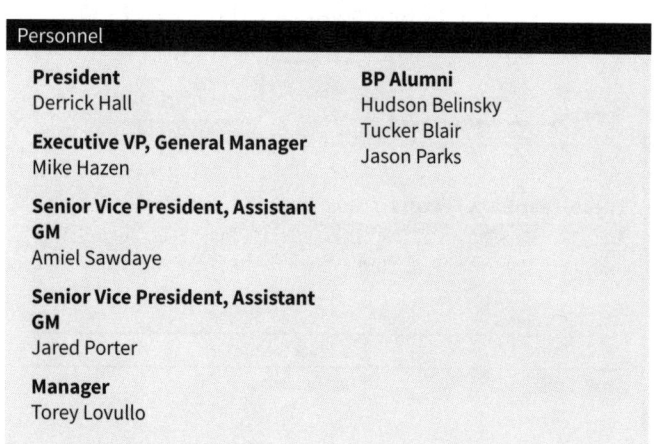

President
Derrick Hall

Executive VP, General Manager
Mike Hazen

Senior Vice President, Assistant GM
Amiel Sawdaye

Senior Vice President, Assistant GM
Jared Porter

Manager
Torey Lovullo

BP Alumni
Hudson Belinsky
Tucker Blair
Jason Parks

are. Every baseball team wants to win the World Series, but some get distracted; they grow fascinated with building a certain type of team, manipulating a certain type of inefficiency that overtakes the value of accumulating talent. The A's are famous for this; the Rockies, likewise, have been obsessed with character; so too were the Diamondbacks, particularly under the Kevin Towers regime, with grit.

3. Crossing the Threshold

This is the part of the story where the hero or heroes leave their idyllic, safe homelands and venture into the unknown. After the spectacular (in the literal, spectacle-based sense) failures of Dave Stewart, control of the team was handed to new general manager Mike Hazen, who was known for being smart but for little else. Given an opportunity to sculpt and imprint his own vision and message on a young, flawed team, Hazen ... made a single trade, sending Jean Segura and *2017 BP Annual* essay protagonist Mitch Haniger to Seattle for Taijuan Walker and Ketel Marte. It was a big trade, to be fair, but not an eventful one: In terms of 2017 production, it turned out to be somewhat of a wash, although Marte's team control probably gives Arizona the slight advantage.

Instead, Hazen chose to move forward quietly with his 93-loss team; his major transactions were signing a pair of sub-replacement-level catchers in Chris Iannetta and Jeff Mathis, as well as a washed-up, painful-to-watch Fernando Rodney to close games. Instead, the organization focused on working with what they had, adding fractions of runs through smart baserunning and tossing around phrases like "pitch framing" never before uttered by the front office. It was a strategy that demanded a remarkable amount of patience, to sort out what the team had and how much they could grow.

It was also, in retrospect, a brilliant move. A roster long considered the apex of stars-and-scrubs watched its cast of secondary characters transform from underwhelming afterthoughts to average, valuable components. Middle infielders like Marte and Chris Owings hit well enough to curb fans' nostalgia for Segura. And despite a down year for the recovering A.J. Pollock, Iannetta's offensive resurgence and quality offense from David Peralta made the entire lineup—not just Paul Goldschmidt and Jake Lamb—a source of consistency. But the story of the 2017 season was on the pitching side, where every promising arm of yesteryear, including Robbie Ray, Patrick Corbin, Archie Bradley and even Randall Delgado, took a step forward together.

4. Supernatural Aid

The hero never truly goes it alone, if only because it would make for terrible dialogue. Besides, things have to get rough here and there, to test the depths of the hero's strength and fortitude, to seem almost too much to bear. In these situations, a god or goddess will often appear to lend a hand and provide guidance, as Athena helps Odysseus by representing his cause on Olympus, or the Great Red Dragon scares off the occasional bad guy in Jeff Smith's *Bone* comics. In our example, divine providence arrived for the Diamondbacks in the form of J.D. Martinez. On the morning of July 18, Arizona was mired in a 1-8 slump and, for the first time since spring, the team's playoff odds were suddenly in doubt. The trade, considered a fairly cheap purchase at the time, proved to be much more than that, as Martinez was one of the best hitters in baseball over the second half.

5. The Road of Trials

Here's where we get our plot: the voyage, the road trip, the dungeon dive, with its episodic difficulties to be surmounted. It's also where we reach the present day, in this allegory. When the Diamondbacks were swept out of the NLDS by the Dodgers, there was hardly even a sense of disappointment; beyond the exhilaration of the regular season, the Dodgers just felt like the natural stopping point of the season. It's fairly clear that the Diamondbacks aren't there yet, shouldn't even be there yet; it's only been a year, after all. Journeys must be long and hard to be rewarding.

Overcoming the trials of the underworld, according to Campbell, requires self-actualization. He writes: "And where we had thought to find an abomination, we shall find a god; where we had thought to slay another, we shall slay ourselves; where we had thought to travel outward, we shall come to the center of our own existence; where we had thought to be alone, we shall be with all the world."

The Dodgers, the champion itself, is just a personal demon, a psychological hurdle. The Diamondbacks must know themselves, fully and completely, to advance. Doing so will require them to rely on their ability to fashion their core of young pitchers and shape second-tier prospects into a lasting juggernaut. They may fail in the mission; the improvement may be a mirage, or one or more may simply get struck down, as the Argonaut Mopsus, slain by a viper grown from a drop of blood from Medusa. These things happen.

6. Apotheosis

Every story reaches a climax, a final test that surpasses and combines all of the trials and lessons on the way. With apologies to the surprising Rockies, the Goliath blocking the Diamondbacks' path to the pennant is clearly the Dodgers, a developmental and financial powerhouse, a foe that seems to hold every possible advantage.

So many movies and stories derive their climaxes from the work of *deus ex machina*, the single bullet or the fortuitous shift that allows the hero a moment of even odds. Baseball, lacking an author, cannot promise such a twist. With a team like the Dodgers, there is no window to time; they, unlike Arizona, can spend their way into and out of windows at will. So the Diamondbacks can't afford to operate as if destiny is on their side; instead, they have to rely on vigilance and control, to set up a perpetual system of development and talent acquisition. When the Dodgers expose their heel, suffer their own bout of injury and misfortune, the Diamondbacks will need to be ready if they are to seize control of the division.

7. The Journey Home

Someday, they win the World Series.

The beautiful and the terrible thing about baseball is that it never ends. After the trophy is wrested from the forces of evil and brought home in celebration, the hero wields the force to bend the world to his or her will, to create life and prosperity for his or her people. This is the goal. But it's always the goal, and there's always another season, and another hero, and another darkness invading the land. Bones break and heal, players get drafted, leave, return, retire. We never run out of baseball, and we are never sated by it.

This stage of the monomyth might be the only one where baseball fails; sports are not designed for denouement. There will be another parade; perhaps Greinke and Goldschmidt will be at its head, or perhaps they will be eaten by the wolves and followed by others. A band of heroes will return to the city, to share their victory and inspiration, to "release again of the flow of life into the body of the world." It's very easy, especially in this current stage, to worry only about that victory. But mythology, and the value of mythology, isn't just about the end; it's about the struggle, the gaining of clarity, the first and the fifth and the 50th steps. Last season, on its own, was a fine step. It deserves to be memorialized.

—Patrick Dubuque is an author of Baseball Prospectus.

Hitters

Nick Ahmed SS Born: 03/15/90 Age: 28 Bats: R Throws: R Height: 6'2" Weight: 195 Origin: Round 2, 2011 Draft (#85 overall)

YEAR	TEAM	LVL	AGE	PA	R	2B	3B	HR	RBI	BB	K	SB	CS	AVG/OBP/SLG	TAv	VORP	BABIP	BRR	FRAA	WARP
2015	ARI	MLB	25	459	49	17	6	9	34	29	81	4	5	.226/.275/.359	.236	12.0	.257	4.6	SS(129): 5.1	1.8
2016	ARI	MLB	26	308	26	9	1	4	20	15	58	5	2	.218/.265/.299	.197	-4.8	.258	2.3	SS(88): 9.4	0.5
2017	ARI	MLB	27	178	24	8	1	6	21	10	39	3	4	.251/.298/.419	.233	1.6	.295	-0.8	SS(48): 3.9	0.5
2018	*ARI*	*MLB*	*28*	*131*	*13*	*6*	*1*	*3*	*13*	*8*	*24*	*2*	*1*	*.236/.283/.361*	*.222*	*1.2*	*.271*	*-0.2*	*SS 1, 2B 0*	*0.0*
2019	*ARI*	*MLB*	*29*	*198*	*22*	*8*	*1*	*5*	*21*	*13*	*39*	*3*	*2*	*.240/.294/.383*	*.238*	*3.1*	*.275*	*1.1*	*SS 2, 2B 0*	*0.6*

Breakout: 3% Improve: 41% Collapse: 10% Attrition: 19% MLB: 88% *Comparables: Donovan Solano, Jonathan Herrera, Adeiny Hechavarria*

The good news: Ahmed hit a bit better than he did in 2016, including more average and a little pop too (though that may have had something to do with the baseball, which totally wasn't juiced at all you guys). That allowed him to post an ever-so-slightly higher WARP.

The bad news: Ahmed fractured his right wrist and played in just 53 games overall. He had surgery on that wrist, which can prove to be a trickier, less predictable comeback trail than most other injuries for hitters. Ahmed's game has always been about defense, though, and fortunately for him the bar for utility-man status offensively is always low.

Gregor Blanco CF Born: 12/24/83 Age: 34 Bats: L Throws: L Height: 5'11" Weight: 175 Origin: International Free Agent, 2000

YEAR	TEAM	LVL	AGE	PA	R	2B	3B	HR	RBI	BB	K	SB	CS	AVG/OBP/SLG	TAv	VORP	BABIP	BRR	FRAA	WARP
2015	SFN	MLB	31	372	59	19	3	5	26	40	59	13	5	.291/.368/.413	.299	27.5	.338	4.3	CF(44): -3.4, LF(38): 3.3	2.7
2016	SFN	MLB	32	274	28	10	4	1	18	29	51	6	3	.224/.309/.311	.237	-0.8	.279	-0.7	RF(34): -1.0, LF(29): -0.3	-0.4
2017	ARI	MLB	33	256	43	10	3	3	13	31	59	15	1	.246/.337/.357	.247	6.3	.321	2.8	LF(44): -2.5, CF(35): -3.5	0.0
2018	*ARI*	*MLB*	*34*	*250*	*30*	*11*	*2*	*4*	*24*	*26*	*51*	*9*	*2*	*.254/.335/.387*	*.241*	*5.9*	*.307*	*1.4*	*CF -4, LF 1*	*0.4*
2019	*ARI*	*MLB*	*35*	*148*	*17*	*6*	*1*	*3*	*15*	*15*	*31*	*5*	*1*	*.243/.324/.370*	*.249*	*3.3*	*.295*	*0.9*	*CF -2, LF 1*	*0.2*

Breakout: 1% Improve: 31% Collapse: 11% Attrition: 18% MLB: 84% *Comparables: Mike Kingery, Sam Fuld, Tony Gonzalez*

Blanco kinda sorta recovered from his disastrous showing at the plate in 2016 and put up a line that more closely resembled his usual self. At the same time, he still didn't hit quite as well as he had in the past, got into just 90 games for the Diamondbacks and had his worst defensive season yet at age 33. Blanco is still theoretically a quality fourth outfielder for a lower-half team, but he's rapidly approaching Perpetual Non-Roster Invitee status.

Socrates Brito RF Born: 09/06/92 Age: 25 Bats: L Throws: L Height: 6'2" Weight: 205 Origin: International Free Agent, 2010

YEAR	TEAM	LVL	AGE	PA	R	2B	3B	HR	RBI	BB	K	SB	CS	AVG/OBP/SLG	TAv	VORP	BABIP	BRR	FRAA	WARP
2015	MOB	AA	22	522	70	17	15	9	57	29	84	20	6	.300/.339/.451	.286	31.1	.346	5.6	RF(63): 12.4, CF(48): 3.3	5.1
2015	ARI	MLB	22	34	5	3	1	0	1	1	7	1	0	.303/.324/.455	.268	1.5	.385	0.5	RF(5): 2.1, CF(1): -0.1	0.4
2016	RNO	AAA	23	317	46	10	8	6	39	13	60	7	6	.294/.322/.439	.265	10.6	.349	1.6	RF(43): 0.3, CF(31): 1.4	1.3
2016	ARI	MLB	23	97	10	3	1	4	12	2	23	2	0	.179/.196/.358	.188	-3.0	.191	1.6	CF(17): -2.2, RF(16): -0.4	-0.4
2017	RNO	AAA	24	318	43	15	8	5	44	22	64	6	1	.291/.336/.449	.260	8.7	.352	0.6	RF(36): -0.3, CF(33): 1.0	0.9
2018	*ARI*	*MLB*	*25*	*205*	*23*	*8*	*4*	*5*	*23*	*8*	*49*	*3*	*1*	*.250/.281/.411*	*.233*	*1.5*	*.305*	*0.5*	*LF 1, RF 1*	*0.2*
2019	*ARI*	*MLB*	*26*	*322*	*37*	*14*	*6*	*10*	*39*	*17*	*80*	*5*	*2*	*.252/.293/.431*	*.252*	*6.2*	*.310*	*0.9*	*LF 1, RF 2*	*1.1*

Breakout: 2% Improve: 8% Collapse: 5% Attrition: 15% MLB: 20% *Comparables: Kyle Waldrop, Jason Coats, Jared Hoying*

SOCRATES: I am a better athlete than this man. Though I missed time with a dislocated finger and didn't even crack September call-ups, I still believe I am a big-league-caliber player. I have physical tools, I can play right field like a Spartan hero. Contact can elude me, but aye, I do what I can with what the gods have given me. My arm has the strength of an ox, and it is the weapon with which I lay waste to those on the basepaths. Some may fancy they know me as a Quad-A type, yet they know nothing, for I could thrive as a fourth outfielder, or even as more if a below-average team gave me a chance to start. DARRYL, SOCRATES' FRIEND: F*** him up, Socrates.

Jasrado Chisholm SS Born: 02/01/98 Age: 20 Bats: L Throws: R Height: 5'11" Weight: 165 Origin: International Free Agent, 2015

YEAR	TEAM	LVL	AGE	PA	R	2B	3B	HR	RBI	BB	K	SB	CS	AVG/OBP/SLG	TAv	VORP	BABIP	BRR	FRAA	WARP
2016	MSO	RK	18	270	42	12	1	9	37	19	73	13	4	.281/.333/.446	.271	15.4	.363	0.6	SS(60): 2.5, 2B(1): 0.0	1.8
2017	KNC	A	19	125	14	5	2	1	12	10	39	3	0	.248/.325/.358	.264	6.3	.371	0.7	SS(29): 0.8	0.7
2018	*ARI*	*MLB*	*20*	*250*	*22*	*10*	*1*	*6*	*26*	*14*	*93*	*1*	*0*	*.195/.246/.329*	*.191*	*-6.5*	*.288*	*-0.1*	*SS 2*	*-0.5*
2019	*ARI*	*MLB*	*21*	*309*	*32*	*13*	*1*	*9*	*33*	*18*	*115*	*1*	*0*	*.206/.258/.351*	*.214*	*-4.7*	*.304*	*-0.3*	*SS 2*	*-0.2*

Breakout: 1% Improve: 5% Collapse: 0% Attrition: 2% MLB: 9% *Comparables: Raul Mondesi, Tim Beckham, Amed Rosario*

The man they call "Jazz" didn't have a euphonic year in his first run at full-season ball. Chisholm never found his tempo at the plate, losing 33 points off his batting average while notably just about keeping pace in OBP, but he's still young. A second attempt at A-ball will likely do him well, and maybe put him on track to Take the A-Train to Phoenix. There's still enough potential here for a good percussive bat with his all-fields approach, and his speed and good glove work should have the guys in the front office Feeling Good if all goes well here. Because of his age and rawness, that may take a while, perhaps four years. It may even Take Five. Who knows. Player development is far from an exact science, but there can sometimes be beauty in just seeing what melodies come about through experimentation.

Daniel Descalso UT Born: 10/19/86 Age: 31 Bats: L Throws: R Height: 5'10" Weight: 190 Origin: Round 3, 2007 Draft (#112 overall)

YEAR	TEAM	LVL	AGE	PA	R	2B	3B	HR	RBI	BB	K	SB	CS	AVG/OBP/SLG	TAv	VORP	BABIP	BRR	FRAA	WARP
2015	COL	MLB	28	209	22	3	2	5	22	20	45	1	2	.205/.283/.324	.225	-1.3	.244	-0.6	SS(33): 0.8, 2B(15): -1.2	-0.2
2016	COL	MLB	29	289	38	12	2	8	38	34	56	3	0	.264/.349/.424	.272	15.4	.305	3.4	SS(31): -6.0, 1B(16): 0.2	1.1
2017	ARI	MLB	30	398	47	16	5	10	51	48	89	4	0	.233/.332/.395	.256	5.1	.283	-3.2	2B(45): 0.9, LF(36): -4.8	0.1
2018	*ARI*	*MLB*	*31*	*331*	*35*	*15*	*2*	*7*	*36*	*33*	*69*	*3*	*1*	*.233/.311/.371*	*.236*	*3.2*	*.278*	*-0.1*	*2B 0, 3B -2*	*-0.2*
2019	*ARI*	*MLB*	*32*	*331*	*39*	*16*	*2*	*8*	*36*	*35*	*71*	*2*	*1*	*.236/.320/.387*	*.250*	*5.2*	*.280*	*-0.3*	*2B 0, 3B -2*	*0.3*

Breakout: 1% Improve: 46% Collapse: 6% Attrition: 19% MLB: 92% *Comparables: Luis Alicea, Bernie Allen, Jerry Hairston*

Descalso played well early on last season, but that went away quickly as the Diamondbacks continued to give him surprisingly regular playing time. He's no longer playing at Coors Field, but Arizona is about as good as it gets for non-Colorado hitter's parks. Descalso is back to hitting like, well, Descalso. He has also been below average on defense for four seasons in a row now, albeit with the usual versatility. Descalso's greatest skill seems to be the ability to not embarrass himself at various positions, which is not inconsequential. There will always be a demand for guys like Descalso, which means he'll probably stay in the league until his bat totally, completely atrophies.

Brandon Drury 2B Born: 08/21/92 Age: 25 Bats: R Throws: R Height: 6'2" Weight: 210 Origin: Round 13, 2010 Draft (#404 overall)

YEAR	TEAM	LVL	AGE	PA	R	2B	3B	HR	RBI	BB	K	SB	CS	AVG/OBP/SLG	TAv	VORP	BABIP	BRR	FRAA	WARP
2015	MOB	AA	22	291	22	14	1	3	36	11	41	4	5	.278/.306/.370	.252	5.1	.312	-0.7	2B(35): 2.1, 3B(33): 2.0	1.0
2015	RNO	AAA	22	276	43	26	0	2	25	21	35	0	2	.331/.384/.458	.279	13.0	.375	-1.0	3B(28): -2.8, 2B(27): -1.6	0.9
2015	ARI	MLB	22	59	3	3	0	2	8	2	8	0	0	.214/.254/.375	.205	-3.0	.217	-1.5	3B(11): -0.6, 2B(6): -0.1	-0.5
2016	ARI	MLB	23	499	59	31	1	16	53	31	100	1	1	.282/.329/.458	.270	18.6	.327	1.9	LF(62): -5.2, RF(32): -1.8	1.0
2017	ARI	MLB	24	480	41	37	2	13	63	28	103	1	1	.267/.317/.447	.262	10.1	.320	-3.9	2B(114): 2.5, 3B(1): -0.2	1.2
2018	*ARI*	*MLB*	*25*	*272*	*29*	*17*	*1*	*7*	*34*	*15*	*54*	*1*	*1*	*.262/.307/.423*	*.249*	*6.8*	*.305*	*-0.6*	*2B 1, 3B -1*	*0.5*
2019	*ARI*	*MLB*	*26*	*372*	*44*	*24*	*0*	*11*	*45*	*23*	*76*	*1*	*1*	*.259/.310/.427*	*.259*	*9.6*	*.303*	*-1.1*	*2B 1, 3B -1*	*1.1*

Breakout: 1% Improve: 53% Collapse: 10% Attrition: 16% MLB: 98% *Comparables: Kolten Wong, Jose Castillo, Josh Barfield*

Drury's bat has always been his carrying tool, so naturally it backed up a bit when he posted his first-ever positive FRAA mark. The end result was roughly the same; a spare-part player with a lot more value to a National League team. As of publication, the Diamondbacks still play in the NL, so that works out well for the former Braves prospect acquired in the January 2013 Justin Upton trade. Drury is younger than you probably think he is, so there's still a chance we see him suddenly start to demolish the ball, but until then he'll be a mediocre quasi-regular.

Reymond Fuentes CF Born: 02/12/91 Age: 27 Bats: L Throws: L Height: 6'0" Weight: 160 Origin: Round 1, 2009 Draft (#28 overall)

YEAR	TEAM	LVL	AGE	PA	R	2B	3B	HR	RBI	BB	K	SB	CS	AVG/OBP/SLG	TAv	VORP	BABIP	BRR	FRAA	WARP
2015	OMA	AAA	24	445	70	10	4	9	46	30	72	29	6	.308/.360/.422	.281	23.9	.356	2.7	CF(53): 5.5, LF(47): 4.1	3.6
2016	KCA	MLB	25	44	2	1	0	0	5	3	8	0	2	.317/.364/.341	.273	1.3	.394	-0.1	RF(9): 0.4, LF(3): -0.1	0.2
2016	OMA	AAA	25	272	32	9	3	0	14	23	62	17	5	.254/.325/.317	.245	5.7	.335	3.7	CF(27): -0.4, LF(20): 0.3	0.8
2017	RNO	AAA	26	192	30	11	3	0	14	12	30	13	1	.343/.385/.440	.266	10.5	.405	3.6	CF(28): -1.4, LF(15): 5.6	1.4
2017	ARI	MLB	26	145	19	1	2	3	9	8	35	4	1	.235/.278/.338	.225	-0.4	.296	0.5	CF(41): -2.5, LF(9): -0.4	-0.3
2018	*ARI*	*MLB*	*27*	*91*	*11*	*4*	*1*	*2*	*9*	*6*	*21*	*4*	*1*	*.264/.316/.380*	*.240*	*1.9*	*.327*	*0.4*	*CF 0*	*0.1*
2019	*ARI*	*MLB*	*28*	*289*	*33*	*11*	*2*	*6*	*30*	*22*	*68*	*12*	*3*	*.264/.326/.390*	*.252*	*7.5*	*.328*	*1.5*	*CF 0*	*0.8*

Breakout: 0% Improve: 21% Collapse: 8% Attrition: 15% MLB: 45% *Comparables: Nyjer Morgan, Craig Gentry, Jarrod Dyson*

Fuentes got into 64 games for Arizona, which isn't an inconsequential number. Unfortunately, those games were more *Superman 64* than *Super Mario 64*. He seemed to be playing with an outdated controller, or maybe on a crappy ROM hack. He couldn't get to the ball and he didn't do a whole lot of damage to it either. We'd say he should try the tutorial again, but this may just be who he is, as past production in the minors and past *Annual* comments will tell you. *Superman 64* may just be a bad game.

Paul Goldschmidt 1B Born: 09/10/87 Age: 30 Bats: R Throws: R Height: 6'3" Weight: 225 Origin: Round 8, 2009 Draft (#246 overall)

YEAR	TEAM	LVL	AGE	PA	R	2B	3B	HR	RBI	BB	K	SB	CS	AVG/OBP/SLG	TAv	VORP	BABIP	BRR	FRAA	WARP
2015	ARI	MLB	27	695	103	38	2	33	110	118	151	21	5	.321/.435/.570	.348	68.8	.382	2.4	1B(157): 17.0	9.2
2016	ARI	MLB	28	705	106	33	3	24	95	110	150	32	5	.297/.411/.489	.311	45.3	.358	1.5	1B(157): 16.1	6.3
2017	ARI	MLB	29	665	117	34	3	36	120	94	147	18	5	.297/.404/.563	.328	58.0	.343	3.7	1B(151): 5.7	6.4
2018	*ARI*	*MLB*	*30*	*628*	*100*	*34*	*2*	*29*	*97*	*91*	*140*	*19*	*4*	*.288/.394/.520*	*.308*	*43.8*	*.340*	*1.4*	*1B 9*	*5.0*
2019	*ARI*	*MLB*	*31*	*575*	*91*	*31*	*1*	*27*	*89*	*86*	*131*	*16*	*4*	*.288/.398/.524*	*.318*	*43.3*	*.342*	*1.6*	*1B 9*	*5.6*

Breakout: 1% Improve: 45% Collapse: 3% Attrition: 9% MLB: 99% *Comparables: Mark Teixeira, Stan Musial, Lance Berkman*

At some point, writing about excellence can get boring. You have to keep finding new ways to make excellence exciting, especially when that excellence is so constant, without any ebb and flow. You have to come up with stuff like "death, taxes and Paul Goldschmidt." "Life, the universe and Paul Goldschmidt." "Bears crapping in the woods, and Paul Goldschmidt."

At a certain point, though, you run out of superlatives and turns of phrase. You run out of ways to say that Goldschmidt is one of the most consistently lethal offensive players in baseball, along with being a good defender and a stunningly good baserunner for a first baseman. There are only so many ways you can say that the man they call "America's First Baseman" (Freddie Freeman couldn't be reached for comment) is the face of the franchise and will likely be for years to come. If the Diamondbacks continue their winning ways, the country as a whole will get a better taste of the show they've been missing in the desert. They'll experience the mind-numbing brilliance of Goldschmidt, and then it'll fade into more of watching paint dry and watching Goldschmidt be exemplary.

Jeremy Hazelbaker LF Born: 08/14/87 Age: 30 Bats: L Throws: R Height: 6'3" Weight: 190 Origin: Round 4, 2009 Draft (#138 overall)

YEAR	TEAM	LVL	AGE	PA	R	2B	3B	HR	RBI	BB	K	SB	CS	AVG/OBP/SLG	TAv	VORP	BABIP	BRR	FRAA	WARP
2015	TUL	AA	27	58	5	2	2	0	2	3	11	6	0	.245/.286/.358	.266	2.0	.310	0.6	LF(8): 0.0, RF(4): -0.1	0.2
2015	SFD	AA	27	168	30	13	3	3	20	18	33	10	0	.308/.394/.503	.300	12.4	.380	2.9	RF(31): -0.9	1.2
2015	MEM	AAA	27	233	38	10	7	10	46	23	60	8	2	.333/.403/.594	.357	27.4	.428	-0.6	RF(52): -2.7, CF(3): -0.3	2.5
2016	MEM	AAA	28	50	8	3	0	1	11	6	12	2	1	.325/.438/.475	.299	2.4	.444	-0.9	CF(6): -0.3, RF(4): 0.2	0.3
2016	SLN	MLB	28	224	35	7	3	12	28	18	64	5	2	.235/.295/.480	.283	9.2	.278	-1.6	LF(52): -2.1, CF(21): -1.2	0.5
2017	RNO	AAA	29	211	31	13	5	6	25	19	57	11	0	.279/.341/.495	.266	7.8	.364	0.7	LF(26): -0.7, CF(25): -0.8	0.6
2017	ARI	MLB	29	61	10	2	2	2	10	9	20	1	0	.346/.443/.577	.341	6.4	.533	-0.4	LF(11): -0.3, RF(8): 0.8	0.6
2018	*ARI*	*MLB*	*30*	*95*	*12*	*4*	*1*	*3*	*12*	*8*	*29*	*3*	*0*	*.248/.314/.446*	*.258*	*2.8*	*.325*	*0.5*	*LF 0*	*0.2*
2019	*ARI*	*MLB*	*31*	*179*	*23*	*7*	*2*	*7*	*23*	*16*	*56*	*5*	*1*	*.240/.315/.441*	*.262*	*4.6*	*.318*	*-0.3*	*LF -1*	*0.4*

Breakout: 5% Improve: 17% Collapse: 10% Attrition: 20% MLB: 49% *Comparables: Justin Ruggiano, Chris Aguila, Laynce Nix*

Hazelnuts aren't the sort of thing you usually find in cookies, but a quick search reveals several different recipes for, you guessed it, hazelnut cookies. They generally call for the hazelnuts to be toasted before being incorporated into the batter. In a turn of fate, it was Hazelbaker who toasted opposing pitchers during his brief work in Arizona. True to form, he struck out a lot, but the raw results are hard to argue with for fill-in work. A role off the bench or as an up-and-down guy indeed seems to be the recipe for success for Hazelbaker, who owns a career .500 SLG in 285 big-league plate appearances. If a front office were to consider combining him with chocolate in some sort of spreadable form, though, who knows what could happen?

Chris Herrmann C Born: 11/24/87 Age: 30 Bats: L Throws: R Height: 6'0" Weight: 200 Origin: Round 6, 2009 Draft (#192 overall)

YEAR	TEAM	LVL	AGE	PA	R	2B	3B	HR	RBI	BB	K	SB	CS	AVG/OBP/SLG	TAv	VORP	BABIP	BRR	FRAA	WARP
2015	ROC	AAA	27	88	9	3	0	1	6	11	13	3	0	.260/.364/.342	.266	3.3	.295	-0.4	C(17): 1.7, LF(1): 0.0	0.5
2015	MIN	MLB	27	113	13	5	1	2	10	7	37	0	0	.146/.214/.272	.186	-2.4	.203	1.0	C(38): -4.8, 1B(2): 0.0	-0.8
2016	RNO	AAA	28	28	3	1	0	0	3	3	8	0	0	.087/.214/.130	.151	-2.1	.125	0.3	C(3): 0.1, LF(2): 0.0	-0.2
2016	ARI	MLB	28	166	21	5	4	6	28	16	44	4	0	.284/.352/.493	.291	13.0	.364	1.1	C(31): -4.9, RF(4): 0.4	0.8
2017	ARI	MLB	29	256	35	7	0	10	27	29	67	5	0	.181/.273/.345	.224	1.2	.207	1.6	C(45): -4.5, LF(22): -2.0	-0.5
2018	*ARI*	*MLB*	*30*	*161*	*18*	*7*	*1*	*4*	*17*	*14*	*42*	*3*	*0*	*.219/.290/.363*	*.226*	*2.1*	*.278*	*0.4*	*C -5, RF 0*	*-0.5*
2019	*ARI*	*MLB*	*31*	*238*	*27*	*10*	*2*	*6*	*25*	*23*	*66*	*3*	*0*	*.211/.289/.360*	*.231*	*1.9*	*.271*	*0.9*	*C -6, RF 0*	*-0.5*

Breakout: 3% Improve: 26% Collapse: 9% Attrition: 25% MLB: 74% *Comparables: Rob Johnson, Carlos Corporan, Geronimo Gil*

Frequently called "The Herrmannator" by the team's Twitter account and by the Arizona broadcasters, the Diamondbacks' third catcher/outfielder/pinch-hitter probably should have requested more than boots, clothes and a motorcycle. Herrmann backslid from a shockingly strong 2016 campaign to slip under replacement level (and the Mendoza line) again. At age 30, this is probably who he is. Because he can play behind the plate and has some pop in his bat, he'll keep getting jobs. It'll take more than hitting .186 to stop a Cyberdyne Systems Model 101 Herrmannator. He'll be back.

YEAR	TEAM	P. COUNT	FRM RUNS	BLK RUNS	THRW RUNS	TOT RUNS
2015	MIN	4431	-4.3	-0.5	0.3	-4.5
2015	ROC	2119	1.5	0.1	0.1	1.7
2016	ARI	4304	-4.8	0.1	0.1	-4.7
2017	ARI	5360	-3.4	-0.2	-0.1	-3.7
2018	*ARI*	*4703*	*-4.1*	*-0.3*	*0.1*	*-4.3*
2019	*ARI*	*6944*	*-5.0*	*-0.3*	*0.1*	*-5.2*

Jake Lamb 3B Born: 10/09/90 Age: 27 Bats: L Throws: R Height: 6'3" Weight: 215 Origin: Round 6, 2012 Draft (#213 overall)

YEAR	TEAM	LVL	AGE	PA	R	2B	3B	HR	RBI	BB	K	SB	CS	AVG/OBP/SLG	TAv	VORP	BABIP	BRR	FRAA	WARP
2015	ARI	MLB	24	390	38	15	5	6	34	36	97	3	2	.263/.331/.386	.263	11.2	.344	-1.7	3B(95): 9.6, 1B(8): 0.4	2.3
2016	ARI	MLB	25	594	81	31	9	29	91	64	154	6	1	.249/.332/.509	.287	37.8	.294	2.3	3B(142): -5.0	3.4
2017	ARI	MLB	26	635	89	30	4	30	105	87	152	6	4	.248/.357/.487	.293	44.8	.287	2.0	3B(144): -10.8	3.4
2018	*ARI*	*MLB*	*27*	*602*	*78*	*30*	*5*	*24*	*84*	*64*	*153*	*5*	*2*	*.250/.333/.459*	*.270*	*26.1*	*.306*	*-0.3*	*3B -3*	*1.7*
2019	*ARI*	*MLB*	*28*	*572*	*78*	*30*	*4*	*24*	*80*	*66*	*147*	*4*	*2*	*.250/.339/.471*	*.282*	*27.6*	*.303*	*0.7*	*3B -2*	*2.8*

Breakout: 4% Improve: 47% Collapse: 3% Attrition: 6% MLB: 98% *Comparables: Edwin Encarnacion, Chase Headley, Kevin Kouzmanoff*

For the second year in a row, Lamb's excellent production hit the skids in the second half. He hit a robust .279/.376/.546 entering the All-Star break, but hovered around the Mendoza line thereafter. It's hard to pinpoint exactly why Lamb has had this happen two years in a row. Perhaps it's undisclosed nagging injuries. He's also still unable to do much of anything against lefty pitchers. This isn't all to say that Lamb is a bad player; he's pretty darn good when he's going right. It's just that "when he's going right" bit that makes him something of a tough nut to crack. Half a year of All-Star production isn't anything to be trifled with, but if he's going to make the leap to full-time greatness he'll need to break his habit of coming in like a lion and going out like, well, a lamb.

Ketel Marte SS Born: 10/12/93 Age: 24 Bats: B Throws: R Height: 6'1" Weight: 165 Origin: International Free Agent, 2010

YEAR	TEAM	LVL	AGE	PA	R	2B	3B	HR	RBI	BB	K	SB	CS	AVG/OBP/SLG	TAv	VORP	BABIP	BRR	FRAA	WARP
2015	TAC	AAA	21	287	41	12	2	3	29	20	32	20	3	.314/.359/.410	.279	19.5	.345	3.3	SS(49): -0.1, 2B(14): 0.2	2.1
2015	SEA	MLB	21	247	25	14	3	2	17	24	43	8	4	.283/.351/.402	.289	15.9	.341	-0.5	SS(51): 4.5, 2B(4): 0.4	2.2
2016	TAC	AAA	22	31	5	2	0	0	2	2	1	2	0	.214/.258/.286	.253	1.2	.214	0.5	SS(5): -0.5	0.1
2016	SEA	MLB	22	466	55	21	2	1	33	18	84	11	5	.259/.287/.323	.219	2.5	.313	2.6	SS(119): -1.5	0.1
2017	RNO	AAA	23	338	62	23	7	6	41	25	34	7	2	.338/.391/.514	.295	31.2	.365	3.8	SS(59): 2.1, CF(5): 1.6	3.5
2017	ARI	MLB	23	255	30	11	2	5	18	29	37	3	1	.260/.345/.395	.267	14.1	.290	1.5	SS(64): -0.1, 3B(3): 0.1	1.4
2018	*ARI*	*MLB*	*24*	*542*	*59*	*30*	*5*	*8*	*56*	*38*	*88*	*12*	*4*	*.275/.326/.402*	*.251*	*21.6*	*.317*	*0.6*	*SS 2*	*1.6*
2019	*ARI*	*MLB*	*25*	*512*	*60*	*30*	*4*	*11*	*57*	*39*	*85*	*11*	*4*	*.283/.339/.432*	*.272*	*26.0*	*.324*	*2.0*	*SS 2*	*3.0*

Breakout: 4% Improve: 49% Collapse: 5% Attrition: 10% MLB: 98% *Comparables: Andrelton Simmons, Ruben Tejada, Jean Segura*

Many comments in this book, including some in this very chapter, are composed largely of puns or jokes based on the name of the player. Some of the best comments in *BP Annual* history have come about this way. Marte will receive no such treatment. He filled in admirably at shortstop following the injury to Nick Ahmed, and shined in Arizona's brief playoff run. It would be a stretch to call Marte a "dynamic" player, but his combination of defense, speed and an adequate bat makes him the sort of guy who can make things happen in a game and is great fun to watch when it's all clicking. It'll be interesting to see what happens between him and Ahmed in spring training. He's just 24, so there's still some time to see if his talent will come to more of a boil, and if that steam translates to even more in-game success. Aw, dang it.

J.D. Martinez RF Born: 08/21/87 Age: 30 Bats: R Throws: R Height: 6'3" Weight: 220 Origin: Round 20, 2009 Draft (#611 overall)

YEAR	TEAM	LVL	AGE	PA	R	2B	3B	HR	RBI	BB	K	SB	CS	AVG/OBP/SLG	TAv	VORP	BABIP	BRR	FRAA	WARP
2015	DET	MLB	27	657	93	33	2	38	102	53	178	3	2	.282/.344/.535	.304	35.1	.339	-3.9	RF(148): -7.5	3.0
2016	TOL	AAA	28	38	3	3	0	0	5	1	11	1	0	.278/.316/.361	.248	0.4	.400	0.5	RF(2): 0.4	0.1
2016	DET	MLB	28	517	69	35	2	22	68	49	128	1	2	.307/.373/.535	.302	24.0	.378	-7.3	RF(118): -11.2	1.3
2017	DET	MLB	29	232	38	13	2	16	39	29	54	2	0	.305/.388/.630	.322	17.9	.338	-1.5	RF(53): -6.3	1.2
2017	ARI	MLB	29	257	47	13	1	29	65	24	74	2	0	.302/.366/.741	.350	26.6	.315	-2.4	RF(60): -3.9	2.3
2018	*ARI*	*MLB*	*30*	*473*	*66*	*28*	*2*	*28*	*80*	*39*	*131*	*3*	*1*	*.281/.343/.546*	*.290*	*24.4*	*.340*	*-3.6*	*RF -8*	*1.8*
2019	*ARI*	*MLB*	*31*	*463*	*69*	*28*	*1*	*26*	*78*	*39*	*129*	*2*	*1*	*.275/.339/.538*	*.301*	*26.0*	*.334*	*-3.6*	*RF -8*	*2.0*

Breakout: 0% Improve: 43% Collapse: 1% Attrition: 8% MLB: 100% *Comparables: Matt Kemp, Reggie Jackson, Carlos Gonzalez*

Perhaps it was an act of divine providence that someone named Just Dingers Martinez would end up playing professional baseball. Public records may indicate that his given name is Julio Daniel, but we know the truth. Martinez has quietly been one of the best right-handed hitters in the game for years now, and the Diamondbacks got him for a song from Detroit at midseason. He touched down in Arizona and promptly did his best to live up to that name of his, which the Diamondbacks' broadcasters were so fond of calling him. He went as far as to have a four-homer game, only the 18th player to ever do so. He also hit for plenty of average, finishing above .300 for the third time in four years. Most impressively he launched 45 homers despite missing 43 games, which makes you wonder what he can do if he plays a full season.

Jeff Mathis C Born: 03/31/83 Age: 35 Bats: R Throws: R Height: 6'0" Weight: 205 Origin: Round 1, 2001 Draft (#33 overall)

YEAR	TEAM	LVL	AGE	PA	R	2B	3B	HR	RBI	BB	K	SB	CS	AVG/OBP/SLG	TAv	VORP	BABIP	BRR	FRAA	WARP
2015	MIA	MLB	32	103	9	4	1	2	12	7	24	0	0	.161/.214/.290	.202	-1.6	.186	-0.2	C(30): 4.4	0.3
2016	MIA	MLB	33	132	12	4	1	2	15	4	36	0	0	.238/.267/.333	.230	1.9	.318	0.0	C(38): 8.4	1.1
2017	ARI	MLB	34	203	13	10	2	2	11	14	61	1	0	.215/.277/.323	.207	-1.5	.309	0.4	C(58): 7.0	0.6
2018	*ARI*	*MLB*	*35*	*307*	*28*	*12*	*1*	*6*	*29*	*20*	*94*	*1*	*0*	*.204/.258/.322*	*.202*	*-3.3*	*.279*	*-0.4*	*C 12*	*0.5*
2019	*ARI*	*MLB*	*36*	*220*	*22*	*9*	*1*	*5*	*21*	*17*	*71*	*0*	*0*	*.202/.266/.328*	*.212*	*-2.4*	*.280*	*0.0*	*C 9*	*0.8*

Breakout: 4% Improve: 34% Collapse: 14% Attrition: 39% MLB: 88%

Comparables: Jose Molina, Paul Bako, Mike Matheny

YEAR	TEAM	P. COUNT	FRM RUNS	BLK RUNS	THRW RUNS	TOT RUNS
2015	JAX	322	0.1	0.0	0.0	0.1
2015	MIA	4146	3.2	0.5	0.1	3.7
2015	NWO	377	0.1	0.0	0.0	0.1
2016	MIA	5038	7.2	0.8	-0.1	7.8
2017	ARI	7723	5.7	-0.5	1.0	6.2
2018	*ARI*	*11784*	*10.1*	*0.4*	*0.7*	*11.3*
2019	*ARI*	*8428*	*8.0*	*0.3*	*0.6*	*8.9*

When you think of defense-first catchers, you think of dudes like Jose Molina. The middle Molina brother is one of the best defensive backstops ever, a true monster of pitch framing who compiled nearly 200 FRAA in his illustrious career despite part-time roles. He also couldn't hit a lick. Mathis has had a worse offensive career than Molina. He has a worse career TAv than almost everyone. Mathis cannot hit. He can, however, catch. He does that very, very well. He's stuck around for 13 seasons now as a backup catcher and pitching staff manager, and teams keep bringing him back and paying him millions of dollars. That's really damn impressive. You go, Jeff Mathis.

John Ryan Murphy C Born: 05/13/91 Age: 27 Bats: R Throws: R Height: 5'11" Weight: 205 Origin: Round 2, 2009 Draft (#76 overall)

YEAR	TEAM	LVL	AGE	PA	R	2B	3B	HR	RBI	BB	K	SB	CS	AVG/OBP/SLG	TAv	VORP	BABIP	BRR	FRAA	WARP
2015	NYA	MLB	24	172	21	9	1	3	14	12	43	0	0	.277/.327/.406	.258	7.2	.357	0.2	C(65): -3.2	0.4
2016	ROC	AAA	25	290	24	14	0	3	39	21	51	0	0	.236/.286/.323	.229	2.0	.274	-1.4	C(80): 17.8	2.0
2016	MIN	MLB	25	90	4	3	0	1	3	5	19	0	0	.146/.193/.220	.162	-5.2	.175	-0.3	C(25): -1.3	-0.7
2017	ROC	AAA	26	218	21	9	0	4	27	22	36	0	0	.222/.298/.330	.225	2.2	.250	1.0	C(53): 19.4	2.1
2017	RNO	AAA	26	75	5	0	0	2	7	7	7	0	0	.284/.351/.373	.247	2.1	.293	-0.4	C(19): 3.0	0.5
2017	ARI	MLB	26	7	0	1	0	0	1	0	1	0	0	.143/.143/.286	.045	-1.3	.167	-0.1	C(5): 0.1	-0.1
2018	*ARI*	*MLB*	*27*	*184*	*19*	*9*	*0*	*5*	*20*	*13*	*40*	*0*	*0*	*.239/.295/.381*	*.232*	*3.8*	*.284*	*-0.4*	*C 4*	*0.6*
2019	*ARI*	*MLB*	*28*	*192*	*22*	*10*	*0*	*5*	*22*	*15*	*45*	*0*	*0*	*.238/.298/.392*	*.242*	*3.8*	*.287*	*-0.1*	*C 4*	*0.9*

Breakout: 9% Improve: 24% Collapse: 23% Attrition: 42% MLB: 69%

Comparables: Rob Johnson, Steve Clevenger, Bryan Holaday

YEAR	TEAM	P. COUNT	FRM RUNS	BLK RUNS	THRW RUNS	TOT RUNS
2015	NYA	6891	-0.7	-1.7	-0.1	-2.5
2016	MIN	3340	0.8	-1.7	0.1	-0.7
2017	ARI	249	0.0	0.1	0.0	0.1
2018	*ARI*	*7041*	*6.1*	*-1.2*	*0.1*	*5.0*
2019	*ARI*	*7345*	*4.7*	*-0.9*	*0.0*	*3.8*

A midseason trade for lefty relief prospect Gabriel Moya brought Murphy from Minnesota to Arizona. More accurately, it brought him from Rochester to Reno, a swap of Triple-A locales. Murphy provides some defensive value, but until he proves he can hit at least a little, he'll continue to be a tweener. Minnesota's decision to trade a now broken-out Aaron Hicks for him in November 2015 looks bad. Since that deal, Hicks has nearly twice as many homers (23) as Murphy has hits (13) in the majors.

Chris Owings SS Born: 08/12/91 Age: 26 Bats: R Throws: R Height: 5'10" Weight: 185 Origin: Round 1, 2009 Draft (#41 overall)

YEAR	TEAM	LVL	AGE	PA	R	2B	3B	HR	RBI	BB	K	SB	CS	AVG/OBP/SLG	TAv	VORP	BABIP	BRR	FRAA	WARP
2015	ARI	MLB	23	552	59	27	5	4	43	26	144	16	4	.227/.264/.322	.213	-7.5	.305	1.9	2B(115): -4.7, SS(35): -5.0	-1.8
2016	ARI	MLB	24	466	52	24	11	5	49	20	87	21	2	.277/.315/.416	.251	14.7	.334	1.9	SS(70): -3.5, CF(49): -1.9	1.0
2017	ARI	MLB	25	386	41	25	1	12	51	17	87	12	2	.268/.299/.442	.266	14.9	.318	-0.6	SS(54): 4.2, RF(25): 1.5	2.1
2018	*ARI*	*MLB*	*26*	*330*	*38*	*17*	*3*	*6*	*33*	*15*	*72*	*11*	*2*	*.257/.291/.395*	*.234*	*4.6*	*.312*	*1.7*	*2B -2, SS 0*	*0.0*
2019	*ARI*	*MLB*	*27*	*397*	*44*	*22*	*3*	*10*	*45*	*20*	*88*	*13*	*3*	*.263/.304/.417*	*.252*	*9.9*	*.317*	*0.8*	*2B -3, SS 0*	*0.7*

Breakout: 6% Improve: 59% Collapse: 11% Attrition: 16% MLB: 97%

Comparables: Adeiny Hechavarria, Freddy Galvis, Marwin Gonzalez

A fractured finger sustained during a bunt attempt put an end to what was easily Owings' best season in the big leagues. It was a good reminder that in due time, everything fractures in its own way. Our faith in humanity. Our belief that Pauly Shore is funny. Our desire to devour any handful of M&M's within reach. Perhaps that third one never truly fractures, or instead just heals rather quickly. Similarly, Owings should be ready for Opening Day following a pair of surgeries on the finger. There's no way of telling whether he's ready to give *Bio-Dome* another try.

David Peralta RF Born: 08/14/87 Age: 30 Bats: L Throws: L Height: 6'1" Weight: 210 Origin: International Free Agent, 2005

YEAR	TEAM	LVL	AGE	PA	R	2B	3B	HR	RBI	BB	K	SB	CS	AVG/OBP/SLG	TAv	VORP	BABIP	BRR	FRAA	WARP
2015	ARI	MLB	27	517	61	26	10	17	78	44	107	9	4	.312/.371/.522	.320	39.7	.368	-1.2	LF(124): 4.6, RF(9): -0.3	4.7
2016	RNO	AAA	28	34	6	4	0	0	2	4	5	0	0	.276/.353/.414	.250	0.2	.320	0.0	RF(9): 0.3	0.1
2016	ARI	MLB	28	183	23	9	5	4	15	8	42	2	0	.251/.295/.433	.253	4.7	.310	2.4	RF(44): 0.0, CF(8): -0.4	0.5
2017	ARI	MLB	29	577	82	31	3	14	57	43	94	8	4	.293/.352/.444	.283	24.6	.333	-0.9	RF(78): 10.0, LF(50): 2.3	3.7
2018	*ARI*	*MLB*	*30*	*594*	*79*	*30*	*7*	*16*	*67*	*40*	*112*	*8*	*3*	*.275/.329/.446*	*.264*	*17.7*	*.318*	*0.2*	*RF 18*	*3.3*
2019	*ARI*	*MLB*	*31*	*516*	*64*	*26*	*6*	*16*	*65*	*39*	*104*	*6*	*3*	*.271/.331/.452*	*.275*	*18.7*	*.316*	*0.0*	*RF 17*	*3.9*

Breakout: 1% Improve: 41% Collapse: 10% Attrition: 18% MLB: 94%

Comparables: Nate Schierholtz, Roger Bernadina, Josh Reddick

Though he didn't hit quite as well as he did in his ridiculous 2015 campaign, simply being on the field for a full season proved more than enough for Peralta to once again provide big value. Peralta didn't hit for his usual power, but his on-base skills and best-ever defense more than compensated. It stands to reason that Arizona hopes he'll hit the ball over the fence again this year. If he does, he's an All-Star and strong "most underrated player in the league" candidate. If he doesn't, he'll still be a pretty darn good player.

A.J. Pollock CF Born: 12/05/87 Age: 30 Bats: R Throws: R Height: 6'1" Weight: 195 Origin: Round 1, 2009 Draft (#17 overall)

YEAR	TEAM	LVL	AGE	PA	R	2B	3B	HR	RBI	BB	K	SB	CS	AVG/OBP/SLG	TAv	VORP	BABIP	BRR	FRAA	WARP
2015	ARI	MLB	27	673	111	39	6	20	76	53	89	39	7	.315/.367/.498	.306	57.9	.338	7.9	CF(151): -7.9	5.3
2016	ARI	MLB	28	46	9	0	0	2	4	5	8	4	0	.244/.326/.390	.252	2.8	.258	1.8	CF(12): 1.5	0.4
2017	ARI	MLB	29	466	73	33	6	14	49	35	71	20	6	.266/.330/.471	.286	28.1	.291	0.7	CF(109): 0.4	2.9
2018	*ARI*	*MLB*	*30*	*585*	*88*	*35*	*5*	*17*	*65*	*44*	*92*	*27*	*7*	*.276/.333/.457*	*.269*	*31.4*	*.305*	*3.4*	*CF -3*	*2.4*
2019	*ARI*	*MLB*	*31*	*483*	*61*	*30*	*4*	*16*	*63*	*37*	*81*	*21*	*6*	*.275/.334/.465*	*.281*	*28.3*	*.305*	*3.3*	*CF -1*	*2.9*

Breakout: 1% Improve: 43% Collapse: 7% Attrition: 3% MLB: 97% *Comparables: Jacoby Ellsbury, Jon Jay, Shane Victorino*

A groin injury prevented Pollock's grand return from being truly grand, but he still offered the usual dynamic power/speed dual threat when he was on the field. Providing nearly 3.0 WARP in just 112 games speaks to the type of player he is, but he has trouble staying in the lineup, having played more than 130 games in just two seasons and having never cracked 100 games in back-to-back years. It's possible that Pollock will never again reach the MVP-caliber heights of his 2015 season, but his all-around game is rare, and a hitter-friendly home ballpark pretties up his raw numbers.

Adam Rosales UT Born: 05/20/83 Age: 35 Bats: R Throws: R Height: 6'2" Weight: 200 Origin: Round 12, 2005 Draft (#362 overall)

YEAR	TEAM	LVL	AGE	PA	R	2B	3B	HR	RBI	BB	K	SB	CS	AVG/OBP/SLG	TAv	VORP	BABIP	BRR	FRAA	WARP
2015	TEX	MLB	32	125	14	4	0	3	7	10	30	4	4	.228/.296/.342	.229	-0.2	.284	0.7	1B(19): 0.5, 2B(19): 1.6	0.1
2016	SDN	MLB	33	248	37	12	3	13	35	29	88	4	0	.229/.319/.495	.287	15.8	.308	1.2	3B(41): 3.3, 2B(36): -1.4	1.9
2017	OAK	MLB	34	223	15	11	0	4	27	10	66	1	1	.234/.273/.346	.225	0.8	.319	-0.1	SS(55): -0.1, 2B(8): -1.5	-0.1
2017	ARI	MLB	34	89	10	5	0	3	9	1	34	0	1	.202/.227/.369	.196	-2.8	.292	0.2	3B(11): 1.0, SS(10): 0.2	-0.2
2018	*ARI*	*MLB*	*35*	*280*	*31*	*13*	*1*	*8*	*31*	*21*	*81*	*3*	*2*	*.228/.292/.388*	*.227*	*3.4*	*.295*	*0.7*	*SS 2, 2B 0*	*0.6*
2019	*ARI*	*MLB*	*36*	*216*	*24*	*9*	*1*	*6*	*23*	*16*	*64*	*2*	*1*	*.217/.283/.365*	*.232*	*1.2*	*.285*	*0.6*	*SS 1, 2B 0*	*0.3*

Breakout: 2% Improve: 29% Collapse: 14% Attrition: 35% MLB: 73% *Comparables: Alex Gonzalez, Clint Barmes, Bill Almon*

For a moment, the world didn't make sense. Rosales wasn't playing for the A's or the Rangers, and he was hitting dingers. Lots of dingers. Well, 13 isn't that many, but it's a lot for Rosales. Then the world was righted once more, and Rosales signed with Oakland. For a time, peace and tranquility seeped back into the realm. There was much joy and celebration. Crops flourished, children were merry, lovers felt closer. Things were as they were meant to be, for Rosales was back where he belonged. Then horror struck, and Rosales was traded to the Diamondbacks. Fire rained from the skies and the screams of the innocent filled the air once more. The harmony had been broken. And there was only despair.

Pavin Smith 1B Born: 02/06/96 Age: 22 Bats: L Throws: L Height: 6'2" Weight: 210 Origin: Round 1, 2017 Draft (#7 overall)

YEAR	TEAM	LVL	AGE	PA	R	2B	3B	HR	RBI	BB	K	SB	CS	AVG/OBP/SLG	TAv	VORP	BABIP	BRR	FRAA	WARP
2017	YAK	A-	21	223	34	15	2	0	27	27	24	2	1	.318/.401/.415	.319	14.6	.363	-1.8	1B(42): 1.0	1.6
2018	*ARI*	*MLB*	*22*	*250*	*23*	*12*	*1*	*6*	*27*	*20*	*62*	*0*	*0*	*.224/.290/.361*	*.215*	*-7.3*	*.279*	*-0.4*	*1B 1*	*-0.7*
2019	*ARI*	*MLB*	*23*	*280*	*32*	*13*	*1*	*8*	*31*	*23*	*69*	*0*	*0*	*.230/.297/.381*	*.240*	*-3.0*	*.282*	*-0.5*	*1B 1*	*-0.3*

Breakout: 9% Improve: 11% Collapse: 2% Attrition: 13% MLB: 15% *Comparables: James Loney, Russ Canzler, Jose Osuna*

Drafting a first baseman with the seventh overall pick usually means one of two things: The team thinks he can hit the snot out of the ball or he can move to a different position. Fortunately, there's a decent amount of evidence that Smith can hit the snot out of the ball. Smith waltzed his way to a .342/.427/.570 line in his junior campaign at Virginia, setting a school single-season RBI record and being named a semifinalist for the Golden Spikes award. He's an advanced bat, he oozes OBP and he took to pro ball very well. There's some guy named Paul Goldschmidt currently at first base in Arizona, but don't be surprised if Smith surfaces in the big leagues quickly. Nobody will ever truly replace Goldy, but Smith's as good a choice to develop as a caddy as anyone.

Yasmany Tomas LF Born: 11/14/90 Age: 27 Bats: R Throws: R Height: 6'2" Weight: 250 Origin: International Free Agent, 2014

YEAR	TEAM	LVL	AGE	PA	R	2B	3B	HR	RBI	BB	K	SB	CS	AVG/OBP/SLG	TAv	VORP	BABIP	BRR	FRAA	WARP
2015	ARI	MLB	24	426	40	19	3	9	48	17	110	5	2	.273/.305/.401	.246	3.2	.354	-0.1	RF(57): -1.8, 3B(31): -2.8	-0.2
2016	ARI	MLB	25	563	72	30	1	31	83	31	136	2	4	.272/.313/.508	.276	19.5	.310	-0.8	RF(91): -10.9, LF(60): -8.8	0.0
2017	ARI	MLB	26	180	19	11	1	8	32	13	50	0	0	.241/.294/.464	.271	5.9	.294	-0.3	LF(42): -7.0	-0.1
2018	*ARI*	*MLB*	*27*	*511*	*62*	*26*	*2*	*22*	*73*	*28*	*129*	*3*	*2*	*.257/.300/.455*	*.255*	*13.8*	*.307*	*-1.0*	*LF -18*	*-0.9*
2019	*ARI*	*MLB*	*28*	*431*	*56*	*23*	*1*	*19*	*61*	*26*	*110*	*2*	*1*	*.256/.303/.460*	*.265*	*12.7*	*.306*	*-0.3*	*LF -15*	*-0.2*

Breakout: 3% Improve: 59% Collapse: 2% Attrition: 9% MLB: 94% *Comparables: Bob Nieman, Randy Elliott, Elston Howard*

Core muscle issues that wound up requiring surgery cut Tomas' season short. Although he had been a good power source in 2016, Arizona clearly got along just fine without him last year. Tomas has always been a bit of a cumbersome fit on the Diamondbacks' roster (or any NL roster, for that matter), and trade rumors are forever swirling. Power as a standalone tool has less value now than at just about any time in baseball history, and Tomas is awful at every other aspect of the sport. Plopped into a different era he might be praised as an "RBI man" and rewarded for slugging 25-30 homers per season, but he's much closer to a replacement-level player than an All-Star.

Christian Walker 1B Born: 03/28/91 Age: 27 Bats: R Throws: R Height: 6'0" Weight: 220 Origin: Round 4, 2012 Draft (#132 overall)

YEAR	TEAM	LVL	AGE	PA	R	2B	3B	HR	RBI	BB	K	SB	CS	AVG/OBP/SLG	TAv	VORP	BABIP	BRR	FRAA	WARP
2015	NOR	AAA	24	592	68	33	1	18	74	49	136	1	3	.257/.324/.423	.262	8.5	.311	1.4	1B(130): -2.8	0.6
2015	BAL	MLB	24	12	0	0	0	0	0	3	4	0	0	.111/.333/.111	.208	-0.4	.200	0.0	1B(2): 0.0	-0.1
2016	NOR	AAA	25	552	64	29	2	18	64	40	138	1	3	.264/.321/.437	.263	11.4	.327	-0.5	LF(90): -6.1, 1B(5): 0.2	0.6
2017	RNO	AAA	26	592	104	34	9	32	114	61	104	5	2	.309/.382/.597	.304	38.8	.327	2.1	1B(119): -6.2, 3B(9): 0.4	3.1
2017	ARI	MLB	26	15	2	1	0	2	2	1	5	0	0	.250/.400/.833	.388	2.4	.200	0.0	1B(1): 0.0	0.2
2018	*ARI*	*MLB*	*27*	*46*	*6*	*2*	*0*	*2*	*6*	*4*	*13*	*0*	*0*	*.247/.313/.456*	*.260*	*1.0*	*.305*	*-0.1*	*1B 0*	*0.0*
2019	*ARI*	*MLB*	*28*	*290*	*39*	*14*	*1*	*14*	*42*	*25*	*84*	*0*	*0*	*.244/.315/.468*	*.271*	*7.5*	*.302*	*-0.6*	*1B -2*	*0.6*

Breakout: 1% Improve: 10% Collapse: 11% Attrition: 17% MLB: 29% *Comparables: Daniel Dorn, Andy Wilkins, Juan Miranda*

After five seasons in the Orioles' farm system, Walker bounced around waivers last spring before ending up at Triple-A for the Diamondbacks. He dominated there, posting huge, PCL-inflated numbers to win league MVP honors before going deep twice in a September call-up to Arizona. He even made the Diamondbacks' postseason roster, but that shouldn't necessarily be taken as a sign that he's in their plans. Something of a tweener without great power or patience before the 2017 breakout, Walker will need to find a new organization if he wants to get consistent at-bats in the majors.

PITCHERS

Anthony Banda LHP Born: 08/10/93 Age: 24 Bats: L Throws: L Height: 6'2" Weight: 190 Origin: Round 10, 2012 Draft (#335 overall)

YEAR	TEAM	LVL	AGE	W	L	SV	G	GS	IP	H	HR	BB/9	K/9	K	GB%	BABIP	WHIP	ERA	DRA	WARP	MPH	CMD	PWR	STM
2015	VIS	A+	21	8	8	0	28	27	151^{2}	150	8	2.3	9.0	152	48%	.336	1.25	3.32	2.62	4.5				
2016	MOB	AA	22	6	2	0	13	13	76^{1}	70	4	3.3	9.9	84	50%	.317	1.28	2.12	1.78	3.0				
2016	RNO	AAA	22	4	4	0	13	13	73^{2}	73	6	3.3	8.3	68	46%	.313	1.36	3.67	3.41	1.6				
2017	RNO	AAA	23	8	7	0	22	22	122	125	15	3.8	8.6	116	43%	.317	1.44	5.39	4.25	1.9				
2017	ARI	MLB	23	2	3	0	8	4	25^{2}	26	1	3.5	8.8	25	39%	.329	1.40	5.96	4.96	0.1	96.5	51	57	66
2018	*ARI*	*MLB*	*24*	*3*	*3*	*0*	*21*	*7*	*51*	*51*	*8*	*3.7*	*9.3*	*54*	*44%*	*.303*	*1.41*	*4.26*	*4.63*	*0.3*	*96.3*	*53*	*59*	*68*
2019	*ARI*	*MLB*	*25*	*8*	*7*	*0*	*61*	*19*	*157*	*145*	*24*	*3.3*	*9.5*	*166*	*44%*	*.318*	*1.29*	*4.25*	*4.85*	*1.0*	*96.1*	*53*	*59*	*69*

Breakout: 13% Improve: 33% Collapse: 19% Attrition: 27% MLB: 58% *Comparables: Nick Tropeano, Ross Stripling, Frankie Montas*

Roger Clemens. Brandon Belt. Andy Pettitte. Patrick Swazye. These are some of the illustrious alumni of San Jacinto College, and the impressive company that Banda is trying to join. He'll at the very least be mentioned among the school's notable attendees after he made the big leagues last year. He's no longer the team's top prospect, though, between his rough season in Reno and Arizona, and the ascension of guys like Jon Duplantier. He's still got plenty of time to take another run or two at the bigs and settle in, so there's still a good chance he'll have more notoriety at San Jacinto than Sean Nolin.

Brad Boxberger RHP Born: 05/27/88 Age: 30 Bats: R Throws: R Height: 6'2" Weight: 205 Origin: Round 1, 2009 Draft (#43 overall)

YEAR	TEAM	LVL	AGE	W	L	SV	G	GS	IP	H	HR	BB/9	K/9	K	GB%	BABIP	WHIP	ERA	DRA	WARP	MPH	CMD	PWR	STM
2015	TBA	MLB	27	4	10	41	69	0	63	54	9	4.6	10.6	74	37%	.292	1.37	3.71	3.26	1.1	95.1	44	48	52
2016	TBA	MLB	28	4	3	0	27	0	24^{1}	23	3	7.0	8.1	22	49%	.294	1.73	4.81	5.21	-0.1	94.5	38	44	34
2017	TBA	MLB	29	4	4	0	30	0	29^{1}	23	4	3.4	12.3	40	46%	.292	1.16	3.38	3.44	0.6	94.2	34	49	41
2018	*ARI*	*MLB*	*30*	*2*	*2*	*6*	*46*	*0*	*49*	*45*	*8*	*4.5*	*10.7*	*58*	*42%*	*.304*	*1.44*	*4.58*	*4.81*	*0.1*	*93.9*	*39*	*47*	*41*
2019	*ARI*	*MLB*	*31*	*2*	*1*	*3*	*45*	*0*	*47^{1}*	*40*	*8*	*4.6*	*10.9*	*57*	*42%*	*.307*	*1.35*	*4.63*	*5.30*	*-0.1*	*93.2*	*37*	*47*	*39*

Breakout: 19% Improve: 41% Collapse: 25% Attrition: 17% MLB: 88% *Comparables: Steve Delabar, Boone Logan, Vinnie Pestano*

Boxberger's closed-front, stiff delivery makes his sheer stuff (average fastball, pretty good changeup) play down a bit, but he spots and mixes it well enough to keep opponents on the defensive. He upped his slider usage in 2017, trying to get fellow righties out more consistently. It didn't work, but it didn't compromise his effectiveness, either. He remains a great reverse-split right-handed reliever, but one who must be used almost like a LOOGY. He reached the end of the line in Tampa Bay, but will now get high-leverage work in Arizona.

Archie Bradley RHP Born: 08/10/92 Age: 25 Bats: R Throws: R Height: 6'4" Weight: 225 Origin: Round 1, 2011 Draft (#7 overall)

YEAR	TEAM	LVL	AGE	W	L	SV	G	GS	IP	H	HR	BB/9	K/9	K	GB%	BABIP	WHIP	ERA	DRA	WARP	MPH	CMD	PWR	STM
2015	ARI	MLB	22	2	3	0	8	8	35^{2}	36	3	5.6	5.8	23	60%	.297	1.63	5.80	6.17	-0.5	94.4	33	54	25
2015	RNO	AAA	22	1	0	0	4	4	21^{1}	26	3	2.1	8.4	20	40%	.359	1.45	2.95	3.53	0.4				
2016	RNO	AAA	23	5	1	0	7	7	40^{2}	26	0	4.0	10.4	47	64%	.289	1.08	1.99	1.19	1.9				
2016	ARI	MLB	23	8	9	0	26	26	141^{2}	154	16	4.3	9.1	143	47%	.338	1.56	5.02	5.18	0.3	95.1	49	52	79
2017	ARI	MLB	24	3	3	1	63	0	73	55	4	2.6	9.7	79	49%	.276	1.04	1.73	3.71	1.2	98.0	51	71	50
2018	*ARI*	*MLB*	*25*	*2*	*2*	*30*	*51*	*0*	*54*	*45*	*5*	*3.7*	*10.3*	*62*	*48%*	*.297*	*1.25*	*2.91*	*3.43*	*0.9*	*95.8*	*49*	*60*	*55*
2019	*ARI*	*MLB*	*26*	*3*	*1*	*32*	*63*	*0*	*67*	*50*	*7*	*3.5*	*10.9*	*81*	*48%*	*.3*	*1.13*	*3.21*	*3.67*	*1.1*	*95.8*	*50*	*60*	*60*

Breakout: 33% Improve: 60% Collapse: 15% Attrition: 13% MLB: 92% *Comparables: Ubaldo Jimenez, Jon Lester, Sonny Gray*

The former seventh overall pick's struggles in a starting role saw him open the year in the bullpen, and boy did it work. Bradley has always had the pure stuff to mow through hitters and quickly found himself doing just that while setting up Fernando Rodney. Bradley became a local star, bounding off the mound and revving up crowds of fans wearing fake bushy Bradley beards. "This is our house!" he shouted to the Chase Field faithful after an overpowering inning against the Dodgers in the home stretch of the playoff run. So rarely has a setup man been so wildly loved by fans. When Bradley hit a two-run triple in the wild card game to help send the Rockies home, it was the pinnacle of absurdity. He isn't starting, but after hearing about the promise of Bradley for years, Arizona fans are getting to see what the hype is all about.

Andrew Chafin LHP Born: 06/17/90 Age: 27 Bats: R Throws: L Height: 6'2" Weight: 225 Origin: Round 1, 2011 Draft (#43 overall)

YEAR	TEAM	LVL	AGE	W	L	SV	G	GS	IP	H	HR	BB/9	K/9	K	GB%	BABIP	WHIP	ERA	DRA	WARP	MPH	CMD	PWR	STM
2015	ARI	MLB	25	5	1	2	66	0	75	56	3	3.6	7.0	58	60%	.248	1.15	2.76	3.39	1.2	95.6	46	56	52
2016	ARI	MLB	26	0	1	0	32	0	22^{2}	22	1	4.4	11.1	28	52%	.368	1.46	6.75	3.30	0.4	96.0	42	57	34
2017	ARI	MLB	27	1	0	0	71	0	51^{1}	48	5	3.7	10.7	61	58%	.326	1.34	3.51	3.60	0.9	95.1	41	51	47
2018	*ARI*	*MLB*	*28*	*2*	*2*	*0*	*46*	*0*	*49*	*41*	*5*	*4.0*	*10.1*	*55*	*52%*	*.295*	*1.29*	*3.35*	*3.82*	*0.6*	*94.9*	*43*	*54*	*44*
2019	*ARI*	*MLB*	*29*	*3*	*1*	*0*	*61*	*0*	*64^{1}*	*49*	*7*	*3.8*	*10.9*	*77*	*52%*	*.301*	*1.18*	*3.50*	*4.00*	*0.8*	*94.5*	*42*	*53*	*43*

Breakout: 19% Improve: 38% Collapse: 25% Attrition: 18% MLB: 84% *Comparables: Alex Colome, Justin Wilson, Ryan Cook*

If you watched a Diamondbacks game in 2017, there was a 44 percent chance you were going to see Chafin and his mustache trot in from the bullpen. Seriously, a Google Images search for "Andrew Chafin mustache" will do a body good in times of need. There's no way of proving whether the mustache helped his utter dominance against left-handers (they hit just .217/.281/.284 against him), or whether it led to righties slugging against him way more than they have over the course of his career. Either way, having a killer mustache seems like a very LOOGY thing to do. We'll see if the Diamondbacks adjust accordingly.

Taylor Clarke RHP Born: 05/13/93 Age: 25 Bats: R Throws: R Height: 6'4" Weight: 200 Origin: Round 3, 2015 Draft (#76 overall)

YEAR	TEAM	LVL	AGE	W	L	SV	G	GS	IP	H	HR	BB/9	K/9	K	GB%	BABIP	WHIP	ERA	DRA	WARP	MPH	CMD	PWR	STM
2015	YAK	A-	22	0	0	3	13	0	21	8	0	1.7	11.6	27	51%	.186	0.57	0.00	1.70	0.8				
2016	KNC	A	23	3	2	0	6	6	28^{2}	24	1	1.6	7.5	24	32%	.277	1.01	2.83	3.96	0.4				
2016	VIS	A+	23	1	1	0	4	4	23	19	3	2.7	8.6	22	31%	.262	1.13	2.74	6.32	-0.2				
2016	MOB	AA	23	8	6	0	17	17	97^{2}	99	9	1.9	6.6	72	38%	.297	1.23	3.59	5.66	-0.7				
2017	WTN	AA	24	9	7	0	21	21	111^{1}	94	7	3.2	8.6	107	40%	.292	1.19	2.91	3.84	1.8				
2017	RNO	AAA	24	3	2	0	6	6	33^{2}	29	8	3.5	8.3	31	34%	.231	1.25	4.81	7.15	-0.5				
2018	*ARI*	*MLB*	*25*	*8*	*7*	*0*	*22*	*22*	*121*	*113*	*22*	*3.3*	*10.1*	*136*	*37%*	*.307*	*1.30*	*4.51*	*5.13*	*0.7*				
2019	*ARI*	*MLB*	*26*	*7*	*9*	*0*	*25*	*25*	*147*	*136*	*28*	*3.3*	*9.7*	*159*	*37%*	*.309*	*1.29*	*4.66*	*5.32*	*0.5*				

Breakout: 11% Improve: 14% Collapse: 13% Attrition: 24% MLB: 32% *Comparables: Red Patterson, Tyler Pill, Roenis Elias*

Clarke is a big horse of a man, which is a good thing to be if your goal is to make the big leagues as a starter. He's got a good fastball and a good slider. Those are other good qualities to have under your belt if you want to be a big-league starter. What he doesn't have is a reliable third offering just yet, which is part of why he got the tar beat out of him in his brief promotion to Triple-A. Solidifying that changeup isn't going to put the tar back into him, but it should somewhat help prevent further tar loss.

Patrick Corbin LHP Born: 07/19/89 Age: 28 Bats: L Throws: L Height: 6'3" Weight: 210 Origin: Round 2, 2009 Draft (#80 overall)

YEAR	TEAM	LVL	AGE	W	L	SV	G	GS	IP	H	HR	BB/9	K/9	K	GB%	BABIP	WHIP	ERA	DRA	WARP	MPH	CMD	PWR	STM
2015	MOB	AA	25	1	0	0	3	3	16^{1}	13	1	2.8	6.1	11	44%	.255	1.10	2.76	4.33	0.1				
2015	ARI	MLB	25	6	5	0	16	16	85	91	9	1.8	8.3	78	48%	.327	1.27	3.60	4.26	0.8	95.0	45	49	52
2016	ARI	MLB	26	5	13	1	36	24	155^{2}	177	24	3.8	7.6	131	55%	.322	1.56	5.15	5.91	-1.1	94.4	48	49	68
2017	ARI	MLB	27	14	13	0	33	32	189^{2}	208	26	2.9	8.4	178	52%	.326	1.42	4.03	4.60	2.0	94.3	58	42	80
2018	*ARI*	*MLB*	*28*	*9*	*10*	*0*	*29*	*29*	*174*	*172*	*23*	*3.1*	*8.6*	*166*	*50%*	*.300*	*1.34*	*3.90*	*4.32*	*1.7*	*93.9*	*53*	*46*	*69*
2019	*ARI*	*MLB*	*29*	*11*	*11*	*0*	*32*	*32*	*202^{1}*	*191*	*26*	*2.9*	*8.5*	*191*	*50%*	*.314*	*1.26*	*3.96*	*4.52*	*2.3*	*93.5*	*54*	*45*	*73*

Breakout: 23% Improve: 58% Collapse: 23% Attrition: 7% MLB: 95% *Comparables: Mat Latos, Jordan Zimmermann, John Danks*

Corbin turned in a nondescript mid-rotation lefty starter season, which is significant for two reasons. From a pure results perspective, he was arguably Arizona's fifth-best starter, which speaks to the team's depth. It's also significant because Corbin has reached All-Star levels of success in the past. This was his first full season back from Tommy John surgery, and DRA was far less fond of his work than the raw results were. A new high in strikeout rate was nice to see, and it didn't come with an offensive amount of walks. If this is who Corbin is now, so be it. Getting your elbow sliced open does things to a man. He's still a valuable asset.

Jorge De La Rosa LHP Born: 04/05/81 Age: 37 Bats: L Throws: L Height: 6'1" Weight: 215 Origin: International Free Agent, 1998

YEAR	TEAM	LVL	AGE	W	L	SV	G	GS	IP	H	HR	BB/9	K/9	K	GB%	BABIP	WHIP	ERA	DRA	WARP	MPH	CMD	PWR	STM
2015	COL	MLB	34	9	7	0	26	26	149	137	17	3.9	8.1	134	54%	.289	1.36	4.17	3.82	2.2	94.6	40	31	68
2016	ABQ	AAA	35	0	0	0	3	3	14^{2}	14	0	4.9	6.8	11	56%	.311	1.50	4.30	6.79	-0.2				
2016	COL	MLB	35	8	9	0	27	24	134	157	23	4.2	7.3	108	49%	.325	1.64	5.51	7.23	-2.9	92.1	36	28	69
2017	ARI	MLB	36	3	1	0	65	0	51^{1}	46	7	3.7	7.9	45	49%	.273	1.31	4.21	5.06	0.1	94.8	29	43	45
2018	*ARI*	*MLB*	*37*	*4*	*3*	*0*	*16*	*10*	*60^{2}*	*58*	*9*	*3.7*	*8.0*	*54*	*49%*	*.302*	*1.37*	*4.62*	*5.24*	*0.2*	*92.2*	*35*	*31*	*57*
2019	*ARI*	*MLB*	*38*	*9*	*10*	*0*	*47*	*25*	*173^{2}*	*169*	*24*	*3.8*	*7.9*	*152*	*49%*	*.315*	*1.39*	*4.64*	*5.28*	*0.5*	*91.3*	*33*	*32*	*55*

Breakout: 11% Improve: 32% Collapse: 27% Attrition: 13% MLB: 81% *Comparables: Miguel Batista, Bob Gibson, Allie Reynolds*

It was jarring to see De La Rosa in a uniform that wasn't black and purple. After so many years in Colorado, the veteran southpaw moved to a (slightly) more forgiving offensive environment. Instead of a boatload of dingers going over the wall, only a truckload of dingers go over the wall in Arizona. He made the best of it, albeit in a mop-up relief role. He doesn't seem to have a whole lot left, but it was a far cry from the disaster that was his last year with the Rockies. De La Rosa is a competent left-hander, so as long as he can throw a fastball without it getting consistently crushed he'll have teams calling his agent.

Rubby De La Rosa RHP Born: 03/04/89 Age: 29 Bats: R Throws: R Height: 6'0" Weight: 210 Origin: International Free Agent, 2007

YEAR	TEAM	LVL	AGE	W	L	SV	G	GS	IP	H	HR	BB/9	K/9	K	GB%	BABIP	WHIP	ERA	DRA	WARP	MPH	CMD	PWR	STM
2015	ARI	MLB	26	14	9	0	32	32	188^{2}	193	32	3.0	7.2	150	51%	.287	1.36	4.67	4.65	1.0	97.9	46	64	75
2016	ARI	MLB	27	4	5	0	13	10	50^{2}	43	8	3.6	9.6	54	54%	.257	1.24	4.26	3.45	1.1	97.5	50	58	17
2017	ARI	MLB	28	0	1	0	9	0	7^{2}	7	2	4.7	14.1	12	39%	.312	1.43	4.70	3.79	0.1	98.9			38
2017	RNO	AAA	28	1	2	0	19	0	20^{1}	17	3	4.0	12.4	28	41%	.304	1.28	3.10	4.17	0.2				
2018	*ARI*	*MLB*	*29*	*2*	*2*	*0*	*7*	*7*	*35^{2}*	*33*	*6*	*3.6*	*10.1*	*40*	*46%*	*.307*	*1.32*	*4.64*	*5.28*	*0.1*	*97.2*	*47*	*62*	*40*
2019	*ARI*	*MLB*	*30*	*9*	*11*	*0*	*29*	*29*	*179^{2}*	*156*	*31*	*3.5*	*10.5*	*209*	*46%*	*.308*	*1.26*	*4.46*	*5.09*	*0.9*	*96.7*	*48*	*61*	*34*

Breakout: 29% Improve: 49% Collapse: 19% Attrition: 18% MLB: 87% *Comparables: Armando Galarraga, Christian Friedrich, Chase Anderson*

The UCL demons and their fel magic came for De La Rosa after a season spent largely trying to work his way back from elbow trouble. A plasma injection only served as a momentary deterrent before he underwent Tommy John surgery and was released in September. Two months later Arizona brought him back into the fold on a two-year minor-league deal that will give him time to spend this season rehabbing his elbow. When healthy, De La Rosa is a decent back-end starter. If nothing else, he's a depth option the team understandably wants to keep in-house.

Randall Delgado RHP Born: 02/09/90 Age: 28 Bats: R Throws: R Height: 6'4" Weight: 220 Origin: International Free Agent, 2006

YEAR	TEAM	LVL	AGE	W	L	SV	G	GS	IP	H	HR	BB/9	K/9	K	GB%	BABIP	WHIP	ERA	DRA	WARP	MPH	CMD	PWR	STM
2015	ARI	MLB	25	8	4	1	64	1	72	63	7	4.1	9.1	73	44%	.290	1.33	3.25	3.58	1.0	96.0	38	49	52
2016	ARI	MLB	26	5	2	0	79	0	75	77	8	4.3	8.2	68	43%	.309	1.51	4.44	5.25	-0.2	94.8	43	48	57
2017	ARI	MLB	27	1	2	1	26	5	62^{2}	60	6	2.0	8.6	60	48%	.302	1.18	3.59	4.28	0.7	96.1	56	55	47
2018	*ARI*	*MLB*	*28*	*2*	*2*	*2*	*51*	*0*	*54*	*50*	*6*	*3.6*	*9.0*	*54*	*45%*	*.296*	*1.33*	*3.69*	*4.10*	*0.5*	*95.0*	*47*	*51*	*52*
2019	*ARI*	*MLB*	*29*	*3*	*1*	*2*	*56*	*0*	*59^{2}*	*50*	*7*	*3.3*	*9.6*	*64*	*45%*	*.305*	*1.21*	*3.67*	*4.19*	*0.7*	*94.6*	*49*	*51*	*52*

Breakout: 24% Improve: 57% Collapse: 15% Attrition: 8% MLB: 92% *Comparables: Sean Marshall, Carlos Villanueva, Kyle McClellan*

After three seasons spent almost entirely as a reliever, Delgado filled several different roles for the Diamondbacks in the first half. He started five times and relieved in 21 other games, mostly faring well in the swingman role. And then he was shut down in mid-July with an elbow injury, throwing his final pitch of the season on July 15. He opted for the rest-and-rehab route rather than immediate Tommy John surgery, but Delgado will now have the dark cloud of arm problems hanging over his head. Again.

Jon Duplantier RHP Born: 07/11/94 Age: 23 Bats: L Throws: R Height: 6'4" Weight: 225 Origin: Round 3, 2016 Draft (#89 overall)

YEAR	TEAM	LVL	AGE	W	L	SV	G	GS	IP	H	HR	BB/9	K/9	K	GB%	BABIP	WHIP	ERA	DRA	WARP	MPH	CMD	PWR	STM
2017	KNC	A	22	6	1	0	13	12	72^{2}	45	4	1.9	9.7	78	52%	.240	0.83	1.24	1.71	3.0				
2017	VIS	A+	22	6	2	0	12	12	63^{1}	46	2	3.8	12.4	87	53%	.324	1.15	1.56	2.07	2.4				
2018	*ARI*	*MLB*	*23*	*5*	*5*	*0*	*16*	*16*	*88*	*77*	*16*	*4.9*	*11.7*	*114*	*43%*	*.318*	*1.42*	*4.61*	*5.26*	*0.4*				
2019	*ARI*	*MLB*	*24*	*9*	*11*	*0*	*29*	*29*	*178^{2}*	*160*	*29*	*4.3*	*10.1*	*201*	*43%*	*.316*	*1.38*	*4.60*	*5.26*	*0.6*				

Breakout: 24% Improve: 40% Collapse: 6% Attrition: 23% MLB: 54% *Comparables: Matt Harvey, Jordan Zimmermann, Eric Surkamp*

There wasn't a lot to write home about down on the farm for Arizona last year, but Duplantier was a very bright spot. A 2016 draftee who fell into the second round because of health concerns, he showed a quality four-pitch mix. While the profile isn't sexy, he's a pretty surefire bet to pitch in the back of a big-league rotation, with a chance for more. These kinds of guys don't grow on trees, and they're valuable commodities. The Diamondbacks will gladly take that, and Duplantier should have an opportunity to rise up the ladder quickly if things go well again in 2018.

Zack Godley RHP Born: 04/21/90 Age: 28 Bats: R Throws: R Height: 6'3" Weight: 240 Origin: Round 10, 2013 Draft (#288 overall)

YEAR	TEAM	LVL	AGE	W	L	SV	G	GS	IP	H	HR	BB/9	K/9	K	GB%	BABIP	WHIP	ERA	DRA	WARP	MPH	CMD	PWR	STM
2015	VIS	A+	25	8	3	0	14	12	75^{1}	64	3	2.3	9.3	78	56%	.300	1.10	2.27	2.09	2.7				
2015	MOB	AA	25	2	1	0	7	5	24^{1}	21	2	3.7	4.4	12	61%	.260	1.27	4.07	5.25	-0.1				
2015	ARI	MLB	25	5	1	0	9	6	36^{2}	29	4	4.2	8.3	34	47%	.272	1.25	3.19	3.97	0.5	93.8	46	27	50
2016	MOB	AA	26	2	5	0	8	8	49^{1}	48	4	2.0	5.7	31	56%	.291	1.20	3.83	3.90	0.7				
2016	RNO	AAA	26	2	1	0	7	6	32^{2}	37	3	4.1	10.5	38	50%	.382	1.59	3.31	2.06	1.2				
2016	ARI	MLB	26	5	4	0	27	9	74^{2}	86	13	3.0	7.2	60	55%	.313	1.49	6.39	4.80	0.4	92.8	30	28	68
2017	RNO	AAA	27	2	1	0	5	3	28	14	0	5.5	9.3	29	68%	.222	1.11	2.57	2.37	1.0				
2017	ARI	MLB	27	8	9	0	26	25	155	124	15	3.1	9.6	165	58%	.280	1.14	3.37	3.14	4.2	93.0	23	26	73
2018	*ARI*	*MLB*	*28*	*9*	*9*	*0*	*28*	*28*	*168*	*153*	*21*	*3.3*	*9.2*	*172*	*53%*	*.296*	*1.27*	*3.72*	*4.12*	*2.0*	*92.5*	*27*	*27*	*66*
2019	*ARI*	*MLB*	*29*	*12*	*11*	*0*	*32*	*32*	*211^{2}*	*171*	*24*	*3.0*	*9.7*	*227*	*53%*	*.299*	*1.14*	*3.58*	*4.08*	*3.3*	*92.1*	*25*	*27*	*69*

Breakout: 17% Improve: 53% Collapse: 17% Attrition: 21% MLB: 88% *Comparables: Josh Collmenter, Adam Warren, Jacob deGrom*

Godley couldn't put the finishing touches on his breakout season, struggling down the stretch and being skipped over for playoff work, but what he did from late April through mid-September warrants plenty of attention. His first 144 innings included a 2.99 ERA and 152 strikeouts along with groundballs in bunches and decent control. Godley was one of 21 starters to throw at least 150 innings and average more than one strikeout per frame, and his ground-ball rate led that group by a wide margin over second-ranked Carlos Martinez. Godley turns 28 just after Opening Day, so there may not be a ton of projection left, but if he can maintain his performance for an entire season he'll likely be perceived as having a big-time breakout by the time you read his comment in next year's book.

Zack Greinke RHP Born: 10/21/83 Age: 34 Bats: R Throws: R Height: 6'2" Weight: 200 Origin: Round 1, 2002 Draft (#6 overall)

YEAR	TEAM	LVL	AGE	W	L	SV	G	GS	IP	H	HR	BB/9	K/9	K	GB%	BABIP	WHIP	ERA	DRA	WARP	MPH	CMD	PWR	STM
2015	LAN	MLB	31	19	3	0	32	32	222^{2}	148	14	1.6	8.1	200	49%	.229	0.84	1.66	2.47	6.9	94.7	59	45	78
2016	ARI	MLB	32	13	7	0	26	26	158^{2}	161	23	2.3	7.6	134	47%	.294	1.27	4.37	3.49	3.4	93.8	72	42	70
2017	ARI	MLB	33	17	7	0	32	32	202^{1}	172	25	2.0	9.6	215	48%	.285	1.07	3.20	3.00	5.8	92.3	61	33	79
2018	*ARI*	*MLB*	*34*	*12*	*11*	*0*	*31*	*31*	207^{2}	*190*	*28*	*2.5*	*8.8*	*204*	*47%*	*.288*	*1.19*	*3.67*	*4.06*	*2.7*	*92.3*	*63*	*38*	*75*
2019	*ARI*	*MLB*	*35*	*13*	*12*	*0*	*32*	*32*	211^{2}	*182*	*27*	*2.4*	*8.8*	*207*	*47%*	*.297*	*1.13*	*3.69*	*4.21*	*3.4*	*91.4*	*63*	*36*	*74*

Breakout: 16% Improve: 43% Collapse: 37% Attrition: 6% MLB: 97% *Comparables: Adam Wainwright, Chris Carpenter, Justin Verlander*

And just like that, Greinke is back. He didn't reach the heights of his absolutely bonkers final season with the Dodgers, but Greinke pitched like the ace he is and put Arizona firmly in contention. He put up his highest K/9 since 2011, lowered his ERA by more than a run compared to 2016 and did it while throwing more than 200 innings in a very hostile pitching environment. DRA shows a less volatile year-by-year progression for the former Cy Young winner, with a sub-3.50 mark every season since 2006. He'll be 34 years old on Opening Day, but there's little reason to think he's close to slowing down in a meaningful way.

David Hernandez RHP Born: 05/13/85 Age: 33 Bats: R Throws: R Height: 6'3" Weight: 245 Origin: Round 16, 2005 Draft (#483 overall)

YEAR	TEAM	LVL	AGE	W	L	SV	G	GS	IP	H	HR	BB/9	K/9	K	GB%	BABIP	WHIP	ERA	DRA	WARP	MPH	CMD	PWR	STM
2015	ARI	MLB	30	1	5	0	40	0	33^{2}	33	6	2.9	8.8	33	40%	.297	1.31	4.28	5.42	-0.3	96.9	44	54	42
2016	PHI	MLB	31	3	4	1	70	0	72^{2}	77	11	4.0	9.9	80	40%	.337	1.50	3.84	4.53	0.4	96.3	38	51	53
2017	ANA	MLB	32	1	0	1	38	0	36^{1}	29	0	2.0	9.2	37	49%	.309	1.02	2.23	3.59	0.6	95.0	46	47	48
2017	ARI	MLB	32	2	1	1	26	0	18^{2}	19	4	0.5	7.2	15	36%	.278	1.07	4.82	4.75	0.1	94.9	46	47	48
2018	*ARI*	*MLB*	*33*	*3*	*1*	*1*	*51*	*0*	53^{2}	*50*	*7*	*3.3*	*9.6*	*57*	*42%*	*.312*	*1.29*	*3.98*	*4.52*	*0.4*	*94.8*	*41*	*49*	*48*
2019	*ARI*	*MLB*	*34*	*2*	*1*	*1*	*38*	*0*	35^{1}	*33*	*5*	*3.5*	*9.3*	*37*	*42%*	*.318*	*1.33*	*4.28*	*4.88*	*0.1*	*94.2*	*41*	*49*	*48*

Breakout: 22% Improve: 42% Collapse: 22% Attrition: 11% MLB: 88% *Comparables: Jason Frasor, Michael Wuertz, Joakim Soria*

"Your task is to write a comment about David Hernandez," they said. "Make it interesting." This presents a quandary. Hernandez had a typical Hernandez season, pitching well for the Angels before a late trade to Arizona, where he was lit up. This is the outcome of Hernandez. It is foretold in ancient tomes, and it comes to pass. He is a righty, he throws hard and occasionally has unremarkable success, sometimes in late innings. "Make it interesting," they said. Okay: Hernandez registered the lowest walk rate of his career by a lot and was much tougher against lefties than he had been in 2016. See? That wasn't so hard.

Yoshihisa Hirano RHP Born: 03/08/84 Age: 34 Bats: R Throws: R Height: 6'0" Weight: 158 Origin: International Free Agent, 2017

YEAR	TEAM	LVL	AGE	W	L	SV	G	GS	IP	H	HR	BB/9	K/9	K	GB%	BABIP	WHIP	ERA	DRA	WARP	MPH	CMD	PWR	STM
2018	*ARI*	*MLB*	*34*	*2*	*2*	*0*	*37*	*0*	*39*	*39*	*6*	*3.1*	*8.4*	*37*	*46%*	*.298*	*1.34*	*4.17*	*4.48*	*0.2*				
2019	*ARI*	*MLB*	*35*	*2*	*1*	*4*	*37*	*1*	*41*	*39*	*5*	*2.9*	*8.8*	*44*	*46%*	*.293*	*1.20*	*3.88*	*4.35*	*0.5*				

Breakout: 13% Improve: 29% Collapse: 36% Attrition: 6% MLB: 86% *Comparables: Matt Belisle, Scott Downs, Bob Howry*

When the Cardinals signed Seung-hwan Oh before the 2016 season, hardly anyone expected The Final Boss to realize his nickname on the mound. Hirano, heading into his age-34 season, has a similar profile and pitch arsenal to Stone Buddha. However, his strikeout rate, which once topped out at 31.4 percent, has declined precipitously for four consecutive seasons, to a below-average 19.6 percent in 2017. Even though his fastball velocity has generally hovered around 92 mph, there's plenty of risk in signing relievers mid-decline.

Yoan Lopez RHP Born: 01/02/93 Age: 25 Bats: R Throws: R Height: 6'3" Weight: 185 Origin: International Free Agent, 2015

YEAR	TEAM	LVL	AGE	W	L	SV	G	GS	IP	H	HR	BB/9	K/9	K	GB%	BABIP	WHIP	ERA	DRA	WARP	MPH	CMD	PWR	STM
2015	MOB	AA	22	1	6	0	10	9	48	46	4	4.5	6.0	32	40%	.290	1.46	4.69	6.69	-0.9				
2016	MOB	AA	23	4	7	0	14	14	62	67	10	4.6	5.2	36	42%	.285	1.60	5.52	9.64	-3.4				
2017	VIS	A+	24	2	0	4	20	0	30^{2}	16	2	2.6	16.4	56	49%	.298	0.82	0.88	1.08	1.4				
2018	*ARI*	*MLB*	*25*	*2*	*2*	*0*	*14*	*6*	36^{1}	*32*	*7*	*4.0*	*11.9*	*48*	*41%*	*.318*	*1.31*	*4.36*	*4.97*	*0.2*				
2019	*ARI*	*MLB*	*26*	*6*	*7*	*1*	*45*	*21*	163^{2}	*136*	*31*	*3.8*	*11.8*	*215*	*41%*	*.315*	*1.26*	*4.37*	*5.00*	*0.7*				

Breakout: 12% Improve: 16% Collapse: 2% Attrition: 12% MLB: 20% *Comparables: Luke Farrell, Justin Thomas, Parker Bridwell*

A weird thing happened last year with Dave Stewart's (arguably) biggest mistake. Lopez was shifted into a full-time relief role at High-A Visalia and absolutely shoved. He only threw 30 innings because of a midseason rotator cuff strain, but Lopez struck out almost half the batters he faced and worked to a 0.88 ERA. The mitigating factor is that we're talking about a 24-year-old in High-A, but he was a major international prospect at one point for a good reason. You can expect to see Lopez try to replicate his success at Double-A this year. He may have been an Alaska-sized mistake at the time, but if this pans out there may yet be a tiny bit of hope for Stewart's Folly.

T.J. McFarland LHP Born: 06/08/89 Age: 29 Bats: L Throws: L Height: 6'3" Weight: 220 Origin: Round 4, 2007 Draft (#137 overall)

YEAR	TEAM	LVL	AGE	W	L	SV	G	GS	IP	H	HR	BB/9	K/9	K	GB%	BABIP	WHIP	ERA	DRA	WARP	MPH	CMD	PWR	STM
2015	NOR	AAA	26	2	3	1	16	9	52^{2}	42	0	2.4	5.3	31	66%	.255	1.06	2.91	4.40	0.5				
2015	BAL	MLB	26	2	2	0	30	0	40^{1}	52	4	4.0	5.8	26	65%	.343	1.74	4.91	4.89	-0.1	94.2	52	51	50
2016	BAL	MLB	27	2	2	0	16	0	24^{2}	33	3	3.6	2.6	7	60%	.333	1.74	6.93	5.34	-0.1	93.9	49	52	34
2016	NOR	AAA	27	1	1	0	8	4	26^{1}	33	3	2.4	3.8	11	63%	.330	1.52	4.44	7.23	-0.6				
2017	RNO	AAA	28	0	0	1	7	0	11	6	0	3.3	7.4	9	81%	.231	0.91	0.00	2.63	0.3				
2017	ARI	MLB	28	4	5	0	43	1	54	65	4	2.8	4.8	29	69%	.323	1.52	5.33	4.36	0.5	92.6	51	50	44
2018	*ARI*	*MLB*	*29*	*2*	*3*	*0*	*51*	*0*	*54*	*61*	*6*	*4.0*	*6.2*	*37*	*59%*	*.310*	*1.58*	*4.78*	*4.93*	*0.0*	*92.6*	*51*	*51*	*42*
2019	*ARI*	*MLB*	*30*	*2*	*1*	*0*	*35*	*0*	36^{2}	*41*	*4*	*3.9*	*6.4*	*26*	*59%*	*.333*	*1.54*	*4.73*	*5.38*	*-0.1*	*92.0*	*50*	*50*	*41*

Breakout: 39% Improve: 51% Collapse: 29% Attrition: 27% MLB: 92% *Comparables: Logan Ondrusek, Adam Warren, Ryan Webb*

McFarland has made something of a career being the second or third lefty in a bullpen. He's a mop-up man or a LOOGY, the guy you go to when there's a five-run difference in the score or the man ahead of him on the depth chart isn't available (and even then the five-run difference doesn't hurt). For one game, though, McFarland started, against the Twins. He recorded one out and allowed seven runs, all earned. Braden Shipley then came in and pitched through the sixth inning. We've all heard of the idea of tandem starters, but folks, maybe the guy who's a starting pitcher should have started the game.

Shelby Miller RHP Born: 10/10/90 Age: 27 Bats: R Throws: R Height: 6'3" Weight: 225 Origin: Round 1, 2009 Draft (#19 overall)

YEAR	TEAM	LVL	AGE	W	L	SV	G	GS	IP	H	HR	BB/9	K/9	K	GB%	BABIP	WHIP	ERA	DRA	WARP	MPH	CMD	PWR	STM
2015	ATL	MLB	24	6	17	0	33	33	205^1	183	13	3.2	7.5	171	49%	.285	1.25	3.02	2.99	5.1	96.7	49	63	78
2016	VIS	A+	25	2	0	0	2	2	12	8	0	0.8	14.2	19	46%	.308	0.75	0.75	1.33	0.6				
2016	RNO	AAA	25	5	1	0	8	8	50^2	55	4	1.8	9.8	55	52%	.367	1.28	3.91	0.91	2.6				
2016	ARI	MLB	25	3	12	0	20	20	101	127	14	3.7	6.2	70	44%	.340	1.67	6.15	7.02	-1.9	95.9	36	57	70
2017	ARI	MLB	26	2	2	0	4	4	22	20	1	4.9	8.2	20	46%	.288	1.45	4.09	6.37	-0.2	97.1	34	62	49
2018	*ARI*	*MLB*	*27*	*1*	*1*	*0*	*4*	*4*	*21*	*20*	*3*	*3.4*	*8.9*	*21*	*46%*	*.295*	*1.31*	*3.78*	*4.17*	*0.2*	*96.0*	*43*	*61*	*64*
2019	*ARI*	*MLB*	*28*	*10*	*11*	*0*	*32*	*32*	*206*	*181*	*28*	*3.1*	*9.0*	*206*	*46%*	*.299*	*1.22*	*4.01*	*4.57*	*1.9*	*95.6*	*39*	*60*	*61*

Breakout: 23% Improve: 49% Collapse: 24% Attrition: 14% MLB: 95% *Comparables: Adam Wainwright, Mat Latos, Matt Cain*

After a disastrous first year with Arizona, Miller looked like he was starting to get back to decency in his first four outings of 2017. Then he left the fourth start with the team trainer. One grim team statement about a "forearm strain" later, Miller was under the knife and getting his UCL replaced. Miller at least had the procedure done early enough in the season that he could theoretically get back on the mound this year and maybe give his team a little help down the stretch, though it's never easy to come back from major surgery.

Robbie Ray LHP Born: 10/01/91 Age: 26 Bats: L Throws: L Height: 6'2" Weight: 195 Origin: Round 12, 2010 Draft (#356 overall)

YEAR	TEAM	LVL	AGE	W	L	SV	G	GS	IP	H	HR	BB/9	K/9	K	GB%	BABIP	WHIP	ERA	DRA	WARP	MPH	CMD	PWR	STM
2015	RNO	AAA	23	2	3	0	9	9	41^2	44	1	5.8	12.3	57	44%	.422	1.70	3.67	2.16	1.5				
2015	ARI	MLB	23	5	12	0	23	23	127^2	121	9	3.5	8.4	119	45%	.311	1.33	3.52	4.36	1.1	96.4	44	62	72
2016	ARI	MLB	24	8	15	0	32	32	174^1	185	24	3.7	11.3	218	47%	.352	1.47	4.90	4.33	2.1	97.2	57	63	79
2017	ARI	MLB	25	15	5	0	28	28	162	116	23	3.9	12.1	218	42%	.267	1.15	2.89	3.61	3.5	96.3	44	54	70
2018	*ARI*	*MLB*	*26*	*9*	*9*	*0*	*29*	*29*	*165^1*	*143*	*23*	*3.6*	*11.5*	*211*	*44%*	*.304*	*1.27*	*3.51*	*3.90*	*2.4*	*96.3*	*50*	*60*	*75*
2019	*ARI*	*MLB*	*27*	*12*	*10*	*0*	*32*	*32*	*210^2*	*167*	*28*	*3.0*	*11.7*	*274*	*44%*	*.315*	*1.13*	*3.36*	*3.85*	*3.6*	*96.1*	*51*	*59*	*75*

Breakout: 28% Improve: 62% Collapse: 12% Attrition: 5% MLB: 95% *Comparables: Gio Gonzalez, Clay Buchholz, Max Scherzer*

All of a sudden, all those jokes about trades are gone. Ray is no longer a punchline, but instead the second part of a one-two punch of front-line starters in tandem with Zack Greinke. Ray was brilliant in 2017. He fanned seemingly every batter who dared cross his path, eclipsing the 200-strikeout mark for the second season in a row, in 10 fewer innings than 2016. The only thing stopping him from a full season of dominance was a terrifying midsummer line drive to the head, from which he thankfully came back strong. Barring another injury, he's going to be one of the scariest pitchers in the National League West for a while to come.

Braden Shipley RHP Born: 02/22/92 Age: 26 Bats: R Throws: R Height: 6'1" Weight: 190 Origin: Round 1, 2013 Draft (#15 overall)

YEAR	TEAM	LVL	AGE	W	L	SV	G	GS	IP	H	HR	BB/9	K/9	K	GB%	BABIP	WHIP	ERA	DRA	WARP	MPH	CMD	PWR	STM
2015	MOB	AA	23	9	11	0	28	27	156^2	147	7	3.2	6.8	118	46%	.294	1.30	3.50	4.48	1.1				
2016	RNO	AAA	24	8	5	0	19	19	119^1	131	7	1.7	5.8	77	47%	.316	1.28	3.70	3.29	2.8				
2016	ARI	MLB	24	4	5	0	13	11	70	80	14	3.6	5.5	43	45%	.300	1.54	5.27	6.81	-1.2	94.2	53	44	77
2017	RNO	AAA	25	7	6	0	19	19	105	129	18	3.6	5.9	69	43%	.326	1.63	5.66	7.22	-1.7				
2017	ARI	MLB	25	0	1	0	10	3	25	31	5	5.4	6.5	18	44%	.317	1.84	5.76	6.49	-0.3	94.9	68	47	62
2018	*ARI*	*MLB*	*26*	*2*	*3*	*0*	*28*	*5*	*51*	*54*	*8*	*3.5*	*7.3*	*41*	*43%*	*.299*	*1.45*	*4.89*	*5.13*	*-0.1*	*94.0*	*59*	*46*	*70*
2019	*ARI*	*MLB*	*27*	*6*	*5*	*0*	*68*	*11*	*124^2*	*122*	*18*	*3.1*	*7.5*	*104*	*43%*	*.307*	*1.32*	*4.55*	*5.17*	*0.3*	*93.8*	*59*	*46*	*70*

Breakout: 27% Improve: 45% Collapse: 12% Attrition: 33% MLB: 69% *Comparables: Shairon Martis, Dustin Moseley, Troy Patton*

Yikes. Shipley got shelled in his 25 innings in the big leagues, and got shelled in many more innings at Triple-A Reno. That's not what you want to see from a former first-round pick with his pedigree, but it's also not as if the Diamondbacks are in desperate need of rotation help right now. That gives Shipley more time to straighten back out again, which the late convert to pitching may need. Don't purge all your Shipley stock from your portfolio just yet, but maybe have your broker on speed dial.

Taijuan Walker RHP Born: 08/13/92 Age: 25 Bats: R Throws: R Height: 6'4" Weight: 235 Origin: Round 1, 2010 Draft (#43 overall)

YEAR	TEAM	LVL	AGE	W	L	SV	G	GS	IP	H	HR	BB/9	K/9	K	GB%	BABIP	WHIP	ERA	DRA	WARP	MPH	CMD	PWR	STM
2015	SEA	MLB	22	11	8	0	29	29	169^2	163	25	2.1	8.3	157	41%	.291	1.20	4.56	3.89	2.4	97.2	52	70	70
2016	TAC	AAA	23	1	0	0	3	3	15	12	1	4.8	3.6	6	55%	.220	1.33	3.60	7.51	-0.4				
2016	SEA	MLB	23	8	11	0	25	25	134^1	129	27	2.5	8.0	119	45%	.267	1.24	4.22	4.28	1.7	97.0	59	60	64
2017	ARI	MLB	24	9	9	0	28	28	157^1	148	17	3.5	8.4	146	50%	.291	1.33	3.49	4.17	2.5	95.6	51	54	70
2018	*ARI*	*MLB*	*25*	*9*	*9*	*0*	*29*	*29*	*153^2*	*140*	*20*	*3.0*	*9.0*	*155*	*46%*	*.291*	*1.24*	*3.73*	*4.13*	*1.8*	*96.2*	*55*	*61*	*70*
2019	*ARI*	*MLB*	*26*	*11*	*10*	*0*	*32*	*32*	*211*	*171*	*24*	*2.7*	*9.4*	*221*	*46%*	*.292*	*1.11*	*3.54*	*4.03*	*3.0*	*95.8*	*55*	*59*	*70*

Breakout: 24% Improve: 56% Collapse: 21% Attrition: 12% MLB: 97% *Comparables: Shelby Miller, David Price, Matt Garza*

Acquired from the Mariners as part of the Jean Segura swap, Walker posted career lows in ERA and home-run rate while looking very much like a fixture of Arizona's rotation for years to come. DRA says he's likely just a mid-rotation dude, and he missed time with an injury once again, but that's a damn fine outcome for Walker given his previous ups and downs. The injury was also a blister issue instead of his usual structural maladies, which is progress. Though he may be destined for a career as a guy with stuff that plays bigger than his results, Walker provides a solid building block for an Arizona staff that needs to produce innings to compensate for a lack of depth.

Lineouts

Hitters

HITTER	POS	TEAM	LVL	AGE	PA	R	2B	3B	HR	RBI	BB	K	SB	CS	AVG/OBP/SLG	TAv	VORP	BABIP	BRR	FRAA	WARP
Oswaldo Arcia	RF	RNO	AAA	26	400	79	25	5	24	87	45	86	0	0	.326/.410/.639	.334	40.6	.367	0.7	RF(42): 2.7, LF(15): -0.3	4.2
Emilio Bonifacio	CF	ATL	MLB	32	44	2	1	1	0	3	1	9	0	0	.132/.150/.211	.164	-3.0	.167	0.3	LF(8): -0.4, RF(2): -0.1	-0.3
	CF	WTN	AA	32	100	15	5	2	1	5	4	15	5	4	.286/.313/.418	.266	1.9	.329	-1.4	CF(13): -3.4, 2B(5): -0.7	-0.2
Kevin Cron	1B	WTN	AA	24	588	76	35	0	25	91	56	134	1	0	.283/.357/.497	.297	28.8	.332	0.8	1B(126): -0.9, 3B(1): 0.0	3.0
Drew Ellis	3B	YAK	A-	21	208	35	8	0	8	23	24	45	3	1	.227/.327/.403	.284	13.0	.258	1.6	3B(40): 4.3	1.8
Anfernee Grier	OF	KNC	A	21	547	69	20	3	4	36	58	114	30	11	.251/.340/.331	.263	17.2	.319	1.4	CF(75): -10.2, LF(40): 2.9	1.0
Domingo Leyba	2B	YAK	A-	21	32	4	1	0	1	6	4	2	0	0	.286/.375/.429	.272	1.9	.280	0.1	SS(6): 2.0	0.4
	2B	WTN	AA	21	64	11	4	0	2	9	5	6	0	0	.276/.344/.448	.278	5.5	.280	1.9	SS(14): -2.2	0.4
Kris Negron	UT	RNO	AAA	31	437	70	17	11	13	64	35	88	13	3	.300/.366/.501	.268	22.7	.356	5.8	RF(33): 3.5, 3B(30): 5.7	3.4
	UT	ARI	MLB	31	31	3	1	0	0	1	4	7	0	0	.160/.300/.200	.223	-2.2	.222	-1.9	SS(5): 0.4, LF(5): -0.1	-0.2
Jack Reinheimer	SS	ARI	MLB	24	5	0	0	0	0	0	0	3	0	0	.000/.000/.000	.026	-1.0	.000	0.0	SS(1): 0.0	-0.1
	SS	RNO	AAA	24	537	87	19	2	4	56	47	86	12	8	.278/.341/.351	.237	13.3	.327	7.2	SS(63): -2.7, 3B(34): -4.7	0.7
Tony Renda	2B	LOU	AAA	26	198	16	7	1	1	19	12	18	2	3	.260/.305/.326	.226	-2.0	.279	0.7	3B(14): 0.8, 2B(13): -2.9	-0.4
	2B	RNO	AAA	26	28	3	2	0	0	1	1	4	1	0	.185/.214/.259	.177	-0.9	.217	0.8	3B(8): 0.4	0.0
Ildemaro Vargas	2B	RNO	AAA	25	535	87	35	4	10	65	30	40	8	3	.312/.355/.462	.286	32.9	.319	1.3	2B(93): 11.8, CF(8): -1.8	4.0
	2B	ARI	MLB	25	13	4	1	0	0	4	0	3	0	0	.308/.308/.385	.214	-0.2	.400	0.1	2B(3): 0.0, 3B(2): -0.1	0.0
Daulton Varsho	C	YAK	A-	20	212	36	16	3	7	39	17	30	7	2	.311/.368/.534	.319	23.5	.338	2.4	C(36): 0.8	2.5
Marcus Wilson	OF	KNC	A	20	447	56	21	5	9	54	55	90	15	7	.295/.383/.446	.301	32.6	.361	2.2	CF(61): 2.5, LF(33): 0.0	3.7

If you want to know the difference between the PCL and the big leagues, **Oswaldo Arcia** hit like Mike Trout in Reno and he never even got called up. He signed with Japan's Nippon Ham Fighters in December. ⚾ Where've you gone, **Emilio Bonifacio**? Benches turn their lonely eyes to you, oo-oo-ooh. God bless your speed, Bonifacio, goodness knows your bat is left and gone away, hey-hey-hey, hey-hey-hey. ⚾ **Kevin Cron**'s second run at Double-A produced a .297 TAv and the Diamondbacks' Minor League Player of the Year award. C.J.'s brother was a 24-year old first baseman at Double-A, but there's *something* here. ⚾ Arizona took third baseman **Drew Ellis** 44th overall last summer out of Louisville and he struggled to make consistent contact in his first exposure to pro pitching. ⚾ A toolsy former 39th overall pick out of Auburn who hit just four homers in A-ball, **Anfernee Grier** needs to do more at the plate if he's going to go anywhere. ⚾ **Domingo Leyba** entered last season as one of the Diamondbacks' top prospects, but then missed nearly the entire year with a shoulder injury that required surgery. ⚾ **Kris Negron** is good enough to thump Triple-A pitching, but hasn't shown an ability to do the same in the bigs. There will be lots of headlines with the phrase "non-roster invitee" and his name in them. ⚾ **Jack Reinheimer** posted a sub-.400 slugging percentage in the PCL in back-to-back seasons, which is an awful lot to overcome to stick in the majors. ⚾ Acquired at midseason from the Reds, **Tony Renda** spent almost all year on the Triple-A disabled list. He does most things decently, but not well enough to be more than a tweener utility type. ⚾ Signed for $2.5 million as a 16-year-old last summer, **Kristian Robinson** is already big and strong and runs like the wind. Oh, and there's pop in the bat, too. ⚾ People will notice when you make as much contact as **Ildemaro Vargas** does, but he may need a bit more thump to land a full-time role. ⚾ **Daulton Varsho**, son of former big-league outfielder Gary Varsho, was the 68th overall pick in the 2017 draft. The college catcher torched Low-A pitchers in his pro debut. ⚾ **Marcus Wilson** lacks power, but he's fast, can play the outfield well and can hit for average with a good eye at the plate. Keep an eye on this guy.

Pitchers

PITCHER	TEAM	LVL	AGE	W	L	SV	G	GS	IP	H	HR	BB/9	K/9	K	GB%	BABIP	WHIP	ERA	DRA	WARP	MPH	CMD	PWR	STM
Jake Barrett	RNO	AAA	25	2	0	3	20	0	22	18	2	4.5	7.8	19	40%	.267	1.32	4.91	5.86	-0.1				
	ARI	MLB	25	1	1	0	28	0	27	27	7	5.0	8.7	26	38%	.274	1.56	5.00	7.09	-0.6	97.3	37	68	46
Silvino Bracho	RNO	AAA	24	3	2	8	33	0	35^{1}	25	8	4.3	12.2	48	34%	.239	1.19	4.08	4.48	0.3				
	ARI	MLB	24	0	0	0	21	0	20^{2}	18	5	3.0	10.9	25	46%	.260	1.21	5.66	4.59	0.1	94.5	45	43	43
J.J. Hoover	RNO	AAA	29	0	0	0	9	0	10^{1}	6	1	6.1	10.5	12	59%	.238	1.26	0.87	4.41	0.1				
	ARI	MLB	29	3	1	0	52	0	41^{1}	47	7	5.7	11.8	54	34%	.367	1.77	3.92	5.43	-0.1	93.6	54	44	47
Matthew Koch	YAK	A-	26	1	0	0	2	2	11	13	2	0.8	7.4	9	41%	.344	1.27	4.91	5.62	0.0				
	ARI	MLB	26	0	0	0	1	0	0	2	0			0	0%	1.000					91.9			22
	RNO	AAA	26	2	2	0	10	10	45	68	11	3.0	5.0	25	45%	.350	1.84	8.40	8.64	-1.4				
Brian Matusz	RNO	AAA	30	0	1	0	11	0	17^{2}	26	3	2.5	6.6	13	37%	.371	1.75	6.11	7.61	-0.4				
Jared Miller	WTN	AA	23	0	3	2	31	0	39^{1}	33	2	4.1	11.7	51	52%	.313	1.30	3.89	2.17	1.2				
	RNO	AAA	23	3	3	1	22	0	31^{1}	16	2	2.9	12.4	43	51%	.215	0.83	1.72	1.88	1.2				
Cody Reed	KNC	A	21	3	2	0	8	8	46^{2}	29	1	2.1	9.4	49	40%	.237	0.86	1.74	2.83	1.3				
	VIS	A+	21	5	6	0	17	17	89^{2}	94	14	3.0	9.0	90	37%	.325	1.38	3.91	7.00	-1.8				
Jimmie Sherfy	RNO	AAA	25	2	1	20	44	0	49	37	6	1.8	11.2	61	35%	.279	0.96	3.12	2.04	1.7				
	ARI	MLB	25	2	0	1	11	0	10^{2}	5	0	1.7	7.6	9	54%	.192	0.66	0.00	4.22	0.1	95.5			44

Shoulder issues kept **Jake Barrett** off the Opening Day roster and he never got back on track, mostly wasting a sophomore season after dropping 30 pounds during the winter. A healthy and in-sync Barrett is good enough to play a part in a big-league bullpen. ⚾ **Silvino Bracho** rediscovered the strikeout in 2017, but poor command and fly-ball tendencies combined to render his up-and-down year more down than up. At this rate he's going to need to find a bigger park to play in, or a sport with a bigger home plate. ⚾ After surfacing in the big leagues in 2016, hard-throwing left-hander **Steve Hathaway** spent all of 2017 on the disabled list with a shoulder injury and was dropped from the 40-man roster. ⚾ That **J.J. Hoover** was able to compile more than 41 innings of work on a Diamondbacks team that won 93 games is quite something, especially after last year's *Annual* made a joke about Hoover vacuums and sucking. ⚾ Asdrubal Cabrera (walk). Yoenis Cespedes (single). Dom Smith (ground-rule double). So came and went **Matt Koch's** only big-league outing of 2017. Enjoy Arby's. ⚾ A former top-five pick who was once thought of as a potential ace and later became an actual useful reliever, **Brian Matusz** is nearing the end of the line. ⚾ **Jared Miller** is one of those lefties whose stuff (low-90s fastball, fringy secondaries) doesn't project to work against big-league hitters, so it's nice that he got to beat up some more minor-league hitters in the meantime. He'll get his shot to prove he's more than the sum of his parts, perhaps as early as 2018. ⚾ This **Cody Reed** still has a chance to be better than the other Cody Reed. Although Cody Reed has already reached the majors and Cody

Reed only just reached High-A, Cody Reed is struggling as a big-league reliever. The Cody Reed race could come down to the wire. **Jimmie Sherfy** looks the part of a late-inning reliever, but the whole high-octane profile is reliant upon him keeping his violently whippy delivery in order. Massachusetts prep player of the year and the 82nd overall pick in last June's draft, **Matt Tabor** throws in the mid-90s and has room in his frame to project more.

LEAGUE LEADERS 2017

MLB Isolated Power – J.D. Martinez, .387

MLB Slugging Percentage – J.D. Martinez, .690

ATLANTA BRAVES

Essay by Russell Carleton

Player comments by Demetrius Bell and BP staff

On May 25, 2017, I took my daughters out to the ballgame at brand new SunTrust Park. The Braves were playing a Thursday afternoon getaway day game against the Pirates and the ever meme-able Bartolo Colon was pitching in what turned out to be one of his last outings as a Brave. Armed with a prepaid parking pass for one of the "official" garages, I set sail for the new home of the Braves around 10:30. I don't live all that far away from the stadium, and so for a noontime game, I figured that would be plenty of time to get myself parked, hop on the shuttle that the Braves promised to have on hand and work my way into the stadium in time for the first pitch.

The problem with SunTrust Park is that its proximity to two major interstates makes it seem like a good place to build a ballpark, until you realize that means it was also a good place for plenty of other commercial development forty years ago. There's a large shopping mall nearby, as well as several office parks, and so the roads and parking infrastructure had already been built to handle shopping and working traffic, rather than ballpark traffic. Unlike building in a part of town where there wasn't much going on, you can't rebuild that infrastructure from the ground up. The planners had to squeeze things in where they could. It doesn't help that the nearest MARTA station is literally in the next county over.

And so, as Bartolo threw his first pitch that day, I was driving past several parking lots that held cars belonging to people who were hard at work while I played hooky. Or at least crawling past them. I was stuck in traffic behind a bunch of other people who were trying to get to that same "official" parking garage in which the Braves had claimed some spaces. By the time I got there and placed my car between those "official" yellow lines, it took another 15 minutes until the shuttle arrived, and even then it dropped us off across the highway from the park, right at the foot of a pedestrian bridge. Crossing a bridge like that isn't a big deal if you're an adult, but when your baseball companions are seven and five, the challenge is a little greater. By the time we reached our seats, it was the third inning and the Pirates already had a 5-0 lead.

That's how the 2017 Atlanta Braves season went. The ballpark was nice enough, but everything else didn't quite fit and it was pretty much over before it started. This was supposed to be the third year in the rebuild—one of awkward growth—after seasons of 95 and 93 losses. Even if no one expected the Braves to have a winning season, there comes a point when you have to show that you're capable of avoiding 90 losses.

The framework for what was *supposed* to happen was pretty clear. Freddie Freeman was the superstar already on the roster. Dansby Swanson—still a rookie by literally one at-bat coming into 2017—was the preseason favorite for NL Rookie of the Year. He was, by midseason, supposed to pair up the middle with 20-year-old *wünderkind* Ozzie Albies. Julio Teheran was supposed to continue to be the 200-inning rock on which the rotation was built. Relievers Arodys Vizcaino and Ian Krol were supposed to mature into bullpen stoppers. And there was supposed to be just oodles of pitching on

BRAVES PROSPECTUS

2017 W-L: 72-90, 3RD IN NL EAST

Pythag	.445	20th	B-Age	28.7	*20th*
RS/G	4.52	20th	P-Age	29.5	*25th*
RA/G	5.07	24th	Salary	$122.6M	*19th*
TAv	.264	14th	M$/MW	$4.6M	*10th*
TAv-P	.278	26th	DL Days	1146	*19th*
FIP	4.52	18th	$ on DL	14%	*15th*
DER	.698	21st			

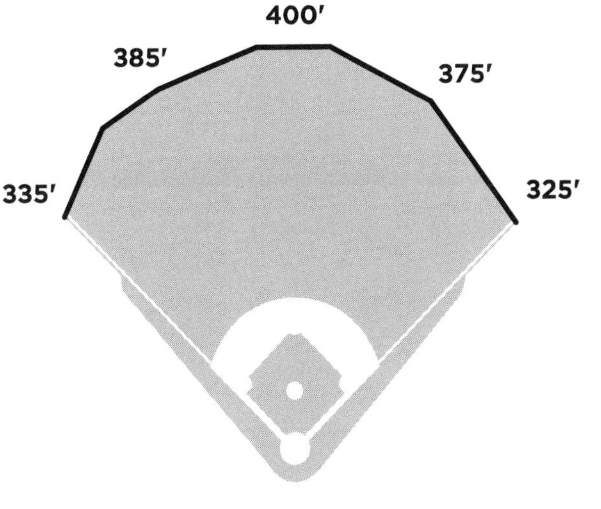

Outfield wall profile: **6′** to **16′**

Three-Year Park Factors

Runs	Runs/RH	Runs/LH	HR/RH	HR/LH
101	95	108	91	108

Top Hitter WARP	5.9 Tyler Flowers
Top Pitcher WARP	3.8 Julio Teheran
Top Prospect	Ronald Acuna

2017 Hit List Ranking

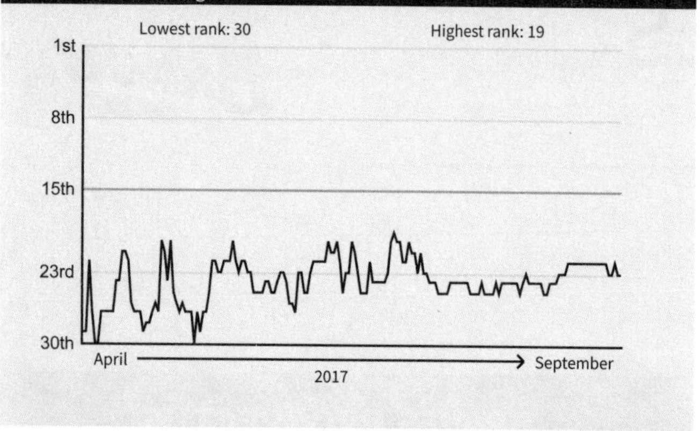

Committed Payroll (in millions)

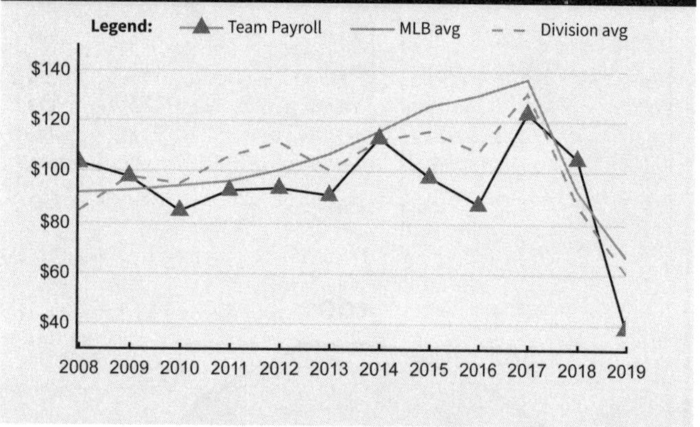

Farm System Ranking

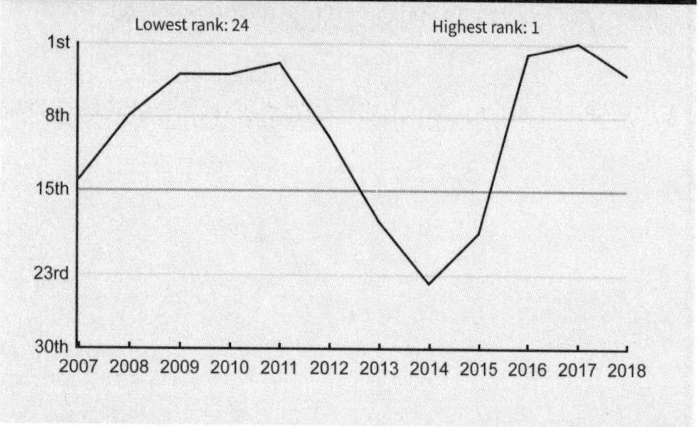

Personnel

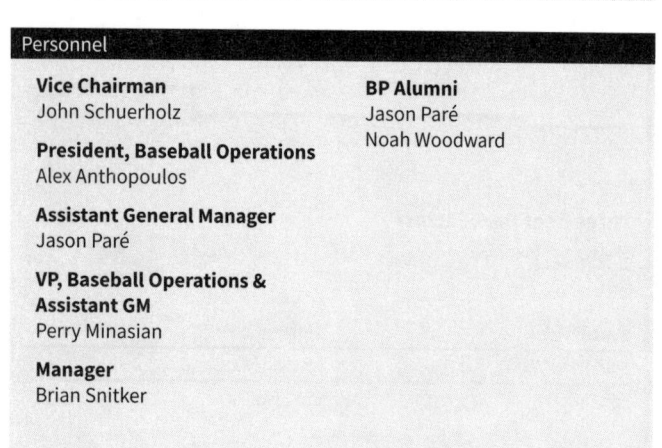

Vice Chairman
John Schuerholz

President, Baseball Operations
Alex Anthopoulos

Assistant General Manager
Jason Paré

VP, Baseball Operations & Assistant GM
Perry Minasian

Manager
Brian Snitker

BP Alumni
Jason Paré
Noah Woodward

its way. Mike Foltynewicz was finally going to put up a strikeout-per-nine rate to rival the number of letters in his name. The first wave of newbies from which the new Maddux/Glavine/Smoltz would be assembled (Sean Newcomb, Matt Wisler, Max Fried, Lucas Sims, Aaron Blair) would arrive. Things were supposed to be looking up.

Freeman put in a performance worthy of the title of superstar, logging a second straight season with an OBP over .400, but he missed six weeks with a broken wrist. Swanson ended up pairing with Albies by midseason, but in a Gwinnett Braves uniform. The new generation of pitchers looked more like Steve Avery and Kent Mercker. It wasn't likely that *everything* Braves fans (and Braves brass) hoped for was going to happen, but looking back over 2017, none of it did.

A young team is like a bag of microwave popcorn. You set the timer for two minutes and spend most of the first minute just watching the bag spin in a circle, not doing anything. But you know that at some point, one of those kernels is going to pop, and that pop is the harbinger of a popping bonanza. But sometimes you get a dud bag. As the clock ticks past the 45-second mark without a pop, you start to worry. I wish I had something reassuring to say to you. Instead, I have more bad news.

The day after the regular season ended, general manager John Coppolella abruptly resigned from his job amidst a catalog of hints, allegations and words left unspoken. Sometimes things don't work out the way you planned them, although I don't think anyone fully expected what happened next, with the Braves losing a dozen prospects whom they had signed in the international market, including the highly touted Kevin Maitan. On top of that, the Braves were hit with sanctions to their international signing bonus pool going forward, meaning that maintaining a steady stream of prospects through that market just got a lot tougher. That's not the greatest news for a rebuilding team.

And while the fallout from the MLB sanctions will dominate the memories of 2017 and probably 2018 for all those Braves fans out there, there was at least one positive thing that happened in 2017, perhaps not for the reason you might think. In fact, perhaps for the opposite reason. The Braves went into 2017 with a rather unorthodox strategy for a rebuilding team: They started signing old players. (That line used to make me giggle when I was younger than those "old" players.) And they traded some younger players. The aforementioned Bartolo Colon was signed, along with fellow quadragenarian R. A. Dickey. Jaime Garcia—remember when he was almost Rookie of the Year in 2010?—was a trade acquisition and the Braves gave up 24-year-old John Gant in the deal. Second baseman Brandon Phillips was gotten in a barter as well and former Phillies stalwart Ryan Howard somehow ended up at Triple-A. At the same time, fourth outfielder Mallex Smith and reliever Shae Simmons were shipped off to Seattle. What were the Braves doing?

Well, for one, Smith was always going to be a fourth outfielder and Simmons a middling middle reliever. They weren't long-term assets, so they were flipped for what they might bring. As to the veterans, the Braves were doing a simple math problem that said they needed to pitch 1,458 innings in 2017, and while it may be tempting to "just play the kids," when they did that in 2016, the kids got smacked around. Even without leading to lasting trauma, that's still a recipe for starts that last 3 1/3 innings and a burned-out bullpen. Then, you have to pitch guys to cover the situation, rather than pitch them in a way that is best for their development. Why not have the veterans cover some of those innings and have the kids develop at Triple-A? If one of the kids took a giant leap in the minors, it's not like anyone was counting on Bartolo going into the Hall of Fame wearing a Braves hat. He could be jettisoned or at least heaved overboard.

But more than that, the Braves knew it would eventually be July. If some miracle had happened and they were in contention, the veterans would be nice to have around. If they were out of it (as it so happened they were), it can be easy to sell other teams on the idea that the veteran you just happen to have is exactly what they need "for the stretch run." Surely enough, the Twins bit on Garcia and the Braves were able to claim Huascar Ynoa as a prize. The Smith/Simmons deal brought back Luiz Gohara, who eventually pitched for the big club by the end of the year. It's not that anyone's expecting either to be an all-star, but prospects don't have to be future all-stars to be worth something.

In 2017, there were 333 players who were in their "cost-controlled" years and logged at least 50 plate appearances. If we take away the top 100 of these players (Aaron Judge, Kris Bryant, etc.) and focus on the ones who probably weren't highly regarded during their prospect days, they still returned an average of about two-tenths of a win to their teams. Do the same thing for pitchers and you get the same result. If the Braves get *that* out of Ynoa or Gohara, they'll have picked up a win or so worth of value out of those guys during their cost-controlled years.

So let's go back over the transactions. The Braves, who knew they weren't going anywhere in 2017, laid down around $30 million for Colon, Dickey, Garcia and Phillips. Garcia was the only player who brought back any sort of trade return. (Phillips was traded at the end of August, but for 29-year-old catcher Tony Sanchez.) For their $30 million, the Braves got whatever value those guys could provide—not all that useful in the context of a lost season—before getting a gift that might just keep on giving. But now looking back on the whole business, it was clear what the Braves were really doing, which was laundering free agent money into buying prospects from other teams. They aren't the first team to use the strategy, but they've been a little more forthright about using it than most. This is the team, after all, that took on Bronson Arroyo's dead contract for the pleasure of receiving Touki Toussaint.

People who talk about such things for a living generally believe that the Braves and White Sox have the most talent-laden farm systems in baseball, with the Braves scoring points based on their extensive depth of guys—even after the sanctions—who look like they'll be "decent." This is how you make that depth happen. It's also one of those trends that in a few years, we'll look back on and realize it was the next big thing and we didn't see it when it was happening.

In the most recent Collective Bargaining Agreement negotiations, owners and players agreed that teams would have a cap on how much they could spend on signing bonuses in the international market. In the previous CBA, they had agreed to one on the Rule 4 draft. Baseball's economics have long favored gathering together talented young players, because as a whole, they tend to produce value at a rate that is much cheaper than that of free agents, even after accounting for the expenses of running a farm system to get them some practice time and for the signing bonuses paid to guys who never make it to the majors. But with the amount of money a team can directly spend on young players capped, perhaps there's a (legal) workaround? If a team is willing to spend $30 million in a fully free-market system, but can only spend $4 million, they can take that extra $26 million and direct it to salaries for "trade chip" guys and then go shopping in July. It's a bit riskier of a plan (the trade chip might get hurt or have an awful first half), but it's a way to spend more money to obtain more young players. They probably won't be A-grade blue chippers, but rather B- and C-level prospects—the kinds that provide the value no one talks about.

So, even if the Braves weren't much to look at on the field in 2017 (and let's be honest, they're not "there" yet for 2018 either), they were at least experimenting with a strategy that might be something new and fun in terms of how rosters are (slowly) constructed. In a few years, someone might look back on Bartolo one more time and smile about the small part he played in the evolution of the game.

—Russell A. Carleton is an author of Baseball Prospectus.

Hitters

Ronald Acuna CF Born: 12/18/97 Age: 20 Bats: R Throws: R Height: 6'0" Weight: 180 Origin: International Free Agent, 2014

YEAR	TEAM	LVL	AGE	PA	R	2B	3B	HR	RBI	BB	K	SB	CS	AVG/OBP/SLG	TAv	VORP	BABIP	BRR	FRAA	WARP
2015	BRA	RK	17	157	31	9	2	3	11	18	23	11	3	.258/.376/.424	.273	8.2	.292	1.1	CF(33): -1.5	0.7
2015	DNV	RK	17	80	10	5	2	1	7	10	19	5	1	.290/.388/.464	.318	8.8	.388	1.2	CF(12): -2.0, RF(6): -0.6	0.6
2016	ROM	A	18	171	27	2	2	4	18	18	28	14	7	.311/.387/.432	.319	17.3	.359	2.9	CF(34): 1.0	2.0
2017	BRV	A+	19	126	21	3	5	3	19	8	40	14	3	.287/.336/.478	.283	7.4	.411	1.2	CF(19): -1.7, RF(9): 0.1	0.6
2017	MIS	AA	19	243	29	14	1	9	30	18	56	19	11	.326/.374/.520	.320	21.6	.396	0.6	CF(34): -0.9, RF(14): -1.4	2.1
2017	GWN	AAA	19	243	38	14	2	9	33	17	48	11	6	.344/.393/.548	.302	17.4	.404	0.0	CF(20): 1.8, RF(20): 2.8	2.2
2018	*ATL*	*MLB*	*20*	*538*	*77*	*24*	*4*	*20*	*69*	*35*	*138*	*26*	*13*	*.269/.320/.450*	*.266*	*18.3*	*.331*	*1.2*	*RF -7, CF -1*	*0.8*
2019	*ATL*	*MLB*	*21*	*552*	*75*	*26*	*3*	*23*	*79*	*41*	*143*	*28*	*13*	*.279/.338/.483*	*.290*	*31.7*	*.344*	*2.3*	*RF -6, CF -1*	*2.7*

Breakout: 11% Improve: 33% Collapse: 0% Attrition: 7% MLB: 34% *Comparables: Byron Buxton, Mike Trout, Delmon Young*

The excitement surrounding Acuña went supernova as he proceeded to treat Triple-A as his own personal playground in his age-19 season. It was as though he viewed every promotion in 2017 as a challenge to get better, and he met each challenge with increased levels of vigor and intensity. What made his improvement even more impressive is the fact that his pitch recognition got even better with each promotion, and the across-the-board plus tools he displayed in 2016 continued to blossom into true deployable weapons as he continued to develop. Acuña didn't receive a call-up to the bigs in 2017, but the conversation has shifted from "we'll see him when he's ready" to "we'll see him when the Braves are ready," which depends on whether the new regime wants to get just the extra year of control out of him or hang on until the specter of Super Two is out of reach. However, once he makes it to the big leagues, he should have his fans singing and dancing like the animated warthog and meerkat who coined the phrase "Hakuna Matata" back before the future star was born.

Lane Adams OF Born: 11/13/89 Age: 28 Bats: R Throws: R Height: 6'3" Weight: 220 Origin: Round 13, 2009 Draft (#392 overall)

YEAR	TEAM	LVL	AGE	PA	R	2B	3B	HR	RBI	BB	K	SB	CS	AVG/OBP/SLG	TAv	VORP	BABIP	BRR	FRAA	WARP
2015	OMA	AAA	25	132	14	5	0	4	13	13	21	2	1	.226/.305/.374	.249	3.5	.239	1.6	CF(21): 2.1, RF(11): -0.4	0.6
2015	NWA	AA	25	414	58	21	3	12	49	36	98	29	6	.298/.360/.466	.291	24.4	.372	2.0	CF(40): -0.2, LF(34): 0.0	2.5
2016	SWB	AAA	26	32	2	1	0	0	3	2	10	0	0	.267/.313/.300	.226	-0.1	.400	0.4	RF(3): 0.2, CF(2): 0.1	0.0
2016	TRN	AA	26	332	49	12	1	6	32	36	84	31	5	.253/.343/.363	.279	16.9	.333	5.0	RF(63): 4.7, LF(10): -0.8	2.2
2016	TEN	AA	26	91	12	6	0	3	19	5	20	9	0	.325/.378/.506	.331	10.2	.400	1.9	RF(16): -1.4, CF(4): 0.1	1.0
2016	IOW	AAA	26	26	3	1	0	1	2	0	5	4	0	.231/.231/.385	.251	0.7	.250	0.5	RF(3): -0.6, LF(3): 0.1	0.0
2017	GWN	AAA	27	194	21	10	2	7	30	15	60	15	3	.264/.320/.461	.278	9.7	.357	0.8	CF(23): 2.1, RF(21): 0.5	1.2
2017	ATL	MLB	27	122	19	4	1	5	20	10	37	10	0	.275/.339/.468	.291	6.9	.368	-0.3	LF(27): 0.4, CF(11): 0.2	0.7
2018	*ATL*	*MLB*	*28*	*171*	*24*	*7*	*1*	*5*	*18*	*13*	*46*	*10*	*1*	*.242/.305/.394*	*.246*	*5.1*	*.310*	*1.7*	*CF 0, LF 1*	*0.5*
2019	*ATL*	*MLB*	*29*	*319*	*40*	*14*	*1*	*11*	*39*	*26*	*88*	*19*	*3*	*.246/.315/.415*	*.263*	*12.5*	*.313*	*3.0*	*CF 1, LF 2*	*1.7*

Breakout: 2% Improve: 10% Collapse: 18% Attrition: 33% MLB: 42% *Comparables: Ryan LaMarre, Matt Carson, Jared Hoying*

They don't call him LA Swiftness on the Twitter machine for nothing. Adams made his return to the big leagues in 2017 (he'd had a spoonful of coffee with the Royals back in 2014), and part of the reason he stuck around was his speed. Statcast's Sprint Speed measured him at 29.1 feet per second, fastest on the Braves until Ozzie Albies showed up. When you put his excellent speed in the pot along with a little pop in his bat and passable defense, you've got a nice stew going for a fourth outfielder.

Ozhaino Albies 2B Born: 01/07/97 Age: 21 Bats: B Throws: R Height: 5'9" Weight: 160 Origin: International Free Agent, 2013

YEAR	TEAM	LVL	AGE	PA	R	2B	3B	HR	RBI	BB	K	SB	CS	AVG/OBP/SLG	TAv	VORP	BABIP	BRR	FRAA	WARP
2015	ROM	A	18	439	64	21	8	0	37	36	56	29	8	.310/.368/.404	.304	41.5	.358	4.7	SS(93): 5.7	5.0
2016	GWN	AAA	19	247	27	11	3	2	20	19	39	9	4	.248/.307/.351	.242	4.9	.290	1.1	SS(33): 1.5, 2B(23): 2.3	0.9
2016	MIS	AA	19	371	56	22	7	4	33	33	57	21	9	.321/.391/.467	.339	44.7	.376	4.5	2B(60): 3.3, SS(22): 2.9	5.5
2017	GWN	AAA	20	448	67	21	8	9	41	28	90	21	2	.285/.330/.440	.281	27.5	.342	3.3	2B(82): 3.8, SS(14): -2.0	2.8
2017	ATL	MLB	20	244	34	9	5	6	28	21	36	8	1	.286/.354/.456	.286	14.2	.316	0.6	2B(57): -2.9	1.1
2018	*ATL*	*MLB*	*21*	*655*	*88*	*30*	*8*	*14*	*65*	*44*	*126*	*22*	*6*	*.268/.321/.418*	*.259*	*26.7*	*.314*	*2.9*	*2B 6*	*2.9*
2019	*ATL*	*MLB*	*22*	*620*	*77*	*31*	*7*	*18*	*77*	*45*	*119*	*21*	*5*	*.276/.334/.454*	*.282*	*35.3*	*.317*	*1.2*	*2B 6*	*4.4*

Breakout: 4% Improve: 28% Collapse: 5% Attrition: 16% MLB: 44% *Comparables: Dilson Herrera, Mookie Betts, Rougned Odor*

It may have come a year later than he wanted, but Albies finally made it to the big leagues in 2017, and it did not take long for him to prove that the tools he displayed in the minors would translate seamlessly into Cobb County cheers. Albies showed off his blazing speed and ability as a plus hitter when he quickly became the team leader in triples, and he also proved that he was a more-than-capable defender at second base. Perhaps the biggest surprise of Albies' ascension was the additional pop he showed both at Triple-A and in the majors—his combined 15 homers was more than double his output over the previous two-and-a-half seasons. And he didn't take the easy way either, as five of his six homers came away from the seemingly comfy confines of SunTrust Park. He should be a consistent top-of-the-lineup talent this season and beyond, serving as a pest at the plate before turning into a blur on the basepaths.

Johan Camargo 3B Born: 12/13/93 Age: 24 Bats: B Throws: R Height: 6'0" Weight: 160 Origin: International Free Agent, 2010

YEAR	TEAM	LVL	AGE	PA	R	2B	3B	HR	RBI	BB	K	SB	CS	AVG/OBP/SLG	TAv	VORP	BABIP	BRR	FRAA	WARP
2015	CAR	A+	21	449	50	15	6	1	32	30	54	4	2	.258/.315/.335	.251	15.6	.294	2.3	SS(130): 4.8	2.2
2016	MIS	AA	22	491	46	26	6	4	43	24	82	1	2	.267/.304/.379	.262	17.3	.317	1.2	2B(64): 2.5, SS(32): -0.4	2.1
2017	GWN	AAA	23	142	17	9	1	4	20	8	22	1	0	.295/.340/.473	.278	8.9	.324	-0.2	SS(31): -6.4, 3B(2): 0.2	0.3
2017	ATL	MLB	23	256	30	21	2	4	27	12	51	0	0	.299/.331/.452	.276	16.4	.364	3.0	3B(43): -0.4, SS(26): 0.6	1.6
2018	*ATL*	*MLB*	*24*	*454*	*44*	*24*	*3*	*9*	*48*	*21*	*88*	*0*	*0*	*.257/.289/.393*	*.234*	*6.1*	*.296*	*-0.7*	*3B -2, SS 0*	*-0.3*
2019	*ATL*	*MLB*	*25*	*523*	*59*	*28*	*3*	*12*	*58*	*29*	*107*	*0*	*0*	*.260/.306/.409*	*.249*	*10.3*	*.301*	*2.6*	*3B -1, SS -1*	*0.9*

Breakout: 5% Improve: 24% Collapse: 10% Attrition: 29% MLB: 60% *Comparables: Omar Quintanilla, Marwin Gonzalez, Freddy Galvis*

You might know Camargo as the poor soul who managed to get injured while simply taking the field before a game. If that's all you know about him, you've missed out on one of the most intriguing stories of 2017. A non-prospect in an organization full of prospects, he was called up as a bench option and ended up starting for the majority of the season. While there's nothing spectacular about his game, Camargo showed that he has staying power by simply excelling at the non-spectacular parts of the game. He also has an absolute cannon of an arm. Now he just needs to avoid those nefarious foul lines that are lurking in 30 MLB stadiums, waiting for their opportunity to strike.

Charlie Culberson INF Born: 04/10/89 Age: 29 Bats: R Throws: R Height: 6'0" Weight: 200 Origin: Round 1, 2007 Draft (#51 overall)

YEAR	TEAM	LVL	AGE	PA	R	2B	3B	HR	RBI	BB	K	SB	CS	AVG/OBP/SLG	TAv	VORP	BABIP	BRR	FRAA	WARP
2016	OKL	AAA	27	285	32	17	2	4	33	18	61	6	5	.260/.310/.385	.248	6.4	.325	-1.1	SS(57): 4.7, 2B(5): 0.5	1.2
2016	LAN	MLB	27	68	6	3	0	1	7	1	13	1	0	.299/.309/.388	.260	3.8	.358	1.6	SS(11): -0.9, 2B(10): -0.8	0.2
2017	OKL	AAA	28	414	37	13	4	4	32	26	68	7	3	.250/.299/.336	.214	-4.2	.294	-0.6	SS(97): 0.8, 3B(7): 0.9	-0.2
2017	LAN	MLB	28	15	0	1	0	0	1	2	4	0	0	.154/.267/.231	.146	-1.2	.222	0.0	SS(11): 0.2, 2B(2): 0.0	-0.1
2018	*ATL*	*MLB*	*29*	*90*	*9*	*4*	*0*	*2*	*9*	*4*	*21*	*1*	*1*	*.232/.272/.347*	*.218*	*-0.5*	*.285*	*-0.1*	*2B 0*	*-0.1*
2019	*ATL*	*MLB*	*30*	*209*	*22*	*9*	*1*	*5*	*21*	*11*	*52*	*2*	*1*	*.230/.275/.357*	*.227*	*-1.0*	*.285*	*-0.2*	*2B 0*	*-0.1*

Breakout: 1% Improve: 15% Collapse: 13% Attrition: 21% MLB: 49% *Comparables: Tommy Manzella, Pedro Florimon, Josh Barfield*

A year after shuffling Scully off the baseball coil in style, Culberson curtain-called his way into regular season at-bats in the bigs again for a fifth season despite a .214 TAv at Triple-A. That would've made for a successful year in its own right, but then things really turned sideways: After Corey Seager wrenched his back in the NLDS, Culberson found himself the unlikeliest of next men up. And as it should be for a player arcing through the fringe-blue skies of a career like Charlie's, he seized the moment. A brilliant five-game performance in the NLCS presaged one of the most exuberant, genuinely joyful sprints around the bases you'll ever see in a classic fall loss. Another season spinning yarns on bus trips to Iowa seemed likely until a December trade sent him to Atlanta, where he'll get to tell those tales on a jumbo jet.

Travis Demeritte 2B Born: 09/30/94 Age: 23 Bats: R Throws: R Height: 6'0" Weight: 180 Origin: Round 1, 2013 Draft (#30 overall)

YEAR	TEAM	LVL	AGE	PA	R	2B	3B	HR	RBI	BB	K	SB	CS	AVG/OBP/SLG	TAv	VORP	BABIP	BRR	FRAA	WARP
2015	HIC	A	20	198	27	12	1	5	19	25	69	10	1	.241/.343/.412	.295	12.7	.371	0.5	2B(43): 6.0, 3B(3): 0.4	2.0
2016	HDS	A+	21	378	73	20	4	25	59	41	125	13	3	.272/.352/.583	.308	34.0	.351	4.7	2B(80): 9.6, 3B(1): 0.0	4.5
2016	CAR	A+	21	152	21	9	5	3	11	26	50	4	1	.250/.384/.476	.303	11.3	.394	0.4	2B(30): 2.1, SS(1): 0.0	1.4
2017	MIS	AA	22	511	62	21	6	15	45	49	134	5	7	.231/.306/.402	.267	19.6	.293	1.8	2B(77): 7.8, 3B(43): 1.4	3.1
2018	*ATL*	*MLB*	*23*	*250*	*29*	*10*	*1*	*10*	*33*	*23*	*87*	*2*	*1*	*.218/.294/.411*	*.239*	*4.2*	*.301*	*-0.2*	*2B 3, 3B 1*	*0.9*
2019	*ATL*	*MLB*	*24*	*360*	*45*	*15*	*2*	*14*	*46*	*34*	*124*	*4*	*2*	*.218/.295/.413*	*.255*	*8.6*	*.300*	*-0.2*	*2B 5, 3B 1*	*1.6*

Breakout: 8% Improve: 20% Collapse: 4% Attrition: 13% MLB: 39% *Comparables: Trevor Story, J.D. Davis, Paul DeJong*

Let's begin with the positives: Demeritte started 2017 by zooming out of the gates and hinting at a breakout season. The power in his bat was on full display, and he was also showing his trademark patience and playing good defense at the keystone to boot. Everything was coming up Milhouse for Demeritte until summer, when he fell into a severe and prolonged slump. The talent is there, but now instead of potentially being at or near the top of the organization, he'll once again be fighting to prove he can cut it at Double-A. If he can find a way to make contact like he did during his hot streak, maybe he's got more than a puncher's chance after all.

Tyler Flowers C Born: 01/24/86 Age: 32 Bats: R Throws: R Height: 6'4" Weight: 260 Origin: Round 33, 2005 Draft (#1007 overall)

YEAR	TEAM	LVL	AGE	PA	R	2B	3B	HR	RBI	BB	K	SB	CS	AVG/OBP/SLG	TAv	VORP	BABIP	BRR	FRAA	WARP
2015	CHA	MLB	29	361	21	12	0	9	39	21	104	0	1	.239/.295/.356	.239	6.2	.320	-1.8	C(110): 11.0, 1B(2): 0.0	1.8
2016	ATL	MLB	30	325	27	18	0	8	41	29	91	0	0	.270/.357/.420	.295	19.9	.366	-6.4	C(81): 5.0	2.6
2017	ATL	MLB	31	370	41	16	0	12	49	31	82	0	1	.281/.378/.445	.309	35.8	.342	-0.2	C(85): 23.5	5.9
2018	*ATL*	*MLB*	*32*	*447*	*48*	*18*	*0*	*13*	*53*	*30*	*131*	*0*	*0*	*.239/.308/.379*	*.244*	*12.6*	*.319*	*-1.2*	*C 20*	*3.0*
2019	*ATL*	*MLB*	*33*	*341*	*40*	*14*	*0*	*9*	*36*	*26*	*101*	*0*	*0*	*.232/.308/.368*	*.249*	*7.3*	*.314*	*-2.0*	*C 17*	*2.7*

Breakout: 6% Improve: 35% Collapse: 9% Attrition: 22% MLB: 93% *Comparables: John Buck, Jason LaRue, Mike Macfarlane*

YEAR	TEAM	P. COUNT	FRM RUNS	BLK RUNS	THRW RUNS	TOT RUNS
2015	CHA	14504	15.2	-2.8	-0.6	11.9
2016	ATL	11338	11.8	-0.8	-4.4	6.6
2017	ATL	12424	25.8	-0.6	-1.1	24.1
2018	*ATL*	*16524*	*26.3*	*-2.0*	*-2.1*	*22.2*
2019	*ATL*	*12589*	*23.2*	*-1.8*	*-1.8*	*19.6*

If there's such a thing as a breakout season that goes under the radar, Flowers' 2017 season qualifies. He finally combined his ability as an elite defender behind the plate with a career year of production while standing next to it. As a result, Flowers played much of the season as a top-10 player, according to WARP. It's a shocking development for a catcher who was initially acquired to serve as a backup, and instead his three-year, $9 million contract—the Braves made the easy decision of picking up his $4 million option for 2018—has turned into one of the game's true bargains. But as much as he's helping his own pitchers with elite-level framing, he might be doing more for other catchers across the league as the first (and biggest) proponent of the Force3 Defender—a catcher's mask specifically engineered to reduce concussions in backstops.

Freddie Freeman 1B Born: 09/12/89 Age: 28 Bats: L Throws: R Height: 6'5" Weight: 220 Origin: Round 2, 2007 Draft (#78 overall)

YEAR	TEAM	LVL	AGE	PA	R	2B	3B	HR	RBI	BB	K	SB	CS	AVG/OBP/SLG	TAv	VORP	BABIP	BRR	FRAA	WARP
2015	ATL	MLB	25	481	62	27	0	18	66	56	98	3	1	.276/.370/.471	.316	32.5	.321	1.4	1B(117): -9.8	2.4
2016	ATL	MLB	26	693	102	43	6	34	91	89	171	6	1	.302/.400/.569	.350	69.6	.370	-0.9	1B(158): -2.9	6.9
2017	ATL	MLB	27	514	84	35	2	28	71	65	95	8	5	.307/.403/.586	.341	53.6	.335	2.7	1B(105): -1.2, 3B(16): -2.4	5.0
2018	*ATL*	*MLB*	*28*	*607*	*87*	*34*	*2*	*25*	*91*	*72*	*122*	*6*	*3*	*.293/.384/.508*	*.306*	*40.2*	*.339*	*-0.9*	*1B -4*	*3.2*
2019	*ATL*	*MLB*	*29*	*549*	*84*	*33*	*1*	*24*	*83*	*70*	*110*	*5*	*2*	*.300/.396/.529*	*.327*	*45.8*	*.345*	*0.7*	*1B -3*	*4.7*

Breakout: 1% Improve: 59% Collapse: 1% Attrition: 2% MLB: 99% *Comparables: Miguel Cabrera, Adrian Gonzalez, Mark Teixeira*

Any questions about whether Freeman could keep hitting at an elite level following his excellent 2016 season were answered emphatically. He started strong in 2017, hitting .341/.461/.748 before an errant fastball struck him on the wrist during his 37th game and robbed him of seven weeks. However, Freeman continued to impress when he returned not only earlier than expected but as a decent third baseman as well. You don't *want* him to be your man at the hot corner, but he showed that he *could* be if the need came up. He may have returned a little too early from the wrist injury and admitted that he was swinging a "wet newspaper" by the tail end of the season. The newspaper will be dry and firm following an offseason in the sun, which should be welcome news for anybody who was concerned and ominous news for the pitchers who will have to once again figure out how to keep him from peppering baseballs all over the diamond.

Adonis Garcia 3B Born: 04/12/85 Age: 33 Bats: R Throws: R Height: 5'9" Weight: 205 Origin: International Free Agent, 2012

YEAR	TEAM	LVL	AGE	PA	R	2B	3B	HR	RBI	BB	K	SB	CS	AVG/OBP/SLG	TAv	VORP	BABIP	BRR	FRAA	WARP
2015	GWN	AAA	30	350	43	17	1	3	47	15	41	5	1	.284/.314/.369	.247	8.1	.314	3.4	3B(66): 2.0, LF(9): 1.2	1.2
2015	ATL	MLB	30	198	20	12	0	10	26	5	35	0	0	.277/.293/.497	.287	11.1	.291	0.1	3B(42): -3.3, LF(10): 0.4	0.9
2016	GWN	AAA	31	80	14	7	0	4	18	3	12	2	1	.356/.413/.616	.367	8.5	.386	-2.0	LF(17): -0.1	0.9
2016	ATL	MLB	31	563	65	29	0	14	65	24	93	3	2	.273/.311/.406	.258	18.5	.308	1.8	3B(123): -11.0, LF(4): -0.3	0.7
2017	ATL	MLB	32	183	19	4	0	5	19	7	23	4	0	.237/.273/.347	.228	-0.4	.247	-0.2	3B(39): -5.6, LF(1): -0.1	-0.6
2018	*ATL*	*MLB*	*33*	*309*	*34*	*15*	*0*	*9*	*38*	*11*	*51*	*3*	*1*	*.264/.297/.408*	*.246*	*6.1*	*.292*	*-0.3*	*LF -1, 3B -2*	*0.0*
2019	*ATL*	*MLB*	*34*	*295*	*34*	*14*	*0*	*9*	*34*	*13*	*50*	*2*	*1*	*.262/.300/.404*	*.253*	*5.4*	*.291*	*0.3*	*LF -1, 3B -1*	*0.3*

Breakout: 1% Improve: 37% Collapse: 12% Attrition: 23% MLB: 79% *Comparables: Yulieski Gurriel, Don Kelly, Andres Blanco*

During Players Weekend last season, Garcia elected to have "La Maravilla" as the nickname on his jersey. "La Maravilla" roughly translates to "The Wonder" in English, and Garcia has to be wondering how 2017 went so wrong. The pop in his bat that he had on full display in

2015 and at times in 2016 completely disappeared last year. His bat was the main attraction keeping him around as a starter and once that went away, he found himself on the bench after returning from a two-month layoff due to finger surgery. If he can return to being an everyday starter—which would require enough power to overcompensate for his below-average hot corner defense—he will have truly earned La Maravilla as a moniker.

Adrian Gonzalez 1B Born: 05/08/82 Age: 36 Bats: L Throws: L Height: 6'2" Weight: 215 Origin: Round 1, 2000 Draft (#1 overall)

YEAR	TEAM	LVL	AGE	PA	R	2B	3B	HR	RBI	BB	K	SB	CS	AVG/OBP/SLG	TAv	VORP	BABIP	BRR	FRAA	WARP
2015	LAN	MLB	33	643	76	33	0	28	90	62	107	0	1	.275/.350/.480	.302	30.8	.294	-2.1	1B(149): 10.9	4.5
2016	LAN	MLB	34	633	69	31	0	18	90	55	117	0	2	.285/.349/.435	.293	28.1	.328	0.3	1B(151): -1.2	2.8
2017	RCU	A+	35	27	4	2	0	0	2	3	2	0	0	.208/.296/.292	.212	-1.1	.227	-0.1	1B(4): 0.6	-0.1
2017	LAN	MLB	35	252	14	17	0	3	30	16	43	0	1	.242/.287/.355	.230	-6.9	.280	-1.8	1B(60): -2.5	-0.9
2018	*LAN*	*MLB*	*36*	*42*	*5*	*2*	*0*	*1*	*5*	*3*	*7*	*0*	*0*	*.265/.327/.423*	*.261*	*1.5*	*.294*	*-0.1*	*1B 0*	*0.1*
2019	*LAN*	*MLB*	*37*	*159*	*20*	*8*	*0*	*5*	*19*	*14*	*29*	*0*	*0*	*.259/.327/.421*	*.268*	*6.6*	*.289*	*-0.2*	-	*0.7*

Breakout: 1% Improve: 26% Collapse: 14% Attrition: 19% MLB: 76% *Comparables: Aubrey Huff, Justin Morneau, Mike Sweeney*

For the big, slow cornermen in our lives, we all know that when it goes, it can go fast. And boy things up and went right quick for the 35-year-old in 2017. PECOTA tried to warn us preseason, slapping a projected career-worst (by a lot) TAv on the Dodgers' aging butter-and-egg man despite a dozen consecutive seasons of consistently healthy, well above-average production. Sure enough, an anemic April previewed a DL stint for a balky elbow in May, and that malady in turn led to a herniated stagger into the trainer's room for two solid months through the dog days. After a brief cameo in the season's final third, he shut it down for good in September and reportedly watched the club's World Series run from Europe. Just one year remains on the seven-year pact he originally signed in Sox red, and with a breaking-down body and Cody Bellinger's first-division emergence, he'll enter a season with wild uncertainty for the first time in a long time.

Ender Inciarte CF Born: 10/29/90 Age: 27 Bats: L Throws: L Height: 5'11" Weight: 190 Origin: International Free Agent, 2008

YEAR	TEAM	LVL	AGE	PA	R	2B	3B	HR	RBI	BB	K	SB	CS	AVG/OBP/SLG	TAv	VORP	BABIP	BRR	FRAA	WARP
2015	ARI	MLB	24	561	73	27	5	6	45	26	58	21	10	.303/.338/.408	.277	27.1	.329	6.5	RF(77): 2.5, LF(47): 7.9	4.1
2016	ATL	MLB	25	578	85	24	7	3	29	45	68	16	7	.291/.351/.381	.274	26.2	.329	0.4	CF(120): 20.9, LF(10): 3.3	5.2
2017	ATL	MLB	26	718	93	27	5	11	57	49	94	22	9	.304/.350/.409	.270	35.6	.339	5.4	CF(156): 10.1	4.6
2018	*ATL*	*MLB*	*27*	*637*	*81*	*26*	*4*	*8*	*55*	*40*	*75*	*20*	*8*	*.288/.333/.390*	*.255*	*24.7*	*.314*	*0.8*	*CF 10*	*2.7*
2019	*ATL*	*MLB*	*28*	*562*	*65*	*23*	*4*	*10*	*59*	*38*	*71*	*16*	*7*	*.289/.339/.407*	*.267*	*24.9*	*.315*	*3.9*	*CF 10*	*3.8*

Breakout: 6% Improve: 44% Collapse: 8% Attrition: 17% MLB: 98% *Comparables: Richie Ashburn, Curt Flood, Mickey Stanley*

When it comes to his defense, Inciarte's past three seasons can be compared to the rise of an underground rapper. He delivered some under-the-radar brilliance in 2015 that real baseball heads got hip to before he hit the mainstream. Then the critical acclaim came with a 2016 season that saw him take home some hardware as he began to make waves in the mainstream. Finally, his 2017 offering may not have been as strong as the follow-up to the debut was, but it was still enough to earn him a trip to the All-Star Game so that he could finally receive the proper admiration from the masses. All the while, he continued to deliver the goods as a leadoff man, to the point where he even ended up getting a 200-hit season under his belt. Just like the underground rapper who made his way to the top, Inciarte figures to keep on delivering the hits in more ways than one as his career continues.

Alex Jackson C Born: 12/25/95 Age: 22 Bats: R Throws: R Height: 6'2" Weight: 215 Origin: Round 1, 2014 Draft (#6 overall)

YEAR	TEAM	LVL	AGE	PA	R	2B	3B	HR	RBI	BB	K	SB	CS	AVG/OBP/SLG	TAv	VORP	BABIP	BRR	FRAA	WARP
2015	CLN	A	19	121	10	6	0	0	13	6	35	1	1	.157/.240/.213	.187	-6.3	.230	0.5	RF(18): -0.1, LF(10): -2.8	-1.0
2015	EVE	A-	19	197	31	11	1	8	25	21	61	2	4	.239/.365/.466	.290	9.9	.326	0.4	RF(38): 5.4, CF(3): 1.1	1.7
2016	CLN	A	20	381	43	20	1	11	55	34	103	2	1	.243/.332/.408	.285	19.0	.317	3.4	RF(54): 6.0, LF(10): 0.3	2.7
2017	BRV	A+	21	282	44	17	0	14	45	13	74	0	1	.272/.333/.502	.306	19.7	.329	-1.3	C(33): -2.1	1.9
2017	MIS	AA	21	120	12	4	0	5	20	10	32	0	0	.255/.317/.427	.267	5.0	.315	-0.1	C(23): -0.1	0.5
2018	*ATL*	*MLB*	*22*	*250*	*27*	*11*	*0*	*10*	*33*	*15*	*82*	*0*	*0*	*.218/.282/.399*	*.231*	*3.8*	*.287*	*-0.6*	*C -8*	*-0.5*
2019	*ATL*	*MLB*	*23*	*288*	*36*	*13*	*0*	*12*	*38*	*19*	*94*	*0*	*0*	*.219/.288/.411*	*.251*	*7.0*	*.288*	*-0.8*	*C -7*	*0.0*

Breakout: 0% Improve: 12% Collapse: 4% Attrition: 14% MLB: 25% *Comparables: Jorge Alfaro, Gary Sanchez, Chris Parmelee*

YEAR	TEAM	P. COUNT	FRM RUNS	BLK RUNS	THRW RUNS	TOT RUNS
2018	*ATL*	*7903*	*-4.2*	*-2.4*	*-1.2*	*-7.8*
2019	*ATL*	*9100*	*-1.7*	*-1.0*	*-0.5*	*-3.3*

The Braves decided to disregard Seattle's opinion and try to remake Jackson into a catcher. He's got the arm to wipe out anybody who thinks about nabbing a base on his watch, but there are plenty of questions regarding whether he can translate that raw skill into actually throwing out runners at will. His framing, while rusty, could eventually become average—though any expectations higher than that have long been washed away. However, even if he has to return to the outfield, his power potential alone should lead him to the majors. He still has a strikeout rate that's high enough to cause some concerns, but when he isn't whiffing he tends to crush whatever he does get a hold of. Should he cut down on the strikeouts, he could potentially become the next in the line of catchers who can rake while doing just enough defensively to stay in the lineup.

Nick Markakis RF Born: 11/17/83 Age: 34 Bats: L Throws: L Height: 6'1" Weight: 215 Origin: Round 1, 2003 Draft (#7 overall)

YEAR	TEAM	LVL	AGE	PA	R	2B	3B	HR	RBI	BB	K	SB	CS	AVG/OBP/SLG	TAv	VORP	BABIP	BRR	FRAA	WARP
2015	ATL	MLB	31	686	73	38	1	3	53	70	83	2	1	.296/.370/.376	.283	25.5	.338	-1.8	RF(153): -7.7	1.9
2016	ATL	MLB	32	684	67	38	0	13	89	71	101	0	2	.269/.346/.397	.275	19.6	.300	-3.1	RF(150): -3.1, 1B(1): 0.1	1.7
2017	ATL	MLB	33	670	76	39	1	8	76	68	110	0	2	.275/.354/.384	.269	20.9	.324	2.1	RF(156): -8.9	1.2
2018	*ATL*	*MLB*	*34*	*575*	*57*	*27*	*0*	*7*	*57*	*51*	*78*	*1*	*1*	*.269/.337/.362*	*.250*	*11.5*	*.303*	*-1.7*	*LF 0, RF -2*	*0.4*
2019	*ATL*	*MLB*	*35*	*525*	*61*	*24*	*0*	*9*	*51*	*48*	*77*	*0*	*0*	*.264/.335/.372*	*.259*	*11.0*	*.298*	*-0.5*	*LF 0, RF -1*	*1.1*

Breakout: 2% Improve: 28% Collapse: 13% Attrition: 20% MLB: 85% *Comparables: Al Spangler, Tommy Holmes, Willard Marshall*

Markakis's third season in Atlanta felt uninspired. Sure, he had a batting average that looks pretty enough on a baseball card, but his power and defense both declined into comfortably below-average territory. If—like we said in last year's edition—Markakis is the fast food option that will tide you over for the time being, at least the Braves know that a Michelin-starred Venezuelan bistro is on the way if they remain patient. You know exactly what you're going to get from Markakis at this stage of his career, which is a body to put in right on a daily basis and a continuous questioning of how you should view a mediocre compiler on the $/win scale. It still feels uninspired.

Dustin Peterson OF Born: 09/10/94 Age: 23 Bats: R Throws: R Height: 6'2" Weight: 210 Origin: Round 2, 2013 Draft (#50 overall)

YEAR	TEAM	LVL	AGE	PA	R	2B	3B	HR	RBI	BB	K	SB	CS	AVG/OBP/SLG	TAv	VORP	BABIP	BRR	FRAA	WARP
2015	CAR	A+	20	498	58	15	2	8	62	44	91	6	3	.251/.317/.348	.253	8.4	.295	2.0	LF(114): -10.5	-0.2
2016	MIS	AA	21	578	65	38	2	12	88	45	100	4	1	.282/.343/.431	.303	37.1	.327	0.1	LF(125): -1.4, CF(4): -1.2	3.7
2017	GWN	AAA	22	346	35	17	1	1	30	27	78	1	2	.248/.318/.318	.229	-4.6	.328	0.1	LF(68): 6.4, RF(9): -0.4	0.1
2018	*ATL*	*MLB*	*23*	*250*	*25*	*12*	*0*	*7*	*29*	*18*	*59*	*0*	*0*	*.246/.308/.395*	*.239*	*2.2*	*.301*	*-0.5*	*LF 1, RF 0*	*0.4*
2019	*ATL*	*MLB*	*24*	*285*	*34*	*15*	*0*	*8*	*32*	*22*	*67*	*0*	*0*	*.245/.312/.395*	*.257*	*5.1*	*.299*	*-0.7*	*LF 1, RF 0*	*0.7*

Breakout: 0% Improve: 3% Collapse: 1% Attrition: 3% MLB: 8% *Comparables: Phil Ervin, Dwight Smith, Jose Osuna*

It seems like Peterson has the tools to potentially carve out a starting role in the majors. The issue is whether he'll hit enough to be a solid starter or just a fourth outfielder. There's power, but not enough for fans in the left-field seats at SunTrust Park to bother picking up their gloves. There's some speed, but the only way he ends up in center is if he gets lost. The floor is major-league quality, but the ceiling isn't going to springboard Peterson to the top of any future Braves depth charts. Of course, a step forward with the bat on top of his solid base of tools could easily float him to the top of the current Braves depth chart given their state of decay in the corners.

Jace Peterson 2B Born: 05/09/90 Age: 28 Bats: L Throws: R Height: 6'0" Weight: 215 Origin: Round 1, 2011 Draft (#58 overall)

YEAR	TEAM	LVL	AGE	PA	R	2B	3B	HR	RBI	BB	K	SB	CS	AVG/OBP/SLG	TAv	VORP	BABIP	BRR	FRAA	WARP
2015	ATL	MLB	25	597	55	23	5	6	52	56	120	12	10	.239/.314/.335	.251	12.4	.296	2.3	2B(144): -3.1	1.0
2016	GWN	AAA	26	110	8	3	2	0	6	11	15	2	2	.186/.275/.258	.194	-4.3	.220	0.2	2B(16): 1.9, CF(10): 0.3	-0.2
2016	ATL	MLB	26	408	45	16	1	7	29	52	69	5	5	.254/.350/.366	.275	16.6	.296	-0.4	2B(87): 3.2, LF(15): -1.2	1.9
2017	GWN	AAA	27	155	20	5	1	2	26	25	26	6	1	.258/.374/.359	.266	7.2	.304	0.8	SS(14): -1.1, 2B(7): 0.3	0.8
2017	ATL	MLB	27	215	15	9	2	2	17	27	48	3	0	.215/.318/.317	.235	1.4	.279	1.4	LF(25): -0.4, 2B(15): 0.0	0.1
2018	*ATL*	*MLB*	*28*	*277*	*34*	*12*	*2*	*5*	*24*	*31*	*54*	*5*	*3*	*.241/.332/.365*	*.237*	*4.9*	*.287*	*0.8*	*SS -1, LF 1*	*0.5*
2019	*ATL*	*MLB*	*29*	*318*	*37*	*13*	*2*	*6*	*31*	*36*	*64*	*5*	*3*	*.239/.330/.362*	*.250*	*6.7*	*.285*	*1.1*	*SS -1, LF 1*	*0.7*

Breakout: 1% Improve: 34% Collapse: 9% Attrition: 19% MLB: 85% *Comparables: Andy LaRoche, Chris Getz, Brian Roberts*

There is a place for Swiss Army knives, but when you have a sharp blade and a full-sized screwdriver, it becomes a lot less useful. Peterson went from being a core component of the Braves in 2015 to a bit player in 2017, and he couldn't even hit enough last year to avoid the shuttle back to Gwinnett. One of the only positives is that Peterson put his value as a utility man on full display by playing every position save for pitcher, catcher and center field. The other is that he managed to end the season on a high note, hitting .325/.460/.475 during September and October. Then again, that's the time of year when hitters face the pitching equivalents of Jace Peterson.

Austin Riley 3B Born: 04/02/97 Age: 21 Bats: R Throws: R Height: 6'3" Weight: 220 Origin: Round 1, 2015 Draft (#41 overall)

YEAR	TEAM	LVL	AGE	PA	R	2B	3B	HR	RBI	BB	K	SB	CS	AVG/OBP/SLG	TAv	VORP	BABIP	BRR	FRAA	WARP
2015	BRA	RK	18	121	18	5	0	7	21	12	37	2	1	.255/.331/.500	.263	4.2	.313	0.3	3B(24): 2.5	0.7
2015	DNV	RK	18	131	18	9	1	5	19	14	28	0	1	.351/.443/.586	.356	18.2	.430	-0.5	3B(29): -3.0	1.5
2016	ROM	A	19	543	68	39	2	20	80	39	147	3	3	.271/.324/.479	.299	33.9	.341	-2.6	3B(122): 3.1	4.1
2017	BRV	A+	20	339	43	10	1	12	47	23	74	0	2	.252/.310/.408	.268	12.8	.289	-0.4	3B(80): -2.5	1.1
2017	MIS	AA	20	203	28	9	1	8	27	20	50	2	0	.315/.389/.511	.329	20.0	.393	-0.5	3B(47): -1.6	2.0
2018	*ATL*	*MLB*	*21*	*47*	*5*	*2*	*0*	*2*	*6*	*3*	*14*	*0*	*0*	*.233/.285/.415*	*.243*	*0.6*	*.299*	*-0.1*	*3B 0*	*0.0*
2019	*ATL*	*MLB*	*22*	*381*	*51*	*18*	*0*	*18*	*55*	*26*	*110*	*0*	*0*	*.251/.307/.458*	*.271*	*13.0*	*.311*	*-1.0*	*3B 0*	*1.4*

Breakout: 5% Improve: 10% Collapse: 5% Attrition: 10% MLB: 23% *Comparables: Ryan McMahon, Corey Seager, Lonnie Chisenhall*

A fair share of prospects in Atlanta's minor-league system received a substantial push up the organizational ladder, and Riley was no exception, closing out the year by crushing the ball in Double-A. Still, Riley has some work to do—both with his hit tool and his defense at the hot corner—to reclaim the sheen of his pro debut. The power is still the calling card, and will play at the major-league level even if his swing-and-miss tendencies don't permit all of it to shine through. However, if you combine that with his continually improving defense (which has coincided with shedding weight off of his frame), Riley could be the tonic that cures the Braves' ailing third-base situation.

Rio Ruiz 3B Born: 05/22/94 Age: 24 Bats: L Throws: R Height: 6'1" Weight: 230 Origin: Round 4, 2012 Draft (#129 overall)

YEAR	TEAM	LVL	AGE	PA	R	2B	3B	HR	RBI	BB	K	SB	CS	AVG/OBP/SLG	TAv	VORP	BABIP	BRR	FRAA	WARP
2015	MIS	AA	21	489	48	21	1	5	46	63	94	2	2	.233/.333/.324	.259	10.9	.288	-2.8	3B(120): 6.7	1.9
2016	GWN	AAA	22	533	52	24	3	10	62	61	116	1	4	.271/.355/.400	.265	14.8	.337	-3.8	3B(119): -7.0	0.8
2016	ATL	MLB	22	7	1	0	1	0	2	0	2	1	0	.286/.286/.571	.251	0.3	.400	0.2	3B(2): -0.1	0.0
2017	GWN	AAA	23	432	48	25	2	16	56	42	110	1	2	.247/.322/.446	.260	13.4	.304	-0.2	3B(91): 2.0, 1B(5): 0.2	1.5
2017	ATL	MLB	23	173	22	5	0	4	19	19	41	1	0	.193/.283/.307	.219	-0.9	.231	0.9	3B(41): 0.6, 1B(2): 0.0	0.0
2018	*ATL*	*MLB*	*24*	*365*	*42*	*16*	*1*	*10*	*41*	*36*	*91*	*1*	*1*	*.233/.311/.385*	*.244*	*3.8*	*.289*	*-0.8*	*3B -1, 1B 0*	*0.0*
2019	*ATL*	*MLB*	*25*	*522*	*65*	*23*	*1*	*17*	*62*	*55*	*135*	*1*	*1*	*.233/.317/.402*	*.258*	*8.9*	*.289*	*-1.2*	*3B -1, 1B -1*	*0.8*

Breakout: 5% Improve: 19% Collapse: 13% Attrition: 25% MLB: 44% *Comparables: Daniel Murphy, Matt Tuiasosopo, Neil Walker*

If you're going to be an up-and-down player, the Braves are a highly convenient organization to be in. It's just a 36-mile drive from Coolray Field, home of the Gwinnett Braves, to SunTrust Park, but the journey took its toll on Ruiz, who lost more than a point of TAv for every mile west. When Adonis Garcia went down with Achilles tendinitis in May, Ruiz's task was simple: hold his own on defense and hit right-handed pitching. He handled the former well enough, but the latter bought him another car ride back east a month later. There's no amount of hot corner defense that can make a .517 OPS against opposite-hand pitching digestible. However, relying on that sample to judge whether he can be a useful platoon bat moving forward—which he can—is about as good an idea as using his 1.429 OPS in 14 plate appearances against southpaws as evidence that he's an everyday player—which he isn't.

Kurt Suzuki C

Born: 10/04/83 Age: 34 Bats: R Throws: R Height: 5'11" Weight: 205 Origin: Round 2, 2004 Draft (#67 overall)

YEAR	TEAM	LVL	AGE	PA	R	2B	3B	HR	RBI	BB	K	SB	CS	AVG/OBP/SLG	TAv	VORP	BABIP	BRR	FRAA	WARP
2015	MIN	MLB	31	479	36	17	0	5	50	29	59	0	0	.240/.296/.314	.216	-1.7	.265	-1.8	C(130): -11.0	-1.4
2016	MIN	MLB	32	373	34	24	1	8	49	18	48	0	0	.258/.301/.403	.238	6.9	.276	-0.9	C(99): -8.4	-0.1
2017	ATL	MLB	33	309	38	13	0	19	50	17	39	0	0	.283/.351/.536	.308	27.3	.268	-2.8	C(77): -1.3	2.6
2018	*ATL*	*MLB*	*34*	*255*	*26*	*12*	*0*	*5*	*26*	*15*	*33*	*0*	*0*	*.251/.306/.366*	*.237*	*5.5*	*.271*	*-0.6*	*C -6*	*-0.2*
2019	*ATL*	*MLB*	*35*	*254*	*29*	*12*	*0*	*6*	*27*	*15*	*35*	*0*	*0*	*.250/.308/.378*	*.246*	*4.9*	*.270*	*-1.1*	*C -5*	*0.0*

Breakout: 1% Improve: 27% Collapse: 18% Attrition: 24% MLB: 86%

Comparables: Brayan Pena, Brian Schneider, Tim McCarver

YEAR	TEAM	P. COUNT	FRM RUNS	BLK RUNS	THRW RUNS	TOT RUNS
2015	MIN	17433	-8.0	1.0	-3.6	-10.6
2016	MIN	13825	-6.8	1.6	-2.5	-7.7
2017	ATL	10594	-3.5	1.1	-0.8	-3.2
2018	*ATL*	*8441*	*-4.7*	*0.8*	*-1.5*	*-5.4*
2019	*ATL*	*8421*	*-5.2*	*0.9*	*-1.6*	*-5.9*

From 2013 to 2016, Suzuki hit a grand total of 21 home runs and his ISO never even came close to .200. Then Suzuki got hip to the times, as he might assume the kids might say, and hit 19 home runs, finished the year with a .254 ISO and ended up forming half of what was the best catching platoon in baseball last season. So what changed? For starters, Suzuki's 46.6 percent fly-ball rate was the highest of his career (he had spent the previous three years well below 40 percent). He also pulled the ball more than ever, which is especially beneficial for Suzuki, who has never hit an opposite-field home run in his major-league career. It wouldn't be safe to bet on a repeat of 2017, but one of the more under-the-radar launch-angle adjusters received a $3.5 million extension for 2018 in September and will once again spell Tyler Flowers in Atlanta.

Dansby Swanson SS

Born: 02/11/94 Age: 24 Bats: R Throws: R Height: 6'1" Weight: 190 Origin: Round 1, 2015 Draft (#1 overall)

YEAR	TEAM	LVL	AGE	PA	R	2B	3B	HR	RBI	BB	K	SB	CS	AVG/OBP/SLG	TAv	VORP	BABIP	BRR	FRAA	WARP
2015	YAK	A-	21	99	19	7	3	1	11	14	14	0	0	.289/.394/.482	.372	17.9	.333	2.5	SS(22): 1.7	2.1
2016	CAR	A+	22	93	14	12	0	1	10	15	13	7	1	.333/.441/.526	.361	14.9	.391	1.0	SS(21): 1.5	1.7
2016	MIS	AA	22	377	54	13	5	8	45	35	71	6	2	.261/.342/.402	.295	29.9	.309	2.0	SS(83): 15.9	4.9
2016	ATL	MLB	22	145	20	7	1	3	17	13	34	3	0	.302/.361/.442	.303	13.1	.383	0.8	SS(37): -2.3	1.1
2017	GWN	AAA	23	45	5	1	0	1	5	6	9	1	0	.237/.356/.342	.274	1.6	.286	-0.9	SS(9): -0.9, 2B(2): -0.2	0.0
2017	ATL	MLB	23	551	59	23	2	6	51	59	120	3	3	.232/.312/.324	.237	13.3	.292	3.2	SS(142): -10.1	0.3
2018	*ATL*	*MLB*	*24*	*553*	*63*	*25*	*3*	*12*	*57*	*52*	*119*	*5*	*2*	*.248/.323/.378*	*.250*	*21.8*	*.303*	*-0.5*	*SS -1*	*1.2*
2019	*ATL*	*MLB*	*25*	*569*	*70*	*27*	*2*	*15*	*65*	*57*	*125*	*5*	*2*	*.255/.334/.407*	*.269*	*27.2*	*.309*	*2.4*	*SS -1*	*2.9*

Breakout: 4% Improve: 53% Collapse: 5% Attrition: 17% MLB: 94%

Comparables: Everth Cabrera, Jurickson Profar, Asdrubal Cabrera

What was supposed to be a season of excitement and wonder for Swanson turned into something you'd see in a psychological thriller film where you watch the twists and turns unfolding in front of you between the gaps in your fingers. Swanson came out of the gate struggling mightily at the plate and never got going, posting numbers that reminded Braves fans of another horror show: Andres Thomas. Those hitting woes combined with suspect defense on seemingly routine plays resulted in Swanson making his first career appearance at Triple-A. He only spent 11 games there before fate intervened in the form of a rogue foul line that took out Johan Camargo. Upon returning to the big leagues, Swanson went from looking completely lost at the plate to somewhat competent—he was hitting .213/.287/.312 before the demotion and hit .268/.360/.348 after coming back. There might be a diamond underneath this rough texture, but the rock still needs to be buffed a bit more before it can begin to shine.

Drew Waters OF

Born: 12/30/98 Age: 19 Bats: B Throws: R Height: 6'2" Weight: 183 Origin: Round 2, 2017 Draft (#41 overall)

YEAR	TEAM	LVL	AGE	PA	R	2B	3B	HR	RBI	BB	K	SB	CS	AVG/OBP/SLG	TAv	VORP	BABIP	BRR	FRAA	WARP
2017	BRA	RK	18	58	13	3	1	2	10	7	11	2	1	.347/.448/.571	.326	7.3	.417	0.8	CF(9): -1.6, RF(3): 0.7	0.6
2017	DNV	RK	18	166	20	11	1	2	14	16	59	4	2	.255/.331/.383	.257	4.0	.409	-1.3	CF(35): -4.6	-0.1
2018	*ATL*	*MLB*	*19*	*250*	*24*	*9*	*0*	*6*	*21*	*16*	*94*	*1*	*0*	*.186/.241/.302*	*.185*	*-10.3*	*.280*	*-0.4*	*CF -2, RF 0*	*-1.3*
2019	*ATL*	*MLB*	*20*	*327*	*34*	*12*	*1*	*9*	*33*	*22*	*117*	*1*	*1*	*.202/.262/.335*	*.215*	*-6.4*	*.294*	*-0.5*	*CF -2, RF 0*	*-0.9*

Breakout: 0% Improve: 6% Collapse: 2% Attrition: 5% MLB: 11%

Comparables: Engel Beltre, Nomar Mazara, Raul Mondesi

The Braves did not need to travel far to find their second-round pick in the 2017 draft, as Waters went to high school only 20 miles north of SunTrust Park. They managed to sign him for slightly under slot value, and if he can realize his potential as a five-tool outfielder, the Braves could end up having even more of a bargain on their hands. He entered pro ball with plus speed and a plus throwing arm, and scouts can dream on above-average hit and power tools to boot. He should be a solid defender in either right or left field, which is a good thing as it's unlikely he'll be able to stay in center for long. It'll be a while before we see Waters in the majors, but he could certainly quench a thirst if he's able to make good on the promise contained within his toolbox.

PITCHERS

Kolby Allard LHP

Born: 08/13/97 Age: 20 Bats: L Throws: L Height: 6'1" Weight: 190 Origin: Round 1, 2015 Draft (#14 overall)

YEAR	TEAM	LVL	AGE	W	L	SV	G	GS	IP	H	HR	BB/9	K/9	K	GB%	BABIP	WHIP	ERA	DRA	WARP	MPH	CMD	PWR	STM
2016	DNV	RK	18	3	0	0	5	5	27^{1}	18	0	1.6	10.9	33	53%	.281	0.84	1.32	1.53	1.3				
2016	ROM	A	18	5	3	0	11	11	60^{1}	54	5	3.0	9.2	62	38%	.312	1.23	3.73	4.97	0.0				
2017	MIS	AA	19	8	11	0	27	27	150	146	11	2.7	7.7	129	44%	.310	1.27	3.18	3.67	2.7				
2018	*ATL*	*MLB*	*20*	*7*	*7*	*0*	*21*	*21*	112^{2}	*107*	*19*	*3.7*	*10.6*	*133*	*39%*	*.324*	*1.36*	*4.23*	*4.89*	*0.9*				
2019	*ATL*	*MLB*	*21*	*9*	*10*	*0*	*29*	*29*	180^{2}	*155*	*31*	*3.3*	*11.0*	*221*	*39%*	*.313*	*1.23*	*4.12*	*4.73*	*1.5*				

Breakout: 4% Improve: 8% Collapse: 2% Attrition: 5% MLB: 10%

Comparables: Jameson Taillon, David Holmberg, Martin Perez

The Braves have developed a reputation for being a bit aggressive in promoting their talented prospects. A prime example is Allard. After he dominated rookie ball and Low-A, it would have seemed like High-A was in his future—especially since he was still months away from turning 20 on Opening Day. Instead, the Braves sent him to Double-A to start 2017, and while he may not have dominated the level, he showed that he belonged. Whether he can keep moving up in 2018 depends on whether he can continue to show great command of his plus fastball—the biggest factor in his ability to adjust to the upper minors. However, the biggest story of his season was that he stayed healthy, as back issues have dogged the lefty since before he was drafted. There's no reason to believe Allard won't continue to make his way through the system and up to the big leagues in relatively quick fashion.

Aaron Blair RHP Born: 05/26/92 Age: 26 Bats: R Throws: R Height: 6'4" Weight: 250 Origin: Round 1, 2013 Draft (#36 overall)

YEAR	TEAM	LVL	AGE	W	L	SV	G	GS	IP	H	HR	BB/9	K/9	K	GB%	BABIP	WHIP	ERA	DRA	WARP	MPH	CMD	PWR	STM
2015	MOB	AA	23	6	3	0	13	13	83^{1}	70	8	2.5	6.9	64	55%	.265	1.12	2.70	2.49	2.6				
2015	RNO	AAA	23	7	2	0	13	12	77	67	5	3.2	6.5	56	48%	.273	1.22	3.16	3.49	1.6				
2016	GWN	AAA	24	5	4	0	13	13	71^{2}	77	4	4.0	8.9	71	50%	.358	1.52	4.65	3.63	1.4				
2016	ATL	MLB	24	2	7	0	15	15	70	82	14	4.4	5.9	46	42%	.304	1.66	7.59	6.97	-1.3	93.2	33	42	62
2017	ATL	MLB	25	0	1	0	1	1	3	5	1	15.0	9.0	3	55%	.400	3.33	15.00	2.79	0.1	93.2			66
2017	GWN	AAA	25	7	9	0	25	25	127^{1}	135	10	4.0	7.4	104	43%	.315	1.50	5.02	6.81	-1.5				
2018	*ATL*	*MLB*	*26*	*2*	*2*	*0*	*6*	*6*	*30*	*29*	*4*	*3.5*	*8.3*	*28*	*44%*	*.295*	*1.36*	*4.20*	*4.67*	*0.2*	*92.8*	*34*	*43*	*65*
2019	*ATL*	*MLB*	*27*	*8*	*11*	*0*	*31*	*31*	*193^{1}*	*185*	*28*	*3.4*	*7.8*	*167*	*44%*	*.303*	*1.34*	*4.59*	*5.28*	*0.6*	*92.6*	*34*	*43*	*66*

Breakout: 22% Improve: 38% Collapse: 16% Attrition: 36% MLB: 73% *Comparables: Bryan Mitchell, Kyle Weiland, Josh Tomlin*

At the end of 2017, the youth movement in Atlanta's rotation was well underway. There were hopes that Blair, the forgotten third guy who came over in the Shelby Miller trade, could have taken part, but it would have been too cruel for the Braves to hit on all three pieces in that deal. He only made one start at the major-league level, and things didn't look too different from what we saw over 15 starts in 2016: His fastball is without distinction and there's nothing in his arsenal that can prevent him from getting hit around. He was decent enough at Triple-A in 2017 to earn one more shot to prove he can stick in the majors, but poor enough that he'll be fortunate to have it come as a starter.

R.A. Dickey RHP Born: 10/29/74 Age: 43 Bats: R Throws: R Height: 6'3" Weight: 215 Origin: Round 1, 1996 Draft (#18 overall)

YEAR	TEAM	LVL	AGE	W	L	SV	G	GS	IP	H	HR	BB/9	K/9	K	GB%	BABIP	WHIP	ERA	DRA	WARP	MPH	CMD	PWR	STM
2015	TOR	MLB	40	11	11	0	33	33	214^{1}	195	25	2.6	5.3	126	43%	.257	1.19	3.91	4.24	2.1	84.6	51	0	81
2016	TOR	MLB	41	10	15	0	30	29	169^{2}	169	28	3.3	6.7	126	42%	.279	1.37	4.46	5.14	0.4	85.4	57	0	73
2017	ATL	MLB	42	10	10	0	31	31	190	193	26	3.2	6.4	136	48%	.290	1.37	4.26	4.65	2.0	85.4	69	0	78
2018	*ATL*	*MLB*	*43*	*9*	*9*	*0*	*25*	*25*	*153*	*156*	*19*	*3.2*	*5.9*	*100*	*45%*	*.296*	*1.38*	*4.64*	*5.37*	*0.4*	*83.4*	*58*	*0*	*74*
2019	*ATL*	*MLB*	*44*	*7*	*8*	*0*	*21*	*21*	*122^{1}*	*123*	*15*	*3.3*	*5.8*	*78*	*45%*	*.298*	*1.37*	*4.67*	*5.37*	*0.4*	*82.8*	*60*	*0*	*72*

Breakout: 7% Improve: 9% Collapse: 36% Attrition: 10% MLB: 69% *Comparables: Tim Wakefield, Kenny Rogers, Jamie Moyer*

For a while, it seemed like Dickey was going to go the way of fellow dinosaur Bartolo Colon and find himself on the waiver wire after a string of poor performances. However, Dickey's knuckleball started to dance again and he started to remind us why pitchers of his ilk can last as long as they do. He nearly reached the 200-inning mark for what would have been the sixth time in the past seven seasons and ended up being one of the relatively stable forces in Atlanta's rotation during 2017. Father Time will come for everybody who puts on a big-league uniform, but it appears that Dickey is determined to keep him off-balance just as he's been keeping most hitters this decade.

Mike Foltynewicz RHP Born: 10/07/91 Age: 26 Bats: R Throws: R Height: 6'4" Weight: 220 Origin: Round 1, 2010 Draft (#19 overall)

YEAR	TEAM	LVL	AGE	W	L	SV	G	GS	IP	H	HR	BB/9	K/9	K	GB%	BABIP	WHIP	ERA	DRA	WARP	MPH	CMD	PWR	STM
2015	GWN	AAA	23	1	6	0	10	10	56^{2}	52	7	4.1	10.0	63	42%	.308	1.38	3.49	2.07	2.1				
2015	ATL	MLB	23	4	6	0	18	15	86^{2}	112	17	3.0	8.0	77	36%	.349	1.63	5.71	5.77	-0.7	99.0	43	69	70
2016	GWN	AAA	24	1	2	0	5	5	27	13	0	4.7	8.3	25	54%	.206	1.00	1.67	3.99	0.4				
2016	ATL	MLB	24	9	5	0	22	22	123^{1}	125	18	2.6	8.1	111	43%	.301	1.30	4.31	4.35	1.4	98.7	49	59	64
2017	ATL	MLB	25	10	13	0	29	28	154	169	20	3.4	8.4	143	42%	.324	1.48	4.79	5.83	-0.4	97.9	58	63	74
2018	*ATL*	*MLB*	*26*	*10*	*11*	*0*	*30*	*30*	*171*	*168*	*22*	*3.2*	*8.7*	*166*	*42%*	*.300*	*1.34*	*3.93*	*4.37*	*1.6*	*98.0*	*54*	*64*	*71*
2019	*ATL*	*MLB*	*27*	*11*	*11*	*0*	*32*	*32*	*206*	*181*	*24*	*2.9*	*9.2*	*210*	*42%*	*.307*	*1.20*	*3.67*	*4.24*	*2.8*	*97.6*	*55*	*63*	*71*

Breakout: 37% Improve: 70% Collapse: 13% Attrition: 11% MLB: 97% *Comparables: Felix Doubront, Luke Hochevar, Ricky Romero*

In a lot of ways, there wasn't much difference between the 2016 and 2017 versions of Foltynewicz. He had stretches where he was able to use his high velocity to overwhelm batters while utilizing his breakers and the occasional change to make it look like he'd scaled the mountain in Atlanta. However, for each good actionable stretch there was an equal and opposite reaction that would force his ERA back up toward the sky. The Braves won nine straight games that Foltenewicz pitched from early June to late July, but lost seven consecutive starts of his to close the season during August and September. A slight uptick in walks helped contribute to a year of lateral movement in overall development. If Folty can find a way to avoid his massive blowups, he can settle in as a solid mid-level rotation guy. Or at the very least, maybe he could just do a better job of avoiding the Cardinals, who socked him for 13 earned runs in less than seven innings last year.

Sam Freeman LHP Born: 06/24/87 Age: 30 Bats: R Throws: L Height: 5'11" Weight: 180 Origin: Round 32, 2008 Draft (#965 overall)

YEAR	TEAM	LVL	AGE	W	L	SV	G	GS	IP	H	HR	BB/9	K/9	K	GB%	BABIP	WHIP	ERA	DRA	WARP	MPH	CMD	PWR	STM
2015	TEX	MLB	28	0	0	0	54	0	38^1	31	4	5.9	9.4	40	50%	.273	1.46	3.05	3.92	0.4	96.7	43	54	46
2016	MIL	MLB	29	0	0	0	7	0	7^2	13	2	10.6	9.4	8	37%	.440	2.87	12.91	5.66	-0.1	97.2			42
2016	CSP	AAA	29	2	1	2	30	3	55^1	63	4	4.6	7.5	46	59%	.351	1.64	5.20	5.38	-0.2				
2017	GWN	AAA	30	3	1	1	9	0	10^1	5	1	5.2	7.0	8	54%	.160	1.06	0.87	4.09	0.1				
2017	ATL	MLB	30	2	0	0	58	0	60	48	3	4.1	8.9	59	58%	.278	1.25	2.55	4.55	0.4	96.7	42	58	51
2018	*ATL*	*MLB*	*31*	*3*	*3*	*2*	*52*	*0*	*54^2*	*53*	*7*	*4.3*	*8.5*	*51*	*52%*	*.297*	*1.45*	*4.39*	*4.67*	*0.1*	*95.9*	*42*	*56*	*46*
2019	*ATL*	*MLB*	*32*	*2*	*1*	*1*	*46*	*0*	*48^1*	*44*	*6*	*4.4*	*8.2*	*44*	*52%*	*.303*	*1.41*	*4.57*	*5.27*	*0.0*	*95.4*	*42*	*57*	*46*

Breakout: 25% Improve: 35% Collapse: 23% Attrition: 23% MLB: 71% *Comparables: Saul Rivera, Anthony Varvaro, Evan Meek*

Life is full of zigzags, and if Freeman zigged when he should have zagged in 2016, he got the motions under control in 2017. The southpaw went from barely being allowed in the Brewers' bullpen during his lone year with Milwaukee to being arguably the Braves' most reliable reliever last season. In what can only be described as a gut punch to his former employers, he was able to keep his walks under control—limiting his self-inflicted damage at a career-best rate. If he can keep the control gains, he'll pass Tom Gorzelanny for the most PWARP of any pitcher drafted out of the University of Kansas, and Braves fans should continue to see Freeman's nasty slider and fiery fastball in a middle-relief role for a while to come.

Max Fried LHP Born: 01/18/94 Age: 24 Bats: L Throws: L Height: 6'4" Weight: 200 Origin: Round 1, 2012 Draft (#7 overall)

YEAR	TEAM	LVL	AGE	W	L	SV	G	GS	IP	H	HR	BB/9	K/9	K	GB%	BABIP	WHIP	ERA	DRA	WARP	MPH	CMD	PWR	STM
2016	ROM	A	22	8	7	0	21	20	103	87	10	4.1	9.8	112	52%	.306	1.30	3.93	3.03	2.5				
2017	MIS	AA	23	2	11	0	19	19	86^2	88	8	4.5	8.8	85	53%	.331	1.51	5.92	3.56	1.7				
2017	ATL	MLB	23	1	1	0	9	4	26	30	3	4.2	7.6	22	65%	.338	1.62	3.81	5.65	-0.1	95.4	46	44	54
2018	*ATL*	*MLB*	*24*	*4*	*6*	*0*	*16*	*16*	*84*	*83*	*14*	*4.4*	*9.4*	*88*	*47%*	*.301*	*1.49*	*4.63*	*5.11*	*0.1*	*95.2*	*47*	*45*	*56*
2019	*ATL*	*MLB*	*25*	*9*	*11*	*0*	*30*	*30*	*189^1*	*174*	*27*	*4.1*	*8.7*	*182*	*47%*	*.308*	*1.37*	*4.56*	*5.25*	*0.7*	*95.0*	*48*	*46*	*56*

Breakout: 17% Improve: 29% Collapse: 6% Attrition: 21% MLB: 37% *Comparables: Mike Foltynewicz, Buck Farmer, Felix Doubront*

After recovering from two seasons lost to Tommy John surgery, Fried made his way through the minor-league ranks and shockingly earned a promotion from Double-A straight to the big leagues in 2017—as a middle reliever, of course. Finally, in September, Fried got a chance to make four starts and acquitted himself well, giving up only seven earned runs in total—though he never threw more than 83 pitches in an outing. He'll have every opportunity to make it into the rotation in 2018, and he's certainly got the tools to stick. His curveball still has the potential to turn your face into a grimace as it turns the opposing batter's knees into Jell-O, and his fastball is a true worm killer, inducing grounders at a near 70 percent clip. He'll need to find that consistency relatively quickly though, as there is a wave of arms coming up behind him.

Luiz Gohara LHP Born: 07/31/96 Age: 21 Bats: L Throws: L Height: 6'3" Weight: 210 Origin: International Free Agent, 2012

YEAR	TEAM	LVL	AGE	W	L	SV	G	GS	IP	H	HR	BB/9	K/9	K	GB%	BABIP	WHIP	ERA	DRA	WARP	MPH	CMD	PWR	STM
2015	EVE	A-	18	3	7	0	14	14	53^2	67	4	5.4	10.4	62	53%	.404	1.84	6.20	3.70	1.0				
2016	EVE	A-	19	2	0	0	3	3	15^1	13	1	1.8	12.3	21	68%	.333	1.04	1.76	1.50	0.7				
2016	CLN	A	19	5	2	0	10	10	54^1	44	1	3.3	9.9	60	52%	.314	1.18	1.82	2.04	2.0				
2017	BRV	A+	20	3	1	0	7	7	36^1	33	0	2.5	9.7	39	58%	.340	1.18	1.98	1.60	1.6				
2017	MIS	AA	20	2	1	0	12	11	52	42	2	3.1	10.4	60	46%	.299	1.15	2.60	2.89	1.4				
2017	GWN	AAA	20	2	2	0	7	7	35^1	31	4	4.1	12.2	48	43%	.318	1.33	3.31	2.54	1.2				
2017	ATL	MLB	20	1	3	0	5	5	29^1	32	2	2.5	9.5	31	37%	.366	1.36	4.91	5.92	-0.1	98.7	48	63	65
2018	*ATL*	*MLB*	*21*	*6*	*7*	*0*	*19*	*19*	*108^1*	*102*	*16*	*4.0*	*10.2*	*123*	*44%*	*.305*	*1.41*	*3.98*	*4.41*	*0.9*	*98.9*	*50*	*66*	*68*
2019	*ATL*	*MLB*	*22*	*10*	*11*	*0*	*31*	*31*	*195^1*	*168*	*29*	*3.6*	*10.4*	*225*	*44%*	*.312*	*1.26*	*4.04*	*4.64*	*1.9*	*98.9*	*51*	*67*	*70*

Breakout: 8% Improve: 21% Collapse: 9% Attrition: 21% MLB: 37% *Comparables: Jaime Garcia, Matt Cain, Noah Syndergaard*

There are aggressive promotions and then there's a riding a rocket ship to the big leagues. Gohara may as well be Buzz Aldrin. Throughout his incredibly rapid rise from High-A ball to the majors in one season, Gohara never looked outmatched at any level, including the bigs. He only made a handful of starts for the Braves, but it was enough to suggest that the big man—his listed weight is, uh, let's just say generous—could miss bats regardless of opponent. Raw stuff has never been an issue for Gohara, whose fastball can hit the upper-90s and whose slider induces enough wind power to make us wonder why Liberty Media hasn't tried to use it as an alternative energy source, but control is the big question mark. He has the potential to be scary good if he can continue to find the strike zone with regularity, which would send him into orbit as a staple of the next good Braves rotation.

Luke Jackson RHP Born: 08/24/91 Age: 26 Bats: R Throws: R Height: 6'2" Weight: 210 Origin: Round 1, 2010 Draft (#45 overall)

YEAR	TEAM	LVL	AGE	W	L	SV	G	GS	IP	H	HR	BB/9	K/9	K	GB%	BABIP	WHIP	ERA	DRA	WARP	MPH	CMD	PWR	STM
2015	ROU	AAA	23	2	3	0	39	5	66^1	62	3	4.7	10.7	79	54%	.335	1.46	4.34	4.09	0.7				
2015	TEX	MLB	23	0	0	0	7	0	6^1	5	1	2.8	8.5	6	53%	.222	1.11	4.26	5.47	-0.1	98.8			48
2016	ROU	AAA	24	1	0	2	16	0	22	13	2	6.1	11.0	27	45%	.244	1.27	2.45	4.24	0.2				
2016	TEX	MLB	24	0	0	0	8	0	11^2	22	4	6.2	2.3	3	33%	.383	2.57	10.80	7.78	-0.4	96.6	46	53	45
2016	FRI	AA	24	0	1	1	20	0	24^1	27	4	6.3	11.8	32	43%	.365	1.81	4.81	4.74	0.0				
2017	GWN	AAA	25	0	3	1	9	4	24^1	26	2	5.9	8.5	23	34%	.338	1.73	6.29	7.17	-0.4				
2017	ATL	MLB	25	2	0	0	43	0	50^2	55	4	3.4	5.9	33	43%	.311	1.46	4.62	5.19	0.0	96.3	30	52	49
2018	*ATL*	*MLB*	*26*	*3*	*3*	*0*	*37*	*6*	*62^2*	*62*	*10*	*4.5*	*9.1*	*63*	*42%*	*.317*	*1.50*	*4.82*	*5.56*	*-0.1*	*96.1*	*34*	*53*	*48*
2019	*ATL*	*MLB*	*27*	*4*	*4*	*0*	*52*	*9*	*106^1*	*98*	*17*	*4.4*	*8.8*	*104*	*42%*	*.305*	*1.41*	*4.84*	*5.56*	*-0.2*	*95.7*	*34*	*53*	*48*

Breakout: 23% Improve: 38% Collapse: 23% Attrition: 29% MLB: 71% *Comparables: Zack Godley, Michael Kirkman, Randor Bierd*

During his short stint in the big leagues in 2016, Jackson's major weaknesses were poor command and a repertoire that lefties feasted upon. To help counteract the latter, he completely abandoned his change in favor of throwing more sliders. The results were mixed, as he limited lefties to a .607 OPS last season, but right-handed batters turned into Edwin Encarnacion against him. A career high in innings is nice, but there's still nothing in his arsenal that will blow hitters away and as such, his strikeout rate isn't great. It's looking more and more like his ceiling is that of an up-and-down reliever who is great to have around if you need to fill out your bullpen, but if he's pitching high-leverage spots, you're either in trouble or angling for a draft pick.

Scott Kazmir LHP Born: 01/24/84 Age: 34 Bats: L Throws: L Height: 6'0" Weight: 195 Origin: Round 1, 2002 Draft (#15 overall)

YEAR	TEAM	LVL	AGE	W	L	SV	G	GS	IP	H	HR	BB/9	K/9	K	GB%	BABIP	WHIP	ERA	DRA	WARP	MPH	CMD	PWR	STM
2015	OAK	MLB	31	5	5	0	18	18	109^{2}	84	7	2.9	8.3	101	48%	.262	1.09	2.38	3.28	2.3	94.7	53	43	73
2015	HOU	MLB	31	2	6	0	13	13	73^{1}	78	13	2.9	6.6	54	40%	.288	1.39	4.17	4.90	0.2	94.4	53	43	73
2016	LAN	MLB	32	10	6	0	26	26	136^{1}	133	21	3.4	8.8	134	42%	.298	1.36	4.56	4.92	0.7	94.4	55	40	61
2017	RCU	A+	33	1	0	0	4	3	12	12	2	4.5	4.5	6	45%	.263	1.50	4.50	7.38	-0.3				
2018	*ATL*	*MLB*	*34*	*1*	*2*	*0*	*5*	*5*	*26*	*29*	*5*	*3.7*	*6.8*	*20*	*42%*	*.295*	*1.49*	*5.07*	*5.60*	*-0.1*	*93.4*	*53*	*41*	*65*
2019	*ATL*	*MLB*	*35*	*8*	*12*	*0*	*29*	*29*	*181^{1}*	*189*	*30*	*3.6*	*6.3*	*127*	*42%*	*.304*	*1.44*	*5.24*	*6.04*	*-0.7*	*92.9*	*53*	*40*	*62*

Breakout: 11% Improve: 46% Collapse: 23% Attrition: 14% MLB: 90% *Comparables: Johan Santana, Wandy Rodriguez, Whitey Ford*

In his 1977 inquiry into the evolution of human intelligence, *The Dragons of Eden*, Carl Sagan talks about the discrepancy between our collective ability to recognize and describe from memory: "Witnesses commonly exhibit a total failure in verbal description of an individual previously encountered," he notes, "but high accuracy in recognizing the same individual when seen again." It's a hypothesis baseball fans will have an opportunity to test in 2018, after Kazmir missed the entire season. A hip injury felled him in spring training, then reared its ugly head again during an abbreviated rehab tour in July. He resurfaced in early September sitting in the low-80s at Rancho Cucamonga, and that, as they say, was that. It's not like he hasn't come back from longer odds before, and with nearly $18 million left on his tab he won't lack for theoretical opportunity to present his case a final time in Atlanta.

Ian Krol LHP Born: 05/09/91 Age: 27 Bats: L Throws: L Height: 6'1" Weight: 210 Origin: Round 7, 2009 Draft (#213 overall)

YEAR	TEAM	LVL	AGE	W	L	SV	G	GS	IP	H	HR	BB/9	K/9	K	GB%	BABIP	WHIP	ERA	DRA	WARP	MPH	CMD	PWR	STM
2015	TOL	AAA	24	1	1	1	28	0	31^{1}	21	0	3.7	9.8	34	56%	.259	1.09	2.30	3.21	0.6				
2015	DET	MLB	24	2	3	0	33	0	28	31	4	5.5	8.4	26	46%	.338	1.71	5.79	4.77	0.0	96.5	42	59	48
2016	GWN	AAA	25	1	2	1	12	0	12^{1}	10	1	4.4	10.2	14	42%	.281	1.30	4.38	3.76	0.2				
2016	ATL	MLB	25	2	0	0	63	0	51	54	4	2.3	9.9	56	59%	.355	1.31	3.18	3.82	0.7	96.3	50	58	52
2017	ATL	MLB	26	2	2	0	51	0	49	50	8	3.9	8.1	44	45%	.307	1.45	5.33	6.07	-0.5	95.0	53	50	43
2018	*ATL*	*MLB*	*27*	*2*	*1*	*1*	*46*	*0*	*48^{1}*	*47*	*6*	*3.8*	*9.3*	*50*	*49%*	*.320*	*1.39*	*4.20*	*4.87*	*0.1*	*95.3*	*51*	*55*	*48*
2019	*ATL*	*MLB*	*28*	*3*	*1*	*1*	*57*	*0*	*50^{1}*	*46*	*7*	*3.4*	*9.4*	*53*	*49%*	*.313*	*1.28*	*4.13*	*4.75*	*0.3*	*94.9*	*52*	*54*	*48*

Breakout: 35% Improve: 56% Collapse: 15% Attrition: 20% MLB: 88% *Comparables: Hector Rondon, Boone Logan, Joe Smith*

All the promise Krol showed in 2016 dissipated last year. This is mostly due to the fastball he relied upon when successful dropping a tick in velocity. Hitters slugged .548 against it, over .150 higher than the previous season. Combine that with the rest of his arsenal being underwhelming, and the unfortunate result was a drop in strikeout rate, a big increase in walk rate and his ERA and DRA both soaring higher and further than one of his hanging sliders. He has gone from being the Braves' main lefty to having his role in a bit of flux, which is right back where he was before 2016. Time is truly a flat circle, especially for relievers.

Brandon McCarthy RHP Born: 07/07/83 Age: 34 Bats: R Throws: R Height: 6'7" Weight: 235 Origin: Round 17, 2002 Draft (#510 overall)

YEAR	TEAM	LVL	AGE	W	L	SV	G	GS	IP	H	HR	BB/9	K/9	K	GB%	BABIP	WHIP	ERA	DRA	WARP	MPH	CMD	PWR	STM
2015	LAN	MLB	31	3	0	0	4	4	23	24	9	1.6	11.3	29	39%	.288	1.22	5.87	4.32	0.2	96.0	62	63	44
2016	RCU	A+	32	0	2	0	4	4	14	21	6	1.3	7.7	12	48%	.326	1.64	7.07	5.40	0.0				
2016	LAN	MLB	32	2	3	0	10	9	40	29	2	5.8	9.9	44	35%	.278	1.38	4.95	5.00	0.2	94.7	31	51	30
2017	LAN	MLB	33	6	4	0	19	16	92^{2}	89	5	2.6	7.0	72	44%	.303	1.25	3.98	4.76	0.8	94.5	55	54	40
2018	*ATL*	*MLB*	*34*	*5*	*6*	*0*	*16*	*16*	*84*	*84*	*11*	*3.4*	*8.5*	*80*	*42%*	*.302*	*1.38*	*4.01*	*4.45*	*0.7*	*93.6*	*49*	*53*	*37*
2019	*ATL*	*MLB*	*35*	*10*	*11*	*0*	*31*	*31*	*198^{1}*	*189*	*25*	*3.3*	*8.7*	*191*	*42%*	*.321*	*1.32*	*4.06*	*4.66*	*1.8*	*92.9*	*48*	*52*	*36*

Breakout: 13% Improve: 47% Collapse: 18% Attrition: 12% MLB: 85% *Comparables: Jason Vargas, Roy Oswalt, J.A. Happ*

After a couple seasons wearing the costume of a four-seam-and-curveballer, McCarthy dropped the most balanced four-pitch mix of his career in 2017, reintroducing the cutter as a primary complement to his two-seamer. The stuff played together well enough, and he controlled contact by inducing swings against pitches out of the zone. He missed a brief stretch in May, but otherwise things were rolling right along the back-end road the Dodgers had paved out for him ... until they weren't. Because they never do with McCarthy. For the fifth time in the last six years he failed to top 140 innings, and he hasn't reached triple-digit innings since arriving in Southern California three years ago. He'll try to embark on his quest for another multi-year deal; getting unstuck from the mud of another loaded rotation depth chart in Los Angeles should help.

A.J. Minter LHP Born: 09/02/93 Age: 24 Bats: L Throws: L Height: 6'0" Weight: 205 Origin: Round 2, 2015 Draft (#75 overall)

YEAR	TEAM	LVL	AGE	W	L	SV	G	GS	IP	H	HR	BB/9	K/9	K	GB%	BABIP	WHIP	ERA	DRA	WARP	MPH	CMD	PWR	STM
2016	MIS	AA	22	1	0	0	18	0	18^{2}	13	0	2.9	14.9	31	46%	.333	1.02	2.41	1.85	0.6				
2017	GWN	AAA	23	1	2	0	17	0	15^{1}	15	1	5.9	10.0	17	30%	.326	1.63	4.70	7.72	-0.4				
2017	ATL	MLB	23	0	1	0	16	0	15	13	1	1.2	15.6	26	34%	.387	1.00	3.00	3.77	0.2	97.0	63	59	34
2018	*ATL*	*MLB*	*24*	*3*	*3*	*1*	*52*	*0*	*54^{2}*	*48*	*9*	*4.2*	*11.5*	*70*	*40%*	*.305*	*1.37*	*4.13*	*4.46*	*0.3*	*96.8*	*65*	*61*	*35*
2019	*ATL*	*MLB*	*25*	*2*	*1*	*0*	*39*	*0*	*41*	*37*	*8*	*3.9*	*10.3*	*47*	*40%*	*.309*	*1.32*	*4.70*	*5.39*	*-0.1*	*96.5*	*65*	*61*	*35*

Breakout: 19% Improve: 31% Collapse: 12% Attrition: 22% MLB: 57% *Comparables: Koda Glover, Ken Giles, Silvino Bracho*

Upon reaching the major leagues, Minter immediately made history for the Braves, becoming the first pitcher since 1913 to avoid giving up a walk in his first 10 appearances. While he may have been doing things that haven't been done since the Deadball Era, Minter's arm is very much alive, and the hitters he subdued in the minors and impressed in the majors are all witnesses to it. Combine his impressive raw stuff with his confidence—his stated goal is to dominate hitters—and you have someone who looks to have the makeup to handle high-leverage situations. Assuming he can stay healthy, he appears destined to do very well with the closing duties that will eventually be bestowed upon him.

Jason Motte RHP Born: 06/22/82 Age: 35 Bats: R Throws: R Height: 6'0" Weight: 205 Origin: Round 19, 2003 Draft (#575 overall)

YEAR	TEAM	LVL	AGE	W	L	SV	G	GS	IP	H	HR	BB/9	K/9	K	GB%	BABIP	WHIP	ERA	DRA	WARP	MPH	CMD	PWR	STM
2015	CHN	MLB	33	8	1	6	57	0	48^1	48	4	2.0	6.3	34	32%	.284	1.22	3.91	5.10	-0.2	97.8	55	80	48
2016	COL	MLB	34	0	1	0	30	0	23^2	28	6	3.0	9.1	24	43%	.319	1.52	4.94	6.60	-0.4	96.1	52	57	31
2017	ATL	MLB	35	1	0	0	46	0	40^2	28	6	4.4	6.0	27	46%	.200	1.18	3.54	4.40	0.4	94.7	42	47	41
2018	*ATL*	*MLB*	*36*	*2*	*1*	*0*	*35*	*0*	*36^2*	*37*	*6*	*3.8*	*7.5*	*31*	*41%*	*.299*	*1.43*	*4.98*	*5.74*	*-0.2*	*94.7*	*48*	*59*	*39*
2019	*ATL*	*MLB*	*37*	*2*	*1*	*0*	*47*	*0*	*41*	*40*	*7*	*3.8*	*7.2*	*33*	*41%*	*.294*	*1.39*	*5.16*	*5.93*	*-0.3*	*93.5*	*45*	*52*	*37*

Breakout: 21% Improve: 40% Collapse: 17% Attrition: 4% MLB: 69% *Comparables: Shawn Camp, Craig Breslow, Matt Herges*

Motte posted a career low in BABIP, which helped him cut his DRA by a third and notch a positive WARP for the first time since 2012. Unfortunately, the fact that Motte still struggled mightily despite having the BABIP gods on his side should tell you all you need to know about the type of season he had. When he did get hit, he got hit hard, and he didn't help his own cause by keeping runners off base the easy way. Relievers who give up plenty of walks and hard contact don't last long, even if they are a former Proven Closer, and that may be the case for Motte.

Kyle Muller LHP Born: 10/07/97 Age: 20 Bats: R Throws: L Height: 6'6" Weight: 225 Origin: Round 2, 2016 Draft (#44 overall)

YEAR	TEAM	LVL	AGE	W	L	SV	G	GS	IP	H	HR	BB/9	K/9	K	GB%	BABIP	WHIP	ERA	DRA	WARP	MPH	CMD	PWR	STM
2016	BRA	RK	18	1	0	0	10	9	27^2	14	0	3.9	12.4	38	55%	.233	0.94	0.65	1.99	1.1				
2017	DNV	RK	19	1	1	0	11	11	47^2	43	5	3.4	9.3	49	40%	.284	1.28	4.15	5.64	0.2				
2018	*ATL*	*MLB*	*20*	*2*	*4*	*0*	*9*	*9*	*35^2*	*39*	*10*	*6.2*	*10.1*	*40*	*37%*	*.329*	*1.78*	*6.54*	*7.51*	*-0.8*				
2019	*ATL*	*MLB*	*21*	*3*	*11*	*0*	*24*	*24*	*143^2*	*165*	*41*	*5.2*	*8.6*	*137*	*37%*	*.332*	*1.73*	*6.88*	*7.87*	*-2.4*				

Breakout: 0% Improve: 0% Collapse: 0% Attrition: 1% MLB: 1% *Comparables: Tyler Chatwood, Timothy Melville, Carlos Carrasco*

The Braves have used most of their top draft picks on pitchers during this current rebuild. While most of those pitchers have climbed quickly up the ladder, Muller spent the vast majority of 2017 in rookie ball, where he didn't exactly set the world on fire. His velocity took a dip, which is concerning since it was already in the low-90s before the draft. The good news is that not every prospect has a clear and linear path to the majors and Muller will be given plenty of time to show why the Braves made him their second-round pick in 2016. Until then, he's a work in progress and the work has only just begun.

Sean Newcomb LHP Born: 06/12/93 Age: 24 Bats: L Throws: L Height: 6'5" Weight: 255 Origin: Round 1, 2014 Draft (#15 overall)

YEAR	TEAM	LVL	AGE	W	L	SV	G	GS	IP	H	HR	BB/9	K/9	K	GB%	BABIP	WHIP	ERA	DRA	WARP	MPH	CMD	PWR	STM
2015	BUR	A	22	1	0	0	7	7	34^1	25	1	5.0	11.8	45	66%	.308	1.28	1.83	1.97	1.3				
2015	INL	A+	22	6	1	0	13	13	65^2	50	2	4.5	11.5	84	49%	.300	1.26	2.47	2.49	2.0				
2015	ARK	AA	22	2	2	0	7	7	36	22	2	6.0	9.8	39	47%	.235	1.28	2.75	4.06	0.4				
2016	MIS	AA	23	8	7	0	27	27	140	113	4	4.6	9.8	152	46%	.302	1.31	3.86	4.04	1.8				
2017	GWN	AAA	24	3	3	0	11	11	57^2	45	3	5.2	11.5	74	41%	.304	1.35	2.97	2.68	1.9				
2017	ATL	MLB	24	4	9	0	19	19	100	100	10	5.1	9.7	108	46%	.327	1.57	4.32	5.66	-0.1	96.2	44	54	73
2018	*ATL*	*MLB*	*25*	*9*	*10*	*0*	*29*	*29*	*153^2*	*136*	*19*	*4.7*	*10.4*	*177*	*44%*	*.299*	*1.42*	*3.99*	*4.42*	*1.3*	*95.9*	*45*	*55*	*75*
2019	*ATL*	*MLB*	*26*	*10*	*10*	*0*	*32*	*32*	*205^1*	*162*	*24*	*3.9*	*10.8*	*247*	*44%*	*.304*	*1.22*	*3.64*	*4.19*	*2.7*	*95.6*	*45*	*55*	*75*

Breakout: 40% Improve: 69% Collapse: 17% Attrition: 29% MLB: 94% *Comparables: Tyson Ross, Jake Arrieta, Rubby De La Rosa*

The book on Newcomb as a prospect was that he had the velocity and the stuff to be a front-end starter but needed to improve his command and cut down on his walks. Once Newcomb made it to the bigs, he brought all of the walks and strikeouts with him. He had the best strikeout rate among Braves starters and the worst walk rate of all Braves pitchers. The only thing preventing him from being the pitcher version of Joey Gallo is his ability to prevent homers—giving up less than a dinger per nine innings in 2017 was an impressive feat. Newcomb is still green but has the potential to ripen quite nicely with a little patience.

Jose Ramirez RHP Born: 01/21/90 Age: 28 Bats: R Throws: R Height: 6'1" Weight: 215 Origin: International Free Agent, 2007

YEAR	TEAM	LVL	AGE	W	L	SV	G	GS	IP	H	HR	BB/9	K/9	K	GB%	BABIP	WHIP	ERA	DRA	WARP	MPH	CMD	PWR	STM
2015	NYA	MLB	25	0	0	0	3	0	3	6	0	12.0	6.0	2	46%	.462	3.33	15.00	7.27	-0.1	98.2	41	62	49
2015	SWB	AAA	25	3	0	10	32	0	49^2	40	1	4.2	10.1	56	46%	.305	1.27	2.90	2.99	1.1				
2015	TAC	AAA	25	1	1	0	9	0	13	16	5	4.8	6.9	10	32%	.282	1.77	9.00	5.26	0.0				
2015	SEA	MLB	25	1	0	0	5	0	4^2	9	0	11.6	5.8	3	43%	.429	3.21	11.57	7.71	-0.2	98.5	41	62	49
2016	GWN	AAA	26	3	2	6	36	0	41^1	34	3	3.9	9.8	45	51%	.292	1.26	2.18	3.42	0.7				
2016	ATL	MLB	26	2	2	0	33	0	32^2	26	2	5.0	9.1	33	35%	.279	1.35	3.58	3.49	0.6	97.9	36	61	52
2017	ATL	MLB	27	2	3	0	68	0	62	45	9	4.2	8.1	56	46%	.226	1.19	3.19	4.11	0.7	98.6	58	72	50
2018	*ATL*	*MLB*	*28*	*3*	*3*	*2*	*52*	*0*	*54^2*	*52*	*7*	*4.5*	*8.7*	*53*	*44%*	*.295*	*1.46*	*4.68*	*4.90*	*0.0*	*97.8*	*51*	*69*	*51*
2019	*ATL*	*MLB*	*29*	*2*	*1*	*1*	*45*	*0*	*47^1*	*40*	*6*	*4.4*	*8.8*	*46*	*44%*	*.293*	*1.33*	*4.37*	*5.02*	*0.1*	*97.4*	*51*	*69*	*51*

Breakout: 30% Improve: 45% Collapse: 12% Attrition: 12% MLB: 67% *Comparables: Cory Rasmus, John Parrish, Michael Kohn*

If you liked what you saw from Ramirez in 2016, you had to have appreciated his efforts in 2017 because it was more of the same stretched out over twice as many innings. Early in the season it seemed like he would take a quantum leap, as he posted a 1.99 ERA through the first two months accompanied by improved control. Then the calendar turned from May to June, and while the strikeout rate remained solid, the high walk rate returned and stuck around for the rest of the season. If he can cut down on the free passes, Ramirez could see high-leverage work in 2018.

Josh Ravin RHP Born: 01/21/88 Age: 30 Bats: R Throws: R Height: 6'4" Weight: 215 Origin: Round 5, 2006 Draft (#144 overall)

YEAR	TEAM	LVL	AGE	W	L	SV	G	GS	IP	H	HR	BB/9	K/9	K	GB%	BABIP	WHIP	ERA	DRA	WARP	MPH	CMD	PWR	STM
2015	LAN	MLB	27	2	1	0	9	0	9^1	13	3	3.9	11.6	12	43%	.370	1.82	6.75	5.49	-0.1	99.4			40
2015	OKL	AAA	27	3	1	3	22	0	28	23	2	5.1	12.2	38	45%	.313	1.39	3.86	3.85	0.3				
2016	LAN	MLB	28	0	0	0	10	0	9^2	2	1	3.7	12.1	13	33%	.059	0.62	0.93	2.41	0.3	98.9			24
2017	OKL	AAA	29	4	0	2	30	0	35^1	29	2	4.8	14.0	55	41%	.342	1.36	4.33	2.67	1.0				
2017	LAN	MLB	29	0	1	1	14	0	16^2	12	4	4.9	10.3	19	38%	.211	1.26	6.48	4.54	0.1	98.4	52	65	47
2018	*ATL*	*MLB*	*30*	*3*	*3*	*0*	*52*	*0*	54^2	*51*	*11*	*4.8*	*11.3*	*69*	*42%*	*.303*	*1.47*	*5.06*	*5.20*	*-0.2*	*97.9*	*52*	*65*	*37*
2019	*ATL*	*MLB*	*31*	*2*	*1*	*0*	*47*	*0*	49^2	*42*	*9*	*4.2*	*11.7*	*65*	*42%*	*.315*	*1.31*	*4.45*	*5.11*	*0.0*	*97.2*	*52*	*65*	*37*

Breakout: 13% Improve: 23% Collapse: 14% Attrition: 19% MLB: 42% *Comparables: Blake Parker, Mike Zagurski, Fernando Cabrera*

Throwing baseballs for a living is hard. It's hard to be consistent with your throws, and it's hard on your body to throw consistently. Ravin again dealt with both perils last year, losing time to groin and hip issues while walking over 12 percent of the hitters he faced at Triple-A. On the plus side, his high-octane heater and pretty good slider both missed bats at an obscene rate when he was able to locate 'em, and he parlayed that stuff into a near doubling of his career innings total in the bigs. Ravin figures to rap at the chamber door of a major-league bullpen again this season, but only in an up-and-down role, and nothing more.

Lucas Sims RHP Born: 05/10/94 Age: 24 Bats: R Throws: R Height: 6'2" Weight: 220 Origin: Round 1, 2012 Draft (#21 overall)

YEAR	TEAM	LVL	AGE	W	L	SV	G	GS	IP	H	HR	BB/9	K/9	K	GB%	BABIP	WHIP	ERA	DRA	WARP	MPH	CMD	PWR	STM
2015	CAR	A+	21	3	4	0	9	9	40	39	2	5.2	8.3	37	47%	.325	1.55	5.18	4.59	0.2				
2015	MIS	AA	21	4	2	0	9	9	47^2	29	1	5.5	10.6	56	48%	.257	1.22	3.21	3.54	0.9				
2016	GWN	AAA	22	2	6	0	11	10	50	56	12	6.7	10.4	58	42%	.333	1.86	7.56	6.81	-0.9				
2016	MIS	AA	22	5	5	0	17	17	91	64	3	5.4	10.0	101	42%	.276	1.31	2.67	5.68	-0.6				
2017	GWN	AAA	23	7	4	0	20	19	115^1	95	19	2.8	10.3	132	35%	.275	1.14	3.75	3.54	2.7				
2017	ATL	MLB	23	3	6	0	14	10	57^2	64	9	3.6	6.9	44	40%	.314	1.51	5.62	5.82	-0.2	93.8	49	39	74
2018	*ATL*	*MLB*	*24*	*2*	*3*	*0*	*8*	*8*	*42*	*39*	*7*	*4.3*	*9.7*	*46*	*40%*	*.294*	*1.40*	*4.55*	*5.02*	*0.1*	*93.6*	*50*	*40*	*76*
2019	*ATL*	*MLB*	*25*	*9*	*11*	*0*	*32*	*32*	202^1	*160*	*31*	*4.2*	*10.5*	*237*	*40%*	*.29*	*1.26*	*4.36*	*5.00*	*1.1*	*93.4*	*51*	*40*	*77*

Breakout: 22% Improve: 45% Collapse: 13% Attrition: 28% MLB: 60% *Comparables: Eric Hurley, Garrett Olson, Neil Ramirez*

If there is someone who represents the progress and accumulation of talent in Atlanta's minor-league system, it's Sims. He went from one of the top arms in the organization to a future bullpen arm with only a chance of possibly cracking into the rotation, despite not having changed himself. He made 10 starts last season, and the next wave of starters aren't quite ready yet, so he'll get an abbreviated shot to become a starter in the bigs. However, the high strikeout rate that he posted at every level in the minors did not make the jump with Sims to the major leagues, and as such, he looked very much like a swingman playing the role of a starter.

Mike Soroka RHP Born: 08/04/97 Age: 20 Bats: R Throws: R Height: 6'5" Weight: 225 Origin: Round 1, 2015 Draft (#28 overall)

YEAR	TEAM	LVL	AGE	W	L	SV	G	GS	IP	H	HR	BB/9	K/9	K	GB%	BABIP	WHIP	ERA	DRA	WARP	MPH	CMD	PWR	STM
2015	BRA	RK	17	0	0	0	4	3	10	5	0	0.9	9.9	11	54%	.208	0.60	1.80	2.38	0.4				
2015	DNV	RK	17	0	2	0	6	6	24	28	0	1.5	9.8	26	53%	.384	1.33	3.75	2.22	1.0				
2016	ROM	A	18	9	9	0	25	24	143	130	3	2.0	7.9	125	52%	.305	1.13	3.02	2.76	3.9				
2017	MIS	AA	19	11	8	0	26	26	153^2	133	10	2.0	7.3	125	49%	.275	1.09	2.75	2.82	4.3				
2018	*ATL*	*MLB*	*20*	*8*	*7*	*0*	*23*	*23*	123^1	*121*	*17*	*3.0*	*8.7*	*119*	*44%*	*.315*	*1.32*	*4.13*	*4.77*	*1.2*				
2019	*ATL*	*MLB*	*21*	*8*	*9*	*0*	*25*	*25*	144^1	*138*	*22*	*2.7*	*8.6*	*138*	*44%*	*.312*	*1.26*	*4.29*	*4.94*	*1.0*				

Breakout: 7% Improve: 11% Collapse: 3% Attrition: 7% MLB: 14% *Comparables: Mike Montgomery, Tyler Danish, Francis Martes*

You would think that throwing a 19-year-old to the wolves in Double-A would be a bit much. That's exactly what the Braves did with Soroka, and this wasn't a mid-season promotion, either. He started the season in Mississippi and repaid the Braves' faith in him by having a great season and earning an All-Star appearance to boot. Soroka rode his well-located low-90s fastball and manicured secondaries to the top of a large group of talented right-handed pitching prospects scattered throughout the organization, well ahead of where a pitcher his age should be when it comes to development. Expect him to keep pitching above his age and experience level, as he brings his good stuff and better command to Triple-A, and potentially beyond, during the 2018 season.

Julio Teheran RHP Born: 01/27/91 Age: 27 Bats: R Throws: R Height: 6'2" Weight: 205 Origin: International Free Agent, 2007

YEAR	TEAM	LVL	AGE	W	L	SV	G	GS	IP	H	HR	BB/9	K/9	K	GB%	BABIP	WHIP	ERA	DRA	WARP	MPH	CMD	PWR	STM
2015	ATL	MLB	24	11	8	0	33	33	200^2	189	27	3.3	7.7	171	42%	.288	1.31	4.04	4.66	1.0	94.3	61	44	79
2016	ATL	MLB	25	7	10	0	30	30	188	157	22	2.0	8.0	167	41%	.260	1.05	3.21	3.61	3.8	94.0	53	42	75
2017	ATL	MLB	26	11	13	0	32	32	188^1	186	31	3.4	7.2	151	41%	.281	1.37	4.49	3.74	3.8	93.7	70	46	79
2018	*ATL*	*MLB*	*27*	*10*	*12*	*0*	*30*	*30*	*180*	*172*	*24*	*3.1*	*7.7*	*155*	*42%*	*.286*	*1.29*	*4.13*	*4.59*	*1.2*	*93.5*	*63*	*45*	*79*
2019	*ATL*	*MLB*	*28*	*11*	*12*	*0*	*32*	*32*	208^1	*181*	*25*	*2.8*	*7.7*	*178*	*42%*	*.285*	*1.18*	*4.04*	*4.64*	*2.1*	*93.1*	*63*	*45*	*78*

Breakout: 20% Improve: 49% Collapse: 30% Attrition: 12% MLB: 97% *Comparables: Mat Latos, John Danks, Vida Blue*

Julio Teheran's 2017 back-of-the-baseball-card stats would make you think that the bottom fell out for him over the last 12 months. He had some stretches of pitching at SunTrust Park that made you think they built the new ballpark in spite of him—his home ERA of 5.86 didn't exactly make him feel welcome at his new digs. However, if you take a look at his DRA, this was the same Teheran—the same former top prospect making good on his promise. Then again, expectations have always been out of control for him, and he's never made that big leap to meet them. The slider is good, but not the type of weapon he really needs to keep right-handers off his fastball. The change is fine, but not the type of weapon he needs to avoid having noticeable platoon splits against him. Without the weight of his promise, you'd appreciate him more as the glue that holds this Atlanta staff together.

Touki Toussaint RHP Born: 06/20/96 Age: 21 Bats: R Throws: R Height: 6'3" Weight: 185 Origin: Round 1, 2014 Draft (#16 overall)

YEAR	TEAM	LVL	AGE	W	L	SV	G	GS	IP	H	HR	BB/9	K/9	K	GB%	BABIP	WHIP	ERA	DRA	WARP	MPH	CMD	PWR	STM
2015	KNC	A	19	2	2	0	7	7	39	31	4	3.5	6.7	29	38%	.243	1.18	3.69	5.77	-0.3				
2015	ROM	A	19	3	5	0	10	10	48^2	40	6	6.1	7.0	38	41%	.252	1.50	5.73	7.22	-1.1				
2016	ROM	A	20	4	8	0	27	24	132^1	105	13	4.8	8.7	128	40%	.263	1.33	3.88	5.68	-1.1				
2017	BRV	A+	21	3	9	0	19	19	105^1	101	8	3.6	10.5	123	45%	.324	1.36	5.04	2.93	2.9				
2017	MIS	AA	21	3	4	0	7	7	39^2	30	3	5.0	10.0	44	38%	.276	1.31	3.18	5.36	-0.1				
2018	*ATL*	*MLB*	*22*	*7*	*9*	*0*	*25*	*25*	*125^1*	*115*	*22*	*4.6*	*10.3*	*144*	*37%*	*.310*	*1.43*	*4.78*	*5.51*	*0.2*				
2019	*ATL*	*MLB*	*23*	*4*	*7*	*0*	*17*	*17*	*102^1*	*92*	*20*	*4.4*	*9.5*	*108*	*37%*	*.297*	*1.38*	*5.22*	*5.97*	*-0.3*				

Breakout: 3% Improve: 6% Collapse: 3% Attrition: 8% MLB: 9% *Comparables: Roman Mendez, Robbie Ray, James Houser*

Touki, Touki, Touki, can't you see? Sometimes your cheese just hypnotize me. And I just love your flashy ways. Guess that's why they broke when your curve swayed. It's still hard to believe that Arizona had the nerve to just give him away to the Braves. Terrible interpolations of classic rap songs aside, there's a lot to like about Toussaint—even if it's been the same stuff we've grown to like at every stop of his minor-league tour. It may seem like he was struggling when you scout the stat line, but his peripherals and advanced stats paint a very different story. Plus, his stuff is still getting better. He's improving with fastball command, even though he's still got a ways to go if he wants to be a starter long-term, and his curveball could definitely be described as notorious. Touki's time to shine will come eventually, but until then the *Sky's The Limit* for this *Bad Boy*.

Arodys Vizcaino RHP Born: 11/13/90 Age: 27 Bats: R Throws: R Height: 6'0" Weight: 230 Origin: International Free Agent, 2007

YEAR	TEAM	LVL	AGE	W	L	SV	G	GS	IP	H	HR	BB/9	K/9	K	GB%	BABIP	WHIP	ERA	DRA	WARP	MPH	CMD	PWR	STM
2015	ATL	MLB	24	3	1	9	36	0	33^2	27	1	3.5	9.9	37	37%	.295	1.19	1.60	2.80	0.8	100.2	45	74	48
2016	ATL	MLB	25	1	4	10	43	0	38^2	37	3	6.1	11.6	50	56%	.333	1.63	4.42	3.30	0.7	100.1	46	62	40
2017	ATL	MLB	26	5	3	14	62	0	57^1	42	7	3.3	10.0	64	38%	.248	1.10	2.83	3.59	1.0	99.0	46	70	46
2018	*ATL*	*MLB*	*27*	*3*	*3*	*25*	*57*	*0*	*60*	*56*	*9*	*4.1*	*10.1*	*67*	*44%*	*.301*	*1.39*	*4.07*	*4.41*	*0.3*	*99.0*	*46*	*69*	*45*
2019	*ATL*	*MLB*	*28*	*2*	*1*	*15*	*48*	*0*	*50^2*	*42*	*8*	*3.9*	*10.6*	*60*	*44%*	*.301*	*1.26*	*4.23*	*4.85*	*0.2*	*98.6*	*46*	*68*	*44*

Breakout: 34% Improve: 49% Collapse: 25% Attrition: 18% MLB: 92% *Comparables: Alexi Ogando, Jordan Walden, Trevor Rosenthal*

Vizcaino was one of the few bright spots in the Atlanta bullpen, as the former Closer of the Future set a career high in saves after he took over the role full time in August. After ascending to closer, he was mostly reliable, but his two worst performances highlighted the two areas he'll need to improve in to be an elite reliever. On August 26, he entered a tie game in the top of the ninth against the Rockies and allowed a Carlos Gonzalez single and back-to-back homers by Charlie Blackmon and DJ LeMahieu before being removed. On September 20, he was called on with the bases loaded and one out in the eighth against the Nationals and went on to walk in three batters in a row before being sent to the showers. Those two blips aside, the stuff is electric and his control continues to improve. And just in time, really, as Vizcaino only has two seasons left before he hits the open market despite barely pitching 150 major-league innings in his career.

Patrick Weigel RHP Born: 07/08/94 Age: 23 Bats: R Throws: R Height: 6'6" Weight: 240 Origin: Round 7, 2015 Draft (#210 overall)

YEAR	TEAM	LVL	AGE	W	L	SV	G	GS	IP	H	HR	BB/9	K/9	K	GB%	BABIP	WHIP	ERA	DRA	WARP	MPH	CMD	PWR	STM
2015	DNV	RK	20	0	3	0	14	14	51^2	53	2	4.5	8.5	49	59%	.325	1.53	4.53	3.73	1.2				
2016	ROM	A	21	10	4	0	22	21	129	92	7	3.3	9.4	135	46%	.264	1.08	2.51	2.37	4.1				
2016	MIS	AA	21	1	2	0	3	3	20^2	9	2	3.5	7.4	17	45%	.143	0.82	2.18	4.39	0.2				
2017	MIS	AA	22	3	0	0	7	7	37^1	32	2	2.7	9.2	38	37%	.300	1.15	2.89	3.75	0.6				
2017	GWN	AAA	22	3	2	0	8	8	41	42	5	3.7	6.6	30	44%	.301	1.44	5.27	7.36	-0.7				
2018	*ATL*	*MLB*	*23*	*4*	*5*	*0*	*15*	*15*	*75^1*	*74*	*13*	*4.2*	*9.0*	*75*	*41%*	*.311*	*1.45*	*4.99*	*5.75*	*-0.1*				
2019	*ATL*	*MLB*	*24*	*7*	*12*	*0*	*29*	*29*	*177^2*	*172*	*34*	*4.2*	*8.5*	*168*	*41%*	*.306*	*1.44*	*5.35*	*6.14*	*-0.8*				

Breakout: 5% Improve: 14% Collapse: 7% Attrition: 14% MLB: 26% *Comparables: Jeff Hoffman, Aaron Blair, John Gant*

Poor Patrick Weigel. He had a breakout year in 2016 and picked up right where he left off by starting 2017 with an early promotion to Gwinnett. Unfortunately his season ended in May following Tommy John surgery. He'll be back at the tail end of 2018, and if he can return to the form that saw him pumping fastballs in the upper-90s and displaying solid command, he'll return to being considered one of the top pitching prospects in Atlanta's system.

Joey Wentz LHP Born: 10/06/97 Age: 20 Bats: L Throws: L Height: 6'5" Weight: 210 Origin: Round 1, 2016 Draft (#40 overall)

YEAR	TEAM	LVL	AGE	W	L	SV	G	GS	IP	H	HR	BB/9	K/9	K	GB%	BABIP	WHIP	ERA	DRA	WARP	MPH	CMD	PWR	STM
2016	BRA	RK	18	0	0	0	4	4	12	3	0	3.8	13.5	18	33%	.167	0.67	0.00	2.04	0.5				
2016	DNV	RK	18	1	4	0	8	8	32	31	0	5.6	9.8	35	26%	.365	1.59	5.06	5.75	0.0				
2017	ROM	A	19	8	3	0	26	26	131^2	99	4	3.1	10.4	152	41%	.293	1.10	2.60	3.15	3.3				
2018	*ATL*	*MLB*	*20*	*5*	*7*	*0*	*20*	*20*	*91^2*	*87*	*18*	*5.6*	*11.0*	*112*	*32%*	*.323*	*1.56*	*5.21*	*6.00*	*-0.4*				
2019	*ATL*	*MLB*	*21*	*5*	*9*	*0*	*23*	*23*	*138^1*	*138*	*28*	*4.9*	*9.7*	*149*	*32%*	*.326*	*1.54*	*5.47*	*6.27*	*-0.8*				

Breakout: 6% Improve: 10% Collapse: 1% Attrition: 6% MLB: 11% *Comparables: Lucas Giolito, Julio Teheran, Justin Nicolino*

After big money out of the draft in 2016 commanded even bigger expectations, 2017 was a big step forward for Wentz—a statement just as true in Philadelphia as it is in Atlanta. The southpaw may have gotten off to a relatively slow start, but he gradually worked on his mechanics and continued to develop the fastball and curveball that will one day lead his repertoire, and then it clicked. From July on, Wentz went on an absolute tear in the Sally League, holding opponents to a .167/.244/.245 line over his last 66-plus innings. And all before his 20th birthday. The most encouraging part of his improvement has been his command and if that continues to get better in 2018, Super Bowl here we come.

Chase Whitley RHP Born: 06/14/89 Age: 28 Bats: R Throws: R Height: 6'4" Weight: 220 Origin: Round 15, 2010 Draft (#475 overall)

YEAR	TEAM	LVL	AGE	W	L	SV	G	GS	IP	H	HR	BB/9	K/9	K	GB%	BABIP	WHIP	ERA	DRA	WARP	MPH	CMD	PWR	STM
2015	SWB	AAA	26	2	0	0	3	3	17	13	0	3.2	6.9	13	35%	.265	1.12	2.12	3.51	0.3				
2015	NYA	MLB	26	1	2	0	4	4	19^1	20	3	2.3	7.4	16	51%	.293	1.29	4.19	5.91	-0.2	91.5	52	24	46
2016	MNT	AA	27	2	1	0	6	6	27^2	17	3	2.6	7.2	22	28%	.194	0.90	2.93	3.83	0.4				
2016	TBA	MLB	27	0	0	0	5	1	14^1	13	2	1.9	9.4	15	42%	.268	1.12	2.51	4.73	0.1	92.7	65	33	34
2017	TBA	MLB	28	2	1	2	41	0	57^1	48	4	2.5	6.8	43	34%	.256	1.12	4.08	4.26	0.6	91.6	50	25	43
2018	*ATL*	*MLB*	*29*	*2*	*2*	*0*	*41*	*0*	*43^2*	*45*	*7*	*3.7*	*7.8*	*38*	*38%*	*.297*	*1.45*	*5.11*	*5.25*	*-0.2*	*91.1*	*53*	*26*	*41*
2019	*ATL*	*MLB*	*30*	*2*	*1*	*0*	*45*	*0*	*48*	*45*	*8*	*3.5*	*8.1*	*43*	*38%*	*.296*	*1.32*	*4.76*	*5.46*	*-0.1*	*90.7*	*52*	*26*	*40*

Breakout: 26% Improve: 49% Collapse: 15% Attrition: 15% MLB: 87% *Comparables: Phil Coke, Matt Guerrier, Aaron Heilman*

The Rays grabbed Whitley on a waiver claim after he had Tommy John surgery in 2015, and when he emerged on the other side of that it was clear they had seen the potential for some new tricks in him. Just not enough potential to avoid placing him back on waivers after the season, losing him to the Braves. He throws from a higher arm slot these days and has been trained in the art of the rising fastball. His changeup differentiates itself from the heater better than it used to, too. Whitley isn't a prototypical short reliever, but his modest velocity and three-pitch attack work fine now that he has a better idea of how to use and disguise it.

Bryse Wilson RHP Born: 12/20/97 Age: 20 Bats: R Throws: R Height: 6'1" Weight: 225 Origin: Round 4, 2016 Draft (#109 overall)

YEAR	TEAM	LVL	AGE	W	L	SV	G	GS	IP	H	HR	BB/9	K/9	K	GB%	BABIP	WHIP	ERA	DRA	WARP	MPH	CMD	PWR	STM
2016	BRA	RK	18	1	1	0	9	6	26^2	16	0	2.7	9.8	29	66%	.250	0.90	0.68	2.04	1.1				
2017	ROM	A	19	10	7	0	26	26	137	105	8	2.4	9.1	139	54%	.272	1.04	2.50	2.13	5.0				
2018	*ATL*	*MLB*	*20*	*6*	*7*	*0*	*20*	*20*	*95^1*	*91*	*18*	*4.1*	*10.2*	*108*	*45%*	*.317*	*1.41*	*4.73*	*5.45*	*0.2*				
2019	*ATL*	*MLB*	*21*	*7*	*10*	*0*	*27*	*27*	*163*	*157*	*31*	*4.2*	*9.2*	*167*	*45%*	*.315*	*1.43*	*5.09*	*5.84*	*-0.3*				

Breakout: 5% Improve: 8% Collapse: 1% Attrition: 6% MLB: 9% *Comparables: Lucas Giolito, Justin Nicolino, Jack Flaherty*

Wilson may have flown under the radar a bit in 2017, but those who paid attention should know he'll deserve any and all praise that starts to come his way. His first full season as a professional went about as well as it possibly could, as he quickly transformed from a future reliever to a potential no. 3 starter. That development came about following a tweak in his mechanics and a display of stamina that saw him consistently go deep in games while keeping his velocity intact. With a fastball that regularly sits in the mid-90s, a steadily improving changeup and a breaking ball that is showing signs of nastiness, Wilson is going to have to resort to jamming if he doesn't want his signal to get picked up.

Matt Wisler RHP Born: 09/12/92 Age: 25 Bats: R Throws: R Height: 6'3" Weight: 205 Origin: Round 7, 2011 Draft (#233 overall)

YEAR	TEAM	LVL	AGE	W	L	SV	G	GS	IP	H	HR	BB/9	K/9	K	GB%	BABIP	WHIP	ERA	DRA	WARP	MPH	CMD	PWR	STM
2015	GWN	AAA	22	3	4	0	12	12	65	68	5	1.8	6.8	49	40%	.307	1.25	4.29	3.14	1.6				
2015	ATL	MLB	22	8	8	0	20	19	109	119	16	3.3	5.9	72	35%	.298	1.46	4.71	5.38	-0.4	95.6	46	51	69
2016	GWN	AAA	23	2	1	0	4	4	26^2	27	3	1.7	7.4	22	52%	.296	1.20	3.71	3.96	0.4				
2016	ATL	MLB	23	7	13	1	27	26	156^2	159	26	2.8	6.6	115	42%	.279	1.33	5.00	5.59	-0.4	95.1	48	48	74
2017	GWN	AAA	24	7	5	0	18	14	93^2	101	7	1.9	6.1	64	44%	.310	1.29	3.56	4.87	0.8				
2017	ATL	MLB	24	0	1	0	20	1	32^1	43	5	3.6	6.1	22	33%	.342	1.73	8.35	7.23	-0.7	94.3	43	44	58
2018	*ATL*	*MLB*	*25*	*2*	*2*	*0*	*24*	*3*	*37*	*39*	*5*	*2.9*	*7.2*	*30*	*41%*	*.296*	*1.35*	*4.29*	*4.65*	*0.2*	*94.8*	*48*	*49*	*68*
2019	*ATL*	*MLB*	*26*	*6*	*4*	*0*	*73*	*8*	*117^2*	*111*	*16*	*2.7*	*7.6*	*99*	*41%*	*.3*	*1.24*	*4.15*	*4.78*	*0.7*	*94.5*	*48*	*49*	*67*

Breakout: 31% Improve: 51% Collapse: 21% Attrition: 26% MLB: 89% *Comparables: David Huff, Dan Haren, Ian Snell*

If there was a season for Wisler to show what he could do, 2017 was it. Unfortunately, he spent most of the year at Triple-A and only got one start in the bigs, while getting the majority of his major-league work in out of the bullpen. He continued to show the same aversion to missing bats that he's showed ever since making it to the bigs in 2015, and his curveball and changeup are nowhere near the weapon that his slider is. Wisler has probably missed the luxurious "starting pitcher" boat, but he still has plenty of chance to hop on the "reliever" dinghy, which fortunately always has available seating.

Kyle Wright RHP Born: 10/02/95 Age: 22 Bats: R Throws: R Height: 6'4" Weight: 200 Origin: Round 1, 2017 Draft (#5 overall)

YEAR	TEAM	LVL	AGE	W	L	SV	G	GS	IP	H	HR	BB/9	K/9	K	GB%	BABIP	WHIP	ERA	DRA	WARP	MPH	CMD	PWR	STM
2017	BRV	A+	21	0	1	0	6	6	11^1	8	0	3.2	7.9	10	61%	.258	1.06	3.18	1.97	0.4				
2018	*ATL*	*MLB*	*22*	*2*	*3*	*0*	*10*	*10*	*35*	*33*	*5*	*4.4*	*9.9*	*39*	*45%*	*.323*	*1.43*	*4.29*	*4.97*	*0.3*				
2019	*ATL*	*MLB*	*23*	*4*	*7*	*0*	*29*	*29*	*179^1*	*175*	*27*	*4.8*	*8.5*	*168*	*45%*	*.318*	*1.51*	*5.01*	*5.76*	*-0.2*				

Breakout: 5% Improve: 7% Collapse: 2% Attrition: 9% MLB: 11% *Comparables: Jon Moscot, Matt Magill, Rudy Owens*

For the third season in a row, the Braves used their number one pick on a pitcher. Wright, the former Vanderbilt ace, was arguably the best overall player in the 2017 draft and received a $7 million signing bonus. What do the Braves hope to get for that investment? A tall-but-lean pitcher with solid command and a fastball that's been known to reach 97 mph at times. Add to that two potentially plus pitches in the form of his curveball and slider with an above-average changeup, and you've got a pitcher with a high floor and potentially dynamic upside. If he does indeed have the Wright stuff, it won't be long before he becomes the new kid on the block in Cobb County.

LINEOUTS

Hitters

HITTER	POS	TEAM	LVL	AGE	PA	R	2B	3B	HR	RBI	BB	K	SB	CS	AVG/OBP/SLG	TAv	VORP	BABIP	BRR	FRAA	WARP
Reid Brignac	3B	FRE	AAA	31	437	53	17	3	13	52	41	116	4	1	.251/.326/.411	.249	11.0	.321	-2.4	SS(107): -5.3, 2B(1): 0.0	0.5

HITTER	POS	TEAM	LVL	AGE	PA	R	2B	3B	HR	RBI	BB	K	SB	CS	AVG/OBP/SLG	TAv	VORP	BABIP	BRR	FRAA	WARP
James Loney	1B	TOL	AAA	33	62	6	1	0	0	2	13	7	0	0	.229/.387/.250	.267	0.8	.262	-0.4	1B(7): 0.3	0.1
Cristian Pache	OF	ROM	A	18	514	60	13	8	0	42	39	104	32	14	.281/.335/.343	.262	22.2	.360	5.8	CF(116): 27.8, RF(2): 0.0	5.3
Tony Sanchez	C	SLC	AAA	29	284	33	13	0	4	40	29	61	1	3	.272/.355/.374	.253	8.0	.343	-3.4	C(68): -9.1, 1B(1): 0.0	-0.1
	C	ATL	MLB	29	1	0	0	0	0	0	0	1	0	0	.000/.000/.000	.062	-0.2	--	0.0		0.0
Danny Santana	CF	MIN	MLB	26	26	3	1	0	1	1	1	8	1	0	.200/.231/.360	.187	-1.2	.250	0.2	LF(8): 0.8, RF(3): 0.0	0.0
	CF	ATL	MLB	26	152	16	9	2	3	22	7	33	6	0	.203/.245/.357	.216	-1.3	.243	2.0	LF(30): 2.7, 2B(7): -0.6	0.0
Preston Tucker	RF	FRE	AAA	26	569	84	20	7	24	96	65	102	2	3	.250/.333/.465	.269	14.7	.263	-0.9	RF(54): -8.9, LF(35): 3.9	1.0

For the first time since 2007, utility infielder **Reid Brignac** spent a year without finding a way into a major-league game. Given his uninspiring PCL batting line and advancing age, perhaps "utility" is too complimentary an adjective these days. ⚾ In May, the Braves thought **James Loney** could fill in for Freddie Freeman. In July, the LG Twins of the KBO thought Loney could fill in for Luis Jimenez. Turns out they were both wrong. ⚾ If you're looking for a speedy, defense-first outfielder, **Cristian Pache** could be your guy in a few years. But if he can tap into a little of his power potential, Pache absolutely *should* be. ⚾ Congratulations are in order for **Tony Sanchez**, who made it back to the majors in 2017. He only had one plate appearance in the one game he played in, but he made it! ⚾ Despite showing no signs of tangible improvement from an awful 2016, **Danny Santana** inexplicably received even more playing time in 2017. It'll be a miracle (or disaster, depending on your outlook) if the trend continues this season. ⚾ Well and truly surpassed by his brother Kyle, **Preston Tucker** never cracked the 2017 Astros' roster. He's likely headed for a two-pronged career as both a Triple-A journeyman and a sidenote on his brother's Baseball-Reference page.

Pitchers

PITCHER	TEAM	LVL	AGE	W	L	SV	G	GS	IP	H	HR	BB/9	K/9	K	GB%	BABIP	WHIP	ERA	DRA	WARP	MPH	CMD	PWR	STM
Ian Anderson	ROM	A	19	4	5	0	20	20	83	69	0	4.7	11.0	101	50%	.345	1.35	3.14	4.65	0.6				
Jesse Biddle	MIS	AA	25	2	4	2	27	0	49^{2}	48	3	2.9	9.6	53	45%	.328	1.29	2.90	3.01	1.1				
Rex Brothers	ATL	MLB	29	4	3	0	27	0	23^{2}	23	3	4.6	12.5	33	39%	.357	1.48	7.23	4.56	0.2	96.9	44	65	42
Mauricio Cabrera	GWN	AAA	23	2	2	3	24	0	26^{1}	26	1	8.5	6.8	20	47%	.312	1.94	7.86	8.56	-0.9				
	MIS	AA	23	1	0	0	14	0	13^{2}	8	0	11.9	9.9	15	44%	.235	1.90	5.27	8.71	-0.6				
Josh Collmenter	ATL	MLB	31	0	2	0	11	0	17	29	7	3.2	9.5	18	36%	.393	2.06	9.00	6.87	-0.3	86.3	64	9	21
	GWN	AAA	31	1	1	0	5	4	20	20	3	2.2	9.4	21	29%	.309	1.25	3.60	4.42	0.3				
Grant Dayton	LAN	MLB	29	1	1	0	29	0	23^{2}	19	5	4.6	7.6	20	33%	.215	1.31	4.94	6.95	-0.5	92.9	37	51	40
Anyelo Gomez	CSC	A	24	0	0	7	10	0	14	10	0	2.6	14.8	23	57%	.333	1.00	1.93	2.44	0.4				
	TAM	A+	24	2	2	2	10	0	17^{2}	15	1	3.1	9.7	19	53%	.292	1.19	2.55	2.89	0.4				
	TRN	AA	24	3	1	0	17	1	36^{2}	26	1	2.7	10.6	43	38%	.291	1.01	1.72	3.85	0.4				
Jason Hursh	MIS	AA	25	0	0	5	10	0	14^{2}	10	0	3.1	6.1	10	52%	.250	1.02	1.23	3.72	0.2				
	ATL	MLB	25	1	0	0	9	0	10^{2}	13	1	3.4	5.9	7	57%	.353	1.59	5.06	6.19	-0.1	96.3			47
	GWN	AAA	25	3	4	0	28	0	37^{2}	53	3	2.9	9.8	41	56%	.413	1.73	5.50	2.88	1.0				
Adam McCreery	ROM	A	24	2	0	2	20	0	31^{2}	26	0	4.3	13.4	47	76%	.351	1.29	2.84	1.46	1.3				
	BRV	A+	24	1	1	5	18	0	30^{2}	21	1	6.8	12.6	43	68%	.294	1.43	2.64	2.47	0.9				
Kris Medlen	BRV	A+	31	1	1	0	2	2	11^{1}	10	1	3.2	4.8	6	49%	.250	1.24	3.97	4.34	0.1				
	MIS	AA	31	1	0	0	2	2	10^{1}	10	0	2.6	7.0	8	59%	.294	1.26	1.74	3.64	0.2				
	GWN	AAA	31	3	7	0	16	16	94^{2}	105	15	2.2	8.0	84	38%	.318	1.35	5.42	4.64	1.1				
Akeel Morris	ATL	MLB	24	0	0	0	8	0	7^{1}	6	0	4.9	11.0	9	32%	.316	1.36	1.23	4.92	0.0	94.6			46
	GWN	AAA	24	1	3	1	30	0	46^{2}	38	3	4.4	10.2	53	35%	.282	1.31	3.09	5.30	0.0				
Eric O'Flaherty	ATL	MLB	32	0	0	0	22	0	18^{1}	20	4	4.4	7.4	15	52%	.291	1.58	7.85	5.79	-0.1	91.8	36	44	39
Ricardo Sanchez	BRV	A+	20	4	12	0	22	21	100	117	10	4.1	9.1	101	45%	.358	1.63	4.95	5.82	-0.7				
Daniel Winkler	GWN	AAA	27	1	0	0	10	0	10	14	2	0.9	10.8	12	39%	.414	1.50	6.30	3.48	0.2				
	ATL	MLB	27	1	1	0	16	0	14^{1}	7	1	3.8	11.3	18	38%	.214	0.91	2.51	3.63	0.2	94.7	50	45	35

The Braves had **Ian Anderson** on a very strict innings limit by the time the 2017 season ended, but it was a successful first run at full-season ball for the 19-year-old jewel of Atlanta's 2016 draft class. ⚾ A former high-profile Phillies prospect, **Jesse Biddle** finally returned to the mound after recovering from Tommy John surgery. After an impressive year as a Double-A reliever, don't be shocked if the southpaw shows up in a major-league bullpen near you in 2018. ⚾ When the Braves cut ties with Big Sexy, they replaced him with Big Rexy. Despite striking out a ton of batters, **Rex Brothers** will likely have to settle for another minor-league deal in 2018. ⚾ Although **Mauricio Cabrera** showed plenty of promise after his initial major-league stint in 2016, it came with the caveat that he needed to show better command. He then proceeded to walk everyone in sight in the minors and never got back to the bigs in 2017. Whoops! ⚾ **Josh Collmenter** managed to turn 19 solid innings at the end of 2016 into a major-league deal. He only made it 17 innings in 2017 before the Braves realized they'd made a huge mistake. ⚾ The obscene strikeout rates and feel-good success of yesteryear faded quickly into the black for **Grant Dayton**, as the southpaw struggled with lingering back and neck issues before blowing out his elbow on a rehab assignment. ⚾ A quintessential Rule 5 pick selected by the Braves in December, **Anyelo Gomez** was a fledging starter in the Yankees system before a full transition to the bullpen in 2017 saw him firing flame emojis out of his right arm. ⚾ The good news for **Jason Hursh** is that he spent more time in the majors in 2017 than he did in 2016. The bad news is that 10 2/3 innings still qualifies as a cameo. ⚾ After spending nearly two seasons recovering from injury, at least **Jacob Lindgren** is still younger than Bryce Harper. ⚾ **Adam McCreery** is no relation to *American Idol* winner and country crooner Scotty McCreery, but he's a 6-foot-8 lefty who struck out a lot of guys in A-ball, making him far more relevant to your baseball interests. ⚾ **Kris Medlen** spent 2017 back in the minors, again showcasing his strong command and underwhelming stuff. At this point, it will be a surprise to see him don a major-league uniform again. ⚾ Finally, **Akeel Morris** got to spend more than a day in the major leagues. He still only made a handful of appearances in 2017, but he got J.D. Martinez out twice, so there was plenty to be proud of. ⚾ The Braves did **Eric O'Flaherty** a solid by purposefully waiting until he reached 10 years of service time before releasing him. You can take away his pitching opportunities, but you can't take away that pension. ⚾ **Ricardo Sanchez** is proof that a 20-year-old prospect can seem old, which is a terrifying concept if you're 21 or above. ⚾ Losing multiple years of your career due to injury is a bummer, but **Dan Winkler** has managed to overcome those injuries and return to action. Here's hoping he doesn't have another year-long rehab stint in his future.

League Leaders 2017

MLB Catcher Framing Runs – Tyler Flowers, 25.1

BALTIMORE ORIOLES

Essay by Russell Carleton

Player comments by Patrick Dubuque and BP staff

Is Buck Showalter a genius?

Let's start with the obvious answer to that one. As far as baseball is concerned, I am someone who can barely tap out "Twinkle Twinkle Little Star" on the piano and he is Mozart. Showalter started his managerial career in Low-A in 1985 with the Oneonta Yankees. He was 29. Seven years later, he was managing another Yankee team, albeit one that played in a somewhat larger city located 165 miles to the southeast. Showalter has literally been managing baseball teams longer than I've been going to baseball games.

Across four stops, he's piloted the Yankees, the Diamondbacks, the Rangers and, since midway through the 2010 season, the Baltimore Orioles. In a neat little bit of symmetry, he won the AL Manager of the Year Award in the 1994, 2004 and 2014 seasons. The Orioles under Showalter have always flummoxed those of us here at *Baseball Prospectus*. We keep picking the Orioles to have a lousy year and they keep not cooperating. How did a team that spent so many years relying on starters like Ubaldo Jimenez, Chris Tillman, Yovani Gallardo, Wei-Yin Chen and Miguel Gonzalez manage to poke their heads into the playoffs even once, much less thrice? (Does the 2016 wild card loss count?) The answer to that question among baseball insiders always seems to come back to the idea that Showalter is a genius. In particular, Showalter commonly gets points for being a genius at *handling a bullpen*.

But is he a genius? Maybe there's something that we at *Baseball Prospectus* are missing. Yeast leavens bread, interacting with the ingredients already in the pan and turns what had been a two-dimensional lump into a 3-D fluffy loaf of goodness by virtue of the carbon dioxide it produces. Perhaps Showalter is the yeast, taking the flour, water and salt-of-the-earth players who wear black and orange and turning them into something more than they appeared to be an hour or so ago? Maybe he's just passing gas.

Warning! Gory Mathematical Details Ahead!

There are twin problems that we run into when we evaluate managers. One is that most teams have only one manager over the course of a season and on the flip side of that coin, it's rare that a manager gets to pilot two different teams in the course of a season. We have no idea whether Showalter would have done anything differently than he did with Baltimore if he had been the manager in Toronto or Tampa or Texas. We have no idea what another manager would have done given the Orioles' roster to work with. It's hard to disentangle how much of a manager's impact—if he has one—is dependent on the players whom he finds on his bench. Maybe one of the reasons Showalter has gotten so much out of his bullpens is that he's had Zach Britton to call on for the past few years. (Again, does the 2016 wild card loss count?)

The second problem is that while a manager makes tactical decisions during a game, there aren't *that* many of them, and it seems that all 30 managers in the game follow the same basic rules

ORIOLES PROSPECTUS

2017 W-L: 75-87, 5TH IN AL EAST

Pythag	.441	24th
RS/G	4.59	16th
RA/G	5.19	27th
TAv	.253	24th
TAv-P	.270	21st
FIP	4.93	28th
DER	.698	19th

B-Age	28.6	*18th*
P-Age	27.9	*10th*
Salary	$164.3M	*10th*
M$/MW	$5.6M	*4th*
DL Days	527	*5th*
$ on DL	12%	*10th*

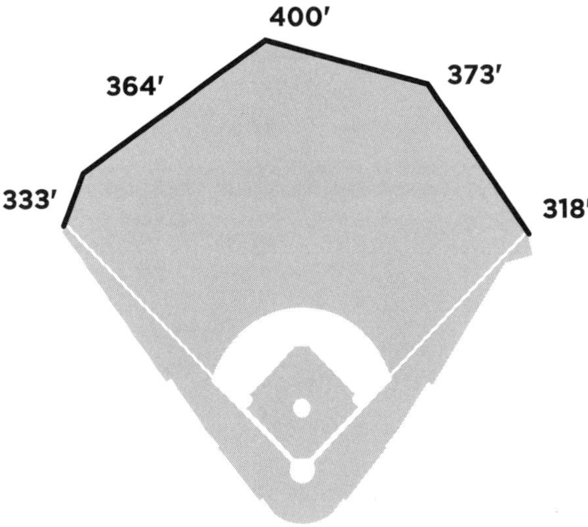

Outfield wall profile: **7′** to **21′**

Three-Year Park Factors

Runs	Runs/RH	Runs/LH	HR/RH	HR/LH
102	101	102	110	106

Top Hitter WARP	4.7 Jonathan Schoop
Top Pitcher WARP	3.6 Dylan Bundy
Top Prospect	Ryan Mountcastle

2017 Hit List Ranking

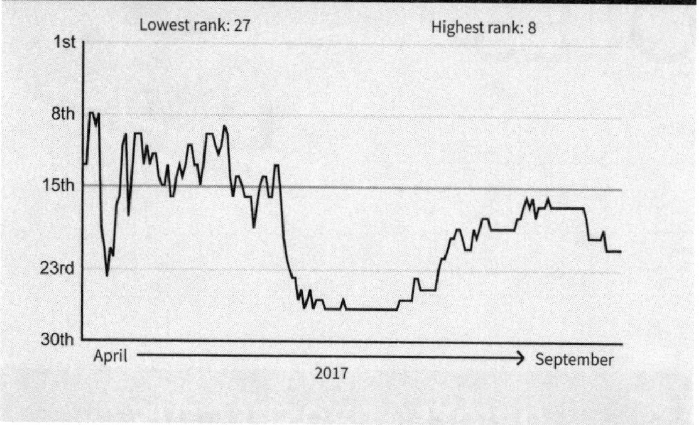

Committed Payroll (in millions)

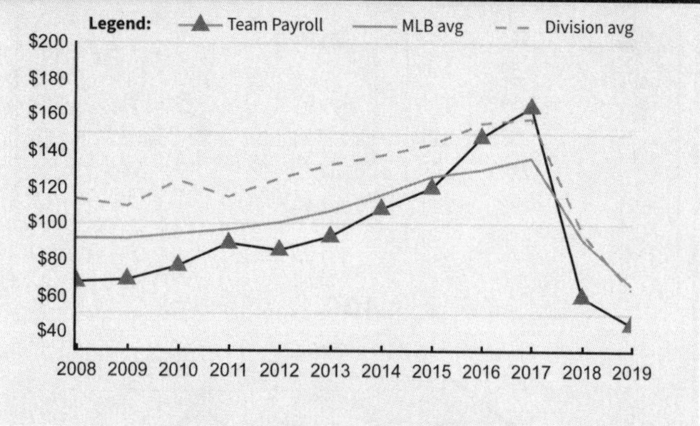

Farm System Ranking

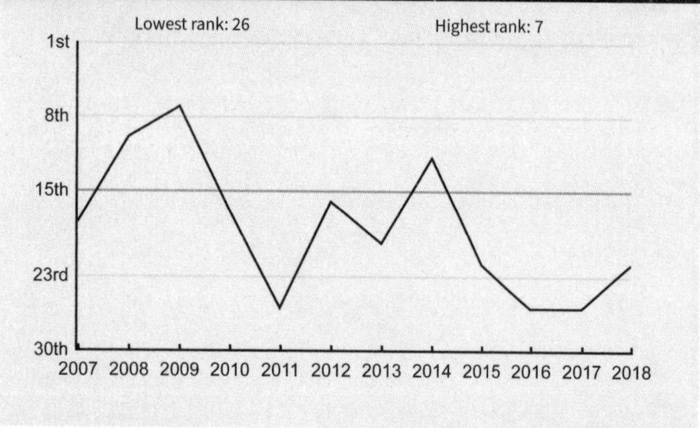

Personnel

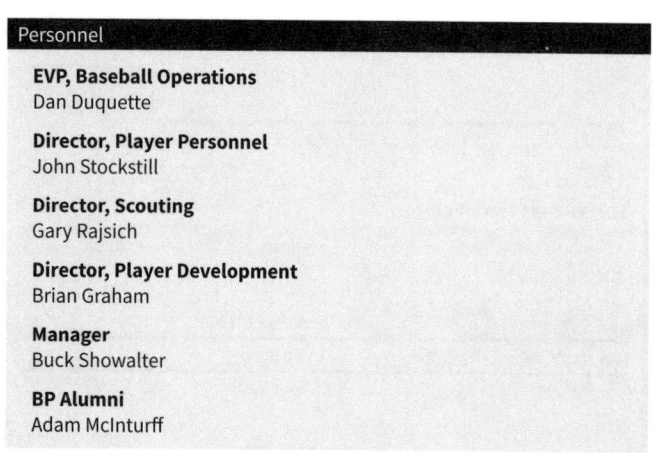

EVP, Baseball Operations
Dan Duquette

Director, Player Personnel
John Stockstill

Director, Scouting
Gary Rajsich

Director, Player Development
Brian Graham

Manager
Buck Showalter

BP Alumni
Adam McInturff

on what to do. So, while Showalter's teams appear to have gotten good results over the years, would a replacement-level manager—perhaps a Triple-A manager or one who had previously been in the hot seat before, but is currently on the waiver wire—have made the same moves? Still, we can look at Showalter's tendencies to see whether he does anything particularly tactically tasty. Maybe he's making a mark there?

For example, one thing a manager does is call for the bunt, when appropriate. In general, bunting gets a frowny face among the sabermetric crowd with the realization that advancing a runner to second is actually less valuable than the out "sacrificed" to get him there. In 2017, Orioles position players tallied 10 sacrifice hits, seventh fewest in MLB. In 2015 and 2016, they placed ninth on that same list. In this case, Showalter is on the good side of the spectrum, but still middle of the pack. When it comes to stolen bases, a team generally needs to be successful on 70 percent of steal attempts to break even. On that count, the lead-footed Orioles had the fewest attempted stolen bases in 2017, with 45. The 29th-place team (the Blue Jays) had more successful steals (53) than the Orioles had attempts. Still, the Orioles did cash in on 71 percent of their attempts, although looking back to 2015 and 2016, Showalter's teams were below the 70 percent mark. He isn't particularly loose or tight when it comes to pitch counts for starters. What exactly does Showalter do differently?

Let's look at this the other way around. We've heard that Showalter is a master at managing a bullpen. Perhaps there's evidence to support the claim. There's a statistic on how "clutch" a player (or a team) has been over some period of time. It's based on the concepts of leverage index and win probability added. We know that a single in the top of the first when the game is tied and there's a runner on second is less important than a single in the bottom of the ninth when the game is tied and there's a runner on second, despite the fact that it's the same single. It's the fact that the latter situation has a higher leverage that's more important. The winner of the game may very well be determined by that single in the ninth. In the first, it's nice to score a run, but there's a lot of baseball left to play. If a manager could somehow pick which situations he wanted his players to save *that* single for, he'd pick the more important situations.

If a hitter (or pitcher or team) can tilt his performance toward those important situations, his "clutch" metric goes up. And so we can look at how clutch Oriole hitters, starters, and relievers have been during the Showalter administration.

Year	Hitters	Starters	Relievers
2011	0.54	-2.11	2.27
2012	1.77	0.70	7.19
2013	5.07	0.51	-2.25
2014	1.71	3.77	2.70
2015	-2.25	1.57	2.27
2016	-1.12	-0.05	8.43
2017	-0.76	0.13	4.29

Here we see that Oriole hitters and starters haven't been particularly good on the clutch metric, but the bullpen has beaten the spread by at least two wins in six of his seven seasons.

As sabermetricians, we (engage "royal we" mode!) tend to discount ideas of "clutch" as an ability because, at least on an individual level, there doesn't seem to be a lot of predictive value in it. Sure, we can say that a player's *performance* was clutch in retrospect, but going forward, an individual player's previous *overall* performance is more predictive of what he'll do in a clutch situation than is his previous performance in high-leverage situations. The best studies of clutch ability generally come back to the same conclusion. There might be some sort of extra ability that certain players have that leads to them coming through when it counts, but it is largely overwhelmed by random noise. I've done a study looking at how teams perform in one-run games and found it's much the same story at the team level.

I think there's a small logical error we risk making here that runs up against the geometry of the game in a way that makes a pretty big difference. Maybe Buck just found some luck over the past few years and what we see in the table above is a man who's riding a hot streak. But if there is *any* skill in there, it's actually a pretty good skill to have. The thing about the bullpen is that it's the one area where a manager gets to match the man to the moment. The batting order dictates who will come up with the game on the line and the manager has no input. The best he can do is pinch-hit, but that's usually a matter of subbing in a bit player. The starter enters the game at the beginning before anyone knows what shape it will take. A manager has the full ability to insert his good relievers into the spots that mean the most to a game. By definition, the bullpen handles the most tender portions of the game. If a manager has a knack for figuring out who handles those best, his genius will be rewarded in an outsized manner.

We often focus on the fact that the R-squared for "noise" is much bigger than the R-squared for "talent" but forget that what really matters is whether the R-squared for "talent" is greater than "zero." Suppose for a moment (to oversimplify how this all works and use some made-up numbers) a manager's actual contribution to performance is that he can move the needle one win in either direction, and that luck can move things five wins in either direction. Luck overwhelms talent in this case, but if Showalter really is a genius at handling a bullpen, then perhaps he's one of those plus-one managers. That's still a win. What if the numbers for how much of a difference being a bullpen wizard can make is even bigger than that?

I can't swear to the fact that getting clutch performances out of a bullpen really is a talent. It's entirely possible that it isn't, but if someone were to have that talent, the Orioles' performance under Showalter would be where it would appear. But now we need to ask a hard question: Why is this also on the record?

Year	Reliever Clutch
1992 (Yankees)	4.28
1993 (Yankees)	-1.40
1994 (Yankees)	-0.07
1995 (Yankees)	-2.55
1998 (Diamondbacks)	-2.35
1999 (Diamondbacks)	-2.19
2000 (Diamondbacks)	-2.11
2003 (Rangers)	2.64
2004 (Rangers)	4.84
2005 (Rangers)	-1.99
2006 (Rangers)	-4.17

Suddenly, Showalter's total body of work doesn't look so amazing anymore. Maybe one could make the case that he figured it all out between leaving the Rangers and joining the Orioles, but that's rather convenient. Suddenly, we're back to "maybe Buck Showalter caught a run of luck" or "maybe Buck Showalter caught Zach Britton."

But what if all of the above are actually correct? What if Buck Showalter really is a bullpen whisperer and really does add value to the Orioles that way? What if he has learned his tricks over time to the point that they are now finally mature? What if the metric we are trying to prove that with really is riddled with noise that might drown out Showalter's virtuoso performance? What if that noise has been randomly running in Showalter's favor for a few years straight? One of the conceits of the sabermetric movement has been the idea that when we are trying to solve some puzzle, the answer must have one part and one part only, and for some reason, we always pick "Oh, it's just randomness."

Is Buck Showalter a genius? I don't know that he is, but in an important distinction, I'm not willing to rule it out.

—Russell A. Carleton is an author of Baseball Prospectus.

Hitters

Tim Beckham SS Born: 01/27/90 Age: 28 Bats: R Throws: R Height: 6'1" Weight: 205 Origin: Round 1, 2008 Draft (#1 overall)

YEAR	TEAM	LVL	AGE	PA	R	2B	3B	HR	RBI	BB	K	SB	CS	AVG/OBP/SLG	TAv	VORP	BABIP	BRR	FRAA	WARP
2015	DUR	AAA	25	45	5	6	0	0	4	5	10	2	1	.308/.378/.462	.285	2.2	.400	-0.3	3B(7): -0.8, 2B(2): 0.2	0.1
2015	TBA	MLB	25	223	24	7	4	9	37	13	69	3	1	.222/.274/.429	.254	3.9	.279	-1.2	2B(38): -1.8, SS(28): -1.8	0.0
2016	TBA	MLB	26	215	25	12	5	5	16	14	67	2	1	.247/.300/.434	.258	5.2	.349	-0.9	SS(25): 1.5, 2B(19): -0.2	0.6
2017	TBA	MLB	27	345	31	5	3	12	36	24	110	5	4	.259/.314/.407	.254	11.0	.357	-0.4	SS(70): -2.2, 2B(17): -0.8	0.8
2017	BAL	MLB	27	230	36	13	2	10	26	12	57	1	1	.306/.348/.523	.292	18.2	.376	0.9	SS(49): 3.2	2.1
2018	*BAL*	*MLB*	*28*	*617*	*79*	*24*	*6*	*18*	*67*	*41*	*164*	*7*	*5*	*.254/.307/.412*	*.250*	*20.2*	*.323*	*-0.3*	*SS 2*	*1.6*
2019	*BAL*	*MLB*	*29*	*525*	*63*	*21*	*5*	*17*	*64*	*38*	*142*	*5*	*4*	*.251/.309/.421*	*.247*	*9.7*	*.317*	*-0.7*	*SS 2*	*1.2*

Breakout: 4% Improve: 48% Collapse: 8% Attrition: 16% MLB: 93% *Comparables: Sean Rodriguez, Bobby Crosby, Danny Espinosa*

The arguments over team chemistry and morale have lessened to a dull roar in baseball circles these days, as advanced statistics have breached the gates of even the staunchest of defenders. These are scientific times. And yet there's still a spirit of mysticism buried deep within baseball, a need for an element that confounds and surprises us, a need for stories like Beckham. The former first overall pick arrived in Baltimore as another of the team's buy-off-the-free-table-now moves at the deadline, and pounded three home runs in his first week in orange. Though the scientists would assert that he was already enjoying his finest season before the trade, there are plenty of reasons to buy into the change-of-scenery narrative. His skill set features some glaring holes (errors, strikeouts, "baserunning") that don't mix well with the fan expectations of being a former number one, and "at the cost of Tobias Meyers" will make those mishaps easier to swallow. Though he's under team control for three more years, he's also not young, so PECOTA sees 2017 as the peak of his abilities. The key will be whether he can build on his improved contact numbers, because good things do happen when he can put wood on the ball. Either way, for the first time in a long time, Beckham is actually exceeding expectations.

Chris Davis 1B Born: 03/17/86 Age: 32 Bats: L Throws: R Height: 6'3" Weight: 230 Origin: Round 5, 2006 Draft (#148 overall)

YEAR	TEAM	LVL	AGE	PA	R	2B	3B	HR	RBI	BB	K	SB	CS	AVG/OBP/SLG	TAv	VORP	BABIP	BRR	FRAA	WARP
2015	BAL	MLB	29	670	100	31	0	47	117	84	208	2	3	.262/.361/.562	.316	43.4	.319	-0.9	1B(111): -5.0, RF(30): -2.5	3.8
2016	BAL	MLB	30	665	99	21	0	38	84	88	219	1	0	.221/.332/.459	.271	14.6	.279	0.3	1B(152): 5.7, RF(3): -0.1	2.1
2017	BAL	MLB	31	524	65	15	1	26	61	61	195	1	1	.215/.309/.423	.250	-2.0	.301	-2.0	1B(125): 4.2, 3B(2): -0.1	0.2
2018	*BAL*	*MLB*	*32*	*580*	*83*	*21*	*1*	*33*	*95*	*68*	*190*	*1*	*1*	*.232/.329/.478*	*.275*	*18.1*	*.294*	*-1.3*	*1B 0*	*1.4*
2019	*BAL*	*MLB*	*33*	*519*	*77*	*19*	*0*	*30*	*81*	*62*	*173*	*0*	*0*	*.227/.325/.469*	*.265*	*8.2*	*.289*	*-0.6*	*1B 0*	*0.9*

Breakout: 1% Improve: 28% Collapse: 4% Attrition: 10% MLB: 99% *Comparables: Ryan Howard, Mike Napoli, Adam Dunn*

Joey Gallo may be the popular symbol of the modern age of baseball—with Rob Deer and Adam Dunn the prophets who foretold a time of binary baseball, success or failure—but Davis isn't far behind in the procession. If you look at his batted-ball numbers, his disappointing 2017 looks like the usual old Chris Davis: same BABIP, same line-drive and fly-ball rates, same hard-hit ratios. It's just getting to that stage in the at-bat that haunts him. Davis had the third-worst contact rate of all qualified hitters last year, and while he's tried to adjust by leaving the bat on his shoulder more, pitchers have duly compensated by throwing more strikes than they have since his pre-arbitration days. Granted, we're talking about a man whose career arc is more of a Ferris wheel, so he could have a four-win season like he does every third year. But if this is what he is now, he'd be better served to literally lean into it, pull the ball all the time and at least accept the 40+ home-run part of his Faustian bargain.

Craig Gentry OF Born: 11/29/83 Age: 34 Bats: R Throws: R Height: 6'2" Weight: 190 Origin: Round 10, 2006 Draft (#298 overall)

YEAR	TEAM	LVL	AGE	PA	R	2B	3B	HR	RBI	BB	K	SB	CS	AVG/OBP/SLG	TAv	VORP	BABIP	BRR	FRAA	WARP
2015	NAS	AAA	31	450	64	13	0	5	25	36	76	25	7	.256/.319/.327	.262	17.8	.301	3.5	CF(101): -0.6	1.8
2015	OAK	MLB	31	56	6	0	2	0	3	4	15	1	1	.120/.196/.200	.184	-2.5	.167	0.4	LF(13): -0.7, CF(8): 0.5	-0.2
2016	ANA	MLB	32	39	2	1	0	0	2	3	6	0	0	.147/.237/.176	.153	-3.8	.179	-0.4	LF(12): 0.9, CF(1): 0.0	-0.3
2016	INL	A+	32	28	3	1	0	0	3	5	4	2	0	.227/.393/.273	.282	2.3	.278	1.1	LF(4): -0.2	0.2
2016	SLC	AAA	32	37	6	1	0	0	1	5	8	4	0	.129/.243/.161	.172	-1.9	.167	0.8	LF(6): -0.6	-0.3
2017	NOR	AAA	33	162	16	6	2	1	16	11	36	6	3	.243/.309/.331	.246	2.5	.315	1.1	RF(23): 5.9, CF(14): -0.2	0.8
2017	BAL	MLB	33	117	17	5	1	2	11	11	24	5	4	.257/.333/.386	.246	1.1	.316	0.3	RF(31): -0.6, LF(30): 1.5	0.2
2018	*BAL*	*MLB*	*34*	*250*	*31*	*8*	*1*	*4*	*20*	*21*	*51*	*11*	*4*	*.242/.315/.345*	*.229*	*0.4*	*.292*	*0.5*	*RF 1, CF 0*	*0.3*
2019	*BAL*	*MLB*	*35*	*107*	*12*	*4*	*1*	*2*	*10*	*9*	*23*	*4*	*2*	*.234/.308/.335*	*.228*	*-0.7*	*.286*	*0.4*	*RF 1, CF 0*	*0.0*

Breakout: 1% Improve: 23% Collapse: 13% Attrition: 24% MLB: 71% *Comparables: Wilson Valdez, Ryan Freel, Jason Bourgeois*

Admit it, you never thought you'd be reading a comment about this guy again. If baseball has miniature positional eras, like the golden age of shortstops with Jeter, Rodriguez, Garciaparra and Tejada, then Gentry was part of a bronze age of fourth outfielders. Emerging from the steroid era, and with defensive metrics clumsily discerning the true value of defensive range, players like Gentry, Peter Bourjos and Jarrod Dyson were making a name for themselves five years ago, or at least accumulating a decent WARP in anonymity. Dyson's still going strong, but otherwise that corps has had a rough time, and shrinking benches have made successors scarce. Gentry managed to put together a halfway decent year with the bat, encouraging memories of the utility outfielder of yore, but the years in exile have robbed his legs of their vigor. He'll have to summon all the best elements of his past if he wants to maintain employment into his mid-thirties.

Adam Hall SS Born: 05/22/99 Age: 19 Bats: R Throws: R Height: 6'0" Weight: 170 Origin: Round 2, 2017 Draft (#60 overall)

YEAR	TEAM	LVL	AGE	PA	R	2B	3B	HR	RBI	BB	K	SB	CS	AVG/OBP/SLG	TAv	VORP	BABIP	BRR	FRAA	WARP
2018	*BAL*	*MLB*	*19*	*250*	*26*	*9*	*0*	*6*	*22*	*14*	*83*	*3*	*1*	*.196/.245/.319*	*.188*	*-7.1*	*.271*	*0.0*	*SS -1*	*-0.8*
2019	*BAL*	*MLB*	*20*	*314*	*34*	*11*	*1*	*9*	*34*	*20*	*100*	*4*	*1*	*.211/.265/.352*	*.211*	*-5.4*	*.283*	*0.2*	*SS -1*	*-0.7*

Breakout: 0% Improve: 4% Collapse: 1% Attrition: 4% MLB: 8% *Comparables: Raul Mondesi, Elvis Andrus, Rougned Odor*

It's not often that the Canadian tundra offers a prospect a massive career opportunity. There's also never been a major-league baseball player born in Bermuda, but Hall, a 2017 second-round pick, looks to end the streak. The 18-year-old shortstop grew up playing basically every sport on the island, including the local equivalent of Little League, but when his baseball prowess became evident (and the country ran out of leagues for him to play in), the government supplied a grant for him to go to London, Ontario, where he was able to play on the Canadian Junior National Team against actual teenagers in front of actual scouts. A torn oblique marred his rookie-league season, but as a prospect Hall offers a little of a lot: enough arm strength and accuracy to stick at short, and maybe enough range. He can use all fields at the plate, but as he adds polish, the main concern is whether he'll be able to add strength to his hitting profile.

J.J. Hardy SS Born: 08/19/82 Age: 35 Bats: R Throws: R Height: 6'1" Weight: 200 Origin: Round 2, 2001 Draft (#56 overall)

YEAR	TEAM	LVL	AGE	PA	R	2B	3B	HR	RBI	BB	K	SB	CS	AVG/OBP/SLG	TAv	VORP	BABIP	BRR	FRAA	WARP
2015	BAL	MLB	32	437	45	14	0	8	37	20	88	0	0	.219/.253/.311	.209	-6.7	.257	-2.1	SS(114): -2.1	-0.9
2016	BAL	MLB	33	438	43	29	0	9	48	26	68	0	0	.269/.309/.407	.246	11.6	.299	-0.4	SS(115): 5.3	1.7
2017	NOR	AAA	34	31	6	1	0	1	3	9	7	0	0	.227/.452/.409	.367	4.4	.286	-0.6	SS(8): -0.1	0.4
2017	BAL	MLB	34	268	24	13	1	4	24	12	48	0	1	.217/.255/.323	.197	-7.8	.252	-1.5	SS(71): 5.8	-0.2
2018	*BAL*	*MLB*	*35*	*292*	*29*	*13*	*0*	*7*	*31*	*17*	*51*	*0*	*0*	*.250/.295/.378*	*.226*	*2.5*	*.280*	*-0.8*	*SS 0*	*0.3*
2019	*BAL*	*MLB*	*36*	*232*	*25*	*10*	*0*	*5*	*24*	*14*	*42*	*0*	*0*	*.244/.290/.366*	*.226*	*-1.2*	*.278*	*-0.7*	*SS 0*	*-0.1*

Breakout: 1% Improve: 36% Collapse: 9% Attrition: 32% MLB: 79% *Comparables: Willie Bloomquist, Jack Wilson, Mike Bordick*

Movies usually end in two ways: the rough cut to black, symbolizing death or completion; or fading out to the crimson sunset or the twinkling city skyline, representing infinity. Life, and baseball, usually ends in a slow descent of periwinkle into navy. Heroism, like daylight, is a finite thing. Hardy devoted a dozen years of his life to battling baseball and largely winning, but the prolonged attrition has clearly set in; he lost half of 2017 to a fractured wrist from a Lance Lynn fastball, but his course had already been set. Hardy's hitting, always reliant on the home run, has little strength left to draw. The former All-Star can still contribute on defense and thus should still be able to find work in the background, appearing randomly and wearing colors, his face a little more lined as he watches first pitches he once might have tried to hit.

Austin Hays RF Born: 07/05/95 Age: 22 Bats: R Throws: R Height: 6'1" Weight: 195 Origin: Round 3, 2016 Draft (#91 overall)

YEAR	TEAM	LVL	AGE	PA	R	2B	3B	HR	RBI	BB	K	SB	CS	AVG/OBP/SLG	TAv	VORP	BABIP	BRR	FRAA	WARP
2016	ABE	A-	20	153	14	9	2	4	21	11	32	4	3	.336/.386/.514	.349	15.7	.410	-0.9	RF(20): 0.3, CF(5): 0.1	1.8
2017	FRD	A+	21	280	42	15	3	16	41	12	40	4	6	.328/.364/.592	.319	25.8	.337	0.7	CF(57): 8.1, RF(4): -0.6	3.5
2017	BOW	AA	21	283	39	17	2	16	54	13	45	1	1	.330/.367/.594	.335	31.3	.345	3.2	CF(31): -3.2, RF(29): -0.4	3.0
2017	BAL	MLB	21	63	4	3	0	1	8	2	16	0	0	.217/.238/.317	.195	-3.2	.273	-0.4	RF(14): -1.6, CF(8): -1.3	-0.6
2018	*BAL*	*MLB*	*22*	*292*	*38*	*13*	*1*	*14*	*43*	*11*	*64*	*1*	*1*	*.270/.302/.483*	*.266*	*10.1*	*.301*	*-0.5*	*LF 0, RF -2*	*0.6*
2019	*BAL*	*MLB*	*23*	*497*	*69*	*23*	*2*	*26*	*78*	*24*	*108*	*2*	*1*	*.275/.317/.502*	*.270*	*15.7*	*.304*	*-1.0*	*LF 0, RF -3*	*1.4*

Breakout: 4% Improve: 34% Collapse: 2% Attrition: 18% MLB: 65% *Comparables: Adam Jones, Matt Kemp, Nick Williams*

On September 7, 2016, Hays was arriving home, having just completed his first professional season with the short-season Aberdeen IronBirds. On September 7, 2017, he was pinch-hitting against the New York Yankees in his first major-league baseball game. Few prospects in recent memory have ascended with the alacrity of the Orioles' newest outfielder, who proved his 2016 success unrepeatable by easily outdoing it. At this point, even a cynic can't project him as worse than an average starter: He has the legs to fake center field and the arm to man right. And while this kind of promotion can often wreak havoc on a player's plate discipline, he's more of the high-contact, low-walk profile that Orioles fans have long since grown used to. What it comes down to is power: Before last season, 32 home runs seemed like a reasonable three-year span. If it's more than an ill-timed career year, and he can maintain even a majority of his slugging in the majors, he could be a star.

Adam Jones CF Born: 08/01/85 Age: 32 Bats: R Throws: R Height: 6'2" Weight: 215 Origin: Round 1, 2003 Draft (#37 overall)

YEAR	TEAM	LVL	AGE	PA	R	2B	3B	HR	RBI	BB	K	SB	CS	AVG/OBP/SLG	TAv	VORP	BABIP	BRR	FRAA	WARP
2015	BAL	MLB	29	581	74	25	3	27	82	24	102	3	1	.269/.308/.474	.259	17.8	.286	1.4	CF(134): 7.5	2.7
2016	BAL	MLB	30	672	86	19	0	29	83	39	115	2	0	.265/.310/.436	.251	17.4	.280	2.7	CF(152): 4.4	2.3
2017	BAL	MLB	31	635	82	28	1	26	73	27	113	2	1	.285/.322/.466	.266	28.0	.312	3.4	CF(147): -4.6	2.3
2018	*BAL*	*MLB*	*32*	*642*	*78*	*25*	*2*	*26*	*91*	*27*	*119*	*3*	*1*	*.271/.308/.449*	*.259*	*26.0*	*.297*	*-0.9*	*CF -1*	*1.6*
2019	*BAL*	*MLB*	*33*	*521*	*67*	*20*	*1*	*22*	*72*	*22*	*104*	*1*	*0*	*.266/.304/.448*	*.251*	*12.4*	*.294*	*1.5*	*CF 0*	*1.3*

Breakout: 1% Improve: 44% Collapse: 2% Attrition: 12% MLB: 99% *Comparables: Aaron Rowand, Torii Hunter, Willie Davis*

One thing that sometimes gets lost in the metrics, but never by managers and fans, is consistency. It helps make it easier to fill out the lineup card, and contributes to the lunch pail mystique that bonds so many in the bleachers to their favorite millionaires. And there's no one in baseball more consistent, year to year, than Jones. Since 2010, he's averaged 152 games, slugged between .450 and .500, and walked about three to five percent of the time. It's like clockwork, particularly that of a very nice, above-average clock. The outspoken Jones has leveled some criticism at advanced statistics (and, indirectly, this very material) by noting that so much of it is inapplicable to the ballplayer, that they get fed these numbers on exit velocities and launch angles after spending their lives perfecting and solidifying their approach. And to some extent, that's true; attention is heaped on players who have retooled their swing, while others just "slump" in anonymity. But it may be time, as Jones nears the end of his current deal, to consider abandoning some of that celebrated consistency. He remains an above-average hitter, despite the eternal flaws, but old age has sapped some of his value by killing his defensive skill in center. He may spend his next contract in left, and at that point, some self-appraisal may be necessary to keep up with all the other Joneses.

Caleb Joseph C Born: 06/18/86 Age: 32 Bats: R Throws: R Height: 6'3" Weight: 180 Origin: Round 7, 2008 Draft (#206 overall)

YEAR	TEAM	LVL	AGE	PA	R	2B	3B	HR	RBI	BB	K	SB	CS	AVG/OBP/SLG	TAv	VORP	BABIP	BRR	FRAA	WARP
2015	BAL	MLB	29	355	38	16	1	11	49	27	72	0	0	.234/.299/.394	.242	7.3	.269	-1.5	C(94): 10.7, 1B(1): 0.1	1.9
2016	NOR	AAA	30	42	2	0	0	0	4	2	5	0	0	.250/.286/.250	.183	-2.5	.286	-0.6	C(7): 0.2	-0.2
2016	BAL	MLB	30	141	7	3	0	0	0	7	28	0	0	.174/.216/.197	.147	-9.4	.221	0.4	C(48): 7.8, 1B(2): 0.0	-0.2
2017	BAL	MLB	31	266	31	14	1	8	28	10	72	0	0	.256/.287/.413	.234	5.4	.328	0.2	C(79): 15.2, 3B(8): -0.1	2.1
2018	*BAL*	*MLB*	*32*	*295*	*30*	*12*	*1*	*7*	*31*	*17*	*70*	*0*	*0*	*.230/.277/.361*	*.223*	*3.0*	*.276*	*-0.6*	*C 12*	*1.2*
2019	*BAL*	*MLB*	*33*	*271*	*30*	*11*	*0*	*8*	*30*	*16*	*67*	*0*	*0*	*.231/.282/.372*	*.224*	*0.0*	*.278*	*-0.3*	*C 12*	*1.3*

Breakout: 3% Improve: 31% Collapse: 13% Attrition: 22% MLB: 89% *Comparables: Chad Moeller, Humberto Quintero, Eli Whiteside*

YEAR	TEAM	P. COUNT	FRM RUNS	BLK RUNS	THRW RUNS	TOT RUNS
2015	BAL	13197	8.9	0.4	1.1	10.4
2016	BAL	6127	6.4	1.3	0.2	7.9
2017	BAL	10556	13.3	3.1	-1.3	15.0
2018	*BAL*	*11623*	*11.2*	*1.8*	*-0.4*	*12.5*
2019	*BAL*	*10667*	*10.0*	*1.6*	*-0.4*	*11.2*

Look, we get it. Pitch-framing metrics have been around for a few years now, long enough to both get used to them and kind of forget about them. And they're so easy to ignore; take Joseph, a blatantly flawed ballplayer, a batter just north of Jeff Mathis territory, a man who got infinity times as many RBI in 2017 as he did the previous year *because the previous year he had zero RBI*. Yet here we are telling you that in half a season of mild positive regression, the Orioles' backup catcher was worth, to his team, as much as Ryan Braun or Miguel Sano. Because he was. It's easy to look at the sometimes enormous value BP puts on pitch framing with skepticism, to say that we're overrating the flick of a wrist as opposed to a good old-fashioned sturdy arm. But Joseph (who has a good arm) got a chance to wield it 32 times in a season, whereas he caught 4,476 pitches. Converting just 1.8 percent of those into extra strikes added 80 to his team's total, putting 80 hitters in more difficult counts. Pitch framing is that important, and there are few in the game better at it than Joseph. It turns out that what fans often describe as the "little things"—bunting, sacrificing the body, getting dirty—aren't really all that little. They're pretty easy to see, actually. Joseph does one truly little thing incredibly well, so little, in fact, that some people can't imagine it exists. It seems grit, in baseball, can be too fine.

Manny Machado 3B Born: 07/06/92 Age: 25 Bats: R Throws: R Height: 6'3" Weight: 185 Origin: Round 1, 2010 Draft (#3 overall)

YEAR	TEAM	LVL	AGE	PA	R	2B	3B	HR	RBI	BB	K	SB	CS	AVG/OBP/SLG	TAv	VORP	BABIP	BRR	FRAA	WARP
2015	BAL	MLB	22	713	102	30	1	35	86	70	111	20	8	.286/.359/.502	.292	47.7	.297	3.4	3B(156): 20.9, SS(7): -0.8	7.3
2016	BAL	MLB	23	696	105	40	1	37	96	48	120	0	3	.294/.343/.533	.292	46.7	.309	0.0	3B(114): 8.6, SS(45): -0.5	5.7
2017	BAL	MLB	24	690	81	33	1	33	95	50	115	9	4	.259/.310/.471	.261	19.4	.265	-4.1	3B(156): -6.2	1.3
2018	*BAL*	*MLB*	*25*	*653*	*97*	*34*	*2*	*27*	*86*	*46*	*105*	*8*	*4*	*.282/.334/.480*	*.277*	*32.8*	*.300*	*-0.9*	*3B 5, SS 0*	*3.2*
2019	*BAL*	*MLB*	*26*	*569*	*81*	*29*	*1*	*27*	*86*	*48*	*96*	*7*	*4*	*.285/.347/.503*	*.280*	*25.9*	*.302*	*0.0*	*3B 5, SS 0*	*3.4*

Breakout: 2% Improve: 72% Collapse: 1% Attrition: 1% MLB: 99% *Comparables: George Brett, Puddin Head Jones, Ryan Zimmerman*

Nothing screams "2012 Baseball Analysis" more than talking about BABIP, but sometimes you don't have a choice. Machado's first disappointing season at the major-league level was propped up by a torrid July and August, when he hit nearly half his home runs and knocked in more than half of his runs. The rest of the year, his profile remained largely consistent: the usual approach, the usual batted ball proliferation, the usual power. What was missing were the singles. Machado's .265 BABIP ranked lowest on the team, driving down all three components of his triple slash. BP's Zach Crizer looked through his batted ball data by launch angle and theorized that the upswing in his power, combined with his pull-happy tendencies, is erasing those unsatisfying little singles that drop ten feet in front of the outfielder, and instead airing them within reach. Nothing screams "1982 Baseball Analysis" more than the suggestion that the star third baseman should abandon the upper deck home run in favor of an all-fields approach, but...

Trey Mancini LF Born: 03/18/92 Age: 26 Bats: R Throws: R Height: 6'4" Weight: 215 Origin: Round 8, 2013 Draft (#249 overall)

YEAR	TEAM	LVL	AGE	PA	R	2B	3B	HR	RBI	BB	K	SB	CS	AVG/OBP/SLG	TAv	VORP	BABIP	BRR	FRAA	WARP
2015	FRD	A+	23	217	28	14	3	8	32	9	35	4	2	.314/.341/.527	.299	10.6	.345	-0.1	1B(51): 2.7	1.4
2015	BOW	AA	23	354	60	29	3	13	57	22	58	2	1	.359/.395/.586	.340	32.5	.400	0.2	1B(75): -0.8	3.4
2016	BOW	AA	24	75	18	4	0	7	14	10	17	0	0	.302/.413/.698	.345	7.8	.308	0.6	1B(15): 0.4	0.9
2016	NOR	AAA	24	536	60	22	5	13	54	48	123	2	2	.280/.349/.427	.281	15.4	.351	-1.9	1B(121): 6.5	2.3
2016	BAL	MLB	24	15	3	1	0	3	5	0	4	0	0	.357/.400/1.071	.435	2.7	.286	-0.1		0.3
2017	BAL	MLB	25	586	65	26	4	24	78	33	139	1	0	.293/.338/.488	.277	21.7	.352	0.9	LF(88): 1.0, 1B(45): -2.1	2.0
2018	*BAL*	*MLB*	*26*	*567*	*72*	*26*	*4*	*24*	*83*	*38*	*136*	*1*	*0*	*.277/.331/.477*	*.275*	*24.7*	*.332*	*-0.8*	*LF 0, 1B 0*	*2.0*
2019	*BAL*	*MLB*	*27*	*549*	*75*	*27*	*3*	*24*	*79*	*41*	*136*	*0*	*0*	*.275/.334/.484*	*.271*	*18.9*	*.332*	*0.2*	*LF 1, 1B 0*	*2.1*

Breakout: 5% Improve: 38% Collapse: 11% Attrition: 22% MLB: 80% *Comparables: Nolan Reimold, Chris Duncan, Corey Dickerson*

Every offseason the Orioles seem to stumble across a contract they can't pass up; last year it was Mark Trumbo, for whom the qualifying offer and a market saturated with power drove down his price considerably. And so he re-signed, despite the fact that the team already had Chris Davis and top prospect Mancini locked into the 1B/DH positions. Mancini appeared to be the odd man out before destroying the ball in spring training, convincing the team that the answer was to accelerate his development by switching him to a position he had never played at the professional level. A pair of two-homer games cemented his spot in the lineup, and after all was said and done ... it actually kind of worked. Mancini's not stellar in the outfield, but Baltimore fans would be excused if they struggled to remember what good corner outfield defense looked like, and the overall batting line sufficed despite a second-half swoon. In the end, he looks like every other Orioles outfielder: subpar plate discipline, good power, below-average glove. Not that a left-field prospect is much more exciting than a first-base prospect, but kudos to Mancini for making himself useful and surviving in the process.

Ryan Mountcastle 3B Born: 02/18/97 Age: 21 Bats: R Throws: R Height: 6'3" Weight: 195 Origin: Round 1, 2015 Draft (#36 overall)

YEAR	TEAM	LVL	AGE	PA	R	2B	3B	HR	RBI	BB	K	SB	CS	AVG/OBP/SLG	TAv	VORP	BABIP	BRR	FRAA	WARP
2015	ORI	RK	18	175	21	7	0	3	14	9	36	10	4	.313/.349/.411	.287	10.9	.381	-1.3	SS(33): 0.0, 3B(3): 0.8	1.1
2015	ABE	A-	18	34	2	0	0	1	5	0	10	0	1	.212/.206/.303	.193	-2.0	.261	-0.5	SS(6): -1.0	-0.3
2016	DEL	A	19	489	53	28	4	10	51	25	95	5	4	.281/.319/.426	.280	25.2	.331	-1.7	SS(105): -21.1	0.5
2017	FRD	A+	20	379	63	35	1	15	47	14	61	8	2	.314/.343/.542	.292	28.6	.343	1.5	SS(76): -12.1	1.7
2017	BOW	AA	20	159	18	13	0	3	15	3	35	0	0	.222/.239/.366	.225	-0.5	.265	0.5	3B(37): -1.1	-0.2
2018	*BAL*	*MLB*	*21*	*250*	*29*	*13*	*0*	*9*	*29*	*7*	*64*	*1*	*0*	*.241/.266/.411*	*.221*	*-0.4*	*.290*	*-0.4*	*SS -5, 3B -1*	*-0.6*
2019	*BAL*	*MLB*	*22*	*313*	*36*	*18*	*0*	*11*	*39*	*12*	*80*	*1*	*1*	*.242/.272/.414*	*.229*	*-1.6*	*.291*	*-0.7*	*SS -6, 3B -1*	*-0.9*

Breakout: 4% Improve: 5% Collapse: 3% Attrition: 24% MLB: 29% *Comparables: Richard Urena, Christian Arroyo, Chris Owings*

Mountcastle made BP's midseason top-50 prospect list, slotting in at no. 41. He probably won't be quite so high on the next one. Two weeks after it came out, he earned a promotion, and cracks quickly surfaced in the foundations. Mountcastle shifted off shortstop to third, where his weak arm was even more exposed, his fielding looked no cleaner and his carrying tool, the steady bat, went through a prolonged slump. Credit the Orioles for thinking positively, and accentuating through their coaching the value of positional versatility, but the truth is that neither position is his natural one: that's left field, where his speed is sufficient, his arm will do the least damage and he can concentrate on the strong hitting skills that will ultimately justify his home on the defensive spectrum. He'll begin the year repeating Double-A, proving himself capable of a renaissance.

Cedric Mullins CF Born: 10/01/94 Age: 23 Bats: B Throws: L Height: 5'8" Weight: 175 Origin: Round 13, 2015 Draft (#403 overall)

YEAR	TEAM	LVL	AGE	PA	R	2B	3B	HR	RBI	BB	K	SB	CS	AVG/OBP/SLG	TAv	VORP	BABIP	BRR	FRAA	WARP
2015	ABE	A-	20	309	34	15	5	2	32	22	33	17	4	.264/.333/.375	.293	20.6	.293	0.9	CF(66): -10.1	1.1
2016	DEL	A	21	559	79	37	10	14	55	37	101	30	6	.273/.321/.464	.299	39.8	.314	2.2	CF(122): 5.0	4.9
2017	BOW	AA	22	350	53	19	1	13	37	27	58	9	7	.265/.319/.460	.275	15.6	.283	0.9	CF(57): 7.3, LF(8): 1.1	2.5
2018	*BAL*	*MLB*	*23*	*250*	*33*	*12*	*1*	*9*	*28*	*15*	*58*	*6*	*3*	*.239/.287/.422*	*.232*	*2.3*	*.275*	*0.1*	*CF 2, LF 0*	*0.5*
2019	*BAL*	*MLB*	*24*	*330*	*40*	*16*	*2*	*13*	*43*	*21*	*77*	*7*	*3*	*.239/.289/.429*	*.238*	*2.2*	*.272*	*0.5*	*CF 3, LF 0*	*0.5*

Breakout: 1% Improve: 10% Collapse: 2% Attrition: 9% MLB: 21% *Comparables: Bryan Petersen, Eddie Rosario, Austin Jackson*

It's hard to put a value on something without comparing it to something else you already know. That's what a big chunk of scouting is: distilling the elements of baseball performance that correlate with success, then overlaying those virtues on the unknown. It's also what we do with new music, romantic interests and fringe-average platoon outfielder types like Mullins. There's suddenly a sizable disparity in the reads on the former 13th-rounder, especially after he skipped a level, jumped straight to Double-A Bowie and held his own. Is the power for real? Will he hit enough to put those legs to use on the basepaths? Maybe. But what he can do, and what few in this organization can do, is play a mean center field. Mullins may have a hard time shaking that fourth-outfielder vibe, and maybe that's what he is. But even then, what a breath of fresh air that would be for the fans who watched far too many games of Trumbo-Jones-Smith. It's almost incomparable.

Jomar Reyes 3B Born: 02/20/97 Age: 21 Bats: R Throws: R Height: 6'3" Weight: 220 Origin: International Free Agent, 2014

YEAR	TEAM	LVL	AGE	PA	R	2B	3B	HR	RBI	BB	K	SB	CS	AVG/OBP/SLG	TAv	VORP	BABIP	BRR	FRAA	WARP
2015	DEL	A	18	335	36	27	4	5	44	18	73	1	0	.278/.334/.440	.309	23.1	.351	-3.4	3B(74): -6.4	1.8
2016	FRD	A+	19	498	53	16	2	10	51	25	102	3	0	.228/.271/.336	.214	-7.8	.269	0.8	3B(122): -4.4	-1.3
2017	ORI	RK	20	31	6	1	0	0	4	1	3	0	0	.464/.484/.500	.331	4.2	.500	0.7	3B(3): 0.7	0.4
2017	FRD	A+	20	193	28	10	1	4	21	8	31	1	0	.302/.333/.434	.254	4.7	.345	0.1	3B(47): 1.5	0.7
2018	*BAL*	*MLB*	*21*	*250*	*23*	*11*	*1*	*7*	*28*	*9*	*66*	*0*	*0*	*.227/.262/.364*	*.209*	*-5.4*	*.284*	*-0.3*	*3B -2*	*-0.8*
2019	*BAL*	*MLB*	*22*	*333*	*37*	*15*	*1*	*10*	*38*	*14*	*87*	*0*	*0*	*.235/.274/.388*	*.227*	*-4.3*	*.291*	*-0.7*	*3B -3*	*-0.7*

Breakout: 0% Improve: 0% Collapse: 0% Attrition: 3% MLB: 3% *Comparables: Neftali Soto, Jefry Marte, Brandon Drury*

There's something about baseball players and walls. Call it confirmation bias if you want, but it feels like there's an athlete losing a boxing match against an indestructible object every season; you never hear about them winning. Is it the product of a temporary sense of invincibility? A natural revulsion against obstacles in general? Should teams install inflatable punching bags in every dugout? The answer is yes, but even then it would be too late for Reyes, who lost three months to his own terrible hubris. The rest of his repeat trip through the Carolina League was pleasant, however, and everything said before remains true: He is very large, can hit very well and will never, ever play third base in the major leagues. He'll move on to Double-A as a 21-year-old in 2018, where he'll seek to learn how to draw walks, play first base and find more constructive ways of displaying frustration.

Joey Rickard OF Born: 05/21/91 Age: 27 Bats: R Throws: L Height: 6'1" Weight: 185 Origin: Round 9, 2012 Draft (#302 overall)

YEAR	TEAM	LVL	AGE	PA	R	2B	3B	HR	RBI	BB	K	SB	CS	AVG/OBP/SLG	TAv	VORP	BABIP	BRR	FRAA	WARP
2015	PCH	A+	24	94	8	3	0	0	12	20	13	3	2	.268/.436/.310	.308	6.0	.322	-0.5	LF(11): -1.8, RF(6): 1.3	0.6
2015	MNT	AA	24	282	38	19	6	2	32	39	42	19	4	.322/.420/.479	.327	26.4	.379	1.5	LF(24): -1.8, RF(19): 3.0	2.8
2015	DUR	AAA	24	104	16	6	2	0	11	10	20	1	0	.360/.437/.472	.334	8.8	.457	-1.3	LF(13): 0.1, RF(11): -0.4	0.8
2016	BAL	MLB	25	282	32	13	0	5	19	18	54	4	1	.268/.319/.377	.241	0.6	.320	0.3	RF(51): -0.8, LF(31): 1.2	-0.1
2017	NOR	AAA	26	58	8	1	0	1	4	11	9	0	0	.191/.345/.277	.243	1.3	.216	1.2	LF(7): 0.5, RF(6): -1.0	0.1
2017	BAL	MLB	26	277	29	15	0	4	19	9	63	8	1	.241/.276/.345	.223	-3.7	.303	0.9	RF(53): 2.9, LF(43): -1.4	-0.2
2018	*BAL*	*MLB*	*27*	*415*	*48*	*20*	*2*	*7*	*41*	*34*	*84*	*10*	*2*	*.260/.325/.381*	*.248*	*7.1*	*.313*	*0.8*	*RF 2, LF 0*	*0.7*
2019	*BAL*	*MLB*	*28*	*402*	*48*	*20*	*1*	*9*	*43*	*37*	*85*	*9*	*2*	*.261/.336/.395*	*.249*	*5.0*	*.317*	*0.6*	*RF 2, LF 0*	*0.8*

Breakout: 3% Improve: 32% Collapse: 8% Attrition: 15% MLB: 75% *Comparables: Roger Bernadina, Shane Victorino, David Murphy*

If you ever get the inclination to drop five bucks on a box of junk wax baseball cards of the '80s, one of the things you might notice as you slide the gum-scented cardboard through your hands is how many mediocre baseball players there used to be. It's not just that there was a generation of bench players whose names faded from history, but that in an era of complete-game starters and mediocre relievers, benches teemed with "utility" outfielders and pinch-hitters. Guys like John Moses, Steve Jeltz and Darnell Coles seemed to stick around for years, despite the fact that they didn't do anything particularly well or terribly, at the plate or on the bases or in the field. They were just there, earning their five-figure salaries and their five-cent baseball cards. That breed of baseball player is dying, but it appears to have at least one holdout in the form of Rickard, who appears to at least have half of that success locked up.

Anthony Santander OF Born: 10/19/94 Age: 23 Bats: B Throws: R Height: 6'2" Weight: 190 Origin: International Free Agent, 2011

YEAR	TEAM	LVL	AGE	PA	R	2B	3B	HR	RBI	BB	K	SB	CS	AVG/OBP/SLG	TAv	VORP	BABIP	BRR	FRAA	WARP
2015	MHV	A-	20	35	6	6	0	3	9	4	8	0	0	.419/.486/.903	.448	6.9	.500	-0.4	RF(3): 0.5	0.8
2015	LKC	A	20	276	46	16	0	10	42	18	53	4	2	.278/.337/.464	.282	13.6	.312	2.2	LF(45): 0.2, RF(10): -0.7	1.4
2016	LYN	A+	21	574	90	42	0	20	95	54	118	10	5	.290/.368/.494	.305	35.3	.339	-1.8	LF(67): -9.5, 1B(9): -0.2	2.5
2017	BOW	AA	22	59	13	5	0	5	14	7	9	0	0	.380/.458/.780	.397	8.5	.378	-0.7	RF(6): 0.0, LF(4): -0.2	0.9
2017	BAL	MLB	22	31	1	3	0	0	2	0	8	0	0	.267/.258/.367	.235	-0.1	.348	0.1	RF(8): 0.7, LF(4): -0.2	0.0
2018	*BAL*	*MLB*	*23*	*193*	*24*	*10*	*0*	*8*	*26*	*12*	*49*	*1*	*0*	*.247/.302/.440*	*.253*	*3.3*	*.293*	*-0.4*	*RF 0, LF -2*	*0.0*
2019	*BAL*	*MLB*	*24*	*358*	*47*	*19*	*0*	*16*	*50*	*24*	*91*	*1*	*1*	*.251/.312/.456*	*.255*	*6.0*	*.299*	*-0.8*	*RF 0, LF -3*	*0.3*

Breakout: 5% Improve: 19% Collapse: 6% Attrition: 11% MLB: 35% *Comparables: Domonic Brown, Kyle Parker, Wladimir Balentien*

Among the great enduring romances of our generation is the blissful marriage of Dan Duquette and the Rule 5 Draft. The consolation round that brought you such names as Rickard, Verrett and Flaherty this time supplied Santander, an athletic July 2 signing out of Venezuela back in 2012. His 2016 season in High-A was legitimately impressive, but the Indians ran out of time developing him thanks to a checkered injury history that left him averaging around 60 games a season. The Orioles scooped him up, and he proceeded to spend the majority of the season recovering from offseason shoulder surgery. If he can ever get healthy, he's hinted at the ability to hit the ball hard from both sides of the plate and handle a corner outfield spot. There are worse lottery tickets, even deferred.

Jonathan Schoop 2B Born: 10/16/91 Age: 26 Bats: R Throws: R Height: 6'1" Weight: 225 Origin: International Free Agent, 2008

YEAR	TEAM	LVL	AGE	PA	R	2B	3B	HR	RBI	BB	K	SB	CS	AVG/OBP/SLG	TAv	VORP	BABIP	BRR	FRAA	WARP
2015	BOW	AA	23	26	3	2	0	3	6	1	6	0	0	.240/.269/.680	.308	1.1	.188	-0.8	2B(7): 0.3	0.2
2015	BAL	MLB	23	321	34	17	0	15	39	9	79	2	0	.279/.306/.482	.271	8.9	.329	-2.9	2B(84): 0.1	1.0
2016	BAL	MLB	24	647	82	38	1	25	82	21	137	1	2	.267/.298/.454	.250	12.3	.305	1.5	2B(162): -2.4	1.0
2017	BAL	MLB	25	675	92	35	0	32	105	35	142	1	0	.293/.338/.503	.280	37.5	.330	4.2	2B(159): 8.2, SS(5): 0.8	4.7
2018	*BAL*	*MLB*	*26*	*610*	*73*	*29*	*1*	*26*	*87*	*25*	*134*	*1*	*1*	*.263/.301/.450*	*.257*	*23.6*	*.299*	*-1.3*	*2B 0*	*1.6*
2019	*BAL*	*MLB*	*27*	*574*	*77*	*28*	*0*	*27*	*84*	*28*	*129*	*1*	*0*	*.265/.310/.472*	*.260*	*19.0*	*.301*	*0.6*	*2B 0*	*2.1*

Breakout: 6% Improve: 54% Collapse: 3% Attrition: 12% MLB: 97% *Comparables: Howie Kendrick, Bret Boone, Jeff Kent*

Not to break the fourth wall too much, but one of the hardest things about writing player comments is avoiding the cautiously optimistic final sentence. It's not easy: The writer wants to provide some piece of summary analysis, yet at the same time maintain that baseball is weird and contains a million variables. So the result is often: "If Player A can fix B, he'll have a great season." It's a perfect conditional statement: prediction without assumption. But here's the thing: Schoop didn't really fix B. He swung a little less and walked a little more, but otherwise his approach and his batted-ball tendencies and velocities remained pretty equal, and he still swung through a lot of balls. He just got better at what he does well, which is hitting the ball hard. We tend to have a bias toward balanced players, guys who shore up the weak spots and adjust, and maybe that's a good way to go about things. But you can also have some weaknesses and still be a very, very good baseball player, and Schoop fits that mold. But if he can start making more contact...

Chance Sisco C Born: 02/24/95 Age: 23 Bats: L Throws: R Height: 6'2" Weight: 195 Origin: Round 2, 2013 Draft (#61 overall)

YEAR	TEAM	LVL	AGE	PA	R	2B	3B	HR	RBI	BB	K	SB	CS	AVG/OBP/SLG	TAv	VORP	BABIP	BRR	FRAA	WARP
2015	FRD	A+	20	300	30	12	3	4	26	33	41	8	1	.308/.387/.422	.299	21.3	.350	-0.7	C(57): -1.3	2.2
2015	BOW	AA	20	84	9	4	0	2	8	9	14	0	1	.257/.337/.392	.268	2.0	.293	-1.9	C(17): -0.1	0.2
2016	BOW	AA	21	479	53	28	1	4	44	59	83	2	2	.320/.406/.422	.297	28.8	.387	-5.7	C(83): -9.8	2.1
2017	NOR	AAA	22	388	47	23	0	7	47	32	99	2	2	.267/.340/.395	.263	22.1	.351	1.9	C(94): 1.7	2.3
2017	BAL	MLB	22	22	3	2	0	2	4	3	7	0	0	.333/.455/.778	.400	3.9	.444	-0.3	C(10): -0.6	0.3
2018	*BAL*	*MLB*	*23*	*250*	*29*	*12*	*1*	*6*	*28*	*24*	*60*	*0*	*0*	*.257/.334/.399*	*.255*	*10.8*	*.322*	*-0.6*	*C -7*	*0.1*
2019	*BAL*	*MLB*	*24*	*430*	*56*	*21*	*1*	*14*	*53*	*46*	*105*	*1*	*0*	*.261/.347/.428*	*.261*	*16.4*	*.324*	*-1.1*	*C -8*	*0.9*

Breakout: 6% Improve: 19% Collapse: 8% Attrition: 23% MLB: 41% *Comparables: Carlos Santana, Hank Conger, Josh Donaldson*

YEAR	TEAM	P. COUNT	FRM RUNS	BLK RUNS	THRW RUNS	TOT RUNS
2015	BOW	2140	0.1	-0.2	0.1	0.0
2017	BAL	653	-0.5	-0.2	-0.1	-0.7
2018	*BAL*	*9093*	*-3.9*	*-0.2*	*-1.1*	*-5.2*
2019	*BAL*	*15623*	*-3.0*	*-0.1*	*-0.9*	*-4.0*

One of the *causes célèbre* of the sabermetric writer is the man born of the wrong time, whose work went unappreciated by the zoo crew talk radio hosts and sixth-beer conversationalists. Bobby Grich, he of the 56.6 career WARP (more than Lou Whitaker!) and non-300-game-winner Mike Mussina are common subjects. But there's also the player who arrives exactly when he was meant to be, and Sisco appears to be of that caliber. Expectations have been tampered slightly for Baltimore's top prospect after he struggled for the first time at Triple-A, but the projections remain basically the same: excellent bat control, quick hands, doubles power. A good hitter for a catcher. And that was always the problem; it was assumed that because of his weak arm, the tools were doomed to be temporary. But in the enlightened times we live in, with devices that order products for us by picking up snippets of conversation, as well as catcher framing, the importance of the arm has been seen as a mirage, and that presentation is all. Sisco improved his framing work in 2017, and while that number can be volatile, it supplies at least some hope that he can hold out as catcher for some of those arbitration years. If that's the case, the Orioles could have themselves a fairly safe, above-average catcher for the next half-decade, and that's worth plenty in any era.

Seth Smith OF Born: 09/30/82 Age: 35 Bats: L Throws: L Height: 6'3" Weight: 210 Origin: Round 2, 2004 Draft (#50 overall)

YEAR	TEAM	LVL	AGE	PA	R	2B	3B	HR	RBI	BB	K	SB	CS	AVG/OBP/SLG	TAv	VORP	BABIP	BRR	FRAA	WARP
2015	SEA	MLB	32	452	54	31	5	12	42	47	99	0	0	.248/.330/.443	.281	20.0	.298	2.6	LF(65): 0.2, RF(55): -1.9	2.0
2016	SEA	MLB	33	438	62	15	0	16	63	48	89	0	0	.249/.342/.415	.262	8.0	.282	-1.2	RF(74): -3.1, LF(35): -1.5	0.3
2017	BAL	MLB	34	373	50	19	0	13	32	36	79	2	0	.258/.340/.433	.261	5.9	.301	-1.4	RF(80): -2.1, LF(12): 0.0	0.4
2018	*BAL*	*MLB*	*35*	*363*	*47*	*19*	*1*	*11*	*41*	*40*	*75*	*1*	*0*	*.254/.343/.426*	*.259*	*9.8*	*.297*	*0.0*	*RF 0, LF 0*	*1.0*
2019	*BAL*	*MLB*	*36*	*283*	*36*	*14*	*1*	*9*	*34*	*32*	*61*	*0*	*0*	*.245/.336/.415*	*.255*	*4.4*	*.289*	*-0.2*	*RF 0, LF 0*	*0.4*

Breakout: 1% Improve: 24% Collapse: 7% Attrition: 27% MLB: 71% *Comparables: Shawn Green, Kosuke Fukudome, Jim King*

Baseball's Favorite Dad had a prototypical Dad-like season, once again contributing a league-average bat despite heavy platooning and an increasingly creaky right field. In fact, Smith became an apt metaphor for the Orioles' own aging, plain-yogurt roster, to the point that the team couldn't trade him in July despite their efforts, and they spent the rest of the year fading into forgettable subadequacy together. We're even running out of metaphors: Vanilla is delicious, and even discounted post-Passover matzos are nourishing. Smith is just kind of there, now. Perhaps it's us: perhaps he's the same Dad, and now we as fans are the teenagers at the movie theater pretending we don't know him. Regardless, for the Orioles in retrospect, the price for his services—one Yovani Gallardo—was certainly right. But at 35 and with a ready replacement in wunderkind Austin Hays, he'll find even part-time employment difficult to locate going forward.

D.J. Stewart LF Born: 11/30/93 Age: 24 Bats: L Throws: R Height: 6'0" Weight: 230 Origin: Round 1, 2015 Draft (#25 overall)

YEAR	TEAM	LVL	AGE	PA	R	2B	3B	HR	RBI	BB	K	SB	CS	AVG/OBP/SLG	TAv	VORP	BABIP	BRR	FRAA	WARP
2015	ABE	A-	21	268	25	8	2	6	24	23	52	4	1	.218/.288/.345	.247	1.1	.250	-0.3	LF(52): -0.1	0.1
2016	DEL	A	22	262	27	12	1	4	25	42	58	16	6	.230/.366/.352	.273	7.3	.294	-1.2	LF(58): 0.2	0.8
2016	FRD	A+	22	240	41	12	2	6	30	36	46	10	3	.279/.389/.448	.282	10.7	.333	0.0	LF(51): 1.0, CF(2): -0.2	1.2
2017	BOW	AA	23	540	80	26	2	21	79	65	87	20	4	.278/.378/.481	.305	37.4	.299	2.1	LF(110): -0.4, RF(4): 0.7	4.1
2018	*BAL*	*MLB*	*24*	*250*	*32*	*10*	*1*	*9*	*32*	*28*	*60*	*6*	*2*	*.234/.331/.417*	*.251*	*6.6*	*.278*	*0.3*	*LF 2, RF 0*	*1.0*
2019	*BAL*	*MLB*	*25*	*302*	*41*	*12*	*1*	*12*	*39*	*34*	*75*	*7*	*2*	*.238/.335/.425*	*.257*	*7.0*	*.285*	*0.5*	*LF 3, RF 0*	*1.1*

Breakout: 2% Improve: 16% Collapse: 12% Attrition: 23% MLB: 36% *Comparables: Phil Ervin, Chad Huffman, Mark Zagunis*

For those about to scout the stat line, we dissuade you. On the surface, it would appear that the former first-rounder finally made good on his promises, kindling the power the O's had hoped for and flashing serious speed. There are a lot of problems remaining between those numbers, however. For someone with 20 stolen bases, Stewart isn't all that athletic, and it requires a fair amount of wishcasting to get him above detriment level in left field. Only his bat will take him where he wants to go, and the scouts cry danger there as well. His swing tends to be flat and mechanical, passing through a single plane, making adjustments on breaking balls a much bigger challenge. Stewart is essentially a first-base prospect who hasn't realized he's a first-base prospect, and for him to become more than a bench bat, he'll have to demonstrate that there's more raw power still locked within, and that those 20 home runs were just the start.

Mark Trumbo DH Born: 01/16/86 Age: 32 Bats: R Throws: R Height: 6'4" Weight: 225 Origin: Round 18, 2004 Draft (#533 overall)

YEAR	TEAM	LVL	AGE	PA	R	2B	3B	HR	RBI	BB	K	SB	CS	AVG/OBP/SLG	TAv	VORP	BABIP	BRR	FRAA	WARP
2015	ARI	MLB	29	184	23	10	3	9	23	10	39	0	0	.259/.299/.506	.282	5.6	.286	-1.5	RF(42): -2.0, 1B(1): 0.0	0.4
2015	SEA	MLB	29	361	39	13	0	13	41	26	93	0	0	.263/.316/.419	.274	11.8	.328	1.9	RF(34): -3.0, 1B(22): 0.1	0.9
2016	BAL	MLB	30	667	94	27	1	47	108	51	170	2	0	.256/.316/.533	.276	18.5	.278	-2.6	RF(95): 2.2, 1B(6): 0.2	2.1
2017	BAL	MLB	31	603	79	22	0	23	65	42	149	1	0	.234/.289/.397	.237	-9.3	.278	-2.3	RF(31): -4.6, 3B(2): 0.0	-1.4
2018	*BAL*	*MLB*	*32*	*571*	*72*	*22*	*1*	*27*	*85*	*42*	*144*	*1*	*0*	*.242/.298/.444*	*.256*	*8.3*	*.280*	*-1.0*	*RF -2*	*0.5*
2019	*BAL*	*MLB*	*33*	*549*	*73*	*21*	*1*	*27*	*78*	*45*	*143*	*0*	*0*	*.237/.301/.444*	*.252*	*7.8*	*.276*	*-1.5*	*RF -1*	*0.7*

Breakout: 2% Improve: 36% Collapse: 7% Attrition: 12% MLB: 93% *Comparables: Craig Monroe, Xavier Nady, Eric Karros*

The world went and passed Trumbo by. There was a time, not so long ago, when the ball was made of granite and right-handed power was a precious commodity: years when a number like 47 home runs felt like a lot of home runs, when we actually felt pleasure when we saw a good old-fashioned dinger instead of just getting annoyed by anything that doesn't clear the wall. But these are jaded times, when Elvis Andrus can hit 20 homers on 22 fly balls, and suddenly we don't need Mark Trumbos anymore, one-dimensional players who picked the wrong dimension. Trumbo still had to play, though, having signed that contract and all, so he went out with the same plate approach as usual, the same plate discipline and contact rates and launch angles. It just didn't work: Usually among the leaders in exit velocity, he lost a few ticks and added a few warning-track flies. We don't have enough of a sample to know how predictive that statistic is, and Trumbo is a studious hitter who has returned to form before. But that form had better include at least 40 homers.

PITCHERS

Keegan Akin LHP Born: 04/01/95 Age: 23 Bats: L Throws: L Height: 6'0" Weight: 225 Origin: Round 2, 2016 Draft (#54 overall)

YEAR	TEAM	LVL	AGE	W	L	SV	G	GS	IP	H	HR	BB/9	K/9	K	GB%	BABIP	WHIP	ERA	DRA	WARP	MPH	CMD	PWR	STM
2016	ABE	A-	21	0	1	0	9	9	26	15	0	2.4	10.0	29	51%	.231	0.85	1.04	2.60	0.8				
2017	FRD	A+	22	7	8	0	21	21	100	89	12	4.1	10.0	111	38%	.307	1.35	4.14	5.19	0.1				
2018	*BAL*	*MLB*	*23*	*4*	*6*	*0*	*16*	*16*	*70^{1}*	*72*	*16*	*4.7*	*10.1*	*79*	*38%*	*.308*	*1.55*	*5.77*	*5.89*	*-0.2*				
2019	*BAL*	*MLB*	*24*	*6*	*11*	*0*	*27*	*27*	*165^{2}*	*175*	*40*	*4.8*	*9.2*	*169*	*38%*	*.301*	*1.59*	*6.25*	*6.41*	*-1.0*				

Breakout: 4% Improve: 4% Collapse: 4% Attrition: 8% MLB: 10% *Comparables: Henry Sosa, Dinelson Lamet, Garrett Olson*

All life is context. If you ran into someone with those height and weight numbers in real life, you probably wouldn't think twice about it. For Akin, it means that every scouting profile includes the word "stocky" by sentence two at the latest. Despite all that, the former second-rounder had a pleasant encore in the minors, striking out batters despite average pitches, and developing consistency. His mechanics are fairly clean and repeatable; his fastball is low-90s but heavy, and he's willing to challenge batters in the zone. It adds up to a fourth-starter profile, which doesn't sound exciting, but: Jeremy Hellickson. Alec Asher. Mike Wright. Tyler Wilson. These are the names of pitchers who have gotten at least a half-dozen starts for the Orioles the last couple of years. As already mentioned, all life is context.

Michael Baumann RHP Born: 09/10/95 Age: 22 Bats: R Throws: R Height: 6'4" Weight: 225 Origin: Round 3, 2017 Draft (#98 overall)

YEAR	TEAM	LVL	AGE	W	L	SV	G	GS	IP	H	HR	BB/9	K/9	K	GB%	BABIP	WHIP	ERA	DRA	WARP	MPH	CMD	PWR	STM
2017	ABE	A-	21	4	2	0	10	9	41^{1}	25	2	4.1	8.9	41	48%	.217	1.06	1.31	3.25	0.9				
2018	*BAL*	*MLB*	*22*	*2*	*3*	*0*	*7*	*7*	*32*	*36*	*8*	*5.9*	*8.8*	*31*	*40%*	*.313*	*1.78*	*6.58*	*6.74*	*-0.4*				
2019	*BAL*	*MLB*	*23*	*5*	*10*	*0*	*26*	*26*	*151*	*169*	*34*	*6.0*	*8.2*	*138*	*40%*	*.31*	*1.79*	*6.64*	*6.82*	*-1.5*				

Comparables: Blake Wood, Evan Reed, Jhonny Nunez

Baumann was one of the dozens of pitchers who posted pretty respectable numbers in the low minors for the Orioles, an indication that either the system is finally in place or that it hasn't broken this particular corps yet. The large human being (not, sadly, the former writer at Baseball Prospectus) has a big body and a big fastball, working in the mid-90s. The trouble is that his secondaries, while good enough for now, threaten to develop without that all-important out pitch the kids are into these days. He has the durability to start, but if the command never surfaces or the changeup fails to develop, he's got a path to the majors as a setup man with a fastball-slider combo. As a writer, he's an unknown but has a high bar to clear.

Cameron Bishop LHP Born: 02/14/96 Age: 22 Bats: L Throws: L Height: 6'4" Weight: 215 Origin: Round 26, 2017 Draft (#788 overall)

YEAR	TEAM	LVL	AGE	W	L	SV	G	GS	IP	H	HR	BB/9	K/9	K	GB%	BABIP	WHIP	ERA	DRA	WARP	MPH	CMD	PWR	STM
2017	ABE	A-	21	1	1	0	8	8	34^{2}	20	1	4.2	9.9	38	51%	.232	1.04	0.78	2.71	1.0				
2018	*BAL*	*MLB*	*22*	*2*	*3*	*0*	*7*	*7*	*32*	*35*	*7*	*5.8*	*9.2*	*32*	*41%*	*.313*	*1.74*	*6.39*	*6.54*	*-0.3*				
2019	*BAL*	*MLB*	*23*	*5*	*10*	*0*	*27*	*27*	*160*	*172*	*35*	*5.4*	*8.5*	*151*	*41%*	*.304*	*1.67*	*6.38*	*6.54*	*-1.2*				

Breakout: 0% Improve: 1% Collapse: 0% Attrition: 0% MLB: 1% *Comparables: Justin Haley, Aaron Blair, Justin Wilson*

One of the underrated sources of drama in the game of baseball: paperwork. From the infamous Carlton Fisk debacle of February 1981, to the Travis Lee accidental nontender of 1996, every so often we get reminded that baseball is won in the desk organizer every bit as much as on the field. Bishop is the latest recipient of organizational incompetence: Scouted as an early-rounder, he strained an oblique and healed his way through his entire senior year. The Orioles took him in the 26th round, but failed to submit their offer by the deadline, forcing them to fork over $600,000 to keep his rights. Bishop held up his part of the inflated bargain, giving up a mere three runs in eight starts, and demonstrating enough raw materials to entice. Whether or not he puts it all together, and it'll be a while before we're sure, he'll almost certainly be one of the most interesting 26th-round draft picks in recent memory. Let's just hope the Orioles don't trade this one for Gerardo Parra as well.

Richard Bleier LHP Born: 04/16/87 Age: 31 Bats: L Throws: L Height: 6'3" Weight: 215 Origin: Round 6, 2008 Draft (#183 overall)

YEAR	TEAM	LVL	AGE	W	L	SV	G	GS	IP	H	HR	BB/9	K/9	K	GB%	BABIP	WHIP	ERA	DRA	WARP	MPH	CMD	PWR	STM
2015	HAR	AA	28	8	3	0	16	15	103	95	6	0.8	3.5	40	65%	.259	1.01	2.45	2.24	3.5				
2015	SYR	AAA	28	6	2	0	12	11	68^{2}	75	0	0.9	3.3	25	65%	.307	1.19	2.75	3.28	1.6				
2016	SWB	AAA	29	2	3	1	12	10	58	66	2	1.7	3.9	25	64%	.318	1.33	3.72	7.27	-1.3				
2016	NYA	MLB	29	0	0	0	23	0	23	20	0	1.6	5.1	13	55%	.270	1.04	1.96	5.22	-0.1	91.7	61	42	41
2017	NOR	AAA	30	0	0	1	8	0	14^{2}	9	0	0.0	9.2	15	70%	.243	0.61	0.61	1.74	0.6				
2017	BAL	MLB	30	2	1	0	57	0	63^{1}	62	6	1.8	3.7	26	69%	.259	1.18	1.99	4.48	0.5	91.1	38	39	50
2018	*BAL*	*MLB*	*31*	*2*	*3*	*0*	*48*	*0*	50^{2}	*52*	*5*	*2.8*	*5.0*	*28*	*59%*	*.290*	*1.34*	*4.19*	*4.33*	*0.5*	*90.4*	*43*	*39*	*46*
2019	*BAL*	*MLB*	*32*	*2*	*1*	*0*	*49*	*0*	52^{1}	*55*	*5*	*2.7*	*4.8*	*28*	*59%*	*.289*	*1.36*	*4.72*	*4.75*	*0.3*	*90.0*	*43*	*39*	*46*

Breakout: 16% Improve: 24% Collapse: 10% Attrition: 13% MLB: 44% *Comparables: Brian Schlitter, Dana Eveland, Dan Otero*

Three years ago, former BP editor-in-chief Ben Lindbergh canvassed the tundra of minor-league veterans to find statistical outliers. Of the 12 he profiled, three made it, two of them pitchers: Ryan Buchter and Bleier, polar opposites. Buchter is a hard-throwing wild lefty; beyond the shared dominant hand the latter is, well, not. The 30-year-old rookie pitches as if the air were gelatin, each pitch dying of boredom before it reaches the plate, and yet the formula worked for the entire season. His pitching style is like that of an undersized boxer; his pitches duck and weave, but mostly duck. PECOTA is unsurprisingly a buzzkill, thanks to a CSAA (called strikes above average) near the bottom of the league. He'll have to find the corners better than he has to keep that walk rate (and more importantly, perhaps, that BABIP) intact, and his chances are remote. Even so, sub-2.00 ERA performances from guys and stories like Bleier are little pearls, and we should appreciate them.

Brad Brach RHP Born: 04/12/86 Age: 32 Bats: R Throws: R Height: 6'6" Weight: 215 Origin: Round 42, 2008 Draft (#1275 overall)

YEAR	TEAM	LVL	AGE	W	L	SV	G	GS	IP	H	HR	BB/9	K/9	K	GB%	BABIP	WHIP	ERA	DRA	WARP	MPH	CMD	PWR	STM
2015	BAL	MLB	29	5	3	1	62	0	79^{1}	57	7	4.3	10.1	89	46%	.263	1.20	2.72	2.56	2.0	96.5	48	59	52
2016	BAL	MLB	30	10	4	2	71	0	79	57	7	2.8	10.5	92	43%	.267	1.04	2.05	2.38	2.3	96.8	54	57	53
2017	BAL	MLB	31	4	5	18	67	0	68	51	7	3.4	9.3	70	42%	.256	1.13	3.18	3.38	1.4	96.4	65	61	50
2018	*BAL*	*MLB*	*32*	*3*	*3*	*2*	*58*	*0*	*61*	*57*	*9*	*3.8*	*9.2*	*63*	*44%*	*.292*	*1.35*	*4.19*	*4.33*	*0.6*	*95.6*	*56*	*59*	*51*
2019	*BAL*	*MLB*	*33*	*2*	*1*	*1*	*48*	*0*	*51*	*47*	*8*	*4.1*	*9.2*	*52*	*44%*	*.289*	*1.38*	*4.82*	*4.86*	*0.2*	*95.2*	*58*	*58*	*51*

Breakout: 24% Improve: 43% Collapse: 20% Attrition: 7% MLB: 89% *Comparables: Jason Frasor, Jesse Crain, Kevin Gregg*

Brach spent half the year filling in at closer for an injured Zach Britton and acquitted himself nicely, then took over the job again at the end of the year and watched as the team gave him a single save opportunity. It's almost as if, on the morning of October 1, the baseball gods looked down on his pitching line and decided: This guy's in danger of no longer being underrated. They smote him with a thunderbolt constructed of BABIP and offseason dreams, and the result—four consecutive line drives followed by two walks—elevated his ERA from 2.53 to 3.18. Regardless, Brach remains one of the best relievers in baseball, and holder of one the league's craziest and most unheralded records in recent history: He has improved his average fastball speed in each of the last six years, from 91.9 to 95, at a time when most pitchers are starting to see their velocity go the other way.

Zach Britton LHP Born: 12/22/87 Age: 30 Bats: L Throws: L Height: 6'3" Weight: 195 Origin: Round 3, 2006 Draft (#85 overall)

YEAR	TEAM	LVL	AGE	W	L	SV	G	GS	IP	H	HR	BB/9	K/9	K	GB%	BABIP	WHIP	ERA	DRA	WARP	MPH	CMD	PWR	STM
2015	BAL	MLB	27	4	1	36	64	0	65^{2}	51	3	1.9	10.8	79	81%	.308	0.99	1.92	1.59	2.4	98.7	52	82	47
2016	BAL	MLB	28	2	1	47	69	0	67	38	1	2.4	9.9	74	80%	.230	0.84	0.54	1.72	2.5	98.6	53	76	48
2017	BAL	MLB	29	2	1	15	38	0	37^{1}	39	1	4.3	7.0	29	75%	.336	1.53	2.89	5.03	0.1	97.3	26	83	39
2018	*BAL*	*MLB*	*30*	*3*	*3*	*30*	*58*	*0*	*61*	*54*	*5*	*3.6*	*8.8*	*61*	*68%*	*.292*	*1.27*	*3.17*	*3.49*	*1.2*	*97.5*	*44*	*80*	*44*
2019	*BAL*	*MLB*	*31*	*3*	*1*	*23*	*57*	*0*	*60*	*52*	*5*	*3.9*	*9.0*	*60*	*68%*	*.294*	*1.30*	*3.94*	*3.95*	*0.8*	*96.9*	*42*	*79*	*43*

Breakout: 25% Improve: 52% Collapse: 33% Attrition: 19% MLB: 92% *Comparables: Pedro Strop, Brandon Webb, Chad Qualls*

On April 15, five saves into the young 2017 season, Britton went on the DL with a strained forearm. The MRI was spotless, and when his return in May went sour, so was the second one. A Zach Britton did finally return on July 5, but not quite the same one as before. It's tempting to treat injuries as binary, to categorize players as "able to play" or "unable to play." But 2016's near-MVP fell between those two extremes; he was able, just not right. The basic numbers looked okay; his velocity wasn't down, his ground-ball rate was its usual unbelievable score. But Britton, one of the most analytically minded players in the game, knew something wasn't working, and the newfangled statistics were backing up the hunch. The strain had tampered with his arm angle, which was preventing him from reaching over the top with his delivery, causing the ball to drive downward toward the plate to earn those precious groundballs. Instead, the spin rate on his world-famous sinker was actually increasing; you'd think spin rate would be good, but in this case it was robbing the pitch of some of its sink. This in turn caused hitters to get more wood on the pitch, increasing the exit velocity on his groundballs and thus driving up his batting average against. It's an ugly chain all borne out of a tiny loss of mechanics, and it looked like Britton was finally getting a handle on things before a knee injury cut his season short. The DRA looks ugly because, as he was dealing with these issues, he had some of the spottiest command in the majors, his strikes getting too much plate. But if anyone can perform the necessary triage on a delivery, it's him.

Dylan Bundy RHP Born: 11/15/92 Age: 25 Bats: B Throws: R Height: 6'1" Weight: 200 Origin: Round 1, 2011 Draft (#4 overall)

YEAR	TEAM	LVL	AGE	W	L	SV	G	GS	IP	H	HR	BB/9	K/9	K	GB%	BABIP	WHIP	ERA	DRA	WARP	MPH	CMD	PWR	STM
2015	BOW	AA	22	0	3	0	8	8	22	21	0	2.0	10.2	25	42%	.356	1.18	3.68	2.77	0.6				
2016	BAL	MLB	23	10	6	0	36	14	109^2	109	18	3.4	8.5	104	37%	.299	1.38	4.02	4.49	0.9	97.0	43	53	54
2017	BAL	MLB	24	13	9	0	28	28	169^2	152	26	2.7	8.1	152	33%	.273	1.20	4.24	3.67	3.6	94.0	45	42	74
2018	*BAL*	*MLB*	*25*	*10*	*11*	*0*	*30*	*30*	*171*	*170*	*30*	*3.3*	*8.6*	*164*	*38%*	*.295*	*1.35*	*4.54*	*4.76*	*1.2*	*94.7*	*45*	*47*	*67*
2019	*BAL*	*MLB*	*26*	*9*	*11*	*0*	*30*	*30*	*187^2*	*185*	*35*	*3.3*	*8.8*	*184*	*38%*	*.294*	*1.35*	*5.10*	*5.18*	*0.9*	*94.5*	*45*	*47*	*67*

Breakout: 20% Improve: 58% Collapse: 20% Attrition: 7% MLB: 100% *Comparables: Yovani Gallardo, Phil Hughes, David Price*

Time is capricious. You can spend a twilight hour pacing a darkened room with a screaming toddler in your arms, a writhing mass of monosyllabic anguish, and it feels like a lifetime; the next day, you'll be helping them move into their college dorm room. Boys and girls become adults in a single instant, either on their eighteenth birthday or, if you're Faulkner, when they shoot a bear. And Bundy, added to the 2016 major-league roster after 38 Double-A innings because the Orioles would literally lose him if they didn't, ended 2017 as their unquestioned best starter. The transition between prospect and veteran is already a blurry line, but for the former blue-chipper, it came in a flash. Years of physical attrition have shaved off a little of the magic from those hazy, luminescent memories of 2012, but the modern version is impressive enough: four strong pitches, a willingness to work every part of the strike zone and a growing command of his full arsenal. Just remember how he looks now, because tomorrow he'll be throwing out ceremonial pitches, graying at the temple, as you think: When did we get so old?

Miguel Castro RHP Born: 12/24/94 Age: 23 Bats: R Throws: R Height: 6'7" Weight: 205 Origin: International Free Agent, 2012

YEAR	TEAM	LVL	AGE	W	L	SV	G	GS	IP	H	HR	BB/9	K/9	K	GB%	BABIP	WHIP	ERA	DRA	WARP	MPH	CMD	PWR	STM
2015	TOR	MLB	20	0	2	4	13	0	12^1	15	2	4.4	8.8	12	41%	.351	1.70	4.38	4.00	0.1	99.5	45	66	43
2015	BUF	AAA	20	1	3	0	13	5	19^2	26	4	5.5	9.6	21	42%	.367	1.93	4.58	4.84	0.0				
2015	ABQ	AAA	20	2	0	0	11	0	13^2	6	0	4.6	6.6	10	57%	.162	0.95	1.32	4.51	0.1				
2015	COL	MLB	20	0	1	0	5	0	5^1	6	2	6.8	10.1	6	25%	.286	1.88	10.12	8.23	-0.2	99.0	45	66	43
2016	COL	MLB	21	0	0	0	19	0	14^2	18	3	3.1	7.4	12	55%	.326	1.57	6.14	5.02	0.0	98.9	42	56	32
2016	ABQ	AAA	21	2	3	0	16	0	15^2	21	5	4.0	8.6	15	49%	.364	1.79	10.34	4.58	0.1				
2017	BOW	AA	22	3	0	0	6	0	24^1	23	1	2.2	4.1	11	49%	.275	1.19	4.44	4.93	0.0				
2017	BAL	MLB	22	3	3	0	39	1	66^1	53	8	3.8	5.2	38	50%	.227	1.22	3.53	5.11	0.1	98.3	39	65	54
2018	*BAL*	*MLB*	*23*	*3*	*4*	*0*	*35*	*8*	*68*	*72*	*11*	*4.2*	*6.8*	*51*	*47%*	*.289*	*1.50*	*5.31*	*5.38*	*-0.1*	*98.4*	*42*	*66*	*45*
2019	*BAL*	*MLB*	*24*	*5*	*5*	*0*	*53*	*11*	*107^1*	*107*	*19*	*4.2*	*7.6*	*91*	*47%*	*.282*	*1.46*	*5.63*	*5.73*	*-0.3*	*98.2*	*41*	*66*	*46*

Breakout: 29% Improve: 47% Collapse: 23% Attrition: 25% MLB: 79% *Comparables: Eric O'Flaherty, Josh Johnson, Jason Vargas*

Castro has been given up on so many times it's easy to forget he just turned 23 as this book was going to print. He's younger than Walker Buehler, younger than Alex Reyes, younger than Lucas Giolito. These names are not, sadly, presented as a demonstration of future promise; they're proof of how quickly a life can calcify. Eight months after Castro was sent to Colorado as one of the major pieces in the Troy Tulowitzki trade, the Rockies essentially gave up on him, shipping him to Baltimore for a PTBNL. The Orioles threw him into losing games, and he pitched well enough until September snuck up and disemboweled his pitching line. They gave him a spot start at the end of the year, and there are rumors that the team would like to see him start in 2018; teams have always whispered about seeing Castro start, and yet they've never given him a chance to actually learn how to be a starter. The fastball remains blistering, if flat, but already it shows signs of wear. In the end, this is probably it for Castro, if only because there was never a chance for him to be anything else.

Stefan Crichton RHP Born: 02/29/92 Age: 26 Bats: R Throws: R Height: 6'3" Weight: 200 Origin: Round 23, 2013 Draft (#699 overall)

YEAR	TEAM	LVL	AGE	W	L	SV	G	GS	IP	H	HR	BB/9	K/9	K	GB%	BABIP	WHIP	ERA	DRA	WARP	MPH	CMD	PWR	STM
2015	DEL	A	23	4	4	4	28	1	66	64	1	1.6	6.8	50	63%	.301	1.15	3.27	2.37	1.9				
2015	FRD	A+	23	0	0	2	7	0	13^1	14	0	0.7	12.1	18	58%	.424	1.12	4.05	1.41	0.5				
2016	BOW	AA	24	2	6	1	48	4	72^1	73	4	3.2	7.6	61	48%	.312	1.37	3.73	3.73	0.9				
2017	BAL	MLB	25	0	0	0	8	0	12^1	26	2	2.9	5.8	8	48%	.500	2.43	8.03	7.79	-0.4	95.9	35	56	45
2017	NOR	AAA	25	7	2	2	29	0	47^2	47	2	2.1	9.4	50	48%	.321	1.22	3.02	2.47	1.5				
2018	*BAL*	*MLB*	*26*	*1*	*1*	*0*	*21*	*0*	*22*	*24*	*4*	*3.7*	*7.6*	*19*	*47%*	*.304*	*1.54*	*4.99*	*4.93*	*0.0*	*95.5*	*36*	*57*	*46*
2019	*BAL*	*MLB*	*27*	*2*	*1*	*0*	*36*	*0*	*38^1*	*42*	*6*	*3.8*	*7.8*	*33*	*47%*	*.313*	*1.53*	*5.28*	*5.36*	*-0.1*	*95.1*	*36*	*57*	*46*

Breakout: 18% Improve: 21% Collapse: 4% Attrition: 17% MLB: 27% *Comparables: Chad Smith, Mark Hamburger, Chad Girodo*

On May 22, 2017, Crichton wound up to pitch and dropped the ball. For two seconds, he just stared at it as it rolled to a stop, like a child that won't brush their teeth. Then he realized where he was and jumped after it to keep the runner from third from scoring, which the runner did anyway, because when you drop the ball midpitch, it's a balk. Every part of this sequence was Crichton's 2017 season with the Orioles.

Kevin Gausman RHP Born: 01/06/91 Age: 27 Bats: L Throws: R Height: 6'3" Weight: 190 Origin: Round 1, 2012 Draft (#4 overall)

YEAR	TEAM	LVL	AGE	W	L	SV	G	GS	IP	H	HR	BB/9	K/9	K	GB%	BABIP	WHIP	ERA	DRA	WARP	MPH	CMD	PWR	STM
2015	NOR	AAA	24	0	1	0	3	3	14	10	2	3.9	9.0	14	51%	.242	1.14	1.29	4.23	0.2				
2015	BAL	MLB	24	4	7	0	25	17	112^{1}	109	17	2.3	8.3	103	46%	.288	1.23	4.25	3.52	2.0	98.7	50	69	58
2016	BAL	MLB	25	9	12	0	30	30	179^{2}	183	28	2.4	8.7	174	46%	.308	1.28	3.61	3.86	3.1	98.2	47	59	80
2017	BAL	MLB	26	11	12	0	34	34	186^{2}	208	29	3.4	8.6	179	44%	.336	1.49	4.68	4.57	2.1	97.4	52	63	81
2018	*BAL*	*MLB*	*27*	*10*	*10*	*0*	*30*	*30*	*171*	*177*	*27*	*3.2*	*8.4*	*159*	*45%*	*.305*	*1.41*	*4.38*	*4.58*	*1.6*	*97.4*	*50*	*63*	*76*
2019	*BAL*	*MLB*	*28*	*10*	*11*	*0*	*30*	*30*	*187^{1}*	*191*	*29*	*3.2*	*8.9*	*185*	*45%*	*.311*	*1.37*	*4.65*	*4.69*	*1.8*	*97.0*	*50*	*62*	*79*

Breakout: 28% Improve: 60% Collapse: 21% Attrition: 10% MLB: 96% *Comparables: Francisco Liriano, Matt Garza, Ricky Nolasco*

When you think about it, the human body is a terrifying thing: a loose amalgam of microscopic parts, and parts of parts, totally reliant on one another to function, almost all of them absolutely necessary to keep your existence from vanishing in a breath. Like pitchers, in many ways. Before the season Gausman appeared as safe as any young arm could be, his innings marshaled, his mechanics and results predictable. Then, he had a 2017 season like a child taking apart a clock radio, as he posted a first-half ERA of 5.85. The peripherals were down, and every time a batter made contact, it seemed like a Charlie Brown-disrobing line drive. The Orioles had no choice but to keep starting him and praying for a miracle. Then, in mid-June, he altered his release point by an inch—and immediately he was his old self again, unleashing a forgotten slider that elicited a whiff nearly 20 percent of the time. It's a heartwarming story, and also a terrifying one, proof that we all might be an inch away from greatness, or collapse.

Mychal Givens RHP Born: 05/13/90 Age: 28 Bats: R Throws: R Height: 6'0" Weight: 210 Origin: Round 2, 2009 Draft (#54 overall)

YEAR	TEAM	LVL	AGE	W	L	SV	G	GS	IP	H	HR	BB/9	K/9	K	GB%	BABIP	WHIP	ERA	DRA	WARP	MPH	CMD	PWR	STM
2015	BOW	AA	25	4	2	15	35	0	57^{1}	38	1	2.5	12.4	79	42%	.289	0.94	1.73	1.15	2.5				
2015	BAL	MLB	25	2	0	0	22	0	30	20	1	1.8	11.4	38	42%	.268	0.87	1.80	2.26	0.9	97.1	60	61	52
2016	BAL	MLB	26	8	2	0	66	0	74^{2}	59	6	4.3	11.6	96	38%	.314	1.27	3.13	3.03	1.7	97.3	43	59	52
2017	BAL	MLB	27	8	1	0	69	0	78^{2}	57	10	2.9	10.1	88	43%	.251	1.04	2.75	2.85	2.0	97.8	42	72	54
2018	*BAL*	*MLB*	*28*	*3*	*3*	*0*	*64*	*0*	*67*	*57*	*9*	*3.5*	*10.6*	*80*	*42%*	*.291*	*1.24*	*3.63*	*3.88*	*1.0*	*96.9*	*45*	*66*	*53*
2019	*BAL*	*MLB*	*29*	*3*	*1*	*0*	*55*	*0*	*58^{1}*	*48*	*8*	*3.8*	*11.0*	*71*	*42%*	*.288*	*1.26*	*4.26*	*4.29*	*0.6*	*96.6*	*43*	*66*	*53*

Breakout: 27% Improve: 40% Collapse: 31% Attrition: 17% MLB: 83% *Comparables: Joey Devine, Danny Farquhar, Aaron Barrett*

Givens' throwing motion is a special thing: He is all parabolas. He bends forward, picks up the left foot and curls in twisting upward, raises the ball aloft like the head of an angry cobra. Then the arm snakes downward into a sidearm and the pitch seems to whip out in the same arc, bending as it crosses the plate too quickly to be real. It's a percussive act, almost the pitching equivalent of swinging a bat. Although a few more of his hits left the yard, 2017 proved to be a step forward in almost every other fashion; his fastball gained a tick, his command improved and even his ground-ball rate rose. Most importantly, that improved fastball gave Givens a tool to chip away at that bane of the side-armer, the dreaded platoon split. It's been a fittingly circuitous path to greatness for the former second-round shortstop, but now that he's almost there, it's been a pleasant journey to behold.

Miguel Gonzalez RHP Born: 09/29/95 Age: 22 Bats: R Throws: R Height: 6'3" Weight: 185 Origin: International Free Agent, 2014

YEAR	TEAM	LVL	AGE	W	L	SV	G	GS	IP	H	HR	BB/9	K/9	K	GB%	BABIP	WHIP	ERA	DRA	WARP	MPH	CMD	PWR	STM
2015	DBA	RK	19	0	5	0	13	7	37^{2}	42	1	7.2	4.5	19	58%	.311	1.91	6.93	9.82	-1.7				
2016	DBA	RK	20	0	3	0	10	6	23^{2}	26	0	10.3	8.0	21	52%	.377	2.24	9.89	8.91	-0.9				
2017	DOR	RK	21	1	1	0	15	0	23^{1}	22	1	7.7	7.7	20	50%	.304	1.80	6.56	9.61	-0.9				
2018	*BAL*	*MLB*	*22*	*0*	*2*	*0*	*14*	*3*	*24^{1}*	*31*	*7*	*15.9*	*7.1*	*19*	*40%*	*.320*	*3.05*	*11.50*	*11.95*	*-2.0*				
2019	*BAL*	*MLB*	*23*	*2*	*3*	*1*	*29*	*7*	*75^{2}*	*99*	*19*	*6.0*	*5.4*	*46*	*40%*	*.314*	*1.97*	*8.13*	*8.38*	*-1.9*				

Comparables: Evan Crawford, Paul Clemens, Tayron Guerrero

Not the Miguel Gonzalez who toiled his way to fourth-starter success with the Orioles between 2012 and 2015, this Gonzalez was an undrafted member of the team's Dominican Summer League squad. Ordinarily, having your name in the *BP Annual* is a measure of honor: an indication not necessarily of making it, but having the potential to make it, at least enough to discuss the appropriate timeline. But it was almost impossible to find the thread where Gonzalez got there; he was a 22-year-old kid who couldn't throw strikes, who got to be a baseball player on the very loosest level of familiarity. He was an Oriole who probably barely knew of Baltimore, at least as anything more than a boy's scattering dream. We will never know more of him than that; driving on the dark Dominican roads of early autumn, an out-of-control truck slammed into the driver's side of his car, and his timelines all ended the following day.

DL Hall LHP Born: 09/19/98 Age: 19 Bats: L Throws: L Height: 6'0" Weight: 180 Origin: Round 1, 2017 Draft (#21 overall)

YEAR	TEAM	LVL	AGE	W	L	SV	G	GS	IP	H	HR	BB/9	K/9	K	GB%	BABIP	WHIP	ERA	DRA	WARP	MPH	CMD	PWR	STM
2017	ORI	RK	18	0	0	0	5	5	10^{1}	10	1	8.7	10.5	12	58%	.360	1.94	6.97	7.72	-0.2				
2018	*BAL*	*MLB*	*19*	*0*	*4*	*0*	*7*	*7*	*26*	*32*	*8*	*13.7*	*8.4*	*25*	*41%*	*.316*	*2.76*	*10.50*	*10.90*	*-1.5*				
2019	*BAL*	*MLB*	*20*	*3*	*8*	*0*	*26*	*26*	*153*	*186*	*34*	*4.6*	*7.0*	*120*	*41%*	*.318*	*1.73*	*6.58*	*6.74*	*-1.2*				

Comparables: Jamie Callahan, Jenrry Mejia, Brad Hand

The Orioles may have gotten a bit of a bargain in Hall, considered the second-best prep lefty heading into the draft, when he fell to the 21st pick in the draft. The question is whether he can break the Curse of Bedard and survive the gauntlet of Orioles pitching development unscathed. For all the risks inherent in going with a high school pitcher, especially one with a foreboding first name, the young man has a fairly high floor: His fastball clocks in at 90-93 mph, and although he's on the short side, there's potential for him to add a few pounds, and ticks, to his profile. He has a changeup that currently can be described as "identifiable as a changeup." But it's the biting, heavy curve that is the main draw, an unqualified out pitch, and the combination is what gets one projected as a mid-rotation starter. He'll have to develop all those things that 18-year-olds struggle with, like fastball command and the ability to balance a checkbook, but he's off to a good start. For now, perhaps Hall's greatest virtue is how few elements there are of his to mess with.

Donnie Hart LHP Born: 09/06/90 Age: 27 Bats: L Throws: L Height: 5'11" Weight: 180 Origin: Round 27, 2013 Draft (#819 overall)

YEAR	TEAM	LVL	AGE	W	L	SV	G	GS	IP	H	HR	BB/9	K/9	K	GB%	BABIP	WHIP	ERA	DRA	WARP	MPH	CMD	PWR	STM
2015	DEL	A	24	1	1	10	19	0	17	14	0	2.1	9.0	17	68%	.280	1.06	2.12	2.30	0.5				
2015	FRD	A+	24	5	1	3	27	0	35	26	0	2.6	7.5	29	61%	.265	1.03	1.03	2.40	1.0				
2016	BOW	AA	25	3	1	4	40	0	46^{1}	41	1	1.4	9.7	50	50%	.325	1.04	2.72	1.64	1.7				
2016	BAL	MLB	25	0	0	0	22	0	18^{1}	12	1	2.9	5.9	12	60%	.212	0.98	0.49	4.06	0.2	89.7	37	24	46
2017	NOR	AAA	26	1	0	0	13	0	15^{1}	17	1	1.2	11.7	20	55%	.390	1.24	2.35	1.54	0.6				
2017	BAL	MLB	26	2	0	0	51	0	43^{2}	48	5	2.7	6.0	29	54%	.309	1.40	3.71	4.35	0.4	88.8	59	13	47
2018	*BAL*	*MLB*	*27*	*2*	*3*	*0*	*53*	*0*	56^{1}	*59*	*8*	*3.8*	*7.0*	*44*	*50%*	*.301*	*1.49*	*4.91*	*4.87*	*0.2*	*88.6*	*55*	*16*	*47*
2019	*BAL*	*MLB*	*28*	*2*	*1*	*0*	*34*	*0*	36^{1}	*39*	*5*	*3.6*	*7.1*	*29*	*50%*	*.305*	*1.48*	*5.04*	*5.11*	*0.0*	*88.3*	*55*	*16*	*47*

Breakout: 21% Improve: 35% Collapse: 20% Attrition: 26% MLB: 66% *Comparables: Daniel Herrera, Zach Putnam, Wes Littleton*

None of it should work. Hart is the antithesis of the modern bullpen arm, an undersized and underpowered 27th-round sidearm lefty whose fastball is among the slowest in the game. The slider is mostly flat and fairly slurvy, and the changeup ... well, he only threw it three times to a hitter without the platoon advantage in 2017 and missed the strike zone all three times. The key to Hart's success is that he has no key to success. With a long stride and that funky, purely halfway arm slot, Hart's lone weapon is his deceptiveness, and he complements it with a total randomization of his very similar pitches; he throws the slider and fastball nearly equally, no matter what the count, and he's not afraid to sprinkle it in against lefties as well. Essentially, he converts every pitch into a coin flip, and by wielding a heavy sinker and staying low, he minimizes the damage on the bets he loses. The good fortune may not last, but it's easy to root for a guy who finds his fortune in a novel way, and helps his team in the process.

Hunter Harvey RHP Born: 12/09/94 Age: 23 Bats: R Throws: R Height: 6'3" Weight: 175 Origin: Round 1, 2013 Draft (#22 overall)

YEAR	TEAM	LVL	AGE	W	L	SV	G	GS	IP	H	HR	BB/9	K/9	K	GB%	BABIP	WHIP	ERA	DRA	WARP	MPH	CMD	PWR	STM
2018	*BAL*	*MLB*	*23*	*2*	*3*	*0*	*8*	*8*	32^{1}	*35*	*9*	*5.4*	*10.1*	*36*	*36%*	*.312*	*1.68*	*6.55*	*6.71*	*-0.4*				
2019	*BAL*	*MLB*	*24*	*5*	*11*	*0*	*27*	*27*	161^{1}	*173*	*44*	*4.8*	*9.8*	*176*	*36%*	*.306*	*1.61*	*6.55*	*6.73*	*-1.3*				

Breakout: 9% Improve: 14% Collapse: 3% Attrition: 15% MLB: 21% *Comparables: Sean Manaea, Dellin Betances, Jered Weaver*

First, the good news: Harvey saw two promotions in the span of a single month. Okay, the real good news, technically, is that he pitched. The bad news is that he made eight starts and threw 18 2/3 innings, in the most Sisyphean display of rehab imaginable. Scouts swear the talent is still there, but after recovery from Tommy John surgery as slow to develop as an Ingmar Bergman film, one is driven to ask exactly where talent even exists. Is it in the sinew, oxidized and rusted over time, an identity set and then worn into unrecognizability? Is it in some hidden pineal gland, eventually lost and locked away forever? Will Harvey ever be Hunter Harvey again, or was he ever? Who knows what Harvey was meant to be, what caused the path to disappear among the weeds. All we know is he'll be back in the spring, starting another game, returning to the dugout after each inning and waiting, waiting for the arm to ache.

Jeremy Hellickson RHP Born: 04/08/87 Age: 31 Bats: R Throws: R Height: 6'1" Weight: 190 Origin: Round 4, 2005 Draft (#118 overall)

YEAR	TEAM	LVL	AGE	W	L	SV	G	GS	IP	H	HR	BB/9	K/9	K	GB%	BABIP	WHIP	ERA	DRA	WARP	MPH	CMD	PWR	STM
2015	ARI	MLB	28	9	12	0	27	27	146	151	22	2.7	7.5	121	45%	.291	1.33	4.62	4.49	1.0	92.2	46	33	63
2016	PHI	MLB	29	12	10	0	32	32	189	173	24	2.1	7.3	154	43%	.274	1.15	3.71	3.91	3.1	92.2	56	37	75
2017	PHI	MLB	30	6	5	0	20	20	112^{1}	111	22	2.4	5.2	65	37%	.255	1.26	4.73	4.71	1.1	91.3	57	32	70
2017	BAL	MLB	30	2	6	0	10	10	51^{2}	49	13	3.0	5.4	31	36%	.225	1.28	6.97	4.45	0.6	91.6	57	32	70
2018	*BAL*	*MLB*	*31*	*7*	*9*	*0*	*24*	*24*	132^{1}	*145*	*25*	*3.1*	*6.3*	*93*	*42%*	*.293*	*1.44*	*5.50*	*5.60*	*0.1*	*91.0*	*54*	*34*	*69*
2019	*BAL*	*MLB*	*32*	*6*	*8*	*0*	*19*	*19*	114^{2}	*126*	*20*	*2.9*	*6.3*	*80*	*42%*	*.294*	*1.42*	*5.45*	*5.53*	*0.2*	*90.6*	*55*	*34*	*70*

Breakout: 8% Improve: 38% Collapse: 21% Attrition: 13% MLB: 85% *Comparables: Carl Pavano, Brian Bannister, Jeff Francis*

Look, it's easy to make jokes. How simple it would be to describe Hellickson as a timeshare poltergeist, moving from team to team, haunting them for their misspent existence. But the painful truth, for weary *Annual* writers and righteous fans, is that the former Rookie of the Year and eternal punchline isn't that bad; he's just a generic four-pitch strike-thrower. Coming over at the deadline, he was a perfect fit for an Orioles team choking on a rotation of Actually That Bad. But Hellickson is doomed to be one of those people who only exist in context: compared to the promise of his youth, compared to the qualifying offer he didn't really deserve and compared to the situation he was brought into. BP had the Orioles at a 2.8 percent chance of making the playoffs when they brought him in, and experts rightly chided the organization for failing to understand themselves and their position. That's hardly Hellickson's fault, and he'll just soldier on, eating innings and never quite living up to expectations, randomly set.

Ubaldo Jimenez RHP Born: 01/22/84 Age: 34 Bats: R Throws: R Height: 6'5" Weight: 210 Origin: International Free Agent, 2001

YEAR	TEAM	LVL	AGE	W	L	SV	G	GS	IP	H	HR	BB/9	K/9	K	GB%	BABIP	WHIP	ERA	DRA	WARP	MPH	CMD	PWR	STM
2015	BAL	MLB	31	12	10	0	32	32	184	182	20	3.3	8.2	168	50%	.309	1.36	4.11	3.86	2.7	93.7	59	45	74
2016	BAL	MLB	32	8	12	1	29	25	142^{1}	150	16	4.6	7.9	125	50%	.318	1.56	5.44	5.15	0.3	92.9	50	42	64
2017	BAL	MLB	33	6	11	0	31	25	142^{2}	169	33	3.7	8.8	139	44%	.329	1.59	6.81	6.68	-1.8	92.7	37	37	69
2018	*BAL*	*MLB*	*34*	*7*	*8*	*0*	*23*	*23*	123^{2}	*136*	*21*	*3.8*	*8.1*	*111*	*47%*	*.313*	*1.52*	*5.15*	*5.22*	*0.7*	*91.9*	*47*	*40*	*68*
2019	*BAL*	*MLB*	*35*	*6*	*8*	*0*	*21*	*21*	*125*	*140*	*22*	*3.9*	*8.0*	*111*	*47%*	*.315*	*1.55*	*5.35*	*5.43*	*0.3*	*91.2*	*43*	*39*	*66*

Breakout: 12% Improve: 38% Collapse: 20% Attrition: 8% MLB: 94% *Comparables: Erik Bedard, A.J. Burnett, Jose Contreras*

The Orioles' version of the Maginot Line completed his four-year, $50 million contract, and the net result was a single win above replacement. After a lifetime of ups and downs, disasters and reinventions, Jimenez was primed to repeat his Cleveland tour and finish with just enough promise to lure a new club to its demise. It never came, as the mercurial righty posted a single month with an ERA below six, 5.96 in May. Perhaps the most mechanically unsound pitcher in all of baseball, Jimenez still has the stuff to miss bats, if he could ever keep his pitches close enough to the plate to trick hitters into swinging at them. The starting rotations of MLB are the world's worst game of musical chairs, so some desperate team will give Jimenez a job and convince themselves that they have the hidden talent to unlock his greatness. Fortunately for them, they won't have to wait four years to find out.

Wade Miley LHP Born: 11/13/86 Age: 31 Bats: L Throws: L Height: 6'0" Weight: 220 Origin: Round 1, 2008 Draft (#43 overall)

YEAR	TEAM	LVL	AGE	W	L	SV	G	GS	IP	H	HR	BB/9	K/9	K	GB%	BABIP	WHIP	ERA	DRA	WARP	MPH	CMD	PWR	STM
2015	BOS	MLB	28	11	11	0	32	32	193^{2}	201	17	3.0	6.8	147	50%	.307	1.37	4.46	3.75	3.1	93.8	59	42	78
2016	SEA	MLB	29	7	8	0	19	19	112	117	18	2.7	6.6	82	48%	.298	1.35	4.98	5.12	0.3	93.3	59	38	70
2016	BAL	MLB	29	2	5	0	11	11	54	70	7	2.5	9.2	55	50%	.389	1.57	6.17	4.40	0.6	92.8	59	38	70
2017	BAL	MLB	30	8	15	0	32	32	157^{1}	179	25	5.3	8.1	142	51%	.332	1.73	5.61	5.23	0.6	93.3	61	40	76
2018	*BAL*	*MLB*	*31*	*8*	*9*	*0*	*25*	*25*	138^{2}	*155*	*21*	*4.1*	*7.2*	*110*	*49%*	*.315*	*1.57*	*5.18*	*5.25*	*0.7*	*92.5*	*59*	*40*	*74*
2019	*BAL*	*MLB*	*32*	*5*	*6*	*0*	*16*	*16*	93^{2}	*105*	*14*	*3.9*	*7.0*	*73*	*49%*	*.318*	*1.56*	*5.19*	*5.25*	*0.4*	*92.0*	*59*	*39*	*73*

Breakout: 13% Improve: 47% Collapse: 26% Attrition: 15% MLB: 94% *Comparables: Gil Meche, Paul Maholm, Matt Garza*

There's not being able to throw strikes, and then there's not being able to throw strikes. On the surface it appeared that Miley's life voyage as a forgettable back-end starter was ruined by a loss of command, as he walked nearly twice as many batters as usual. However, using CSAA (caught strikes above average), we can look at balls and strikes not as binary events but as probabilities: the strike straight down the middle as opposed to one off the edge, earning the call. Miley's 3.1 percent CSAA ranked fourth among full-time starters, which sounds good (he got more strikes called than other pitchers!) but presages a dark tale. Miley's stuff, never intimidating, has deteriorated to the point where he can't risk throwing anything hittable, and instead has to nibble like hell at the edges and pray for the call. It's an interesting strategy, given the circumstances, but not an especially hopeful one.

Darren O'Day RHP Born: 10/22/82 Age: 35 Bats: R Throws: R Height: 6'4" Weight: 220 Origin: Undrafted Free Agent, 2006

YEAR	TEAM	LVL	AGE	W	L	SV	G	GS	IP	H	HR	BB/9	K/9	K	GB%	BABIP	WHIP	ERA	DRA	WARP	MPH	CMD	PWR	STM
2015	BAL	MLB	32	6	2	6	68	0	65^{1}	47	5	1.9	11.3	82	36%	.278	0.93	1.52	2.71	1.6	89.1	78	20	50
2016	BAL	MLB	33	3	1	3	34	0	31	25	6	3.8	11.0	38	34%	.260	1.23	3.77	3.74	0.4	88.3	71	30	24
2017	BAL	MLB	34	2	3	2	64	0	60^{1}	41	8	3.6	11.3	76	48%	.256	1.08	3.43	1.94	2.2	89.0	86	21	48
2018	*BAL*	*MLB*	*35*	*3*	*4*	*2*	*69*	*0*	*73*	*64*	*11*	*3.9*	*10.1*	*82*	*42%*	*.284*	*1.29*	*4.25*	*4.38*	*0.6*	*87.7*	*79*	*22*	*40*
2019	*BAL*	*MLB*	*36*	*3*	*1*	*1*	*52*	*0*	*55*	*47*	*9*	*3.9*	*10.0*	*61*	*42%*	*.277*	*1.29*	*4.79*	*4.85*	*0.2*	*87.0*	*79*	*23*	*38*

Breakout: 17% Improve: 33% Collapse: 32% Attrition: 13% MLB: 88% *Comparables: Matt Thornton, Heath Bell, Francisco Cordero*

Anthony Young. Bob Feller. Dooley Womack. Curt Schilling. One thing they have in common: They all have more career saves than O'Day, one of the best and most underrated relief pitchers of the past decade. The king of the eighth inning recovered from an injury-plagued 2016 to post perhaps his finest season yet, and his career splits embody the spirit of Orioles Bullpen Magic: He performs better in the second half of the season, better in late innings, better in high-leverage situations. Some were skeptical of the four-year, $31 million contract the team awarded him, but at least halfway through, he's earned it. If you're in the mood for nitpicking, you could point to his rising contact rates. Or note that decline might be hidden in the recent leaguewide strikeout boom. Or just remind people that he's a 35-year-old side-arming middle reliever. But the odds are better than even that he'll be good again next year, and the odds are even better that most people won't even notice.

Ofelky Peralta RHP Born: 04/20/97 Age: 21 Bats: R Throws: R Height: 6'5" Weight: 195 Origin: International Free Agent, 2013

YEAR	TEAM	LVL	AGE	W	L	SV	G	GS	IP	H	HR	BB/9	K/9	K	GB%	BABIP	WHIP	ERA	DRA	WARP	MPH	CMD	PWR	STM
2015	ORI	RK	18	0	2	0	11	10	25^{2}	20	0	6.7	10.9	31	47%	.294	1.52	5.61	5.22	0.2				
2016	DEL	A	19	8	5	0	23	23	103^{1}	87	3	5.2	8.8	101	39%	.301	1.42	4.01	8.64	-4.6				
2017	FRD	A+	20	2	10	0	26	26	104^{2}	109	8	7.4	8.2	95	37%	.328	1.86	5.42	10.42	-6.3				
2018	*BAL*	*MLB*	*21*	*4*	*9*	*0*	*22*	*22*	86^{2}	*93*	*18*	*8.5*	*9.3*	*89*	*35%*	*.314*	*2.02*	*7.03*	*7.22*	*-1.5*				
2019	*BAL*	*MLB*	*22*	*4*	*7*	*0*	*19*	*19*	112^{2}	*121*	*26*	*4.3*	*8.9*	*112*	*35%*	*.303*	*1.55*	*6.06*	*6.21*	*-0.5*				

Comparables: Jairo Labourt, Shawn Morimando, Timothy Melville

In 2016, a teenaged Peralta managed to hold his own against the Sally League despite employing the rare strategy of walking more batters than he technically faced. The Orioles looked at results, decided to let it ride, and 2017 was the result. Peralta shares the physique of Keegan Akin but made the wise choice of being five inches taller. That and an upper-90s fastball are the sum of his current virtues. Unfortunately, constant survival mode has hampered his ability to develop any kind of breaking ball, and his mechanics between upper and lower halves remind one of someone being sucked into a vortex in a cheap science fiction movie. The result is a reliever who needs a batting average against below .200 to get by; it's not perhaps the truest path to success.

Tanner Scott LHP Born: 07/22/94 Age: 23 Bats: R Throws: L Height: 6'2" Weight: 220 Origin: Round 6, 2014 Draft (#181 overall)

YEAR	TEAM	LVL	AGE	W	L	SV	G	GS	IP	H	HR	BB/9	K/9	K	GB%	BABIP	WHIP	ERA	DRA	WARP	MPH	CMD	PWR	STM
2015	ABE	A-	20	4	0	0	9	1	21^{1}	16	0	5.1	13.1	31	64%	.340	1.31	3.38	3.71	0.3				
2015	DEL	A	20	0	3	2	9	2	21	19	0	4.3	12.4	29	57%	.373	1.38	4.29	2.69	0.6				
2016	FRD	A+	21	4	2	5	29	0	48^{1}	22	1	7.8	11.7	63	59%	.198	1.32	4.47	3.74	0.7				
2016	BOW	AA	21	1	2	0	14	0	16	18	0	8.4	10.1	18	64%	.429	2.06	5.62	7.96	-0.6				
2017	BOW	AA	22	0	2	0	24	24	69	45	2	6.0	11.3	87	54%	.281	1.32	2.22	4.20	0.8				
2017	BAL	MLB	22	0	0	0	2	0	1^{2}	2	0	10.8	10.8	2	20%	.400	2.40	10.80	2.82	0.0	100.1			37
2018	*BAL*	*MLB*	*23*	*2*	*3*	*0*	*22*	*6*	48^{2}	*42*	*8*	*6.1*	*11.0*	*60*	*50%*	*.299*	*1.57*	*4.79*	*4.92*	*0.2*	*100.0*			*38*
2019	*BAL*	*MLB*	*24*	*6*	*6*	*0*	*58*	*15*	133^{1}	*120*	*22*	*5.2*	*10.7*	*159*	*50%*	*.298*	*1.48*	*5.09*	*5.17*	*0.4*	*99.8*			*39*

Breakout: 19% Improve: 25% Collapse: 8% Attrition: 21% MLB: 35% *Comparables: Akeel Morris, Jose Leclerc, Scott Elbert*

Scott has both the physique and the arm of a taut rubber band; he can seemingly throw 100 mph with the flick of his left wrist. Unfortunately, that's about the total of the young man's arsenal. Command and secondaries have been twin downfalls, so the Orioles took the interesting step of having him start games and go three innings, despite the fact that Scott is unquestionably a reliever. The thinking was that by forcing him to conserve his efforts, it would encourage him to pitch more and throw less, and the results were faintly encouraging. Progress still needs to be made, particularly with a slider incapable of fooling anyone who chooses to sit on it, but the hope is that Scott can tap into his athleticism and take at least one more step forward.

Cody Sedlock RHP Born: 06/19/95 Age: 22 Bats: R Throws: R Height: 6'3" Weight: 190 Origin: Round 1, 2016 Draft (#27 overall)

YEAR	TEAM	LVL	AGE	W	L	SV	G	GS	IP	H	HR	BB/9	K/9	K	GB%	BABIP	WHIP	ERA	DRA	WARP	MPH	CMD	PWR	STM
2016	ABE	A-	21	0	1	0	9	9	27	16	1	4.3	8.3	25	60%	.200	1.07	3.00	3.57	0.5				
2017	FRD	A+	22	4	5	0	20	20	90	119	11	3.6	6.9	69	48%	.356	1.72	5.90	6.29	-1.1				
2018	*BAL*	*MLB*	*23*	*3*	*6*	*0*	*16*	*16*	*67^1*	*80*	*15*	*5.0*	*7.6*	*57*	*44%*	*.316*	*1.74*	*6.29*	*6.43*	*-0.6*				
2019	*BAL*	*MLB*	*24*	*4*	*8*	*0*	*21*	*21*	*121^1*	*143*	*27*	*4.7*	*7.5*	*102*	*44%*	*.315*	*1.71*	*6.30*	*6.45*	*-0.8*				

Breakout: 3% Improve: 6% Collapse: 0% Attrition: 1% MLB: 7% *Comparables: Ross Ohlendorf, Patrick Light, Sergio Romo*

A common misconception of stamina, in part cemented by Nintendo baseball games, is that when pitchers get tired they just start throwing slower. Some do, but it's not Sedlock's main problem. He was a reliever during his first two years of college, and the Orioles were careful to limit his innings in his second year of pro ball, hoping to build up the workload while he developed a changeup to go with his promising slider and curve. But as he pitched deeper into games, it was his mechanics and not his velocity that wore down—to the detriment of his command and, eventually, his health. The book's nowhere near closed on Sedlock yet, as he's young for a college grad, but the obstacles he's faced in development make a bullpen role appear more and more likely.

Chris Tillman RHP Born: 04/15/88 Age: 30 Bats: R Throws: R Height: 6'5" Weight: 200 Origin: Round 2, 2006 Draft (#49 overall)

YEAR	TEAM	LVL	AGE	W	L	SV	G	GS	IP	H	HR	BB/9	K/9	K	GB%	BABIP	WHIP	ERA	DRA	WARP	MPH	CMD	PWR	STM
2015	BAL	MLB	27	11	11	0	31	31	173	176	20	3.3	6.2	120	46%	.294	1.39	4.99	4.81	0.6	94.4	44	49	71
2016	BAL	MLB	28	16	6	0	30	30	172	155	19	3.5	7.3	140	42%	.282	1.28	3.77	4.29	2.1	94.6	45	48	72
2017	BAL	MLB	29	1	7	0	24	19	93	125	24	4.9	6.1	63	39%	.334	1.89	7.84	7.97	-2.5	92.5	39	36	56
2018	*BAL*	*MLB*	*30*	*6*	*8*	*0*	*19*	*19*	*106^2*	*116*	*19*	*4.0*	*6.5*	*77*	*43%*	*.293*	*1.53*	*5.70*	*5.81*	*-0.1*	*93.2*	*43*	*45*	*65*
2019	*BAL*	*MLB*	*31*	*7*	*10*	*0*	*24*	*24*	*141^1*	*154*	*25*	*3.8*	*6.6*	*103*	*43%*	*.297*	*1.52*	*5.72*	*5.82*	*-0.2*	*92.7*	*42*	*43*	*63*

Breakout: 7% Improve: 33% Collapse: 37% Attrition: 12% MLB: 92% *Comparables: Brad Penny, Jason Jennings, Travis Wood*

There's a certain amount of synecdoche that goes along with any baseball analysis, and it goes double for pitchers. This paragraph, for example, is ostensibly about Tillman, who suffered through a miserable 2017. But it's actually about his shoulder, the shoulder that forced him to miss a chunk of 2016, an injury he rushed back from to push his team to a wild card berth, and which never really healed in the following offseason. The team gave him injections, shots and some old-timey elixirs, and allowed him a month to rehab in the minors. But it was clear that the Chris Tillman who returned, or at least the shoulder of said Tillman, wasn't the same one Orioles fans took for granted. Everything spelled disaster: the velocity, the command, the mechanics, the results. He got behind in counts by missing his first pitches, then got his strikes clobbered in the resulting hitter's counts. And the team, with no alternatives, would throw him out there again five days later. Tillman the man swore that Tillman the arm was fine despite all evidence, and there's no way to know just how much either will rebound in 2018. Another offseason may be all it takes, but any prospective buyers should be careful letting their eyes drift too far up the career stat line: Those belong to a different Chris Tillman.

Alex Wells LHP Born: 02/27/97 Age: 21 Bats: L Throws: L Height: 6'1" Weight: 190 Origin: International Free Agent, 2015

YEAR	TEAM	LVL	AGE	W	L	SV	G	GS	IP	H	HR	BB/9	K/9	K	GB%	BABIP	WHIP	ERA	DRA	WARP	MPH	CMD	PWR	STM
2016	ABE	A-	19	4	5	0	13	13	62^2	48	1	1.3	7.2	50	46%	.269	0.91	2.15	2.46	2.0				
2017	DEL	A	20	11	5	0	25	25	140	118	16	0.6	7.3	113	43%	.251	0.91	2.38	2.38	4.7				
2018	*BAL*	*MLB*	*21*	*5*	*7*	*0*	*19*	*19*	*98^1*	*107*	*22*	*2.8*	*8.0*	*87*	*38%*	*.300*	*1.40*	*5.43*	*5.52*	*0.2*				
2019	*BAL*	*MLB*	*22*	*6*	*10*	*0*	*23*	*23*	*133*	*151*	*33*	*3.6*	*7.9*	*117*	*38%*	*.302*	*1.53*	*6.21*	*6.36*	*-0.9*				

Breakout: 2% Improve: 2% Collapse: 2% Attrition: 4% MLB: 5% *Comparables: Matt Harrison, Vance Worley, Zach Lee*

Wells watched his identical twin brother Lachlan sign with the Twins in 2014, but after giving him a two-year head start, Alex is making up for lost time. A begoggled soft-tossing Australian left-hander, Wells built on his success in rookie ball with an impressive 11.3-to-1 strikeout-to-walk ratio in the South Atlantic League. He did so despite wielding a fastball south of 90 mph and a looping curveball that can only earn strikes through charity. The changeup, though, is impressive and he can throw it for strikes against batters on both sides of the plate, which forgives a lot of other problems. There isn't much projection left for the fastball, and the Orioles aren't exactly renowned for coaxing great new pitches out of their arms, so Wells' success will come down to how much he can maintain that deception as he moves up the ladder. Whether he does or not, it'll be easy to root for him.

Gabriel Ynoa RHP Born: 05/26/93 Age: 25 Bats: R Throws: R Height: 6'2" Weight: 205 Origin: International Free Agent, 2009

YEAR	TEAM	LVL	AGE	W	L	SV	G	GS	IP	H	HR	BB/9	K/9	K	GB%	BABIP	WHIP	ERA	DRA	WARP	MPH	CMD	PWR	STM
2015	BIN	AA	22	9	9	0	25	24	152^1	157	14	1.8	4.8	82	47%	.283	1.23	3.90	4.41	1.2				
2016	LVG	AAA	23	12	5	0	25	25	154^1	170	15	2.3	4.5	78	48%	.300	1.36	3.97	4.57	1.4				
2016	NYN	MLB	23	1	0	0	10	3	18^1	26	0	3.4	8.3	17	51%	.413	1.80	6.38	5.36	0.0	95.4	46	49	70
2017	NOR	AAA	24	6	9	0	21	21	106^1	129	8	2.0	6.1	72	44%	.333	1.44	5.25	5.52	0.2				
2017	BAL	MLB	24	2	3	0	9	4	34^2	39	5	2.1	6.8	26	39%	.318	1.36	4.15	5.13	0.1	95.5	39	51	63
2018	*BAL*	*MLB*	*25*	*7*	*8*	*0*	*23*	*23*	*115*	*129*	*18*	*2.9*	*5.9*	*76*	*44%*	*.298*	*1.45*	*4.79*	*5.01*	*0.5*	*95.2*	*42*	*52*	*68*
2019	*BAL*	*MLB*	*26*	*8*	*11*	*0*	*29*	*29*	*181*	*198*	*30*	*2.7*	*6.4*	*129*	*44%*	*.297*	*1.40*	*5.26*	*5.33*	*0.5*	*94.9*	*42*	*52*	*68*

Breakout: 25% Improve: 32% Collapse: 11% Attrition: 38% MLB: 53% *Comparables: Ty Blach, Josh Geer, Ryan Merritt*

With an arm motion like a slap from a white linen glove, wielding a repertoire of pitches as deceptive (and as scary) as a second-rate Shyamalan film, Ynoa fought his way against hitters who appeared to have been given the script beforehand. Lacking any semblance of an out pitch, he tends to avoid overusing his decent, if flat, mid-90s fastball. Instead he tries to scrape the edges with his middling slider and change, although if he's going to miss, he'll miss for strikes. That he found the success he did rested in his ability to not beat himself, or really anyone else; instead, he just threw pitches over the plate and let God play his dice. Put together, Ynoa has all the makings of a reliable swingman, a position he was finally granted after struggling early in the year in Triple-A. He's certainly worth what the Orioles didn't pay for him, and the Mets almost certainly wish they could have that trade back.

Lineouts

Hitters

HITTER	POS	TEAM	LVL	AGE	PA	R	2B	3B	HR	RBI	BB	K	SB	CS	AVG/OBP/SLG	TAv	VORP	BABIP	BRR	FRAA	WARP
Pedro Alvarez	3B	NOR	AAA	30	595	60	31	1	26	89	42	137	1	0	.239/.294/.442	.251	1.5	.271	-0.3	1B(52): 1.3, RF(42): -2.9	0.0
	3B	BAL	MLB	30	34	4	1	0	1	4	2	10	0	0	.313/.353/.438	.283	0.9	.429	-0.3	1B(2): 0.2	0.1
Jaycob Brugman	OF	OAK	MLB	25	162	12	2	0	3	12	18	38	1	2	.266/.346/.343	.264	4.5	.340	-1.2	CF(40): -2.5, LF(4): -0.1	0.2
	OF	NAS	AAA	25	172	17	5	1	1	9	19	28	3	1	.275/.355/.340	.270	6.6	.331	0.0	CF(19): -3.5, LF(11): -0.5	0.2
Trevor Craport	UT	ABE	A-	20	209	31	15	3	3	30	21	36	4	1	.302/.388/.469	.330	22.2	.357	0.5	3B(42): 3.7, 1B(3): -0.1	2.6
Ryan Flaherty	3B	BOW	AA	30	49	18	3	0	2	6	10	3	0	0	.395/.531/.632	.363	7.7	.394	1.3	2B(4): -0.2, 3B(4): 0.1	0.8
	3B	BAL	MLB	30	43	5	1	0	0	4	4	10	0	0	.211/.302/.237	.224	0.5	.286	0.7	2B(12): 0.0, SS(5): -0.3	0.0
Johnny Giavotella	2B	NOR	AAA	29	379	43	22	4	5	45	34	41	4	3	.306/.368/.441	.294	23.2	.329	0.2	2B(43): 4.3, LF(6): -0.5	2.6
	2B	BAL	MLB	29	10	0	0	0	0	0	0	4	1	0	.100/.100/.100	.083	-1.5	.167	0.1	2B(5): -0.3	-0.2
Chris Johnson	3B	ABE	A-	32	27	2	0	0	1	1	5	9	0	0	.182/.333/.318	.249	0.3	.250	-0.1	3B(5): 0.1	0.0
	3B	NOR	AAA	32	264	32	17	2	10	36	11	75	1	0	.301/.330/.506	.279	12.1	.389	0.7	3B(18): -2.4, 1B(13): -1.5	0.7
Jesus Montero	DH	NOR	AAA	27	51	1	1	0	0	3	2	14	0	1	.143/.176/.163	.109	-7.8	.200	0.2	1B(6): -0.5, P(1): 0.0	-0.8
Ruben Tejada	SS	SWB	AAA	27	148	22	7	0	6	21	15	17	0	2	.269/.345/.462	.267	7.1	.266	0.8	3B(14): -0.3, SS(12): -1.1	0.6
	SS	BAL	MLB	27	124	17	6	0	0	5	8	15	0	0	.230/.293/.283	.196	-3.4	.265	-0.1	SS(36): -2.4, 3B(6): -0.5	-0.6
	SS	NOR	AAA	27	51	9	3	0	0	2	4	4	0	0	.311/.392/.378	.279	3.1	.341	0.0	SS(10): 0.5, 3B(4): -0.2	0.3
Austin Wynns	C	BOW	AA	26	434	54	19	1	10	46	52	64	1	0	.281/.377/.419	.278	25.6	.314	0.6	C(90): -1.9	2.6

Pedro Alvarez wasn't called on to be Pedro Alvarez much in 2017, but when the time came, he was ready. He will always be ready. Ten years from now, he'll be ready, available to come to your corporate function, slug .450 and do absolutely nothing else. Visa and Mastercard accepted. ⚾ **Jaycob Brugman** had a decent enough debut to keep him in the mix for future reserve outfielder work, which is more than can be said for many 17th-round picks. ⚾ **Trevor Craport** played catcher and pitcher in college, so naturally in his first pro season he saw time at third, first, DH and even an inning at short. Perhaps more importantly, he hit, earning himself a chance to serve at second, left field and Human Resources director this year. ⚾ Timing is more important than all the talent in the world. Consider poor **Ryan Flaherty**, who, heading into his walk year, hurt his shoulder in spring and lost the chance to get extensive playing time in the wake of J.J. Hardy's injury. ⚾ **Johnny Giavotella** spent 2017 doing what he does best: playing well in Triple-A. As with Petagines past, there comes a time when every misused minor leaguer ages beyond his unused usefulness, and after ten years, Johnny's appears to be up. It maybe could have been a heck of a ride. ⚾ The sad thing is that if **Chris Johnson** hadn't broken his arm on an HBP in early April, he might have gotten some MLB service time, and we might have gotten more Shortstop Machado. Pitchers would have gotten to face Chris Johnson. In other words, we all lost. ⚾ In a parallel universe, **Jesus Montero** spent his age-27 season happily slugging away in front of adoring major-league crowds. In this universe, at Triple-A Norfolk, he allowed more walks than he drew and he was released more times than he homered. ⚾ All prospects go to the same place; all ride the bus, and to the bus all return. **Ruben Tejada** spent his youth in the sun. Now he is the injury replacement, soon to be the injury replacement's replacement. Then: no more. Do not weep over the inevitable. ⚾ What happens when you're 22, at a college party, and the one sober dude making drinks for everyone starts combining random ingredients: "Hey, try this! It's middle-infielder batting profile plus slow-footed catcher. I call it ... an **Austin Wynns**." Is it drinkable because the guy's a genius? Or have you just had too many to taste it?

Pitchers

PITCHER	TEAM	LVL	AGE	W	L	SV	G	GS	IP	H	HR	BB/9	K/9	K	GB%	BABIP	WHIP	ERA	DRA	WARP	MPH	CMD	PWR	STM
Jayson Aquino	BAL	MLB	24	1	2	0	4	2	13^{1}	15	4	4.1	8.8	13	44%	.282	1.58	7.43	5.47	0.0	91.2	37	26	63
	NOR	AAA	24	3	10	0	21	21	114^{2}	125	11	3.2	7.0	89	50%	.318	1.45	4.24	4.65	1.3				
Alec Asher	NOR	AAA	25	3	3	0	10	10	50^{1}	62	6	2.7	6.4	36	45%	.337	1.53	4.65	5.97	-0.1				
	BAL	MLB	25	2	5	0	24	6	60	61	10	3.5	7.1	47	38%	.287	1.40	5.25	5.39	0.0	92.5	50	38	60
Nestor Cortes	TRN	AA	22	5	0	0	18	7	52	35	3	3.5	7.8	45	31%	.235	1.06	2.60	4.30	0.5				
	SWB	AAA	22	2	4	0	11	6	48^{1}	40	0	2.0	10.6	57	41%	.317	1.06	1.49	2.27	1.7				
Andrew Faulkner	NOR	AAA	24	3	0	0	34	0	38^{2}	30	1	5.6	8.1	35	43%	.279	1.40	2.79	6.60	-0.5				
Brenan Hanifee	ABE	A-	19	7	3	0	12	12	68^{2}	65	2	1.6	5.8	44	59%	.289	1.12	2.75	1.99	2.5				
David Hess	BOW	AA	23	11	9	0	27	26	154^{1}	137	16	3.1	7.2	123	32%	.269	1.23	3.85	4.60	1.0				
Chris Lee	NOR	AAA	24	5	6	0	27	20	116^{1}	144	11	4.2	6.4	83	53%	.339	1.70	5.11	5.94	-0.4				
Jesus Liranzo	BOW	AA	22	3	4	2	31	12	65	54	12	6.0	10.4	75	27%	.271	1.49	4.85	7.51	-2.0				
Zac Lowther	ABE	A-	21	2	2	0	12	11	54^{1}	35	1	1.8	12.4	75	47%	.283	0.85	1.66	0.71	2.8				
Timothy Melville	ROC	AAA	27	4	3	0	11	10	66^{2}	48	5	3.1	8.6	64	36%	.246	1.07	2.70	4.45	0.9				
	MIN	MLB	27	0	1	0	1	1	3^{1}	4	1	8.1	10.8	4	50%	.333	2.10	13.50	3.23	0.1	95.9			49
	SDN	MLB	27	0	0	0	2	0	2^{1}	3	0	11.6	11.6	3	17%	.500	2.57	7.71	7.75	-0.1	96.5			49
Yefrey Ramirez	TRN	AA	23	10	3	0	18	18	92^{1}	78	9	3.7	8.9	91	36%	.284	1.26	3.41	6.02	-0.9				
	BOW	AA	23	5	0	0	6	6	32	27	6	3.1	7.3	26	28%	.250	1.19	3.66	5.60	-0.2				
Logan Verrett	BAL	MLB	27	2	0	0	4	0	10^{2}	11	3	2.5	7.6	9	39%	.267	1.31	4.22	3.50	0.2	92.8			49
	NOR	AAA	27	2	6	5	40	2	60	56	9	3.3	7.3	49	39%	.266	1.30	5.10	7.14	-1.2				
Tyler Wilson	BAL	MLB	27	2	2	0	9	1	15^{1}	22	3	2.3	5.3	9	39%	.358	1.70	7.04	6.35	-0.2	92.8	33	49	63
	NOR	AAA	27	7	8	0	20	20	114	128	10	2.8	5.4	68	46%	.313	1.43	4.74	6.20	-0.6				
Mike Wright	NOR	AAA	27	4	6	0	16	16	83	81	6	2.8	7.7	71	46%	.301	1.29	3.69	4.31	1.2				
	BAL	MLB	27	0	0	0	13	0	25	26	5	2.5	10.1	28	44%	.318	1.32	5.76	4.14	0.3	96.2	75	59	52
Jimmy Yacabonis	NOR	AAA	25	4	0	11	41	0	61^{1}	30	0	4.1	7.0	48	49%	.184	0.95	1.32	3.17	1.4				
	BAL	MLB	25	2	0	0	14	0	20^{2}	18	2	6.1	3.5	8	47%	.242	1.55	4.35	6.90	-0.4	96.9	36	65	51

After eight years in the minors and two cups of coffee, at least **Jayson Aquino** is still starting. It's the Quad-A koan, the baseball equivalent of one-hand clapping: What is a replacement player who doesn't replace anyone? ⚾ Prior to the deadline, **Alec Asher** served as the team's sixth starter; afterward, he did not. The burly right-hander made an effort, swapping out his slider for a cutter and relying more on a sinker, but for all the tinkering, he could not deny his own swingman essence. ⚾ Future LOOGY **Nestor Cortes** rarely tops 90 mph with his fastball, relying instead on a funky delivery and short arm action. The eye-popping numbers he posted as a swingman between Trenton and Scranton caught the attention of the Orioles, who scooped him up in the Rule 5 draft. ⚾ On the road to being a LOOGY, the only thing a southpaw who can touch the mid-90s needs to avoid is walking too many batters. For **Andrew Faulkner**, there's always next year. ⚾ A former fourth-rounder, **Brenan Hanifee** is still a blank slate, but at his height, it's a lot of slate. Consider it a name to tuck away for later, but at least it's a fairly easy one to remember. ⚾ It's not uncommon for prospects to repeat a level, but **David Hess** took the instruction to extremes: he basically had the same exact season, aided by a little more batted ball luck. There's still a good chance he winds up in the O's bullpen, and a non-zero chance that he's trapped in the saddest conceivable time loop. ⚾ The Orioles watched Chris Tillman, Ubaldo Jimenez and Wade Miley start half the team's games. Then they looked at **Chris Lee**, their top pitching prospect in Norfolk, and thought, "Nah, let's keep running with the guys we have." ⚾ Despite being a sleeper candidate to reach the majors in 2017, **Jesus Liranzo** failed to make his own surprise ascension, as he struggled with command during a repeat engagement at Double-A Bowie. ⚾ **Zac Lowther** is the kind of Low-A pitcher designed to get out Low-A batters, armed with a fringy fastball that breaks late and crosses up unsuspecting hitters. What's encouraging is that he's proven more accurate than advertised, so the ingredients for a contact pitcher are beginning to coalesce. ⚾ Like Rich Hill, **Tim Melville** was signed out of independent ball after pitching for the Long Island Ducks. Unlike Hill, Melville was not great upon reaching the big leagues, allowing eight runs and 13 baserunners in 5 2/3 innings. ⚾ The Yankees needed room on their 40-man roster, and the Orioles needed an excuse not to waste money on international signings, so the latter found themselves in possession of one **Yefrey Ramirez**, a converted shortstop who took to pitching quickly. ⚾ **Logan Verrett** didn't have his most noteworthy season, pitching less than a dozen major-league innings and getting outrighted in September. He did get to pitch to Aaron Judge, so that's fun. Well, for Aaron Judge, at least. ⚾ For a couple years now, **Tyler Wilson** has served as the gun the Orioles throw at the enemy after they've run out of bullets. There's no real sin in being a mediocre pitch-to-contact righty, but if you're looking his name up midseason because he's somehow back in the rotation, from us here in the past, accept our condolences. ⚾ The editors of the *Annual* have declared that we can't leave the **Mike Wright** lineout blank, so this next sentence will have to serve in its stead. The fact that he didn't start a game in 2017, after doing so 21 times over the previous two seasons, is a small credit to the Orioles' roster construction. ⚾ You don't know **Jimmy Yacabonis**. Yet in another sense you do: He's what baseball is becoming, an interchangeable fastball-slider reliever designed to face a couple of batters, consumed for the life in his arm and then discarded.

LEAGUE LEADERS 2017

MLB Catcher Blocking Runs – Caleb Joseph, 2.9

BOSTON RED SOX

Essay by Alex Speier

Player comments by Ben Carsley and BP staff

Entering the 2015 season, the Red Sox elected to build their rotation around an idea rather than an ace. With Jon Lester having been dealt at the previous year's trade deadline and the Cubs outbidding the Sox for his services in free agency, the team constructed a rotation of starters with clear similarities of strengths.

In Clay Buchholz, Rick Porcello, Justin Masterson, Wade Miley and Joe Kelly, the team hoped to build around pitchers who employed arsenals heavy on two-seam fastballs to take advantage of an expanding bottom of the strike zone. If effective, the group seemed poised to benefit from catchers with excellent framing skills at the bottom of the zone (Christian Vazquez, Ryan Hanigan) while efficiently turning groundballs into outs thanks to the aggressive use of shifts. In some ways, the Sox hoped to replicate the integrated pitching program of the Pirates to succeed in the AL East.

The plan failed spectacularly for a multitude of reasons, with the Red Sox slouching through a second straight last-place finish. Yet perhaps the most interesting of those reasons was one that went well beyond standard evaluations of any individual pitchers: The baseball environment fundamentally changed, in a way that prompted the Red Sox to overhaul their pitching strategy completely by the 2017 season.

The pitches at the bottom of the strike zone that had rendered offense anemic during the first half of the decade suddenly started prompting batters to salivate. Opposing hitters were no longer trying to survive against pitches in that area—instead, they started hunting them with cruel intentions, with batters looking to lift pitches down in the zone and drive them in the air.

Those batted balls that were launched in the air were clearing the fences with greater and greater frequency, a reflection of both the type of contact being made and almost certainly the composition of the baseball. In late-2015, a home-run scarcity became a gamewide home-run binge. The Red Sox had to crumple their designs for how to build a pitching staff and, in many ways, start over.

"I'm constantly monitoring the league from a macro perspective [to see], are there any anomalies around the league? That spike in home runs in 2015 was very interesting. There wasn't an immediate reason or catalyst," said Brian Bannister, who was promoted from a scouting position to become the Red Sox' director of pitching analysis and development in late-2015. "Any time data becomes public and it becomes part of a common conversation, you see a lot more adopters. Everyone adopts the strategy.

"With the increase in home runs, with all the talk about launch angle and exit velo—new lingo that had been around since 2012 but not publicized too much—you start to look at, OK, how are hitters going to react to this information? And then you're always trying to zig when everyone else zags." In 2015, the Red Sox got run over when they zigged and the rest of the league zagged over them. Over the last two seasons, the team has attempted to return the favor.

In 2017, according to Baseball Savant, a major-league-high 21.8

RED SOX PROSPECTUS

2017 W-L: 93-69, 1st in AL East

Pythag	.575	8th	B-Age	27.3	*7th*
RS/G	4.85	10th	P-Age	28.4	*16th*
RA/G	4.12	5th	Salary	$197.0M	*3rd*
TAv	.254	23rd	M$/MW	$4.1M	*14th*
TAv-P	.248	4th	DL Days	1390	*26th*
FIP	3.75	3rd	$ on DL	22%	*26th*
DER	.698	20th			

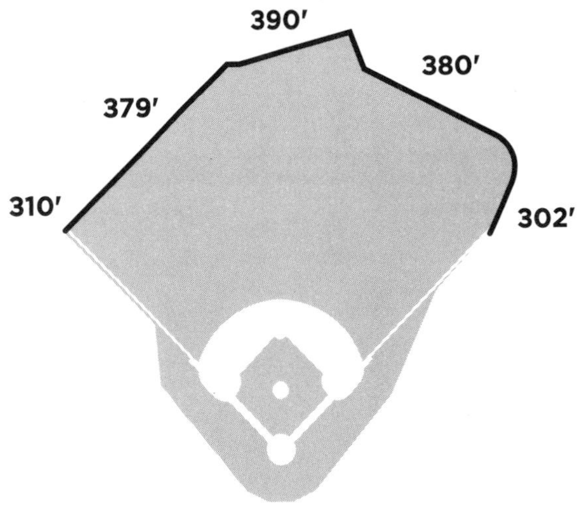

Outfield wall profile: **3′** to **37′**

Three-Year Park Factors

Runs	Runs/RH	Runs/LH	HR/RH	HR/LH
105	107	103	103	89

Top Hitter WARP	7.2 Chris Sale
Top Pitcher WARP	7.6 Chris Sale
Top Prospect	Jason Groome

2017 Hit List Ranking

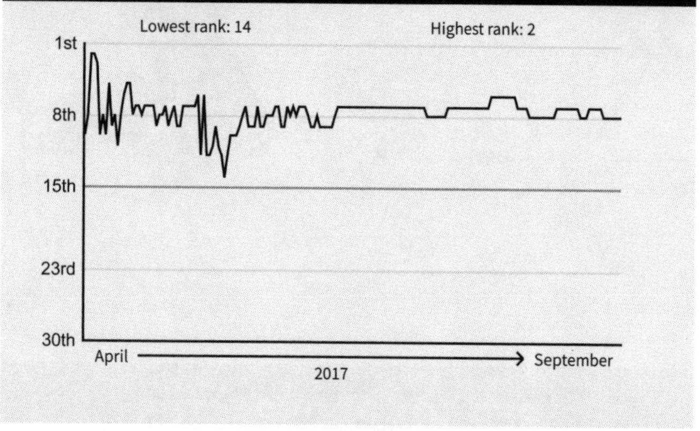

Committed Payroll (in millions)

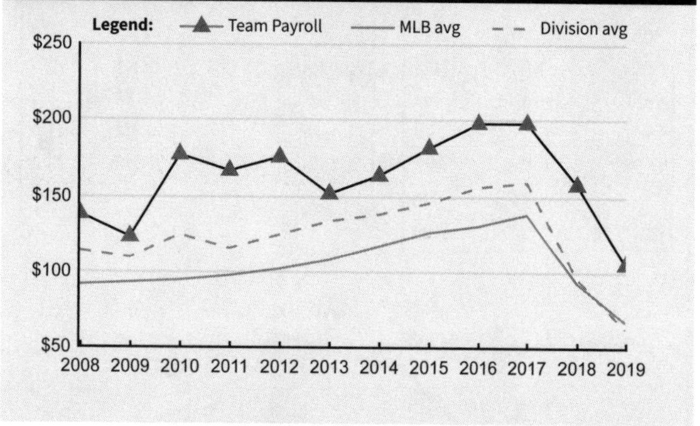

Farm System Ranking

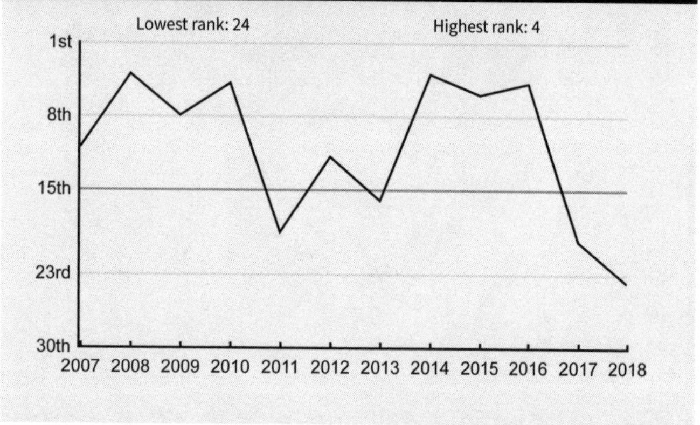

Personnel

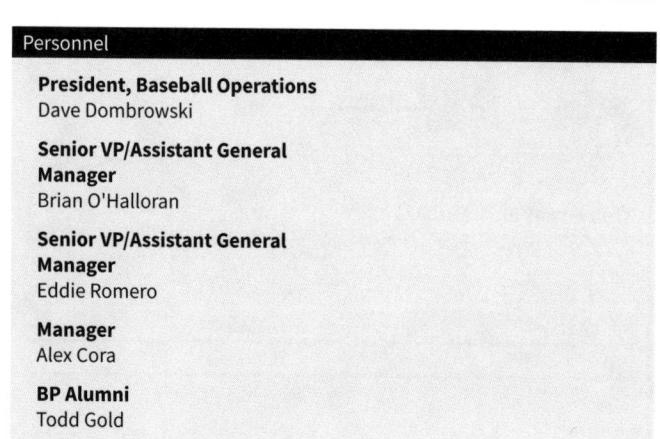

President, Baseball Operations
Dave Dombrowski

Senior VP/Assistant General Manager
Brian O'Halloran

Senior VP/Assistant General Manager
Eddie Romero

Manager
Alex Cora

BP Alumni
Todd Gold

percent of the Red Sox' pitches were four-seamers in either the upper third of the strike zone or outside of the upper half of it. Pitchers who had traditionally worked down in the zone with two-seamers were applying completely altered plans of attack.

Part of the overhaul reflected a change of personnel, with a staff anchored by Chris Sale and Craig Kimbrel unleashing comets that crossed the plate above hitters' belt buckles. Yet the change in the Sox' plan of attack went beyond just those pitchers who arrived in Boston with an arsenal that emphasized elevated fastballs.

Joe Kelly broke into the majors with the Cardinals focusing on east-west movement with his two-seam fastball while trying to work down in the strike zone. From 2013 to 2015, he threw roughly seven sinkers for every four-seamer he fired toward the plate. But in 2016, with a move from the rotation to the bullpen, he shifted his attack to feature primarily—and sometimes exclusively—four-seamers up in the zone.

Rick Porcello likewise evolved from a pitcher who broke into the big leagues as a precocious 20-year-old throwing almost nothing but two-seamers (amazingly, as a rookie starter in 2009, he relied on his sinker 60 percent of the time) into someone who spread the strike zone vertically with a relatively even split of four- and two-seamers in 2017. While he became more vulnerable at times to homers because of that strategy, at its best, he also employed the increasingly unpredictable arsenal to win a Cy Young Award in 2016.

Yet the poster child of the movement may have been even less obvious than Kelly or Porcello, both key members of the Red Sox' 2015 rotation blueprint. Blaine Boyer had the lowest strikeout rate in the big leagues (9.2 percent) among the 385 pitchers who worked at least 40 innings in 2016. Even with a relatively effective season in which he consistently induced weak contact, the veteran right-hander found it hard to find employment entering 2017. Eventually, the Braves signed Boyer to a minor-league deal before cutting him in April, with the Sox signing a 35-year-old (he turned 36 in July) who was determined to make a career transition.

"I was almost strictly sinkers [in 2016], the year before that and the year before that," Boyer explained. "One of the reasons I had such a hard time locking down a place to go in the offseason was because my strikeouts were low. I figured, 'Well, let's see what happens if I add four-seamers.' In spring training, I started. It took a while to get used to it. Then when I came over [to Boston], it was, 'That's all we do.' I went from one opposite end of the spectrum to another."

Boyer went from a pitcher who rarely contemplated his four-seamer to one who threw it more than three times as often as his sinker. His strikeout rate roughly doubled, from 9.2 percent in 2016 to 18.5 percent in 2017. His rapid evolution underscored the degree to which individual players and the game as a whole are willing to change fundamentally in response to on-field incentives. Even with a perfectly respectable 3.95 ERA in 2016 (albeit a 5.38 DRA), Boyer found it sufficiently difficult to land a job that he completely overhauled a pitch mix that had kept him in the big leagues for the prior three years.

He's not alone. Nor is the Red Sox' shift from a team that attacked the bottom of the strike zone to one that tried to entice opposing hitters to chase pitches above it an isolated incident.

The volume of information has destabilized the game in fascinating ways. Small changes can have huge impacts with teams either left wheezing behind (the last-place 2015 Red Sox) or benefiting from being on the crest of a wave (the first-place 2017 Red Sox).

The timetable for change throughout the game has become compressed. The speed with which information—both Statcast-driven data and scouting analysis—is being disseminated has amplified its importance and potential impact, to the point where teams must search constantly for their narrow competitive advantages yet remain responsive to the idea that a perceived edge may soon become a disadvantage.

"The game was pretty constant for decades, I feel like. We had, during the steroid era, a change in the hitters, but for the most part, the game was pretty constant," suggested Bannister. "And now that analytics are such a huge part, we see this chaotic environment where everything is changing all the time. Year-to-year, you don't quite know what you'll get. You have to operate in a predictive sense and try to predict what the trends are going to be, but it's becoming more like the stock market, where you have to take strategies but then be flexible enough to change if you realize it's not working.

"That's the fun part, but it requires more and more monitoring of what's actually happening. You can't just assume the game is static and what we do now is going to work next week, next month or next year. You have to be really flexible, both hitters and pitchers."

That idea comes with plenty of risks. Adjustments made to capitalize on one game state may quickly become dated. Particularly with their minor leaguers, teams face a conundrum about whether to tailor their philosophies to benefit from conditions that may not exist by the time the players reach the big leagues.

What if, for instance, a team trains its minor leaguers to drive the ball in the air, only to have a change in ball composition turn those players into a bunch of guys with warning track power, and the virtual elimination of opposite-field homers? What if the elevation of the bottom of the strike zone fundamentally alters the relative strengths and weaknesses of hitters and pitchers? What if a pitch clock leads to a diminished number of shifts (in an effort to combat the fatigue of panting fielders running back and forth between positions on the diamond), resulting in an increase to the value of groundballs?

Teams can't know how the game will change—but they can be certain that it will change, and that those clubs unwilling to consign one year's blueprint to the scrap heap may find themselves trampled by a stampede of rivals.

—Alex Speier covers the Red Sox for the Boston Globe.

Hitters

Andrew Benintendi LF Born: 07/06/94 Age: 23 Bats: L Throws: L Height: 5'10" Weight: 170 Origin: Round 1, 2015 Draft (#7 overall)

YEAR	TEAM	LVL	AGE	PA	R	2B	3B	HR	RBI	BB	K	SB	CS	AVG/OBP/SLG	TAv	VORP	BABIP	BRR	FRAA	WARP
2015	LOW	A-	20	153	19	2	4	7	15	25	15	7	1	.290/.408/.540	.317	15.0	.279	1.6	CF(31): 8.4	2.5
2015	GRN	A	20	86	17	5	0	4	16	10	9	3	2	.351/.430/.581	.374	13.5	.355	1.0	CF(18): -2.5	1.2
2016	SLM	A+	21	155	30	13	7	1	32	15	9	8	2	.341/.413/.563	.343	18.0	.354	-0.2	CF(30): 5.5	2.4
2016	PME	AA	21	263	40	18	5	8	44	24	30	8	7	.295/.357/.515	.304	19.4	.308	0.7	CF(53): 0.1, LF(4): 1.9	2.3
2016	BOS	MLB	21	118	16	11	1	2	14	10	25	1	0	.295/.359/.476	.284	5.0	.367	-0.6	LF(29): 0.9, CF(5): -0.2	0.6
2017	BOS	MLB	22	658	84	26	1	20	90	70	112	20	5	.271/.352/.424	.262	18.5	.301	1.4	LF(123): -0.5, CF(30): 0.0	1.8
2018	*BOS*	*MLB*	*23*	*606*	*88*	*31*	*4*	*18*	*69*	*58*	*103*	*16*	*5*	*.273/.346/.446*	*.273*	*28.5*	*.305*	*1.0*	*LF 0, CF 1*	*2.5*
2019	*BOS*	*MLB*	*24*	*594*	*81*	*32*	*3*	*21*	*79*	*62*	*103*	*16*	*5*	*.276/.357/.471*	*.276*	*25.4*	*.306*	*0.4*	*LF 1, CF 1*	*2.9*

Breakout: 5% Improve: 61% Collapse: 2% Attrition: 11% MLB: 94% *Comparables: Jose Tabata, Mookie Betts, Gordon Beckham*

If Benintendi didn't live up to your expectations in 2017, the fault lies with you and with you alone. In his first full season in the majors, Benintendi joined the 20/20 club, hit his way into the heart of the Red Sox order and proved to be a capable defender in both left and center field. He finished second in AL ROY voting, but first among people from this planet (there is no way Aaron Judge is from earth). Benintendi showed more power than scouts once believed existed in his wiry frame, and while his platoon splits were noticeable, he flashed the ability to make adjustments against same-side pitching as the year went on. There's still room for improvement here—especially on the bases, where Benintendi became one of the poster boys of Boston's frustrating penchant for running into outs. But all in all, Benintendi proved he's ready to serve as an above-average regular for many years, and he's got a dash of star potential as well.

Mookie Betts RF Born: 10/07/92 Age: 25 Bats: R Throws: R Height: 5'9" Weight: 180 Origin: Round 5, 2011 Draft (#172 overall)

YEAR	TEAM	LVL	AGE	PA	R	2B	3B	HR	RBI	BB	K	SB	CS	AVG/OBP/SLG	TAv	VORP	BABIP	BRR	FRAA	WARP
2015	BOS	MLB	22	654	92	42	8	18	77	46	82	21	6	.291/.341/.479	.291	40.4	.310	2.3	CF(133): 12.1, RF(11): -0.9	5.5
2016	BOS	MLB	23	730	122	42	5	31	113	49	80	26	4	.318/.363/.534	.296	48.3	.322	8.7	RF(157): 24.8	7.5
2017	BOS	MLB	24	712	101	46	2	24	102	77	79	26	3	.264/.344/.459	.276	31.5	.268	6.2	RF(153): 24.0	5.6
2018	*BOS*	*MLB*	*25*	*621*	*85*	*36*	*4*	*19*	*81*	*54*	*74*	*23*	*4*	*.293/.355/.477*	*.288*	*38.6*	*.308*	*2.8*	*RF 15*	*4.9*
2019	*BOS*	*MLB*	*26*	*580*	*81*	*36*	*3*	*22*	*82*	*55*	*74*	*21*	*4*	*.302/.368/.507*	*.292*	*35.8*	*.316*	*4.4*	*RF 15*	*5.6*

Breakout: 1% Improve: 53% Collapse: 1% Attrition: 3% MLB: 100% *Comparables: Tony Gwynn, Nick Markakis, Jason Heyward*

The only way Betts could've improved upon his 2016 season was by winning the AL MVP award. By that insane standard his 2017 season was a letdown, but by any conventional metric it was excellent. Once again, Betts excelled on the bases and in the field. FRAA pegs him as one of the very best defenders in the game, and given how effortlessly he plays Fenway's notorious right field, it's tough to disagree. Where Betts took a small step back was at the plate. His lower average seems to largely be a function of BABIP—he actually hit the ball harder than in 2016—but the power drop-off is harder to explain away. Still, Betts finished in the top 15 in baseball in BWARP, and he didn't turn 25 until October. He is still very clearly the best player on the Red Sox and one of the best players in baseball, and the Win Dance Repeat movement he helped start is one of the game's elite celebrations. Someone just needs to tell him that Salt Bae is a terrible meme.

Xander Bogaerts SS Born: 10/01/92 Age: 25 Bats: R Throws: R Height: 6'1" Weight: 210 Origin: International Free Agent, 2009

YEAR	TEAM	LVL	AGE	PA	R	2B	3B	HR	RBI	BB	K	SB	CS	AVG/OBP/SLG	TAv	VORP	BABIP	BRR	FRAA	WARP
2015	BOS	MLB	22	654	84	35	3	7	81	32	101	10	2	.320/.355/.421	.266	34.3	.372	4.8	SS(156): -1.6	3.5
2016	BOS	MLB	23	719	115	34	1	21	89	58	123	13	4	.294/.356/.446	.267	38.4	.335	3.3	SS(157): -11.9	2.7
2017	BOS	MLB	24	635	94	32	6	10	62	56	116	15	1	.273/.343/.403	.259	31.9	.327	5.5	SS(146): -9.2	2.3
2018	*BOS*	*MLB*	*25*	*639*	*83*	*30*	*3*	*12*	*63*	*48*	*118*	*11*	*2*	*.280/.338/.407*	*.263*	*34.5*	*.330*	*0.7*	*SS -10*	*1.5*
2019	*BOS*	*MLB*	*26*	*568*	*71*	*28*	*2*	*14*	*65*	*47*	*107*	*10*	*2*	*.283/.347/.426*	*.265*	*25.7*	*.333*	*3.2*	*SS -9*	*1.8*

Breakout: 1% Improve: 60% Collapse: 2% Attrition: 2% MLB: 100% *Comparables: Jose Reyes, Starlin Castro, Jean Segura*

Edgar Renteria. Alex Gonzalez. Julio Lugo. Nick Green. Marco Scutaro. Mike Aviles. Stephen Drew. Those are the seven shortstops the Red Sox relied on as primary starters in the decade between Nomar Garciaparra and Xander Bogaerts. You would think that'd buy Bogaerts a long leash, but this is Boston, so you'd be wrong. In a way, Red Sox Nation's frustration with Bogaerts is understandable. He has so much talent that watching him struggle as he did for much of 2017 is tough, even if the wrist injury he suffered in early July was an obvious limiting factor. Bogaerts has too much power to only hit 10 homers, and too quick a bat to only hit .273, yet here we are. But even Bogaerts at his worst was the 16th best shortstop in the majors by BWARP, and he's now a 25-year-old who has averaged three wins over the last three seasons. Bogaerts might not be Carlos Correa or Corey Seager, but he's only a tier below those players at his peak and still a serviceable everyday shortstop at his valley. If the Sox allow him to reach free agency after 2019, you can bet some team will pay richly for Bogaerts to end their own shortstop drought.

Jackie Bradley CF Born: 04/19/90 Age: 28 Bats: L Throws: R Height: 5'10" Weight: 200 Origin: Round 1, 2011 Draft (#40 overall)

YEAR	TEAM	LVL	AGE	PA	R	2B	3B	HR	RBI	BB	K	SB	CS	AVG/OBP/SLG	TAv	VORP	BABIP	BRR	FRAA	WARP
2015	PAW	AAA	25	318	38	18	1	9	29	30	44	4	4	.305/.382/.472	.320	29.1	.336	-0.2	CF(67): -2.1, RF(2): 0.2	2.8
2015	BOS	MLB	25	255	43	17	4	10	43	27	69	3	0	.249/.335/.498	.280	12.8	.310	2.0	RF(32): 3.5, CF(27): -1.7	2.1
2016	BOS	MLB	26	636	94	30	7	26	87	63	143	9	2	.267/.349/.486	.273	31.1	.312	3.0	CF(156): 9.1	4.2
2017	BOS	MLB	27	541	58	19	3	17	63	48	124	8	3	.245/.323/.402	.257	19.3	.294	3.8	CF(132): -7.3	1.2
2018	*BOS*	*MLB*	*28*	*530*	*65*	*25*	*4*	*15*	*61*	*47*	*126*	*7*	*2*	*.245/.322/.408*	*.256*	*20.9*	*.302*	*0.2*	*CF -4*	*1.1*
2019	*BOS*	*MLB*	*29*	*500*	*63*	*23*	*3*	*16*	*60*	*49*	*122*	*6*	*2*	*.243/.328/.416*	*.254*	*14.2*	*.299*	*2.3*	*CF -3*	*1.3*

Breakout: 0% Improve: 45% Collapse: 8% Attrition: 17% MLB: 95% *Comparables: Nate McLouth, Desmond Jennings, Milton Bradley*

Back in 2016, we wrote that Bradley's inconsistency made it hard to properly evaluate him as a hitter. Fast-forward two years and that streakiness has become his defining offensive quality. Bradley hit .283/.355/.439 in June, July and August. He also hit .217/.317/.417 in April and May, then .172/.328/.280 in September, because he's Jackie Bradley. With some players, you can tell when they're about to get hot. They'll hit the ball the other way, or swing earlier in the count, or jump on hanging breakers, etc. Good luck finding a pattern with Bradley; he simply is and isn't a good hitter at any interchangeable moment, a sort of Schrödinger's offensive threat. When you add up his outstanding glove and his hot streaks, Bradley still ends up being a fairly valuable player. But he gets so cold it's a wonder little blue mountains don't start glowing on his jersey, and when that happens, boy is Bradley tough to watch.

Rusney Castillo CF Born: 07/09/87 Age: 30 Bats: R Throws: R Height: 5'9" Weight: 195 Origin: International Free Agent, 2014

YEAR	TEAM	LVL	AGE	PA	R	2B	3B	HR	RBI	BB	K	SB	CS	AVG/OBP/SLG	TAv	VORP	BABIP	BRR	FRAA	WARP
2015	PAW	AAA	27	172	17	7	0	3	17	14	28	10	2	.282/.337/.385	.291	9.2	.323	0.0	CF(17): 1.9, RF(16): -1.3	1.0
2015	BOS	MLB	27	289	35	10	2	5	29	13	54	4	5	.253/.288/.359	.213	-6.4	.298	1.3	RF(48): 4.4, LF(24): 4.8	0.3
2016	BOS	MLB	28	8	4	1	0	0	0	0	3	0	0	.250/.250/.375	.214	0.2	.400	0.4	LF(2): -0.5, RF(1): 0.0	0.0
2016	PAW	AAA	28	429	55	20	5	2	34	24	68	9	3	.263/.309/.354	.252	13.1	.310	4.6	CF(86): 10.1, LF(8): -1.8	2.3
2017	PAW	AAA	29	369	52	22	0	15	43	11	51	14	2	.314/.350/.507	.296	29.0	.332	3.0	CF(73): 4.7, RF(7): 0.6	3.3
2018	*BOS*	*MLB*	*30*	*250*	*32*	*12*	*1*	*6*	*26*	*14*	*49*	*6*	*2*	*.270/.317/.417*	*.247*	*7.7*	*.315*	*1.4*	*CF 4, RF 0*	*1.3*
2019	*BOS*	*MLB*	*31*	*210*	*24*	*10*	*1*	*6*	*24*	*12*	*43*	*4*	*2*	*.262/.310/.407*	*.246*	*4.2*	*.307*	*1.2*	*CF 3, RF 0*	*0.8*

Breakout: 0% Improve: 11% Collapse: 11% Attrition: 23% MLB: 54% *Comparables: Elian Herrera, Jason Bourgeois, Bubba Crosby*

His prohibitive contract aside, two things are prying Castillo's window with the Red Sox open: his Triple-A performance and the fact that Alex Cora would be his new manager. Castillo hit quite well at Pawtucket last season, striking out less and hitting for substantially more power than he'd previously shown. As for Cora, he has managed Castillo in winter ball and has been a vocal supporter. So what's the big holdup? Castillo's $10-plus million AAV contract would count against the luxury tax if he were added back to the 40-man, so his shot at redemption would come with a hefty price tag. With Chris Young departing for free agency, the Red Sox could have a spot open for a fourth outfielder, and it would make sense for that player to be right-handed. Lots of players fit that profile, though, and not all of them cost eight figures.

Lorenzo Cedrola OF Born: 01/12/98 Age: 20 Bats: R Throws: R Height: 5'11" Weight: 170 Origin: International Free Agent, 2015

YEAR	TEAM	LVL	AGE	PA	R	2B	3B	HR	RBI	BB	K	SB	CS	AVG/OBP/SLG	TAv	VORP	BABIP	BRR	FRAA	WARP
2015	DRX	RK	17	312	61	8	7	1	31	23	33	27	7	.321/.420/.415	.324	38.7	.362	5.9	CF(63): -0.2	3.8
2016	RSX	RK	18	238	33	14	1	2	21	11	28	9	4	.290/.350/.393	.288	13.7	.323	-1.1	CF(48): 4.0, RF(3): -0.3	1.7
2017	GRN	A	19	379	47	18	3	4	34	11	48	19	7	.285/.322/.387	.275	17.5	.319	1.2	CF(75): -7.1, RF(14): 3.0	1.4
2018	*BOS*	*MLB*	*20*	*250*	*28*	*11*	*1*	*5*	*22*	*7*	*56*	*6*	*2*	*.243/.279/.363*	*.217*	*-1.5*	*.296*	*0.1*	*CF -2, RF 0*	*-0.4*
2019	*BOS*	*MLB*	*21*	*335*	*35*	*15*	*2*	*7*	*35*	*11*	*73*	*8*	*3*	*.252/.290/.377*	*.230*	*-0.4*	*.304*	*0.6*	*CF -3, RF 0*	*-0.4*

Breakout: 2% Improve: 9% Collapse: 0% Attrition: 3% MLB: 10% *Comparables: Gorkys Hernandez, Cedric Hunter, Engel Beltre*

It says a lot about the current state of the Red Sox farm system that Cedrola is now one of the more interesting guys in it, but don't overlook what that says about Cedrola, too. A premium athlete who can fly around the outfield and on the bases, the young Venezuelan could get to the majors on the strength of his glove alone. He's a pure slap hitter at present, pretty much never walking, striking out or hitting for power, but some scouts like the bat-to-ball ability and think he could grow into at least playable pop. You won't see Cedrola on any top-101 lists this offseason, but he's a guy who'll be worth watching until Dave Dombrowski trades him for, like, Luke Gregerson in two years.

Michael Chavis 3B Born: 08/11/95 Age: 22 Bats: R Throws: R Height: 5'10" Weight: 210 Origin: Round 1, 2014 Draft (#26 overall)

YEAR	TEAM	LVL	AGE	PA	R	2B	3B	HR	RBI	BB	K	SB	CS	AVG/OBP/SLG	TAv	VORP	BABIP	BRR	FRAA	WARP
2015	GRN	A	19	471	56	29	1	16	58	29	144	8	5	.223/.277/.405	.244	2.2	.293	-1.2	3B(68): 3.7, SS(1): -0.1	0.6
2016	GRN	A	20	312	30	11	3	8	35	22	74	3	1	.244/.321/.391	.270	13.2	.303	1.3	3B(68): -0.4	1.4
2016	SLM	A+	20	27	5	0	0	0	1	2	7	1	0	.160/.222/.160	.180	-0.8	.222	1.1	3B(2): -0.7	-0.2
2017	SLM	A+	21	250	50	17	2	17	55	19	57	1	0	.318/.388/.641	.348	28.7	.360	1.3	3B(24): -1.6	2.9
2017	PME	AA	21	274	39	18	0	14	39	20	56	1	0	.250/.310/.492	.279	11.9	.265	0.1	3B(39): -0.5, SS(1): 0.0	1.2
2018	*BOS*	*MLB*	*22*	*250*	*27*	*12*	*0*	*11*	*34*	*14*	*78*	*0*	*0*	*.223/.275/.419*	*.232*	*-0.1*	*.283*	*-0.4*	*3B -1, 1B 0*	*-0.1*
2019	*BOS*	*MLB*	*23*	*355*	*44*	*16*	*1*	*16*	*49*	*21*	*113*	*1*	*0*	*.223/.277/.426*	*.237*	*-1.5*	*.283*	*-0.8*	*3B -1, 1B 0*	*-0.3*

Breakout: 3% Improve: 21% Collapse: 4% Attrition: 23% MLB: 39% *Comparables: Ryan McMahon, Renato Nunez, Matt Davidson*

Chavis enjoyed a breakout campaign in 2017. Boston's 2014 first-rounder finally stayed both healthy and productive for a full season. He mashed in High-A like a prospect with his pedigree should, then handled the jump to Portland, showcasing above-average power with a very respectable strikeout rate. The one drawback? Chavis keeps moving further down the defensive spectrum. Drafted as a shortstop who was likely to move to second or third, he's now a third baseman who's likely to shift to first or left field. He's got enough pop and a good enough hit tool that serving in an everyday role as such isn't out of the question, though.

Rajai Davis OF Born: 10/19/80 Age: 37 Bats: R Throws: R Height: 5'10" Weight: 195 Origin: Round 38, 2001 Draft (#1134 overall)

YEAR	TEAM	LVL	AGE	PA	R	2B	3B	HR	RBI	BB	K	SB	CS	AVG/OBP/SLG	TAv	VORP	BABIP	BRR	FRAA	WARP
2015	DET	MLB	34	370	55	16	11	8	30	22	76	18	8	.258/.306/.440	.263	11.0	.308	0.9	CF(46): -1.0, LF(39): -2.0	0.8
2016	CLE	MLB	35	495	74	23	2	12	48	33	106	43	6	.249/.306/.388	.238	6.3	.299	3.7	CF(80): 3.5, LF(66): 1.4	1.2
2017	OAK	MLB	36	328	49	17	2	5	18	26	70	26	6	.233/.294/.353	.220	-1.5	.288	2.4	CF(79): -3.4, LF(19): -1.7	-0.7
2017	BOS	MLB	36	38	7	2	0	0	2	1	13	3	1	.250/.289/.306	.208	-1.0	.391	0.1	LF(6): -0.5, CF(4): -0.3	-0.2
2018	*BOS*	*MLB*	*37*	*370*	*50*	*18*	*3*	*6*	*29*	*23*	*78*	*28*	*7*	*.250/.302/.369*	*.228*	*3.3*	*.305*	*1.5*	*CF -2, LF 0*	*0.2*
2019	*BOS*	*MLB*	*38*	*298*	*30*	*14*	*2*	*4*	*28*	*18*	*65*	*21*	*6*	*.243/.295/.356*	*.227*	*0.2*	*.301*	*1.8*	*CF -1, LF 0*	*-0.1*

Breakout: 2% Improve: 31% Collapse: 12% Attrition: 26% MLB: 77% *Comparables: Bill Bruton, Russ Snyder, Willie McGee*

Don't ya just hate when you accidentally buy something you don't need? The Red Sox sent anonymous minor-league outfielder Rafael Rincones to the A's for Davis on August 23. They proceeded to give Davis just 38 plate appearances through the remainder of the year. It's sort of hard to blame them; Davis proved in 2017 that the only tool he has left is his speed. FRAA hated him in center field. His .218 TAv ranked 40th out of 41 among center fielders with at least 200 PA (sorry, Adam Engel). Davis can still be a fourth or preferably fifth outfielder as long as he retains his speed, but the second that goes, well, at least he'll always have that World Series bomb off of Aroldis Chapman!

Rafael Devers 3B Born: 10/24/96 Age: 21 Bats: L Throws: R Height: 6'0" Weight: 195 Origin: International Free Agent, 2013

YEAR	TEAM	LVL	AGE	PA	R	2B	3B	HR	RBI	BB	K	SB	CS	AVG/OBP/SLG	TAv	VORP	BABIP	BRR	FRAA	WARP
2015	GRN	A	18	508	71	38	1	11	70	24	84	3	2	.288/.329/.443	.282	25.1	.326	1.6	3B(72): -8.9	1.7
2016	SLM	A+	19	546	64	32	8	11	71	40	94	18	6	.282/.335/.443	.276	25.1	.328	-1.2	3B(117): 22.2	4.9
2017	PME	AA	20	320	48	19	3	18	56	31	55	0	3	.300/.369/.575	.318	26.8	.316	-0.7	3B(58): 4.6	3.4
2017	PAW	AAA	20	38	6	1	0	2	4	3	8	0	0	.400/.447/.600	.361	5.6	.480	0.1	3B(8): -2.1	0.3
2017	BOS	MLB	20	240	34	14	0	10	30	18	57	3	1	.284/.338/.482	.275	12.0	.342	0.2	3B(56): 4.9	1.7
2018	*BOS*	*MLB*	*21*	*592*	*69*	*31*	*3*	*21*	*79*	*34*	*139*	*4*	*2*	*.258/.302/.438*	*.255*	*15.6*	*.308*	*-0.9*	*3B 6*	*1.6*
2019	*BOS*	*MLB*	*22*	*619*	*81*	*34*	*2*	*25*	*86*	*41*	*141*	*4*	*2*	*.270/.321/.470*	*.264*	*17.9*	*.317*	*-0.1*	*3B 7*	*2.7*

Breakout: 6% Improve: 19% Collapse: 7% Attrition: 21% MLB: 42% *Comparables: Maikel Franco, Lonnie Chisenhall, Dilson Herrera*

The Red Sox have developed lots of special young hitters over the past few years, but what Devers did in 2017 is remarkable even by Boston's lofty standards. Despite entering the season with no experience above High-A, Devers ended it batting seventh for the Red Sox in the ALDS. The Sox made an earnest attempt not to rush him, giving all sorts of riff-raff playing time at third base. But by late July, they had to accept that Devers was too good for the minor leagues. He proved that point by finishing in the top 20 in TAv among third basemen with 240 PA, doing so before he turned 21 years old. Devers' swing is as sweet as his face is young, and he's got a chance for double-plus game power as he grows into his already-thick body. He's also got the arm and instincts for third, though his range leaves something to be desired. That's nitpicking, though; Devers is an above-average MLB hitter right now, and if he reaches his ceiling he could occupy the cleanup spot in Boston's lineup for the better part of the next decade.

Daniel Flores C Born: 10/21/00 Age: 17 Bats: B Throws: R Height: 6'1" Weight: 182 Origin: International Free Agent, 2016

On Wednesday, November 8, Daniel Flores passed away due to complications from treatment he was receiving for testicular cancer. He was just 17. A few months earlier, Flores signed with the Red Sox for $3.1 million out of Venezuela as the crown jewel of their 2017 J2 class. On the field, he was a defensively gifted catcher with offensive potential as a switch-hitter who received rave reviews for his work ethic. We don't need to tell you that who he was off the field matters more. Saying Flores was taken before his time is inadequate; it's true of everyone we lose to cancer, and does not do the tragedy of losing a 17-year-old justice. Instead, we can honor Flores' memory by extending our best wishes and love to his family, reminding our own loved ones to seek preventative care and, if within our means, donating to an organization that fights pediatric cancer.

Marco Hernandez INF Born: 09/06/92 Age: 25 Bats: L Throws: R Height: 6'0" Weight: 200 Origin: International Free Agent, 2009

YEAR	TEAM	LVL	AGE	PA	R	2B	3B	HR	RBI	BB	K	SB	CS	AVG/OBP/SLG	TAv	VORP	BABIP	BRR	FRAA	WARP
2015	PME	AA	22	294	30	21	4	5	31	9	49	4	2	.326/.349/.482	.289	18.1	.382	-1.9	SS(67): -3.0	1.6
2015	PAW	AAA	22	190	27	9	2	4	22	8	39	1	0	.271/.300/.409	.266	6.1	.324	-1.2	SS(22): -4.3, 2B(15): -0.6	0.1
2016	PAW	AAA	23	237	26	7	4	5	29	12	51	4	2	.309/.343/.444	.291	14.8	.381	-0.5	SS(22): -2.5, 2B(20): 0.7	1.1
2016	BOS	MLB	23	56	11	1	0	1	5	5	10	1	0	.294/.357/.373	.246	0.7	.350	-0.2	2B(14): -0.6, 3B(10): -0.1	0.0
2017	BOS	MLB	24	60	7	3	0	0	2	1	15	0	1	.276/.300/.328	.216	-1.0	.372	-0.3	3B(9): 0.0, 2B(6): 1.7	0.0
2018	*BOS*	*MLB*	*25*	*119*	*13*	*6*	*1*	*3*	*13*	*5*	*28*	*1*	*0*	*.273/.305/.412*	*.247*	*3.2*	*.339*	*-0.1*	*2B 1*	*0.3*
2019	*BOS*	*MLB*	*26*	*291*	*33*	*13*	*2*	*8*	*34*	*15*	*70*	*2*	*1*	*.270/.309/.419*	*.245*	*4.6*	*.335*	*-0.2*	*2B 2*	*0.8*

Breakout: 8% Improve: 27% Collapse: 11% Attrition: 33% MLB: 59% *Comparables: Ryon Healy, Ryan Wheeler, Danny Valencia*

It's easy to forget, now that we're officially in the Rafael Devers Era, but at one point in 2017 it looked like Hernandez would play a big role in Boston. With Brock Holt injured and Pablo Sandoval being Pablo Sandoval, the Red Sox were in dire need of a third baseman. They turned to Hernandez, a smooth-swinging utility infielder who had acquitted himself well in his brief MLB time in 2016. Unfortunately, Hernandez injured his non-throwing shoulder on May 4, and that was that. He needed surgery to stabilize the joint and missed the rest of the season, meaning that when the Red Sox yelled "Marco," no one responded (we've all been there). Hernandez isn't a star, but he's a competent hitter and a passable defensive option at third, short and second. That last part could be key for a Red Sox team that expects to be without Dustin Pedroia until May or June.

Brock Holt UT Born: 06/11/88 Age: 30 Bats: L Throws: R Height: 5'10" Weight: 180 Origin: Round 9, 2009 Draft (#265 overall)

YEAR	TEAM	LVL	AGE	PA	R	2B	3B	HR	RBI	BB	K	SB	CS	AVG/OBP/SLG	TAv	VORP	BABIP	BRR	FRAA	WARP
2015	BOS	MLB	27	509	56	27	6	2	45	46	97	8	1	.280/.349/.379	.256	14.5	.350	3.8	2B(58): 0.9, 3B(33): -1.5	1.6
2016	PAW	AAA	28	30	2	2	0	0	2	5	5	0	0	.320/.433/.400	.302	2.3	.400	0.2	LF(6): 1.5, SS(2): 0.1	0.4
2016	BOS	MLB	28	324	45	16	0	7	34	27	58	4	3	.255/.322/.383	.246	5.1	.294	1.7	LF(64): 5.4, 3B(17): 1.9	1.2
2017	PAW	AAA	29	77	9	1	0	3	9	6	14	0	0	.214/.286/.357	.244	0.4	.226	0.1	LF(7): 1.3, 3B(4): 0.1	0.2
2017	BOS	MLB	29	164	20	6	0	0	7	19	34	2	1	.200/.305/.243	.214	-3.0	.259	0.6	2B(31): 0.1, LF(10): 0.7	-0.2
2018	*BOS*	*MLB*	*30*	*173*	*17*	*7*	*1*	*1*	*16*	*14*	*32*	*3*	*1*	*.257/.319/.345*	*.239*	*3.3*	*.310*	*0.0*	*2B 0, LF 1*	*0.2*
2019	*BOS*	*MLB*	*31*	*226*	*25*	*10*	*1*	*3*	*21*	*19*	*44*	*3*	*1*	*.256/.324/.356*	*.238*	*2.3*	*.311*	*1.1*	*2B 0, LF 1*	*0.4*

Breakout: 1% Improve: 38% Collapse: 9% Attrition: 18% MLB: 88% *Comparables: Jonathan Herrera, Eric Sogard, Ryan Freel*

For the second straight year Holt was sidelined by concussion issues, but this time they limited him for the majority of the season. The former All-Star (remember that?) was placed on the DL on April 21 and didn't return to the bigs until July 16. He made cameos at all the corners, but Holt's primary duty upon rejoining the Red Sox was to fill in as Dustin Pedroia's replacement at second. Turns out the Sox might've been better off with a one-legged Pedroia, as Holt hit .198/.307/.267 from August 1 onward. It's unclear if Holt's non-follicular skills are naturally leaving him or if his concussion troubles are expediting the process. If the latter is true and a full offseason of R&R helps, Holt could emerge as an important part of a 2018 Red Sox team that will be without Pedroia until at least May. But the smart bet is that the halcyon days of Brock Holt: Superstar Super Sub are over, and that's a shame.

Sandy Leon C Born: 03/13/89 Age: 29 Bats: B Throws: R Height: 5'10" Weight: 225 Origin: International Free Agent, 2007

YEAR	TEAM	LVL	AGE	PA	R	2B	3B	HR	RBI	BB	K	SB	CS	AVG/OBP/SLG	TAv	VORP	BABIP	BRR	FRAA	WARP
2015	PAW	AAA	26	111	8	4	0	1	13	10	23	0	1	.263/.342/.333	.258	4.6	.333	0.6	C(21): 2.0	0.7
2015	BOS	MLB	26	128	8	2	0	0	3	7	28	0	1	.184/.238/.202	.170	-6.3	.244	-0.5	C(37): -3.2, 3B(1): 0.0	-1.0
2016	PAW	AAA	27	130	12	3	1	2	13	11	24	0	0	.243/.315/.339	.234	1.4	.286	-0.1	C(29): 6.2, 1B(1): 0.0	0.8
2016	BOS	MLB	27	283	36	17	2	7	35	23	66	0	0	.310/.369/.476	.293	20.7	.392	-1.5	C(74): -4.0	1.7
2017	BOS	MLB	28	301	32	14	0	7	39	25	74	0	0	.225/.290/.354	.226	-1.9	.280	-5.2	C(84): 4.2	0.2
2018	*BOS*	*MLB*	*29*	*220*	*21*	*9*	*1*	*4*	*21*	*19*	*50*	*0*	*0*	*.228/.297/.335*	*.227*	*1.9*	*.283*	*-0.5*	*C 0*	*0.0*
2019	*BOS*	*MLB*	*30*	*326*	*36*	*13*	*1*	*7*	*32*	*30*	*79*	*0*	*0*	*.221/.297/.344*	*.226*	*-1.2*	*.273*	*-2.3*	*C 1*	*-0.1*

Breakout: 4% Improve: 26% Collapse: 15% Attrition: 33% MLB: 70% *Comparables: Craig Tatum, Rob Johnson, Martin Maldonado*

The main attraction with Leon will always be his defense. He's great against the run and an average blocker. According to our catching stats, Leon was a good framer in 2017, too. But that's the standard backup-catcher kit. What makes Leon a little more interesting is his penchant for catching fire at the plate for a few weeks every season. Last year it was May 6 through July 1. For those glorious three and a half fortnights, Leon hit .290/.350/.473 in 104 PA. Outside of that stretch he was as pathetic with a bat in his hands as anyone this side of Danny DeVito's Penguin. Alas, that's why Leon remains a decent no. 2 backstop and nothing more, but his hot streaks remain as fun as they are random.

YEAR	TEAM	P. COUNT	FRM RUNS	BLK RUNS	THRW RUNS	TOT RUNS
2015	BOS	4770	-4.7	-0.2	0.4	-4.5
2015	PAW	2961	2.1	0.0	0.1	2.2
2016	BOS	9517	-4.5	-0.5	1.1	-3.9
2017	BOS	11373	3.3	0.3	1.9	5.5
2018	*BOS*	*8123*	*-0.4*	*-0.2*	*1.0*	*0.3*
2019	*BOS*	*12046*	*-0.5*	*-0.3*	*1.1*	*0.3*

Deven Marrero INF Born: 08/25/90 Age: 27 Bats: R Throws: R Height: 6'1" Weight: 195 Origin: Round 1, 2012 Draft (#24 overall)

YEAR	TEAM	LVL	AGE	PA	R	2B	3B	HR	RBI	BB	K	SB	CS	AVG/OBP/SLG	TAv	VORP	BABIP	BRR	FRAA	WARP
2015	PAW	AAA	24	419	49	13	1	6	29	33	87	12	5	.256/.316/.344	.257	17.9	.315	2.7	SS(90): 5.9, 2B(8): -1.1	2.4
2015	BOS	MLB	24	56	8	0	0	1	3	3	19	2	1	.226/.268/.283	.202	-0.7	.333	0.8	3B(13): 0.2, SS(6): 0.3	0.0
2016	PAW	AAA	25	388	30	11	1	1	27	22	90	10	3	.198/.245/.242	.184	-15.1	.259	-0.2	SS(92): 2.8, 3B(2): 0.0	-1.2
2016	BOS	MLB	25	14	0	0	0	0	0	2	5	0	0	.083/.214/.083	.134	-1.4	.143	0.0	2B(6): -0.5, 3B(4): 0.0	-0.2
2017	PAW	AAA	26	194	17	13	0	3	14	6	52	1	4	.240/.266/.361	.225	0.1	.315	-0.2	SS(40): -1.6, 2B(7): 0.8	-0.1
2017	BOS	MLB	26	188	32	9	0	4	27	12	61	5	0	.211/.259/.333	.215	-2.2	.296	0.4	3B(53): 1.7, 2B(11): 0.0	-0.1
2018	*BOS*	*MLB*	*27*	*97*	*10*	*4*	*0*	*2*	*9*	*6*	*27*	*2*	*1*	*.225/.274/.329*	*.217*	*-0.5*	*.299*	*0.0*	*2B 0, SS 0*	*-0.1*
2019	*BOS*	*MLB*	*28*	*294*	*31*	*12*	*0*	*6*	*28*	*21*	*85*	*5*	*2*	*.222/.281/.337*	*.217*	*-4.0*	*.297*	*0.3*	*2B 0, SS 0*	*-0.3*

Breakout: 8% Improve: 25% Collapse: 15% Attrition: 33% MLB: 54% *Comparables: Robert Andino, Nick Noonan, Ray Olmedo*

What could we write that would do Marrero's glove work justice? He's got a strong arm, sure hands and quick reflexes. He can pick it at second or short. He was impressive at the hot corner when the Sox played him there for a month before turning to Rafael Devers. But perhaps nothing speaks to the caliber of Marrero's leather quite like the fact that he was ever allowed to bat at all. Watching Marrero at the plate is like replaying every Theon Greyjoy torture scene on a loop. It's like getting a deep cavity filled without novocaine. Marrero's attempts at providing some punch from the right were so ineffective even Britt McHenry feels bad for him. Marrero is good organizational depth, but if anyone ever gives him 188 PA again they should answer for it at The Hague.

Mitch Moreland 1B Born: 09/06/85 Age: 32 Bats: L Throws: L Height: 6'2" Weight: 230 Origin: Round 17, 2007 Draft (#530 overall)

YEAR	TEAM	LVL	AGE	PA	R	2B	3B	HR	RBI	BB	K	SB	CS	AVG/OBP/SLG	TAv	VORP	BABIP	BRR	FRAA	WARP
2015	TEX	MLB	29	515	51	27	0	23	85	32	112	1	0	.278/.330/.482	.284	15.4	.317	-2.1	1B(120): -7.9	0.8
2016	TEX	MLB	30	503	49	21	0	22	60	35	118	1	0	.233/.298/.422	.244	-6.2	.266	-3.0	1B(139): 3.8	-0.2
2017	BOS	MLB	31	576	73	34	0	22	79	57	120	0	1	.246/.326/.443	.260	3.5	.278	-2.7	1B(138): 5.7, P(1): 0.0	1.0
2018	*BOS*	*MLB*	*32*	*432*	*52*	*22*	*0*	*15*	*54*	*34*	*98*	*1*	*0*	*.243/.309/.417*	*.252*	*1.8*	*.285*	*-1.0*	*1B -1*	*0.0*
2019	*BOS*	*MLB*	*33*	*464*	*59*	*23*	*0*	*17*	*59*	*39*	*111*	*0*	*0*	*.242/.313/.424*	*.250*	*-1.6*	*.286*	*-2.1*	*1B 0*	*-0.2*

Breakout: 6% Improve: 35% Collapse: 7% Attrition: 17% MLB: 85% *Comparables: Ryan Zimmerman, Xavier Nady, Daryl Boston*

Moreland is a $12 bottle of wine, or a Certified Pre-Owned Toyota Camry, or a pair of Dockers dress shoes: perfectly serviceable and utterly unremarkable. The #OffensiveThreatMitchMoreland hashtag aside, Moreland came to the Red Sox with a reputation as a strong defender and tolerable down-the-order hitter. He was as advertised. FRAA likes Moreland despite his so-so scooping ability, and he earned another Gold Glove finalist spot. As for the offense, well, Moreland's TAv was 23rd out of the 28 first basemen who saw at least 400 PA. That's fine for a guy who signed for just $5.5 million. The problem for the Red Sox is Moreland ranked fourth in TAv on his own team, and he batted fourth or fifth over 100 times. If cast in more of a complementary role, Moreland can be useful. If he is one of the linchpins of your offense, well, that's how you end up underperforming your projected runs totals by a few dozen. Boston re-signed him to a two-year deal in December. Enjoy your Camry!

Eduardo Nunez UT Born: 06/15/87 Age: 31 Bats: R Throws: R Height: 6'0" Weight: 195 Origin: International Free Agent, 2004

YEAR	TEAM	LVL	AGE	PA	R	2B	3B	HR	RBI	BB	K	SB	CS	AVG/OBP/SLG	TAv	VORP	BABIP	BRR	FRAA	WARP
2015	MIN	MLB	28	204	23	14	1	4	20	12	29	8	4	.282/.327/.431	.262	7.1	.314	0.8	SS(27): 2.3, 3B(16): -1.2	0.9
2016	MIN	MLB	29	396	49	15	1	12	47	15	58	27	6	.296/.325/.439	.264	20.7	.320	4.8	SS(51): -1.8, 3B(33): -0.1	1.9
2016	SFN	MLB	29	199	24	9	3	4	20	14	30	13	4	.269/.327/.418	.271	10.1	.302	1.4	3B(48): 3.8, SS(4): -0.3	1.4
2017	SFN	MLB	30	318	37	21	0	4	31	12	29	18	5	.308/.334/.417	.273	18.8	.328	4.4	3B(49): -0.1, LF(19): 2.4	2.0
2017	BOS	MLB	30	173	23	12	0	8	27	6	25	6	2	.321/.353/.539	.305	12.0	.341	-1.2	2B(26): -0.8, SS(5): 0.0	1.2
2018	*BOS*	*MLB*	*31*	*483*	*66*	*25*	*3*	*11*	*46*	*26*	*73*	*26*	*7*	*.281/.324/.422*	*.249*	*15.0*	*.312*	*2.8*	*3B 0, 2B -1*	*1.6*
2019	*BOS*	*MLB*	*32*	*464*	*52*	*24*	*2*	*10*	*50*	*25*	*72*	*23*	*7*	*.268/.312/.401*	*.245*	*8.8*	*.298*	*3.4*	*3B 0, 2B -1*	*0.9*

Breakout: 2% Improve: 32% Collapse: 12% Attrition: 14% MLB: 91% *Comparables: Bubba Phillips, Joe Randa, Carney Lansford*

Once again, none of it makes sense. Nunez returned to his pre-breakout ways for the first half of 2017, posting an empty average and using his speed to carve out an everyday role with the Giants despite his poor glove. The Red Sox needed some infield insurance and the asking price for Nunez was awfully low, so he made sense as a deadline acquisition. But once in Boston, Nunez rediscovered his 2016 All-Star ways. He doubled his ISO after heading east. He hit the ball harder and pulled it more. He even looked kind of sort of okayish at second base. Unfortunately, Nunez played just once after September 9 thanks to a knee injury. He returned for the ALDS but fell to the ground in pain trying to run out a groundball in his first at-bat, done for the series and the season. Nunez now enters free agency coming off of two strong years, but he's a speed-based player with a recent leg injury who's on the wrong side of 30. He's got more red flags than a Moroccan parade, but are you really willing to bet against him at this point?

Josh Ockimey 1B Born: 10/18/95 Age: 22 Bats: L Throws: R Height: 6'1" Weight: 215 Origin: Round 5, 2014 Draft (#164 overall)

YEAR	TEAM	LVL	AGE	PA	R	2B	3B	HR	RBI	BB	K	SB	CS	AVG/OBP/SLG	TAv	VORP	BABIP	BRR	FRAA	WARP
2015	LOW	A-	19	229	30	13	3	4	38	25	78	2	2	.266/.349/.422	.277	4.9	.408	-1.6	1B(47): -3.9	0.1
2016	GRN	A	20	499	60	25	1	18	62	88	129	3	1	.226/.367/.425	.294	23.0	.284	1.8	1B(101): -3.2	2.2
2017	SLM	A+	21	425	56	20	2	11	63	66	110	1	4	.275/.388/.438	.301	21.3	.362	-0.7	1B(82): -2.6	2.0
2017	PME	AA	21	121	12	7	0	3	11	17	33	0	0	.272/.372/.427	.276	2.6	.368	-0.5	1B(21): 0.2	0.3
2018	*BOS*	*MLB*	*22*	*250*	*27*	*10*	*0*	*8*	*30*	*33*	*82*	*0*	*0*	*.215/.319/.378*	*.239*	*-1.4*	*.301*	*-0.5*	*1B -1*	*-0.3*
2019	*BOS*	*MLB*	*23*	*385*	*50*	*16*	*0*	*13*	*46*	*51*	*123*	*0*	*0*	*.218/.323/.390*	*.245*	*-2.2*	*.298*	*-1.0*	*1B -1*	*-0.4*

Breakout: 2% Improve: 16% Collapse: 4% Attrition: 15% MLB: 32% *Comparables: Chris Parmelee, Matt Olson, Jon Singleton*

Ockimey came to Portland to walk, homer and strike out, and friends, he was all out of homers. In Salem, where he posted a .301 TAv as a 21-year-old, Ockimey looked straight out of Central Casting for a first base prospect. He's big, he's got a ton of natural raw, he strikes out too much and he can't run or field a lick. The first two factors work in his favor, and he's got a good enough work ethic that he might end up mitigating that last point as well. Ockimey won't be able to outwork the swing-and-miss, though; it's who he is, and the same long, leveraged swing that could one day produce plus game power also leaves him vulnerable to the K. If it all clicks for Ockimey, he could hit for enough power to become a second-division regular. If not, it's tough to envision a role for him unless the majors expand to 28-man rosters.

Dustin Pedroia 2B Born: 08/17/83 Age: 34 Bats: R Throws: R Height: 5'9" Weight: 175 Origin: Round 2, 2004 Draft (#65 overall)

YEAR	TEAM	LVL	AGE	PA	R	2B	3B	HR	RBI	BB	K	SB	CS	AVG/OBP/SLG	TAv	VORP	BABIP	BRR	FRAA	WARP
2015	BOS	MLB	31	425	46	19	1	12	42	38	51	2	2	.291/.356/.441	.271	14.9	.308	-0.4	2B(92): 2.7	1.9
2016	BOS	MLB	32	698	105	36	1	15	74	61	73	7	4	.318/.376/.449	.274	26.4	.339	-2.0	2B(152): -2.7	2.4
2017	BOS	MLB	33	463	46	19	0	7	62	49	48	4	3	.293/.369/.392	.266	9.5	.315	-5.7	2B(98): -0.1	1.0
2018	*BOS*	*MLB*	*34*	*447*	*55*	*21*	*1*	*6*	*40*	*40*	*52*	*4*	*3*	*.285/.348/.385*	*.262*	*17.4*	*.313*	*-1.1*	*2B 0*	*1.5*
2019	*BOS*	*MLB*	*35*	*379*	*45*	*17*	*0*	*6*	*38*	*37*	*49*	*2*	*2*	*.276/.345/.382*	*.254*	*8.1*	*.304*	*-1.6*	*2B 1*	*0.9*

Breakout: 3% Improve: 35% Collapse: 8% Attrition: 15% MLB: 89% *Comparables: Placido Polanco, Mark Loretta, Ian Kinsler*

Way back in 2007, Pedroia ended any hopes Alex Cora had at remaining an everyday player, emerging to become the AL Rookie of the Year. Now it might be time for Cora to end Pedroia's everyday-player status in return. Boston's preeminent sparkplug has averaged just 121 games over the past four years, battling injuries to his hands, wrists, hamstrings and now most seriously to his knee. We'd heard reports that Pedroia's left knee was balky even before Manny Machado slammed into it in April. Who knows exactly how much damage that slide did, but Pedroia's knee worsened to the point where he needed offseason surgery to repair it. The most optimistic estimates suggest he won't return to action until May or June.

Even if Pedroia were slated to start 2018 on time, Cora would be wise to make some changes because Pedroia looks every bit the part of a 34-year-old second baseman. He is now a below-average runner, his unfailing belief that he can always take the extra bag adding to Boston's overall base-running malaise. FRAA has his glove at just around average, and while the eye test suggests he might still be a tick better, he's no longer elite (though some metrics disagree). Couple those losses with power output that fluctuates between "surprisingly decent" and "almost nonexistent," and Pedroia's once well-rounded skill set has quickly whittled down to his eye at the plate and his preternatural bat-to-ball ability.

When healthy, Pedroia is still good enough to play often for a contender. He can still reach base at a solid clip, make some splash plays on the dirt and provide on-field leadership. But time waits for no man, and it is especially cruel to second basemen. Pedroia no longer belongs in the top third of a good lineup, and he should no longer be asked or expected to play every day. He needs time off. He needs time at DH. And he needs to admit when his injuries limit his effectiveness. Everything we know about Pedroia suggests he won't enjoy this new reality, but perhaps he can remember the example his new manager set for him back in 2007. For the good of his own career and the good of the Red Sox's chances through the end of his contract in 2021, he needs to.

Hanley Ramirez DH Born: 12/23/83 Age: 34 Bats: R Throws: R Height: 6'2" Weight: 235 Origin: International Free Agent, 2000

YEAR	TEAM	LVL	AGE	PA	R	2B	3B	HR	RBI	BB	K	SB	CS	AVG/OBP/SLG	TAv	VORP	BABIP	BRR	FRAA	WARP
2015	BOS	MLB	31	430	59	12	1	19	53	21	71	6	3	.249/.291/.426	.252	5.0	.257	0.0	LF(92): -15.3, 3B(1): 0.0	-1.1
2016	BOS	MLB	32	620	81	28	1	30	111	60	120	9	3	.286/.361/.505	.280	16.3	.315	-2.8	1B(133): -10.4	0.6
2017	BOS	MLB	33	553	58	24	0	23	62	51	116	1	3	.242/.320/.429	.253	-0.2	.272	-1.8	1B(18): -1.1	-0.1
2018	*BOS*	*MLB*	*34*	*602*	*77*	*28*	*1*	*22*	*82*	*52*	*113*	*7*	*3*	*.266/.335/.446*	*.273*	*18.8*	*.299*	*-1.0*	*1B -1*	*1.6*
2019	*BOS*	*MLB*	*35*	*458*	*60*	*21*	*1*	*17*	*60*	*42*	*91*	*4*	*2*	*.258/.332/.440*	*.264*	*12.3*	*.291*	*-1.1*	*1B -1*	*1.2*

Breakout: 0% Improve: 31% Collapse: 3% Attrition: 14% MLB: 93% *Comparables: Kendrys Morales, Aubrey Huff, Adrian Gonzalez*

The Red Sox really needed Ramirez to be good in 2017, and he let them down. David Ortiz's retirement left Ramirez as the premier slugger in Boston's lineup. He was supposed to provide power, some innings at first base and a stabilizing presence in a young lineup. Instead, he posted the second-worst TAv of his career—just a tick better than 2015. A shoulder injury limited Ramirez to 18 games at first base, and while that might not be such a bad thing defensively, it killed whatever flexibility the Sox were hoping to gain at the DH position post-Ortiz. At the plate, Ramirez took a step back in almost every way imaginable, and while you can blame BABIP for some of that, he just didn't look right all year. Ramirez tried to pull the ball more but hit the ball hard less often, all while whiffing at the highest rate of his career. That's a disastrous combination, and given his injury history and age, it's tough to see this ending well. Ramirez has a vesting option that pays him $22 million in 2019 if he gets 497 PA in 2018. Expect the Sox to do all they can to prevent him from reaching that mark.

Blake Swihart C Born: 04/03/92 Age: 26 Bats: B Throws: R Height: 6'1" Weight: 200 Origin: Round 1, 2011 Draft (#26 overall)

YEAR	TEAM	LVL	AGE	PA	R	2B	3B	HR	RBI	BB	K	SB	CS	AVG/OBP/SLG	TAv	VORP	BABIP	BRR	FRAA	WARP
2015	PAW	AAA	23	80	7	3	0	0	11	6	14	1	1	.311/.363/.351	.270	2.5	.383	-1.4	C(16): 1.7	0.4
2015	BOS	MLB	23	309	47	17	1	5	31	18	77	4	2	.274/.319/.392	.241	10.1	.359	2.4	C(83): -8.7	0.1
2016	PAW	AAA	24	122	13	4	0	1	8	17	17	2	1	.243/.344/.311	.247	2.1	.276	-0.2	C(15): 0.3, LF(11): 1.4	0.4
2016	BOS	MLB	24	74	9	0	3	0	5	11	17	0	1	.258/.365/.355	.247	0.5	.348	-0.6	LF(13): 1.0, C(6): -1.4	0.0
2017	RSX	RK	25	38	6	2	0	0	2	8	8	2	0	.167/.342/.233	.205	-1.9	.227	0.0	1B(4): 0.1, C(2): 0.0	-0.2
2017	PAW	AAA	25	212	22	6	1	4	23	13	54	1	0	.190/.246/.292	.197	-8.1	.239	-1.7	C(43): 5.2, 1B(3): 0.2	-0.3
2017	BOS	MLB	25	7	1	0	0	0	0	2	3	0	0	.200/.429/.200	.240	-0.1	.500	-0.2	C(4): -0.4	0.0
2018	*BOS*	*MLB*	*26*	*197*	*20*	*8*	*1*	*3*	*18*	*16*	*48*	*2*	*1*	*.244/.309/.354*	*.236*	*1.2*	*.314*	*-0.2*	*LF 2, C 0*	*0.0*
2019	*BOS*	*MLB*	*27*	*173*	*20*	*7*	*1*	*4*	*18*	*16*	*43*	*1*	*1*	*.243/.317/.374*	*.239*	*1.1*	*.310*	*0.5*	*LF 1, C 0*	*0.2*

Breakout: 13% Improve: 47% Collapse: 15% Attrition: 29% MLB: 90% *Comparables: Christian Vazquez, Lou Marson, Jeff Mathis*

YEAR	TEAM	P. COUNT	FRM RUNS	BLK RUNS	THRW RUNS	TOT RUNS
2015	BOS	11445	-5.5	-3.5	0.2	-8.8
2015	PAW	2261	0.5	0.1	0.0	0.6
2015	PME	133	0.0	0.0	0.0	0.0
2016	BOS	908	-0.7	-0.7	0.0	-1.4
2017	BOS	187	0.0	-0.4	0.0	-0.4
2018	*BOS*	*1227*	*-0.2*	*-0.2*	*0.0*	*-0.5*
2019	*BOS*	*1076*	*-0.2*	*-0.2*	*0.0*	*-0.3*

Swihart was still a Red Sox when we sent this book to press, but by the time it gets to your doorstep there's a good chance that will no longer be the case. Entering his age-26 season and now out of options, Swihart only has a few paths left toward a career in Boston. He could start playing better defense behind the plate and supplant Sandy Leon as the backup. He could get more reps at the corners and hope to become a super-utility option. He could, uh, suddenly emerge as a dominant left-handed reliever? None of these doors will be open to Swihart if he can't stay healthy, and that was a major issue for the former top prospect once again in 2017. Swihart missed time with a finger injury and ankle inflammation, and those maladies contributed to his atrocious offensive output at Pawtucket. The Sox now have to choose between selling low on Swihart or banking on a return to his 2015 form, and neither option seems particularly enticing.

Sam Travis 1B Born: 08/27/93 Age: 24 Bats: R Throws: R Height: 6'0" Weight: 205 Origin: Round 2, 2014 Draft (#67 overall)

YEAR	TEAM	LVL	AGE	PA	R	2B	3B	HR	RBI	BB	K	SB	CS	AVG/OBP/SLG	TAv	VORP	BABIP	BRR	FRAA	WARP
2015	SLM	A+	21	278	35	15	4	5	40	26	43	10	6	.313/.378/.467	.306	17.6	.356	2.0	1B(46): 2.3	2.2
2015	PME	AA	21	281	35	17	2	4	38	33	34	9	6	.300/.384/.436	.297	15.9	.332	2.7	1B(63): 8.7	2.7
2016	PAW	AAA	22	190	26	10	0	6	29	15	40	1	0	.272/.332/.434	.283	7.8	.320	1.4	1B(34): 2.1	1.0
2017	PAW	AAA	23	342	40	14	0	6	24	37	57	6	2	.270/.351/.375	.259	-0.1	.315	-3.5	1B(58): -0.1	0.0
2017	BOS	MLB	23	83	13	6	0	0	1	6	23	1	0	.263/.325/.342	.217	-3.8	.377	-1.0	1B(21): 0.2	-0.4
2018	*BOS*	*MLB*	*24*	*131*	*15*	*7*	*0*	*3*	*14*	*12*	*28*	*2*	*1*	*.262/.332/.396*	*.257*	*1.7*	*.320*	*-0.1*	*1B 1*	*0.2*
2019	*BOS*	*MLB*	*25*	*352*	*44*	*18*	*1*	*10*	*41*	*34*	*79*	*4*	*2*	*.265/.340/.422*	*.260*	*4.0*	*.324*	*-0.3*	*1B 4*	*0.8*

Breakout: 5% Improve: 21% Collapse: 9% Attrition: 24% MLB: 43% *Comparables: Chris Parmelee, Chris Marrero, Mike Carp*

Did Travis take a step forward or a step back in 2017? On the one hand, he cut his strikeout rate and bumped his walk rate in Triple-A, didn't embarrass himself in the majors and earned your uncle's respect by continuing to eschew batting gloves. He seemed fully recovered from his ACL injury, too. On the other hand, Travis hit for even less power than he had in 2016, and while his Pawtucket production was solid, it was hardly remarkable. The Red Sox re-signed Mitch Moreland to a two-year deal in December, so Travis might've missed his window to prove he belongs at Fenway on an everyday basis. He didn't look overwhelmed facing MLB pitching, though, so perhaps he'll become familiar with the Providence-to-Boston Commuter Rail line.

Christian Vazquez C Born: 08/21/90 Age: 27 Bats: R Throws: R Height: 5'9" Weight: 195 Origin: Round 9, 2008 Draft (#292 overall)

YEAR	TEAM	LVL	AGE	PA	R	2B	3B	HR	RBI	BB	K	SB	CS	AVG/OBP/SLG	TAv	VORP	BABIP	BRR	FRAA	WARP
2016	PAW	AAA	25	171	19	9	0	2	16	15	31	2	0	.270/.345/.368	.269	9.4	.325	0.3	C(41): 5.2	1.5
2016	BOS	MLB	25	184	21	9	1	1	12	10	39	0	0	.227/.277/.308	.198	-4.0	.288	-0.7	C(56): 6.0	0.2
2017	BOS	MLB	26	345	43	18	2	5	32	17	64	7	2	.290/.330/.404	.244	7.0	.348	-3.3	C(95): 10.6, 3B(2): 0.0	1.8
2018	*BOS*	*MLB*	*27*	*378*	*39*	*19*	*1*	*5*	*35*	*25*	*74*	*4*	*1*	*.260/.314/.362*	*.240*	*9.4*	*.315*	*-0.2*	*C 10*	*1.7*
2019	*BOS*	*MLB*	*28*	*391*	*43*	*20*	*1*	*6*	*38*	*28*	*81*	*4*	*1*	*.257/.315/.372*	*.237*	*3.8*	*.312*	*-2.0*	*C 10*	*1.5*

Breakout: 3% Improve: 42% Collapse: 9% Attrition: 18% MLB: 91% *Comparables: Tony Cruz, Yorvit Torrealba, James McCann*

YEAR	TEAM	P. COUNT	FRM RUNS	BLK RUNS	THRW RUNS	TOT RUNS
2016	BOS	7176	6.7	-0.8	-0.1	5.8
2017	BOS	13558	9.9	0.8	2.3	13.1
2018	*BOS*	*14786*	*10.4*	*0.1*	*1.4*	*11.8*
2019	*BOS*	*15303*	*9.5*	*0.1*	*1.3*	*10.8*

Last year's *Annual* comment suggested Vazquez consult with a sorceress to resurrect his bat. You're welcome for the sage advice, Christian. Vazquez benefited from a .348 BABIP to post the best TAv of his short career, but there were real improvements in his approach, too. Vazquez went the other way with the ball more than ever and cut down on his strikeouts. Pair those advancements with the stellar defensive metrics you'd expect from a guy with Vazquez's reputation and you get a solid starting catcher. We've long joked about Vazquez being a secret member of the Molina family, but our Similarity Index spits out a different, equally interesting name as Vazquez's top comp: Jonathan Lucroy. That might be a tad optimistic, but if Vazquez keeps stealing strikes behind the plate and sporadically homering off of the game's best relievers (this year it was Cody Allen), the Sox will take it.

Chris Young LF Born: 09/05/83 Age: 34 Bats: R Throws: R Height: 6'2" Weight: 200 Origin: Round 16, 2001 Draft (#493 overall)

YEAR	TEAM	LVL	AGE	PA	R	2B	3B	HR	RBI	BB	K	SB	CS	AVG/OBP/SLG	TAv	VORP	BABIP	BRR	FRAA	WARP
2015	NYA	MLB	31	356	53	20	1	14	42	30	73	3	1	.252/.320/.453	.272	9.4	.283	-2.0	RF(76): -3.6, LF(55): -2.2	0.3
2016	PAW	AAA	32	25	2	2	0	0	2	1	7	0	0	.217/.280/.304	.205	-1.1	.313	-0.1	LF(4): 0.6	-0.1
2016	BOS	MLB	32	227	29	18	0	9	24	21	50	4	2	.276/.352/.498	.281	9.6	.326	-0.2	LF(63): -1.2, CF(3): -0.5	0.9
2017	BOS	MLB	33	276	30	12	2	7	25	30	55	3	2	.235/.322/.387	.247	1.2	.275	-0.1	LF(39): -5.0, RF(8): 0.8	-0.3
2018	*BOS*	*MLB*	*34*	*253*	*30*	*13*	*1*	*8*	*30*	*24*	*57*	*3*	*2*	*.240/.318/.414*	*.249*	*4.7*	*.285*	*-0.6*	*LF -1, RF 0*	*0.5*
2019	*BOS*	*MLB*	*35*	*215*	*26*	*11*	*1*	*6*	*25*	*20*	*50*	*2*	*1*	*.230/.307/.393*	*.242*	*0.6*	*.276*	*-0.4*	*LF -1, RF 0*	*0.0*

Breakout: 0% Improve: 25% Collapse: 20% Attrition: 24% MLB: 87% *Comparables: Eric Byrnes, Cody Ross, Ryan Doumit*

Heading into the season, Young looked like the perfect complement to the Red Sox's trio of starting outfielders. If Young had played at his 2016 level that might've been true, but instead he took the biggest step back this side of Twitter. Young posted a .210 TAv against southpaws despite a career mark of .314. He also lost a step in the field, and if Young can't hit lefties or play defense, well, we're running out of reasons to keep Young employed—the Red Sox clearly agree, having left him off the postseason roster. He's just one year removed from being useful and he's in phenomenal shape, so Young deserves another shot to latch on somewhere as a reserve. He's starting to look more like his age than his last name, though.

PITCHERS

Fernando Abad LHP
Born: 12/17/85 Age: 32 Bats: L Throws: L Height: 6'1" Weight: 220 Origin: International Free Agent, 2002

YEAR	TEAM	LVL	AGE	W	L	SV	G	GS	IP	H	HR	BB/9	K/9	K	GB%	BABIP	WHIP	ERA	DRA	WARP	MPH	CMD	PWR	STM
2015	OAK	MLB	29	2	2	0	62	0	47^2	45	11	3.6	8.5	45	41%	.264	1.34	4.15	5.35	-0.4	94.5	49	40	45
2016	MIN	MLB	30	1	4	1	39	0	34	27	2	3.7	7.7	29	46%	.269	1.21	2.65	6.49	-0.6	94.5	44	36	41
2016	BOS	MLB	30	0	2	0	18	0	12^2	13	2	5.7	8.5	12	38%	.297	1.66	6.39	6.17	-0.2	95.4	44	36	41
2017	BOS	MLB	31	2	1	1	48	0	43^2	40	4	2.9	7.6	37	46%	.286	1.24	3.30	3.91	0.6	94.0	57	35	39
2018	*BOS*	*MLB*	*32*	*2*	*1*	*1*	*34*	*0*	36^1	*36*	*4*	*4.0*	*8.0*	*32*	*44%*	*.298*	*1.42*	*4.39*	*4.80*	*0.1*	*93.4*	*50*	*36*	*41*
2019	*BOS*	*MLB*	*33*	*3*	*1*	*1*	*54*	*0*	44^1	*45*	*6*	*4.5*	*8.1*	*40*	*44%*	*.304*	*1.52*	*4.62*	*5.04*	*0.1*	*93.0*	*50*	*35*	*40*

Breakout: 23% Improve: 39% Collapse: 32% Attrition: 16% MLB: 89% *Comparables: Matt Wise, Kevin Jepsen, Craig Breslow*

Look, we all know where this comment wants to go, but the obvious route wouldn't be fair to our subject's most recent performance. Because in 2017, he was Fernando Aserviceable. Some of the walk issues that plagued Abad in his first stint with the Red Sox dissipated, and he threw his changeup more and his curveball less, nearly halving his DRA in the process. The Red Sox somehow let Abad face more right-handers than left-handers, which is a definite win for the #FireFarrell crowd, but Abad's splits weren't as crazy as in years past. After never truly earning his last manager's trust, he will look to ascend into higher-leverage work under Alex Cora. He has almost nowhere to go but up; according to FanGraphs, Abad had the 13th-lowest Leverage Index score among relievers who threw at least 40 innings in 2017.

Matt Barnes RHP
Born: 06/17/90 Age: 27 Bats: R Throws: R Height: 6'4" Weight: 210 Origin: Round 1, 2011 Draft (#19 overall)

YEAR	TEAM	LVL	AGE	W	L	SV	G	GS	IP	H	HR	BB/9	K/9	K	GB%	BABIP	WHIP	ERA	DRA	WARP	MPH	CMD	PWR	STM
2015	PAW	AAA	25	1	1	0	17	5	37^2	36	3	5.3	9.8	41	42%	.320	1.54	4.06	4.62	0.2				
2015	BOS	MLB	25	3	4	0	32	2	43	56	9	3.1	8.2	39	42%	.351	1.65	5.44	5.30	-0.3	97.7	45	60	51
2016	BOS	MLB	26	4	3	1	62	0	66^2	62	6	4.2	9.6	71	46%	.318	1.39	4.05	4.27	0.5	99.1	42	60	49
2017	BOS	MLB	27	7	3	1	70	0	69^2	57	7	3.6	10.7	83	50%	.298	1.22	3.88	3.22	1.5	96.8	52	52	52
2018	*BOS*	*MLB*	*28*	*2*	*2*	*2*	*44*	*0*	*46*	*43*	*4*	*4.1*	*9.8*	*50*	*46%*	*.306*	*1.40*	*3.38*	*3.97*	*0.6*	*97.2*	*47*	*57*	*51*
2019	*BOS*	*MLB*	*29*	*3*	*1*	*2*	*54*	*0*	57^1	*51*	*6*	*3.8*	*10.5*	*67*	*46%*	*.307*	*1.30*	*3.46*	*3.78*	*0.9*	*96.9*	*48*	*56*	*51*

Breakout: 32% Improve: 52% Collapse: 19% Attrition: 19% MLB: 86% *Comparables: Andrew Bailey, Phil Coke, Juan Gutierrez*

The polite way to phrase the question is "How much does a former first-rounder need to produce to justify his draft slot?" If we're among friends, the real question is "Has Barnes done enough to avoid being labeled a bust?" Barnes was the 19th overall pick back in 2011 and was projected to be a fast-moving mid-rotation starter, or at the very least a dominant reliever. Instead he's just slightly better than your run-of-the-mill, medium-leverage bullpen guy. He's got a big fastball that features little movement. He's got a good curveball that he can't always throw for strikes. He was solid enough early in the season to serve as the primary setup man and bad enough in September to get left off the postseason roster. If Barnes hadn't been a first-round pick, you wouldn't know him apart from 60 other guys in the majors with his profile. This might seem harsh since Barnes just had his best season by WARP. It's just that Barnes' best isn't special.

Jalen Beeks LHP
Born: 07/10/93 Age: 24 Bats: L Throws: L Height: 5'11" Weight: 195 Origin: Round 12, 2014 Draft (#374 overall)

YEAR	TEAM	LVL	AGE	W	L	SV	G	GS	IP	H	HR	BB/9	K/9	K	GB%	BABIP	WHIP	ERA	DRA	WARP	MPH	CMD	PWR	STM
2015	GRN	A	21	9	7	0	26	26	145^2	156	17	1.7	6.2	100	46%	.298	1.26	4.32	3.47	3.0				
2016	SLM	A+	22	4	4	0	13	13	67^1	67	9	3.2	7.4	55	43%	.294	1.35	3.07	2.94	2.0				
2016	PME	AA	22	5	4	0	13	13	65^1	72	6	3.9	7.7	56	35%	.330	1.53	4.68	5.03	0.0				
2017	PME	AA	23	5	1	0	9	9	49^1	35	3	4.0	10.6	58	51%	.276	1.16	2.19	2.47	1.6				
2017	PAW	AAA	23	6	7	0	17	17	95^2	86	10	3.1	9.1	97	45%	.291	1.24	3.86	3.09	2.7				
2018	*BOS*	*MLB*	*24*	*2*	*2*	*0*	*5*	*5*	*26*	*27*	*4*	*3.6*	*8.3*	*24*	*41%*	*.296*	*1.45*	*4.44*	*5.06*	*0.1*				
2019	*BOS*	*MLB*	*25*	*8*	*11*	*0*	*29*	*29*	178^1	*188*	*29*	*3.6*	*8.1*	*160*	*41%*	*.304*	*1.46*	*4.76*	*5.20*	*0.8*				

Breakout: 12% Improve: 24% Collapse: 17% Attrition: 36% MLB: 47% *Comparables: Erick Fedde, John Ely, Adam Morgan*

An unheralded southpaw drafted out of Arkansas in 2014, Beeks climbed the pecking order of Red Sox minor-league arms with a strong 2017 campaign. Despite being relatively short and stocky—he doesn't fit the bill of your typical starting pitcher prospect—Beeks throws a low-to-mid-90s fastball with good life and a slider that's aided by his unorthodox, deceptive delivery. That combination really clipped Double-A batters' wings, but what about hitters who can make adjustments more quickly? Beeks proved toucan play at that game, improving his command as he reached Pawtucket. Scouts haven't exactly flocked to Beeks' outings, and we shouldn't be so gullible as to believe he's a prime-time prospect now. But Beeks has positioned himself to serve as a capable swingman for the Red Sox in 2018. That's why the Sox added him to the 40-man this winter, and for a 12th-rounder, that's something to preen about.

Blaine Boyer RHP
Born: 07/11/81 Age: 36 Bats: R Throws: R Height: 6'3" Weight: 225 Origin: Round 3, 2000 Draft (#100 overall)

YEAR	TEAM	LVL	AGE	W	L	SV	G	GS	IP	H	HR	BB/9	K/9	K	GB%	BABIP	WHIP	ERA	DRA	WARP	MPH	CMD	PWR	STM
2015	MIN	MLB	33	3	6	1	68	0	65	62	5	2.6	4.6	33	49%	.270	1.25	2.49	4.34	0.3	95.5	44	54	49
2016	MIL	MLB	34	2	4	1	61	0	66	80	4	2.3	3.5	26	51%	.325	1.47	3.95	5.38	-0.3	95.1	48	51	47
2017	PAW	AAA	35	0	2	2	11	0	15^1	13	0	4.1	7.0	12	47%	.289	1.30	2.93	3.18	0.3				
2017	BOS	MLB	35	1	1	0	32	0	41^1	50	3	3.0	7.2	33	37%	.370	1.55	4.35	5.44	-0.1	95.8	52	52	42
2018	*BOS*	*MLB*	*36*	*2*	*1*	*0*	*45*	*0*	47^2	*55*	*6*	*3.8*	*5.9*	*31*	*45%*	*.315*	*1.58*	*4.91*	*5.37*	*-0.1*	*94.1*	*47*	*51*	*44*
2019	*BOS*	*MLB*	*37*	*1*	*0*	*0*	*21*	*0*	*23*	*27*	*3*	*3.8*	*5.7*	*15*	*45%*	*.309*	*1.58*	*5.00*	*5.47*	*-0.1*	*93.5*	*48*	*50*	*43*

Breakout: 21% Improve: 38% Collapse: 24% Attrition: 6% MLB: 64% *Comparables: Matt Lindstrom, Luis Ayala, Javier Lopez*

The year is 2020. You're bored and you love baseball, so you've decided to hop on Sporcle and take the "name the 2017 Red Sox" quiz. You're doing well—you've got all the starting pitchers, the whole lineup, some key bench guys and even Josh Rutledge—holy crap, you remembered Josh Rutledge! But now you've moved on to the bullpen and, uh oh, things are getting dicier. You nailed Kimbrel and Kelly and Barnes, of course, and oh yeah, this was the year Brandon Workman came back, too. You remember the Addison Reed trade, and the multiple LOOGYs named Robby/ie. But who is supposed to occupy this last blank spot? Who threw more innings than Steven Wright or Carson Smith, but fewer than Heath Hembree or Fernando Abad? Was it Brad Ziegler? Wrong year. Alexi Ogando? Getting colder. Manny Delcarmen? You're not even trying now. Errrrr. The buzzer went off, the clock ticked down to zero, and you only missed one name. You forgot Blaine Boyer, and when you take the quiz again in four months, you'll forget him then, too.

Jay Groome LHP Born: 08/23/98 Age: 19 Bats: L Throws: L Height: 6'6" Weight: 220 Origin: Round 1, 2016 Draft (#12 overall)

YEAR	TEAM	LVL	AGE	W	L	SV	G	GS	IP	H	HR	BB/9	K/9	K	GB%	BABIP	WHIP	ERA	DRA	WARP	MPH	CMD	PWR	STM
2017	LOW	A-	18	0	2	0	3	3	11	5	0	4.1	11.5	14	58%	.208	0.91	1.64	2.44	0.4				
2017	GRN	A	18	3	7	0	11	11	44^1	44	6	5.1	11.8	58	55%	.355	1.56	6.70	3.52	0.9				
2018	*BOS*	*MLB*	*19*	*2*	*3*	*0*	*10*	*10*	38^1	*39*	*8*	*5.8*	*10.7*	*46*	*43%*	*.323*	*1.68*	*5.65*	*6.12*	*-0.2*				
2019	*BOS*	*MLB*	*20*	*6*	*9*	*0*	*29*	*29*	175^2	*175*	*32*	*4.6*	*10.1*	*196*	*43%*	*.312*	*1.51*	*4.87*	*5.29*	*0.5*				

Comparables: Jordan Lyles, Roberto Osuna, Danny Duffy

There's no way to comb over the troubles Groome had in 2017. The 12th overall pick in 2016 was already currying favors with scouts headed into the season, ranking as one of the best left-handed prospects in baseball. But while he was expected to clean up in the low minors, injuries stymied his first full professional season. Groome missed time early in the year with a lat injury, and was then shut down for good in August with a left forearm strain. It's tempting to brush away those concerns because Groome did not end up needing Tommy John surgery, and when on the mound, he flashed future top-of-the-rotation stuff. You hate to hear about elbow issues with any potential stud, though, and Groome's walk rate reveals that he's not yet the most stable man when it comes to command and control. Also, it's pronounced "Grom," but what were we going to do with that?

Heath Hembree RHP Born: 01/13/89 Age: 29 Bats: R Throws: R Height: 6'4" Weight: 210 Origin: Round 5, 2010 Draft (#168 overall)

YEAR	TEAM	LVL	AGE	W	L	SV	G	GS	IP	H	HR	BB/9	K/9	K	GB%	BABIP	WHIP	ERA	DRA	WARP	MPH	CMD	PWR	STM
2015	PAW	AAA	26	0	5	8	29	0	31^2	23	1	2.8	9.1	32	36%	.265	1.04	2.27	2.28	0.9				
2015	BOS	MLB	26	2	0	0	22	0	25^1	25	5	3.2	5.3	15	30%	.260	1.34	3.55	5.81	-0.3	97.7	43	68	43
2016	PAW	AAA	27	0	0	8	13	0	13^1	6	0	2.0	14.9	22	38%	.250	0.68	0.68	1.48	0.5				
2016	BOS	MLB	27	4	1	0	38	0	51	51	6	3.0	8.3	47	38%	.294	1.33	2.65	4.59	0.2	96.5	49	56	43
2017	BOS	MLB	28	2	3	0	62	0	62	72	10	2.6	10.2	70	42%	.360	1.45	3.63	5.96	-0.5	97.4	43	60	49
2018	*BOS*	*MLB*	*29*	*2*	*2*	*0*	*35*	*0*	*37*	*37*	*5*	*3.4*	*8.8*	*36*	*40%*	*.303*	*1.39*	*4.01*	*4.48*	*0.3*	*96.4*	*45*	*60*	*46*
2019	*BOS*	*MLB*	*30*	*2*	*1*	*0*	*48*	*0*	50^2	*49*	*7*	*3.8*	*9.3*	*52*	*40%*	*.301*	*1.39*	*4.17*	*4.56*	*0.4*	*96.1*	*45*	*59*	*46*

Breakout: 22% Improve: 50% Collapse: 11% Attrition: 14% MLB: 81% *Comparables: Shawn Kelley, Matt Reynolds, Pedro Baez*

We tend to roll our eyes at players who are hostile toward advanced statistics, but if Hembree acted as such it'd simply be self-preservation. The right-hander's surface-level numbers don't look too bad: an unremarkable ERA, a solid strikeout rate, etc. But DRA tells us Hembree was awful last season, actively hurting the Red Sox when on the mound. Hembree served as a traveling dinger machine last year, and his well-documented struggles against lefties (.277 TAv) continued. But for the first time in his career, Hembree was bad against righties, too (.281 TAv). Odds are his same-side struggles are an aberration, and there's value in Hembree's ability to log innings, but he seems destined for a career as the 24th or 25th guy on a roster. He also still looks too much like the love child of Animal the Muppet and John Lackey, which is a fairly major flaw.

Tanner Houck RHP Born: 06/29/96 Age: 21 Bats: R Throws: R Height: 6'5" Weight: 220 Origin: Round 1, 2017 Draft (#24 overall)

YEAR	TEAM	LVL	AGE	W	L	SV	G	GS	IP	H	HR	BB/9	K/9	K	GB%	BABIP	WHIP	ERA	DRA	WARP	MPH	CMD	PWR	STM
2017	LOW	A-	21	0	3	0	10	10	22^1	21	0	3.2	10.1	25	49%	.333	1.30	3.63	3.17	0.5				
2018	*BOS*	*MLB*	*22*	*2*	*3*	*0*	*9*	*9*	32^2	*36*	*6*	*4.6*	*9.0*	*33*	*40%*	*.325*	*1.63*	*5.49*	*5.96*	*-0.1*				
2019	*BOS*	*MLB*	*23*	*4*	*8*	*0*	*27*	*27*	162^2	*177*	*32*	*4.9*	*8.7*	*158*	*40%*	*.314*	*1.64*	*5.56*	*6.04*	*-0.4*				

Breakout: 1% Improve: 2% Collapse: 0% Attrition: 1% MLB: 2% *Comparables: Braden Shipley, Steven Brault, Myles Jaye*

The sun-loving brother of Pale Houck, Tanner is a big, right-handed starter out of the University of Missouri, who can run his heavy fastball up to the high-90s but pitched most often in the 92-95 range as a junior. He's got an ideal build for a starting pitcher, showed decent command as an undergrad and gets positive reviews for his demeanor on the mound. The fine folks at *Baseball America* labeled Houck "the second coming of Jake Peavy," which is pretty high praise and a great sign for Sox fans and duck boat salesmen alike. So why'd Houck fall all the way to the 24th pick in last year's draft? He lacks an impact secondary pitch at present and has a high-effort delivery, which may limit him to a bullpen role. Houck could move fast as a potential impact reliever, but he's still got mid-rotation upside, so expect the Sox to give him at least a season to try and figure it out as a starter.

Joe Kelly RHP Born: 06/09/88 Age: 29 Bats: R Throws: R Height: 6'1" Weight: 190 Origin: Round 3, 2009 Draft (#98 overall)

YEAR	TEAM	LVL	AGE	W	L	SV	G	GS	IP	H	HR	BB/9	K/9	K	GB%	BABIP	WHIP	ERA	DRA	WARP	MPH	CMD	PWR	STM
2015	PAW	AAA	27	1	1	0	4	4	19	14	1	2.8	8.5	18	58%	.265	1.05	2.84	3.10	0.5				
2015	BOS	MLB	27	10	6	0	25	25	134^1	145	15	3.3	7.4	110	46%	.319	1.44	4.82	4.54	0.9	98.6	54	68	69
2016	PAW	AAA	28	1	1	2	17	4	35	29	1	1.5	11.8	46	57%	.341	1.00	1.54	1.63	1.4				
2016	BOS	MLB	28	4	0	0	20	6	40	44	5	5.4	10.8	48	48%	.358	1.70	5.18	4.11	0.5	100.4	43	64	43
2017	BOS	MLB	29	4	1	0	54	0	58	42	3	4.2	8.1	52	51%	.252	1.19	2.79	4.59	0.4	100.9	44	79	45
2018	*BOS*	*MLB*	*30*	*3*	*2*	*2*	*48*	*0*	*51*	*46*	*4*	*3.8*	*8.9*	*51*	*48%*	*.295*	*1.31*	*3.37*	*3.96*	*0.7*	*98.9*	*48*	*71*	*50*
2019	*BOS*	*MLB*	*31*	*3*	*1*	*1*	*52*	*0*	55^1	*50*	*6*	*3.8*	*8.9*	*55*	*48%*	*.293*	*1.32*	*3.87*	*4.24*	*0.6*	*99.1*	*45*	*72*	*46*

Breakout: 12% Improve: 46% Collapse: 33% Attrition: 14% MLB: 92% *Comparables: Tyson Ross, Clay Buchholz, Doug Fister*

If we've said it once, we've said it a million times: Joe Kelly Has Great Luck. Wait, what? Despite the offensive outbreak around him, Kelly posted the lowest homer rate, second-lowest BABIP and third-best strand rate of his career in 2017. That would seem to make him a prime regression candidate, but hold your horses, because Kelly isn't just fortunate, he also had Great Stuff™. Kelly's *average* fastball velocity in 2017 was a ridiculous 99.3 mph, good for the fastest mark among qualified relievers not named Aroldis Chapman. Despite that uptick in velo, Kelly didn't look like he was overthrowing the ball as much as in years past. His strikeout rate fell a bit, but so too did his walk rate, and that tradeoff seemed to work for him (though DRA is not impressed). Kelly missed some time with a hamstring strain in July, but he was a big part of why the Red Sox's bullpen finished a surprising second in the American League in ERA.

Craig Kimbrel RHP Born: 05/28/88 Age: 30 Bats: R Throws: R Height: 6'0" Weight: 210 Origin: Round 3, 2008 Draft (#96 overall)

YEAR	TEAM	LVL	AGE	W	L	SV	G	GS	IP	H	HR	BB/9	K/9	K	GB%	BABIP	WHIP	ERA	DRA	WARP	MPH	CMD	PWR	STM
2015	SDN	MLB	27	4	2	39	61	0	59^{1}	40	6	3.3	13.2	87	46%	.276	1.04	2.58	2.15	1.8	99.5	43	77	47
2016	BOS	MLB	28	2	6	31	57	0	53	28	4	5.1	14.1	83	31%	.242	1.09	3.40	2.21	1.7	99.7	43	67	43
2017	BOS	MLB	29	5	0	35	67	0	69	33	6	1.8	16.4	126	37%	.260	0.68	1.43	1.89	2.5	99.8	59	78	50
2018	*BOS*	*MLB*	*30*	*3*	*2*	*38*	*48*	*0*	*51*	*34*	*6*	*3.3*	*14.1*	*80*	*39%*	*.289*	*1.04*	*2.31*	*2.91*	*1.3*	*98.9*	*50*	*74*	*47*
2019	*BOS*	*MLB*	*31*	*3*	*1*	*45*	*58*	*0*	*62*	*44*	*9*	*3.8*	*14.3*	*99*	*39%*	*.291*	*1.13*	*3.32*	*3.60*	*1.1*	*98.5*	*52*	*73*	*47*

Breakout: 24% Improve: 41% Collapse: 28% Attrition: 9% MLB: 89% *Comparables: Greg Holland, Rich Gossage, B.J. Ryan*

The Red Sox fans who give Red Sox fans a bad reputation will only want to talk about Kimbrel's disappointing ALDS Game 3 outing. But more enlightened New Englanders will realize that Kimbrel treated them to legitimate greatness in 2017. Had he struck out just one more hitter, Kimbrel would've fanned (Chris Traeger voice) *literally* 50 percent of those foolish enough to enter the batter's box in his presence. Seriously, Kimbrel struck out more batters in 69 super nice innings than Dallas Keuchel did in 145, or than Zach Davies did in 191. Kimbrel also cut his walk rate by eight percentage points. And he blew just four saves in 39 chances. And he made seven multi-inning appearances. Kimbrel didn't just have one of the best seasons of any reliever in 2017, he had one of the most dominant reliever campaigns in recent history. See? Not all Dombrowski's reliever trades turn out badly.

Travis Lakins RHP Born: 06/29/94 Age: 23 Bats: R Throws: R Height: 6'1" Weight: 180 Origin: Round 6, 2015 Draft (#171 overall)

YEAR	TEAM	LVL	AGE	W	L	SV	G	GS	IP	H	HR	BB/9	K/9	K	GB%	BABIP	WHIP	ERA	DRA	WARP	MPH	CMD	PWR	STM
2016	SLM	A+	22	6	3	0	19	18	91	111	8	3.6	7.8	79	41%	.355	1.62	5.93	4.81	0.7				
2017	SLM	A+	23	5	0	0	7	7	38	32	2	3.1	10.2	43	44%	.309	1.18	2.61	2.53	1.2				
2017	PME	AA	23	0	4	0	8	8	30^{1}	34	2	6.2	5.6	19	48%	.337	1.81	6.23	7.73	-0.9				
2018	*BOS*	*MLB*	*24*	*4*	*4*	*0*	*13*	*13*	61^{1}	*66*	*9*	*4.2*	*9.0*	*61*	*40%*	*.327*	*1.54*	*4.78*	*5.20*	*0.3*				
2019	*BOS*	*MLB*	*25*	*7*	*10*	*0*	*27*	*27*	164^{1}	*181*	*28*	*4.7*	*8.3*	*151*	*40%*	*.319*	*1.62*	*5.17*	*5.63*	*0.0*				

Breakout: 3% Improve: 6% Collapse: 2% Attrition: 5% MLB: 9% *Comparables: Rob Rasmussen, Thad Weber, Charlie Furbush*

Boy, the Red Sox love prospects named "Travis," huh? Since he was signed to an overslot deal in 2015, we've been hearing how Lakins was rawer and had more upside than many collegiate right-handers. Both sentiments proved true in 2017, as Lakins torched High-A before Double-A hitters returned the favor. In Salem, Lakins used a four-pitch repertoire headlined by a low-to-mid-90s fastball to strike out nearly 28 percent of the batters he faced. Once in Portland, Lakins' command left him, and his opposition pounced. But the real problem? He ended 2017 the same way he ended 2016—on the DL with a stress fracture in his right elbow. If Lakins can stay healthy and rediscover the command that let him dominate the Carolina League (yes, those are two big ifs), a future at the back of an MLB rotation is in play. A shift to the bullpen is looking more and more likely, though.

Bryan Mata RHP Born: 05/03/99 Age: 19 Bats: R Throws: R Height: 6'3" Weight: 160 Origin: International Free Agent, 2016

YEAR	TEAM	LVL	AGE	W	L	SV	G	GS	IP	H	HR	BB/9	K/9	K	GB%	BABIP	WHIP	ERA	DRA	WARP	MPH	CMD	PWR	STM
2016	DRX	RK	17	4	4	0	14	14	61	54	2	2.8	9.0	61	51%	.319	1.20	2.80	2.10	2.5				
2017	GRN	A	18	5	6	0	17	17	77	75	3	3.0	8.6	74	53%	.333	1.31	3.74	4.18	1.0				
2018	*BOS*	*MLB*	*19*	*3*	*5*	*0*	*13*	*13*	59^{1}	*65*	*12*	*4.6*	*9.5*	*62*	*42%*	*.325*	*1.61*	*5.49*	*5.96*	*-0.2*				
2019	*BOS*	*MLB*	*20*	*6*	*9*	*0*	*24*	*24*	142^{1}	*157*	*28*	*4.5*	*8.3*	*131*	*42%*	*.313*	*1.61*	*5.51*	*6.00*	*-0.4*				

Comparables: Noah Syndergaard, Jayson Aquino, Manny Banuelos

Nothing Mata has done in his career looks terribly special until you realize he doesn't turn 19 until May. Viewed through that lens, he deserves praise for already surpassing 130 career innings, and for holding his own in Greenville despite barely being old enough to vote. Mata is thinner than a Whippet and lacks a premium fastball, but he has a projectable body and a good feel for pitching. His ceiling falls short of sky-high, and he's even riskier than your average starting pitching prospect due to his age and size. But Mata has passed every test he's been given on the mound at an age when most are worried about the SATs or AP exams, and that's all you can ask for.

Drew Pomeranz LHP Born: 11/22/88 Age: 29 Bats: R Throws: L Height: 6'6" Weight: 240 Origin: Round 1, 2010 Draft (#5 overall)

YEAR	TEAM	LVL	AGE	W	L	SV	G	GS	IP	H	HR	BB/9	K/9	K	GB%	BABIP	WHIP	ERA	DRA	WARP	MPH	CMD	PWR	STM
2015	OAK	MLB	26	5	6	3	53	9	86	71	8	3.2	8.6	82	43%	.266	1.19	3.66	3.66	1.3	94.5	51	49	53
2016	SDN	MLB	27	8	7	0	17	17	102	67	8	3.6	10.1	115	50%	.240	1.06	2.47	3.17	2.6	93.5	43	38	71
2016	BOS	MLB	27	3	5	0	14	13	68^{2}	70	14	3.1	9.3	71	47%	.306	1.37	4.59	4.20	0.9	94.0	43	38	71
2017	BOS	MLB	28	17	6	0	32	32	173^{2}	166	19	3.6	9.0	174	45%	.310	1.35	3.32	3.86	3.3	93.5	43	41	76
2018	*BOS*	*MLB*	*29*	*10*	*9*	*0*	*28*	*28*	*159*	*152*	*20*	*3.5*	*8.8*	*156*	*46%*	*.297*	*1.35*	*3.90*	*4.48*	*1.7*	*93.1*	*44*	*41*	*69*
2019	*BOS*	*MLB*	*30*	*10*	*10*	*0*	*30*	*30*	192^{1}	*175*	*23*	*3.7*	*9.1*	*195*	*46%*	*.294*	*1.32*	*3.94*	*4.31*	*2.6*	*92.6*	*43*	*40*	*71*

Breakout: 21% Improve: 42% Collapse: 19% Attrition: 9% MLB: 94% *Comparables: Carlos Carrasco, Tyson Ross, Zach McAllister*

Once you become a whipping boy for the Boston shock jocks, it can be hard to change the narrative that you're soft, overpaid, selfish or whatever other Cardinal Sports Sin you stand accused of. But Pomeranz did so in 2017, shaking off his shaky start as a Red Sox and turning in a gem of a season. Despite starting the year on the DL with a left forearm flexor strain, Pomeranz was reliable and durable once joining the team in mid-April. He finished second on the Red Sox in PWARP, third in innings pitched, third among starters in DRA and, if you're into this sort of thing, tied for first in wins. He emerged as the type of legitimate no. 2/3 starter you might give up a top-50 prospect for, and huh, would you look at that, Anderson Espinoza ended up needing Tommy John surgery. Pomeranz stands poised for a big payday if he stays healthy again in 2018, because we now have two seasons worth of starts that tell us he's a damn fine pitcher.

Rick Porcello RHP Born: 12/27/88 Age: 29 Bats: R Throws: R Height: 6'5" Weight: 205 Origin: Round 1, 2007 Draft (#27 overall)

YEAR	TEAM	LVL	AGE	W	L	SV	G	GS	IP	H	HR	BB/9	K/9	K	GB%	BABIP	WHIP	ERA	DRA	WARP	MPH	CMD	PWR	STM
2015	BOS	MLB	26	9	15	0	28	28	172	196	25	2.0	7.8	149	47%	.332	1.36	4.92	4.58	1.0	94.2	58	47	70
2016	BOS	MLB	27	22	4	0	33	33	223	193	23	1.3	7.6	189	44%	.269	1.01	3.15	3.09	5.8	93.9	61	43	85
2017	BOS	MLB	28	11	17	0	33	33	203^1	236	38	2.1	8.0	181	40%	.322	1.40	4.65	5.51	0.1	93.9	61	43	86
2018	*BOS*	*MLB*	*29*	*12*	*10*	*0*	*30*	*30*	*180*	*186*	*25*	*2.6*	*7.5*	*151*	*43%*	*.302*	*1.33*	*4.05*	*4.66*	*1.5*	*93.3*	*60*	*44*	*82*
2019	*BOS*	*MLB*	*30*	*11*	*11*	*0*	*30*	*30*	*189^2*	*200*	*26*	*2.5*	*7.8*	*164*	*43%*	*.312*	*1.33*	*4.10*	*4.50*	*2.3*	*92.9*	*61*	*43*	*84*

Breakout: 10% Improve: 37% Collapse: 22% Attrition: 6% MLB: 97% *Comparables: Joe Blanton, Kris Medlen, Roy Oswalt*

You'll recall that it was Ben Cherington who brought Porcello to the Red Sox back in 2014. That's the same Cherington who masterminded teams that finished in last place or won the World Series with no in between. Porcello embodies that type of wild fluctuation. Coming off a season in which he earned the AL Cy Young, Porcello was barely replacement level in 2017. Nothing about who Porcello is changed—there was no velocity drop or shift in repertoire or major injury. He just pitched worse, missing his spots more frequently and suffering from more than his fair share of bad luck. Porcello's BABIP was well above league average, and while he's always been a little homer-happy, his 2017 rate was the most extreme of his career. That being said, Porcello's strategy of getting hitters to chase high fastballs is one that's prone to producing extreme results—especially with a juiced ball—so it's hard to say whether he'll regress to the mean or whether this Jekyll-and-Hyde act is his new norm.

David Price LHP Born: 08/26/85 Age: 32 Bats: L Throws: L Height: 6'5" Weight: 215 Origin: Round 1, 2007 Draft (#1 overall)

YEAR	TEAM	LVL	AGE	W	L	SV	G	GS	IP	H	HR	BB/9	K/9	K	GB%	BABIP	WHIP	ERA	DRA	WARP	MPH	CMD	PWR	STM
2015	DET	MLB	29	9	4	0	21	21	146	133	13	1.8	8.5	138	41%	.293	1.11	2.53	2.73	4.1	96.5	67	54	83
2015	TOR	MLB	29	9	1	0	11	11	74^1	57	4	2.2	10.5	87	44%	.283	1.01	2.30	2.45	2.3	97.2	67	54	83
2016	BOS	MLB	30	17	9	0	35	35	230	227	30	2.0	8.9	228	45%	.310	1.20	3.99	3.31	5.4	95.5	72	45	89
2017	BOS	MLB	31	6	3	0	16	11	74^2	65	8	2.9	9.2	76	40%	.278	1.19	3.38	4.37	1.0	96.0	63	56	42
2018	*BOS*	*MLB*	*32*	*9*	*8*	*0*	*24*	*24*	*144*	*144*	*20*	*2.9*	*8.6*	*138*	*42%*	*.303*	*1.35*	*3.93*	*4.52*	*1.5*	*95.1*	*68*	*50*	*67*
2019	*BOS*	*MLB*	*33*	*10*	*10*	*0*	*30*	*30*	*184^1*	*187*	*26*	*2.8*	*8.6*	*175*	*42%*	*.307*	*1.33*	*4.08*	*4.46*	*2.3*	*94.4*	*68*	*48*	*64*

Breakout: 13% Improve: 33% Collapse: 36% Attrition: 9% MLB: 91% *Comparables: Zack Greinke, Justin Verlander, Chris Carpenter*

Block out all the noise for a second. Forget about the spat with Dennis Eckersley or the tiff with reporter Evan Drellich or the ridiculous "is Price faking his injury" propaganda from the mouth-breathers. Just look at Price's performance, and be honest: You didn't realize he was that decent in 2017, did you? *Days of Price's Life* has become Boston's leading drama when the Pats aren't playing, but when the big lefty was actually on the mound last season he was a good pitcher. Sure, the giant caveat here is that Price threw just 74 2/3 innings, and 8 2/3 of them came in relief. It was outstanding relief work, but that won't cut it when you're making $30 million a year. Nonetheless, when healthy, Price proved he's still mostly the guy the Red Sox invested in. That's one question answered, but two big ones remain. First, will Price's left elbow allow him to log 200 innings in a season? And second, does Price hate Boston enough to opt out of his contract after 2018 even if it will cost him money? Tune in next time to find out.

Addison Reed RHP Born: 12/27/88 Age: 29 Bats: L Throws: R Height: 6'4" Weight: 230 Origin: Round 3, 2010 Draft (#95 overall)

YEAR	TEAM	LVL	AGE	W	L	SV	G	GS	IP	H	HR	BB/9	K/9	K	GB%	BABIP	WHIP	ERA	DRA	WARP	MPH	CMD	PWR	STM
2015	RNO	AAA	26	1	1	5	11	0	10^1	8	1	4.4	9.6	11	48%	.250	1.26	1.74	3.60	0.2				
2015	ARI	MLB	26	2	2	3	38	0	40^2	47	2	3.1	7.5	34	41%	.344	1.50	4.20	4.60	0.1	94.8	54	57	50
2015	NYN	MLB	26	1	1	1	17	0	15^1	11	1	2.9	10.0	17	50%	.270	1.04	1.17	3.02	0.3	95.0	54	57	50
2016	NYN	MLB	27	4	2	1	80	0	77^2	60	4	1.5	10.5	91	42%	.286	0.94	1.97	2.90	1.8	94.8	63	59	54
2017	NYN	MLB	28	1	2	19	48	0	49	49	6	1.1	8.8	48	38%	.307	1.12	2.57	5.08	0.0	93.7	57	54	54
2017	BOS	MLB	28	1	1	0	29	0	27	16	5	3.0	9.3	28	47%	.175	0.93	3.33	2.36	0.8	94.6	57	54	54
2018	*BOS*	*MLB*	*29*	*3*	*1*	*4*	*58*	*0*	*61^2*	*59*	*7*	*3.2*	*9.4*	*64*	*42%*	*.301*	*1.31*	*3.92*	*4.28*	*0.6*	*93.8*	*58*	*56*	*53*
2019	*BOS*	*MLB*	*30*	*2*	*1*	*3*	*44*	*0*	*43*	*41*	*6*	*3.3*	*9.4*	*45*	*42%*	*.301*	*1.33*	*3.95*	*4.33*	*0.4*	*93.4*	*59*	*56*	*53*

Breakout: 19% Improve: 42% Collapse: 39% Attrition: 13% MLB: 96% *Comparables: Drew Storen, Hector Rondon, Joe Black*

The thing about Boston is that you have to make a good first impression. See Price, David. Reed failed to do so on August 1 when, in his first outing for the Red Sox, he coughed up a homer. Three subsequent scoreless outings almost had Red Sox Nation feeling comfortable, but then Reed imploded in his first appearance against the Yankees, and you can guess how that went over in homes north of Hartford. The truth is Reed was fine in Boston, but his suddenly homerriffic ways didn't play as well in Fenway as they did in Citi Field, oddly enough. As Reed's 153 innings over the past two seasons suggest, he remains one of baseball's most durable setup men, and he's a passable closer as well. But his next team will have to decide if Reed's sizeable workload is indicative of a rubber arm or an arm that's about to fall off.

Eduardo Rodriguez LHP Born: 04/07/93 Age: 25 Bats: L Throws: L Height: 6'2" Weight: 220 Origin: International Free Agent, 2010

YEAR	TEAM	LVL	AGE	W	L	SV	G	GS	IP	H	HR	BB/9	K/9	K	GB%	BABIP	WHIP	ERA	DRA	WARP	MPH	CMD	PWR	STM
2015	PAW	AAA	22	4	3	0	8	8	48^1	46	2	1.3	8.2	44	50%	.321	1.10	2.98	1.82	1.9				
2015	BOS	MLB	22	10	6	0	21	21	121^2	120	13	2.7	7.2	98	45%	.290	1.29	3.85	4.31	1.1	96.8	54	64	69
2016	PAW	AAA	23	0	4	0	7	7	38	33	6	1.7	5.7	24	43%	.233	1.05	3.08	4.00	0.6				
2016	BOS	MLB	23	3	7	0	20	20	107	99	16	3.4	8.4	100	33%	.278	1.30	4.71	4.15	1.5	96.1	51	58	65
2017	PAW	AAA	24	0	1	0	2	2	10^1	10	0	4.4	10.5	12	38%	.385	1.45	4.35	4.52	0.1				
2017	BOS	MLB	24	6	7	0	25	24	137^1	126	19	3.3	9.8	150	36%	.299	1.28	4.19	3.61	3.0	95.0	55	57	68
2018	*BOS*	*MLB*	*25*	*6*	*5*	*0*	*16*	*16*	*91*	*88*	*13*	*3.2*	*9.1*	*92*	*40%*	*.299*	*1.34*	*3.91*	*4.49*	*0.9*	*95.5*	*55*	*60*	*69*
2019	*BOS*	*MLB*	*26*	*10*	*10*	*0*	*30*	*30*	*192^2*	*183*	*29*	*3.1*	*9.7*	*208*	*40%*	*.303*	*1.29*	*4.01*	*4.38*	*2.4*	*95.1*	*55*	*59*	*69*

Breakout: 27% Improve: 59% Collapse: 18% Attrition: 16% MLB: 98% *Comparables: Tyler Skaggs, Jaime Garcia, Matt Garza*

In Rodriguez's first nine starts, he posted a 2.77 ERA, held batters to a .209/.290/.362 line and looked like a bona fide no. 3 MLB starter.

Then, June 1 happened. Rodriguez slipped during warmups and suffered another subluxation of his right knee. He got bombed in his start that night, missed six weeks and was never as effective upon his return. In the 14 appearances E-Rod made after coming off the DL, his ERA was close to 5.00 and his problems with the long ball resurfaced. Rodriguez's knee is predisposed to this type of injury—it's his third as a professional—so in October, he tried to do something about it. Rodriguez underwent patellofemoral ligament reconstruction in the hope of stabilizing his pesky joint once and for all. The bad news is the surgery should keep E-Rod out for the early part of 2018, but if it ensures his long-term health, the Red Sox will take the trade-off. Still, it seems cruel that the first good arm Boston has developed in forever would have so many problems with his legs.

Robbie Ross LHP Born: 06/24/89 Age: 28 Bats: L Throws: L Height: 5'11" Weight: 215 Origin: Round 2, 2008 Draft (#57 overall)

YEAR	TEAM	LVL	AGE	W	L	SV	G	GS	IP	H	HR	BB/9	K/9	K	GB%	BABIP	WHIP	ERA	DRA	WARP	MPH	CMD	PWR	STM
2015	BOS	MLB	26	0	2	6	54	0	60^2	59	7	3.0	7.9	53	51%	.295	1.30	3.86	4.60	0.1	95.1	42	48	49
2016	BOS	MLB	27	3	2	0	54	0	55^1	47	2	3.7	9.1	56	51%	.302	1.27	3.25	3.88	0.7	96.0	43	49	42
2017	BOS	MLB	28	0	0	0	8	0	9	12	0	5.0	9.0	9	46%	.429	1.89	7.00	6.24	-0.1	93.2			40
2018	*BOS*	*MLB*	*29*	*2*	*1*	*0*	*21*	*3*	*33^2*	*34*	*4*	*4.2*	*8.7*	*32*	*47%*	*.319*	*1.48*	*4.46*	*4.85*	*0.2*	*94.7*	*43*	*49*	*43*
2019	*BOS*	*MLB*	*30*	*4*	*3*	*0*	*53*	*6*	*90*	*93*	*13*	*4.7*	*8.9*	*89*	*47%*	*.318*	*1.55*	*4.86*	*5.30*	*0.1*	*94.4*	*43*	*49*	*42*

Breakout: 32% Improve: 52% Collapse: 23% Attrition: 17% MLB: 93% *Comparables: Jeff Bennett, Sean Burnett, Jared Burton*

Ross was a nonfactor in 2017 thanks to illness (the flu), arm trouble (left elbow inflammation) and back issues (he needed lumbar spine surgery in August). Problems with health care, the left wing and a backbone? Folks, Ross' nickname may as well be Paul Ryan. Ross elected to become a free agent rather than accept an outright assignment in November; given Boston's crowded bullpen, it's tough to blame him. The bards will not sing of Ross' time in Boston, but he was a solid contributor for the better part of three seasons. Considering he was acquired for the low, low cost of one Anthony Ranaudo, that's a win for Boston, albeit a minor one.

Chris Sale LHP Born: 03/30/89 Age: 29 Bats: L Throws: L Height: 6'6" Weight: 180 Origin: Round 1, 2010 Draft (#13 overall)

YEAR	TEAM	LVL	AGE	W	L	SV	G	GS	IP	H	HR	BB/9	K/9	K	GB%	BABIP	WHIP	ERA	DRA	WARP	MPH	CMD	PWR	STM
2015	CHA	MLB	26	13	11	0	31	31	208^2	185	23	1.8	11.8	274	43%	.323	1.09	3.41	2.59	6.2	98.4	61	56	80
2016	CHA	MLB	27	17	10	0	32	32	226^2	190	27	1.8	9.3	233	42%	.279	1.04	3.34	3.04	6.0	97.0	65	50	85
2017	BOS	MLB	28	17	8	0	32	32	214^1	165	24	1.8	12.9	308	40%	.301	0.97	2.90	2.37	7.6	97.4	42	51	85
2018	*BOS*	*MLB*	*29*	*14*	*8*	*0*	*29*	*29*	*203*	*168*	*26*	*2.3*	*11.6*	*255*	*42%*	*.301*	*1.10*	*2.96*	*3.44*	*4.6*	*96.8*	*54*	*52*	*84*
2019	*BOS*	*MLB*	*30*	*14*	*10*	*0*	*32*	*32*	*202^2*	*171*	*26*	*2.2*	*11.6*	*261*	*42%*	*.304*	*1.08*	*3.06*	*3.36*	*5.5*	*96.3*	*52*	*51*	*84*

Breakout: 12% Improve: 35% Collapse: 15% Attrition: 3% MLB: 98% *Comparables: Roger Clemens, Erik Bedard, Jose Rijo*

Want to endear yourself to a tough fan base? Have the type of April Sale did in his inaugural season with the Red Sox. In five April starts composed of 37 2/3 innings, Sale allowed five earned runs, struck out 52 batters and posted a 1.19 ERA. It was the beginning of a dominant campaign from Sale, and an especially absurd first half. Sale became the second Red Sox ever to strike out 300 batters in a season (the first was Pedro, of course), and just the fourth pitcher ever to reach that milestone in his first season with a new team. He posted the second-most PWARP in the majors and second-best DRA among AL starters en route to a second-place AL Cy Young finish. The elephant in the room is that Sale faded down the stretch. His ERA in August and September was north of 4.00, and his first-ever playoff start in the ALDS was a disaster. That shouldn't diminish what Sale accomplished in the first four months of the season, but it's fair to wonder if Sale would be best served dialing it back a bit in an effort to hold up for an entire regular season and, the Red Sox hope, a few starts beyond.

Robby Scott LHP Born: 08/29/89 Age: 28 Bats: B Throws: L Height: 6'3" Weight: 220 Origin: International Free Agent, 2011

YEAR	TEAM	LVL	AGE	W	L	SV	G	GS	IP	H	HR	BB/9	K/9	K	GB%	BABIP	WHIP	ERA	DRA	WARP	MPH	CMD	PWR	STM
2015	PME	AA	25	1	1	0	25	2	43^2	32	3	2.7	8.5	41	37%	.240	1.03	2.06	3.24	0.8				
2015	PAW	AAA	25	1	1	1	13	1	31^2	47	5	2.6	7.7	27	45%	.385	1.77	7.67	4.05	0.3				
2016	PAW	AAA	26	4	3	0	32	6	78	57	9	1.6	8.4	73	31%	.240	0.91	2.54	1.67	3.0				
2016	BOS	MLB	26	1	0	0	7	0	6	6	0	3.0	7.5	5	50%	.333	1.33	0.00	4.14	0.1	89.9			42
2017	BOS	MLB	27	2	1	0	57	0	35^2	22	7	3.3	7.8	31	44%	.172	0.98	3.79	3.68	0.6	90.8	41	26	42
2018	*BOS*	*MLB*	*28*	*2*	*2*	*0*	*31*	*0*	*32*	*32*	*5*	*3.4*	*8.1*	*29*	*39%*	*.293*	*1.36*	*4.57*	*4.92*	*0.1*	*90.1*	*41*	*26*	*42*
2019	*BOS*	*MLB*	*29*	*2*	*1*	*0*	*37*	*0*	*39^1*	*39*	*6*	*3.3*	*8.1*	*35*	*39%*	*.297*	*1.36*	*4.52*	*4.95*	*0.1*	*89.8*	*41*	*26*	*42*

Breakout: 15% Improve: 24% Collapse: 11% Attrition: 24% MLB: 44% *Comparables: Matt Daley, Michael Mariot, Mitch Stetter*

It takes about 55 minutes to drive from Pawtucket to Boston in moderate traffic. Scott got to know the route well in 2017, as he fell victim to the dreaded "still has options left" curse. The LOOGY with the feel-good story was solid enough in his limited MLB time, holding lefties to a .119/.224/.303 line without embarrassing himself against righties. But for whatever reason he was rarely called upon in high-leverage spots, and Fernando Abad got considerably more work despite being Fernando Abad. Assuming offseason surgery to clean up his left elbow doesn't derail him, Scott should be in line for more innings in 2018. That being said, he does have options left...

Carson Smith RHP Born: 10/19/89 Age: 28 Bats: R Throws: R Height: 6'6" Weight: 215 Origin: Round 8, 2011 Draft (#243 overall)

YEAR	TEAM	LVL	AGE	W	L	SV	G	GS	IP	H	HR	BB/9	K/9	K	GB%	BABIP	WHIP	ERA	DRA	WARP	MPH	CMD	PWR	STM
2015	SEA	MLB	25	2	5	13	70	0	70	49	2	2.8	11.8	92	66%	.292	1.01	2.31	2.16	2.1	95.9	40	46	51
2016	BOS	MLB	26	0	0	0	3	0	2^2	2	0	3.4	6.8	2	75%	.250	1.12	0.00	3.97	0.0	94.5			
2017	BOS	MLB	27	0	0	1	8	0	6^2	7	0	2.7	9.4	7	61%	.389	1.35	1.35	5.79	0.0	93.5			36
2018	*BOS*	*MLB*	*28*	*2*	*2*	*0*	*48*	*0*	*51*	*49*	*5*	*4.4*	*9.0*	*51*	*52%*	*.307*	*1.48*	*3.94*	*4.43*	*0.4*	*95.0*	*40*	*46*	*42*
2019	*BOS*	*MLB*	*29*	*2*	*1*	*0*	*40*	*0*	*42*	*43*	*6*	*5.0*	*9.3*	*43*	*52%*	*.315*	*1.57*	*4.66*	*5.08*	*0.1*	*94.2*	*40*	*46*	*39*

Breakout: 34% Improve: 48% Collapse: 21% Attrition: 16% MLB: 84% *Comparables: A.J. Ramos, Steve Cishek, Jeremy Jeffress*

Life is all about how you spin things, ya know? Smith nearly tripled his MLB workload for the Red Sox last season. He struck out 26 percent of the batters he faced. He was even on the postseason roster! I mean sure, Smith didn't make it back from his Tommy John recovery until September 5, and yeah, he wasn't very good in October. But why'd you have to bring all that stuff up, you buzzkill? The most important thing is Smith looked like himself down the stretch, and that means he should be in position to help build the bridge to Craig Kimbrel in 2018. At the very least he has a head start on Tyler Thornburg.

Tyler Thornburg RHP Born: 09/29/88 Age: 29 Bats: R Throws: R Height: 5'11" Weight: 190 Origin: Round 3, 2010 Draft (#96 overall)

YEAR	TEAM	LVL	AGE	W	L	SV	G	GS	IP	H	HR	BB/9	K/9	K	GB%	BABIP	WHIP	ERA	DRA	WARP	MPH	CMD	PWR	STM
2015	CSP	AAA	26	2	7	0	17	17	88^2	106	16	3.7	5.8	57	42%	.315	1.60	5.28	4.91	0.4				
2015	MIL	MLB	26	0	2	0	24	0	34^1	31	7	3.1	8.9	34	35%	.253	1.25	3.67	5.60	-0.4	95.2	40	44	60
2016	MIL	MLB	27	8	5	13	67	0	67	38	6	3.4	12.1	90	36%	.229	0.94	2.15	2.69	1.7	96.4	46	52	49
2018	*BOS*	*MLB*	*29*	*2*	*2*	*0*	*35*	*0*	*37*	*34*	*5*	*3.8*	*9.3*	*38*	*39%*	*.294*	*1.33*	*3.88*	*4.39*	*0.3*	*95.4*	*44*	*50*	*54*
2019	*BOS*	*MLB*	*30*	*2*	*1*	*0*	*46*	*0*	*48^2*	*49*	*7*	*3.5*	*6.9*	*37*	*39%*	*.283*	*1.39*	*4.68*	*5.12*	*0.1*	*95.2*	*45*	*51*	*52*

Breakout: 27% Improve: 58% Collapse: 14% Attrition: 14% MLB: 88% *Comparables: Jon Rauch, Aaron Heilman, Rich Hill*

Defense Against the Dark Arts professors, Spinal Tap drummers and Browns quarterbacks tremble at the thought of having Dave Dombrowski acquire them to serve as the primary setup man for the Red Sox. Before the 2016 season, Dealin' Dave sent Wade Miley and spare parts to the Mariners for Carson Smith, who threw just 2 2/3 innings before blowing out his elbow. That stunk, but when the sunk cost is Wade Miley, people move on. But when Davey With The Good Hair sent Travis Shaw and Mauricio Dubon to the Brewers for Thornburg before the 2017 season, his mistake proved more costly. Thornburg's shoulder acted up in spring training and never got better, and by June he needed thoracic outlet surgery. Meanwhile, Shaw hit .273/.349/.513 for Milwaukee while Boston third baseman posted a -.456 TAv and committed 563 errors (all stats approximate) before Rafael Devers arrived. Also, Shaw's 31 homers would've been tops for a Red Sox team that finished last in the AL in taters. Yikes. If Thornburg recovers, he can play a key role in the 2018 bullpen, but that's a big if. Given how fickle even healthy relievers are, it's probably smart to bet the under on the number of high-leverage innings Thornburg will see next season. It would also probably be smart to stop trading so aggressively for relievers.

Brandon Workman RHP Born: 08/13/88 Age: 29 Bats: R Throws: R Height: 6'5" Weight: 235 Origin: Round 2, 2010 Draft (#57 overall)

YEAR	TEAM	LVL	AGE	W	L	SV	G	GS	IP	H	HR	BB/9	K/9	K	GB%	BABIP	WHIP	ERA	DRA	WARP	MPH	CMD	PWR	STM
2016	PME	AA	27	0	0	0	4	0	10	15	3	6.3	4.5	5	48%	.324	2.20	9.00	5.90	-0.1				
2017	PAW	AAA	28	4	1	2	18	0	29	16	1	4.0	10.9	35	46%	.234	1.00	1.55	2.72	0.8				
2017	BOS	MLB	28	1	1	0	33	0	39^2	37	7	2.5	8.4	37	44%	.283	1.21	3.18	4.26	0.4	94.7	58	46	45
2018	*BOS*	*MLB*	*29*	*2*	*2*	*0*	*35*	*0*	*37*	*38*	*7*	*4.6*	*8.9*	*37*	*43%*	*.296*	*1.53*	*5.41*	*5.70*	*-0.2*	*94.0*	*58*	*46*	*45*
2019	*BOS*	*MLB*	*30*	*2*	*1*	*0*	*34*	*0*	*36^2*	*36*	*6*	*5.0*	*7.9*	*32*	*43%*	*.29*	*1.55*	*5.23*	*5.69*	*-0.2*	*93.6*	*58*	*46*	*45*

Breakout: 21% Improve: 46% Collapse: 16% Attrition: 24% MLB: 74% *Comparables: Kevin Gregg, Brad Peacock, Brad Lincoln*

Workman went more than three full years between MLB appearances, but he finally fought his way back to "The Show" in 2017. For the most part, he looked just like the pitcher he was before he underwent Tommy John surgery in 2015. He featured a low-90s fastball with late life, a big ol' Uncle Charlie and decent command. Workman also demonstrated a penchant for giving up the long ball, so it's nice to know that some things never change. Boston's bullpen figures to be crowded in 2018, but Workman has enough to offer as a middle-innings guy who doesn't crumble in high-leverage spots that he should stick around. Plus, maybe people will stop complaining about his World Series at-bat now that John Farrell is gone.

Steven Wright RHP Born: 08/30/84 Age: 33 Bats: R Throws: R Height: 6'2" Weight: 215 Origin: Round 2, 2006 Draft (#56 overall)

YEAR	TEAM	LVL	AGE	W	L	SV	G	GS	IP	H	HR	BB/9	K/9	K	GB%	BABIP	WHIP	ERA	DRA	WARP	MPH	CMD	PWR	STM
2015	PAW	AAA	30	2	5	0	8	8	52	55	2	2.6	7.3	42	51%	.331	1.35	3.81	3.96	0.8				
2015	BOS	MLB	30	5	4	0	16	9	72^2	67	12	3.3	6.4	52	45%	.252	1.29	4.09	3.91	0.9	88.2	51	0	62
2016	BOS	MLB	31	13	6	0	24	24	156^2	138	12	3.3	7.3	127	46%	.279	1.24	3.33	3.99	2.5	87.7	49	0	71
2017	BOS	MLB	32	1	3	0	5	5	24	40	9	1.9	4.9	13	43%	.365	1.88	8.25	8.41	-0.8	86.9	61	0	45
2018	*BOS*	*MLB*	*33*	*7*	*8*	*0*	*19*	*19*	*114*	*130*	*19*	*3.5*	*5.6*	*71*	*44%*	*.298*	*1.54*	*5.14*	*5.84*	*-0.6*	*86.7*	*50*	*0*	*57*
2019	*BOS*	*MLB*	*34*	*9*	*12*	*0*	*29*	*29*	*177^2*	*198*	*27*	*3.2*	*5.6*	*111*	*44%*	*.297*	*1.47*	*5.05*	*5.53*	*0.2*	*86.1*	*50*	*0*	*56*

Breakout: 16% Improve: 38% Collapse: 17% Attrition: 7% MLB: 79% *Comparables: D.J. Carrasco, Scott Feldman, Scott Downs*

The most notable thing Wright did in 2017 was undergo the same knee surgery Dustin Pedroia ended up needing, only in May instead of October. Unlike Pedroia, Wright should be ready for the start of the season, but also unlike Pedroia, few people seem to care. How quickly we forget that Wright was an All-Star in 2016, posting a 2.18 ERA through his first 15 starts that year. Of course, how quickly we forgot back then that Wright had been pretty nondescript as a starter up until his random breakout. The Red Sox don't have a ton of sure things in their rotation behind Chris Sale, so Wright could get another shot to stick as a starter. He's about as lucky as pre-Season 7 Garry Gergich though, so don't hold your breath.

LINEOUTS

Hitters

HITTER	POS	TEAM	LVL	AGE	PA	R	2B	3B	HR	RBI	BB	K	SB	CS	AVG/OBP/SLG	TAv	VORP	BABIP	BRR	FRAA	WARP
Cole Brannen	OF	RSX	Rk	18	168	23	2	0	0	7	30	37	9	1	.231/.383/.246	.227	0.5	.320	1.6	CF(37): -1.0, LF(1): 0.2	0.0
Bryce Brentz	LF	PAW	AAA	28	494	75	21	1	31	85	42	109	1	1	.271/.334/.529	.298	31.5	.293	0.8	LF(56): 0.8, RF(45): -0.4	3.1
Bobby Dalbec	3B	RSX	Rk	22	32	3	1	0	0	2	5	9	1	0	.259/.375/.296	.209	-0.5	.389	0.7	3B(4): -0.5	-0.1
	3B	GRN	A	22	329	48	15	0	13	39	36	123	4	5	.246/.345/.437	.275	12.8	.383	-2.0	3B(67): -2.3	1.1
Tzu-Wei Lin	SS	PME	AA	23	184	31	9	3	5	19	20	27	8	2	.302/.379/.491	.305	17.1	.333	1.8	SS(35): 1.1, CF(6): 0.5	2.0
	SS	PAW	AAA	23	154	12	5	1	2	9	11	28	2	4	.227/.283/.319	.222	-1.8	.270	-0.6	CF(20): -1.0, SS(9): -0.3	-0.3
	SS	BOS	MLB	23	66	7	0	2	0	2	9	17	1	1	.268/.369/.339	.267	2.8	.385	0.0	2B(10): 0.1, 3B(9): -0.2	0.3

HITTER	POS	TEAM	LVL	AGE	PA	R	2B	3B	HR	RBI	BB	K	SB	CS	AVG/OBP/SLG	TAv	VORP	BABIP	BRR	FRAA	WARP
Jhonny Peralta	3B	SLN	MLB	35	58	3	0	0	0	0	4	13	0	0	.204/.259/.204	.185	-4.2	.268	-1.5	3B(15): -0.6	-0.5
	3B	PAW	AAA	35	41	4	1	0	2	5	0	11	0	0	.200/.195/.375	.202	-1.9	.214	0.0	3B(3): 0.0	-0.2
Josh Rutledge	3B	BOS	MLB	28	118	10	2	1	0	9	9	31	1	0	.224/.297/.262	.206	-3.2	.316	-0.1	3B(20): 0.0, 2B(16): 0.3	-0.3
	3B	PAW	AAA	28	29	2	1	0	1	1	4	10	0	0	.120/.241/.280	.182	-2.7	.143	-0.9	3B(3): -0.1, 2B(3): 0.1	-0.3
Joshua Tobias	2B	SLM	A+	24	97	16	7	0	2	11	8	16	4	2	.345/.412/.494	.330	7.5	.406	-1.8	2B(17): -1.0	0.7
	2B	PME	AA	24	367	32	19	0	3	34	19	72	4	3	.268/.321/.352	.259	5.6	.330	-3.5	2B(80): -4.3	0.1

A second-round pick last June, **Cole Brannen** is a speedy prep outfielder out of Georgia who the Red Sox signed to an over-slot deal. We are fairly confident he is not just a parody account of former Hawaii quarterback Colt Brennan. **Bryce Brentz** hit .279/.380/.577 against lefties in Pawtucket. If the Sox decide to go with a cheap bench he could be in the mix, but given his historical trouble with guns Brentz should be kept away from Jackie Bradley's arm. 2016 second-rounder **C.J. Chatham** hit over .300 between rookie ball and the Sally League! (Just don't read the fine print, which reveals he did so in only 21 plate appearances thanks to hamstring problems.) **Bobby Dalbec**'s walk-up song should be Duke Ellington's "It Don't Mean a Thing" because it's about missing swings. He continues to make Joey Gallo look like Ichiro. The Red Sox signed 16-year-old shortstop **Danny Diaz** out of Venezuela for $1.6 million during the most recent J2 period. Scouts love his power potential and alliterative name, but not his chances of sticking at short. As a free agent who signed for $2.05 million out of Taiwan back in 2012—the largest bonus ever for a Taiwanese position player at the time—**Tzu-Wei Lin**'s calling cards are his plus glove and defensive versatility. A shortstop by trade, he also saw reps at second, third and center field across three levels in 2017, including the majors. Enron stock declined more gently than **Jhonny Peralta**. He was released by the Cardinals on June 13, then by the Red Sox exactly one month later. **Josh Rutledge** is a bat-first backup infielder who has had trouble both staying healthy and hitting well for the past two years, so he's gonna need a pretty good elevator pitch this offseason. **Josh Tobias** posted a .259 TAv in Portland as a defensively-challenged 24-year-old. He still had a better year than Clay Buchholz.

Pitchers

PITCHER	TEAM	LVL	AGE	W	L	SV	G	GS	IP	H	HR	BB/9	K/9	K	GB%	BABIP	WHIP	ERA	DRA	WARP	MPH	CMD	PWR	STM
Trey Ball	PME	AA	23	7	12	0	25	24	124^{2}	161	17	4.1	7.4	103	44%	.373	1.75	5.27	7.10	-2.9				
Ty Buttrey	PAW	AAA	24	1	1	0	10	0	17^{2}	21	2	5.1	9.2	18	53%	.358	1.75	7.64	4.26	0.2				
	PME	AA	24	1	4	4	30	0	46	39	1	4.5	11.0	56	50%	.339	1.35	3.72	3.69	0.6				
Roenis Elias	PAW	AAA	28	1	4	0	7	7	34	43	9	2.4	6.6	25	33%	.312	1.53	6.62	7.46	-0.6				
	BOS	MLB	28	0	0	0	1	0	0^{1}	0	0	27.0	27.0	1	0%	.000	3.00	0.00			93.5			18
Justin Haley	MIN	MLB	26	0	0	1	10	0	18	22	3	3.0	7.0	14	38%	.333	1.56	6.00	5.14	0.0	92.3	64	42	41
	ROC	AAA	26	1	0	0	5	4	17^{1}	17	3	1.6	5.7	11	49%	.269	1.15	3.63	2.96	0.5				
	PAW	AAA	26	1	2	0	7	7	44	35	7	1.4	7.2	35	42%	.237	0.95	2.66	2.97	1.3				
Darwinzon Hernandez	GRN	A	20	4	5	0	23	23	103^{1}	85	8	4.3	10.1	116	50%	.292	1.30	4.01	4.09	1.4				
Williams Jerez	PME	AA	25	2	0	4	29	0	51^{1}	50	3	3.0	8.2	47	47%	.324	1.31	3.16	4.17	0.4				
	PAW	AAA	25	0	2	0	9	0	12	9	3	4.5	7.5	10	47%	.194	1.25	3.75	4.60	0.1				
Brian Johnson	BOS	MLB	26	2	0	0	5	5	27	32	5	2.7	7.0	21	38%	.310	1.48	4.33	5.14	0.1	89.8	53	18	57
	PAW	AAA	26	3	4	0	17	17	90^{1}	82	10	2.8	7.0	70	39%	.271	1.22	3.09	3.62	2.0				
Kyle Kendrick	BOS	MLB	32	0	2	0	2	2	8^{1}	18	1	3.2	3.2	3	49%	.447	2.52	12.96	7.77	-0.2	93.2			52
	PAW	AAA	32	5	7	0	18	18	101^{2}	114	24	1.4	5.9	67	40%	.286	1.28	5.67	4.72	1.1				
Austin Maddox	PME	AA	26	0	1	2	10	0	13^{1}	9	0	3.4	5.4	8	37%	.237	1.05	1.35	5.52	-0.1				
	PAW	AAA	26	2	2	6	27	0	36	22	2	5.2	9.5	38	33%	.227	1.19	3.50	6.41	-0.4				
	BOS	MLB	26	0	0	0	13	0	17^{1}	13	1	1.0	7.3	14	28%	.240	0.87	0.52	4.90	0.1	96.9	62	60	45
Kyle Martin	BOS	MLB	26	0	0	0	2	0	2^{1}	2	1	7.7	3.9	1	62%	.143	1.71	3.86	8.92	-0.1	94.2			40
	PAW	AAA	26	0	4	1	33	0	53^{2}	56	7	4.4	8.4	50	33%	.318	1.53	4.36	7.53	-1.3				
Roniel Raudes	SLM	A+	19	4	7	0	23	23	116	134	14	3.4	7.4	95	34%	.339	1.53	4.50	6.98	-2.3				
Michael Shawaryn	GRN	A	22	3	2	0	10	10	53^{1}	44	5	2.2	13.2	78	42%	.331	1.07	3.88	2.26	1.9				
	SLM	A+	22	5	5	0	16	16	81^{1}	71	10	3.9	10.1	91	34%	.289	1.30	3.76	4.68	0.6				
James Shepherd	PAW	AAA	24	1	5	2	34	1	59^{2}	59	5	2.7	10.3	68	46%	.340	1.29	4.07	2.23	2.0				
Ben Taylor	BOS	MLB	24	0	1	1	14	0	17^{1}	20	3	4.7	9.3	18	28%	.340	1.67	5.19	5.46	-0.1	94.5	55	54	28
	PAW	AAA	24	0	0	2	12	0	13^{1}	7	2	3.4	8.1	12	47%	.156	0.90	2.70	3.38	0.3				
Hector Velazquez	PAW	AAA	28	8	4	0	19	19	102	78	7	2.1	7.0	79	45%	.251	1.00	2.21	2.99	3.0				
	BOS	MLB	28	3	1	0	8	3	24^{2}	21	4	2.6	6.9	19	44%	.258	1.14	2.92	4.55	0.2	92.0	55	42	51

Hey so remember how **Trey Ball** was considered a two-way prospect when he was drafted seventh overall in 2013? That's good, because hooo boy he can't pitch. **Ty Buttrey** is a big boy with a big fastball and big-time command problems. He can miss bats, but he'll be stuck churning through Triple-A hitters until he limits his walks. The good news is Carson Smith has now thrown more innings for the Red Sox than **Roenis Elias**. The bad news is that's because Elias has logged just eight innings for Boston after battling injuries during most of 2017. Potential middle reliever **Justin Haley** had the shortest and most ill-fated career at the Twins since Robb Stark. Minnesota returned the Rule 5 pick to Boston in July. He's got a long way to go before he evolves into a major leaguer, but **Darwinzon Hernandez** keeps surviving as he climbs the ladder. High-A should prove a good test of his adaptability. The development path is likely to take its time for the 2015 high school draftee, but given his size **Bryan Hudson** might be worth the wait. They say that forcing a child to use their non-dominant hand can be bad for their health and psyche, but **Williams Jerez** got himself added to Boston's 40-man roster pretty much just because he throws left-handed, so ... He may still have rookie eligibility, but **Brian Johnson** is too old and has been too ineffective to be considered a prospect. The stuff won't play up out of the bullpen, so Quad-A starting depth appears to be his present and future role. How do you think **Kyle Kendrick** fared for his two starts in the AL East? Don't look at the stats, just go with your gut on this one. Yep. Yep, you're right. **Austin Maddox** is blessed with a name straight out of an Elmore Leonard book, a good fastball and fortuitous timing. He waited until the majors to stop throwing so many balls, which is how he made the playoff roster over other relievers you've actually heard of. The Red Sox have a host of serviceable but nondescript righty relievers who could ride the Pawtucket-to-Boston shuttle in 2018. **Kyle Martin** is the tallest among them. Back-end starter prospect **Roniel Raudes** spent much of the season as the youngest pitcher in the Carolina League. He kept his head above water, but if we're going with that analogy let's just say plenty of waves hit him in the forehead. A big right-hander with an even bigger arm, **Alex Scherff** fell to the fifth round in the draft due to signability concerns. The Red Sox lured him away from college with a deal about $400,000 over slot, and they'll now work to iron out his mechanics in the hope that one day he can be the new Scherff in town. He might be able to get major-league righties out right now in a relief role, but **Mike Shawaryn** has just enough upside as a starter that the Red Sox will keep him in the rotation at present. Portland looms large as his next challenge. ⚾ **Chandler Shepherd** didn't distinguish himself as a reliever at Pawtucket last year, but that didn't stop the Sox from putting him on their 40-man roster and stretching him out as a starter in Mexico this winter. ⚾ For someone named **Ben Taylor**, he sure had trouble working with stitches. The righty reliever missed plenty of bats in his first 17 major-league innings, but he missed the plate a whole lot, too. ⚾ After spending seven seasons pitching in the Mexican League, right-hander **Hector Velazquez** signed with the Red Sox for $30,000 and ended up making three major-league starts. They were unremarkable, but for an anonymous 28-year-old swingman that's sort of a compliment, no?

League Leaders 2017

MLB cFIP – Craig Kimbrel, 43.6

MLB Strikeout Rate – Craig Kimbrel, 49.6%

MLB Strikeouts – Chris Sale, 308

MLB DRA, Relievers – Craig Kimbrel, 1.89

CHICAGO CUBS

Essay by Brett Taylor

Player comments by Matt Sussman, Jared Wyllys and BP staff

You know what was a great show? *Homeland.*

I say "was" a great show because I couldn't offer you the foggiest opinion of what the show is today (is it still on?), and I couldn't tell you with a straight face that I didn't eventually come to hate what it became.

For those of you unaware, give me a couple spoiler-free moments: *Homeland* recounts the return of a marine to the United States after years of being held in captivity by al-Qaeda. It's an emotional, tense, exciting and thoughtful look at what that might be like. Or, well, it was. So much of the early brilliance of *Homeland* was entirely wrapped up in its central story line—the return of that marine, and his relationship with the CIA analyst who believes he is not what he seems.

To the showrunners' credit, they managed to play that story line out to tremendous effect over the first two seasons. Then the show's premise story line naturally played itself out, and it struggled to find footing in Season Three. In fact, it was the reliance on that original story line that ultimately choked out the show's efforts to find success in other directions in Season Three.

Third seasons, I guess, are hard that way. If the highest and best version of your show has a natural arc through two seasons, turning that corner in the third will, at best, look like a pale imitation of what came before. At worst, the very thing that drove the excellence in the first two seasons will prove to be something of a noose in the third.

In the Cubs' third season, those plot holes started to show.

The story that was the Cubs' 2016 World Series title actually started many years before, in the development process, and the narrower arc that lands with the championship as the payoff began no later than the 2015 season. Joe Maddon and Jon Lester came to Chicago. Kris Bryant, Addison Russell and Kyle Schwarber arrived. Kyle Hendricks emerged. Jake Arrieta dominated.

From there, the same story lines carried forward into 2016, accelerating to their scripted conclusion: The best team in baseball wins its first World Series in 108 years. Where would any storyteller go from there?

It was not only a philosophical issue for Cubs fans who'd defined themselves for a lifetime in a certain way they no longer saw in the mirror, it was a practical issue for the Cubs' players, coaching staff and front office. How do you keep that magic going for another season, particularly when the key story line that propelled your success was almost completely wrung out?

I'm speaking, of course, of the Cubs' sublime starting pitching in 2015 and 2016. (Not what you were expecting?)

Although the young bats always got the bulk of the ballyhoo during the Cubs' rebuild, so much of the team's actual success in the

CUBS PROSPECTUS

2017 W-L: 92-70, 1st in NL Central

Pythag	.579	7th	B-Age	26.8	*4th*
RS/G	5.07	4th	P-Age	30.7	*30th*
RA/G	4.29	7th	Salary	$172.2M	*6th*
TAv	.271	6th	M$/MW	$3.6M	*18th*
TAv-P	.251	8th	DL Days	267	*2nd*
FIP	4.21	10th	$ on DL	6%	*4th*
DER	.715	6th			

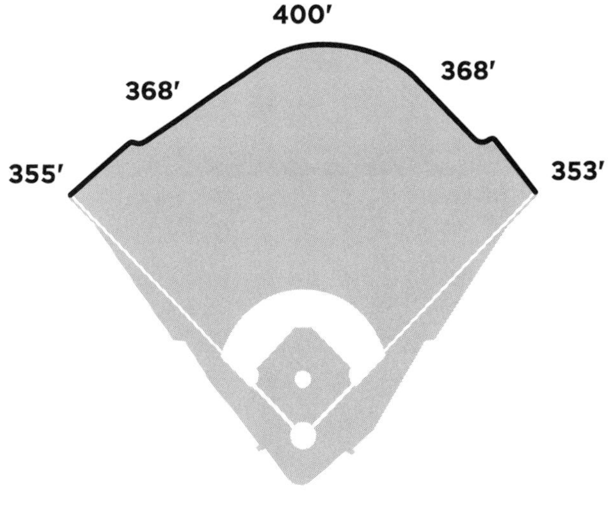

Outfield wall profile: **11′6″** to **15′**

Three-Year Park Factors

Runs	Runs/RH	Runs/LH	HR/RH	HR/LH
99	103	94	109	94

Top Hitter WARP	6.6 Kris Bryant
Top Pitcher WARP	3.5 Kyle Hendricks
Top Prospect	Adbert Alzolay

2017 Hit List Ranking

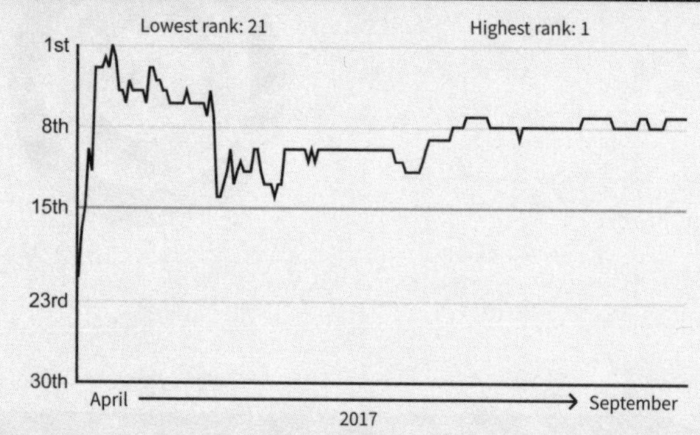

Committed Payroll (in millions)

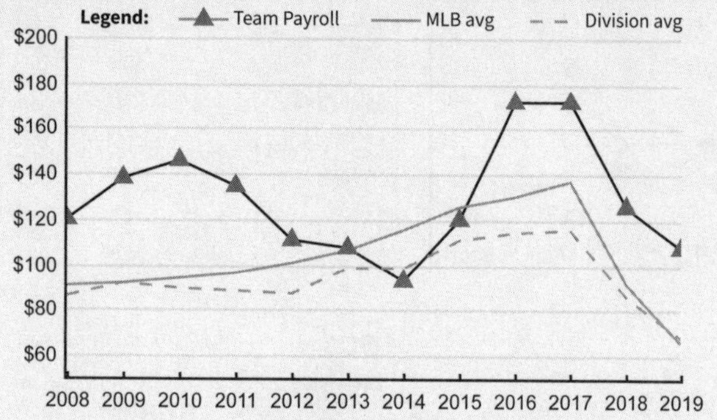

Farm System Ranking

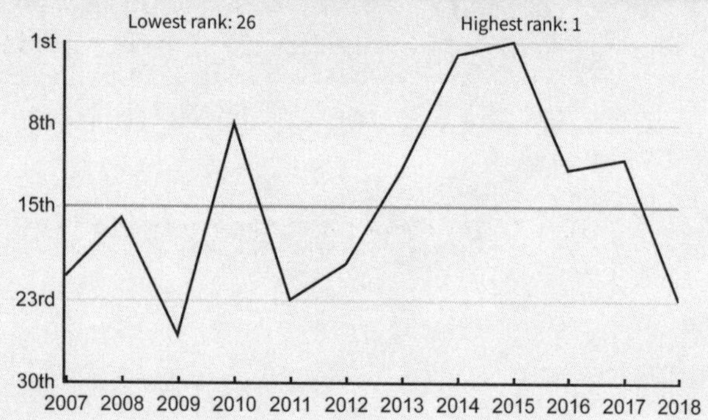

Personnel

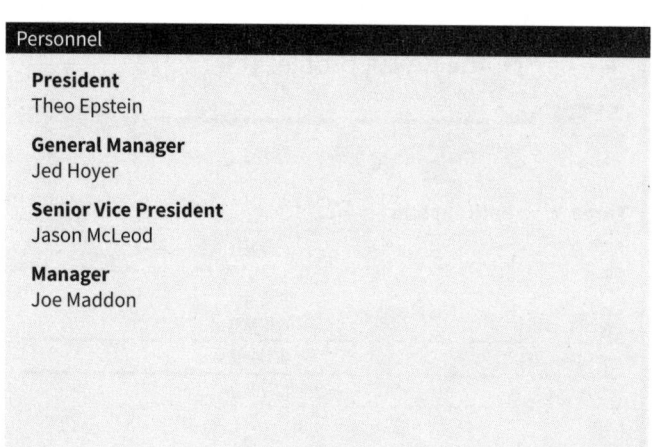

President
Theo Epstein

General Manager
Jed Hoyer

Senior Vice President
Jason McLeod

Manager
Joe Maddon

first two seasons of their arc was built on the arms—specifically, the incredible health and results of the starting rotation.

In 2015, the Cubs had four starting pitchers make at least 31 starts and reach 170 innings in the regular season: Arrieta (33 starts, 229 IP), Lester (32, 205), Hendricks (32, 180) and Jason Hammel (31, 171). The starters posted a 3.41 DRA, best in the National League, and just 0.03 and 0.04 points behind the Indians and Rays, respectively, at the top of the MLB heap.

In 2016, it was even more remarkable. Four of five Cubs starting pitchers made at least 29 starts and threw at least 170 innings, and the fifth made 30 starts and just barely missed 170 innings: Lester (32 starts, 203 IP), Arrieta (31, 197), Hendricks (30, 190), John Lackey (29, 188) and Hammel (30, 167). That season, despite the limited pool of starters on which they relied so heavily, the Cubs posted the best DRA in baseball, at 3.72.

It's no surprise, then, that the Cubs won 97 and 103 games in 2015 and 2016. The next year, the Cubs ambled to a sub-.500 record at the All-Star break like an overserved patron dismounting the throne at his favorite watering hole. It took a stellar second-half pace to get them to 92 wins by the time the postseason rolled around. With time and an outside perspective, folks will remember the 2017 season as a success for the Cubs (90-plus wins, another NL Central crown, a third straight NLCS), but ask any fan who lived it and they'll tell you that the thing just wasn't right from Day 1.

After it was over, we were left to wonder: What happened? How did such a behemoth seemingly fall so far, even if only in the way the season felt? Sure, the "World Series hangover" stuff has a lot of layers of truth and impact, but you should still be able to spot the (relative) struggles on the field and in the numbers. For the Cubs, it wasn't really in the bats. That 2015 club scored a perfectly league-average 4.25 runs per game. As the offensive tide of the Juiced Ball Era started to lift all ships in 2016 (and the young talent developed), the Cubs scored 4.99 runs per game in 2016, second best in the NL.

In 2017, the Cubs' 5.07 runs scored per game was once again second best in the NL, behind only the Coors Field-aided Rockies (5.09). Offense, by and large, did not slumber for the Cubs. What failed them in 2017 was the very thing that pushed them so well (and that they pushed so hard) in 2015 and 2016: the productivity and durability of the starting pitchers.

In 2017, the Cubs' starters posted a 4.43 DRA, nearly a run higher than in 2015-2016, and only ninth best in baseball. Moreover, the team saw just two starting pitchers reach the 170-inning mark with the Cubs, none exceeding Lester's 181. Only three starting pitchers made 30 starts.[1]

In total, starting pitchers logged 947 innings for the Cubs in 2015. The next year, that figure rose to 989 innings, which was the most in the NL. In 2017? Cubs starters accounted for just 888 innings, 15th most in baseball. Some of the change was philosophical, though Maddon hardly shifted his approach to starters *that* dramatically from 2016 to 2017. Instead, the bulk of the drop-off was thanks to bouts of ineffectiveness in the rotation and injuries that forced the Cubs to routinely call upon lesser starters.

It's worth noting that after their remarkable run of health in 2015 and 2016, the Cubs saw every member of the Opening Day rotation spend time on the disabled list in 2017. The lack of durability and productivity in the rotation had something of a compounding effect, too, as the bullpen seemed to pay the price, wearing down by the end of the year despite performing nearly as well overall in 2017 (4.07 DRA) as in 2015 (4.01) and 2016 (3.88). On the whole, the Cubs' 559 bullpen innings in 2017 were sixth most in the NL, and an absurd leap from the 471 innings they logged in 2016—*least* in the NL.

When the entire bullpen throws more innings (in some cases substantially more) in a given season than the year before, of course some fatigue is to be expected. To the extent recency bias screams to Cubs fans that the "problem" in 2017 was the bullpen, let this discussion disabuse you of that notion. A great deal of the lack of bullpen productivity is rightly laid at the feet of the rotation.

In 2015, the Cubs had the best group of pitchers in the NL, netting 23.2 WARP. In 2016, the Cubs had the best group of pitchers in baseball, netting 26.2 WARP. In 2017, however, Cubs pitchers netted just 19.8 WARP, ninth best in baseball. That's not bad, and together with the offense it helped the Cubs win 92 games. But on the heels of the two years that preceded it, things simply didn't feel as solid overall for the club in 2017. And they weren't.

It's also worth noting that the starting pitching slide in 2017 wasn't entirely on the rotation. After posting a fantastic 2.41 Park-Adjusted Defensive Efficiency in 2015 and a historically absurd 6.38 in 2016 (Washington came in second at just 1.70!), the Cubs were at 1.41 in 2017, sixth in baseball. Stellar defense gets those pitchers back to the dugout a little earlier, and the cumulative impact of an inferior defense in 2017 contributed to the grind.

There's one more parallel to wring out of the Cubs-as-TV-show metaphor, and it's probably the most important one from a fan perspective. When a TV show soars so very high in its early seasons, later years are often dubbed disappointing primarily within the context of the expectations that those tremendous early seasons generated. There are no sabermetric statistics or aging curves that tell us most TV shows are bound to regress as they go on—and that the perception of regression will be exacerbated by the quality of the early years—but we should know the score by now. Like a baseball team that overproduced for a couple thrilling seasons, the comedown thereafter is as inevitable as it is unfair.

For the Cubs, that means a third straight season winning 90-plus games and reaching the NLCS is viewed as the kind of disappointment meriting a write-up that compares it to a TV show I stopped faithfully watching because its third season was not what I'd hoped it would be. Which, of course, is nuts. Thankfully, the parallel ends here, as three-year arcs in the baseball world are but blips in the overall show. Even if the third season has a tough job living up to the two that preceded it, I think I'm gonna keep watching.

Notes

1. Jose Quintana pitched 189 innings spread over 32 starts split between the White Sox and Cubs, but the midseason trade to acquire him only underscores the Cubs' needs in the rotation at the time.

—Brett Taylor covers the Cubs for Bleacher Nation.

Hitters

Aramis Ademan SS Born: 09/13/98 Age: 19 Bats: L Throws: R Height: 5'11" Weight: 160 Origin: International Free Agent, 2015

YEAR	TEAM	LVL	AGE	PA	R	2B	3B	HR	RBI	BB	K	SB	CS	AVG/OBP/SLG	TAv	VORP	BABIP	BRR	FRAA	WARP
2016	DCH	RK	17	248	37	5	4	0	16	34	28	17	9	.254/.366/.316	.265	12.4	.293	1.1	SS(52): -1.6	1.1
2017	EUG	A-	18	183	23	9	4	4	27	14	30	10	6	.286/.365/.466	.336	19.0	.331	-3.5	SS(38): -1.0	1.8
2017	SBN	A	18	134	13	6	1	3	15	4	24	4	2	.244/.269/.378	.241	2.9	.275	0.1	SS(29): -5.0	-0.2
2018	*CHN*	*MLB*	*19*	*250*	*31*	*10*	*1*	*7*	*25*	*14*	*64*	*5*	*3*	*.224/.275/.374*	*.211*	*-1.1*	*.273*	*-0.1*	*SS -3*	*-0.4*
2019	*CHN*	*MLB*	*20*	*389*	*47*	*15*	*3*	*14*	*48*	*25*	*94*	*8*	*5*	*.239/.295/.411*	*.245*	*7.6*	*.284*	*0.4*	*SS -5*	*0.3*

Breakout: 0% Improve: 4% Collapse: 1% Attrition: 8% MLB: 12% *Comparables: Wilmer Flores, Raul Mondesi, Rougned Odor*

Now is the time to start celebrating the prowess of Ademan, so you can say you were into him before it was cool. The shortstop turned 19 after his first full pro season, and between short-season Eugene and South Bend in the Midwest League he was good, but not enough that everyone is hip to him yet. He has the right combination of skills—a little power, some speed, the ability to hit for extra bases *and* he's a middle infielder—to keep him from staying off the radar for long. So declare yourself an Ademan hipster while you still can.

Albert Almora CF Born: 04/16/94 Age: 24 Bats: R Throws: R Height: 6'2" Weight: 190 Origin: Round 1, 2012 Draft (#6 overall)

YEAR	TEAM	LVL	AGE	PA	R	2B	3B	HR	RBI	BB	K	SB	CS	AVG/OBP/SLG	TAv	VORP	BABIP	BRR	FRAA	WARP
2015	TEN	AA	21	452	69	26	4	6	46	32	47	8	4	.272/.327/.400	.271	17.8	.291	1.2	CF(69): 3.2, LF(18): -0.3	2.3
2016	IOW	AAA	22	336	46	18	3	4	43	9	44	10	3	.303/.317/.416	.285	22.5	.336	3.8	CF(69): -0.5, LF(6): 1.5	2.4
2016	CHN	MLB	22	117	14	9	1	3	14	5	20	0	0	.277/.308/.455	.267	5.2	.315	0.9	CF(33): -0.1, LF(8): 1.7	0.7
2017	CHN	MLB	23	323	39	18	1	8	46	19	53	1	0	.298/.338/.445	.267	15.9	.338	3.2	CF(104): -1.0, RF(1): 0.0	1.5
2018	*CHN*	*MLB*	*24*	*475*	*54*	*26*	*2*	*12*	*55*	*23*	*75*	*4*	*1*	*.274/.311/.426*	*.252*	*16.8*	*.302*	*-0.3*	*CF 1*	*1.1*
2019	*CHN*	*MLB*	*25*	*453*	*55*	*26*	*2*	*14*	*57*	*26*	*73*	*4*	*1*	*.279/.323/.450*	*.270*	*20.5*	*.305*	*2.4*	*CF 2*	*2.4*

Breakout: 8% Improve: 45% Collapse: 5% Attrition: 14% MLB: 82% *Comparables: Odubel Herrera, Ender Inciarte, Billy Hamilton*

He'll always have Scoring The Game-Winning Run In A World Series Game 7, but look for Almora to expand beyond that trivia question into playing way more outfield, possibly in a true starting role. He gets the job done against the left-handers, and he's a fan favorite. But then again, aren't most fourth outfielders? His subjectively intense but empirically okay defense doesn't shout first-division center fielder, though development of more walks and/or extra bases could force the issue. He's young and going to be in outfields for several years, but figuring out his ceiling is the tricky part.

Alex Avila C Born: 01/29/87 Age: 31 Bats: L Throws: R Height: 5'11" Weight: 210 Origin: Round 5, 2008 Draft (#163 overall)

YEAR	TEAM	LVL	AGE	PA	R	2B	3B	HR	RBI	BB	K	SB	CS	AVG/OBP/SLG	TAv	VORP	BABIP	BRR	FRAA	WARP
2015	DET	MLB	28	219	21	5	0	4	13	40	66	0	1	.191/.339/.287	.235	-1.0	.278	-3.3	C(44): -9.8, 1B(23): -0.1	-1.2
2016	CHR	AAA	29	30	4	1	0	1	3	6	7	0	0	.333/.467/.500	.325	2.7	.438	-0.1	C(5): -0.1	0.3
2016	CHA	MLB	29	209	19	6	0	7	11	38	78	0	0	.213/.359/.373	.266	8.3	.341	-2.2	C(54): -7.9	0.0
2017	DET	MLB	30	264	30	11	0	11	32	43	80	0	1	.274/.394/.475	.288	16.2	.380	-1.5	C(50): -9.0, 1B(16): -0.9	0.6
2017	CHN	MLB	30	112	11	2	1	3	17	19	40	0	0	.239/.369/.380	.261	5.6	.388	0.5	C(28): -1.3, 1B(3): 0.2	0.4
2018	*CHN*	*MLB*	*31*	*324*	*38*	*11*	*0*	*10*	*36*	*50*	*105*	*0*	*1*	*.220/.345/.377*	*.246*	*8.4*	*.315*	*-1.8*	*C -14, 1B -1*	*-0.6*
2019	*CHN*	*MLB*	*32*	*308*	*40*	*10*	*0*	*9*	*34*	*46*	*104*	*0*	*0*	*.216/.338/.368*	*.254*	*7.0*	*.317*	*-1.7*	*C -13, 1B -1*	*-0.7*

Breakout: 4% Improve: 39% Collapse: 12% Attrition: 22% MLB: 95% *Comparables: Chris Snyder, Geovany Soto, Chris Iannetta*

Avila's All-Star season in 2011 will always stand out on his stats page as a miraculous aberration, but 2017 was a reasonable facsimile. His power to all fields has returned, and with no concussion concerns for miles, his brief reunion in Detroit impressed his dad so much that the Tigers' general manager traded him to a contender for an impressive return. Avila should by all accounts be a platoon catcher, as lefties bother him a whole bunch, and his durability will always be a yellow flag until he hangs up the catcher's mask and begins the front-office portion of his baseball career.

YEAR	TEAM	P. COUNT	FRM RUNS	BLK RUNS	THRW RUNS	TOT RUNS
2015	DET	5969	-7.7	-1.2	0.1	-8.8
2015	TOL	361	-0.1	0.0	0.0	-0.1
2016	CHA	7394	-6.5	0.0	-0.6	-7.1
2017	DET	6716	-9.2	0.6	0.2	-8.5
2017	CHN	3507	-1.5	-0.1	0.1	-1.6
2018	*CHN*	*9702*	*-11.8*	*-0.5*	*-0.2*	*-12.5*
2019	*CHN*	*9229*	*-11.8*	*-0.5*	*-0.2*	*-12.5*

Javier Baez INF Born: 12/01/92 Age: 25 Bats: R Throws: R Height: 6'0" Weight: 190 Origin: Round 1, 2011 Draft (#9 overall)

YEAR	TEAM	LVL	AGE	PA	R	2B	3B	HR	RBI	BB	K	SB	CS	AVG/OBP/SLG	TAv	VORP	BABIP	BRR	FRAA	WARP
2015	IOW	AAA	22	313	49	14	2	13	61	21	76	17	3	.324/.385/.527	.330	35.5	.402	1.7	SS(40): 2.2, 2B(19): 1.5	4.0
2015	CHN	MLB	22	80	4	6	0	1	4	4	24	1	2	.289/.325/.408	.268	2.0	.412	-1.1	2B(17): -0.5, 3B(11): 1.9	0.4
2016	CHN	MLB	23	450	50	19	1	14	59	15	108	12	3	.273/.314/.423	.275	20.2	.336	-0.7	3B(62): 1.1, 2B(59): 2.7	2.5
2017	CHN	MLB	24	508	75	24	2	23	75	30	144	10	3	.273/.317/.480	.274	30.0	.345	4.4	2B(80): -1.3, SS(73): -6.6	2.3
2018	*CHN*	*MLB*	*25*	*536*	*71*	*23*	*1*	*22*	*74*	*30*	*154*	*13*	*4*	*.255/.304/.443*	*.253*	*18.0*	*.322*	*0.7*	*2B 1, 3B 3*	*1.6*
2019	*CHN*	*MLB*	*26*	*514*	*68*	*24*	*1*	*23*	*73*	*30*	*147*	*12*	*4*	*.256/.309/.457*	*.265*	*19.8*	*.320*	*1.3*	*2B 1, 3B 3*	*2.5*

Breakout: 2% Improve: 55% Collapse: 9% Attrition: 16% MLB: 98% *Comparables: Jhonny Peralta, Wilson Betemit, Travis Fryman*

Baez is one of the most electric middle infielders in the game, with a plate discipline that routinely short circuits. He had 15 unintentional walks on the year, and his second one didn't come until June 6, in his 165th plate appearance of the season. The sudden power and outrageous defense compensates, of course. He split time between second base and shortstop out of necessity, which pretty much torpedoes one's chances of taking home any postseason hardware (even though the metrics were bullish on his value). It would have been fun to see Baez pull it off like he does any of his tags, picks, throws or relays. It would also be fun to dedicate 300 pages of this *Annual* to a Baez defensive highlights flip book.

Kris Bryant 3B Born: 01/04/92 Age: 26 Bats: R Throws: R Height: 6'5" Weight: 230 Origin: Round 1, 2013 Draft (#2 overall)

YEAR	TEAM	LVL	AGE	PA	R	2B	3B	HR	RBI	BB	K	SB	CS	AVG/OBP/SLG	TAv	VORP	BABIP	BRR	FRAA	WARP
2015	IOW	AAA	23	33	7	1	0	3	10	2	9	2	0	.321/.364/.679	.408	6.6	.333	0.5	3B(7): -1.0	0.6
2015	CHN	MLB	23	650	87	31	5	26	99	77	199	13	4	.275/.369/.488	.317	58.0	.378	2.3	3B(144): -3.3, LF(8): -0.4	5.9
2016	CHN	MLB	24	699	121	35	3	39	102	75	154	8	5	.292/.385/.554	.350	86.5	.332	3.4	3B(107): 1.5, LF(60): 1.1	9.1
2017	CHN	MLB	25	665	111	38	4	29	73	95	128	7	5	.295/.409/.537	.326	69.6	.334	1.9	3B(144): -3.9, RF(7): 0.2	6.6
2018	*CHN*	*MLB*	*26*	*628*	*105*	*31*	*3*	*30*	*91*	*76*	*147*	*8*	*4*	*.281/.381/.520*	*.305*	*50.8*	*.333*	*-0.7*	*3B -3, LF 0*	*4.1*
2019	*CHN*	*MLB*	*27*	*574*	*91*	*29*	*2*	*30*	*93*	*74*	*140*	*7*	*4*	*.282/.388/.537*	*.318*	*50.8*	*.335*	*2.0*	*3B -2, LF 0*	*5.3*

Breakout: 1% Improve: 57% Collapse: 0% Attrition: 5% MLB: 100% *Comparables: Evan Longoria, David Wright, Eddie Mathews*

Not since Jeff Dunham's entire routine did a hand bother someone so much. Bryant's hand sprain last summer wasn't bad enough to sideline him, but it does lay as the most likely reason for the home-run drop in a season of spikes. He might as well have been in a cast next to the swimming pool. But the young 2016 MVP is still the league's best third baseman and proved he can angst his way through an All-Star season that 95 percent of the league can't accomplish even with two strong titanium hands. The underlying skill is his discipline; his strikeouts went down for the third straight season. At this rate he'll be down to zero strikeouts on the season by the time he's 49, at which point he'll probably have another MVP award or two.

Victor Caratini C Born: 08/17/93 Age: 24 Bats: B Throws: R Height: 6'1" Weight: 215 Origin: Round 2, 2013 Draft (#65 overall)

YEAR	TEAM	LVL	AGE	PA	R	2B	3B	HR	RBI	BB	K	SB	CS	AVG/OBP/SLG	TAv	VORP	BABIP	BRR	FRAA	WARP
2015	MYR	A+	21	453	39	31	1	4	53	49	75	0	0	.257/.342/.372	.266	15.6	.303	-3.2	C(86): -0.6, 1B(12): -0.4	1.6
2016	TEN	AA	22	480	57	25	2	6	47	54	80	2	1	.291/.375/.405	.290	29.3	.341	-1.5	C(82): -9.1, 1B(30): -0.1	2.2
2017	IOW	AAA	23	326	50	27	3	10	61	27	48	1	0	.342/.393/.558	.319	34.0	.375	1.4	C(50): -4.3, 1B(30): 0.7	3.0
2017	CHN	MLB	23	66	6	3	0	1	2	4	13	0	0	.254/.333/.356	.241	0.5	.311	-0.4	C(12): -0.5, 1B(8): 0.1	0.0
2018	*CHN*	*MLB*	*24*	*189*	*22*	*10*	*1*	*5*	*22*	*17*	*39*	*0*	*0*	*.262/.334/.415*	*.256*	*8.3*	*.311*	*-0.4*	*C -8*	*-0.2*
2019	*CHN*	*MLB*	*25*	*383*	*49*	*21*	*1*	*12*	*47*	*36*	*84*	*0*	*0*	*.262/.338/.434*	*.270*	*18.1*	*.312*	*-0.9*	*C -11*	*0.7*

Breakout: 6% Improve: 20% Collapse: 18% Attrition: 29% MLB: 60% *Comparables: Jonathan Lucroy, John Jaso, Jeff Clement*

Sometimes playing extremely well at Triple-A doesn't mean you forge an easy path to the majors. Caratini, a former second-round pick of the Braves who tore up the PCL in 2017, has the misfortune of sitting behind Willson Contreras on the Cubs' catching depth chart. The good news for Caratini is that Alex Avila is a goner in free agency, so if the Cubs don't opt for a veteran backstop presence in 2018, he should get a chance to stick with the big-league club this season.

YEAR	TEAM	P. COUNT	FRM RUNS	BLK RUNS	THRW RUNS	TOT RUNS
2017	CHN	1182	-0.8	0.4	0.0	-0.3
2018	*CHN*	*6890*	*-6.5*	*0.4*	*-0.5*	*-6.6*
2019	*CHN*	*13978*	*-5.9*	*0.4*	*-0.4*	*-6.0*

Willson Contreras C Born: 05/13/92 Age: 26 Bats: R Throws: R Height: 6'1" Weight: 210 Origin: International Free Agent, 2009

YEAR	TEAM	LVL	AGE	PA	R	2B	3B	HR	RBI	BB	K	SB	CS	AVG/OBP/SLG	TAv	VORP	BABIP	BRR	FRAA	WARP
2015	TEN	AA	23	521	71	34	4	8	75	57	62	4	4	.333/.413/.478	.322	48.6	.370	-0.6	C(75): -6.6, 3B(8): -0.5	4.5
2016	IOW	AAA	24	240	40	16	3	9	43	28	32	4	4	.353/.442/.593	.378	38.1	.382	-0.9	C(45): -4.5	3.5
2016	CHN	MLB	24	283	33	14	1	12	35	26	67	2	2	.282/.357/.488	.302	21.5	.339	-0.9	C(57): 6.1, LF(24): -2.5	2.6
2017	CHN	MLB	25	428	50	21	0	21	74	45	98	5	4	.276/.356/.499	.302	34.2	.319	-3.9	C(108): -2.7, 1B(5): 0.0	3.1
2018	*CHN*	*MLB*	*26*	*523*	*71*	*27*	*2*	*21*	*76*	*51*	*105*	*5*	*4*	*.284/.362/.484*	*.290*	*39.7*	*.326*	*-1.2*	*C -7*	*2.8*
2019	*CHN*	*MLB*	*27*	*500*	*71*	*25*	*1*	*21*	*71*	*51*	*104*	*4*	*3*	*.277/.360/.483*	*.296*	*35.8*	*.318*	*-2.2*	*C -6*	*3.3*

Breakout: 4% Improve: 44% Collapse: 11% Attrition: 13% MLB: 95% *Comparables: Travis d'Arnaud, Buster Posey, Chris Shelton*

YEAR	TEAM	P. COUNT	FRM RUNS	BLK RUNS	THRW RUNS	TOT RUNS
2015	TEN	10381	-5.9	1.3	-0.8	-5.4
2016	CHN	6569	4.3	1.4	0.8	6.5
2017	CHN	14005	-6.3	0.5	-1.0	-6.8
2018	*CHN*	*18045*	*-8.7*	*1.2*	*-0.4*	*-7.9*
2019	*CHN*	*17237*	*-7.7*	*1.1*	*-0.3*	*-7.0*

Contreras might be the most exciting catcher the Cubs have seen in 20 years, becoming just the second to hit 20 or more homers in a season for the club since 1995. He's definitely the most balanced, swinging the stick more than well enough to widen the dangerous nougat center of a batting order, while using that throwing arm to keep baserunners uncomfortable at all bases, especially first (as Jose Lobaton learned in the NLDS Game 5, eventually, after review). He did lose a month to a dreaded hamstring injury, but assuming the muscle behaves this year he should be one of fantasy's and reality's most attractive backstops.

Mike Freeman SS Born: 08/04/87 Age: 30 Bats: L Throws: R Height: 6'0" Weight: 190 Origin: Round 11, 2010 Draft (#331 overall)

YEAR	TEAM	LVL	AGE	PA	R	2B	3B	HR	RBI	BB	K	SB	CS	AVG/OBP/SLG	TAv	VORP	BABIP	BRR	FRAA	WARP
2015	RNO	AAA	27	435	79	23	5	3	41	34	51	10	0	.317/.371/.422	.266	17.3	.357	3.7	RF(37): -3.1, 2B(29): 3.1	1.2
2016	RNO	AAA	28	384	56	17	6	1	24	38	75	11	1	.317/.387/.411	.283	23.2	.402	3.8	2B(71): 7.1, CF(11): -0.5	3.0
2016	ARI	MLB	28	11	0	0	0	0	0	2	5	0	0	.000/.182/.000	.081	-1.7	.000	0.0	RF(1): -0.1, LF(1): 0.0	-0.2
2016	TAC	AAA	28	119	15	6	0	3	15	13	19	1	0	.305/.378/.448	.298	8.1	.345	-0.1	2B(21): -0.5, SS(3): 0.0	0.9
2016	SEA	MLB	28	13	1	1	0	0	1	0	2	0	0	.385/.385/.462	.277	0.1	.455	-0.5	2B(5): 0.1, SS(2): 0.0	0.0
2017	SEA	MLB	29	34	3	0	0	1	1	4	9	0	0	.067/.176/.167	.137	-3.4	.050	0.2	2B(3): -0.2, 1B(3): 0.3	-0.3
2017	TAC	AAA	29	67	12	3	1	1	9	7	10	2	0	.350/.418/.483	.313	6.6	.408	0.7	2B(9): 0.5, 3B(6): -0.1	0.7
2017	LAN	MLB	29	5	0	0	0	0	0	0	2	0	0	.000/.000/.000	-.019	-1.3	.000	0.0	3B(1): 0.0	-0.1
2017	OKL	AAA	29	139	17	4	2	0	16	13	31	5	0	.306/.384/.372	.256	5.8	.407	1.5	3B(14): -0.1, SS(14): 1.7	0.6
2017	IOW	AAA	29	88	10	3	0	2	6	7	19	3	0	.273/.345/.390	.275	4.0	.333	-0.6	SS(11): -0.1, 3B(7): -1.3	0.2
2017	CHN	MLB	29	27	3	2	0	0	0	2	8	0	0	.160/.222/.240	.167	-1.7	.235	-0.1	SS(10): 0.0, 2B(3): 0.0	-0.2
2018	*CHN*	*MLB*	*30*	*250*	*30*	*10*	*2*	*5*	*23*	*23*	*56*	*4*	*0*	*.254/.328/.374*	*.234*	*3.7*	*.317*	*0.4*	*SS 3, 3B 0*	*0.8*
2019	*CHN*	*MLB*	*31*	*262*	*30*	*10*	*2*	*5*	*26*	*24*	*59*	*3*	*0*	*.249/.322/.368*	*.246*	*4.1*	*.311*	*0.2*	*SS 3, 3B 0*	*0.8*

Breakout: 2% Improve: 9% Collapse: 8% Attrition: 20% MLB: 32% *Comparables: Mike McCoy, Chase d'Arnaud, Brian Barden*

Freeman got his call-up in September thanks to Addison Russell's lingering foot injury and managed to stick around through the final weeks of the season because of 40-man roster expansion. If Ben Zobrist were boiled down to pure grit and a more close-cropped beard, that's Freeman. He wore six different uniforms in 2017, splitting time between the Dodgers, Mariners, Cubs and their respective Pacific Coast League affiliates, so he is something of a budget travel connoisseur. At age 30 he's hardly guaranteed an extended MLB opportunity as a utility man, but his career .377 on-base percentage in four seasons at Triple-A suggests he warrants one.

Ian Happ OF Born: 08/12/94 Age: 23 Bats: B Throws: R Height: 6'0" Weight: 205 Origin: Round 1, 2015 Draft (#9 overall)

YEAR	TEAM	LVL	AGE	PA	R	2B	3B	HR	RBI	BB	K	SB	CS	AVG/OBP/SLG	TAv	VORP	BABIP	BRR	FRAA	WARP
2015	EUG	A-	20	130	26	8	1	4	11	23	28	9	0	.283/.408/.491	.355	19.4	.347	2.7	CF(28): -5.1	1.5
2015	SBN	A	20	165	24	9	3	5	22	17	39	1	1	.241/.315/.448	.277	6.1	.288	-0.1	LF(14): 0.6, RF(12): -1.2	0.7
2016	MYR	A+	21	293	37	16	3	7	42	48	69	10	3	.296/.410/.475	.320	26.1	.381	0.2	2B(50): -3.1, LF(6): 0.0	2.4
2016	TEN	AA	21	274	35	14	0	8	31	20	60	6	2	.262/.318/.415	.271	9.8	.310	0.4	2B(42): -0.6, LF(7): 0.7	0.9
2017	IOW	AAA	22	116	21	6	0	9	25	11	27	2	1	.298/.362/.615	.342	13.8	.319	0.0	2B(16): 1.2, CF(6): 1.0	1.6
2017	CHN	MLB	22	413	62	17	3	24	68	39	129	8	4	.253/.328/.514	.284	25.2	.316	3.1	CF(54): 0.8, 2B(44): 0.1	2.1
2018	*CHN*	*MLB*	*23*	*449*	*62*	*19*	*2*	*21*	*66*	*42*	*129*	*7*	*3*	*.245/.319/.462*	*.264*	*21.2*	*.303*	*0.0*	*CF -2, 2B 0*	*1.3*
2019	*CHN*	*MLB*	*24*	*521*	*73*	*22*	*2*	*26*	*77*	*53*	*152*	*9*	*4*	*.245/.327/.469*	*.274*	*26.2*	*.303*	*2.6*	*CF -2, 2B 0*	*2.6*

Breakout: 4% Improve: 36% Collapse: 9% Attrition: 16% MLB: 75% *Comparables: Oswaldo Arcia, Javier Baez, Evan Longoria*

Joe Maddon has no doubt been searching for his next Ben Zobrist, since the one he has is way past his warranty. The toolsy Happ isn't a perfect facsimile (though he is a switch-hitter), but he has been shifted about the field (because shift Happ ins), from second base to left field to center field, and it wouldn't be a surprise if down the road he found his way to the infield corners. He won't win any fielding awards, but quantity over quality is a nice skill to have, especially when you can mash like he does, and it keeps him in the lineup by any means necessary.

Jason Heyward RF Born: 08/09/89 Age: 28 Bats: L Throws: L Height: 6'5" Weight: 240 Origin: Round 1, 2007 Draft (#14 overall)

YEAR	TEAM	LVL	AGE	PA	R	2B	3B	HR	RBI	BB	K	SB	CS	AVG/OBP/SLG	TAv	VORP	BABIP	BRR	FRAA	WARP
2015	SLN	MLB	25	610	79	33	4	13	60	56	90	23	3	.293/.359/.439	.294	37.0	.329	6.1	RF(144): 16.0, CF(10): 2.0	5.9
2016	CHN	MLB	26	592	61	27	1	7	49	54	93	11	4	.230/.306/.325	.237	-2.6	.266	-0.4	RF(131): -0.2, CF(24): 2.8	0.0
2017	CHN	MLB	27	481	59	15	4	11	59	41	67	4	4	.259/.326/.389	.254	8.6	.284	1.9	RF(120): 10.1, CF(13): 1.0	2.0
2018	*CHN*	*MLB*	*28*	*528*	*66*	*24*	*2*	*12*	*57*	*52*	*78*	*11*	*4*	*.263/.342/.402*	*.258*	*14.7*	*.292*	*0.3*	*RF 5*	*1.6*
2019	*CHN*	*MLB*	*29*	*470*	*59*	*21*	*1*	*13*	*54*	*47*	*74*	*8*	*3*	*.260/.339/.409*	*.267*	*14.9*	*.287*	*1.7*	*RF 6*	*2.2*

Breakout: 3% Improve: 59% Collapse: 7% Attrition: 16% MLB: 95% *Comparables: Ryan Sweeney, Gene Larkin, Matt Lawton*

Heyward's defensive numbers and perfectly vanilla batting lines suggest one of those outfielders who bounces from team to team, with fans huddling around the space heater every winter thinking their team should just sign Heyward. Of course, the conversation on him cannot be left without mentioning that megacontract—he's still owed another $134 million through 2023—which he absolutely earned. At his current production level (and with four straight Gold Glove awards under his belt) he'll get 500 at-bats per year as long as he shows up for work. Last year he rebounded from 2016 a little, but if Heyward can ever drive more balls upward and outward, his contract wouldn't look so wayward.

Jon Jay OF Born: 03/15/85 Age: 33 Bats: L Throws: L Height: 5'11" Weight: 195 Origin: Round 2, 2006 Draft (#74 overall)

YEAR	TEAM	LVL	AGE	PA	R	2B	3B	HR	RBI	BB	K	SB	CS	AVG/OBP/SLG	TAv	VORP	BABIP	BRR	FRAA	WARP
2015	SLN	MLB	30	245	25	5	1	1	10	19	36	0	2	.210/.306/.257	.214	-4.3	.246	-0.1	CF(54): 1.2, LF(17): -0.1	-0.4
2016	SDN	MLB	31	373	49	26	1	2	26	19	78	2	0	.291/.339/.389	.271	18.0	.371	3.1	CF(72): -1.9, RF(9): 0.1	1.7
2017	CHN	MLB	32	433	65	18	3	2	34	37	80	6	2	.296/.374/.375	.267	16.8	.368	2.4	LF(64): -3.6, CF(54): -4.8	0.7
2018	*CHN*	*MLB*	*33*	*396*	*46*	*17*	*1*	*5*	*34*	*31*	*74*	*4*	*2*	*.270/.346/.372*	*.243*	*8.9*	*.323*	*1.6*	*CF -1, LF -2*	*0.6*
2019	*CHN*	*MLB*	*34*	*398*	*46*	*16*	*1*	*5*	*37*	*32*	*76*	*3*	*1*	*.264/.342/.360*	*.254*	*9.6*	*.318*	*1.6*	*CF -1, LF -2*	*0.7*

Breakout: 3% Improve: 31% Collapse: 20% Attrition: 29% MLB: 87% *Comparables: Eddie Milner, Jacoby Ellsbury, Bill Tuttle*

They won't be building a Hall of Second-Division Starters Fame anytime soon, since brick-and-mortar is a big investment and only gadget stores really have the capital for it. But Jay would be a first-balloter. Yes, his colonial name helps one remember, but he's had a fine career, going into his ninth year, playing a capable center field and keeping his batting average at an impressive level during a time when everyone's swinging for the fences. He won't do much else for you, but playing center field is hard and not every team can share Austin Jackson at the same time.

Tommy La Stella INF Born: 01/31/89 Age: 29 Bats: L Throws: R Height: 5'11" Weight: 180 Origin: Round 8, 2011 Draft (#266 overall)

YEAR	TEAM	LVL	AGE	PA	R	2B	3B	HR	RBI	BB	K	SB	CS	AVG/OBP/SLG	TAv	VORP	BABIP	BRR	FRAA	WARP
2015	TEN	AA	26	41	9	3	0	0	3	3	1	0	0	.250/.325/.333	.261	0.4	.257	-0.7	2B(5): 0.4, 3B(4): 0.9	0.2
2015	IOW	AAA	26	38	3	2	1	1	6	4	3	0	0	.333/.395/.545	.313	2.2	.333	-0.7	2B(5): 0.1	0.2
2015	CHN	MLB	26	75	4	6	0	1	11	5	7	2	0	.269/.324/.403	.269	2.2	.283	-0.4	2B(14): 0.5, 3B(12): -0.7	0.2
2016	IOW	AAA	27	46	6	2	0	1	3	2	9	0	0	.273/.304/.386	.223	-0.2	.324	0.4	3B(6): 0.9, 2B(4): -0.6	0.0
2016	CHN	MLB	27	169	17	12	1	2	11	18	27	0	1	.270/.357/.405	.287	8.0	.319	-1.8	3B(33): -3.3, 2B(9): -0.9	0.4
2017	IOW	AAA	28	121	14	2	0	1	6	10	22	0	1	.218/.281/.264	.199	-3.8	.261	1.0	2B(22): 0.3, 3B(4): 0.0	-0.3
2017	CHN	MLB	28	151	18	8	0	5	22	20	18	0	0	.288/.389/.472	.310	11.6	.298	-0.7	2B(21): -2.4, 3B(18): -0.5	0.9
2018	*CHN*	*MLB*	*29*	*136*	*15*	*6*	*0*	*2*	*14*	*14*	*18*	*0*	*0*	*.259/.341/.377*	*.249*	*2.0*	*.286*	*-0.3*	*3B -2, 1B 0*	*0.0*
2019	*CHN*	*MLB*	*30*	*197*	*24*	*9*	*0*	*4*	*20*	*21*	*28*	*0*	*0*	*.258/.345/.386*	*.260*	*3.5*	*.285*	*-0.9*	*3B -3, 1B 0*	*0.1*

Breakout: 5% Improve: 36% Collapse: 15% Attrition: 23% MLB: 94% *Comparables: Luis Rodriguez, Eric Sogard, Johnny Giavotella*

Only Joey Votto had more plate appearances, a lower strikeout rate and a higher walk rate than La Stella last year, a fact that he will now mention at every soirée he attends for the rest of his life. La Stella and the Cubs haven't always seen eye-to-eye regarding his role (or his proximity to Iowa), but he's served as an excellent part-time asset, hitting .276/.363/.429 over three seasons and filling in when needed at second base and third base.

Rene Rivera C Born: 07/31/83 Age: 34 Bats: R Throws: R Height: 5'10" Weight: 215 Origin: Round 2, 2001 Draft (#49 overall)

YEAR	TEAM	LVL	AGE	PA	R	2B	3B	HR	RBI	BB	K	SB	CS	AVG/OBP/SLG	TAv	VORP	BABIP	BRR	FRAA	WARP
2015	TBA	MLB	31	319	16	14	0	5	26	11	86	0	0	.178/.213/.275	.176	-15.5	.230	-2.8	C(107): 5.1, 1B(7): -0.1	-1.1
2016	LVG	AAA	32	29	3	1	0	0	5	2	3	0	0	.280/.357/.320	.290	0.7	.318	-1.5	C(8): 0.3	0.1
2016	NYN	MLB	32	207	12	4	0	6	26	16	54	0	0	.222/.291/.341	.239	3.8	.276	-1.0	C(59): 10.5, 1B(1): 0.0	1.5
2017	NYN	MLB	33	187	15	4	0	8	23	9	54	0	1	.230/.278/.391	.232	1.1	.283	-2.1	C(52): 2.8, 1B(1): -0.2	0.4
2017	CHN	MLB	33	50	8	5	0	2	12	5	16	0	0	.341/.408/.591	.327	5.2	.500	-0.7	C(19): -3.2	0.2
2018	*CHN*	*MLB*	*34*	*250*	*26*	*11*	*0*	*7*	*28*	*17*	*62*	*0*	*0*	*.239/.297/.387*	*.221*	*1.4*	*.290*	*-1.5*	*C 3, 1B 0*	*0.5*
2019	*CHN*	*MLB*	*35*	*202*	*23*	*8*	*0*	*6*	*22*	*14*	*53*	*0*	*0*	*.227/.287/.372*	*.229*	*0.0*	*.278*	*-1.3*	*C 3, 1B 0*	*0.3*

Breakout: 7% Improve: 30% Collapse: 17% Attrition: 27% MLB: 81% *Comparables: Humberto Quintero, Chad Moeller, Vance Wilson*

YEAR	TEAM	P. COUNT	FRM RUNS	BLK RUNS	THRW RUNS	TOT RUNS
2015	TBA	12905	4.7	-0.5	1.3	5.5
2016	NYN	7602	7.8	-0.6	1.2	8.4
2017	NYN	7418	2.7	-0.9	0.4	2.2
2017	CHN	2027	-2.2	-1.4	0.5	-3.0
2018	*CHN*	*9907*	*2.8*	*-1.1*	*0.8*	*2.5*
2019	*CHN*	*8000*	*2.4*	*-1.0*	*0.7*	*2.2*

Proving anyone can look like Mike Piazza for a month, the most typecast backup defensive catcher in recent memory rode a 50-plate-appearance stint with the Cubs to an OPS of nearly 1.000. We know it's a small sample because his typical defensive numbers also looked Piazzan. The uplifting part of this story is that Rivera—who once had to wait five years between big-league stints, including time with a Puerto Rican semiprofessional team—has recorded only eight minor-league games in the past four seasons. It was an odd year, but he'll no doubt continue to ride the bench, throw out the occasional foolish baserunner and bat eighth if he's lucky.

Anthony Rizzo 1B Born: 08/08/89 Age: 28 Bats: L Throws: L Height: 6'3" Weight: 240 Origin: Round 6, 2007 Draft (#204 overall)

YEAR	TEAM	LVL	AGE	PA	R	2B	3B	HR	RBI	BB	K	SB	CS	AVG/OBP/SLG	TAv	VORP	BABIP	BRR	FRAA	WARP
2015	CHN	MLB	25	701	94	38	3	31	101	78	105	17	6	.278/.387/.512	.328	48.4	.289	-5.1	1B(160): 1.4	5.3
2016	CHN	MLB	26	676	94	43	4	32	109	74	108	3	5	.292/.385/.544	.334	56.5	.309	-1.2	1B(154): 11.4, 2B(1): -0.2	7.0
2017	CHN	MLB	27	691	99	32	3	32	109	91	90	10	4	.273/.392/.507	.304	36.3	.273	-3.2	1B(157): 14.4, 2B(10): -0.3	5.1
2018	*CHN*	*MLB*	*28*	*655*	*97*	*34*	*2*	*30*	*100*	*77*	*104*	*8*	*4*	*.273/.376/.503*	*.295*	*32.9*	*.286*	*-0.9*	*1B 6*	*3.8*
2019	*CHN*	*MLB*	*29*	*566*	*89*	*30*	*1*	*28*	*89*	*73*	*92*	*6*	*3*	*.276/.388/.523*	*.312*	*35.3*	*.287*	*-2.2*	*1B 6*	*4.4*

Breakout: 0% Improve: 46% Collapse: 3% Attrition: 4% MLB: 98% *Comparables: Billy Butler, Todd Helton, Nick Johnson*

Of all the things the league is, it's not a place where first basemen are en vogue, so Rizzo's accomplishments remain somewhat overlooked, despite consistent numbers that match most everyone at his station. He's one half of the most marketable corner-infield tandem in recent memory. He crowds the plate. He clears the bases. He even keeps runners at first base and makes the infield defense better. For a player this consistent, there are just no concerns in his late-twenties. Just set it and forget it. In the six seasons since the Cubs acquired Rizzo from the Padres for Andrew Cashner and Kyung-Min Na (move over, Brock-for-Broglio), he ranks 10th in Runs Created among all MLB hitters, and only Mike Trout, Paul Goldschmidt, Miguel Cabrera and Andrew McCutchen have more plate appearances and a higher on-base percentage.

Addison Russell SS Born: 01/23/94 Age: 24 Bats: R Throws: R Height: 6'0" Weight: 200 Origin: Round 1, 2012 Draft (#11 overall)

YEAR	TEAM	LVL	AGE	PA	R	2B	3B	HR	RBI	BB	K	SB	CS	AVG/OBP/SLG	TAv	VORP	BABIP	BRR	FRAA	WARP
2015	IOW	AAA	21	46	7	4	0	1	9	1	7	1	0	.318/.326/.477	.298	2.7	.351	-0.8	SS(6): -1.0, 2B(5): 0.3	0.2
2015	CHN	MLB	21	523	60	29	1	13	54	42	149	4	3	.242/.307/.389	.252	10.3	.324	-1.7	2B(86): 7.0, SS(61): -2.6	1.6
2016	CHN	MLB	22	598	67	25	3	21	95	55	135	5	1	.238/.321/.417	.275	33.6	.277	-0.2	SS(148): 3.6	3.8
2017	CHN	MLB	23	385	52	21	3	12	43	29	91	2	1	.239/.304/.418	.254	13.7	.289	-0.3	SS(101): 3.4	1.7
2018	*CHN*	*MLB*	*24*	*589*	*70*	*30*	*2*	*20*	*76*	*49*	*141*	*4*	*2*	*.246/.318/.422*	*.252*	*20.9*	*.299*	*-0.6*	*SS 4*	*1.9*
2019	*CHN*	*MLB*	*25*	*509*	*66*	*26*	*1*	*19*	*66*	*47*	*125*	*4*	*2*	*.246/.324/.434*	*.264*	*18.6*	*.298*	*-0.6*	*SS 4*	*2.5*

Breakout: 4% Improve: 55% Collapse: 1% Attrition: 9% MLB: 98% *Comparables: Ernie Banks, Dale Sveum, Denis Menke*

The extra month of highly tense, cold, micromanaged baseball took its toll on a number of Cubs, Russell among the thick of the group. He took a slightly more aggressive approach, which effected nothing but a smaller walk rate. On the bright side, his premium defense will be with him for some time. And while he's a ways from being one of the greatest offensive shortstops, he showed he was up for the moment when he laced a go-ahead double off Max Scherzer in Game 5 of the NLDS. If he ever can reach base a little more, he could be Jimmy Rollins. Right now he's angling for the new J.J. Hardy role—the worthwhile starter you keep forgetting still plays.

Kyle Schwarber LF Born: 03/05/93 Age: 25 Bats: L Throws: R Height: 6'0" Weight: 235 Origin: Round 1, 2014 Draft (#4 overall)

YEAR	TEAM	LVL	AGE	PA	R	2B	3B	HR	RBI	BB	K	SB	CS	AVG/OBP/SLG	TAv	VORP	BABIP	BRR	FRAA	WARP
2015	TEN	AA	22	243	39	10	1	13	39	42	49	1	0	.320/.438/.579	.371	35.5	.365	0.3	C(37): 3.7	4.2
2015	IOW	AAA	22	67	7	7	1	3	10	7	23	0	0	.333/.403/.633	.385	11.5	.500	0.1	C(15): 0.1	1.2
2015	CHN	MLB	22	273	52	6	1	16	43	36	77	3	3	.246/.355/.487	.307	23.0	.293	3.4	LF(41): -3.1, C(21): -1.6	1.9
2016	CHN	MLB	23	5	0	0	0	0	0	1	2	0	0	.000/.200/.000	.099	-0.7	.000	0.0	LF(2): 0.0	-0.1
2017	IOW	AAA	24	44	9	1	0	4	9	8	12	0	0	.343/.477/.714	.385	6.9	.421	-0.1	LF(9): -1.5	0.5
2017	CHN	MLB	24	486	67	16	1	30	59	59	150	1	1	.211/.315/.467	.266	14.1	.244	0.6	LF(110): 2.8, C(4): 0.0	1.7
2018	*CHN*	*MLB*	*25*	*569*	*94*	*20*	*2*	*33*	*87*	*72*	*163*	*3*	*2*	*.244/.346/.494*	*.283*	*34.5*	*.292*	*-0.9*	*LF -8*	*1.9*
2019	*CHN*	*MLB*	*26*	*501*	*79*	*18*	*1*	*30*	*82*	*67*	*144*	*2*	*1*	*.245/.353/.506*	*.295*	*32.8*	*.292*	*2.1*	*LF -6*	*2.9*

Breakout: 1% Improve: 58% Collapse: 5% Attrition: 6% MLB: 99% *Comparables: Joc Pederson, Jorge Soler, Ryan Klesko*

YEAR	TEAM	P. COUNT	FRM RUNS	BLK RUNS	THRW RUNS	TOT RUNS
2015	CHN	2400	-0.8	-0.2	-0.2	-1.3
2015	IOW	1863	0.7	-0.1	0.0	0.5
2015	TEN	4884	5.5	-1.1	-1.2	3.2

In the batter's box, Schwarber has the presence and power of an RPG miniboss. In left field, he has the grace and polish of a DOS text adventure. Pitchers cast mute on him for much of last year, forcing the Cubs' hand into demoting him to Triple-A in late June with a .168 batting average. Schwarber returned two weeks later and hit .255/.338/.565 with 18 homers in 65 games down the stretch. He reached 30 homers on the season for the first time at age 24, but the man without a position is just going to be in the lineup to bash and possibly write letters begging the commissioner's office to institute the designated hitter in both leagues. Chasing around a fast-moving white sphere near a hidden brick wall can be hazardous to one's health.

Chesny Young UT Born: 10/06/92 Age: 25 Bats: R Throws: R Height: 6'0" Weight: 170 Origin: Round 14, 2014 Draft (#409 overall)

YEAR	TEAM	LVL	AGE	PA	R	2B	3B	HR	RBI	BB	K	SB	CS	AVG/OBP/SLG	TAv	VORP	BABIP	BRR	FRAA	WARP
2015	SBN	A	22	122	23	5	1	0	14	12	7	9	3	.315/.385/.380	.275	7.9	.333	2.7	2B(26): 0.9, SS(4): -0.8	0.9
2015	MYR	A+	22	452	65	18	3	1	30	45	44	12	5	.321/.394/.388	.301	31.2	.358	2.6	3B(23): 0.6, 2B(21): -1.4	3.1
2016	TEN	AA	23	553	60	25	2	4	37	57	64	16	14	.303/.376/.387	.282	24.2	.340	-2.9	2B(58): -0.3, 3B(35): -1.8	2.3
2017	IOW	AAA	24	475	56	20	0	1	33	33	70	7	6	.256/.311/.311	.232	-2.7	.299	-2.6	2B(52): -4.9, SS(30): 0.0	-0.6
2018	*CHN*	*MLB*	*25*	*250*	*30*	*11*	*1*	*5*	*23*	*22*	*43*	*4*	*3*	*.265/.333/.381*	*.239*	*3.8*	*.306*	*-0.6*	*2B -1, SS 0*	*0.3*
2019	*CHN*	*MLB*	*26*	*307*	*36*	*12*	*1*	*6*	*31*	*26*	*52*	*4*	*3*	*.262/.329/.379*	*.254*	*6.4*	*.300*	*-0.5*	*2B -1, SS 0*	*0.5*

Breakout: 3% Improve: 6% Collapse: 23% Attrition: 33% MLB: 42% *Comparables: Tony Renda, Jake Elmore, Cole Figueroa*

Young had better have Jeimer Candelario on speed dial, because he could tell him a few things about being blocked on the Cubs' depth chart by top-tier talent. Even with a respectable season at Triple-A Iowa last year, the second baseman is blocked by Addison Russell and #ElMago, so Young has a good chance to be a PCL All-Star for several more years unless, as the Tigers did with Candelario, another team comes to his rescue.

Ben Zobrist UT Born: 05/26/81 Age: 37 Bats: B Throws: R Height: 6'3" Weight: 210 Origin: Round 6, 2004 Draft (#184 overall)

YEAR	TEAM	LVL	AGE	PA	R	2B	3B	HR	RBI	BB	K	SB	CS	AVG/OBP/SLG	TAv	VORP	BABIP	BRR	FRAA	WARP
2015	OAK	MLB	34	271	39	20	2	6	33	33	26	1	1	.268/.354/.447	.298	15.9	.277	-0.2	2B(34): -0.1, LF(27): -0.9	1.6
2015	KCA	MLB	34	264	37	16	1	7	23	29	30	2	3	.284/.364/.453	.293	16.0	.299	1.2	2B(35): -2.2, LF(18): -1.4	1.3
2016	CHN	MLB	35	631	94	31	3	18	76	96	82	6	4	.272/.386/.446	.306	49.2	.290	3.9	2B(119): -7.2, LF(27): -1.6	4.0
2017	CHN	MLB	36	496	58	20	3	12	50	54	71	2	2	.232/.318/.375	.249	5.2	.251	-1.3	2B(81): -2.0, LF(36): -0.2	0.2
2018	*CHN*	*MLB*	*37*	*448*	*58*	*22*	*2*	*9*	*44*	*52*	*60*	*4*	*2*	*.260/.348/.398*	*.259*	*16.6*	*.284*	*-0.9*	*2B -3, RF -1*	*0.8*
2019	*CHN*	*MLB*	*38*	*355*	*44*	*18*	*1*	*8*	*39*	*42*	*52*	*2*	*1*	*.252/.345/.398*	*.265*	*12.4*	*.277*	*0.8*	*2B -2, RF 0*	*1.0*

Breakout: 0% Improve: 34% Collapse: 13% Attrition: 13% MLB: 82% *Comparables: Marco Scutaro, Chase Utley, Mark Loretta*

It's funny how ages and wages never arise in a player discussion when he's so consistent and versatile, and helps three different teams break World Series droughts. Then suddenly a year like 2017 rolls around and holy hamburgers how is Zobrist already 37 years old? And he's making *how* much this year? Joe Maddon's favorite Swiss Army knife had his worst offensive season since 2007, back when he wasn't *Ben Zobrist* but instead another Quad-A shortstop in the Devil Rays' organization. His wrist bothered him, and according to many scientists, you need good wrists to swing the bat. If nagging injuries aren't the reason for his offensive decline, Zobrist is quickly going to become the world's most expensive Willie Bloomquist impersonator.

PITCHERS

Jose Albertos RHP Born: 11/07/98 Age: 19 Bats: R Throws: R Height: 6'1" Weight: 185 Origin: International Free Agent, 2015

YEAR	TEAM	LVL	AGE	W	L	SV	G	GS	IP	H	HR	BB/9	K/9	K	GB%	BABIP	WHIP	ERA	DRA	WARP	MPH	CMD	PWR	STM
2017	EUG	A-	18	2	1	0	8	8	34^{2}	24	0	3.6	10.9	42	58%	.264	1.10	2.86	2.22	1.2				
2018	*CHN*	*MLB*	*19*	*2*	*2*	*0*	*8*	*8*	34^{1}	*33*	*7*	*5.3*	*10.2*	*39*	*42%*	*.317*	*1.56*	*5.44*	*6.03*	*-0.2*				
2019	*CHN*	*MLB*	*20*	*6*	*11*	*0*	*28*	*28*	173^{1}	*165*	*32*	*4.8*	*9.0*	*174*	*42%*	*.311*	*1.49*	*5.51*	*6.12*	*-0.7*				

Comparables: Keury Mella, Tyler Glasnow, Domingo German

Albertos is arguably one of the two best arms in the Cubs' system, but until he pitches a full season as a professional and isn't, you know, 18 years old, it's wise to temper expectations for now. If he does pan out, Albertos sports a plus fastball and two potentially plus off-speed pitches in his curveball and changeup, so the makeup is there for a legitimate starter. Just be prepared to wait until after the next presidential election.

Adbert Alzolay RHP Born: 03/01/95 Age: 23 Bats: R Throws: R Height: 6'0" Weight: 179 Origin: International Free Agent, 2012

YEAR	TEAM	LVL	AGE	W	L	SV	G	GS	IP	H	HR	BB/9	K/9	K	GB%	BABIP	WHIP	ERA	DRA	WARP	MPH	CMD	PWR	STM
2015	EUG	A-	20	6	2	0	12	3	53	29	5	2.5	8.3	49	38%	.183	0.83	2.04	3.61	0.8				
2016	SBN	A	21	9	4	0	22	20	120^{1}	119	9	2.1	6.1	81	44%	.292	1.22	4.34	5.34	-0.5				
2017	MYR	A+	22	7	1	0	15	15	81^{2}	65	8	2.4	8.6	78	39%	.263	1.07	2.98	3.82	1.4				
2017	TEN	AA	22	0	3	0	7	7	32^{2}	27	0	3.3	8.3	30	36%	.297	1.19	3.03	4.38	0.3				
2018	*CHN*	*MLB*	*23*	*6*	*5*	*1*	*35*	*15*	95^{2}	*94*	*19*	*3.6*	*9.1*	*97*	*36%*	*.303*	*1.37*	*5.01*	*5.53*	*-0.2*				
2019	*CHN*	*MLB*	*24*	*4*	*6*	*0*	*21*	*15*	111^{2}	*108*	*23*	*3.7*	*9.1*	*113*	*36%*	*.308*	*1.38*	*5.42*	*6.00*	*-0.5*				

Breakout: 5% Improve: 7% Collapse: 10% Attrition: 17% MLB: 22% *Comparables: Ricardo Pinto, Jonathan Holder, John Gast*

Along with Jose Albertos, Alzolay makes up the cream of the crop of arms in the Cubs' system. He made it to Double-A in 2017, but the Cubs are still treating him with kid gloves, often spacing out his starts by six days at a time, limiting him to 80 pitches per start in the second half of the season and shutting him down altogether late in the year.

Jake Arrieta RHP Born: 03/06/86 Age: 32 Bats: R Throws: R Height: 6'4" Weight: 225 Origin: Round 5, 2007 Draft (#159 overall)

YEAR	TEAM	LVL	AGE	W	L	SV	G	GS	IP	H	HR	BB/9	K/9	K	GB%	BABIP	WHIP	ERA	DRA	WARP	MPH	CMD	PWR	STM
2015	CHN	MLB	29	22	6	0	33	33	229	150	10	1.9	9.3	236	58%	.246	0.86	1.77	2.07	8.2	97.0	39	56	82
2016	CHN	MLB	30	18	8	0	31	31	197^{1}	138	16	3.5	8.7	190	54%	.241	1.08	3.10	3.29	4.7	96.3	34	60	79
2017	CHN	MLB	31	14	10	0	30	30	168^{1}	150	23	2.9	8.7	163	46%	.279	1.22	3.53	4.24	2.5	93.8	35	51	72
2018	*CHN*	*MLB*	*32*	*10*	*7*	*0*	*24*	*24*	*147*	*118*	*19*	*3.1*	*9.4*	*154*	*50%*	*.278*	*1.15*	*3.91*	*4.28*	*2.2*	*94.6*	*35*	*55*	*76*
2019	*CHN*	*MLB*	*33*	*11*	*10*	*0*	*29*	*29*	*180*	*145*	*23*	*3.1*	*9.3*	*185*	*50%*	*.286*	*1.15*	*4.05*	*4.44*	*2.4*	*93.8*	*34*	*54*	*75*

Breakout: 11% Improve: 30% Collapse: 34% Attrition: 11% MLB: 90% *Comparables: Roy Halladay, Zack Greinke, Ryan Dempster*

Arrieta has taken a big step backward in each of the last two seasons, regressing into a curious middle-of-the-rotation starter relying on well-located sinkers instead of crafty cutters and sweeping sliders. With the entire coterie of pitching metrics trending in the wrong direction for him, it was a suboptimal time to have a walk year, but former Cy Young winners will always have a (highly paid) home in a rotation. It speaks to how awesome Arrieta was in 2015 that he could see his strikeout, walk, home-run and ground-ball rates all slip dramatically in back-to-back seasons and still come out the other side as a perfectly solid, three-WARP pitcher. There isn't much room left for similar slides in 2018 and 2019, though, which is what makes him such a risky long-term investment.

Eddie Butler RHP Born: 03/13/91 Age: 27 Bats: R Throws: R Height: 6'2" Weight: 180 Origin: Round 1, 2012 Draft (#46 overall)

YEAR	TEAM	LVL	AGE	W	L	SV	G	GS	IP	H	HR	BB/9	K/9	K	GB%	BABIP	WHIP	ERA	DRA	WARP	MPH	CMD	PWR	STM
2015	COL	MLB	24	3	10	0	16	16	79^{1}	102	13	4.8	5.0	44	51%	.333	1.82	5.90	6.69	-1.5	96.2	42	60	66
2015	ABQ	AAA	24	2	6	0	11	11	63^{1}	71	6	3.6	5.3	37	54%	.314	1.52	5.40	4.52	0.6				
2016	ABQ	AAA	25	8	3	0	15	15	89	93	9	2.6	3.5	35	50%	.271	1.34	4.45	7.72	-2.4				
2016	COL	MLB	25	2	5	0	17	9	64	87	13	3.0	6.6	47	48%	.354	1.69	7.17	6.56	-1.0	96.2	44	55	65
2017	CHN	MLB	26	4	3	0	13	11	54^{2}	50	4	4.6	4.9	30	45%	.266	1.43	3.95	7.41	-1.1	95.4	42	58	55
2017	IOW	AAA	26	2	0	0	8	8	45^{2}	49	1	2.4	5.9	30	45%	.329	1.34	2.17	5.80	0.0				
2018	*CHN*	*MLB*	*27*	*5*	*5*	*0*	*45*	*8*	*81*	*85*	*11*	*3.8*	*6.3*	*57*	*47%*	*.292*	*1.47*	*5.08*	*5.04*	*0.0*	*95.4*	*43*	*58*	*62*
2019	*CHN*	*MLB*	*28*	*6*	*5*	*0*	*63*	*10*	*117*	*114*	*15*	*3.6*	*6.6*	*86*	*47%*	*.3*	*1.37*	*4.87*	*5.39*	*0.0*	*95.0*	*43*	*57*	*61*

Breakout: 19% Improve: 39% Collapse: 12% Attrition: 23% MLB: 66% *Comparables: Shawn Hill, Nick Tepesch, Casey Coleman*

Butler was benevolently rescued from the parameters of Denver after serving up tray after delicious tray of hors d'oeuvres and poor curves. He briefly held a Cubs rotation spot after the customary Triple-A hot month in April. But the ability to make the batter walk back to the dugout in disgust still isn't there, nor is the confidence to throw strikes at the major-league level, and he finished the year in Iowa (before truly finishing the year on the disabled list). It may be high time for the former first-round pick to move to the bullpen and see if that helps his very hittable fastball dodge more maple.

Tyler Chatwood RHP Born: 12/16/89 Age: 28 Bats: R Throws: R Height: 6'0" Weight: 185 Origin: Round 2, 2008 Draft (#74 overall)

YEAR	TEAM	LVL	AGE	W	L	SV	G	GS	IP	H	HR	BB/9	K/9	K	GB%	BABIP	WHIP	ERA	DRA	WARP	MPH	CMD	PWR	STM
2016	COL	MLB	26	12	9	0	27	27	158	147	15	4.0	6.7	117	58%	.286	1.37	3.87	4.67	1.3	94.8	52	59	69
2017	COL	MLB	27	8	15	1	33	25	147^{2}	136	20	4.7	7.3	120	59%	.283	1.44	4.69	4.77	1.3	96.4	43	63	66
2018	*CHN*	*MLB*	*28*	*9*	*7*	*0*	*24*	*24*	*136*	*126*	*15*	*4.1*	*7.8*	*119*	*53%*	*.288*	*1.36*	*4.28*	*4.41*	*1.2*	*95.1*	*47*	*62*	*68*
2019	*CHN*	*MLB*	*29*	*10*	*11*	*0*	*32*	*32*	204^{2}	*174*	*21*	*3.8*	*7.6*	*174*	*53%*	*.288*	*1.27*	*4.37*	*4.82*	*1.6*	*94.8*	*47*	*61*	*67*

Breakout: 13% Improve: 38% Collapse: 32% Attrition: 9% MLB: 94% *Comparables: Jhoulys Chacin, Barry Zito, Carlos Zambrano*

Harken back, if you will, to a time before the Rockies had starting pitching options; let's say, oh, I don't know, 1993-2016. Way back then, a guy like Chatwood represented Plan A for the Rox. Sure, he has two Tommy Johns on his résumé, and sure, his career Coors ERA is nearly two full runs higher than his respectable road ERA of 3.31. But uninspired competence was once as good as it got on the mound in Colorado, and in some ways, Chatwood was its poster boy. We saw more of the same from him in 2017: bad at home, solid-to-good on the road and sometimes injured. That would've been good enough for the first 25 years of Rockies baseball, but thanks to the emergence of some young starters, Colorado didn't have to bid for Chatwood's services in free agency. The Cubs gave him a three-year, $38 million deal in December. Like most pitchers, he'll be far better off away from Coors.

Steve Cishek RHP Born: 06/18/86 Age: 31 Bats: R Throws: R Height: 6'6" Weight: 215 Origin: Round 5, 2007 Draft (#166 overall)

YEAR	TEAM	LVL	AGE	W	L	SV	G	GS	IP	H	HR	BB/9	K/9	K	GB%	BABIP	WHIP	ERA	DRA	WARP	MPH	CMD	PWR	STM
2015	MIA	MLB	29	2	6	3	32	0	32	37	2	3.9	7.9	28	49%	.350	1.59	4.50	4.30	0.2	93.1	59	38	48
2015	SLN	MLB	29	0	0	1	27	0	23^1	18	2	5.0	7.7	20	43%	.254	1.33	2.31	4.45	0.1	93.2	59	38	48
2016	SEA	MLB	30	4	6	25	62	0	64	44	8	3.0	10.7	76	45%	.242	1.02	2.81	2.67	1.7	93.9	62	34	48
2017	SEA	MLB	31	1	1	1	23	0	20	13	3	3.2	6.8	15	61%	.185	1.00	3.15	2.60	0.6	92.1	57	28	44
2017	TBA	MLB	31	2	1	0	26	0	24^2	13	0	2.6	9.5	26	52%	.220	0.81	1.09	2.24	0.8	92.4	57	28	44
2018	*CHN*	*MLB*	*32*	*2*	*2*	*0*	*42*	*0*	*44*	*42*	*6*	*4.2*	*8.6*	*42*	*47%*	*.295*	*1.43*	*4.57*	*4.57*	*0.2*	*92.2*	*59*	*33*	*46*
2019	*CHN*	*MLB*	*33*	*2*	*1*	*0*	*45*	*0*	*47^2*	*43*	*6*	*4.3*	*8.4*	*45*	*47%*	*.3*	*1.38*	*4.75*	*5.27*	*0.0*	*91.8*	*59*	*31*	*45*

Breakout: 18% Improve: 37% Collapse: 21% Attrition: 8% MLB: 90% *Comparables: Francisco Cordero, Jason Frasor, Scot Shields*

After a report during the World Series that pitchers for both the Dodgers and the Astros found the specially made balls to be slicker than their regular-season forebears, Cishek tweeted that it "must feel like throwing a wet bar of soap considering they felt like cue balls" in the regular season. Indeed, the pitchers who went on the record with that opinion in October cited an inability to throw their slider as effectively, and Cishek (whose slider usage in the second half of 2016 had been north of 60 percent) did use his slider less in 2017. He didn't suffer any ill effects from the change, though. In fact, his career-best ground-ball rate suggests that hitters felt like they were hitting cue balls, too. While platoon-sensitive, Cishek is a very valuable middle reliever.

Oscar De La Cruz RHP Born: 03/04/95 Age: 23 Bats: R Throws: R Height: 6'4" Weight: 200 Origin: International Free Agent, 2012

YEAR	TEAM	LVL	AGE	W	L	SV	G	GS	IP	H	HR	BB/9	K/9	K	GB%	BABIP	WHIP	ERA	DRA	WARP	MPH	CMD	PWR	STM
2015	EUG	A-	20	6	3	0	13	13	73	56	4	2.1	9.0	73	41%	.271	1.00	2.84	2.52	2.3				
2016	SBN	A	21	1	2	0	6	6	27^2	22	0	2.6	11.4	35	43%	.328	1.08	3.25	2.07	1.0				
2017	MYR	A+	22	4	3	0	12	12	54^2	55	6	2.1	7.7	47	42%	.308	1.24	3.46	5.13	0.1				
2018	*CHN*	*MLB*	*23*	*3*	*3*	*0*	*9*	*9*	*45^1*	*46*	*9*	*3.7*	*9.3*	*47*	*37%*	*.314*	*1.42*	*5.15*	*5.69*	*0.0*				
2019	*CHN*	*MLB*	*24*	*7*	*12*	*0*	*29*	*29*	*180^2*	*178*	*37*	*3.7*	*9.1*	*182*	*37%*	*.315*	*1.39*	*5.44*	*6.03*	*-0.7*				

Breakout: 5% Improve: 5% Collapse: 2% Attrition: 9% MLB: 9% *Comparables: Braden Shipley, James Houser, Michael Stutes*

There's every reason to believe De La Cruz could rival Jose Albertos and Adbert Alzolay as one of the most electric arms the Cubs have waiting in the wings, but his injury concerns are standing in the way. De La Cruz pitched well in April and May before being shut down until August, when he made a two-inning rehab appearance. De La Cruz was scheduled to pitch in the Arizona Fall League but then was scratched. It will be hard to remain bullish on De La Cruz unless he can pitch a full season.

Brian Duensing LHP Born: 02/22/83 Age: 35 Bats: L Throws: L Height: 6'0" Weight: 200 Origin: Round 3, 2005 Draft (#84 overall)

YEAR	TEAM	LVL	AGE	W	L	SV	G	GS	IP	H	HR	BB/9	K/9	K	GB%	BABIP	WHIP	ERA	DRA	WARP	MPH	CMD	PWR	STM
2015	MIN	MLB	32	4	1	1	55	0	48^2	46	5	3.9	4.4	24	53%	.265	1.38	4.25	4.90	-0.1	93.9	47	39	41
2016	OMA	AAA	33	1	0	2	12	0	20^1	16	0	2.2	8.4	19	50%	.276	1.03	3.10	3.78	0.3				
2016	BAL	MLB	33	1	0	0	14	0	13^1	13	2	2.0	6.8	10	26%	.275	1.20	4.05	6.59	-0.2	94.4	37	42	26
2017	CHN	MLB	34	1	1	0	68	0	62^1	58	6	2.6	8.8	61	49%	.306	1.22	2.74	4.08	0.8	93.6	53	35	51
2018	*CHN*	*MLB*	*35*	*2*	*1*	*1*	*48*	*0*	*50^1*	*49*	*7*	*3.7*	*7.9*	*44*	*47%*	*.304*	*1.38*	*4.44*	*4.89*	*0.2*	*92.6*	*49*	*36*	*39*
2019	*CHN*	*MLB*	*36*	*2*	*1*	*0*	*32*	*0*	*31^1*	*30*	*4*	*3.7*	*7.7*	*27*	*47%*	*.308*	*1.37*	*4.70*	*5.18*	*0.0*	*91.9*	*49*	*35*	*39*

Breakout: 24% Improve: 43% Collapse: 18% Attrition: 11% MLB: 72% *Comparables: Javier Lopez, Matt Lindstrom, Blaine Boyer*

Duensing's first successful year as a reliever was the direct result of trusting his changeup. He always had a fine one dating back to his years as a Twins rotation participant—he somehow made multiple playoff starts for Minnesota—but finally began throwing it to righties *and* lefties, wiping out his platoon splits and becoming a popular selection for Joe Maddon in the postseason. He'll still come in just to face the occasional ornery lefty because managers love strolling to dirt hills to interrupt the passage of time, but he's good for anywhere between one and six outs.

Carl Edwards Jr. RHP Born: 09/03/91 Age: 26 Bats: R Throws: R Height: 6'3" Weight: 170 Origin: Round 48, 2011 Draft (#1464 overall)

YEAR	TEAM	LVL	AGE	W	L	SV	G	GS	IP	H	HR	BB/9	K/9	K	GB%	BABIP	WHIP	ERA	DRA	WARP	MPH	CMD	PWR	STM
2015	TEN	AA	23	2	2	4	13	0	23^2	11	1	6.5	13.7	36	67%	.222	1.18	2.66	2.31	0.7				
2015	IOW	AAA	23	3	1	2	23	0	31^2	15	0	6.8	11.1	39	44%	.221	1.23	2.84	2.92	0.7				
2015	CHN	MLB	23	0	0	0	5	0	4^2	3	0	5.8	7.7	4	58%	.250	1.29	3.86	3.14	0.1	96.0			40
2016	IOW	AAA	24	1	1	1	24	0	25^1	17	1	6.0	12.4	35	40%	.286	1.34	4.26	3.61	0.4				
2016	CHN	MLB	24	0	1	2	36	0	36	15	4	3.5	13.0	52	51%	.162	0.81	3.75	2.46	1.0	97.6	48	59	46
2017	CHN	MLB	25	5	4	0	73	0	66^1	29	6	5.2	12.8	94	46%	.193	1.01	2.98	2.70	1.8	96.8	38	62	52
2018	*CHN*	*MLB*	*26*	*3*	*2*	*5*	*51*	*0*	*53*	*38*	*6*	*5.1*	*12.3*	*74*	*46%*	*.278*	*1.26*	*3.60*	*3.81*	*0.7*	*96.6*	*42*	*62*	*48*
2019	*CHN*	*MLB*	*27*	*3*	*1*	*3*	*58*	*0*	*61^1*	*41*	*8*	*4.6*	*12.4*	*84*	*46%*	*.286*	*1.17*	*3.81*	*4.20*	*0.7*	*96.4*	*42*	*62*	*49*

Breakout: 39% Improve: 55% Collapse: 28% Attrition: 15% MLB: 91% *Comparables: Kevin Siegrist, Carson Smith, Kevin Quackenbush*

Edwards is the first pitcher in major-league history to throw two seasons of at least 35 innings while allowing fewer than four hits per nine innings, and he did it in consecutive years. It's an arbitrary point, sure, so slide the query back to 30 innings: same results. Now to 25 innings: no change. Go all the way down to 20, and another name shows up: Craig Kimbrel, now that his brief rookie year is factored in. It's unprecedented but not the entire story. Back to the original result, of all 35-inning, sub-four H/9 seasons (and there have been 11, all but one since 2009), Edwards gave up the most walks and produced the worst FIP. The league usually figures out relievers at some point, so his command will be the difference between the seventh and the ninth inning.

Luke Farrell RHP Born: 06/07/91 Age: 27 Bats: L Throws: R Height: 6'6" Weight: 210 Origin: Round 6, 2013 Draft (#174 overall)

YEAR	TEAM	LVL	AGE	W	L	SV	G	GS	IP	H	HR	BB/9	K/9	K	GB%	BABIP	WHIP	ERA	DRA	WARP	MPH	CMD	PWR	STM
2015	WIL	A+	24	2	0	2	7	3	29^{2}	27	0	1.8	12.4	41	44%	.380	1.11	3.03	1.28	1.3				
2015	NWA	AA	24	5	3	0	19	16	93^{1}	89	7	2.8	6.3	65	40%	.285	1.26	3.09	3.81	1.4				
2016	OMA	AAA	25	6	3	0	19	14	91	85	12	4.0	7.7	78	42%	.283	1.37	3.76	4.35	1.0				
2017	KCA	MLB	26	0	0	0	1	1	2^{2}	7	1	10.1	6.8	2	38%	.500	3.75	16.88	7.52	-0.1	92.2	55	39	61
2017	OMA	AAA	26	7	4	0	17	16	97^{1}	89	13	3.1	8.7	94	34%	.288	1.25	4.07	4.81	0.9				
2017	LOU	AAA	26	1	2	0	4	3	14^{2}	14	2	6.8	11.0	18	29%	.308	1.70	9.82	6.06	-0.1				
2017	CIN	MLB	26	0	0	0	9	0	10^{1}	5	1	6.1	6.1	7	38%	.143	1.16	2.61	5.33	0.0	93.1	55	39	61
2018	*CHN*	*MLB*	*27*	*2*	*2*	*0*	*10*	*5*	*31*	*34*	*7*	*4.2*	*8.3*	*29*	*38%*	*.297*	*1.55*	*5.65*	*5.76*	*-0.2*	*92.5*	*56*	*39*	*62*
2019	*CHN*	*MLB*	*28*	*7*	*11*	*0*	*27*	*27*	*164^{2}*	*162*	*31*	*3.5*	*8.5*	*156*	*38%*	*.308*	*1.37*	*5.21*	*5.78*	*-0.2*	*92.0*	*56*	*39*	*62*

Breakout: 19% Improve: 22% Collapse: 11% Attrition: 24% MLB: 37% *Comparables: Chris Narveson, Fabio Castro, Asher Wojciechowski*

What a wild year it was for Farrell. He started the year in Triple-A, his second stint at the level. He made his major-league debut later in the summer, with his father and then-Red Sox manager John in attendance. He was then immediately demoted back to Triple-A, designated for assignment and eventually picked up by the Reds. Cincinnati shifted him into the bullpen, and he got to play in front of his father again—though this time John was in the opponents' dugout. After the season, his father was fired from his job and Luke was claimed on waivers by the Cubs.

Justin Grimm RHP Born: 08/16/88 Age: 29 Bats: R Throws: R Height: 6'3" Weight: 210 Origin: Round 5, 2010 Draft (#166 overall)

YEAR	TEAM	LVL	AGE	W	L	SV	G	GS	IP	H	HR	BB/9	K/9	K	GB%	BABIP	WHIP	ERA	DRA	WARP	MPH	CMD	PWR	STM
2015	CHN	MLB	26	3	5	3	62	0	49^{2}	31	4	4.7	12.1	67	46%	.255	1.15	1.99	2.84	1.1	97.8	35	55	49
2016	CHN	MLB	27	2	1	0	68	0	52^{2}	47	5	3.9	11.1	65	42%	.321	1.33	4.10	3.77	0.7	96.5	49	44	46
2017	IOW	AAA	28	0	1	3	10	0	11^{2}	10	2	3.9	13.9	18	52%	.320	1.29	3.86	2.91	0.3				
2017	CHN	MLB	28	1	2	1	50	0	55^{1}	47	12	4.4	9.6	59	41%	.263	1.34	5.53	5.48	-0.2	96.5	40	53	49
2018	*CHN*	*MLB*	*29*	*3*	*3*	*0*	*51*	*0*	*53*	*49*	*8*	*4.2*	*10.6*	*64*	*43%*	*.301*	*1.38*	*4.24*	*4.32*	*0.4*	*96.1*	*42*	*51*	*48*
2019	*CHN*	*MLB*	*30*	*2*	*1*	*0*	*50*	*0*	*53^{2}*	*44*	*8*	*4.2*	*10.7*	*63*	*43%*	*.303*	*1.29*	*4.42*	*4.88*	*0.2*	*95.6*	*43*	*49*	*48*

Breakout: 32% Improve: 55% Collapse: 22% Attrition: 12% MLB: 88% *Comparables: Neftali Feliz, David Hernandez, Juan Cruz*

Missing: one fastball, often used. Description: mid-90s and all over the place. Last seen with: a decent curveball. Has also been spotted in Triple-A a few times, as well as the outfield seats probably more than it should. No known distinguishing marks or features that you wouldn't see on any other pitch dinged with high exit velocity. If located, please return to Justin Grimm, 123 Waiver Wire Boulevard, Baseballtown, USA.

Thomas Hatch RHP Born: 09/29/94 Age: 23 Bats: R Throws: R Height: 6'1" Weight: 190 Origin: Round 3, 2016 Draft (#104 overall)

YEAR	TEAM	LVL	AGE	W	L	SV	G	GS	IP	H	HR	BB/9	K/9	K	GB%	BABIP	WHIP	ERA	DRA	WARP	MPH	CMD	PWR	STM
2017	MYR	A+	22	5	11	0	26	26	124^{2}	126	2	3.6	9.1	126	46%	.347	1.41	4.04	3.66	2.4				
2018	*CHN*	*MLB*	*23*	*6*	*5*	*0*	*18*	*18*	*89^{1}*	*87*	*13*	*4.4*	*9.5*	*94*	*41%*	*.324*	*1.46*	*4.52*	*4.99*	*0.6*				
2019	*CHN*	*MLB*	*24*	*6*	*11*	*0*	*27*	*27*	*160^{2}*	*164*	*28*	*4.8*	*8.4*	*150*	*41%*	*.324*	*1.56*	*5.53*	*6.14*	*-0.7*				

Breakout: 6% Improve: 10% Collapse: 3% Attrition: 11% MLB: 17% *Comparables: John Gant, Steven Matz, Giovanni Soto*

Elbow issues kept Hatch from pitching in 2015 and dropped his draft stock the following year, but the Cubs took him in the third round with their first pick of the 2016 draft and may have gotten a steal anyway. After a slow start in the Carolina League last year, Hatch put together a sturdy finish to his first full professional season. Most importantly, he pitched 120-plus innings without health issues—an obvious concern given his absence from the mound in his sophomore year at Oklahoma State and the Cubs' decision to shut him down after drafting him.

Kyle Hendricks RHP Born: 12/07/89 Age: 28 Bats: R Throws: R Height: 6'3" Weight: 190 Origin: Round 8, 2011 Draft (#264 overall)

YEAR	TEAM	LVL	AGE	W	L	SV	G	GS	IP	H	HR	BB/9	K/9	K	GB%	BABIP	WHIP	ERA	DRA	WARP	MPH	CMD	PWR	STM
2015	CHN	MLB	25	8	7	0	32	32	180	166	17	2.2	8.4	167	54%	.296	1.16	3.95	3.26	3.9	90.7	81	34	70
2016	CHN	MLB	26	16	8	0	31	30	190	142	15	2.1	8.1	170	50%	.250	0.98	2.13	3.00	5.1	90.2	79	38	72
2017	CHN	MLB	27	7	5	0	24	24	139^{2}	126	17	2.6	7.9	123	52%	.281	1.19	3.03	3.31	3.5	87.6	76	20	62
2018	*CHN*	*MLB*	*28*	*12*	*8*	*0*	*29*	*29*	*165^{1}*	*149*	*19*	*2.9*	*8.4*	*154*	*50%*	*.288*	*1.22*	*3.76*	*3.87*	*2.5*	*88.9*	*79*	*31*	*68*
2019	*CHN*	*MLB*	*29*	*12*	*10*	*0*	*33*	*33*	*214^{2}*	*172*	*21*	*2.4*	*8.7*	*208*	*50%*	*.287*	*1.07*	*3.51*	*3.86*	*3.6*	*88.3*	*78*	*29*	*67*

Breakout: 21% Improve: 46% Collapse: 24% Attrition: 12% MLB: 96% *Comparables: Dallas Keuchel, Garrett Richards, Brandon Webb*

The career year two seasons ago should keep Hendricks from being confused with Kyle Kendrick. His midseason return after missing over a month with an inflamed middle finger not only allowed him to express all of his emotions visually, but also helped him regain his velocity (if that's what you called it in the first place), and he posted a 2.19 second-half ERA—pretty close to that of his Cy Young bronze finalist season. It's so hard to trust someone barely scraping 90 mph on the radar in the rotation for so long, but it's not unprecedented and it's all Hendricks has. Basically, save all your unused Jered Weaver jokes for Hendricks in 10 years when he's still pitching for the expansion Calgary Grizzly Sox or whomever.

John Lackey RHP Born: 10/23/78 Age: 39 Bats: R Throws: R Height: 6'6" Weight: 235 Origin: Round 2, 1999 Draft (#68 overall)

YEAR	TEAM	LVL	AGE	W	L	SV	G	GS	IP	H	HR	BB/9	K/9	K	GB%	BABIP	WHIP	ERA	DRA	WARP	MPH	CMD	PWR	STM
2015	SLN	MLB	36	13	10	0	33	33	218	211	21	2.2	7.2	175	48%	.295	1.21	2.77	4.22	2.2	94.4	50	51	79
2016	CHN	MLB	37	11	8	0	29	29	188^1	146	23	2.5	8.6	180	44%	.255	1.06	3.35	4.00	2.9	94.4	57	46	74
2017	CHN	MLB	38	12	12	0	31	30	170^2	165	36	2.8	7.9	149	43%	.268	1.28	4.59	5.20	0.7	92.8	53	35	72
2018	*CHN*	*MLB*	*39*	*9*	*7*	*0*	*23*	*23*	*142*	*134*	*22*	*3.0*	*7.7*	*121*	*44%*	*.290*	*1.28*	*4.63*	*5.09*	*0.8*	*92.2*	*52*	*42*	*72*
2019	*CHN*	*MLB*	*40*	*10*	*11*	*0*	*28*	*28*	*170*	*162*	*25*	*2.8*	*7.3*	*137*	*44%*	*.299*	*1.26*	*4.69*	*5.17*	*0.9*	*91.4*	*52*	*39*	*70*

Breakout: 8% Improve: 30% Collapse: 9% Attrition: 1% MLB: 76% *Comparables: Hiroki Kuroda, Kevin Brown, Roger Clemens*

As Lackey nears the end of a memorable career spanning two decades and three World Series championships, there's not much more to learn about him as a pitcher. All the clichés about getting the most out of his stuff to stifle batters at an advanced age and having the reputation of a big-game pitcher apply. But we did learn one new thing: Absolutely, under no circumstances, should Lackey be used in relief. It makes sense: 446 career starts under one's belt will lock a man into a routine, no doubt. His postseason bullpen meltdown shouldn't be the reason for concern, but his reduced velocity and 5.00-plus DRA? Yeah, that'll do it.

Jon Lester LHP Born: 01/07/84 Age: 34 Bats: L Throws: L Height: 6'4" Weight: 240 Origin: Round 2, 2002 Draft (#57 overall)

YEAR	TEAM	LVL	AGE	W	L	SV	G	GS	IP	H	HR	BB/9	K/9	K	GB%	BABIP	WHIP	ERA	DRA	WARP	MPH	CMD	PWR	STM
2015	CHN	MLB	31	11	12	0	32	32	205	183	16	2.1	9.1	207	50%	.304	1.12	3.34	3.01	5.0	94.3	81	45	78
2016	CHN	MLB	32	19	5	0	32	32	202^2	154	21	2.3	8.7	197	48%	.256	1.02	2.44	3.26	4.9	94.4	67	51	78
2017	CHN	MLB	33	13	8	0	32	32	180^2	179	26	3.0	9.0	180	48%	.310	1.32	4.33	3.94	3.3	92.7	69	38	78
2018	*CHN*	*MLB*	*34*	*13*	*9*	*0*	*28*	*28*	*196*	*186*	*26*	*3.0*	*8.6*	*187*	*47%*	*.293*	*1.28*	*4.01*	*4.13*	*2.4*	*92.6*	*70*	*43*	*77*
2019	*CHN*	*MLB*	*35*	*13*	*12*	*0*	*32*	*32*	*207^2*	*181*	*24*	*2.8*	*8.5*	*195*	*47%*	*.299*	*1.19*	*3.95*	*4.34*	*3.1*	*91.9*	*67*	*43*	*76*

Breakout: 15% Improve: 49% Collapse: 21% Attrition: 10% MLB: 97% *Comparables: Andy Pettitte, Justin Verlander, Cliff Lee*

Lester has made more starts than any other pitcher in the last 10 years, because his threshold for the disabled list is apparently lymphoma or worse. The first scientist to determine how to keep a pitcher healthy for his career will win the Nobel Prize and also a job with the Mets. Lester's durability is proving him to be worth his huge deal with the Cubs, and while he did hit a 10-year low in innings and FIP (buoyed by a slightly swollen walk rate), he looks fresh and ready for another 32 starts in the middle of the rotation. Of course, we buried the lede: Lester picked off a runner, in the postseason no less. We're mentioning that here, because including it in Ryan Zimmerman's comment just seems cruel.

Dillon Maples RHP Born: 05/09/92 Age: 26 Bats: R Throws: R Height: 6'2" Weight: 225 Origin: Round 14, 2011 Draft (#429 overall)

YEAR	TEAM	LVL	AGE	W	L	SV	G	GS	IP	H	HR	BB/9	K/9	K	GB%	BABIP	WHIP	ERA	DRA	WARP	MPH	CMD	PWR	STM
2015	SBN	A	23	1	1	1	15	0	30^1	28	2	3.6	5.6	19	63%	.286	1.32	4.15	5.60	-0.3				
2016	SBN	A	24	1	2	9	19	0	25	18	1	3.6	6.1	17	76%	.233	1.12	3.24	5.64	-0.3				
2017	MYR	A+	25	4	0	3	21	0	31^1	21	2	4.3	12.6	44	65%	.288	1.15	2.01	1.52	1.2				
2017	TEN	AA	25	1	1	6	14	0	13^2	11	0	7.2	18.4	28	64%	.440	1.61	3.29	1.53	0.5				
2017	IOW	AAA	25	1	2	4	17	0	18^1	12	1	5.4	13.7	28	63%	.297	1.25	1.96	2.11	0.6				
2017	CHN	MLB	25	0	0	0	6	0	5^1	6	0	10.1	18.6	11	50%	.600	2.25	10.12	2.49	0.2	98.2			49
2018	*CHN*	*MLB*	*26*	*1*	*1*	*0*	*14*	*0*	*14^2*	*15*	*2*	*6.0*	*9.4*	*15*	*56%*	*.302*	*1.68*	*5.68*	*5.48*	*-0.1*	*97.8*			*50*
2019	*CHN*	*MLB*	*27*	*2*	*1*	*0*	*39*	*0*	*41^2*	*40*	*6*	*4.4*	*9.7*	*45*	*56%*	*.33*	*1.44*	*4.75*	*5.25*	*0.0*	*97.4*			*50*

Breakout: 23% Improve: 28% Collapse: 6% Attrition: 19% MLB: 37% *Comparables: Victor Garate, Jake Diekman, Phillippe Aumont*

The former promising starter bottomed out over the last few years with various injuries and overall substandard performances, unable to advance past High-A at age 24. He was ready to hang it up last year, but as he told the *Des Moines Register*, his father, who was fertilizing his lawn at the time, talked him out of it. Good advice, dad. Maples sought out some career advice and added a low-90s cutter to his existing high-90s fastball and curveball, though he barely used the yakker in his September call-up. He struggled with command but has the arsenal to be bullpen material this year.

Dakota Mekkes RHP Born: 11/06/94 Age: 23 Bats: R Throws: R Height: 6'7" Weight: 252 Origin: Round 10, 2016 Draft (#314 overall)

YEAR	TEAM	LVL	AGE	W	L	SV	G	GS	IP	H	HR	BB/9	K/9	K	GB%	BABIP	WHIP	ERA	DRA	WARP	MPH	CMD	PWR	STM
2016	EUG	A-	21	1	1	0	9	0	17	11	1	2.1	11.1	21	54%	.250	0.88	2.12	2.26	0.5				
2017	SBN	A	22	3	0	4	18	0	31	14	1	4.1	13.6	47	41%	.228	0.90	0.58	2.40	0.9				
2017	MYR	A+	22	5	2	3	24	0	42^1	25	0	4.3	9.6	45	39%	.240	1.06	1.28	3.69	0.6				
2018	*CHN*	*MLB*	*23*	*2*	*1*	*2*	*48*	*0*	*50^2*	*46*	*11*	*5.1*	*11.1*	*62*	*38%*	*.309*	*1.48*	*5.29*	*5.85*	*-0.6*				
2019	*CHN*	*MLB*	*24*	*1*	*0*	*1*	*18*	*0*	*31^2*	*29*	*7*	*4.6*	*10.0*	*35*	*38%*	*.307*	*1.43*	*5.50*	*6.10*	*-0.3*				

Breakout: 6% Improve: 8% Collapse: 1% Attrition: 3% MLB: 10% *Comparables: Tommy Kahnle, Keith Butler, Lester Oliveros*

Mekkes doesn't use his height to create downward plane on his pitches, pushing his prodigious frame toward the batter instead, and it's working: He didn't allow a run in June and July last year, and his stock in the Cubs' system is rising fast. Though his fastball tops out at 93 mph, the release point and deception in his delivery can make it appear much faster to opposing hitters. Remember his name to impress your friends when the dinner party conversation inevitably turns to dark-horse candidates for the 2019 Cubs bullpen.

Alec Mills RHP Born: 11/30/91 Age: 26 Bats: R Throws: R Height: 6'4" Weight: 190 Origin: Round 22, 2012 Draft (#673 overall)

YEAR	TEAM	LVL	AGE	W	L	SV	G	GS	IP	H	HR	BB/9	K/9	K	GB%	BABIP	WHIP	ERA	DRA	WARP	MPH	CMD	PWR	STM
2015	WIL	A+	23	7	7	0	21	21	113^1	122	3	1.1	8.8	111	52%	.350	1.20	3.02	1.73	4.6				
2016	NWA	AA	24	1	2	0	12	12	67^2	57	2	1.6	9.0	68	44%	.314	1.02	2.39	1.21	3.2				
2016	OMA	AAA	24	4	3	0	12	11	58	62	8	2.9	8.4	54	47%	.323	1.40	4.19	3.15	1.4				
2016	KCA	MLB	24	0	0	0	3	0	3^1	3	0	13.5	10.8	4	44%	.333	2.40	13.50	2.68	0.1	94.2			56
2017	IOW	AAA	25	2	0	0	3	3	14	12	0	1.9	4.5	7	47%	.255	1.07	3.21	3.27	0.4				
2018	*CHN*	*MLB*	*26*	*3*	*3*	*0*	*22*	*8*	*54^2*	*58*	*8*	*3.6*	*7.5*	*46*	*45%*	*.302*	*1.47*	*4.70*	*4.77*	*0.2*	*93.8*			*57*
2019	*CHN*	*MLB*	*27*	*7*	*7*	*0*	*57*	*19*	*152*	*153*	*23*	*3.2*	*7.7*	*131*	*45%*	*.317*	*1.36*	*4.81*	*5.31*	*0.3*	*93.3*			*57*

Breakout: 24% Improve: 35% Collapse: 12% Attrition: 26% MLB: 63% *Comparables: Tim Cooney, Ross Stripling, Chris Stratton*

Once upon a time, Mills was a pitcher the Cubs acquired to potentially fill gaps in their 2017 rotation, but that time never came. An ankle injury in April sidelined him until late August, when the right-hander rehabbed with High-A Myrtle Beach. The obvious hope is that Mills can stay healthy this year, as the Cubs are likely to need more rotation help in 2018.

Mike Montgomery LHP Born: 07/01/89 Age: 28 Bats: L Throws: L Height: 6'5" Weight: 215 Origin: Round 1, 2008 Draft (#36 overall)

YEAR	TEAM	LVL	AGE	W	L	SV	G	GS	IP	H	HR	BB/9	K/9	K	GB%	BABIP	WHIP	ERA	DRA	WARP	MPH	CMD	PWR	STM
2015	SEA	MLB	25	4	6	0	16	16	90	92	11	3.7	6.4	64	53%	.291	1.43	4.60	5.25	-0.2	93.4	45	34	68
2015	TAC	AAA	25	4	3	0	11	11	65^1	59	3	2.6	8.0	58	51%	.299	1.19	4.13	3.28	1.5				
2016	SEA	MLB	26	3	4	0	32	2	61^2	49	3	2.6	7.9	54	59%	.272	1.09	2.34	3.20	1.3	96.4	37	43	51
2016	CHN	MLB	26	1	1	0	17	5	38^1	30	5	4.7	8.9	38	61%	.258	1.30	2.82	3.78	0.6	95.5	37	43	51
2017	CHN	MLB	27	7	8	3	44	14	130^2	103	10	3.8	6.9	100	59%	.253	1.21	3.38	4.29	1.6	94.1	46	40	60
2018	*CHN*	*MLB*	*28*	*10*	*8*	*0*	*26*	*26*	*148*	*138*	*16*	*3.5*	*7.8*	*128*	*55%*	*.289*	*1.31*	*4.10*	*4.22*	*1.6*	*94.0*	*43*	*40*	*59*
2019	*CHN*	*MLB*	*29*	*11*	*11*	*0*	*32*	*32*	*208*	*172*	*22*	*3.2*	*8.1*	*188*	*55%*	*.287*	*1.19*	*4.08*	*4.49*	*2.3*	*93.8*	*43*	*41*	*57*

Breakout: 10% Improve: 38% Collapse: 27% Attrition: 18% MLB: 89% *Comparables: Alex Colome, Adam Warren, Josh Collmenter*

Montgomery is a true swingman in a hopeless maelstrom of roster construction where teams just hope for the best out of their 25th man, but that's to be expected of left-handed relievers who pump the strike zone with low-90s material and no real platoon split. He's a useful person to have warming up down there, whether you need five emergency innings, nine outs in the middle or just one more out in a World Series Game 7. For his major-league career—which didn't get going until 2015, at age 25—Montgomery has a 4.20 ERA in 37 starts compared to a 2.29 ERA in 72 relief appearances, although his strikeout rate is nearly identical (18 percent vs. 19 percent) in both roles.

Brandon Morrow RHP Born: 07/26/84 Age: 33 Bats: R Throws: R Height: 6'3" Weight: 205 Origin: Round 1, 2006 Draft (#5 overall)

YEAR	TEAM	LVL	AGE	W	L	SV	G	GS	IP	H	HR	BB/9	K/9	K	GB%	BABIP	WHIP	ERA	DRA	WARP	MPH	CMD	PWR	STM
2015	SDN	MLB	30	2	0	0	5	5	33	29	3	1.9	6.3	23	48%	.280	1.09	2.73	3.91	0.5	96.3	53	54	8
2016	LEL	A+	31	0	1	0	2	2	11^2	15	1	2.3	6.2	8	41%	.368	1.54	6.94	8.03	-0.3				
2016	SAN	AA	31	1	1	0	2	2	10^1	18	3	3.5	3.5	4	40%	.375	2.13	7.84	6.62	-0.2				
2016	ELP	AAA	31	0	0	2	12	2	21	29	2	3.9	9.0	21	52%	.403	1.81	6.43	3.34	0.4				
2016	SDN	MLB	31	1	0	0	18	0	16	19	2	1.7	4.5	8	47%	.309	1.38	1.69	5.13	0.0	97.1	47	52	36
2017	OKL	AAA	32	0	5	6	20	0	20	25	5	2.2	9.9	22	56%	.339	1.50	7.20	2.96	0.5				
2017	LAN	MLB	32	6	0	2	45	0	43^2	31	0	1.9	10.3	50	46%	.282	0.92	2.06	3.17	1.0	99.6	44	74	48
2018	*CHN*	*MLB*	*33*	*3*	*3*	*30*	*51*	*0*	*53*	*54*	*8*	*3.6*	*8.5*	*51*	*46%*	*.305*	*1.42*	*4.37*	*4.40*	*0.3*	*97.2*	*46*	*64*	*34*
2019	*CHN*	*MLB*	*34*	*2*	*1*	*23*	*49*	*0*	*51^2*	*48*	*7*	*3.2*	*8.2*	*47*	*46%*	*.309*	*1.28*	*4.41*	*4.87*	*0.2*	*96.9*	*44*	*67*	*38*

Breakout: 22% Improve: 39% Collapse: 16% Attrition: 19% MLB: 66% *Comparables: Carlos Torres, Tim Stauffer, Jorge Sosa*

Well, well, well, lookie what we have here. The recipient of a minor-league deal last winter on the heels of yet another injury-abbreviated season, Morrow *finally* managed to stay healthy and air it out for a full year in the bullpen. The result? A three-tick jump in sitting velocity, the best strikeout rate of his career and utter and complete domination of left-handed batters. He announced his presence with authority after arriving in Los Angeles from Double-A in late May, racking up 11 straight scoreless outings to start his season. By October he'd emerged as both the primary bridge to Kenley Time and the unlikeliest of everyday workhorses. The fumes on which he ran by Game 5 of the World Series caught fire in an ill-timed explosion, but he otherwise acquitted himself masterfully under the bright lights—conveniently in time to lock down a two-year, $21 million contract from the Cubs in December.

Jose Quintana LHP Born: 01/24/89 Age: 29 Bats: R Throws: L Height: 6'1" Weight: 220 Origin: International Free Agent, 2006

YEAR	TEAM	LVL	AGE	W	L	SV	G	GS	IP	H	HR	BB/9	K/9	K	GB%	BABIP	WHIP	ERA	DRA	WARP	MPH	CMD	PWR	STM
2015	CHA	MLB	26	9	10	0	32	32	206^1	218	16	1.9	7.7	177	48%	.327	1.27	3.36	3.99	2.7	94.1	52	40	81
2016	CHA	MLB	27	13	12	0	32	32	208	192	22	2.2	7.8	181	41%	.293	1.16	3.20	3.65	4.1	94.6	64	46	82
2017	CHA	MLB	28	4	8	0	18	18	104^1	98	14	3.5	9.4	109	45%	.301	1.32	4.49	3.83	2.0	93.3	50	42	79
2017	CHN	MLB	28	7	3	0	14	14	84^1	72	9	2.2	10.5	98	48%	.300	1.10	3.74	3.90	1.6	94.0	50	42	79
2018	*CHN*	*MLB*	*29*	*12*	*8*	*0*	*29*	*29*	*174*	*161*	*22*	*2.9*	*9.3*	*179*	*45%*	*.298*	*1.25*	*3.74*	*3.84*	*2.7*	*93.4*	*55*	*43*	*80*
2019	*CHN*	*MLB*	*30*	*12*	*11*	*0*	*32*	*32*	*204^2*	*179*	*25*	*2.7*	*9.3*	*212*	*45%*	*.31*	*1.18*	*3.81*	*4.19*	*3.0*	*93.1*	*56*	*43*	*80*

Breakout: 7% Improve: 33% Collapse: 24% Attrition: 7% MLB: 98% *Comparables: Josh Johnson, Hyun-jin Ryu, Matt Cain*

Quintana is no longer the circuit's best-kept secret as a sweet-throwing lefty on a sour team, as he was unsurprisingly the focal point in Chicago's biggest crosstown trade since George Bell for Sammy Sosa. Down the stretch he showed he could pitch anywhere in the Windy City as long as there was a mound of dirt somewhere. The list of 30-and-under lefties with a better adjusted ERA than Quintana is short: Clayton Kershaw, Chris Sale and Madison Bumgarner. Although he did get maimed in his first postseason experience, his regular-season numbers are excruciatingly consistent to the point that the US Naval Observatory is considering using his DRA to regulate its clock.

Drew Smyly LHP Born: 06/13/89 Age: 28 Bats: L Throws: L Height: 6'3" Weight: 190 Origin: Round 2, 2010 Draft (#68 overall)

YEAR	TEAM	LVL	AGE	W	L	SV	G	GS	IP	H	HR	BB/9	K/9	K	GB%	BABIP	WHIP	ERA	DRA	WARP	MPH	CMD	PWR	STM
2015	DUR	AAA	26	0	2	0	3	3	10^2	13	2	5.1	11.0	13	34%	.367	1.78	8.44	4.20	0.1				
2015	TBA	MLB	26	5	2	0	12	12	66^2	58	11	2.7	10.4	77	39%	.283	1.17	3.11	3.37	1.4	92.8	48	34	34
2016	TBA	MLB	27	7	12	0	30	30	175^1	174	32	2.5	8.6	167	33%	.291	1.27	4.88	4.83	1.1	92.7	54	38	74
2018	*CHN*	*MLB*	*29*	*2*	*2*	*0*	*7*	*7*	*36^2*	*33*	*6*	*3.2*	*9.6*	*39*	*38%*	*.300*	*1.27*	*4.38*	*4.82*	*0.3*	*92.1*	*53*	*37*	*57*
2019	*CHN*	*MLB*	*30*	*9*	*12*	*0*	*30*	*30*	*188^1*	*197*	*32*	*2.6*	*7.0*	*146*	*38%*	*.31*	*1.33*	*4.99*	*5.51*	*0.2*	*91.8*	*53*	*38*	*63*

Breakout: 18% Improve: 42% Collapse: 24% Attrition: 5% MLB: 98% *Comparables: Dennis Leonard, Jered Weaver, Homer Bailey*

Acquired from the Rays for three minor leaguers in a significant mid-winter swap, Smyly was a late addition to the United States' pitching staff for the World Baseball Classic. After returning to Mariners' camp in late March, he exhibited symptoms of what manager Scott Servais called a "soggy arm." Diagnosed with a left flexor strain, Smyly tried the rehab route, but ultimately was forced to go under the knife with Tommy John surgery in July. This knocked Smyly out of commission for all of 2017 and will keep him out of action for some of 2018 as well. It's difficult to draw a facial expression on this situation that would convey positive feelings and/or emotions.

Pedro Strop RHP Born: 06/13/85 Age: 32 Bats: R Throws: R Height: 6'1" Weight: 220 Origin: International Free Agent, 2002

YEAR	TEAM	LVL	AGE	W	L	SV	G	GS	IP	H	HR	BB/9	K/9	K	GB%	BABIP	WHIP	ERA	DRA	WARP	MPH	CMD	PWR	STM
2015	CHN	MLB	30	2	6	3	76	0	68	39	5	3.8	10.7	81	53%	.225	1.00	2.91	2.66	1.7	97.5	22	50	52
2016	CHN	MLB	31	2	2	0	54	0	47^1	27	4	2.9	11.4	60	61%	.221	0.89	2.85	2.23	1.5	97.0	29	42	38
2017	CHN	MLB	32	5	4	0	69	0	60^1	45	4	3.9	9.7	65	61%	.270	1.18	2.83	3.42	1.2	97.2	34	59	49
2018	*CHN*	*MLB*	*33*	*3*	*2*	*5*	*51*	*0*	*53*	*46*	*6*	*4.0*	*9.6*	*58*	*54%*	*.286*	*1.28*	*3.79*	*3.96*	*0.6*	*96.2*	*29*	*51*	*46*
2019	*CHN*	*MLB*	*34*	*3*	*1*	*3*	*55*	*0*	*58^2*	*46*	*7*	*4.0*	*9.1*	*60*	*54%*	*.28*	*1.22*	*4.30*	*4.73*	*0.3*	*95.6*	*31*	*52*	*44*

Breakout: 19% Improve: 38% Collapse: 38% Attrition: 10% MLB: 95% *Comparables: Francisco Cordero, Scot Shields, Jason Isringhausen*

Strop continues to throw the same upper-90s heat year after year out of the bullpen, and only Matt LeBlanc has made a better career living in 97 for so long. He did hit a road bump, though, despite the velo remaining consistent: The fastball isn't putting away as many batters. It was instead slugged pretty hard and wasn't much of an out pitch. His slider remains the finishing move of choice, his "how you doin'," if you will, though strikeouts and walks both went in the wrong direction. Maybe it was a 60-inning fluke, especially since righties were the only ones who had added success, because don't forget Strop's mother always warned him there'd be sample sizes like this, when it hasn't been his pitch, his inning, his appearance or even his year.

Jen-Ho Tseng RHP Born: 10/03/94 Age: 23 Bats: L Throws: R Height: 6'1" Weight: 195 Origin: International Free Agent, 2013

YEAR	TEAM	LVL	AGE	W	L	SV	G	GS	IP	H	HR	BB/9	K/9	K	GB%	BABIP	WHIP	ERA	DRA	WARP	MPH	CMD	PWR	STM
2015	MYR	A+	20	7	7	0	22	22	119	115	5	2.3	6.6	87	40%	.301	1.22	3.55	3.75	1.9				
2016	TEN	AA	21	6	8	0	22	22	113^1	138	12	2.5	5.5	69	49%	.327	1.50	4.29	4.99	0.1				
2017	TEN	AA	22	7	3	0	15	15	90^1	79	7	2.4	8.3	83	41%	.281	1.14	2.99	3.88	1.4				
2017	IOW	AAA	22	6	1	0	9	9	55	48	5	2.3	6.4	39	55%	.264	1.13	1.80	3.09	1.6				
2017	CHN	MLB	22	1	0	0	2	1	6	5	2	3.0	12.0	8	33%	.231	1.17	7.50	5.82	0.0	93.5			62
2018	*CHN*	*MLB*	*23*	*2*	*2*	*0*	*10*	*5*	*29*	*32*	*5*	*3.3*	*7.5*	*25*	*43%*	*.297*	*1.43*	*4.84*	*4.93*	*0.1*	*93.4*			*64*
2019	*CHN*	*MLB*	*24*	*8*	*10*	*0*	*28*	*28*	*172*	*164*	*28*	*3.0*	*8.1*	*156*	*43%*	*.303*	*1.29*	*4.79*	*5.29*	*0.5*	*93.2*			*65*

Breakout: 12% Improve: 15% Collapse: 13% Attrition: 26% MLB: 33% *Comparables: Zach McAllister, Dallas Beeler, Kyle Hendricks*

A jewel of the Cubs' minor-league system with multiple Minor League Pitcher of the Year awards to prove it (2014 and 2017), Tseng got a surprise September call-up for a spot start. Though his individual performance that day (3 IP, 5 H, 5 R, 6 K) wasn't cause for ecstatic enthusiasm, there is reason to remain bullish. In both the Double-A Southern League and Triple-A Pacific Coast League last season, Tseng showed off his above-average ability to keep hitters from making hard contact, and with the big-league rotation in Chicago becoming more of a question mark in 2018, Tseng is a realistic option to eventually take a spot.

Koji Uehara RHP Born: 04/03/75 Age: 43 Bats: R Throws: R Height: 6'2" Weight: 195 Origin: International Free Agent, 2009

YEAR	TEAM	LVL	AGE	W	L	SV	G	GS	IP	H	HR	BB/9	K/9	K	GB%	BABIP	WHIP	ERA	DRA	WARP	MPH	CMD	PWR	STM
2015	BOS	MLB	40	2	4	25	43	0	40^1	28	3	2.0	10.5	47	29%	.248	0.92	2.23	2.72	1.0	89.1	62	10	45
2016	BOS	MLB	41	2	3	7	50	0	47	34	8	2.1	12.1	63	27%	.260	0.96	3.45	2.70	1.2	88.8	53	25	37
2017	CHN	MLB	42	3	4	2	49	0	43	38	7	2.5	10.5	50	26%	.284	1.16	3.98	3.78	0.7	87.9	57	23	41
2018	*CHN*	*MLB*	*43*	*2*	*1*	*2*	*36*	*0*	*37^2*	*33*	*7*	*3.4*	*9.7*	*41*	*32%*	*.286*	*1.25*	*4.49*	*4.95*	*0.1*	*86.6*	*54*	*20*	*39*
2019	*CHN*	*MLB*	*44*	*2*	*1*	*2*	*52*	*0*	*48^2*	*43*	*10*	*3.5*	*9.6*	*52*	*32%*	*.29*	*1.27*	*5.01*	*5.54*	*-0.2*	*85.7*	*52*	*22*	*37*

Breakout: 14% Improve: 19% Collapse: 14% Attrition: 16% MLB: 50% *Comparables: Takashi Saito, Hoyt Wilhelm, Satchel Paige*

Every year we have to wonder whether this will be the last season for Uehara. He told the *Chicago Tribune* last March that he wanted to last 10 years in the majors, and he's gotten through nine so far, so do the math. Now for some tougher ones: He debuted in his mid-thirties, in the same calendar year as Madison Bumgarner. He throws over 90 mph about as often as he cuts in front of nuns in line at the emergency room. And he's averaged at least 10 strikeouts per nine innings each year this decade. (The complete list of others: David Robertson, Kenley Jansen, Craig Kimbrel, Aroldis Chapman.) The real question for Uehara is not where in the bullpen he belongs, but rather why stop at 10 seasons?

Justin Wilson LHP Born: 08/18/87 Age: 30 Bats: L Throws: L Height: 6'2" Weight: 205 Origin: Round 5, 2008 Draft (#144 overall)

YEAR	TEAM	LVL	AGE	W	L	SV	G	GS	IP	H	HR	BB/9	K/9	K	GB%	BABIP	WHIP	ERA	DRA	WARP	MPH	CMD	PWR	STM
2015	NYA	MLB	27	5	0	0	74	0	61	49	3	3.0	9.7	66	46%	.301	1.13	3.10	3.78	0.7	97.6	37	76	51
2016	DET	MLB	28	4	5	1	66	0	58^2	61	6	2.6	10.0	65	56%	.340	1.33	4.14	3.56	0.9	97.7	40	64	47
2017	DET	MLB	29	3	4	13	42	0	40^1	22	5	3.6	12.3	55	38%	.210	0.94	2.68	4.62	0.2	97.1	31	72	49
2017	CHN	MLB	29	1	0	0	23	0	17^2	18	0	9.7	12.7	25	37%	.391	2.09	5.09	4.89	0.1	97.0	31	72	49
2018	*CHN*	*MLB*	*30*	*3*	*2*	*0*	*51*	*0*	*53*	*47*	*8*	*3.9*	*11.0*	*66*	*46%*	*.297*	*1.30*	*4.02*	*4.14*	*0.5*	*96.6*	*35*	*70*	*49*
2019	*CHN*	*MLB*	*31*	*2*	*1*	*0*	*48*	*0*	*50^1*	*43*	*9*	*4.2*	*10.5*	*59*	*46%*	*.305*	*1.31*	*4.72*	*5.20*	*0.0*	*96.2*	*34*	*69*	*48*

Breakout: 28% Improve: 45% Collapse: 29% Attrition: 10% MLB: 93% *Comparables: Luke Gregerson, Sparky Lyle, Steve Cishek*

While the Tigers' trade of Justin Verlander reinvigorated his career, the flip of Wilson to the Cubs seemed to dash his stock value on arrival. He earned the closer role in Detroit after K-Rod accidentally threw ninth-inning batting practice for a week, and Wilson became a highly valued lefty. But his fastball command spiked the walk rate and he was rarely given high-leverage innings. He was entrusted with two-thirds of a postseason inning in which the Cubs were down five runs. When he pitched the ninth inning in Detroit he was wicked, but to get his own closer entrance music again he'll have to climb that ladder of trust once more.

Lineouts

Hitters

HITTER	POS	TEAM	LVL	AGE	PA	R	2B	3B	HR	RBI	BB	K	SB	CS	AVG/OBP/SLG	TAv	VORP	BABIP	BRR	FRAA	WARP
David Bote	2B	TEN	AA	24	536	65	30	3	14	59	49	101	5	2	.272/.353/.438	.291	30.9	.318	1.0	2B(107): 5.7, RF(9): 1.2	4.0
Charcer Burks	OF	TEN	AA	22	535	67	21	3	10	40	69	107	16	12	.270/.370/.395	.282	23.3	.329	-0.8	LF(87): -1.5, CF(34): -2.9	2.1
Taylor Davis	C	IOW	AAA	27	406	41	27	1	6	62	37	45	0	3	.297/.357/.429	.276	19.2	.318	-2.0	C(59): 11.2, 1B(26): -1.3	2.8
	C	CHN	MLB	27	13	1	1	0	0	1	0	4	0	0	.231/.231/.308	.194	-0.8	.333	-0.2	3B(2): 0.0, 1B(2): 0.0	-0.1
Wladimir Galindo	3B	SBN	A	20	177	21	11	0	4	19	14	40	1	1	.290/.350/.432	.282	6.6	.364	-1.2	3B(25): 0.0, 1B(15): 0.2	0.7
Jacob Hannemann	OF	TEN	AA	26	141	17	9	1	1	6	14	44	6	3	.180/.286/.295	.228	1.3	.273	1.7	CF(34): -1.1	0.0
	OF	IOW	AAA	26	322	40	23	1	5	26	24	69	23	3	.265/.324/.404	.258	10.6	.327	0.9	CF(72): 1.5, RF(3): 0.0	1.2
	OF	SEA	MLB	26	20	3	0	0	1	1	0	4	0	1	.150/.150/.300	.140	-2.4	.133	-0.5	CF(7): 0.0, LF(2): -0.1	-0.2
Eddy Martinez	OF	MYR	A+	22	502	59	11	2	14	61	31	78	6	6	.244/.297/.366	.255	3.7	.265	-2.6	RF(64): 4.6, LF(27): -0.4	0.9
Bijan Rademacher	LF	IOW	AAA	26	329	38	16	2	7	46	36	64	3	2	.294/.375/.436	.284	12.8	.356	-2.9	RF(56): -1.8, LF(27): 0.8	1.1
Carlos Sepulveda	2B	MYR	A+	20	125	13	2	0	0	7	11	19	0	1	.196/.272/.214	.200	-5.9	.234	-0.8	2B(12): 1.7	-0.4
	2B	CUB	Rk	20	41	6	2	0	0	4	4	4	0	1	.324/.390/.378	.336	6.2	.364	0.9	2B(8): 1.0	0.6
Jemile Weeks	2B	IOW	AAA	30	259	31	18	2	2	24	28	32	4	0	.235/.316/.358	.247	4.6	.263	1.9	2B(40): -0.7, LF(7): 0.3	0.4
D.J. Wilson	OF	SBN	A	20	348	56	16	8	9	45	33	89	15	7	.229/.309/.419	.272	20.4	.292	5.9	CF(83): -6.4, LF(1): -0.1	1.5
Mark Zagunis	LF	CHN	MLB	24	18	0	0	0	0	1	4	6	2	0	.000/.222/.000	.162	-0.9	.000	0.6	RF(4): -0.3	-0.1
	LF	IOW	AAA	24	408	59	21	1	13	55	70	93	4	3	.267/.404/.455	.298	24.4	.333	-1.7	LF(53): 1.1, RF(39): -3.4	2.2

JUSTIN TIMBERLAKE: He's **David Bote** and, he don't run fast and, he can hit more than your average young second baseman. Was king of the AFL, born in '93 though, if you want him to start, then you're sure not Theoooooooh. T-PAIN: YEAHHHHH YEAH YEAH. ⚾ **Charcer Burks** is young enough that he might realize his evident potential yet, but he has organizational depth written all over him. Last season was his best yet, but even with that it's hard to muster much excitement for the 23-year-old outfielder. ⚾ Google "**Taylor Davis** Can't Take His Eyes Off You" for an enjoyable viral video of the catcher/corner infielder being innately aware of the camera at all times. Do not Google his numbers that project him as organizational depth. ⚾ **Wladimir Galindo** spent most of his first full season on the disabled list, but when healthy he handled the Midwest League—usually a significant challenge to young players stepping out of the developmental leagues or short-season ball—with aplomb. ⚾ He has developed into a decent defensive outfielder and has good base-running instincts, but Hawaii-born **Jacob Hannemann** will have difficulty sticking in the majors due to a lack of power. ⚾ The shine is beginning to wear off on **Eddy Martinez**, who was once one of the jewels of the system. He's gotten a bit old for his level and the numbers aren't there, leaving him looking like organizational depth. ⚾ Former pitcher **Bijan Rademacher** committed to the outfield when he was drafted. Though his progression through the minors has been slow, he would be a good addition to most any outfield, even if it isn't the one in Chicago. ⚾ **Carlos Sepulveda**'s injury-shortened 2017 campaign belies his real talent. He torched the Midwest League in 2016 and has the ability to be a middle-infield asset in a few years. ⚾ It takes every fiber of a scout's being to watch **Jemile Weeks** try to reinvent himself as a utility player in the minor leagues and simply not write down "more like Jemile Days." ⚾ Want a dark-horse candidate for a Cubs outfield prospect? **D.J. Wilson** is your guy. He has speed and can hit for extra bases but has so far struggled to hit for average. Hedge your bet here. ⚾ The Cubs chose to protect **Mark Zagunis** from the Rule 5 draft, and it may or may not be because he has the ability to draw walks at a rate that makes Kevin Youkilis tip his cap. Without that, however, Zagunis might just be Quad-A fodder.

Pitchers

PITCHER	TEAM	LVL	AGE	W	L	SV	G	GS	IP	H	HR	BB/9	K/9	K	GB%	BABIP	WHIP	ERA	DRA	WARP	MPH	CMD	PWR	STM
Cory Abbott	EUG	A-	21	0	0	0	5	5	14	14	1	1.9	11.6	18	31%	.371	1.21	3.86	4.35	0.1				
Dario Alvarez	TEX	MLB	28	2	0	0	20	0	16^1	19	1	7.7	9.4	17	44%	.367	2.02	2.76	5.60	-0.1	93.9	31	31	39
	ROU	AAA	28	2	0	0	18	1	27	24	3	3.3	12.0	36	40%	.339	1.26	2.33	2.54	0.8				
Jake Buchanan	IOW	AAA	27	2	2	0	8	8	41^2	49	5	4.1	6.3	29	51%	.324	1.63	4.75	3.71	0.9				
	CIN	MLB	27	0	0	0	5	0	14^1	24	1	4.4	2.5	4	59%	.371	2.16	8.16	7.22	-0.3	90.9	72	29	60
	RNO	AAA	27	5	0	0	11	11	61^1	61	2	1.3	5.6	38	52%	.292	1.14	4.26	3.17	1.7				
Bailey Clark	EUG	A-	22	2	4	0	11	11	44^2	45	1	5.6	8.9	44	46%	.333	1.63	3.83	7.42	-1.1				
Trevor Clifton	TEN	AA	22	5	8	0	21	21	100^1	112	8	4.0	7.7	86	36%	.343	1.56	5.20	5.62	-0.5				
Brendon Little	EUG	A-	20	0	2	0	6	6	16^1	21	2	5.0	6.6	12	45%	.339	1.84	9.37	8.41	-0.6				

PITCHER	TEAM	LVL	AGE	W	L	SV	G	GS	IP	H	HR	BB/9	K/9	K	GB%	BABIP	WHIP	ERA	DRA	WARP	MPH	CMD	PWR	STM
Cory Mazzoni	ELP	AAA	27	1	0	1	14	0	20^{1}	18	0	1.3	13.7	31	50%	.375	1.03	0.89	1.38	0.9				
	SDN	MLB	27	0	0	0	6	0	8	17	5	4.5	4.5	4	40%	.375	2.62	13.50	9.77	-0.4	94.9			41
Erling Moreno	SBN	A	20	2	4	0	14	14	64	56	3	4.4	8.0	57	62%	.312	1.36	4.22	2.81	1.8				
Jose Paulino	SBN	A	22	7	6	0	27	22	123^{2}	125	6	3.1	6.8	94	53%	.316	1.35	4.51	4.30	1.4				
Randy Rosario	MIN	MLB	23	0	0	0	2	0	2^{1}	7	1	0.0	7.7	2	67%	.545	3.00	30.86	8.22	-0.1	96.2			42
	CHT	AA	23	1	0	1	32	0	57^{1}	57	4	3.6	7.1	45	51%	.312	1.40	4.08	5.34	-0.4				
Michael Rucker	SBN	A	23	0	0	1	7	0	12^{2}	7	1	0.0	15.6	22	33%	.261	0.55	1.42	1.74	0.5				
	MYR	A+	23	5	5	1	20	15	93^{1}	82	5	2.0	8.9	92	48%	.302	1.10	2.51	2.38	3.1				
Justin Steele	MYR	A+	21	6	7	0	20	20	98^{2}	100	6	3.3	7.5	82	50%	.315	1.38	2.92	5.06	0.2				
Jake Stinnett	TEN	AA	25	0	1	0	9	0	14^{2}	6	0	3.7	8.6	14	58%	.182	0.82	0.61	3.00	0.3				
Keegan Thompson	EUG	A-	22	1	2	0	7	1	19	15	1	1.9	10.9	23	40%	.298	1.00	2.37	3.06	0.4				
Duane Underwood	TEN	AA	22	13	7	0	25	24	138	130	13	3.3	6.4	98	45%	.282	1.30	4.43	5.40	-0.4				
Rob Zastryzny	IOW	AAA	25	2	3	1	14	7	47	50	7	2.7	7.7	40	50%	.305	1.36	5.94	3.19	1.2				
	CHN	MLB	25	0	0	0	4	0	13	19	2	4.8	7.6	11	51%	.415	2.00	8.31	5.80	-0.1	91.7	57	38	28

Chicago's second-round pick out of Loyola Marymount last June, **Cory Abbott** had no trouble missing bats at Low-A in his pro debut. ⚾ **Dario Alvarez** may not be good, but he's left-handed and gets swings and misses with his slide piece, so general managers will keep giving him deals well into the 2020s, and managers will keep using him to play Russian roulette against Bryce Harper. ⚾ **Jake Buchanan** owns a career 5.7 K/9 in more than 900 minor-league innings. In related news, he got whacked right good in his big-league cameo with the Reds last year. ⚾ **Bailey Clark** has the stuff to be a decent reliever, but it's worrisome that his velocity ticked down late in the 2017 season. ⚾ Just a year ago, **Trevor Clifton** would have been in serious consideration for one of the better arms in the Cubs' system, but his velocity dropped and his ERA doubled. ⚾ Drafted 30th overall out of LSU last June, **Alex Lange** agreed to a below-slot deal with the Cubs after some "issues" were found in his pre-signing physical. ⚾ Armed with a plus fastball and a good curveball, junior college left-hander **Brendon Little** was drafted by the Cubs at no. 27 overall. ⚾ **Cory Mazzoni** has allowed 38 runs in 16 2/3 big-league innings but gave up just two runs in 30 1/3 minor-league innings last season. He is the human embodiment of the line between Triple-A and the majors. ⚾ His injury history is a concern, but **Erling Moreno** could project as a back-of-the-rotation starter with two potentially plus pitches in his fastball and changeup. ⚾ **Jose Paulino** has good command, but his fastball lacks much snap and is a little too slow (high-80s) to properly complement his quality changeup. ⚾ **Armando Rivero** spent all of 2017 on Atlanta's disabled list and was promptly outrighted once the season ended. The Cubs declined to take him back, so the future for this Cuban reliever is very murky. ⚾ **Randy Rosario** induced lots of groundballs and held lefties to a .599 OPS at Double-A last year, so the Cubs claimed him on waivers from the Twins in the hope he can duplicate that at Wrigley Field (or at least Triple-A Iowa). ⚾ With a funky delivery and a deceptive fastball, **Michael Rucker** just needs to develop his breaking pitches and he'll have a shot at continuing as a starter. ⚾ Tommy John surgery robbed us of a complete season from **Justin Steele**, who was showing a resurgence at High-A in 2017. He might be gone until 2019, but bet big on Steele if his fastball stays in the mid-90s when he returns. ⚾ Once one of the better arms in the system, **Jake Stinnett** didn't pitch until mid-July, but he got to Double-A and allowed just a single run in 14 innings. ⚾ **Keegan Thompson** is intriguing for his plus curveball and his four-pitch repertoire, but his fastball needs to come along if he's going to be more than a back-end starter. ⚾ **Duane Underwood** pitched a fully healthy season for the first time, and though he probably lacks a good enough fastball and the command needed to pan out as a starter, his plus slider might pair well enough with his heater if he moves to the bullpen. ⚾ Some pitchers with short names have injuries of muscles that are difficult to spell. **Rob Zastryzny** missed two months with a sore lat. Whether he makes the rotation in the spring will determine how often sportswriters will stop copying and pasting his name into articles.

CHICAGO WHITE SOX

Essay by David Roth

Player comments by Nick Schaefer, Collin Whitchurch and BP staff

Every day, millions of Americans get out of bed, do their best to lash down and whip together and spot-clean their weary and multiply compromised selves into something approaching a presentable public shape, and then wrap the resulting mess in a suit. Most of these people dress this way because they have to do it for work, or because some other obligation compels them to do so. They are not heroes, really, or at least not any more heroic than any of the many other people who simply and uncomplainingly do what needs doing whether they want to do it or not. Some of these people in suits help people and others work to make the lives of vulnerable people even more parlous; a lot of them are just lawyers. But there is one fundamental truth about people in suits that is germane to our purposes here: You do not necessarily want one of those People In Suits to be the best thing about your favorite baseball team.

All things being equal, it would be natural for baseball fans to prefer, say, an overachieving max-effort outfielder or a brilliant and aesthetically unconventional mega-ace or even a less brilliant and more conventional ace-of-convenience to someone wearing a suit, and not only because the first options are baseball players and the last is just someone wearing a suit. Barring some sort of menswear fetish, the only reason fans would choose the person in the suit would be the absence of actual compelling baseball players to care about instead. This is nothing against people who wear suits to work. It's just that you don't see them legging out triples or throwing complete-game two-hitters very often. I myself follow the game fairly closely and can't remember the last time someone in a suit struck out Jose Bautista with the bases loaded in an important game. You might have to go back to the '90s for that.

All of which is to say that, for everything Rick Hahn has accomplished as the general manager of the White Sox in the last year, his most remarkable achievement is strangely easy to miss. Hahn has overseen the wholesale dismantling of a flawed team with some legitimately compelling stars—charismatic and productive position players, super-aces and crypto-aces and dominant bullpen contributors—by trading not just franchise cornerstones but more or less every major leaguer who could bring back any sort of value in return. He started this by trading Chris Sale, the team's—and quite possibly the league's—best pitcher, on December 6, 2016, and flipping outfielder Adam Eaton to the Nationals the next day. Then, with periodic breaks for waiver deadlines and, we can only assume, sleeping and eating, Hahn just kept going.

All of these moves cleared a great deal of salary from the books, but they weren't done with that in mind. The point was to bring back the biggest and best assortment of prospects possible, and in that Hahn unquestionably succeeded. The young players who came on board—Yoan Moncada, Reynaldo Lopez, Eloy Jimenez, Michael Kopech, Lucas Giolito, Blake Rutherford and other names that will be recognizable to even less obsessive prospector types— are for the most part still beings of pure potential; only a handful have

WHITE SOX PROSPECTUS

2017 W-L: 67-95, 4TH IN AL CENTRAL

Pythag	.429	26th	B-Age	26.7	3rd
RS/G	4.36	23rd	P-Age	28.8	19th
RA/G	5.06	23rd	Salary	$97.8M	23rd
TAv	.250	29th	M$/MW	$4.5M	11th
TAv-P	.267	20th	DL Days	1161	20th
FIP	5.14	30th	$ on DL	11%	9th
DER	.719	3rd			

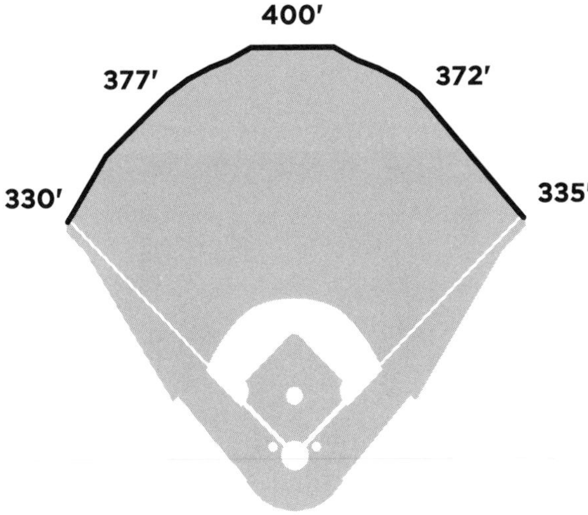

Outfield wall profile: **8'**

Three-Year Park Factors

Runs	Runs/RH	Runs/LH	HR/RH	HR/LH
97	97	96	104	111

Top Hitter WARP	3.9 Jose Abreu
Top Pitcher WARP	2.0 Jose Quintana
Top Prospect	Eloy Jimenez

2017 Hit List Ranking

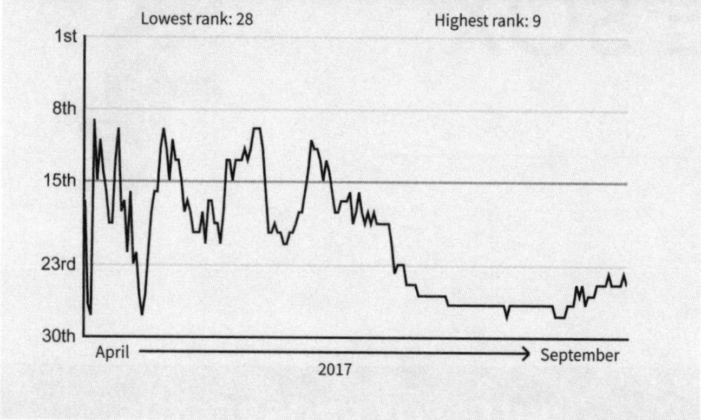

Committed Payroll (in millions)

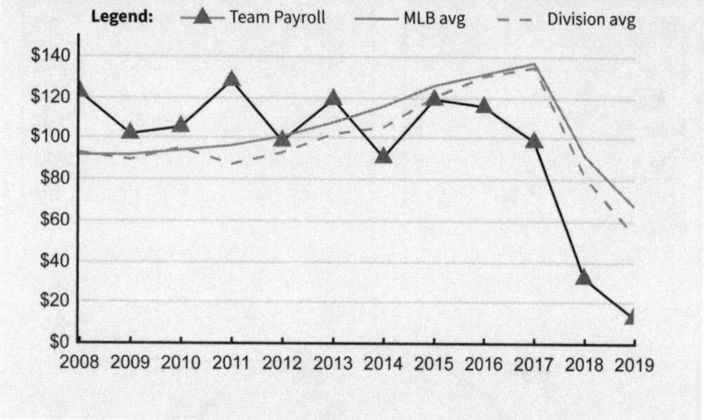

Farm System Ranking

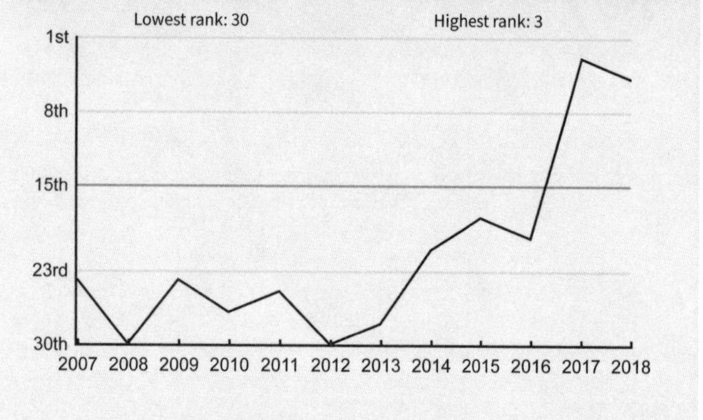

Personnel

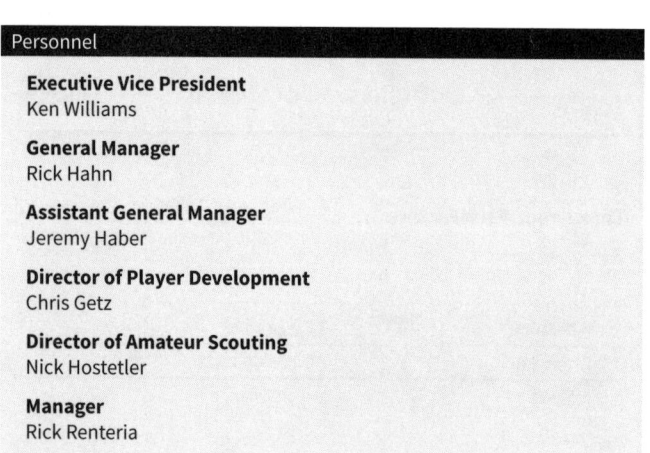

Executive Vice President
Ken Williams

General Manager
Rick Hahn

Assistant General Manager
Jeremy Haber

Director of Player Development
Chris Getz

Director of Amateur Scouting
Nick Hostetler

Manager
Rick Renteria

even sniffed the bigs yet. The sell-off is either over or nearly over, if only because there is not much left for Hahn to sell. One or more of these young players will, at some point in the future, slip the surly bonds of the prospect rankings and become the best things about the White Sox.

It is not at all unprecedented for a GM to do what Hahn did. There are names for it, and various templates for the various ways in which GMs have gone about doing it in different situations and leagues. It is not even unusual for the Person In Suit overseeing all that transactional carnage to emerge as something like a hero in real time; Philadelphia 76ers fans talk about the deposed author of that team's historically fulsome rebuilding process with a reverence typically reserved for 13th-century religious martyrs. But for all the dishonor associated with tanking, for all the noxious political echoes of burning down the present to set up some fantastical and abstracted future, for all the risk in asking fans to believe in things presently unseen and quite possibly nonexistent, Hahn and the White Sox somehow enter the 2018 season—that is, the season after one in which the team lost 95 games—with a fan base that is more hopeful than it has been in years. Maybe not for this year, although given that hope is a free and renewable resource it's hard to see why not, but certainly for the ones after that. In time, this will be a matter of seeing how well all of those prospects—Hahn added a total of 20 during the 2017 season—deliver on their significant individual and collective promise.

For now, though, it's about believing in a man wearing a suit. It's true that there aren't that many more appealing options in uniform. But also the White Sox have, in the last year, become something significantly more abstract than the average team. They will play 162 games in 2018, just like everyone else. They may even play them well. But Rick Hahn's White Sox, in this moment, are as much an idea as they are a baseball team. All of those ideas—the idea of a team built this way out of prospects like these, and the possible futures of that team—are much more fun to think about than they have been in some time. That is not the final goal, of course. But if this team and its architect accomplish nothing else, they have already done something significant—turned a mediocre, topped-out team into one of the most fascinating fantasy objects in Major League Baseball.

It's not that White Sox fans chose Rick Hahn over Chris Sale or Adam Eaton or Jose Quintana or Todd Frazier or David Robertson or Dan Jennings or (uh) Melky Cabrera or (significantly louder uh) Tyler Clippard; these are reasonable people, or at least unreasonable in the same unreasonable ways that all fans are, and so they would not make that choice. It's that they understood those moves in the broader context in which they were made. They looked at the players the White Sox had and decided that they would trust someone in a suit to swap that particular present for players who might deliver a different sort of future—through a series of trades that would, in the near term, deliver a significantly more excruciating present.

"When we set off down this path, we were ambitious," Hahn told the *Chicago Tribune* in September 2017. "We knew we had some premium assets at the big-league level, so we were very ambitious in terms of our expectations about what we were going to bring back." Hahn left the present out of that statement, but that's only polite—it was going to be bad, right up until the future arrived. This was the deal: Believe in a brighter future enough to trust that suffering in the present might eventually be worth it, and might even someday redeem that suffering in spades.

Like many teams, the White Sox have been in between for some time; like most teams, they seemed not to know what to do about that. Since Hahn took over as GM in 2012 and for years before that, the roster was an archipelago of quality players surrounded by some wide and boggy shallows; during those seasons, the team mostly tried to fill the spaces between well enough to get from 75 wins to 85. Some of the team's topped-out top-heaviness was budget-related, but a great deal of it owed to a farm system that had stopped producing the sort of cost-effective young talent that might have filled in those gaps. After all those years of constructing another series of rickety bridges and potholed causeways, Hahn finally decided to just flood the whole thing.

The result, in 2017, was a season spent deeply if intentionally underwater, and well under .500. The first of the team's big prospects arrived—Moncada was called up for good in July, Lopez and Giolito and 2015 first-round pick Carson Fulmer at various points in August—and proceeded to get acclimated, with varying degrees of awkwardness, through some months of deeply meaningless games. When White Sox fans look back on the dark days, they will trade these names of the misfits and randos who were on hand in 2017 with the same dorky ecstasy that obsessives discuss the more obscure outer-canon figures in the *Star Wars* universe. There is a George Lucas-esque combination of musicality and overdetermination to some of these names—Yolmer Sanchez and Omar Narvaez and Aaron Bummer and Jace Fry and Al Alburquerque. Some of these players fall more on the hard sci-fi side of the spectrum—Adam Engel and his floridly psychedelic OPS+ of 39 in 336 plate appearances, Chris Volstad making major-league starts for the first time since Barack Obama's first term in office, Dylan Covey allowing 20 home runs in 70 innings. None of this mattered, really, and boy did it ever feel that way.

But there is more than one kind of losing, and if all of the losing the White Sox did in 2017 felt lighter and goofier and more illusory than it had in the years before, it was because the team and its fans were already living in the future. Hahn was the star of the season because his transactions were, in a real sense, the best show in town. But the extent to which fans embraced it—and when you can go online and buy T-shirts reading HAHNSIGHT IS 2020, with the zeroes replaced with World Series trophies, it's safe to say they've embraced it—reflected not just the desperation of the Aaron Bummer present, but a conscious decision not to live there.

While the Sox figure to be closer in 2018 to whatever their future will look like, it's tough to know if they will actually have arrived there. It seems likely that the promising young players who arrived at the end of last season will be there at the beginning of this one, and that alone will provide a better reason to watch than anything on offer in 2017. Whatever additional growing pains might await Lopez and Fulmer and Giolito, they will assuredly not be more painful to watch than the work Derek Holland, Mike Pelfrey and the aforementioned Covey did in creating the incandescently toxic Superfund site that was the team's 2017 rotation. The team will be in no rush to promote Jimenez, who will be 21 for the 2018 season, or Kopech, who will turn 22 around Opening Day, but both showed signs last season of being talents that make it difficult, or even foolish, to be too patient. The big-league roster is still mostly holes, and for all the promise presently percolating up through the system there is still the sense that the White Sox have another year or so of Figuring Things Out ahead.

Prospects being prospects and baseball being baseball, it's hard to know when or if the White Sox will ever get there. The farm system is stocked with brilliant pitching prospects, but also there is no such thing as a pitching prospect; the premium hitting prospects might turn out to be anything, but they also might just turn out to be a bunch of tall guys with good baseball names. Hahn has spoken about the team being at the end of Stage One of this process, but while it's clear that Stage Two will mainly be a matter of player development, it's hard to say how many stages are ahead. "There are different challenges along the way when you're rebuilding to transition to get those guys to the big leagues to eventually winning," Cubs GM Jed Hoyer told the *Chicago Tribune* in November. "Certainly, (with) the beginning part of the process, the talent accumulation part, they have done a really good job." That's important, but it's not everything.

This is one of the frustrating things about the future, but it coexists with one of the best things about it—to live in the future is, in a certain sense, to escape the unpleasantness of waking up here in the present. Before the 2017 season and during it, the White Sox realized their particular present wasn't worth risking the future over. They are, as the 2018 season looms, still very much in between—not where they were, but not yet where they're headed.

It's hard to know what the next stage of figuring things out will look like or how many stages will follow before this team gets wherever it's going. But it seems safe to say that, as with last year's exercise in on-the-job training, it won't really matter much. When Hahn decided to burn down the present to bet on the future, he wasn't just making deals that turned one of baseball's worst farm systems into one of its best. In a practical sense, of course, that is just what he did. But, in a broader sense, he turned a team stuck scuffling for a marginal advantage in the present into one working toward a bigger advantage in the future.

More than that, though, he made room for a grander and more ambitious sort of belief. The White Sox could well win a lot of games with all of the talent that Hahn accumulated over the last year and change. They also might not—the pitching prospects might all turn out to be relievers, the hitters might not be hitters at all.

This year, and in years to come, the team that Hahn made will become whatever it will become. They might be great, or they might be something less than that. What they will never be, for better or worse, is more exciting and full of promise than what they are right now—a team that is so supremely unfinished, so suffused with possibility and comprised so fully of faith and hope and the sweetest sort of anticipation that it could be anything we could imagine. It could, for all we know, be even more than that. Or less. Anyway, it's fun to think about. That doesn't sound remarkable, I know. But it is.

—David Roth is an editor for Deadspin.

HITTERS

Jose Abreu 1B Born: 01/29/87 Age: 31 Bats: R Throws: R Height: 6'3" Weight: 255 Origin: International Free Agent, 2013

YEAR	TEAM	LVL	AGE	PA	R	2B	3B	HR	RBI	BB	K	SB	CS	AVG/OBP/SLG	TAv	VORP	BABIP	BRR	FRAA	WARP
2015	CHA	MLB	28	668	88	34	3	30	101	39	140	0	0	.290/.347/.502	.291	23.7	.333	-2.9	1B(115): 6.2	3.2
2016	CHA	MLB	29	695	67	32	1	25	100	47	125	0	2	.293/.353/.468	.283	21.8	.327	-1.7	1B(152): 7.1	3.0
2017	CHA	MLB	30	675	95	43	6	33	102	35	119	3	0	.304/.354/.552	.295	33.0	.330	0.8	1B(139): 5.5	3.9
2018	*CHA*	*MLB*	*31*	*636*	*86*	*32*	*3*	*29*	*99*	*42*	*124*	*2*	*1*	*.289/.349/.505*	*.291*	*30.6*	*.322*	*-1.0*	*1B 4*	*3.1*
2019	*CHA*	*MLB*	*32*	*562*	*79*	*29*	*2*	*26*	*84*	*38*	*116*	*0*	*0*	*.279/.341/.497*	*.278*	*17.1*	*.314*	*-1.1*	*1B 3*	*2.2*

Breakout: 1% Improve: 36% Collapse: 4% Attrition: 4% MLB: 95% *Comparables: Kendrys Morales, Ted Kluszewski, Corey Hart*

Despite a power resurgence giving credence to the theory his down 2016 could be attributed to injury rather than a real loss of skill, Abreu was never the subject of serious trade rumors in 2017 and enjoyed his best season since his prodigious rookie year. The last veteran standing on offense took to the role of team leader and mentor like a duck to water. That, paired with the bounce-back in performance, could force the White Sox to make some tough decisions about how his contract lines up with their next competitive window. Power is up all over the majors, but Abreu's hit tool continues to separate him from generic dinger-dependent first basemen and gives hope that he may age more gracefully than it looked this time last year.

Micker Adolfo RF Born: 09/11/96 Age: 21 Bats: R Throws: R Height: 6'3" Weight: 200 Origin: International Free Agent, 2013

YEAR	TEAM	LVL	AGE	PA	R	2B	3B	HR	RBI	BB	K	SB	CS	AVG/OBP/SLG	TAv	VORP	BABIP	BRR	FRAA	WARP
2015	WSX	RK	18	93	14	3	1	0	10	6	25	3	2	.253/.323/.313	.244	1.3	.356	0.7	RF(12): 0.0, CF(9): -0.6	0.1
2016	KAN	A	19	265	30	13	1	5	21	14	88	0	1	.219/.269/.340	.246	0.7	.318	0.0	RF(61): 8.9, CF(2): -0.2	1.0
2017	KAN	A	20	473	60	28	2	16	68	31	149	2	0	.264/.331/.453	.287	17.3	.366	-4.1	RF(102): -12.2	0.5
2018	*CHA*	*MLB*	*21*	*250*	*24*	*10*	*0*	*9*	*30*	*13*	*95*	*0*	*0*	*.202/.255/.360*	*.207*	*-7.4*	*.293*	*-0.4*	*RF -3*	*-1.1*
2019	*CHA*	*MLB*	*22*	*312*	*35*	*12*	*1*	*12*	*37*	*17*	*115*	*0*	*0*	*.207/.263/.376*	*.218*	*-7.9*	*.294*	*-0.7*	*RF -3*	*-1.2*

Breakout: 0% Improve: 1% Collapse: 0% Attrition: 4% MLB: 4% *Comparables: Marcell Ozuna, Willy Garcia, Yorman Rodriguez*

In the mid-to-late '90s, when *Men In Black* delighted audiences everywhere, the White Sox made a habit of churning out power-hitting position players. Fast-forward to the mid-2000s and we had the execrable *Men In Black 2* and the White Sox's dismal inability to produce any hitters whatsoever. The colossal Adolfo initially looked like a continuation of those busts, needing three tries to get out of rookie ball. But, just as *Men In Black 3* rallied to be a solid offering, Adolfo went from having a self-described "no approach" to "an approach" in 2017 and posted adequate numbers in Low-A. The massive power and howitzer arm are still there, but his eye and plan at the plate must continue to improve exponentially, as his bat speed is not a strength. Some hope beats no hope any day.

Tim Anderson SS Born: 06/23/93 Age: 25 Bats: R Throws: R Height: 6'1" Weight: 185 Origin: Round 1, 2013 Draft (#17 overall)

YEAR	TEAM	LVL	AGE	PA	R	2B	3B	HR	RBI	BB	K	SB	CS	AVG/OBP/SLG	TAv	VORP	BABIP	BRR	FRAA	WARP
2015	BIR	AA	22	550	79	21	12	5	46	24	114	49	13	.312/.350/.429	.289	46.9	.391	10.9	SS(110): 0.7	5.2
2016	CHR	AAA	23	256	39	10	2	4	20	8	58	11	4	.304/.325/.409	.262	10.9	.384	0.1	SS(52): -1.5	1.0
2016	CHA	MLB	23	431	57	22	6	9	30	13	117	10	2	.283/.306/.432	.248	16.6	.375	4.0	SS(98): -4.7	1.2
2017	CHA	MLB	24	606	72	26	4	17	56	13	162	15	1	.257/.276/.402	.233	10.6	.328	2.1	SS(145): -11.7	-0.1
2018	*CHA*	*MLB*	*25*	*629*	*81*	*26*	*7*	*16*	*64*	*19*	*165*	*19*	*4*	*.265/.289/.409*	*.241*	*18.6*	*.336*	*3.0*	*SS -8*	*0.4*
2019	*CHA*	*MLB*	*26*	*570*	*66*	*25*	*5*	*19*	*71*	*21*	*155*	*17*	*4*	*.262/.294/.433*	*.244*	*12.6*	*.331*	*2.7*	*SS -7*	*0.6*

Breakout: 4% Improve: 55% Collapse: 8% Attrition: 19% MLB: 98% *Comparables: Danny Santana, Ian Desmond, Ronny Cedeno*

Anderson's margin for error has always been slim, and his success or failure both at the plate and in the field were always going to be contingent on whether his raw tools and athleticism would translate into actual skills. His 2017 was rife with struggles, none more so than the May death of his best friend, which reminded observers that sometimes life throws curveballs more difficult than anything he'll face in the batter's box. While the extent to which Anderson's personal life dictated his struggles on the field is unquantifiable, his last two months of the season—in which he improved his OPS by 180 points—showed why his ceiling remains that of a solid regular at a key defensive position.

Luis Alexander Basabe OF Born: 08/26/96 Age: 21 Bats: B Throws: R Height: 6'0" Weight: 160 Origin: International Free Agent, 2012

YEAR	TEAM	LVL	AGE	PA	R	2B	3B	HR	RBI	BB	K	SB	CS	AVG/OBP/SLG	TAv	VORP	BABIP	BRR	FRAA	WARP
2015	LOW	A-	18	256	36	8	3	7	23	32	67	15	4	.243/.340/.401	.273	13.5	.315	4.1	CF(28): 4.8, RF(25): 5.9	2.9
2016	GRN	A	19	451	61	24	8	12	52	40	116	25	5	.258/.325/.447	.285	26.3	.330	2.7	CF(98): 11.6	4.1
2017	WNS	A+	20	435	52	12	5	5	36	49	104	17	6	.221/.320/.320	.245	10.0	.292	4.4	CF(78): 0.1, RF(10): -0.4	1.0
2018	*CHA*	*MLB*	*21*	*250*	*31*	*9*	*2*	*7*	*24*	*21*	*78*	*6*	*2*	*.209/.282/.359*	*.217*	*-1.1*	*.280*	*0.6*	*CF 2, RF 1*	*0.2*
2019	*CHA*	*MLB*	*22*	*381*	*45*	*14*	*4*	*12*	*45*	*33*	*118*	*9*	*3*	*.218/.293/.389*	*.233*	*1.1*	*.289*	*1.2*	*CF 3, RF 1*	*0.6*

Breakout: 2% Improve: 5% Collapse: 0% Attrition: 4% MLB: 6% *Comparables: Daniel Fields, Teoscar Hernandez, Michael Saunders*

Unlike the return on the Adam Eaton trade, the four prospects who came back in exchange for Chris Sale were easy to sort in terms of shine. As the obvious third piece, Basabe lives somewhere in the yawning chasm between Michael Kopech and Victor Diaz. Basabe is toolsy, but not as toolsy as, say, Luis Robert. He was somewhat disappointing last year, but not in any serious way considering he was a 20-year-old in High-A. There's still the starter kit here for a good defensive center fielder who hits enough to be a useful contributor, but it's going to take some time.

Rob Brantly C Born: 07/14/89 Age: 28 Bats: L Throws: R Height: 6'1" Weight: 195 Origin: Round 3, 2010 Draft (#100 overall)

YEAR	TEAM	LVL	AGE	PA	R	2B	3B	HR	RBI	BB	K	SB	CS	AVG/OBP/SLG	TAv	VORP	BABIP	BRR	FRAA	WARP
2015	BIR	AA	25	121	13	6	1	4	22	3	14	0	1	.325/.347/.496	.290	7.3	.343	-1.5	C(29): -4.9	0.3
2015	CHR	AAA	25	94	11	3	0	4	16	5	17	0	0	.291/.319/.465	.269	2.4	.309	-1.3	C(14): -1.1	0.1
2015	CHA	MLB	25	36	3	1	0	1	6	2	8	0	0	.121/.167/.242	.154	-2.2	.120	0.0	C(14): -2.3	-0.5
2016	TAC	AAA	26	315	34	13	1	14	43	8	53	0	1	.244/.268/.432	.263	11.5	.253	-0.8	C(60): 2.8, 3B(1): 0.0	1.5
2017	LOU	AAA	27	179	21	6	1	5	16	9	25	3	2	.298/.335/.435	.265	8.2	.324	-0.8	C(39): -4.8	0.3
2017	CHR	AAA	27	142	18	5	0	5	30	11	14	0	1	.286/.373/.454	.281	7.4	.279	-2.6	C(35): 3.5	1.1
2017	CHA	MLB	27	36	4	1	0	2	5	3	14	0	0	.290/.389/.516	.307	2.6	.467	-0.3	C(6): -0.2, P(1): 0.0	0.2
2018	*CHA*	*MLB*	*28*	*250*	*27*	*10*	*1*	*10*	*33*	*13*	*51*	*1*	*0*	*.245/.295/.422*	*.236*	*5.8*	*.272*	*-0.4*	*C -8, 1B 0*	*-0.2*
2019	*CHA*	*MLB*	*29*	*201*	*25*	*7*	*0*	*8*	*26*	*11*	*42*	*0*	*0*	*.237/.288/.419*	*.237*	*2.4*	*.260*	*-0.5*	*C -5, 1B 0*	*-0.3*

Breakout: 5% Improve: 25% Collapse: 15% Attrition: 34% MLB: 72% *Comparables: Shawn Riggans, Austin Romine, Bryan Holaday*

YEAR	TEAM	P. COUNT	FRM RUNS	BLK RUNS	THRW RUNS	TOT RUNS
2015	BIR	3932	-5.4	-0.2	-0.2	-5.8
2015	CHA	1468	-2.0	-0.1	0.1	-2.1
2015	CHR	1994	-1.0	-0.1	0.1	-1.0
2017	CHA	675	-0.5	0.4	0.0	-0.1
2018	*CHA*	*8904*	*-5.8*	*-1.5*	*0.0*	*-7.2*
2019	*CHA*	*7148*	*-2.6*	*-0.7*	*0.0*	*-3.2*

Brantly posted gaudy offensive numbers for the White Sox last year in an extremely small sample, much as he had for the Marlins back in 2012. The problem is that between those two brief outbursts, he flopped hard in 2013 and was largely forgotten over the next three seasons, notching only 14 big-league games and getting waived twice. He doesn't turn 29 until the All-Star break, so technically there's still time for him to carve out a career, but he won't be able to play the youth card much longer. The question of whether Brantly's future lies as an organization's second- or third-best catcher is largely academic. On the bright side, and perhaps no less academic, he's the best backstop drafted out of UC Riverside since Troy Percival.

Jake Burger 3B Born: 04/10/96 Age: 22 Bats: R Throws: R Height: 6'2" Weight: 210 Origin: Round 1, 2017 Draft (#11 overall)

YEAR	TEAM	LVL	AGE	PA	R	2B	3B	HR	RBI	BB	K	SB	CS	AVG/OBP/SLG	TAv	VORP	BABIP	BRR	FRAA	WARP
2017	KAN	A	21	200	21	9	2	4	27	13	28	0	1	.271/.335/.409	.279	9.5	.300	-0.2	3B(42): -0.8	0.9
2018	*CHA*	*MLB*	*22*	*250*	*26*	*10*	*1*	*8*	*30*	*16*	*58*	*0*	*0*	*.234/.292/.393*	*.230*	*0.1*	*.277*	*-0.3*	*3B -1*	*-0.1*
2019	*CHA*	*MLB*	*23*	*238*	*29*	*10*	*1*	*8*	*29*	*16*	*56*	*0*	*0*	*.237/.299/.406*	*.240*	*0.3*	*.278*	*-0.5*	*3B -1*	*-0.1*

Breakout: 9% Improve: 18% Collapse: 5% Attrition: 22% MLB: 29% *Comparables: Miguel Andujar, Jefry Marte, Ryan Wheeler*

The White Sox drafted the beefy Burger in the first round hoping his colossal college power numbers would translate to the majors. The meat of Burger's production will come in that form, but the White Sox hope the toppings will include some cheese (a strong throwing arm), lettuce (good bat-to-ball skills), and tomato (uh ... keen sense of the strike zone). Burger may never be a deluxe prospect given that he'll be limited to the corner-infield positions, and there are legitimate concerns about how he'll hold up at third base as his already robust frame fills out. But if he can grasp the finer aspects of the game to go along with his sizzling power, he'll make some serious bacon.

Welington Castillo C Born: 04/24/87 Age: 31 Bats: R Throws: R Height: 5'10" Weight: 220 Origin: International Free Agent, 2004

YEAR	TEAM	LVL	AGE	PA	R	2B	3B	HR	RBI	BB	K	SB	CS	AVG/OBP/SLG	TAv	VORP	BABIP	BRR	FRAA	WARP
2015	CHN	MLB	28	47	5	2	0	2	5	3	12	0	0	.163/.234/.349	.233	0.6	.172	0.0	C(9): 0.5	0.1
2015	SEA	MLB	28	28	3	0	0	0	2	1	5	0	0	.160/.179/.160	.134	-2.4	.182	0.0	C(5): -0.5	-0.3
2015	ARI	MLB	28	303	34	13	1	17	50	21	75	0	0	.255/.317/.496	.284	19.2	.286	-0.9	C(74): -8.3	1.2
2016	ARI	MLB	29	457	41	24	0	14	68	33	121	2	0	.264/.322/.423	.266	18.6	.337	-4.5	C(107): -10.3	0.9
2017	BAL	MLB	30	365	44	11	0	20	53	22	97	0	0	.282/.323/.490	.272	20.3	.336	-0.7	C(88): 7.4	2.8
2018	*CHA*	*MLB*	*31*	*452*	*55*	*18*	*1*	*17*	*57*	*32*	*114*	*1*	*0*	*.247/.308/.414*	*.252*	*16.8*	*.299*	*-0.9*	*C -5*	*0.9*
2019	*CHA*	*MLB*	*32*	*387*	*49*	*15*	*0*	*15*	*49*	*28*	*101*	*0*	*0*	*.242/.308/.412*	*.246*	*7.8*	*.296*	*-1.8*	*C -3*	*0.5*

Breakout: 3% Improve: 31% Collapse: 19% Attrition: 21% MLB: 97% *Comparables: John Buck, Ozzie Virgil, Mike Macfarlane*

YEAR	TEAM	P. COUNT	FRM RUNS	BLK RUNS	THRW RUNS	TOT RUNS
2015	CHN	1119	0.3	0.3	0.0	0.6
2015	SEA	860	-0.8	0.4	0.0	-0.4
2015	ARI	10394	-9.6	1.1	0.0	-8.5
2016	ARI	15918	-9.4	-1.5	3.1	-7.8
2017	BAL	13481	3.7	1.1	3.1	7.9
2018	*CHA*	*16644*	*-5.9*	*0.3*	*2.7*	*-3.0*
2019	*CHA*	*14232*	*-5.4*	*0.2*	*2.4*	*-2.7*

In 2015, Castillo was flipped by the Mariners to the Diamondbacks for Mark Trumbo in a salary dump; in 2016, his new team nontendered him; he then went on to sign the Orioles Memorial One-Year Under-Market Contract™ and enjoy the best season of his career. It was a fantastic season for the backstop in every way except in terms of testicles, as foul tips sent him to the hospital on two separate occasions with contusions. Those sad evenings, a bout of shoulder tightness and the existence of tough right-handed pitching limited him to less than a hundred games, and that's what a team should expect out of him. But the days of him being a cheap addition might be over: Castillo's framing skills have slowly crept from damaging to acceptable, which combined with a strong arm makes him a decent enough catcher. All he needs is the Steve Yeager of groin protection to invent a new cup, and he'll be ready for another fine season in 2018.

Zack Collins C Born: 02/06/95 Age: 23 Bats: L Throws: R Height: 6'3" Weight: 220 Origin: Round 1, 2016 Draft (#10 overall)

YEAR	TEAM	LVL	AGE	PA	R	2B	3B	HR	RBI	BB	K	SB	CS	AVG/OBP/SLG	TAv	VORP	BABIP	BRR	FRAA	WARP
2016	WNS	A+	21	153	24	7	0	6	18	33	39	0	0	.258/.418/.467	.302	10.8	.333	-0.4	C(18): -0.6	1.0
2017	WNS	A+	22	426	63	18	3	17	48	76	118	0	2	.223/.365/.443	.283	22.6	.282	-2.6	C(63): 1.5	2.6
2017	BIR	AA	22	45	7	2	0	2	5	11	11	0	0	.235/.422/.471	.324	4.8	.286	-0.1	C(11): -2.0	0.3
2018	*CHA*	*MLB*	*23*	*250*	*31*	*8*	*1*	*10*	*33*	*40*	*81*	*0*	*0*	*.208/.339/.407*	*.253*	*10.3*	*.277*	*-0.4*	*C -16*	*-0.7*
2019	*CHA*	*MLB*	*24*	*308*	*43*	*11*	*1*	*13*	*40*	*48*	*98*	*0*	*0*	*.209/.337/.409*	*.254*	*9.1*	*.275*	*-0.6*	*C -14*	*-0.5*

Breakout: 8% Improve: 17% Collapse: 7% Attrition: 18% MLB: 45% *Comparables: Derek Norris, Matt Olson, Travis Shaw*

YEAR	TEAM	P. COUNT	FRM RUNS	BLK RUNS	THRW RUNS	TOT RUNS
2018	*CHA*	*8568*	*-13.7*	*-1.8*	*0.3*	*-15.1*
2019	*CHA*	*10558*	*-4.9*	*-0.6*	*0.1*	*-5.4*

Going into the 2016 draft, scouts generally liked Collins' bat, but didn't see him as a catcher and worried his bat wouldn't stand out at first base or designated hitter. Two years later he's made it to Double-A and hasn't veered far from that forecast. The patience and power are still there, although he has dedicated the offseason to smoothing a hitch out of his swing, which may help his bat-to-ball skills. The defense has improved enough that he's much closer to the majors and hasn't been moved off the position, but he hasn't gotten so much better that one can confidently pencil him in behind the plate just yet. Tyler Flowers and Kevan Smith are encouraging examples of the White Sox's ability to coach up the receiving skills of gigantic catchers, and if Collins can pull it off he still has an outside chance at being a special player.

Matt Davidson 3B Born: 03/26/91 Age: 27 Bats: R Throws: R Height: 6'3" Weight: 230 Origin: Round 1, 2009 Draft (#35 overall)

YEAR	TEAM	LVL	AGE	PA	R	2B	3B	HR	RBI	BB	K	SB	CS	AVG/OBP/SLG	TAv	VORP	BABIP	BRR	FRAA	WARP
2015	CHR	AAA	24	602	63	22	0	23	74	62	191	1	0	.203/.293/.375	.237	-0.4	.264	-3.6	3B(130): 14.6, SS(2): -0.1	1.4
2016	CHR	AAA	25	326	35	20	0	10	46	32	86	0	0	.268/.349/.444	.271	10.7	.346	-2.6	3B(66): 6.7, 1B(6): 0.1	1.8
2016	CHA	MLB	25	2	1	0	0	0	1	0	1	0	0	.500/.500/.500	.352	0.1	1.000	-0.1		0.0
2017	CHA	MLB	26	443	43	16	1	26	68	19	165	0	1	.220/.260/.452	.233	-7.9	.285	-3.4	3B(34): -1.9, 1B(19): -1.2	-1.1
2018	*CHA*	*MLB*	*27*	*504*	*58*	*21*	*1*	*21*	*69*	*40*	*168*	*0*	*0*	*.216/.286/.406*	*.238*	*-3.3*	*.287*	*-1.1*	*1B -2, 3B 1*	*-0.6*
2019	*CHA*	*MLB*	*28*	*535*	*69*	*23*	*1*	*24*	*72*	*46*	*182*	*0*	*0*	*.218/.294/.417*	*.239*	*-2.4*	*.291*	*-2.4*	*1B -2, 3B 1*	*-0.4*

Breakout: 1% Improve: 12% Collapse: 11% Attrition: 18% MLB: 32% *Comparables: Jeff Baker, Victor Diaz, Alex Liddi*

Guys who are good at whacking dingers but little else will always have a place in our hearts, but where they fit into a team's long-term plans is, well, dependent on the team. Davidson went from top prospect to someone whose contact issues had him toiling in Triple-A far longer than anyone might've expected, and then he became a regular for the White Sox at age 26. He's more first baseman/designated hitter than third baseman, and one-dimensional offense makes it tough to envision a future in which he's more than the right side of a platoon. But at least aesthetically speaking, you could do a lot worse than "dude who mashes lots of taters."

Nick Delmonico 4C Born: 07/12/92 Age: 25 Bats: L Throws: R Height: 6'2" Weight: 230 Origin: Round 6, 2011 Draft (#185 overall)

YEAR	TEAM	LVL	AGE	PA	R	2B	3B	HR	RBI	BB	K	SB	CS	AVG/OBP/SLG	TAv	VORP	BABIP	BRR	FRAA	WARP
2015	BIR	AA	22	253	26	24	0	3	26	25	52	2	1	.238/.313/.386	.261	8.7	.292	1.1	3B(59): 6.7	1.7
2016	BIR	AA	23	159	25	14	2	10	31	13	33	1	0	.338/.397/.676	.374	15.7	.384	-4.3	1B(30): 0.4, 3B(3): 0.1	1.8
2016	CHR	AAA	23	295	32	16	0	7	30	29	74	2	0	.246/.320/.388	.254	3.4	.311	-1.8	3B(39): 0.4, RF(17): 0.5	0.7
2017	CHR	AAA	24	429	55	18	3	12	45	46	73	4	2	.262/.347/.421	.269	20.0	.296	2.9	3B(73): -1.4, LF(13): -0.6	1.8
2017	CHA	MLB	24	166	25	4	0	9	23	23	31	2	0	.262/.373/.482	.295	10.0	.277	0.9	LF(27): 2.8, 1B(4): -0.6	1.2
2018	*CHA*	*MLB*	*25*	*364*	*45*	*17*	*1*	*14*	*49*	*35*	*85*	*2*	*0*	*.246/.324/.435*	*.263*	*10.7*	*.290*	*-0.4*	*LF 5*	*1.3*
2019	*CHA*	*MLB*	*26*	*448*	*59*	*20*	*2*	*18*	*60*	*45*	*108*	*2*	*1*	*.245/.326/.442*	*.260*	*10.8*	*.289*	*-0.6*	*LF 6*	*1.9*

Breakout: 9% Improve: 28% Collapse: 15% Attrition: 42% MLB: 77% *Comparables: Jefry Marte, Yamaico Navarro, Ryan Rua*

Delmonico was the type of out-of-nowhere revelation organizations like the Cardinals or Dodgers usually discover—certainly not a White Sox team that has struggled to develop hitting prospects since the George W. Bush administration. As a journeyman with a mixed track record in the minors, his true hitting talent lies somewhere between his 1.000 OPS in August and his .600 OPS in September, though that describes most hitters. He's also a work in progress in left field—his most likely landing spot defensively—but if all else fails, his smoldering good looks and marquee-ready moniker may help him transition to Hollywood when his playing days are done.

Adam Engel CF Born: 12/09/91 Age: 26 Bats: R Throws: R Height: 6'2" Weight: 210 Origin: Round 19, 2013 Draft (#573 overall)

YEAR	TEAM	LVL	AGE	PA	R	2B	3B	HR	RBI	BB	K	SB	CS	AVG/OBP/SLG	TAv	VORP	BABIP	BRR	FRAA	WARP
2015	WNS	A+	23	608	90	23	9	7	43	62	132	65	11	.251/.335/.369	.259	27.6	.321	10.3	CF(136): -1.1	2.9
2016	WNS	A+	24	64	15	6	1	0	5	7	11	6	0	.327/.413/.473	.319	9.6	.409	3.6	CF(12): -0.9, LF(2): -0.2	0.9
2016	BIR	AA	24	357	56	18	9	4	25	39	70	31	9	.255/.352/.412	.288	26.1	.319	5.8	CF(71): -2.0	2.6
2016	CHR	AAA	24	161	19	6	2	3	16	10	50	8	5	.242/.298/.369	.235	-0.1	.344	-0.1	CF(25): 4.9, LF(16): -2.1	0.3
2017	CHR	AAA	25	192	20	12	2	8	19	19	51	4	3	.218/.312/.461	.270	9.8	.262	1.8	CF(33): -0.3, LF(13): 1.9	1.1
2017	CHA	MLB	25	336	34	11	3	6	21	19	117	8	1	.166/.235/.282	.199	-9.3	.247	1.4	CF(95): 8.0, LF(1): 0.0	-0.1
2018	*CHA*	*MLB*	*26*	*385*	*48*	*15*	*4*	*9*	*37*	*31*	*115*	*16*	*5*	*.210/.283/.356*	*.225*	*1.3*	*.279*	*2.2*	*CF 2*	*0.2*
2019	*CHA*	*MLB*	*27*	*498*	*57*	*19*	*5*	*14*	*54*	*44*	*153*	*21*	*6*	*.209/.294/.369*	*.227*	*-0.8*	*.279*	*1.5*	*CF 4*	*0.3*

Breakout: 3% Improve: 30% Collapse: 14% Attrition: 22% MLB: 55% *Comparables: Gorkys Hernandez, Choo Freeman, Abraham Almonte*

There should be a spot for a player with Engel's skill set. A plus defender in center field with plus-plus speed, Engel profiles as an ideal fourth outfielder/defensive replacement/pinch-runner. What makes this far from a certainty is that he has yet to display any prolonged stretches of competency with the bat. The darling of the 2015 Arizona Fall League whiffed at a 31 percent clip in Triple-A in 2016 and followed that up with a 35 percent strikeout rate in his first look at the majors. The glove and speed are such that Engel merely needs to be run-of-the-mill "bad" in the hitting department to warrant rostering, but right now he's far from even that. He turned 26 during the offseason, so there may not be as much development left as you think.

Avisail Garcia RF Born: 06/12/91 Age: 27 Bats: R Throws: R Height: 6'4" Weight: 240 Origin: International Free Agent, 2007

YEAR	TEAM	LVL	AGE	PA	R	2B	3B	HR	RBI	BB	K	SB	CS	AVG/OBP/SLG	TAv	VORP	BABIP	BRR	FRAA	WARP
2015	CHA	MLB	24	601	66	17	2	13	59	36	141	7	7	.257/.309/.365	.245	0.6	.320	-0.3	RF(130): 3.5	0.4
2016	CHA	MLB	25	453	59	18	2	12	51	34	115	4	4	.245/.307/.385	.247	2.4	.309	2.0	RF(46): 6.1, LF(11): 0.0	0.9
2017	CHA	MLB	26	561	75	27	5	18	80	33	111	5	3	.330/.380/.506	.293	29.1	.392	-0.5	RF(132): 7.3	3.7
2018	*CHA*	*MLB*	*27*	*589*	*70*	*23*	*4*	*18*	*74*	*38*	*133*	*6*	*4*	*.275/.329/.428*	*.264*	*18.1*	*.333*	*-0.8*	*RF 2*	*1.6*
2019	*CHA*	*MLB*	*28*	*533*	*68*	*21*	*3*	*18*	*67*	*37*	*125*	*5*	*3*	*.276/.334/.440*	*.263*	*13.6*	*.337*	*0.7*	*RF 3*	*1.8*

Breakout: 1% Improve: 53% Collapse: 2% Attrition: 7% MLB: 97% *Comparables: Hunter Pence, Alex Rios, Derek Bell*

As Garcia began his unexpected tear at the plate to start the 2017 season, you had to excuse regular viewers of the Avi Experience for being pessimistic while patiently waiting for his fall back to mediocrity. Well, it never happened. The massive right fielder once dubbed "Little Miggy" began hitting for both power and average. When you consider that his 90th percentile outcome from PECOTA was a 2.5 WARP season, the 3.6 he posted was unfathomable. So how did he do it? Many thought Garcia's best route to longevity was to sell out for power, as his desire in the past to use all fields led to an abundance of weak groundballs and pop-ups. But while his contact rate stayed the same, it was good contact, and while his power numbers weren't overwhelming in an environment where a record number of dingers were being launched, he was still able to post a career-high ISO while somehow maintaining a batting average second only to Jose Altuve's in the American League. His defense also improved to the point of competence, even if it still leaves a lot to be desired. The stench of Garcia's first five seasons hasn't completely been washed off, and there's some evidence that a sky-high BABIP means he'll come crashing back to earth at some point, but his improvements in 2017 have reopened the door to all of the enticing possibilities that come with his profile.

Leury Garcia OF Born: 03/18/91 Age: 27 Bats: B Throws: R Height: 5'8" Weight: 170 Origin: International Free Agent, 2007

YEAR	TEAM	LVL	AGE	PA	R	2B	3B	HR	RBI	BB	K	SB	CS	AVG/OBP/SLG	TAv	VORP	BABIP	BRR	FRAA	WARP
2015	CHR	AAA	24	385	57	19	3	3	31	20	66	30	12	.298/.340/.395	.260	16.0	.357	3.0	SS(43): 0.2, CF(22): 6.3	2.4
2015	CHA	MLB	24	15	0	0	0	0	1	1	7	1	0	.214/.267/.214	.171	-0.2	.429	0.7	CF(4): -0.5, SS(3): -0.1	-0.1
2016	CHR	AAA	25	342	45	9	4	6	35	24	64	18	8	.313/.367/.426	.275	16.9	.378	1.3	LF(28): 1.2, SS(25): -1.1	2.1
2016	CHA	MLB	25	50	6	1	1	1	5	1	13	2	1	.229/.260/.354	.214	-0.4	.294	0.4	CF(16): -1.1	-0.2
2017	CHA	MLB	26	326	41	15	2	9	33	13	69	8	5	.270/.316/.423	.252	7.2	.321	0.5	CF(51): 3.5, LF(24): 0.3	1.2
2018	*CHA*	*MLB*	*27*	*554*	*67*	*20*	*4*	*12*	*54*	*29*	*133*	*21*	*9*	*.248/.292/.374*	*.231*	*3.3*	*.306*	*1.4*	*LF -2, CF 2*	*0.0*
2019	*CHA*	*MLB*	*28*	*495*	*56*	*18*	*4*	*12*	*54*	*31*	*122*	*18*	*9*	*.250/.305/.391*	*.234*	*1.3*	*.308*	*1.7*	*LF -1, CF 2*	*0.3*

Breakout: 3% Improve: 29% Collapse: 9% Attrition: 21% MLB: 70% *Comparables: Chris Duffy, Choo Freeman, Tony Gwynn*

As an unheralded former prospect whose career batting line was downright pitcheresque, the fact that Garcia even had a chance to make the 25-man roster out of spring training said more about the state of the White Sox's center-field situation than about his ability. Despite this, Garcia has always been the type of player you could envision having a long and sustainable career given his skill set. A plus runner and plus defender at a number of positions, he improved his contact skills and morphed from afterthought into something that looked like a first-division center fielder for more than half the season.

Willy Garcia OF Born: 09/04/92 Age: 25 Bats: R Throws: R Height: 6'2" Weight: 215 Origin: International Free Agent, 2010

YEAR	TEAM	LVL	AGE	PA	R	2B	3B	HR	RBI	BB	K	SB	CS	AVG/OBP/SLG	TAv	VORP	BABIP	BRR	FRAA	WARP
2015	ALT	AA	22	224	26	7	2	5	29	11	47	3	2	.314/.353/.441	.280	7.1	.381	-2.2	LF(38): 7.1, CF(11): -0.3	1.5
2015	IND	AAA	22	291	36	11	4	10	38	12	76	1	4	.246/.285/.424	.251	-0.1	.305	-3.0	RF(47): 4.1, CF(13): 1.9	0.9
2016	IND	AAA	23	499	53	30	4	6	43	31	131	5	9	.245/.293/.366	.244	0.8	.326	0.1	RF(124): 5.1, CF(3): -0.5	0.7
2017	CHR	AAA	24	134	20	6	0	5	20	18	38	1	0	.286/.396/.473	.301	9.3	.386	0.3	RF(20): -2.0, CF(7): 1.7	0.9
2017	CHA	MLB	24	119	15	5	3	2	12	11	31	0	0	.238/.305/.400	.251	1.3	.311	-0.3	RF(17): 0.5, LF(13): -0.3	0.2
2018	*CHA*	*MLB*	*25*	*93*	*10*	*4*	*1*	*3*	*11*	*6*	*27*	*0*	*1*	*.237/.292/.400*	*.243*	*1.1*	*.309*	*-0.2*	*LF 1, RF 0*	*0.1*
2019	*CHA*	*MLB*	*26*	*302*	*37*	*13*	*2*	*11*	*38*	*23*	*88*	*2*	*2*	*.238/.304/.418*	*.247*	*2.3*	*.309*	*-0.5*	*LF 3, RF 0*	*0.6*

Breakout: 3% Improve: 15% Collapse: 9% Attrition: 26% MLB: 45% *Comparables: Aaron Altherr, Alex Castellanos, Rymer Liriano*

Garcia was a scrap-heap find who didn't hit well but wouldn't have been the worst player at his position in the majors by any means. He's also got the tools to play a good corner outfield, with a highlight-reel, rail-gun of an arm, and he was working on being able to play center field in a pinch to boost his utility. A horrifying collision in which he broke his jaw on Yoan Moncada's knee punched a hole in his season and cut his playing time to almost nothing. The scenarios where he puts it all together and becomes a regular are vanishingly scarce, but if he can play center field once or twice a week he could certainly be a role player and contributor off the bench.

Casey Gillaspie 1B Born: 01/25/93 Age: 25 Bats: B Throws: L Height: 6'4" Weight: 240 Origin: Round 1, 2014 Draft (#20 overall)

YEAR	TEAM	LVL	AGE	PA	R	2B	3B	HR	RBI	BB	K	SB	CS	AVG/OBP/SLG	TAv	VORP	BABIP	BRR	FRAA	WARP
2015	BGR	A	22	268	37	11	0	16	44	28	43	4	0	.278/.358/.530	.307	12.5	.275	-3.1	1B(60): 1.5	1.5
2015	PCH	A+	22	45	3	0	1	1	4	4	9	0	0	.146/.222/.268	.181	-3.8	.161	-0.7	1B(12): -0.6	-0.5
2016	MNT	AA	23	357	51	21	0	11	41	58	79	5	1	.270/.387/.454	.314	20.4	.327	-2.6	1B(77): 2.0	2.4
2016	DUR	AAA	23	203	27	13	2	7	23	22	38	0	1	.307/.389/.520	.313	14.5	.358	1.2	1B(45): -0.3	1.5
2017	DUR	AAA	24	395	45	15	2	9	44	36	77	1	1	.227/.296/.357	.245	-4.1	.261	-1.5	1B(86): -6.0	-1.0
2017	CHR	AAA	24	120	17	5	0	6	18	14	23	0	0	.210/.300/.429	.250	0.1	.208	0.2	1B(22): -0.6	-0.1
2018	*CHA*	*MLB*	*25*	*250*	*31*	*11*	*1*	*11*	*35*	*28*	*59*	*0*	*0*	*.241/.329/.447*	*.259*	*4.2*	*.277*	*-0.4*	*1B -1*	*0.3*
2019	*CHA*	*MLB*	*26*	*387*	*53*	*17*	*1*	*17*	*54*	*42*	*91*	*0*	*0*	*.240/.326/.449*	*.261*	*4.3*	*.275*	*-0.8*	*1B -2*	*0.3*

Breakout: 7% Improve: 21% Collapse: 8% Attrition: 28% MLB: 43% *Comparables: Travis Shaw, Chris McGuiness, Tommy Medica*

Casey Gillaspie is still just "Conor's brother," as opposed to the other way around, particularly within the parts of White Sox Twitter where the elder Gillaspie developed a devoted following after three spectacularly average seasons on the South Side. The younger Gillaspie entered pro ball with a more promising pedigree, and his advanced plate discipline is what helped him reach Triple-A just two years after he was drafted. The offensive threshold for first basemen is such that he might not be more than a second-division starter, but his ability to adjust gives him a higher ceiling than you'd expect from a player traded for Dan Jennings. He still has a chance to one day transform into "The Good Gillaspie."

Alen Hanson UT Born: 10/22/92 Age: 25 Bats: B Throws: R Height: 5'11" Weight: 170 Origin: International Free Agent, 2009

YEAR	TEAM	LVL	AGE	PA	R	2B	3B	HR	RBI	BB	K	SB	CS	AVG/OBP/SLG	TAv	VORP	BABIP	BRR	FRAA	WARP
2015	IND	AAA	22	529	66	17	12	6	43	37	91	35	12	.263/.313/.387	.254	9.3	.311	-1.6	2B(111): 10.3, 3B(7): 0.4	2.0
2016	IND	AAA	23	478	58	15	7	8	32	32	78	36	15	.266/.318/.389	.255	12.3	.307	2.2	2B(67): -8.5, LF(26): -0.3	0.4
2016	PIT	MLB	23	33	5	1	0	0	1	2	5	2	1	.226/.273/.258	.208	-0.4	.269	0.5	2B(8): -0.4	-0.1
2017	PIT	MLB	24	59	8	0	2	0	1	2	9	2	1	.193/.220/.263	.173	-4.5	.229	-0.9	2B(15): 0.0, RF(2): -0.1	-0.5
2017	CHA	MLB	24	175	28	9	1	4	10	10	43	9	2	.231/.276/.375	.225	-0.5	.284	1.7	RF(18): -1.6, 2B(13): -0.1	0.0
2018	*CHA*	*MLB*	*25*	*250*	*36*	*9*	*3*	*7*	*25*	*17*	*54*	*14*	*5*	*.248/.303/.416*	*.235*	*2.9*	*.285*	*0.2*	*2B 0, RF -1*	*0.3*
2019	*CHA*	*MLB*	*26*	*396*	*48*	*14*	*5*	*13*	*49*	*29*	*83*	*22*	*9*	*.251/.311/.428*	*.245*	*6.2*	*.285*	*1.3*	*2B 1, RF -1*	*0.6*

Breakout: 3% Improve: 22% Collapse: 15% Attrition: 29% MLB: 62% *Comparables: Cory Spangenberg, Donovan Solano, Tyler Pastornicky*

The White Sox added Hanson to their never-ending collection of post-hype prospects when they plucked him off waivers from the Pirates last June. Hanson emerged as a legit top 101 prospect in 2012 when scouts saw a shortstop with plus speed who regularly hit the gaps and showed a surprising amount of MMMpop. Then he just kind of ... stopped. Since getting his first taste of the majors in 2016 he's actualized the "R" in WARP. His speed is still there, but he's far too strikeout prone, and when he does make contact it's more of a one-hit wonder than a pop sensation. Hanson is still young enough to carve out a career as a useful utility guy, but if he doesn't figure it out soon he'll likely wind up playing in the *Middle of Nowhere*.

Eloy Jimenez RF Born: 11/27/96 Age: 21 Bats: R Throws: R Height: 6'4" Weight: 205 Origin: International Free Agent, 2013

YEAR	TEAM	LVL	AGE	PA	R	2B	3B	HR	RBI	BB	K	SB	CS	AVG/OBP/SLG	TAv	VORP	BABIP	BRR	FRAA	WARP
2015	EUG	A-	18	250	36	10	0	7	33	15	43	3	2	.284/.328/.418	.300	15.1	.321	-0.2	LF(46): -4.8, RF(8): 3.1	1.4
2016	SBN	A	19	464	65	40	3	14	81	25	94	8	3	.329/.369/.532	.320	35.7	.391	-0.3	LF(86): -4.6, RF(11): 0.4	3.4
2017	MYR	A+	20	174	23	6	2	8	32	18	35	0	0	.271/.351/.490	.302	10.0	.304	-0.3	LF(13): 0.3, RF(6): -0.1	1.1
2017	WNS	A+	20	122	20	11	1	8	26	12	21	0	2	.345/.410/.682	.353	14.0	.370	0.4	RF(19): -0.6	1.4
2017	BIR	AA	20	73	11	5	0	3	7	5	16	1	1	.353/.397/.559	.364	9.0	.429	0.1	RF(15): -1.0	0.9
2018	*CHA*	*MLB*	*21*	*136*	*16*	*7*	*1*	*6*	*20*	*7*	*35*	*0*	*0*	*.255/.297/.459*	*.255*	*2.1*	*.304*	*-0.3*	*RF 0*	*0.1*
2019	*CHA*	*MLB*	*22*	*427*	*59*	*23*	*1*	*21*	*65*	*26*	*104*	*1*	*1*	*.270/.318/.497*	*.267*	*12.3*	*.314*	*-0.9*	*RF 0*	*1.4*

Breakout: 7% Improve: 15% Collapse: 6% Attrition: 15% MLB: 32% *Comparables: Nomar Mazara, Caleb Gindl, Domingo Santana*

Scouts have been drooling over Jimenez's power potential since he signed with the Cubs as an international free agent, and he continued to impress as he mashed through High-A while switching Chicago parent clubs along the way. His success earned him a late-season promotion to Double-A, his first shot at the high minors, and it was more of the same. It's not just the power, though. Jimenez is more of a free swinger than your prototypical power hitter, but he has the hit tool to make it work. There remain questions about whether his body will hold up to the rigors of outfield play as he ages, but if he continues to mash his way through the high minors he could get his first major-league audition as soon as this year. The upside here is a pure, classic, middle-of-the-order, MVP-caliber bat.

Rymer Liriano RF Born: 06/20/91 Age: 27 Bats: R Throws: R Height: 6'0" Weight: 230 Origin: International Free Agent, 2008

YEAR	TEAM	LVL	AGE	PA	R	2B	3B	HR	RBI	BB	K	SB	CS	AVG/OBP/SLG	TAv	VORP	BABIP	BRR	FRAA	WARP
2015	ELP	AAA	24	549	85	31	3	14	64	64	132	18	8	.292/.383/.460	.290	30.0	.376	2.5	RF(102): 16.4, CF(20): -0.7	4.7
2017	CHR	AAA	26	500	67	15	3	17	52	42	133	7	4	.256/.323/.416	.251	4.5	.325	0.3	RF(92): 5.1, LF(10): 0.8	1.0
2017	CHA	MLB	26	46	4	2	0	1	6	5	14	1	0	.220/.304/.341	.228	-0.4	.308	0.2	LF(12): -0.1, RF(7): -0.2	-0.1
2018	*CHA*	*MLB*	*27*	*250*	*29*	*10*	*1*	*8*	*30*	*24*	*74*	*4*	*2*	*.237/.318/.404*	*.244*	*3.0*	*.314*	*-0.1*	*RF 2, LF 1*	*0.6*
2019	*CHA*	*MLB*	*28*	*249*	*31*	*10*	*1*	*8*	*30*	*24*	*75*	*4*	*2*	*.235/.320/.400*	*.245*	*1.6*	*.314*	*0.0*	*RF 2, LF 1*	*0.5*

Breakout: 6% Improve: 19% Collapse: 10% Attrition: 22% MLB: 39% *Comparables: Sean Halton, Joe Benson, Lane Adams*

With the rebuild in full force, plenty of plate appearances promised to be up for grabs on the South Side, and Liriano made sense as a dice roll on freely available talent. Only a few years ago he was a consensus top 101 prospect, cresting as high as no. 39 overall on BP's list. Unfortunately, he lost a whole year after a terrifying injury incurred when he was hit in the head with a pitch. He posted pedestrian numbers at Triple-A Charlotte and was released after the season. It wouldn't be the craziest comeback story even in recent memory if Liriano caught on as a major leaguer another year removed from injury, but at his age it's an uphill battle.

Yoan Moncada 2B Born: 05/27/95 Age: 23 Bats: B Throws: R Height: 6'2" Weight: 205 Origin: International Free Agent, 2015

YEAR	TEAM	LVL	AGE	PA	R	2B	3B	HR	RBI	BB	K	SB	CS	AVG/OBP/SLG	TAv	VORP	BABIP	BRR	FRAA	WARP
2015	GRN	A	20	363	61	19	3	8	38	42	83	49	3	.278/.380/.438	.312	35.7	.353	7.6	2B(71): -5.4	3.2
2016	SLM	A+	21	284	57	25	3	4	34	45	60	36	8	.307/.427/.496	.320	32.0	.395	6.2	2B(58): -1.7	3.1
2016	PME	AA	21	207	37	6	3	11	28	27	64	9	4	.277/.379/.531	.309	16.4	.373	0.6	2B(34): -4.8, 3B(10): 0.8	1.3
2016	BOS	MLB	21	20	3	1	0	0	1	1	12	0	0	.211/.250/.263	.189	-0.5	.571	0.3	3B(5): 0.2	0.0
2017	CHR	AAA	22	361	57	9	3	12	36	49	102	17	8	.282/.377/.447	.276	16.8	.379	-0.1	2B(80): 1.4	1.8
2017	CHA	MLB	22	231	31	8	2	8	22	29	74	3	2	.231/.338/.412	.254	4.2	.325	-0.7	2B(54): 5.8	1.0
2018	*CHA*	*MLB*	*23*	*576*	*88*	*20*	*4*	*20*	*64*	*68*	*181*	*21*	*7*	*.233/.331/.410*	*.259*	*22.3*	*.320*	*1.6*	*2B 1*	*2.1*
2019	*CHA*	*MLB*	*24*	*553*	*74*	*20*	*3*	*21*	*70*	*67*	*177*	*20*	*7*	*.231/.331/.419*	*.254*	*15.2*	*.315*	*0.6*	*2B 1*	*1.8*

Breakout: 6% Improve: 26% Collapse: 10% Attrition: 19% MLB: 61% *Comparables: Andy Marte, Jon Singleton, Dilson Herrera*

There are a lot of things about Moncada that are obvious. The guy has a cartoonishly athletic build with ridiculous musculature and plenty of speed. But, as much as we know not to overrate small sample sizes and not to ignore context, Moncada's rough and brief 2016 debut in Boston threw cold water on his seemingly inexorable rise to stardom. And while the concerns about his batting average remain after his first season in Chicago, he exhibited an excellent eye, spitting on close pitches even with two strikes, and a patient approach that bordered on self-sabotaging passivity. As he got more comfortable with major-league pitching and attacking his pitch through his rookie year, the talent started to win out. The difference between Moncada being a good player, a great player and an MVP candidate hinges on just how much his bat-to-ball skills can progress. With his patience, power and speed, it's a safe bet that he's a quality major leaguer at a minimum.

Omar Narvaez C Born: 02/10/92 Age: 26 Bats: L Throws: R Height: 5'11" Weight: 215 Origin: International Free Agent, 2008

YEAR	TEAM	LVL	AGE	PA	R	2B	3B	HR	RBI	BB	K	SB	CS	AVG/OBP/SLG	TAv	VORP	BABIP	BRR	FRAA	WARP
2015	WNS	A+	23	385	38	10	0	1	27	40	31	1	0	.274/.352/.313	.247	10.5	.297	-0.8	C(96): 2.2	1.4
2016	BIR	AA	24	49	4	2	0	0	5	4	8	0	0	.222/.286/.267	.208	-1.6	.270	-1.1	C(13): -0.2	-0.2
2016	CHR	AAA	24	156	14	6	0	2	11	9	17	0	0	.245/.292/.329	.210	0.1	.264	1.5	C(39): -4.4	-0.4
2016	CHA	MLB	24	117	13	4	0	1	10	14	14	0	0	.267/.350/.337	.261	5.0	.295	-0.5	C(34): -4.1	0.1
2017	CHA	MLB	25	295	23	10	0	2	14	38	45	0	0	.277/.373/.340	.246	8.3	.330	-1.0	C(83): -10.7, 1B(1): 0.0	-0.2
2018	*CHA*	*MLB*	*26*	*125*	*13*	*5*	*0*	*2*	*12*	*13*	*19*	*0*	*0*	*.253/.331/.352*	*.241*	*3.5*	*.286*	*-0.3*	*C -5*	*-0.2*
2019	*CHA*	*MLB*	*27*	*250*	*30*	*9*	*0*	*5*	*25*	*27*	*41*	*0*	*0*	*.252/.336/.369*	*.242*	*4.6*	*.285*	*-0.6*	*C -8*	*-0.4*

Breakout: 5% Improve: 40% Collapse: 14% Attrition: 27% MLB: 80% *Comparables: Josh Thole, Tucker Barnhart, Christian Vazquez*

YEAR	TEAM	P. COUNT	FRM RUNS	BLK RUNS	THRW RUNS	TOT RUNS
2016	CHA	4399	-1.6	-0.8	-1.0	-3.4
2017	CHA	11422	-7.8	-1.1	-0.5	-9.4
2018	*CHA*	*4852*	*-3.4*	*-0.4*	*-0.2*	*-4.0*
2019	*CHA*	*9706*	*-5.3*	*-0.7*	*-0.3*	*-6.3*

Narvaez owns a lofty 12.6 percent walk rate in just over 400 big-league plate appearances. That's higher than the career mark of Kevin Youkilis, dubbed "The Greek God of Walks" in *Moneyball*. Cute small-sample stats aside, Narvaez hasn't demonstrated a similar ability in the minors, where his walk rate is a more pedestrian 10 percent in over 1,700 plate appearances. He also hasn't shown power at any level, with a slugging percentage south of .340 both in the bigs and down on the farm. He packs all the wallop of legendary sluggers Dee Gordon, Jose Peraza and Denard Span. On the defensive side, Narvaez has posted poor framing numbers in his limited big-league tenure, which isn't a strong selling point. Still, as a catcher with plus on-base skills, he could have value if he learns to steal the occasional strike for his batterymates.

Luis Robert OF Born: 08/03/97 Age: 20 Bats: R Throws: R Height: 6'3" Weight: 185 Origin: International Free Agent, 2017

YEAR	TEAM	LVL	AGE	PA	R	2B	3B	HR	RBI	BB	K	SB	CS	AVG/OBP/SLG	TAv	VORP	BABIP	BRR	FRAA	WARP
2017	DWS	RK	19	114	17	8	1	3	14	22	23	12	3	.310/.491/.536	.367	21.2	.397	2.5	CF(19): -0.5	1.9
2018	*CHA*	*MLB*	*20*	*250*	*27*	*9*	*1*	*7*	*26*	*21*	*85*	*7*	*2*	*.194/.272/.331*	*.204*	*-4.6*	*.271*	*0.4*	*CF -2*	*-0.7*
2019	*CHA*	*MLB*	*21*	*247*	*28*	*9*	*1*	*7*	*26*	*23*	*80*	*7*	*2*	*.199/.285/.345*	*.219*	*-3.0*	*.272*	*0.7*	*CF -2*	*-0.5*

Breakout: 1% Improve: 4% Collapse: 0% Attrition: 3% MLB: 6% *Comparables: Joe Benson, Cedric Hunter, Chris Parmelee*

Robert is an extreme version of what makes prospect watching so intoxicating and so dangerous. An immensely toolsy athlete who has annihilated overmatched competition in Cuba and the Dominican Summer League, Robert has also uncorked 80-grade run times, conjuring visions of dazzling center field defense and electric, complete offense. The reality is, he has yet to be tested against Low-A, and questions about how his athleticism will translate in-game against domestic, professional competition abound. With the massive influx of talent to the organization, Robert is simultaneously perilously hyped and flying under the radar. Accordingly, there is a massive range of possibilities as to what you might read in this space even as soon as next year.

Blake Rutherford OF Born: 05/02/97 Age: 21 Bats: L Throws: R Height: 6'3" Weight: 195 Origin: Round 1, 2016 Draft (#18 overall)

YEAR	TEAM	LVL	AGE	PA	R	2B	3B	HR	RBI	BB	K	SB	CS	AVG/OBP/SLG	TAv	VORP	BABIP	BRR	FRAA	WARP
2016	YAT	RK	19	30	3	1	0	1	3	4	6	0	0	.240/.333/.400	.321	2.8	.263	0.0	CF(6): -1.1	0.2
2016	PUL	RK	19	100	13	7	4	2	9	9	24	0	2	.382/.440/.618	.370	14.7	.500	0.0	CF(14): -1.7, LF(2): -0.2	1.3
2017	CSC	A	20	304	41	20	2	2	30	25	55	9	4	.281/.342/.391	.280	11.0	.341	-2.6	CF(39): -5.6, LF(13): -0.5	0.4
2017	KAN	A	20	136	11	5	0	0	5	13	21	1	0	.213/.289/.254	.204	-4.8	.257	-0.1	CF(13): -1.3, LF(10): -0.3	-0.7
2018	*CHA*	*MLB*	*21*	*250*	*24*	*11*	*1*	*6*	*27*	*19*	*65*	*1*	*1*	*.222/.283/.356*	*.214*	*-3.1*	*.281*	*-0.3*	*CF -4, LF 0*	*-0.9*
2019	*CHA*	*MLB*	*22*	*361*	*41*	*15*	*2*	*10*	*39*	*29*	*91*	*2*	*1*	*.229/.294/.375*	*.228*	*-2.8*	*.285*	*-0.4*	*CF -6, LF -1*	*-1.1*

Breakout: 1% Improve: 4% Collapse: 2% Attrition: 4% MLB: 6% *Comparables: Che-Hsuan Lin, Domonic Brown, Abraham Almonte*

Unlike say, Eloy Jimenez, Rutherford does not and has not inspired confidence about what, exactly, he is or will be. From draft day to the present, those who believe in Rutherford think he'll be an asset on offense with a batting-average-driven profile while playing good defense in an outfield corner. Doubters see only an average hit tool with unremarkable power and unremarkable defense from a position that is at the bad end of the defensive spectrum. Depending on what you think Tommy Kahnle will do, one can understand being excited to get this caliber of prospect by bundling assets, but the realistic hope here is for a nice regular and not a star.

Tyler Saladino INF Born: 07/20/89 Age: 28 Bats: R Throws: R Height: 6'0" Weight: 200 Origin: Round 7, 2010 Draft (#218 overall)

YEAR	TEAM	LVL	AGE	PA	R	2B	3B	HR	RBI	BB	K	SB	CS	AVG/OBP/SLG	TAv	VORP	BABIP	BRR	FRAA	WARP
2015	CHR	AAA	25	231	28	7	2	4	29	22	33	25	2	.255/.332/.372	.256	7.9	.277	1.7	SS(34): 2.3, 3B(2): -0.3	1.0
2015	CHA	MLB	25	254	33	6	4	4	20	12	51	8	2	.225/.267/.335	.210	-3.3	.269	1.1	3B(60): 5.1, SS(11): -0.7	0.1
2016	CHA	MLB	26	319	33	14	0	8	38	13	62	11	5	.282/.315/.409	.251	8.5	.329	1.1	2B(41): 1.9, SS(32): 0.4	1.4
2017	CHA	MLB	27	281	23	9	2	0	10	23	67	5	4	.178/.254/.229	.181	-14.2	.242	1.1	2B(26): 1.2, 3B(22): 4.3	-0.9
2018	*CHA*	*MLB*	*28*	*276*	*32*	*10*	*2*	*5*	*26*	*19*	*57*	*9*	*3*	*.237/.295/.358*	*.230*	*2.7*	*.281*	*0.7*	*3B 3, 2B 1*	*0.4*
2019	*CHA*	*MLB*	*29*	*337*	*38*	*12*	*2*	*8*	*36*	*24*	*72*	*10*	*4*	*.240/.303/.377*	*.233*	*1.7*	*.283*	*1.4*	*3B 4, 2B 2*	*0.7*

Breakout: 1% Improve: 42% Collapse: 10% Attrition: 20% MLB: 91% *Comparables: Darwin Barney, Willie Bloomquist, DJ LeMahieu*

Saladino lost his mesmerizing mustache, and with it any semblance of the surprisingly productive utility player he had turned into in 2016. As a competent defender at every infield position with the ability to hold his own in either corner outfield spot, his ability to stick was always going to come down to how his bat developed. At 26, it looked like things had finally clicked, but a year later we're left wondering whether that was merely an aberration after a season in which he battled injuries concurrent with a season-long slump at the plate. Either way, grow the mustache back just to be safe.

Yolmer Sanchez 2B Born: 06/29/92 Age: 26 Bats: B Throws: R Height: 5'11" Weight: 185 Origin: International Free Agent, 2009

YEAR	TEAM	LVL	AGE	PA	R	2B	3B	HR	RBI	BB	K	SB	CS	AVG/OBP/SLG	TAv	VORP	BABIP	BRR	FRAA	WARP
2015	CHR	AAA	23	137	17	10	0	2	17	4	28	5	2	.344/.368/.466	.281	7.4	.426	0.6	2B(26): -0.6, SS(3): 1.2	0.8
2015	CHA	MLB	23	420	40	23	1	5	31	19	81	2	2	.224/.268/.326	.218	-5.0	.270	1.5	2B(117): -2.0	-0.7
2016	CHR	AAA	24	260	31	11	2	8	29	17	55	10	4	.255/.309/.421	.244	1.8	.299	-1.5	2B(45): -0.5, SS(16): 1.8	0.3
2016	CHA	MLB	24	163	15	9	1	4	21	5	42	0	1	.208/.236/.357	.210	-4.9	.257	-1.2	2B(33): -1.8, 3B(6): 0.3	-0.7
2017	CHA	MLB	25	534	63	19	8	12	59	35	111	8	9	.267/.319/.413	.254	13.2	.321	0.9	2B(78): -0.3, 3B(52): 3.2	1.6
2018	*CHA*	*MLB*	*26*	*554*	*59*	*24*	*5*	*12*	*60*	*31*	*118*	*9*	*6*	*.250/.295/.385*	*.236*	*4.9*	*.297*	*-0.6*	*3B 3, SS 0*	*0.3*
2019	*CHA*	*MLB*	*27*	*535*	*62*	*23*	*4*	*14*	*61*	*35*	*120*	*8*	*6*	*.251/.306/.404*	*.240*	*3.1*	*.299*	*1.0*	*3B 4, SS 0*	*0.8*

Breakout: 7% Improve: 53% Collapse: 13% Attrition: 24% MLB: 95% *Comparables: Donovan Solano, Ronny Cedeno, DJ LeMahieu*

Years ago, Yolmer still went by "Carlos" Sanchez and was a 20-year-old who hit his way to Triple-A by way of obliterating the Southern League. A switch-hitter who could handle shortstop in a pinch and looked like a plus glove at second base, there was a lot to like, even if his ceiling was limited. Then he got blown away in his first three looks at the majors, failing to get his OPS above .600, and it looked like

Sanchez would be one of the dozens of failed bats from the last decade. The rebuild, though, meant the White Sox could afford to give him one more shot, and in his age-25 season he converted his skills into roughly league-average offense to pair with his defensive versatility and high-energy personality. Beloved in the clubhouse, he looks like he's back on track to be a solid bench piece or stopgap infielder.

Kevan Smith C Born: 06/28/88 Age: 30 Bats: R Throws: R Height: 6'4" Weight: 230 Origin: Round 7, 2011 Draft (#231 overall)

YEAR	TEAM	LVL	AGE	PA	R	2B	3B	HR	RBI	BB	K	SB	CS	AVG/OBP/SLG	TAv	VORP	BABIP	BRR	FRAA	WARP
2015	CHR	AAA	27	361	41	13	2	6	36	29	66	0	1	.260/.330/.370	.246	8.8	.309	-1.5	C(93): -7.6	0.1
2016	CHR	AAA	28	205	18	9	0	8	24	16	36	0	0	.219/.291/.399	.225	-0.2	.229	-1.1	C(43): -2.1	-0.2
2016	CHA	MLB	28	16	2	0	0	0	0	0	6	0	0	.125/.125/.125	.121	-1.0	.200	0.7	C(6): -0.1	-0.1
2017	CHR	AAA	29	62	10	6	0	0	15	6	9	0	0	.377/.435/.491	.289	5.4	.435	0.5	C(13): 0.2	0.5
2017	CHA	MLB	29	294	23	17	0	4	30	9	46	0	0	.283/.309/.388	.237	6.5	.323	0.5	C(79): -7.7	-0.1
2018	*CHA*	*MLB*	*30*	*58*	*6*	*3*	*0*	*1*	*6*	*4*	*12*	*0*	*0*	*.246/.300/.380*	*.236*	*1.6*	*.287*	*-0.1*	*C -2*	*-0.1*
2019	*CHA*	*MLB*	*31*	*243*	*27*	*10*	*1*	*6*	*26*	*15*	*52*	*0*	*0*	*.239/.294/.371*	*.227*	*1.5*	*.281*	*0.4*	*C -6*	*-0.5*

Breakout: 4% Improve: 21% Collapse: 9% Attrition: 22% MLB: 54%

Comparables: Bobby Wilson, Mike Nickeas, Steve Clevenger

YEAR	TEAM	P. COUNT	FRM RUNS	BLK RUNS	THRW RUNS	TOT RUNS
2015	CHR	12953	-3.9	-1.2	-1.5	-6.6
2016	CHA	396	-0.3	0.2	0.0	-0.1
2017	CHA	10862	-0.5	-1.3	-3.7	-5.4
2018	*CHA*	*2239*	*-0.8*	*-0.3*	*-0.3*	*-1.4*
2019	*CHA*	*9369*	*-2.2*	*-0.8*	*-0.8*	*-3.8*

Catchers are already weird. Smith is weird, even for a catcher. He's older than you'd think for a rookie, but his framing has improved significantly since becoming a pro to the point of being solid in that regard. He also hit for better contact than one might have expected. Unfortunately, he rates out as a ghastly defender otherwise, and in an era where utility infielders are popping 20-plus home runs, the big, former quarterback's bat was oddly punchless. If he can shore up his blocking and throwing, and runs into a few more dingers, he could elevate himself beyond a serviceable backup. Then again, if every player could simply fix his weaknesses baseball would look a lot different.

Geovany Soto C Born: 01/20/83 Age: 35 Bats: R Throws: R Height: 6'1" Weight: 225 Origin: Round 11, 2001 Draft (#318 overall)

YEAR	TEAM	LVL	AGE	PA	R	2B	3B	HR	RBI	BB	K	SB	CS	AVG/OBP/SLG	TAv	VORP	BABIP	BRR	FRAA	WARP
2015	CHA	MLB	32	210	20	8	0	9	21	21	63	0	1	.219/.301/.406	.255	7.3	.278	-0.4	C(73): -1.8	0.6
2016	SLC	AAA	33	38	2	4	0	1	8	1	7	0	0	.194/.216/.389	.199	-1.3	.214	-0.2	C(7): 0.1	-0.1
2016	ANA	MLB	33	86	11	5	0	4	9	6	21	0	0	.269/.321/.487	.270	5.0	.321	0.2	C(23): -1.2, 3B(1): 0.0	0.4
2017	CHA	MLB	34	48	5	0	0	3	9	4	10	0	0	.190/.271/.405	.229	-0.6	.167	-1.3	C(13): -2.7	-0.3
2018	*CHA*	*MLB*	*35*	*250*	*29*	*11*	*0*	*10*	*32*	*23*	*72*	*0*	*0*	*.230/.304/.418*	*.240*	*7.4*	*.285*	*-0.4*	*C -6*	*0.1*
2019	*CHA*	*MLB*	*36*	*47*	*6*	*2*	*0*	*2*	*6*	*4*	*14*	*0*	*0*	*.219/.293/.394*	*.233*	*0.4*	*.279*	*-0.1*	*C -1*	*-0.1*

Breakout: 1% Improve: 25% Collapse: 19% Attrition: 23% MLB: 82%

Comparables: David Ross, Ramon Castro, Jason Varitek

YEAR	TEAM	P. COUNT	FRM RUNS	BLK RUNS	THRW RUNS	TOT RUNS
2015	CHA	7902	-0.5	0.1	0.0	-0.5
2016	ANA	3086	0.0	-0.2	-0.5	-0.7
2017	CHA	1709	-2.3	-0.1	-0.3	-2.6
2018	*CHA*	*9423*	*-4.6*	*-0.2*	*-0.5*	*-5.3*
						-1.2

Soto was reacquired before last season as the lone veteran amid a group of backup-caliber backstops. He went from battling knee injuries in 2016 to having arthroscopic elbow surgery that cost him basically all of 2017. He can still handle the bat, but as an aging, injury-prone catcher his days appear numbered.

PITCHERS

Chris Beck RHP Born: 09/04/90 Age: 27 Bats: R Throws: R Height: 6'3" Weight: 225 Origin: Round 2, 2012 Draft (#76 overall)

YEAR	TEAM	LVL	AGE	W	L	SV	G	GS	IP	H	HR	BB/9	K/9	K	GB%	BABIP	WHIP	ERA	DRA	WARP	MPH	CMD	PWR	STM
2015	CHA	MLB	24	0	1	0	1	1	6	10	0	6.0	4.5	3	50%	.417	2.33	6.00	5.23	0.0	94.5			47
2015	CHR	AAA	24	3	2	0	10	10	54^1	50	3	2.3	6.6	40	46%	.281	1.18	3.15	3.45	1.1				
2016	CHR	AAA	25	5	4	0	22	7	66^1	77	5	3.4	6.8	50	50%	.348	1.54	4.21	5.53	-0.3				
2016	CHA	MLB	25	2	2	0	25	0	25^1	31	3	6.0	7.1	20	48%	.346	1.89	6.39	5.50	-0.2	96.9	48	54	51
2017	CHA	MLB	26	2	1	0	57	0	64^2	73	16	4.7	5.8	42	42%	.288	1.65	6.40	8.12	-2.1	96.1	50	57	52
2018	*CHA*	*MLB*	*27*	*1*	*1*	*0*	*15*	*0*	*16*	*16*	*3*	*4.3*	*7.1*	*13*	*45%*	*.291*	*1.49*	*5.36*	*5.27*	*0.0*	*95.7*	*50*	*57*	*51*
2019	*CHA*	*MLB*	*28*	*2*	*1*	*0*	*40*	*0*	*42*	*43*	*6*	*4.4*	*7.8*	*36*	*45%*	*.301*	*1.52*	*5.16*	*5.36*	*-0.1*	*95.6*	*50*	*57*	*52*

Breakout: 20% Improve: 35% Collapse: 11% Attrition: 24% MLB: 58%

Comparables: Ben Hendrickson, John Koronka, Carlos Frias

The right-hander was ready and willing to go at the White Sox's beck and call, leading the team in bullpen innings. That's about the only positivity that can be gleaned from another season in which the converted starting pitcher's lively fastball consistently missed the strike zone. Beck's workload was almost entirely based on the White Sox jettisoning every reliever with any value before the trade deadline, and he'll likely play out the rest of his career as little more than minor-league depth.

Aaron Bummer LHP Born: 09/21/93 Age: 24 Bats: L Throws: L Height: 6'3" Weight: 200 Origin: Round 19, 2014 Draft (#558 overall)

YEAR	TEAM	LVL	AGE	W	L	SV	G	GS	IP	H	HR	BB/9	K/9	K	GB%	BABIP	WHIP	ERA	DRA	WARP	MPH	CMD	PWR	STM
2017	WNS	A+	23	0	2	2	8	0	11	10	2	2.5	12.3	15	59%	.296	1.18	4.91	2.59	0.3				
2017	BIR	AA	23	1	3	3	17	1	33	29	2	4.4	9.3	34	56%	.318	1.36	3.00	3.49	0.5				
2017	CHA	MLB	23	1	3	0	30	0	22	13	4	6.1	7.0	17	57%	.167	1.27	4.50	5.77	-0.1	95.0	31	50	49
2018	*CHA*	*MLB*	*24*	*1*	*1*	*0*	*25*	*0*	*26*	*26*	*5*	*5.5*	*9.4*	*28*	*47%*	*.293*	*1.57*	*5.56*	*5.49*	*-0.1*	*94.8*	*32*	*52*	*50*
2019	*CHA*	*MLB*	*25*	*2*	*1*	*0*	*35*	*0*	37^2	*37*	*6*	*5.5*	*7.8*	*32*	*47%*	*.286*	*1.60*	*5.85*	*6.08*	*-0.3*	*94.6*	*32*	*52*	*51*

Breakout: 20% Improve: 27% Collapse: 8% Attrition: 25% MLB: 45%

Comparables: Wesley Wright, Chris Resop, Chance Ruffin

Most 19th-round picks wouldn't be blue if they managed a lineout in the *BP Annual*. Bummer has earned his very own paragraph already, even after missing 2015 to Tommy John surgery, which was a drag. But, that'll happen when you throw mid-to-high-90s with your left hand, and despite his struggles in the majors last year he could still wind up as a setup man. That would be quite the opposite of a disappointment.

Dylan Cease RHP Born: 12/28/95 Age: 22 Bats: R Throws: R Height: 6'2" Weight: 190 Origin: Round 6, 2014 Draft (#169 overall)

YEAR	TEAM	LVL	AGE	W	L	SV	G	GS	IP	H	HR	BB/9	K/9	K	GB%	BABIP	WHIP	ERA	DRA	WARP	MPH	CMD	PWR	STM
2015	CUB	RK	19	1	2	0	11	8	24	12	0	6.0	9.4	25	66%	.207	1.17	2.62	4.91	0.2				
2016	EUG	A-	20	2	0	0	12	12	44^{2}	27	1	5.0	13.3	66	55%	.295	1.16	2.22	1.69	1.9				
2017	SBN	A	21	1	2	0	13	13	51^{2}	39	2	4.5	12.9	74	46%	.339	1.26	2.79	2.90	1.4				
2017	KAN	A	21	0	8	0	9	9	41^{2}	35	1	3.9	11.2	52	43%	.330	1.27	3.89	3.48	0.9				
2018	*CHA*	*MLB*	*22*	*3*	*6*	*0*	*17*	*17*	*65*	*62*	*15*	*6.8*	*11.3*	*82*	*42%*	*.303*	*1.70*	*6.06*	*6.31*	*-0.4*				
2019	*CHA*	*MLB*	*23*	*5*	*10*	*0*	*25*	*25*	*150*	*153*	*37*	*6.1*	*10.7*	*178*	*42%*	*.309*	*1.70*	*6.36*	*6.65*	*-1.1*				

Breakout: 11% Improve: 18% Collapse: 4% Attrition: 16% MLB: 26% *Comparables: Michael Stutes, Trevor May, Radhames Liz*

The fact that Cease arrived on the South Side alongside Eloy Jimenez takes a lot of the pressure and attention off of him, and makes his volatile, high-upside profile a much more worthwhile risk. Cease has touched 100 mph and now sits mid-to-high-90s, flashes a gorgeous curve and has even shown the ability to throw a good changeup from time to time. Unfortunately, his 93 innings last year more than doubled his previous career high, he's already had Tommy John surgery and he ended the year with shoulder fatigue. There's a perfect world where he becomes an ace, but it's hard to imagine him consistently throwing 150-plus innings a year. Fortunately, a fallback of dominant reliever is never bad, especially with bullpens absorbing a higher percentage of innings nowadays.

Dylan Covey RHP Born: 08/14/91 Age: 26 Bats: R Throws: R Height: 6'2" Weight: 195 Origin: Round 4, 2013 Draft (#131 overall)

YEAR	TEAM	LVL	AGE	W	L	SV	G	GS	IP	H	HR	BB/9	K/9	K	GB%	BABIP	WHIP	ERA	DRA	WARP	MPH	CMD	PWR	STM
2015	STO	A+	23	8	9	0	26	26	140^{1}	135	13	2.8	6.4	100	60%	.282	1.27	3.59	4.56	0.9				
2016	MID	AA	24	2	1	0	6	6	29^{1}	21	2	5.2	8.0	26	61%	.247	1.30	1.84	5.25	-0.1				
2017	CHA	MLB	25	0	7	0	18	12	70	83	20	4.4	5.3	41	49%	.296	1.67	7.71	7.61	-1.6	94.6	38	50	37
2018	*CHA*	*MLB*	*26*	*3*	*4*	*0*	*10*	*10*	*53*	*59*	*11*	*4.4*	*6.7*	*39*	*50%*	*.296*	*1.62*	*5.67*	*6.01*	*-0.4*	*94.2*	*39*	*51*	*38*
2019	*CHA*	*MLB*	*27*	*6*	*7*	*0*	*52*	*16*	*133^{1}*	*144*	*24*	*4.2*	*7.1*	*105*	*50%*	*.299*	*1.55*	*5.66*	*5.88*	*-0.5*	*93.9*	*39*	*51*	*38*

Breakout: 23% Improve: 34% Collapse: 11% Attrition: 26% MLB: 50% *Comparables: David Buchanan, Burke Badenhop, Zach Jackson*

Covey remaining on Chicago's 25-man roster for the duration of last season is undoubtedly good news for the front office, as they can now keep the Rule 5 pick from the A's as minor-league depth instead of returning him to the organization from which he was selected. The author's ability to successfully frame Covey's season in a positive manner is as surprising as that random May start in which he struck out nine Padres, which is more than he had in his first four starts combined. Perhaps not coincidentally, the Padres rostered three Rule 5 picks themselves.

Tyler Danish RHP Born: 09/12/94 Age: 23 Bats: R Throws: R Height: 6'0" Weight: 200 Origin: Round 2, 2013 Draft (#55 overall)

YEAR	TEAM	LVL	AGE	W	L	SV	G	GS	IP	H	HR	BB/9	K/9	K	GB%	BABIP	WHIP	ERA	DRA	WARP	MPH	CMD	PWR	STM
2015	BIR	AA	20	8	12	0	26	26	142	175	13	3.8	5.7	90	56%	.347	1.65	4.50	5.72	-1.1				
2016	BIR	AA	21	3	7	0	12	12	75^{1}	71	3	1.9	5.6	47	57%	.281	1.15	4.42	4.13	0.9				
2016	CHA	MLB	21	0	0	0	3	0	1^{2}	6	0	16.2	0.0	0	44%	.667	5.40	10.80	9.61	-0.1	93.8			57
2016	CHR	AAA	21	1	3	0	7	5	29^{1}	39	0	3.1	6.4	21	54%	.382	1.67	5.83	5.75	-0.2				
2017	CHA	MLB	22	1	0	0	1	1	5	3	0	10.8	10.8	6	36%	.273	1.80	0.00	2.97	0.1	91.3			69
2017	CHR	AAA	22	4	14	0	26	25	138^{1}	175	18	3.1	4.6	71	52%	.318	1.60	5.47	3.94	2.6				
2018	*CHA*	*MLB*	*23*	*3*	*3*	*0*	*22*	*7*	*51*	*57*	*7*	*3.6*	*5.9*	*34*	*50%*	*.300*	*1.53*	*4.87*	*5.00*	*0.2*	*91.7*			*66*
2019	*CHA*	*MLB*	*24*	*7*	*6*	*0*	*58*	*16*	*140^{1}*	*145*	*18*	*3.4*	*7.1*	*110*	*50%*	*.299*	*1.42*	*4.76*	*4.93*	*0.8*	*91.5*			*67*

Breakout: 14% Improve: 16% Collapse: 8% Attrition: 19% MLB: 26% *Comparables: Zeke Spruill, Kyle Ryan, Dallas Beeler*

Danish generated a bit of excitement in 2014 when he burst onto the scene to more than hold his own at High-A. The former second-round pick found himself in Double-A just two years after being drafted out of high school, but his development has kind of hit a wall since then. It's not outside the realm of possibility that a pitcher who misses bats as infrequently as Danish does can find a spot in a major-league rotation, but his ceiling at this point is probably that of a back-end starter.

Dane Dunning RHP Born: 12/20/94 Age: 23 Bats: R Throws: R Height: 6'4" Weight: 200 Origin: Round 1, 2016 Draft (#29 overall)

YEAR	TEAM	LVL	AGE	W	L	SV	G	GS	IP	H	HR	BB/9	K/9	K	GB%	BABIP	WHIP	ERA	DRA	WARP	MPH	CMD	PWR	STM
2016	AUB	A-	21	3	2	0	7	7	33^{2}	26	1	1.9	7.8	29	65%	.263	0.98	2.14	2.33	1.2				
2017	KAN	A	22	2	0	0	4	4	26	13	0	0.7	11.4	33	64%	.224	0.58	0.35	1.13	1.3				
2017	WNS	A+	22	6	8	0	22	22	118	114	15	2.7	10.3	135	52%	.316	1.27	3.51	2.68	3.6				
2018	*CHA*	*MLB*	*23*	*6*	*7*	*0*	*20*	*20*	*103*	*100*	*21*	*3.7*	*9.9*	*113*	*47%*	*.296*	*1.38*	*5.07*	*5.23*	*0.5*				
2019	*CHA*	*MLB*	*24*	*6*	*9*	*0*	*22*	*22*	*126^{2}*	*130*	*26*	*4.3*	*9.3*	*131*	*47%*	*.301*	*1.51*	*5.60*	*5.83*	*-0.2*				

Breakout: 12% Improve: 19% Collapse: 6% Attrition: 24% MLB: 32% *Comparables: Nick Tropeano, Burch Smith, Pierce Johnson*

For the consensus third piece coming back to Chicago in the Adam Eaton deal, Dunning is an impressive pitching prospect in his own right. Don't let the glasses fool you: The 6-foot-4, thickly built right-hander is extremely competitive on the mound, such that the label of "bulldog" seems to be his destiny. (Somewhere, Jake Peavy nods in approval, undoubtedly chewing a piece of rawhide). With three potential plus pitches and a good idea of what he's doing on the mound, Dunning seems a fairly safe bet as far as pitching prospects go, although his ceiling appears to be that of an innings-eating mid-rotation arm rather than anything resembling an ace. Still, when all is said and done, Washington may be most melancholy about parting with this Dane.

Danny Farquhar RHP Born: 02/17/87 Age: 31 Bats: R Throws: R Height: 5'9" Weight: 185 Origin: Round 10, 2008 Draft (#309 overall)

YEAR	TEAM	LVL	AGE	W	L	SV	G	GS	IP	H	HR	BB/9	K/9	K	GB%	BABIP	WHIP	ERA	DRA	WARP	MPH	CMD	PWR	STM
2015	TAC	AAA	28	1	1	3	27	1	38	40	3	2.4	9.7	41	38%	.359	1.32	3.08	2.41	1.1				
2015	SEA	MLB	28	1	8	1	43	0	51	53	9	3.0	8.5	48	40%	.306	1.37	5.12	3.80	0.5	95.2	49	50	56
2016	DUR	AAA	29	4	2	2	32	0	38	33	2	2.1	5.7	24	48%	.270	1.11	3.32	6.71	-0.8				
2016	TBA	MLB	29	1	0	0	35	0	35^1	33	8	3.8	11.7	46	41%	.294	1.36	3.06	3.01	0.8	94.7	40	48	51
2017	TBA	MLB	30	2	2	0	37	0	35	28	2	5.7	8.5	33	47%	.280	1.43	4.11	3.18	0.8	94.5	43	49	49
2017	CHA	MLB	30	2	0	0	15	0	14^1	11	1	3.8	7.5	12	37%	.238	1.19	4.40	4.94	0.0	95.0	43	49	49
2018	*CHA*	*MLB*	*31*	*3*	*3*	*0*	*56*	*0*	*58*	*60*	*10*	*4.2*	*8.5*	*55*	*43%*	*.298*	*1.47*	*5.09*	*5.04*	*0.1*	*94.0*	*43*	*49*	*51*
2019	*CHA*	*MLB*	*32*	*2*	*1*	*0*	*40*	*0*	*42^1*	*42*	*7*	*4.2*	*8.5*	*40*	*43%*	*.297*	*1.46*	*5.20*	*5.39*	*-0.1*	*93.4*	*42*	*48*	*50*

Breakout: 32% Improve: 43% Collapse: 22% Attrition: 22% MLB: 79% *Comparables: David Carpenter, Will Ohman, Al Alburquerque*

Farquhar was one of a good number of random arms used to help ride out the season after the White Sox traded every reliever with any value in their never-ending quest to build the best farm system known to man. As far as veteran bullpenners in an otherwise lost season go, he served his purpose inasmuch as he fit the definition of "not a trainwreck." But Farquhar's White Sox legacy will likely go down as "most commonly missed name in the Sporcle quiz on the 2017 White Sox roster."

Jace Fry LHP Born: 07/09/93 Age: 24 Bats: L Throws: L Height: 6'1" Weight: 190 Origin: Round 3, 2014 Draft (#77 overall)

YEAR	TEAM	LVL	AGE	W	L	SV	G	GS	IP	H	HR	BB/9	K/9	K	GB%	BABIP	WHIP	ERA	DRA	WARP	MPH	CMD	PWR	STM
2015	WNS	A+	21	1	8	0	10	10	52	60	1	2.9	6.8	39	54%	.339	1.48	3.63	3.61	0.9				
2017	BIR	AA	23	2	1	3	33	0	45^1	36	1	4.8	10.3	52	59%	.307	1.32	2.78	3.30	0.8				
2017	CHA	MLB	23	0	0	0	11	0	6^2	12	1	6.8	4.1	3	39%	.407	2.55	10.80	6.66	-0.1	95.5			38
2018	*CHA*	*MLB*	*24*	*1*	*1*	*0*	*25*	*0*	*26*	*26*	*3*	*4.5*	*9.1*	*27*	*46%*	*.299*	*1.47*	*4.36*	*4.48*	*0.2*	*95.3*			*39*
2019	*CHA*	*MLB*	*25*	*2*	*1*	*0*	*34*	*0*	*36*	*36*	*5*	*5.4*	*8.8*	*35*	*46%*	*.301*	*1.59*	*5.19*	*5.39*	*-0.1*	*95.0*			*40*

Breakout: 22% Improve: 29% Collapse: 11% Attrition: 26% MLB: 47% *Comparables: Osiris Matos, Randor Bierd, Luis Castillo*

Good news, everyone! Despite undergoing two Tommy John surgeries Fry still defied the odds and made it to the majors. The second one tapped out any flickering hopes that he could start, but he is left-handed and throws in the mid-90s, so it wouldn't take much Don Cooper magic to find something here. Modern bullpens are big, and one can imagine Fry getting plenty of run after a surprising late-season promotion in 2017. If he gets enough plane on his fastball without too many walks, Fry could still sculpt a career for himself. He could also be sent back to the minors to get more work if space is needed.

Carson Fulmer RHP Born: 12/13/93 Age: 24 Bats: R Throws: R Height: 6'0" Weight: 195 Origin: Round 1, 2015 Draft (#8 overall)

YEAR	TEAM	LVL	AGE	W	L	SV	G	GS	IP	H	HR	BB/9	K/9	K	GB%	BABIP	WHIP	ERA	DRA	WARP	MPH	CMD	PWR	STM
2015	WNS	A+	21	0	0	0	8	8	22	16	2	3.7	10.2	25	43%	.269	1.14	2.05	3.61	0.4				
2016	BIR	AA	22	4	9	0	17	17	87	82	7	5.3	9.3	90	45%	.310	1.53	4.76	6.31	-1.3				
2016	CHA	MLB	22	0	2	0	8	0	11^2	12	2	5.4	7.7	10	44%	.312	1.63	8.49	4.50	0.1	95.3	12	47	58
2016	CHR	AAA	22	2	1	0	4	4	16	14	1	2.8	7.9	14	61%	.289	1.19	3.94	3.73	0.3				
2017	CHR	AAA	23	7	9	0	25	25	126	132	18	4.6	6.9	96	46%	.297	1.56	5.79	5.77	-0.1				
2017	CHA	MLB	23	3	1	0	7	5	23^1	16	4	5.0	7.3	19	31%	.190	1.24	3.86	5.97	-0.1	94.6	54	48	69
2018	*CHA*	*MLB*	*24*	*6*	*9*	*0*	*23*	*23*	*115*	*115*	*20*	*4.6*	*8.4*	*108*	*42%*	*.293*	*1.51*	*5.03*	*5.34*	*0.1*	*94.6*	*43*	*49*	*66*
2019	*CHA*	*MLB*	*25*	*8*	*11*	*0*	*29*	*29*	*181*	*174*	*31*	*4.2*	*8.9*	*179*	*42%*	*.289*	*1.43*	*5.15*	*5.35*	*0.5*	*94.4*	*44*	*49*	*67*

Breakout: 19% Improve: 31% Collapse: 18% Attrition: 26% MLB: 58% *Comparables: Dustin McGowan, Brad Hand, Andy Oliver*

Fulmer's stuff, build and mechanics scream "reliever." The White Sox have been swimming upstream with this since day one, but their track record is such with pitchers that perhaps he can beat the odds. To wit, Fulmer displayed a dynamic cutter in his final few outings of the season, which, paired with his ability to hold mid-90s velocity over multiple innings, may yet allow him to Hail Mary his way into a rotation. Still, even as fans excitedly passed around GIFs of Fulmer generating big swings and misses, the same clips showed him missing the target by a couple of feet. Fortunately, even the vast majority of analysts who believe this is a reliever tend to think he'd be quite good at it.

Lucas Giolito RHP Born: 07/14/94 Age: 23 Bats: R Throws: R Height: 6'6" Weight: 255 Origin: Round 1, 2012 Draft (#16 overall)

YEAR	TEAM	LVL	AGE	W	L	SV	G	GS	IP	H	HR	BB/9	K/9	K	GB%	BABIP	WHIP	ERA	DRA	WARP	MPH	CMD	PWR	STM
2015	POT	A+	20	3	5	0	13	11	69^2	65	1	2.6	11.1	86	54%	.352	1.22	2.71	1.17	3.2				
2015	HAR	AA	20	4	2	0	8	8	47^1	48	2	3.2	8.6	45	56%	.341	1.37	3.80	3.00	1.2				
2016	HAR	AA	21	5	3	0	14	14	71	67	2	4.3	9.1	72	53%	.323	1.42	3.17	3.69	1.2				
2016	SYR	AAA	21	1	2	0	7	7	37^1	31	3	2.4	9.6	40	56%	.298	1.10	2.17	2.36	1.3				
2016	WAS	MLB	21	0	1	0	6	4	21^1	26	7	5.1	4.6	11	42%	.271	1.78	6.75	7.58	-0.6	96.1	46	55	61
2017	CHR	AAA	22	6	10	0	24	24	128^2	122	17	4.1	9.4	134	45%	.312	1.41	4.48	2.85	4.0				
2017	CHA	MLB	22	3	3	0	7	7	45^1	31	8	2.4	6.8	34	47%	.189	0.95	2.38	5.28	0.2	94.1	46	45	75
2018	*CHA*	*MLB*	*23*	*9*	*11*	*0*	*28*	*28*	*159*	*155*	*27*	*4.0*	*9.1*	*161*	*46%*	*.295*	*1.42*	*4.58*	*4.85*	*1.0*	*94.6*	*48*	*50*	*71*
2019	*CHA*	*MLB*	*24*	*9*	*11*	*0*	*29*	*29*	*181^1*	*170*	*31*	*3.6*	*9.9*	*200*	*46%*	*.295*	*1.33*	*4.73*	*4.90*	*1.4*	*94.4*	*48*	*50*	*72*

Breakout: 27% Improve: 47% Collapse: 10% Attrition: 26% MLB: 69% *Comparables: Jon Niese, Luke Weaver, Daniel Norris*

Giolito doesn't throw 100 mph anymore. He didn't when the White Sox acquired him, hadn't in some time and frankly, given the other two arms that came over from Washington with him, it would be bizarre if either team was acting like he was still That Guy who was in the global no. 1 prospect conversation once upon a time. He works 91-94 now, he still flashes his plus curve, his changeup took big strides in 2017 and he's been working on adding a slider to his repertoire. Giolito gets good reviews for his thoughtfulness and pitchability, won't turn 24 until July and will start the year in the major-league rotation. He's not going to be the ace he looked like he might be years ago, but if he were the Nationals never would have traded him in the first place.

Alec Hansen RHP Born: 10/10/94 Age: 23 Bats: R Throws: R Height: 6'7" Weight: 235 Origin: Round 2, 2016 Draft (#49 overall)

YEAR	TEAM	LVL	AGE	W	L	SV	G	GS	IP	H	HR	BB/9	K/9	K	GB%	BABIP	WHIP	ERA	DRA	WARP	MPH	CMD	PWR	STM
2016	GRF	RK	21	2	0	0	7	7	36^2	12	3	2.9	14.5	59	52%	.161	0.65	1.23	1.11	1.9				
2016	KAN	A	21	0	1	0	2	2	11	11	0	3.3	9.0	11	53%	.344	1.36	2.45	3.08	0.3				
2017	KAN	A	22	7	3	0	13	13	72^2	57	3	2.8	11.4	92	32%	.292	1.10	2.48	3.14	1.8				
2017	WNS	A+	22	4	5	0	11	11	58^1	42	5	3.9	12.7	82	38%	.296	1.15	2.93	2.48	1.9				
2017	BIR	AA	22	0	0	0	2	2	10^1	15	0	2.6	14.8	17	36%	.536	1.74	4.35	3.53	0.2				
2018	*CHA*	*MLB*	*23*	*5*	*8*	*0*	*20*	*20*	*101^2*	*95*	*28*	*4.7*	*12.3*	*139*	*38%*	*.299*	*1.46*	*5.80*	*6.05*	*-0.4*				
2019	*CHA*	*MLB*	*24*	*6*	*9*	*0*	*22*	*22*	*131*	*136*	*35*	*4.6*	*10.7*	*156*	*38%*	*.308*	*1.55*	*6.10*	*6.40*	*-0.9*				

Breakout: 17% Improve: 25% Collapse: 3% Attrition: 21% MLB: 35% *Comparables: Trevor May, James McDonald, Christian Garcia*

It's been a whirlwind of a journey for Hansen over the last two years. He went from potential top-five pick in the 2016 draft to someone whose stock plummeted after a disastrous junior season at Oklahoma, then to a potential revival project, to a bona fide prospect, jumping three levels during the 2017 season and putting himself squarely in the White Sox's future plans. Hansen's improvement can best be attributed to improved command and a refinement of his changeup, giving him four pitches he's shown comfort using regularly. He's a pitcher, so of course there are no guarantees, but the quick development he's shown increases the likelihood that the Alec Hansen pitch face will be seen at major-league ballparks much sooner than initially thought.

Derek Holland LHP Born: 10/09/86 Age: 31 Bats: B Throws: L Height: 6'2" Weight: 215 Origin: Round 25, 2006 Draft (#748 overall)

YEAR	TEAM	LVL	AGE	W	L	SV	G	GS	IP	H	HR	BB/9	K/9	K	GB%	BABIP	WHIP	ERA	DRA	WARP	MPH	CMD	PWR	STM
2015	TEX	MLB	28	4	3	0	10	10	58^2	59	11	2.6	6.3	41	43%	.281	1.30	4.91	5.27	-0.1	95.8	59	50	20
2016	ROU	AAA	29	0	0	0	3	3	10	11	1	3.6	7.2	8	58%	.312	1.50	4.50	4.95	0.0				
2016	TEX	MLB	29	7	9	0	22	20	107^1	116	15	2.9	5.6	67	38%	.295	1.41	4.95	5.62	-0.3	94.5	60	46	50
2017	CHA	MLB	30	7	14	0	29	26	135	156	31	5.0	6.9	104	39%	.307	1.71	6.20	7.46	-2.8	93.1	57	36	69
2018	*CHA*	*MLB*	*31*	*6*	*9*	*0*	*23*	*23*	*115^2*	*124*	*22*	*4.1*	*7.1*	*91*	*42%*	*.293*	*1.53*	*5.68*	*5.88*	*-0.2*	*93.1*	*58*	*41*	*50*
2019	*CHA*	*MLB*	*32*	*5*	*7*	*0*	*19*	*19*	*110^2*	*122*	*20*	*3.7*	*7.2*	*88*	*42%*	*.303*	*1.51*	*5.47*	*5.68*	*0.0*	*92.5*	*58*	*40*	*56*

Breakout: 11% Improve: 50% Collapse: 18% Attrition: 21% MLB: 85% *Comparables: Jason Vargas, John Danks, Vicente Padilla*

On paper, the signing made a lot of sense. The White Sox tried to pick up every piece of a pitcher we used to love, leveraging Don Cooper and their reputation for keeping pitchers healthy to get necessary innings, and maybe rebuild Holland's value for the trade deadline. For a few months it looked like they'd successfully ridden the circus wheel with this Derek wrapped in white. Then the wings fell off, and although he stayed healthy, from mid-May until his September release opposing batters got even healthier, slashing .322/.417/.595 with seemingly 1,945 RBIs. He didn't mean to make you cry, with bats that sing and dingers fly, but now he rides the waivers flame and won't be coming back again.

David Holmberg LHP Born: 07/19/91 Age: 26 Bats: R Throws: L Height: 6'3" Weight: 245 Origin: Round 2, 2009 Draft (#71 overall)

YEAR	TEAM	LVL	AGE	W	L	SV	G	GS	IP	H	HR	BB/9	K/9	K	GB%	BABIP	WHIP	ERA	DRA	WARP	MPH	CMD	PWR	STM
2015	CIN	MLB	23	1	4	0	6	6	28^1	36	10	5.1	4.8	15	44%	.280	1.84	7.62	8.64	-1.2	90.0	51	28	68
2015	LOU	AAA	23	7	7	0	21	19	120^1	142	14	3.1	5.3	71	45%	.322	1.52	4.34	6.61	-1.8				
2016	BIR	AA	24	6	6	0	19	19	114^1	112	7	2.2	5.8	74	52%	.292	1.22	3.70	4.04	1.5				
2016	CHR	AAA	24	2	3	0	9	9	54^1	51	6	2.3	5.5	33	49%	.271	1.20	4.14	3.60	1.1				
2017	CHR	AAA	25	3	1	0	10	4	32^1	26	4	2.2	6.7	24	49%	.244	1.05	2.78	2.73	1.0				
2017	CHA	MLB	25	2	4	0	37	7	57^2	63	12	5.3	5.2	33	44%	.273	1.68	4.68	6.70	-0.9	89.2	48	18	52
2018	*CHA*	*MLB*	*26*	*4*	*6*	*0*	*24*	*14*	*87^2*	*93*	*16*	*3.8*	*6.3*	*62*	*45%*	*.286*	*1.48*	*5.62*	*5.81*	*-0.2*	*89.0*	*50*	*21*	*59*
2019	*CHA*	*MLB*	*27*	*7*	*9*	*0*	*32*	*21*	*142^2*	*151*	*24*	*3.5*	*6.6*	*105*	*45%*	*.29*	*1.44*	*5.37*	*5.58*	*0.0*	*88.6*	*49*	*19*	*57*

Breakout: 29% Improve: 46% Collapse: 15% Attrition: 33% MLB: 67% *Comparables: Zach Jackson, Mitchell Boggs, Craig Stammen*

Holmberg was among a number of replacement-level arms to eat innings for the White Sox in 2017, even making a handful of starts. While not yet an old dog, he was nonetheless unable to learn any new tricks, as his low velocity and average breaking stuff translated into another season with more walks than strikeouts and a home-run rate higher than any competitive team, along with many slow-pitch softball teams, would be comfortable with.

Gregory Infante RHP Born: 07/10/87 Age: 30 Bats: R Throws: R Height: 6'2" Weight: 215 Origin: International Free Agent, 2006

YEAR	TEAM	LVL	AGE	W	L	SV	G	GS	IP	H	HR	BB/9	K/9	K	GB%	BABIP	WHIP	ERA	DRA	WARP	MPH	CMD	PWR	STM
2015	BUF	AAA	27	1	2	7	45	0	48^2	43	3	5.9	7.6	41	48%	.290	1.54	2.77	8.63	-2.0				
2016	LEH	AAA	28	2	1	0	9	1	17	17	3	6.4	6.4	12	36%	.298	1.71	5.82	10.03	-1.0				
2016	REA	AA	28	4	2	0	30	1	44^2	49	4	4.6	10.7	53	46%	.363	1.61	4.84	3.70	0.6				
2017	CHR	AAA	29	0	1	3	12	0	15	7	0	4.8	10.8	18	28%	.219	1.00	1.80	4.21	0.2				
2017	CHA	MLB	29	2	1	0	52	0	54^2	45	4	3.3	8.1	49	37%	.272	1.19	3.13	4.74	0.3	97.3	34	58	51
2018	*CHA*	*MLB*	*30*	*2*	*3*	*0*	*51*	*0*	*53*	*55*	*10*	*4.9*	*8.6*	*51*	*40%*	*.297*	*1.57*	*5.75*	*5.69*	*-0.4*	*96.5*	*34*	*58*	*51*
2019	*CHA*	*MLB*	*31*	*1*	*0*	*0*	*32*	*0*	*33^1*	*35*	*7*	*4.7*	*8.4*	*31*	*40%*	*.303*	*1.58*	*5.86*	*6.10*	*-0.3*	*96.0*	*34*	*58*	*51*

Breakout: 13% Improve: 21% Collapse: 8% Attrition: 18% MLB: 34% *Comparables: Cesar Jimenez, Joe Paterson, Dalier Hinojosa*

You're having breakfast in your kitchen and checking a box score for the White Sox in September 2017, thinking to yourself, "Oh cool, there's someone else named Greg Infante in the majors? I wonder what happened to the old one." Then a stranger leans through your open window with overly dilated pupils and shouts, "IT'S THE SAME GUY!" You are scared to your core, but this well-informed eccentric goes on to explain that Infante's high-90s, lively fastball has been harnessed juuuuuuuuussssst enough by Don Cooper to at least, for the moment, yield a usable reliever. The two of you discuss Infante for a few more minutes and then return to your respective lives, with a newfound respect for one another and the universe's potential to turn retreads into fire-balling setup men with seemingly no rhyme or reason.

Nate Jones RHP Born: 01/28/86 Age: 32 Bats: R Throws: R Height: 6'5" Weight: 220 Origin: Round 5, 2007 Draft (#179 overall)

YEAR	TEAM	LVL	AGE	W	L	SV	G	GS	IP	H	HR	BB/9	K/9	K	GB%	BABIP	WHIP	ERA	DRA	WARP	MPH	CMD	PWR	STM
2015	CHA	MLB	29	2	2	0	19	0	19	12	5	2.8	12.8	27	49%	.206	0.95	3.32	2.53	0.5	100.0	47	68	39
2016	CHA	MLB	30	5	3	3	71	0	70^{2}	48	7	1.9	10.2	80	47%	.243	0.89	2.29	2.25	2.2	99.2	49	63	49
2017	CHA	MLB	31	1	0	0	11	0	11^{2}	9	1	4.6	11.6	15	59%	.308	1.29	2.31	3.12	0.3	98.3	49	64	46
2018	*CHA*	*MLB*	*32*	*2*	*2*	*8*	*41*	*0*	*42*	*37*	*5*	*3.9*	*9.9*	*47*	*48%*	*.291*	*1.31*	*3.88*	*4.12*	*0.5*	*98.2*	*48*	*63*	*45*
2019	*CHA*	*MLB*	*33*	*2*	*1*	*4*	*50*	*0*	*53*	*46*	*8*	*4.1*	*9.9*	*58*	*48%*	*.284*	*1.32*	*4.58*	*4.72*	*0.3*	*97.6*	*48*	*62*	*46*

Breakout: 23% Improve: 38% Collapse: 27% Attrition: 4% MLB: 93% *Comparables: Jose Valverde, Rafael Soriano, Brian Fuentes*

Jones uses his 6-foot-5 frame and his "I will hold this ball in the sky and smite you with it" motion to generate high-90s velocity and a brutal slider to phenomenal results. The downside is that after an oddly heavy workload in a 99-loss season in 2013, Jones underwent Tommy John surgery. Last year was another lost season due to nerve repositioning surgery in his elbow. If he's healthy, Jones is a legitimate late-inning relief option, which is a particularly good result given his pedigree, but the first part of this sentence inspires less confidence than his ability to get hitters out when he's able to take the mound.

Michael Kopech RHP Born: 04/30/96 Age: 22 Bats: R Throws: R Height: 6'3" Weight: 205 Origin: Round 1, 2014 Draft (#33 overall)

YEAR	TEAM	LVL	AGE	W	L	SV	G	GS	IP	H	HR	BB/9	K/9	K	GB%	BABIP	WHIP	ERA	DRA	WARP	MPH	CMD	PWR	STM
2015	GRN	A	19	4	5	0	16	15	65	53	2	3.7	9.7	70	47%	.313	1.23	2.63	2.92	1.7				
2016	SLM	A+	20	4	1	0	11	11	52	25	1	5.0	14.2	82	45%	.273	1.04	2.25	1.07	2.6				
2017	BIR	AA	21	8	7	0	22	22	119^{1}	77	6	4.5	11.7	155	42%	.272	1.15	2.87	2.34	4.0				
2017	CHR	AAA	21	1	1	0	3	3	15	15	0	3.0	10.2	17	35%	.375	1.33	3.00	3.93	0.3				
2018	*CHA*	*MLB*	*22*	*3*	*4*	*0*	*24*	*9*	*63*	*54*	*10*	*5.2*	*11.4*	*81*	*40%*	*.294*	*1.42*	*4.39*	*4.60*	*0.5*				
2019	*CHA*	*MLB*	*23*	*7*	*8*	*0*	*55*	*19*	*149^{2}*	*130*	*28*	*4.8*	*11.7*	*194*	*40%*	*.298*	*1.40*	*4.92*	*5.11*	*0.7*				

Breakout: 17% Improve: 31% Collapse: 6% Attrition: 19% MLB: 50% *Comparables: Carlos Rodon, Tyler Glasnow, Carl Edwards Jr.*

Kopech has an ideal build, an 80-grade fastball and a slider that flashes double-plus. After a few months of pitching at the highest level of his career for more innings than he ever had, he started to look like he'd hit a wall, struggling mightily midseason. Then he appeared to consciously take a little off his fastball in a bid for more command, morphed into a fire-breathing dragon and eviscerated Double-A until he was promoted to Triple-A for three starts. Although the walks dropped as he progressed, they're still an issue—both command and control may ultimately relegate him to relief, and all of the general pitcher caveats apply. That said, Kopech may arrive in the majors as a starter as soon as 2018.

Reynaldo Lopez RHP Born: 01/04/94 Age: 24 Bats: R Throws: R Height: 6'0" Weight: 185 Origin: International Free Agent, 2012

YEAR	TEAM	LVL	AGE	W	L	SV	G	GS	IP	H	HR	BB/9	K/9	K	GB%	BABIP	WHIP	ERA	DRA	WARP	MPH	CMD	PWR	STM
2015	POT	A+	21	6	7	0	19	19	99	93	5	2.5	8.5	94	47%	.321	1.22	4.09	2.82	2.7				
2016	HAR	AA	22	3	5	0	14	14	76^{1}	69	7	2.9	11.8	100	43%	.320	1.23	3.18	1.34	3.4				
2016	SYR	AAA	22	2	2	0	5	5	33	21	6	2.7	7.1	26	33%	.174	0.94	3.27	5.19	0.1				
2016	WAS	MLB	22	5	3	0	11	6	44	47	4	4.5	8.6	42	43%	.326	1.57	4.91	4.19	0.5	98.7	47	55	65
2017	CHR	AAA	23	6	7	0	22	22	121	101	16	3.6	9.7	131	38%	.270	1.24	3.79	3.36	3.1				
2017	CHA	MLB	23	3	3	0	8	8	47^{2}	49	7	2.6	5.7	30	30%	.271	1.32	4.72	7.34	-0.9	97.6	59	59	73
2018	*CHA*	*MLB*	*24*	*9*	*11*	*0*	*28*	*28*	*159*	*156*	*29*	*3.7*	*9.0*	*160*	*39%*	*.291*	*1.39*	*4.66*	*4.93*	*0.8*	*97.9*	*55*	*59*	*72*
2019	*CHA*	*MLB*	*25*	*9*	*11*	*0*	*30*	*30*	*186*	*177*	*37*	*3.5*	*9.7*	*200*	*39%*	*.286*	*1.34*	*5.11*	*5.29*	*0.7*	*97.6*	*55*	*59*	*72*

Breakout: 24% Improve: 64% Collapse: 11% Attrition: 19% MLB: 85% *Comparables: Travis Wood, Vincent Velasquez, Jon Gray*

Lopez entered 2017 with a new organization but the same doubts about his future as a starter. After a mostly successful stint at Triple-A, he spent the latter two months of the season with the big club, and questions remain. What has always made Lopez an enticing prospect is his ability to miss bats, but he went through an odd four-start stretch at the end of the season in which he failed to strike out more than two batters in any outing. Further puzzling is that he was effective in the run-prevention department anyway. The sample size for Lopez at the major-league level is still small enough that he'll have his fair share of opportunities to stick as a starter. The zip on his fastball and plus curve make him more than capable of doing so.

Juan Minaya RHP Born: 09/18/90 Age: 27 Bats: R Throws: R Height: 6'4" Weight: 210 Origin: International Free Agent, 2008

YEAR	TEAM	LVL	AGE	W	L	SV	G	GS	IP	H	HR	BB/9	K/9	K	GB%	BABIP	WHIP	ERA	DRA	WARP	MPH	CMD	PWR	STM
2015	CCH	AA	24	1	0	1	29	0	44^{1}	43	2	3.2	9.7	48	40%	.345	1.33	3.25	3.42	0.7				
2015	FRE	AAA	24	0	0	0	6	0	10^{1}	6	0	4.4	9.6	11	50%	.273	1.06	0.87	3.58	0.2				
2016	FRE	AAA	25	1	3	0	17	0	25^{1}	25	1	3.6	6.8	19	51%	.308	1.38	3.91	4.90	0.0				
2016	CHR	AAA	25	4	3	1	17	0	26^{2}	23	2	3.4	9.4	28	48%	.288	1.24	3.38	2.61	0.7				
2016	CHA	MLB	25	1	0	0	11	0	10^{1}	10	0	4.4	5.2	6	24%	.294	1.45	4.35	4.80	0.0	96.6			39
2017	CHR	AAA	26	1	0	0	13	0	19	17	0	2.4	7.1	15	45%	.293	1.16	1.42	4.23	0.2				
2017	CHA	MLB	26	3	2	9	40	0	43^{2}	38	7	4.1	10.5	51	34%	.304	1.33	4.53	5.44	-0.1	95.7	42	56	49
2018	*CHA*	*MLB*	*27*	*3*	*3*	*5*	*56*	*0*	*58*	*57*	*10*	*4.0*	*9.4*	*62*	*40%*	*.301*	*1.43*	*4.71*	*4.76*	*0.2*	*95.4*	*43*	*57*	*45*
2019	*CHA*	*MLB*	*28*	*2*	*1*	*14*	*43*	*0*	*45*	*43*	*8*	*4.0*	*9.5*	*47*	*40%*	*.296*	*1.41*	*5.02*	*5.19*	*0.0*	*95.0*	*42*	*57*	*45*

Breakout: 20% Improve: 29% Collapse: 15% Attrition: 35% MLB: 54% *Comparables: Warner Madrigal, Caleb Thielbar, Jose Ascanio*

Minaya is 27. He throws 95 mph and also has a slider. His command isn't very good. His peripherals are a little worse than his slightly below-average ERA. He was acquired off waivers. It makes sense that he's in a major-league bullpen, but it would make just as much sense if a team tried to replace him at every opportunity. Maybe the White Sox see something in his delivery or off-speed stuff that they think can improve to make him average instead of below average. Maybe not. He's clearly better than Chris Beck, although that's hardly a ringing endorsement.

Mike Pelfrey RHP Born: 01/14/84 Age: 34 Bats: R Throws: R Height: 6'7" Weight: 240 Origin: Round 1, 2005 Draft (#9 overall)

YEAR	TEAM	LVL	AGE	W	L	SV	G	GS	IP	H	HR	BB/9	K/9	K	GB%	BABIP	WHIP	ERA	DRA	WARP	MPH	CMD	PWR	STM
2015	MIN	MLB	31	6	11	0	30	30	164^2	198	11	2.5	4.7	86	53%	.334	1.48	4.26	5.27	-0.4	96.0	59	58	68
2016	DET	MLB	32	4	10	0	24	22	119	160	15	3.5	4.2	56	52%	.347	1.73	5.07	6.96	-2.2	95.3	45	53	57
2017	CHA	MLB	33	3	12	0	34	21	120	127	25	4.7	5.9	79	50%	.276	1.58	5.93	5.59	-0.1	93.7	66	43	64
2018	*CHA*	*MLB*	*34*	*5*	*9*	*0*	*22*	*22*	*109^1*	*128*	*18*	*4.0*	*5.5*	*66*	*50%*	*.308*	*1.62*	*5.73*	*5.91*	*-0.3*	*93.8*	*57*	*50*	*62*
2019	*CHA*	*MLB*	*35*	*5*	*7*	*0*	*18*	*18*	*106^1*	*133*	*18*	*3.6*	*5.3*	*63*	*50%*	*.322*	*1.65*	*5.76*	*5.96*	*-0.3*	*92.9*	*56*	*47*	*60*

Breakout: 7% Improve: 45% Collapse: 17% Attrition: 11% MLB: 88% *Comparables: Jason Marquis, Jake Westbrook, Jeff Suppan*

Yes, the newspapers were right: runs were general all over Chicago. They were falling softly upon the Bog of Dick Allen and, farther eastward, softly falling into the dark mutinous Lake Michigan waves. They were falling, too, upon every part of the lonely bullpen where Michael Pelfrey lay buried. They lay thickly drifted in the crooked numbers and home runs, on the walls of the little outfield, in the barren gaps. His soul swooned slowly as he heard the runs falling faintly through the universe and faintly falling, like the descent of their last end, upon all the living and the dead.

Jake Petricka RHP Born: 06/05/88 Age: 30 Bats: R Throws: R Height: 6'5" Weight: 220 Origin: Round 2, 2010 Draft (#63 overall)

YEAR	TEAM	LVL	AGE	W	L	SV	G	GS	IP	H	HR	BB/9	K/9	K	GB%	BABIP	WHIP	ERA	DRA	WARP	MPH	CMD	PWR	STM
2015	CHA	MLB	27	4	3	2	62	0	52	56	2	3.1	5.7	33	66%	.325	1.42	3.63	3.63	0.7	97.2	49	68	46
2016	CHA	MLB	28	0	0	0	9	0	8	8	1	9.0	7.9	7	71%	.304	2.00	4.50	2.80	0.2	97.4			
2017	CHA	MLB	29	1	1	0	27	0	25^2	39	6	2.1	9.1	26	48%	.398	1.75	7.01	6.56	-0.4	97.0	56	66	30
2018	*CHA*	*MLB*	*30*	*1*	*0*	*1*	*32*	*0*	*33^2*	*35*	*6*	*4.3*	*7.6*	*29*	*52%*	*.300*	*1.52*	*5.29*	*5.46*	*-0.1*	*96.4*	*52*	*67*	*36*
2019	*CHA*	*MLB*	*31*	*2*	*0*	*1*	*34*	*0*	*32^2*	*36*	*6*	*5.0*	*7.8*	*28*	*52%*	*.31*	*1.65*	*5.84*	*6.07*	*-0.3*	*95.8*	*54*	*66*	*33*

Breakout: 30% Improve: 54% Collapse: 24% Attrition: 19% MLB: 84% *Comparables: Bryan Morris, Dan Jennings, Chad Qualls*

With a mid-90s bowling-ball sinker, Petricka profiled as an unusual, good-but-not-great middle reliever. Given that he's now two full years removed from his most recent healthy season, it's not clear that he still has the arsenal that was once viable. The White Sox aren't at the phase of the rebuild yet where they're going to give up on prospects as starters and shunt them into the bullpen, but that time is not as far off as one might think, and Petricka may be hard pressed to hang on to a spot.

Zach Putnam RHP Born: 07/03/87 Age: 30 Bats: R Throws: R Height: 6'2" Weight: 220 Origin: Round 5, 2008 Draft (#171 overall)

YEAR	TEAM	LVL	AGE	W	L	SV	G	GS	IP	H	HR	BB/9	K/9	K	GB%	BABIP	WHIP	ERA	DRA	WARP	MPH	CMD	PWR	STM
2015	CHA	MLB	27	3	3	0	49	0	48^2	42	7	4.4	11.8	64	47%	.310	1.36	4.07	2.55	1.2	92.4	44	13	40
2016	CHA	MLB	28	1	0	0	25	0	27^1	25	2	3.6	9.9	30	41%	.324	1.32	2.30	2.96	0.6	92.5	37	13	38
2017	CHA	MLB	29	0	0	0	7	0	8^2	2	0	1.0	9.3	9	56%	.111	0.35	1.04	2.56	0.3	92.1			
2018	*CHA*	*MLB*	*30*	*2*	*1*	*0*	*33*	*0*	*35*	*30*	*4*	*4.3*	*10.1*	*39*	*45%*	*.291*	*1.33*	*4.08*	*4.16*	*0.4*	*91.7*	*41*	*13*	*39*
2019	*CHA*	*MLB*	*31*	*2*	*1*	*0*	*39*	*0*	*41^2*	*38*	*7*	*4.7*	*10.3*	*48*	*45%*	*.298*	*1.42*	*4.71*	*4.87*	*0.2*	*91.1*	*39*	*13*	*38*

Breakout: 30% Improve: 50% Collapse: 29% Attrition: 20% MLB: 93% *Comparables: Brian Wilson, Jake Diekman, Steve Cishek*

What if we told you the White Sox had claimed a 26-year-old Triple-A right-handed reliever off waivers whose repertoire consisted of spamming a mid-80s splitter? What if we told you this pitcher would then strike out 149 batters over 139 innings with an ERA of 2.71 across the next few seasons? Well, it's true, and that's Putnam. Unfortunately, whether you believe it or not, Tommy John surgery meant a second straight season cut short by injury, and his durability is now a serious question.

Carlos Rodon LHP Born: 12/10/92 Age: 25 Bats: L Throws: L Height: 6'3" Weight: 235 Origin: Round 1, 2014 Draft (#3 overall)

YEAR	TEAM	LVL	AGE	W	L	SV	G	GS	IP	H	HR	BB/9	K/9	K	GB%	BABIP	WHIP	ERA	DRA	WARP	MPH	CMD	PWR	STM
2015	CHR	AAA	22	1	0	0	2	2	10	8	0	3.6	11.7	13	42%	.333	1.20	3.60	2.67	0.3				
2015	CHA	MLB	22	9	6	0	26	23	139^1	130	11	4.6	9.0	139	49%	.315	1.44	3.75	4.92	0.2	97.1	32	59	66
2016	CHA	MLB	23	9	10	0	28	28	165	176	23	2.9	9.2	168	44%	.330	1.39	4.04	4.28	2.0	97.5	41	57	72
2017	CHR	AAA	24	0	3	0	3	3	13^2	17	0	4.6	7.2	11	50%	.354	1.76	9.22	4.98	0.1				
2017	CHA	MLB	24	2	5	0	12	12	69^1	64	12	4.0	9.9	76	45%	.297	1.37	4.15	5.22	0.3	96.4	42	55	58
2018	*CHA*	*MLB*	*25*	*8*	*8*	*0*	*24*	*24*	*136*	*129*	*20*	*3.6*	*9.8*	*150*	*45%*	*.302*	*1.36*	*4.01*	*4.23*	*1.8*	*96.8*	*39*	*58*	*66*
2019	*CHA*	*MLB*	*26*	*10*	*11*	*0*	*30*	*30*	*186*	*182*	*30*	*3.6*	*9.7*	*200*	*45%*	*.306*	*1.38*	*4.68*	*4.81*	*1.6*	*96.6*	*42*	*58*	*66*

Breakout: 23% Improve: 56% Collapse: 17% Attrition: 11% MLB: 100% *Comparables: Scott Kazmir, Madison Bumgarner, Joba Chamberlain*

Rodon showcased in his 12 starts everything that made him one of the more enticing pitching prospects in baseball. The problem? He only made 12 starts. Last season was supposed to be a breakout year for the former no. 3 pick after he cut his walk rate nearly in half between his rookie and sophomore campaigns. Instead, he missed the first three months of the season with bursitis and was shut down again in September, ultimately having arthroscopic surgery on his left shoulder. Rodon has shown enough talent when healthy to maintain the hope that he'll turn into a dependable no. 2 starter, but we've sung this song enough over the years to know predicting that would be foolish.

Jose Ruiz RHP Born: 10/21/94 Age: 23 Bats: R Throws: R Height: 6'1" Weight: 190 Origin: International Free Agent, 2011

YEAR	TEAM	LVL	AGE	W	L	SV	G	GS	IP	H	HR	BB/9	K/9	K	GB%	BABIP	WHIP	ERA	DRA	WARP	MPH	CMD	PWR	STM
2016	TRI	A-	21	2	0	2	9	0	10^2	3	0	1.7	10.1	12	71%	.143	0.47	0.00	2.67	0.3				
2017	SDN	MLB	22	0	0	0	1	0	1	0	0	9.0	9.0	1	50%	.000	1.00	0.00	4.67	0.0	95.9			44
2017	LEL	A+	22	1	2	2	44	0	49^2	57	7	4.5	8.2	45	33%	.345	1.65	5.98	9.02	-2.4				
2018	*CHA*	*MLB*	*23*	*1*	*0*	*1*	*34*	*0*	*36^1*	*39*	*10*	*5.5*	*9.3*	*38*	*40%*	*.296*	*1.67*	*6.68*	*6.97*	*-0.7*	*95.8*			*46*
2019	*CHA*	*MLB*	*24*	*1*	*0*	*1*	*27*	*0*	*30^2*	*30*	*7*	*5.1*	*9.0*	*31*	*40%*	*.304*	*1.54*	*5.92*	*6.87*	*-0.6*	*95.6*			*46*

Comparables: Rhiner Cruz, Steve Cishek, Phil Klein

Ruiz was the crown jewel of the Padres 2011 international class when he signed for $1.1 million. Unfortunately, he could never hit, spending five years flailing at stateside pitching and never graduating from A-ball. But he featured a plus arm from behind the dish, so after some "success" with Christian Bethancourt, the Padres tried another catcher-to-pitcher conversion with Ruiz and ... well, he still throws hard off the mound, inducing plenty of whiffs with a mid-90s fastball. Next step: figure out where it's going.

James Shields RHP Born: 12/20/81 Age: 36 Bats: R Throws: R Height: 6'3" Weight: 215 Origin: Round 16, 2000 Draft (#466 overall)

YEAR	TEAM	LVL	AGE	W	L	SV	G	GS	IP	H	HR	BB/9	K/9	K	GB%	BABIP	WHIP	ERA	DRA	WARP	MPH	CMD	PWR	STM
2015	SDN	MLB	33	13	7	0	33	33	202^{1}	189	33	3.6	9.6	216	47%	.299	1.33	3.91	4.65	1.0	93.6	48	35	81
2016	SDN	MLB	34	2	7	0	11	11	67^{1}	69	9	3.6	7.6	57	48%	.316	1.43	4.28	5.59	-0.2	92.5	49	35	79
2016	CHA	MLB	34	4	12	0	22	22	114^{1}	139	31	4.3	6.1	78	38%	.296	1.70	6.77	7.16	-2.4	93.1	49	35	79
2017	CHR	AAA	35	0	3	0	3	3	14	13	0	1.9	9.0	14	48%	.325	1.14	3.21	2.78	0.4				
2017	CHA	MLB	35	5	7	0	21	21	117	116	27	4.1	7.9	103	40%	.270	1.44	5.23	4.72	1.1	91.9	48	24	60
2018	*CHA*	*MLB*	*36*	*9*	*13*	*0*	*28*	*28*	*176*	*188*	*36*	*4.0*	*7.6*	*149*	*43%*	*.293*	*1.51*	*5.36*	*5.69*	*-0.6*	*91.5*	*47*	*31*	*70*
2019	*CHA*	*MLB*	*37*	*9*	*12*	*0*	*28*	*28*	*173*	*184*	*33*	*4.0*	*7.7*	*148*	*43%*	*.297*	*1.50*	*5.58*	*5.79*	*-0.3*	*90.6*	*47*	*29*	*67*

Breakout: 18% Improve: 43% Collapse: 16% Attrition: 15% MLB: 75% *Comparables: Kevin Millwood, Jeff Fassero, Cory Lidle*

If you view Shields' 2017 season through rose-colored glasses, you see a pitcher who ate innings for a rebuilding White Sox team while providing valuable veteran mentorship to the club's plethora of young pitchers. The story goes that he even gave Lucas Giolito some key pointers while rehabbing at Triple-A Charlotte! If you take off those glasses, suddenly your eyes are pried open like Alex DeLarge and you're forced to watch highlights of Fernando Tatis Jr. until you're driven to insanity. And at the end of it all you're out $27 million.

Michael Ynoa RHP Born: 09/24/91 Age: 26 Bats: R Throws: R Height: 6'7" Weight: 210 Origin: International Free Agent, 2008

YEAR	TEAM	LVL	AGE	W	L	SV	G	GS	IP	H	HR	BB/9	K/9	K	GB%	BABIP	WHIP	ERA	DRA	WARP	MPH	CMD	PWR	STM
2015	WNS	A+	23	0	2	6	28	0	38	37	2	3.8	9.5	40	44%	.337	1.39	2.61	2.64	0.9				
2016	CHR	AAA	24	1	3	4	18	0	23^{2}	25	2	4.6	7.6	20	33%	.324	1.56	4.56	6.41	-0.4				
2016	CHA	MLB	24	1	0	0	23	0	30	20	0	5.1	9.0	30	40%	.241	1.23	3.00	4.01	0.3	97.0	37	59	38
2017	CHA	MLB	25	1	0	0	22	0	29	28	4	6.8	7.1	23	35%	.276	1.72	5.90	7.18	-0.6	94.6	31	47	32
2018	*CHA*	*MLB*	*26*	*2*	*1*	*0*	*35*	*0*	*36^{2}*	*35*	*5*	*4.9*	*8.6*	*35*	*39%*	*.288*	*1.49*	*5.24*	*5.41*	*-0.1*	*95.3*	*34*	*53*	*35*
2019	*CHA*	*MLB*	*27*	*1*	*1*	*0*	*31*	*0*	*41^{1}*	*41*	*7*	*4.2*	*8.7*	*40*	*39%*	*.3*	*1.47*	*5.20*	*5.40*	*-0.1*	*95.0*	*34*	*53*	*35*

Breakout: 33% Improve: 49% Collapse: 15% Attrition: 22% MLB: 65% *Comparables: Steve Schmoll, Gary Majewski, Jeremy Jeffress*

Ynoa has a lot going for him. He's tall, handsome, throws hard and has been a millionaire since he was a teenager. And, despite the fact that he has been on the radar screen since he was 16 years old, he only turned 26 last September. That's where the good news ends. Coming off a year in which he missed some bats and kept the ball in the park, he got crushed for a few months, got hurt for a few months and then finished with a whimper at Triple-A. Velocity and a name will keep you around for a while, but he sure feels more like organizational filler than anything else at this point.

LINEOUTS

Hitters

HITTER	POS	TEAM	LVL	AGE	PA	R	2B	3B	HR	RBI	BB	K	SB	CS	AVG/OBP/SLG	TAv	VORP	BABIP	BRR	FRAA	WARP
Alex Call	OF	WNS	A+	22	45	2	3	1	0	5	3	11	2	1	.244/.311/.366	.265	-0.3	.333	-1.3	RF(2): 0.6	0.0
	OF	WSX	Rk	22	61	8	1	0	0	6	7	5	1	0	.059/.180/.078	.121	-9.5	.063	-0.4	CF(6): 1.0, RF(4): -1.0	-0.9
	OF	KAN	A	22	168	24	9	1	3	22	16	33	2	2	.248/.333/.386	.264	3.9	.300	-0.6	CF(14): -0.1, RF(11): 0.1	0.4
Ryan Cordell	OF	CSP	AAA	25	292	49	18	5	10	45	25	65	9	4	.284/.349/.506	.270	11.9	.339	1.6	RF(29): 0.0, LF(15): 0.2	1.2
Jameson Fisher	OF	KAN	A	23	265	35	14	5	3	36	31	59	2	2	.269/.365/.417	.292	15.2	.345	1.1	LF(52): 2.1	1.8
	OF	WNS	A+	23	271	33	16	1	7	32	27	55	3	4	.221/.320/.387	.259	6.5	.260	1.1	LF(57): -3.6	0.3
Alfredo Gonzalez	C	BIR	AA	24	249	22	6	1	4	24	29	41	4	4	.208/.306/.301	.239	6.5	.238	1.0	C(71): 13.1	2.1
Courtney Hawkins	CF	KAN	A	23	32	2	4	0	0	1	2	11	0	1	.357/.400/.500	.345	2.9	.588	-0.3	LF(2): -0.1	0.3
	CF	BIR	AA	23	322	33	8	1	10	27	21	105	0	0	.190/.252/.325	.215	-9.3	.253	-0.5	LF(61): -4.4	-1.5
Jacob May	OF	CHA	MLB	25	42	2	0	0	0	3	3	17	0	0	.056/.150/.056	.096	-5.7	.105	0.3	CF(10): -0.7, LF(3): -0.1	-0.7
	OF	CHR	AAA	25	467	54	10	5	4	27	30	112	31	8	.248/.307/.325	.219	-5.8	.331	1.0	CF(92): -4.8, LF(17): 0.7	-1.0
Daniel Palka	OF	ROC	AAA	25	362	47	13	3	11	42	27	80	1	2	.274/.329/.431	.263	9.4	.329	1.2	RF(61): 3.6, LF(25): 0.1	1.3
Jake Peter	2B	BIR	AA	24	322	35	12	1	4	21	26	80	9	4	.270/.340/.361	.268	12.0	.360	1.2	2B(56): -2.3, 3B(8): 0.9	1.2
	2B	CHR	AAA	24	194	28	7	2	9	28	15	44	2	2	.292/.351/.506	.277	10.3	.344	1.2	2B(41): -0.8, LF(2): -0.2	0.9
Tito Polo	OF	TAM	A+	22	259	42	10	6	4	20	16	62	20	6	.289/.346/.434	.284	13.9	.376	1.6	LF(23): -0.4, CF(23): 0.1	1.4
	OF	TRN	AA	22	64	14	4	1	1	17	6	8	7	1	.382/.460/.545	.373	10.3	.435	1.5	LF(7): 0.6, CF(2): -0.5	1.1
	OF	BIR	AA	22	79	10	4	2	0	7	5	15	7	3	.278/.342/.389	.266	5.8	.351	3.0	CF(20): 1.3	0.8
Gavin Sheets	1B	KAN	A	21	218	16	10	0	3	25	20	34	0	0	.266/.346/.365	.271	2.3	.308	-2.4	1B(50): -2.1	0.0
Evan Skoug	C	KAN	A	21	76	6	0	2	2	7	8	29	0	0	.154/.263/.308	.218	-0.1	.229	-0.1	C(20): 1.1	0.1

Alex Call missed most of 2017 with rib injuries. His calling card was his statistical performance in college and the hope that he could hang in center field. ⚾ **Ryan Cordell**'s numbers probably should have been better as a 25-year-old in the hitter-friendly PCL and Colorado Springs, but if healthy he projects as a solid fourth outfielder. ⚾ **Jameson Fisher** is a polished college bat who held his own at both A-ball stops, but is unlikely to be more than a backup at the highest level. ⚾ **Alfredo Gonzalez** hasn't hit at any level above High-A, but his defensive reputation gives him a decent shot at making it to the majors as a backup catcher. ⚾ **Courtney Hawkins** is the last vestige of an era when the White Sox drafted toolsy outfielders, only for them to subsequently fail in spectacular fashion. At least we *think* he's the last. ⚾ **Jacob May** surprisingly made the Opening Day roster, only to find himself back at Triple-A Charlotte shortly after the calendar switched over to his namesake month. ⚾ The White Sox are betting the broken finger that cost **Daniel Palka** half a season also caused his power outage. Since that's his only tool and his future is approximately half-past now, they had better be right. **Jake Peter** is a slap-hitting second-base prospect who doesn't slap quite enough to merit much excitement. Aptly, his name rhymes with "Fake Jeter." Should **Tito Polo** exceed expectations and become anything more than a fourth outfielder, it will leave New Yorkers lamenting, "Hahn robbed the Yanks of Tito!" **Gavin Sheets** was drafted as a power-heavy college first baseman outside of the first round. Sometimes these guys muscle their way to relevance, but you really, really have to hit to do that. **Evan Skoug**'s ceiling is a catcher who can mash, but after contact issues and defensive questions plagued his senior season at TCU, that ceiling would dwarf Willis Tower. **Charlie Tilson** is a classic fringe, defense-and-speed fourth outfielder, with the fun added wrinkle that his lower body keeps breaking all the time and we have no idea what will happen if he ever gets healthy.

Pitchers

PITCHER	TEAM	LVL	AGE	W	L	SV	G	GS	IP	H	HR	BB/9	K/9	K	GB%	BABIP	WHIP	ERA	DRA	WARP	MPH	CMD	PWR	STM
Spencer Adams	BIR	AA	21	7	15	0	26	26	152^2	171	19	2.4	6.7	113	49%	.314	1.38	4.42	3.77	2.6				
Zack Burdi	CHR	AAA	22	0	4	7	29	0	33^1	30	2	4.6	13.8	51	51%	.359	1.41	4.05	1.68	1.3				
Ian Clarkin	TAM	A+	22	4	5	0	15	14	75^2	71	4	3.0	6.9	58	56%	.303	1.27	2.62	3.56	1.5				
	WNS	A+	22	0	0	0	3	3	11	7	1	6.5	4.1	5	47%	.194	1.36	2.45	5.61	0.0				
Bernardo Flores	KAN	A	21	8	4	0	14	14	78	73	5	1.5	8.1	70	50%	.308	1.10	3.00	3.27	1.8				
	WNS	A+	21	2	3	0	9	9	40^1	43	5	4.2	7.4	33	41%	.309	1.54	4.24	5.70	-0.2				
Brad Goldberg	CHA	MLB	27	0	0	0	11	0	12	14	2	10.5	2.2	3	49%	.293	2.33	8.25	8.49	-0.4	98.1	27	70	45
	CHR	AAA	27	3	2	5	30	0	40^1	40	2	4.9	10.5	47	42%	.352	1.54	3.35	4.77	0.2				
Jordan Guerrero	BIR	AA	23	7	12	0	25	25	146^1	150	8	2.6	8.4	136	47%	.333	1.32	4.18	2.64	4.4				
A.J. Puckett	WIL	A+	22	9	7	0	20	20	108^1	107	7	3.8	8.1	98	51%	.313	1.41	3.90	4.93	0.4				
	WNS	A+	22	1	0	0	5	5	27^1	35	2	1.6	6.9	21	48%	.379	1.46	4.28	5.34	0.0				
Jordan Stephens	BIR	AA	24	3	7	0	16	16	91^2	84	4	3.4	8.1	83	43%	.309	1.30	3.14	4.30	1.0				
Thyago Vieira	ARK	AA	23	2	3	2	29	0	36^1	30	1	3.7	8.7	35	49%	.293	1.24	3.72	4.61	0.1				
	SEA	MLB	23	0	0	0	1	0	1	0	0	0.0	9.0	1	50%	.000	0.00	0.00	2.55	0.0	100.7			43
	TAC	AAA	23	0	1	2	12	0	17^2	18	1	3.6	5.6	11	53%	.298	1.42	4.58	6.56	-0.2				

Spencer Adams still has youth, athleticism, build and control on his side, but some day he's going to have to miss some more bats or he'll lose the benefit of the doubt. For a rehabbing relief prospect, **Zack Burdi** is about as safe as they come. He throws triple-digit heat and should profile as a late-inning reliever in 2019, unless his Tommy John surgery recovery goes poorly. **Ian Clarkin** has had a few arm injuries between now and when he excited a whole lot of Yankees fans. He's working on a cutter, but he has yet to clear 100 innings in a professional season. **Bernardo Flores** could be a diamond in the rough, as a lefty with a plus fastball and interesting changeup, but there's a long road between him and the majors. According to wrestling lore, WCW and WWE champion Bill Goldberg began his career with a record of 173-0. The unrelated **Brad Goldberg**'s career hasn't started quite as well, so the White Sox are probably asking "Who's Next?" **Jordan Guerrero**, a big lefty whose best secondary pitch is a changeup, may wind up being a nifty find as a fifth starter. **A.J. Puckett** is a big, physical right-hander, but lacks a wipeout breaking pitch, which can serve to Kirby your enthusiasm. **Jordan Stephens** was a clever buy-low pick in the 2015 fifth round as he came off Tommy John surgery. He profiles as a potential back-end starter or middle reliever. With the combination of near-triple-digit heat and a solid slider, **Thyago Vieira** has the potential to be a bullpen weapon if he can harness his command, which is something that can be said about dozens of other minor-league relievers.

CINCINNATI REDS

Essay by Mo Bjonski

Player comments by Matt Collins and BP staff

In a sport steeped in its history and tradition, few teams claim a closer link to the fabric of the game than the Cincinnati Reds. Baseball's first team, the Reds began playing professionally in the early days of the Grant administration. They are charter members of the National League, the franchise of Bench and Morgan and Larkin and Votto, home of the Big Red Machine, and host of the two and a half hour Opening Day parade that unofficially rings in the new season.

FC Cincinnati plays in the second division of America's fledgling soccer pyramid. The club is two years old and its best players make a few grand per month; none of them will get into any Hall of Fame without a ticket. For now, they play in Nippert Stadium, a charming but century-old college football stadium tucked into the University of Cincinnati campus.

On Wednesday, August 23, 2017, the Reds hosted the defending World Series champion Chicago Cubs. In front of 15,355 spectators, many of whom donned Cubbie blue, the visitors raced out to an early 9-0 lead and never looked back. Seven days earlier, FC Cincinnati met the New York Red Bulls in a US Open Cup match at Nippert. The game had only been scheduled a month earlier: It wasn't even listed on the little pocket schedules fans can grab in gas stations around town, yet more than 33,000 supporters showed up anyway. FC Cincinnati lost a 3-2 heartbreaker, but the rabid fans saw their scrappy upstarts nearly beat one of American soccer's premier franchises.

The games described above are part of a larger attendance pattern. Despite their stadium situation, FC Cincinnati topped 30,000 fans on multiple occasions and averaged only 981 fewer fans per game than the Reds. There are mitigating circumstances, of course: Soccer tickets are cheap and the sport's relatively sparse schedule turns each match into an event. But contrast a day at Great American Ball Park—sleepy affairs where the attendance figures sure aren't *under*reported—with the exuberant and youthful energy pulsating through Nippert Stadium and the comparison doesn't look good for the ol' ballclub.

What the hell is going on here?

For fans alarmed that the national pastime is on the cusp of taking a backseat to, in Jack Kemp's infamous words, that "European socialist sport," a deep breath is in order. Even with a rainy few years at the box office, the Reds are a healthy organization. They're charging hundreds, not dozens, of dollars for premium seats; even in a rebuilding year, the club ran an Opening Day payroll north of $90 million. The Reds are second on talk radio in the city, behind the Bengals but comfortably ahead of FC Cincinnati, college sports and everything else. A survey of local fans and media personalities suggests that Votto is the most popular athlete in town.

Change, however, does not strike dramatically overnight. It creeps from the margins, and it's not crazy to think that soccer has

REDS PROSPECTUS

2017 W-L: 68-94, 5TH IN NL CENTRAL

Pythag	.431	25th
RS/G	4.65	14th
RA/G	5.36	29th
TAv	.269	10th
TAv-P	.285	29th
FIP	5.09	29th
DER	.704	13th

B-Age	27.2	*6th*
P-Age	27.7	*8th*
Salary	$95.4M	*25th*
M$/MW	$4.1M	*13th*
DL Days	1253	*23rd*
$ on DL	18%	*20th*

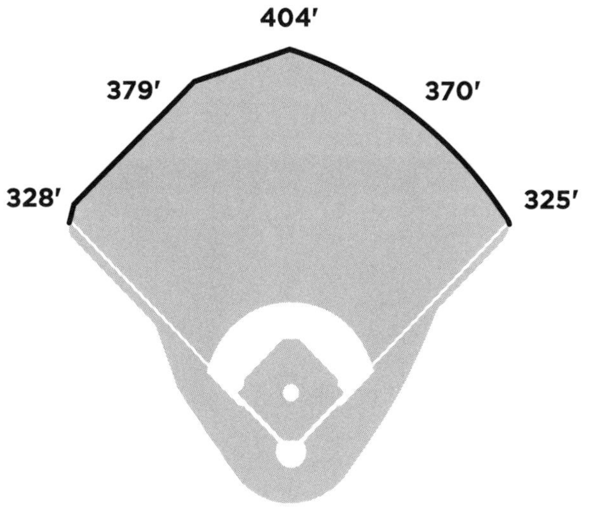

Outfield wall profile: **8′** to **12′**

Three-Year Park Factors

Runs	Runs/RH	Runs/LH	HR/RH	HR/LH
102	100	104	104	109

Top Hitter WARP	8.0 Joey Votto
Top Pitcher WARP	2.2 Luis Castillo
Top Prospect	Nick Senzel

2017 Hit List Ranking

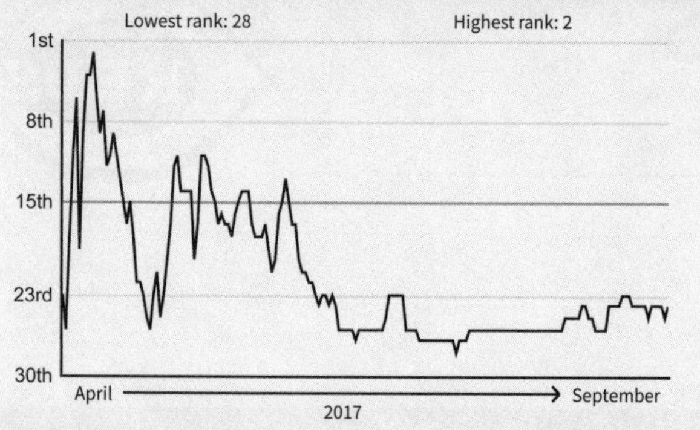

Committed Payroll (in millions)

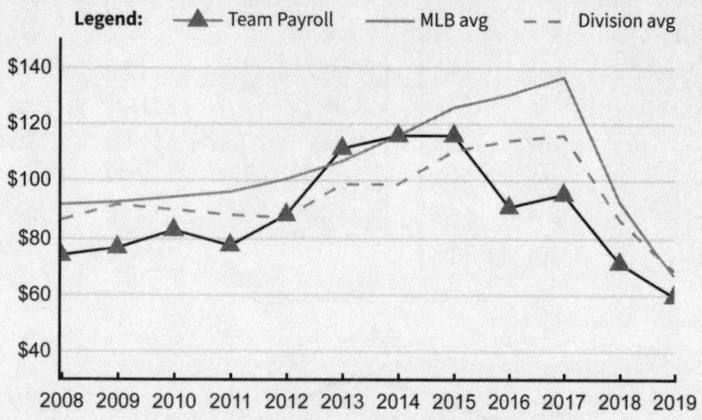

Farm System Ranking

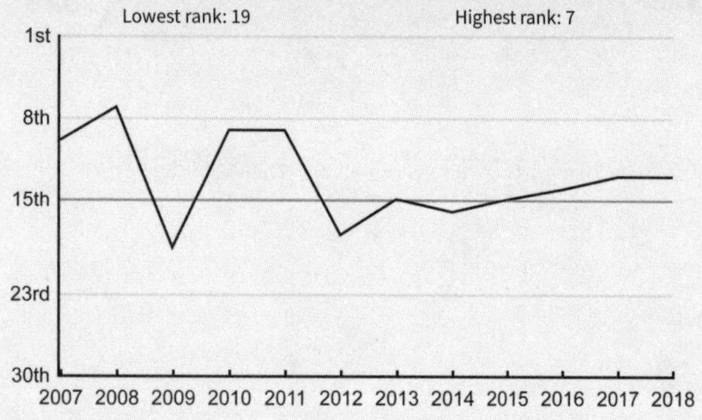

Personnel

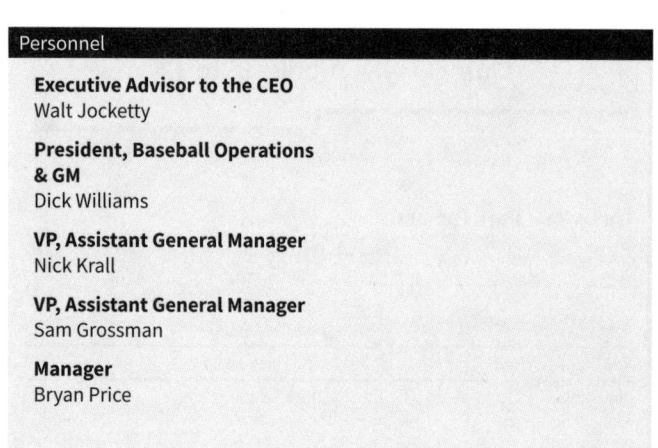

Executive Advisor to the CEO
Walt Jocketty

President, Baseball Operations & GM
Dick Williams

VP, Assistant General Manager
Nick Krall

VP, Assistant General Manager
Sam Grossman

Manager
Bryan Price

already siphoned away a few of MLB's fans and dollars. That this is happening in Cincinnati is a bit surprising, given that FC Cincinnati is just a couple of years old and isn't even part of Major League Soccer. But MLS clubs in Seattle and Atlanta outdrew the Mariners and Braves last year, and while it's a bit of an apples-to-chocolate comparison, Orlando's fledgling soccer franchise has captured eyeballs and fan enthusiasm in ways that Derek Jeter can only dream about.

Baseball and soccer season overlap significantly in the United States, and soccer is particularly appealing to the younger generation of fans that baseball so obviously covets. Baseball is the more popular game, but these sports will jockey for some of the same fan attention in the coming years, and *fútbol* has a knack for gaining traction in cities with middling baseball clubs. Soon enough, baseball probably won't be able to credibly claim it monopolizes July on the sports calendar.

At the local level, the best way to stop writers from speculating about whether the shiny new soccer team is sapping enthusiasm from the hometown nine is for the baseball team to win some baseball games. The Reds, needless to say, haven't done much of that lately. Since their defeat in the wild card round of the 2013 playoffs, the Reds have posted four consecutive losing seasons and have lost at least 94 games in each of the past three years.

There have been a few bright spots during the rebuild. The maturation process for Eugenio Suarez was long, but he finally broke out in 2017. It's fair to point out that most of his offensive production came in his hitter-friendly home stadium, but those dingers count too, and he bopped 21 of them there. More encouragingly, his walk rate surged and he played better defensively. It's too early to say whether Jesse Winker will be able to replicate the power he flashed in a 47-game audition last season, but even if he never slugs .530 again, he has the bat-to-ball and on-base skills to stay in the Reds' outfield for a long time. Votto is still Votto.

While Cincinnati's pitchers have taken a battering in recent seasons, a few of the franchise's young arms emerged as viable long-term starters last year. After another rough start to the season, Robert Stephenson strung a few quality outings together down the stretch, posting a 3.30 ERA with encouraging peripherals over his final 12 games. Sal Romano emerged from relative obscurity and pitched well enough to earn a job in the 2018 rotation. Best of all, Luis Castillo quietly established himself as one of the most exciting young pitchers in baseball. Sporting a triple-digit fastball and a devastating sinking changeup, he struck out 98 hitters in 89 innings. He also showed some aptitude for keeping opposing batters in the yard, a welcome development for a pitching staff that finished dead last in the National League in home runs allowed for the second year in a row.

Cincinnati's developmental machine has proven it can produce big leaguers. The more relevant challenge, however, will be producing *enough* of them to compete in the NL Central, and it's an arduous mission. Despite a few positive development stories, a more careful look at the roster and the broader context in which the Reds find themselves suggests that their rebuild will likely spiral into a rainy decade.

This is partly beyond Cincinnati's control. No one can blame management for geography; it's just bad luck that the Reds are forced to compete against the exceedingly competent Cardinals, the suddenly contending Brewers and a fully awakened giant in Chicago. Chicago and St. Louis ran payrolls exceeding $170 million and $150 million, respectively, and they'll have bigger financial muscles to flex than Cincinnati can ever hope to sustain. The three aforementioned clubs are also deep in good young players and are poised to have a vise grip on the division for years to come.

To bust out of the basement, the Reds will need to develop big-league contributors more efficiently. Castillo, Stephenson, Suarez and Winker are a good start, but they represent a fraction of the star power Cincinnati will need to compete in the division. Worse, a number of the unproven arms that the Reds needed to take a step forward last season flopped or were saddled with injuries. Brandon Finnegan walked 13 hitters in 13 innings and then missed most of the season with shoulder problems. Cody Reed lost his velocity and stopped throwing strikes. Amir Garrett's three-month experiment with avoiding the corners of the plate led to as many walks and dingers as you would expect. It's not necessarily *fair* that the Reds need to hit on more of their top prospects than the average club, but it's their only plausible route to contention. There's quite a bit riding on those three to return to their minor-league form, and for the jewels remaining in the system (Nick Senzel, Tyler Mahle, Taylor Trammell, etc.) to produce.

Some of those farmhands will see the field for Cincinnati in 2018, but even in a best-case scenario, it's hard to imagine this roster coalescing into a playoff team. Baseball has a way of making its analysts look like dummies, and an 88-win season from the Reds this year wouldn't be much more surprising than what Minnesota or Milwaukee pulled off a year ago. But the smart money is on another losing season, and if consensus wisdom prevails, success for Cincinnati in 2018 should be measured in something other than wins and losses. Given that premise, two questions linger over the 2018 team: Will any of the players on the roster still be in town for the next good Reds team? And will this team be fun to watch in the interim?

The answer to the former question, alas, is probably not. The top of the NL Central is so stacked that even with a relatively prosperous developmental cycle, it's easy to forecast a scenario where the Reds have to deal their current crop of young talent to augment the *next* wave. Undoubtedly, that would be tough to stomach for a fan base that hasn't won a playoff series since 1995. Expect plenty of images from Reds games to show up on the @EmptySeatsPics Twitter feed.

That doesn't mean the Reds will be boring. For those blessed with a high threshold for losing baseball, Cincinnati has plenty of fun players. Diehards already know that every trip Votto makes to the plate is a spectacle. His mastery of the strike zone and control of each at-bat is unparalleled in the modern game, and even casual fans can appreciate a .320 hitter who hits homers and brings his lunchpail to work 162 times per year. Billy Hamilton, too, is worth the price of admission. For a team trying to win, his lack of power and .300 OBP is an obstacle; for fans hoping to enjoy a day at the park, a .300 OBP and a bunch of singles means that, in any given game, they have a pretty good shot at seeing baseball's fastest man work his magic on the basepaths. Anyone who likes watching youngsters find their footing will have plenty of players to root for, as Senzel will likely join Stephenson and Castillo for the latter part of the season. Plus, spectators will see plenty of dingers—the Reds bashed 117 at home last year, second most among National League teams—and it's hard to imagine the bullpen pitching any *worse* this year than in the last two seasons.

In the absence of realistic playoff ambitions, the challenge for Reds fans is to find enjoyment in the fun players they have and the brand of baseball their park affords. It's a reality that should resonate with, of all people, soccer fans. Soccer is a game built on aesthetics, where graceful and spellbinding play is as appreciated as the three points that accompany a victory; just ask Tony Pulis, an otherwise successful manager in the English Premier League who was nonetheless sacked by Stoke City in part for playing an ugly, brutish style of football.

In a sense, the Reds and FC Cincinnati have swapped part of the identities typically associated with teams in their respective sports. For all of the energy at Nippert Stadium, the squad on the field plays the kind of workmanlike game typically found in a lower-level league. Meanwhile, the Reds have plenty of eye-popping talent but, by major-league standards, few eyes at the ballpark to watch them. Ultimately, Cincinnati sports fans will have ample opportunity to see big-league stars and a big-league environment this summer—they just won't get them at the same time.

Not that there's anything wrong with that. Cincy's enduring connection to the earliest days of baseball is undoubtedly something to celebrate, and the city's startlingly warm embrace of soccer is pretty neat, too. Perhaps the fortunes of the Reds and FC Cincinnati will dovetail well together. There's no reason Cincinnati can't take pride in both of its clubs.

—Mo Bjonski is an author of Baseball Prospectus.

Hitters

Aristides Aquino RF Born: 04/22/94 Age: 24 Bats: R Throws: R Height: 6'4" Weight: 220 Origin: International Free Agent, 2011

YEAR	TEAM	LVL	AGE	PA	R	2B	3B	HR	RBI	BB	K	SB	CS	AVG/OBP/SLG	TAv	VORP	BABIP	BRR	FRAA	WARP
2015	BIL	RK	21	54	7	1	3	2	13	2	9	0	1	.308/.333/.558	.284	2.0	.341	-0.4	RF(11): 0.6	0.2
2015	DYT	A	21	249	25	9	3	5	27	11	53	6	1	.234/.281/.364	.236	0.1	.280	2.0	RF(60): 1.5	0.2
2016	DAY	A+	22	526	69	26	12	23	79	34	104	11	7	.273/.327/.519	.282	22.8	.304	1.3	RF(123): 29.7	5.4
2017	PEN	AA	23	504	54	20	6	17	56	39	145	9	3	.216/.282/.397	.240	-2.6	.274	-0.9	RF(128): 9.1	0.7
2018	*CIN*	*MLB*	*24*	*250*	*28*	*10*	*2*	*11*	*34*	*14*	*75*	*3*	*1*	*.219/.271/.423*	*.227*	*-1.4*	*.270*	*0.2*	*RF 2*	*0.1*
2019	*CIN*	*MLB*	*25*	*294*	*37*	*11*	*3*	*14*	*41*	*18*	*88*	*3*	*1*	*.222/.276/.436*	*.249*	*2.9*	*.271*	*0.2*	*RF 3, LF 0*	*0.6*

Breakout: 9% Improve: 15% Collapse: 0% Attrition: 15% MLB: 20% *Comparables: Hunter Renfroe, Roger Kieschnick, Zoilo Almonte*

Aquino had everything you look for in a prospect heading into the 2017 season: a name that just won't quit and loud tools that anyone could dream on, provided everything came together. He finally had his breakout season in 2016 at High-A when he harnessed his swing enough to put up strong numbers in Daytona. This was the year for him to take his real leap forward and become a legitimate prospect. Unfortunately, baseball is really hard and it's not always so easy to keep your gains. Aquino struggled to make contact against more advanced Double-A pitchers and his strikeout rate soared, putting his future at risk. He's still young enough to dream on, but he'll need to put his nightmare season behind him if he wants to become the greatest Aristides in baseball history.

Tucker Barnhart C Born: 01/07/91 Age: 27 Bats: B Throws: R Height: 5'11" Weight: 192 Origin: Round 10, 2009 Draft (#299 overall)

YEAR	TEAM	LVL	AGE	PA	R	2B	3B	HR	RBI	BB	K	SB	CS	AVG/OBP/SLG	TAv	VORP	BABIP	BRR	FRAA	WARP
2015	CIN	MLB	24	274	23	9	0	3	13	25	45	0	1	.252/.324/.326	.245	10.1	.294	2.4	C(73): 3.2, RF(1): 0.2	1.4
2016	CIN	MLB	25	420	34	23	1	7	51	36	72	1	0	.257/.323/.379	.254	14.6	.299	-1.7	C(108): 1.4	1.7
2017	CIN	MLB	26	423	26	24	2	7	44	42	68	4	0	.270/.347/.403	.266	20.9	.312	-1.6	C(110): -1.2	2.0
2018	*CIN*	*MLB*	*27*	*376*	*40*	*17*	*1*	*7*	*37*	*34*	*63*	*2*	*0*	*.248/.318/.366*	*.239*	*10.6*	*.283*	*-0.4*	*C -1*	*0.5*
2019	*CIN*	*MLB*	*28*	*396*	*47*	*19*	*1*	*9*	*43*	*39*	*70*	*1*	*0*	*.253/.330/.392*	*.257*	*13.8*	*.287*	*-0.5*	*C 0*	*1.5*

Breakout: 7% Improve: 44% Collapse: 7% Attrition: 18% MLB: 98% *Comparables: Dioner Navarro, Kevin Higgins, Steve Nicosia*

YEAR	TEAM	P. COUNT	FRM RUNS	BLK RUNS	THRW RUNS	TOT RUNS
2015	CIN	10131	1.9	0.4	0.2	2.5
2015	LOU	676	0.0	0.0	0.1	0.0
2016	CIN	16074	-4.2	2.3	1.7	-0.3
2017	CIN	15640	-9.4	2.3	4.6	-2.5
2018	*CIN*	*14362*	*-6.1*	*1.7*	*1.9*	*-2.4*
2019	*CIN*	*15115*	*-6.3*	*1.8*	*2.0*	*-2.5*

All Barnhart has done over his career is outperform expectations. He was a tenth-round pick out of high school who slowly made his way through the minors without much fanfare. He finally broke into the majors but was seen as nothing more than a glove-first backup. Injuries to Devin Mesoraco kept giving Barnhart chances, and he just kept getting a little better, culminating in a 2017 campaign that combined his strong-enough defensive profile with the best offensive performance of his career. Though he's still not hitting for power, his newfound patience and improved bat-to-ball skills make him a viable primary catcher. The Reds saw enough in September to lock him up through 2022. If Barnhart keeps improving as he has through his entire career he'll be one of the biggest steals in baseball, a fine piece of irony given that he's the hardest catcher in baseball against whom to steal.

Alex Blandino INF Born: 11/06/92 Age: 25 Bats: R Throws: R Height: 6'0" Weight: 190 Origin: Round 1, 2014 Draft (#29 overall)

YEAR	TEAM	LVL	AGE	PA	R	2B	3B	HR	RBI	BB	K	SB	CS	AVG/OBP/SLG	TAv	VORP	BABIP	BRR	FRAA	WARP
2015	DAY	A+	22	342	46	18	2	7	35	31	56	7	10	.294/.370/.438	.317	32.3	.338	0.5	SS(68): -0.6, 2B(6): 0.0	3.4
2015	PEN	AA	22	138	15	7	0	3	18	18	21	2	2	.235/.350/.374	.283	8.5	.261	0.3	SS(24): 1.9, 2B(6): -0.4	1.1
2016	PEN	AA	23	465	52	18	0	8	37	55	114	14	5	.232/.333/.337	.262	12.2	.302	-2.0	2B(74): -5.1, 3B(30): 1.2	0.9
2017	PEN	AA	24	236	31	22	0	6	31	32	49	3	4	.259/.374/.462	.292	12.8	.315	-1.6	2B(39): 1.8, 3B(18): 2.1	1.8
2017	LOU	AAA	24	237	29	14	1	6	20	32	37	1	3	.270/.390/.444	.285	11.7	.305	-2.8	2B(29): -1.8, 3B(26): 0.5	1.1
2018	*CIN*	*MLB*	*25*	*59*	*7*	*3*	*0*	*2*	*7*	*6*	*14*	*1*	*0*	*.234/.330/.402*	*.255*	*2.0*	*.284*	*-0.1*	*SS 0*	*0.2*
2019	*CIN*	*MLB*	*26*	*295*	*39*	*15*	*0*	*10*	*37*	*35*	*73*	*3*	*2*	*.240/.342/.423*	*.273*	*12.4*	*.293*	*-0.7*	*SS 1*	*1.4*

Breakout: 1% Improve: 11% Collapse: 10% Attrition: 22% MLB: 43% *Comparables: Scott Sizemore, Colin Walsh, Cord Phelps*

Blandino's heavy regression in 2016 made all of our worst nightmares come true in terms of using his name as a pun. I mean, the man has "bland" right in his name, he needs to make sure he does *something* well enough to avoid the cruel jokes that he's likely heard since kindergarten. Fortunately, the former first-round pick rediscovered his power stroke in 2017 and is on the cusp of the majors. He's still going to hear those jokes for the rest of his life, but he's doing everything in his power to make sure they don't define his career.

Adam Duvall LF Born: 09/04/88 Age: 29 Bats: R Throws: R Height: 6'1" Weight: 215 Origin: Round 11, 2010 Draft (#348 overall)

YEAR	TEAM	LVL	AGE	PA	R	2B	3B	HR	RBI	BB	K	SB	CS	AVG/OBP/SLG	TAv	VORP	BABIP	BRR	FRAA	WARP
2015	SAC	AAA	26	437	60	25	2	26	80	25	91	4	1	.281/.325/.547	.304	30.4	.299	1.1	3B(46): -5.1, 1B(45): 2.0	2.7
2015	LOU	AAA	26	104	11	4	0	4	7	6	23	1	0	.189/.260/.358	.212	-4.6	.206	-1.1	LF(16): 0.8, 1B(8): 2.1	-0.2
2015	CIN	MLB	26	72	6	2	0	5	9	6	26	0	0	.219/.306/.484	.286	3.7	.273	0.4	LF(15): -0.7, 1B(4): 0.0	0.3
2016	CIN	MLB	27	608	85	31	6	33	103	41	164	6	5	.241/.297/.498	.285	24.5	.275	-3.8	LF(137): 11.9, RF(6): -1.1	3.7
2017	CIN	MLB	28	647	78	37	3	31	99	39	170	5	3	.249/.301/.480	.279	25.0	.290	-2.2	LF(151): 6.9, 1B(3): 0.0	3.2
2018	*CIN*	*MLB*	*29*	*594*	*79*	*27*	*3*	*32*	*93*	*38*	*158*	*5*	*3*	*.237/.295/.473*	*.260*	*16.3*	*.271*	*-0.6*	*LF 4, 1B 1*	*1.8*
2019	*CIN*	*MLB*	*30*	*569*	*77*	*27*	*2*	*31*	*88*	*39*	*156*	*4*	*2*	*.234/.294/.472*	*.267*	*15.8*	*.269*	*-1.7*	*LF 5, 1B 1*	*2.3*

Breakout: 7% Improve: 36% Collapse: 3% Attrition: 10% MLB: 83% *Comparables: Ryan Raburn, Casper Wells, Rick Ankiel*

Duvall is a nondescript hitter. His overall offensive production is about average. He hits for a fair amount of power, but so does pretty much everyone in today's game. He strikes out a bunch, but not enough for it to garner attention like Chris Davis or Aaron Judge. He has a plus glove but plays left field, a position near the bottom rung of the defensive spectrum. In baseball, however, nondescript isn't necessarily a bad thing. Despite not standing out in any one area, Duvall served as a major-league cleanup hitter all year long and figures to have a major-league job for the foreseeable future. He's doing a hell of a lot better than most of us.

Phil Ervin OF Born: 07/15/92 Age: 25 Bats: R Throws: R Height: 5'10" Weight: 207 Origin: Round 1, 2013 Draft (#27 overall)

YEAR	TEAM	LVL	AGE	PA	R	2B	3B	HR	RBI	BB	K	SB	CS	AVG/OBP/SLG	TAv	VORP	BABIP	BRR	FRAA	WARP
2015	DAY	A+	22	475	68	18	0	12	63	53	83	30	7	.242/.338/.375	.277	23.1	.271	4.2	LF(83): 10.3, CF(26): 1.1	3.7
2015	PEN	AA	22	66	7	3	0	2	8	13	15	4	3	.235/.409/.412	.296	2.5	.294	-1.5	LF(12): -0.3, CF(5): 1.2	0.4
2016	PEN	AA	23	505	71	22	3	13	45	65	88	36	10	.239/.362/.399	.312	38.8	.271	1.2	LF(76): 2.3, CF(31): -1.2	4.3
2017	LOU	AAA	24	408	46	20	2	7	40	37	83	23	6	.256/.328/.380	.251	7.2	.315	0.6	LF(56): 8.8, CF(40): -3.1	1.2
2017	CIN	MLB	24	64	8	2	0	3	10	4	15	4	1	.259/.317/.448	.287	4.6	.300	1.1	CF(9): -0.6, RF(5): -0.4	0.4
2018	*CIN*	*MLB*	*25*	*189*	*27*	*8*	*1*	*6*	*22*	*20*	*43*	*9*	*3*	*.233/.325/.404*	*.256*	*7.2*	*.273*	*0.9*	*CF 0*	*0.6*
2019	*CIN*	*MLB*	*26*	*396*	*52*	*17*	*1*	*15*	*50*	*42*	*93*	*18*	*6*	*.235/.328/.420*	*.269*	*17.1*	*.275*	*2.1*	*CF 0*	*1.9*

Breakout: 8% Improve: 25% Collapse: 16% Attrition: 31% MLB: 52% *Comparables: Jaff Decker, Shane Peterson, Garin Cecchini*

Ervin has been a professional since 2013 and is coming out of his age-24 season, but it's still not at all clear what kind of player he's going to be. Staring into his 2017 won't make you more likely to see the sailboat, either. Most of the season was spent putting together his worst minor-league campaign since 2014, but he still got the call to the majors at the end of the year. There, he regained all the power he didn't show off in the minors and gave some reason to believe he can be a major-league regular. The reality, though, is that there's a reason they don't have Magic Eye pictures at the mall anymore.

Stuart Fairchild CF Born: 03/17/96 Age: 22 Bats: R Throws: R Height: 6'0" Weight: 190 Origin: Round 2, 2017 Draft (#38 overall)

YEAR	TEAM	LVL	AGE	PA	R	2B	3B	HR	RBI	BB	K	SB	CS	AVG/OBP/SLG	TAv	VORP	BABIP	BRR	FRAA	WARP
2017	BIL	RK	21	234	36	5	4	3	23	19	35	12	4	.304/.393/.412	.272	13.0	.355	1.8	CF(43): -9.4, RF(5): -0.6	0.4
2018	*CIN*	*MLB*	*22*	*250*	*22*	*8*	*1*	*6*	*24*	*14*	*78*	*3*	*1*	*.194/.252/.313*	*.188*	*-9.3*	*.263*	*-0.1*	*CF -3, RF 0*	*-1.3*
2019	*CIN*	*MLB*	*23*	*232*	*24*	*8*	*1*	*6*	*23*	*13*	*72*	*2*	*1*	*.201/.257/.329*	*.209*	*-5.9*	*.270*	*0.0*	*CF -3, RF 0*	*-0.9*

Breakout: 0% Improve: 1% Collapse: 1% Attrition: 2% MLB: 2% *Comparables: Aaron Altherr, Alfredo Marte, Michael Taylor*

You don't know about me, but I bet you want to. The Reds' second-round pick in the 2017 draft, Fairchild put together a strong showing in his professional debut, impressing scouts with his ability to drive the ball in advanced rookie ball. At 22, it may not be fair to call him a child, but he's one of a growing group of young kids in the Reds organization—and you can generally find them eating at one of the two

Denny's in Billings, where it's always a perfect night for breakfast at midnight.

Jose Israel Garcia SS Born: 04/05/98 Age: 20 Bats: R Throws: R Height: 6'2" Weight: 175 Origin: International Free Agent, 2017

The Reds continued their aggressive rebuild over the summer in the international market, and Garcia could end up being one of their best prospects acquired in recent years. The Cuban signee was welcomed to the US with a $5 million bonus, and he provides a relatively high floor with athleticism and plus speed to go with the tools to turn into a strong defensive shortstop. There is some work to do both in the field and at the plate, but that's to be expected from an 18-year-old. If Garcia can reach his full potential, we're talking about a strong defender at a premium position who can make an impact on the bases and provide gap-to-gap power.

Scooter Gennett 2B Born: 05/01/90 Age: 28 Bats: L Throws: R Height: 5'10" Weight: 185 Origin: Round 16, 2009 Draft (#496 overall)

YEAR	TEAM	LVL	AGE	PA	R	2B	3B	HR	RBI	BB	K	SB	CS	AVG/OBP/SLG	TAv	VORP	BABIP	BRR	FRAA	WARP
2015	CSP	AAA	25	79	12	7	1	2	11	4	10	0	1	.307/.342/.507	.276	2.7	.333	-0.7	2B(17): -0.2	0.3
2015	MIL	MLB	25	391	42	18	4	6	29	12	68	1	3	.264/.294/.381	.233	0.8	.309	1.1	2B(108): -2.7	-0.2
2016	MIL	MLB	26	542	58	30	1	14	56	38	114	8	1	.263/.317/.412	.262	14.6	.315	-0.8	2B(127): 4.8	2.0
2017	CIN	MLB	27	497	80	22	3	27	97	30	114	3	2	.295/.342/.531	.299	32.7	.339	-1.4	2B(99): -8.9, 3B(10): -0.2	2.1
2018	*CIN*	*MLB*	*28*	*524*	*59*	*25*	*3*	*15*	*65*	*29*	*100*	*5*	*2*	*.269/.313/.428*	*.254*	*17.9*	*.308*	*-0.5*	*2B -4*	*0.9*
2019	*CIN*	*MLB*	*29*	*518*	*65*	*25*	*3*	*18*	*67*	*34*	*101*	*4*	*2*	*.272/.323/.451*	*.272*	*23.0*	*.308*	*-0.4*	*2B -4*	*2.1*

Breakout: 2% Improve: 46% Collapse: 5% Attrition: 5% MLB: 97% *Comparables: Orlando Hudson, Omar Infante, Ryan Flaherty*

Perhaps nothing better represents the home-run revolution of 2017 than Gennett's performance on June 6: The second baseman, a late addition to the lineup in left field that day, became the 17th player in major-league history to hit four home runs in a game. Given that he had 35 career homers coming into the year and was claimed off waivers a week before the season started, it was startling at the time. It still is, based on the rarity of the event, but it's also indicative of the strides he has made at the plate. Thanks to a more patient approach, more loft in his swing and more emphasis to use his pull side, Gennett was one of the most improved players in the league in 2017. His defense took a major step back, but if his gains with the wood can hold moving forward, he finally has a bat that can play somewhere besides the middle infield.

Billy Hamilton CF Born: 09/09/90 Age: 27 Bats: B Throws: R Height: 6'0" Weight: 160 Origin: Round 2, 2009 Draft (#57 overall)

YEAR	TEAM	LVL	AGE	PA	R	2B	3B	HR	RBI	BB	K	SB	CS	AVG/OBP/SLG	TAv	VORP	BABIP	BRR	FRAA	WARP
2015	CIN	MLB	24	454	56	8	3	4	28	28	75	57	8	.226/.274/.289	.215	4.2	.264	10.9	CF(110): 1.7	0.6
2016	CIN	MLB	25	460	69	19	3	3	17	36	93	58	8	.260/.321/.343	.236	13.4	.329	10.5	CF(115): 9.5	2.4
2017	CIN	MLB	26	633	85	17	11	4	38	44	133	59	13	.247/.299/.335	.227	4.7	.313	6.6	CF(137): 5.2	1.0
2018	*CIN*	*MLB*	*27*	*638*	*94*	*21*	*6*	*7*	*42*	*43*	*124*	*65*	*13*	*.243/.292/.340*	*.220*	*5.6*	*.289*	*10.5*	*CF 1*	*0.4*
2019	*CIN*	*MLB*	*28*	*540*	*55*	*18*	*5*	*8*	*50*	*38*	*109*	*52*	*11*	*.237/.292/.346*	*.226*	*5.1*	*.281*	*8.3*	*CF 2*	*0.7*

Breakout: 0% Improve: 42% Collapse: 9% Attrition: 21% MLB: 88% *Comparables: Willy Taveras, Michael Bourn, Billy Burns*

People have a tendency to look too hard for all-time greatness, and the pursuit can cause them to miss the simple pleasures in life. This happens with movies, television, music and just about everything that can be judged, including baseball players. Hamilton could use some serious improvement at the plate, and if he got on base a little more often he could use his best qualities to an even greater degree than he does. There's a good chance that won't happen, but Hamilton still provides unmatched electricity on the bases and is one of the best and most exciting glove men at one of the most important positions on the diamond. At a certain point, it's best to stop worrying about his flaws and just appreciate the excitement he provides.

Dilson Herrera 2B Born: 03/03/94 Age: 24 Bats: R Throws: R Height: 5'10" Weight: 210 Origin: International Free Agent, 2010

YEAR	TEAM	LVL	AGE	PA	R	2B	3B	HR	RBI	BB	K	SB	CS	AVG/OBP/SLG	TAv	VORP	BABIP	BRR	FRAA	WARP
2015	LVG	AAA	21	364	68	23	2	11	50	28	59	13	9	.327/.382/.511	.294	25.1	.369	2.7	2B(78): 2.0	2.8
2015	NYN	MLB	21	103	7	3	1	3	6	11	23	2	0	.211/.311/.367	.259	2.7	.250	0.2	2B(29): 2.1	0.5
2016	LVG	AAA	22	389	61	24	2	13	55	27	72	6	7	.276/.327/.462	.261	11.0	.313	0.5	2B(75): -4.7	0.6
2016	LOU	AAA	22	80	10	0	2	2	9	11	15	1	2	.266/.372/.422	.312	6.4	.306	0.1	2B(16): -0.1	0.6
2017	LOU	AAA	23	265	31	9	1	7	42	15	61	2	4	.264/.312/.397	.255	3.9	.322	-1.7	2B(55): 0.8, 3B(3): 0.2	0.5
2018	*CIN*	*MLB*	*24*	*216*	*27*	*9*	*1*	*7*	*26*	*17*	*50*	*3*	*2*	*.250/.312/.419*	*.252*	*6.6*	*.296*	*-0.4*	*2B 0, SS 0*	*0.5*
2019	*CIN*	*MLB*	*25*	*349*	*45*	*15*	*2*	*13*	*46*	*29*	*82*	*5*	*4*	*.252/.321/.437*	*.267*	*13.1*	*.296*	*-0.5*	*2B 0, SS 0*	*1.4*

Breakout: 4% Improve: 28% Collapse: 10% Attrition: 30% MLB: 56% *Comparables: Jason Kipnis, Joey Wendle, Devon Travis*

It's incredible that Herrera is only entering his age-24 season when you consider the arc his career has already undergone. He's been a pro since 2010. He's been traded twice, both times in August for some valuable, late-season veteran help. He's been everything from a sleeper to a top prospect to a disappointment to a post-hype candidate. And yet, he's the same age as some of the top prospects in baseball. Herrera's skill set doesn't scream future star, since he's a second-base-only player who has seen his power drop and contact skills fade as the years have gone on. Still, he's young, and after everything he's been through so early in his career it seems time for him to settle in as a solid, unspectacular bench piece on a fringe contender.

Patrick Kivlehan 4C Born: 12/22/89 Age: 28 Bats: R Throws: R Height: 6'2" Weight: 223 Origin: Round 4, 2012 Draft (#131 overall)

YEAR	TEAM	LVL	AGE	PA	R	2B	3B	HR	RBI	BB	K	SB	CS	AVG/OBP/SLG	TAv	VORP	BABIP	BRR	FRAA	WARP
2015	TAC	AAA	25	518	58	25	1	22	73	36	113	14	3	.256/.313/.453	.272	11.7	.289	-5.4	LF(48): 1.9, 1B(30): -0.1	1.1
2016	ROU	AAA	26	155	17	8	0	1	16	11	36	2	2	.184/.252/.262	.195	-6.6	.238	0.9	3B(17): -1.8, 1B(16): -0.2	-0.9
2016	TAC	AAA	26	166	21	8	2	8	25	8	49	2	2	.293/.327/.522	.318	14.3	.380	0.2	3B(24): -0.6, LF(7): 0.1	1.4
2016	SDN	MLB	26	19	5	0	0	1	2	2	9	0	0	.250/.368/.438	.301	1.0	.500	-0.1	RF(4): -0.8, LF(1): -0.1	0.0
2016	ELP	AAA	26	78	8	2	1	3	8	5	23	1	0	.306/.351/.486	.287	4.6	.413	1.1	1B(11): -0.2, LF(7): -1.2	0.3
2016	CIN	MLB	26	5	0	0	0	0	0	0	2	0	0	.000/.000/.000	-.000	-1.2	.000	0.0	RF(2): 0.6	-0.1
2017	CIN	MLB	27	204	23	5	1	9	26	22	61	1	2	.208/.304/.399	.256	4.6	.257	0.6	RF(29): 1.2, 1B(12): -0.4	0.4
2018	*CIN*	*MLB*	*28*	*250*	*29*	*9*	*1*	*11*	*33*	*19*	*74*	*3*	*1*	*.224/.291/.413*	*.236*	*1.6*	*.281*	*0.3*	*RF -2, 3B 0*	*-0.1*
2019	*CIN*	*MLB*	*29*	*338*	*42*	*13*	*1*	*14*	*44*	*26*	*101*	*3*	*2*	*.222/.289/.412*	*.249*	*4.0*	*.278*	*0.5*	*RF -2, 3B 0*	*0.1*

Breakout: 2% Improve: 10% Collapse: 19% Attrition: 34% MLB: 47% *Comparables: Brett Carroll, Scott Cousins, Joe Borchard*

If you want to know how hard it is to succeed in the majors, look at Kivlehan's career. He spent most of his college life playing in the secondary for the Rutgers football team before taking up baseball in his senior year. Clearly, he was a natural talent as he took home Big East Player of the Year and was a fourth-round draft pick. Kivlehan then did nothing but hit in the minors but couldn't get a chance to play at the highest level on a consistent basis until 2017. And when he got to the majors, he did everything right from hitting for power to drawing walks. Despite all that, a severe lack of contact made Kivlehan a below-average player and will likely prevent him from being more than a bench bat.

Devin Mesoraco C Born: 06/19/88 Age: 30 Bats: R Throws: R Height: 6'1" Weight: 229 Origin: Round 1, 2007 Draft (#15 overall)

YEAR	TEAM	LVL	AGE	PA	R	2B	3B	HR	RBI	BB	K	SB	CS	AVG/OBP/SLG	TAv	VORP	BABIP	BRR	FRAA	WARP
2015	CIN	MLB	27	51	2	1	1	0	2	5	9	1	0	.178/.275/.244	.203	-1.0	.222	0.3	C(6): -1.0	-0.2
2016	CIN	MLB	28	55	2	1	0	0	1	5	10	0	1	.140/.218/.160	.146	-4.6	.175	-0.6	C(13): -2.4	-0.7
2017	PEN	AA	29	55	4	1	0	1	3	6	10	0	0	.170/.291/.255	.228	-0.3	.194	-0.6	C(11): -0.4	-0.1
2017	CIN	MLB	29	165	17	5	1	6	14	18	38	1	0	.213/.321/.390	.253	5.2	.245	-0.8	C(40): -2.3	0.3
2018	*CIN*	*MLB*	*30*	*208*	*27*	*8*	*1*	*8*	*27*	*19*	*44*	*1*	*1*	*.238/.320/.418*	*.256*	*9.0*	*.269*	*-0.4*	*C -7*	*0.0*
2019	*CIN*	*MLB*	*31*	*192*	*25*	*8*	*0*	*7*	*25*	*18*	*42*	*1*	*0*	*.236/.320/.417*	*.263*	*7.6*	*.269*	*-0.4*	*C -6*	*0.2*

Breakout: 1% Improve: 42% Collapse: 6% Attrition: 13% MLB: 94% *Comparables: Ryan Doumit, Welington Castillo, Matt Wieters*

YEAR	TEAM	P. COUNT	FRM RUNS	BLK RUNS	THRW RUNS	TOT RUNS
2015	CIN	777	-0.4	-0.2	0.0	-0.7
2016	CIN	2035	-1.9	-0.2	0.0	-2.2
2017	CIN	5242	-4.6	1.4	-0.4	-3.6
2018	*CIN*	*7149*	*-7.2*	*0.3*	*-0.3*	*-7.2*
2019	*CIN*	*6603*	*-6.1*	*0.3*	*-0.3*	*-6.1*

Baseball has the ability to completely devastate anyone at any time for no reason with little warning. It's the most wonderful game, and at the same time the biggest bummer. Consider Mesoraco, a former top prospect who finally broke out back in 2014 and looked poised to become one of the top offensive catchers in baseball for years to come. Injuries limited him to 39 games combined over the next two seasons, and a foot injury shelved him last August after he appeared in a whopping 56 contests. It's hard to tell whether his lackluster performance was due to eroding skill or rust; either way, his past looks brighter than his future. Sometimes, baseball sucks.

Jose Peraza MI Born: 04/30/94 Age: 24 Bats: R Throws: R Height: 6'0" Weight: 196 Origin: International Free Agent, 2010

YEAR	TEAM	LVL	AGE	PA	R	2B	3B	HR	RBI	BB	K	SB	CS	AVG/OBP/SLG	TAv	VORP	BABIP	BRR	FRAA	WARP
2015	GWN	AAA	21	427	52	10	7	3	37	15	35	26	7	.294/.318/.379	.253	9.6	.311	0.9	2B(81): -1.4, CF(13): -2.5	0.5
2015	OKL	AAA	21	94	11	3	1	1	5	2	10	7	0	.289/.304/.378	.263	4.7	.316	1.6	2B(14): 0.1, SS(4): -0.5	0.4
2015	LAN	MLB	21	25	3	1	1	0	1	2	2	3	0	.182/.250/.318	.224	0.4	.200	0.7	2B(6): 0.6, CF(1): 0.0	0.1
2016	LOU	AAA	22	322	40	15	3	2	21	21	43	10	7	.281/.333/.375	.263	14.8	.324	1.5	SS(58): -3.6, CF(6): -0.1	1.2
2016	CIN	MLB	22	256	25	8	2	3	25	7	33	21	10	.324/.352/.411	.271	10.9	.361	-0.8	SS(31): -1.0, CF(13): -1.3	0.8
2017	CIN	MLB	23	518	50	9	4	5	37	20	70	23	8	.259/.297/.324	.227	-0.1	.293	0.6	2B(77): 2.3, SS(55): 0.6	0.3
2018	*CIN*	*MLB*	*24*	*624*	*84*	*20*	*6*	*11*	*55*	*27*	*86*	*29*	*11*	*.271/.306/.386*	*.238*	*13.6*	*.296*	*2.8*	*SS -8*	*0.2*
2019	*CIN*	*MLB*	*25*	*560*	*65*	*18*	*6*	*13*	*62*	*28*	*79*	*27*	*11*	*.279/.323/.411*	*.257*	*18.6*	*.302*	*1.1*	*SS -7*	*1.3*

Breakout: 6% Improve: 37% Collapse: 10% Attrition: 17% MLB: 77% *Comparables: Alexi Casilla, Emmanuel Burriss, Yolmer Sanchez*

Peraza is simultaneously the type of player on whom you give up too soon and the type for whom you wait too long. On the one hand, the athletic infielder is coming off his age-23 season despite already having three stints in the majors. On the other, he doesn't draw walks, doesn't hit for power and isn't particularly great at shortstop—though that wasn't much of a concern while Zack Cozart was around. He certainly deserves more chances to prove his .361 BABIP in 2016 was closer to the real Peraza than last year's sub-.300 mark, but his athleticism and versatility will likely make him more of an intriguing bench piece rather than the strong regular the Dodgers and Reds thought they were getting when they acquired him.

Scott Schebler RF Born: 10/06/90 Age: 27 Bats: L Throws: R Height: 6'0" Weight: 228 Origin: Round 26, 2010 Draft (#802 overall)

YEAR	TEAM	LVL	AGE	PA	R	2B	3B	HR	RBI	BB	K	SB	CS	AVG/OBP/SLG	TAv	VORP	BABIP	BRR	FRAA	WARP
2015	OKL	AAA	24	485	57	16	9	13	50	40	93	15	2	.241/.322/.410	.275	21.0	.278	2.3	RF(48): -4.2, CF(38): 3.0	2.1
2015	LAN	MLB	24	40	6	0	0	3	4	3	13	2	1	.250/.325/.500	.325	3.8	.300	0.4	LF(7): -0.3, RF(6): -0.1	0.4
2016	LOU	AAA	25	319	40	18	8	13	43	19	59	2	0	.311/.370/.564	.329	29.9	.352	-1.7	CF(49): 3.1, LF(16): -1.1	3.2
2016	CIN	MLB	25	282	36	12	2	9	40	19	59	2	4	.265/.330/.432	.267	10.0	.312	1.7	RF(41): 4.2, CF(18): -2.5	1.1
2017	CIN	MLB	26	531	63	25	2	30	67	39	125	5	3	.233/.307/.484	.278	20.6	.248	-0.2	RF(120): -4.7, CF(15): 0.9	1.7
2018	*CIN*	*MLB*	*27*	*493*	*67*	*20*	*5*	*22*	*69*	*36*	*112*	*6*	*3*	*.245/.317/.460*	*.265*	*16.8*	*.279*	*0.0*	*RF -6, LF 0*	*0.7*
2019	*CIN*	*MLB*	*28*	*505*	*70*	*21*	*4*	*24*	*74*	*41*	*115*	*5*	*3*	*.249/.326/.476*	*.280*	*22.8*	*.281*	*1.4*	*RF -5, LF 0*	*2.0*

Breakout: 5% Improve: 44% Collapse: 8% Attrition: 17% MLB: 89% *Comparables: Shin-Soo Choo, Josh Reddick, Travis Buck*

In a season full of forgettable 30-homer seasons, Schebler's might have been the most forgettable. His extremely underwhelming RBI total was mostly the result of 76 percent of his dingers coming with the bases empty, and only twice all season did he move the Reds' win expectancy by more than 15 percent with one swing. That said, the power he put on full blast in 2017 was not a creation of Great American Ballpark either, as 17 of his 30 homers came on the road. Unfortunately, when he's not hitting home runs he's not doing much else. Even assuming his BABIP drop-off in 2017 was bad luck, he hasn't shown the patience to take the big step forward he needs to secure a role on the next good Reds team. There's nothing wrong with being a perfectly average major-league player, though—especially before hitting arbitration. But with Jesse Winker hot on his tail, Schebler might not have much longer to prove he's worth remembering.

Nick Senzel 3B Born: 06/29/95 Age: 23 Bats: R Throws: R Height: 6'1" Weight: 205 Origin: Round 1, 2016 Draft (#2 overall)

YEAR	TEAM	LVL	AGE	PA	R	2B	3B	HR	RBI	BB	K	SB	CS	AVG/OBP/SLG	TAv	VORP	BABIP	BRR	FRAA	WARP
2016	BIL	RK	21	41	3	1	0	0	4	6	5	3	0	.152/.293/.182	.195	-1.5	.172	0.1	3B(10): 1.0	0.0
2016	DYT	A	21	251	38	23	3	7	36	32	49	15	7	.329/.415/.567	.362	34.0	.392	1.6	3B(56): 3.2	4.1
2017	DAY	A+	22	272	41	26	2	4	31	23	54	9	2	.305/.371/.476	.312	24.2	.378	1.3	3B(60): 5.1	3.1
2017	PEN	AA	22	235	40	14	1	10	34	26	43	5	4	.340/.413/.560	.342	26.5	.391	-0.5	3B(56): 1.7	3.0
2018	*CIN*	*MLB*	*23*	*250*	*32*	*14*	*1*	*10*	*34*	*23*	*61*	*4*	*2*	*.263/.336/.467*	*.267*	*10.1*	*.318*	*-0.2*	*3B 3*	*1.4*
2019	*CIN*	*MLB*	*24*	*374*	*50*	*21*	*1*	*15*	*51*	*35*	*94*	*6*	*3*	*.261/.334/.463*	*.283*	*18.0*	*.318*	*-0.1*	*3B 4*	*2.4*

Breakout: 9% Improve: 24% Collapse: 8% Attrition: 21% MLB: 58% *Comparables: Paul DeJong, Brett Wallace, Alex Liddi*

Senzel was the most exciting prospect in the Reds system for all of a year before they went out and made a huge splash in the 2017 draft, but that'll be fine with the young third baseman. The 2016 second overall pick came out of college extremely polished and has done nothing in the minors to prove that he's not one of the more major-league-ready draftees in recent memory. He isn't particularly special in one specific area of the game, but he's very good at just about everything. Senzel's 2017 season was cut short by vertigo, possibly the result of climbing so quickly through the system. Barring something unforeseen, he'll make his major-league debut in 2018, and all signs point toward him being a staple in the lineup for a long time.

Jose Siri CF Born: 07/22/95 Age: 22 Bats: R Throws: R Height: 6'2" Weight: 175 Origin: International Free Agent, 2012

YEAR	TEAM	LVL	AGE	PA	R	2B	3B	HR	RBI	BB	K	SB	CS	AVG/OBP/SLG	TAv	VORP	BABIP	BRR	FRAA	WARP
2015	CIN	RK	19	175	34	7	9	3	19	3	64	9	2	.246/.259/.444	.236	2.5	.375	2.2	CF(30): 0.4, RF(7): -0.9	0.1
2016	DYT	A	20	87	5	3	0	0	3	2	34	3	2	.145/.163/.181	.124	-8.9	.240	0.6	CF(17): 1.7, RF(9): -0.2	-0.8
2016	BIL	RK	20	255	52	12	8	10	35	8	66	17	4	.320/.348/.560	.314	25.2	.404	3.9	RF(33): 4.6, CF(21): 5.4	3.5
2017	DYT	A	21	552	92	24	11	24	76	33	130	46	12	.293/.341/.530	.306	48.9	.349	7.4	CF(103): 15.7, RF(9): 1.5	6.9
2018	*CIN*	*MLB*	*22*	*250*	*35*	*9*	*2*	*10*	*27*	*10*	*85*	*11*	*3*	*.218/.253/.400*	*.212*	*-1.4*	*.286*	*1.4*	*CF 5, RF 0*	*0.4*
2019	*CIN*	*MLB*	*23*	*300*	*34*	*11*	*3*	*12*	*38*	*14*	*101*	*13*	*4*	*.219/.259/.404*	*.231*	*1.7*	*.289*	*2.3*	*CF 6, RF 0*	*0.9*

Breakout: 8% Improve: 11% Collapse: 4% Attrition: 13% MLB: 22% *Comparables: Teoscar Hernandez, Franchy Cordero, David Dahl*

One of the most exciting prospects in baseball, Siri made a name for himself in 2017, his first full professional season. The outfielder jumped onto the prospect map during the summer when he put together a 39-game hit streak that had fans from all over the country following along by the end. That wasn't a fluke, either. His absurd bat speed will allow him to hit at any level, and he pairs that with athleticism to make him a monster both in the outfield and on the basepaths. Perhaps the most exciting aspect of his future, though, is the possibility of tens of thousands of iPhones going off every time his name is announced over the loudspeakers.

Eugenio Suarez 3B Born: 07/18/91 Age: 26 Bats: R Throws: R Height: 5'11" Weight: 213 Origin: International Free Agent, 2008

YEAR	TEAM	LVL	AGE	PA	R	2B	3B	HR	RBI	BB	K	SB	CS	AVG/OBP/SLG	TAv	VORP	BABIP	BRR	FRAA	WARP
2015	LOU	AAA	23	238	30	9	2	8	25	26	40	3	4	.256/.348/.438	.285	16.1	.282	0.5	SS(55): -2.9	1.3
2015	CIN	MLB	23	398	42	19	2	13	48	17	94	4	1	.280/.315/.446	.283	24.9	.341	0.3	SS(96): -2.7, 3B(1): 0.0	2.4
2016	CIN	MLB	24	627	78	25	2	21	70	51	155	11	5	.248/.317/.411	.258	19.8	.304	0.7	3B(151): 2.0, SS(2): -0.3	2.2
2017	CIN	MLB	25	632	87	25	2	26	82	84	147	4	5	.260/.367/.461	.294	38.8	.309	-4.7	3B(153): -1.9, SS(1): 0.0	3.7
2018	*CIN*	*MLB*	*26*	*586*	*74*	*24*	*2*	*21*	*77*	*54*	*139*	*7*	*4*	*.250/.327/.427*	*.262*	*18.4*	*.299*	*-0.9*	*3B -2*	*1.2*
2019	*CIN*	*MLB*	*27*	*546*	*74*	*24*	*2*	*23*	*74*	*54*	*130*	*6*	*4*	*.253/.335/.452*	*.278*	*22.7*	*.297*	*-1.0*	*3B -1*	*2.3*

Breakout: 1% Improve: 52% Collapse: 2% Attrition: 11% MLB: 98% *Comparables: Edwin Encarnacion, Hank Blalock, Alex Gordon*

Everyone knows it's easier to perform at your job when you're comfortable. Suarez finally was in 2017, and it showed. After spending the early parts of his career as a subpar defensive player tasked with filling in for plus defensive shortstops, he finally got a chance to start every day at the hot corner in 2016. It took a year to settle in, but in his age-25 season he showed the best strike zone judgment of his career en route to a healthy uptick in walks as well as power. It didn't hurt that he played in a great hitters park, as 21 of his 26 home runs came on the banks of the Ohio River. He never got uncomfortable, either, even in the toughest situations. Suarez was at his best in high-leverage spots and was the third-best hitter in all of baseball with the bases loaded. Reaching arbitration for the first time this winter, he picked a hell of a time to get comfortable.

Taylor Trammell LF Born: 09/13/97 Age: 20 Bats: L Throws: L Height: 6'2" Weight: 195 Origin: Round 1, 2016 Draft (#35 overall)

YEAR	TEAM	LVL	AGE	PA	R	2B	3B	HR	RBI	BB	K	SB	CS	AVG/OBP/SLG	TAv	VORP	BABIP	BRR	FRAA	WARP
2016	BIL	RK	18	254	39	9	6	2	34	23	57	24	7	.303/.374/.421	.284	15.1	.396	2.7	LF(39): 0.5, CF(11): 2.1	1.7
2017	DYT	A	19	571	80	24	10	13	77	71	123	41	12	.281/.368/.450	.304	41.3	.345	3.1	LF(104): -3.7, CF(17): -0.9	3.8
2018	*CIN*	*MLB*	*20*	*250*	*29*	*9*	*2*	*7*	*27*	*23*	*73*	*9*	*3*	*.224/.298/.374*	*.228*	*1.0*	*.295*	*0.8*	*LF 1, CF 0*	*0.2*
2019	*CIN*	*MLB*	*21*	*387*	*47*	*15*	*3*	*12*	*45*	*38*	*108*	*15*	*5*	*.232/.310/.395*	*.254*	*9.0*	*.299*	*1.8*	*LF 1, CF 0*	*1.1*

Breakout: 4% Improve: 15% Collapse: 0% Attrition: 7% MLB: 17% *Comparables: Jesse Winker, Victor Robles, Ramon Flores*

Though Trammell was drafted 35th overall in 2016, he was more highly regarded than that and was paid accordingly—his $3.2 million bonus was more than the recommended slot for the 12th overall pick. The outfield prospect is always going to get by mostly on his athleticism, which led him to cross the 40-steal plateau at an efficient rate. However, the bat will determine whether he lives up to his tools, and he has done nothing in his two years in the minors to show that he can't make the most of his talent. Odd draft quirks allowed the Reds to pick Trammell relatively late, and so far he looks like a bargain.

Joey Votto 1B Born: 09/10/83 Age: 34 Bats: L Throws: R Height: 6'2" Weight: 220 Origin: Round 2, 2002 Draft (#44 overall)

YEAR	TEAM	LVL	AGE	PA	R	2B	3B	HR	RBI	BB	K	SB	CS	AVG/OBP/SLG	TAv	VORP	BABIP	BRR	FRAA	WARP
2015	CIN	MLB	31	695	95	33	2	29	80	143	135	11	3	.314/.459/.541	.360	69.2	.371	-5.7	1B(156): 1.3	7.6
2016	CIN	MLB	32	677	101	34	2	29	97	108	120	8	1	.326/.434/.550	.341	58.6	.366	-4.1	1B(154): -1.1	5.9
2017	CIN	MLB	33	707	106	34	1	36	100	134	83	5	1	.320/.454/.578	.354	70.1	.321	-6.9	1B(162): 9.5	8.0
2018	*CIN*	*MLB*	*34*	*645*	*98*	*28*	*2*	*25*	*94*	*115*	*114*	*6*	*2*	*.291/.422/.496*	*.313*	*42.5*	*.328*	*-0.5*	*1B 2*	*4.6*
2019	*CIN*	*MLB*	*35*	*606*	*97*	*26*	*1*	*25*	*88*	*109*	*111*	*4*	*1*	*.287/.419/.501*	*.323*	*43.0*	*.323*	*-4.7*	*1B 2*	*4.9*

Breakout: 1% Improve: 27% Collapse: 5% Attrition: 2% MLB: 98% *Comparables: Todd Helton, Albert Pujols, Lance Berkman*

If some non-mad scientist were to build a robot whose sole job was to hit baseballs at the most productive and most efficient rate possible, the closest human equivalent would be Votto. The first baseman is never going to be the most popular player in the league—hell, he's never even been the most popular player in his own city despite being the best player on the team for his entire career—and he's never going to be the guy kids around the country emulate at the plate. His home runs aren't going to fill up SportsCenter, and most of his production is the kind that you don't really think all that much about. And yet, at the end of every season, he is among the very best hitters in baseball and gets there without any major blemishes in his game showing through.

As if that alone isn't scary enough for his opponents, Votto has found a way to *get even better.* The star hitter already had some of the best plate discipline in recent memory, but in 2017 he started swinging more at better pitches and less frequently at pitches out of the zone. This helped him join the launch-angle revolution, giving him more power than he's shown in seven years, while also cutting his strikeout rate to a career-low 11.7 percent. Oh, and this all took place in his age-33 season. Maybe Votto *is* that robot created by the non-mad scientist.

Jesse Winker OF Born: 08/17/93 Age: 24 Bats: L Throws: L Height: 6'3" Weight: 215 Origin: Round 1, 2012 Draft (#49 overall)

YEAR	TEAM	LVL	AGE	PA	R	2B	3B	HR	RBI	BB	K	SB	CS	AVG/OBP/SLG	TAv	VORP	BABIP	BRR	FRAA	WARP
2015	PEN	AA	21	526	69	24	2	13	55	74	83	8	4	.282/.390/.433	.308	33.7	.320	-2.0	LF(83): -4.9, RF(40): -2.9	2.8
2016	LOU	AAA	22	448	39	22	0	3	45	59	59	0	0	.303/.397/.384	.288	20.4	.347	-1.0	RF(52): 1.0, LF(46): -2.3	2.0
2017	LOU	AAA	23	347	33	22	0	2	41	38	46	2	4	.314/.395/.408	.289	14.5	.359	-3.2	RF(70): 2.8, LF(3): 0.4	1.7
2017	CIN	MLB	23	137	21	7	0	7	15	15	24	1	1	.298/.375/.529	.313	9.7	.322	-0.6	RF(25): -1.4, LF(2): -0.3	0.8
2018	*CIN*	*MLB*	*24*	*396*	*49*	*19*	*1*	*11*	*49*	*46*	*71*	*2*	*1*	*.270/.360/.426*	*.273*	*16.2*	*.309*	*-1.0*	*RF -2, LF -1*	*1.1*
2019	*CIN*	*MLB*	*25*	*505*	*71*	*25*	*0*	*18*	*66*	*62*	*95*	*2*	*1*	*.277/.371/.457*	*.293*	*28.0*	*.316*	*-1.3*	*RF -2, LF -1*	*2.7*

Breakout: 5% Improve: 30% Collapse: 18% Attrition: 28% MLB: 72% *Comparables: Carlos Quentin, L.J. Hoes, Ramon Flores*

Winker, a former first-round pick and two-time BP top-100 prospect, finally made his major-league debut in 2017. The bat was never a concern; he always showed great plate discipline and had strong bat-to-ball abilities, but he had never shown much power in the minors, a major red flag for a guy who didn't profile to play anything besides left field. Then, Winker got called up and a funny thing happened: The dude hit for a ton of power. It was only 137 plate appearances, but the ball was flying off his bat, leaving some to wonder if he's one of those guys who just needed the assistance of major-league advanced scouting. His park and the home-run bonanza around the league aided that power spike, but Winker may yet be able to slug his way to an above-average career at in the corner of somebody's outfield.

PITCHERS

Tim Adleman RHP Born: 11/13/87 Age: 30 Bats: R Throws: R Height: 6'5" Weight: 225 Origin: Round 24, 2010 Draft (#718 overall)

YEAR	TEAM	LVL	AGE	W	L	SV	G	GS	IP	H	HR	BB/9	K/9	K	GB%	BABIP	WHIP	ERA	DRA	WARP	MPH	CMD	PWR	STM
2015	PEN	AA	27	9	10	0	27	26	150	134	7	2.9	6.8	113	47%	.290	1.22	2.64	3.22	3.4				
2016	LOU	AAA	28	3	1	0	10	10	56^2	52	4	1.6	6.0	38	47%	.277	1.09	2.38	3.57	1.2				
2016	CIN	MLB	28	4	4	0	13	13	69^2	64	13	2.6	6.1	47	40%	.252	1.21	4.00	6.09	-0.6	93.5	50	42	50
2017	CIN	MLB	29	5	11	0	30	20	122^1	124	29	3.8	7.9	108	36%	.282	1.43	5.52	6.24	-1.0	91.8	57	38	62
2018	*CIN*	*MLB*	*30*	*6*	*7*	*0*	*32*	*17*	*107*	*107*	*21*	*3.6*	*7.8*	*93*	*42%*	*.299*	*1.40*	*5.38*	*5.83*	*-0.4*	*91.6*	*55*	*39*	*56*
2019	*CIN*	*MLB*	*31*	*4*	*6*	*0*	*22*	*14*	93^1	*91*	*17*	*3.5*	*7.8*	*81*	*42%*	*.302*	*1.36*	*5.46*	*5.89*	*-0.3*	*91.2*	*55*	*39*	*56*

Breakout: 13% Improve: 18% Collapse: 20% Attrition: 21% MLB: 43% *Comparables: Philip Humber, Dylan Axelrod, Josh Hancock*

Adleman stuck in the majors for essentially the entire 2017 season, an impressive accomplishment for a guy who once spent two years in indy ball. It's a testament to Adleman's hard work that his ultimate goal came true, but unfortunately, the only impressive part of his game is his propensity for allowing homers. It seems strange to say since he is coming off a near-6.00-ERA season, but 2017 will be the peak of his baseball career, at least on this side of the Pacific. He'll spend 2018 in Korea, pitching for the Samsung Lions, who praised his durability and work ethic when they signed him in November.

Bronson Arroyo RHP Born: 02/24/77 Age: 41 Bats: R Throws: R Height: 6'4" Weight: 190 Origin: Round 3, 1995 Draft (#69 overall)

YEAR	TEAM	LVL	AGE	W	L	SV	G	GS	IP	H	HR	BB/9	K/9	K	GB%	BABIP	WHIP	ERA	DRA	WARP	MPH	CMD	PWR	STM
2017	CIN	MLB	40	3	6	0	14	14	71	94	23	2.4	5.7	45	32%	.305	1.59	7.35	8.30	-2.2	86.1	59	0	55
2018	*CIN*	*MLB*	*41*	*2*	*4*	*0*	*9*	*9*	47^1	*59*	*15*	*4.1*	*5.6*	*30*	*38%*	*.300*	*1.69*	*7.74*	*8.49*	*-1.5*	*84.5*	*57*	*0*	*53*
2019	*CIN*	*MLB*	*42*	*5*	*14*	*0*	*26*	*26*	152^2	*186*	*38*	*4.5*	*4.2*	*72*	*38%*	*.304*	*1.72*	*7.64*	*8.33*	*-4.3*	*83.7*	*56*	*0*	*52*

Breakout: 7% Improve: 34% Collapse: 13% Attrition: 7% MLB: 68% *Comparables: Woody Williams, David Wells, Sal Maglie*

After missing two consecutive seasons due to injury, Arroyo finally made it back on the field in 2017. The results were decidedly awful, and injury would once again cut his season short, but it didn't matter. He made it back. Everyone knew the end was near for Arroyo, once the model of health and durability on the mound. Nobody would have been surprised, nor would they have blamed him, if he had hung it up after one of his setbacks. Arroyo had to make it back, though. Opponents surely appreciated his presence, but so did those who have been watching him and his crazy leg kick since 2000. After being shut down with a shoulder strain in June, Arroyo hinted that 2017 would be his final season, and he confirmed it a few months later. Arroyo won't make the Hall of Fame and will be forgotten by many, but the league is losing one of the coolest players in the game, the last active member of the curse-breaking 2004 Red Sox, and a fan favorite everywhere he landed over his 16-year career.

Homer Bailey RHP Born: 05/03/86 Age: 32 Bats: R Throws: R Height: 6'4" Weight: 223 Origin: Round 1, 2004 Draft (#7 overall)

YEAR	TEAM	LVL	AGE	W	L	SV	G	GS	IP	H	HR	BB/9	K/9	K	GB%	BABIP	WHIP	ERA	DRA	WARP	MPH	CMD	PWR	STM
2015	CIN	MLB	29	0	1	0	2	2	11^1	16	3	3.2	2.4	3	59%	.317	1.76	5.56	6.44	-0.2	94.5			45
2016	LOU	AAA	30	1	2	0	7	7	24	31	7	3.4	7.1	19	54%	.312	1.67	5.62	4.87	0.1				
2016	CIN	MLB	30	2	3	0	6	6	23	35	2	2.7	10.6	27	47%	.452	1.83	6.65	5.23	0.0	96.0	51	51	22
2017	CIN	MLB	31	6	9	0	18	18	91	112	11	4.2	6.6	67	46%	.346	1.69	6.43	7.72	-2.2	95.4	42	53	62
2018	*CIN*	*MLB*	*32*	*9*	*11*	*0*	*27*	*27*	*162*	*172*	*27*	*3.8*	*7.1*	*129*	*48%*	*.297*	*1.48*	*5.12*	*5.20*	*-0.1*	*94.5*	*43*	*52*	*44*
2019	*CIN*	*MLB*	*33*	*9*	*13*	*0*	*30*	*30*	*185^2*	*184*	*30*	*3.6*	*6.6*	*135*	*48%*	*.297*	*1.40*	*5.51*	*5.94*	*-0.6*	*93.8*	*43*	*52*	*44*

Breakout: 15% Improve: 47% Collapse: 24% Attrition: 18% MLB: 88% *Comparables: Gavin Floyd, Edinson Volquez, Vicente Padilla*

We hadn't seen a fully healthy Bailey since Iggy Azalea and Charli XCX were topping the charts through the summer of 2014. He finally returned for a significant stretch in 2017, though it came after missing almost three months to start the year. The veteran righty struggled to rack up strikeouts, struggled even more to find the zone and generally looked nothing like the player who earned a six-year extension from the Reds before that last good season. But he nearly threw 100 innings, which makes last year a rousing success for the former elite prospect. For the Reds, however, it was a different story: Bailey is still owed $49 million over the next two seasons. His $/WARP would have looked respectable in 2017 if you just ignored that pesky negative sign.

Austin Brice RHP Born: 06/19/92 Age: 25 Bats: R Throws: R Height: 6'4" Weight: 235 Origin: Round 9, 2010 Draft (#287 overall)

YEAR	TEAM	LVL	AGE	W	L	SV	G	GS	IP	H	HR	BB/9	K/9	K	GB%	BABIP	WHIP	ERA	DRA	WARP	MPH	CMD	PWR	STM
2015	JAX	AA	23	6	9	0	25	25	125^1	114	11	5.0	9.1	127	34%	.307	1.46	4.67	5.30	-0.3				
2016	JAX	AA	24	4	7	2	27	13	93^1	79	5	2.8	7.6	79	47%	.280	1.16	2.89	3.01	2.2				
2016	MIA	MLB	24	0	1	0	15	0	14	9	2	3.2	9.0	14	53%	.194	1.00	7.07	2.90	0.3	96.6	74	56	54
2017	LOU	AAA	25	1	2	1	15	0	21^1	23	0	3.8	8.9	21	46%	.365	1.50	3.80	4.05	0.3				
2017	CIN	MLB	25	0	0	0	22	0	32^2	33	6	1.9	7.2	26	50%	.284	1.22	4.96	4.75	0.2	95.6	58	56	45
2018	*CIN*	*MLB*	*26*	*3*	*3*	*0*	*54*	*0*	*57*	*53*	*8*	*4.2*	*9.0*	*57*	*43%*	*.293*	*1.41*	*4.71*	*4.61*	*0.2*	*95.5*	*63*	*57*	*50*
2019	*CIN*	*MLB*	*27*	*2*	*1*	*0*	*46*	*0*	*48^1*	*43*	*7*	*4.1*	*9.1*	*49*	*43%*	*.302*	*1.35*	*4.91*	*5.29*	*0.0*	*95.2*	*63*	*57*	*50*

Breakout: 15% Improve: 25% Collapse: 14% Attrition: 34% MLB: 51% *Comparables: Dustin Nippert, Tyler Cravy, Kyle Weiland*

In all likelihood, Brice will be remembered as some guy who was also involved in the deal that sent Luis Castillo to the Reds. A big righty with a mid-to-high-90s fastball to go with a wicked slider, Brice can miss bats and get groundballs. A home-run problem might hold him back from being a true late-inning reliever, but he could be a weapon out of the bullpen. And yet, knowing how baseball goes, that's not what's going to lead his Wikipedia page at any point in his career.

Luis Castillo RHP Born: 12/12/92 Age: 25 Bats: R Throws: R Height: 6'2" Weight: 190 Origin: International Free Agent, 2012

YEAR	TEAM	LVL	AGE	W	L	SV	G	GS	IP	H	HR	BB/9	K/9	K	GB%	BABIP	WHIP	ERA	DRA	WARP	MPH	CMD	PWR	STM
2015	GRB	A	22	4	3	4	25	7	63^1	59	1	2.7	9.0	63	53%	.326	1.23	2.98	1.89	2.4				
2015	JUP	A+	22	2	3	0	10	9	43^2	44	3	2.9	6.4	31	52%	.308	1.33	3.50	4.39	0.4				
2016	JUP	A+	23	8	4	0	23	21	117^2	95	2	1.4	7.0	91	50%	.271	0.96	2.07	2.29	4.2				
2016	JAX	AA	23	0	2	0	3	3	14	12	1	4.5	7.7	12	42%	.262	1.36	3.86	5.76	-0.1				
2017	PEN	AA	24	4	4	0	14	14	80^1	68	5	1.5	9.1	81	42%	.293	1.01	2.58	2.49	2.6				
2017	CIN	MLB	24	3	7	0	15	15	89^1	64	11	3.2	9.9	98	60%	.247	1.07	3.12	3.36	2.2	98.7	48	69	74
2018	*CIN*	*MLB*	*25*	*7*	*8*	*0*	*24*	*24*	*127*	*121*	*19*	*3.2*	*8.8*	*124*	*46%*	*.293*	*1.29*	*4.29*	*4.33*	*1.2*	*98.4*	*49*	*71*	*76*
2019	*CIN*	*MLB*	*26*	*10*	*11*	*0*	*32*	*32*	*208^2*	*178*	*27*	*2.8*	*9.1*	*210*	*46%*	*.296*	*1.17*	*4.13*	*4.42*	*2.3*	*98.1*	*49*	*71*	*76*

Breakout: 26% Improve: 62% Collapse: 16% Attrition: 21% MLB: 86% *Comparables: Nick Tropeano, Tyler Duffey, A.J. Griffin*

At first, Castillo seemed destined to be confused with the long-time Marlins second baseman. Then, he was involved in a botched trade that sent him from Miami to San Diego and back to Miami in the span of four days. He was subsequently dealt to Cincinnati, where his career took a massive leap forward and Castillo started to show that he's not destined to be remembered as anything other than a great pitcher. After mowing down Southern League hitters to start the year, he was promoted to the majors and used his big velocity and strong secondaries to show he's among the most intriguing young pitchers in the game. Against all odds, he may be the best Luis Castillo we've ever seen.

Rookie Davis RHP Born: 04/29/93 Age: 25 Bats: R Throws: R Height: 6'5" Weight: 255 Origin: Round 14, 2011 Draft (#449 overall)

YEAR	TEAM	LVL	AGE	W	L	SV	G	GS	IP	H	HR	BB/9	K/9	K	GB%	BABIP	WHIP	ERA	DRA	WARP	MPH	CMD	PWR	STM
2015	TAM	A+	22	6	6	0	19	19	97^1	94	4	1.7	9.7	105	47%	.327	1.15	3.70	1.47	4.2				
2015	TRN	AA	22	2	1	0	6	5	33^1	38	1	2.2	6.5	24	47%	.343	1.38	4.32	3.68	0.5				
2016	LOU	AAA	23	0	2	0	5	4	24	38	3	2.6	5.6	15	43%	.389	1.88	7.50	6.70	-0.4				
2016	PEN	AA	23	10	3	0	19	19	101	88	10	2.7	5.5	62	49%	.254	1.17	2.94	6.58	-1.8				
2017	PEN	AA	24	0	0	0	3	3	13^2	12	2	4.0	7.2	11	43%	.250	1.32	4.61	5.09	0.0				
2017	LOU	AAA	24	4	4	0	11	11	60^1	68	10	1.9	8.1	54	33%	.320	1.34	4.77	5.31	0.3				
2017	CIN	MLB	24	1	3	0	7	6	24	38	7	5.2	7.5	20	46%	.387	2.17	8.62	8.65	-0.8	94.1	51	53	50
2018	*CIN*	*MLB*	*25*	*1*	*2*	*0*	*14*	*3*	*27^1*	*29*	*5*	*3.6*	*8.3*	*25*	*42%*	*.300*	*1.49*	*5.38*	*5.28*	*-0.1*	*93.8*	*52*	*54*	*51*
2019	*CIN*	*MLB*	*26*	*6*	*6*	*0*	*65*	*13*	*131*	*126*	*24*	*3.3*	*8.7*	*126*	*42%*	*.307*	*1.33*	*5.13*	*5.54*	*-0.1*	*93.5*	*52*	*54*	*52*

Breakout: 13% Improve: 20% Collapse: 14% Attrition: 34% MLB: 38% *Comparables: Wei-Chung Wang, Jon Moscot, David Pauley*

We've been waiting for this moment since 2011: Rookie Davis was finally a rookie in 2017. Part of the haul for Aroldis Chapman, he made his major-league debut in April and struck out the first batter he faced. Alas, the good times ended there, as the second batter took him deep and he couldn't find any semblance of command. Then again, Davis only tossed 24 innings in the majors, meaning he has another shot at being a Rookie of the Year contender. Reds fans deserve that, even if Davis himself doesn't.

Brandon Finnegan LHP Born: 04/14/93 Age: 25 Bats: L Throws: L Height: 5'11" Weight: 212 Origin: Round 1, 2014 Draft (#17 overall)

YEAR	TEAM	LVL	AGE	W	L	SV	G	GS	IP	H	HR	BB/9	K/9	K	GB%	BABIP	WHIP	ERA	DRA	WARP	MPH	CMD	PWR	STM
2015	NWA	AA	22	0	1	1	5	3	13	10	1	8.3	9.0	13	42%	.257	1.69	2.77	7.92	-0.5				
2015	KCA	MLB	22	3	0	0	14	0	24^1	16	3	4.8	7.8	21	59%	.213	1.19	2.96	3.27	0.5	96.0	47	57	52
2015	OMA	AAA	22	0	2	0	6	4	14	17	1	4.5	12.2	19	46%	.421	1.71	7.07	3.15	0.3				
2015	LOU	AAA	22	0	3	0	8	8	30^1	31	3	5.0	8.9	30	45%	.318	1.58	6.23	3.87	0.5				
2015	CIN	MLB	22	2	2	0	6	4	23^2	21	5	3.0	9.1	24	52%	.262	1.23	4.18	4.34	0.1	94.6	47	57	52
2016	CIN	MLB	23	10	11	0	31	31	172	150	29	4.4	7.6	145	41%	.256	1.36	3.98	5.15	0.4	94.6	53	52	74
2017	CIN	MLB	24	1	1	0	4	4	13	9	1	9.0	11.1	16	53%	.276	1.69	4.15	4.28	0.2	96.0	47	61	6
2018	*CIN*	*MLB*	*25*	*7*	*8*	*0*	*24*	*24*	*120*	*107*	*17*	*4.4*	*9.1*	*121*	*45%*	*.284*	*1.35*	*4.48*	*4.53*	*0.9*	*94.5*	*53*	*55*	*41*
2019	*CIN*	*MLB*	*26*	*9*	*11*	*0*	*32*	*32*	*206^2*	*161*	*29*	*4.0*	*9.7*	*224*	*45%*	*.28*	*1.22*	*4.45*	*4.78*	*1.5*	*94.2*	*54*	*55*	*38*

Breakout: 28% Improve: 55% Collapse: 16% Attrition: 11% MLB: 96% *Comparables: Johnny Cueto, Andrew Miller, David Price*

In a year that saw many young pitchers step up and give Reds fans hope for the future, perhaps their most exciting young arm heading into the season barely got to play. Finnegan started the year with a bang, tossing seven shutout innings with nine strikeouts. He made a couple of early exits after that first start before hitting the disabled list, making one more short start before undergoing season-ending shoulder surgery. In his brief time in the majors during 2017, Finnegan flashed the stuff that makes him so intriguing—a mid-90s fastball and a nasty, late-breaking slider boring in front the left side—but the injury also played into his long-term role concerns. He's still only 25 so there is time to watch Finnegan begin again, but the fear is he may be another young Reds starter on the Raisel Iglesias/Michael Lorenzen path.

Amir Garrett LHP Born: 05/03/92 Age: 26 Bats: R Throws: L Height: 6'5" Weight: 228 Origin: Round 22, 2011 Draft (#685 overall)

YEAR	TEAM	LVL	AGE	W	L	SV	G	GS	IP	H	HR	BB/9	K/9	K	GB%	BABIP	WHIP	ERA	DRA	WARP	MPH	CMD	PWR	STM
2015	DAY	A+	23	9	7	0	26	26	140^1	117	4	3.5	8.5	133	45%	.298	1.23	2.44	3.59	2.5				
2016	PEN	AA	24	5	3	0	13	12	77	51	0	3.3	9.1	78	50%	.252	1.03	1.75	3.21	1.7				
2016	LOU	AAA	24	2	5	0	12	11	67^2	48	6	4.1	7.2	54	49%	.231	1.17	3.46	4.44	0.7				
2017	LOU	AAA	25	2	4	0	14	14	67^2	79	7	3.2	8.1	61	41%	.346	1.52	5.72	6.11	-0.3				
2017	CIN	MLB	25	3	8	0	16	14	70^2	74	23	5.1	8.0	63	44%	.264	1.61	7.39	7.85	-1.8	94.4	41	46	64
2018	*CIN*	*MLB*	*26*	*3*	*4*	*0*	*19*	*8*	*53*	*53*	*9*	*4.3*	*8.6*	*52*	*44%*	*.292*	*1.44*	*5.15*	*5.14*	*0.0*	*94.0*	*42*	*47*	*65*
2019	*CIN*	*MLB*	*27*	*8*	*9*	*0*	*54*	*22*	*164^2*	*145*	*26*	*3.8*	*8.7*	*160*	*44%*	*.295*	*1.30*	*4.91*	*5.29*	*0.4*	*93.7*	*42*	*47*	*65*

Breakout: 19% Improve: 34% Collapse: 15% Attrition: 40% MLB: 55% *Comparables: Manny Banuelos, Joel Hanrahan, Philip Humber*

Most of us don't end up where we thought we'd be back when we were getting out of high school. Some accomplish their dreams, but most of us schmucks dream of saving the world or making a boatload of money but end up in a middling job with student loans, back problems, less hair where we wanted more and vice versa. Garrett, a top basketball recruit out of high school about to start playing for a storied St. John's program, is the rare professional baseball player who isn't where he thought he'd be after high school either. Eventually, Plan A didn't work out and he is now a major-league pitcher. Well, sort of. He's still raw and his first taste of the highest level showed what a true lack of command can mean—he turned all right-handed hitters into Cody Bellinger and all left-handed hitters into Kris Bryant, so at least he was an equal opportunity giver. But even if this is the peak of his career, his Plan B is a helluva lot better than most of ours.

Hunter Greene RHP Born: 08/06/99 Age: 18 Bats: R Throws: R Height: 6'4" Weight: 197 Origin: Round 1, 2017 Draft (#2 overall)

Greene is one of the more exciting prospects to come into the league through the MLB draft in quite some time. The high school wunderkind is a superb athlete who has the talent to stick at shortstop long-term defensively and plenty of projection in his bat. Yet, it's unlikely he'll ever actually see time at the position in the majors. Usually when you say a high-end pick is unlikely to stick at shortstop it is because he'll have to move down the defensive spectrum. In Greene's case, it's because he can scrape triple digits on the mound as well. The big righty can sit in the mid-90s with his fastball and has the potential for at least one plus breaking ball. In a world where baseball teams were capable of thinking outside of the box, we could be staring down a new era of two-way players with Greene, Shohei Ohtani and Rays prospect Brendan McKay. In this world, fear will once again rule the day.

Vladimir Gutierrez RHP Born: 09/18/95 Age: 22 Bats: R Throws: R Height: 6'0" Weight: 190 Origin: International Free Agent, 2016

YEAR	TEAM	LVL	AGE	W	L	SV	G	GS	IP	H	HR	BB/9	K/9	K	GB%	BABIP	WHIP	ERA	DRA	WARP	MPH	CMD	PWR	STM
2017	DAY	A+	21	7	8	0	19	19	103	108	10	1.7	8.2	94	42%	.320	1.23	4.46	2.86	2.9				
2018	*CIN*	*MLB*	*22*	*4*	*5*	*0*	*14*	*14*	*73^2*	*74*	*14*	*3.0*	*9.1*	*75*	*39%*	*.315*	*1.34*	*4.76*	*5.14*	*0.4*				
2019	*CIN*	*MLB*	*23*	*7*	*12*	*0*	*29*	*29*	*175*	*176*	*36*	*4.5*	*8.5*	*166*	*39%*	*.312*	*1.51*	*5.92*	*6.43*	*-1.4*				

Breakout: 13% Improve: 17% Collapse: 4% Attrition: 19% MLB: 23% *Comparables: Aaron Nola, Jeanmar Gomez, Adam Wilk*

Gutierrez was signed out of Cuba for $4.75 million and acclimated himself nicely to the States in 2017. Now that he has a full season under his belt, expect him to be pushed a bit more quickly after showing that he had little trouble with High-A hitters in his age-21 season. He still needs some work, particularly in developing his changeup into a solid third pitch, but he is looking like a strong addition to the Reds farm system.

Ariel Hernandez RHP
Born: 03/02/92 Age: 26 Bats: R Throws: R Height: 6'4" Weight: 230 Origin: International Free Agent, 2008

YEAR	TEAM	LVL	AGE	W	L	SV	G	GS	IP	H	HR	BB/9	K/9	K	GB%	BABIP	WHIP	ERA	DRA	WARP	MPH	CMD	PWR	STM
2015	YAK	A-	23	1	1	2	22	0	22^1	18	1	8.5	12.9	32	40%	.327	1.75	6.04	6.66	-0.5				
2016	DYT	A	24	0	1	2	18	0	31^1	11	0	5.7	11.5	40	55%	.164	0.99	2.59	3.28	0.5				
2016	DAY	A+	24	3	1	3	25	0	30^2	18	1	5.6	10.0	34	50%	.227	1.21	1.76	3.87	0.4				
2017	PEN	AA	25	2	0	1	24	0	33	18	0	5.5	10.6	39	46%	.254	1.15	2.18	3.69	0.4				
2017	LOU	AAA	25	1	2	0	15	0	17	14	1	10.1	10.1	19	59%	.302	1.94	5.29	5.08	0.0				
2017	CIN	MLB	25	0	0	0	19	0	24^1	14	6	8.1	10.7	29	44%	.157	1.48	5.18	6.26	-0.3	99.5	43	76	51
2018	*CIN*	*MLB*	*26*	*1*	*1*	*0*	*16*	*0*	*17*	*15*	*3*	*7.4*	*10.6*	*20*	*43%*	*.291*	*1.70*	*6.16*	*5.88*	*-0.2*	*99.1*	*44*	*77*	*52*
2019	*CIN*	*MLB*	*27*	*2*	*1*	*0*	*49*	*0*	51^2	*43*	*8*	*4.3*	*9.5*	*54*	*43%*	*.289*	*1.31*	*4.98*	*5.36*	*-0.1*	*98.8*	*44*	*77*	*52*

Breakout: 14% Improve: 19% Collapse: 12% Attrition: 18% MLB: 35% *Comparables: Stephen Pryor, Kyle Barraclough, Jose Dominguez*

Hernandez has come a long way from indy ball in 2014, and the Reds made a hell of a discovery when they selected him in the minor-league portion of the 2015 Rule 5 draft. The righty can dial his fastball up to 100 mph, which is increasingly becoming a requirement to be part of a major-league bullpen. Although he rode that fastball to the majors in 2017, he quickly learned that to succeed at the highest level you need more than a wicked fastball. You also need control.

Jared Hughes RHP
Born: 07/04/85 Age: 32 Bats: R Throws: R Height: 6'7" Weight: 240 Origin: Round 4, 2006 Draft (#110 overall)

YEAR	TEAM	LVL	AGE	W	L	SV	G	GS	IP	H	HR	BB/9	K/9	K	GB%	BABIP	WHIP	ERA	DRA	WARP	MPH	CMD	PWR	STM
2015	PIT	MLB	29	3	1	0	76	0	67	70	3	2.6	4.8	36	65%	.306	1.33	2.28	4.19	0.4	95.2	42	66	52
2016	PIT	MLB	30	1	1	1	67	0	59^1	62	6	3.3	5.2	34	59%	.295	1.42	3.03	4.30	0.5	95.6	27	66	51
2017	MIL	MLB	31	5	3	1	67	0	59^2	49	4	3.6	7.2	48	63%	.278	1.22	3.02	3.89	0.8	95.1	38	65	47
2018	*CIN*	*MLB*	*32*	*3*	*3*	*0*	*59*	*0*	*62*	*63*	*8*	*4.1*	*6.5*	*46*	*57%*	*.292*	*1.46*	*5.13*	*4.91*	*0.0*	*94.3*	*35*	*65*	*49*
2019	*CIN*	*MLB*	*33*	*2*	*1*	*0*	*41*	*0*	*44*	*43*	*6*	*3.7*	*6.4*	*31*	*57%*	*.3*	*1.38*	*4.94*	*5.53*	*-0.2*	*93.8*	*33*	*65*	*48*

Breakout: 20% Improve: 40% Collapse: 24% Attrition: 13% MLB: 87% *Comparables: Burke Badenhop, Jim Johnson, Matt Albers*

For the first time in his career, Hughes threw his sinking fastball less than 80 percent of the time. He began throwing his slider more frequently, at the behest of Brewers pitching coach Derek Johnson, and it paid major dividends. Hughes become an integral part of the Brewers' bullpen after getting waived by Pittsburgh in the spring and saw his swinging-strike rate jump from 9.6 percent to 11.3 percent. His 7.2 K/9 was his highest since his brief rookie campaign in 2011. Reintroducing the slider hasn't made Hughes usable against left-handed hitters, but it did help him hold righties to a .203 average with just one homer. In other words, Hughes remains a ROOGY, just a better one than he was 12 months ago.

Raisel Iglesias RHP
Born: 01/04/90 Age: 28 Bats: R Throws: R Height: 6'2" Weight: 188 Origin: International Free Agent, 2014

YEAR	TEAM	LVL	AGE	W	L	SV	G	GS	IP	H	HR	BB/9	K/9	K	GB%	BABIP	WHIP	ERA	DRA	WARP	MPH	CMD	PWR	STM
2015	LOU	AAA	25	1	3	0	6	6	29	26	4	2.5	6.5	21	53%	.250	1.17	3.41	4.25	0.3				
2015	CIN	MLB	25	3	7	0	18	16	95^1	81	11	2.6	9.8	104	48%	.286	1.14	4.15	3.22	2.1	95.4	42	48	55
2016	CIN	MLB	26	3	2	6	37	5	78^1	63	7	3.0	9.5	83	43%	.275	1.14	2.53	3.53	1.4	97.9	41	53	43
2017	CIN	MLB	27	3	3	28	63	0	76	57	5	3.2	10.9	92	43%	.287	1.11	2.49	3.70	1.2	98.6	43	65	51
2018	*CIN*	*MLB*	*28*	*3*	*3*	*25*	*59*	*0*	*62*	*51*	*7*	*3.4*	*10.5*	*73*	*44%*	*.285*	*1.18*	*3.30*	*3.47*	*1.0*	*96.9*	*42*	*57*	*50*
2019	*CIN*	*MLB*	*29*	*3*	*1*	*18*	*62*	*0*	65^1	*50*	*8*	*3.4*	*10.4*	*76*	*44%*	*.29*	*1.14*	*4.00*	*4.26*	*0.7*	*97.1*	*42*	*59*	*48*

Breakout: 17% Improve: 35% Collapse: 34% Attrition: 11% MLB: 93% *Comparables: Alexi Ogando, Kris Medlen, Josh Johnson*

After two years of withering under the weight of a starter's workload, Iglesias finally got his first full season as a reliever and did not disappoint. Sticking with short bursts, his average fastball velocity ticked up again and his command was much less of an issue. Eventually named closer, he proved he'll be a capable one for the foreseeable future. Yet right now Iglesias sits as a potential bellwether—like fellow Cuban-turned-Red Aroldis Chapman a half-decade ago—for the closer's role in general. Bryan Price showed more creativity than any other manager in 2017, allowing Iglesias to rack up eight saves in which he recorded at least six outs—the most in a season since Danny Graves in 1999 (for the Reds, coincidentally). Will this be a step toward using Iglesias as a true fireman, someone who could pitch multiple innings at any spot and toss 100-120 innings out of the bullpen every year? More likely than not, he'll settle in as a standard-issue bullpen ace and be another point of reference when the next failed starter proves capable of high-quality multi-inning appearances.

Michael Lorenzen RHP
Born: 01/04/92 Age: 26 Bats: R Throws: R Height: 6'3" Weight: 217 Origin: Round 1, 2013 Draft (#38 overall)

YEAR	TEAM	LVL	AGE	W	L	SV	G	GS	IP	H	HR	BB/9	K/9	K	GB%	BABIP	WHIP	ERA	DRA	WARP	MPH	CMD	PWR	STM
2015	LOU	AAA	23	4	2	0	6	6	43	34	3	1.7	4.0	19	49%	.231	0.98	1.88	4.20	0.5				
2015	CIN	MLB	23	4	9	0	27	21	113^1	131	18	4.5	6.6	83	42%	.322	1.66	5.40	6.80	-2.4	97.1	37	61	66
2016	CIN	MLB	24	2	1	0	35	0	50	41	5	2.3	8.6	48	64%	.277	1.08	2.88	3.08	1.1	98.6	45	57	45
2017	CIN	MLB	25	8	4	2	70	0	83	78	9	3.7	8.7	80	57%	.295	1.35	4.45	4.27	0.8	97.9	41	62	56
2018	*CIN*	*MLB*	*26*	*3*	*3*	*3*	*54*	*0*	*57*	*51*	*6*	*3.8*	*9.0*	*57*	*53%*	*.292*	*1.31*	*3.91*	*3.98*	*0.6*	*97.4*	*41*	*62*	*56*
2019	*CIN*	*MLB*	*27*	*3*	*1*	*2*	*58*	*0*	61^2	*50*	*7*	*3.4*	*9.5*	*65*	*53%*	*.3*	*1.19*	*3.97*	*4.24*	*0.6*	*97.4*	*42*	*62*	*54*

Breakout: 30% Improve: 64% Collapse: 12% Attrition: 14% MLB: 85% *Comparables: Dustin McGowan, Brandon McCarthy, Noah Lowry*

Lorenzen is, in many ways, a valuable asset in relief. He can throw a ton and go multiple innings, as he did in 20 of his 70 appearances last year. He can deal heat and has added more movement since shifting to the bullpen. He gets a ton of groundballs, which is even more valuable the longer he stays in Cincinnati. There's just ... something missing. He misses plenty of bats, but he hasn't been able to take his game to the next level by finding that near-elite strikeout rate seen throughout bullpens all over baseball. He still has time to do it, but relievers are ever-depreciating assets staring down the write-off. Even at his current skill level, Lorenzen and his power sinker can play a useful bullpen role, but his continued inability to take the next step can be frustrating.

Tyler Mahle RHP Born: 09/29/94 Age: 23 Bats: R Throws: R Height: 6'3" Weight: 210 Origin: Round 7, 2013 Draft (#225 overall)

YEAR	TEAM	LVL	AGE	W	L	SV	G	GS	IP	H	HR	BB/9	K/9	K	GB%	BABIP	WHIP	ERA	DRA	WARP	MPH	CMD	PWR	STM
2015	DYT	A	20	13	8	0	27	26	152	145	7	1.5	8.0	135	53%	.313	1.12	2.43	2.16	5.5				
2016	DAY	A+	21	8	3	0	13	13	79^{1}	58	6	1.9	8.6	76	48%	.255	0.95	2.50	2.41	2.8				
2016	PEN	AA	21	6	3	0	14	14	71^{1}	78	12	2.5	8.2	65	42%	.320	1.37	4.92	2.68	2.1				
2017	PEN	AA	22	7	3	0	14	14	85	57	5	1.8	9.2	87	42%	.245	0.87	1.59	1.73	3.5				
2017	LOU	AAA	22	3	4	0	10	10	59^{1}	52	4	2.0	7.7	51	42%	.281	1.10	2.73	2.61	2.0				
2017	CIN	MLB	22	1	2	0	4	4	20	19	0	4.9	6.3	14	56%	.302	1.50	2.70	5.06	0.1	95.5	59	55	70
2018	*CIN*	*MLB*	*23*	*4*	*4*	*0*	*35*	*8*	*71*	*69*	*12*	*3.5*	*8.4*	*67*	*43%*	*.291*	*1.35*	*4.82*	*4.77*	*0.2*	*95.4*	*61*	*57*	*73*
2019	*CIN*	*MLB*	*24*	*6*	*6*	*0*	*63*	*13*	*131^{1}*	*116*	*22*	*3.1*	*9.1*	*133*	*43%*	*.296*	*1.22*	*4.75*	*5.10*	*0.5*	*95.2*	*62*	*57*	*74*

Breakout: 17% Improve: 32% Collapse: 13% Attrition: 22% MLB: 54% *Comparables: Liam Hendriks, Zach Davies, Michael Bowden*

Mahle separated himself from the pack in 2017, starting in Double-A and ending in the major-league rotation. In between, he tossed a perfect game in the minors, gained a couple ticks on his fastball and posted an ERA under 3.00 at all three levels he appeared. Mahle has some work to do, particularly in terms of his command, as nearly five walks per nine won't cut it given his natural stuff. But he went from a fringe prospect at the start of 2017 to an active major-league starter by the end of it, and that's an impressive leap for the pitching-starved Reds.

Deck McGuire RHP Born: 06/23/89 Age: 28 Bats: R Throws: R Height: 6'6" Weight: 220 Origin: Round 1, 2010 Draft (#11 overall)

YEAR	TEAM	LVL	AGE	W	L	SV	G	GS	IP	H	HR	BB/9	K/9	K	GB%	BABIP	WHIP	ERA	DRA	WARP	MPH	CMD	PWR	STM
2015	TUL	AA	26	4	2	1	18	9	71	58	5	2.4	8.4	66	39%	.277	1.08	3.55	2.79	1.9				
2015	OKL	AAA	26	5	4	0	12	9	65^{2}	70	6	2.3	7.3	53	44%	.337	1.32	3.84	3.06	1.6				
2016	MEM	AAA	27	7	11	0	26	26	134	134	22	3.4	7.5	111	39%	.294	1.37	5.10	4.64	1.1				
2017	PEN	AA	28	9	9	0	28	27	168	125	13	3.1	9.1	170	40%	.263	1.08	2.79	2.39	5.6				
2017	CIN	MLB	28	1	1	0	6	2	13^{2}	10	1	1.3	7.2	11	26%	.220	0.88	2.63	3.21	0.3	94.7	57	52	72
2018	*TOR*	*MLB*	*29*	*1*	*1*	*0*	*3*	*3*	*15*	*15*	*3*	*4.0*	*8.4*	*14*	*38%*	*.293*	*1.47*	*5.47*	*5.60*	*-0.1*	*94.0*	*57*	*52*	*72*
2019	*TOR*	*MLB*	*30*	*8*	*12*	*0*	*30*	*30*	*186^{2}*	*181*	*36*	*3.6*	*8.2*	*169*	*38%*	*.301*	*1.37*	*5.51*	*5.94*	*-0.5*	*93.5*	*57*	*52*	*72*

Breakout: 4% Improve: 7% Collapse: 9% Attrition: 15% MLB: 20% *Comparables: Hiram Burgos, Bruce Billings, Chad Reineke*

McGuire is a former 11th overall pick who has been through it all as a professional baseball player. He has been in five different organizations since 2010, having been traded for cash once, cut once and allowed to hit minor-league free agency twice. Last year he started striking batters out without sacrificing too much command, which was enough to finally get him to the majors in September after over 1,000 minor-league innings. If only we could all be so persistent.

Wandy Peralta LHP Born: 07/27/91 Age: 26 Bats: L Throws: L Height: 6'0" Weight: 220 Origin: International Free Agent, 2009

YEAR	TEAM	LVL	AGE	W	L	SV	G	GS	IP	H	HR	BB/9	K/9	K	GB%	BABIP	WHIP	ERA	DRA	WARP	MPH	CMD	PWR	STM
2015	PEN	AA	23	7	7	0	29	20	116^{2}	129	7	4.6	6.2	80	49%	.330	1.62	5.09	8.09	-4.3				
2016	PEN	AA	24	0	1	0	13	0	17^{2}	17	1	1.5	10.2	20	50%	.327	1.13	3.06	2.85	0.4				
2016	LOU	AAA	24	4	1	3	37	2	58	44	2	3.6	5.9	38	61%	.249	1.16	2.33	4.61	0.3				
2016	CIN	MLB	24	0	0	0	10	0	7^{1}	11	1	8.6	6.1	5	46%	.400	2.45	8.59	6.53	-0.1	97.5			51
2017	CIN	MLB	25	3	4	0	69	0	64^{2}	53	8	3.3	7.9	57	56%	.260	1.19	3.76	4.58	0.4	98.0	38	60	49
2018	*CIN*	*MLB*	*26*	*3*	*3*	*2*	*54*	*0*	*57*	*55*	*7*	*4.2*	*8.1*	*51*	*51%*	*.295*	*1.42*	*4.52*	*4.45*	*0.3*	*97.6*	*39*	*61*	*51*
2019	*CIN*	*MLB*	*27*	*2*	*1*	*1*	*45*	*0*	*47^{1}*	*42*	*6*	*4.0*	*8.5*	*45*	*51%*	*.303*	*1.32*	*4.49*	*4.82*	*0.2*	*97.3*	*39*	*61*	*51*

Breakout: 40% Improve: 53% Collapse: 12% Attrition: 35% MLB: 70% *Comparables: Ryan Pressly, Ryan Tucker, Jim Johnson*

On the surface, there wasn't anything special about Peralta's first full season in the majors. He induced a ton of groundballs, but combined that with pedestrian true-outcome rates and a fine but unspectacular ERA. In a Reds bullpen with other intriguing, young arms, Peralta was easy to miss, but he's setting himself up to surprise people in his second full season. Despite the mediocre strikeout rate, Peralta had one of the highest swinging strike rates in baseball, finishing the year between Felipe Rivero and Brad Hand. A lefty with a power sinker, two strong secondaries, the ability to miss bats and induce groundballs? If he can find a way to hone his command just a tad, Rodriguez won't be the first Wandy you think of for much longer.

Cody Reed LHP Born: 04/15/93 Age: 25 Bats: L Throws: L Height: 6'5" Weight: 228 Origin: Round 2, 2013 Draft (#46 overall)

YEAR	TEAM	LVL	AGE	W	L	SV	G	GS	IP	H	HR	BB/9	K/9	K	GB%	BABIP	WHIP	ERA	DRA	WARP	MPH	CMD	PWR	STM
2015	WIL	A+	22	5	5	1	13	10	67^{1}	62	3	2.4	8.7	65	46%	.309	1.19	2.14	2.73	1.9				
2015	NWA	AA	22	2	2	0	5	5	28^{2}	26	3	2.5	6.0	19	45%	.258	1.19	3.45	4.75	0.1				
2015	PEN	AA	22	6	2	0	8	8	49^{2}	39	1	2.9	10.9	60	50%	.311	1.11	2.17	1.79	2.0				
2016	CIN	MLB	23	0	7	0	10	10	47^{2}	67	12	3.6	8.1	43	54%	.364	1.80	7.36	5.31	0.0	95.8	47	50	59
2016	LOU	AAA	23	6	4	0	13	13	73	71	6	2.5	8.0	65	52%	.314	1.25	3.08	1.96	2.8				
2017	LOU	AAA	24	4	9	0	21	20	106^{1}	105	7	5.2	8.6	102	50%	.328	1.56	3.55	5.16	0.6				
2017	CIN	MLB	24	1	1	1	12	1	17^{2}	11	3	9.7	8.7	17	65%	.200	1.70	5.09	5.49	-0.1	96.2	36	53	59
2018	*CIN*	*MLB*	*25*	*3*	*3*	*0*	*33*	*6*	*58*	*55*	*8*	*4.4*	*9.3*	*61*	*48%*	*.302*	*1.45*	*4.57*	*4.55*	*0.3*	*95.6*	*45*	*52*	*60*
2019	*CIN*	*MLB*	*26*	*6*	*5*	*0*	*70*	*11*	*127^{2}*	*112*	*16*	*3.8*	*9.6*	*136*	*48%*	*.315*	*1.30*	*4.40*	*4.73*	*0.9*	*95.4*	*44*	*52*	*61*

Breakout: 33% Improve: 54% Collapse: 19% Attrition: 49% MLB: 86% *Comparables: T.J. House, Blake Wood, Bobby Parnell*

Reed is the perfect reminder of how hard it is to pitch in the major leagues and how important it is to throw strikes. It sounds obvious, and it is, but we've seen many talented pitchers flame out in the majors because they couldn't get the ball over the plate on a consistent basis. For the second straight year, Reed's command kept him from reaching his potential in the majors, with his control issues carrying over to Triple-A in 2017. There's too much talent here to give up on, but a major adjustment is needed if Reed is going to become the mid-rotation pitcher that's in there somewhere.

Sal Romano RHP Born: 10/12/93 Age: 24 Bats: L Throws: R Height: 6'5" Weight: 270 Origin: Round 23, 2011 Draft (#715 overall)

YEAR	TEAM	LVL	AGE	W	L	SV	G	GS	IP	H	HR	BB/9	K/9	K	GB%	BABIP	WHIP	ERA	DRA	WARP	MPH	CMD	PWR	STM
2015	DAY	A+	21	6	5	0	19	18	104	103	2	2.9	6.8	79	59%	.318	1.31	3.46	3.42	2.1				
2015	PEN	AA	21	0	4	0	7	7	23	35	4	4.7	3.5	9	47%	.348	2.04	10.96	8.82	-1.0				
2016	PEN	AA	22	6	11	0	27	27	156	157	10	2.0	8.3	144	49%	.320	1.22	3.52	2.42	5.0				
2017	LOU	AAA	23	1	4	0	10	10	49^1	49	1	3.1	5.8	32	50%	.298	1.34	3.47	4.93	0.4				
2017	CIN	MLB	23	5	8	0	16	16	87	91	9	3.8	7.6	73	53%	.314	1.47	4.45	5.86	-0.3	97.1	57	65	60
2018	*CIN*	*MLB*	*24*	*7*	*8*	*0*	*23*	*23*	*121*	*125*	*16*	*3.5*	*7.9*	*106*	*48%*	*.303*	*1.43*	*4.35*	*4.38*	*1.1*	*96.9*	*59*	*67*	*62*
2019	*CIN*	*MLB*	*25*	*10*	*11*	*0*	*32*	*32*	*203^1*	*185*	*24*	*3.2*	*8.5*	*192*	*48%*	*.309*	*1.27*	*4.28*	*4.59*	*1.9*	*96.7*	*59*	*67*	*62*

Breakout: 25% Improve: 47% Collapse: 10% Attrition: 33% MLB: 69% *Comparables: Felipe Rivero, Jeanmar Gomez, Trevor Bell*

We constantly joke about this being the era where you can find a 95-and-a-slider pitcher under the cushions of your couch. And while Romano has a frame that's not conducive to being inconspicuous behind that holiday-themed throw pillow, he's more of a quarter than your typical nickel or penny. The Long Island native showed in 2017 that when pressed into a starting role he had enough of a change to hold his own—though the magic faded by the end of the season as Romano threw 34 changeups in September to left-handed batters and got exactly zero swings-and-misses. Without a reliable third pitch, it will be tough for Romano be more than a starter in a pinch, but as a reliever, he could be a late-inning option without needing to rely on more than just his high-octane fastball and nasty slider. Fortunately for him, Romano will likely get plenty of leash in 2018 to prove he can work through his issues to remain in the rotation long-term.

Antonio Santillan RHP Born: 04/15/97 Age: 21 Bats: R Throws: R Height: 6'3" Weight: 240 Origin: Round 2, 2015 Draft (#49 overall)

YEAR	TEAM	LVL	AGE	W	L	SV	G	GS	IP	H	HR	BB/9	K/9	K	GB%	BABIP	WHIP	ERA	DRA	WARP	MPH	CMD	PWR	STM
2015	CIN	RK	18	0	2	0	8	7	19^2	15	1	5.0	8.7	19	40%	.275	1.32	5.03	5.39	0.1				
2016	BIL	RK	19	1	0	0	8	8	39	32	4	3.7	10.6	46	46%	.292	1.23	3.92	2.51	1.4				
2016	DYT	A	19	2	3	0	7	7	30^1	27	3	7.1	11.3	38	38%	.338	1.68	6.82	3.99	0.4				
2017	DYT	A	20	9	8	0	25	24	128	104	9	3.9	9.0	128	45%	.281	1.25	3.38	3.61	2.5				
2018	*CIN*	*MLB*	*21*	*5*	*8*	*0*	*21*	*21*	*94^2*	*94*	*22*	*6.1*	*10.1*	*106*	*36%*	*.313*	*1.67*	*6.19*	*6.77*	*-1.2*				
2019	*CIN*	*MLB*	*22*	*4*	*9*	*0*	*21*	*21*	*121^1*	*118*	*29*	*5.4*	*9.9*	*133*	*36%*	*.314*	*1.57*	*6.34*	*6.92*	*-1.4*				

Breakout: 2% Improve: 4% Collapse: 0% Attrition: 5% MLB: 6% *Comparables: Matt Magill, Dan Cortes, Vincent Velasquez*

Santillan and his power fastball/curveball combination acclimated well to his first full season as a professional, and we saw a lot of what makes him one of the more intriguing pitching prospects in the game. There are enough flaws and rawness in his game that he's far from an elite prospect, but with his big body that's now synonymous with Texan righties and his potentially elite fastball, he's racking up strikeouts at every level. His command falls into the "can get lower-level hitters out" bucket, and he'll have to start honing it more as he works his way up. There are still question marks around his future, but Santillan is one to start following now, because there's real potential for him to take off in 2018.

Kevin Shackelford RHP Born: 04/07/89 Age: 29 Bats: R Throws: R Height: 6'5" Weight: 210 Origin: Round 21, 2010 Draft (#639 overall)

YEAR	TEAM	LVL	AGE	W	L	SV	G	GS	IP	H	HR	BB/9	K/9	K	GB%	BABIP	WHIP	ERA	DRA	WARP	MPH	CMD	PWR	STM
2015	PEN	AA	26	2	4	3	35	0	38^2	45	1	4.0	5.8	25	68%	.341	1.60	3.72	6.49	-0.8				
2016	PEN	AA	27	1	0	0	10	0	13	11	1	2.8	7.6	11	47%	.270	1.15	1.38	4.29	0.1				
2016	LOU	AAA	27	1	2	8	25	0	31^1	25	1	3.7	5.7	20	55%	.250	1.21	2.30	7.06	-0.8				
2017	LOU	AAA	28	3	1	12	35	0	47	33	2	3.4	11.7	61	50%	.282	1.09	1.53	2.29	1.5				
2017	CIN	MLB	28	0	0	0	26	0	30^2	30	6	3.8	11.2	38	58%	.320	1.40	4.70	3.87	0.4	96.2	41	59	51
2018	*CIN*	*MLB*	*29*	*3*	*3*	*0*	*54*	*0*	*57*	*57*	*9*	*4.4*	*8.7*	*55*	*51%*	*.302*	*1.49*	*5.09*	*4.89*	*0.0*	*95.5*	*41*	*59*	*51*
2019	*CIN*	*MLB*	*30*	*2*	*1*	*0*	*42*	*0*	*45*	*41*	*6*	*3.9*	*8.6*	*43*	*51%*	*.309*	*1.35*	*4.81*	*5.17*	*0.0*	*94.9*	*41*	*59*	*51*

Breakout: 13% Improve: 15% Collapse: 16% Attrition: 22% MLB: 34% *Comparables: Ross Wolf, Mike Ekstrom, Jon Link*

Shackelford is one of the best obscure stories in baseball. The former Brewers 21st-round pick did a lot of nothing in their farm system before being sent to Cincinnati as a throw-in for Jonathan Broxton. He continued to do more of the same in the Reds' system, getting plenty of groundballs with his sinking fastball but not much else. Last year he started dominating Triple-A competition, striking out almost 12 batters per nine innings—a more than 50 percent increase over his previous career-high—all while maintaining the ground-ball rate. He finally got his first call to the majors, and eventually earned high-leverage spots toward the end of the year. With a high-velocity sinker and a slider that induced whiffs on over half the swings it saw, Shackelford isn't a blip on the radar. We may have missed the story as it was unfolding, but he'll stick around long enough for us to all discuss and appreciate his rapid ascension.

Robert Stephenson RHP Born: 02/24/93 Age: 25 Bats: R Throws: R Height: 6'2" Weight: 200 Origin: Round 1, 2011 Draft (#27 overall)

YEAR	TEAM	LVL	AGE	W	L	SV	G	GS	IP	H	HR	BB/9	K/9	K	GB%	BABIP	WHIP	ERA	DRA	WARP	MPH	CMD	PWR	STM
2015	PEN	AA	22	4	7	0	14	14	78^1	53	8	4.9	10.2	89	39%	.249	1.23	3.68	3.25	1.7				
2015	LOU	AAA	22	4	4	0	11	11	55^2	51	2	4.4	8.2	51	41%	.306	1.40	4.04	6.32	-0.6				
2016	LOU	AAA	23	8	9	0	24	24	136^2	115	17	4.7	7.9	120	42%	.259	1.36	4.41	8.76	-5.3				
2016	CIN	MLB	23	2	3	0	8	8	37	41	9	4.6	7.5	31	35%	.299	1.62	6.08	5.39	0.0	95.7	37	53	74
2017	LOU	AAA	24	1	2	0	8	7	40^1	27	8	2.9	10.0	45	40%	.200	0.99	3.79	2.52	1.4				
2017	CIN	MLB	24	5	6	1	25	11	84^2	81	12	5.6	9.1	86	41%	.300	1.58	4.68	5.61	-0.2	96.0	44	53	58
2018	*CIN*	*MLB*	*25*	*6*	*8*	*0*	*23*	*23*	*115*	*105*	*19*	*4.5*	*9.5*	*121*	*40%*	*.287*	*1.40*	*4.79*	*4.88*	*0.4*	*95.6*	*43*	*54*	*67*
2019	*CIN*	*MLB*	*26*	*9*	*11*	*0*	*32*	*32*	*203*	*165*	*30*	*4.0*	*10.0*	*225*	*40%*	*.288*	*1.25*	*4.57*	*4.92*	*1.2*	*95.4*	*43*	*54*	*67*

Breakout: 33% Improve: 50% Collapse: 23% Attrition: 46% MLB: 81% *Comparables: Boof Bonser, Radhames Liz, Matt Boyd*

If there were ever a player on whom you would bet being a late-bloomer, it'd be Stephenson. The former first-round pick has been in the Reds organization since 2012 and has consistently shown some of the best stuff in the minors. Even in his major-league auditions it's clear that he can miss bats at the highest level. Unfortunately, one thing that isn't clear is whether he can hit the strike zone on a consistent basis. The hope was that an increased focus on his secondaries would help him keep his walks under control, but he threw fewer fastballs than ever in 2017 and still walked more than six batters per nine innings. He had more problems out of the bullpen: In 26 2/3 relief innings, hitters crushed him to the tune of a .303/.398/.578 line. The stuff is still too much to give up on though, and Stephenson will get an almost infinite number of chances to fail.

Drew Storen RHP Born: 08/11/87 Age: 30 Bats: B Throws: R Height: 6'1" Weight: 195 Origin: Round 1, 2009 Draft (#10 overall)

YEAR	TEAM	LVL	AGE	W	L	SV	G	GS	IP	H	HR	BB/9	K/9	K	GB%	BABIP	WHIP	ERA	DRA	WARP	MPH	CMD	PWR	STM
2015	WAS	MLB	27	2	2	29	58	0	55	45	4	2.6	11.0	67	44%	.301	1.11	3.44	2.70	1.3	96.3	61	48	48
2016	TOR	MLB	28	1	3	3	38	0	33^1	43	6	2.7	8.6	32	48%	.363	1.59	6.21	4.02	0.4	94.1	53	37	43
2016	SEA	MLB	28	3	0	0	19	0	18^1	13	1	1.5	7.9	16	54%	.235	0.87	3.44	4.71	0.1	94.0	53	37	43
2017	CIN	MLB	29	4	2	1	58	0	54^2	57	7	3.8	7.9	48	49%	.316	1.46	4.45	4.22	0.6	91.8	51	25	49
2018	*CIN*	*MLB*	*30*	*2*	*1*	*1*	*46*	*0*	*48^2*	*44*	*7*	*3.7*	*9.3*	*50*	*47%*	*.305*	*1.33*	*4.49*	*4.84*	*0.2*	*92.9*	*54*	*34*	*47*
2019	*CIN*	*MLB*	*31*	*2*	*1*	*1*	*45*	*0*	*41^1*	*37*	*6*	*3.9*	*8.8*	*41*	*47%*	*.305*	*1.34*	*4.91*	*5.27*	*0.0*	*92.0*	*52*	*31*	*46*

Breakout: 30% Improve: 47% Collapse: 23% Attrition: 10% MLB: 86% *Comparables: Juan Rincon, Andrew Bailey, Joakim Soria*

For Storen, there was but one bright moment in 2017: On June 23 he returned to his old stomping grounds in Washington with boos raining down on him and retired the only batter he faced, Anthony Rendon. It was wonderful for the veteran righty to get that bit of closure against a city that has come to hate him, despite his 3.02 ERA over six seasons with the Nationals. Other than that, the year was a disaster. His fastball lost a few ticks, his strikeouts dropped, his walk rate rose and he continued to allow home runs. Finally, as the overripe cherry on top of a horrible year, he tore his UCL and will likely miss the entire 2018 season after undergoing Tommy John surgery. Fortunately, while he spends the next year resting and rehabbing, he'll be able to look back on those four magical pitches on that Friday evening against his former team and smile.

Asher Wojciechowski RHP Born: 12/21/88 Age: 29 Bats: R Throws: R Height: 6'4" Weight: 235 Origin: Round 1, 2010 Draft (#41 overall)

YEAR	TEAM	LVL	AGE	W	L	SV	G	GS	IP	H	HR	BB/9	K/9	K	GB%	BABIP	WHIP	ERA	DRA	WARP	MPH	CMD	PWR	STM
2015	HOU	MLB	26	0	1	0	5	3	16^1	23	2	3.9	8.8	16	21%	.389	1.84	7.16	7.46	-0.5	93.5	46	43	62
2015	FRE	AAA	26	8	4	0	20	20	115^1	129	13	3.2	6.8	87	38%	.319	1.47	4.92	4.75	0.7				
2016	FRE	AAA	27	2	2	0	5	5	25^1	29	1	4.6	7.8	22	22%	.341	1.66	5.33	10.67	-1.6				
2016	JAX	AA	27	1	0	0	2	2	10^2	9	0	0.8	7.6	9	25%	.281	0.94	2.53	3.90	0.2				
2016	NWO	AAA	27	2	3	0	13	10	49^2	61	10	4.3	5.8	32	40%	.315	1.71	5.26	9.55	-2.4				
2017	LOU	AAA	28	2	0	0	8	5	30^2	24	2	2.3	10.3	35	28%	.275	1.04	2.05	3.30	0.8				
2017	CIN	MLB	28	4	3	0	25	8	62^1	71	14	2.7	9.2	64	32%	.324	1.44	6.50	5.19	0.1	93.8	63	46	50
2018	*BAL*	*MLB*	*29*	*1*	*1*	*0*	*2*	*2*	*10*	*11*	*2*	*3.9*	*8.1*	*9*	*34%*	*.294*	*1.51*	*5.73*	*5.87*	*-0.1*	*93.1*	*61*	*46*	*54*
2019	*BAL*	*MLB*	*30*	*7*	*12*	*0*	*29*	*29*	*180*	*184*	*39*	*3.5*	*8.0*	*159*	*34%*	*.307*	*1.41*	*5.85*	*6.31*	*-1.1*	*92.9*	*62*	*46*	*52*

Breakout: 14% Improve: 22% Collapse: 12% Attrition: 27% MLB: 42% *Comparables: Everett Teaford, Seth Etherton, Andrew Albers*

Wojciechowski has lived a fascinating life, spending parts of his childhood in Florida, Michigan and the Dominican Republic. He also spent a large chunk of his younger years in Romania, which is where he learned to play baseball. Those circumstances are even more unique because there has never been a major-league pitcher born in the eastern European country. And it's a good thing he's unique off the field because, well, on the mound there isn't much separating him from a hundred other arms you won't remember in three years. Like Tostitos salsa his heat is mild and unimpressive, leading to mundane strikeout and walk rates and too many home runs. Other than his cosmopolitan background and the fact he shares a surname with our favorite labor lawyer, Wojciechowski is about what you'd expect from every other middling pitcher in 2017.

Lineouts

Hitters

HITTER	POS	TEAM	LVL	AGE	PA	R	2B	3B	HR	RBI	BB	K	SB	CS	AVG/OBP/SLG	TAv	VORP	BABIP	BRR	FRAA	WARP
Jeter Downs	SS	BIL	Rk	18	209	31	3	3	6	29	27	32	8	5	.267/.370/.424	.269	11.0	.288	-1.5	SS(50): -4.5	0.6
Tyler Goeddel	OF	PEN	AA	24	256	30	15	1	5	21	33	44	9	3	.243/.367/.393	.280	11.6	.285	0.8	LF(50): 0.0, CF(15): -0.7	1.2
	OF	LOU	AAA	24	214	23	9	2	1	15	19	40	7	2	.277/.352/.361	.256	6.0	.347	1.3	CF(24): -1.9, LF(20): 2.8	0.6
Shedric Long	2B	DAY	A+	21	279	37	16	1	13	36	27	63	6	3	.312/.380/.543	.313	21.3	.368	-1.1	2B(62): 5.4	2.8
	2B	PEN	AA	21	160	13	6	2	3	14	19	31	3	1	.227/.319/.362	.261	1.8	.271	-2.4	2B(39): -1.7	0.0
Chris Okey	C	DAY	A+	22	363	27	10	1	3	28	32	104	2	1	.185/.265/.249	.195	-11.3	.260	-1.5	C(82): -0.9, LF(1): 0.0	-1.3
D.J. Peterson	1B	TAC	AAA	25	421	47	17	2	12	54	32	75	6	2	.264/.323/.414	.254	6.4	.298	0.7	1B(51): -0.4, 3B(43): -1.6	0.4
	1B	CHR	AAA	25	97	9	2	0	4	9	10	21	0	0	.198/.281/.360	.213	-2.1	.213	0.0	3B(22): -0.1, 1B(1): 0.0	-0.2
Alfredo Rodriguez	SS	DAY	A+	23	516	52	14	0	2	36	25	79	11	9	.253/.294/.294	.218	-3.1	.297	-1.1	SS(115): 11.1	0.9
Tyler Stephenson	C	DYT	A	20	348	39	22	0	6	50	44	58	2	1	.278/.374/.414	.290	19.8	.322	-2.6	C(53): -3.9	1.7
Stuart Turner	C	LOU	AAA	25	64	2	0	0	0	3	3	14	0	1	.237/.297/.237	.187	-3.8	.311	-0.9	C(11): -3.7	-0.7
	C	CIN	MLB	25	89	4	3	0	2	7	5	22	0	0	.134/.182/.244	.140	-6.8	.153	0.5	C(28): -2.6	-0.9
Scott Van Slyke	LF	LAN	MLB	30	48	6	1	0	2	3	7	15	1	0	.122/.250/.293	.217	-0.6	.125	0.6	LF(11): -0.8, 1B(9): 0.6	-0.1
	LF	OKL	AAA	30	209	30	12	0	5	20	19	54	1	1	.242/.332/.390	.262	2.1	.315	-1.1	1B(38): -0.1, RF(5): 0.1	0.2
	LF	LOU	AAA	30	57	5	3	0	1	3	7	12	2	0	.146/.263/.271	.197	-3.0	.167	0.4	1B(13): 0.4	-0.3

The Reds' second-round pick, **Jeter Downs** will look back fondly at how things turned out if he can put together a career comparable to his namesake's down years. ⚾ After struggling in his first major-league season, **Tyler Goeddel** returned to the minors and failed to pick up where he left off, instead putting up a performance better suited for the NFL commissioner who shares his name's pronunciation. ⚾ **Shedric Long** looks to be a major success story in the

12th round with strong bat-to-ball skills and enough tools to stick long-term at second base. He just needs to clear one last hurdle in the high-minors. **Chris Okey**, a 2016 second-round pick, struggled in an aggressive placement immediately after being drafted, and continued to struggle in 2017 as the Reds continued to push him through the system. He might be Okey if they slow his development. **D.J. Peterson's** name isn't cool enough for an actual disc jockey and his bat probably isn't good enough to be a major-league regular. **Alfredo Rodriguez** was signed to a massive contract out of Cuba, and while it's not the worst international amateur free agent deal in recent memory, that this even needs to be clarified should tell you how it's worked out thus far. **Tyler Stephenson**, a former 11th overall pick, can't catch a break. He was finally starting to hit for the first time in his minor-league career, but then his 2017 was cut short by a thumb injury. Another injury to Devin Mesoraco allowed **Stuart Turner** to stick as a Rule 5 pick despite being the third-worst hitter in baseball among those receiving at least 80 plate appearances. **Scott Van Slyke** continued his slide from lefty-masher to irrelevance, and after a midseason trade to Cincinnati he couldn't even muster a chance on the major-league roster of one of the worst teams in baseball.

Pitchers

PITCHER	TEAM	LVL	AGE	W	L	SV	G	GS	IP	H	HR	BB/9	K/9	K	GB%	BABIP	WHIP	ERA	DRA	WARP	MPH	CMD	PWR	STM
Barrett Astin	CIN	MLB	25	0	0	0	6	0	8	9	2	7.9	2.2	2	63%	.250	2.00	6.75	7.01	-0.2	93.6			42
	LOU	AAA	25	3	4	0	26	3	48^{2}	71	4	4.1	8.1	44	46%	.411	1.91	6.10	7.85	-1.3				
Alejandro Chacin	LOU	AAA	24	0	3	1	44	0	69^{1}	63	4	3.5	8.2	63	45%	.292	1.30	2.60	3.65	1.2				
	CIN	MLB	24	0	0	0	6	0	6	11	2	6.0	9.0	6	36%	.450	2.50	10.50	4.99	0.0	89.7			51
Kyle Crockett	COH	AAA	25	5	5	4	51	0	48	42	2	2.1	9.2	49	59%	.305	1.10	3.38	0.93	2.3				
	CLE	MLB	25	0	0	0	4	0	1^{2}	4	0	5.4	10.8	2	57%	.571	3.00	10.80	10.54	-0.1	90.4			46
Jumbo Diaz	TBA	MLB	33	1	4	0	31	0	30	32	4	4.5	8.4	28	36%	.315	1.57	5.70	3.66	0.5	98.5	46	59	40
	FRE	AAA	33	1	0	3	12	0	12^{1}	11	1	3.6	8.0	11	42%	.286	1.30	2.92	5.78	-0.1				
Scott Feldman	CIN	MLB	34	7	7	0	21	21	111^{1}	116	21	2.8	7.5	93	46%	.300	1.36	4.77	5.05	0.6	91.2	67	35	58
Jacob Heatherly	CIN	Rk	19	2	1	0	9	6	30^{2}	26	3	4.7	7.6	26	59%	.261	1.37	2.93	4.57	0.4				
Jimmy Herget	PEN	AA	23	1	3	16	24	0	29^{2}	22	1	3.6	13.3	44	32%	.323	1.15	2.73	1.88	1.0				
	LOU	AAA	23	3	1	9	28	0	32^{1}	30	4	2.5	7.8	28	38%	.283	1.21	3.06	3.14	0.8				
Jose Lopez	DAY	A+	23	2	4	0	9	9	50^{2}	50	3	2.5	8.5	48	47%	.329	1.26	2.84	3.08	1.3				
	PEN	AA	23	7	2	0	17	15	96^{1}	64	9	3.3	8.9	95	44%	.231	1.03	2.43	2.55	3.0				
Keury Mella	PEN	AA	23	4	10	1	27	26	134	135	14	2.9	7.3	109	47%	.300	1.33	4.30	4.65	0.8				
	CIN	MLB	23	0	0	0	2	0	4	5	1	4.5	2.2	1	31%	.267	1.75	6.75	10.04	-0.2	97.4			61
Tanner Rainey	DAY	A+	24	2	2	9	39	0	45	21	4	4.4	15.4	77	47%	.230	0.96	3.80	1.16	2.0				
	PEN	AA	24	1	1	4	14	0	17	8	2	5.8	14.3	27	62%	.222	1.12	1.59	3.16	0.3				
Jesus Reyes	DAY	A+	24	6	5	0	15	15	85^{2}	80	8	2.8	7.0	67	60%	.290	1.25	3.78	2.31	3.0				
	PEN	AA	24	2	4	0	10	10	51^{2}	55	3	3.5	7.7	44	68%	.344	1.45	3.31	2.91	1.4				
Josh Smith	OAK	MLB	29	2	1	0	26	0	35	35	3	3.9	6.4	25	46%	.296	1.43	4.89	4.04	0.4	93.1	51	35	50
	NAS	AAA	29	4	1	1	19	2	41^{1}	33	4	2.4	9.6	44	35%	.276	1.06	3.70	3.49	0.8				
Jackson Stephens	LOU	AAA	23	7	10	0	26	25	139	156	16	3.3	7.1	110	45%	.321	1.49	4.92	5.66	0.1				
	CIN	MLB	23	2	1	0	7	4	25	19	6	3.2	7.6	21	36%	.203	1.12	4.68	5.78	-0.1	95.3	55	50	72
Zachary Weiss	DAY	A+	25	2	1	1	10	0	13	8	1	1.4	13.2	19	41%	.269	0.77	2.08	1.77	0.5				
	PEN	AA	25	2	4	9	24	0	28	22	2	3.5	11.9	37	49%	.294	1.18	2.89	2.60	0.7				

Barrett Astin, who is still not a brand of luxury yachts, made Cincinnati's Opening Day roster and pitched four scoreless outings before two consecutive three-run drubbings resulted in a permanent vacation to Louisville and an eventual DFA in September. **Alejandro Chacin** utilizes a three-quarters arm slot to help overshadow his lack of dominant stuff out of the bullpen, but no arm slot will be enough to give him a long career without an improvement in either stuff or command. **Kyle Crockett** grew up to be an honest-to-goodness major-league pitcher and last year ended his season, and perhaps his big-league career, by striking out Efren Navarro; truly, that's one heck of an accomplishment (the growing up to pitch in the majors part, not the striking out Efren Navarro part). Instead of building off his strong 2016, **Anthony DeSclafani** felt elbow discomfort at the start of spring training and ended up missing almost the entire season. "The bigger they are, the harder they fall." Hefty (and well-nicknamed) righty **Jumbo Diaz** saw his peripherals fall hard in half a season with Tampa Bay, and by the end of 2017 he was in a familiar position: closing in a Triple-A bullpen. **Scott Feldman** has made a career of finding his way into the back of rotations around the league, but after losing his ability to keep the ball on the ground it could prove challenging to find yet another back of the rotation in which to roam. **Jacob Heatherly** started his 2017 with a decent chance of being a first-round pick, but some slight regression led the southpaw to fall into Cincinnati's lap in the third round. **Jimmy Herget** pairs a funky delivery that gives his pitches huge movement with the mustache you tried to grow when you got your fake ID, and that's been enough to lead him to the cusp of a major-league debut. The Reds had to wait for **Jose Lopez**, who was recovering from Tommy John when they drafted him, but he's been worth it and is now climbing through the ranks thanks to a strong repertoire and a deceptive delivery. **Keury Mella** had another lackluster year in the minors in 2017, and it's only a matter of time until he's converted to a full-time reliever. The Reds decided to put **Tanner Rainey**, a former college closer, back in the bullpen in 2017 and the righty rewarded them with absurd strikeout numbers in short stints that better hid his lack of control. As an oldish starting pitcher prospect without crazy stuff, **Jesus Reyes** needs to be on point with his command at all times to succeed. Unfortunately for Reds fans, his stint in Double-A revealed that Jesus walks. Andrew McCutchen, Anthony Rizzo and Kris Bryant are a combined 1-for-22 against **Josh Smith**, who unfortunately struggles against mere mortals. **Jackson Stephens** continued doing just enough to get by in 2017, eventually leading to his first major-league call-up, where once again he did just enough to get by. A former first round pick who has yet to pitch above Double-A, **Nick Travieso** can't miss bats, has seen a downturn in command, missed all of 2017 with injury and was outrighted off the 40-man after the season. Other than that, things are going great. **Zack Weiss** looked like exactly what the Reds needed: a reliever who could strike batters out and avoid walks. Then his arm got sore, he missed two years of development and the Reds missed him in turn. An encouraging second half earned him a 40-man roster spot.

LEAGUE LEADERS 2017

MLB Walk Rate – Joey Votto, 18.95%

MLB On-Base Percentage – Joey Votto, .454

MLB Catcher Throwing Runs - Tucker Barnhart, 4.6

CLEVELAND INDIANS

Essay by Travis Sawchik

Player comments by Ken Funck and BP staff

There is a Catch-22 when it comes to small markets and starting pitching. To compete without quality, cost-controlled starting pitching is nearly impossible, but acquiring it is difficult and no type of player carries more inherent risk than a pitching prospect.

For instance, the Cubs followed something of an NBA-tanking model and used their premium draft picks on "safer" position players. They filled in pitching holes with expensive free agents like Jon Lester and John Lackey en route to a World Series title. Small-market teams cannot follow such a model. The Pirates made a historic commitment to pitching in the 2009-2011 drafts, handing out over-slot bonuses to projectable arms and taking pitchers with 22 of their top 30 selections in the first 10 rounds. It's had mixed results, as only two of those pitchers—Gerrit Cole (first overall pick in 2011) and Jameson Taillon (second overall pick in 2010)—stuck in the rotation.

With player evaluation becoming more a science than an art, with performance projections and dollar-per-win estimates in the public sphere often very much in line with teams' own valuations and with all teams having the access to the player- and pitch-tracking data, it's become more difficult to identify value in the free agent and trade markets. This makes the rotation and success of the small-market Cleveland Indians so fascinating.

The Indians have developed one of the game's best starting staffs. It performed at a historic level last season, ranking 15th all-time in single-season rotation WAR (23.1), according to FanGraphs' leaderboards. The staff propelled them to two straight division titles, as well as an AL-record winning streak and the best record in the league last season. It's a starting staff that led the majors in WAR and surplus value. It's a staff that was put together without requiring one first-round pick or significant free agent contract be expended on a starting pitcher. It's a staff that stands a good chance of allowing the Indians to compete into the next decade as perhaps the lone small-market power for the foreseeable future in a landscape dominated more and more by large-market super teams.

The Indians' entire starting rotation is controlled through at least 2020. The starting five are projected to produce $336 million in surplus value over the next three seasons, according to FanGraphs' surplus calculator. What the Indians have built has been remarkable and the process is something others—like former lieutenant Derek Falvey, now in Minnesota—are undoubtedly trying to recreate. How did the Indians do it?

Riding the Wave

Late last season, reporting for *The Athletic*, I approached Corey Kluber in a quiet, mostly empty Profession Field clubhouse to understand what he was up to. Kluber was in the midst of an incredible strikeout binge.

His stuff hadn't really changed. His velocity was stable, as was the movement on his wipeout breaking ball. But he was pitching differently. He had never thrown his signature breaking ball more

INDIANS PROSPECTUS

2017 W-L: 102-60, 1st in AL Central

Pythag	.665	1st	B-Age	28.1	*12th*
RS/G	5.05	6th	P-Age	28.9	*20th*
RA/G	3.48	1st	Salary	$124.1M	*18th*
TAv	.269	11th	M$/MW	$2.0M	*27th*
TAv-P	.230	1st	DL Days	705	*7th*
FIP	3.30	1st	$ on DL	13%	*12th*
DER	.696	24th			

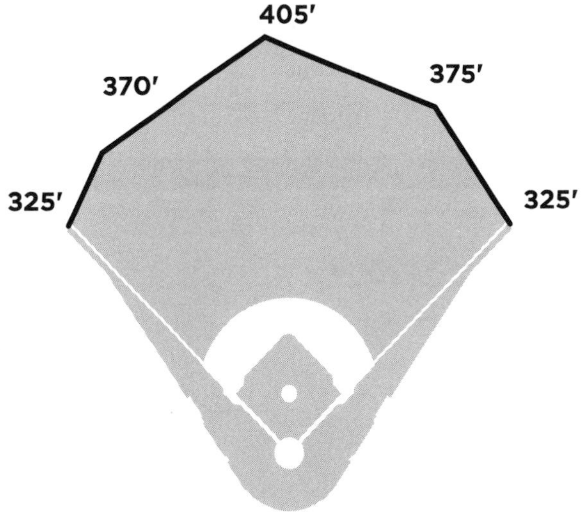

Outfield wall profile: **9'** to **19'**

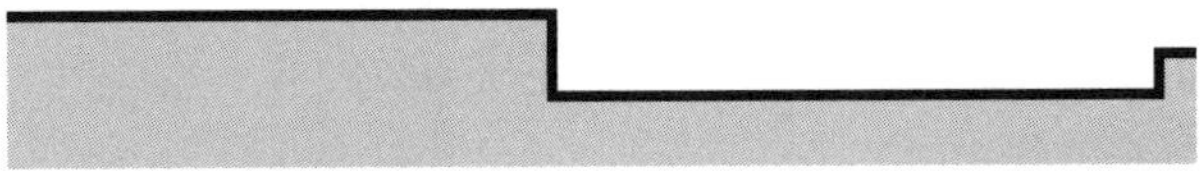

Three-Year Park Factors

Runs	Runs/RH	Runs/LH	HR/RH	HR/LH
106	101	111	99	105

Top Hitter WARP	6.3 Jose Ramirez
Top Pitcher WARP	8.0 Corey Kluber
Top Prospect	Francisco Mejia

2017 Hit List Ranking

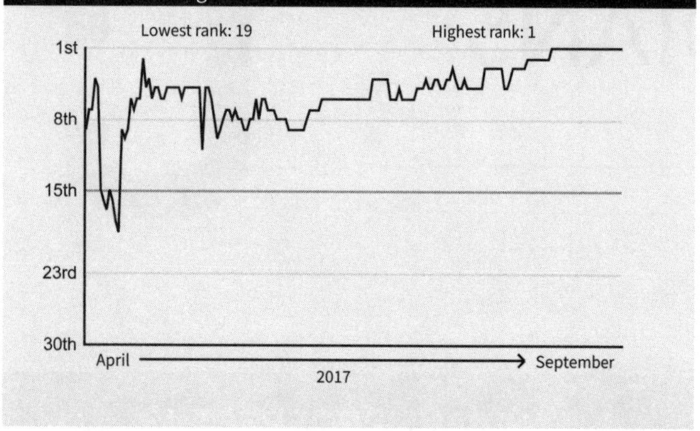

Committed Payroll (in millions)

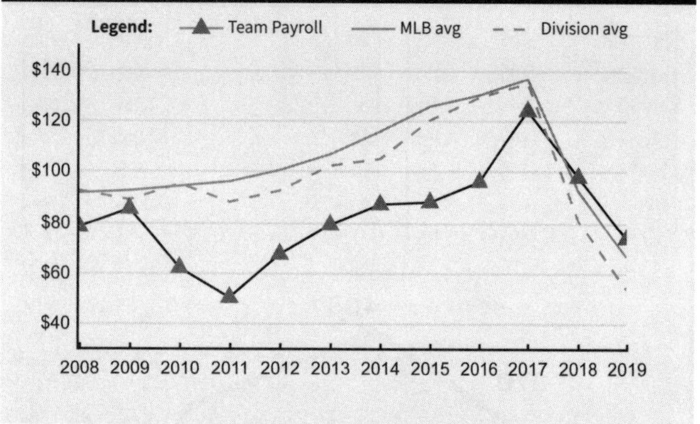

Farm System Ranking

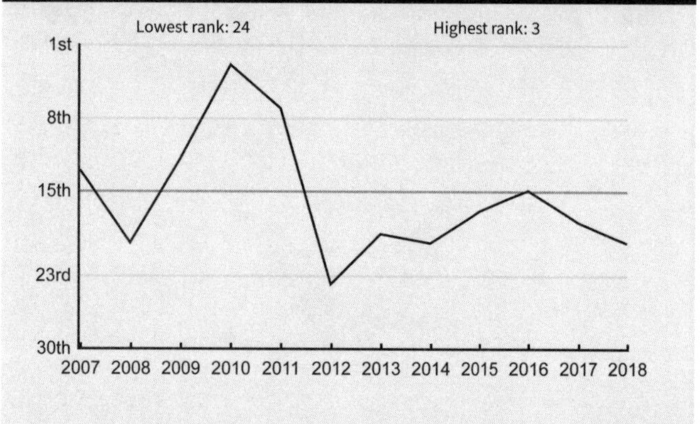

Personnel

President
Chris Antonetti

General Manager
Mike Chernoff

Assistant General Manager
Carter Hawkins

Manager
Terry Francona

BP Alumni
Ethan Purser
Steffan Segui
Keith Woolner

often. His rise in strikeout rate strongly correlated with the pitch's usage. In 2017, Kluber's breaking ball was the second-best pitch in baseball—45.1 runs above average, according to linear weights—trailing only Justin Verlander's fastball (45.6 runs). According to Baseball Prospectus' leaderboards, the pitch averaged 48.85 percent whiffs per swing—sixth in the majors—and batters hit .112 against the pitch.

Kluber said he hadn't changed, batters had. Between starts the focused, seemingly emotionless Kluber closely studies opponents. More and more, he'd seen batters try to gear up for extra power, more willing to miss.

"I'm not sure it's as much me doing anything different as much as it is guys just don't care about striking out," Kluber told me. "I think it goes hand-and-hand ... Guys a lot of times don't really make adjustments. They go up there swinging for the fences. More times more than not [the breaking ball] is the best pitch to take advantage of that."

But it wasn't just Kluber relying more often on his biting breaker that seems to dart at a 90-degree angle, it was a number of Indians pitchers relying more on their curveballs. Trevor Bauer's turnaround in 2017 was in part tied to relying more on his sharp-breaking, 12-6 curveball. Mike Clevinger added a curve en route to becoming a pitcher who now looks like something much more valuable than rotation depth.

The Indians were the best curveball-throwing rotation of all time, recording an MLB-record 56.3 runs above average with the pitch, according to linear weights. (The no. 2 team all time? The 2016 Indians. The no. 4 team? The 2015 Indians.) It's the starting rotation's curveball and slider usage that explains how it became the first staff to average better than 10 strikeouts per nine innings (10.08) for a season in the game's history.

And that usage and effectiveness was no accident. Former Indians pitching coach Mickey Callaway is now attempting to bring this format to the Mets as a first-time manager. "I think the key to pitching is to pitch with your best stuff," said Callaway at the Winter Meetings in December. "In Cleveland, every one of our starters had a nasty curveball. So they threw their best pitch, and it wasn't necessarily us teaching curveballs and stressing curveballs. It was just us stressing their best pitch and their best weapon against hitters."

The traditional baseball tenet that a pitcher must pitch off his fastball as a primary pitch was discarded. While some individuals like Rich Hill have arrived at this conclusion on their own, the Indians arrived there as an organization.

"[Conventional wisdom] is so ingrained. It was kind of a hump for me to get over that your fastball doesn't have to be your primary pitch," former starting pitcher turned elite reliever Andrew Miller told me last season, regarding the early stages of his career. "It was getting over almost being afraid to throw a 2-0, 2-1 or 3-1 slider because I'd come back to the dugout and the pitching coach would go 'Why the hell did you do that? You should have thrown a baseball down and away."

Miller, Kluber, Bauer and every other Indians pitcher never had to worry about Callaway berating them for unconventional pitch usage. And the breaking ball usage increase follows a familiar pattern: The Indians have consistently gotten more out of pitchers they have acquired.

Patience as a Virtue

In the spring of 2014, Carlos Carrasco looked like he would never fulfill his potential and live up to his former top-100-prospect pedigree. In the winter of 2011-2012, Bauer was testing the patience of many in Arizona when the Diamondbacks traded him less than 12 months after selecting him third overall in the draft. Both became success stories in Cleveland.

The Indians moved Carrasco to the bullpen in 2014, where they hoped he would learn to pitch more aggressively. The club also had him pitch exclusively from the stretch. That mind-set change and simplification of mechanics allowed him to emerge as one of the most talented starting pitchers in the game.

The Indians did not try to change Bauer. He still engages in his unusual long-toss program before games, tossing balls from foul pole to foul pole. He is still committed to his weighted-ball program. The Indians did not try to force an esoteric, round peg into a square, organizational hole. While the Diamondbacks struggled to understand and communicate with Bauer, he praised the communication skills of some within the Indians' organization, particularly Falvey, the person Bauer says he was closest to in the organization.

Each player learns and comprehends information differently, and Falvey seemed to understand that. For instance, Bauer explained to me how he learns differently, citing Robert Nideffer's attention model to explain why he has trouble grasping traditional coaching.

"People say, the best way to throw a pitch down in the zone is to throw it down in the zone. I'm like 'What?'" Bauer said. "I know [through] reading and studying that conscious thought is a huge detractor from performance. ... A narrow-external focus is your best performance mindset. Narrow-internal is the worst. ... I have the best chance of executing that pitch [through narrow-external focus]. The worst chance I have is 'OK, I have to move this way to execute this pitch.' Things like that where I think about it differently than how people say it."

The Indians have also tried to communicate and teach using tools players are comfortable with, which are increasingly tools of technology.

Said Callaway of working with younger pitchers in Cleveland: "The good thing is today's player likes technology. If you use technology, they're going to love it and find it intriguing. It kind of is not boring throughout the day. So there's that. ... I think the main thing [in instruction] is showing them that it's going to help their performance, and that's what we're all about. We want to win games. We want our players to be the best they can be, and that's what we're trying to accomplish with all of these little things. And they may seem tedious, but sometimes those smaller things, paying attention to those smaller, tedious tasks is what it takes to win. ... When players know that it's going to help them, they're going to do it."

The Indians were patient with Bauer and were ultimately rewarded in the second half of 2017 when he, in part, adopted the club's pitching philosophy of throwing his best pitch more often. The Indians were rewarded for not quitting on Bauer as the Diamondbacks had. The Indians were rewarded for not quitting on Carrasco when others might have. Even their ace, Kluber, a two-time Cy Young Award winner, was a project who added a two-seamer at Triple-A Columbus. The Indians haven't given up on young arms and have found ways to build upon their strengths and minimize their weaknesses.

Low Risk, High Reward

Josh Tomlin (19th round in 2006) and Ryan Merritt (16th round in 2011) were the only starting pitchers drafted by the Indians who made starts for the club in 2017. They haven't had a first-rounder pitch for the club since their 2009 pick Alex White did it in 2011. The Indians traded for this staff. They traded for Kluber. They traded for Carrasco. They traded for Bauer. They traded for Clevinger. Danny Salazar was signed as an amateur out of the Dominican Republic. The Indians have done exceptionally well in finding starting pitchers of value in the trade market.

A team hopes to extract a talent like Carrasco or Bauer when moving a big game piece like Cliff Lee or Shin-Soo Choo, though it took some time for Carrasco to become Carrasco and for Bauer to begin to live up to his pedigree. Still, both trades have become long-term, surplus-value-adding deals for the club. It's the Kluber and Clevinger trades that are particularly worthy of exploration. The Indians were able to find upside arms and acquired them for a relatively low cost.

Kluber was a fourth-round pick by Padres in the 2007 out of Stetson University. He never made a *Baseball America* or Baseball Prospectus top-100 prospect list. What he did was post an 18 percent K-BB mark or better at stops in Low-A, High-A and Double-A while advancing through the Padres' system. His K-BB% marks were similar to that of Homer Bailey, a consensus top-10 prospect in 2008. But Kluber didn't have a first-round pedigree. When the Indians acquired him, he didn't have his present arsenal, though he did come with the same workhorse frame and pitching makeup. Kluber was worth taking a chance on then, when the Indians sent Jake Westbrook to the Cardinals in a three-team deal.

Clevinger was another fourth-round pick, from another small program, who had never been ranked as a top-100 prospect, but who had a projectable frame and struck out batters at a 29.4 percent rate in Low-A and a 23 percent rate in High-A in the Angels' system before the Indians acquired him in 2014 in a waiver deal for Vinny Pestano. "He was striking out a hitter an inning (58 in 55 innings)," Indians general manager Mike Chernoff told the *Cleveland Plain Dealer*. "We felt with some changes to his delivery, he could throw a little harder and get more depth on his breaking ball. There were some ingredients for him to succeed."

Clevinger's acquisition is a success story, as is Kluber's, each being discovered and built through a blend of analytics, scouting and development. In both cases, there was little risk and great reward.

Health

Even the most talented arm does nothing for a club if it's not healthy, and this is another separator for the Indians. They've largely kept their best pitchers healthy. Over the last five years seasons, according to research by Eno Sarris and Jeff Zimmerman, the Indians rank second in fewest days lost to the disabled list. Their strength and training staffs have been on the cutting edge of preventive health practices and kinesiology, and the Indians keep adding to their progressive front office and field staff.

For instance, in 2016 the Indians hired Matt Blake—a private pitching instructor in New Hampshire—to be a sort of "liaison" between the front office and coaches and players, as he described to the *Concord (N.H.) Monitor*. According to the *Monitor*, Blake specializes in "philosophies and individualized training regimens rooted deep in anatomy and kinesiology, and tried to develop positive habits for athletes on and off the field."

Good health is no accident. Callaway saw to that in Cleveland and gave some insights into the approach he plans to implement with the Mets:

"You have to condition yourself to do something. Rest isn't always the best thing, especially if you haven't conditioned yourself the right way to go out there and deal with the rigors of throwing 200 innings and 115 pitches a game. We're going to condition guys to be able to do that, and then we'll rest and recover in between those good workouts.

"Have we prepared and looked and see what does this guy's stuff do? We're going to be monitoring guys' stuff in real time throughout the game. So it's not necessarily just at 100 pitches or 90 pitches. We're going to know if his arm slot's dropping and things like that in real-time hopefully."

Building a historic, cost-controlled staff that could keep the Indians relevant and as division contenders into the next decade wasn't easy. Arriving there required prescient evaluation, effective development and good fortune. The results are difficult to replicate, but lessons from the process can be learned.

—Travis Sawchik is a writer for FanGraphs and The Athletic.

Hitters

Greg Allen CF Born: 03/15/93 Age: 25 Bats: B Throws: R Height: 6'0" Weight: 175 Origin: Round 6, 2014 Draft (#188 overall)

YEAR	TEAM	LVL	AGE	PA	R	2B	3B	HR	RBI	BB	K	SB	CS	AVG/OBP/SLG	TAv	VORP	BABIP	BRR	FRAA	WARP
2015	LKC	A	22	564	83	27	2	7	45	53	57	43	16	.273/.368/.382	.287	36.4	.297	4.2	CF(116): 0.9, RF(6): -0.1	4.0
2016	LYN	A+	23	432	93	16	4	4	31	58	51	38	7	.298/.424/.402	.309	49.4	.338	13.1	CF(92): 15.9	6.7
2016	AKR	AA	23	174	26	7	3	3	13	19	27	7	6	.290/.399/.441	.310	16.1	.336	2.3	CF(36): 4.0	2.2
2017	AKR	AA	24	303	37	16	1	2	24	22	55	21	2	.264/.344/.357	.268	12.8	.319	1.5	CF(67): -6.3, RF(1): -0.1	0.7
2017	CLE	MLB	24	39	7	1	0	1	6	2	8	1	0	.229/.282/.343	.226	0.5	.259	0.7	CF(21): -0.8, LF(5): -0.1	0.0
2018	*CLE*	*MLB*	*25*	*236*	*29*	*10*	*1*	*4*	*24*	*19*	*45*	*11*	*3*	*.243/.324/.367*	*.243*	*4.2*	*.285*	*1.1*	*LF 0, RF -1*	*0.2*
2019	*CLE*	*MLB*	*26*	*410*	*51*	*18*	*2*	*10*	*44*	*38*	*82*	*18*	*5*	*.247/.341/.391*	*.248*	*6.9*	*.287*	*2.1*	*LF 1, RF -1*	*0.7*

Breakout: 3% Improve: 20% Collapse: 5% Attrition: 23% MLB: 37% *Comparables: Che-Hsuan Lin, Rafael Ortega, Todd Cunningham*

There's plenty to like about Allen, a switch-hitting center fielder who oozes athleticism. He's a plus defender with a strong arm and a blur on the basepaths, swiping bags at a high rate of success and taking the extra base. At the plate he flashes a balanced, line-drive stroke, gap power and a patient approach that helps him get on base at a solid rate. The broken hamate bone that shelved him last summer may have cost him the surprising thump he showed in his breakout 2016 season, but at age 25 he's not about to turn into Aaron Judge. Allen looks to be an above-average fourth outfielder and bench bat who can provide some occasional spark at the top of the lineup.

Abraham Almonte OF Born: 06/27/89 Age: 29 Bats: B Throws: R Height: 5'9" Weight: 210 Origin: International Free Agent, 2005

YEAR	TEAM	LVL	AGE	PA	R	2B	3B	HR	RBI	BB	K	SB	CS	AVG/OBP/SLG	TAv	VORP	BABIP	BRR	FRAA	WARP
2015	ELP	AAA	26	282	43	18	2	4	35	33	46	11	4	.275/.361/.414	.285	17.0	.325	1.3	CF(59): -10.3, LF(3): -0.5	0.6
2015	SDN	MLB	26	62	6	3	0	0	4	5	19	1	1	.204/.271/.259	.215	-3.0	.314	-1.8	LF(6): -1.0, CF(6): -0.5	-0.5
2015	CLE	MLB	26	196	30	9	5	5	20	16	33	6	0	.264/.321/.455	.264	7.7	.296	1.2	CF(50): 3.5	1.2
2016	COH	AAA	27	33	6	2	1	1	4	5	4	2	0	.444/.545/.704	.413	5.7	.500	-0.5	CF(6): -0.2	0.6
2016	CLE	MLB	27	194	24	20	1	1	22	8	42	8	0	.264/.294/.401	.229	-2.4	.331	-0.2	RF(36): 3.5, LF(34): -2.4	-0.2
2017	COH	AAA	28	92	11	6	1	2	6	15	13	3	1	.260/.380/.442	.266	4.5	.290	2.0	CF(7): -0.9, RF(6): -0.7	0.3
2017	CLE	MLB	28	195	26	8	3	3	14	20	46	2	1	.233/.314/.366	.242	1.6	.298	1.1	RF(32): -3.2, LF(20): -0.2	-0.2
2018	*CLE*	*MLB*	*29*	*104*	*12*	*5*	*1*	*2*	*10*	*9*	*23*	*3*	*1*	*.249/.314/.384*	*.245*	*1.9*	*.305*	*0.3*	*LF -1, CF -1*	*0.0*
2019	*CLE*	*MLB*	*30*	*203*	*23*	*10*	*1*	*4*	*21*	*19*	*46*	*4*	*1*	*.241/.316/.381*	*.238*	*0.7*	*.295*	*-0.1*	*LF -2, CF -1*	*-0.3*

Breakout: 1% Improve: 21% Collapse: 17% Attrition: 31% MLB: 63% *Comparables: Collin Cowgill, Brian Bogusevic, Travis Buck*

Remember that time your cousin visited and you took him to that Indian buffet down the block for lunch, and after wandering perplexed past the chicken tikka masala and paneer he sat down with a plate full of pale, dry chicken wings? So you told him those don't look very good, and he said they probably aren't very good, but at least he knows they won't be awful? That's Almonte's role on Cleveland's outfield menu. He's adequate in the field and on the basepaths, and won't get the bat knocked out of his hands, but he's never good enough to warrant second helpings. If that sounds like a replacement-level player to you, you're an astute observer of the baseball landscape, because eventually every team that wants to win a championship tries the paneer.

Yonder Alonso 1B Born: 04/08/87 Age: 31 Bats: L Throws: R Height: 6'1" Weight: 230 Origin: Round 1, 2008 Draft (#7 overall)

YEAR	TEAM	LVL	AGE	PA	R	2B	3B	HR	RBI	BB	K	SB	CS	AVG/OBP/SLG	TAv	VORP	BABIP	BRR	FRAA	WARP
2015	SDN	MLB	28	402	50	18	1	5	31	42	48	2	5	.282/.361/.381	.271	6.3	.313	-2.0	1B(102): 3.7, 3B(2): 0.0	1.1
2016	OAK	MLB	29	532	52	34	0	7	56	45	74	3	1	.253/.316/.367	.245	-2.0	.284	0.2	1B(145): 6.5, 3B(7): -0.5	0.4
2017	OAK	MLB	30	371	52	17	0	22	49	50	88	1	0	.266/.369/.527	.294	16.8	.301	-0.2	1B(96): -2.7	1.4
2017	SEA	MLB	30	150	20	5	0	6	18	18	30	1	0	.265/.353/.439	.265	2.4	.302	-0.1	1B(39): -2.8	0.0
2018	*CLE*	*MLB*	*31*	*446*	*51*	*23*	*0*	*11*	*53*	*44*	*71*	*3*	*1*	*.264/.337/.408*	*.258*	*6.3*	*.294*	*-0.9*	*1B -2*	*0.1*
2019	*CLE*	*MLB*	*32*	*446*	*57*	*22*	*0*	*13*	*52*	*47*	*76*	*2*	*1*	*.260/.340/.413*	*.254*	*2.1*	*.291*	*-0.4*	*1B -2*	*0.0*

Breakout: 2% Improve: 38% Collapse: 3% Attrition: 12% MLB: 85% *Comparables: Casey Kotchman, Sean Casey, Ed Kranepool*

There arguably isn't a hitter more emblematic of the launch-angle/fly-ball revolution than Alonso. A busted former first-round pick with a career .387 slugging percentage and a .118 isolated power entering 2017, Alonso made a mechanical adjustment last spring, taking a bigger stride into the pitch but more importantly finishing his swing at a higher angle. The change paid immediate dividends. Alonso posted a .275/.372/.562 first-half line and earned his first trip to the All-Star game at age 30. Alas, the change didn't stick, and Alonso's fly-ball rate dropped from 49 percent in the first half to 36 percent in the second. Alonso most likely spent the offseason looking hither and yon, trying to recapture the mechanics that led to his first-half breakout, in the hope of returning to form.

Will Benson RF Born: 06/16/98 Age: 20 Bats: L Throws: L Height: 6'5" Weight: 225 Origin: Round 1, 2016 Draft (#14 overall)

YEAR	TEAM	LVL	AGE	PA	R	2B	3B	HR	RBI	BB	K	SB	CS	AVG/OBP/SLG	TAv	VORP	BABIP	BRR	FRAA	WARP
2016	CLE	RK	18	184	31	10	3	6	27	22	60	10	2	.209/.321/.424	.276	9.1	.293	2.5	RF(39): -2.0	0.7
2017	MHV	A-	19	236	29	8	5	10	36	31	80	7	1	.238/.347/.475	.285	10.6	.339	0.1	RF(56): -2.4	0.8
2018	*CLE*	*MLB*	*20*	*250*	*26*	*8*	*1*	*9*	*29*	*22*	*95*	*3*	*1*	*.188/.264/.348*	*.206*	*-7.1*	*.275*	*0.1*	*RF -1*	*-0.9*
2019	*CLE*	*MLB*	*21*	*353*	*42*	*13*	*1*	*13*	*42*	*34*	*129*	*4*	*1*	*.200/.283/.372*	*.223*	*-6.2*	*.287*	*0.1*	*RF -2*	*-0.9*

Breakout: 2% Improve: 7% Collapse: 0% Attrition: 4% MLB: 9% *Comparables: Chris Parmelee, Nomar Mazara, Caleb Gindl*

It's all about the projection with Benson, the massive prep outfielder whom the Indians tabbed as their top pick in 2016. His first full summer as a pro featured plenty of growing pains, as pitchers often exploited his long swing and he struggled to make contact. When he did, though, it had *that sound,* hinting at the plus power that can carry him to the big leagues. Benson's glove won't win any awards, but he moves better than you would expect from someone his size and should be able to stick in an outfield corner. He has plenty of work to do at the plate, but plenty of time in which to do it.

Bobby Bradley 1B Born: 05/29/96 Age: 22 Bats: L Throws: R Height: 6'1" Weight: 225 Origin: Round 3, 2014 Draft (#97 overall)

YEAR	TEAM	LVL	AGE	PA	R	2B	3B	HR	RBI	BB	K	SB	CS	AVG/OBP/SLG	TAv	VORP	BABIP	BRR	FRAA	WARP
2015	LKC	A	19	465	62	15	4	27	92	56	148	3	0	.269/.361/.529	.314	28.1	.352	-2.1	1B(101): 4.7	3.5
2016	LYN	A+	20	572	82	23	1	29	102	75	170	3	0	.235/.344/.466	.288	23.4	.293	0.2	1B(116): -6.4	1.7
2017	AKR	AA	21	532	66	25	3	23	89	55	122	3	3	.251/.331/.465	.287	17.3	.287	-2.6	1B(123): -6.3	1.2
2018	*CLE*	*MLB*	*22*	*66*	*9*	*2*	*0*	*3*	*9*	*6*	*22*	*0*	*0*	*.221/.298/.436*	*.251*	*0.4*	*.283*	*-0.1*	*1B -1*	*-0.1*
2019	*CLE*	*MLB*	*23*	*331*	*47*	*13*	*1*	*18*	*51*	*34*	*107*	*0*	*0*	*.226/.310/.465*	*.256*	*1.8*	*.283*	*-0.7*	*1B -3*	*-0.1*

Breakout: 1% Improve: 27% Collapse: 3% Attrition: 15% MLB: 48% *Comparables: Matt Olson, Chris Carter, Anthony Rizzo*

It's partially about the projection with Bradley, the bulky prep infielder whom the Indians tabbed as their third pick in 2014. His first full summer in the high minors featured a few growing pains, as pitchers often exploited his awkward swing and he struggled to make contact. When he did, though, it had *that sound*, and as he's matured he's proven he can turn his massive power potential into game-day bombs. Bradley isn't athletic and his glove won't win any awards, as he's at best a below-average fielder and a slug on the basepaths who may slide to DH at the highest level. He draws walks but not enough to post a high on-base percentage, so he'll have to absolutely mash to provide value. Bradley has plenty of work to do at the plate, and less time than Will Benson in which to do it.

Michael Brantley LF Born: 05/15/87 Age: 31 Bats: L Throws: L Height: 6'2" Weight: 200 Origin: Round 7, 2005 Draft (#205 overall)

YEAR	TEAM	LVL	AGE	PA	R	2B	3B	HR	RBI	BB	K	SB	CS	AVG/OBP/SLG	TAv	VORP	BABIP	BRR	FRAA	WARP
2015	CLE	MLB	28	596	68	45	0	15	84	60	51	15	1	.310/.379/.480	.294	28.9	.318	-3.2	LF(101): 3.6, CF(28): -4.0	3.1
2016	CLE	MLB	29	43	5	2	0	0	7	3	6	1	0	.231/.279/.282	.207	-1.0	.265	0.4	LF(11): 0.3	-0.1
2017	CLE	MLB	30	375	47	20	1	9	52	31	50	11	1	.299/.357/.444	.275	13.8	.325	-0.6	LF(87): 5.3	1.9
2018	*CLE*	*MLB*	*31*	*533*	*66*	*31*	*2*	*12*	*63*	*44*	*55*	*14*	*1*	*.294/.354/.440*	*.273*	*22.7*	*.310*	*1.6*	*LF 5*	*2.7*
2019	*CLE*	*MLB*	*32*	*314*	*40*	*18*	*0*	*8*	*38*	*28*	*36*	*7*	*1*	*.290/.355/.446*	*.269*	*9.8*	*.306*	*-0.9*	*LF 3*	*1.4*

Breakout: 0% Improve: 41% Collapse: 5% Attrition: 13% MLB: 95% *Comparables: Mike Greenwell, Gregg Jefferies, Dale Mitchell*

Brantley returned from the shoulder ailments that cost him most of 2016 and posted a solid comeback year, making his second All-Star squad before hurting his ankle running down a fly ball in early August. Surgery followed in October, possibly jeopardizing his availability for Opening Day. A healthy Brantley ranks among the league's better left fielders, with tremendous contact skills, a solid batting eye, gap power and outstanding base-stealing acumen. He's also a leader in the clubhouse and an ambassador in the community, which helped sway Cleveland's decision to bet $12 million on his option year. As he enters his early-thirties his walk and strikeout numbers are moving in the wrong direction, his defense is no longer stellar and his health is a question mark, but given the Tribe's gaping outfield voids, the talent he still flashes and the intangibles he brings, Brantley is a risk worth taking.

Jay Bruce RF Born: 04/03/87 Age: 31 Bats: L Throws: L Height: 6'3" Weight: 225 Origin: Round 1, 2005 Draft (#12 overall)

YEAR	TEAM	LVL	AGE	PA	R	2B	3B	HR	RBI	BB	K	SB	CS	AVG/OBP/SLG	TAv	VORP	BABIP	BRR	FRAA	WARP
2015	CIN	MLB	28	649	72	35	4	26	87	58	145	9	5	.226/.294/.434	.261	9.0	.251	-2.7	RF(150): 3.1	1.3
2016	CIN	MLB	29	402	60	22	6	25	80	27	83	4	2	.265/.316/.559	.301	24.4	.275	0.5	RF(95): -2.8, CF(1): 0.0	2.2
2016	NYN	MLB	29	187	14	5	0	8	19	17	43	0	0	.219/.294/.391	.251	-0.5	.246	-2.1	RF(43): -2.3	-0.3
2017	NYN	MLB	30	448	61	20	0	29	75	39	102	0	1	.256/.321/.520	.297	25.5	.271	0.1	RF(92): 2.4, 1B(11): -0.1	2.8
2017	CLE	MLB	30	169	21	9	2	7	26	18	37	1	0	.248/.331/.477	.277	6.6	.283	0.4	RF(41): -2.6, 1B(1): 0.0	0.4
2018	*CLE*	*MLB*	*31*	*574*	*71*	*29*	*2*	*27*	*84*	*51*	*140*	*5*	*2*	*.244/.312/.465*	*.256*	*12.3*	*.280*	*-0.9*	*RF 1, 1B 0*	*1.4*
2019	*CLE*	*MLB*	*32*	*531*	*70*	*27*	*2*	*24*	*75*	*47*	*132*	*3*	*2*	*.240/.308/.455*	*.253*	*5.7*	*.279*	*-0.9*	*RF 1, 1B 0*	*0.7*

Breakout: 3% Improve: 42% Collapse: 9% Attrition: 10% MLB: 92% *Comparables: Xavier Nady, Richard Hidalgo, Eric Hinske*

After his impressive first half in Queens, Bruce came to the Indians in a straightforward salary dump, and the veteran lefty provided his new employers with some straightforward Jay Bruce production. His Cleveland numbers were a match for his career .249/.319/.472 line and .278 TAv, as he hit dingers, drove in runs and leaked value from his sketchy right-field glove exactly as expected. Bruce is an old-school run producer, which some take as a pejorative but which perfectly describes his ability to stay healthy and drive the ball. Since 2010, he's seventh in home runs and eighth in RBIs in all of baseball, but his low walk and contact rates lead to far more outs than a truly elite bat, and his generally indifferent defense drags down his value. Bruce isn't the star that he impersonates when he's on one of his patented hot streaks, but if you catch him at the right time he can carry a lineup.

Yu-Cheng Chang SS Born: 08/18/95 Age: 22 Bats: R Throws: R Height: 6'1" Weight: 175 Origin: International Free Agent, 2013

YEAR	TEAM	LVL	AGE	PA	R	2B	3B	HR	RBI	BB	K	SB	CS	AVG/OBP/SLG	TAv	VORP	BABIP	BRR	FRAA	WARP
2015	LKC	A	19	440	52	16	4	9	52	27	103	5	6	.232/.293/.361	.260	20.1	.288	2.8	SS(99): 11.0	3.3
2016	LYN	A+	20	477	78	30	8	13	70	45	110	11	3	.259/.332/.463	.285	35.1	.316	2.9	SS(104): 0.0	3.6
2017	AKR	AA	21	508	72	24	5	24	66	52	134	11	4	.220/.312/.461	.282	33.6	.254	2.3	SS(119): 20.3	5.8
2018	*CLE*	*MLB*	*22*	*250*	*28*	*11*	*2*	*10*	*33*	*19*	*76*	*3*	*1*	*.217/.285/.414*	*.233*	*4.6*	*.274*	*0.0*	*SS 5, 2B 0*	*1.1*
2019	*CLE*	*MLB*	*23*	*388*	*50*	*17*	*2*	*18*	*54*	*31*	*117*	*4*	*2*	*.222/.293/.438*	*.244*	*6.7*	*.274*	*0.1*	*SS 8*	*1.6*

Breakout: 2% Improve: 22% Collapse: 4% Attrition: 16% MLB: 32% *Comparables: Derek Dietrich, Trevor Story, Nick Franklin*

If we asked you to close your eyes and imagine a Three True Outcomes slugger, you almost certainly wouldn't picture a mid-sized Taiwanese shortstop with good wheels and a name that causes an old Aretha Franklin hit to run through your head, but that's Chang in a nutshell. Last year in Double-A he showed enough improvement with the glove that there's a chance he might stick at the six, with sure hands and a strong arm making up for subpar range. There's plenty of swing-and-miss in his game—perhaps too much—but the thunder in his bat is no mirage and should play even if he has to move to third base. Only a chain of fools would argue he'll ever play every day in Cleveland, but Chang has the chain of tools to be a second-division starter somewhere else.

Lonnie Chisenhall OF Born: 10/04/88 Age: 29 Bats: L Throws: R Height: 6'2" Weight: 190 Origin: Round 1, 2008 Draft (#29 overall)

YEAR	TEAM	LVL	AGE	PA	R	2B	3B	HR	RBI	BB	K	SB	CS	AVG/OBP/SLG	TAv	VORP	BABIP	BRR	FRAA	WARP
2015	COH	AAA	26	171	18	13	0	3	21	11	35	1	0	.280/.329/.420	.256	2.0	.342	-2.0	3B(32): -1.4, RF(4): 1.3	0.2
2015	CLE	MLB	26	362	38	19	1	7	44	23	69	4	1	.246/.294/.372	.238	2.5	.288	1.6	RF(51): 5.3, 3B(50): 2.4	1.1
2016	CLE	MLB	27	418	43	25	5	8	57	23	70	6	0	.286/.328/.439	.260	7.5	.328	-0.3	RF(118): 1.2, 1B(3): 0.0	0.9
2017	COH	AAA	28	28	4	2	0	1	4	0	6	1	0	.370/.357/.556	.283	1.3	.429	0.0	LF(4): -0.6, RF(2): -0.3	0.0
2017	CLE	MLB	28	270	34	17	1	12	53	25	55	2	2	.288/.360/.521	.288	12.6	.326	-1.5	RF(45): -1.6, CF(19): -0.2	1.2
2018	*CLE*	*MLB*	*29*	*465*	*55*	*26*	*2*	*12*	*54*	*32*	*90*	*5*	*1*	*.262/.317/.421*	*.252*	*8.4*	*.303*	*-0.2*	*RF 2*	*0.8*
2019	*CLE*	*MLB*	*30*	*375*	*44*	*21*	*1*	*10*	*44*	*27*	*78*	*3*	*1*	*.256/.314/.415*	*.243*	*1.0*	*.299*	*-0.2*	*RF 2*	*0.3*

Breakout: 3% Improve: 45% Collapse: 11% Attrition: 19% MLB: 95% *Comparables: Kevin Mench, Nate Schierholtz, David Peralta*

The most memorable moment of Chisenhall's season was his infamous bat-knob hit-by-pitch in Game 2 of the ALDS, but let's not forget the welts he raised during the first half. Chisenhall was slashing .305/.376/.578 and punishing lefties for the first time in his career before injuring his calf in early July, though his post-return September slump dragged his overall numbers down. A more discriminating approach clearly helped him, as Chisenhall saw more pitches than ever before, put a charge into the ones he could handle and took his walks when the strikes never arrived. Like all mere mortals he's no center fielder, but he's adequate in right and can play first base in a pinch. A career-high rate of home runs per fly ball point to likely regression in his power numbers, but with enough playing time Lonnie Baseball should launch 15-20 bombs and serve as a valuable lefty bat in an outfield corner.

Yandy Diaz 3B Born: 08/08/91 Age: 26 Bats: R Throws: R Height: 6'2" Weight: 185 Origin: International Free Agent, 2013

YEAR	TEAM	LVL	AGE	PA	R	2B	3B	HR	RBI	BB	K	SB	CS	AVG/OBP/SLG	TAv	VORP	BABIP	BRR	FRAA	WARP
2015	AKR	AA	23	564	61	13	5	7	55	78	65	8	7	.315/.412/.408	.306	40.2	.350	-2.3	3B(122): -9.8	3.3
2016	AKR	AA	24	110	13	0	1	2	14	24	16	6	2	.286/.445/.381	.324	9.5	.328	-0.7	3B(22): -1.1, 2B(1): 0.0	0.9
2016	COH	AAA	24	416	53	22	3	7	44	47	70	5	1	.325/.399/.461	.300	28.9	.381	2.1	3B(30): -0.8, RF(28): 5.3	3.8
2017	COH	AAA	25	374	56	17	1	5	33	60	56	1	2	.350/.454/.460	.316	34.5	.412	1.1	3B(42): -3.4, LF(21): 0.7	3.2
2017	CLE	MLB	25	179	25	8	1	0	13	21	35	2	0	.263/.352/.327	.244	1.9	.336	-0.4	3B(40): -0.9, LF(3): -0.2	0.1
2018	*CLE*	*MLB*	*26*	*246*	*29*	*10*	*1*	*5*	*27*	*32*	*47*	*1*	*1*	*.281/.376/.406*	*.276*	*10.1*	*.338*	*-0.3*	*3B -2*	*0.7*
2019	*CLE*	*MLB*	*27*	*432*	*58*	*19*	*2*	*10*	*50*	*58*	*83*	*2*	*1*	*.289/.386/.436*	*.278*	*18.6*	*.345*	*-0.6*	*3B -3*	*1.7*

Breakout: 3% Improve: 30% Collapse: 18% Attrition: 24% MLB: 59% *Comparables: Rob Refsnyder, Matt Carpenter, Ty Kelly*

We learned a lot about Diaz last year. He's fast, but not much of a basestealer. He's not an outfielder, but looks plenty smooth at third base. He has nothing left to prove at Triple-A. His plate discipline, contact skills and all-fields approach translate well to the big leagues. But mostly, we learned he hits the ball very, very hard. Diaz ranked eighth on the Statcast exit velocity leaderboard, spooning with Giancarlo Stanton and Paul Goldschmidt. He hit the hardest groundballs in the league by a wide margin—and therein lies the rub. Diaz ranks among the most ground-ball-centric hitters in baseball, which can lead to high batting averages and on-base percentages but virtually no extra-base hits. A player with that much juice in his bat shouldn't post an Isolated Power lower than Dee Gordon and Ben Revere. He's already 26, so big changes may be too much to expect, but if Diaz can add the word "loft" to his vocabulary, watch out.

Edwin Encarnacion 1B Born: 01/07/83 Age: 35 Bats: R Throws: R Height: 6'1" Weight: 230 Origin: Round 9, 2000 Draft (#274 overall)

YEAR	TEAM	LVL	AGE	PA	R	2B	3B	HR	RBI	BB	K	SB	CS	AVG/OBP/SLG	TAv	VORP	BABIP	BRR	FRAA	WARP
2015	TOR	MLB	32	624	94	31	0	39	111	77	98	3	2	.277/.372/.557	.324	43.5	.267	-1.6	1B(59): 0.1	4.7
2016	TOR	MLB	33	702	99	34	0	42	127	87	138	2	0	.263/.357/.529	.291	28.7	.270	-0.4	1B(75): -2.8	2.7
2017	CLE	MLB	34	669	96	20	1	38	107	104	133	2	0	.258/.377/.504	.297	27.6	.271	-5.2	1B(23): -0.6	2.7
2018	*CLE*	*MLB*	*35*	*609*	*90*	*26*	*1*	*33*	*100*	*76*	*105*	*2*	*0*	*.262/.358/.503*	*.293*	*31.0*	*.267*	*-1.0*	*1B -1*	*2.8*
2019	*CLE*	*MLB*	*36*	*553*	*84*	*24*	*0*	*30*	*87*	*68*	*101*	*0*	*0*	*.259/.355/.498*	*.281*	*22.8*	*.268*	*-2.0*	*1B -1*	*2.4*

Breakout: 1% Improve: 27% Collapse: 2% Attrition: 9% MLB: 96% *Comparables: Lance Berkman, Vladimir Guerrero, Stan Musial*

Since the start of the 2012 season, Encarnacion has been a model of consistent offensive production and durability. No other human has faced the best pitchers in the world at least 500 times in each of the last six years and posted a TAv of at least .290. (Mike Trout has, too, but we're limiting this to humans.) Like Albert Pujols at a similar age, Encarnacion has become more of an all-or-nothing hitter with a declining batting average and a lack of doubles eroding his slugging percentage. Unlike Pujols, Encarnacion has maintained his walk rate and continues to post high on-base percentages, giving hope that he can stare down Father Time longer than Prince Albert could. Whether he'll be worth his $20 million option in 2020 at the age of 37 is another matter entirely.

Yan Gomes C Born: 07/19/87 Age: 30 Bats: R Throws: R Height: 6'2" Weight: 215 Origin: Round 10, 2009 Draft (#310 overall)

YEAR	TEAM	LVL	AGE	PA	R	2B	3B	HR	RBI	BB	K	SB	CS	AVG/OBP/SLG	TAv	VORP	BABIP	BRR	FRAA	WARP
2015	CLE	MLB	27	389	38	22	0	12	45	13	104	0	0	.231/.267/.391	.237	6.7	.285	-0.7	C(91): -3.0	0.4
2016	CLE	MLB	28	264	22	11	1	9	34	9	69	0	0	.167/.201/.327	.179	-7.4	.189	2.3	C(73): -6.8	-1.5
2017	CLE	MLB	29	383	43	15	0	14	56	31	99	0	0	.232/.309/.399	.244	13.1	.283	1.7	C(103): 3.2	1.6
2018	*CLE*	*MLB*	*30*	*262*	*30*	*13*	*1*	*9*	*32*	*15*	*64*	*0*	*0*	*.242/.293/.411*	*.243*	*9.1*	*.292*	*-0.5*	*C -3*	*0.3*
2019	*CLE*	*MLB*	*31*	*277*	*33*	*14*	*1*	*10*	*34*	*18*	*70*	*0*	*0*	*.236/.293/.411*	*.237*	*4.7*	*.284*	*0.6*	*C -2*	*0.3*

Breakout: 2% Improve: 33% Collapse: 6% Attrition: 16% MLB: 94% *Comparables: John Buck, Nick Hundley, Matt Nokes*

YEAR	TEAM	P. COUNT	FRM RUNS	BLK RUNS	THRW RUNS	TOT RUNS
2015	CLE	12205	-2.4	-0.5	0.0	-2.9
2015	COH	303	0.1	0.0	0.0	0.1
2016	CLE	9256	-5.4	-0.3	0.2	-5.6
2017	CLE	13358	0.7	0.4	2.2	3.4
2018	*CLE*	*9100*	*-2.5*	*-0.1*	*0.7*	*-1.9*
2019	*CLE*	*9612*	*-2.8*	*-0.2*	*0.8*	*-2.2*

After two years filled with enough bleak misfortune to fill an Edward Gorey anthology, it was nice to see Gomes healthy and productive last year. Battery mates love him for his plus framing skills, blocking abilities and rocket arm that controls the running game as well as any backstop in baseball. Coaches, teammates and fans love him for his work ethic, toughness and leadership. Opposing pitchers love him for his tendency to offer at pitches outside the zone and swing through hittable fastballs, though Gomes did show a little more selectivity and drew a few more walks last year. He'll never be the offensive force his 2014 breakout may have presaged, but his solid work behind the dish makes him well worth his reasonable contract.

Erik Gonzalez UT Born: 08/31/91 Age: 26 Bats: R Throws: R Height: 6'3" Weight: 195 Origin: International Free Agent, 2008

YEAR	TEAM	LVL	AGE	PA	R	2B	3B	HR	RBI	BB	K	SB	CS	AVG/OBP/SLG	TAv	VORP	BABIP	BRR	FRAA	WARP
2015	AKR	AA	23	327	38	18	4	6	46	11	56	10	5	.280/.304/.421	.263	14.2	.321	0.5	SS(71): 4.2	2.0
2015	COH	AAA	23	261	32	6	3	3	23	15	47	8	2	.223/.277/.311	.221	2.3	.266	2.7	SS(62): 8.4	1.1
2016	COH	AAA	24	460	62	31	1	11	53	19	88	12	10	.296/.329/.450	.279	27.3	.349	0.5	SS(90): 0.2, 2B(8): -1.5	2.7
2016	CLE	MLB	24	17	2	0	0	0	0	1	8	0	1	.313/.353/.313	.235	0.2	.625	0.1	SS(8): 0.0, 2B(5): -0.1	0.0
2017	COH	AAA	25	170	21	4	3	6	13	7	53	5	1	.256/.286/.431	.237	2.4	.343	0.3	SS(26): -0.7, 2B(9): -0.5	0.1
2017	CLE	MLB	25	115	18	6	0	4	11	3	37	1	2	.255/.272/.418	.228	-1.3	.343	-1.0	2B(36): -0.5, SS(11): 0.1	-0.2
2018	*CLE*	*MLB*	*26*	*90*	*11*	*4*	*1*	*3*	*10*	*4*	*23*	*2*	*1*	*.250/.282/.403*	*.237*	*1.7*	*.309*	*-0.1*	*SS 0, 2B 0*	*0.1*
2019	*CLE*	*MLB*	*27*	*295*	*34*	*14*	*1*	*10*	*36*	*14*	*78*	*6*	*4*	*.249/.289/.415*	*.237*	*2.6*	*.307*	*0.0*	*SS 2, 2B -1*	*0.4*

Breakout: 6% Improve: 29% Collapse: 8% Attrition: 28% MLB: 50% *Comparables: Tyler Greene, Chase d'Arnaud, J.J. Furmaniak*

Gonzalez is a true shortstop whose glove can be plugged in anywhere on the diamond and whose bat can generate surprising pop. Here's the problem, though: he can hit a little, but he can also miss *a lot*. Gonzalez continually expands the zone and struck out in nearly a third of his plate appearances last year while treating walks like an admission of failure. His hacktastic approach is doomed to be forever exploited by the best pitchers in the world, making him a utility option at best and organizational depth at worst.

Brandon Guyer OF Born: 01/28/86 Age: 32 Bats: R Throws: R Height: 6'2" Weight: 200 Origin: Round 5, 2007 Draft (#157 overall)

YEAR	TEAM	LVL	AGE	PA	R	2B	3B	HR	RBI	BB	K	SB	CS	AVG/OBP/SLG	TAv	VORP	BABIP	BRR	FRAA	WARP
2015	TBA	MLB	29	385	51	21	2	8	28	25	61	10	4	.265/.359/.413	.279	17.1	.303	1.6	LF(60): 4.6, RF(41): -4.0	1.8
2016	TBA	MLB	30	249	27	12	1	7	18	12	42	2	1	.241/.347/.406	.280	9.7	.268	-0.8	LF(25): 0.0, CF(18): -0.5	0.9
2016	CLE	MLB	30	96	12	5	0	2	14	7	13	1	1	.333/.438/.469	.302	6.4	.379	0.2	LF(26): 2.1, RF(7): 0.1	0.9
2017	CLE	MLB	31	192	23	7	1	2	20	15	43	2	0	.236/.326/.327	.243	0.8	.303	0.3	RF(37): 2.5, LF(33): -1.1	0.2
2018	*CLE*	*MLB*	*32*	*166*	*19*	*8*	*1*	*3*	*18*	*11*	*30*	*2*	*1*	*.261/.345/.394*	*.261*	*5.0*	*.304*	*0.0*	*RF -1, LF 1*	*0.4*
2019	*CLE*	*MLB*	*33*	*165*	*20*	*8*	*1*	*3*	*18*	*12*	*32*	*2*	*1*	*.252/.343/.394*	*.254*	*2.7*	*.296*	*0.2*	*RF 0, LF 1*	*0.3*

Breakout: 3% Improve: 36% Collapse: 3% Attrition: 16% MLB: 92% *Comparables: David DeJesus, Kosuke Fukudome, Nick Markakis*

Baseball's reigning King of Pain couldn't quite duplicate his otherworldly hit-by-pitch tallies of recent seasons, but still ranked among the league leaders in plunkings per plate appearance. Which is all good fun, but Guyer's .282/.379/.449 career line against lefties betrays his true calling as the short side of an outfield platoon. Last year he wasn't up to the task, posting a mundane .256 TAv against portsiders, but a wrist ailment culminating in offseason surgery was the likely culprit. With a plethora of lefty outfielders littering their big-league roster, the Tribe needs a healthy Guyer this spring to help balance their lineup.

Austin Jackson OF Born: 02/01/87 Age: 31 Bats: R Throws: R Height: 6'1" Weight: 205 Origin: Round 8, 2005 Draft (#259 overall)

YEAR	TEAM	LVL	AGE	PA	R	2B	3B	HR	RBI	BB	K	SB	CS	AVG/OBP/SLG	TAv	VORP	BABIP	BRR	FRAA	WARP
2015	TAC	AAA	28	42	4	1	0	0	1	4	12	1	0	.263/.333/.289	.229	-0.2	.385	0.4	CF(4): -1.1	-0.1
2015	SEA	MLB	28	448	46	18	3	8	38	24	107	15	9	.272/.312/.387	.255	8.3	.348	-2.6	CF(107): 5.0	1.4
2015	CHN	MLB	28	79	10	7	0	1	10	5	19	2	1	.236/.304/.375	.247	0.9	.308	0.2	RF(22): 1.1, CF(8): -0.6	0.1
2016	CHA	MLB	29	203	24	12	2	0	18	17	39	2	1	.254/.318/.343	.234	0.4	.319	-0.4	CF(54): -1.2	-0.1
2017	COH	AAA	30	29	2	3	0	1	4	2	6	2	0	.333/.379/.556	.285	1.4	.400	0.0	CF(3): -0.2, RF(2): -0.2	0.1
2017	CLE	MLB	30	318	46	19	3	7	35	33	64	3	1	.318/.387/.482	.293	20.9	.385	1.6	CF(38): -2.0, LF(38): 0.1	1.9
2018	*CLE*	*MLB*	*31*	*280*	*34*	*15*	*2*	*5*	*26*	*24*	*63*	*6*	*2*	*.265/.330/.397*	*.244*	*5.5*	*.332*	*-0.1*	*CF -1, LF 0*	*0.5*
2019	*CLE*	*MLB*	*32*	*224*	*25*	*12*	*1*	*4*	*23*	*18*	*51*	*4*	*2*	*.257/.320/.389*	*.242*	*1.6*	*.321*	*0.0*	*CF -1, LF 0*	*0.1*

Breakout: 0% Improve: 43% Collapse: 7% Attrition: 14% MLB: 91% *Comparables: Eric Byrnes, Coco Crisp, Jacob Brumfield*

Jackson was one of the year's most successful non-roster invitees last spring. Injuries and ineffectiveness in the Cleveland outfield thrust him into a much bigger role than the organization likely anticipated, and A-Jax responded with his best season in years. He filled Brandon Guyer's shoes and then some, tattooing lefties to the tune of a .331 TAv, holding his own against righties and playing solid outfield defense peppered with the occasional highlight-reel catch. Credit Terry Francona for spotting him wisely and giving him the platoon advantage in a career-best 44 percent of his plate appearances, and credit Jackson for seeing more pitches and drawing more walks than in his Tigers heyday. The humbug in us requires we point out his .385 batting average on balls in play is unsustainable, but Jackson showed he can still function as a genuine starting center fielder, and there aren't many of those around.

Nolan Jones 3B Born: 05/07/98 Age: 20 Bats: L Throws: R Height: 6'4" Weight: 185 Origin: Round 2, 2016 Draft (#55 overall)

YEAR	TEAM	LVL	AGE	PA	R	2B	3B	HR	RBI	BB	K	SB	CS	AVG/OBP/SLG	TAv	VORP	BABIP	BRR	FRAA	WARP
2016	CLE	RK	18	134	10	5	2	0	9	23	49	3	1	.257/.388/.339	.279	7.7	.459	0.2	3B(28): 4.6, SS(5): 0.2	1.2
2017	MHV	A-	19	265	41	18	3	4	33	43	60	1	0	.317/.430/.482	.325	27.8	.417	1.7	3B(53): 0.0	2.8
2018	*CLE*	*MLB*	*20*	*250*	*23*	*10*	*1*	*6*	*26*	*27*	*83*	*0*	*0*	*.201/.289/.328*	*.211*	*-4.9*	*.290*	*-0.4*	*3B 0*	*-0.6*
2019	*CLE*	*MLB*	*21*	*344*	*40*	*15*	*1*	*9*	*36*	*37*	*113*	*0*	*0*	*.210/.299/.351*	*.225*	*-5.2*	*.297*	*-0.7*	*3B 0*	*-0.6*

Breakout: 2% Improve: 6% Collapse: 0% Attrition: 4% MLB: 8% *Comparables: Matt Davidson, Jeimer Candelario, Matt Dominguez*

When a toolsy prospect starts capitalizing on his natural skills the development staff notices, and when a youngster starts controlling the strike zone they smile. When a teenager like Mr. Jones does both in his first pro season, it puts a wiggle in their stride. A long and lean prep shortstop converted to third base, Jones laid waste to the New York-Penn League last summer while showing gap power that could become plus as he fills out. There's some swing-and-miss in his game, but he showed better contact skills than expected and displayed a patient approach far beyond his years. Defensively he's raw and error prone, but his arm and athleticism give him a chance to stick on the left side of the infield. If Jones begins sanding away some of the rough edges and duplicates his patience-and-power routine throughout a full season, expect him to vault up the prospect charts.

Jason Kipnis 2B Born: 04/03/87 Age: 31 Bats: L Throws: R Height: 5'11" Weight: 195 Origin: Round 2, 2009 Draft (#63 overall)

YEAR	TEAM	LVL	AGE	PA	R	2B	3B	HR	RBI	BB	K	SB	CS	AVG/OBP/SLG	TAv	VORP	BABIP	BRR	FRAA	WARP
2015	CLE	MLB	28	641	86	43	7	9	52	57	107	12	8	.303/.372/.451	.290	35.3	.356	0.9	2B(124): -5.4	3.2
2016	CLE	MLB	29	688	91	41	4	23	82	60	146	15	3	.275/.343/.469	.264	24.1	.324	3.0	2B(151): 10.6	3.6
2017	CLE	MLB	30	373	43	25	0	12	35	28	71	6	2	.232/.291/.414	.252	6.6	.256	-0.7	2B(75): 1.0, CF(11): -1.1	0.7
2018	*CLE*	*MLB*	*31*	*641*	*85*	*35*	*4*	*14*	*64*	*59*	*127*	*14*	*4*	*.260/.331/.408*	*.257*	*23.9*	*.308*	*0.6*	*2B 2*	*2.0*
2019	*CLE*	*MLB*	*32*	*466*	*56*	*25*	*2*	*11*	*52*	*44*	*96*	*9*	*3*	*.254/.329/.404*	*.248*	*9.9*	*.301*	*1.0*	*2B 1*	*1.2*

Breakout: 2% Improve: 48% Collapse: 5% Attrition: 7% MLB: 96% *Comparables: Orlando Hudson, Mark Ellis, Brian Roberts*

A lifetime of baseball fandom brings with it the bittersweet knowledge that you will be following the game far longer than the incredible athletes in front of you will be able to play it at the highest level. This means you're forced to suffer alongside a series of heroes as they struggle against the indignity of diminished skills and eventually, inevitably, succumb. And then it happens again, with a new group of heroes. Which brings us to Kipnis, grinder extraordinaire and the beating heart of the Cleveland franchise who soldiered through shoulder and hamstring woes, the loss of his spot at the keystone and a late-season center-field tryout to put up some of the worst numbers of his career. It's fair to attribute last year's struggles at the plate to injury and random chance; after all, Kipnis has bounced back from bad seasons before, and may very well do so again. But the aging curve for second basemen is notoriously cruel, and much of Kipnis' value comes from being a solid all-around hitter and adequate fielder at a premium defensive position. Put him at first base or in an outfield corner—center field is likely a bridge too far—and he's at best just another dirty uniform, albeit an important one for other, less tangible reasons. A healthy Kipnis may thrive this year, at the pivot or elsewhere, but he may not. We'll watch and cheer either way, because he's worth it.

Francisco Lindor SS Born: 11/14/93 Age: 24 Bats: B Throws: R Height: 5'11" Weight: 190 Origin: Round 1, 2011 Draft (#8 overall)

YEAR	TEAM	LVL	AGE	PA	R	2B	3B	HR	RBI	BB	K	SB	CS	AVG/OBP/SLG	TAv	VORP	BABIP	BRR	FRAA	WARP
2015	COH	AAA	21	262	26	11	5	2	22	25	38	9	7	.284/.350/.402	.271	13.6	.328	0.4	SS(56): -1.3	1.3
2015	CLE	MLB	21	438	50	22	4	12	51	27	69	12	2	.313/.353/.482	.286	27.7	.348	-0.6	SS(98): 3.3	3.3
2016	CLE	MLB	22	684	99	30	3	15	78	57	88	19	5	.301/.358/.435	.270	40.4	.324	5.5	SS(155): 19.3	6.2
2017	CLE	MLB	23	723	99	44	4	33	89	60	93	15	3	.273/.337/.505	.280	48.4	.275	2.1	SS(158): 3.8	5.2
2018	*CLE*	*MLB*	*24*	*690*	*100*	*35*	*5*	*21*	*81*	*55*	*95*	*17*	*5*	*.288/.344/.463*	*.276*	*44.3*	*.305*	*1.3*	*SS 8*	*4.4*
2019	*CLE*	*MLB*	*25*	*625*	*86*	*33*	*4*	*24*	*88*	*54*	*92*	*15*	*4*	*.294/.358/.493*	*.279*	*35.5*	*.309*	*1.9*	*SS 8*	*4.7*

Breakout: 1% Improve: 54% Collapse: 3% Attrition: 6% MLB: 100% *Comparables: J.J. Hardy, Xander Bogaerts, Troy Tulowitzki*

He can turn the world on with his smile. He can take a nothing play and suddenly make it all seem worthwhile. In these angry and polarized times it's nice to know we can all agree on Lindor, and if some day we get to see him spin around and toss his cap in the air after a championship win, the ensuing joy-quake could heal our nation. Or not, but there's no denying that Lindor is one of the game's greatest gifts. Last year he spent more time looking for pitches to drive, resulting in a huge increase in fly balls and home runs, and a concurrent drop in BABIP and on-base percentage. As he continues to grow into his power and make more adjustments it wouldn't be surprising to see his batting average creep back up, making him a high-contact slugger who also happens to be a Gold Glove shortstop, clubhouse leader and world-class jersey-seller working on a cheap contract. Stay healthy, Mr. Smile.

Francisco Mejia C Born: 10/27/95 Age: 22 Bats: B Throws: R Height: 5'10" Weight: 180 Origin: International Free Agent, 2012

YEAR	TEAM	LVL	AGE	PA	R	2B	3B	HR	RBI	BB	K	SB	CS	AVG/OBP/SLG	TAv	VORP	BABIP	BRR	FRAA	WARP
2015	LKC	A	19	446	45	13	0	9	53	38	78	4	1	.243/.324/.345	.259	15.1	.281	-1.8	C(94): 4.4	2.1
2016	LKC	A	20	259	41	17	3	7	51	15	39	1	0	.347/.384/.531	.329	29.7	.388	2.3	C(52): 1.5	3.4
2016	LYN	A+	20	184	22	12	1	4	29	13	24	1	2	.333/.380/.488	.308	16.8	.366	-0.1	C(35): 0.6	1.8
2017	AKR	AA	21	383	52	21	2	14	52	24	53	7	2	.297/.346/.490	.302	32.4	.311	1.5	C(71): 2.6, 3B(1): -0.1	3.8
2017	CLE	MLB	21	14	1	0	0	0	1	1	3	0	0	.154/.214/.154	.146	-1.7	.200	-0.3	C(3): 0.0	-0.2
2018	*CLE*	*MLB*	*22*	*158*	*18*	*8*	*0*	*5*	*19*	*8*	*33*	*1*	*0*	*.256/.301/.420*	*.248*	*4.6*	*.295*	*-0.2*	*C -3, 3B -1*	*0.0*
2019	*CLE*	*MLB*	*23*	*305*	*40*	*15*	*1*	*12*	*41*	*20*	*65*	*1*	*0*	*.261/.317/.452*	*.256*	*8.5*	*.296*	*-0.5*	*C -3, 3B -1*	*0.5*

Breakout: 10% Improve: 27% Collapse: 11% Attrition: 33% MLB: 52% *Comparables: Hank Conger, Gary Sanchez, Austin Romine*

YEAR	TEAM	P. COUNT	FRM RUNS	BLK RUNS	THRW RUNS	TOT RUNS
2017	CLE	40	0.0	0.0	0.0	0.0
2018	*CLE*	*3438*	*-2.2*	*-0.2*	*-0.2*	*-2.6*
2019	*CLE*	*6644*	*-1.9*	*-0.2*	*-0.2*	*-2.3*

The consensus top catching prospect in baseball, Mejia excelled at the plate and improved behind the dish in Double-A before making his big-league debut last September. A switch-hitter with a quick, balanced stroke from both sides of the plate, Mejia shows plus contact skills that lead to high batting averages and solid in-game power with the potential for more to come. It's an offensive profile that would play anywhere on the diamond, but a catcher with that bat could be a perennial All-Star. Mejia is an athletic and strong-armed receiver who has worked hard to improve defensively, though he's unlikely to win any Gold Gloves back there. The Tribe tried him out at third base last fall to give him some defensive versatility, but he isn't an instinctive infielder and his future lies behind the plate. It's a bright one.

Tyler Naquin CF Born: 04/24/91 Age: 27 Bats: L Throws: R Height: 6'2" Weight: 195 Origin: Round 1, 2012 Draft (#15 overall)

YEAR	TEAM	LVL	AGE	PA	R	2B	3B	HR	RBI	BB	K	SB	CS	AVG/OBP/SLG	TAv	VORP	BABIP	BRR	FRAA	WARP
2015	AKR	AA	24	160	16	12	1	1	10	15	24	7	1	.348/.419/.468	.336	15.5	.410	-1.4	CF(33): 1.5	1.8
2015	COH	AAA	24	218	34	13	0	6	17	25	49	6	2	.263/.353/.430	.269	9.2	.323	0.8	CF(47): 2.9	1.2
2016	COH	AAA	25	79	6	3	1	1	8	8	15	1	2	.286/.354/.400	.288	3.1	.345	-1.6	CF(15): 1.3, RF(2): -0.1	0.4
2016	CLE	MLB	25	365	52	18	5	14	43	36	112	6	3	.296/.372/.514	.285	18.0	.411	-2.3	CF(105): -8.2, RF(4): -0.4	1.0
2017	COH	AAA	26	330	42	14	4	10	51	30	71	5	2	.298/.359/.475	.284	18.4	.358	0.9	CF(49): 10.8, RF(23): -1.1	2.7
2017	CLE	MLB	26	40	4	2	0	0	1	2	9	0	1	.216/.250/.270	.207	-1.4	.276	-0.2	CF(11): -0.4, RF(8): -0.5	-0.2
2018	*CLE*	*MLB*	*27*	*64*	*8*	*3*	*0*	*2*	*8*	*6*	*17*	*1*	*0*	*.261/.333/.428*	*.262*	*2.4*	*.337*	*0.0*	*CF 0*	*0.2*
2019	*CLE*	*MLB*	*28*	*251*	*33*	*13*	*2*	*8*	*32*	*25*	*68*	*3*	*2*	*.263/.342/.445*	*.262*	*7.3*	*.339*	*-0.8*	*CF -1*	*0.7*

Breakout: 5% Improve: 42% Collapse: 9% Attrition: 19% MLB: 83% *Comparables: Cody Ross, Ryan Ludwick, Jordan Danks*

Naquin followed up his woeful 2016 stretch run with a punchless April, leading to a quick demotion to Triple-A, a sore back and an ongoing attempt to play his way back into the club's good graces. Long branded a tweener who lacked the range for center field or the power for an outfield corner, Naquin's defensive misadventures have seemingly confirmed the former and his recent difficulties handling high heat have cut into his offensive numbers whenever he gets the call. His window was always going to be a narrow one, with a Cleveland roster already littered with lefty corner men and true center fielders like Greg Allen and Bradley Zimmer coming up behind him, so Naquin is likely a fourth outfielder going forward, perhaps in another city.

Roberto Perez C Born: 12/23/88 Age: 29 Bats: R Throws: R Height: 5'11" Weight: 220 Origin: Round 33, 2008 Draft (#1011 overall)

YEAR	TEAM	LVL	AGE	PA	R	2B	3B	HR	RBI	BB	K	SB	CS	AVG/OBP/SLG	TAv	VORP	BABIP	BRR	FRAA	WARP
2015	CLE	MLB	26	226	30	9	1	7	21	33	64	0	0	.228/.348/.402	.257	8.4	.304	-0.8	C(69): 6.9	1.6
2016	CLE	MLB	27	184	14	6	1	3	17	23	44	0	0	.183/.285/.294	.218	0.2	.229	-0.2	C(61): 10.1	1.1
2017	CLE	MLB	28	248	22	12	0	8	38	26	71	0	1	.207/.291/.373	.232	3.7	.266	-0.6	C(71): 14.4	1.8
2018	*CLE*	*MLB*	*29*	*290*	*33*	*12*	*1*	*8*	*32*	*34*	*78*	*0*	*0*	*.227/.316/.378*	*.242*	*8.6*	*.288*	*-0.6*	*C 14*	*2.0*
2019	*CLE*	*MLB*	*30*	*283*	*35*	*12*	*1*	*8*	*32*	*37*	*79*	*0*	*0*	*.225/.329/.385*	*.241*	*5.1*	*.287*	*-0.5*	*C 14*	*2.1*

Breakout: 3% Improve: 42% Collapse: 8% Attrition: 15% MLB: 91% *Comparables: Hank Conger, Nick Hundley, Brian Schneider*

YEAR	TEAM	P. COUNT	FRM RUNS	BLK RUNS	THRW RUNS	TOT RUNS
2015	CLE	8759	4.3	2.0	1.2	7.4
2016	CLE	7261	7.7	1.3	1.2	10.2
2016	CLE	7261	7.7	1.3	1.2	10.2
2017	CLE	9658	12.5	1.8	0.5	14.8
2018	*CLE*	*11203*	*11.8*	*2.3*	*1.1*	*15.2*
2019	*CLE*	*10925*	*10.4*	*2.0*	*1.0*	*13.5*

Perez will be the first one to tell you that the job title is "catcher," not "hitter." The man they call Robocop had best hope the league never implements robo-umps, costing him the opportunity to capitalize on human frailty and steal strikes at an elite rate. His framing skills, along with a rocket arm that shoots down runners with the temerity to cross his line of death, allow his defense to outweigh one of the least potent bats in the game. At the plate Perez is patient to the point of passivity, drawing a few walks but rarely driving the ball. His defensive chops make him a solid big-league backup, but if he's your primary starter you're settling.

Jose Ramirez 3B Born: 09/17/92 Age: 25 Bats: B Throws: R Height: 5'9" Weight: 165 Origin: International Free Agent, 2009

YEAR	TEAM	LVL	AGE	PA	R	2B	3B	HR	RBI	BB	K	SB	CS	AVG/OBP/SLG	TAv	VORP	BABIP	BRR	FRAA	WARP
2015	COH	AAA	22	195	29	13	2	1	12	17	9	15	4	.293/.354/.408	.268	9.1	.303	1.6	2B(28): 1.8, SS(10): -0.5	1.0
2015	CLE	MLB	22	355	50	14	3	6	27	32	39	10	4	.219/.291/.340	.238	5.2	.232	1.0	SS(46): -4.3, 2B(33): 2.5	0.5
2016	CLE	MLB	23	618	84	46	3	11	76	44	62	22	7	.312/.363/.462	.274	31.4	.333	4.7	3B(117): -2.6, LF(48): -0.8	2.8
2017	CLE	MLB	24	645	107	56	6	29	83	52	69	17	5	.318/.374/.583	.315	57.2	.319	0.2	3B(88): 6.0, 2B(71): -0.1	6.3
2018	*CLE*	*MLB*	*25*	*624*	*76*	*37*	*5*	*14*	*72*	*46*	*68*	*20*	*7*	*.281/.333/.435*	*.263*	*24.8*	*.294*	*1.6*	*3B -3, 2B 1*	*1.9*
2019	*CLE*	*MLB*	*26*	*543*	*66*	*33*	*4*	*14*	*66*	*43*	*64*	*17*	*6*	*.281/.340/.451*	*.262*	*17.2*	*.294*	*2.1*	*3B -2, 2B 1*	*1.9*

Breakout: 2% Improve: 54% Collapse: 2% Attrition: 7% MLB: 98% *Comparables: Sean Burroughs, Blake DeWitt, Aaron Hill*

If Jason Kipnis and Francisco Lindor are the heart and soul of the Cleveland lineup, Ramirez has become its hyperactive battery pack. Few expected him to fully match his 2016 breakout, let alone top it, but Ramirez was an even better player in just about every way last year. His defense at third base was stellar and he was solid filling in at the pivot, so much so that he may just stay there. At the plate he made an effort to turn on the ball and grew into a *bona fide* slugger; if last year's ball was juiced Ramirez was a clear beneficiary, as his average exit velocity didn't increase but his rate of home runs per fly ball more than doubled. A little more carry meant a lot more bombs, while his speed and aggressive baserunning helped him tally a league-leading 56 doubles. Duplicating this in 2018 will be a tall order, but then again, we all said that last spring.

Giovanny Urshela 3B Born: 10/11/91 Age: 26 Bats: R Throws: R Height: 6'0" Weight: 215 Origin: International Free Agent, 2008

YEAR	TEAM	LVL	AGE	PA	R	2B	3B	HR	RBI	BB	K	SB	CS	AVG/OBP/SLG	TAv	VORP	BABIP	BRR	FRAA	WARP
2015	COH	AAA	23	84	12	5	1	3	9	3	12	0	0	.272/.298/.469	.245	1.5	.288	0.6	3B(17): 3.0	0.5
2015	CLE	MLB	23	288	25	8	1	6	21	18	58	0	1	.225/.279/.330	.217	-4.8	.266	-1.4	3B(80): 7.4	0.3
2016	COH	AAA	24	491	54	24	1	8	57	15	58	0	0	.274/.294/.380	.236	-1.6	.294	-4.3	3B(104): 6.4, SS(5): -0.3	0.5
2017	COH	AAA	25	325	34	12	1	6	34	20	45	0	0	.266/.321/.374	.241	1.1	.294	-3.5	3B(60): 0.3, SS(16): 1.0	0.2
2017	CLE	MLB	25	165	14	7	0	1	15	8	22	0	0	.224/.262/.288	.197	-5.9	.256	-0.5	3B(60): 0.9, SS(5): -0.1	-0.5
2018	*CLE*	*MLB*	*26*	*68*	*7*	*3*	*0*	*2*	*8*	*3*	*11*	*0*	*0*	*.250/.292/.377*	*.234*	*0.2*	*.282*	*-0.1*	*3B 1*	*0.0*
2019	*CLE*	*MLB*	*27*	*297*	*34*	*14*	*1*	*9*	*34*	*18*	*53*	*0*	*0*	*.253/.301/.402*	*.239*	*0.1*	*.283*	*-0.7*	*3B 3*	*0.4*

Breakout: 6% Improve: 36% Collapse: 12% Attrition: 27% MLB: 63% *Comparables: Hernan Perez, Matt Dominguez, Tyler Saladino*

Urshela's defense at the hot corner doesn't just border on the sublime, it sometimes barges right in and takes a selfie eating a hoagie in the sublime's breakfast nook. Given his soft hands, strong and accurate arm, continent-spanning range, plus instincts and flair for the dramatic, it's easy to see why Terry Francona felt comfortable penciling his glove into the Cleveland lineup down the stretch and in the playoffs. What's also easy to see is that Urshela is simply never going to be a good major-league hitter, as he's already spent 11 seasons proving he'll never be a good minor-league hitter. He's a nice bench piece on a team that's already flush with them, but Urshela should never be given 300 out-making opportunities in a season.

Bradley Zimmer CF Born: 11/27/92 Age: 25 Bats: L Throws: R Height: 6'5" Weight: 220 Origin: Round 1, 2014 Draft (#21 overall)

YEAR	TEAM	LVL	AGE	PA	R	2B	3B	HR	RBI	BB	K	SB	CS	AVG/OBP/SLG	TAv	VORP	BABIP	BRR	FRAA	WARP
2015	LYN	A+	22	335	60	17	3	10	39	37	77	32	5	.308/.403/.493	.322	31.3	.388	3.1	CF(41): 7.4, RF(22): 0.3	4.2
2015	AKR	AA	22	214	24	9	1	6	24	18	54	12	2	.219/.313/.374	.257	4.8	.273	-0.2	CF(42): 0.6	0.6
2016	AKR	AA	23	407	58	20	6	14	53	56	115	33	13	.253/.371/.471	.304	30.6	.341	1.8	CF(76): -0.6, RF(9): 2.0	3.5
2016	COH	AAA	23	150	18	5	0	1	9	21	56	5	1	.242/.349/.305	.245	1.4	.423	-0.7	CF(36): 1.2	0.3
2017	COH	AAA	24	144	22	11	2	5	14	14	43	9	3	.294/.371/.532	.300	10.1	.405	-0.6	CF(26): 3.6, RF(8): 0.5	1.4
2017	CLE	MLB	24	332	41	15	2	8	39	26	99	18	1	.241/.307/.385	.245	6.8	.328	1.6	CF(97): 9.6	1.6
2018	*CLE*	*MLB*	*25*	*500*	*71*	*22*	*3*	*15*	*55*	*50*	*158*	*26*	*6*	*.233/.321/.401*	*.253*	*16.1*	*.323*	*3.4*	*CF 7*	*2.2*
2019	*CLE*	*MLB*	*26*	*538*	*68*	*25*	*3*	*18*	*65*	*55*	*172*	*27*	*6*	*.234/.323/.410*	*.249*	*11.1*	*.324*	*1.4*	*CF 9*	*2.2*

Breakout: 5% Improve: 23% Collapse: 10% Attrition: 28% MLB: 68% *Comparables: Trayvon Robinson, Michael Taylor, Kirk Nieuwenhuis*

Zimmer spent his rookie season showing off the tools that could make him an All-Star: plus speed on the bases and in the field, terrific defensive instincts, a cannon arm and solid lefty power. He also revealed the one thing that can still get in his way: what Brooks Baseball labels "an exceptionally high likelihood to swing and miss," especially facing soft stuff and spin. Zimmer got off to a great start after his call-up in mid-May, but pitchers quickly learned how to exploit his contact woes and held him to a .211/.273/.335 line with strikeouts in nearly a third of his plate appearances after the calendar flipped to July. Zimmer's game has always featured plenty of whiff, but in the minors he walked enough to make up for it. Baseball is a game of adjustments, and if Zimmer can come back healthy from his late-season hand fracture and either make more contact or draw more free passes, his speed and defense can make him an asset in the center pasture.

PITCHERS

Brady Aiken LHP Born: 08/16/96 Age: 21 Bats: L Throws: L Height: 6'4" Weight: 205 Origin: Round 1, 2015 Draft (#17 overall)

YEAR	TEAM	LVL	AGE	W	L	SV	G	GS	IP	H	HR	BB/9	K/9	K	GB%	BABIP	WHIP	ERA	DRA	WARP	MPH	CMD	PWR	STM
2016	CLE	RK	19	0	4	0	9	8	24	32	1	4.9	13.1	35	54%	.449	1.88	7.12	3.15	0.7				
2016	MHV	A-	19	2	1	0	5	5	22^1	20	3	3.2	8.9	22	43%	.266	1.25	4.43	3.23	0.5				
2017	LKC	A	20	5	13	0	27	27	132	134	12	6.9	6.1	89	51%	.312	1.78	4.77	8.17	-4.4				
2018	*CLE*	*MLB*	*21*	*4*	*9*	*0*	*20*	*20*	*91^2*	*108*	*22*	*8.2*	*8.2*	*83*	*41%*	*.322*	*2.10*	*7.44*	*7.94*	*-2.3*				
2019	*CLE*	*MLB*	*22*	*3*	*6*	*0*	*14*	*14*	*85*	*98*	*19*	*4.2*	*7.6*	*72*	*41%*	*.315*	*1.62*	*5.79*	*6.26*	*-0.4*				

Comparables: Cam Bedrosian, Nick Gardewine, Enrique Burgos

Most Low-A pitchers who walk more batters than they whiff don't merit a full comment in this book, but Aiken isn't most pitchers. The former first overall pick once described in a national publication as "Peyton Manning on a surfboard" completed his first spin in a full-season league, and while merely completing the season healthy is a notable achievement for a Tommy John survivor, the results were uniformly abysmal. Aiken obviously struggled to control his pitches, let alone command them, and his fastball velocity remained stuck in second gear. The young lefty gets high marks for his makeup; so do we, and perhaps you do too. But if none of us have a fastball that can get out of the upper eighties, the odds of any of us thriving in a big-league rotation are equally low.

Cody Allen RHP Born: 11/20/88 Age: 29 Bats: R Throws: R Height: 6'1" Weight: 210 Origin: Round 23, 2011 Draft (#698 overall)

YEAR	TEAM	LVL	AGE	W	L	SV	G	GS	IP	H	HR	BB/9	K/9	K	GB%	BABIP	WHIP	ERA	DRA	WARP	MPH	CMD	PWR	STM
2015	CLE	MLB	26	2	5	34	70	0	69^1	56	2	3.2	12.9	99	35%	.342	1.17	2.99	2.31	2.0	97.1	49	61	51
2016	CLE	MLB	27	3	5	32	67	0	68	41	8	3.6	11.5	87	48%	.232	1.00	2.51	3.05	1.5	96.5	48	55	49
2017	CLE	MLB	28	3	7	30	69	0	67^1	57	9	2.8	12.3	92	34%	.304	1.16	2.94	3.26	1.4	95.5	45	50	51
2018	*CLE*	*MLB*	*29*	*3*	*3*	*30*	*60*	*0*	*63*	*55*	*10*	*3.6*	*11.4*	*80*	*40%*	*.297*	*1.27*	*3.64*	*4.12*	*0.7*	*95.6*	*47*	*54*	*50*
2019	*CLE*	*MLB*	*30*	*3*	*1*	*20*	*52*	*0*	*54^2*	*45*	*10*	*4.0*	*11.6*	*70*	*40%*	*.282*	*1.27*	*4.33*	*4.69*	*0.3*	*95.0*	*46*	*53*	*50*

Breakout: 17% Improve: 43% Collapse: 34% Attrition: 5% MLB: 97% *Comparables: Troy Percival, Lee Smith, John Wetteland*

When discussing the best relievers in the game Allen is rarely mentioned, but when you consider where he ranks since his first full season in 2013 it's clear that he is among the most reliably dominant. He has the third-most relief appearances during that time, posting the seventh-best FIP and eighth-highest WARP. Only Craig Kimbrel, Dellin Betances, Kenley Jansen and David Robertson better Allen's 32.4 percent strikeout rate. He's also younger than any reliever ahead of him on any of those lists and his overall salary has been roughly a third of what the others have earned. Allen's hard curveball is among the game's filthiest pitches, and his high-spin four-seamer is difficult to barrel. Riches will soon find him, but Allen has been one of the game's quietest bargains for half a decade.

Trevor Bauer RHP Born: 01/17/91 Age: 27 Bats: R Throws: R Height: 6'1" Weight: 190 Origin: Round 1, 2011 Draft (#3 overall)

YEAR	TEAM	LVL	AGE	W	L	SV	G	GS	IP	H	HR	BB/9	K/9	K	GB%	BABIP	WHIP	ERA	DRA	WARP	MPH	CMD	PWR	STM
2015	CLE	MLB	24	11	12	0	31	30	176	152	23	4.0	8.7	170	41%	.276	1.31	4.55	3.71	2.9	95.6	59	49	71
2016	CLE	MLB	25	12	8	0	35	28	190	179	20	3.3	8.0	168	49%	.292	1.31	4.26	4.51	1.8	96.2	51	48	78
2017	CLE	MLB	26	17	9	0	32	31	176^1	181	25	3.1	10.0	196	47%	.337	1.37	4.19	4.58	1.9	96.1	61	44	77
2018	*CLE*	*MLB*	*27*	*13*	*8*	*0*	*30*	*30*	*171*	*161*	*22*	*3.5*	*9.1*	*174*	*46%*	*.298*	*1.34*	*3.80*	*4.27*	*2.2*	*95.5*	*58*	*47*	*77*
2019	*CLE*	*MLB*	*28*	*11*	*10*	*0*	*31*	*31*	*193^1*	*179*	*24*	*3.3*	*9.4*	*203*	*46%*	*.301*	*1.29*	*3.84*	*4.16*	*2.9*	*95.3*	*57*	*46*	*78*

Breakout: 22% Improve: 49% Collapse: 23% Attrition: 9% MLB: 90% *Comparables: Gio Gonzalez, Chad Gaudin, Danny Duffy*

Drone builder. Chess player. Twitter ranter. Self-analyzer. Bauer labels himself accurately (and redundantly) as "one of the most scientific baseball players in MLB" and endeavors to absorb and apply the lessons of statistical analysis, biomechanics, performance psychology and numerous other disciplines to his life and career. It's impossible for us to know whether all, some or none of those things contributed to his improvement last season, but improve he did. Bauer's curveball was tremendous and he threw it more than ever last year, while cutting back on his tendency to play pitch-type bingo every night. His strikeout rate spiked, settling into the upper tiers of major-league starters. If he stays healthy and continues this level of performance—and at this very moment he's reading something that he believes will help him do so—he won't be an ace, but he'll be within shouting distance.

Carlos Carrasco RHP Born: 03/21/87 Age: 31 Bats: R Throws: R Height: 6'3" Weight: 212 Origin: International Free Agent, 2003

YEAR	TEAM	LVL	AGE	W	L	SV	G	GS	IP	H	HR	BB/9	K/9	K	GB%	BABIP	WHIP	ERA	DRA	WARP	MPH	CMD	PWR	STM
2015	CLE	MLB	28	14	12	0	30	30	183^{2}	154	18	2.1	10.6	216	53%	.304	1.07	3.63	2.35	6.0	97.5	50	61	70
2016	CLE	MLB	29	11	8	0	25	25	146^{1}	134	21	2.1	9.2	150	50%	.289	1.15	3.32	3.14	3.7	96.8	53	53	63
2017	CLE	MLB	30	18	6	0	32	32	200	173	21	2.1	10.2	226	47%	.307	1.10	3.29	3.36	4.9	96.3	47	50	78
2018	*CLE*	*MLB*	*31*	*13*	*8*	*0*	*29*	*29*	*174*	*161*	*25*	*2.7*	*9.9*	*191*	*48%*	*.299*	*1.23*	*3.54*	*3.99*	*2.8*	*95.9*	*49*	*53*	*71*
2019	*CLE*	*MLB*	*32*	*12*	*10*	*0*	*31*	*31*	197^{2}	*180*	*27*	*2.5*	*10.0*	*219*	*48%*	*.3*	*1.19*	*3.63*	*3.93*	*3.5*	*95.3*	*49*	*51*	*71*

Breakout: 16% Improve: 40% Collapse: 27% Attrition: 7% MLB: 91% *Comparables: Corey Kluber, Adam Wainwright, David Price*

While Trevor Bauer may be trying to cross the border into true ace country, Carrasco has already been there for several years. His stuff ranks among the best, most varied and most aesthetically pleasing in the game, featuring mid-90s heat, a big-breaking bender, a righty-killing slider and a lefty-taming changeup, though Carrasco can and will throw any pitch to anyone at any time. His only question mark has been durability, but a healthy Carrasco took 32 dominating turns last year and hit the 200-inning mark for the first time. Working on what has turned out to be a ludicrously affordable deal with club options through 2020, Carrasco has quietly become one of the game's most valuable assets.

Mike Clevinger RHP Born: 12/21/90 Age: 27 Bats: R Throws: R Height: 6'4" Weight: 210 Origin: Round 4, 2011 Draft (#135 overall)

YEAR	TEAM	LVL	AGE	W	L	SV	G	GS	IP	H	HR	BB/9	K/9	K	GB%	BABIP	WHIP	ERA	DRA	WARP	MPH	CMD	PWR	STM
2015	AKR	AA	24	9	8	0	27	26	158	127	8	2.3	8.3	145	37%	.272	1.06	2.73	2.94	4.1				
2016	COH	AAA	25	11	1	0	17	17	93	78	8	3.4	9.4	97	40%	.293	1.22	3.00	2.72	2.8				
2016	CLE	MLB	25	3	3	0	17	10	53	50	8	4.9	8.5	50	40%	.288	1.49	5.26	5.41	-0.1	96.1	44	53	64
2017	COH	AAA	26	3	2	0	7	7	34	28	3	3.7	10.1	38	40%	.298	1.24	2.65	2.56	1.2				
2017	CLE	MLB	26	12	6	0	27	21	121^{2}	92	13	4.4	10.1	137	40%	.274	1.25	3.11	3.88	2.3	94.4	54	42	69
2018	*CLE*	*MLB*	*27*	*6*	*5*	*0*	*16*	*16*	*91*	*86*	*14*	*4.0*	*9.2*	*93*	*40%*	*.293*	*1.40*	*4.18*	*4.69*	*0.7*	*94.4*	*52*	*45*	*68*
2019	*CLE*	*MLB*	*28*	*10*	*11*	*0*	*30*	*30*	*189*	*176*	*29*	*3.9*	*9.1*	*191*	*40%*	*.287*	*1.37*	*4.49*	*4.86*	*1.5*	*94.1*	*52*	*45*	*68*

Breakout: 29% Improve: 57% Collapse: 18% Attrition: 20% MLB: 92% *Comparables: J.A. Happ, John Maine, Ramon Ramirez*

With his freedom rock hair Clevinger may resemble a young Mitch Kramer on the mound, but he has more than enough stuff to leave batsmen dazed and confused. Used primarily as a starter last year, he relied more on his power curve and slider, working up and down and getting plenty of awkward swings, although his changeup didn't keep lefties from subjecting him to a good paddling. His low-90s fastball doesn't shatter bats like a bowling ball hitting a windshield but it's a solid pitch, helping him to post an elite strikeout rate. Clevinger doesn't carry solid control, though, and it would be a lot cooler if he did, as his high walk rate will always be a concern. Still, Clevinger should be capable of holding onto a job in a rotation, which is a better option than working for the city to put money in your pocket.

Nick Goody RHP Born: 07/06/91 Age: 26 Bats: R Throws: R Height: 5'11" Weight: 195 Origin: Round 6, 2012 Draft (#217 overall)

YEAR	TEAM	LVL	AGE	W	L	SV	G	GS	IP	H	HR	BB/9	K/9	K	GB%	BABIP	WHIP	ERA	DRA	WARP	MPH	CMD	PWR	STM
2015	TRN	AA	23	1	1	4	29	0	41^{2}	29	2	3.0	12.7	59	35%	.287	1.03	1.73	1.02	1.9				
2015	SWB	AAA	23	1	1	4	14	0	20^{2}	14	0	3.0	10.9	25	30%	.280	1.02	1.31	2.07	0.7				
2015	NYA	MLB	23	0	0	0	7	0	5^{2}	6	0	4.8	4.8	3	47%	.316	1.59	4.76	3.81	0.1	93.6			45
2016	SWB	AAA	24	0	1	5	18	0	23^{1}	12	4	1.5	13.5	35	33%	.182	0.69	1.93	0.97	1.1				
2016	NYA	MLB	24	0	0	0	27	0	29	30	7	3.7	10.6	34	25%	.311	1.45	4.66	5.97	-0.3	93.1	43	39	42
2017	CLE	MLB	25	1	2	0	56	0	54^{2}	39	7	3.3	11.9	72	29%	.269	1.08	2.80	3.45	1.0	93.1	49	38	46
2018	*CLE*	*MLB*	*26*	*3*	*2*	*0*	*51*	*0*	53^{2}	*48*	*10*	*3.8*	*11.4*	*68*	*33%*	*.297*	*1.32*	*4.24*	*4.60*	*0.3*	*92.7*	*48*	*39*	*45*
2019	*CLE*	*MLB*	*27*	*2*	*1*	*0*	*48*	*0*	50^{2}	*43*	*10*	*3.7*	*11.9*	*67*	*33%*	*.286*	*1.25*	*4.36*	*4.72*	*0.3*	*92.4*	*48*	*39*	*45*

Breakout: 29% Improve: 45% Collapse: 18% Attrition: 25% MLB: 79% *Comparables: Fernando Cabrera, Chad Orvella, Tony Sipp*

Just how good were Indians pitchers at missing bats last year? Goody posted the 26th-highest strikeout rate in baseball (minimum 40 innings), yet ranked only fifth on his own staff and was left off the playoff roster. The former Yankees farmhand thrived in his first season in Cleveland, unleashing a plus slider that had always produced plenty of whiffs in the minors and proved to be surprisingly effective against hitters of all stripes. Short, two-pitch right-handers are often expected to be platoon liabilities, with some reason. Goody may not be able to keep missing bats at such an elite level, but should be able to settle in as a solid middle relief option with late-inning upside.

Corey Kluber RHP Born: 04/10/86 Age: 32 Bats: R Throws: R Height: 6'4" Weight: 215 Origin: Round 4, 2007 Draft (#134 overall)

YEAR	TEAM	LVL	AGE	W	L	SV	G	GS	IP	H	HR	BB/9	K/9	K	GB%	BABIP	WHIP	ERA	DRA	WARP	MPH	CMD	PWR	STM
2015	CLE	MLB	29	9	16	0	32	32	222	189	22	1.8	9.9	245	44%	.297	1.05	3.49	2.61	6.5	95.2	56	49	80
2016	CLE	MLB	30	18	9	0	32	32	215	170	22	2.4	9.5	227	46%	.271	1.06	3.14	3.04	5.7	94.8	51	48	83
2017	CLE	MLB	31	18	4	0	29	29	203^{2}	141	21	1.6	11.7	265	46%	.267	0.87	2.25	2.05	8.0	94.0	60	38	77
2018	*CLE*	*MLB*	*32*	*15*	*8*	*0*	*29*	*29*	194^{1}	*169*	*25*	*2.6*	*10.2*	*221*	*45%*	*.296*	*1.17*	*3.25*	*3.67*	*3.9*	*93.6*	*55*	*44*	*79*
2019	*CLE*	*MLB*	*33*	*13*	*10*	*0*	*32*	*32*	*203*	*171*	*24*	*2.4*	*10.2*	*231*	*45%*	*.293*	*1.11*	*3.25*	*3.53*	*4.9*	*93.0*	*55*	*42*	*78*

Breakout: 13% Improve: 31% Collapse: 37% Attrition: 6% MLB: 92% *Comparables: Zack Greinke, Justin Verlander, Roger Clemens*

Don't call it a curveball. Don't call it a slider. Just call it the most fearsome weapon in any starter's arsenal and leave it at that. Kluber rode his ethereal spinner to his second Cy Young Award last year, throwing it more and more as the season wore on and setting career bests in just about everything you can measure. After sitting out May with a sore back, he returned to post the most dominant stretch of his career, featuring a 224/23 K/BB ratio over 166 innings. His two poor postseason starts set off klaxons for those with concerns about overuse, but his efficiency has always enabled him to work deep into games without high pitch counts. Kluber will be 35 when his team-friendly contract expires after the 2021 season; last year's hardware added a few million in incentive bonuses to the total cost, but we're sure the Indians don't mind.

Boone Logan LHP Born: 08/13/84 Age: 33 Bats: R Throws: L Height: 6'5" Weight: 215 Origin: Round 20, 2002 Draft (#600 overall)

YEAR	TEAM	LVL	AGE	W	L	SV	G	GS	IP	H	HR	BB/9	K/9	K	GB%	BABIP	WHIP	ERA	DRA	WARP	MPH	CMD	PWR	STM
2015	COL	MLB	30	0	3	0	60	0	35^{1}	40	3	4.3	11.2	44	45%	.374	1.61	4.33	5.16	-0.2	95.5	47	40	41
2016	COL	MLB	31	2	5	1	66	0	46^{1}	27	4	3.9	11.1	57	51%	.221	1.01	3.69	2.86	1.1	95.5	49	42	44
2017	CLE	MLB	32	1	0	0	38	0	21	20	2	3.9	12.0	28	51%	.353	1.38	4.71	4.78	0.1	95.5	35	40	38
2018	*CLE*	*MLB*	*33*	*2*	*1*	*1*	*33*	*0*	34^{2}	*31*	*4*	*4.2*	*10.3*	*39*	*47%*	*.307*	*1.38*	*4.10*	*4.36*	*0.2*	*94.4*	*44*	*40*	*40*
2019	*CLE*	*MLB*	*34*	*3*	*1*	*2*	*70*	*0*	45^{2}	*43*	*7*	*4.7*	*9.9*	*50*	*47%*	*.306*	*1.47*	*4.51*	*4.88*	*0.2*	*93.9*	*43*	*40*	*40*

Breakout: 23% Improve: 46% Collapse: 26% Attrition: 8% MLB: 92% *Comparables: Jose Valverde, Michael Gonzalez, Roberto Hernandez*

Logan's run of seasons in which he's struck out more than a batter per inning has now reached seven, and should continue well into his thirties so long as he's healthy and spotted correctly. He's evolved into a true LOOGY, facing 2.4 batters per appearance last year—fewer than any pitcher in baseball other than fellow lefty specialist Marc Rzepczynski. Back problems cut his season short in July and the Indians found a cheaper alternative in Tyler Olson, sending Logan back onto the free agent market. His slider is still poison to same-side batters, so he should be coming soon to a bullpen near you.

Evan Marshall RHP Born: 04/18/90 Age: 28 Bats: R Throws: R Height: 6'2" Weight: 225 Origin: Round 4, 2011 Draft (#124 overall)

YEAR	TEAM	LVL	AGE	W	L	SV	G	GS	IP	H	HR	BB/9	K/9	K	GB%	BABIP	WHIP	ERA	DRA	WARP	MPH	CMD	PWR	STM
2015	ARI	MLB	25	0	2	0	13	0	13^{1}	20	3	3.4	4.7	7	51%	.370	1.88	6.07	5.14	-0.1	96.3	39	60	48
2015	RNO	AAA	25	3	2	0	31	0	32^{1}	47	1	3.6	7.0	25	66%	.380	1.86	6.40	6.06	-0.4				
2016	ARI	MLB	26	0	1	0	15	0	15^{1}	28	2	4.7	5.3	9	57%	.441	2.35	8.80	4.92	0.0	95.7	45	48	43
2016	RNO	AAA	26	1	1	0	33	0	33^{1}	36	1	4.3	7.6	28	48%	.340	1.56	4.59	6.42	-0.6				
2017	SEA	MLB	27	0	0	0	6	0	7^{2}	12	1	5.9	4.7	4	34%	.393	2.22	9.39	5.05	0.0	94.7			22
2017	TAC	AAA	27	1	0	1	13	1	21^{2}	28	4	2.9	10.8	26	61%	.400	1.62	4.15	2.70	0.6				
2018	*CLE*	*MLB*	*28*	*1*	*1*	*0*	*31*	*0*	32^{1}	*38*	*5*	*4.4*	*7.9*	*28*	*50%*	*.339*	*1.68*	*4.95*	*5.27*	*0.0*	*95.0*	*43*	*53*	*36*
2019	*CLE*	*MLB*	*29*	*1*	*0*	*0*	*30*	*0*	*32*	*38*	*5*	*4.5*	*7.5*	*27*	*50%*	*.329*	*1.68*	*5.18*	*5.61*	*-0.1*	*94.4*	*44*	*50*	*33*

Breakout: 24% Improve: 39% Collapse: 11% Attrition: 24% MLB: 60% *Comparables: Josh Edgin, Caleb Thielbar, Bryan Morris*

Claimed on waivers from the Diamondbacks in early April, Marshall rode the Seattle-Tacoma shuttle for a month before he blew out a hamstring in early May, spent nearly three months on the disabled list, and finally was demoted to the minors to stay in August. As injury-marred as 2017 was, it doesn't compare to 2015, when a line drive hit Marshall in the head and nearly ended his career. Marshall's low-strikeout, high-contact profile isn't a great fit in today's high-strikeout environment, but given his medical history Marshall is happy just to have an opportunity to step on the field every day.

Zach McAllister RHP Born: 12/08/87 Age: 30 Bats: R Throws: R Height: 6'6" Weight: 240 Origin: Round 3, 2006 Draft (#104 overall)

YEAR	TEAM	LVL	AGE	W	L	SV	G	GS	IP	H	HR	BB/9	K/9	K	GB%	BABIP	WHIP	ERA	DRA	WARP	MPH	CMD	PWR	STM
2015	CLE	MLB	27	4	4	1	61	1	69	70	7	3.0	11.0	84	46%	.346	1.35	3.00	3.19	1.3	97.9	60	72	50
2016	CLE	MLB	28	3	2	0	53	2	52^{1}	53	6	4.0	9.3	54	35%	.318	1.45	3.44	5.05	0.0	96.6	56	63	44
2017	CLE	MLB	29	2	2	0	50	0	62	53	8	3.0	9.6	66	37%	.294	1.19	2.61	5.13	0.0	97.3	62	71	43
2018	*CLE*	*MLB*	*30*	*2*	*2*	*0*	*42*	*0*	*44*	*40*	*6*	*3.8*	*9.9*	*48*	*40%*	*.298*	*1.34*	*3.77*	*4.22*	*0.5*	*96.5*	*59*	*69*	*45*
2019	*CLE*	*MLB*	*31*	*2*	*1*	*0*	*48*	*0*	50^{2}	*47*	*8*	*4.0*	*10.6*	*60*	*40%*	*.304*	*1.37*	*4.29*	*4.64*	*0.3*	*96.0*	*59*	*68*	*44*

Breakout: 14% Improve: 44% Collapse: 28% Attrition: 9% MLB: 90% *Comparables: Kris Medlen, David Phelps, A.J. Burnett*

While the term "innings-eater" is usually reserved for mediocre but durable starting pitchers, McAllister certainly qualifies as a bullpen version. Since becoming a full-time reliever three years ago, the hulking right-hander has averaged 61 unspectacular, low-leverage innings per season; only Dustin McGowan and Dan Otero have entered games with less on the line than McAllister. That's not to say Z-Mac doesn't have his uses beyond saving other, more valuable arms from overuse, as his mid-90s heater and power curve can make same-side hitters look silly and his strikeout rate is solid. Yet another sign that the Indians' bullpen is more overqualified than a campus cabbie.

Triston McKenzie RHP Born: 08/02/97 Age: 20 Bats: R Throws: R Height: 6'5" Weight: 165 Origin: Round 1, 2015 Draft (#42 overall)

YEAR	TEAM	LVL	AGE	W	L	SV	G	GS	IP	H	HR	BB/9	K/9	K	GB%	BABIP	WHIP	ERA	DRA	WARP	MPH	CMD	PWR	STM
2015	CLE	RK	17	1	1	0	4	3	12	4	0	2.2	12.8	17	48%	.174	0.58	0.75	2.03	0.5				
2016	MHV	A-	18	4	3	0	9	9	49^{1}	31	2	2.9	10.0	55	37%	.248	0.95	0.55	2.44	1.6				
2016	LKC	A	18	2	2	0	6	6	34	27	2	1.6	13.0	49	40%	.333	0.97	3.18	1.04	1.6				
2017	LYN	A+	19	12	6	0	25	25	143	105	14	2.8	11.7	186	43%	.283	1.05	3.46	2.30	5.0				
2018	*CLE*	*MLB*	*20*	*7*	*6*	*0*	*19*	*19*	105^{1}	*96*	*20*	*4.2*	*11.7*	*136*	*37%*	*.310*	*1.38*	*4.55*	*4.85*	*1.0*				
2019	*CLE*	*MLB*	*21*	*7*	*9*	*0*	*24*	*24*	*139*	*127*	*30*	*4.2*	*12.2*	*188*	*37%*	*.307*	*1.38*	*4.71*	*5.10*	*0.8*				

Breakout: 8% Improve: 10% Collapse: 2% Attrition: 6% MLB: 13% *Comparables: Zach Braddock, Shelby Miller, Tyler Glasnow*

McKenzie spent much of last summer as a teenager laying waste to the Carolina League, unleashing a fastball that can reach the mid-90s and a potential plus curveball that helped him strike out more than a man per inning. The only fly in the ointment at this point is his thin physique, as most scouts feel he'll need to start filling out and bulking up to maintain his velocity deeper into games and develop enough stamina to support a starter's workload. We can't decide whether it's McKenzie's inability to gain weight or the Indians' concern that their healthy and productive 20-year-old might need to grow a little to become yet another frontline starter that would draw less empathy from your average middle-aged Twins fan.

Ryan Merritt LHP Born: 02/21/92 Age: 26 Bats: L Throws: L Height: 6'0" Weight: 180 Origin: Round 16, 2011 Draft (#488 overall)

YEAR	TEAM	LVL	AGE	W	L	SV	G	GS	IP	H	HR	BB/9	K/9	K	GB%	BABIP	WHIP	ERA	DRA	WARP	MPH	CMD	PWR	STM
2015	AKR	AA	23	10	7	0	22	22	141	145	8	1.0	5.7	89	44%	.304	1.14	3.51	1.71	5.7				
2015	COH	AAA	23	2	0	0	5	5	30	38	1	1.8	4.8	16	49%	.343	1.47	4.20	3.99	0.4				
2016	COH	AAA	24	11	8	0	24	24	143^{1}	156	15	1.4	5.8	92	40%	.307	1.25	3.70	2.44	4.8				
2016	CLE	MLB	24	1	0	0	4	1	11	6	0	0.0	4.9	6	55%	.194	0.55	1.64	5.16	0.0	90.1			61
2017	COH	AAA	25	10	5	0	19	18	116	116	19	1.9	6.6	85	45%	.286	1.22	3.03	2.76	3.7				
2017	CLE	MLB	25	2	0	0	5	4	20^{2}	26	0	1.7	3.0	7	55%	.333	1.45	1.74	7.37	-0.4	89.3	60	10	64
2018	*CLE*	*MLB*	*26*	*3*	*3*	*0*	*28*	*5*	*50*	*55*	*7*	*2.9*	*6.1*	*35*	*43%*	*.295*	*1.40*	*4.59*	*4.95*	*0.2*	*89.2*	*61*	*10*	*64*
2019	*CLE*	*MLB*	*27*	*6*	*5*	*0*	*66*	*11*	*122^{2}*	*132*	*17*	*2.4*	*6.3*	*86*	*43%*	*.299*	*1.34*	*4.44*	*4.80*	*0.8*	*88.9*	*61*	*10*	*64*

Breakout: 24% Improve: 36% Collapse: 7% Attrition: 24% MLB: 60% *Comparables: Austin Pruitt, Tim Cooney, Josh Geer*

The short description of Merritt is that he'd fit in nicely at no. 8 on a mid-aughties Twins prospect list. But you came here for the long description, so we're happy to tell you he's a walk-allergic pitch-to-contact lefty with a high-80s fastball, a wide assortment of off-speed junk and an ability to generate ground-ball outs. Merritt knows how to pitch and can fool 'em down on the farm, but prolonged exposure to the best hitters in the world would not be a good idea. He's a worthy Triple-A insurance policy.

Julian Merryweather RHP Born: 10/14/91 Age: 26 Bats: R Throws: R Height: 6'4" Weight: 200 Origin: Round 5, 2014 Draft (#158 overall)

YEAR	TEAM	LVL	AGE	W	L	SV	G	GS	IP	H	HR	BB/9	K/9	K	GB%	BABIP	WHIP	ERA	DRA	WARP	MPH	CMD	PWR	STM
2015	LKC	A	23	2	3	1	21	4	70^{2}	89	6	1.5	8.8	69	48%	.366	1.43	4.08	2.79	1.8				
2016	LYN	A+	24	8	2	0	11	11	61	47	4	2.2	8.6	58	56%	.262	1.02	1.03	1.55	2.7				
2016	AKR	AA	24	5	4	0	13	13	74	75	6	2.1	7.4	61	44%	.297	1.24	3.89	3.55	1.4				
2017	AKR	AA	25	4	2	0	9	9	50^{2}	37	3	1.8	9.2	52	50%	.254	0.93	3.38	1.92	2.0				
2017	COH	AAA	25	3	7	0	16	16	78	105	13	2.9	8.8	76	45%	.388	1.67	6.58	4.62	0.9				
2018	*CLE*	*MLB*	*26*	*1*	*1*	*0*	*14*	*0*	*14^{2}*	*15*	*2*	*3.3*	*8.8*	*14*	*44%*	*.298*	*1.38*	*4.24*	*4.60*	*0.1*				
2019	*CLE*	*MLB*	*27*	*2*	*1*	*0*	*48*	*0*	*50^{1}*	*51*	*7*	*2.9*	*9.1*	*51*	*44%*	*.308*	*1.33*	*4.18*	*4.52*	*0.4*				

Breakout: 18% Improve: 30% Collapse: 12% Attrition: 32% MLB: 46% *Comparables: Simon Castro, Vidal Nuno, Chase Anderson*

Merryweather showed enough in his first season in the high minors to earn a spot on the 40-man roster, though he still has plenty to prove. His stuff isn't electric by any means, but Merryweather can pump his fastball up into the mid-90s, his curveball can flash plus and his changeup is more than just a show-me offering. Triple-A hitters lit into him down the stretch, but there's enough here to suggest he could survive at the back of a big-league rotation. Or more likely not, as big-league rosters aren't exactly teeming with guys who hadn't mastered Triple-A by the age of 26.

Andrew Miller LHP Born: 05/21/85 Age: 33 Bats: L Throws: L Height: 6'7" Weight: 205 Origin: Round 1, 2006 Draft (#6 overall)

YEAR	TEAM	LVL	AGE	W	L	SV	G	GS	IP	H	HR	BB/9	K/9	K	GB%	BABIP	WHIP	ERA	DRA	WARP	MPH	CMD	PWR	STM
2015	NYA	MLB	30	3	2	36	60	0	61^{2}	33	5	2.9	14.6	100	50%	.241	0.86	2.04	1.95	2.0	97.6	57	49	47
2016	NYA	MLB	31	6	1	9	44	0	45^{1}	28	5	1.4	15.3	77	55%	.284	0.77	1.39	1.85	1.6	98.2	52	43	50
2016	CLE	MLB	31	4	0	3	26	0	29	14	3	0.6	14.3	46	58%	.212	0.55	1.55	1.63	1.1	97.5	52	43	50
2017	CLE	MLB	32	4	3	2	57	0	62^{2}	31	3	3.0	13.6	95	42%	.233	0.83	1.44	2.32	2.0	96.9	57	45	45
2018	*CLE*	*MLB*	*33*	*3*	*2*	*5*	*55*	*0*	*58*	*44*	*8*	*3.1*	*13.0*	*85*	*47%*	*.289*	*1.09*	*2.70*	*3.28*	*1.2*	*96.4*	*55*	*45*	*47*
2019	*CLE*	*MLB*	*34*	*3*	*1*	*3*	*63*	*0*	*67^{1}*	*51*	*11*	*3.2*	*13.1*	*98*	*47%*	*.286*	*1.11*	*3.45*	*3.74*	*1.1*	*95.8*	*54*	*44*	*46*

Breakout: 17% Improve: 41% Collapse: 35% Attrition: 8% MLB: 94% *Comparables: B.J. Ryan, Francisco Cordero, Robb Nen*

Perhaps the most impressive thing about Cleveland's record-setting win streak last August was that they did it without Miller, who remains perhaps the most impressive thing about any bullpen. Over the last five seasons the towering lefty has posted a 41 percent whiff rate compared to a seven percent walk rate, all while pitching anytime, anywhere and for however long his manager has asked. Scouring his peripherals for bad news (like his small drop in strikeouts and increase in walks last year) is like looking for dirt under a Lamborghini's floor mats. Hitters rarely look as helpless as they do flailing away at Miller's slider, and if his late-season knee soreness was just a blip we should expect plenty more jaw-dropping GIFs for years to come.

Tyler Olson LHP Born: 10/02/89 Age: 28 Bats: R Throws: L Height: 6'3" Weight: 195 Origin: Round 7, 2013 Draft (#207 overall)

YEAR	TEAM	LVL	AGE	W	L	SV	G	GS	IP	H	HR	BB/9	K/9	K	GB%	BABIP	WHIP	ERA	DRA	WARP	MPH	CMD	PWR	STM
2015	SEA	MLB	25	1	1	0	11	0	13^{1}	18	2	6.8	5.4	8	48%	.364	2.10	5.40	6.96	-0.4	91.0			44
2015	TAC	AAA	25	3	5	1	25	6	54^{1}	61	7	2.8	8.8	53	46%	.329	1.44	4.47	2.50	1.6				
2016	NYA	MLB	26	0	0	0	1	0	2^{2}	3	0	6.8	0.0	0	27%	.273	1.88	6.75	8.15	-0.1	90.1			29
2016	SWB	AAA	26	1	2	0	11	3	27^{1}	31	2	2.6	6.9	21	53%	.341	1.43	5.27	3.90	0.4				
2016	COH	AAA	26	1	0	0	9	0	10^{2}	12	1	5.1	8.4	10	29%	.333	1.69	5.91	2.95	0.3				
2017	COH	AAA	27	2	0	2	34	0	42	28	7	2.6	11.6	54	43%	.241	0.95	3.21	1.83	1.6				
2017	CLE	MLB	27	1	0	1	30	0	20	13	0	2.7	8.1	18	54%	.250	0.95	0.00	4.38	0.2	90.3	58	11	46
2018	*CLE*	*MLB*	*28*	*3*	*2*	*2*	*51*	*0*	*53^{2}*	*52*	*8*	*4.1*	*8.9*	*53*	*44%*	*.301*	*1.43*	*4.44*	*4.76*	*0.2*	*89.9*	*58*	*11*	*40*
2019	*CLE*	*MLB*	*29*	*2*	*1*	*1*	*43*	*0*	*46*	*44*	*6*	*4.2*	*9.3*	*47*	*44%*	*.305*	*1.44*	*4.49*	*4.85*	*0.2*	*89.4*	*58*	*11*	*39*

Breakout: 20% Improve: 37% Collapse: 14% Attrition: 23% MLB: 54% *Comparables: Eric Surkamp, Arnold Leon, Darin Downs*

Two years ago in these pages we noted that Olson's seven intentional walks in 13 1/3 innings was a rate that was unlikely to ever be surpassed. This year, we can state unequivocally that no one will ever work at least 20 innings and better his 0.00 ERA. Olson's freakish ability to set all-time records isn't his only talent, though. Last year the Indians plugged him into their lefty-specialist role in late July and never looked back. Same-side hitters slashed .162/.244/.216 against Olson, and while he was also dominant against righties that seems less likely to last. Olson's best pitch is his big-bending curve, which he mixes in with a sinker and changeup to keep hitters off his combustible high-80s fastball. There's a reasonable chance he turns back into a pumpkin this year, but at least his name is in the record books.

Dan Otero RHP

Born: 02/19/85 Age: 33 Bats: R Throws: R Height: 6'3" Weight: 205 Origin: Round 21, 2007 Draft (#644 overall)

YEAR	TEAM	LVL	AGE	W	L	SV	G	GS	IP	H	HR	BB/9	K/9	K	GB%	BABIP	WHIP	ERA	DRA	WARP	MPH	CMD	PWR	STM
2015	NAS	AAA	30	2	0	0	15	2	27^{2}	23	1	1.3	6.2	19	60%	.262	0.98	1.95	3.02	0.6				
2015	OAK	MLB	30	2	4	0	41	0	46^{2}	64	7	1.2	5.4	28	50%	.354	1.50	6.75	4.61	0.1	92.1	67	49	48
2016	CLE	MLB	31	5	1	1	62	0	70^{2}	54	2	1.3	7.3	57	64%	.260	0.91	1.53	2.92	1.7	92.9	63	56	47
2017	CLE	MLB	32	3	0	0	52	0	60	63	6	1.4	5.7	38	65%	.302	1.20	2.85	4.41	0.5	91.6	56	50	42
2018	*CLE*	*MLB*	*33*	*3*	*2*	*0*	*51*	*0*	*53^{2}*	*55*	*5*	*3.0*	*6.3*	*38*	*56%*	*.297*	*1.37*	*3.84*	*4.28*	*0.5*	*91.2*	*60*	*51*	*45*
2019	*CLE*	*MLB*	*34*	*2*	*1*	*0*	*49*	*0*	*51^{2}*	*53*	*6*	*2.8*	*6.4*	*37*	*56%*	*.296*	*1.34*	*4.13*	*4.48*	*0.4*	*90.7*	*59*	*52*	*44*

Breakout: 24% Improve: 43% Collapse: 27% Attrition: 10% MLB: 86% *Comparables: Mariano Rivera, Burke Badenhop, Jim Johnson*

The Cleveland bullpen is bursting with pitchers at the extreme ends of performance leaderboards, and Otero is yet another. Last year his fly-ball percentage ranked among the lowest in the majors, while his home runs per fly ball ranked among the highest. And as our old friend Sam Miller pointed out at ESPN, Otero has the lowest career ERA of any Indians pitcher in the live-ball era. Otero relies on his sinker, obviously, to generate shoals of groundballs. He doesn't walk anybody, doesn't strike anybody out, doesn't give up runs and in a loaded Cleveland 'pen rarely gets to pitch in high-leverage situations. Is Otero truly a great reliever? That depends on what you believe about falling trees in empty forests.

Danny Salazar RHP

Born: 01/11/90 Age: 28 Bats: R Throws: R Height: 6'0" Weight: 195 Origin: International Free Agent, 2006

YEAR	TEAM	LVL	AGE	W	L	SV	G	GS	IP	H	HR	BB/9	K/9	K	GB%	BABIP	WHIP	ERA	DRA	WARP	MPH	CMD	PWR	STM
2015	CLE	MLB	25	14	10	0	30	30	185	156	23	2.6	9.5	195	45%	.278	1.13	3.45	3.15	4.3	97.9	44	66	74
2016	CLE	MLB	26	11	6	0	25	25	137^{1}	121	16	4.1	10.6	161	49%	.307	1.34	3.87	3.63	2.7	97.5	47	61	64
2017	CLE	MLB	27	5	6	0	23	19	103	94	14	3.8	12.7	145	39%	.343	1.34	4.28	3.55	2.3	97.2	48	61	55
2018	*CLE*	*MLB*	*28*	*9*	*6*	*0*	*42*	*19*	*132^{2}*	*119*	*20*	*3.8*	*11.0*	*162*	*44%*	*.303*	*1.32*	*3.71*	*4.17*	*1.8*	*97.0*	*47*	*63*	*63*
2019	*CLE*	*MLB*	*29*	*9*	*9*	*0*	*28*	*28*	*166^{1}*	*148*	*25*	*3.6*	*11.2*	*208*	*44%*	*.307*	*1.29*	*3.89*	*4.22*	*2.5*	*96.5*	*47*	*62*	*61*

Breakout: 22% Improve: 53% Collapse: 22% Attrition: 7% MLB: 91% *Comparables: Max Scherzer, Brandon Morrow, Francisco Liriano*

Salazar has long been a tease, with raw stuff that matches any in baseball, but is continually undermined by fleeting control, spectral command and inconsistent health. Salazar's mid-90s heater and baffling splitter can be overpowering, and were during a midseason stretch between his June shoulder woes and late-August elbow soreness, yet you can never shake the feeling that another bout of wildness or another nagging injury is just an inning or a pitch away. If Salazar can ever put things together over a full season he could win a major award, but right now his career sits stalled in an excelsior-filled crate marked *Fragile*.

Josh Tomlin RHP

Born: 10/19/84 Age: 33 Bats: R Throws: R Height: 6'1" Weight: 190 Origin: Round 19, 2006 Draft (#581 overall)

YEAR	TEAM	LVL	AGE	W	L	SV	G	GS	IP	H	HR	BB/9	K/9	K	GB%	BABIP	WHIP	ERA	DRA	WARP	MPH	CMD	PWR	STM
2015	COH	AAA	30	1	2	0	4	4	21^{1}	25	3	0.4	7.2	17	43%	.328	1.22	4.22	2.59	0.7				
2015	CLE	MLB	30	7	2	0	10	10	65^{2}	47	13	1.1	7.8	57	39%	.199	0.84	3.02	4.62	0.4	91.2	54	41	53
2016	CLE	MLB	31	13	9	0	30	29	174	187	36	1.0	6.1	118	44%	.276	1.19	4.40	4.74	1.2	89.9	83	43	69
2017	CLE	MLB	32	10	9	0	26	26	141	166	23	0.9	7.0	109	42%	.329	1.28	4.98	5.10	0.7	89.1	71	27	59
2018	*CLE*	*MLB*	*33*	*11*	*9*	*0*	*29*	*29*	*165^{1}*	*180*	*30*	*2.5*	*6.6*	*122*	*42%*	*.294*	*1.36*	*4.63*	*5.19*	*0.4*	*88.7*	*73*	*35*	*60*
2019	*CLE*	*MLB*	*34*	*10*	*11*	*0*	*31*	*31*	*193^{2}*	*208*	*33*	*1.7*	*6.4*	*138*	*42%*	*.291*	*1.26*	*4.54*	*4.92*	*1.4*	*88.1*	*75*	*34*	*61*

Breakout: 19% Improve: 43% Collapse: 20% Attrition: 12% MLB: 85% *Comparables: Dan Haren, Jon Lieber, Jim Bunning*

Tomlin is a control freak in the pitching sense of the term, as he has taken the art of strike-throwing to an unnatural extreme by allowing more home runs than walks in each of the last four seasons. Yet in another sense he must be anything but a control freak, as his low-strikeout, pitch-to-contact style makes him more reliant on the work of others than most any pitcher in baseball. Tomlin has fringy stuff, but his steady contribution at the end of the Cleveland rotation and in the clubhouse made picking up his 2018 option a no-brainer. Having him available as a swingman is a security blanket Terry Francona will appreciate having.

LINEOUTS

Hitters

HITTER	POS	TEAM	LVL	AGE	PA	R	2B	3B	HR	RBI	BB	K	SB	CS	AVG/OBP/SLG	TAv	VORP	BABIP	BRR	FRAA	WARP
Brandon Barnes	CF	NWO	AAA	31	451	55	22	2	11	49	31	114	15	6	.276/.331/.420	.271	21.1	.353	2.6	CF(83): 1.1, 1B(16): 3.8	2.6
Conner Capel	OF	LKC	A	20	492	73	22	7	22	61	43	108	15	10	.246/.316/.478	.278	24.1	.275	5.0	RF(67): -0.6, LF(26): 0.2	2.3
Willi Castro	SS	LYN	A+	20	510	69	24	3	11	58	28	90	19	9	.290/.337/.424	.284	34.8	.336	1.6	SS(116): 5.0	4.2
Gavin Collins	3B	LKC	A	21	159	23	5	1	8	19	14	30	0	0	.270/.340/.489	.283	9.2	.286	0.0	3B(34): 2.7, C(7): 0.1	1.3
	3B	LYN	A+	21	162	18	16	0	4	35	13	45	1	1	.275/.340/.472	.317	13.0	.361	-1.4	3B(34): 0.7	1.4
Oscar Gonzalez	OF	MHV	A-	19	246	20	16	0	3	34	5	61	0	0	.283/.301/.388	.245	-0.7	.366	-1.7	LF(38): -3.2, RF(15): 2.1	-0.2
Eric Haase	C	AKR	AA	24	381	59	17	5	26	59	44	116	4	2	.258/.349/.574	.332	41.9	.313	2.2	C(58): 0.7	4.6
Quentin Holmes	CF	CLE	Rk	17	169	22	5	3	2	15	8	61	5	4	.182/.220/.289	.195	-7.2	.278	0.7	CF(36): -5.2	-1.1
Logan Ice	C	LKC	A	22	367	38	10	1	11	42	42	74	1	1	.228/.320/.370	.251	8.4	.258	-2.8	C(81): -2.6	0.6
Michael Martinez	UT	CLE	MLB	34	14	1	1	0	0	0	2	5	0	1	.364/.462/.455	.320	0.7	.667	-0.6	3B(6): 0.1, 2B(3): 0.2	0.1
	UT	TBA	MLB	34	29	1	0	0	0	0	3	10	0	0	.077/.172/.077	.101	-4.1	.125	0.0	2B(8): 0.0, 3B(3): 0.0	-0.4
	UT	COH	AAA	34	229	29	16	2	0	20	13	35	4	2	.277/.317/.371	.229	1.2	.330	1.9	CF(24): 4.4, 2B(17): -1.1	0.4
Rob Refsnyder	2B	NYA	MLB	26	40	3	1	1	0	0	3	8	2	0	.135/.200/.216	.158	-3.5	.172	0.0	LF(8): -0.8, 1B(4): -0.4	-0.5

HITTER	POS	TEAM	LVL	AGE	PA	R	2B	3B	HR	RBI	BB	K	SB	CS	AVG/OBP/SLG	TAv	VORP	BABIP	BRR	FRAA	WARP
	2B	SWB	AAA	26	159	20	11	2	2	12	15	30	2	1	.312/.390/.464	.298	10.4	.380	0.1	2B(18): -2.5, 1B(9): -0.8	0.7
	2B	TOR	MLB	26	58	5	1	0	0	0	5	9	2	1	.196/.281/.216	.178	-3.5	.238	0.0	2B(18): 1.8, 1B(2): 0.0	-0.2
Daniel Robertson	OF	CLE	MLB	31	88	9	4	1	1	7	7	3	0	1	.225/.287/.338	.211	-3.8	.224	-1.1	RF(17): 0.0, LF(10): 1.5	-0.3
	OF	COH	AAA	31	231	29	8	0	1	16	21	35	12	6	.321/.383/.373	.267	7.8	.382	0.6	LF(41): 1.7, CF(8): 0.8	1.0
Nellie Rodriguez	1B	COH	AAA	23	433	38	14	0	17	49	53	181	0	0	.170/.271/.342	.210	-2.7	.260	-0.8	1B(108): -1.8	-2.2
Eric Stamets	SS	AKR	AA	25	50	7	3	1	1	5	8	13	2	0	.325/.429/.525	.346	7.2	.444	1.2	3B(10): -0.4, SS(3): -0.7	0.7
	SS	COH	AAA	25	380	49	23	0	15	47	30	87	8	0	.251/.324/.455	.264	20.6	.294	2.4	SS(91): 6.8, 2B(10): 0.3	2.7
Melvin Upton	OF	SAC	AAA	32	49	4	1	0	1	4	4	14	0	0	.244/.306/.333	.230	-0.1	.333	0.1	CF(10): -0.8	-0.1

Even if **Brandon Barnes** never plays another MLB game, you still can't take the time he recorded a pair of inside-the-park home runs in the same month away from him. I mean, you could try, but you'd have to catch him first. The Indians challenged **Conner Capel** with a Midwest League assignment in his first full pro season and the Texas prep prospect responded, flashing speed, a strong arm and a quick bat with surprising game-day power; he may not stick in center field, but he's a gamer. Switch-hitting shortstops with bat-to-ball skills and gap power were a hot Cyber Monday item, so the Indians were wise to stash **Willi Castro** on the 40-man roster last fall before other teams came shopping; he's likely a utility player, but that sure beats selling Lady Kenmores. Former Mississippi State catcher **Gavin Collins** spent his first pro season learning to man the hot corner and flashing patience and power in the low minors; his glove has miles to go before it sleeps, so his bat has promises to keep. International bonus baby **Oscar Gonzalez** is a bipedal toolshed and was a New York-Penn League All-Star outfielder last summer, but he walks less frequently than an astronaut in space. He'll need to tone down his aggressive approach if he wants to earn any more helmet stickers. **Eric Haase** slugged his way onto the 40-man roster after an impressive spin through Double-A; he's not an exceptional receiver, nor is he Ryan Doumit, which means his patient approach and power bat could carry him all the way to Cleveland. Top pick **Quentin Holmes** struggled at the plate in his pro debut, but the Indians hope his blistering speed, center-field glove and plus makeup will carry him far. **Logan Ice** flashed plus catch-and-throw skills and drew a few walks during his full-season debut, but struggled to make hard contact. Future contributors to this book fervently hope his defense and leadership eventually make him a pension-holder in the International Brotherhood of Backup Catchers, because seriously, Logan Ice. A Cleveland summer wouldn't be complete without an evening stroll along the lakefront, drifting in the lazy river at Cedar Point, mosquito bites and the local nine trading away and then re-signing **Michael Martinez**. Does **Rob Refsnyder** need to play every day to finally show his skills as a quasi-versatile utility man? If you're his family member, you'd answer yes. Over the last four seasons, punchless fifth outfielder **Daniel Robertson** has made brief visits to Texas, Anaheim, Seattle and Cleveland. So has your retired Aunt June, who is parlaying her Amtrak rewards credit card into a clockwise circumnavigation of the country; maybe they'll meet up on the east coast this summer. No, **Nellie Rodriguez** isn't a long-lost Bluth sibling given up for adoption at an early age, although seeing a bat-only first-base prospect strike out in over 40 percent of his Triple-A plate appearances certainly made us feel like we were binge-watching *Arrested Development*. Home cooking clearly agrees with **Eric Stamets**, as the Ohio native long known for his high-quality leatherwork finally made enough noise at the plate in Akron and Columbus to earn a spot on the 40-man roster. There are worse utility infielders currently cluttering big-league benches. **Melvin Upton** cashed a $16.05 million check from the Padres and received another $1 million from the Blue Jays, all while appearing in 12 Triple-A contests for the Giants. With no guaranteed salary for 2018, he'll have to earn his pay by winning a bench job this year.

Pitchers

PITCHER	TEAM	LVL	AGE	W	L	SV	G	GS	IP	H	HR	BB/9	K/9	K	GB%	BABIP	WHIP	ERA	DRA	WARP	MPH	CMD	PWR	STM
Shane Bieber	LKC	A	22	2	3	0	5	5	29	34	1	0.3	9.6	31	45%	.375	1.21	3.10	2.42	1.0				
	LYN	A+	22	6	1	0	14	14	90	95	5	0.4	8.2	82	50%	.340	1.10	3.10	2.24	3.2				
	AKR	AA	22	2	1	0	9	9	54^{1}	56	2	0.8	8.1	49	50%	.331	1.12	2.32	1.89	2.1				
Lisalverto Bonilla	LOU	AAA	27	3	4	2	18	8	62^{2}	61	6	3.3	8.5	59	48%	.309	1.34	3.59	3.12	1.7				
	CIN	MLB	27	1	3	0	10	4	36^{2}	42	8	5.4	6.9	28	48%	.304	1.75	8.10	5.89	-0.2	93.9	47	39	58
Craig Breslow	MIN	MLB	36	1	1	0	30	0	31	38	4	3.5	5.2	18	43%	.318	1.61	5.23	6.64	-0.5	91.4	52	32	37
	CLE	MLB	36	0	0	0	7	0	4^{1}	3	0	4.2	10.4	5	33%	.333	1.15	4.15	5.95	0.0	90.4	52	32	37
Leonel Campos	BUF	AAA	29	3	0	9	26	0	32^{2}	20	2	3.9	10.7	39	35%	.234	1.04	1.65	3.26	0.7				
	TOR	MLB	29	0	0	0	13	0	13^{2}	11	2	5.3	9.9	15	39%	.265	1.39	2.63	4.85	0.0	94.4	29	43	36
Aaron Civale	LKC	A	22	2	4	0	10	10	57	64	2	0.8	8.4	53	55%	.358	1.21	4.58	2.03	2.2				
	LYN	A+	22	11	2	0	17	17	107^{2}	96	11	0.8	7.4	88	49%	.276	0.98	2.59	2.35	3.7				
Joseph Colon	COH	AAA	27	0	0	6	28	0	32^{2}	33	4	5.0	9.4	34	33%	.319	1.56	4.13	7.77	-0.9				
Juan Hillman	LKC	A	20	7	10	0	26	26	137^{2}	158	22	3.1	6.6	101	42%	.316	1.50	6.08	6.28	-1.6				
Shawn Morimando	COH	AAA	24	10	9	0	26	26	159^{1}	177	22	3.2	7.2	128	41%	.320	1.47	4.41	5.61	0.2				
Adam Plutko	COH	AAA	25	7	12	0	24	22	135^{2}	153	24	3.5	6.8	103	33%	.319	1.52	5.90	8.14	-3.6				

Once and future swingman **Cody Anderson** underwent Tommy John surgery last spring but hopes to compete for a bullpen job in Cleveland, which is rather like picking up a bass for the first time in a year and auditioning for a spot with The Beatles. Josh Tomlin Fan Club president **Shane Bieber** allowed more bombs than free passes in the low minors before his walk rate soared to 2.3 percent in Double-A. With impeccable control, a fastball with some giddy-up and a career 15/1 K/BB ratio he's worth watching. Big-league lefties hit .348/.430/.682 in 81 plate appearances against **Lisalverto Bonilla** last year. Rey Fuentes took him deep. Yes, *that* Rey Fuentes. It was your typical man pitches poorly, man invests in 3-D camera and spends offseason reinventing his delivery, man generates interest and signs a minor-league contract, man pitches even worse story for **Craig Breslow** last year, although he may still have his uses as a LOOGY. Despite pitching reasonably well, **Leonel Campos** was recalled and optioned *seven* times in 2017. His pitches go all over the place, so it only seems fitting that he should, too. Josh Tomlin Fan Club vice president **Aaron Civale** allowed one more walk than bomb in his full-season debut. Early-round college starters are expected to carve up the low minors, so we'll have to see if his sinker/slider combo can work against more advanced hitters this summer. With a name befitting the cartoon narrator of a digestive system filmstrip, **Joe Colon** might know enough biology to understand how the Selective Androgen Receptor Modulator actually works; if he didn't also know it was a banned PED that would lead to his second suspension, he should have asked his old pal Freddie Rules. **Juan Hillman** struggled with his command and didn't miss many bats in his Midwest League debut, but chin up, there's plenty of time for him to leverage his low-90s fastball and developing off-speed stuff into the back of a rotation. One-time Cardinals top pick **Rob Kaminsky** only made one start last summer before being shut down with arm problems; he'll need to get healthy and then figure out something to retire hitters beyond his plus curveball before he'll earn a more interesting sobriquet than "one-time Cardinals top pick." If **Shawn Morimando** gets another opportunity beyond the four-plus innings he spent slinging his low-velo four-pitch mix in the Cleveland bullpen last summer, he will certainly lower his career 3.00 WHIP, but probably not enough to earn even more opportunities. If **Adam Plutko** gets another opportunity beyond the three-plus innings he spent slinging his low-velo four-pitch mix in the Cleveland bullpen last summer, he will certainly lower his career 1.91 WHIP, but probably not enough to earn even more opportunities.

LEAGUE LEADERS 2017

MLB Walk Rate – Dan Otero, 2.1%

MLB ERA, Starters – Corey Kluber, 2.25

MLB WHIP – Corey Kluber, 0.869

MLB DRA, Starters – Corey Kluber, 2.05

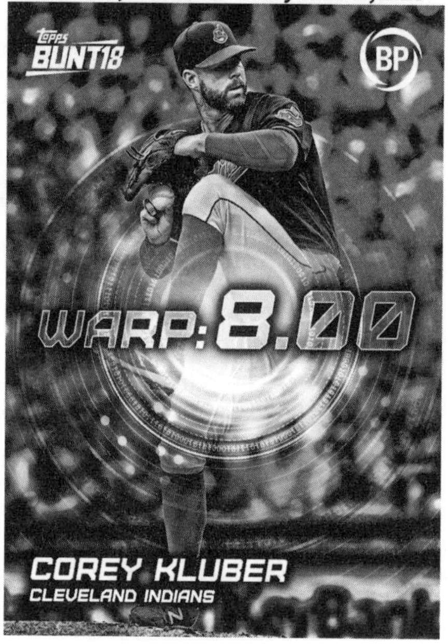

MLB WARP, Pitchers – Corey Kluber, 8.0

COLORADO ROCKIES

Essay by Robert O'Connell

Player comments by Ben Carsley and BP staff

Plenty of ballparks seem sprung from their teams' essences. Fenway Park has the extensive history and the even-more-extensive awareness of it—that sense that it's after awe dressed as fellowship. Dodger Stadium has the careless beauty, the late-arriving crowds, the beach balls and thin palms and smog-filtered sunsets. Kaufmann Stadium is electric when it's full and familiar when it's empty. Tropicana Field is slapdash; Yankee Stadium, fascist.

One park, though, seems not only to reflect its tenants' fortunes but to control them. Thinking about the Colorado Rockies, ever since 1995, has meant thinking about Coors Field. The stadium—a mile high and roomy in the power alleys—is more famous than any player who has played in it. Its characteristics are well-known, at this point, but they'll always be the story: The thin air makes baseballs fly far and fast, and the small nation-state beyond the infield gives them plenty of room to land. In Colorado, batting averages tick up and ERAs swell. Hitters break out of slumps and pitchers leave early. A three-run inning isn't worth standing up for.

Coors is most commonly understood as something to be investigated, an area of research. To the team that calls it home, it presents a yearly challenge: to assemble a roster that can take advantage of its benefits without wilting under its pressures. Batters are brought in on the cheap, in the hope that the heady environment will turn them around; pitchers fit the latest hypotheses about surviving in such a climate. To outside observers tasked with evaluating players—from opposing general managers to analysts to anyone watching on TV and trying to figure out exactly how impressive that homer was—it's a constant riddle. How much of the action is actually the location?

Coors is so synonymous with stat-stuffing that it can be hard to think of in aesthetic terms, as a place and not a kind of synthetic baseball add-on. But it *is* a place, like any of those places listed above. It sits in Denver, at the edge of the Rocky Mountains, and it distills its region to the appropriate degree. During day games, it has that too-clear quality of light; during night games, it has fans huddled in hoodies. Its dusks are of the sort found only in that time zone—big, lysergic blots of purple and orange. As an envious Plains Stater, I get an aspirational sunburn and altitude headache just seeing it on TV. Even the hard line drives and flat breaking balls, before they become data points, contribute to the vibe; this a land of angles, not curves.

Whether the 2018 Colorado Rockies "solve" Coors Field—whether they wring a net benefit from a place that alternates between blessing and curse every half-inning—is an open question, and a stale one. What's more interesting about this team is how fully it fits the place it's usually resigned to battling. Coors is Colorado; Colorado is glorious, all-day fun. And when their best players are playing their best, these Rockies are pretty much the same.

ROCKIES PROSPECTUS

2017 W-L: 87-75, 3RD IN NL WEST

Pythag	.541	9th	B-Age	28.3	*16th*
RS/G	5.09	3rd	P-Age	26.2	*1st*
RA/G	4.67	14th	Salary	$127.8M	*16th*
TAv	.265	12th	M$/MW	$2.9M	*22nd*
TAv-P	.262	15th	DL Days	792	*9th*
FIP	4.34	15th	$ on DL	7%	*5th*
DER	.694	26th			

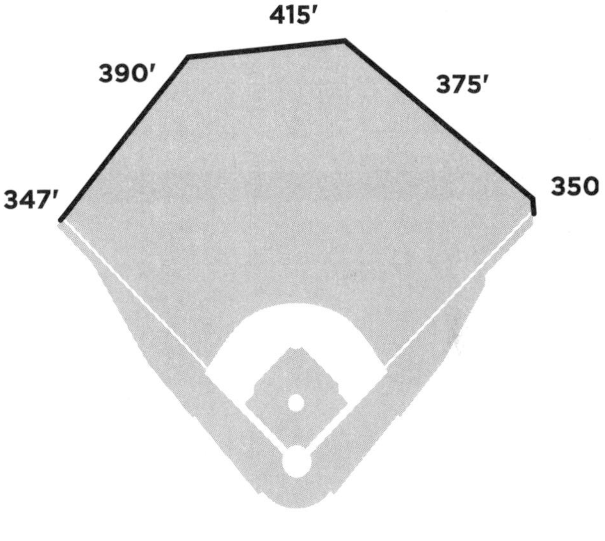

Outfield wall profile: **8′** to **14′**

Three-Year Park Factors

Runs	Runs/RH	Runs/LH	HR/RH	HR/LH
114	116	112	108	108

Top Hitter WARP	7.9 Charlie Blackmon
Top Pitcher WARP	2.3 Jon Gray
Top Prospect	Brendan Rodgers

2017 Hit List Ranking

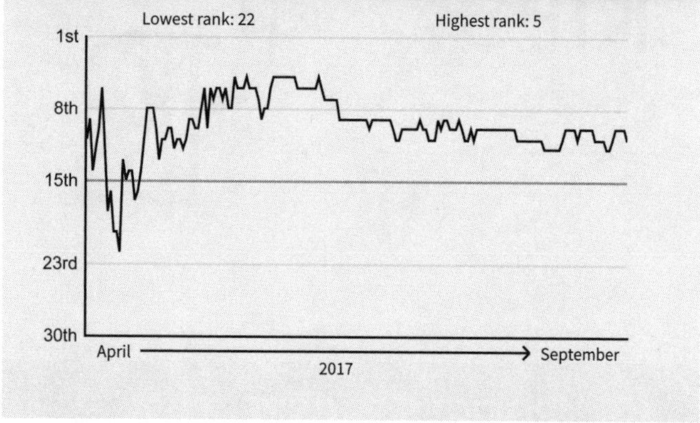

Committed Payroll (in millions)

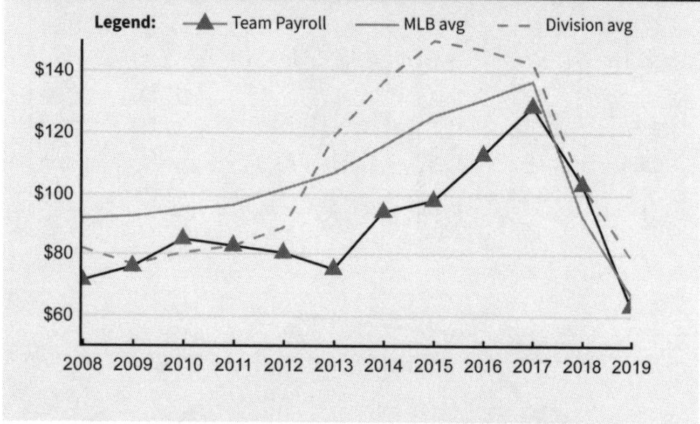

Farm System Ranking

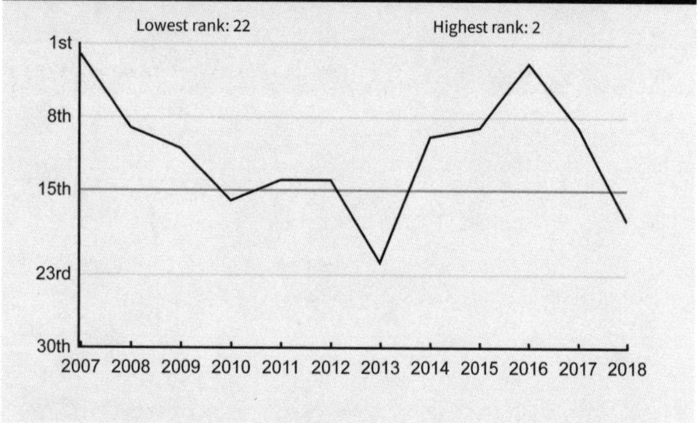

Personnel

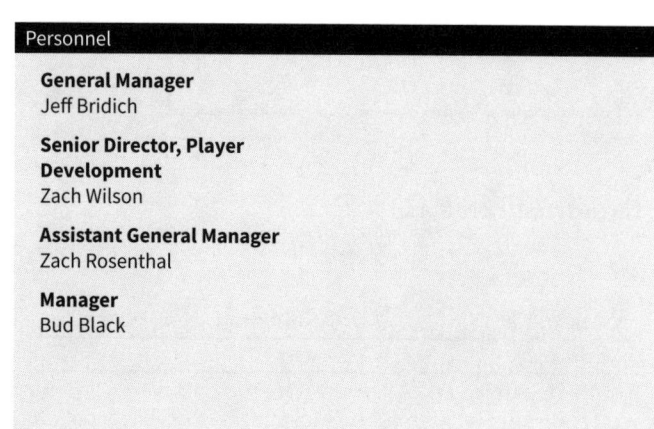

General Manager
Jeff Bridich

Senior Director, Player Development
Zach Wilson

Assistant General Manager
Zach Rosenthal

Manager
Bud Black

⚾ ⚾ ⚾

In 2017, the Rockies broke a string of six consecutive losing seasons and seven straight playoff-less Octobers, reaching a goofily thrilling all-NL West wild card game against the Arizona Diamondbacks, which Colorado lost 11-8. The consensus version of how they righted the ship goes like this. The offense, while broadly disappointing, was helped along by Coors enough to score in those familiar Colorado bursts (Mark Reynolds hit 30 homers, 19 before July). A starting rotation full of junior fireballers—the latest thinking is that fastballs fare better than soft stuff at elevation—acquitted itself well, with three rookies winning at least ten games and the team allowing 103 fewer runs than it had the year before. New manager Bud Black proved a steady hand, a squad used to wallowing in slumps was able to break out of them and incremental improvement resulted. The Rockies won 87 games, the right number for a team that does a few things marginally better.

The truer-feeling version, though, goes like this: A heretofore distracted baseball universe finally saw what fun stuff was going on in Colorado and smiled on it. The Rockies' principals—the often literally unbelievable third baseman Nolan Arenado, the shaggy-maned and sweet-swinging center fielder Charlie Blackmon—did in 2017 what they have been doing for a little while now. They played baseball not only expertly but *righteously*, according to my almost certainly outdated understanding of mountain-bum vernacular. They were good enough to secure wins and fun enough to redeem losses. They built MVP cases and team identity in equal measure.

There may be players as entertaining as Arenado, but there are none as plainly thrilling, none who register in quite the same adrenal way. In the right-handed batter's box, waiting for the pitch, he has a nervous rocking rhythm, a palpable impatience. His swing is pure torque, and it can send a baseball anywhere. Arenado's defense is in a class of its own, of course, but even were he not the uncontested best third baseman in the sport, he would still be the one most worth watching. He treats everything hit his way like it's a dare, leaping after liners, dropping his hand to snatch up even hard-hit groundballs. From any angle, his arm is strong and accurate to an absolute degree. He has a knack for amazing you twice: once when he tries to make a play, and again when he pulls it off.

On June 18 of last year, Arenado hit for the cycle in Coors against San Francisco. The home run came last, a three-run job that doubled as a ninth-inning walk-off. The announcers calling the game went appropriately apoplectic—"a cycle for the ages!" et cetera—but really, it was almost expected. Arenado plays like that's the point: to do it all, all the time.

Blackmon, meanwhile, supplies the Rockies with a languid, cruising counterpoint. This is not to say he produces at any less severe a clip than Arenado; a .332 TAv in 2017 won him a second straight Silver Slugger Award and advanced his argument for being the NL's best leadoff hitter. It is just that Blackmon seems to exist in a state of self-summary, as if you're watching a highlight reel in real time. His face stays set, behind the island-stranded beard and roadie mullet, and his legs stay balanced. His swing looks like a tennis player's warm-up backhand. Blackmon is forever scooping fastballs the other way (a league-leading 213 hits last year), forever sliding feet-first into third (a league-leading 14 triples), forever trotting home (a league-leading 137 runs).

It's hard to single out a specific instance of Blackmon excellence. Indeed, he is most impressive before his bat even touches the ball. He features that combination of batting stance and reputation—the former square and relaxed, the latter growing daily—that makes you wonder what possible combination of pitches could get him out. Blackmon has the coordination to go with a slider away and the strength to pull a fastball halfway up the bleachers. More to the point, he has the classic leadoff hitter's indifference to which the pitcher chooses. He probably covers as much daily distance as anyone in the sport, roaming in Coors' spacious center field and constantly reaching base, and he makes it look like the pleasantest sort of work.

Arenado and Blackmon are joined by a cast of oddballs. DJ LeMahieu, the much-too-tall second baseman, fields grounders by loping over and crumpling on top of them like a dropped bedsheet; somehow, this technique works pretty well. Jon Gray has a mean slider and a ghostly stare. Reynolds will hit three homers in a game and then, for the rest of the month, hold his helmet in his hands and wear his bat on his head.

Then there are the players whose shortcomings are impossible to disguise as eccentricity. Ian Desmond, last offseason's splurge, was miserable in his first year in Colorado, posting a negative WARP. Trevor Story, still trying to recapture the magic of his first week in the majors, led the NL in strikeouts. It's hard not to see, in them, one of Coors' fabled effects: the too-big swing, the outsized power-number ambition.

The Rockies will be too wonky in some spots—and simply too bad in others—to seriously challenge the Dodgers in 2018. Standings-wise, their best-case scenario is probably a repeat of last year: coasting in LA's wake to a wild card berth, with maybe the added bonus of a home game this time around. They will spend another year tracking and refining their young starting pitchers, building their knowledge about how to survive in baseball's toughest pitching park.

The six or so months between Opening Day and whatever conclusions the end of the season brings, though, will offer daily chances to forget all about long-term franchise plans and altitude-mitigation strategies. Arenado and Blackmon alone make the Rockies a plenty good time—which means they're right where they're supposed to be.

—Robert O'Connell is a writer for The Athletic.

Hitters

Alexi Amarista UT Born: 04/06/89 Age: 29 Bats: L Throws: R Height: 5'6" Weight: 160 Origin: International Free Agent, 2007

YEAR	TEAM	LVL	AGE	PA	R	2B	3B	HR	RBI	BB	K	SB	CS	AVG/OBP/SLG	TAv	VORP	BABIP	BRR	FRAA	WARP
2015	SDN	MLB	26	357	28	10	4	3	30	24	55	5	1	.204/.257/.287	.205	-5.2	.232	0.9	SS(85): 3.1, LF(11): -0.5	-0.3
2016	ELP	AAA	27	55	9	3	0	1	4	4	8	1	0	.333/.382/.458	.302	4.3	.366	-0.2	SS(9): -1.0, 2B(2): 0.0	0.3
2016	SDN	MLB	27	150	9	2	0	0	11	8	26	9	2	.257/.295/.271	.208	-5.1	.313	-1.6	2B(28): 1.5, SS(12): 0.3	-0.5
2017	COL	MLB	28	176	22	10	0	3	19	7	38	1	0	.238/.269/.351	.209	-3.7	.291	0.0	2B(19): -0.4, SS(18): -0.1	-0.7
2018	*COL*	*MLB*	*29*	*250*	*27*	*10*	*2*	*5*	*24*	*17*	*39*	*6*	*1*	*.252/.303/.374*	*.215*	*-1.6*	*.280*	*-0.1*	*SS 0, 2B 1*	*-0.2*
2019	*COL*	*MLB*	*30*	*131*	*14*	*5*	*1*	*3*	*13*	*9*	*21*	*2*	*1*	*.245/.296/.364*	*.227*	*-0.6*	*.272*	*-0.1*	*SS 0, 2B 0*	*-0.1*

Breakout: 3% Improve: 51% Collapse: 5% Attrition: 20% MLB: 88% *Comparables: Tim Foli, Cesar Gutierrez, Sam Dente*

Amarista played every position but catcher, first base, pitcher and hitter in 2017. Unfortunately, he's gone from posting TAvs in the .240s to posting TAvs in the .200s, and he's stopped running, too. Considering he's entering his age-29 season it's likely we've already seen Amarista's best work at the plate—and here's a reminder that best is a relative term. Swiss Army Knives have value in a vacuum, but if you were told you could only save 25 of your possessions, would a dull Swiss Army knife make the cut?

Nolan Arenado 3B Born: 04/16/91 Age: 27 Bats: R Throws: R Height: 6'2" Weight: 205 Origin: Round 2, 2009 Draft (#59 overall)

YEAR	TEAM	LVL	AGE	PA	R	2B	3B	HR	RBI	BB	K	SB	CS	AVG/OBP/SLG	TAv	VORP	BABIP	BRR	FRAA	WARP
2015	COL	MLB	24	665	97	43	4	42	130	34	110	2	5	.287/.323/.575	.299	47.1	.284	1.5	3B(157): 21.8	7.4
2016	COL	MLB	25	696	116	35	6	41	133	68	103	2	3	.294/.362/.570	.304	52.5	.293	-0.9	3B(160): 23.0	7.8
2017	COL	MLB	26	680	100	43	7	37	130	62	106	3	2	.309/.373/.586	.317	63.0	.320	-0.5	3B(157): 5.0	6.8
2018	*COL*	*MLB*	*27*	*599*	*81*	*35*	*4*	*29*	*96*	*43*	*92*	*2*	*2*	*.281/.334/.519*	*.278*	*30.7*	*.288*	*-1.2*	*3B 9*	*3.4*
2019	*COL*	*MLB*	*28*	*562*	*80*	*34*	*3*	*29*	*89*	*44*	*89*	*2*	*2*	*.278/.335/.523*	*.287*	*29.7*	*.284*	*0.3*	*3B 9*	*4.2*

Breakout: 9% Improve: 47% Collapse: 4% Attrition: 12% MLB: 99% *Comparables: Adrian Beltre, Pablo Sandoval, Richie Hebner*

On June 18, Arenado hit a walkoff home run against the Giants to complete the cycle. In the ensuing celebration, Charlie Blackmon's helmet gave Arenado a nasty cut above his left eye. It resulted in a powerful image; a bloody and defiant Arenado surrounded by adoring teammates after single-handedly vanquishing one of their most prominent foes. It signified a changing of the guard, as if Arenado was screaming "We're for real now. We're here to stay." And so the Rockies were, thanks in large part to another elite performance from their all-world third baseman. Arenado posted twice the BWARP of the next-best third baseman in the National League. He set new career highs in hits, doubles, every triple-slash component and TAv. He won his third straight Gold Glove and third-straight Silver Slugger, made his third straight All-Star team and finished in the top five in NL MVP voting for the second straight season. Somehow, he just keeps getting better. Arenado is no longer underrated; he is properly appreciated as one of the 10-or-so best players in the game, and the Rockies should make retaining his services for as long as possible their top priority.

Charlie Blackmon CF Born: 07/01/86 Age: 31 Bats: L Throws: L Height: 6'3" Weight: 210 Origin: Round 2, 2008 Draft (#72 overall)

YEAR	TEAM	LVL	AGE	PA	R	2B	3B	HR	RBI	BB	K	SB	CS	AVG/OBP/SLG	TAv	VORP	BABIP	BRR	FRAA	WARP
2015	COL	MLB	28	682	93	31	9	17	58	46	112	43	13	.287/.347/.450	.272	31.1	.325	3.4	CF(147): -4.9, LF(14): -1.2	2.7
2016	COL	MLB	29	641	111	35	5	29	82	43	102	17	9	.324/.381/.552	.311	57.4	.350	4.2	CF(138): -7.1	5.2
2017	COL	MLB	30	725	137	35	14	37	104	65	135	14	10	.331/.399/.601	.332	79.2	.371	1.6	CF(158): 0.0	7.9
2018	*COL*	*MLB*	*31*	*628*	*95*	*28*	*6*	*21*	*75*	*43*	*110*	*19*	*9*	*.286/.342/.469*	*.269*	*32.0*	*.317*	*0.8*	*CF -4*	*2.2*
2019	*COL*	*MLB*	*32*	*565*	*74*	*25*	*5*	*20*	*75*	*40*	*105*	*15*	*8*	*.280/.341/.466*	*.274*	*27.9*	*.312*	*2.5*	*CF -3*	*2.7*

Breakout: 0% Improve: 45% Collapse: 6% Attrition: 5% MLB: 93% *Comparables: Angel Pagan, Vernon Wells, Alex Rios*

Pick a statistic other than stolen bases: Blackmon set a career-high for it in 2017. Already an excellent everyday starter, Blackmon took the leap last year, emerging as one of the best players in the game and a legitimate MVP candidate. He finished first in homers, triples, total bases, RBI and batting average among center fielders, and second in OBP and TAv behind some guy named Mike Trout. Blackmon made his second All-Star Game, won his second Silver Slugger award, played good-to-passable defense in center and finished fifth in an NL MVP race in which he easily could've placed second or third—he and teammate Nolan Arenado (who placed fourth) split some votes. This is all excellent news for Blackmon, who is set to hit the free-agent market next winter after his age-31 season. It's a mixed bag for the Rockies, who got to benefit from Blackmon's performance but who probably realize it will take in excess of $100 million to keep Chuck Nazty beyond this summer.

David Dahl OF Born: 04/01/94 Age: 24 Bats: L Throws: R Height: 6'2" Weight: 195 Origin: Round 1, 2012 Draft (#10 overall)

YEAR	TEAM	LVL	AGE	PA	R	2B	3B	HR	RBI	BB	K	SB	CS	AVG/OBP/SLG	TAv	VORP	BABIP	BRR	FRAA	WARP
2015	NBR	AA	21	302	46	16	3	6	24	11	72	22	7	.278/.304/.417	.265	14.8	.352	5.0	CF(62): -4.5, RF(3): -0.4	1.1
2016	HFD	AA	22	332	53	21	2	13	45	39	85	16	5	.278/.367/.500	.311	28.6	.351	3.7		3.4
2016	ABQ	AAA	22	68	17	6	2	5	16	6	11	1	2	.484/.529/.887	.426	14.4	.543	0.8	CF(11): -1.3, LF(3): 0.8	1.4
2016	COL	MLB	22	237	42	12	4	7	24	15	59	5	0	.315/.359/.500	.289	14.5	.404	2.1	LF(54): -2.4, CF(6): 0.3	1.3
2017	ABQ	AAA	23	74	12	2	2	2	14	3	17	1	1	.243/.274/.414	.230	0.1	.294	0.7	LF(6): -0.2, CF(6): -0.3	-0.1
2018	*COL*	*MLB*	*24*	*328*	*44*	*16*	*3*	*12*	*42*	*23*	*90*	*9*	*3*	*.265/.317/.454*	*.257*	*10.4*	*.337*	*0.9*	*LF -2, RF 0*	*0.5*
2019	*COL*	*MLB*	*25*	*365*	*47*	*18*	*3*	*14*	*50*	*28*	*103*	*10*	*3*	*.266/.324/.468*	*.270*	*13.9*	*.342*	*1.3*	*LF -2, RF 0*	*1.2*

Breakout: 6% Improve: 32% Collapse: 20% Attrition: 33% MLB: 74% *Comparables: Fernando Martinez, Randal Grichuk, Victor Diaz*

We've wondered for a while now if Dahl is injury prone or just unlucky. Unfortunately, the answer seems to be "both." Stuff like the 2015 collision that cost him his spleen? That could happen to any baseball player, and we can't dock Dahl for it. But the hamstring injury that ate up his 2013 season, or the stress reaction in Dahl's ribs and back that prevented him from recording a single MLB plate appearance in 2017? Those kinds of lingering injuries are harder to explain away. When on the field, Dahl has one of the more exciting skill sets in baseball. "When on the field" is a pretty important part of that sentiment, though, and Dahl makes Carlos Gonzalez look like Cal Ripken. He hasn't exactly inspired confidence in his ability to hold up to the rigors of a 162-game campaign, but the silver lining here is that he turns 24 just after Opening Day.

Ian Desmond OF Born: 09/20/85 Age: 32 Bats: R Throws: R Height: 6'3" Weight: 215 Origin: Round 3, 2004 Draft (#84 overall)

YEAR	TEAM	LVL	AGE	PA	R	2B	3B	HR	RBI	BB	K	SB	CS	AVG/OBP/SLG	TAv	VORP	BABIP	BRR	FRAA	WARP
2015	WAS	MLB	29	641	69	27	2	19	62	45	187	13	5	.233/.290/.384	.254	23.7	.307	2.5	SS(155): -1.6	2.4
2016	TEX	MLB	30	677	107	29	3	22	86	44	160	21	6	.285/.335/.446	.261	26.2	.350	5.5	CF(130): -4.3, LF(29): -1.2	2.1
2017	COL	MLB	31	373	47	11	1	7	40	24	87	15	4	.274/.326/.375	.244	3.7	.345	2.7	LF(66): -2.7, 1B(27): -2.5	-0.1
2018	*COL*	*MLB*	*32*	*575*	*72*	*25*	*3*	*18*	*70*	*40*	*147*	*17*	*5*	*.259/.313/.419*	*.246*	*5.2*	*.323*	*1.5*	*1B -12, LF -1*	*-1.2*
2019	*COL*	*MLB*	*33*	*419*	*50*	*19*	*2*	*14*	*51*	*30*	*110*	*11*	*4*	*.249/.307/.414*	*.252*	*4.4*	*.312*	*2.4*	*1B -8, LF 0*	*-0.5*

Breakout: 4% Improve: 32% Collapse: 11% Attrition: 24% MLB: 91% *Comparables: Eli Marrero, Melvin Upton, Al Martin*

The five-year, $70 million contract the Rockies gave Desmond last offseason never made much sense. It's true that $14 million a season isn't star-level money anymore, and a player with Desmond's versatility can be useful. But the Rockies aren't known for their overflowing coffers. They are known for their good hitters at the positions Desmond primarily plays, and oh geez, this is getting awkward. Maybe Colorado would've found a way to make it work in 2017, but injuries largely made Desmond's square-peg-in-round-hole-iness a moot point: He played in just 95 games thanks to a broken hand and a recurring right calf strain. When healthy, Desmond made 66 starts in left field, but he didn't hit as well as Gerardo Parra. He also made 27 appearances at first base, but he didn't hit as well as Mark Reynolds. There should be more opportunity for Desmond in 2018; Reynolds and Carlos Gonzalez are free agents, and heck, if you want to get imaginative, Trevor Story's no sure thing either. The Rockies got a pretty poor ROI from Desmond in year one, though, and it sure looks like they could stand to allocate $14 million elsewhere.

Carlos Gonzalez RF Born: 10/17/85 Age: 32 Bats: L Throws: L Height: 6'1" Weight: 220 Origin: International Free Agent, 2002

YEAR	TEAM	LVL	AGE	PA	R	2B	3B	HR	RBI	BB	K	SB	CS	AVG/OBP/SLG	TAv	VORP	BABIP	BRR	FRAA	WARP
2015	COL	MLB	29	608	87	25	2	40	97	46	133	2	0	.271/.325/.540	.284	24.4	.284	-0.1	RF(151): -3.8	2.2
2016	COL	MLB	30	632	87	42	2	25	100	46	129	2	2	.298/.350/.505	.276	23.0	.346	1.4	RF(148): -4.5	1.9
2017	COL	MLB	31	534	72	34	0	14	57	56	119	3	0	.262/.339/.423	.260	10.8	.318	1.1	RF(125): -4.9	0.6
2018	*COL*	*MLB*	*32*	*521*	*66*	*27*	*2*	*24*	*78*	*46*	*125*	*2*	*1*	*.262/.327/.483*	*.258*	*14.1*	*.305*	*0.6*	*RF -4*	*1.1*
2019	*COL*	*MLB*	*33*	*425*	*57*	*20*	*1*	*19*	*60*	*37*	*104*	*1*	*0*	*.249/.314/.455*	*.261*	*9.6*	*.290*	*0.3*	*RF -3*	*0.7*

Breakout: 1% Improve: 37% Collapse: 6% Attrition: 13% MLB: 95% *Comparables: Scott Hairston, Cody Ross, Matt Kemp*

Gonzalez posted 22 WARP during his nine-year Rockies career. He made three All-Star teams, won three Gold Gloves, was named a Silver Slugger three times and once finished in the top three in MVP voting. Yet for many of those seasons, the Rockies stunk. That's why it's such a shame that CarGo's Rockies career is likely ending just as Colorado is becoming a contender. Gonzalez regressed across the board in 2017, posting his worst ISO since his rookie season, his second-worst TAv as a Rockie and his worst FRAA ever. CarGo has long been a better hitter against righties than lefties and a better hit at home than on the road, but those splits have become even more pronounced. It seems Gonzalez's days as an impact player are over, and many doubted he would've been quite as good in a different environment to begin with. That being said, if the price is right he can provide value as a strong-side platoon corner outfielder. Hopefully he can do so for a good team because CarGo deserves better than to become Nick Markakis 2.0.

Garrett Hampson MI Born: 10/10/94 Age: 23 Bats: R Throws: R Height: 5'11" Weight: 185 Origin: Round 3, 2016 Draft (#81 overall)

YEAR	TEAM	LVL	AGE	PA	R	2B	3B	HR	RBI	BB	K	SB	CS	AVG/OBP/SLG	TAv	VORP	BABIP	BRR	FRAA	WARP
2016	BOI	A-	21	312	43	14	8	2	44	48	56	36	4	.301/.404/.441	.323	36.7	.366	4.6	SS(64): 8.2, 2B(1): -0.2	4.7
2017	LNC	A+	22	603	113	24	12	8	70	56	77	51	14	.326/.387/.462	.283	41.1	.364	7.5	2B(71): -0.4, SS(56): 7.3	5.1
2018	*COL*	*MLB*	*23*	*250*	*34*	*10*	*2*	*5*	*22*	*22*	*52*	*13*	*4*	*.255/.321/.392*	*.231*	*5.0*	*.305*	*1.3*	*2B 0, SS 1*	*0.7*
2019	*COL*	*MLB*	*24*	*336*	*39*	*14*	*3*	*8*	*37*	*30*	*68*	*18*	*5*	*.258/.325/.404*	*.253*	*11.0*	*.305*	*2.6*	*2B 0, SS 2*	*1.4*

Breakout: 5% Improve: 12% Collapse: 2% Attrition: 10% MLB: 22% *Comparables: Logan Watkins, Tim Locastro, Tony Renda*

Man, it's about time the Rockies developed a toolsy middle-infield prospect. Hampson has flown under the radar since being drafted in the third round in 2016 but has straight mashed since entering the professional world. He's got a prototypical leadoff profile, with a short, compact swing and plus speed, as evidenced by his 87 steals in less than 1,000 career PA. He's splitting time at second and short right now, but Hampson profiles better at the keystone thanks to an underwhelming arm. All the usual caveats about scouting the stats for Rockies prospects apply, but Hampson is ready for Double-A at the very least. A future as a first-division regular is in play here, as is someone overdrafting Hampson in your dynasty league.

Sam Hilliard OF Born: 02/21/94 Age: 24 Bats: L Throws: L Height: 6'5" Weight: 225 Origin: Round 15, 2015 Draft (#437 overall)

YEAR	TEAM	LVL	AGE	PA	R	2B	3B	HR	RBI	BB	K	SB	CS	AVG/OBP/SLG	TAv	VORP	BABIP	BRR	FRAA	WARP
2015	GJR	RK	21	262	45	13	8	7	42	36	55	12	4	.306/.397/.532	.302	20.4	.372	3.3	RF(53): 2.2	2.2
2016	ASH	A	22	527	71	23	5	17	83	56	150	30	12	.267/.348/.449	.276	20.3	.357	2.2	LF(62): 0.1, RF(56): -0.6	2.1
2017	LNC	A+	23	597	95	23	7	21	92	50	154	37	17	.300/.360/.487	.277	24.8	.384	3.9	RF(85): 6.6, LF(30): 5.1	3.8
2018	*COL*	*MLB*	*24*	*250*	*31*	*9*	*2*	*8*	*29*	*21*	*81*	*9*	*4*	*.227/.293/.394*	*.223*	*-2.0*	*.309*	*0.4*	*RF 0, LF 1*	*-0.2*
2019	*COL*	*MLB*	*25*	*327*	*40*	*12*	*2*	*12*	*40*	*28*	*107*	*12*	*5*	*.234/.299/.407*	*.243*	*2.2*	*.317*	*1.1*	*RF 0, LF 1*	*0.3*

Breakout: 5% Improve: 9% Collapse: 0% Attrition: 9% MLB: 11% *Comparables: Jai Miller, Scott Cousins, Alex Castellanos*

We know what you're thinking: "Man, it's about time the Rockies had an outfield prospect emerge from relative obscurity." Well, play it again, Sam. A former 15th-rounder, Hilliard is the latest in a long line of unheralded toolsy outfielders who've made names for themselves in a hitter-friendly minor-league park. Hilliard did so by joining the 20/30 club and riding a friendly BABIP to post a shiny .300 average. If you scout the stat sheet, he looks like a future star. Here comes that pesky other shoe; Hilliard struck out in over a quarter of his plate appearances, he was worse against same-side pitching and he played the entire season as a 23-year-old in High-A. There's enough power, speed and glove here for Hilliard to carve out a role as a platoon guy, but enough questions about the hit tool for arms in the upper minors to stay his progress rather quickly. Stay tuned.

Chris Iannetta C Born: 04/08/83 Age: 35 Bats: R Throws: R Height: 6'0" Weight: 230 Origin: Round 4, 2004 Draft (#110 overall)

YEAR	TEAM	LVL	AGE	PA	R	2B	3B	HR	RBI	BB	K	SB	CS	AVG/OBP/SLG	TAv	VORP	BABIP	BRR	FRAA	WARP
2015	ANA	MLB	32	317	28	10	0	10	34	41	83	0	1	.188/.293/.335	.230	3.3	.225	-0.8	C(85): 12.6, 1B(2): 0.0	1.7
2016	SEA	MLB	33	338	23	14	0	7	24	38	83	0	0	.210/.303/.329	.231	0.2	.266	-5.1	C(93): -15.6	-1.6
2017	ARI	MLB	34	316	38	19	0	17	43	37	87	0	0	.254/.354/.511	.300	25.7	.308	-2.0	C(78): 6.5, 3B(1): 0.0	3.2
2018	*COL*	*MLB*	*35*	*352*	*43*	*16*	*1*	*10*	*40*	*47*	*88*	*0*	*0*	*.231/.340/.389*	*.252*	*12.1*	*.292*	*-0.7*	*C -2*	*0.8*
2019	*COL*	*MLB*	*36*	*284*	*37*	*12*	*0*	*9*	*32*	*39*	*74*	*0*	*0*	*.223/.336/.384*	*.256*	*7.8*	*.283*	*-1.8*	*C -1*	*0.7*

Breakout: 1% Improve: 27% Collapse: 12% Attrition: 26% MLB: 81% *Comparables: Jason Varitek, Ed Bailey, Carl Sawatski*

YEAR	TEAM	P. COUNT	FRM RUNS	BLK RUNS	THRW RUNS	TOT RUNS
2015	ANA	11581	13.1	-0.8	-0.6	11.8
2016	SEA	13011	-13.8	-1.4	0.8	-14.4
2017	ARI	10626	6.1	-0.8	0.2	5.4
2018	*COL*	*11602*	*0.1*	*-1.1*	*0.0*	*-1.0*
2019	*COL*	*9373*	*0.1*	*-1.0*	*0.0*	*-0.9*

We're pretty sure nobody had "Chris Iannetta is good again" in their 2017 predictions pool. And yet, a career high in slugging percentage and a return to strong framing numbers propelled Iannetta to his best season yet. The Diamondbacks had lots of little moves that helped propel them to the playoffs, but the new front-office regime picking up Iannetta on the cheap may be the most underrated one. Also of note: He hasn't topped a .750 OPS in back-to-back seasons since 2008-2009, but until last year he hadn't cracked an .800 OPS in any season since then either.

DJ LeMahieu 2B Born: 07/13/88 Age: 29 Bats: R Throws: R Height: 6'4" Weight: 215 Origin: Round 2, 2009 Draft (#79 overall)

YEAR	TEAM	LVL	AGE	PA	R	2B	3B	HR	RBI	BB	K	SB	CS	AVG/OBP/SLG	TAv	VORP	BABIP	BRR	FRAA	WARP
2015	COL	MLB	26	620	85	21	5	6	61	50	107	23	3	.301/.358/.388	.253	16.9	.362	4.9	2B(149): -0.6	1.8
2016	COL	MLB	27	635	104	32	8	11	66	66	80	11	7	.348/.416/.495	.298	44.1	.388	2.0	2B(146): -1.2	4.4
2017	COL	MLB	28	682	95	28	4	8	64	59	90	6	5	.310/.374/.409	.268	27.9	.351	3.4	2B(153): 20.5	4.8
2018	*COL*	*MLB*	*29*	*615*	*75*	*25*	*5*	*7*	*53*	*49*	*97*	*10*	*5*	*.286/.342/.386*	*.248*	*19.7*	*.330*	*-0.1*	*2B 5*	*1.8*
2019	*COL*	*MLB*	*30*	*561*	*65*	*23*	*4*	*9*	*56*	*47*	*95*	*7*	*4*	*.280/.343/.392*	*.257*	*18.5*	*.325*	*2.3*	*2B 5*	*2.6*

Breakout: 1% Improve: 50% Collapse: 8% Attrition: 12% MLB: 98% *Comparables: Jerry Lumpe, Jim Gantner, Bob Randall*

The onus is no longer on LeMahieu to prove he's legit; it's on you to prove he isn't. Every year, LeMahieu seems to find something to get better at. In 2015, he improved as a hitter and basestealer. In 2016, well, he became a better hitter again, and even added some power. And in 2017? LeMahieu posted some truly eye-popping defensive statistics that justified his second Gold Glove. We hear the phrase "the sum of the parts is greater than the whole" a lot in scouting, but with LeMahieu, it's true. He has no real flaws as a player other than a lack of pop, and given the environment he plays in and his supporting cast, it's tough to imagine the Rockies mind very much. He may not be one of the game's truly elite second baseman, but LeMahieu is just one tier below. Only Jose Altuve and Daniel Murphy have produced more BWARP at the position over the past two seasons, a fact LeMahieu's agent is likely to bring up when he reaches the market after 2018.

Jonathan Lucroy C Born: 06/13/86 Age: 32 Bats: R Throws: R Height: 6'0" Weight: 200 Origin: Round 3, 2007 Draft (#101 overall)

YEAR	TEAM	LVL	AGE	PA	R	2B	3B	HR	RBI	BB	K	SB	CS	AVG/OBP/SLG	TAv	VORP	BABIP	BRR	FRAA	WARP
2015	MIL	MLB	29	415	51	20	3	7	43	36	64	1	0	.264/.326/.391	.254	12.0	.297	-2.4	C(86): 0.4, 1B(7): 0.1	1.3
2016	MIL	MLB	30	376	48	17	3	13	50	33	70	5	0	.299/.359/.482	.297	32.1	.340	2.0	C(82): 6.7, 1B(6): -0.6	3.9
2016	TEX	MLB	30	168	19	7	0	11	31	14	30	0	0	.276/.345/.539	.297	12.8	.279	-1.1	C(44): 2.0	1.5
2017	TEX	MLB	31	306	27	15	0	4	27	19	32	1	0	.242/.297/.338	.217	0.0	.259	1.0	C(66): -13.5, 1B(1): 0.0	-1.4
2017	COL	MLB	31	175	18	6	3	2	13	27	19	0	0	.310/.429/.437	.292	13.9	.341	-0.2	C(44): -6.0	0.8
2018	*COL*	*MLB*	*32*	*464*	*53*	*26*	*3*	*13*	*59*	*44*	*65*	*2*	*0*	*.283/.353/.454*	*.260*	*23.7*	*.307*	*-0.3*	*C -9, 1B 0*	*1.7*
2019	*COL*	*MLB*	*33*	*443*	*55*	*22*	*2*	*11*	*52*	*42*	*65*	*1*	*0*	*.271/.343/.427*	*.266*	*19.4*	*.298*	*-0.6*	*C -8, 1B 0*	*1.2*

Breakout: 0% Improve: 29% Collapse: 10% Attrition: 17% MLB: 98% *Comparables: Darrin Fletcher, Yadier Molina, Del Crandall*

YEAR	TEAM	P. COUNT	FRM RUNS	BLK RUNS	THRW RUNS	TOT RUNS
2015	MIL	12038	1.1	0.6	-1.0	0.6
2016	MIL	11622	3.6	2.1	2.2	7.9
2016	TEX	5788	0.4	-0.2	2.2	2.4
2017	TEX	9640	-12.4	-1.0	0.6	-12.8
2017	COL	5958	-5.2	-1.3	0.0	-6.5
2018	*COL*	*15707*	*-9.6*	*-0.1*	*1.3*	*-8.5*
2019	*COL*	*15003*	*-9.6*	*-0.1*	*1.3*	*-8.5*

If you loved the original with Kate Hudson and Matthew McConaughey, hopefully you checked out the sequel Lucroy starred in last year: *How to Lose a Free Agent Megadeal in 10 Weeks*. Coming off one of the best seasons of his career in 2016, Lucroy looked poised to enjoy a big walk year in the hitter-friendly confines of Globe Life Park. Instead, he posted a miserable .217 TAv for the Rangers and was sold off to the Rockies for the low cost of a player to be named later (outfield prospect Pedro Gonzalez, it turns out). Lucroy was much better offensively with the Rockies, so perhaps he saved some face, but what's likely to trouble teams more than Lucroy's struggles at the plate are his sudden difficulties behind it. Historically a top performer in Framing Runs, Lucroy dropped to -17.7 last season, and we scored him as a below-average blocker, too. That means teams that want to bid on him have a tough question to answer: Is he a potential bargain coming off a rough year, or was 2017 the beginning of the end for one of baseball's premier backstops?

Ryan McMahon 3B Born: 12/14/94 Age: 23 Bats: L Throws: R Height: 6'2" Weight: 185 Origin: Round 2, 2013 Draft (#42 overall)

YEAR	TEAM	LVL	AGE	PA	R	2B	3B	HR	RBI	BB	K	SB	CS	AVG/OBP/SLG	TAv	VORP	BABIP	BRR	FRAA	WARP
2015	MOD	A+	20	556	85	43	6	18	75	49	153	6	13	.300/.372/.520	.358	72.9	.401	1.5	3B(129): 24.7	10.6
2016	HFD	AA	21	535	49	27	5	12	75	55	161	11	6	.242/.325/.399	.265	14.7	.338	1.3		1.9
2017	HFD	AA	22	205	28	16	2	6	32	20	39	7	0	.326/.390/.536	.317	15.8	.381	0.0		1.7
2017	ABQ	AAA	22	314	46	23	2	14	56	21	53	4	3	.374/.411/.612	.318	24.3	.416	-2.9	1B(36): 1.1, 2B(24): 2.4	2.6
2017	COL	MLB	22	24	2	1	0	0	1	5	5	0	0	.158/.333/.211	.201	0.3	.214	1.4	1B(7): 0.2, 2B(4): 0.0	0.1
2018	*COL*	*MLB*	*23*	*252*	*31*	*14*	*2*	*8*	*33*	*22*	*71*	*3*	*1*	*.261/.327/.448*	*.259*	*6.5*	*.342*	*-0.2*	*1B 0, 3B 2*	*0.7*
2019	*COL*	*MLB*	*24*	*450*	*60*	*26*	*3*	*17*	*61*	*43*	*126*	*5*	*2*	*.267/.339/.470*	*.276*	*16.7*	*.344*	*-0.3*	*1B 0, 3B 3*	*2.2*

Breakout: 5% Improve: 20% Collapse: 7% Attrition: 22% MLB: 41% *Comparables: Rhys Hoskins, Jerry Sands, Ryan Lavarnway*

Few people outside of the cable news industry had a better 2017 than McMahon. After a rough 2016 season that saw him stall out a bit in Double-A, McMahon reemerged as one of the better prospects in the game, reaching the majors well before his 23rd birthday. McMahon cut down on his strikeouts while further tapping into his power in Hartford and Albuquerque, and even added some defensive versatility by making 43 appearances at second base. All the usual caveats about inflated offensive stats for Rockies prospects apply here, but McMahon's improved plate discipline should travel, as should his pop. That's good, because McMahon faces an uphill battle for playing time at second or third if he remains in Colorado.

Tom Murphy C Born: 04/03/91 Age: 27 Bats: R Throws: R Height: 6'1" Weight: 220 Origin: Round 3, 2012 Draft (#105 overall)

YEAR	TEAM	LVL	AGE	PA	R	2B	3B	HR	RBI	BB	K	SB	CS	AVG/OBP/SLG	TAv	VORP	BABIP	BRR	FRAA	WARP
2015	NBR	AA	24	294	36	17	1	13	44	23	80	5	2	.249/.320/.468	.272	14.8	.306	0.1	C(58): -1.7	1.4
2015	ABQ	AAA	24	136	19	9	2	7	19	5	43	0	1	.271/.301/.535	.266	6.9	.350	0.8	C(27): -1.2	0.6
2015	COL	MLB	24	39	5	1	0	3	9	4	10	0	0	.257/.333/.543	.281	3.0	.273	0.5	C(11): -2.3	0.1
2016	ABQ	AAA	25	322	53	26	7	19	59	16	78	1	1	.327/.361/.647	.321	31.6	.386	-2.2	C(69): 2.0	3.5
2016	COL	MLB	25	49	8	2	0	5	13	4	19	1	0	.273/.347/.659	.290	2.8	.350	-0.7	C(12): 0.4	0.3
2017	ABQ	AAA	26	154	22	10	1	4	19	9	56	0	0	.255/.312/.426	.230	0.9	.390	-0.7	C(34): 0.9	0.2
2017	COL	MLB	26	26	1	1	0	0	1	2	9	0	0	.042/.115/.083	.113	-2.7	.067	0.2	C(8): 0.3	-0.2
2018	*COL*	*MLB*	*27*	*88*	*11*	*4*	*1*	*4*	*13*	*6*	*29*	*0*	*0*	*.239/.293/.464*	*.249*	*2.9*	*.312*	*-0.1*	*C -1*	*0.1*
2019	*COL*	*MLB*	*28*	*256*	*35*	*14*	*1*	*14*	*39*	*18*	*87*	*1*	*0*	*.240/.301/.485*	*.264*	*9.7*	*.316*	*-0.4*	*C -3*	*0.8*

Breakout: 1% Improve: 13% Collapse: 9% Attrition: 16% MLB: 38% *Comparables: Kelly Shoppach, Zach Walters, Victor Diaz*

YEAR	TEAM	P. COUNT	FRM RUNS	BLK RUNS	THRW RUNS	TOT RUNS
2015	ABQ	4087	-0.6	-0.3	-0.3	-1.3
2015	COL	1584	-1.9	-0.2	-0.1	-2.2
2015	NBR	7358	0.3	-1.4	0.5	-0.6
2016	COL	1415	0.2	0.1	0.1	0.4
2017	COL	1031	-0.5	0.5	-0.1	-0.1
2018	*COL*	*2322*	*-1.0*	*-0.3*	*0.0*	*-1.3*
2019	*COL*	*6760*	*-1.0*	*-0.3*	*0.0*	*-1.3*

Catching prospects, man. Murphy has a lot of swing-and-miss to his game, and he's only an adequate defender, but the dude posted an OPS north of 1.000 at Triple-A in 2016; he was ready for the majors. But what did we forget about Murphy? What's the one thing we know to be true of every Rockies prospect? No, no, we're not talking about the inflated minor-league numbers; we're talking about the injuries. Murphy broke his forearm in March. That kept him out of action until early June and is part of the reason he played in just 50 games between Albuquerque and Denver. Jonathan Lucroy is a free agent and it's still not clear that Tony Wolters can hit, so Murphy should get a shot this year. We've said that before, though. They oughta name a law after this guy or something.

Dom Nunez C Born: 01/17/95 Age: 23 Bats: L Throws: R Height: 6'0" Weight: 175 Origin: Round 6, 2013 Draft (#169 overall)

YEAR	TEAM	LVL	AGE	PA	R	2B	3B	HR	RBI	BB	K	SB	CS	AVG/OBP/SLG	TAv	VORP	BABIP	BRR	FRAA	WARP
2015	ASH	A	20	441	61	23	0	13	53	53	55	7	7	.282/.373/.448	.281	27.3	.298	-0.8	C(99): -1.5	2.7
2016	MOD	A+	21	450	44	13	2	10	51	49	91	8	1	.241/.321/.362	.261	20.7	.284	1.6	C(93): 5.1	2.7
2017	HFD	AA	22	364	37	10	1	11	28	53	83	7	1	.202/.335/.354	.260	15.1	.238	0.0		1.6
2018	*COL*	*MLB*	*23*	*250*	*28*	*9*	*1*	*9*	*31*	*27*	*60*	*1*	*0*	*.226/.316/.394*	*.230*	*4.7*	*.266*	*-0.2*	*C 2*	*0.8*
2019	*COL*	*MLB*	*24*	*276*	*36*	*11*	*1*	*10*	*34*	*31*	*65*	*2*	*0*	*.230/.323/.405*	*.250*	*7.6*	*.268*	*-0.3*	*C 2*	*1.0*

Breakout: 2% Improve: 20% Collapse: 3% Attrition: 21% MLB: 30% *Comparables: Victor Caratini, Christian Vazquez, David Freitas*

YEAR	TEAM	P. COUNT	FRM RUNS	BLK RUNS	THRW RUNS	TOT RUNS
2018	*COL*	*9005*	*2.1*	*-0.2*	*0.0*	*2.0*
2019	*COL*	*9958*	*0.9*	*-0.1*	*0.0*	*0.8*

This was supposed to be the sequel to the Tony Wolters story: *Converted Catcher II, Tokyo Drift*, if you will. A former infielder, Nunez earns positive reviews for his work ethic, athleticism and his still-developing chops behind the plate. His offensive abilities don't require reviews because his line speaks for itself. To be fair to Nunez, the backstop hit .260/.356/.416 from August 1 on. To be fair to realists, that means he hit .182 from April through July. Nunez has a demonstrated history of getting better the longer he stays at a level, but his offensive output is declining with each rung of the ladder he climbs. A future as a backup backstop is probably the safest outcome to bet on here, though once upon a time Nick Hundley OPSed over .800 in Coors, so...

Gerardo Parra LF Born: 05/06/87 Age: 31 Bats: L Throws: L Height: 5'11" Weight: 210 Origin: International Free Agent, 2004

YEAR	TEAM	LVL	AGE	PA	R	2B	3B	HR	RBI	BB	K	SB	CS	AVG/OBP/SLG	TAv	VORP	BABIP	BRR	FRAA	WARP
2015	MIL	MLB	28	351	53	24	5	9	31	20	57	9	3	.328/.369/.517	.309	23.1	.372	-1.8	LF(46): -2.0, CF(31): 0.1	2.3
2015	BAL	MLB	28	238	30	12	0	5	20	8	35	5	1	.237/.268/.357	.218	-5.3	.259	-0.1	RF(47): -0.5, CF(10): 1.1	-0.4
2016	COL	MLB	29	381	45	27	3	7	39	9	73	6	4	.253/.271/.399	.215	-1.7	.297	-1.1	LF(60): 1.8, 1B(19): 0.4	-1.1
2017	COL	MLB	30	425	56	24	1	10	71	20	67	2	5	.309/.341/.452	.267	9.6	.343	-2.5	LF(82): 3.7, RF(22): -0.1	1.3
2018	*COL*	*MLB*	*31*	*519*	*54*	*28*	*3*	*10*	*56*	*28*	*88*	*7*	*5*	*.268/.309/.401*	*.236*	*-1.2*	*.306*	*-0.8*	*RF -6*	*-0.9*
2019	*COL*	*MLB*	*32*	*470*	*55*	*26*	*3*	*11*	*54*	*31*	*82*	*6*	*4*	*.275/.327/.427*	*.258*	*7.0*	*.312*	*-1.6*	*RF -5*	*0.3*

Breakout: 2% Improve: 40% Collapse: 11% Attrition: 22% MLB: 87% *Comparables: Mackey Sasser, Billy Hatcher, B.J. Surhoff*

According to Wikipedia, the term "dead cat bounce" has only been around since 1985, and it was referencing the Malaysian stock market. Weird, right? You were probably expecting it to be from Confucius or something. Anyway, Parra was much better in his second season with the Rockies. He was solid against right-handers, played good defense in the corners and tied his previous career-high in homers. So why the negative vibe? Parra is a career .247/.303/.322 hitter against southpaws, but he hit .347/.377/.429 against them in 2017. The problem is his BABIP vs. lefties was .413, so this is less a case of a player learning how to conquer his weaknesses and more a case of flat-out good luck. Parra cost his team runs on the bases, going just 2-for-7 in steals, and the Rockies know he can't be trusted in center anymore. Add it all up, and you get a player more likely to repeat his 2016 swoon than his 2017 rebound.

Jordan Patterson OF Born: 02/12/92 Age: 26 Bats: L Throws: L Height: 6'4" Weight: 215 Origin: Round 4, 2013 Draft (#109 overall)

YEAR	TEAM	LVL	AGE	PA	R	2B	3B	HR	RBI	BB	K	SB	CS	AVG/OBP/SLG	TAv	VORP	BABIP	BRR	FRAA	WARP
2015	MOD	A+	23	339	62	26	12	10	43	19	88	9	6	.304/.378/.568	.358	45.8	.400	6.8	RF(52): -3.5, LF(9): -0.2	4.6
2015	NBR	AA	23	202	26	19	0	7	32	11	42	9	4	.286/.342/.503	.302	12.6	.336	1.0	RF(23): 4.4, 1B(21): 0.9	1.9
2016	ABQ	AAA	24	495	75	24	7	14	61	47	118	10	0	.293/.376/.480	.281	19.6	.370	1.5	RF(76): 15.6, 1B(38): 0.4	3.7
2016	COL	MLB	24	19	1	1	0	0	2	1	1	0	1	.444/.474/.500	.323	0.9	.471	-0.6	RF(5): -0.3, LF(2): -0.2	0.1
2017	ABQ	AAA	25	542	78	32	7	26	92	36	128	3	5	.283/.348/.539	.275	16.4	.330	-0.2	1B(84): 0.7, RF(39): -1.7	1.5
2018	*COL*	*MLB*	*26*	*57*	*7*	*3*	*1*	*2*	*7*	*4*	*16*	*1*	*0*	*.253/.323/.452*	*.258*	*1.4*	*.320*	*0.0*	*1B 0*	*0.1*
2019	*COL*	*MLB*	*27*	*305*	*40*	*16*	*3*	*12*	*42*	*24*	*86*	*3*	*1*	*.248/.325/.461*	*.268*	*8.1*	*.316*	*-0.2*	*1B 1*	*1.0*

Breakout: 4% Improve: 15% Collapse: 4% Attrition: 28% MLB: 38% *Comparables: Matt Clark, Mark Hamilton, Matthew Brown*

Being a Rockies prospect giveth and being a Rockies prospect taketh away. Patterson has power and can mash the hell out of right-handed pitchers. Favorable ballparks and genuine, truck-commercial-voice-over-type strength have helped Patterson put up some shiny numbers in the minors, and it's easy to envision him crushing many a tater into the Denver sky. But you know who else can crush many taters in Coors? Lots and lots of guys, many of whom aren't limited to a corner, aren't platoon bats and have already proven they can hit major-league pitching. Patterson's skill set would play up more in Coors than anywhere else, but it isn't a particularly unique profile, which makes the margin for error so much thinner with the Rockies than it likely would be anywhere else. *Catch-22* was a frustrating read, huh?

Mark Reynolds 1B Born: 08/03/83 Age: 34 Bats: R Throws: R Height: 6'2" Weight: 220 Origin: Round 16, 2004 Draft (#476 overall)

YEAR	TEAM	LVL	AGE	PA	R	2B	3B	HR	RBI	BB	K	SB	CS	AVG/OBP/SLG	TAv	VORP	BABIP	BRR	FRAA	WARP
2015	SLN	MLB	31	432	35	21	2	13	48	44	121	2	3	.230/.315/.398	.253	-1.2	.300	-4.5	1B(100): 1.6, 3B(22): -0.9	-0.1
2016	COL	MLB	32	441	61	24	0	14	53	42	112	1	2	.282/.356/.450	.275	8.9	.361	-2.6	1B(115): 1.6, 2B(1): 0.0	1.1
2017	COL	MLB	33	593	82	22	1	30	97	69	175	2	1	.267/.352/.487	.284	18.3	.343	-2.9	1B(138): -11.9, LF(1): 0.0	0.6
2018	*COL*	*MLB*	*34*	*527*	*64*	*20*	*1*	*22*	*72*	*57*	*154*	*2*	*2*	*.237/.323/.428*	*.247*	*0.2*	*.301*	*-2.7*	*1B -3, 3B 0*	*-0.3*
2019	*COL*	*MLB*	*35*	*459*	*61*	*16*	*1*	*19*	*60*	*51*	*136*	*1*	*1*	*.230/.319/.415*	*.256*	*1.2*	*.295*	*-2.4*	*1B -3, 3B 0*	*-0.2*

Breakout: 1% Improve: 29% Collapse: 14% Attrition: 23% MLB: 88% *Comparables: Jim Hickman, Chili Davis, Candy Maldonado*

Back in 2013, former BP Editor-in-Chief Sam Miller wrote a piece called "Baseball's Greatest Hoax." It's composed of several thousand words and a few dozen gifs that make a tongue-in-cheek case that Mark Reynolds is actually blind, and it's a bit of a cult favorite among the baseballing Internet. Well, turns out the joke's on us, because Reynolds isn't blind at all; in fact, he's a visionary. Baseball in 2017 was all about socking dongers and unapologetically striking out. That means Reynolds has simply been ahead of his time, a sort of genius hipster among sentient windmills. Unexpectedly pressed into an everyday role, Reynolds posted his best TAv since 2009 and launched more homers than any season since 2011. Sure, he still struck out more than Dustin from *Stranger Things*, and yes, only nine of his taters came away from Coors, but 30 homers is 30 homers. Reynolds did enough at the plate that some power-hungry team will give him a look this offseason, though a Rockies reunion would make sense for both sides.

Brendan Rodgers SS Born: 08/09/96 Age: 21 Bats: R Throws: R Height: 6'0" Weight: 180 Origin: Round 1, 2015 Draft (#3 overall)

YEAR	TEAM	LVL	AGE	PA	R	2B	3B	HR	RBI	BB	K	SB	CS	AVG/OBP/SLG	TAv	VORP	BABIP	BRR	FRAA	WARP
2015	GJR	RK	18	159	22	8	2	3	20	15	37	4	3	.273/.340/.420	.267	7.6	.346	0.5	SS(29): 9.8	1.7
2016	ASH	A	19	491	73	31	0	19	73	35	98	6	3	.281/.342/.480	.282	21.9	.319	-2.5	SS(56): 0.0, 2B(24): 0.9	2.5
2017	HFD	AA	20	164	20	5	0	6	17	8	36	0	2	.260/.323/.413	.265	6.4	.306	-0.5		0.7
2017	LNC	A+	20	236	44	21	3	12	47	6	35	2	1	.387/.407/.671	.327	26.4	.413	0.9	SS(47): -5.6, 2B(4): -0.6	2.1
2018	*COL*	*MLB*	*21*	*250*	*31*	*12*	*1*	*10*	*32*	*12*	*64*	*0*	*0*	*.253/.299/.446*	*.239*	*5.7*	*.303*	*-0.5*	*SS -1, 2B 0*	*0.6*
2019	*COL*	*MLB*	*22*	*328*	*43*	*17*	*1*	*14*	*46*	*18*	*83*	*0*	*0*	*.258/.309/.461*	*.262*	*11.1*	*.307*	*-0.8*	*SS -1, 2B 0*	*1.1*

Breakout: 6% Improve: 10% Collapse: 4% Attrition: 23% MLB: 35% *Comparables: Franklin Barreto, Addison Russell, Corey Seager*

What do you think about when you think of top-shelf Rockies prospects? Big-time bats? Tons of athleticism? Aggressive approaches? Injuries galore? Check and check and check and check. Rodgers isn't just the best Rockies prospect; he is the most Rockies prospect, a five-tool talent who's battled boo-boos and who'd swing at a live grenade if you threw one nearish the plate. Rodgers began the season on the DL with a minor hand injury, then hit .400—yes, .400—in 222 PA in Lancaster (it's Lancaster, but still). The Rockies had no choice but to promote him to Hartford, and Rodgers held his own there for about six weeks before returning to the DL with a quad injury. Rodgers has a rocket arm and an elite hit tool. He also just turned 21 in August, so even if there are some questions about his game power, patience and defense at short, we're talking about a consensus top-10 prospect in the game. He may very well force the issue and make the majors this season, and at this point seeing him in Colorado by 2019 looks like a given.

Trevor Story SS Born: 11/15/92 Age: 25 Bats: R Throws: R Height: 6'1" Weight: 210 Origin: Round 1, 2011 Draft (#45 overall)

YEAR	TEAM	LVL	AGE	PA	R	2B	3B	HR	RBI	BB	K	SB	CS	AVG/OBP/SLG	TAv	VORP	BABIP	BRR	FRAA	WARP
2015	NBR	AA	22	300	46	20	6	10	40	35	73	15	2	.281/.373/.523	.330	35.3	.350	3.4	SS(50): 3.3, 2B(12): -0.2	4.3
2015	ABQ	AAA	22	275	37	20	4	10	40	16	68	7	1	.277/.324/.504	.282	18.5	.341	2.4	SS(35): 2.1, 3B(14): -0.2	2.1
2016	COL	MLB	23	415	67	21	4	27	72	35	130	8	5	.272/.341/.567	.288	31.2	.343	2.1	SS(96): 0.8	3.3
2017	COL	MLB	24	555	68	32	3	24	82	49	191	7	2	.239/.308/.457	.261	28.6	.332	4.2	SS(142): -0.4	2.8
2018	*COL*	*MLB*	*25*	*530*	*72*	*27*	*4*	*25*	*79*	*45*	*167*	*9*	*3*	*.245/.314/.474*	*.262*	*27.9*	*.319*	*0.6*	*SS 0*	*2.0*
2019	*COL*	*MLB*	*26*	*516*	*71*	*26*	*3*	*26*	*78*	*47*	*162*	*9*	*3*	*.244/.319/.482*	*.272*	*27.0*	*.314*	*3.0*	*SS 0*	*2.9*

Breakout: 0% Improve: 55% Collapse: 7% Attrition: 10% MLB: 97% *Comparables: Randal Grichuk, Mark Reynolds, Oswaldo Arcia*

The Similarity Index is a fickle mistress. It will take a guy like Story and tease you with comps like Paul Goldschmidt, Chris Davis and Jake Lamb. Then you'll scroll down a little and see Mike Olt, Will Middlebrooks and Brandon Wood bandied about. Story has already enjoyed more MLB success than that second, scarier trio, but he sure doubled down on his Trevor Story-ness in 2017, posting the third-highest strikeout rate among qualified batters. Only Davis and Joey Gallo struck out more, and while Story is a more valuable defender than either of those hackers, he doesn't hit for quite as much power, either. As long as Story can hang at shortstop he's got value, but he's already only an average defender; if he slides to second or third, teams will have less patience for his contact issues. Then again, Story need only look at his teammate Mark Reynolds to see how long a leash prodigious power affords a man, so we're still a long way off from seeing how this Story ends.

Raimel Tapia RF Born: 02/04/94 Age: 24 Bats: L Throws: L Height: 6'2" Weight: 160 Origin: International Free Agent, 2010

YEAR	TEAM	LVL	AGE	PA	R	2B	3B	HR	RBI	BB	K	SB	CS	AVG/OBP/SLG	TAv	VORP	BABIP	BRR	FRAA	WARP
2015	MOD	A+	21	593	74	34	9	12	71	24	105	26	10	.305/.333/.467	.317	47.6	.350	-0.7	CF(74): 3.0, LF(46): 0.4	5.5
2016	HFD	AA	22	457	79	20	5	8	34	25	49	17	14	.323/.363/.450	.287	25.2	.349	1.4		3.8
2016	ABQ	AAA	22	110	14	5	5	0	14	2	12	6	3	.346/.355/.490	.261	2.9	.379	0.0	CF(12): 1.9, LF(8): 1.3	0.6
2016	COL	MLB	22	41	4	0	0	0	3	2	11	3	0	.263/.293/.263	.191	-0.4	.357	1.2	CF(9): 0.2, LF(2): -0.2	0.0
2017	ABQ	AAA	23	277	45	20	8	2	30	13	42	12	2	.369/.397/.529	.294	18.8	.432	-0.1	CF(48): 0.1, LF(5): -0.6	1.7
2017	COL	MLB	23	171	27	12	2	2	16	8	36	5	2	.288/.329/.425	.252	4.0	.361	1.6	RF(22): -3.0, LF(18): -1.3	-0.1
2018	*COL*	*MLB*	*24*	*494*	*59*	*25*	*6*	*10*	*52*	*22*	*93*	*15*	*6*	*.284/.316/.427*	*.246*	*11.2*	*.334*	*1.1*	*LF -1, CF 1*	*0.6*
2019	*COL*	*MLB*	*25*	*524*	*61*	*28*	*7*	*13*	*62*	*27*	*102*	*15*	*7*	*.286/.326/.448*	*.262*	*17.1*	*.334*	*2.7*	*LF -1, CF 1*	*1.9*

Breakout: 8% Improve: 31% Collapse: 9% Attrition: 20% MLB: 58% *Comparables: Peter Bourjos, Felix Pie, Dave Sappelt*

Everything Raimel Tapia did in 2017 was extremely Raimel Tapia, both for better and for worse. We'll start with the negatives. He hit just four homers between Triple-A and the majors. He took fewer walks than a *WALL-E* human. He was just okay defensively in the outfield. But because he's Raimel Tapia, he also hit nearly .370 in Albuquerque and nearly .290 in Colorado. When it comes to Tapia, our Similarity Index might as well just spit out a ¯_(ツ)_/¯. His approach at the plate shouldn't work, but it does, just as scouts have been telling us it would for years. Tapia is on the right track, but admittedly he'll need to keep hitting close to .300 or add some power to be a no-doubt everyday player. You'd think the "add some power" part would be easier, but with Tapia it's the "hit .300" part that's the safer bet.

Michael Tauchman OF Born: 12/03/90 Age: 27 Bats: L Throws: L Height: 6'2" Weight: 200 Origin: Round 10, 2013 Draft (#289 overall)

YEAR	TEAM	LVL	AGE	PA	R	2B	3B	HR	RBI	BB	K	SB	CS	AVG/OBP/SLG	TAv	VORP	BABIP	BRR	FRAA	WARP
2015	NBR	AA	24	563	62	23	6	3	43	47	69	25	13	.294/.355/.381	.281	25.3	.334	0.7	LF(60): 3.1, CF(38): 2.4	3.0
2016	ABQ	AAA	25	527	72	24	7	1	51	40	77	23	10	.286/.342/.373	.243	11.1	.337	5.4	CF(93): 2.4, LF(21): 5.1	1.8
2017	ABQ	AAA	26	475	82	30	8	16	80	40	73	16	7	.331/.386/.555	.296	35.3	.361	2.5	CF(62): 1.3, LF(34): 5.7	4.0
2017	COL	MLB	26	32	2	0	1	0	2	5	10	1	2	.222/.344/.296	.220	-1.0	.353	-0.5	RF(3): -0.1, LF(3): -0.1	-0.2
2018	*COL*	*MLB*	*27*	*91*	*11*	*4*	*1*	*2*	*9*	*7*	*17*	*3*	*1*	*.263/.323/.393*	*.243*	*1.1*	*.312*	*0.1*	*RF 0*	*0.0*
2019	*COL*	*MLB*	*28*	*275*	*32*	*13*	*2*	*6*	*30*	*23*	*54*	*8*	*4*	*.265/.330/.406*	*.256*	*5.7*	*.313*	*0.5*	*RF -1*	*0.5*

Breakout: 2% Improve: 15% Collapse: 5% Attrition: 11% MLB: 28% *Comparables: Craig Gentry, Ryan Lollis, Matt Angle*

Tauchman started the year as a relative unknown and ended the year on the postseason roster, so at least 2017 will be remembered fondly by one person. He has always been able to hit for average and has always had speed, plus he's a capable defender at all three outfield spots. But before 2017, he had generated about as much power as a first-generation Prius, which was frustrating given his size. Some work with Triple-A manager Glenallen Hill allowed Tauchman to tap into his natural pop, and he now has the profile of a solid fourth or fifth outfielder. Unfortunately the Rockies have like 90 guys who fit that bill, but at least Tauchman has put himself in contention for some more major-league at-bats.

Patrick Valaika UT Born: 09/09/92 Age: 25 Bats: R Throws: R Height: 5'11" Weight: 200 Origin: Round 9, 2013 Draft (#259 overall)

YEAR	TEAM	LVL	AGE	PA	R	2B	3B	HR	RBI	BB	K	SB	CS	AVG/OBP/SLG	TAv	VORP	BABIP	BRR	FRAA	WARP
2015	NBR	AA	22	512	57	25	5	8	57	30	117	19	7	.235/.281/.361	.240	11.1	.292	4.5	SS(62): -1.1, 2B(33): 2.0	1.2
2016	HFD	AA	23	474	66	33	3	13	67	28	95	8	9	.269/.314/.450	.275	25.9	.315	2.1		2.3
2016	ABQ	AAA	23	115	8	8	1	1	13	2	28	2	0	.209/.226/.327	.194	-3.3	.265	0.6	SS(15): 0.7, 2B(9): 1.5	-0.1
2016	COL	MLB	23	19	3	1	0	1	2	0	8	0	0	.263/.263/.474	.274	0.5	.400	-0.4	3B(6): 0.1, 2B(5): -0.1	0.0
2017	ABQ	AAA	24	50	6	2	1	1	11	4	11	0	0	.267/.327/.422	.237	1.1	.333	0.5	SS(9): 0.3, 1B(2): 0.0	0.1
2017	COL	MLB	24	195	28	11	0	13	40	7	53	0	0	.258/.284/.533	.273	11.2	.291	2.1	SS(22): -0.6, 3B(19): -0.1	1.0
2018	*COL*	*MLB*	*25*	*321*	*35*	*16*	*2*	*11*	*40*	*16*	*86*	*4*	*2*	*.235/.272/.410*	*.224*	*0.9*	*.288*	*-0.1*	*SS -1, 2B 1*	*-0.2*
2019	*COL*	*MLB*	*26*	*501*	*60*	*27*	*3*	*19*	*65*	*30*	*135*	*6*	*3*	*.240/.287/.435*	*.243*	*7.0*	*.290*	*1.4*	*SS -1, 2B 1*	*0.8*

Breakout: 3% Improve: 22% Collapse: 7% Attrition: 25% MLB: 46% *Comparables: Donnie Murphy, Juan Diaz, Charlie Culberson*

The Rockies' third-round pick way back in 2013, Valaika made the most of the MLB playing time he saw in 2017. Defensively, he appeared at first, second, third, shortstop and left field, so here is your obligatory Ben Zobrist reference. Offensively, he hit 13 bombs, proving that some of the power he showed in Double-A in 2016 is real and also that the ball is definitely juiced. Pat now has a commanding 1.5 career WARP lead over his brother Chris, who finished his time in the majors with a -0.5 mark. That could make the holidays a little awkward, but our Similarity Index says that Pat's number one comp is Chris, so the family dynamics here are truly complex.

Forrest Wall 2B Born: 11/20/95 Age: 22 Bats: L Throws: R Height: 6'0" Weight: 176 Origin: Round 1, 2014 Draft (#35 overall)

YEAR	TEAM	LVL	AGE	PA	R	2B	3B	HR	RBI	BB	K	SB	CS	AVG/OBP/SLG	TAv	VORP	BABIP	BRR	FRAA	WARP
2015	ASH	A	19	416	57	16	10	7	46	41	72	23	9	.280/.355/.438	.284	22.1	.329	1.4	2B(92): 1.6	2.5
2016	MOD	A+	20	521	57	16	4	6	56	41	97	22	11	.264/.329/.355	.267	18.2	.319	0.6	2B(117): -4.5	1.4
2017	LNC	A+	21	98	17	4	1	3	16	9	16	5	3	.299/.361/.471	.267	5.9	.333	2.4	CF(17): 0.5, 2B(2): -0.2	0.6
2018	*COL*	*MLB*	*22*	*250*	*31*	*9*	*2*	*6*	*24*	*19*	*59*	*7*	*3*	*.239/.299/.383*	*.218*	*-0.9*	*.289*	*0.2*	*CF 0, LF 0*	*-0.1*
2019	*COL*	*MLB*	*23*	*264*	*31*	*10*	*2*	*7*	*29*	*21*	*62*	*7*	*4*	*.244/.308/.393*	*.241*	*3.0*	*.295*	*0.6*	*CF 0, LF 0*	*0.3*

Breakout: 0% Improve: 9% Collapse: 3% Attrition: 9% MLB: 15% *Comparables: Mason Williams, Gerardo Parra, Darrell Ceciliani*

Wall was expected to move quickly for a prep bat when he was drafted 35th overall in 2014, but injuries, ineffectiveness and a positional switch have stayed his progress. The 21-year-old was supposed to repeat High-A after a lackluster 2016, but he lasted just 98 PA before suffering a season-ending shoulder injury. How did he hurt his arm, you ask? By running into a literal wall in the most ironic injury since Angel Pagan was cursed by a witch. Wall still has the tools to put up solid numbers—especially in hitter-friendly Lancaster—but he's less exciting in center field than he was at second, and he's not very exciting at all if he can't stay on the field. Let's keep Viserion away from him, too.

Colton Welker 3B Born: 10/09/97 Age: 20 Bats: R Throws: R Height: 6'2" Weight: 195 Origin: Round 4, 2016 Draft (#110 overall)

YEAR	TEAM	LVL	AGE	PA	R	2B	3B	HR	RBI	BB	K	SB	CS	AVG/OBP/SLG	TAv	VORP	BABIP	BRR	FRAA	WARP
2016	GJR	RK	18	227	38	15	2	5	36	13	28	6	4	.329/.366/.490	.314	20.3	.356	-0.4	3B(48): -5.8	1.5
2017	ASH	A	19	279	32	18	1	6	33	18	42	5	7	.350/.401/.500	.308	19.7	.399	-1.6	3B(52): -7.3	1.3
2018	*COL*	*MLB*	*20*	*250*	*26*	*12*	*1*	*7*	*30*	*14*	*59*	*1*	*1*	*.252/.298/.408*	*.227*	*-0.9*	*.305*	*-0.6*	*3B -6*	*-0.8*
2019	*COL*	*MLB*	*21*	*337*	*41*	*18*	*1*	*11*	*42*	*19*	*75*	*2*	*2*	*.263/.309/.435*	*.255*	*5.5*	*.311*	*-0.8*	*3B -8*	*-0.3*

Breakout: 8% Improve: 15% Collapse: 0% Attrition: 4% MLB: 17% *Comparables: Cheslor Cuthbert, Rafael Devers, Matt Dominguez*

A 2016 fourth-rounder who signed a well-over-slot deal, Welker put in work justifying his $855,000 price tag by mashing in Asheville. Welker generally receives solid marks for his defense at third base, has strong bat-to-ball skills and could grow into plus power as well. He's a Rockies prospect, so of course he missed two months with an injury (strained groin, for those counting at home), but when Welker was on the field, he shined. He's another good half-season or so from emerging as a household name among prospect enthusiasts, at which point he can look forward to being unfairly compared to Nolan Arenado for the rest of his life.

Tony Wolters C Born: 06/09/92 Age: 26 Bats: L Throws: R Height: 5'10" Weight: 200 Origin: Round 3, 2010 Draft (#87 overall)

YEAR	TEAM	LVL	AGE	PA	R	2B	3B	HR	RBI	BB	K	SB	CS	AVG/OBP/SLG	TAv	VORP	BABIP	BRR	FRAA	WARP
2015	AKR	AA	23	271	23	7	2	2	17	21	63	3	2	.209/.290/.280	.219	1.3	.273	1.8	C(56): 13.5, SS(3): 0.2	1.6
2016	COL	MLB	24	230	27	15	2	3	30	21	53	4	1	.259/.327/.395	.249	8.4	.336	0.7	C(59): 7.6, 2B(7): -0.1	1.6
2017	ABQ	AAA	25	58	6	5	1	2	9	3	15	0	1	.259/.310/.500	.270	3.6	.324	0.3	C(13): 1.8	0.5
2017	COL	MLB	25	266	30	8	1	0	16	33	55	0	1	.240/.341/.284	.218	0.9	.316	0.5	C(77): -2.1, 2B(4): 0.1	-0.1
2018	*COL*	*MLB*	*26*	*249*	*26*	*11*	*1*	*4*	*23*	*23*	*59*	*2*	*1*	*.235/.311/.349*	*.226*	*4.1*	*.299*	*-0.3*	*C 2*	*0.3*
2019	*COL*	*MLB*	*27*	*270*	*31*	*12*	*2*	*6*	*27*	*28*	*67*	*2*	*1*	*.234/.320/.369*	*.241*	*5.6*	*.296*	*0.3*	*C 2*	*0.9*

Breakout: 13% Improve: 55% Collapse: 16% Attrition: 29% MLB: 92% *Comparables: Carlos Perez, Christian Vazquez, Francisco Cervelli*

YEAR	TEAM	P. COUNT	FRM RUNS	BLK RUNS	THRW RUNS	TOT RUNS
2015	AKR	7755	10.5	-0.1	2.7	13.1
2016	COL	8341	8.7	-0.1	0.5	9.0
2017	COL	9693	-3.8	-0.6	1.1	-3.3
2018	*COL*	*9420*	*1.8*	*-0.5*	*0.8*	*2.1*
2019	*COL*	*10202*	*1.8*	*-0.5*	*0.8*	*2.1*

If we take the macro view, Wolters is still a success story. But if we zoom in a bit we'll see that he was a disappointment in 2017. His steps backward at the plate aren't terribly concerning—Wolters still showed a good eye, and it's possible that some of his offensive drop-off resulted from a concussion he suffered in May. The bigger cause for concern is Wolters' regression *behind* the plate. Our advanced metrics say he was a below-average framer and blocker last season, which is a stark change from his 2016 numbers. Wolters remained strong against the run and has earned a reputation as a guy pitchers like throwing to, so this could just be a blip on the radar. He goes from "good story" to "eminently replaceable" if his glove isn't a plus, though, so Wolters needs to rediscover his magic quickly if he wants to stick.

PITCHERS

Yency Almonte RHP Born: 06/04/94 Age: 24 Bats: B Throws: R Height: 6'3" Weight: 205 Origin: Round 17, 2012 Draft (#537 overall)

YEAR	TEAM	LVL	AGE	W	L	SV	G	GS	IP	H	HR	BB/9	K/9	K	GB%	BABIP	WHIP	ERA	DRA	WARP	MPH	CMD	PWR	STM
2015	KAN	A	21	8	4	0	17	16	92^2	92	8	2.5	6.9	71	45%	.295	1.27	3.88	3.87	1.5				
2015	WNS	A+	21	3	3	0	7	6	44^2	28	1	2.4	7.9	39	52%	.231	0.90	2.42	2.68	1.3				
2016	HFD	AA	22	3	1	0	5	5	30	22	4	4.8	6.6	22	37%	.212	1.27	3.00	7.78	-1.0				
2016	MOD	A+	22	8	9	0	22	22	138^1	124	14	2.5	8.7	134	47%	.285	1.18	3.71	2.77	4.3				
2017	HFD	AA	23	5	3	0	14	14	76^1	58	4	3.7	8.4	71	45%	.267	1.17	2.00	4.25	0.8				
2017	ABQ	AAA	23	3	1	0	8	7	35	41	7	5.4	5.7	22	50%	.321	1.77	4.89	9.28	-1.4				
2018	*COL*	*MLB*	*24*	*1*	*1*	*0*	*15*	*0*	*16*	*15*	*2*	*4.0*	*8.8*	*16*	*43%*	*.294*	*1.38*	*4.66*	*4.67*	*0.0*				
2019	*COL*	*MLB*	*25*	*3*	*1*	*0*	*52*	*0*	55^1	*47*	*8*	*3.4*	*8.9*	*54*	*43%*	*.29*	*1.24*	*4.54*	*4.98*	*0.1*				

Breakout: 6% Improve: 15% Collapse: 9% Attrition: 18% MLB: 27% *Comparables: Domingo German, Williams Perez, Clayton Mortensen*

Don't look now, but the Rockies might have learned how to develop pitching prospects. Almonte was largely an afterthought when the Angels traded him to the White Sox and when the White Sox traded him to the Rockies, but now he's a borderline top-100 prospect. The hard-throwing righty pitched well in Double-A Hartford, showing off a mid-90s fastball and a nice slider. Reports suggest his changeup is still a work in progress, but he does show some feel for it. Almonte could move to the bullpen if the cambio never comes around (stop us if you've heard that before), but he holds his velocity deep into his outings and has been able to turn over high-minors lineups thus far, so he should get every chance to start. Unless of course the Rockies already have enough quality starters, which is strangely starting to look like a real possibility.

Tyler Anderson LHP Born: 12/30/89 Age: 28 Bats: L Throws: L Height: 6'4" Weight: 210 Origin: Round 1, 2011 Draft (#20 overall)

YEAR	TEAM	LVL	AGE	W	L	SV	G	GS	IP	H	HR	BB/9	K/9	K	GB%	BABIP	WHIP	ERA	DRA	WARP	MPH	CMD	PWR	STM
2016	HFD	AA	26	1	1	0	2	2	10	6	0	1.8	9.9	11	59%	.222	0.80	1.80	3.23	0.2				
2016	ABQ	AAA	26	1	1	0	3	3	17	15	1	3.2	6.9	13	48%	.286	1.24	2.12	4.66	0.1				
2016	COL	MLB	26	5	6	0	19	19	114^1	119	12	2.2	7.8	99	53%	.319	1.29	3.54	4.47	1.2	93.7	63	37	66
2017	ABQ	AAA	27	0	2	0	4	2	12^1	14	0	2.9	9.5	13	35%	.412	1.46	4.38	5.11	0.1				
2017	COL	MLB	27	6	6	0	17	15	86	88	16	2.7	8.5	81	46%	.304	1.33	4.81	4.87	0.7	93.9	52	40	42
2018	*COL*	*MLB*	*28*	*9*	*9*	*0*	*26*	*26*	*156*	*153*	*23*	*3.1*	*8.5*	*147*	*45%*	*.298*	*1.33*	*4.16*	*4.34*	*1.5*	*93.2*	*58*	*39*	*53*
2019	*COL*	*MLB*	*29*	*11*	*12*	*0*	*31*	*31*	199^2	*186*	*27*	*3.3*	*8.0*	*178*	*45%*	*.306*	*1.30*	*4.47*	*4.90*	*1.5*	*92.8*	*58*	*39*	*53*

Breakout: 21% Improve: 52% Collapse: 20% Attrition: 23% MLB: 93% *Comparables: Josh Outman, Joe Saunders, Jacob deGrom*

Anderson might've missed his window. Back when he was drafted 20th overall in 2011, the Rockies needed pitching help badly. That's why, despite his limited upside, you could understand why Colorado went with the Oregon product; he was supposed to be a fast riser, and he was supposed to be safe. Alas, Anderson is a pitcher. Thanks in part to elbow issues that cost him all of 2015 and a knee injury that sidelined him in 2017, the lefty has thrown just 243 innings over the past three seasons. He wasn't as effective in the majors as he was during his rookie campaign, and now the Rockies actually have options in the rotation. Anderson could still be good enough to serve as a no. 4 or 5 starter when healthy, but there's a lot of risk here for such a pedestrian reward. He doesn't have the type of stuff that would play up in relief either, so if Anderson wants to remain a Rockie (c'mon now, just play along), logging more innings would seem to be his only option.

Chad Bettis RHP Born: 04/26/89 Age: 29 Bats: R Throws: R Height: 6'1" Weight: 200 Origin: Round 2, 2010 Draft (#76 overall)

YEAR	TEAM	LVL	AGE	W	L	SV	G	GS	IP	H	HR	BB/9	K/9	K	GB%	BABIP	WHIP	ERA	DRA	WARP	MPH	CMD	PWR	STM
2015	ABQ	AAA	26	3	2	0	7	7	39	41	5	2.3	7.6	33	47%	.319	1.31	3.46	3.05	1.0				
2015	COL	MLB	26	8	6	0	20	20	115	120	11	3.3	7.7	98	53%	.313	1.41	4.23	3.88	1.6	95.7	54	50	65
2016	COL	MLB	27	14	8	0	32	32	186	204	22	2.9	6.7	138	54%	.310	1.41	4.79	4.63	1.5	94.8	62	49	78
2017	ABQ	AAA	28	0	3	0	4	4	18^2	22	2	2.9	5.3	11	55%	.312	1.50	4.82	4.60	0.2				
2017	COL	MLB	28	2	4	0	9	9	46^1	52	8	2.1	5.8	30	50%	.293	1.36	5.05	5.73	-0.1	92.4	55	37	50
2018	*COL*	*MLB*	*29*	*8*	*10*	*0*	*28*	*28*	*140*	*150*	*20*	*3.4*	*6.8*	*106*	*50%*	*.301*	*1.46*	*4.56*	*4.76*	*0.7*	*94.0*	*59*	*47*	*63*
2019	*COL*	*MLB*	*30*	*9*	*11*	*0*	*30*	*30*	191^2	*194*	*25*	*3.1*	*7.0*	*148*	*50%*	*.311*	*1.36*	*4.61*	*5.05*	*1.0*	*93.4*	*60*	*46*	*62*

Breakout: 26% Improve: 45% Collapse: 24% Attrition: 15% MLB: 93% *Comparables: Brian Bannister, John Maine, David Phelps*

Wins and losses aren't terribly descriptive stats when it comes to pitching, but they are when it comes to fighting cancer, and friends, Bettis is now 1-0. He was diagnosed with testicular cancer in November 2016 and underwent surgery to have one of his testicles removed. Doctors believed he'd be ready for the beginning of the season, but then found that the cancer had spread to his lymph nodes, which meant he spent the better part of his spring enduring treatment. Thankfully, Bettis made a full recovery, and in the latest bit of evidence that athletes aren't like the rest of us, he was back on the mound in the majors on August 14. Analyzing the nine starts he made upon his return seems trivial. What matters is that Bettis is healthy and should be fully ready to compete for a spot in a suddenly crowded Rockies rotation.

Ryan Castellani RHP Born: 04/01/96 Age: 22 Bats: R Throws: R Height: 6'4" Weight: 220 Origin: Round 2, 2014 Draft (#48 overall)

YEAR	TEAM	LVL	AGE	W	L	SV	G	GS	IP	H	HR	BB/9	K/9	K	GB%	BABIP	WHIP	ERA	DRA	WARP	MPH	CMD	PWR	STM
2015	ASH	A	19	2	7	0	27	27	113^1	134	5	2.3	7.5	94	49%	.348	1.44	4.45	3.43	2.4				
2016	MOD	A+	20	7	8	0	26	26	167^2	156	8	2.7	7.6	142	55%	.302	1.23	3.81	3.39	4.0				
2017	HFD	AA	21	9	12	0	27	27	157^1	163	16	2.7	7.6	132	47%	.309	1.33	4.81	3.90	2.4				
2018	*COL*	*MLB*	*22*	*9*	*8*	*0*	*26*	*26*	*135*	*146*	*21*	*3.4*	*8.4*	*126*	*45%*	*.334*	*1.46*	*4.57*	*5.04*	*0.9*				
2019	*COL*	*MLB*	*23*	*5*	*7*	*0*	*18*	*18*	*107*	*110*	*19*	*3.4*	*8.7*	*103*	*45%*	*.327*	*1.40*	*5.06*	*5.56*	*0.1*				

Breakout: 20% Improve: 29% Collapse: 5% Attrition: 21% MLB: 39% *Comparables: Eduardo Rodriguez, David Holmberg, Ian Krol*

The Rockies have been aggressive with Castellani since drafting him 48th overall in 2014, routinely asking him to face older competition and to shoulder a heavy workload for someone his age. The right-hander finally met his match pitching as a 21-year-old at Double-A. Castellani struck out and walked batters at about the same clip as he did in the California League, but Yard Goats opponents (lol) were able to square up his pitches more often. The righty's homer rate spiked, his ERA ballooned and, worst of all, he had to spend a lot of time in Connecticut. Castellani could spend all of 2018 back at Double-A and still be ahead of the curve, and his sinker-led four-pitch mix still gives him the ceiling of a mid-rotation starter. It might be time for the Rockies to ease up on the gas pedal, though you could argue it's wise to stress-test guys who'll be asked to pitch in Coors.

Wade Davis RHP Born: 09/07/85 Age: 32 Bats: R Throws: R Height: 6'5" Weight: 225 Origin: Round 3, 2004 Draft (#75 overall)

YEAR	TEAM	LVL	AGE	W	L	SV	G	GS	IP	H	HR	BB/9	K/9	K	GB%	BABIP	WHIP	ERA	DRA	WARP	MPH	CMD	PWR	STM
2015	KCA	MLB	29	8	1	17	69	0	67^{1}	33	3	2.7	10.4	78	39%	.200	0.79	0.94	1.98	2.2	98.4	60	66	50
2016	KCA	MLB	30	2	1	27	45	0	43^{1}	33	0	3.3	9.8	47	48%	.300	1.13	1.87	2.95	1.0	97.8	42	56	35
2017	CHN	MLB	31	4	2	32	59	0	58^{2}	39	6	4.3	12.1	79	42%	.262	1.14	2.30	2.99	1.4	96.1	59	52	47
2018	*COL*	*MLB*	*32*	*2*	*1*	*23*	*46*	*0*	48^{2}	*42*	*6*	*3.8*	*10.9*	*59*	*43%*	*.324*	*1.30*	*3.71*	*4.09*	*0.6*	*96.3*	*55*	*56*	*43*
2019	*COL*	*MLB*	*33*	*3*	*1*	*27*	*55*	*0*	*55*	*45*	*8*	*4.0*	*10.6*	*65*	*43%*	*.306*	*1.27*	*4.31*	*4.74*	*0.3*	*95.5*	*53*	*54*	*42*

Breakout: 17% Improve: 34% Collapse: 24% Attrition: 7% MLB: 92% *Comparables: Scot Shields, Pedro Strop, Jesse Crain*

The most famous conversion in baseball since Pedro Cerrano to Christianity lost a little more zip on his fastball and his fallibility began to emerge. Consider: In his first three years as an all-world reliever, Davis gave up three home runs total. Last year in a tie game in August he gave up back-to-back home runs to Paul Goldschmidt and J.D. Martinez. The emperor was exposed, but it's not like he doesn't have any close (get it?), as his cutters and curves still rack up the strikeouts. Maybe the novelty of a lowly fifth starter becoming a ninth-inning guru has finally worn off, because Davis is now nothing more than just a very good closer (who just got very well paid).

Mike Dunn LHP Born: 05/23/85 Age: 33 Bats: L Throws: L Height: 6'0" Weight: 215 Origin: Round 33, 2004 Draft (#999 overall)

YEAR	TEAM	LVL	AGE	W	L	SV	G	GS	IP	H	HR	BB/9	K/9	K	GB%	BABIP	WHIP	ERA	DRA	WARP	MPH	CMD	PWR	STM
2015	MIA	MLB	30	2	5	0	72	0	54	46	6	4.8	10.8	65	40%	.301	1.39	4.50	3.61	0.7	96.7	39	61	50
2016	MIA	MLB	31	6	1	0	51	0	42^{1}	43	5	2.3	8.1	38	30%	.319	1.28	3.40	5.57	-0.3	95.8	49	56	47
2017	COL	MLB	32	5	1	0	68	0	50^{1}	43	8	5.0	10.2	57	34%	.276	1.41	4.47	6.28	-0.6	93.8	42	44	47
2018	*COL*	*MLB*	*33*	*3*	*3*	*2*	*57*	*0*	*60*	*60*	*11*	*4.2*	*9.3*	*62*	*37%*	*.303*	*1.49*	*5.03*	*4.94*	*0.0*	*94.1*	*43*	*52*	*47*
2019	*COL*	*MLB*	*34*	*2*	*1*	*1*	*35*	*0*	37^{2}	*37*	*7*	*4.6*	*9.5*	*40*	*37%*	*.32*	*1.50*	*5.39*	*5.91*	*-0.3*	*93.2*	*43*	*49*	*46*

Breakout: 21% Improve: 43% Collapse: 23% Attrition: 10% MLB: 92% *Comparables: John Axford, Joakim Soria, Armando Benitez*

What is there to say about Dunn that hasn't been said about the six-day-old Kung Pao Chicken in the back of your fridge that you forgot about, sniffed, thought better of and then decided to eat anyway? Sure, that food was relatively tasty once upon a time. It was never gonna be good for you, and once you factor in the delivery fee, taxes and tip it probably wasn't worth buying in the first place. But it filled an immediate need, ya know? Or so you thought. You hate throwing food away, but you probably hate how you feel after eating that past-its-prime MSG bomb more, huh? You would've been better off accepting the sunk cost. Anyway, Dunn's velocity dropped, he walked almost 13 percent of the batters he faced and lefties posted a .349 OBP against him. He's still owed $15 million if you include his 2020 buyout, but do you really wanna reheat this and roll the dice again?

Carlos Estevez RHP Born: 12/28/92 Age: 25 Bats: R Throws: R Height: 6'4" Weight: 210 Origin: International Free Agent, 2011

YEAR	TEAM	LVL	AGE	W	L	SV	G	GS	IP	H	HR	BB/9	K/9	K	GB%	BABIP	WHIP	ERA	DRA	WARP	MPH	CMD	PWR	STM
2015	MOD	A+	22	5	0	5	14	0	19^{2}	12	0	2.3	11.4	25	55%	.286	0.86	1.37	1.98	0.6				
2015	NBR	AA	22	0	3	13	34	0	36	39	2	2.2	10.8	43	42%	.363	1.33	4.50	1.76	1.3				
2016	COL	MLB	23	3	7	11	63	0	55	50	6	4.6	9.7	59	45%	.297	1.42	5.24	5.03	0.0	100.0	49	71	49
2017	ABQ	AAA	24	1	4	4	33	0	33^{2}	23	2	2.7	9.1	34	60%	.253	0.98	1.34	1.79	1.3				
2017	COL	MLB	24	5	0	0	35	0	32^{1}	39	3	3.9	8.6	31	47%	.360	1.64	5.57	6.42	-0.4	98.8	49	80	50
2018	*COL*	*MLB*	*25*	*1*	*1*	*0*	*26*	*0*	27^{1}	*26*	*3*	*4.1*	*9.3*	*28*	*46%*	*.307*	*1.45*	*4.04*	*4.19*	*0.2*	*99.2*	*50*	*77*	*51*
2019	*COL*	*MLB*	*26*	*2*	*1*	*0*	*41*	*0*	43^{2}	*41*	*5*	*4.0*	*9.5*	*46*	*46%*	*.331*	*1.39*	*4.21*	*4.62*	*0.3*	*99.0*	*50*	*77*	*51*

Breakout: 18% Improve: 34% Collapse: 31% Attrition: 30% MLB: 77% *Comparables: Jake Barrett, Daniel Herrera, Kyle Crockett*

The Rockies did their best to keep Estevez away from high-leverage situations by bringing in a ton of bullpen talent last offseason, and that proved wise. Estevez was so ineffective through his first 13 outings that he was banished to Albuquerque in early May. A few brief call-ups aside, he stayed there until September. It's not just that Estevez issues too many walks; he misses in the zone with his fastball and slider far too often. His raw stuff is too much for Triple-A bats to handle, but big-league hitters are less intimidated by the whole Wild Thing routine. Estevez was better in the big leagues in September and the Rockies are slated to lose some key bullpen pieces, so he should get more chances in 2018. Just don't be surprised if he ends up closing by June or back in the minors by May; both outcomes seem equally plausible.

Kyle Freeland LHP Born: 05/14/93 Age: 25 Bats: L Throws: L Height: 6'3" Weight: 170 Origin: Round 1, 2014 Draft (#8 overall)

YEAR	TEAM	LVL	AGE	W	L	SV	G	GS	IP	H	HR	BB/9	K/9	K	GB%	BABIP	WHIP	ERA	DRA	WARP	MPH	CMD	PWR	STM
2015	MOD	A+	22	3	2	0	7	7	39^{2}	48	5	1.8	4.3	19	49%	.314	1.41	4.76	5.92	-0.4				
2016	HFD	AA	23	5	7	0	14	14	88^{1}	84	9	2.5	5.2	51	53%	.268	1.23	3.87	3.78	1.4				
2016	ABQ	AAA	23	6	3	0	12	12	73^{2}	81	7	2.3	7.0	57	55%	.330	1.36	3.91	3.62	1.5				
2017	COL	MLB	24	11	11	0	33	28	156	169	17	3.6	6.2	107	56%	.308	1.49	4.10	5.91	-0.6	93.6	58	52	68
2018	*COL*	*MLB*	*25*	*9*	*9*	*0*	*26*	*26*	*148*	*154*	*18*	*3.4*	*6.7*	*110*	*50%*	*.298*	*1.42*	*4.36*	*4.55*	*1.1*	*93.3*	*59*	*53*	*70*
2019	*COL*	*MLB*	*26*	*10*	*11*	*0*	*32*	*32*	*203*	*192*	*22*	*3.1*	*7.2*	*162*	*50%*	*.307*	*1.29*	*4.27*	*4.69*	*1.9*	*93.1*	*60*	*53*	*70*

Breakout: 22% Improve: 57% Collapse: 16% Attrition: 22% MLB: 92% *Comparables: Martin Perez, Aaron Laffey, Sean Marshall*

Freeland impressed big-time from April through July. The former first-rounder posted a 3.71 ERA in his first 121 1/3 big league innings, and Rockies fans had visions of a long-term no. 3 starter dancing in their heads. Seriously, the last time a group of mountain-dwelling peoples were *that* captivated by Freeland, Cliven Bundy almost got shot. Then August happened. Freeland had to leave his first start of the month in the first inning because of a groin injury. He came back on August 15, but in the 34 1/3 innings he threw for the rest of the season, he coughed up an ERA of 5.50 and walked 19 batters in the process. Who knows whether the groin did Freeland in, his super-skinny frame wore down at the 120-inning mark or hitters simply adjusted. It's not like Freeland has much margin for error to begin with, what with his low-strikeout, high-contact approach. He certainly showed enough as a rookie to be given another few chances in the rotation, but he didn't do quite enough to remove the "potential reliever" tag for good, either.

Jon Gray RHP Born: 11/05/91 Age: 26 Bats: R Throws: R Height: 6'4" Weight: 235 Origin: Round 1, 2013 Draft (#3 overall)

YEAR	TEAM	LVL	AGE	W	L	SV	G	GS	IP	H	HR	BB/9	K/9	K	GB%	BABIP	WHIP	ERA	DRA	WARP	MPH	CMD	PWR	STM
2015	ABQ	AAA	23	6	6	0	21	20	114^{1}	129	9	3.2	8.7	110	44%	.350	1.49	4.33	3.77	2.0				
2015	COL	MLB	23	0	2	0	9	9	40^{2}	52	4	3.1	8.9	40	46%	.384	1.62	5.53	5.51	-0.2	97.4	55	60	68
2016	COL	MLB	24	10	10	0	29	29	168	153	18	3.2	9.9	185	45%	.309	1.26	4.61	3.95	2.7	97.9	35	56	74
2017	COL	MLB	25	10	4	0	20	20	110^{1}	113	10	2.4	9.1	112	49%	.336	1.30	3.67	3.67	2.3	97.8	60	64	53
2018	*COL*	*MLB*	*26*	*10*	*9*	*0*	*28*	*28*	*159*	*152*	*19*	*3.3*	*9.3*	*165*	*46%*	*.305*	*1.33*	*3.70*	*3.85*	*2.4*	*97.4*	*48*	*61*	*65*
2019	*COL*	*MLB*	*27*	*11*	*10*	*0*	*32*	*32*	*206*	*186*	*25*	*2.9*	*9.4*	*216*	*46%*	*.319*	*1.22*	*3.81*	*4.16*	*2.9*	*97.2*	*48*	*61*	*64*

Breakout: 27% Improve: 58% Collapse: 20% Attrition: 9% MLB: 86% *Comparables: Daniel Hudson, Brandon Beachy, J.P. Howell*

Gray is a good Rorschach Test for a question that's plagued baseball since the invention of the modern five-man rotation: What is an ace? Do you believe an ace is simply the best pitcher on a team? If so, Gray fits the bill. For the second year in a row, he posted the most PWARP on the Rockies by a long shot, as well as the best DRA among the team's starters. Gray started on Opening Day and, disastrous results aside, he started the NL wild card play-in game. Whether the Rockies wanted to make a first impression or needed to put it all on the line, Gray was the alpha and the omega.

Do you believe an ace needs to be among the elite of the elite year in and year out, a True Ace, if you will? Then Gray isn't yet close to who you want him to be. He had the 34th best DRA and 54th most PWARP among pitchers with at least 100 innings. He missed 10 weeks with a broken foot. His road ERA was north of 4.00. And man, that playoff start. Gray gave up seven hits and four runs to the Diamondbacks, recording just four outs in Colorado's first playoff game since 2009. True Aces need to perform in October, and Gray is 0-for-1.

And now the toughest questions of all: Should we lower our standards for Rockies aces? The pitching hellscape that is Coors Field has spit up and chewed out enough promising arms that, despite his warts, Gray very well could end up being the best pitcher in franchise history. Still, the Rox must be hoping that for once they won't have to grade on a curve. Gray has the stuff, the tenacity and enough time on his side to emerge as the first True Ace to wear a Rockies uniform. Frankly, the Baseball Gods owe them as much.

Jeff Hoffman RHP Born: 01/08/93 Age: 25 Bats: R Throws: R Height: 6'5" Weight: 225 Origin: Round 1, 2014 Draft (#9 overall)

YEAR	TEAM	LVL	AGE	W	L	SV	G	GS	IP	H	HR	BB/9	K/9	K	GB%	BABIP	WHIP	ERA	DRA	WARP	MPH	CMD	PWR	STM
2015	DUN	A+	22	3	3	0	11	11	56	59	4	2.4	6.1	38	53%	.329	1.32	3.21	5.48	-0.3				
2015	NHP	AA	22	0	0	0	2	2	11^{2}	9	0	1.5	6.2	8	43%	.257	0.94	1.54	3.09	0.3				
2015	NBR	AA	22	2	2	0	7	7	36^{1}	27	3	2.5	7.2	29	58%	.242	1.02	3.22	3.18	0.8				
2016	ABQ	AAA	23	6	9	0	22	22	118^{2}	117	11	3.3	9.4	124	44%	.325	1.36	4.02	2.77	3.5				
2016	COL	MLB	23	0	4	0	8	6	31^{1}	37	7	4.9	6.3	22	51%	.297	1.72	4.88	7.07	-0.6	96.8	42	52	65
2017	ABQ	AAA	24	3	3	0	10	10	49^{2}	44	3	3.4	8.5	47	46%	.285	1.27	4.71	2.92	1.5				
2017	COL	MLB	24	6	5	0	23	16	99^{1}	106	15	3.6	7.4	82	42%	.304	1.47	5.89	5.98	-0.5	96.5	47	57	66
2018	*COL*	*MLB*	*25*	*4*	*5*	*0*	*13*	*13*	*68*	*69*	*10*	*3.6*	*8.0*	*62*	*45%*	*.297*	*1.41*	*4.43*	*4.63*	*0.4*	*96.3*	*47*	*57*	*67*
2019	*COL*	*MLB*	*26*	*9*	*10*	*0*	*30*	*30*	188^{2}	*165*	*25*	*3.1*	*8.6*	*181*	*45%*	*.296*	*1.22*	*4.23*	*4.65*	*1.7*	*96.1*	*47*	*57*	*67*

Breakout: 37% Improve: 67% Collapse: 11% Attrition: 17% MLB: 93% *Comparables: Wade Davis, Chris Tillman, Jordan Zimmermann*

The crown jewel of the Troy Tulowitzki deal, Hoffman looked ready to take the leap after a 2016 season that saw him pitch decently in Triple-A and hold his own in the majors. Instead, Hoffman continued to exhibit symptoms of Joe Kelly Syndrome, proving to be far more hittable than his mid-90s fastball and beauty of a curveball suggest he should be. The former first-rounder still struggles to locate his pitches on a consistent basis, and he walked too many batters in Colorado and Albuquerque alike—that's how a dude with Hoffman's talent ends up with a DRA around 6.00. After a brief return to Triple-A in mid-August, Hoffman was summoned back to the majors as a reliever in September. He coughed up 11 earned runs in 7 2/3 innings out of the 'pen, and it's back to the drawing board for 2018. He could still be a good mid-rotation starter, or it could turn out that neither side won the Tulo trade.

Greg Holland RHP Born: 11/20/85 Age: 32 Bats: R Throws: R Height: 5'10" Weight: 205 Origin: Round 10, 2007 Draft (#306 overall)

YEAR	TEAM	LVL	AGE	W	L	SV	G	GS	IP	H	HR	BB/9	K/9	K	GB%	BABIP	WHIP	ERA	DRA	WARP	MPH	CMD	PWR	STM
2015	KCA	MLB	29	3	2	32	48	0	44^{2}	39	2	5.2	9.9	49	51%	.319	1.46	3.83	2.98	0.9	96.7	53	49	40
2017	COL	MLB	31	3	6	41	61	0	57^{1}	40	7	4.1	11.0	70	41%	.252	1.15	3.61	3.42	1.1	95.3	35	44	45
2018	*COL*	*MLB*	*32*	*2*	*1*	*25*	*38*	*0*	39^{2}	*36*	*5*	*4.1*	*10.2*	*45*	*43%*	*.314*	*1.35*	*4.12*	*4.54*	*0.3*	*94.8*	*41*	*45*	*43*
2019	*COL*	*MLB*	*33*	*2*	*1*	*27*	*42*	*0*	*40*	*38*	*7*	*4.9*	*8.8*	*39*	*43%*	*.306*	*1.48*	*5.41*	*5.95*	*-0.3*	*94.0*	*37*	*44*	*43*

Breakout: 18% Improve: 39% Collapse: 23% Attrition: 8% MLB: 92% *Comparables: Francisco Cordero, Michael Gonzalez, Brendan Donnelly*

The narrative is that Holland had a terrible second half and that his performance was in many ways a microcosm of Colorado's struggles. If you zoom out to first- vs. second-half splits, that looks true. But dive a little deeper into his second-half swoon and you'll see that he wasn't bad for the entire half, he was just atrocious in August. Holland's ERAs in July and September? They were 2.25 and 1.86, respectively. But August? Oh god, August: He allowed 14 earned runs in 9 1/3 innings and four of the seven homers he coughed up all year. Those innings count, of course, and if we could magically wave away every player's worst outings, well, every player would be better. But Holland didn't slowly bleed out after June; he patched himself up and was back to being very good, if not a little tired-looking, down the stretch. He remains a risky play going forward, but his upside is clearly intact.

Sam Howard LHP Born: 03/05/93 Age: 25 Bats: R Throws: L Height: 6'3" Weight: 170 Origin: Round 3, 2014 Draft (#82 overall)

YEAR	TEAM	LVL	AGE	W	L	SV	G	GS	IP	H	HR	BB/9	K/9	K	GB%	BABIP	WHIP	ERA	DRA	WARP	MPH	CMD	PWR	STM
2015	ASH	A	22	11	9	0	25	25	134	131	8	2.1	8.2	122	55%	.310	1.22	3.43	2.21	4.8				
2016	HFD	AA	23	5	6	0	16	16	90^1	113	11	2.8	6.7	67	38%	.333	1.56	3.99	5.89	-0.9				
2016	MOD	A+	23	4	3	0	11	11	65^2	43	3	3.3	10.0	73	40%	.247	1.02	2.47	2.78	2.0				
2017	HFD	AA	24	1	4	0	9	9	46^1	31	5	1.9	7.8	40	39%	.208	0.88	2.33	2.85	1.3				
2017	ABQ	AAA	24	4	4	0	15	14	81	82	6	3.7	7.1	64	41%	.309	1.42	3.89	6.45	-0.7				
2018	*COL*	*MLB*	*25*	*1*	*1*	*0*	*15*	*0*	*16*	*16*	*2*	*3.8*	*8.4*	*15*	*40%*	*.295*	*1.41*	*4.72*	*4.72*	*0.0*				
2019	*COL*	*MLB*	*26*	*2*	*1*	*0*	*46*	*0*	*49*	*45*	*8*	*3.7*	*8.3*	*45*	*40%*	*.296*	*1.33*	*4.91*	*5.39*	*-0.1*				

Breakout: 16% Improve: 27% Collapse: 10% Attrition: 26% MLB: 44% *Comparables: Myles Jaye, Adam Warren, Tyler Wagner*

Howard has moved quickly since being drafted in the third round out of Georgia Southern in 2014, reaching Triple-A as a 24-year-old last June. He fits the bill of your standard advanced college lefty—good command, strong changeup, underwhelming breaker, etc—which allowed him to carve up the minors until he reached Albuquerque. At Triple-A, Howard struggled with his command and missed fewer bats. DRA believes he was utter garbage as an Isotope, but ERA and FIP tell a kinder, if still not inspiring, story. Hey, at least he wasn't the worst Howard on his own team (this might be the last Ryan Howard dig in *BP Annual* history, so enjoy)! A better second stint in the PCL could have Sam knocking on the door to the majors this season, but in an organization that suddenly has some pitching depth he's unlikely to be used as more than a spot starter.

Peter Lambert RHP Born: 04/18/97 Age: 21 Bats: R Throws: R Height: 6'2" Weight: 185 Origin: Round 2, 2015 Draft (#44 overall)

YEAR	TEAM	LVL	AGE	W	L	SV	G	GS	IP	H	HR	BB/9	K/9	K	GB%	BABIP	WHIP	ERA	DRA	WARP	MPH	CMD	PWR	STM
2015	GJR	RK	18	0	4	0	8	8	31^1	29	3	3.2	7.5	26	54%	.263	1.28	3.45	3.59	0.8				
2016	ASH	A	19	5	8	0	26	26	126	125	7	2.4	7.7	108	47%	.324	1.25	3.93	2.79	3.4				
2017	LNC	A+	20	9	8	0	26	26	142^1	147	18	1.9	8.3	131	43%	.321	1.24	4.17	3.14	3.5				
2018	*COL*	*MLB*	*21*	*7*	*8*	*0*	*23*	*23*	*116*	*125*	*23*	*3.6*	*8.7*	*112*	*40%*	*.328*	*1.48*	*5.04*	*5.55*	*0.1*				
2019	*COL*	*MLB*	*22*	*5*	*8*	*0*	*20*	*20*	118^2	*119*	*25*	*3.5*	*8.6*	*114*	*40%*	*.316*	*1.39*	*5.41*	*5.94*	*-0.4*				

Breakout: 4% Improve: 4% Collapse: 0% Attrition: 4% MLB: 5% *Comparables: Michael Pineda, Jeremy Hellickson, Miguel Almonte*

The 44th overall pick back in 2015, Lambert has quickly risen through the ranks thanks to an advanced changeup and solid fastball that he controls well. His Lancaster ERA doesn't look pretty, but his DRA tells a more encouraging story, and if he's going to be a Rockies pitcher, well, he'd better get used to that dichotomy. So why isn't there more buzz surrounding a guy who looks ready to take on Double-A before he can legally order a beverage named after his future home park? Despite boasting an advanced feel for his stuff, Lambert also lacks much further projection. That leads scouts to peg him as more of a back-end starter than the type of mid-rotation workhorse you might imagine just by looking at his stats. The Rockies used to stick guys like that in the middle of their rotations anyway, but they've begun to elevate their standards.

German Marquez RHP Born: 02/22/95 Age: 23 Bats: R Throws: R Height: 6'1" Weight: 185 Origin: International Free Agent, 2011

YEAR	TEAM	LVL	AGE	W	L	SV	G	GS	IP	H	HR	BB/9	K/9	K	GB%	BABIP	WHIP	ERA	DRA	WARP	MPH	CMD	PWR	STM
2015	PCH	A+	20	7	13	0	26	23	139	147	6	1.9	6.7	104	41%	.320	1.27	3.56	4.09	1.6				
2016	HFD	AA	21	9	6	0	21	21	135^2	124	9	2.2	8.4	126	48%	.304	1.16	2.85	1.76	5.4				
2016	ABQ	AAA	21	2	0	0	5	5	31	30	5	1.7	8.4	29	45%	.298	1.16	4.35	2.66	1.0				
2016	COL	MLB	21	1	1	0	6	3	20^2	28	2	2.6	6.5	15	55%	.361	1.65	5.23	5.68	-0.1	96.8	46	50	73
2017	ABQ	AAA	22	0	0	0	3	2	10	8	2	0.0	16.2	18	53%	.353	0.80	2.70	1.05	0.5				
2017	COL	MLB	22	11	7	0	29	29	162	174	25	2.7	8.2	147	47%	.316	1.38	4.39	5.88	-0.5	97.5	33	60	73
2018	*COL*	*MLB*	*23*	*10*	*9*	*0*	*28*	*28*	*159*	*159*	*22*	*2.9*	*8.8*	*156*	*44%*	*.303*	*1.33*	*3.93*	*4.10*	*2.0*	*97.3*	*35*	*61*	*76*
2019	*COL*	*MLB*	*24*	*11*	*10*	*0*	*31*	*31*	*197*	*178*	*26*	*2.5*	*9.3*	*203*	*44%*	*.311*	*1.18*	*3.91*	*4.28*	*2.6*	*97.2*	*36*	*62*	*76*

Breakout: 22% Improve: 55% Collapse: 12% Attrition: 17% MLB: 85% *Comparables: Aaron Nola, Brian Matusz, Alex White*

It's a little cliché at this point to say that all the best Marquezes are German, but our protagonist proved that point in 2017. Sure, he wasn't the starting DH for the AL All-Star team, but Marquez held his own as a 22-year-old rookie starter in one of the least forgiving environments imaginable. He gave up too many homers to right-handed hitters and he gave up a few too many homers at home, but again, he was just 22, and hey, welcome to life at Coors. There's no premium upside here, but Marquez is ready to play the part of affordable innings-eater for many years to come, and there's evidence to suggest he could be something more if he starts throwing to better receivers. It's crazy how fast the Rockies got good at developing guys like this.

Jake McGee LHP Born: 08/06/86 Age: 31 Bats: L Throws: L Height: 6'3" Weight: 230 Origin: Round 5, 2004 Draft (#135 overall)

YEAR	TEAM	LVL	AGE	W	L	SV	G	GS	IP	H	HR	BB/9	K/9	K	GB%	BABIP	WHIP	ERA	DRA	WARP	MPH	CMD	PWR	STM
2015	TBA	MLB	28	1	2	6	39	0	37^1	27	3	1.9	11.6	48	39%	.276	0.94	2.41	2.93	0.8	98.1	51	71	39
2016	COL	MLB	29	2	3	15	57	0	45^2	56	9	3.2	7.5	38	41%	.338	1.58	4.73	7.42	-1.3	96.5	54	60	43
2017	COL	MLB	30	0	2	3	62	0	57^1	47	4	2.5	9.1	58	40%	.287	1.10	3.61	4.33	0.5	97.2	56	76	46
2018	*COL*	*MLB*	*31*	*2*	*2*	*0*	*46*	*0*	*49*	*49*	*8*	*3.6*	*9.4*	*51*	*42%*	*.302*	*1.38*	*4.49*	*4.54*	*0.2*	*96.3*	*54*	*69*	*43*
2019	*COL*	*MLB*	*32*	*2*	*1*	*0*	*44*	*0*	*47*	*44*	*8*	*3.7*	*9.6*	*50*	*42%*	*.317*	*1.34*	*4.74*	*5.19*	*0.0*	*95.7*	*54*	*69*	*44*

Breakout: 29% Improve: 44% Collapse: 28% Attrition: 10% MLB: 91% *Comparables: Sergio Romo, Joakim Soria, Steve Cishek*

That's more like it. After a moderately disastrous first season with the Rockies, McGee was one of the few institutions to actually rebound in 2017. McGee's average fastball velocity ticked back up above 95, and on a related note his fastball usage ticked back up above 90 percent. Name a positive sign you want to see from a reliever—lower walk rate, higher swinging strike percentage, better HR/FB—and odds are McGee obliged. Unless you want to see "better second-half splits," that is, but we digress. McGee did miss a little time with a back strain, but we didn't hear anything about his once-painful left elbow. That means he's poised to make some noise in free agency, though his utter dependence on his fastball and his shakier second half should give teams pause when considering going beyond a two-

or three-year pact.

Scott Oberg RHP Born: 03/13/90 Age: 28 Bats: R Throws: R Height: 6'2" Weight: 205 Origin: Round 15, 2012 Draft (#468 overall)

YEAR	TEAM	LVL	AGE	W	L	SV	G	GS	IP	H	HR	BB/9	K/9	K	GB%	BABIP	WHIP	ERA	DRA	WARP	MPH	CMD	PWR	STM
2015	COL	MLB	25	3	4	1	64	0	58^1	58	10	4.8	6.8	44	56%	.286	1.53	5.09	4.42	0.2	97.7	29	60	52
2016	ABQ	AAA	26	1	0	9	27	0	29^2	16	1	3.3	10.9	36	54%	.234	0.91	2.43	1.79	1.1				
2016	COL	MLB	26	1	1	1	24	0	26	26	3	3.8	6.9	20	56%	.295	1.42	5.19	4.99	0.0	97.2	44	56	48
2017	COL	MLB	27	0	1	0	66	0	58^1	70	4	3.7	8.5	55	58%	.367	1.61	4.94	5.84	-0.4	98.1	30	65	50
2018	*COL*	*MLB*	*28*	*2*	*2*	*0*	*46*	*0*	*49*	*49*	*6*	*4.0*	*8.1*	*44*	*53%*	*.305*	*1.45*	*4.24*	*4.36*	*0.3*	*97.2*	*32*	*62*	*50*
2019	*COL*	*MLB*	*29*	*2*	*1*	*0*	*49*	*0*	*51^2*	*47*	*6*	*3.9*	*8.7*	*50*	*53%*	*.313*	*1.34*	*4.26*	*4.67*	*0.3*	*96.9*	*33*	*63*	*50*

Breakout: 18% Improve: 42% Collapse: 25% Attrition: 21% MLB: 87% *Comparables: Kevin Jepsen, Ryan Pressly, Jose Arredondo*

The good news is the relatively anonymous Oberg pitched well enough in the regular season that the Rockies felt comfortable handing him the ball in the NL wild card game. The bad news is it was already 4-0 Diamondbacks when Oberg took the mound; the worse news is it was only the second inning. But our hero struck out Paul Goldschmidt and J.D. Martinez back-to-back to stop the bleeding, keeping the Rockies in the game. That was pretty much the only remarkable thing about Oberg's 2017 season, but fanning a perennial MVP candidate and the hottest hitter on the planet in October ain't no joke. The Rockies would likely prefer to not have to use Oberg so early in a game should they make the playoffs again, but at least they know he's up to the challenge if needed.

Adam Ottavino RHP Born: 11/22/85 Age: 32 Bats: B Throws: R Height: 6'5" Weight: 220 Origin: Round 1, 2006 Draft (#30 overall)

YEAR	TEAM	LVL	AGE	W	L	SV	G	GS	IP	H	HR	BB/9	K/9	K	GB%	BABIP	WHIP	ERA	DRA	WARP	MPH	CMD	PWR	STM
2015	COL	MLB	29	1	0	3	10	0	10^1	3	0	1.7	11.3	13	63%	.158	0.48	0.00	2.05	0.3	98.1			
2016	COL	MLB	30	1	3	7	34	0	27	18	3	2.3	11.7	35	62%	.250	0.93	2.67	2.82	0.7	96.3	45	46	42
2017	COL	MLB	31	2	3	0	63	0	53^1	48	8	6.6	10.6	63	40%	.310	1.63	5.06	4.84	0.2	96.3	20	47	48
2018	*COL*	*MLB*	*32*	*3*	*3*	*35*	*52*	*0*	*54^2*	*52*	*10*	*4.6*	*10.5*	*64*	*46%*	*.306*	*1.48*	*4.76*	*4.75*	*0.1*	*95.5*	*26*	*46*	*45*
2019	*COL*	*MLB*	*33*	*2*	*1*	*24*	*41*	*0*	*43^2*	*41*	*7*	*4.2*	*10.1*	*49*	*46%*	*.329*	*1.41*	*4.83*	*5.29*	*0.0*	*94.9*	*26*	*46*	*45*

Breakout: 17% Improve: 42% Collapse: 21% Attrition: 8% MLB: 93% *Comparables: Fernando Rodney, Francisco Cordero, Pedro Feliciano*

Only two relievers threw at least 50 innings and walked more than 16 percent of the batters they faced in 2017: Dellin Betances and Ottavino. In his first full season back from Tommy John surgery, Ottavino took the concept of high-strikeout, high-walk reliever to its logical extreme. Only 53 percent of the batters Ottavino faced didn't strike out, walk, homer or reach via hit-by-pitch. That's how a guy with Ottavino's stuff ends up with a DRA flirting with 5.00. Ottavino's fastball is down about a mile-per-hour or so since his pre-surgery days, but he still chucks in the mid-90s. Velocity isn't the issue here, command is, and that means Ottavino has the ceiling of an elite closer and the floor of a guy who's back in Albuquerque by June.

Riley Pint RHP Born: 11/06/97 Age: 20 Bats: R Throws: R Height: 6'4" Weight: 195 Origin: Round 1, 2016 Draft (#4 overall)

YEAR	TEAM	LVL	AGE	W	L	SV	G	GS	IP	H	HR	BB/9	K/9	K	GB%	BABIP	WHIP	ERA	DRA	WARP	MPH	CMD	PWR	STM
2016	GJR	RK	18	1	5	0	11	11	37	43	2	5.6	8.8	36	60%	.383	1.78	5.35	4.44	0.5				
2017	ASH	A	19	2	11	0	22	22	93	96	3	5.7	7.6	79	60%	.325	1.67	5.42	5.52	-0.3				
2018	*COL*	*MLB*	*20*	*4*	*7*	*0*	*17*	*17*	*69^2*	*78*	*14*	*7.7*	*8.7*	*68*	*46%*	*.337*	*1.97*	*6.60*	*7.34*	*-1.3*				
2019	*COL*	*MLB*	*21*	*3*	*7*	*0*	*17*	*17*	*97^2*	*106*	*18*	*6.2*	*7.7*	*84*	*46%*	*.331*	*1.78*	*6.50*	*7.15*	*-1.1*				

Comparables: Scott Elbert, Juan Minaya, Patrick Schuster

To say Pint is a high-risk, high-reward pitching prospect is to say that betting it all on black is a gamble; it understates the two potential outcomes entirely. Pint, Colorado's first-round pick in the 2016 draft, can run his fastball up to triple digits and drop a hammer on hitters who are all geared up for his premium velo. He can also the leave the ball over the middle of the plate or miss the plate entirely, which is how a guy with his stuff ends up with an ERA north of 5.00 in Asheville. "Projectable, hard-throwing righty with command issues" is a standard prospect profile, but Pint's ceiling is special. His floor is also somewhere in Death Valley, and we haven't even talked about the trials and tribulations that come with pitching in Coors yet. He could be Noah Syndergaard. He could be Nathan Eovaldi. He could be Trevor Rosenthal. He could be Daniel Bard. He could never make it out of Double-A. Basically, who Pint will become is anyone's gu(inn)ess.

Chad Qualls RHP Born: 08/17/78 Age: 39 Bats: R Throws: R Height: 6'4" Weight: 235 Origin: Round 2, 2000 Draft (#67 overall)

YEAR	TEAM	LVL	AGE	W	L	SV	G	GS	IP	H	HR	BB/9	K/9	K	GB%	BABIP	WHIP	ERA	DRA	WARP	MPH	CMD	PWR	STM
2015	HOU	MLB	36	3	5	4	60	0	49^1	46	6	1.6	8.4	46	61%	.288	1.11	4.38	3.00	1.0	94.2	50	46	44
2016	COL	MLB	37	2	0	0	44	0	32^2	43	5	2.5	6.1	22	55%	.328	1.59	5.23	5.86	-0.3	92.5	54	46	35
2017	COL	MLB	38	1	1	0	19	0	16^2	17	3	2.7	5.9	11	59%	.264	1.32	5.40	6.84	-0.3	92.8	51	52	37
2018	*COL*	*MLB*	*39*	*2*	*1*	*0*	*33*	*0*	*34^2*	*38*	*5*	*3.8*	*7.2*	*28*	*52%*	*.325*	*1.51*	*4.63*	*5.11*	*0.0*	*91.7*	*50*	*46*	*37*
2019	*COL*	*MLB*	*40*	*2*	*1*	*0*	*48*	*0*	*40^1*	*43*	*6*	*3.6*	*6.6*	*30*	*52%*	*.317*	*1.47*	*5.08*	*5.58*	*-0.2*	*90.5*	*50*	*46*	*35*

Breakout: 18% Improve: 37% Collapse: 14% Attrition: 10% MLB: 69% *Comparables: Bob Wickman, Darren Oliver, Gene Garber*

Let's not talk about the 2017 version of Qualls. Let's remember the good times instead: From 2005 through 2008 he produced 7.5 WARP. That's about as good as it gets for a non-elite reliever. In 2005 he threw 13 postseason innings, only surrendering three runs. He held batters to a .219 average in 2008. Hell, as recently as 2014 his DRA was below 3.00! Qualls has been traded for good major leaguers who you've actually heard of, guys like Jose Valverde and Casey McGehee. He fell down that one time and made us all laugh. Qualls had a nice career, and it stinks that his (likely) undignified end came via a midseason DFA from the Rockies as a 38-year-old. At least Colorado gave him $6 million over the past two years for his troubles. We should all be so lucky.

Chris Rusin LHP Born: 10/22/86 Age: 31 Bats: L Throws: L Height: 6'2" Weight: 195 Origin: Round 4, 2009 Draft (#140 overall)

YEAR	TEAM	LVL	AGE	W	L	SV	G	GS	IP	H	HR	BB/9	K/9	K	GB%	BABIP	WHIP	ERA	DRA	WARP	MPH	CMD	PWR	STM
2015	ABQ	AAA	28	3	2	0	7	6	34^{1}	47	6	2.9	4.7	18	54%	.325	1.69	6.29	5.88	-0.2				
2015	COL	MLB	28	6	10	0	24	22	131^{2}	170	19	2.8	5.9	86	53%	.339	1.60	5.33	6.19	-1.8	91.9	59	26	69
2016	COL	MLB	29	3	5	0	29	7	84^{1}	82	5	2.5	7.4	69	61%	.308	1.25	3.74	4.32	0.8	91.7	48	35	42
2017	COL	MLB	30	5	1	2	60	0	85	75	9	2.0	7.5	71	60%	.277	1.11	2.65	4.07	1.0	92.6	34	34	52
2018	*COL*	*MLB*	*31*	*3*	*2*	*0*	*52*	*0*	54^{2}	*53*	*5*	*3.2*	*7.8*	*48*	*55%*	*.301*	*1.34*	*3.66*	*3.89*	*0.6*	*91.3*	*47*	*31*	*53*
2019	*COL*	*MLB*	*32*	*3*	*1*	*0*	*52*	*0*	55^{1}	*52*	*5*	*3.0*	*7.7*	*47*	*55%*	*.315*	*1.28*	*3.95*	*4.32*	*0.5*	*91.0*	*42*	*33*	*49*

Breakout: 15% Improve: 36% Collapse: 22% Attrition: 18% MLB: 73% *Comparables: Chris Sampson, Luis Mendoza, Jorge Campillo*

When you think of "career year" you think of a breakout, right? A good player taking the jump to elite or an everyday guy making an All-Star team. Those are the most exciting cases, sure, but your average middle relievers/swingmen have personal bests too. In 2017, the Rockies stopped asking Rusin to spot start. On a related note, he posted the highest strikeout rate, lowest walk rate, best ERA, best DRA, most appearances and the lowest WHIP of his career. Rusin threw his changeup a bit more and stopped throwing his curveball altogether. But on the whole, not much about the veteran's repertoire changed; he just did better. You might not remember Rusin's 2017 campaign years, months or even days from now, but he will. May it continue to bring him peace and satisfaction.

Antonio Senzatela RHP Born: 01/21/95 Age: 23 Bats: R Throws: R Height: 6'1" Weight: 180 Origin: International Free Agent, 2011

YEAR	TEAM	LVL	AGE	W	L	SV	G	GS	IP	H	HR	BB/9	K/9	K	GB%	BABIP	WHIP	ERA	DRA	WARP	MPH	CMD	PWR	STM
2015	MOD	A+	20	9	9	0	26	26	154	131	10	1.9	8.4	143	47%	.282	1.06	2.51	2.80	4.2				
2016	HFD	AA	21	4	1	0	7	7	34^{2}	27	1	2.3	7.0	27	44%	.265	1.04	1.82	3.68	0.6				
2017	COL	MLB	22	10	5	0	36	20	134^{2}	128	18	3.1	6.8	102	50%	.280	1.30	4.68	5.77	-0.4	96.9	38	65	62
2018	*COL*	*MLB*	*23*	*5*	*5*	*0*	*39*	*13*	92^{1}	*87*	*11*	*3.3*	*8.2*	*84*	*45%*	*.294*	*1.30*	*3.94*	*4.11*	*1.0*	*96.8*	*39*	*67*	*64*
2019	*COL*	*MLB*	*24*	*7*	*7*	*0*	*60*	*18*	149^{2}	*133*	*20*	*3.1*	*8.9*	*148*	*45%*	*.308*	*1.23*	*4.20*	*4.60*	*1.3*	*96.7*	*40*	*68*	*65*

Breakout: 21% Improve: 49% Collapse: 19% Attrition: 28% MLB: 81% *Comparables: Vin Mazzaro, Zach Duke, Robert Gsellman*

If life is truly all about timing, pour one out for Senzatela. In most years, what he did for the Rockies as a rookie starter would've made him the talk of the town among baseball-lovers. But Senzatela picked 2017 to emerge, which means he had to share the spotlight. Senzatela wasn't quite as good or well-known as fellow rookie starter Kyle Freeland. And he wasn't quite as good or as young as fellow rookie starter German Marquez. Heck, even fellow rookie starter Jeff Hoffman got more headlines because of his pedigree. Senzatela probably has the lowest upside of Colorado's up-and-coming crop of young arms, which is part of why he spent some of his time in the majors as a reliever. In truth, he was far more effective in that role. But at almost any other point in Rockies history, what Senzatela did as a rookie would've been good enough to earn a spot in the next season's rotation. That might not be so anymore, proving that in so many ways, life as a Rockies pitching prospect just isn't fair.

Bryan Shaw RHP Born: 11/08/87 Age: 30 Bats: B Throws: R Height: 6'1" Weight: 220 Origin: Round 2, 2008 Draft (#73 overall)

YEAR	TEAM	LVL	AGE	W	L	SV	G	GS	IP	H	HR	BB/9	K/9	K	GB%	BABIP	WHIP	ERA	DRA	WARP	MPH	CMD	PWR	STM
2015	CLE	MLB	27	3	3	2	74	0	64	59	8	2.7	7.6	54	47%	.279	1.22	2.95	3.56	0.9	94.3	43	55	51
2016	CLE	MLB	28	2	5	1	75	0	66^{2}	56	8	3.8	9.3	69	56%	.284	1.26	3.24	3.00	1.5	95.9	46	62	53
2017	CLE	MLB	29	4	6	3	79	0	76^{2}	71	5	2.6	8.6	73	57%	.311	1.21	3.52	4.47	0.6	96.5	52	73	55
2018	*COL*	*MLB*	*30*	*3*	*3*	*1*	*52*	*0*	54^{2}	*52*	*6*	*3.6*	*8.5*	*51*	*52%*	*.298*	*1.36*	*3.98*	*4.14*	*0.5*	*95.0*	*48*	*65*	*53*
2019	*COL*	*MLB*	*31*	*2*	*1*	*1*	*48*	*0*	50^{1}	*45*	*6*	*4.0*	*8.4*	*47*	*52%*	*.309*	*1.34*	*4.40*	*4.76*	*0.2*	*95.0*	*49*	*67*	*53*

Breakout: 28% Improve: 53% Collapse: 29% Attrition: 13% MLB: 96% *Comparables: John Franco, Eric O'Flaherty, Sparky Lyle*

When a reporter from the entertainment section of the Cleveland Plain Dealer asked Shaw about his post-retirement plans, the rubber-armed reliever declared that "culinary school is a possibility." Which is a little ironic, as the self-proclaimed foodie clearly enjoys a wide variety of cuisine, but when he takes the mound his menu is as narrow and vanilla as they come. Shaw threw his high-velo cutter 88 percent of the time last year, abetted by nothing more than his sweeping slider and his infectious smile (YMMV, Indians fans). And like death and taxes, hitters knew what was coming but usually couldn't do much about it. Shaw once again led baseball in appearances last year, working in the middle innings, but his stuff would play just fine in a setup role.

LINEOUTS

Hitters

HITTER	POS	TEAM	LVL	AGE	PA	R	2B	3B	HR	RBI	BB	K	SB	CS	AVG/OBP/SLG	TAv	VORP	BABIP	BRR	FRAA	WARP
Stephen Cardullo	OF	COL	MLB	29	32	2	0	0	0	3	3	7	0	0	.143/.250/.143	.215	-1.1	.190	-0.3	LF(6): -0.2, RF(2): 0.0	-0.1
	OF	ABQ	AAA	29	31	6	3	0	0	5	4	4	1	1	.308/.419/.423	.265	0.3	.364	-0.4	LF(4): 0.1, 1B(4): -0.3	0.0
	OF	BOI	A-	29	38	8	2	0	1	5	5	5	0	1	.242/.342/.394	.263	1.2	.259	0.5	LF(3): -0.4, 1B(3): -0.4	0.0
	OF	HFD	AA	29	153	17	5	1	4	17	22	22	1	0	.195/.318/.344	.246	0.3	.206	-0.7		0.0
Noel Cuevas	OF	ABQ	AAA	25	528	79	17	12	15	79	25	102	16	3	.312/.353/.487	.266	22.5	.368	7.3	RF(67): -3.6, CF(30): -2.8	1.3
Yonathan Daza	OF	LNC	A+	23	569	93	34	11	3	87	30	88	31	8	.341/.376/.466	.285	36.7	.397	7.8	CF(75): 3.0, RF(46): 5.4	4.8
Ryan Hanigan	C	ABQ	AAA	36	69	9	3	0	0	8	10	16	0	0	.264/.362/.321	.255	2.0	.333	-1.0	C(16): 1.6	0.4
	C	COL	MLB	36	112	9	2	0	2	12	8	26	0	0	.267/.324/.347	.226	1.0	.338	-0.2	C(30): -8.9	-0.8
Ryan Howard	1B	GWN	AAA	37	42	1	0	0	1	5	2	11	0	0	.184/.238/.263	.187	-3.4	.222	-0.4	1B(1): 0.0	-0.3
	1B	ABQ	AAA	37	54	5	4	0	3	8	0	17	0	0	.192/.185/.442	.186	-3.8	.206	0.1	1B(10): -0.3	-0.4
Daniel Montano	OF	DRO	Rk	18	217	32	14	3	3	39	24	39	9	7	.270/.355/.423	.256	1.2	.327	-3.4	RF(30): 2.5, CF(19): 2.7	0.6
Brian Mundell	1B	LNC	A+	23	301	44	16	1	12	59	35	44	0	1	.299/.379/.504	.295	15.1	.319	1.4	1B(52): 2.0	1.8
	1B	HFD	AA	23	203	30	12	0	3	19	25	26	1	1	.302/.394/.424	.297	9.0	.336	-0.8		1.0

HITTER	POS	TEAM	LVL	AGE	PA	R	2B	3B	HR	RBI	BB	K	SB	CS	AVG/OBP/SLG	TAv	VORP	BABIP	BRR	FRAA	WARP
Tyler Nevin	3B	BOI	A-	20	30	4	3	0	1	5	0	9	0	1	.233/.233/.433	.232	-0.1	.300	0.1	3B(3): 0.0, 1B(2): -0.2	0.0
	3B	ASH	A	20	335	45	18	3	7	47	27	56	10	5	.305/.364/.456	.294	18.7	.349	1.3	1B(32): 1.6, 3B(23): -2.5	1.9
Chris Rabago	C	LNC	A+	24	361	52	18	8	1	43	35	53	25	8	.272/.350/.393	.252	14.6	.319	2.1	C(86): 0.9	1.6
Wes Rogers	OF	LNC	A+	23	521	94	37	7	9	82	45	85	70	12	.319/.377/.488	.283	29.4	.368	4.8	LF(71): -0.4, CF(46): -6.1	2.4
Ryan Vilade	SS	GJR	Rk	18	146	23	3	2	5	21	27	31	5	5	.308/.438/.496	.292	12.9	.378	0.4	SS(30): -2.1	1.0

Backup outfielder **Stephen Cardullo** continued to be a better story than player, but that'd be true even if he hit .300. He super didn't though. ⚾ **Fadriel Cruz** is a raw, toolsy shortstop from the Dominican Republic who the Rockies popped for $650,000 as a J2 signing. If he follows the traditional development path for Rockies shortstops, he'll emerge as a third baseman with a plus hit tool and bad medicals in a year or so. ⚾ **Noel Cuevas** is a 26-year-old outfielder who was added to the Rockies' 40-man this offseason. If they run into a roster crunch he's likely to be the first Noel they cut, at which point your uncle will remind you that the War on Christmas is real. ⚾ **Yonathan Daza** will turn 24 in February, but 2018 will already be his eighth season in the Rockies system. He's a glove-first center fielder with wheels who just won the Cal League batting title, though that overstates his offensive prowess. ⚾ Oft-injured **Ryan Hanigan** has played in just 71 games over the past two years, and that's not all by design. He's had a nice career and looks like Droopy Dog in a charming way, but how many more teams will opt for a backup catcher who always needs a backup himself? ⚾ Don't think about how sad it is that **Ryan Howard**'s awesome career limped to a finish in Albuquerque. Think about how much fun Prime Ryan Howard would've been in Coors instead. ⚾ Former J2 super-signee **Daniel Montano** had a more successful second stint in the DSL, upgrading his MLB ETA to sometime around the iPhone 14. ⚾ Now that **Brian Mundell** has crushed it in Double-A, we should tell you he's isn't your average first-base prospect. Well, he's just as flawed, but with the standard accompanying power and hit tool grades flipped, basically. ⚾ After missing most of 2016 with hamstring injuries, **Tyler Nevin** (yes, Phil's son) hit well as a 20-year-old in Asheville. He's got a long swing and is already spending time at first base, but he has real power potential. Hmm, that sounds familiar. ⚾ Anonymous 24-year-old catcher **Chris Rabago** stole 25 bases in High-A last year. He's basically the Cal League's Jason Kendall. ⚾ Outfield prospect **Wes Rogers** stole 70 bases in Lancaster, with an 85 percent success rate. Scouts love his wheels and think the bat-to-ball is real, but Rogers faces questions about his power that can't be answered until he plays in a more legitimate home park. ⚾ Rated by our good friends at Baseball America as the no. 22 prospect among this year's J2 crop, **Ezequiel Tovar** is a Venezuelan shortstop with lots of tools. He is younger than iTunes. ⚾ The Rockies really went out of their comfort zone when they drafted **Ryan Vilade**, a power-hitting shortstop who'll probably have to move to third base, with the 48th overall pick. He's the reigning Gatorade Oklahoma player of the year, but Powerade is comparatively down on him.

Pitchers

PITCHER	TEAM	LVL	AGE	W	L	SV	G	GS	IP	H	HR	BB/9	K/9	K	GB%	BABIP	WHIP	ERA	DRA	WARP	MPH	CMD	PWR	STM
Shane Carle	ABQ	AAA	25	3	5	1	36	3	62	74	8	3.2	7.3	50	45%	.344	1.55	5.37	5.40	0.0				
	COL	MLB	25	0	0	0	3	0	4	6	1	0.0	9.0	4	27%	.357	1.50	6.75	4.83	0.0	95.0			44
Jairo Diaz	COL	MLB	26	0	0	0	4	0	5	12	0	9.0	3.6	2	59%	.545	3.40	9.00	6.51	-0.1	99.8			27
	ABQ	AAA	26	0	1	3	20	0	18	16	1	3.5	8.5	17	56%	.306	1.28	5.00	3.85	0.3				
Tommy Doyle	GJR	Rk	21	3	3	3	20	0	21	29	2	4.3	7.7	18	59%	.365	1.86	5.14	4.88	0.2				
Breiling Eusebio	BOI	A-	20	3	0	0	3	3	17	10	0	2.1	11.6	22	58%	.278	0.82	1.59	1.78	0.7				
	ASH	A	20	3	3	0	8	8	40^1	44	3	3.6	6.9	31	52%	.328	1.49	4.46	5.21	0.0				
Will Gaddis	GJR	Rk	21	3	1	0	11	9	44^1	66	6	1.4	5.3	26	53%	.380	1.65	5.68	4.98	0.5				
Zachary Jemiola	BOI	A-	23	1	0	0	3	3	11^1	13	0	4.0	6.4	8	53%	.342	1.59	3.97	4.91	0.0				
	ABQ	AAA	23	5	5	0	16	15	81^2	104	13	4.2	4.4	40	46%	.316	1.74	6.83	9.32	-3.2				
Zac Rosscup	CHN	MLB	29	0	0	0	1	0	0^2	0	0	0.0	0.0	0	50%	.000	0.00	0.00	11.14	0.0	93.8			37
	IOW	AAA	29	2	2	1	17	1	27^2	21	3	2.6	12.7	39	37%	.305	1.05	2.60	2.32	0.9				
	ABQ	AAA	29	0	0	1	12	0	12^2	8	1	2.8	10.7	15	36%	.233	0.95	2.13	3.29	0.3				
	COL	MLB	29	0	0	0	9	0	7	9	2	0.0	12.9	10	32%	.412	1.29	5.14	5.34	0.0	94.3			37
Jesus Tinoco	LNC	A+	22	11	4	0	24	24	140^2	157	19	3.2	6.8	107	45%	.318	1.47	4.67	5.94	-1.1				

Future up-and-down reliever **Shane Carle** gave up three earned runs in his first four MLB innings, but if the world ends tomorrow he can brag about making the majors in whatever lies beyond. ⚾ After missing all of 2016 thanks to Tommy John, **Jairo Diaz** pitched 25 innings across three levels before ending the year on the DL with a sore elbow. Somewhere, Sisyphus shrugs. ⚾ The Rockies made former Cavaliers fireman **Tommy Doyle** the 70th overall pick in the draft. He could move quickly as a reliever, or he could be the most disappointing Virginia closer since Robert E. Lee. ⚾ **Breiling Eusebio** is rawer than high-end sushi but is left-handed and can throw in the mid-90s. Couple those qualities with a power curveball and you get a guy who could make beat writers complain about having to spell his name for years to come. ⚾ The Rockies' third-round pick and reigning Southern Conference pitcher of the year, **Will Gaddis** throws a heavy sinker and pounds the zone. He's a bit undersized, but scouts like his moxie. He'll need it in Coors. ⚾ Ground-ball specialist **Rayan Gonzalez** has enough talent that the Rockies kept him on their 40-man roster despite the Tommy John surgery he endured in March, but not so much talent that you've heard of him before. ⚾ In his first stint in Triple-A, **Zach Jemiola** learned the hard way that the problem with pitching to contact is sometimes that contact is hard. ⚾ **Mike Nikorak** missed the entire season recovering from Tommy John surgery. Thus far it's proven to be the only strategy that stops him from giving out walks. ⚾ Oh so you think that just because you bought this book you're a big baseball fan? Bet you can't tell us who the Rockies traded to the Cubs for **Zac Rosscup**, an oldish potential LOOGY, on June 26. It was Matt Carasiti, you charlatan. ⚾ **Jesus Tinoco** is essentially a prep school garage band; he's got flashy tools and loud stuff but can't do anything good with either.

League Leaders 2017

MLB Runs – Charlie Blackmon, 137

MLB VORP – Charlie Blackmon, 79.1

DETROIT TIGERS

Essay by Zachary Levine

Player comments by Ashley Varela and BP staff

Uninteresting gets you nowhere in life, so let's make the 2018 Tigers interesting, and for the 2018 Tigers to be interesting, it will take 21 more wins. Luckily, they don't have to look far to find the inspiration for that number.

Twenty-one more wins takes them from last year's forgettable 64 up to 85—the number hit last season by their division rival Twins, who snuck into October at a good-enough 85-77 just months after utilizing the no. 1 pick in the draft. Of course, the Twins, while ahead of schedule, at least were known to have had a positive first derivative to their trajectory. They were young in a good way throughout the lineup and turned out to be good in a young way, with enough veteran help on the pitching side to get them to the pseudo-playoffs.

But in this everybody-into-the-pool era, we've seen stranger things than a 21-win improvement from a last-place team. The Plexiglas principle—that you don't get that bad without some unfortunate and naturally reversible things going against you—is generally to thank. Since the no. 1 overall pick started going to the team with the worst record in baseball, only the exaggeratedly tanking Astros failed to improve by at least eight games the following season.

Chart 1: Year-to-year improvement/regression of worst teams in baseball

Year	Worst Team	Record	Next Year	Change
2016	Twins	59-103	85-77	26
2015	Phillies	63-99	71-91	8
2014	Diamondbacks	64-98	79-93	15
2013	Astros	51-111	70-92	19
2012	Astros	55-107	51-111	-4
2011	Astros	56-106	55-107	-1
2010	Pirates	57-105	72-90	15
2009	Nationals	59-103	69-93	10

We've seen stranger things than this path, so let's take a shot at it. Starting with the baseline of their lowly 64 wins in 2017, here's one recipe for 85 wins and a surprisingly fun fall in Detroit.

Start: 64 wins

Natural improvement to their Pythagorean expected record: +2 wins (66)

Natural improvement from that to their third-order record: +1 win (67)

Let's start with easiest things first, sort of like the Tigers' 2018 schedule, which results in a six-game homestand against the Pirates and Royals to get Project 21 off to a potentially good start.

The Tigers underachieved their true performance by three games last year—two to get to their true runs scored and runs allowed, and one more from that to their raw offensive and baserunner prevention output. In reality, we should probably add another three or so, because this team will need a lot of luck to have a prayer for 85

TIGERS PROSPECTUS

2017 W-L: 64-98, 5TH IN AL CENTRAL

Pythag	.406	29th	B-Age	29.7	*28th*
RS/G	4.54	18th	P-Age	28.3	*15th*
RA/G	5.52	30th	Salary	$199.8M	*2nd*
TAv	.250	28th	M$/MW	$12.0M	*1st*
TAv-P	.270	22nd	DL Days	259	*1st*
FIP	4.70	25th	$ on DL	6%	*2nd*
DER	.680	30th			

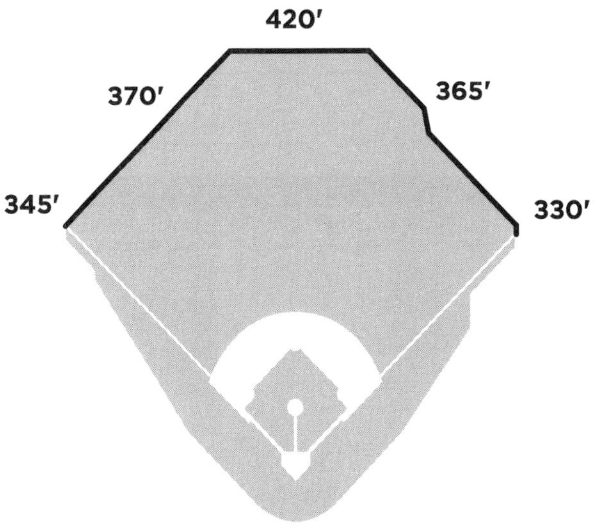

Outfield wall profile: **6'10"** to **14'**

Three-Year Park Factors

Runs	Runs/RH	Runs/LH	HR/RH	HR/LH
101	101	101	101	103

Top Hitter WARP	4.3 Justin Upton
Top Pitcher WARP	4.7 Justin Verlander
Top Prospect	Franklin Perez

2017 Hit List Ranking

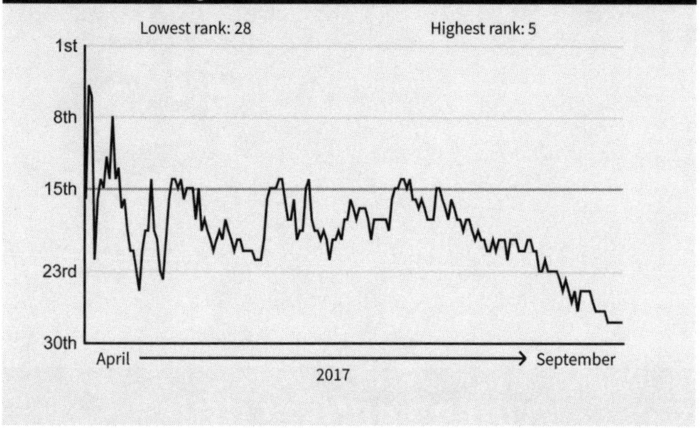

Committed Payroll (in millions)

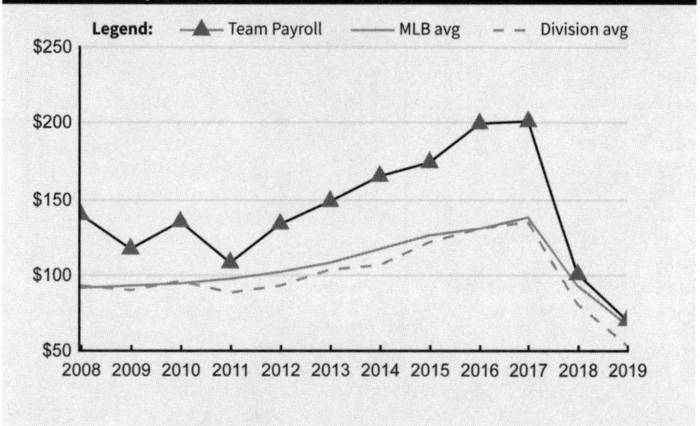

Farm System Ranking

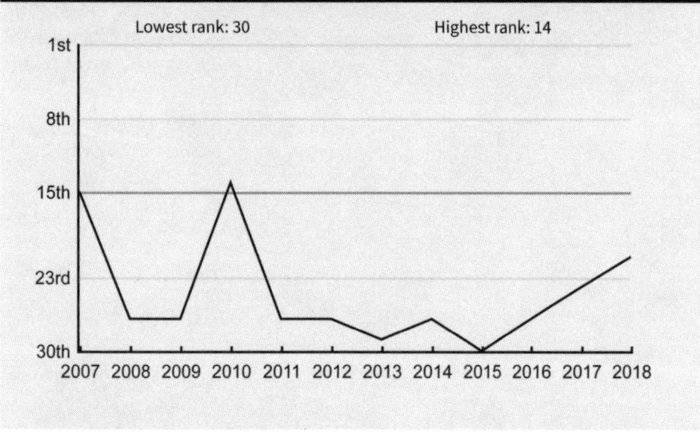

Personnel

EVP, General Manager
Al Avila

VP, Assistant General Manager
David Chadd

VP, Assistant General Manager
John Westhoff

Manager
Ron Gardenhire

wins and even normal good teams that make the playoffs generally outperform their expected win percentages. But we like a challenge, so we roll on, unfortified by luck.

Jordan Zimmermann being decent: +3 wins (70)

Pretty much anything other than the worst version of himself would get you to a couple wins, and throw in a third for returning a little closer to his Nationals-level performance after a season of no real velocity change.

The old guys—OR—the power of replacement level: +4 wins (74)

This is where we really stop correcting and start optimism-ing.

No, Miguel Cabrera and Victor Martinez, the subjects of all previous years' doomsaying essays who were liabilities even before the financial liabilities, aren't projected to be significantly better at 35 and 39. So these three wins of optimism aren't coming from a pure WARP-to-WARP projection. It's things like maybe they'll do the Albert Pujols and be bad but drive in a ton of runs (starring, uh, Nick Castellanos as Mike Trout?). Maybe Cabrera, through no change in ability, will have better than a .588 OPS in "late and close" situations.

Or maybe this is still a story of replacement level, as the two veterans, who played 130 and 107 games last year, will begin to be phased out, either through injury or conscious decision. There will be a point in the near future when we learn what the new Tigers regime's approach is to sunk cost, and a season that turns out to have more hope than expected wouldn't be the worst time.

Chad Bell. Chad Bell?: +2 wins (76)

Something would have to go very wrong for the Tigers or very right for Bell to get this depths-of-the-depth-chart option anywhere near the starter's spot on the lineup card. No American League pitcher contributed as much negative value in as few innings as Bell last year. And while Bell is a microcosm of the larger failures of a pitching staff that was the league's worst with or without Justin Verlander, just finding anything for those back-of-the-rotation and swingman spots is enough to get us thinking respectability at this point.

Give up on giving up: +4 wins (80)

As optimistic as this exercise is, we have to acknowledge that there are some things that start this season undeniably worse, so in addition to starting at the depths of the league-worst 68-94, we have to give ourselves a 10-game handicap. We'll address why specifically -10 later, but this is the effect of the trades they made last year and the contributions of players who are no longer here.

However, if in the season we're constructing, this team heads into the trade deadline pushing .500, you won't get those 10 wins. You also won't have to deal with that post-July 31 horror show that saw just about the worst that could happen to a team in terms of non-competitiveness.

Even if the Tigers play only .500 baseball to end the season, they'd have a nice +14 over the 20-48 they suffered through following the J.D. Martinez trade. And while .500 is optimistic, in any scenario where they're headed to a potential wild card spot, you could see some additions around the edges.

Cleveland and Kansas City's regression: +2 wins (82)

The 2017 Tigers went 14-24 against these two teams, both of which should be worse with the turn of the calendar. Cleveland will by Plexiglas alone and Kansas City by defections at the end of an era. Some of the fruits of these for Detroit overlap with the August/September improvements for which we've already accounted, but there may be a couple more to steal against these teams this year.

Defense at the key positions +3 wins (85)

The hidden flaw of the Tigers last year—not that it wasn't obviously bad but that it wasn't the combination of obviously bad and obviously well paid—was behind the plate. Much of what made the Tigers' catching as a whole the worst in the American League was framing, the most hidden skill and one that had to contribute to the league-worst pitching staff.

Chart 2: Positions and Ranks in WARP

Position	2017 WARP	AL Rank
C	-0.9	15th
1B	-1	15th
2B	1.3	11th
3B	1.6	11th
SS	-0.4	15th
LF	4.9	1st
CF	-0.2	15th
RF	0.4	12th
DH	-0.9	14th

James McCann has never been a spectacular or even a good framer, but he's capable of much better than the 15 runs his framing cost the Tigers last year: In his three major-league seasons, he's gone (-15, 0, -15). Stick with the rhyme scheme on his framing, add another one or two for the hope that shortstop Jose Iglesias just had a down year and didn't really lose a step, and all of this ought to clean up the ERA numbers and get us to 85.

See you Tuesday night at Yankee Stadium.

Uninteresting gets you nowhere in life, so let's make the 2018 Tigers interesting, and for the 2018 Tigers to be interesting, it will take 21 fewer wins. Luckily, they don't have to look far to find the inspiration for that number.

These very same Tigers in 2003 went 43-119, which represented the most losses in American League history. They are the worst team anyone younger than Cecil Fielder has ever experienced in their lifetime. And it's made all the more impressive by their ascent to the World Series three years later. Those 2003 Tigers broke the game. They were last in scoring and second-to-last in runs allowed. They played 18 different teams and had a winning record against none of them. They'll be remembered long after the 2017 Tigers are forgotten.

What fun is 64-98 when you can make a little history, so let's make history.

Start: 64 wins

Direct consequences of last season's three big departures: -10 wins (54)

We'll start off easy here with the most obvious reason the Tigers will be less good:

- Justin Verlander: 4.7 WARP for the Tigers alone in 2017. Gone.
- Justin Upton – 4.3 WARP for the Tigers alone in 2017. Gone.
- J.D. Martinez – 1.2 WARP for the Tigers alone in 2017. Gone.

So, what if the bullpen is actually worse: -4 wins (50)

The last mentioned personage of the three-Justin-trade season was Wilson, whose mid-2017 exit is just one reason why the T****s' b*****n (family publication here) might pull off an even worse disaster this season.

The impact of a bullpen being worse isn't easy to measure because a straight WARP calculation would—among other shortcomings—tend to give full credit for games the Tigers were or would have been already out of anyway. And in this scenario there are plenty of those. So instead, let's go with how much worse it could get by Win Probability Added, where Justin Wilson was actually a decent +1.4. The bullpen could sink even lower with Shane Greene on the anchor leg and not much else.

One might be tempted to think that a terrible team can't possibly have a historically low bullpen WPA—after all, how much can the bullpen eat away at your win probability when the starters and the lineup don't give you any win probability? But you'd be surprised. The worst bullpen WPA of the last five seasons belongs to the worst team of the last five seasons—the 2013 Astros, who explored the depths of the American League with the bullpen responsible by that measure for 8.5 extra losses.

Chart 3: Worst bullpen WPAs in the last five seasons

Year	Team	Bullpen WPA
2013	Astros	-8.5
2015	Athletics	-8.3
2014	Rockies	-7.4
2013	Cubs	-6.2
2014	White Sox	-6
2016	Rockies	-5.8
2017	Athletics	-5.1
2017	Tigers	-4.6

If the Tigers pull off something like that instead of the "only" -4.6 WPA of last season, this could go from bad to historically bad. And that's the goal here.

Another trade deadline: -4 wins (46)

Speaking of those 2013 Astros, they hold another key to any pursuit the Tigers might be making of the all-time lows. When the Astros of the early part of the decade broke it all down, they didn't just trade guys like Carlos Lee, Brett Myers and others at the end of deals. They traded Michael Bourn—a year-and-a-half from free agency—and Hunter Pence—two-and-a-half years years away. Ultimately even pre-arbitration guys like Jarred Cosart were on the block for prospects.

How deep do the Tigers go? Ian Kinsler already headed upward and westward in the offseason and that's probably at least a one-win downgrade. But is a player like Castellanos too advanced to have a spot on the next good Tigers team? Is lone pitching bright spot Michael Fulmer too valuable to a contender to resist with all the service time remaining? There may be nothing left, and August and September of last year could look like the good old days.

Maybe luck or something: -2 wins (44)

This is getting hard, so we need that luck that we'd been saving. Seriously, they once won only 43 games (and they had to win five of their last six to even reach that total!)? How is that possible? That team, like all extremely terrible ones, underperformed its theoretical record, in this case by about a half-dozen wins. We'll take two here and the forecast makes it seem like we're in good shape.

Rainout of the September 16 game vs. Cleveland. Not made up: -1 win (43)

No more mutual off days, a clinched division against a clinched no. 1 pick and really, why bother anyway?

—Zachary Levine is a Baseball Prospectus contributor and covered the Astros for the Houston Chronicle from 2009-2012.

Hitters

Miguel Cabrera 1B
Born: 04/18/83 Age: 35 Bats: R Throws: R Height: 6'4" Weight: 240 Origin: International Free Agent, 1999

YEAR	TEAM	LVL	AGE	PA	R	2B	3B	HR	RBI	BB	K	SB	CS	AVG/OBP/SLG	TAv	VORP	BABIP	BRR	FRAA	WARP
2015	DET	MLB	32	511	64	28	1	18	76	77	82	1	1	.338/.440/.534	.333	38.2	.384	-3.0	1B(107): 6.9	4.8
2016	DET	MLB	33	679	92	31	1	38	108	75	116	0	0	.316/.393/.563	.308	36.2	.336	-3.8	1B(147): 3.4, 3B(1): -0.1	4.1
2017	DET	MLB	34	529	50	22	0	16	60	54	110	0	1	.249/.329/.399	.243	-1.2	.292	-6.6	1B(115): -1.7	-1.2
2018	*DET*	*MLB*	*35*	*603*	*84*	*29*	*1*	*26*	*92*	*67*	*104*	*1*	*1*	*.300/.381/.505*	*.296*	*29.4*	*.331*	*-1.5*	*1B 0*	*2.9*
2019	*DET*	*MLB*	*36*	*525*	*77*	*26*	*1*	*22*	*76*	*58*	*95*	*0*	*0*	*.295/.376/.498*	*.282*	*16.2*	*.329*	*-3.6*	*1B 0*	*1.8*

Breakout: 1% Improve: 28% Collapse: 2% Attrition: 9% MLB: 96% *Comparables: Paul Konerko, Vladimir Guerrero, Lance Berkman*

Things get pretty bleak once we realize that we cannot delay the day of reckoning, only our consciousness of its inevitable approach. Cabrera pushed it away for as long as he could, gritting his teeth through bursts of back tightness that curtailed his swing, shortchanged his starts and fed into career-worst numbers at the plate. An MRI exam eventually uncovered several herniated discs in his spine, perhaps foreshadowing a full-time gig at designated hitter or a simple change in offseason regimen. Provided Cabrera can work his way back from what Brad Ausmus characterized as a lifelong affliction, he might very well regard this as little more than a blip on the radar of a phenomenal career. He hit the ball harder, and often better, than his poor BABIP and ugly overall numbers suggest, but at age 35 nothing is guaranteed.

Daz Cameron OF
Born: 01/15/97 Age: 21 Bats: R Throws: R Height: 6'2" Weight: 185 Origin: Round 1, 2015 Draft (#37 overall)

YEAR	TEAM	LVL	AGE	PA	R	2B	3B	HR	RBI	BB	K	SB	CS	AVG/OBP/SLG	TAv	VORP	BABIP	BRR	FRAA	WARP
2015	AST	RK	18	87	14	2	0	0	6	9	18	13	4	.222/.326/.250	.262	4.7	.286	2.0	CF(17): -1.5	0.3
2015	GRV	RK	18	124	20	2	3	0	11	16	31	11	6	.272/.372/.350	.296	9.4	.384	0.6	CF(22): 2.6, LF(6): -0.5	1.1
2016	QUD	A	19	87	5	2	2	0	6	8	33	4	3	.143/.221/.221	.170	-5.6	.244	0.1	CF(10): -0.6, LF(6): -0.3	-0.7
2016	TCV	A-	19	89	13	3	1	2	14	6	26	8	2	.278/.352/.418	.286	4.7	.392	0.0	CF(15): 0.0, LF(2): -0.3	0.5
2017	QUD	A	20	511	79	29	8	14	73	45	108	32	12	.271/.349/.466	.298	38.2	.323	3.1	CF(110): 1.8, RF(4): 0.1	4.1
2018	*DET*	*MLB*	*21*	*250*	*32*	*10*	*2*	*7*	*24*	*17*	*75*	*9*	*4*	*.219/.283/.372*	*.216*	*-1.2*	*.290*	*0.4*	*CF 1, LF 0*	*0.0*
2019	*DET*	*MLB*	*22*	*356*	*42*	*15*	*3*	*11*	*42*	*25*	*106*	*13*	*6*	*.229/.294/.402*	*.232*	*1.2*	*.300*	*1.4*	*CF 1, LF 0*	*0.3*

Breakout: 2% Improve: 4% Collapse: 0% Attrition: 3% MLB: 5% *Comparables: Daniel Fields, Teoscar Hernandez, Michael Saunders*

At some point, you have to cleave family legacy from future potential. Cameron dazzled in his sophomore Single-A season, and while his father's power stroke may linger out of reach in the long term, his own exceptional speed is the calling card that should get him a full-time gig in center field by 2019, if not sooner. If nothing else, he'll certainly get more of an opportunity in Detroit than he would have in Houston.

Jeimer Candelario 3B
Born: 11/24/93 Age: 24 Bats: B Throws: R Height: 6'1" Weight: 210 Origin: International Free Agent, 2010

YEAR	TEAM	LVL	AGE	PA	R	2B	3B	HR	RBI	BB	K	SB	CS	AVG/OBP/SLG	TAv	VORP	BABIP	BRR	FRAA	WARP
2015	MYR	A+	21	343	42	25	3	5	39	20	62	0	1	.270/.318/.415	.270	13.2	.320	-0.5	3B(77): -8.6	0.5
2015	TEN	AA	21	182	21	10	1	5	25	22	21	0	0	.291/.379/.462	.306	14.1	.308	0.2	3B(44): -3.6	1.1
2016	TEN	AA	22	244	30	17	1	4	23	32	46	0	0	.219/.324/.367	.247	4.2	.261	0.0	3B(54): 2.7, 1B(2): -0.3	0.7
2016	CHN	MLB	22	14	0	0	0	0	0	2	5	0	0	.091/.286/.091	.178	-0.5	.167	0.2	3B(3): -0.4	-0.1
2016	IOW	AAA	22	309	44	22	3	9	54	38	53	0	2	.333/.417/.542	.353	40.9	.383	1.7	3B(67): -0.8, 1B(10): 1.1	4.2
2017	CHN	MLB	23	36	2	2	0	1	3	1	12	0	0	.152/.222/.303	.196	-1.2	.200	0.2	3B(9): 0.9, 1B(1): 0.0	0.0
2017	IOW	AAA	23	330	39	27	3	12	52	41	72	0	0	.266/.361/.507	.307	23.1	.315	-4.5	3B(70): 5.0, 1B(16): -0.7	2.7
2017	TOL	AAA	23	128	13	9	1	3	19	5	32	1	0	.264/.297/.430	.249	0.8	.333	-1.9	3B(28): -1.5	-0.1
2017	DET	MLB	23	106	16	7	0	2	13	12	18	0	0	.330/.406/.468	.288	6.9	.392	0.2	3B(27): -2.4	0.4
2018	*DET*	*MLB*	*24*	*509*	*59*	*30*	*3*	*16*	*67*	*47*	*112*	*0*	*0*	*.258/.332/.442*	*.262*	*15.2*	*.308*	*-0.9*	*3B -4, 1B 0*	*0.8*
2019	*DET*	*MLB*	*25*	*548*	*72*	*32*	*3*	*20*	*73*	*54*	*121*	*0*	*0*	*.258/.336/.459*	*.260*	*11.4*	*.303*	*-1.2*	*3B -3, 1B 0*	*0.9*

Breakout: 4% Improve: 23% Collapse: 20% Attrition: 31% MLB: 65% *Comparables: James Darnell, Marcus Semien, Cody Asche*

Too much can be made of a bright, bat-first prospect with a good head for defense and the ability to tweak his approach against big-league competition. Too much can be made of a record-snapping triple play, a hot bat in the middle of a cold season, a third baseman not named Nick Castellanos. Context matters, kids, and while Candelario's third big-league tryout looked like a smashing success, his lofty batting average and fistful of defensive gems also papered over a dismal Tigers season and their gaping hole at the hot corner. His breakout efforts should merit an extended look in the spring, even if his less-impressive minor-league output preludes future struggles.

Nick Castellanos 3B
Born: 03/04/92 Age: 26 Bats: R Throws: R Height: 6'4" Weight: 210 Origin: Round 1, 2010 Draft (#44 overall)

YEAR	TEAM	LVL	AGE	PA	R	2B	3B	HR	RBI	BB	K	SB	CS	AVG/OBP/SLG	TAv	VORP	BABIP	BRR	FRAA	WARP
2015	DET	MLB	23	595	42	33	6	15	73	39	152	0	3	.255/.303/.419	.251	10.3	.322	-2.4	3B(145): 1.5	1.3
2016	DET	MLB	24	447	54	25	4	18	58	28	111	1	1	.285/.331/.496	.278	18.4	.345	-3.9	3B(108): -3.3	1.6
2017	DET	MLB	25	665	73	36	10	26	101	41	142	4	5	.272/.320/.490	.267	22.5	.313	-2.6	3B(129): -7.7, RF(21): -6.0	0.9
2018	*DET*	*MLB*	*26*	*614*	*80*	*33*	*5*	*20*	*73*	*41*	*136*	*3*	*3*	*.268/.319/.450*	*.257*	*12.5*	*.318*	*-1.1*	*RF -23, 3B -1*	*-1.3*
2019	*DET*	*MLB*	*27*	*566*	*72*	*33*	*4*	*21*	*77*	*42*	*126*	*2*	*2*	*.269/.325/.471*	*.258*	*8.6*	*.317*	*-2.3*	*RF -20, 3B -*	*-1.3*

Breakout: 3% Improve: 52% Collapse: 2% Attrition: 10% MLB: 97% *Comparables: Hank Blalock, Wilson Betemit, Edwin Encarnacion*

In the second installment of Judith Martin's acclaimed series, *Miss Manners' Basic Training: The Right Thing to Say*, Martin advises her readers to embrace simple, tactful platitudes when thrust into a delicate situation. Her wise counsel would have behooved Brad Ausmus when Castellanos shifted to the outfield in September, prompting the skipper to blurt, "He actually thinks he's going to be good out there." As Miss Manners also points out, the decorous response is not always the most truthful one, and in this case Ausmus' thinly veiled snark was spot on. Castellanos flailed his way to a career-worst FRAA, proving no more adept at orchestrating fly-ball routes than gloving the occasional zinger at the hot corner. His bat kept him off the bench more often than not, however, and he might be on the cusp of another offensive breakout after turning in his first 20-homer performance and leading the league in triples.

Tyler Collins OF Born: 06/06/90 Age: 28 Bats: L Throws: L Height: 5'11" Weight: 215 Origin: Round 6, 2011 Draft (#197 overall)

YEAR	TEAM	LVL	AGE	PA	R	2B	3B	HR	RBI	BB	K	SB	CS	AVG/OBP/SLG	TAv	VORP	BABIP	BRR	FRAA	WARP
2015	TOL	AAA	25	218	21	10	0	2	20	22	40	9	2	.247/.330/.332	.243	2.0	.298	1.1	RF(17): 1.8, LF(17): 1.2	0.3
2015	DET	MLB	25	207	18	11	3	4	25	13	43	2	1	.266/.316/.417	.255	2.8	.324	0.0	LF(37): 2.1, RF(7): -1.2	0.4
2016	TOL	AAA	26	281	29	7	0	7	30	20	69	4	1	.214/.274/.323	.208	-8.7	.262	0.4	LF(38): -1.3, RF(16): 5.8	-0.2
2016	DET	MLB	26	151	14	2	3	4	15	13	38	1	1	.235/.305/.382	.238	0.1	.295	-0.5	CF(29): 1.2, LF(13): 0.2	0.0
2017	TOL	AAA	27	296	29	14	2	9	46	29	72	11	2	.288/.358/.462	.284	15.3	.359	0.6	RF(49): -1.6, CF(20): -0.6	1.3
2017	DET	MLB	27	169	18	4	1	5	14	18	55	0	4	.193/.278/.333	.213	-4.7	.264	-0.9	CF(26): 1.4, RF(17): -0.8	-0.4
2018	*DET*	*MLB*	*28*	*250*	*29*	*9*	*1*	*8*	*31*	*22*	*63*	*4*	*2*	*.243/.313/.409*	*.236*	*1.9*	*.297*	*-0.1*	*RF -1, CF 0*	*0.1*
2019	*DET*	*MLB*	*29*	*364*	*45*	*13*	*2*	*13*	*44*	*31*	*96*	*5*	*3*	*.236/.306/.403*	*.235*	*-0.5*	*.293*	*0.1*	*RF -1, CF 0*	*-0.1*

Breakout: 4% Improve: 17% Collapse: 17% Attrition: 34% MLB: 57% *Comparables: Brett Carroll, Bryan Petersen, Joe Mather*

It's an old adage that has haunted many a journeyman and Quad-A hitter: "Always a backup, never a starter." Collins filled in the gaps for the Tigers for a fourth straight season, answering the call when Brad Ausmus needed a stopgap for his beleaguered outfield or when shortstop Jose Iglesias found himself temporarily stranded during Hurricane Irma. A nagging rib injury and sub-Mendoza line production did little to convince the club that he was leading-man material, and he faded into the background as seamlessly as Judy Greer in a mid-2000s romcom.

Derek Hill CF Born: 12/30/95 Age: 22 Bats: R Throws: R Height: 6'2" Weight: 195 Origin: Round 1, 2014 Draft (#23 overall)

YEAR	TEAM	LVL	AGE	PA	R	2B	3B	HR	RBI	BB	K	SB	CS	AVG/OBP/SLG	TAv	VORP	BABIP	BRR	FRAA	WARP
2015	WMI	A	19	235	33	6	5	0	16	20	44	25	7	.238/.305/.314	.258	7.6	.298	1.2	CF(51): 2.5	1.1
2016	WMI	A	20	415	66	17	6	1	31	24	105	35	6	.266/.312/.349	.261	16.6	.361	6.6	CF(54): -6.7, RF(33): 5.1	1.7
2017	TGW	RK	21	61	11	1	1	1	7	10	15	7	0	.163/.300/.286	.245	1.5	.206	1.2	CF(7): 0.7	0.2
2017	WMI	A	21	168	28	8	6	1	21	16	38	12	5	.285/.367/.444	.310	14.9	.374	2.2	CF(23): 0.1	1.6
2017	LAK	A+	21	38	3	1	0	0	2	5	10	10	0	.194/.324/.226	.276	3.0	.286	1.5	CF(6): 0.0	0.3
2018	*DET*	*MLB*	*22*	*250*	*31*	*9*	*3*	*5*	*20*	*15*	*73*	*13*	*3*	*.224/.276/.349*	*.209*	*-2.3*	*.299*	*1.8*	*CF -2*	*-0.5*
2019	*DET*	*MLB*	*23*	*289*	*30*	*11*	*3*	*6*	*29*	*19*	*86*	*16*	*4*	*.228/.284/.362*	*.220*	*-1.4*	*.306*	*2.7*	*CF -3*	*-0.4*

Breakout: 2% Improve: 13% Collapse: 2% Attrition: 15% MLB: 16% *Comparables: Xavier Avery, Trayvon Robinson, Darrell Ceciliani*

Tommy John surgery can be a career-killer at any level, but in Hill's case it just snuffed out the last vestige of his power. He returned in the second half of the season with a newly constructed elbow and a .300-plus TAv, enough to temporarily silence the critics during a brief audition in the Midwest League. His speed is still his best asset, however, and he cuts an imposing figure in center field with plus defense and highlight-reel catches aching for a Statcast breakdown. Once he proves capable of making consistent contact, he'll be a threat at the plate and on the field.

Jose Iglesias SS Born: 01/05/90 Age: 28 Bats: R Throws: R Height: 5'11" Weight: 185 Origin: International Free Agent, 2009

YEAR	TEAM	LVL	AGE	PA	R	2B	3B	HR	RBI	BB	K	SB	CS	AVG/OBP/SLG	TAv	VORP	BABIP	BRR	FRAA	WARP
2015	DET	MLB	25	454	44	17	3	2	23	25	44	11	8	.300/.347/.370	.252	10.1	.330	-4.3	SS(119): -6.7	0.4
2016	DET	MLB	26	513	57	26	0	4	32	28	50	7	4	.255/.306/.336	.234	8.6	.276	1.2	SS(136): 14.2	2.4
2017	DET	MLB	27	489	56	33	1	6	54	21	65	7	4	.255/.288/.369	.221	4.4	.285	3.7	SS(130): -4.8	0.0
2018	*DET*	*MLB*	*28*	*537*	*58*	*26*	*3*	*7*	*50*	*28*	*61*	*9*	*5*	*.276/.320/.379*	*.239*	*13.0*	*.300*	*-0.7*	*SS 1*	*0.7*
2019	*DET*	*MLB*	*29*	*513*	*59*	*26*	*2*	*9*	*54*	*31*	*60*	*8*	*5*	*.280/.332/.402*	*.243*	*8.7*	*.300*	*0.5*	*SS 1*	*1.1*

Breakout: 1% Improve: 38% Collapse: 9% Attrition: 12% MLB: 96% *Comparables: Luis Aparicio, Elvis Andrus, Alcides Escobar*

When you come across someone with a singular, spectacular talent, it's difficult to criticize their shortcomings without feeling like a jerk. Iglesias is one such someone. His defensive wizardry has repeatedly placed him in the same conversation as Hall of Fame-worthy shortstops, but when it comes to swinging the bat his lack of patience and power starts to lessen his appeal. Last season, FRAA didn't love his inexplicable struggles with routine plays and WARP didn't love his decline at the plate. He's slipping ever so slightly, and while that may not have raised alarms a year ago, there are younger, more well-rounded infielders waiting to step out from the shadows of the dugout and take their place in the sun.

Omar Infante 2B Born: 12/26/81 Age: 36 Bats: R Throws: R Height: 5'11" Weight: 195 Origin: International Free Agent, 1999

YEAR	TEAM	LVL	AGE	PA	R	2B	3B	HR	RBI	BB	K	SB	CS	AVG/OBP/SLG	TAv	VORP	BABIP	BRR	FRAA	WARP
2015	KCA	MLB	33	455	39	23	7	2	44	9	69	2	2	.220/.234/.318	.202	-14.8	.255	-0.8	2B(124): -6.2	-2.3
2016	KCA	MLB	34	149	16	9	1	0	11	9	23	0	0	.239/.279/.321	.233	2.4	.278	2.5	2B(39): 0.7	0.3
2016	GWN	AAA	34	116	8	5	1	1	9	3	16	0	1	.209/.226/.300	.205	-3.7	.232	-0.1	2B(26): 0.3	-0.4
2017	TOL	AAA	35	523	46	31	0	3	37	24	50	3	6	.282/.315/.364	.244	5.0	.306	-0.7	2B(118): 2.4, SS(3): 0.2	0.7
2018	*DET*	*MLB*	*36*	*250*	*23*	*12*	*2*	*4*	*24*	*12*	*34*	*1*	*1*	*.258/.293/.375*	*.216*	*-0.6*	*.282*	*0.3*	*2B -1, 3B 0*	*-0.2*
2019	*DET*	*MLB*	*37*	*109*	*11*	*5*	*1*	*2*	*10*	*5*	*16*	*0*	*0*	*.247/.284/.359*	*.217*	*-1.3*	*.272*	*0.2*	*2B -1, 3B 0*	*-0.2*

Breakout: 4% Improve: 36% Collapse: 11% Attrition: 21% MLB: 76% *Comparables: Aaron Miles, Miguel Cairo, Denny Hocking*

It's been a year full of "almosts" for Infante, who was stashed away at Triple-A Toledo while the Tigers began a laborious evaluation of their infield options. He almost broke camp in the spring, but found himself blocked by Ian Kinsler; he almost brought his TAv back to .250, but was ensnared by a high strikeout rate and what can only be characterized as an absolute dearth of power. At age 36, those "almosts" are starting to sound a lot like "never."

Jacoby Jones CF Born: 05/10/92 Age: 26 Bats: R Throws: R Height: 6'2" Weight: 205 Origin: Round 3, 2013 Draft (#87 overall)

YEAR	TEAM	LVL	AGE	PA	R	2B	3B	HR	RBI	BB	K	SB	CS	AVG/OBP/SLG	TAv	VORP	BABIP	BRR	FRAA	WARP
2015	BRD	A+	23	423	48	18	3	10	58	31	113	14	4	.253/.313/.396	.261	14.3	.330	-1.8	SS(84): 10.3	2.7
2015	ERI	AA	23	160	26	7	2	6	20	17	52	10	3	.250/.331/.463	.282	11.4	.337	1.5	SS(37): 3.7	1.6
2016	ERI	AA	24	89	11	6	2	4	20	10	23	2	1	.312/.393/.597	.337	9.2	.392	-0.3	3B(9): -0.5, CF(9): 1.1	1.1
2016	TOL	AAA	24	324	33	14	5	3	23	25	97	11	4	.243/.309/.356	.246	6.9	.349	1.8	CF(57): -5.3, 3B(22): -1.3	0.0
2016	DET	MLB	24	28	3	3	0	0	2	0	12	0	0	.214/.214/.321	.171	-1.2	.375	0.5	3B(6): 0.0, CF(5): -0.2	-0.1
2017	TOL	AAA	25	393	57	19	2	9	44	33	104	12	4	.245/.314/.387	.260	15.5	.322	3.6	CF(76): 3.2, LF(7): 0.2	1.9
2017	DET	MLB	25	154	14	3	1	3	13	9	65	6	2	.170/.240/.270	.174	-8.0	.288	1.1	CF(51): 2.3, RF(1): 0.0	-0.6
2018	*DET*	*MLB*	*26*	*579*	*71*	*23*	*5*	*16*	*63*	*43*	*187*	*15*	*5*	*.225/.290/.382*	*.230*	*3.8*	*.312*	*1.5*	*CF 4, LF 0*	*0.3*
2019	*DET*	*MLB*	*27*	*537*	*64*	*23*	*4*	*18*	*64*	*44*	*173*	*14*	*5*	*.227/.300/.398*	*.233*	*1.2*	*.309*	*1.4*	*CF 4, LF 0*	*0.6*

Breakout: 4% Improve: 17% Collapse: 9% Attrition: 23% MLB: 41% *Comparables: Jordan Danks, Matt Den Dekker, Brett Eibner*

"The starting point of all achievement is desire," Napoleon Hill wrote in his cult-inspiring bestseller, *Think and Grow Rich*. And while Jones had desire in spades, he's still waiting to reap the results. He logged 16 games in the majors before a Justin Haley fastball rearranged his face, and returned to close out the first half with a .137 batting average and a ticket to Triple-A. His emergence in the second half established him as the Tigers' best defensive option in center field, but continued struggles at the plate doomed him to finish the year with the first sub-Mendoza line performance of his career. At this point, he'd be wise to heed another of Hill's maxims: "If you can't do great things, do small things in a great way."

Dawel Lugo INF Born: 12/31/94 Age: 23 Bats: R Throws: R Height: 6'0" Weight: 190 Origin: International Free Agent, 2012

YEAR	TEAM	LVL	AGE	PA	R	2B	3B	HR	RBI	BB	K	SB	CS	AVG/OBP/SLG	TAv	VORP	BABIP	BRR	FRAA	WARP
2015	DUN	A+	20	276	16	9	2	2	21	9	49	1	3	.219/.258/.292	.207	-7.5	.262	-3.8	SS(67): 1.6	-0.6
2015	LNS	A	20	132	15	6	1	2	23	5	24	3	1	.336/.348/.451	.284	8.4	.386	0.1	SS(29): 1.9	1.1
2015	KNC	A	20	86	12	1	1	0	3	4	13	2	2	.333/.372/.370	.272	2.2	.397	-1.5	SS(14): -0.8, 2B(2): -0.4	0.1
2016	VIS	A+	21	333	61	14	5	13	42	15	41	2	1	.314/.348/.514	.303	28.6	.328	2.5	3B(60): -3.5, SS(14): 2.0	2.8
2016	MOB	AA	21	177	24	9	2	4	20	4	15	1	1	.306/.322/.451	.287	13.3	.318	2.7	3B(41): 4.7, SS(10): 0.4	2.0
2017	WTN	AA	22	369	40	21	4	7	43	21	51	1	0	.282/.325/.428	.271	14.1	.310	-1.7	3B(77): 4.5, SS(10): -0.4	2.0
2017	ERI	AA	22	188	18	6	1	6	22	12	21	2	1	.269/.314/.417	.256	3.3	.275	-1.5	3B(29): -1.1, 2B(13): 0.6	0.3
2018	*DET*	*MLB*	*23*	*250*	*26*	*11*	*2*	*9*	*33*	*9*	*46*	*0*	*0*	*.264/.294/.436*	*.237*	*2.6*	*.293*	*-0.2*	*3B 1, 2B 0*	*0.4*
2019	*DET*	*MLB*	*24*	*374*	*44*	*16*	*3*	*13*	*47*	*14*	*68*	*0*	*0*	*.264/.296/.434*	*.241*	*1.9*	*.293*	*-0.5*	*3B 1, 2B 0*	*0.4*

Breakout: 5% Improve: 20% Collapse: 11% Attrition: 25% MLB: 53% *Comparables: Giovanny Urshela, Henry Rodriguez, Brent Morel*

Maybe you were one of those kids who got marked down in math class for not "showing your work." You knew how to arrive at the correct answer, but your problem-solving methods didn't exactly conform to conventional standards. Later, you'd learn that it wasn't enough to just know how to do something; you also have to figure out how to do it correctly. Lugo has that kind of natural talent at the plate. He knows how to swing for the fences, how to angle line drives and dismantle a Double-A strike zone, but his approach lacks refinement and patience, to say nothing of his subpar baserunning. That aggression, however effective in the Eastern League, may not translate well to the majors, in which case Lugo's average arm and defensive flexibility will become his biggest selling points.

Dixon Machado MI Born: 02/22/92 Age: 26 Bats: R Throws: R Height: 6'1" Weight: 170 Origin: International Free Agent, 2008

YEAR	TEAM	LVL	AGE	PA	R	2B	3B	HR	RBI	BB	K	SB	CS	AVG/OBP/SLG	TAv	VORP	BABIP	BRR	FRAA	WARP
2015	TOL	AAA	23	567	61	22	1	4	48	36	85	15	3	.261/.313/.332	.230	6.7	.305	2.0	SS(125): -5.7, 3B(2): -0.1	0.1
2015	DET	MLB	23	78	6	3	0	0	5	7	14	1	0	.235/.307/.279	.208	-1.6	.296	-0.7	SS(24): -0.8	-0.3
2016	TOL	AAA	24	569	59	28	2	4	48	58	75	17	5	.266/.349/.356	.259	23.1	.305	0.7	SS(130): 12.5, 2B(4): 0.2	3.7
2016	DET	MLB	24	13	1	0	0	0	0	3	4	0	0	.100/.308/.100	.183	0.1	.167	0.6	SS(6): 0.5, 2B(2): 0.0	0.1
2017	DET	MLB	25	181	17	5	1	1	11	10	32	1	0	.259/.302/.319	.220	-3.3	.311	-2.0	SS(32): -2.3, 2B(27): 2.8	-0.3
2018	*DET*	*MLB*	*26*	*501*	*55*	*20*	*2*	*9*	*49*	*38*	*85*	*8*	*2*	*.257/.314/.370*	*.235*	*4.6*	*.292*	*0.3*	*2B 12, 3B 0*	*1.4*
2019	*DET*	*MLB*	*27*	*448*	*54*	*19*	*1*	*11*	*50*	*37*	*82*	*7*	*2*	*.259/.326/.398*	*.238*	*2.0*	*.290*	*-1.6*	*2B 11, 3B 0*	*1.4*

Breakout: 5% Improve: 39% Collapse: 9% Attrition: 28% MLB: 69% *Comparables: Ben Zobrist, Cliff Pennington, Brian Dozier*

With a glove-first profile, a bat that runs lukewarm and three years of team control left, Machado proved the perfect test subject for Brad Ausmus' thought experiment in 2017. As a renowned Austrian physicist once theorized, a rookie is both useful and useless to their team until they're pulled off of Schrödinger's bench. Ausmus was content to keep Machado in that grey area for the majority of the season, despite his proven defensive flexibility and what looked like a slight upward trend at the plate. He may be the shortstop of the future, but playing second string to Jose Iglesias' flashier glove work and Ian Kinsler's power stroke did little to prove his capabilities as an everyday player.

Mikie Mahtook OF Born: 11/30/89 Age: 28 Bats: R Throws: R Height: 6'1" Weight: 200 Origin: Round 1, 2011 Draft (#31 overall)

YEAR	TEAM	LVL	AGE	PA	R	2B	3B	HR	RBI	BB	K	SB	CS	AVG/OBP/SLG	TAv	VORP	BABIP	BRR	FRAA	WARP
2015	DUR	AAA	25	418	35	27	3	4	45	22	98	10	1	.249/.304/.366	.251	3.1	.323	-2.0	RF(43): -1.5, CF(34): 7.4	0.8
2015	TBA	MLB	25	115	22	5	1	9	19	6	31	4	3	.295/.351/.619	.352	12.2	.338	-0.6	LF(16): 0.3, CF(13): -0.9	1.4
2016	DUR	AAA	26	120	16	5	3	1	7	12	24	5	1	.305/.383/.438	.288	6.9	.383	0.6	CF(11): -1.1, RF(9): 1.9	0.8
2016	TBA	MLB	26	196	16	9	0	3	11	7	68	0	1	.195/.231/.292	.184	-11.6	.287	-1.2	LF(26): -0.9, CF(23): 0.5	-1.2
2017	DET	MLB	27	379	50	15	6	12	38	23	79	6	0	.276/.330/.457	.268	15.6	.324	1.6	CF(67): -1.6, RF(25): -1.7	1.1
2018	*DET*	*MLB*	*28*	*557*	*73*	*26*	*6*	*16*	*61*	*32*	*136*	*8*	*2*	*.254/.308/.419*	*.247*	*10.4*	*.315*	*0.8*	*LF 1, RF -1*	*0.7*
2019	*DET*	*MLB*	*29*	*474*	*57*	*24*	*4*	*15*	*59*	*29*	*119*	*6*	*2*	*.254/.311/.433*	*.245*	*4.3*	*.314*	*0.2*	*LF 1, RF -1*	*0.6*

Breakout: 1% Improve: 38% Collapse: 11% Attrition: 24% MLB: 83% *Comparables: Roger Bernadina, Brian Anderson, Lorenzo Cain*

Opportunity and hard work are the breeding grounds of a true breakthrough, which is exactly what Mahtook experienced during his first full season in Detroit. Fresh off of his second stint as Tampa Bay's fourth outfielder, Mahtook started tweaking his swing, getting under the ball and scaling back a high strikeout rate to prolong his at-bats. It helped that he was healthy for the better part of his 2017 campaign, and when the Tigers jettisoned Alex Avila and J.D. Martinez halfway through the year, their absence paved the way for the first starting gig of his career. While there are precious few guarantees during a full-scale rebuild, Mahtook's proven transformation and remarkably affordable contract should at least merit another formal tryout in the spring.

Leonys Martin OF Born: 03/06/88 Age: 30 Bats: L Throws: R Height: 6'2" Weight: 200 Origin: International Free Agent, 2011

YEAR	TEAM	LVL	AGE	PA	R	2B	3B	HR	RBI	BB	K	SB	CS	AVG/OBP/SLG	TAv	VORP	BABIP	BRR	FRAA	WARP
2015	ROU	AAA	27	43	7	3	0	2	4	5	4	2	1	.297/.372/.541	.343	5.8	.281	0.8	CF(8): 2.5, RF(1): 0.0	0.9
2015	TEX	MLB	27	310	26	12	0	5	25	16	69	14	5	.219/.264/.313	.210	-4.6	.270	1.4	CF(92): 11.6	0.7
2016	SEA	MLB	28	576	72	17	3	15	47	44	149	24	6	.247/.306/.378	.244	10.7	.313	2.5	CF(143): 9.6	2.1
2017	SEA	MLB	29	122	12	2	1	3	8	5	29	6	4	.174/.221/.287	.179	-7.7	.205	-0.4	CF(15): -0.7, RF(15): 2.8	-0.6
2017	TAC	AAA	29	388	63	24	5	11	39	21	89	25	6	.306/.346/.492	.288	25.3	.376	1.1	CF(82): 16.2	4.0
2017	CHN	MLB	29	16	2	1	0	0	1	3	4	1	0	.154/.313/.231	.203	-0.5	.222	0.1	CF(5): 0.0, RF(4): -0.4	-0.3
2018	*DET*	*MLB*	*30*	*235*	*29*	*9*	*2*	*5*	*24*	*15*	*52*	*11*	*4*	*.255/.305/.383*	*.233*	*2.8*	*.309*	*1.3*	*CF 4*	*0.5*
2019	*DET*	*MLB*	*31*	*315*	*37*	*12*	*3*	*8*	*35*	*22*	*72*	*14*	*5*	*.257/.313/.402*	*.235*	*2.4*	*.311*	*1.2*	*CF 6*	*0.9*

Breakout: 4% Improve: 50% Collapse: 8% Attrition: 13% MLB: 92% *Comparables: Corey Patterson, Cameron Maybin, Franklin Gutierrez*

Martin's bat never developed as hoped, but his speed and defense have kept him in the majors (albeit with a few detours to Triple-A). His limited but clear value became obvious last season when the Cubs acquired him from the Mariners for the stretch drive simply to do some running and catching. Martin will be asked to do a lot more this season on a one-year deal with the Tigers, but that speaks more to Detroit's full-scale rebuilding effort than any remaining upside for the 30-year-old.

Victor Martinez DH Born: 12/23/78 Age: 39 Bats: B Throws: R Height: 6'2" Weight: 210 Origin: International Free Agent, 1996

YEAR	TEAM	LVL	AGE	PA	R	2B	3B	HR	RBI	BB	K	SB	CS	AVG/OBP/SLG	TAv	VORP	BABIP	BRR	FRAA	WARP
2015	DET	MLB	36	485	39	20	0	11	64	31	52	0	0	.245/.301/.366	.232	-11.9	.253	-3.5	1B(10): 0.5	-1.2
2016	DET	MLB	37	610	65	22	0	27	86	50	90	0	0	.289/.351/.476	.274	5.6	.303	-9.6	1B(5): 0.0	0.6
2017	DET	MLB	38	435	38	16	0	10	47	36	63	0	0	.255/.324/.372	.235	-11.9	.280	-4.9		-1.2
2018	*DET*	*MLB*	*39*	*592*	*68*	*25*	*1*	*17*	*73*	*46*	*68*	*0*	*0*	*.274/.334/.417*	*.254*	*2.5*	*.286*	*-1.3*		*0.5*
2019	*DET*	*MLB*	*40*	*453*	*56*	*19*	*1*	*14*	*54*	*34*	*57*	*0*	*0*	*.268/.326/.415*	*.245*	*-4.8*	*.281*	*-4.7*	-	*-0.5*

Breakout: 0% Improve: 20% Collapse: 13% Attrition: 14% MLB: 69% *Comparables: Rusty Staub, Scott Hatteberg, Todd Helton*

Jim Abbott could whip a fastball over the corner of the plate and brush off a bunt attempt with a deft barehanded play. Dave Stevens could sprint down a college football field using only his arms, darting under the legs of opposing linemen who didn't know how to block someone who reached three feet, two inches at his full height. Plenty of athletes have proven themselves capable, if not outstanding, without hands and legs and all kinds of extraneous body parts. A working heart, however, is one of those non-negotiable items, and when an irregular heartbeat landed Martinez in the hospital and led to season-ending surgery the question facing the five-time All-Star wasn't how soon he can return to the field, but whether he would be able to return at all.

James McCann C Born: 06/13/90 Age: 28 Bats: R Throws: R Height: 6'2" Weight: 210 Origin: Round 2, 2011 Draft (#76 overall)

YEAR	TEAM	LVL	AGE	PA	R	2B	3B	HR	RBI	BB	K	SB	CS	AVG/OBP/SLG	TAv	VORP	BABIP	BRR	FRAA	WARP
2015	DET	MLB	25	425	32	18	5	7	41	16	90	0	1	.264/.297/.387	.230	1.2	.325	-4.7	C(112): -14.6	-1.4
2016	TOL	AAA	26	27	2	0	0	0	2	5	6	0	0	.091/.259/.091	.206	-0.5	.125	0.2	C(4): -0.3	-0.1
2016	DET	MLB	26	373	31	9	1	12	48	23	109	0	1	.221/.272/.358	.210	-4.3	.283	-2.0	C(99): 3.0	-0.1
2017	DET	MLB	27	391	39	14	2	13	49	26	89	1	0	.253/.318/.415	.251	13.4	.300	-0.9	C(103): -22.1	-0.9
2018	*DET*	*MLB*	*28*	*525*	*55*	*22*	*3*	*13*	*61*	*30*	*121*	*1*	*1*	*.252/.302/.392*	*.236*	*10.9*	*.307*	*-0.7*	*C -19*	*-1.2*
2019	*DET*	*MLB*	*29*	*470*	*56*	*20*	*2*	*14*	*55*	*29*	*113*	*1*	*0*	*.250/.306/.401*	*.235*	*3.9*	*.304*	*-2.4*	*C -16*	*-1.3*

Breakout: 7% Improve: 35% Collapse: 14% Attrition: 21% MLB: 87% *Comparables: Jesus Flores, Hank Conger, Ronny Paulino*

YEAR	TEAM	P. COUNT	FRM RUNS	BLK RUNS	THRW RUNS	TOT RUNS
2015	DET	15395	-15.1	0.9	1.8	-12.4
2016	DET	13823	0.1	1.1	3.6	4.8
2017	DET	14626	-15.0	-2.8	-0.8	-18.6
2018	*DET*	*19733*	*-15.9*	*-0.8*	*1.4*	*-15.3*
2019	*DET*	*17669*	*-13.6*	*-0.7*	*1.2*	*-13.1*

At some point, an experiment has to end—or, at the very least, show some signs of progression. You have to collect the data, refine your hypothesis and make adjustments. You can't let your test subject run wild, crumbling at the first sight of a right-handed pitcher and doing the second-worst job of framing pitches in the entire AL Central division, despite showing some life behind the dish only a year ago. You can't ignore the data that suggests your test subject is putting up the best offensive numbers of his career, nor should you overlook the mounting evidence in favor of a platoon with a younger, more capable defender. Once you've carefully sifted through four years of lusterless run production and inconsistent defensive metrics, you might also want to spend some time rebranding your experiment: "Convert Backup Catcher to Starter?" and "James McCann: Catcher of the Future?" just don't ring true the way they used to.

Steven Moya RF Born: 08/09/91 Age: 26 Bats: L Throws: R Height: 6'7" Weight: 260 Origin: Undrafted Free Agent, 2008

YEAR	TEAM	LVL	AGE	PA	R	2B	3B	HR	RBI	BB	K	SB	CS	AVG/OBP/SLG	TAv	VORP	BABIP	BRR	FRAA	WARP
2015	LAK	A+	23	42	3	3	0	3	8	1	13	0	0	.275/.286/.575	.291	2.1	.320	0.1	RF(9): 0.2	0.2
2015	TOL	AAA	23	535	53	30	0	20	74	27	162	5	4	.240/.283/.420	.242	-1.8	.312	-0.5	RF(97): -9.0, LF(13): 0.3	-1.1
2015	DET	MLB	23	25	1	0	1	0	0	3	10	0	0	.182/.280/.273	.199	-1.4	.333	-0.3	RF(5): 0.3, LF(2): 1.7	0.1
2016	TOL	AAA	24	426	60	23	3	20	66	15	96	3	0	.284/.310/.501	.277	15.2	.327	-0.3	RF(72): -3.1, LF(21): -3.9	0.8
2016	DET	MLB	24	100	9	4	2	5	11	5	38	0	1	.255/.290/.500	.249	-0.8	.365	-1.5	RF(18): 0.5, LF(8): -0.2	0.0
2017	TOL	AAA	25	162	12	2	2	7	15	11	61	3	0	.166/.222/.344	.180	-11.4	.217	0.8	RF(21): -1.2	-1.2
2017	ERI	AA	25	246	23	10	1	11	35	19	65	2	0	.246/.305/.446	.261	3.1	.293	-1.3	RF(58): -2.7	0.1
2018	*DET*	*MLB*	*26*	*250*	*30*	*11*	*1*	*13*	*38*	*12*	*81*	*2*	*1*	*.239/.279/.467*	*.238*	*1.0*	*.301*	*-0.1*	*RF -2*	*-0.1*
2019	*DET*	*MLB*	*27*	*298*	*39*	*13*	*1*	*16*	*45*	*16*	*96*	*2*	*1*	*.238/.283/.466*	*.241*	*-0.1*	*.299*	*-0.2*	*RF -2*	*-0.2*

Breakout: 8% Improve: 12% Collapse: 11% Attrition: 21% MLB: 30% *Comparables: Brad Glenn, John Mayberry, Mike Wilson*

A magician's disappearing act is rendered all the more astonishing upon the sudden reappearance of the vanished victim. Moya had audiences fooled when his power bat and major-league gig went missing last spring, but by September it was evident that neither would be returning anytime soon. Unless he figures out how to boost his contact and walk rates to pre-2017 levels—or, barring that, fine-tune his glove work enough to compensate for an inexplicable lack of power—he might find a brighter future awaiting him in amateur stage magic than professional baseball.

Alex Presley OF Born: 07/25/85 Age: 32 Bats: L Throws: L Height: 5'10" Weight: 195 Origin: Round 8, 2006 Draft (#230 overall)

YEAR	TEAM	LVL	AGE	PA	R	2B	3B	HR	RBI	BB	K	SB	CS	AVG/OBP/SLG	TAv	VORP	BABIP	BRR	FRAA	WARP
2015	HOU	MLB	29	13	1	0	0	0	1	1	5	0	0	.250/.308/.250	.210	-0.4	.429	0.0	LF(4): -0.3, RF(1): -0.4	-0.1
2015	FRE	AAA	29	367	48	14	1	3	49	27	41	15	4	.292/.345/.367	.253	7.8	.324	2.0	CF(41): 5.5, RF(28): -0.7	1.2
2016	CSP	AAA	30	35	5	2	1	1	3	3	7	1	0	.344/.400/.563	.318	3.3	.417	0.3	LF(4): 1.1, CF(3): -0.1	0.4
2016	MIL	MLB	30	129	12	2	0	3	11	11	25	0	2	.198/.271/.293	.218	-2.7	.225	0.0	RF(13): 1.7, LF(12): -0.9	-0.2
2016	DET	MLB	30	5	0	0	0	0	0	0	0	0	0	.200/.200/.200	.143	-0.4	.200	0.0	CF(2): 0.0, LF(1): 0.2	0.0
2016	TOL	AAA	30	193	23	10	3	3	14	18	27	4	6	.296/.365/.444	.278	8.9	.331	0.3	CF(22): 2.9, LF(21): -0.7	1.1
2017	TOL	AAA	31	185	26	6	1	2	9	12	36	4	2	.216/.284/.299	.223	-2.2	.264	0.3	CF(23): -0.7, LF(18): 2.7	-0.1
2017	DET	MLB	31	264	30	10	3	3	20	15	49	5	0	.314/.354/.416	.255	3.8	.383	-0.8	RF(36): -3.0, CF(19): -3.0	-0.3
2018	*DET*	*MLB*	*32*	*277*	*33*	*10*	*2*	*6*	*26*	*20*	*51*	*5*	*2*	*.264/.321/.390*	*.233*	*1.0*	*.306*	*-0.5*	*CF 0, RF -1*	*0.1*
2019	*DET*	*MLB*	*33*	*311*	*35*	*11*	*2*	*7*	*32*	*23*	*61*	*4*	*2*	*.253/.311/.376*	*.230*	*-2.3*	*.297*	*-0.4*	*CF 0, RF -1*	*-0.3*

Breakout: 4% Improve: 26% Collapse: 14% Attrition: 34% MLB: 70% *Comparables: Jason Ellison, Tike Redman, Tony Gwynn*

Ever the resilient Quad-A journeyman, Presley heated up at precisely the right moment to earn another cup of coffee in the majors. In fact, he stuck around for a whole pot of brew, providing the Tigers with a decent outfield stopgap and a not-too-shabby batting line in the wake of Justin Upton's and J.D. Martinez's midseason departures. A sizzling BABIP and .250-ish TAv isn't enough to forecast a full-scale breakthrough, however, and Presley has a long way to go before he'll find himself penciled into any starting lineup on a daily basis.

Christin Stewart LF Born: 12/10/93 Age: 24 Bats: L Throws: R Height: 6'0" Weight: 205 Origin: Round 1, 2015 Draft (#34 overall)

YEAR	TEAM	LVL	AGE	PA	R	2B	3B	HR	RBI	BB	K	SB	CS	AVG/OBP/SLG	TAv	VORP	BABIP	BRR	FRAA	WARP
2015	TGR	RK	21	26	5	2	1	1	2	3	5	2	1	.364/.462/.682	.401	5.1	.438	0.4	LF(6): 0.6	0.6
2015	ONE	A-	21	59	7	2	2	2	11	5	18	0	0	.245/.322/.490	.315	4.0	.313	-0.6	LF(13): -0.3	0.4
2015	WMI	A	21	216	29	9	4	7	31	18	45	3	2	.286/.375/.492	.316	15.9	.338	-0.5	LF(39): -5.9	1.1
2016	LAK	A+	22	442	60	22	1	24	68	74	105	3	1	.264/.403/.534	.323	32.4	.306	-6.6	LF(94): -15.2	1.8
2016	ERI	AA	22	100	17	2	0	6	19	12	26	0	0	.218/.310/.448	.275	4.1	.232	0.7	LF(22): 0.9	0.5
2017	ERI	AA	23	555	67	29	3	28	86	56	138	3	0	.256/.335/.501	.297	31.1	.294	-0.8	LF(120): -10.4	2.2
2018	*DET*	*MLB*	*24*	*250*	*32*	*11*	*1*	*13*	*39*	*26*	*73*	*0*	*0*	*.237/.326/.475*	*.261*	*8.5*	*.288*	*-0.3*	*LF -5*	*0.4*
2019	*DET*	*MLB*	*25*	*369*	*54*	*17*	*2*	*20*	*57*	*40*	*108*	*0*	*0*	*.241/.333/.487*	*.265*	*10.5*	*.295*	*-0.6*	*LF -7*	*0.4*

Breakout: 6% Improve: 24% Collapse: 15% Attrition: 23% MLB: 50% *Comparables: Daniel Dorn, Jerry Sands, Kyle Parker*

Superman is incapacitated by kryptonite, Daredevil can't handle unexpected noise pollution, Thor can't be separated from Mjolnir for more than 60 seconds and the Flash faces certain death whenever he runs too fast. Every superhero is foiled by something, from the terrifying to the mundane, and for home-run connoisseur and on-base wizard Christin Stewart, that weakness materialized in the outfield. While his burgeoning power at the plate obscured his defensive shortcomings in Double-A, he'll need to round out his skill set to become the hero Motor City needs.

PITCHERS

Tyler Alexander LHP Born: 07/14/94 Age: 23 Bats: R Throws: L Height: 6'2" Weight: 200 Origin: Round 2, 2015 Draft (#65 overall)

YEAR	TEAM	LVL	AGE	W	L	SV	G	GS	IP	H	HR	BB/9	K/9	K	GB%	BABIP	WHIP	ERA	DRA	WARP	MPH	CMD	PWR	STM
2015	ONE	A-	20	0	2	0	12	12	37	17	3	1.2	8.0	33	67%	.151	0.59	0.97	2.25	1.3				
2016	LAK	A+	21	6	7	0	19	18	102	87	7	1.4	7.2	82	57%	.268	1.01	2.21	1.69	4.4				
2016	ERI	AA	21	2	1	0	6	6	34^{1}	36	4	1.0	6.0	23	49%	.302	1.17	3.15	2.88	0.9				
2017	ERI	AA	22	8	9	0	27	26	138^{1}	178	20	1.5	7.8	120	41%	.356	1.45	5.07	3.65	2.5				
2018	*DET*	*MLB*	*23*	*6*	*9*	*0*	*24*	*24*	*115*	*142*	*24*	*3.0*	*7.4*	*95*	*46%*	*.327*	*1.57*	*5.54*	*5.58*	*0.1*				
2019	*DET*	*MLB*	*24*	*6*	*9*	*0*	*22*	*22*	*131^{2}*	*156*	*30*	*2.7*	*7.2*	*106*	*46%*	*.312*	*1.49*	*5.85*	*5.95*	*-0.4*				

Breakout: 8% Improve: 13% Collapse: 9% Attrition: 20% MLB: 25% *Comparables: Edwin Escobar, Sean Gilmartin, A.J. Cole*

What Alexander lacks in raw power, he compensates for with exceptional control of a four-pitch repertoire. Poor command hurt him last year, as Eastern League hitters routinely pounced on his 50-grade stuff and he plummeted to a career-worst home-run rate. While he doesn't have the wow factor a big-league team covets in a pitching prospect, his ability to stay healthy and post consistent numbers while shouldering a full workload should keep him on track for another promotion.

Sandy Baez RHP Born: 11/25/93 Age: 24 Bats: R Throws: R Height: 6'2" Weight: 180 Origin: International Free Agent, 2011

YEAR	TEAM	LVL	AGE	W	L	SV	G	GS	IP	H	HR	BB/9	K/9	K	GB%	BABIP	WHIP	ERA	DRA	WARP	MPH	CMD	PWR	STM
2015	ONE	A-	21	3	4	0	14	14	65^{1}	73	4	3.0	7.2	52	41%	.343	1.45	4.13	4.81	0.4				
2016	WMI	A	22	7	9	0	21	21	113^{1}	125	7	2.2	7.0	88	40%	.337	1.35	3.81	5.79	-1.1				
2017	LAK	A+	23	6	7	0	17	17	88^{2}	88	7	2.4	9.3	92	39%	.328	1.26	3.86	3.89	1.4				
2017	ERI	AA	23	0	1	0	2	2	10	9	3	4.5	11.7	13	36%	.273	1.40	4.50	3.61	0.2				
2018	*DET*	*MLB*	*24*	*4*	*6*	*0*	*16*	*16*	80^{2}	*99*	*18*	*3.7*	*8.2*	*74*	*35%*	*.336*	*1.65*	*5.80*	*5.85*	*-0.1*				
2019	*DET*	*MLB*	*25*	*6*	*9*	*0*	*24*	*24*	138^{2}	*164*	*31*	*3.6*	*8.4*	*130*	*35%*	*.326*	*1.58*	*5.87*	*5.97*	*-0.4*				

Breakout: 10% Improve: 15% Collapse: 3% Attrition: 14% MLB: 20% *Comparables: Jerad Eickhoff, Jeff Ferrell, Angel Sanchez*

We're still shaking the Magic-8 Ball to predict Baez's big-league future, and the die just shifted from "outlook good" to "reply hazy try again." It's not that Baez doesn't have the arm strength or the stuff to carve up the strike zone—just ask the High-A hitters who shook hands with his triple-digit four-seamer—but rather that he lacks the consistent command and plus secondary pitches to support it. While he understandably didn't get a September call-up in 2017, his end-of-year promotion to Double-A suggests that he's still showing enough potential to advance toward that elusive rotation spot.

Matt Boyd LHP Born: 02/02/91 Age: 27 Bats: L Throws: L Height: 6'3" Weight: 215 Origin: Round 6, 2013 Draft (#175 overall)

YEAR	TEAM	LVL	AGE	W	L	SV	G	GS	IP	H	HR	BB/9	K/9	K	GB%	BABIP	WHIP	ERA	DRA	WARP	MPH	CMD	PWR	STM
2015	NHP	AA	24	6	1	0	12	12	73^{2}	39	3	2.2	8.6	70	24%	.199	0.77	1.10	2.27	2.5				
2015	TOR	MLB	24	0	2	0	2	2	6^{2}	15	5	1.4	9.4	7	43%	.435	2.40	14.85	8.36	-0.3	94.8	46	39	68
2015	BUF	AAA	24	3	1	0	6	6	39	32	5	1.4	8.5	37	41%	.260	0.97	2.77	3.06	1.0				
2015	DET	MLB	24	1	4	0	11	10	50^{2}	56	12	3.4	6.4	36	32%	.297	1.48	6.57	7.44	-1.4	94.6	46	39	68
2016	TOL	AAA	25	2	5	0	11	11	64	53	5	2.5	8.0	57	42%	.271	1.11	2.25	2.50	2.1				
2016	DET	MLB	25	6	5	0	20	18	97^{1}	97	17	2.7	7.6	82	39%	.286	1.29	4.53	5.84	-0.6	94.3	50	43	70
2017	TOL	AAA	26	3	3	0	8	8	51	35	7	2.3	9.4	53	39%	.224	0.94	2.82	2.83	1.6				
2017	DET	MLB	26	6	11	0	26	25	135	157	18	3.5	7.3	110	40%	.330	1.56	5.27	5.50	0.1	94.3	38	39	79
2018	*DET*	*MLB*	*27*	*7*	*9*	*0*	*24*	*24*	*127*	*130*	*21*	*3.2*	*7.8*	*111*	*39%*	*.295*	*1.39*	*4.64*	*4.74*	*1.0*	*93.9*	*43*	*41*	*74*
2019	*DET*	*MLB*	*28*	*8*	*11*	*0*	*29*	*29*	*179*	*185*	*28*	*3.8*	*7.7*	*154*	*39%*	*.296*	*1.46*	*5.21*	*5.27*	*0.7*	*93.6*	*43*	*41*	*75*

Breakout: 31% Improve: 59% Collapse: 13% Attrition: 16% MLB: 89% *Comparables: Juan Nicasio, Anthony Reyes, John Maine*

"Always leave them wanting more" seems like a fitting mantra for Boyd, whose late-season resurgence finally left him looking the part of a bona fide no. 3 starter. The Tigers got the best stuff out of him in September, when he pulled his WARP out of the red and tossed his first shutout with a streamlined delivery, lower release point and drastic reduction in fastball usage. He's still at his most efficient when leading with his signature changeup, and might even be on the cusp of finding true consistency once he learns to control the ball better and limit free passes. There's no doubt Boyd's limited success will set him up for an encore performance in 2018, but whether he emerges from spring training as a solid mid-rotation contributor or a crafty bullpen piece remains to be seen.

Beau Burrows RHP Born: 09/18/96 Age: 21 Bats: R Throws: R Height: 6'2" Weight: 200 Origin: Round 1, 2015 Draft (#22 overall)

YEAR	TEAM	LVL	AGE	W	L	SV	G	GS	IP	H	HR	BB/9	K/9	K	GB%	BABIP	WHIP	ERA	DRA	WARP	MPH	CMD	PWR	STM
2015	TGR	RK	18	1	0	0	10	9	28	18	0	3.5	10.6	33	42%	.277	1.04	1.61	3.00	0.9				
2016	WMI	A	19	6	4	0	21	20	97	87	2	2.8	6.2	67	42%	.283	1.21	3.15	6.06	-1.3				
2017	LAK	A+	20	4	3	0	11	11	58^{2}	45	3	1.7	9.5	62	45%	.298	0.95	1.23	2.32	2.0				
2017	ERI	AA	20	6	4	0	15	15	76^{1}	79	5	3.9	8.8	75	40%	.339	1.47	4.72	6.13	-0.9				
2018	*DET*	*MLB*	*21*	*1*	*1*	*0*	*3*	*3*	*15*	*15*	*3*	*4.0*	*9.0*	*16*	*37%*	*.296*	*1.48*	*4.72*	*4.83*	*0.1*				
2019	*DET*	*MLB*	*22*	*8*	*11*	*0*	*29*	*29*	*177*	*178*	*35*	*4.1*	*9.6*	*188*	*37%*	*.304*	*1.46*	*5.42*	*5.51*	*0.2*				

Breakout: 5% Improve: 8% Collapse: 1% Attrition: 5% MLB: 9% *Comparables: Jose Berrios, Michael Pineda, John Lamb*

There are certain things in which you may presume a man named Beau Burrows to excel: pouring a perfectly balanced herbal infusion at afternoon tea, the unironic use of the phrase "by Jove," penning a series of quaint children's books, demonstrating the proper form of *bartitsu*. There are other things in which you may presume a young pitcher, also by the name of Beau Burrows, does not excel: pairing a 95-mph heater with an equally developed changeup and slider, controlling his pitches, missing bats. For every shortcoming, however, the upside is that much brighter. A sparkling sub-3.00 DRA and improved walk and strikeout rates propelled him to Double-A in his age-20 season, where he continued to showcase his stuff and dodged bats with his first no-hit attempt. While he may not have a future in children's literature or the complex art of Victorian street-fighting, Burrows could hit his ceiling as a mid-rotation starter.

Alex Faedo RHP Born: 11/12/95 Age: 22 Bats: R Throws: R Height: 6'5" Weight: 225 Origin: Round 1, 2017 Draft (#18 overall)

Faedo was drafted by the Tigers in the 40th round out of high school, but headed to the University of Florida rather than signing. The decision worked out pretty well, as he starred for the Gators and then was picked again by Detroit last June, this time 18th overall. Faedo offers the promise of three plus pitches, led by an excellent slider, but his velocity has varied along with some health issues (namely arthroscopic surgery on both knees in September 2016). He should move quickly through the Tigers' system and has rotation-leading potential.

Buck Farmer RHP Born: 02/20/91 Age: 27 Bats: L Throws: R Height: 6'4" Weight: 225 Origin: Round 5, 2013 Draft (#156 overall)

YEAR	TEAM	LVL	AGE	W	L	SV	G	GS	IP	H	HR	BB/9	K/9	K	GB%	BABIP	WHIP	ERA	DRA	WARP	MPH	CMD	PWR	STM
2015	TOL	AAA	24	7	3	0	16	16	86^2	85	6	2.6	7.9	76	44%	.306	1.27	4.15	2.56	2.7				
2015	DET	MLB	24	0	4	0	14	5	40^1	53	10	3.8	5.4	24	48%	.326	1.74	7.36	6.84	-0.9	95.2	44	50	56
2016	TOL	AAA	25	5	6	0	20	20	100	106	11	2.5	8.4	93	47%	.326	1.34	3.96	2.74	3.0				
2016	DET	MLB	25	0	1	0	14	1	29^1	25	4	6.1	8.3	27	52%	.266	1.53	4.60	3.51	0.5	95.5	65	53	60
2017	TOL	AAA	26	6	4	0	21	21	123^2	133	9	2.3	8.3	114	43%	.343	1.33	3.93	3.50	2.9				
2017	DET	MLB	26	5	5	0	11	11	48	55	9	3.8	9.2	49	34%	.336	1.56	6.75	5.85	-0.1	93.9	58	46	73
2018	*DET*	*MLB*	*27*	*3*	*5*	*0*	*25*	*10*	*69*	*76*	*12*	*3.4*	*7.6*	*59*	*43%*	*.306*	*1.51*	*4.96*	*4.98*	*0.3*	*94.1*	*57*	*49*	*65*
2019	*DET*	*MLB*	*28*	*7*	*8*	*0*	*52*	*19*	*149*	*156*	*25*	*3.3*	*8.4*	*138*	*43%*	*.309*	*1.42*	*5.02*	*5.09*	*0.7*	*93.7*	*60*	*49*	*67*

Breakout: 36% Improve: 58% Collapse: 7% Attrition: 20% MLB: 69% *Comparables: Brandon Workman, Chase Anderson, Tyler Lyons*

In a game of constant, incremental adjustments, major-league hitters are finding it far easier to adapt to Farmer's pitch repertoire than he is to their bats. That's not a promising trend for an aging no. 5 starter who's out of minor-league options. His flashes of brilliance—a 13 2/3-inning scoreless streak, sharper secondary pitches, a pleasing strikeout-to-walk ratio—were just that, and he couldn't hang onto his rotation spot long enough to shed the "swingman" label.

Jeff Ferrell RHP Born: 11/23/90 Age: 27 Bats: R Throws: R Height: 6'4" Weight: 205 Origin: Round 26, 2010 Draft (#793 overall)

YEAR	TEAM	LVL	AGE	W	L	SV	G	GS	IP	H	HR	BB/9	K/9	K	GB%	BABIP	WHIP	ERA	DRA	WARP	MPH	CMD	PWR	STM
2015	ERI	AA	24	0	0	12	17	1	27	21	4	1.3	11.7	35	32%	.279	0.93	1.67	1.42	1.1				
2015	TOL	AAA	24	0	1	4	11	0	11^1	8	3	4.0	7.9	10	36%	.179	1.15	4.76	4.13	0.1				
2015	DET	MLB	24	0	0	0	9	0	11^1	12	3	3.2	4.8	6	40%	.243	1.41	6.35	6.47	-0.2	95.3			33
2017	TOL	AAA	26	2	1	2	41	0	46^2	39	1	2.7	9.8	51	48%	.304	1.14	2.51	2.69	1.3				
2017	DET	MLB	26	0	0	0	11	0	9^1	17	2	4.8	5.8	6	34%	.417	2.36	6.75	6.85	-0.2	95.6			50
2018	*DET*	*MLB*	*27*	*2*	*2*	*0*	*24*	*5*	*45^1*	*49*	*7*	*3.7*	*9.1*	*46*	*38%*	*.327*	*1.49*	*4.56*	*4.56*	*0.5*	*95.0*			*44*
2019	*DET*	*MLB*	*28*	*6*	*5*	*0*	*59*	*12*	*122*	*124*	*20*	*3.7*	*9.5*	*129*	*38%*	*.313*	*1.43*	*4.82*	*4.88*	*0.7*	*94.5*			*47*

Breakout: 22% Improve: 31% Collapse: 13% Attrition: 18% MLB: 48% *Comparables: Mike Burns, Daniel McCutchen, Seth Lugo*

No fun-sized statistical sample should be trusted point-blank, but it sure seemed like Ferrell was onto something good after posting compelling numbers in consecutive Double-A and Triple-A gigs last summer. His dynamic fastball/changeup pairing and sub-3.00 ERAs earned him another look in Detroit's bullpen, but he only lasted a month in the majors before a Ryon Healy comebacker brought his callback to its untimely end. Given his limited playing time and history of shoulder injuries, he'll still need to clear a few hurdles to be seen as anything but expendable pitching depth.

Mike Fiers RHP Born: 06/15/85 Age: 32 Bats: R Throws: R Height: 6'2" Weight: 200 Origin: Round 22, 2009 Draft (#676 overall)

YEAR	TEAM	LVL	AGE	W	L	SV	G	GS	IP	H	HR	BB/9	K/9	K	GB%	BABIP	WHIP	ERA	DRA	WARP	MPH	CMD	PWR	STM
2015	MIL	MLB	30	5	9	0	21	21	118	117	14	3.3	9.2	121	41%	.316	1.36	3.89	4.73	0.5	91.8	43	33	74
2015	HOU	MLB	30	2	1	0	10	9	62^1	45	10	3.0	8.5	59	39%	.217	1.06	3.32	3.85	0.9	92.2	43	33	74
2016	HOU	MLB	31	11	8	0	31	30	168^2	187	26	2.2	7.2	134	44%	.313	1.36	4.48	5.48	-0.2	91.9	42	30	72
2017	HOU	MLB	32	8	10	0	29	28	153^1	157	32	3.6	8.6	146	43%	.300	1.43	5.22	5.32	0.4	91.4	55	28	71
2018	*DET*	*MLB*	*33*	*7*	*9*	*0*	*24*	*24*	*127*	*136*	*23*	*3.4*	*7.6*	*108*	*43%*	*.298*	*1.45*	*4.97*	*5.10*	*0.4*	*90.7*	*47*	*30*	*71*
2019	*DET*	*MLB*	*34*	*8*	*11*	*0*	*29*	*29*	*180^2*	*188*	*31*	*3.3*	*7.8*	*157*	*43%*	*.296*	*1.40*	*5.21*	*5.29*	*0.6*	*90.2*	*48*	*29*	*70*

Breakout: 15% Improve: 43% Collapse: 22% Attrition: 16% MLB: 84% *Comparables: Aaron Harang, J.A. Happ, Claudio Vargas*

In 2014, Fiers ended Giancarlo Stanton's season with a fastball that shattered the slugger's face. Despite his obvious distress at the injury, later in the game he was back working inside and plunked Reed Johnson when another fastball went awry. Three years later, in the midst of his weakest season, Fiers fired a fastball up and in at former teammate Luis Valbuena in retaliation for a bat flip, and was suspended five games as a result. More than most pitchers, Fiers knew what damage an errant fastball could do, and yet he delivered one out of frustration anyway. Perhaps it's because hitters like Valbuena have started launching dingers at Stantonesque rates, and increased homer allowance has shifted Fiers from mid-rotation starter to the type of guy who gets left off a World Series roster.

Michael Fulmer RHP Born: 03/15/93 Age: 25 Bats: R Throws: R Height: 6'3" Weight: 210 Origin: Round 1, 2011 Draft (#44 overall)

YEAR	TEAM	LVL	AGE	W	L	SV	G	GS	IP	H	HR	BB/9	K/9	K	GB%	BABIP	WHIP	ERA	DRA	WARP	MPH	CMD	PWR	STM
2015	BIN	AA	22	6	2	0	15	15	86	73	3	2.4	8.7	83	52%	.293	1.12	1.88	2.43	2.8				
2015	ERI	AA	22	4	1	0	6	6	31^2	27	4	2.0	9.4	33	48%	.287	1.07	2.84	2.36	1.0				
2016	TOL	AAA	23	1	1	0	3	3	15^1	16	3	2.9	11.7	20	49%	.325	1.37	4.11	2.60	0.5				
2016	DET	MLB	23	11	7	0	26	26	159	136	16	2.4	7.5	132	51%	.268	1.12	3.06	3.53	3.3	97.3	54	56	71
2017	DET	MLB	24	10	12	0	25	25	164^2	150	13	2.2	6.2	114	51%	.273	1.15	3.83	3.56	3.7	97.7	57	66	73
2018	*DET*	*MLB*	*25*	*10*	*11*	*0*	*30*	*30*	*180*	*178*	*20*	*2.9*	*7.3*	*146*	*49%*	*.294*	*1.31*	*4.04*	*4.12*	*2.7*	*97.2*	*57*	*63*	*74*
2019	*DET*	*MLB*	*26*	*11*	*10*	*0*	*31*	*31*	*195*	*188*	*24*	*2.5*	*8.0*	*174*	*49%*	*.296*	*1.25*	*4.19*	*4.22*	*2.9*	*97.0*	*57*	*63*	*74*

Breakout: 23% Improve: 54% Collapse: 20% Attrition: 16% MLB: 94% *Comparables: Sonny Gray, Marcus Stroman, Justin Masterson*

Losing Justin Verlander was bound to sting regardless of timing or circumstance, but make no mistake: Fulmer is no poor man's ace. He improved on a sterling rookie campaign, collecting groundballs with a potent changeup-sinker and a wipeout slider. His DRA was nothing special and his strikeout rate looked fair to middling (given his propensity for inducing soft contact, we'd expect little else), but he more than doubled the value of the Tigers' rotation in the midst of an injury-shortened season. Frequent bouts of finger numbness gave way to ulnar nerve transposition surgery in September, robbing Fulmer of a month of starts as the club played it safe with their no. 1 arm. All signs still point to a long and award-worthy career, however, and one that won't cost the Tigers a pretty penny for years to come.

Shane Greene RHP Born: 11/17/88 Age: 29 Bats: R Throws: R Height: 6'4" Weight: 210 Origin: Round 15, 2009 Draft (#465 overall)

YEAR	TEAM	LVL	AGE	W	L	SV	G	GS	IP	H	HR	BB/9	K/9	K	GB%	BABIP	WHIP	ERA	DRA	WARP	MPH	CMD	PWR	STM
2015	DET	MLB	26	4	8	0	18	16	83^2	103	13	2.9	5.4	50	46%	.325	1.55	6.88	6.60	-1.5	94.2	49	43	60
2015	TOL	AAA	26	1	1	0	7	7	35	37	2	2.8	5.4	21	44%	.304	1.37	3.86	5.65	-0.1				
2016	DET	MLB	27	5	4	2	50	3	60^1	58	3	3.3	8.8	59	48%	.327	1.33	5.82	4.13	0.6	96.2	36	44	46
2017	DET	MLB	28	4	3	9	71	0	67^2	50	6	4.5	9.7	73	49%	.265	1.24	2.66	4.19	0.7	96.4	54	53	51
2018	*DET*	*MLB*	*29*	*2*	*3*	*35*	*51*	*0*	*54*	*53*	*6*	*4.1*	*8.7*	*52*	*46%*	*.307*	*1.44*	*3.87*	*3.98*	*0.7*	*95.0*	*47*	*47*	*52*
2019	*DET*	*MLB*	*30*	*2*	*1*	*31*	*48*	*0*	*51^1*	*49*	*5*	*4.0*	*9.6*	*54*	*46%*	*.314*	*1.39*	*4.07*	*4.11*	*0.6*	*95.1*	*47*	*49*	*50*

Breakout: 30% Improve: 51% Collapse: 19% Attrition: 22% MLB: 88% *Comparables: Brian Duensing, Josh Outman, Mitchell Boggs*

The most maddening things in life are those that thrive without the appearance of logic or reason. We have an insatiable appetite for knowledge; we want to understand why the slow, erratic flight of a knuckleball confounds hitters; we crave an explanation for the career trajectories of players built like Jose Altuve and Bartolo Colon, and marvel at their distinct and undeniable successes. Greene has long confused both analysts and batters with an exceptional strand rate and less-than-exceptional stuff. He graduated from swingman to innings muncher to closer, taking the spot vacated first by Francisco Rodriguez and then by trade chip Justin Wilson. His walk rate has never been optimal and frequently dipped toward career lows, but he continued to generate swings and misses with a solid cutter and fringe-average slider. Greene has the poise needed to handle a high-leverage role and the ERA and strikeout rate needed to look good doing it, but will undoubtedly face stiff competition.

Blaine Hardy LHP Born: 03/14/87 Age: 31 Bats: L Throws: L Height: 6'2" Weight: 215 Origin: Round 22, 2008 Draft (#655 overall)

YEAR	TEAM	LVL	AGE	W	L	SV	G	GS	IP	H	HR	BB/9	K/9	K	GB%	BABIP	WHIP	ERA	DRA	WARP	MPH	CMD	PWR	STM
2015	DET	MLB	28	5	3	0	70	0	61^1	61	2	3.2	8.1	55	42%	.319	1.35	3.08	4.92	-0.2	91.0	49	17	51
2016	TOL	AAA	29	1	0	1	32	0	31^1	20	1	1.4	5.5	19	56%	.213	0.80	1.72	4.51	0.2				
2016	DET	MLB	29	1	0	0	21	0	25^2	25	2	4.2	7.0	20	49%	.295	1.44	3.51	5.64	-0.2	91.1	38	29	43
2017	TOL	AAA	30	7	3	3	34	2	40^2	32	1	1.1	10.0	45	48%	.304	0.91	3.10	1.57	1.7				
2017	DET	MLB	30	1	0	0	35	0	33^1	46	7	3.5	7.6	28	34%	.361	1.77	5.94	8.32	-1.2	91.3	47	24	52
2018	*DET*	*MLB*	*31*	*2*	*3*	*0*	*51*	*0*	*54*	*56*	*8*	*3.5*	*7.4*	*44*	*44%*	*.295*	*1.43*	*4.97*	*4.84*	*0.2*	*90.3*	*45*	*22*	*48*
2019	*DET*	*MLB*	*32*	*2*	*1*	*0*	*39*	*0*	*41^2*	*44*	*8*	*3.6*	*7.4*	*34*	*44%*	*.293*	*1.47*	*5.51*	*5.59*	*-0.2*	*89.8*	*44*	*24*	*48*

Breakout: 25% Improve: 34% Collapse: 19% Attrition: 21% MLB: 66% *Comparables: Evan Meek, Cory Gearrin, Will Harris*

It's not the clothes that make the man: It's time, opportunity and a curveball that just won't quit. All three were in short supply for the second-string lefty Hardy, who razed the International League with a sub-2.00 DRA before bottoming out in the majors. Blame it on poor command of his changeup, a curveball that induced far more swings than misses or the leaguewide spike in home runs, but the Tigers never carved out a permanent role for their soft-tossing middle reliever, and Hardy's monthly trips to Comerica Park were never long enough to yield consistent results.

Joe Jimenez RHP Born: 01/17/95 Age: 23 Bats: R Throws: R Height: 6'3" Weight: 220 Origin: Undrafted Free Agent, 2013

YEAR	TEAM	LVL	AGE	W	L	SV	G	GS	IP	H	HR	BB/9	K/9	K	GB%	BABIP	WHIP	ERA	DRA	WARP	MPH	CMD	PWR	STM
2015	WMI	A	20	5	1	17	40	0	43	23	2	2.3	12.8	61	34%	.239	0.79	1.47	1.08	1.9				
2016	LAK	A+	21	0	0	10	17	0	17^1	5	0	2.6	14.5	28	36%	.179	0.58	0.00	1.06	0.8				
2016	ERI	AA	21	3	2	12	21	0	20^2	12	0	3.5	14.8	34	24%	.316	0.97	2.18	2.30	0.6				
2016	TOL	AAA	21	0	1	8	17	0	15^2	9	1	2.3	9.2	16	38%	.205	0.83	2.30	4.25	0.1				
2017	TOL	AAA	22	1	1	4	26	0	25	19	1	4.3	13.0	36	43%	.340	1.24	1.44	2.06	0.9				
2017	DET	MLB	22	0	2	0	24	0	19	31	4	4.3	8.1	17	37%	.403	2.11	12.32	6.43	-0.3	97.2	42	65	41
2018	*DET*	*MLB*	*23*	*2*	*3*	*0*	*51*	*0*	*54*	*49*	*8*	*4.2*	*10.7*	*64*	*36%*	*.304*	*1.40*	*4.14*	*4.20*	*0.6*	*97.1*	*44*	*67*	*42*
2019	*DET*	*MLB*	*24*	*2*	*1*	*1*	*50*	*0*	*52^2*	*48*	*9*	*3.7*	*11.0*	*65*	*36%*	*.298*	*1.32*	*4.59*	*4.63*	*0.3*	*96.9*	*44*	*68*	*43*

Breakout: 18% Improve: 25% Collapse: 14% Attrition: 22% MLB: 46% *Comparables: Corey Knebel, Eduardo Sanchez, Jon Meloan*

Say it with me now: There's no such thing as a pitching prospect, and there's *really* no such thing as a relief pitching prospect. Jimenez's output didn't align with the elite billing he received at the start of the season, but his location issues and temporary velocity drop are just part and parcel of a premature call-up. His fastball still sits mid-to-upper-90s and his slider generates more whiffs than any other offering thanks to the righty's deceptive three-quarters arm slot. Given time to adjust, he'll fill in nicely as the Tigers' closer once Shane Greene's walk-prone approach catches up with him.

Arcenio Leon RHP Born: 09/22/86 Age: 31 Bats: R Throws: R Height: 6'3" Weight: 222 Origin: International Free Agent, 2005

YEAR	TEAM	LVL	AGE	W	L	SV	G	GS	IP	H	HR	BB/9	K/9	K	GB%	BABIP	WHIP	ERA	DRA	WARP	MPH	CMD	PWR	STM
2015	CHR	AAA	28	1	0	1	9	0	11^1	20	2	6.4	9.5	12	50%	.500	2.47	11.91	6.00	-0.1				
2017	DET	MLB	30	0	0	0	6	0	6^2	7	0	8.1	2.7	2	52%	.304	1.95	12.15	6.79	-0.1	97.4			42
2017	TOL	AAA	30	1	2	10	26	0	22^1	15	2	5.2	8.5	21	52%	.206	1.25	5.24	4.68	0.1				
2018	*DET*	*MLB*	*31*	*1*	*0*	*0*	*30*	*0*	*32*	*36*	*5*	*5.1*	*7.4*	*26*	*47%*	*.314*	*1.70*	*5.66*	*5.71*	*-0.2*	*96.5*			*42*
2019	*DET*	*MLB*	*32*	*1*	*0*	*0*	*28*	*0*	*33^2*	*37*	*6*	*5.3*	*6.9*	*26*	*47%*	*.303*	*1.69*	*6.05*	*6.16*	*-0.3*	*95.7*			*41*

Breakout: 9% Improve: 15% Collapse: 3% Attrition: 10% MLB: 19% *Comparables: Steve Green, Tony Pena, Jon Link*

Leon had the Tigers' feel-good story of the year. The journeyman righty topped off a dozen years in the minors with his long-awaited debut, made possible after retooling an unwieldy fastball during a stint in the Mexican League. He emerged as a legitimate relief option in Detroit, but his heater was undercut by chronic command issues that prematurely capped his run in the bigs. Leon enters his age-31 season with fewer than 10 major-league innings under his belt, and his happy beginning may also have been a bittersweet ending.

Artie Lewicki RHP Born: 04/08/92 Age: 26 Bats: R Throws: R Height: 6'3" Weight: 195 Origin: Round 8, 2014 Draft (#250 overall)

YEAR	TEAM	LVL	AGE	W	L	SV	G	GS	IP	H	HR	BB/9	K/9	K	GB%	BABIP	WHIP	ERA	DRA	WARP	MPH	CMD	PWR	STM
2015	WMI	A	23	3	4	0	15	15	79^{1}	87	4	2.8	8.7	77	41%	.352	1.41	3.52	4.01	1.1				
2016	LAK	A+	24	2	1	0	5	3	21^{2}	21	0	2.5	8.3	20	62%	.323	1.25	3.32	2.75	0.6				
2016	ERI	AA	24	1	7	0	12	12	67^{1}	67	4	1.7	7.6	57	53%	.307	1.19	3.48	3.46	1.3				
2017	ERI	AA	25	9	4	0	20	20	110	107	5	2.0	7.4	90	43%	.302	1.19	3.76	2.74	3.2				
2017	TOL	AAA	25	5	0	0	5	5	31	28	2	2.0	9.6	33	48%	.329	1.13	2.03	2.60	1.0				
2017	DET	MLB	25	0	1	0	4	1	10^{1}	19	1	3.5	5.2	6	40%	.439	2.23	6.10	7.58	-0.3	94.3			66
2018	*DET*	*MLB*	*26*	*2*	*2*	*0*	*6*	*6*	*34*	*38*	*6*	*3.3*	*7.2*	*27*	*43%*	*.300*	*1.53*	*4.99*	*5.12*	*0.1*	*93.9*			*67*
2019	*DET*	*MLB*	*27*	*9*	*11*	*0*	*28*	*28*	*173^{2}*	*199*	*30*	*3.0*	*7.3*	*141*	*43%*	*.315*	*1.48*	*5.26*	*5.33*	*0.6*	*93.5*			*67*

Breakout: 20% Improve: 30% Collapse: 17% Attrition: 38% MLB: 57% *Comparables: Eric Jokisch, Ross Stripling, Cory Luebke*

Maybe Lewicki will be the second coming of Justin Verlander, or maybe he'll just be the guy who got to test drive the front of the rotation for a few ill-fated afternoons in September. Inasmuch as aces are born, not made, the answer already seems clear. Tommy John surgery in 2013 and a fastball that brushes 94 mph on a good day are the mile markers down the path of long relief, though there's still time to reach that mid-rotation ceiling if he reverses course in 2018.

Grayson Long RHP Born: 05/27/94 Age: 24 Bats: R Throws: R Height: 6'5" Weight: 230 Origin: Round 3, 2015 Draft (#104 overall)

YEAR	TEAM	LVL	AGE	W	L	SV	G	GS	IP	H	HR	BB/9	K/9	K	GB%	BABIP	WHIP	ERA	DRA	WARP	MPH	CMD	PWR	STM
2015	ORM	RK	21	0	0	0	13	12	19^{2}	19	1	4.6	10.1	22	57%	.346	1.47	5.03	3.61	0.5				
2016	BUR	A	22	3	3	0	8	8	40	27	2	3.6	10.1	45	40%	.258	1.08	1.58	2.47	1.2				
2016	ANG	RK	22	0	1	0	4	4	11	13	0	4.1	8.2	10	32%	.382	1.64	6.55	4.62	0.1				
2016	INL	A+	22	2	1	0	3	3	14	14	5	2.6	9.6	15	32%	.281	1.29	5.14	4.57	0.1				
2017	INL	A+	23	0	2	0	3	3	12	14	0	3.0	10.5	14	54%	.400	1.50	4.50	4.21	0.1				
2017	MOB	AA	23	8	6	0	23	23	121^{2}	100	7	2.8	8.2	111	34%	.283	1.13	2.52	3.94	1.8				
2018	*DET*	*MLB*	*24*	*5*	*8*	*0*	*23*	*23*	*96*	*109*	*22*	*4.4*	*9.2*	*98*	*36%*	*.321*	*1.62*	*5.89*	*5.95*	*-0.3*				
2019	*DET*	*MLB*	*25*	*5*	*8*	*0*	*22*	*22*	*131*	*143*	*30*	*4.4*	*8.6*	*125*	*36%*	*.302*	*1.58*	*6.22*	*6.33*	*-0.7*				

Breakout: 7% Improve: 20% Collapse: 12% Attrition: 24% MLB: 38% *Comparables: Ben Lively, John Ely, Adam Morgan*

Acquired from the Angels in the late-season Justin Upton trade/contract dump, Long is a nice addition to a Tigers' farm system that simply needed some quality depth. A former third-round pick out of Texas A&M, the big right-hander works with a low-90s fastball. His slider is a good second offering and could allow his overall stuff to play up as a reliever, but for now he'll likely get an opportunity to snag a spot at the back of the rotation.

Matt Manning RHP Born: 01/28/98 Age: 20 Bats: R Throws: R Height: 6'6" Weight: 190 Origin: Round 1, 2016 Draft (#9 overall)

YEAR	TEAM	LVL	AGE	W	L	SV	G	GS	IP	H	HR	BB/9	K/9	K	GB%	BABIP	WHIP	ERA	DRA	WARP	MPH	CMD	PWR	STM
2016	TGW	RK	18	0	2	0	10	10	29^{1}	27	2	2.1	14.1	46	38%	.379	1.16	3.99	1.06	1.5				
2017	ONE	A-	19	2	2	0	9	9	33^{1}	27	0	3.8	9.7	36	31%	.310	1.23	1.89	5.15	0.0				
2017	WMI	A	19	2	0	0	5	5	17^{2}	14	0	5.6	13.2	26	49%	.341	1.42	5.60	3.30	0.4				
2018	*DET*	*MLB*	*20*	*2*	*4*	*0*	*10*	*10*	*37*	*42*	*11*	*5.3*	*10.8*	*45*	*34%*	*.332*	*1.73*	*6.53*	*6.61*	*-0.4*				
2019	*DET*	*MLB*	*21*	*4*	*10*	*0*	*27*	*27*	*158^{2}*	*175*	*42*	*4.8*	*10.0*	*175*	*34%*	*.316*	*1.64*	*6.47*	*6.60*	*-1.0*				

Breakout: 4% Improve: 4% Collapse: 0% Attrition: 1% MLB: 5% *Comparables: Trevor May, Alex Reyes, Jarrod Parker*

Manning scored the Tigers' top slot in the 2016 draft with a double-plus fastball (almost unheard of for someone who spent the majority of his high school career on the basketball court), and while his slight frame, rough mechanics and limited experience were woven into one giant red flag, the Tigers found his upside as a potential no. 2 starter irresistible. Manning hasn't lost his prospect status to injuries or declining velocity, and that's largely because he hasn't pitched very much at all. It takes time to gather experience and it takes experience to showcase consistency and right now, the 20-year-old flamethrower has neither. His electric four-seamer provided the step stool he needed to reach Low-A, but his inability to miss bats with his curveball and changeup highlighted a troubling volatility. Should he continue to smooth out his delivery and tighten up his secondary offerings, Manning still has plenty of time to make good on the promise Detroit saw.

Edward Mujica RHP Born: 05/10/84 Age: 34 Bats: R Throws: R Height: 6'3" Weight: 220 Origin: International Free Agent, 2001

YEAR	TEAM	LVL	AGE	W	L	SV	G	GS	IP	H	HR	BB/9	K/9	K	GB%	BABIP	WHIP	ERA	DRA	WARP	MPH	CMD	PWR	STM
2015	BOS	MLB	31	1	1	0	11	0	13^{2}	15	3	2.0	5.3	8	55%	.293	1.32	4.61	4.97	0.0	92.5	41	38	40
2015	OAK	MLB	31	2	4	1	38	0	33^{2}	37	7	1.1	5.9	22	46%	.286	1.22	4.81	4.89	-0.1	92.9	41	38	40
2016	LEH	AAA	32	0	3	23	36	0	39	42	3	0.9	6.2	27	45%	.298	1.18	3.69	2.87	0.9				
2016	OMA	AAA	32	1	0	2	9	0	12	17	2	1.5	10.5	14	34%	.417	1.58	8.25	2.03	0.4				
2017	DET	MLB	33	0	0	0	5	0	6^{1}	11	4	0.0	9.9	7	30%	.368	1.74	9.95	7.81	-0.2	93.2			50
2017	TOL	AAA	33	1	1	21	56	0	56	51	4	1.4	7.4	46	41%	.280	1.07	2.57	2.70	1.6				
2018	*DET*	*MLB*	*34*	*2*	*1*	*1*	*46*	*0*	*49^{1}*	*60*	*9*	*3.0*	*6.3*	*35*	*42%*	*.317*	*1.55*	*5.41*	*5.45*	*-0.1*	*91.7*	*40*	*37*	*46*
2019	*DET*	*MLB*	*35*	*1*	*0*	*0*	*26*	*0*	*26^{2}*	*32*	*5*	*3.0*	*6.1*	*18*	*42%*	*.309*	*1.53*	*5.71*	*5.79*	*-0.2*	*90.6*	*40*	*37*	*47*

Breakout: 23% Improve: 31% Collapse: 14% Attrition: 10% MLB: 57% *Comparables: Jamie Walker, Blaine Boyer, Joel Peralta*

After pinballing around the minors for most of 2016, Mujica resurfaced with the Tigers when Michael Fulmer took to the disabled list in August. Never intended to be much more than a temporary scapegoat for the worst bullpen in baseball, the veteran righty had trouble missing bats with his splitter and finished his stint with a bloated DRA—his worst mark in 11 years. Mujica tried to compensate for poor command and lack of firepower with outstanding control, refusing to walk a single batter during his six-inning gig in the majors and distributing just nine free passes in nearly 60 innings in Triple-A. While he'd be lucky to snag another full-time position at this stage in his career, his long tenure, past success and low walk rate make him an intriguing option for teams in need of organizational depth.

Daniel Norris LHP Born: 04/25/93 Age: 25 Bats: L Throws: L Height: 6'2" Weight: 195 Origin: Round 2, 2011 Draft (#74 overall)

YEAR	TEAM	LVL	AGE	W	L	SV	G	GS	IP	H	HR	BB/9	K/9	K	GB%	BABIP	WHIP	ERA	DRA	WARP	MPH	CMD	PWR	STM
2015	TOR	MLB	22	1	1	0	5	5	23^{1}	23	3	4.6	6.9	18	32%	.294	1.50	3.86	4.05	0.3	94.6	45	50	63
2015	BUF	AAA	22	3	10	0	16	16	90^{2}	96	5	4.1	7.7	78	46%	.325	1.51	4.27	5.50	-0.2				
2015	DET	MLB	22	2	1	0	8	8	36^{2}	30	6	1.7	6.6	27	47%	.222	1.01	3.68	4.95	0.1	95.6	45	50	63
2016	TOL	AAA	23	5	7	0	14	14	73^{1}	78	2	3.4	9.4	77	57%	.358	1.45	4.54	3.17	1.8				
2016	DET	MLB	23	4	2	0	14	13	69^{1}	75	10	2.9	9.2	71	38%	.327	1.40	3.38	4.79	0.4	96.0	52	55	67
2017	TOL	AAA	24	0	4	0	6	6	14	22	3	10.3	11.6	18	50%	.442	2.71	12.21	7.90	-0.3				
2017	DET	MLB	24	5	8	0	22	18	101^{2}	120	12	3.9	7.6	86	40%	.344	1.61	5.31	6.17	-0.7	94.8	43	50	58
2018	*DET*	*MLB*	*25*	*6*	*9*	*0*	*24*	*24*	*120*	*131*	*18*	*4.0*	*8.0*	*107*	*44%*	*.310*	*1.57*	*4.67*	*4.78*	*0.8*	*94.9*	*47*	*53*	*64*
2019	*DET*	*MLB*	*26*	*8*	*9*	*0*	*27*	*27*	*164*	*176*	*25*	*3.4*	*8.5*	*155*	*44%*	*.315*	*1.45*	*4.77*	*4.82*	*1.3*	*94.7*	*47*	*53*	*64*

Breakout: 41% Improve: 73% Collapse: 12% Attrition: 15% MLB: 95% *Comparables: Jordan Zimmermann, Felix Doubront, Sean Manaea*

You've heard this story before: It's the one about a young, talented starter whose career gets corrupted by chronic injuries. Sometimes he rebounds, develops a new pitch, shifts to the bullpen. Sometimes he fades from the spotlight altogether. Norris is trying desperately to avoid the latter after his 2017 run was shortened by lingering quad and groin injuries, not a full year after he battled through an oblique strain and fractured vertebrae. The loss of strength in his right leg impacted both his delivery and command, feeding into declining walk and strikeout rates as he struggled to stay ahead of hitters with a weakening fastball. When healthy, however, the lefty has been lights-out in the no. 2 spot, and 2018 could be the year he finally begins to subvert an upsetting narrative.

Zac Reininger RHP Born: 01/28/93 Age: 25 Bats: B Throws: R Height: 6'3" Weight: 170 Origin: Round 8, 2013 Draft (#246 overall)

YEAR	TEAM	LVL	AGE	W	L	SV	G	GS	IP	H	HR	BB/9	K/9	K	GB%	BABIP	WHIP	ERA	DRA	WARP	MPH	CMD	PWR	STM
2015	ERI	AA	22	0	2	0	9	0	12^{1}	19	3	5.1	6.6	9	37%	.372	2.11	10.22	5.61	-0.1				
2015	LAK	A+	22	1	0	3	7	0	13^{1}	8	0	3.4	5.4	8	50%	.211	0.98	0.00	4.77	0.0				
2017	LAK	A+	24	1	1	0	17	0	28	22	2	1.9	8.4	26	55%	.270	1.00	3.86	2.60	0.8				
2017	ERI	AA	24	1	1	1	16	0	24^{1}	13	0	3.0	10.7	29	40%	.245	0.86	1.48	2.53	0.7				
2017	TOL	AAA	24	1	0	1	9	0	11^{1}	7	0	3.2	4.0	5	38%	.206	0.97	1.59	5.17	0.0				
2017	DET	MLB	24	0	0	0	10	0	9^{2}	16	3	2.8	4.7	5	41%	.361	1.97	7.45	6.86	-0.2	96.6			47
2018	*DET*	*MLB*	*25*	*1*	*2*	*0*	*36*	*0*	*37*	*42*	*8*	*5.2*	*7.7*	*32*	*40%*	*.299*	*1.68*	*6.21*	*5.96*	*-0.4*	*96.3*			*48*
2019	*DET*	*MLB*	*26*	*1*	*0*	*0*	*27*	*0*	28^{2}	*31*	*6*	*4.8*	*7.8*	*25*	*40%*	*.301*	*1.63*	*6.17*	*6.28*	*-0.3*	*96.0*			*48*

Breakout: 13% Improve: 15% Collapse: 5% Attrition: 12% MLB: 23% *Comparables: Angel Nesbitt, Chad Smith, Osiris Matos*

We don't need to tell you this is Reininger's first rodeo. You can see it in his eyes—wide as those of a 6-year-old who finally met the height requirement for Space Mountain—and his tight-lipped smile. Or maybe he's just thinking back to his first major-league brawl (another rodeo of sorts), when he ducked behind the umpire moments before Gary Sanchez sucker punched Miguel Cabrera. On the mound, however, he carries the presence and pitch selection of an old-timer. His fastball plays up to 98 mph and he complements it with a solid, albeit inconsistent slider. If he can polish his off-speed stuff and keep hittable pitches away from the heart of the strike zone, he might just see a full season of eye-popping brawls and setup opportunities in 2018.

Bruce Rondon RHP Born: 12/09/90 Age: 27 Bats: R Throws: R Height: 6'3" Weight: 275 Origin: International Free Agent, 2007

YEAR	TEAM	LVL	AGE	W	L	SV	G	GS	IP	H	HR	BB/9	K/9	K	GB%	BABIP	WHIP	ERA	DRA	WARP	MPH	CMD	PWR	STM
2015	TOL	AAA	24	2	2	1	13	0	12^{2}	16	1	4.3	9.9	14	44%	.375	1.74	7.11	3.60	0.2				
2015	DET	MLB	24	1	0	5	35	0	31	31	3	5.5	10.5	36	44%	.329	1.61	5.81	3.39	0.5	101.1	36	75	48
2016	TOL	AAA	25	2	2	9	22	0	21^{2}	23	1	6.6	12.5	30	44%	.407	1.80	3.74	4.49	0.1				
2016	DET	MLB	25	5	2	0	37	0	36^{1}	23	5	3.0	11.1	45	34%	.228	0.96	2.97	3.46	0.6	100.8	35	63	45
2017	DET	MLB	26	1	3	1	21	0	15^{2}	21	1	5.7	12.6	22	40%	.476	1.98	10.91	4.23	0.2	99.5	41	65	50
2017	TOL	AAA	26	2	1	1	38	0	36^{2}	34	2	6.1	10.6	43	31%	.330	1.61	2.70	7.49	-0.9				
2018	*DET*	*MLB*	*27*	*2*	*1*	*1*	*44*	*0*	*46*	*48*	*8*	*5.0*	*10.4*	*53*	*39%*	*.327*	*1.59*	*5.00*	*5.02*	*0.1*	*100.1*	*37*	*68*	*48*
2019	*DET*	*MLB*	*28*	*2*	*1*	*1*	*33*	*0*	30^{2}	*32*	*6*	*4.7*	*9.9*	*33*	*39%*	*.314*	*1.57*	*5.52*	*5.61*	*-0.1*	*99.6*	*38*	*66*	*48*

Breakout: 41% Improve: 51% Collapse: 13% Attrition: 26% MLB: 78% *Comparables: Tony Sipp, Shawn Tolleson, David Aardsma*

The probability of spinning a natural Yahtzee on the first try has been roughly estimated around .00077 percent. Most competitors don't just fling the dice once, however; they try gripping the dice with the desired numbers on top, skipping them across a low-friction surface to reduce the spin or bowling them along the side to get the numbers to align just so. The Tigers revealed a similar optimism with Rondon, flinging him and his untamed high-90s heat into improbable late-inning situations over and over again to see if he'd come up precision and control. Even the most amateur gambler could have predicted the outcome: Rondon flamed out in just four months, tumbling back down to Triple-A after posting a 10.00-plus ERA and knocking down Mike Moustakas in an ill-advised midseason brawl. Since the probability of Rondon throwing two consecutive strikes has also been roughly estimated around .00077 percent, it's difficult to imagine any team choosing to roll with him again in 2018.

Kyle Ryan LHP Born: 09/25/91 Age: 26 Bats: L Throws: L Height: 6'5" Weight: 215 Origin: Round 12, 2010 Draft (#373 overall)

YEAR	TEAM	LVL	AGE	W	L	SV	G	GS	IP	H	HR	BB/9	K/9	K	GB%	BABIP	WHIP	ERA	DRA	WARP	MPH	CMD	PWR	STM
2015	TOL	AAA	23	4	9	0	17	17	103	117	3	2.9	5.5	63	61%	.335	1.46	4.19	5.39	-0.1				
2015	DET	MLB	23	2	4	0	16	6	56^{1}	60	9	3.2	4.8	30	49%	.288	1.42	4.47	6.59	-1.1	90.8	55	31	65
2016	DET	MLB	24	4	2	0	56	0	55^{2}	48	2	2.4	5.7	35	57%	.269	1.13	3.07	5.06	-0.1	91.7	33	43	46
2017	DET	MLB	25	0	0	0	8	0	5^{2}	9	0	11.1	1.6	1	52%	.429	2.82	7.94	4.69	0.0	92.1			49
2017	TOL	AAA	25	3	1	0	48	0	45^{1}	55	5	5.4	7.7	39	54%	.365	1.81	4.96	6.22	-0.5				
2018	*DET*	*MLB*	*26*	*3*	*2*	*0*	*20*	*5*	46^{2}	*51*	*6*	*4.3*	*6.8*	*35*	*51%*	*.316*	*1.58*	*5.00*	*5.03*	*0.3*	*91.0*	*44*	*38*	*53*
2019	*DET*	*MLB*	*27*	*7*	*7*	*0*	*55*	*15*	130^{1}	*140*	*18*	*4.2*	*6.7*	*97*	*51%*	*.306*	*1.55*	*5.35*	*5.44*	*0.1*	*90.9*	*38*	*41*	*50*

Breakout: 25% Improve: 46% Collapse: 18% Attrition: 29% MLB: 77% *Comparables: Andrew Chafin, Drew VerHagen, Carlos Frias*

Unless you happen to be a 10-year-old prodigy tasked with decimating alien colonies from a remote asteroid, it's fair to say that no simulation ever fully prepares you for reality. Even so, every spring some benchwarmer turns in a .400 average and someone gets their hopes up that this year will be different. That illusion faded all too quickly for the Tigers, who kept Ryan on a short leash after it became evident that his abnormally low walk rate and careful pitch location would not be following him out of the Grapefruit League. He spent the rest of the year kicking around Triple-A in middle relief, but never looked dominant enough to unseat such bullpen luminaries as Blaine Hardy and Daniel Stumpf. Expect Ryan to pop up somewhere in camp this spring, if only as a depth piece, but don't be surprised if his shiny preseason stats fizzle out on another big-league stage.

Anibal Sanchez RHP Born: 02/27/84 Age: 34 Bats: R Throws: R Height: 6'0" Weight: 205 Origin: International Free Agent, 2001

YEAR	TEAM	LVL	AGE	W	L	SV	G	GS	IP	H	HR	BB/9	K/9	K	GB%	BABIP	WHIP	ERA	DRA	WARP	MPH	CMD	PWR	STM
2015	DET	MLB	31	10	10	0	25	25	157	152	29	2.8	7.9	138	41%	.278	1.28	4.99	4.02	2.0	94.5	55	44	72
2016	DET	MLB	32	7	13	0	35	26	153^{1}	171	30	3.1	7.9	135	41%	.317	1.46	5.87	6.29	-1.7	93.8	45	45	69
2017	TOL	AAA	33	0	2	0	4	4	15^{2}	17	3	2.9	11.5	20	46%	.350	1.40	4.60	2.39	0.6				
2017	DET	MLB	33	3	7	0	28	17	105^{1}	139	26	2.5	8.9	104	36%	.354	1.59	6.41	6.53	-1.2	92.6	52	35	59
2018	*DET*	*MLB*	*34*	*6*	*8*	*0*	*20*	*20*	*111^{1}*	*133*	*23*	*3.3*	*7.9*	*98*	*40%*	*.323*	*1.56*	*5.51*	*5.55*	*0.2*	*92.5*	*49*	*41*	*65*
2019	*DET*	*MLB*	*35*	*8*	*10*	*0*	*26*	*26*	*150^{2}*	*172*	*31*	*3.1*	*7.7*	*129*	*40%*	*.31*	*1.48*	*5.53*	*5.62*	*0.1*	*91.7*	*48*	*40*	*63*

Breakout: 14% Improve: 37% Collapse: 21% Attrition: 6% MLB: 91% *Comparables: Josh Beckett, James Shields, A.J. Burnett*

There are always those people who take particular pride in the glory of their high school days. They revel in the basketball games and yearbook committees, the glitzy prom nights and underfunded drama productions. No matter how many years tick by, they remain spellbound by nostalgia and past success, especially when the present is a more dark and foreboding place. Sanchez may not yearn for halcyon days spent at U.E. Colegio San Pedro Alejandro, but there's a certain kind of wistfulness one assumes while looking back at his peak years in Detroit. These days, though, he's looking less and less like his old self. His fastball velocity began dipping into the low-90s and he didn't create enough separation with his off-speed pitches to consistently fool hitters. His ongoing struggles won't be the Tigers' burden to bear next spring, but like old high school chums, they'll still share some fond memories together.

Warwick Saupold RHP Born: 01/16/90 Age: 28 Bats: R Throws: R Height: 6'1" Weight: 195 Origin: International Free Agent, 2012

YEAR	TEAM	LVL	AGE	W	L	SV	G	GS	IP	H	HR	BB/9	K/9	K	GB%	BABIP	WHIP	ERA	DRA	WARP	MPH	CMD	PWR	STM
2015	ERI	AA	25	5	6	1	23	15	103^{1}	102	5	3.1	6.2	71	48%	.302	1.34	4.01	5.43	-0.5				
2015	TOL	AAA	25	1	2	0	6	3	20^{1}	14	1	2.7	10.2	23	40%	.283	0.98	4.43	2.89	0.5				
2016	DET	MLB	26	1	1	0	6	0	9^{2}	17	0	2.8	9.3	10	54%	.486	2.07	7.45	4.93	0.0	94.7			45
2016	TOL	AAA	26	7	2	0	18	11	74^{1}	64	3	2.7	6.1	50	55%	.277	1.16	2.30	5.14	0.1				
2017	TOL	AAA	27	2	0	0	7	7	40^{1}	38	2	3.8	7.4	33	48%	.308	1.36	2.90	4.73	0.4				
2017	DET	MLB	27	3	2	0	45	0	62^{2}	64	9	4.5	6.3	44	44%	.289	1.52	4.88	6.28	-0.8	94.3	45	46	58
2018	*DET*	*MLB*	*28*	*2*	*3*	*0*	*51*	*0*	*54*	*54*	*7*	*4.0*	*7.1*	*43*	*47%*	*.295*	*1.45*	*4.86*	*4.75*	*0.2*	*93.8*	*45*	*46*	*53*
2019	*DET*	*MLB*	*29*	*2*	*1*	*0*	*43*	*0*	*46*	*47*	*6*	*3.8*	*7.4*	*38*	*47%*	*.298*	*1.44*	*4.92*	*5.00*	*0.1*	*93.4*	*45*	*46*	*52*

Breakout: 15% Improve: 29% Collapse: 10% Attrition: 19% MLB: 43% *Comparables: Ben Hendrickson, Luis Mendoza, Graham Godfrey*

Nothing about Saupold suggests he has the stuff to miss major-league bats. His repertoire skews fringe-average, his command tends to glitch up in the zone and his peripherals took a nosedive in the second half due to overuse. Still, there's something about him that hitters just can't put their finger (or their lumber, at least before the break) on, and if his workload gets scaled back in 2018 he might yet pose a legitimate threat in long relief.

Daniel Stumpf LHP Born: 01/04/91 Age: 27 Bats: L Throws: L Height: 6'2" Weight: 200 Origin: Round 9, 2012 Draft (#283 overall)

YEAR	TEAM	LVL	AGE	W	L	SV	G	GS	IP	H	HR	BB/9	K/9	K	GB%	BABIP	WHIP	ERA	DRA	WARP	MPH	CMD	PWR	STM
2015	NWA	AA	24	5	4	3	42	1	70^{2}	55	6	3.9	9.7	76	57%	.271	1.22	3.57	2.79	1.7				
2016	PHI	MLB	25	0	0	0	7	0	5	9	1	3.6	3.6	2	38%	.400	2.20	10.80	8.27	-0.2	95.1			23
2016	NWA	AA	25	2	0	1	14	0	21^{1}	14	0	1.7	11.0	26	55%	.264	0.84	2.11	2.23	0.6				
2017	TOL	AAA	26	1	2	0	24	0	21^{1}	19	3	2.1	11.0	26	47%	.320	1.12	3.38	2.57	0.6				
2017	DET	MLB	26	0	1	0	55	0	37^{2}	37	5	3.6	7.9	33	43%	.305	1.38	3.82	6.45	-0.5	95.2	43	52	51
2018	*DET*	*MLB*	*27*	*3*	*3*	*0*	*56*	*0*	*59*	*57*	*9*	*3.8*	*9.1*	*60*	*47%*	*.302*	*1.41*	*4.61*	*4.56*	*0.4*	*94.7*	*44*	*53*	*39*
2019	*DET*	*MLB*	*28*	*2*	*1*	*0*	*44*	*0*	*47*	*45*	*8*	*3.9*	*9.4*	*49*	*47%*	*.299*	*1.39*	*4.88*	*4.95*	*0.1*	*94.3*	*43*	*53*	*39*

Breakout: 23% Improve: 42% Collapse: 12% Attrition: 35% MLB: 65% *Comparables: Carlos Fisher, David Rollins, Michael Mariot*

Although Stumpf may have clowned around as Rudolph during the Tigers' annual rookie dress-up day, he was hardly a guiding light for the bullpen. The fact that he's a cheap lefty with decent stuff and a shiny ERA only serves to illuminate the dilapidated state of the Tigers' pitching staff. As a two-time Rule 5 pick, he's also beaten the odds.

Alex Wilson RHP Born: 11/03/86 Age: 31 Bats: R Throws: R Height: 6'0" Weight: 215 Origin: Round 2, 2009 Draft (#77 overall)

YEAR	TEAM	LVL	AGE	W	L	SV	G	GS	IP	H	HR	BB/9	K/9	K	GB%	BABIP	WHIP	ERA	DRA	WARP	MPH	CMD	PWR	STM
2015	DET	MLB	28	3	3	2	59	1	70	61	5	1.4	4.9	38	53%	.258	1.03	2.19	4.36	0.3	94.5	47	48	51
2016	DET	MLB	29	4	0	0	62	0	73	68	5	2.6	6.0	49	45%	.285	1.22	2.96	4.25	0.6	93.9	50	48	51
2017	DET	MLB	30	2	5	2	66	0	60	67	7	2.2	6.3	42	42%	.311	1.37	4.50	5.20	0.0	94.0	68	51	49
2018	*DET*	*MLB*	*31*	*2*	*3*	*0*	*51*	*0*	*54*	*61*	*8*	*3.5*	*5.8*	*35*	*45%*	*.299*	*1.51*	*5.32*	*5.09*	*0.0*	*93.2*	*56*	*49*	*50*
2019	*DET*	*MLB*	*32*	*2*	*1*	*1*	*38*	*0*	*40^{1}*	*45*	*6*	*3.4*	*5.8*	*26*	*45%*	*.297*	*1.49*	*5.47*	*5.55*	*-0.1*	*92.7*	*58*	*49*	*49*

Breakout: 29% Improve: 46% Collapse: 21% Attrition: 16% MLB: 81% *Comparables: Brandon Kintzler, Burke Badenhop, Ryan Webb*

Miley Cyrus may relish the climb more than the view from the top of whatever metaphorical mountain she's facing, but the same couldn't be said for Wilson, whose relentless uphill battles spanned the personal (skin cancer on the bridge of his nose; a fibula that fractured on Joe Mauer's 103.8-mph comebacker) and professional (a miraculously hittable cutter; a four-game suspension for beaning Todd Frazier; a career-worst DRA coupled with a striking loss of command). There's little to suggest that Wilson won't be able to return in the spring as durable and versatile as ever, but if there's any certainty in life, it's that there will always be another mountain to move.

Jordan Zimmermann RHP Born: 05/23/86 Age: 32 Bats: R Throws: R Height: 6'2" Weight: 225 Origin: Round 2, 2007 Draft (#67 overall)

YEAR	TEAM	LVL	AGE	W	L	SV	G	GS	IP	H	HR	BB/9	K/9	K	GB%	BABIP	WHIP	ERA	DRA	WARP	MPH	CMD	PWR	STM
2015	WAS	MLB	29	13	10	0	33	33	201^{2}	204	24	1.7	7.3	164	44%	.302	1.20	3.66	4.37	1.7	95.2	57	53	77
2016	TOL	AAA	30	0	1	0	5	5	20^{1}	19	2	1.8	4.9	11	46%	.270	1.13	1.33	4.38	0.2				
2016	DET	MLB	30	9	7	0	19	18	105^{1}	118	14	2.2	5.6	66	44%	.304	1.37	4.87	5.14	0.3	94.3	54	46	50
2017	DET	MLB	31	8	13	0	29	29	160	204	29	2.5	5.8	103	35%	.330	1.55	6.07	6.32	-1.3	93.5	49	44	70
2018	*DET*	*MLB*	*32*	*10*	*13*	*0*	*30*	*30*	*189*	*220*	*36*	*2.8*	*6.0*	*126*	*41%*	*.302*	*1.48*	*5.23*	*5.37*	*0.1*	*93.3*	*52*	*47*	*64*
2019	*DET*	*MLB*	*33*	*9*	*12*	*0*	*28*	*28*	*172^{2}*	*207*	*33*	*2.5*	*5.5*	*106*	*41%*	*.305*	*1.48*	*5.69*	*5.78*	*-0.2*	*92.5*	*50*	*45*	*62*

Breakout: 7% Improve: 39% Collapse: 26% Attrition: 10% MLB: 85% *Comparables: Bronson Arroyo, Shaun Marcum, Freddy Garcia*

If you listen carefully, you can hear the clanking of chains—or, more accurately, the $74 million rattling around Zimmermann's ankles as he shuffles through the last three years of his contract. The veteran righty was a ghost-like presence in the Tigers' rotation, spooking batters with a reworked slider one day and vanishing fastball velocity the next. In the end, he was done in by chronic neck pain and the worst ERA by a starting pitcher (minimum 29 starts) in franchise history, and finished his season the same way he began it: unproductive and overpaid. He barely resembles the two-time All-Star who so often pitched so well for the Nationals.

Lineouts

Hitters

HITTER	POS	TEAM	LVL	AGE	PA	R	2B	3B	HR	RBI	BB	K	SB	CS	AVG/OBP/SLG	TAv	VORP	BABIP	BRR	FRAA	WARP
Jim Adduci	LF	DET	MLB	32	93	14	6	2	1	10	10	27	1	1	.241/.323/.398	.253	0.1	.345	-0.9	RF(26): 1.1	0.1
	LF	TOL	AAA	32	239	32	13	1	4	27	20	59	10	3	.288/.343/.414	.267	10.0	.372	2.8	RF(24): -0.8, LF(15): -1.2	0.8
Sergio Alcantara	INF	VIS	A+	20	378	44	15	2	3	28	34	57	11	10	.279/.344/.362	.271	19.3	.327	-0.2	SS(85): 4.0	2.5
	INF	LAK	A+	20	143	18	4	1	0	7	14	23	4	3	.230/.307/.278	.236	1.2	.282	-1.0	SS(35): 0.1	0.1
Jose Azocar	OF	LAK	A+	21	456	38	10	6	3	37	14	122	12	6	.220/.246/.292	.201	-14.8	.297	0.9	CF(81): -5.2, RF(38): 0.1	-2.1
Mike Gerber	RF	ERI	AA	24	394	62	22	2	13	45	39	85	10	6	.291/.363/.477	.297	27.4	.349	1.2	CF(83): -6.7	2.2
Niko Goodrum	UT	ROC	AAA	25	499	71	25	5	13	66	30	119	11	7	.265/.309/.425	.258	16.6	.326	4.4	RF(47): 3.3, 2B(37): -4.2	1.4
	UT	MIN	MLB	25	18	1	0	0	0	0	1	10	0	0	.059/.111/.059	.075	-2.9	.143	0.2	2B(8): -0.4, RF(1): 0.0	-0.3
Grayson Greiner	C	ERI	AA	24	371	34	20	1	14	42	38	72	0	0	.241/.323/.436	.264	13.8	.266	-3.0	C(90): 21.5	3.8
John Hicks	C	TOL	AAA	27	218	21	10	1	7	35	4	54	5	3	.269/.281/.428	.251	5.4	.325	-0.5	C(37): 2.7, 1B(11): -0.8	0.6
	C	DET	MLB	27	190	25	12	0	6	22	13	51	2	1	.266/.326/.439	.250	1.1	.342	-1.0	1B(26): -0.4, C(18): 0.4	0.1
Bryan Holaday	C	TOL	AAA	29	347	31	20	0	12	50	22	54	0	3	.269/.325/.450	.272	18.1	.286	-3.2	C(90): 0.0, 3B(3): 0.0	1.8
	C	DET	MLB	29	29	1	2	0	0	2	0	1	0	0	.241/.241/.310	.161	-1.2	.250	0.5	C(11): -2.6, 2B(1): 0.0	-0.4
Efren Navarro	1B	TOL	AAA	31	558	61	23	2	10	61	71	101	2	3	.276/.370/.395	.273	15.9	.328	1.7	1B(105): 2.6, LF(5): -1.0	1.7
	1B	DET	MLB	31	69	9	1	1	2	2	8	21	0	1	.230/.319/.377	.235	-0.5	.316	0.6	1B(20): 0.8	0.0
Derek Norris	C	TBA	MLB	28	198	21	5	0	9	24	12	48	1	0	.201/.258/.380	.230	2.4	.214	-0.7	C(53): -3.9	-0.1
Isaac Paredes	INF	SBN	A	18	384	49	25	0	7	49	29	54	2	1	.264/.343/.401	.272	17.4	.294	-1.0	SS(70): -2.7, 3B(7): 2.5	1.8
	INF	WMI	A	18	133	16	3	0	4	21	13	13	0	0	.217/.323/.348	.229	0.1	.214	-0.5	SS(22): -2.4, 3B(5): 1.4	0.0
Victor Reyes	OF	WTN	AA	22	516	59	29	5	4	51	27	80	18	9	.292/.332/.399	.258	10.5	.342	0.1	RF(83): 5.0, CF(57): 10.9	2.8
Reynaldo Rivera	OF	ONE	A-	20	207	16	9	1	2	26	18	55	3	1	.187/.261/.280	.224	-7.7	.246	-2.8	RF(30): -4.5, 1B(12): -1.4	-1.4
Jake Rogers	C	QUD	A	22	116	17	7	1	6	15	9	28	1	0	.255/.336/.520	.306	10.2	.290	0.3	C(21): 0.8	1.2
	C	BCA	A+	22	367	43	18	3	12	55	44	72	13	8	.265/.357/.457	.306	29.9	.302	-0.8	C(24): 2.6	3.4
Brendan Ryan	SS	TOL	AAA	35	408	46	20	0	4	28	45	74	5	7	.236/.323/.326	.243	11.8	.286	1.6	SS(112): 0.5, P(1): 0.0	1.2
Jarrod Saltalamacchia	C	TOR	MLB	32	26	1	0	0	0	0	1	16	0	0	.040/.077/.040	.059	-5.3	.111	-1.0	C(7): -1.5	-0.7
	C	BUF	AAA	32	129	8	6	0	1	5	17	51	0	0	.162/.271/.243	.210	-5.9	.283	-0.4	C(3): -0.1	-0.6
A.J. Simcox	SS	ERI	AA	23	474	55	22	5	8	36	27	72	12	5	.250/.293/.378	.246	10.6	.281	-1.5	SS(121): 1.9, 2B(1): 0.0	1.4

Jim Adduci looked lost at the plate more times than Matt Damon has gotten sidetracked in deep space. He got back to the majors for the first time since 2014, but a return looks even less likely. ⚾ If **Sergio Alcantara** can hit .200 in the majors, his defense, baserunning and plate discipline would be enough to make him a useful player. The fact that we have to include that provision tells you just about everything you need to know. ⚾ It's not that **Jose Azocar** lacks a hit tool, it's that he treated it with all the finesse and self-restraint of a child unwrapping a Red Ryder Carbine Action 200-Shot Range Model BB gun on Christmas morning; until he learns to temper an aggressive approach, he's bound to shoot his eye out sooner or later. ⚾ **Mike Gerber** is still as well-rounded as they come, with the above-average speed, arm and defensive versatility needed to enhance a major-league outfield if given a chance. ⚾ Speedy switch-hitter **Niko Goodrum** was in "The Show" for 28 days last year, hitting white balls for batting practice and toting a glove for every position, but his career .712 OPS in the minors is light even for a steady utility man. ⚾ Yes, **Grayson Greiner** is actually a good catching prospect and not a character on a CW show. ⚾ And the award for Best Supporting Actor in a Limited Series goes to **John Hicks**, who parlayed a gruesome hit-by-pitch off of James McCann's left hand into a compelling 60-game stint in the majors. Perhaps next year he can go out for the leading role. ⚾ "We'll see" is the cruelest way of saying something is never going to happen. For **Bryan Holaday**, it might be time to admit that all those "maybes" and "not just yets" he's been hearing from the Tigers are covering for a harsher reality. **Efren Navarro** harnessed his first major-league gig since 2014, but had the misfortune of landing on a team with Miguel Cabrera ensconced at first base. He's a solid hitter, but lacks the power to make a real impact. The less said about **Derek Norris**, the better. There's an argument to be made that he should have been finished in affiliated baseball, but Al Avila and the Tigers disagreed. **Isaac Paredes** spent last season holding his own at Low-A as one of the youngest players in the league, but with a move away from shortstop looking likely his bat will have to develop more than expected to make a long-term impact. **Victor Reyes** is a natural line-drive hitter who lacks power and needs to mature into some plate discipline. The Tigers nabbed him with the first pick in the Rule 5 draft and hope he can mature quickly enough to help plug the gaping hole in their outfield. **Reynaldo Rivera** is no Shohei Ohtani, to be sure, and his potential at the plate has garnered more interest than his status as a two-way prospect. His first foray into pro ball exposed raw mechanics and a middling defensive profile. **Jake Rogers** has a good defensive tool set behind the plate and some pop, but the former third-round draft pick projects as a backup unless his hit tool improves. Don't let him entice you with whispers of Fielding Bible Awards and whiz-bang double play highlights from 2011. There are better, less fringy fish in the utility man sea than a 36-year-old **Brendan Ryan**. Channeling his inner Chumbawamba, **Jarrod Saltalamacchia** was quite the one-hit wonder in 2017. Despite recording just a single base knock, he impressively amassed more strikeouts (16) than letters in his record-long last name (14). He might not get up again. When you need a smooth soprano saxophone to soften the antiseptic atmosphere of a hospital waiting room, you play Kenny G. When you need a guy with plus defense up the middle and a bat that tops out around .250, you play **A.J. Simcox**. Thankfully, you rarely need either of those things.

Pitchers

PITCHER	TEAM	LVL	AGE	W	L	SV	G	GS	IP	H	HR	BB/9	K/9	K	GB%	BABIP	WHIP	ERA	DRA	WARP	MPH	CMD	PWR	STM
Victor Alcantara	ERI	AA	24	1	2	1	30	2	54^{2}	46	1	5.6	9.4	57	60%	.312	1.46	3.46	4.91	-0.1				
	TOL	AAA	24	0	1	0	9	1	20	22	0	5.4	7.2	16	54%	.338	1.70	4.05	6.16	-0.2				
	DET	MLB	24	0	0	0	6	0	7^{1}	12	1	4.9	6.1	5	54%	.407	2.18	8.59	4.86	0.0	94.6			49
Chad Bell	TOL	AAA	28	2	4	0	7	7	34^{1}	34	3	2.6	8.1	31	40%	.323	1.28	3.41	4.19	0.6				
	DET	MLB	28	0	3	0	28	4	62^{1}	81	12	4.5	8.2	57	47%	.363	1.80	6.93	8.03	-1.9	94.6	39	50	51
Enrique Burgos	RNO	AAA	26	1	1	1	11	0	13	15	2	7.6	9.0	13	45%	.342	2.00	6.23	8.01	-0.4				
	GWN	AAA	26	0	1	2	24	0	22^{1}	13	1	6.0	10.5	26	40%	.235	1.25	5.24	5.36	0.0				
Ryan Carpenter	ABQ	AAA	26	10	9	0	27	25	156	161	19	2.2	9.3	161	45%	.332	1.28	4.15	2.39	5.6				
Kyle Funkhouser	WMI	A	23	4	1	0	7	7	31^{1}	30	3	3.7	14.1	49	56%	.403	1.37	3.16	2.11	1.2				
	LAK	A+	23	1	1	0	5	5	31^{1}	23	1	1.7	9.8	34	57%	.275	0.93	1.72	1.35	1.4				
Bryan Garcia	WMI	A	22	1	2	9	14	0	14^{1}	12	0	2.5	17.0	27	36%	.429	1.12	3.14	1.86	0.5				
	ERI	AA	22	1	1	8	17	0	18^{2}	7	1	3.9	11.6	24	35%	.167	0.80	0.96	3.56	0.3				
	TOL	AAA	22	1	0	0	14	0	13^{1}	10	1	5.4	8.1	12	40%	.265	1.35	4.05	6.52	-0.2				
Eduardo Jimenez	WMI	A	22	1	1	6	21	0	34^{1}	21	0	2.6	11.5	44	53%	.269	0.90	1.05	2.21	1.1				
	LAK	A+	22	0	1	6	13	0	16^{1}	21	2	2.8	8.8	16	35%	.365	1.59	4.41	5.43	-0.1				
Logan Kensing	TOL	AAA	34	3	3	0	66	0	74^{1}	71	3	3.0	6.9	57	56%	.311	1.29	2.54	4.12	0.9				
Jairo Labourt	LAK	A+	23	0	0	0	8	0	13^{2}	8	0	2.0	14.5	22	62%	.308	0.80	0.66	1.21	0.6				
	ERI	AA	23	1	1	4	21	0	30^{2}	23	3	2.1	10.6	36	47%	.278	0.98	2.64	2.41	0.9				
	TOL	AAA	23	0	0	0	16	0	22	12	1	9.4	8.6	21	48%	.200	1.59	2.45	6.67	-0.3				
	DET	MLB	23	0	0	0	6	0	6	4	0	10.5	6.0	4	41%	.235	1.83	4.50	3.29	0.1	95.8			49
Gerson Moreno	LAK	A+	21	1	0	8	21	0	22^{1}	19	1	3.2	12.1	30	44%	.333	1.21	2.01	2.57	0.6				
	ERI	AA	21	0	3	0	20	0	28	23	4	5.5	11.6	36	54%	.284	1.43	6.43	4.67	0.0				
Franklin Perez	BCA	A+	19	4	2	2	12	10	54^{1}	38	4	2.7	8.8	53	38%	.236	0.99	2.98	3.73	0.9				
	CCH	AA	19	2	1	1	7	6	32	33	2	3.1	7.0	25	35%	.316	1.38	3.09	6.67	-0.6				
Adam Ravenelle	ERI	AA	24	0	5	1	42	0	52^{1}	59	8	3.6	8.4	49	50%	.342	1.53	5.16	4.78	0.0				
Austin Sodders	WMI	A	22	7	0	0	11	11	64^{1}	49	2	1.8	9.1	65	44%	.290	0.96	1.40	3.47	1.4				
	LAK	A+	22	4	5	0	12	12	74^{2}	55	0	2.0	6.9	57	38%	.252	0.96	2.17	3.99	1.1				
Gregory Soto	WMI	A	22	10	1	0	18	18	96	70	3	5.1	10.9	116	45%	.295	1.29	2.25	4.48	0.9				
	LAK	A+	22	2	1	0	5	5	28	27	1	3.5	9.0	28	56%	.351	1.36	2.25	3.44	0.6				
Spencer Turnbull	LAK	A+	24	7	3	0	15	15	82^{2}	68	3	2.7	7.0	64	52%	.280	1.12	3.05	3.41	1.8				
	ERI	AA	24	0	3	0	4	4	20^{1}	22	1	3.5	9.7	22	58%	.356	1.48	6.20	3.59	0.4				
Drew VerHagen	TOL	AAA	26	7	7	0	19	19	97^{1}	108	7	4.0	6.4	69	46%	.329	1.55	4.90	5.86	-0.2				
	DET	MLB	26	0	3	0	24	2	34^{1}	42	10	2.4	6.6	25	51%	.317	1.49	5.77	6.00	-0.3	95.5	42	50	63

Raw power alone does not a reliever make. **Victor Alcantara** brought the heat but none of the command or control required to temper it, and finished the season more of a liability than a genuine threat. A lefty with a mid-90s fastball and chronic control issues, **Chad Bell** finally made his big-league debut after a seven-year circuit in the minors. The other hard-throwing righty the Braves purchased from the Diamondbacks, **Enrique Burgos** started his Braves career with 11 straight scoreless appearances. The next 13, uh, were enough to strand him in Gwinnett and send him straight to free agency after the season. Look, when it comes down to it, the 2018 Detroit Tigers are going to give up five runs a game, and minor-league free agent **Ryan Carpenter** is as qualified to distribute them as anyone else. An elbow strain clouded the second half of **Kyle Funkhouser**'s sophomore campaign, in which he looked every bit the mid-rotation starter with an upper-90s fastball. His big-league ETA may be delayed, but he isn't ready to give up the funk just yet. Bryan Garcia tunneled through the Tigers' system with all the delicacy of a bull in a Chihuly museum, logging 55 innings across four separate levels. **Eduardo Jimenez** showed improved control in 2017, but tried to put it to use in the worst possible way—he threw a ball at an opposing pitcher during a brawl in Dayton, earning himself a 30-game suspension. **Logan Kensing** is like that seasonal IPA your hipster buddy can't stop raving about: You've probably never heard of him, but he's good in limited quantities. After taming an erratic delivery and transitioning to the bullpen, **Jairo Labourt** transformed into the fantasy reliever every manager dreams of—in High-A, that is. Elsewhere, he struggled to fool hitters with a plus fastball/slider combo, and his appalling lack of control spelled trouble. **Gerson Moreno** has an undeniable future in flame-throwing, but he'll need to locate his pitches and sharpen his slider before he starts firing triple-digit bullets through major-league strike zones. Part of the package of Astros prospects headed to Detroit in the Justin Verlander deal, **Franklin Perez** has a plus fastball with promising off-speed stuff, giving him a chance to develop into more than a mid-rotation starter. **Adam Ravenelle** continued to enchant scouts with a high-90s fastball and plus slider, but chronic command issues and an inability to fool lefties undercut his chances of jumping to Triple-A. **Austin Sodders** understands what Yogi Berra put best: Ninety percent of this game is half mental. He spent a year honing the big-league mentality needed to weather both slumps and streaks, and complemented a still-developing arsenal with pinpoint command and a superb stat line. Much like the premature explosion of an aerial firework shell, **Gregory Soto**'s fastball only lights up batters when he knows how to control it. A cluster of shoulder and elbow issues lengthened **Spencer Turnbull**'s path to the majors, but the flame-throwing righty got somewhat back on track with a tweaked delivery, refined control and a midseason promotion to Double-A. **Drew VerHagen** flexed his swingman capabilities when a bout of ulnar neuritis decommissioned Michael Fulmer in August, but even a brand-new slider wasn't enough to keep him in the rotation full time.

HOUSTON ASTROS

Essay by Meg Rowley

Player comments by Bryan Grosnick and BP staff

It's quite a hard trick to win at least 101 games, and harder still to win a World Series. Since 1901, only 31 teams have done both in the same season. It's a damned difficult business. Teams like that generally inspire a lot of "How?" questions. Teams like the 2017 Houston Astros, predicated as they are on a Process, engage us with the "How?" all along the way. The "How?" matters a lot: for the Astros looking to repeat, for other teams looking to copy their success, for fans looking to watch the game smarter. The "How?" matters. The "How?" is people and math and bad labor practices. But we shouldn't underestimate how much the "How?" depends, when pressed, on being able to stop at a yellow light. I'll explain.

At Johns Hopkins University, there is a group of researchers who examine the human brain's stop system. Measuring the brainwaves of 21 human subjects (and one monkey), the researchers asked their subjects to home in on a point on a screen. After a time, another target appeared on the boundary of the screen. Sometimes, the researchers allowed their subjects to glance at the new target, but occasionally the subjects received a visual cue to keep their gaze fixed on their original point of focus. Part of their brain was already preparing the series of neural signals required to shift their gaze, even as another recognized that the researchers were asking them to pump the brakes, to change plans midstream. It is, as it turns out, an incredibly complex process. Multiple parts of the brain have to work together in tenths of seconds, and sometimes the cue just arrived too late for the signals to be overridden; the subjects failed. They looked where they shouldn't have.

It's an experience with which we're all familiar. As one of the study's architects put it in a December 2017 interview on National Public Radio, it's like when you're driving toward an intersection and find the light turning yellow. You decide to accelerate to catch the light—perhaps you're late delivering your quarterly projections. Your brain starts to do the work of accelerating, and it's only then that you see the cop car. A different part of your brain rapidly processes that accelerating will mean a ticket. You want to tap your brakes instead. You know you shouldn't hit the gas. But you do it anyway, feeling sort of queasy. Your brain has betrayed you; the signal has already been sent. You run the light. You look at the part of the screen you shouldn't look at. The stop system is faulty. Baseball's neuropathways can work in a similar fashion, if on a slower schedule. Front offices are forever laying out plans, a process—*the* Process. Sometimes, things go wrong; teams have to react to stimulus. Long contracts sour prematurely; prospects develop too slowly, or not at all. Arms blow out. There's bad batted ball luck; there's a cop at the intersection. Presented with bumps in the road, and having already set a plan in motion, the team can't adapt in time; the stop system fails. Windows of contention close, and general managers go in search of new work. Every World Series

ASTROS PROSPECTUS

2017 W-L: 101-61, 1st in AL West

Pythag	.617	4th
RS/G	5.53	1st
RA/G	4.32	9th
TAv	.280	1st
TAv-P	.248	6th
FIP	3.88	6th
DER	.699	18th

B-Age	28.8	*22nd*
P-Age	28.5	*17th*
Salary	$124.3M	*17th*
M$/MW	$2.1M	*26th*
DL Days	855	*12th*
$ on DL	10%	*7th*

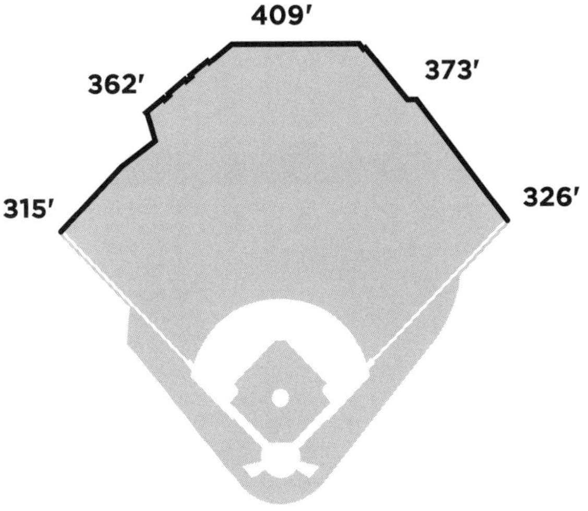

Outfield wall profile: **5′** to **25′**

Three-Year Park Factors

Runs	Runs/RH	Runs/LH	HR/RH	HR/LH
95	93	97	102	103

Top Hitter WARP	6.4 Jose Altuve
Top Pitcher WARP	4.7 Dallas Keuchel
Top Prospect	Forrest Whitley

2017 Hit List Ranking

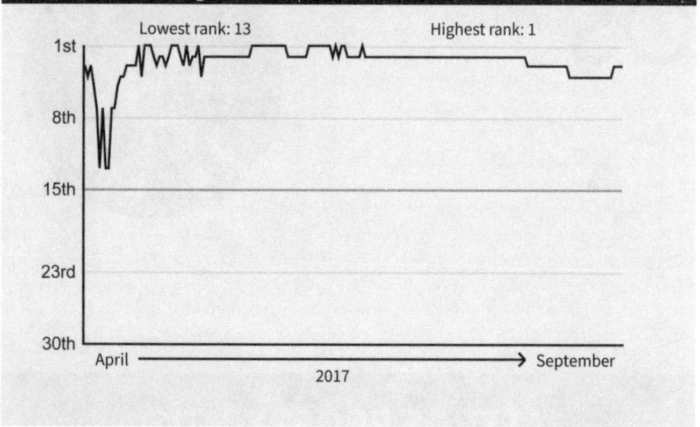

Committed Payroll (in millions)

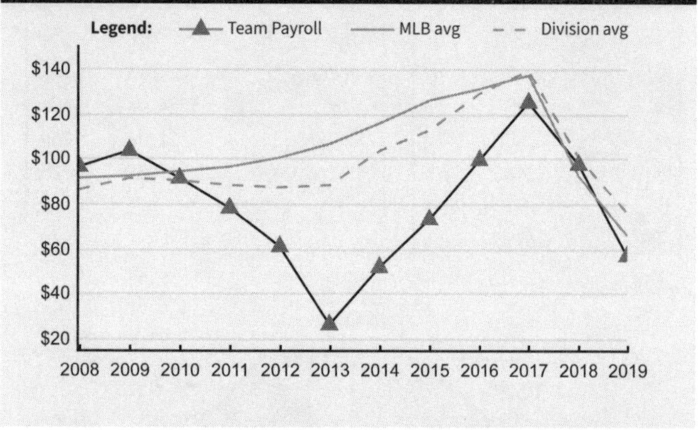

Farm System Ranking

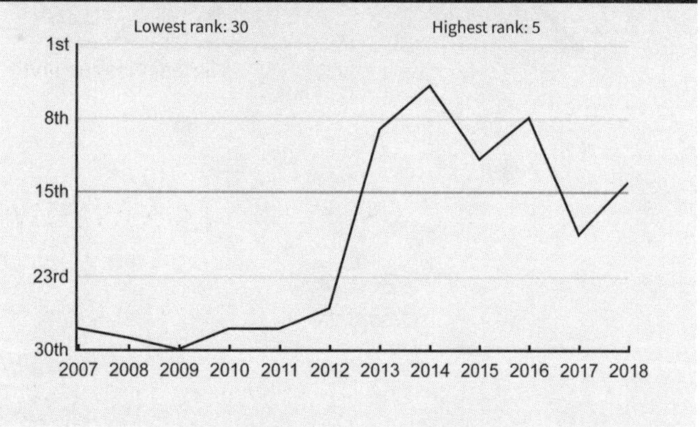

Personnel

General Manager
Jeff Luhnow

AGM, Scouting & Player Development
Mike Elias

Special Assistant, Process Improvement
Sig Mejdal

Director, International
Oz Ocampo

Manager
A.J. Hinch

BP Alumni
Mike Fast
Kevin Goldstein
Ronit Shah
Colin Wyers

is a miracle, set in motion by drafts and births and decisions to play baseball instead of do other things, all smashing up against the drafts and births and decisions to play baseball that other people have made. Even very good, very smart franchises, with talent and treasure, lose; the Dodgers didn't throw a parade in November. To understand Houston's victory is then an exercise in defining where the plan worked, but also in seeing where its failure was acceptable, absorbable. It's seeing how the stop system succeeded, how the Process bobbed and weaved and got a little squirrely. Diverging from their Protestant brethren, Catholics believe that man isn't saved by faith alone: He must also be saved by good works. The Astros didn't win by mere Process alone: They were saved by good works along the way. They were saved by quick thinking at yellow lights.

It's hard to think of a team that wins 101 games as ever being uncomfortable. Teams that win 101 games breathe easy. They luxuriate in calm. They strut. They don't worry about the police car waiting for them to blow through a yellow; they have green lights all the way.

In the first half, the Astros won 60 games. They scored 162 more runs than their opponents. Jose Altuve had 116 hits, just part of an eventual MVP case. Brad Peacock and Charlie Morton turned in improbably good performances. Among American League staffs, their starters trailed only the Indians and Red Sox in FIP. In between bits of fuss and notion in the batter's box, Marwin Gonzalez was playing his way past his loftiest projections. George Springer was thumping. Carlos Correa dazzled. Going into the All-Star break, the Astros led the American League West by 16 1/2 games; they had 10 games on the next-best American League team. Like a plucky band of rebels in some space drama, the rest of the league could only look on tensely as they realized that the Process had arrived. The juggernaut was here.

At some point, a team that wins 101 games stops worrying about the particulars of the regular season and turns its attention to October. One has to get from 60 to 101 wins, of course, but very good teams find their way to that. The stakes of any given game shift to the big contest and home-field advantage; injuries are measured less in terms of players' return to regular action, and more in terms of their postseason availability. At some point, 101-win teams don't fret that they had an off day. Except when they do.

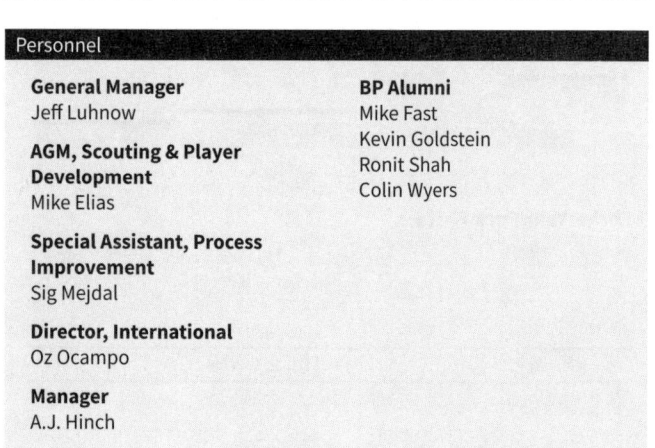

On June 5, Dallas Keuchel went on the disabled list; when he was activated on July 28, he didn't look his usual dominant self. The staff flagged. Correa went out on July 18 with a torn ligament in his thumb; Gonzalez and Alex Bregman filled in ably but they weren't *Carlos Correa*. The Astros went 11-17 in August. They approached a yellow light. No tanking team executes a perfect rebuild, however good their process. As days ticked by on the 2017 calendar, others registered in the rearview: June 6, 2013, the day the Astros drafted Mark Appel over Kris Bryant. March 22, 2014, the day the Astros released J.D. Martinez. October 14, 2015, the day the Royals defeated the Astros 7-2 in the ALDS. September 28, 2016, the day the Astros were eliminated from postseason contention. We never know which days on the baseball calendar will matter until we do. But with the benefit of hindsight, we know that August 31, 2017, was a day that mattered. That was the day the Astros sent prospects Daz Cameron, Franklin Perez and Jake Rogers to the Tigers for Justin Verlander. Verlander wasn't part of the plan. He isn't cheap, homegrown talent. He isn't young. But he was what the Astros needed, and the true triumph of the process wasn't just in drafting and developing well, or in deploying analytics. It was in the stop system. It was in the ability to adapt. It was in not becoming trapped in previous detours, in previous bad dates. It was in seeing the peril of too many scrambles through stoplights, but also in knowing when perhaps it makes sense to just say screw it, and risk a dash. ***

At some point, every 101-win team resets. They have to go get a new first win. The Astros' first win of the postseason came against the Red Sox. Verlander beat Chris Sale, in Houston. Their fourth win came with Keuchel on the mound; the Yankees lost 2-1. Their seventh win was a Charlie Morton start; Lance McCullers got the save. McCullers would start their first World Series win against the Dodgers; Morton would stand on the mound for the final out of the World Series, a Corey Seager groundout to Altuve.

They'll start this year in need of their first win, but carrying with them a few characters they didn't expect to meet—or see do nearly so well—and a shiny trophy. All because, among other things, Charlie Morton got Corey Seager to ground out. Adaptation is good, and process is perhaps better, but sometimes things just work out better than you thought they would. To be a 101-win team and win a World Series, they almost have to. ***

The cruel thing about being a team as good as the 2017 Astros is that now everyone has expectations. The "How?" has to ride again; no one is content with one World Series title, even though they ought to be. One World Series title, just *one*, is amazing. But we want more. We want to take this baby out and see what she can do when we open her up on the road. We expect she's gonna purr. We expect to see the Astros back in the fall classic. They've had a process and shown an ability to pump the breaks when they see the light turning yellow, or take a side street no one knows, and to have the good luck to avoid a few jam-ups on the freeway that sunk lesser franchises. They've been saved by their good works; they positioned themselves for salvation by a process, a payoff of faith in a thing yet seen.The Astros have shown they can adapt, and they'll have to. Otherwise it's just early exits and traffic tickets from here on out.

—Meg Rowley is an author of Baseball Prospectus.

Hitters

Jose Altuve 2B Born: 05/06/90 Age: 28 Bats: R Throws: R Height: 5'6" Weight: 165 Origin: International Free Agent, 2007

YEAR	TEAM	LVL	AGE	PA	R	2B	3B	HR	RBI	BB	K	SB	CS	AVG/OBP/SLG	TAv	VORP	BABIP	BRR	FRAA	WARP
2015	HOU	MLB	25	689	86	40	4	15	66	33	67	38	13	.313/.353/.459	.285	32.6	.329	-2.0	2B(153): -2.8	3.2
2016	HOU	MLB	26	717	108	42	5	24	96	60	70	30	10	.338/.396/.531	.321	66.3	.347	3.2	2B(148): -7.2, SS(1): 0.0	6.1
2017	HOU	MLB	27	662	112	39	4	24	81	58	84	32	6	.346/.410/.547	.322	64.0	.370	2.7	2B(149): -0.1	6.4
2018	*HOU*	*MLB*	*28*	*665*	*89*	*39*	*3*	*15*	*79*	*43*	*69*	*32*	*8*	*.315/.364/.463*	*.288*	*47.8*	*.333*	*2.9*	*2B -6*	*3.8*
2019	*HOU*	*MLB*	*29*	*594*	*78*	*34*	*2*	*16*	*75*	*43*	*64*	*27*	*8*	*.313/.369/.474*	*.286*	*37.0*	*.329*	*1.7*	*2B -5*	*3.4*

Breakout: 0% Improve: 48% Collapse: 3% Attrition: 1% MLB: 99% *Comparables: Dustin Pedroia, Bill Madlock, Roberto Alomar*

The baseball Internet is at its best when it's equal parts weird and celebratory; one of the finest examples of this is HowManyAltuves.com, a site that calculates distance based on the height of the Astros' diminutive second baseman. Long known for his stature and his energy, Altuve surged to a professional apex last season. The numbers are, in a word, astronomical; his .346 batting average is a throwback to the years when the batting title was synonymous with the most talented players in the game, and the power production from such a compact package still amazes every time he squares up a ball and sends it flying. No other player in the game does exactly what Altuve does; he is likely the best contact hitter in the sport, an on-base force, powerful and one of the game's top baserunners. And after years of toiling through the tough times in Houston, clawing up from not-even-a-prospect status, he's reached new heights as the American League MVP and a World Series champion. You can use Altuves to measure distance, but in baseball the answer to "How many Altuves?" is this: *just one*.

Yordan Alvarez OF Born: 06/27/97 Age: 21 Bats: L Throws: L Height: 6'5" Weight: 225 Origin: International Free Agent, 2016

YEAR	TEAM	LVL	AGE	PA	R	2B	3B	HR	RBI	BB	K	SB	CS	AVG/OBP/SLG	TAv	VORP	BABIP	BRR	FRAA	WARP
2016	DAR	RK	19	57	7	2	1	1	4	12	7	2	1	.341/.474/.500	.376	8.1	.378	0.1	1B(4): -0.2	0.8
2017	QUD	A	20	139	26	6	0	9	33	23	36	2	0	.360/.468/.658	.383	18.2	.449	-1.6	LF(13): -1.5, 1B(7): 0.0	1.8
2017	BCA	A+	20	252	19	11	3	3	36	19	41	6	1	.277/.329/.393	.273	7.0	.316	-0.2	1B(9): -0.4, LF(6): 2.6	1.0
2018	*HOU*	*MLB*	*21*	*250*	*28*	*10*	*1*	*9*	*32*	*21*	*64*	*1*	*0*	*.242/.310/.417*	*.246*	*3.0*	*.295*	*-0.2*	*LF -2, 1B 0*	*0.1*
2019	*HOU*	*MLB*	*22*	*338*	*44*	*15*	*1*	*13*	*44*	*31*	*83*	*2*	*0*	*.251/.325/.435*	*.260*	*6.1*	*.303*	*-0.3*	*LF -3, 1B 0*	*0.3*

Breakout: 5% Improve: 15% Collapse: 3% Attrition: 14% MLB: 29% *Comparables: Jesse Winker, Andrew Lambo, Fernando Martinez*

To start the 2017 season, Alvarez did as much damage in the Quad Cities as the 1980s farm crisis. With an OPS over 1.100 in 32 games, the burly youngster was moved up to tougher competition in Buies Creek at midseason. It only takes a cursory look at his size and his batting practice displays to see the potential for top-tier power production. He turns 21 in June, so there's plenty of room to grow his raw power into game power, and if he can resist growing out of an outfield corner, he could be a rare high-impact corner outfielder. If not, he'll have to hope his bat can carry him out of the swampy ground of first-base-only sluggers.

Carlos Beltran DH Born: 04/24/77 Age: 41 Bats: B Throws: R Height: 6'1" Weight: 215 Origin: Round 2, 1995 Draft (#49 overall)

YEAR	TEAM	LVL	AGE	PA	R	2B	3B	HR	RBI	BB	K	SB	CS	AVG/OBP/SLG	TAv	VORP	BABIP	BRR	FRAA	WARP
2015	NYA	MLB	38	531	57	34	1	19	67	45	85	0	0	.276/.337/.471	.280	18.9	.297	-0.4	RF(123): -15.4	0.4
2016	NYA	MLB	39	387	50	21	0	22	64	22	70	0	0	.304/.344/.546	.293	16.3	.321	-2.6	RF(60): -1.7	1.5
2016	TEX	MLB	39	206	23	12	0	7	29	13	31	1	0	.280/.325/.451	.252	-1.2	.303	-2.0	RF(9): -0.5	-0.2
2017	HOU	MLB	40	509	60	29	0	14	51	33	102	0	0	.231/.283/.383	.233	-8.9	.263	-0.6	LF(13): -0.7, RF(1): -0.1	-1.0
2018	*HOU*	*MLB*	*41*	*495*	*53*	*26*	*1*	*17*	*63*	*35*	*96*	*1*	*0*	*.250/.304/.420*	*.242*	*2.6*	*.280*	*-1.4*	*LF -2, RF 0*	*0.0*
2019	*HOU*	*MLB*	*42*	*361*	*41*	*18*	*0*	*11*	*41*	*24*	*73*	*0*	*0*	*.234/.285/.387*	*.230*	*-5.6*	*.266*	*-1.2*	*LF -2, RF 0*	*-0.8*

Breakout: 0% Improve: 15% Collapse: 8% Attrition: 21% MLB: 54% *Comparables: George Brett, Eddie Murray, Hal McRae*

During the middle of the season, Brian McCann led the team in a faux funeral for Beltran's well-traveled outfield glove. Perhaps they should have buried his bat in a nearby grave, as Beltran didn't provide the offensive firepower the Astros had hoped for. But even as the curtain closed on his MLB career, a new narrative was given life: *Carlos Beltran, clubhouse hero*. The nine-time All-Star was lauded for his influence on players like Carlos Correa, and even parlayed his reputation into an interview to succeed Joe Girardi as manager of the Yankees. After the Astros' World Series win, Beltran announced his retirement from the game, going out on top after attaining the peak he'd worked toward for nearly two decades. If McCann, other teammates or anyone who studied his time in baseball wants to lay his 17-year career to rest, the only suitable location to hold services is in Cooperstown, New York.

Alex Bregman 3B Born: 03/30/94 Age: 24 Bats: R Throws: R Height: 6'0" Weight: 180 Origin: Round 1, 2015 Draft (#2 overall)

YEAR	TEAM	LVL	AGE	PA	R	2B	3B	HR	RBI	BB	K	SB	CS	AVG/OBP/SLG	TAv	VORP	BABIP	BRR	FRAA	WARP
2015	QUD	A	21	133	18	5	0	1	13	17	13	5	2	.259/.368/.330	.263	7.9	.283	2.4	SS(26): 3.0	1.2
2015	LNC	A+	21	178	19	8	4	3	21	12	17	8	4	.319/.364/.475	.289	10.3	.336	-2.0	SS(37): -2.0	0.9
2016	CCH	AA	22	285	54	16	2	14	46	42	26	5	3	.297/.415/.559	.353	38.9	.286	1.6	SS(51): -3.4, 3B(11): 1.4	4.0
2016	FRE	AAA	22	83	17	6	0	6	15	5	12	2	1	.333/.373/.641	.353	10.0	.333	-1.2	SS(14): 2.1, LF(3): -0.1	1.2
2016	HOU	MLB	22	217	31	13	3	8	34	15	52	2	0	.264/.313/.478	.270	9.6	.317	0.5	3B(40): 0.9, SS(6): -0.1	1.1
2017	HOU	MLB	23	626	88	39	5	19	71	55	97	17	5	.284/.352/.475	.282	34.8	.311	-1.5	3B(132): 8.7, SS(30): -2.9	4.1
2018	*HOU*	*MLB*	*24*	*643*	*95*	*35*	*5*	*23*	*79*	*58*	*108*	*13*	*4*	*.271/.342/.467*	*.281*	*34.5*	*.296*	*0.7*	*3B 6, SS 0*	*3.8*
2019	*HOU*	*MLB*	*25*	*578*	*81*	*31*	*3*	*25*	*83*	*57*	*102*	*12*	*4*	*.272/.350/.491*	*.284*	*28.6*	*.294*	*-0.6*	*3B 7, SS 0*	*3.8*

Breakout: 3% Improve: 53% Collapse: 3% Attrition: 8% MLB: 99% *Comparables: Maikel Franco, Mike Moustakas, Anthony Rendon*

Before the season, Bregman was a popular name in trade discussions because the young infielder showed off the talent during his 2016 debut to one day be a star. The only questions were how quickly he'd be able to make the leap, and how high he'd fly. As it turns out, the Astros were right in not dealing him for present value, because Bregman emerged slightly ahead of schedule, improving his contact rate and lowering his strikeouts while continuing to pull the ball for power. Now it appears he's got the full Anthony Rendon starter kit, which is a pretty great baseline for any team's best infielder. It's just that on the Astros, despite his youth, his skills and his potential, he's only the team's third-best infielder.

Gilberto Celestino OF Born: 02/13/99 Age: 19 Bats: R Throws: L Height: 6'0" Weight: 170 Origin: International Free Agent, 2015

YEAR	TEAM	LVL	AGE	PA	R	2B	3B	HR	RBI	BB	K	SB	CS	AVG/OBP/SLG	TAv	VORP	BABIP	BRR	FRAA	WARP
2016	DAR	RK	17	165	22	9	3	2	17	25	23	9	2	.279/.388/.434	.305	12.6	.316	-0.8	CF(37): -0.1	1.2
2016	AST	RK	17	65	7	3	1	0	2	8	16	6	1	.200/.308/.291	.244	0.5	.275	-0.2	CF(16): -4.0	-0.3
2017	GRV	RK	18	261	38	10	2	4	24	22	59	10	2	.268/.331/.379	.252	11.0	.339	5.3	CF(43): 2.7, RF(8): 0.1	1.2
2018	*HOU*	*MLB*	*19*	*250*	*26*	*9*	*1*	*6*	*22*	*16*	*83*	*3*	*1*	*.195/.248/.319*	*.194*	*-7.9*	*.271*	*0.0*	*CF -1, RF 0*	*-1.0*
2019	*HOU*	*MLB*	*20*	*364*	*39*	*14*	*2*	*10*	*38*	*25*	*114*	*4*	*1*	*.211/.269/.352*	*.216*	*-6.5*	*.284*	*0.2*	*CF -2, RF 0*	*-0.9*

Breakout: 0% Improve: 6% Collapse: 2% Attrition: 5% MLB: 11% *Comparables: Engel Beltre, Nomar Mazara, Raul Mondesi*

Outfielder-turned-raconteur Fernando Perez insists there are two very different skills a hitter can develop: the ability to hunt for fastballs and the ability to hit adaptively. Young and toolsy, Celestino is already starting to show some affinity for the former, but the more challenging latter skill is something he'll have to work hard to improve. Right now, he hasn't figured out how to recognize spin or develop a big-league approach, but that's understandable; he's a 19-year-old with no pro experience beyond rookie ball. With dynamite tools already in hand—or more accurately *in foot*; he's crazy fast and looks to develop nice defensive chops in center field—he has a relatively high floor as a reserve outfielder. If he can learn to take the adaptive approach to hitting, he might one day be a star, but if he can't ... well, a floor like Fernando Perez's brief career sounds about right.

Carlos Correa SS Born: 09/22/94 Age: 23 Bats: R Throws: R Height: 6'4" Weight: 215 Origin: Round 1, 2012 Draft (#1 overall)

YEAR	TEAM	LVL	AGE	PA	R	2B	3B	HR	RBI	BB	K	SB	CS	AVG/OBP/SLG	TAv	VORP	BABIP	BRR	FRAA	WARP
2015	CCH	AA	20	133	25	15	2	7	32	15	25	15	0	.385/.459/.726	.387	22.2	.447	0.0	SS(28): 4.5	2.9
2015	FRE	AAA	20	113	19	6	1	3	12	12	14	3	1	.276/.345/.449	.281	4.8	.286	-2.3	SS(24): -4.8	0.0
2015	HOU	MLB	20	432	52	22	1	22	68	40	78	14	4	.279/.345/.512	.295	32.1	.296	0.4	SS(99): -7.4	2.6
2016	HOU	MLB	21	660	76	36	3	20	96	75	139	13	3	.274/.361/.451	.297	53.7	.328	1.8	SS(153): -4.5	5.1
2017	HOU	MLB	22	481	82	25	1	24	84	53	92	2	1	.315/.391/.550	.320	47.4	.352	-3.0	SS(108): -1.4	4.6
2018	*HOU*	*MLB*	*23*	*615*	*87*	*33*	*2*	*26*	*91*	*64*	*119*	*11*	*3*	*.285/.362/.496*	*.302*	*54.9*	*.322*	*0.3*	*SS -3*	*4.6*
2019	*HOU*	*MLB*	*24*	*549*	*84*	*30*	*2*	*26*	*86*	*64*	*105*	*10*	*2*	*.292/.378/.527*	*.309*	*46.7*	*.323*	*-0.1*	*SS -2*	*4.8*

Breakout: 4% Improve: 64% Collapse: 0% Attrition: 0% MLB: 99% *Comparables: Miguel Cabrera, Jason Heyward, Ryan Zimmerman*

Just how good is Correa? Despite missing over a month after thumb surgery, baseball's most marketable young star provided output at a rate awfully similar to that of teammate and AL MVP Jose Altuve, while improving every aspect of his game from plate discipline to power. Just how young is the co-face of the game's most successful franchise? Of the top 100 hitters by True Average last season, only one (Cody Bellinger) was younger than Correa. And just how joyous is he? His effervescence in victory makes him all the more beloved, his post-World Series wedding proposal was a fitting capper and his continued charity work in the offseason is a blessing. Coming off his first championship and a top-flight season, the question isn't what one of the game's brightest stars will do next, it's what *won't* he do next?

J.D. Davis 3B Born: 04/27/93 Age: 25 Bats: R Throws: R Height: 6'3" Weight: 225 Origin: Round 3, 2014 Draft (#75 overall)

YEAR	TEAM	LVL	AGE	PA	R	2B	3B	HR	RBI	BB	K	SB	CS	AVG/OBP/SLG	TAv	VORP	BABIP	BRR	FRAA	WARP
2015	LNC	A+	22	552	93	28	3	26	101	54	157	5	2	.289/.370/.520	.294	34.1	.374	-1.3	3B(117): -1.9	3.5
2016	CCH	AA	23	539	61	34	1	23	81	45	143	1	3	.268/.334/.485	.301	34.0	.331	-2.6	3B(101): -6.1, LF(4): 0.3	3.0
2017	CCH	AA	24	388	49	18	0	21	60	31	90	5	2	.279/.340/.510	.310	29.9	.317	-0.5	3B(73): 6.1, 1B(3): -0.2	3.9
2017	FRE	AAA	24	73	10	5	0	5	18	9	18	0	0	.295/.370/.623	.332	7.8	.317	-0.4	3B(13): 2.1, 1B(4): 0.0	1.0
2017	HOU	MLB	24	68	8	4	0	4	7	4	20	1	1	.226/.279/.484	.254	1.7	.256	-0.2	3B(22): 0.5, P(2): 0.0	0.3
2018	*HOU*	*MLB*	*25*	*67*	*9*	*3*	*0*	*3*	*9*	*5*	*21*	*0*	*0*	*.236/.301/.445*	*.261*	*2.0*	*.299*	*-0.1*	*3B 0*	*0.1*
2019	*HOU*	*MLB*	*26*	*303*	*41*	*13*	*0*	*15*	*43*	*26*	*96*	*1*	*1*	*.233/.306/.448*	*.257*	*5.9*	*.300*	*-0.7*	*3B 0*	*0.7*

Breakout: 8% Improve: 29% Collapse: 12% Attrition: 36% MLB: 62% *Comparables: Mike Olt, Richie Shaffer, Mat Gamel*

The Astros used three position players as pitchers last season: Nori Aoki, Tyler White and Davis. One of these things is not like the other.

Formerly a closer for Cal State Fullerton, the big righty struck out three of the seven batters he faced, so he technically led the vaunted Houston pitching staff in strikeout percentage last season, out-whiffing Ken Giles and Justin Verlander. Punchouts have always been part of the package with Davis, but usually as part of his real job as a power-hitting, big-swinging third baseman. He's hit at every level in the minors, though strikeout questions and a late start have dogged him as he's climbed the ranks. He's got a chance to earn a spot on the Astros' bench as a part-time reliever/bench bat, and yet who'd have thought that strikeouts would be his saving grace, rather than his fatal flaw?

Derek Fisher LF Born: 08/21/93 Age: 24 Bats: L Throws: R Height: 6'3" Weight: 205 Origin: Round 1, 2014 Draft (#37 overall)

YEAR	TEAM	LVL	AGE	PA	R	2B	3B	HR	RBI	BB	K	SB	CS	AVG/OBP/SLG	TAv	VORP	BABIP	BRR	FRAA	WARP
2015	QUD	A	21	171	32	11	1	6	24	19	37	8	2	.305/.386/.510	.326	15.7	.370	-0.5	CF(30): -3.0, LF(3): -0.8	1.3
2015	LNC	A+	21	398	74	10	7	16	63	47	95	23	5	.262/.354/.471	.295	27.7	.314	4.3	LF(43): -1.4, CF(35): -1.6	2.7
2016	CCH	AA	22	448	54	13	4	16	59	74	128	23	7	.245/.373/.431	.303	30.0	.329	-0.5	CF(70): -7.9, RF(19): -1.2	2.2
2016	FRE	AAA	22	118	17	8	0	5	17	9	26	5	0	.290/.347/.505	.308	8.2	.338	-0.6	RF(13): -1.6, CF(13): -0.9	0.6
2017	FRE	AAA	23	384	63	26	1	21	66	35	74	16	10	.318/.384/.583	.312	32.4	.352	-0.8	CF(53): -5.4, LF(17): 2.3	2.9
2017	HOU	MLB	23	166	21	4	1	5	17	17	54	3	3	.212/.307/.356	.234	-1.4	.299	-0.5	LF(38): 1.2, RF(12): 0.1	0.0
2018	*HOU*	*MLB*	*24*	*333*	*48*	*13*	*2*	*13*	*42*	*36*	*97*	*10*	*4*	*.234/.321/.425*	*.263*	*12.0*	*.300*	*0.3*	*LF 4, RF 0*	*1.3*
2019	*HOU*	*MLB*	*25*	*455*	*60*	*18*	*2*	*18*	*60*	*48*	*140*	*13*	*6*	*.228/.316/.423*	*.255*	*9.5*	*.299*	*0.9*	*LF 6, RF 0*	*1.6*

Breakout: 5% Improve: 30% Collapse: 15% Attrition: 22% MLB: 60% *Comparables: Joe Benson, Brett Jackson, Bradley Zimmer*

Fisher is a strange and fascinating player. Over the past three seasons he's put up solid offensive numbers at Lancaster, Corpus Christi and Fresno, displaying power and patience in abundance. At the same time, those standout skills sometime put the holes in his game into sharp relief. Despite top-end speed and athleticism, Fisher remains a terrible outfielder. He runs poor routes and plays center field because his arm may not be cut out for a corner, not because he's a plus defender. In addition, the speed hasn't translated to actual production on the basepaths. There's no doubt Fisher contains tantalizing potential, as before his strikeout-laden MLB debut he had cut down on his whiffs considerably in the upper minors. Yet until we see him take a final step or two forward in the majors, Fisher might be more of a high-risk bench bat curiosity than a productive regular.

Evan Gattis C Born: 08/18/86 Age: 31 Bats: R Throws: R Height: 6'4" Weight: 270 Origin: Round 23, 2010 Draft (#704 overall)

YEAR	TEAM	LVL	AGE	PA	R	2B	3B	HR	RBI	BB	K	SB	CS	AVG/OBP/SLG	TAv	VORP	BABIP	BRR	FRAA	WARP
2015	HOU	MLB	28	604	66	20	11	27	88	30	119	0	1	.246/.285/.463	.262	7.7	.264	0.0	LF(11): -1.7	0.6
2016	CCH	AA	29	42	8	2	0	5	10	1	4	0	0	.375/.405/.800	.432	8.2	.323	0.1	C(4): 0.1	0.9
2016	HOU	MLB	29	499	58	19	0	32	72	43	127	2	1	.251/.319/.508	.290	27.6	.273	-0.1	C(55): -1.3	2.7
2017	HOU	MLB	30	325	41	22	0	12	55	18	50	0	1	.263/.311/.457	.253	8.5	.278	0.0	C(49): -0.2, 1B(1): 0.0	0.8
2018	*HOU*	*MLB*	*31*	*467*	*62*	*21*	*2*	*23*	*69*	*29*	*101*	*1*	*1*	*.250/.302/.470*	*.268*	*17.4*	*.272*	*-0.8*	*C -2*	*1.2*
2019	*HOU*	*MLB*	*32*	*416*	*55*	*18*	*1*	*21*	*61*	*27*	*96*	*0*	*0*	*.239/.297/.460*	*.258*	*11.9*	*.263*	*0.0*	*C -1*	*1.2*

Breakout: 1% Improve: 32% Collapse: 13% Attrition: 11% MLB: 98% *Comparables: John Buck, Ryan Doumit, Gene Oliver*

YEAR	TEAM	P. COUNT	FRM RUNS	BLK RUNS	THRW RUNS	TOT RUNS
2016	HOU	7151	2.1	-4.4	1.3	-1.0
2017	HOU	7026	2.5	-0.6	-1.8	0.1
2018	*HOU*	*4751*	*1.3*	*-1.9*	*-0.1*	*-0.8*
2019	*HOU*	*4230*	*1.1*	*-1.7*	*-0.1*	*-0.7*

Last season was kind of a bear for El Oso Blanco. In part, that's because of a sequence of injuries, and in part it's because the big man's power production was, well, bearish. After he spent a higher percentage of games behind the dish than usual, maybe it's time to ask whether his injuries and offense are related. Last season was chock full of catcher concussions, and Gattis suffered one of his own in August—after returning he posted an awful .203/.230/.322 line. The stats show that he's a decent enough defensive catcher—though he doesn't exactly look the part—but he may need to give up the tools of ignorance to save his health and his bat.

Marwin Gonzalez UT Born: 03/14/89 Age: 29 Bats: B Throws: R Height: 6'1" Weight: 205 Origin: International Free Agent, 2005

YEAR	TEAM	LVL	AGE	PA	R	2B	3B	HR	RBI	BB	K	SB	CS	AVG/OBP/SLG	TAv	VORP	BABIP	BRR	FRAA	WARP
2015	HOU	MLB	26	370	44	18	1	12	34	16	74	4	5	.279/.317/.442	.261	10.8	.326	0.7	1B(43): 2.0, SS(32): -1.3	1.4
2016	HOU	MLB	27	518	55	26	3	13	51	22	118	12	6	.254/.293/.401	.245	0.1	.311	-1.4	1B(92): 0.7, 3B(22): 0.6	0.2
2017	HOU	MLB	28	515	67	34	0	23	90	49	99	8	3	.303/.377/.530	.303	36.5	.343	-0.8	LF(47): -3.5, SS(38): -1.7	3.1
2018	*HOU*	*MLB*	*29*	*468*	*57*	*24*	*1*	*13*	*54*	*28*	*93*	*8*	*4*	*.263/.310/.418*	*.255*	*11.9*	*.302*	*-0.5*	*LF -2, 2B 0*	*0.6*
2019	*HOU*	*MLB*	*30*	*505*	*62*	*26*	*1*	*16*	*62*	*34*	*107*	*7*	*4*	*.257/.314/.425*	*.253*	*8.4*	*.296*	*-0.2*	*LF -1, 2B 0*	*0.7*

Breakout: 5% Improve: 44% Collapse: 8% Attrition: 18% MLB: 93% *Comparables: Reed Johnson, Keith Moreland, Andy Dirks*

Call it slow-playing, but no major-league regular took more time between pitches in 2017 than Gonzalez. As Jeff Sullivan of FanGraphs pointed out this offseason, the most unexpected breakout of the Astros' season came slowly on both micro and macro levels, with Gonzalez rearranging the dirt and adjusting his gear before rearranging baseballs and adjusting everyone's image of what kind of player he could be. For years, he was a do-it-all utility man without standout contact or power tools, and his walk rate made it appear that he was bereft of patience. But after a season in which he obliterated right-handed pitching and spit on more pitches than ever before, it's become clear that patience is both a virtue that he's developed and virtue from which the Astros have benefited. Good things come to those who wait.

Yulieski Gurriel 1B Born: 06/09/84 Age: 34 Bats: R Throws: R Height: 6'0" Weight: 190 Origin: International Free Agent, 2016

YEAR	TEAM	LVL	AGE	PA	R	2B	3B	HR	RBI	BB	K	SB	CS	AVG/OBP/SLG	TAv	VORP	BABIP	BRR	FRAA	WARP
2016	HOU	MLB	32	137	13	7	0	3	15	5	12	1	1	.262/.292/.385	.223	-3.0	.267	-1.2	3B(21): -0.8, 1B(5): 0.1	-0.4
2017	HOU	MLB	33	564	69	43	1	18	75	22	62	3	2	.299/.332/.486	.282	18.0	.308	-1.7	1B(131): 8.4, 3B(7): -0.3	2.6
2018	*HOU*	*MLB*	*34*	*552*	*61*	*34*	*1*	*15*	*69*	*24*	*71*	*4*	*2*	*.274/.311/.434*	*.261*	*8.7*	*.290*	*-1.0*	*1B 7*	*1.3*
2019	*HOU*	*MLB*	*35*	*435*	*51*	*27*	*0*	*13*	*53*	*20*	*64*	*2*	*1*	*.270/.310/.433*	*.255*	*2.2*	*.292*	*-1.2*	*1B 5*	*0.8*

Breakout: 1% Improve: 32% Collapse: 9% Attrition: 21% MLB: 86% *Comparables: Nomar Garciaparra, Juan Rivera, Ross Gload*

After fighting off younger first-base competitors last year, Gurriel is leaving a bit of an opening for another hitter to supplant him when he serves a five-game suspension to start 2018. (In case you forgot, Gurriel threw out an offensive gesture and comment toward Yu Darvish in the midst of the World Series.) However, if the team's incumbent first sacker hits as well as he did last season, the Astros will find some way to get him into the lineup every day. Though he may be allergic to walks, the pineapple-haired longtime Cuban superstar displayed a line-drive stroke and plenty of power during his second season in the big leagues. If he can get out of his own way, he's likely to force his other competition out of the way as well.

Jake Marisnick CF Born: 03/30/91 Age: 27 Bats: R Throws: R Height: 6'4" Weight: 220 Origin: Round 3, 2009 Draft (#104 overall)

YEAR	TEAM	LVL	AGE	PA	R	2B	3B	HR	RBI	BB	K	SB	CS	AVG/OBP/SLG	TAv	VORP	BABIP	BRR	FRAA	WARP
2015	HOU	MLB	24	372	46	15	4	9	36	18	105	24	9	.236/.281/.383	.243	7.3	.310	3.1	CF(99): 5.3, LF(16): 2.2	1.6
2016	FRE	AAA	25	28	3	2	0	0	1	1	10	1	1	.185/.214/.259	.168	-2.0	.294	-0.1	CF(6): 0.4, RF(2): 0.1	-0.1
2016	HOU	MLB	25	311	40	18	1	5	21	16	83	10	5	.209/.257/.331	.216	-6.2	.275	-1.1	CF(74): 8.8, LF(26): 1.4	0.4
2017	HOU	MLB	26	259	50	10	0	16	35	20	90	9	4	.243/.319/.496	.275	13.7	.320	1.4	CF(93): -5.1, LF(6): 0.3	0.9
2018	*HOU*	*MLB*	*27*	*283*	*37*	*12*	*1*	*8*	*29*	*14*	*77*	*12*	*5*	*.233/.280/.382*	*.233*	*3.4*	*.293*	*1.0*	*CF 1, LF 1*	*0.3*
2019	*HOU*	*MLB*	*28*	*308*	*35*	*14*	*1*	*9*	*36*	*17*	*86*	*13*	*5*	*.231/.286/.389*	*.231*	*1.1*	*.291*	*1.3*	*CF 2, LF 1*	*0.4*

Breakout: 7% Improve: 44% Collapse: 5% Attrition: 17% MLB: 90% *Comparables: Franklin Gutierrez, Brian Anderson, Luis Matos*

It's all about timing. As an anchor of the Mark Buerhle trade in 2012, the toolsy Marisnick was beholden to unrealistic expectations he was unlikely to fulfill. But as a defensive replacement on the forward-thinking Astros, he found a niche. When his low-OBP offense and the 'Stros' glut of talented outfielders began to set off alarm bells that his job was in jeopardy, timing saved him: the trend of low-power hitters suddenly bashing dingers swept him up and led to career highs in every important offensive category. Of course, fate giveth and fate taketh away—he shattered his hand in September and missed out on the Astros' postseason run—but he'll enter 2018 with slightly more upside just in time to command a reasonable arbitration raise and prolong his reputation as a player with potential.

Cameron Maybin OF Born: 04/04/87 Age: 31 Bats: R Throws: R Height: 6'3" Weight: 215 Origin: Round 1, 2005 Draft (#10 overall)

YEAR	TEAM	LVL	AGE	PA	R	2B	3B	HR	RBI	BB	K	SB	CS	AVG/OBP/SLG	TAv	VORP	BABIP	BRR	FRAA	WARP
2015	ATL	MLB	28	555	65	18	2	10	59	45	102	23	6	.267/.327/.370	.264	22.2	.316	3.5	CF(139): 1.0	2.5
2016	TOL	AAA	29	100	14	9	0	2	11	14	17	4	1	.188/.310/.365	.236	0.0	.212	0.8	CF(9): 0.3	0.0
2016	DET	MLB	29	391	65	14	5	4	43	36	69	15	6	.315/.383/.418	.277	23.9	.383	5.1	CF(91): -1.1	2.4
2017	ANA	MLB	30	387	57	19	1	6	22	48	78	29	5	.235/.333/.351	.247	9.9	.289	4.9	LF(45): 2.6, CF(42): 1.5	1.4
2017	HOU	MLB	30	63	6	1	1	4	13	3	16	4	3	.186/.226/.441	.237	-0.1	.179	-0.4	CF(15): -0.4, LF(5): -0.3	-0.1
2018	*HOU*	*MLB*	*31*	*426*	*57*	*18*	*2*	*9*	*38*	*41*	*87*	*20*	*6*	*.250/.325/.382*	*.246*	*12.1*	*.299*	*3.0*	*LF 3, CF 1*	*1.7*
2019	*HOU*	*MLB*	*32*	*383*	*44*	*17*	*2*	*8*	*40*	*36*	*80*	*16*	*5*	*.243/.317/.375*	*.244*	*6.8*	*.291*	*3.1*	*LF 3, CF 1*	*1.1*

Breakout: 0% Improve: 39% Collapse: 4% Attrition: 14% MLB: 87% *Comparables: Ryan Freel, Gregor Blanco, Rajai Davis*

In Detroit he played so well
But hurt himself when he fell
After that wasn't swell
So just trade him away

LA seemed like a good fit
Now Justin Upton's in it
Though Angels liked his mitt
They just gave him away

Houston was knowin'
They'd need bases stolen
Rosters started growin'
So they claimed him though he's 30!

Then the World Series
Game 2 is crazy
In extra innings
It's Cameron Maybin!

He got a rally
Going baby
By stealing bases
Go Cameron Maybin!

Once he came into their life
His bat was so bad
The Astros knew that
His bat was so, so bad

But when he came into their life
They told him "run fast"
And he could do that
He could still run so fast

He's still productive
When he stays healthy
Good speed and glove work
That's Cameron Maybin!

But his next contract
Won't be too wealthy
Still can't hit much
He's Cameron Maybin!

Brian McCann C Born: 02/20/84 Age: 34 Bats: L Throws: R Height: 6'3" Weight: 225 Origin: Round 2, 2002 Draft (#64 overall)

YEAR	TEAM	LVL	AGE	PA	R	2B	3B	HR	RBI	BB	K	SB	CS	AVG/OBP/SLG	TAv	VORP	BABIP	BRR	FRAA	WARP
2015	NYA	MLB	31	535	68	15	1	26	94	52	97	0	0	.232/.320/.437	.270	23.3	.235	-4.5	C(126): 0.3, 1B(10): -0.1	2.5
2016	NYA	MLB	32	492	56	13	0	20	58	54	99	1	0	.242/.335/.413	.256	11.7	.269	-3.9	C(92): 10.9, 1B(3): -0.6	2.3
2017	HOU	MLB	33	399	47	12	1	18	62	38	58	1	0	.241/.323/.436	.262	19.2	.237	-0.2	C(95): -3.7	1.5
2018	*HOU*	*MLB*	*34*	*512*	*65*	*16*	*1*	*21*	*67*	*45*	*91*	*1*	*0*	*.235/.313/.413*	*.256*	*20.1*	*.249*	*-0.9*	*C 0*	*1.7*
2019	*HOU*	*MLB*	*35*	*375*	*49*	*12*	*0*	*15*	*48*	*33*	*70*	*0*	*0*	*.229/.306/.406*	*.247*	*7.3*	*.243*	*-2.1*	*C 1*	*0.9*

Breakout: 0% Improve: 37% Collapse: 9% Attrition: 13% MLB: 89%

Comparables: Gary Carter, Ramon Hernandez, Bill Freehan

YEAR	TEAM	P. COUNT	FRM RUNS	BLK RUNS	THRW RUNS	TOT RUNS
2015	NYA	17347	-3.6	0.7	1.2	-1.6
2016	NYA	12380	9.2	2.7	-0.5	11.4
2017	HOU	13673	0.0	-0.4	-2.3	-2.6
2018	*HOU*	*16670*	*1.2*	*1.1*	*-1.0*	*1.3*
2019	*HOU*	*12200*	*1.1*	*1.0*	*-0.9*	*1.1*

Before pitch framing was cool—or at least quantified—there was McCann. At his peak he was one of the best in the game at both blocking and framing, and even in his later years he's been at least good at both. Not so in 2017, when after he came to the Astros his defensive numbers crashed and he showed his age behind the dish. Of course, that's only half the story; his offensive output was steady and solid as usual, despite the lowest number of plate appearances he'd seen since his age-21 debut season. (Oh, and that veteran leadership he was acquired to provide? You can't argue with a World Series win.) He's on the downside of a great career, but he's still an average backstop at this stage.

Colin Moran 3B Born: 10/01/92 Age: 25 Bats: L Throws: R Height: 6'4" Weight: 204 Origin: Round 1, 2013 Draft (#6 overall)

YEAR	TEAM	LVL	AGE	PA	R	2B	3B	HR	RBI	BB	K	SB	CS	AVG/OBP/SLG	TAv	VORP	BABIP	BRR	FRAA	WARP
2015	CCH	AA	22	417	47	25	2	9	67	43	79	1	0	.306/.381/.459	.293	24.9	.365	-0.6	3B(78): 0.4	2.7
2016	FRE	AAA	23	511	50	18	1	10	69	47	124	3	2	.259/.329/.368	.248	5.0	.332	-4.6	3B(109): 5.1, SS(2): -0.3	1.0
2016	HOU	MLB	23	25	1	1	0	0	2	1	8	0	0	.130/.200/.174	.089	-3.4	.200	0.1	3B(8): 0.8	-0.3
2017	FRE	AAA	24	338	53	15	1	18	63	31	55	0	3	.308/.373/.543	.307	27.4	.323	-0.3	3B(57): 0.3, 1B(15): -1.7	2.5
2017	HOU	MLB	24	12	3	0	1	1	3	1	1	0	0	.364/.417/.818	.379	2.5	.333	0.6	1B(4): -0.1, 3B(3): -0.2	0.2
2018	*HOU*	*MLB*	*25*	*103*	*13*	*4*	*0*	*3*	*12*	*8*	*26*	*0*	*0*	*.243/.309/.402*	*.250*	*1.1*	*.300*	*-0.2*	*3B 0, 1B -1*	*0.0*
2019	*HOU*	*MLB*	*26*	*320*	*41*	*14*	*1*	*12*	*41*	*29*	*83*	*0*	*0*	*.247/.318/.424*	*.254*	*3.9*	*.304*	*-0.8*	*3B 0, 1B -2*	*0.2*

Breakout: 6% Improve: 16% Collapse: 11% Attrition: 34% MLB: 42%

Comparables: Matthew Duffy, Adam Duvall, Taylor Green

Purgatory, limbo, the land between. In baseball, we call it Quad-A. For now, Moran resides there as a hitter who appears ready for regular action but is rapidly aging out of prospect status and without anywhere to play. The good news is that he was having a solid season at Fresno before being called up by the Astros in July. The bad news is that after he ripped off two solid games, a foul ball ricocheted off his face and sent him to the hospital with a gruesome injury. There shouldn't be any lasting effects—he returned to the big club in September to get reps in—but the injury robbed the former no. 6 overall pick of a precious chance to play his way out of the space between minors and majors.

Josh Reddick RF Born: 02/19/87 Age: 31 Bats: L Throws: R Height: 6'2" Weight: 195 Origin: Round 17, 2006 Draft (#523 overall)

YEAR	TEAM	LVL	AGE	PA	R	2B	3B	HR	RBI	BB	K	SB	CS	AVG/OBP/SLG	TAv	VORP	BABIP	BRR	FRAA	WARP
2015	OAK	MLB	28	582	67	25	4	20	77	49	65	10	2	.272/.333/.449	.287	24.9	.278	-0.1	RF(143): -6.7, CF(1): 0.0	1.9
2016	NAS	AAA	29	26	2	1	0	1	1	1	6	0	0	.120/.154/.280	.138	-2.9	.111	0.0	RF(3): 0.2	-0.3
2016	OAK	MLB	29	272	33	11	1	8	28	28	34	5	0	.296/.368/.449	.300	18.0	.317	2.1	RF(68): 3.0	2.2
2016	LAN	MLB	29	167	20	6	0	2	9	11	22	3	3	.258/.307/.335	.240	-0.7	.290	-0.3	RF(42): 0.8	0.0
2017	HOU	MLB	30	540	77	34	4	13	82	43	72	7	3	.314/.363/.484	.296	33.4	.339	2.5	RF(102): -1.5, LF(48): -1.1	3.0
2018	*HOU*	*MLB*	*31*	*562*	*67*	*27*	*4*	*16*	*70*	*48*	*87*	*7*	*3*	*.267/.330/.428*	*.268*	*21.0*	*.292*	*0.0*	*RF -1, LF 0*	*1.6*
2019	*HOU*	*MLB*	*32*	*477*	*60*	*22*	*2*	*16*	*59*	*43*	*80*	*5*	*2*	*.259/.327/.430*	*.262*	*12.4*	*.283*	*0.9*	*RF 0, LF 0*	*1.4*

Breakout: 0% Improve: 38% Collapse: 7% Attrition: 14% MLB: 89%

Comparables: David DeJesus, Nick Markakis, Ben Francisco

How do you reconcile a HR/FB rate in the bottom 10th percentile among qualified hitters with a True Average worthy of mashers like Justin Upton and Edwin Encarnacion? Start with the no-brainer of contact ability and patience, then start cracking line-drive doubles; Reddick had one of the highest line-drive rates in baseball, with nearly a quarter of his balls in play resembling frozen ropes. After that, get lucky against lefties. After barely squeaking by southpaws for years, Reddick finally mustered a .384 BABIP against them last season. This talented outfielder's profile has continued to change and adapt as he's earned his veteran status, but if Reddick keeps making hard contact while reaching base, he could continue being an above-average regular even as his lauded defensive abilities start to decline.

A.J. Reed 1B Born: 05/10/93 Age: 25 Bats: L Throws: L Height: 6'4" Weight: 275 Origin: Round 2, 2014 Draft (#42 overall)

YEAR	TEAM	LVL	AGE	PA	R	2B	3B	HR	RBI	BB	K	SB	CS	AVG/OBP/SLG	TAv	VORP	BABIP	BRR	FRAA	WARP
2015	LNC	A+	22	385	75	16	4	23	81	59	73	0	0	.346/.449/.638	.360	43.5	.385	1.2	1B(64): 3.1	5.1
2015	CCH	AA	22	237	38	14	1	11	46	27	49	0	0	.332/.405/.571	.334	15.5	.383	-4.5	1B(32): -1.7	1.5
2016	FRE	AAA	23	296	42	22	1	15	50	32	67	0	0	.291/.368/.556	.323	20.1	.337	-2.4	1B(46): 2.2	2.3
2016	HOU	MLB	23	141	11	3	0	3	8	18	48	0	0	.164/.270/.262	.200	-7.2	.236	-0.2	1B(35): -2.0	-1.0
2017	HOU	MLB	24	6	0	0	0	0	0	0	1	0	0	.000/.000/.000	.012	-1.5	.000	0.0	1B(1): 0.0	-0.1
2017	FRE	AAA	24	556	89	24	0	34	104	72	146	0	0	.261/.358/.525	.284	17.8	.299	-3.1	1B(109): -4.0	1.3
2018	*HOU*	*MLB*	*25*	*68*	*9*	*3*	*0*	*3*	*10*	*8*	*19*	*0*	*0*	*.238/.327/.459*	*.273*	*2.0*	*.292*	*-0.1*	*1B 0*	*0.1*
2019	*HOU*	*MLB*	*26*	*290*	*42*	*13*	*0*	*15*	*43*	*34*	*87*	*0*	*0*	*.239/.331/.470*	*.271*	*6.3*	*.297*	*-0.7*	*1B -1*	*0.5*

Breakout: 5% Improve: 37% Collapse: 4% Attrition: 19% MLB: 67% *Comparables: Chris Carter, Brandon Allen, Aaron Judge*

In the interest of not burying the lede, know that Reed led all of minor-league baseball in home runs last season, banging 34 dingers. Better yet, it was a repeat of prior success–back in 2015 he also hit 34 bombs, most in MiLB. The first time, that was a sign of surging potential, but the second time? Now it tells us this oversized slugger might make Triple-A his ceiling. Given how much trouble he's had against breaking stuff, it's possible that he can't make enough adjustments at the highest level, and the Astros haven't seemed interested in giving him an extended look. Expect a stretch of playing time in 2018–either in Houston or abroad–that will give this hulk the chance to prove he's either the second coming of Russell Branyan or the second coming of Matt LaPorta.

George Springer RF Born: 09/19/89 Age: 28 Bats: R Throws: R Height: 6'3" Weight: 215 Origin: Round 1, 2011 Draft (#11 overall)

YEAR	TEAM	LVL	AGE	PA	R	2B	3B	HR	RBI	BB	K	SB	CS	AVG/OBP/SLG	TAv	VORP	BABIP	BRR	FRAA	WARP
2015	HOU	MLB	25	451	59	19	2	16	41	50	109	16	4	.276/.367/.459	.299	27.7	.342	2.3	RF(93): 5.6, CF(10): 0.6	3.6
2016	HOU	MLB	26	744	116	29	5	29	82	88	178	9	10	.261/.359/.457	.280	29.4	.317	1.2	RF(147): 20.1, CF(1): 0.0	5.1
2017	HOU	MLB	27	629	112	29	0	34	85	64	111	5	7	.283/.367/.522	.297	40.7	.297	0.5	CF(84): 2.6, RF(78): 0.7	4.4
2018	*HOU*	*MLB*	*28*	*656*	*104*	*27*	*2*	*29*	*87*	*73*	*155*	*10*	*7*	*.262/.356/.470*	*.290*	*44.6*	*.309*	*-1.4*	*CF 2, RF 2*	*4.1*
2019	*HOU*	*MLB*	*29*	*565*	*83*	*24*	*2*	*26*	*82*	*67*	*137*	*7*	*5*	*.260/.359/.477*	*.286*	*32.4*	*.308*	*1.4*	*CF 2, RF 2*	*4.0*

Breakout: 1% Improve: 51% Collapse: 1% Attrition: 2% MLB: 99% *Comparables: Josh Hamilton, Grady Sizemore, Matt Kemp*

The model for the-now famous 2014 *Sports Illustrated* cover story predicting the Astros' 2017 World Series win could not have been chosen more perfectly. The *SI* story itself was more about Sig Mejdal and Jeff Luhnow, and the team at the time was led by Jose Altuve and Dallas Keuchel, but the excitement and energy of Springer and fellow rookie Jonathan Singleton (oops) were a big part of the positive vibes bouncing off Houston in the summer of '14. Cut to three-and-a-half years later, and Springer was the ultimate clutch hitter for the World Series champions. He has come into his own as a dangerous power hitter and solid outfield defender at just the right time, while also showing a flair for the dramatic on the game's biggest stage. Having conquered the lofty expectations set by a bold cover story several years ago, the World Series MVP can turn his attention to the unwritten future ahead, which appears to be incredibly bright.

Max Stassi C Born: 03/15/91 Age: 27 Bats: R Throws: R Height: 5'10" Weight: 200 Origin: Round 4, 2009 Draft (#123 overall)

YEAR	TEAM	LVL	AGE	PA	R	2B	3B	HR	RBI	BB	K	SB	CS	AVG/OBP/SLG	TAv	VORP	BABIP	BRR	FRAA	WARP
2015	FRE	AAA	24	328	37	8	2	13	43	26	93	1	1	.211/.279/.384	.238	9.0	.257	2.2	C(83): 14.5	2.4
2015	HOU	MLB	24	17	4	0	0	1	2	1	5	0	0	.400/.438/.600	.340	2.6	.556	0.5	C(10): -0.5	0.2
2016	FRE	AAA	25	266	21	12	1	7	32	20	65	1	0	.230/.294/.374	.233	5.1	.287	1.1	C(66): 8.5	1.4
2016	HOU	MLB	25	13	1	0	0	0	0	0	5	0	0	.077/.077/.077	.047	-2.3	.125	-0.1	C(8): -0.5	-0.3
2017	FRE	AAA	26	287	54	14	0	12	33	38	67	1	1	.266/.383/.473	.302	26.2	.321	-0.2	C(65): 10.1	3.5
2017	HOU	MLB	26	31	5	1	0	2	4	6	4	0	0	.167/.323/.458	.247	0.9	.105	0.0	C(11): 0.3, 1B(1): 0.0	0.1
2018	*HOU*	*MLB*	*27*	*61*	*7*	*2*	*0*	*2*	*7*	*4*	*17*	*0*	*0*	*.218/.282/.382*	*.236*	*1.4*	*.273*	*-0.1*	*C 0*	*0.1*
2019	*HOU*	*MLB*	*28*	*154*	*18*	*6*	*0*	*6*	*19*	*11*	*46*	*0*	*0*	*.212/.279/.384*	*.230*	*0.9*	*.267*	*-0.4*	*C 1*	*0.2*

Breakout: 5% Improve: 14% Collapse: 11% Attrition: 25% MLB: 34% *Comparables: Johnny Monell, Brett Nicholas, Jose Lobaton*

YEAR	TEAM	P. COUNT	FRM RUNS	BLK RUNS	THRW RUNS	TOT RUNS
2015	FRE	11665	16.2	-0.4	0.1	15.9
2015	HOU	760	-0.6	0.2	0.0	-0.4
2016	HOU	491	-0.5	0.1	0.0	-0.4
2017	HOU	1029	0.1	0.3	0.0	0.4
2018	*HOU*	*2313*	*0.9*	*-0.1*	*-0.1*	*0.7*
2019	*HOU*	*5836*	*1.3*	*-0.1*	*-0.2*	*1.0*

The beat goes on. For five consecutive years, Stassi has surfaced in Houston for just a handful of plate appearances. This time, there were 31 glorious PAs—a new personal record!—but the days of prospect status and over-slot bonuses are long past. But lo! Something finally changed last season, as he started posting solid offensive numbers during his long run at Triple-A Fresno. While he's unlikely to ever become the two-way threat the Athletics drafted him to be, now we can imagine him as a solid defense-first backup or maybe even a second-division starter. That is, if he ever gets more than 50 plate appearances to prove his worth.

Myles Straw OF Born: 10/17/94 Age: 23 Bats: R Throws: R Height: 5'10" Weight: 180 Origin: Round 12, 2015 Draft (#349 overall)

YEAR	TEAM	LVL	AGE	PA	R	2B	3B	HR	RBI	BB	K	SB	CS	AVG/OBP/SLG	TAv	VORP	BABIP	BRR	FRAA	WARP
2015	GRV	RK	20	248	47	10	3	0	13	29	51	22	9	.268/.355/.344	.304	25.9	.348	6.3	CF(32): 10.8, LF(20): 3.9	4.0
2016	QUD	A	21	307	40	14	6	0	22	29	58	17	10	.374/.432/.470	.334	29.1	.472	0.3	RF(24): 4.4, CF(21): 2.5	4.6
2016	LNC	A+	21	90	21	4	0	1	5	11	17	4	2	.303/.393/.395	.279	6.4	.373	2.7	RF(7): 1.1, CF(5): -0.6	0.9
2017	BCA	A+	22	533	81	17	7	1	41	87	70	36	9	.295/.412/.373	.323	53.6	.347	5.5	CF(32): 6.9, RF(12): 7.2	7.4
2017	CCH	AA	22	54	9	0	0	0	3	7	9	2	0	.239/.340/.239	.251	1.7	.297	0.6	CF(11): -1.0, LF(2): 0.7	0.1
2018	*HOU*	*MLB*	*23*	*250*	*32*	*9*	*2*	*4*	*21*	*28*	*57*	*8*	*3*	*.255/.341/.370*	*.248*	*6.5*	*.320*	*0.4*	*CF 2, RF 1*	*1.1*
2019	*HOU*	*MLB*	*24*	*369*	*44*	*13*	*2*	*7*	*38*	*41*	*82*	*11*	*4*	*.261/.346/.385*	*.257*	*10.0*	*.323*	*1.1*	*CF 3, RF 1*	*1.7*

Breakout: 2% Improve: 20% Collapse: 6% Attrition: 14% MLB: 35% *Comparables: Boog Powell, Mallex Smith, Ezequiel Carrera*

No serious prospect pedigree. Outfield routes more tangled than your daughter's hair. Less power than the AAA battery in your old flashlight. And *the highest WARP for 2017 in all of minor-league baseball*. Straw achieved this incredible feat through a combination of approach, speed and very favorable defensive metrics, and literally no one thinks he'll repeat this feat any time in the future. But if you're one to dream, perhaps you might believe that this eye-popping walk rate could withstand the challenges of upper-minors seasoning? If so, this straw will stir a very special drink, but for now it's hard to imagine him as anything more than a trick of the light and a statistical oddity.

Garrett Stubbs C Born: 05/26/93 Age: 25 Bats: L Throws: R Height: 5'10" Weight: 175 Origin: Round 8, 2015 Draft (#229 overall)

YEAR	TEAM	LVL	AGE	PA	R	2B	3B	HR	RBI	BB	K	SB	CS	AVG/OBP/SLG	TAv	VORP	BABIP	BRR	FRAA	WARP
2015	TCV	A-	22	42	5	0	0	0	2	7	3	2	0	.235/.366/.235	.272	2.3	.258	-0.1	C(10): -0.4	0.2
2015	QUD	A	22	103	15	5	0	0	5	14	2	1	0	.274/.370/.333	.268	5.8	.274	0.4	C(25): 0.3	0.6
2016	LNC	A+	23	244	35	13	0	6	38	29	37	10	3	.291/.385/.442	.279	14.2	.323	1.0	C(37): 1.1	1.6
2016	CCH	AA	23	137	23	9	1	4	16	14	11	5	0	.325/.401/.517	.338	18.0	.330	1.4	C(30): -2.7	1.7
2017	CCH	AA	24	300	36	13	0	4	25	32	44	8	0	.236/.324/.331	.246	10.0	.269	2.3	C(64): 6.8	1.8
2017	FRE	AAA	24	91	11	5	0	0	12	11	15	3	0	.221/.341/.286	.218	1.6	.274	1.9	C(19): 0.2	0.2
2018	*HOU*	*MLB*	*25*	*250*	*27*	*12*	*0*	*6*	*27*	*26*	*48*	*4*	*0*	*.234/.322/.374*	*.239*	*7.4*	*.271*	*0.2*	*C -3*	*0.5*
2019	*HOU*	*MLB*	*26*	*273*	*32*	*14*	*0*	*7*	*29*	*27*	*54*	*4*	*1*	*.236/.319/.380*	*.243*	*5.7*	*.274*	*0.1*	*C -2*	*0.4*

Breakout: 6% Improve: 17% Collapse: 4% Attrition: 22% MLB: 35%

Comparables: Jordan Pacheco, Ramon Cabrera, Chris Herrmann

YEAR	TEAM	P. COUNT	FRM RUNS	BLK RUNS	THRW RUNS	TOT RUNS
2015	TCV	1306	-0.5	0.0	0.4	-0.2
2018	*HOU*	*8795*	*-3.8*	*0.2*	*-0.1*	*-3.7*
2019	*HOU*	*9612*	*-1.6*	*0.1*	*-0.1*	*-1.6*

Though he's running out of time as a prospect and his scouting report is peppered with concerns about his bat and his size, Stubbs should be going to sleep at night and waking up in the morning thinking about one player: Austin Barnes. Like Barnes, this undersized backstop has excellent defensive bona fides and a terrific approach, as well as the athleticism to pick up a different glove and head to the middle infield or outfield if needed. What prevents Stubbs from reaching a Barnes-in-2017 ceiling are questions about his contact ability that cropped up during an uninspiring run at both Corpus Christi and Fresno last season. The odds are stacked against this backstop becoming a big-league force, but if one vertically challenged catcher with an unorthodox profile could do it, why can't Stubbs?

Kyle Tucker OF Born: 01/17/97 Age: 21 Bats: L Throws: R Height: 6'4" Weight: 190 Origin: Round 1, 2015 Draft (#5 overall)

YEAR	TEAM	LVL	AGE	PA	R	2B	3B	HR	RBI	BB	K	SB	CS	AVG/OBP/SLG	TAv	VORP	BABIP	BRR	FRAA	WARP
2015	AST	RK	18	133	19	3	2	2	13	9	14	4	2	.208/.267/.317	.251	4.4	.219	3.4	RF(17): -1.8, CF(4): 0.8	0.3
2015	GRV	RK	18	121	11	9	0	1	20	7	15	14	2	.286/.322/.393	.259	2.7	.316	0.6	RF(26): 4.2, CF(1): -0.1	0.7
2016	QUD	A	19	428	43	19	5	6	56	40	75	31	9	.276/.348/.402	.282	20.9	.322	1.3	CF(61): -5.2, LF(17): -0.3	1.7
2016	LNC	A+	19	69	13	6	2	3	13	10	6	1	3	.339/.435/.661	.347	8.0	.340	0.2	RF(6): -0.1, LF(4): 0.2	0.8
2017	BCA	A+	20	206	31	12	4	9	43	24	45	13	5	.288/.379/.554	.353	21.1	.336	-3.1	RF(16): -1.8, CF(7): 1.2	2.2
2017	CCH	AA	20	318	39	21	1	16	47	22	64	8	4	.265/.325/.512	.294	19.5	.286	1.2	CF(37): -5.3, RF(18): -1.4	1.4
2018	*HOU*	*MLB*	*21*	*250*	*32*	*12*	*1*	*10*	*33*	*19*	*63*	*7*	*3*	*.238/.302/.439*	*.250*	*6.3*	*.281*	*0.2*	*CF -2, RF -1*	*0.3*
2019	*HOU*	*MLB*	*22*	*417*	*55*	*21*	*2*	*18*	*58*	*35*	*102*	*12*	*5*	*.245/.315/.458*	*.262*	*12.7*	*.286*	*0.9*	*CF -4, RF -1*	*0.8*

Breakout: 9% Improve: 19% Collapse: 4% Attrition: 14% MLB: 31%

Comparables: Christian Yelich, Joc Pederson, Clint Frazier

As the last top-five draft choice the Astros will likely make for a while, Tucker's under pressure to thrive. Fortunately, the young outfielder had a solid 2017 and is proving that good things come to those who wait. To wit, his advanced approach boosted his on-base percentage, while his emerging power (25 dingers) is making him look like the total offensive package. Is it possible that big-league pitchers could make him look passive rather than patient? Sure. Will he have plenty of time to prove himself as he works out the kinks in the upper minors? Definitely; the Astros are already loaded with good outfielders. If Houston's fans can mimic the team's Minor League Player of the Year's willingness to wait for his shot, they could be very happy with the end result.

Tyler White 1B Born: 10/29/90 Age: 27 Bats: R Throws: R Height: 5'11" Weight: 225 Origin: Round 33, 2013 Draft (#977 overall)

YEAR	TEAM	LVL	AGE	PA	R	2B	3B	HR	RBI	BB	K	SB	CS	AVG/OBP/SLG	TAv	VORP	BABIP	BRR	FRAA	WARP
2015	CCH	AA	24	236	33	6	0	7	40	42	35	1	0	.284/.415/.426	.297	14.9	.313	0.2	3B(45): -2.6, 1B(3): -0.2	1.3
2015	FRE	AAA	24	259	37	19	1	7	59	42	38	0	1	.362/.467/.559	.354	25.5	.412	-3.0	1B(25): -1.5, 3B(3): -0.1	2.4
2016	FRE	AAA	25	190	28	4	1	13	29	16	30	1	1	.241/.305/.500	.282	5.8	.221	-1.2	1B(24): 0.9, LF(3): -0.3	0.7
2016	HOU	MLB	25	276	24	16	0	8	28	23	65	1	0	.217/.286/.378	.236	-3.7	.258	-0.1	1B(58): -2.5, 3B(3): 0.0	-0.7
2017	FRE	AAA	26	497	84	22	1	25	89	47	101	7	3	.300/.371/.528	.303	39.9	.334	0.5	3B(50): 8.3, 2B(21): -0.2	4.8
2017	HOU	MLB	26	67	7	6	0	3	10	4	16	0	1	.279/.328/.525	.303	4.5	.326	0.4	1B(19): -1.5, 2B(4): 0.1	0.2
2018	*HOU*	*MLB*	*27*	*163*	*22*	*7*	*0*	*7*	*22*	*17*	*37*	*1*	*0*	*.250/.332/.446*	*.273*	*5.6*	*.290*	*-0.3*		*0.5*
2019	*HOU*	*MLB*	*28*	*325*	*46*	*15*	*0*	*14*	*46*	*36*	*75*	*1*	*1*	*.250/.339/.456*	*.272*	*9.5*	*.289*	*0.1*	-	*1.0*

Breakout: 8% Improve: 38% Collapse: 17% Attrition: 23% MLB: 71%

Comparables: Josh Donaldson, Scott Sizemore, Scott Moore

After the Astros won the World Series, White did a good turn by paying for a high school pizza party to celebrate the championship. And despite limited run with the big club, the Western Carolina product should be pretty happy with the way things turned out last season. Not only did he inflict another beating on Triple-A pitchers, he held his own during a few short stints in the majors, finally channeling some of the power once promised. No, he didn't carry forward the walk rate that once made him so interesting to those who scout the stat line, but the 27-year-old has earned at least one more chance to graduate from Fresno.

Pitchers

Rogelio Armenteros RHP Born: 06/30/94 Age: 23 Bats: R Throws: R Height: 6'1" Weight: 215 Origin: International Free Agent, 2014

YEAR	TEAM	LVL	AGE	W	L	SV	G	GS	IP	H	HR	BB/9	K/9	K	GB%	BABIP	WHIP	ERA	DRA	WARP	MPH	CMD	PWR	STM
2015	TCV	A-	21	2	2	0	12	9	44	44	3	3.5	8.2	40	49%	.315	1.39	4.09	3.86	0.7				
2015	QUD	A	21	1	0	0	3	3	17	9	1	3.7	11.1	21	36%	.211	0.94	2.65	3.35	0.4				
2016	QUD	A	22	0	2	0	4	3	18^{2}	12	0	1.4	9.6	20	67%	.245	0.80	1.93	2.04	0.7				
2016	LNC	A+	22	6	4	1	19	16	90^{1}	87	13	3.7	10.7	107	39%	.323	1.37	4.18	3.22	2.3				
2016	CCH	AA	22	2	0	0	3	3	18^{1}	17	1	2.0	6.4	13	36%	.308	1.15	1.96	3.65	0.3				
2017	CCH	AA	23	2	3	1	14	10	65^{1}	49	3	2.6	10.2	74	42%	.284	1.04	1.93	2.78	1.8				
2017	FRE	AAA	23	8	1	0	10	10	58^{1}	42	5	2.9	11.1	72	50%	.276	1.05	2.16	1.72	2.5				
2018	*HOU*	*MLB*	*24*	*1*	*0*	*0*	*9*	*0*	*9*	*8*	*1*	*3.9*	*10.2*	*11*	*41%*	*.290*	*1.28*	*4.02*	*4.36*	*0.1*				
2019	*HOU*	*MLB*	*25*	*3*	*1*	*1*	*51*	*0*	*54*	*45*	*8*	*4.0*	*10.7*	*64*	*41%*	*.281*	*1.27*	*4.31*	*4.60*	*0.4*				

Breakout: 23% Improve: 46% Collapse: 13% Attrition: 32% MLB: 64% *Comparables: Jake McGee, Alex Meyer, David Huff*

Ten games at Fresno does not a Top 101 prospect make, but it's getting harder and harder to ignore Armenteros and his increasingly impressive body of work. He's polished for his age—perhaps an artifact of his time pitching in Cuba—and his sinking fastball and curveball give him two solid weapons that he has used to dismantle minor-league hitters. He'll need to improve his changeup to hold off lefties, but a repeat engagement in the PCL this season could be the final step before Armenteros takes his place in a big-league rotation.

J.B. Bukauskas RHP Born: 10/11/96 Age: 21 Bats: R Throws: R Height: 6'0" Weight: 196 Origin: Round 1, 2017 Draft (#15 overall)

YEAR	TEAM	LVL	AGE	W	L	SV	G	GS	IP	H	HR	BB/9	K/9	K	GB%	BABIP	WHIP	ERA	DRA	WARP	MPH	CMD	PWR	STM
2018	*HOU*	*MLB*	*21*	*2*	*2*	*0*	*14*	*5*	31^{2}	*36*	*7*	*6.3*	*8.1*	*28*	*41%*	*.313*	*1.83*	*6.46*	*6.94*	*-0.5*				
2019	*HOU*	*MLB*	*22*	*3*	*5*	*0*	*26*	*14*	*120*	*135*	*24*	*5.3*	*7.7*	*102*	*41%*	*.31*	*1.72*	*6.02*	*6.44*	*-0.8*				

Comparables: David Hernandez, Ryan Pressly, Jason Garcia

It's all too easy to simplify a pitcher down to his most critical body part; sometimes we even refer to a hurler as an "arm." But in the case of this former Tar Heel, perhaps it would be more prudent to focus on the rest of his anatomy. Blessed with high-end velocity, Bukauskas has trouble engaging his lower half during his delivery—which might be the key reason his command improves and his breaking ball has a broader shape as the game goes on. When and if his hips catch up with his arm, he'll have the chance to be something special.

Tyler Clippard RHP Born: 02/14/85 Age: 33 Bats: R Throws: R Height: 6'3" Weight: 200 Origin: Round 9, 2003 Draft (#274 overall)

YEAR	TEAM	LVL	AGE	W	L	SV	G	GS	IP	H	HR	BB/9	K/9	K	GB%	BABIP	WHIP	ERA	DRA	WARP	MPH	CMD	PWR	STM
2015	OAK	MLB	30	1	3	17	37	0	38^{2}	25	3	4.9	8.8	38	22%	.214	1.19	2.79	3.74	0.4	93.6	46	33	53
2015	NYN	MLB	30	4	1	2	32	0	32^{1}	24	5	2.8	7.2	26	24%	.209	1.05	3.06	4.18	0.2	93.9	46	33	53
2016	ARI	MLB	31	2	3	1	40	0	37^{2}	34	7	3.6	11.0	46	34%	.310	1.30	4.30	5.47	-0.2	93.3	38	33	49
2016	NYA	MLB	31	2	3	2	29	0	25^{1}	20	3	3.9	9.2	26	32%	.258	1.22	2.49	4.38	0.2	93.8	38	33	49
2017	NYA	MLB	32	1	5	1	40	0	36^{1}	28	7	4.7	10.4	42	35%	.236	1.29	4.95	3.25	0.8	92.3	64	22	50
2017	CHA	MLB	32	1	1	2	11	0	10	8	0	4.5	10.8	12	30%	.296	1.30	1.80	2.08	0.3	92.8	64	22	50
2017	HOU	MLB	32	0	2	2	16	0	14	11	3	4.5	11.6	18	36%	.242	1.29	6.43	3.16	0.3	91.6	64	22	50
2018	*HOU*	*MLB*	*33*	*2*	*1*	*2*	*50*	*0*	52^{2}	*46*	*9*	*4.2*	*9.1*	*53*	*35%*	*.264*	*1.33*	*4.98*	*5.34*	*0.0*	*92.0*	*50*	*28*	*50*
2019	*HOU*	*MLB*	*34*	*2*	*1*	*1*	*36*	*0*	*34*	*31*	*6*	*4.4*	*8.8*	*33*	*35%*	*.265*	*1.39*	*5.30*	*5.65*	*-0.2*	*91.4*	*52*	*27*	*49*

Breakout: 19% Improve: 43% Collapse: 31% Attrition: 8% MLB: 94% *Comparables: Jerry Blevins, Hideki Okajima, Damaso Marte*

Fate is fickle, especially when you're a veteran relief pitcher. The ability to time your hot and cold streaks can be the difference between toiling in obscurity and bringing home a World Series ring. Clippard managed to sandwich a brilliant 11-game run in Chicago between disappointing stints with the two teams that met in the ALCS. For the rest of the season, he was the prototypical catch-your-breath reliever, walking too many despite getting more extra called strikes than all but eight other pitchers, and giving up far too many homers. For one month, the bespectacled wonder kept the ball in the park, and it was glorious.

Chris Devenski RHP Born: 11/13/90 Age: 27 Bats: R Throws: R Height: 6'3" Weight: 210 Origin: Round 25, 2011 Draft (#771 overall)

YEAR	TEAM	LVL	AGE	W	L	SV	G	GS	IP	H	HR	BB/9	K/9	K	GB%	BABIP	WHIP	ERA	DRA	WARP	MPH	CMD	PWR	STM
2015	CCH	AA	24	7	4	2	24	17	119^{2}	117	12	2.5	7.8	104	34%	.300	1.25	3.01	2.00	4.3				
2016	HOU	MLB	25	4	4	1	48	5	108^{1}	79	4	1.7	8.6	104	34%	.271	0.91	2.16	3.36	2.1	95.6	56	39	53
2017	HOU	MLB	26	8	5	4	62	0	80^{2}	50	11	2.9	11.2	100	41%	.220	0.94	2.68	3.40	1.6	95.5	51	39	52
2018	*HOU*	*MLB*	*27*	*3*	*2*	*0*	*51*	*0*	54^{1}	*45*	*6*	*3.1*	*9.9*	*60*	*38%*	*.286*	*1.17*	*3.20*	*3.67*	*0.9*	*95.1*	*54*	*39*	*53*
2019	*HOU*	*MLB*	*28*	*3*	*1*	*1*	*63*	*0*	67^{1}	*54*	*8*	*3.2*	*10.3*	*77*	*38%*	*.279*	*1.15*	*3.55*	*3.76*	*1.1*	*94.8*	*54*	*39*	*53*

Breakout: 30% Improve: 58% Collapse: 13% Attrition: 14% MLB: 86% *Comparables: Ramon Ramirez, Justin Grimm, Andrew Bailey*

After Andrew Miller's incredible success at the end of the 2016 season, the hot new thing for sabermetrically inclined writers was to try to pick out a "new" Miller. Pitching multiple innings and punching out hitters for the analytically inclined Astros made Devenski one of the consensus favorites to help redefine the multi-inning fireman role. To kick off the year, he was absolutely glorious: Not only were his first two relief appearances four innings each, but he ended April having struck out more than half the batters he faced. However, by the time the second half of the season began, Devenski already looked like the victim of burnout and lost effectiveness despite maintaining fastball velocity. He's likely to come back in 2018 as a good, albeit normal late-inning reliever.

Michael Feliz RHP Born: 06/28/93 Age: 24 Bats: R Throws: R Height: 6'4" Weight: 230 Origin: International Free Agent, 2010

YEAR	TEAM	LVL	AGE	W	L	SV	G	GS	IP	H	HR	BB/9	K/9	K	GB%	BABIP	WHIP	ERA	DRA	WARP	MPH	CMD	PWR	STM
2015	LNC	A+	22	1	1	0	8	5	32^{2}	30	2	3.3	9.1	33	48%	.298	1.29	4.41	3.52	0.6				
2015	CCH	AA	22	6	3	1	15	12	78^{2}	52	5	2.3	8.0	70	43%	.228	0.92	2.17	3.19	1.7				
2015	HOU	MLB	22	0	0	0	5	0	8	9	2	4.5	7.9	7	38%	.292	1.62	7.88	5.18	0.0	96.7			47
2016	HOU	MLB	23	8	1	0	47	0	65	55	10	3.0	13.2	95	42%	.315	1.18	4.43	3.57	1.0	98.1	37	57	48
2017	HOU	MLB	24	4	2	0	46	0	48	53	8	4.1	13.1	70	31%	.381	1.56	5.62	5.01	0.1	98.1	47	72	40
2018	*HOU*	*MLB*	*25*	*2*	*2*	*0*	*37*	*0*	*39*	*34*	*6*	*3.6*	*11.4*	*50*	*39%*	*.296*	*1.25*	*3.66*	*4.07*	*0.5*	*97.7*	*43*	*66*	*45*
2019	*HOU*	*MLB*	*26*	*3*	*1*	*0*	*56*	*0*	*59*	*49*	*10*	*3.6*	*12.2*	*80*	*39%*	*.292*	*1.22*	*4.02*	*4.28*	*0.6*	*97.6*	*43*	*66*	*45*

Breakout: 40% Improve: 65% Collapse: 14% Attrition: 19% MLB: 89% *Comparables: Anthony Reyes, Vincent Velasquez, Jake Odorizzi*

After another year of whipping his slider past all sorts of hitters, it looks like Feliz's Frisbee is the real deal; his 13.1 K/9 was 10th among MLB relievers with 40 or more innings. While that's a great sign, everything else didn't go quite as well as his slick breaking ball. Both his ERA and DRA placed him right around replacement level, as he struggled with control and gave up loads of hard contact. If Feliz can rein in any one or all of the hits, walks or homers, he'll be well on his way to a job as a closer.

Ken Giles RHP Born: 09/20/90 Age: 27 Bats: R Throws: R Height: 6'2" Weight: 205 Origin: Round 7, 2011 Draft (#241 overall)

YEAR	TEAM	LVL	AGE	W	L	SV	G	GS	IP	H	HR	BB/9	K/9	K	GB%	BABIP	WHIP	ERA	DRA	WARP	MPH	CMD	PWR	STM
2015	PHI	MLB	24	6	3	15	69	0	70	59	2	3.2	11.2	87	47%	.311	1.20	1.80	2.76	1.6	99.8	44	70	52
2016	HOU	MLB	25	2	5	15	69	0	65^{2}	60	8	3.4	14.0	102	41%	.349	1.29	4.11	2.33	2.0	100.0	41	57	50
2017	HOU	MLB	26	1	3	34	63	0	62^{2}	44	4	3.0	11.9	83	45%	.290	1.04	2.30	3.20	1.4	99.7	46	67	47
2018	*HOU*	*MLB*	*27*	*3*	*2*	*30*	*51*	*0*	54^{1}	*45*	*7*	*3.4*	*11.7*	*71*	*44%*	*.299*	*1.20*	*2.92*	*3.41*	*1.1*	*99.3*	*44*	*65*	*50*
2019	*HOU*	*MLB*	*28*	*3*	*1*	*28*	*57*	*0*	60^{2}	*50*	*9*	*3.5*	*12.0*	*81*	*44%*	*.295*	*1.21*	*3.70*	*3.91*	*0.9*	*99.0*	*44*	*63*	*49*

Breakout: 26% Improve: 48% Collapse: 30% Attrition: 12% MLB: 99% *Comparables: Sean Doolittle, Cody Allen, Francisco Rodriguez*

Conventional wisdom states that having an elite closer makes a world of difference in the postseason, but Giles proved the exception to that rule. During the playoffs, Houston's bullpen fell to pieces and it nearly cost them a championship, with Giles feeling the sting worst of all. His playoff ERA of 11.74 was astonishing given that his regular-season numbers were almost perfectly in line with his excellent career rates. By the end of October, he was mostly a nonfactor. His slider is still as potent as any weapon in the game, but a short run of not-quite-dominance may have the Astros looking for more late-inning assistance. Timing, they say, is everything.

Anthony Gose LHP Born: 08/10/90 Age: 27 Bats: L Throws: L Height: 6'1" Weight: 190 Origin: Round 2, 2008 Draft (#51 overall)

YEAR	TEAM	LVL	AGE	W	L	SV	G	GS	IP	H	HR	BB/9	K/9	K	GB%	BABIP	WHIP	ERA	DRA	WARP	MPH	CMD	PWR	STM
2017	LAK	A+	26	0	2	0	11	0	10^{2}	7	0	5.1	11.8	14	42%	.292	1.22	7.59	3.82	0.1				
2018	*HOU*	*MLB*	*27*	*1*	*0*	*1*	*31*	*0*	*33*	*30*	*6*	*5.4*	*10.2*	*37*	*47%*	*.278*	*1.49*	*5.44*	*5.84*	*-0.2*				
2019	*Out of baseball*																							

Breakout: 4% Improve: 6% Collapse: 3% Attrition: 5% MLB: 9% *Comparables: Rafael Martin, Jumbo Diaz, Brad Goldberg*

Ah yes, the old "if you can't fix an ailing outfielder, turn him into a relief pitcher" trick. Gose threw his weight behind the idea, rattling off a first-pitch fastball that glowed 99 mph on the radar gun and prompted some high praise from the Tigers, who pronounced his delivery clean and his curveball good. That's not to say he's on the cusp of morphing into Rafael Soriano anytime soon. Florida State League hitters ran roughshod over his first 11 relief appearances, coaxing nearly one run per inning while the lefty struggled to pair his high-octane stuff with some semblance of control. The Astros and old friend Kevin Goldstein liked his upside on the mound enough to take him in the Rule 5 draft as a pitcher.

Will Harris RHP Born: 08/28/84 Age: 33 Bats: R Throws: R Height: 6'4" Weight: 250 Origin: Round 9, 2006 Draft (#258 overall)

YEAR	TEAM	LVL	AGE	W	L	SV	G	GS	IP	H	HR	BB/9	K/9	K	GB%	BABIP	WHIP	ERA	DRA	WARP	MPH	CMD	PWR	STM
2015	HOU	MLB	30	5	5	2	68	0	71	42	8	2.8	8.6	68	52%	.192	0.90	1.90	2.42	1.9	94.2	52	55	51
2016	HOU	MLB	31	1	2	12	66	0	64	52	3	2.1	9.7	69	59%	.293	1.05	2.25	2.63	1.7	94.6	49	51	49
2017	HOU	MLB	32	3	2	2	46	0	45^{1}	37	7	1.4	10.3	52	49%	.270	0.97	2.98	3.75	0.7	93.2	52	48	38
2018	*HOU*	*MLB*	*33*	*3*	*2*	*3*	*47*	*0*	49^{1}	*44*	*7*	*3.1*	*9.3*	*51*	*50%*	*.287*	*1.23*	*3.73*	*4.12*	*0.6*	*93.0*	*50*	*51*	*44*
2019	*HOU*	*MLB*	*34*	*3*	*1*	*2*	*54*	*0*	*57*	*50*	*8*	*3.2*	*9.2*	*59*	*50%*	*.278*	*1.23*	*4.21*	*4.46*	*0.5*	*92.4*	*50*	*49*	*43*

Breakout: 19% Improve: 39% Collapse: 34% Attrition: 11% MLB: 89% *Comparables: Luke Gregerson, Scot Shields, J.J. Putz*

From out of nowhere (read: the bullpens of iffy Colorado and Arizona teams) to a first All-Star game just shy of his 32nd birthday in 2016, it was going to be hard for Harris to top his breakout season. Despite improving both his strikeout and walk rates in 2017, Harris dealt with another new event for him: his first disabled list stint, thanks to shoulder pain. Around the injury, and despite the improved peripherals, he allowed more balls in the air, which meant more balls out of the park. By the time the World Series rolled around, Harris was one of the dudes A.J. Hinch avoided, and he didn't look nearly as sharp in his limited October innings. He's likely to keep his late-inning role, but a recent history of fading as the year drags on might make him better suited to shut down opposing hitters in April and May rather than in September and October.

James Hoyt RHP Born: 09/30/86 Age: 31 Bats: R Throws: R Height: 6'6" Weight: 230 Origin: Undrafted Free Agent, 2013

YEAR	TEAM	LVL	AGE	W	L	SV	G	GS	IP	H	HR	BB/9	K/9	K	GB%	BABIP	WHIP	ERA	DRA	WARP	MPH	CMD	PWR	STM
2015	FRE	AAA	28	0	1	9	47	0	49	48	1	2.0	12.1	66	40%	.362	1.20	3.49	1.91	1.7				
2016	FRE	AAA	29	4	3	29	49	0	55	29	2	3.1	15.2	93	67%	.276	0.87	1.64	1.08	2.4				
2016	HOU	MLB	29	1	1	0	22	0	22	16	5	3.7	11.5	28	55%	.229	1.14	4.50	2.87	0.5	95.7	45	40	52
2017	FRE	AAA	30	2	0	4	13	0	14	10	1	3.9	11.6	18	52%	.281	1.14	1.93	2.86	0.4				
2017	HOU	MLB	30	1	0	0	43	0	49^{1}	51	7	2.6	12.0	66	40%	.361	1.32	4.38	3.51	0.9	94.7	39	38	47
2018	*HOU*	*MLB*	*31*	*1*	*1*	*0*	*23*	*0*	24^{2}	*22*	*4*	*3.4*	*11.1*	*31*	*47%*	*.298*	*1.28*	*3.99*	*4.34*	*0.2*	*94.1*	*40*	*38*	*49*
2019	*HOU*	*MLB*	*32*	*2*	*1*	*1*	*49*	*0*	52^{1}	*47*	*9*	*3.6*	*11.2*	*65*	*47%*	*.3*	*1.30*	*4.35*	*4.62*	*0.3*	*93.7*	*40*	*38*	*49*

Breakout: 16% Improve: 25% Collapse: 23% Attrition: 13% MLB: 57% *Comparables: Jason Bulger, Jim Henderson, Blake Wood*

From the Yuma Scorpions to the Olmecas de Tabasco to the World Series champions, Hoyt is starting to establish himself as more than just a great story. Only one right-handed reliever managed to get more swings outside of the zone than this late-blooming slider artist. With that note in the plus column, opposing hitters did punish him on the rare occasion when they caught up with his offerings; he allowed soft contact only 13 percent of the time and opposing batters racked up hits. With another successful season in the books, Hoyt's no longer a curiosity. He's a threat to batting lines everywhere.

Dallas Keuchel LHP Born: 01/01/88 Age: 30 Bats: L Throws: L Height: 6'3" Weight: 205 Origin: Round 7, 2009 Draft (#221 overall)

YEAR	TEAM	LVL	AGE	W	L	SV	G	GS	IP	H	HR	BB/9	K/9	K	GB%	BABIP	WHIP	ERA	DRA	WARP	MPH	CMD	PWR	STM
2015	HOU	MLB	27	20	8	0	33	33	232	185	17	2.0	8.4	216	62%	.269	1.02	2.48	2.23	7.9	91.8	81	36	83
2016	HOU	MLB	28	9	12	0	26	26	168	168	20	2.6	7.7	144	58%	.304	1.29	4.55	3.83	3.0	90.6	65	38	76
2017	HOU	MLB	29	14	5	0	23	23	145^{2}	116	15	2.9	7.7	125	68%	.256	1.12	2.90	2.65	4.7	90.4	74	34	62
2018	*HOU*	*MLB*	*30*	*13*	*8*	*0*	*29*	*29*	*174*	*164*	*18*	*3.1*	*7.4*	*144*	*59%*	*.293*	*1.29*	*3.81*	*4.19*	*2.4*	*90.2*	*73*	*36*	*72*
2019	*HOU*	*MLB*	*31*	*11*	*11*	*0*	*31*	*31*	196^{2}	*185*	*21*	*3.0*	*7.5*	*164*	*59%*	*.291*	*1.27*	*4.03*	*4.26*	*2.8*	*89.5*	*70*	*36*	*69*

Breakout: 11% Improve: 43% Collapse: 40% Attrition: 19% MLB: 95% *Comparables: Brandon Webb, Johnny Cueto, Roy Halladay*

The Astros came out of the gate strong last year, and a key reason was the astonishing abilities of their bearded ace. He pitched to a league-leading 1.84 ERA before a pinched nerve in his neck pushed him to the disabled list. On returning, he couldn't quite dominate the same way, but the sinker specialist still maintained the league's highest ground-ball rate among starters. During the playoffs, the pain in the neck was for his opponents, mostly because he upped his game and struck out opposing hitters 28 percent of the time. After the team's World Series parade, Kid Keuchy revealed that he had struggled with a foot injury in the second half, and there's a kernel of old baseball wisdom that sinker-wielding starters break down faster than their counterparts. Perhaps a durability issue is starting to crop up, which would be a shame; the Astros stand a much better chance of staying on top if their signature southpaw can remain upright and effective.

Francisco Liriano LHP Born: 10/26/83 Age: 34 Bats: L Throws: L Height: 6'2" Weight: 225 Origin: International Free Agent, 2000

YEAR	TEAM	LVL	AGE	W	L	SV	G	GS	IP	H	HR	BB/9	K/9	K	GB%	BABIP	WHIP	ERA	DRA	WARP	MPH	CMD	PWR	STM
2015	PIT	MLB	31	12	7	0	31	31	186^{2}	155	15	3.4	9.9	205	54%	.293	1.21	3.38	3.16	4.3	95.4	53	43	73
2016	PIT	MLB	32	6	11	0	21	21	113^{2}	115	19	5.5	9.2	116	54%	.308	1.62	5.46	4.84	0.7	95.5	55	47	72
2016	TOR	MLB	32	2	2	0	10	8	49^{1}	42	7	2.9	9.5	52	52%	.267	1.18	2.92	4.59	0.4	95.9	55	47	72
2017	TOR	MLB	33	6	5	0	18	18	82^{2}	91	11	4.7	8.1	74	44%	.327	1.62	5.88	5.58	-0.1	94.5	49	46	54
2017	HOU	MLB	33	0	2	0	20	0	14^{1}	14	0	6.3	6.9	11	54%	.341	1.67	4.40	4.25	0.2	96.1	49	46	54
2018	*HOU*	*MLB*	*34*	*6*	*6*	*0*	*18*	*18*	98^{1}	*97*	*14*	*4.1*	*8.6*	*93*	*49%*	*.299*	*1.45*	*4.80*	*5.14*	*0.6*	*94.2*	*52*	*45*	*64*
2019	*HOU*	*MLB*	*35*	*9*	*11*	*0*	*29*	*29*	*177*	*178*	*27*	*4.0*	*8.5*	*167*	*49%*	*.302*	*1.46*	*4.77*	*5.07*	*1.0*	*93.6*	*51*	*45*	*61*

Breakout: 14% Improve: 48% Collapse: 23% Attrition: 11% MLB: 95% *Comparables: CC Sabathia, Doug Davis, Andy Pettitte*

While we never know quite what to expect when Liriano takes the hill, 2017 was a bit of a wild card even by his standards. After a rough go of it north of the border to start the season, he was dealt to the Astros and moved to the bullpen to serve as the team's key left-handed reliever. Despite laying off his changeup and leaning more heavily on his sinker-slider combo, hitters didn't seem fazed by his uptick in velocity, and his command was the same enigma as always. Perhaps a little practice in the close-and-late role will help him settle in as a solid relief option, but this experiment was one of the few that didn't pay dividends for Houston last year.

Francis Martes RHP Born: 11/24/95 Age: 22 Bats: R Throws: R Height: 6'1" Weight: 225 Origin: International Free Agent, 2012

YEAR	TEAM	LVL	AGE	W	L	SV	G	GS	IP	H	HR	BB/9	K/9	K	GB%	BABIP	WHIP	ERA	DRA	WARP	MPH	CMD	PWR	STM
2015	QUD	A	19	3	2	2	10	8	52	33	1	2.2	7.8	45	48%	.229	0.88	1.04	3.39	1.1				
2015	LNC	A+	19	4	1	0	6	5	35	31	1	2.1	9.5	37	55%	.309	1.11	2.31	1.84	1.4				
2015	CCH	AA	19	1	0	0	3	3	14^{2}	19	2	4.3	9.8	16	30%	.386	1.77	4.91	4.42	0.1				
2016	CCH	AA	20	9	6	0	25	22	125^{1}	104	4	3.4	9.4	131	45%	.296	1.20	3.30	4.42	1.0				
2017	FRE	AAA	21	0	2	0	8	8	32^{1}	40	5	7.8	10.6	38	39%	.380	2.10	5.29	8.87	-1.1				
2017	HOU	MLB	21	5	2	0	32	4	54^{1}	51	7	5.1	11.4	69	44%	.328	1.51	5.80	4.08	0.7	97.8	44	60	52
2018	*HOU*	*MLB*	*22*	*3*	*2*	*0*	*25*	*6*	49^{2}	*45*	*7*	*4.4*	*10.1*	*56*	*42%*	*.297*	*1.40*	*4.15*	*4.51*	*0.4*	*97.8*	*46*	*63*	*54*
2019	*HOU*	*MLB*	*23*	*7*	*6*	*0*	*66*	*14*	*138*	*120*	*20*	*4.0*	*11.0*	*169*	*42%*	*.298*	*1.31*	*4.18*	*4.43*	*1.4*	*97.7*	*46*	*63*	*55*

Breakout: 27% Improve: 37% Collapse: 11% Attrition: 23% MLB: 64% *Comparables: Chris Tillman, Mat Latos, Jenrry Mejia*

Last year's no. 1 Astros prospect was the season's minor disappointment. By spending much of the season toiling in the bullpen without distinguishing himself, Martes has lost both his prospect status and some of his shine. But after rocketing through the minors in a manner befitting the name of his franchise, he lost control more literally than figuratively. He walked plenty of hitters in both Fresno and the majors, where his new status was "garbage-time reliever." The season wasn't a complete wash—he did maintain his ability to chuck his slider for a swing and miss almost one out of every five times—but now he'll need a good long look in the Triple-A rotation to determine what kind of pitcher he'll become. Will he rise to the top of a rotation or fall to the back of the bullpen?

Lance McCullers RHP Born: 10/02/93 Age: 24 Bats: L Throws: R Height: 6'1" Weight: 205 Origin: Round 1, 2012 Draft (#41 overall)

YEAR	TEAM	LVL	AGE	W	L	SV	G	GS	IP	H	HR	BB/9	K/9	K	GB%	BABIP	WHIP	ERA	DRA	WARP	MPH	CMD	PWR	STM
2015	CCH	AA	21	3	1	1	7	5	32	16	1	3.9	13.5	48	42%	.234	0.94	0.56	1.77	1.2				
2015	HOU	MLB	21	6	7	0	22	22	125^{2}	106	10	3.1	9.2	129	48%	.288	1.19	3.22	3.32	2.6	97.4	40	54	63
2016	HOU	MLB	22	6	5	0	14	14	81	80	5	5.0	11.8	106	59%	.383	1.54	3.22	2.77	2.4	97.0	46	45	47
2017	HOU	MLB	23	7	4	0	22	22	118^{2}	114	8	3.0	10.0	132	62%	.330	1.30	4.25	3.52	2.7	96.5	36	46	55
2018	*HOU*	*MLB*	*24*	*12*	*6*	*0*	*26*	*26*	*148*	*128*	*13*	*3.6*	*10.2*	*169*	*54%*	*.303*	*1.28*	*3.22*	*3.55*	*3.2*	*96.7*	*41*	*50*	*56*
2019	*HOU*	*MLB*	*25*	*11*	*9*	*0*	*30*	*30*	*187^{2}*	*162*	*19*	*3.6*	*10.8*	*224*	*54%*	*.309*	*1.27*	*3.48*	*3.67*	*3.7*	*96.4*	*41*	*48*	*55*

Breakout: 27% Improve: 67% Collapse: 11% Attrition: 16% MLB: 97% *Comparables: Rich Harden, Phil Hughes, Alex Wood*

McCullers' curveball is a work of art. During Game 7 of the ALCS, the Texan crafted a perfect tessellation of bent shapes, working almost exclusively in that medium and creating a mosaic so stunning that it silenced even the Yankees' bats. Only Dellin Betances (a reliever) and Bronson Arroyo (a trickster) threw their benders more frequently than McCullers did, and it earned him a *Sports Illustrated* cover story even as pundits posited him as a Cy Young candidate. Of course, his offerings give his work another thing in common with grand works of art: fragility. McCullers is perhaps the platonic ideal of today's pitcher, as his combo of reliance on breaking balls and difficulty staying healthy occasionally overshadows his raw brilliance. But for the time being, critics should consider placing his Uncle Charlie in the Louvre with Noah Syndergaard's slider and Aroldis Chapman's fastball—you know, the other modern classics.

Collin McHugh RHP Born: 06/19/87 Age: 30 Bats: R Throws: R Height: 6'2" Weight: 190 Origin: Round 18, 2008 Draft (#554 overall)

YEAR	TEAM	LVL	AGE	W	L	SV	G	GS	IP	H	HR	BB/9	K/9	K	GB%	BABIP	WHIP	ERA	DRA	WARP	MPH	CMD	PWR	STM
2015	HOU	MLB	28	19	7	0	32	32	203^{2}	207	19	2.3	7.6	171	47%	.310	1.28	3.89	4.12	2.3	92.7	38	25	78
2016	HOU	MLB	29	13	10	0	33	33	184^{2}	206	25	2.6	8.6	177	43%	.339	1.41	4.34	4.72	1.3	92.6	43	27	78
2017	CCH	AA	30	0	0	0	4	4	15	18	1	2.4	6.6	11	57%	.340	1.47	3.60	4.17	0.2				
2017	HOU	MLB	30	5	2	0	12	12	63^{1}	62	7	2.8	8.8	62	33%	.312	1.29	3.55	3.75	1.3	91.7	52	29	30
2018	*HOU*	*MLB*	*31*	*6*	*5*	*0*	*27*	*13*	*92*	*95*	*14*	*3.1*	*8.1*	*84*	*42%*	*.300*	*1.38*	*4.41*	*4.80*	*0.6*	*91.6*	*43*	*27*	*58*
2019	*HOU*	*MLB*	*32*	*9*	*10*	*0*	*26*	*26*	*153^{2}*	*161*	*24*	*3.2*	*7.7*	*132*	*42%*	*.303*	*1.40*	*4.77*	*5.07*	*1.0*	*91.1*	*44*	*27*	*53*

Breakout: 13% Improve: 34% Collapse: 30% Attrition: 12% MLB: 91% *Comparables: Bronson Arroyo, Shaun Marcum, Jordan Zimmermann*

We don't often expect to see a pitcher return from elbow injury rehab with a new and improved slider, of all things, but one good turn deserves another. When McHugh missed the first three months of the season, it gave teammate Brad Peacock the chance to shine in a starting role, and in exchange, Peacock passed along his signature pitch to his recovering teammate. When he returned in July, McHugh pushed his own sweeping slider as a weapon against right-handed hitters. His new pitch was immediately his best swing-and-miss offering, which is saying something given his history of getting whiffs with his curveball and his changeup. Now he's back right where he left off: a solid mid-rotation hand.

Charlie Morton RHP Born: 11/12/83 Age: 34 Bats: R Throws: R Height: 6'5" Weight: 235 Origin: Round 3, 2002 Draft (#95 overall)

YEAR	TEAM	LVL	AGE	W	L	SV	G	GS	IP	H	HR	BB/9	K/9	K	GB%	BABIP	WHIP	ERA	DRA	WARP	MPH	CMD	PWR	STM
2015	IND	AAA	31	1	1	0	2	2	13^{1}	13	0	2.7	11.5	17	60%	.371	1.27	2.03	1.90	0.5				
2015	PIT	MLB	31	9	9	0	23	23	129	137	13	2.9	6.7	96	60%	.309	1.38	4.81	4.25	1.3	94.4	59	46	66
2016	PHI	MLB	32	1	1	0	4	4	17^{1}	15	1	4.2	9.9	19	66%	.326	1.33	4.15	3.02	0.5	96.5	53	52	37
2017	HOU	MLB	33	14	7	0	25	25	146^{2}	125	14	3.1	10.0	163	53%	.295	1.19	3.62	3.46	3.4	96.6	42	58	66
2018	*HOU*	*MLB*	*34*	*12*	*7*	*0*	*26*	*26*	*156*	*145*	*19*	*3.4*	*8.7*	*150*	*54%*	*.297*	*1.32*	*3.91*	*4.31*	*2.0*	*94.7*	*47*	*53*	*55*
2019	*HOU*	*MLB*	*35*	*10*	*11*	*0*	*30*	*30*	*187^{2}*	*180*	*26*	*3.8*	*8.7*	*182*	*54%*	*.3*	*1.37*	*4.48*	*4.75*	*1.8*	*94.3*	*44*	*55*	*53*

Breakout: 14% Improve: 50% Collapse: 18% Attrition: 11% MLB: 94% *Comparables: Andy Pettitte, Gavin Floyd, Whitey Ford*

Morton's comment in last year's *Annual* closed with this sentence: "Somewhere out there, perhaps there's a multiverse where a healthy Charlie Morton consistently throws 190-200 innings, is a 3-4 WARP pitcher and is appreciated on his own merits." Folks, we've slipped through the wormhole and arrived in Charlie's dimension. The Astros made a small bet on the journeyman right-hander and it paid off big after he built on his abortive season in Philly. Injury issues still kept him from going deep into games or making 30 starts, but his curveball shut down the left-handed hitters that were previously the bane of his existence. Perhaps 2018 will bring a fast trip back to reality, but if he can stay strong for another full season he'll bring home a contract that's much more lucrative than the one that brought him to Houston.

Joe Musgrove RHP Born: 12/04/92 Age: 25 Bats: R Throws: R Height: 6'5" Weight: 265 Origin: Round 1, 2011 Draft (#46 overall)

YEAR	TEAM	LVL	AGE	W	L	SV	G	GS	IP	H	HR	BB/9	K/9	K	GB%	BABIP	WHIP	ERA	DRA	WARP	MPH	CMD	PWR	STM
2015	QUD	A	22	4	1	0	5	3	25^{2}	22	0	0.4	8.1	23	51%	.293	0.90	0.70	2.30	0.8				
2015	LNC	A+	22	4	0	0	6	4	30	28	2	0.3	12.9	43	52%	.366	0.97	2.40	1.51	1.3				
2015	CCH	AA	22	4	0	1	8	7	45	35	7	1.2	6.6	33	45%	.219	0.91	2.20	4.17	0.5				
2016	CCH	AA	23	2	1	0	6	4	26^{1}	19	1	1.0	10.3	30	49%	.265	0.84	0.34	1.10	1.2				
2016	FRE	AAA	23	5	3	0	10	10	59	60	8	1.1	8.7	57	55%	.317	1.14	3.81	2.08	2.2				
2016	HOU	MLB	23	4	4	0	11	10	62	59	9	2.3	8.0	55	43%	.289	1.21	4.06	4.61	0.5	94.6	40	38	58
2017	HOU	MLB	24	7	8	2	38	15	109^{1}	117	18	2.3	8.1	98	46%	.316	1.33	4.77	5.76	-0.4	95.7	43	46	56
2018	*HOU*	*MLB*	*25*	*5*	*4*	*0*	*50*	*8*	*84*	*77*	*11*	*2.8*	*8.8*	*83*	*46%*	*.291*	*1.22*	*3.80*	*4.17*	*1.0*	*95.1*	*43*	*45*	*58*
2019	*HOU*	*MLB*	*26*	*7*	*5*	*0*	*75*	*11*	*130^{2}*	*120*	*18*	*2.3*	*8.9*	*130*	*46%*	*.291*	*1.17*	*3.83*	*4.07*	*1.8*	*94.9*	*43*	*45*	*58*

Breakout: 29% Improve: 57% Collapse: 17% Attrition: 19% MLB: 94% *Comparables: David Huff, Dan Haren, Kevin Slowey*

As a starter to begin the season, Musgrove was tuned up. As a relief pitcher in the second half, he was tuned in. In September he even went so far as to resist walking a single batter in 11 innings of work. But despite his later-season effectiveness, the playoffs were just as sketchy as his April, and he coughed up six runs in 6 2/3 innings when A.J. Hinch was forced to use him in October. Nevertheless, this big righty gets to go down in history as the guy who got the win during one of the wildest World Series games ever after giving up three runs in Game 5. With all of the other talent in Houston, he's more likely to find work in relief than get another crack at the rotation, but his combo of versatility and command makes him a valuable part of the staff.

David Paulino RHP Born: 02/06/94 Age: 24 Bats: R Throws: R Height: 6'7" Weight: 215 Origin: International Free Agent, 2010

YEAR	TEAM	LVL	AGE	W	L	SV	G	GS	IP	H	HR	BB/9	K/9	K	GB%	BABIP	WHIP	ERA	DRA	WARP	MPH	CMD	PWR	STM
2015	QUD	A	21	3	2	0	5	5	28^{2}	21	0	2.2	10.0	32	47%	.292	0.98	1.57	2.04	1.1				
2015	LNC	A+	21	1	1	1	6	5	29^{1}	24	1	3.1	9.2	30	40%	.295	1.16	4.91	4.67	0.1				
2016	AST	RK	22	0	0	0	3	3	12	9	0	1.5	10.5	14	75%	.281	0.92	0.75	2.14	0.5				
2016	CCH	AA	22	5	2	1	14	9	64	47	3	1.5	10.1	72	40%	.280	0.91	1.83	2.07	2.2				
2016	FRE	AAA	22	0	2	0	3	3	14	16	1	3.9	12.9	20	45%	.385	1.57	3.86	3.04	0.4				
2016	HOU	MLB	22	0	1	0	3	1	7	6	0	3.9	2.6	2	44%	.261	1.29	5.14	8.21	-0.2	94.8			35
2017	FRE	AAA	23	0	1	0	3	3	14	11	3	5.8	8.4	13	28%	.216	1.43	4.50	7.94	-0.3				
2017	HOU	MLB	23	2	0	0	6	6	29	36	8	2.2	10.6	34	33%	.359	1.48	6.52	6.52	-0.3	94.0	37	35	45
2018	*HOU*	*MLB*	*24*	*2*	*2*	*0*	*17*	*3*	*30^{2}*	*29*	*6*	*3.7*	*9.9*	*34*	*38%*	*.294*	*1.35*	*4.66*	*4.94*	*0.1*	*93.9*	*38*	*36*	*42*
2019	*HOU*	*MLB*	*25*	*6*	*5*	*0*	*66*	*11*	*122^{1}*	*110*	*23*	*3.4*	*10.6*	*144*	*38%*	*.29*	*1.27*	*4.54*	*4.85*	*0.7*	*93.7*	*38*	*36*	*42*

Breakout: 32% Improve: 62% Collapse: 10% Attrition: 22% MLB: 86% *Comparables: Jon Gray, Matt Harvey, Michael Feliz*

When a young player misses time thanks to an injury or suspension, their team doesn't just lose out on performance, the player also misses out on critical development time. So everyone lost when Paulino—possessor of a serious heater but sketchy secondary stuff—got slapped with an 80-game suspension after testing positive for an anabolic steroid. Besides the ignominy of a failed test and the specter of a full-season suspension looming if he slips again, the tall righty may have cost himself a chance to nudge his way into a rotation. The 2018 season will be a make-or-break year, and unless he can figure out a decent second pitch he'll find himself in the 'pen or on the fringes of domestic pro ball.

Brad Peacock RHP Born: 02/02/88 Age: 30 Bats: R Throws: R Height: 6'1" Weight: 210 Origin: Round 41, 2006 Draft (#1231 overall)

YEAR	TEAM	LVL	AGE	W	L	SV	G	GS	IP	H	HR	BB/9	K/9	K	GB%	BABIP	WHIP	ERA	DRA	WARP	MPH	CMD	PWR	STM
2015	HOU	MLB	27	0	1	0	1	1	5	5	0	3.6	5.4	3	31%	.312	1.40	5.40	3.51	0.1	92.3			0
2016	FRE	AAA	28	5	6	0	22	21	117	122	11	3.1	9.2	119	44%	.335	1.38	4.23	3.14	2.9				
2016	HOU	MLB	28	0	1	0	10	5	31^{2}	21	6	4.0	8.0	28	41%	.190	1.11	3.69	5.37	0.0	94.1	44	39	64
2017	HOU	MLB	29	13	2	0	34	21	132	100	10	3.9	11.0	161	44%	.286	1.19	3.00	2.83	3.9	93.9	55	38	60
2018	*HOU*	*MLB*	*30*	*8*	*6*	*0*	*27*	*18*	*112*	*104*	*16*	*4.1*	*9.0*	*113*	*42%*	*.290*	*1.37*	*4.35*	*4.75*	*0.8*	*93.2*	*53*	*38*	*46*
2019	*HOU*	*MLB*	*31*	*10*	*10*	*0*	*29*	*29*	*183^{1}*	*162*	*25*	*3.8*	*9.0*	*184*	*42%*	*.28*	*1.30*	*4.37*	*4.64*	*1.9*	*92.7*	*53*	*38*	*55*

Breakout: 19% Improve: 46% Collapse: 20% Attrition: 15% MLB: 87% *Comparables: Rich Hill, Corey Kluber, Collin McHugh*

Ever wonder why some pitchers get second and third and fourth chances to start? It's usually because they have some combination of eye-popping stuff and poor command. Peacock was no exception, but after bouncing in and out of the majors for the better part of six seasons, he had about run out of chances before adjusting his arm slot. That minor tweak gave him a slider that disappears from the zone like David Copperfield making the Statue of Liberty blink out of existence, and his focus on that one magical pitch finally completed his transformation from Quad-A swingman to one of the league's most fearsome hurlers. There are issues still, as Peacock has hardly ever faced a lineup more than twice in a game and he looked gassed by the end of the season. It doesn't matter how many chances you blow in baseball, so long as you make the most of your last one.

Hector Rondon RHP Born: 02/26/88 Age: 30 Bats: R Throws: R Height: 6'3" Weight: 230 Origin: International Free Agent, 2004

YEAR	TEAM	LVL	AGE	W	L	SV	G	GS	IP	H	HR	BB/9	K/9	K	GB%	BABIP	WHIP	ERA	DRA	WARP	MPH	CMD	PWR	STM
2015	CHN	MLB	27	6	4	30	72	0	70	55	4	1.9	8.9	69	53%	.268	1.00	1.67	2.51	1.8	99.0	51	65	51
2016	CHN	MLB	28	2	3	18	54	0	51	42	8	1.4	10.2	58	49%	.274	0.98	3.53	2.55	1.4	98.5	68	61	39
2017	CHN	MLB	29	4	1	0	61	0	57^{1}	50	10	3.1	10.8	69	48%	.292	1.22	4.24	3.57	1.0	98.3	61	66	47
2018	*HOU*	*MLB*	*30*	*2*	*2*	*0*	*42*	*0*	*44*	*39*	*7*	*3.2*	*10.0*	*49*	*48%*	*.289*	*1.24*	*3.97*	*4.32*	*0.4*	*97.8*	*60*	*64*	*45*
2019	*HOU*	*MLB*	*31*	*3*	*1*	*0*	*53*	*0*	*55^{2}*	*50*	*9*	*3.4*	*9.9*	*61*	*48%*	*.285*	*1.27*	*4.21*	*4.63*	*0.4*	*97.3*	*62*	*64*	*44*

Breakout: 31% Improve: 45% Collapse: 25% Attrition: 9% MLB: 92% *Comparables: Luke Gregerson, Keith Foulke, Sparky Lyle*

In *The Iliad*, the Greek hero Hector is slain at the end by Achilles, who then proceeds to drag his lifeless body around on a chariot for 12 days. This is not necessarily what happened to Rondon, but he did fall out of Joe Maddon's good graces when it came to any sort of high-leverage inning, and last year he was left off the postseason roster entirely. That walk rate did get Trojan horsed, especially against left-handers, and while he did endure a couple arm injuries, the velocity hasn't shown it. He doesn't look comfortable setting up the closer—the job he lost for no great reason other than Aroldis Chapman and then Wade Davis appeared—and that's going to hurt his stock, which is weird since Hector in Ancient Greek literally means "to hold."

Joe Smith RHP Born: 03/22/84 Age: 34 Bats: R Throws: R Height: 6'2" Weight: 205 Origin: Round 3, 2006 Draft (#94 overall)

YEAR	TEAM	LVL	AGE	W	L	SV	G	GS	IP	H	HR	BB/9	K/9	K	GB%	BABIP	WHIP	ERA	DRA	WARP	MPH	CMD	PWR	STM
2015	ANA	MLB	31	5	5	5	70	0	65^{1}	64	4	2.6	7.9	57	54%	.317	1.27	3.58	3.46	1.0	90.8	72	35	50
2016	ANA	MLB	32	1	4	6	38	0	37^{2}	36	4	3.1	6.0	25	57%	.283	1.30	3.82	4.89	0.0	90.6	63	37	42
2016	CHN	MLB	32	1	1	0	16	0	14^{1}	11	4	3.1	9.4	15	36%	.219	1.12	2.51	4.91	0.0	90.6	63	37	42
2017	TOR	MLB	33	3	0	0	38	0	35^{2}	30	3	2.5	12.9	51	44%	.342	1.12	3.28	1.98	1.3	90.6	50	35	44
2017	CLE	MLB	33	0	0	1	21	0	18^{1}	16	1	0.0	9.8	20	60%	.306	0.87	3.44	2.73	0.5	90.1	50	35	44
2018	*HOU*	*MLB*	*34*	*3*	*2*	*0*	*47*	*0*	*49^{1}*	*44*	*7*	*3.3*	*9.5*	*52*	*49%*	*.291*	*1.26*	*3.92*	*4.28*	*0.5*	*89.5*	*60*	*35*	*44*
2019	*HOU*	*MLB*	*35*	*3*	*1*	*0*	*53*	*0*	*56^{2}*	*50*	*8*	*3.3*	*9.5*	*60*	*49%*	*.29*	*1.25*	*4.13*	*4.38*	*0.5*	*88.9*	*56*	*35*	*43*

Breakout: 11% Improve: 28% Collapse: 41% Attrition: 5% MLB: 87% *Comparables: J.P. Howell, Jonathan Papelbon, Jim Johnson*

Quick: Of all the high-octane arms on the Cleveland staff, who put up the lowest FIP in 2017? Yeah, sure, it was Andrew Miller. But would you believe that the anonymous Mr. Smith finished a close second? Of course you would, since you're reading this and we therefore know you are a tremendously insightful and well-informed baseball fan already aware that the veteran side-armer is one of the most consistently productive relievers in the game. Smith's low-velo sinker-slider approach induces plenty of groundballs and has held righties to a .215/.281/.305 line over his 11-year career, and there's no reason to think he'll stop anytime soon.

Justin Verlander RHP Born: 02/20/83 Age: 35 Bats: R Throws: R Height: 6'5" Weight: 225 Origin: Round 1, 2004 Draft (#2 overall)

YEAR	TEAM	LVL	AGE	W	L	SV	G	GS	IP	H	HR	BB/9	K/9	K	GB%	BABIP	WHIP	ERA	DRA	WARP	MPH	CMD	PWR	STM
2015	DET	MLB	32	5	8	0	20	20	133^1	113	13	2.2	7.6	113	37%	.267	1.09	3.38	3.27	2.9	96.5	63	54	66
2016	DET	MLB	33	16	9	0	34	34	227^2	171	30	2.3	10.0	254	35%	.255	1.00	3.04	2.66	7.0	96.8	65	53	88
2017	DET	MLB	34	10	8	0	28	28	172	153	23	3.5	9.2	176	34%	.283	1.28	3.82	3.10	4.7	97.3	62	61	86
2017	HOU	MLB	34	5	0	0	5	5	34	17	4	1.3	11.4	43	32%	.194	0.65	1.06	3.97	0.6	97.3	62	61	86
2018	*HOU*	*MLB*	*35*	*14*	*9*	*0*	*31*	*31*	*195^1*	*184*	*32*	*3.1*	*8.9*	*194*	*37%*	*.289*	*1.28*	*4.24*	*4.67*	*1.6*	*95.7*	*62*	*56*	*80*
2019	*HOU*	*MLB*	*36*	*11*	*12*	*0*	*30*	*30*	*189^1*	*180*	*32*	*3.4*	*8.6*	*182*	*37%*	*.287*	*1.34*	*4.76*	*5.06*	*1.2*	*95.2*	*62*	*56*	*82*

Breakout: 11% Improve: 31% Collapse: 39% Attrition: 9% MLB: 89% *Comparables: Adam Wainwright, Jason Schmidt, Roy Halladay*

Everyone's life is a sequence of millions of little decision points. Years ago, Verlander made so many decisions along his path that created the pitcher he was in 2017: extra pitching practice instead of video games, another round at the gym instead of another round at the bar. His decisions made him one of the greatest pitchers of his generation, and kept him working at an elite level into his age-34 season. Another decision point changed his career, perhaps more than any other to this point: the decision to accept the trade to Houston just minutes before the deadline in August. Beyond the #HoustonStrong and "the Astros needed a veteran starter" narratives, he was every inch the dominant ace through five regular-season games and six playoff appearances. Having earned the ring he's been striving for his entire career, all the following decision points seem just a little sweeter. "Where should I go on my honeymoon? How will I follow up such an incredible season? And what should I say during my Hall of Fame induction speech?"

Forrest Whitley RHP Born: 09/15/97 Age: 20 Bats: R Throws: R Height: 6'7" Weight: 240 Origin: Round 1, 2016 Draft (#17 overall)

YEAR	TEAM	LVL	AGE	W	L	SV	G	GS	IP	H	HR	BB/9	K/9	K	GB%	BABIP	WHIP	ERA	DRA	WARP	MPH	CMD	PWR	STM
2016	GRV	RK	18	0	1	0	4	4	11^1	11	0	2.4	10.3	13	53%	.344	1.24	3.18	2.94	0.3				
2017	QUD	A	19	2	3	0	12	10	46^1	42	2	4.1	13.0	67	37%	.388	1.36	2.91	3.63	0.9				
2017	BCA	A+	19	3	1	0	7	6	31^1	28	2	2.6	14.4	50	40%	.394	1.18	3.16	2.14	1.1				
2017	CCH	AA	19	0	0	0	4	2	14^2	8	1	2.5	16.0	26	48%	.292	0.82	1.84	1.89	0.6				
2018	*HOU*	*MLB*	*20*	*4*	*4*	*0*	*23*	*13*	*64^1*	*60*	*14*	*4.7*	*12.2*	*87*	*37%*	*.318*	*1.46*	*5.03*	*5.40*	*0.2*				
2019	*HOU*	*MLB*	*21*	*5*	*7*	*0*	*30*	*21*	*144^2*	*140*	*31*	*4.7*	*11.6*	*186*	*37%*	*.316*	*1.48*	*5.16*	*5.51*	*0.1*				

Breakout: 8% Improve: 10% Collapse: 3% Attrition: 5% MLB: 13% *Comparables: Tyler Glasnow, Zach Braddock, Clayton Kershaw*

The Astros' top prospect absolutely crushed his first full season in affiliated ball as he climbed the ranks. Whitley took three steps from the Quad Cities to Buies Creek to Corpus Christi, improving his numbers at every stop. It makes sense that he would thrive in the upper minors; for a prep arm, he's a bit of a pitchability prodigy with three pitches that flash plus as well as the height to fill out over time. Of course he hasn't proven the ability to log a big-league workload—over 23 appearances last year, he didn't even crack 95 innings—but it's hard to find more than four or five pitching prospects with the combination of floor and upside that Whitley might one day bring to Houston.

LINEOUTS

Hitters

HITTER	POS	TEAM	LVL	AGE	PA	R	2B	3B	HR	RBI	BB	K	SB	CS	AVG/OBP/SLG	TAv	VORP	BABIP	BRR	FRAA	WARP
Jonathan Arauz	SS	QUD	A	18	149	23	3	2	0	4	20	18	0	1	.220/.331/.276	.242	2.8	.257	-0.3	SS(32): -1.3, 2B(4): -0.4	0.1
	SS	TCV	A-	18	135	16	7	1	1	11	12	29	1	0	.264/.341/.364	.266	6.5	.341	0.2	SS(28): -3.1, 3B(5): -0.4	0.3
Tim Federowicz	C	SAC	AAA	29	314	34	19	0	9	43	30	65	3	0	.300/.366/.463	.286	22.2	.362	-1.7	C(73): 4.6, 1B(2): 0.0	2.6
	C	SFN	MLB	29	14	3	0	0	2	3	1	4	0	0	.231/.286/.692	.302	1.4	.143	0.2	C(6): 0.1, 1B(1): 0.0	0.1
Tony Kemp	2B	FRE	AAA	25	554	95	23	9	10	62	35	43	24	7	.329/.375/.470	.297	38.7	.344	0.4	2B(97): -10.2, CF(10): -0.2	2.6
	2B	HOU	MLB	25	39	6	1	0	0	4	1	5	1	0	.216/.256/.243	.173	-1.7	.250	0.9	LF(10): -0.4, CF(4): -0.2	-0.2
Jason Martin	OF	BCA	A+	21	198	34	11	2	7	29	20	42	9	5	.287/.354/.494	.313	13.6	.333	-1.6	LF(14): 1.1, CF(8): -2.2	1.3
	OF	CCH	AA	21	320	38	24	3	11	37	19	82	7	6	.273/.319/.483	.282	14.0	.343	1.1	LF(57): -6.8	0.8
J.J. Matijevic	INF	TCV	A-	21	222	34	14	0	6	27	18	60	11	3	.240/.302/.400	.255	4.0	.307	0.8	LF(44): -5.3, 1B(1): 0.0	-0.1
	INF	QUD	A	21	26	2	0	0	1	4	1	9	0	1	.125/.192/.250	.161	-2.6	.143	-0.2		-0.3
Freudis Nova	SS	DAR	Rk	17	190	30	6	0	4	16	15	33	8	3	.247/.342/.355	.278	8.9	.287	-2.1	SS(19): 0.0, 3B(8): -1.0	0.7
Chuckie Robinson	C	QUD	A	22	468	69	32	2	15	77	31	98	7	1	.274/.330/.463	.289	30.7	.324	-0.2	C(80): 5.3, 1B(3): 0.2	3.8
Miguelangel Sierra	SS	TCV	A-	19	208	15	8	1	4	13	17	62	6	1	.178/.260/.297	.222	-2.9	.240	-2.3	SS(43): -4.6, 2B(15): 1.8	-0.6
Jon Singleton	1B	CCH	AA	25	500	55	20	0	18	62	107	132	3	0	.205/.376/.397	.286	15.2	.253	-3.2	1B(77): 7.5	2.4

Athletic 19-year-old shortstop **Jonathan Arauz** needs to do something to perk up his bat to crack prospect lists and make it to "The Show." A 50-game suspension for stimulant use was probably not the right way to add some pep to his offensive game. ⚾ When a big-league catcher goes down and the Triple-A reserve is ordered overnight, **Tim Federowicz** (aka FedEx) lives to deliver. ⚾ As much as the Astros would like to relive the Jose Altuve experience with **Tony Kemp**, that small ship has sailed. Though fleet and able to draw a walk, he hasn't displayed enough bat or defense to be anything other than a sixth infielder or Triple-A depth. ⚾ Left-handed masher **Jason Martin** continues to slowly progress up the ranks in the Astros' system, topping out at Double-A, where he had twice as many extra-base hits as walks. It's appropriate that he's got a fairly vanilla name; given the holes in his game, it's already hard enough to separate him from the rest of Houston's outfield depth. ⚾ University of Arizona standout **J.J. Matijevic** excelled in his final year of college

(.383/.436/.633) but struggled in his first partial season of pro ball. With no position and no clear path to the majors, this former Wildcat is a current wild card. ⚾ A nova is a false star, a supernova is an exploding star and a **Freudis Nova** is a hyper-talented teenage shortstop who could one day become a star. (It's just a bit too on-the-nose that he's an Astro.) P.S. Now you are an astronomer. ⚾ Despite little fanfare, catcher **Chuckie Robinson** was the best player on the Midwest League champion Quad Cities River Bandits in his first full pro season. Given his launching-pad swing and ability to wear shin guards, there's potential that he'll make the majors. ⚾ After two seasons of solid performance in rookie ball, everything went backward for young shortstop prospect **Miguelangel Sierra**. The tools are still there, but his bat needs to at least cross the Mendoza line. ⚾ **Jon Singleton** is entering the final year of the infamous contract extension that he signed before ever reaching the majors. He spent all of 2017 at Double-A Corpus Christi, and it's unlikely a second big-league contract will ever materialize.

Pitchers

PITCHER	TEAM	LVL	AGE	W	L	SV	G	GS	IP	H	HR	BB/9	K/9	K	GB%	BABIP	WHIP	ERA	DRA	WARP	MPH	CMD	PWR	STM
Dean Deetz	CCH	AA	23	4	2	0	8	6	39^{2}	27	3	2.0	9.5	42	46%	.253	0.91	1.82	2.62	1.2				
	FRE	AAA	23	3	4	0	17	10	45	46	5	8.2	11.0	55	40%	.353	1.93	6.40	8.22	-1.3				
Riley Ferrell	CCH	AA	23	2	2	4	36	0	52	51	2	2.4	9.5	55	52%	.348	1.25	3.81	2.93	1.2				
Reymin Guduan	FRE	AAA	25	5	7	1	39	0	46	61	4	2.7	9.2	47	50%	.401	1.63	5.87	4.23	0.5				
	HOU	MLB	25	0	0	0	22	0	16	24	1	6.8	9.0	16	55%	.426	2.25	7.88	6.34	-0.2	97.0	35	63	49
Jandel Gustave	HOU	MLB	24	0	0	0	6	0	5	5	0	12.6	3.6	2	50%	.312	2.40	5.40	4.65	0.0	97.8			
Corbin Martin	TCV	A-	21	0	1	1	8	3	27^{2}	20	1	2.6	12.4	38	63%	.297	1.01	2.60	1.34	1.1				
Cionel Perez	QUD	A	21	4	3	2	12	9	55^{1}	52	2	2.8	8.9	55	51%	.331	1.25	4.39	3.37	1.2				
	BCA	A+	21	2	1	0	5	4	25^{1}	27	1	1.8	6.4	18	46%	.325	1.26	2.84	4.24	0.3				
	CCH	AA	21	0	0	0	4	3	13	15	1	3.5	6.9	10	33%	.341	1.54	5.54	6.16	-0.2				
Hector Perez	QUD	A	21	1	1	0	4	3	18	9	2	5.5	12.0	24	51%	.200	1.11	2.50	2.92	0.5				
	BCA	A+	21	6	5	2	21	14	89^{1}	69	6	6.8	10.5	104	55%	.300	1.52	3.63	4.50	0.7				
Brady Rodgers	FRE	AAA	26	2	0	0	3	3	16^{1}	14	0	0.6	6.1	11	60%	.292	0.92	1.10	3.12	0.5				
Elian Rodriguez	DAR	Rk	20	0	3	0	9	9	25^{1}	26	1	10.7	6.8	19	62%	.385	2.21	7.46	9.80	-0.9				
Tony Sipp	HOU	MLB	33	0	1	0	46	0	37^{1}	36	8	3.9	9.4	39	50%	.277	1.39	5.79	5.70	-0.2	92.2	46	32	38
Trent Thornton	CCH	AA	23	1	2	0	4	3	16^{1}	25	2	0.0	7.2	13	57%	.377	1.53	6.06	3.85	0.2				
	FRE	AAA	23	8	4	0	21	20	115	137	12	1.8	6.9	88	47%	.338	1.39	5.09	3.20	3.1				
Framber Valdez	BCA	A+	23	2	3	1	13	9	61^{1}	41	3	4.3	10.7	73	57%	.257	1.14	2.79	2.32	2.0				
	CCH	AA	23	5	5	0	12	9	49	60	4	4.2	9.7	53	60%	.394	1.69	5.88	4.24	0.5				

Here are the (**Dean**) **Deetz**: flashy three-pitch stuff and loads of strikeouts, but nothing remotely resembling control. He walked almost a batter per inning at Triple-A and is almost certainly now a candidate for a relief conversion. ⚾ It was a September to remember for former TCU closer **Riley Ferrell**: 16 punchouts, three hits and zero walks in 10 glorious innings. With his 2016 shoulder surgery in the rear-view mirror, all signs point to a shot at a big-league bullpen. ⚾ For one shining moment, control-challenged **Reymin Guduan** found the strike zone at Triple-A Fresno. Of course, he lost that command as soon as he hit the majors, so maybe Reymin *Bad*uan? ⚾ Scramble the letters in the name of flame-throwing reliever **Jandel Gustave** and you can get *unsalvaged jet*. That seems rather appropriate, as his season crashed and burned after a slow start and Tommy John surgery in April. ⚾ Former Aggie and 2017 second-round pick **Corbin Martin** dominated in a brief showing after signing, but as a college starter he's kind of supposed to. Without any true plus offerings, he profiles as more of a back-end starter, but there's room to grow. ⚾ Diminutive Cuban lefty **Cionel Perez** may have lost half of his original signing bonus thanks to contract drama, but what he lacks in stacks he made up for with a rapid ascent through three levels of Houston's system in a single season. ⚾ Any minor-league starting pitcher who averages more than a strikeout per inning is an exciting prospect; any minor-league starting pitcher who walks almost seven batters per nine innings is probably not a starting pitcher for much longer. See you in the bullpen, **Hector Perez**. ⚾ Last April, **Brady Rodgers** hit the "young potential back-of-the-rotation starter" trifecta in limited action. He a) displayed impeccable control, b) limited earned runs and c) blew out his UCL, scuttling what could have been his breakout season. ⚾ High-profile international signing **Elian Rodriguez** got off to a rough start in his pro debut. Unfortunately, it's just another example of a Cuban named Elian having a rough go of things in the US. ⚾ **Tony Sipp** signed a three-year, $18 million contract before the 2016 season, and as the old saying goes, hindsight is 20/20: He's given up 20 homers in 81 innings since then and he's about 20 minutes away from finding himself out of the majors. ⚾ Lanky right-hander **Trent Thornton** is enough of a talent to serve as Triple-A starter depth, but might not be cut out for extended major-league duty. While he walks remarkably few hitters, his long levers and athleticism haven't translated to punchouts just yet. ⚾ Signed out of the Dominican Republic at the ripe old age of 21, **Framber Valdez** is a left-hander with a heavy fastball that sits in the mid-90s.

League Leaders 2017

MLB Batting Average – Jose Altuve, .346

KANSAS CITY ROYALS

Essay by Christina Kahrl

Player comments by Zack Crizer and BP staff

You're reading this now, not a year ago, and not in July 2017 around the trade deadline, so you know what the Royals' circumstance is. The future is a veritable nuclear winter on the diamond. Sure, you've survived, and sure, something resembling normality might seem possible. Something even resembling the Royals will take the field in front of fans animated by happy memories of 2015 in the seasons to come. For a while yet, you'll recognize a few familiar names on the roster, so it won't be all zombies and fleshy-headed mutants. And between the brief glimpses of sunlight you'll get from Danny Duffy's starts during this long, self-inflicted chill, you can hope that Alex Gordon's contract burns warmly enough to keep you from freezing.

You also know what got you to this point. Flags fly forever, and the pennants and title from the Royals' 2014-2015 peak own a permanent place in baseball history. They delivered memories and glory to animate the imagination, the picture-postcard-perfect payoff on the investment of millions of Royals fans across decades of waiting, and an object lesson in DIY franchise-building and player development. The Royals earned their place in the landscape of possibilities, a team for middle-class America that reached for and achieved its dream.

Which is why you can perhaps also honor their kamikaze run of 2017 for being entirely in character with the organization, while lamenting their lost opportunity to pivot into an actual rebuild. But that's projecting millennial wisdom onto a franchise pursuing a Baby Boomer-style narcissistic worship of the present.

And so it's come to this, and the Royals only have themselves to blame. They went into the 2017 season bidding to make a last run at the postseason with this team, with these Royals. They'd added players to their core, in part to compensate for the tragic loss of Yordano Ventura the previous winter. But they also knew that Eric Hosmer, Lorenzo Cain and Mike Moustakas (and Alcides Escobar if you want to be so generous as to put him on their level) were all outbound free agents to be after the season. Everyone from owner David Glass and general manager Dayton Moore on down to the batboys and beer vendors came into 2017 knowing this was effectively the endpoint of their recent run at relevance.

Moore knew full well what that meant, having elected to keep the team together going into Opening Day: If the Royals stayed in the race early, he wouldn't have to be a seller at the trade deadline. He might even be a buyer, looking to milk this last season for one final October appearance. He might end this stretch of franchise history on an up note. And put a playoff-experienced team in the postseason, and who's to say what might happen?

Except that didn't happen. The Royals didn't even start out strong, but they wanted it so badly that they stuck with it, cresting to seven games above .500 at the end of July, only to reap the worst of all possible rewards while pursuing the siren's song of the playoffs' play-in game as a wild card, and failing to get even that far. They died with their cleats on. There will be no tomorrows, not ones

ROYALS PROSPECTUS

2017 W-L: 80-82, 3RD IN AL CENTRAL

Pythag	.444	21st	B-Age	28.9	*23rd*
RS/G	4.33	24th	P-Age	30.3	*29th*
RA/G	4.88	20th	Salary	$143.0M	*15th*
TAv	.252	26th	M$/MW	$4.1M	*16th*
TAv-P	.264	18th	DL Days	732	*8th*
FIP	4.40	17th	$ on DL	5%	*1st*
DER	.697	22nd			

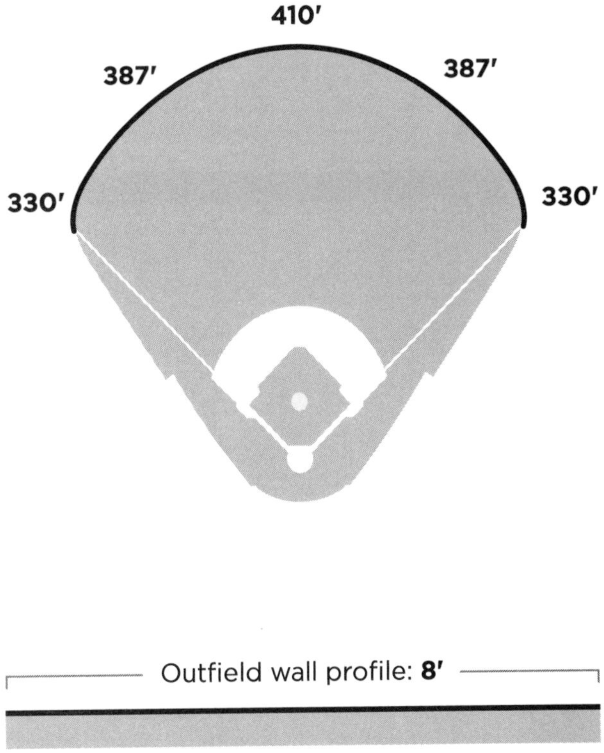

Three-Year Park Factors

Runs	Runs/RH	Runs/LH	HR/RH	HR/LH
101	103	99	88	93

Top Hitter WARP	5.6 Lorenzo Cain
Top Pitcher WARP	3.5 Jason Vargas
Top Prospect	Seuly Matias

2017 Hit List Ranking

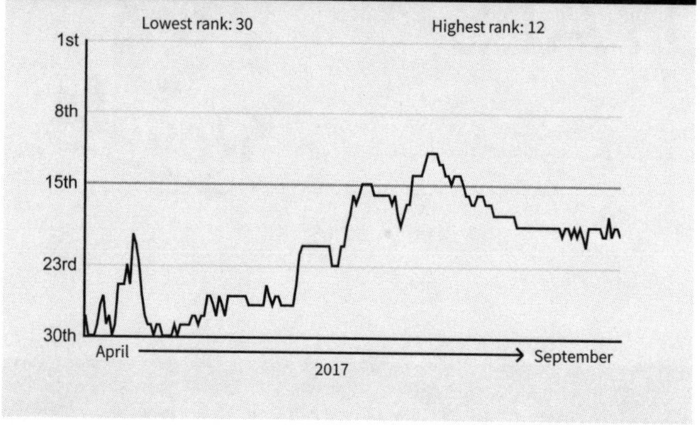

Committed Payroll (in millions)

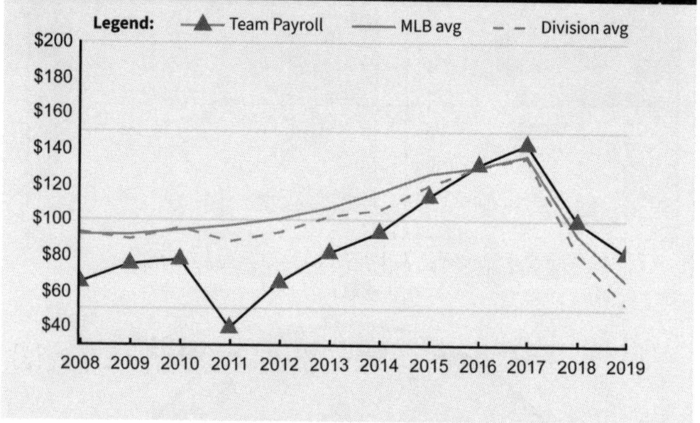

Farm System Ranking

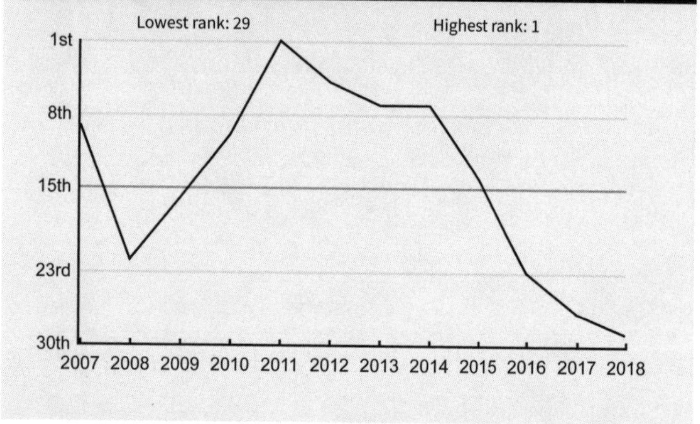

Personnel

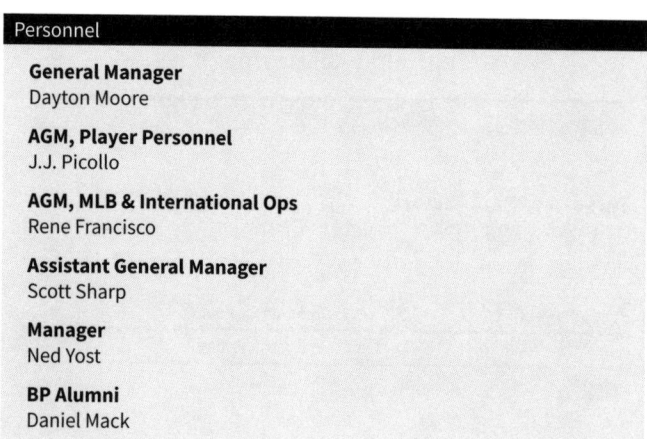

General Manager
Dayton Moore

AGM, Player Personnel
J.J. Picollo

AGM, MLB & International Ops
Rene Francisco

Assistant General Manager
Scott Sharp

Manager
Ned Yost

BP Alumni
Daniel Mack

with any meaning, only penalties.

For the next several seasons, the Royals will exist as baseball's object lesson of what happens to a middle-class franchise that doesn't leverage the tail end of its control of the players it can't keep when the opportunity is there, and that is doomed by its desperate need to cling to familiar comforts and old goals. If Billy Beane perhaps traded Josh Donaldson too soon, this is what the opposite of that looks like—no meaningless playoff appearance *and* no prospects to show for ambitions run rancid.

It's all the more bitter coming from a GM and an organization that should have long since internalized the lesson of swapping before it was too late. The seeds of their 2015 title were sown not just in Moore's earliest drafts as GM (landing Moustakas in 2007 and Hosmer in 2008), but in swapping Zack Greinke in December 2010 to get Cain and Escobar (plus Jeremy Jeffress and Jake Odorizzi). However long Moore has been a convenient whipping boy in sabermetric circles, he'd bet on his talent and won *and* made the hard trades before. You can simultaneously condemn and respect his reservations this time around, having won through patience. But now the price for that failure must be paid.

Sadly—for competitive balance in the industry, as well as for paying customers in their market—the Royals' future is essentially aimless, expensive and almost certainly unfortunate. Now that their core talent has scattered itself across the game through free agency, you're nevertheless left with a team with a payroll that might approach $120 million, while being worth considerably less.

That's already a lot of money to spend for a team. For that kind of payroll, you might hope the Royals would at least have a dead-cat bounce left in them, something like Ed Wade's 2008 Astros and their 86 wins before that franchise's unavoidable reckoning with the wrecking ball. You shouldn't bet on seeing that from the 2018 Royals. Moore had to overbid to gain the services of complementary pieces like Jason Hammel and Joakim Soria, and massively overpaid and bet far too high on the contributions they'd get from Alex Gordon and Ian Kennedy. Even if Glass suddenly wanted to open his checkbook and reimplant the aging heart of this team by re-signing some or all of that Hosmer/Cain/Moose trio, projections suggest they'd be hard-pressed to repeat even last season's 80 wins. That's the fading light of their sunniest scenario. We've already seen the bounce.

Which means they'll be expensive and bad, perhaps lingering in the AL Central standings for a year more above the White Sox and their already impressive rebuild, as well as a Tigers franchise already burrowing deep into their own long night. After 2018 the Royals can cut some costs by skipping out on their mutual options with Hammel, Soria and Brandon Moss—assuming any of those three haven't been dealt first—at which point a new era of even more anonymous Royals should begin. But nobody's going to trade useful talent to rent those three, not in an era where prospect value is at a premium. And nobody's going to trade good stuff for Gordon, even were he inclined to be dealt now that he has 10-and-5 rights to block a deal.

Several factors combine to make this bleak scenario even more grim, and the rebuild even more painful. First, the Royals possess just two talents who might yield any number of difference-making prospects in return—Duffy and Salvador Perez, both signed through 2021. Done right and with the right circumstances in terms of starter-hungry contenders, Duffy's return via in-season trade might yield a package of prospects much like Jose Quintana's did from the Cubs for the White Sox last summer. It would also remove one of the last remaining reasons to watch Royals baseball for the discriminating fan, but a cynic's view of the matter is that whoever's investing in season tickets from this point forward is already committed to rooting for the laundry.

As bleak as that sounds, it's recognizably worse still. There's something bittersweet about the fact that Moore wasn't allowed to chew off a limb, escape his deal (which runs through 2020) and instead prematurely skedaddle back to the Braves organization that launched his career in the wake of Atlanta's front-office scandal. You can admire his readiness to follow the trail John Schuerholz blazed decades earlier out of Kansas City to avoid a reckoning with what he'd wrought. But the other circumstance of Moore's making is the depressing state of the Royals' farm system, exacerbated by their failure to throw in the towel last summer and reap something, anything to shore up their prospect inventory.

You could argue that "the process" generated just this one wave of impact talent in Kansas City, because there's very little help on the way. To Moore's credit, that's the hangover effect of trades that worked in the heat of 2015—like sending Sean Manaea to the A's for Ben Zobrist, or Brandon Finnegan to the Reds for Johnny Cueto—but the organization collectively has to accept responsibility for so many bad bets since, leaving the cupboard relatively bare. There's no inventory to shore up a major-league roster stocked with fourth starters and fading hitters. Trading Perez would make room for Cam Gallagher behind the plate, but they're left hoping for things like Raul Mondesi Jr. or Jorge Soler finally coming around.

Deeper down in the system, the outlook doesn't get any better. If you were pinning your hopes for the future on Kyle Zimmer, Bubba Starling or Josh Staumont, you should probably stop. It's a system overstocked on low-upside first basemen. The Royals had to absorb a two-year penalty on signing international signing bonuses, which finally disappears this summer, but which contributes to their empty player-development pipeline for the near future.

From among their younger crop of highly rated prep pitchers picked in early rounds in recent years, 2015 first-rounders Ashe Russell and Nolan Watson have already imploded (or in Russell's case, almost literally disappeared when he stepped away from the game in 2017 after struggling his first two years). Their best pitching prospect might be 2014 first-rounder Foster Griffin. He's projected as an eventual no. 4 starter, which probably defines what upside looks like in Kansas City these days—aspiring to participate, not star.

Participate, not star. It's a projection that captures the Royals' future, a legacy of thwarted ambitions born of former glory. You can't hate them for what they're about to become or what they failed to do to minimize the damage, but in a near-term future likely to be dominated by a shrinking group of super teams armed to win for years to come, participation is all they can look forward to, unless or until Moore proves that "the process" was not a one-and-done, generational feat to celebrate as a symptom of one of the game's most competitive eras. If he can do that, his legacy will be more than the combination of redemptive success and cautionary tale it has now become. But in the meantime, baby, it's cold outside.

—Christina Kahrl is a co-founder of Baseball Prospectus and MLB senior editor for ESPN.com.

Hitters

Cody Asche OF Born: 06/30/90 Age: 28 Bats: L Throws: R Height: 6'1" Weight: 205 Origin: Round 4, 2011 Draft (#151 overall)

YEAR	TEAM	LVL	AGE	PA	R	2B	3B	HR	RBI	BB	K	SB	CS	AVG/OBP/SLG	TAv	VORP	BABIP	BRR	FRAA	WARP
2015	LEH	AAA	25	67	7	3	0	1	3	6	9	0	0	.295/.358/.393	.270	1.1	.333	-1.0	LF(15): -1.0	0.0
2015	PHI	MLB	25	456	41	22	3	12	39	26	111	1	2	.245/.294/.395	.248	4.1	.304	-2.1	LF(63): -2.5, 3B(51): -2.6	-0.1
2016	LEH	AAA	26	123	20	8	0	6	15	11	26	1	0	.279/.350/.514	.306	9.2	.316	0.7	LF(16): 2.7, 3B(7): -0.5	1.2
2016	PHI	MLB	26	218	22	15	0	4	18	18	54	3	1	.213/.284/.350	.239	0.7	.271	0.5	LF(57): 1.8	0.3
2017	CHA	MLB	27	62	5	1	0	1	4	3	21	0	0	.105/.177/.175	.131	-7.8	.143	-0.1	1B(2): -0.2, 3B(1): 0.0	-0.8
2017	CHR	AAA	27	347	42	15	1	14	57	49	75	4	1	.292/.392/.495	.306	23.5	.343	-0.7	LF(26): 0.0, RF(13): -1.7	2.0
2018	*KCA*	*MLB*	*28*	*250*	*28*	*13*	*1*	*8*	*31*	*21*	*59*	*1*	*1*	*.249/.317/.420*	*.247*	*3.5*	*.301*	*-0.3*	*LF 0, 1B 0*	*0.2*
2019	*KCA*	*MLB*	*29*	*196*	*24*	*10*	*0*	*6*	*23*	*17*	*48*	*1*	*0*	*.241/.311/.404*	*.245*	*0.5*	*.294*	*-0.3*	*LF 0, 1B 0*	*0.0*

Breakout: 6% Improve: 41% Collapse: 9% Attrition: 26% MLB: 83% *Comparables: Matt LaPorta, Mark Canha, Ryan Garko*

Having exhausted his opportunities in Philadelphia, Asche bounced from one rebuilding team to another and promptly mashed his way to a roster spot in spring training. The shortcomings that plagued Asche during his time with the Phillies were quickly realized in Chicago as well, and after an abbreviated tenure with the big club, he spent the duration of his season in Triple-A Charlotte. An oldish corner outfielder, Asche has neither displayed the ability to handle major-league pitching nor proven competent with his glove. All that glitters is not gold. And though not all those who wander are lost, some of them are.

Jorge Bonifacio RF Born: 06/04/93 Age: 25 Bats: R Throws: R Height: 6'1" Weight: 195 Origin: International Free Agent, 2009

YEAR	TEAM	LVL	AGE	PA	R	2B	3B	HR	RBI	BB	K	SB	CS	AVG/OBP/SLG	TAv	VORP	BABIP	BRR	FRAA	WARP
2015	NWA	AA	22	536	60	30	2	17	64	42	126	3	2	.240/.305/.416	.256	7.1	.287	0.1	RF(97): -5.8, LF(18): -1.3	0.0
2016	OMA	AAA	23	558	82	22	6	19	86	51	130	6	2	.277/.351/.461	.290	29.3	.339	1.2	RF(72): 13.8, LF(50): 7.0	5.1
2017	OMA	AAA	24	57	6	2	2	3	12	6	8	0	0	.314/.386/.608	.317	3.9	.325	-0.9	RF(9): 0.1, LF(3): 0.0	0.4
2017	KCA	MLB	24	422	55	15	1	17	40	35	118	1	1	.255/.320/.432	.255	5.3	.324	-0.1	RF(92): -9.8, LF(9): -0.5	-0.5
2018	*KCA*	*MLB*	*25*	*566*	*74*	*23*	*3*	*20*	*67*	*44*	*148*	*2*	*1*	*.243/.307/.420*	*.252*	*10.3*	*.300*	*-0.6*	*RF -8*	*-0.2*
2019	*KCA*	*MLB*	*26*	*569*	*74*	*25*	*3*	*22*	*75*	*49*	*151*	*2*	*1*	*.248/.319/.439*	*.255*	*9.1*	*.305*	*0.0*	*RF -7*	*0.2*

Breakout: 4% Improve: 30% Collapse: 11% Attrition: 26% MLB: 67% *Comparables: Josh Reddick, Fernando Martinez, Tyler Colvin*

It's hard to classify not-quite-league-average production as a roaring success, but it was worth at least a contented-face emoji. The long-known and occasionally heralded Bonifacio made his major-league debut in 2017 (yes, really) and won playing time in the outfield with his bat (possibly by virtue of simply having one, compared to Jorge Soler). But in all seriousness, he's still just 24 years old and has more than 400 plate appearances under his belt as a serviceable major leaguer, posting an OPS above .720 in five of six months as a rookie. If he is what he seems to be, everyone will probably be perfectly happy. And at least in 2017, the Good Face powers did extend to his stat page, where his batting average and True Average matched up perfectly.

Drew Butera C Born: 08/09/83 Age: 34 Bats: R Throws: R Height: 6'1" Weight: 200 Origin: Round 5, 2005 Draft (#149 overall)

YEAR	TEAM	LVL	AGE	PA	R	2B	3B	HR	RBI	BB	K	SB	CS	AVG/OBP/SLG	TAv	VORP	BABIP	BRR	FRAA	WARP
2015	ANA	MLB	31	21	3	0	0	0	0	0	2	0	1	.190/.190/.190	.180	-1.0	.211	-0.2	C(7): -0.5, 1B(3): 0.0	-0.2
2015	KCA	MLB	31	99	6	3	0	1	5	6	24	0	0	.198/.266/.267	.202	-2.6	.262	-1.0	C(42): -2.1, 1B(5): 0.0	-0.5
2016	KCA	MLB	32	133	18	10	1	4	16	8	36	0	0	.285/.328/.480	.268	6.0	.373	-1.1	C(51): 0.1, P(2): 0.0	0.6
2017	KCA	MLB	33	177	18	4	1	3	14	12	41	0	0	.227/.284/.319	.223	1.2	.286	-0.1	C(74): -6.7, 1B(4): -0.2	-0.6
2018	*KCA*	*MLB*	*34*	*126*	*12*	*5*	*1*	*2*	*12*	*8*	*29*	*0*	*0*	*.219/.273/.325*	*.212*	*-0.3*	*.269*	*-0.2*	*C -4*	*-0.6*
2019	*KCA*	*MLB*	*35*	*127*	*13*	*5*	*0*	*2*	*12*	*9*	*31*	*0*	*0*	*.213/.275/.327*	*.208*	*-2.3*	*.264*	*-0.4*	*C -4*	*-0.7*

Breakout: 7% Improve: 37% Collapse: 13% Attrition: 27% MLB: 82%

Comparables: Chad Moeller, Humberto Quintero, Gary Bennett

YEAR	TEAM	P. COUNT	FRM RUNS	BLK RUNS	THRW RUNS	TOT RUNS
2015	ANA	933	-0.7	0.3	0.0	-0.4
2015	KCA	3765	-2.8	-0.2	0.2	-2.8
2016	KCA	5369	1.4	-0.4	-0.1	0.9
2017	KCA	7350	-7.3	1.7	-0.1	-5.7
2018	*KCA*	*5108*	*-3.5*	*0.4*	*-0.1*	*-3.3*
2019	*KCA*	*5164*	*-4.0*	*0.4*	*-0.1*	*-3.7*

This was perhaps his last chance. He had fought through an oblique injury to get here, to the World Baseball Classic, to this game against Venezuela and Royals starting catcher Salvador Perez. Now Butera, backup to baseball's sturdiest backstop, was running, and the ball was live, and it was the ninth inning, and Perez was standing near the plate, vulnerable. See, Butera had come home in the eighth—tying the game—but the throw hadn't even been chucked in from center field by the time he approached his target. An opportunity foiled. This time, Butera was going for it. He was, after all, the potential winning run—it wouldn't look too suspicious. Even with a bobble by the cutoff man, Butera was clearly doomed. So his teammate, his tormentor, was stationed far in front of the plate, nearly outside of the left-handed batters' box, when Butera arrived. He barrel rolled into Perez's knees, and the postseason hero went down in a heap. Concern was expressed, regrets. It was all executed perfectly. Perez, though, proved even more resilient than expected. Butera got into more games than he had in any season since 2011, but never owned up to his plot.

Melky Cabrera OF Born: 08/11/84 Age: 33 Bats: B Throws: L Height: 5'10" Weight: 210 Origin: International Free Agent, 2001

YEAR	TEAM	LVL	AGE	PA	R	2B	3B	HR	RBI	BB	K	SB	CS	AVG/OBP/SLG	TAv	VORP	BABIP	BRR	FRAA	WARP
2015	CHA	MLB	30	683	70	36	2	12	77	40	88	3	0	.273/.314/.394	.253	6.3	.297	-2.6	LF(150): -7.2	-0.1
2016	CHA	MLB	31	646	70	42	5	14	86	47	69	2	0	.296/.345/.455	.270	15.7	.314	-4.3	LF(147): -6.6	0.9
2017	CHA	MLB	32	428	54	17	0	13	56	25	52	0	0	.295/.336/.436	.263	8.6	.310	-2.2	LF(92): -5.7	0.3
2017	KCA	MLB	32	238	24	13	2	4	29	11	22	1	2	.269/.303/.399	.238	-0.3	.280	0.6	RF(46): -6.2, LF(12): -0.6	-0.7
2018	*KCA*	*MLB*	*33*	*622*	*63*	*32*	*3*	*12*	*70*	*41*	*74*	*2*	*1*	*.284/.331/.415*	*.252*	*12.5*	*.304*	*-2.4*	*LF -4, RF -6*	*0.3*
2019	*KCA*	*MLB*	*34*	*531*	*60*	*25*	*2*	*10*	*55*	*35*	*65*	*1*	*0*	*.273/.321/.396*	*.247*	*3.0*	*.295*	*-2.2*	*LF -3, RF -5*	*-0.6*

Breakout: 4% Improve: 35% Collapse: 6% Attrition: 15% MLB: 85%

Comparables: Mike Greenwell, Shannon Stewart, Frank Catalanotto

Ever wonder why fast food restaurants dot even the street corners of major cities with bustling, interesting food scenes? It's because of familiarity. Yes, the new taco stand around the corner is run by a chef on the acclaimed "33 Under 33" list, but you don't know how your stomach will take beef tongue laced with Sriracha, and you're still going to be in close quarters with co-workers for another four hours. Sometimes, you just need to know what you're getting. Cabrera won't be worth saving or bringing up at a dinner party, but he will happily rescue someone facing a disconcerting dilemma at a corner outfield spot, as he's done with a fast-food-like consistency for the past decade.

Lorenzo Cain CF Born: 04/13/86 Age: 32 Bats: R Throws: R Height: 6'2" Weight: 205 Origin: Round 17, 2004 Draft (#496 overall)

YEAR	TEAM	LVL	AGE	PA	R	2B	3B	HR	RBI	BB	K	SB	CS	AVG/OBP/SLG	TAv	VORP	BABIP	BRR	FRAA	WARP
2015	KCA	MLB	29	604	101	34	6	16	72	37	98	28	6	.307/.361/.477	.301	45.4	.347	4.0	CF(136): 17.7, RF(5): -0.4	6.7
2016	KCA	MLB	30	434	56	19	1	9	56	31	84	14	5	.287/.339/.408	.258	13.1	.341	2.2	CF(72): 7.9, RF(29): 0.4	2.2
2017	KCA	MLB	31	645	86	27	5	15	49	54	100	26	2	.300/.363/.440	.280	36.6	.340	2.4	CF(151): 19.5	5.6
2018	*KCA*	*MLB*	*32*	*565*	*66*	*27*	*3*	*12*	*62*	*42*	*108*	*21*	*4*	*.281/.340/.417*	*.258*	*23.9*	*.333*	*2.2*	*CF 15*	*4.3*
2019	*KCA*	*MLB*	*33*	*509*	*59*	*24*	*3*	*11*	*55*	*36*	*102*	*17*	*4*	*.272/.328/.404*	*.253*	*13.8*	*.325*	*2.2*	*CF 14*	*3.0*

Breakout: 1% Improve: 42% Collapse: 2% Attrition: 12% MLB: 93%

Comparables: Michael Bourn, Reed Johnson, Angel Pagan

Like John McClane in *Die Hard*, Cain wasn't exactly young when we met him. Thus, the imagination must strain to envision his physically demanding style of play spawning too many sequels to a 6.7-WARP season in 2015. For his part, Cain came out with a vengeance in 2017, producing a bounce-back campaign to reduce his injury-riddled 2016 to a mere blip on the radar. The truth is that it's all guesswork. You think his primo athleticism makes Cain ageless. That snooty critic you can't stand deems him a one-off phenomenon. But, well, money talks. There will always be an audience for a dynamic center fielder with a recognizable face who just might hit 15 homers and steal 25 bases on demand.

Cheslor Cuthbert 3B Born: 11/16/92 Age: 25 Bats: R Throws: R Height: 6'1" Weight: 190 Origin: International Free Agent, 2009

YEAR	TEAM	LVL	AGE	PA	R	2B	3B	HR	RBI	BB	K	SB	CS	AVG/OBP/SLG	TAv	VORP	BABIP	BRR	FRAA	WARP
2015	OMA	AAA	22	438	55	22	1	11	51	37	60	5	2	.277/.339/.421	.275	16.4	.302	-1.8	3B(75): 4.6, 1B(25): 0.4	2.2
2015	KCA	MLB	22	50	6	2	1	1	8	4	9	0	0	.217/.280/.370	.236	0.1	.250	-0.2	3B(17): 1.1, 1B(1): 0.0	0.1
2016	OMA	AAA	23	107	15	4	1	7	28	11	14	0	1	.333/.402/.624	.377	14.8	.324	-1.4	3B(21): -2.0, 1B(3): 0.0	1.3
2016	KCA	MLB	23	510	49	28	1	12	46	32	96	2	0	.274/.318/.413	.250	5.9	.320	-5.1	3B(127): -2.1	0.4
2017	OMA	AAA	24	68	10	3	1	4	9	7	11	0	0	.271/.353/.559	.297	4.7	.267	0.0	3B(10): 0.6, 1B(2): -0.2	0.5
2017	KCA	MLB	24	153	10	7	0	2	18	9	39	0	0	.231/.275/.322	.221	-1.6	.301	0.2	3B(44): 0.6, 1B(6): 0.0	-0.1
2018	*KCA*	*MLB*	*25*	*506*	*58*	*24*	*2*	*14*	*59*	*37*	*94*	*2*	*1*	*.260/.315/.411*	*.255*	*9.3*	*.297*	*-0.8*	*3B 0, 1B 0*	*0.8*
2019	*KCA*	*MLB*	*26*	*412*	*51*	*21*	*1*	*13*	*50*	*33*	*78*	*1*	*0*	*.261/.322/.427*	*.254*	*4.7*	*.297*	*-2.3*	*3B 1, 1B 0*	*0.6*

Breakout: 1% Improve: 55% Collapse: 7% Attrition: 13% MLB: 96%

Comparables: Matt Duffy, Wilmer Flores, Lonnie Chisenhall

When word of Cuthbert's presence on earth reached Dodgers pitcher and tweet maestro Brandon McCarthy in 2016, he posited that "no more made-up name has ever existed." His 19 homers between Triple-A and the majors that year were undoubtedly enough to increase the universe's chances of spawning more Cheslors. Given that Cuthbert has now spent more than 200 games in the majors, McCarthy's statement would be dismissed by many present-day baseball fans as untrue—a turn 'round the league will do that. But his on-base percentage will have to start with something other than a two if he hopes to permanently strip the tweet of a valid point.

Donald Dewees OF Born: 09/29/93 Age: 24 Bats: L Throws: L Height: 5'11" Weight: 204 Origin: Round 2, 2015 Draft (#47 overall)

YEAR	TEAM	LVL	AGE	PA	R	2B	3B	HR	RBI	BB	K	SB	CS	AVG/OBP/SLG	TAv	VORP	BABIP	BRR	FRAA	WARP
2015	EUG	A-	21	303	42	14	1	5	30	14	54	19	7	.266/.306/.376	.270	13.4	.311	2.5	CF(42): 1.6, LF(16): 1.8	1.8
2016	SBN	A	22	410	65	15	12	3	54	29	51	17	5	.282/.337/.414	.288	30.0	.316	7.7	CF(74): -1.8, LF(15): 2.0	3.3
2016	MYR	A+	22	167	25	10	2	2	19	10	36	14	0	.289/.339/.423	.289	13.5	.360	3.2	CF(33): 3.7	1.8
2017	NWA	AA	23	524	67	24	6	9	52	46	81	20	8	.272/.340/.407	.274	23.0	.309	0.8	CF(107): 3.7, LF(14): 0.3	2.9
2018	*KCA*	*MLB*	*24*	*250*	*31*	*11*	*3*	*6*	*24*	*17*	*53*	*6*	*2*	*.242/.298/.392*	*.231*	*2.8*	*.284*	*0.6*	*CF 2, LF 1*	*0.7*
2019	*KCA*	*MLB*	*25*	*401*	*46*	*18*	*4*	*11*	*46*	*29*	*88*	*10*	*3*	*.245/.305/.406*	*.240*	*4.5*	*.289*	*1.3*	*CF 3, LF 2*	*1.1*

Breakout: 12% Improve: 19% Collapse: 5% Attrition: 25% MLB: 36% *Comparables: Abraham Almonte, Jon Jay, Charlie Blackmon*

In a full season at Double-A, following a trade from the Cubs for right-hander Alec Mills, Dewees kept hitting and even walked a bit more. Any and all trips to first base are likely to prove useful for the speedy Dewees, thief of 20 bases in 2017. He might be destined for (stop me if you've heard this before) fourth-outfielder status, but there's also a chance that his perpetually solid batting average turns into something more. He got into nine homers at Double-A and the more advanced pitching didn't noticeably ding his bat-to-ball skills.

Hunter Dozier RF Born: 08/22/91 Age: 26 Bats: R Throws: R Height: 6'4" Weight: 220 Origin: Round 1, 2013 Draft (#8 overall)

YEAR	TEAM	LVL	AGE	PA	R	2B	3B	HR	RBI	BB	K	SB	CS	AVG/OBP/SLG	TAv	VORP	BABIP	BRR	FRAA	WARP
2015	NWA	AA	23	523	65	27	1	12	53	45	151	6	2	.213/.281/.349	.241	3.8	.283	-0.7	3B(115): -4.2	0.0
2016	NWA	AA	24	110	14	8	0	8	21	14	23	4	0	.305/.400/.642	.365	14.5	.328	0.1	3B(19): -0.3, LF(6): -1.3	1.4
2016	OMA	AAA	24	434	65	36	1	15	54	40	100	3	1	.294/.357/.506	.304	31.6	.358	0.9	3B(63): -6.6, RF(14): 1.0	2.6
2016	KCA	MLB	24	21	4	1	0	0	1	2	8	0	0	.211/.286/.263	.236	-0.2	.364	0.0	RF(7): -0.2	0.0
2017	OMA	AAA	25	96	11	6	1	4	12	9	37	1	1	.226/.313/.464	.281	3.8	.341	-0.3	RF(10): -0.1, 3B(7): -0.3	0.3
2018	*KCA*	*MLB*	*26*	*253*	*29*	*13*	*1*	*8*	*30*	*21*	*75*	*1*	*0*	*.231/.296/.402*	*.245*	*2.3*	*.303*	*-0.3*	*3B -3, 1B 1*	*-0.1*
2019	*KCA*	*MLB*	*27*	*369*	*46*	*20*	*1*	*14*	*47*	*34*	*109*	*2*	*1*	*.234/.308/.423*	*.249*	*2.6*	*.303*	*-0.6*	*3B -4, 1B 1*	*0.0*

Breakout: 9% Improve: 18% Collapse: 10% Attrition: 21% MLB: 33% *Comparables: John Mayberry, Brent Clevlen, Carlos Moncrief*

An oblique strain and then a broken wrist derailed Dozier's 2017, which was unfortunate timing for the college shortstop turned blocked corner infielder turned prospective corner outfielder. His draft position (no. 8 overall as part of a mechanism to sign a later pick, left-hander Sean Manaea) always placed some undue weight on his shoulders. All of that sounds worse when it's put together like that. So sure, at age 26, it would seem his chances of turning into a star like his Kansas City corner forebears are slim. Still, Dozier was an excellent hitter at Triple-A in 2016. If he needs reps to sort some things out, he might just be in the right organization.

Alcides Escobar SS Born: 12/16/86 Age: 31 Bats: R Throws: R Height: 6'1" Weight: 185 Origin: International Free Agent, 2003

YEAR	TEAM	LVL	AGE	PA	R	2B	3B	HR	RBI	BB	K	SB	CS	AVG/OBP/SLG	TAv	VORP	BABIP	BRR	FRAA	WARP
2015	KCA	MLB	28	662	76	20	5	3	47	26	75	17	5	.257/.293/.320	.224	8.4	.286	5.3	SS(148): 7.0	1.7
2016	KCA	MLB	29	682	57	24	6	7	55	27	96	17	4	.261/.292/.350	.227	5.8	.295	0.4	SS(162): 0.8	0.7
2017	KCA	MLB	30	629	71	36	5	6	54	15	102	4	7	.250/.272/.357	.223	3.1	.291	0.6	SS(162): 10.0	1.3
2018	*KCA*	*MLB*	*31*	*601*	*64*	*26*	*4*	*7*	*47*	*25*	*88*	*12*	*5*	*.256/.292/.353*	*.217*	*2.4*	*.286*	*1.4*	*SS 4*	*0.7*
2019	*KCA*	*MLB*	*32*	*539*	*52*	*23*	*4*	*6*	*48*	*24*	*81*	*10*	*4*	*.251/.289/.347*	*.219*	*-3.6*	*.282*	*1.6*	*SS 4*	*0.0*

Breakout: 4% Improve: 27% Collapse: 11% Attrition: 15% MLB: 84% *Comparables: Sam Dente, Alfredo Griffin, Bill Russell*

Since 2014, the contemporary golden era for the Royals, the slick-fielding Escobar has been a constant presence at shortstop, and nearly as constant a presence atop the lineup. Which is just the requisite prelude to this: Escobar has recorded 1,917 outs in that time frame, fourth most in the game. Being atop that list isn't necessarily a bad thing—in fact, the list is populated mostly by top-of-the-order hitters who impact the game with power. Escobar, of course, does not do that. He just makes outs, prodigiously. Sporting a .644 OPS, he's taken 2,593 turns at the plate since 2014, which is 435 more than the next hitter with an OPS of .650 or worse (Billy Hamilton) and 881 more than the third-most overextended bat (J.J. Hardy). How many undeserved plate appearances did he accumulate? Well, that's open to interpretation, but don't be surprised if #EskyMagic allows him to add to his total in 2018.

Alex Gordon LF Born: 02/10/84 Age: 34 Bats: L Throws: R Height: 6'1" Weight: 220 Origin: Round 1, 2005 Draft (#2 overall)

YEAR	TEAM	LVL	AGE	PA	R	2B	3B	HR	RBI	BB	K	SB	CS	AVG/OBP/SLG	TAv	VORP	BABIP	BRR	FRAA	WARP
2015	OMA	AAA	31	37	6	2	0	1	5	8	6	0	0	.429/.568/.607	.428	5.9	.524	-1.1	LF(4): 1.0	0.7
2015	KCA	MLB	31	422	40	18	0	13	48	49	92	2	5	.271/.377/.432	.299	23.2	.327	-1.7	LF(101): 4.2	2.9
2016	KCA	MLB	32	506	62	16	2	17	40	52	148	8	1	.220/.312/.380	.240	1.6	.288	1.2	LF(126): -3.1	-0.2
2017	KCA	MLB	33	541	52	20	2	9	45	45	126	7	4	.208/.293/.315	.223	-8.8	.261	-0.2	LF(140): 2.8, CF(15): -0.9	-0.7
2018	*KCA*	*MLB*	*34*	*598*	*69*	*23*	*2*	*15*	*67*	*57*	*139*	*8*	*4*	*.239/.323/.377*	*.249*	*12.2*	*.294*	*-0.4*	*LF -1*	*0.6*
2019	*KCA*	*MLB*	*35*	*507*	*62*	*20*	*2*	*14*	*56*	*50*	*126*	*5*	*3*	*.234/.323/.379*	*.244*	*3.9*	*.293*	*0.0*	*LF 0*	*0.4*

Breakout: 1% Improve: 30% Collapse: 21% Attrition: 25% MLB: 88% *Comparables: Willie Harris, Jose Cruz Jr., Rickie Weeks*

Gordon provided a stress test for headline writers' grasp on the concept of irony on September 19, when one of his nine measly long balls turned out to be the one to break the all-time, MLB-wide single-season home-run record. See, two years into a $72 million contract that the Royals certainly regret at this point, Gordon wasn't just a rare hitter who didn't benefit from the supercharged power environment. He literally posted the lowest slugging percentage of any qualified player. Much like rain on your wedding day, that is merely an incredibly depressing coincidence. And if Gordon's bat doesn't bounce back, the fact that he's one of the last Royals building blocks still in Kansas City could be plenty depressing as well.

Terrance Gore OF Born: 06/08/91 Age: 27 Bats: R Throws: R Height: 5'7" Weight: 165 Origin: Round 20, 2011 Draft (#606 overall)

YEAR	TEAM	LVL	AGE	PA	R	2B	3B	HR	RBI	BB	K	SB	CS	AVG/OBP/SLG	TAv	VORP	BABIP	BRR	FRAA	WARP
2015	NWA	AA	24	259	42	4	1	0	16	26	50	39	2	.284/.367/.311	.256	8.8	.366	4.1	LF(51): 0.3, CF(21): -3.0	0.7
2015	KCA	MLB	24	4	1	0	0	0	0	0	1	3	0	.000/.250/.000	.147	0.6	.000	0.9	LF(4): -0.5	0.0
2016	NWA	AA	25	302	31	2	1	0	11	26	58	44	5	.233/.314/.249	.233	5.7	.303	5.4	CF(70): 5.0, LF(15): -0.1	1.1
2016	KCA	MLB	25	3	6	0	0	0	0	0	1	11	2	.000/.000/.000	.025	-0.5	.000	0.1	LF(2): 0.0	-0.1
2017	NWA	AA	26	62	9	1	0	0	1	2	13	8	0	.254/.279/.271	.195	-1.2	.326	1.4	LF(10): 1.5, CF(7): -0.3	0.0
2017	OMA	AAA	26	192	29	3	3	1	10	16	38	13	3	.247/.321/.319	.234	2.1	.310	2.5	LF(30): 1.1, CF(29): 0.7	0.4
2017	KCA	MLB	26	5	2	0	0	0	0	1	2	2	2	.000/.200/.000	.121	-0.4	.000	0.3	LF(2): -0.2	-0.1
2018	*KCA*	*MLB*	*27*	*29*	*3*	*1*	*0*	*0*	*2*	*2*	*7*	*3*	*0*	*.224/.281/.286*	*.207*	*-0.1*	*.283*	*0.4*	*CF 0*	*0.0*
2019	*KCA*	*MLB*	*28*	*179*	*18*	*4*	*1*	*2*	*14*	*14*	*44*	*16*	*3*	*.223/.297/.300*	*.209*	*-1.4*	*.281*	*2.8*	*CF 3*	*0.1*

Breakout: 4% Improve: 10% Collapse: 2% Attrition: 9% MLB: 15% *Comparables: Kyle Hudson, Rich Thompson, Ryan Strausborger*

Here's a distinction Gore likely already holds: Among non-pitchers, he's the most famous active baseball player without a major-league hit. Here's another distinction he *probably* holds: He's the current member of the Royals most likely to play in the 2018 postseason. Okay, maybe not quite the most likely, but he's only three October trots to first base from moving into a tie for yet another distinction: the all-time postseason pinch-run appearance record! Also: Did you know that Quintin Berry has seen the field in more postseason games than Ian Desmond? Speed—a good, distinctive thing to have.

Eric Hosmer 1B Born: 10/24/89 Age: 28 Bats: L Throws: L Height: 6'4" Weight: 225 Origin: Round 1, 2008 Draft (#3 overall)

YEAR	TEAM	LVL	AGE	PA	R	2B	3B	HR	RBI	BB	K	SB	CS	AVG/OBP/SLG	TAv	VORP	BABIP	BRR	FRAA	WARP
2015	KCA	MLB	25	667	98	33	5	18	93	61	108	7	3	.297/.363/.459	.289	28.1	.336	2.7	1B(154): 3.6, RF(1): 0.0	3.4
2016	KCA	MLB	26	667	80	24	1	25	104	57	132	5	3	.266/.328/.433	.261	7.6	.301	0.1	1B(154): -2.2	0.6
2017	KCA	MLB	27	671	98	31	1	25	94	66	104	6	1	.318/.385/.498	.302	35.1	.351	-1.3	1B(157): 0.6	3.6
2018	*KCA*	*MLB*	*28*	*630*	*76*	*31*	*2*	*21*	*83*	*58*	*108*	*5*	*2*	*.288/.353/.459*	*.273*	*21.2*	*.322*	*0.4*	*1B 0*	*2.3*
2019	*KCA*	*MLB*	*29*	*559*	*78*	*27*	*1*	*21*	*77*	*55*	*97*	*4*	*1*	*.290/.360/.476*	*.281*	*19.4*	*.322*	*0.3*	*1B 0*	*2.1*

Breakout: 0% Improve: 49% Collapse: 0% Attrition: 6% MLB: 96% *Comparables: Kent Hrbek, Paul Konerko, Mike Sweeney*

Golden boy of a golden moment, Hosmer could feasibly be Justin Timberlake or Nick Carter. He's always had the hits and the boyish good looks, always been the face that pops out of a crowd at the bar. For these reasons, not entirely tangible, he's always been the headliner. Living this sort of charmed life requires some luck, but also a serious knack for timing. Hosmer has it. He ripped off his first great offensive season at age 27 and promptly stepped into the spotlight of free agency, which had threatened to correct the popular but misinformed notion that he'd had four great offensive seasons. Let's quit playing games here: There are 29 active first-base-playing dudes who have hit more than 25 homers in a season, and even more who have slugged .500. Hosmer? Not one of them. The park didn't help. Fine. He still runs a ground-ball rate that would make slap-hitting second basemen blush. The fact is some stars have staying power, and others are never the same after the band breaks up. His second act may yet be shockingly successful and lucrative, but it's far from a given.

Whit Merrifield 2B Born: 01/24/89 Age: 29 Bats: R Throws: R Height: 6'0" Weight: 195 Origin: Round 9, 2010 Draft (#269 overall)

YEAR	TEAM	LVL	AGE	PA	R	2B	3B	HR	RBI	BB	K	SB	CS	AVG/OBP/SLG	TAv	VORP	BABIP	BRR	FRAA	WARP
2015	OMA	AAA	26	594	83	29	5	5	38	39	66	32	9	.265/.317/.364	.241	8.4	.292	6.0	2B(57): 4.7, LF(39): 4.0	1.9
2016	OMA	AAA	27	304	46	19	0	8	29	22	55	20	2	.266/.321/.423	.278	14.4	.302	1.5	2B(40): 1.5, 1B(9): -0.5	1.5
2016	KCA	MLB	27	332	44	22	3	2	29	19	72	8	3	.283/.323/.392	.253	6.0	.361	-0.2	2B(65): 2.2, LF(13): 1.9	1.1
2017	OMA	AAA	28	37	6	4	0	3	9	1	4	1	1	.412/.432/.794	.399	5.5	.393	-1.3	2B(6): 0.3, 3B(1): 0.0	0.6
2017	KCA	MLB	28	630	80	32	6	19	78	29	88	34	8	.288/.324/.460	.272	26.8	.308	1.7	2B(132): -0.2, RF(10): -1.9	2.5
2018	*KCA*	*MLB*	*29*	*624*	*84*	*32*	*4*	*12*	*57*	*35*	*104*	*27*	*7*	*.262/.306/.396*	*.246*	*16.5*	*.298*	*3.3*	*2B 4, 3B 0*	*1.8*
2019	*KCA*	*MLB*	*30*	*585*	*66*	*28*	*2*	*14*	*64*	*36*	*104*	*24*	*7*	*.254/.305/.394*	*.238*	*6.6*	*.287*	*1.2*	*2B 4, 3B 0*	*1.2*

Breakout: 4% Improve: 26% Collapse: 24% Attrition: 29% MLB: 73% *Comparables: Matt Tolbert, Alberto Gonzalez, Ramiro Pena*

Like a plucky *Downton Abbey* extra accidentally earning an arc, Whitley David Merrifield one-upped his already admirable 2016 cameo as "player in the majors" and ... led the American League in stolen bases? He hit 19 homers and batted .288? Well then. It's an unlikely development for a 28-year-old who walked off the 2010 College World Series for the University of South Carolina in what appeared to be the highlight of his career. Despite the tendency of such fanciful success stories to subside as quickly as they appear, Merrifield doesn't present huge regression red flags. His BABIP was just .308, and while his homer-per-fly-ball rate exceeded his track record, it was nothing special for the majors in 2017, matching teammate Lorenzo Cain's exactly. There is a fragile but real chance that he's here to stay.

Raul Mondesi SS Born: 07/27/95 Age: 22 Bats: B Throws: R Height: 6'1" Weight: 185 Origin: International Free Agent, 2011

YEAR	TEAM	LVL	AGE	PA	R	2B	3B	HR	RBI	BB	K	SB	CS	AVG/OBP/SLG	TAv	VORP	BABIP	BRR	FRAA	WARP
2015	NWA	AA	19	338	36	11	5	6	33	17	88	19	6	.243/.279/.372	.239	5.7	.316	0.8	SS(63): -1.9, 2B(18): -3.2	0.1
2016	WIL	A+	20	39	5	2	1	1	4	2	11	2	0	.243/.282/.432	.246	1.5	.320	0.9	SS(6): 0.5	0.2
2016	NWA	AA	20	131	20	5	1	5	17	13	30	17	1	.259/.331/.448	.297	10.5	.305	1.0	SS(21): 2.1, 2B(6): 0.4	1.4
2016	OMA	AAA	20	61	9	2	4	1	9	2	19	5	0	.304/.328/.536	.312	7.1	.444	1.4	SS(12): 0.6, 2B(2): 0.1	0.8
2016	KCA	MLB	20	149	16	1	3	2	13	6	48	9	1	.185/.231/.281	.190	-5.1	.271	1.5	2B(42): -4.4, SS(7): -0.1	-1.0
2017	OMA	AAA	21	357	52	20	8	13	52	18	86	21	3	.305/.340/.539	.297	30.9	.373	1.3	SS(71): 2.2, 2B(10): 0.1	3.2
2017	KCA	MLB	21	60	4	1	0	1	3	3	22	5	2	.170/.214/.245	.162	-5.8	.267	-1.4	2B(14): 0.1, SS(9): 0.1	-0.6
2018	*KCA*	*MLB*	*22*	*484*	*63*	*17*	*7*	*13*	*49*	*24*	*140*	*28*	*5*	*.234/.268/.390*	*.227*	*5.7*	*.298*	*5.4*	*SS 4*	*0.8*
2019	*KCA*	*MLB*	*23*	*539*	*63*	*20*	*8*	*19*	*68*	*33*	*155*	*32*	*6*	*.243/.293/.432*	*.240*	*9.1*	*.302*	*2.1*	*SS 4*	*1.4*

Breakout: 5% Improve: 25% Collapse: 5% Attrition: 13% MLB: 33% *Comparables: Derek Dietrich, Tim Beckham, Chris Owings*

Now a full two years from his strange introduction to the baseball world during the 2015 World Series, Mondesi still hasn't provided a substantial regular-season accounting of his abilities. He did not stick in Kansas City as expected in 2017, but deserves plaudits for taking a step forward offensively at Triple-A while weathering both the loss of his friend Yordano Ventura and the uncertainty surrounding his father, who faced and was eventually convicted of criminal corruption charges back home in the Dominican Republic. Mondesi will likely get his chance in the majors in 2018, hopefully under sunnier personal skies, as the Royals hope he can be part of their next core.

Brandon Moss 1B Born: 09/16/83 Age: 34 Bats: L Throws: R Height: 6'1" Weight: 210 Origin: Round 8, 2002 Draft (#238 overall)

YEAR	TEAM	LVL	AGE	PA	R	2B	3B	HR	RBI	BB	K	SB	CS	AVG/OBP/SLG	TAv	VORP	BABIP	BRR	FRAA	WARP
2015	CLE	MLB	31	375	36	17	1	15	50	32	106	0	0	.217/.288/.407	.244	-3.2	.265	-3.4	RF(79): 2.4, 1B(10): 1.2	0.1
2015	SLN	MLB	31	151	11	7	1	4	8	17	42	0	1	.250/.344/.409	.271	2.1	.337	-1.7	1B(32): -0.3, LF(10): -0.3	0.1
2016	SLN	MLB	32	464	66	19	2	28	67	39	141	1	0	.225/.300/.484	.279	16.2	.261	-0.3	1B(64): 1.7, LF(58): 2.2	2.0
2017	KCA	MLB	33	401	41	14	0	22	50	37	128	2	0	.207/.279/.428	.240	-4.5	.248	-0.7	1B(14): 0.0, LF(5): -1.1	-0.6
2018	*KCA*	*MLB*	*34*	*586*	*74*	*23*	*2*	*27*	*85*	*55*	*170*	*2*	*0*	*.225/.305/.433*	*.254*	*5.6*	*.276*	*-0.7*	*1B 6, LF -1*	*0.9*
2019	*KCA*	*MLB*	*35*	*419*	*55*	*16*	*1*	*19*	*57*	*42*	*128*	*0*	*0*	*.215/.299/.421*	*.244*	*-3.0*	*.266*	*-1.7*	*1B 4, LF 0*	*0.1*

Breakout: 1% Improve: 27% Collapse: 12% Attrition: 20% MLB: 85% *Comparables: Richie Sexson, Marcus Thames, Tony Clark*

Moss' success as a slugger in Oakland might have created some belief that he possessed a special immunity to the power-melting effects of a place like Kansas City. The leaguewide power spike might have provided optimism, too. But, no, the changing climate of the game instead rendered his power inconsequential and further highlighted his rising strikeout levels. He has walloped his way off the slope toward irrelevance before, but age 34 isn't typically kind to his profile of production. This variety of Moss could be facing extinction if drastic action isn't taken.

Mike Moustakas 3B Born: 09/11/88 Age: 29 Bats: L Throws: R Height: 6'0" Weight: 215 Origin: Round 1, 2007 Draft (#2 overall)

YEAR	TEAM	LVL	AGE	PA	R	2B	3B	HR	RBI	BB	K	SB	CS	AVG/OBP/SLG	TAv	VORP	BABIP	BRR	FRAA	WARP
2015	KCA	MLB	26	614	73	34	1	22	82	43	76	1	2	.284/.348/.470	.291	35.9	.294	-1.3	3B(146): 6.8	4.6
2016	KCA	MLB	27	113	12	6	0	7	13	9	13	0	1	.240/.301/.500	.281	5.4	.214	-0.7	3B(26): -0.4	0.5
2017	KCA	MLB	28	598	75	24	0	38	85	34	94	0	0	.272/.314/.521	.275	26.3	.263	-1.6	3B(127): -7.4	1.9
2018	*NYA*	*MLB*	*29*	*503*	*62*	*23*	*1*	*20*	*67*	*35*	*75*	*1*	*1*	*.254/.310/.437*	*.259*	*13.4*	*.263*	*-1.3*	*3B -3, 1B 0*	*0.7*
2019	*NYA*	*MLB*	*30*	*464*	*61*	*22*	*0*	*20*	*64*	*36*	*74*	*0*	*0*	*.250/.313/.447*	*.255*	*7.4*	*.258*	*-0.9*	*3B -2*	*0.6*

Breakout: 1% Improve: 41% Collapse: 8% Attrition: 13% MLB: 96% *Comparables: Pablo Sandoval, Jorge Cantu, Buddy Bell*

The Eddie Murphy of extreme hitter adjustments, Moustakas fulfilled his prospect promise–in a way–by becoming Mr. Opposite Field in 2015. After missing nearly all of 2016 with injuries, he came out in his contract year and ... became Sir-Hack-A-Lot? He swung nearly 55 percent of the time, keeping company with Javier Baez and Carlos Gomez in the second tier of swing-happy hitters who aren't quite ready to go full Adam Jones. Oh, and the whole opposite-field thing vanished into thin air. In a testament to his natural hitting ability, his strikeout and walk numbers didn't let on that anything quite that drastic had occurred. Maybe, just maybe, Moose should get an adaptability merit badge for sensing the power-aiding changes in the offensive environment and tailoring his swing to top Steve Balboni's long-held franchise homer record. You'd expect the 29-year-old Moustakas to have a more defined character as a player hitting free agency, but succeeding in multiple ways sure beats failing. Lends a nice air of suspense to the 2019 version of his comment, to boot.

Paulo Orlando RF Born: 11/01/85 Age: 32 Bats: R Throws: R Height: 6'2" Weight: 210 Origin: International Free Agent, 2005

YEAR	TEAM	LVL	AGE	PA	R	2B	3B	HR	RBI	BB	K	SB	CS	AVG/OBP/SLG	TAv	VORP	BABIP	BRR	FRAA	WARP
2015	OMA	AAA	29	182	20	11	0	3	17	8	32	9	0	.276/.309/.394	.256	5.5	.321	2.1	CF(18): -0.9, RF(11): 0.6	0.9
2015	KCA	MLB	29	251	31	14	6	7	27	5	53	3	3	.249/.269/.444	.254	3.4	.291	0.1	RF(45): -1.9, LF(37): 2.1	0.5
2016	KCA	MLB	30	484	52	24	4	5	43	13	105	14	3	.302/.329/.405	.257	10.0	.380	1.0	RF(89): -1.8, CF(37): -1.2	0.7
2017	NWA	AA	31	47	4	1	0	0	3	6	7	0	0	.341/.426/.366	.299	2.6	.412	0.1	RF(6): 0.2, CF(1): -0.1	0.3
2017	OMA	AAA	31	129	14	10	0	2	19	9	26	2	2	.293/.357/.431	.279	6.0	.360	0.4	RF(14): 0.7, CF(8): 0.1	0.7
2017	KCA	MLB	31	90	9	3	0	2	6	1	20	1	1	.198/.225/.302	.185	-3.9	.234	0.9	RF(20): -0.5, CF(18): -1.9	-0.6
2018	*KCA*	*MLB*	*32*	*521*	*55*	*25*	*4*	*8*	*50*	*19*	*114*	*11*	*4*	*.258/.291/.375*	*.235*	*5.5*	*.317*	*0.6*	*CF -9*	*-0.8*
2019	*KCA*	*MLB*	*33*	*326*	*35*	*16*	*2*	*6*	*34*	*13*	*75*	*6*	*2*	*.259/.295/.389*	*.235*	*1.6*	*.320*	*0.7*	*CF -5*	*-0.4*

Breakout: 0% Improve: 39% Collapse: 16% Attrition: 30% MLB: 84% *Comparables: Jeff Francoeur, Corey Patterson, Gerald Williams*

It's not a misprint: Orlando logged significant playing time in 2016 while collecting 105 strikeouts alongside just 13 walks. The question marks finally caught up to him in 2017, derailing whatever good vibes came from those two partial seasons of mostly palatable play. They punctuated fairly pressing inquiries such as: "How was there a corner outfielder in the majors who hasn't hit more than 10 homers in a season since 2010 (at Double-A)?" And: "No, seriously, how?" The speed and defense mostly still play, though, so he may not be done yet.

Brayan Pena C Born: 01/07/82 Age: 36 Bats: B Throws: R Height: 5'9" Weight: 240 Origin: International Free Agent, 2000

YEAR	TEAM	LVL	AGE	PA	R	2B	3B	HR	RBI	BB	K	SB	CS	AVG/OBP/SLG	TAv	VORP	BABIP	BRR	FRAA	WARP
2015	CIN	MLB	33	367	17	17	0	0	18	29	34	2	0	.273/.334/.324	.242	5.3	.303	-3.5	C(86): -8.8, 1B(5): -0.1	-0.4
2016	SFD	AA	34	33	2	0	0	0	0	1	4	0	0	.188/.212/.188	.146	-4.3	.214	-1.6	C(5): -0.4, 1B(1): 0.0	-0.5
2016	SLN	MLB	34	14	0	1	0	0	0	1	2	0	0	.154/.214/.231	.176	-0.7	.182	0.0	C(3): -1.2, 1B(1): 0.0	-0.2
2017	OMA	AAA	35	134	8	3	0	0	15	6	7	1	0	.274/.308/.298	.196	-4.6	.286	-1.5	C(37): -5.3, P(5): -0.1	-1.0
2018	*KCA*	*MLB*	*36*	*250*	*22*	*11*	*1*	*2*	*21*	*14*	*29*	*1*	*0*	*.258/.302/.344*	*.219*	*0.6*	*.282*	*-1.4*	*C -10, 1B 0*	*-1.0*
2019	*KCA*	*MLB*	*37*	*7*	*1*	*0*	*0*	*0*	*1*	*0*	*1*	*0*	*0*	*.255/.299/.332*	*.220*	*0.0*	*.281*	*0.0*	*C -1, 1B 0*	*-0.1*

Breakout: 2% Improve: 23% Collapse: 13% Attrition: 32% MLB: 72% *Comparables: Bob Boone, Del Crandall, Ryan Hanigan*

YEAR	TEAM	P. COUNT	FRM RUNS	BLK RUNS	THRW RUNS	TOT RUNS
2015	CIN	12480	-6.2	0.4	-2.0	-7.8
2016	SLN	277	-0.3	-0.8	-0.1	-1.2
2018	*KCA*	*8721*	*-7.7*	*-0.4*	*-1.2*	*-9.3*
2019	*KCA*	*257*	*-1.0*	*0.0*	*-0.2*	*-1.2*

Perhaps tired of his eternal backup catcher role, Peña seized a little portion of the spotlight at Triple-A Omaha. He appeared as a relief pitcher in five games, trotting out an incredible eephus pitch that took so long to reach the plate that he finished his motion and stood there, both feet on the ground, in his own unique version of the textbook "ready to field" position for what seemed like several seconds before the ball ever completed its journey. And for however long it was, everyone was watching him. And it was glorious.

Salvador Perez C Born: 05/10/90 Age: 28 Bats: R Throws: R Height: 6'3" Weight: 240 Origin: International Free Agent, 2006

YEAR	TEAM	LVL	AGE	PA	R	2B	3B	HR	RBI	BB	K	SB	CS	AVG/OBP/SLG	TAv	VORP	BABIP	BRR	FRAA	WARP
2015	KCA	MLB	25	553	52	25	0	21	70	13	82	1	0	.260/.280/.426	.251	16.0	.270	-2.5	C(139): -8.6, 1B(1): 0.0	0.8
2016	KCA	MLB	26	546	57	28	2	22	64	22	119	0	0	.247/.288/.438	.245	12.7	.280	-2.7	C(128): -5.3, 1B(1): 0.0	0.8
2017	KCA	MLB	27	499	57	24	1	27	80	17	95	1	0	.268/.297/.495	.259	19.5	.280	-1.3	C(115): -12.2	0.7
2018	*KCA*	*MLB*	*28*	*574*	*65*	*27*	*2*	*21*	*77*	*23*	*94*	*1*	*0*	*.263/.297/.436*	*.253*	*20.7*	*.283*	*-0.9*	*C -13*	*0.3*
2019	*KCA*	*MLB*	*29*	*501*	*62*	*23*	*1*	*20*	*66*	*24*	*87*	*0*	*0*	*.256/.297/.436*	*.248*	*10.3*	*.274*	*-2.1*	*C -10*	*0.0*

Breakout: 2% Improve: 43% Collapse: 9% Attrition: 14% MLB: 100%

Comparables: Wilson Ramos, Rich Gedman, Dave Valle

YEAR	TEAM	P. COUNT	FRM RUNS	BLK RUNS	THRW RUNS	TOT RUNS
2015	KCA	19339	-7.5	0.6	0.5	-6.5
2016	KCA	18379	-12.8	2.9	5.6	-4.3
2017	KCA	15629	-11.8	1.3	0.1	-10.4
2018	*KCA*	*17962*	*-14.2*	*1.8*	*1.8*	*-10.6*
2019	*KCA*	*15668*	*-12.7*	*1.6*	*1.6*	*-9.5*

For the first time since 2012, Perez played fewer than 130 games. It's probably just correlation, but he also put up his best True Average since 2013, setting a new career-high in slugging percentage despite his swing rate becoming even more prodigious. The defense is what it is at this point. Perez doesn't frame very well, but he does fine with everything else and certainly carries the glowing reputation as a stud catcher. Whether he's turning teammates into Instagram phenoms or adopting Rally Mantises, his presence behind the plate and in this clubhouse is likely to be among the most consistent things about the franchise moving forward, as he's under team control through 2021.

Jorge Soler RF Born: 02/25/92 Age: 26 Bats: R Throws: R Height: 6'4" Weight: 215 Origin: International Free Agent, 2012

YEAR	TEAM	LVL	AGE	PA	R	2B	3B	HR	RBI	BB	K	SB	CS	AVG/OBP/SLG	TAv	VORP	BABIP	BRR	FRAA	WARP
2015	CHN	MLB	23	404	39	18	1	10	47	32	121	3	1	.262/.324/.399	.263	7.7	.361	-0.2	RF(95): -8.8	-0.1
2016	TEN	AA	24	42	4	0	0	0	2	11	11	0	0	.167/.381/.167	.246	0.1	.250	0.0	LF(6): -0.5	0.0
2016	CHN	MLB	24	264	37	9	0	12	31	31	66	0	0	.238/.333/.436	.293	13.9	.276	-0.4	LF(53): -2.7, RF(7): -1.1	1.0
2017	OMA	AAA	25	327	49	9	0	24	59	50	82	1	0	.267/.388/.564	.317	25.3	.293	-2.0	RF(39): -0.4, LF(23): 3.0	2.7
2017	KCA	MLB	25	110	7	5	0	2	6	12	36	0	0	.144/.245/.258	.172	-8.6	.203	-0.3	RF(15): -1.6, LF(7): 0.8	-0.9
2018	*KCA*	*MLB*	*26*	*561*	*72*	*24*	*2*	*23*	*79*	*61*	*152*	*1*	*0*	*.244/.330/.442*	*.269*	*16.9*	*.303*	*-0.9*	*RF -3*	*1.1*
2019	*KCA*	*MLB*	*27*	*414*	*57*	*18*	*1*	*18*	*57*	*48*	*112*	*1*	*0*	*.245/.336/.446*	*.266*	*12.5*	*.303*	*-0.5*	*RF -2*	*1.1*

Breakout: 4% Improve: 49% Collapse: 6% Attrition: 12% MLB: 89%

Comparables: Travis Snider, Oswaldo Arcia, Derek Dietrich

Finally! Freed from Chicago's crowded outfield and given consistent at-bats with which to work, Soler blasted 24 homers and struck out just 25 percent of the time! At last! What's that? He did that in Triple-A Omaha? Without providing much evidence that his shaky combo of power and whiffs can play in the majors? The 2017 campaign was, once again, nothing to write home about for one of the more disappointing Cuban prospects. In the context of costly "sluggers" entering their age-26 seasons—especially those traded for the services of Wade Davis—no news is not good news. Soler has even more to prove now than he did before, and he's running out of time to prove it.

Bubba Starling CF Born: 08/03/92 Age: 25 Bats: R Throws: R Height: 6'4" Weight: 210 Origin: Round 1, 2011 Draft (#5 overall)

YEAR	TEAM	LVL	AGE	PA	R	2B	3B	HR	RBI	BB	K	SB	CS	AVG/OBP/SLG	TAv	VORP	BABIP	BRR	FRAA	WARP
2015	WIL	A+	22	51	6	4	0	2	12	7	17	2	1	.386/.471/.614	.388	7.9	.600	-0.1	CF(11): -0.1	0.8
2015	NWA	AA	22	367	51	19	4	10	32	30	91	4	5	.254/.318/.426	.272	15.0	.319	0.9	CF(75): -3.6, RF(9): -0.3	1.2
2016	NWA	AA	23	255	28	15	1	5	23	15	81	10	1	.185/.251/.322	.219	-2.4	.257	1.3	CF(51): 2.7, RF(8): 0.9	0.1
2016	OMA	AAA	23	176	14	8	0	2	17	7	64	1	0	.181/.213/.265	.180	-1.9	.277	-1.2	CF(44): 6.3, RF(1): -0.2	-0.5
2017	OMA	AAA	24	303	35	14	1	7	21	19	65	5	4	.248/.303/.381	.248	1.3	.301	-2.2	RF(40): 7.7, CF(37): 3.5	1.2
2018	*KCA*	*MLB*	*25*	*58*	*6*	*3*	*0*	*1*	*6*	*3*	*17*	*1*	*0*	*.214/.266/.349*	*.219*	*-0.3*	*.287*	*0.0*	*CF 0*	*-0.1*
2019	*KCA*	*MLB*	*26*	*273*	*30*	*13*	*1*	*8*	*30*	*19*	*84*	*3*	*2*	*.217/.277/.371*	*.225*	*-2.0*	*.289*	*-0.1*	*CF 0*	*-0.2*

Breakout: 1% Improve: 2% Collapse: 1% Attrition: 3% MLB: 4%

Comparables: Jared Hoying, Joey Butler, Brandon Barnes

A .248 True Average for Triple-A Omaha is not going to be enough to rekindle hopes of Starling finding a major-league bat, especially considering its status as an improvement over 2016. What might be encouraging is his improving strikeout rate—down to a career-low 21.5 percent. But in the organization of the defense-first fourth outfielder, Starling is going to have to do more than whip around some Triple-A pitching to stand out. From both a performance and age standpoint, the former no. 5 overall pick's days as a legit prospect may be over.

Chase Vallot C Born: 08/21/96 Age: 21 Bats: R Throws: R Height: 6'0" Weight: 215 Origin: Round 1, 2014 Draft (#40 overall)

YEAR	TEAM	LVL	AGE	PA	R	2B	3B	HR	RBI	BB	K	SB	CS	AVG/OBP/SLG	TAv	VORP	BABIP	BRR	FRAA	WARP
2015	LEX	A	18	333	46	13	3	13	40	41	105	1	0	.219/.331/.427	.274	11.7	.291	-2.8	C(44): -8.4	0.3
2016	ROY	RK	19	35	5	1	0	2	2	3	14	0	0	.133/.257/.367	.222	-0.5	.143	0.0	C(5): 0.1	0.0
2016	LEX	A	19	330	37	20	0	13	44	39	118	0	0	.246/.367/.463	.305	25.7	.372	0.6	C(53): -4.1	2.4
2017	WIL	A+	20	355	34	22	0	12	37	64	127	0	0	.231/.380/.438	.300	21.6	.363	-4.5	C(53): -3.7	1.9
2018	*KCA*	*MLB*	*21*	*250*	*27*	*9*	*0*	*9*	*31*	*29*	*99*	*0*	*0*	*.192/.300/.370*	*.230*	*3.9*	*.295*	*-0.4*	*C -1*	*0.3*
2019	*KCA*	*MLB*	*22*	*331*	*43*	*14*	*1*	*13*	*41*	*39*	*128*	*0*	*0*	*.200/.309/.387*	*.240*	*4.3*	*.302*	*-0.8*	*C -1*	*0.3*

Breakout: 5% Improve: 11% Collapse: 4% Attrition: 5% MLB: 18%

Comparables: Derek Norris, Matt Olson, Ryan McMahon

A 21-year-old catcher wielding an extreme Three True Outcomes approach against High-A pitching is a very confusing thing. In an interview, Vallot once said that the major leaguer who reminds him of himself is Mike Napoli, whose evolution is a nice frame for trying to peer into the future of this young backstop. Worst-case scenario: He washes out quickly as dingers and walks cease to outweigh whiffs and stagnant defense. However, he is already a disciplined hitter—seriously, that's an 18 percent walk rate—who nonetheless strikes out a ton. The shape of his inevitable growth, physically and skills-wise, will determine where he ends up. He posted a .380 on-base percentage as one of the 20 youngest regulars at his level. Vallot still has time to clear up the confusion, in one way or another.

Pitchers

Scott Alexander LHP Born: 07/10/89 Age: 28 Bats: L Throws: L Height: 6'2" Weight: 190 Origin: Round 6, 2010 Draft (#179 overall)

YEAR	TEAM	LVL	AGE	W	L	SV	G	GS	IP	H	HR	BB/9	K/9	K	GB%	BABIP	WHIP	ERA	DRA	WARP	MPH	CMD	PWR	STM
2015	OMA	AAA	25	2	3	14	41	0	63^{1}	48	5	2.4	7.1	50	64%	.243	1.03	2.56	4.10	0.6				
2015	KCA	MLB	25	0	0	0	4	0	6	5	0	4.5	4.5	3	72%	.278	1.33	4.50	3.69	0.1	95.0			43
2016	OMA	AAA	26	2	0	1	22	0	30	32	2	3.0	7.2	24	67%	.323	1.40	3.00	4.85	0.0				
2016	KCA	MLB	26	0	0	0	17	0	19	24	1	3.3	7.6	16	69%	.383	1.63	3.32	4.12	0.2	94.1	57	53	37
2017	KCA	MLB	27	5	4	4	58	0	69	62	3	3.7	7.7	59	73%	.306	1.30	2.48	3.81	1.0	95.0	39	76	51
2018	*LAN*	*MLB*	*28*	*3*	*2*	*0*	*50*	*0*	*52*	*51*	*5*	*3.6*	*7.7*	*45*	*61%*	*.297*	*1.36*	*3.76*	*4.25*	*0.4*	*94.3*	*43*	*72*	*45*
2019	*LAN*	*MLB*	*29*	*2*	*1*	*0*	*44*	*0*	*46^{2}*	*47*	*4*	*3.6*	*7.0*	*36*	*61%*	*.301*	*1.40*	*4.18*	*4.44*	*0.4*	*93.9*	*42*	*72*	*45*

Breakout: 28% Improve: 37% Collapse: 20% Attrition: 17% MLB: 69% *Comparables: Ehren Wassermann, Andrew Triggs, Jeremy Jeffress*

It's hard to tell if Alexander's name is more reminiscent of an off-Broadway musical star, a poet or a shockingly wealthy candidate for the House of Representatives. What we can tell: He throws with his left hand, has a prodigious ground-ball rate, generates enough strikeouts and has an upward trajectory on his resume. That might just sound like closer material in Kansas City, at least these days. He already earned the ninth-inning call from manager Ned Yost in several of the garbage-time games of 2017, and Alexander will be given every chance to show that his solid campaign—which included better work versus righties than lefties—was for real.

Miguel Almonte RHP Born: 04/04/93 Age: 25 Bats: R Throws: R Height: 6'2" Weight: 210 Origin: International Free Agent, 2010

YEAR	TEAM	LVL	AGE	W	L	SV	G	GS	IP	H	HR	BB/9	K/9	K	GB%	BABIP	WHIP	ERA	DRA	WARP	MPH	CMD	PWR	STM
2015	NWA	AA	22	4	4	0	17	17	67	65	4	3.6	7.4	55	43%	.307	1.37	4.03	4.90	0.2				
2015	OMA	AAA	22	2	2	0	11	6	36^{2}	33	3	3.7	10.1	41	43%	.323	1.31	5.40	3.77	0.6				
2015	KCA	MLB	22	0	2	0	9	0	8^{2}	7	4	7.3	10.4	10	52%	.158	1.62	6.23	2.72	0.2	98.9			56
2016	OMA	AAA	23	3	7	0	21	12	60	63	5	6.3	8.6	57	49%	.335	1.75	5.55	8.72	-2.4				
2016	NWA	AA	23	2	1	0	11	0	16	24	4	2.2	8.4	15	41%	.400	1.75	7.31	4.60	0.0				
2017	NWA	AA	24	1	0	0	7	6	29	22	2	1.9	10.9	35	41%	.294	0.97	1.86	3.26	0.6				
2017	KCA	MLB	24	0	0	0	2	0	2	5	0	9.0	0.0	0	50%	.500	3.50	13.50	9.36	-0.1	96.7			33
2017	OMA	AAA	24	0	1	0	9	3	18	20	1	3.5	8.5	17	46%	.388	1.50	1.50	5.48	0.0				
2018	*KCA*	*MLB*	*25*	*3*	*4*	*0*	*23*	*8*	*61*	*61*	*9*	*4.4*	*8.8*	*60*	*43%*	*.302*	*1.50*	*4.81*	*5.02*	*0.2*	*98.0*			*43*
2019	*KCA*	*MLB*	*26*	*7*	*7*	*0*	*53*	*18*	*144*	*145*	*24*	*4.2*	*9.5*	*151*	*43%*	*.311*	*1.47*	*4.87*	*5.16*	*0.6*	*97.6*			*39*

Breakout: 19% Improve: 27% Collapse: 15% Attrition: 35% MLB: 48% *Comparables: Alex Colome, Josh Collmenter, Tom Koehler*

The riddles of Almonte: 1. How, two years after a poor showing in his cup of coffee as a reliever, did he suddenly dominate Double-A as a starter? 2. This guy throws mid-90s heat? 3. Come on, is he actually a starter? 4. Can he harness some of his abilities in the majors?

(Answer key: 1. He was 24. 2. Yes, but rarely in the direction he intends. 3. Probably a reliever. 4. If you want a crystal ball, you need to buy a different box of cereal.)

Scott Blewett RHP Born: 04/10/96 Age: 22 Bats: R Throws: R Height: 6'6" Weight: 210 Origin: Round 2, 2014 Draft (#56 overall)

YEAR	TEAM	LVL	AGE	W	L	SV	G	GS	IP	H	HR	BB/9	K/9	K	GB%	BABIP	WHIP	ERA	DRA	WARP	MPH	CMD	PWR	STM
2015	LEX	A	19	3	5	0	18	18	81^{1}	88	6	2.7	6.6	60	48%	.317	1.38	5.20	3.80	1.4				
2016	LEX	A	20	8	11	0	25	25	129^{1}	138	10	3.5	8.4	121	47%	.338	1.46	4.31	3.52	2.4				
2017	WIL	A+	21	7	10	0	27	27	152^{2}	153	16	3.1	7.6	129	47%	.302	1.34	4.07	4.18	1.9				
2018	*KCA*	*MLB*	*22*	*6*	*9*	*0*	*24*	*24*	*122*	*139*	*23*	*4.1*	*7.9*	*107*	*42%*	*.317*	*1.60*	*5.47*	*5.79*	*-0.1*				
2019	*KCA*	*MLB*	*23*	*4*	*6*	*0*	*16*	*16*	*95*	*104*	*19*	*4.0*	*8.3*	*88*	*42%*	*.31*	*1.54*	*5.43*	*5.76*	*-0.1*				

Breakout: 3% Improve: 4% Collapse: 0% Attrition: 4% MLB: 5% *Comparables: Braden Shipley, Kyle Lobstein, Vance Worley*

This is a name to remember and root for. Why? Well, he's a cold-weather pitcher from Baldwinsville, New York—an underdog story, if you please. When he was drafted, the newspaper in nearby Syracuse ran a photo on its website in which Blewett was smiling and hugging his beaming mother, who stands only about as high as his sternum. Hugs his mom despite being a relative giant! Ah, but there is another reason: The universe, cruel in its obvious yet dogged maneuvering, is trying to pull the young man named Blewett into the bullpen. An imposing righty who will turn 22 in April, he possesses a good fastball that played in High-A as he added almost 25 innings to his workload and registered a solid strikeout rate. A fork in the road is coming, though. His curveball can be quite good, but it's not the most consistent offering. His changeup is just kind of ... there. Only by showing significant improvement in his secondary offerings can he save us from the puns.

Ryan Buchter LHP Born: 02/13/87 Age: 31 Bats: L Throws: L Height: 6'4" Weight: 258 Origin: Round 33, 2005 Draft (#984 overall)

YEAR	TEAM	LVL	AGE	W	L	SV	G	GS	IP	H	HR	BB/9	K/9	K	GB%	BABIP	WHIP	ERA	DRA	WARP	MPH	CMD	PWR	STM
2015	OKL	AAA	28	0	0	3	27	0	32^{2}	27	0	4.4	10.7	39	39%	.321	1.32	1.65	2.85	0.8				
2015	IOW	AAA	28	2	0	0	16	0	18	9	0	4.5	11.5	23	44%	.231	1.00	2.00	3.06	0.4				
2016	SDN	MLB	29	3	0	1	67	0	63	34	4	4.4	11.1	78	21%	.227	1.03	2.86	3.62	1.0	94.6	65	68	52
2017	SDN	MLB	30	3	3	1	42	0	38^{1}	28	7	4.2	11.0	47	33%	.239	1.20	3.05	4.39	0.3	94.3	46	64	51
2017	KCA	MLB	30	1	0	0	29	0	27	16	3	2.7	6.0	18	32%	.173	0.89	2.67	4.76	0.1	94.0	46	64	51
2018	*KCA*	*MLB*	*31*	*2*	*2*	*0*	*49*	*0*	*51*	*46*	*7*	*4.1*	*9.6*	*55*	*34%*	*.284*	*1.32*	*4.43*	*4.58*	*0.3*	*93.5*	*54*	*65*	*51*
2019	*KCA*	*MLB*	*32*	*2*	*1*	*1*	*48*	*0*	*51*	*44*	*8*	*4.4*	*9.3*	*53*	*34%*	*.272*	*1.35*	*4.84*	*5.13*	*0.1*	*93.1*	*54*	*65*	*51*

Breakout: 24% Improve: 34% Collapse: 24% Attrition: 19% MLB: 68% *Comparables: Jason Bulger, Cory Gearrin, Will Harris*

Part of the pitching reinforcements shipped from San Diego to Kansas City before the deadline, Buchter didn't match the 2016 performance that put him on the map—mostly because of dingers, go figure. However, the lefty with the high-spin, whiff-inducing four-seamer did manage to keep his head above water upon introduction to the American League. It's more than the rest of that trade's triumvirate can boast. Deployed properly, that fastball will earn him roster spots, and possibly midseason plane tickets, for several years to come.

Trevor Cahill RHP Born: 03/01/88 Age: 30 Bats: R Throws: R Height: 6'4" Weight: 240 Origin: Round 2, 2006 Draft (#66 overall)

YEAR	TEAM	LVL	AGE	W	L	SV	G	GS	IP	H	HR	BB/9	K/9	K	GB%	BABIP	WHIP	ERA	DRA	WARP	MPH	CMD	PWR	STM
2015	ATL	MLB	27	0	3	0	15	3	26^1	36	2	3.8	4.8	14	64%	.354	1.78	7.52	4.47	0.1	94.1	47	44	46
2015	OKL	AAA	27	1	3	0	6	6	28^2	32	3	4.4	5.3	17	51%	.299	1.60	6.28	5.22	0.0				
2015	CHN	MLB	27	1	0	0	11	0	17	8	2	2.6	11.6	22	63%	.182	0.76	2.12	2.92	0.4	95.2	47	44	46
2016	IOW	AAA	28	0	3	0	6	6	19^2	25	3	5.5	11.4	25	53%	.407	1.88	4.58	4.51	0.2				
2016	CHN	MLB	28	4	4	0	50	1	65^2	49	7	4.8	9.0	66	57%	.246	1.28	2.74	3.98	0.8	95.1	35	44	53
2017	SDN	MLB	29	4	3	0	11	11	61	58	6	3.5	10.6	72	58%	.329	1.34	3.69	3.84	1.1	93.1	38	34	44
2017	KCA	MLB	29	0	0	0	10	3	23	33	10	8.2	5.9	15	54%	.319	2.35	8.22	5.32	0.1	93.3	38	34	44
2018	*KCA*	*MLB*	*30*	*4*	*4*	*0*	*35*	*10*	*74^2*	*76*	*10*	*4.3*	*8.3*	*69*	*53%*	*.310*	*1.50*	*4.75*	*5.01*	*0.5*	*93.3*	*38*	*39*	*47*
2019	*KCA*	*MLB*	*31*	*5*	*5*	*0*	*45*	*14*	*123^2*	*126*	*16*	*4.0*	*8.7*	*120*	*53%*	*.314*	*1.47*	*4.45*	*4.72*	*0.9*	*92.8*	*37*	*38*	*47*

Breakout: 16% Improve: 46% Collapse: 15% Attrition: 9% MLB: 83% *Comparables: Ross Detwiler, Jeff Niemann, Tom Gorzelanny*

In 2013, a Department of Transportation spokesperson told the *Seattle Times* that airlines must compensate passengers for "provable loss." The compensation is capped, however, at $3,300 for domestic flights. So even if he can pin down the company and keep them from slipping through a legal loophole, Cahill is probably not going to recover the value of the effectiveness lost in his travels from San Diego to Kansas City. Doubts will be abundant now, with his performance hitting the skids the moment anyone started paying attention again, but the 2017 disappearance of production is all the more frustrating because his time in the bullpen really does seem to have shifted his approach in a positive direction. There's still upside here, but the question marks are many and varied.

Danny Duffy LHP Born: 12/21/88 Age: 29 Bats: L Throws: L Height: 6'3" Weight: 205 Origin: Round 3, 2007 Draft (#96 overall)

YEAR	TEAM	LVL	AGE	W	L	SV	G	GS	IP	H	HR	BB/9	K/9	K	GB%	BABIP	WHIP	ERA	DRA	WARP	MPH	CMD	PWR	STM
2015	KCA	MLB	26	7	8	1	30	24	136^2	137	15	3.5	6.7	102	41%	.298	1.39	4.08	5.46	-0.7	97.0	40	57	63
2016	KCA	MLB	27	12	3	0	42	26	179^2	163	27	2.1	9.4	188	37%	.291	1.14	3.51	3.73	3.3	97.8	49	55	72
2017	KCA	MLB	28	9	10	0	24	24	146^1	143	13	2.5	8.0	130	41%	.309	1.26	3.81	3.85	2.8	94.8	47	42	64
2018	*KCA*	*MLB*	*29*	*8*	*9*	*0*	*24*	*24*	*136*	*135*	*19*	*2.9*	*7.7*	*117*	*41%*	*.293*	*1.31*	*4.24*	*4.54*	*1.3*	*95.8*	*46*	*50*	*66*
2019	*KCA*	*MLB*	*30*	*10*	*11*	*0*	*31*	*31*	*193*	*190*	*26*	*2.8*	*7.9*	*169*	*41%*	*.294*	*1.29*	*4.28*	*4.54*	*2.1*	*95.3*	*47*	*49*	*67*

Breakout: 12% Improve: 36% Collapse: 23% Attrition: 6% MLB: 96% *Comparables: Alex Cobb, Chris Tillman, Josh Johnson*

The video is a little slice of life. It's Duffy, only half of his figure in the frame, casually tossing a full water bottle up above a table and watching it stick the landing right on its green cap. It's on his Twitter, @Duffkc41, from April 9, 2017. *Haters will say it's fake*, goes the caption.

March 23, directed at Eric Hosmer, shortly after Team USA won the World Baseball Classic: *Been at this for awhile now! Dope way to start my 10th season calling you my brother! Lets take it back to the K.*

March 29, with photo of a wristband honoring Yordano Ventura: *This year is for you kid. #RIPACE.*

Early morning hours of April 26, after the Royals' sixth straight loss dropped them to 7-13: *We will pull together and come out of this. Reason for concern, but i dare somebody to count us out.*

June 12: *Yoo @Mooose_8 and i were officially drafted a decade ago. We're old dawg.*

June 18, in the midst of a Royals hot streak: *This team, man.*

June 24: *Every year yall count us out. & late june, every year, we flip that switch. And the networks jump on board (eye-roll emoji) .. we never left, you guys.* Three minutes later: *...none of us have vacay plans in october. Dont sleep on the boys.*

Duffy went on the disabled list on August 26, as the season fell apart. While in Kansas City to get an MRI, he was arrested for DUI when he fell asleep at the wheel of his car in a Burger King drive-thru. In early November, after several months of mostly retweeting charities, Duffy posted a picture of his dog on an empty beach: *Rough times make you more appreciative of the good times.*

Whether Duffy returns with his defiant optimism intact, it's hard to say, but two seasons and 326 innings of excellent starting pitching say he is likely to remain a useful rotation piece. A decade of trials and tribulations as a professional baseball player rarely feels this human. So if nothing else, count on Duffy to be a sympathetic, sometimes flawed and exceedingly real character in a pastime that can seem both too big and too small to be simply an entertainment product.

Neftali Feliz RHP Born: 05/02/88 Age: 30 Bats: R Throws: R Height: 6'3" Weight: 235 Origin: International Free Agent, 2005

YEAR	TEAM	LVL	AGE	W	L	SV	G	GS	IP	H	HR	BB/9	K/9	K	GB%	BABIP	WHIP	ERA	DRA	WARP	MPH	CMD	PWR	STM
2015	ROU	AAA	27	0	1	0	10	0	11	15	1	3.3	9.0	11	23%	.368	1.73	7.36	5.04	0.0				
2015	TEX	MLB	27	1	2	6	18	0	19^2	24	2	4.1	7.3	16	36%	.344	1.68	4.58	5.04	-0.1	97.1	54	64	47
2015	DET	MLB	27	2	2	4	30	0	28^1	33	3	2.9	7.3	23	40%	.353	1.48	7.62	4.75	0.0	98.6	54	64	47
2016	PIT	MLB	28	4	2	2	62	0	53^2	40	10	3.5	10.2	61	38%	.240	1.14	3.52	3.60	0.8	99.3	51	65	48
2017	MIL	MLB	29	1	5	8	29	0	27	23	8	5.0	7.0	21	35%	.211	1.41	6.00	6.44	-0.4	98.4	54	68	47
2017	KCA	MLB	29	1	0	0	20	0	19	17	1	3.8	7.6	16	38%	.291	1.32	4.74	6.63	-0.3	97.8	54	68	47
2018	*KCA*	*MLB*	*30*	*2*	*1*	*1*	*37*	*0*	*39*	*39*	*7*	*4.1*	*7.9*	*34*	*39%*	*.288*	*1.46*	*5.33*	*5.63*	*-0.1*	*97.7*	*53*	*66*	*47*
2019	*KCA*	*MLB*	*31*	*2*	*1*	*1*	*42*	*0*	*41^2*	*42*	*8*	*4.2*	*7.8*	*36*	*39%*	*.289*	*1.49*	*5.45*	*5.79*	*-0.3*	*97.4*	*52*	*66*	*47*

Breakout: 21% Improve: 51% Collapse: 12% Attrition: 12% MLB: 79% *Comparables: Santiago Casilla, Manny Acosta, David Carpenter*

The Brewers' attempt to build up the former All-Star closer's value did not work. The strikeout rate uptick from 2016 didn't hold, while the control problems very much did. Still, despite seemingly being around forever, Feliz won't turn 30 years old until May and still has that golden ticket known as velocity. If you just muttered "eh, I can work with that," you might be a pitching coach. Feliz has the third-most saves (72) in baseball history through age 23, but now seems unlikely to reach even double that number for his career.

Brian Flynn LHP Born: 04/19/90 Age: 28 Bats: L Throws: L Height: 6'7" Weight: 250 Origin: Round 7, 2011 Draft (#227 overall)

YEAR	TEAM	LVL	AGE	W	L	SV	G	GS	IP	H	HR	BB/9	K/9	K	GB%	BABIP	WHIP	ERA	DRA	WARP	MPH	CMD	PWR	STM
2016	OMA	AAA	26	2	1	0	9	4	23^{2}	22	1	4.6	10.6	28	66%	.350	1.44	3.04	3.58	0.4				
2016	KCA	MLB	26	1	2	0	36	1	55^{1}	38	5	3.7	7.2	44	57%	.223	1.10	2.60	3.82	0.7	95.4	44	55	44
2017	OMA	AAA	27	5	3	0	22	4	50	68	10	2.2	9.0	50	46%	.369	1.60	5.40	4.53	0.5				
2017	KCA	MLB	27	0	0	0	1	0	2^{1}	3	0	0.0	0.0	0	38%	.375	1.29	3.86	7.43	-0.1	94.2			44
2018	*KCA*	*MLB*	*28*	*2*	*2*	*0*	*49*	*0*	*51*	*51*	*7*	*3.5*	*8.5*	*49*	*47%*	*.302*	*1.39*	*4.40*	*4.55*	*0.3*	*94.8*	*44*	*55*	*44*
2019	*KCA*	*MLB*	*29*	*2*	*1*	*0*	*42*	*0*	*44^{2}*	*45*	*6*	*4.2*	*8.1*	*40*	*47%*	*.305*	*1.48*	*4.73*	*5.02*	*0.1*	*94.4*	*44*	*55*	*44*

Breakout: 26% Improve: 44% Collapse: 13% Attrition: 27% MLB: 66% *Comparables: Blake Treinen, Duane Below, Eric Surkamp*

The Brian Flynn Addendum, henceforth, prohibits ball-playing employees of the Kansas City Royals from working, climbing, walking on or traversing roofs whose integrity could be appraised, by a reasonable person, as questionable. Further, activity on all roofs of structures unintended for dwelling or business purposes—such as barns, er, uh, barns—will be banned under the addendum. The club shall be entitled to withhold an appropriate amount of compensation from employees in the event that an injury preventing baseball activity is suffered in the course of a violation of the addendum.

Onelki Garcia LHP Born: 08/02/89 Age: 28 Bats: L Throws: L Height: 6'3" Weight: 225 Origin: Round 3, 2012 Draft (#113 overall)

YEAR	TEAM	LVL	AGE	W	L	SV	G	GS	IP	H	HR	BB/9	K/9	K	GB%	BABIP	WHIP	ERA	DRA	WARP	MPH	CMD	PWR	STM
2015	BIR	AA	25	1	0	0	13	0	17^{2}	19	0	3.6	12.2	24	45%	.388	1.47	5.09	2.64	0.4				
2015	CHR	AAA	25	0	1	3	25	0	38^{1}	45	3	5.2	11.3	48	50%	.389	1.75	4.70	3.73	0.5				
2017	NWA	AA	27	0	0	0	2	2	10^{1}	11	2	0.9	5.2	6	58%	.265	1.16	2.61	3.81	0.2				
2017	OMA	AAA	27	7	3	0	20	10	75	84	6	3.8	7.6	63	50%	.333	1.55	5.04	4.69	0.7				
2017	KCA	MLB	27	0	1	0	2	1	6	12	2	7.5	3.0	2	56%	.435	2.83	13.50	8.69	-0.2	95.2			54
2018	*KCA*	*MLB*	*28*	*1*	*1*	*0*	*15*	*0*	*15*	*15*	*2*	*4.4*	*8.1*	*14*	*47%*	*.301*	*1.54*	*4.88*	*4.93*	*0.0*	*94.6*			*54*
2019	*KCA*	*MLB*	*29*	*2*	*1*	*0*	*40*	*0*	*42^{2}*	*45*	*6*	*4.2*	*8.0*	*38*	*47%*	*.313*	*1.52*	*4.67*	*4.97*	*0.1*	*94.1*			*54*

Breakout: 10% Improve: 19% Collapse: 17% Attrition: 24% MLB: 38% *Comparables: Darin Downs, Seth Frankoff, Justin Thomas*

Once upon a time—2013, to be exact—Garcia was a top 10 Dodgers prospect. The Cuban southpaw got a cup of coffee in LA before his prospect star was dimmed by injury. He managed to reawaken his major-league career with the Royals in 2017, only to step into a nightmare. His first outing was a mop-up appearance during an Indians romp. Okay, fine, he then got his first big-league start! But he gave up four runs to the Twins while recording just one out. It was the shortest debut start since the Rangers threw 19-year-old Wilson Alvarez to the wolves in 1989. Alvarez gave up three runs without retiring anyone before he was pulled from that game, but eventually became a steady starter—an All-Star. He just had to wait another two years for the chance.

Foster Griffin LHP Born: 07/27/95 Age: 22 Bats: R Throws: L Height: 6'3" Weight: 200 Origin: Round 1, 2014 Draft (#28 overall)

YEAR	TEAM	LVL	AGE	W	L	SV	G	GS	IP	H	HR	BB/9	K/9	K	GB%	BABIP	WHIP	ERA	DRA	WARP	MPH	CMD	PWR	STM
2015	LEX	A	19	4	6	0	22	22	102^{2}	123	8	3.1	6.2	71	55%	.337	1.54	5.44	4.71	0.6				
2016	LEX	A	20	1	4	0	7	7	37^{1}	35	3	2.2	7.0	29	60%	.281	1.18	3.38	3.89	0.5				
2016	WIL	A+	20	5	10	0	20	20	95^{1}	130	9	4.1	7.2	76	47%	.376	1.81	6.23	5.59	-0.1				
2017	WIL	A+	21	4	2	0	10	10	56^{2}	43	2	3.2	9.5	60	43%	.279	1.11	2.86	3.88	0.9				
2017	NWA	AA	21	11	5	0	18	18	104^{2}	108	11	2.9	7.0	81	46%	.311	1.36	3.61	4.16	1.3				
2018	*KCA*	*MLB*	*22*	*7*	*10*	*0*	*26*	*26*	*126^{2}*	*144*	*22*	*4.0*	*7.7*	*108*	*44%*	*.320*	*1.58*	*5.29*	*5.59*	*0.1*				
2019	*KCA*	*MLB*	*23*	*4*	*5*	*0*	*14*	*14*	*82^{2}*	*91*	*15*	*4.0*	*8.2*	*75*	*44%*	*.315*	*1.54*	*5.27*	*5.60*	*0.0*				

Breakout: 5% Improve: 10% Collapse: 2% Attrition: 13% MLB: 15% *Comparables: Jose Urena, Max Povse, Ronald Herrera*

Individual pitch nicknames should be a thing. Not like how everyone with a 12-to-6 curveball throws a "hammer." No, more like: Griffin's fastball is called The Fringe. The lefty controls the zone well and has displayed worm-killing ability at times, but every report on him nonetheless is obliged to mention that his fastball doesn't have much giddy-up. It is fringe-average, and wouldn't even be there if he threw with his right hand. Still, after experiencing a modicum of success over a very full 2017 season that included a promotion to Double-A, Griffin has increased the chances that he will one day get to see what major-league hitters would call it. For his sake, we hope it isn't "Lunch."

Jason Hammel RHP Born: 09/02/82 Age: 35 Bats: R Throws: R Height: 6'6" Weight: 225 Origin: Round 10, 2002 Draft (#284 overall)

YEAR	TEAM	LVL	AGE	W	L	SV	G	GS	IP	H	HR	BB/9	K/9	K	GB%	BABIP	WHIP	ERA	DRA	WARP	MPH	CMD	PWR	STM
2015	CHN	MLB	32	10	7	0	31	31	170^{2}	158	23	2.1	9.1	172	41%	.288	1.16	3.74	4.13	1.9	94.4	46	43	69
2016	CHN	MLB	33	15	10	0	30	30	166^{2}	148	25	2.9	7.8	144	44%	.267	1.21	3.83	5.10	0.5	94.3	45	43	69
2017	KCA	MLB	34	8	13	0	32	32	180^{1}	209	26	2.4	7.2	145	38%	.318	1.43	5.29	4.78	1.6	93.5	53	40	79
2018	*KCA*	*MLB*	*35*	*9*	*12*	*0*	*30*	*30*	*171*	*183*	*27*	*3.0*	*6.8*	*130*	*42%*	*.296*	*1.41*	*4.76*	*5.11*	*0.6*	*92.8*	*48*	*41*	*72*
2019	*KCA*	*MLB*	*36*	*9*	*11*	*0*	*30*	*30*	*185^{2}*	*195*	*30*	*2.8*	*6.9*	*142*	*42%*	*.291*	*1.36*	*4.85*	*5.15*	*1.0*	*92.1*	*48*	*40*	*72*

Breakout: 16% Improve: 40% Collapse: 19% Attrition: 12% MLB: 85% *Comparables: John Lackey, Kevin Millwood, Johan Santana*

It used to be that Hammel Time stopped promptly at the All-Star break. To look at the ugly ERA, you'd be tempted to say that it never really got started in Kansas City, but the underlying numbers say he's probably still the league-average arm that has taken the mound every fifth day for four years in a row. If his (mostly newfound) durability somehow remains intact into his mid-thirties, you probably won't hear the Royals complaining about a down year and he might be in another rotation altogether.

Kelvin Herrera RHP Born: 12/31/89 Age: 28 Bats: R Throws: R Height: 5'10" Weight: 200 Origin: International Free Agent, 2006

YEAR	TEAM	LVL	AGE	W	L	SV	G	GS	IP	H	HR	BB/9	K/9	K	GB%	BABIP	WHIP	ERA	DRA	WARP	MPH	CMD	PWR	STM
2015	KCA	MLB	25	4	3	0	72	0	69^{2}	52	5	3.4	8.3	64	46%	.249	1.12	2.71	2.67	1.7	101.0	34	86	52
2016	KCA	MLB	26	2	6	12	72	0	72	57	6	1.5	10.8	86	46%	.290	0.96	2.75	2.43	2.1	99.7	57	60	51
2017	KCA	MLB	27	3	3	26	64	0	59^{1}	60	9	3.0	8.5	56	47%	.295	1.35	4.25	4.42	0.5	99.3	51	78	48
2018	*KCA*	*MLB*	*28*	*3*	*3*	*25*	*54*	*0*	*57*	*53*	*7*	*3.2*	*8.4*	*53*	*46%*	*.289*	*1.29*	*3.95*	*4.20*	*0.6*	*99.3*	*49*	*74*	*50*
2019	*KCA*	*MLB*	*29*	*2*	*1*	*16*	*49*	*0*	*51^{2}*	*48*	*7*	*3.4*	*8.5*	*49*	*46%*	*.286*	*1.31*	*4.43*	*4.69*	*0.3*	*98.7*	*52*	*71*	*50*

Breakout: 27% Improve: 47% Collapse: 27% Attrition: 10% MLB: 90% *Comparables: Drew Storen, Addison Reed, Jordan Walden*

For a while, it looked as though the hearty parade of Royals would never cease. What with the bloodline being surprisingly strong and the territory providing a distinct strategic advantage, maybe the succession plan had indeed gone smoothly yet again. When Prince Wade II ascended to a more grandiose post by the shores of the famous breeze-throwing lake, nothing was certain. Yet the newly appointed Prince Kelvin (the first, not to be confused with Prince Kelvim) took control seamlessly. Until things started to go wrong. Prized commodities began fleeing at never-before-seen rates. Rumors swirled that Kelvin was weak, that the line established by King Greg XIII was shaky. It was officially toppled on September 8, 2017, when the always instrumental bureaucrat known as Yost suddenly wielded his immense power and removed Prince Kelvin, bringing a close to one of the Kingdom of the Ninth's longest eras of peace. When word of the turmoil reached the twittering peasants, one less than earnest reaction incited an immediate scuffle.

Jake Junis RHP Born: 09/16/92 Age: 25 Bats: R Throws: R Height: 6'2" Weight: 225 Origin: Round 29, 2011 Draft (#876 overall)

YEAR	TEAM	LVL	AGE	W	L	SV	G	GS	IP	H	HR	BB/9	K/9	K	GB%	BABIP	WHIP	ERA	DRA	WARP	MPH	CMD	PWR	STM
2015	WIL	A+	22	5	11	0	26	26	155^{2}	145	11	1.7	7.1	123	38%	.294	1.12	3.64	3.88	2.2				
2016	NWA	AA	23	9	7	0	21	21	119	110	12	2.0	8.8	117	43%	.302	1.15	3.25	2.93	3.1				
2016	OMA	AAA	23	1	3	0	6	6	30	39	6	2.1	7.8	26	41%	.367	1.53	7.20	3.78	0.5				
2017	OMA	AAA	24	3	5	0	12	12	71	61	6	1.9	10.9	86	37%	.307	1.07	2.92	1.82	3.0				
2017	KCA	MLB	24	9	3	0	20	16	98^{1}	101	15	2.3	7.3	80	42%	.294	1.28	4.30	4.70	0.9	93.1	47	38	69
2018	*KCA*	*MLB*	*25*	*7*	*9*	*0*	*23*	*23*	*131*	*138*	*23*	*3.0*	*7.9*	*115*	*39%*	*.300*	*1.40*	*4.69*	*5.02*	*0.6*	*92.8*	*48*	*39*	*71*
2019	*KCA*	*MLB*	*26*	*10*	*11*	*0*	*30*	*30*	*184^{2}*	*197*	*30*	*2.6*	*8.2*	*169*	*39%*	*.31*	*1.36*	*4.56*	*4.84*	*1.5*	*92.5*	*48*	*39*	*71*

Breakout: 21% Improve: 43% Collapse: 21% Attrition: 43% MLB: 81% *Comparables: Chad Bettis, Hector Noesi, Joe Wieland*

Dominant at Triple-A and quietly quite good in the majors once he ramped up his slider usage in August, Junis has established himself as a viable big-league pitcher. What he has not established is whether he prefers to go by Jake or Jakob. If you believe a *Kansas City Star* account of his emergence in which Ned Yost compared his disposition to that of a "dead fish" and "Corey Kluber," then the unassuming Jake seems the way to go. On the other hand, adult contemporary radio data suggests that a name like Jakob might keep him on the radar longer if 2017 turns out to be his peak. Wait, that's not why "One Headlight" is still playing on the radio?

Nate Karns RHP Born: 11/25/87 Age: 30 Bats: R Throws: R Height: 6'3" Weight: 225 Origin: Round 12, 2009 Draft (#352 overall)

YEAR	TEAM	LVL	AGE	W	L	SV	G	GS	IP	H	HR	BB/9	K/9	K	GB%	BABIP	WHIP	ERA	DRA	WARP	MPH	CMD	PWR	STM
2015	TBA	MLB	27	7	5	0	27	26	147	132	19	3.4	8.9	145	43%	.285	1.28	3.67	3.49	2.8	94.6	42	45	66
2016	SEA	MLB	28	6	2	1	22	15	94^{1}	95	11	4.3	9.6	101	43%	.327	1.48	5.15	4.36	1.0	95.8	39	44	56
2017	KCA	MLB	29	2	2	0	9	8	45^{1}	41	9	2.6	10.1	51	48%	.283	1.19	4.17	4.21	0.7	95.1	47	45	48
2018	*KCA*	*MLB*	*30*	*7*	*9*	*0*	*23*	*23*	*131*	*127*	*18*	*3.6*	*9.0*	*131*	*45%*	*.298*	*1.37*	*4.22*	*4.51*	*1.3*	*94.4*	*42*	*44*	*55*
2019	*KCA*	*MLB*	*31*	*10*	*10*	*0*	*30*	*30*	*190^{2}*	*180*	*26*	*3.4*	*9.5*	*201*	*45%*	*.301*	*1.33*	*4.20*	*4.45*	*2.3*	*94.0*	*42*	*44*	*53*

Breakout: 18% Improve: 42% Collapse: 20% Attrition: 17% MLB: 75% *Comparables: Matt Shoemaker, Chris Narveson, Dustin Nippert*

One of the thousands affected by Jerry Dipoto trades last winter, Karns took noteworthy steps forward in strikeout rate and walk rate. However, he was bitten by the homer bug despite moving from one pitcher-friendly ballpark to another. His season ended (due to injury) before the opposing forces could decide on a prevailing direction. Luckily, Karns will probably get more chances to figure it out since he is no longer Dipoto trade fodder. There is serious strikeout ability here, which is just about the best possible starting point for a pitcher.

Ian Kennedy RHP Born: 12/19/84 Age: 33 Bats: R Throws: R Height: 6'0" Weight: 200 Origin: Round 1, 2006 Draft (#21 overall)

YEAR	TEAM	LVL	AGE	W	L	SV	G	GS	IP	H	HR	BB/9	K/9	K	GB%	BABIP	WHIP	ERA	DRA	WARP	MPH	CMD	PWR	STM
2015	SDN	MLB	30	9	15	0	30	30	168^{1}	166	31	2.8	9.3	174	41%	.301	1.30	4.28	4.85	0.5	93.8	58	46	70
2016	KCA	MLB	31	11	11	0	33	33	195^{2}	173	33	3.0	8.5	184	34%	.268	1.22	3.68	4.46	2.0	94.5	59	51	81
2017	KCA	MLB	32	5	13	0	30	30	154	143	34	3.6	7.7	131	36%	.257	1.32	5.38	5.68	-0.2	93.6	55	48	68
2018	*KCA*	*MLB*	*33*	*9*	*13*	*0*	*29*	*29*	*174*	*181*	*32*	*3.5*	*7.7*	*149*	*38%*	*.293*	*1.43*	*5.06*	*5.43*	*-0.1*	*93.0*	*57*	*48*	*72*
2019	*KCA*	*MLB*	*34*	*10*	*12*	*0*	*29*	*29*	*181*	*186*	*30*	*3.5*	*7.7*	*155*	*38%*	*.293*	*1.42*	*4.98*	*5.29*	*0.7*	*92.5*	*56*	*48*	*72*

Breakout: 23% Improve: 48% Collapse: 14% Attrition: 8% MLB: 88% *Comparables: Edwin Jackson, Tim Lincecum, J.A. Happ*

Who said baseball can't be enjoyed in a timely fashion? Clearly no one familiar with the Ian Kennedy Experience. Here, you can be in on the secret. Ready? Take in the first three innings of his next start. Check the box score after those three innings, where you will inevitably find a zero in the opposing team's hits column. Now, turn off the TV or leave the ballpark and go about your day, ignoring the five runs he'll give up in the next two innings or so. Don't check the score, but do be sure to have mobile notifications of some sort turned on, so you can occasionally be electrified by the thought that you saw the beginning of something special.

Seth Maness RHP Born: 10/14/88 Age: 29 Bats: R Throws: R Height: 6'0" Weight: 190 Origin: Round 11, 2011 Draft (#350 overall)

YEAR	TEAM	LVL	AGE	W	L	SV	G	GS	IP	H	HR	BB/9	K/9	K	GB%	BABIP	WHIP	ERA	DRA	WARP	MPH	CMD	PWR	STM
2015	SLN	MLB	26	4	2	3	76	0	63^1	77	7	1.8	6.5	46	58%	.345	1.42	4.26	4.56	0.1	91.6	60	39	51
2016	SLN	MLB	27	2	2	0	29	0	31^2	34	2	2.3	4.5	16	58%	.296	1.33	3.41	4.40	0.2	90.2	64	43	33
2017	KCA	MLB	28	1	0	0	8	0	9^2	16	3	1.9	3.7	4	54%	.361	1.86	3.72	5.57	0.0	88.9			42
2017	OMA	AAA	28	2	2	2	24	0	47	63	7	1.5	6.7	35	48%	.359	1.51	6.13	3.76	0.8				
2018	*KCA*	*MLB*	*29*	*2*	*1*	*0*	*42*	*0*	44^2	*52*	*6*	*3.5*	*5.9*	*29*	*50%*	*.315*	*1.57*	*5.16*	*5.47*	*-0.1*	*90.1*	*62*	*41*	*41*
2019	*KCA*	*MLB*	*30*	*2*	*1*	*0*	*33*	*0*	*36*	*42*	*6*	*3.5*	*5.8*	*23*	*50%*	*.31*	*1.56*	*5.24*	*5.58*	*-0.1*	*89.3*	*62*	*42*	*39*

Breakout: 30% Improve: 52% Collapse: 26% Attrition: 20% MLB: 90% *Comparables: Brandon Lyon, Anthony Swarzak, Tommy Hunter*

Maness is worth rooting for if only to witness a test of surgical naming conventions in the Internet age. As of right now, the procedure that allowed him to overcome a torn ulnar collateral ligament in less than a year is known as "primary repair." The name, so far as the general baseball-watching public is concerned, only exists in the service of explaining why Maness is different. The last time this strategy was employed, Tommy John gave his name to a certain type of scar and a sort of dour, half-realized state of mind. The open question, then, is less about his performance and more about whether Maness' moniker possesses the cache and cadence to infiltrate the collective baseball psyche.

Brandon Maurer RHP Born: 07/03/90 Age: 27 Bats: R Throws: R Height: 6'5" Weight: 230 Origin: Round 23, 2008 Draft (#702 overall)

YEAR	TEAM	LVL	AGE	W	L	SV	G	GS	IP	H	HR	BB/9	K/9	K	GB%	BABIP	WHIP	ERA	DRA	WARP	MPH	CMD	PWR	STM
2015	SDN	MLB	24	7	4	0	53	0	51	39	3	2.6	6.9	39	48%	.243	1.06	3.00	3.15	0.9	97.9	33	53	50
2016	SDN	MLB	25	0	5	13	71	0	69^2	65	7	3.0	9.3	72	39%	.297	1.26	4.52	4.33	0.5	98.4	47	55	53
2017	SDN	MLB	26	1	4	20	42	0	39^1	39	4	1.8	8.7	38	44%	.315	1.19	5.72	5.95	-0.3	98.6	52	64	50
2017	KCA	MLB	26	2	2	2	26	0	20	34	4	4.9	9.4	21	33%	.435	2.25	8.10	6.48	-0.3	98.8	52	64	50
2018	*KCA*	*MLB*	*27*	*3*	*3*	*3*	*54*	*0*	*57*	*56*	*7*	*3.5*	*8.5*	*54*	*42%*	*.303*	*1.39*	*4.04*	*4.28*	*0.6*	*97.9*	*47*	*59*	*52*
2019	*KCA*	*MLB*	*28*	*2*	*1*	*2*	*48*	*0*	51^1	*49*	*7*	*3.6*	*9.0*	*51*	*42%*	*.301*	*1.36*	*4.21*	*4.47*	*0.4*	*97.7*	*49*	*60*	*52*

Breakout: 31% Improve: 58% Collapse: 20% Attrition: 14% MLB: 96% *Comparables: Carlos Villanueva, Randall Delgado, Kyle McClellan*

Maurer was the rural juror of baseball's 2017 season, a plot point introduced solely to create an arc of confusion. Look, 20 saves for the Padres and a midseason trade to an aspiring contender! Wait, he was bad? Holy ... does that ERA start with a five? It got worse? How fast can you get DFA'd after tallying that many saves? *Looks up Ernesto Frieri transaction log.* Never mind. Let's not discuss that. Let's talk about how you concoct a last name that verbally mirrors that of the Minnesota Twins' franchise player yet includes two Rs on paper.

Peter Moylan RHP Born: 12/02/78 Age: 39 Bats: R Throws: R Height: 6'2" Weight: 225 Origin: International Free Agent, 1996

YEAR	TEAM	LVL	AGE	W	L	SV	G	GS	IP	H	HR	BB/9	K/9	K	GB%	BABIP	WHIP	ERA	DRA	WARP	MPH	CMD	PWR	STM
2015	GWN	AAA	36	2	0	6	27	0	28^2	22	1	2.8	7.5	24	57%	.269	1.08	3.14	2.77	0.7				
2015	ATL	MLB	36	1	0	0	22	0	10^1	12	1	0.0	7.0	8	69%	.314	1.16	3.48	4.21	0.1	92.6			45
2016	OMA	AAA	37	1	1	5	12	0	12^2	8	0	3.6	7.1	10	59%	.235	1.03	0.71	5.38	-0.1				
2016	KCA	MLB	37	2	0	0	50	0	44^2	42	4	3.2	6.9	34	63%	.281	1.30	3.43	4.23	0.4	92.6	50	36	45
2017	KCA	MLB	38	0	0	0	79	0	59^1	40	4	3.8	7.0	46	62%	.221	1.10	3.49	2.52	1.8	91.8	65	27	50
2018	*KCA*	*MLB*	*39*	*2*	*1*	*0*	*45*	*0*	47^1	*47*	*4*	*4.1*	*6.3*	*33*	*56%*	*.291*	*1.46*	*4.74*	*5.02*	*0.1*	*90.6*	*58*	*29*	*46*
2019	*KCA*	*MLB*	*40*	*2*	*1*	*0*	*42*	*0*	34^1	*35*	*4*	*3.9*	*5.9*	*23*	*56%*	*.289*	*1.46*	*4.82*	*5.13*	*0.0*	*89.9*	*57*	*29*	*45*

Breakout: 17% Improve: 39% Collapse: 18% Attrition: 12% MLB: 76% *Comparables: Scott Atchison, Jamey Wright, Doug Brocail*

He looks like a high school gym teacher, grooms his facial hair like an early '90s NASCAR driver and talks like Crocodile Dundee, but Moylan still pitches a lot like a poor man's peak Brad Ziegler. That may not exactly sound like the dream, but this is a 39-year-old several seasons removed from taking a minor-league coaching job, only to return from the brink and log successful major-league innings. That's a ripsnorter of a career, and there's a trail of befuddled right-handed hitters to prove it.

Wily Peralta RHP Born: 05/08/89 Age: 29 Bats: R Throws: R Height: 6'1" Weight: 255 Origin: International Free Agent, 2005

YEAR	TEAM	LVL	AGE	W	L	SV	G	GS	IP	H	HR	BB/9	K/9	K	GB%	BABIP	WHIP	ERA	DRA	WARP	MPH	CMD	PWR	STM
2015	MIL	MLB	26	5	10	0	20	20	108^2	130	14	3.1	5.0	60	53%	.320	1.54	4.72	6.34	-1.6	97.1	46	60	52
2016	CSP	AAA	27	1	3	0	10	10	41^1	55	5	3.7	8.5	39	56%	.391	1.74	6.31	3.95	0.7				
2016	MIL	MLB	27	7	11	0	23	23	127^2	152	19	3.0	6.6	93	52%	.336	1.53	4.86	5.11	0.4	97.6	66	57	72
2017	MIL	MLB	28	5	4	0	19	8	57^1	73	10	5.0	8.2	52	46%	.362	1.83	7.85	6.16	-0.5	97.8	60	61	47
2017	CSP	AAA	28	1	0	1	13	0	16	13	0	5.6	5.6	10	57%	.255	1.44	3.38	6.86	-0.3				
2018	*KCA*	*MLB*	*29*	*4*	*4*	*0*	*45*	*6*	73^1	*78*	*9*	*4.0*	*6.9*	*56*	*49%*	*.303*	*1.52*	*4.80*	*4.94*	*0.2*	*96.8*	*59*	*59*	*57*
2019	*KCA*	*MLB*	*30*	*5*	*4*	*0*	*62*	*8*	102^2	*110*	*13*	*3.8*	*7.1*	*81*	*49%*	*.311*	*1.50*	*4.65*	*4.95*	*0.5*	*96.6*	*62*	*59*	*57*

Breakout: 33% Improve: 51% Collapse: 21% Attrition: 15% MLB: 93% *Comparables: Jon Niese, Felix Doubront, Wandy Rodriguez*

Human beings adore things that go fast: high-speed trains, cars, jets, cheetahs—anything. Sports are no different. It's why the Minnesota Vikings took Troy Williamson with the seventh pick of the 2005 NFL Draft. Never mind that he wasn't actually a very good receiver; he could fly. Similarly, Peralta had been a potential breakout star for the Brewers for the better part of three years. He only had two pitches, struggled to find the strike zone and didn't miss bats, but his mid- to upper-90s sinker was irresistible, and he had decent stretches (like the second half of 2016) where the BABIP was kind. Everything finally unraveled in 2017. Peralta couldn't find the strike zone, throw his slider effectively or hold his spot in the Brewers' rotation. The old adage that "relievers are just failed starters" didn't apply to the righty, either, as he had an 11.94 ERA out of the bullpen last year. Maybe he can still adjust to the 'pen with an entire spring training to establish a routine and embrace the role, but if he can't find more and better strikes, the former top-101 prospect's career could mirror Williamson's a little too closely.

Eric Skoglund LHP

Born: 10/26/92 Age: 25 Bats: L Throws: L Height: 6'7" Weight: 200 Origin: Round 3, 2014 Draft (#92 overall)

YEAR	TEAM	LVL	AGE	W	L	SV	G	GS	IP	H	HR	BB/9	K/9	K	GB%	BABIP	WHIP	ERA	DRA	WARP	MPH	CMD	PWR	STM
2015	WIL	A+	22	6	3	0	15	15	84^1	83	2	1.2	7.0	66	50%	.314	1.11	3.52	2.76	2.4				
2016	NWA	AA	23	7	10	0	27	27	156^1	135	19	2.2	7.7	134	44%	.263	1.11	3.45	1.95	5.9				
2017	OMA	AAA	24	4	5	0	19	19	100^2	110	14	2.6	9.1	102	42%	.331	1.38	4.11	3.22	2.7				
2017	KCA	MLB	24	1	2	0	7	5	18	30	2	6.0	7.0	14	39%	.431	2.33	9.50	9.24	-0.8	94.1	31	48	57
2018	*KCA*	*MLB*	*25*	*4*	*5*	*0*	*25*	*10*	*72*	*77*	*13*	*3.3*	*7.7*	*62*	*42%*	*.298*	*1.43*	*4.92*	*5.15*	*0.2*	*93.8*	*32*	*49*	*58*
2019	*KCA*	*MLB*	*26*	*8*	*8*	*0*	*51*	*20*	*150^2*	*160*	*26*	*3.4*	*8.0*	*134*	*42%*	*.305*	*1.44*	*4.90*	*5.21*	*0.6*	*93.5*	*32*	*49*	*59*

Breakout: 16% Improve: 28% Collapse: 18% Attrition: 40% MLB: 58% *Comparables: Bryan Augenstein, Kyle McPherson, Alec Asher*

If you got to pick when to pitch the game of your life, would you maximize the ecstasy of your first big-league start? Or would the knowledge that it's all downhill from there scare you away? Write that question down to maybe ask Skoglund in 10 years. The lanky lefty's very first outing saw him spin 6 1/3 scoreless innings against the Tigers and Justin Verlander. Problem was, that grand entrance didn't change the fact that he doesn't miss many bats. A string of rough starts followed, including a four-out, seven-run disaster upon his return from Triple-A in August. He's a tall southpaw, so there will be opportunity. Either way, he will always have May 30, 2017.

Joakim Soria RHP

Born: 05/18/84 Age: 34 Bats: R Throws: R Height: 6'3" Weight: 200 Origin: International Free Agent, 2001

YEAR	TEAM	LVL	AGE	W	L	SV	G	GS	IP	H	HR	BB/9	K/9	K	GB%	BABIP	WHIP	ERA	DRA	WARP	MPH	CMD	PWR	STM
2015	DET	MLB	31	3	1	23	43	0	41	32	8	2.4	7.9	36	46%	.222	1.05	2.85	3.38	0.6	95.2	64	47	52
2015	PIT	MLB	31	0	0	1	29	0	26^2	23	0	2.7	9.4	28	41%	.329	1.16	2.03	3.47	0.4	94.7	64	47	52
2016	KCA	MLB	32	5	8	1	70	0	66^2	70	10	3.6	9.2	68	52%	.323	1.46	4.05	3.94	0.8	95.2	48	50	51
2017	KCA	MLB	33	4	3	1	59	0	56	49	1	3.2	10.3	64	58%	.329	1.23	3.70	3.07	1.3	94.7	44	45	46
2018	*CHA*	*MLB*	*34*	*3*	*3*	*25*	*51*	*0*	*53*	*50*	*6*	*3.6*	*9.0*	*54*	*50%*	*.296*	*1.34*	*3.72*	*3.97*	*0.7*	*93.8*	*50*	*47*	*48*
2019	*CHA*	*MLB*	*35*	*3*	*1*	*0*	*49*	*0*	*52^1*	*49*	*6*	*3.8*	*8.4*	*49*	*50%*	*.293*	*1.37*	*4.23*	*4.47*	*0.4*	*93.3*	*46*	*46*	*47*

Breakout: 9% Improve: 22% Collapse: 48% Attrition: 7% MLB: 89% *Comparables: Jose Valverde, Akinori Otsuka, Scot Shields*

The return to his Kansas City stomping grounds bore belated fruit for Soria, who posted what was arguably his best season since 2014 thanks to a rise in ground-ball rate and slicing his homers allowed from 10 to one. At age 33, and having pitched in precisely three postseason games (all ill-fated), he likely has enough left in the tank to take another spin through the circuit of noncommittal contenders seeking relief help. Soria is closer to again being the preinjury bullpen anchor of 2007-2011 than last season's ERA would suggest, assuming there's not another injury ahead.

Josh Staumont RHP

Born: 12/21/93 Age: 24 Bats: R Throws: R Height: 6'3" Weight: 200 Origin: Round 2, 2015 Draft (#64 overall)

YEAR	TEAM	LVL	AGE	W	L	SV	G	GS	IP	H	HR	BB/9	K/9	K	GB%	BABIP	WHIP	ERA	DRA	WARP	MPH	CMD	PWR	STM
2015	IDA	RK	21	3	1	1	14	1	31^1	18	0	6.9	14.6	51	70%	.316	1.34	3.16	1.63	1.3				
2016	WIL	A+	22	2	10	0	18	15	73	62	3	8.3	11.6	94	46%	.328	1.77	5.05	6.84	-1.2				
2016	NWA	AA	22	2	1	0	11	11	50^1	42	2	6.6	13.1	73	42%	.364	1.57	3.04	4.25	0.5				
2017	OMA	AAA	23	3	8	0	16	15	76	64	14	7.5	11.0	93	41%	.279	1.67	6.28	9.92	-3.5				
2017	NWA	AA	23	3	4	0	10	10	48^2	42	2	6.3	8.3	45	36%	.308	1.56	4.44	8.83	-2.1				
2018	*KCA*	*MLB*	*24*	*5*	*8*	*0*	*34*	*20*	*104*	*95*	*19*	*7.9*	*11.6*	*134*	*43%*	*.309*	*1.79*	*5.99*	*6.31*	*-0.9*				
2019	*KCA*	*MLB*	*25*	*3*	*4*	*0*	*16*	*11*	*76*	*71*	*13*	*5.3*	*10.4*	*87*	*43%*	*.302*	*1.53*	*5.11*	*5.41*	*0.1*				

Breakout: 11% Improve: 20% Collapse: 7% Attrition: 17% MLB: 30% *Comparables: Nick Hagadone, Mauricio Robles, Samuel Deduno*

Blessed with 100-mph heat, the 24-year-old Staumont always had a shot at a starring role. Doubt he thought it would be as the addled mind at the center of *Inception 2*, though. As unlikely a baseball movie as you're likely to come across, it explores the uneasy and previously unfathomable nature of a world in which hitters know more about the incoming pitch than the man who threw it. Though visually stimulating and technologically advanced, the film is being panned for plopping a predictable resolution onto its novel premise—with the intercranial interlopers planting thoughts of the bullpen, or perhaps a simplified delivery, in Staumont's mind following a season that saw a demotion to Double-A.

Jason Vargas LHP

Born: 02/02/83 Age: 35 Bats: L Throws: L Height: 6'0" Weight: 215 Origin: Round 2, 2004 Draft (#68 overall)

YEAR	TEAM	LVL	AGE	W	L	SV	G	GS	IP	H	HR	BB/9	K/9	K	GB%	BABIP	WHIP	ERA	DRA	WARP	MPH	CMD	PWR	STM
2015	KCA	MLB	32	5	2	0	9	9	43	46	5	2.5	5.7	27	41%	.297	1.35	3.98	4.74	0.2	90.3	68	25	22
2016	OMA	AAA	33	0	2	0	3	3	13^2	16	3	0.7	11.9	18	35%	.382	1.24	5.93	2.58	0.4				
2016	KCA	MLB	33	0	0	0	3	3	12	8	1	2.2	8.2	11	36%	.219	0.92	2.25	3.85	0.2	89.0	62	25	29
2017	KCA	MLB	34	18	11	0	32	32	179^2	181	27	2.9	6.7	134	41%	.289	1.33	4.16	3.83	3.5	87.5	55	9	74
2018	*KCA*	*MLB*	*35*	*6*	*9*	*0*	*23*	*23*	*124^1*	*140*	*22*	*3.4*	*6.6*	*92*	*40%*	*.303*	*1.51*	*5.40*	*5.72*	*0.0*	*86.8*	*56*	*11*	*45*
2019	*KCA*	*MLB*	*36*	*5*	*7*	*0*	*19*	*19*	*109^2*	*122*	*19*	*3.0*	*6.5*	*79*	*40%*	*.298*	*1.45*	*5.19*	*5.52*	*0.2*	*86.0*	*54*	*10*	*50*

Breakout: 11% Improve: 35% Collapse: 22% Attrition: 14% MLB: 84% *Comparables: Kevin Millwood, Kyle Lohse, Tim Hudson*

Rorschach test time: In this shockingly complete season—which followed two wipeouts comprising 12 starts in total—what would you identify as the "return" of Vargas? Would it be his April 7 start that kicked off a run of outings involving one run or fewer? Or would it be May 17, against the Yankees? That's when he gave up six runs in four innings and began a stretch of, uh, the rest of the season that featured a 4.95 ERA and worse peripherals than ever. If you ignore the inflated win total not much about Vargas has changed, which could actually be viewed as a compliment given his recent injury history.

Lineouts

Hitters

HITTER	POS	TEAM	LVL	AGE	PA	R	2B	3B	HR	RBI	BB	K	SB	CS	AVG/OBP/SLG	TAv	VORP	BABIP	BRR	FRAA	WARP
Billy Burns	OF	KCA	MLB	27	6	1	0	0	0	0	0	1	0	1	.167/.167/.167	.116	-0.9	.200	-0.2	CF(4): -0.1, RF(1): 0.0	-0.1
	OF	OMA	AAA	27	414	50	7	4	0	22	44	60	24	11	.285/.369/.328	.251	9.8	.341	1.5	CF(66): 3.0, LF(29): 4.1	1.6
D.J. Burt	2B	WIL	A+	21	445	52	19	5	0	29	64	101	32	13	.227/.347/.307	.247	8.5	.310	3.3	2B(89): -2.9	0.6
Samir Duenez	1B	NWA	AA	21	566	65	23	2	17	75	37	116	10	3	.252/.304/.402	.245	-4.8	.293	-1.6	1B(104): -17.4	-2.4
Cameron Gallagher	C	OMA	AAA	24	282	26	13	0	5	37	18	33	0	1	.292/.336/.400	.247	5.2	.317	-4.1	C(71): 9.5	1.4
	C	KCA	MLB	24	27	2	1	0	1	5	3	4	0	0	.250/.333/.417	.244	0.4	.263	-0.4	C(13): -0.4	0.0
Elier Hernandez	OF	WIL	A+	22	131	15	7	3	4	27	4	35	1	0	.306/.336/.508	.299	9.1	.395	0.9	CF(13): 0.1, RF(11): -1.7	0.8
	OF	NWA	AA	22	70	8	4	0	1	10	4	14	0	3	.339/.391/.452	.326	5.8	.417	-0.2	RF(10): 0.5, LF(3): -0.8	0.6
Khalil Lee	OF	LEX	A	19	532	71	24	6	17	61	65	171	20	18	.237/.344/.430	.276	19.9	.338	-2.2	CF(67): -6.2, RF(52): 4.3	1.9
Nicky Lopez	SS	WIL	A+	22	324	42	12	7	2	27	36	23	14	8	.295/.376/.407	.297	25.6	.315	0.8	SS(58): 4.4	3.2
	SS	NWA	AA	22	253	26	6	1	0	11	16	29	7	4	.259/.312/.293	.235	4.4	.296	2.2	SS(33): -2.9, 2B(25): 2.5	0.4
Seuly Matias	OF	BNC	Rk	18	246	27	13	3	7	36	16	72	2	1	.243/.297/.423	.254	3.9	.318	0.7	RF(52): 9.2	1.2
Oliver Nunez	2B	BNC	Rk	22	249	44	10	3	2	20	22	36	19	4	.321/.389/.421	.286	19.2	.375	1.3	3B(27): -3.5, 2B(17): -2.2	1.1
Ryan O'Hearn	1B	OMA	AAA	23	463	48	26	1	18	53	45	119	1	0	.252/.325/.450	.263	4.4	.309	-2.5	1B(75): -1.2, RF(5): -0.2	0.3
	1B	NWA	AA	23	76	7	1	1	4	11	10	20	0	0	.258/.355/.485	.285	3.0	.310	0.1	1B(8): 0.3, LF(5): -0.6	0.3
Nick Pratto	1B	ROY	Rk	18	230	25	15	3	4	34	24	58	10	4	.247/.330/.414	.260	2.1	.319	-0.8	1B(48): 5.2	0.7
Frank Schwindel	1B	NWA	AA	25	147	17	13	0	6	25	6	17	0	0	.350/.374/.577	.323	9.2	.359	-1.7	1B(12): 0.5	1.0
	1B	OMA	AAA	25	406	51	30	0	17	72	10	68	0	1	.321/.340/.528	.293	17.8	.353	-1.7	1B(54): 1.2	1.8
Ramon Torres	2B	OMA	AAA	24	317	43	10	1	6	41	15	32	17	4	.292/.325/.393	.247	7.0	.308	-0.3	SS(47): -2.2, 2B(27): -0.8	0.4
	2B	KCA	MLB	24	79	9	3	0	0	4	4	12	1	0	.243/.291/.284	.198	-3.5	.290	-0.8	2B(20): 0.6, 3B(12): 0.2	-0.3
Meibrys Viloria	C	LEX	A	20	398	42	25	0	8	52	25	79	4	3	.259/.313/.394	.241	8.4	.310	-0.4	C(92): -0.5	0.8
Zach Walters	1B	LOU	AAA	27	48	3	3	0	0	2	1	14	0	0	.174/.208/.239	.160	-5.1	.250	-0.2	1B(8): 0.5	-0.4
	1B	NWA	AA	27	96	12	3	0	1	8	5	21	1	0	.211/.250/.278	.211	-3.3	.261	-0.5	3B(11): -0.3, 1B(5): -0.5	-0.4

Do you think **Billy Burns** looked on wistfully, longingly, when the A's reacquired their on-again, off-again prospect Boog Powell? The speed merchant who drew some attention in 2015 languished in the minors in 2017, waiting for a chance to steal a little piece of the spotlight once again. ⚾ D.J. Bert is a strange, alternate-universe *Sesame Street* storyline unlikely to see the light of day. **D.J. Burt** is a strange, speed-based utility prospect unlikely to reach base if forced to use his bat. ⚾ Once intriguing because he paired low strikeout rates with some power potential, **Samir Duenez** couldn't keep the same sort of contact tune going during a full season at Double-A. If the contact abilities don't pop, he probably doesn't have the power to find his groove at first base. ⚾ A 25-year-old who can stick at catcher, and thus likely find some work in the majors, **Cam Gallagher** turned his first home run into a grand slam. Compared to smashing watermelons with a mallet for money, it's quite an impressive career achievement. ⚾ An injury-shortened 2017 saw **Elier Hernandez** add some line drives and some power, recouping a little bit of the prospect sheen that he had as a promising international signing and earning an Arizona Fall League roster spot. ⚾ **Khalil Lee**'s first full season as a pro didn't assuage contact concerns, but it did further showcase his athletic prowess and eyebrow-raising power potential. As a 19-year-old, the 2016 third rounder stroked 17 homers in A-ball, with a fair number of walks providing reassurance that everything is headed in the right direction. ⚾ Playing excellent defense at shortstop while simultaneously running a .376 OBP is a great way to get noticed. That's exactly what **Nicky Lopez** did in 324 High-A plate appearances before taking some lumps at Double-A. He doesn't have much power, but the defensive ability and a high-contact bat make him a classic utility prospect. ⚾ **Seuly Matias** is just 19 years old and drawing positive reports for his pop, athleticism and pitch recognition in rookie-ball. The visions of a slugging right fielder (the arm is there) are easy to muster. The seemingly inevitable contact issue is present too, but Matias showed improvement in 2017. It's okay to be excited. Just, you know, remember he's 19. ⚾ Lest you conclude that a 22-year-old with a stellar OBP in rookie-ball isn't worth your time, know that **Oliver Nunez** doesn't fret over first impressions. On August 22, he grounded out twice in the first inning before hitting for the cycle. ⚾ **Ryan O'Hearn** isn't going to set the world ablaze, but with the big club in flux and better-known prospects struggling, he can harbor legitimate thoughts of seeing Kansas City in 2018, even if his power-and-patience *modus operandi* didn't play quite as well at Triple-A. ⚾ A baby-faced high schooler taken in the first round as a first-base prospect, **Nick Pratto** is described as an advanced, natural hitter. He'll need to work to keep those labels because of his defensive home, but it's too early to feel anything except hope. ⚾ If you like first basemen who don't strike out or walk, but do post batting averages north of .320, you apparently work for the Royals. Either that, or your baseball knowledge is built around **Frank Schwindel** and the 2017 Omaha Storm Chasers. ⚾ **Ramon Torres** does a little of this and a little of that, but neither this nor that usually involves a bat. ⚾ His full-season debut understandably stripped **Meibrys Viloria**'s numbers of some luster, but he is still a very young catcher who might just be able to hit after a strong rookie-ball showing in 2016. ⚾ If **Zach Walters** never plays in the big leagues again, you may still be able to identify the era in which he played simply by knowing that he has the fifth-lowest career batting average of any non-pitcher to hit 10 home runs.

Pitchers

PITCHER	TEAM	LVL	AGE	W	L	SV	G	GS	IP	H	HR	BB/9	K/9	K	GB%	BABIP	WHIP	ERA	DRA	WARP	MPH	CMD	PWR	STM
Scott Barlow	OKL	AAA	24	1	3	0	7	7	32^1	37	6	6.4	10.0	36	37%	.333	1.86	7.24	7.07	-0.5				
	TUL	AA	24	6	3	0	19	19	107^1	60	9	3.1	10.4	124	45%	.211	0.90	2.10	2.01	4.1				
Samuel Gaviglio	SEA	MLB	27	3	5	0	12	11	62^1	63	15	3.0	5.8	40	49%	.265	1.35	4.62	5.64	-0.1	90.3	46	31	62
	TAC	AAA	27	3	6	0	13	13	72	72	5	1.5	7.1	57	54%	.302	1.17	3.88	2.13	2.8				
	KCA	MLB	27	1	0	0	4	2	12	13	1	3.8	6.8	9	56%	.316	1.50	3.00	8.19	-0.4	91.0	46	31	62
Tim Hill	NWA	AA	27	1	2	4	36	0	69	76	2	2.5	9.8	75	62%	.372	1.38	4.17	1.75	2.5				
Brad Keller	WTN	AA	21	10	9	0	26	26	130^2	142	7	3.9	7.6	111	51%	.339	1.52	4.68	4.67	0.8				

PITCHER	TEAM	LVL	AGE	W	L	SV	G	GS	IP	H	HR	BB/9	K/9	K	GB%	BABIP	WHIP	ERA	DRA	WARP	MPH	CMD	PWR	STM
Richard Lovelady	WIL	A+	21	1	0	7	21	0	33^1	18	0	1.1	11.1	41	70%	.237	0.66	1.08	1.23	1.4				
	NWA	AA	21	3	2	3	21	0	33^1	28	1	3.5	9.7	36	50%	.310	1.23	2.16	2.85	0.8				
Andres Machado	WIL	A+	24	6	7	2	21	9	73^1	88	8	1.7	8.8	72	42%	.359	1.39	5.03	3.89	1.1				
	OMA	AAA	24	2	2	0	7	7	34^2	30	6	4.4	9.9	38	39%	.279	1.36	3.63	5.50	0.1				
	KCA	MLB	24	0	0	0	2	0	3^2	10	2	7.4	2.5	1	50%	.444	3.55	22.09	9.42	-0.2	97.4			58
Kevin McCarthy	OMA	AAA	25	1	1	2	25	0	32	32	3	2.5	4.8	17	58%	.296	1.28	3.09	5.04	0.1				
	KCA	MLB	25	1	0	0	33	0	45	50	4	2.6	5.4	27	55%	.303	1.40	3.20	5.81	-0.3	94.3	47	52	49
Corey Ray	NWA	AA	24	6	12	0	29	29	143	170	20	3.7	5.9	93	43%	.321	1.60	5.41	7.58	-4.1				
Burch Smith	PCH	A+	27	3	1	0	9	8	37	26	1	4.9	8.0	33	35%	.255	1.24	2.43	5.71	-0.2				
	DUR	AAA	27	2	1	0	3	3	16^1	9	2	2.2	10.5	19	46%	.200	0.80	1.65	2.65	0.5				
Eric Stout	OMA	AAA	24	5	2	5	45	1	69^1	58	4	3.8	7.3	56	40%	.270	1.25	2.99	6.22	-0.7				
Jace Vines	LEX	A	22	9	5	3	19	14	100	96	6	2.1	5.7	63	58%	.285	1.19	3.42	3.64	1.8				
	WIL	A+	22	3	3	0	7	7	40	41	2	3.4	4.5	20	58%	.300	1.40	3.60	4.04	0.6				
Kyle Zimmer	OMA	AAA	25	0	0	3	20	2	32^2	35	4	4.4	9.4	34	28%	.337	1.56	5.79	7.42	-0.7				

Scott Barlow impressed enough in his second go-round at Double-A—he fell five innings short of being the qualifying ERA leader in the Texas League—that the Royals grabbed the minor-league free agent and gave him a spot on the 40-man. It would be easy to label **Sam Gaviglio** as a Quad-A starter and move along. It would also be easy to stop and gawk at an actual, functional pitcher who was waived by the 2017 Seattle Mariners. Upon reading that the 27-year-old was added to the 40-man roster in November, Royals fans muttered "What the **Tim Hill**?" to themselves. **Brad Keller**'s first taste of Double-A was often a struggle, but the big right-hander is still just 22 years old and has the stuff to be a major leaguer. The Reds took him in the Rule 5 draft and traded him to Kansas City. As if it could be any other way given his name, **Richard Lovelady** is a surprisingly impressive side-arming left-handed relief prospect. A Venezuelan righty who started 2017 at High-A, **Andres Machado** brought fire in the form of a mid-90s fastball. Maybe he wasn't ready for his surprise September call-up, but the ascent earned him a spot on the Royals' radar. Three-pitch righty **Kevin McCarthy** became a fixture in the Royals' bullpen by July, out of necessity. Having taken that opportunity and submitted one of the lowest reliever strikeout rates in the majors, he will have to find some new tricks to sustain the steady diet of big-league innings. **Corey Ray**'s serviceable strikeout numbers did not follow him to Double-A, and now it will take a serious breakout for the 25-year-old to reclaim his one-time status as the most famous professional baseball player named Corey Ray. **Ashe Russell**, the Royals' first-round pick in 2015, was held back at extended spring training and eventually took a leave of absence—a mental break. If it summons echoes of Zack Greinke in 2006, that's understandable. We should not be expecting the same type of baseball career, but can instead hope for better days for Russell the person, and maybe, eventually, for Russell the pitcher. **Burch Smith** spent nearly two-and-a-half years on the disabled list after Tommy John surgery, but returned during the 2017 season and was impressive enough between Charlotte and Durham to get himself plucked in the Rule 5 draft. If he sticks with the Royals, he'll see his first major-league action since 2013. Left Hand Milk Stout has a 4.2 rating on Beer Advocate. Left-hander **Eric Stout** had a 4.24 FIP as a reliever in Triple-A. How deep does this conspiracy go?! A solidly built Texas A&M product, **Jace Vines**' very good results don't come with many strikeouts at all and ... yep, he's a sinkerballer. Also: His middle name is Addison, raising the question of why he isn't in the Cubs organization. Having pitched most of 2017 in relief at Triple-A, **Kyle Zimmer** left an August appearance after throwing low-80s fastballs. A laundry list of injuries have conspired to rob the college product and former no. 5 overall pick, now 26 years old, of development time.

League Leaders 2017

MLB Ground-ball Rate – Scott Alexander, 73.0%

LOS ANGELES ANGELS

Essay by Pedro Moura

Player comments by Mark Barry and BP staff

Rarely is any ballplayer as good at the end of a free agent contract as he was at the start. This is due to aging and to MLB's owner-driven process that allows only veterans to reach free agency.

The simple response would be to front-load most every free agent contract, so as to more appropriately compensate players for their current performance. But nobody does that. It's one of the oddities of MLB operations, exemplified by the Angels' salvo to start their surprising 2017-2018 offseason.

Twelve hours after the Astros won the World Series, the Angels announced an updated agreement with 30-year-old slugging left fielder Justin Upton, saving themselves more than $10 million between the 2018 and 2019 seasons. That coupon, of course, comes due later. In 2022, for which he hadn't previously been under contract, Upton will make $28 million. Aging curves inform us he's unlikely to even be average at that point.

Like many of their competitors within the industry, the Angels are renouncing the future for the present, hoping that their now will prove more spectacular than anyone else speculates. It makes sense: They have Mike Trout under contract for three more seasons. They will try to keep him forever, but so will several other teams. All they can do now is assemble a talented team around him. That has been difficult, given their steady payroll restraints in the range of $165 million, one-sixth of which is tied up in a sub-replacement player for the foreseeable future. Shohei Ohtani's choice to spend six years in Anaheim clearly changes the calculus.

It's not as if third-year general manager Billy Eppler had better routes available after falling five wins short of the playoffs. As of November, his task was to win or risk being fired. There is no more efficient way to do the former immediately than to acquire good players at below-market rates, and Upton at $16 million in 2018 qualifies.

Viewed that way, the Angels are an apt facsimile for our society, if only our society could conjure up an Ohtani. They have shoved back their commitments as far as possible for so long. Now, the only way they can hope to complete the tasks held over is to nudge today's responsibilities back to tomorrow, every day. Their teams in 2018 and beyond will be the result of a continuous, vicious cycle that started with the signing of Gary Matthews Jr. on Thanksgiving Eve 2006.

Until then, the Angels had been the model franchise of the previous half-decade. They won a title, made the playoffs three times and averaged more than 90 wins per season. Then they signed Matthews to a heavily back-loaded disaster of a five-year deal. Fed up with two seasons still to go, they absorbed almost all of the remaining money to send him to New York.

Next was Vernon Wells, whose heavily back-loaded deal they inherited from Toronto in an unfathomably terrible trade. With two seasons still to go on that, the Angels again absorbed almost all of

ANGELS PROSPECTUS

2017 W-L: 80-82, 2ND IN AL WEST

Pythag	.501	13th	B-Age	29.9	*29th*
RS/G	4.38	22nd	P-Age	29.1	*23rd*
RA/G	4.38	12th	Salary	$166.4M	*7th*
TAv	.250	27th	M$/MW	$4.8M	*8th*
TAv-P	.256	10th	DL Days	1312	*25th*
FIP	4.40	16th	$ on DL	17%	*19th*
DER	.711	9th			

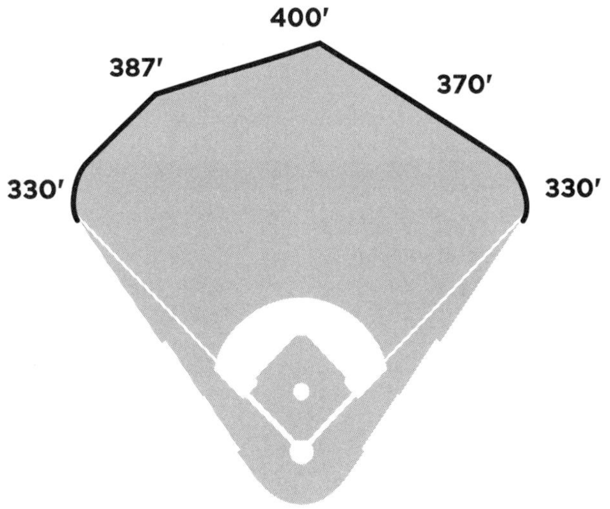

Outfield wall profile: **4'6" to 18'**

Three-Year Park Factors

Runs	Runs/RH	Runs/LH	HR/RH	HR/LH
96	96	96	101	97

Top Hitter WARP	6.6 Mike Trout
Top Pitcher WARP	2.4 Yusmeiro Petit
Top Prospect	Jordon Adell

2017 Hit List Ranking

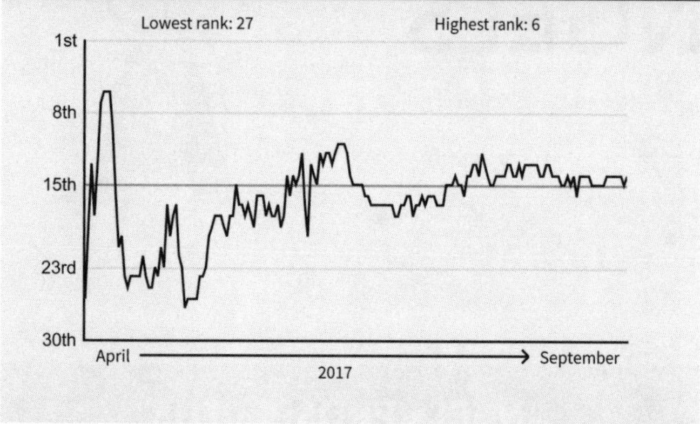

Committed Payroll (in millions)

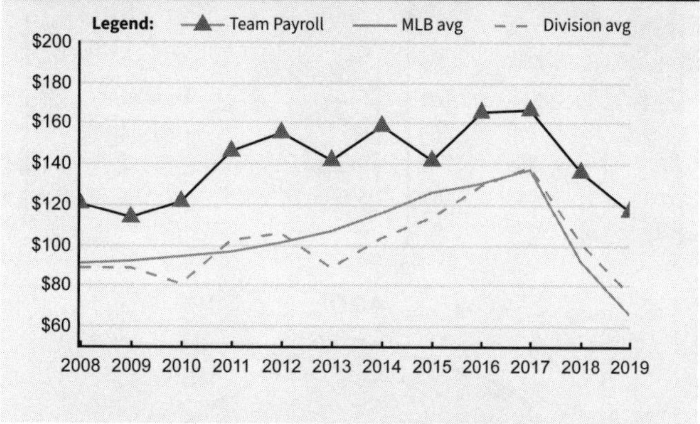

Farm System Ranking

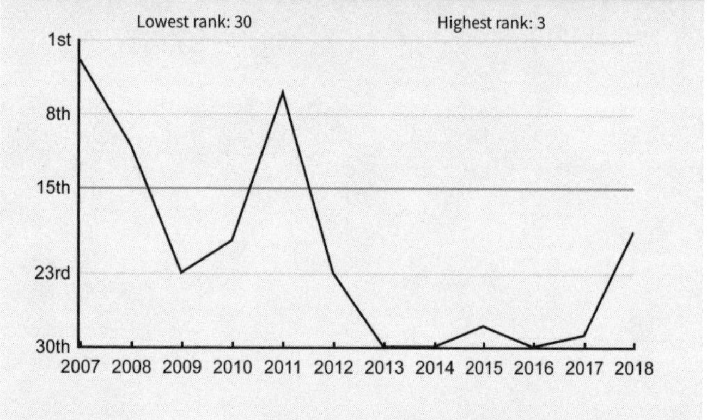

Personnel

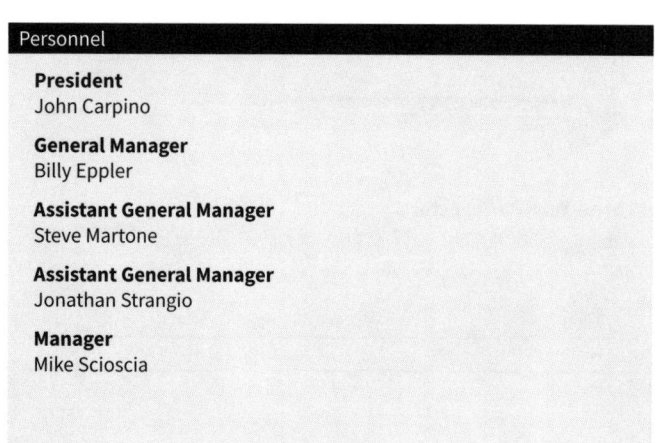

President
John Carpino

General Manager
Billy Eppler

Assistant General Manager
Steve Martone

Assistant General Manager
Jonathan Strangio

Manager
Mike Scioscia

the remaining money to send him to New York.

In between, they decided—on the same December 2011 day—to back-load long-term contracts for both C.J. Wilson and Albert Pujols. Ignoring whether they ever should have agreed to pay those players one-third of a billion dollars and focusing instead on the structure of said deals, the Angels saved $17.5 million in 2012 by not evenly splitting the money on each. But they cost themselves $6.5 million in 2017.

Deployed in a prudent manner, that $6.5 million could have vaulted the Angels into the American League's last playoff position. Yet, the Angels' approach is not unique. Teams have landed on success by traversing Back Load Boulevard, the 2014 and 2015 Kansas City Royals being particular practitioners.

Over the four offseasons that preceded this one, more than 70 percent of the 167 multi-year agreements between MLB teams and players contained at least some back-loading. Fewer than 5 percent contained any front-loading at all, and most of those were minute. The rest of the contracts were even splits throughout. (These numbers, calculated via Baseball-Reference.com, do not count the stateside arrivals of international free agents such as Yasmany Tomas, Yuli Gurriel and Yaisel Sierra.)

Only twice in the last four years had any team committed significantly more up-front money to a big-league free agent. In the 2013-2014 offseason, both Jhonny Peralta's four-year pact with St. Louis and Scott Feldman's three-year contract with Houston emphasized the present. In 2014, Peralta received 29.2 percent of the value of his four-year deal, while Feldman received 40 percent of the value of his three-year deal.

Each time, the structure seemed to function as intended for the club. The players were better at first. Near the end, their lower salaries made it more palatable for the teams to get rid of them, which in both cases they did.

Gurriel was not included in the above calculations but represents another example of a so-far-successful front-loaded contract. Understanding their budget limitations and that their top pre-arbitration players would soon command larger sums, the Astros agreed to pay Gurriel $14.4 million in 2017. He'll get only $8.4 million in 2020, when he'll be 36 and George Springer, Carlos Correa and Alex Bregman will be drawing significant salaries. The Astros arranged the deal with the rest of their roster in mind. To date, it has worked.

That, many league executives agree while speaking anonymously, is the primary instance where front-loading fits, when a team's unused payroll space cannot carry over between seasons and a stock of newly established talent makes contention possible. Philadelphia's pact with Carlos Santana and Milwaukee's union with Jhoulys Chacin, both reached in December, exemplify that theory. And those executives cite an array of rationales for why the practice is not more popular.

For one, teams signing free agents to multi-year contracts are generally good, or at least better than those teams that are sitting out the market while rebuilding. That situates the signing club on a more certain position along the win-curve cycle where every franchise must fit. Most everyone will be bad at some point. When you are going to be good, you want to be able to maximize that good and magnify the certainty you are pushing your club into playoff position.

For another, leaguewide inflation is an unrelenting beast. Estimates of its value vary, but even at something like 5 percent annually, $24 million in 2022 is worth less than $20 million in 2018. Thus, if a deal called for a player to make $20 million a season for the next five seasons, it would essentially be a front-loaded contract by another name. The team would functionally spend less at the end than the beginning.

And, of course, inflation within the sport far outpaces the overall rate of the United States dollar, so it's not as meaningful to the player and agent. $20 million is still $20 million. Four percent of $20 million is still $800,000. While the net present value difference between Upton's new deal and his old one is quite small, the new deal will forever be listed as worth $17.5 million more.

One agent who has counseled a client who signed a front-loaded contract said that most of the players he represents do not concern themselves with net present value. Their evaluations are centered on the stated total and where that places them among their peers. From the player's perspective, a secondary benefit of a back-loaded contract is that it can serve as a *de facto* no-trade clause, a benefit that typically must be negotiated. Upton's deal contains a real no-trade clause, too, but the money due him on the back end mostly covers that possibility.

Another factor must be mentioned: General managers are rarely signed beyond four or five seasons, and assistant executives typically work on even shorter contracts. To keep their jobs, their focus cannot be on the next decade. They must be able to rationalize their decisions to their owners, or maybe their next employers. That's all.

In the cases of Peralta and Feldman, the decision to front-load did not actually help as much as it appeared. In August 2016, the Astros sold off Feldman to save money after they signed Gurriel days earlier. In June 2017, the Cardinals cut Peralta, a decision made easier by his smaller salary. But they would have saved money if his deal had been traditionally back-loaded, because of the net-present-value factor. When a team acquires a player for a stated cost over a given time frame, it is acquiring the sum of his value produced throughout that time frame. To some degree, the distribution of that value is irrelevant.

This is not a concept exclusive to baseball among American professional sports. The NBA prohibits significant raises within free agent contracts; the NFL's many non-guaranteed contracts render front-loading a separate notion altogether. But NHL teams made front-loading a leaguewide trend late last decade, so much so that the league drew up a new rule preventing it.

More than a dozen NHL teams signed players to contracts spanning roughly a dozen years, with small salaries in the final seasons so as to lower the deal's average annual value and arrest themselves under the salary cap. It's not a direct parallel to baseball, which has no cap, but the Angels have long operated as if the luxury-tax threshold is an unofficial cap, despite owner Arte Moreno's persistent protestations to that point. Other teams conduct their business the same way.

In Anaheim, Mike Scioscia has presided over all of this: the rush to the top and the slow descent toward the bottom. He has been on the job six years longer than any of his managerial counterparts. At season's end, Scioscia will have managed almost exactly one-third of the franchise's games. Since he last won a playoff game in 2009, 23 teams have won at least one.

2018 will be the last year of Scioscia's 10-year, $50-million contract, which, fittingly, is also back-loaded. His rapport with Eppler has so far been absent the strife that permeated his relationship with Jerry Dipoto, the former general manager who resigned in a huff, but eventually, the bill will come due. It always does. For the Angels, even with Ohtani, even with an improving farm system, that will be in 2021 and 2022, unless Trout re-signs. If they make the playoffs a time or two before that, make one October run, maybe the forthcoming lean years will be worth it. More likely, they will not. The surviving peak of their win cycle pales in comparison to the Astros' apparent capabilities in the American League West.

That is tough, albeit anticipatable, luck. For more than a decade now, the Angels have done their best to slough off payment. Graced with corresponding financial freedom, Eppler has assembled a talented roster that should be able to snag a wild-card spot.

There is scant time left to push back anything else.

—Pedro Moura covers the Angels for the Los Angeles Times.

Hitters

Jordon Adell OF Born: 04/08/99 Age: 19 Bats: R Throws: R Height: 6'2" Weight: 195 Origin: Round 1, 2017 Draft (#10 overall)

YEAR	TEAM	LVL	AGE	PA	R	2B	3B	HR	RBI	BB	K	SB	CS	AVG/OBP/SLG	TAv	VORP	BABIP	BRR	FRAA	WARP
2017	ANG	RK	18	132	18	6	6	4	21	10	32	5	0	.288/.351/.542	.309	11.8	.361	1.9		1.1
2017	ORM	RK	18	90	25	5	2	1	9	4	17	3	2	.376/.411/.518	.304	6.5	.463	0.4		0.6
2018	*ANA*	*MLB*	*19*	*250*	*22*	*8*	*1*	*7*	*25*	*11*	*85*	*1*	*0*	*.195/.232/.322*	*.191*	*-12.8*	*.270*	*-0.2*		*-1.4*
2019	*ANA*	*MLB*	*20*	*305*	*32*	*10*	*1*	*9*	*33*	*15*	*99*	*2*	*1*	*.211/.253/.353*	*.212*	*-10.8*	*.284*	*-0.2*	*-*	*-1.2*

Breakout: 0% Improve: 5% Collapse: 2% Attrition: 4% MLB: 10% *Comparables: Nomar Mazara, Raul Mondesi, Engel Beltre*

Hello, it's me
I was wondering if after all these years you'd like to see
A top prospect with everything
They say I have some decent wheels
But I ain't done much stealing

Hello, can you hear me?
I'm here to save the system, starting in the rookie league
Picked in the top 10, with all the sheen
I've got raw power and some patience, and I'm only just a teen.

There's such a difference between us
I was a workout star.

Hello from the other side
I'm gonna hit lots of big flies
I'm still raw and youthful, so please give me some time
But I'll leave you breathless, when I run down that line.

Hello from the outside
It's just the start of a fun ride
I'll tell you I'm sorry, for striking out that one time

But it don't matter it clearly doesn't tear you apart anymore.

Kole Calhoun RF Born: 10/14/87 Age: 30 Bats: L Throws: L Height: 5'10" Weight: 205 Origin: Round 8, 2010 Draft (#264 overall)

YEAR	TEAM	LVL	AGE	PA	R	2B	3B	HR	RBI	BB	K	SB	CS	AVG/OBP/SLG	TAv	VORP	BABIP	BRR	FRAA	WARP
2015	ANA	MLB	27	686	78	23	2	26	83	45	164	4	1	.256/.308/.422	.267	13.8	.304	-2.3	RF(157): 14.0, 1B(1): 0.0	3.0
2016	ANA	MLB	28	672	91	35	5	18	75	67	118	2	3	.271/.348/.438	.277	23.5	.309	0.1	RF(154): -6.7	1.7
2017	ANA	MLB	29	654	77	23	2	19	71	71	134	5	1	.244/.333/.392	.259	11.0	.284	-0.6	RF(154): 10.0	2.1
2018	*ANA*	*MLB*	*30*	*641*	*76*	*26*	*3*	*20*	*81*	*56*	*129*	*4*	*2*	*.257/.326/.421*	*.265*	*19.3*	*.296*	*-0.7*	*RF 3*	*1.9*
2019	*ANA*	*MLB*	*31*	*555*	*72*	*23*	*2*	*19*	*70*	*54*	*118*	*2*	*1*	*.253/.330/.426*	*.263*	*12.5*	*.293*	*-0.8*	*RF 4*	*1.8*

Breakout: 2% Improve: 39% Collapse: 8% Attrition: 15% MLB: 98% *Comparables: Josh Reddick, Austin Kearns, John Wockenfuss*

Between innings of a sleepy, September battle, in an attempt to keep fans from staring at their phones, scoreboard entertainment played *Name That Tune* with several Angels players. Classic rock songs drew high praise and beaming grins, but when Disney blasted over the speakers, it was met only with quizzical glances. Until Kole Calhoun. The Sun Devil belted out a couple lyrics before correctly identifying "Let it Go" to raucous applause from the crowd. Unfortunately Calhoun likely wishes he could let it go, with "it" being the 2017 season. It was his bat that was frozen this year, with Calhoun producing the lowest slugging percentage of his career as a full-time player. An icy BABIP could have something to do with the outfielder's offensive plummet, but Calhoun hit more groundballs last year than any season previously, a problem he'll need to rectify to reestablish himself as a borderline all star. On the bright side, the former Gold Glove winner's putrid 2016 in the field seems to be in the rear-view mirror, as Calhoun once again ranked as one of the best defensive right fielders in the game.

Kaleb Cowart 3B Born: 06/02/92 Age: 26 Bats: B Throws: R Height: 6'3" Weight: 225 Origin: Round 1, 2010 Draft (#18 overall)

YEAR	TEAM	LVL	AGE	PA	R	2B	3B	HR	RBI	BB	K	SB	CS	AVG/OBP/SLG	TAv	VORP	BABIP	BRR	FRAA	WARP
2015	INL	A+	23	221	32	14	4	2	23	22	43	10	2	.242/.326/.387	.273	10.9	.298	1.7	3B(42): 5.9, SS(4): -0.1	1.8
2015	SLC	AAA	23	253	35	13	3	6	45	29	64	2	1	.323/.395/.491	.296	17.0	.422	0.3	3B(49): -1.7, LF(5): 0.5	1.7
2015	ANA	MLB	23	52	8	2	0	1	4	5	19	1	1	.174/.255/.283	.195	-1.7	.269	0.0	3B(33): 1.1	-0.1
2016	SLC	AAA	24	458	58	34	5	9	58	37	100	18	4	.280/.340/.452	.269	16.2	.347	-1.1	3B(65): 1.5, 1B(15): -0.8	1.6
2016	ANA	MLB	24	87	8	4	0	1	8	0	23	0	0	.176/.184/.259	.148	-6.9	.226	0.5	3B(21): 1.0, 2B(15): 0.0	-0.6
2017	SLC	AAA	25	414	65	25	1	12	57	44	73	19	5	.311/.383/.482	.285	27.5	.359	3.7	3B(45): -2.7, 2B(35): -1.0	2.3
2017	ANA	MLB	25	117	18	5	1	3	11	10	28	4	2	.225/.313/.382	.234	1.1	.282	0.9	2B(30): 1.5, 3B(24): -0.4	0.2
2018	*ANA*	*MLB*	*26*	*30*	*4*	*1*	*0*	*1*	*3*	*2*	*8*	*1*	*0*	*.232/.298/.376*	*.242*	*0.8*	*.294*	*0.1*	*2B 0*	*0.0*
2019	*ANA*	*MLB*	*27*	*279*	*33*	*13*	*1*	*8*	*32*	*24*	*76*	*7*	*2*	*.233/.304/.391*	*.243*	*5.1*	*.298*	*1.2*	*2B -1*	*0.4*

Breakout: 9% Improve: 40% Collapse: 7% Attrition: 32% MLB: 61% *Comparables: Ryan Flaherty, Danny Richar, Darnell Sweeney*

Cowart has the Triple-A thing all figured out. During his three seasons at Salt Lake, the former first-round pick has slashed .301/.368/.472, dominating the opposition. While Smith's Ballpark does play as a middle-of-the-road venue in the notoriously hitter-friendly PCL, that's a little like saying Wendy's serves the healthiest fast food. The ball's gonna fly. The problem for Cowart has been the transition to the big-league roster. If you're a realist, you'll note that he has shown decent chops with the glove both to the left and right of Andrelton Simmons, which could solidify his chances of a utility-role future. If you're an optimist, you'll note that the Georgia native improved enough at the plate to finally have a "2" at the outset of his TAv. If you're an anarchist, you'll note that he was a first-round pick not only as a third baseman, but also as a pitcher—and that ship hasn't sailed yet. But if you're a fun-fact enthusiast, you'll probably just note that of his five career homers, his first and last both came with one out in the bottom of the fifth inning on August 22, two years apart, and move on.

Zack Cozart SS Born: 08/12/85 Age: 32 Bats: R Throws: R Height: 6'0" Weight: 204 Origin: Round 2, 2007 Draft (#79 overall)

YEAR	TEAM	LVL	AGE	PA	R	2B	3B	HR	RBI	BB	K	SB	CS	AVG/OBP/SLG	TAv	VORP	BABIP	BRR	FRAA	WARP
2015	CIN	MLB	29	214	28	10	1	9	28	14	29	3	3	.258/.310/.459	.288	15.1	.258	0.8	SS(52): 0.8	1.7
2016	CIN	MLB	30	508	67	28	2	16	50	37	84	4	1	.252/.308/.425	.253	20.4	.274	3.1	SS(111): 2.6	2.4
2017	CIN	MLB	31	507	80	24	7	24	63	62	78	3	0	.297/.385/.548	.321	51.1	.312	-2.8	SS(112): 1.3	5.3
2018	*ANA*	*MLB*	*32*	*547*	*60*	*23*	*3*	*14*	*60*	*35*	*87*	*4*	*1*	*.244/.294/.385*	*.244*	*9.8*	*.266*	*-0.1*	*SS 0, 3B 0*	*0.4*
2019	*ANA*	*MLB*	*33*	*421*	*48*	*18*	*2*	*12*	*47*	*29*	*72*	*2*	*1*	*.244/.301/.392*	*.242*	*3.3*	*.268*	*0.3*	*SS 0*	*0.4*

Breakout: 1% Improve: 29% Collapse: 14% Attrition: 14% MLB: 97% *Comparables: Edgar Renteria, Jason Bartlett, Alexei Ramirez*

Generally speaking, donkeys do not provide promising symbolism. The primary synonym for donkey is *ass*, which also brings to mind the animal's association with the concept of blind, unreasoned stubbornness and with a political party noted for tragic losses in winnable elections. For Cozart, however, his 2017 season will always be associated with the foal that now resides in his backyard, and there's little doubt he feels anything but pride for that. You see, Joey Votto told his then-teammate that if he made his first career All-Star Game, he'd get him a donkey, and on the back of a revamped approach at the plate that preached patience, the stellar defensive shortstop had a breakout season. He showed off unprecedented power to go with vastly improved on-base skills and landed that All-Star Game invitation. Votto's gift is ostensibly for the enjoyment of his entire family, but for Cozart it's a reminder of how he worked his donkey off to earn his big free-agent payday. The newly minted Angel wasn't too stubborn to accept a move to third base, where he'll team with Andrelton Simmons to form the best defensive left side in the game.

C.J. Cron 1B Born: 01/05/90 Age: 28 Bats: R Throws: R Height: 6'4" Weight: 235 Origin: Round 1, 2011 Draft (#17 overall)

YEAR	TEAM	LVL	AGE	PA	R	2B	3B	HR	RBI	BB	K	SB	CS	AVG/OBP/SLG	TAv	VORP	BABIP	BRR	FRAA	WARP
2015	SLC	AAA	25	98	15	10	2	6	23	4	14	0	0	.323/.347/.667	.314	5.0	.324	-1.4	1B(16): -1.4	0.4
2015	ANA	MLB	25	404	37	17	1	16	51	17	82	3	1	.262/.300/.439	.262	6.3	.293	1.4	1B(58): -0.5	0.6
2016	ANA	MLB	26	445	51	25	2	16	69	24	75	2	3	.278/.325/.467	.282	12.4	.302	-2.0	1B(97): 2.6	1.5
2017	SLC	AAA	27	96	11	6	0	4	23	7	15	1	0	.268/.344/.488	.275	2.7	.273	0.0	1B(19): 0.9	0.4
2017	ANA	MLB	27	373	39	14	1	16	56	22	96	3	2	.248/.305/.437	.261	2.3	.296	-2.1	1B(98): 4.1	0.6
2018	*ANA*	*MLB*	*28*	*567*	*71*	*26*	*2*	*22*	*75*	*31*	*120*	*4*	*2*	*.254/.304/.439*	*.261*	*9.7*	*.289*	*-0.9*	*1B 1*	*0.8*
2019	*ANA*	*MLB*	*29*	*472*	*61*	*21*	*1*	*20*	*65*	*29*	*108*	*2*	*1*	*.252/.307/.447*	*.259*	*6.0*	*.289*	*-0.7*	*1B 1*	*0.8*

Breakout: 2% Improve: 41% Collapse: 2% Attrition: 14% MLB: 93% *Comparables: Mitch Moreland, Matt Adams, Mike Jacobs*

When analyzing Cron, one is reminded of vanilla ice cream, room temperature water and *The Big Bang Theory*. They're all fine, but there is usually a better option available. The former Ute dealt with foot and wrist injuries in 2017, likely contributing to his struggles at the plate, which included a career-high strikeout rate. However, it's yet to be seen whether that's a feature or a bug, since Cron's strong second half—he slugged .512 with 14 homers after the break—saw a strikeout rate five percentage points higher than his first. Worst-case scenario, Cron helps save the team from having to play Albert Pujols in the field, which is both alarming and sad all at once.

Yunel Escobar 3B Born: 11/02/82 Age: 35 Bats: R Throws: R Height: 6'2" Weight: 215 Origin: Round 2, 2005 Draft (#75 overall)

YEAR	TEAM	LVL	AGE	PA	R	2B	3B	HR	RBI	BB	K	SB	CS	AVG/OBP/SLG	TAv	VORP	BABIP	BRR	FRAA	WARP
2015	WAS	MLB	32	591	75	25	1	9	56	45	70	2	2	.314/.375/.415	.284	30.7	.347	-0.8	3B(134): -22.3	0.9
2016	ANA	MLB	33	567	68	28	1	5	39	40	67	0	3	.304/.355/.391	.260	18.2	.339	-0.1	3B(129): -5.9	1.3
2017	ANA	MLB	34	381	43	20	1	7	31	29	51	1	4	.274/.333/.397	.248	7.1	.305	-0.7	3B(87): -5.9	0.1
2018	*ANA*	*MLB*	*35*	*396*	*45*	*17*	*0*	*7*	*36*	*31*	*53*	*1*	*2*	*.271/.334/.378*	*.249*	*8.4*	*.300*	*-0.2*	*3B -11*	*-0.2*
2019	*ANA*	*MLB*	*36*	*348*	*39*	*14*	*0*	*5*	*33*	*27*	*48*	*1*	*1*	*.262/.324/.358*	*.244*	*2.4*	*.291*	*-0.1*	*3B -9*	*-0.7*

Breakout: 2% Improve: 26% Collapse: 11% Attrition: 28% MLB: 85% *Comparables: Carney Lansford, Placido Polanco, Bill Spiers*

Relying on Escobar as an everyday infielder in 2018 would be a little bit like asking Kendall Jenner to represent you in court: You're going to get bad defense. For the fifth straight year (and seventh of the last eight), Escobar struggled to be even average defensively, and despite strong contact skills, he displayed the type of power most commonly associated with backup catchers. Only five players hit groundballs at a higher clip than the Cuban export, so he'll need to continue to rely on BABIP luck if he wants to have a role on a roster, let alone one that expects to contend.

David Fletcher MI Born: 05/31/94 Age: 24 Bats: R Throws: R Height: 5'10" Weight: 175 Origin: Round 6, 2015 Draft (#195 overall)

YEAR	TEAM	LVL	AGE	PA	R	2B	3B	HR	RBI	BB	K	SB	CS	AVG/OBP/SLG	TAv	VORP	BABIP	BRR	FRAA	WARP
2015	BUR	A	21	135	18	4	1	1	10	12	13	6	1	.283/.358/.358	.263	8.2	.311	2.6	SS(29): 1.9, 2B(3): 0.4	1.1
2015	ORM	RK	21	180	28	12	4	0	30	16	9	11	4	.331/.391/.456	.293	15.9	.346	1.3	SS(37): -1.2	1.4
2016	INL	A+	22	355	42	12	1	3	31	22	43	15	3	.275/.321/.346	.254	11.7	.307	1.6	SS(47): -6.2, 2B(28): -0.2	0.5
2016	ARK	AA	22	83	10	6	0	0	6	3	13	1	0	.300/.325/.375	.277	5.0	.358	0.6	SS(18): 2.3	0.8
2017	MOB	AA	23	272	32	14	1	1	22	21	30	12	5	.276/.341/.354	.270	10.0	.308	-1.5	2B(34): 1.0, SS(28): 0.0	1.2
2017	SLC	AAA	23	217	27	6	1	2	17	6	25	8	1	.254/.285/.322	.216	-0.5	.281	2.3	SS(26): 0.2, 2B(22): 0.2	0.0
2018	*ANA*	*MLB*	*24*	*250*	*29*	*10*	*1*	*5*	*22*	*12*	*44*	*6*	*2*	*.245/.289/.361*	*.225*	*2.3*	*.277*	*0.3*	*2B 0, SS -1*	*0.2*
2019	*ANA*	*MLB*	*25*	*343*	*38*	*14*	*1*	*9*	*37*	*18*	*62*	*8*	*2*	*.244/.290/.376*	*.235*	*2.8*	*.275*	*0.6*	*2B 0, SS -1*	*0.2*

Breakout: 3% Improve: 12% Collapse: 5% Attrition: 28% MLB: 37% *Comparables: Ramon Torres, Darwin Barney, Brian Dozier*

If you like grit, baseball IQ and a general David Eckstein-y sensibility, Fletcher is your man. He hits, but not a ton. He plays a couple of positions, but isn't elite anywhere. He doesn't strike out at all, but doesn't walk much either. If a late-season promotion to Triple-A Salt Lake is any indication, Fletcher could see a homecoming as a utility player some time in 2018, as an 1,100-foot homer to right field at Angel Stadium would bounce off Route 57 and into the town of Orange, where he was born. Of course, he's not a great candidate to hit it there, as his power sits somewhere between imaginary and, well, David Eckstein.

Nolan Fontana MI Born: 06/06/91 Age: 27 Bats: L Throws: R Height: 5'11" Weight: 195 Origin: Round 2, 2012 Draft (#61 overall)

YEAR	TEAM	LVL	AGE	PA	R	2B	3B	HR	RBI	BB	K	SB	CS	AVG/OBP/SLG	TAv	VORP	BABIP	BRR	FRAA	WARP
2015	FRE	AAA	24	456	56	21	6	3	40	74	99	6	11	.241/.369/.357	.278	24.1	.317	0.1	SS(57): -6.2, 2B(31): -1.0	1.9
2016	CCH	AA	25	44	4	4	0	0	4	8	5	1	0	.278/.409/.389	.280	2.4	.323	-0.1	SS(9): 1.2	0.4
2016	FRE	AAA	25	407	35	15	0	3	27	32	108	4	3	.195/.268/.262	.208	-4.4	.266	2.5	SS(77): -5.5, 2B(27): 1.8	-0.8
2017	SLC	AAA	26	453	82	26	4	10	51	75	97	14	2	.271/.396/.449	.296	39.5	.338	4.7	SS(40): 1.7, 2B(37): -2.8	4.0
2017	ANA	MLB	26	23	1	0	0	1	1	3	8	1	1	.050/.174/.200	.137	-2.4	.000	-0.1	2B(9): -0.6	-0.3
2018	*ANA*	*MLB*	*27*	*93*	*10*	*3*	*0*	*2*	*8*	*12*	*25*	*1*	*1*	*.202/.304/.316*	*.231*	*0.5*	*.267*	*-0.1*	*2B 0, 3B 1*	*0.1*
2019	*ANA*	*MLB*	*28*	*257*	*29*	*10*	*1*	*5*	*24*	*33*	*73*	*3*	*2*	*.201/.311/.328*	*.229*	*-0.9*	*.264*	*-0.2*	*2B 0, 3B 2*	*0.1*

Breakout: 2% Improve: 9% Collapse: 6% Attrition: 9% MLB: 19% *Comparables: Josh Prince, Jack Hannahan, Mike Fontenot*

The Astros waived Fontana after a 2016 Triple-A experience worse than Hawkins, Indiana, during a Demogorgon invasion. As a prospect, the former Florida Gator hung his hat on drawing walks and making enough contact to get by, but Fontana truly went Upside Down in 2016. He rebounded nicely in his new digs with his best season as a professional at Triple-A Salt Lake, where he returned to his standard-issue excellent plate discipline, even picking up some scattered time with the big club, including taking Kyle Barraclough deep for his first MLB hit. At publication time it is still his only MLB hit. He'll need to be more season two Will Byers than season one Will Byers if he wants to keep a job in the big leagues. Stranger things have happened.

Juan Graterol C Born: 02/14/89 Age: 29 Bats: R Throws: R Height: 6'1" Weight: 205 Origin: International Free Agent, 2005

YEAR	TEAM	LVL	AGE	PA	R	2B	3B	HR	RBI	BB	K	SB	CS	AVG/OBP/SLG	TAv	VORP	BABIP	BRR	FRAA	WARP
2015	SWB	AAA	26	72	8	1	0	1	9	1	10	0	0	.200/.208/.257	.159	-5.2	.217	-0.8	C(20): 0.0	-0.5
2016	SLC	AAA	27	246	24	10	0	2	23	10	27	2	1	.300/.340/.370	.235	2.3	.330	-1.7	C(61): 0.8	0.3
2016	ANA	MLB	27	15	2	2	0	0	3	0	3	0	0	.286/.286/.429	.243	-0.5	.364	-0.9	C(9): 0.3	0.0
2017	ANA	MLB	28	87	5	4	0	0	10	1	13	0	0	.202/.207/.250	.169	-3.8	.233	0.5	C(47): 4.2	0.0
2018	*ANA*	*MLB*	*29*	*90*	*8*	*4*	*0*	*1*	*8*	*3*	*15*	*0*	*0*	*.238/.273/.336*	*.221*	*0.7*	*.272*	*-0.2*	*C 0*	*0.0*
2019	*ANA*	*MLB*	*30*	*169*	*17*	*7*	*0*	*3*	*16*	*7*	*31*	*0*	*0*	*.231/.272/.340*	*.216*	*-1.6*	*.265*	*-0.4*	*C 0*	*-0.2*

Breakout: 1% Improve: 13% Collapse: 13% Attrition: 30% MLB: 47%

Comparables: Bryan Holaday, Humberto Quintero, Rocky Gale

YEAR	TEAM	P. COUNT	FRM RUNS	BLK RUNS	THRW RUNS	TOT RUNS
2015	SWB	2599	0.3	0.1	0.0	0.4
2015	TRN	606	0.3	0.0	0.0	0.3
2016	ANA	694	-0.1	0.5	-0.1	0.3
2017	ANA	4016	1.8	2.0	0.6	4.4
2018	*ANA*	*3583*	*-0.3*	*0.5*	*0.0*	*0.3*
2019	*ANA*	*6709*	*-0.3*	*0.6*	*0.0*	*0.3*

As a backup backstop, Graterol spent most of 2017 seemingly trying to avoid one thing. He presumably despises *The Walking Dead* (don't even get him started on *Fear the Walking Dead*), he loves yo-yoing but refuses to walk the dog and when Aerosmith and Run DMC told him to "Walk This Way," he politely declined. When Doc Holliday asked if someone walked over his grave, it sure wasn't Graterol, who drew *one walk* in 87 plate appearances, tied for the lowest total in baseball. (Shouts to Paulo Orlando, who accomplished the same feat with three additional trips to the plate.) Added bonus: He also hates runs.

Jahmai Jones OF Born: 08/04/97 Age: 20 Bats: R Throws: R Height: 6'0" Weight: 215 Origin: Round 2, 2015 Draft (#70 overall)

YEAR	TEAM	LVL	AGE	PA	R	2B	3B	HR	RBI	BB	K	SB	CS	AVG/OBP/SLG	TAv	VORP	BABIP	BRR	FRAA	WARP
2015	ANG	RK	17	183	28	6	2	2	20	17	33	16	7	.244/.330/.344	.271	10.8	.294	2.7	CF(38): -2.3, RF(2): -0.3	0.8
2016	ORM	RK	18	226	49	12	3	3	20	21	29	19	6	.321/.404/.459	.320	23.1	.364	1.3	CF(41): -4.2, RF(4): -0.5	2.0
2016	BUR	A	18	70	8	1	0	1	10	5	13	1	0	.242/.294/.306	.213	-1.3	.286	0.2	CF(8): -0.7, RF(4): 1.8	0.0
2017	BUR	A	19	387	54	18	4	9	30	32	63	18	7	.272/.338/.425	.286	27.0	.309	5.7	CF(65): -3.4, LF(16): 0.5	2.5
2017	INL	A+	19	191	32	11	3	5	17	13	43	9	6	.302/.368/.488	.311	17.6	.379	2.0	CF(37): -9.7, LF(3): -0.5	0.8
2018	*ANA*	*MLB*	*20*	*250*	*31*	*10*	*1*	*7*	*25*	*15*	*65*	*6*	*3*	*.228/.283/.374*	*.228*	*1.3*	*.279*	*0.0*	*CF -4, LF 0*	*-0.4*
2019	*ANA*	*MLB*	*21*	*336*	*40*	*13*	*1*	*11*	*40*	*22*	*84*	*8*	*4*	*.236/.295/.394*	*.242*	*3.6*	*.284*	*0.4*	*CF -6, LF 0*	*-0.3*

Breakout: 4% Improve: 18% Collapse: 0% Attrition: 9% MLB: 20%

Comparables: Victor Robles, Jose Tabata, Joe Benson

There's a scene in *Lawrence of Arabia* that opens with a desert. Just the desert. Undulating dunes stretching as far as the eye can see. Then, from nowhere, there's a speck of color on the horizon. It's Lawrence (you know, Lawrence ... of Arabia) leading the cavalry. For the Angels, Jones is that figure, with their farm system obviously playing the role of the desert. The former second-round pick emerged as a bona fide top prospect in 2017, pairing a stellar slash line across two levels with more tools than a Craftsman aisle. Jones is still young, sure, but raves about his makeup point to the baseballer from a football family being the real deal, and capable of bringing much needed water to the Angels' arid landscape.

Ian Kinsler 2B Born: 06/22/82 Age: 36 Bats: R Throws: R Height: 6'0" Weight: 200 Origin: Round 17, 2003 Draft (#496 overall)

YEAR	TEAM	LVL	AGE	PA	R	2B	3B	HR	RBI	BB	K	SB	CS	AVG/OBP/SLG	TAv	VORP	BABIP	BRR	FRAA	WARP
2015	DET	MLB	33	675	94	35	7	11	73	43	80	10	6	.296/.342/.428	.269	25.1	.323	2.1	2B(153): 0.1	2.7
2016	DET	MLB	34	679	117	29	4	28	83	45	115	14	6	.288/.348/.484	.285	40.2	.314	4.7	2B(151): 3.0	4.5
2017	DET	MLB	35	613	90	25	3	22	52	55	86	14	5	.236/.313/.412	.240	9.0	.244	4.7	2B(135): 1.0	1.0
2018	*ANA*	*MLB*	*36*	*645*	*83*	*28*	*2*	*16*	*64*	*40*	*92*	*13*	*5*	*.253/.306/.387*	*.250*	*22.6*	*.274*	*0.1*	*2B 1*	*1.5*
2019	*ANA*	*MLB*	*37*	*516*	*59*	*21*	*1*	*13*	*56*	*34*	*82*	*9*	*4*	*.242/.300/.377*	*.239*	*8.1*	*.266*	*2.8*	*2B 1*	*1.0*

Breakout: 0% Improve: 34% Collapse: 9% Attrition: 17% MLB: 77%

Comparables: Mark Ellis, Brandon Phillips, Tony Graffanino

Kinsler's glove has a great solo act going. It started the second-most double plays in the league and netted the AL's fourth-best FRAA among qualified keystone players. It looks great in a highlight reel and, while perhaps not Gold Glove–worthy, has a shelf life of three to four more years under the right circumstances. Unfortunately, baseball is more of a double act, and though Kinsler's defense may be compelling, his offense makes a poor scene partner. Whatever precipitated his renascence in 2016 did not rear its head a second time, and a sharp decline and strained hamstring left the veteran infielder looking more his age and less the offensive juggernaut the Tigers were hoping to see. He'd make a great opener for some young middle-infield hotshot (sadly the Angels have none), but his days as a headliner may be over soon enough.

Kevin Maitan INF Born: 02/12/00 Age: 18 Bats: B Throws: R Height: 6'2" Weight: 190 Origin: International Free Agent, 2016

YEAR	TEAM	LVL	AGE	PA	R	2B	3B	HR	RBI	BB	K	SB	CS	AVG/OBP/SLG	TAv	VORP	BABIP	BRR	FRAA	WARP
2017	BRA	RK	17	37	5	3	0	0	3	2	10	1	0	.314/.351/.400	.262	1.7	.440	0.3	SS(5): -1.7	0.0
2017	DNV	RK	17	139	10	5	1	2	15	9	39	1	0	.220/.273/.323	.220	-1.4	.295	-0.7	SS(30): 0.9	0.0
2018	*ANA*	*MLB*	*18*	*250*	*19*	*8*	*0*	*6*	*24*	*11*	*90*	*0*	*0*	*.183/.222/.293*	*.178*	*-10.4*	*.265*	*-0.4*	*SS -1*	*-1.3*
2019	*ANA*	*MLB*	*19*	*259*	*24*	*9*	*1*	*6*	*25*	*11*	*95*	*0*	*0*	*.184/.219/.306*	*.184*	*-12.6*	*.264*	*-0.4*	*SS -1*	*-1.5*

Comparables: Raul Mondesi, Wilmer Flores

The prized prospect of Atlanta's now-controversial haul of international signings got his first taste of pro ball in 2017, and if you were expecting the kid who's been compared to Chipper Jones and Miguel Cabrera to set the world on fire in a similar manner, you came away disappointed. Instead, Maitan's rookie-league stats were underwhelming, and there was also a bit of concern about the weight he put on during the season. It then becomes no surprise that after entering the season with dreams of sticking at shortstop long-term, we sit now pondering how far he could fall on the defensive spectrum before he hits the ground. At this stage in a prospect's career you can throw the stats out the window if the flashes of star potential are bright enough and when Maitan showed flashes, they could still blind a bat. Of course, those flashes will be coming in another organization because of the punishment handed down to the Braves by MLB for violating international free agency rules. Atlanta's loss is Anaheim's gain.

Martin Maldonado C

Born: 08/16/86 Age: 31 Bats: R Throws: R Height: 6'0" Weight: 230 Origin: Round 27, 2004 Draft (#803 overall)

YEAR	TEAM	LVL	AGE	PA	R	2B	3B	HR	RBI	BB	K	SB	CS	AVG/OBP/SLG	TAv	VORP	BABIP	BRR	FRAA	WARP
2015	MIL	MLB	28	256	19	7	0	4	22	23	65	0	1	.210/.282/.293	.208	-2.6	.272	-0.5	C(74): 4.4, 1B(1): 0.0	0.2
2016	MIL	MLB	29	253	21	7	0	8	21	35	56	1	0	.202/.332/.351	.245	6.5	.234	-1.1	C(69): 5.1	1.2
2017	ANA	MLB	30	471	43	19	1	14	38	15	119	0	2	.221/.276/.368	.224	2.0	.273	-2.4	C(137): 22.8, 1B(1): 0.0	2.5
2018	*ANA*	*MLB*	*31*	*425*	*44*	*15*	*1*	*11*	*43*	*30*	*108*	*1*	*1*	*.209/.279/.335*	*.222*	*3.4*	*.256*	*-1.0*	*C 13*	*1.2*
2019	*ANA*	*MLB*	*32*	*402*	*45*	*14*	*0*	*11*	*42*	*32*	*103*	*0*	*0*	*.207/.287/.340*	*.222*	*-1.4*	*.252*	*-1.1*	*C 13*	*1.3*

Breakout: 3% Improve: 37% Collapse: 14% Attrition: 22% MLB: 94%

Comparables: Rich Gedman, Haywood Sullivan, Yorvit Torrealba

YEAR	TEAM	P. COUNT	FRM RUNS	BLK RUNS	THRW RUNS	TOT RUNS
2015	MIL	10023	5.3	0.6	0.7	6.6
2016	MIL	9275	2.0	1.3	2.1	5.4
2017	ANA	18609	18.4	0.8	3.0	22.2
2018	*ANA*	*16539*	*11.4*	*1.2*	*2.2*	*14.8*
2019	*ANA*	*15629*	*11.0*	*1.1*	*2.2*	*14.3*

Need protection for that original Rembrandt on the wall? What about help pinning your crime on someone else? Or to tell a story within a story that explains the overarching story? Maldonado had a great year framing, ranking fourth best in the league at stealing strikes behind the plate. He also added plenty of strikes while holding a bat, as he saw first-pitch strikes 66 percent of the time—fifth most in baseball—and was attacked often, not just early. This caused the patience Maldonado had previously displayed in short spurts to all but disappear, and he sputtered to a .539 OPS in the second half. In other words, he hit like a defense-first catcher.

Brandon Marsh OF

Born: 12/18/97 Age: 20 Bats: L Throws: R Height: 6'4" Weight: 210 Origin: Round 2, 2016 Draft (#60 overall)

YEAR	TEAM	LVL	AGE	PA	R	2B	3B	HR	RBI	BB	K	SB	CS	AVG/OBP/SLG	TAv	VORP	BABIP	BRR	FRAA	WARP
2017	ORM	RK	19	192	47	13	5	4	44	9	35	10	2	.350/.396/.548	.295	16.5	.417	3.2	RF(26): -1.9, CF(11): 1.6	1.5
2018	*ANA*	*MLB*	*20*	*250*	*25*	*9*	*1*	*6*	*21*	*10*	*83*	*3*	*1*	*.193/.230/.310*	*.185*	*-11.7*	*.267*	*0.0*	*RF 0, CF 0*	*-1.3*
2019	*ANA*	*MLB*	*21*	*284*	*28*	*10*	*1*	*8*	*29*	*12*	*91*	*3*	*1*	*.205/.245/.336*	*.203*	*-10.1*	*.276*	*0.1*	*RF 0, CF 0*	*-1.1*

Breakout: 0% Improve: 1% Collapse: 0% Attrition: 1% MLB: 2%

Comparables: Avisail Garcia, Chris Parmelee, Engel Beltre

If you add three letters to Marsh's name, you get a former Pro Bowl wide receiver. If you add three tools to his arsenal, you get, like, eight tools, which would be a record. A back injury kept him off the field after signing in 2016, but Marsh raked in the Pioneer League last season, flashing the skills and raw ability that led the Angels to pop the Georgia native in the second round. Even with fewer than 200 professional plate appearances to his name, Marsh offers the projectability and promise of a potential star, and could be a force to be reckoned with as he enters full-season ball in 2018.

Cliff Pennington UT

Born: 06/15/84 Age: 34 Bats: B Throws: R Height: 5'11" Weight: 195 Origin: Round 1, 2005 Draft (#21 overall)

YEAR	TEAM	LVL	AGE	PA	R	2B	3B	HR	RBI	BB	K	SB	CS	AVG/OBP/SLG	TAv	VORP	BABIP	BRR	FRAA	WARP
2015	ARI	MLB	31	157	15	3	0	1	10	16	29	3	0	.237/.314/.281	.216	-2.4	.290	-0.6	SS(24): 2.9, 3B(12): -0.1	0.1
2015	TOR	MLB	31	92	9	3	0	2	11	11	20	0	0	.160/.270/.280	.218	-0.9	.182	0.5	2B(22): 1.7, 3B(6): 0.0	0.1
2016	SLC	AAA	32	26	3	2	1	0	3	3	4	0	0	.304/.385/.478	.266	0.7	.368	-0.1	SS(2): -0.1, 2B(2): 0.2	0.1
2016	ANA	MLB	32	188	18	4	2	3	10	13	55	1	0	.209/.265/.308	.202	-5.3	.289	0.1	2B(58): -2.4, SS(17): 1.1	-0.7
2017	ANA	MLB	33	217	23	6	0	3	21	16	58	3	1	.253/.306/.330	.244	5.2	.333	1.9	2B(47): 1.6, 3B(18): -0.1	0.6
2018	*ANA*	*MLB*	*34*	*250*	*25*	*8*	*1*	*4*	*22*	*22*	*58*	*3*	*1*	*.228/.302/.323*	*.221*	*0.7*	*.284*	*0.5*	*2B 0, SS 1*	*0.2*
2019	*ANA*	*MLB*	*35*	*213*	*22*	*6*	*1*	*3*	*18*	*20*	*51*	*2*	*1*	*.214/.293/.302*	*.216*	*-2.9*	*.271*	*0.3*	*2B 0, SS 1*	*-0.2*

Breakout: 3% Improve: 27% Collapse: 20% Attrition: 35% MLB: 82%

Comparables: Brendan Ryan, Johnny Berardino, Mickey Morandini

There's no sugarcoating it: Pennington was dreadful in the first year of his two-year deal with the Angels. He was much better last year, taking the contract from terrible to slightly less terrible. Originally signed to bolster the defense as a utility guy, the former Texas A&M Aggie saw his glove dropped off a, well, you know, last year. He rebounded with slightly above-average production at three infield spots in 2017, making him a much better bet to land somewhere in a similar role.

Brandon Phillips 2B

Born: 06/28/81 Age: 37 Bats: R Throws: R Height: 6'0" Weight: 211 Origin: Round 2, 1999 Draft (#57 overall)

YEAR	TEAM	LVL	AGE	PA	R	2B	3B	HR	RBI	BB	K	SB	CS	AVG/OBP/SLG	TAv	VORP	BABIP	BRR	FRAA	WARP
2015	CIN	MLB	34	623	69	19	2	12	70	27	68	23	3	.294/.328/.395	.270	24.7	.315	2.3	2B(141): 0.5, SS(1): 0.0	2.7
2016	CIN	MLB	35	584	74	34	1	11	64	18	68	14	8	.291/.320/.416	.266	17.5	.312	-1.4	2B(138): -4.2	1.4
2017	ATL	MLB	36	499	68	27	1	11	52	19	57	10	8	.291/.329/.423	.263	18.1	.313	2.2	2B(88): -3.4, 3B(25): -1.6	1.3
2017	ANA	MLB	36	105	13	7	0	2	8	2	16	1	0	.255/.269/.382	.224	-0.7	.286	0.3	2B(24): -0.4	-0.1
2018	*ANA*	*MLB*	*37*	*563*	*58*	*24*	*1*	*12*	*59*	*23*	*79*	*12*	*6*	*.262/.299/.380*	*.236*	*9.1*	*.285*	*0.4*	*2B -1, 3B -1*	*0.7*
2019	*ANA*	*MLB*	*38*	*472*	*50*	*20*	*1*	*10*	*48*	*19*	*69*	*9*	*5*	*.255/.292/.368*	*.233*	*2.0*	*.280*	*0.6*	*2B -1, 3B -1*	*0.0*

Breakout: 1% Improve: 21% Collapse: 10% Attrition: 17% MLB: 59%

Comparables: Orlando Cabrera, Cookie Rojas, Jim Gantner

Phillips held out as long as possible on the trade market before finally agreeing to a deal sending the veteran second baseman to Atlanta. He liked the first taste so much, he agreed to *another* deal at the August deadline, spending the last month of the season on the West Coast. Dat Dude lived up to his reputation, making tons of contact, but he was about as miscast as a table setter as Daniel Day-Lewis playing Billy Madison, or a reality game show host being president. The four-time Gold Glove winner saw his defense slip once again last season, but he can still hit and run a little, keeping his bid for the Hall of Pretty Good alive.

Albert Pujols DH Born: 01/16/80 Age: 38 Bats: R Throws: R Height: 6'3" Weight: 240 Origin: Round 13, 1999 Draft (#402 overall)

YEAR	TEAM	LVL	AGE	PA	R	2B	3B	HR	RBI	BB	K	SB	CS	AVG/OBP/SLG	TAv	VORP	BABIP	BRR	FRAA	WARP
2015	ANA	MLB	35	661	85	22	0	40	95	50	72	5	3	.244/.307/.480	.279	17.9	.217	-1.0	1B(95): 6.1, 3B(1): 0.0	2.6
2016	ANA	MLB	36	650	71	19	0	31	119	49	75	4	0	.268/.323/.457	.274	11.8	.260	-3.8	1B(28): -1.1	1.1
2017	ANA	MLB	37	636	53	17	0	23	101	37	93	3	0	.241/.286/.386	.225	-17.8	.249	-1.2	1B(6): -0.6	-1.8
2018	*ANA*	*MLB*	*38*	*426*	*51*	*15*	*0*	*17*	*58*	*28*	*54*	*2*	*1*	*.245/.298/.417*	*.253*	*4.7*	*.243*	*-0.6*		*0.3*
2019	*ANA*	*MLB*	*39*	*415*	*53*	*15*	*0*	*18*	*55*	*28*	*58*	*1*	*0*	*.241/.296/.419*	*.248*	*0.1*	*.241*	*-1.3*	-	*0.0*

Breakout: 0% Improve: 15% Collapse: 17% Attrition: 18% MLB: 62% *Comparables: Carlos Lee, Victor Martinez, Rico Carty*

In *The Incredibles*, Mr. Incredible was the greatest superhero in the world. He was beloved and adored, and perhaps most importantly, he was, well, important. Then, he got older. He got a little less athletic and a little less imposing. His decline was a stark reminder that primes dissipate, skills erode and things end. We might not be ready to live in a world where Albert Pujols is less incredible, yet here we are. He didn't strike fear into the hearts of opposing pitchers last season, drawing walks at the lowest rate of his career. Nagging foot injuries sapped even more speed from his arsenal, turning lasers off the wall into long singles. His -1.8 WARP is the second-worst season by a Hall of Famer since 1950, and the fact that he needed no qualifiers in this sentence makes it all the more uncomfortable. Mr. Incredible reinvented himself and once again found success and adulation late in his career. Pujols still has opportunities to reinvent himself, but he's running out of ways to be incredible.

Ben Revere OF Born: 05/03/88 Age: 30 Bats: L Throws: R Height: 5'9" Weight: 175 Origin: Round 1, 2007 Draft (#28 overall)

YEAR	TEAM	LVL	AGE	PA	R	2B	3B	HR	RBI	BB	K	SB	CS	AVG/OBP/SLG	TAv	VORP	BABIP	BRR	FRAA	WARP
2015	PHI	MLB	27	388	49	13	6	1	26	19	36	24	5	.298/.334/.374	.268	18.0	.328	5.9	LF(56): 2.7, CF(42): 0.0	2.1
2015	TOR	MLB	27	246	35	9	1	1	19	13	28	7	2	.319/.354/.381	.268	10.9	.355	3.9	LF(56): -7.0, CF(1): -0.1	0.4
2016	WAS	MLB	28	375	44	9	7	2	24	18	34	14	5	.217/.260/.300	.201	-8.5	.234	3.0	CF(74): -1.2, LF(25): 0.0	-1.0
2017	ANA	MLB	29	308	37	13	2	1	20	15	25	21	6	.275/.308/.344	.238	5.0	.296	4.9	LF(78): -0.3, CF(6): 0.4	0.5
2018	*ANA*	*MLB*	*30*	*305*	*37*	*10*	*3*	*3*	*23*	*14*	*31*	*17*	*4*	*.278/.315/.365*	*.237*	*6.5*	*.298*	*3.3*	*LF 1, CF 0*	*0.8*
2019	*ANA*	*MLB*	*31*	*278*	*29*	*8*	*3*	*3*	*25*	*14*	*29*	*14*	*4*	*.271/.312/.359*	*.238*	*3.7*	*.291*	*3.4*	*LF 1, CF 0*	*0.5*

Breakout: 2% Improve: 36% Collapse: 13% Attrition: 17% MLB: 94% *Comparables: Mike Felder, Endy Chavez, Rudy Law*

Much of Revere's 2016 was a wash due to a nagging oblique injury that cost him most of the season. He was back with a vengeance last year, returning to his Ben Revere-y self. If there was a fly-ball revolution taking place across baseball, Revere didn't get the memo, as the speedster beat the ball into the ground like he was trying to win all the tickets at Whack-a-Mole, with fewer than 20 percent of the lefty's batted balls making it into the air. With Revere, you're looking for speed, and speed alone. He did wreak havoc on the basepaths last season, but if he loses a step at all, it could be a long, bumpy path down a dirt road, as there's a thin line between fourth outfielder and TV color guy.

Andrelton Simmons SS Born: 09/04/89 Age: 28 Bats: R Throws: R Height: 6'2" Weight: 200 Origin: Round 2, 2010 Draft (#70 overall)

YEAR	TEAM	LVL	AGE	PA	R	2B	3B	HR	RBI	BB	K	SB	CS	AVG/OBP/SLG	TAv	VORP	BABIP	BRR	FRAA	WARP
2015	ATL	MLB	25	583	60	23	2	4	44	39	48	5	3	.265/.321/.338	.248	17.0	.285	0.7	SS(147): 10.4	2.9
2016	ANA	MLB	26	483	48	22	2	4	44	28	38	10	1	.281/.324/.366	.249	15.3	.298	0.8	SS(124): 6.2	2.2
2017	ANA	MLB	27	647	77	38	2	14	69	47	67	19	6	.278/.331/.421	.262	31.8	.291	2.7	SS(158): 16.1	4.8
2018	*ANA*	*MLB*	*28*	*625*	*66*	*27*	*3*	*11*	*64*	*39*	*56*	*12*	*4*	*.259/.308/.373*	*.248*	*21.9*	*.269*	*0.5*	*SS 7*	*2.1*
2019	*ANA*	*MLB*	*29*	*570*	*65*	*25*	*2*	*12*	*60*	*41*	*53*	*10*	*4*	*.261/.318/.387*	*.250*	*14.2*	*.269*	*1.1*	*SS 6*	*2.2*

Breakout: 1% Improve: 38% Collapse: 7% Attrition: 8% MLB: 98% *Comparables: Elvis Andrus, Bobby Valentine, Alex Arias*

Every year, typically following a game featuring a handful of superhuman, highlight-reel defensive plays, someone will write a piece touting Simmons' MVP candidacy. These pieces always include the caveat, "Well, if he could just hit a little bit..." Well, Simmons hit a little bit last year. The Curaçao native had the seventh-highest TAv among AL shortstops, and the third-most doubles and stolen bases to boot. Pair the offensive upgrade with perennial otherworldly wizardry with the glove—he led all shortstops in FRAA and has been in the top five for five consecutive years—and you get, well, an MVP candidate.

Matt Thaiss 1B Born: 05/06/95 Age: 23 Bats: L Throws: R Height: 6'0" Weight: 195 Origin: Round 1, 2016 Draft (#16 overall)

YEAR	TEAM	LVL	AGE	PA	R	2B	3B	HR	RBI	BB	K	SB	CS	AVG/OBP/SLG	TAv	VORP	BABIP	BRR	FRAA	WARP
2016	ORM	RK	21	71	16	7	1	2	12	4	4	2	4	.338/.394/.569	.324	4.7	.339	-1.0	1B(15): 0.7	0.5
2016	BUR	A	21	226	24	12	3	4	31	22	28	1	0	.276/.351/.427	.290	5.2	.302	-3.6	1B(43): 5.5	1.2
2017	INL	A+	22	385	46	13	4	8	48	40	59	4	3	.265/.353/.399	.282	13.0	.299	0.5	1B(78): 2.8	1.7
2017	MOB	AA	22	221	29	14	0	1	25	37	50	4	3	.292/.412/.388	.309	12.0	.389	-1.2	1B(46): -1.5	1.1
2018	*ANA*	*MLB*	*23*	*250*	*26*	*10*	*1*	*7*	*28*	*25*	*56*	*1*	*1*	*.235/.319/.380*	*.245*	*0.3*	*.283*	*-0.4*	*1B 2*	*0.2*
2019	*ANA*	*MLB*	*24*	*384*	*48*	*17*	*1*	*12*	*45*	*41*	*86*	*2*	*1*	*.237/.326/.399*	*.255*	*2.1*	*.281*	*-0.7*	*1B 2*	*0.5*

Breakout: 6% Improve: 13% Collapse: 4% Attrition: 12% MLB: 20% *Comparables: Max Muncy, David Cooper, Mike Carp*

It's hard to make waves as a first-base-only prospect, as the major-league potential begins and ends with the ability to hit, and hit a lot. Fortunately Thaiss can hit. The former Virginia Cavalier showed an advanced approach across two levels last season, making a ton of contact to pair with impressive walk rates. The problem is that, like a thirsty Midwesterner, he's devoid of pop. Without some semblance of power, Thaiss will have to flash pretty extremely with the hit and glove tools to be worthy of a starting job at the big-league level, and while the former is further ahead than the latter it is a tough row to hoe.

Mike Trout CF Born: 08/07/91 Age: 26 Bats: R Throws: R Height: 6'2" Weight: 235 Origin: Round 1, 2009 Draft (#25 overall)

YEAR	TEAM	LVL	AGE	PA	R	2B	3B	HR	RBI	BB	K	SB	CS	AVG/OBP/SLG	TAv	VORP	BABIP	BRR	FRAA	WARP
2015	ANA	MLB	23	682	104	32	6	41	90	92	158	11	7	.299/.402/.590	.353	83.5	.344	1.6	CF(156): 10.0	10.0
2016	ANA	MLB	24	681	123	32	5	29	100	116	137	30	7	.315/.441/.550	.355	90.7	.371	4.8	CF(148): -6.8	8.7
2017	ANA	MLB	25	507	92	25	3	33	72	94	90	22	4	.306/.442/.629	.360	69.0	.318	0.0	CF(108): -3.5	6.6
2018	*ANA*	*MLB*	*26*	*666*	*122*	*32*	*6*	*34*	*102*	*98*	*140*	*22*	*6*	*.296/.409/.559*	*.334*	*79.5*	*.339*	*2.1*	*CF -3*	*7.2*
2019	*ANA*	*MLB*	*27*	*584*	*99*	*28*	*4*	*32*	*101*	*91*	*125*	*19*	*5*	*.300/.416/.578*	*.337*	*66.9*	*.340*	*2.2*	*CF -1*	*7.1*

Breakout: 1% Improve: 59% Collapse: 0% Attrition: 2% MLB: 100% *Comparables: Mickey Mantle, Frank Thomas, Willie Mays*

How do you even begin to talk about someone like Trout? You could humanize him, spinning anecdotes about his Philadelphia Eagles fandom or fascination with meteorology. You could try to bring him down a peg, citing his poor choice of haircuts last season or his campy, wholesome performances in Subway commercials. But all of these avenues just feel ... wrong. It begins and ends with excellence. Trout is still only 26 years old, so any discussion of which Hall of Famers he has already passed in WARP and which ones he might pass next is only going to get more obnoxious. For the second consecutive season, Millville, New Jersey's favorite son led all of baseball in TAv (he has finished in the top three in each of his first six full seasons) and was perhaps en route to his best season as a big leaguer when injury struck.

On May 28, Trout tore a ligament in his thumb on a headfirst slide, costing him about a month and a half. It was his first major injury. At the time of "The Slide," baseball's wunderkind led the American League in slugging percentage, OPS and walks, and was tied for the league lead in homers. We've basically reached the point where only injuries can stop Trout from leading the pack in the MVP race (he still finished seventh in WARP last season, second in the AL), a race that he remained a participant in despite having roughly 150 fewer plate appearance than his counterparts.

We spend a lot of words in this book making jokes, but sometimes we just need to sit back and bask in the excellence. Mike Trout has been excellent. Mike Trout is excellent. There's little reason to believe that Mike Trout won't be excellent in the future, as he takes his rightful position among history's greatest ballplayers. In today's climate it's easy to be hyperbolic about recent success stories, but it's hard to be hyperbolic about Mike Trout. Let's enjoy it. But also, let's try to fix that haircut for 2018, shall we?

Justin Upton LF Born: 08/25/87 Age: 30 Bats: R Throws: R Height: 6'2" Weight: 205 Origin: Round 1, 2005 Draft (#1 overall)

YEAR	TEAM	LVL	AGE	PA	R	2B	3B	HR	RBI	BB	K	SB	CS	AVG/OBP/SLG	TAv	VORP	BABIP	BRR	FRAA	WARP
2015	SDN	MLB	27	620	85	26	3	26	81	68	159	19	5	.251/.336/.454	.294	37.3	.304	3.8	LF(146): -6.6	3.3
2016	DET	MLB	28	626	81	28	2	31	87	50	179	9	4	.246/.310/.465	.260	16.3	.301	2.4	LF(146): -5.4, CF(6): 0.0	1.1
2017	DET	MLB	29	520	81	37	0	28	94	57	147	10	5	.279/.362/.542	.297	31.4	.351	-0.6	LF(124): 11.9	4.3
2017	ANA	MLB	29	115	19	7	0	7	15	17	33	4	0	.245/.357/.531	.292	7.6	.293	1.1	LF(27): -2.5	0.5
2018	*ANA*	*MLB*	*30*	*615*	*86*	*28*	*1*	*28*	*89*	*62*	*165*	*13*	*5*	*.248/.328/.459*	*.276*	*32.1*	*.301*	*0.1*	*LF 2*	*2.8*
2019	*ANA*	*MLB*	*31*	*541*	*76*	*25*	*1*	*26*	*78*	*57*	*148*	*10*	*4*	*.246/.329/.462*	*.273*	*22.1*	*.299*	*1.6*	*LF 3*	*2.7*

Breakout: 4% Improve: 56% Collapse: 6% Attrition: 6% MLB: 99% *Comparables: Jason Bay, Pat Burrell, Todd Hundley*

The great American poet Jay Z spent many hours philosophizing about gifts and curses. For Upton, his athleticism and prodigious, natural talent clashing with weighty, outlandish expectations can be described in just that way. For his major-league career, the former first-overall pick owns a .290 TAv and more than 250 homers. Last season marked one of the best yet for the veteran, as he feasted with runners in scoring position, slashing .336/.440/.643 in 168 plate appearances. Upton also graded as a positive asset in the outfield for the first time since Obama's first term. Yet somehow each of Upton's great seasons *feels* slightly underwhelming. See how the universe works? It's a gift and a curse.

Luis Valbuena 3B Born: 11/30/85 Age: 32 Bats: L Throws: R Height: 5'10" Weight: 215 Origin: International Free Agent, 2002

YEAR	TEAM	LVL	AGE	PA	R	2B	3B	HR	RBI	BB	K	SB	CS	AVG/OBP/SLG	TAv	VORP	BABIP	BRR	FRAA	WARP
2015	HOU	MLB	29	493	62	18	0	25	56	50	106	1	0	.224/.310/.438	.267	18.2	.235	1.9	3B(99): -6.8, 1B(31): 1.9	1.4
2016	HOU	MLB	30	342	38	17	1	13	40	44	81	1	1	.260/.357/.459	.290	19.4	.315	-1.4	3B(81): 5.9, 1B(8): 0.3	2.6
2017	ANA	MLB	31	401	42	15	0	22	65	48	106	0	2	.199/.294/.432	.250	4.5	.210	-0.6	3B(59): 1.6, 1B(48): -0.3	0.6
2018	*ANA*	*MLB*	*32*	*176*	*21*	*7*	*0*	*7*	*23*	*20*	*38*	*0*	*0*	*.227/.318/.411*	*.260*	*4.6*	*.256*	*-0.5*	*3B -1, 1B 0*	*0.2*
2019	*ANA*	*MLB*	*33*	*267*	*36*	*11*	*0*	*11*	*35*	*33*	*61*	*0*	*0*	*.227/.325/.419*	*.261*	*5.4*	*.258*	*0.0*	*3B -1, 1B 0*	*0.4*

Breakout: 4% Improve: 41% Collapse: 6% Attrition: 6% MLB: 98% *Comparables: Chase Headley, Robin Ventura, Morgan Ensberg*

Only one regular hit below .200 in 2017 and still managed a positive WARP. Guess who it was? This might sound reductive and obvious, but sometimes Valbuena hits, and when he does, he's a pretty good player—though he won't kill you even when he doesn't. He also played well at the hot corner, despite being signed primarily to stand at the cold corner against right-handed pitching. As a walking embodiment of the second-division regular, Valbuena has a knack for showing up (and departing) *just before* a team gets good, with stints on the Indians, Cubs and Astros right before their respective playoff runs. That said, he played for the Mariners briefly back in 2008, so there clearly has to be some sort of minimum-plate-appearance thing going on here. Just another thing for fans to blame Jack Z for.

Taylor Ward C Born: 12/14/93 Age: 24 Bats: R Throws: R Height: 6'1" Weight: 200 Origin: Round 1, 2015 Draft (#26 overall)

YEAR	TEAM	LVL	AGE	PA	R	2B	3B	HR	RBI	BB	K	SB	CS	AVG/OBP/SLG	TAv	VORP	BABIP	BRR	FRAA	WARP
2015	ORM	RK	21	141	20	4	1	2	19	29	8	5	2	.349/.489/.459	.333	14.8	.360	-3.1	C(29): -0.2	1.4
2015	BUR	A	21	103	10	3	0	1	12	10	15	1	1	.348/.412/.413	.296	7.8	.408	0.1	C(20): -0.7	0.8
2016	INL	A+	22	529	61	11	0	10	56	48	81	0	0	.249/.323/.337	.240	9.4	.279	1.4	C(90): 4.2	1.4
2017	INL	A+	23	247	32	11	1	6	30	35	43	0	0	.242/.348/.391	.262	11.0	.275	1.3	C(42): -0.8	1.1
2017	MOB	AA	23	145	14	3	0	3	19	22	17	0	0	.286/.400/.387	.304	11.4	.307	0.3	C(21): -3.9	0.8
2018	*ANA*	*MLB*	*24*	*250*	*26*	*8*	*0*	*7*	*28*	*25*	*52*	*0*	*0*	*.229/.309/.361*	*.233*	*4.7*	*.263*	*-0.5*	*C -14*	*-1.0*
2019	*ANA*	*MLB*	*25*	*288*	*35*	*9*	*0*	*9*	*33*	*28*	*60*	*0*	*0*	*.231/.310/.379*	*.242*	*4.5*	*.262*	*-0.8*	*C -12*	*-0.8*

Breakout: 3% Improve: 9% Collapse: 9% Attrition: 13% MLB: 22%

Comparables: Austin Barnes, Chris Herrmann, Steve Clevenger

YEAR	TEAM	P. COUNT	FRM RUNS	BLK RUNS	THRW RUNS	TOT RUNS
2018	*ANA*	*8307*	*-12.5*	*-0.9*	*-0.3*	*-13.6*
2019	*ANA*	*9561*	*-6.1*	*-0.4*	*-0.1*	*-6.6*

When the Halos drafted Ward, many were hoping for a Love Story. With the 24-year-old remaining unspectacular behind the dish after a couple of years in the system, he was looking more and more like a Blank Space. While comments like that could foster Bad Blood, Ward was able to Shake It Off offensively, displaying a strong eye at the plate and the ability to make lots of contact, albeit without much power. Hopefully this doesn't sound too Mean, but Ward likely is destined to be a backup catcher in the big leagues. If you think some of those references feel a little forced, you're right. We should've just left a Blank Space.

Eric Young OF Born: 05/25/85 Age: 33 Bats: B Throws: R Height: 5'10" Weight: 195 Origin: Round 30, 2003 Draft (#887 overall)

YEAR	TEAM	LVL	AGE	PA	R	2B	3B	HR	RBI	BB	K	SB	CS	AVG/OBP/SLG	TAv	VORP	BABIP	BRR	FRAA	WARP
2015	ATL	MLB	30	85	7	4	2	0	5	6	17	3	0	.169/.229/.273	.184	-3.5	.217	0.5	CF(16): -0.1, LF(13): -0.5	-0.4
2015	GWN	AAA	30	280	36	6	3	1	27	33	43	23	3	.248/.349/.312	.245	6.7	.298	5.2	LF(44): 7.7, 2B(11): 0.6	1.5
2015	LVG	AAA	30	27	1	2	0	0	1	4	2	3	1	.261/.370/.348	.275	1.6	.286	0.5	LF(6): 0.4, CF(3): -0.4	0.2
2015	NYN	MLB	30	9	9	0	0	0	0	0	1	3	2	.000/.111/.000	.063	-0.7	.000	0.8	LF(5): -0.2, RF(2): 0.1	-0.1
2016	CSP	AAA	31	329	48	9	2	3	30	31	51	23	6	.263/.338/.339	.253	6.6	.308	1.9	LF(44): 1.1, RF(36): -1.3	0.5
2016	NYA	MLB	31	1	2	0	0	0	0	0	0	1	0	.000/.000/.000	.016	-0.1	.000	0.1	CF(2): 0.1	0.0
2017	SLC	AAA	32	385	67	15	5	8	52	33	56	20	7	.305/.375/.449	.278	19.6	.345	2.0	CF(37): -5.5, LF(27): 2.7	1.7
2017	ANA	MLB	32	125	24	5	0	4	16	5	31	12	3	.264/.336/.418	.278	6.6	.333	1.0	LF(22): 0.8, CF(15): -1.0	0.6
2018	*ANA*	*MLB*	*33*	*250*	*32*	*8*	*2*	*4*	*19*	*20*	*50*	*15*	*4*	*.232/.304/.341*	*.225*	*0.9*	*.274*	*1.1*	*CF -2, LF 2*	*0.1*
2019	*ANA*	*MLB*	*34*	*226*	*24*	*7*	*2*	*4*	*20*	*18*	*47*	*12*	*4*	*.228/.299/.332*	*.223*	*-1.5*	*.271*	*1.3*	*CF -2, LF 2*	*-0.2*

Breakout: 2% Improve: 23% Collapse: 15% Attrition: 30% MLB: 67%

Comparables: Kerry Robinson, Craig Gentry, Jason Bourgeois

Imagine being tossed Superman's cape with the instructions, "Go replace the Man of Steel." When Mike Trout went down in late May, the Angels flung a uniform at Young, and the second-generation journeyman filled in surprisingly well. He can fake it as an everyday outfielder, but at this point, if a team is using him as anything more than a pinch-runner, something has gone horribly wrong in Metropolis.

PITCHERS

Jose Alvarez LHP Born: 05/06/89 Age: 29 Bats: L Throws: L Height: 5'11" Weight: 190 Origin: International Free Agent, 2005

YEAR	TEAM	LVL	AGE	W	L	SV	G	GS	IP	H	HR	BB/9	K/9	K	GB%	BABIP	WHIP	ERA	DRA	WARP	MPH	CMD	PWR	STM
2015	ANA	MLB	26	4	3	0	64	0	67	58	5	3.1	7.9	59	52%	.277	1.21	3.49	3.75	0.8	93.3	60	33	49
2016	ANA	MLB	27	1	3	0	64	0	57^{1}	71	4	2.4	8.0	51	46%	.362	1.50	3.45	4.69	0.2	92.9	61	35	49
2017	SLC	AAA	28	0	0	0	9	0	11^{2}	10	0	1.5	7.7	10	44%	.294	1.03	2.31	3.52	0.2				
2017	ANA	MLB	28	0	3	1	64	0	48^{2}	50	7	2.2	8.3	45	39%	.309	1.27	3.88	4.79	0.2	92.8	63	38	49
2018	*ANA*	*MLB*	*29*	*3*	*4*	*0*	*64*	*0*	*67*	*64*	*9*	*3.4*	*8.3*	*62*	*45%*	*.290*	*1.32*	*4.13*	*4.44*	*0.5*	*92.3*	*61*	*36*	*49*
2019	*ANA*	*MLB*	*30*	*3*	*1*	*0*	*53*	*0*	*55^{2}*	*50*	*7*	*3.4*	*8.7*	*54*	*45%*	*.283*	*1.28*	*4.34*	*4.50*	*0.4*	*91.8*	*62*	*36*	*49*

Breakout: 35% Improve: 59% Collapse: 16% Attrition: 16% MLB: 92%

Comparables: Phil Coke, Matt Guerrier, Vinnie Chulk

Alvarez was the first lefty out of the bullpen for manager Mike Scioscia in 2017, but that's a little like using peppermint schnapps in your chili because there was nothing else in the spice cabinet. The veteran Venezuelan once again soaked up appearances in relief, and once against managed to be fine-ish. He was especially afflicted with the homeritis going around the league, surrendering the most long balls in any season since his rookie year in 2013. While he won't be confused for Andrew Miller any time soon, he does throw with his left arm, which should guarantee his job security until at least the 2032 Summer Olympics.

Andrew Bailey RHP Born: 05/31/84 Age: 34 Bats: R Throws: R Height: 6'3" Weight: 240 Origin: Round 6, 2006 Draft (#188 overall)

YEAR	TEAM	LVL	AGE	W	L	SV	G	GS	IP	H	HR	BB/9	K/9	K	GB%	BABIP	WHIP	ERA	DRA	WARP	MPH	CMD	PWR	STM
2015	TRN	AA	31	1	0	2	11	0	14^{1}	6	0	3.8	10.7	17	42%	.194	0.84	0.63	2.45	0.4				
2015	SWB	AAA	31	0	0	4	9	0	12^{1}	12	1	2.2	9.5	13	35%	.333	1.22	2.19	2.96	0.3				
2015	NYA	MLB	31	0	1	0	10	0	8^{2}	9	2	5.2	6.2	6	43%	.286	1.62	5.19	5.77	-0.1	95.5			32
2016	PHI	MLB	32	3	1	0	33	0	32^{1}	32	6	4.2	9.2	33	41%	.292	1.45	6.40	4.31	0.2	94.4	61	47	45
2016	ANA	MLB	32	0	0	6	12	0	11^{1}	9	1	1.6	6.4	8	46%	.235	0.97	2.38	5.61	-0.1	94.5	61	47	45
2017	ANA	MLB	33	2	0	0	4	0	4	1	0	0.0	4.5	2	27%	.091	0.25	0.00	6.97	-0.1	91.4			
2018	*ANA*	*MLB*	*34*	*1*	*0*	*2*	*32*	*0*	*34*	*35*	*6*	*3.7*	*7.2*	*27*	*41%*	*.284*	*1.44*	*5.53*	*5.86*	*-0.2*	*93.1*	*60*	*46*	*39*
2019	*ANA*	*MLB*	*35*	*2*	*1*	*2*	*37*	*0*	*39^{2}*	*42*	*8*	*3.9*	*6.6*	*29*	*41%*	*.282*	*1.49*	*5.83*	*6.10*	*-0.4*	*92.3*	*59*	*46*	*40*

Breakout: 20% Improve: 31% Collapse: 14% Attrition: 12% MLB: 60%

Comparables: Jim Henderson, Mark Lowe, David Aardsma

Signed to bolster a bumpy bullpen, Bailey competed for the closer job in spring training. Unfortunately for the Staten Islander, that's as competitive as it got in 2017, with multiple trips to the disabled list limiting Bailey to only four innings before an August shoulder strain put him on the shelf for good. The veteran will once again toss his line into the free agent pond heading into 2018, still five saves short of triple digits for his career.

Jaime Barria RHP Born: 07/18/96 Age: 21 Bats: R Throws: R Height: 6'1" Weight: 210 Origin: International Free Agent, 2013

YEAR	TEAM	LVL	AGE	W	L	SV	G	GS	IP	H	HR	BB/9	K/9	K	GB%	BABIP	WHIP	ERA	DRA	WARP	MPH	CMD	PWR	STM
2015	ANG	RK	18	3	0	0	7	6	36	40	0	0.8	7.8	31	57%	.351	1.19	2.00	2.17	1.4				
2015	ORM	RK	18	2	4	0	8	8	33^1	45	4	1.9	8.1	30	45%	.380	1.56	6.21	3.96	0.7				
2016	BUR	A	19	8	6	0	25	25	117	133	6	1.6	6.0	78	44%	.323	1.32	3.85	4.68	0.5				
2017	INL	A+	20	4	3	0	11	11	65^1	48	6	1.8	7.9	57	35%	.236	0.93	2.48	3.90	1.0				
2017	MOB	AA	20	1	6	0	12	12	61^2	62	8	2.2	6.9	47	29%	.284	1.25	3.21	5.02	0.1				
2017	SLC	AAA	20	2	0	0	3	3	14^2	11	0	1.8	8.0	13	29%	.262	0.95	2.45	5.46	0.0				
2018	*ANA*	*MLB*	*21*	*6*	*9*	*0*	*22*	*22*	*112*	*119*	*23*	*3.1*	*7.4*	*93*	*36%*	*.290*	*1.40*	*5.47*	*5.79*	*-0.1*				
2019	*ANA*	*MLB*	*22*	*5*	*8*	*0*	*19*	*19*	112^2	*124*	*28*	*3.0*	*7.9*	*98*	*36%*	*.293*	*1.44*	*6.00*	*6.28*	*-0.7*				

Breakout: 2% Improve: 2% Collapse: 1% Attrition: 4% MLB: 5% *Comparables: Adalberto Mejia, Jen-Ho Tseng, Gabriel Ynoa*

Outpitching your peripherals can certainly be a skill, and Barria will need to bank on said skill, as his ERA (low) and DRA (high) paint very different pictures of the soft-tossing righty's success in 2017. Let's call him the anti-Clint Eastwood because Barria did not have trouble with the curve last season, riding an improved bender to productive results. His fastball won't blow anyone away, but he commands it well and pairs it with an excellent change. It's a workable enough arsenal that the two-time recipient of the Angels' Minor League Pitcher of the Year honors could get the chance to provide rotation depth as early as this season. That would make his day.

Cam Bedrosian RHP Born: 10/02/91 Age: 26 Bats: R Throws: R Height: 6'0" Weight: 230 Origin: Round 1, 2010 Draft (#29 overall)

YEAR	TEAM	LVL	AGE	W	L	SV	G	GS	IP	H	HR	BB/9	K/9	K	GB%	BABIP	WHIP	ERA	DRA	WARP	MPH	CMD	PWR	STM
2015	SLC	AAA	23	1	1	3	24	0	35^2	32	0	3.5	10.6	42	54%	.348	1.29	2.78	2.27	1.1				
2015	ANA	MLB	23	1	0	0	34	0	33^1	40	3	5.1	9.2	34	45%	.378	1.77	5.40	4.18	0.2	97.0	48	62	50
2016	ANA	MLB	24	2	0	1	45	0	40^1	30	1	3.1	11.4	51	52%	.309	1.09	1.12	2.53	1.1	97.6	48	59	48
2017	ANA	MLB	25	6	5	6	48	0	44^2	41	5	3.4	10.7	53	45%	.313	1.30	4.43	3.47	0.8	95.4	44	51	41
2018	*ANA*	*MLB*	*26*	*2*	*3*	*5*	*53*	*0*	*56*	*51*	*7*	*3.7*	*10.2*	*64*	*46%*	*.303*	*1.33*	*3.56*	*3.98*	*0.7*	*96.1*	*47*	*57*	*46*
2019	*ANA*	*MLB*	*27*	*3*	*1*	*3*	*50*	*0*	52^2	*47*	*7*	*4.2*	*10.7*	*62*	*46%*	*.303*	*1.36*	*4.32*	*4.46*	*0.4*	*95.7*	*46*	*56*	*46*

Breakout: 36% Improve: 48% Collapse: 27% Attrition: 25% MLB: 84% *Comparables: Bruce Rondon, David Robertson, Daniel Schlereth*

It took a few seasons for Bedrosian to evolve from Closer of the Future to plain old Closer, but only one groin injury for him to get Wally Pipp'd by a committee, and eventually Blake Parker. When he returned in June, he had lost a tick on his fastball and spent the next six weeks getting nickel-and-dimed into a near-5.00 ERA. His luck would have balanced out over the remainder of the season if not for an unfortunate final appearance against the Mariners on September 30. He entered with a 3.43 ERA, but three singles followed by back-to-back homers by Kyle Seager and Yonder Alonso caused it to rise by a full run. His swinging-strike rate, the highest of his career, bodes well for Bedrosian's continued claim to the closer throne, but he'll need to put together a full season of health before he's viewed as one of the game's better late-inning relievers.

Parker Bridwell RHP Born: 08/02/91 Age: 26 Bats: R Throws: R Height: 6'4" Weight: 185 Origin: Round 9, 2010 Draft (#268 overall)

YEAR	TEAM	LVL	AGE	W	L	SV	G	GS	IP	H	HR	BB/9	K/9	K	GB%	BABIP	WHIP	ERA	DRA	WARP	MPH	CMD	PWR	STM
2015	BOW	AA	23	4	5	0	18	18	97	96	7	3.5	8.6	93	40%	.320	1.38	3.99	5.06	0.0				
2016	BOW	AA	24	1	1	1	18	7	55^2	56	7	4.5	6.1	38	43%	.283	1.51	4.53	6.34	-0.9				
2016	BAL	MLB	24	0	0	0	2	0	3^1	5	2	2.7	8.1	3	27%	.333	1.80	13.50	8.44	-0.1	94.6			41
2016	NOR	AAA	24	1	0	0	4	0	10	4	1	0.9	12.6	14	47%	.167	0.50	1.80	2.35	0.3				
2017	SLC	AAA	25	2	3	0	6	5	27^1	26	2	2.6	7.9	24	52%	.300	1.24	4.28	3.16	0.7				
2017	ANA	MLB	25	10	3	0	21	20	121	115	19	2.2	5.4	73	39%	.262	1.20	3.64	5.12	0.6	93.9	47	39	64
2018	*ANA*	*MLB*	*26*	*6*	*8*	*1*	*33*	*20*	120^2	*124*	*23*	*3.4*	*7.5*	*100*	*41%*	*.288*	*1.41*	*5.39*	*5.70*	*-0.1*	*93.5*	*48*	*40*	*55*
2019	*ANA*	*MLB*	*27*	*4*	*6*	*0*	*19*	*14*	94^2	*98*	*18*	*3.4*	*7.4*	*78*	*41%*	*.289*	*1.41*	*5.39*	*5.63*	*0.0*	*93.2*	*48*	*40*	*55*

Breakout: 23% Improve: 46% Collapse: 19% Attrition: 39% MLB: 77% *Comparables: Shairon Martis, Kyle Lobstein, Josh Tomlin*

Bridwell exchanged his avian wings for those of the celestial variety, after a trade sent the Texan from Baltimore to Anaheim. The righty stepped into the decimated Halo rotation and provided solid depth, riding a five-pitch mix and inducing plenty of soft contact. There's a definite ceiling for Bridwell and his paltry strikeout rates, but there's always a need for back-end starters, and his 2017 is proof that he can handle the role.

Jesse Chavez RHP Born: 08/21/83 Age: 34 Bats: R Throws: R Height: 6'2" Weight: 175 Origin: Round 42, 2002 Draft (#1252 overall)

YEAR	TEAM	LVL	AGE	W	L	SV	G	GS	IP	H	HR	BB/9	K/9	K	GB%	BABIP	WHIP	ERA	DRA	WARP	MPH	CMD	PWR	STM
2015	OAK	MLB	31	7	15	1	30	26	157	164	18	2.8	7.8	136	45%	.312	1.35	4.18	3.69	2.6	94.1	71	53	69
2016	TOR	MLB	32	1	2	0	39	0	41^1	43	9	2.2	9.1	42	46%	.309	1.28	4.57	4.60	0.2	95.6	72	59	48
2016	LAN	MLB	32	1	0	0	23	0	25^2	28	3	2.8	7.4	21	39%	.325	1.40	4.21	4.00	0.3	94.9	72	59	48
2017	ANA	MLB	33	7	11	0	38	21	138	148	28	2.9	7.8	119	42%	.306	1.40	5.35	4.95	0.8	93.1	73	45	64
2018	*ANA*	*MLB*	*34*	*5*	*6*	*0*	*37*	*14*	103^2	*111*	*19*	*3.3*	*7.5*	*86*	*43%*	*.300*	*1.44*	*5.23*	*5.53*	*0.1*	*92.7*	*71*	*50*	*59*
2019	*ANA*	*MLB*	*35*	*7*	*8*	*1*	*44*	*18*	*139*	*152*	*25*	*3.4*	*7.3*	*113*	*43%*	*.303*	*1.48*	*5.31*	*5.53*	*0.0*	*92.1*	*71*	*48*	*57*

Breakout: 12% Improve: 38% Collapse: 23% Attrition: 9% MLB: 88% *Comparables: Phil Niekro, Gavin Floyd, Kevin Millwood*

In one version of Marvel comics, Steve Rogers becomes disillusioned with the United States, abandons his Captain America suit and shield and becomes Nomad, a man without a country. Forced to rely on heightened physiology and guile, Nomad has varying degrees of success before returning to the shield. Having now pitched for seven different MLB teams, which excludes his three-week stint in Tampa during the 2009-10 offseason, Chavez has become baseball's Nomad, shifting between personas as a starter and long reliever. The veteran righty struggled to suppress homers, but otherwise provided his typical league-average production and his reverse role split—Chavez, both for his career and in 2017, has been about a half run better in the rotation than he has been coming out of the bullpen.

Andrew Heaney LHP Born: 06/05/91 Age: 27 Bats: L Throws: L Height: 6'2" Weight: 195 Origin: Round 1, 2012 Draft (#9 overall)

YEAR	TEAM	LVL	AGE	W	L	SV	G	GS	IP	H	HR	BB/9	K/9	K	GB%	BABIP	WHIP	ERA	DRA	WARP	MPH	CMD	PWR	STM
2015	SLC	AAA	24	6	2	0	14	14	78^{1}	95	2	2.9	8.5	74	48%	.372	1.53	4.71	3.31	1.8				
2015	ANA	MLB	24	6	4	0	18	18	105^{2}	99	9	2.4	6.6	78	41%	.284	1.20	3.49	4.72	0.5	94.1	55	43	73
2016	ANA	MLB	25	0	1	0	1	1	6	7	2	0.0	10.5	7	44%	.312	1.17	6.00	6.13	-0.1	94.3			
2017	ANG	RK	26	0	1	0	3	3	10^{1}	11	0	0.9	13.1	15	42%	.423	1.16	1.74	2.55	0.4				
2017	SLC	AAA	26	1	1	0	3	3	17^{1}	17	2	2.1	7.3	14	39%	.306	1.21	3.12	4.42	0.2				
2017	ANA	MLB	26	1	2	0	5	5	21^{2}	27	12	3.7	11.2	27	34%	.283	1.66	7.06	5.01	0.1	94.2	57	47	44
2018	*ANA*	*MLB*	*27*	*4*	*9*	*0*	*40*	*19*	*79*	*80*	*18*	*3.6*	*9.0*	*80*	*40%*	*.290*	*1.40*	*5.19*	*5.59*	*-0.3*	*93.7*	*56*	*45*	*56*
2019	*ANA*	*MLB*	*28*	*5*	*6*	*0*	*56*	*17*	143^{2}	*144*	*33*	*3.3*	*8.9*	*142*	*40%*	*.285*	*1.37*	*5.59*	*5.84*	*-0.4*	*93.2*	*57*	*46*	*51*

Breakout: 35% Improve: 59% Collapse: 16% Attrition: 18% MLB: 90% *Comparables: Josh Collmenter, Jacob deGrom, David Phelps*

Despite a return bumpier than Oceanic Flight 815, Heaney showed some promise in five starts back from Tommy John surgery. The former Oklahoma State standout added velocity, running his sinker up to 97 mph and getting groundballs over 60 percent of the time with the pitch. We're grading on the biggest of curves, as aside from participation, not much went right for Heaney last season. The southpaw gave up more big flies than a David Cronenberg film, surrendering one more dinger in his abbreviated 2017 than he did in his previous two seasons as an Angel combined. Shoulder discomfort shut him down for good in late September, but Heaney should be back and ready to take his turn come Opening Day.

Jim Johnson RHP Born: 06/27/83 Age: 34 Bats: R Throws: R Height: 6'6" Weight: 250 Origin: Round 5, 2001 Draft (#143 overall)

YEAR	TEAM	LVL	AGE	W	L	SV	G	GS	IP	H	HR	BB/9	K/9	K	GB%	BABIP	WHIP	ERA	DRA	WARP	MPH	CMD	PWR	STM
2015	ATL	MLB	32	2	3	9	49	0	48	45	2	2.6	6.2	33	64%	.295	1.23	2.25	4.13	0.3	96.5	42	61	52
2015	LAN	MLB	32	0	3	1	23	0	18^{2}	32	3	2.9	8.2	17	65%	.446	2.04	10.12	3.78	0.2	96.9	42	61	52
2016	ATL	MLB	33	2	6	20	65	0	64^{2}	57	3	2.8	9.5	68	56%	.314	1.19	3.06	3.15	1.4	96.1	51	53	49
2017	ATL	MLB	34	6	3	22	61	0	56^{2}	59	8	4.0	9.7	61	49%	.317	1.48	5.56	3.98	0.7	95.0	59	53	46
2018	*ANA*	*MLB*	*35*	*2*	*4*	*4*	*53*	*0*	*56*	*58*	*7*	*3.7*	*7.8*	*49*	*52%*	*.305*	*1.46*	*4.44*	*4.69*	*0.3*	*94.6*	*51*	*54*	*48*
2019	*ANA*	*MLB*	*36*	*2*	*1*	*2*	*41*	*0*	43^{1}	*46*	*6*	*3.6*	*7.6*	*37*	*52%*	*.312*	*1.48*	*4.94*	*5.12*	*0.1*	*93.8*	*53*	*52*	*46*

Breakout: 25% Improve: 42% Collapse: 22% Attrition: 12% MLB: 79% *Comparables: Matt Lindstrom, Ryan Madson, Matt Guerrier*

Johnson's 2017 is a prime example of what happens when the stat test and the eye test don't align at all. The stats will tell you that he had a perfectly fine season. However, the eye test will tell you that the veteran pitcher's age-34 campaign could be best described as "tumultuous." Johnson's season was going as expected until August, when the bottom fell out—which is ironic since his sinker decided to do exactly the opposite—as it seemed as though he had completely forgotten how to locate the strike zone. As a result, his ERA and FIP for the month of August reached the unenviable heights of 16.71 and 8.01, respectively. He earned his diminished role in Atlanta's bullpen last season, but he'll have a shot at returning to the forefront in 2018, albeit elsewhere. Traded to the Angels just after Thanksgiving, Johnson will be thankful if this latest trip to the West Coast ends up better than his previous two.

Alex Meyer RHP Born: 01/03/90 Age: 28 Bats: R Throws: R Height: 6'9" Weight: 225 Origin: Round 1, 2011 Draft (#23 overall)

YEAR	TEAM	LVL	AGE	W	L	SV	G	GS	IP	H	HR	BB/9	K/9	K	GB%	BABIP	WHIP	ERA	DRA	WARP	MPH	CMD	PWR	STM
2015	MIN	MLB	25	0	0	0	2	0	2^{2}	4	2	10.1	10.1	3	22%	.286	2.62	16.88	5.08	0.0	98.6			55
2015	ROC	AAA	25	4	5	0	38	8	92	101	4	4.7	9.8	100	47%	.372	1.62	4.79	4.85	0.2				
2016	ROC	AAA	26	1	1	1	3	2	17^{1}	11	0	2.1	9.9	19	54%	.268	0.87	1.04	1.98	0.7				
2016	MIN	MLB	26	0	1	0	2	1	3^{2}	8	1	9.8	12.3	5	36%	.538	3.27	12.27	2.81	0.1	97.6	33	56	9
2016	ANA	MLB	26	1	2	0	5	5	21^{2}	17	2	5.4	10.0	24	40%	.273	1.38	4.57	5.35	0.0	97.7	33	56	9
2017	SLC	AAA	27	0	1	0	5	5	24	30	4	3.4	11.6	31	48%	.406	1.62	6.00	2.81	0.7				
2017	ANA	MLB	27	4	5	0	13	13	67^{1}	48	6	5.6	10.0	75	47%	.255	1.34	3.74	4.62	0.7	98.0	30	62	56
2018	*ANA*	*MLB*	*28*	*4*	*4*	*0*	*24*	*13*	73^{1}	*67*	*10*	*4.1*	*10.1*	*82*	*45%*	*.302*	*1.38*	*4.36*	*4.59*	*0.9*	*97.4*	*31*	*61*	*40*
2019	*ANA*	*MLB*	*29*	*5*	*6*	*0*	*28*	*17*	120^{1}	*109*	*16*	*4.1*	*10.3*	*138*	*45%*	*.304*	*1.36*	*4.29*	*4.44*	*1.3*	*97.0*	*31*	*61*	*38*

Breakout: 24% Improve: 47% Collapse: 15% Attrition: 27% MLB: 71% *Comparables: Mike Bolsinger, Eric Surkamp, Nate Karns*

It's a tale as old as time: A former first-round pick and top-20 prospect flashes incredible stuff, then struggles and is moved to the bullpen before finally getting thrown in as part of a blockbuster Hector Santiago-for-Ricky Nolasco deal. Then a funny thing happened. An unexpected twist to the story, if you will. Meyer was pretty good for the Halos in 2017. He walked almost everyone, sure, but he also littered the field with strikeouts thanks to a fastball he could pump up to 100 mph and a power curve that generated plenty of whiffs. Things were finally looking up for Meyer until a torn labrum ended his 2017 season. And his 2018 season. It's a tale as old as time.

Keynan Middleton RHP Born: 09/12/93 Age: 24 Bats: R Throws: R Height: 6'2" Weight: 185 Origin: Round 3, 2013 Draft (#95 overall)

YEAR	TEAM	LVL	AGE	W	L	SV	G	GS	IP	H	HR	BB/9	K/9	K	GB%	BABIP	WHIP	ERA	DRA	WARP	MPH	CMD	PWR	STM
2015	BUR	A	21	6	11	0	26	26	125^{2}	148	15	3.4	6.3	88	40%	.336	1.55	5.30	7.94	-4.0				
2016	INL	A+	22	1	1	0	25	0	36^{1}	22	7	5.0	13.9	56	34%	.227	1.16	3.72	2.09	1.2				
2016	ARK	AA	22	0	0	6	13	0	15	11	1	2.4	10.8	18	42%	.270	1.00	1.20	3.06	0.3				
2016	SLC	AAA	22	0	1	2	8	0	14^{2}	14	1	2.5	8.6	14	48%	.302	1.23	4.91	4.25	0.1				
2017	SLC	AAA	23	0	0	2	10	0	12^{2}	11	0	2.8	5.7	8	36%	.282	1.18	2.84	5.99	-0.1				
2017	ANA	MLB	23	6	1	3	64	0	58^{1}	60	11	2.8	9.7	63	38%	.318	1.34	3.86	4.39	0.5	99.2	42	73	53
2018	*ANA*	*MLB*	*24*	*2*	*4*	*0*	*59*	*0*	*62*	*61*	*11*	*3.8*	*9.1*	*63*	*38%*	*.295*	*1.40*	*4.95*	*5.08*	*0.0*	*99.0*	*43*	*75*	*55*
2019	*ANA*	*MLB*	*25*	*2*	*1*	*0*	*42*	*0*	44^{2}	*41*	*9*	*4.0*	*9.5*	*47*	*38%*	*.282*	*1.36*	*5.13*	*5.35*	*-0.1*	*98.8*	*44*	*76*	*55*

Breakout: 21% Improve: 29% Collapse: 4% Attrition: 21% MLB: 42% *Comparables: Ian Krol, Juan Oviedo, Logan Kensing*

It was a big year for K. Middletons. Keynan made his big-league debut for the Halos, acquitting himself well and entrenching himself as a potential ninth-inning option for the club. His cousin [not fact checked] Kate, the Duchess of Cambridge, is expecting her third child, entrenching herself as not only a fashionista but a philanthropic icon the world over. So, pretty much the same thing. The younger Middleton started folding a changeup into his arsenal late in the season—he had scrapped the pitch after spring training—and had success, jumping straight into a 33 percent whiff rate during September. With a more diverse pitch mix to go with his heater that can scrape 101 mph, the right-hander could be looking at a coronation in 2018.

Ricky Nolasco RHP Born: 12/13/82 Age: 35 Bats: R Throws: R Height: 6'2" Weight: 235 Origin: Round 4, 2001 Draft (#108 overall)

YEAR	TEAM	LVL	AGE	W	L	SV	G	GS	IP	H	HR	BB/9	K/9	K	GB%	BABIP	WHIP	ERA	DRA	WARP	MPH	CMD	PWR	STM
2015	MIN	MLB	32	5	2	0	9	8	37^{1}	50	3	3.4	8.4	35	42%	.392	1.71	6.75	3.80	0.6	93.5	47	34	0
2016	MIN	MLB	33	4	8	0	21	21	124^{2}	139	18	2.1	6.7	93	43%	.315	1.35	5.13	4.42	1.3	93.7	50	35	80
2016	ANA	MLB	33	4	6	0	11	11	73	63	8	1.8	6.3	51	46%	.257	1.07	3.21	4.05	1.1	93.0	50	35	80
2017	ANA	MLB	34	6	15	0	33	33	181	205	35	2.9	7.1	143	41%	.311	1.45	4.92	6.00	-0.9	92.8	53	31	78
2018	*ANA*	*MLB*	*35*	*8*	*11*	*0*	*27*	*27*	*154^{2}*	*171*	*26*	*3.1*	*6.7*	*116*	*43%*	*.303*	*1.44*	*5.11*	*5.40*	*0.5*	*91.9*	*50*	*32*	*58*
2019	*ANA*	*MLB*	*36*	*4*	*5*	*0*	*13*	*13*	*78^{2}*	*89*	*13*	*2.9*	*6.3*	*55*	*43%*	*.307*	*1.45*	*5.08*	*5.28*	*0.3*	*91.4*	*50*	*32*	*69*

Breakout: 13% Improve: 34% Collapse: 13% Attrition: 12% MLB: 81% *Comparables: Carl Pavano, Bartolo Colon, Josh Beckett*

The veteran right-hander "let it eat" last season, and by eat, of course we mean innings. Nolasco dutifully took the ball every fifth day for the Halos, a noble feat that wasn't matched by any of his staffmates. His production, however, was reminiscent of another famed Angels' righty, Mel Clark, immortalized in the documentary *Angels in the Outfield*. On July 1, perhaps with a little help from above, Nolasco fired a divine gem, a complete-game shutout of the Mariners, fanning seven batters while surrendering only three hits. It was a Hollywood ending. Unfortunately, the season didn't end there. In his next start, the native Californian got bombed for eight runs in an inning and two thirds. We'll have to cut that out of the movie. Additionally, by logging "only" 181 innings, Nolasco fell about 20 innings short of vesting a $13 million option for 2018. We'll cut that part out too.

Bud Norris RHP Born: 03/02/85 Age: 33 Bats: R Throws: R Height: 6'0" Weight: 215 Origin: Round 6, 2006 Draft (#189 overall)

YEAR	TEAM	LVL	AGE	W	L	SV	G	GS	IP	H	HR	BB/9	K/9	K	GB%	BABIP	WHIP	ERA	DRA	WARP	MPH	CMD	PWR	STM
2015	BAL	MLB	30	2	9	0	18	11	66^{1}	84	14	3.4	6.8	50	44%	.329	1.64	7.06	5.58	-0.5	96.3	55	60	51
2015	SDN	MLB	30	1	2	0	20	0	16^{2}	16	1	3.2	11.3	21	61%	.349	1.32	5.40	3.90	0.2	97.8	55	60	51
2016	ATL	MLB	31	3	7	0	22	10	70^{1}	68	6	3.6	7.7	60	53%	.302	1.36	4.22	4.34	0.8	96.0	46	51	59
2016	LAN	MLB	31	3	3	0	13	9	42^{2}	48	8	4.4	8.9	42	45%	.328	1.62	6.54	5.44	-0.1	95.8	46	51	59
2017	ANA	MLB	32	2	6	19	60	3	62	56	8	3.9	10.7	74	45%	.310	1.34	4.21	4.02	0.8	95.5	39	48	48
2018	*ANA*	*MLB*	*33*	*3*	*3*	*2*	*23*	*9*	*61^{2}*	*60*	*9*	*3.6*	*8.7*	*60*	*46%*	*.300*	*1.38*	*4.62*	*4.87*	*0.5*	*94.9*	*46*	*52*	*52*
2019	*ANA*	*MLB*	*34*	*8*	*8*	*5*	*54*	*20*	*154^{2}*	*154*	*24*	*3.4*	*8.9*	*153*	*46%*	*.304*	*1.38*	*4.64*	*4.80*	*1.2*	*94.3*	*43*	*50*	*52*

Breakout: 15% Improve: 52% Collapse: 16% Attrition: 13% MLB: 88% *Comparables: Ervin Santana, Jason Hammel, John Lackey*

Raise your hand if you had Bud Norris becoming a major-league closer. You're all liars. All of you. Most starters-turned-relievers cut down on their pitch mixes, featuring only their best offerings. Norris calls those guys underachievers. None of the journeyman righty's four pitches are standouts, but the whole is better than the sum of its parts, leading to an above-average 13 percent swinging strike rate in his relief appearances. You probably still don't feel good about seeing Norris when the bullpen door opens in the ninth inning, but he does now have Closer Experience™, which we all know means more than it should.

Shohei Ohtani RHP Born: 07/05/94 Age: 23 Bats: L Throws: R Height: 6'4" Weight: 205 Origin: International Free Agent, 2017

YEAR	TEAM	LVL	AGE	W	L	SV	G	GS	IP	H	HR	BB/9	K/9	K	GB%	BABIP	WHIP	ERA	DRA	WARP	MPH	CMD	PWR	STM
2018	*ANA*	*MLB*	*23*	*8*	*10*	*0*	*24*	*24*	*144*	*129*	*18*	*2.7*	*9.3*	*148*	*46%*	*.291*	*1.19*	*3.55*	*3.91*	*2.5*				
2019	*ANA*	*MLB*	*24*	*9*	*7*	*0*	*23*	*23*	*151*	*126*	*18*	*2.4*	*10.1*	*170*	*47%*	*.299*	*1.10*	*3.33*	*3.71*	*3.1*				

Breakout: 26% Improve: 61% Collapse: 19% Attrition: 6% MLB: 97% *Comparables: Felix Hernandez, Jose Fernandez, Dwight Gooden*

Ohtani is like a unicorn: something that theoretically exists only in fairy tales. A pitcher who throws a triple-digit heater and pairs it with two double-plus pitches while mashing taters at the plate, with speed to boot, sounds more mythical than horned horses. Astronomically speaking, he's Halley's Comet. You're unlikely to see it more than once in a lifetime. After changing our understanding of baseball on one side of the Pacific Ocean, now he's set to do the same on the other, and he has all the skills necessary to do so. That said, don't let the hype fly higher than it should. Unlike most of the NPB players who've made the jump to the big leagues, Ohtani is still a work in progress, an unfinished product. He'll need time to adjust to a whole new level of competition—especially at the plate. But once he does, he could be the single most fascinating superstar in the game—you know, aside from the one who will track down fly balls in center field while Ohtani is on the mound.

Blake Parker RHP Born: 06/19/85 Age: 32 Bats: R Throws: R Height: 6'3" Weight: 225 Origin: Round 16, 2006 Draft (#479 overall)

YEAR	TEAM	LVL	AGE	W	L	SV	G	GS	IP	H	HR	BB/9	K/9	K	GB%	BABIP	WHIP	ERA	DRA	WARP	MPH	CMD	PWR	STM
2016	TAC	AAA	31	1	2	19	38	0	39^{2}	24	4	2.5	12.7	56	44%	.256	0.88	2.72	0.99	1.8				
2016	SEA	MLB	31	0	0	0	1	0	1	1	0	9.0	0.0	0	75%	.250	2.00	0.00	6.61	0.0	94.4	50	40	42
2016	NYA	MLB	31	1	0	1	16	0	16^{1}	16	1	4.4	8.3	15	49%	.312	1.47	4.96	5.67	-0.1	94.2	50	40	42
2017	ANA	MLB	32	3	3	8	71	0	67^{1}	40	7	2.1	11.5	86	48%	.229	0.83	2.54	2.57	1.9	95.0	56	50	51
2018	*ANA*	*MLB*	*33*	*2*	*4*	*25*	*53*	*0*	*56*	*52*	*8*	*3.6*	*9.3*	*59*	*43%*	*.286*	*1.30*	*4.03*	*4.38*	*0.5*	*93.8*	*54*	*47*	*46*
2019	*ANA*	*MLB*	*34*	*2*	*1*	*16*	*46*	*0*	*49*	*45*	*8*	*4.3*	*8.9*	*48*	*43%*	*.278*	*1.39*	*5.04*	*5.23*	*0.0*	*93.2*	*54*	*47*	*46*

Breakout: 17% Improve: 40% Collapse: 34% Attrition: 13% MLB: 89% *Comparables: Fernando Rodriguez, Grant Balfour, Mike Adams*

Despite having a name that calls to mind the protagonist of some ill-advised John Hughes sequel like *Seventeen Candles*, Parker finally found a role that suits him the best as a new-age fireman reliever. At age 32 he spent the entire season on a big-league roster for the first time in his career and rewarded the Angels for their commitment, adding 2 mph to his fastball and posting the 12th-best cFIP of any reliever in baseball. Parker's success can in part be traced back to his decision to all but scrap his curveball in favor of a splitter that he now throws almost a third of the time, getting whiffs nearly 25 percent of the time, third best in all of baseball. It's cool to see a guy not only succeed after 10 years of starts and stops, but transform himself into a key piece of what looks to be a very strong bullpen in 2018.

J.C. Ramirez RHP

Born: 08/16/88 Age: 29 Bats: R Throws: R Height: 6'4" Weight: 250 Origin: International Free Agent, 2005

YEAR	TEAM	LVL	AGE	W	L	SV	G	GS	IP	H	HR	BB/9	K/9	K	GB%	BABIP	WHIP	ERA	DRA	WARP	MPH	CMD	PWR	STM
2015	ARI	MLB	26	1	1	0	12	0	15^{1}	15	1	2.3	6.5	11	62%	.298	1.24	4.11	4.47	0.0	97.7	46	68	47
2015	RNO	AAA	26	0	1	1	23	0	25	22	0	3.6	6.5	18	55%	.282	1.28	2.88	4.40	0.1				
2015	TAC	AAA	26	1	1	0	14	0	18	17	2	3.5	9.0	18	40%	.312	1.33	2.50	4.41	0.1				
2015	SEA	MLB	26	0	1	0	8	0	8^{1}	10	2	7.6	5.4	5	17%	.286	2.04	7.56	6.37	-0.2	99.1	46	68	47
2016	CIN	MLB	27	1	3	1	27	0	32^{1}	35	7	2.5	7.8	28	57%	.295	1.36	6.40	4.48	0.2	98.9	32	70	56
2016	ANA	MLB	27	2	1	1	43	0	46^{1}	42	5	2.5	6.0	31	55%	.259	1.19	2.91	3.75	0.7	99.6	32	70	56
2017	ANA	MLB	28	11	10	0	27	24	147^{1}	149	21	3.0	6.4	105	52%	.292	1.34	4.15	4.68	1.4	97.7	40	58	69
2018	*ANA*	*MLB*	*29*	*7*	*11*	*0*	*24*	*24*	*127*	*136*	*21*	*3.2*	*6.4*	*91*	*50%*	*.293*	*1.43*	*4.83*	*5.31*	*0.1*	*97.5*	*38*	*62*	*59*
2019	*ANA*	*MLB*	*30*	*8*	*11*	*0*	*28*	*28*	*174^{1}*	*187*	*29*	*3.5*	*6.6*	*128*	*50%*	*.294*	*1.46*	*5.34*	*5.54*	*0.2*	*97.1*	*38*	*61*	*61*

Breakout: 39% Improve: 55% Collapse: 24% Attrition: 21% MLB: 91% *Comparables: Jim Johnson, Tanner Scheppers, Anthony Swarzak*

Ramirez, one of only three current major leaguers from Nicaragua, was the most consistent Angels starter during the 2017 season, which says more about the rotation than it does about Ramirez. It wasn't always pretty for the journeyman right-hander, but outside of a forgettable June, Ramirez rode a high-90s fastball to what should have been a 2018 rotation spot written in ink. Sadly, the run of excellent mediocrity came to a screeching halt in mid-August when Ramirez suffered a partially torn UCL. He opted for stem-cell treatment, à la his teammate, Garrett Richards, with the hopes of returning to the rotation in 2018. Pencil it is then.

Garrett Richards RHP

Born: 05/27/88 Age: 30 Bats: R Throws: R Height: 6'3" Weight: 210 Origin: Round 1, 2009 Draft (#42 overall)

YEAR	TEAM	LVL	AGE	W	L	SV	G	GS	IP	H	HR	BB/9	K/9	K	GB%	BABIP	WHIP	ERA	DRA	WARP	MPH	CMD	PWR	STM
2015	ANA	MLB	27	15	12	0	32	32	207^{1}	181	20	3.3	7.6	176	56%	.274	1.24	3.65	2.96	5.2	97.8	40	63	80
2016	ANA	MLB	28	1	3	0	6	6	34^{2}	31	2	3.9	8.8	34	47%	.302	1.33	2.34	3.15	0.9	98.5	46	62	50
2017	ANA	MLB	29	0	2	0	6	6	27^{2}	18	1	2.3	8.8	27	55%	.233	0.90	2.28	3.28	0.7	97.2	55	63	0
2018	*ANA*	*MLB*	*30*	*11*	*13*	*0*	*30*	*30*	*189*	*172*	*20*	*3.5*	*8.1*	*170*	*50%*	*.286*	*1.29*	*3.78*	*4.17*	*2.7*	*97.0*	*43*	*63*	*37*
2019	*ANA*	*MLB*	*31*	*11*	*11*	*0*	*30*	*30*	*191^{2}*	*178*	*27*	*3.5*	*8.4*	*179*	*50%*	*.284*	*1.32*	*4.61*	*4.76*	*1.9*	*96.3*	*46*	*62*	*28*

Breakout: 11% Improve: 45% Collapse: 39% Attrition: 20% MLB: 95% *Comparables: Brandon Webb, Johnny Cueto, Roy Halladay*

The 2017 season was unkind to the Angels' ace, yet there were a lot of positives when he did step between the foul lines. First and foremost, he pitched. Richards blamed his injuries in part on his changeup, so he hip-pocketed the pitch in favor of a slider that was one of the hardest in the league. It was a successful approach for Richards: The slider induced groundballs around a 75 percent clip and generated a 21 percent whiff rate, which, as the bald bard Larry David might say, is prettay, prettay, prettay good. As always with Richards, it will be more about health than anything else, but here's hoping 2018 brings the former Oklahoma Sooner good tidings because a healthy Garrett Richards is a fun Garrett Richards.

Matt Shoemaker RHP

Born: 09/27/86 Age: 31 Bats: R Throws: R Height: 6'2" Weight: 225 Origin: Undrafted Free Agent, 2008

YEAR	TEAM	LVL	AGE	W	L	SV	G	GS	IP	H	HR	BB/9	K/9	K	GB%	BABIP	WHIP	ERA	DRA	WARP	MPH	CMD	PWR	STM
2015	ANA	MLB	28	7	10	0	25	24	135^{1}	135	24	2.3	7.7	116	42%	.285	1.26	4.46	4.50	0.9	93.5	41	40	59
2016	ANA	MLB	29	9	13	0	27	27	160	166	18	1.7	8.0	143	42%	.315	1.23	3.88	3.58	3.3	94.4	50	42	73
2017	ANA	MLB	30	6	3	0	14	14	77^{2}	73	15	3.2	8.0	69	40%	.278	1.30	4.52	5.15	0.4	93.9	48	40	51
2018	*ANA*	*MLB*	*31*	*8*	*12*	*0*	*26*	*26*	*156*	*158*	*25*	*2.9*	*7.8*	*135*	*42%*	*.293*	*1.33*	*4.42*	*4.87*	*0.9*	*93.2*	*47*	*41*	*60*
2019	*ANA*	*MLB*	*32*	*10*	*11*	*0*	*30*	*30*	*188^{1}*	*190*	*31*	*2.9*	*7.9*	*166*	*42%*	*.293*	*1.33*	*4.84*	*5.02*	*1.3*	*92.8*	*48*	*41*	*60*

Breakout: 22% Improve: 52% Collapse: 18% Attrition: 16% MLB: 89% *Comparables: Colby Lewis, Josh Towers, Brett Myers*

There are two ways to look at Shoemaker's 2017 campaign. On the one hand, it's a miracle that he came back to pitch after his 2016 season was cut short by a line drive that fractured his skull and required surgery to stop the bleeding in his brain. On the other, The Cobbler (more a foil to Batman than to batsmen) followed up his stellar breakout with something of a dud, seeing huge spikes in both walks and homers, en route to his worst season as a member of the Angels' rotation. It's always great to see the glass as half full; however, the hand that holds the glass—and the same one Shoemaker uses to grip his vicious splitter—was out of commission much of the last four months of 2017, as a forearm injury derailed and eventually ended his season.

Tyler Skaggs LHP

Born: 07/13/91 Age: 26 Bats: L Throws: L Height: 6'4" Weight: 215 Origin: Round 1, 2009 Draft (#40 overall)

YEAR	TEAM	LVL	AGE	W	L	SV	G	GS	IP	H	HR	BB/9	K/9	K	GB%	BABIP	WHIP	ERA	DRA	WARP	MPH	CMD	PWR	STM
2016	SLC	AAA	24	3	2	0	7	7	32^{1}	19	2	2.2	12.5	45	39%	.246	0.84	1.67	1.31	1.5				
2016	ANA	MLB	24	3	4	0	10	10	49^{2}	51	5	4.2	9.1	50	44%	.331	1.49	4.17	4.98	0.2	95.7	53	43	31
2017	SLC	AAA	25	0	1	0	3	3	10	14	0	5.4	6.3	7	54%	.400	2.00	8.10	6.52	-0.1				
2017	ANA	MLB	25	2	6	0	16	16	85	90	13	3.0	8.0	76	42%	.318	1.39	4.55	4.71	0.8	94.0	61	39	41
2018	*ANA*	*MLB*	*26*	*7*	*10*	*0*	*23*	*23*	*121*	*119*	*17*	*3.5*	*8.7*	*117*	*42%*	*.297*	*1.37*	*4.16*	*4.59*	*1.1*	*94.2*	*59*	*41*	*37*
2019	*ANA*	*MLB*	*27*	*9*	*11*	*0*	*29*	*29*	*179*	*183*	*27*	*4.0*	*8.1*	*161*	*42%*	*.3*	*1.47*	*4.96*	*5.16*	*0.8*	*93.9*	*59*	*41*	*37*

Breakout: 34% Improve: 68% Collapse: 14% Attrition: 11% MLB: 92% *Comparables: Dallas Braden, Matt Garza, Patrick Corbin*

If you looked up "serviceable" in the dictionary, there might be a picture of Skaggs next to the definition. However, that picture would also likely be accompanied by an asterisk stating "if healthy." Staying on the mound has been the biggest hurdle for the native Californian, who has flashed brilliance during his last two abbreviated seasons, but hasn't translated it into sustained success. The Angels kept Skaggs on a short pitch count all season—only allowing him to throw 90 pitches during five of his 16 starts—but it didn't stop him from missing three months anyway. Already the southpaw has missed time with injuries to his shoulder, thigh, bicep, oblique and, of course, elbow, leading to his 2014 Tommy John surgery. Millennials really are breaking everything.

Huston Street RHP Born: 08/02/83 Age: 34 Bats: R Throws: R Height: 6'0" Weight: 205 Origin: Round 1, 2004 Draft (#40 overall)

YEAR	TEAM	LVL	AGE	W	L	SV	G	GS	IP	H	HR	BB/9	K/9	K	GB%	BABIP	WHIP	ERA	DRA	WARP	MPH	CMD	PWR	STM
2015	ANA	MLB	31	3	3	40	62	0	62^1	52	7	2.9	8.2	57	36%	.263	1.16	3.18	3.53	0.9	91.6	63	21	48
2016	ANA	MLB	32	3	2	9	26	0	22^1	31	5	4.8	5.6	14	38%	.351	1.93	6.45	5.42	-0.1	90.9	45	31	25
2017	ANA	MLB	33	0	0	0	4	0	4	2	0	2.2	6.8	3	36%	.182	0.75	0.00	2.71	0.1	90.4			
2018	*ANA*	*MLB*	*34*	*2*	*0*	*6*	*33*	*0*	*34^1*	*33*	*6*	*4.1*	*7.2*	*28*	*39%*	*.275*	*1.42*	*5.36*	*5.67*	*-0.1*	*90.2*	*56*	*24*	*34*
2019	*ANA*	*MLB*	*35*	*2*	*0*	*7*	*36*	*0*	*35^1*	*37*	*7*	*5.0*	*6.2*	*24*	*39%*	*.272*	*1.59*	*6.41*	*6.72*	*-0.6*	*89.2*	*51*	*26*	*30*

Breakout: 10% Improve: 23% Collapse: 37% Attrition: 8% MLB: 83% *Comparables: Guillermo Mota, Jason Motte, Aaron Fultz*

It was truly a season for the ages. Against all odds, Street dominated the competition, not allowing a single run for the entire season. Of course, that season didn't begin until late June. And sadly, it ended less than two weeks later. At 34 years old, Street's velocity seems to be going the way of former teammate Jered Weaver's, and the former Longhorn doesn't strike guys out the way he used to. Still, he's been pretty-to-very good for 12 seasons, and there's something poetic about a Texas gunslinger shooting until he doesn't have any bullets left.

Nick Tropeano RHP Born: 08/27/90 Age: 27 Bats: R Throws: R Height: 6'4" Weight: 200 Origin: Round 5, 2011 Draft (#160 overall)

YEAR	TEAM	LVL	AGE	W	L	SV	G	GS	IP	H	HR	BB/9	K/9	K	GB%	BABIP	WHIP	ERA	DRA	WARP	MPH	CMD	PWR	STM
2015	SLC	AAA	24	3	6	0	16	16	88	97	9	3.7	9.8	96	42%	.353	1.51	4.81	3.70	1.6				
2015	ANA	MLB	24	3	2	0	8	7	37^2	40	2	2.4	9.1	38	42%	.342	1.33	3.82	3.25	0.8	93.4	47	37	57
2016	ANA	MLB	25	3	2	0	13	13	68^1	70	14	4.1	9.0	68	36%	.309	1.48	3.56	5.95	-0.5	93.4	39	37	47
2018	*ANA*	*MLB*	*27*	*2*	*2*	*0*	*6*	*6*	*35*	*33*	*6*	*3.5*	*9.0*	*35*	*40%*	*.291*	*1.34*	*4.76*	*5.02*	*0.3*	*92.9*	*42*	*37*	*52*
2019	*ANA*	*MLB*	*28*	*8*	*11*	*0*	*29*	*29*	*175^1*	*191*	*34*	*2.9*	*6.7*	*131*	*40%*	*.294*	*1.42*	*5.42*	*5.65*	*0.0*	*92.6*	*40*	*37*	*50*

Breakout: 36% Improve: 56% Collapse: 16% Attrition: 28% MLB: 85% *Comparables: J.A. Happ, Jacob deGrom, Matt Barnes*

What is there to say about Tropeano that hasn't already been said about Alex Meyer? Or Matt Shoemaker? Or Garrett Richards? Or C.J. Wilson? The Stony Brook product spent the entire 2017 season on the shelf recovering from Tommy John surgery. While he allows a few too many fly balls for comfort in this homerrific climate, Tropeano could be a useful back-end starter for the Halos when he returns in 2018.

Lineouts

Hitters

HITTER	POS	TEAM	LVL	AGE	PA	R	2B	3B	HR	RBI	BB	K	SB	CS	AVG/OBP/SLG	TAv	VORP	BABIP	BRR	FRAA	WARP
Dustin Ackley	LF	SLC	AAA	29	505	66	27	3	6	59	54	71	3	2	.261/.340/.376	.247	-1.5	.295	0.0	1B(16): 0.7, LF(7): -0.1	-0.1
Michael Bourn	OF	NOR	AAA	34	51	8	0	2	0	0	10	8	3	0	.220/.373/.317	.283	4.6	.273	1.9	CF(6): -0.8, LF(3): 0.0	0.4
	OF	SLC	AAA	34	106	15	2	1	2	9	8	16	4	5	.260/.317/.365	.221	-2.6	.295	-0.7	CF(10): -2.1, LF(6): -0.4	-0.4
Ramon Flores	OF	ANA	MLB	25	9	0	0	0	0	1	0	1	0	0	.125/.111/.125	.120	-1.2	.125	0.0	RF(3): 0.5	-0.1
	OF	SLC	AAA	25	493	65	21	5	10	71	68	70	12	2	.312/.409/.460	.301	33.5	.353	0.2	RF(51): 4.1, LF(31): -3.0	3.5
Nick Franklin	2B	MIL	MLB	26	89	7	2	1	2	10	5	19	2	0	.195/.258/.317	.224	-1.8	.230	-0.6	LF(16): 3.7, RF(2): 0.4	0.2
	2B	ANA	MLB	26	30	2	1	0	0	2	5	3	0	0	.125/.300/.167	.188	-1.2	.143	0.2	2B(8): 0.3, LF(3): -0.2	-0.1
Michael Hermosillo	OF	INL	A+	22	64	5	6	0	0	2	9	15	5	2	.321/.438/.434	.316	4.1	.447	-1.3	CF(9): -2.3, LF(3): -0.3	0.2
	OF	MOB	AA	22	340	40	13	2	4	26	40	73	21	9	.248/.361/.353	.284	15.2	.316	-2.0	CF(52): -2.3, RF(13): 2.3	1.7
	OF	SLC	AAA	22	129	20	6	1	5	16	7	28	9	2	.287/.341/.487	.271	5.1	.337	0.3	LF(14): -0.1, CF(10): 0.6	0.6
Jefry Marte	3B	ANA	MLB	26	145	10	5	0	4	14	13	34	1	0	.173/.269/.307	.207	-7.7	.200	-2.1	1B(28): -0.8, 3B(10): 0.6	-0.7
	3B	SLC	AAA	26	205	26	10	0	9	39	17	32	6	1	.265/.332/.465	.266	4.5	.276	-0.1	1B(31): -0.7, 3B(11): -1.3	0.2
Jacob Pearson	OF	ANG	Rk	19	176	20	7	1	0	13	15	37	5	3	.226/.302/.284	.222	-4.5	.297	-0.8	LF(30): 0.8, CF(9): 0.8	-0.3
Carlos Perez	C	SLC	AAA	26	300	40	18	3	5	40	32	38	4	1	.352/.423/.502	.305	24.6	.392	-3.6	C(58): 0.3	2.4
	C	ANA	MLB	26	21	1	0	0	1	3	1	6	0	0	.100/.143/.250	.132	-1.9	.077	0.0	C(10): -0.2	-0.2
Leonardo Rivas	SS	BUR	A	19	116	24	5	0	0	7	20	22	8	1	.267/.412/.322	.305	12.5	.348	2.8	SS(21): 1.7, 2B(4): -0.2	1.5
	SS	ORM	Rk	19	183	37	6	4	2	29	39	22	11	0	.299/.462/.445	.297	18.5	.339	1.7	SS(28): 3.3, 2B(8): -0.2	1.9
Shane Robinson	OF	SLC	AAA	32	385	64	21	5	2	47	28	37	15	1	.319/.370/.425	.281	21.7	.347	2.8	CF(33): 3.7, RF(27): 5.6	3.0
	OF	ANA	MLB	32	35	7	0	0	0	1	3	5	2	0	.194/.257/.194	.199	-0.1	.222	1.3	RF(8): 0.3, CF(5): 0.1	0.0
Harrison Wenson	C	ORM	Rk	22	167	34	8	0	13	48	25	38	0	0	.286/.413/.639	.308	17.5	.294	-0.2	C(29): -0.3, 1B(1): 0.1	1.6
Nonie Williams	SS	ANG	Rk	19	185	22	3	2	1	15	14	53	11	3	.220/.286/.280	.205	-4.8	.313	0.8	SS(31): -0.2	-0.4

Like Kris Humphries, Rebecca Black and Let's Rock Elmo, add **Dustin Ackley** to the list of things that were much more popular in 2011. It hurts to admit, but not more than the torn labrum that sapped the remaining morsels of power from the former top pick. ⚾ The Orioles thought **Michael Bourn** so nice, they released him twice. As Abraham Lincoln once said, "The mystic chords of memory will swell when again touched, as surely they will be, by the better angels of our nature." Well, two months later those better Angels released him too. ⚾ Upon receiving a $1.2 million signing bonus as the Angels' biggest international free agent splash in 2017, **Trent Deveaux**, a Bahamian outfielder, said he'd compete with Mike Trout for center field in three years, so we know he's not lacking confidence in either himself or the Halos' chances of re-signing Trout after the 2020 season. ⚾ **Ramon Flores** rebounded from a ghastly 2016 stint with the Brewers' big club by raking at Triple-A Salt Lake. It's possible the term "Quad-A" player was created specifically for the journeyman outfielder. ⚾ Last year's *Annual* touted **Nick Franklin** as a boom or bust hitter, and that sentiment certainly remained true in 2017, though perhaps without boom. The former first-rounder hit below the Mendoza Line for two separate clubs, producing a slash line that could only be considered impressive for a pitcher. ⚾ A little more power and patience would be nice, but even still, **Michael Hermosillo** had a solid 2017 season, floating through three levels while displaying strong speed and contact skills. ⚾ Last year in this space we said that **Jefry Marte** "doesn't draw walks but is finally showing the thump that's long been expected from him" and he rewarded us by losing the thump. ⚾ The Angels tossed a cool million dollars to outfielder **Jacob Pearson** to pry him out of his commitment to LSU, which is a reminder to youngsters everywhere that sometimes it pays not go to college. Just kidding, kids. Stay in school.

Don't do drugs. The three years with the Angels have been The (relatively) Good, The Bad and The Ugly for **Carlos Perez**, who once again saw his playing time cut due to inconsistency at the dish. If he doesn't start hitting soon, he won't be The Man With No Name, he'll be the man with no team. Tipping the scales at an unassuming 150 pounds, **Leonardo Rivas** will probably need to show ID before entering the stadium, but the young middle infielder has a great idea at the plate, and flashes more speed than *Reqiuem for a Dream*. In previous iterations of this compendium, **Shane Robinson** has been described as a 25th man, Quad-A outfielder, fifth outfielder, sixth outfielder, backup outfielder and diminutive outfielder, and yeah, that sounds about right. **Raidel Uceta**'s name anagrams smoothly to "acute derail," which, perhaps not coincidentally, accurately sums up what happened when Internet searches for him turned up empty. The 2017 J2 outfielder will look to tap into that SEO power when he makes his debut in 2018. Drafted as a college senior in the 24th round, **Harrison Wenson** made an immediate impact behind the dish in the Pioneer League, smacking 13 homers in his first 36 games. Over the course of a full season, the pace roughly translates to all of the homers. The Angels bet on raw strength and speed when they went over slot to pop **Nonie Williams** in the third round of the 2016 draft, but the shortstop needs more time to cook to be considered even medium rare.

Pitchers

PITCHER	TEAM	LVL	AGE	W	L	SV	G	GS	IP	H	HR	BB/9	K/9	K	GB%	BABIP	WHIP	ERA	DRA	WARP	MPH	CMD	PWR	STM
Manny Banuelos	SLC	AAA	26	5	6	0	39	9	95	107	4	4.6	8.1	85	48%	.350	1.64	4.93	6.31	-0.9				
Luke Bard	CHT	AA	26	4	3	5	33	0	52^{1}	50	4	3.4	13.4	78	35%	.380	1.34	2.58	2.58	1.4				
	ROC	AAA	26	0	0	0	8	0	13	13	1	2.8	14.5	21	30%	.400	1.31	3.46	3.71	0.2				
Vicente Campos	SLC	AAA	24	0	2	0	6	5	16^{1}	23	2	6.6	5.0	9	33%	.382	2.14	8.27	12.02	-1.1				
Jesus Castillo	BUR	A	21	1	1	0	4	4	19	13	1	0.9	10.4	22	54%	.267	0.79	2.37	2.28	0.7				
	INL	A+	21	8	3	0	16	15	82	86	13	2.0	8.1	74	57%	.309	1.27	3.62	2.18	2.9				
	MOB	AA	21	0	2	0	5	5	23^{2}	27	2	2.3	8.4	22	55%	.347	1.39	3.04	2.23	0.8				
Dayan Diaz	HOU	MLB	28	1	1	0	10	1	13	17	3	2.8	13.8	20	41%	.452	1.62	9.00	2.59	0.4	95.5	56	56	47
	FRE	AAA	28	4	3	2	35	0	48	47	3	3.4	9.8	52	43%	.336	1.35	4.12	3.10	1.1				
Deolis Guerra	SLC	AAA	28	4	1	2	31	0	41	26	3	1.8	9.0	41	46%	.228	0.83	1.98	2.15	1.4				
	ANA	MLB	28	2	2	0	19	0	25	20	4	4.3	7.9	22	37%	.239	1.28	4.68	4.44	0.2	92.9	34	28	44
Jason Gurka	SWB	AAA	29	0	0	0	13	0	16^{2}	25	4	1.1	10.8	20	62%	.412	1.62	5.40	2.04	0.6				
	SLC	AAA	29	3	1	1	30	0	34	29	1	2.9	9.5	36	56%	.318	1.18	2.12	2.23	1.1				
	ANA	MLB	29	0	0	0	3	0	0^{2}	2	0	13.5	0.0	0	0%	.500	4.50	0.00	11.44	0.0	92.5			43
Jake Jewell	INL	A+	24	0	1	0	3	3	16	11	1	1.7	8.4	15	62%	.227	0.88	2.25	2.15	0.6				
	MOB	AA	24	7	8	0	24	23	124^{2}	136	14	3.0	5.8	81	57%	.311	1.42	4.84	5.22	-0.1				
Eduardo Paredes	MOB	AA	22	0	0	1	9	0	12^{2}	11	0	2.8	12.1	17	38%	.344	1.18	1.42	2.75	0.3				
	SLC	AAA	22	1	0	2	25	0	37	27	3	4.1	9.2	38	34%	.253	1.19	2.92	5.03	0.1				
	ANA	MLB	22	0	1	1	18	0	22^{1}	21	2	2.4	6.9	17	50%	.297	1.21	4.43	4.49	0.2	94.7	50	52	48
Felix Pena	IOW	AAA	27	2	1	6	24	0	39	42	6	3.2	10.6	46	42%	.346	1.44	5.54	4.18	0.5				
	CHN	MLB	27	1	0	0	25	0	34^{1}	35	8	4.7	9.7	37	35%	.300	1.54	5.24	5.61	-0.2	96.0	33	56	47
Brooks Pounders	ANA	MLB	26	1	0	0	11	0	10^{1}	17	4	4.4	10.5	12	28%	.406	2.13	10.45	7.91	-0.3	94.2	40	46	48
	SLC	AAA	26	2	2	6	38	2	51^{1}	42	6	2.6	8.6	49	40%	.257	1.11	2.63	3.64	0.9				
Noe Ramirez	BOS	MLB	27	0	0	0	2	0	4^{2}	3	2	1.9	7.7	4	23%	.091	0.86	3.86	6.39	-0.1	91.2	49	18	45
	PAW	AAA	27	3	3	5	33	0	48^{2}	40	7	3.0	10.5	57	35%	.284	1.15	3.51	2.75	1.3				
	ANA	MLB	27	0	0	0	10	0	8^{1}	3	0	4.3	10.8	10	65%	.176	0.84	2.16	2.43	0.3	91.4	49	18	45
Chris Rodriguez	ORM	Rk	18	4	1	0	8	8	32^{1}	35	1	1.9	8.9	32	46%	.343	1.30	6.40	4.38	0.6				
	BUR	A	18	1	2	0	6	6	24^{2}	32	1	2.6	8.8	24	54%	.403	1.58	5.84	3.96	0.4				
Fernando Salas	NYN	MLB	32	1	2	0	48	0	45	60	7	4.0	9.4	47	47%	.379	1.78	6.00	5.87	-0.4	92.9	53	47	49
	ANA	MLB	32	1	0	0	13	0	13^{2}	7	0	1.3	5.9	9	58%	.184	0.66	2.63	5.24	0.0	91.7	53	47	49
Troy Scribner	SLC	AAA	25	11	4	0	20	19	103^{1}	100	13	3.3	9.0	103	38%	.306	1.34	4.35	3.43	2.5				
	ANA	MLB	25	2	1	0	10	4	23^{2}	17	7	3.8	6.8	18	25%	.161	1.14	4.18	5.59	0.0	89.6	41	23	63
Jose Valdez	ANA	MLB	27	0	0	0	1	0	1	1	1	9.0	9.0	1	33%	.000	2.00	18.00	9.85	-0.1	96.2	30	60	45
	SLC	AAA	27	1	1	1	10	0	12	10	0	3.8	11.2	15	44%	.312	1.25	6.00	4.73	0.1				
	ELP	AAA	27	2	3	0	23	0	28^{2}	34	2	3.5	9.4	30	39%	.368	1.57	5.02	3.91	0.4				
	SDN	MLB	27	0	0	0	13	0	17	20	7	2.1	8.5	16	30%	.283	1.41	7.94	7.66	-0.5	97.6	30	60	45
Blake Wood	CIN	MLB	31	1	4	0	55	0	57^{1}	64	5	4.6	9.7	62	55%	.364	1.62	5.65	4.61	0.4	97.5	42	63	54
	ANA	MLB	31	2	0	0	17	0	17	20	3	2.1	11.6	22	49%	.386	1.41	4.76	5.94	-0.1	97.0	42	63	54
Daniel Wright	ANA	MLB	26	0	1	0	5	2	19^{2}	21	1	3.7	5.0	11	33%	.317	1.47	4.58	5.56	0.0	92.3	43	30	58
	SLC	AAA	26	6	10	0	19	18	92^{2}	112	17	3.4	5.9	61	42%	.308	1.59	6.99	8.05	-2.4				

It seems impossible that **Manny Banuelos** is just 26 years old, but the former top prospect and Tommy John recoveree had enough success in Triple-A last year to latch on as an emergency starter somewhere. Six years and nearly as many arm injuries after being a Twins first-round pick out of Georgia Tech, **Luke Bard** finally reached Triple-A and got snatched up by the Angels in the Rule 5 draft. **Vicente Campos** missed a huge chunk of the season recovering from a fractured forearm. That hurt. What also hurt: the righty's 8.22 ERA in 23 innings. Once projected as a first-round arm, **Griffin Canning** slipped to 47th overall in the 2017 draft due to medical concerns. When healthy, the former UCLA Bruin boasts a heater that can touch the mid-90s, with a curveball and changeup that make him one of the most intriguing arms in the system. Since coming over from the Cubs' organization, **Jesus Castillo** has added a couple of ticks to his fastball, thanks in large part to adding a few pounds on his slight frame. While he's not a huge strikeout asset, he gets a lot of groundballs and has fared well according to cFIP and DRA. The Angels nabbed **Dayan Diaz** off waivers in September from an Astros team overflowing with relief arms. The Colombian ramps his heater up to 97 while featuring a smoke show of a slider that can hit the low-90s. I guess you could say he spits that hot fire. DAYAN, DAYAN, DAYAN. **Deolis Guerra** saw his walk rate nearly quadruple during the 10 weeks it took him to go from surprisingly solid bullpen cog in 2016 to unclaimed through waivers. Apparently relievers are pretty volatile. Who knew? When **Jason Gurka** went from Coors Field to Angel Stadium it was like trading a unicycle with a flat tire for a Honda Civic. Those things, like left-handed pitchers, run forever, you know. **Jake Jewell** pitched well in three games at Inland Empire. Once upon a time that would've made him the (puts on sunglasses) Crown Jewell of the Angels' system, but Double-A hitters were less accommodating. There won't be any **Paredes** for **Eduardo**'s 2017 season (that was so, so bad, I'm sorry), as the young Venezuelan couldn't translate his gaudy minor-league strikeout numbers into big-league success in his first go-around. Auxiliary bullpen cast member **Felix Pena** has a sweet slider but a fastball that is much sweeter to batters before he gets a chance to bury it in the strike zone. **Brooks Pounders** has accrued about a fourth of a season's worth of service time on the back of a mid-90s fastball, a slider and a spot on the 40-man. I guess that makes him a quarter Pounders, or an ex-Royal with cheese if you're nasty. **Noe Ramirez** gave up nine dingers in 30 2/3 innings with the Red Sox before being shipped west, where he managed to hold opponents homerless in almost nine innings of work. He's the best Boston to Los Angeles success story since Matt Damon. **Chris Rodriguez**, the Angels' fourth-round pick in 2016, was promoted to the Midwest League a couple of weeks after his 19th birthday and held his own there thanks to a well-rounded four-pitch mix. The year is 2049. **Fernando Salas** rides a three-pitch mix to a mediocre first half before being claimed by the Angels for the stretch run. The sun sets in the west. With the rotation in shambles, the Angels called on **Troy Scribner** to make four starts for the big club. Unfortunately, in those starts he tossed only 16 2/3 innings and gave up six homers. D'oh. **Nate Smith**'s career has had more stops and starts than a city block without synced traffic lights. The southpaw once again lost most of his season to nagging injuries, but was impressive in ultra short bursts. He'll once again hope to travel uninterrupted to the big club for a 2018 debut. **Jose Valdez** faced 48 right-handed batters in the big leagues last year and allowed 11 extra-base hits, including six homers. They're gonna miss him when he's gone. Although **Blake Wood**'s sinker touches 99 mph, putting in a waiver claim on a Reds reliever feels a little like ordering sushi from the gas station. Do you like lima beans and hate pizza? Do you like walks and hate strikeouts? Then **Daniel Wright** is your man. His changeup is kinda good, so at least there's that.

League Leaders 2017

MLB OPS – Mike Trout, 1.071

MLB True Average – Mike Trout, .360

LOS ANGELES DODGERS

Essay by Grant Brisbee

Player comments by Wilson Karaman and BP staff

The Dodgers might or might not win the World Series in the next decade. They might win three pennants, they might win five championships or they might be eliminated in the NLDS in 10 straight seasons. The rough one-in-eight odds of the postseason would suggest something similar to the Braves of the '90s (multiple pennants, one championship), but you can adjust those estimates upward or downward according to your tastes.

That doesn't really matter, though. It's interesting to wonder about the Dodgers' fate in future World Series, but only in the general sense of, "Gee, I wonder who's going to win the World Series this year." It's not interesting to dwell on it, to assume that the organization's existence still needs to be justified.

To put it another way, if you're comparing any team to the Braves of the '90s and intending it to be an insult, you're baseballing all wrong. Stop that.

No, if you want a really interesting discussion topic about the Los Angeles Dodgers—baseball's richest, smartest team—don't ask how many championships they're going to win or lose. Ask yourself this: "Will the Dodgers ever be bad again?"

I'm talking, like, ever. Will they have a disappointing regular season before Clayton Kershaw retires? Before Cody Bellinger retires? Before California slides into the ocean?

I'm skeptical.

If we define "bad" as under .500, we know it's not going to be this year. Baseball is strange, baseball is implausible, baseball is forever running through a crowded train station with an open parachute and a flaming rainbow wig. But baseball ain't that weird. The Dodgers will win more games than they lose in 2018. The old conventional wisdom posits that any team is just a few injuries away from oblivion. The new conventional wisdom notes that the Dodgers have *had* those injuries, year after year. Their best pitcher goes down for a month or two at a time, and they win. Their best hitter goes down, and they win. A key contributor drifts off into the abyss, and they bring up his replacement for the next decade.

There are three legs to the argument that the Dodgers will be good for the next twenty or thirty years.

Money is the obvious elephant in the room. It's a gold-plated, jewel-encrusted elephant, and it's lifting its tail, and, uh oh, buddy, it looks like more jewels are coming. Boy, this sure is a hard elephant to ignore. But it's easy to get sucked into everything else before remembering that the Dodgers are here by the graces of Guggenheim Partners. They have Yasiel Puig because they outbid the world on a hunch. They have Alex Wood because they signed Hector Olivera on a similar hunch and could afford to dump half of his contract months later. They still have Kershaw and Kenley Jansen because they're one of the six or seven teams that can afford to.

Point of order, though: They didn't win the NL pennant with the help of an obvious mercenary. The lineup didn't feature Robinson

DODGERS PROSPECTUS

2017 W-L: 104-58, 1st in NL West

Pythag	.627	2nd	B-Age	27.8	*9th*
RS/G	4.75	12th	P-Age	29.7	*27th*
RA/G	3.58	2nd	Salary	$241.1M	*1st*
TAv	.280	2nd	M$/MW	$4.1M	*15th*
TAv-P	.244	3rd	DL Days	1657	*30th*
FIP	3.68	2nd	$ on DL	27%	*29th*
DER	.719	2nd			

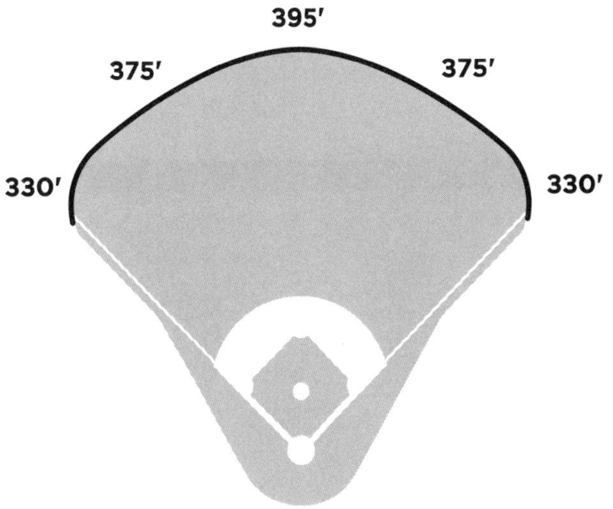

Outfield wall profile: **4′** to **8′**

Three-Year Park Factors

Runs	Runs/RH	Runs/LH	HR/RH	HR/LH
96	93	99	96	107

Top Hitter WARP	5.9 Justin Turner
Top Pitcher WARP	4.4 Clayton Kershaw
Top Prospect	Walker Buehler

2017 Hit List Ranking

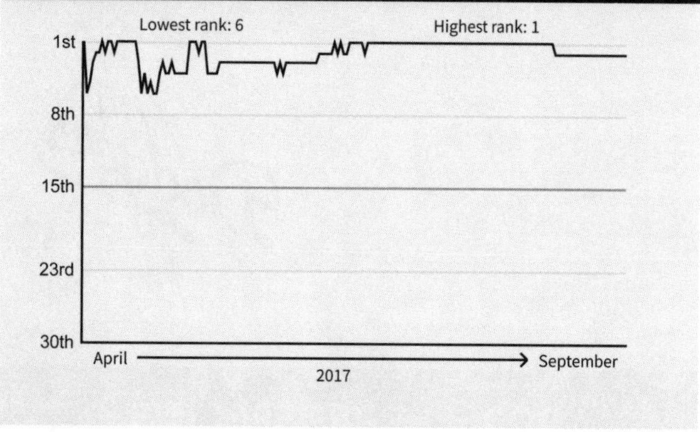

Committed Payroll (in millions)

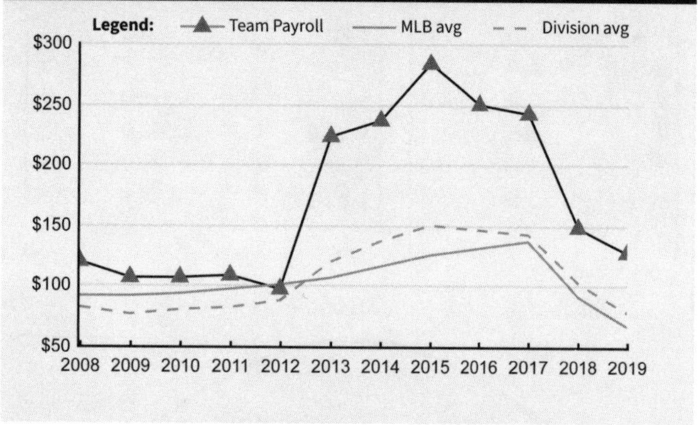

Farm System Ranking

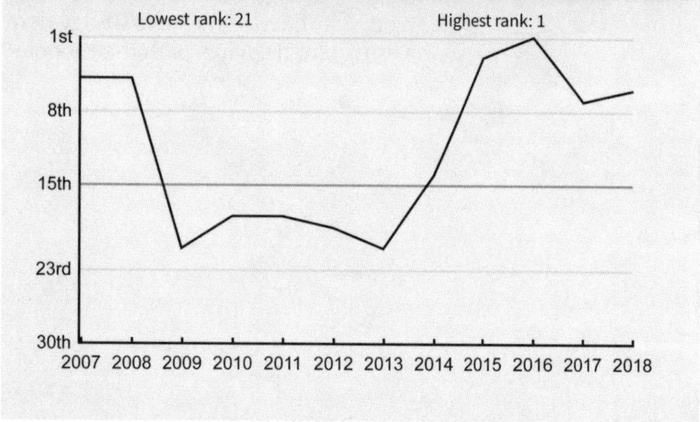

Personnel

President, Baseball Operations
Andrew Friedman

General Manager
Farhan Zaidi

SVP, Baseball Operations
Josh Byrnes

Manager
Dave Roberts

Cano, and the rotation wasn't retrofitted with Max Scherzer. The lineup was either homegrown (Corey Seager, Puig, Bellinger) or stuffed with the winnings of unfair trades (Yasmani Grandal, Austin Barnes, Chris Taylor). The one free agent regular was Justin Turner, and he hardly counts as a traditional mercenary.

Really, you have to get to the back of the rotation to find the obvious fruits of the money tree, with Brandon McCarthy and Kenta Maeda combining for 227 well-compensated innings, but it's not like you wouldn't find similar contracts on the Twins, Braves or Mariners. Spending money on the open market isn't what made the Dodgers great.

Spending money to *keep* their players, though ... well, that's different. The Dodgers could afford to give traditional money to an nontraditional player like Rich Hill, and they could gamble on an over-30 enigma like Turner. Kershaw and Jansen are the obvious points of reference, but the roster is filled with players who are paid handsomely to continue their Dodgers career, right down to Chase Utley, the Silver Fox, who quietly contributed 1.3 WARP after he was brought back.

And they'll get to do this indefinitely. Seager ain't goin' nowhere as long as the Dodgers want him around, and the same goes with Bellinger. Kershaw has an opt-out clause in his contract after the 2018 season, but do you think the Yankees are quietly stashing spare change to lure him away? Forget it. He's just going to get the old contract torn up and replaced on the same letterhead.

The money advantage isn't necessarily going to buy them Mike Trout in a couple years. It will, however, allow them to keep whatever players they've weaponized in his stead.

After money, the second leg is technically the Dodgers' farm system, except we know those are ephemeral and mysterious. A couple years of promotions, blown drafts and aggressive trades can rip a hole right through the best organizations, so it's not smart to assume they'll keep pumping out stars like it's no big deal. No, the second leg of the Dodgers' perpetual success is **the system**, man. That is, the system that guarantees young players will be underpaid for six or seven years, which is when they're likeliest to be their most productive.

It used to be that this system was how teams like the A's, Twins and Rays could still trade body blows with the richer teams in their divisions, and it still helps with the competitive balance of baseball generally. But the Dodgers, more than any of their peers, have pounced on the advantage that comes with a rich team spitting out prospects. Seager isn't just one of the game's greatest shortstops: He's a human escape-a-financial-blunder card. Because he'll be underpaid for the next few years, the Dodgers will feel comfortable giving $50 million to whatever round peg they source for their next round hole. Because if that idea fails, it's okay. Seager will pick up part of the tab.

Bellinger isn't just one of the most spectacular and productive examples of modern baseball; he's a reason the Dodgers felt comfortable paying market price to bring Turner, Hill and Jansen back. They feel comfortable with the idea that they'll have an all-star making Nick Punto money for a few seasons. There's a reason the Dodgers didn't cash out these guys for whatever Brian Dozier or David Price was dangled in front of them. Now they get to reap the rewards for several years.

When it's time for Seager and Bellinger to get their paydays, to cast off the yoke of indentured servitude and become a part of the veteran class, there will be players behind them, ready to subsidize it all. These future youngsters might not be all-stars, but they'll give the Dodgers a buffer they don't need. Just because they don't need it, though, doesn't mean they won't take advantage of it, over and over again.

The idea of the system and the benefits of a robust farm bleed into the final leg of this argument, and that's the **smarts** of this whole operation. I'm not just talking about the eggheads pulling strings in air-conditioned offices, though the Dodgers' executives are clearly among the class of baseball. I'm talking about the people who could look at a lump of Chris Taylor clay and help sculpt it into art, the people who made a compelling argument as to why Brandon Morrow would be a low-risk, high-reward option for a high-stakes bullpen. Up and down the organization, there's evidence of the angles the Dodgers spotted before other teams, the buried treasure that was available to all 30 teams, but secured by just one.

It's not just the spring invites and under-the-radar trades, either. Bellinger didn't just appear, fully formed, from the top five picks in a loaded draft. He was scouted and secured, developed and sharpened. He might have been the same whip-swinging power ogre if he came up through the Giants' system, but would you bet even $20 on that? This goes for Seager, or for Walker Buehler if he breaks through in 2018, and it applies to the prospects they actually do trade after overcoming their perennially disadvantageous draft position again and again.

Now, any crowing about the foundation and eternal success of the Los Angeles Dodgers should begin with an acknowledgment of what was inherited by the current front office. They had Kershaw. They had Puig. Seager was in the system. Jansen was moved out from behind the plate. The 2017 Dodgers weren't a Bugatti built from scratch out of parts ordered off the Internet. The chassis, engine and transmission were in place, and that's a serious head start.

Still, if you want to dumb it down, the secret of the Dodgers' success goes something like this: They're better at acquiring baseball players than other teams. They're better at fixing the players that are broken, and they're better at polishing the ones with imperfections. And after they hoard all of these talented players, they're better at keeping them around for as long as it takes.

This is how a team can win 43 games out of 50. This is how a team can win 104 games and still feel a sense of disappointment. This, all of this, is how it's possible to look at a franchise and assume that they'll be good in 25 years, when they'll be powered by Copy Bellinger, who hasn't even been born yet. If the Dodgers had just one of these three legs—the money, the pipeline and the smarts—they would be a fearsome organization. As is, I don't see how this stool can wobble.

Unfortunately, we have to bring it back to that first paragraph, in which we danced around the idea that the Dodgers most certainly did not win the World Series in 2017. Just as they haven't won it since their manager was in high school. Since *Super Mario Bros. 3* was released. I can go on. Email me.

At the end of this particular season, the Dodgers didn't win 11 postseason games because ... [*opens envelope*] ... Yu Darvish had two absolutely abominable outings at the worst possible time? Oh, come on. How are they supposed to prepare for that? The money allowed the Dodgers to slap Darvish's salary, luxury tax and all, onto their payroll. The system is why the Rangers coveted the Dodgers' sweet, sweet prospects. And the smarts are why the Dodgers could build a team that could effortlessly slide an ace behind their other ace and steamroll through the first two rounds of the postseason.

None of that could help them when the previously excellent baseball player took a momentary break from being excellent. It's been a problem in previous Octobers. It might be a problem this October. There's only so much a team can do.

Returning to that question about when the Dodgers will be bad again, there's an obvious comparison. The last time the Yankees finished under .500 was 1992, which was so long ago, it felt like the Dodgers had *just* won the World Series. Since then, the Yankees have spent, developed, fleeced and persevered, and right when it looked like they would be forced into a rebuilding phase, they nearly won the pennant themselves. That's 25 seasons without sucking, and it doesn't look like they're going to start now.

That's the Dodgers, except I think they're even better prepared. They've had a chance to study what happens to a team that relies on a wild, careening, free-spending approach to building a roster. They've learned what happens when a team gets too loose with its prospects and is sucked into win-now quicksand. They're going to take everything that made the Yankees impervious for a quarter-century and improve upon it.

That seems like an unqualified success to me, and it will continue indefinitely. Just how you and everyone in the greater Los Angeles area measure success, well, that's going to be a heckuva lot different. There are regrets. There are what-ifs. Mistakes were made. The 2017 experience wasn't nearly as magical as it should or could have been.

The Dodgers won't be bad again, though. And if they're not bad, they're good. And if they're good, they have a chance to trudge right back up that hill. And as long as they're trudging, with their money, youth and smarts, they'll have a much better chance than just about any other team in baseball.

They'll have that much better chance for years. The better chance is all an organization can ask for. The Dodgers might or might not win the World Series in the next decade, after all.

But they probably will.

—Grant Brisbee is a writer for SB Nation.

HITTERS

Austin Barnes C Born: 12/28/89 Age: 28 Bats: R Throws: R Height: 5'10" Weight: 190 Origin: Round 9, 2011 Draft (#283 overall)

YEAR	TEAM	LVL	AGE	PA	R	2B	3B	HR	RBI	BB	K	SB	CS	AVG/OBP/SLG	TAv	VORP	BABIP	BRR	FRAA	WARP
2015	OKL	AAA	25	335	40	17	2	9	42	35	36	12	2	.315/.389/.479	.333	38.6	.331	-1.5	C(78): 17.8	5.8
2015	LAN	MLB	25	37	4	2	0	0	1	6	6	1	0	.207/.361/.276	.257	1.1	.261	-0.2	C(11): 1.0, 3B(1): 0.0	0.2
2016	OKL	AAA	26	385	59	22	5	6	39	43	53	18	3	.295/.380/.443	.308	38.3	.335	3.3	C(63): 16.0, 2B(15): 1.3	5.6
2016	LAN	MLB	26	37	3	1	0	0	2	5	9	0	0	.156/.270/.188	.187	-1.0	.217	0.3	C(9): 0.2, 2B(7): -0.2	-0.1
2017	LAN	MLB	27	262	35	15	2	8	38	39	43	4	1	.289/.408/.486	.325	29.5	.329	0.5	C(55): 10.5, 2B(21): -0.1	4.0
2018	*LAN*	*MLB*	*28*	*364*	*48*	*18*	*2*	*10*	*42*	*41*	*61*	*8*	*2*	*.262/.353/.424*	*.277*	*25.3*	*.294*	*0.6*	*C 16*	*3.7*
2019	*LAN*	*MLB*	*29*	*337*	*45*	*16*	*1*	*11*	*41*	*41*	*61*	*7*	*2*	*.257/.355/.432*	*.289*	*24.1*	*.289*	*0.5*	*C 15*	*4.2*

Breakout: 6% Improve: 23% Collapse: 13% Attrition: 24% MLB: 73%

Comparables: John Jaso, J.R. Towles, Ryan Lavarnway

YEAR	TEAM	P. COUNT	FRM RUNS	BLK RUNS	THRW RUNS	TOT RUNS
2015	LAN	1229	0.5	0.5	-0.1	0.9
2015	OKL	10507	18.9	0.3	0.1	19.3
2016	LAN	819	0.4	0.0	0.0	0.3
2017	LAN	7057	10.3	1.3	-0.5	11.2
2018	*LAN*	*13399*	*18.5*	*0.9*	*-0.8*	*18.6*
2019	*LAN*	*12395*	*15.5*	*0.7*	*-0.6*	*15.6*

Since arriving from Miami in the Dee Gordon deal a few years back, Barnes has quietly and steadily evolved into the poster child of the Dodgers' penchant for developing athletic catchers. The mitt was dynamite by virtually all measurements, and in a testament to his agility he managed to log 76 innings at second base when he wasn't saving runs behind the dish. His advanced approach played well in his first sustained look at big-league pitching, with consistent gap-to-gap contact bolstering a surge in slugging. On a WARP-by-PA rate basis, he produced the second most value of any catcher in baseball. It all came to a head when he rode a hot second half to a borderline-unfathomable unseating of one of the league's most productive incumbents come playoff time. With two more pre-arbitration seasons to come, Barnes will enter 2018 as a delightful bargain for the leveraged Dodgers, and a primary driver of a classic Good Problem To Have for the team's catching depth chart.

Cody Bellinger 1B Born: 07/13/95 Age: 22 Bats: L Throws: L Height: 6'4" Weight: 210 Origin: Round 4, 2013 Draft (#124 overall)

YEAR	TEAM	LVL	AGE	PA	R	2B	3B	HR	RBI	BB	K	SB	CS	AVG/OBP/SLG	TAv	VORP	BABIP	BRR	FRAA	WARP
2015	RCU	A+	19	544	97	33	4	30	103	52	150	10	2	.264/.336/.538	.315	39.9	.314	2.5	1B(91): 8.8, CF(26): -0.1	5.3
2016	TUL	AA	20	465	61	17	1	23	65	59	94	8	2	.263/.359/.484	.313	32.0	.287	1.0	1B(81): 0.7, LF(13): 1.2	3.5
2017	OKL	AAA	21	77	15	4	0	5	15	9	22	7	0	.343/.429/.627	.341	9.0	.450	0.8	1B(16): 1.0, CF(2): -0.5	0.9
2017	LAN	MLB	21	548	87	26	4	39	97	64	146	10	3	.267/.352/.581	.331	48.6	.299	-0.2	1B(93): 0.7, LF(39): -2.4	4.8
2018	*LAN*	*MLB*	*22*	*610*	*93*	*26*	*2*	*37*	*103*	*64*	*165*	*10*	*2*	*.249/.329/.509*	*.287*	*27.7*	*.285*	*0.5*	*1B 4*	*2.9*
2019	*LAN*	*MLB*	*23*	*597*	*94*	*26*	*2*	*38*	*103*	*69*	*157*	*10*	*3*	*.254/.343/.529*	*.309*	*38.3*	*.287*	*0.3*	*1B 4*	*4.6*

Breakout: 4% Improve: 50% Collapse: 2% Attrition: 9% MLB: 83% *Comparables: Giancarlo Stanton, Jay Bruce, Travis Snider*

While not quite on the level of Isaac Hayes rolling up in his chandelier-laden '77 Cadillac Fleetwood in *Escape From New York*, Bellinger nonetheless made an entrance for the ages. The scouting reports pretty much nailed the fundamentals: Where evaluators had wondered about Bellinger's ability to handle the high hard stuff with his long, uppercut swing, he did indeed whiff a *ton* up the ladder. But there was more than enough boom to offset the busts, as he slugged .602 against elevated pitches en route to taking the lunch money of NL hurlers of both left- and right-handed persuasion with startling consistency for five straight months after a late-April promotion. The plate discipline translated, too, and his rare speed and athleticism for a first baseman allowed for versatile deployment onto the outfield grass. Instant stardom at 21 is a tough act, but Bellinger sure looks the part of an A-Number One building block for the Dodgers.

Yusniel Diaz OF Born: 10/07/96 Age: 21 Bats: R Throws: R Height: 6'1" Weight: 195 Origin: International Free Agent, 2015

YEAR	TEAM	LVL	AGE	PA	R	2B	3B	HR	RBI	BB	K	SB	CS	AVG/OBP/SLG	TAv	VORP	BABIP	BRR	FRAA	WARP
2016	RCU	A+	19	348	47	8	7	8	54	29	71	7	8	.272/.333/.418	.269	8.7	.326	-2.1	CF(34): -6.1, RF(15): -0.7	0.3
2017	RCU	A+	20	374	42	15	3	8	39	35	73	7	9	.278/.343/.414	.264	8.6	.328	-1.0	CF(29): 1.8, RF(26): -1.2	1.0
2017	TUL	AA	20	118	15	8	0	3	13	10	29	2	5	.333/.390/.491	.302	6.5	.434	-0.8	RF(26): -0.5, CF(5): -0.1	0.6
2018	*LAN*	*MLB*	*21*	*250*	*26*	*10*	*1*	*7*	*29*	*19*	*66*	*3*	*3*	*.232/.291/.383*	*.231*	*-0.3*	*.290*	*-0.8*	*RF 0, CF -1*	*-0.1*
2019	*LAN*	*MLB*	*22*	*378*	*46*	*16*	*2*	*13*	*47*	*31*	*100*	*4*	*5*	*.238/.302/.412*	*.257*	*7.3*	*.295*	*-0.7*	*RF 0, CF -2*	*0.6*

Breakout: 3% Improve: 11% Collapse: 3% Attrition: 11% MLB: 20% *Comparables: Jorge Bonifacio, Jose Tabata, Rymer Liriano*

Chapter Two of Diaz's stateside career got off to a slow start, as multiple, significant swing overhauls curtailed his early comfort and stifled his production during a return trip to High-A. But once the new moving parts clicked into place in late May, he was off and running: A .396/.438/.673 June presaged a promotion to Tulsa, where he raked as one of the younger regulars in the Texas League. The development hasn't been especially linear, but there's been a lot of it in a little time, and it has produced impressive progress through the fits and starts. His across-the-board skill set will likely undergo additional refinement at Double-A to start the 2018 campaign, with a cup of big-league Joe very much on the table by September.

Andre Ethier LF Born: 04/10/82 Age: 36 Bats: L Throws: L Height: 6'2" Weight: 210 Origin: Round 2, 2003 Draft (#62 overall)

YEAR	TEAM	LVL	AGE	PA	R	2B	3B	HR	RBI	BB	K	SB	CS	AVG/OBP/SLG	TAv	VORP	BABIP	BRR	FRAA	WARP
2015	LAN	MLB	33	445	54	20	7	14	53	43	75	2	3	.294/.366/.486	.314	29.0	.330	-2.7	RF(80): -2.5, LF(51): -0.2	2.8
2016	RCU	A+	34	35	7	4	0	0	3	1	6	0	0	.290/.343/.419	.291	2.0	.346	0.3	RF(3): 0.0, LF(2): -0.3	0.2
2016	LAN	MLB	34	26	2	1	0	1	2	2	6	0	0	.208/.269/.375	.235	-0.2	.235	-0.1	LF(4): -0.7	-0.1
2017	LAN	MLB	35	38	3	1	0	2	3	4	10	0	0	.235/.316/.441	.271	1.4	.273	0.0	LF(8): -1.2	0.0
2018	*LAN*	*MLB*	*36*	*250*	*27*	*12*	*2*	*6*	*29*	*25*	*49*	*1*	*1*	*.252/.333/.410*	*.256*	*6.6*	*.295*	*-0.8*	*LF -3, RF 0*	*0.4*
2019														*Out of baseball*						

Breakout: 0% Improve: 31% Collapse: 6% Attrition: 15% MLB: 68% *Comparables: David DeJesus, Johnny Damon, Mark DeRosa*

To burn out, or to fade away: an eternal question of preference in demise. Unfortunately for Ethier's pursuit of Dodger franchise history, the issue was more or less settled outside of his hands (and more specifically in his tibial and lower-back regions). He has been an at-times sneaky generational player for the 21st-century Dodgers, a homegrown Hollywood pseudo-star bought out of late-prime free agency into careerist comfort. The injuries robbed him of likely top-ten standing in all-time games played for those donning Dodger Blue. But even a faded "Daddy" still dots the top 20 in most of the club's career counting stat leaderboards. Regardless of style, the demise is of course eventual, and a declined option in November means his career in Los Angeles has likely ended after an oh-so-close run at a ring.

Logan Forsythe 2B Born: 01/14/87 Age: 31 Bats: R Throws: R Height: 6'1" Weight: 205 Origin: Round 1, 2008 Draft (#46 overall)

YEAR	TEAM	LVL	AGE	PA	R	2B	3B	HR	RBI	BB	K	SB	CS	AVG/OBP/SLG	TAv	VORP	BABIP	BRR	FRAA	WARP
2015	TBA	MLB	28	615	69	33	2	17	68	55	111	9	4	.281/.359/.444	.290	29.7	.323	-2.9	2B(126): -4.8, 1B(26): 0.6	2.8
2016	TBA	MLB	29	567	76	24	4	20	52	46	127	6	6	.264/.333/.444	.277	24.9	.314	0.6	2B(118): -7.9	1.8
2017	LAN	MLB	30	439	56	19	0	6	36	69	109	3	2	.224/.351/.327	.262	14.3	.299	0.5	2B(80): 4.8, 3B(42): -0.1	1.9
2018	*LAN*	*MLB*	*31*	*428*	*51*	*19*	*2*	*11*	*47*	*42*	*93*	*4*	*3*	*.245/.326/.390*	*.258*	*15.6*	*.294*	*-0.7*	*2B -2, 3B 1*	*1.0*
2019	*LAN*	*MLB*	*32*	*370*	*45*	*16*	*1*	*10*	*41*	*38*	*84*	*3*	*2*	*.236/.322/.385*	*.261*	*11.8*	*.284*	*-0.2*	*2B -1, 3B 1*	*1.2*

Breakout: 2% Improve: 44% Collapse: 5% Attrition: 8% MLB: 95% *Comparables: Orlando Hudson, Mark Ellis, Dick McAuliffe*

It was a year of transition for Forsythe, who wandered back west to Los Angeles in a January 2017 trade from Tampa, and at times he appeared stuck in the middle. He swung the bat less often than any other hitter to log 400 plate appearances, and while his walk rate ballooned, the passivity cost him his power. Coming off back-to-back seasons slugging .444, he stopped pulling the ball with any semblance of authority. Instead, lower-half injuries and deep counts forced reactive swings and an up-the-middle, ground-ball-heavier approach. Still, with Forsythe's snappy leather at second and an on-base clip of .435 in October, it's hard to imagine Dodger brass getting *too* upset—especially with a wholly reasonable $9 million club option for 2019 at their whim.

Yasmani Grandal C Born: 11/08/88 Age: 29 Bats: B Throws: R Height: 6'1" Weight: 235 Origin: Round 1, 2010 Draft (#12 overall)

YEAR	TEAM	LVL	AGE	PA	R	2B	3B	HR	RBI	BB	K	SB	CS	AVG/OBP/SLG	TAv	VORP	BABIP	BRR	FRAA	WARP
2015	LAN	MLB	26	426	43	12	0	16	47	65	92	0	1	.234/.353/.403	.276	20.4	.268	-4.0	C(107): 22.7, 1B(6): -0.1	4.6
2016	LAN	MLB	27	457	49	14	1	27	72	64	116	1	3	.228/.339/.477	.299	33.1	.250	-5.1	C(115): 30.8, 1B(4): 0.4	6.6
2017	LAN	MLB	28	482	50	27	0	22	58	40	130	0	1	.247/.308/.459	.272	25.8	.298	-2.6	C(117): 19.3	4.5
2018	*LAN*	*MLB*	*29*	*313*	*40*	*13*	*0*	*13*	*44*	*40*	*77*	*1*	*1*	*.230/.329/.426*	*.266*	*15.2*	*.269*	*-0.9*	*C 16*	*2.9*
2019	*LAN*	*MLB*	*30*	*400*	*56*	*16*	*0*	*17*	*53*	*54*	*100*	*0*	*0*	*.230/.336/.427*	*.278*	*19.9*	*.271*	*-2.6*	*C 20*	*4.4*

Breakout: 2% Improve: 40% Collapse: 7% Attrition: 13% MLB: 98% *Comparables: Miguel Montero, Chris Iannetta, Alex Avila*

YEAR	TEAM	P. COUNT	FRM RUNS	BLK RUNS	THRW RUNS	TOT RUNS
2015	LAN	13767	23.3	-0.8	0.0	22.5
2016	LAN	15887	25.6	0.3	0.5	26.5
2017	LAN	16211	17.6	-1.2	1.2	17.7
2018	*LAN*	*9601*	*15.0*	*-0.4*	*0.5*	*15.0*
2019	*LAN*	*12276*	*18.2*	*-0.5*	*0.6*	*18.3*

It's not often you see an elite defensive catcher hit 22 home runs and lose his job during a World Series run, but such was Grandal's unlikely fate. When he was at the dish and not behind it the strikeouts piled up, the exit velocity slowed and he stopped getting on base as often. All combined with noticeably poor performance in higher-leverage situations, the offensive production was lean and low for much of the season's push. And come shoving time his icy lumber was chilling on the October bench in favor of a former understudy doing everything he could do, and doing it better. It was an inglorious turn in what otherwise has been a nice prime run for the 29-year-old. He'll enter his walk year with questions and a lot to prove.

Curtis Granderson OF Born: 03/16/81 Age: 37 Bats: L Throws: R Height: 6'1" Weight: 200 Origin: Round 3, 2002 Draft (#80 overall)

YEAR	TEAM	LVL	AGE	PA	R	2B	3B	HR	RBI	BB	K	SB	CS	AVG/OBP/SLG	TAv	VORP	BABIP	BRR	FRAA	WARP
2015	NYN	MLB	34	682	98	33	2	26	70	91	151	11	6	.259/.364/.457	.314	49.2	.305	1.3	RF(149): 1.3, CF(2): 0.7	5.5
2016	NYN	MLB	35	633	88	24	5	30	59	74	130	4	2	.237/.335/.464	.296	37.7	.254	1.3	RF(110): 3.1, CF(36): -4.4	3.8
2017	NYN	MLB	36	395	58	22	3	19	52	53	90	4	2	.228/.334/.481	.294	26.4	.251	1.5	CF(59): -8.4, RF(30): 1.9	2.0
2017	LAN	MLB	36	132	16	2	0	7	12	18	33	2	0	.161/.288/.366	.258	2.9	.153	0.2	LF(26): -3.2, RF(8): 0.2	0.0
2018	*LAN*	*MLB*	*37*	*516*	*72*	*22*	*2*	*21*	*63*	*63*	*121*	*6*	*2*	*.228/.327/.429*	*.258*	*18.8*	*.262*	*1.1*	*CF -10, RF 1*	*1.1*
2019	*LAN*	*MLB*	*38*	*403*	*52*	*16*	*1*	*15*	*49*	*50*	*97*	*3*	*2*	*.213/.315/.396*	*.260*	*11.4*	*.249*	*0.9*	*CF -8, RF 0*	*0.5*

Breakout: 0% Improve: 22% Collapse: 12% Attrition: 11% MLB: 80% *Comparables: Brady Anderson, Ken Griffey, Bernie Williams*

The Grandy Man could not, at least not for the Dodgers. After a miserable April, he caught fire in May and hit .263/.383/.570 over his next 300 plate appearances before heading west in a late-August waiver deal. The curtains may not have dropped altogether after he left the shadows of Flushing, but they sure drooped. He hit a few Dodger dingers, and that was well and dandy, but after an overmatched drag to the pennant he was left to spectate for his third World Series loss. One of the perennial "good guys" of the game, Granderson will take his slowing bat and decayed defense in search of one more legacy crack at a farewell title in 2018.

Franklin Gutierrez RF Born: 02/21/83 Age: 35 Bats: R Throws: R Height: 6'2" Weight: 200 Origin: International Free Agent, 2000

YEAR	TEAM	LVL	AGE	PA	R	2B	3B	HR	RBI	BB	K	SB	CS	AVG/OBP/SLG	TAv	VORP	BABIP	BRR	FRAA	WARP
2015	TAC	AAA	32	209	34	12	0	7	31	23	43	2	0	.317/.402/.500	.315	16.8	.379	1.2	LF(29): 0.1, CF(1): 0.3	1.8
2015	SEA	MLB	32	189	27	11	0	15	35	14	54	0	0	.292/.354/.620	.334	16.8	.340	-0.7	LF(42): 3.7, RF(4): -0.2	2.2
2016	SEA	MLB	33	283	33	9	0	14	39	29	85	1	0	.246/.329/.452	.272	9.9	.309	1.2	RF(64): -4.6, LF(9): 0.1	0.6
2017	LAN	MLB	34	63	8	3	0	1	8	7	16	0	1	.232/.317/.339	.234	0.6	.308	0.8	LF(17): -1.5	-0.1
2018	*LAN*	*MLB*	*35*	*250*	*30*	*11*	*0*	*11*	*35*	*21*	*74*	*1*	*0*	*.236/.306/.437*	*.253*	*7.0*	*.295*	*0.4*	*LF 1, RF 0*	*0.9*
2019	*LAN*	*MLB*	*36*	*98*	*12*	*4*	*0*	*4*	*13*	*8*	*29*	*0*	*0*	*.228/.296/.418*	*.258*	*2.3*	*.288*	*0.1*	*LF 0, RF 0*	*0.3*

Breakout: 1% Improve: 21% Collapse: 10% Attrition: 26% MLB: 81% *Comparables: Justin Ruggiano, Marcus Thames, Josh Hamilton*

Sixteen years and some-odd days after John Hancocking his first professional contract with the Dodgers, Gutierrez signed on a blue dotted line again last winter amid the team's search up, down and sideways for a solution—*any* solution—to cure what had fatally ailed it against left-handed pitching. The theory behind the reunion was sound enough, as the flashes of brilliance and death to assorted flying things that had marked Gutierrez's when-healthy career included a noteworthy résumé of southpaw slaying. But Gutierrez sagged under the weight of inactivity as the team's 25th man, logging just eight starts in the season's first two months and recording just a single multi-hit game before a rare and chronic back condition flared up and foisted him onto the shelf for good in late June. As he heads into another round of free agency, it's quite possible his days of playing under a guaranteed contract are numbered.

Enrique Hernandez CF Born: 08/24/91 Age: 26 Bats: R Throws: R Height: 5'11" Weight: 200 Origin: Round 6, 2009 Draft (#191 overall)

YEAR	TEAM	LVL	AGE	PA	R	2B	3B	HR	RBI	BB	K	SB	CS	AVG/OBP/SLG	TAv	VORP	BABIP	BRR	FRAA	WARP
2015	OKL	AAA	23	64	6	2	0	1	9	4	14	1	0	.169/.219/.254	.187	-2.2	.200	0.6	SS(8): -0.4, CF(4): -0.1	-0.3
2015	LAN	MLB	23	218	24	12	2	7	22	11	46	0	2	.307/.346/.490	.315	18.2	.364	0.1	2B(20): 1.1, CF(19): -1.5	1.9
2016	LAN	MLB	24	244	25	8	0	7	18	28	64	2	0	.190/.283/.324	.240	0.5	.234	-0.9	LF(41): 2.6, CF(22): -0.7	0.3
2017	LAN	MLB	25	342	46	24	2	11	37	41	80	3	0	.215/.308/.421	.265	14.5	.254	2.6	CF(34): 5.8, LF(28): 0.7	2.3
2018	*LAN*	*MLB*	*26*	*414*	*48*	*21*	*2*	*12*	*48*	*36*	*85*	*3*	*1*	*.240/.308/.404*	*.253*	*13.7*	*.277*	*-0.3*	*2B 2, LF 1*	*1.4*
2019	*LAN*	*MLB*	*27*	*348*	*43*	*19*	*1*	*12*	*43*	*33*	*73*	*2*	*1*	*.242/.317/.422*	*.268*	*13.8*	*.277*	*0.5*	*2B 2, LF 1*	*1.9*

Breakout: 8% Improve: 57% Collapse: 7% Attrition: 15% MLB: 99% *Comparables: Khalil Greene, Didi Gregorius, Brandon Crawford*

We all play certain roles in life, it's just that some of us have the good fortune to have the contours and limits of those roles spelled out in painfully obvious detail. Such is the case of Kiké, a player who does some things well, does some other things not very well at all and shows precious middle ground between the two extremes. After a down year in 2016, he came back with a vengeance to reestablish himself as a vital member of the 25-man in Los Angeles, appearing once again at every position but the battery and throwing down a .310 TAv against southpaws. That was more than enough to offset a putrid .499 OPS against righties, though he managed to blur the lines a *bit* with a back-breaking grand slam off a right-hander amid an epic three-homer outburst in the pennant-clincher. With the first arbitrated pay raise of his career in pocket, he figures to line up in a similar role again for the Azul in 2018.

Ibandel Isabel 1B Born: 06/20/95 Age: 23 Bats: R Throws: R Height: 6'4" Weight: 225 Origin: International Free Agent, 2013

YEAR	TEAM	LVL	AGE	PA	R	2B	3B	HR	RBI	BB	K	SB	CS	AVG/OBP/SLG	TAv	VORP	BABIP	BRR	FRAA	WARP
2015	DOD	RK	20	165	29	7	4	5	26	13	57	5	1	.295/.354/.497	.288	4.6	.443	-2.4	1B(44): -1.6	0.3
2016	OGD	RK	21	132	19	6	2	5	29	15	36	0	2	.351/.432/.570	.334	11.9	.473	-0.2	1B(28): -2.5	0.9
2016	GRL	A	21	98	17	5	1	7	15	9	41	1	2	.273/.347/.591	.332	8.3	.425	0.4	1B(15): 0.3	0.9
2017	RCU	A+	22	492	62	16	1	28	87	40	172	0	2	.259/.327/.489	.281	14.3	.354	-1.2	1B(113): -8.4	0.6
2018	*LAN*	*MLB*	*23*	*250*	*29*	*8*	*1*	*13*	*34*	*17*	*99*	*0*	*0*	*.207/.266/.413*	*.230*	*-3.7*	*.291*	*-0.5*	*1B -2*	*-0.7*
2019	*LAN*	*MLB*	*24*	*267*	*33*	*9*	*1*	*12*	*36*	*21*	*105*	*0*	*0*	*.206/.274/.402*	*.242*	*-2.5*	*.297*	*-0.7*	*1B -2*	*-0.5*

Breakout: 3% Improve: 13% Collapse: 2% Attrition: 11% MLB: 26% *Comparables: Xavier Scruggs, Paul Goldschmidt, Greg Halman*

Talib Kweli once framed the fight to cope with overwhelming oppositional forces in terms of finding beauty in the hideous, and those with the opportunity to view an Isabel at-bat are well-served by the advice. Rare is the human being with the strength and barrel velocity to damage a baseball as he can; rarer still is the professional hitter who so consistently winds himself tighter than the ball itself on the back end of an empty swing. And his max-effort assaults yield these contorted, buckled postures much more often than they launch rocket ships into space. He produces negative value on the bases and takes more away on the dirt. The deck is stacked, the odds are long, the oppositional forces overwhelming. But man, those dingers are beautiful things.

Matt Kemp LF Born: 09/23/84 Age: 33 Bats: R Throws: R Height: 6'4" Weight: 210 Origin: Round 6, 2003 Draft (#181 overall)

YEAR	TEAM	LVL	AGE	PA	R	2B	3B	HR	RBI	BB	K	SB	CS	AVG/OBP/SLG	TAv	VORP	BABIP	BRR	FRAA	WARP
2015	SDN	MLB	30	648	80	31	3	23	100	39	147	12	2	.265/.312/.443	.273	21.2	.311	1.8	RF(149): 4.6	2.8
2016	SDN	MLB	31	431	54	24	0	23	69	16	100	0	0	.262/.285/.489	.269	11.0	.288	-0.4	RF(97): -5.3	0.6
2016	ATL	MLB	31	241	35	15	0	12	39	20	56	1	0	.280/.336/.519	.307	18.3	.316	1.5	LF(54): 0.0	1.9
2017	ATL	MLB	32	467	47	23	1	19	64	27	99	0	2	.276/.318/.463	.261	7.3	.318	-3.4	LF(103): -14.5	-0.7
2018	*LAN*	*MLB*	*33*	*479*	*57*	*25*	*0*	*21*	*67*	*33*	*117*	*3*	*1*	*.256/.307/.453*	*.255*	*13.8*	*.301*	*-0.3*	*LF -10*	*0.4*
2019	*LAN*	*MLB*	*34*	*403*	*49*	*19*	*0*	*15*	*51*	*28*	*104*	*2*	*1*	*.235/.290/.412*	*.251*	*5.8*	*.283*	*-0.3*	*LF -8*	*-0.3*

Breakout: 0% Improve: 24% Collapse: 11% Attrition: 9% MLB: 92% *Comparables: Scott Hairston, Cody Ross, Joe Rudi*

By now, we all know the book on Kemp. He'll give you a half season where he'll hit well enough to make you forget about his statuesque defense in left field, and then a half season that reminds you why multiple teams are currently paying him. However, Kemp threw a plot twist into the 2017 chapter. Instead of starting the season cold and finishing it hot, he started by raking at the plate before injuries and a general lack of production soured his season in a hurry. If he ends up in the American League, he could still be a DH somewhere, but his time as a dependable outfielder is likely done.

Joc Pederson OF Born: 04/21/92 Age: 26 Bats: L Throws: L Height: 6'1" Weight: 220 Origin: Round 11, 2010 Draft (#352 overall)

YEAR	TEAM	LVL	AGE	PA	R	2B	3B	HR	RBI	BB	K	SB	CS	AVG/OBP/SLG	TAv	VORP	BABIP	BRR	FRAA	WARP
2015	LAN	MLB	23	585	67	19	1	26	54	92	170	4	7	.210/.346/.417	.287	32.9	.262	0.3	CF(147): -22.1	1.2
2016	LAN	MLB	24	476	64	26	0	25	68	63	130	6	2	.246/.352/.495	.310	35.5	.296	-3.6	CF(132): -2.2	3.4
2017	OKL	AAA	25	71	8	1	0	3	9	5	14	1	0	.169/.225/.323	.191	-4.1	.163	-0.2	LF(10): 3.7, CF(4): 0.8	0.0
2017	LAN	MLB	25	323	44	20	0	11	35	39	68	4	3	.212/.331/.407	.266	14.2	.241	1.8	CF(92): -9.0, LF(4): -0.4	0.5
2018	*LAN*	*MLB*	*26*	*536*	*77*	*21*	*1*	*25*	*77*	*77*	*145*	*8*	*5*	*.226/.346/.441*	*.277*	*29.7*	*.273*	*-1.0*	*CF -12, LF 0*	*1.2*
2019	*LAN*	*MLB*	*27*	*439*	*64*	*17*	*0*	*20*	*61*	*66*	*119*	*6*	*4*	*.225/.351/.442*	*.288*	*25.7*	*.269*	*-0.1*	*CF -9, LF 0*	*1.8*

Breakout: 6% Improve: 61% Collapse: 2% Attrition: 5% MLB: 97% *Comparables: Grady Sizemore, Nick Swisher, Carlos Quentin*

Pederson continued to evolve as a hitter in 2017, and his season reminds us that evolution can often be as messy as the middle finger of an aye-aye lemur. After flashing glimpses of a Trot Nixonian palate of skills in 2016, Pederson failed to progress at the dish. He cratered in August, precipitating an embarrassing demotion to the minors in August. After responding poorly in a 17-game run at Oklahoma City, he backed his way into the postseason mix despite a similarly uninspiring September. One thing led to another, and suddenly he was manning the strong side of a left-field platoon deep in October. Naturally, he took full advantage with a 1.344 OPS across 20 trips to the World Series dish. That big-stage breakout should have his confidence riding high into 2018, though he still can't hit lefties and it remains to be seen whether he can lay off equally confident high ones he'll see again aplenty from the righties.

DJ Peters CF Born: 12/12/95 Age: 22 Bats: R Throws: R Height: 6'6" Weight: 225 Origin: Round 4, 2016 Draft (#131 overall)

YEAR	TEAM	LVL	AGE	PA	R	2B	3B	HR	RBI	BB	K	SB	CS	AVG/OBP/SLG	TAv	VORP	BABIP	BRR	FRAA	WARP
2016	OGD	RK	20	302	63	24	3	13	48	35	66	5	3	.351/.437/.615	.375	46.4	.432	0.5	CF(31): 4.5, RF(28): -3.6	4.6
2017	RCU	A+	21	587	91	29	5	27	82	64	189	3	3	.276/.372/.514	.306	42.8	.385	0.9	CF(80): -3.4, LF(18): -1.0	4.1
2018	*LAN*	*MLB*	*22*	*250*	*28*	*10*	*1*	*11*	*34*	*23*	*88*	*0*	*0*	*.217/.300/.412*	*.245*	*4.9*	*.299*	*-0.5*	*CF -1, LF 0*	*0.4*
2019	*LAN*	*MLB*	*23*	*370*	*49*	*15*	*1*	*16*	*50*	*36*	*126*	*0*	*0*	*.221/.308/.423*	*.266*	*11.5*	*.299*	*-0.9*	*CF -2, LF -1*	*1.0*

Breakout: 1% Improve: 27% Collapse: 4% Attrition: 14% MLB: 45% *Comparables: Lewis Brinson, Domingo Santana, Chris Young*

Youth is a time for extremes, a truism that Peters frequently attempted to push to its limits at High-A last year. He is a large man, comparable in physicality and plate-side demeanor to a budding Jayson Werth for the next generation. And while a spry athleticism underlies his movements, length often bedevils them. His swing, unbridled and powerful, can struggle to migrate from Point A to B efficiently enough to catch a halfway-decent fastball. And he'll offer his share of helping hands to the pitchers by obliging their trickery outside the zone, often with unhinged flails. When he does catch one with the barrel, however, it turns around in a hurry. Plus-or-better pop pairs with solid speed, quality instincts and improving reads in center, along with enough arm strength to accommodate a likely eventual shift to right. It's a classic slugging profile, provided maturity curbs some of his enthusiasm.

Yasiel Puig RF Born: 12/07/90 Age: 27 Bats: R Throws: R Height: 6'2" Weight: 240 Origin: International Free Agent, 2012

YEAR	TEAM	LVL	AGE	PA	R	2B	3B	HR	RBI	BB	K	SB	CS	AVG/OBP/SLG	TAv	VORP	BABIP	BRR	FRAA	WARP
2015	LAN	MLB	24	311	30	12	3	11	38	26	66	3	3	.255/.322/.436	.286	14.7	.296	1.4	RF(78): -0.4	1.5
2016	OKL	AAA	25	75	12	3	1	4	12	6	8	0	1	.348/.400/.594	.348	5.2	.351	-3.0	RF(17): 0.0	0.5
2016	LAN	MLB	25	368	45	14	2	11	45	24	74	5	2	.263/.323/.416	.274	13.7	.306	1.4	RF(90): 5.3, LF(5): 0.0	2.0
2017	LAN	MLB	26	570	72	24	2	28	74	64	100	15	6	.263/.346/.487	.296	27.8	.274	-4.3	RF(145): 9.1	3.7
2018	*LAN*	*MLB*	*27*	*541*	*75*	*25*	*4*	*21*	*76*	*51*	*106*	*11*	*5*	*.272/.349/.472*	*.288*	*29.2*	*.307*	*-0.1*	*RF 5*	*3.2*
2019	*LAN*	*MLB*	*28*	*515*	*73*	*25*	*3*	*22*	*74*	*52*	*102*	*9*	*5*	*.275/.357/.488*	*.305*	*35.0*	*.309*	*-0.4*	*RF 6*	*4.4*

Breakout: 0% Improve: 57% Collapse: 7% Attrition: 6% MLB: 99% *Comparables: Hunter Pence, George Springer, Andre Ethier*

Stranger, let us tell you: Sometimes there's a Wild Horse, and well, he's the man for his time and place. The path certainly hasn't been a straight one; from the rocky Straights of Florida on up, it's been pretty far from it, actually. But in an electric 2017 season, Puig supercharged to a next level of performance and showmanship. Under the tutelage of hitting coach Turner Ward, Puig finally found discipline. He jumped his walk rate to a career high by staying off soft chasers, and just as importantly put the reins on his aggressiveness against fastballs in harder-to-reach parts of the zone. After posting the numbers of a legitimate superstar in the second half, Puig galloped and wagged his way to the pennant before Astros pitchers finally managed to tame him for a spell in the Series. Still just 27, he'll enter the season as one of the most dynamic players in the game, and with a chance to blow the roof off his final arbitration number.

Edwin Rios 1B Born: 04/21/94 Age: 24 Bats: L Throws: R Height: 6'3" Weight: 220 Origin: Round 6, 2015 Draft (#192 overall)

YEAR	TEAM	LVL	AGE	PA	R	2B	3B	HR	RBI	BB	K	SB	CS	AVG/OBP/SLG	TAv	VORP	BABIP	BRR	FRAA	WARP
2015	OGD	RK	21	75	8	7	0	3	13	7	29	0	0	.235/.307/.471	.253	0.6	.361	-0.8	3B(14): -0.2, 1B(3): -0.2	0.0
2016	GRL	A	22	128	17	8	1	6	13	8	44	3	1	.252/.305/.487	.297	7.6	.348	0.0	3B(20): -0.1, 1B(9): 0.6	0.9
2016	RCU	A+	22	188	37	11	1	16	46	8	35	0	0	.367/.394/.712	.387	30.3	.383	1.0	3B(20): 1.1, 1B(18): 0.9	3.3
2016	TUL	AA	22	135	14	7	0	5	17	8	31	0	0	.254/.304/.434	.271	5.3	.292	0.1	3B(28): 0.8, 1B(4): 0.2	0.7
2017	TUL	AA	23	332	47	21	0	15	62	17	69	1	1	.317/.358/.533	.308	23.6	.363	0.9	3B(38): -4.1, 1B(28): 1.8	2.3
2017	OKL	AAA	23	190	23	13	0	9	29	18	42	0	1	.296/.368/.533	.297	8.7	.345	-2.6	1B(33): 0.6, 3B(9): -1.0	0.8
2018	*LAN*	*MLB*	*24*	*250*	*30*	*13*	*0*	*13*	*38*	*14*	*71*	*0*	*0*	*.253/.300/.477*	*.259*	*5.9*	*.305*	*-0.6*	*1B 2, 3B -1*	*0.7*
2019	*LAN*	*MLB*	*25*	*357*	*48*	*19*	*0*	*18*	*53*	*23*	*101*	*0*	*0*	*.255/.308/.476*	*.279*	*12.6*	*.311*	*-1.0*	*1B 3, 3B -2*	*1.5*

Breakout: 8% Improve: 20% Collapse: 13% Attrition: 26% MLB: 41% *Comparables: Matt Clark, Neftali Soto, Matt Adams*

Rios has managed to defy the conventions of his profile thus far, continuing to hit for massive power up through the high minors despite modest bat speed, an aggressive approach and a bunch of length into the zone. He's done it by leveraging that length better than most, with a gorgeously balanced, fluid swing that delivers his barrel at an angle capable of producing majestic, carrying fly balls. Provided his best-in-the-system raw power translates, the rest of it isn't going to matter much. And that's a welcome thing for his fans, as despite continuing to see reps at the hot corner his defensive lot is much more likely that of a passable first baseman. The bat's the thing here, and so far it has proven up to the task of carrying him to the doorstep of a big-league career.

Keibert Ruiz C Born: 07/20/98 Age: 19 Bats: B Throws: R Height: 6'0" Weight: 200 Origin: International Free Agent, 2015

YEAR	TEAM	LVL	AGE	PA	R	2B	3B	HR	RBI	BB	K	SB	CS	AVG/OBP/SLG	TAv	VORP	BABIP	BRR	FRAA	WARP
2015	DDO	RK	16	159	14	8	1	1	19	8	15	4	2	.300/.340/.387	.289	10.6	.328	-2.3	C(43): 0.7	1.1
2016	DOD	RK	17	39	5	4	1	0	15	3	4	0	0	.485/.513/.667	.416	7.4	.516	-0.8	C(7): -0.1	0.7
2016	OGD	RK	17	206	28	18	2	2	33	12	23	0	0	.354/.393/.503	.308	17.0	.389	-1.6	C(35): -1.2	1.6
2017	GRL	A	18	251	34	16	1	2	24	18	30	0	0	.317/.372/.423	.296	15.6	.355	-3.2	C(49): -0.9	1.5
2017	RCU	A+	18	160	24	7	1	6	27	7	23	0	0	.315/.344/.497	.297	13.0	.333	0.0	C(37): -0.3	1.3
2018	*LAN*	*MLB*	*19*	*250*	*24*	*12*	*0*	*7*	*29*	*10*	*53*	*0*	*0*	*.247/.281/.392*	*.228*	*3.8*	*.289*	*-0.5*	*C 0*	*0.5*
2019	*LAN*	*MLB*	*20*	*390*	*47*	*19*	*1*	*13*	*49*	*19*	*78*	*0*	*0*	*.266/.304/.431*	*.264*	*16.0*	*.303*	*-0.8*	*C 1*	*1.8*

Breakout: 0% Improve: 8% Collapse: 2% Attrition: 8% MLB: 16% *Comparables: Freddie Freeman, Wilmer Flores, Rougned Odor*

If baseball player archetypes were collected onto a breakfast menu, switch-hitting catchers would most definitely be a well-made eggs Benedict. A lot has to come together to make it work, but when you get that Hollandaise popping with a proper dash of cayenne, and the eggs are poached all puffy-like, and there's a nice hearty, gently toasted English muffin underlining the whole thing ... mmph. Such is the promise for Ruiz, who thrived at High-A after a midseason promotion at the shockingly tender age of 18. He's got lightning in his wrists, with excellent bat speed and advanced framing the chief products at present. The standard slow-simmer caveats apply to Ruiz, just the same as any other precocious talent, but all the ingredients of a top-tier catching prospect are here (insert DroolingHomer.gif).

Corey Seager SS Born: 04/27/94 Age: 24 Bats: L Throws: R Height: 6'4" Weight: 220 Origin: Round 1, 2012 Draft (#18 overall)

YEAR	TEAM	LVL	AGE	PA	R	2B	3B	HR	RBI	BB	K	SB	CS	AVG/OBP/SLG	TAv	VORP	BABIP	BRR	FRAA	WARP
2015	TUL	AA	21	86	17	7	1	5	15	5	11	1	1	.375/.407/.675	.393	15.2	.385	0.5	SS(15): 0.1, 3B(4): -0.2	1.6
2015	OKL	AAA	21	464	64	30	2	13	61	32	65	3	0	.278/.332/.451	.285	32.4	.298	2.2	SS(90): 7.9, 3B(15): 0.9	4.2
2015	LAN	MLB	21	113	17	8	1	4	17	14	19	2	0	.337/.425/.561	.356	15.3	.387	0.4	SS(21): 1.6, 3B(6): 0.6	1.9
2016	LAN	MLB	22	687	105	40	5	26	72	54	133	3	3	.308/.365/.512	.320	73.1	.355	2.7	SS(155): -8.8	6.6
2017	LAN	MLB	23	613	85	33	0	22	77	67	131	4	2	.295/.375/.479	.307	58.5	.352	2.2	SS(138): -1.8	5.7
2018	*LAN*	*MLB*	*24*	*635*	*93*	*35*	*2*	*24*	*83*	*54*	*122*	*4*	*2*	*.284/.349/.481*	*.289*	*50.1*	*.321*	*-1.1*	*SS -3*	*3.7*
2019	*LAN*	*MLB*	*25*	*575*	*83*	*32*	*1*	*26*	*85*	*55*	*111*	*3*	*2*	*.286/.358/.503*	*.308*	*50.5*	*.319*	*1.7*	*SS -3*	*5.2*

Breakout: 3% Improve: 62% Collapse: 0% Attrition: 2% MLB: 100% *Comparables: Troy Tulowitzki, Pablo Sandoval, Hanley Ramirez*

Players who notch top-three MVP seasons as rookies tend to set themselves up for unreasonably high expectations, but Seager managed to not disappoint in a stellar encore performance. Another good-enough effort at shortstop will forestall for another year, maybe more, talk of a wander down the defensive spectrum. Paired with a top-three TAv at the position, the effort drove a best-in-class WARP among six-spotters. His contact rate backed up a bit in the service of hitting balls in the air more often, but other than picking nits on the margins of that, Seager displayed encouraging growth across the board. He's already halfway to his brother's career WARP total in about a third as many games, and appears poised to anchor the roster for at least the next several years.

Chris Taylor UT Born: 08/29/90 Age: 27 Bats: R Throws: R Height: 6'1" Weight: 195 Origin: Round 5, 2012 Draft (#161 overall)

YEAR	TEAM	LVL	AGE	PA	R	2B	3B	HR	RBI	BB	K	SB	CS	AVG/OBP/SLG	TAv	VORP	BABIP	BRR	FRAA	WARP
2015	SEA	MLB	24	102	9	3	1	0	1	6	31	3	2	.170/.220/.223	.172	-5.4	.254	-0.6	SS(28): -0.6, 2B(4): -0.2	-0.7
2015	TAC	AAA	24	396	56	20	6	4	32	50	61	16	8	.300/.391/.429	.280	22.8	.355	-0.4	SS(72): 3.8, 2B(13): -0.8	2.6
2016	SEA	MLB	25	3	0	0	0	0	0	0	2	0	0	.333/.333/.333	.234	0.0	1.000	0.0	SS(1): -0.3	0.0
2016	TAC	AAA	25	280	41	19	4	3	29	29	49	12	5	.312/.387/.457	.294	20.7	.378	0.0	SS(50): 2.1, 2B(7): -1.3	2.2
2016	OKL	AAA	25	64	7	6	2	0	8	6	16	5	0	.368/.438/.544	.345	9.2	.512	1.0	SS(13): -1.2, 3B(2): -0.1	0.8
2016	LAN	MLB	25	62	8	2	2	1	7	4	13	0	0	.207/.258/.362	.207	-0.7	.250	0.7	3B(10): -0.1, 2B(7): -0.5	-0.2
2017	OKL	AAA	26	49	8	2	2	1	5	5	5	1	2	.233/.327/.442	.267	2.8	.243	0.6	SS(5): 0.5, CF(3): 0.2	0.3
2017	LAN	MLB	26	568	85	34	5	21	72	50	142	17	4	.288/.354/.496	.309	50.3	.361	4.4	CF(49): -2.2, LF(48): 6.6	5.7
2018	*LAN*	*MLB*	*27*	*692*	*93*	*35*	*7*	*14*	*67*	*62*	*162*	*20*	*7*	*.260/.330/.406*	*.263*	*30.0*	*.329*	*1.5*	*LF 9, CF -1*	*3.0*
2019	*LAN*	*MLB*	*28*	*554*	*66*	*29*	*5*	*12*	*61*	*55*	*131*	*16*	*6*	*.261/.339/.414*	*.276*	*27.5*	*.331*	*2.5*	*LF 8, CF -1*	*3.7*

Breakout: 3% Improve: 39% Collapse: 6% Attrition: 14% MLB: 86% *Comparables: Abraham Almonte, Lorenzo Cain, Jon Jay*

Taylor entered his age-26 season with 0.9 career WARP, collecting dust on the shelf, then proceeded to rewrite the whole damn book. Chalk it up to another confluence of natural talent and newfound Dodgerness; the analytic Blues have shown an uncanny ability to tweak and twist with fringy-looking acquisitions to great success, and Taylor might be the best example yet. Swing changes unlocked never-seen power to the pull side, and after going five for his first nine and seizing a more-or-less everyday role by early May, he never stopped hitting. By the season's second half his versatility and shiny new thump at the top of the lineup made him one of the more indispensable players in the league, and he'll enter 2018 under full pre-arbitration control for a final time with one of the best cost-benefits in baseball.

Trayce Thompson OF Born: 03/15/91 Age: 27 Bats: R Throws: R Height: 6'3" Weight: 217 Origin: Round 2, 2009 Draft (#61 overall)

YEAR	TEAM	LVL	AGE	PA	R	2B	3B	HR	RBI	BB	K	SB	CS	AVG/OBP/SLG	TAv	VORP	BABIP	BRR	FRAA	WARP
2015	CHR	AAA	24	417	53	23	4	13	39	23	79	11	5	.260/.304/.441	.259	13.1	.295	1.5	CF(94): 3.8, RF(5): 2.5	1.9
2015	CHA	MLB	24	135	17	8	3	5	16	13	26	1	0	.295/.363/.533	.308	10.6	.341	1.5	RF(18): 0.2, LF(12): 0.7	1.1
2016	LAN	MLB	25	262	31	11	0	13	32	26	66	5	1	.225/.302/.436	.271	11.8	.255	2.5	CF(32): -0.1, RF(28): -2.8	0.6
2017	OKL	AAA	26	369	44	12	6	9	33	26	93	3	5	.212/.269/.363	.218	-6.7	.264	1.0	CF(47): -4.3, RF(34): 1.8	-0.8
2017	LAN	MLB	26	55	6	2	1	1	2	6	23	0	0	.122/.218/.265	.175	-3.4	.200	0.0	CF(9): -0.6, RF(8): -0.3	-0.5
2018	*LAN*	*MLB*	*27*	*145*	*17*	*6*	*1*	*5*	*18*	*11*	*37*	*2*	*1*	*.222/.282/.400*	*.241*	*2.4*	*.268*	*0.0*	*LF -2, RF 0*	*-0.1*
2019	*LAN*	*MLB*	*28*	*246*	*30*	*11*	*2*	*9*	*32*	*21*	*64*	*3*	*2*	*.225/.294/.419*	*.257*	*6.2*	*.269*	*1.0*	*LF -3, RF 0*	*0.4*

Breakout: 4% Improve: 34% Collapse: 9% Attrition: 20% MLB: 76% *Comparables: Ryan Kalish, Will Venable, Mikie Mahtook*

It's easy to bracket our thinking about season-ending injuries strictly in terms of the blow they strike to immediate productivity. Yet Thompson's case serves as a cautionary reminder that there's often more to it than that. Requisite months removed from two fractured vertebrae that derailed a once-promising 2016 campaign, Thompson returned to the field ostensibly healthy. He didn't play like a new man, though, or at least in any kind of affirming, "he's back!" kind of way. On the contrary, he struggled mightily throughout his time at Triple-A, and he looked no more comfortable across 55 sporadic plate appearances in Los Angeles. With an ever-more-crowded outfield depth chart around him, it'll be that much higher of a hill to climb to get back into the mix for regular at-bats this summer.

Justin Turner 3B Born: 11/23/84 Age: 33 Bats: R Throws: R Height: 5'11" Weight: 205 Origin: Round 7, 2006 Draft (#204 overall)

YEAR	TEAM	LVL	AGE	PA	R	2B	3B	HR	RBI	BB	K	SB	CS	AVG/OBP/SLG	TAv	VORP	BABIP	BRR	FRAA	WARP
2015	LAN	MLB	30	439	55	26	1	16	60	36	71	5	2	.294/.370/.491	.321	39.9	.321	1.2	3B(100): -1.3, 1B(10): -0.1	4.2
2016	LAN	MLB	31	622	79	34	3	27	90	48	107	4	1	.275/.339/.493	.309	49.2	.293	-1.7	3B(144): -4.8, 1B(1): 0.0	4.6
2017	LAN	MLB	32	543	72	32	0	21	71	59	56	7	1	.322/.415/.530	.347	63.9	.326	-3.2	3B(121): -5.5	5.9
2018	*LAN*	*MLB*	*33*	*622*	*80*	*33*	*1*	*21*	*84*	*53*	*97*	*6*	*2*	*.282/.355/.460*	*.287*	*35.9*	*.308*	*-0.5*	*3B -7*	*2.6*
2019	*LAN*	*MLB*	*34*	*542*	*74*	*30*	*1*	*19*	*72*	*47*	*87*	*4*	*1*	*.283/.358/.469*	*.300*	*34.8*	*.308*	*-1.3*	*3B -5*	*3.3*

Breakout: 0% Improve: 31% Collapse: 2% Attrition: 5% MLB: 94% *Comparables: David Wright, Aramis Ramirez, Carlos Guillen*

The fly-ball revolution was definitely televised, if only to a certain percentage of Southern California homes with a certain cable subscription. For those fortunate few, however, it was a real treat to watch the ginger Animal doppelgänger at the heart of the Dodgers' powerful lineup put on a fireworks display above Chavez Ravine every night. And talk about a revolutionary effort: Turner dramatically altered his approach, ultimately taking more walks than he suffered strikeouts. He nearly put up more extra-base hits than whiffs, too, as he continued a now four-year trend of driving a whole bunch more balls in the air. The glove gets mixed reviews from assorted defensive metrics, but given the evolution of the bat into an elite asset, LA has to be feeling cautiously optimistic about the three years remaining on his deal, even as he wades further into over-30 waters.

Chase Utley 2B Born: 12/17/78 Age: 39 Bats: L Throws: R Height: 6'1" Weight: 195 Origin: Round 1, 2000 Draft (#15 overall)

YEAR	TEAM	LVL	AGE	PA	R	2B	3B	HR	RBI	BB	K	SB	CS	AVG/OBP/SLG	TAv	VORP	BABIP	BRR	FRAA	WARP
2015	PHI	MLB	36	282	23	12	1	5	30	22	35	3	0	.217/.284/.333	.240	0.5	.227	-1.1	2B(62): -1.8, 1B(4): -0.1	-0.2
2015	LAN	MLB	36	141	14	9	1	3	9	10	29	1	0	.202/.291/.363	.241	0.6	.237	-0.4	2B(26): 1.9, 3B(3): -0.1	0.2
2016	LAN	MLB	37	565	79	26	3	14	52	40	115	2	2	.252/.319/.396	.273	21.6	.299	-1.1	2B(134): 1.1, 3B(1): 0.0	2.3
2017	LAN	MLB	38	353	43	20	4	8	34	32	57	6	1	.236/.324/.405	.268	13.9	.264	2.0	2B(80): -1.7, 1B(17): 0.2	1.2
2018	*LAN*	*MLB*	*39*	*374*	*44*	*18*	*2*	*9*	*37*	*29*	*64*	*4*	*1*	*.237/.308/.383*	*.238*	*5.8*	*.266*	*-0.1*	*2B -1, 1B 0*	*0.6*
2019	*LAN*	*MLB*	*40*	*256*	*28*	*11*	*1*	*6*	*26*	*20*	*45*	*2*	*1*	*.223/.294/.357*	*.238*	*1.5*	*.250*	*-0.2*	*2B 0, 1B 0*	*0.1*

Breakout: 0% Improve: 20% Collapse: 13% Attrition: 20% MLB: 63% *Comparables: Craig Counsell, Jamey Carroll, Red Schoendienst*

Utley's borderline Hall-of-Fame career pulled into some of its final stops in 2017, and the sparks of carrying production that he'd scraped to life in 2016 largely smoldered a year later. He still managed to get drilled by nine pitches and make one of the season's most unexpectedly spectacular catches to preserve Rich Hill's nine-inning no-hitter, though. It's been cool to see The Man from Long Beach's career wind up in hometown blue some 20 years after he rejected them for the lighter collegiate shade as a second-round prep shortstop. The salty aftertaste of Game 7 swishing around the gums may coax a final run at glory, but the Cooperstown clock will starting ticking soon enough regardless.

Alex Verdugo CF Born: 05/15/96 Age: 22 Bats: L Throws: L Height: 6'0" Weight: 205 Origin: Round 2, 2014 Draft (#62 overall)

YEAR	TEAM	LVL	AGE	PA	R	2B	3B	HR	RBI	BB	K	SB	CS	AVG/OBP/SLG	TAv	VORP	BABIP	BRR	FRAA	WARP
2015	GRL	A	19	444	50	23	2	5	42	17	53	13	5	.295/.325/.394	.258	10.9	.326	-0.7	CF(89): 16.3, RF(11): 1.4	3.0
2015	RCU	A+	19	96	20	9	2	4	19	4	12	1	0	.385/.406/.659	.372	14.1	.408	0.4	CF(23): 2.1	1.8
2016	TUL	AA	20	529	58	23	1	13	63	44	67	2	6	.273/.336/.407	.275	20.8	.292	-1.2	CF(91): -1.2, RF(30): -0.2	2.1
2017	OKL	AAA	21	495	67	27	4	6	62	52	50	9	3	.314/.389/.436	.289	32.0	.340	3.1	CF(59): -5.5, RF(46): 3.1	2.9
2017	LAN	MLB	21	25	1	0	0	1	1	2	4	0	1	.174/.240/.304	.189	-1.2	.167	-0.1	CF(6): -0.7, LF(3): 0.3	-0.2
2018	*LAN*	*MLB*	*22*	*274*	*29*	*13*	*1*	*7*	*31*	*19*	*45*	*2*	*1*	*.255/.309/.392*	*.248*	*4.6*	*.285*	*-0.5*	*RF -1, LF 0*	*0.1*
2019	*LAN*	*MLB*	*23*	*481*	*58*	*24*	*2*	*14*	*57*	*37*	*81*	*3*	*2*	*.262/.321/.419*	*.267*	*14.3*	*.290*	*-0.9*	*RF -1, LF 0*	*1.3*

Breakout: 6% Improve: 26% Collapse: 8% Attrition: 27% MLB: 45% *Comparables: Manuel Margot, Ben Revere, Michael Brantley*

Prospects with multiple 70-grade tools aren't especially common, particularly when one of those tools is the elusive hit. But if Verdugo's bat pans all the way out he might be that guy. His arm will certainly do its part, and judging by his demolition of PCL pitching at age 21, the stick should be favored to follow suit. It remains a mystery in this stimulated era of long-ball offense what Verdugo's power numbers might look like as a modern-day big leaguer, but he's a good enough hitter to grow into an everyday role whether the pop comes or not. He'll try to force the issue of a longer audition on a short timeline in 2018.

PITCHERS

Yadier Alvarez RHP Born: 03/07/96 Age: 22 Bats: R Throws: R Height: 6'3" Weight: 175 Origin: International Free Agent, 2015

YEAR	TEAM	LVL	AGE	W	L	SV	G	GS	IP	H	HR	BB/9	K/9	K	GB%	BABIP	WHIP	ERA	DRA	WARP	MPH	CMD	PWR	STM
2016	DOD	RK	20	1	1	0	5	5	20	9	0	4.5	11.7	26	64%	.200	0.95	1.80	2.50	0.7				
2016	GRL	A	20	3	2	0	9	9	39^{1}	31	1	2.5	12.6	55	50%	.326	1.07	2.29	1.32	1.8				
2017	RCU	A+	21	2	4	1	14	11	59^{1}	61	3	3.8	9.3	61	51%	.335	1.45	5.31	4.54	0.4				
2017	TUL	AA	21	2	2	0	7	7	33	29	1	6.8	9.8	36	56%	.318	1.64	3.55	4.99	0.1				
2018	*LAN*	*MLB*	*22*	*5*	*5*	*0*	*18*	*18*	*79*	*67*	*12*	*4.2*	*10.9*	*95*	*45%*	*.305*	*1.32*	*4.18*	*4.77*	*0.7*				
2019	*LAN*	*MLB*	*23*	*6*	*9*	*0*	*27*	*27*	*161*	*144*	*28*	*4.7*	*9.9*	*177*	*45%*	*.307*	*1.42*	*4.87*	*5.61*	*0.0*				

Breakout: 6% Improve: 15% Collapse: 3% Attrition: 13% MLB: 23% *Comparables: David Paulino, Mauricio Robles, Dan Cortes*

Where Alvarez's stateside debut in 2016 served largely to inflate the imaginations of ceiling hounds, 2017's follow-up campaign checked on the realities of a still-maturing 21-year-old. His high-end velocity remained among the easiest in all of the minors, and his slider still tantalized with bouts of dazzling bite, but his simple mechanics belied a peculiar inability to repeat his throwing motion and command the baseball consistently. The fastball lacked movement in larger doses, the slider came and went, and the changeup still lagged. Prospect development is rarely a linear endeavor, of course, and the sky-high ceiling is still there—he's just tethered a bit tighter to the floor than anticipated a year ago.

Luis Avilan LHP Born: 07/19/89 Age: 28 Bats: L Throws: L Height: 6'2" Weight: 225 Origin: International Free Agent, 2005

YEAR	TEAM	LVL	AGE	W	L	SV	G	GS	IP	H	HR	BB/9	K/9	K	GB%	BABIP	WHIP	ERA	DRA	WARP	MPH	CMD	PWR	STM
2015	ATL	MLB	25	2	4	0	50	0	37^{2}	35	4	2.4	7.4	31	49%	.284	1.19	3.58	3.48	0.5	95.8	57	51	48
2015	LAN	MLB	25	0	1	0	23	0	15^{2}	13	2	2.9	10.3	18	55%	.275	1.15	5.17	3.03	0.3	95.5	57	51	48
2016	OKL	AAA	26	0	3	4	33	0	34	35	3	4.2	9.8	37	49%	.337	1.50	4.24	5.74	-0.3				
2016	LAN	MLB	26	3	0	0	27	0	19^{2}	12	0	4.6	12.8	28	55%	.286	1.12	3.20	2.29	0.6	94.4	49	37	44
2017	LAN	MLB	27	2	3	0	61	0	46	42	2	4.3	10.2	52	56%	.342	1.39	2.93	3.19	1.0	94.3	44	36	46
2018	*CHA*	*MLB*	*28*	*3*	*3*	*0*	*51*	*0*	*53*	*48*	*7*	*4.4*	*9.4*	*56*	*49%*	*.290*	*1.37*	*4.18*	*4.35*	*0.5*	*94.2*	*49*	*41*	*46*
2019	*CHA*	*MLB*	*29*	*3*	*1*	*0*	*53*	*0*	56^{1}	*46*	*7*	*4.1*	*9.8*	*61*	*49%*	*.3*	*1.28*	*4.09*	*4.69*	*0.3*	*93.6*	*46*	*38*	*46*

Breakout: 22% Improve: 43% Collapse: 26% Attrition: 18% MLB: 92% *Comparables: Bryan Shaw, Bobby Jenks, Robbie Ross*

It's not often you see a LOOGY come into a given game and throw his changeup at all to left-handed hitters, let alone feature the dang thing over his fastball. Yet that's just how Avilan rolled in 2017, and it worked like a charm. The pitch moves considerably less on either plane than a typical cambio and features just average velocity separation from his four-seamer, yet same-handed batters managed to hit just .132 against the pitch, while coming up empty on two out of every five swings. He still struggles to keep the ball in the strike zone consistently, and health remains a question mark after a sore shoulder put the kibosh on his postseason plans, but southpaws who sit 93 with an additional out pitch tend to survive anything short of the Apocalypse, so it should surprise no one if we're still writing about Avilan in the *2028 Annual*.

Pedro Baez RHP Born: 03/11/88 Age: 30 Bats: R Throws: R Height: 6'0" Weight: 230 Origin: International Free Agent, 2007

YEAR	TEAM	LVL	AGE	W	L	SV	G	GS	IP	H	HR	BB/9	K/9	K	GB%	BABIP	WHIP	ERA	DRA	WARP	MPH	CMD	PWR	STM
2015	LAN	MLB	27	4	2	0	52	0	51	47	4	1.9	10.6	60	41%	.326	1.14	3.35	2.94	1.1	99.8	44	78	43
2016	LAN	MLB	28	3	2	0	73	0	74	52	11	2.7	10.1	83	44%	.233	1.00	3.04	3.16	1.5	99.2	49	70	52
2017	LAN	MLB	29	3	6	0	66	0	64	56	9	4.1	9.0	64	35%	.267	1.33	2.95	5.17	0.0	98.6	55	77	52
2018	*LAN*	*MLB*	*30*	*3*	*2*	*0*	*55*	*0*	*58*	*55*	*10*	*3.5*	*9.4*	*61*	*41%*	*.288*	*1.32*	*4.56*	*4.90*	*0.0*	*98.3*	*51*	*74*	*50*
2019	*LAN*	*MLB*	*31*	*2*	*1*	*1*	*47*	*0*	50^{1}	*42*	*9*	*3.1*	*9.6*	*53*	*41%*	*.283*	*1.19*	*4.39*	*5.04*	*0.1*	*97.8*	*52*	*74*	*51*

Breakout: 23% Improve: 45% Collapse: 16% Attrition: 15% MLB: 80% *Comparables: Craig Breslow, Jerry Blevins, Brad Brach*

Back in May of aught-seven, Officer Edward Sanchez of Dearborn, Michigan, seized some marijuana while on patrol and pocketed it. He brought it home, baked a big ol' pile of it into some brownies, and then he and his wife ate a plate full of the first weed brownies they'd ever had. How many brownies did they eat? And how many herbs were in the brownies? "I don't know," a panic-stricken Sanchez frantically warned the 911 dispatcher he'd just called. "We made brownies, and I think we're dead. I really do."

Now, the dispatcher's 80-grade training is on point throughout this call. She plays him like the stoned fiddle he is, and has the entire situation on lock not three minutes in, save for living in Dearborn, Michigan, and not having the score of the Red Wings game at the ready. But with the stakes still less certain, early on in the call, she has the young corporal checking with concern on the vitality of his potentially-overdosing-on-marijuana-somehow wife. She's okay, he reports, but "time is going by really, really ... really ... really slowly."

Still two-and-two, by the way. Deuces wild here in the seventh, as Baez comes set.

Walker Buehler RHP Born: 07/28/94 Age: 23 Bats: R Throws: R Height: 6'2" Weight: 175 Origin: Round 1, 2015 Draft (#24 overall)

YEAR	TEAM	LVL	AGE	W	L	SV	G	GS	IP	H	HR	BB/9	K/9	K	GB%	BABIP	WHIP	ERA	DRA	WARP	MPH	CMD	PWR	STM
2017	RCU	A+	22	0	0	0	5	5	16^{1}	8	0	2.8	14.9	27	57%	.267	0.80	1.10	1.65	0.7				
2017	TUL	AA	22	2	2	0	11	11	49	40	5	2.8	11.8	64	52%	.315	1.12	3.49	1.54	2.1				
2017	OKL	AAA	22	1	1	1	12	3	23^{1}	19	1	4.2	13.1	34	62%	.333	1.29	4.63	1.50	1.0				
2017	LAN	MLB	22	1	0	0	8	0	9^{1}	11	2	7.7	11.6	12	67%	.409	2.04	7.71	6.36	-0.1	99.5			49
2018	*LAN*	*MLB*	*23*	*4*	*3*	*0*	*10*	*10*	*53*	*47*	*9*	*4.6*	*10.8*	*64*	*48%*	*.295*	*1.39*	*4.27*	*4.87*	*0.2*	*99.4*			*51*
2019	*LAN*	*MLB*	*24*	*10*	*11*	*0*	*32*	*32*	*202^{2}*	*164*	*29*	*4.1*	*10.1*	*227*	*48%*	*.294*	*1.27*	*4.27*	*4.92*	*1.3*	*99.2*			*51*

Breakout: 28% Improve: 53% Collapse: 15% Attrition: 20% MLB: 79% *Comparables: Edwin Diaz, Matt Moore, Aroldis Chapman*

A season that started at High-A ended with a first few sips of September Joe for the top Dodgers prospect. Despite the wild success of that ride, it did end perhaps a bit prematurely. Seeking to both cap the Tommy John survivor's workload and audition the kid for a role of late-inning playoff dominance, Los Angeles converted the young fireballer to relief in time for his big-league debut. The stuff was there when he stepped on the hallowed Chavez hump, but playoff-caliber command of it didn't materialize as hoped, and October will have to call again another day. Fortunately, Buehler figures to have his opportunities. His top-of-the-scale gas and hard curve anchor a potentially front-end arsenal, and he'll position well to build an innings bump in his second full season removed from the knife.

Tony Cingrani LHP Born: 07/05/89 Age: 28 Bats: L Throws: L Height: 6'4" Weight: 214 Origin: Round 3, 2011 Draft (#114 overall)

YEAR	TEAM	LVL	AGE	W	L	SV	G	GS	IP	H	HR	BB/9	K/9	K	GB%	BABIP	WHIP	ERA	DRA	WARP	MPH	CMD	PWR	STM
2015	LOU	AAA	25	0	1	0	9	6	24^{2}	20	2	4.0	11.7	32	45%	.310	1.26	1.82	2.08	0.9				
2015	CIN	MLB	25	0	3	0	35	1	33^{1}	31	3	6.8	10.5	39	41%	.329	1.68	5.67	4.53	0.1	94.7	55	62	42
2016	CIN	MLB	26	2	5	17	65	0	63	54	5	5.3	7.0	49	48%	.277	1.44	4.14	4.95	0.0	96.7	52	67	48
2017	CIN	MLB	27	0	0	0	25	0	23^{1}	25	9	2.3	9.3	24	43%	.271	1.33	5.40	6.72	-0.4	95.9	47	69	39
2017	LAN	MLB	27	0	0	0	22	0	19^{1}	15	1	2.8	13.0	28	42%	.333	1.09	2.79	3.48	0.4	96.2	47	69	39
2018	*LAN*	*MLB*	*28*	*3*	*2*	*0*	*45*	*0*	*47*	*40*	*7*	*3.9*	*10.3*	*55*	*44%*	*.284*	*1.26*	*3.84*	*4.33*	*0.3*	*95.5*	*51*	*67*	*43*
2019	*LAN*	*MLB*	*29*	*3*	*1*	*0*	*55*	*0*	*58*	*45*	*8*	*4.2*	*10.4*	*67*	*44%*	*.287*	*1.24*	*4.13*	*4.75*	*0.3*	*95.4*	*50*	*68*	*43*

Breakout: 22% Improve: 47% Collapse: 25% Attrition: 6% MLB: 89% *Comparables: Jonathan Sanchez, Juan Cruz, Brandon Morrow*

A six-foot-four southpaw who sits 95 with plane is *always* interesting, even when he hasn't put together an above-average season in more than four years and his DRA is lining up to kick the extra point. The Dodgers saw something they liked despite the top-line failures, poaching him as a cheap fixer-upper in July. And fix him up they did: He immediately started throwing many more sliders, while moving his fastball north and pinning it more consistently arm-side. Voila! Over his 22 games in Pantone 294 he racked up the strikeouts while cutting that bloated DRA nearly in half. With two more years of club control and a run of gnarly statistical output denting his arbitration comps, Cingrani stands capable of providing excellent middle relief at even more excellent value for the next couple seasons.

Yu Darvish RHP Born: 08/16/86 Age: 31 Bats: R Throws: R Height: 6'5" Weight: 220 Origin: International Free Agent, 2012

YEAR	TEAM	LVL	AGE	W	L	SV	G	GS	IP	H	HR	BB/9	K/9	K	GB%	BABIP	WHIP	ERA	DRA	WARP	MPH	CMD	PWR	STM
2016	FRI	AA	29	1	1	0	5	5	20	14	1	3.2	10.8	24	50%	.277	1.05	2.25	2.88	0.5				
2016	TEX	MLB	29	7	5	0	17	17	100^{1}	81	12	2.8	11.8	132	40%	.290	1.12	3.41	3.11	2.6	97.1	38	56	55
2017	TEX	MLB	30	6	9	0	22	22	137	115	20	3.0	9.7	148	42%	.275	1.17	4.01	3.02	3.9	96.5	42	59	78
2017	LAN	MLB	30	4	3	0	9	9	49^{2}	44	7	2.4	11.1	61	45%	.308	1.15	3.44	3.24	1.3	96.4	42	59	78
2018	*LAN*	*MLB*	*31*	*11*	*7*	*0*	*26*	*26*	*154^{2}*	*124*	*22*	*2.9*	*10.6*	*183*	*42%*	*.288*	*1.12*	*3.74*	*4.25*	*2.4*	*95.8*	*41*	*58*	*67*
2019	*LAN*	*MLB*	*32*	*10*	*11*	*0*	*30*	*30*	*187^{2}*	*162*	*26*	*3.4*	*8.8*	*184*	*42%*	*.292*	*1.25*	*4.24*	*4.87*	*1.5*	*95.3*	*40*	*58*	*67*

Breakout: 20% Improve: 53% Collapse: 21% Attrition: 9% MLB: 93% *Comparables: Max Scherzer, John Smoltz, Jake Peavy*

High tonight, low tomorrow ... and precipitation is expected. That was Tom Waits' emotional weather report a long time ago, and boy does Darvish know what that tune is singing. Baseball is a game of failure, of course, but there's a difference between everyday, run-of-the-mill failure, and spectacular, naked failure on the game's biggest stage. Los Angeles acquired Darvish nearly 14 months after his return from Tommy John surgery, amid a period of some uncertainty in his career; the stuff looked more or less like a robust ghost of its former self, yet he hadn't missed quite as many bats quite as consistently over the first half of his first full season back. He'd been good, but he hadn't been great—or at least as great as he'd been before. The Dodgers took the plunge anyway, and he settled into some kind of September groove in Chavez Ravine before waltzing right on through all National League comers. But where the lights shine the brightest, the memories are the most vivid. It was an unceremonious cast into the waters of free agency for the right-hander, who'll test the open market for the first time in his storied career looking to escape the most unpleasant of vice grips on his mental health.

Josh Fields RHP
Born: 08/19/85 Age: 32 Bats: R Throws: R Height: 6'0" Weight: 195 Origin: Round 1, 2008 Draft (#20 overall)

YEAR	TEAM	LVL	AGE	W	L	SV	G	GS	IP	H	HR	BB/9	K/9	K	GB%	BABIP	WHIP	ERA	DRA	WARP	MPH	CMD	PWR	STM
2015	HOU	MLB	29	4	1	0	54	0	50^{2}	39	2	3.4	11.9	67	37%	.308	1.14	3.55	2.77	1.2	97.1	49	60	48
2016	HOU	MLB	30	0	0	0	15	0	15^{2}	23	2	1.7	11.5	20	31%	.457	1.66	6.89	5.74	-0.1	97.0	46	52	47
2016	FRE	AAA	30	1	0	1	23	0	27^{1}	19	0	2.3	10.5	32	46%	.279	0.95	1.65	2.07	0.9				
2016	LAN	MLB	30	1	0	0	22	0	19^{1}	20	2	3.7	10.2	22	41%	.333	1.45	2.79	3.59	0.3	97.4	46	52	47
2017	LAN	MLB	31	5	0	2	57	0	57	40	10	2.4	9.5	60	30%	.219	0.96	2.84	4.34	0.5	97.0	52	66	45
2018	*LAN*	*MLB*	*32*	*3*	*2*	*0*	*50*	*0*	*52*	*50*	*10*	*3.6*	*10.1*	*59*	*38%*	*.295*	*1.34*	*4.45*	*4.83*	*0.0*	*96.1*	*49*	*60*	*46*
2019	*LAN*	*MLB*	*33*	*2*	*1*	*1*	*40*	*0*	*42*	*38*	*8*	*3.7*	*9.9*	*47*	*38%*	*.302*	*1.32*	*4.84*	*5.56*	*-0.2*	*95.6*	*49*	*60*	*45*

Breakout: 20% Improve: 40% Collapse: 27% Attrition: 4% MLB: 87% *Comparables: Shawn Kelley, Scott Williamson, Mike Dunn*

Since joining the Dodgers in a midseason deal back in 2016, Fields has outperformed his FIP and DRA by more than a run by precariously balancing an extreme amount of sometimes-scary fly-ball contact with a healthy dose of bat-missing. A poster child for the Dodgers' elevation-heavy pitching attack, he comes right at hitters, challenging up in the zone with lively 96-mph gas that holds its plane. The strategy is not without its pitfalls, particularly in the modern era where the world is a Coors Field-lookin' vampire: Fields gave up some of the loudest exit velocity and longest contact on average of any reliever last year, let alone any successful one. Despite his built-in susceptibilities to the allure of the long ball, he figures to slot right back into a reasonably priced middle-relief role in 2018.

Rich Hill LHP
Born: 03/11/80 Age: 38 Bats: L Throws: L Height: 6'5" Weight: 220 Origin: Round 4, 2002 Draft (#112 overall)

YEAR	TEAM	LVL	AGE	W	L	SV	G	GS	IP	H	HR	BB/9	K/9	K	GB%	BABIP	WHIP	ERA	DRA	WARP	MPH	CMD	PWR	STM
2015	SYR	AAA	35	2	2	0	25	0	21^{2}	12	1	8.7	13.3	32	54%	.262	1.52	2.91	3.32	0.4				
2015	PAW	AAA	35	3	2	0	5	5	32^{1}	27	3	2.5	8.1	29	48%	.282	1.11	2.78	3.53	0.6				
2015	BOS	MLB	35	2	1	0	4	4	29	14	2	1.6	11.2	36	51%	.197	0.66	1.55	2.83	0.8	92.7	51	21	41
2016	OAK	MLB	36	9	3	0	14	14	76	55	2	3.3	10.7	90	51%	.290	1.09	2.25	2.83	2.2	93.0	55	28	42
2016	LAN	MLB	36	3	2	0	6	6	34^{1}	22	2	1.3	10.2	39	38%	.244	0.79	1.83	3.61	0.7	92.2	55	28	42
2017	LAN	MLB	37	12	8	0	25	25	135^{2}	99	18	3.3	11.0	166	39%	.261	1.09	3.32	4.16	2.1	90.7	43	21	61
2018	*LAN*	*MLB*	*38*	*10*	*6*	*0*	*24*	*24*	*136*	*118*	*19*	*3.3*	*10.2*	*155*	*44%*	*.291*	*1.23*	*3.63*	*4.15*	*1.6*	*90.1*	*47*	*23*	*48*
2019	*LAN*	*MLB*	*39*	*11*	*11*	*0*	*32*	*32*	*207^{1}*	*169*	*28*	*3.2*	*10.0*	*231*	*44%*	*.296*	*1.17*	*3.89*	*4.47*	*2.3*	*89.3*	*46*	*23*	*49*

Breakout: 23% Improve: 36% Collapse: 22% Attrition: 5% MLB: 81% *Comparables: Roger Clemens, Allie Reynolds, Hoyt Wilhelm*

Armed with the first multi-year contract of his fascinating career at 37, Hill showed why the Dodgers made him rich. Blister issues foiled him early, but once he got rolling he again proved that he's just tough to do much of anything with. After threatening to drop a slider into the mix in spring training, he quickly settled in to his standard one-two punch. And despite a couple missing ticks, it was a lethal combination once again. He whiffed over 30 percent of the hitters he faced, while masterfully controlling the exit velocities of the ones who did manage to get a piece. He also showed himself to be a tough [expletive] to boot, taking a fastball off the neck during a botched bunt attempt in an August start and staying in the game for two more scoreless frames. The Dodgers were careful to limit his exposure to third looks, a pattern taken to the extreme in four postseason starts during which he finished five just once. Expect more of the same in the second of Hill's three gloriously contracted years, and enjoy rooting for the old man.

Kenley Jansen RHP
Born: 09/30/87 Age: 30 Bats: B Throws: R Height: 6'5" Weight: 275 Origin: International Free Agent, 2004

YEAR	TEAM	LVL	AGE	W	L	SV	G	GS	IP	H	HR	BB/9	K/9	K	GB%	BABIP	WHIP	ERA	DRA	WARP	MPH	CMD	PWR	STM
2015	LAN	MLB	27	2	1	36	54	0	52^{1}	33	6	1.4	13.8	80	36%	.260	0.78	2.41	2.13	1.6	95.6	49	67	48
2016	LAN	MLB	28	3	2	47	71	0	68^{2}	35	4	1.4	13.6	104	33%	.238	0.67	1.83	1.94	2.4	96.6	52	73	49
2017	LAN	MLB	29	5	0	41	65	0	68^{1}	44	5	0.9	14.4	109	40%	.291	0.75	1.32	2.34	2.2	95.7	64	73	48
2018	*LAN*	*MLB*	*30*	*4*	*2*	*40*	*60*	*0*	*63*	*46*	*8*	*2.6*	*13.3*	*94*	*38%*	*.291*	*1.00*	*2.18*	*2.75*	*1.6*	*95.2*	*56*	*72*	*48*
2019	*LAN*	*MLB*	*31*	*4*	*2*	*47*	*76*	*0*	*80^{2}*	*55*	*11*	*2.2*	*13.2*	*118*	*38%*	*.298*	*0.93*	*2.72*	*3.12*	*1.8*	*94.9*	*58*	*72*	*48*

Breakout: 23% Improve: 40% Collapse: 27% Attrition: 8% MLB: 91% *Comparables: Rich Gossage, Rafael Soriano, David Robertson*

John Keats once opined that a thing of beauty is a joy forever, and he was right. When Jansen threw 20 pitches in an inning, 17 of 'em were 93-to-94-mph cut fastballs—blazing darts that hooked hard and late to the glove side and held their vertical line better than just about any other cut fastball. The pitch poured from the heaven's brink again in 2017, one of the most dominant in all the world. But what really brought Jansen to the next level was the slider. It's a rare pitch to be sure, but upon deployment it coaxed many more whiffs last year than it had in 2016. And when you've got as little room to improve as Jansen, that's a pretty big deal. He'll enter the second year of his five-year deal in Keats-approved fashion, full of sweet dreams and health and quiet breathing.

Jair Jurrjens RHP
Born: 01/29/86 Age: 32 Bats: R Throws: R Height: 6'1" Weight: 200 Origin: International Free Agent, 2003

YEAR	TEAM	LVL	AGE	W	L	SV	G	GS	IP	H	HR	BB/9	K/9	K	GB%	BABIP	WHIP	ERA	DRA	WARP	MPH	CMD	PWR	STM
2015	ABQ	AAA	29	2	5	0	17	14	70^{2}	105	9	2.9	5.0	39	41%	.368	1.81	6.88	6.82	-1.3				
2017	OKL	AAA	31	4	3	0	11	10	54^{1}	63	6	3.0	7.3	44	44%	.335	1.49	4.64	6.80	-0.7				
2018	*LAN*	*MLB*	*32*	*2*	*2*	*0*	*8*	*8*	*38*	*40*	*6*	*3.1*	*7.1*	*30*	*41%*	*.307*	*1.41*	*4.94*	*5.64*	*0.0*				
2019	*LAN*	*MLB*	*33*	*6*	*12*	*0*	*27*	*27*	*159^{2}*	*180*	*29*	*4.3*	*6.1*	*108*	*41%*	*.315*	*1.60*	*5.72*	*6.59*	*-1.4*				

Breakout: 5% Improve: 8% Collapse: 1% Attrition: 5% MLB: 11% *Comparables: Thad Weber, Greg Smith, Anthony Lerew*

Yes, you're reading this right, he was still kicking around the high minors last season. "Was" is the operative word in that sentence; Jurrjens hasn't toed a big-league rubber since 2014, and after struggling through an injury-riddled campaign in the Chinese Professional Baseball League in 2016, it appeared he might just be done with the whole professional baseball player thing. But he looked marginally less done while pitching for Team Netherlands in the World Baseball Classic last spring, and the effort was enough to net him a minor-league reclamation contract. Fifty-some-odd mediocre innings at Triple-A and a PED suspension later, however, and a return test of international waters seems the likeliest next landing spot for the greatest starting pitcher in Curacao's history.

Clayton Kershaw LHP Born: 03/19/88 Age: 30 Bats: L Throws: L Height: 6'4" Weight: 228 Origin: Round 1, 2006 Draft (#7 overall)

YEAR	TEAM	LVL	AGE	W	L	SV	G	GS	IP	H	HR	BB/9	K/9	K	GB%	BABIP	WHIP	ERA	DRA	WARP	MPH	CMD	PWR	STM
2015	LAN	MLB	27	16	7	0	33	33	232^2	163	15	1.6	11.6	301	52%	.281	0.88	2.13	2.09	8.3	95.8	55	51	81
2016	LAN	MLB	28	12	4	0	21	21	149	97	8	0.7	10.4	172	51%	.254	0.72	1.69	2.13	5.5	95.1	51	47	52
2017	LAN	MLB	29	18	4	0	27	27	175	136	23	1.5	10.4	202	49%	.267	0.95	2.31	3.30	4.4	94.3	63	45	68
2018	*LAN*	*MLB*	*30*	*15*	*7*	*0*	*28*	*28*	*187*	*146*	*21*	*2.1*	*10.5*	*219*	*49%*	*.276*	*0.98*	*2.80*	*3.23*	*4.2*	*94.2*	*57*	*47*	*66*
2019	*LAN*	*MLB*	*31*	*15*	*10*	*0*	*34*	*34*	*225^2*	*157*	*24*	*1.5*	*10.5*	*264*	*49%*	*.273*	*0.87*	*2.72*	*3.10*	*6.2*	*93.6*	*58*	*46*	*63*

Breakout: 13% Improve: 45% Collapse: 37% Attrition: 11% MLB: 95% *Comparables: Greg Maddux, Johnny Cueto, Roy Halladay*

There isn't much left to say about Kershaw's brilliant performance. For a seventh straight year he put up one of the five best seasons of any National League pitcher, as told by Cy Young voters. And that'd likely be seven straight top-*three* finishes if he'd just stayed healthy in 2016. But therein lies the rub: For the third time in four years Kershaw missed time with injury, and most alarmingly it was a second straight back issue. With over 2,000 total big-league innings on the odometer, any carpool of consecutive foundational injuries blares reggaeton alarms out the windows as it cruises by—especially since he's owed another nine guaranteed figures. The big Texan rebounded to dominate for most of his first World Series run, though the sting of a lost four-run lead in pivotal swing Game 5 leaves another mark. He'll shuffle into his third decade still in search of an elusive ring to tie off a résumé that tells the tale of one of the greatest pitching runs the game has ever seen.

Tom Koehler RHP Born: 06/29/86 Age: 31 Bats: R Throws: R Height: 6'3" Weight: 235 Origin: Round 18, 2008 Draft (#538 overall)

YEAR	TEAM	LVL	AGE	W	L	SV	G	GS	IP	H	HR	BB/9	K/9	K	GB%	BABIP	WHIP	ERA	DRA	WARP	MPH	CMD	PWR	STM
2015	MIA	MLB	29	11	14	0	32	31	187^1	180	22	3.7	6.6	137	49%	.283	1.37	4.08	4.85	0.5	94.6	43	43	73
2016	MIA	MLB	30	9	13	0	33	33	176^2	176	22	4.2	7.5	147	44%	.298	1.47	4.33	5.18	0.4	94.4	46	40	76
2017	MIA	MLB	31	1	5	0	12	12	55^2	67	15	4.7	7.1	44	41%	.313	1.72	7.92	7.53	-1.3	94.3	48	43	56
2017	NWO	AAA	31	1	1	0	7	6	37^2	30	4	3.1	13.1	55	46%	.310	1.14	1.67	1.99	1.5				
2017	TOR	MLB	31	0	2	0	15	1	17	16	1	3.2	9.5	18	47%	.312	1.29	2.65	6.58	-0.2	94.9	48	43	56
2018	*LAN*	*MLB*	*32*	*5*	*4*	*0*	*43*	*8*	*79*	*76*	*12*	*4.0*	*8.3*	*73*	*44%*	*.289*	*1.39*	*4.62*	*5.04*	*0.0*	*93.5*	*45*	*41*	*66*
2019	*LAN*	*MLB*	*33*	*7*	*5*	*0*	*71*	*12*	*134^1*	*115*	*19*	*3.7*	*8.5*	*127*	*44%*	*.289*	*1.26*	*4.81*	*5.05*	*0.5*	*93.1*	*46*	*41*	*65*

Breakout: 11% Improve: 46% Collapse: 20% Attrition: 12% MLB: 84% *Comparables: Edinson Volquez, Jason Hammel, Roberto Hernandez*

Little-known fact: American Standard makes the official toilet of the Toronto Blue Jays. Better-known fact: Tom Koehler's last name sounds conspicuously like a popular American toilet maker. When the team acquired Koehler in late August, pundits joked that Big Toilet wouldn't be happy with it. Despite posting a 4.70 ERA over 420 innings in the two-and-a-half seasons prior, Koehler pitched well in Toronto, making him difficult to remove. In particular, his velocity played up in the bullpen; he was touching 96 mph regularly for the first time since early 2015. Given his age and lack of remarkable secondary stuff, it's unlikely that there's much hidden talent left in the tank, but apparently the Dodgers saw something they liked when they signed him in December.

Kenta Maeda RHP Born: 04/11/88 Age: 30 Bats: R Throws: R Height: 6'1" Weight: 175 Origin: International Free Agent, 2016

YEAR	TEAM	LVL	AGE	W	L	SV	G	GS	IP	H	HR	BB/9	K/9	K	GB%	BABIP	WHIP	ERA	DRA	WARP	MPH	CMD	PWR	STM
2016	LAN	MLB	28	16	11	0	32	32	175^2	150	20	2.6	9.2	179	45%	.283	1.14	3.48	3.18	4.4	92.5	62	30	72
2017	LAN	MLB	29	13	6	1	29	25	134^1	121	22	2.3	9.4	140	40%	.278	1.15	4.22	3.89	2.5	93.3	62	33	60
2018	*LAN*	*MLB*	*30*	*9*	*6*	*0*	*24*	*24*	*127*	*115*	*18*	*2.8*	*9.2*	*131*	*42%*	*.287*	*1.20*	*3.73*	*4.27*	*1.3*	*92.1*	*62*	*31*	*65*
2019	*LAN*	*MLB*	*31*	*10*	*11*	*0*	*32*	*32*	*204^2*	*181*	*28*	*3.2*	*7.9*	*180*	*42%*	*.288*	*1.24*	*4.34*	*4.98*	*1.2*	*91.8*	*62*	*31*	*65*

Breakout: 9% Improve: 37% Collapse: 31% Attrition: 10% MLB: 96% *Comparables: John Lackey, Zack Greinke, Shaun Marcum*

Second acts are often tough, and while Maeda largely held his own, he crumbled a bit at the margins. He was thrice the victim of Dodger rotation largesse, first serving a dubious 10-day DL stint in May for a "tight hamstring" that just so happened to accommodate Hyun-Jin Ryu's return. After enjoying a gentle, temporary workload in the bullpen while a next wave of overcrowding crashed in June, he found himself outside the rotation again in October. He looked right at home in the role, however. His hard slider ate righties alive, and he yielded just one run in more than ten knockout innings with tantalizingly played-up stuff. His incentive-laden deal is weighted heavily toward bulk, giving the Dodgers something else to ponder for the future. One sure thing is that it will be the Dodgers doing the pondering, as they'll control his consistently above-average services on the cheap and flexible until 2024.

Dustin May RHP Born: 09/06/97 Age: 20 Bats: R Throws: R Height: 6'6" Weight: 180 Origin: Round 3, 2016 Draft (#101 overall)

YEAR	TEAM	LVL	AGE	W	L	SV	G	GS	IP	H	HR	BB/9	K/9	K	GB%	BABIP	WHIP	ERA	DRA	WARP	MPH	CMD	PWR	STM
2016	DOD	RK	18	0	1	1	10	6	30^1	37	0	1.2	10.1	34	57%	.394	1.35	3.86	2.04	1.2				
2017	GRL	A	19	9	6	0	23	23	123	121	8	1.9	8.3	113	52%	.306	1.20	3.88	2.36	4.2				
2017	RCU	A+	19	0	0	0	2	1	11	6	0	0.8	12.3	15	60%	.240	0.64	0.82	1.98	0.4				
2018	*LAN*	*MLB*	*20*	*6*	*6*	*0*	*29*	*18*	*101^1*	*97*	*19*	*3.3*	*9.5*	*108*	*44%*	*.306*	*1.32*	*4.70*	*5.36*	*0.2*				
2019	*LAN*	*MLB*	*21*	*6*	*8*	*0*	*27*	*22*	*146^2*	*142*	*27*	*3.5*	*8.9*	*145*	*44%*	*.311*	*1.35*	*4.90*	*5.64*	*-0.1*				

Breakout: 4% Improve: 5% Collapse: 1% Attrition: 3% MLB: 7% *Comparables: Henderson Alvarez, Jameson Taillon, Vicente Campos*

Bronson Arroyo may have hung 'em up, but the ghost of his frame and delivery lingers on in May. The young redhead's affectionate "Gingergaard" moniker is something of a misnomer, as despite the length and locks, the Dodgers' former third-rounder lacks projection for true Thor-ian bulk and top-end velocity. His gas ain't bad, though, working consistently into the mid-90s with a strong bore into the kitchen of right-handed hitters. And he pairs it with an exciting slider that can tantalize on the same plane as his two-seamer before veering sharp and late in the opposite direction. Standard questions about durability for a skinny guy, command projection for a tall guy and third-pitch development for ... well, just about every young starter, figure to dog him throughout the growth process, but there's a sassy kind of mid-rotation upside here.

Trevor Oaks RHP Born: 03/26/93 Age: 25 Bats: R Throws: R Height: 6'3" Weight: 220 Origin: Round 7, 2014 Draft (#219 overall)

YEAR	TEAM	LVL	AGE	W	L	SV	G	GS	IP	H	HR	BB/9	K/9	K	GB%	BABIP	WHIP	ERA	DRA	WARP	MPH	CMD	PWR	STM
2015	GRL	A	22	5	5	0	18	16	102	84	3	1.2	5.1	58	64%	.252	0.96	2.56	3.52	2.0				
2015	RCU	A+	22	3	0	0	5	5	23^2	28	2	1.9	6.1	16	54%	.333	1.39	3.04	4.36	0.2				
2016	RCU	A+	23	1	1	0	4	4	25	26	1	1.1	7.9	22	60%	.352	1.16	3.60	2.35	0.9				
2016	TUL	AA	23	8	1	0	10	10	63	56	1	1.3	5.4	38	65%	.276	1.03	2.14	3.08	1.5				
2016	OKL	AAA	23	5	1	0	10	10	63	64	7	1.3	6.9	48	58%	.300	1.16	3.00	2.50	2.1				
2017	OKL	AAA	24	4	3	0	16	15	84	87	5	1.9	7.7	72	52%	.336	1.25	3.64	2.27	3.1				
2018	*KCA*	*MLB*	*25*	*1*	*1*	*0*	*29*	*0*	*31*	*29*	*3*	*3.0*	*7.1*	*25*	*52%*	*.291*	*1.28*	*3.96*	*4.22*	*0.3*				
2019	*KCA*	*MLB*	*26*	*10*	*11*	*0*	*33*	*33*	*213^1*	*187*	*27*	*2.2*	*7.6*	*179*	*52%*	*.287*	*1.12*	*3.94*	*4.51*	*2.0*				

Breakout: 24% Improve: 38% Collapse: 7% Attrition: 31% MLB: 54% *Comparables: Ryan Merritt, Ty Blach, Matt Andriese*

Oaks missed nearly all of July and August with an oblique injury, which was unfortunate, as he had been cruising toward a likely big-league debut when the pitching gods cashed that check. A plus two-seamer headlines a workable and deep arsenal, and he commands his pitches consistently down in the zone. Some of what he lacks in bat-missing secondaries he makes up for by burning hella worms, though after his ground-ball rate took a step back at Triple-A it's less clear that the best hitters will struggle to get their barrels under his ball. He won't fail for shying away from the challenge, however, and his consistency in executing around the zone should keep him in the hunt for rotation spots around baseball for many years to come.

Henry Owens LHP Born: 07/21/92 Age: 25 Bats: L Throws: L Height: 6'6" Weight: 220 Origin: Round 1, 2011 Draft (#36 overall)

YEAR	TEAM	LVL	AGE	W	L	SV	G	GS	IP	H	HR	BB/9	K/9	K	GB%	BABIP	WHIP	ERA	DRA	WARP	MPH	CMD	PWR	STM
2015	PAW	AAA	22	3	8	0	21	21	122^1	84	7	4.1	7.6	103	41%	.233	1.14	3.16	4.84	0.6				
2015	BOS	MLB	22	4	4	0	11	11	63	62	7	3.4	7.1	50	37%	.293	1.37	4.57	4.96	0.1	92.5	48	31	74
2016	PAW	AAA	23	10	7	0	24	24	137^2	107	13	5.3	8.8	135	36%	.266	1.37	3.53	6.53	-1.9				
2016	BOS	MLB	23	0	2	0	5	5	22	23	5	8.2	8.6	21	31%	.321	1.95	6.95	6.23	-0.2	92.6	53	32	71
2017	PAW	AAA	24	4	5	0	14	14	69	57	6	7.8	9.4	72	33%	.283	1.70	3.91	10.82	-3.8				
2017	PME	AA	24	3	6	0	12	12	57	40	2	8.7	7.7	49	39%	.257	1.67	4.58	9.83	-3.2				
2018	*LAN*	*MLB*	*25*	*2*	*2*	*0*	*5*	*5*	*25*	*22*	*4*	*5.5*	*9.9*	*27*	*37%*	*.290*	*1.44*	*4.76*	*5.41*	*-0.1*	*92.3*	*51*	*32*	*74*
2019	*LAN*	*MLB*	*26*	*6*	*8*	*0*	*20*	*20*	*117^1*	*107*	*21*	*3.4*	*8.9*	*116*	*37%*	*.296*	*1.29*	*4.82*	*5.50*	*0.2*	*92.0*	*53*	*33*	*74*

Breakout: 16% Improve: 34% Collapse: 16% Attrition: 27% MLB: 58% *Comparables: Dustin Nippert, Jose Capellan, Charlie Haeger*

Portland, Maine, is a really cool city. It's very walkable, it has great seafood and it's home to some incredible craft beer. It packs a ton of New England charm without Massachusetts' aggressiveness, New Hampshire's inferiority complex or Connecticut's New York-ness. There are worse ways to spend your summer than hanging out in Portland, but Owens probably didn't feel that way in July. The former top prospect was demoted back to Double-A after a particularly rough stretch in Pawtucket that saw him walk 48 batters in 47 1/3 innings, issuing eight free passes in two of his final three starts. Even though it feels like we've been talking about Owens forever, he's still just 25. There's still time for it to click. That time is running out, though. His low-90s fastball and deception-based changeup won't necessarily translate well to the bullpen, so cutting down his walks is Owens' only shot.

Hyun-jin Ryu LHP Born: 03/25/87 Age: 31 Bats: R Throws: L Height: 6'3" Weight: 250 Origin: International Free Agent, 2013

YEAR	TEAM	LVL	AGE	W	L	SV	G	GS	IP	H	HR	BB/9	K/9	K	GB%	BABIP	WHIP	ERA	DRA	WARP	MPH	CMD	PWR	STM
2016	RCU	A+	29	1	1	0	5	5	18	15	2	0.5	7.0	14	45%	.241	0.89	2.00	3.22	0.5				
2016	LAN	MLB	29	0	1	0	1	1	4^2	8	1	3.9	7.7	4	50%	.412	2.14	11.57	7.60	-0.1	92.7			29
2017	LAN	MLB	30	5	9	1	25	24	126^2	128	22	3.2	8.2	116	48%	.299	1.37	3.77	4.99	0.8	92.3	61	22	56
2018	*LAN*	*MLB*	*31*	*8*	*6*	*0*	*21*	*21*	*111^1*	*113*	*19*	*3.1*	*8.0*	*99*	*44%*	*.294*	*1.35*	*4.37*	*4.97*	*0.2*	*91.5*	*61*	*22*	*44*
2019	*LAN*	*MLB*	*32*	*9*	*12*	*0*	*30*	*30*	*189^1*	*186*	*29*	*3.5*	*7.1*	*149*	*44%*	*.301*	*1.37*	*4.79*	*5.51*	*0.2*	*91.0*	*60*	*22*	*44*

Breakout: 9% Improve: 42% Collapse: 32% Attrition: 10% MLB: 93% *Comparables: Homer Bailey, Matt Garza, Jason Hammel*

One of the greatest luxuries of wealth is patience, and the Dodgers were rewarded for exercising theirs through Ryu's various recoveries. He was gone, and then, like a gentle breeze wafting through an open window under an obsidian sky, he was back, starting 24 more games than you remember him starting. It was a return uncannily lacking in triumph, and yet it was as steady and valuable as any best-case scenario could've predicted. Although he effectively hadn't set foot on a big-league mound since the last mid-term election, Ryu's stuff looked reasonably intact. He even added a shiny new cutter into the mix, and it wasn't half bad! The performance was weird, though. He worked behind constantly, and gave up some dingers and walks for his trouble, yet he managed to skirt the damning DRA that ensued and prevent runs at just a nominally below-average rate. He'll enter his walk year looking to carve out a niche for his thirties as quality rotation depth.

Brock Stewart RHP Born: 10/03/91 Age: 26 Bats: L Throws: R Height: 6'3" Weight: 210 Origin: Round 6, 2014 Draft (#189 overall)

YEAR	TEAM	LVL	AGE	W	L	SV	G	GS	IP	H	HR	BB/9	K/9	K	GB%	BABIP	WHIP	ERA	DRA	WARP	MPH	CMD	PWR	STM
2015	GRL	A	23	2	2	0	7	7	38	38	4	1.4	9.0	38	36%	.324	1.16	2.84	2.86	1.1				
2015	RCU	A+	23	2	4	0	18	12	63	75	6	2.6	9.3	65	42%	.365	1.48	5.43	4.80	0.2				
2016	RCU	A+	24	2	0	0	2	2	11	5	0	1.6	8.2	10	44%	.185	0.64	0.82	2.94	0.3				
2016	OKL	AAA	24	4	0	0	9	9	50^2	41	4	1.1	9.6	54	44%	.278	0.93	2.49	1.36	2.3				
2016	TUL	AA	24	3	4	0	10	10	59^1	41	0	1.7	9.9	65	46%	.275	0.88	1.37	1.37	2.7				
2016	LAN	MLB	24	2	2	0	7	5	28	33	7	3.9	8.0	25	44%	.317	1.61	5.79	5.87	-0.2	95.9	39	53	58
2017	OKL	AAA	25	0	1	0	5	5	17^1	19	2	1.6	13.0	25	42%	.415	1.27	3.12	2.66	0.6				
2017	LAN	MLB	25	0	0	1	17	4	34^1	28	4	5.0	7.6	29	43%	.255	1.37	3.41	5.35	0.0	94.7	43	50	35
2018	*LAN*	*MLB*	*26*	*6*	*4*	*0*	*15*	*15*	*79*	*75*	*12*	*3.2*	*9.1*	*80*	*41%*	*.294*	*1.29*	*3.92*	*4.48*	*0.6*	*94.8*	*42*	*52*	*46*
2019	*LAN*	*MLB*	*27*	*10*	*11*	*0*	*32*	*32*	*210*	*176*	*29*	*2.8*	*9.4*	*220*	*41%*	*.294*	*1.15*	*3.82*	*4.38*	*2.3*	*94.5*	*42*	*52*	*46*

Breakout: 30% Improve: 52% Collapse: 16% Attrition: 22% MLB: 83% *Comparables: Nick Tropeano, Josh Collmenter, Rafael Perez*

Though his season's start was unduly delayed by a bum shoulder, Stewart was able to quickly pitch himself back into the anticipated fray once healthy, rejoining the big-league club after rehab work in June. A reasonably successful campaign swinging between the rotation and the middle innings followed, albeit one checkered by uncharacteristic nibbling and wildness at times. The son of a scout, Stewart has high baseball IQ that shines through in the form of clean, repeatable mechanics and strong pitchability. The stuff ain't bad either, with a mid-90s heater, hard slider and solid change. He may struggle to crack the rotation for a sustained stretch given the Dodgers' depth, but he'd be well-suited for the opportunity on the merits of his true talent.

Ross Stripling RHP Born: 11/23/89 Age: 28 Bats: R Throws: R Height: 6'3" Weight: 210 Origin: Round 5, 2012 Draft (#176 overall)

YEAR	TEAM	LVL	AGE	W	L	SV	G	GS	IP	H	HR	BB/9	K/9	K	GB%	BABIP	WHIP	ERA	DRA	WARP	MPH	CMD	PWR	STM
2015	TUL	AA	25	3	6	0	13	13	67^{1}	61	7	2.5	7.4	55	55%	.281	1.19	3.88	3.01	1.7				
2016	OKL	AAA	26	0	2	0	5	4	16^{2}	20	2	1.1	9.2	17	38%	.360	1.32	3.78	4.04	0.2				
2016	LAN	MLB	26	5	9	0	22	14	100	96	10	2.7	6.7	74	52%	.283	1.26	3.96	4.16	1.3	93.3	59	35	51
2017	LAN	MLB	27	3	5	2	49	2	74^{1}	69	10	2.3	9.0	74	51%	.294	1.18	3.75	4.03	1.0	94.5	64	37	48
2018	*LAN*	*MLB*	*28*	*4*	*3*	*0*	*65*	*0*	*68*	*61*	*8*	*3.3*	*8.7*	*66*	*49%*	*.289*	*1.26*	*3.55*	*4.08*	*0.7*	*93.3*	*62*	*36*	*50*
2019	*LAN*	*MLB*	*29*	*3*	*1*	*0*	*63*	*0*	66^{2}	*54*	*7*	*3.0*	*9.2*	*68*	*49%*	*.294*	*1.14*	*3.51*	*4.02*	*0.9*	*93.0*	*62*	*36*	*49*

Breakout: 20% Improve: 53% Collapse: 14% Attrition: 25% MLB: 85% *Comparables: Joe Saunders, Aaron Heilman, Alfredo Aceves*

Stripling got kind of lost in the mix there for a while, despite always being a pretty consistently interesting pitching prospect. Tommy John'll do that to a man. Before going under the knife, he'd been twice drafted in the top nine rounds, even peeking into the team's top-ten prospect list back in 2014. After logging a second straight season of 70-plus innings in the bigs, it's safe to say he's found his niche. He can really spin the ball, with two bending secondaries that worked to flummox left-handed hitters more than righties. He missed his share of barrels, coaxing a solid rate of grounders alongside ample weak contact in the air. Dingers took a bite out of his numbers, but overall it was a stellar effort providing swing value through the middle frames. Getting those innings homegrown and cheap is a must for any team, even one with pockets as deep as the Dodgers, and Stripling figures to see more opportunity in the role while arbitration remains a figment of future days.

Julio Urias LHP Born: 08/12/96 Age: 21 Bats: L Throws: L Height: 6'0" Weight: 215 Origin: International Free Agent, 2012

YEAR	TEAM	LVL	AGE	W	L	SV	G	GS	IP	H	HR	BB/9	K/9	K	GB%	BABIP	WHIP	ERA	DRA	WARP	MPH	CMD	PWR	STM
2015	TUL	AA	18	3	4	0	13	13	68^{1}	53	4	2.0	9.7	74	47%	.282	1.00	2.77	1.68	2.8				
2016	OKL	AAA	19	5	1	0	11	7	45	31	2	1.6	9.8	49	54%	.269	0.87	1.40	1.53	1.9				
2016	LAN	MLB	19	5	2	0	18	15	77	81	5	3.6	9.8	84	45%	.358	1.45	3.39	4.35	0.9	95.4	57	44	54
2017	LAN	MLB	20	0	2	0	5	5	23^{1}	23	1	5.4	4.2	11	43%	.293	1.59	5.40	6.91	-0.3	95.2	45	44	46
2017	OKL	AAA	20	3	0	0	6	6	31^{1}	20	1	4.3	9.2	32	47%	.253	1.12	2.59	3.75	0.7				
2018	*LAN*	*MLB*	*21*	*4*	*3*	*0*	*12*	*12*	54^{2}	*47*	*5*	*3.6*	*9.6*	*58*	*45%*	*.305*	*1.26*	*3.62*	*4.11*	*0.9*	*95.5*	*56*	*46*	*52*
2019	*LAN*	*MLB*	*22*	*9*	*9*	*0*	*31*	*31*	196^{2}	*164*	*23*	*3.2*	*10.1*	*221*	*45%*	*.31*	*1.19*	*3.57*	*4.09*	*2.4*	*95.4*	*57*	*47*	*53*

Breakout: 22% Improve: 38% Collapse: 6% Attrition: 22% MLB: 55% *Comparables: Madison Bumgarner, Clayton Kershaw, Tyler Skaggs*

There isn't much in the game that depresses the soul more than a young player of immense talent and unbridled potential blowing out before he finds his bearings at the big-league level. Unfortunately, so it went for the left-handed wunderkind, who tore the anterior capsule of his throwing shoulder on a June 10 pitch and went under the knife the following month for a procedure that will likely keep him out of vigorous competition until 2019. It was a devastating and ironic blow for a player whose pitch stress was monitored so acutely throughout his rapid summit of the system. The Dodgers said all the right things about the success of his surgery, but the realistic outcome of such operations remains a glaring unknown. The club will cross its fingers and hope a World Series run and extreme youth will prove a potent enough salve to keep the kid's spirits up until he can start chucking it again in the late summer months of 2018.

Tony Watson LHP Born: 05/30/85 Age: 33 Bats: L Throws: L Height: 6'4" Weight: 220 Origin: Round 9, 2007 Draft (#278 overall)

YEAR	TEAM	LVL	AGE	W	L	SV	G	GS	IP	H	HR	BB/9	K/9	K	GB%	BABIP	WHIP	ERA	DRA	WARP	MPH	CMD	PWR	STM
2015	PIT	MLB	30	4	1	1	77	0	75^{1}	55	3	2.0	7.4	62	50%	.251	0.96	1.91	3.11	1.4	96.3	65	64	53
2016	PIT	MLB	31	2	5	15	70	0	67^{2}	52	10	2.7	7.7	58	46%	.232	1.06	3.06	4.08	0.7	95.5	55	55	50
2017	PIT	MLB	32	5	3	10	47	0	46^{2}	57	7	2.7	6.8	35	46%	.333	1.52	3.66	6.25	-0.6	95.0	44	56	51
2017	LAN	MLB	32	2	1	0	24	0	20	15	2	2.7	8.1	18	62%	.241	1.05	2.70	4.17	0.2	95.2	44	56	51
2018	*LAN*	*MLB*	*33*	*3*	*1*	*7*	*58*	*0*	61^{2}	*52*	*8*	*3.0*	*8.0*	*55*	*47%*	*.272*	*1.17*	*4.25*	*4.83*	*0.2*	*94.5*	*53*	*57*	*51*
2019	*LAN*	*MLB*	*34*	*2*	*1*	*5*	*42*	*0*	40^{1}	*34*	*6*	*3.3*	*7.5*	*33*	*47%*	*.272*	*1.21*	*4.51*	*5.16*	*0.0*	*93.8*	*49*	*55*	*50*

Breakout: 22% Improve: 44% Collapse: 35% Attrition: 9% MLB: 93% *Comparables: Joe Smith, Mariano Rivera, Casey Janssen*

The Dodgers didn't exactly play coy with their in-season lefty-acquisition strategy: Similar to fellow arrival Tony Cingrani, Watson came over on the heels of a lackluster first half, started throwing a different pitch mix to different zones and suddenly pitched much better. He skied his ground-ball rate by working off a heavy two-seamer, which is a thing that can happen when you sit 94 with above-average wiggle. He performed well situationally at both championship levels in October, too. It was a fortuitous turn for the free-agent-to-be, and he'll hit the open market with both high-leverage street cred and a rejuvenated nasty from the arm-side that gets paid.

Mitch White RHP Born: 12/28/94 Age: 23 Bats: R Throws: R Height: 6'4" Weight: 207 Origin: Round 2, 2016 Draft (#65 overall)

YEAR	TEAM	LVL	AGE	W	L	SV	G	GS	IP	H	HR	BB/9	K/9	K	GB%	BABIP	WHIP	ERA	DRA	WARP	MPH	CMD	PWR	STM
2016	GRL	A	21	0	0	0	8	4	16	3	0	3.4	11.2	20	72%	.094	0.56	0.00	2.13	0.5				
2017	RCU	A+	22	2	1	0	9	9	38^{2}	26	0	3.7	11.4	49	64%	.286	1.09	3.72	1.50	1.7				
2017	TUL	AA	22	1	1	0	7	7	28	17	2	4.2	10.0	31	51%	.217	1.07	2.57	4.13	0.3				
2018	*LAN*	*MLB*	*23*	*4*	*3*	*0*	*19*	*13*	55^{2}	*44*	*8*	*3.9*	*11.2*	*69*	*49%*	*.291*	*1.21*	*3.98*	*4.53*	*0.7*				
2019	*LAN*	*MLB*	*24*	*6*	*8*	*0*	*37*	*27*	192^{2}	*154*	*28*	*3.8*	*10.2*	*219*	*49%*	*.292*	*1.23*	*4.15*	*4.77*	*1.0*				

Breakout: 22% Improve: 39% Collapse: 11% Attrition: 24% MLB: 58% *Comparables: Drew Smyly, Zack Wheeler, Blake Snell*

The Dodgers paid 60 percent of slot value to grab White in the second round of 2016 after he'd undergone Tommy John surgery and worked as a reliever in college. His three-pitch mix is not a traditional one for a right-handed starter, but his fastball, cutter and curve all flash plus ceilings. There's a good bit of gap between present and potential, however, as he missed out on almost a third of the season's development again last year. He was in the black for the rest of it, however, holding batters through Double-A to a paltry .172/.271/.229 line. Durability looms as a pressing question, and getting through a full season's workload will be high on the priority list for 2018.

Alex Wood LHP Born: 01/12/91 Age: 27 Bats: R Throws: L Height: 6'4" Weight: 215 Origin: Round 2, 2012 Draft (#85 overall)

YEAR	TEAM	LVL	AGE	W	L	SV	G	GS	IP	H	HR	BB/9	K/9	K	GB%	BABIP	WHIP	ERA	DRA	WARP	MPH	CMD	PWR	STM
2015	ATL	MLB	24	7	6	0	20	20	119^{1}	132	8	2.7	6.8	90	49%	.332	1.41	3.54	5.31	-0.3	91.9	59	36	73
2015	LAN	MLB	24	5	6	0	12	12	70^{1}	66	7	2.9	6.3	49	57%	.280	1.27	4.35	3.86	1.0	91.0	59	36	73
2016	LAN	MLB	25	1	4	0	14	10	60^{1}	56	5	3.0	9.8	66	55%	.319	1.26	3.73	3.25	1.4	92.7	66	39	9
2017	LAN	MLB	26	16	3	0	27	25	152^{1}	123	15	2.2	8.9	151	54%	.267	1.06	2.72	3.44	3.6	94.0	57	40	62
2018	*LAN*	*MLB*	*27*	*10*	*6*	*0*	*24*	*24*	*136*	*122*	*15*	*2.8*	*9.1*	*139*	*52%*	*.292*	*1.20*	*3.29*	*3.78*	*2.2*	*92.5*	*60*	*39*	*48*
2019	*LAN*	*MLB*	*28*	*12*	*10*	*0*	*33*	*33*	*214*	*170*	*22*	*2.5*	*9.5*	*226*	*52%*	*.293*	*1.07*	*3.27*	*3.74*	*3.9*	*92.6*	*60*	*40*	*43*

Breakout: 19% Improve: 52% Collapse: 22% Attrition: 8% MLB: 96% *Comparables: Hyun-jin Ryu, Jose Quintana, Mark Buehrle*

Wood flashed some untapped potential during an injury-abbreviated 2016 arrival in Los Angeles and picked right on up tapping it for the first three and a half months. Assigned to relief calls out of the gate, Wood saw his velocity spike hard in the bullpen. Both his whiff and worm-burning rates climbed correspondingly, and just kept right on going through a transition back to the rotation. Despite—or perhaps because of—the era, his season will be remembered for an uncanny run of 11 straight wins to start the year. That's in part because his second half was wholly forgettable, however: His velocity continued to slide, the groundballs grew wings and 90 extra innings looked to take their toll. A redemptive shove in the Series put a cork in it, but he'll enter 2018 mired in some uncertainty as to which version of himself will show up.

Lineouts

Hitters

HITTER	POS	TEAM	LVL	AGE	PA	R	2B	3B	HR	RBI	BB	K	SB	CS	AVG/OBP/SLG	TAv	VORP	BABIP	BRR	FRAA	WARP
Matt Beaty	1B	TUL	AA	24	481	61	31	1	15	69	35	54	3	3	.326/.378/.505	.304	30.8	.343	0.2	1B(55): 2.3, 3B(49): -0.7	3.5
O'Koyea Dickson	OF	OKL	AAA	27	458	70	22	1	24	76	44	97	4	1	.246/.328/.484	.272	14.0	.262	-1.0	LF(59): 1.1, RF(23): -0.4	1.4
	OF	LAN	MLB	27	9	0	0	0	0	0	2	2	0	0	.143/.333/.143	.196	-0.4	.200	0.0	LF(5): -0.3	-0.1
Kyle Farmer	C	TUL	AA	26	141	21	7	0	3	18	16	13	1	0	.339/.411/.468	.304	11.6	.358	0.1	C(19): -0.7, 3B(11): -0.3	1.2
	C	OKL	AAA	26	240	32	16	1	7	38	13	36	0	4	.305/.354/.480	.269	12.6	.339	0.6	C(32): 2.3, 3B(18): 0.5	1.5
	C	LAN	MLB	26	20	1	1	0	0	2	0	3	0	0	.300/.300/.350	.215	-0.7	.353	-0.3	3B(4): 0.0, C(3): 0.1	0.0
Jose Fernandez	2B	TUL	AA	29	369	47	16	0	16	64	24	33	0	2	.306/.366/.498	.297	20.7	.300	-1.2	2B(57): -4.6, 1B(10): 0.6	1.8
Starling Heredia	OF	DOD	Rk	18	32	8	2	2	2	9	4	7	0	0	.429/.500/.857	.416	7.0	.526	-0.3	LF(4): -0.3, CF(2): 0.0	0.6
	OF	OGD	Rk	18	92	21	11	1	4	17	10	24	5	4	.427/.489/.732	.368	15.3	.574	0.8	LF(8): -1.2, RF(5): -0.7	1.2
	OF	GRL	A	18	110	14	6	1	1	8	10	38	5	1	.212/.291/.323	.235	1.6	.333	2.6	RF(11): -0.8, LF(8): -0.6	0.0
Drew Jackson	SS	RCU	A+	23	298	48	16	2	8	30	34	67	14	6	.254/.367/.429	.291	20.2	.316	1.7	SS(29): 1.9, 2B(25): 1.3	2.5
	SS	TUL	AA	23	130	22	5	1	1	10	11	28	7	2	.234/.346/.324	.261	6.7	.305	2.9	2B(23): 1.7, SS(4): 0.5	0.9
Jeren Kendall	CF	GRL	A	21	155	21	5	7	2	18	13	42	5	8	.221/.290/.400	.251	1.8	.299	-0.6	CF(24): 3.5, RF(5): -0.4	0.5
Tim Locastro	INF	TUL	AA	24	420	69	21	4	8	31	22	56	22	5	.285/.366/.429	.286	29.7	.317	5.4	CF(46): -2.2, SS(31): -3.9	2.4
	INF	OKL	AAA	24	115	18	10	0	2	9	6	12	12	2	.388/.443/.544	.345	15.9	.422	1.7	2B(22): -2.0, LF(8): 0.0	1.3
	INF	LAN	MLB	24	1	0	0	0	0	0	0	0	1	0	.000/.000/.000	.018	-0.3	.000	0.0	LF(2): -0.1	0.0
Gavin Lux	SS	GRL	A	19	501	68	14	8	7	39	56	88	27	10	.244/.331/.362	.257	19.3	.288	3.4	SS(65): 3.8, 2B(43): 4.0	2.8
Johan Mieses	OF	RCU	A+	21	129	25	17	0	8	27	10	38	0	0	.353/.411/.707	.377	17.1	.465	-1.4	CF(12): 1.2, LF(10): 1.1	2.0
	OF	TUL	AA	21	329	34	7	0	16	36	27	116	0	0	.160/.246/.347	.224	-5.1	.190	-1.9	CF(71): -0.7, RF(21): -0.2	-0.6
Max Muncy	1B	OKL	AAA	26	379	62	20	1	12	44	54	84	3	6	.309/.414/.491	.316	35.9	.387	2.0	3B(53): 0.3, 1B(22): 1.9	3.5
Peter O'Brien	OF	OMA	AAA	26	115	10	1	1	3	6	9	31	0	0	.162/.235/.276	.198	-6.2	.197	0.0	LF(10): 2.4, 1B(9): 1.3	-0.2
	OF	ROU	AAA	26	55	6	1	0	2	7	6	19	0	0	.188/.273/.333	.218	-1.8	.250	-0.1	LF(7): -0.1, 3B(1): 0.0	-0.2
	OF	TUL	AA	26	172	23	11	0	9	26	16	78	0	0	.219/.297/.465	.253	0.3	.368	-0.4	1B(27): 0.3, LF(6): -0.7	0.0
Rob Segedin	1B	OKL	AAA	28	101	13	7	0	4	15	4	16	0	1	.320/.347/.515	.304	6.0	.351	-1.2	3B(9): -0.4, 1B(8): 1.4	0.8
	1B	LAN	MLB	28	20	3	2	0	0	1	0	7	0	0	.200/.200/.300	.182	-0.7	.308	0.5	1B(6): 0.0, 3B(5): -0.1	-0.1
Will Smith	C	RCU	A+	22	305	38	15	3	11	43	37	71	6	2	.232/.355/.448	.281	16.6	.273	-2.0	C(55): 2.6, 3B(6): -1.0	1.9
Andrew Toles	CF	LAN	MLB	25	102	17	3	0	5	15	5	16	0	1	.271/.314/.458	.274	4.3	.280	0.2	LF(21): 0.2, CF(10): 0.1	0.5

You know that guy with the boring but sneaky-helpful profile? He can play any of the corners, hit a little, take a walk, pull an occasional grooved fastball over the wall ... maybe even start a season's worth of games for Oakland someday? **Matt Beaty** knows that guy. A former 12th-round pick with some pop and paid minor-league dues, **O'Koyea Dickson** earned an inaugural cup of big-league coffee and a story to tell after ripping his first career hit off Madison Bumgarner. He'll spend 2018 in Japan. After sewing another solid season in the high minors, **Kyle Farmer** harvested a magical big-league debut with a walk-off double in his first at-bat. A decent defender with a solid hit tool, he figures to remain a fixture on the organizational depth chart for a while at Triple-A. **Jose Miguel Fernandez** did about what you'd expect a polished 29-year-old to do with the bat in Double-A, but defensive struggles kept the Cuban import moored in minor-league no-man's-land and a mysterious ending to his season led to his release in November. Generally 18-year-olds who could body-double Juan Uribe aren't what evaluators would call "prospects," but **Starling Heredia** has a whole bunch of athleticism hidden in that body, and his star-caliber hit and power tools flashed some signs in rookie ball last year. **Drew Jackson** switched organizations, abandoned the Stanford Swing and put together a nice little season up through Double-A to reestablish himself as an interesting six-spot prospect after a down year in 2016. The Dodgers' 2017 first-rounder, **Jeren Kendall** can run, catch and throw, and if he can set aside concerns about his bat he has a profile capable of one day catching Jason atop the Kendall games-played leaderboard. A utility guy with a nifty little speed-and-contact profile, **Tim Locastro** parlayed a solid season in the high minors into an unexpected cup of September coffee. The Dodgers may have the **Gavin Lux**-ury to be patient with their first-rounder from 2016, but after an underwhelming full-season debut and swirling questions about his future at the six, a strong showing in 2018 would help alleviate some creeping doubts about his future. ⚾ There's a bunch of pop in his bat, but Johan swings and **Johan Mieses** so often that Double-A pitchers were able to exploit him mercilessly on both sides of a midseason demotion to High-A. ⚾ **Max Muncy** munched on Triple-A pitching, but that's about where his bat maxes out. ⚾ **Peter O'Brien** brought his dingers-and-donuts routine to four different franchises last year, but with an increasing number of the strikeout-laden latter filling out his box scores it is unclear from where his next opportunity might come. ⚾ An uplifting, feel-good 2016 gave way to an injury-riddled pile of frustration for **Rob Segedin** in 2017; before a wrist injury felled him for much of the campaign, his versatility and Triple-A dominance had portended a cushy position on the organizational depth chart and plenty of opportunity for big-league contribution. ⚾ **Will Smith** be able to successfully transition his solid contact skills and steadily improving glove to Double-A? Alas, a broken wrist suffered on a hit-by-pitch in his inaugural game at the level will leave us all pondering that question until the athletic backstop resumes play next spring. ⚾ Author of one of the better feel-good redemption stories of 2016, **Andrew Toles** got off to another solid start in his second big-league season before blowing out his knee in early May.

Pitchers

PITCHER	TEAM	LVL	AGE	W	L	SV	G	GS	IP	H	HR	BB/9	K/9	K	GB%	BABIP	WHIP	ERA	DRA	WARP	MPH	CMD	PWR	STM
Dylan Baker	AKR	AA	25	0	1	0	13	0	12^2	15	1	0.7	7.1	10	45%	.341	1.26	2.84	3.81	0.1				
Fabio Castillo	OKL	AAA	28	4	8	1	22	16	84^1	77	9	3.3	9.1	85	36%	.298	1.28	4.27	5.14	0.4				
	LAN	MLB	28	0	0	0	2	0	1^1	3	0	6.8	13.5	2	40%	.600	3.00	13.50	5.26	0.0	98.1			49
Caleb Ferguson	RCU	A+	20	9	4	0	25	24	122^1	113	6	4.0	10.3	140	46%	.335	1.37	2.87	4.71	0.8				
Wilmer Font	OKL	AAA	27	10	8	0	25	25	134^1	114	11	2.3	11.9	178	39%	.315	1.11	3.42	1.68	5.8				
	LAN	MLB	27	0	0	0	3	0	3^2	7	2	9.8	7.4	3	27%	.385	3.00	17.18	9.00	-0.2	96.5			65
Adam Liberatore	LAN	MLB	30	0	0	0	4	0	3^1	3	0	5.4	13.5	5	62%	.375	1.50	2.70	4.56	0.0	94.3			4
	OKL	AAA	30	0	1	0	10	0	11^2	9	0	0.8	7.7	10	36%	.273	0.86	2.31	4.97	0.0				
Justin Masterson	OKL	AAA	32	11	6	0	26	25	141^2	129	7	4.2	8.9	140	52%	.309	1.38	4.13	4.11	2.4				
Edward Paredes	TUL	AA	30	0	2	1	24	0	32	33	1	3.4	12.7	45	53%	.416	1.41	2.81	2.36	0.9				
	OKL	AAA	30	2	1	0	11	0	12	4	0	4.5	15.8	21	37%	.211	0.83	0.75	2.53	0.4				
	LAN	MLB	30	1	0	0	10	0	8^1	8	1	0.0	11.9	11	40%	.368	0.96	3.24	6.47	-0.1	91.9			38
Dennis Santana	RCU	A+	21	5	6	0	17	14	85^2	87	5	2.3	9.7	92	50%	.340	1.27	3.57	2.74	2.5				
	TUL	AA	21	3	1	0	7	7	32^2	32	2	6.3	10.2	37	52%	.337	1.68	5.51	4.94	0.1				
Josh Sborz	TUL	AA	23	8	8	0	24	24	116^2	106	8	4.3	6.2	81	46%	.275	1.39	3.86	6.40	-1.7				
Jordan Sheffield	GRL	A	22	3	7	0	20	20	89^1	86	9	4.2	9.2	91	43%	.320	1.43	4.03	4.80	0.5				
	RCU	A+	22	0	2	0	5	4	18	23	2	7.5	9.0	18	40%	.375	2.11	8.00	9.40	-0.9				
Yaisel Sierra	TUL	AA	26	5	0	4	26	0	49^2	47	1	2.9	11.6	64	53%	.357	1.27	2.54	2.46	1.4				
	OKL	AAA	26	0	1	0	13	0	21^1	22	2	6.3	8.4	20	64%	.323	1.73	4.22	4.14	0.3				

Sometimes an 80-grade name is all it takes to garner a second chance, though in the case of former second-rounder **Stetson Allie**, a 94-mph heater didn't hurt either in a successful first foray back into mound work. ⚾ Dropped from the Indians' 40-man roster following Tommy John surgery and a rocky rehab, **Dylan Baker** has the velocity to be a late-inning bullpen arm but has barely pitched enough above the low minors to know much else for certain about his potential. ⚾ He may not have the cheekbones to grace the cover of a romance novel or the acting chops to feign surprise at the pinnacle of human engineering in sprayable dairy form, but for the rest of his life **Fabio Castillo** will be able to tell anyone who'll listen that he was a major-league pitcher once upon a time. ⚾ Sure, why not? **Ike Davis** is a pitcher now! Five years removed from a 32-homer campaign in Queens, the former Sun Devil closer touched 92 from the left side in a six-game trial run in the Arizona League. ⚾ Southpaw **Caleb Ferguson** rode a solid heater and plus-flashing hook to one of the better pitching seasons in the high-octane California League, pacing the circuit's qualified starters in ERA and whiff rate. ⚾ Not only did **Wilmer Font** manage to stay healthy, he also harnessed his delivery for one of the first sustained stretches in his career, and the results were fantastic: four whiffs for every three innings pitched at Triple-A and a second crack at major-league hitters. ⚾ First **Yimi Garcia** broke out in 2015, then he just broke. After missing the year recovering from Tommy John surgery, he's now thrown barely eight innings since that storied rookie season. ⚾ Would-be LOOGY **Adam Liberatore** was unable to liberate himself from injury in 2017, as groin and forearm issues limited him to just four spring appearances before an eventual September rehab shutdown. ⚾ The only Jamaican-born hurler in big-league history, **Justin Masterson** didn't exactly pop style all season in Oklahoma City, but he did manage to stay reasonably healthy and effective as a starter all year. ⚾ So after a decade of wandering from minor league city to minor league state, and to Indy ball, and back again, **Edward Paredes** charges in from the Dodgers bullpen like he owns the place and is lights out in nine of his 10 games. Go figure! ⚾ Converted shortstop **Dennis Santana** still throws like a middle infielder on the run, but he managed to control his 96-mph gas and developing secondaries well enough to dominate A-ball hitters and cut a path toward eventual big-league bullpen work. ⚾ **Josh Sborz**'s particular struggles to throw strikes and miss left-handed bats at Double-A foreshadowed a likely conversion to situational relief work, where his explosive heater and solid slider will have a better chance to play with modest control. ⚾ **Jordan Sheffield** struck out a batter an inning as a starter across two levels of A-ball in his first full season, and he has the stuff, command and delivery of a future high-leverage bullpen asset. ⚾ The Dodgers' $30 million bet on **Yaisel Sierra** was starting to look at least a little less catastrophic when he was dominating in Double-A relief, but subsequent struggles at Oklahoma City raised more questions about whether the club can coax a big-league future out of the not-*that*-young right-hander. ⚾ **Albert Suarez** bumped his curveball usage and struck out 26 percent of the batters he faced over the last two months of 2017. With more than 100 league-average innings under his belt, he looks like a viable swingman or middle reliever.

League Leaders 2017

MLB ERA, Relievers – Kenley Jansen, 1.31

NL Rookie Hitter WARP – Cody Bellinger, 4.79

MLB Wins – Clayton Kershaw, 18

MIAMI MARLINS

Essay by Erik Malinowski

Player comments by George Bissell and BP staff

As you get older, it's easier to accept the prevailing wisdom that fandom, in all its forms, is a largely futile endeavor. You can hope the realization never comes, but it is inevitable and hits you hard. It's a cumulative condition, but no fan base is immune. No amount of World Series titles or homegrown stud prospects can delay its onset; the epiphany finds you, in its own way. For some groups, the moment will be quick, maybe even dulled in due time. For others—such as those poor souls who root for the Miami Marlins—the condition is chronic and can often be cruel.

First, a question: Why does a team fall out of favor with its fans? Losing is almost always the primary reason, but there are organizations that smooth out these rough patches in performance, either through community outreach or by elevating fresh-faced up-and-comers into singular attractions all their own. But losing, above all, is the surest way to breed fan revolt or (even worse) apathy. You lose games by losing your best players, and that's where the psychology of it all starts to become a critical part of the equation.

Another one: Why do players leave? The most frequent reason is that, after years of toiling through cost-controlled contracts and one annual arbitration decision after another, and after the fans have invested no small amount of emotion into them being *here* on *my* team, they attain their well-earned status as free agents. Your favorite player will almost certainly break your heart simply by doing what is best for himself and his family. This has happened or will happen to everyone who loves baseball. We cheer such an exercising of one's agency, even as we feel it dampen our collective spirits.

But what happens when management accelerates that sequence of events by trading players before their stated intentions are fulfilled? There's an element of smart business to this, but fans are utterly irrational about such things. It's a far easier situation to grasp when, say, a franchise has been openly feuding with a superstar who is a year away from such contractual freedom, and in this way you better understand why teams leak unflattering comments on background to their preferred beat writers. Either way, the expectations have been set: This player isn't coming back in a year, so—as painful as this might be—it's best to get something in return for him now while we can.

What if your favorite team regularly flouted such norms? Now that's a dicier proposition. Think about rooting for a team that regularly executed splashy free agent moves, only to renege on those explicit commitments within a year's time. Sure, maybe the team underperformed, and maybe there were chemistry issues. Rosters need time to jell; no team is a juggernaut fresh out of the box. But a basic lack of trust that your executives and coaching staff can make such arrangements work will foster some very real and damning trust issues between the team and its fans (to say nothing of the players themselves, who are little more than well-compensated yet discardable employees in these back-and-forths).

Now what if this was in your team's DNA, regardless of which

MARLINS PROSPECTUS

2017 W-L: 77-85, 2nd in NL East

Pythag	.473	17th	B-Age	28.1	*11th*
RS/G	4.80	11th	P-Age	28.6	*18th*
RA/G	5.07	25th	Salary	$115.4M	*20th*
TAv	.273	3rd	M$/MW	$3.5M	*19th*
TAv-P	.278	25th	DL Days	834	*11th*
FIP	4.70	26th	$ on DL	26%	*28th*
DER	.702	14th			

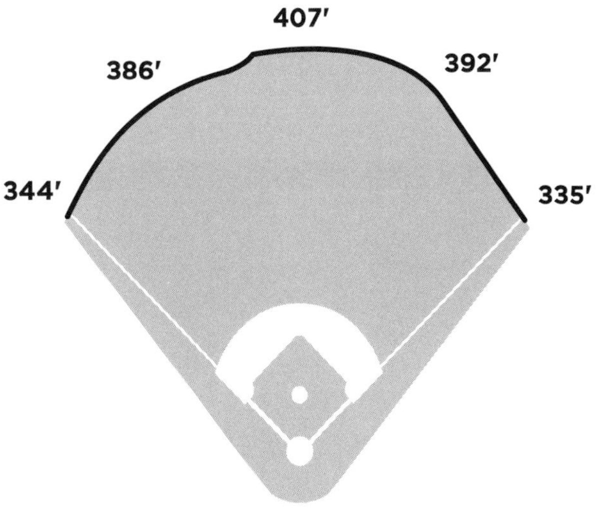

Outfield wall profile: **7'** to **11.5'**

Three-Year Park Factors

Runs	Runs/RH	Runs/LH	HR/RH	HR/LH
94	94	93	89	92

Top Hitter WARP	8.5 Giancarlo Stanton
Top Pitcher WARP	2.2 Dan Straily
Top Prospect	Magneuris Sierra

2017 Hit List Ranking

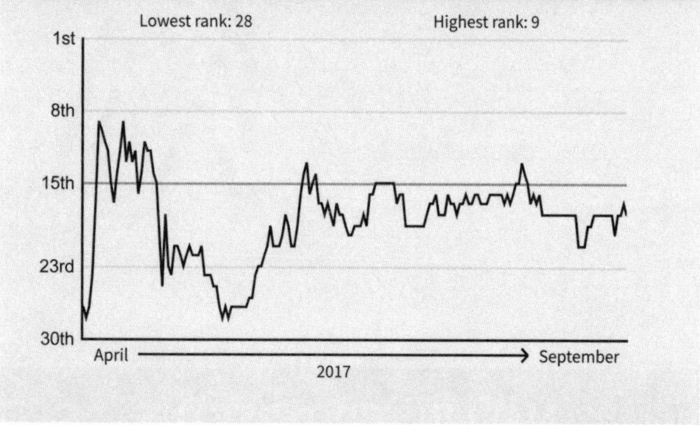

Committed Payroll (in millions)

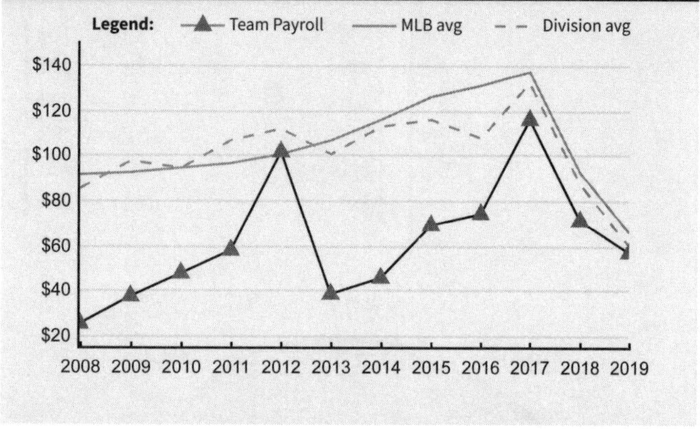

Farm System Ranking

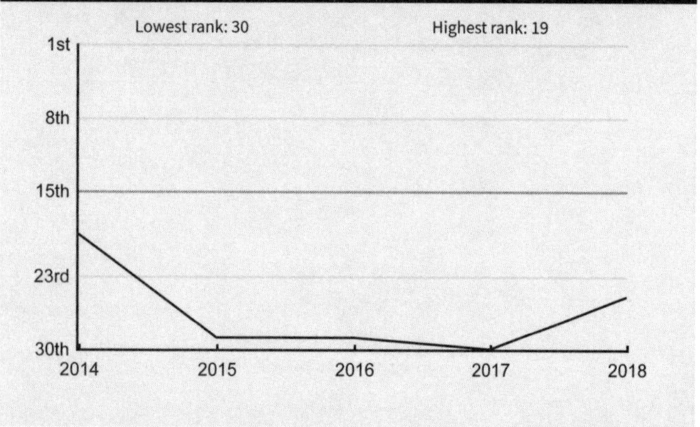

Personnel

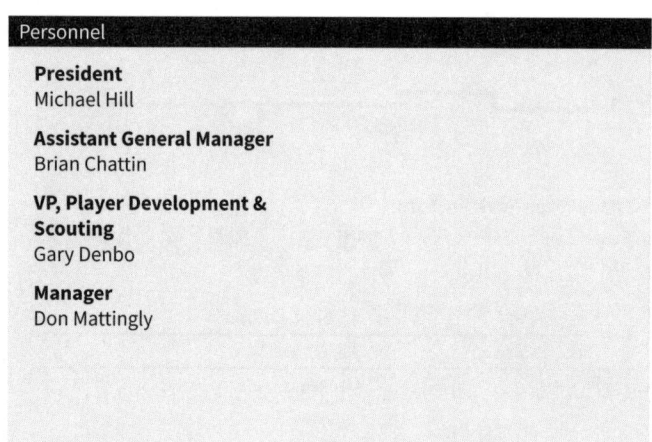

President
Michael Hill

Assistant General Manager
Brian Chattin

VP, Player Development & Scouting
Gary Denbo

Manager
Don Mattingly

ownership group controlled the payroll? Imagine, in your lifetime, enjoying the euphoria of two World Series titles only to watch the whole operation unravel at warp speed within a few weeks of receiving a champagne-fueled congratulation from the commissioner. That feeling of profound deflation affects you on a visceral level. Ideally, such continuous trauma can serve a purpose, either to help you build up personal defenses for the next time it happens—and there's always a next time, isn't there?—or even to prepare yourself for the day when a new owner comes in and sweeps out such abhorrent approaches to personnel.

But what do you do if the new owners come in and *don't* change the culture? A deep-pocketed savior lurking in the background and a Hall of Fame partner standing at the fore sounds like the perfect duo to transform a diseased workplace culture that has spent years alienating fans and players alike, but new bosses have an impressive way of falling short of whatever hopes we heap upon them. What we, as sports fans, conveniently forget about owners is that (a) they are not our friends in any way and (b) they bought a team with one priority above all others: to make money. That means revenues have to outpace expenses. It's simple, painful math. And it's doesn't take a Stanford MBA to know that one surefire way to cut expenses is to deal the guy with a decade (and up to $295 million) left on his contract.

And what does losing such an icon do to your outlook? Your brain automatically goes back to all the memories he has created since emerging eight years ago. But beyond the scattered pockets of joy, this player has suffered right along with you, through the personal pain of taking a fastball to the skull and the existential grief of losing a teammate who was just scratching the outer edges of his immense talents. Yes, his 59 dingers and other Ruthian power numbers from a year ago are now gone, but so is the locker room leadership and the instant national credibility he helped create and the way he made other players more potent and, of course, that chiseled face, often angling out from the beyond his helmet faceguard with a smile firmly affixed. There is no easy, enjoyable or fair way to trade away your newly crowned Most Valuable Player; your only goal is to survive such an occurrence.

Do you think about the young, cheap prospects that are coming back in such a transaction? You may read breathless quotes about how such a deal was vital for stability's sake, how they had to regroup for the future and that investing so much capital in one player was ultimately a misguided way of running a franchise. But the price will feel agonizingly steep, and it should. Those players coming back won't be in the majors for years, if ever. (Think back a decade to the Miguel Cabrera trade: Andrew Miller didn't become Andrew Miller until the year before he hit free agency, we're still waiting for Cameron Maybin to turn into a star and Burke Badenhop hasn't made up the difference.) And so you know deep down that move was all about money, and that knowledge is what kills a sliver of your fandom all over again.

And what about the other pieces that are in place? You might need to consider their immediate vulnerability before expecting them to fill this newly created emotional void. There's the dynamic leadoff hitter who stole 60 bases. There's the left fielder who smashed 37 homers and is entering his age-27 season. Then there's the first baseman who broke out with a .902 OPS. Hell, even your catcher mashed 17 dingers, and you know things are humming along when that happens out of the blue. If most of them stick around, it's enough to spawn some nebulous sense of hope, but then you think back to who this team is and what it has done to you not just in the past but very much in the present. And then you remember that no one is safe from the cascading whims of a front office operating solely along the bottom line. Soon, the leadoff hitter and that other power source in the outfield are fading into the background like Dave and Linda McFly, while Marty is on the phone with his agent discussing how to leak a trade request.

How does this uncertainty and near-guaranteed potential for

future heartaches affect a perspective on baseball that was crafted years before such worries had to be considered? Of course, it doesn't take away the long-etched memory of enjoying the sport with full-throated fervor as a child during a brisk April evening, the chill of the bleachers stinging your nether regions as your limbs slowly lose sensation. These nights form the subfloor of our entire approach to sports. As such, they are the unsullied and integral underpinnings to our very being, but everything built atop those early days is fair game. Baseball gets far more complicated the more familiar it becomes to you. It requires effort to keep loving baseball in the same way. Before long, the innocence has been thoroughly washed away and you must reckon with this long-term relationship as you would any other in your adult life.

Even if that's the reality for most any baseball fan of a certain age, why must it always be so acute in South Florida? Two decades ago, the offseason was a bloodbath. The same thing happened a few years later, and some years after that. In all, the franchise has lost 100 games as many times as it has raised a championship pennant; excise those four years and behold the theme-park version of the dreaded treadmill of mediocrity. And still, for an organization that has largely been defined by its blandness to be constantly sabotaged by player losses—be they through means within their control or not—feels like a special kind of sports hell. It's been said that you should root for players and not teams, yet some organizations prove that maxim to be a losing proposition either way.

Maybe there's an upside to all this? If you understand the past, you can't say you were unprepared for what nightmares may come. And it's not like there were no rewards to be reaped. Several years rooting for one of the best sluggers of the modern day isn't nothing. Holding onto the fleeting memory of feeling your own knees buckle inward while watching one of the most dynamic young pitchers in a generation drop a soul-crushing curve down the middle isn't nothing. Getting to revel in the surreal hilarity of the "home run sculpture" every time someone goes yard may not alone be worth the price of admission on any given day, but it isn't nothing.

With so much to take into account, how do you even prepare for the 2018 season and beyond? By not expecting anything. It's a perverse philosophy as applied to sports, but when an organization has proven itself so unreliable compared to its public promises and so injurious to your psyche as a fan, it's all you can do to protect yourself. It's anathema to what drives people into the throes of fandom, but this baseball team is unlike any other. It forces you—more than any other franchise—to ask questions that often produce uncomfortable answers.

Then, one day, you finally get to the most central question of all: *Why do I keep doing this?*

—Erik Malinowski is a freelance writer and editor, and the author of "Betaball: How Silicon Valley and Science Built One of the Greatest Basketball Teams in History."

HITTERS

Brian Anderson 3B Born: 05/19/93 Age: 25 Bats: R Throws: R Height: 6'3" Weight: 185 Origin: Round 3, 2014 Draft (#76 overall)

YEAR	TEAM	LVL	AGE	PA	R	2B	3B	HR	RBI	BB	K	SB	CS	AVG/OBP/SLG	TAv	VORP	BABIP	BRR	FRAA	WARP
2015	JUP	A+	22	530	50	22	2	8	62	40	109	2	2	.235/.304/.340	.269	19.3	.287	-0.9	3B(121): 3.6	2.5
2016	JUP	A+	23	207	27	12	2	3	25	22	38	3	0	.302/.377/.440	.300	13.9	.364	-1.5	3B(47): 8.5	2.3
2016	JAX	AA	23	345	38	9	1	8	40	36	59	0	0	.243/.330/.359	.269	13.7	.274	0.2	3B(85): 12.7	2.8
2017	JAX	AA	24	361	53	14	3	14	55	36	71	1	1	.251/.341/.450	.287	19.6	.277	-1.3	3B(82): 9.0	3.1
2017	NWO	AAA	24	137	21	7	0	8	26	12	27	0	1	.339/.416/.602	.368	20.7	.376	-0.4	3B(30): 1.5	2.2
2017	MIA	MLB	24	95	11	7	1	0	8	10	28	0	0	.262/.337/.369	.265	4.6	.386	1.0	3B(25): -2.2	0.2
2018	*MIA*	*MLB*	*25*	*395*	*44*	*15*	*2*	*12*	*49*	*33*	*95*	*0*	*0*	*.239/.312/.398*	*.253*	*9.1*	*.290*	*-0.7*	*3B 5*	*1.2*
2019	*MIA*	*MLB*	*26*	*483*	*62*	*19*	*2*	*18*	*61*	*44*	*120*	*0*	*0*	*.243/.322/.420*	*.271*	*16.1*	*.294*	*-1.0*	*3B 7*	*2.6*

Breakout: 6% Improve: 18% Collapse: 15% Attrition: 39% MLB: 51% *Comparables: Jefry Marte, Adam Duvall, Matthew Duffy*

A 2014 third-round selection, Anderson began the year at Double-A Jacksonville, but rapidly evolved into the quintessential high-floor, cost-controlled, second-division regular that every modern front office covets. He's a quality hitter with a solid foundation of on-base skills and a swing geared toward generating line drives and fly balls. He possesses enough raw power to punish mistakes in the zone and didn't look overmatched in a late-season cameo. The rising leaguewide home-run tide lifts all boats, so it's not unrealistic to project Anderson to pop 15-to-20 homers per year in the current landscape. There are some lingering questions regarding his defense at the hot corner, but he's got a big-time arm, which may be enough to compensate for his lack of experience. He's unlikely to blossom into a star, but he's the type of indispensable role player that provides plenty of value to a contending team and a badly needed victory for Miami from a player-development standpoint.

Justin Bour 1B Born: 05/28/88 Age: 30 Bats: L Throws: R Height: 6'3" Weight: 265 Origin: Round 25, 2009 Draft (#770 overall)

YEAR	TEAM	LVL	AGE	PA	R	2B	3B	HR	RBI	BB	K	SB	CS	AVG/OBP/SLG	TAv	VORP	BABIP	BRR	FRAA	WARP
2015	NWO	AAA	27	62	8	1	0	1	5	11	6	1	0	.275/.403/.353	.283	2.3	.295	0.2	1B(13): -0.1	0.2
2015	MIA	MLB	27	446	42	20	0	23	73	34	101	0	0	.262/.321/.479	.289	13.2	.294	-4.1	1B(111): -6.4	0.7
2016	MIA	MLB	28	321	35	12	1	15	51	38	56	0	0	.264/.349/.475	.307	17.7	.278	-1.1	1B(82): -5.1	1.3
2017	MIA	MLB	29	429	52	18	0	25	83	47	95	1	0	.289/.366/.536	.321	30.2	.322	-1.8	1B(102): -10.0	2.0
2018	*MIA*	*MLB*	*30*	*554*	*74*	*22*	*1*	*25*	*83*	*53*	*108*	*1*	*0*	*.266/.337/.465*	*.277*	*16.7*	*.291*	*-1.1*	*1B -9*	*0.6*
2019	*MIA*	*MLB*	*31*	*469*	*67*	*18*	*0*	*23*	*69*	*48*	*96*	*0*	*0*	*.257/.334/.466*	*.285*	*15.6*	*.280*	*-2.5*	*1B -7*	*0.9*

Breakout: 1% Improve: 38% Collapse: 7% Attrition: 19% MLB: 90% *Comparables: Lyle Overbay, Kendrys Morales, Matthew Lecroy*

An unexpected metamorphosis against left-handed pitching served as the catalyst fueling Bour's breakout campaign, as he blossomed into a legitimate middle-of-the-order bopper. Blessed with a mammoth physical frame, he's always had staggering raw power, but a lengthy track record of futility against southpaws seemed destined to relegate him to a permanent cold-corner platoon role. That changed in 2017, as he posted a more respectable .253/.327/.483 line against lefties, but the main attraction still lives with his platoon advantage, as Bour continued to turn right-handed pitchers into Robert Baratheon. If we're nitpicking, he isn't a total disaster at first base, but Jon Heyman has seen orange traffic cones with more range. His career has had its fair share of strange twists and turns, but Bour has finally arrived as an everyday slugger and, well, you know the damn words.

Starlin Castro 2B Born: 03/24/90 Age: 28 Bats: R Throws: R Height: 6'2" Weight: 230 Origin: International Free Agent, 2006

YEAR	TEAM	LVL	AGE	PA	R	2B	3B	HR	RBI	BB	K	SB	CS	AVG/OBP/SLG	TAv	VORP	BABIP	BRR	FRAA	WARP
2015	CHN	MLB	25	578	52	23	2	11	69	21	91	5	5	.265/.296/.375	.243	9.2	.298	-2.2	SS(109): 2.7, 2B(38): 1.7	1.5
2016	NYA	MLB	26	610	63	29	1	21	70	24	118	4	0	.270/.300/.433	.250	8.1	.305	-2.1	2B(150): 1.3, SS(3): -0.5	0.9
2017	SWB	AAA	27	25	4	0	0	1	2	1	4	0	0	.333/.360/.458	.274	1.3	.368	0.4	2B(4): 0.1	0.1
2017	NYA	MLB	27	473	66	18	1	16	63	23	93	2	0	.300/.338/.454	.269	18.2	.347	0.5	2B(109): -4.9	1.3
2018	*MIA*	*MLB*	*28*	*609*	*74*	*26*	*2*	*14*	*61*	*30*	*106*	*4*	*2*	*.269/.309/.394*	*.249*	*16.6*	*.307*	*-0.8*	*2B 1*	*1.2*
2019	*MIA*	*MLB*	*29*	*555*	*65*	*24*	*1*	*15*	*63*	*31*	*101*	*2*	*1*	*.267/.312/.404*	*.259*	*16.4*	*.304*	*-1.2*	*2B 1*	*1.9*

Breakout: 0% Improve: 46% Collapse: 8% Attrition: 9% MLB: 97% *Comparables: Al Kozar, Omar Infante, Carlos Garcia*

Castro was on fire to start the season (not literally; that would hurt!), but just as his strong first half was ending he suffered a hamstring injury that affected him until September. He came back after the All-Star break but quickly returned to the disabled list. It's a shame, because he was laying off pitches outside the strike zone that he used to flail at, posting numbers that looked like those from his early Cubs days. After returning for good in late August, the old Castro who'd swing at pitches in the opposite batter's box also made an appearance. His 2017 will still be regarded as a solid campaign, but it would have been nice to see what could have been if it weren't for that darn hamstring.

Garrett Cooper 1B Born: 12/25/90 Age: 27 Bats: R Throws: R Height: 6'6" Weight: 230 Origin: Round 6, 2013 Draft (#182 overall)

YEAR	TEAM	LVL	AGE	PA	R	2B	3B	HR	RBI	BB	K	SB	CS	AVG/OBP/SLG	TAv	VORP	BABIP	BRR	FRAA	WARP
2015	BRV	A+	24	470	55	32	2	8	54	35	88	1	1	.294/.356/.436	.305	26.1	.352	0.2	1B(114): -7.5	2.0
2015	BLX	AA	24	36	3	2	1	0	5	7	2	0	0	.552/.639/.690	.502	8.4	.593	-1.0	1B(5): 0.0, RF(4): -1.1	0.8
2016	BLX	AA	25	329	27	22	1	4	49	20	55	3	3	.299/.350/.419	.305	16.5	.351	-2.5	1B(59): -0.3, RF(16): 0.6	1.7
2016	CSP	AAA	25	139	17	5	0	5	20	10	20	0	0	.276/.331/.433	.231	-2.3	.291	0.1	1B(22): 0.1, LF(11): -1.1	-0.3
2017	CSP	AAA	26	320	64	29	0	17	82	33	48	0	0	.366/.428/.652	.329	25.9	.386	-2.3	1B(73): 4.3	2.9
2017	NYA	MLB	26	45	3	5	1	0	6	1	12	0	0	.326/.333/.488	.276	1.3	.438	0.0	1B(13): 0.0	0.1
2018	*MIA*	*MLB*	*27*	*203*	*23*	*11*	*1*	*6*	*26*	*15*	*44*	*0*	*0*	*.270/.329/.439*	*.269*	*6.4*	*.320*	*-0.4*	*1B 0*	*0.5*
2019	*MIA*	*MLB*	*28*	*296*	*39*	*16*	*1*	*11*	*39*	*24*	*67*	*0*	*0*	*.268/.331/.456*	*.284*	*11.8*	*.316*	*-0.7*	*1B 0*	*1.3*

Breakout: 2% Improve: 16% Collapse: 14% Attrition: 20% MLB: 36% *Comparables: Luis Antonio Jimenez, Clint Robinson, Justin Bour*

When Cooper, acquired in a trade that sent reliever to Tyler Webb to the Brewers, made his major-league debut for the Yankees at Fenway Park in July, he was the eighth (of what would eventually be 11) player to start at first base for New York in 2017. After the Yankees traded for Todd Frazier, Cooper served as the backup for Chase Headley at first base and hit well before developing left hamstring tendinitis in mid-August. After that, he was optioned to Triple-A Scranton and stayed there when Greg Bird returned. Cooper is the one guy who didn't fall victim to the first baseman curse that felled Tyler Austin and Bird, but he'll have to make his MLB memories away from New York.

Derek Dietrich 3B Born: 07/18/89 Age: 28 Bats: L Throws: R Height: 6'0" Weight: 205 Origin: Round 2, 2010 Draft (#79 overall)

YEAR	TEAM	LVL	AGE	PA	R	2B	3B	HR	RBI	BB	K	SB	CS	AVG/OBP/SLG	TAv	VORP	BABIP	BRR	FRAA	WARP
2015	NWO	AAA	25	224	25	13	2	7	27	15	45	0	2	.260/.357/.458	.305	15.2	.303	-0.7	2B(35): -4.7, 1B(8): -0.8	1.2
2015	MIA	MLB	25	289	38	14	3	10	24	23	65	0	2	.256/.346/.456	.301	19.3	.303	0.8	LF(46): -3.7, 3B(26): 0.4	1.7
2016	MIA	MLB	26	412	39	20	5	7	42	32	84	1	0	.279/.374/.425	.308	29.7	.343	-1.1	2B(75): -0.3, 1B(16): -0.1	3.0
2017	MIA	MLB	27	464	56	22	5	13	53	36	98	0	1	.249/.334/.424	.275	22.6	.294	0.5	3B(103): -7.6, 2B(10): 0.3	1.5
2018	*MIA*	*MLB*	*28*	*322*	*43*	*13*	*3*	*10*	*37*	*24*	*71*	*1*	*1*	*.247/.334/.424*	*.267*	*13.5*	*.292*	*-0.4*	*3B -2, LF 0*	*0.9*
2019	*MIA*	*MLB*	*29*	*440*	*59*	*19*	*3*	*16*	*58*	*35*	*99*	*0*	*0*	*.245/.338/.443*	*.282*	*21.5*	*.286*	*0.1*	*3B -3, LF 1*	*2.1*

Breakout: 1% Improve: 54% Collapse: 4% Attrition: 14% MLB: 95% *Comparables: Chase Headley, Todd Frazier, Trevor Plouffe*

Nobody has been hit by more pitches over the last two seasons than Dietrich, who has been drilled an absurd 42 times. Some phenomena lack simple or convincing explanations. This isn't one of them. If he's going to pry the vaunted "King of the HBP" crown away from Brandon Guyer, it'll take a few more years of dedication, nerves of steel to remain motionless in the face of oncoming projectiles and more ice than Elsa's castle. An ideal platoon player, Dietrich has hit a robust .254/.344/.438 against right-handed pitching for his career. His righty-mashing tendencies and trademark defensive versatility will continue to make him a quality bench bat with decent pop for years to come.

A.J. Ellis C Born: 04/09/81 Age: 37 Bats: R Throws: R Height: 6'2" Weight: 225 Origin: Round 18, 2003 Draft (#541 overall)

YEAR	TEAM	LVL	AGE	PA	R	2B	3B	HR	RBI	BB	K	SB	CS	AVG/OBP/SLG	TAv	VORP	BABIP	BRR	FRAA	WARP
2015	LAN	MLB	34	217	24	9	0	7	21	32	38	0	0	.238/.355/.403	.293	13.6	.265	-2.7	C(62): -1.5	1.3
2016	LAN	MLB	35	161	8	5	0	1	13	16	24	1	1	.194/.285/.252	.202	-2.5	.226	-0.1	C(46): -0.1	-0.3
2016	PHI	MLB	35	35	3	3	0	1	9	3	7	1	0	.313/.371/.500	.328	3.1	.375	-0.9	C(11): -1.3	0.2
2017	MIA	MLB	36	163	17	5	0	6	14	12	29	0	0	.210/.298/.371	.237	1.9	.222	-1.6	C(39): -4.4	-0.3
2018	*MIA*	*MLB*	*37*	*250*	*27*	*9*	*0*	*6*	*25*	*30*	*44*	*1*	*0*	*.224/.326/.347*	*.236*	*5.3*	*.252*	*-1.5*	*C -6*	*-0.1*
2019	*MIA*	*MLB*	*38*	*89*	*10*	*3*	*0*	*2*	*8*	*11*	*17*	*0*	*0*	*.212/.315/.328*	*.242*	*1.2*	*.244*	*-0.6*	*C -3*	*-0.2*

Breakout: 1% Improve: 28% Collapse: 4% Attrition: 12% MLB: 70% *Comparables: Del Crandall, Carlos Ruiz, Jason Kendall*

YEAR	TEAM	P. COUNT	FRM RUNS	BLK RUNS	THRW RUNS	TOT RUNS
2015	LAN	7583	-5.4	0.0	1.0	-4.4
2016	LAN	6050	-0.8	-0.6	-0.1	-1.4
2016	PHI	1303	-0.9	-0.4	-0.2	-1.5
2017	MIA	5473	-4.6	0.0	0.0	-4.6
2018	*MIA*	*9147*	*-7.2*	*-0.5*	*0.0*	*-7.6*
2019	*MIA*	*3259*	*-4.6*	*-0.3*	*0.0*	*-4.9*

If you thought 2017's scariest horror film involved a bloodthirsty clown, you might want to check the tape on Ellis. There's no way to sugarcoat it. He ranked 40th in TAv among catchers with at least 150 plate appearances and his defensive metrics receded faster than Bradley Whitford's hairline. He's never been a pitch-framing savant, but his receiving skills finally dropped through the floor. Perhaps the only thing he accomplished was removing any doubt that he's completely washed up. Ellis deserves credit for being a veteran leader and a positively chilled-out dad in the clubhouse. Institutional memory is an invaluable commodity, but after years of on-field decline, it's fair to wonder how much longer his tangible impact on clubhouse chemistry still warrants a big-league roster spot.

Thomas Jones CF Born: 12/09/97 Age: 20 Bats: R Throws: R Height: 6'4" Weight: 195 Origin: Round 3, 2016 Draft (#84 overall)

YEAR	TEAM	LVL	AGE	PA	R	2B	3B	HR	RBI	BB	K	SB	CS	AVG/OBP/SLG	TAv	VORP	BABIP	BRR	FRAA	WARP
2016	MRL	RK	18	80	11	3	1	0	6	11	20	6	2	.234/.380/.313	.277	5.6	.341	1.5	CF(19): -0.9	0.5
2017	BAT	A-	19	292	31	10	4	2	21	34	94	7	6	.181/.315/.282	.235	-1.8	.283	-2.3	CF(54): -2.1, RF(7): 0.0	-0.5
2018	*MIA*	*MLB*	*20*	*250*	*23*	*7*	*1*	*5*	*22*	*22*	*89*	*3*	*2*	*.179/.266/.285*	*.192*	*-8.4*	*.268*	*-0.3*	*CF -2, RF 0*	*-1.1*
2019	*MIA*	*MLB*	*21*	*285*	*30*	*9*	*1*	*6*	*26*	*28*	*98*	*3*	*2*	*.186/.281/.300*	*.216*	*-5.4*	*.273*	*-0.2*	*CF -2, RF 0*	*-0.8*

Breakout: 1% Improve: 3% Collapse: 0% Attrition: 2% MLB: 4% *Comparables: Joe Benson, Cedric Hunter, Ramon Flores*

It's not unusual for the Marlins to have athletic, raw and toolsy outfield prospects. Most of the time, they're littered throughout the organization like California references in Red Hot Chili Peppers lyrics. Jones, a 2016 third-round selection, isn't just a toolbox in the crowd, he's a spiritual successor for those who still sing about the potential five-tool ability of Jai Miller. Jones is capable of thunderballs in BP but led the New York-Penn League with 94 strikeouts, which would sound a lot better if he were a pitcher. At least he has the potential to stick in the green, green grass of center field long-term. Given his prolonged struggles, you might say he'll stay (in extended spring) until tomorrow to get some additional seasoning before venturing out into the cold, harsh world of full-season ball.

Braxton Lee CF Born: 08/23/93 Age: 24 Bats: L Throws: R Height: 5'10" Weight: 185 Origin: Round 12, 2014 Draft (#367 overall)

YEAR	TEAM	LVL	AGE	PA	R	2B	3B	HR	RBI	BB	K	SB	CS	AVG/OBP/SLG	TAv	VORP	BABIP	BRR	FRAA	WARP
2015	PCH	A+	21	422	48	7	1	0	24	36	67	23	13	.281/.347/.305	.261	13.6	.340	0.7	CF(113): 20.7	3.7
2016	MNT	AA	22	431	35	12	3	0	25	30	58	13	10	.209/.269/.256	.213	-8.2	.245	-0.1	CF(102): 2.7, LF(6): -0.6	-0.6
2017	MNT	AA	23	298	47	9	3	2	16	29	56	12	11	.321/.391/.401	.286	20.3	.400	3.5	CF(67): 10.0	3.3
2017	JAX	AA	23	263	34	12	0	1	21	36	48	8	2	.294/.398/.364	.284	16.9	.369	2.9	CF(58): 7.6	2.6
2018	*MIA*	*MLB*	*24*	*251*	*27*	*8*	*1*	*3*	*21*	*20*	*52*	*6*	*4*	*.247/.305/.334*	*.229*	*0.3*	*.297*	*-0.3*	*CF 2, RF 0*	*0.1*
2019	*MIA*	*MLB*	*25*	*437*	*49*	*14*	*2*	*8*	*42*	*37*	*92*	*10*	*7*	*.251/.320/.357*	*.244*	*4.6*	*.299*	*0.0*	*CF 4, RF 0*	*0.9*

Breakout: 8% Improve: 17% Collapse: 6% Attrition: 17% MLB: 31% *Comparables: Matt Angle, Denard Span, Darin Mastroianni*

Acquired by Miami from the Rays in exchange for Adeiny Hechavarria in late June, Lee racked up all of the hits en route to a Southern League batting title, while also finishing among the league leaders in runs scored, on-base percentage and stolen bases. With an approach geared toward generating line drives and worm burners, Lee offers almost nothing in the power department. In just over 400 career minor-league games, he's hit a grand total of three home runs. A plus defender in center field with a rocket arm, he'll need to maximize his tools to have a shot at an everyday role. Realistically, he fits the mold of a tough-as-nails grinder that eventually settles in as a fourth or fifth outfielder.

Ynmanol Marinez SS Born: 04/12/01 Age: 17 Bats: R Throws: R Height: 6'0" Weight: 170 Origin: International Free Agent, 2017

It's been five years since the Marlins spent over $600,000 on a July 2 prospect, so it doesn't require the services of Sherlock Holmes to figure out why they haven't landed an impact prospect on the international market since Francis Martes (for $78,000) back in 2012. Instead of merely dipping their toes back into international waters with a bevy of low-cost, spread-the-risk moves, the front office elected to ride or die with Marinez. There are more unknowns here than in an algebra textbook, but the highly touted, slick-fielding Dominican shortstop commanded a whopping $1.5 million last July. It's the first seven-figure signing bonus handed out by the organization since they inked a Venezuelan shortstop named Miguel Cabrera in 1999. That decision worked out well.

Brian Miller CF Born: 08/20/95 Age: 22 Bats: L Throws: R Height: 6'1" Weight: 186 Origin: Round 1, 2017 Draft (#36 overall)

YEAR	TEAM	LVL	AGE	PA	R	2B	3B	HR	RBI	BB	K	SB	CS	AVG/OBP/SLG	TAv	VORP	BABIP	BRR	FRAA	WARP
2017	GRB	A	21	258	42	17	1	1	28	23	35	21	6	.322/.384/.416	.290	15.7	.374	0.9	CF(35): 1.9, RF(13): -0.4	1.9
2018	*MIA*	*MLB*	*22*	*250*	*31*	*11*	*1*	*5*	*21*	*20*	*55*	*10*	*3*	*.240/.303/.353*	*.225*	*0.4*	*.294*	*0.6*	*CF 2, RF 0*	*0.3*
2019	*MIA*	*MLB*	*23*	*230*	*26*	*10*	*1*	*4*	*23*	*19*	*51*	*10*	*3*	*.246/.311/.364*	*.245*	*3.6*	*.302*	*1.0*	*CF 2, RF 0*	*0.6*

Breakout: 1% Improve: 13% Collapse: 4% Attrition: 13% MLB: 23% *Comparables: Gerardo Parra, Ryan Sweeney, Ender Inciarte*

Remember that *Seinfeld* episode where George Costanza resolves to start doing the opposite? If every instinct you have is wrong, then the opposite would have to be right. That's the exact philosophy Miami's front office employed with their second-round selection last June. Instead of going back to the wishing well with their standing order of tuna on toast—high-risk, extremely raw, multi-sport high school athlete with a long developmental track ahead—the Marlins ordered their version of chicken salad on untoasted rye. He's a polished left-handed collegiate bat with a disciplined, contact-oriented, line-drive approach. A throwback top-of-the-order table-setter, Miller should move quickly through the Marlins' barren system.

Tyler Moore 1B Born: 01/30/87 Age: 31 Bats: R Throws: R Height: 6'2" Weight: 220 Origin: Round 16, 2008 Draft (#481 overall)

YEAR	TEAM	LVL	AGE	PA	R	2B	3B	HR	RBI	BB	K	SB	CS	AVG/OBP/SLG	TAv	VORP	BABIP	BRR	FRAA	WARP
2015	WAS	MLB	28	200	14	12	0	6	27	11	45	0	0	.203/.250/.364	.230	-4.2	.234	-1.8	1B(39): -2.9, LF(20): -1.7	-0.9
2016	GWN	AAA	29	106	10	5	0	3	14	7	28	0	0	.229/.276/.375	.243	-0.9	.284	-0.3	1B(12): 0.0, LF(7): -0.5	-0.1
2017	NWO	AAA	30	46	3	2	0	1	7	7	11	0	0	.231/.348/.359	.276	1.7	.296	0.4	1B(11): 0.1	0.2
2017	MIA	MLB	30	203	17	14	0	6	30	10	56	0	0	.230/.267/.401	.243	-0.1	.287	0.1	1B(45): -0.5, LF(7): -0.6	-0.2
2018	*MIA*	*MLB*	*31*	*250*	*26*	*12*	*0*	*9*	*31*	*21*	*67*	*0*	*0*	*.231/.300/.400*	*.238*	*-0.9*	*.287*	*-0.5*	*1B -1, LF -1*	*-0.4*
2019	*MIA*	*MLB*	*32*	*269*	*32*	*12*	*0*	*9*	*32*	*22*	*75*	*0*	*0*	*.225/.292/.386*	*.245*	*-1.0*	*.282*	*-0.7*	*1B -1, LF -1*	*-0.4*

Breakout: 6% Improve: 25% Collapse: 12% Attrition: 27% MLB: 67% *Comparables: Travis Ishikawa, Mike Jacobs, Jeff Liefer*

An Amazon press release made the bold claim that Tyler Moore was the "Most Searched for Player in Baseball" by users of its Alexa digital home assistant product last year. The prospect of interacting with machines (and billion-dollar corporations) solely through voice technology in a *Blade Runner 2049* dystopian future is both exhilarating and terrifying. Not only can Alexa understand and reply to questions and commands within seconds, it also has the capability to distinguish between multiple voices. Yet, its failure to differentiate queries for deceased actress Mary Tyler Moore and a 30-year-old pinch-hitting specialist from Mississippi is quite alarming. Based on this evidence, we can draw several conclusions:

1. There are zero baseball fans employed in Amazon's PR department.
2. Your future sex robot is definitely going to strangle you.
3. Jeff Bezos should buy BP and rename it Bezos Prospectus.
4. If Alexa worked correctly, she would tell you that Moore has been a sub-replacement-level performer for virtually his entire career and was mercifully ousted from Miami's 40-man roster at the end of last season.

James Nelson 3B Born: 10/18/97 Age: 20 Bats: R Throws: R Height: 6'2" Weight: 180 Origin: Round 15, 2016 Draft (#443 overall)

YEAR	TEAM	LVL	AGE	PA	R	2B	3B	HR	RBI	BB	K	SB	CS	AVG/OBP/SLG	TAv	VORP	BABIP	BRR	FRAA	WARP
2016	MRL	RK	18	180	26	10	0	1	24	14	30	7	3	.284/.344/.364	.277	9.8	.338	0.6	3B(40): 1.4	1.1
2017	GRB	A	19	432	41	31	3	7	59	26	106	6	2	.309/.354/.456	.296	27.0	.399	-0.9	3B(80): 4.0	3.2
2018	*MIA*	*MLB*	*20*	*250*	*22*	*11*	*1*	*5*	*26*	*14*	*76*	*0*	*0*	*.229/.277/.350*	*.215*	*-3.9*	*.313*	*-0.4*	*3B 1*	*-0.3*
2019	*MIA*	*MLB*	*21*	*356*	*39*	*17*	*1*	*9*	*38*	*21*	*104*	*0*	*0*	*.238/.287/.371*	*.240*	*0.0*	*.317*	*-0.8*	*3B 2*	*0.2*

Breakout: 3% Improve: 9% Collapse: 0% Attrition: 3% MLB: 10% *Comparables: Jefry Marte, Rafael Devers, Cheslor Cuthbert*

In the land of the blind, the one-eyed Cyclops is king, yet Nelson's meteoric rise has still flown under the radar in the Marlins' wasteland of a farm system. Nelson smoked 41 extra-base hits at Low-A Greensboro last season. His age and offensive production at a premium defensive position bode well for his future. At the same time, striking out nearly a quarter of the time isn't ideal, and he's also a fringe defender at third base with an erratic throwing arm. If Nelson can curb his free-swinging ways while adding some power as he adds weight to his frame, there is plenty of reason for enthusiasm.

Rafael Ortega OF Born: 05/15/91 Age: 27 Bats: L Throws: R Height: 5'11" Weight: 160 Origin: International Free Agent, 2008

YEAR	TEAM	LVL	AGE	PA	R	2B	3B	HR	RBI	BB	K	SB	CS	AVG/OBP/SLG	TAv	VORP	BABIP	BRR	FRAA	WARP
2015	MEM	AAA	24	502	66	22	6	2	42	55	71	17	6	.286/.367/.378	.286	26.4	.336	-0.6	CF(88): 20.0, LF(22): 2.3	5.2
2016	SLC	AAA	25	341	47	18	7	4	31	15	39	14	8	.317/.348/.453	.269	9.4	.350	-1.4	LF(40): 5.0, CF(22): -0.8	1.4
2016	ANA	MLB	25	202	24	8	0	1	16	13	23	8	3	.232/.283/.292	.210	-5.5	.261	0.1	LF(46): 1.8, CF(10): -0.8	-0.4
2017	ELP	AAA	26	472	69	31	7	6	53	46	49	26	7	.317/.383/.468	.288	24.6	.345	-1.9	CF(37): -5.3, LF(34): 2.2	2.2
2018	*MIA*	*MLB*	*27*	*250*	*32*	*11*	*2*	*4*	*22*	*21*	*40*	*9*	*3*	*.263/.328/.387*	*.243*	*4.4*	*.299*	*-0.1*	*CF 1, LF 0*	*0.6*
2019	*MIA*	*MLB*	*28*	*304*	*34*	*13*	*3*	*5*	*30*	*26*	*50*	*10*	*4*	*.260/.325/.381*	*.256*	*7.2*	*.297*	*0.4*	*CF 1, LF 0*	*1.0*

Breakout: 3% Improve: 16% Collapse: 8% Attrition: 16% MLB: 40% *Comparables: L.J. Hoes, Skip Schumaker, Matt Angle*

The line between prospect and Quad-A veteran becomes awfully fuzzy when you reach a player like Ortega, who features an unusually nomadic background, strong minor-league stats and minimal big-league playing time. On the one hand, the center fielder has three strong Triple-A seasons under his belt. On the other, he was atrocious in a 2016 big-league audition, so it's hard to get overly excited about a standout minor-league performance. Still, he is only a year older than Aaron Judge, never strikes out and, save for power, boasts strong skills across the board. Ortega isn't going to replicate those minor-league numbers at the highest level, but that doesn't mean he can't be a useful up-and-down fifth outfielder for a shallow team.

Martin Prado 3B Born: 10/27/83 Age: 34 Bats: R Throws: R Height: 6'0" Weight: 215 Origin: International Free Agent, 2001

YEAR	TEAM	LVL	AGE	PA	R	2B	3B	HR	RBI	BB	K	SB	CS	AVG/OBP/SLG	TAv	VORP	BABIP	BRR	FRAA	WARP
2015	MIA	MLB	31	551	52	22	2	9	63	37	68	1	0	.288/.338/.394	.283	29.2	.313	0.2	3B(124): -0.6, 2B(11): -0.2	3.0
2016	MIA	MLB	32	658	70	37	3	8	75	49	69	2	2	.305/.359/.417	.288	39.9	.331	0.2	3B(150): -3.1	3.8
2017	JUP	A+	33	25	0	1	0	0	0	3	5	0	0	.273/.360/.318	.277	1.4	.353	0.2	3B(8): -0.1	0.1
2017	MIA	MLB	33	147	13	9	0	2	12	6	22	0	0	.250/.279/.357	.221	-2.2	.282	-1.0	3B(34): -1.2	-0.3
2018	*MIA*	*MLB*	*34*	*585*	*59*	*25*	*2*	*10*	*62*	*38*	*68*	*2*	*1*	*.275/.325/.382*	*.253*	*14.4*	*.298*	*-1.0*	*LF -1, 3B -1*	*0.7*
2019	*MIA*	*MLB*	*35*	*329*	*38*	*15*	*1*	*6*	*34*	*24*	*42*	*0*	*0*	*.272/.329/.390*	*.262*	*8.5*	*.297*	*-0.2*	*LF 0, 3B 0*	*0.9*

Breakout: 0% Improve: 31% Collapse: 10% Attrition: 19% MLB: 86% *Comparables: Jose Reyes, Yunel Escobar, Kevin Seitzer*

In *The Color of Money*, Paul Newman as Fast Eddie Felson reflects on his retirement from pool hustling, saying, "It was over for me before it ever really got started." Prado has to be feeling the same way after an injury-marred campaign in which he lasted just 37 games—his lowest total since 2008—before undergoing season-ending knee surgery in July. The 13-year-veteran began the year on the disabled list after his hamstring pull in the World Baseball Classic and went back on the shelf in early May when he reaggravated it. Given his advanced age and bloated contract, as well as the presence of a younger (cheaper) in-house alternative in top prospect Brian Anderson, he could easily fall victim to the new regime's cost-cutting mission. Regardless of where he ends up, Prado is a certifiable veteran leader—both on the field and in the clubhouse—that nearly every franchise would love to have mentoring their young nucleus. At the right price, of course.

J.T. Realmuto C Born: 03/18/91 Age: 27 Bats: R Throws: R Height: 6'1" Weight: 210 Origin: Round 3, 2010 Draft (#104 overall)

YEAR	TEAM	LVL	AGE	PA	R	2B	3B	HR	RBI	BB	K	SB	CS	AVG/OBP/SLG	TAv	VORP	BABIP	BRR	FRAA	WARP
2015	MIA	MLB	24	467	49	21	7	10	47	19	70	8	4	.259/.290/.406	.260	20.4	.285	0.5	C(118): -14.5	0.6
2016	MIA	MLB	25	545	60	31	0	11	48	28	100	12	4	.303/.343/.428	.282	38.0	.357	1.6	C(129): -4.4	3.5
2017	MIA	MLB	26	579	68	31	5	17	65	36	106	8	2	.278/.332/.451	.279	37.8	.318	1.0	C(126): 14.2, 1B(9): 0.3	5.2
2018	*MIA*	*MLB*	*27*	*581*	*76*	*27*	*4*	*15*	*61*	*34*	*99*	*10*	*3*	*.273/.320/.420*	*.261*	*30.5*	*.310*	*0.5*	*C -3*	*2.1*
2019	*MIA*	*MLB*	*28*	*538*	*66*	*25*	*4*	*16*	*65*	*37*	*96*	*9*	*3*	*.267/.322/.431*	*.273*	*29.8*	*.301*	*1.0*	*C -2*	*3.1*

Breakout: 8% Improve: 45% Collapse: 5% Attrition: 11% MLB: 96% *Comparables: Jonathan Lucroy, Wilson Ramos, Ronny Paulino*

YEAR	TEAM	P. COUNT	FRM RUNS	BLK RUNS	THRW RUNS	TOT RUNS
2015	MIA	16187	-14.3	-0.2	0.2	-14.3
2015	NWO	416	0.1	0.0	0.0	0.0
2016	MIA	18935	-12.9	1.8	2.1	-9.0
2017	MIA	18959	3.8	1.6	0.9	6.4
2018	*MIA*	*20799*	*-7.7*	*1.2*	*1.0*	*-5.5*
2019	*MIA*	*19267*	*-7.0*	*1.1*	*0.9*	*-5.0*

According to BP's defensive metrics, Realmuto graded out as one of the worst defensive catchers in baseball between 2015 and 2016—costing Miami nearly 24 runs as a result of poor framing, blocking and throwing. Success is always an adjustment away. The former high school quarterback and converted infielder has always had impressive athleticism and physical tools, but it's taken years to refine his technique behind the plate. In his second season under the guidance of catching coach Brian Schneider, the Oklahoma native's work ethic began to pay off: In addition to saving the Marlins nearly seven runs with his glove work, he graded out as the 11th-best defensive catcher last season. Realmuto's dramatic improvements on the defensive end of the spectrum have transformed him from a prolific, offense-oriented catcher into a potential franchise cornerstone.

Joshua Riddle SS Born: 10/12/91 Age: 26 Bats: L Throws: R Height: 6'1" Weight: 180 Origin: Round 13, 2013 Draft (#382 overall)

YEAR	TEAM	LVL	AGE	PA	R	2B	3B	HR	RBI	BB	K	SB	CS	AVG/OBP/SLG	TAv	VORP	BABIP	BRR	FRAA	WARP
2015	JUP	A+	23	198	30	6	1	0	9	11	29	7	3	.270/.311/.314	.274	12.9	.321	2.7	SS(42): 4.4	1.9
2015	JAX	AA	23	189	26	6	1	5	20	8	24	0	0	.289/.323/.422	.293	13.7	.306	0.3	SS(42): -4.7	1.0
2016	JAX	AA	24	429	49	18	4	3	51	33	72	5	1	.278/.332/.368	.269	20.0	.331	1.0	SS(71): 1.0, 2B(21): -0.2	2.2
2016	NWO	AAA	24	57	4	2	0	1	2	1	9	1	0	.268/.281/.357	.253	1.0	.304	-0.8	SS(13): -1.8, 2B(1): 0.0	-0.1
2017	NWO	AAA	25	64	9	4	1	2	6	1	8	1	0	.286/.297/.476	.284	4.2	.302	-0.3	SS(16): 0.9	0.5
2017	MIA	MLB	25	247	20	13	1	3	31	12	50	0	2	.250/.282/.355	.232	4.1	.300	0.7	SS(69): 1.5	0.6
2018	*MIA*	*MLB*	*26*	*431*	*43*	*18*	*2*	*9*	*44*	*22*	*84*	*2*	*1*	*.253/.289/.372*	*.234*	*8.9*	*.296*	*-0.6*	*SS -3*	*0.0*
2019	*MIA*	*MLB*	*27*	*465*	*51*	*18*	*2*	*11*	*49*	*27*	*102*	*2*	*1*	*.244/.290/.372*	*.238*	*6.4*	*.290*	*1.2*	*SS -3*	*0.4*

Breakout: 5% Improve: 35% Collapse: 11% Attrition: 29% MLB: 65% *Comparables: Brian Dozier, Chin-lung Hu, Omar Quintanilla*

Adeiny Hechavarria's persistent injury issues forced the Marlins to rely on Riddle as their starting shortstop by early May. He delivered from a defensive standpoint, grading out as an above-average fielder before undergoing season-ending shoulder surgery to repair a torn labrum in July. Although Riddle lacks a true carrying tool, he doesn't have any glaring weaknesses either. A short, compact swing enables him to spray line drives to all fields, but it isn't geared for power. He isn't a burner, but he's a better runner than his stolen-base figures would have you infer. Riddle's defensive versatility makes him a viable, cost-controlled everyday option during Miami's embarrassing teardown, though he may be best suited in a complementary role as a multi-position specialist for a major-league team.

Miguel Rojas SS Born: 02/24/89 Age: 29 Bats: R Throws: R Height: 5'11" Weight: 195 Origin: International Free Agent, 2005

YEAR	TEAM	LVL	AGE	PA	R	2B	3B	HR	RBI	BB	K	SB	CS	AVG/OBP/SLG	TAv	VORP	BABIP	BRR	FRAA	WARP
2015	NWO	AAA	26	275	32	15	4	3	23	13	26	2	5	.301/.343/.430	.285	17.9	.324	-0.4	SS(63): 7.1, 3B(1): 0.2	2.6
2015	MIA	MLB	26	157	13	7	1	1	17	11	16	0	1	.282/.329/.366	.273	9.4	.307	1.9	SS(32): -1.9, 2B(9): -0.6	0.8
2016	MIA	MLB	27	214	27	12	0	1	14	11	27	2	1	.247/.288/.325	.217	-2.1	.280	0.7	2B(45): -0.6, 1B(41): 1.8	0.2
2017	JUP	A+	28	30	3	2	0	0	2	3	1	0	1	.308/.400/.385	.307	2.5	.320	0.3	2B(3): -0.4, SS(2): 0.0	0.3
2017	MIA	MLB	28	306	37	16	2	1	26	27	32	2	1	.290/.361/.375	.272	21.1	.324	4.6	SS(77): -0.2, 3B(15): -0.2	2.1
2018	*MIA*	*MLB*	*29*	*194*	*19*	*8*	*1*	*2*	*17*	*13*	*24*	*1*	*1*	*.259/.311/.352*	*.238*	*5.2*	*.284*	*-0.4*	*SS 1, 2B -1*	*0.2*
2019	*MIA*	*MLB*	*30*	*255*	*28*	*11*	*1*	*4*	*24*	*18*	*37*	*1*	*1*	*.252/.311/.359*	*.244*	*5.8*	*.279*	*1.8*	*SS 1, 2B -1*	*0.6*

Breakout: 4% Improve: 39% Collapse: 13% Attrition: 24% MLB: 89% *Comparables: Angel Sanchez, Paul Janish, Jonathan Herrera*

Rojas is the Mark Ruffalo of everyday shortstops: sensational in a supporting role, but overmatched as a leading man. He's a utility infielder straight out of Central Casting; a grinder who consistently plays above his raw tools in a "whole is greater than the sum of his parts" sense. There have never been any questions regarding his defensive ability, and Rojas' bat finally woke up after years in hibernation during a two-month audition as the Marlins' everyday shortstop to close out last season. He also showed himself to be a very deft baserunner, finishing first in baseball in baserunning runs among players with fewer than 10 steals. More importantly, he took home the team's annual Dion Waiters Heat Check Award, going 4-for-5 and finishing a homer shy of the first cycle in franchise history on September 30. Where is Erik Goeddel when you need him?

Magneuris Sierra OF Born: 04/07/96 Age: 22 Bats: L Throws: L Height: 5'11" Weight: 160 Origin: International Free Agent, 2012

YEAR	TEAM	LVL	AGE	PA	R	2B	3B	HR	RBI	BB	K	SB	CS	AVG/OBP/SLG	TAv	VORP	BABIP	BRR	FRAA	WARP
2015	PEO	A	19	190	19	1	3	1	7	7	52	4	5	.191/.219/.247	.177	-11.8	.260	-1.2	CF(50): 5.6	-0.7
2015	JCY	RK	19	239	38	8	0	3	15	19	42	15	2	.315/.371/.394	.285	15.6	.378	1.0	CF(53): 6.1	2.1
2016	PEO	A	20	562	78	29	4	3	60	22	97	31	17	.307/.335/.395	.280	28.9	.367	1.6	CF(121): 3.3	3.5
2017	PMB	A+	21	89	16	3	4	0	9	7	15	3	5	.272/.337/.407	.265	4.1	.333	1.1	CF(19): 0.6	0.5
2017	SFD	AA	21	353	32	18	3	1	35	20	59	17	5	.269/.313/.352	.238	3.5	.323	3.6	RF(34): 0.5, LF(26): 2.1	0.9
2017	SLN	MLB	21	64	10	0	0	0	5	4	14	2	2	.317/.359/.317	.272	3.2	.413	0.8	RF(8): 0.7, CF(7): -1.3	0.3
2018	*MIA*	*MLB*	*22*	*422*	*44*	*15*	*3*	*5*	*35*	*19*	*100*	*12*	*6*	*.239/.272/.330*	*.214*	*-8.8*	*.302*	*0.3*	*RF 5, CF 0*	*-0.6*
2019	*MIA*	*MLB*	*23*	*506*	*53*	*19*	*4*	*9*	*50*	*26*	*117*	*15*	*8*	*.249/.291/.365*	*.235*	*-1.5*	*.308*	*1.1*	*RF 7, CF 0*	*0.6*

Breakout: 2% Improve: 8% Collapse: 6% Attrition: 14% MLB: 18% *Comparables: Eury Perez, Gorkys Hernandez, Charlie Tilson*

With the rest of the outfielders on the 40-man roster up to their necks in quicksand, the Cardinals called up Sierra all the way from A-ball to cover for a few days in May. He got a hit in all seven games he played on his way to going 11-for-30, and was sent to Double-A upon his return to the minors. Sierra continued to do well in short call-up stints in June and July, but didn't hit much down on the farm, and even the MLB success hints at the deficit in his offensive game: All 19 of his hits were singles. Despite the lack of in-game power, he's very toolsy and athletic, with a center-field defensive profile. Sierra was traded to Miami in the Marcell Ozuna deal, and his future might look a lot like former Marlin Juan Pierre's past.

Ichiro Suzuki RF Born: 10/22/73 Age: 44 Bats: L Throws: R Height: 5'11" Weight: 175 Origin: International Free Agent, 2000

YEAR	TEAM	LVL	AGE	PA	R	2B	3B	HR	RBI	BB	K	SB	CS	AVG/OBP/SLG	TAv	VORP	BABIP	BRR	FRAA	WARP
2015	MIA	MLB	41	438	45	5	6	1	21	31	51	11	5	.229/.282/.279	.218	-6.1	.257	3.5	RF(73): 8.5, LF(30): -0.2	0.1
2016	MIA	MLB	42	365	48	15	5	1	22	30	42	10	2	.291/.354/.376	.266	8.5	.329	-1.7	RF(54): -1.9, CF(14): -0.7	0.9
2017	MIA	MLB	43	215	19	6	0	3	20	17	35	1	1	.255/.318/.332	.234	-3.0	.297	-2.7	RF(16): -0.1, CF(10): -1.3	-0.2
2018	*MIA*	*MLB*	*44*	*250*	*27*	*7*	*2*	*2*	*18*	*18*	*37*	*5*	*2*	*.256/.312/.331*	*.220*	*-2.6*	*.293*	*-0.2*	*RF 2, LF 1*	*0.0*
2019	*MIA*	*MLB*	*45*	*152*	*14*	*4*	*1*	*1*	*11*	*10*	*24*	*3*	*1*	*.243/.294/.303*	*.217*	*-3.4*	*.285*	*-0.1*	*RF 1, LF 0*	*-0.2*

Breakout: 0% Improve: 21% Collapse: 0% Attrition: 12% MLB: 56% *Comparables: Omar Vizquel, Enos Slaughter, Pete Rose*

According to Wharton professor Adam Grant, "The hallmark of originality is rejecting the default and exploring whether a better option exists." Originals are nonconformists. They analyze the world around them and ask if it could be improved. After eclipsing the 3,000-hit plateau and recording nearly 4,500 combined between Japan and America, Ichiro didn't just embrace his newfound part-time role, he owned it. At 43, he decided to embark on a new, original challenge: become the most prolific pinch hitter of all-time. Despite falling one hit shy of matching John Vander Wal's 1995 single-season record of 28 pinch-hits, Ichiro's 109 pinch-hit appearances is a record that may never be broken. He's repeatedly stated that he wants to play until he's 50, and we can only hope there is enough of Tom Brady's avocado ice cream to make that a reality.

Tomas Telis C Born: 06/18/91 Age: 27 Bats: B Throws: R Height: 5'8" Weight: 220 Origin: International Free Agent, 2007

YEAR	TEAM	LVL	AGE	PA	R	2B	3B	HR	RBI	BB	K	SB	CS	AVG/OBP/SLG	TAv	VORP	BABIP	BRR	FRAA	WARP
2015	ROU	AAA	24	300	43	15	1	5	25	14	31	1	2	.291/.327/.404	.251	6.2	.313	-1.3	C(50): -0.4, 1B(3): 0.1	0.6
2015	TEX	MLB	24	12	1	0	0	0	2	0	1	0	0	.182/.250/.182	.194	-0.6	.200	-0.3	C(4): -0.9	-0.2
2015	NWO	AAA	24	55	3	0	0	0	4	5	6	2	0	.333/.389/.333	.284	4.3	.372	0.5	C(12): -8.1	-0.4
2015	MIA	MLB	24	29	1	0	0	0	0	1	3	0	0	.148/.207/.148	.171	-2.3	.167	-0.7	C(7): -1.7	-0.4
2016	NWO	AAA	25	368	46	16	3	6	45	27	42	4	2	.310/.362/.429	.292	24.3	.338	0.5	C(55): -22.5, 1B(25): 0.2	0.2
2016	MIA	MLB	25	13	1	0	0	1	4	0	2	0	0	.308/.308/.538	.311	0.7	.300	-0.4	C(3): -0.2	0.1
2017	NWO	AAA	26	306	39	14	2	5	31	18	29	5	0	.279/.326/.396	.263	12.1	.293	0.2	C(45): -1.5, 1B(15): -0.9	0.9
2017	MIA	MLB	26	111	13	5	3	0	9	3	10	0	0	.240/.279/.346	.238	-0.1	.263	0.6	1B(28): -1.3, C(6): -0.3	-0.2
2018	*MIA*	*MLB*	*27*	*96*	*10*	*4*	*1*	*2*	*9*	*5*	*13*	*1*	*0*	*.265/.306/.371*	*.243*	*3.0*	*.291*	*0.0*	*C -6*	*-0.4*
2019	*MIA*	*MLB*	*28*	*198*	*22*	*8*	*1*	*4*	*20*	*12*	*30*	*1*	*0*	*.265/.316/.386*	*.256*	*6.6*	*.295*	*-0.2*	*C -10*	*-0.4*

Breakout: 6% Improve: 15% Collapse: 18% Attrition: 32% MLB: 55% *Comparables: Ramon Cabrera, Jose Morales, Rob Johnson*

If legendary plate discipline earned Kevin Youkilis the *Moneyball*-era moniker "The Greek God of Walks," Telis is the Statcast-era's "Yugoslavian Peasant of Free Passes." He's walked only five times in 236 career plate appearances since 2014. To put that in perspective, Joey Votto walked five times in one game last season. Of the 3,135 position players to accrue at least 200 plate appearances in the last half century, Matt McBride, Joe Cannon and Alejandro Sanchez are the only hitters to walk fewer times. That stat is crazier than anything you'll find on Aubrey Huff's Twitter timeline. On the plus side, Telis has a contact-oriented approach and rarely strikes out. He's a quality receiver with solid intangibles and a perfectly viable backup catcher.

YEAR	TEAM	P. COUNT	FRM RUNS	BLK RUNS	THRW RUNS	TOT RUNS
2015	ROU	7286	-4.9	0.3	2.3	-2.3
2015	TEX	402	-1.1	0.3	0.0	-0.8
2015	MIA	557	-1.8	0.2	0.0	-1.6
2015	NWO	1789	-7.4	-0.2	-0.2	-7.8
2016	MIA	213	-0.1	0.1	0.0	-0.1
2017	MIA	329	-0.4	0.1	-0.1	-0.3
2018	*MIA*	*3525*	*-5.9*	*0.1*	*0.0*	*-5.8*
2019	*MIA*	*7256*	*-8.4*	*0.1*	*0.1*	*-8.2*

Christopher Torres INF Born: 02/06/98 Age: 20 Bats: B Throws: R Height: 5'11" Weight: 170 Origin: International Free Agent, 2014

YEAR	TEAM	LVL	AGE	PA	R	2B	3B	HR	RBI	BB	K	SB	CS	AVG/OBP/SLG	TAv	VORP	BABIP	BRR	FRAA	WARP
2015	MCO	RK	17	274	40	8	3	2	30	51	56	20	9	.251/.399/.344	.283	19.6	.327	0.9	SS(53): 0.8, 2B(11): 0.2	2.0
2016	MRN	RK	18	189	31	9	4	0	17	19	44	12	4	.257/.337/.359	.283	13.0	.350	0.1	SS(44): 4.8	1.8
2017	EVE	A-	19	220	44	8	6	6	22	25	64	13	3	.238/.324/.435	.277	15.5	.323	2.7	SS(44): -5.9, 3B(1): -0.2	1.0
2018	*MIA*	*MLB*	*20*	*250*	*29*	*8*	*1*	*5*	*20*	*24*	*83*	*7*	*3*	*.191/.269/.309*	*.200*	*-3.8*	*.271*	*0.5*	*SS 0, 3B 0*	*-0.4*
2019	*MIA*	*MLB*	*21*	*303*	*33*	*9*	*2*	*7*	*29*	*30*	*100*	*9*	*3*	*.200/.281/.325*	*.222*	*-1.1*	*.281*	*0.9*	*SS 0, 3B 0*	*-0.1*

Breakout: 1% Improve: 6% Collapse: 0% Attrition: 2% MLB: 8% *Comparables: Tim Beckham, Amed Rosario, Delino DeShields*

After missing the first half of the season with a shoulder injury, Torres initially struggled upon his return, particularly in the power department. After a brief adjustment period Torres flashed the raw pop that scouts hoped he would develop, slugging .513 over his final 129 plate appearances in the Northwest League and hitting half of his homers in his last five games. Torres' high strikeout rate remains a concern, but his lively bat will push him up the ladder and keep him in the conversation for a future major-league role. There is enough risk and variability in his profile to create a wide range of outcomes, and Torres could be anything from an everyday starting shortstop to a future utility infielder.

Christian Yelich LF Born: 12/05/91 Age: 26 Bats: L Throws: R Height: 6'3" Weight: 195 Origin: Round 1, 2010 Draft (#23 overall)

YEAR	TEAM	LVL	AGE	PA	R	2B	3B	HR	RBI	BB	K	SB	CS	AVG/OBP/SLG	TAv	VORP	BABIP	BRR	FRAA	WARP
2015	MIA	MLB	23	525	63	30	2	7	44	47	101	16	5	.300/.366/.416	.288	27.8	.370	1.4	LF(103): 5.0, CF(36): -3.3	3.2
2016	MIA	MLB	24	659	78	38	3	21	98	72	138	9	4	.298/.376/.483	.318	56.6	.356	2.2	LF(120): -5.0, CF(31): 0.0	5.3
2017	MIA	MLB	25	695	100	36	2	18	81	80	137	16	2	.282/.369/.439	.292	46.4	.336	0.8	CF(155): -17.2	2.9
2018	*MIA*	*MLB*	*26*	*639*	*81*	*30*	*3*	*16*	*77*	*68*	*130*	*14*	*4*	*.281/.361/.431*	*.279*	*36.7*	*.338*	*0.7*	*CF -9, LF 0*	*2.2*
2019	*MIA*	*MLB*	*27*	*558*	*75*	*27*	*2*	*17*	*70*	*62*	*117*	*12*	*3*	*.282/.366/.449*	*.294*	*36.7*	*.338*	*1.2*	*CF -7, LF 0*	*3.2*

Breakout: 4% Improve: 62% Collapse: 2% Attrition: 7% MLB: 99% *Comparables: Chet Lemon, Melvin Upton, Grady Sizemore*

Has there ever been a more obvious candidate to enroll in Launch Angle University? We've seen what it can do for others like J.D. Martinez, Justin Turner and Daniel Murphy. That troika of late bloomers evolved into bona fide superstars once they changed their approach at the plate and have been among the most vocal advocates at the forefront of the fly-ball revolution ever since. After 15 seasons of *NCIS*, we still don't know how Gibbs gets the boat out of the basement, yet that mystery pales in comparison to Yelich's batted-ball profile. Among qualified hitters, he ranked sixth in ground-ball rate last season. Only slap-hitter and route-runner extraordinaire Nori Aoki has burned a higher percentage of worms than Yelich since his 2013 debut. The crazy thing is that he's already a star, a middle-of-the-order force with a penchant for scorching line drives in every direction. He started hitting more fly balls in the second half last season. If that carries over into 2018, look out.

PITCHERS

Sandy Alcantara RHP Born: 09/07/95 Age: 22 Bats: R Throws: R Height: 6'4" Weight: 170 Origin: International Free Agent, 2013

YEAR	TEAM	LVL	AGE	W	L	SV	G	GS	IP	H	HR	BB/9	K/9	K	GB%	BABIP	WHIP	ERA	DRA	WARP	MPH	CMD	PWR	STM
2015	CRD	RK	19	4	4	0	12	12	64^{1}	59	3	2.8	7.1	51	59%	.298	1.23	3.22	3.68	1.5				
2016	PEO	A	20	5	7	0	17	17	90^{1}	78	4	4.5	11.9	119	46%	.333	1.36	4.08	2.28	3.0				
2016	PMB	A+	20	0	4	0	6	6	32^{1}	25	0	3.9	9.5	34	52%	.294	1.21	3.62	4.36	0.4				
2017	SFD	AA	21	7	5	0	25	22	125^{1}	125	13	3.9	7.6	106	46%	.305	1.43	4.31	6.04	-1.3				
2017	SLN	MLB	21	0	0	0	8	0	8^{1}	9	2	6.5	10.8	10	26%	.333	1.80	4.32	4.81	0.0	100.6			60
2018	*SLN*	*MLB*	*22*	*2*	*3*	*0*	*27*	*3*	*40*	*40*	*6*	*4.6*	*9.0*	*40*	*42%*	*.300*	*1.50*	*5.05*	*5.09*	*0.0*	*100.6*			*63*
2019	*SLN*	*MLB*	*23*	*4*	*3*	*0*	*61*	*6*	93^{1}	*89*	*15*	*4.6*	*8.9*	*93*	*42%*	*.316*	*1.46*	*5.07*	*5.67*	*-0.3*	*100.5*			*64*

Breakout: 8% Improve: 9% Collapse: 3% Attrition: 9% MLB: 12% *Comparables: Tony Sipp, Michael Stutes, Carlos Carrasco*

After an explosive 2016, Alcantara backed up a touch in 2017 despite making his major-league debut. He attacks hitters with an upper-90s fastball that couples with a high-end spin rate to give it the ceiling of an elite offering. Why isn't it there already? It doesn't move as much as you'd like, which has resulted in Alcantara getting hit harder than his raw stuff would indicate. His breaking ball is a solid secondary option, but he struggles with consistency and could benefit from throwing it in a higher velocity band. The changeup, on the other hand, arrives too firmly in the low-90s, and he would do well to widen the velocity gap between it and the fastball. Lack of a true third offering and the effort in his mechanics mean Alcantara might be a bullpen candidate in the long run, though he'll get plenty of chances to start thanks to his stuff, frame and move to Miami.

Kyle Barraclough RHP Born: 05/23/90 Age: 28 Bats: R Throws: R Height: 6'3" Weight: 225 Origin: Round 7, 2012 Draft (#240 overall)

YEAR	TEAM	LVL	AGE	W	L	SV	G	GS	IP	H	HR	BB/9	K/9	K	GB%	BABIP	WHIP	ERA	DRA	WARP	MPH	CMD	PWR	STM
2015	PMB	A+	25	1	0	4	11	0	15	9	0	5.4	13.8	23	32%	.290	1.20	0.60	2.79	0.3				
2015	SFD	AA	25	2	0	8	23	0	24^{2}	19	0	7.3	10.2	28	49%	.302	1.58	3.28	4.83	0.0				
2015	MIA	MLB	25	2	1	0	25	0	24^{1}	12	1	6.7	11.1	30	34%	.224	1.23	2.59	3.19	0.4	97.8	32	58	50
2016	MIA	MLB	26	6	3	0	75	0	72^{2}	45	1	5.4	14.0	113	55%	.301	1.22	2.85	2.08	2.4	98.0	46	51	58
2017	MIA	MLB	27	6	2	1	66	0	66	53	5	5.2	10.4	76	46%	.291	1.38	3.00	3.92	0.9	96.4	35	50	52
2018	*MIA*	*MLB*	*28*	*2*	*3*	*3*	*51*	*0*	53^{2}	*47*	*6*	*5.0*	*10.8*	*64*	*47%*	*.299*	*1.42*	*3.91*	*4.13*	*0.5*	*96.6*	*40*	*52*	*54*
2019	*MIA*	*MLB*	*29*	*3*	*1*	*2*	*50*	*0*	53^{1}	*43*	*6*	*5.1*	*10.9*	*65*	*47%*	*.315*	*1.38*	*4.02*	*4.57*	*0.4*	*96.3*	*40*	*51*	*54*

Breakout: 32% Improve: 48% Collapse: 23% Attrition: 13% MLB: 83% *Comparables: A.J. Ramos, Brian Wilson, Joey Devine*

Omnipresent control issues are the lone bugaboo for Barraclough, a classic power pitcher with a blazing fastball/wipeout slider combo. He's one of the most extreme Two True Outcomes pitchers in baseball history, having faced 690 major-league hitters in his career, with a staggering 46.2 percent of those plate appearances ending in either a strikeout or a walk. That's a rate bested only by contemporaries like Craig Kimbrel, Aroldis Chapman, Kenley Jansen and Dellin Betances. He also owns the highest strikeout rate of any pitcher to ever walk more than five batters per nine innings. Barraclough is nearly unhittable when his command is on, yet there are some warning signs in his profile. He missed time with a shoulder impingement and lost nearly 2 mph off his average fastball velocity upon his return. Barraclough's raw talent is unquestioned, but it remains to be seen whether he can scale back his wildness enough to anchor a major-league bullpen.

Jeff Brigham RHP Born: 02/16/92 Age: 26 Bats: R Throws: R Height: 6'0" Weight: 200 Origin: Round 4, 2014 Draft (#129 overall)

YEAR	TEAM	LVL	AGE	W	L	SV	G	GS	IP	H	HR	BB/9	K/9	K	GB%	BABIP	WHIP	ERA	DRA	WARP	MPH	CMD	PWR	STM
2015	RCU	A+	23	4	5	0	17	14	68	78	8	4.8	8.5	64	57%	.340	1.68	5.96	4.42	0.5				
2015	JUP	A+	23	2	2	0	6	5	33^{2}	34	0	2.4	5.9	22	52%	.324	1.28	1.87	4.68	0.1				
2016	JUP	A+	24	7	8	1	27	23	122^{2}	115	6	3.4	8.2	112	41%	.307	1.32	4.04	3.54	2.6				
2017	JUP	A+	25	4	2	0	11	11	59	49	2	3.1	8.1	53	44%	.287	1.17	2.90	3.84	1.0				
2018	*MIA*	*MLB*	*26*	*3*	*4*	*0*	*18*	*11*	*59*	*60*	*10*	*4.2*	*8.6*	*57*	*42%*	*.319*	*1.49*	*5.02*	*5.66*	*-0.1*				
2019	*MIA*	*MLB*	*27*	*4*	*7*	*0*	*21*	*17*	114^{2}	*119*	*20*	*4.0*	*8.1*	*103*	*42%*	*.323*	*1.48*	*5.22*	*5.93*	*-0.3*				

Breakout: 3% Improve: 5% Collapse: 2% Attrition: 6% MLB: 8% *Comparables: Sammy Solis, Chris Dwyer, Nik Turley*

Not every trade involving a high-risk prospect ends up working out for the team giving up big-league talent, but the Marlins have to be encouraged with what they've seen from the healthy version of Brigham, the hard-throwing righty acquired from the Dodgers for Mat Latos in 2015. The issue? The oft-injured Washington native could be the model for a 21st-century Operation mobile app. He has already had Tommy John surgery and was limited to just 11 starts in High-A thanks to a laundry list of maladies including shoulder tendinitis—which cost him two months to begin the year—and a season-ending oblique strain in late July. Given his advanced age, major durability concerns and a power fastball/slider combo, he's an obvious reliever conversion candidate.

Edward Cabrera RHP Born: 04/13/98 Age: 20 Bats: R Throws: R Height: 6'4" Weight: 175 Origin: International Free Agent, 2015

YEAR	TEAM	LVL	AGE	W	L	SV	G	GS	IP	H	HR	BB/9	K/9	K	GB%	BABIP	WHIP	ERA	DRA	WARP	MPH	CMD	PWR	STM
2016	MRL	RK	18	2	6	0	11	7	47	54	1	1.9	5.4	28	41%	.331	1.36	4.21	6.60	-0.5				
2017	BAT	A-	19	1	3	0	13	6	35^2	42	1	2.0	8.1	32	55%	.350	1.40	5.30	3.92	0.5				
2018	*MIA*	*MLB*	*20*	*2*	*2*	*0*	*18*	*5*	*34*	*38*	*7*	*4.0*	*7.6*	*29*	*39%*	*.325*	*1.57*	*5.54*	*6.27*	*-0.5*				
2019	*MIA*	*MLB*	*21*	*3*	*4*	*0*	*25*	*11*	107^1	*116*	*20*	*4.3*	*7.0*	*83*	*39%*	*.317*	*1.55*	*5.81*	*6.61*	*-1.0*				

Comparables: Jeanmar Gomez, Jarlin Garcia, Justin De Fratus

Signed for $100,000 out of the Dominican Republic in 2015, Cabrera established himself as one of the most intriguing pitching prospects in the Marlins organization when he jumped to short-season Batavia last summer. Despite being one of the youngest pitchers in the New York-Penn League, he struck out nearly a batter per inning, displayed pinpoint control and allowed just one homer over 35 2/3 innings. The 6-foot-4 righty owns a solid three-pitch mix, headlined by a mid-90s fastball, and could add even more velocity as he continues to develop physically. He's still a jump to hyperspace away from Miami, but Cabrera has earned the nebulous mid-rotation starter projection.

Wei-Yin Chen LHP Born: 07/21/85 Age: 32 Bats: R Throws: L Height: 6'0" Weight: 200 Origin: International Free Agent, 2012

YEAR	TEAM	LVL	AGE	W	L	SV	G	GS	IP	H	HR	BB/9	K/9	K	GB%	BABIP	WHIP	ERA	DRA	WARP	MPH	CMD	PWR	STM
2015	BAL	MLB	29	11	8	0	31	31	191^1	192	28	1.9	7.2	153	43%	.290	1.22	3.34	4.46	1.4	94.3	56	49	74
2016	MIA	MLB	30	5	5	0	22	22	123^1	134	22	1.8	7.3	100	42%	.302	1.28	4.96	5.07	0.4	93.5	62	46	47
2017	MIA	MLB	31	2	1	0	9	5	33	25	3	2.5	6.8	25	39%	.234	1.03	3.82	4.19	0.5	92.4	54	43	0
2018	*MIA*	*MLB*	*32*	*6*	*9*	*0*	*23*	*23*	*121*	*122*	*17*	*2.9*	*7.5*	*102*	*42%*	*.293*	*1.32*	*4.35*	*4.62*	*0.8*	*92.8*	*58*	*47*	*34*
2019	*MIA*	*MLB*	*33*	*9*	*11*	*0*	*31*	*31*	199^1	*193*	*29*	*2.8*	*7.2*	*159*	*42%*	*.301*	*1.28*	*4.51*	*5.12*	*0.9*	*92.0*	*58*	*45*	*26*

Breakout: 8% Improve: 41% Collapse: 25% Attrition: 10% MLB: 87% *Comparables: Freddy Garcia, Ben Sheets, Brandon McCarthy*

It's hard to tell who lost more zip on his fastball after signing a big-money deal in free agency: Wei-Yin Chen or Bill Simmons. The southpaw was a bigger flop than HBO's *Any Given Wednesday* in his Marlins debut back in 2016. Not only was he sidelined two months with a partially torn UCL, he also recorded the highest DRA of his career and lost nearly a full mile per hour in average velocity off his fastball. On the heels of a second consecutive injury-marred campaign in which he was limited to just nine appearances—missing nearly four months due to lingering elbow discomfort—Chen's long-term health is a serious question mark, and Tommy John feels like a growing inevitability. Most teams would write him off as a sunk cost, but Miami remains on the hook for an additional $65 million, thanks to a series of lucrative player options and bonuses that won't expire until 2021. If he can get healthy, the Taiwanese lefty mixes five quality pitches and has the talent to return to form as a low-risk middle-of-the-rotation anchor. If he can't, god only knows how Derek Jeter is going to dispose of him.

Adam Conley LHP Born: 05/24/90 Age: 28 Bats: L Throws: L Height: 6'3" Weight: 200 Origin: Round 2, 2011 Draft (#72 overall)

YEAR	TEAM	LVL	AGE	W	L	SV	G	GS	IP	H	HR	BB/9	K/9	K	GB%	BABIP	WHIP	ERA	DRA	WARP	MPH	CMD	PWR	STM
2015	NWO	AAA	25	9	3	0	19	18	107	85	4	3.4	6.8	81	48%	.265	1.17	2.52	4.12	1.4				
2015	MIA	MLB	25	4	1	0	15	11	67	65	7	2.8	7.9	59	41%	.304	1.28	3.76	3.62	1.1	95.2	54	49	69
2016	MIA	MLB	26	8	6	0	25	25	133^1	125	13	4.2	8.4	124	41%	.300	1.40	3.85	4.91	0.7	94.3	57	52	58
2017	NWO	AAA	27	3	3	0	12	12	62^1	69	7	3.6	5.9	41	39%	.310	1.51	5.49	7.92	-1.5				
2017	MIA	MLB	27	8	8	0	22	20	102^2	114	19	3.7	6.3	72	42%	.295	1.52	6.14	6.76	-1.4	91.9	42	41	74
2018	*MIA*	*MLB*	*28*	*6*	*9*	*0*	*23*	*23*	*121*	*120*	*16*	*3.6*	*7.6*	*103*	*42%*	*.294*	*1.39*	*4.45*	*4.73*	*0.6*	*92.9*	*51*	*47*	*68*
2019	*MIA*	*MLB*	*29*	*9*	*11*	*0*	*31*	*31*	*200*	*181*	*25*	*3.5*	*7.7*	*171*	*42%*	*.297*	*1.30*	*4.38*	*4.97*	*1.2*	*92.4*	*50*	*47*	*67*

Breakout: 16% Improve: 47% Collapse: 16% Attrition: 33% MLB: 84% *Comparables: Joe Saunders, Josh Outman, Clay Hensley*

Conley has experienced a precipitous decline in the run-prevention department over each of the past two seasons. The southpaw finished 130th in DRA among pitchers with at least 100 innings in 2017. Only Matt Moore, Jharel Cotton, Derek Holland and the sentient remains of Matt Cain were hit harder. After Conley allowed 18 runs over a three-start span in early May, Miami finally pulled the plug and banished him from the rotation. It turned out to be a temporary exile, as a tornado of injuries devastated the Marlins' alternatives and forced them to give him 14 second-half starts. He lost nearly 2 mph off his fastball in 2017 and simply doesn't miss enough bats to compensate for lackluster control. His days as a conventional starter appear to be over. Yet, it's common knowledge that lefties are afforded nine lives. He's used up a few of his already, but he may be better suited for a bullpen role. If he regains some life on his heater in shorter stints, Conley could still provide value as a multi-inning reliever.

Odrisamer Despaigne RHP Born: 04/04/87 Age: 31 Bats: R Throws: R Height: 6'0" Weight: 200 Origin: International Free Agent, 2014

YEAR	TEAM	LVL	AGE	W	L	SV	G	GS	IP	H	HR	BB/9	K/9	K	GB%	BABIP	WHIP	ERA	DRA	WARP	MPH	CMD	PWR	STM
2015	SDN	MLB	28	5	9	0	34	18	125^2	142	17	2.3	4.9	69	53%	.298	1.38	5.80	6.12	-1.7	94.1	45	47	58
2016	BAL	MLB	29	0	2	0	16	0	27^1	32	3	4.9	5.6	17	38%	.337	1.72	5.60	6.72	-0.5	95.2	48	56	56
2016	NOR	AAA	29	1	9	0	18	17	88^1	91	5	2.8	7.1	70	53%	.319	1.34	3.87	5.06	0.3				
2016	MIA	MLB	29	0	0	0	3	0	3	4	0	3.0	0.0	0	50%	.333	1.67	9.00	4.21	0.0	94.3	48	56	56
2017	NWO	AAA	30	2	4	2	20	10	70	62	6	3.1	6.3	49	52%	.271	1.23	3.09	4.26	1.0				
2017	MIA	MLB	30	2	3	1	18	8	58^1	57	3	3.7	4.8	31	38%	.280	1.39	4.01	6.40	-0.6	94.2	51	59	60
2018	*MIA*	*MLB*	*31*	*2*	*3*	*0*	*51*	*0*	53^2	*54*	*6*	*3.6*	*6.5*	*39*	*47%*	*.291*	*1.40*	*4.71*	*4.77*	*0.1*	*93.4*	*47*	*53*	*58*
2019	*MIA*	*MLB*	*32*	*2*	*1*	*0*	*46*	*0*	48^2	*47*	*5*	*3.5*	*6.6*	*36*	*47%*	*.301*	*1.34*	*4.39*	*4.99*	*0.1*	*93.0*	*49*	*55*	*58*

Breakout: 15% Improve: 38% Collapse: 21% Attrition: 19% MLB: 75% *Comparables: Lucas Harrell, Luis Mendoza, Samuel Deduno*

The journeyman Cuban junkballer finally stumbled upon an oasis, serving as the Marlins' default back-of-the-rotation innings-eater down the stretch. Afforded an extended opportunity, the soft-tossing righty posted his lowest ERA since a 2014 debut with San Diego that turned out to be a harbinger of nothing. It remains to be seen whether his late-season success was a more of the same, a cruel Potemkin mirage. We know that DRA didn't buy into his performance last season, but no matter what the metrics say, we can collectively appreciate that Despaigne has gotten every ounce out of his fringy stuff.

Brian Ellington RHP Born: 08/04/90 Age: 27 Bats: R Throws: R Height: 6'3" Weight: 215 Origin: Round 16, 2012 Draft (#497 overall)

YEAR	TEAM	LVL	AGE	W	L	SV	G	GS	IP	H	HR	BB/9	K/9	K	GB%	BABIP	WHIP	ERA	DRA	WARP	MPH	CMD	PWR	STM
2015	JAX	AA	24	4	1	0	25	0	43	28	0	2.7	9.8	47	37%	.259	0.95	2.51	2.57	1.1				
2015	MIA	MLB	24	2	1	0	23	0	25	17	1	4.7	6.5	18	39%	.225	1.20	2.88	3.08	0.5	99.5	42	73	45
2016	NWO	AAA	25	1	0	2	32	0	34^{2}	17	2	6.8	14.0	54	31%	.238	1.24	3.12	2.50	1.0				
2016	MIA	MLB	25	4	2	0	32	0	33	27	2	4.4	8.7	32	31%	.281	1.30	2.45	3.76	0.5	100.4	42	74	50
2017	NWO	AAA	26	1	0	5	20	0	23^{2}	11	3	4.2	13.7	36	39%	.186	0.93	2.28	3.13	0.6				
2017	MIA	MLB	26	1	1	0	42	0	44^{2}	48	7	7.1	9.7	48	38%	.333	1.86	7.25	6.05	-0.4	100.0	41	84	53
2018	*MIA*	*MLB*	*27*	*1*	*2*	*0*	*30*	*0*	*32*	*29*	*5*	*5.0*	*10.0*	*36*	*37%*	*.296*	*1.47*	*4.86*	*4.88*	*0.0*	*99.5*	*42*	*80*	*51*
2019	*MIA*	*MLB*	*28*	*2*	*1*	*0*	*43*	*0*	*45*	*38*	*7*	*4.6*	*9.8*	*49*	*37%*	*.299*	*1.36*	*4.61*	*5.23*	*0.0*	*99.3*	*42*	*81*	*52*

Breakout: 24% Improve: 37% Collapse: 13% Attrition: 22% MLB: 65% *Comparables: Jared Burton, Scott Oberg, Brandon Cunniff*

Ellington boasts the classic middle reliever starter kit. He can touch triple digits with his fastball, but hasn't shown enough command of his secondary offerings—or an ability to consistently throw strikes—to merit consideration in high-leverage situations. As he discovered last season, handing out free passes at an alarming rate and serving up home runs are the fastest routes to the pit of misery (and New Orleans). If Ellington can regain his confidence, there is more than enough salvageable talent to make him a worthwhile restoration project; after all, 100 is still 100.

Jarlin Garcia LHP Born: 01/18/93 Age: 25 Bats: L Throws: L Height: 6'3" Weight: 215 Origin: International Free Agent, 2010

YEAR	TEAM	LVL	AGE	W	L	SV	G	GS	IP	H	HR	BB/9	K/9	K	GB%	BABIP	WHIP	ERA	DRA	WARP	MPH	CMD	PWR	STM
2015	JUP	A+	22	3	5	0	18	18	97	96	4	2.1	6.4	69	41%	.303	1.23	3.06	7.36	-2.7				
2015	JAX	AA	22	1	3	0	7	7	36^{2}	38	4	4.2	8.6	35	41%	.324	1.50	4.91	4.23	0.4				
2016	JAX	AA	23	1	3	0	9	9	39^{2}	38	4	2.5	6.1	27	48%	.274	1.24	4.54	4.79	0.1				
2017	MIA	MLB	24	1	2	0	68	0	53^{1}	47	6	2.9	7.1	42	41%	.263	1.20	4.72	5.72	-0.3	95.8	49	49	49
2018	*MIA*	*MLB*	*25*	*2*	*2*	*0*	*46*	*0*	*48^{1}*	*48*	*7*	*3.8*	*7.9*	*43*	*42%*	*.295*	*1.42*	*4.82*	*4.86*	*0.0*	*95.5*	*50*	*50*	*50*
2019	*MIA*	*MLB*	*26*	*2*	*1*	*0*	*48*	*0*	*50^{2}*	*46*	*7*	*3.6*	*8.2*	*46*	*42%*	*.297*	*1.30*	*4.53*	*5.14*	*0.0*	*95.3*	*50*	*50*	*51*

Breakout: 21% Improve: 36% Collapse: 17% Attrition: 47% MLB: 68% *Comparables: Billy Buckner, Jeff Karstens, Yorman Bazardo*

Despite being met with more resistance than a McDonald's employee informing rabid *Rick and Morty* fans that they ran out of Szechuan sauce, Garcia wasn't a complete failure in his first taste of the big leagues. A converted starter, he led the Marlins with 68 relief appearances and his three-pitch mix played up out of the bullpen. Garcia proved particularly adept at cleaning up other pitcher's messes. Of the 42 runners he inherited, only 19 percent crossed the plate. He appeared to wear down as the season progressed and his overall numbers took a substantial hit when he allowed 13 earned runs over his final 11 appearances. There's talk of a potential return to the rotation in 2018, but regardless of the role Miami envisions for Garcia, he's shown enough already to inspire confidence in his long-term outlook. He'll just have to tamp down that .783 OPS allowed to right-handed batters if he wants to the opportunity to face more of them.

Braxton Garrett LHP Born: 08/05/97 Age: 20 Bats: L Throws: L Height: 6'3" Weight: 190 Origin: Round 1, 2016 Draft (#7 overall)

YEAR	TEAM	LVL	AGE	W	L	SV	G	GS	IP	H	HR	BB/9	K/9	K	GB%	BABIP	WHIP	ERA	DRA	WARP	MPH	CMD	PWR	STM
2017	GRB	A	19	1	0	0	4	4	15^{1}	13	3	3.5	9.4	16	49%	.250	1.24	2.93	4.44	0.2				
2018	*MIA*	*MLB*	*20*	*2*	*3*	*0*	*8*	*8*	*34^{2}*	*36*	*8*	*4.6*	*9.6*	*37*	*41%*	*.319*	*1.56*	*5.75*	*6.49*	*-0.3*				
2019	*MIA*	*MLB*	*21*	*6*	*10*	*0*	*29*	*29*	*176^{2}*	*177*	*34*	*4.7*	*8.3*	*163*	*41%*	*.312*	*1.53*	*5.53*	*6.29*	*-1.0*				

Breakout: 4% Improve: 4% Collapse: 0% Attrition: 1% MLB: 5% *Comparables: Luiz Gohara, Jarrod Parker, Jack Flaherty*

Garrett, the seventh overall selection in the 2016 draft, possesses the highest ceiling of any prospect in the Marlins system. He made just four starts at Low-A Greensboro before his elbow began barking and remains a tantalizing unknown after undergoing Tommy John surgery last June. Before the injury, he featured a low-90s fastball and a dynamic curveball that he could throw in any count or situation, either for a called strike or for a chase out of the zone. But while Tommy John surgery is common these days, it's far from routine. There's a strong possibility that Garrett doesn't throw a pitch until 2019, and it's going to take time for his stuff to get all the way back, assuming it even does.

Merandy Gonzalez RHP Born: 10/09/95 Age: 22 Bats: R Throws: R Height: 6'0" Weight: 216 Origin: International Free Agent, 2013

YEAR	TEAM	LVL	AGE	W	L	SV	G	GS	IP	H	HR	BB/9	K/9	K	GB%	BABIP	WHIP	ERA	DRA	WARP	MPH	CMD	PWR	STM
2015	MTS	RK	19	2	1	0	4	2	22	9	1	1.2	10.2	25	56%	.163	0.55	2.05	1.97	0.9				
2015	KNG	RK	19	2	2	0	9	7	44^{2}	40	1	3.8	7.9	39	55%	.302	1.32	2.82	3.67	1.0				
2016	BRO	A-	20	6	3	0	14	14	69	65	2	3.5	9.3	71	54%	.337	1.33	2.87	3.10	1.7				
2017	COL	A	21	8	1	0	11	11	69^{2}	50	3	1.7	8.4	65	43%	.253	0.90	1.55	3.88	1.1				
2017	SLU	A+	21	4	2	0	6	6	36^{1}	33	1	2.0	5.9	24	43%	.271	1.13	2.23	3.63	0.7				
2017	JUP	A+	21	1	0	1	5	3	24^{1}	18	0	1.8	5.2	14	56%	.247	0.95	1.11	3.60	0.5				
2018	*MIA*	*MLB*	*22*	*5*	*7*	*0*	*18*	*18*	*96^{1}*	*97*	*18*	*4.1*	*8.6*	*92*	*42%*	*.311*	*1.46*	*5.13*	*5.78*	*-0.2*				
2019	*MIA*	*MLB*	*23*	*7*	*10*	*0*	*24*	*24*	*142^{1}*	*140*	*27*	*4.1*	*8.6*	*135*	*42%*	*.312*	*1.44*	*5.31*	*6.02*	*-0.6*				

Breakout: 9% Improve: 12% Collapse: 0% Attrition: 9% MLB: 15% *Comparables: Scott Diamond, Robert Whalen, Jayson Aquino*

Despite the recent arrival of several intriguing pitching prospects, Gonzalez—acquired from the Mets for closer A.J. Ramos at the 2017 trade deadline—has a chance to rise quickly. He allowed three runs or less in 18 of his 20 starts across two minor-league levels and posted an even shinier ERA at High-A Jupiter after joining the Marlins system in August. Ostensibly being developed as a starter, Gonzalez features a naturally cutting fastball, a slider and a curveball. His changeup remains a work in progress, and most scouts believe he's a future reliever. Gonzalez was added to Miami's 40-man roster in the offseason, and it's only a matter of time before he's knocking on the door of the big leagues. A move to the bullpen would expedite that timeline.

Jorge Guzman RHP Born: 01/28/96 Age: 22 Bats: R Throws: R Height: 6'2" Weight: 182 Origin: International Free Agent, 2014

YEAR	TEAM	LVL	AGE	W	L	SV	G	GS	IP	H	HR	BB/9	K/9	K	GB%	BABIP	WHIP	ERA	DRA	WARP	MPH	CMD	PWR	STM
2015	DAR	RK	19	0	2	0	4	4	13^{1}	19	1	5.4	5.4	8	51%	.360	2.03	7.43	8.26	-0.4				
2015	DAS	RK	19	2	1	0	9	7	33	36	1	4.1	5.2	19	50%	.287	1.55	4.91	7.27	-0.5				
2016	AST	RK	20	1	1	0	7	4	17^{1}	4	0	5.2	13.0	25	77%	.129	0.81	3.12	2.73	0.6				
2016	GRV	RK	20	2	3	0	6	4	22^{2}	25	1	2.8	11.5	29	56%	.387	1.41	4.76	2.23	0.8				
2017	STA	A-	21	5	3	0	13	13	66^{2}	51	4	2.4	11.9	88	55%	.311	1.03	2.30	1.19	3.1				
2018	*MIA*	*MLB*	*22*	*2*	*4*	*0*	*16*	*10*	47^{2}	*50*	*11*	*5.3*	*9.9*	*53*	*44%*	*.326*	*1.64*	*5.87*	*6.62*	*-0.6*				
2019	*MIA*	*MLB*	*23*	*5*	*9*	*0*	*33*	*23*	160^{2}	*157*	*34*	*4.1*	*9.4*	*167*	*44%*	*.315*	*1.44*	*5.45*	*6.19*	*-0.8*				

Breakout: 1% Improve: 1% Collapse: 2% Attrition: 3% MLB: 3% *Comparables: Adam Warren, Kyle Weiland, Patrick Light*

One winter can change everything. In November, Guzman was a bit lost in the shuffle among one of the game's best farm systems; even a fastball that cracks triple digits doesn't change the fact that short-season pitchers with no off-speed stuff don't often make a team's top-10 prospect list. Then he was traded for the best player in Marlins history, destined to be remembered by both Miami and New York fans even if he never gets a sniff of the majors. Instead of the gentle expectations that come with being one of many talented Yankees pitching prospects, Guzman now must shoulder the significant weight of having been traded for Giancarlo Stanton.

Tyler Kolek RHP Born: 12/15/95 Age: 22 Bats: R Throws: R Height: 6'5" Weight: 260 Origin: Round 1, 2014 Draft (#2 overall)

YEAR	TEAM	LVL	AGE	W	L	SV	G	GS	IP	H	HR	BB/9	K/9	K	GB%	BABIP	WHIP	ERA	DRA	WARP	MPH	CMD	PWR	STM
2015	GRB	A	19	4	10	0	25	25	108^{2}	108	7	5.1	6.7	81	51%	.298	1.56	4.56	6.83	-2.1				
2018	*MIA*	*MLB*	*22*	*-1*	*5*	*-0*	*6*	*6*	*22*	*26*	*6*	*23.7*	*7.5*	*18*	*42%*	*.325*	*3.80*	*13.62*	*15.75*	*-2.5*				
2019	*MIA*	*MLB*	*23*	*5*	*10*	*0*	*28*	*28*	167^{2}	*183*	*28*	*3.0*	*6.2*	*116*	*42%*	*.315*	*1.42*	*5.58*	*6.36*	*-0.8*				

Breakout: 3% Improve: 3% Collapse: 1% Attrition: 2% MLB: 4% *Comparables: Elvin Ramirez, Shawn Morimando, Esmil Rogers*

The second overall pick in the 2014 draft, Kolek has seen his odyssey to greatness take a rather depressing detour and has become the latest high-profile exhibit on why a franchise shouldn't gamble on a high-risk project with a top-five pick. It's too early to call him a total bust, but the odds of him reaching the ceiling many envisioned are virtually nonexistent. He's missed nearly two full seasons of valuable development time recovering from Tommy John surgery, and for a raw arm with a lot of work to do on his secondary offerings, that alone could be crippling. If the triple-digit velocity, which once inspired Paul Bunyanesque tales and defined his Texas high school career, doesn't return, the floor is deeper than a mine shaft.

Dustin McGowan RHP Born: 03/24/82 Age: 36 Bats: R Throws: R Height: 6'3" Weight: 235 Origin: Round 1, 2000 Draft (#33 overall)

YEAR	TEAM	LVL	AGE	W	L	SV	G	GS	IP	H	HR	BB/9	K/9	K	GB%	BABIP	WHIP	ERA	DRA	WARP	MPH	CMD	PWR	STM
2015	PHI	MLB	33	1	2	0	14	1	23^{1}	29	7	7.7	8.1	21	42%	.314	2.10	6.94	6.08	-0.4	97.3	29	67	49
2015	LEH	AAA	33	2	2	15	31	1	39^{2}	41	2	5.4	6.4	28	45%	.300	1.64	4.08	9.93	-2.2				
2016	MIA	MLB	34	1	3	1	55	0	67	49	7	4.4	8.5	63	55%	.241	1.22	2.82	2.96	1.5	97.7	25	61	48
2017	MIA	MLB	35	8	2	0	63	0	77^{2}	77	13	3.1	7.4	64	52%	.286	1.34	4.75	4.77	0.3	95.5	37	56	51
2018	*MIA*	*MLB*	*36*	*3*	*2*	*1*	*53*	*2*	63^{2}	*61*	*8*	*4.3*	*7.4*	*53*	*49%*	*.296*	*1.44*	*4.77*	*5.39*	*-0.1*	*95.1*	*31*	*58*	*48*
2019	*MIA*	*MLB*	*37*	*2*	*1*	*0*	*33*	*1*	45^{1}	*43*	*6*	*4.7*	*7.4*	*37*	*49%*	*.296*	*1.46*	*4.98*	*5.66*	*-0.2*	*94.4*	*31*	*57*	*48*

Breakout: 20% Improve: 44% Collapse: 13% Attrition: 4% MLB: 64% *Comparables: Hector Carrasco, Shawn Camp, D.J. Carrasco*

The fact that Seattle is still without an NBA franchise is almost as incomprehensible as McGowan's rebirth in a low-leverage, mop-up specialist role. When the SuperSonics played their final game in 2008, McGowan was a fresh-faced 25-year-old coming off a career-high 27 starts for Toronto. In the decade since, he's persevered through more physical issues and surgical procedures than Shaquille O'Neal and Penny Hardaway combined, making just 32 starts during that span. In 2017, McGowan entered games in which the Marlins were either tied or losing 41 times, and only David Robertson racked up more wins in relief than his eight. In last year's *Annual* we wrote: "Between his injury history and his public struggle with Type-1 diabetes—he wears an insulin pump during games—it's amazing that he's still here at all, let alone thriving at age 34." Father Time will eventually win this battle, but rather than forecast his inevitable decline, let's take a moment to marvel at the fact that McGowan continues to defy the odds every year.

Nick Neidert RHP Born: 11/20/96 Age: 21 Bats: R Throws: R Height: 6'1" Weight: 180 Origin: Round 2, 2015 Draft (#60 overall)

YEAR	TEAM	LVL	AGE	W	L	SV	G	GS	IP	H	HR	BB/9	K/9	K	GB%	BABIP	WHIP	ERA	DRA	WARP	MPH	CMD	PWR	STM
2015	MRN	RK	18	0	2	0	11	11	35^{1}	25	1	2.3	5.9	23	67%	.235	0.96	1.53	3.27	1.0				
2016	CLN	A	19	7	3	0	19	19	91	75	7	1.3	6.8	69	41%	.262	0.97	2.57	3.90	1.2				
2017	MOD	A+	20	10	3	0	19	19	104^{1}	95	7	1.5	9.4	109	43%	.318	1.07	2.76	2.97	2.8				
2017	ARK	AA	20	1	3	0	6	6	23^{1}	33	4	1.9	5.0	13	47%	.341	1.63	6.56	4.64	0.1				
2018	*MIA*	*MLB*	*21*	*6*	*7*	*0*	*22*	*22*	101^{1}	*103*	*17*	*3.3*	*8.3*	*93*	*41%*	*.310*	*1.39*	*4.81*	*5.42*	*0.2*				
2019	*MIA*	*MLB*	*22*	*6*	*9*	*0*	*25*	*25*	147^{2}	*141*	*27*	*2.9*	*8.6*	*141*	*41%*	*.304*	*1.28*	*4.82*	*5.47*	*0.2*				

Breakout: 4% Improve: 4% Collapse: 1% Attrition: 5% MLB: 7% *Comparables: Vicente Campos, Jeremy Hellickson, Brandon Maurer*

In baseball lingo, "numbers don't tell the whole story" is commonly proffered as an excuse when a player's numbers are subpar or worse. On the surface, Neidert's 6.56 ERA in six late-season starts at Double-A Arkansas following promotion is simply a lousy performance against more advanced competition that rings the alarm bells. The reality is that the rest of Neidert's 2017 campaign was strong, and he was a 20-year-old frequently squaring off against more advanced competition. Neidert doesn't light up the radar guns, but he draws raves for his pinpoint command and a herky-jerky delivery that makes it difficult for batters to pick up what he's throwing down. He'll get plenty of chances to prove that last year's hiccup at Arkansas was a small-sample-size fluke and not a harbinger of bad things to come.

Justin Nicolino LHP Born: 11/22/91 Age: 26 Bats: L Throws: L Height: 6'3" Weight: 195 Origin: Round 2, 2010 Draft (#80 overall)

YEAR	TEAM	LVL	AGE	W	L	SV	G	GS	IP	H	HR	BB/9	K/9	K	GB%	BABIP	WHIP	ERA	DRA	WARP	MPH	CMD	PWR	STM
2015	NWO	AAA	23	7	7	0	20	20	115	134	11	2.3	4.9	63	52%	.324	1.42	3.52	4.17	1.5				
2015	MIA	MLB	23	5	4	0	12	12	74	72	8	2.4	2.8	23	46%	.259	1.24	4.01	6.10	-0.9	91.8	57	32	71
2016	NWO	AAA	24	7	6	0	14	14	85	87	10	1.4	5.2	49	54%	.282	1.18	4.13	2.35	2.9				
2016	MIA	MLB	24	3	6	0	18	13	79^{1}	96	8	2.3	4.2	37	49%	.317	1.46	4.99	6.36	-0.9	92.4	57	39	66
2017	NWO	AAA	25	5	5	0	14	14	79	75	10	2.7	5.8	51	45%	.269	1.25	3.19	4.54	1.0				
2017	MIA	MLB	25	2	3	0	20	8	48	66	8	3.8	4.9	26	48%	.333	1.79	5.06	7.83	-1.3	92.3	54	34	60
2018	*MIA*	*MLB*	*26*	*3*	*5*	*0*	*33*	*8*	*72*	*79*	*10*	*3.4*	*5.6*	*45*	*48%*	*.296*	*1.47*	*5.03*	*5.17*	*-0.1*	*91.8*	*57*	*36*	*66*
2019	*MIA*	*MLB*	*27*	*7*	*7*	*0*	*66*	*15*	*144*	*143*	*18*	*3.0*	*6.1*	*97*	*48%*	*.301*	*1.32*	*4.51*	*5.13*	*0.5*	*91.6*	*57*	*37*	*65*

Breakout: 37% Improve: 53% Collapse: 9% Attrition: 32% MLB: 75% *Comparables: Eddie Butler, Carlos Frias, Casey Coleman*

After oscillating between the majors and the minors, and between the rotation and the bullpen, Nicolino has begun to straddle the razor-thin line dividing relevancy and irrelevancy. Yet he's still not a threat to fall off the grid entirely and resurface as a Cinnabon manager in Omaha like Saul Goodman. Nicolino remains relatively young, cost-controlled and left-handed, after all. Yet the disintegration of his once-pinpoint control and a truly historic inability to miss bats are huge red flags in his long-term profile. Over the last three seasons, Nicolino has struck out just 3.84 batters per nine, which is lower than all but seven pitchers since 1998.

Chris O'Grady LHP Born: 04/17/90 Age: 28 Bats: R Throws: L Height: 6'4" Weight: 225 Origin: Round 10, 2012 Draft (#327 overall)

YEAR	TEAM	LVL	AGE	W	L	SV	G	GS	IP	H	HR	BB/9	K/9	K	GB%	BABIP	WHIP	ERA	DRA	WARP	MPH	CMD	PWR	STM
2015	ARK	AA	25	0	5	4	38	0	49	42	5	1.8	8.6	47	48%	.278	1.06	3.31	1.98	1.6				
2016	SLC	AAA	26	2	1	0	22	2	34^{2}	41	3	3.1	6.2	24	44%	.352	1.53	4.15	5.07	0.0				
2016	ARK	AA	26	7	1	1	15	8	61	64	3	1.5	7.4	50	44%	.332	1.21	2.80	2.53	1.8				
2017	NWO	AAA	27	3	5	0	12	9	54^{2}	44	7	2.5	8.9	54	43%	.264	1.08	3.29	2.88	1.6				
2017	MIA	MLB	27	2	1	0	13	6	33	33	4	4.9	8.2	30	36%	.315	1.55	4.36	7.02	-0.6	88.9	45	14	45
2018	*MIA*	*MLB*	*28*	*4*	*6*	*0*	*15*	*15*	*79*	*81*	*13*	*3.3*	*8.3*	*73*	*42%*	*.298*	*1.40*	*4.66*	*4.94*	*0.2*	*88.4*	*45*	*14*	*45*
2019	*MIA*	*MLB*	*29*	*9*	*11*	*0*	*31*	*31*	*198*	*188*	*30*	*3.2*	*8.6*	*188*	*42%*	*.312*	*1.30*	*4.43*	*5.03*	*1.1*	*87.9*	*45*	*14*	*45*

Breakout: 20% Improve: 34% Collapse: 13% Attrition: 22% MLB: 50% *Comparables: Arnold Leon, A.J. Murray, Eric Surkamp*

Does O'Grady's sudden emergence seem a tad fluky? You bet. He walked five batters per nine and his DRA was nearly three runs higher than his actual ERA. It's easy to dismiss the southpaw's colossal strikeout rate as a total mirage because he throws a mid-80s fastball and relies on mixing speeds and locations, but it was propped up by being death on lefties due to deception and angle—they only mustered a .502 OPS against him. After being unceremoniously released by the Angels in April, O'Grady languished at Triple-A New Orleans for months before being called up by Miami in July. He wasn't completely overmatched in a six-start stint until a strained oblique sidelined him in early August. He lost his rotation spot but reemerged as a legitimate weapon out of the bullpen in late September, posting seven scoreless appearances to close out the year. While he lacks an electrifying arsenal and a glamorous role, O'Grady has proven that he can be a valuable big-league asset. Ignore him at your own peril.

Dillon Peters LHP Born: 08/31/92 Age: 25 Bats: L Throws: L Height: 5'9" Weight: 195 Origin: Round 10, 2014 Draft (#287 overall)

YEAR	TEAM	LVL	AGE	W	L	SV	G	GS	IP	H	HR	BB/9	K/9	K	GB%	BABIP	WHIP	ERA	DRA	WARP	MPH	CMD	PWR	STM
2015	MRL	RK	22	1	1	0	4	4	13^{1}	10	0	2.0	8.8	13	42%	.303	0.98	0.68	3.39	0.4				
2015	BAT	A-	22	0	3	0	7	7	31^{2}	40	2	2.8	7.7	27	58%	.345	1.58	4.83	2.77	0.9				
2016	JUP	A+	23	11	6	0	20	20	106	102	2	1.4	7.6	89	60%	.316	1.11	2.46	2.10	4.1				
2016	JAX	AA	23	3	0	0	4	4	22^{2}	17	2	1.6	6.4	16	54%	.231	0.93	1.99	3.00	0.6				
2017	JUP	A+	24	1	0	0	2	2	10^{2}	5	0	1.7	7.6	9	59%	.185	0.66	0.00	2.43	0.4				
2017	JAX	AA	24	6	2	0	9	9	45^{2}	33	1	2.2	7.9	40	46%	.258	0.96	1.97	2.43	1.5				
2017	MIA	MLB	24	1	2	0	6	6	31^{1}	32	3	5.5	7.8	27	63%	.330	1.63	5.17	6.09	-0.2	93.4	36	32	36
2018	*MIA*	*MLB*	*25*	*7*	*9*	*0*	*23*	*23*	*131*	*130*	*17*	*3.5*	*8.0*	*116*	*49%*	*.298*	*1.39*	*4.37*	*4.64*	*0.8*	*93.1*	*37*	*33*	*37*
2019	*MIA*	*MLB*	*26*	*10*	*11*	*0*	*31*	*31*	*199^{1}*	*184*	*23*	*3.1*	*7.9*	*174*	*49%*	*.304*	*1.27*	*4.13*	*4.70*	*1.8*	*92.8*	*37*	*33*	*37*

Breakout: 25% Improve: 42% Collapse: 12% Attrition: 36% MLB: 69% *Comparables: Jeff Manship, Wade Miley, T.J. House*

The Double-A Jacksonville Jumbo Shrimp are a minor-league affiliate straight out of a Michael Scott focus group, but nobody embraced the concept and excelled more than Peters during their inaugural season. The 5-foot-9 lefty spent last summer stifling Southern League lineups with his deceptive three-pitch mix before making the seamless transition to the big-league rotation in early September. A southpaw with a metric ton of moxie, a low-90s fastball and an angry curveball to dominate minor-league lineups, Peters proved in his brief exposure to major-league hitters that he needs to refine his command if he's going to survive as a starter. He's the type of prospect that flies under the radar—and limbo sticks—because of his size, but he projects as a durable back-end starter for years to come.

Trevor Richards RHP Born: 05/15/93 Age: 25 Bats: R Throws: R Height: 6'2" Weight: 190 Origin: Undrafted Free Agent, 2016

YEAR	TEAM	LVL	AGE	W	L	SV	G	GS	IP	H	HR	BB/9	K/9	K	GB%	BABIP	WHIP	ERA	DRA	WARP	MPH	CMD	PWR	STM
2016	BAT	A-	23	0	0	0	3	1	10^{2}	9	1	1.7	12.7	15	28%	.333	1.03	1.69	1.94	0.4				
2016	GRB	A	23	2	3	0	8	8	43^{2}	29	3	2.9	7.8	38	47%	.222	0.98	2.68	3.33	0.9				
2017	JUP	A+	24	7	4	0	13	11	70^{2}	54	2	1.5	10.3	81	62%	.284	0.93	2.17	0.71	3.7				
2017	JAX	AA	24	5	7	0	14	14	75^{1}	67	4	2.2	9.2	77	50%	.297	1.13	2.87	1.96	2.9				
2018	*MIA*	*MLB*	*25*	*1*	*1*	*0*	*3*	*3*	*17*	*16*	*3*	*3.3*	*9.2*	*18*	*43%*	*.296*	*1.31*	*4.26*	*4.51*	*0.1*				
2019	*MIA*	*MLB*	*26*	*10*	*12*	*0*	*31*	*31*	*200^{1}*	*180*	*27*	*3.5*	*8.3*	*185*	*43%*	*.298*	*1.28*	*4.38*	*4.97*	*1.2*				

Breakout: 17% Improve: 36% Collapse: 11% Attrition: 29% MLB: 58% *Comparables: P.J. Walters, Matt Bowman, Kyle Gibson*

In the era of prospect proliferation, it's rare when a legitimate talent goes completely undiscovered. Undrafted following his collegiate career at Division II Drury University, Richards pitched for the Gateway Grizzlies of the Frontier League until signing with Miami in July

2016. In 27 games split between High-A Jupiter and Double-A Jacksonville, Richards led the Marlins' minor-league system in both ERA (2.53) and strikeouts (158) over 146 innings. He's gone from usable innings-eater, to quality organizational depth, to potential major-league swingman. Not too shabby for a first full-season in affiliated baseball.

Trevor Rogers LHP Born: 11/13/97 Age: 20 Bats: L Throws: L Height: 6'6" Weight: 185 Origin: Round 1, 2017 Draft (#13 overall)

"Clyde Bruckman's Final Repose" is one of the most iconic episodes of *The X-Files*. There's an infamous scene where Scully lectures an overeager Mulder: "The human mind naturally seeks meaningful patterns and configurations in things that don't inherently have any. Given the suggestion of a particular image, you can't help but see that shape somewhere." Scouting director Stan Meek described the 13th overall selection in last year's draft to reporters as a cross between Randy Johnson and Mark Mulder. "He's kind of in the loose, lanky mold," Meek told the *Miami Herald*. "We just liked how the body worked, the way the arm looked. We liked his delivery. He's 6-foot-6, loose and a strike-thrower." The Marlins see what they want to see in Rogers: a potential ace. The issue with lofty expectations is that you run the risk of burying a prospect under the weight of them. The New Mexico native hasn't even thrown a professional pitch yet and already turned 20 just a few months ago. Rogers is just the latest entry in a series of high-risk first-round selections over the last decade for Miami.

Drew Steckenrider RHP Born: 01/10/91 Age: 27 Bats: R Throws: R Height: 6'5" Weight: 215 Origin: Round 8, 2012 Draft (#257 overall)

YEAR	TEAM	LVL	AGE	W	L	SV	G	GS	IP	H	HR	BB/9	K/9	K	GB%	BABIP	WHIP	ERA	DRA	WARP	MPH	CMD	PWR	STM
2015	GRB	A	24	1	3	0	10	5	39^{1}	38	2	3.9	7.8	34	47%	.316	1.40	2.75	3.34	0.8				
2015	JUP	A+	24	4	3	1	15	8	56^{2}	59	2	4.0	7.0	44	56%	.324	1.48	3.18	4.38	0.4				
2016	JUP	A+	25	0	0	1	6	0	10	2	0	1.8	15.3	17	64%	.143	0.40	0.00	1.46	0.4				
2016	JAX	AA	25	1	0	6	24	0	30^{1}	12	0	3.0	11.6	39	54%	.197	0.73	1.48	1.55	1.2				
2016	NWO	AAA	25	0	1	7	10	0	11^{2}	11	1	5.4	11.6	15	52%	.333	1.54	5.40	2.67	0.3				
2017	NWO	AAA	26	0	1	5	26	0	33^{1}	18	3	2.2	11.9	44	43%	.217	0.78	1.62	1.20	1.5				
2017	MIA	MLB	26	1	1	1	37	0	34^{2}	30	4	4.7	14.0	54	43%	.347	1.38	2.34	3.34	0.7	96.8	59	69	51
2018	*MIA*	*MLB*	*27*	*2*	*3*	*0*	*51*	*0*	53^{2}	*49*	*8*	*4.4*	*10.5*	*62*	*46%*	*.299*	*1.40*	*4.39*	*4.51*	*0.2*	*96.3*	*60*	*70*	*52*
2019	*MIA*	*MLB*	*28*	*3*	*1*	*0*	*51*	*0*	53^{2}	*45*	*8*	*3.9*	*10.8*	*64*	*46%*	*.307*	*1.27*	*4.11*	*4.65*	*0.3*	*95.9*	*60*	*70*	*52*

Breakout: 21% Improve: 38% Collapse: 21% Attrition: 27% MLB: 67% *Comparables: Pedro Strop, Lester Oliveros, Brandon Gomes*

Not since the halcyon days of shaggy-haired backstop Jarrod Saltalamacchia or legendary Panthers goalie John Van Biesbrouck have South Florida residents seen a name stretched this wide across the back of a jersey. A tall, physical specimen, Steckenrider leans heavily on a blistering fastball that sits comfortably in the 95-to-98-mph range and complements it with the occasional mid-80s slider. He was borderline unhittable in a brief stint at Triple-A and turned heads with an eye-popping strikeout rate at the big-league level. Stop me if you've heard this before: If he can iron out his control issues, he's got the raw stuff required to close.

Dan Straily RHP Born: 12/01/88 Age: 29 Bats: R Throws: R Height: 6'2" Weight: 220 Origin: Round 24, 2009 Draft (#723 overall)

YEAR	TEAM	LVL	AGE	W	L	SV	G	GS	IP	H	HR	BB/9	K/9	K	GB%	BABIP	WHIP	ERA	DRA	WARP	MPH	CMD	PWR	STM
2015	FRE	AAA	26	10	9	0	22	22	122^{2}	147	13	1.8	9.1	124	33%	.356	1.40	4.77	2.18	4.3				
2015	HOU	MLB	26	0	1	0	4	3	16^{2}	16	2	4.3	7.6	14	42%	.275	1.44	5.40	5.53	-0.1	91.3	45	28	61
2016	CIN	MLB	27	14	8	0	34	31	191^{1}	154	31	3.4	7.6	162	34%	.239	1.19	3.76	5.03	0.7	91.8	49	36	78
2017	MIA	MLB	28	10	9	0	33	33	181^{2}	176	31	3.0	8.4	170	36%	.288	1.30	4.26	4.51	2.2	92.1	48	33	77
2018	*MIA*	*MLB*	*29*	*8*	*12*	*0*	*30*	*30*	*171*	*164*	*27*	*3.1*	*8.4*	*160*	*36%*	*.286*	*1.29*	*4.42*	*4.69*	*0.9*	*91.3*	*48*	*34*	*73*
2019	*MIA*	*MLB*	*30*	*10*	*12*	*0*	*32*	*32*	205^{1}	*176*	*28*	*3.2*	*8.4*	*192*	*36%*	*.285*	*1.21*	*4.26*	*4.83*	*1.6*	*91.0*	*48*	*34*	*75*

Breakout: 28% Improve: 50% Collapse: 20% Attrition: 17% MLB: 91% *Comparables: Chris Young, Vidal Nuno, Chase Anderson*

In 1867, U.S. Secretary of State William H. Seward purchased Alaska from Russia for $7.2 million. At the time, it was extremely controversial, met with harsh criticism and skeptics mocked it openly as "Seward's Folly." He was eventually vindicated by the discovery of gold and oil, but not before his death in 1872. The trade that sent fire-balling right-hander Luis Castillo to Cincinnati for Straily may ultimately be remembered as "Hill's Folly" in Miami. It's too early to render a final decision, but the early returns are not promising. To his credit, Straily held up his end of the bargain, making a team-high 33 starts last season. Meanwhile, Castillo looked like a potential ace as a rookie and returned just as much big-league value in half the innings.

Junichi Tazawa RHP Born: 06/06/86 Age: 32 Bats: R Throws: R Height: 5'11" Weight: 200 Origin: International Free Agent, 2008

YEAR	TEAM	LVL	AGE	W	L	SV	G	GS	IP	H	HR	BB/9	K/9	K	GB%	BABIP	WHIP	ERA	DRA	WARP	MPH	CMD	PWR	STM
2015	BOS	MLB	29	2	7	3	61	0	58^{2}	65	5	2.0	8.6	56	42%	.349	1.33	4.14	4.02	0.5	95.9	47	54	49
2016	BOS	MLB	30	3	2	0	53	0	49^{2}	47	9	2.5	9.8	54	40%	.292	1.23	4.17	3.94	0.6	95.0	46	42	40
2017	MIA	MLB	31	3	5	0	55	0	55^{1}	55	8	3.6	6.2	38	38%	.280	1.39	5.69	5.22	0.0	94.1	48	44	47
2018	*MIA*	*MLB*	*32*	*2*	*3*	*0*	*56*	*0*	*59*	*64*	*10*	*3.8*	*7.6*	*50*	*42%*	*.301*	*1.51*	*5.41*	*5.35*	*-0.3*	*93.9*	*47*	*46*	*45*
2019	*MIA*	*MLB*	*33*	*2*	*1*	*1*	*41*	*0*	43^{2}	*43*	*8*	*3.6*	*7.9*	*38*	*42%*	*.3*	*1.38*	*5.05*	*5.74*	*-0.3*	*93.2*	*47*	*43*	*44*

Breakout: 17% Improve: 35% Collapse: 37% Attrition: 7% MLB: 91% *Comparables: Jon Rauch, Donnie Moore, Edward Mujica*

The Japanese right-hander gobbled up nearly 300 high-leverage relief innings over a five-year period from 2012 to 2016. That effort turned out to be a herculean eating challenge reminiscent of the time *Man vs. Food* host Adam Richman consumed 15 dozen oysters during a single sitting. From a physical standpoint, Tazawa emerged relatively unscathed. Yet he was a shell of his former self by the end of his time in Boston and wasn't the same in his Marlins debut last season. His average fastball velocity declined for the third consecutive season and he posted the worst single-season strikeout and walk rates of his major-league career. He's endured more abuse than a *Westworld* host and the backbreaking workload has clearly sapped his overall effectiveness. Fortunately, veteran relievers with his relative youth and playoff experience don't have to look far to find their next meal.

Jose Urena RHP Born: 09/12/91 Age: 26 Bats: R Throws: R Height: 6'2" Weight: 200 Origin: International Free Agent, 2008

YEAR	TEAM	LVL	AGE	W	L	SV	G	GS	IP	H	HR	BB/9	K/9	K	GB%	BABIP	WHIP	ERA	DRA	WARP	MPH	CMD	PWR	STM
2015	NWO	AAA	23	6	1	0	11	11	67^{2}	65	4	2.5	5.5	41	54%	.292	1.24	2.66	4.37	0.7				
2015	MIA	MLB	23	1	5	0	20	9	61^{2}	73	5	3.6	4.1	28	49%	.319	1.59	5.25	5.87	-0.6	97.1	56	60	55
2016	NWO	AAA	24	3	3	0	12	12	48^{1}	41	4	3.9	7.6	41	46%	.278	1.28	3.17	5.35	0.0				
2016	MIA	MLB	24	4	9	1	28	12	83^{2}	91	11	3.1	6.2	58	49%	.297	1.43	6.13	4.68	0.6	97.7	48	63	62
2017	MIA	MLB	25	14	7	0	34	28	169^{2}	152	26	3.4	6.0	113	44%	.249	1.27	3.82	5.29	0.5	97.3	51	60	72
2018	*MIA*	*MLB*	*26*	*7*	*11*	*0*	*26*	*26*	*156*	*156*	*21*	*3.5*	*6.7*	*116*	*46%*	*.289*	*1.38*	*4.64*	*4.93*	*0.4*	*97.0*	*52*	*62*	*66*
2019	*MIA*	*MLB*	*27*	*11*	*12*	*0*	*32*	*32*	202^{2}	*185*	*25*	*3.2*	*7.4*	*166*	*46%*	*.295*	*1.27*	*4.36*	*4.95*	*1.4*	*96.7*	*51*	*62*	*68*

Breakout: 28% Improve: 53% Collapse: 7% Attrition: 19% MLB: 90% *Comparables: Nick Martinez, Jeremy Sowers, Travis Wood*

There's a reason major studios release superhero movie after superhero movie. Audiences clamor for them and compare them against both the previous version and the original comics or series. No one in South Florida was clamoring for another Nate Eovaldi, but Urena continued to do his best impression of the frustrating fireballer by racking up innings while being unable to consistently use his secondary stuff to miss bats. While the surface stats may inspire some long-term confidence, the underlying metrics tell a different story. The gap between his 3.82 ERA and uninspiring 5.29 DRA was the sixth highest of any starter, and despite the heat emojis on his fastball, Urena recorded the ninth-lowest strikeout rate of any pitcher with at least 150 innings in 2017. It's too early to render a final verdict, but his fly-ball tendencies and pedestrian strikeout potential do not play well in the current landscape, even if they play well enough in Marlins Park.

Edinson Volquez RHP Born: 07/03/83 Age: 34 Bats: R Throws: R Height: 6'0" Weight: 220 Origin: International Free Agent, 2001

YEAR	TEAM	LVL	AGE	W	L	SV	G	GS	IP	H	HR	BB/9	K/9	K	GB%	BABIP	WHIP	ERA	DRA	WARP	MPH	CMD	PWR	STM
2015	KCA	MLB	31	13	9	0	34	33	200^{1}	190	16	3.2	7.0	155	47%	.290	1.31	3.55	4.11	2.3	96.3	49	47	79
2016	KCA	MLB	32	10	11	0	34	34	189^{1}	217	23	3.6	6.6	139	52%	.319	1.55	5.37	5.27	0.2	96.0	44	45	82
2017	MIA	MLB	33	4	8	0	17	17	92^{1}	78	8	5.2	7.9	81	49%	.278	1.42	4.19	3.76	1.9	95.0	46	49	58
2018	*MIA*	*MLB*	*34*	*5*	*6*	*0*	*16*	*16*	91^{1}	*92*	*11*	*4.2*	*7.4*	*75*	*49%*	*.310*	*1.47*	*4.63*	*5.23*	*0.4*	*94.7*	*45*	*46*	*70*
2019	*MIA*	*MLB*	*35*	*10*	*11*	*0*	*30*	*30*	188^{1}	*184*	*22*	*4.0*	*7.5*	*156*	*49%*	*.313*	*1.42*	*4.49*	*5.11*	*1.0*	*94.1*	*44*	*46*	*68*

Breakout: 13% Improve: 47% Collapse: 20% Attrition: 12% MLB: 93% *Comparables: Whitey Ford, Scott Feldman, C.J. Wilson*

One of the lone bright spots in a year where everything seemed to go wrong for Miami, Volquez fired the only no-hitter of the entire 2017 season on June 3. He walked two batters and needed just 98 pitches to finish off the "Maddux"—a shutout on fewer than 100 pitches—against a high-powered Diamondbacks lineup. The fact that he was pitching through pain virtually the entire time made the feat even more surreal. On just his third pitch of the afternoon, Volquez was involved in an ugly collision while covering first base. "I thought I broke my ankle," he told reporters after the game. If you're a believer in the supernatural, it's entirely possible that the 33-year-old had some help from his former Royals teammate Yordano Ventura—who passed away in an offseason car accident—to summon the strength to continue. After striking out the side in the ninth inning, Volquez dedicated the no-hitter to both Ventura and former Miami ace Jose Fernandez, a fitting tribute to a pair of immensely talented young pitchers who lost their lives in tragic fashion. "They're watching right now, what happened today," Volquez said. "And they must feel really happy right now."

Nick Wittgren RHP Born: 05/29/91 Age: 27 Bats: R Throws: R Height: 6'2" Weight: 210 Origin: Round 9, 2012 Draft (#287 overall)

YEAR	TEAM	LVL	AGE	W	L	SV	G	GS	IP	H	HR	BB/9	K/9	K	GB%	BABIP	WHIP	ERA	DRA	WARP	MPH	CMD	PWR	STM
2015	NWO	AAA	24	1	6	19	51	0	62^{1}	58	6	1.2	9.2	64	35%	.302	1.06	3.03	1.37	2.5				
2016	NWO	AAA	25	1	0	2	10	0	12^{2}	6	1	2.8	7.8	11	39%	.167	0.79	1.42	3.78	0.2				
2016	MIA	MLB	25	4	3	0	48	0	51^{2}	50	6	1.7	7.3	42	41%	.286	1.16	3.14	4.88	0.1	94.6	61	59	47
2017	MIA	MLB	26	3	1	0	38	0	42^{1}	46	5	2.8	9.1	43	32%	.339	1.39	4.68	5.27	0.0	94.0	48	56	48
2018	*MIA*	*MLB*	*27*	*2*	*3*	*0*	*51*	*0*	53^{2}	*53*	*8*	*3.2*	*9.0*	*54*	*38%*	*.300*	*1.34*	*4.25*	*4.41*	*0.3*	*93.8*	*55*	*58*	*48*
2019	*MIA*	*MLB*	*28*	*3*	*1*	*0*	*51*	*0*	53^{2}	*50*	*8*	*3.0*	*9.4*	*56*	*38%*	*.311*	*1.26*	*4.20*	*4.77*	*0.3*	*93.5*	*54*	*58*	*48*

Breakout: 17% Improve: 37% Collapse: 20% Attrition: 26% MLB: 76% *Comparables: Cory Wade, Daniel Herrera, Nick Vincent*

Astrophysicists estimate that roughly 80 percent of the universe's mass consists of material that we cannot directly observe, known as dark matter. Wittgren is baseball's equivalent: an obscure, unheralded middle reliever. Unless you're a hardcore Purdue Boilermakers fan—or play in a crazy-deep NL-only fantasy league—you probably aren't even aware of his existence. Despite wearing the figurative cloak of invisibility, he delivered 94 innings of replacement-level performance in Miami over the last two years before undergoing surgery to remove bone chips from his elbow in September. Wittgren pounds the strike zone with a three-pitch repertoire, spearheaded by a consistent low-90s fastball, and has the look of a future seventh-inning reliever.

Brad Ziegler RHP Born: 10/10/79 Age: 38 Bats: R Throws: R Height: 6'4" Weight: 220 Origin: Round 20, 2003 Draft (#595 overall)

YEAR	TEAM	LVL	AGE	W	L	SV	G	GS	IP	H	HR	BB/9	K/9	K	GB%	BABIP	WHIP	ERA	DRA	WARP	MPH	CMD	PWR	STM
2015	ARI	MLB	35	0	3	30	66	0	68	48	3	2.2	4.8	36	74%	.220	0.96	1.85	2.40	1.9	86.4	78	13	48
2016	ARI	MLB	36	2	3	18	36	0	38^{1}	41	1	3.5	6.3	27	66%	.333	1.46	2.82	2.54	1.1	85.9	77	22	49
2016	BOS	MLB	36	2	4	4	33	0	29^{2}	26	1	3.3	9.4	31	64%	.312	1.25	1.52	2.93	0.7	86.9	77	22	49
2017	MIA	MLB	37	1	4	10	53	0	47	57	1	3.1	5.0	26	65%	.346	1.55	4.79	2.75	1.3	84.5	74	0	41
2018	*MIA*	*MLB*	*38*	*3*	*3*	*30*	*56*	*0*	*59*	*62*	*5*	*4.4*	*4.6*	*30*	*60%*	*.292*	*1.55*	*5.12*	*5.09*	*-0.1*	*84.4*	*74*	*12*	*44*
2019	*MIA*	*MLB*	*39*	*2*	*1*	*17*	*41*	*0*	43^{1}	*43*	*4*	*4.2*	*4.7*	*23*	*60%*	*.294*	*1.47*	*5.06*	*5.77*	*-0.3*	*83.6*	*73*	*11*	*43*

Breakout: 25% Improve: 37% Collapse: 23% Attrition: 5% MLB: 87% *Comparables: Javier Lopez, Scott Downs, Mariano Rivera*

Nothing new to see here. Ziegler remains the same old veteran side-winding, extreme ground-ball pitcher who relies entirely on deception and movement to survive. He's still utilizing a three-pitch package fronted by a mid-80s sinker, Frisbee slider and straight changeup. By DRA, his core skills appear intact despite a decreasing strikeout rate and continually slipping velocity—he only touched 86 mph once throughout the entire season. At some point, the stuff will decline enough that his numbers will slip, but the Marlins have nine million reasons to hope it doesn't happen in 2018. Take a moment to marvel at his remarkable consistency and longevity because he could go flying off a building at any moment like Captain Queenan in *The Departed*.

Lineouts

Hitters

HITTER	POS	TEAM	LVL	AGE	PA	R	2B	3B	HR	RBI	BB	K	SB	CS	AVG/OBP/SLG	TAv	VORP	BABIP	BRR	FRAA	WARP
Cristhian Adames	SS	COL	MLB	25	14	1	0	0	0	0	1	6	0	0	.000/.071/.000	.055	-2.5	.000	0.1	SS(1): -0.1, 2B(1): 0.0	-0.3
	SS	ABQ	AAA	25	362	47	19	6	11	52	29	68	3	4	.263/.317/.461	.256	9.9	.294	0.0	2B(49): -2.9, 3B(33): -2.6	0.5
Mike Aviles	SS	NWO	AAA	36	196	22	8	2	1	24	10	24	1	2	.292/.326/.376	.268	6.2	.325	-1.2	3B(24): -3.1, 1B(9): -0.4	0.1
	SS	MIA	MLB	36	97	5	2	0	1	8	6	15	0	0	.233/.298/.291	.214	-2.3	.271	-1.2	SS(15): 0.9, 3B(6): -0.1	-0.1
Christian Colon	2B	KCA	MLB	28	19	1	0	0	0	0	1	3	0	0	.176/.222/.176	.123	-2.1	.214	0.1	2B(6): 0.8	-0.1
	2B	MIA	MLB	28	38	3	1	0	0	0	4	7	0	0	.152/.243/.182	.166	-2.1	.192	0.4	3B(10): 0.7, 2B(4): 0.3	-0.1
	2B	NWO	AAA	28	177	17	8	0	1	13	16	26	6	3	.302/.379/.376	.291	10.1	.358	-1.5	3B(17): -2.0, 2B(16): 0.4	0.7
Austin Dean	LF	JAX	AA	23	251	29	14	4	4	30	14	46	3	1	.282/.323/.427	.293	14.3	.333	0.9	LF(53): -2.8, RF(3): -0.5	1.2
Jake Elmore	2B	BUF	AAA	30	357	23	6	2	1	36	38	54	11	7	.231/.321/.273	.225	-4.4	.272	0.7	LF(48): 1.9, 2B(16): -3.1	-0.2
	2B	NWO	AAA	30	59	6	3	0	0	5	6	5	1	1	.269/.345/.327	.245	1.0	.298	0.1	2B(11): -0.2, 3B(3): -0.2	0.1
Stone Garrett	LF	JUP	A+	21	399	37	24	1	4	29	21	126	8	1	.212/.257/.314	.227	-3.8	.307	1.6	LF(41): 3.3, RF(25): -2.8	-0.4
Grant Green	3B	WAS	MLB	29	3	0	0	0	0	0	0	2	0	0	.000/.000/.000	-.008	-0.8	.000	0.0	2B(2): -0.1	-0.1
	3B	SYR	AAA	29	144	11	5	0	0	2	14	34	0	2	.246/.319/.285	.233	-1.6	.333	-2.0	3B(30): -0.8, 2B(8): -0.3	-0.3
	3B	CHR	AAA	29	101	9	7	0	1	10	10	19	0	1	.211/.287/.322	.218	-2.3	.254	-0.2	3B(15): -1.6, LF(9): -0.6	-0.4
	3B	NWO	AAA	29	50	4	1	0	0	8	3	9	1	1	.304/.340/.326	.258	0.2	.368	-0.5	1B(10): 1.0, 3B(2): 0.0	0.1
Brayan Hernandez	RF	EVE	A-	19	112	9	2	4	2	15	7	26	4	1	.252/.306/.408	.267	2.5	.320	-1.6	CF(25): -5.8, RF(1): 1.8	-0.2
	RF	BAT	A-	19	64	9	2	3	0	3	2	14	0	0	.271/.302/.407	.252	0.3	.348	-0.7	RF(7): 0.0, CF(6): -0.6	-0.1
Destin Hood	LF	NWO	AAA	27	254	36	8	1	14	41	31	66	5	1	.260/.349/.498	.291	11.0	.305	-3.1	LF(48): -4.6, RF(8): 1.2	0.7
Steve Lombardozzi	2B	MIA	MLB	28	8	0	0	0	0	0	0	2	0	0	.000/.000/.000	-.008	-2.0	.000	0.0	2B(2): -0.1	-0.2
	2B	NWO	AAA	28	445	53	16	2	2	18	38	60	13	6	.274/.337/.339	.242	5.3	.317	1.5	2B(72): -2.4, 3B(16): 0.9	0.3
Riley Mahan	2B	GRB	A	21	27	4	1	0	1	4	0	7	0	0	.259/.259/.407	.219	-0.5	.316	0.0	2B(6): -0.1	-0.1
Austin Nola	C	JAX	AA	27	197	21	7	0	2	25	25	26	3	2	.250/.352/.327	.253	6.2	.284	-0.4	C(46): 0.4, 1B(1): -0.1	0.7
	C	NWO	AAA	27	105	7	4	0	1	6	10	16	0	0	.202/.287/.281	.204	-2.5	.233	-1.0	C(29): -4.8	-0.7
John Norwood	RF	JAX	AA	24	539	68	17	4	19	62	59	134	4	4	.285/.367/.459	.293	23.1	.359	-4.3	RF(122): 4.4, CF(2): -0.2	2.9
Yefri Perez	CF	JAX	AA	26	293	31	6	6	0	15	37	57	10	4	.169/.280/.242	.206	-6.0	.220	1.4	CF(46): -1.1, 2B(15): -1.7	-1.0
Chad Wallach	C	LOU	AAA	25	243	28	12	0	9	18	13	62	1	0	.226/.280/.398	.227	0.8	.271	-1.0	C(57): 2.4, 1B(8): -0.6	0.3
	C	CIN	MLB	25	11	0	0	0	0	0	0	5	0	0	.091/.091/.091	.072	-1.7	.167	0.0	C(3): 0.1, 1B(1): 0.0	-0.2

Christian Adames continues to look at home in Triple-A and overwhelmed in the majors. But hey, Albuquerque is the sixth-fastest-growing mid-sized city in the US! ⚾ At 36 years old, **Mike Aviles** was the elder statesman of the Pacific Coast League last season. He's carved out a unique niche as the proverbial "break glass in case of emergency" veteran roster filler who ends up with way too much major-league playing time. ⚾ If his career were an episode of *American Pickers*, **Christian Colon** would be the baseball equivalent of a rusted Indian motorcycle buried in a flyover state backyard. He's an ideal, low-risk reclamation project for a franchise in asset accumulation mode. ⚾ Just as Jim Gaffigan always seemed predestined to star in minivan commercials, **Austin Dean** is finally on the precipice of fulfilling his destiny as a gritty, contact-oriented, light-hitting fifth outfielder. ⚾ Just when Derek Jeter thought he had finally gotten away from Alex Rodriguez by purchasing the Marlins, he was informed that they had drafted his long-time rival's nephew, **Joe Dunand**, in the second round last June. ⚾ Unlike the majority of Americans threatening to move to Canada on Twitter following the presidential election, utility man **Jake Elmore** actually tried to leave by signing with Toronto, but he only made it as far north as Buffalo before being relocated to New Orleans in August. ⚾ The sample size is still small, but research now shows that being stabbed by a teammate can cause you to stop hitting, as **Stone Garrett** continued the slide that started toward the end of 2016 throughout his year in the Florida State League. ⚾ **Grant Green** is one of six position players to suit up with both Mike Trout and Bryce Harper since 2011. If the 30-year-old journeyman infielder absorbed any of their talent through osmosis, he's done a remarkable job keeping it a secret. ⚾ The centerpiece of the deal that jettisoned David Phelps to Seattle at the trade deadline, **Brayan Hernandez** remains a high-risk, long-term project in center field. ⚾ Nearly a decade after turning down a scholarship to play football at Alabama, oft-injured, lefty-mashing outfielder **Destin Hood** reversed his splits in 2017, finally breaking through against righties before being sidelined by injury and outrighted off the 40-man. ⚾ Veteran grinder **Steve Lombardozzi** lasted just four days on Miami's injury plagued roster, going 0-for-8 at the dish, before being banished to Triple-A. According to Statcast, that qualifies as the quickest hook of the Anthony Scaramucci era. ⚾ The Marlins eagerly plucked one of the more enticing middle-infield bats in the entire draft, Kentucky second baseman **Riley Mahan**, with the 89th overall selection last June. Scouts are split on whether he possesses the defensive chops to stick at the keystone long-term, but his loose, fluid, left-handed swing is a carrying tool. ⚾ A middle infielder his first five minor-league seasons, **Austin Nola** is still learning the nuances of receiving, blocking and framing after shifting behind the plate full-time last offseason. If he succeeds, he will finally join his younger brother Aaron in the big-leagues. ⚾ **John Norwood** has always flashed plus raw power, a strong arm and enough speed to be an asset defensively in right field, but he needs to stop chasing spin out of the zone if he's ever going to garner fourth-outfielder consideration. ⚾ **Yefri Perez** is Terrance Gore without the publicity. He couldn't hit water if he fell out of a boat, but his blazing speed is off the metaphorical charts and he could latch on as a designated runner with random playoff contenders for years to come. ⚾ **Isael Soto** fractured his foot in spring training and missed the entire 2017 campaign. He's an extremely raw corner outfielder, and the massive chunk of lost development time further amplifies the contact risk in his profile and puts his future in jeopardy. ⚾ **Chad Wallach**'s father Tim was one of the better players of the '80s, and Chad is one of the better players of the 2010s, if you're talking in relation to the general population of the world.

Pitchers

PITCHER	TEAM	LVL	AGE	W	L	SV	G	GS	IP	H	HR	BB/9	K/9	K	GB%	BABIP	WHIP	ERA	DRA	WARP	MPH	CMD	PWR	STM
Andy Beltre	JUP	A+	23	0	1	3	13	0	17^2	9	1	2.0	10.2	20	42%	.200	0.74	1.02	2.59	0.5				
	JAX	AA	23	4	0	0	28	0	34	32	2	4.0	11.9	45	33%	.337	1.38	3.44	3.83	0.4				
Hunter Cervenka	MIA	MLB	27	0	0	0	5	0	4^2	1	0	15.4	11.6	6	50%	.125	1.93	15.43	4.13	0.1	94.5			44
	NWO	AAA	27	1	4	0	44	0	39^1	38	7	5.9	8.9	39	46%	.290	1.63	4.58	7.71	-1.0				
Miguel Del Pozo	JUP	A+	24	2	0	0	12	0	16^2	12	0	2.7	9.2	17	50%	.273	1.02	0.54	3.25	0.3				
Severino Gonzalez	JAX	AA	24	5	5	3	31	5	61	59	9	1.8	5.6	38	41%	.263	1.16	4.28	4.53	0.3				
	NWO	AAA	24	0	3	3	13	2	19^1	26	2	2.3	8.4	18	34%	.364	1.60	6.52	6.40	-0.2				
Javy Guerra	NWO	AAA	31	2	4	2	35	0	51^2	46	7	3.7	7.7	44	42%	.273	1.30	4.70	4.51	0.4				
	MIA	MLB	31	1	1	0	16	0	21	23	2	3.0	5.1	12	52%	.313	1.43	3.00	7.33	-0.5	94.3	60	45	46
Tayron Guerrero	JAX	AA	26	0	1	0	17	0	16	14	3	7.9	12.4	22	41%	.306	1.75	3.38	4.11	0.1				
	NWO	AAA	26	3	2	0	13	0	15^1	12	2	7.0	6.5	11	44%	.217	1.57	5.87	8.12	-0.5				
Colton Hock	BAT	A-	21	1	3	0	7	1	17^2	22	2	6.1	6.6	13	32%	.351	1.92	6.62	10.07	-1.0				
Jeff Locke	JAX	AA	29	1	0	0	2	2	11^1	13	1	1.6	9.5	12	58%	.375	1.32	2.38	2.37	0.4				
	MIA	MLB	29	0	5	0	7	7	32	42	4	4.2	7.3	26	45%	.355	1.78	8.16	5.71	0.0	92.3	61	36	49
Pablo Lopez	MOD	A+	21	5	8	0	19	18	100	113	6	1.2	8.0	89	51%	.341	1.26	5.04	2.25	3.5				
	JUP	A+	21	0	3	0	8	6	45^1	42	0	1.4	6.4	32	59%	.307	1.08	2.18	2.72	1.3				
James Needy	JUP	A+	26	3	2	0	7	7	36^1	23	0	3.0	8.2	33	43%	.247	0.96	1.73	3.73	0.7				
	JAX	AA	26	0	1	0	2	2	10	10	1	2.7	9.0	10	37%	.310	1.30	4.50	4.27	0.1				
Victor Payano	JAX	AA	24	1	1	1	9	0	12^2	7	0	7.1	14.9	21	38%	.292	1.34	3.55	4.49	0.0				
	NWO	AAA	24	4	3	0	28	2	52^2	37	5	5.5	10.1	59	36%	.258	1.31	3.42	5.08	0.2				
Cody Poteet	MRL	Rk	22	0	1	0	4	4	14	11	0	1.3	7.7	12	65%	.256	0.93	3.21	0.85	0.7				
	JUP	A+	22	3	7	0	16	14	80	84	2	2.6	4.5	40	51%	.308	1.34	4.16	5.21	0.0				
Caleb Smith	SWB	AAA	25	9	1	0	18	17	98	75	7	2.6	8.9	97	42%	.264	1.05	2.39	3.17	2.7				
	NYA	MLB	25	0	1	0	9	2	18^2	21	4	4.8	8.7	18	28%	.315	1.66	7.71	5.53	0.0	95.5	48	44	57
Alex Wimmers	MIN	MLB	28	0	0	0	6	0	7^1	8	2	9.8	8.6	7	35%	.286	2.18	4.91	5.66	0.0	93.1			42
	ROC	AAA	28	7	3	7	34	0	47^1	33	5	2.1	9.1	48	32%	.237	0.93	3.23	3.62	0.9				
Vance Worley	NWO	AAA	29	2	5	0	8	8	44^2	53	4	2.2	4.4	22	51%	.322	1.43	4.43	6.48	-0.4				
	MIA	MLB	29	2	6	1	24	12	71^2	99	9	3.8	6.3	50	49%	.378	1.80	6.91	6.78	-1.0	91.9	58	40	56

Andy Beltre has the stuff to pitch out of a big-league bullpen, as his prodigious fastball routinely flirts with triple digits and he backs it up with a hard biting slider. ⚾ **Hunter Cervenka** credits a heart-to-heart conversation with Triple-A manager Arnie Beyeler for resuscitating a career that has spanned four big-league organizations and a stint with the independent leagues' Sugar Land Skeeters. Veteran LOOGYs live forever in the Statcast era, which means persistent control issues are his only roadblock to immortality. ⚾ Left-handed reliever **Miguel Del Pozo** allowed just two earned runs during the 2017 minor-league regular season before the Marlins sent him to the AFL and he promptly gave up 11 in just seven innings. No confirmation yet as to whether Derek Jeter asked the southpaw for his money back. ⚾ It's telling that **Severino Gonzalez** couldn't crack a Miami bullpen that logged the most innings (612) in baseball last season. ⚾ Veteran righty **Javy Guerra** is the textbook example of a flotsam and jetsam Quad-A reliever that doesn't strike out enough batters to avoid languishing in roster bubble purgatory. ⚾ Towering 6-foot-8 right-hander **Tayron Guerrero** brandishes a blistering fastball, which routinely touches triple digits, but has more trouble hitting his target than a replacement-level stormtrooper. ⚾ The Marlins tabbed Stanford closer **Colton Hock**, a 6-foot-5 righty who shattered the program's single-season saves record, with their fourth-round selection last June. It's hard to gloss over his struggles in the New York-Penn League, but he has the polish and pedigree to make the jump to full-season ball in short order. ⚾ There was reason for optimism that a reunion with pitching guru Jim Benedict could revitalize former All-Star southpaw **Jeff Locke**, but those hopes were quickly dashed after he posted an ERA higher than the model number on a Boeing jet in nine major-league starts. ⚾ Plucked from the Mariners system via trade, **Pablo Lopez** would rather eat glass than issue free passes and throws enough quality strikes that you can dream on him as a future swingman. ⚾ After selling off whatever assets weren't nailed down this offseason, the Marlins adding **James Needy** to the 40-man roster in November just felt a little too on the nose. ⚾ Southpaw **Victor Payano** embraced the latest hipster trend, successfully converting to a multi-inning relief role, and ping-ponged from Jacksonville to New Orleans. Unfortunately, his horrific fastball command remained fully intact at each stop. ⚾ A fourth-round selection out of UCLA, **Cody Poteet** was one of the youngest collegiate pitchers in the entire 2015 draft class. While his raw stuff isn't overpowering, he locates an 88-92 mph fastball well and displays an uncanny knack for inducing weak contact. ⚾ Before being called up to the Yankees to replace Michael Pineda on the roster, **Caleb Smith** was lights out in Triple-A, but he had trouble with major-league hitters. He made two starts and couldn't get out of the fourth inning in either one. ⚾ Right-hander **Alex Wimmers** posted solid numbers in the Rochester 'pen but was torched during his brief sojourn in the bigs; the odds are good we'll just cut-and-paste this comment next year. ⚾ **Vance Worley** posted the fourth-worst ERA of the 204 hurlers to log at least 70 innings. As Ernest Hemingway wrote in *The Old Man and the Sea*, "A man can be destroyed but not defeated." He'll get another shot as a sinker/cutter combo swingman, but The Vanimal is clearly on the endangered species list.

LEAGUE LEADERS 2017

MLB Base-Running Runs – Dee Gordon, 8.4

MLB RBI – Giancarlo Stanton, 132

MLB WARP, Hitters – Giancarlo Stanton, 8.55

MLB Home Runs – Giancarlo Stanton, 59

MLB Stolen Bases – Dee Gordon, 60

MILWAUKEE BREWERS

Essay by Adam McCalvy

Player comments by J.P. Breen and BP staff

"Don't fuck it up."

It was a surprising opening statement for what would become one of baseball's most surprising teams. Those four words were uttered during the Brewers' first full-squad meeting of spring training from the mouth of Mark Attanasio, the super-competitive but soft-spoken club owner who made his fortune in finance. Around the room, jaws dropped. Even manager Craig Counsell didn't know Attanasio was going to say it.

But this wasn't an owner demanding a championship. Quite the contrary: Attanasio, who had approved the Brewers' deep dive into rebuilding less than two years earlier and hired David Stearns to be baseball's youngest general manager and execute it, dropped his four-letter bomb with a smile. It was meant as a reminder that while even the most optimistic projections for 2017 did not put the Brewers in the postseason, there were advantages inherent in playing for a franchise entering its second full year of rebuilding.

"For me, this year, the opportunity is unmistakable," Attanasio told reporters after the meeting broke up. "There's a group of guys who are going to be part of this next push and who are going to be part of the next playoff team, and that's exciting. So they have to seize it.

"For the first time in 13 years I may have dropped an F-bomb: 'Don't eff it up.'"

You know by now that the 2017 Brewers did not eff it up. Counsell and company built a 5 1/2 game lead over the sputtering Cubs and the rest of the National League Central by the All-Star break. When Chicago charged in the second half to take the division, the Brewers held on in the wild card race until Game 161 on the final day of September: They blew a 6-0 lead at Busch Stadium, lost to the Cardinals and were eliminated from postseason contention.

How did this happen? The most bullish preseason projection from Baseball Prospectus put Milwaukee at 78 wins. Oddsmaker Bovada set the Brewers' over/under at 69.5 wins. One projection model gave them a 1.1 percent chance of reaching the postseason.

Let's set aside the "how" question and ask another: Was it a good thing?

Rebuilding requires commitment, as the past three World Series champions have shown. The 2015 Royals, 2016 Cubs and 2017 Astros reached the sport's zenith only because they spent long years at or near its nadir, flipping what proven assets they had for top prospects while hoarding high draft picks over a succession of seasons.

The Royals were already bad when they hired Dayton Moore as GM in 2006, with Zack Greinke (sixth overall pick in 2002) and Alex Gordon (second overall in 2005) already in the system as a result. Moore added Mike Moustakas (second overall in 2007) and Eric

BREWERS PROSPECTUS

2017 W-L: 86-76, 2ND IN NL CENTRAL

Pythag	.523	11th	B-Age	27.3	*8th*
RS/G	4.52	20th	P-Age	28.3	*14th*
RA/G	4.30	8th	Salary	$63.1M	*30th*
TAv	.265	13th	M$/MW	$1.3M	*30th*
TAv-P	.263	16th	DL Days	477	*4th*
FIP	4.25	13th	$ on DL	15%	*16th*
DER	.702	15th			

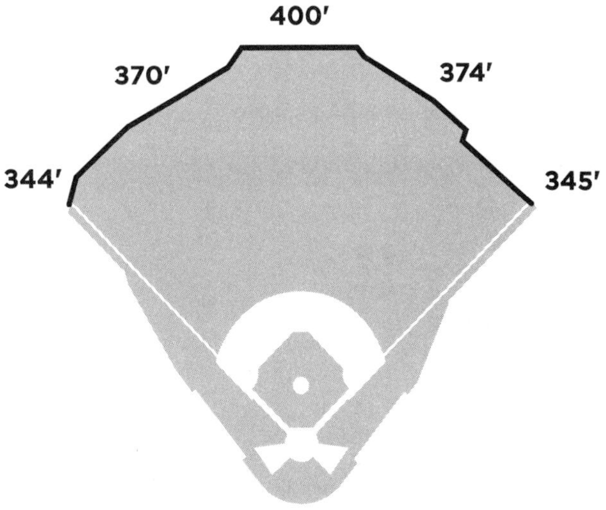

Outfield wall profile: **8'**

Three-Year Park Factors

Runs	Runs/RH	Runs/LH	HR/RH	HR/LH
102	101	103	106	117

Top Hitter WARP	4.2 Travis Shaw
Top Pitcher WARP	3.9 Jimmy Nelson
Top Prospect	Lewis Brinson

2017 Hit List Ranking

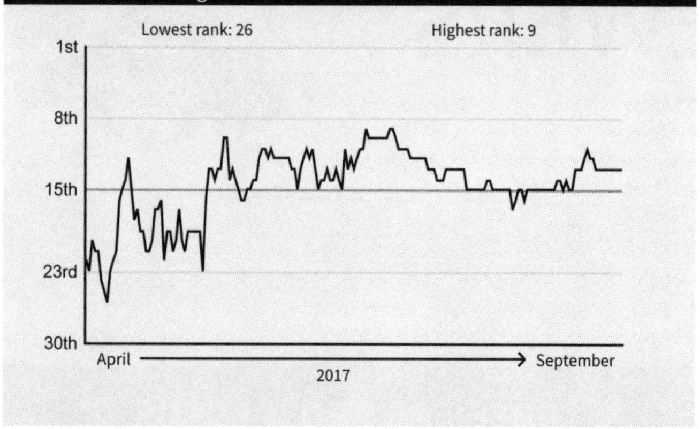

Committed Payroll (in millions)

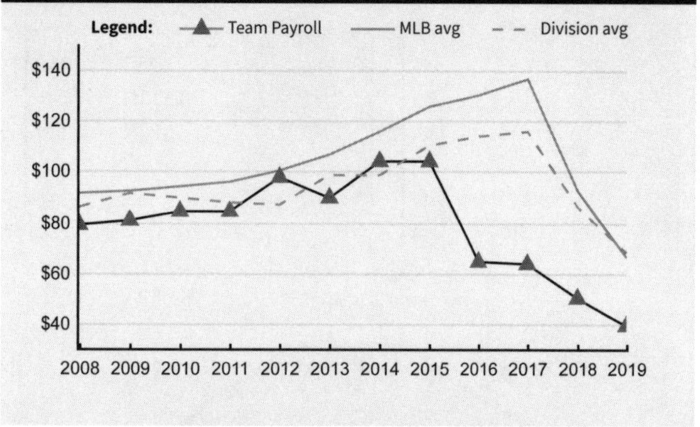

Farm System Ranking

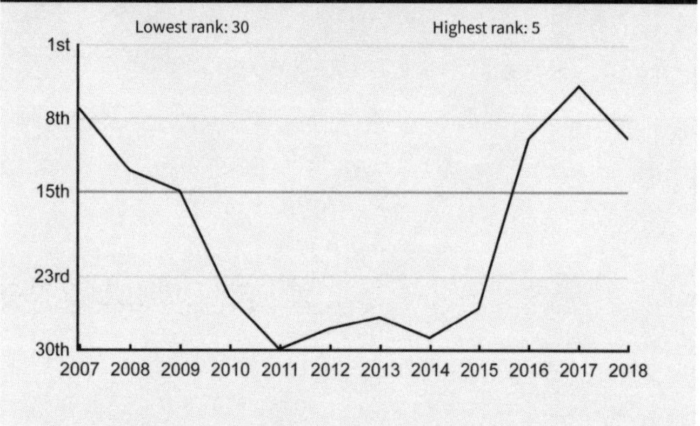

Personnel

General Manager
David Stearns

VP, Assistant General Manager
Matt Arnold

Senior Advisor
Doug Melvin

Manager
Craig Counsell

BP Alumni
James Fisher
Brendan Gawlowski
Greg Goldstein
Mike Groopman
Shawn Hoffman
Matt Kleine
Will Siskel
Dan Turkenkopf

Hosmer (third overall in 2008), and all of those players had a hand in lifting Kansas City—Greinke by virtue of netting Lorenzo Cain and Alcides Escobar in a December 2010 trade with the Brewers—to back-to-back World Series appearances.

While the Royals were popping champagne, the Cubs and Astros were emerging from their own rebuilds. Theo Epstein in Chicago and Jeff Luhnow in Houston each took over following the 2011 season, oversaw drafts beginning in 2012, and had their teams in the playoffs by 2015.

Here's how those years looked in Houston:

Year	Top pick	Player
2012	1	Carlos Correa
2013	1	Mark Appel
~~2014~~	~~1~~	~~Brady Aiken~~
2015	2	Alex Bregman
2015	5	Kyle Tucker

Three out of five ain't bad. Correa and Bregman are two of the brightest young players in the game, while Tucker, although technically not the Astros' top pick that year, is their top hitting prospect.

Here are those years for the Cubs:

Year	Top pick	Player
2012	6	Albert Almora
2013	2	Kris Bryant
2014	4	Kyle Schwarber
2015	9	Ian Happ

We'll see what Schwarber's ultimate future holds, but that's a pretty solid 4-for-4.

(It bears noting that, like Moore, Epstein and Luhnow were helped by their predecessors. In the 2011 draft, the Cubs landed Javier Baez with the ninth overall pick and the Astros took George Springer 11th. It takes a village to build a winner.)

In all three places, patience was required, and it paid off.

Now, consider the Brewers.

They were coming off a 96-win regular season and a six-game NLCS against the eventual champion Cardinals in 2011 when Epstein and Luhnow were taking over, and remained in competitive mode all the way through 2014, when they led the NL Central for 150 days only to collapse late and miss the playoffs.

When the Brewers lost 21 of their first 30 games in 2015, Attanasio finally succumbed to rebuilding. He replaced manager Ron Roenicke with Counsell, a hometown guy with a winning pedigree but no managerial experience. Weeks later, veteran GM Doug Melvin began to break apart Counsell's roster. After a trade that would have netted the Mets' Zack Wheeler was nixed by New York, Melvin made the biggest single move of the Brewers' rebuild, sending Carlos Gomez and Mike Fiers to the Astros for four prospects, all of whom would make it to Milwaukee within the ensuing two years: outfielders Domingo Santana and Brett Phillips and pitchers Josh Hader and Adrian Houser. A day later, Melvin flipped free agent-to-be Gerardo Parra to the Orioles for right-hander Zach Davies.

Once the trade deadline was cleared, Melvin announced he would transition into an advisory role after 13 seasons as GM. His replacement was 30-year-old Astros assistant general manager Stearns, a Harvard graduate who'd already amassed experience in the commissioner's office and some of baseball's most forward-thinking front offices, including Pittsburgh, Cleveland and Houston.

Stearns doggedly refused to put a timetable on the rebuild, but Brewers fans could turn on their televisions and watch the Cubs and Astros play postseason games on the heels of a process that took four or five years.

So it came as no surprise when Stearns continued the process Melvin had begun. Within his first 15 months on the job, Stearns dealt Adam Lind, Jean Segura, Khris Davis, Aaron Hill, Jeremy Jeffress, Jonathan Lucroy, Will Smith and Tyler Thornburg in swaps that netted at least one minor-league prospect. And Stearns was deep into talks to trade Ryan Braun to the Dodgers at the August 31, 2016, deadline, only to run out of time.

It was all according to the script written by the Royals, Cubs and Astros, including the Brewers' 94-loss season in 2015. That finish translated to the fifth overall draft pick in 2016. University of Louisville outfielder Corey Ray went directly into the top 10 of every Brewers prospect list.

Then came 73 wins in 2016, which was not exactly tanking but still netted the Brewers a top-10 pick. They took UC Irvine second baseman Keston Hiura ninth overall, and he went into to Milwaukee's top 10, too.

Then came 2017, when rebuilding went off the rails.

Were the Brewers bad enough, long enough, for their rebuilding project to work?

Melvin and Stearns generally get good reviews for the prospects they netted in trades, but the process was far more condensed than the rebuilds in Kansas City, Chicago and Houston. It spanned barely more than 17 months—from July 23, 2015, when Melvin made the first "sell" move of the rebuild by shipping Aramis Ramirez to the Pirates, to the December 6, 2016, trade that sent Thornburg to the Red Sox for prospects plus then-unproven third baseman Travis Shaw.

Remember all those single-digit draft picks in Houston and Chicago? Because the Brewers never got bad enough before pushing back into contention, those picks will be missing in Milwaukee. In 2012, coming off 96 wins and a trip to the NLCS, the Brewers drafted 27th. In 2013, they forfeited their first-round pick to sign free agent Kyle Lohse.

Here are the years since then:

Year	Top pick	Player
2014	12	Kodi Medeiros
2015	15	Trent Grisham (formerly Trent Clark)
2016	5	Corey Ray
2017	9	Keston Hiura
2018	21	???

There are plenty of examples of great draft picks outside of the top 20 overall. You just won't find many at no. 21, where Rick Sutcliffe (Dodgers, 1974) and Jason Varitek (1993, Twins) are the most valuable pitcher and position player ever selected. Next on the position player list is Gorman Thomas, the outfielder picked 21st overall in 1969 by the Seattle Pilots, who were less than a year away from moving to Milwaukee and becoming the Brewers.

So, barring a major regression, the Brewers will have to take their next step without any more super-premium draft picks for a while. And the Cubs' window doesn't seem likely to close anytime soon.

As the Brewers showed in 2017, anything is possible.

"It's a position nobody expected us to be in," said Braun, the only player remaining from Milwaukee's last playoff team in 2011. "It's such a unique learning experience to play games of this magnitude with this intensity, and to just understand that when you continue to compete and put yourself in a position to win, over time, you'll come through."

Said Attanasio: "It was not expected this season. Or, if somebody did expect it, I'd like to know who it was. Maybe Craig Counsell might have expected it. Craig said, 'Don't put any limits on the team,' and then David adopted that way of speaking. That certainly worked here."

It started with Attanasio's four-letter word.

"It's funny," said Counsell, "because right after, I told the room we've had some good conversations about being direct with our conversation. I said, 'Guys, that's a great example of direct communication.'"

Everybody laughed.

"That's raising the standards, I think. I'm a fan of that," Counsell said.

—Adam McCalvy covers the Brewers for MLB.com.

Hitters

Jesus Aguilar 1B Born: 06/30/90 Age: 28 Bats: R Throws: R Height: 6'3" Weight: 250 Origin: International Free Agent, 2007

YEAR	TEAM	LVL	AGE	PA	R	2B	3B	HR	RBI	BB	K	SB	CS	AVG/OBP/SLG	TAv	VORP	BABIP	BRR	FRAA	WARP
2015	COH	AAA	25	570	57	29	1	19	93	47	115	0	0	.267/.332/.439	.254	-1.1	.305	-3.4	1B(98): -3.8	-0.5
2015	CLE	MLB	25	20	0	1	0	0	2	0	7	0	0	.316/.350/.368	.256	-0.2	.500	-0.3	1B(4): -0.1	0.0
2016	COH	AAA	26	578	62	26	0	30	92	53	110	0	0	.247/.319/.472	.268	7.8	.255	-3.0	1B(120): -1.0, 3B(2): 0.3	0.7
2016	CLE	MLB	26	6	0	0	0	0	0	0	1	0	0	.000/.000/.000	-.027	-1.7	.000	0.0	1B(7): -0.3	-0.2
2017	MIL	MLB	27	311	40	15	2	16	52	25	94	0	0	.265/.331/.505	.284	12.7	.337	0.4	1B(77): 1.2, 3B(1): 0.0	1.4
2018	*MIL*	*MLB*	*28*	*339*	*42*	*15*	*1*	*15*	*48*	*30*	*86*	*0*	*0*	*.242/.314/.440*	*.260*	*7.8*	*.288*	*-0.7*	*1B -1*	*0.4*
2019	*MIL*	*MLB*	*29*	*437*	*59*	*20*	*0*	*19*	*60*	*43*	*116*	*0*	*0*	*.239/.320/.443*	*.270*	*11.8*	*.289*	*-0.1*	*1B -1*	*1.1*

Breakout: 7% Improve: 21% Collapse: 10% Attrition: 27% MLB: 48% *Comparables: Bryan LaHair, Jason Rogers, Nate Freiman*

The past century has seen countless innovations: the microwave, the Internet, gak and the fidget spinner. In baseball, we've witnessed the rebirth of the right-handed first baseman. According to Stuart Miller of the *New York Times*, 92 percent of everyday first basemen were left-handed in 1928. Left-handed first basemen, the theory went, made defensive duties much easier, whether it was fielding a grounder in the hole or throwing around a runner to second base. Since the turn of the century, though, the number of lefties at first base has hovered between 25 and 40 percent—largely due to increased platooning. Aguilar is very much a creature of 21st-century baseball and has benefited from this philosophical switch. His glove work consistently begs the question, but the 27-year-old still hit .301/.365/.524 against southpaws. Thus, despite a dismal second half, he posted a near .900 OPS against opposite-handed pitching, and if one is really feeling charitable, one could expect his surprisingly high strikeout rate to drop, given his sub-20-percent strikeout rate in the minors since the beginning of 2013. The Venezuelan slugger fulfilled his duties in 2017 and seems to have carved out a useful major-league niche, one that has only recently become available to part-time players.

Orlando Arcia SS Born: 08/04/94 Age: 23 Bats: R Throws: R Height: 6'0" Weight: 165 Origin: International Free Agent, 2010

YEAR	TEAM	LVL	AGE	PA	R	2B	3B	HR	RBI	BB	K	SB	CS	AVG/OBP/SLG	TAv	VORP	BABIP	BRR	FRAA	WARP
2015	BLX	AA	20	552	74	37	7	8	69	30	73	25	8	.307/.347/.453	.294	41.5	.343	1.3	SS(123): 15.9, 2B(3): 0.2	6.2
2016	CSP	AAA	21	440	59	19	6	8	53	29	77	15	8	.267/.320/.403	.249	12.2	.312	-0.5	SS(92): 6.8, 2B(7): 0.7	2.0
2016	MIL	MLB	21	216	21	10	3	4	17	15	47	8	0	.219/.273/.358	.217	-1.6	.267	-1.0	SS(53): 3.8	0.2
2017	MIL	MLB	22	548	56	17	2	15	53	36	100	14	7	.277/.324/.407	.262	26.8	.317	2.1	SS(152): 6.8	3.4
2018	*MIL*	*MLB*	*23*	*522*	*63*	*23*	*4*	*14*	*57*	*28*	*104*	*14*	*5*	*.256/.298/.404*	*.247*	*16.5*	*.298*	*0.8*	*SS 8*	*1.9*
2019	*MIL*	*MLB*	*24*	*548*	*67*	*25*	*4*	*18*	*68*	*34*	*108*	*15*	*6*	*.265/.313/.434*	*.268*	*24.0*	*.303*	*0.7*	*SS 8*	*3.5*

Breakout: 9% Improve: 52% Collapse: 9% Attrition: 20% MLB: 90% *Comparables: Ketel Marte, Hanley Ramirez, Everth Cabrera*

After scuffling in his major-league debut, Arcia made the jump in his sophomore campaign. He was the fourth-best shortstop in the National League, according to WARP, and was the NL's youngest player at the position (min. 200 PA). Not ignoring that fact that he occasionally booted routine plays, Arcia proved to be a game-saver in the field. The off-balance, whirling play to nab John Jaso to end a close July game against the Pirates particularly stands out; however, his expansive range helped him tally the best FRAA among National League shortstops in his age-22 season. For many, though, the exquisite glove work was expected. The 15-homer campaign with an above-average TAv caught the league by surprise, especially after an offensively decaffeinated cup of coffee in 2016. The alleged juiced ball likely aided his jump in productivity, but his 8.1 percent contact-rate jump at pitches inside the zone also surely helped. Many scouts liked the projectability of his bat in Double-A as a 20-year-old. If his contact and power increases remain, Arcia has a legitimate chance to be a five-win player in 2018.

Jett Bandy C Born: 03/26/90 Age: 28 Bats: R Throws: R Height: 6'4" Weight: 235 Origin: Round 31, 2011 Draft (#945 overall)

YEAR	TEAM	LVL	AGE	PA	R	2B	3B	HR	RBI	BB	K	SB	CS	AVG/OBP/SLG	TAv	VORP	BABIP	BRR	FRAA	WARP
2015	SLC	AAA	25	344	47	21	0	11	60	16	63	0	0	.291/.347/.466	.272	17.6	.329	-1.5	C(84): 0.5	1.8
2015	ANA	MLB	25	2	1	0	0	1	1	0	0	0	0	.500/.500/2.000	.770	1.1	.000	0.0	C(1): 0.0	0.1
2016	SLC	AAA	26	105	13	7	0	2	21	2	19	2	1	.274/.314/.411	.263	1.8	.312	-2.7	C(21): 1.2	0.3
2016	ANA	MLB	26	231	23	9	0	8	25	11	38	1	0	.234/.281/.392	.242	4.2	.246	-2.0	C(68): 2.4	0.7
2017	CSP	AAA	27	51	7	2	0	2	14	5	5	0	1	.310/.412/.500	.265	1.7	.306	-0.6	C(9): -1.1	0.1
2017	MIL	MLB	27	188	14	6	0	6	18	15	51	1	0	.207/.287/.349	.227	0.1	.259	-1.9	C(50): -3.9	-0.4
2018	*MIL*	*MLB*	*28*	*66*	*7*	*3*	*0*	*2*	*8*	*4*	*15*	*0*	*0*	*.236/.297/.398*	*.243*	*1.7*	*.273*	*-0.1*	*C -1*	*0.0*
2019	*MIL*	*MLB*	*29*	*187*	*23*	*8*	*0*	*7*	*23*	*12*	*42*	*1*	*0*	*.232/.301/.405*	*.252*	*4.6*	*.265*	*-1.2*	*C -3*	*0.2*

Breakout: 8% Improve: 33% Collapse: 12% Attrition: 36% MLB: 80% *Comparables: Martin Maldonado, Jason Jaramillo, JD Closser*

YEAR	TEAM	P. COUNT	FRM RUNS	BLK RUNS	THRW RUNS	TOT RUNS
2015	ANA	16	0.0	0.1	0.0	0.0
2015	SLC	11935	1.9	0.4	-1.0	1.4
2016	ANA	8749	-1.2	1.5	1.9	2.2
2017	MIL	6970	-3.1	-0.6	-0.7	-4.5
2018	*MIL*	*2510*	*-0.9*	*0.0*	*0.0*	*-0.9*
2019	*MIL*	*7125*	*-1.9*	*0.0*	*0.0*	*-1.9*

Bandy surprised everyone with a .300-plus batting average in April; however, much like The Bravery's self-titled debut that featured the smash hit "An Honest Mistake," the rest of the performance stunk. The 27-year-old catcher hit just .158/.252/.233 with five extra-base hits once the calendar flipped past the season's first month—making it a truly Swollen Summer. To put that in perspective, there were 11 pitchers (min. 50 plate appearances) who compiled a better slugging percentage than Bandy's post-April mark of .233. He should be thankful, just for his own ego's sake, that none of those 11 pitchers were in his own dugout.

Ryan Braun LF Born: 11/17/83 Age: 34 Bats: R Throws: R Height: 6'2" Weight: 205 Origin: Round 1, 2005 Draft (#5 overall)

YEAR	TEAM	LVL	AGE	PA	R	2B	3B	HR	RBI	BB	K	SB	CS	AVG/OBP/SLG	TAv	VORP	BABIP	BRR	FRAA	WARP
2015	MIL	MLB	31	568	87	27	3	25	84	54	115	24	4	.285/.356/.498	.298	34.3	.322	3.5	RF(130): -11.7	2.4
2016	MIL	MLB	32	564	80	23	3	30	91	46	98	16	5	.305/.365/.538	.316	45.7	.326	1.4	LF(127): -3.7, RF(2): -0.1	4.3
2017	MIL	MLB	33	425	58	28	2	17	52	38	76	12	4	.268/.336/.487	.283	20.1	.292	0.5	LF(95): -4.0	1.6
2018	*MIL*	*MLB*	*34*	*498*	*69*	*24*	*3*	*20*	*69*	*41*	*101*	*14*	*4*	*.266/.331/.461*	*.274*	*24.5*	*.302*	*1.1*	*LF -4*	*1.6*
2019	*MIL*	*MLB*	*35*	*433*	*58*	*20*	*2*	*17*	*59*	*39*	*93*	*11*	*4*	*.260/.330/.454*	*.280*	*20.9*	*.298*	*1.1*	*LF -3*	*1.9*

Breakout: 0% Improve: 29% Collapse: 10% Attrition: 18% MLB: 93% *Comparables: Billy Williams, Rondell White, Dusty Baker*

As Braun approaches his mid-thirties, few consider him to be an elite outfielder in the National League any longer. His various injuries will probably limit him to 500 PA in a given year; however, people should be careful to read too much into his "mere" .283 TAv. His peripherals varied little between his banner 2016 and his disappointing 2017. What did change, though, was his batted-ball luck. His .292 BABIP was the lowest of his 11-year-career without a difference in ground-ball rate, strikeout rate or his spray chart. Even his .218 ISO was roughly average for him over the last five seasons. Don't sleep on Braun. He might have a couple All-Star seasons in him yet.

Lewis Brinson CF Born: 05/08/94 Age: 24 Bats: R Throws: R Height: 6'3" Weight: 195 Origin: Round 1, 2012 Draft (#29 overall)

YEAR	TEAM	LVL	AGE	PA	R	2B	3B	HR	RBI	BB	K	SB	CS	AVG/OBP/SLG	TAv	VORP	BABIP	BRR	FRAA	WARP
2015	HDS	A+	21	298	51	22	7	13	42	31	64	13	6	.337/.416/.628	.363	39.9	.402	0.9	CF(51): -1.6, LF(7): 1.0	4.2
2015	FRI	AA	21	121	14	8	1	6	23	6	28	2	1	.291/.328/.545	.301	7.9	.333	-0.3	CF(22): 3.8, LF(3): 0.4	1.3
2015	ROU	AAA	21	37	9	1	0	1	4	7	6	3	0	.433/.541/.567	.428	7.6	.522	0.3	LF(7): 0.1, CF(1): -0.1	0.8
2016	FRI	AA	22	326	46	14	6	11	40	17	64	11	4	.237/.280/.431	.245	3.6	.264	-0.4	CF(65): -0.4, RF(5): -1.1	0.2
2016	CSP	AAA	22	93	14	9	0	4	20	2	21	4	2	.382/.387/.618	.323	8.9	.455	-0.1	CF(23): 6.0	1.5
2017	MIL	MLB	23	55	2	0	1	2	3	7	17	1	0	.106/.236/.277	.182	-3.4	.107	-0.5	CF(8): 0.5, LF(8): -0.1	-0.3
2017	CSP	AAA	23	340	66	22	4	13	48	32	62	11	5	.331/.400/.562	.299	26.9	.377	1.6	CF(61): 1.1, RF(6): -0.1	3.0
2018	*MIL*	*MLB*	*24*	*297*	*40*	*14*	*2*	*12*	*39*	*21*	*75*	*7*	*3*	*.250/.309/.449*	*.262*	*11.0*	*.300*	*0.4*	*CF 2, LF -1*	*1.0*
2019	*MIL*	*MLB*	*25*	*428*	*56*	*20*	*3*	*18*	*59*	*33*	*114*	*10*	*4*	*.247/.311/.456*	*.272*	*17.5*	*.300*	*0.8*	*CF 3, LF -1*	*2.1*

Breakout: 9% Improve: 28% Collapse: 11% Attrition: 21% MLB: 55% *Comparables: Joe Benson, Kyle Parker, Bradley Zimmer*

Brinson seems to be a sure-fire prospect. He's been ranked in the top 20 for the last two seasons and he's there again this year—you can check for yourself at the end of this book. He looks the part in center field and has compiled gaudy Triple-A numbers. There's more risk here than meets the eye, though. His 18.2 percent strikeout rate hides a long swing with ample holes, something that was on display in his brief big-league debut. Brinson still carries an impact profile, even if his batting average hovers around .250, but his adjustment period in the majors may be longer than most people assume.

Keon Broxton CF Born: 05/07/90 Age: 28 Bats: R Throws: R Height: 6'3" Weight: 195 Origin: Round 3, 2009 Draft (#95 overall)

YEAR	TEAM	LVL	AGE	PA	R	2B	3B	HR	RBI	BB	K	SB	CS	AVG/OBP/SLG	TAv	VORP	BABIP	BRR	FRAA	WARP
2015	ALT	AA	25	204	35	12	4	3	26	19	51	11	6	.302/.365/.464	.292	16.0	.395	3.5	CF(43): 4.4, RF(1): -0.3	2.2
2015	IND	AAA	25	367	51	15	8	7	42	47	105	28	9	.256/.352/.423	.275	14.8	.356	0.1	LF(46): 5.0, CF(31): -2.5	2.0
2015	PIT	MLB	25	2	3	0	0	0	0	0	1	1	1	.000/.000/.000	.001	-0.1	.000	0.1	RF(1): 0.0, CF(1): 0.0	0.0
2016	CSP	AAA	26	199	30	11	7	8	26	20	60	18	8	.287/.362/.562	.306	15.5	.391	0.3	CF(38): 4.4, LF(4): -0.4	2.1
2016	MIL	MLB	26	244	28	10	1	9	19	36	88	23	4	.242/.354/.430	.278	13.2	.373	1.3	CF(68): 0.5	1.4
2017	CSP	AAA	27	34	4	2	0	1	7	7	8	4	0	.385/.500/.577	.318	3.9	.500	0.5	CF(7): -0.8	0.3
2017	MIL	MLB	27	463	66	15	4	20	49	40	175	21	7	.220/.299/.420	.257	17.1	.323	3.6	CF(139): -8.1	0.9
2018	*MIL*	*MLB*	*28*	*359*	*53*	*13*	*3*	*13*	*41*	*38*	*126*	*21*	*6*	*.223/.310/.406*	*.251*	*11.5*	*.323*	*2.6*	*CF -4*	*0.6*
2019	*MIL*	*MLB*	*29*	*483*	*60*	*18*	*4*	*16*	*58*	*53*	*172*	*27*	*9*	*.221/.311/.397*	*.255*	*14.6*	*.324*	*2.7*	*CF -4*	*1.2*

Breakout: 3% Improve: 35% Collapse: 14% Attrition: 20% MLB: 78% *Comparables: Kirk Nieuwenhuis, Ryan Church, Casper Wells*

Scientists posit that climate change has caused an increased frequency of extreme weather events: worse droughts, heavier downpours, higher temperatures, etc. Though not in the climate-change models, that phenomenon seems to have affected Broxton's production at the plate. In his first 24 games, he hit .194/.275/.319. In his next 18 games, he mashed to the tune of a .352/.387/.620 slash line. That outburst was directly followed by a 16-game slump, in which he hit .082/.196/.204 with 23 strikeouts. Then, true to form, Broxton feasted again with a .353/.414/.843 slash line over 16 games, a stretch that included seven homers. Just when journalists were once again trying to determine "what changed," he went 3-for-50 over his next 18 games and this time ended the streak with a trip to Colorado Springs. The Brewers promptly recalled him in August, after which he once again went on a tear, hitting .281/.361/.594 over his next 21 contests. Of course, just to drive the point home, Broxton closed the year with a .158/.250/.175 slash line over his final 30 games. It was feast or famine. It was an arid drought or a torrential downpour. It was everything scientists have been warning humanity about, just on a baseball field, and it similarly left fans and front-office folks feeling helpless.

Michael Choice LF Born: 11/10/89 Age: 28 Bats: R Throws: R Height: 6'0" Weight: 230 Origin: Round 1, 2010 Draft (#10 overall)

YEAR	TEAM	LVL	AGE	PA	R	2B	3B	HR	RBI	BB	K	SB	CS	AVG/OBP/SLG	TAv	VORP	BABIP	BRR	FRAA	WARP
2015	TEX	MLB	25	1	0	0	0	0	0	0	1	0	0	.000/.000/.000	.011	-0.2	--	0.0	RF(1): -0.1	0.0
2015	ROU	AAA	25	447	53	25	1	12	60	32	115	2	0	.244/.309/.399	.261	8.7	.310	0.6	LF(62): -10.8, RF(16): -1.1	-0.3
2015	COH	AAA	25	62	5	5	0	1	7	5	22	1	0	.204/.306/.352	.236	-1.1	.323	-0.5	RF(8): 1.1, LF(2): 0.3	0.0
2016	COH	AAA	26	276	33	11	0	14	39	14	81	0	1	.246/.304/.456	.277	5.9	.302	-2.8	LF(16): 0.3, RF(12): -1.6	0.5
2017	NOR	AAA	27	32	1	1	0	0	2	5	9	1	0	.038/.219/.077	.156	-2.6	.059	0.4	LF(8): -0.7, RF(2): -0.2	-0.3
2017	BLX	AA	27	195	26	13	0	9	29	18	49	0	1	.272/.349/.503	.315	13.7	.328	-0.3	RF(38): -4.2, LF(2): 0.1	1.0
2018	*MIL*	*MLB*	*28*	*250*	*28*	*11*	*0*	*9*	*32*	*21*	*71*	*0*	*0*	*.228/.307/.404*	*.243*	*2.2*	*.289*	*-0.5*	*RF -5, LF -1*	*-0.4*
2019	*MIL*	*MLB*	*29*	*199*	*25*	*9*	*0*	*8*	*25*	*17*	*57*	*0*	*0*	*.228/.304/.408*	*.257*	*3.1*	*.289*	*-0.5*	*RF -4, LF -1*	*-0.2*

Breakout: 1% Improve: 9% Collapse: 16% Attrition: 30% MLB: 41% *Comparables: Joe Mather, Michael Ryan, Brian Bogusevic*

When studying immigration flows, it's well-understood that individuals or families are more likely to follow previously used routes and networks. People go places because others have gone there before. Choice, who joined the Brewers' organization in May, opted for the Eric Thames Development Path™. The former top prospect launched five homers in his final week with Double-A Biloxi and promptly signed a deal with the Nexen Heroes of the KBO, for whom he hit .307/.390/.653 with 17 homers in 46 games. Perhaps he'll be the next former "failed prospect" to demolish the ball in Korea for a few years and return to the states with a multi-million-dollar contract in his back pocket.

Isan Diaz MI Born: 05/27/96 Age: 22 Bats: L Throws: R Height: 5'10" Weight: 185 Origin: Round 2, 2014 Draft (#70 overall)

YEAR	TEAM	LVL	AGE	PA	R	2B	3B	HR	RBI	BB	K	SB	CS	AVG/OBP/SLG	TAv	VORP	BABIP	BRR	FRAA	WARP
2015	MSO	RK	19	312	58	25	6	13	51	34	65	12	7	.360/.436/.640	.365	49.1	.434	-1.3	SS(64): -1.5, 2B(5): 0.2	4.7
2016	WIS	A	20	587	71	34	5	20	75	72	148	11	8	.264/.358/.469	.287	37.7	.332	2.5	SS(90): -0.1, 2B(41): 1.0	4.2
2017	CAR	A+	21	455	59	20	0	13	54	62	121	9	3	.222/.334/.376	.262	14.5	.283	0.1	2B(58): -1.9, SS(32): -4.8	0.8
2018	*MIL*	*MLB*	*22*	*250*	*28*	*10*	*0*	*9*	*31*	*26*	*80*	*1*	*1*	*.212/.299/.391*	*.233*	*3.5*	*.282*	*-0.4*	*2B 0, SS -1*	*0.3*
2019	*MIL*	*MLB*	*23*	*356*	*46*	*15*	*1*	*15*	*46*	*38*	*114*	*2*	*1*	*.216/.303/.409*	*.253*	*8.4*	*.282*	*-0.6*	*2B -1, SS -1*	*0.7*

Breakout: 1% Improve: 26% Collapse: 3% Attrition: 15% MLB: 37% *Comparables: Ian Happ, Yoan Moncada, Matt Davidson*

It's been two years since Diaz torched the Pioneer League and became a prospect-watcher darling. He seemingly offered power, speed, average and a decent middle-infield defensive profile. When the Brewers traded for Diaz prior to the 2016 season, a couple of organizations had lofty grades on his potential hit tool. The story of the last two years, though, has been an erosion of confidence in those hit-tool projections. He understands the strike zone, leading to an attractive walk rate, but the combination of an uppercut swing path and an aggressive mentality has led to more strikeouts than expected. Unless his approach changes, Diaz profiles best as a power/patience middle infielder, à la Trevor Story or Ian Happ. The good news: Those types of players are valuable and occasional All-Stars, and the numbers should bounce back away from Five County Stadium, one of the toughest offensive environments in High-A. Diaz remains one of the more exciting second-base prospects in the minors.

Mauricio Dubon SS Born: 07/19/94 Age: 23 Bats: R Throws: R Height: 6'0" Weight: 160 Origin: Round 26, 2013 Draft (#773 overall)

YEAR	TEAM	LVL	AGE	PA	R	2B	3B	HR	RBI	BB	K	SB	CS	AVG/OBP/SLG	TAv	VORP	BABIP	BRR	FRAA	WARP
2015	GRN	A	20	262	43	12	3	4	29	18	34	18	4	.301/.354/.428	.294	23.3	.337	6.3	2B(38): 9.1, SS(18): 1.0	3.6
2015	SLM	A+	20	269	27	9	0	1	18	23	38	12	3	.274/.343/.325	.240	6.6	.320	2.1	SS(52): -2.3, 2B(5): 0.1	0.5
2016	SLM	A+	21	279	53	11	3	0	29	33	25	24	4	.306/.387/.379	.289	25.6	.338	5.5	SS(61): -11.6	1.4
2016	PME	AA	21	270	48	20	6	6	40	11	36	6	3	.339/.371/.538	.301	25.7	.374	4.1	SS(62): -5.7	2.2
2017	BLX	AA	22	304	34	14	0	2	24	25	42	31	9	.276/.338/.351	.245	6.6	.319	0.3	SS(53): 5.4, 2B(20): 3.0	1.6
2017	CSP	AAA	22	244	40	15	0	6	33	14	34	7	6	.272/.320/.420	.229	-0.1	.297	-0.4	SS(30): -1.0, 2B(27): 3.5	0.2
2018	*MIL*	*MLB*	*23*	*62*	*8*	*3*	*0*	*1*	*6*	*4*	*12*	*3*	*1*	*.249/.295/.380*	*.235*	*1.2*	*.289*	*0.2*	*SS 0, 2B 1*	*0.1*
2019	*MIL*	*MLB*	*24*	*266*	*31*	*11*	*1*	*7*	*30*	*18*	*53*	*11*	*4*	*.246/.302/.390*	*.245*	*5.8*	*.282*	*1.2*	*SS -2, 2B 4*	*0.8*

Breakout: 8% Improve: 26% Collapse: 11% Attrition: 25% MLB: 47% *Comparables: Jack Reinheimer, Ozzie Martinez, Cristhian Adames*

Dubon personifies why scouting is an art, rather than a science. On the surface, he's a slightly built, light-hitting utility player. He's a guy who shows some speed, but only had a 61 percent success rate when swiping bases. For those scouts who have sat on him for numerous viewings, though, all of that misses the point. Dubon has above-average makeup, meshing well with teammates and showing real behind-the-scenes effort to improve. He doesn't hit for power, but can sting the ball to all fields and hit for average. His walk rate has plummeted since reaching Double-A, but he still has an idea of what he's doing at the plate. He also offers quality defense at multiple positions up the middle of the diamond. From an outsider's perspective, that may sound like a quality utility man; however, some scouts (and Matt Collins) will continue to insist that he'll be something more than that.

Lucas Erceg 3B Born: 05/01/95 Age: 23 Bats: L Throws: R Height: 6'3" Weight: 200 Origin: Round 2, 2016 Draft (#46 overall)

YEAR	TEAM	LVL	AGE	PA	R	2B	3B	HR	RBI	BB	K	SB	CS	AVG/OBP/SLG	TAv	VORP	BABIP	BRR	FRAA	WARP
2016	HEL	RK	21	115	17	8	1	2	22	8	16	8	1	.400/.452/.552	.339	14.0	.460	0.6	3B(20): 0.3	1.4
2016	WIS	A	21	180	17	9	3	7	29	12	38	1	3	.281/.328/.497	.294	10.1	.325	-0.8	3B(37): -0.6	1.0
2017	CAR	A+	22	538	66	33	1	15	81	35	95	2	3	.256/.307/.417	.259	12.2	.287	-1.6	3B(85): -0.6	1.2
2018	*MIL*	*MLB*	*23*	*250*	*26*	*12*	*1*	*9*	*33*	*13*	*62*	*0*	*0*	*.235/.278/.413*	*.228*	*-0.7*	*.278*	*-0.5*	*3B -2*	*-0.3*
2019	*MIL*	*MLB*	*24*	*372*	*45*	*19*	*0*	*14*	*48*	*23*	*92*	*0*	*0*	*.237/.286/.419*	*.249*	*3.6*	*.280*	*-1.0*	*3B -3*	*0.0*

Breakout: 1% Improve: 27% Collapse: 7% Attrition: 19% MLB: 45% *Comparables: Cody Asche, Neil Walker, Ryan Wheeler*

Erceg's yearlong numbers may not inspire long-term confidence, but the left-handed slugger impressed many as the year wore on. Scouts like his traditional third-base profile and many have raved about his makeup, as evidenced by the Brewers' willingness to challenge him in spring training and also promote him for the Triple-A playoffs. It also helped that he hit .290/.343/.470 in his final 86 games, of course.

Mario Feliciano C Born: 11/20/98 Age: 19 Bats: R Throws: R Height: 6'1" Weight: 195 Origin: Round 2, 2016 Draft (#75 overall)

YEAR	TEAM	LVL	AGE	PA	R	2B	3B	HR	RBI	BB	K	SB	CS	AVG/OBP/SLG	TAv	VORP	BABIP	BRR	FRAA	WARP
2016	BRR	RK	17	127	16	5	3	0	16	7	19	2	2	.265/.307/.359	.263	4.7	.310	-0.3	C(20): -0.6	0.4
2017	WIS	A	18	446	47	16	2	4	36	34	72	10	2	.251/.320/.331	.246	10.8	.297	1.4	C(78): -2.8	0.8
2018	*MIL*	*MLB*	*19*	*250*	*26*	*10*	*1*	*5*	*22*	*14*	*61*	*1*	*0*	*.222/.272/.340*	*.207*	*-1.8*	*.276*	*-0.3*	*C -1*	*-0.3*
2019	*MIL*	*MLB*	*20*	*361*	*40*	*14*	*1*	*9*	*39*	*23*	*83*	*1*	*0*	*.241/.297/.376*	*.243*	*6.4*	*.293*	*-0.5*	*C -1*	*0.6*

Breakout: 0% Improve: 7% Collapse: 2% Attrition: 7% MLB: 13% *Comparables: Francisco Pena, Rougned Odor, Carlos Triunfel*

It's not often that a catcher with a .651 OPS ends the campaign as a breakout prospect. The Brewers showed confidence in Feliciano by shoving him into full-season ball in Wisconsin at just 18 years old. When he hit .292/.347/.431 in April, area scouts began paying a bit more attention to the former Competitive Balance B pick. The defensive skill set is raw, but he's a very good athlete for a catcher and flashes legitimate ability behind the dish. Some think he could be an average corner outfielder, if necessary; however, Feliciano's attractiveness comes from his combination of catching potential and projectable bat. He offers bat speed, a bit of power, and an idea of how to approach an at-bat. It's still raw at his age, but few catching prospects have the athleticism to be an asset defensively behind the plate and the raw hitting ability to carry a non-catching profile. Minor-league catchers notoriously blossom more slowly than other position players, due to the extra time that must be devoted to learning how to handle a pitching staff and call games, but he's a potential everyday starter at the major-league level. If you want to sound like a cool prospect insider to your many friends, tell them you're very high on Feliciano. A couple of years down the road, they may look at you like you're a genius.

Jake Gatewood 1B Born: 09/25/95 Age: 22 Bats: R Throws: R Height: 6'5" Weight: 190 Origin: Round 1, 2014 Draft (#41 overall)

YEAR	TEAM	LVL	AGE	PA	R	2B	3B	HR	RBI	BB	K	SB	CS	AVG/OBP/SLG	TAv	VORP	BABIP	BRR	FRAA	WARP
2015	HEL	RK	19	238	38	23	1	6	41	18	68	3	5	.274/.331/.476	.279	14.0	.366	-1.0	SS(51): -1.9	1.2
2015	WIS	A	19	193	16	5	1	4	16	14	65	5	0	.209/.275/.316	.226	0.3	.306	-0.8	SS(52): -4.0	-0.4
2016	WIS	A	20	524	70	33	0	14	64	18	141	3	2	.240/.268/.391	.241	3.9	.303	0.6	3B(93): -1.2, 1B(26): 0.5	0.3
2017	CAR	A+	21	470	66	36	1	11	53	43	132	7	5	.269/.340/.438	.281	15.5	.364	-0.7	1B(71): 0.4, 3B(10): -0.1	1.7
2017	BLX	AA	21	100	9	4	2	4	9	8	29	3	0	.239/.300/.457	.257	2.6	.305	-0.1	3B(21): -0.4	0.2
2018	*MIL*	*MLB*	*22*	*250*	*24*	*12*	*0*	*8*	*30*	*13*	*88*	*1*	*0*	*.209/.253/.369*	*.209*	*-8.1*	*.289*	*-0.3*	*1B 0, 3B 0*	*-0.9*
2019	*MIL*	*MLB*	*23*	*330*	*37*	*15*	*1*	*11*	*38*	*19*	*118*	*2*	*1*	*.212/.263/.374*	*.228*	*-6.5*	*.299*	*-0.5*	*1B 0, 3B 0*	*-0.7*

Breakout: 1% Improve: 2% Collapse: 1% Attrition: 3% MLB: 3% *Comparables: Brandon Allen, Brandon Snyder, Neftali Soto*

Everyone is familiar with the Best Shape of His Life (BSOHL) puff pieces that get rolled out every spring. Related, a handful of stories about guys getting LASIK surgery come out every year, along with subsequent articles about how so-and-so is going to improve at the dish with his new superhuman eyesight. It rarely happens. Gatewood doesn't fit comfortably into that narrative. The supplemental-first-round pick in 2014 wore contact lenses for the first time in his life and immediately posted the best walk rate of his young career. The strikeout rate remained reasonable and the batting average started creeping up, and the Brewers rewarded him—and not the other high-profile position prospects on the Carolina Mudcats—with a Double-A promotion. Of course, Gatewood also retooled his swing. His posture is different, his hands drop deeper during his load, and his back knee and hips remain in a better hitting position. It's difficult to ascertain whether Gatewood's improvement has stemmed from the significant swing changes or the contact lenses, but it's likely a combination of the two. Either way, Gatewood is translating his physical gifts into in-game skills. Some scouts, on draft day, thought he'd never be able to hit for a meaningful average. It's not there yet, but the California native is trending in the right direction.

Trent Grisham OF Born: 11/01/96 Age: 21 Bats: L Throws: L Height: 6'0" Weight: 205 Origin: Round 1, 2015 Draft (#15 overall)

YEAR	TEAM	LVL	AGE	PA	R	2B	3B	HR	RBI	BB	K	SB	CS	AVG/OBP/SLG	TAv	VORP	BABIP	BRR	FRAA	WARP
2015	BRR	RK	18	200	34	7	6	1	16	30	36	20	5	.309/.422/.442	.315	19.2	.388	0.4	CF(40): -0.6, LF(1): 1.7	2.0
2015	HEL	RK	18	52	5	0	0	1	5	9	8	5	3	.310/.431/.381	.291	2.7	.364	-0.8	CF(12): -1.8	0.1
2016	WIS	A	19	262	27	15	2	2	24	37	68	5	10	.231/.346/.344	.249	0.2	.325	-4.0	CF(49): 1.4, LF(10): -1.6	0.0
2017	CAR	A+	20	569	78	21	6	8	45	98	141	37	5	.223/.360/.348	.263	14.9	.299	1.6	RF(44): 1.5, LF(34): -0.5	1.8
2018	*MIL*	*MLB*	*21*	*250*	*32*	*9*	*1*	*5*	*21*	*34*	*76*	*8*	*3*	*.199/.312/.328*	*.222*	*-1.4*	*.276*	*0.6*	*RF -1, LF -1*	*-0.4*
2019	*MIL*	*MLB*	*22*	*377*	*46*	*14*	*2*	*10*	*39*	*52*	*113*	*12*	*4*	*.207/.321/.357*	*.246*	*4.8*	*.281*	*1.4*	*RF -1, LF -1*	*0.2*

Breakout: 0% Improve: 3% Collapse: 0% Attrition: 0% MLB: 3% *Comparables: Michael Reed, Aaron Hicks, Brandon Nimmo*

Scouting prospects is a bit like scouring hundreds of musical tracks for the next great hit. Maybe it's heart-wrenching lyrics, an earworm of a beat or a killer guitar solo, but a good song must stand out somehow. For the former first-rounder, scouts are desperately searching for what makes him potentially special. It was supposed to be his hit tool, but even with his new conventional batting grip, he's rocking a Chris Carter-esque batting average. Projecting double-digit homers appears to be a stretch, even with a juiced ball. Defensively, he's probably a left fielder, which squeezes the margin for error everywhere else. It's too early to resign his demo to the trash bin, as the Brewers pushed him to High-A at just 20 years old, but the former first-round pick is flirting dangerously with prospect obscurity. He officially changed his last name from Clark to Grisham in November after his mother, so perhaps that will help. It worked for Robert Zimmerman.

Monte Harrison OF Born: 08/10/95 Age: 22 Bats: R Throws: R Height: 6'3" Weight: 220 Origin: Round 2, 2014 Draft (#50 overall)

YEAR	TEAM	LVL	AGE	PA	R	2B	3B	HR	RBI	BB	K	SB	CS	AVG/OBP/SLG	TAv	VORP	BABIP	BRR	FRAA	WARP
2015	WIS	A	19	184	18	6	2	2	11	14	77	6	4	.148/.246/.247	.184	-8.0	.265	1.0	CF(42): -5.9, RF(4): 0.0	-1.5
2015	HEL	RK	19	119	20	4	2	3	13	14	23	14	2	.299/.410/.474	.330	14.3	.361	1.1	CF(25): 3.5, RF(3): 0.0	1.7
2016	BRR	RK	20	25	4	1	1	0	1	4	4	0	0	.211/.375/.368	.295	1.9	.267	0.1	CF(5): 0.9	0.3
2016	WIS	A	20	298	34	11	1	6	37	20	97	8	3	.221/.294/.337	.232	0.4	.321	1.0	CF(48): -0.7, RF(14): 1.0	0.1
2017	WIS	A	21	261	32	12	1	11	32	29	70	11	3	.265/.359/.475	.307	21.8	.333	1.3	CF(62): 1.6	2.4
2017	CAR	A+	21	252	41	16	1	10	35	14	69	16	1	.278/.341/.487	.305	21.2	.358	3.3	CF(27): -1.8, RF(18): -1.3	2.0
2018	*MIL*	*MLB*	*22*	*250*	*27*	*9*	*1*	*9*	*29*	*16*	*93*	*5*	*1*	*.200/.267/.359*	*.214*	*-2.5*	*.287*	*0.4*	*CF 0, RF 1*	*-0.2*
2019	*MIL*	*MLB*	*23*	*299*	*34*	*12*	*1*	*10*	*34*	*21*	*110*	*7*	*2*	*.201/.272/.362*	*.229*	*-1.0*	*.291*	*0.6*	*CF 0, RF 1*	*0.0*

Breakout: 3% Improve: 8% Collapse: 3% Attrition: 8% MLB: 17% *Comparables: Tommy Pham, Trayce Thompson, Michael Saunders*

It finally happened. The former high-school football star had flashed freakish ability on the diamond, but injuries kept derailing the hype train. Harrison remained healthy in 2017 and mashed. He is physically built like a Mack truck, has plus raw power that's beginning to translate to in-game situations and seemingly glides around the bases. Our prospect team has tabbed him as a potential Role 7 player, and he's perhaps the most exciting prospect that few casual followers have ever heard of. That will almost certainly change after the upcoming season.

Keston Hiura 2B Born: 08/02/96 Age: 21 Bats: R Throws: R Height: 5'11" Weight: 190 Origin: Round 1, 2017 Draft (#9 overall)

YEAR	TEAM	LVL	AGE	PA	R	2B	3B	HR	RBI	BB	K	SB	CS	AVG/OBP/SLG	TAv	VORP	BABIP	BRR	FRAA	WARP
2017	BRR	RK	20	72	18	3	5	4	18	6	13	0	2	.435/.500/.839	.426	16.6	.500	0.5		1.5
2017	WIS	A	20	115	14	11	2	0	15	7	24	2	0	.333/.374/.476	.326	10.3	.422	1.1	2B(3): -0.4	1.0
2018	*MIL*	*MLB*	*21*	*250*	*23*	*11*	*1*	*6*	*27*	*14*	*72*	*0*	*0*	*.223/.273/.362*	*.215*	*-5.5*	*.294*	*-0.3*	*2B 0*	*-0.6*
2019	*MIL*	*MLB*	*22*	*235*	*26*	*11*	*1*	*6*	*26*	*14*	*68*	*0*	*0*	*.228/.281/.377*	*.236*	*-1.7*	*.299*	*-0.4*	*2B 0*	*-0.2*

Breakout: 0% Improve: 0% Collapse: 0% Attrition: 2% MLB: 2% *Comparables: Jose Osuna, Dominic Smith, Matt Davidson*

Hiura may have gone ninth overall in the 2017 draft, but the University of California Irvine star arguably had the best pure swing of anyone selected throughout the three-day event. He makes loud contact to all fields and straight-up raked in his professional debut. Questions about the defensive profile stem from elbow troubles; he has seemingly avoided Tommy John surgery for now—even the Brewers weren't sure if he'd need it when they drafted him—but it's still an awkward throwing motion. With plus makeup and a potentially special bat, he's a first-division starter if he can even be remotely average at second base, and maybe even if he can't. It's that latter part that scared off eight teams in the draft. If Hiura flashes a decent arm in the spring, though, he'll soar up prospect lists. Because no one doubts he's gonna hit.

Hernan Perez UT Born: 03/26/91 Age: 27 Bats: R Throws: R Height: 6'1" Weight: 215 Origin: International Free Agent, 2007

YEAR	TEAM	LVL	AGE	PA	R	2B	3B	HR	RBI	BB	K	SB	CS	AVG/OBP/SLG	TAv	VORP	BABIP	BRR	FRAA	WARP
2015	DET	MLB	24	34	1	0	0	0	0	1	11	1	0	.061/.088/.061	.039	-6.6	.091	-0.3	3B(8): 0.0, 2B(5): -0.1	-0.7
2015	MIL	MLB	24	238	13	15	2	1	21	4	48	4	1	.270/.281/.365	.227	-1.9	.335	-1.3	3B(72): 0.4, 2B(14): -1.0	-0.3
2016	CSP	AAA	25	67	10	4	1	1	11	3	10	2	0	.339/.364/.484	.289	4.4	.385	0.4	2B(10): -0.8, 3B(6): 0.1	0.4
2016	MIL	MLB	25	430	50	18	3	13	56	18	94	34	7	.272/.302/.428	.273	19.8	.322	3.0	3B(60): -0.5, RF(36): 3.6	2.4
2017	MIL	MLB	26	458	47	19	3	14	51	20	79	13	4	.259/.289/.414	.249	9.4	.286	2.4	LF(53): 2.5, 3B(31): 3.4	1.3
2018	*MIL*	*MLB*	*27*	*310*	*35*	*14*	*2*	*7*	*32*	*12*	*57*	*13*	*3*	*.256/.284/.385*	*.231*	*2.4*	*.292*	*1.6*	*2B -1, 3B 1*	*0.0*
2019	*MIL*	*MLB*	*28*	*455*	*50*	*21*	*3*	*12*	*51*	*21*	*88*	*18*	*5*	*.254/.290/.397*	*.242*	*5.3*	*.290*	*1.4*	*2B -2, 3B 1*	*0.5*

Breakout: 8% Improve: 29% Collapse: 11% Attrition: 24% MLB: 74% *Comparables: Josh Anderson, Felix Pie, Matt Szczur*

Perez does a lot of things. He doesn't do anything particularly well, but he does a lot of things. He hits for some power. He steals a few bases. He plays multiple infield positions. He plays multiple outfield positions. He hits for a decent average. Unfortunately the Venezuelan has been a below-average hitter as measured by TAv since he arrived in Milwaukee, and his hyper-aggressive approach led to the sixth-highest swing rate in baseball (min. 400 PA) last season. People salivating over his massive second half in 2016 focused too much on the raw power-speed numbers and forgot to interrogate the broader offensive profile. He's a free-swinging utility fielder who occasionally runs into one and provides some pop off the bench. What he doesn't appear to be, though, is a super-sub who deserves 450+ plate appearances on a competitive ball club. He's a useful cog who derives most of his value from his glove, though most of his defensive value sneakily came from 337 innings in left field, a position his offensive profile cannot hope to carry nor one that teams prioritize in a utility fielder. That does leave one wondering: How much practical value undergirds his overall valuation that puts him as a one- or two-win player?

Brett Phillips CF Born: 05/30/94 Age: 24 Bats: L Throws: R Height: 6'0" Weight: 185 Origin: Round 6, 2012 Draft (#189 overall)

YEAR	TEAM	LVL	AGE	PA	R	2B	3B	HR	RBI	BB	K	SB	CS	AVG/OBP/SLG	TAv	VORP	BABIP	BRR	FRAA	WARP
2015	LNC	A+	21	322	68	19	7	15	53	22	64	8	6	.320/.379/.588	.328	33.6	.368	3.0	CF(53): 1.4, RF(9): 0.3	3.8
2015	CCH	AA	21	145	22	8	4	1	18	8	26	7	2	.321/.372/.463	.294	11.6	.393	2.6	CF(28): 6.3, RF(3): 0.7	2.0
2015	BLX	AA	21	98	14	7	3	0	6	14	30	2	1	.250/.361/.413	.286	6.3	.385	0.8	CF(22): 3.9	1.1
2016	BLX	AA	22	517	60	14	6	16	62	67	154	12	7	.229/.332/.397	.278	24.9	.311	1.5	CF(102): 0.6, RF(19): 0.0	2.7
2017	CSP	AAA	23	432	79	23	10	19	78	45	129	9	1	.305/.377/.567	.295	30.1	.412	2.1	RF(52): -3.2, CF(49): 3.9	3.1
2017	MIL	MLB	23	98	9	3	0	4	12	9	34	5	0	.276/.351/.448	.293	6.7	.408	0.3	CF(26): 4.8, RF(9): -0.3	1.1
2018	*MIL*	*MLB*	*24*	*251*	*32*	*10*	*3*	*9*	*31*	*23*	*81*	*4*	*1*	*.234/.307/.420*	*.252*	*7.3*	*.319*	*0.5*	*CF 2, RF 0*	*0.7*
2019	*MIL*	*MLB*	*25*	*401*	*50*	*16*	*4*	*15*	*51*	*37*	*134*	*7*	*2*	*.232/.308/.426*	*.260*	*11.9*	*.320*	*0.9*	*CF 3, RF 0*	*1.6*

Breakout: 6% Improve: 20% Collapse: 10% Attrition: 23% MLB: 43% *Comparables: Brett Jackson, Joe Benson, Bradley Zimmer*

Scouting stat lines is inherently dangerous, with Phillips being the latest example. He mashed for two years before failing to eclipse the .230 mark in 2016. That low average prompted many publications to drop Phillips from their Brewers' top-10 lists, but not *Baseball Prospectus*, who ranked the center fielder at no. 6 in the organization, citing his volatility due to a fringe-average hit tool but lauding his athleticism, power and patience. Phillips delivered. Undoubtedly aided by the Rocky Mountain run environment in Colorado Springs, the man nicknamed "Maverick" posted a .944 OPS and played his way onto the major-league squad. There, he showed the good and the bad of what he is. Phillips displayed his cannon of a right arm, once hitting 104 mph on a throw from center field to nail David Freese at home plate. He also exhibited power, patience and a penchant for the strikeout. The Florida native hit .295/.368/.487 against righties, showing everything a big-league team would want in a highly productive platoon player.

Manny Pina C Born: 06/05/87 Age: 31 Bats: R Throws: R Height: 6'0" Weight: 215 Origin: International Free Agent, 2004

YEAR	TEAM	LVL	AGE	PA	R	2B	3B	HR	RBI	BB	K	SB	CS	AVG/OBP/SLG	TAv	VORP	BABIP	BRR	FRAA	WARP
2015	TOL	AAA	28	292	28	19	0	7	39	24	34	2	0	.305/.379/.461	.288	20.5	.327	0.3	C(66): 0.3	2.1
2016	CSP	AAA	29	262	35	21	3	5	43	17	39	1	1	.329/.371/.506	.296	17.8	.371	-3.4	C(57): -7.7	1.0
2016	MIL	MLB	29	81	4	4	0	2	12	10	15	0	1	.254/.346/.394	.263	2.4	.296	-1.2	C(17): -0.9	0.2
2017	MIL	MLB	30	359	45	21	0	9	43	20	79	2	0	.279/.327/.424	.262	16.8	.339	-0.6	C(102): 0.5	1.7
2018	*MIL*	*MLB*	*31*	*245*	*27*	*13*	*0*	*7*	*30*	*16*	*50*	*1*	*0*	*.260/.317/.413*	*.253*	*9.7*	*.304*	*-0.5*	*C -5*	*0.2*
2019	*MIL*	*MLB*	*32*	*282*	*34*	*15*	*0*	*9*	*34*	*20*	*63*	*0*	*0*	*.248/.312/.413*	*.257*	*9.4*	*.292*	*-0.7*	*C -6*	*0.4*

Breakout: 1% Improve: 20% Collapse: 18% Attrition: 25% MLB: 77% *Comparables: Robinson Chirinos, Rene Rivera, Robby Hammock*

YEAR	TEAM	P. COUNT	FRM RUNS	BLK RUNS	THRW RUNS	TOT RUNS
2015	TOL	8894	-1.3	0.3	2.5	1.4
2016	MIL	2273	-0.6	-0.2	-0.1	-0.9
2017	MIL	12774	-3.5	0.6	1.8	-1.1
2018	*MIL*	*8440*	*-5.2*	*0.0*	*0.8*	*-4.3*
2019	*MIL*	*9715*	*-5.9*	*0.0*	*1.0*	*-4.9*

A slew of breakout performances fueled the 2017 Brewers' surprise run at the NL playoffs. Pina's two-win season has been overlooked by both fans and the broader baseball community alike, but the 30-year-old rookie had recently been nothing more than an afterthought for both the Tigers and the Brewers. Detroit included him as a PTBNL in the 2015 K-Rod deal. The Brewers, for their part, didn't appear to consider Pina a long- or short-term solution, acquiring both Andrew Susac and Jett Bandy in the year following his arrival. Pina outplayed them both in 2017 and grabbed the everyday catcher role by the scruff of the neck. His overall value numbers suffered because he was a poor pitch framer, but he showed competency with the bat and boasts a big arm to control the running game. At the very least, Pina is a quality backup catcher in the big leagues, though he showed that there is no shame in giving him 300 plate appearances.

Corey Ray OF Born: 09/22/94 Age: 23 Bats: L Throws: L Height: 5'11" Weight: 185 Origin: Round 1, 2016 Draft (#5 overall)

YEAR	TEAM	LVL	AGE	PA	R	2B	3B	HR	RBI	BB	K	SB	CS	AVG/OBP/SLG	TAv	VORP	BABIP	BRR	FRAA	WARP
2016	BRV	A+	21	254	24	13	2	5	17	20	54	9	5	.247/.307/.385	.252	2.4	.299	-1.9	CF(40): -3.3	-0.1
2017	CAR	A+	22	503	56	29	4	7	48	48	156	24	10	.238/.311/.367	.254	7.7	.346	-2.5	CF(69): 5.5, RF(21): 0.9	1.5
2018	*MIL*	*MLB*	*23*	*250*	*31*	*11*	*1*	*7*	*23*	*19*	*83*	*7*	*3*	*.208/.271/.351*	*.211*	*-3.5*	*.290*	*0.2*	*CF 1, RF 0*	*-0.3*
2019	*MIL*	*MLB*	*24*	*324*	*36*	*15*	*1*	*9*	*35*	*26*	*105*	*9*	*4*	*.215/.282/.366*	*.232*	*0.1*	*.298*	*0.7*	*CF 1, RF 0*	*0.2*

Breakout: 0% Improve: 7% Collapse: 3% Attrition: 9% MLB: 10% *Comparables: Michael Taylor, Daniel Fields, Aaron Altherr*

As the no. 5 pick in the 2016 draft, Ray has largely disappointed, yet scouts remain split. Pessimists will point out that he struck out over 30 percent of the time last year, hit for next-to-no power and hasn't sniffed .250 as a professional. Optimists, however, will point to his vast defensive improvement, the fact that he may stick in center and his premium athleticism. It's also possible that 2016 knee surgery contributed to his inability to incorporate his lower half into his swing. Next year will prove be a key litmus test for the former Louisville Cardinal star.

Domingo Santana RF

Born: 08/05/92 Age: 25 Bats: R Throws: R Height: 6'5" Weight: 220 Origin: International Free Agent, 2009

YEAR	TEAM	LVL	AGE	PA	R	2B	3B	HR	RBI	BB	K	SB	CS	AVG/OBP/SLG	TAv	VORP	BABIP	BRR	FRAA	WARP
2015	HOU	MLB	22	42	6	2	0	2	8	2	17	2	1	.256/.310/.462	.256	0.9	.400	0.3	RF(9): -0.2, LF(3): -0.8	0.0
2015	FRE	AAA	22	326	62	18	3	16	59	48	91	1	4	.320/.426/.582	.348	36.0	.429	0.6	RF(59): -5.3, LF(1): 0.2	3.1
2015	CSP	AAA	22	85	13	5	1	2	18	6	17	1	1	.380/.424/.544	.319	6.9	.467	-0.1	LF(14): -1.3, RF(4): -0.3	0.5
2015	MIL	MLB	22	145	14	5	0	6	18	18	46	2	0	.231/.345/.421	.299	9.6	.310	0.6	CF(23): -2.9, RF(16): -1.4	0.5
2016	WIS	A	23	28	4	0	0	1	3	4	5	0	0	.174/.321/.304	.243	-0.1	.176	0.0	RF(4): -0.2	0.0
2016	MIL	MLB	23	281	34	14	0	11	32	32	91	2	3	.256/.345/.447	.287	14.8	.359	1.6	RF(62): -5.0, LF(4): -0.4	1.0
2017	MIL	MLB	24	607	88	29	0	30	85	73	178	15	4	.278/.371/.505	.306	40.5	.363	0.2	RF(144): -7.6	3.3
2018	*MIL*	*MLB*	*25*	*581*	*89*	*25*	*1*	*24*	*74*	*67*	*182*	*9*	*4*	*.253/.346/.450*	*.278*	*27.1*	*.345*	*-0.5*	*RF -10*	*1.3*
2019	*MIL*	*MLB*	*26*	*569*	*82*	*26*	*1*	*25*	*81*	*70*	*176*	*9*	*4*	*.258/.355/.468*	*.295*	*33.7*	*.346*	*1.1*	*RF -8*	*2.8*

Breakout: 2% Improve: 53% Collapse: 4% Attrition: 7% MLB: 92% *Comparables: Oswaldo Arcia, Jonny Gomes, Joc Pederson*

Santana boasts an alluring profile: a legit 30-homer bat with a .275 average and an above-average walk rate—all at just 25 years old. The plate discipline is real, too, as evidenced by his 26.5 percent swing rate at pitches outside the zone (30 percent is the league-average mark). The problem, though, is that Santana carries significant defensive risk and has big holes in his swing. His 51.9 percent contact rate at pitches in the strike zone was ninth worst in all of baseball, which explains how he strikes out 29.3 percent of the time without a penchant for chasing. It comes down to this: Can Santana maintain a crazy-high BABIP? His career average is .354, and his .363 BABIP in 2017 was the sixth-highest in baseball. If he can sustain such a BABIP, he could be a perennial three- or four-win player. If that number drops, he's basically Khris Davis in right field—a decent two-win player but nothing to build around.

Travis Shaw 3B

Born: 04/16/90 Age: 28 Bats: L Throws: R Height: 6'4" Weight: 230 Origin: Round 9, 2011 Draft (#292 overall)

YEAR	TEAM	LVL	AGE	PA	R	2B	3B	HR	RBI	BB	K	SB	CS	AVG/OBP/SLG	TAv	VORP	BABIP	BRR	FRAA	WARP
2015	PAW	AAA	25	322	29	12	2	5	30	26	54	0	1	.249/.318/.356	.251	2.8	.289	-1.3	3B(43): 4.2, 1B(31): -2.9	0.5
2015	BOS	MLB	25	248	31	10	0	13	36	18	57	0	1	.270/.327/.487	.278	6.2	.304	-1.0	1B(55): -0.3, 3B(8): 0.4	0.7
2016	BOS	MLB	26	530	63	34	2	16	71	43	133	5	1	.242/.306/.421	.246	5.7	.299	-0.8	3B(105): 7.4, 1B(50): 2.3	1.6
2017	MIL	MLB	27	606	84	34	1	31	101	60	138	10	0	.273/.349/.513	.289	41.5	.312	3.2	3B(143): 0.9, 1B(1): 0.0	4.2
2018	*MIL*	*MLB*	*28*	*592*	*75*	*29*	*2*	*24*	*82*	*51*	*140*	*6*	*1*	*.248/.317/.443*	*.260*	*18.8*	*.291*	*-0.1*	*3B 3, 1B 0*	*1.8*
2019	*MIL*	*MLB*	*29*	*560*	*75*	*28*	*1*	*25*	*78*	*51*	*137*	*4*	*1*	*.244/.318/.453*	*.271*	*19.8*	*.285*	*0.1*	*3B 4, 1B 0*	*2.6*

Breakout: 1% Improve: 46% Collapse: 4% Attrition: 9% MLB: 98% *Comparables: Todd Frazier, Kevin Kouzmanoff, Wilson Betemit*

It's cliché to say player development is nonlinear and players should be allowed to fail without an organization giving up on them. Teams often embrace that ideology in the minors. At the major-league level, though, competitive teams can rarely afford to extend a long leash to struggling players. After surprising many in 2015, Shaw earned 530 plate appearances the following season and mostly slumped at the plate. Boston functionally gave up on him, sending him (and three others) to Milwaukee in the Tyler Thornburg trade. The Brewers had no expectations of winning and no internal options at third base, meaning Shaw had the perfect environment in which to continue his development. The 27-year-old slumped a bit in August and September, but over the course of the year, he mashed. His year-end numbers looked eerily similar to those of his 2015 rookie campaign, but in more than twice as many plate appearances. Scouts will say that countless professionals failed at the big-league level because they didn't have the luxury of time—time to fail, learn, adjust and succeed. Teams without expectations, like the 2017 Brewers, offer the rare long big-league leash. Shaw took advantage of it.

Eric Sogard 2B

Born: 05/22/86 Age: 32 Bats: L Throws: R Height: 5'9" Weight: 180 Origin: Round 2, 2007 Draft (#81 overall)

YEAR	TEAM	LVL	AGE	PA	R	2B	3B	HR	RBI	BB	K	SB	CS	AVG/OBP/SLG	TAv	VORP	BABIP	BRR	FRAA	WARP
2015	OAK	MLB	29	401	40	12	3	1	37	23	50	6	1	.247/.294/.304	.224	-0.9	.283	2.2	2B(96): 5.9, SS(17): 0.0	0.5
2017	CSP	AAA	31	107	30	8	0	3	17	15	12	5	0	.330/.421/.516	.294	6.9	.351	-0.2	2B(15): -0.2, 3B(3): 0.0	0.7
2017	MIL	MLB	31	299	37	15	1	3	18	45	37	3	3	.273/.393/.378	.283	14.1	.311	-2.9	2B(60): -2.1, SS(26): -0.2	1.2
2018	*MIL*	*MLB*	*32*	*310*	*36*	*14*	*1*	*3*	*24*	*28*	*43*	*5*	*2*	*.251/.323/.344*	*.238*	*5.8*	*.283*	*-0.1*	*2B 1, SS 0*	*0.4*
2019	*MIL*	*MLB*	*33*	*237*	*27*	*11*	*1*	*3*	*22*	*23*	*34*	*3*	*1*	*.249/.328/.355*	*.249*	*5.0*	*.280*	*-0.1*	*2B 1, SS 0*	*0.6*

Breakout: 2% Improve: 31% Collapse: 7% Attrition: 14% MLB: 90% *Comparables: Dave Cash, Felix Millan, Rich Dauer*

Life lesson: If you perform well enough early at a new job, very few people notice when you begin coasting home. Sogard hit .338/.449/.500 with 12 doubles and three homers in his first 41 games. Before going on the DL for a short stint, he became the Brewers' starting second baseman and leadoff hitter. That blistering start hid the fact that he took a nosedive in his final 53 games with a .202/.331/.244 slash line. If you're looking at the .331 and telling yourself that's decent, you're the glass-half-full type that this world needs. Everyone else is busy looking at that .575 OPS and wondering if the juiced-ball theory is nothing but an Alex Jones-type sham.

Eric Thames 1B

Born: 11/10/86 Age: 31 Bats: L Throws: R Height: 6'0" Weight: 210 Origin: Round 7, 2008 Draft (#219 overall)

YEAR	TEAM	LVL	AGE	PA	R	2B	3B	HR	RBI	BB	K	SB	CS	AVG/OBP/SLG	TAv	VORP	BABIP	BRR	FRAA	WARP
2017	MIL	MLB	30	551	83	26	4	31	63	75	163	4	2	.247/.359/.518	.304	29.4	.309	-2.7	1B(108): -2.2, LF(25): -1.8	2.5
2018	*MIL*	*MLB*	*31*	*515*	*73*	*21*	*2*	*26*	*79*	*65*	*152*	*4*	*2*	*.235/.339/.468*	*.278*	*18.9*	*.294*	*-0.4*	*1B -1, LF 0*	*1.7*
2019	*MIL*	*MLB*	*32*	*507*	*74*	*21*	*2*	*26*	*76*	*65*	*152*	*3*	*1*	*.232/.339/.468*	*.285*	*19.3*	*.290*	*-1.7*	*1B 0, LF 0*	*2.0*

Breakout: 6% Improve: 37% Collapse: 8% Attrition: 10% MLB: 97% *Comparables: Fred McGriff, Richie Sexson, Mark McGwire*

People look at Thames' body-builder physique and his gaudy home-run totals, and they assume that his success in Korea stemmed from raw power and tiny ballparks. In truth, Korean baseball fans dubbed the Pepperdine alum "God" because he retooled his swing, dedicated himself to an intensive stretching regime and obsessed about plate discipline. Thames' 11-homer April and subsequent struggles had many tossing him aside as an early-season fluke. But that's dangerous. In September, he told the *Milwaukee Journal Sentinel* he was relearning the strike zone, which was smaller and stayed below the belt in Korea. That same month, he hit .328/.431/.574 in 22 games. Digging deeper, we see that Thames clearly adjusted to pitches above the belt. In the upper-third of the zone, he had a 20-plus-percent whiff rate between April and July. After August 1, according to Brooks Baseball, it dropped to under 10 percent. That adjustment translated to massive production in September. It will be fascinating to see whether he can carry that into 2018, replicating his Korean adjustment experience.

Jonathan Villar 2B Born: 05/02/91 Age: 27 Bats: B Throws: R Height: 6'1" Weight: 215 Origin: International Free Agent, 2008

YEAR	TEAM	LVL	AGE	PA	R	2B	3B	HR	RBI	BB	K	SB	CS	AVG/OBP/SLG	TAv	VORP	BABIP	BRR	FRAA	WARP
2015	FRE	AAA	24	313	59	13	5	5	32	27	77	35	9	.271/.342/.407	.276	24.0	.359	6.7	SS(59): -4.4, 3B(6): -0.4	1.9
2015	HOU	MLB	24	128	18	7	1	2	11	10	29	7	2	.284/.339/.414	.270	5.2	.360	-0.4	SS(22): 1.3, 3B(12): 1.1	0.8
2016	MIL	MLB	25	679	92	38	3	19	63	79	174	62	18	.285/.369/.457	.291	44.9	.373	-2.4	SS(108): 5.5, 3B(42): -4.1	4.7
2017	MIL	MLB	26	436	49	18	1	11	40	30	132	23	8	.241/.293/.372	.242	5.8	.330	1.6	2B(98): 2.7, CF(6): -0.1	0.8
2018	*MIL*	*MLB*	*27*	*423*	*64*	*18*	*3*	*10*	*38*	*38*	*117*	*30*	*9*	*.246/.312/.384*	*.244*	*9.2*	*.322*	*3.3*	*2B -1, 3B -1*	*0.8*
2019	*MIL*	*MLB*	*28*	*465*	*56*	*20*	*3*	*12*	*52*	*46*	*131*	*32*	*10*	*.244/.321/.398*	*.256*	*13.3*	*.320*	*0.5*	*2B 0, 3B -1*	*1.3*

Breakout: 6% Improve: 34% Collapse: 11% Attrition: 17% MLB: 92% *Comparables: Danny Espinosa, Chris Burke, Luis Gonzalez*

When can you safely characterize a breakout as a one-year fluke? Villar lit up the National League in 2016, putting up monster offensive numbers that made him a five-win player at a premium position. Fast-forward 12 months, and he wasn't much better than replacement level, playing himself out of a starting role. His walk rate declined, while his strikeout and chase rates increased. Thus, the development of his approach suddenly vanished without reason. The Dominican Republic native also looked lost against lefties to the tune of a .607 OPS, despite a career 50-point OPS split in the opposite direction. Evaluating Villar is tricky because some of the improvements disappeared, while some of the mainstays of his profile vanished. So, again, was 2016 or 2017 the actual fluke?

Stephen Vogt C Born: 11/01/84 Age: 33 Bats: L Throws: R Height: 6'0" Weight: 225 Origin: Round 12, 2007 Draft (#365 overall)

YEAR	TEAM	LVL	AGE	PA	R	2B	3B	HR	RBI	BB	K	SB	CS	AVG/OBP/SLG	TAv	VORP	BABIP	BRR	FRAA	WARP
2015	OAK	MLB	30	511	58	21	3	18	71	56	97	0	2	.261/.341/.443	.286	23.7	.290	-7.0	C(99): -11.1, 1B(25): -1.2	1.2
2016	OAK	MLB	31	532	54	30	2	14	56	35	83	0	0	.251/.305/.406	.262	19.0	.275	-3.0	C(113): -13.5, 1B(1): 0.0	0.6
2017	OAK	MLB	32	174	12	8	1	4	20	16	31	0	1	.217/.287/.357	.228	-0.4	.244	-1.7	C(43): -4.0, LF(1): -0.1	-0.4
2017	MIL	MLB	32	129	13	7	0	8	20	5	25	0	0	.254/.281/.508	.282	7.1	.256	-1.8	C(38): 7.2	1.4
2018	*MIL*	*MLB*	*33*	*377*	*43*	*17*	*2*	*13*	*49*	*30*	*69*	*0*	*0*	*.255/.316/.427*	*.257*	*14.6*	*.284*	*-0.8*	*C -8*	*0.5*
2019	*MIL*	*MLB*	*34*	*339*	*43*	*15*	*1*	*13*	*44*	*27*	*66*	*0*	*0*	*.250/.312/.431*	*.264*	*11.9*	*.278*	*-2.7*	*C -7*	*0.6*

Breakout: 1% Improve: 40% Collapse: 6% Attrition: 17% MLB: 87% *Comparables: Dioner Navarro, Josh Bard, Robinson Chirinos*

YEAR	TEAM	P. COUNT	FRM RUNS	BLK RUNS	THRW RUNS	TOT RUNS
2015	OAK	13004	-8.9	-0.7	0.7	-8.9
2016	OAK	15068	-10.8	-1.7	0.0	-12.5
2017	OAK	5443	-1.6	0.2	-1.6	-3.1
2017	MIL	4322	8.2	1.1	-2.1	7.2
2018	*MIL*	*12956*	*-4.0*	*-0.7*	*-1.2*	*-5.9*
2019	*MIL*	*11660*	*-3.8*	*-0.6*	*-1.1*	*-5.6*

Vogt sits at the end of your neighborhood bar, except he plies his trade behind the plate with a helmet, a chest pad and shin guards. He looks grizzled, as if he's 45, except he's just 33. Everything—his swing, his base running, his throwing—looks labored, yet it somehow works well enough because he wills it to work enough. Vogt has something important to tell you about hard work, about friendship, about communication, about trust ... about life. Just like that guy at the end of the bar.

Neil Walker 2B Born: 09/10/85 Age: 32 Bats: B Throws: R Height: 6'3" Weight: 210 Origin: Round 1, 2004 Draft (#11 overall)

YEAR	TEAM	LVL	AGE	PA	R	2B	3B	HR	RBI	BB	K	SB	CS	AVG/OBP/SLG	TAv	VORP	BABIP	BRR	FRAA	WARP
2015	PIT	MLB	29	603	69	32	3	16	71	44	110	4	1	.269/.328/.427	.274	25.7	.306	1.8	2B(146): 4.9	3.3
2016	NYN	MLB	30	458	57	9	1	23	55	42	84	3	1	.282/.347/.476	.300	31.2	.302	0.3	2B(111): 2.6	3.5
2017	NYN	MLB	31	299	40	13	2	10	36	27	47	0	1	.264/.339/.442	.279	12.6	.286	-1.5	2B(68): -5.0, 1B(3): 0.0	0.8
2017	MIL	MLB	31	149	19	8	0	4	13	28	30	0	1	.267/.409/.433	.305	10.0	.326	-0.7	2B(27): -1.1, 1B(14): 0.0	0.9
2018	*MIL*	*MLB*	*32*	*426*	*52*	*19*	*2*	*17*	*58*	*40*	*79*	*2*	*1*	*.260/.338/.451*	*.262*	*18.1*	*.286*	*-0.1*	*2B 0, 1B 0*	*2.0*
2019	*MIL*	*MLB*	*33*	*361*	*48*	*15*	*1*	*14*	*47*	*33*	*68*	*1*	*1*	*.255/.331/.436*	*.272*	*15.3*	*.281*	*-0.1*	*2B 0, 1B 0*	*1.6*

Breakout: 2% Improve: 38% Collapse: 2% Attrition: 6% MLB: 96% *Comparables: Brian Roberts, Orlando Hudson, Aaron Hill*

In baseball, there's something simultaneously comforting and forgettable about year-to-year consistency. Walker owns a .282 TAv over his nine-year major-league career, and he was right #onbrand with a .287 mark in 2017 between New York and Milwaukee. He's a reliable, veteran second baseman who has long been above average with the stick. Yet he's never made an All-Star squad, and there's a 75 percent chance the average baseball fan would guess he still plays for the Pittsburgh Pirates. Too many people focus on upside and breakout potential in baseball. Too many people advocate for the buy-low move, in the hopes of looking like geniuses six months down the road. More people need to embrace boring, dependable signings, like Walker will almost certainly prove to be in his first shot at free agency.

PITCHERS

Chase Anderson RHP Born: 11/30/87 Age: 30 Bats: R Throws: R Height: 6'1" Weight: 200 Origin: Round 9, 2009 Draft (#276 overall)

YEAR	TEAM	LVL	AGE	W	L	SV	G	GS	IP	H	HR	BB/9	K/9	K	GB%	BABIP	WHIP	ERA	DRA	WARP	MPH	CMD	PWR	STM
2015	ARI	MLB	27	6	6	0	27	27	152^{2}	158	18	2.4	6.5	111	44%	.302	1.30	4.30	5.21	-0.2	94.3	48	44	63
2016	MIL	MLB	28	9	11	0	31	30	151^{2}	155	28	3.1	7.1	120	38%	.287	1.37	4.39	6.00	-1.1	93.6	59	42	67
2017	MIL	MLB	29	12	4	0	25	25	141^{1}	113	14	2.6	8.5	133	41%	.265	1.09	2.74	4.05	2.4	94.9	59	45	61
2018	*MIL*	*MLB*	*30*	*11*	*10*	*0*	*29*	*29*	*174*	*167*	*26*	*3.0*	*8.3*	*160*	*42%*	*.290*	*1.28*	*4.33*	*4.54*	*1.3*	*93.5*	*56*	*44*	*63*
2019	*MIL*	*MLB*	*31*	*11*	*12*	*0*	*32*	*32*	208^{1}	*181*	*28*	*2.7*	*8.4*	*195*	*42%*	*.292*	*1.17*	*4.12*	*4.61*	*2.1*	*93.1*	*58*	*43*	*63*

Breakout: 12% Improve: 36% Collapse: 26% Attrition: 12% MLB: 85% *Comparables: Joe Saunders, Dustin McGowan, Jeff Niemann*

Thanks to a quality changeup, Anderson had always been a reverse-split guy. Righties torched the former ninth-round pick in 2016, to the tune of a .310/.369/.566 line, and previous years told a similar story. In 2017, though, they hit a meager .220/.290/.389 against him. While a velocity increase has helped, a new grip on his curveball seems to have been an "Uh oh, Happy learned how to putt" moment. Opponents only hit .167 (with an .056 ISO) against his curveball, which he threw more than 20 percent of the time to righties. He rarely hung the pitch, and it was one of the biggest reasons he became an above-average starter in 2017. There are questions about the sustainability of his success and whether his velocity spike proves long-lasting; however, the biggest news for Anderson was that he finally figured out how to retire righties.

Jacob Barnes RHP

Born: 04/14/90 Age: 28 Bats: R Throws: R Height: 6'2" Weight: 220 Origin: Round 14, 2011 Draft (#431 overall)

YEAR	TEAM	LVL	AGE	W	L	SV	G	GS	IP	H	HR	BB/9	K/9	K	GB%	BABIP	WHIP	ERA	DRA	WARP	MPH	CMD	PWR	STM
2015	BLX	AA	25	4	5	0	39	6	75	74	2	3.6	10.1	84	53%	.362	1.39	3.36	2.05	2.5				
2016	CSP	AAA	26	2	1	1	17	0	22^{1}	14	1	2.8	9.3	23	54%	.245	0.94	1.21	3.14	0.5				
2016	MIL	MLB	26	0	1	1	27	0	26^{2}	24	1	2.0	8.8	26	49%	.315	1.12	2.70	3.28	0.5	97.9	44	60	36
2017	MIL	MLB	27	3	4	2	73	0	72	57	8	4.1	10.0	80	54%	.272	1.25	4.00	3.39	1.4	98.7	54	69	53
2018	*MIL*	*MLB*	*28*	*3*	*3*	*2*	*58*	*0*	*61*	*54*	*7*	*4.1*	*9.7*	*67*	*49%*	*.295*	*1.32*	*3.80*	*4.02*	*0.6*	*97.9*	*52*	*68*	*46*
2019	*MIL*	*MLB*	*29*	*3*	*1*	*2*	*60*	*0*	*63^{1}*	*50*	*7*	*3.5*	*10.0*	*70*	*49%*	*.298*	*1.18*	*3.76*	*4.21*	*0.7*	*97.6*	*52*	*67*	*46*

Breakout: 22% Improve: 40% Collapse: 19% Attrition: 20% MLB: 73% *Comparables: Sammy Solis, Michael Blazek, Blake Treinen*

Barnes is a bit of a cross between Joe Nathan and Derrick Turnbow on the mound. He combines the demeanor of Nathan—snarling and huffing at opposing hitters—with the sudden, quick and violent delivery Brewers fans have long associated with Turnbow. However, Barnes has a raw arsenal that outweighs anything Turnbow—or even Nathan, frankly—ever offered. He pairs an upper-90s fastball with a devastating slider that regularly sits in the low-90s. Opposing teams only hit .181 against his slider all year, and his swinging-strike rate (15.6 percent) ranked in the top-20 among qualified pitchers. In terms of raw stuff, he occasionally looked better than teammate Corey Knebel, but control issues have kept Barnes from being anywhere near as effective as the current closer.

Corbin Burnes RHP

Born: 10/22/94 Age: 23 Bats: R Throws: R Height: 6'3" Weight: 205 Origin: Round 4, 2016 Draft (#111 overall)

YEAR	TEAM	LVL	AGE	W	L	SV	G	GS	IP	H	HR	BB/9	K/9	K	GB%	BABIP	WHIP	ERA	DRA	WARP	MPH	CMD	PWR	STM
2016	WIS	A	21	3	0	0	9	5	28^{2}	20	1	5.0	9.7	31	64%	.275	1.26	2.20	4.12	0.3				
2017	CAR	A+	22	5	0	0	10	10	60	37	1	2.4	8.4	56	54%	.243	0.88	1.05	1.81	2.4				
2017	BLX	AA	22	3	3	0	16	16	85^{2}	66	2	2.1	8.8	84	51%	.279	1.00	2.10	2.30	2.9				
2018	*MIL*	*MLB*	*23*	*1*	*1*	*0*	*3*	*3*	*15*	*14*	*2*	*3.8*	*9.7*	*17*	*47%*	*.295*	*1.32*	*4.35*	*4.58*	*0.1*				
2019	*MIL*	*MLB*	*24*	*9*	*11*	*0*	*31*	*31*	*201^{2}*	*167*	*30*	*4.0*	*9.5*	*213*	*47%*	*.293*	*1.27*	*4.49*	*5.04*	*1.1*				

Breakout: 21% Improve: 40% Collapse: 18% Attrition: 30% MLB: 65% *Comparables: Carl Edwards Jr., David Paulino, Zack Wheeler*

A three-year starter at St. Mary's (CA), Burnes improved his peripherals each year and showed better stuff as a junior. He dropped to the fourth round due to questions about his future role, his top-end velocity and his off-speed efficacy; however, after 181 1/3 professional innings, he's arguably a top-50 prospect. Burnes has worked with Brewers' pitching coaches to incorporate his lower half more into his delivery, and it appears to have paid dividends. His fastball now touches 97 mph, and his slider has become a legitimate swing-and-miss pitch. The right-hander also throws a solid changeup and a get-me-over curveball. What brings it all together, though, is his plus control and his no-shit approach on the mound. Burnes owns a career 1.74 ERA across four levels in his professional career and could see a big-league promotion in 2018 if his success continues.

Jhoulys Chacin RHP

Born: 01/07/88 Age: 30 Bats: R Throws: R Height: 6'3" Weight: 215 Origin: International Free Agent, 2004

YEAR	TEAM	LVL	AGE	W	L	SV	G	GS	IP	H	HR	BB/9	K/9	K	GB%	BABIP	WHIP	ERA	DRA	WARP	MPH	CMD	PWR	STM
2015	COH	AAA	27	1	3	0	7	7	42	39	3	3.2	5.4	25	45%	.271	1.29	3.21	5.06	0.1				
2015	RNO	AAA	27	6	3	0	13	13	86^{2}	79	3	3.1	6.5	63	51%	.292	1.26	3.22	2.79	2.5				
2015	ARI	MLB	27	2	1	0	5	4	26^{2}	24	4	3.4	7.1	21	51%	.263	1.27	3.38	6.68	-0.5	90.9	46	23	68
2016	ATL	MLB	28	1	2	0	5	5	26^{2}	29	4	2.7	9.1	27	50%	.321	1.39	5.40	4.17	0.3	92.4	46	41	65
2016	ANA	MLB	28	5	6	0	29	17	117^{1}	124	10	3.6	7.1	92	52%	.316	1.46	4.68	4.52	1.0	93.9	46	41	65
2017	SDN	MLB	29	13	10	0	32	32	180^{1}	157	19	3.6	7.6	153	50%	.272	1.27	3.89	4.13	2.9	93.2	49	37	75
2018	*MIL*	*MLB*	*30*	*8*	*8*	*0*	*24*	*24*	*136*	*128*	*17*	*3.5*	*7.9*	*121*	*49%*	*.288*	*1.30*	*4.24*	*4.44*	*1.1*	*92.5*	*48*	*38*	*70*
2019	*MIL*	*MLB*	*31*	*10*	*12*	*0*	*32*	*32*	*206*	*176*	*26*	*3.3*	*8.0*	*184*	*49%*	*.285*	*1.22*	*4.18*	*4.86*	*1.5*	*92.2*	*48*	*38*	*70*

Breakout: 9% Improve: 42% Collapse: 31% Attrition: 13% MLB: 89% *Comparables: Tanner Roark, Clay Buchholz, Alexi Ogando*

There are no shortage of reasons to fall in love with a city like San Diego, whether it's the weather, the beaches, the beer or the world-renowned zoo. And when a place is special to you, that place can sometimes return the favor—just ask Chacin. When starting at home in 2017, the journeyman had a 1.79 ERA, the best in baseball. He somehow managed to chuck his four-seamer faster than he ever had before, a feat all the more impressive in the context of the sub-90 wilderness in which he'd wandered throughout 2014 and 2015. The velocity spike helped, but the best season of his career arguably owed more to the embrace of his strengths: Chacin became a true fastball/slider pitcher, throwing one of those two pitches more than 70 percent of the time in 2017, after going above 50 percent only once before last season. His road ERA of 6.53 was fifth worst in baseball. Either that didn't go into his brochure or the Brewers missed it. They inked him to a two-year deal in December.

Zach Davies RHP

Born: 02/07/93 Age: 25 Bats: R Throws: R Height: 6'0" Weight: 155 Origin: Round 26, 2011 Draft (#785 overall)

YEAR	TEAM	LVL	AGE	W	L	SV	G	GS	IP	H	HR	BB/9	K/9	K	GB%	BABIP	WHIP	ERA	DRA	WARP	MPH	CMD	PWR	STM
2015	NOR	AAA	22	5	6	0	19	18	101^{1}	91	4	2.9	7.2	81	54%	.290	1.22	2.84	3.69	1.8				
2015	CSP	AAA	22	1	2	0	5	5	27	38	2	4.0	7.0	21	57%	.391	1.85	5.00	2.57	0.8				
2015	MIL	MLB	22	3	2	0	6	6	34	26	2	4.0	6.4	24	58%	.245	1.21	3.71	3.47	0.7	90.9	61	29	67
2016	MIL	MLB	23	11	7	0	28	28	163^{1}	166	20	2.1	7.4	135	47%	.302	1.25	3.97	4.24	2.1	91.4	81	35	72
2017	MIL	MLB	24	17	9	0	33	33	191^{1}	204	20	2.6	5.8	124	51%	.302	1.35	3.90	4.00	3.4	91.2	73	31	80
2018	*MIL*	*MLB*	*25*	*10*	*10*	*0*	*28*	*28*	*168*	*168*	*19*	*3.1*	*7.4*	*138*	*49%*	*.298*	*1.35*	*4.09*	*4.28*	*1.7*	*91.0*	*77*	*33*	*76*
2019	*MIL*	*MLB*	*26*	*12*	*11*	*0*	*32*	*32*	*207*	*192*	*23*	*2.5*	*7.9*	*182*	*49%*	*.308*	*1.21*	*3.83*	*4.28*	*2.8*	*90.8*	*78*	*33*	*78*

Breakout: 22% Improve: 51% Collapse: 22% Attrition: 14% MLB: 94% *Comparables: Martin Perez, Daniel Hudson, Tom Gorzelanny*

Despite two consecutive big-league seasons with a sub-4.00 ERA, Davies had a disastrous four-game start to the 2017 season that had Brewers fans ready to throw in the towel. After allowing 18 runs in his first 19 2/3 frames, though, Davies cruised with a 3.41 ERA over his final 171 2/3 innings. He's an intelligent hurler who mixes his four-pitch repertoire in all four quadrants, rarely hurting himself with free passes or too many home runs. As a soft-tossing changeup specialist, he's the epitome of a starting profile that flies under the radar because it doesn't look like the standard of success we've defined for this generation of pitchers. It's almost magical, in a sense. With two eyes you see a lack of velocity. With three you could see impeccable command and his 3.2 percent CSAA. With two eyes you see a person who could make a seamless cameo on *The Big Bang Theory*. With three you would see a quality mid-rotation starter with a career 4.05 DRA.

Yovani Gallardo RHP Born: 02/27/86 Age: 32 Bats: R Throws: R Height: 6'2" Weight: 205 Origin: Round 2, 2004 Draft (#46 overall)

YEAR	TEAM	LVL	AGE	W	L	SV	G	GS	IP	H	HR	BB/9	K/9	K	GB%	BABIP	WHIP	ERA	DRA	WARP	MPH	CMD	PWR	STM
2015	TEX	MLB	29	13	11	0	33	33	184^{1}	193	15	3.3	5.9	121	51%	.303	1.42	3.42	4.55	1.2	93.2	67	43	77
2016	NOR	AAA	30	1	0	0	2	2	10	5	2	3.6	9.0	10	32%	.130	0.90	3.60	4.06	0.1				
2016	BAL	MLB	30	6	8	0	23	23	118	126	16	4.7	6.5	85	44%	.304	1.58	5.42	6.33	-1.3	92.9	53	44	58
2017	SEA	MLB	31	5	10	1	28	22	130^{2}	138	24	4.1	6.5	94	45%	.286	1.52	5.72	5.69	-0.2	94.2	54	44	63
2018	*MIL*	*MLB*	*32*	*2*	*2*	*0*	*5*	*5*	*28*	*30*	*4*	*3.8*	*7.1*	*22*	*45%*	*.295*	*1.46*	*4.90*	*5.15*	*0.0*	*92.6*	*57*	*43*	*64*
2019	*MIL*	*MLB*	*33*	*10*	*12*	*0*	*31*	*31*	*196^{2}*	*187*	*27*	*3.4*	*7.1*	*154*	*45%*	*.297*	*1.33*	*4.96*	*5.28*	*0.6*	*92.5*	*54*	*43*	*62*

Breakout: 10% Improve: 48% Collapse: 21% Attrition: 12% MLB: 88% *Comparables: Barry Zito, Carlos Zambrano, Brad Penny*

Without the benefit of context, "good news" sounds like cause for celebration. But context matters, as there is a significant difference between doubling your investment on a penny stock versus making a mint on your Google shares. Last season Gallardo's velocity spiked to its highest since 2011, but this "good news" was tempered by the fact that his results were still extremely poor. The main culprit was more balls left in the strike zone than any season since 2009. "Peak Gallardo" would be worth rostering by any major-league team, and it's perhaps appropriate that the Brewers, the last club to see said peak, signed him to a one-year deal in December.

Matt Garza RHP Born: 11/26/83 Age: 34 Bats: R Throws: R Height: 6'4" Weight: 220 Origin: Round 1, 2005 Draft (#25 overall)

YEAR	TEAM	LVL	AGE	W	L	SV	G	GS	IP	H	HR	BB/9	K/9	K	GB%	BABIP	WHIP	ERA	DRA	WARP	MPH	CMD	PWR	STM
2015	MIL	MLB	31	6	14	0	26	25	148^{2}	176	23	3.5	6.3	104	47%	.319	1.57	5.63	6.18	-2.0	95.1	53	49	67
2016	WIS	A	32	0	2	0	3	3	11^{1}	13	1	0.8	7.9	10	56%	.364	1.24	4.76	3.77	0.2				
2016	MIL	MLB	32	6	8	0	19	19	101^{2}	117	11	3.2	6.2	70	57%	.311	1.50	4.51	5.77	-0.5	94.7	52	53	61
2017	MIL	MLB	33	6	9	0	24	22	114^{2}	121	17	3.5	6.2	79	42%	.287	1.45	4.94	5.46	0.1	93.8	53	45	57
2018	*MIL*	*MLB*	*34*	*6*	*7*	*0*	*18*	*18*	*101^{2}*	*107*	*16*	*3.5*	*7.0*	*79*	*48%*	*.307*	*1.45*	*5.01*	*5.62*	*0.0*	*93.3*	*52*	*48*	*60*
2019	*MIL*	*MLB*	*35*	*8*	*11*	*0*	*27*	*27*	*159^{1}*	*170*	*25*	*3.5*	*6.6*	*116*	*48%*	*.314*	*1.46*	*5.15*	*5.76*	*-0.2*	*92.6*	*51*	*47*	*58*

Breakout: 10% Improve: 48% Collapse: 18% Attrition: 12% MLB: 91% *Comparables: Jake Westbrook, Jason Vargas, Jason Marquis*

Garza has declining stuff and mediocre command. In last year's *Annual* we pointed out that the right-hander posted a 50-plus-percent ground-ball rate for the first time in his career, citing that as a positive development on which to build. That silver lining is now gone, and we're left with a mid-thirties pitcher without any clear strength and growing weaknesses. That's not a CV header primed to generate many clicks on LinkedIn.

Junior Guerra RHP Born: 01/16/85 Age: 33 Bats: R Throws: R Height: 6'0" Weight: 205 Origin: International Free Agent, 2001

YEAR	TEAM	LVL	AGE	W	L	SV	G	GS	IP	H	HR	BB/9	K/9	K	GB%	BABIP	WHIP	ERA	DRA	WARP	MPH	CMD	PWR	STM
2015	BIR	AA	30	2	3	0	5	3	19^{2}	15	2	1.8	11.9	26	48%	.325	0.97	2.29	1.63	0.8				
2015	CHA	MLB	30	0	0	0	3	0	4	7	1	2.2	6.8	3	57%	.462	2.00	6.75	2.91	0.1	96.7			48
2015	CHR	AAA	30	2	4	7	26	8	63^{2}	44	5	4.1	11.2	79	44%	.260	1.15	3.39	2.21	2.1				
2016	CSP	AAA	31	0	2	0	5	5	26^{2}	18	2	3.7	8.4	25	40%	.235	1.09	4.05	3.32	0.6				
2016	MIL	MLB	31	9	3	0	20	20	121^{2}	94	10	3.2	7.4	100	47%	.250	1.13	2.81	4.01	1.9	95.5	34	52	62
2017	CSP	AAA	32	2	2	0	6	6	30	27	0	3.6	6.0	20	47%	.303	1.30	2.10	6.62	-0.3				
2017	MIL	MLB	32	1	4	0	21	14	70^{1}	61	18	5.5	8.6	67	36%	.236	1.48	5.12	7.03	-1.2	93.9	37	49	48
2018	*MIL*	*MLB*	*33*	*4*	*4*	*0*	*11*	*11*	*66*	*62*	*11*	*3.9*	*8.7*	*64*	*43%*	*.287*	*1.33*	*4.67*	*4.91*	*0.2*	*93.8*	*35*	*50*	*52*
2019	*MIL*	*MLB*	*34*	*11*	*12*	*0*	*32*	*32*	*205*	*173*	*30*	*3.5*	*8.5*	*194*	*43%*	*.28*	*1.23*	*4.56*	*5.11*	*1.1*	*93.3*	*35*	*50*	*52*

Breakout: 11% Improve: 35% Collapse: 18% Attrition: 14% MLB: 69% *Comparables: Daisuke Matsuzaka, Clay Hensley, Eric Stults*

Never let the facts get in the way of a good narrative, right? Guerra proved to be one of the most heartwarming stories of 2016. After stints in the Mexican League, the American Association, and even Italy, the right-hander became the ace of the 2016 Brewers' rotation as a 31-year-old rookie. DRA, however, saw through the shiny narrative, and it proved prescient in 2017. Guerra injured his calf in April and never could find the strike zone once he returned; his signature split-fingered fastball was the most fickle of the bunch. If he rediscovers the form that made him successful as a rookie, perhaps he can work his way back into a big-league rotation. Considering how long it took the first time, it doesn't seem wise to expect a rebound in 2018.

Josh Hader LHP Born: 04/07/94 Age: 24 Bats: L Throws: L Height: 6'3" Weight: 185 Origin: Round 19, 2012 Draft (#582 overall)

YEAR	TEAM	LVL	AGE	W	L	SV	G	GS	IP	H	HR	BB/9	K/9	K	GB%	BABIP	WHIP	ERA	DRA	WARP	MPH	CMD	PWR	STM
2015	CCH	AA	21	3	3	1	17	10	65^{1}	60	5	3.3	9.5	69	42%	.301	1.29	3.17	3.29	1.4				
2015	BLX	AA	21	1	4	0	7	7	38^{2}	27	3	2.6	11.6	50	47%	.282	0.98	2.79	1.79	1.5				
2016	BLX	AA	22	2	1	0	11	11	57	38	1	3.0	11.5	73	41%	.291	1.00	0.95	1.47	2.5				
2016	CSP	AAA	22	1	7	0	14	14	69	63	5	4.7	11.5	88	43%	.345	1.43	5.22	2.78	2.0				
2017	CSP	AAA	23	3	4	0	12	12	52	49	14	5.4	8.8	51	37%	.265	1.54	5.37	8.03	-1.3				
2017	MIL	MLB	23	2	3	0	35	0	47^{2}	25	4	4.2	12.8	68	36%	.233	0.99	2.08	3.79	0.7	96.8	46	69	54
2018	*MIL*	*MLB*	*24*	*3*	*3*	*0*	*63*	*0*	*67*	*53*	*10*	*4.3*	*11.6*	*86*	*40%*	*.282*	*1.25*	*3.99*	*4.18*	*0.6*	*96.6*	*47*	*71*	*56*
2019	*MIL*	*MLB*	*25*	*3*	*1*	*0*	*62*	*0*	65^{1}	*47*	*9*	*3.8*	*11.5*	*84*	*40%*	*.281*	*1.13*	*3.92*	*4.40*	*0.6*	*96.4*	*48*	*71*	*56*

Breakout: 23% Improve: 58% Collapse: 16% Attrition: 20% MLB: 81% *Comparables: Henry Owens, Eric Surkamp, Vincent Velasquez*

Hader blew away the opposition in his rookie campaign, compiling a 36.2 percent strikeout rate. More importantly for the Brewers, the lefty stabilized a bullpen that tested various implosion techniques throughout May and June. The crazy thing, though, was that he dominated with one pitch. Only six pitchers (min. 40 IP) threw their fastball more often than Hader, but the pitch still finished the season with an 18.1 percent whiff rate. Even Kenley Jansen's famous cutter only whiffs batters 13 percent of the time. Hader might move to the rotation in 2018. If he does, he'll need to throw his fastball less often and prove he can consistently retire right-handers. He'll also need to show that his skinny frame and unorthodox delivery can hold up over five-plus innings every fifth day, and that he can sequence better when seeing hitters multiple times in the same game. The stuff is there—he even flashed a decent changeup down the stretch—but there's still a good chance Hader winds up a high-leverage reliever. Judging from his 2017 performance, though, that can still be an impact role.

Jeremy Jeffress RHP Born: 09/21/87 Age: 30 Bats: R Throws: R Height: 6'0" Weight: 205 Origin: Round 1, 2006 Draft (#16 overall)

YEAR	TEAM	LVL	AGE	W	L	SV	G	GS	IP	H	HR	BB/9	K/9	K	GB%	BABIP	WHIP	ERA	DRA	WARP	MPH	CMD	PWR	STM
2015	MIL	MLB	27	5	0	0	72	0	68	64	5	2.9	8.9	67	60%	.314	1.26	2.65	3.41	1.1	97.7	36	67	51
2016	MIL	MLB	28	2	2	27	47	0	44^{2}	45	2	2.2	7.1	35	59%	.312	1.25	2.22	3.34	0.8	98.3	45	63	43
2016	TEX	MLB	28	1	0	0	12	0	13^{1}	10	0	4.7	4.7	7	70%	.270	1.27	2.70	3.48	0.2	96.9	45	63	43
2017	TEX	MLB	29	1	2	0	39	0	40^{2}	49	8	4.2	6.4	29	56%	.328	1.67	5.31	6.12	-0.4	96.4	48	60	49
2017	MIL	MLB	29	4	0	0	22	1	24^{2}	24	2	5.5	8.0	22	65%	.301	1.58	3.65	7.60	-0.7	96.7	48	60	49
2018	*MIL*	*MLB*	*30*	*3*	*3*	*2*	*54*	*0*	56^{2}	*57*	*7*	*4.1*	*7.6*	*48*	*55%*	*.303*	*1.47*	*4.57*	*4.63*	*0.2*	*96.5*	*44*	*62*	*47*
2019	*MIL*	*MLB*	*31*	*2*	*1*	*1*	*44*	*0*	*47*	*45*	*5*	*4.0*	*7.7*	*40*	*55%*	*.318*	*1.40*	*4.44*	*4.98*	*0.1*	*96.0*	*46*	*61*	*47*

Breakout: 27% Improve: 53% Collapse: 23% Attrition: 16% MLB: 87% *Comparables: Chad Qualls, Dan Jennings, Marc Rzepczynski*

Jeffress finding success after a midseason trade back to Milwaukee has a nice narrative baked into it. He started working his way back into leverage situations, showing high-90s velocity and that old swagger. His quasi-renaissance was more than just a return to comfortable confines, though. The right-hander started leaning on his splitter, upward of 27 percent of the time in September. He'd never even thrown it 10 percent of the time prior to the July trade, but it was a devastating pitch for him. It's one of the reasons he posted a 65.3 percent ground-ball rate with the Brewers, which would've been good enough for sixth in all of baseball (min. 50 IP). The warts remain—he still can't find the strike zone with any meaningful consistency—but Jeffress's splitter gives him a legitimate new weapon with which to miss bats and erase the extra baserunners he'll inevitably allow via the walk.

Corey Knebel RHP Born: 11/26/91 Age: 26 Bats: R Throws: R Height: 6'4" Weight: 220 Origin: Round 1, 2013 Draft (#39 overall)

YEAR	TEAM	LVL	AGE	W	L	SV	G	GS	IP	H	HR	BB/9	K/9	K	GB%	BABIP	WHIP	ERA	DRA	WARP	MPH	CMD	PWR	STM
2015	CSP	AAA	23	1	2	6	16	0	15^{1}	14	1	4.1	12.9	22	42%	.371	1.37	4.70	1.92	0.5				
2015	MIL	MLB	23	0	0	0	48	0	50^{1}	44	8	3.0	10.4	58	50%	.290	1.21	3.22	3.41	0.8	97.5	44	60	50
2016	CSP	AAA	24	1	0	2	11	2	13^{2}	5	0	2.0	9.2	14	66%	.172	0.59	1.32	2.08	0.5				
2016	MIL	MLB	24	1	4	2	35	0	32^{2}	32	3	4.4	10.5	38	43%	.333	1.47	4.68	4.55	0.2	97.7	60	60	46
2017	MIL	MLB	25	1	4	39	76	0	76	48	6	4.7	14.9	126	39%	.311	1.16	1.78	2.44	2.3	98.9	59	70	56
2018	*MIL*	*MLB*	*26*	*3*	*3*	*37*	*58*	*0*	*61*	*48*	*8*	*4.2*	*12.6*	*86*	*44%*	*.297*	*1.25*	*3.37*	*3.67*	*0.9*	*98.0*	*57*	*67*	*52*
2019	*MIL*	*MLB*	*27*	*3*	*1*	*33*	*60*	*0*	63^{1}	*44*	*9*	*4.2*	*12.9*	*90*	*44%*	*.299*	*1.16*	*3.65*	*4.09*	*0.8*	*97.9*	*59*	*68*	*52*

Breakout: 32% Improve: 54% Collapse: 25% Attrition: 9% MLB: 92% *Comparables: Ken Giles, Rex Brothers, Sean Doolittle*

So much about Knebel's life screams "Texas": He was born in Denton, went to college at UT-Austin, stands 6-foot-4 and has a four-seamer that touches triple digits to go with a curveball that falls off the table. That profile helped Knebel become one of the best relievers in baseball in 2017. He posted the 12th-best DRA and sixth-best cFIP of any major-league pitcher (min. 50 IP), which suggests his breakout performance wasn't a fluke. He tied with Craig Kimbrel for the most strikeouts by a reliever and had two more than teammate Zach Davies notched in his 33 starts. Despite his background Knebel is a die-hard Packers fan, which may endear him to the good people of Milwaukee, although perhaps not as much as his dominance in the ninth.

Caden Lemons RHP Born: 12/02/98 Age: 19 Bats: R Throws: R Height: 6'6" Weight: 175 Origin: Round 2, 2017 Draft (#46 overall)

YEAR	TEAM	LVL	AGE	W	L	SV	G	GS	IP	H	HR	BB/9	K/9	K	GB%	BABIP	WHIP	ERA	DRA	WARP	MPH	CMD	PWR	STM
2018	*MIL*	*MLB*	*19*	*1*	*3*	*0*	*7*	*7*	32^{1}	*37*	*11*	*5.5*	*7.9*	*28*	*39%*	*.293*	*1.76*	*7.55*	*8.53*	*-1.0*				
2019	*MIL*	*MLB*	*20*	*2*	*6*	*0*	*25*	*25*	146^{2}	*149*	*31*	*5.3*	*7.0*	*115*	*39%*	*.288*	*1.61*	*6.41*	*7.22*	*-2.0*				

Comparables: Deolis Guerra, Adrian Houser, David Holmberg

The lanky Lemons resembles a Stretch Armstrong figurine more than a major-league pitcher, but his long levers and quick arm enticed the Brewers to spend $1.45 million and a second-round pick on him in June. The right-hander already boasts a fastball in the mid-90s, and the organization feels he has more in the tank. As Scouting Director Tod Johnson told MLB.com, "He throws hard now, and we think he's going to throw really hard in the future." Expect Lemons to move at a glacial pace through the ranks—and expect his command to be shaky as he tries to figure out how to control his long limbs—but few young arms have his kind of extreme projectability.

Jorge Lopez RHP Born: 02/10/93 Age: 25 Bats: R Throws: R Height: 6'3" Weight: 195 Origin: Round 2, 2011 Draft (#70 overall)

YEAR	TEAM	LVL	AGE	W	L	SV	G	GS	IP	H	HR	BB/9	K/9	K	GB%	BABIP	WHIP	ERA	DRA	WARP	MPH	CMD	PWR	STM
2015	BLX	AA	22	12	5	0	24	24	143^{1}	105	9	3.3	8.6	137	54%	.259	1.10	2.26	2.88	3.8				
2015	MIL	MLB	22	1	1	0	2	2	10	14	0	4.5	9.0	10	57%	.467	1.90	5.40	4.93	0.0	96.0			58
2016	CSP	AAA	23	1	7	0	17	16	79^{1}	101	12	6.2	7.5	66	58%	.355	1.97	6.81	6.65	-1.2				
2016	BLX	AA	23	2	4	0	8	8	45^{1}	45	5	3.2	9.3	47	48%	.323	1.35	3.97	2.83	1.2				
2017	MIL	MLB	24	0	0	0	1	0	2	4	0	4.5	0.0	0	44%	.444	2.50	4.50	7.65	-0.1	96.1			58
2017	BLX	AA	24	8	8	7	39	13	103^{2}	92	7	3.3	9.1	105	49%	.301	1.25	4.25	3.50	1.9				
2018	*MIL*	*MLB*	*25*	*1*	*1*	*0*	*8*	*3*	*20*	*19*	*3*	*4.2*	*9.4*	*21*	*48%*	*.299*	*1.46*	*4.80*	*4.96*	*0.0*	*95.7*			*59*
2019	*MIL*	*MLB*	*26*	*7*	*8*	*1*	*57*	*19*	153^{2}	*143*	*24*	*4.0*	*9.6*	*164*	*48%*	*.321*	*1.38*	*4.67*	*5.24*	*0.4*	*95.3*			*60*

Breakout: 14% Improve: 20% Collapse: 18% Attrition: 40% MLB: 49% *Comparables: Matt Shoemaker, Daniel Winkler, Francisco Cruceta*

It's been a winding road for the former top-100 prospect. Lopez officially shifted to the bullpen in June, where his fastball and hammer curve perhaps profile best. However, poor control remains his bugaboo and has prevented his quality stuff from playing at the big-league level. The Brewers' pitcher-unfriendly Triple-A affiliate in Colorado Springs was thought to be one of the reasons for his downfall in 2016, so Lopez spent much of last season in Biloxi. A successful August prompted a big-league return in September, though the right-hander only appeared in a single game. While Lopez's big-league future may be murky, the best news of the 2017 campaign came when he and his family successfully managed to leave Puerto Rico following Hurricane Maria.

Kodi Medeiros LHP Born: 05/25/96 Age: 22 Bats: L Throws: L Height: 6'2" Weight: 180 Origin: Round 1, 2014 Draft (#12 overall)

YEAR	TEAM	LVL	AGE	W	L	SV	G	GS	IP	H	HR	BB/9	K/9	K	GB%	BABIP	WHIP	ERA	DRA	WARP	MPH	CMD	PWR	STM
2015	WIS	A	19	4	5	1	25	16	93^{1}	79	0	3.9	9.1	94	65%	.307	1.27	4.44	3.08	2.3				
2016	BRV	A+	20	4	12	0	23	22	85	102	4	6.7	6.8	64	55%	.356	1.94	5.93	10.45	-4.8				
2017	CAR	A+	21	8	9	1	27	18	128^{1}	115	7	3.7	8.5	121	48%	.299	1.31	4.98	4.45	1.1				
2018	*MIL*	*MLB*	*22*	*6*	*7*	*1*	*40*	*19*	*105*	*103*	*17*	*5.2*	*9.5*	*111*	*48%*	*.323*	*1.56*	*5.05*	*5.69*	*-0.3*				
2019	*MIL*	*MLB*	*23*	*3*	*5*	*0*	*21*	*14*	*101*	*98*	*18*	*4.7*	*9.5*	*107*	*48%*	*.324*	*1.49*	*5.32*	*5.99*	*-0.4*				

Breakout: 6% Improve: 7% Collapse: 0% Attrition: 7% MLB: 11% *Comparables: Victor Alcantara, Robert Whalen, Jayson Aquino*

Medeiros possesses many major-league qualities as a pitcher: He spins a nasty slider, severely suppresses home runs and is a lefty with low-90s velocity. Such a package should give him a high floor as a big-league reliever, with intriguing upside as a late-inning guy if enough clicks. Fairly or not, as an unexpected first-round pick, the story with Medeiros has always been what he lacks. His slight frame and side-armed delivery make it unlikely that he'll stick as a starter. Moreover, his control often has a "Dick Cheney while hunting" vibe to it. The latter could cause him to stall out in the upper minors—he has never posted an ERA below 4.44 in his professional career—but his positive qualities still should help him give left-handed hitters fits out of the big-league bullpen someday.

Jimmy Nelson RHP Born: 06/05/89 Age: 29 Bats: R Throws: R Height: 6'6" Weight: 250 Origin: Round 2, 2010 Draft (#64 overall)

YEAR	TEAM	LVL	AGE	W	L	SV	G	GS	IP	H	HR	BB/9	K/9	K	GB%	BABIP	WHIP	ERA	DRA	WARP	MPH	CMD	PWR	STM
2015	MIL	MLB	26	11	13	0	30	30	177^{1}	163	18	3.3	7.5	148	52%	.285	1.29	4.11	4.20	1.9	96.0	39	54	73
2016	MIL	MLB	27	8	16	0	32	32	179^{1}	186	25	4.3	7.0	140	51%	.299	1.52	4.62	5.83	-1.0	95.5	30	59	78
2017	MIL	MLB	28	12	6	0	29	29	175^{1}	171	16	2.5	10.2	199	51%	.340	1.25	3.49	3.58	3.9	95.5	47	56	76
2018	*MIL*	*MLB*	*29*	*2*	*2*	*0*	*6*	*6*	*34*	*31*	*4*	*3.1*	*9.5*	*36*	*50%*	*.296*	*1.25*	*3.74*	*3.91*	*0.5*	*95.0*	*39*	*57*	*76*
2019	*MIL*	*MLB*	*30*	*11*	*10*	*0*	*32*	*32*	*208*	*173*	*22*	*3.0*	*9.5*	*220*	*50%*	*.303*	*1.17*	*3.66*	*4.10*	*3.0*	*94.7*	*39*	*57*	*76*

Breakout: 27% Improve: 47% Collapse: 27% Attrition: 18% MLB: 95% *Comparables: Joe Kelly, Tyson Ross, Roberto Hernandez*

It's an old adage that baseball is a game of adjustments. While insightful, such a statement often mistakenly implies immediacy: that players make adjustments and different results closely follow. For some pitchers, like Nelson, the statistical improvements don't reflect the work behind-the-scenes for the better part of a year. Nelson shortened his delivery in the summer of 2016, slowed his tempo, and strengthened his legs to enhance his stability on the mound. As he struggled to implement the changes that year, the right-hander posted a 6.10 ERA in the second half. In 2017, though, things came together. The mechanical tweaks helped keep his arm path more consistent, leading to a career-best 6.6 percent walk rate and a massive jump in his strikeouts. The whiff rate on his curve alone jumped over six percentage points (to 15.3 percent), giving him three legitimate swing-and-miss pitches and a repertoire that worked against righties and lefties alike. Nelson credits pitching coach Derek Johnson for many of his mechanical improvements, but it's a credit to both Nelson and the Brewers that they remained patient and committed to the changes. They refused to panic when the results dramatically worsened. As a reward to both parties, Nelson now looks to be a legitimate number-two starter, depending on how a fluke base-running-related shoulder injury recovers over the offseason.

Luis Ortiz RHP Born: 09/22/95 Age: 22 Bats: R Throws: R Height: 6'3" Weight: 230 Origin: Round 1, 2014 Draft (#30 overall)

YEAR	TEAM	LVL	AGE	W	L	SV	G	GS	IP	H	HR	BB/9	K/9	K	GB%	BABIP	WHIP	ERA	DRA	WARP	MPH	CMD	PWR	STM
2015	HIC	A	19	4	1	0	13	13	50	45	1	1.6	8.3	46	45%	.306	1.08	1.80	3.35	1.1				
2016	HDS	A+	20	3	2	0	7	6	27^{2}	23	4	2.0	9.1	28	51%	.264	1.05	2.60	2.67	0.9				
2016	FRI	AA	20	1	4	1	9	8	39^{2}	47	3	1.6	7.7	34	47%	.352	1.36	4.08	2.61	1.2				
2016	BLX	AA	20	2	2	0	6	6	23^{1}	26	2	3.9	6.2	16	33%	.316	1.54	1.93	6.51	-0.4				
2017	BLX	AA	21	4	7	0	22	20	94^{1}	79	12	3.5	7.5	79	36%	.258	1.23	4.01	4.84	0.3				
2018	*MIL*	*MLB*	*22*	*1*	*1*	*0*	*3*	*3*	*15*	*15*	*3*	*3.3*	*8.7*	*15*	*39%*	*.296*	*1.38*	*4.79*	*5.05*	*0.0*				
2019	*MIL*	*MLB*	*23*	*8*	*11*	*0*	*31*	*31*	196^{1}	*181*	*37*	*2.9*	*9.1*	*199*	*39%*	*.302*	*1.24*	*4.74*	*5.32*	*0.5*				

Breakout: 5% Improve: 10% Collapse: 3% Attrition: 12% MLB: 18% *Comparables: Steve Garrison, Jon Moscot, Rudy Owens*

Scouts have talked about Ortiz for so long that it seems scientifically impossible that he only turned 22 years old last September. The mediocre ERA and prospect fatigue have slightly devalued the right-hander's stock value, but he still possesses the mid-rotation starter kit. Ortiz has an effective low-90s fastball that can show higher when he needs it, backing it with a tight slider and fringy changeup. The

Brewers babied him a bit, only allowing him to go more than five innings five times, but he also struggled with a hamstring injury over the summer. The question remains as to whether the Brewers have been protecting his arm or he simply doesn't have the stamina to pitch deep into contests. If the training wheels come off and Ortiz can handle a 120-plus-inning campaign with solid run-prevention numbers, he'll reappear on top-prospect lists in a hurry. Unless, of course, he loses that eligibility.

Freddy Peralta RHP Born: 06/04/96 Age: 22 Bats: R Throws: R Height: 5'11" Weight: 175 Origin: International Free Agent, 2013

YEAR	TEAM	LVL	AGE	W	L	SV	G	GS	IP	H	HR	BB/9	K/9	K	GB%	BABIP	WHIP	ERA	DRA	WARP	MPH	CMD	PWR	STM
2015	MRN	RK	19	2	3	0	11	9	57	52	1	1.3	10.6	67	53%	.333	1.05	4.11	1.68	2.6				
2016	WIS	A	20	4	1	2	16	8	60	45	3	3.6	11.6	77	35%	.292	1.15	2.85	3.31	1.1				
2016	BRV	A+	20	0	3	0	8	2	22	27	4	4.9	8.2	20	51%	.365	1.77	5.73	5.17	0.0				
2017	CAR	A+	21	1	3	0	12	8	56^{1}	39	6	5.0	12.5	78	39%	.268	1.24	3.04	3.49	1.1				
2017	BLX	AA	21	2	5	1	13	11	63^{2}	38	2	4.4	12.9	91	44%	.267	1.08	2.26	2.15	2.3				
2018	*MIL*	*MLB*	*22*	*1*	*1*	*0*	*19*	*0*	*20*	*17*	*3*	*4.7*	*11.8*	*27*	*38%*	*.295*	*1.36*	*4.47*	*4.57*	*0.1*				
2019	*MIL*	*MLB*	*23*	*2*	*1*	*0*	*49*	*0*	*52*	*42*	*9*	*4.2*	*11.5*	*66*	*38%*	*.307*	*1.28*	*4.45*	*5.01*	*0.1*				

Breakout: 17% Improve: 25% Collapse: 4% Attrition: 14% MLB: 33% *Comparables: Tommy Hanson, Christian Friedrich, Daniel Norris*

Peralta doesn't look the part. If he says he's six-foot, he's probably lying, and he's slightly built. His fastball isn't overpowering, nor is his control remarkable, but struck out 33.4 percent of the batters he faced in 2017. Why? Everything moves. The fastball sits in the low-90s, but sinks, cuts, dives and seemingly disappears on hitters. It has a high spin rate, which augments the deception he naturally gets from his mechanics. But Peralta also has a late-breaking slider and an idea of what he's doing on the mound. While it's not a profile without warts, it's one that could potentially start at the big-league level. The fastball might not be big enough for a back-end relief role, but he's a young man with a growing track record and a good idea how to pitch off a deceptively good fastball.

Nick Ramirez LHP Born: 08/01/89 Age: 28 Bats: L Throws: L Height: 6'3" Weight: 225 Origin: Round 4, 2011 Draft (#131 overall)

YEAR	TEAM	LVL	AGE	W	L	SV	G	GS	IP	H	HR	BB/9	K/9	K	GB%	BABIP	WHIP	ERA	DRA	WARP	MPH	CMD	PWR	STM
2017	BLX	AA	27	7	4	3	48	0	79	56	4	2.7	6.4	56	49%	.230	1.01	1.37	4.28	0.5				
2018	*MIL*	*MLB*	*28*	*2*	*1*	*2*	*49*	*0*	*52*	*51*	*8*	*3.6*	*7.8*	*45*	*42%*	*.300*	*1.38*	*4.82*	*5.41*	*-0.2*				
2019	*MIL*	*MLB*	*29*	*1*	*0*	*1*	*18*	*0*	*29^{2}*	*31*	*5*	*5.0*	*6.0*	*20*	*42%*	*.303*	*1.60*	*6.02*	*6.77*	*-0.5*				

Breakout: 3% Improve: 5% Collapse: 2% Attrition: 4% MLB: 7% *Comparables: Jean Machi, Jordan De Jong, Nick Christiani*

A former fourth-round draft pick out of Cal State Fullerton, Ramirez possesses all the right tools to become a bona fide Milwaukee cult hero as the Millennial Brooks Kieschnick. The southpaw transitioned to the mound after six years as a slugging first baseman and held left-handed hitters to a .512 OPS (we know what you're thinking, but he held righties to a .565 OPS). What's more, Ramirez still clobbered a couple of pinch-hit homers, just to remind fans that the monster who hit 35 collegiate homers in 617 at-bats still needs to eat.

Brent Suter LHP Born: 08/29/89 Age: 28 Bats: L Throws: L Height: 6'5" Weight: 195 Origin: Round 31, 2012 Draft (#965 overall)

YEAR	TEAM	LVL	AGE	W	L	SV	G	GS	IP	H	HR	BB/9	K/9	K	GB%	BABIP	WHIP	ERA	DRA	WARP	MPH	CMD	PWR	STM
2015	BLX	AA	25	5	3	0	20	11	83	71	2	3.6	6.9	64	48%	.296	1.25	1.95	3.10	1.9				
2015	CSP	AAA	25	3	1	0	6	6	35^{1}	35	4	1.5	4.8	19	48%	.277	1.16	3.31	4.18	0.4				
2016	CSP	AAA	26	6	6	2	26	15	110^{2}	129	5	1.1	6.1	75	41%	.348	1.29	3.50	2.83	3.1				
2016	MIL	MLB	26	2	2	0	14	2	21^{2}	25	3	2.1	6.2	15	44%	.328	1.38	3.32	7.99	-0.7	86.9	63	27	57
2017	CSP	AAA	27	3	1	0	10	8	36^{2}	42	5	2.0	9.3	38	46%	.359	1.36	4.42	2.50	1.3				
2017	MIL	MLB	27	3	2	0	22	14	81^{2}	83	8	2.4	7.1	64	46%	.306	1.29	3.42	4.93	0.5	88.2	63	22	55
2018	*MIL*	*MLB*	*28*	*6*	*6*	*0*	*37*	*13*	*99*	*104*	*14*	*3.1*	*7.3*	*81*	*44%*	*.302*	*1.40*	*4.54*	*4.68*	*0.5*	*87.4*	*63*	*23*	*56*
2019	*MIL*	*MLB*	*29*	*8*	*8*	*0*	*59*	*20*	*159^{1}*	*163*	*21*	*2.7*	*7.4*	*131*	*44%*	*.322*	*1.32*	*4.32*	*4.83*	*1.1*	*87.0*	*63*	*23*	*56*

Breakout: 19% Improve: 36% Collapse: 17% Attrition: 26% MLB: 59% *Comparables: Andrew Albers, A.J. Schugel, Chris Heston*

Suter's best known for his "Raptor Run"—just Google it—but the left-hander plugged a massive midseason hole in the Brewers' rotation once Chase Anderson went down with an oblique injury. He posted a 3.45 ERA as a starter despite barely cracking 85 mph with the fastball and helped Milwaukee remain in the wild card race until late September. Suter lacks a long-term starter profile, though, as his raw stuff gives him a razor-thin margin: Opposing teams hit .286/.304/.477 the second time they saw him and an even more robust .386/.449/.636 the third time. Lefties only hit .192/.259/.282 on the year against Suter, though, so he could carve out a big-league career as a LOOGY.

Wei-Chung Wang LHP Born: 04/25/92 Age: 26 Bats: L Throws: L Height: 6'2" Weight: 185 Origin: International Free Agent, 2011

YEAR	TEAM	LVL	AGE	W	L	SV	G	GS	IP	H	HR	BB/9	K/9	K	GB%	BABIP	WHIP	ERA	DRA	WARP	MPH	CMD	PWR	STM
2015	BRV	A+	23	10	6	0	25	25	139^{2}	146	9	2.5	5.9	91	44%	.303	1.32	3.54	4.90	0.3				
2016	BLX	AA	24	6	5	0	19	19	107^{1}	102	7	2.8	7.6	91	47%	.310	1.26	3.52	3.58	2.0				
2016	CSP	AAA	24	1	3	0	5	5	26	32	2	0.7	8.0	23	34%	.366	1.31	4.85	4.67	0.2				
2017	CSP	AAA	25	6	2	1	47	0	57	57	6	1.9	7.6	48	49%	.300	1.21	2.05	3.55	1.1				
2017	MIL	MLB	25	0	0	0	8	0	1^{1}	5	1	0.0	13.5	2	43%	.667	3.75	13.50	10.14	-0.1	95.8			45
2018	*MIL*	*MLB*	*26*	*2*	*2*	*0*	*44*	*0*	*46*	*46*	*6*	*3.2*	*8.1*	*42*	*44%*	*.299*	*1.35*	*4.27*	*4.40*	*0.3*	*95.4*			*46*
2019	*MIL*	*MLB*	*27*	*3*	*1*	*0*	*53*	*0*	*56^{2}*	*52*	*7*	*2.9*	*8.0*	*50*	*44%*	*.303*	*1.24*	*4.12*	*4.61*	*0.4*	*94.9*			*46*

Breakout: 19% Improve: 31% Collapse: 17% Attrition: 36% MLB: 52% *Comparables: Pat Misch, Tyler Olson, Chris Rusin*

Wang transitioned to a relief role in 2017 and finally earned a return to the big-league club with a September call-up. He dominated opposing batters in the hitter-friendly Pacific Coast League but failed to record an out in four of his eight appearances with the Brewers. What should we take from such a small sample? Perhaps it's a sign that his fastball/slider combination fits better in Triple-A. Perhaps it means absolutely nothing, and a southpaw touching 94 mph deserves another serious look in spring.

Aaron Wilkerson RHP Born: 05/24/89 Age: 29 Bats: R Throws: R Height: 6'3" Weight: 190 Origin: Undrafted Free Agent, 2014

YEAR	TEAM	LVL	AGE	W	L	SV	G	GS	IP	H	HR	BB/9	K/9	K	GB%	BABIP	WHIP	ERA	DRA	WARP	MPH	CMD	PWR	STM
2015	GRN	A	26	0	0	0	5	1	17	17	2	2.6	9.0	17	46%	.326	1.29	4.76	4.01	0.2				
2015	SLM	A+	26	7	2	0	17	12	79	62	0	2.4	9.7	85	40%	.305	1.05	2.96	1.35	3.5				
2015	PME	AA	26	4	1	0	7	7	40^2	28	0	2.9	7.7	35	40%	.252	1.01	2.66	3.14	1.0				
2016	PME	AA	27	2	1	0	8	8	44^1	28	2	2.8	9.7	48	48%	.236	0.95	1.83	1.78	1.8				
2016	PAW	AAA	27	4	2	0	9	8	48	41	5	2.1	10.1	54	32%	.286	1.08	2.44	1.36	2.2				
2016	CSP	AAA	27	2	6	0	11	11	54^2	67	5	2.6	9.4	57	38%	.371	1.52	6.42	2.50	1.8				
2017	BLX	AA	28	11	4	0	24	24	142^1	117	12	2.3	9.0	143	37%	.285	1.07	3.16	2.32	4.8				
2017	MIL	MLB	28	1	0	0	3	2	10^1	6	1	0.9	6.1	7	48%	.179	0.68	3.48	1.84	0.4	91.8			61
2018	*MIL*	*MLB*	*29*	*2*	*3*	*0*	*16*	*6*	*40^1*	*40*	*7*	*3.5*	*9.0*	*40*	*38%*	*.296*	*1.38*	*4.86*	*5.00*	*0.0*	*91.2*			*61*
2019	*MIL*	*MLB*	*30*	*7*	*8*	*0*	*59*	*20*	*160^2*	*151*	*27*	*3.0*	*8.5*	*152*	*38%*	*.303*	*1.27*	*4.65*	*5.22*	*0.4*	*90.6*			*61*

Breakout: 7% Improve: 11% Collapse: 13% Attrition: 18% MLB: 32% *Comparables: Hiram Burgos, Ryan Verdugo, Brad Mills*

Wilkerson was a relatively unknown minor-league journeyman before starting the Brewers' final game of the year and carrying a perfect game into the seventh inning. He pitched at Cumberland University and, after going undrafted, spent time in three different independent leagues in 2013 and 2014 before getting his first taste of affiliated ball. The former Red Sox prospect came to the Brewers in the very well-known Aaron Hill deal in 2016. He throws four average pitches, controls the zone and has an idea how to pitch. It's unclear how his approach can translate to the majors, especially once teams get multiple looks at him. Plus, as it often is with this type of pitcher, Wilkerson's margin for error with his command will likely be minuscule. Still, the fact that we're talking about Wilkerson as a potential no. 5 starter at the major-league level is a success in itself, considering his journey to this point.

Brandon Woodruff RHP Born: 02/10/93 Age: 25 Bats: L Throws: R Height: 6'4" Weight: 215 Origin: Round 11, 2014 Draft (#326 overall)

YEAR	TEAM	LVL	AGE	W	L	SV	G	GS	IP	H	HR	BB/9	K/9	K	GB%	BABIP	WHIP	ERA	DRA	WARP	MPH	CMD	PWR	STM
2015	BRV	A+	22	4	7	0	21	19	109^2	112	2	2.7	5.8	71	44%	.316	1.32	3.45	5.74	-0.9				
2016	BRV	A+	23	4	1	0	8	8	44^1	33	2	2.0	9.9	49	52%	.277	0.97	1.83	1.80	1.9				
2016	BLX	AA	23	10	8	0	20	20	113^2	88	4	2.4	9.8	124	49%	.286	1.04	3.01	1.93	4.3				
2017	CSP	AAA	24	6	5	0	16	16	75^1	78	8	3.0	8.4	70	49%	.323	1.37	4.30	3.46	1.8				
2017	MIL	MLB	24	2	3	0	8	8	43	43	5	2.9	6.7	32	50%	.292	1.33	4.81	5.67	0.0	96.3	54	58	54
2018	*MIL*	*MLB*	*25*	*8*	*8*	*0*	*23*	*23*	*131*	*127*	*18*	*3.3*	*8.4*	*122*	*45%*	*.294*	*1.33*	*4.30*	*4.51*	*1.0*	*96.0*	*55*	*59*	*55*
2019	*MIL*	*MLB*	*26*	*10*	*11*	*0*	*32*	*32*	*204*	*183*	*27*	*3.1*	*8.4*	*191*	*45%*	*.3*	*1.24*	*4.23*	*4.75*	*1.7*	*95.7*	*55*	*60*	*56*

Breakout: 16% Improve: 44% Collapse: 21% Attrition: 32% MLB: 75% *Comparables: Tim Cooney, Steven Brault, Rafael Montero*

Woodruff is a prototypical big-bodied innings-eater who throws gas; he took a massive step forward in 2016, forcing his way into the Brewers' 2017 plans. Unfortunately, the former Mississippi State star injured his hamstring while warming up for his major-league debut and never got back on track with any consistency. Shaky command—specifically the ability to locate quality strikes within the strike zone—held him back in 2017. He has the tools to be a no. 3 starter, but as with many young pitchers, though, the development of his ability to separate strikes from *good* strikes will determine whether he sticks in the rotation or transitions to a late-inning relief role.

LINEOUTS

Hitters

HITTER	POS	TEAM	LVL	AGE	PA	R	2B	3B	HR	RBI	BB	K	SB	CS	AVG/OBP/SLG	TAv	VORP	BABIP	BRR	FRAA	WARP
Quintin Berry	OF	ROC	AAA	32	40	5	1	1	0	0	4	11	1	2	.194/.275/.278	.213	-0.9	.280	0.0	CF(11): -1.9, LF(3): -0.3	-0.3
	OF	CSP	AAA	32	48	9	1	0	2	3	5	9	2	0	.286/.375/.452	.236	1.2	.323	1.0	CF(9): 1.5	0.3
	OF	MIL	MLB	32	3	0	0	0	0	0	0	2	2	1	.000/.000/.000	-.014	-1.0	.000	-0.2	LF(2): 0.0, CF(1): 0.0	-0.1
Ivan De Jesus	INF	CSP	AAA	30	466	67	30	4	7	65	33	75	3	2	.345/.407/.488	.280	23.7	.405	-0.2	3B(65): -1.6, 1B(23): 0.9	2.3
KJ Harrison	C	HEL	Rk	20	214	38	14	0	10	33	23	55	0	0	.308/.388/.546	.298	17.5	.382	1.3	C(17): -0.2	1.6
Tristen Lutz	OF	HEL	Rk	18	111	23	1	1	6	16	12	21	2	4	.333/.432/.559	.315	10.6	.373	-1.1	CF(22): -1.6	0.8
	OF	BRR	Rk	18	76	12	4	3	3	11	4	21	1	0	.279/.347/.559	.265	3.0	.364	0.1	CF(11): 0.5, LF(4): -1.2	0.2
Kirk Nieuwenhuis	OF	MIL	MLB	29	31	3	1	0	1	1	4	15	0	0	.115/.258/.269	.203	-0.9	.200	0.0	CF(7): -0.5, LF(3): -0.1	-0.2
	OF	CSP	AAA	29	247	32	12	0	4	33	38	67	5	0	.244/.362/.361	.247	0.5	.338	-0.4	RF(29): -2.9, LF(15): 0.0	-0.3
Jacob Nottingham	C	BLX	AA	22	385	37	21	2	9	48	37	87	7	3	.209/.326/.369	.263	13.0	.255	-3.0	C(83): 6.3, 1B(13): -0.8	2.0
Yadiel Rivera	SS	MIL	MLB	25	2	0	0	0	0	0	0	1	0	0	.000/.000/.000	.007	-0.5	.000	0.0	3B(1): 0.0	0.0
	SS	CSP	AAA	25	414	45	15	3	5	43	30	104	5	2	.218/.282/.314	.194	-12.9	.287	0.0	SS(96): 7.6, 3B(7): -0.3	-0.5
Andrew Susac	C	CSP	AAA	27	202	22	10	0	8	35	26	53	0	0	.205/.307/.404	.230	0.8	.237	-1.5	C(45): -1.8	-0.1
	C	MIL	MLB	27	12	0	0	0	0	0	0	6	0	0	.083/.083/.083	.066	-1.8	.167	0.1	C(2): -0.3	-0.2
Je'Von Ward	OF	BRR	Rk	17	132	15	6	0	0	15	9	39	2	7	.276/.326/.325	.228	-3.4	.405	-1.5	LF(15): -0.9, RF(11): -2.2	-0.6

Quintin Berry is who Terrance Gore wants to be when he grows up: he owns a .000/.000/.000 line with four stolen bases since 2014, yet has been a part of five September playoff runs with five different teams in his career. ⚾ **Ivan De Jesus** posted an .894 OPS in Triple-A, and it wasn't even good enough to rank in the league's top 30. Pump some of that Pacific Coast League baseball directly into the veins. ⚾ Milwaukee inked Dominican outfielder **Larry Ernesto** to a $1.7 million bonus in July, making him the Brewers' most expensive international signing of the 2017 J2 period and potentially the first player with the last name Ernesto to make The Show. ⚾ **KJ Harrison** was the fourth Hawaii-born player drafted by the Brewers in as many seasons. With a polished swing, better-than-expected pop and a chance to stick behind the dish, he could be the best of the bunch. ⚾ **Tristen Lutz** looks the part of a power-hitting right fielder and mashed after being selected in Competitive Balance Round A. If he doesn't swing and miss too much in his full-season debut, he'll be a top-10 organization prospect (no matter the organization) by June. **Kirk Nieuwenhuis** is a Three True Outcome player: 46.6 percent of his career plate appearances have ended in a strikeout, walk or home run. Unfortunately, the proportions are all wrong. **Jacob Nottingham** improved his TAv a little in a second run at Double-A pitching but still wasn't great. He came to Milwaukee in 2016, billed as a bat-first catching prospect with defensive deficiencies, but now appears to be as utterly miscast for that role as John Wayne was for the role of Genghis Khan in *The Conqueror*. While everyone debates the merits of bringing the designated hitter to the National League, **Yadiel Rivera** and his .596 Triple-A OPS recently started a change.org petition for a new designated fielder position. **Carlos Rodriguez**, a 16-year-old Dominican signee who has shown quality bat-to-ball skill in games, continues the Brewers' long-term international strategy of only committing six-figure bonuses to position players. **Andrew Susac** was a talented catching prospect, hopelessly blocked by a perennial All-Star in San Francisco. Milwaukee freed him, only to discover why so many football fans love the backup quarterback until he plays. **Je'Von Ward** is mostly known for being the nephew of former Bears safety Mark Carrier, but the 6-foot-5 center fielder possesses a projectable power/speed combination that could eventually blitz him up prospect lists.

Pitchers

PITCHER	TEAM	LVL	AGE	W	L	SV	G	GS	IP	H	HR	BB/9	K/9	K	GB%	BABIP	WHIP	ERA	DRA	WARP	MPH	CMD	PWR	STM
Michael Blazek	MIL	MLB	28	0	1	0	5	1	8^{2}	12	6	1.0	7.3	7	31%	.261	1.50	8.31	6.59	-0.1	95.5			51
	CSP	AAA	28	3	4	2	26	13	85	87	5	3.5	7.0	66	49%	.318	1.41	3.71	4.00	1.5				
Marcos Diplan	CAR	A+	20	7	8	0	26	22	125^{2}	126	11	5.1	8.5	119	48%	.327	1.57	5.23	5.76	-0.8				
Oliver Drake	BAL	MLB	30	0	0	0	3	0	3^{1}	6	0	8.1	8.1	3	67%	.500	2.70	8.10	4.46	0.0	92.9	48	39	49
	MIL	MLB	30	3	5	1	61	0	52^{2}	57	6	3.8	10.1	59	49%	.349	1.50	4.44	4.66	0.3	93.5	48	39	49
David Goforth	MIL	MLB	28	0	0	0	1	0	1	0	0	9.0	0.0	0	33%	.000	1.00	0.00	2.88	0.0	95.7			46
	CSP	AAA	28	3	4	5	48	0	54^{1}	57	7	4.3	6.3	38	56%	.292	1.53	3.98	6.21	-0.5				
Taylor Jungmann	MIL	MLB	27	0	0	0	1	0	0^{2}	2	0	13.5	13.5	1	67%	.667	4.50	13.50	5.18	0.0	92.1			59
	BLX	AA	27	1	2	0	9	6	33	35	5	4.6	8.5	31	51%	.330	1.58	4.36	4.62	0.2				
	CSP	AAA	27	9	2	0	17	15	90^{1}	69	4	3.9	8.2	82	48%	.271	1.20	2.59	4.04	1.6				
Josh Pennington	WIS	A	21	1	3	0	9	9	30^{1}	24	4	2.4	8.6	29	45%	.244	1.05	2.97	3.50	0.6				
Cody Ponce	CAR	A+	23	8	8	0	22	22	120	130	14	1.9	7.1	94	42%	.312	1.29	3.38	4.72	0.8				
	BLX	AA	23	2	1	0	3	3	17^{2}	10	0	2.5	4.6	9	54%	.200	0.85	1.53	4.07	0.2				
Rob Scahill	MIL	MLB	30	1	3	0	18	0	22^{1}	21	3	4.0	4.0	10	54%	.254	1.39	4.43	6.03	-0.2	95.1	42	63	41
	CSP	AAA	30	0	1	10	27	0	25^{2}	24	1	1.4	6.7	19	60%	.299	1.09	1.40	3.21	0.6				
Trey Supak	WIS	A	21	2	2	0	8	7	41	21	1	2.2	11.6	53	36%	.235	0.76	1.76	2.61	1.3				
	CAR	A+	21	3	4	1	15	11	72^{1}	65	12	3.5	7.1	57	34%	.261	1.29	4.60	5.86	-0.6				
Carlos Torres	MIL	MLB	34	4	4	1	67	0	72^{2}	78	10	4.1	6.9	56	48%	.309	1.53	4.21	6.14	-0.8	95.1	61	66	52
Tyler Webb	SWB	AAA	26	3	1	1	21	0	33^{1}	33	3	0.8	12.7	47	52%	.366	1.08	3.24	1.38	1.4				
	NYA	MLB	26	0	0	0	7	0	6	3	1	6.0	7.5	5	57%	.154	1.17	4.50	4.01	0.1	92.4			47
	MIL	MLB	26	0	0	0	2	0	2	6	1	4.5	13.5	3	22%	.625	3.50	9.00	8.05	-0.1	92.7			47
	CSP	AAA	26	1	2	0	17	0	16^{2}	21	4	3.8	9.2	17	59%	.362	1.68	6.48	3.93	0.2				
Taylor Williams	BLX	AA	25	0	2	0	22	14	46^{2}	42	2	4.1	11.0	57	48%	.339	1.35	3.09	4.10	0.5				
	MIL	MLB	25	0	0	0	5	0	4^{2}	4	0	3.9	7.7	4	43%	.286	1.29	1.93	5.39	0.0	97.1			28

Everything in Colorado Springs is high: the mountains, the students, **Michael Blazek**'s WHIP ... everything. **Marcos Diplan** is a diminutive, two-pitch hurler with significant control problems. He'll likely continue to be developed as a starter, as numerous scouts adore his arm, but something in his profile needs to change. He ain't getting any taller, either, so that limits his avenues for improvement. **Oliver Drake** doesn't look the part of a major-league pitcher. He employs an awkward, body-contorting, over-the-top delivery, sort of like the mythic Sidd Finch but without the superhuman velocity or good results. **David Goforth** is undoubtedly familiar with Mary Shelley's "And now, once again, I bid my hideous progeny go forth and prosper." Shaky fastball command has precluded the latter part from coming to pass. Continuing his Tommy John rehab, **Adrian Houser** returned to the mound in July and represented the Brewers in the Arizona Fall League. The right-hander surprised scouts with a mid-90s fastball and a tight mid-80s breaker that missed bats. **Taylor Jungmann** made one big-league appearance in 2017. He walked one, hit a dude, served up a couple of hits and allowed a run. The right-hander was exactly replacement level, though, which means he objectively improved on the previous year. **Josh Pennington** came to Milwaukee in the Tyler Thornburg deal and coincidentally has the Thornburg Starter Kit: a small frame, an upper-90s fastball, a tight curveball that flashes and a troublesome injury history. **Cody Ponce** possesses a potential four-pitch repertoire, featuring a nasty high-80s cutter, but occasionally suffers from Michael Pineda Syndrome: a pitcher who pounds the strike zone with good stuff but too often throws too few *good* strikes and gets hammered. **Rob Scahill** may have gotten demoted in late July, but the right-hander still managed to post the lowest strikeout rate (10.3 percent) of any pitcher in the National League with a minimum of 20 innings pitched. **Trey Supak** is a big southern boy with a mid-90s fastball and a 12-to-6 hammer, which reflexively should make every Wisconsinite swoon over a certain Louisianan hurler who once whiffed 18 batters in a complete-game victory on May 16, 2004. **Carlos Torres** is a cautionary tale for why a velocity spike doesn't immediately equal improved results. His fastball velocity increased 2.2 mph, but his strikeout rate dropped, his walk rate jumped, his home-run rate rose and his DRA ballooned to well below replacement level. **Tyler Webb** celebrated his Brewers debut by serving up a grand slam on his first pitch, which may not have been best way for the University of South Carolina product and minor-league control artist to demonstrate his efficiency. **Devin Williams** underwent Tommy John surgery in March 2017, pushing back his fabled "breakout campaign" yet again. But it's coming. Noted scout @BrewersFan491762 has predicted it every year since 2014. **Taylor Williams**, a hard-throwing fastball/slider reliever, made his major-league debut in September after not allowing a single earned run in August. The former top-10 prospect struck out 10 and walked none in that stretch.

MINNESOTA TWINS

Essay by John Bonnes

Player comments by Ken Funck and BP staff

The Twins' 2017 season was a 26-game improvement over their 2016 season, the biggest year-to-year improvement in franchise history. Twins fans can commiserate as much as any fan base, but they've been fairly blessed with regular Big Leap seasons. In their six decades in Minnesota, the Twins have shot up at least 15 wins from the previous year eight times, with only the 1970s failing to provide that season of hope.

A closer look at Big Leap seasons tells the story of the franchise—of four generations of competitive teams. Sometimes, hope was fleeting. Sometimes, it ushered in intriguing summers. On two occasions, it led to championships. Expanding the scope a little, to the top 10 Big Leaps, the seasons fall into four categories. Here they are, sorted by category, partly to see what fits best for the 2017 Twins, and partly because I want to jump around these generations chronologically, like a Tarantino film.

The Mirage Year

These are the teams that make the list for most improved, but it's mainly because the years before them were so bad. And that's saying something, because both years in this category were absolutely devastating to the franchise, despite the improvement.

1996 (+22 games) – The 1996 team improved by 22 games in part because the 1995 team only played 144 games (due to the strike), but this year would still belong in the top 10 if gauging by winning percentage. Still, it didn't feel like a Big Leap, despite Paul Molitor coming home, Chuck Knoblauch being in his prime and Brad Radke teetering on the verge of greatness.

The team only won 78 games, finished fourth in the AL Central and had fallen 10 games back of Cleveland by May 19 (and never got closer). But it was worse than that. The season felt like it ended before it began, when Kirby Puckett woke up one morning at spring training and couldn't see. In retrospect, that year was probably the high-water mark for the generation that was supposed to follow the Puckett/Kent Hrbek core. When the team regressed in 1997, Knoblauch demanded a trade, and the rebuild to the third generation of competitive Twins teams began.

1982 (+19 games) – This year absolutely does not belong on this list. Yes, in terms of wins, the 1982 Twins improved by 19, which is the sixth-highest leap in franchise history. But 1981 was a strike-shortened year. In terms of winning percentage, the 1982 Twins, which won just 60 games, were actually worse than the 1981 team, and even that doesn't do this disaster of a year justice. So why even mention it? Because it's a great excuse to look at the starting point for the second generation of competitive Twins teams.

The Metrodome's first year was 1982. Its inaugural contest drew 52,279 fans amid much pageantry. The next night? The club drew 5,213. By the *end of the first week*, owner Calvin Griffith realized he had made a huge mistake and started dismantling the team, trading Roy Smalley to the Yankees. He completed two more fire-sale trades by the middle of May. That stadium dominated the direction of the

TWINS PROSPECTUS

2017 W-L: 85-77, 2ND IN AL CENTRAL

Pythag	.516	12th	B-Age	27.1	*5th*
RS/G	5.03	7th	P-Age	29.6	*26th*
RA/G	4.86	19th	Salary	$108.1M	*21st*
TAv	.258	18th	M$/MW	$2.6M	*23rd*
TAv-P	.259	13th	DL Days	946	*16th*
FIP	4.69	24th	$ on DL	20%	*22nd*
DER	.704	12th			

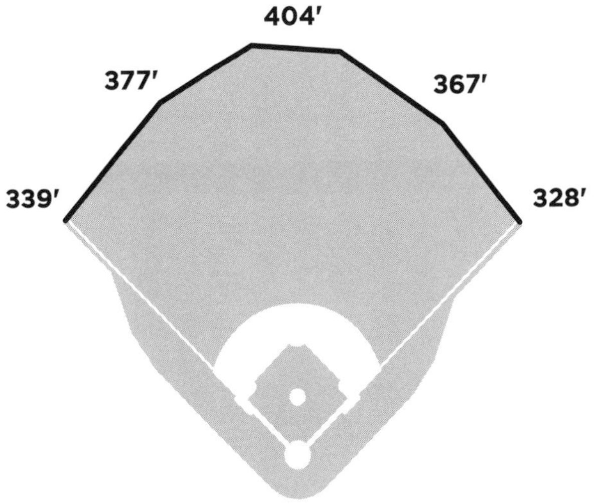

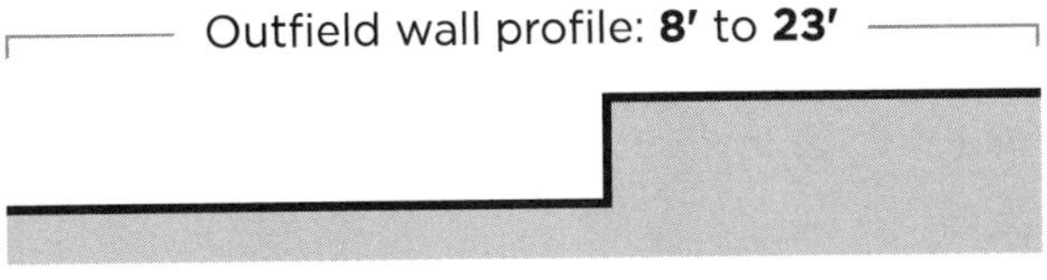

Three-Year Park Factors

Runs	Runs/RH	Runs/LH	HR/RH	HR/LH
101	102	100	106	98

Top Hitter WARP	4.7 Brian Dozier
Top Pitcher WARP	4.3 Ervin Santana
Top Prospect	Royce Lewis

2017 Hit List Ranking

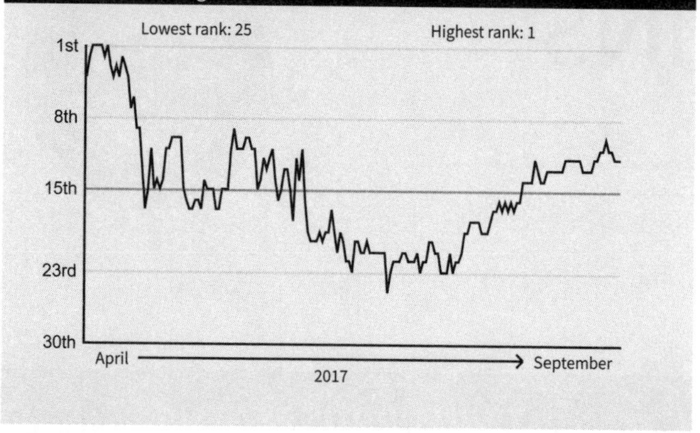

Committed Payroll (in millions)

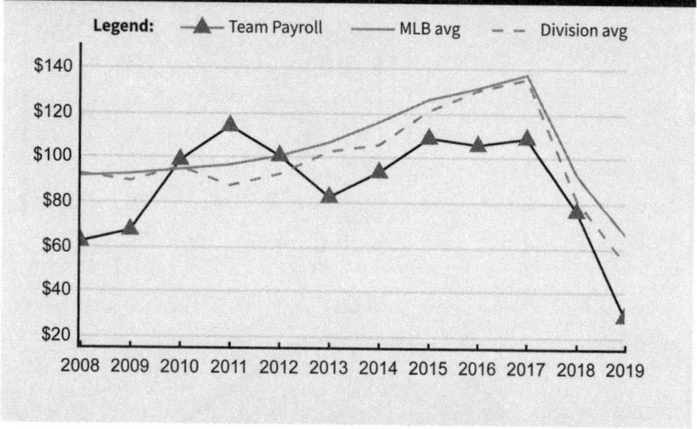

Farm System Ranking

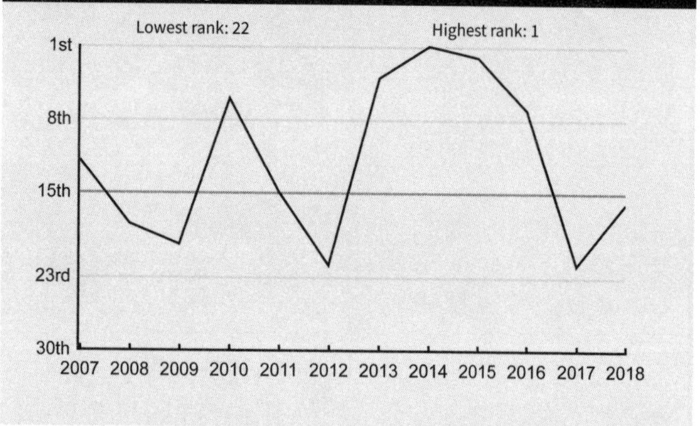

Personnel

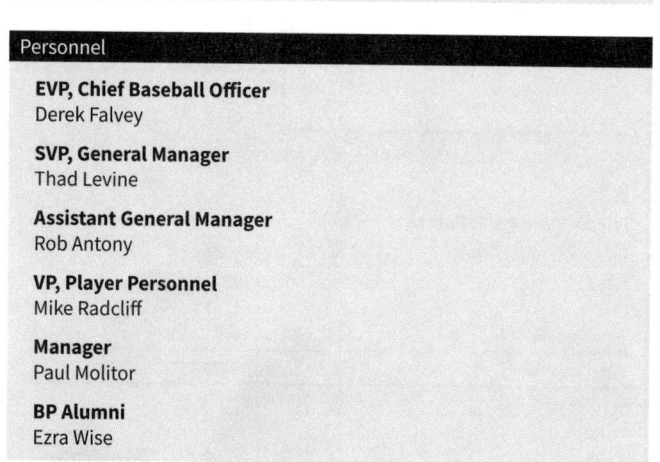

EVP, Chief Baseball Officer
Derek Falvey

SVP, General Manager
Thad Levine

Assistant General Manager
Rob Antony

VP, Player Personnel
Mike Radcliff

Manager
Paul Molitor

BP Alumni
Ezra Wise

team for the next 30 years, causing them to almost move several times and almost be contracted once. But 1982 also started a youth movement: Frank Viola, Kent Hrbek, Gary Gaetti and Tom Brunansky all debuted. The Metrodome and those youngsters would combine five years later for a magical season. They eventually led to two championships.

There is a touch of mirage to the 2017 season, in that it shines overly brightly against 2016's darkness. But that 59-win 2016 team, in retrospect, looks like the real mirage. They performed below preseason expectations, had a win total way lower than their run differential and had roughly the same roster as the 2015 and 2017 teams. Regardless, 1982 shows the "game improvement" metric is truly a lie sometimes, so instead we'll use winning percentage for the rest of this list.

The Tease Year

1984 (+11 games, +6.8%) – Almost every generation of successful Twins teams has had a tease year, in which they entice but ultimately fall short. This is usually followed by a year or two that makes fans wonder if it was a mirage year.

The youth movement that launched in 1982 added a speedy, light-hitting (zero homers in 583 plate appearances) center fielder named Kirby Puckett in 1984. It was a down year for the AL West, and as a result the Twins' 80-75 record with a week left to play put them in first place. However, instead of winning a division championship, they lost their last six games, including *blowing a 10-run lead* in their elimination game.

Understandably, with a close call and a young improving core, expectations were sky high for the next year. But they failed to reach .500 and there was a coaching change. Failure was followed by a coaching change again in 1986, this time accompanied by a change in management. And a change in ownership. People lose their jobs (and minds) after a tease year.

1967 – The 1967 season doesn't make this list because it was a great year in the midst of many very good seasons, so there was no Big Leap. However, for the first generation of competitive Twins teams, it fits the tease year in a lot of ways. The Twins were in first place with two games left to play, but lost both in gut-wrenching fashion. The success was partially driven by talented youth—this was Rod Carew's debut year. Expectations were high as a result, but instead the 1968 season stunk (mostly because of injuries), and the manager, Cal Ermer, got canned. Which led to a legendary rookie manager and a breakthrough season, but more on that later.

2015 (+13 games, +8.0%) – Like 1984, the 2015 Twins found themselves on the edge of a postseason spot late in the season, this time just one game back of a wild card spot going into the final series. Like the 1984 team, they were swept in that series and missed the playoffs. Still, it looked like the fourth Twins competitive wave had arrived.

Again, as with the 1984 team, expectations were lofty headed into the following season. The Twins failed (spectacularly) to reach .500 and there was a change, but this time it went further up the ladder than the manager. In fact, ownership decreed that the manager must be retained by the new general manager: a rare case where a manager oversees a tease year *and* a sunrise year, unless you want to count this next season as both.

2001 (+16 games, +9.9%) – The Twins entered 2001 with a *total* payroll of $24 million and were riding eight consecutive losing seasons. That streak ended when they won 85 games. However, they went 30-45 in the second half and blew a postseason spot. Manager Tom Kelly resigned. Ownership announced it would be the franchise's last year, because MLB was contracting the team. It looked like the third generation of competitive Twins teams might end before it even began. So it's hard to count 2001 as a sunrise season.

But it kind of was, or at least it wasn't a classic tease year, because the Twins didn't take a step backward in 2002; they improved by nine games, to 94 wins. Still, 2002 feels like the sunrise year, because that's when a young core—which included Torii Hunter, Johan Santana and David Ortiz—finally clicked under new manager Ron Gardenhire. So we'll leave 2001 in the tease-year category, with the point being that even in retrospect, it's hard to tell. This is proven by the next year on this list, even though it happened four decades and two generations earlier.

The Sunrise Year

1962 (+21 games, +12.4%) – In the franchise's second year in Minnesota, this team announced that the decades of Washington Senators futility was over and that a generation of winning had arrived. It did so with a bang, as Harmon Killebrew hit a league-leading 48 home runs. Killebrew, Bob Allison, Jim Kaat and Earl Battey—plus a sprinkle of Tony Oliva—led the Twins to 91 wins under new manager Sam Mele. But it was a different time: There were no divisions in the AL, and 91 wins didn't earn them a postseason spot. (That same total didn't earn them a spot the next year, either.) Still, being the second-best team in the league is good enough to avoid the "tease" category. But the real elite years were yet to come.

1987 (+14 games, +8.7%) – *Magic*. That was the *Minneapolis Star Tribune* headline the day after the Twins' first World Series title, and no other Twins season gets that label. It included going from worst-to-first, sporting the best home record in MLB and winning Minnesota's first championship in any major sport. They had a hell of a run in October, but it was far from an elite team; they won six more regular-season games in (an almost universally lamented) 1988 season than they did in 1987. No, this was the breakthrough year that announced a competitive window was opening. It just also happened to be the year the team won a championship, because ... magic.

2017 (+26 games, +16.1%). Let's put this here, for now. All the ingredients are there, to be sure: young core, new management, breakthrough future stars. It could be the second tease year for this generation of Twins players. It would also be the only tease year where the team made the postseason. Plus, it will be difficult to take a step backward in a division where three teams are clearly rebuilding.

The Elite Year

1965 (+23 games, +14.2%) – The 1965 team played at a level far above that of the teams before and after, winning 102 games despite dealing with a boatload of injuries, but this is not the result of any major moves or breakthrough rookies. Perhaps the biggest addition was assistant coach Billy Martin, widely credited with tutoring Zoilo Versalles into a career year that earned him the AL MVP. Beyond that, this team was just a number of guys playing at an elite level: Oliva was an MVP contender, Killebrew's 25 home runs included one versus the Yankees that ranks among the most dramatic in Twins history and right-hander Mudcat Grant won 20 games for the first and only time in his career. A World Series Game 7 shutout by Sandy Koufax (on two days' rest, no less) was all that separated the team from immortality.

1969 (+18 games, +11.1%) – The first generation got more than one elite year. After a few frustrating second-place finishes and a 1968 season that went completely off the rails due to injuries, the Twins promoted their Triple-A manager to take over the team. It was Billy Martin's first MLB managerial job, and it went about as you would expect. On the one hand, the team—which still had a core that included Killebrew, Oliva and Carew in their primes—played aggressive, winning baseball. On the other, Martin battled management and literally knocked out his own 20-game winner in a bar fight. But they were an elite team, winning 99 and 98 games over the next two years, only to be knocked out by the Orioles.

2006 (+13 games, +8.1%) – An early playoff exit tarnishes the elite year of the third generation of Twins teams, too. A common narrative about the 2002-2010 Twins is that they weren't especially strong teams and they benefited from playing in a fairly weak division, but that wasn't the case in 2006. The 96-win Twins won the division over a Tigers team that won 95. The White Sox won 90 and got to watch October on TV. The AL Central was stacked in 1996. The Twins didn't make any significant moves before the season, but both Justin Morneau and Joe Mauer fulfilled their potential, winning the MVP and batting title, respectively. Joining them with hardware were Gold Glove center fielder Torii Hunter and Cy Young winner Johan Santana. They went 72-38 after June 1, a 106-win pace. (Plus, that was the year Francisco Liriano was unhittable but needed Tommy John surgery. Not that I'm bitter.) The 2006 team was swept out of the playoffs in the ALDS by Oakland and perhaps unjustly labeled as being no different than any other Twins team of that decade. This was the high point of the arc of that third generation, and it was short-circuited by a three-game slump.

1991 (+21 games, +12.9%) – The 1991 Twins won 95 games during the regular season but provided their fans with a couple legendary moments en route to the franchise's second championship. This was the best season of the second generation, and its postseason success has led to reverence. Still, these Twins won the fewest regular-season games of any of the elite teams on this list. And unlike the others, this team was influenced by a number of moves made before the season. Jack Morris was signed as a free agent. So was Chili Davis, who led the lineup in OPS. The remarkable season was also keyed by breakout performances from starting pitcher Scott Erickson and second baseman Chuck Knoblauch.

This fourth generation will now be looking for its own elite season. History suggests the Twins are on their way, with organizational changes (like 1969) and a young core that needs to start peaking together (like 1965). But the next step will require some additions, either from outside the organization (like 1991) or from within (2006). The elite year might not be around the corner, but it's on the horizon. Twins fans should be ready for that next Big Leap.

—John Bonnes covers the Twins for Twins Daily.

HITTERS

Ehire Adrianza UT
Born: 08/21/89 Age: 28 Bats: B Throws: R Height: 6'1" Weight: 170 Origin: International Free Agent, 2006

YEAR	TEAM	LVL	AGE	PA	R	2B	3B	HR	RBI	BB	K	SB	CS	AVG/OBP/SLG	TAv	VORP	BABIP	BRR	FRAA	WARP
2015	SAC	AAA	25	195	16	6	1	3	15	17	37	6	1	.316/.384/.415	.294	15.1	.389	0.3	SS(43): 2.4, 2B(1): 0.1	1.8
2015	SFN	MLB	25	134	11	7	1	0	11	15	20	3	2	.186/.303/.265	.225	-0.4	.226	-0.1	SS(20): 0.1, 2B(20): 0.6	0.1
2016	SJO	A+	26	36	8	3	0	5	11	2	4	0	0	.333/.361/.879	.353	4.4	.240	-0.2	SS(5): 0.2, 3B(1): 0.0	0.5
2016	SAC	AAA	26	37	6	2	0	1	3	2	4	1	3	.257/.297/.400	.262	1.2	.267	-0.2	3B(5): -0.8, SS(3): -0.1	0.0
2016	SFN	MLB	26	71	3	2	0	2	7	2	13	0	1	.254/.299/.381	.250	0.9	.292	-0.8	SS(13): 0.8, 3B(7): -0.2	0.2
2017	ROC	AAA	27	44	1	0	0	0	3	6	11	0	1	.216/.326/.216	.206	-1.6	.308	-0.1	LF(4): 1.0, SS(2): 0.3	0.0
2017	MIN	MLB	27	186	30	9	2	2	24	16	25	8	1	.265/.324/.383	.252	6.3	.291	1.6	SS(29): 3.0, LF(17): 1.5	1.2
2018	*MIN*	*MLB*	*28*	*217*	*25*	*9*	*1*	*4*	*21*	*19*	*39*	*5*	*2*	*.251/.318/.373*	*.236*	*2.7*	*.288*	*0.2*	*LF 1, SS 1*	*0.4*
2019	*MIN*	*MLB*	*29*	*266*	*31*	*11*	*2*	*6*	*28*	*23*	*51*	*6*	*3*	*.249/.325/.383*	*.235*	*0.7*	*.287*	*0.2*	*LF 2, SS 1*	*0.5*

Breakout: 5% Improve: 26% Collapse: 13% Attrition: 25% MLB: 69% *Comparables: Kevin Frandsen, Angel Sanchez, Brandon Fahey*

This is a very simple game. You throw the ball. You catch the ball. You hit the ball. And if you are outstanding at the first two, aren't full-on embarrassing at the third, can bat from both sides of the plate and patrol both sides of the infield, you can make a nice living on today's three-man bench. Adrianza flirted with competence at the plate last year, helping him post the fifth-highest WARP among Twins hitters, but that was surely just a summer fling. He can draw the occasional walk, slap a few singles and swipe a bag or two, but familiarity with his offensive game inevitably leads to contempt. Still, Adrianza's leather remains as slick as they come and should earn him plenty of work as a stopgap shortstop and utility man.

Byron Buxton CF
Born: 12/18/93 Age: 24 Bats: R Throws: R Height: 6'2" Weight: 190 Origin: Round 1, 2012 Draft (#2 overall)

YEAR	TEAM	LVL	AGE	PA	R	2B	3B	HR	RBI	BB	K	SB	CS	AVG/OBP/SLG	TAv	VORP	BABIP	BRR	FRAA	WARP
2015	CHT	AA	21	268	44	7	12	6	37	26	51	20	2	.283/.351/.489	.305	22.4	.332	2.4	CF(59): 14.6	4.0
2015	ROC	AAA	21	59	11	3	1	1	8	4	12	2	1	.400/.441/.545	.377	9.7	.500	0.9	CF(11): 1.5	1.1
2015	MIN	MLB	21	138	16	7	1	2	6	6	44	2	2	.209/.250/.326	.214	-0.9	.301	1.3	CF(44): 6.5	0.6
2016	ROC	AAA	22	209	41	11	3	11	24	14	58	7	0	.305/.359/.568	.327	23.7	.382	2.9	CF(47): -2.2	2.2
2016	MIN	MLB	22	331	44	19	6	10	38	23	118	10	2	.225/.284/.430	.246	10.3	.329	4.9	CF(92): 6.4	1.7
2017	MIN	MLB	23	511	69	14	6	16	51	38	150	29	1	.253/.314/.413	.247	17.0	.339	7.4	CF(137): 25.5	4.3
2018	*MIN*	*MLB*	*24*	*565*	*77*	*22*	*8*	*19*	*69*	*41*	*166*	*24*	*3*	*.251/.309/.439*	*.252*	*23.0*	*.327*	*4.8*	*CF 17*	*3.4*
2019	*MIN*	*MLB*	*25*	*547*	*70*	*21*	*7*	*21*	*74*	*44*	*161*	*23*	*3*	*.251/.318/.455*	*.253*	*18.6*	*.323*	*6.4*	*CF 17*	*3.9*

Breakout: 3% Improve: 50% Collapse: 8% Attrition: 7% MLB: 95% *Comparables: Matt Kemp, Marcell Ozuna, Melvin Upton*

Buxton's natural athleticism may be the stuff of legend among scouts, but it's his makeup, coachability and work ethic that have many still expecting superstardom despite his early-career struggles at the plate. Consider Buxton's defense, which was already outstanding before Twins coaches presented him with metrics stressing the importance of better first-step quickness. The young center fielder spent the offseason working hard to improve his jumps, and the results were a career's worth of highlight-reel plays in a single summer and a well-deserved Gold Glove award. Given Buxton's virtuoso defense and blinding speed on the basepaths even modest success at the plate will land him among the league's most valuable players, and there too you can find promising signs. After another woeful first half he simplified his swing mechanics via frequent adjustments under the watchful eye of hitting coach James Rowson, made more contact and started to unlock his burgeoning power, leading to a .300/.347/.546 second-half line. His bat has teased us before, but given his combination of youth, talent and determination don't be surprised if this is the year Buxton takes his game to another level.

Jason Castro C
Born: 06/18/87 Age: 31 Bats: L Throws: R Height: 6'3" Weight: 215 Origin: Round 1, 2008 Draft (#10 overall)

YEAR	TEAM	LVL	AGE	PA	R	2B	3B	HR	RBI	BB	K	SB	CS	AVG/OBP/SLG	TAv	VORP	BABIP	BRR	FRAA	WARP
2015	HOU	MLB	28	375	38	19	0	11	31	33	115	0	0	.211/.283/.365	.231	4.5	.280	-1.2	C(103): 9.6	1.5
2016	HOU	MLB	29	376	41	16	3	11	32	45	123	2	1	.210/.307/.377	.239	7.4	.297	-1.3	C(111): 15.8, 1B(3): -0.2	2.4
2017	MIN	MLB	30	407	49	22	0	10	47	45	108	0	0	.242/.333/.388	.247	13.0	.318	-0.4	C(108): 2.7	1.6
2018	*MIN*	*MLB*	*31*	*452*	*52*	*22*	*1*	*13*	*52*	*44*	*126*	*1*	*0*	*.234/.314/.393*	*.242*	*13.3*	*.306*	*-0.8*	*C 7*	*1.6*
2019	*MIN*	*MLB*	*32*	*398*	*49*	*20*	*1*	*13*	*47*	*38*	*113*	*0*	*0*	*.236/.314/.402*	*.240*	*6.2*	*.307*	*-0.9*	*C 7*	*1.5*

Breakout: 5% Improve: 36% Collapse: 16% Attrition: 20% MLB: 96% *Comparables: Ramon Castro, Ozzie Virgil, John Buck*

YEAR	TEAM	P. COUNT	FRM RUNS	BLK RUNS	THRW RUNS	TOT RUNS
2015	HOU	14019	10.0	-1.0	1.0	10.0
2016	HOU	14976	16.3	0.0	-0.9	15.4
2017	MIN	14556	3.3	0.2	0.0	3.4
2018	*MIN*	*17068*	*9.7*	*-0.9*	*-0.2*	*8.5*
2019	*MIN*	*15014*	*8.8*	*-0.8*	*-0.2*	*7.8*

Castro has built his career playing Ben Kenobi to every umpire's Tatooine stormtrooper, subtly suggesting that each pitch near the plate is just the strike they're looking for. The former Astro hasn't hit much since his 2013 breakout, didn't hit much last year for the Twins and likely won't hit much ever again, but his pitch-framing prowess and plus defense consistently make him far more valuable to his real-life employers than to your fantasy roster. After years ranking among the league's leading strike-stealers Castro was merely good last season, but his work behind the dish still netted Minnesota the equivalent of a two-win upgrade from his predecessor, Kurt Suzuki. As long as he keeps that up, the Twins will be happy to stick him at the bottom of the order and let their other young Jedi provide the offensive fireworks.

Brian Dozier 2B Born: 05/15/87 Age: 31 Bats: R Throws: R Height: 5'11" Weight: 200 Origin: Round 8, 2009 Draft (#252 overall)

YEAR	TEAM	LVL	AGE	PA	R	2B	3B	HR	RBI	BB	K	SB	CS	AVG/OBP/SLG	TAv	VORP	BABIP	BRR	FRAA	WARP
2015	MIN	MLB	28	704	101	39	4	28	77	61	148	12	4	.236/.307/.444	.260	23.1	.261	4.8	2B(157): -8.2	1.6
2016	MIN	MLB	29	691	104	35	5	42	99	61	138	18	2	.268/.340/.546	.291	41.4	.280	1.1	2B(151): -2.2	4.0
2017	MIN	MLB	30	705	106	30	4	34	93	78	141	16	7	.271/.359/.498	.280	37.0	.300	2.2	2B(152): 9.7	4.7
2018	*MIN*	*MLB*	*31*	*679*	*104*	*32*	*4*	*28*	*86*	*69*	*135*	*16*	*5*	*.249/.333/.456*	*.266*	*34.1*	*.276*	*1.0*	*2B -2*	*2.5*
2019	*MIN*	*MLB*	*32*	*538*	*73*	*24*	*2*	*23*	*73*	*56*	*112*	*11*	*4*	*.242/.329/.445*	*.255*	*16.1*	*.268*	*1.7*	*2B -1*	*1.6*

Breakout: 0% Improve: 47% Collapse: 2% Attrition: 4% MLB: 98% *Comparables: Rickie Weeks, Kelly Johnson, Don Money*

Data point no. 12,356 that more baseball fans are buying into modern methods of building a winner: The Twins *didn't* trade away their gritty, popular, defensively slick second baseman coming off a 40-bomb season, and a noticeable segment of the fan base was vocally disappointed last spring. Instead, Dozier stayed in Minnesota and enjoyed his best all-around campaign, proving that his 2016 power surge was no fluke while posting career highs in batting average and on-base percentage and winning a Gold Glove award. He made a concerted effort to drive the ball to center and right field last summer, and while he remains one of the league's most pull-heavy hitters he's no longer lapping the field—a development that should help his offensive profile as he moves into his thirties. Second basemen tend to age worse than Oliver Stone flicks, but Dozier may well retain his power bat long enough to be worth his upcoming free agent bonanza.

Eduardo Escobar INF Born: 01/05/89 Age: 29 Bats: B Throws: R Height: 5'10" Weight: 185 Origin: International Free Agent, 2006

YEAR	TEAM	LVL	AGE	PA	R	2B	3B	HR	RBI	BB	K	SB	CS	AVG/OBP/SLG	TAv	VORP	BABIP	BRR	FRAA	WARP
2015	MIN	MLB	26	446	48	31	4	12	58	28	86	2	3	.262/.309/.445	.266	15.4	.301	-1.4	SS(71): -6.0, LF(35): 4.1	1.5
2016	MIN	MLB	27	377	32	14	2	6	37	21	72	1	3	.236/.280/.338	.209	-3.3	.280	1.7	SS(71): 1.0, 3B(23): -1.2	-0.4
2017	MIN	MLB	28	499	62	16	5	21	73	33	98	5	1	.254/.309/.449	.255	14.8	.279	2.3	3B(79): -5.1, SS(16): -0.5	0.9
2018	*MIN*	*MLB*	*29*	*423*	*47*	*22*	*3*	*11*	*48*	*28*	*83*	*3*	*2*	*.255/.307/.410*	*.241*	*6.8*	*.296*	*-0.5*	*3B -9, SS -1*	*-0.7*
2019	*MIN*	*MLB*	*30*	*392*	*46*	*20*	*3*	*11*	*46*	*29*	*81*	*2*	*1*	*.251/.310/.415*	*.238*	*2.0*	*.291*	*0.8*	*3B -7, SS -1*	*-0.6*

Breakout: 3% Improve: 50% Collapse: 7% Attrition: 13% MLB: 90% *Comparables: Phil Garner, Joe Crede, Brandon Inge*

Escobar fully embraced the fly-ball revolution last season and spent the year swinging for the fences, lopping more than five percent off his already low ground-ball rate and raising his profile by launching a career-high 21 homers. The thing about revolutions, though, is they always bring change, but not always for the better. His new approach traded doubles for home runs and ground-ball singles for fly-ball outs, which cancelled out to produce the same level of mediocre offense we've grown to expect from him. Escobar remains one of the league's better backup infielders, a switch-hitter with an adequate glove who can smooth over a short-term hole in the lineup, but likely he'd be stretched as an everyday player on a contending team.

Mitch Garver C Born: 01/15/91 Age: 27 Bats: R Throws: R Height: 6'1" Weight: 220 Origin: Round 9, 2013 Draft (#260 overall)

YEAR	TEAM	LVL	AGE	PA	R	2B	3B	HR	RBI	BB	K	SB	CS	AVG/OBP/SLG	TAv	VORP	BABIP	BRR	FRAA	WARP
2015	FTM	A+	24	520	46	24	1	4	58	69	82	5	3	.245/.356/.333	.275	24.7	.287	1.1	C(77): -0.2, 1B(14): -0.8	2.6
2016	CHT	AA	25	407	44	25	0	11	66	43	86	1	3	.257/.334/.419	.278	18.4	.305	0.3	C(46): 7.3, 1B(14): -0.9	2.7
2016	ROC	AAA	25	84	6	5	0	1	8	7	21	0	0	.329/.381/.434	.305	7.0	.436	0.4	C(14): 0.1, 1B(2): -0.1	0.7
2017	ROC	AAA	26	372	56	29	0	17	45	50	85	2	0	.291/.387/.541	.319	40.3	.347	0.2	C(67): 4.3, LF(14): 0.9	4.4
2017	MIN	MLB	26	52	5	1	3	0	3	6	15	0	0	.196/.288/.348	.212	-1.1	.290	0.2	C(13): -1.3, 1B(3): 0.3	-0.2
2018	*MIN*	*MLB*	*27*	*118*	*14*	*6*	*0*	*4*	*15*	*13*	*29*	*0*	*0*	*.244/.332/.422*	*.258*	*5.5*	*.301*	*-0.2*	*C -1*	*0.3*
2019	*MIN*	*MLB*	*28*	*240*	*32*	*12*	*1*	*9*	*31*	*28*	*60*	*0*	*0*	*.243/.334/.430*	*.255*	*7.4*	*.297*	*-0.6*	*C -2*	*0.6*

Breakout: 6% Improve: 16% Collapse: 11% Attrition: 24% MLB: 39% *Comparables: Chris Gimenez, Jose Lobaton, Johnny Monell*

YEAR	TEAM	P. COUNT	FRM RUNS	BLK RUNS	THRW RUNS	TOT RUNS
2017	MIN	832	-1.1	-0.1	0.0	-1.2
2018	*MIN*	*4349*	*-0.6*	*-0.5*	*0.0*	*-1.0*
2019	*MIN*	*8831*	*-0.7*	*-0.5*	*0.0*	*-1.2*

A longtime minor-league receiver with decent catch-and-throw skills and a whiff of framing magic, Garver unexpectedly laid waste to Triple-A pitching last year and earned the organization's Minor League Player of the Year award and a month-long stint caddying for the big club. The New Mexico product has always done a good job of controlling the strike zone and has started to show some power, making his righty bat a nice complement to incumbent catcher Jason Castro. The organization also handed him some outfield and first base reps, giving him a good shot to break camp this spring as Minnesota's backup catcher/outfield platoon mate/heartwarming tale of grit and determination.

Chris Gimenez C Born: 12/27/82 Age: 35 Bats: R Throws: R Height: 6'2" Weight: 230 Origin: Round 19, 2004 Draft (#557 overall)

YEAR	TEAM	LVL	AGE	PA	R	2B	3B	HR	RBI	BB	K	SB	CS	AVG/OBP/SLG	TAv	VORP	BABIP	BRR	FRAA	WARP
2015	ROU	AAA	32	277	28	10	0	6	33	24	62	2	0	.243/.315/.356	.254	3.0	.298	-2.3	C(26): 0.4, 1B(20): -1.2	0.3
2015	TEX	MLB	32	113	19	6	1	5	14	10	19	2	0	.255/.330/.490	.279	7.1	.270	0.1	C(36): -0.4	0.7
2016	FRI	AA	33	29	3	0	0	1	4	3	8	0	0	.240/.345/.360	.244	0.2	.313	-0.3	C(5): 0.1	0.0
2016	CLE	MLB	33	155	17	4	0	4	11	10	41	0	0	.216/.272/.331	.206	-2.4	.274	-1.0	C(59): -2.2, 1B(4): 0.0	-0.5
2017	MIN	MLB	34	225	28	9	0	7	16	33	60	1	0	.220/.350/.382	.249	6.1	.286	-1.4	C(59): 3.2, 1B(7): 0.0	0.9
2018	*MIN*	*MLB*	*35*	*250*	*27*	*10*	*1*	*6*	*26*	*27*	*59*	*1*	*0*	*.227/.319/.364*	*.228*	*3.2*	*.278*	*-0.8*	*C 0, 1B 0*	*0.4*
2019	*MIN*	*MLB*	*36*	*243*	*28*	*9*	*1*	*5*	*24*	*29*	*60*	*0*	*0*	*.216/.317/.341*	*.225*	*-0.7*	*.270*	*-0.9*	*C 0, 1B 0*	*-0.1*

Breakout: 1% Improve: 31% Collapse: 13% Attrition: 31% MLB: 71% *Comparables: Corky Miller, Chris Widger, Chad Moeller*

Gimenez was the best Gimenez he could be last year. The veteran backstop played solid defense, got on base, hit a few bombs, took the mound to finish off six blowout losses—the most by a position player in at least a half-century—and engaged in all manner of clubhouse goofery to keep Minnesota's youngsters loose during a tense playoff run. For pulling the same schtick David Ross wound up *Dancing With The Stars*, whereas Gimenez was *Queueing With The Scrubs* after being outrighted in November. No one ever said baseball is fair, but Gimenez has a good chance of spending at least one more summer as a backup catcher and professional teammate.

YEAR	TEAM	P. COUNT	FRM RUNS	BLK RUNS	THRW RUNS	TOT RUNS
2015	ROU	3578	0.4	0.1	0.1	0.5
2015	TEX	4512	0.4	-0.5	-0.6	-0.7
2016	CLE	6271	-3.0	0.3	-0.2	-2.8
2017	MIN	8144	3.5	0.2	0.6	4.2
2018	*MIN*	*8930*	*-0.3*	*0.0*	*0.0*	*-0.4*
2019	*MIN*	*8692*	*-0.2*	*0.0*	*0.0*	*-0.3*

Nick Gordon SS Born: 10/24/95 Age: 22 Bats: L Throws: R Height: 6'0" Weight: 160 Origin: Round 1, 2014 Draft (#5 overall)

YEAR	TEAM	LVL	AGE	PA	R	2B	3B	HR	RBI	BB	K	SB	CS	AVG/OBP/SLG	TAv	VORP	BABIP	BRR	FRAA	WARP
2015	CDR	A	19	535	79	23	7	1	58	39	88	25	8	.277/.336/.360	.258	23.0	.333	2.9	SS(118): 7.9	3.3
2016	FTM	A+	20	494	56	23	6	3	52	23	87	19	13	.291/.335/.386	.277	25.2	.353	-2.9	SS(103): 4.1, 2B(2): -0.1	3.0
2017	CHT	AA	21	578	80	29	8	9	66	53	134	13	7	.270/.341/.408	.279	33.7	.347	1.1	SS(104): 0.4, 2B(14): 0.4	3.7
2018	*MIN*	*MLB*	*22*	*250*	*30*	*12*	*2*	*6*	*25*	*16*	*63*	*4*	*2*	*.252/.305/.400*	*.235*	*4.9*	*.319*	*0.0*	*SS 2, 2B 0*	*0.8*
2019	*MIN*	*MLB*	*23*	*389*	*46*	*18*	*4*	*11*	*46*	*27*	*95*	*6*	*3*	*.257/.316/.420*	*.248*	*8.2*	*.320*	*0.2*	*SS 3, 2B 0*	*1.3*

Breakout: 4% Improve: 25% Collapse: 6% Attrition: 18% MLB: 38% *Comparables: Nick Franklin, Marcus Semien, Eugenio Suarez*

From a John Keats prospect report filed late last summer, under the heading *Ode on a Gordon Urn*: "Beauty is youth, youth beauty. That is all ye know on earth, and all ye need to know." Put another way, a minor-league baseball season can be a grind, especially to a 21-year-old facing advanced pitching for the first time. So don't make too much of Gordon's god-awful second half, and don't let it overshadow his .302/.370/.464 line at the break. The former top-five pick has started drawing walks and tapping into his lefty power potential, and still projects as a steady glove at shortstop and a burner on the basepaths. There's plenty of time for Gordon to grow into a solid regular, but superstardom is likely a bridge too far. As Keats himself noted in the same report: "What pipes and timbrels? What wild ecstasy?"

Zach Granite CF Born: 09/17/92 Age: 25 Bats: L Throws: L Height: 6'1" Weight: 175 Origin: Round 14, 2013 Draft (#410 overall)

YEAR	TEAM	LVL	AGE	PA	R	2B	3B	HR	RBI	BB	K	SB	CS	AVG/OBP/SLG	TAv	VORP	BABIP	BRR	FRAA	WARP
2015	CDR	A	22	83	17	5	1	0	5	12	6	7	1	.358/.463/.463	.358	11.9	.393	1.8	LF(13): 2.3, CF(4): 0.1	1.5
2015	FTM	A+	22	441	59	10	4	1	26	41	63	21	12	.249/.328/.304	.250	8.5	.294	1.7	CF(64): 5.9, LF(39): 5.7	2.2
2016	CHT	AA	23	584	86	18	8	4	52	42	43	56	14	.295/.347/.382	.276	33.8	.312	8.2	CF(108): 7.3, LF(18): 0.8	4.5
2017	ROC	AAA	24	313	46	16	4	5	29	24	34	15	6	.338/.392/.475	.304	25.9	.371	0.0	CF(70): 6.9	3.2
2017	MIN	MLB	24	107	14	2	0	1	13	12	9	2	2	.237/.321/.290	.201	-2.7	.250	0.7	CF(24): 1.1, LF(8): -0.2	-0.2
2018	*MIN*	*MLB*	*25*	*178*	*25*	*7*	*2*	*4*	*16*	*14*	*25*	*8*	*3*	*.273/.327/.402*	*.248*	*4.9*	*.297*	*0.8*	*CF 1, LF 2*	*0.6*
2019	*MIN*	*MLB*	*26*	*391*	*48*	*15*	*4*	*10*	*46*	*33*	*58*	*18*	*6*	*.277/.342/.430*	*.253*	*10.2*	*.300*	*2.2*	*CF 3, LF 4*	*1.8*

Breakout: 5% Improve: 34% Collapse: 8% Attrition: 32% MLB: 57% *Comparables: Todd Cunningham, Travis Jankowski, A.J. Pollock*

A fourth outfielder/John Wayne squad member straight out of Central Casting, Granite is a Staten Island native (though John Ford would change that to Brooklyn) with great wheels and a plus glove who hit his way onto the Twins' roster last summer. His lefty stroke is geared for contact and line drives, not power, but Granite controls the zone well, stays within himself and works his way on base. All the ingredients are here for a long and valuable bench career peppered with talk-radio cries for more playing time than would be good for him.

Robbie Grossman OF Born: 09/16/89 Age: 28 Bats: B Throws: L Height: 6'0" Weight: 215 Origin: Round 6, 2008 Draft (#174 overall)

YEAR	TEAM	LVL	AGE	PA	R	2B	3B	HR	RBI	BB	K	SB	CS	AVG/OBP/SLG	TAv	VORP	BABIP	BRR	FRAA	WARP
2015	HOU	MLB	25	54	7	2	0	1	5	5	17	0	0	.143/.222/.245	.182	-2.6	.194	0.4	LF(17): -2.2, RF(4): -0.2	-0.5
2015	FRE	AAA	25	408	54	16	1	5	37	55	85	14	8	.254/.354/.349	.252	3.8	.318	-1.3	LF(75): 2.2, CF(7): 1.5	0.8
2016	COH	AAA	26	139	14	5	0	6	13	21	25	3	1	.256/.370/.453	.285	5.4	.279	-1.6	CF(19): -1.4, LF(10): 1.8	0.6
2016	MIN	MLB	26	389	49	19	1	11	37	55	96	2	3	.280/.386/.443	.287	18.0	.364	-0.2	LF(75): -5.4, CF(1): 0.0	1.3
2017	MIN	MLB	27	456	62	22	1	9	45	67	79	3	1	.246/.361/.380	.260	5.1	.287	-1.9	RF(35): -1.6, LF(18): -1.2	0.2
2018	*MIN*	*MLB*	*28*	*265*	*32*	*11*	*1*	*5*	*27*	*34*	*59*	*3*	*2*	*.250/.348/.375*	*.253*	*3.8*	*.312*	*-0.4*	*LF -1*	*0.2*
2019	*MIN*	*MLB*	*29*	*390*	*49*	*17*	*1*	*10*	*42*	*51*	*92*	*4*	*2*	*.246/.348/.388*	*.249*	*5.2*	*.307*	*-0.5*	*LF -1*	*0.4*

Breakout: 3% Improve: 32% Collapse: 9% Attrition: 20% MLB: 81% *Comparables: Kevin Youkilis, Yonder Alonso, Ryan Garko*

Most hitters treat the strike zone like a gladiatorial arena where they're paid to land blows and win glory. Grossman is more like a security guard, ready and able to fend off a pitch that intrudes into his area but more than happy to end his uneventful shift with a leisurely stroll to first base. Each year he ranks among the league leaders in taking pitches and coaxing walks, posting high on-base percentages that can fuel the top of a lineup. His patient but punchless approach would be perfect for a middle infielder, but Grossman instead patrols the outfield corners like the DH he frequently is, eroding his value to near replacement level. Working at the bottom of the defensive spectrum in today's power-packed offensive environment makes employing Grossman a stopgap, not a solution.

Wander Javier SS Born: 12/29/98 Age: 19 Bats: R Throws: R Height: 6'1" Weight: 165 Origin: International Free Agent, 2015

YEAR	TEAM	LVL	AGE	PA	R	2B	3B	HR	RBI	BB	K	SB	CS	AVG/OBP/SLG	TAv	VORP	BABIP	BRR	FRAA	WARP
2016	DTW	RK	17	30	7	3	0	2	6	4	5	0	0	.308/.400/.654	.371	4.0	.316	-1.0	SS(8): -0.4	0.4
2017	ELZ	RK	18	180	34	13	1	4	22	19	49	4	3	.299/.383/.471	.283	15.3	.410	1.9	SS(36): -6.5	0.8
2018	*MIN*	*MLB*	*19*	*250*	*26*	*9*	*1*	*7*	*24*	*17*	*86*	*1*	*0*	*.197/.255/.333*	*.192*	*-6.5*	*.277*	*-0.4*	*SS -2*	*-1.0*
2019	*MIN*	*MLB*	*20*	*327*	*37*	*12*	*1*	*10*	*37*	*24*	*108*	*1*	*1*	*.212/.275/.368*	*.216*	*-4.8*	*.290*	*-0.5*	*SS -3*	*-0.9*

Breakout: 0% Improve: 5% Collapse: 2% Attrition: 6% MLB: 10% *Comparables: Raul Mondesi, Nomar Mazara, Elvis Andrus*

The Twins unleashed Javier, a top international signee back in 2015, on the Appalachian League last summer to great acclaim. A potential five-tool shortstop, Javier impressed scouts with a surprisingly advanced approach for a teenager making his stateside debut. He flashed good instincts and plenty of arm for the left side of the infield, and a quick stick with power potential at the plate. In a system flush with middle-infield prospects Javier has as much upside as any of them, and if he continues to progress in his full-season debut he may well find himself ranked among the game's top prospects.

Max Kepler RF Born: 02/10/93 Age: 25 Bats: L Throws: L Height: 6'4" Weight: 205 Origin: International Free Agent, 2009

YEAR	TEAM	LVL	AGE	PA	R	2B	3B	HR	RBI	BB	K	SB	CS	AVG/OBP/SLG	TAv	VORP	BABIP	BRR	FRAA	WARP
2015	FTM	A+	22	26	4	2	0	0	0	2	5	1	0	.250/.308/.333	.277	1.2	.316	0.4	RF(5): -0.2	0.1
2015	CHT	AA	22	482	76	32	13	9	71	67	63	18	4	.322/.416/.531	.341	55.7	.359	8.0	1B(37): -0.2, RF(31): 3.6	6.9
2015	MIN	MLB	22	7	0	0	0	0	0	0	3	0	0	.143/.143/.143	.114	-0.9	.250	0.0	RF(2): 0.1	-0.1
2016	ROC	AAA	23	128	16	4	6	1	19	16	14	1	1	.282/.367/.455	.292	7.5	.309	0.7	RF(26): 1.9, CF(6): 0.4	1.0
2016	MIN	MLB	23	447	52	20	2	17	63	42	93	6	2	.235/.309/.424	.254	6.3	.261	0.9	RF(108): 3.6, CF(4): -0.1	1.0
2017	MIN	MLB	24	568	67	32	2	19	69	47	114	6	1	.243/.312/.425	.247	1.2	.276	-2.2	RF(138): 5.2, CF(13): 0.3	0.7
2018	*MIN*	*MLB*	*25*	*600*	*74*	*30*	*6*	*19*	*78*	*58*	*114*	*8*	*2*	*.257/.333/.445*	*.264*	*17.4*	*.292*	*0.6*	*RF 3*	*1.9*
2019	*MIN*	*MLB*	*26*	*551*	*73*	*27*	*5*	*20*	*74*	*55*	*109*	*7*	*2*	*.257/.336/.459*	*.261*	*11.3*	*.290*	*-0.6*	*RF 4*	*1.7*

Breakout: 4% Improve: 59% Collapse: 3% Attrition: 12% MLB: 99% *Comparables: Travis Buck, Ryan Sweeney, Elijah Dukes*

Whatever pixie dust kissed Minnesota's young hitters down the stretch last year must have floated right past Kepler, who posted a .216/.284/.351 line over the season's last month. After his September swoon the young German's numbers were a near-perfect *doppelgänger* for his rookie year, which depending on your capacity for *schadenfreude*, is either stagnation or consolidation. We prefer the latter, as it's hard to watch Kepler's pretty lefty swing and not envision even better things to come. His *weltschmerz*-inducing .176/.242/.279 line against same-side pitching seems to beg for a platoon partner, but Kepler did fine against lefties in the minors so here, too, patience is in order. He's not destined for stardom, but once he starts holding his own against portsiders and polishes up his defense Kepler will be a solid cog in a contender's outfield.

Royce Lewis SS Born: 06/05/99 Age: 19 Bats: R Throws: R Height: 6'2" Weight: 188 Origin: Round 1, 2017 Draft (#1 overall)

YEAR	TEAM	LVL	AGE	PA	R	2B	3B	HR	RBI	BB	K	SB	CS	AVG/OBP/SLG	TAv	VORP	BABIP	BRR	FRAA	WARP
2017	TWI	RK	18	159	38	6	2	3	17	19	17	15	2	.271/.390/.414	.282	16.3	.292	4.6	SS(32): -0.9	1.4
2017	CDR	A	18	80	16	2	1	1	10	6	16	3	1	.296/.363/.394	.286	6.5	.364	1.0	SS(17): 1.9	0.9
2018	*MIN*	*MLB*	*19*	*250*	*29*	*10*	*1*	*7*	*24*	*18*	*68*	*4*	*1*	*.223/.286/.362*	*.215*	*-0.1*	*.285*	*0.1*	*SS 2*	*0.2*
2019	*MIN*	*MLB*	*20*	*362*	*44*	*14*	*2*	*12*	*43*	*28*	*93*	*6*	*2*	*.239/.306/.402*	*.237*	*3.9*	*.295*	*0.4*	*SS 2*	*0.7*

Breakout: 0% Improve: 5% Collapse: 1% Attrition: 12% MLB: 16% *Comparables: Carlos Correa, Elvis Andrus, Jurickson Profar*

The top overall pick in last summer's draft, Lewis launched his initial pro season by going deep in his first career plate appearance and ended it looking perfectly comfortable as a teenager in a full-season league. Blessed with paint-peeling speed and a quick bat that should develop significant power, Lewis showcased a discriminating eye and looks to be a steady defender at shortstop. He's got all the tools needed to build a big-league career, and the makeup needed to put them to their best use. It may be early, but it's okay to get excited.

Joe Mauer 1B Born: 04/19/83 Age: 35 Bats: L Throws: R Height: 6'5" Weight: 225 Origin: Round 1, 2001 Draft (#1 overall)

YEAR	TEAM	LVL	AGE	PA	R	2B	3B	HR	RBI	BB	K	SB	CS	AVG/OBP/SLG	TAv	VORP	BABIP	BRR	FRAA	WARP
2015	MIN	MLB	32	666	69	34	2	10	66	67	112	2	1	.265/.338/.380	.258	2.7	.309	-2.6	1B(137): -1.7	0.1
2016	MIN	MLB	33	576	68	22	4	11	49	79	93	2	0	.261/.363/.389	.259	3.1	.301	-2.2	1B(95): -2.7	0.0
2017	MIN	MLB	34	597	69	36	1	7	71	66	83	2	1	.305/.384/.417	.274	8.5	.349	-6.6	1B(125): 1.6	1.0
2018	*MIN*	*MLB*	*35*	*549*	*68*	*27*	*2*	*8*	*50*	*63*	*94*	*2*	*1*	*.272/.357/.383*	*.258*	*5.6*	*.322*	*-0.8*	*1B 0*	*0.5*
2019	*MIN*	*MLB*	*36*	*485*	*59*	*23*	*1*	*8*	*48*	*58*	*86*	*0*	*0*	*.268/.357/.386*	*.252*	*0.1*	*.318*	*-2.8*	*1B 0*	*0.0*

Breakout: 4% Improve: 26% Collapse: 6% Attrition: 30% MLB: 81% *Comparables: Doug Mientkiewicz, Greg Brock, Gates Brown*

It was heartwarming to watch a rejuvenated Mauer bat over .300, reach base at a clip reminiscent of his pre-concussion days, play sterling defense and lead his hometown nine back into the playoffs last season. So we feel bad pointing out that Minnesota's first baseman, playing in a hitter-friendly ballpark during a year when the league launched more home runs than ever before, went deep only seven times and ranked among the dregs at his position in both WARP and TAv. It's nearly impossible to provide value at the bottom of the defensive spectrum unless there's significant thunder in your bat, which explains why the last first baseman to keep his job while matching Mauer's run of four seasons with fewer than a dozen home runs was some cat named Rod Carew. Mauer's contract is set to expire this fall, and the Twins will be faced with some hard choices on what to pay and how to play their local hero should he want to return.

Jorge Polanco SS Born: 07/05/93 Age: 24 Bats: B Throws: R Height: 5'11" Weight: 200 Origin: International Free Agent, 2009

YEAR	TEAM	LVL	AGE	PA	R	2B	3B	HR	RBI	BB	K	SB	CS	AVG/OBP/SLG	TAv	VORP	BABIP	BRR	FRAA	WARP
2015	ROC	AAA	21	94	7	6	0	0	6	4	10	1	0	.284/.309/.352	.231	0.8	.313	0.2	SS(19): -0.5	0.0
2015	MIN	MLB	21	12	1	0	0	0	1	2	1	1	0	.300/.417/.300	.270	0.9	.333	0.3	SS(4): -0.5	0.0
2015	CHT	AA	21	431	55	17	3	6	47	35	63	18	10	.289/.346/.393	.261	18.0	.330	1.5	SS(83): 2.6, 2B(8): -0.5	2.2
2016	ROC	AAA	22	325	32	14	6	9	39	27	51	5	4	.276/.335/.457	.287	17.5	.304	0.3	2B(64): 5.7, 3B(2): 0.2	2.4
2016	MIN	MLB	22	270	24	15	4	4	27	17	46	4	3	.282/.332/.424	.259	9.3	.328	-0.7	SS(47): -1.9, 3B(9): -0.8	0.6
2017	MIN	MLB	23	544	60	30	3	13	74	41	78	13	5	.256/.313/.410	.248	17.1	.278	0.8	SS(130): -9.2	0.8
2018	*MIN*	*MLB*	*24*	*580*	*67*	*27*	*5*	*14*	*66*	*42*	*99*	*12*	*6*	*.264/.318/.411*	*.246*	*17.7*	*.298*	*0.3*	*SS -2, 2B 0*	*1.0*
2019	*MIN*	*MLB*	*25*	*581*	*71*	*28*	*5*	*16*	*70*	*47*	*104*	*12*	*6*	*.271/.332/.437*	*.252*	*15.1*	*.307*	*0.3*	*SS -2, 2B 0*	*1.4*

Breakout: 5% Improve: 39% Collapse: 9% Attrition: 22% MLB: 87% *Comparables: Didi Gregorius, Jurickson Profar, Enrique Hernandez*

It's hard to believe that the Polanco putting on a laser show while batting third in a contender's September lineup is the same guy who was slashing .213/.265/.305 on August 1, but there's no video evidence proving otherwise. What we can see, however, is the positive effect of improved pitch recognition on his production. As the season wore on Polanco concentrated on laying off pitches out of the zone, worked himself into better counts and found pitches to drive. Every hitting coach alive preaches this—including the Twins' James Rowson—but to Polanco's credit he didn't just nod along, he went out and did it. For the year his swing rate on pitches out of the zone fell nearly seven percent compared to 2016, one of the biggest drops in the league, and his results improved because of it. His arm is stretched at shortstop, but he makes all the routine plays and some of the spectacular ones, so the Twins will be fine with the more judicious version of Polanco until Javier/Gordon/Lewis comes along.

Brent Rooker OF Born: 11/01/94 Age: 23 Bats: R Throws: R Height: 6'3" Weight: 215 Origin: Round 1, 2017 Draft (#35 overall)

YEAR	TEAM	LVL	AGE	PA	R	2B	3B	HR	RBI	BB	K	SB	CS	AVG/OBP/SLG	TAv	VORP	BABIP	BRR	FRAA	WARP
2017	ELZ	RK	22	99	19	5	0	7	17	11	21	2	2	.282/.364/.588	.308	8.9	.288	0.6	LF(17): 0.4	0.8
2017	FTM	A+	22	162	23	6	0	11	35	16	47	0	0	.280/.364/.552	.332	12.8	.341	-1.5	LF(16): -2.6, 1B(11): -0.4	1.0
2018	*MIN*	*MLB*	*23*	*250*	*31*	*9*	*1*	*13*	*38*	*20*	*79*	*0*	*0*	*.233/.302/.457*	*.247*	*3.6*	*.291*	*-0.4*	*LF -2, 1B 0*	*0.1*
2019	*MIN*	*MLB*	*24*	*226*	*31*	*9*	*1*	*12*	*33*	*18*	*70*	*0*	*0*	*.237/.306/.457*	*.250*	*1.9*	*.295*	*-0.5*	*LF -2, 1B 0*	*0.0*

Breakout: 6% Improve: 19% Collapse: 3% Attrition: 12% MLB: 36% *Comparables: Corey Dickerson, Nick Williams, Jamie Romak*

Rooker put on a fireworks display after the Twins nabbed him late in the first round of last year's draft. The Mississippi State alum understandably pounded rookie-league pitching, but the fact that he kept it up after a challenging promotion to High-A underscores the potential in his lumber. Rooker's grip-it-and-rip-it approach will lead to high strikeout totals, but he's willing to wait out a pitcher who won't challenge him in the zone and accept his walks. His defense in the outfield corners isn't quite a Trumbo-class disaster, but most scouts expect a full-time move to first base, where his bat will play just fine. If he can show the same thump against more advanced pitching this summer, Rooker could start taking aim at the Target Field scoreboard as soon as September.

Eddie Rosario LF Born: 09/28/91 Age: 26 Bats: L Throws: R Height: 6'1" Weight: 180 Origin: Round 4, 2010 Draft (#135 overall)

YEAR	TEAM	LVL	AGE	PA	R	2B	3B	HR	RBI	BB	K	SB	CS	AVG/OBP/SLG	TAv	VORP	BABIP	BRR	FRAA	WARP
2015	ROC	AAA	23	100	11	2	1	3	12	5	17	1	1	.242/.280/.379	.248	0.5	.267	-0.5	CF(11): -0.8, RF(10): -0.3	-0.1
2015	MIN	MLB	23	474	60	18	15	13	50	15	118	11	6	.267/.289/.459	.252	9.8	.332	4.1	LF(86): 12.6, RF(34): -0.4	2.4
2016	ROC	AAA	24	169	26	14	0	7	25	7	25	5	3	.319/.343/.538	.303	13.3	.338	1.1	CF(29): 2.6, RF(9): 3.0	1.9
2016	MIN	MLB	24	354	52	17	2	10	32	12	91	5	2	.269/.295/.421	.248	9.0	.338	4.4	LF(57): 0.7, CF(37): -1.9	0.8
2017	MIN	MLB	25	589	79	33	2	27	78	35	106	9	8	.290/.328/.507	.271	18.1	.312	-1.6	LF(138): -5.1, RF(16): 0.2	1.3
2018	*MIN*	*MLB*	*26*	*578*	*73*	*28*	*6*	*22*	*79*	*29*	*122*	*10*	*6*	*.274/.310/.469*	*.257*	*18.6*	*.314*	*-0.1*	*LF -1, RF -1*	*1.0*
2019	*MIN*	*MLB*	*27*	*555*	*73*	*28*	*5*	*24*	*81*	*33*	*119*	*9*	*6*	*.277/.320/.491*	*.259*	*15.2*	*.314*	*2.5*	*LF -1, RF -1*	*1.5*

Breakout: 6% Improve: 59% Collapse: 2% Attrition: 13% MLB: 94% *Comparables: Cody Asche, Delmon Young, George Bell*

If you were one of the top hundred or so humans blessed with the ability to barrel up a baseball thrown anywhere near you, imagine how difficult it must be not to swing. Or don't imagine it; just watch and feel the yearning that radiates from Rosario as he impatiently awaits his next chance to put a charge into one. His hit tool and plus bat speed have long struggled to overcome his impatient approach, but as last summer wore on Rosario started learning to separate pitches he *can* hit from those he *should* hit. His .292/.331/.558 second-half line was the product of fewer strikeouts, more walks and better counts in which to unleash the surprising juice he can generate to all fields. If Rosario can maintain at least some semblance of selectivity and tighten up the sloppy defense that undermines his cannon arm, he can be an above-average major-league outfielder. If not, he'll remain a hyper-talented out-maker who looks more valuable than he actually is.

Miguel Sano 3B Born: 05/11/93 Age: 25 Bats: R Throws: R Height: 6'4" Weight: 260 Origin: International Free Agent, 2009

YEAR	TEAM	LVL	AGE	PA	R	2B	3B	HR	RBI	BB	K	SB	CS	AVG/OBP/SLG	TAv	VORP	BABIP	BRR	FRAA	WARP
2015	CHT	AA	22	286	55	18	1	15	48	38	68	5	1	.274/.374/.544	.332	30.4	.315	1.0	3B(63): -1.1	3.2
2015	MIN	MLB	22	335	46	17	1	18	52	53	119	1	1	.269/.385/.530	.314	17.7	.396	-4.0	3B(9): -0.4, 1B(2): 0.0	1.9
2016	ROC	AAA	23	30	3	1	0	2	2	5	10	0	0	.160/.300/.440	.239	0.3	.154	0.2	3B(5): -0.5, RF(1): -0.2	0.0
2016	MIN	MLB	23	495	57	22	1	25	66	54	178	1	0	.236/.319/.462	.262	13.6	.329	2.0	3B(42): 6.5, RF(38): -1.9	1.9
2017	MIN	MLB	24	483	75	15	2	28	77	54	173	0	0	.264/.352/.507	.282	22.4	.375	-2.0	3B(82): -5.9, 1B(9): 1.2	1.8
2018	*MIN*	*MLB*	*25*	*610*	*87*	*24*	*2*	*32*	*97*	*74*	*207*	*1*	*0*	*.245/.341/.483*	*.277*	*24.0*	*.332*	*-0.9*	*3B -2, 1B 1*	*2.1*
2019	*MIN*	*MLB*	*26*	*535*	*82*	*22*	*1*	*31*	*86*	*70*	*180*	*1*	*0*	*.246/.349/.500*	*.275*	*19.8*	*.329*	*-1.5*	*3B -1, 1B 1*	*2.1*

Breakout: 3% Improve: 65% Collapse: 3% Attrition: 6% MLB: 97% *Comparables: Mark Reynolds, Kris Bryant, Mike Schmidt*

Sano spent most of last season drawing walks, swinging through pitches and launching whatever he squares up into orbit—in other words, doing exactly what we expect from him—until his latest Three True Outcomes master class came to an abrupt end in August. A foul ball off his shin led to a stress reaction that virtually sidelined him the rest of the way, eventually requiring the permanent insertion of a titanium rod to resolve. He should be ready to go by spring training, but this latest in a series of injuries to dog him has fans, media and even manager Paul Molitor wondering whether a little more dedicated conditioning could help keep the big man on the field. Sano is a preternaturally gifted slugger who has become the beating heart of Minnesota's lineup before his 25th birthday. To a great extent it's up to him how long he can remain there.

Kennys Vargas 1B Born: 08/01/90 Age: 27 Bats: B Throws: R Height: 6'5" Weight: 290 Origin: Undrafted Free Agent, 2009

YEAR	TEAM	LVL	AGE	PA	R	2B	3B	HR	RBI	BB	K	SB	CS	AVG/OBP/SLG	TAv	VORP	BABIP	BRR	FRAA	WARP
2015	CHT	AA	24	151	20	3	2	7	24	26	32	0	0	.287/.417/.516	.339	13.0	.333	-0.7	1B(27): 2.3	1.7
2015	ROC	AAA	24	151	20	6	0	6	22	26	39	0	0	.279/.411/.475	.325	10.8	.359	-1.0	1B(26): 0.9	1.2
2015	MIN	MLB	24	184	18	4	0	5	17	9	54	0	0	.240/.277/.349	.212	-7.7	.319	-1.1	1B(18): 0.2	-0.8
2016	ROC	AAA	25	402	41	16	1	15	58	66	89	1	0	.233/.361/.424	.296	16.1	.270	-3.1	1B(77): -2.3	1.4
2016	MIN	MLB	25	177	27	11	0	10	20	24	57	0	0	.230/.333/.500	.275	2.9	.291	-1.7	1B(32): -2.1	0.1
2017	ROC	AAA	26	211	26	8	1	9	28	31	53	0	0	.253/.360/.461	.294	7.5	.305	-2.8	1B(29): -2.0	0.5
2017	MIN	MLB	26	264	33	13	0	11	41	20	77	0	0	.253/.314/.444	.248	0.7	.325	1.1	1B(40): 0.5	0.1
2018	*MIN*	*MLB*	*27*	*308*	*40*	*12*	*1*	*13*	*44*	*34*	*82*	*0*	*0*	*.247/.335/.444*	*.266*	*7.0*	*.303*	*-0.6*	*1B 0*	*0.5*
2019	*MIN*	*MLB*	*28*	*339*	*48*	*14*	*1*	*16*	*48*	*40*	*91*	*0*	*0*	*.246/.340/.456*	*.263*	*6.8*	*.301*	*-0.7*	*1B 0*	*0.7*

Breakout: 5% Improve: 33% Collapse: 15% Attrition: 25% MLB: 67% *Comparables: Brett Wallace, Mike Carp, Mark Canha*

A hulking switch-hitter with prodigious power and a long swing born to be exploited, Vargas looks for all the world like a Three True Outcomes beast. He even plays like one in the high minors, but when he rides the shuttle to MSP he inevitably forgets to pack his walking stick. Vargas has earned a free pass in 7.6 percent of his major-league plate appearances, less than half his Triple-A walk rate, which lowers his on-base percentage below the acceptable threshold for a whiff-loving, iron-gloved first baseman or designated hitter. The Twins keep hoping someone can fill their gaping DH power void, but Vargas continues to make too many outs to keep the job.

PITCHERS

Matt Belisle RHP Born: 06/06/80 Age: 38 Bats: R Throws: R Height: 6'3" Weight: 230 Origin: Round 2, 1998 Draft (#52 overall)

YEAR	TEAM	LVL	AGE	W	L	SV	G	GS	IP	H	HR	BB/9	K/9	K	GB%	BABIP	WHIP	ERA	DRA	WARP	MPH	CMD	PWR	STM
2015	SLN	MLB	35	1	1	0	34	0	33^{2}	34	1	4.0	6.7	25	55%	.314	1.46	2.67	4.57	0.1	93.5	63	44	27
2016	WAS	MLB	36	0	0	0	40	0	46	43	2	1.4	6.3	32	49%	.285	1.09	1.76	4.82	0.1	93.9	53	46	39
2017	MIN	MLB	37	2	2	9	62	0	60^{1}	48	7	3.3	8.1	54	43%	.253	1.16	4.03	3.47	1.1	93.1	73	40	47
2018	*MIN*	*MLB*	*38*	*2*	*1*	*2*	*44*	*0*	*47*	*50*	*7*	*4.1*	*6.9*	*36*	*46%*	*.301*	*1.53*	*5.15*	*5.24*	*0.0*	*91.9*	*63*	*41*	*38*
2019	*MIN*	*MLB*	*39*	*1*	*0*	*1*	*24*	*0*	*24^{2}*	*28*	*4*	*4.0*	*6.3*	*17*	*46%*	*.298*	*1.56*	*5.82*	*5.97*	*-0.2*	*91.2*	*63*	*41*	*40*

Breakout: 23% Improve: 33% Collapse: 24% Attrition: 8% MLB: 81% *Comparables: David Weathers, Kyle Farnsworth, Francisco Cordero*

Relying on a pitch-to-contact guy like Belisle to close games for a playoff contender may have been the most unlikely baseball scenario since *Air Bud: Seventh Inning Fetch*, yet the veteran reliever was pure, unadulterated Disney down the stretch last fall. He held opponents to a solid .239/.326/.384 line through July, but when the deadline trade of Brandon Kintzler moved Belisle to the ninth inning, that dropped to .164/.203/.328, and he started striking out everyone in sight. The old dog used the same tricks that had helped him build a solid career in middle relief, but the league suddenly started missing his hittable pitches and posted an unsustainably low .179 BABIP down the stretch. Front offices are too smart nowadays to expect (and pay for) a sequel, but Belisle remains a solid seventh-inning option whose clubhouse leadership and veteran moxie will help his stuff play up.

Jose Berrios RHP Born: 05/27/94 Age: 24 Bats: R Throws: R Height: 6'0" Weight: 185 Origin: Round 1, 2012 Draft (#32 overall)

YEAR	TEAM	LVL	AGE	W	L	SV	G	GS	IP	H	HR	BB/9	K/9	K	GB%	BABIP	WHIP	ERA	DRA	WARP	MPH	CMD	PWR	STM
2015	CHT	AA	21	8	3	0	15	15	90^{2}	77	6	2.4	9.1	92	49%	.296	1.11	3.08	1.87	3.5				
2015	ROC	AAA	21	6	2	0	12	12	75^{2}	59	6	1.7	9.9	83	40%	.277	0.96	2.62	1.44	3.3				
2016	ROC	AAA	22	10	5	0	17	17	111^{1}	74	8	2.9	10.1	125	45%	.254	0.99	2.51	1.89	4.4				
2016	MIN	MLB	22	3	7	0	14	14	58^{1}	74	12	5.4	7.6	49	39%	.344	1.87	8.02	6.77	-0.9	95.9	46	52	69
2017	ROC	AAA	23	3	0	0	6	6	39^{2}	24	2	1.8	8.8	39	40%	.214	0.81	1.13	2.26	1.5				
2017	MIN	MLB	23	14	8	0	26	25	145^{2}	131	15	3.0	8.6	139	41%	.289	1.23	3.89	3.62	3.2	95.9	41	52	76
2018	*MIN*	*MLB*	*24*	*11*	*9*	*0*	*30*	*30*	*171*	*161*	*24*	*3.3*	*9.1*	*173*	*42%*	*.296*	*1.32*	*3.95*	*4.18*	*2.4*	*95.7*	*44*	*54*	*75*
2019	*MIN*	*MLB*	*25*	*10*	*10*	*0*	*31*	*31*	*194^{2}*	*179*	*29*	*2.9*	*9.7*	*210*	*42%*	*.296*	*1.25*	*4.30*	*4.37*	*2.5*	*95.5*	*44*	*54*	*76*

Breakout: 23% Improve: 64% Collapse: 14% Attrition: 15% MLB: 92% *Comparables: Michael Pineda, Jarrod Parker, Daniel Hudson*

The Berrios your prospect-junkie friend has long been telling you about finally arrived at Target Field last summer, and he was well worth the wait. The last Twins pitchers to start at least 25 games and post a higher strikeout rate than Berrios did last summer were Francisco Liriano and Johan Santana; the last one before them was ... no one, ever. Berrios dropped his arm slot, moved to the third-base side of the rubber and made a few other mechanical adjustments after his disastrous 2016, resulting in more fastball spin, better command and more first-pitch strikes. Getting ahead in the count is always important but especially so for Berrios, whose sweeping curveball can be one of the game's most fearsome weapons when batters are in the hole and can't afford to take a strike. He needs to work on his changeup to give lefties something else to worry about, but it's easy to see Berrios is Minnesota's first homegrown pitcher with front-line potential in a long time.

Buddy Boshers LHP Born: 05/09/88 Age: 30 Bats: L Throws: L Height: 6'3" Weight: 205 Origin: Round 4, 2008 Draft (#139 overall)

YEAR	TEAM	LVL	AGE	W	L	SV	G	GS	IP	H	HR	BB/9	K/9	K	GB%	BABIP	WHIP	ERA	DRA	WARP	MPH	CMD	PWR	STM
2016	ROC	AAA	28	1	1	2	22	0	26	18	1	3.8	10.0	29	48%	.266	1.12	1.04	3.51	0.4				
2016	MIN	MLB	28	2	0	0	37	0	36	35	3	1.8	9.2	37	48%	.308	1.17	4.25	3.54	0.6	94.2	62	37	45
2017	ROC	AAA	29	0	0	0	18	0	14^{2}	16	1	4.9	9.2	15	52%	.366	1.64	3.68	4.43	0.1				
2017	MIN	MLB	29	1	0	0	38	0	35	37	7	2.6	7.2	28	47%	.283	1.34	4.89	4.48	0.3	91.6	54	25	43
2018	*MIN*	*MLB*	*30*	*2*	*2*	*0*	*40*	*0*	*42*	*44*	*6*	*4.0*	*7.8*	*37*	*45%*	*.300*	*1.49*	*4.76*	*4.79*	*0.2*	*92.0*	*57*	*30*	*44*
2019	*MIN*	*MLB*	*31*	*2*	*1*	*0*	*33*	*0*	*35^{1}*	*40*	*6*	*4.5*	*6.6*	*26*	*45%*	*.307*	*1.64*	*5.66*	*5.80*	*-0.2*	*91.6*	*57*	*30*	*44*

Breakout: 19% Improve: 38% Collapse: 16% Attrition: 20% MLB: 67% *Comparables: Doug Slaten, Chaz Roe, Cory Gearrin*

Of all the things manager Paul Molitor did or didn't get right last year, nothing seemed to annoy Twins Twitter as much as his handling of Boshers. Everyone knows "The Waterboy" can be effective against same-side hitters but should be hidden from righties for the same reason firecrackers are hidden from children, so the Internet howls could be heard from Albert Lea to Grand Marais whenever Boshers was left in to face a righty slugger in a key situation. He has limited lefties to a career .245/.277/.344 line, so if spotted wisely Boshers may be able to hold on as a serviceable but not dominant specialist for a few more years.

Alan Busenitz RHP Born: 08/22/90 Age: 27 Bats: R Throws: R Height: 6'1" Weight: 180 Origin: Round 25, 2013 Draft (#757 overall)

YEAR	TEAM	LVL	AGE	W	L	SV	G	GS	IP	H	HR	BB/9	K/9	K	GB%	BABIP	WHIP	ERA	DRA	WARP	MPH	CMD	PWR	STM
2015	ARK	AA	24	1	5	0	16	8	53^1	80	7	2.7	6.4	38	52%	.395	1.80	6.75	4.41	0.4				
2015	INL	A+	24	0	2	2	21	0	46^1	49	2	3.1	8.5	44	50%	.353	1.40	3.30	3.83	0.5				
2016	ARK	AA	25	0	1	3	24	0	32^2	29	2	1.4	8.8	32	52%	.318	1.04	1.93	2.76	0.8				
2016	SLC	AAA	25	0	1	0	10	0	13	16	1	3.5	9.0	13	42%	.375	1.62	7.62	4.29	0.1				
2017	ROC	AAA	26	3	0	2	24	0	35^1	19	0	2.5	9.9	39	43%	.235	0.82	1.78	2.14	1.2				
2017	MIN	MLB	26	1	1	0	28	0	31^2	22	4	2.6	6.5	23	38%	.212	0.98	1.99	4.98	0.1	97.0	55	64	45
2018	*MIN*	*MLB*	*27*	*2*	*3*	*0*	*50*	*0*	*53*	*56*	*9*	*3.9*	*8.0*	*47*	*43%*	*.305*	*1.50*	*4.93*	*4.93*	*0.1*	*96.5*	*56*	*65*	*46*
2019	*MIN*	*MLB*	*28*	*2*	*1*	*0*	*37*	*0*	39^1	*43*	*6*	*4.0*	*8.2*	*36*	*43%*	*.316*	*1.53*	*5.18*	*5.31*	*0.0*	*96.1*	*56*	*65*	*46*

Breakout: 17% Improve: 25% Collapse: 10% Attrition: 26% MLB: 41% *Comparables: Travis Schlichting, C.J. Riefenhauser, Tim Wood*

A former 25th-round pick from Kennesaw State, Busenitz has ridden his mid-90s fastball from small college obscurity through late-round anonymity and minor-league drudgery to major-league relevancy. His heater may lack the late movement or steep downward plane that distinguishes the great ones, but it arrives in a hurry with a lot of spin and can overpower hitters who aren't geared up to match it. Busenitz posted a glittering ERA in the Minnesota 'pen that belied a mundane FIP more indicative of his subpar strikeout rate and sketchy secondary stuff. Still, he doesn't hand out many walks and his velocity can spackle over a lot of other flaws, so Busenitz is a solid, low-cost choice to pop mitts in the middle innings.

Bartolo Colon RHP Born: 05/24/73 Age: 45 Bats: R Throws: R Height: 5'11" Weight: 285 Origin: International Free Agent, 1993

YEAR	TEAM	LVL	AGE	W	L	SV	G	GS	IP	H	HR	BB/9	K/9	K	GB%	BABIP	WHIP	ERA	DRA	WARP	MPH	CMD	PWR	STM
2015	NYN	MLB	42	14	13	0	33	31	194^2	217	25	1.1	6.3	136	44%	.307	1.24	4.16	5.32	-0.6	92.8	66	53	72
2016	NYN	MLB	43	15	8	0	34	33	191^2	200	24	1.5	6.0	128	45%	.291	1.21	3.43	5.45	-0.2	92.1	70	59	74
2017	ATL	MLB	44	2	8	0	13	13	63	92	11	2.9	6.0	42	48%	.360	1.78	8.14	6.04	-0.3	91.5	73	49	64
2017	MIN	MLB	44	5	6	0	15	15	80	100	17	1.7	5.3	47	42%	.307	1.44	5.18	6.65	-1.0	91.3	73	49	64
2018	*MIN*	*MLB*	*45*	*7*	*8*	*0*	*21*	*21*	125^2	*160*	*19*	*2.8*	*5.1*	*71*	*44%*	*.322*	*1.59*	*5.20*	*5.28*	*0.6*	*89.9*	*67*	*51*	*66*
2019	*MIN*	*MLB*	*46*	*5*	*6*	*0*	*15*	*15*	87^1	*112*	*14*	*2.6*	*5.1*	*49*	*44%*	*.323*	*1.57*	*5.35*	*5.46*	*0.2*	*88.9*	*67*	*50*	*64*

Breakout: 9% Improve: 18% Collapse: 7% Attrition: 0% MLB: 28% *Comparables: David Wells, Tim Wakefield, Jamie Moyer*

When the end finally comes, if it hasn't already, it will surprise no one, yet it will surprise everyone. Big Sexy has been working his mojo nearly as long as bumblebees have taken flight and with just as much visual wonderment, with each successful season in his forties certainly being his last until the moment it became clear it wasn't. If his late-career success has been a magic trick, it's been one of the Penn and Teller variety where you know exactly how it works—in this case, throw nothing but slow fastballs exactly where you want to throw them—and the entertainment comes from watching the talent, precision and audacity necessary to pull it off. Last year's Minnesota stint wasn't quite as disastrous as his sojourn in Atlanta, but for the first time Colon truly pitched like a replacement-level veteran whose curtain is finally coming down. Unless, of course, it isn't.

John Curtiss RHP Born: 04/05/93 Age: 25 Bats: R Throws: R Height: 6'4" Weight: 200 Origin: Round 6, 2014 Draft (#170 overall)

YEAR	TEAM	LVL	AGE	W	L	SV	G	GS	IP	H	HR	BB/9	K/9	K	GB%	BABIP	WHIP	ERA	DRA	WARP	MPH	CMD	PWR	STM
2015	CDR	A	22	3	3	2	16	7	46	62	10	2.0	8.6	44	39%	.371	1.57	6.07	4.16	0.5				
2016	FTM	A+	23	0	2	3	38	0	53	42	0	3.9	11.5	68	39%	.326	1.23	3.06	1.96	1.9				
2017	CHT	AA	24	2	0	13	21	0	25	12	0	4.3	12.6	35	52%	.231	0.96	0.72	1.99	0.8				
2017	ROC	AAA	24	0	0	6	18	0	24^1	11	0	3.7	12.2	33	46%	.212	0.86	1.85	2.12	0.8				
2017	MIN	MLB	24	0	0	0	9	0	8^2	9	2	2.1	10.4	10	24%	.304	1.27	8.31	5.10	0.0	97.0			42
2018	*MIN*	*MLB*	*25*	*2*	*2*	*0*	*40*	*0*	*42*	*39*	*6*	*4.7*	*10.2*	*48*	*40%*	*.303*	*1.47*	*4.29*	*4.43*	*0.3*	*96.7*			*43*
2019	*MIN*	*MLB*	*26*	*2*	*1*	*0*	*46*	*0*	*49*	*46*	*8*	*4.2*	*10.5*	*57*	*40%*	*.305*	*1.40*	*4.61*	*4.70*	*0.3*	*96.4*			*43*

Breakout: 19% Improve: 25% Collapse: 15% Attrition: 36% MLB: 46% *Comparables: Santiago Casilla, Ben Heller, Jeff Beliveau*

Curtiss parlayed a dominant season closing in the high minors into a September cup of coffee, and while big-league hitters knocked him around a bit there's a lot to like here. An Academic All-American at the University of Texas, Curtiss survived Tommy John surgery, thoracic outlet surgery and the Brontë sisters with his top-shelf fastball velocity intact. After another bout of elbow soreness scuppered Minnesota's plans to make him into a starter he's been lights out in the 'pen. His mid-90s heater can be overpowering and his hard-breaking slider generates plenty of awkward swings, as Curtiss whiffed more than a third of the batters he faced last year and dominated hitters on both sides of the plate. If he can apply enough ice to reduce his swollen walk rate, Curtiss has more than enough stuff to function as a serviceable setup man.

Tyler Duffey RHP Born: 12/27/90 Age: 27 Bats: R Throws: R Height: 6'3" Weight: 220 Origin: Round 5, 2012 Draft (#160 overall)

YEAR	TEAM	LVL	AGE	W	L	SV	G	GS	IP	H	HR	BB/9	K/9	K	GB%	BABIP	WHIP	ERA	DRA	WARP	MPH	CMD	PWR	STM
2015	CHT	AA	24	2	2	0	8	8	52^{2}	46	0	2.1	9.2	54	54%	.322	1.10	2.56	1.88	2.0				
2015	ROC	AAA	24	5	6	0	14	14	85^{1}	73	1	1.9	7.2	68	47%	.276	1.07	2.53	2.80	2.4				
2015	MIN	MLB	24	5	1	0	10	10	58	56	4	3.1	8.2	53	51%	.315	1.31	3.10	3.63	1.0	93.3	52	35	74
2016	ROC	AAA	25	1	1	0	5	5	30^{2}	24	4	3.5	7.3	25	35%	.238	1.17	2.93	4.64	0.2				
2016	MIN	MLB	25	9	12	0	26	26	133	167	25	2.2	7.7	114	49%	.339	1.50	6.43	4.65	1.1	93.2	50	39	70
2017	MIN	MLB	26	2	3	1	56	0	71	79	9	2.3	8.5	67	50%	.326	1.37	4.94	3.64	1.2	93.8	60	44	48
2018	*MIN*	*MLB*	*27*	*3*	*3*	*0*	*60*	*0*	*63*	*61*	*7*	*3.3*	*8.3*	*59*	*47%*	*.296*	*1.32*	*3.72*	*3.99*	*0.8*	*93.0*	*54*	*40*	*63*
2019	*MIN*	*MLB*	*28*	*3*	*1*	*0*	*56*	*0*	*59*	*54*	*7*	*3.0*	*8.9*	*58*	*47%*	*.293*	*1.25*	*3.97*	*4.04*	*0.8*	*92.7*	*54*	*41*	*60*

Breakout: 33% Improve: 62% Collapse: 13% Attrition: 12% MLB: 90% *Comparables: Anthony DeSclafani, Liam Hendriks, Matt Andriese*

"This is the primordial soup from which middle relievers and swingmen evolve." So we wrote before Duffey's 2015 season, and after two up-and-down seasons in the rotation and a move to the 'pen, that's exactly what he's grown into. His four-seamer found another gear in relief and started missing bats, pairing nicely with his often-baffling curveball to produce an improved strikeout rate while keeping his walks in check. Duffey's ERA was nothing to write home about, but his peripherals had plenty to say, describing a young man poised to join the likes of Adam Warren and Craig Stammen as a successful multi-inning reliever and occasional spot starter. Not bad for a guy we once described as discrete organic matter floating in a warm sea.

Zach Duke LHP Born: 04/19/83 Age: 35 Bats: L Throws: L Height: 6'2" Weight: 210 Origin: Round 20, 2001 Draft (#594 overall)

YEAR	TEAM	LVL	AGE	W	L	SV	G	GS	IP	H	HR	BB/9	K/9	K	GB%	BABIP	WHIP	ERA	DRA	WARP	MPH	CMD	PWR	STM
2015	CHA	MLB	32	3	6	1	71	0	60^{2}	47	9	4.7	9.8	66	59%	.264	1.30	3.41	3.68	0.7	92.0	47	29	51
2016	CHA	MLB	33	2	0	1	53	0	37^{2}	31	2	3.8	10.0	42	65%	.299	1.25	2.63	2.98	0.9	92.4	56	38	52
2016	SLN	MLB	33	0	1	1	28	0	23^{1}	17	0	5.0	10.0	26	60%	.293	1.29	1.93	4.26	0.2	92.1	56	38	52
2017	SLN	MLB	34	1	1	0	27	0	18^{1}	13	3	2.9	5.9	12	52%	.196	1.04	3.93	4.98	0.0	89.7	64	21	41
2018	*MIN*	*MLB*	*35*	*1*	*1*	*0*	*25*	*0*	*26*	*27*	*4*	*4.6*	*7.6*	*22*	*54%*	*.296*	*1.53*	*5.06*	*5.02*	*0.0*	*90.5*	*53*	*31*	*46*
2019	*MIN*	*MLB*	*36*	*2*	*1*	*0*	*36*	*0*	*38*	*39*	*6*	*4.7*	*7.5*	*32*	*54%*	*.299*	*1.56*	*5.10*	*5.70*	*-0.2*	*89.9*	*55*	*32*	*45*

Breakout: 22% Improve: 36% Collapse: 24% Attrition: 14% MLB: 76% *Comparables: Kiko Calero, Jose Veras, Akinori Otsuka*

When Matt Albers recorded his first save in 12 years, it made Internet cult headlines. Another drought less mentioned was when Albers pitched in his first postseason, thereby passing the dubious torch of "active pitcher with the most appearances without a playoff appearance" to the Duke, who didn't really ask for this label and why would he. All he's trying to do is recoup from Tommy John surgery; he got two months of time in with the Cardinals, but the velocity didn't come back. That's not vitally important for a lefty reliever, but if the days of throwing 90 mph are behind him he may not be able to help a team reach the playoffs, forever carrying that torch until he hangs it up.

Dietrich Enns LHP Born: 05/16/91 Age: 27 Bats: L Throws: L Height: 6'1" Weight: 210 Origin: Round 19, 2012 Draft (#607 overall)

YEAR	TEAM	LVL	AGE	W	L	SV	G	GS	IP	H	HR	BB/9	K/9	K	GB%	BABIP	WHIP	ERA	DRA	WARP	MPH	CMD	PWR	STM
2015	YAT	RK	24	1	0	0	3	3	11^{1}	6	0	4.8	11.9	15	72%	.240	1.06	0.00	3.28	0.3				
2015	TAM	A+	24	1	1	0	10	9	47^{1}	27	0	2.7	7.6	40	40%	.206	0.87	0.76	3.48	0.9				
2016	TRN	AA	25	7	2	0	12	12	70	55	3	3.9	9.5	74	35%	.297	1.21	1.93	3.29	1.5				
2016	SWB	AAA	25	7	2	1	14	10	65	47	3	3.6	6.9	50	42%	.253	1.12	1.52	4.36	0.7				
2017	SWB	AAA	26	1	1	0	7	7	39^{1}	30	1	2.3	8.5	37	45%	.271	1.02	2.29	3.10	1.1				
2017	MIN	MLB	26	0	0	0	2	1	4	7	2	2.2	4.5	2	39%	.312	2.00	6.75	6.29	0.0	91.1			21
2017	ROC	AAA	26	0	1	1	3	1	11^{2}	13	2	3.1	6.9	9	39%	.324	1.46	2.31	3.85	0.2				
2018	*MIN*	*MLB*	*27*	*6*	*6*	*0*	*16*	*16*	*91*	*94*	*15*	*4.0*	*7.7*	*78*	*41%*	*.295*	*1.48*	*4.74*	*5.03*	*0.4*	*90.6*			*21*
2019	*MIN*	*MLB*	*28*	*9*	*11*	*0*	*29*	*29*	*177^{2}*	*184*	*31*	*3.9*	*7.7*	*151*	*41%*	*.295*	*1.47*	*5.40*	*5.53*	*0.2*	*90.1*			*21*

Breakout: 13% Improve: 26% Collapse: 19% Attrition: 23% MLB: 53% *Comparables: Carlos Torres, Warwick Saupold, Jacob Barnes*

Minnesota's quick flip of the recently acquired Jaime Garcia raised some eyebrows at the trade deadline last summer, but the Twins are hopeful that the Enns will justify the means. The former Yankees farmhand has plus lefty velocity and a deep assortment of off-speed stuff that he's used to run roughshod over the minor leagues, striking out more than a man per inning and posting a career 1.88 ERA. Of course, Enns did much of that damage as a polished college product dominating green competition in the bus leagues, so it's fair to question how much of his success will translate to Target Field. Injuries have chipped away at his development time and he'll likely wind up in relief, but the Twins can use all the live arms they can get.

Dillon Gee RHP Born: 04/28/86 Age: 32 Bats: R Throws: R Height: 6'1" Weight: 205 Origin: Round 21, 2007 Draft (#663 overall)

YEAR	TEAM	LVL	AGE	W	L	SV	G	GS	IP	H	HR	BB/9	K/9	K	GB%	BABIP	WHIP	ERA	DRA	WARP	MPH	CMD	PWR	STM
2015	SLU	A+	29	0	0	0	2	2	10^{1}	9	0	0.0	10.5	12	59%	.333	0.87	0.87	1.65	0.4				
2015	NYN	MLB	29	0	3	0	8	7	39^{2}	55	5	2.5	5.7	25	53%	.355	1.66	5.90	6.46	-0.7	92.2	48	33	63
2015	LVG	AAA	29	8	3	0	14	14	88^{1}	105	7	1.8	6.4	63	45%	.338	1.39	4.58	3.64	1.7				
2016	KCA	MLB	30	8	9	0	33	14	125	146	24	2.7	6.4	89	42%	.309	1.46	4.68	6.01	-1.2	92.5	49	35	60
2017	ROU	AAA	31	3	4	0	9	9	51	53	5	2.3	7.6	43	42%	.306	1.29	3.88	3.57	1.2				
2017	TEX	MLB	31	0	0	0	4	1	13	17	4	4.2	6.9	10	44%	.333	1.77	4.15	4.31	0.1	92.4	59	32	57
2017	ROC	AAA	31	3	1	0	5	5	27	24	1	1.0	6.7	20	35%	.291	1.00	2.00	4.28	0.4				
2017	MIN	MLB	31	3	2	1	14	3	36^{1}	37	4	2.2	7.7	31	44%	.314	1.27	3.22	4.50	0.3	92.5	59	32	57
2018	*MIN*	*MLB*	*32*	*6*	*6*	*0*	*31*	*16*	*104^{2}*	*121*	*19*	*3.3*	*6.5*	*76*	*43%*	*.308*	*1.52*	*5.41*	*5.51*	*0.1*	*91.5*	*51*	*34*	*59*
2019	*MIN*	*MLB*	*33*	*4*	*5*	*0*	*17*	*12*	*83^{2}*	*97*	*15*	*3.0*	*6.5*	*60*	*43%*	*.307*	*1.50*	*5.52*	*5.66*	*-0.1*	*91.0*	*51*	*33*	*58*

Breakout: 18% Improve: 47% Collapse: 23% Attrition: 19% MLB: 88% *Comparables: Tim Stauffer, Brandon Morrow, Chris Narveson*

The English language can be so baffling. For example, it's correct to say that Gee found himself in the bullpen last summer after a long career spent mostly as a starter. At the same time, it's not at all correct to say that Gee *found himself* in the bullpen last summer, as he didn't suddenly start lobbing thunderbolts and whiffleballs and grow into a fire-breathing closer. Instead, he relied on his usual assortment of low-velo junk to not quite achieve adequacy in Texas before his June release, and achieve adequacy in Minnesota afterward. If Gee's repertoire were as baffling as the English language he'd probably find himself back in the rotation; since it's not, he'll likely get another chance to *find himself* in a bullpen this summer.

Kyle Gibson RHP Born: 10/23/87 Age: 30 Bats: R Throws: R Height: 6'6" Weight: 215 Origin: Round 1, 2009 Draft (#22 overall)

YEAR	TEAM	LVL	AGE	W	L	SV	G	GS	IP	H	HR	BB/9	K/9	K	GB%	BABIP	WHIP	ERA	DRA	WARP	MPH	CMD	PWR	STM
2015	MIN	MLB	27	11	11	0	32	32	194^2	186	18	3.0	6.7	145	56%	.287	1.29	3.84	3.29	4.1	94.5	55	46	78
2016	MIN	MLB	28	6	11	0	25	25	147^1	175	20	3.4	6.4	104	50%	.330	1.56	5.07	5.44	-0.1	93.6	54	44	69
2017	ROC	AAA	29	1	2	0	3	3	17^1	13	1	2.6	11.9	23	60%	.308	1.04	2.08	2.07	0.7				
2017	MIN	MLB	29	12	10	0	29	29	158	182	24	3.4	6.9	121	52%	.328	1.53	5.07	6.30	-1.3	94.4	55	46	74
2018	*MIN*	*MLB*	*30*	*10*	*10*	*0*	*29*	*29*	*153^2*	*167*	*22*	*3.6*	*6.5*	*110*	*51%*	*.302*	*1.51*	*4.64*	*4.92*	*0.8*	*93.4*	*55*	*45*	*73*
2019	*MIN*	*MLB*	*31*	*8*	*11*	*0*	*28*	*28*	*172^1*	*189*	*27*	*3.7*	*6.7*	*128*	*51%*	*.305*	*1.51*	*5.38*	*5.51*	*0.2*	*92.9*	*54*	*45*	*72*

Breakout: 11% Improve: 44% Collapse: 28% Attrition: 12% MLB: 90% *Comparables: Doug Fister, Clay Buchholz, Brandon McCarthy*

Gibson was awful out of the gate last spring but, like so many of his teammates, was at his best down the stretch. The Twins won all six of his September starts while the veteran righty posted a 3.28 ERA and held opponents to a .248/.302/.388 line, helping to propel his team to the wild card game. Unfortunately, the rest of the season also happened, during which Gibson once again proved that his greatest strength is his willingness to take the ball, and his greatest weakness is his inability to then throw it past someone. His strikeout, walk and home-run rates are all subpar, and as he enters his thirties that's not about to change. Innings-eaters have their uses, but you'll know the Twins are serious title contenders once theirs isn't also the no. 3 starter.

Stephen Gonsalves LHP Born: 07/08/94 Age: 23 Bats: L Throws: L Height: 6'5" Weight: 213 Origin: Round 4, 2013 Draft (#110 overall)

YEAR	TEAM	LVL	AGE	W	L	SV	G	GS	IP	H	HR	BB/9	K/9	K	GB%	BABIP	WHIP	ERA	DRA	WARP	MPH	CMD	PWR	STM
2015	CDR	A	20	6	1	0	9	9	55	29	2	2.5	12.6	77	41%	.243	0.80	1.15	1.09	2.7				
2015	FTM	A+	20	7	2	0	15	15	79^1	66	2	4.3	6.2	55	39%	.270	1.31	2.61	7.82	-2.6				
2016	FTM	A+	21	5	4	0	11	11	65^2	43	2	2.7	9.0	66	48%	.248	0.96	2.33	2.26	2.4				
2016	CHT	AA	21	8	1	0	13	13	74^1	43	1	4.5	10.8	89	38%	.255	1.08	1.82	3.56	1.4				
2017	CHT	AA	22	8	3	0	15	15	87^1	67	7	2.4	9.9	96	35%	.270	1.03	2.68	3.39	1.9				
2017	ROC	AAA	22	1	2	0	5	4	22^2	27	4	3.2	8.7	22	34%	.343	1.54	5.56	5.84	0.0				
2018	*MIN*	*MLB*	*23*	*4*	*4*	*0*	*20*	*10*	*63*	*60*	*11*	*3.8*	*9.6*	*68*	*37%*	*.293*	*1.37*	*4.48*	*4.69*	*0.5*				
2019	*MIN*	*MLB*	*24*	*8*	*10*	*0*	*27*	*27*	*162^2*	*151*	*31*	*3.9*	*10.0*	*181*	*37%*	*.288*	*1.36*	*5.09*	*5.22*	*0.7*				

Breakout: 28% Improve: 42% Collapse: 11% Attrition: 23% MLB: 59% *Comparables: Jacob Faria, Dylan Bundy, Jon Gray*

Now *this* is what a no. 3 starter looks like. Gonsalves has marched steadily through the minors and polished off Double-A last summer before dipping his toe in the International League. Along the way he's flashed solid command of a low-90s fastball along with a plus changeup that proofs him against huge platoon splits and a curveball that's more than just a show-me pitch. Gonsalves has an ideal starter's frame and an easy three-quarters delivery that he repeats well, allowing him to command his offerings to both sides of the plate. If he keeps his normal schedule and makes strides with his control he should solve Triple-A by Independence Day and could be a boost to the rotation down the stretch.

Trevor Hildenberger RHP Born: 12/15/90 Age: 27 Bats: R Throws: R Height: 6'2" Weight: 211 Origin: Round 22, 2014 Draft (#650 overall)

YEAR	TEAM	LVL	AGE	W	L	SV	G	GS	IP	H	HR	BB/9	K/9	K	GB%	BABIP	WHIP	ERA	DRA	WARP	MPH	CMD	PWR	STM
2015	CDR	A	24	2	1	14	28	0	45	24	0	1.0	11.8	59	68%	.238	0.64	0.80	0.87	2.1				
2015	FTM	A+	24	1	1	3	13	0	19	15	0	0.9	9.9	21	65%	.312	0.89	3.32	1.69	0.7				
2016	CHT	AA	25	2	3	16	32	0	38^2	21	2	1.4	10.5	45	61%	.211	0.70	0.70	1.37	1.6				
2017	ROC	AAA	26	2	1	6	21	0	30^2	27	1	2.3	10.3	35	56%	.321	1.14	2.05	1.81	1.2				
2017	MIN	MLB	26	3	3	1	37	0	42	38	4	1.3	9.4	44	60%	.304	1.05	3.21	2.50	1.2	93.2	52	26	49
2018	*MIN*	*MLB*	*27*	*3*	*3*	*2*	*55*	*0*	*58*	*56*	*8*	*3.4*	*9.2*	*60*	*54%*	*.299*	*1.34*	*3.92*	*4.15*	*0.7*	*92.7*	*53*	*26*	*50*
2019	*MIN*	*MLB*	*28*	*3*	*1*	*2*	*52*	*0*	*55^1*	*52*	*7*	*3.0*	*9.5*	*58*	*54%*	*.302*	*1.27*	*4.13*	*4.20*	*0.6*	*92.3*	*53*	*26*	*50*

Breakout: 24% Improve: 38% Collapse: 24% Attrition: 22% MLB: 82% *Comparables: Hunter Strickland, Sergio Romo, Nick Vincent*

Hildenberger never got much prospect love while posting video-game numbers in the minor leagues due to his advanced age and gimmicky side-arm delivery. However, once he started opening institutional-sized cans of whoop-ass au gratin and pouring them over shamefaced big leaguers, the world started to pay attention. Especially Paul Molitor, who became a glutton for the best thing on his bullpen menu and ordered up a Triple Meat Hildenberger as often as he could down the stretch. His unorthodox delivery helps his slow-and-slower routine, but so does the lack of spin that makes his pitches "heavy." Hildenberger's low-90s sinker gets extra tumble into the bottom of the zone, while his changeup plummets below it, causing hitters to swing over the top or pound it into the ground. Yet he manages to avoid ball four, posting a strikeout-to-walk ratio that rests comfortably between Corey Kluber and Chris Sale. The Twins have seen their share of bullpen comets flame out, including side-armers (see: Neshek, Pat), but Hildenberger just may have the goods to stick around a while.

Phil Hughes RHP

Born: 06/24/86 Age: 31 Bats: R Throws: R Height: 6'5" Weight: 240 Origin: Round 1, 2004 Draft (#23 overall)

YEAR	TEAM	LVL	AGE	W	L	SV	G	GS	IP	H	HR	BB/9	K/9	K	GB%	BABIP	WHIP	ERA	DRA	WARP	MPH	CMD	PWR	STM
2015	MIN	MLB	29	11	9	0	27	25	155^{1}	184	29	0.9	5.4	94	37%	.304	1.29	4.40	5.62	-1.0	93.1	58	48	61
2016	MIN	MLB	30	1	7	0	12	11	59	76	11	2.0	5.2	34	36%	.323	1.51	5.95	6.98	-1.1	92.5	61	47	47
2017	MIN	MLB	31	4	3	0	14	9	53^{2}	72	12	2.2	6.4	38	30%	.333	1.58	5.87	7.12	-1.0	91.6	56	35	41
2018	*MIN*	*MLB*	*32*	*1*	*2*	*0*	*5*	*5*	*25*	*31*	*6*	*3.1*	*5.8*	*16*	*36%*	*.298*	*1.62*	*5.59*	*5.92*	*-0.2*	*91.6*	*58*	*43*	*48*
2019	*MIN*	*MLB*	*33*	*6*	*11*	*0*	*27*	*27*	*159*	*209*	*37*	*2.9*	*5.5*	*97*	*36%*	*.318*	*1.63*	*6.31*	*6.48*	*-1.2*	*90.9*	*57*	*41*	*45*

Breakout: 10% Improve: 40% Collapse: 27% Attrition: 6% MLB: 87% *Comparables: Brad Radke, Don Newcombe, Freddy Garcia*

Hughes started last season in the rotation but began experiencing the same numbing symptoms that led to his 2016 thoracic outlet surgery. Rest and a move to the bullpen didn't help, so the former Yankee went under the knife again last August to try to correct things once and for all. When he was on the mound Hughes showed his usual propensity for the long ball alongside diminished velocity, so what he'll be if he can return this year is an open question. All that's certain is that the Twins owe him $26.4 million through 2019 as part of an ill-advised Terry Ryan extension, money we're sure Hughes would much rather earn on the bump than in the whirlpool.

Myles Jaye RHP

Born: 12/28/91 Age: 26 Bats: B Throws: R Height: 6'3" Weight: 170 Origin: Round 17, 2010 Draft (#516 overall)

YEAR	TEAM	LVL	AGE	W	L	SV	G	GS	IP	H	HR	BB/9	K/9	K	GB%	BABIP	WHIP	ERA	DRA	WARP	MPH	CMD	PWR	STM
2015	BIR	AA	23	12	9	0	26	26	147^{2}	135	8	2.9	6.3	104	48%	.284	1.23	3.29	4.47	1.1				
2016	ERI	AA	24	4	8	0	21	21	122^{2}	127	11	2.1	7.6	104	53%	.311	1.27	4.04	3.59	2.2				
2016	TOL	AAA	24	1	4	0	7	7	39	30	2	2.8	7.2	31	51%	.248	1.08	3.69	5.52	-0.1				
2017	ERI	AA	25	1	7	0	14	14	71^{1}	77	8	2.9	9.2	73	49%	.333	1.40	4.29	4.03	1.0				
2017	TOL	AAA	25	3	6	0	11	11	60^{1}	71	3	3.4	6.3	42	55%	.342	1.56	3.58	5.47	0.2				
2017	DET	MLB	25	1	2	0	5	2	12^{2}	18	2	7.1	2.8	4	50%	.308	2.21	12.08	7.07	-0.2	91.8	30	38	70
2018	*MIN*	*MLB*	*26*	*8*	*8*	*0*	*23*	*23*	129^{1}	*140*	*21*	*3.4*	*7.5*	*108*	*48%*	*.306*	*1.46*	*4.98*	*5.06*	*0.9*	*91.4*	*31*	*39*	*71*
2019	*MIN*	*MLB*	*27*	*4*	*5*	*0*	*13*	*13*	*76*	*83*	*12*	*3.7*	*7.2*	*61*	*48%*	*.306*	*1.50*	*5.31*	*5.44*	*0.2*	*91.0*	*31*	*39*	*72*

Breakout: 25% Improve: 38% Collapse: 11% Attrition: 30% MLB: 55% *Comparables: Zeke Spruill, Mitch Talbot, Tyler Wagner*

What do you do with a 25-year-old righty who compensates for passable stuff with above-average command? If you're the Tigers, you chuck him at the Indians right in the middle of their 22-game winning streak. That worked about as well as pumping the brakes on a patch of black ice: Jaye spun out in a blowout loss and never fully recovered, bruising his chances of making the rotation with a seven-something DRA and a walk rate that nearly rivaled Andrew Romine's.

Felix Jorge RHP

Born: 01/02/94 Age: 24 Bats: R Throws: R Height: 6'2" Weight: 170 Origin: International Free Agent, 2011

YEAR	TEAM	LVL	AGE	W	L	SV	G	GS	IP	H	HR	BB/9	K/9	K	GB%	BABIP	WHIP	ERA	DRA	WARP	MPH	CMD	PWR	STM
2015	CDR	A	21	6	7	0	23	22	142	118	11	2.0	7.2	114	47%	.267	1.06	2.79	3.30	3.2				
2016	FTM	A+	22	9	3	0	14	14	93	76	3	1.1	7.5	77	52%	.280	0.94	1.55	2.40	3.3				
2016	CHT	AA	22	3	5	0	11	11	74^{1}	83	7	1.5	3.9	32	52%	.306	1.28	4.12	5.05	0.0				
2017	MIN	MLB	23	1	0	0	2	2	7^{2}	14	4	2.3	4.7	4	27%	.385	2.09	10.57	8.88	-0.3	94.2			70
2017	CHT	AA	23	10	3	0	22	22	134^{2}	142	11	2.5	6.6	99	51%	.316	1.33	3.54	3.37	2.9				
2017	ROC	AAA	23	0	1	0	3	3	14^{1}	19	3	1.9	5.7	9	50%	.356	1.53	5.02	4.85	0.1				
2018	*MIN*	*MLB*	*24*	*3*	*3*	*0*	*13*	*8*	*50*	*57*	*9*	*3.2*	*6.4*	*36*	*45%*	*.299*	*1.49*	*4.84*	*5.06*	*0.2*	*94.0*			*72*
2019	*MIN*	*MLB*	*25*	*8*	*10*	*0*	*25*	*25*	145^{1}	*156*	*25*	*3.1*	*6.9*	*112*	*45%*	*.299*	*1.42*	*5.25*	*5.38*	*0.4*	*93.7*			*73*

Breakout: 12% Improve: 20% Collapse: 3% Attrition: 15% MLB: 23% *Comparables: Abe Alvarez, Barry Enright, Todd Redmond*

A poised right-hander who embodies the stereotype of the old regime's pitching philosophy, Jorge fills the zone with his four-pitch assortment and lets his fielders do the work. His low-90s fastball has missed fewer and fewer bats as he's faced more advanced hitters, and his off-speed stuff is often solid but never spectacular. Jorge made his big-league debut last summer but didn't stick, and is about to be passed by the more electric arms littering the system below him. He's a possible future swingman and a probable Triple-A insurance policy.

Zack Littell RHP

Born: 10/05/95 Age: 22 Bats: R Throws: R Height: 6'4" Weight: 220 Origin: Round 11, 2013 Draft (#327 overall)

YEAR	TEAM	LVL	AGE	W	L	SV	G	GS	IP	H	HR	BB/9	K/9	K	GB%	BABIP	WHIP	ERA	DRA	WARP	MPH	CMD	PWR	STM
2015	CLN	A	19	3	6	0	21	21	112^{2}	121	4	2.4	6.7	84	54%	.324	1.34	3.91	3.34	2.5				
2016	CLN	A	20	5	5	0	16	16	97^{2}	94	5	1.9	8.8	95	51%	.332	1.18	2.76	2.41	3.1				
2016	BAK	A+	20	8	1	0	12	11	68	64	3	1.7	8.1	61	49%	.311	1.13	2.51	2.75	2.1				
2017	TAM	A+	21	9	1	0	13	11	71^{1}	65	4	1.9	7.2	57	55%	.302	1.12	1.77	2.70	2.1				
2017	TRN	AA	21	5	0	0	7	7	44	37	3	1.6	10.6	52	52%	.304	1.02	2.05	1.62	1.9				
2017	CHT	AA	21	5	0	0	7	7	41^{2}	33	1	3.9	7.1	33	55%	.274	1.22	2.81	3.19	1.0				
2018	*MIN*	*MLB*	*22*	*2*	*2*	*0*	*5*	*5*	*28*	*30*	*5*	*3.6*	*7.4*	*23*	*46%*	*.298*	*1.50*	*4.63*	*4.90*	*0.2*				
2019	*MIN*	*MLB*	*23*	*9*	*11*	*0*	*29*	*29*	183^{2}	*187*	*31*	*3.3*	*8.6*	*175*	*46%*	*.303*	*1.38*	*4.98*	*5.09*	*1.0*				

Breakout: 19% Improve: 26% Collapse: 9% Attrition: 27% MLB: 46% *Comparables: Luke Weaver, Casey Kelly, Liam Hendriks*

Littell was Minnesota's headlining return in last summer's Garcia-to-Gotham asset liquidation, at least as much as a low-velocity right-hander just reaching Double-A can be a headliner. Scouting the stat line is supposed to be a no-no and pitcher wins aren't particularly eloquent, but Littell's downright impressive 19-1 record last year is hard to ignore. His raw stuff—two fastball varieties that barely reach 90, curveball, slider and changeup—is an analog throwback in today's digital age, but his terrific command and feel for pitching gets the most out of it. Arms like Littell usually plateau in the high minors or spend a few years as a big-league swingman, but once in a while extreme pitchability and command are enough for a mid-rotation starter. Triple-A hitters should sort that out for us this summer.

Trevor May RHP Born: 09/23/89 Age: 28 Bats: R Throws: R Height: 6'5" Weight: 240 Origin: Round 4, 2008 Draft (#136 overall)

YEAR	TEAM	LVL	AGE	W	L	SV	G	GS	IP	H	HR	BB/9	K/9	K	GB%	BABIP	WHIP	ERA	DRA	WARP	MPH	CMD	PWR	STM
2015	MIN	MLB	25	8	9	0	48	16	114^{2}	127	11	2.0	8.6	110	41%	.340	1.33	4.00	3.72	1.7	96.8	50	55	58
2016	MIN	MLB	26	2	2	0	44	0	42^{2}	39	7	3.6	12.7	60	32%	.317	1.31	5.27	3.13	0.9	96.7	49	52	41
2018	*MIN*	*MLB*	*28*	*1*	*1*	*0*	*25*	*0*	*26*	*25*	*4*	*3.5*	*10.1*	*30*	*39%*	*.300*	*1.32*	*3.69*	*3.96*	*0.4*	*96.2*	*50*	*54*	*49*
2019	*MIN*	*MLB*	*29*	*2*	*1*	*0*	*42*	*0*	44^{2}	*47*	*7*	*3.1*	*7.8*	*39*	*39%*	*.304*	*1.41*	*4.90*	*5.02*	*0.1*	*95.8*	*50*	*53*	*46*

Breakout: 36% Improve: 63% Collapse: 11% Attrition: 23% MLB: 89% *Comparables: Rich Hill, Chris Young, Tyler Thornburg*

The answer to the question of whether May should spend 2017 as a starter or reliever turned out to be "none of the above" after the big right-hander underwent Tommy John surgery last March. He should be back on the mound later this summer, and if his four-pitch mix survived the knife he could help out in either role. May's fastball plays up in relief and he's more likely to be above-average there, but starters are inherently more valuable. It's a difficult story problem to solve, but if May is eased back into the 'pen to protect his arm and starts to thrive, the Twins may find it hard not to just leave him there.

Adalberto Mejia LHP Born: 06/20/93 Age: 24 Bats: R Throws: L Height: 6'3" Weight: 195 Origin: International Free Agent, 2011

YEAR	TEAM	LVL	AGE	W	L	SV	G	GS	IP	H	HR	BB/9	K/9	K	GB%	BABIP	WHIP	ERA	DRA	WARP	MPH	CMD	PWR	STM
2015	RIC	AA	22	5	2	0	12	9	51^{1}	38	2	3.2	6.7	38	46%	.238	1.09	2.45	3.73	0.8				
2016	RIC	AA	23	3	2	0	11	11	65	48	4	2.2	8.0	58	48%	.251	0.98	1.94	2.37	2.1				
2016	SAC	AAA	23	4	1	0	7	7	40^{2}	42	5	2.4	9.5	43	42%	.327	1.30	4.20	2.33	1.4				
2016	MIN	MLB	23	0	0	0	1	0	2^{1}	5	0	3.9	0.0	0	42%	.417	2.57	7.71	7.37	-0.1	93.2			59
2016	ROC	AAA	23	2	2	0	4	4	26^{1}	28	3	1.0	8.5	25	33%	.329	1.18	3.76	2.51	0.9				
2017	ROC	AAA	24	1	1	0	6	6	28^{2}	26	1	1.9	6.9	22	51%	.294	1.12	2.83	2.66	0.9				
2017	MIN	MLB	24	4	7	0	21	21	98	110	13	4.0	7.8	85	41%	.328	1.57	4.50	5.09	0.5	94.2	51	45	58
2018	*MIN*	*MLB*	*25*	*8*	*8*	*0*	*24*	*24*	*127*	*135*	*20*	*3.6*	*7.5*	*106*	*42%*	*.301*	*1.47*	*4.53*	*4.80*	*0.9*	*93.9*	*52*	*46*	*60*
2019	*MIN*	*MLB*	*26*	*9*	*10*	*0*	*30*	*30*	184^{2}	*188*	*28*	*3.4*	*8.2*	*169*	*42%*	*.302*	*1.40*	*4.82*	*4.92*	*1.3*	*93.6*	*52*	*46*	*60*

Breakout: 26% Improve: 55% Collapse: 16% Attrition: 27% MLB: 89% *Comparables: Zach McAllister, Justin Germano, Juan Nicasio*

Mejia sported one of baseball's shortest leashes during his rookie season, and didn't do much to earn more slack. Only Josh Tomlin averaged fewer pitches per start, as Mejia finished six innings in just four starts all year, none of them in the second half. A biceps strain cost him a full month and when he did take the mound Mejia issued far too many walks and bleacher souvenirs to make up for his nondescript strikeout rate. The hulking lefty has decent stuff, featuring two- and four-seam fastballs that reach the low-90s and a workable slider and changeup, but lacks the control and command to do much with it. He's young enough to improve and work his way into the middle of the rotation, particularly given that control and command were often billed as his strengths in the minors.

Glen Perkins LHP Born: 03/02/83 Age: 35 Bats: L Throws: L Height: 6'0" Weight: 205 Origin: Round 1, 2004 Draft (#22 overall)

YEAR	TEAM	LVL	AGE	W	L	SV	G	GS	IP	H	HR	BB/9	K/9	K	GB%	BABIP	WHIP	ERA	DRA	WARP	MPH	CMD	PWR	STM
2015	MIN	MLB	32	3	5	32	60	0	57	58	9	1.6	8.5	54	34%	.297	1.19	3.32	4.51	0.1	96.1	57	58	45
2016	MIN	MLB	33	0	0	0	2	0	2	5	0	4.5	13.5	3	38%	.625	3.00	9.00	5.46	0.0	93.5			
2017	MIN	MLB	34	0	0	0	8	0	5^{2}	8	0	7.9	3.2	2	38%	.333	2.29	9.53	7.70	-0.2	92.3			27
2018	*MIN*	*MLB*	*35*	*1*	*0*	*1*	*30*	*0*	*32*	*35*	*5*	*5.0*	*7.4*	*27*	*39%*	*.306*	*1.64*	*5.61*	*5.72*	*-0.2*	*94.2*	*56*	*57*	*33*
2019	*MIN*	*MLB*	*36*	*1*	*0*	*1*	*24*	*0*	23^{2}	*29*	*5*	*5.0*	*6.7*	*18*	*39%*	*.315*	*1.78*	*6.69*	*6.90*	*-0.4*	*92.6*	*55*	*56*	*30*

Breakout: 19% Improve: 44% Collapse: 26% Attrition: 14% MLB: 86% *Comparables: Justin Speier, Jason Motte, Brian Fuentes*

"Am I disappointed that I can't contribute to our team this year while getting paid a shit ton of money? Yes, it makes me sick." So said Perkins—All-Star closer, Minnesota native, longtime pitcher for the local college and pro teams and all-around solid guy—in June 2016. As it turned out Perkins would spend almost all of 2017 trying to work his way back from the shoulder ailments that have plagued his career, only to struggle in a few low-leverage outings before his emotional one-out appearance on the season's final Saturday. Minnesota understandably declined the final year of Perkins' team-friendly contract, so his career may be done. He was the brightest spot on some pretty bleak Twins teams, so it was particularly sad that Perkins couldn't play a bigger role once they finally earned some relevance. Rest assured you earned every penny, Glen, and then some.

Michael Pineda RHP Born: 01/18/89 Age: 29 Bats: R Throws: R Height: 6'7" Weight: 260 Origin: International Free Agent, 2005

YEAR	TEAM	LVL	AGE	W	L	SV	G	GS	IP	H	HR	BB/9	K/9	K	GB%	BABIP	WHIP	ERA	DRA	WARP	MPH	CMD	PWR	STM
2015	NYA	MLB	26	12	10	0	27	27	160^{2}	176	21	1.2	8.7	156	50%	.332	1.23	4.37	3.30	3.4	95.7	44	50	65
2016	NYA	MLB	27	6	12	0	32	32	175^{2}	184	27	2.7	10.6	207	46%	.340	1.35	4.82	3.52	3.7	96.9	39	50	75
2017	NYA	MLB	28	8	4	0	17	17	96^{1}	103	20	2.0	8.6	92	52%	.302	1.29	4.39	4.72	0.9	95.9	46	49	60
2018	*MIN*	*MLB*	*29*	*6*	*5*	*0*	*17*	*17*	93^{2}	*98*	*14*	*2.8*	*8.8*	*92*	*48%*	*.316*	*1.37*	*4.31*	*4.35*	*1.4*	*95.6*	*42*	*50*	*66*
2019	*MIN*	*MLB*	*30*	*10*	*10*	*0*	*30*	*30*	*188*	*197*	*26*	*2.7*	*8.9*	*186*	*48%*	*.318*	*1.35*	*4.26*	*4.32*	*2.5*	*95.4*	*42*	*49*	*66*

Breakout: 22% Improve: 45% Collapse: 23% Attrition: 4% MLB: 93% *Comparables: James Shields, Ricky Nolasco, Ervin Santana*

Every year you'd hear the same thing. "Maybe this is the year Pineda will put it all together." "Maybe he'll stay healthy." "Maybe he'll figure things out." "Maybe he'll stop giving up home runs on 0-2 pitches." And every year, the Yankees and their fans would be disappointed by Pineda's inconsistent performance. In 2016, he threw a career high in innings. In 2017, Pineda's season was cut short in July when a partial tear in his UCL was discovered and he underwent Tommy John surgery. His Yankees career ended like it began, with a season-ending injury. The Twins signed him in December in the hope that he can contribute in 2019.

Ryan Pressly RHP Born: 12/15/88 Age: 29 Bats: R Throws: R Height: 6'3" Weight: 210 Origin: Round 11, 2007 Draft (#354 overall)

YEAR	TEAM	LVL	AGE	W	L	SV	G	GS	IP	H	HR	BB/9	K/9	K	GB%	BABIP	WHIP	ERA	DRA	WARP	MPH	CMD	PWR	STM
2015	ROC	AAA	26	0	2	0	7	0	10	6	1	5.4	13.5	15	35%	.263	1.20	4.50	2.71	0.3				
2015	MIN	MLB	26	3	2	0	27	0	27^{2}	27	0	3.9	7.2	22	49%	.318	1.41	2.93	4.23	0.2	97.0	29	49	47
2016	MIN	MLB	27	6	7	1	72	0	75^{1}	79	8	2.7	8.0	67	41%	.311	1.35	3.70	4.51	0.4	98.0	17	55	54
2017	ROC	AAA	28	2	0	4	7	0	10	5	0	4.5	13.5	15	55%	.250	1.00	0.90	3.29	0.2				
2017	MIN	MLB	28	2	3	0	57	0	61^{1}	52	10	2.8	9.0	61	52%	.264	1.16	4.70	4.40	0.5	97.8	29	59	49
2018	*MIN*	*MLB*	*29*	*2*	*2*	*0*	*50*	*0*	*53*	*52*	*7*	*3.8*	*8.6*	*51*	*46%*	*.297*	*1.39*	*4.17*	*4.35*	*0.5*	*97.1*	*23*	*56*	*50*
2019	*MIN*	*MLB*	*30*	*2*	*1*	*0*	*42*	*0*	*44*	*42*	*6*	*4.2*	*9.0*	*44*	*46%*	*.3*	*1.42*	*4.73*	*4.82*	*0.2*	*96.8*	*23*	*57*	*51*

Breakout: 34% Improve: 54% Collapse: 27% Attrition: 23% MLB: 95% *Comparables: Jared Burton, Joe Smith, Jeff Bennett*

Pressly punched a June ticket to Rochester after some early-season struggles, but returned to post another solid campaign in the Minnesota ‘pen. His overall peripherals were a spot-on Pressly impression slightly updated for last year's run environment: a few more walks, a few more strikeouts and a truckload of extra home runs. Pressly allowed fewer fly balls last year, but more of them left the park, a development that comes with the tagline "Welcome to 2017" and may very well disappear on its own. While he's never found the potion to cure his big platoon splits, and likely never will, his mid-90s, high-spin heater, curve and slider usually leave same-side hitters muttering to themselves. Pressly remains a reliable seventh-inning arm, which is a scarcer commodity than most people think.

Fernando Rodney RHP Born: 03/18/77 Age: 41 Bats: R Throws: R Height: 5'11" Weight: 230 Origin: International Free Agent, 1997

YEAR	TEAM	LVL	AGE	W	L	SV	G	GS	IP	H	HR	BB/9	K/9	K	GB%	BABIP	WHIP	ERA	DRA	WARP	MPH	CMD	PWR	STM
2015	SEA	MLB	38	5	5	16	54	0	50^{2}	51	8	4.4	7.6	43	51%	.295	1.50	5.68	4.07	0.4	98.0	56	59	50
2015	CHN	MLB	38	2	0	0	14	0	12	8	1	3.0	11.2	15	57%	.259	1.00	0.75	4.83	0.0	97.0	56	59	50
2016	SDN	MLB	39	0	1	17	28	0	28^{2}	13	0	3.8	10.4	33	60%	.210	0.87	0.31	3.39	0.5	97.3	38	53	49
2016	MIA	MLB	39	2	3	8	39	0	36^{2}	41	5	6.1	10.1	41	54%	.360	1.80	5.89	3.67	0.5	97.6	38	53	49
2017	ARI	MLB	40	5	4	39	61	0	55^{1}	40	3	4.2	10.6	65	54%	.274	1.19	4.23	3.11	1.3	96.7	47	56	46
2018	*MIN*	*MLB*	*41*	*3*	*3*	*35*	*55*	*0*	*58*	*58*	*7*	*4.7*	*8.4*	*54*	*51%*	*.301*	*1.52*	*4.26*	*4.41*	*0.5*	*95.4*	*44*	*54*	*46*
2019	*MIN*	*MLB*	*42*	*2*	*1*	*21*	*38*	*0*	40^{2}	*41*	*6*	*5.0*	*8.4*	*38*	*51%*	*.303*	*1.57*	*4.67*	*5.34*	*0.0*	*94.4*	*42*	*52*	*45*

Breakout: 16% Improve: 38% Collapse: 20% Attrition: 10% MLB: 64% *Comparables: Darren Oliver, Larry Andersen, Mike Stanton*

Another year, another season of The Fernando Rodney Experience. Finishing one short of 40 saves at age 40 is an impressive feat, even if Rodney's typically erratic pitching sent him through some wild hills and valleys. His ERA meandered from 12.60 ERA in April to 0.00 in May and June to 9.00 in July before settling in at a less extreme 2.91 over the final two months. Rodney will never not make it interesting for his team, but he's had a hell of a career and is now one of 28 pitchers to reach 300 saves. His one-year deal to close in Minnesota ensures we haven't seen nearly the last of Rodney, and in a way it's hard to think of this insane game without him and his arrows.

Taylor Rogers LHP Born: 12/17/90 Age: 27 Bats: L Throws: L Height: 6'3" Weight: 170 Origin: Round 11, 2012 Draft (#340 overall)

YEAR	TEAM	LVL	AGE	W	L	SV	G	GS	IP	H	HR	BB/9	K/9	K	GB%	BABIP	WHIP	ERA	DRA	WARP	MPH	CMD	PWR	STM
2015	ROC	AAA	24	11	12	0	28	27	174	190	9	2.3	6.5	126	53%	.330	1.34	3.98	2.37	5.8				
2016	ROC	AAA	25	0	1	0	7	2	18	24	1	3.0	7.5	15	44%	.365	1.67	4.50	4.10	0.2				
2016	MIN	MLB	25	3	1	0	57	0	61^{1}	63	7	2.3	9.4	64	51%	.326	1.29	3.96	4.31	0.5	95.0	53	40	52
2017	MIN	MLB	26	7	3	0	69	0	55^{2}	52	6	3.4	7.9	49	46%	.291	1.31	3.07	4.97	0.1	94.7	59	46	48
2018	*MIN*	*MLB*	*27*	*2*	*2*	*5*	*45*	*0*	*47*	*47*	*6*	*3.7*	*8.2*	*44*	*47%*	*.304*	*1.42*	*4.01*	*4.22*	*0.5*	*94.4*	*57*	*44*	*50*
2019	*MIN*	*MLB*	*28*	*2*	*1*	*3*	*47*	*0*	49^{1}	*49*	*6*	*3.6*	*8.7*	*48*	*47%*	*.31*	*1.40*	*4.46*	*4.56*	*0.4*	*94.1*	*57*	*44*	*50*

Breakout: 28% Improve: 43% Collapse: 16% Attrition: 22% MLB: 77% *Comparables: Tyler Anderson, Randy Wells, Matt Andriese*

Now that Rogers is working exclusively from the bullpen his hard sinker continues to show some real giddy-up and his curveball can torture left-handed hitters, who posted a .173/.253/.307 line against him last summer. But righties sprinted to the plate to face him, since his changeup didn't scare anyone and his curveball got tattooed to the tune of a .619 slugging percentage, continuing a career-long issue that stretches back to his minor-league days as a starter. Rogers needs to find something—anything—that makes righties uncomfortable posthaste if he wants to avoid the slow train to LOOGY town.

Fernando Romero RHP Born: 12/24/94 Age: 23 Bats: R Throws: R Height: 6'0" Weight: 215 Origin: International Free Agent, 2011

YEAR	TEAM	LVL	AGE	W	L	SV	G	GS	IP	H	HR	BB/9	K/9	K	GB%	BABIP	WHIP	ERA	DRA	WARP	MPH	CMD	PWR	STM
2016	CDR	A	21	4	1	0	5	5	28	18	0	1.6	8.0	25	53%	.250	0.82	1.93	2.76	0.8				
2016	FTM	A+	21	5	2	0	11	11	62^{1}	48	1	1.4	9.4	65	58%	.288	0.93	1.88	1.48	2.8				
2017	CHT	AA	22	11	9	0	24	23	125	124	4	3.2	8.6	120	54%	.328	1.35	3.53	3.96	1.8				
2018	*MIN*	*MLB*	*23*	*7*	*6*	*0*	*19*	*19*	101^{2}	*102*	*14*	*3.3*	*9.3*	*105*	*47%*	*.314*	*1.36*	*4.23*	*4.27*	*1.6*				
2019	*MIN*	*MLB*	*24*	*6*	*8*	*0*	*21*	*21*	*124*	*132*	*19*	*3.9*	*8.3*	*115*	*47%*	*.314*	*1.51*	*5.07*	*5.19*	*0.6*				

Breakout: 14% Improve: 22% Collapse: 11% Attrition: 29% MLB: 42% *Comparables: Adam Warren, Matt Andriese, Simon Castro*

Romero flashed the ability to command his electric arsenal with results to match in his Double-A debut. The burly right-hander dominated older hitters with his moving mid-90s heat, plus slide piece and improving changeup, before inexplicably struggling in his last three starts. He landed on the disabled list with a shoulder impingement, the latest in a litany of arm troubles that have derailed his promising career. Romero has the stuff and the skill to make his living in the middle of a big-league rotation if his arm can bear up to the workload; if not, his stuff will play nicely in the late innings.

Ervin Santana RHP Born: 12/12/82 Age: 35 Bats: R Throws: R Height: 6'2" Weight: 175 Origin: International Free Agent, 2000

YEAR	TEAM	LVL	AGE	W	L	SV	G	GS	IP	H	HR	BB/9	K/9	K	GB%	BABIP	WHIP	ERA	DRA	WARP	MPH	CMD	PWR	STM
2015	ROC	AAA	32	3	0	0	3	3	20^2	17	2	1.7	4.8	11	41%	.242	1.02	1.74	5.08	0.1				
2015	MIN	MLB	32	7	5	0	17	17	108	104	12	3.0	6.8	82	43%	.285	1.30	4.00	4.12	1.2	95.8	51	47	65
2016	MIN	MLB	33	7	11	0	30	30	181^1	168	19	2.6	7.4	149	44%	.285	1.22	3.38	3.72	3.4	95.6	46	46	74
2017	MIN	MLB	34	16	8	0	33	33	211^1	177	31	2.6	7.1	167	43%	.245	1.13	3.28	3.74	4.3	95.0	52	46	83
2018	*MIN*	*MLB*	*35*	*11*	*10*	*0*	*29*	*29*	182^2	*191*	*28*	*3.2*	*6.5*	*132*	*43%*	*.289*	*1.39*	*4.64*	*4.91*	*1.0*	*94.1*	*49*	*45*	*74*
2019	*MIN*	*MLB*	*36*	*10*	*12*	*0*	*30*	*30*	*184*	*188*	*28*	*3.4*	*6.4*	*132*	*43%*	*.283*	*1.40*	*5.22*	*5.34*	*0.7*	*93.5*	*48*	*45*	*75*

Breakout: 13% Improve: 37% Collapse: 31% Attrition: 8% MLB: 87% *Comparables: Hiroki Kuroda, Adam Wainwright, David Cone*

Santana's season ended in a predictable way during Minnesota's wild card elimination game, as the most homer-prone no. 1 starter in baseball facing the league's most power-packed lineup allowed two shots into the league's shortest porch to turn an early 3-0 lead into a 4-3 deficit. The real news in that sentence isn't the home runs; it's that Santana somehow remains a no. 1 starter given his age, stuff and tendencies during the most homer-happy run environment in baseball history. His repertoire—low-90s fastball and slider with a changeup mixed in against lefties—is as exciting and cutting edge as a *Gunsmoke* marathon, but Santana commands it well, coaxes weak contact and generally manages to avoid the big inning despite all of those big flies. He was an All-Star last year, yet pitched progressively worse as the season wore on, posting his worst FIP in years despite his stellar ERA. Santana won't be able to outpitch his peripherals forever, and as he enters his late-thirties the day is fast approaching when the wheels will truly come off.

Hector Santiago LHP Born: 12/16/87 Age: 30 Bats: R Throws: L Height: 6'0" Weight: 215 Origin: Round 30, 2006 Draft (#915 overall)

YEAR	TEAM	LVL	AGE	W	L	SV	G	GS	IP	H	HR	BB/9	K/9	K	GB%	BABIP	WHIP	ERA	DRA	WARP	MPH	CMD	PWR	STM
2015	ANA	MLB	27	9	9	0	33	32	180^2	156	29	3.5	8.1	162	31%	.252	1.26	3.59	5.47	-0.9	93.8	51	43	75
2016	ANA	MLB	28	10	4	0	22	22	120^2	104	20	4.3	8.0	107	40%	.257	1.33	4.25	5.63	-0.4	95.3	57	49	78
2016	MIN	MLB	28	3	6	0	11	11	61^1	65	13	3.2	5.4	37	28%	.264	1.42	5.58	7.03	-1.2	93.8	57	49	78
2017	MIN	MLB	29	4	8	0	15	14	70^1	70	15	4.0	6.5	51	32%	.263	1.44	5.63	7.93	-1.8	93.0	37	41	49
2017	ROC	AAA	29	1	2	0	7	7	23^2	21	4	6.5	9.5	25	27%	.270	1.61	5.32	7.32	-0.4				
2018	*MIN*	*MLB*	*30*	*5*	*7*	*0*	*18*	*18*	*94*	*98*	*20*	*4.1*	*7.8*	*81*	*35%*	*.285*	*1.50*	*5.78*	*5.91*	*-0.2*	*93.3*	*50*	*45*	*65*
2019	*MIN*	*MLB*	*31*	*6*	*9*	*0*	*22*	*22*	127^1	*138*	*26*	*4.2*	*7.6*	*107*	*35%*	*.294*	*1.54*	*5.97*	*6.14*	*-0.6*	*93.0*	*50*	*46*	*63*

Breakout: 8% Improve: 31% Collapse: 35% Attrition: 14% MLB: 89% *Comparables: Jason Jennings, Kip Wells, Wade Miller*

Since coming to the Twins in the summer of 2016, Santiago has started 25 games and posted a 5.61 ERA and even worse secondary numbers—in some cases, the worst in baseball. He's been bad, is what we're saying here, but maybe there was a reason. Santiago's campaign was cut short by back issues, so perhaps some of his struggles were due to injury, but his high walk rate and propensity for gopher balls had him walking a razor line even at his best. Expect him to pop up on non-roster invite lists for the next few years.

Lineouts

Hitters

HITTER	POS	TEAM	LVL	AGE	PA	R	2B	3B	HR	RBI	BB	K	SB	CS	AVG/OBP/SLG	TAv	VORP	BABIP	BRR	FRAA	WARP
Akil Baddoo	CF	TWI	Rk	18	86	18	4	3	1	10	9	13	4	0	.267/.360/.440	.267	3.6	.311	0.9	CF(8): -0.7	0.3
	CF	ELZ	Rk	18	157	39	15	2	3	19	27	19	5	4	.357/.478/.579	.359	25.7	.400	0.8	CF(28): -4.2	1.9
Andrew Bechtold	3B	ELZ	Rk	21	175	33	10	1	2	19	27	40	0	0	.299/.406/.424	.282	11.9	.390	0.6	3B(39): -4.6	0.7
Travis Blankenhorn	INF	CDR	A	20	508	68	22	11	13	69	47	119	13	2	.251/.343/.441	.282	30.2	.312	5.1	3B(55): -5.9, 2B(43): -1.2	2.4
Lewin Diaz	1B	CDR	A	20	508	47	33	1	12	68	25	80	2	1	.292/.329/.444	.276	11.6	.322	-2.2	1B(110): 3.0	1.5
Jose Miranda	MI	ELZ	Rk	19	247	43	8	2	11	43	16	24	2	3	.283/.340/.484	.294	16.5	.272	-0.8	2B(37): 5.6, 3B(1): 0.0	2.0
Jermaine Palacios	SS	CDR	A	20	276	52	13	6	11	39	12	46	9	8	.320/.362/.544	.315	29.7	.356	2.6	SS(62): 2.1	3.3
	SS	FTM	A+	20	263	30	8	4	2	28	10	53	11	7	.269/.303/.359	.235	5.1	.332	1.3	SS(62): -0.4	0.5
Anthony Recker	C	ATL	MLB	33	7	1	0	0	0	0	0	1	0	0	.143/.143/.143	.070	-1.4	.167	-0.3	C(4): -0.3	-0.2
	C	GWN	AAA	33	156	20	8	1	4	10	11	48	1	0	.223/.301/.381	.237	3.0	.307	0.1	C(37): -5.8	-0.3
	C	ROC	AAA	33	78	9	9	0	0	8	4	15	0	0	.286/.333/.414	.279	4.9	.351	-0.6	C(19): -3.7	0.1
LaMonte Wade	OF	CHT	AA	23	519	74	22	3	7	67	76	71	9	2	.292/.397/.408	.306	35.2	.328	-0.1	LF(57): 7.2, CF(31): 1.2	4.7

High school heartthrob **Akil Baddoo** showed surprising polish in his Appalachian League debut, walking more than he struck out and barreling up everything in sight. His final destination is probably left field, but his combination of patience and power will still make him an asset there. ⚾ Junior College heartthrob **Andrew Bechtold** showed the polish you'd expect in his Appalachian League debut, controlling the strike zone and barreling up everything in sight. He has sure hands and a plus arm at the hot corner, with enough power potential to be an asset there. ⚾ By god his name may sound like a fictional character in one of Norm MacDonald's long-form jokes, you know, but **Travis Blankenhorn**'s hit tool and power potential from the left side of the infield and the plate is nothing to laugh at. ⚾ If his swing grows along with his frame and the doubles he mashed in his full-season debut start leaving the yard, he can be a big league first baseman. If not, the Coen Brothers will title their award-winning film documenting his struggles *Inside* ***Lewin Diaz***. ⚾ After his eye-opening 2016 pro debut, first-round pick **Alex Kirilloff** lost a full year of development time recovering from Tommy John surgery; the Twins still expect him to grow into a prototypical right fielder. ⚾ First baseman **Joe Maloney** hit 35 home runs in 99 games on his way to the MVP award in the independent Can-Am League. A minor-league contract and a job at Double-A feels like just about the correct reward. He's organizational depth, but fun organizational depth! ⚾ While **Jose Miranda**'s bat didn't remain silent in his productive spin through the Appalachian League, the court of public opinion says he won't stick in the middle infield; his glove, arm and right-handed power potential should play just fine at third base. ⚾ As if the Twins need another shortstop prospect, **Jermaine Palacios** showed surprising pop, plus instincts and a slick glove while working his way up to High-A and might someday find work on a big-league bench. ⚾ So you're telling me that whole Jaime Garcia thing was just a ploy to get **Anthony Recker** behind the plate in Rochester? Those new front-office guys are totally next level, dude. ⚾ **LaMonte Wade** in Double-A: .292/.397/.408, 14.6 percent walk rate. Robbie Grossman in Double-A: .266/.376/.410, 13.3 percent walk rate. You've never seen them together, have you? Have you?

Pitchers

PITCHER	TEAM	LVL	AGE	W	L	SV	G	GS	IP	H	HR	BB/9	K/9	K	GB%	BABIP	WHIP	ERA	DRA	WARP	MPH	CMD	PWR	STM
Blayne Enlow	TWI	Rk	18	3	0	0	6	1	20^{1}	10	1	1.8	8.4	19	56%	.176	0.69	1.33	1.11	0.9				
Brusdar Graterol	TWI	Rk	18	2	0	0	5	2	19^{1}	10	1	1.9	9.8	21	58%	.205	0.72	1.40	1.88	0.8				
	ELZ	Rk	18	2	1	0	5	5	20^{2}	16	1	3.9	10.5	24	59%	.300	1.21	3.92	2.37	0.7				
Chris Heston	TAC	AAA	29	2	1	0	6	6	31^{2}	26	2	3.1	8.0	28	49%	.286	1.17	3.41	3.53	0.7				
	SEA	MLB	29	0	1	0	2	1	5	14	3	9.0	5.4	3	31%	.478	3.80	19.80	5.87	0.0	88.7			38
	MIN	MLB	29	0	0	0	1	0	1	1	0	0.0	0.0	0	50%	.250	1.00	0.00	9.54	0.0	90.0			38
	ROC	AAA	29	0	3	0	8	6	27	56	8	5.0	4.0	12	46%	.444	2.63	10.00	9.35	-1.1				
Gabriel Moya	WTN	AA	22	4	1	17	34	0	43^{2}	22	1	2.5	14.0	68	44%	.259	0.78	0.82	1.43	1.8				
	CHT	AA	22	2	0	7	13	0	14^{2}	8	1	1.8	11.7	19	44%	.212	0.75	0.61	1.27	0.6				
	MIN	MLB	22	0	0	1	7	0	6^{1}	5	2	2.8	7.1	5	32%	.176	1.11	4.26	2.90	0.2	92.2			44
Jake Reed	ROC	AAA	24	1	0	5	22	0	30^{2}	24	1	3.2	7.3	25	45%	.280	1.14	2.05	4.00	0.4				
Alex Robinson	CDR	A	22	2	5	2	28	0	38	29	2	3.6	12.1	51	53%	.303	1.16	2.84	2.80	0.9				
	FTM	A+	22	4	0	0	13	0	17^{1}	14	1	6.8	14.0	27	46%	.382	1.56	4.67	3.66	0.2				
Drew Rucinski	MIN	MLB	28	0	0	0	2	0	4^{1}	10	2	4.2	10.4	5	50%	.571	2.77	10.38	4.27	0.0	93.5			44
	ROC	AAA	28	2	6	2	37	2	63	54	3	1.4	8.1	57	55%	.291	1.02	2.57	2.34	2.0				
Aaron Slegers	ROC	AAA	24	15	4	0	24	24	148^{1}	154	11	1.8	7.2	119	45%	.312	1.23	3.40	3.22	4.0				
	MIN	MLB	24	0	1	0	4	3	15^{1}	12	3	3.5	5.3	9	46%	.200	1.17	6.46	5.56	0.0	92.8	36	46	66
Kohl Stewart	CHT	AA	22	5	6	0	16	16	77	72	4	5.3	6.1	52	48%	.296	1.52	4.09	6.10	-0.9				
Lewis Thorpe	FTM	A+	21	3	4	0	16	15	77	62	3	3.6	9.8	84	39%	.304	1.21	2.69	4.33	0.8				
Adam Wilk	LVG	AAA	29	2	3	0	6	6	32	40	5	1.4	8.2	29	42%	.354	1.41	5.91	4.33	0.5				
	NYN	MLB	29	0	1	0	1	1	3^{2}	8	3	2.5	4.9	2	35%	.357	2.45	12.27	10.90	-0.2	89.0	57	24	48
	ROC	AAA	29	1	0	0	3	2	12^{1}	15	2	2.2	4.4	6	30%	.310	1.46	4.38	7.94	-0.3				
	MIN	MLB	29	0	1	0	3	1	10^{1}	16	3	7.0	5.2	6	45%	.351	2.32	7.84	7.19	-0.2	89.8	57	24	48

J.T. Chargois was in line to be a key cog in the Twins' bullpen, but instead missed most of the year with a stress reaction in his elbow. If healthy his upper-90s gas and sharp slider can get high-leverage outs, but that's a big if. ⚾ Signed away from LSU with an above-slot bonus as a third-round pick, Canadian high school right-hander **Blayne Enlow** had an impressive rookie-ball debut. ⚾ Venezuelan teenager **Brusdar Graterol** returned from Tommy John surgery and showed surprising command of his upper-90s fastball and developing off-speed stuff. There be dragons between Joe O'Brien Field and Target Plaza, and he may wind up in the 'pen, but his raw stuff is undeniable. ⚾ In less than six months, soft-tossing **Chris Heston** passed from the Giants to the Dodgers to the Mariners to the Twins, a game best described as Lukewarm Potato. ⚾ Former top-10 pick **Tyler Jay** lost much of the year to the neck and shoulder problems that have dogged him, before recovering his mid-90s heat in the Arizona Fall League. If he can stay healthy and regain his plus slider he might build a nice career in the bullpen, but his days as a starter are likely over. ⚾ Acquired from the Diamondbacks for John Ryan Murphy, left-hander **Gabriel Moya** boasts a plus changeup, crazy mound energy and an impressive track record in the minors. ⚾ Shortly after surfacing in the Twins' bullpen as a certified LOOGY, **Ryan O'Rourke**'s elbow went sproing and he missed all of 2017 after Tommy John surgery. ⚾ This particular **Jake Reed** can't run a skinny post but he can chuck a baseball 97 mph and get righties to chase his slider. ⚾ **Alex Robinson** toted his high-90s fastball to High-A last summer, continued to pile up strikeouts, improved his control grade from "Abysmal" to "Diet Cherry Abysmal" and can now be considered a serious bullpen prospect. ⚾ **Drew Rucinski** inched closer to earning a pension with a few more days of service time in Minnesota last summer, and if he keeps posting sub-3.00 FIPs at Triple-A he just might get there. ⚾ Towering right-hander **Aaron Slegers** doesn't have great stuff, but he earned Minnesota's Minor League Pitcher of the Year award and made three starts for the big club. His walk-averse approach might have been more valued under the old regime, but nowadays he's more likely to be kept behind glass at Triple-A. ⚾ We've included an entry for **Kohl Stewart** this year out of habit rather than necessity, but we promise we'll wake you if the former top-five pick ever starts missing bats. ⚾ A hearty "good on ya" to **Lewis Thorpe**, who returned from two seasons lost to a litany of woes (mononucleosis, elbow surgery, maybe let's just say funnel spider bites) to post solid numbers at High-A. If he can improve his command and pass the Double-A exam he could grow into a mid-rotation starter. ⚾ You can add **Adam Wilk** to the list of people who should be allowed to smack Matt Harvey in the kisser, as the latter's sudden suspension last May forced the former to fly through five states in 24 hours before taking his lumps in a sleep-deprived emergency start.

NEW YORK METS

Essay by Bryan Grosnick

Player comments by Kate Feldman and BP staff

April 30, 2017: Noah Syndergaard tears his right latissimus muscle.

It's the last day of the first month of the season, and suddenly the Mets are out of contention. Despite the back-to-back postseason appearances, and despite being exactly 18 months away from the World Series, the Mets can no longer be considered a serious playoff threat thanks to one damaged bit of muscle. Of course blame can be shared; ownership didn't pay to bring in new talent where the team needed it most—the bullpen and the infield—despite playing in the largest market in baseball. By the end of that fateful game, the Mets had lost to the Nationals by 18 runs, were 10-14 on the season and were without their most impactful player.

Ted Berg extolled Syndergaard's virtues in glorious detail in last year's *Annual*, and nothing has changed since then; you know the salient details. The most talented right-handed pitcher in baseball, Thor had (and has) an electric fastball, devastating slider and the weight of colossal expectations stretched across his ample shoulders. Though the team had already suffered setbacks with starters Seth Lugo and Steven Matz to begin the season, others were replaceable given the Mets' depth of seven starting pitchers. There was no replacing a star of Syndergaard's caliber.

Things fall apart, the center cannot hold. (Jacob deGrom did sublime work in the face of a decomposing rotation, but one excellent starting pitcher does not a contender make.) While the Mets' front office's decision to just rerun the 2016 roster might have kept the Mets out of contention even if their big, blonde ace stayed upright and shoving, it's possible the Mets would have flailed and failed anyway. When you build your team around pitching—even pitching as great as Syndergaard and deGrom—you are building beachfront property, subject to incredible views but also fickle winds and tides.

Can you blame the Mets for building around pitching, the team's unquestioned strength? That's how they won their two World Series: Tom Seaver and Jerry Koosman and Doc Gooden and Sid Fernandez and great young starters. Mets fireball pitching in their hurler-supporting stadiums has been a tradition over 55 years. Maybe the only problem was that their history of pitching excellence dovetailed with a more recent history of injury susceptibility. To contend, they needed everything to go right; when Noah Syndergaard missed most of the season, the first and most important thing went wrong.

June 12, 2017: Yoenis Cespedes leaves a game during the fifth inning with a sore left heel. He would return to the lineup the next day.

Syndergaard's injury was a haymaker, an unexpected blow that set the Mets and their fans reeling, a Panic City breaking news bulletin. Cespedes' injury—or rather series of injuries—was familiar, expected, predictable. Despite his incredible athleticism, he has faced more than his share of lower body injuries, and they have become part and parcel of the *La Potencia* experience. It is rote to

METS PROSPECTUS

2017 W-L: 70-92, 4th in NL East

Pythag	.423	27th	B-Age	29.0	*24th*
RS/G	4.54	18th	P-Age	27.2	*4th*
RA/G	5.33	28th	Salary	$154.4M	*12th*
TAv	.271	7th	M$/MW	$6.5M	*3rd*
TAv-P	.288	30th	DL Days	1289	*24th*
FIP	4.60	21st	$ on DL	30%	*30th*
DER	.681	29th			

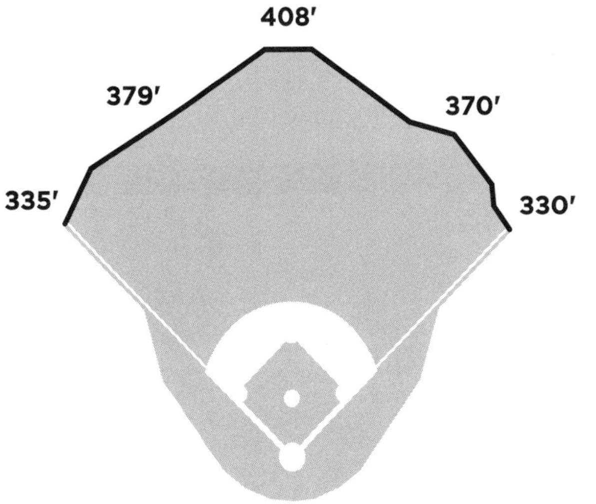

Outfield wall profile: **8'**

Three-Year Park Factors

Runs	Runs/RH	Runs/LH	HR/RH	HR/LH
96	93	101	96	102

Top Hitter WARP	4.6 Michael Conforto
Top Pitcher WARP	5.9 Jacob deGrom
Top Prospect	Andres Gimenez

2017 Hit List Ranking

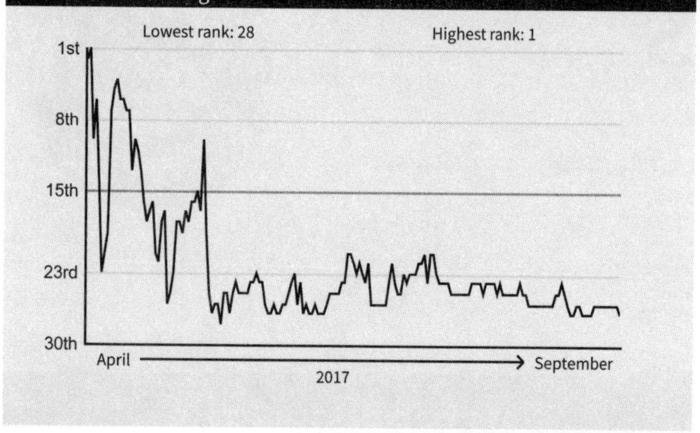

Committed Payroll (in millions)

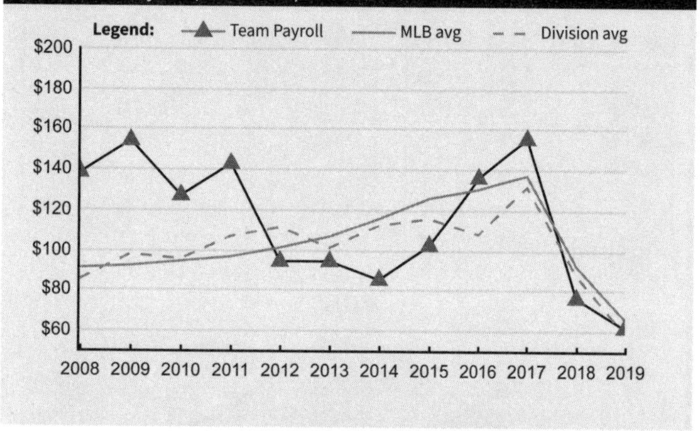

Farm System Ranking

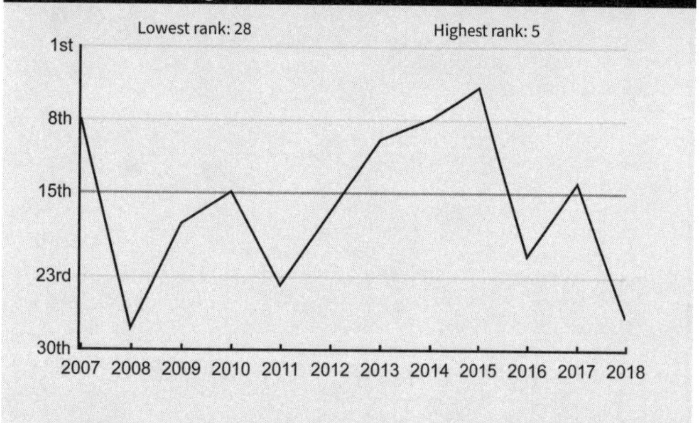

Personnel

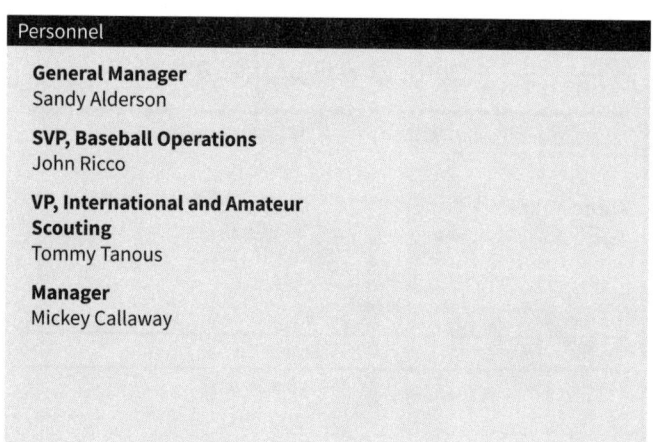

General Manager
Sandy Alderson

SVP, Baseball Operations
John Ricco

VP, International and Amateur Scouting
Tommy Tanous

Manager
Mickey Callaway

expect him to miss games here and there, and dull to hear of a 10-day disabled list stint. By the middle of June, after already so many major and minor maladies had hampered the team, every narrative about the Mets was subsumed into *the Mets cannot stay healthy*. Cespedes was no exception.

It is hard to fault a player for his injuries, and harder still for worsening them in an attempt to help the team while playing hurt; it is far easier to fault the team for overusing a player or assigning an improper diagnosis. At this point in the season, the Mets had suffered such a laundry list of injuries—three starting pitchers, a closer and four offensive starters—that it almost seemed to be desperation that caused them to at least field the team's best remaining player, even if he was not right. Over the course of the season, the Mets would habitually avoid using the disabled list until the last possible moment, preferring to play short-handed or use the walking wounded.

Within five days of this "mild heel issue," Asdrubal Cabrera, Neil Walker, Juan Lagares and Josh Smoker would hit the 10-day DL in another wave of minor injuries. Even as the team avoided the loss of their other superstar, and even as Michael Conforto embarked on a breakout season, the team was greatly diminished. We had to change the way we refer to a collection of wounded ballplayers, giving it the kind of colorful name that we often use to name groups of birds: a *flock* of seagulls, a *murder* of crows ... a *mets* of injured baseball players. Cespedes would play on and ultimately return to the disabled list. It was inevitable. The last of the Mets' trifecta of famous superstars—the least valuable of the three, but a huge name nonetheless—was about to suffer his own breakdown.

June 16, 2017: Matt Harvey is diagnosed with a fracture in his scapula (after Terry Collins described him as suffering from a "tired arm") and placed on the disabled list.

We all knew there was something wrong with Harvey; the only question was to what degree. Harvey had heralded the newest age of Mets pitching dominance in 2013, and his fall from grace was aggressive. Tommy John surgery late in that season was disheartening and disorienting, but survivable; thoracic outlet syndrome is a career-killer. Pitchers hardly ever recover from that and resume their old effectiveness, and the team's Dark Knight was no exception. After a mildly encouraging April, Harvey pitched to an uncharacteristic 5.25 ERA through his first 13 starts, throwing only 58 pitches in the last of them. The once-dominant hurler had nothing resembling the command or the stuff that made him a sensation, or even the adequacy that made him a solid mid-rotation starter in 2015. Why not? Former manager Terry Collins said in a press conference that Harvey was dealing with a tired arm, but in reality, he had a fracture in his scapula.

The past two years have inundated us with "alternate facts" and "fake news," gross attempts to reframe reality to our liking despite all evidence to the contrary. But I'll be damned if there isn't something very appealing about controlling our own narratives—science and objectivity be damned. When Collins is told to spin Harvey's continued missteps on the field as something they are not, we feel a little better, even though we know the truth is something darker and more hopeless. Mets fans *want* Harvey to be fine, despite all evidence to the contrary. The Wilpons and the front office *want* Harvey to be fine. Matt Harvey wants to be fine. It is just a tired arm, nothing to see here.

Harvey returned in September and gave up 28 earned runs in less than 23 innings. He was not fine.

July 24, 2017: Zack Wheeler is placed on the 10-day disabled list with a "stress reaction" in his right arm.

Follow baseball for long enough and you become familiar with the common injuries that crop up: *UCL tear. Hamstring strain.*

Concussion. Even *tired arm* and *fractured scapula*. Obsess over transactions, cover a team like a beat reporter, or become a fantasy maven and you start recognizing the minutiae. *Biceps tendinitis is code for "he'll need Tommy John surgery soon." Meniscus tears are less worrisome than ACL tears. Elbow injuries are bad for pitchers, but shoulder injuries are worse.* Even still, once in a while something comes up that you haven't seen or heard before. Like *stress reaction*.

For the past several seasons, the Mets have been the butt of jokes due to a failure to properly diagnose and rehab injuries; their medical staff has been widely derided. I wonder if the line between Harvey and Wheeler is the line between disingenuousness and incompetence. With Harvey, I believe the team had a general idea of what was going on and failed—for whatever reason—to disclose it to the public. With Wheeler, I got the impression that the team did or does not quite understand what is wrong. It's impossible to tell for sure, however, because the team has banished all goodwill and benefit of the doubt over years of saying everything is fine when the wolves are at the gate. The Mets, seeking to rearchitect their approach to injury, eventually moved on from trainer Ray Ramirez. That might bring some optimism for the next season, but in the case of Wheeler, perhaps too much damage has already been done for anyone to become too hopeful about 2018.

August 23, 2017: Michael Conforto dislocates his left shoulder and tears his posterior shoulder capsule during a routine swing.

Syndergaard's lat tear meant the death of a very specific brand of hope: It was the end of the serious possibility that the Mets could make a playoff run. But Conforto's shoulder injury hit the fan base like a hammer because it felt like the death of all hope. Of course that is overstating things; baseball is overflowing with teams returning rapidly even from the worst of circumstances (Miami Marlins excluded). The loss of the Mets' best young player and 2017 All-Star was so spontaneous and arresting because it took place on what appeared to be a perfectly harmless swing of the bat. Where there were rumblings about a potential arm injury hanging over Syndergaard's head, there was no warning about a potential Conforto injury.

Now, the Mets are likely to be without Conforto for the start of the 2018 season. In some ways, that's fine because the team would have likely projected as average at best going into this new year; a few months of even a thunderous young hitter might not tip the scale to a serious degree. But the seriousness of Conforto's injury lays the groundwork for a diminished bat and a hitter that may never return to the previous level of performance. Shoulder injuries are not predictable, and although it's eminently possible that he returns at a high level, it also opens up the possibility that a vibrant young star may never return to the level we imagine of him. That's especially disheartening because, well, it's not like Conforto's the only Met in that boat.

August 28, 2017: David Wright ends his rehabilitation assignment due to recurring shoulder pain.

Five days later, we see the best-case scenario for Michael Conforto, as Wright—a beloved Met and All-Star who spends his entire career with the team and fans that embrace him—slouches toward retirement. No one who followed Wright's injury issues and recovery seriously had any notions about the third baseman returning to make a difference during the Mets' abortive 2017 season, but his setback stings all the same. Time wears away at all players, except perhaps Julio Franco, and all we want to see is a player hold off the end as long as possible. For Wright, the end is likely here. To witness this in someone so representative of the franchise hurts.

September 2, 2017: Wilmer Flores breaks his nose after fouling a pitch into his face.

Wright symbolizes the Mets in one way, Flores and his particular close to the season symbolize them in another. It wasn't the worst injury and it wasn't even the *last* injury, but this was a more than fitting denouement to the Mets' season of wounds. For a team that figuratively could not seem to get out of its own way, one of the Mets' last few young stalwarts—a player whose Mets-ness was exemplified with his breakdown at the thought of being dealt at the 2015 deadline—does the seemingly impossible and hits a ball directly into his own face.

This injury wasn't the impetus for the team to fire the training staff and kick Collins to the curb. It didn't cause the team to sell off all their veterans for middle relief prospects at each trade deadline. All those moves were in various stages before one utility infielder accidentally crushed his own nose. This injury just brought back a feeling Mets fans are well used to, best described as "LOLMets." It's a feeling that the team is hapless, helpless, the second-class citizens of a first-class city. They're a joke. It comes from years of jokes on Seinfeld and standing in the shadow of the Yankees and misguided Bobby Bonilla contracts and awful ownership and everything else negative in 55 years of baseball. This is a team that cannot get out of its own way, and this was just the most literal representation of "not getting out of your own way."

Now it is 2018, and things have changed. A new manager, Mickey Callaway, likely brings a new philosophy from the analytically driven Indians. Amed Rosario brings a thrill to the field and the basepaths like a young Jose Reyes did back in the early part of the decade. Syndergaard flashed his old dominance in a September surprise. Most of all, it seems impossible that the team will suffer such an extraordinary stretch of injuries once again.

But the biggest predictor of future injuries is past injuries, and the Mets are still built from the broken bones of pitchers and position players alike. There is new hope, but there is also the potential to again be derailed. Beyond that, the fan base has been injured so many times not only by the little disappointments that built up over 2017, but also by the previous seasons, that it can feel like waiting for the other shoe to drop, despite all the recent success and stars like Thor and Conforto and (maybe) Rosario. Like Flores, Mets fans seem to be unable to get out of their own way, desperately wanting to live and die with the team but unable to stay upright amid all the little wounds. It's a new year, but 2017 left scars in its wake.

—Bryan Grosnick is an author of Baseball Prospectus.

Hitters

Nori Aoki RF

Born: 01/05/82 Age: 36 Bats: L Throws: R Height: 5'9" Weight: 180 Origin: International Free Agent, 2012

YEAR	TEAM	LVL	AGE	PA	R	2B	3B	HR	RBI	BB	K	SB	CS	AVG/OBP/SLG	TAv	VORP	BABIP	BRR	FRAA	WARP
2015	SFN	MLB	33	392	42	12	3	5	26	30	25	14	5	.287/.353/.380	.272	11.2	.298	-1.3	LF(86): -0.2, RF(2): -0.4	1.1
2016	TAC	AAA	34	108	17	5	0	1	7	8	13	4	0	.323/.374/.406	.305	8.9	.357	1.5	LF(21): -3.4, CF(3): -0.1	0.6
2016	SEA	MLB	34	467	63	24	4	4	28	34	45	7	9	.283/.349/.388	.269	14.8	.309	0.1	LF(99): 4.2, CF(15): -1.1	1.8
2017	HOU	MLB	35	224	28	12	1	2	19	15	29	5	2	.272/.323/.371	.233	-3.9	.303	-2.3	LF(56): -0.3, RF(16): -1.7	-0.7
2017	TOR	MLB	35	34	4	1	0	3	8	1	5	0	0	.281/.294/.594	.312	2.5	.240	0.0	RF(8): -0.8, LF(3): 1.3	0.3
2017	NYN	MLB	35	116	16	7	1	0	8	13	10	5	0	.284/.371/.373	.270	3.2	.315	-0.4	RF(23): 0.3, LF(5): 0.0	0.3
2018	*NYN*	*MLB*	*36*	*383*	*46*	*15*	*2*	*5*	*32*	*31*	*39*	*10*	*4*	*.270/.339/.370*	*.246*	*6.0*	*.288*	*-1.0*	*LF 0, RF -2*	*0.3*
2019	*NYN*	*MLB*	*37*	*293*	*32*	*11*	*1*	*3*	*26*	*23*	*32*	*6*	*3*	*.261/.330/.352*	*.254*	*4.6*	*.281*	*-0.5*	*LF 0, RF -2*	*0.2*

Breakout: 0% Improve: 22% Collapse: 10% Attrition: 24% MLB: 69% *Comparables: Juan Pierre, Manny Mota, Darryl Hamilton*

Imagine that you're an MLB GM in desperate need of a reliable corner outfielder that won't cost much. Good news, Aoki is always available! Claimed off waivers by the Astros in the offseason, the veteran recorded his 2,000th professional hit in June, then was traded six weeks later to the Blue Jays after playing his way off the team. Within a month, his play perked up but he was still designated for assignment. Five days later he became a Met because all the other Mets were gone. With an eight-game hit streak to begin his career in orange and blue, Aoki continued to be exactly what he always has been: an on-base machine with limited other skills. This year he'll likely be a little less effective and a little older, but still available for a bargain-basement price.

Asdrubal Cabrera INF

Born: 11/13/85 Age: 32 Bats: B Throws: R Height: 6'0" Weight: 205 Origin: International Free Agent, 2002

YEAR	TEAM	LVL	AGE	PA	R	2B	3B	HR	RBI	BB	K	SB	CS	AVG/OBP/SLG	TAv	VORP	BABIP	BRR	FRAA	WARP
2015	TBA	MLB	29	551	66	28	5	15	58	36	107	6	3	.265/.315/.430	.261	21.4	.306	-0.4	SS(136): -8.4	1.4
2016	NYN	MLB	30	568	65	30	1	23	62	38	103	5	1	.280/.336/.474	.298	45.7	.310	0.1	SS(135): -4.2	4.3
2017	NYN	MLB	31	540	66	32	0	14	59	50	83	3	2	.280/.351/.434	.285	31.1	.310	-2.2	SS(45): -0.2, 3B(44): -1.1	2.8
2018	*NYN*	*MLB*	*32*	*610*	*78*	*30*	*2*	*17*	*65*	*44*	*110*	*5*	*2*	*.252/.313/.405*	*.254*	*15.5*	*.285*	*-0.7*	*3B -8, 2B -1*	*0.2*
2019	*NYN*	*MLB*	*33*	*515*	*63*	*26*	*1*	*16*	*62*	*41*	*97*	*3*	*1*	*.254/.320/.418*	*.267*	*16.0*	*.286*	*-0.7*	*3B -6, 2B -1*	*1.0*

Breakout: 0% Improve: 35% Collapse: 11% Attrition: 10% MLB: 96% *Comparables: Edgar Renteria, Jhonny Peralta, J.J. Hardy*

As the Mets shipped off almost every other tradeable veteran at midseason, Cabrera stuck around even after complaining about a move off shortstop and reportedly requesting a deal. Despite the grumblings, the team's reluctant infielder delivered another solid offensive season laden with doubles. Cabrera drew more bases on balls and had fewer whiffs than in the past, delivering the best walk-to-strikeout ratio of his career. He also obliterated left-handed pitching to the tune of a .392/.434/.512 slash line. Regardless of team or position, Cabrera puts up essentially the same numbers every year, and there's no reason to believe he'll stop now.

Gavin Cecchini MI

Born: 12/22/93 Age: 24 Bats: R Throws: R Height: 6'2" Weight: 196 Origin: Round 1, 2012 Draft (#12 overall)

YEAR	TEAM	LVL	AGE	PA	R	2B	3B	HR	RBI	BB	K	SB	CS	AVG/OBP/SLG	TAv	VORP	BABIP	BRR	FRAA	WARP
2015	BIN	AA	21	485	64	26	4	7	51	42	55	3	4	.317/.377/.442	.300	36.2	.348	-2.3	SS(109): 2.5	4.2
2016	LVG	AAA	22	499	71	27	2	8	55	48	55	4	1	.325/.390/.448	.274	25.2	.357	-2.1	SS(105): -11.7, 2B(3): 1.2	1.5
2016	NYN	MLB	22	7	2	2	0	0	2	0	2	0	0	.333/.429/.667	.642	2.5	.500	0.0	SS(2): 0.0	0.3
2017	LVG	AAA	23	497	68	27	3	6	39	40	61	5	4	.267/.329/.380	.232	0.3	.298	-0.2	2B(80): -7.1, SS(30): -2.7	-0.9
2017	NYN	MLB	23	82	4	2	0	1	7	4	19	0	1	.208/.256/.273	.181	-3.9	.263	0.6	2B(20): -1.9	-0.6
2018	*NYN*	*MLB*	*24*	*240*	*25*	*10*	*1*	*5*	*24*	*19*	*41*	*1*	*1*	*.253/.313/.372*	*.244*	*5.3*	*.290*	*-0.5*	*2B -3, SS 0*	*0.0*
2019	*NYN*	*MLB*	*25*	*370*	*44*	*16*	*1*	*10*	*41*	*32*	*67*	*1*	*1*	*.254/.322/.395*	*.260*	*10.7*	*.289*	*-0.7*	*2B -5, SS 0*	*0.6*

Breakout: 10% Improve: 18% Collapse: 6% Attrition: 19% MLB: 40% *Comparables: Daniel Descalso, Brad Emaus, Eric Sogard*

He's the friend you go to prom with because your crush didn't ask. He's the guy you jokingly promise to marry if you're both still single at 40. He certainly doesn't make your heart race or give you goosebumps. He's just there. And he's fine. You'd think that since they had an opening at second base after July, the Mets might've been willing to settle and give Cecchini a chance to prove he's more than just a stand-in. Alas, the 23-year-old stayed on the bench for most of September, as good a sign as any that the Mets just aren't that into him.

Yoenis Cespedes LF

Born: 10/18/85 Age: 32 Bats: R Throws: R Height: 5'10" Weight: 220 Origin: International Free Agent, 2012

YEAR	TEAM	LVL	AGE	PA	R	2B	3B	HR	RBI	BB	K	SB	CS	AVG/OBP/SLG	TAv	VORP	BABIP	BRR	FRAA	WARP
2015	DET	MLB	29	427	62	28	2	18	61	19	87	3	4	.293/.323/.506	.293	23.1	.331	0.6	LF(99): 13.0	3.9
2015	NYN	MLB	29	249	39	14	4	17	44	14	54	4	1	.287/.337/.604	.334	25.1	.306	0.6	CF(40): -2.4, LF(35): 0.8	2.5
2016	NYN	MLB	30	543	72	25	1	31	86	51	108	3	1	.280/.354/.530	.326	48.4	.298	-1.9	LF(80): 7.7, CF(63): -5.2	5.2
2017	NYN	MLB	31	321	46	17	2	17	42	26	61	0	1	.292/.352/.540	.313	23.9	.316	-1.1	LF(74): 2.9	2.7
2018	*NYN*	*MLB*	*32*	*601*	*78*	*28*	*3*	*28*	*91*	*39*	*127*	*4*	*2*	*.262/.315/.477*	*.274*	*28.0*	*.291*	*-0.9*	*LF 10*	*3.3*
2019	*NYN*	*MLB*	*33*	*465*	*63*	*21*	*1*	*23*	*68*	*34*	*105*	*2*	*1*	*.250/.310/.467*	*.278*	*19.9*	*.279*	*-0.4*	*LF 8*	*3.0*

Breakout: 1% Improve: 34% Collapse: 3% Attrition: 13% MLB: 96% *Comparables: Alfonso Soriano, Benny Ayala, Willie Horton*

Already a superstar, Cespedes decreased his strikeouts and increased his walks in 2017. He averaged a home run every five games. He played decent outfield defense and his arm held up. His legs, on the other hand, did not hold up. He only suited up for half the season, much of which he spent hobbling around the bases. Once such a dynamic athlete, La Potencia has become the dad who can't mow the lawn anymore because his hips hurt or can't walk the dog because his hamstring's acting up. "The Circle of Life" isn't *just* the big man's former walk-up music, it's supposed to move us through despair and hope. At the same time, the circle wears us down until it's time for the next person to come along and take their place. Let's hope that he can fight time and his body a little longer.

Michael Conforto LF Born: 03/01/93 Age: 25 Bats: L Throws: R Height: 6'1" Weight: 215 Origin: Round 1, 2014 Draft (#10 overall)

YEAR	TEAM	LVL	AGE	PA	R	2B	3B	HR	RBI	BB	K	SB	CS	AVG/OBP/SLG	TAv	VORP	BABIP	BRR	FRAA	WARP
2015	SLU	A+	22	206	25	12	0	7	28	17	26	0	1	.283/.350/.462	.292	9.0	.294	-1.7	LF(41): 6.9	1.7
2015	BIN	AA	22	197	21	12	3	5	26	23	35	1	0	.312/.396/.503	.312	12.0	.368	-2.4	LF(45): -0.1	1.3
2015	NYN	MLB	22	194	30	14	0	9	26	17	39	0	1	.270/.335/.506	.315	15.0	.297	0.6	LF(50): 2.8	1.9
2016	LVG	AAA	23	144	30	8	2	9	28	13	18	2	2	.422/.483/.727	.381	20.1	.446	-1.1	LF(18): 0.4, CF(6): -1.3	2.1
2016	NYN	MLB	23	348	38	21	1	12	42	36	89	2	1	.220/.310/.414	.271	12.6	.267	1.2	LF(73): 0.8, RF(9): 0.7	1.4
2017	NYN	MLB	24	440	72	20	1	27	68	57	113	2	0	.279/.384/.555	.336	47.8	.328	1.4	LF(52): 3.9, CF(43): -6.4	4.6
2018	*NYN*	*MLB*	*25*	*594*	*82*	*29*	*2*	*28*	*92*	*62*	*135*	*3*	*1*	*.263/.347/.488*	*.288*	*34.8*	*.301*	*-1.0*	*RF -5, LF 0*	*2.5*
2019	*NYN*	*MLB*	*26*	*526*	*78*	*27*	*1*	*27*	*82*	*58*	*119*	*2*	*1*	*.266/.355/.504*	*.306*	*37.4*	*.302*	*1.2*	*RF -3, LF 0*	*3.8*

Breakout: 1% Improve: 50% Collapse: 4% Attrition: 6% MLB: 98% *Comparables: Jorge Soler, Carlos Gonzalez, Anthony Rizzo*

Had Brandon Nimmo not started the season injured, this 2017 All-Star would likely have opened 2017 in Triple-A. But thanks to this twist of fate, Conforto found himself the Mets' fourth outfielder to open the season. It wasn't long before he forced his way into the starting lineup because, well, he put up a TAv that was good for ninth in baseball—just three points shy of crosstown phenom Aaron Judge. That's not shabby for a dude who was almost buried in Las Vegas despite previously proving himself to be a top-shelf hitter. He also emerged as the team's center fielder, which was just a touch more unexpected than his hitting so well. But, like most other Mets, he was hurt; at the end of June it was a bone bruise that never sent him to the DL but that kept him off the field and from hitting his best. But in August, Conforto suffered a far more serious—and far more absurd—injury: On a normal, routine swing he dislocated his shoulder and tore his posterior capsule. The start of his 2018 is in jeopardy despite all the talent in the world, so in a weird way he's back to where he started last season.

Travis d'Arnaud C Born: 02/10/89 Age: 29 Bats: R Throws: R Height: 6'2" Weight: 210 Origin: Round 1, 2007 Draft (#37 overall)

YEAR	TEAM	LVL	AGE	PA	R	2B	3B	HR	RBI	BB	K	SB	CS	AVG/OBP/SLG	TAv	VORP	BABIP	BRR	FRAA	WARP
2015	NYN	MLB	26	268	31	14	1	12	41	23	49	0	0	.268/.340/.485	.312	25.0	.289	-0.1	C(64): 11.2	3.9
2016	SLU	A+	27	38	3	2	0	0	5	9	5	1	0	.310/.474/.379	.311	2.7	.375	-0.2	C(3): 0.0	0.3
2016	NYN	MLB	27	276	27	7	0	4	15	19	50	0	0	.247/.307/.323	.239	6.2	.293	-0.3	C(73): 7.3	1.4
2017	NYN	MLB	28	376	39	19	1	16	57	23	59	0	0	.244/.293/.443	.261	15.4	.250	-2.2	C(93): 7.3, 2B(1): 0.0	2.3
2018	*NYN*	*MLB*	*29*	*488*	*58*	*23*	*1*	*16*	*60*	*40*	*81*	*0*	*0*	*.250/.315/.418*	*.258*	*22.5*	*.271*	*-0.9*	*C 10*	*2.8*
2019	*NYN*	*MLB*	*30*	*466*	*60*	*21*	*1*	*18*	*60*	*41*	*82*	*0*	*0*	*.251/.321/.432*	*.271*	*22.6*	*.272*	*-1.2*	*C 10*	*3.6*

Breakout: 2% Improve: 34% Collapse: 7% Attrition: 18% MLB: 94% *Comparables: Brian Schneider, Dioner Navarro, Jonathan Lucroy*

YEAR	TEAM	P. COUNT	FRM RUNS	BLK RUNS	THRW RUNS	TOT RUNS
2015	BIN	438	0.2	0.0	0.0	0.2
2015	LVG	249	0.1	0.0	0.0	0.1
2015	NYN	9002	11.5	0.4	0.1	12.0
2016	NYN	10281	7.2	1.0	-2.5	5.7
2017	NYN	13404	6.7	0.8	-2.7	4.8
2018	*NYN*	*17974*	*12.0*	*0.8*	*-2.7*	*10.1*
2019	*NYN*	*17158*	*10.3*	*0.7*	*-2.3*	*8.6*

August 17, 2017: Travis d'Arnaud started at third base after Wilmer Flores and Jose Reyes were both late scratches. This could have been problematic for the career-long catcher, so after a few plays he switched with Asdrubal Cabrera and moved to *second base*, which isn't any easier. They switched back. And switched again. Twenty-three times they traded positions, every time to get d'Arnaud as far away from a potential batted ball as possible. He made just one play: a pop-up from Todd Frazier that he handled cleanly. It was a game of musical chairs that would have been hilarious had it not been so pathetic. It was also completely emblematic of a disastrous Mets season that had seen everything go wrong. Never mind the fact that d'Arnaud didn't just survive his experiment at second and third base, he was one of the few Mets that improved his batting line over 2016. He's a fine catcher so long as he stays healthy, but on that day he was a hauntingly perfect representation of the circus the team had become.

Phillip Evans INF Born: 09/10/92 Age: 25 Bats: R Throws: R Height: 5'10" Weight: 223 Origin: Round 15, 2011 Draft (#462 overall)

YEAR	TEAM	LVL	AGE	PA	R	2B	3B	HR	RBI	BB	K	SB	CS	AVG/OBP/SLG	TAv	VORP	BABIP	BRR	FRAA	WARP
2015	SLU	A+	22	280	19	14	3	0	32	24	44	2	2	.234/.300/.313	.239	2.7	.280	0.8	2B(41): -5.8, 3B(33): 1.8	-0.2
2016	SLU	A+	23	33	3	0	0	0	2	5	3	0	0	.143/.273/.143	.186	-1.9	.160	0.1	3B(3): 0.1, 2B(2): 0.5	-0.1
2016	BIN	AA	23	386	50	30	0	8	39	19	60	1	1	.335/.374/.485	.304	30.4	.384	0.7	SS(39): 0.6, 2B(32): -4.0	3.1
2017	LVG	AAA	24	510	58	26	3	11	56	42	79	2	3	.279/.341/.418	.252	11.6	.316	-0.6	3B(66): 1.4, 2B(29): -0.2	0.8
2017	NYN	MLB	24	38	4	2	0	0	1	4	8	0	0	.303/.395/.364	.269	1.8	.400	0.3	3B(6): -0.8, 2B(2): 0.3	0.1
2018	*NYN*	*MLB*	*25*	*140*	*15*	*7*	*0*	*3*	*15*	*9*	*29*	*0*	*0*	*.246/.301/.377*	*.242*	*1.8*	*.294*	*-0.3*	*3B 0, LF -1*	*0.1*
2019	*NYN*	*MLB*	*26*	*307*	*36*	*14*	*0*	*8*	*35*	*22*	*67*	*0*	*0*	*.247/.307/.393*	*.256*	*5.6*	*.295*	*-0.8*	*3B 1, LF -1*	*0.6*

Breakout: 0% Improve: 8% Collapse: 10% Attrition: 18% MLB: 26% *Comparables: Andrew Burns, Ryan Rohlinger, Casey McGehee*

Evans was headed home for the offseason, staring straight into minor-league free agency, when the Mets surprisingly added him to the 40-man roster and brought him to the big leagues, where he doubled up on the shocks by recording double-digit hits despite limited playing time. With solid minor-league stats and a $650,000 signing bonus in his rear-view, it shouldn't be *that* strange a thought for Evans to hold his own as a bat-first reserve infielder in the majors. He'll return to the Mets on a minor-league deal this year and look for a way to reprise his game of peek-a-boo in Queens during 2018.

Wilmer Flores INF Born: 08/06/91 Age: 26 Bats: R Throws: R Height: 6'3" Weight: 205 Origin: International Free Agent, 2007

YEAR	TEAM	LVL	AGE	PA	R	2B	3B	HR	RBI	BB	K	SB	CS	AVG/OBP/SLG	TAv	VORP	BABIP	BRR	FRAA	WARP
2015	NYN	MLB	23	510	55	22	0	16	59	19	63	0	1	.263/.295/.408	.262	19.2	.273	-0.1	SS(103): -1.3, 2B(37): 2.5	2.2
2016	NYN	MLB	24	335	38	14	0	16	49	23	48	1	1	.267/.319/.469	.305	21.9	.268	-2.4	3B(51): -4.0, 1B(27): 0.4	2.0
2017	NYN	MLB	25	362	42	17	1	18	52	17	54	1	1	.271/.307/.488	.278	16.1	.270	-0.6	3B(55): 0.2, 1B(29): -0.2	1.5
2018	*NYN*	*MLB*	*26*	*569*	*66*	*27*	*1*	*22*	*78*	*27*	*81*	*1*	*1*	*.266/.304/.442*	*.261*	*20.0*	*.275*	*-1.4*	*2B 2, 1B 0*	*1.7*
2019	*NYN*	*MLB*	*27*	*412*	*54*	*20*	*1*	*18*	*59*	*23*	*62*	*1*	*1*	*.269/.313/.467*	*.279*	*18.9*	*.276*	*-0.9*	*2B 2, 1B 0*	*2.2*

Breakout: 2% Improve: 41% Collapse: 5% Attrition: 16% MLB: 91% *Comparables: Matt Duffy, Lonnie Chisenhall, Scooter Gennett*

The One Where Wilmer Finally Develops once again turned into The One Where Wilmer Got Hurt so yeah, this one's a rerun. While the *not-actually-a-shortstop* shortstop has always found success against southpaws, Flores finally managed to put up average numbers against righties in 2017, posting a .262/.306/.459 line when not graced with the platoon advantage. (That also brought us ever closer to an answer to "Will they or won't they ... give him a chance to play everyday?") In early September, Flores broke his nose in sitcomesque fashion when he fouled a ball off his face. He was shut down for the year.

Andres Gimenez SS Born: 09/04/98 Age: 19 Bats: L Throws: R Height: 5'11" Weight: 176 Origin: International Free Agent, 2015

YEAR	TEAM	LVL	AGE	PA	R	2B	3B	HR	RBI	BB	K	SB	CS	AVG/OBP/SLG	TAv	VORP	BABIP	BRR	FRAA	WARP
2016	MET	RK	17	141	24	10	4	1	17	21	13	7	1	.360/.461/.544	.389	28.1	.388	2.1	SS(29): 7.1	3.5
2016	DME	RK	17	134	28	10	0	2	21	25	9	6	7	.340/.478/.500	.367	20.0	.344	-0.9	SS(19): -2.9, 2B(12): -1.1	1.6
2017	COL	A	18	399	50	9	4	4	31	28	61	14	8	.265/.346/.349	.273	22.4	.310	0.7	SS(89): 6.6	3.0
2018	*NYN*	*MLB*	*19*	*250*	*30*	*9*	*1*	*7*	*24*	*18*	*58*	*3*	*2*	*.234/.305/.373*	*.233*	*4.3*	*.282*	*-0.3*	*SS 3*	*0.8*
2019	*NYN*	*MLB*	*20*	*439*	*56*	*16*	*2*	*15*	*54*	*35*	*95*	*6*	*4*	*.252/.326/.418*	*.269*	*18.9*	*.292*	*-0.2*	*SS 6*	*2.7*

Breakout: 0% Improve: 7% Collapse: 1% Attrition: 28% MLB: 35% *Comparables: Jurickson Profar, Carlos Correa, Elvis Andrus*

Literally a decade younger than Columbia teammate Tim Tebow, Gimenez is less of a ratings draw but far more relevant to the Mets' future. His stock rose in 2017, as he was stateside for the first time in his professional career and displayed all the traits that made him a former top international signee. Grading the 19-year-old is challenging; so far he looks like a lock to stay at shortstop but hasn't managed to tap into any power, though both of those things could change at any time. Gimenez will join St. Lucie in the spring as the organization's top prospect.

Luis Guillorme MI Born: 09/27/94 Age: 23 Bats: L Throws: R Height: 5'9" Weight: 199 Origin: Round 10, 2013 Draft (#296 overall)

YEAR	TEAM	LVL	AGE	PA	R	2B	3B	HR	RBI	BB	K	SB	CS	AVG/OBP/SLG	TAv	VORP	BABIP	BRR	FRAA	WARP
2015	SAV	A	20	523	67	16	0	0	55	54	70	18	8	.318/.391/.354	.305	44.9	.374	0.4	SS(120): 7.6	5.6
2016	SLU	A+	21	505	47	16	2	1	46	43	63	4	2	.263/.332/.315	.245	9.9	.303	0.1	SS(72): -1.6, 2B(52): 4.0	1.3
2017	BIN	AA	22	558	70	20	0	1	43	72	55	4	3	.283/.376/.331	.268	25.8	.316	3.4	2B(69): 4.1, SS(58): -2.1	3.0
2018	*NYN*	*MLB*	*23*	*61*	*6*	*2*	*0*	*1*	*5*	*6*	*11*	*0*	*0*	*.246/.314/.333*	*.237*	*1.2*	*.287*	*-0.1*	*SS 0*	*0.1*
2019	*NYN*	*MLB*	*24*	*346*	*41*	*13*	*0*	*7*	*36*	*34*	*61*	*1*	*0*	*.259/.336/.376*	*.262*	*11.7*	*.295*	*-0.9*	*SS 1*	*1.4*

Breakout: 3% Improve: 13% Collapse: 2% Attrition: 7% MLB: 22% *Comparables: Tony Renda, Tim Locastro, Joe Panik*

The legend of the *Best Defensive Infielder In All The Land* went national during spring training with a life-saving bat grab in the dugout that you need to see to believe. (Teammate Brandon Nimmo, on the other hand, ran directly into the line of fire.) When not snatching bats out of the air off the field, Guillorme—a 10th-round pick back in 2013—snatched most of the balls on it and continued to show off his defensive prowess in Binghamton. That, combined with his .376 OBP, is enough to ignore a stark lack of power. The Mets haven't recently put a high priority on defense, so any middle infielder who can turn a clean double play is a sight for sore eyes ... but rest assured, Guillorme's glove really is that good.

Desmond Jennings CF Born: 10/30/86 Age: 31 Bats: R Throws: R Height: 6'2" Weight: 210 Origin: Round 10, 2006 Draft (#289 overall)

YEAR	TEAM	LVL	AGE	PA	R	2B	3B	HR	RBI	BB	K	SB	CS	AVG/OBP/SLG	TAv	VORP	BABIP	BRR	FRAA	WARP
2015	DUR	AAA	28	25	2	2	0	0	0	4	5	0	0	.143/.280/.238	.183	-1.5	.188	0.1	LF(4): -0.2	-0.2
2015	TBA	MLB	28	108	9	2	1	1	7	8	17	5	3	.268/.324/.340	.254	1.1	.309	-0.7	LF(21): 1.7, CF(10): -0.9	0.2
2016	TBA	MLB	29	225	22	7	1	7	20	21	58	2	0	.200/.281/.350	.226	-1.7	.243	0.4	LF(33): 2.0, CF(30): -4.2	-0.4
2017	LVG	AAA	30	229	32	5	4	8	25	20	43	3	3	.237/.301/.415	.233	1.2	.259	1.5	CF(35): 0.6, LF(11): 0.4	0.4
2018	*NYN*	*MLB*	*31*	*250*	*28*	*11*	*1*	*7*	*28*	*24*	*53*	*5*	*2*	*.239/.318/.392*	*.243*	*4.6*	*.279*	*-0.3*	*CF -3, LF 1*	*0.3*
2019	*NYN*	*MLB*	*32*	*51*	*6*	*2*	*0*	*1*	*6*	*5*	*11*	*1*	*0*	*.231/.308/.383*	*.252*	*1.0*	*.270*	*0.0*	*CF -1, LF 0*	*0.1*

Breakout: 0% Improve: 44% Collapse: 8% Attrition: 15% MLB: 87% *Comparables: Nyjer Morgan, Gregor Blanco, Rajai Davis*

Baseball is an exercise in failure. In Little League, they tell you that if you fail seven out of every 10 tries, you'll make it to the majors. Fail just six out of every 10 tries in the big leagues and you become a legend. Everyone fails eventually; how long a player holds off failure determines how we remember him 25 years later.

Jennings failed quietly, despite loud tools. He was a top-10 prospect in all of baseball while with Tampa Bay and enjoyed a breakout rookie season in 2009. But even that could be seen as something of a failure: He was average, not a star, and at the plate the former phenom failed in seven or eight tries out of 10. Injuries, age and loss of talent caught up with him, and failure came a bit more often, as he couldn't get on the field and couldn't hit the few times when he did.

After being dumped by the Rays in August 2016, Jennings bounced into and out of Cincinnati before being picked up by the Mets last April as Triple-A depth. Even in the comfortable offensive environment of Las Vegas, he failed too often and was released in June. Now, probably done with professional baseball, Jennings can perhaps focus on the fact that reaching the big leagues at all made him an unmitigated success despite all those small failures.

Juan Lagares CF Born: 03/17/89 Age: 29 Bats: R Throws: R Height: 6'1" Weight: 215 Origin: International Free Agent, 2006

YEAR	TEAM	LVL	AGE	PA	R	2B	3B	HR	RBI	BB	K	SB	CS	AVG/OBP/SLG	TAv	VORP	BABIP	BRR	FRAA	WARP
2015	NYN	MLB	26	465	47	16	5	6	41	16	87	7	3	.259/.289/.358	.245	8.0	.308	1.4	CF(137): -1.1, RF(2): -0.3	0.7
2016	NYN	MLB	27	160	15	7	2	3	9	11	27	4	2	.239/.301/.380	.245	2.4	.274	0.1	CF(68): 1.4, RF(2): 0.1	0.4
2017	BIN	AA	28	29	3	0	0	0	0	0	6	0	0	.241/.241/.241	.163	-1.7	.304	0.4	CF(7): 0.0	-0.2
2017	NYN	MLB	28	272	37	16	2	3	15	14	56	7	3	.250/.296/.365	.234	3.3	.309	1.9	CF(85): 5.0	0.8
2018	*NYN*	*MLB*	*29*	*347*	*41*	*15*	*3*	*5*	*30*	*17*	*68*	*8*	*3*	*.255/.295/.366*	*.236*	*5.0*	*.304*	*0.4*	*CF -1, RF 0*	*0.1*
2019	*NYN*	*MLB*	*30*	*291*	*32*	*14*	*2*	*6*	*30*	*17*	*60*	*6*	*3*	*.256/.305/.384*	*.249*	*5.9*	*.305*	*0.9*	*CF 0, RF 0*	*0.6*

Breakout: 1% Improve: 44% Collapse: 9% Attrition: 17% MLB: 91% *Comparables: Leonys Martin, Corey Patterson, Cameron Maybin*

Unlike most injury-riddled regulars in the Mets' organization, Lagares isn't a pitcher. But just like most injury-riddled regulars in the Mets' organization, his health has threatened to derail a promising career. The former Gold Glove center fielder spent a significant portion of 2017 on the disabled list, but his defensive metrics rebounded nicely to an FRAA of 5.0 over just 94 games. The offense still leaves a little to be desired—he had a reverse split last year and his .610 OPS against lefties was over 100 points lower than his career mark—but if Lagares can continue chasing down balls in the outfield, that four-year, $23 million contract extension might not be the black hole it once appeared to be.

Desmond Lindsay CF Born: 01/15/97 Age: 21 Bats: R Throws: R Height: 5'11" Weight: 196 Origin: Round 2, 2015 Draft (#53 overall)

YEAR	TEAM	LVL	AGE	PA	R	2B	3B	HR	RBI	BB	K	SB	CS	AVG/OBP/SLG	TAv	VORP	BABIP	BRR	FRAA	WARP
2015	MTS	RK	18	81	10	4	2	1	6	11	21	3	2	.304/.400/.464	.317	8.1	.426	0.7	CF(16): 0.0	0.8
2015	BRO	A-	18	53	3	3	0	0	7	7	19	0	1	.200/.308/.267	.240	-0.6	.346	-1.0	CF(14): -3.8	-0.5
2016	BRO	A-	19	134	18	5	0	4	17	20	26	3	1	.297/.418/.450	.344	15.3	.358	-0.1	CF(29): -3.8	1.2
2017	COL	A	20	251	40	10	1	8	30	33	77	4	2	.220/.327/.388	.265	11.1	.298	2.2	CF(62): 2.2	1.4
2018	*NYN*	*MLB*	*21*	*250*	*26*	*8*	*0*	*8*	*29*	*27*	*87*	*0*	*0*	*.198/.287/.349*	*.221*	*-0.7*	*.279*	*-0.4*	*CF -1*	*-0.2*
2019	*NYN*	*MLB*	*22*	*313*	*38*	*11*	*1*	*11*	*37*	*34*	*106*	*1*	*0*	*.206/.296/.374*	*.244*	*3.5*	*.284*	*-0.6*	*CF -1*	*0.2*

Breakout: 3% Improve: 5% Collapse: 0% Attrition: 3% MLB: 6% *Comparables: Clint Frazier, Daniel Fields, Trayce Thompson*

Most evaluators said they wanted to see a full season of Lindsay before passing judgment on the prep star. Well, it's three seasons later and everyone is still waiting. The second-round draft pick out of Out-of-Door Academy still has legendary bat speed, but only played half a season before undergoing elbow surgery in late July. Before his injury he hit a career-high eight home runs in Columbia as a full-time center fielder, but his inability to stay on the field has to be a growing concern. Let's see if we have to repeat this same *Annual* comment next year or if he shows himself out the door.

Jose Lobaton C Born: 10/21/84 Age: 33 Bats: B Throws: R Height: 6'1" Weight: 205 Origin: International Free Agent, 2002

YEAR	TEAM	LVL	AGE	PA	R	2B	3B	HR	RBI	BB	K	SB	CS	AVG/OBP/SLG	TAv	VORP	BABIP	BRR	FRAA	WARP
2015	WAS	MLB	30	155	11	4	0	3	20	15	40	0	0	.199/.279/.294	.226	1.1	.253	-0.5	C(42): 3.5	0.5
2016	WAS	MLB	31	114	10	3	1	3	8	12	18	0	0	.232/.319/.374	.257	3.4	.253	-1.4	C(38): 1.5	0.5
2017	WAS	MLB	32	158	11	3	0	4	11	14	35	0	0	.170/.248/.277	.197	-1.5	.194	1.6	C(50): -1.9	-0.3
2018	*NYN*	*MLB*	*33*	*64*	*6*	*2*	*0*	*1*	*6*	*6*	*15*	*0*	*0*	*.221/.291/.332*	*.228*	*1.0*	*.271*	*-0.1*	*C 0*	*0.0*
2019	*NYN*	*MLB*	*34*	*67*	*8*	*2*	*0*	*2*	*7*	*6*	*17*	*0*	*0*	*.215/.295/.337*	*.236*	*0.8*	*.268*	*-0.1*	*C 0*	*0.1*

Breakout: 3% Improve: 39% Collapse: 8% Attrition: 24% MLB: 90% *Comparables: Chris Cannizzaro, Jeff Reed, Gerald Laird*

YEAR	TEAM	P. COUNT	FRM RUNS	BLK RUNS	THRW RUNS	TOT RUNS
2015	WAS	5681	4.5	-0.1	-0.3	4.0
2016	WAS	4509	2.4	0.3	0.1	2.8
2017	WAS	6575	-2.4	0.8	-1.0	-2.6
2018	*NYN*	*2481*	*0.0*	*0.1*	*-0.1*	*0.0*
2019	*NYN*	*2584*	*0.0*	*0.2*	*-0.2*	*0.1*

Matt Wieters didn't exactly set a high bar at catcher last season—an extremely low bar, as one of the worst starting catchers in the majors, actually—but it was still too high for his backup, Lobaton, to clear. Both Nationals backstops had career-worst offensive seasons, but at least Wieters had the decency to crack a TAv of .200, if only by a bit. Lobaton had the edge on him in catching metrics, but when you're talking about two players ranked solidly in the bottom half of eligible guys, that edge doesn't feel so meaningful. Generally, it's not a great way to sail off into free agency; specifically, given that his last plate appearance of the year ended with him getting picked off on a ticky-tacky replay call in Game 5 of the NLDS, it's *really* not a great way to do so.

Tomas Nido C Born: 04/12/94 Age: 24 Bats: R Throws: R Height: 6'0" Weight: 210 Origin: Round 8, 2012 Draft (#260 overall)

YEAR	TEAM	LVL	AGE	PA	R	2B	3B	HR	RBI	BB	K	SB	CS	AVG/OBP/SLG	TAv	VORP	BABIP	BRR	FRAA	WARP
2015	SAV	A	21	335	39	14	2	6	40	12	86	1	1	.259/.284/.372	.256	10.7	.332	-1.5	C(75): 6.2	1.8
2016	SLU	A+	22	370	38	23	2	7	46	19	42	0	1	.320/.357/.459	.294	27.8	.344	-2.4	C(88): 4.8	3.3
2017	BIN	AA	23	404	41	19	1	8	60	30	63	0	0	.232/.287/.354	.227	4.3	.255	2.4	C(82): 25.2	3.2
2017	NYN	MLB	23	10	0	1	0	0	3	0	2	0	0	.300/.300/.400	.244	0.2	.375	-0.1	C(3): 0.2	0.0
2018	*NYN*	*MLB*	*24*	*250*	*24*	*11*	*0*	*8*	*30*	*13*	*59*	*0*	*0*	*.235/.277/.389*	*.225*	*3.1*	*.278*	*-0.5*	*C 14*	*1.9*
2019	*NYN*	*MLB*	*25*	*235*	*26*	*11*	*0*	*8*	*28*	*12*	*55*	*0*	*0*	*.236/.277/.395*	*.241*	*3.7*	*.278*	*-0.6*	*C 10*	*1.5*

Breakout: 7% Improve: 26% Collapse: 4% Attrition: 26% MLB: 31% *Comparables: Tony Cruz, Luis Exposito, Tim Federowicz*

YEAR	TEAM	P. COUNT	FRM RUNS	BLK RUNS	THRW RUNS	TOT RUNS
2017	NYN	379	0.0	0.2	0.0	0.2
2018	*NYN*	*8839*	*13.4*	*0.4*	*0.3*	*14.1*
2019	*NYN*	*8293*	*6.0*	*0.2*	*0.1*	*6.3*

A year removed from the Florida State League batting title, Nido found a new way to lead his league, posting the highest Adjusted FRAA among all Double-A catchers on the strength of terrific pitch-framing statistics. This reinforces previous beliefs that he has the tools to be a solid defensive backstop in the majors with some power, though he needs to refine his approach and other secondary skills before he gets there. Well, technically he's already there—he earned a September call-up—but even if those adjustments never come, he'll stick around Citi Field for at least half a decade or so in a Rene Rivera-like role.

Brandon Nimmo CF Born: 03/27/93 Age: 25 Bats: L Throws: R Height: 6'3" Weight: 207 Origin: Round 1, 2011 Draft (#13 overall)

YEAR	TEAM	LVL	AGE	PA	R	2B	3B	HR	RBI	BB	K	SB	CS	AVG/OBP/SLG	TAv	VORP	BABIP	BRR	FRAA	WARP
2015	BIN	AA	22	302	26	12	3	2	16	26	55	0	2	.279/.354/.368	.266	6.1	.343	-3.9	CF(57): -2.7, RF(10): 1.0	0.4
2015	LVG	AAA	22	112	19	3	1	3	8	18	20	5	4	.264/.393/.418	.284	6.3	.304	0.9	RF(17): 4.3, CF(13): -0.2	1.0
2016	LVG	AAA	23	444	72	25	8	11	61	46	73	7	8	.352/.423/.541	.304	35.3	.411	2.8	CF(65): 2.6, LF(23): 1.6	4.1
2016	NYN	MLB	23	80	12	1	0	1	6	6	20	0	0	.274/.338/.329	.267	2.0	.365	-0.4	LF(13): -0.2, RF(7): -0.1	0.2
2017	LVG	AAA	24	198	23	12	1	3	17	33	49	0	0	.227/.364/.368	.262	5.2	.306	-1.0	CF(31): -4.8, RF(12): 2.2	0.2
2017	NYN	MLB	24	215	26	11	1	5	21	33	60	2	0	.260/.379/.418	.295	12.2	.360	-0.9	LF(32): 3.0, CF(12): 0.5	1.6
2018	*NYN*	*MLB*	*25*	*592*	*76*	*23*	*3*	*13*	*58*	*68*	*143*	*4*	*3*	*.246/.339/.383*	*.259*	*18.4*	*.313*	*-0.9*	*CF -7, RF 1*	*1.0*
2019	*NYN*	*MLB*	*26*	*557*	*72*	*23*	*3*	*16*	*64*	*67*	*139*	*4*	*3*	*.247/.346/.406*	*.277*	*23.3*	*.313*	*-1.9*	*CF -6, RF 2*	*2.2*

Breakout: 7% Improve: 48% Collapse: 12% Attrition: 35% MLB: 84% *Comparables: Desmond Jennings, Ryan Kalish, Aaron Hicks*

Someone, in an attempt to get a photograph of Nimmo frowning, flipped his smile upside down using one of those Snapchat filters. Somehow, his grin only got brighter. With a chance to play every day after the trade deadline, the 2011 first-round pick couldn't stop getting on base, so why shouldn't he smile? A walk rate that floated up near the 20 percent range during the season's final month put Nimmo in illustrious company, and he rarely chased pitches out of the strike zone—his 18.6 percent swing rate on such offerings was the lowest in baseball (min. 200 PA). Even with an unsustainable BABIP, Nimmo remains a good bet to get on base, at least against righties. His .404 OBP with the platoon advantage dwarfed his .292 OBP without it, and he'll need to shrink that gap if he wants to be an everyday outfielder. At the very least, we know he can smile.

Kevin Plawecki C Born: 02/26/91 Age: 27 Bats: R Throws: R Height: 6'2" Weight: 210 Origin: Round 1, 2012 Draft (#35 overall)

YEAR	TEAM	LVL	AGE	PA	R	2B	3B	HR	RBI	BB	K	SB	CS	AVG/OBP/SLG	TAv	VORP	BABIP	BRR	FRAA	WARP
2015	LVG	AAA	24	90	7	5	1	1	9	3	12	0	0	.224/.267/.341	.198	-3.8	.250	-1.7	C(20): -0.3, 1B(1): 0.0	-0.4
2015	NYN	MLB	24	258	18	9	0	3	21	17	60	0	0	.219/.280/.296	.241	4.7	.277	-1.6	C(70): 11.2	1.7
2016	LVG	AAA	25	207	27	11	0	8	40	13	19	0	1	.300/.348/.484	.278	9.9	.297	-1.9	C(41): 4.1, 1B(5): 0.2	1.5
2016	NYN	MLB	25	151	6	6	0	1	11	17	33	0	0	.197/.298/.265	.228	2.3	.255	0.3	C(45): 6.2	0.9
2017	LVG	AAA	26	275	37	17	1	9	45	16	38	0	0	.328/.375/.514	.292	21.8	.350	-1.4	C(63): 9.5	3.0
2017	NYN	MLB	26	118	11	5	0	3	13	14	17	1	0	.260/.364/.400	.289	8.6	.284	-0.3	C(29): -3.0, P(2): 0.0	0.3
2018	*NYN*	*MLB*	*27*	*154*	*16*	*6*	*0*	*4*	*18*	*11*	*29*	*0*	*0*	*.242/.309/.375*	*.248*	*4.8*	*.278*	*-0.3*	*C 1*	*0.5*
2019	*NYN*	*MLB*	*28*	*193*	*23*	*8*	*0*	*5*	*21*	*15*	*40*	*0*	*0*	*.234/.304/.373*	*.250*	*4.2*	*.273*	*-0.5*	*C 2*	*0.6*

Breakout: 2% Improve: 37% Collapse: 11% Attrition: 24% MLB: 85% *Comparables: Hank Conger, Lou Marson, JD Closser*

YEAR	TEAM	P. COUNT	FRM RUNS	BLK RUNS	THRW RUNS	TOT RUNS
2015	LVG	2811	0.0	0.0	0.0	-0.1
2015	NYN	9093	11.2	0.4	-0.3	11.3
2016	NYN	5670	5.9	0.9	-0.2	6.6
2017	NYN	3842	-2.9	0.6	-0.5	-2.8
2018	*NYN*	*3629*	*1.3*	*0.2*	*-0.2*	*1.3*
2019	*NYN*	*4540*	*1.4*	*0.2*	*-0.2*	*1.4*

It seemed, for a while at least, that Plawecki was the backstop of the future in Flushing, a contact hitter who would hit enough to keep him behind the plate. However, his bat never made it to the majors, which happens both more often than you'd think and more than some prospect writers would like to admit. Instead he became a backup behind the oft-injured Travis d'Arnaud because even a catcher with a .237 TAv in his first two major-league seasons is valuable if he's cheap enough. That's what Plawecki was until 2017, when suddenly his bat showed up. In just 37 major-league games—he had been disappointing enough that the Mets gave most of his playing time to Rene Rivera—he showed some pop and cut down drastically on his strikeouts despite not changing his approach or his batted-ball profile. If the real Plawecki sits halfway between his 2016 and 2017 seasons offensively, there's still a reasonable argument to be made that he should start behind the plate for the Mets in 2018 due to his track record of strong framing skills.

Jose Reyes SS Born: 06/11/83 Age: 35 Bats: B Throws: R Height: 6'0" Weight: 195 Origin: International Free Agent, 1999

YEAR	TEAM	LVL	AGE	PA	R	2B	3B	HR	RBI	BB	K	SB	CS	AVG/OBP/SLG	TAv	VORP	BABIP	BRR	FRAA	WARP
2015	TOR	MLB	32	311	36	17	0	4	34	17	38	16	2	.285/.322/.385	.252	12.5	.315	2.6	SS(69): -2.9	1.0
2015	COL	MLB	32	208	21	8	2	3	19	9	24	8	4	.259/.291/.368	.224	1.4	.281	0.4	SS(47): 0.6	0.2
2016	ABQ	AAA	33	40	7	0	0	2	2	7	4	3	0	.303/.425/.485	.311	4.0	.296	0.2	SS(9): -1.0	0.3
2016	BIN	AA	33	33	6	1	0	0	2	3	3	1	1	.207/.273/.241	.230	-0.3	.222	-0.3	3B(7): -0.4	-0.1
2016	NYN	MLB	33	279	45	13	4	8	24	23	49	9	2	.267/.326/.443	.285	18.2	.302	1.6	3B(50): -2.6, SS(13): 0.1	1.6
2017	NYN	MLB	34	561	75	25	7	15	58	50	79	24	6	.246/.315/.413	.266	27.0	.263	2.7	SS(80): -3.6, 3B(36): 1.3	2.1
2018	*NYN*	*MLB*	*35*	*481*	*63*	*20*	*2*	*10*	*44*	*36*	*68*	*21*	*5*	*.263/.318/.392*	*.242*	*13.4*	*.285*	*2.1*	*SS -1, 3B 0*	*1.2*
2019	*NYN*	*MLB*	*36*	*355*	*40*	*14*	*1*	*7*	*37*	*26*	*51*	*14*	*4*	*.256/.311/.376*	*.250*	*9.2*	*.279*	*1.8*	*SS -1, 3B 0*	*0.8*

Breakout: 1% Improve: 34% Collapse: 7% Attrition: 19% MLB: 78% *Comparables: Jerry Hairston, Orlando Cabrera, Luis Aparicio*

With playing time to spare and questions about the true talent levels of Wilmer Flores, Matt Reynolds and even Gavin Cecchini, Terry Collins instead stuck with Reyes because he was a veteran or because he was an old friend or because he used to be a star. A year removed from a half-season suspension for alleged domestic violence, Reyes put up a dreadful .215/.284/.370 first half before rebounding in July and played out the season as one of the only productive–or healthy–players on the team. True to the orange and blue, his second tenure in Flushing also saw Reyes notch his 2,000th career hit and 500th career stolen base.

Matt Reynolds UT Born: 12/03/90 Age: 27 Bats: R Throws: R Height: 6'1" Weight: 198 Origin: Round 2, 2012 Draft (#71 overall)

YEAR	TEAM	LVL	AGE	PA	R	2B	3B	HR	RBI	BB	K	SB	CS	AVG/OBP/SLG	TAv	VORP	BABIP	BRR	FRAA	WARP
2015	LVG	AAA	24	490	70	32	5	6	65	32	92	13	4	.267/.319/.402	.247	13.5	.319	2.4	SS(92): 5.1, 2B(11): -0.8	1.8
2016	LVG	AAA	25	299	43	15	2	2	24	26	64	9	2	.264/.336/.357	.229	0.9	.340	0.5	3B(30): 0.4, SS(29): -1.9	0.1
2016	NYN	MLB	25	96	11	8	0	3	13	4	34	0	1	.225/.266/.416	.256	3.4	.327	0.2	SS(21): 0.2, 3B(7): -0.1	0.4
2017	LVG	AAA	26	144	27	9	0	4	14	16	30	2	2	.320/.396/.484	.292	9.5	.394	-0.2	CF(11): 0.0, LF(11): 1.5	1.0
2017	NYN	MLB	26	130	12	1	2	1	5	14	37	0	1	.230/.326/.301	.238	1.1	.333	0.2	3B(23): -1.5, SS(10): 0.2	-0.1
2018	*NYN*	*MLB*	*27*	*134*	*14*	*6*	*1*	*2*	*12*	*10*	*35*	*2*	*1*	*.225/.290/.339*	*.227*	*0.4*	*.294*	*-0.1*	*3B 0, 2B 0*	*-0.1*
2019	*NYN*	*MLB*	*28*	*260*	*28*	*11*	*1*	*5*	*25*	*21*	*70*	*3*	*2*	*.223/.294/.347*	*.236*	*1.0*	*.291*	*0.5*	*3B 0, 2B 0*	*0.1*

Breakout: 3% Improve: 19% Collapse: 12% Attrition: 23% MLB: 38% *Comparables: Travis Metcalf, Taylor Featherston, Jeff Bianchi*

In the ill-fated "Mets Take Manhattan" sequel, Reynolds played the role of "utility guy who stands at most positions and doesn't embarrass himself too badly at the plate." (In other words, he was the new Eric Campbell.) Luckily for both Reynolds and the Mets, he cleared Campbell's admittedly low bar. His below-average bat makes him miscast as a left fielder—which is where he found himself too often in 2017—but as a backup infielder with a little on-base ability, Reynolds will likely use that supporting role to launch a long and unspectacular run in the majors.

T.J. Rivera INF Born: 10/27/88 Age: 29 Bats: R Throws: R Height: 6'1" Weight: 203 Origin: Undrafted Free Agent, 2011

YEAR	TEAM	LVL	AGE	PA	R	2B	3B	HR	RBI	BB	K	SB	CS	AVG/OBP/SLG	TAv	VORP	BABIP	BRR	FRAA	WARP
2015	LVG	AAA	26	196	26	17	1	2	21	7	25	0	0	.306/.345/.443	.260	5.0	.346	-0.8	3B(31): 2.3, 2B(17): -2.9	0.4
2015	BIN	AA	26	234	37	10	0	5	27	12	22	1	1	.341/.380/.455	.290	15.6	.363	1.2	2B(22): 0.4, SS(17): 1.7	2.0
2016	LVG	AAA	27	442	67	31	1	11	85	23	54	3	3	.353/.393/.516	.301	32.1	.383	1.1	3B(69): 0.1, 2B(14): 0.1	3.4
2016	NYN	MLB	27	113	10	4	1	3	16	3	17	0	0	.333/.345/.476	.325	10.1	.360	-0.5	2B(26): -1.0, 3B(9): -0.5	0.9
2017	NYN	MLB	28	231	27	13	1	5	27	9	32	1	0	.290/.330/.430	.279	9.7	.318	-0.6	3B(28): 0.1, 1B(20): 0.1	0.9
2018	*NYN*	*MLB*	*29*	*64*	*7*	*3*	*0*	*2*	*7*	*3*	*10*	*0*	*0*	*.279/.317/.415*	*.260*	*1.0*	*.312*	*-0.1*	*1B -1*	*0.0*
2019	*NYN*	*MLB*	*30*	*235*	*28*	*11*	*0*	*7*	*28*	*11*	*41*	*0*	*0*	*.274/.318/.421*	*.268*	*4.3*	*.306*	*-0.6*	*1B -2*	*0.3*

Breakout: 1% Improve: 16% Collapse: 9% Attrition: 23% MLB: 50% *Comparables: Terry Tiffee, Greg Dobbs, Brent Morel*

There are players who have defied being late-round draft picks, guys like Mike Piazza and John Smoltz and Albert Pujols. Pedigree doesn't mean everything. Rivera, however, doesn't even wear that badge of honor; no one picked his name on draft day at all. The Bronx native was signed as an undrafted free agent and has done nothing but hit at every level since 2011, including, to everyone's surprise, the majors. He continued hitting in 2017, picking up semi-regular playing time until his season was ended by a different TJ—Tommy John surgery. He won't return to Queens until at least the second half of 2018, but he's done enough to establish himself as a quality major leaguer on the strength of that potent hit tool. Pedigree doesn't mean everything, but bat control just might.

Amed Rosario SS Born: 11/20/95 Age: 22 Bats: R Throws: R Height: 6'2" Weight: 189 Origin: International Free Agent, 2012

YEAR	TEAM	LVL	AGE	PA	R	2B	3B	HR	RBI	BB	K	SB	CS	AVG/OBP/SLG	TAv	VORP	BABIP	BRR	FRAA	WARP
2015	SLU	A+	19	417	41	20	5	0	25	23	73	12	4	.257/.307/.335	.240	8.8	.316	0.9	SS(102): 13.3	2.4
2016	SLU	A+	20	290	27	10	8	3	40	21	36	13	6	.309/.359/.442	.299	24.0	.345	0.5	SS(60): -0.4	2.4
2016	BIN	AA	20	237	38	14	5	2	31	19	51	6	2	.341/.392/.481	.302	20.9	.433	1.7	SS(53): -4.9	1.7
2017	LVG	AAA	21	425	66	19	7	7	58	23	67	19	6	.328/.367/.466	.281	29.8	.377	1.4	SS(88): 2.0, 3B(6): -0.2	3.1
2017	NYN	MLB	21	170	16	4	4	4	10	3	49	7	3	.248/.271/.394	.217	0.5	.330	1.0	SS(45): -0.3	0.0
2018	*NYN*	*MLB*	*22*	*539*	*61*	*21*	*6*	*11*	*54*	*26*	*127*	*15*	*6*	*.254/.295/.383*	*.241*	*14.7*	*.318*	*1.5*	*SS 1*	*1.0*
2019	*NYN*	*MLB*	*23*	*566*	*65*	*22*	*6*	*14*	*64*	*34*	*132*	*16*	*6*	*.260/.309/.409*	*.260*	*21.4*	*.319*	*2.0*	*SS 1*	*2.4*

Breakout: 4% Improve: 34% Collapse: 4% Attrition: 14% MLB: 46% *Comparables: Orlando Arcia, Alen Hanson, Tim Beckham*

The last great Mets prospect in a depleted farm system, Rosario started last season with a stellar Twitter account and a beautiful, positive hashtag catchphrase: "#DontBeSurprisedBeReady". What he *didn't* have was anything to prove in the minors, but the Mets still saw fit to leave him in Las Vegas until late July, perhaps because he wasn't ready (he was), perhaps because Sandy Alderson didn't want to put too much pressure on him to lift a sinking team (he didn't) or perhaps because it was too late for him to make a difference (he couldn't). When Rosario did get the call, he displayed occasional signs of life at the plate, and his defense was eye-opening for Mets fans who had grown too accustomed to the likes of Jose Reyes, Asdrubal Cabrera and Wilmer Flores at the six. (Oh, and he showed his speed as the fifth-fastest runner in MLB according to Statcast's Sprint Speed leaderboards.) He is ready, and no one should be surprised.

Dominic Smith 1B Born: 06/15/95 Age: 23 Bats: L Throws: L Height: 6'0" Weight: 239 Origin: Round 1, 2013 Draft (#11 overall)

YEAR	TEAM	LVL	AGE	PA	R	2B	3B	HR	RBI	BB	K	SB	CS	AVG/OBP/SLG	TAv	VORP	BABIP	BRR	FRAA	WARP
2015	SLU	A+	20	497	58	33	0	6	79	35	75	2	1	.305/.354/.417	.279	7.6	.351	-6.5	1B(104): 9.1	1.8
2016	BIN	AA	21	542	64	29	2	14	91	50	74	2	1	.302/.367/.457	.292	17.6	.329	-5.3	1B(106): 1.1	2.0
2017	LVG	AAA	22	500	77	34	2	16	76	39	87	1	1	.330/.386/.519	.293	21.8	.380	-2.4	1B(107): 6.6	2.8
2017	NYN	MLB	22	183	17	6	0	9	26	14	49	0	0	.198/.262/.395	.230	-3.4	.218	0.3	1B(46): -5.5	-0.9
2018	*NYN*	*MLB*	*23*	*536*	*61*	*26*	*0*	*18*	*70*	*38*	*116*	*0*	*0*	*.258/.314/.423*	*.258*	*7.4*	*.302*	*-1.3*	*1B 2*	*0.6*
2019	*NYN*	*MLB*	*24*	*586*	*78*	*30*	*0*	*24*	*80*	*46*	*128*	*0*	*0*	*.265/.326/.456*	*.280*	*18.3*	*.306*	*-1.6*	*1B 2*	*2.2*

Breakout: 6% Improve: 21% Collapse: 5% Attrition: 21% MLB: 40% *Comparables: Chris Marrero, Nick Evans, Max Kepler*

Mr. Smith came to Flushing and proved nothing. Known in the minors for good glove work and far less power than you'd want from a first baseman, the former first-round draft pick initially struggled to adapt to the majors after his August call-up. In a baffling turn, he was suddenly a power hitter with a batting average that floated around the Mendoza line with starkly below-average defense—the exact opposite of what anyone expected. With little competition in-house, Smith will likely get a good chunk of 2018 to prove that his abysmal performance in his debut was just a period of adjustment and not a harbinger of things to come, but at the very least his .194 slugging percentage against southpaws should put him squarely on the bench when the likes of Gio Gonzalez and Jon Lester come to town.

Travis Taijeron RF Born: 01/20/89 Age: 29 Bats: R Throws: R Height: 6'2" Weight: 224 Origin: Round 18, 2011 Draft (#552 overall)

YEAR	TEAM	LVL	AGE	PA	R	2B	3B	HR	RBI	BB	K	SB	CS	AVG/OBP/SLG	TAv	VORP	BABIP	BRR	FRAA	WARP
2015	LVG	AAA	26	478	67	22	3	25	71	65	147	2	2	.274/.393/.536	.303	27.5	.367	-2.3	RF(112): -2.1, LF(10): -0.4	2.6
2016	LVG	AAA	27	541	86	42	5	19	88	67	166	1	3	.275/.372/.512	.293	28.9	.381	0.8	RF(120): 7.7, LF(2): 0.3	3.8
2017	LVG	AAA	28	533	75	32	3	25	78	70	146	2	1	.272/.383/.525	.292	30.1	.346	0.2	RF(105): 3.6, LF(15): -1.3	3.1
2017	NYN	MLB	28	59	3	2	0	1	3	5	24	0	0	.173/.271/.269	.205	-2.2	.296	0.0	RF(15): -2.2	-0.4
2018	*NYN*	*MLB*	*29*	*250*	*30*	*10*	*1*	*11*	*34*	*31*	*88*	*0*	*0*	*.217/.329/.422*	*.258*	*6.2*	*.307*	*-0.4*	*RF 0, LF 0*	*0.7*
2019	*NYN*	*MLB*	*30*	*313*	*43*	*13*	*1*	*13*	*41*	*39*	*112*	*0*	*0*	*.216/.329/.422*	*.272*	*9.9*	*.310*	*-0.8*	*RF 0, LF 0*	*1.1*

Breakout: 7% Improve: 20% Collapse: 7% Attrition: 19% MLB: 42% *Comparables: Mike Wilson, Joe Koshansky, Brad Snyder*

It's easy to forget, especially when watching truly bad baseball, that these men are the best of the best. They made it out of Little League, out of high school, out of training facilities and showcases and college and rookie ball. Only 750 men break camp on opening day, and a few hundred more filter in and out of MLB over the season. That's all. Baseball is a world of small sample sizes, and the success stories are the smallest sample of all. Taijeron is a success story because he made it to the majors after six years of steady but boring production in the minors. Sure, his chance only came due to injuries, and his 40.7 percent strikeout rate won't make it easy for him to get another one, but on September 8, 2017, Taijeron hit a home run in the major leagues. He made it.

Tim Tebow OF Born: 08/14/87 Age: 30 Bats: L Throws: L Height: 6'3" Weight: 250 Origin: Undrafted Free Agent, 2010

YEAR	TEAM	LVL	AGE	PA	R	2B	3B	HR	RBI	BB	K	SB	CS	AVG/OBP/SLG	TAv	VORP	BABIP	BRR	FRAA	WARP
2017	COL	A	29	244	29	14	1	3	23	24	69	0	1	.220/.311/.336	.266	4.9	.308	-1.0	LF(44): -10.3	-0.6
2017	SLU	A+	29	242	21	10	1	5	29	19	57	2	1	.231/.307/.356	.239	-5.0	.290	-3.8	LF(33): -5.7, CF(3): 0.0	-1.1
2018	*NYN*	*MLB*	*30*	*250*	*23*	*9*	*0*	*7*	*26*	*20*	*81*	*0*	*0*	*.198/.270/.328*	*.209*	*-5.7*	*.273*	*-0.5*	*LF -6, CF 0*	*-1.3*
2019	*NYN*	*MLB*	*31*	*190*	*21*	*7*	*0*	*5*	*19*	*15*	*63*	*0*	*0*	*.198/.271/.334*	*.223*	*-3.3*	*.276*	*-0.5*	*LF -5, CF 0*	*-0.9*

Breakout: 3% Improve: 5% Collapse: 7% Attrition: 15% MLB: 21% *Comparables: Andres Torres, Nick Gorneault, Doug Clark*

Whether you consider Tebow's first season in professional baseball a success depends on what you were looking for. As a 29-year-old outfielder in Low-A and High-A, he underperformed even the most meager expectations with terrible plate discipline and an inability to tap into the power that was supposed to be his strongest tool. But as a money grab, he was a wild success, drawing a 21 percent increase in attendance for the Fireflies and a 37 percent jump for the St. Lucie Mets. He pulled in more than $1.5 million from ticket sales, concessions, parking and other revenue streams. None of that matters if the money never sees the field, but Tebow's usefulness was always going to be about ROI, not RBI.

David Wright 3B Born: 12/20/82 Age: 35 Bats: R Throws: R Height: 6'0" Weight: 205 Origin: Round 1, 2001 Draft (#38 overall)

YEAR	TEAM	LVL	AGE	PA	R	2B	3B	HR	RBI	BB	K	SB	CS	AVG/OBP/SLG	TAv	VORP	BABIP	BRR	FRAA	WARP
2015	SLU	A+	32	33	5	0	0	0	1	5	6	0	0	.321/.424/.321	.330	3.5	.409	0.2	3B(7): -2.1	0.1
2015	NYN	MLB	32	174	24	7	0	5	17	22	36	2	1	.289/.379/.434	.315	17.1	.351	2.5	3B(38): -4.2	1.4
2016	NYN	MLB	33	164	18	8	0	7	14	26	55	3	2	.226/.350/.438	.298	10.8	.320	-0.8	3B(36): -0.8	1.0
2018	*NYN*	*MLB*	*35*	*250*	*33*	*11*	*1*	*7*	*27*	*26*	*52*	*4*	*2*	*.265/.345/.422*	*.263*	*9.0*	*.314*	*0.5*	*3B -4*	*0.6*
2019														*Out of baseball*						

Breakout: 0% Improve: 25% Collapse: 12% Attrition: 20% MLB: 90% *Comparables: Melvin Mora, Mark DeRosa, Jhonny Peralta*

Wright played in three games in 2017; MiLB Gameday didn't even record the third one. He made 10 plate appearances, singled once into center field and struck out five times. (He reached base on one of those strikeouts.) No one actually cared about his OBP, because Wright's story isn't about the games themselves anymore. His story is about a Hall-of-Fame career derailed by injury. His story is about expensive contracts that would have—and should have—been even more expensive if they qualified his worth to his fans. His story is about strength and power and frailty and MRIs and physical therapists. His story is about spinal stenosis now.

That's who Wright is now: the man with spinal stenosis. Eventually fans will forget the walk-off single in the 2009 World Baseball Classic elimination game that turned him into Captain America. They'll forget the fist pump in September 2015 at Nationals Park and they'll forget the home run in Game 3 of the World Series. Heck, even Gameday forgot his third and final game of 2017. The stats will fade, the moments will fade, even the way his career ends will fade. All the baseball will fade, but Wright will still be stuck with the injury, the spinal stenosis. The least we can do is remember his story.

PITCHERS

Jerry Blevins LHP Born: 09/06/83 Age: 34 Bats: L Throws: L Height: 6'6" Weight: 190 Origin: Round 17, 2004 Draft (#516 overall)

YEAR	TEAM	LVL	AGE	W	L	SV	G	GS	IP	H	HR	BB/9	K/9	K	GB%	BABIP	WHIP	ERA	DRA	WARP	MPH	CMD	PWR	STM
2015	NYN	MLB	31	1	0	0	7	0	5	0	0	0.0	7.2	4	55%	.000	0.00	0.00	3.46	0.1	92.0			
2016	NYN	MLB	32	4	2	2	73	0	42	36	4	3.2	11.1	52	47%	.302	1.21	2.79	3.98	0.5	91.5	70	30	44
2017	NYN	MLB	33	6	0	1	75	0	49	43	4	4.4	12.7	69	42%	.336	1.37	2.94	2.74	1.3	90.4	53	11	49
2018	*NYN*	*MLB*	*34*	*3*	*3*	*2*	*52*	*0*	*55*	*50*	*8*	*4.5*	*9.9*	*61*	*44%*	*.293*	*1.40*	*4.41*	*4.61*	*0.2*	*89.8*	*59*	*18*	*46*
2019	*NYN*	*MLB*	*35*	*2*	*1*	*1*	*46*	*0*	*49*	*43*	*8*	*4.3*	*9.4*	*51*	*44%*	*.296*	*1.34*	*4.81*	*5.37*	*-0.1*	*89.2*	*58*	*18*	*46*

Breakout: 7% Improve: 24% Collapse: 51% Attrition: 5% MLB: 91% *Comparables: Heath Bell, Francisco Cordero, Jose Valverde*

In one of the more tumultuous Mets bullpens to date, Blevins was a saving grace for those looking for some stability or sanity. Terry Collins continued to deploy him as a LOOGY, and he flourished in that role, posting a career-high 31.8 percent strikeout rate even as the walks simultaneously rose. He also embraced a bizarre fan attraction to both him and his bowties with an SNY segment called "Hello, Jerry" in which he gave terrible life advice on everything from dance moves to Justin Bieber. Best of all, for the second straight year he didn't slip off a curb and break his arm!

Chasen Bradford RHP Born: 08/05/89 Age: 28 Bats: R Throws: R Height: 6'1" Weight: 229 Origin: Round 35, 2011 Draft (#1062 overall)

YEAR	TEAM	LVL	AGE	W	L	SV	G	GS	IP	H	HR	BB/9	K/9	K	GB%	BABIP	WHIP	ERA	DRA	WARP	MPH	CMD	PWR	STM
2015	LVG	AAA	25	5	4	7	53	0	63^{2}	86	3	2.0	6.5	46	53%	.377	1.57	4.10	4.18	0.5				
2016	LVG	AAA	26	5	3	5	56	0	65^{2}	84	5	1.8	7.4	54	50%	.361	1.48	4.80	3.19	1.3				
2017	LVG	AAA	27	1	1	11	33	0	35^{2}	47	3	1.8	7.1	28	57%	.361	1.51	4.04	4.05	0.5				
2017	NYN	MLB	27	2	0	0	28	0	33^{2}	30	3	3.5	7.2	27	55%	.270	1.28	3.74	4.69	0.2	92.5	47	48	49
2018	*NYN*	*MLB*	*28*	*2*	*2*	*0*	*33*	*0*	*35*	*37*	*5*	*3.0*	*7.0*	*27*	*50%*	*.302*	*1.42*	*4.40*	*4.60*	*0.1*	*91.9*	*47*	*48*	*49*
2019	*NYN*	*MLB*	*29*	*2*	*1*	*0*	*45*	*0*	*47^{1}*	*49*	*6*	*3.0*	*6.9*	*36*	*50%*	*.316*	*1.38*	*4.49*	*5.02*	*0.1*	*91.5*	*47*	*48*	*49*

Breakout: 11% Improve: 18% Collapse: 17% Attrition: 18% MLB: 42% *Comparables: Mike McClendon, Dean Kiekhefer, Preston Guilmet*

One letter makes all the difference. *Chase* Bradford sounds like someone who wore puka shells, had floppy blond hair that covered one eye and skipped school when the waves were too good to pass up. Chase was beloved for no reason other than because there was no reason not to be. Everything was easy for him. *Chasen* Bradford sounds like someone who went to boarding school until 10th grade, when his parents suddenly pulled him out and brought him home under mysterious circumstances. No one knew where Chasen's father's wealth came from; there were rumors of a murdered relative, a government payoff ... but no one dared ask.

Either way, the guy who pitches for the Mets is a replacement-level, ground-ball-inducing reliever who isn't as interesting as his name might have you believe. Maybe if batters were chasen more of his pitches, things would be different.

Jamie Callahan RHP Born: 08/24/94 Age: 23 Bats: R Throws: R Height: 6'2" Weight: 230 Origin: Round 2, 2012 Draft (#87 overall)

YEAR	TEAM	LVL	AGE	W	L	SV	G	GS	IP	H	HR	BB/9	K/9	K	GB%	BABIP	WHIP	ERA	DRA	WARP	MPH	CMD	PWR	STM
2015	GRN	A	20	7	6	3	31	6	89^{1}	94	4	3.3	9.5	94	44%	.342	1.42	4.53	3.22	1.8				
2016	SLM	A+	21	5	3	7	36	0	65^{2}	53	1	5.2	8.6	63	44%	.287	1.39	3.29	5.60	-0.4				
2017	PME	AA	22	4	1	2	10	0	13	8	0	0.0	13.8	20	44%	.296	0.62	1.38	1.99	0.4				
2017	PAW	AAA	22	1	1	4	22	0	29	28	2	4.0	11.2	36	38%	.347	1.41	4.03	4.03	0.4				
2017	LVG	AAA	22	1	1	1	9	0	10	12	2	3.6	9.0	10	42%	.345	1.60	1.80	5.84	-0.1				
2017	NYN	MLB	22	0	0	0	9	0	6^{2}	7	0	1.4	6.8	5	58%	.292	1.20	4.05	6.54	-0.1	97.1			43
2018	*NYN*	*MLB*	*23*	*1*	*1*	*0*	*24*	*0*	*25*	*24*	*4*	*4.7*	*10.0*	*28*	*40%*	*.301*	*1.47*	*4.54*	*4.70*	*0.1*	*97.0*			*45*
2019	*NYN*	*MLB*	*24*	*2*	*1*	*1*	*49*	*0*	*52^{1}*	*45*	*8*	*4.1*	*10.4*	*60*	*40%*	*.31*	*1.31*	*4.36*	*4.88*	*0.2*	*96.8*			*45*

Breakout: 12% Improve: 13% Collapse: 4% Attrition: 10% MLB: 18% *Comparables: Chase Anderson, Seth Rosin, Jeremy Horst*

The expensive-veteran-for-a-random-middle-reliever roulette wheel brought back Callahan—among others—when the Mets sent Addison Reed to Boston in July. The former second-round draft pick has a fastball that gets grounders, and with a passable defense behind him, that could be enough to make him a viable bullpen piece. Unfortunately for Callahan, "passable defense" is a big ask when playing in Flushing. Perhaps he should get Amed Rosario a nice present during spring training?

Jacob deGrom RHP Born: 06/19/88 Age: 29 Bats: L Throws: R Height: 6'4" Weight: 180 Origin: Round 9, 2010 Draft (#272 overall)

YEAR	TEAM	LVL	AGE	W	L	SV	G	GS	IP	H	HR	BB/9	K/9	K	GB%	BABIP	WHIP	ERA	DRA	WARP	MPH	CMD	PWR	STM
2015	NYN	MLB	27	14	8	0	30	30	191	149	16	1.8	9.7	205	48%	.271	0.98	2.54	2.65	5.5	97.7	62	62	72
2016	NYN	MLB	28	7	8	0	24	24	148	142	15	2.2	8.7	143	47%	.312	1.20	3.04	4.14	2.1	96.3	58	54	66
2017	NYN	MLB	29	15	10	0	31	31	201^{1}	180	28	2.6	10.7	239	48%	.305	1.19	3.53	2.92	5.9	97.2	60	61	82
2018	*NYN*	*MLB*	*30*	*11*	*10*	*0*	*29*	*29*	*174*	*151*	*21*	*2.7*	*9.9*	*192*	*47%*	*.292*	*1.16*	*3.39*	*3.67*	*3.0*	*96.3*	*60*	*59*	*74*
2019	*NYN*	*MLB*	*31*	*12*	*10*	*0*	*33*	*33*	*215^{2}*	*170*	*26*	*2.4*	*10.0*	*240*	*47%*	*.294*	*1.06*	*3.42*	*3.82*	*3.9*	*95.8*	*59*	*58*	*74*

Breakout: 12% Improve: 45% Collapse: 29% Attrition: 9% MLB: 95% *Comparables: Jake Arrieta, Carlos Carrasco, David Price*

It's time. There have been hints for years, starting with his 2014 Rookie of the Year season, building to an All-Star 2015 and Cy Young Award votes, but it's time for deGrom to don the game's most prestigious label. There are no hard-and-fast benchmarks for what makes an ace, no strikeout number or ERA or home-run rate, but you're supposed to know one when you see one. Some people think that you need to pitch 200 innings to be an ace, and he did that. He put up more than 200 strikeouts too, if that's what makes an ace. The only criticism you might levy against him is that his home-run rate went up, but so did that of every other pitcher in the league.

An ace looks like Clayton Kershaw, but an ace also looks like Max Scherzer, Chris Sale, or Madison Bumgarner. Jacob deGrom looks like an ace too, and its finally time—as we've suggested in each of the last two *Annuals*—to start calling him one.

Justin Dunn RHP Born: 09/22/95 Age: 22 Bats: R Throws: R Height: 6'2" Weight: 195 Origin: Round 1, 2016 Draft (#19 overall)

YEAR	TEAM	LVL	AGE	W	L	SV	G	GS	IP	H	HR	BB/9	K/9	K	GB%	BABIP	WHIP	ERA	DRA	WARP	MPH	CMD	PWR	STM
2016	BRO	A-	20	1	1	0	11	8	30	25	1	3.0	10.5	35	46%	.320	1.17	1.50	3.14	0.7				
2017	SLU	A+	21	5	6	0	20	16	95^{1}	101	5	4.5	7.1	75	44%	.322	1.56	5.00	5.69	-0.6				
2018	*NYN*	*MLB*	*22*	*4*	*5*	*0*	*26*	*14*	*73*	*77*	*14*	*5.0*	*9.1*	*74*	*39%*	*.328*	*1.61*	*5.48*	*6.14*	*-0.6*				
2019	*NYN*	*MLB*	*23*	*4*	*6*	*0*	*22*	*16*	*115*	*119*	*23*	*4.8*	*8.5*	*108*	*39%*	*.321*	*1.56*	*5.77*	*6.48*	*-0.9*				

Breakout: 0% Improve: 0% Collapse: 1% Attrition: 1% MLB: 1% *Comparables: Anthony Ortega, Josh Outman, Michael Ynoa*

Not every highly touted Mets pitching prospect immediately becomes a star with increased velocity and a knock-your-socks-off slider. Dunn, a former first-round pick, followed up a solid debut with a disastrous sophomore season. After posting a 6.89 ERA over his first seven starts, the former Boston College product found himself pitching out of the bullpen for a brief time in St. Lucie. Plenty of talent evaluators had him pegged as a reliever going into the draft, and his stuff looked a little better in short bursts, but not every failed starter eventually finds success in relief.

Jeurys Familia RHP Born: 10/10/89 Age: 28 Bats: R Throws: R Height: 6'3" Weight: 240 Origin: International Free Agent, 2007

YEAR	TEAM	LVL	AGE	W	L	SV	G	GS	IP	H	HR	BB/9	K/9	K	GB%	BABIP	WHIP	ERA	DRA	WARP	MPH	CMD	PWR	STM
2015	NYN	MLB	25	2	2	43	76	0	78	59	6	2.2	9.9	86	61%	.272	1.00	1.85	2.27	2.3	100.1	42	80	54
2016	NYN	MLB	26	3	4	51	78	0	77^{2}	63	1	3.6	9.7	84	66%	.304	1.21	2.55	2.58	2.1	98.8	29	71	55
2017	NYN	MLB	27	2	2	6	26	0	24^{2}	21	1	5.5	9.1	25	61%	.290	1.46	4.38	5.04	0.0	97.9	39	80	26
2018	*NYN*	*MLB*	*28*	*3*	*3*	*31*	*57*	*0*	*60*	*52*	*6*	*4.1*	*9.5*	*63*	*57%*	*.292*	*1.33*	*3.55*	*3.90*	*0.7*	*98.5*	*35*	*76*	*43*
2019	*NYN*	*MLB*	*29*	*3*	*1*	*24*	*56*	*0*	*59*	*47*	*7*	*4.2*	*9.9*	*65*	*57%*	*.3*	*1.27*	*4.00*	*4.47*	*0.5*	*97.8*	*33*	*75*	*40*

Breakout: 28% Improve: 49% Collapse: 17% Attrition: 13% MLB: 95% *Comparables: Hector Rondon, Bryan Shaw, Bobby Jenks*

Five days before the Mets opened their 2017 season, Familia was suspended without pay for the first 15 games for violating the league's personal conduct policy; five months earlier, he had been arrested for assault after an alleged domestic violence incident involving his wife, Bianca Rivas, the mother of his child. Charges were dropped when Rivas failed to cooperate, but Rob Manfred still saw fit to hand down the suspension. The rest of 2017 also went poorly for Familia—he didn't pitch well before a blood clot in his right shoulder cost him most of the season—but that seems to matter less in light of his off-field actions.

Chris Flexen RHP Born: 07/01/94 Age: 23 Bats: R Throws: R Height: 6'3" Weight: 250 Origin: Round 14, 2012 Draft (#440 overall)

YEAR	TEAM	LVL	AGE	W	L	SV	G	GS	IP	H	HR	BB/9	K/9	K	GB%	BABIP	WHIP	ERA	DRA	WARP	MPH	CMD	PWR	STM
2015	BRO	A-	20	0	2	0	3	2	12^{1}	15	0	5.8	9.5	13	60%	.395	1.86	5.11	3.81	0.2				
2015	SAV	A	20	4	0	0	6	5	33^{2}	28	0	1.9	8.8	33	48%	.301	1.04	1.87	2.64	1.0				
2016	SLU	A+	21	10	9	0	25	25	134	125	6	3.4	6.4	95	50%	.287	1.31	3.56	5.05	0.6				
2017	SLU	A+	22	0	0	0	3	3	12^{2}	12	1	2.1	9.2	13	54%	.306	1.18	2.13	3.05	0.3				
2017	BIN	AA	22	6	1	0	7	7	48^{2}	28	4	1.3	9.2	50	55%	.203	0.72	1.66	1.55	2.1				
2017	NYN	MLB	22	3	6	0	14	9	48	62	11	6.6	6.8	36	42%	.342	2.02	7.88	8.01	-1.3	94.7	42	51	54
2018	*NYN*	*MLB*	*23*	*3*	*4*	*0*	*10*	*10*	*53*	*52*	*8*	*3.9*	*8.3*	*49*	*45%*	*.293*	*1.40*	*4.53*	*4.90*	*0.2*	*94.6*	*44*	*53*	*56*
2019	*NYN*	*MLB*	*24*	*10*	*11*	*0*	*32*	*32*	207^{1}	*173*	*29*	*3.3*	*9.1*	*209*	*45%*	*.288*	*1.20*	*4.24*	*4.75*	*1.6*	*94.5*	*44*	*53*	*57*

Breakout: 20% Improve: 29% Collapse: 10% Attrition: 31% MLB: 49% *Comparables: Brad Hand, Jeanmar Gomez, Casey Coleman*

In early September, Flexen was coming off the second consecutive start in which he served up seven earned runs. He was clearly in over his head, having been promoted in July not because he was ready, but because his arm was still intact, which was more than could be said for the rest of the organization's pitchers. Manager Terry Collins had no sympathy. "You've got to go out there and battle through some stuff," he said of the young pitcher and his 7.85 ERA. So Flexen kept battling, this time out of the bullpen, where his stuff flashed better right up until it didn't.

Maybe Collins was right; maybe this was a learning experience and Flexen fought through to the other side. Maybe Flexen was promoted too early and he needs more seasoning in the minors. Maybe patience is something afforded only to the lucky.

Robert Gsellman RHP Born: 07/18/93 Age: 24 Bats: R Throws: R Height: 6'4" Weight: 205 Origin: Round 13, 2011 Draft (#402 overall)

YEAR	TEAM	LVL	AGE	W	L	SV	G	GS	IP	H	HR	BB/9	K/9	K	GB%	BABIP	WHIP	ERA	DRA	WARP	MPH	CMD	PWR	STM
2015	SLU	A+	21	6	0	0	8	8	51	37	1	1.9	6.5	37	61%	.250	0.94	1.76	2.94	1.3				
2015	BIN	AA	21	7	7	0	16	16	92^{1}	89	4	2.5	4.8	49	54%	.277	1.25	3.51	4.62	0.5				
2016	BIN	AA	22	3	4	0	11	11	66^{1}	57	2	2.0	6.5	48	57%	.282	1.09	2.71	3.26	1.5				
2016	LVG	AAA	22	1	5	0	9	9	48^{2}	56	8	3.0	7.4	40	55%	.318	1.48	5.73	4.17	0.7				
2016	NYN	MLB	22	4	2	0	8	7	44^{2}	42	1	3.0	8.5	42	57%	.325	1.28	2.42	4.18	0.6	96.1	42	56	65
2017	BIN	AA	23	1	0	0	4	4	12^{1}	15	0	3.6	6.6	9	76%	.366	1.62	2.92	3.62	0.2				
2017	NYN	MLB	23	8	7	0	25	22	119^{2}	138	17	3.2	6.2	82	51%	.303	1.50	5.19	6.21	-0.9	94.7	55	55	64
2018	*NYN*	*MLB*	*24*	*7*	*8*	*0*	*23*	*23*	*131*	*132*	*16*	*3.3*	*7.1*	*104*	*51%*	*.293*	*1.36*	*4.20*	*4.54*	*0.9*	*94.8*	*54*	*57*	*66*
2019	*NYN*	*MLB*	*25*	*11*	*11*	*0*	*32*	*32*	206^{1}	*184*	*22*	*2.9*	*7.9*	*181*	*51%*	*.299*	*1.21*	*3.90*	*4.36*	*2.5*	*94.6*	*54*	*57*	*67*

Breakout: 20% Improve: 52% Collapse: 18% Attrition: 24% MLB: 84% *Comparables: Jenrry Mejia, Erasmo Ramirez, Alex Sanabia*

Before the season, BP's prospect team positioned Gsellman as a top-20 prospect and boy, has there been fallout. He followed up a life-changing major-league debut with a barely passable 2017 and now we're left asking whether this season will be a sophomore slump (although it's hard to imagine him doing much worse) or comeback of the year. But this ain't a scene, it's an arms race, and Gsellman's skyrocketing home-run rate would have been enough to push the team to say "thnks fr th mmrs" if not for the fact that the Mets had few other viable options. Instead of becoming one of America's suitehearts, instead of a headfirst slide into Cooperstown, his season boiled down to "I don't care" when confronted about his attitude by Sandy Alderson. He turned it around a little and flirted with a sub-5.00 ERA by the end of September, but all he got was this stupid comment written about him.

Matt Harvey RHP Born: 03/27/89 Age: 29 Bats: R Throws: R Height: 6'4" Weight: 215 Origin: Round 1, 2010 Draft (#7 overall)

YEAR	TEAM	LVL	AGE	W	L	SV	G	GS	IP	H	HR	BB/9	K/9	K	GB%	BABIP	WHIP	ERA	DRA	WARP	MPH	CMD	PWR	STM
2015	NYN	MLB	26	13	8	0	29	29	189^{1}	156	18	1.8	8.9	188	49%	.273	1.02	2.71	2.86	5.0	98.8	57	68	70
2016	NYN	MLB	27	4	10	0	17	17	92^{2}	111	8	2.4	7.4	76	44%	.353	1.47	4.86	4.81	0.6	97.4	51	58	58
2017	NYN	MLB	28	5	7	0	19	18	92^{2}	110	21	4.6	6.5	67	46%	.307	1.69	6.70	7.40	-1.9	95.9	60	58	49
2018	*NYN*	*MLB*	*29*	*7*	*7*	*0*	*19*	*19*	*114*	*113*	*16*	*3.2*	*7.9*	*100*	*45%*	*.295*	*1.35*	*4.23*	*4.57*	*0.8*	*96.8*	*57*	*62*	*57*
2019	*NYN*	*MLB*	*30*	*11*	*12*	*0*	*32*	*32*	204^{1}	*190*	*27*	*2.9*	*8.0*	*182*	*45%*	*.303*	*1.25*	*4.26*	*4.77*	*1.8*	*95.9*	*56*	*59*	*55*

Breakout: 9% Improve: 39% Collapse: 23% Attrition: 7% MLB: 94% *Comparables: Matt Garza, Yovani Gallardo, Mark Buehrle*

What happens when a superhero loses his powers? What does it look like when a genius loses his mind? What does one do when a pitcher loses his stuff? Harvey was going to be good, or great or legendary but he spent most of 2017 as none of those things. On the field, he'd lost what once made him magical. His velocity was down across the board and the impeccable control was gone. What remains of the once and future king?

Apparently, more drama than is required from a newly mortal starter. A hurricane of controversies in mid-May began with a skipped start and ended with a team suspension, a broken heart and a "hostile environment" at Citi Field from fans who once whispered his name reverently. A fastball that tops out at 93 mph and six-run, four-inning outings probably aren't worth the headache.

Seth Lugo RHP Born: 11/17/89 Age: 28 Bats: R Throws: R Height: 6'4" Weight: 225 Origin: Round 34, 2011 Draft (#1032 overall)

YEAR	TEAM	LVL	AGE	W	L	SV	G	GS	IP	H	HR	BB/9	K/9	K	GB%	BABIP	WHIP	ERA	DRA	WARP	MPH	CMD	PWR	STM
2015	BIN	AA	25	6	5	0	19	19	109	108	8	2.5	8.0	97	44%	.307	1.27	3.80	3.35	2.3				
2015	LVG	AAA	25	2	2	0	5	5	27	27	3	1.7	10.0	30	43%	.324	1.19	4.00	1.75	1.1				
2016	LVG	AAA	26	3	4	0	21	14	73^{1}	103	10	2.5	7.6	62	46%	.375	1.68	6.50	2.08	2.7				
2016	NYN	MLB	26	5	2	0	17	8	64	49	7	3.0	6.3	45	46%	.230	1.09	2.67	5.29	0.0	95.9	47	49	62
2017	BIN	AA	27	1	1	0	2	2	13	14	1	1.4	10.4	15	54%	.382	1.23	2.77	2.91	0.4				
2017	NYN	MLB	27	7	5	0	19	18	101^{1}	114	13	2.2	7.5	85	43%	.325	1.37	4.71	4.73	0.9	93.8	52	42	59
2018	*NYN*	*MLB*	*28*	*5*	*6*	*0*	*16*	*16*	*91*	*93*	*14*	*3.0*	*8.0*	*81*	*44%*	*.296*	*1.35*	*4.31*	*4.66*	*0.5*	*93.9*	*51*	*44*	*61*
2019	*NYN*	*MLB*	*29*	*11*	*11*	*0*	*32*	*32*	*206*	*187*	*28*	*2.6*	*8.3*	*191*	*44%*	*.299*	*1.20*	*4.15*	*4.63*	*2.0*	*93.6*	*51*	*44*	*60*

Breakout: 32% Improve: 56% Collapse: 13% Attrition: 31% MLB: 78% *Comparables: Brad Lincoln, Marco Estrada, Ariel Miranda*

After an out-of-nowhere 2016 debut that astonished even his biggest fans—presumably his parents—Lugo came back down to earth in a season riddled with injuries. (Sound familiar?) He missed the first two months with a tear in his elbow ligament, maybe caused by, exacerbated by or entirely unrelated to his heroics for the Puerto Rican team during the World Baseball Classic. However, the injury issues aren't to blame for his spike in ERA and hits allowed—that's just the variation that comes with a back-end starting pitcher who allows too much contact, and according to DRA he was actually better in 2017. With his long-term durability in the rotation an open question, it's worth noting that he only completed the seventh inning once in 18 starts.

Steven Matz LHP Born: 05/29/91 Age: 27 Bats: R Throws: L Height: 6'2" Weight: 200 Origin: Round 2, 2009 Draft (#72 overall)

YEAR	TEAM	LVL	AGE	W	L	SV	G	GS	IP	H	HR	BB/9	K/9	K	GB%	BABIP	WHIP	ERA	DRA	WARP	MPH	CMD	PWR	STM
2015	LVG	AAA	24	7	4	0	15	14	90^{1}	69	6	3.1	9.4	94	57%	.278	1.11	2.19	0.95	4.4				
2015	BIN	AA	24	1	0	0	2	2	11^{1}	2	0	1.6	7.9	10	56%	.080	0.35	0.00	1.98	0.4				
2015	NYN	MLB	24	4	0	0	6	6	35^{2}	34	4	2.5	8.6	34	49%	.300	1.23	2.27	4.75	0.1	96.6	50	54	56
2016	NYN	MLB	25	9	8	0	22	22	132^{1}	129	14	2.1	8.8	129	54%	.312	1.21	3.40	3.93	2.2	96.0	55	51	65
2017	LVG	AAA	26	0	1	0	3	3	13^{1}	13	3	1.4	11.5	17	35%	.323	1.12	6.75	3.04	0.4				
2017	NYN	MLB	26	2	7	0	13	13	66^{2}	83	12	2.6	6.5	48	49%	.329	1.53	6.07	5.55	0.0	94.5	53	44	55
2018	*NYN*	*MLB*	*27*	*5*	*4*	*0*	*14*	*14*	*76^{2}*	*76*	*11*	*3.0*	*9.0*	*77*	*49%*	*.324*	*1.33*	*4.10*	*4.58*	*0.9*	*95.1*	*54*	*49*	*59*
2019	*NYN*	*MLB*	*28*	*11*	*11*	*0*	*32*	*32*	*209*	*187*	*28*	*2.6*	*9.1*	*211*	*49%*	*.31*	*1.19*	*3.93*	*4.39*	*2.5*	*94.7*	*55*	*49*	*60*

Breakout: 28% Improve: 54% Collapse: 17% Attrition: 10% MLB: 88% *Comparables: Jeff Niemann, Jacob deGrom, Matt Andriese*

Long Island's brightest star finished the season with more than 30 fewer innings than 2014 Mets reliever Carlos Torres ... in case you were looking for *another* distressing fact about the 2017 Mets' pitching staff. In March, there was elbow discomfort, then irritation, then a flexor tendon strain. In August, it was irritation in the ulnar nerve of his left elbow that eventually led to nerve transposition surgery. In between, Matz looked nothing like the brilliant starter the Mets had seen for the previous two seasons, and every performance indicator went the wrong way: Strikeouts were down, while walks, home runs and hits were up. Before last year, the question about Matz was always his health; when he was healthy, he was good. Last year, he was neither. He still has a chance to rebound in 2018, but eventually you stop being able to put Humpty Dumpty back together again.

Tommy Milone LHP Born: 02/16/87 Age: 31 Bats: L Throws: L Height: 6'0" Weight: 220 Origin: Round 10, 2008 Draft (#301 overall)

YEAR	TEAM	LVL	AGE	W	L	SV	G	GS	IP	H	HR	BB/9	K/9	K	GB%	BABIP	WHIP	ERA	DRA	WARP	MPH	CMD	PWR	STM
2015	ROC	AAA	28	4	0	0	5	5	38^{2}	25	2	0.7	10.9	47	47%	.261	0.72	0.70	0.74	2.0				
2015	MIN	MLB	28	9	5	1	24	23	128^{2}	128	17	2.5	6.4	91	44%	.279	1.27	3.92	4.38	1.1	90.0	70	28	65
2016	ROC	AAA	29	4	0	0	7	7	48^{2}	41	4	0.7	7.6	41	43%	.268	0.92	1.66	1.52	2.1				
2016	MIN	MLB	29	3	5	0	19	12	69^{1}	84	15	2.9	6.4	49	48%	.308	1.53	5.71	6.73	-1.1	89.7	56	32	50
2017	MIL	MLB	30	1	0	1	6	3	21	29	6	0.9	6.9	16	35%	.333	1.48	6.43	6.88	-0.3	89.1	75	25	34
2017	BIN	AA	30	1	0	0	4	4	20	26	8	0.9	4.9	11	27%	.273	1.40	4.95	6.28	-0.3				
2017	NYN	MLB	30	0	3	0	11	5	27^{1}	36	9	4.0	7.2	22	36%	.318	1.76	8.56	6.11	-0.2	89.0	75	25	34
2018	*NYN*	*MLB*	*31*	*3*	*5*	*0*	*12*	*12*	*66^{2}*	*75*	*16*	*3.2*	*7.5*	*55*	*41%*	*.310*	*1.49*	*5.73*	*6.40*	*-0.6*	*88.8*	*67*	*28*	*47*
2019	*NYN*	*MLB*	*32*	*8*	*12*	*0*	*29*	*29*	*177^{1}*	*189*	*39*	*2.8*	*7.2*	*142*	*41%*	*.303*	*1.38*	*5.58*	*6.25*	*-1.1*	*88.2*	*65*	*28*	*43*

Breakout: 14% Improve: 43% Collapse: 12% Attrition: 18% MLB: 74% *Comparables: Josh Tomlin, Dillon Gee, Josh Towers*

Why do some people watch car wrecks? After the Mets claimed Milone off of waivers from the Brewers in May, it becomes easier to understand. The left-hander was the replacement for Adam Wilk, who was the replacement for Matt Harvey. His recent performance had been even worse than his 4.14 career ERA hinted, but now this guy was suddenly a member of the "Best. Rotation. Ever?" He threw 12 innings before getting hurt, then returned in August to play out the stretch. Milone's tenure with the team was a slow-motion accident playing out in full view of everyone. Why watch someone at their lowest moment after that blown tire or fender bender? To remind yourself that things can always be worse.

Rafael Montero RHP Born: 10/17/90 Age: 27 Bats: R Throws: R Height: 6'0" Weight: 185 Origin: International Free Agent, 2011

YEAR	TEAM	LVL	AGE	W	L	SV	G	GS	IP	H	HR	BB/9	K/9	K	GB%	BABIP	WHIP	ERA	DRA	WARP	MPH	CMD	PWR	STM
2015	NYN	MLB	24	0	1	0	5	1	10	9	0	4.5	11.7	13	50%	.321	1.40	4.50	3.51	0.2	95.0			5
2016	LVG	AAA	25	4	6	0	16	16	80	111	12	4.5	7.7	68	46%	.375	1.89	7.20	4.50	0.8				
2016	BIN	AA	25	4	3	0	9	9	49	35	4	3.5	7.3	40	51%	.233	1.10	2.20	3.78	0.8				
2016	NYN	MLB	25	0	1	0	9	3	19	23	4	7.6	9.5	20	37%	.358	2.05	8.05	5.82	-0.1	95.0	62	47	71
2017	LVG	AAA	26	0	2	0	5	5	29	18	3	3.7	11.5	37	52%	.238	1.03	2.48	1.60	1.3				
2017	NYN	MLB	26	5	11	0	34	18	119	141	12	5.1	8.6	114	50%	.366	1.75	5.52	5.02	0.6	95.3	60	51	69
2018	*NYN*	*MLB*	*27*	*3*	*4*	*0*	*22*	*8*	*57*	*57*	*8*	*4.7*	*8.4*	*54*	*45%*	*.299*	*1.54*	*4.83*	*5.08*	*0.0*	*94.8*	*61*	*51*	*54*
2019	*NYN*	*MLB*	*28*	*8*	*8*	*0*	*59*	*20*	*158*	*145*	*20*	*3.9*	*8.4*	*148*	*45%*	*.309*	*1.36*	*4.43*	*4.96*	*0.9*	*94.5*	*61*	*51*	*64*

Breakout: 35% Improve: 55% Collapse: 19% Attrition: 20% MLB: 90% *Comparables: David Phelps, Brandon Claussen, J.A. Happ*

Rafael Montero is a no. 7 pitcher in a deep rotation or a long man out of the bullpen. Due to a series of unfortunate events—not the life-changing Lemony Snicket books, the terrible Jim Carrey movie or the excellent Neil Patrick Harris series—Montero ostensibly became the Mets' no. 2 starter in June. (So much for that "legendary" 2017 rotation.)

No real no. 2 starter should allow nearly five walks per nine and twice as many hits, but nothing was as bad as Montero's ability to inspire hope in the foolish. He'd spend a start or two making you believe he was on the verge of figuring it out (August 30 in Cincinnati: 8 1/3 scoreless innings with eight strikeouts) before getting shellacked (September 4 at home: 5 1/3 innings, four runs, five walks) his next time out. He could have been worse, but his lack of control and consistency is deeply unfortunate.

David Peterson LHP Born: 09/03/95 Age: 22 Bats: L Throws: L Height: 6'6" Weight: 240 Origin: Round 1, 2017 Draft (#20 overall)

YEAR	TEAM	LVL	AGE	W	L	SV	G	GS	IP	H	HR	BB/9	K/9	K	GB%	BABIP	WHIP	ERA	DRA	WARP	MPH	CMD	PWR	STM
2018	*NYN*	*MLB*	*22*	*2*	*3*	*0*	*8*	*8*	*34*	*38*	*7*	*4.6*	*8.8*	*33*	*42%*	*.330*	*1.61*	*5.61*	*6.28*	*-0.2*				
2019	*NYN*	*MLB*	*23*	*3*	*7*	*0*	*29*	*29*	*177^{2}*	*174*	*33*	*5.0*	*8.6*	*169*	*42%*	*.311*	*1.53*	*5.53*	*6.21*	*-0.8*				

Breakout: 1% Improve: 1% Collapse: 0% Attrition: 1% MLB: 1% *Comparables: Myles Jaye, Steven Brault, Adam Warren*

First, Peterson spent two years as a mediocre pitcher for the University of Oregon. Next, he rapidly transformed into one of the best collegiate southpaws in the country and was drafted 20th overall by the Mets. Finally, he faced exactly 16 batters in his first professional season. You can't judge a prospect on 16 batters faced, but here's what we do know: His fastball sat 89-92 in college, which only works if you throw with your left hand (he does!) or you're Bartolo Colon (he's not!). His slider and changeup are passable and he can throw a curve, even if it doesn't do it all that much. All the Mets can do is cross their fingers that the upward progression is real. We'll know more if he can stay on the field, which is never a given with this organization.

A.J. Ramos RHP Born: 09/20/86 Age: 31 Bats: R Throws: R Height: 5'10" Weight: 200 Origin: Round 21, 2009 Draft (#638 overall)

YEAR	TEAM	LVL	AGE	W	L	SV	G	GS	IP	H	HR	BB/9	K/9	K	GB%	BABIP	WHIP	ERA	DRA	WARP	MPH	CMD	PWR	STM
2015	MIA	MLB	28	2	4	32	71	0	70^{1}	45	6	3.3	11.1	87	44%	.252	1.01	2.30	2.38	2.0	95.8	49	42	51
2016	MIA	MLB	29	1	4	40	67	0	64	52	1	4.9	10.3	73	39%	.309	1.36	2.81	3.06	1.4	95.4	51	35	50
2017	MIA	MLB	30	2	4	20	40	0	39^{2}	30	4	5.0	10.7	47	42%	.271	1.31	3.63	3.23	0.9	94.5	47	32	48
2017	NYN	MLB	30	0	0	7	21	0	19	19	3	5.7	11.8	25	40%	.340	1.63	4.74	2.11	0.6	94.7	47	32	48
2018	*NYN*	*MLB*	*31*	*3*	*3*	*8*	*57*	*0*	*60*	*52*	*7*	*4.5*	*10.0*	*67*	*42%*	*.287*	*1.35*	*4.02*	*4.29*	*0.4*	*94.3*	*49*	*35*	*49*
2019	*NYN*	*MLB*	*32*	*3*	*1*	*4*	*53*	*0*	*56^{2}*	*44*	*7*	*4.5*	*10.6*	*66*	*42%*	*.296*	*1.29*	*4.14*	*4.64*	*0.3*	*93.7*	*48*	*34*	*49*

Breakout: 23% Improve: 38% Collapse: 34% Attrition: 14% MLB: 93% *Comparables: Francisco Cordero, Wade Davis, Tyler Clippard*

Much like the Confederate army, Ramos struggled with his command once he ventured over the Mason-Dixon line and his appearance came as something of a surprise. In the midst of shipping off most of the team's available veterans, the Mets acquired a Proven Closer to slot into the role with Addison Reed heading to Boston and Jeurys Familia rehabbing an injury. In Queens, Ramos was in some ways an exaggerated version of himself—more walks, more strikeouts, more homers. In other ways, he was just trying to fit in with his new environment. His slider usage went from under 40 percent to over 50 percent, and he even threw in a bout of biceps tendinitis for good measure. Given how badly the Mets need stability at the back end of their bullpen, the team must be hoping that Ramos both adapts to his new surroundings and doesn't.

Hansel Robles RHP Born: 08/13/90 Age: 27 Bats: R Throws: R Height: 5'11" Weight: 185 Origin: International Free Agent, 2008

YEAR	TEAM	LVL	AGE	W	L	SV	G	GS	IP	H	HR	BB/9	K/9	K	GB%	BABIP	WHIP	ERA	DRA	WARP	MPH	CMD	PWR	STM
2015	NYN	MLB	24	4	3	0	57	0	54	37	8	3.0	10.2	61	34%	.227	1.02	3.67	3.45	0.8	98.7	41	75	47
2016	NYN	MLB	25	6	4	1	68	0	77^{2}	69	7	4.2	9.8	85	31%	.307	1.35	3.48	4.07	0.8	98.8	39	61	54
2017	LVG	AAA	26	0	1	4	18	0	23^{1}	27	5	5.4	8.5	22	36%	.319	1.76	5.79	8.58	-0.8				
2017	NYN	MLB	26	7	5	0	46	0	56^{2}	47	10	4.6	9.5	60	35%	.259	1.34	4.92	5.40	-0.1	97.0	49	66	54
2018	*NYN*	*MLB*	*27*	*2*	*2*	*0*	*47*	*0*	*50*	*44*	*7*	*4.1*	*9.9*	*55*	*36%*	*.290*	*1.34*	*4.34*	*4.55*	*0.2*	*97.6*	*44*	*67*	*53*
2019	*NYN*	*MLB*	*28*	*2*	*1*	*0*	*51*	*0*	*53^{2}*	*44*	*8*	*4.1*	*9.9*	*59*	*36%*	*.292*	*1.28*	*4.47*	*5.01*	*0.1*	*97.2*	*44*	*65*	*54*

Breakout: 29% Improve: 53% Collapse: 13% Attrition: 22% MLB: 81% *Comparables: Jensen Lewis, David Hernandez, Fernando Nieve*

The new Robles is pretty much the same as the old Robles—so many blazing fastballs—only this time he's packing even more home runs. The hard-throwing righty got off to a terrible start, giving up 13 walks and 15 runs in 21 2/3 innings before being demoted to Triple-A in late May, quite the fall for someone who had been a reliable part of the Mets' bullpen over the previous two years. His return to Flushing later in the season went slightly better, but no cringeworthy stat was quite as bad as his habit of pointing at 450-foot fly balls into the Coca-Cola Corner. Did he expect Jay Bruce to grow to enormous size and catch balls that were well on their way out of the park, or was it just wishful thinking?

Paul Sewald RHP Born: 05/26/90 Age: 28 Bats: R Throws: R Height: 6'3" Weight: 207 Origin: Round 10, 2012 Draft (#320 overall)

YEAR	TEAM	LVL	AGE	W	L	SV	G	GS	IP	H	HR	BB/9	K/9	K	GB%	BABIP	WHIP	ERA	DRA	WARP	MPH	CMD	PWR	STM
2015	BIN	AA	25	3	0	24	44	0	51^1	34	3	1.8	9.8	56	44%	.246	0.86	1.75	0.96	2.3				
2016	LVG	AAA	26	5	3	19	56	0	65^2	58	9	2.9	11.0	80	38%	.295	1.20	3.29	2.06	2.2				
2017	NYN	MLB	27	0	6	0	57	0	65^1	58	8	2.9	9.5	69	35%	.287	1.21	4.55	3.51	1.2	93.2	54	46	52
2018	*NYN*	*MLB*	*28*	*2*	*2*	*0*	*47*	*0*	*50*	*47*	*9*	*3.6*	*9.8*	*54*	*38%*	*.293*	*1.34*	*4.75*	*4.87*	*0.0*	*92.6*	*54*	*46*	*52*
2019	*NYN*	*MLB*	*29*	*2*	*1*	*0*	*50*	*0*	*53*	*46*	*10*	*3.4*	*9.9*	*58*	*38%*	*.293*	*1.24*	*4.67*	*5.22*	*0.0*	*92.3*	*54*	*46*	*52*

Breakout: 18% Improve: 27% Collapse: 23% Attrition: 24% MLB: 65% *Comparables: Evan Scribner, Sam Demel, Brad Brach*

A grand goes a long way. $1,000 buys you an iPhone X. It buys you a cruise to the Caribbean or nine days at Disney World or (for all the millennials out there) 235 pieces of avocado toast. $1,000 apparently also bought the Mets the rights to Sewald. An upfront investment of a stack buys you a 2.21 ERA through June 1. It buys you a 92-mph fastball thrown almost two-thirds of the time and a changeup that has shown some promise, even though it is rarely seen. It buys you 65 1/3 innings, more than any other Mets reliever. It buys you 57 appearances out of the bullpen, second only to Jerry Blevins. It doesn't buy you anything spectacular, but it buys you enough.

Josh Smoker LHP Born: 11/26/88 Age: 29 Bats: L Throws: L Height: 6'2" Weight: 246 Origin: Round 1, 2007 Draft (#31 overall)

YEAR	TEAM	LVL	AGE	W	L	SV	G	GS	IP	H	HR	BB/9	K/9	K	GB%	BABIP	WHIP	ERA	DRA	WARP	MPH	CMD	PWR	STM
2015	SLU	A+	26	1	0	6	14	0	21^1	12	1	2.5	11.0	26	50%	.216	0.84	1.69	1.80	0.7				
2015	BIN	AA	26	1	0	0	21	0	21	16	0	4.7	11.1	26	50%	.308	1.29	3.00	3.53	0.3				
2016	LVG	AAA	27	3	2	3	52	0	57	66	5	2.8	12.8	81	46%	.409	1.47	4.11	0.90	2.7				
2016	NYN	MLB	27	3	0	0	20	0	15^1	16	4	2.3	14.7	25	31%	.387	1.30	4.70	3.12	0.3	98.1	56	56	54
2017	NYN	MLB	28	1	2	0	54	0	56^1	64	10	5.1	10.9	68	45%	.351	1.70	5.11	5.62	-0.3	96.3	41	53	51
2018	*NYN*	*MLB*	*29*	*2*	*2*	*0*	*47*	*0*	*50*	*49*	*8*	*4.3*	*10.3*	*57*	*44%*	*.309*	*1.47*	*4.58*	*4.73*	*0.1*	*95.9*	*43*	*53*	*52*
2019	*NYN*	*MLB*	*30*	*2*	*1*	*0*	*45*	*0*	*48*	*44*	*8*	*3.8*	*9.9*	*53*	*44%*	*.317*	*1.35*	*4.55*	*5.09*	*0.1*	*95.5*	*43*	*53*	*52*

Breakout: 17% Improve: 33% Collapse: 14% Attrition: 19% MLB: 63% *Comparables: Brad Brach, Louis Coleman, Jesse Chavez*

In 2016, Smoker's strikeout rate rivaled those of Andrew Miller and Craig Kimbrel. He didn't quite live up to those numbers last season—nor did anyone expect him to—and a doubling of his walk rate leaves something to be desired, but all of that means less than just playing in the majors. (Remember, this Georgia native played in the independent leagues as recently as 2014.) With a replacement-level 2017, no one would dare make the Rich Hill comparison, but there's still a little upside here, and Smoker's story—unlike so many in baseball—is one of hope and a little bit of luck. All the best comeback stories are.

Anthony Swarzak RHP Born: 09/10/85 Age: 32 Bats: R Throws: R Height: 6'4" Weight: 215 Origin: Round 2, 2004 Draft (#61 overall)

YEAR	TEAM	LVL	AGE	W	L	SV	G	GS	IP	H	HR	BB/9	K/9	K	GB%	BABIP	WHIP	ERA	DRA	WARP	MPH	CMD	PWR	STM
2015	CLE	MLB	29	0	0	0	10	0	13^1	18	1	2.7	8.8	13	39%	.395	1.65	3.38	3.93	0.1	95.1			36
2016	SWB	AAA	30	1	4	7	15	6	46^2	47	4	1.5	8.3	43	45%	.323	1.18	3.86	2.66	1.4				
2016	NYA	MLB	30	1	2	0	26	0	31	28	10	2.0	9.0	31	46%	.240	1.13	5.52	3.96	0.4	95.8	65	46	42
2017	CHA	MLB	31	4	3	1	41	0	48^1	37	2	2.4	9.7	52	40%	.294	1.03	2.23	3.09	1.1	95.9	63	50	54
2017	MIL	MLB	31	2	1	1	29	0	29	21	4	2.8	12.1	39	51%	.270	1.03	2.48	3.32	0.6	96.3	63	50	54
2018	*NYN*	*MLB*	*32*	*3*	*3*	*0*	*57*	*0*	*60*	*57*	*9*	*3.5*	*9.2*	*61*	*44%*	*.295*	*1.33*	*4.44*	*4.63*	*0.2*	*95.0*	*63*	*49*	*45*
2019	*NYN*	*MLB*	*33*	*3*	*1*	*0*	*52*	*0*	*55^2*	*48*	*8*	*3.4*	*9.0*	*56*	*44%*	*.299*	*1.25*	*4.34*	*4.86*	*0.2*	*94.5*	*63*	*48*	*47*

Breakout: 23% Improve: 42% Collapse: 26% Attrition: 9% MLB: 85% *Comparables: Todd Coffey, Matt Lindstrom, Kevin Gregg*

In the late 19th century, America struggled to cope with an unpredictable, industrializing economy. Everyday people both amassed fortunes and lost everything with seemingly little rhyme or reason. This arbitrary and chaotic economic environment became known as the Freaks of Fortune—an explanatory term to explain the unexplainable. Jonathan Levy wrote a great history on this phenomenon, but he might as well have been explaining the middle-relief market. Swarzak inked a minor-league contract with the White Sox in January 2017 after 26 disastrous appearances with the Bronx Bombers the previous year. Suddenly, the right-hander found an extra tick on his fastball, struck out 30 percent of the batters he faced and was a top-20 qualified reliever in terms of ERA. After the Brewers acquired him in July, Swarzak pitched in high-leverage situations during a postseason race, still posting quality numbers. He scored a multi-year, multi-million-dollar contract with the Mets at 32 years old. Because that's how relievers apparently work these days. Journeymen randomly become high-leverage studs, but who knows how long guys like Swarzak can capture "it." It's the freaks of fortune, man, just roll with it.

Noah Syndergaard RHP Born: 08/29/92 Age: 25 Bats: L Throws: R Height: 6'6" Weight: 240 Origin: Round 1, 2010 Draft (#38 overall)

YEAR	TEAM	LVL	AGE	W	L	SV	G	GS	IP	H	HR	BB/9	K/9	K	GB%	BABIP	WHIP	ERA	DRA	WARP	MPH	CMD	PWR	STM
2015	LVG	AAA	22	3	0	0	5	5	29^2	20	2	2.4	10.3	34	52%	.261	0.94	1.82	1.65	1.2				
2015	NYN	MLB	22	9	7	0	24	24	150	126	19	1.9	10.0	166	48%	.279	1.05	3.24	2.67	4.3	99.5	53	66	68
2016	NYN	MLB	23	14	9	0	31	30	183^2	168	11	2.1	10.7	218	52%	.334	1.15	2.60	2.47	6.1	100.5	51	66	75
2017	NYN	MLB	24	1	2	0	7	7	30^1	29	0	0.9	10.1	34	59%	.337	1.05	2.97	3.46	0.7	100.0	56	72	0
2018	*NYN*	*MLB*	*25*	*11*	*8*	*0*	*26*	*26*	*163*	*141*	*14*	*2.8*	*10.3*	*187*	*50%*	*.301*	*1.18*	*2.89*	*3.12*	*3.9*	*99.8*	*53*	*68*	*43*
2019	*NYN*	*MLB*	*26*	*13*	*10*	*0*	*33*	*33*	*214^1*	*175*	*20*	*2.2*	*10.5*	*251*	*50%*	*.315*	*1.06*	*2.91*	*3.25*	*5.3*	*99.7*	*53*	*69*	*37*

Breakout: 27% Improve: 60% Collapse: 18% Attrition: 11% MLB: 98% *Comparables: Jaime Garcia, Tyler Skaggs, Drew Smyly*

Syndergaard—perhaps better than any other analogy—truly represents the Mets. This long-haired boy from Texas with a triple-digit four-seamer and 93-mph slider was going to put up legendary numbers. The best pitcher in New York was going to compete with Clayton Kershaw and Max Scherzer for the Cy Young. The undisputed ace was going to lead a brilliant young rotation to the playoffs for the third straight year—and deeper than just a wild card game this time. The guy they call Thor claimed to have put on 17 pounds of muscle in the offseason, subsisting on his Bowl of Doom made of sweet potato hash, bacon, buffalo, venison sausage, avocado and scrambled eggs. And in the end, he threw just 27 1/3 innings before being shut down in late April with a torn right lat. Then he barely made it back for the last two weeks of the season to get some reps and sell some tickets. Syndergaard, much like his 2017 New York Mets team, was barely here.

Thomas Szapucki LHP Born: 06/12/96 Age: 21 Bats: R Throws: L Height: 6'2" Weight: 181 Origin: Round 5, 2015 Draft (#149 overall)

YEAR	TEAM	LVL	AGE	W	L	SV	G	GS	IP	H	HR	BB/9	K/9	K	GB%	BABIP	WHIP	ERA	DRA	WARP	MPH	CMD	PWR	STM
2016	KNG	RK	20	2	1	0	5	5	29	16	2	2.8	14.6	47	46%	.255	0.86	0.62	1.02	1.5				
2016	BRO	A-	20	2	2	0	4	4	23	10	0	4.3	15.3	39	46%	.256	0.91	2.35	1.15	1.1				
2017	COL	A	21	1	2	0	6	6	29	24	0	3.1	8.4	27	44%	.304	1.17	2.79	3.95	0.4				
2018	*NYN*	*MLB*	*22*	*2*	*3*	*0*	*6*	*6*	*33*^{2}	*35*	*7*	*5.1*	*10.1*	*38*	*38%*	*.329*	*1.60*	*5.52*	*6.18*	*-0.2*				
2019	*NYN*	*MLB*	*23*	*7*	*12*	*0*	*27*	*27*	*164*	*165*	*34*	*5.3*	*9.9*	*180*	*38%*	*.33*	*1.60*	*5.80*	*6.50*	*-1.4*				

Breakout: 5% Improve: 7% Collapse: 5% Attrition: 9% MLB: 12% *Comparables: Michael Stutes, Carson Fulmer, Tony Sipp*

A breakout 2016 saw Szapucki become one of the top left-handed pitching prospects in the low minors. Last year he became a True Met when he missed the first two months of 2017 with a shoulder impingement and then underwent Tommy John surgery in July after making only six starts. It would be nice to say this is just an 18-month speed bump and he'll be as good as new in 2019, but the injuries are worrisome. TINSTAAPP.

Zack Wheeler RHP Born: 05/30/90 Age: 28 Bats: L Throws: R Height: 6'4" Weight: 195 Origin: Round 1, 2009 Draft (#6 overall)

YEAR	TEAM	LVL	AGE	W	L	SV	G	GS	IP	H	HR	BB/9	K/9	K	GB%	BABIP	WHIP	ERA	DRA	WARP	MPH	CMD	PWR	STM
2017	NYN	MLB	27	3	7	0	17	17	86^{1}	97	15	4.2	8.4	81	48%	.332	1.59	5.21	7.04	-1.4	96.6	51	62	54
2018	*NYN*	*MLB*	*28*	*7*	*9*	*0*	*23*	*23*	*131*	*128*	*21*	*3.9*	*8.3*	*121*	*43%*	*.291*	*1.40*	*4.60*	*4.97*	*0.3*	*96.0*	*51*	*62*	*54*
2019	*NYN*	*MLB*	*29*	*9*	*12*	*0*	*30*	*30*	*184*^{2}	*177*	*28*	*4.5*	*7.3*	*150*	*43%*	*.296*	*1.45*	*5.27*	*5.90*	*-0.5*	*95.5*	*51*	*62*	*54*

Breakout: 21% Improve: 51% Collapse: 25% Attrition: 13% MLB: 93% *Comparables: Ricky Romero, Matt Moore, Trevor Cahill*

For a while, Wheeler was a revelation. After missing two full seasons following Tommy John surgery, just getting back on the mound was an achievement, and the Georgia native blew past expectations. He came back as the same shooting star hurler who looked to be coming into his own back in 2014. He gave up a few more hits and a few more home runs and a few more walks, but his four-seamer still sat at 95 and his slider still hit 89 even with two years of rust on his elbow. Then, in mid-June, he suffered two terrible outings before hitting the DL, came back, and then hit the pine in July with a "stress reaction" in his right upper arm. Suddenly, he was on the list of players shut down for the season at the end of August. All this goes goes to show that while Wheeler sometimes fits the mold of a mid-rotation starter, his redemption story has hit another pause as we wait for him to play.

LINEOUTS

Hitters

HITTER	POS	TEAM	LVL	AGE	PA	R	2B	3B	HR	RBI	BB	K	SB	CS	AVG/OBP/SLG	TAv	VORP	BABIP	BRR	FRAA	WARP
Peter Alonso	1B	SLU	A+	22	346	45	23	0	16	58	25	64	3	4	.286/.361/.516	.299	11.6	.314	-5.8	1B(78): 3.2	1.6
	1B	BIN	AA	22	47	7	4	1	2	5	2	7	0	0	.311/.340/.578	.322	3.3	.333	-0.1	1B(5): 0.1	0.4
Wuilmer Becerra	OF	SLU	A+	22	519	49	16	2	4	44	36	132	16	5	.267/.332/.335	.246	-2.3	.361	-3.1	RF(47): -3.9, LF(40): -8.6	-1.6
Jayce Boyd	LF	LVG	AAA	26	278	39	18	1	11	46	26	47	3	0	.297/.371/.512	.288	15.2	.326	1.2	LF(38): -1.2	1.4
Alejandro De Aza	OF	SYR	AAA	33	212	30	11	0	4	19	25	30	2	0	.280/.368/.403	.268	7.4	.316	1.0	RF(32): 1.9, LF(22): -0.4	0.8
	OF	WAS	MLB	33	70	8	2	3	0	9	3	16	1	0	.194/.224/.323	.216	-1.5	.250	0.1	RF(14): -0.6, LF(13): 1.4	-0.1
Ali Sanchez	C	COL	A	20	200	20	3	0	1	15	13	26	2	3	.231/.288/.264	.234	2.7	.263	-1.0	C(55): 0.3	0.3
Luis Santana	MI	MET	Rk	17	287	47	12	8	3	52	34	22	16	4	.325/.430/.481	.299	26.0	.346	2.4	2B(61): 1.0, SS(4): 0.4	2.5
Travis Snider	OF	ROU	AAA	29	413	50	24	0	9	44	49	91	2	2	.294/.375/.435	.288	21.6	.367	0.8	LF(44): 3.6, RF(40): -3.7	2.1
	OF	LVG	AAA	29	72	9	2	1	1	8	7	15	0	1	.308/.375/.415	.273	2.4	.388	-0.1	RF(8): -1.1, LF(7): 1.5	0.3
Jhoan Urena	3B	SLU	A+	22	522	72	34	2	11	62	60	114	17	3	.282/.364/.437	.281	23.8	.351	-1.1	3B(89): 0.7, 1B(25): 1.3	2.7
	3B	LVG	AAA	22	48	5	0	1	3	8	4	16	1	0	.227/.292/.477	.239	-0.5	.280	-0.1	1B(10): -0.7, LF(1): 0.0	-0.1
Mark Vientos	SS	MTS	Rk	17	193	22	12	0	4	24	14	42	0	2	.259/.316/.397	.255	6.3	.313	0.8	SS(19): -1.6, 3B(14): 0.1	0.4

University of Florida alumnus and first baseman **Pete Alonso** hit well enough at St. Lucie to earn a promotion to Binghamton at the end of August. Best of all, he still has never had to wear team colors other than orange and blue. ⚾ Coming off labrum surgery in July 2016, **Wuilmer Becerra** resumed his old ways, which is *not* a compliment. He struck out in more than a quarter of his at-bats, something that was always a major concern, even as his power continued its downward spiral. ⚾ For the first time in a six-year professional career, **Jayce Boyd** discovered some power, putting up a .512 slugging percentage with 11 home runs in Las Vegas. But 26 is old for a power surge, and "Travis Taijeron without the homers" is a tough sell. ⚾ **Alejandro de Aza** has four A's in his name, which is fitting, as his true talent level is AAAA. ⚾ **Adrian Hernandez** walked out of the international signing period with a $1.5 million check and rave reviews about pull-side power and above-average speed. ⚾ Switch-hitting infielder **Ronny Mauricio** signed for $2.1 million last July, breaking the Mets' international signing record previously held by Amed Rosario. Don't be surprised, be ready for massive expectations, Ronny! ⚾ The question about **Ali Sanchez**, the best pitch-framer in the Mets' organization, has been whether he can hit. Last year didn't provide any answers, especially after he missed the entire second half with a fractured hamate bone in his left hand. ⚾ After signing for $200,000 at just 16 years old, **Luis Santana** followed up a solid debut with a stellar 2017 while repeating the Dominican Summer League. The 5'8" middle infielder walked more than he struck out and even added some power. ⚾ **Travis Snider** went from top prospect in the Blue Jays organization to 20-year-old rookie to one of the more inconsistent players in the majors to outfield depth in Las Vegas. There's a novel in there somewhere. ⚾ **Jhoan Urena**, a quintessential "bat has to make up for the lack of defense" third baseman, still doesn't have the bat. ⚾ **Mark Vientos**, the Mets' second-round draft pick in 2017, is expected to drift over to third base eventually. "Eventually" is a long way away, as he was too young to buy lottery tickets for his entire first season in pro ball.

Pitchers

PITCHER	TEAM	LVL	AGE	W	L	SV	G	GS	IP	H	HR	BB/9	K/9	K	GB%	BABIP	WHIP	ERA	DRA	WARP	MPH	CMD	PWR	STM
Tyler Bashlor	SLU	A+	24	2	2	10	34	0	35	33	1	5.4	15.7	61	39%	.438	1.54	4.89	3.22	0.7				
	BIN	AA	24	1	0	3	12	0	14^{2}	7	0	2.5	14.1	23	41%	.259	0.75	0.00	2.21	0.5				
Gerson Bautista	SLM	A+	22	3	2	4	27	0	45^{1}	54	2	5.6	10.5	53	41%	.388	1.81	5.16	5.84	-0.5				
	SLU	A+	22	0	1	5	10	0	14^{1}	10	0	1.9	12.6	20	55%	.323	0.91	1.26	1.64	0.5				
P.J. Conlon	BIN	AA	23	8	9	1	28	22	136	130	14	2.5	7.1	108	43%	.289	1.24	3.38	3.71	2.3				
Nabil Crismatt	SLU	A+	22	6	13	0	26	25	145^{2}	161	17	2.2	8.8	142	42%	.333	1.35	3.95	4.93	0.5				
Josh Edgin	NYN	MLB	30	0	1	1	46	0	37	39	3	4.4	6.6	27	49%	.319	1.54	3.65	6.20	-0.4	92.7	48	34	45
Harol Gonzalez	COL	A	22	9	8	0	20	20	126^{1}	123	11	2.6	6.5	91	45%	.293	1.27	3.56	5.47	-0.3				
	SLU	A+	22	0	1	0	3	3	11^{1}	10	2	2.4	7.1	9	32%	.222	1.15	3.18	5.04	0.0				
Jordan Humphreys	COL	A	21	10	1	0	11	11	69^{2}	41	2	1.2	10.3	80	40%	.241	0.72	1.42	1.84	2.8				
	SLU	A+	21	0	0	0	2	2	11	17	1	2.5	2.5	3	30%	.348	1.82	4.09	7.00	-0.2				
Kevin McGowan	LVG	AAA	25	6	5	4	47	1	65	63	8	3.5	7.9	57	39%	.281	1.35	4.15	7.46	-1.5				
	NYN	MLB	25	0	0	0	8	0	8^{2}	8	2	6.2	8.3	8	35%	.250	1.62	5.19	3.54	0.2	94.4			49
Marcos Molina	SLU	A+	22	2	3	0	5	5	28^{2}	17	1	1.6	7.2	23	49%	.213	0.77	1.26	2.04	1.1				
	BIN	AA	22	3	7	0	13	12	78	77	5	2.4	7.3	63	47%	.304	1.26	3.92	4.05	1.0				
Corey Oswalt	BIN	AA	23	12	5	0	24	24	134^{1}	118	9	2.7	8.0	119	49%	.290	1.18	2.28	3.88	2.1				
Tyler Pill	BIN	AA	27	1	0	0	2	2	10^{1}	11	0	0.9	2.6	3	53%	.306	1.16	0.00	4.07	0.1				
	LVG	AAA	27	4	3	0	13	13	80^{1}	83	8	2.5	5.6	50	48%	.291	1.31	3.47	4.90	0.7				
	NYN	MLB	27	0	3	0	7	3	22	22	3	4.1	6.5	16	54%	.279	1.45	5.32	6.05	-0.1	91.4	49	30	62
Jacob Rhame	OKL	AAA	24	0	2	2	41	0	48	52	6	1.9	10.3	55	34%	.351	1.29	4.31	3.66	0.8				
	NYN	MLB	24	1	1	0	9	0	9	12	2	7.0	7.0	7	39%	.345	2.11	9.00	8.80	-0.4	96.4			46
Adonis Uceta	COL	A	23	4	0	11	29	0	43	23	0	3.3	9.8	47	38%	.225	0.91	1.26	3.56	0.7				
	SLU	A+	23	0	0	2	8	0	10^{2}	5	1	2.5	12.7	15	40%	.211	0.75	0.84	2.53	0.3				
Stephen Villines	BRO	A-	21	1	1	1	11	0	19	13	1	0.5	14.2	30	52%	.308	0.74	1.89	0.63	0.9				

Two years removed from a two-year Tommy John recovery process, **Tyler Bashlor** put up an obscene 15.7 K/9 in St. Lucie. Although he was old for High-A, the former $500,000 JuCo sign looks like he could be a major-league reliever. **Gerson Bautista** throws 100! That's about all he can do, but if you can do only one thing in baseball, that's a good one. **P.J. Conlon**, a 13th-round pick out of the University of San Diego in 2015, is looking to become the first player born in Belfast, Northern Ireland, to reach the big leagues since Irish McIlveen did it more than a century ago. **Nabil Crismatt**'s WBC start for Team Colombia didn't go as he (or the team) would have hoped with three innings pitched, three hits and two earned runs. It did, however, put the young righty on the international stage even before his solid full season in St. Lucie. **Josh Edgin** never really made it back from a 2015 Tommy John surgery and followed up a disappointing 2016 with a slightly-less-disappointing-but-still-less-than-impressive 2017. Despite his adequacy, he was designated for assignment in July and outrighted to Las Vegas because no other team wanted a LOOGY who let lefties hit .280/.372/.400. Listed at 5'11" and 178 pounds, **Harol Gonzalez**'s eventual success in the majors is less important than the potential for a photo op standing next to Noah Syndergaard. A major-league veteran and living proof that fringy lefties can stick around for 12 years, the grand **Tom Gorzelanny** Experiment likely came to an end after 7 2/3 innings in the Mets' minor-league system. **Jordan Humphreys** had a 6.9 strikeout-to-walk ratio in 80 2/3 innings at Low-A and High-A in 2017 before undergoing Tommy John surgery in August. **Kevin McGowan** has the long, lustrous hair to make it as a member of the Mets pitching staff. The on-field qualifications, however, are coming along a little slower. **Marcos Molina** still could find his way back after Tommy John surgery, but a DRA over 4.00 in Binghamton isn't the best sign. Hope springs eternal, but patience? Not so much. All pitching prospects in the Mets' organization break, so maybe **Corey Oswalt**—who won Eastern League Pitcher of the Year despite being classified as a marginal prospect—has a shot at staying on the mound. There's a world in which **Tyler Pill**, an organizational arm promoted to replace a failing Rafael Montero, flourished during his opportunity and won the love and admiration of Mets fans. This is not that world. The only thing separating **Jacob Rhame**, a hard-throwing right-hander acquired from the Dodgers in the Curtis Granderson trade, from the cabal of similar arms the Mets received at the 2017 trade deadline is the fact that he wears glasses. Early returns on **Adonis Uceta**'s move to the bullpen showed an uptick in results. Reportedly, his coaches told him not to worry about his regression after reaching Binghamton, saying: "Hey, u-set-a high bar." Tenth-round draft pick **Steve Villines** put up a sparkly ERA in his professional debut and gave up as many home runs as walks—one—over 27 1/3 innings.

NEW YORK YANKEES

Essay by Steven Goldman

Player comments by Stacey Gotsulias and BP staff

For baseball teams, as in life, the long view, perhaps even the geologic view, is necessary if one is to maintain a sense of hope about anything. In the midst of the Cold War, it seemed as if the superpower standoff would last forever, but it persisted for a relatively brief 46 years. The drip-drip-drip of Watergate was excruciating in its seeming open-endedness, but from burglary to resignation the crisis spanned just over 24 months. The dark polyester night in which disco dominated the charts lasted only a half-dozen years. And in 2016, the New York Yankees, a team long held in the grip of a dead man's veterans-only, never-surrender-even-when-you've-already-lost mania, traded its veterans, rebuilt the farm system and started over.

If the turnaround from 2016 to 2017 had been merely cosmetic it would have been a success. All the Yankees had to do was tease a promising future, show some youth and dynamism. Instead, the team—whose player-development philosophy was once exemplified by George Steinbrenner III asking an error-prone kid, "What the hell were you doing last night? Jesus Christ! You looked like a monkey trying to f*** a football out there!"—made its longest postseason run in seven years behind the Rookie of the Year, a 24-year-old catcher and a 23-year-old Cy Young candidate. As hard as it is to accept, George Harrison spoke the truth when he sang, "All things must pass."

The 2016 edition was a drab affair, a team retro-mortgaged to the 2009 championship due to the lingering *Man Who Came to Dinner* presence of Alex Rodriguez, Mark Teixeira and, somewhat more profitably, CC Sabathia. The remaining lineup was overpopulated by drab 32-year-olds like Brian McCann, Chase Headley, Brett Gardner and Jacoby Ellsbury—despite playing in a ballpark that gives away home runs the way banks used to give away toasters, the team finished 11th in the American League in that category. Long-term project pitchers like Nathan Eovaldi and Michael Pineda refused to evolve or stay healthy, and what good there was on the club—principally relievers Aroldis Chapman and Andrew Miller—was dealt for prospects.

Even then, one of the team's most promising young players, former first-round pick Aaron Judge, struggled badly, as did Luis Severino, the best young starting pitcher. With the club puttering along at .500 through the end of June, there was almost no reason to watch the team until kid catcher Gary Sanchez came up in August and re-embodied Kevin Maas as a legitimate prospect.

What was supposed to ensue was a rebuilding year. Instead, the Yankees made it all the way to the seventh game of the ALCS, coming within an unlikely Charlie Morton/Lance McCullers shutout of ejecting the eventual World Series winners from the playoffs. The Yankees won 91 games in the regular season; their Pythagorean record suggests that with added luck (or minus Tyler Clippard) they might have won 100. For this to transpire, a number of unlikely evolutions had to take place. For the team to continue on the path back to the World Series, those evolutions will have to continue.

YANKEES PROSPECTUS

2017 W-L: 91-71, 2ND IN AL EAST

Pythag	.622	3rd	B-Age	28.6	*19th*
RS/G	5.30	2nd	P-Age	27.5	*7th*
RA/G	4.07	4th	Salary	$196.4M	*4th*
TAv	.272	5th	M$/MW	$4.3M	*12th*
TAv-P	.239	2nd	DL Days	824	*10th*
FIP	3.85	5th	$ on DL	12%	*11th*
DER	.720	1st			

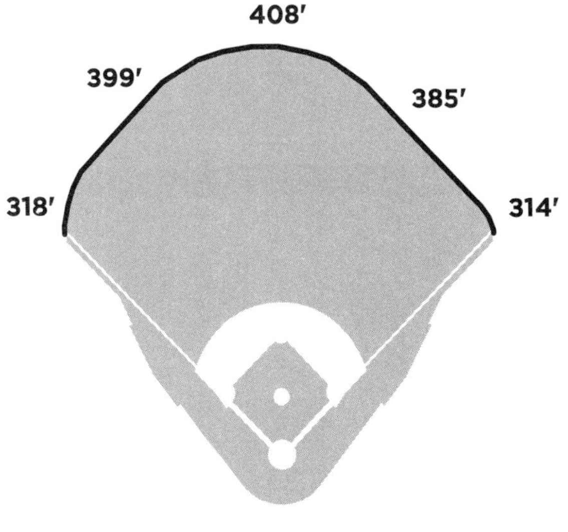

Outfield wall profile: **8′**

Three-Year Park Factors

Runs	Runs/RH	Runs/LH	HR/RH	HR/LH
101	100	102	111	120

Top Hitter WARP	7.3 Aaron Judge
Top Pitcher WARP	5.4 Luis Severino
Top Prospect	Gleyber Torres

2017 Hit List Ranking

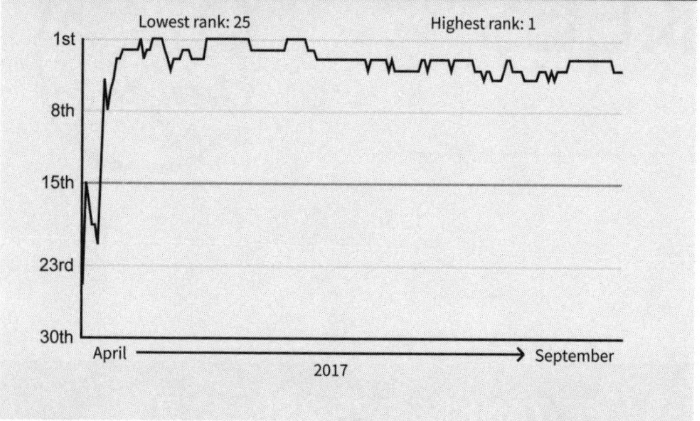

Committed Payroll (in millions)

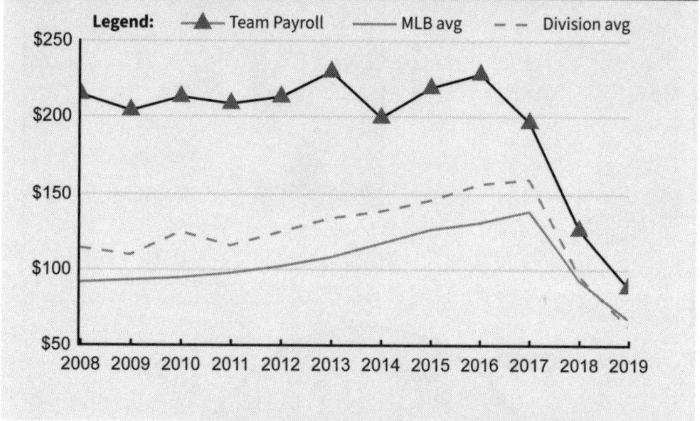

Farm System Ranking

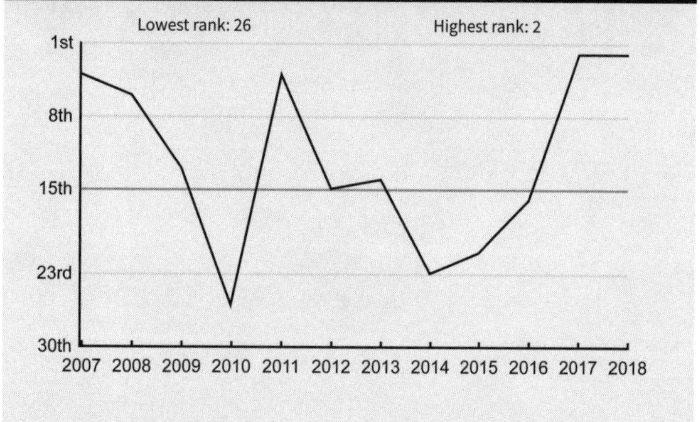

Personnel

General Manager
Brian Cashman

SVP, Assistant General Manager
Jean Afterman

Assistant General Manager
Michael Fishman

VP, Baseball Operations
Tim Naehring

Manager
Aaron Boone

In order of future sustainability:

- Judge had to master the strike zone given his massive size and tendency to chase low pitches. He did that, in a manner of speaking, leading the American League in strikeouts, walks and home runs while maintaining a batting average over .300 in four of the season's six months. To do that while striking out 208 times, he had to hit .357 on balls in play. It was a high but not prohibitive number, and allowance must be made for Judge being a unique physical specimen whose great strength generated the highest average exit velocity in baseball (94.9 mph).
- There is no value in pitcher win-loss records, but there was still something arresting in seeing Severino follow up his strong 11-start 2015 debut with an 8.50 ERA and 0-8 record in a further 11 starts in 2016. Remanded to the bullpen, he dominated, allowing only eight hits in 23 1/3 innings. Given that Severino's changeup had been a far weaker offering than his fastball and slider, as well as his stressful mechanics, the Yankees would have been forgiven had they forever consigned him to relief work. Instead, Severino spent the offseason working to perfect his changeup, received tutelage on his mechanics from no less than old team rival Pedro Martinez and maintained the best average fastball velocity in the bigs (97.6 mph). The resultant season was, on a WARP basis, the best by a homegrown Yankees starter since Chien-Ming Wang's 2006, as well as the best by any Yankees starting pitcher 25 or younger (long a rare breed on a club that loved veterans, forsaking all others) since Andy Pettitte's 1997.
- Several other near miracles had to take place for the pitching staff to coalesce into one of the best aggregations in team history: Masahiro Tanaka had to recover from a dozen early starts in which his command deserted him—2.3 home runs per nine innings leaving the park—and allay concerns that an arm ever on the edge of destruction was healthy; Sabathia continued his late-career renaissance as a 6-foot-6 soft-tosser; busted starter Chad Green emerged as a weapon out of the bullpen; midseason relief (re)acquisitions David Robertson and Tommy Kahnle pitched impeccably; Jordan Montgomery, a not particularly heralded prospect, turned in a representative performance at the back of the rotation, even after theoretically better pitchers had been acquired.
- The Yankees had won without a quality first baseman before (see 1941 rookie Johnny Sturm's 568-plate appearance .239/.293/.300 season), but it's a lot easier doing it the other way. Greg Bird's 103 games on the disabled list meant the team had to patch with Chris Carter, Matt Holliday, Rob Refsnyder, Ji-Man Choi, Garrett Cooper, Tyler Austin and even, for four nihilism-inspiring games, Austin Romine. Bird returned in surprisingly good form, hitting .253/.316/.575 with eight home runs in 98 plate appearances, but even before that the position had been stabilized by Chase Headley, who had been pushed off of third base by the acquisition of Todd Frazier. In 2015 and 2016, Headley had had nigh-identical, and identically disappointing, seasons, averaging.256/.327/.376 between the two campaigns. As of his move across the diamond, he was still going on in the same old way, hitting .257/.339/.368. As if liberated by the relocation, he hit .294/.369/.461 over the remainder of the season.

After all of that, the offseason conventional wisdom seemed to be,

"And on the seventh day both God and Brian Cashman rested." As if lolling in tryptophan slumber after an unexpectedly large turkey dinner, the punditocracy adopted a complacency accepting that all the Yankees had to do to repeat or exceed their 2017 performance was to sign the best starting pitcher available and the rest would again fall into place. Instead, the Yankees swung the biggest deal of the winter, acquiring reigning NL MVP Giancarlo Stanton from old friend Derek Jeter and the forever-rebuilding Marlins.

In doing so they parted with starting second baseman Starlin Castro (and his contract), potentially freeing up the position for top prospect Gleyber Torres. Assuming Torres picks up where he left off following Tommy John surgery, the Yankees will soon be under pressure to promote him. And perhaps soon after that they'll do the same with another top prospect, third baseman Miguel Andujar, who hit .315/.352/.498 in a season split between Double-A and Triple-A. There is an incredible amount of young talent in New York or soon on its way, and adding Stanton to that mix is as scary as seeing him back-to-back with Judge in a lineup.

One position at which the Yankees made a point of flaunting just how many choices they had is manager; the team headed into December without a replacement for Joe Girardi and the list of candidates in a state of seemingly constant expansion. In the aftermath of the team's decision not to extend Girardi's contract, the pursuit of a new skipper was turned into something resembling a reality show, with press availabilities directly following the interviews and the club seemingly open to consideration of anyone from momentary Yankees turned broadcasters like Aaron Boone to players just off the field such as Carlos Beltran.

It all seemed designed to convey just how superfluous the organization considers the manager in our current Age of the Front Office. Baseball has grown up a great deal in recent years, having traveled light-years from the mystique of foundational managers like Connie Mack and John McGraw. They are now mere extensions of the general manager's will, and whereas Girardi clearly had a doghouse when it came to certain players, it seems certain that Boone will not have that prerogative.

That's not to say Girardi was all or even mostly bad. He had his rigidities, particularly in terms of bullpen construction and usage, but he could be surprisingly open-minded in other regards, such as batting orders that saw Judge and Sanchez split 60 games in the second spot and Didi Gregorius take 42 games as the cleanup hitter. Stanton's arrival means Boone won't have to be as creative, but Girardi trying to mass some of his most potent and/or patient hitters at the top of the order followed by a batter who would just put the ball in play was not without merit. It worked in one sense; Gregorius hit .327/.351/.535 with men on, but because the cleanup hitter leads off an inning the second-most times of any hitter on the team, it was not an unalloyed success—Gregorius lost his focus at such times and went to hacking, batting .168/.208/.299.

Nevertheless, Girardi too has now gone the way of the Soviet Union, the Commodore 64 and the days in which the Yankees would have traded Judge for the present-day equivalent of Ken Phelps. That's progress, and moving on from the ex-catcher with the nervous, snickering laugh may prove to be progress as well. These are disconcerting times—all periods of upheaval are, whether one is in sympathy with them or not—but the Yankees now most resemble the best version of themselves, the deep, farm-sustained team that dominated baseball in the 1940s and 1950s, with several in-their-prime superstars around which to build.

They still have a way to go before they become the next Cubs or Astros, but it might happen—or maybe it already has. Remember that Pythagorean record of 100-62. Remember that BP's third-order projected record had them at 106-56. A great deal will depend on the kids' further development and decisions they make about players like Torres, but the potential is there for them to convert that record from a paper projection to an on-the-field reality as soon as this year. Yes, all things must pass, including a nine-year World Series drought.

—Steven Goldman is the former editor-in-chief of Baseball Prospectus and the host of the "Infinite Inning" podcast.

Hitters

Miguel Andujar 3B Born: 03/02/95 Age: 23 Bats: R Throws: R Height: 6'0" Weight: 215 Origin: International Free Agent, 2011

YEAR	TEAM	LVL	AGE	PA	R	2B	3B	HR	RBI	BB	K	SB	CS	AVG/OBP/SLG	TAv	VORP	BABIP	BRR	FRAA	WARP
2015	TAM	A+	20	520	54	24	5	8	57	29	90	12	1	.243/.288/.363	.254	14.7	.282	2.8	3B(115): -9.2	0.6
2016	TAM	A+	21	251	34	10	2	10	41	18	30	1	3	.283/.343/.474	.287	14.6	.289	0.0	3B(51): 4.1	1.9
2016	TRN	AA	21	319	28	16	2	2	42	21	42	2	1	.266/.323/.358	.269	12.3	.296	0.5	3B(64): -2.6	1.0
2017	TRN	AA	22	272	30	23	1	7	52	12	38	2	3	.312/.342/.494	.307	19.1	.338	-1.6	3B(55): -4.5	1.6
2017	SWB	AAA	22	250	36	13	1	9	30	17	33	3	0	.317/.364/.502	.300	20.1	.333	0.3	3B(57): -1.4	1.8
2017	NYA	MLB	22	8	0	2	0	0	4	1	0	1	0	.571/.625/.857	.474	2.0	.571	0.0	3B(3): 0.0	0.2
2018	*NYA*	*MLB*	*23*	*99*	*12*	*5*	*0*	*3*	*12*	*5*	*20*	*0*	*0*	*.253/.298/.427*	*.252*	*2.2*	*.285*	*-0.1*	*3B -1*	*0.1*
2019	*NYA*	*MLB*	*24*	*376*	*48*	*19*	*1*	*15*	*51*	*23*	*77*	*2*	*1*	*.258/.308/.449*	*.256*	*6.8*	*.289*	*-0.6*	*3B -3*	*0.4*

Breakout: 3% Improve: 31% Collapse: 7% Attrition: 20% MLB: 52% *Comparables: Colin Moran, Jedd Gyorko, Neil Walker*

If you blinked, you may have missed Andujar's Yankees debut in June. He went 3-for-4 with four RBIs and was promptly sent back to the minors but made a good enough impression to be brought back up when rosters expanded in September. While sometimes overlooked within a very deep, talented farm system, Andujar has plenty of upside after taking a big step forward offensively last season between Double- and Triple-A. He has a chance to stick at third base, but could get caught as a tweener depending on how his bat continues to develop.

Tyler Austin 1B Born: 09/06/91 Age: 26 Bats: R Throws: R Height: 6'2" Weight: 220 Origin: Round 13, 2010 Draft (#415 overall)

YEAR	TEAM	LVL	AGE	PA	R	2B	3B	HR	RBI	BB	K	SB	CS	AVG/OBP/SLG	TAv	VORP	BABIP	BRR	FRAA	WARP
2015	SWB	AAA	23	299	33	8	0	4	27	26	81	8	1	.235/.309/.311	.227	-3.5	.317	1.8	RF(54): -0.4, LF(10): -0.9	-0.5
2015	TRN	AA	23	86	8	5	2	2	8	8	16	3	2	.260/.337/.455	.260	2.2	.305	0.8	RF(17): 3.4	0.6
2016	TRN	AA	24	210	22	10	1	4	29	30	46	1	1	.260/.367/.395	.277	7.2	.326	1.2	1B(37): 0.1, LF(7): -1.5	0.6
2016	SWB	AAA	24	234	39	24	0	13	49	32	59	5	0	.323/.415/.637	.359	26.9	.400	-0.2	1B(39): -3.5, RF(4): -0.3	2.4
2016	NYA	MLB	24	90	7	3	0	5	12	7	36	1	0	.241/.300/.458	.261	1.4	.357	0.3	1B(27): 1.9, RF(3): 0.0	0.3
2017	SWB	AAA	25	190	29	14	1	10	32	18	52	0	0	.275/.342/.544	.286	5.7	.336	-2.1	1B(23): 0.6, RF(4): 0.4	0.6
2017	NYA	MLB	25	46	4	2	0	2	8	4	17	0	0	.225/.283/.425	.267	0.4	.304	-0.5	1B(8): 0.0, RF(7): -0.5	0.0
2018	*NYA*	*MLB*	*26*	*98*	*13*	*4*	*0*	*4*	*13*	*10*	*30*	*1*	*0*	*.238/.319/.438*	*.262*	*2.0*	*.308*	*-0.1*	*1B 0*	*0.1*
2019	*NYA*	*MLB*	*27*	*285*	*38*	*13*	*1*	*12*	*39*	*30*	*88*	*2*	*1*	*.234/.320/.441*	*.257*	*3.4*	*.304*	*-0.3*	*1B 0*	*0.4*

Breakout: 3% Improve: 21% Collapse: 13% Attrition: 35% MLB: 64% *Comparables: Mat Gamel, Brandon Allen, Tommy Medica*

First base seemed to be cursed for the Yankees in 2017. Any player who dared to don pinstripes and set foot near the position or even have his name mentioned as a possible backup was doomed. Greg Bird was out for an extended period of time, and Austin suffered a very similar injury, fracturing his left ankle on a foul tip during spring training, which put him on the shelf until June. Then after playing in four games he injured his right hamstring and was out again until August. It was a lost season for Austin, who was hoping to build on his 2016 and become a mainstay. Now he's looking up at Bird on the depth chart.

Greg Bird 1B Born: 11/09/92 Age: 25 Bats: L Throws: R Height: 6'4" Weight: 220 Origin: Round 5, 2011 Draft (#179 overall)

YEAR	TEAM	LVL	AGE	PA	R	2B	3B	HR	RBI	BB	K	SB	CS	AVG/OBP/SLG	TAv	VORP	BABIP	BRR	FRAA	WARP
2015	TRN	AA	22	212	29	16	0	6	29	24	30	1	1	.258/.358/.445	.302	12.4	.279	1.2	1B(41): 2.1	1.6
2015	SWB	AAA	22	150	15	7	1	6	23	11	27	0	0	.301/.353/.500	.304	7.1	.333	-1.3	1B(29): 0.3	0.7
2015	NYA	MLB	22	178	26	9	0	11	31	19	53	0	0	.261/.343/.529	.312	9.3	.319	-1.4	1B(46): 0.9	1.1
2017	SWB	AAA	24	59	12	4	0	3	7	11	9	0	0	.298/.424/.574	.334	4.6	.306	-1.0	1B(10): 0.9	0.5
2017	NYA	MLB	24	170	20	7	0	9	28	19	42	0	0	.190/.288/.422	.261	1.2	.194	-1.0	1B(46): -1.1	0.0
2018	*NYA*	*MLB*	*25*	*577*	*77*	*27*	*1*	*28*	*88*	*61*	*138*	*0*	*0*	*.246/.332/.468*	*.276*	*17.8*	*.280*	*-1.3*	*1B 0*	*1.6*
2019	*NYA*	*MLB*	*26*	*431*	*64*	*21*	*0*	*24*	*68*	*46*	*105*	*0*	*0*	*.251/.338/.494*	*.277*	*11.6*	*.283*	*-1.8*	*1B 0*	*1.3*

Breakout: 4% Improve: 54% Collapse: 4% Attrition: 15% MLB: 93% *Comparables: Brandon Belt, Tommy Joseph, Justin Morneau*

Greg Bird swinging in the dead of night, take these broken wings and learn to fly. Or in this case, broken ankle. Poor Bird: After missing all of 2016 with a shoulder injury he had a great spring training before hurting his ankle on the last day in Tampa. He had a dreadful first few weeks of the season and eventually went on the disabled list in May, undergoing surgery in July. After fears that he was lost for the season, Bird returned to the team in late August for the stretch run and quickly earned manager Joe Girardi's confidence. All your life you were only waiting for the moment to arise. Maybe it finally will in 2018.

Jacoby Ellsbury CF Born: 09/11/83 Age: 34 Bats: L Throws: L Height: 6'1" Weight: 195 Origin: Round 1, 2005 Draft (#23 overall)

YEAR	TEAM	LVL	AGE	PA	R	2B	3B	HR	RBI	BB	K	SB	CS	AVG/OBP/SLG	TAv	VORP	BABIP	BRR	FRAA	WARP
2015	NYA	MLB	31	501	66	15	2	7	33	35	86	21	9	.257/.318/.345	.249	13.3	.301	4.2	CF(110): -7.9	0.6
2016	NYA	MLB	32	626	71	24	5	9	56	54	84	20	8	.263/.330/.374	.246	12.3	.295	2.3	CF(148): -14.5	-0.2
2017	NYA	MLB	33	409	65	20	4	7	39	41	63	22	3	.264/.348/.402	.266	16.4	.304	1.4	CF(97): -5.8	1.1
2018	*NYA*	*MLB*	*34*	*181*	*24*	*7*	*1*	*3*	*16*	*15*	*29*	*7*	*2*	*.258/.322/.373*	*.246*	*4.8*	*.294*	*0.8*	*CF -2, LF 0*	*0.1*
2019	*NYA*	*MLB*	*35*	*179*	*21*	*7*	*1*	*4*	*18*	*16*	*30*	*7*	*2*	*.249/.319/.374*	*.240*	*2.2*	*.283*	*1.0*	*CF -2, LF 0*	*0.0*

Breakout: 1% Improve: 33% Collapse: 8% Attrition: 18% MLB: 86% *Comparables: Mike Kingery, Angel Pagan, Darryl Hamilton*

Although Ellsbury's star lost its luster many years ago, he enjoyed a small resurgence in 2017. The fact that a .266 TAv qualifies as a resurgence reminds us how far he has fallen, not that the Yankees—who are still paying him at levels appropriate to a 2011-2014 performance he seldom achieves these days even in short bursts—need reminding. He suffered a concussion and a sprained neck in late May after crashing into the wall at Yankee Stadium while making a catch. That collision seemed to affect Ellsbury for a long time, and he was relegated to the bench. Once the effects wore off he was useful for the Yankees during their second-half push toward the playoffs, with a .293/.384/.467 line over the final two months making his overall numbers look somewhat respectable in a "better than the last two years" kind of way. Ellsbury still doesn't hit for power (.392 SLG since 2012), but he'll get on base and steal one from time to time.

Estevan Florial OF Born: 11/25/97 Age: 20 Bats: L Throws: R Height: 6'1" Weight: 185 Origin: International Free Agent, 2015

YEAR	TEAM	LVL	AGE	PA	R	2B	3B	HR	RBI	BB	K	SB	CS	AVG/OBP/SLG	TAv	VORP	BABIP	BRR	FRAA	WARP
2015	DYA	RK	17	266	51	11	8	7	53	30	61	15	5	.313/.394/.527	.323	29.2	.389	2.9	CF(38): 3.4, RF(10): -0.4	3.2
2016	PUL	RK	18	268	36	10	1	7	25	28	78	10	2	.225/.315/.364	.252	5.1	.305	0.0	CF(43): 0.1, LF(6): -0.8	0.4
2017	CSC	A	19	389	64	21	5	11	43	41	124	17	7	.297/.373/.483	.315	31.7	.431	-0.7	CF(62): -2.1, LF(13): 2.9	3.4
2017	TAM	A+	19	87	13	2	2	2	14	9	24	6	1	.303/.368/.461	.307	7.3	.404	0.7	CF(18): 0.4	0.8
2018	*NYA*	*MLB*	*20*	*250*	*28*	*8*	*1*	*9*	*30*	*21*	*92*	*5*	*2*	*.212/.278/.378*	*.223*	*-0.2*	*.307*	*0.3*	*CF 0, RF 0*	*0.0*
2019	*NYA*	*MLB*	*21*	*389*	*48*	*14*	*2*	*14*	*48*	*35*	*136*	*8*	*3*	*.226/.297/.404*	*.239*	*3.0*	*.320*	*0.8*	*CF 0, RF 0*	*0.3*

Breakout: 4% Improve: 14% Collapse: 0% Attrition: 5% MLB: 15% *Comparables: Lewis Brinson, Domingo Santana, Byron Buxton*

Called by some the prospect who made Blake Rutherford expendable, Florial had a breakout 2017 campaign between Charleston and Tampa at age 19. He oozes tools, including big-time power, and could have the bat to remain an impact player even if he eventually moves away from center field. Before any of that happens he'll have to conquer High-A, and his strikeout rate will be worth keeping an eye on as a barometer of his overall development. There's definite All-Star potential here, but the road may not be a smooth one.

Clint Frazier OF Born: 09/06/94 Age: 23 Bats: R Throws: R Height: 6'1" Weight: 190 Origin: Round 1, 2013 Draft (#5 overall)

YEAR	TEAM	LVL	AGE	PA	R	2B	3B	HR	RBI	BB	K	SB	CS	AVG/OBP/SLG	TAv	VORP	BABIP	BRR	FRAA	WARP
2015	LYN	A+	20	588	88	36	3	16	72	68	125	15	7	.285/.377/.465	.297	34.5	.348	-2.3	CF(93): -5.5, RF(35): 0.5	3.2
2016	AKR	AA	21	391	56	25	1	13	48	41	86	13	4	.276/.356/.469	.298	24.2	.331	1.4	RF(31): -0.5, LF(26): 2.1	2.9
2016	SWB	AAA	21	108	17	2	3	3	7	7	30	0	0	.228/.278/.396	.248	1.6	.294	0.8	LF(13): -0.7, RF(6): 1.5	0.2
2017	SWB	AAA	22	320	46	19	2	12	42	37	69	9	2	.256/.344/.473	.277	14.4	.291	1.8	LF(38): 1.2, RF(29): -1.3	1.4
2017	NYA	MLB	22	142	16	9	4	4	17	7	43	1	0	.231/.268/.448	.242	1.0	.307	0.8	LF(30): -3.0, RF(7): 0.4	-0.2
2018	*NYA*	*MLB*	*23*	*241*	*30*	*11*	*1*	*9*	*32*	*22*	*66*	*4*	*1*	*.236/.309/.428*	*.257*	*5.6*	*.293*	*0.2*	*RF -1, LF 0*	*0.3*
2019	*NYA*	*MLB*	*24*	*468*	*61*	*23*	*3*	*18*	*62*	*47*	*129*	*7*	*2*	*.239/.320/.440*	*.257*	*10.0*	*.298*	*0.4*	*RF -1, LF -1*	*0.9*

Breakout: 5% Improve: 21% Collapse: 9% Attrition: 18% MLB: 48% *Comparables: David Dahl, Michael Saunders, Chad Huffman*

On a hot July day in a game against Milwaukee, a young player with flaming red hair stepped to the plate with his team down 3-2 in the bottom of the ninth, and deposited a 1-0 fastball into the left field seats for a thrilling, walk-off win. He rounded the bases as the fans cheered, tossed his helmet in the air and was showered with Gatorade as he crossed the plate. That was Frazier's sixth game in the majors. Even though he didn't stay that hot and his season was interrupted by an oblique strain, Yankees fans got a glimpse of Frazier's quick, explosive bat and perhaps of their future.

Todd Frazier 3B Born: 02/12/86 Age: 32 Bats: R Throws: R Height: 6'3" Weight: 220 Origin: Round 1, 2007 Draft (#34 overall)

YEAR	TEAM	LVL	AGE	PA	R	2B	3B	HR	RBI	BB	K	SB	CS	AVG/OBP/SLG	TAv	VORP	BABIP	BRR	FRAA	WARP
2015	CIN	MLB	29	678	82	43	1	35	89	44	137	13	8	.255/.309/.498	.293	41.7	.271	-1.1	3B(155): 1.7	4.6
2016	CHA	MLB	30	666	89	21	0	40	98	64	163	15	5	.225/.302/.464	.266	27.2	.236	2.4	3B(149): -2.4, 1B(7): -1.1	2.4
2017	CHA	MLB	31	335	41	15	0	16	44	48	71	4	3	.207/.328/.432	.267	12.0	.214	-0.4	3B(67): 2.2, 1B(4): 0.5	1.5
2017	NYA	MLB	31	241	33	4	1	11	32	35	54	0	0	.222/.365/.423	.268	10.2	.244	0.2	3B(66): 1.0	1.1
2018	*NYA*	*MLB*	*32*	*559*	*75*	*22*	*1*	*28*	*82*	*54*	*127*	*10*	*4*	*.238/.321/.457*	*.262*	*19.8*	*.261*	*0.2*	*3B -1, 1B 0*	*2.1*
2019	*NYA*	*MLB*	*33*	*520*	*72*	*20*	*1*	*25*	*74*	*51*	*121*	*8*	*4*	*.235/.319/.446*	*.260*	*13.0*	*.261*	*0.4*	*3B -1, 1B 0*	*1.3*

Breakout: 3% Improve: 45% Collapse: 7% Attrition: 8% MLB: 98% *Comparables: Chase Headley, David Freese, Morgan Ensberg*

Being traded to New York changed his location but didn't improve Frazier's offense. He continued to hit home runs and not much else, just like he did in 2016. But hey, he wasn't the only one to do that in 2017. He also fit in immediately with his Yankees teammates and started a new rally cry thanks to an angry Mets fan who disapproved when Frazier hit a three-run home run at Citi Field during the Yankees-Rays series after Hurricane Irma struck Florida. The man in question gave him a thumbs down, and the thumbs down became Frazier's thing. Roger Ebert would have been so proud.

Brett Gardner LF Born: 08/24/83 Age: 34 Bats: L Throws: L Height: 5'11" Weight: 195 Origin: Round 3, 2005 Draft (#109 overall)

YEAR	TEAM	LVL	AGE	PA	R	2B	3B	HR	RBI	BB	K	SB	CS	AVG/OBP/SLG	TAv	VORP	BABIP	BRR	FRAA	WARP
2015	NYA	MLB	31	656	94	26	3	16	66	68	135	20	5	.259/.343/.399	.264	22.6	.312	4.7	LF(119): 0.7, CF(40): -2.2	2.3
2016	NYA	MLB	32	634	80	22	6	7	41	70	106	16	4	.261/.351/.362	.254	14.8	.310	5.2	LF(147): 14.3, CF(3): -0.1	3.0
2017	NYA	MLB	33	682	96	26	4	21	63	72	122	23	5	.264/.350/.428	.271	25.4	.300	1.4	LF(122): 12.6, CF(22): 0.2	3.8
2018	*NYA*	*MLB*	*34*	*649*	*86*	*24*	*5*	*13*	*61*	*64*	*131*	*19*	*5*	*.251/.328/.383*	*.251*	*19.1*	*.297*	*2.2*	*LF 8, CF -2*	*1.9*
2019	*NYA*	*MLB*	*35*	*518*	*62*	*19*	*4*	*12*	*55*	*55*	*112*	*13*	*4*	*.242/.330/.381*	*.245*	*7.4*	*.290*	*2.5*	*LF 7, CF -1*	*1.4*

Breakout: 0% Improve: 33% Collapse: 15% Attrition: 20% MLB: 90% *Comparables: Jose Cardenal, David Murphy, Shannon Stewart*

If you want an example of someone who benefited from the home-run spike of 2017, Gardner reached the 20 home-run plateau for the first time in his career at age 33. He also stole more bases in 2017 than he had in his previous four seasons and continued to grind out plate appearances (and his usual .350 on-base percentage) as one of the least likely hitters in baseball to swing at non-strikes. Gardner, who is now one of the grizzled old veterans on a Yankees squad filled with youth, helped lead the team into contention in a year that was supposed to be a rebuild.

Didi Gregorius SS Born: 02/18/90 Age: 28 Bats: L Throws: R Height: 6'3" Weight: 205 Origin: International Free Agent, 2007

YEAR	TEAM	LVL	AGE	PA	R	2B	3B	HR	RBI	BB	K	SB	CS	AVG/OBP/SLG	TAv	VORP	BABIP	BRR	FRAA	WARP
2015	NYA	MLB	25	578	57	24	2	9	56	33	85	5	3	.265/.318/.370	.251	18.8	.297	1.0	SS(155): 1.1	2.1
2016	NYA	MLB	26	597	68	32	2	20	70	19	82	7	1	.276/.304/.447	.257	26.8	.290	4.2	SS(153): -5.6	2.2
2017	NYA	MLB	27	570	73	27	0	25	87	25	70	3	1	.287/.318/.478	.282	39.0	.287	1.9	SS(135): 4.9	4.4
2018	*NYA*	*MLB*	*28*	*636*	*71*	*27*	*3*	*18*	*77*	*38*	*94*	*5*	*2*	*.262/.311/.410*	*.253*	*26.7*	*.282*	*-0.3*	*SS 1*	*1.7*
2019	*NYA*	*MLB*	*29*	*556*	*69*	*25*	*2*	*18*	*68*	*38*	*85*	*4*	*1*	*.264/.322/.424*	*.254*	*16.9*	*.283*	*1.8*	*SS 1*	*1.9*

Breakout: 0% Improve: 45% Collapse: 6% Attrition: 7% MLB: 98% *Comparables: Brandon Crawford, Yuniesky Betancourt, Erick Aybar*

Gregorius hit his prime in 2017 and he did so in a big way, breaking Derek Jeter's record for the most home runs by a Yankees shortstop in a single season and spending much of the year batting cleanup in the league's most powerful lineup. The fourth spot may not be his home often in the future, but general manager Brian Cashman snagging Gregorius for Shane Greene was an underrated key to the Yankees' quicker-than-expected turnaround. Gregorius has cut down on his strikeouts while remaining aggressive at the plate, stepping into Jeter's massive shoes and making a name for himself as a fan favorite as well.

Aaron Hicks CF Born: 10/02/89 Age: 28 Bats: B Throws: R Height: 6'1" Weight: 202 Origin: Round 1, 2008 Draft (#14 overall)

YEAR	TEAM	LVL	AGE	PA	R	2B	3B	HR	RBI	BB	K	SB	CS	AVG/OBP/SLG	TAv	VORP	BABIP	BRR	FRAA	WARP
2015	ROC	AAA	25	168	26	13	4	3	20	17	30	2	1	.342/.405/.544	.344	20.3	.407	1.4	CF(24): 4.9, RF(9): -0.1	2.5
2015	MIN	MLB	25	390	48	11	3	11	33	34	66	13	3	.256/.323/.398	.253	7.4	.285	-0.9	CF(88): 6.5, RF(16): -0.8	1.5
2016	NYA	MLB	26	361	32	13	1	8	31	30	68	3	4	.217/.281/.336	.220	-6.8	.248	0.3	RF(86): -0.7, LF(25): 2.7	-0.3
2017	NYA	MLB	27	361	54	18	0	15	52	51	67	10	5	.266/.372/.475	.286	22.1	.290	2.0	CF(52): -0.7, LF(22): -1.3	1.8
2018	*NYA*	*MLB*	*28*	*451*	*56*	*18*	*2*	*12*	*49*	*49*	*96*	*9*	*5*	*.236/.320/.386*	*.250*	*12.8*	*.278*	*-0.1*	*CF 4*	*1.2*
2019	*NYA*	*MLB*	*29*	*393*	*50*	*16*	*2*	*12*	*46*	*46*	*87*	*7*	*4*	*.234/.326/.401*	*.249*	*7.7*	*.275*	*0.5*	*CF 4*	*1.2*

Breakout: 0% Improve: 45% Collapse: 7% Attrition: 16% MLB: 90% *Comparables: David DeJesus, Desmond Jennings, Leonys Martin*

Hicks had a strange age-27 season, putting together a strong first half and then mostly disappearing in the wake of injuries after the break, only to jump past Jacoby Ellsbury as manager Joe Girardi's preferred center fielder down the stretch. Stealing Hicks from Minnesota for John Ryan Murphy is a huge Brian Cashman victory, and if Hicks repeats his 2017 production while remaining healthy, the deal could look even better for the Yankees. Hicks is only a few years removed from being a top 101 prospect, and an improved approach at the plate has allowed his hit tool to play up without sacrificing the power and patience he always showed with the Twins.

Kyle Higashioka C Born: 04/20/90 Age: 28 Bats: R Throws: R Height: 6'1" Weight: 200 Origin: Round 7, 2008 Draft (#230 overall)

YEAR	TEAM	LVL	AGE	PA	R	2B	3B	HR	RBI	BB	K	SB	CS	AVG/OBP/SLG	TAv	VORP	BABIP	BRR	FRAA	WARP
2015	TAM	A+	25	331	25	18	2	5	36	22	49	0	0	.254/.305/.375	.262	11.3	.287	-3.5	C(88): -3.1	0.9
2016	TRN	AA	26	256	31	15	0	11	51	26	42	0	1	.293/.355/.509	.313	22.4	.305	-2.0	C(61): 12.2	3.7
2016	SWB	AAA	26	160	24	9	0	10	30	12	31	0	1	.250/.306/.514	.275	7.3	.252	-1.9	C(36): 4.3	1.2
2017	NYA	MLB	27	20	2	0	0	0	0	2	6	0	0	.000/.100/.000	.142	-1.6	.000	-0.1	C(8): 0.7	-0.1
2017	SWB	AAA	27	57	5	4	0	2	11	4	7	0	0	.264/.316/.453	.255	2.2	.273	-0.2	C(14): 4.6	0.7
2018	*NYA*	*MLB*	*28*	*60*	*8*	*3*	*0*	*3*	*8*	*5*	*13*	*0*	*0*	*.238/.296/.441*	*.251*	*2.4*	*.263*	*-0.1*	*C 1*	*0.2*
2019	*NYA*	*MLB*	*29*	*229*	*31*	*11*	*0*	*11*	*33*	*19*	*52*	*0*	*0*	*.240/.305/.449*	*.251*	*6.2*	*.266*	*-0.6*	*C 2*	*0.9*

Breakout: 2% Improve: 9% Collapse: 12% Attrition: 23% MLB: 38% *Comparables: Jeremy Brown, Johnny Monell, Hector Gimenez*

YEAR	TEAM	P. COUNT	FRM RUNS	BLK RUNS	THRW RUNS	TOT RUNS
2015	SWB	633	-0.2	0.0	0.0	-0.2
2017	NYA	813	0.8	0.0	0.0	0.7
2018	*NYA*	*2226*	*1.2*	*-0.2*	*-0.2*	*0.9*
2019	*NYA*	*8500*	*1.4*	*-0.2*	*-0.2*	*1.0*

Higashioka served as Austin Romine's backup when starter Gary Sanchez was injured at the beginning of the season. To say he didn't do much for the Yankees would be an understatement. Higgy went hitless in 20 plate appearances and didn't fare much better in the minors, making for a tough all-around season marred by injuries. He is too old to be a prospect and needs to stay healthy, but Higashioka has shown enough power in the minors to get at least a couple more looks as a backup catcher somewhere.

Matt Holliday DH Born: 01/15/80 Age: 38 Bats: R Throws: R Height: 6'4" Weight: 240 Origin: Round 7, 1998 Draft (#210 overall)

YEAR	TEAM	LVL	AGE	PA	R	2B	3B	HR	RBI	BB	K	SB	CS	AVG/OBP/SLG	TAv	VORP	BABIP	BRR	FRAA	WARP
2015	SLN	MLB	35	277	24	16	1	4	35	39	49	2	1	.279/.394/.410	.299	14.7	.335	-1.4	LF(64): -6.5	0.9
2016	SLN	MLB	36	426	48	20	1	20	62	35	71	0	0	.246/.322/.461	.279	15.4	.253	-1.1	LF(84): -5.6, 1B(10): 0.8	1.1
2017	TAM	A+	37	30	1	1	0	0	5	3	5	0	0	.240/.333/.280	.222	-0.9	.286	0.0	1B(1): 0.1	-0.1
2017	NYA	MLB	37	427	50	18	0	19	64	46	114	1	0	.231/.316/.432	.259	2.7	.273	-1.3	1B(8): 0.5	0.3
2018	*NYA*	*MLB*	*38*	*409*	*50*	*18*	*0*	*16*	*55*	*45*	*83*	*1*	*0*	*.249/.342/.436*	*.263*	*9.3*	*.281*	*-1.0*	*1B 2*	*1.2*
2019	*NYA*	*MLB*	*39*	*274*	*36*	*12*	*0*	*10*	*35*	*29*	*58*	*0*	*0*	*.240/.331/.417*	*.256*	*2.2*	*.274*	*-0.8*	*1B 1*	*0.4*

Breakout: 0% Improve: 14% Collapse: 17% Attrition: 24% MLB: 72% *Comparables: Hideki Matsui, Bobby Abreu, Johnny Damon*

Holliday's 2017 started off well. He was hitting and serving as a mentor to the young Yankees position players before being felled by a mysterious virus in June. After that, the veteran's season was a series of disabled list trips and awful plate appearances. Still, he mashed a few big home runs, including one off Red Sox closer Craig Kimbrel in July and another off Red Sox ace Chris Sale in August. Holliday's days as a star are over, and part-time first baseman/designated hitters often have a hard time finding gigs, but he could stick around for another season or two bashing left-handed pitching.

Aaron Judge RF Born: 04/26/92 Age: 26 Bats: R Throws: R Height: 6'7" Weight: 282 Origin: Round 1, 2013 Draft (#32 overall)

YEAR	TEAM	LVL	AGE	PA	R	2B	3B	HR	RBI	BB	K	SB	CS	AVG/OBP/SLG	TAv	VORP	BABIP	BRR	FRAA	WARP
2015	TRN	AA	23	280	36	16	3	12	44	24	70	1	0	.284/.350/.516	.316	23.0	.345	2.6	RF(52): 11.1	3.7
2015	SWB	AAA	23	260	27	10	0	8	28	29	74	6	2	.224/.308/.373	.247	0.8	.289	-0.2	RF(50): 8.8, CF(8): -0.4	0.9
2016	SWB	AAA	24	410	62	18	1	19	65	47	98	5	0	.270/.366/.489	.311	31.4	.319	2.8	RF(66): 19.6, LF(7): -0.7	5.1
2016	NYA	MLB	24	95	10	2	0	4	10	9	42	0	1	.179/.263/.345	.222	-2.5	.282	-0.5	RF(27): -3.2	-0.6
2017	NYA	MLB	25	678	128	24	3	52	114	127	208	9	4	.284/.422/.627	.339	68.5	.357	-0.1	RF(141): 4.4	7.3
2018	*NYA*	*MLB*	*26*	*625*	*107*	*22*	*2*	*37*	*96*	*86*	*194*	*6*	*2*	*.246/.356/.503*	*.294*	*38.0*	*.310*	*-0.5*	*RF 4*	*3.9*
2019	*NYA*	*MLB*	*27*	*620*	*101*	*23*	*1*	*39*	*105*	*91*	*189*	*6*	*2*	*.249/.365/.523*	*.293*	*35.0*	*.306*	*0.0*	*RF 5*	*4.3*

Breakout: 4% Improve: 48% Collapse: 9% Attrition: 9% MLB: 90% *Comparables: George Springer, Jabari Blash, Giancarlo Stanton*

All rise. This court is now in session. Today we are here to prove that Aaron James Judge, outfielder for the New York Yankees did, in fact, have an excellent season. In 2016, the knock on Judge was that although he hit the ball hard and far, he didn't do it often. If it wasn't a straight fastball over the plate, he'd look like Pedro Cerrano flailing away. In 2017, Judge still got fooled at times, leading the league in strikeouts and going through a deep second-half slump, but he also crushed and crushed often. Judge routinely blasted monster homers with relative ease and was far from a lumbering, all-or-nothing slugger, drawing tons of walks, making numerous impressive catches in right field and even contributing on the bases. When he went through the slump his attitude never changed. He continued to answer questions from the media without letting any frustrations he may have had show. And when he snapped out of that slump, he victimized baseballs again at a torrid pace, setting rookie records in home runs and walks while leading the American League in both categories. So while his many strikeouts were troubling, his selectivity at the plate should be celebrated. If there are no further statements, this court is now adjourned until next season.

Austin Romine C Born: 11/22/88 Age: 29 Bats: R Throws: R Height: 6'1" Weight: 220 Origin: Round 2, 2007 Draft (#94 overall)

YEAR	TEAM	LVL	AGE	PA	R	2B	3B	HR	RBI	BB	K	SB	CS	AVG/OBP/SLG	TAv	VORP	BABIP	BRR	FRAA	WARP
2015	SWB	AAA	26	366	38	19	0	7	49	22	53	0	1	.260/.311/.379	.254	13.2	.289	1.3	C(75): 5.3, 1B(10): -0.7	1.8
2015	NYA	MLB	26	2	0	0	0	0	0	0	0	0	0	.000/.000/.000	.020	-0.4	.000	0.0	1B(1): 0.2	0.0
2016	NYA	MLB	27	176	17	11	0	4	26	7	31	1	0	.242/.269/.382	.217	-0.6	.271	-0.1	C(50): -3.1, 1B(6): -0.2	-0.4
2017	NYA	MLB	28	252	19	9	1	2	21	16	57	0	0	.218/.272/.293	.208	-4.8	.277	-1.8	C(67): 2.4, 1B(12): 0.7	-0.2
2018	*NYA*	*MLB*	*29*	*129*	*13*	*6*	*0*	*3*	*13*	*8*	*28*	*0*	*0*	*.231/.279/.355*	*.223*	*1.1*	*.273*	*-0.3*	*C 0*	*-0.1*
2019	*NYA*	*MLB*	*30*	*239*	*26*	*10*	*0*	*6*	*25*	*15*	*55*	*0*	*0*	*.223/.274/.360*	*.219*	*-1.8*	*.263*	*-0.8*	*C 0*	*-0.2*

Breakout: 2% Improve: 25% Collapse: 16% Attrition: 31% MLB: 67%

Comparables: Omir Santos, Craig Tatum, Bryan Holaday

YEAR	TEAM	P. COUNT	FRM RUNS	BLK RUNS	THRW RUNS	TOT RUNS
2015	SWB	10657	7.2	-0.1	-0.3	6.8
2016	NYA	5754	-1.8	-0.1	-0.5	-2.4
2017	NYA	8705	4.1	-0.3	-1.2	2.6
2018	*NYA*	*4893*	*0.8*	*-0.2*	*-0.6*	*0.0*
2019	*NYA*	*9059*	*1.1*	*-0.3*	*-0.8*	*0.0*

Thanks to an injury in early April that kept Gary Sanchez out for close to a month, Romine started 17 games behind the plate and hit .314 with two home runs. After that, he served as the backup and was used sparingly. In the second half, Romine's crowning achievement wasn't a hit or nailing a runner at second base or even being a part of a close play at home, though it did take place around home plate. It was standing up to Miguel Cabrera on a crazy day at Comerica Field when the Yankees and Tigers got into three separate skirmishes.

Gary Sanchez C Born: 12/02/92 Age: 25 Bats: R Throws: R Height: 6'2" Weight: 230 Origin: International Free Agent, 2009

YEAR	TEAM	LVL	AGE	PA	R	2B	3B	HR	RBI	BB	K	SB	CS	AVG/OBP/SLG	TAv	VORP	BABIP	BRR	FRAA	WARP
2015	TRN	AA	22	254	33	14	0	12	36	18	50	6	0	.262/.319/.476	.297	19.2	.285	-0.6	C(54): 4.3	2.5
2015	SWB	AAA	22	146	17	9	0	6	26	11	28	1	2	.295/.349/.500	.292	10.3	.330	-0.2	C(29): 2.5	1.3
2015	NYA	MLB	22	2	0	0	0	0	0	0	1	0	0	.000/.000/.000	.033	-0.4	.000	0.0		0.0
2016	SWB	AAA	23	313	39	21	1	10	50	21	45	7	1	.282/.339/.468	.299	25.1	.302	-0.9	C(64): 10.8	3.7
2016	NYA	MLB	23	229	34	12	0	20	42	24	57	1	0	.299/.376/.657	.332	23.5	.317	-1.2	C(36): 2.0	2.6
2017	NYA	MLB	24	525	79	20	0	33	90	40	120	2	1	.278/.345/.531	.297	44.8	.304	2.3	C(104): 1.8, 1B(2): 0.0	4.7
2018	*NYA*	*MLB*	*25*	*580*	*86*	*27*	*1*	*35*	*99*	*46*	*132*	*4*	*1*	*.269/.334/.521*	*.292*	*47.3*	*.296*	*-0.8*	*C 4*	*4.4*
2019	*NYA*	*MLB*	*26*	*552*	*87*	*27*	*0*	*35*	*97*	*47*	*125*	*3*	*1*	*.276/.346/.543*	*.293*	*40.7*	*.300*	*0.5*	*C 4*	*4.9*

Breakout: 2% Improve: 53% Collapse: 4% Attrition: 7% MLB: 98%

Comparables: Paul Goldschmidt, Justin Morneau, Brandon Belt

YEAR	TEAM	P. COUNT	FRM RUNS	BLK RUNS	THRW RUNS	TOT RUNS
2015	SWB	3954	2.7	0.1	0.1	2.8
2015	TRN	7918	2.8	0.4	1.2	4.4
2016	NYA	5290	1.6	-1.4	1.2	1.4
2017	NYA	14363	3.5	-2.6	2.2	3.0
2018	*NYA*	*17025*	*4.5*	*-1.9*	*2.1*	*4.7*
2019	*NYA*	*16213*	*4.0*	*-1.7*	*1.8*	*4.1*

Complaints about Sanchez's defense—and more specifically his blocking, since his framing is perfectly fine—too often overshadow what has been phenomenal offensive production for a young catcher. After missing the first month of last season with an injury, Sanchez released The Kraken on his way to leading major-league catchers in homers. For many teams Sanchez would be *the* player around which they build for years to come, and the fact that he's merely one of several promising young sluggers in New York speaks more to the Yankees' bright future than to any blemishes on his résumé. He has MVP-caliber upside and is already better than most people seem to think. Sanchez's 53 homers through 177 career games are the fourth most in baseball history behind only Rudy York, Mark McGwire and teammate Aaron Judge.

Giancarlo Stanton RF Born: 11/08/89 Age: 28 Bats: R Throws: R Height: 6'6" Weight: 245 Origin: Round 2, 2007 Draft (#76 overall)

YEAR	TEAM	LVL	AGE	PA	R	2B	3B	HR	RBI	BB	K	SB	CS	AVG/OBP/SLG	TAv	VORP	BABIP	BRR	FRAA	WARP
2015	MIA	MLB	25	318	47	12	1	27	67	34	95	4	2	.265/.346/.606	.353	34.8	.294	0.5	RF(71): 7.9	4.6
2016	MIA	MLB	26	470	56	20	1	27	74	50	140	0	0	.240/.326/.489	.307	31.2	.290	0.4	RF(106): 2.4	3.5
2017	MIA	MLB	27	692	123	32	0	59	132	85	163	2	2	.281/.376/.631	.348	76.7	.288	-0.1	RF(149): 8.4	8.5
2018	*NYA*	*MLB*	*28*	*581*	*95*	*24*	*1*	*41*	*109*	*73*	*160*	*3*	*1*	*.258/.357/.551*	*.307*	*42.2*	*.293*	*-1.1*	*RF 1, LF 0*	*3.9*
2019	*NYA*	*MLB*	*29*	*555*	*94*	*23*	*0*	*39*	*102*	*74*	*153*	*2*	*1*	*.256/.361/.553*	*.299*	*37.3*	*.290*	*0.2*	*RF 1, LF 0*	*4.2*

Breakout: 1% Improve: 47% Collapse: 1% Attrition: 4% MLB: 100%

Comparables: Ralph Kiner, Jose Canseco, Darryl Strawberry

For nearly a decade, the entire baseball universe was left to speculate upon the stratospheric heights Stanton could reach, if he could just stay healthy for an entire season. We finally got the long-awaited answer when Stanton avoided significant injury and played a career-high 159 games in 2017. He led the major leagues in slugging percentage, home runs and RBI en route to being crowned the National League's Most Valuable Player. After becoming the first hitter to threaten Roger Maris (or Barry Bonds) in the Statcast Era, what do you do for an encore? When you reach the top, there is no more upside, just fluctuation.

With 10 years and $295 million remaining on his contract, Stanton stands on the precipice of historical greatness. Only seven hitters have racked up more home runs than Stanton's 267 through his age-27 season: Alex Rodriguez, Jimmie Foxx, Eddie Mathews, Ken Griffey Jr., Albert Pujols, Mickey Mantle and Mel Ott. There is no metric to quantify the rare, unexplainable magnetism that a truly transcendent athlete like Stanton possesses. His otherworldly physical strength forces us to constantly question the limits of human performance. With every violent swing, there is a chance that we will witness something that has never happened before. Is this the moment when the unthinkable become a reality? That unpredictability is what turns greatness into lore, although in hindsight we probably should have seen his trade to the Yankees coming.

Gleyber Torres SS Born: 12/13/96 Age: 21 Bats: R Throws: R Height: 6'1" Weight: 175 Origin: International Free Agent, 2013

YEAR	TEAM	LVL	AGE	PA	R	2B	3B	HR	RBI	BB	K	SB	CS	AVG/OBP/SLG	TAv	VORP	BABIP	BRR	FRAA	WARP
2015	SBN	A	18	514	53	24	5	3	62	43	108	22	13	.293/.353/.386	.266	22.1	.373	-2.0	SS(119): -9.5	1.3
2016	MYR	A+	19	409	62	23	3	9	47	42	87	19	10	.275/.359/.433	.282	26.1	.341	0.2	SS(87): 0.6	2.7
2016	TAM	A+	19	138	19	6	2	2	19	16	23	2	3	.254/.341/.385	.279	5.2	.299	-2.9	SS(27): -0.9, 2B(1): 0.0	0.4
2017	TRN	AA	20	139	22	10	1	5	18	17	21	5	4	.273/.367/.496	.326	15.5	.295	1.3	SS(19): 2.2, 3B(6): 0.8	2.0
2017	SWB	AAA	20	96	9	4	1	2	16	13	26	2	2	.309/.406/.457	.309	7.1	.426	-1.8	3B(9): 1.8, SS(9): 1.0	0.9
2018	*NYA*	*MLB*	*21*	*445*	*54*	*18*	*2*	*12*	*48*	*37*	*121*	*9*	*6*	*.233/.299/.381*	*.240*	*7.6*	*.299*	*-0.7*	*2B -3, 3B 0*	*0.2*
2019	*NYA*	*MLB*	*22*	*492*	*61*	*22*	*2*	*17*	*60*	*46*	*133*	*10*	*7*	*.241/.317/.414*	*.249*	*9.6*	*.305*	*-0.2*	*2B -3, 3B 0*	*0.8*

Breakout: 5% Improve: 9% Collapse: 1% Attrition: 12% MLB: 24% *Comparables: Nick Franklin, Franklin Barreto, Eugenio Suarez*

During their horrendous June, things got even worse for the Yankees at Triple-A when Torres injured his left elbow on a play at the plate. What was first thought to be a hyperextension turned into a torn ulnar collateral ligament, and he was lost for the season after undergoing Tommy John surgery. Torres performed well at both Double-A Trenton and Triple-A Scranton before he was hurt, and it looked like he could be called up to the big club at some point (there was talk before the season that he might make the Opening Day roster). The injury was to his non-throwing elbow and he should be ready for spring training, potentially with a chance to snag an Opening Day job.

Ronald Torreyes INF Born: 09/02/92 Age: 25 Bats: R Throws: R Height: 5'8" Weight: 151 Origin: International Free Agent, 2010

YEAR	TEAM	LVL	AGE	PA	R	2B	3B	HR	RBI	BB	K	SB	CS	AVG/OBP/SLG	TAv	VORP	BABIP	BRR	FRAA	WARP
2015	FRE	AAA	22	72	7	1	0	0	5	1	9	0	1	.200/.211/.214	.157	-6.4	.230	-0.7	2B(13): -1.2, SS(5): -0.5	-0.8
2015	NHP	AA	22	54	4	2	0	0	9	4	2	2	0	.140/.204/.180	.134	-5.6	.146	-0.1	2B(14): -0.7, SS(1): 0.0	-0.7
2015	TUL	AA	22	274	39	13	2	4	19	20	23	3	3	.293/.348/.410	.289	19.7	.308	1.6	SS(48): 0.4, 2B(7): -0.9	2.0
2015	OKL	AAA	22	53	10	2	1	0	3	2	4	0	0	.306/.340/.388	.281	2.8	.326	-0.1	2B(7): -0.7, SS(5): 1.4	0.4
2015	LAN	MLB	22	8	1	1	0	0	1	1	1	0	0	.333/.429/.500	.328	0.8	.400	0.0	2B(4): 0.2, 3B(3): 0.0	0.1
2016	NYA	MLB	23	168	20	7	4	1	12	10	20	2	1	.258/.305/.374	.249	4.6	.289	0.9	3B(34): 4.3, SS(15): -1.2	0.7
2017	NYA	MLB	24	336	35	15	1	3	36	11	43	2	0	.292/.314/.375	.240	5.3	.326	1.3	2B(54): 0.8, SS(36): 0.5	0.9
2018	*NYA*	*MLB*	*25*	*274*	*28*	*12*	*2*	*4*	*27*	*14*	*36*	*2*	*1*	*.265/.302/.379*	*.240*	*5.9*	*.289*	*-0.1*	*2B -1, 3B 2*	*0.3*
2019	*NYA*	*MLB*	*26*	*352*	*40*	*16*	*2*	*7*	*38*	*21*	*49*	*2*	*1*	*.270/.317/.401*	*.245*	*5.9*	*.293*	*0.8*	*2B -1, 3B 2*	*0.7*

Breakout: 5% Improve: 50% Collapse: 9% Attrition: 26% MLB: 94% *Comparables: Steve Lombardozzi, Alexi Casilla, Aaron Hill*

Torreyes, or Toe as his teammates call him, was the smallest guy on the team but came up big several times in 2017. While Didi Gregorius missed most of April with a shoulder injury, Toe batted .313 (albeit an empty .313) in his place. He also filled in at other spots around the infield and became part of Aaron Judge's home-run celebration, when Gregorius would pick him up and place him on his shoulder so he could high-five the much taller slugger. He's never going to be a full-time player, but Torreyes is one of those guys you like having around because every once in a while he'll find a way to help your team win or at least give someone a high-five.

Tyler Wade MI Born: 11/23/94 Age: 23 Bats: L Throws: R Height: 6'1" Weight: 185 Origin: Round 4, 2013 Draft (#134 overall)

YEAR	TEAM	LVL	AGE	PA	R	2B	3B	HR	RBI	BB	K	SB	CS	AVG/OBP/SLG	TAv	VORP	BABIP	BRR	FRAA	WARP
2015	TAM	A+	20	418	51	11	5	2	28	39	65	31	15	.280/.349/.353	.274	23.1	.331	2.3	SS(72): 5.4, 2B(24): -0.9	3.0
2015	TRN	AA	20	117	6	4	0	1	3	2	24	2	1	.204/.224/.265	.198	-2.6	.250	0.3	SS(28): -1.3	-0.4
2016	TRN	AA	21	583	90	16	7	5	27	66	103	27	8	.259/.352/.349	.271	37.6	.317	11.0	SS(91): -5.6, 2B(38): 0.0	3.5
2017	SWB	AAA	22	388	68	22	4	7	31	38	75	26	5	.310/.382/.460	.288	30.3	.375	3.0	SS(54): -2.3, 2B(13): 2.8	3.4
2017	NYA	MLB	22	63	7	4	0	0	2	5	19	1	1	.155/.222/.224	.173	-3.3	.231	0.7	2B(15): -0.8, SS(7): 0.0	-0.5
2018	*NYA*	*MLB*	*23*	*96*	*12*	*3*	*1*	*2*	*10*	*9*	*22*	*4*	*1*	*.240/.311/.370*	*.241*	*2.3*	*.296*	*0.4*	*2B 0*	*0.1*
2019	*NYA*	*MLB*	*24*	*308*	*37*	*11*	*2*	*8*	*34*	*29*	*74*	*12*	*4*	*.240/.316/.383*	*.240*	*4.9*	*.295*	*1.4*	*2B -1*	*0.5*

Breakout: 5% Improve: 30% Collapse: 6% Attrition: 21% MLB: 49% *Comparables: Chris Taylor, Greg Garcia, Yamaico Navarro*

Wade spent most of the season at Triple-A learning how to play a bunch of positions. The idea was to turn him into a Ben Zobrist type who can play anywhere in a pinch. When Wade came up to the majors, he didn't hit a lot, but he was much more impressive at the plate for Scranton. It's easy to project Wade as a utility man, but he has enough upside to make that the fallback plan rather than the ceiling.

PITCHERS

Albert Abreu RHP Born: 09/26/95 Age: 22 Bats: R Throws: R Height: 6'2" Weight: 175 Origin: International Free Agent, 2013

YEAR	TEAM	LVL	AGE	W	L	SV	G	GS	IP	H	HR	BB/9	K/9	K	GB%	BABIP	WHIP	ERA	DRA	WARP	MPH	CMD	PWR	STM
2015	GRV	RK	19	2	3	1	13	7	46^{2}	35	2	4.1	9.8	51	46%	.282	1.20	2.51	2.86	1.4				
2016	QUD	A	20	2	8	4	21	14	90	62	5	4.9	10.4	104	49%	.264	1.23	3.50	3.44	1.6				
2016	LNC	A+	20	1	0	0	3	2	11^{2}	12	2	6.9	8.5	11	41%	.312	1.80	5.40	5.74	0.0				
2017	CSC	A	21	1	0	0	3	2	14^{2}	9	1	1.8	13.5	22	61%	.296	0.82	1.84	2.54	0.5				
2017	TAM	A+	21	1	3	0	9	9	34^{1}	33	2	3.9	8.1	31	48%	.316	1.40	4.19	4.17	0.4				
2018	*NYA*	*MLB*	*22*	*3*	*3*	*0*	*19*	*9*	*50^{1}*	*46*	*10*	*5.4*	*10.1*	*56*	*41%*	*.290*	*1.52*	*5.42*	*5.65*	*-0.1*				
2019	*NYA*	*MLB*	*23*	*4*	*7*	*0*	*26*	*18*	*134^{2}*	*136*	*28*	*5.5*	*10.4*	*155*	*41%*	*.31*	*1.62*	*5.78*	*6.04*	*-0.5*				

Breakout: 4% Improve: 5% Collapse: 4% Attrition: 6% MLB: 8% *Comparables: Juan Jaime, Duane Below, Charlie Furbush*

Abreu, the big get in the Brian McCann deal, missed a large chunk of the season with a shoulder injury. He was out from early June until the end of August before coming back strong for Tampa. He improved his command, which had previously given him problems. A power pitcher, his fastball usually hangs around the mid-90s and he's been known to touch the high-90s. He also has a changeup, a slider and a curveball, the latter of which is his best secondary offering. Hopefully the shoulder injury won't be a nagging problem for the young right-hander, because few prospects can boast better raw stuff.

Chance Adams RHP Born: 08/10/94 Age: 23 Bats: R Throws: R Height: 6'1" Weight: 210 Origin: Round 5, 2015 Draft (#153 overall)

YEAR	TEAM	LVL	AGE	W	L	SV	G	GS	IP	H	HR	BB/9	K/9	K	GB%	BABIP	WHIP	ERA	DRA	WARP	MPH	CMD	PWR	STM
2015	CSC	A	20	1	1	0	5	0	11^2	7	0	3.1	12.3	16	64%	.250	0.94	3.09	2.39	0.3				
2015	TAM	A+	20	1	0	0	5	0	14	12	0	1.3	10.3	16	38%	.324	1.00	1.29	2.16	0.4				
2016	TAM	A+	21	5	0	0	12	12	57^2	41	4	2.3	11.4	73	42%	.276	0.97	2.65	1.43	2.7				
2016	TRN	AA	21	8	1	0	13	12	69^2	35	5	3.1	9.2	71	47%	.181	0.85	2.07	2.74	2.0				
2017	TRN	AA	22	4	0	0	6	6	35	23	2	3.9	8.2	32	43%	.228	1.09	1.03	4.54	0.3				
2017	SWB	AAA	22	11	5	0	21	21	115^1	81	9	3.4	8.0	103	42%	.236	1.08	2.89	3.33	3.0				
2018	*NYA*	*MLB*	*23*	*2*	*2*	*0*	*5*	*5*	*28*	*26*	*5*	*3.8*	*9.3*	*30*	*41%*	*.287*	*1.28*	*4.48*	*4.74*	*0.2*				
2019	*NYA*	*MLB*	*24*	*10*	*11*	*0*	*31*	*31*	*198^1*	*156*	*35*	*3.6*	*10.3*	*227*	*41%*	*.255*	*1.18*	*4.58*	*4.76*	*1.7*				

Breakout: 21% Improve: 41% Collapse: 24% Attrition: 36% MLB: 71% *Comparables: Carl Edwards Jr., Dylan Bundy, Zack Wheeler*

The Yankees took a chance on Adams and he's made his way through their system quickly. He's now the Yankees' top pitching prospect in a system overflowing with promising young arms. After Adams started the year 4-0 at Trenton, he earned a trip up to Scranton and had a strong showing in Triple-A as well. The short, stocky right-hander has a plus fastball and a good slider, and his results have been excellent every step along the way. He'll likely make his MLB debut this season and could slot into the middle of the rotation long term.

Dellin Betances RHP Born: 03/23/88 Age: 30 Bats: R Throws: R Height: 6'8" Weight: 265 Origin: Round 8, 2006 Draft (#254 overall)

YEAR	TEAM	LVL	AGE	W	L	SV	G	GS	IP	H	HR	BB/9	K/9	K	GB%	BABIP	WHIP	ERA	DRA	WARP	MPH	CMD	PWR	STM
2015	NYA	MLB	27	6	4	9	74	0	84	45	6	4.3	14.0	131	49%	.257	1.01	1.50	1.83	2.9	99.7	39	60	56
2016	NYA	MLB	28	3	6	12	73	0	73	54	5	3.5	15.5	126	56%	.353	1.12	3.08	1.79	2.7	100.8	45	51	53
2017	NYA	MLB	29	3	6	10	66	0	59^2	29	3	6.6	15.1	100	49%	.252	1.22	2.87	3.03	1.4	100.2	45	61	50
2018	*NYA*	*MLB*	*30*	*4*	*3*	*5*	*65*	*0*	*69*	*48*	*8*	*4.4*	*13.5*	*104*	*49%*	*.288*	*1.19*	*3.05*	*3.42*	*1.4*	*99.5*	*43*	*57*	*52*
2019	*NYA*	*MLB*	*31*	*3*	*1*	*2*	*56*	*0*	*59^1*	*44*	*9*	*3.6*	*13.3*	*87*	*49%*	*.285*	*1.14*	*3.71*	*3.79*	*0.9*	*99.2*	*44*	*56*	*51*

Breakout: 22% Improve: 38% Collapse: 32% Attrition: 14% MLB: 89% *Comparables: Greg Holland, Carlos Marmol, A.J. Ramos*

When Betances is on, he is a joy to watch and is one of the best relievers in baseball. He freezes batters with his devastating curveball, while his plus fastball produces feeble swings. But when Betances is off, any semblance of command vanishes. He'll hit batters, walk batters and look completely lost on the mound. It doesn't help that Betances is tall and lanky, so when his rhythm is out of sorts it's very noticeable. By the end of last season Joe Giardi had zero faith in Betances, who had previously filled in admirably at closer when Aroldis Chapman was injured. The talent is undeniable, but harnessing it for six months consistently is a challenge.

Luis Cessa RHP Born: 04/25/92 Age: 26 Bats: R Throws: R Height: 6'0" Weight: 205 Origin: International Free Agent, 2008

YEAR	TEAM	LVL	AGE	W	L	SV	G	GS	IP	H	HR	BB/9	K/9	K	GB%	BABIP	WHIP	ERA	DRA	WARP	MPH	CMD	PWR	STM
2015	BIN	AA	23	7	4	0	13	13	77^1	77	2	2.0	7.1	61	50%	.315	1.22	2.56	2.05	2.8				
2015	LVG	AAA	23	0	3	0	5	5	24^1	40	3	1.5	8.9	24	56%	.425	1.81	8.51	2.05	0.9				
2015	TOL	AAA	23	1	3	0	7	7	37^2	46	2	3.6	8.1	34	49%	.376	1.62	5.97	4.42	0.4				
2016	SWB	AAA	24	6	3	0	15	14	77^1	66	8	2.7	8.0	69	47%	.278	1.15	3.03	3.66	1.5				
2016	NYA	MLB	24	4	4	0	17	9	70^1	64	16	1.8	5.9	46	45%	.233	1.11	4.35	4.56	0.6	97.5	46	48	59
2017	SWB	AAA	25	4	6	0	14	13	78^1	75	7	3.0	7.7	67	48%	.304	1.29	3.45	4.18	1.3				
2017	NYA	MLB	25	0	3	0	10	5	36	36	7	4.2	7.5	30	46%	.282	1.47	4.75	5.07	0.1	97.8	43	49	59
2018	*NYA*	*MLB*	*26*	*4*	*3*	*0*	*31*	*8*	*67*	*67*	*11*	*3.4*	*8.0*	*60*	*46%*	*.294*	*1.39*	*4.62*	*4.76*	*0.4*	*97.2*	*46*	*49*	*60*
2019	*NYA*	*MLB*	*27*	*7*	*6*	*0*	*62*	*15*	*136*	*135*	*23*	*3.4*	*8.3*	*126*	*46%*	*.291*	*1.36*	*4.96*	*5.13*	*0.5*	*96.9*	*45*	*49*	*60*

Breakout: 17% Improve: 36% Collapse: 22% Attrition: 41% MLB: 69% *Comparables: Sean Gilmartin, Brad Lincoln, Kyle Lobstein*

Some of the problems that plagued Cessa in 2016 plagued him again in 2017. He has a penchant for surrendering the long ball, which is bad for someone who came out of the bullpen in half of his appearances. He moved into the starting rotation when CC Sabathia went on the disabled list with a hamstring strain and didn't step up. Later, when Masahiro Tanaka was injured, Cessa made two more starts and injured his back, ending the season with a dubious streak of 12 straight winless starts.

Aroldis Chapman LHP Born: 02/28/88 Age: 30 Bats: L Throws: L Height: 6'4" Weight: 212 Origin: International Free Agent, 2010

YEAR	TEAM	LVL	AGE	W	L	SV	G	GS	IP	H	HR	BB/9	K/9	K	GB%	BABIP	WHIP	ERA	DRA	WARP	MPH	CMD	PWR	STM
2015	CIN	MLB	27	4	4	33	65	0	66^1	43	3	4.5	15.7	116	38%	.331	1.15	1.63	1.93	2.2	103.0	47	92	50
2016	NYA	MLB	28	3	0	20	31	0	31^1	20	2	2.3	12.6	44	38%	.273	0.89	2.01	2.02	1.1	104.1	37	85	48
2016	CHN	MLB	28	1	1	16	28	0	26^2	12	0	3.4	15.5	46	59%	.261	0.82	1.01	2.16	0.9	104.2	37	85	48
2017	NYA	MLB	29	4	3	22	52	0	50^1	37	3	3.6	12.3	69	48%	.298	1.13	3.22	3.34	1.0	102.4	45	92	42
2018	*NYA*	*MLB*	*30*	*3*	*2*	*40*	*51*	*0*	*54*	*41*	*6*	*3.5*	*12.7*	*77*	*44%*	*.295*	*1.15*	*2.66*	*3.02*	*1.3*	*102.3*	*43*	*89*	*46*
2019	*NYA*	*MLB*	*31*	*3*	*1*	*41*	*53*	*0*	*55^2*	*46*	*9*	*4.0*	*12.6*	*78*	*44%*	*.297*	*1.26*	*4.05*	*4.16*	*0.7*	*101.9*	*42*	*88*	*45*

Breakout: 23% Improve: 37% Collapse: 32% Attrition: 9% MLB: 89% *Comparables: Greg Holland, Carlos Marmol, David Robertson*

Chapman still throws the hardest of anyone in baseball—in fact, there's a filter on Statcast you can use to remove him from the list so he doesn't take up the first 30 slots. One of those 30 pitches was hit out of the park by Red Sox rookie Rafael Devers on August 13 in what ended up being a Yankees loss, and six days later Chapman was removed from the closer role. It was as if someone was sent from the future and stole Chapman's mojo while he was sleeping. He looked completely lost and uncomfortable on the mound. Some thought that it was from overuse during the 2016 playoffs, but Chapman worked his way back into ninth-inning duties and looked like his old self in September. Maybe it was just a blip. The Yankees hope so: They have him for four more years.

Jaime Garcia LHP Born: 07/08/86 Age: 31 Bats: L Throws: L Height: 6'2" Weight: 215 Origin: Round 22, 2005 Draft (#680 overall)

YEAR	TEAM	LVL	AGE	W	L	SV	G	GS	IP	H	HR	BB/9	K/9	K	GB%	BABIP	WHIP	ERA	DRA	WARP	MPH	CMD	PWR	STM
2015	SLN	MLB	28	10	6	0	20	20	129^{2}	106	6	2.1	6.7	97	62%	.267	1.05	2.43	3.05	3.1	92.3	41	39	59
2016	SLN	MLB	29	10	13	0	32	30	171^{2}	179	26	3.0	7.9	150	58%	.305	1.37	4.67	4.89	0.9	93.1	44	44	71
2017	ATL	MLB	30	4	7	0	18	18	113	108	12	3.3	6.8	85	56%	.287	1.32	4.30	5.30	0.3	92.6	32	42	67
2017	MIN	MLB	30	1	0	0	1	1	6^{2}	8	0	4.1	9.4	7	47%	.421	1.65	4.05	5.38	0.0	92.5	32	42	67
2017	NYA	MLB	30	0	3	0	8	8	37^{1}	41	6	4.8	8.9	37	54%	.327	1.63	4.82	3.96	0.7	92.1	32	42	67
2018	*NYA*	*MLB*	*31*	*8*	*8*	*0*	*23*	*23*	*132^{1}*	*126*	*18*	*3.4*	*7.6*	*112*	*55%*	*.283*	*1.32*	*4.57*	*4.70*	*1.5*	*91.8*	*38*	*42*	*66*
2019	*NYA*	*MLB*	*32*	*9*	*10*	*0*	*26*	*26*	*156^{2}*	*153*	*22*	*3.3*	*7.6*	*133*	*55%*	*.289*	*1.35*	*4.71*	*4.85*	*1.4*	*91.5*	*37*	*42*	*67*

Breakout: 15% Improve: 55% Collapse: 20% Attrition: 12% MLB: 94% *Comparables: Wandy Rodriguez, Jon Lester, Francisco Liriano*

Garcia started the year with the Braves, made a pit stop in Minnesota for six days and finally landed in the Bronx, where he pitched 37 innings of not-so-great ball and failed to reach the sixth inning in any of his eight starts. Injuries and aging have put a dent in Garcia's raw stuff, but he's also been healthier and more durable in recent years. Now, as he moves into his thirties, he looks like a third or fourth starter whose success depends on lots of groundballs and the avoidance of trouble against right-handed sluggers.

Domingo German RHP Born: 08/04/92 Age: 25 Bats: R Throws: R Height: 6'2" Weight: 175 Origin: International Free Agent, 2009

YEAR	TEAM	LVL	AGE	W	L	SV	G	GS	IP	H	HR	BB/9	K/9	K	GB%	BABIP	WHIP	ERA	DRA	WARP	MPH	CMD	PWR	STM
2016	CSC	A	23	1	1	0	5	5	26	15	2	0.7	6.2	18	43%	.186	0.65	3.12	3.54	0.5				
2016	TAM	A+	23	0	2	0	5	5	23^{2}	26	1	3.4	7.6	20	45%	.342	1.48	3.04	4.31	0.3				
2017	TRN	AA	24	1	4	0	6	6	33	32	4	2.7	10.4	38	50%	.318	1.27	3.00	3.11	0.8				
2017	SWB	AAA	24	7	2	0	14	13	76^{1}	59	5	2.6	9.6	81	46%	.274	1.06	2.83	2.95	2.2				
2017	NYA	MLB	24	0	1	0	7	0	14^{1}	11	1	5.7	11.3	18	54%	.294	1.40	3.14	2.87	0.4	98.4	50	56	54
2018	*NYA*	*MLB*	*25*	*2*	*2*	*0*	*37*	*0*	*39*	*35*	*6*	*3.5*	*9.5*	*42*	*42%*	*.287*	*1.28*	*4.23*	*4.39*	*0.3*	*98.1*	*51*	*57*	*55*
2019	*NYA*	*MLB*	*26*	*2*	*1*	*0*	*47*	*0*	*49^{2}*	*45*	*7*	*4.3*	*8.7*	*48*	*42%*	*.281*	*1.39*	*4.92*	*5.11*	*0.1*	*97.8*	*51*	*58*	*56*

Breakout: 17% Improve: 41% Collapse: 17% Attrition: 35% MLB: 65% *Comparables: Alec Mills, Tim Cooney, Steven Brault*

German started the year in the minors and did a nice enough job that the Yankees called him up in June. He was primarily used in a mop-up role, but did pretty well when called upon to stop the bleeding. German has excellent raw stuff, maintaining mid-90s velocity deep into Triple-A starts, but often struggles to keep his mechanics fluid. Command has also been an issue since Tommy John surgery in 2015, perhaps sending him to the bullpen for a setup role eventually.

Sonny Gray RHP Born: 11/07/89 Age: 28 Bats: R Throws: R Height: 5'10" Weight: 190 Origin: Round 1, 2011 Draft (#18 overall)

YEAR	TEAM	LVL	AGE	W	L	SV	G	GS	IP	H	HR	BB/9	K/9	K	GB%	BABIP	WHIP	ERA	DRA	WARP	MPH	CMD	PWR	STM
2015	OAK	MLB	25	14	7	0	31	31	208	166	17	2.6	7.3	169	53%	.255	1.08	2.73	2.97	5.2	95.6	42	56	78
2016	OAK	MLB	26	5	11	0	22	22	117	133	18	3.2	7.2	94	54%	.319	1.50	5.69	4.11	1.7	95.1	55	52	49
2017	OAK	MLB	27	6	5	0	16	16	97	84	8	2.8	8.7	94	58%	.285	1.18	3.43	3.49	2.3	94.8	45	53	74
2017	NYA	MLB	27	4	7	0	11	11	65^{1}	55	11	3.7	8.1	59	48%	.246	1.26	3.72	2.95	1.9	94.6	45	53	74
2018	*NYA*	*MLB*	*28*	*13*	*8*	*0*	*29*	*29*	*174*	*166*	*24*	*3.3*	*8.0*	*155*	*52%*	*.287*	*1.30*	*4.16*	*4.38*	*2.0*	*94.5*	*47*	*54*	*67*
2019	*NYA*	*MLB*	*29*	*11*	*11*	*0*	*31*	*31*	*195^{2}*	*179*	*26*	*3.0*	*8.3*	*182*	*52%*	*.283*	*1.25*	*4.32*	*4.44*	*2.5*	*94.0*	*48*	*53*	*65*

Breakout: 20% Improve: 44% Collapse: 28% Attrition: 12% MLB: 96% *Comparables: Alex Cobb, Johnny Cueto, Alexi Ogando*

In the movie *San Andreas*, The Rock hovers his helicopter over a building that's about to collapse after a major earthquake has struck Los Angeles. On top of the building is his ex-wife, who has somehow survived calamity after calamity. Of course, he's not only able to see her on top of the building but he's also able to save her. She eventually gets into the helicopter with him, a little worse for the wear but alive. She's Sonny Gray, the A's were the collapsing building and the Yankees were The Rock. The Yankees swooped in and rescued Gray from wasting away in Oakland, thrust him into a playoff race and he thrived. He pitched in 2017 more like he did in 2015, and most importantly he stayed healthy. With Gray and Luis Severino, the Yankees have the front end of their rotation locked up for a while.

Chad Green RHP Born: 05/24/91 Age: 27 Bats: L Throws: R Height: 6'3" Weight: 210 Origin: Round 11, 2013 Draft (#336 overall)

YEAR	TEAM	LVL	AGE	W	L	SV	G	GS	IP	H	HR	BB/9	K/9	K	GB%	BABIP	WHIP	ERA	DRA	WARP	MPH	CMD	PWR	STM
2015	ERI	AA	24	5	14	0	27	27	148^{2}	170	9	2.6	8.3	137	51%	.351	1.43	3.93	3.05	3.7				
2016	SWB	AAA	25	7	6	0	16	16	94^{2}	68	3	2.0	9.5	100	50%	.271	0.94	1.52	2.12	3.5				
2016	NYA	MLB	25	2	4	1	12	8	45^{2}	49	12	3.0	10.2	52	44%	.314	1.40	4.73	5.89	-0.3	97.1	45	50	64
2017	SWB	AAA	26	2	1	0	5	5	26^{2}	32	1	3.7	11.1	33	53%	.397	1.61	4.72	3.11	0.7				
2017	NYA	MLB	26	5	0	0	40	1	69	34	4	2.2	13.4	103	28%	.236	0.74	1.83	2.66	1.9	97.5	56	68	53
2018	*NYA*	*MLB*	*27*	*3*	*2*	*0*	*51*	*0*	*54*	*45*	*8*	*3.3*	*11.3*	*68*	*43%*	*.293*	*1.20*	*3.36*	*3.68*	*0.9*	*96.9*	*53*	*62*	*59*
2019	*NYA*	*MLB*	*28*	*3*	*1*	*0*	*55*	*0*	*58^{2}*	*49*	*9*	*3.2*	*11.7*	*76*	*43%*	*.297*	*1.20*	*3.83*	*3.96*	*0.8*	*96.6*	*53*	*62*	*58*

Breakout: 34% Improve: 56% Collapse: 16% Attrition: 25% MLB: 81% *Comparables: Matt Barnes, David Purcey, Junichi Tazawa*

Kermit the Frog once sang, "It's not easy being green," but that was not the case for Chad, who seemed to come out of nowhere and become one of the best relievers in baseball. Green's numbers put him in the conversation with top-tier relievers like Craig Kimbrel and Kenley Jansen. Once an unreliable starter who lacked a third pitch, Green is now one of the most dependable guys in the Yankees' bullpen. Everything came together for him in 2017, as he turned into a strikeout machine, with Joe Girardi deploying him early and often to put out fires.

Jonathan Holder RHP Born: 06/09/93 Age: 24 Bats: R Throws: R Height: 6'2" Weight: 235 Origin: Round 6, 2014 Draft (#182 overall)

YEAR	TEAM	LVL	AGE	W	L	SV	G	GS	IP	H	HR	BB/9	K/9	K	GB%	BABIP	WHIP	ERA	DRA	WARP	MPH	CMD	PWR	STM
2015	TAM	A+	22	7	5	0	19	18	103^1	92	3	1.8	6.8	78	42%	.281	1.09	2.44	2.83	2.8				
2016	TRN	AA	23	3	1	10	28	0	41	27	2	1.5	13.0	59	45%	.298	0.83	2.20	1.37	1.7				
2016	SWB	AAA	23	2	0	6	12	0	20^1	7	1	0.0	15.5	35	42%	.188	0.34	0.89	0.75	1.0				
2016	NYA	MLB	23	0	0	0	8	0	8^1	8	1	4.3	5.4	5	37%	.269	1.44	5.40	4.56	0.0	94.7			42
2017	SWB	AAA	24	0	0	1	12	0	16	15	1	4.5	11.8	21	40%	.359	1.44	1.69	3.36	0.3				
2017	NYA	MLB	24	1	1	0	37	0	39^1	45	5	1.8	9.2	40	42%	.348	1.35	3.89	4.53	0.3	93.5	49	30	42
2018	*NYA*	*MLB*	*25*	*1*	*1*	*0*	*23*	*0*	*24*	*23*	*4*	*3.4*	*9.7*	*26*	*41%*	*.293*	*1.30*	*4.04*	*4.23*	*0.3*	*93.4*	*50*	*31*	*43*
2019	*NYA*	*MLB*	*26*	*3*	*1*	*1*	*53*	*0*	*56*	*49*	*9*	*3.1*	*10.5*	*65*	*41%*	*.289*	*1.22*	*4.31*	*4.46*	*0.5*	*93.2*	*50*	*31*	*43*

Breakout: 31% Improve: 57% Collapse: 18% Attrition: 24% MLB: 82% *Comparables: Josh Lindblom, Jose Ascanio, Jess Todd*

Holder got his first extended opportunity in the majors at age 24 and showed that his track record of minor-league dominance was no fluke, although he never fully secured Joe Girardi's faith in him as a viable setup man. He should get a chance to convince Aaron Boone in 2018 and has the raw stuff to stick in a relatively high-leverage role. In addition to his good work in a half-season with the Yankees, the right-hander posted a sub-2.00 ERA and 122 strikeouts in 81 innings at Double- and Triple-A the past two seasons.

Tommy Kahnle RHP Born: 08/07/89 Age: 28 Bats: R Throws: R Height: 6'1" Weight: 235 Origin: Round 5, 2010 Draft (#175 overall)

YEAR	TEAM	LVL	AGE	W	L	SV	G	GS	IP	H	HR	BB/9	K/9	K	GB%	BABIP	WHIP	ERA	DRA	WARP	MPH	CMD	PWR	STM
2015	COL	MLB	25	0	1	2	36	0	33^1	31	3	7.6	10.5	39	59%	.329	1.77	4.86	3.56	0.5	99.1	38	65	51
2015	ABQ	AAA	25	1	3	6	21	0	27	19	3	4.0	9.3	28	38%	.235	1.15	4.67	5.02	0.0				
2016	CHR	AAA	26	1	1	7	23	0	27	17	0	4.0	12.0	36	48%	.283	1.07	3.00	2.26	0.8				
2016	CHA	MLB	26	0	1	1	29	0	27^1	21	2	6.6	8.2	25	50%	.264	1.50	2.63	4.03	0.3	99.3	34	69	41
2017	CHA	MLB	27	1	3	0	37	0	36	28	3	1.8	15.0	60	43%	.352	0.97	2.50	2.91	0.9	99.7	40	78	49
2017	NYA	MLB	27	1	1	0	32	0	26^2	25	1	3.4	12.1	36	40%	.364	1.31	2.70	2.62	0.8	99.3	40	78	49
2018	*NYA*	*MLB*	*28*	*3*	*2*	*0*	*51*	*0*	*54*	*43*	*7*	*3.9*	*11.4*	*69*	*45%*	*.287*	*1.22*	*3.47*	*3.78*	*0.8*	*98.8*	*38*	*74*	*47*
2019	*NYA*	*MLB*	*29*	*3*	*1*	*0*	*53*	*0*	*56^1*	*45*	*9*	*4.7*	*11.8*	*74*	*45%*	*.288*	*1.32*	*4.33*	*4.48*	*0.5*	*98.5*	*38*	*75*	*46*

Breakout: 35% Improve: 52% Collapse: 21% Attrition: 14% MLB: 87% *Comparables: Brian Wilson, Joey Devine, A.J. Ramos*

Acquired at midseason from the White Sox in a deal that also netted the Yankees a reunion with David Robertson, Kahnle slid into a secondary setup role and made himself at home in a bullpen full of similarly huge strikeout rates. The biggest change for Kahnle last season was vastly improved control, which allowed his always outstanding raw stuff to take the forefront. Kahnle seemed to hit a wall late in the season, but he was acquired to be more than a second-half pickup and won't be eligible for free agency until after 2020.

Jordan Montgomery LHP Born: 12/27/92 Age: 25 Bats: L Throws: L Height: 6'6" Weight: 225 Origin: Round 4, 2014 Draft (#122 overall)

YEAR	TEAM	LVL	AGE	W	L	SV	G	GS	IP	H	HR	BB/9	K/9	K	GB%	BABIP	WHIP	ERA	DRA	WARP	MPH	CMD	PWR	STM
2015	CSC	A	22	4	3	0	9	9	43^2	36	1	2.5	11.3	55	47%	.327	1.10	2.68	1.78	1.8				
2015	TAM	A+	22	6	5	0	16	15	90^2	82	4	2.4	7.6	77	53%	.293	1.17	3.08	2.99	2.3				
2016	TRN	AA	23	9	4	0	19	19	102^1	94	5	3.2	8.5	97	45%	.299	1.27	2.55	3.54	1.9				
2016	SWB	AAA	23	5	1	0	6	6	37	28	0	2.2	9.0	37	56%	.286	1.00	0.97	2.81	1.1				
2017	NYA	MLB	24	9	7	0	29	29	155^1	140	21	3.0	8.3	144	42%	.275	1.23	3.88	4.36	2.1	93.4	37	31	68
2018	*NYA*	*MLB*	*25*	*11*	*8*	*0*	*26*	*26*	*148*	*143*	*24*	*3.4*	*8.7*	*143*	*44%*	*.292*	*1.34*	*4.32*	*4.56*	*1.4*	*93.1*	*38*	*32*	*70*
2019	*NYA*	*MLB*	*26*	*10*	*11*	*0*	*30*	*30*	*191*	*186*	*32*	*3.3*	*8.9*	*190*	*44%*	*.294*	*1.33*	*4.69*	*4.84*	*1.6*	*92.9*	*38*	*32*	*70*

Breakout: 25% Improve: 59% Collapse: 22% Attrition: 16% MLB: 95% *Comparables: Andrew Heaney, Jesse Hahn, Alex Cobb*

Early in his first full season, Montgomery drew comparisons to Andy Pettitte—lefty from the South, not overpowering. Montgomery doesn't rely on his fastball, he likes to throw a curveball and a sinker. Those comparisons to Pettitte were perhaps premature and unfair, but Gumby still had a solid first season as a starter. There were some bumps in the road, as Montgomery pitched more innings than he ever had before, but he ultimately proved he could pitch with the big boys.

David Robertson RHP Born: 04/09/85 Age: 33 Bats: R Throws: R Height: 5'11" Weight: 195 Origin: Round 17, 2006 Draft (#524 overall)

YEAR	TEAM	LVL	AGE	W	L	SV	G	GS	IP	H	HR	BB/9	K/9	K	GB%	BABIP	WHIP	ERA	DRA	WARP	MPH	CMD	PWR	STM
2015	CHA	MLB	30	6	5	34	60	0	63^1	46	7	1.8	12.2	86	38%	.275	0.93	3.41	2.11	2.0	94.7	60	51	47
2016	CHA	MLB	31	5	3	37	62	0	62^1	53	6	4.6	10.8	75	47%	.307	1.36	3.47	2.89	1.5	94.5	57	51	47
2017	CHA	MLB	32	4	2	13	31	0	33^1	21	4	3.0	12.7	47	43%	.250	0.96	2.70	2.14	1.1	93.2	40	38	48
2017	NYA	MLB	32	5	0	1	30	0	35	14	2	3.1	13.1	51	56%	.182	0.74	1.03	2.30	1.1	93.7	40	38	48
2018	*NYA*	*MLB*	*33*	*3*	*3*	*5*	*56*	*0*	*59*	*46*	*8*	*3.8*	*11.6*	*76*	*45%*	*.287*	*1.21*	*3.35*	*3.67*	*1.0*	*93.1*	*50*	*45*	*47*
2019	*NYA*	*MLB*	*34*	*3*	*1*	*3*	*57*	*0*	*60^1*	*47*	*9*	*4.1*	*11.6*	*77*	*45%*	*.277*	*1.24*	*4.20*	*4.31*	*0.6*	*92.5*	*47*	*43*	*47*

Breakout: 19% Improve: 44% Collapse: 37% Attrition: 8% MLB: 96% *Comparables: Brian Fuentes, J.J. Putz, Jonathan Papelbon*

Reunited and it feels so good. The Yankees got their Alabama boy back in late July when they had enough of Tyler Clippard's shenanigans. When the Bombers made the move for Robertson, Tommy Kahnle and Todd Frazier, it showed that they were serious about contending in 2017. Robertson, who was closing for the White Sox, happily accepted his setup role in the Yankees' bullpen and posted some of the best numbers of his career. His strikeouts per nine innings were above 10.0 for the 10th straight season and his ERA was its lowest since 2011. Although he's a luxury item for New York, Robertson would be the best reliever on many other teams.

CC Sabathia LHP
Born: 07/21/80 Age: 37 Bats: L Throws: L Height: 6'6" Weight: 300 Origin: Round 1, 1998 Draft (#20 overall)

YEAR	TEAM	LVL	AGE	W	L	SV	G	GS	IP	H	HR	BB/9	K/9	K	GB%	BABIP	WHIP	ERA	DRA	WARP	MPH	CMD	PWR	STM
2015	NYA	MLB	34	6	10	0	29	29	167^1	188	28	2.7	7.4	137	48%	.317	1.42	4.73	4.97	0.2	93.0	65	37	68
2016	NYA	MLB	35	9	12	0	30	30	179^2	172	22	3.3	7.6	152	52%	.288	1.32	3.91	4.36	2.1	93.4	66	45	75
2017	NYA	MLB	36	14	5	0	27	27	148^2	139	21	3.0	7.3	120	51%	.276	1.27	3.69	4.52	1.7	92.9	58	34	62
2018	*NYA*	*MLB*	*37*	*11*	*9*	*0*	*28*	*28*	*159*	*170*	*24*	*3.5*	*6.9*	*123*	*49%*	*.298*	*1.46*	*4.66*	*4.90*	*0.9*	*91.7*	*61*	*38*	*66*
2019	*NYA*	*MLB*	*38*	*9*	*11*	*0*	*29*	*29*	181^1	*192*	*26*	*3.5*	*7.4*	*149*	*49%*	*.305*	*1.44*	*4.87*	*5.02*	*1.2*	*91.1*	*60*	*38*	*65*

Breakout: 7% Improve: 31% Collapse: 23% Attrition: 11% MLB: 76% *Comparables: Jose Contreras, Andy Pettitte, John Lackey*

There's a reason people are romantic about baseball, and it's stories like Sabathia's. After years of injury woes people writing him off, and after trying to figure out how to go from a power pitcher to crafty lefty, Sabathia actually did it. And he did it in a big way. He wasn't mowing people down and he didn't pitch to a minuscule ERA in 2017, but he did regain his form as the stopper he was in his early years with New York. Sabathia was undefeated in 10 starts following a Yankees loss in 2017. He was old reliable again, with the emphasis on old.

Luis Severino RHP
Born: 02/20/94 Age: 24 Bats: R Throws: R Height: 6'2" Weight: 215 Origin: International Free Agent, 2011

YEAR	TEAM	LVL	AGE	W	L	SV	G	GS	IP	H	HR	BB/9	K/9	K	GB%	BABIP	WHIP	ERA	DRA	WARP	MPH	CMD	PWR	STM
2015	TRN	AA	21	2	2	0	8	8	38	32	2	2.4	11.4	48	46%	.319	1.11	3.32	1.47	1.7				
2015	SWB	AAA	21	7	0	0	11	11	61^1	40	0	2.5	7.3	50	42%	.237	0.93	1.91	2.59	1.9				
2015	NYA	MLB	21	5	3	0	11	11	62^1	53	9	3.2	8.1	56	51%	.265	1.20	2.89	3.16	1.4	97.8	45	59	65
2016	SWB	AAA	22	8	1	0	13	12	77^1	75	4	2.1	9.1	78	46%	.321	1.20	3.49	2.70	2.3				
2016	NYA	MLB	22	3	8	0	22	11	71	78	11	3.2	8.4	66	45%	.324	1.45	5.83	3.93	1.1	99.0	43	60	65
2017	NYA	MLB	23	14	6	0	31	31	193^1	150	21	2.4	10.7	230	50%	.272	1.04	2.98	3.05	5.4	99.5	48	65	78
2018	*NYA*	*MLB*	*24*	*13*	*7*	*0*	*29*	*29*	*174*	*151*	*22*	*3.0*	*10.1*	*195*	*47%*	*.291*	*1.19*	*3.45*	*3.62*	*3.6*	*99.0*	*48*	*65*	*73*
2019	*NYA*	*MLB*	*25*	*12*	*9*	*0*	*31*	*31*	193^2	*161*	*25*	*2.6*	*10.8*	*232*	*47%*	*.29*	*1.12*	*3.58*	*3.65*	*4.0*	*98.9*	*48*	*66*	*74*

Breakout: 30% Improve: 65% Collapse: 11% Attrition: 18% MLB: 96% *Comparables: Marcus Stroman, Carlos Martinez, Rich Harden*

Any questions about Severino were answered in 2017 when the young right-hander made the starting rotation out of spring training and became the Yankees' ace. The Severino of 2016 who couldn't win as a starter was gone and a new Severino emerged with confidence and a bit of swagger on the mound. There were some clunkers, but there were also starts that were either spoiled by his offense not showing up or by his bullpen blowing leads. Sevy was the guy Yankees fans wanted on the mound in big games, although he struggled more than expected in the playoffs after a big regular-season workload. He was one of the best starters in the league whether you focus on stuff, traditional numbers or advanced metrics, and it's easy to see Severino staying atop the Yankees' rotation for a long time.

Chasen Shreve LHP
Born: 07/12/90 Age: 27 Bats: L Throws: L Height: 6'4" Weight: 195 Origin: Round 11, 2010 Draft (#344 overall)

YEAR	TEAM	LVL	AGE	W	L	SV	G	GS	IP	H	HR	BB/9	K/9	K	GB%	BABIP	WHIP	ERA	DRA	WARP	MPH	CMD	PWR	STM
2015	NYA	MLB	24	6	2	0	59	0	58^1	49	10	5.1	9.9	64	47%	.273	1.41	3.09	3.95	0.5	93.5	45	37	49
2016	SWB	AAA	25	0	0	0	13	1	16^2	4	1	3.8	10.8	20	46%	.094	0.66	1.62	3.75	0.2				
2016	NYA	MLB	25	2	1	1	37	0	33	29	8	3.5	9.0	33	44%	.247	1.27	5.18	4.08	0.3	93.8	38	38	38
2017	SWB	AAA	26	1	0	1	9	0	11^1	7	0	2.4	15.1	19	48%	.333	0.88	1.59	2.38	0.4				
2017	NYA	MLB	26	4	1	0	44	0	45^1	35	8	5.0	11.5	58	37%	.252	1.32	3.77	3.14	1.0	94.3	34	39	44
2018	*NYA*	*MLB*	*27*	*1*	*1*	*0*	*23*	*0*	*24*	*22*	*5*	*4.3*	*10.6*	*29*	*43%*	*.291*	*1.38*	*4.82*	*4.85*	*0.1*	*93.4*	*39*	*39*	*44*
2019	*NYA*	*MLB*	*28*	*2*	*1*	*0*	*44*	*0*	*47*	*42*	*10*	*4.3*	*10.9*	*57*	*43%*	*.281*	*1.37*	*5.12*	*5.33*	*-0.1*	*93.3*	*37*	*39*	*43*

Breakout: 37% Improve: 49% Collapse: 19% Attrition: 29% MLB: 84% *Comparables: Tony Sipp, David Aardsma, Shawn Kelley*

Two players named Chasen played in the major leagues in 2017. Both were relievers who played for New York teams and hailed from Las Vegas. The Yankees' Chasen had a much improved season over 2016, but rode the Scranton Shuttle between Triple-A and the Bronx. He didn't see many high-leverage innings out of the 'pen with the Yankees and didn't pitch at all in the postseason.

Masahiro Tanaka RHP
Born: 11/01/88 Age: 29 Bats: R Throws: R Height: 6'3" Weight: 215 Origin: International Free Agent, 2014

YEAR	TEAM	LVL	AGE	W	L	SV	G	GS	IP	H	HR	BB/9	K/9	K	GB%	BABIP	WHIP	ERA	DRA	WARP	MPH	CMD	PWR	STM
2015	NYA	MLB	26	12	7	0	24	24	154	126	25	1.6	8.1	139	48%	.243	0.99	3.51	2.88	4.0	94.6	57	37	61
2016	NYA	MLB	27	14	4	0	31	31	199^2	179	22	1.6	7.4	165	49%	.271	1.08	3.07	3.21	4.9	93.6	59	38	79
2017	NYA	MLB	28	13	12	0	30	30	178^1	180	35	2.1	9.8	194	50%	.306	1.24	4.74	3.66	3.8	94.0	55	32	73
2018	*NYA*	*MLB*	*29*	*13*	*8*	*0*	*29*	*29*	182^2	*173*	*28*	*2.6*	*8.4*	*171*	*48%*	*.287*	*1.23*	*4.05*	*4.26*	*2.4*	*93.3*	*57*	*35*	*72*
2019	*NYA*	*MLB*	*30*	*12*	*11*	*0*	*31*	*31*	*199*	*183*	*26*	*2.2*	*8.5*	*188*	*48%*	*.285*	*1.16*	*4.03*	*4.12*	*3.3*	*92.9*	*57*	*35*	*74*

Breakout: 14% Improve: 41% Collapse: 18% Attrition: 2% MLB: 97% *Comparables: Cole Hamels, Zack Greinke, Ben Sheets*

Some sort of *Freaky Friday* body switch must have occurred last season, because it seemed as if Tanaka became an amalgamation of Michael Pineda and Nathan Eovaldi. The Yankees didn't know which Tanaka they were going to get from start to start. They could get the Tanaka who would pitch a shutout against the Red Sox or they could get the Tanaka who struggled to make it out of the second inning after surrendering four home runs to the Astros. He could still strike out batters, setting a new career high, but he also set a new career high in home runs allowed. Rather than opt out of his contract and become a free agent at age 29, Tanaka decided to remain in the Bronx for the next three seasons. If healthy, his secondary numbers suggest a 2018 bounce-back is likely.

Dillon Tate RHP Born: 05/01/94 Age: 24 Bats: R Throws: R Height: 6'2" Weight: 195 Origin: Round 1, 2015 Draft (#4 overall)

YEAR	TEAM	LVL	AGE	W	L	SV	G	GS	IP	H	HR	BB/9	K/9	K	GB%	BABIP	WHIP	ERA	DRA	WARP	MPH	CMD	PWR	STM
2016	HIC	A	22	3	3	0	17	16	65	78	5	3.7	7.6	55	44%	.376	1.62	5.12	6.47	-1.2				
2016	CSC	A	22	1	0	0	7	0	17^{1}	21	1	3.1	7.8	15	57%	.351	1.56	3.12	6.23	-0.3				
2017	TAM	A+	23	6	0	0	9	9	58^{1}	48	4	2.3	7.1	46	61%	.262	1.08	2.62	1.53	2.6				
2017	TRN	AA	23	1	2	0	4	4	25	23	3	3.2	6.1	17	56%	.270	1.28	3.24	3.67	0.4				
2018	*NYA*	*MLB*	*24*	*4*	*4*	*0*	*20*	*13*	*68*	*68*	*12*	*4.0*	*8.4*	*63*	*47%*	*.295*	*1.44*	*5.13*	*5.32*	*0.2*				
2019	*NYA*	*MLB*	*25*	*6*	*9*	*0*	*31*	*24*	155^{2}	*163*	*26*	*4.7*	*8.0*	*139*	*47%*	*.304*	*1.57*	*5.48*	*5.71*	*-0.1*				

Breakout: 5% Improve: 5% Collapse: 2% Attrition: 5% MLB: 7% *Comparables: Jason Berken, Joe Martinez, Pat Misch*

If the Yankees gave out a Comeback Player of the Year award to their prospects, Tate would have gotten it. They were hoping for a rebound, and boy did he deliver, regaining his fastball velocity and getting his slider working again. His future role is unclear, because even last season he was anything but consistent, but the former no. 4 overall pick is once again on track to reach the majors.

Adam Warren RHP Born: 08/25/87 Age: 30 Bats: R Throws: R Height: 6'1" Weight: 224 Origin: Round 4, 2009 Draft (#135 overall)

YEAR	TEAM	LVL	AGE	W	L	SV	G	GS	IP	H	HR	BB/9	K/9	K	GB%	BABIP	WHIP	ERA	DRA	WARP	MPH	CMD	PWR	STM
2015	NYA	MLB	27	7	7	1	43	17	131^{1}	114	10	2.7	7.1	104	46%	.278	1.16	3.29	3.34	2.6	95.4	58	43	60
2016	CHN	MLB	28	3	2	0	29	1	35	31	7	4.9	6.9	27	44%	.242	1.43	5.91	5.45	-0.2	95.3	51	41	50
2016	NYA	MLB	28	4	2	0	29	0	30^{1}	28	4	3.0	7.4	25	45%	.282	1.25	3.26	5.30	-0.1	94.9	51	41	50
2017	NYA	MLB	29	3	2	1	46	0	57^{1}	35	4	2.4	8.5	54	44%	.208	0.87	2.35	2.53	1.7	94.1	70	34	40
2018	*NYA*	*MLB*	*30*	*2*	*2*	*0*	*42*	*0*	44^{1}	*42*	*7*	*3.8*	*8.2*	*41*	*44%*	*.283*	*1.33*	*4.55*	*4.63*	*0.3*	*94.2*	*59*	*40*	*48*
2019	*NYA*	*MLB*	*31*	*2*	*1*	*0*	*44*	*0*	46^{2}	*45*	*8*	*4.4*	*8.4*	*43*	*44%*	*.286*	*1.44*	*5.16*	*5.35*	*-0.1*	*93.6*	*60*	*38*	*46*

Breakout: 22% Improve: 52% Collapse: 28% Attrition: 12% MLB: 94% *Comparables: Jim Johnson, Eric O'Flaherty, Peter Moylan*

Warren made a change to his repertoire last season, throwing his slider more than his fastball, and in doing so he ended up being one of the most underrated relievers in the league before back problems sidelined him down the stretch. New York has no shortage of high-end relief options, making Warren a relative afterthought with an uncertain role, but he has setup-caliber stuff and the results to match with a lifetime 3.29 ERA out of the bullpen.

Lineouts

Hitters

HITTER	POS	TEAM	LVL	AGE	PA	R	2B	3B	HR	RBI	BB	K	SB	CS	AVG/OBP/SLG	TAv	VORP	BABIP	BRR	FRAA	WARP
Jabari Blash	RF	ELP	AAA	27	291	53	16	1	20	62	48	88	3	2	.285/.419/.617	.318	24.5	.367	0.2	RF(59): 8.4	3.2
	RF	SDN	MLB	27	195	24	6	0	5	16	28	66	1	2	.213/.333/.341	.254	3.6	.319	0.8	RF(33): 0.1, LF(18): -1.7	0.2
Jake Cave	OF	TRN	AA	24	140	19	13	2	5	18	10	33	1	0	.266/.317/.516	.292	6.4	.319	-1.0	LF(17): 0.8, CF(7): -0.5	0.7
	OF	SWB	AAA	24	297	47	13	3	15	38	18	82	1	3	.324/.367/.554	.312	25.2	.414	0.5	CF(30): -1.8, RF(25): 2.2	2.5
Ji-Man Choi	1B	NYA	MLB	26	18	2	1	0	2	5	2	5	0	0	.267/.333/.733	.334	1.3	.222	-0.3	1B(6): 0.2	0.1
	1B	SWB	AAA	26	338	42	25	1	15	69	39	86	3	1	.288/.373/.538	.304	22.2	.351	1.7	1B(57): 4.3	2.6
Thairo Estrada	MI	TRN	AA	21	542	72	19	4	6	48	34	56	8	11	.301/.353/.392	.289	32.9	.327	-2.2	SS(82): -0.3, 2B(23): -0.5	3.5
Wilkerman Garcia	SS	STA	A-	19	277	27	10	3	1	20	12	72	8	9	.222/.256/.296	.221	-2.9	.299	-2.6	SS(65): -3.4, 2B(1): 0.0	-0.6
Kyle Holder	SS	TAM	A+	23	442	41	16	2	4	44	26	62	4	3	.271/.317/.350	.251	11.5	.310	0.2	SS(64): 0.5, 3B(26): 4.2	1.7
Billy McKinney	OF	TRN	AA	22	276	34	16	4	6	29	30	45	2	1	.250/.339/.431	.289	13.4	.277	0.3	RF(50): 12.4, LF(7): -1.1	2.9
	OF	SWB	AAA	22	224	32	13	3	10	35	9	49	0	0	.306/.336/.541	.295	12.7	.353	-0.7	LF(26): 0.1, RF(26): 1.6	1.4
Donny Sands	C	CSC	A	21	314	31	17	0	2	45	21	53	0	5	.269/.323/.350	.258	9.0	.321	-4.6	C(76): -6.7	0.2
	C	TAM	A+	21	68	9	5	0	2	10	5	10	1	1	.306/.353/.484	.301	7.0	.333	1.1	C(17): -0.6	0.7
Nick Solak	2B	TAM	A+	22	406	56	17	4	10	44	53	76	13	4	.301/.397/.460	.322	38.4	.357	2.5	2B(92): 1.4	4.2
	2B	TRN	AA	22	132	16	9	1	2	9	10	24	1	1	.286/.344/.429	.292	8.3	.340	0.5	2B(27): 2.0	1.1
Donovan Solano	INF	SWB	AAA	29	405	44	29	0	4	48	24	60	1	0	.282/.329/.391	.250	6.1	.324	-0.8	2B(59): 2.3, 3B(28): 2.4	1.1
Mason Williams	CF	NYA	MLB	25	17	3	0	0	0	1	1	2	2	0	.250/.294/.250	.204	0.0	.286	0.5	CF(5): -0.4, RF(1): -0.1	0.0
	CF	SWB	AAA	25	437	44	10	3	2	30	28	66	19	5	.263/.309/.318	.217	-5.5	.306	3.3	CF(64): 3.7, LF(19): 0.8	-0.1

Jabari Blash owns a career .807 OPS against lefties at the big-league level, which is exciting until you notice his .574 OPS against righties. **Jake Cave** can rake and it finally looks like he put it all together with a solid campaign in Scranton, but knee problems have likely ruled him out as a center fielder. Signed as a 16-year-old, **Roberto Chirinos** is a middle infielder with speed who will need plenty of time to develop his bat. **Ji-Man Choi** hit a home run in his first two games and got Yankees fans excited. Then it all went away as quickly as it appeared, with the Todd Frazier trade pushing him out of the team's plans. After starting the year at Captain's Camp, **Thairo Estrada** went on to have a productive season for Trenton, playing well on both sides of the ball and making the Eastern League All-Star team. One word often used to describe **Anthony Garcia** is "hulking." The Yankees like what they see from the switch-hitting outfielder and expect him to develop into a power hitter with some speed on the bases. Luis Sojo says that shortstop **Wilkerman Garcia** has the tools to be a good player but that he needs to "clean it up." Luckily, there's plenty of time for the young Venezuelan to work on his game. Known more for his defense, **Kyle Holder** improved his offense last season for the Tampa Yankees. He probably won't ever hit 20 home runs, but he's a solid defender who could become solid at the plate as well. Traded by the A's and by the Cubs, outfielder **Billy McKinney** is still trying to make it to the majors six years after being a first-round pick known for his bat. Venezuelan signee **Everson Pereira** is a center fielder with speed and a good arm, while his bat is mostly projection for now. Former third baseman **Donny Sands** is adjusting slowly to catcher after previously never having played there at any level, but the Charleston coaching staff gave him positive reviews for his work ethic. Hitting is the easy part for **Nick Solak**, who slashes line drives all over the field. Where he plays defensively is less certain, in part due to a weak arm. **Donovan Solano** had a solid season with Scranton in 2017, but his chances of returning to the majors are dwindling as he enters his thirties. **Mason Williams** just didn't pan out. It happens. It also didn't help that there were a number of younger, better outfielders ahead of him in the line to board the Scranton Shuttle.

Pitchers

PITCHER	TEAM	LVL	AGE	W	L	SV	G	GS	IP	H	HR	BB/9	K/9	K	GB%	BABIP	WHIP	ERA	DRA	WARP	MPH	CMD	PWR	STM
Domingo Acevedo	TAM	A+	23	0	4	0	7	7	41^1	49	5	2.0	11.3	52	54%	.393	1.40	4.57	1.74	1.7				
	SWB	AAA	23	1	1	0	2	2	12^1	12	0	5.8	5.8	8	35%	.300	1.62	4.38	6.27	-0.1				
	TRN	AA	23	5	1	0	14	14	79^1	65	8	1.9	9.3	82	37%	.282	1.03	2.38	3.05	2.0				
J.P. Feyereisen	TRN	AA	24	0	0	3	13	0	20	14	2	3.6	8.1	18	39%	.245	1.10	2.70	5.14	-0.1				
	SWB	AAA	24	2	3	1	24	0	43^1	35	3	4.2	8.7	42	43%	.281	1.27	3.53	5.96	-0.3				
Giovanny Gallegos	SWB	AAA	25	4	2	5	28	0	43^1	28	4	2.3	14.3	69	32%	.286	0.90	2.08	1.66	1.7				
	NYA	MLB	25	0	1	0	16	0	20^1	21	3	2.2	9.7	22	37%	.316	1.28	4.87	4.73	0.1	95.3	53	54	42
J.R. Graham	SWB	AAA	27	0	1	1	18	0	20^1	32	3	4.9	10.2	23	46%	.446	2.11	6.64	5.83	-0.1				
Ben Heller	SWB	AAA	25	5	4	6	41	0	56^1	34	6	3.4	13.1	82	44%	.252	0.98	2.88	1.95	2.0				
	NYA	MLB	25	1	0	0	9	0	11	5	0	4.9	7.4	9	50%	.179	1.00	0.82	4.05	0.1	96.6			45
Jonathan Loaisiga	YAN	Rk	22	0	1	0	6	6	13^2	10	1	1.3	9.9	15	58%	.257	0.88	2.63	1.28	0.7				
	STA	A-	22	1	0	0	4	4	17	7	0	0.5	9.5	18	51%	.171	0.47	0.53	1.48	0.7				
Freicer Perez	CSC	A	21	10	3	0	24	24	123^2	96	5	3.3	8.5	117	45%	.272	1.14	2.84	4.86	0.6				
Matt Sauer	YAT	Rk	18	0	2	0	6	6	11^2	13	0	6.2	9.3	12	44%	.361	1.80	5.40	6.96	-0.1				
Justus Sheffield	TRN	AA	21	7	6	0	17	17	93^1	94	14	3.2	7.9	82	48%	.293	1.36	3.18	3.78	1.5				

Domingo Acevedo has big-time velocity, a huge frame and a violent delivery. This combination seemingly has him destined for the bullpen long term, but for now the Yankees still view him as a potential starter. ⚾ Acquired in 2016 as part of the Andrew Miller trade, **J.P. Feyereisen** has struggled to throw enough strikes to earn a promotion to New York. ⚾ **Giovanny Gallegos**, who pitched for Mexico in the World Baseball Classic, has topped a dozen strikeouts per nine innings in back-to-back minor-league seasons and held his own in a brief debut with the Yankees. ⚾ **J.R. Graham** made his MLB debut with the Twins as a Rule 5 pick in 2015, but injuries and poor performances cast doubt on his ability to reach the majors again. ⚾ **Ben Heller**, part of the Andrew Miller deal in 2016, served as little more than emergency depth for the Yankees last season, getting briefly called up from Triple-A whenever they were short on available arms. ⚾ The Yankees signed former Giants prospect **Jonathan Loaisiga** as a minor-league free agent in 2016, and he promptly blew out his elbow after one start. His return from Tommy John surgery only consisted of 11 starts in the lowest rungs of the minors, but his fastball/curveball combo was impressive enough to get a surprise 40-man add. ⚾ It was a bit of a lost year for **Nolan Martinez**, who only pitched in nine games during his first professional season because of a rotator cuff injury. Still, that's a Hall of Fame name. ⚾ Young **Frecier Perez**'s stuff has been compared to that of Pedro Martinez and his build has been compared to that of Dellin Betances. If he's anything like those two guys, the Yankees have something special. ⚾ High school right-hander **Matt Sauer** got twice the slot recommended value for a second-round draft pick, signing for $2.5 million before a brief pro debut in rookie-ball. ⚾ New York snagged South Carolina ace **Clarke Schmidt** in the first round of last June's draft despite his recent Tommy John surgery and a recovery timetable that likely limits his development until 2019. ⚾ Lefty **Justus Sheffield** spent two months on the disabled list in 2017, but still finished tied for second on the Trenton Thunder's strikeout list with 82.

League Leaders 2017

MLB Fastball Velocity – Aroldis Chapman, 102.2

AL Rookie Hitter WARP – Aaron Judge, 7.40

AL Rookie Pitcher WARP – Chad Green, 1.94

OAKLAND ATHLETICS

Essay by Matt Trueblood

Player comments by Jason Wojciechowski and BP staff

Northern California didn't become the epicenter of the United States's 21st-century economy by taking everyone at their word. Innovation blooms where skepticism and rationalism rule. It's not an accident that the West Coast Offense, Moneyball and Betaball all cropped up in the Bay Area. Demand is more sensitive to success in that region than in most, which makes winning a prerequisite for profitability, so teams push harder to overcome their disadvantages and find the (drink) market inefficiency that produces results to which the fans respond.

The same is true when it comes to ballpark financing. The Giants are the only team within living memory to lose their game of chicken with local authorities and end up footing (give or take) the full bill for their new stadium, and given how hard the Giants played that game (they nearly moved, count 'em, three times), that's telling. The A's have learned from that, which is why their process of finding footing for a new ballpark has been a painstaking, fits-and-starts affair.

It seems like that all began to change—like the project really found the traction it needed to get moving—when Lew Wolff sold his stake in the team late in 2016, making John Fisher the managing general partner. Fisher hired Dave Kaval as the new club president that November, and Chris Giles as the new Chief Operating Officer in July 2017. Together, the three did what the team had largely failed to do during Wolff's turn as head owner: aggressively market themselves to a broader swath of the Bay Area and demonstrate their own investment in the future of the franchise.

That any new ballpark for the A's would be privately financed was a given, at least once Wolff's dream of relocating to San Jose was permanently thwarted. Even with that premise, many of the locations the team initially explored ("initially" is a funny word, since the true initiation of this search was well over a decade ago now and some proposed sites seem lost in the haze of the past) were non-starters. The team found a small handful of at least semi-viable sites, though, and as 2017 progressed, their focus (and the focus of so many who have followed the endeavor) narrowed, until they found one to which they were willing to commit.

Nothing could better illustrate the fraught predicament the Athletics face than the fact that they decided what they call The Peralta Site is the most feasible option. The site in question actually sits on part of the property of Laney College, in the Peralta Community College District. To get clearance from any official body to build the ballpark, the team will need to find, purchase and prepare the replacement space the college needs if it surrenders that land. That's the easiest step, too. Assuming they can swing it, the A's then need to determine the extent of a known plume of underground pollution beneath the site, and may or may not be obligated to clean it up.

Then, they would need to overcome what will be significant community opposition: The adjacent neighborhoods of Chinatown and Eastlake are among the only ones that have resisted

ATHLETICS PROSPECTUS

2017 W-L: 75-87, 5th in AL West

Pythag	.447	19th	B-Age	28.7	*21st*
RS/G	4.56	17th	P-Age	27.5	*6th*
RA/G	5.10	26th	Salary	$81.7M	*27th*
TAv	.258	19th	M$/MW	$2.5M	*24th*
TAv-P	.264	19th	DL Days	978	*17th*
FIP	4.54	19th	$ on DL	6%	*3rd*
DER	.705	11th			

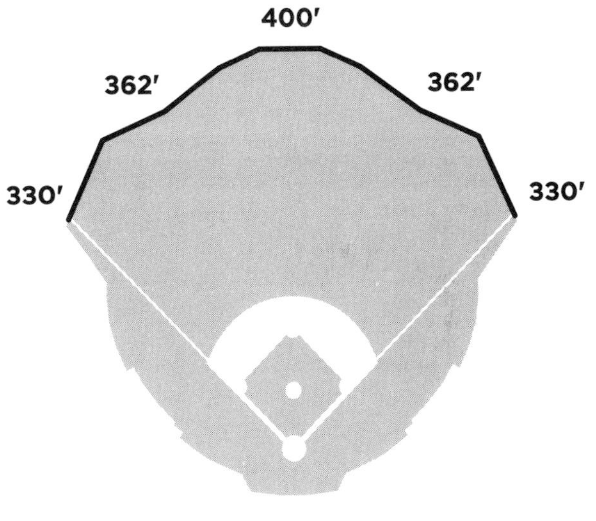

Outfield wall profile: **8'** to **15'**

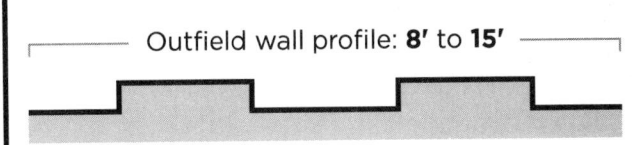

Three-Year Park Factors

Runs	Runs/RH	Runs/LH	HR/RH	HR/LH
99	99	97	93	91

Top Hitter WARP	2.7 Matt Chapman
Top Pitcher WARP	2.3 Sonny Gray
Top Prospect	A.J. Puk

2017 Hit List Ranking

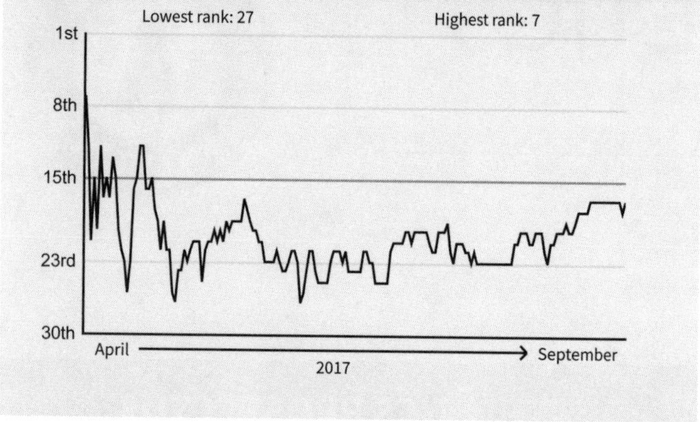

Committed Payroll (in millions)

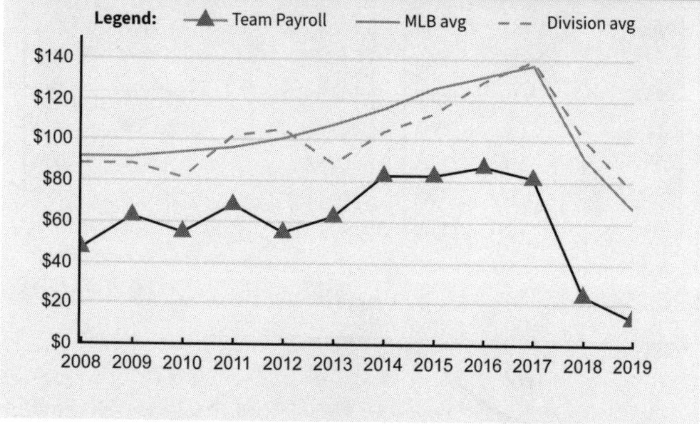

Farm System Ranking

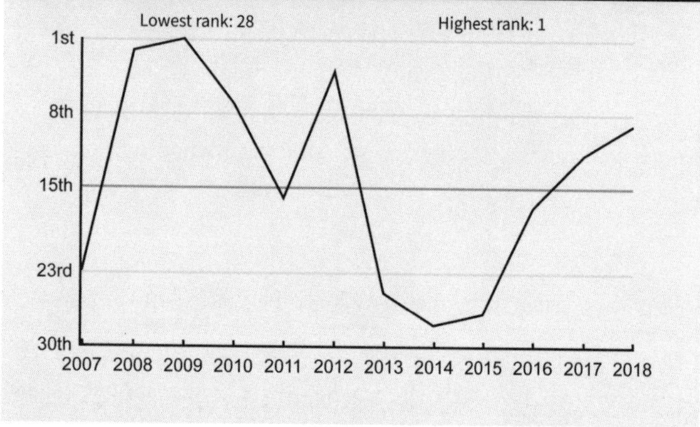

Personnel

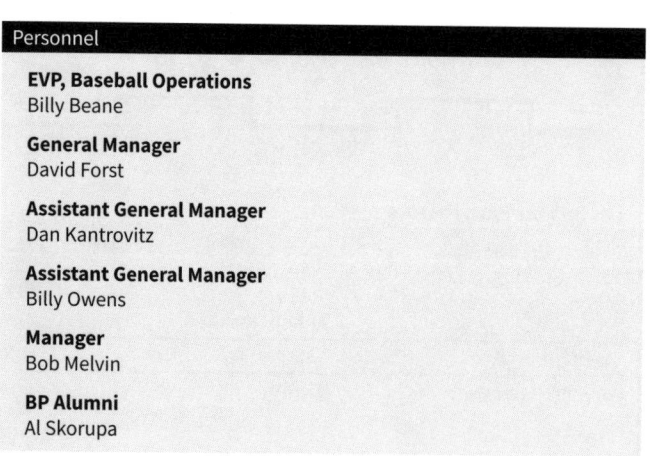

EVP, Baseball Operations
Billy Beane

General Manager
David Forst

Assistant General Manager
Dan Kantrovitz

Assistant General Manager
Billy Owens

Manager
Bob Melvin

BP Alumni
Al Skorupa

gentrification over the last decade, and both are loathe to risk that by allowing this project. The team sold the city council, Mayor Libby Schaaf and numerous stakeholders in East Oakland (where the Coliseum is, and from which they'll be considerably removed if this move happens) on the plan by promising to invest huge amounts in housing (especially affordable housing) and other civic projects, both near the new stadium and, in the long run, in place of the Coliseum. That's a lot of promises, and while the people of Oakland are listening earnestly for now, they'll want the team to back those promises with either concrete action or some firm guarantee before moving forward. It's not at all clear that the team has reckoned with the full scope of the investment it would take to make this work, or that they have the wherewithal to actually plunk down all the requisite dollars when the time comes.

If and when the A's do pass those tests, they're still looking at a stadium site rather shy on parking space. The most credible early estimates of the stadium's capacity, footprint and orientation bring other questions into focus. The stadium could have an even smaller footprint than Minnesota's Target Field, which is itself a minor miracle of civil engineering. It could hold fewer fans than any other park in the majors. It could back right up, along the left-field line especially, to a busy highway, creating potential aesthetic issues. This, remember, is the site the A's have picked over the two other options they identified as finalists. Skepticism is still the watchword.

Similarly, the fans will cast a cold eye toward the team's self-proclaimed on-field rebuild over the coming year or two. Billy Beane and David Forst aren't the darlings of the saber-savvy baseball crowd anymore; they surrendered that status when they traded Josh Donaldson. In fact, the entire deconstruction of the 2012-14 club that went to three straight postseasons has been a subject of consistent scorn ever since it happened. Now that the team appears poised to remain in this rebuilding phase for some time, it only seems to be intensifying.

There are at least two reasons not to import the healthy skepticism about the viability and desirability of the stadium project to the project of making the A's winners again. One is that, given a generous assumption here or there about the parameters within which they were working, Beane and Forst didn't do so badly when it came to managing that three-year window, or the move past it. To wit:

- They took a risk by trading Addison Russell to get Jeff Samardzija and Jason Hammel, in 2014. However, those two not only stabilized the team's rotation enough to get them to the wild card game, but yielded a player (Marcus Semien, the main return for Samardzija after the season) who has delivered virtually the same WARP (6.9) as Russell has (7.2) over the three seasons since.
- Their efforts to keep the team afloat in 2015 and 2016 paid off—just not directly. The talent they received for Ben Zobrist (Sean Manaea) is more valuable, and has been more valuable over the last one and a half seasons, than the talent they gave up for him (Daniel Robertson, Boog Powell and John Jaso). Scott Kazmir turned into Jacob Nottingham and Daniel Mengden, and then Nottingham turned into Khris Davis. Signing Rich Hill paid off, too, when they were able to flip him and Josh Reddick for three promising hurlers who remain part of the team's pitching plan.
- Ryan Madson, previously a curious two-year bullpen commitment, formed a package with Sean Doolittle and netted the team a solid prospect, in third baseman Sheldon Neuse.

Now, Oakland's payroll has risen over the last three years, and given that, one might fairly have expected them to identify Donaldson as a pillar of their winning team and retain him, at least a year longer than they did, or to have gotten more for him than they did. Even so, one player they got in that deal (Franklin Barreto) still has a chance to blossom into their regular second baseman, while another (Kendall Graveman) has been worth close to four wins over the last two seasons, in just under 300 innings of work.

In 2017, a few other players who seem to have vital roles in the team's future also took their places, or established them more firmly. Matt Chapman asserted himself as perhaps (Nolan Arenado notwithstanding) the best defensive third baseman in baseball and flashed enough offensive prowess to make that defense playable. Manaea had a sophomore season that, while marred by a rough second half, showed he can pitch near the front of their rotation. Matt Olson made the loudest entry of all, of course, with a power onslaught even 2017's juiced balls can't explain away. There's no championship core here, not yet, but the outline of one is coming into focus.

The draft played out perfectly for them, too. They took one high-upside high school hitter (Austin Beck) in the first round, then were able to gobble up a second one (California prep shortstop Nick Allen) in the third. Allen had fallen due to his bonus demands, but because they took two college hitters in whom they believed with their sandwich and second-round picks, the A's had the pool money necessary to meet those demands. It's a reminder of the extent to which the last two Collective Bargaining Agreements have helped small-market teams make the most of the draft. In the bad old days, the team would sell players headed toward free agency for pennies on the dollar, preferring whatever prospect help (or mere salary relief) they could get over the prospect of having another pick to play with, but also another mouth to feed in a system that only loosely and poorly controlled bonus figures. Now, the A's get an extra pick for free, via the competitive balance lottery, and the system gives them more leverage in negotiations with players like Allen.

The second reason to believe the A's can make this rebuild work, and even make it work quickly, has relatively little to do with the A's: The AL West opens up a bit in the near future. Little evidence suggests that either the Mariners or the Angels are building systematically toward sustained success. Rather, it seems as though both are trying to make the most of the next two or three years, while the stars they have under contract are still good enough to make them at least fringe contenders. The Rangers are young, but not materially younger or better than the A's. In fact, the A's had a better third-order winning percentage (.480 to .474) than Texas, and for that matter, the 16th-best third-order mark in baseball.

Houston's juggernaut, of course, isn't going anywhere. The A's have a clear path to becoming and remaining the second-best team in the division over the next few seasons, though, and once you get that far, you're just waiting for the right break to overtake that top club. In recent moves (most notably the Sonny Gray trade, which saw them take a chance on two players recovering from serious injuries), the Oakland front office has shown an appetite for risk that isn't typical of them. They're betting on ceiling, because if they're going to be better than the Astros anytime between now and the tentative opening of their new ballpark in 2023, it's going to be thanks to a long shot that pays off in a huge way.

None of that is to say there aren't serious problems with the plan the team has developed here. There are. For 2018, they figure to be as they were in 2017: much better than casual observers think, but not good enough to really win anything. Given how wide open the American League playoff picture is, one could argue that they're letting a real shot at a wild card elude them. Any team in the league's murky middle, these days, will inevitably draw some criticism for not choosing one side of the fence and riding hard on it. It doesn't look like the A's intend to undertake that kind of rebuild. They might fairly believe that, because Bay Area fans aren't generally interested in losers and don't buy into the company line, there's a risk of alienating fans by announcing an intention to slow down in their pursuit of victories.

Suddenly, the watchword here isn't skepticism, but risk. That's the story of a small-market team determined to remain relevant in MLB today, and it's the story of Silicon Valley, too. It's even the story of this team's effort to make a ballpark project that faces unique challenges and that could come with an unprecedented price tag (for the franchise) a viable one. Some teams, in some places, have the luxury of operating almost without risk. They could pay down the top payroll in baseball without selling a single ticket. They could lose a key player to career-altering injury or fail to develop a top draft pick into much of anything, and make up for it with their wallets. That will never be the case in Oakland. The A's believe they must take the risks associated with the move and the rebuild to draw somewhat closer to those teams for whom risk is just a word, and they're probably right. As it so often goes, however, even mitigating long-term risk will require taking a bunch of short-term ones, and having most of them pay off.

—Matthew Trueblood is an author of Baseball Prospectus.

Hitters

Lazaro Armenteros OF Born: 05/22/99 Age: 19 Bats: R Throws: R Height: 6'0" Weight: 182 Origin: International Free Agent, 2016

YEAR	TEAM	LVL	AGE	PA	R	2B	3B	HR	RBI	BB	K	SB	CS	AVG/OBP/SLG	TAv	VORP	BABIP	BRR	FRAA	WARP
2017	DAT	RK	18	26	6	0	0	0	1	3	9	2	2	.167/.385/.167	.258	1.8	.300	0.9	CF(6): 1.5	0.3
2017	ATH	RK	18	181	24	9	4	4	22	16	48	10	1	.288/.376/.474	.284	12.4	.387	2.8	LF(27): 4.3, CF(2): -0.5	1.5
2018	*OAK*	*MLB*	*19*	*250*	*24*	*9*	*1*	*7*	*25*	*14*	*90*	*4*	*1*	*.188/.245/.319*	*.191*	*-9.2*	*.270*	*0.1*	*LF 2, CF 0*	*-0.8*
2019	*OAK*	*MLB*	*20*	*327*	*36*	*12*	*1*	*10*	*36*	*20*	*111*	*6*	*2*	*.206/.267/.355*	*.214*	*-7.2*	*.285*	*0.4*	*LF 3, CF 0*	*-0.5*

Breakout: 0% Improve: 6% Collapse: 2% Attrition: 6% MLB: 12% *Comparables: Nomar Mazara, Engel Beltre, Raul Mondesi*

They call him Lazarito. The Cuban outfielder signed with the A's for $3 million in July 2016 as part of their big year of spending that put them well into the penalties (and, along with the same spending pattern by many other teams, led to a rules change in the next round of CBA bargaining). The now-19-year-old got some stateside complex time in the Arizona League last year and put up numbers with a nice sheen of all-around ability, but, outside of pointing out the 27 percent strikeout rate, we're not going to scout the stat line. We will instead mention that the hype around his athleticism has been utterly out of control: It's not hard to find articles about Armenteros that invoke Bo Jackson, Bryce Harper, Yoenis Cespedes and, no joke, Willie Mays. Take a deep breath, remember how many guys with Cespedes' tools didn't make it, and wish the kid good luck. (Still, he *does* have top-of-the-charts upside, and he's not steak tartare: The A's have commented on his mature approach at the plate.)

Franklin Barreto MI Born: 02/27/96 Age: 22 Bats: R Throws: R Height: 5'10" Weight: 190 Origin: International Free Agent, 2012

YEAR	TEAM	LVL	AGE	PA	R	2B	3B	HR	RBI	BB	K	SB	CS	AVG/OBP/SLG	TAv	VORP	BABIP	BRR	FRAA	WARP
2015	STO	A+	19	364	50	22	3	13	47	15	67	8	3	.302/.333/.500	.318	35.7	.337	0.6	SS(86): -15.0	2.2
2016	MID	AA	20	507	63	25	3	10	50	36	90	30	15	.281/.340/.413	.274	27.5	.330	3.1	SS(81): -10.7, 2B(33): -3.1	1.5
2017	NAS	AAA	21	510	63	19	7	15	54	27	141	15	8	.290/.339/.456	.283	34.1	.384	0.3	SS(83): -3.3, 2B(25): -2.6	2.7
2017	OAK	MLB	21	76	10	1	2	2	6	5	33	2	0	.197/.250/.352	.219	0.2	.333	0.7	SS(11): 0.3, 2B(10): 0.2	0.1
2018	*OAK*	*MLB*	*22*	*180*	*23*	*8*	*2*	*6*	*21*	*9*	*49*	*5*	*2*	*.249/.294/.414*	*.247*	*5.4*	*.316*	*0.2*	*SS -1, 2B -2*	*0.1*
2019	*OAK*	*MLB*	*23*	*434*	*54*	*19*	*4*	*16*	*57*	*26*	*118*	*12*	*6*	*.254/.307/.440*	*.253*	*12.2*	*.317*	*1.0*	*SS -3, 2B -4*	*0.6*

Breakout: 2% Improve: 34% Collapse: 3% Attrition: 16% MLB: 52% *Comparables: Alen Hanson, Derek Dietrich, Dilson Herrera*

Some things a prospect just can't control. "Jed Lowrie playing too well to cut, but not well enough to trade" is one of those things. "Chad Pinder posting a .200-plus ISO in the majors" is another. So it's no shame that Barreto didn't ascend to a full-time spot at second base midway through 2017 the way it once seemed he might. But some things can be laid at the prospect's feet, like a strikeout rate just shy of 30 percent between Triple-A and the majors. For a hitter who has always put the bat on the ball, and who will need to hit for average to succeed because he won't walk, steal, defend or hit for power at top-notch levels, that sudden propensity to whiff is worrisome. Still, Barreto had a fine season at Triple-A, and whatever else he is or is not, he's 22, and there's plenty here to keep seeing an above-average major-leaguer, if something short of a star.

Austin Beck OF Born: 11/21/98 Age: 19 Bats: R Throws: R Height: 6'1" Weight: 200 Origin: Round 1, 2017 Draft (#6 overall)

YEAR	TEAM	LVL	AGE	PA	R	2B	3B	HR	RBI	BB	K	SB	CS	AVG/OBP/SLG	TAv	VORP	BABIP	BRR	FRAA	WARP
2017	ATH	RK	18	174	23	7	4	2	28	17	51	7	1	.211/.293/.349	.229	0.5	.294	1.8	CF(33): 1.3	0.2
2018	*OAK*	*MLB*	*19*	*250*	*22*	*9*	*1*	*6*	*24*	*14*	*90*	*3*	*1*	*.182/.232/.305*	*.181*	*-10.8*	*.263*	*0.1*	*CF -1*	*-1.3*
2019	*OAK*	*MLB*	*20*	*317*	*33*	*11*	*2*	*9*	*33*	*20*	*109*	*4*	*1*	*.199/.254/.339*	*.204*	*-9.1*	*.279*	*0.3*	*CF -1*	*-1.1*

Breakout: 0% Improve: 6% Collapse: 2% Attrition: 5% MLB: 10% *Comparables: Engel Beltre, Nomar Mazara, Francisco Pena*

There's perhaps more uncertainty about what Beck is and what he will become than with most top-10 picks in this age of year-round, all-data-all-the-time baseball because he missed the summer 2016 amateur showcases due to a knee injury. He's also a tools-first guy, less polished than we've come to expect from A's draft picks. His speed has him in center field for now, but we all get slower once we're not teenagers, so put your money on him ending up in right; he's got plenty of arm for the position. All of that is ancillary, though, because the main question is this: Will he hit? The raw power is plus, but you can't go yard unless you can put the barrel on the ball against a human pitcher who very much wants you *not* to put the barrel on the ball, and Beck is still a resounding "maybe" on that front.

Mark Canha OF Born: 02/15/89 Age: 29 Bats: R Throws: R Height: 6'2" Weight: 210 Origin: Round 7, 2010 Draft (#227 overall)

YEAR	TEAM	LVL	AGE	PA	R	2B	3B	HR	RBI	BB	K	SB	CS	AVG/OBP/SLG	TAv	VORP	BABIP	BRR	FRAA	WARP
2015	OAK	MLB	26	485	61	22	3	16	70	33	96	7	2	.254/.315/.426	.270	12.4	.289	0.8	1B(75): -2.0, LF(58): 5.3	1.7
2016	OAK	MLB	27	44	4	0	0	3	6	0	20	0	1	.122/.140/.341	.164	-3.6	.105	-0.1	1B(5): 0.2, RF(3): -0.3	-0.4
2017	NAS	AAA	28	317	52	25	3	12	50	34	62	4	0	.283/.373/.529	.324	32.7	.323	3.3	RF(61): -2.7, CF(8): 0.9	3.0
2017	OAK	MLB	28	187	16	13	1	5	14	7	56	2	0	.208/.262/.382	.221	-2.9	.274	0.3	RF(22): -0.9, LF(20): -0.8	-0.6
2018	*OAK*	*MLB*	*29*	*171*	*21*	*9*	*1*	*6*	*23*	*12*	*41*	*2*	*0*	*.239/.306/.430*	*.256*	*2.6*	*.284*	*0.0*	*1B 0*	*0.2*
2019	*OAK*	*MLB*	*30*	*266*	*34*	*14*	*1*	*11*	*35*	*21*	*67*	*2*	*1*	*.235/.306/.434*	*.251*	*2.5*	*.279*	*0.3*	*1B 0*	*0.3*

Breakout: 4% Improve: 35% Collapse: 6% Attrition: 11% MLB: 83% *Comparables: Jeremy Hermida, Will Venable, Craig Monroe*

Like a long line of Rule 5 picks before him, it's starting to become clear why Canha was available for drafting in 2015. While he was surprisingly good that season, hitting just enough to be a useful three-corners player, losing 2016 to injury did not help his argument for a regular roster spot last year on an A's team with a variety of better and/or younger options. He did add center field to his résumé, but about the most you can say is that he tries real real hard. He'd sure love to be a major-leaguer, but he just canha do it; he dinha have the power.

Chris Carter DH Born: 12/18/86 Age: 31 Bats: R Throws: R Height: 6'4" Weight: 245 Origin: Round 15, 2005 Draft (#455 overall)

YEAR	TEAM	LVL	AGE	PA	R	2B	3B	HR	RBI	BB	K	SB	CS	AVG/OBP/SLG	TAv	VORP	BABIP	BRR	FRAA	WARP
2015	HOU	MLB	28	460	50	17	0	24	64	57	151	1	2	.199/.307/.427	.266	4.5	.244	-2.7	1B(115): -0.8	0.4
2016	MIL	MLB	29	644	84	27	1	41	94	76	206	3	1	.222/.321/.499	.288	20.2	.260	-4.9	1B(155): -11.9	0.9
2017	NYA	MLB	30	208	20	5	1	8	26	20	76	0	0	.201/.284/.370	.230	-4.2	.284	0.0	1B(56): 0.5, RF(2): -0.1	-0.4
2017	NAS	AAA	30	154	21	5	1	9	22	19	49	0	0	.252/.357/.511	.306	8.8	.324	-0.7	1B(24): -1.9	0.7
2018	*OAK*	*MLB*	*31*	*305*	*40*	*12*	*1*	*17*	*47*	*35*	*103*	*1*	*1*	*.217/.314/.460*	*.259*	*4.1*	*.275*	*-1.4*	*1B -2, RF 0*	*0.2*
2019	*OAK*	*MLB*	*32*	*339*	*48*	*14*	*1*	*18*	*51*	*39*	*114*	*1*	*0*	*.214/.312/.451*	*.256*	*1.3*	*.271*	*-1.6*	*1B -3, RF 0*	*-0.1*

Breakout: 5% Improve: 42% Collapse: 7% Attrition: 11% MLB: 96% *Comparables: Mark Reynolds, Cecil Fielder, Craig Wilson*

Carter led the National League in games played, homers and strikeouts in 2016, struggled to find a landing place that winter, got cut by the Yankees in July and played out the rest of the year in Nashville. He hit fine there, as you would expect Carter to do in Triple-A. He can probably kick around the minors and/or Japan for another five to seven years if he wants, making a good, if not life-changing, living. His other option is to grow a thick beard, start going by his given first name (Vernon) and head to indie ball, where some college coach moonlighting as a scout can discover him and give him a fresh start, without the expectations of 2016's 40 homers or his turn-of-the-decade top-prospect rankings weighing him down. Glasses might help.

Matt Chapman 3B Born: 04/28/93 Age: 25 Bats: R Throws: R Height: 6'0" Weight: 210 Origin: Round 1, 2014 Draft (#25 overall)

YEAR	TEAM	LVL	AGE	PA	R	2B	3B	HR	RBI	BB	K	SB	CS	AVG/OBP/SLG	TAv	VORP	BABIP	BRR	FRAA	WARP
2015	STO	A+	22	352	60	21	3	23	57	39	79	4	1	.250/.341/.566	.335	37.5	.257	0.6	3B(77): 10.9	5.2
2016	MID	AA	23	504	78	26	4	29	83	59	147	7	4	.244/.335/.521	.297	35.4	.293	1.8	3B(100): 14.6, SS(10): 3.6	5.8
2016	NAS	AAA	23	85	14	1	1	7	13	9	26	0	0	.197/.282/.513	.302	6.7	.186	0.2	3B(18): 2.1	0.9
2017	NAS	AAA	24	204	30	6	2	16	30	25	63	5	4	.257/.348/.589	.318	20.3	.293	-0.1	3B(49): 7.2	2.7
2017	OAK	MLB	24	326	39	23	2	14	40	32	92	0	3	.234/.313/.472	.272	14.1	.290	-1.0	3B(84): 12.6	2.7
2018	*OAK*	*MLB*	*25*	*566*	*82*	*25*	*3*	*32*	*88*	*58*	*174*	*4*	*3*	*.226/.308/.482*	*.268*	*22.2*	*.272*	*-1.0*	*3B 17*	*3.5*
2019	*OAK*	*MLB*	*26*	*532*	*77*	*23*	*3*	*31*	*85*	*57*	*171*	*4*	*3*	*.221/.308/.484*	*.263*	*14.2*	*.268*	*-0.4*	*3B 17*	*3.3*

Breakout: 2% Improve: 31% Collapse: 12% Attrition: 23% MLB: 72% *Comparables: Mike Olt, Pedro Alvarez, Dallas McPherson*

Chapman's raw power has never been in question; what remained to be seen was whether enough of it would play in major-league games for a team to stomach his prodigious whiffitude and let his sterling glove and sonic-boom arm carry him to the nightly highlight reel. If last year's .238 isolated power holds up, then question answered. It's worth noting that Chapman had an adjustment period to the majors: He didn't get his batting average permanently above .200 until his 29th game. It doesn't mean he's definitely, for sure, 100 percent off-peak Brooks Robinson, but it's a more heartening trend line than a surprise explosion followed by a downward spiral of pitchers adjusting and exploiting weaknesses. He also plays extremely hard and got ejected from a game in September for arguing with Angels catcher Juan Graterol over alleged sign-stealing, so if you're looking for a new redass to love, then in the immortal words of Stephen A. Smith: Take a look, y'all.

Khris Davis LF Born: 12/21/87 Age: 30 Bats: R Throws: R Height: 5'10" Weight: 195 Origin: Round 7, 2009 Draft (#226 overall)

YEAR	TEAM	LVL	AGE	PA	R	2B	3B	HR	RBI	BB	K	SB	CS	AVG/OBP/SLG	TAv	VORP	BABIP	BRR	FRAA	WARP
2015	MIL	MLB	27	440	54	16	2	27	66	44	122	6	2	.247/.323/.505	.286	19.0	.285	-1.3	LF(108): -5.0	1.5
2016	OAK	MLB	28	610	85	24	2	42	102	42	166	1	2	.247/.307/.524	.287	23.9	.270	-3.3	LF(93): 0.2	2.5
2017	OAK	MLB	29	652	91	28	1	43	110	73	195	4	0	.247/.336/.528	.289	32.3	.290	-0.2	LF(116): -8.9	2.4
2018	*OAK*	*MLB*	*30*	*599*	*84*	*27*	*2*	*34*	*98*	*51*	*161*	*4*	*1*	*.242/.314/.491*	*.276*	*21.8*	*.277*	*-0.7*	*LF -1*	*1.9*
2019	*OAK*	*MLB*	*31*	*546*	*80*	*26*	*1*	*33*	*89*	*49*	*150*	*2*	*1*	*.241/.317/.501*	*.273*	*20.2*	*.276*	*-1.5*	*LF 0*	*2.2*

Breakout: 3% Improve: 49% Collapse: 5% Attrition: 8% MLB: 99% *Comparables: Jonny Gomes, Jason Bay, Willie Stargell*

"Khrush" (which, let's just be honest, that's a terrible nickname) seems likely to do what he does for a few more years yet: dongers for days (he trails The Mighty Giancarlo Stanton by just one for the big-league lead over the last two years), whiffs for weeks (second in that as well, behind Chris Davis, his brother from ... well, a whole other family) and throws for pterodactyls (as in, put a dinosaur in left field and you're more likely to see an assist than you are from Davis). He also has an appealingly off-kilter energy that defies easy categorization; that has not made its way into WARP yet, but with three straight last-place finishes, A's fans have needed something to latch onto. Davis is worthy of their love.

Dustin Fowler CF Born: 12/29/94 Age: 23 Bats: L Throws: L Height: 6'0" Weight: 195 Origin: Round 18, 2013 Draft (#554 overall)

YEAR	TEAM	LVL	AGE	PA	R	2B	3B	HR	RBI	BB	K	SB	CS	AVG/OBP/SLG	TAv	VORP	BABIP	BRR	FRAA	WARP
2015	CSC	A	20	256	35	9	3	4	31	11	47	18	7	.307/.340/.419	.295	15.8	.365	-0.2	CF(48): -3.5	1.3
2015	TAM	A+	20	262	29	11	3	1	39	15	43	12	6	.289/.328/.370	.267	11.6	.345	2.3	CF(61): -0.1, RF(2): -0.1	1.2
2016	TRN	AA	21	574	67	30	15	12	88	22	86	25	11	.281/.311/.458	.277	29.1	.313	3.5	CF(119): -10.0, RF(3): -0.6	2.0
2017	SWB	AAA	22	313	49	19	8	13	43	15	63	13	5	.293/.329/.542	.289	18.1	.335	-0.7	CF(40): -4.5, RF(14): -1.1	1.4
2018	*OAK*	*MLB*	*23*	*95*	*12*	*5*	*1*	*3*	*11*	*4*	*21*	*3*	*1*	*.254/.284/.438*	*.245*	*2.5*	*.296*	*0.4*	*CF -2*	*0.0*
2019	*OAK*	*MLB*	*24*	*314*	*38*	*16*	*5*	*12*	*43*	*15*	*70*	*11*	*4*	*.259/.297/.466*	*.253*	*8.5*	*.299*	*1.5*	*CF -5*	*0.4*

Breakout: 4% Improve: 18% Collapse: 4% Attrition: 17% MLB: 38% *Comparables: Josh Reddick, Austin Jackson, Eddie Rosario*

Every baseball journey is unique, which is one of the joys of the sport, but Fowler's stands out from the crowd. He was born in Cadwell, Georgia, a town of about 500 souls, and drafted in the 18th round by the Yankees, who bought him out of his commitment to Georgia Southern. Despite the non-premium pedigree, New York moved him quickly, putting him in Low-A at 19, giving him a midyear promotion to High-A at 20 and pushing him up a level a year since, leading to an early-season call to the big stage last season, whereupon he promptly ruptured his right patella tendon crashing into a wall in his first major-league inning. Hence the stat line you see above, which registers an MLB game played but not a single plate appearance. Then the A's acquired Fowler in the Sonny Gray trade despite the significant uncertainty surrounding his ability to recover completely.

Before the injury, Fowler was a well-rounded lefty with good speed and the classic problem of well-rounded outfielders everywhere: Is he just a tweener? In his case, the concern is less about a lack of power, and more about whether he'll get on base enough because of his aggressive approach. The A's are better stocked at the corners than up the middle, so Fowler should get a chance or six to fail in center unless he shows up in the spring hobbling. The service time he accrued on the disabled list last year hopefully lowers the incentive for the A's to dick him around to avoid Super Two payouts or "early" free agency, and should allow them to decide in April whether he's ready or not as a pure baseball matter.

Dustin Garneau C Born: 08/13/87 Age: 30 Bats: R Throws: R Height: 6'0" Weight: 200 Origin: Round 19, 2009 Draft (#571 overall)

YEAR	TEAM	LVL	AGE	PA	R	2B	3B	HR	RBI	BB	K	SB	CS	AVG/OBP/SLG	TAv	VORP	BABIP	BRR	FRAA	WARP
2015	ABQ	AAA	27	340	44	16	0	15	61	28	44	2	1	.274/.335/.475	.267	16.3	.274	-0.9	C(78): -1.8	1.5
2015	COL	MLB	27	76	6	3	0	2	8	6	14	0	0	.157/.224/.286	.205	-0.5	.167	0.3	C(22): -4.7	-0.6
2016	ABQ	AAA	28	211	31	11	0	15	35	16	43	2	0	.292/.367/.595	.312	20.4	.302	0.2	C(47): -0.1	2.1
2016	COL	MLB	28	75	7	6	0	1	6	6	22	0	0	.235/.293/.368	.235	0.0	.326	-1.4	C(23): -2.7	-0.3
2017	COL	MLB	29	74	5	7	0	1	6	4	24	0	0	.206/.260/.353	.217	0.9	.302	0.8	C(22): -2.6	-0.2
2017	ABQ	AAA	29	144	24	9	2	10	26	13	22	0	1	.281/.347/.617	.301	13.8	.265	0.2	C(36): -2.0	1.2
2017	OAK	MLB	29	52	5	1	0	1	3	8	12	0	0	.159/.288/.250	.205	-0.9	.194	-0.3	C(18): 0.5	0.0
2018	*OAK*	*MLB*	*30*	*97*	*12*	*4*	*0*	*4*	*13*	*8*	*23*	*0*	*0*	*.226/.292/.421*	*.249*	*3.7*	*.255*	*-0.2*	*C -3*	*0.0*
2019	*OAK*	*MLB*	*31*	*200*	*26*	*9*	*0*	*9*	*27*	*17*	*49*	*0*	*0*	*.226/.297/.430*	*.248*	*4.9*	*.256*	*-0.3*	*C -5*	*0.0*

Breakout: 6% Improve: 21% Collapse: 7% Attrition: 19% MLB: 51%

Comparables: Chris Gimenez, Anthony Recker, Mike Rivera

YEAR	TEAM	P. COUNT	FRM RUNS	BLK RUNS	THRW RUNS	TOT RUNS
2015	ABQ	11185	-5.9	-0.2	0.6	-5.5
2015	COL	2947	-5.1	0.1	0.1	-4.9
2016	COL	2680	-2.7	-0.1	0.1	-2.8
2017	COL	2719	-1.7	-0.8	0.0	-2.5
2017	OAK	2146	0.7	-0.5	0.3	0.4
2018	*OAK*	*3667*	*-2.9*	*-0.3*	*0.1*	*-3.0*
2019	*OAK*	*7569*	*-3.7*	*-0.3*	*0.1*	*-3.9*

Josh Phegley's anemic bat and late-summer oblique injury opened the door for Garneau, claimed off waivers from the Rockies in August, to take the A's right-handed-backup-catcher spot, but he didn't exactly seize the day. He has raked in Albuquerque, but your fourth cousin Jerry would hit .220/.310/.400 there, so it's no surprise Garneau's hitting hasn't translated to the bigs. His framing and blocking don't grade out as anything better than mediocre either, so even if he wins a big-league job, he's probably just holding it for the next guy. If that's in Oakland, the next guy is Sean Murphy.

Matt Joyce OF Born: 08/03/84 Age: 33 Bats: L Throws: R Height: 6'2" Weight: 205 Origin: Round 12, 2005 Draft (#360 overall)

YEAR	TEAM	LVL	AGE	PA	R	2B	3B	HR	RBI	BB	K	SB	CS	AVG/OBP/SLG	TAv	VORP	BABIP	BRR	FRAA	WARP
2015	SLC	AAA	30	43	3	1	0	2	6	5	9	0	0	.333/.419/.528	.328	3.8	.385	0.1	LF(7): -0.5	0.3
2015	ANA	MLB	30	284	17	12	1	5	21	30	67	0	3	.174/.272/.291	.217	-6.1	.215	0.5	LF(64): -0.5, RF(2): -0.1	-0.7
2016	PIT	MLB	31	293	45	10	1	13	42	59	67	1	1	.242/.403/.463	.306	22.6	.285	2.6	RF(43): -1.7, LF(26): -0.3	2.1
2017	OAK	MLB	32	544	78	33	0	25	68	66	113	4	1	.243/.335/.473	.270	17.9	.263	1.9	RF(115): 0.7, LF(24): 2.5	2.1
2018	*OAK*	*MLB*	*33*	*634*	*86*	*29*	*2*	*21*	*71*	*81*	*139*	*4*	*2*	*.231/.332/.405*	*.259*	*21.1*	*.270*	*-1.4*	*LF 0*	*1.3*
2019	*OAK*	*MLB*	*34*	*481*	*63*	*22*	*1*	*16*	*58*	*65*	*112*	*2*	*1*	*.226/.333/.406*	*.254*	*10.7*	*.266*	*1.8*	*LF 1*	*1.3*

Breakout: 1% Improve: 27% Collapse: 7% Attrition: 11% MLB: 96%

Comparables: Trot Nixon, David DeJesus, Jim King

Joyce was suspended for two games in August for shouting an anti-gay slur at a fan. His apology, to his credit, was not of the "sorry if anyone was offended" variety, but after-the-fact words, or even actions, are not enough: Every time something like this happens, it's another reminder to any closeted player, coach, scout or executive that no Supreme Court rulings or legislative acts can erase decades of toxic culture. Vile enough words emanate from the bleachers—black players in particular continue to report horrendous treatment—that one could wish all players would be making every effort to welcome and defend each other regardless of their orientation. It will get better, but in 2018, we should not be speaking about this in the future tense.

Joyce had a perfectly decent year afield and at the plate (he set career highs in several offensive categories), but he's now at the age where a little bit of slippage in pitch recognition or bat speed can start the domino effect that takes players right out of the league.

Jed Lowrie 2B Born: 04/17/84 Age: 34 Bats: B Throws: R Height: 6'0" Weight: 180 Origin: Round 1, 2005 Draft (#45 overall)

YEAR	TEAM	LVL	AGE	PA	R	2B	3B	HR	RBI	BB	K	SB	CS	AVG/OBP/SLG	TAv	VORP	BABIP	BRR	FRAA	WARP
2015	HOU	MLB	31	263	35	14	0	9	30	28	43	1	0	.222/.312/.400	.263	10.6	.233	1.2	3B(47): -6.5, SS(17): 1.0	0.5
2016	OAK	MLB	32	369	30	12	1	2	27	26	65	0	0	.263/.314/.322	.229	-2.9	.316	-1.1	2B(82): 2.0, SS(2): 0.0	-0.1
2017	OAK	MLB	33	645	86	49	3	14	69	73	100	0	1	.277/.360/.448	.276	25.7	.314	-2.4	2B(136): -3.5, 3B(1): 0.2	2.2
2018	*OAK*	*MLB*	*34*	*540*	*55*	*31*	*2*	*10*	*59*	*48*	*87*	*1*	*0*	*.258/.326/.391*	*.251*	*16.4*	*.294*	*-1.1*	*2B -2*	*1.0*
2019	*OAK*	*MLB*	*35*	*461*	*53*	*26*	*2*	*10*	*49*	*44*	*80*	*0*	*0*	*.249/.324/.391*	*.244*	*6.6*	*.285*	*-0.8*	*2B -1*	*0.6*

Breakout: 1% Improve: 32% Collapse: 8% Attrition: 23% MLB: 88%

Comparables: Todd Walker, Aaron Hill, Skip Schumaker

Lowrie was supposed to be a placeholder for the A's, manning second base semicompetently until Franklin Barreto was ready to ascend to the position, the unspoken transition period being whatever day in the summer would allow the A's to avoid granting Barreto Super Two status. Instead Lowrie went out and had his best season since 2013, the kind of doubles-upon-doubles year he was supposed to be providing for the last decade. He credited full health for the bounce-back; PECOTA doesn't know anything about that, but it can certainly draw some inferences based on Lowrie's recent playing time, his age and his position. You'd do well to draw those same inferences if you're a fantasy player, or a GM looking to make a trade. And if you're the latter, well, get your nose out of a book and go watch a baseball game.

Jorge Mateo SS Born: 06/23/95 Age: 23 Bats: R Throws: R Height: 6'0" Weight: 190 Origin: International Free Agent, 2012

YEAR	TEAM	LVL	AGE	PA	R	2B	3B	HR	RBI	BB	K	SB	CS	AVG/OBP/SLG	TAv	VORP	BABIP	BRR	FRAA	WARP
2015	CSC	A	20	409	51	18	8	2	33	36	80	71	15	.268/.338/.378	.277	25.5	.338	4.1	SS(79): -1.0	2.6
2015	TAM	A+	20	91	15	5	3	0	7	7	18	11	2	.321/.374/.452	.313	10.6	.409	2.3	SS(20): -0.1	1.1
2016	TAM	A+	21	507	65	16	9	8	47	33	108	36	15	.254/.306/.379	.244	11.8	.313	3.2	SS(62): -5.1, 2B(40): -0.6	0.6
2017	TAM	A+	22	297	39	16	8	4	11	16	79	28	3	.240/.288/.400	.251	15.3	.321	7.6	SS(42): 2.9, CF(22): -0.8	1.8
2017	TRN	AA	22	140	26	9	3	4	26	15	32	11	7	.300/.381/.525	.333	16.9	.372	1.6	SS(16): 1.1, 2B(5): 0.4	1.9
2017	MID	AA	22	147	25	5	7	4	20	9	33	13	3	.292/.333/.518	.301	14.1	.356	2.2	SS(30): 0.8	1.6
2018	*OAK*	*MLB*	*23*	*250*	*36*	*10*	*4*	*7*	*23*	*15*	*72*	*16*	*5*	*.229/.279/.400*	*.225*	*4.3*	*.296*	*2.1*	*SS 1, CF 0*	*0.6*
2019	*OAK*	*MLB*	*24*	*354*	*40*	*14*	*5*	*11*	*42*	*22*	*101*	*22*	*7*	*.229/.283/.408*	*.234*	*5.8*	*.294*	*4.0*	*SS 2, CF 0*	*0.8*

Breakout: 18% Improve: 37% Collapse: 5% Attrition: 20% MLB: 45%

Comparables: Junior Lake, Derek Dietrich, Tim Anderson

The A's needed another good middle-infield prospect like they needed a hole in the bat, but they got Mateo from the Yankees in the Sonny Gray trade anyway, then watched him continue tearing up Double-A the same way he had in Trenton before the deal. The steals, on the basis of true 80-grade speed, are the exciting part (don't run for your calculator: Last year's total was 52 out of 65, an 80 percent success rate), but he's also a good bet to remain at an up-the-middle position (inconsistency at shortstop and the realities of the A's depth chart mean you should bet on center field, though it's worth noting that he played exclusively at short for Midland) and he has more pop than your average string-bean speedster. Think The Flash after he learns how to punch bad guys real hard and throw lightning: Just because the superpower is speed doesn't mean he's one-dimensional.

Bruce Maxwell C

Born: 12/20/90 Age: 27 Bats: L Throws: R Height: 6'1" Weight: 250 Origin: Round 2, 2012 Draft (#62 overall)

YEAR	TEAM	LVL	AGE	PA	R	2B	3B	HR	RBI	BB	K	SB	CS	AVG/OBP/SLG	TAv	VORP	BABIP	BRR	FRAA	WARP
2015	MID	AA	24	381	32	16	0	2	48	39	54	0	1	.243/.321/.308	.220	-3.0	.282	-1.4	C(78): 14.3	1.2
2016	NAS	AAA	25	219	27	12	0	10	41	24	38	1	0	.321/.393/.539	.334	25.8	.354	-1.1	C(60): 15.5	4.3
2016	OAK	MLB	25	101	8	6	1	1	14	8	24	0	0	.283/.337/.402	.265	4.9	.368	0.3	C(29): -0.9	0.4
2017	NAS	AAA	26	93	11	9	0	2	14	8	14	0	0	.286/.344/.464	.272	4.8	.319	-0.2	C(19): 3.0	0.8
2017	OAK	MLB	26	253	21	12	0	3	22	31	63	0	0	.237/.329/.333	.230	2.3	.316	-1.4	C(74): -4.6	-0.2
2018	*OAK*	*MLB*	*27*	*412*	*45*	*20*	*1*	*9*	*44*	*39*	*91*	*0*	*0*	*.240/.313/.377*	*.242*	*12.2*	*.292*	*-0.9*	*C 0*	*0.8*
2019	*OAK*	*MLB*	*28*	*366*	*43*	*18*	*0*	*10*	*40*	*36*	*89*	*0*	*0*	*.234/.311/.381*	*.237*	*4.7*	*.289*	*-0.7*	*C 1*	*0.6*

Breakout: 4% Improve: 28% Collapse: 20% Attrition: 30% MLB: 73%

Comparables: JD Closser, Jason Jaramillo, Steve Clevenger

YEAR	TEAM	P. COUNT	FRM RUNS	BLK RUNS	THRW RUNS	TOT RUNS
2015	MID	10748	15.7	1.3	-0.9	16.0
2016	OAK	3366	-0.5	-0.1	-0.1	-0.7
2017	OAK	9289	-1.3	-1.6	0.4	-2.5
2018	*OAK*	*15551*	*4.0*	*-0.7*	*0.0*	*3.3*
2019	*OAK*	*13828*	*3.2*	*-0.5*	*0.0*	*2.6*

In late September, Maxwell joined a movement that had already taken significant hold in professional football by kneeling for the national anthem. Boos were heard during the A's season-closing series in Texas, but Maxwell joined the protest so late in the year that it is hard to know how, or even whether, things will progress, particularly in the context of a league with about one-tenth the African-American representation of the NFL. In the games, Maxwell stepped directly into Stephen Vogt's role as the primary starting catcher after the A's designated Vogt for assignment in June. Years ago, Nichols' Law of Catcher Defense plus Maxwell's minor-league reputation might have led us to call him a defense-first backstop; now, our framing and blocking stats say he's taking just as much off the table behind the plate as he is at it. That reputation will get him more chances, and he's a big boy who ought to hit for more power than he did last year, but even with the platoon advantage, he's going to have to improve *something* to be more than a Quad-A shuttle passenger. Maxwell clouded his future further by drunkenly pointing a gun at a Postmates driver in the offseason. He was charged with aggravated assault; at press time, his legal situation had not been resolved, but the A's believed he would still be their starting catcher.

Kevin Merrell SS

Born: 12/14/95 Age: 22 Bats: L Throws: R Height: 6'1" Weight: 180 Origin: Round 1, 2017 Draft (#33 overall)

YEAR	TEAM	LVL	AGE	PA	R	2B	3B	HR	RBI	BB	K	SB	CS	AVG/OBP/SLG	TAv	VORP	BABIP	BRR	FRAA	WARP
2017	VER	A-	21	140	27	5	1	2	9	9	22	10	3	.320/.362/.424	.317	18.3	.365	4.1	SS(28): 0.4	1.9
2018	*OAK*	*MLB*	*22*	*250*	*30*	*10*	*1*	*7*	*23*	*14*	*69*	*6*	*2*	*.216/.265/.354*	*.208*	*-1.7*	*.273*	*0.3*	*SS 1*	*-0.1*
2019	*OAK*	*MLB*	*23*	*222*	*24*	*9*	*1*	*6*	*25*	*14*	*60*	*5*	*2*	*.224/.276/.371*	*.222*	*-1.0*	*.280*	*0.5*	*SS 1*	*0.0*

Breakout: 1% Improve: 7% Collapse: 5% Attrition: 9% MLB: 13%

Comparables: Orlando Calixte, Ian Desmond, Pete Kozma

Merrell, who the A's picked 33rd overall last year out of South Florida, hopes to profile like Jorge Mateo, as a speedy shortstop/center fielder with enough in his bat to actualize the wheels. Mateo probably has a better shot at staying at shortstop, though, as Merrell's issues there stem from his physical tools rather than focus and inconsistency. Merrell also lacks Mateo's pop, which is not to say that he gets the bat knocked out of his hands, and he has shown the selectivity at the plate that could help him profile as a legitimate leadoff man. It's worth noting that Merrell is only six months younger than Mateo, so his first full season in the minors will be the big test: Can he be Wally West to Mateo's Barry Allen, or is he more Bart Allen, Barry's very fast but ultimately short-lived grandson?

Sean Murphy C

Born: 10/10/94 Age: 23 Bats: R Throws: R Height: 6'3" Weight: 215 Origin: Round 3, 2016 Draft (#83 overall)

YEAR	TEAM	LVL	AGE	PA	R	2B	3B	HR	RBI	BB	K	SB	CS	AVG/OBP/SLG	TAv	VORP	BABIP	BRR	FRAA	WARP
2016	VER	A-	21	85	10	1	0	2	7	9	12	1	0	.237/.318/.329	.251	3.1	.258	0.4	C(20): 0.4	0.4
2017	STO	A+	22	178	22	11	0	9	26	11	33	0	0	.297/.343/.527	.301	14.9	.323	0.2	C(40): -0.4	1.5
2017	MID	AA	22	217	25	7	0	4	22	21	34	0	0	.209/.288/.309	.223	1.7	.232	0.6	C(51): 4.3	0.6
2018	*OAK*	*MLB*	*23*	*250*	*27*	*11*	*0*	*9*	*32*	*19*	*56*	*0*	*0*	*.232/.295/.410*	*.236*	*6.2*	*.263*	*-0.4*	*C -3*	*0.4*
2019	*OAK*	*MLB*	*24*	*226*	*28*	*10*	*0*	*8*	*28*	*18*	*51*	*0*	*0*	*.234/.298/.412*	*.241*	*3.8*	*.268*	*-0.5*	*C -1*	*0.3*

Breakout: 4% Improve: 25% Collapse: 4% Attrition: 23% MLB: 37%

Comparables: Jonathan Lucroy, Josh Donaldson, John Ryan Murphy

YEAR	TEAM	P. COUNT	FRM RUNS	BLK RUNS	THRW RUNS	TOT RUNS
2018	*OAK*	*8932*	*-1.7*	*-1.0*	*-1.0*	*-3.7*
2019	*OAK*	*8061*	*-0.5*	*-0.3*	*-0.3*	*-1.0*

Murphy was the A's third-round pick in 2016 out of Wright State. The profile behind the plate is everything you could hope for: athleticism, blocking, receiving, a 70-grade arm, even dreamy pop times that cause the arm to play up, not that it needs it. The offense ... well, someone has to bat ninth. Murphy is strong and will hit some homers solely on that basis, and he's not up at the plate hacking at whatever nonsense the pitchers want to give him, but the hit tool is a tool for a reason and Murphy doesn't have one that would normally get someone to the majors. Still, with all we've learned about catcher defense in the last few years, there's more hope than ever for this profile. Think Austin Hedges or Martin Maldonado as full-time, legitimate, above-average major-leaguers who don't hit a lick. It's a long shot, but it's not a non-shot.

Sheldon Neuse INF Born: 12/10/94 Age: 23 Bats: R Throws: R Height: 6'0" Weight: 195 Origin: Round 2, 2016 Draft (#58 overall)

YEAR	TEAM	LVL	AGE	PA	R	2B	3B	HR	RBI	BB	K	SB	CS	AVG/OBP/SLG	TAv	VORP	BABIP	BRR	FRAA	WARP
2016	AUB	A-	21	141	16	5	3	1	11	13	26	2	2	.230/.305/.341	.259	3.9	.280	-0.4	3B(26): 1.9, SS(6): 1.0	0.7
2017	HAG	A	22	321	40	19	3	9	51	25	66	12	5	.291/.349/.469	.313	27.2	.347	-1.9	SS(43): -2.9, 3B(33): 6.6	3.2
2017	STO	A+	22	94	21	3	0	7	22	9	25	2	0	.386/.457/.675	.398	16.8	.490	0.4	3B(10): -1.5, SS(8): -0.4	1.6
2017	MID	AA	22	75	9	4	0	0	6	6	21	0	0	.373/.427/.433	.287	4.7	.532	0.3	3B(18): 1.4, 1B(1): -0.4	0.6
2018	*OAK*	*MLB*	*23*	*250*	*28*	*11*	*1*	*9*	*32*	*18*	*72*	*2*	*1*	*.241/.299/.414*	*.241*	*4.5*	*.309*	*-0.2*	*3B 1, SS -1*	*0.5*
2019	*OAK*	*MLB*	*24*	*366*	*46*	*16*	*1*	*14*	*47*	*27*	*104*	*3*	*1*	*.243/.302/.424*	*.248*	*5.5*	*.307*	*-0.3*	*3B 2, SS -1*	*0.7*

Breakout: 5% Improve: 23% Collapse: 3% Attrition: 11% MLB: 38% *Comparables: Adam Duvall, Paul DeJong, Will Middlebrooks*

Neuse is a beefy third baseman the A's acquired from Washington in the Sean Doolittle/Ryan Madson trade last summer. He's a better defender than you'd think by simply looking at him, especially if you only see a headshot: Like so many of us, he suffers from Really Large Face Syndrome. It's not clear where he'd play given the A's current and future infield, but there's time for that to sort itself out; while he reached Double-A last year, he'll have to perform for a full season in the high minors before the A's start shifting the puzzle pieces around to slot him in. There's reason for optimism, though, specifically in the above-average bat speed that should let him hit enough to reach the majors.

Renato Nunez 3B Born: 04/04/94 Age: 24 Bats: R Throws: R Height: 6'1" Weight: 220 Origin: International Free Agent, 2010

YEAR	TEAM	LVL	AGE	PA	R	2B	3B	HR	RBI	BB	K	SB	CS	AVG/OBP/SLG	TAv	VORP	BABIP	BRR	FRAA	WARP
2015	MID	AA	21	416	62	23	0	18	61	28	66	1	0	.278/.332/.480	.277	14.9	.293	-0.9	3B(49): -0.7, 1B(16): -0.5	1.5
2016	NAS	AAA	22	550	61	20	2	23	75	31	119	2	0	.228/.278/.412	.262	16.8	.249	0.9	3B(89): -1.2, LF(12): -0.5	1.6
2016	OAK	MLB	22	15	0	0	0	0	1	0	3	0	0	.133/.133/.133	.089	-3.1	.167	-0.7		-0.3
2017	NAS	AAA	23	533	74	27	2	32	78	47	141	2	1	.249/.319/.518	.281	23.5	.279	-1.5	LF(48): -7.0, 3B(44): -4.7	1.1
2017	OAK	MLB	23	16	1	0	0	1	3	1	8	0	0	.200/.250/.400	.224	-0.5	.333	-0.2	LF(3): -0.2, 3B(1): 0.2	-0.1
2018	*OAK*	*MLB*	*24*	*197*	*25*	*8*	*1*	*10*	*29*	*12*	*52*	*0*	*0*	*.230/.282/.451*	*.250*	*3.4*	*.259*	*-0.4*	*3B -1, LF -2*	*-0.1*
2019	*OAK*	*MLB*	*25*	*423*	*58*	*20*	*1*	*23*	*66*	*30*	*116*	*0*	*0*	*.238/.298/.476*	*.257*	*7.2*	*.273*	*-0.9*	*3B -2, LF -4*	*0.2*

Breakout: 6% Improve: 25% Collapse: 10% Attrition: 23% MLB: 43% *Comparables: Corey Dickerson, Scott Schebler, Daniel Dorn*

Nuñez was a bonus baby back in 2010, signing for $2.2 million, and he still has the Right-Handed Power™ that got him that money: His first big-league homer, last September in Arlington, was an opposite-field shot on a two-strike fastball low and away. There's enough here at present for a four-corners, all-or-nothing reserve bat, especially if he can make his way to the National League. A step forward in pitch discernment could make him a second-division starter, though if we're being honest, we're probably talking about a step on the order of Neil Armstrong.

Matt Olson 1B Born: 03/29/94 Age: 24 Bats: L Throws: R Height: 6'5" Weight: 230 Origin: Round 1, 2012 Draft (#47 overall)

YEAR	TEAM	LVL	AGE	PA	R	2B	3B	HR	RBI	BB	K	SB	CS	AVG/OBP/SLG	TAv	VORP	BABIP	BRR	FRAA	WARP
2015	MID	AA	21	585	82	37	0	17	75	105	139	5	1	.249/.388/.438	.285	22.2	.311	-0.4	1B(62): 12.4, RF(59): 16.0	5.5
2016	NAS	AAA	22	540	69	34	1	17	60	71	132	1	0	.235/.335/.422	.279	15.5	.289	-2.9	RF(81): -3.0, 1B(49): 3.9	1.7
2016	OAK	MLB	22	28	3	1	0	0	0	7	4	0	0	.095/.321/.143	.194	-1.6	.118	-0.2	RF(5): -0.7, 1B(4): -0.1	-0.2
2017	NAS	AAA	23	343	56	16	1	23	60	45	83	3	0	.272/.367/.568	.326	29.2	.298	-0.1	1B(73): -0.8, 3B(1): -0.2	2.7
2017	OAK	MLB	23	216	33	2	0	24	45	22	60	0	0	.259/.352/.651	.315	15.4	.238	0.3	1B(43): 4.7, RF(12): 2.8	2.3
2018	*OAK*	*MLB*	*24*	*593*	*82*	*27*	*1*	*31*	*92*	*76*	*165*	*0*	*0*	*.230/.333/.466*	*.274*	*19.2*	*.272*	*-1.2*	*1B 6*	*2.1*
2019	*OAK*	*MLB*	*25*	*547*	*82*	*26*	*0*	*29*	*84*	*77*	*154*	*0*	*0*	*.229/.342/.476*	*.274*	*14.8*	*.270*	*-0.1*	*1B 6*	*2.2*

Breakout: 6% Improve: 30% Collapse: 23% Attrition: 28% MLB: 67% *Comparables: A.J. Reed, Rhys Hoskins, Paul Goldschmidt*

Sorry, *how* many homers in *how* many plate appearances? (Hint: Cast your eyes upward an inch.) Olson hit more round-trippers than anyone in baseball as a percentage of trips to the plate (min. 33 PA) and he did it while striking out in the Wil Myers/Javy Baez range, substantially less often than Gods of Whiffs like Chris Davis and Joey Gallo. But don't go multiplying his WARP by 2.5 and declaring Olson an MVP just yet: A winter of pitchers, catchers and coaches watching video may do them wonders at avoiding more embarrassing 440-foot dongs, especially since hitters this tall tend to have substantial holes. Olson also did an alarming amount of his damage against inferior September competition, but even in this Oprah-giving-away-cars atmosphere for dingers, what he did last year was special enough to justify optimism going forward. A fun fact: Only 20 players in MLB history have slugged .650 in a season of at least 200 PA, and 18 of those did it more than once, the 19th being Olson and the 20th being J.D. Martinez, who also reached the plateau just last year. Ergo, Matt Olson will slug .650 again. QED.

Chad Pinder UT Born: 03/29/92 Age: 26 Bats: R Throws: R Height: 6'2" Weight: 195 Origin: Round 2, 2013 Draft (#71 overall)

YEAR	TEAM	LVL	AGE	PA	R	2B	3B	HR	RBI	BB	K	SB	CS	AVG/OBP/SLG	TAv	VORP	BABIP	BRR	FRAA	WARP
2015	MID	AA	23	522	71	32	2	15	86	28	103	7	5	.317/.361/.486	.288	34.4	.374	-0.1	SS(112): -18.6	1.7
2016	NAS	AAA	24	465	72	23	3	14	51	25	108	5	1	.258/.310/.425	.278	31.4	.312	4.5	SS(98): -4.2, 2B(4): -0.9	2.7
2016	OAK	MLB	24	55	4	4	0	1	4	3	14	0	0	.235/.273/.373	.230	0.4	.297	0.4	2B(13): 0.1, SS(7): -0.2	0.0
2017	NAS	AAA	25	71	3	2	1	1	2	6	23	2	1	.266/.338/.375	.259	0.6	.400	-1.5	2B(8): 0.1, SS(4): -0.3	0.0
2017	OAK	MLB	25	309	36	15	1	15	42	18	92	2	1	.238/.292/.457	.261	6.9	.292	-1.8	RF(35): -0.4, SS(22): 1.6	0.8
2018	*OAK*	*MLB*	*26*	*92*	*11*	*4*	*0*	*3*	*12*	*5*	*25*	*1*	*0*	*.245/.292/.426*	*.250*	*2.7*	*.305*	*-0.1*	*2B -1, SS 0*	*0.1*
2019	*OAK*	*MLB*	*27*	*309*	*38*	*16*	*1*	*12*	*40*	*18*	*86*	*2*	*1*	*.245/.300/.431*	*.249*	*5.9*	*.307*	*-0.6*	*2B -3, SS -1*	*0.2*

Breakout: 10% Improve: 28% Collapse: 12% Attrition: 19% MLB: 56% *Comparables: Victor Diaz, Cody Ross, Brennan Boesch*

Pinder came up through the A's minor-league system as a multi-position infielder, then added the outfield to his CV last year. His defensive skills were surprisingly portable, and his arm in particular plays everywhere. This is important because it is increasingly clear that he's not going to make enough contact, or make up the lack of contact in walks, to be a regular at any position, or a Zobristian supersub. The power plays, though, and makes him a dangerous option off the bench, someone who can pinch-hit for nearly any spot without necessitating a second substitution or a series of position switches on defense. He can also get plenty of work covering injuries and days off. One does dread, though, giving modern front offices an excuse to carry yet another pitcher in the bullpen.

Stephen Piscotty RF Born: 01/14/91 Age: 27 Bats: R Throws: R Height: 6'3" Weight: 210 Origin: Round 1, 2012 Draft (#36 overall)

YEAR	TEAM	LVL	AGE	PA	R	2B	3B	HR	RBI	BB	K	SB	CS	AVG/OBP/SLG	TAv	VORP	BABIP	BRR	FRAA	WARP
2015	MEM	AAA	24	372	54	28	2	11	41	46	62	5	6	.272/.366/.475	.309	23.2	.304	-2.3	RF(61): 6.1, LF(10): -0.9	2.9
2015	SLN	MLB	24	256	29	15	4	7	39	20	56	2	1	.305/.359/.494	.314	16.4	.372	-1.9	LF(55): -5.6, RF(15): -1.0	1.0
2016	SLN	MLB	25	649	86	35	3	22	85	51	133	7	5	.273/.343/.457	.291	30.1	.319	-2.1	RF(146): -2.3, CF(10): 0.1	2.9
2017	MEM	AAA	26	38	7	3	0	4	7	6	7	0	0	.313/.421/.781	.405	6.9	.286	0.0	RF(6): -0.2	0.6
2017	SLN	MLB	26	401	40	16	1	9	39	52	87	3	6	.235/.342/.367	.252	1.6	.286	-2.5	RF(99): -0.9	0.1
2018	*OAK*	*MLB*	*27*	*503*	*62*	*26*	*3*	*17*	*65*	*49*	*110*	*5*	*4*	*.255/.335/.439*	*.272*	*17.4*	*.302*	*-1.2*	*RF -1*	*1.5*
2019	*OAK*	*MLB*	*28*	*441*	*58*	*23*	*2*	*15*	*56*	*45*	*97*	*4*	*4*	*.255/.339/.439*	*.268*	*11.4*	*.302*	*-1.6*	*RF 0*	*1.2*

Breakout: 1% Improve: 47% Collapse: 7% Attrition: 9% MLB: 99% *Comparables: Travis Snider, Dexter Fowler, Andre Ethier*

Has it ever felt like everyone else got a party invite except you? Bully for you! Parties are boring and socially awkward. But Piscotty did not get the memo that 2017 was the year of the breakout Cardinals outfielder. In fact, the former top 101 prospect bottomed out in August to the point that he was optioned to Triple-A Memphis to figure out why the ol' stick just isn't producing like it used to. A couple of disabled list trips throughout the season for a maladious hamstring didn't help the rhythm at all, and the only good news from the injury is that it finally gave Tommy Pham playing time. The lame hammy could be related to the evaporated power, and if so, a clean bill of health might be enough to give Piscotty the breakout season he was waiting for a year later than everyone else. Showing up late to the party is still cool. Besides, it's not his fault they moved it to Oakland at the last minute.

Boog Powell CF Born: 01/14/93 Age: 25 Bats: L Throws: L Height: 5'10" Weight: 185 Origin: Round 20, 2012 Draft (#619 overall)

YEAR	TEAM	LVL	AGE	PA	R	2B	3B	HR	RBI	BB	K	SB	CS	AVG/OBP/SLG	TAv	VORP	BABIP	BRR	FRAA	WARP
2015	MNT	AA	22	276	44	6	6	1	22	29	38	11	8	.328/.408/.416	.302	19.8	.385	1.6	CF(34): -0.3, RF(17): 3.8	2.5
2015	DUR	AAA	22	246	22	10	3	2	18	32	41	7	6	.257/.360/.364	.259	3.4	.309	-2.3	CF(29): 3.5, LF(22): -0.3	0.7
2016	TAC	AAA	23	277	39	9	2	3	27	22	42	10	6	.270/.326/.359	.249	5.8	.311	0.5	CF(61): 1.4	0.7
2017	SEA	MLB	24	43	6	0	0	0	2	6	9	0	0	.194/.310/.194	.216	-1.1	.259	0.0	LF(8): 0.7, RF(1): 0.0	-0.1
2017	TAC	AAA	24	239	46	9	2	6	33	28	27	11	5	.340/.416/.490	.320	23.1	.364	0.9	RF(25): -1.0, CF(24): -1.7	1.9
2017	OAK	MLB	24	92	18	5	0	3	10	9	21	0	1	.321/.380/.494	.305	8.9	.390	1.7	CF(28): 2.1	1.1
2018	*OAK*	*MLB*	*25*	*447*	*54*	*17*	*4*	*9*	*46*	*42*	*84*	*10*	*6*	*.264/.333/.396*	*.255*	*14.6*	*.307*	*-0.2*	*CF 1*	*1.2*
2019	*OAK*	*MLB*	*26*	*524*	*65*	*21*	*5*	*13*	*60*	*53*	*102*	*11*	*7*	*.267/.344/.417*	*.258*	*15.0*	*.311*	*0.2*	*CF 2*	*1.8*

Breakout: 8% Improve: 45% Collapse: 4% Attrition: 35% MLB: 72% *Comparables: Brett Gardner, Abraham Almonte, Ezequiel Carrera*

One would not think that Herschel Mack Powell IV would need a nickname, especially a stolen nickname, but even the grumpiest among us have to admit amusement at this 5-foot-10 center fielder carrying the same moniker as the behemoth first baseman–turned–barbecue proprietor, particularly after New Boog hit his first career big-league homer into Original Boog's 'cue stand at Camden Yards. Between Boog the Younger's size, visible choking up on the bat and willingness to wait a pitcher out, you'd peg him as a slapper, but he swings the bat hard and should hit for enough power to keep pitchers honest. The 2017 BABIP at Triple-A and with Oakland is fake news; once you leach off that helium he's looking at a fourth-outfielder career, one whose hot streaks might sometimes convince teams to start him in center. Or he could slug .194 for the rest of his life. Or he could get caught with PEDs for a third time. If we could see the future, it wouldn't be the future; death would be conquered and life would be meaningless.

Marcus Semien SS Born: 09/17/90 Age: 27 Bats: R Throws: R Height: 6'0" Weight: 195 Origin: Round 6, 2011 Draft (#201 overall)

YEAR	TEAM	LVL	AGE	PA	R	2B	3B	HR	RBI	BB	K	SB	CS	AVG/OBP/SLG	TAv	VORP	BABIP	BRR	FRAA	WARP
2015	OAK	MLB	24	601	65	23	7	15	45	42	132	11	5	.257/.310/.405	.253	20.5	.312	0.8	SS(152): -4.4	1.7
2016	OAK	MLB	25	621	72	27	2	27	75	51	139	10	2	.238/.300/.435	.266	32.2	.268	2.6	SS(159): 1.0	3.4
2017	OAK	MLB	26	386	53	19	1	10	40	38	85	12	1	.249/.325/.398	.254	18.2	.300	3.9	SS(85): -1.5	1.7
2018	*OAK*	*MLB*	*27*	*593*	*84*	*27*	*4*	*20*	*68*	*56*	*131*	*12*	*3*	*.248/.321/.426*	*.261*	*30.0*	*.291*	*1.2*	*SS -1*	*2.1*
2019	*OAK*	*MLB*	*28*	*503*	*65*	*23*	*3*	*18*	*65*	*50*	*113*	*10*	*2*	*.247/.324/.435*	*.259*	*18.7*	*.289*	*2.1*	*SS -1*	*1.9*

Breakout: 1% Improve: 40% Collapse: 8% Attrition: 11% MLB: 97% *Comparables: Khalil Greene, Bobby Crosby, Sean Rodriguez*

Semien missed the first half of 2017 with a broken wrist (his first extended absence since a bout of shoulder tendinitis at High-A in 2012) and had the classic wrist-injury lingering effects when he returned: Check that drop in power compared to 2016. Semien himself didn't talk about it, but Susan Slusser reported late in the season that a scout thought his swing was more controlled and that he was hunting pitches to hit more than he had in the past. And wouldn't you know it: a near–10 percent walk rate, a career best. Semien is young enough for optimism that he can combine his 2016 power and defense with his 2017 patience and reach a new level. Even that wouldn't push him to Lindor/Seager/Correa heights, but even without putting the entire package together, he's a comfortably above-average shortstop, a guy whose name you write in thick Sharpie on your roster-planning chart in November before figuring out the rest of the team.

PITCHERS

Raul Alcantara RHP
Born: 12/04/92 Age: 25 Bats: R Throws: R Height: 6'4" Weight: 220 Origin: International Free Agent, 2009

YEAR	TEAM	LVL	AGE	W	L	SV	G	GS	IP	H	HR	BB/9	K/9	K	GB%	BABIP	WHIP	ERA	DRA	WARP	MPH	CMD	PWR	STM
2015	STO	A+	22	0	2	0	15	15	48^2	54	3	1.5	5.4	29	46%	.319	1.27	3.88	4.19	0.5				
2016	MID	AA	23	5	6	0	17	17	90	100	11	2.7	7.3	73	50%	.322	1.41	4.80	3.46	1.8				
2016	NAS	AAA	23	4	0	0	8	8	45^2	38	1	0.6	6.3	32	39%	.272	0.90	1.18	2.93	1.3				
2016	OAK	MLB	23	1	3	0	5	5	22^1	31	9	1.6	5.6	14	41%	.306	1.57	7.25	7.21	-0.5	95.7	51	56	65
2017	NAS	AAA	24	1	2	4	18	3	33^2	36	0	1.9	5.9	22	44%	.321	1.28	2.67	5.28	0.1				
2017	OAK	MLB	24	1	2	0	8	4	24	22	5	4.5	4.5	12	49%	.224	1.42	7.12	6.57	-0.3	97.1	50	62	33
2018	*OAK*	*MLB*	*25*	*2*	*2*	*0*	*32*	*0*	34^1	*34*	*4*	*3.3*	*7.1*	*27*	*44%*	*.290*	*1.35*	*4.52*	*4.67*	*0.2*	*96.2*	*52*	*61*	*48*
2019	*OAK*	*MLB*	*26*	*2*	*1*	*0*	*43*	*0*	*46*	*45*	*7*	*3.3*	*7.0*	*36*	*44%*	*.282*	*1.35*	*4.85*	*5.08*	*0.1*	*96.0*	*52*	*61*	*48*

Breakout: 24% Improve: 34% Collapse: 14% Attrition: 42% MLB: 62% *Comparables: Braden Shipley, Bobby Livingston, Yorman Bazardo*

It feels terrible to write off a 25-year-old with a mid-90s fastball, but Alcántara simply has not looked like a big-league pitcher the last two years, either in his stints in the majors or in his high-minors performance; he's had shiny Triple-A ERAs, but you have to miss *some* bats. He is out of minor-league options, and was outrighted off the 40-man roster last year before being added back in September. Whether he's on the A's by the time you read this is anybody's guess, and if he's on anybody's 40-man, he's probably the first guy cut when someone new needs to be added. It's a cruel portion of the baseball life cycle; you're making more money than you would selling insurance or coaching high school, but you're effectively a peripatetic temp covering for an injury cascade here, a disastrous set of performances there, hoping you're not sitting at home with your fidget spinner and Netflix for *too* long before the next bullpen/data-entry job arises.

Henderson Alvarez RHP
Born: 04/18/90 Age: 28 Bats: R Throws: R Height: 6'0" Weight: 205 Origin: International Free Agent, 2007

YEAR	TEAM	LVL	AGE	W	L	SV	G	GS	IP	H	HR	BB/9	K/9	K	GB%	BABIP	WHIP	ERA	DRA	WARP	MPH	CMD	PWR	STM
2015	MIA	MLB	25	0	4	0	4	4	22^1	28	1	2.8	3.6	9	60%	.318	1.57	6.45	4.58	0.1	93.6	46	47	0
2015	JUP	A+	25	0	1	0	3	3	11^1	11	0	1.6	6.4	8	57%	.297	1.15	1.59	4.13	0.1				
2016	NAS	AAA	26	1	0	0	5	5	18^2	17	3	2.9	8.2	17	48%	.275	1.23	3.86	3.86	0.3				
2016	STO	A+	26	0	1	0	5	5	13^1	17	1	1.4	4.7	7	55%	.348	1.42	4.72	4.60	0.1				
2017	LEH	AAA	27	2	0	0	3	3	19	19	1	2.8	3.8	8	47%	.286	1.32	2.84	4.71	0.2				
2017	PHI	MLB	27	0	1	0	3	3	14^2	14	2	6.8	3.7	6	46%	.250	1.70	4.30	7.63	-0.3	93.1	48	51	40
2018	*OAK*	*MLB*	*28*	*2*	*2*	*0*	*6*	*6*	*34*	*37*	*6*	*3.8*	*5.8*	*22*	*47%*	*.291*	*1.51*	*5.57*	*5.87*	*-0.1*	*92.8*	*47*	*50*	*25*
2019	*OAK*	*MLB*	*29*	*7*	*13*	*0*	*29*	*29*	*179*	*196*	*34*	*3.5*	*5.7*	*113*	*47%*	*.307*	*1.48*	*5.83*	*6.44*	*-1.4*	*92.2*	*48*	*50*	*32*

Breakout: 11% Improve: 39% Collapse: 30% Attrition: 14% MLB: 92% *Comparables: Aaron Cook, Jhoulys Chacin, Chien-Ming Wang*

One of baseball's best young pitchers as recently as 2014, Alvarez spent most of the next two-and-a-half years on transaction logs with "(shoulder)" as the refrain. He'd pop up for a couple starts here and there before going back on the shelf for a few months, never showing signs of life, let alone glimpses of his former self. Alvarez ended up at the last refuge for the failing former major leaguer last July—other members of the 2017 Long Island Ducks included Lew Ford, Ruben Gotay, Nolan Reimold, John Lannan, Eric Gagne, David Aardsma and star of *The Only Rule Is It Has to Work* Fehlandt Lentini—but he threw well enough to earn a minor-league deal with the Phillies. After giving him three healthy Triple-A starts, they plopped Alvarez into the September rotation. His stuff hasn't quite rebounded, but stringing together a few healthy months is a big step in the right direction, and he's certainly young enough that there might be a second act if the shoulder continues to play nice.

Santiago Casilla RHP
Born: 07/25/80 Age: 37 Bats: R Throws: R Height: 6'0" Weight: 210 Origin: International Free Agent, 2000

YEAR	TEAM	LVL	AGE	W	L	SV	G	GS	IP	H	HR	BB/9	K/9	K	GB%	BABIP	WHIP	ERA	DRA	WARP	MPH	CMD	PWR	STM
2015	SFN	MLB	34	4	2	38	67	0	58	51	6	3.6	9.6	62	48%	.298	1.28	2.79	3.42	0.9	95.9	54	49	48
2016	SFN	MLB	35	2	5	31	62	0	58	50	8	2.9	10.1	65	50%	.292	1.19	3.57	3.59	0.9	96.0	64	46	45
2017	OAK	MLB	36	4	5	16	63	0	59	58	8	3.4	8.7	57	40%	.301	1.36	4.27	5.16	0.0	95.6	40	56	47
2018	*OAK*	*MLB*	*37*	*3*	*3*	*10*	*54*	*0*	*57*	*54*	*9*	*3.7*	*8.2*	*52*	*45%*	*.287*	*1.36*	*4.94*	*4.98*	*0.1*	*94.4*	*50*	*50*	*45*
2019	*OAK*	*MLB*	*38*	*2*	*1*	*4*	*40*	*0*	*43*	*42*	*8*	*4.0*	*8.0*	*38*	*45%*	*.283*	*1.42*	*5.39*	*5.63*	*-0.2*	*93.7*	*48*	*50*	*45*

Breakout: 14% Improve: 28% Collapse: 32% Attrition: 16% MLB: 76% *Comparables: Jason Isringhausen, Grant Balfour, Francisco Cordero*

When you're a cash-strapped team going nowhere fast in the standings, it is definitely a good idea to throw a two-year contract at a 36-year-old reliever, as the A's did last year. Casilla was a perfectly good reliever for a decade in both Oakland and San Francisco, and he took a sharp right turn from grounders to strikeouts in 2015, but last year he did the thing that many 36-year-old relievers do: not pitch very well. Batters spit on Casilla's slider, instead waiting to crush the sinkers that he was all too willing to leave in the middle of the zone. They put the pitch in the air to great effect, with a .602 slugging percentage to prove it. Thereby does one become a fly-ball pitcher; thereby does one become a replacement-level pitcher.

Simon Castro RHP Born: 04/09/88 Age: 30 Bats: R Throws: R Height: 6'5" Weight: 230 Origin: International Free Agent, 2006

YEAR	TEAM	LVL	AGE	W	L	SV	G	GS	IP	H	HR	BB/9	K/9	K	GB%	BABIP	WHIP	ERA	DRA	WARP	MPH	CMD	PWR	STM
2015	ABQ	AAA	27	5	5	0	36	0	57	53	6	3.2	11.7	74	40%	.326	1.28	3.79	1.85	2.0				
2015	COL	MLB	27	2	0	0	11	0	10^{1}	11	0	4.4	7.8	9	56%	.344	1.55	6.10	6.35	-0.2	94.2			45
2016	ABQ	AAA	28	0	5	10	50	0	53^{1}	52	5	2.0	9.8	58	49%	.324	1.20	3.38	1.98	1.8				
2017	NAS	AAA	29	3	5	4	33	0	38	24	3	5.0	14.9	63	46%	.284	1.18	3.32	1.85	1.4				
2017	OAK	MLB	29	1	3	0	26	0	37	32	7	3.4	8.5	35	34%	.263	1.24	4.38	5.35	-0.1	96.3	47	66	50
2018	*OAK*	*MLB*	*30*	*3*	*1*	*1*	*57*	*0*	60^{2}	*55*	*10*	*3.7*	*10.2*	*69*	*43%*	*.294*	*1.32*	*4.71*	*4.95*	*0.2*	*95.2*	*47*	*66*	*48*
2019	*OAK*	*MLB*	*31*	*1*	*1*	*0*	*28*	*0*	*35*	*32*	*6*	*3.6*	*10.1*	*39*	*43%*	*.291*	*1.30*	*4.70*	*4.91*	*0.1*	*94.7*	*47*	*66*	*49*

Breakout: 12% Improve: 22% Collapse: 12% Attrition: 18% MLB: 41% *Comparables: Michael Broadway, Blake Parker, Mike Zagurski*

Castro first reached Triple-A way back in 2010, and was a top-100 prospect before both the 2010 and 2011 seasons, but finally managed his first substantial big-league pot of coffee last year. He's a monster reliever in the minors now (check that strikeout rate for Nashville last year), but it only translated to shrug-your-shoulders middle-relief work in the big leagues. There's something of Tyson Ross in his low-effort, fling-it-up-there delivery, as well as in his seeming to have little idea of where the ball is going. He's a good illustration of the difference between control, in the sense of pounding the strike zone, and command *within* the zone. His stuff is good enough to overwhelm Triple-A hitters, but leaving that same stuff in hittable areas in the majors results in things like a homer every five innings. Teams can do worse in middle relief, but *good* teams don't. Castro is out of options, and was outrighted off the 40-man in November, so don't be surprised to see him pitch for four different organizations this year.

Jharel Cotton RHP Born: 01/19/92 Age: 26 Bats: R Throws: R Height: 5'11" Weight: 195 Origin: Round 20, 2012 Draft (#626 overall)

YEAR	TEAM	LVL	AGE	W	L	SV	G	GS	IP	H	HR	BB/9	K/9	K	GB%	BABIP	WHIP	ERA	DRA	WARP	MPH	CMD	PWR	STM
2015	RCU	A+	23	1	0	0	4	2	22^{1}	14	1	2.8	11.3	28	30%	.265	0.94	1.61	2.46	0.6				
2015	TUL	AA	23	5	2	0	11	8	62^{2}	49	4	3.0	10.2	71	49%	.296	1.12	2.30	2.74	1.7				
2016	OKL	AAA	24	8	5	0	22	16	97^{1}	80	17	3.0	11.0	119	42%	.268	1.15	4.90	1.92	3.8				
2016	NAS	AAA	24	3	1	0	6	6	38^{1}	28	3	1.6	8.5	36	43%	.248	0.91	2.82	2.30	1.3				
2016	OAK	MLB	24	2	0	0	5	5	29^{1}	20	4	1.2	7.1	23	36%	.198	0.82	2.15	4.55	0.3	94.5	56	35	66
2017	NAS	AAA	25	3	0	0	4	3	21^{1}	15	3	1.7	11.8	28	43%	.261	0.89	2.95	2.73	0.7				
2017	OAK	MLB	25	9	10	0	24	24	129	133	28	3.7	7.3	105	38%	.281	1.44	5.58	7.14	-2.2	94.7	33	39	67
2018	*OAK*	*MLB*	*26*	*7*	*8*	*0*	*24*	*24*	*120*	*115*	*23*	*3.3*	*9.0*	*121*	*40%*	*.287*	*1.31*	*4.64*	*4.97*	*0.6*	*94.3*	*37*	*39*	*68*
2019	*OAK*	*MLB*	*27*	*9*	*11*	*0*	*31*	*31*	195^{2}	*171*	*34*	*3.2*	*9.2*	*200*	*40%*	*.268*	*1.23*	*4.69*	*4.90*	*1.3*	*94.0*	*37*	*39*	*68*

Breakout: 24% Improve: 44% Collapse: 16% Attrition: 34% MLB: 88% *Comparables: Angel Guzman, Matt Boyd, Wade LeBlanc*

Well, that was miserable. Turns out he's *not* a sub-.200 BABIP pitcher? Cotton had spent years outpitching his size (sorry, but he's not 5-foot-11) and pedigree (undrafted out of high school, eventually signed as a 20th-round pick), but it all tumbled harder than his change in his first extended exposure to the majors, and the baseball gods added injury to insult, knocking him around with summer blister problems and late-September elbow soreness. If you look at Cotton's ground-ball rate, homers allowed and velocity and think you've got him figured out ... well, you might not be wrong. His fastball finishes up in the zone far too often for someone without overwhelming velocity or movement, and batters teed off. An uptick in command, resulting in a downtick in location, will be necessary if he wants to be a starter; if he can add enough speed in short bursts to survive in hitters' locations, maybe there's a high-leverage reliever here, because the changeup is nasty either way.

Daniel Coulombe LHP Born: 10/26/89 Age: 28 Bats: L Throws: L Height: 5'10" Weight: 190 Origin: Round 25, 2012 Draft (#776 overall)

YEAR	TEAM	LVL	AGE	W	L	SV	G	GS	IP	H	HR	BB/9	K/9	K	GB%	BABIP	WHIP	ERA	DRA	WARP	MPH	CMD	PWR	STM
2015	LAN	MLB	25	0	0	0	5	0	8^{1}	9	0	6.5	7.6	7	48%	.333	1.80	7.56	5.45	-0.1	92.0	40	30	44
2015	OKL	AAA	25	3	1	1	38	0	41^{1}	35	1	5.2	8.9	41	50%	.309	1.43	3.27	5.17	-0.1				
2015	OAK	MLB	25	0	0	0	9	0	7^{2}	8	0	3.5	4.7	4	64%	.320	1.43	3.52	6.01	-0.1	91.9	40	30	44
2016	NAS	AAA	26	0	0	0	20	0	25	18	0	2.2	12.6	35	60%	.327	0.96	1.08	1.95	0.9				
2016	OAK	MLB	26	3	1	0	35	0	47^{2}	37	6	3.2	10.2	54	64%	.267	1.13	4.53	3.27	0.9	92.7	45	27	45
2017	OAK	MLB	27	2	2	0	72	0	51^{2}	46	4	3.8	6.8	39	57%	.280	1.32	3.48	5.50	-0.2	92.6	33	22	48
2018	*OAK*	*MLB*	*28*	*2*	*2*	*0*	*49*	*0*	*51*	*50*	*6*	*4.0*	*8.2*	*47*	*53%*	*.295*	*1.41*	*4.40*	*4.57*	*0.3*	*92.0*	*38*	*25*	*46*
2019	*OAK*	*MLB*	*29*	*2*	*1*	*0*	*48*	*0*	50^{2}	*47*	*6*	*4.0*	*8.5*	*48*	*53%*	*.286*	*1.37*	*4.55*	*4.74*	*0.3*	*91.7*	*38*	*24*	*47*

Breakout: 22% Improve: 38% Collapse: 23% Attrition: 18% MLB: 73% *Comparables: Pedro Strop, Derrick Turnbow, Mark Melancon*

Coulombe is an undersized lefty with a junkball approach: He threw a fastball just a third of the time last year; a big, slow curve and a slider that moves almost exclusively down made up another third each. He doesn't have an extreme release point or other obvious deception mechanism that marks him as a clear LOOGY, but he sure pitched like one, getting pasted by righties for an .851 OPS. Still, with 14 bullpen spots available, teams have an easier time than ever making room for players with Coulombe's skill set, particularly because his grounder-oriented approach lends itself to every manager's favorite outcome: the rally-killing double play. You'll forget everything about him as soon as you finish reading this comment, and he'll only make an impact in the weirdest fantasy leagues, but he could also get 10 years in the majors doing the exact thing he did over the last two.

Ryan Dull RHP Born: 10/02/89 Age: 28 Bats: R Throws: R Height: 5'9" Weight: 175 Origin: Round 32, 2012 Draft (#979 overall)

YEAR	TEAM	LVL	AGE	W	L	SV	G	GS	IP	H	HR	BB/9	K/9	K	GB%	BABIP	WHIP	ERA	DRA	WARP	MPH	CMD	PWR	STM
2015	MID	AA	25	3	1	12	35	0	45	29	1	2.6	10.4	52	44%	.262	0.93	0.60	1.65	1.7				
2015	NAS	AAA	25	0	1	0	12	0	16	10	1	1.7	11.8	21	35%	.250	0.81	1.12	2.15	0.5				
2015	OAK	MLB	25	1	2	1	13	0	17	12	4	3.2	8.5	16	39%	.200	1.06	4.24	4.46	0.1	92.9	43	37	50
2016	OAK	MLB	26	5	5	3	70	0	74^1	50	10	1.8	8.8	73	34%	.209	0.87	2.42	2.76	1.9	92.9	57	44	52
2017	OAK	MLB	27	2	2	0	49	0	42	37	7	3.4	9.6	45	41%	.283	1.26	5.14	2.96	1.0	93.3	58	36	40
2018	*OAK*	*MLB*	*28*	*2*	*2*	*0*	*32*	*0*	34^1	*32*	*5*	*3.8*	*9.1*	*35*	*39%*	*.285*	*1.32*	*4.68*	*4.79*	*0.1*	*92.5*	*57*	*41*	*47*
2019	*OAK*	*MLB*	*29*	*3*	*1*	*0*	*53*	*0*	55^2	*48*	*9*	*3.3*	*9.4*	*58*	*39%*	*.267*	*1.23*	*4.61*	*4.81*	*0.3*	*92.2*	*57*	*40*	*46*

Breakout: 31% Improve: 43% Collapse: 27% Attrition: 18% MLB: 84% *Comparables: Sergio Romo, Santiago Casilla, Vinnie Pestano*

Dull was the A's breakout reliever in 2016, finishing with a top-20 season among relief pitchers by WARP, but he saw his ERA double last year. What happened? DRA says nothing, at least of his doing. Perhaps more alarming than his performance was his right-knee strain, which cost him just over two months. At his less-than-ideal size, he goes max effort to achieve even low-90s velocity; if that causes more strain on his body, his time as an effective major leaguer could be shorter than his results dictate. One hopes this was just a blip, because it's a lot of fun watching the mighty mite whiff the best hitters in the world with his superb slider.

Parker Dunshee RHP Born: 02/12/95 Age: 23 Bats: R Throws: R Height: 6'1" Weight: 205 Origin: Round 7, 2017 Draft (#201 overall)

YEAR	TEAM	LVL	AGE	W	L	SV	G	GS	IP	H	HR	BB/9	K/9	K	GB%	BABIP	WHIP	ERA	DRA	WARP	MPH	CMD	PWR	STM
2017	VER	A-	22	1	0	0	12	9	38^1	15	0	1.9	10.6	45	46%	.185	0.60	0.00	1.43	1.6				
2018	*OAK*	*MLB*	*23*	*2*	*2*	*0*	*15*	*6*	33^2	*34*	*8*	*4.1*	*10.0*	*37*	*38%*	*.307*	*1.47*	*5.58*	*5.89*	*-0.2*				
2019	*OAK*	*MLB*	*24*	*3*	*5*	*0*	*27*	*15*	*124*	*132*	*29*	*4.8*	*8.7*	*121*	*38%*	*.301*	*1.60*	*6.23*	*6.56*	*-0.9*				

Breakout: 4% Improve: 4% Collapse: 2% Attrition: 6% MLB: 7% *Comparables: Brayan Villarreal, Michael Blazek, Brooks Pounders*

Dunshee was a seventh-round senior sign out of Wake Forest. You'd expect such a pitcher to dominate short-season ball, but there's domination and then there's not allowing a single run in 38 1/3 (regular-season) innings while giving up exactly one extra-base hit. About that parenthetical: He got blown up for seven runs in 3 1/3 innings across two playoff outings and took the loss in the championship-deciding game. Oops. The straight, 90-mph fastball and "well, they exist" slider and changeup are why Dunshee lasted until the part of the draft where teams save cap room that they can apply to their top picks. This is Dunshee's first Annual comment, but since there's a decent chance it's also his last, we've got to get it all in now: His name anagrams to Darker Pusheen.

Daniel Gossett RHP Born: 11/13/92 Age: 25 Bats: R Throws: R Height: 6'2" Weight: 185 Origin: Round 2, 2014 Draft (#65 overall)

YEAR	TEAM	LVL	AGE	W	L	SV	G	GS	IP	H	HR	BB/9	K/9	K	GB%	BABIP	WHIP	ERA	DRA	WARP	MPH	CMD	PWR	STM
2015	BLT	A	22	5	13	0	27	27	144^2	151	16	3.2	7.0	112	49%	.305	1.40	4.73	5.27	-0.1				
2016	STO	A+	23	4	1	0	9	9	46	40	4	2.5	10.4	53	54%	.295	1.15	3.33	2.24	1.7				
2016	MID	AA	23	5	5	0	16	16	94	75	4	2.4	9.0	94	59%	.284	1.06	2.49	2.90	2.5				
2016	NAS	AAA	23	1	0	0	2	2	13^2	10	0	2.0	2.6	4	57%	.227	0.95	1.98	4.76	0.1				
2017	NAS	AAA	24	4	4	0	14	14	76^1	70	6	2.8	8.4	71	52%	.292	1.23	3.66	2.28	2.8				
2017	OAK	MLB	24	4	11	0	18	18	91^1	116	21	3.1	7.1	72	45%	.328	1.61	6.11	6.61	-1.1	93.0	43	38	73
2018	*OAK*	*MLB*	*25*	*8*	*9*	*0*	*26*	*26*	*137*	*145*	*23*	*3.5*	*7.5*	*114*	*47%*	*.296*	*1.45*	*4.75*	*5.10*	*0.5*	*92.7*	*44*	*39*	*75*
2019	*OAK*	*MLB*	*26*	*9*	*11*	*0*	*30*	*30*	186^1	*188*	*29*	*3.2*	*7.9*	*164*	*47%*	*.295*	*1.37*	*4.70*	*4.91*	*1.3*	*92.4*	*44*	*39*	*75*

Breakout: 27% Improve: 51% Collapse: 14% Attrition: 40% MLB: 82% *Comparables: Hayden Penn, Nick Tepesch, Christian Friedrich*

The listed height and weight above seem generous; watching him pitch, one simply cannot buy that Gossett is as tall as Matt Joyce, or that he has filled out enough to weigh 185, or that he has even gone through puberty. Gossett does generate more velocity from his frame than you might think possible, which is why he was a major-college pitcher (Clemson) and a second-round pick, but his fastball is straight, which is why hitters teed off on him last year: His homers allowed extrapolate to 46 in a 200-inning season. Gossett peppers the bottom of the zone from an overhead slot, but his command has to be perfect, and Joe E. Brown covered the subject of perfection decades ago. If he doesn't add something to his game (turning one of his secondaries into a killer, adding some wiggle to his fastball, finally getting his growth spurt), he's probably a reliever soon enough, and not a high-leverage one.

Kendall Graveman RHP Born: 12/21/90 Age: 27 Bats: R Throws: R Height: 6'2" Weight: 200 Origin: Round 8, 2013 Draft (#235 overall)

YEAR	TEAM	LVL	AGE	W	L	SV	G	GS	IP	H	HR	BB/9	K/9	K	GB%	BABIP	WHIP	ERA	DRA	WARP	MPH	CMD	PWR	STM
2015	NAS	AAA	24	2	1	0	4	4	24^1	20	1	3.3	5.2	14	64%	.241	1.19	1.85	4.40	0.2				
2015	OAK	MLB	24	6	9	0	21	21	115^2	126	15	3.0	6.0	77	51%	.302	1.42	4.05	4.70	0.5	93.3	53	43	66
2016	OAK	MLB	25	10	11	0	31	31	186	196	22	2.3	5.2	108	53%	.290	1.31	4.11	4.41	2.0	95.3	57	55	74
2017	NAS	AAA	26	0	1	0	3	3	10	18	1	3.6	6.3	7	46%	.425	2.20	7.20	5.64	0.0				
2017	OAK	MLB	26	6	4	0	19	19	105^1	114	12	2.7	6.0	70	52%	.313	1.39	4.19	4.16	1.7	95.4	77	63	50
2018	*OAK*	*MLB*	*27*	*8*	*8*	*0*	*23*	*23*	*121*	*129*	*16*	*3.2*	*5.9*	*79*	*50%*	*.295*	*1.43*	*4.61*	*4.93*	*0.6*	*94.4*	*63*	*56*	*63*
2019	*OAK*	*MLB*	*28*	*9*	*10*	*0*	*29*	*29*	181^1	*192*	*24*	*3.0*	*6.3*	*126*	*50%*	*.298*	*1.39*	*4.79*	*4.99*	*1.1*	*94.4*	*66*	*58*	*62*

Breakout: 18% Improve: 43% Collapse: 18% Attrition: 15% MLB: 81% *Comparables: Joe Blanton, Erasmo Ramirez, Jeremy Sowers*

Hopes that Graveman could take a step forward from 2016's mid-rotation high-contact sinkerballer routine were derailed by a shoulder strain that cost him two and a half months in the summer, and he was the same pitcher even when he was healthy. He has added heat since the start of his big-league career and throws his main fastball 93-94 mph now, which, even in this age when your grandma comes roaring out of the bullpen throwing 97, is top-quintile sinker velocity for a starter. His strikeout rate is capped by his all-fastball approach, though: Fastballs, by and large, *set up* strikeouts; they don't finish them off. Example: Sonny Gray's elite whiff rate on his sinker is the same as CC Sabathia's well-below-average rate on his slider. The solution for Graveman isn't to throw his changeup more, though, because his changeup isn't good enough to throw more. Ballplayers aren't toasters, so he could improve the pitch, but if you're a betting person, bet on mid-rotation high-contact sinkerballing for years to come. If you're not a betting person, well, live a little.

Chris Hatcher RHP Born: 01/12/85 Age: 33 Bats: R Throws: R Height: 6'1" Weight: 200 Origin: Round 5, 2006 Draft (#155 overall)

YEAR	TEAM	LVL	AGE	W	L	SV	G	GS	IP	H	HR	BB/9	K/9	K	GB%	BABIP	WHIP	ERA	DRA	WARP	MPH	CMD	PWR	STM
2015	LAN	MLB	30	3	5	4	49	0	39	35	4	3.0	10.4	45	44%	.307	1.23	3.69	3.20	0.7	98.1	57	68	42
2016	LAN	MLB	31	5	4	0	37	0	40^2	40	8	4.6	9.5	43	45%	.296	1.50	5.53	4.41	0.3	97.8	54	57	44
2017	LAN	MLB	32	0	1	0	26	0	36^2	37	7	2.9	10.6	43	28%	.312	1.34	4.66	4.74	0.2	95.9	46	51	46
2017	OAK	MLB	32	1	1	1	23	0	23	21	3	3.5	7.8	20	43%	.269	1.30	3.52	4.79	0.1	95.6	46	51	46
2018	*OAK*	*MLB*	*33*	*3*	*3*	*0*	*54*	*0*	*57*	*59*	*11*	*4.1*	*8.9*	*57*	*41%*	*.298*	*1.48*	*5.39*	*5.38*	*-0.2*	*95.8*	*50*	*55*	*44*
2019	*OAK*	*MLB*	*34*	*2*	*1*	*0*	*38*	*0*	39^2	*40*	*8*	*4.4*	*9.1*	*40*	*41%*	*.296*	*1.51*	*5.51*	*5.77*	*-0.2*	*95.0*	*48*	*53*	*44*

Breakout: 22% Improve: 32% Collapse: 26% Attrition: 22% MLB: 72% *Comparables: Justin Miller, Joel Peralta, Mark Lowe*

Just imagine where the Dodgers would be without Chris Hatcher. Games 2 and 5 of the World Series, wild extra-inning affairs that they only won by the skin of their teeth en route to their first championship since 1988, could have gone entirely differently if the $200 million squad needed to rely on, say, an overmatched Brandon McCarthy or a clearly gassed Brandon Morrow to try to get through the Astros' marauding lineup. Why, the trophy might be in Houston were it not for Hatcher pitching key innings despite not being one of the team's premium relievers!

taps earpiece What's that? *stares into the camera* I'm sorry, it appears Hatcher, who will never be either more or less than a perfectly adequate middle reliever, was traded to Oakland in August for a half-million dollars worth of international bonus slot money.

Liam Hendriks RHP Born: 02/10/89 Age: 29 Bats: R Throws: R Height: 6'0" Weight: 200 Origin: International Free Agent, 2007

YEAR	TEAM	LVL	AGE	W	L	SV	G	GS	IP	H	HR	BB/9	K/9	K	GB%	BABIP	WHIP	ERA	DRA	WARP	MPH	CMD	PWR	STM
2015	TOR	MLB	26	5	0	0	58	0	64^2	59	3	1.5	9.9	71	49%	.322	1.08	2.92	3.12	1.2	97.8	37	66	47
2016	OAK	MLB	27	0	4	0	53	0	64^2	69	6	1.9	9.9	71	42%	.344	1.28	3.76	3.35	1.2	96.8	49	67	47
2017	OAK	MLB	28	4	2	1	70	0	64	57	7	3.2	11.0	78	41%	.303	1.25	4.22	4.21	0.7	96.3	52	69	52
2018	*OAK*	*MLB*	*29*	*3*	*3*	*2*	*65*	*0*	*68*	*61*	*8*	*3.2*	*10.4*	*80*	*44%*	*.300*	*1.25*	*3.30*	*3.67*	*1.1*	*96.2*	*48*	*68*	*49*
2019	*OAK*	*MLB*	*30*	*3*	*1*	*2*	*60*	*0*	63^1	*54*	*8*	*3.1*	*10.9*	*77*	*44%*	*.298*	*1.19*	*3.57*	*3.70*	*1.1*	*95.6*	*50*	*68*	*49*

Breakout: 32% Improve: 62% Collapse: 13% Attrition: 12% MLB: 97% *Comparables: Wilton Lopez, Phil Coke, Tony Watson*

Year Three of Hendriks as full-time major-league reliever went about the same as the first two, putting aside the usual small-sample foibles inherent in That Bullpen Life: same two-pitch approach, same 95-mph velocity, same bat-missing slider, same ability to pitch to batters of any handedness. The walk-rate increase might foretell a downfall, but it's also an extra free pass every three weeks. Foibles. At 29 and with three seasons of moderate workload behind him, the all-time second-best Oakland reliever from Australia should keep on performing competent middle-leverage relief 'til the wallabies come home. Maybe this year he cuts the walk rate back to his previous norm, or he takes a step backward by allowing a couple of homers, or he pitches better but gets unluckier sequencing, or there's an entirely creepy disappearance of some turn-of-the-century schoolgirls and their teacher during a picnic in Victoria. You know, the little shifts around the same central concept.

Grant Holmes RHP Born: 03/22/96 Age: 22 Bats: L Throws: R Height: 6'1" Weight: 215 Origin: Round 1, 2014 Draft (#22 overall)

YEAR	TEAM	LVL	AGE	W	L	SV	G	GS	IP	H	HR	BB/9	K/9	K	GB%	BABIP	WHIP	ERA	DRA	WARP	MPH	CMD	PWR	STM
2015	GRL	A	19	6	4	0	24	24	103^1	86	6	4.7	10.2	117	44%	.307	1.35	3.14	3.26	2.4				
2016	RCU	A+	20	8	4	1	20	18	105^1	103	6	3.7	8.5	100	53%	.316	1.39	4.02	3.00	2.9				
2016	STO	A+	20	3	3	0	6	5	28^2	44	4	3.1	7.5	24	60%	.408	1.88	6.91	3.08	0.8				
2017	MID	AA	21	11	12	0	29	24	148^1	149	15	3.7	9.1	150	46%	.328	1.42	4.49	3.97	2.0				
2018	*OAK*	*MLB*	*22*	*8*	*9*	*0*	*25*	*25*	125^1	*122*	*21*	*4.2*	*9.7*	*135*	*44%*	*.305*	*1.45*	*4.86*	*5.11*	*0.8*				
2019	*OAK*	*MLB*	*23*	*5*	*7*	*0*	*18*	*18*	*108*	*109*	*21*	*4.0*	*9.7*	*116*	*44%*	*.307*	*1.45*	*5.11*	*5.34*	*0.3*				

Breakout: 13% Improve: 15% Collapse: 6% Attrition: 18% MLB: 23% *Comparables: Simon Castro, Carlos Carrasco, Josh Lindblom*

Holmes has a good ballplayer name, a majestic mop on his head, a powerful frame that hopefully leads to durability ... and a mid-rotation upside that makes him a top prospect now but that means in a couple of years he'll be forgettable, a face in the crowd in the majors. Sorry, bud; that's just how it goes in this game. The concerns for years have been not enough changeup and not enough control to really excel in the rotation, and not enough physical projection to make a conversion to flamethrowing relief beast likely. Those issues remained last year. He manipulates his fastball (a little more cut here, a little more run there) and curve (switching up the depth, velocity and sweep) so his two main pitches can play more like a full arsenal, and he's young, but at a certain point wishing for more is insulting to the (quite good!) player Holmes already is. The A's have plenty of back-end pitching depth, so they should be able to give him a full season at Triple-A to finish off his development if they want to.

James Kaprielian RHP Born: 03/02/94 Age: 24 Bats: R Throws: R Height: 6'4" Weight: 200 Origin: Round 1, 2015 Draft (#16 overall)

YEAR	TEAM	LVL	AGE	W	L	SV	G	GS	IP	H	HR	BB/9	K/9	K	GB%	BABIP	WHIP	ERA	DRA	WARP	MPH	CMD	PWR	STM
2016	TAM	A+	22	2	1	0	3	3	18	8	1	1.5	11.0	22	70%	.179	0.61	1.50	1.37	0.8				
2018	*OAK*	*MLB*	*24*	*2*	*2*	*0*	*7*	*7*	34^2	*33*	*6*	*4.1*	*9.8*	*38*	*46%*	*.304*	*1.42*	*4.75*	*4.99*	*0.3*				
2019	*OAK*	*MLB*	*25*	*6*	*10*	*0*	*25*	*25*	*150*	*170*	*34*	*3.3*	*7.7*	*129*	*46%*	*.305*	*1.49*	*5.74*	*6.02*	*-0.5*				

Breakout: 22% Improve: 33% Collapse: 16% Attrition: 34% MLB: 53% *Comparables: Bud Norris, Erick Fedde, P.J. Walters*

"He's that guy the A's traded their best player for even though he had a major injury," we'll say five years from now, and we won't know if we mean Dustin Fowler or Kaprielian. It's all fun and trivia games if the lanky righty makes it back to full strength from his springtime Tommy John surgery, because, while he was drafted as a polished-college-starter type in 2015, he's got ace upside now due to a velocity bump as a professional and excellent secondaries. He didn't pitch all year, of course, and he missed most of 2016 with a forearm strain as well, so it's hard to know what to expect, especially if you start worrying about whether the injuries are not merely correlated with the uptick in velocity but caused by it.

Jesus Luzardo LHP Born: 09/30/97 Age: 20 Bats: L Throws: L Height: 6'1" Weight: 205 Origin: Round 3, 2016 Draft (#94 overall)

YEAR	TEAM	LVL	AGE	W	L	SV	G	GS	IP	H	HR	BB/9	K/9	K	GB%	BABIP	WHIP	ERA	DRA	WARP	MPH	CMD	PWR	STM
2017	NAT	RK	19	1	0	0	3	3	13^{2}	14	1	0.0	9.9	15	33%	.342	1.02	1.32	2.57	0.5				
2017	ATH	RK	19	0	1	0	4	3	11^{2}	9	0	0.8	10.0	13	58%	.290	0.86	1.54	2.15	0.5				
2017	VER	A-	19	1	0	0	5	5	18	12	1	2.0	10.0	20	53%	.250	0.89	2.00	1.07	0.9				
2018	*OAK*	*MLB*	*20*	*2*	*3*	*0*	*8*	*8*	*33^{2}*	*36*	*8*	*3.7*	*9.3*	*35*	*39%*	*.308*	*1.47*	*5.55*	*5.86*	*-0.1*				
2019	*OAK*	*MLB*	*21*	*5*	*10*	*0*	*26*	*26*	*151^{1}*	*165*	*36*	*4.8*	*8.4*	*141*	*39%*	*.3*	*1.63*	*6.35*	*6.68*	*-1.2*				

Breakout: 3% Improve: 3% Collapse: 0% Attrition: 1% MLB: 4% *Comparables: Luiz Gohara, Kyle Lobstein, Luis Severino*

Luzardo was a big-time prep prospect, a mid-90s lefty with a good changeup, before Tommy John surgery wiped out his senior season in March 2016. The Nationals took him in the third round anyway, paid him like a high second-rounder and got him back on the mound for three games in the Gulf Coast League last year before trading him to the A's as part of the haul for Ryan Madson and Sean Doolittle. His grand totals for his professional debut: 48 strikeouts to five walks in 43 innings. Not bad for a post-surgery teen. Don't expect to see Luzardo set loose on the Midwest League—even 20-year-olds *without* an injury history have their workloads carefully managed these days—but keep an eye out anyway, because he came back from his rehab still flashing the stuff to establish himself as a serious prospect. Trivia: Luzardo was born in Peru before his family moved to Florida when he was a baby; Peru has never had a major leaguer and might never have had a minor leaguer (though records are sketchy when you go back more than a few decades).

Sean Manaea LHP Born: 02/01/92 Age: 26 Bats: R Throws: L Height: 6'5" Weight: 245 Origin: Round 1, 2013 Draft (#34 overall)

YEAR	TEAM	LVL	AGE	W	L	SV	G	GS	IP	H	HR	BB/9	K/9	K	GB%	BABIP	WHIP	ERA	DRA	WARP	MPH	CMD	PWR	STM
2015	WIL	A+	23	1	0	0	4	4	19^{2}	22	0	1.8	10.1	22	44%	.407	1.32	3.66	1.96	0.7				
2015	MID	AA	23	6	0	0	7	7	42^{2}	34	3	3.2	10.8	51	40%	.301	1.15	1.90	2.50	1.3				
2016	NAS	AAA	24	2	0	0	3	3	18	16	1	2.0	10.5	21	54%	.319	1.11	1.50	2.63	0.6				
2016	OAK	MLB	24	7	9	0	25	24	144^{2}	135	20	2.3	7.7	124	46%	.281	1.19	3.86	3.92	2.4	95.2	53	49	65
2017	OAK	MLB	25	12	10	0	29	29	158^{2}	167	18	3.1	7.9	140	44%	.318	1.40	4.37	4.61	1.7	93.7	38	44	71
2018	*OAK*	*MLB*	*26*	*9*	*8*	*0*	*26*	*26*	*137*	*134*	*19*	*3.1*	*8.9*	*137*	*44%*	*.300*	*1.33*	*4.00*	*4.29*	*1.8*	*94.0*	*45*	*47*	*70*
2019	*OAK*	*MLB*	*27*	*10*	*10*	*0*	*30*	*30*	*191*	*186*	*27*	*3.1*	*9.0*	*192*	*44%*	*.302*	*1.32*	*4.30*	*4.47*	*2.1*	*93.7*	*44*	*47*	*70*

Breakout: 34% Improve: 66% Collapse: 16% Attrition: 12% MLB: 95% *Comparables: Patrick Corbin, Jordan Zimmermann, Ricky Nolasco*

Manaea is a good reminder that events unknown to us outside the lines can have a great effect within them. He had a decent enough season in a vacuum, but in light of his prospect pedigree and promising 2016, it was disappointing. He suffered an alarming velocity drop and wasn't fully healthy, so he wound up pitching like a back-of-the-rotation type rather than taking another step toward reaching his no. 2 upside. Then, in late September, he revealed that he had lost 25 pounds over a couple of months in the spring after new ADD medication suppressed his appetite. If he can get his body and his velocity back to where he wants them this year, and avoids repeats of 2017's back and shoulder troubles, there's reason to hope for a leap both in quality (as he returns to his 2016 level of stuff paired with the experience of pitching with diminished capacity) and quantity, summing to a solid, utterly unflashy, but still important rotation anchor.

Daniel Mengden RHP Born: 02/19/93 Age: 25 Bats: R Throws: R Height: 6'2" Weight: 190 Origin: Round 4, 2014 Draft (#106 overall)

YEAR	TEAM	LVL	AGE	W	L	SV	G	GS	IP	H	HR	BB/9	K/9	K	GB%	BABIP	WHIP	ERA	DRA	WARP	MPH	CMD	PWR	STM
2015	QUD	A	22	4	1	0	8	6	38^{2}	30	1	1.9	8.4	36	49%	.274	0.98	1.16	2.77	1.1				
2015	LNC	A+	22	2	1	1	10	8	49^{2}	59	4	3.3	8.7	48	46%	.367	1.55	5.26	3.29	1.1				
2015	STO	A+	22	4	2	0	8	8	42^{1}	39	6	2.1	8.7	41	53%	.275	1.16	4.25	3.31	0.9				
2016	MID	AA	23	2	0	0	4	4	23	15	0	4.7	11.0	28	51%	.283	1.17	0.78	3.32	0.5				
2016	NAS	AAA	23	8	2	0	13	13	75^{1}	54	4	2.0	8.0	67	50%	.246	0.94	1.67	2.13	2.8				
2016	OAK	MLB	23	2	9	0	14	14	72	83	9	4.1	8.9	71	42%	.344	1.61	6.50	5.82	-0.4	95.5	50	46	73
2017	NAS	AAA	24	2	4	0	9	9	41	40	5	4.0	8.8	40	43%	.307	1.41	4.17	5.01	0.3				
2017	OAK	MLB	24	3	2	0	7	7	43	36	6	1.9	6.1	29	40%	.240	1.05	3.14	5.31	0.1	94.0	40	41	40
2018	*OAK*	*MLB*	*25*	*4*	*3*	*0*	*10*	*10*	*57*	*57*	*9*	*3.6*	*8.1*	*51*	*44%*	*.294*	*1.40*	*4.47*	*4.80*	*0.4*	*94.6*	*47*	*45*	*56*
2019	*OAK*	*MLB*	*26*	*10*	*11*	*0*	*30*	*30*	*191^{2}*	*181*	*31*	*3.4*	*8.6*	*183*	*44%*	*.284*	*1.32*	*4.71*	*4.91*	*1.4*	*94.4*	*47*	*45*	*56*

Breakout: 27% Improve: 60% Collapse: 19% Attrition: 25% MLB: 93% *Comparables: Travis Wood, Chris Tillman, Dan Straily*

Mengden has a sweet mustache, an old-timey windup and some of the tighest pants this side of Justin Verlander (paired with, let's just say it, a lot more badonk than Verlander brings to the center-field camera). All of which is to avoid the subject of his actual pitching, because very little about his major-league performance, or his stuff-and-command profile, suggests that he actually belongs at that level. Three no-runs starts out of five September outings, including one complete game, might give hope for 2018, but ignore the wild ERA swing over the last two seasons and look instead at his FIP and DRA, or browse to your favorite PITCHf/x site: Mengden, fun as he is to watch, is your eighth starter, someone who can, pitcher arms being what they are, grab a few starts while the team surgeon is drowning in viscera; if he's pitching in the rotation by the organization's choice, especially anywhere above the no. 5 slot, it's a clear sign of trouble.

Frankie Montas RHP Born: 03/21/93 Age: 25 Bats: R Throws: R Height: 6'2" Weight: 255 Origin: International Free Agent, 2009

YEAR	TEAM	LVL	AGE	W	L	SV	G	GS	IP	H	HR	BB/9	K/9	K	GB%	BABIP	WHIP	ERA	DRA	WARP	MPH	CMD	PWR	STM
2015	BIR	AA	22	5	5	0	23	23	112	89	3	3.9	8.7	108	43%	.282	1.22	2.97	4.30	1.1				
2015	CHA	MLB	22	0	2	0	7	2	15	14	1	5.4	12.0	20	38%	.361	1.53	4.80	2.69	0.4	99.8	37	68	55
2016	OKL	AAA	23	0	0	0	4	3	11^{1}	12	0	1.6	11.9	15	63%	.400	1.24	2.38	3.17	0.3				
2017	OAK	MLB	24	1	1	0	23	0	32	39	10	5.6	10.1	36	36%	.349	1.84	7.03	7.30	-0.8	100.1	45	77	46
2017	NAS	AAA	24	0	2	0	9	8	29^{1}	25	4	2.1	11.4	37	53%	.296	1.09	5.22	1.30	1.4				
2018	*OAK*	*MLB*	*25*	*3*	*3*	*0*	*54*	*0*	*57*	*50*	*8*	*3.8*	*10.3*	*65*	*45%*	*.292*	*1.30*	*4.08*	*4.32*	*0.5*	*99.7*	*44*	*77*	*51*
2019	*OAK*	*MLB*	*26*	*3*	*1*	*0*	*54*	*0*	*57^{2}*	*47*	*9*	*3.5*	*11.5*	*73*	*45%*	*.287*	*1.22*	*4.11*	*4.29*	*0.6*	*99.4*	*46*	*78*	*49*

Breakout: 37% Improve: 64% Collapse: 15% Attrition: 35% MLB: 92% *Comparables: Antonio Bastardo, Bud Norris, Scott Elbert*

Montas has always had great upside, most likely as a shutdown closer. He made the A's 2017 Opening Day roster as a multi-inning reliever, but quickly became more of a multi-walk, multi-hit, multi-homer reliever. He was farmed out in June, came back to the majors for 10 days in July in which he pitched just twice (poorly) and got optioned again. At this point in the narrative, you recall his injury history and say, with hope in your voice, "At least he stayed healthy?" Sorry: He hit the minor-league DL with an oblique injury in August. He's out of options now, though he can still be outrighted off the 40-man roster once without being exposed to waivers; if his two most frequent fastball locations remain Outside The Zone and Dead Center Of The Zone, expect that outright to be used this year, 99 mph heat or no. He's still just 25, and the A's replaced pitching coach Curt Young with Scott Emerson around the same time they demoted Montas last year, so there's room to hope for command improvements sufficient to translate that heat into results.

Emilio Pagan RHP Born: 05/07/91 Age: 27 Bats: L Throws: R Height: 6'3" Weight: 210 Origin: Round 10, 2013 Draft (#297 overall)

YEAR	TEAM	LVL	AGE	W	L	SV	G	GS	IP	H	HR	BB/9	K/9	K	GB%	BABIP	WHIP	ERA	DRA	WARP	MPH	CMD	PWR	STM
2015	BAK	A+	24	3	8	8	42	0	78^1	63	5	3.1	10.1	88	35%	.289	1.15	2.53	3.74	0.9				
2016	WTN	AA	25	4	1	9	18	0	30^2	19	1	3.2	13.2	45	32%	.269	0.98	1.17	1.52	1.2				
2016	TAC	AAA	25	1	2	1	23	0	34^1	28	6	4.7	10.2	39	32%	.268	1.34	3.67	4.38	0.2				
2017	TAC	AAA	26	2	1	5	23	0	31^2	19	0	2.3	10.2	36	29%	.241	0.85	2.56	4.24	0.4				
2017	SEA	MLB	26	2	3	0	34	0	50^1	39	7	1.4	10.0	56	23%	.258	0.93	3.22	3.95	0.7	95.5	52	58	50
2018	*OAK*	*MLB*	*27*	*2*	*2*	*0*	*43*	*0*	*45^2*	*42*	*9*	*3.6*	*10.2*	*52*	*32%*	*.289*	*1.32*	*4.80*	*4.88*	*0.1*	*95.0*	*53*	*59*	*51*
2019	*OAK*	*MLB*	*28*	*2*	*1*	*0*	*45*	*0*	*47^1*	*45*	*10*	*3.5*	*10.4*	*55*	*32%*	*.289*	*1.33*	*5.07*	*5.29*	*0.0*	*94.7*	*53*	*59*	*51*

Breakout: 13% Improve: 26% Collapse: 16% Attrition: 31% MLB: 61% *Comparables: Evan Scribner, Michael Schwimer, Chris Hatcher*

Pagan overcame the command issues that plagued him in 2016 at Triple-A and found himself with a regular role in the Seattle bullpen for good in July. Initially used as a long reliever for multi-inning stints, a 21 1/3-inning streak with only one run allowed led to a more prominent late-inning role. When everything is working, Pagan pounds the zone with a rising fastball that generates lots of swings and misses and weak pop-ups. When he catches the fat part of the zone, there's a lot of hard contact and projectiles leaving the yard in short order. Pagan has shown that he has enough raw stuff to survive, but the question is whether he'll be able to develop a secondary pitch and become more than just a guy in the middle innings.

Yusmeiro Petit RHP Born: 11/22/84 Age: 33 Bats: R Throws: R Height: 6'1" Weight: 255 Origin: International Free Agent, 2001

YEAR	TEAM	LVL	AGE	W	L	SV	G	GS	IP	H	HR	BB/9	K/9	K	GB%	BABIP	WHIP	ERA	DRA	WARP	MPH	CMD	PWR	STM
2015	SFN	MLB	30	1	1	1	42	1	76	75	11	1.8	7.0	59	34%	.278	1.18	3.67	5.73	-0.9	90.7	55	25	42
2016	WAS	MLB	31	3	5	1	36	1	62	67	12	2.2	7.1	49	44%	.291	1.32	4.50	5.72	-0.5	90.9	68	33	35
2017	ANA	MLB	32	5	2	4	60	1	91^1	69	9	1.8	10.0	101	34%	.267	0.95	2.76	2.84	2.4	91.2	82	25	53
2018	*OAK*	*MLB*	*33*	*3*	*3*	*0*	*52*	*3*	*66*	*65*	*12*	*3.2*	*8.3*	*61*	*39%*	*.288*	*1.34*	*4.86*	*4.95*	*0.2*	*90.0*	*71*	*27*	*44*
2019	*OAK*	*MLB*	*34*	*4*	*2*	*0*	*62*	*3*	*81^1*	*79*	*15*	*3.1*	*8.2*	*74*	*39%*	*.282*	*1.32*	*4.96*	*5.18*	*0.1*	*89.6*	*74*	*27*	*44*

Breakout: 19% Improve: 35% Collapse: 29% Attrition: 22% MLB: 85% *Comparables: Casey Fien, Jesse Chavez, Tyler Walker*

Like tacos and the weather, Petit is better on the West Coast. After spending an uneventful and frustrating season in the nation's capital, the veteran right hander spent the off-season going, going, back, back, to Cali, Cali. Petit was an ace out of the bullpen for the Halos, and was one of only two relievers in baseball to inherit at least 10 runners and strand them all. He did so in part by leaning heavily on his change, eschewing groundballs in favor of striking everyone out. His 2.7 percent called strike above average (CSAA) rate was 10th best in baseball for pitchers with at least 50 innings. After signing with the A's in December, Petit will remain in the Golden State, along with the good tacos and weather.

A.J. Puk LHP Born: 04/25/95 Age: 23 Bats: L Throws: L Height: 6'7" Weight: 220 Origin: Round 1, 2016 Draft (#6 overall)

YEAR	TEAM	LVL	AGE	W	L	SV	G	GS	IP	H	HR	BB/9	K/9	K	GB%	BABIP	WHIP	ERA	DRA	WARP	MPH	CMD	PWR	STM
2016	VER	A-	21	0	4	0	10	10	32^2	23	0	3.3	11.0	40	51%	.271	1.07	3.03	2.12	1.2				
2017	STO	A+	22	4	5	0	14	11	61	44	1	3.4	14.5	98	42%	.336	1.10	3.69	1.58	2.6				
2017	MID	AA	22	2	5	0	13	13	64	64	2	3.5	12.1	86	48%	.380	1.39	4.36	2.26	2.2				
2018	*OAK*	*MLB*	*23*	*6*	*6*	*0*	*21*	*21*	*92*	*84*	*16*	*4.3*	*11.3*	*115*	*41%*	*.309*	*1.40*	*4.57*	*4.81*	*0.9*				
2019	*OAK*	*MLB*	*24*	*7*	*9*	*0*	*27*	*27*	*159^1*	*154*	*29*	*4.1*	*10.0*	*178*	*41%*	*.304*	*1.43*	*4.91*	*5.13*	*0.7*				

Breakout: 26% Improve: 45% Collapse: 6% Attrition: 19% MLB: 60% *Comparables: James Paxton, Matt Moore, Matt Harvey*

Even big-time college starters like Puk, the A's elfin (as in the orc-slaughtering Tolkien variety, not Keebler) 2016 first-rounder from Florida, can get knocked around in the five-runs-per-game Cal League, but Puk missed so many bats that the environment couldn't hurt him. He followed that up by passing his first high-minors test with flying colors as well. The main question, for all that, hasn't changed: Will he gain the fastball command that allows him to be more than a thrower in the big leagues, or will he suffer from Tall Dude Mechanics Syndrome? His stuff, including a 70-grade fastball and a vicious slider that will make some good hitters look very silly, is good enough to make him a major-leaguer even if he *is* just a thrower, but the good pitchers fight their battles on fields of their choosing: at the edges, and wherever the hitter isn't looking. The throwers cede the terms of engagement to the offense and hope their superior firepower overwhelms. If Puk treats Triple-A hitters the way he has treated everyone else, we may start seeing his tactical capabilities this summer.

Logan Shore RHP Born: 12/28/94 Age: 23 Bats: R Throws: R Height: 6'2" Weight: 215 Origin: Round 2, 2016 Draft (#47 overall)

YEAR	TEAM	LVL	AGE	W	L	SV	G	GS	IP	H	HR	BB/9	K/9	K	GB%	BABIP	WHIP	ERA	DRA	WARP	MPH	CMD	PWR	STM
2016	VER	A-	21	0	2	0	7	7	21	17	1	3.0	9.0	21	50%	.262	1.14	2.57	3.37	0.5				
2017	STO	A+	22	2	5	1	17	14	72^2	81	5	2.0	9.2	74	54%	.350	1.33	4.09	2.35	2.4				
2018	*OAK*	*MLB*	*23*	*4*	*4*	*0*	*19*	*13*	*58^1*	*59*	*10*	*3.7*	*9.4*	*61*	*43%*	*.308*	*1.42*	*4.79*	*5.04*	*0.4*				
2019	*OAK*	*MLB*	*24*	*5*	*8*	*0*	*28*	*24*	*159^1*	*166*	*29*	*4.3*	*8.9*	*158*	*43%*	*.309*	*1.52*	*5.21*	*5.45*	*0.2*				

Breakout: 9% Improve: 14% Collapse: 12% Attrition: 25% MLB: 31% *Comparables: Scott Diamond, Garrett Richards, Rookie Davis*

Shore was the A's 2016 second-round pick out of Florida, where he was the Friday-night starter over A.J. Puk. (This is one of those fun facts that will be mentioned in his Annual comment every year for as long as they're both A's.) They're twins in the Danny DeVito-Arnold Schwarzenegger sense: lefty vs. righty; big arm vs. low-velocity command guy; high ceiling/low floor vs. this-is-what-he-is-and-that's-fine. Shore's game is keeping hitters off-balance by moving the ball around the zone and fouling up their timing with an excellent changeup. He missed two months at High-A with a lat strain last year, but should advance to Double-A Midland, where he'll try to stay on track for a fourth-starter future. A guy with his profile probably benefits more than many from getting out of the Cal League and pitching in front of better, more consistent defenses on better, more consistent infield surfaces.

Blake Treinen RHP Born: 06/30/88 Age: 29 Bats: R Throws: R Height: 6'5" Weight: 225 Origin: Round 7, 2011 Draft (#226 overall)

YEAR	TEAM	LVL	AGE	W	L	SV	G	GS	IP	H	HR	BB/9	K/9	K	GB%	BABIP	WHIP	ERA	DRA	WARP	MPH	CMD	PWR	STM
2015	SYR	AAA	27	0	0	0	5	0	12	6	0	0.8	10.5	14	71%	.214	0.58	0.00	2.14	0.4				
2015	WAS	MLB	27	2	5	0	60	0	67^{2}	62	4	4.3	8.6	65	65%	.328	1.39	3.86	3.25	1.2	98.9	36	73	51
2016	WAS	MLB	28	4	1	1	73	0	67	51	5	4.2	8.5	63	67%	.280	1.22	2.28	3.26	1.3	98.1	28	64	49
2017	WAS	MLB	29	0	2	3	37	0	37^{2}	48	3	3.1	7.6	32	62%	.381	1.62	5.73	5.03	0.1	99.0	44	76	53
2017	OAK	MLB	29	3	4	13	35	0	38	32	3	2.8	9.9	42	60%	.299	1.16	2.13	3.53	0.7	98.9	44	76	53
2018	*OAK*	*MLB*	*30*	*3*	*3*	*25*	*59*	*0*	*62*	*57*	*6*	*3.8*	*8.9*	*62*	*59%*	*.300*	*1.33*	*3.53*	*3.87*	*0.9*	*97.9*	*37*	*71*	*51*
2019	*OAK*	*MLB*	*31*	*3*	*1*	*15*	*50*	*0*	*53*	*48*	*5*	*4.3*	*9.2*	*54*	*59%*	*.303*	*1.38*	*4.15*	*4.31*	*0.5*	*97.5*	*37*	*71*	*51*

Breakout: 24% Improve: 53% Collapse: 24% Attrition: 19% MLB: 89% *Comparables: Matt Lindstrom, Jared Hughes, Tom Wilhelmsen*

Treinen was the major-league piece coming back to the A's in the Sean Doolittle/Ryan Madson trade. He's not a full, drop-in replacement for either pitcher (the days of Billy Beane getting Dan Haren back for Mark Mulder are long gone), but if you cover up his ugly (albeit BABIP-fueled) first half with Washington last year, he looks like a dang good reliever, particularly when you watch him throw 97-mph sinkers and 89-mph sliders with movement that should not be permissible at that velocity. The knock has always been control, but check out the chop in walk rate last year: He did it! He's the guy this Annual has been writing about for literally two decades, the "if he can cut his walk rate while maintaining everything else, he'll be great" guy. Congratulations to him, to us and to everyone involved. Last one out, please hit the lights.

Andrew Triggs RHP Born: 03/16/89 Age: 29 Bats: R Throws: R Height: 6'4" Weight: 220 Origin: Round 19, 2012 Draft (#583 overall)

YEAR	TEAM	LVL	AGE	W	L	SV	G	GS	IP	H	HR	BB/9	K/9	K	GB%	BABIP	WHIP	ERA	DRA	WARP	MPH	CMD	PWR	STM
2015	BOW	AA	26	0	2	17	43	0	61	42	0	1.6	10.3	70	61%	.286	0.87	1.03	1.70	2.2				
2016	NAS	AAA	27	2	1	2	16	0	18^{1}	16	0	2.5	10.3	21	59%	.314	1.15	2.95	2.93	0.4				
2016	OAK	MLB	27	1	1	0	24	6	56^{1}	56	5	2.1	8.8	55	52%	.315	1.22	4.31	3.19	1.3	92.6	47	39	47
2017	OAK	MLB	28	5	6	0	12	12	65^{1}	68	9	2.6	6.9	50	49%	.294	1.33	4.27	3.55	1.5	91.1	41	23	53
2018	*OAK*	*MLB*	*29*	*9*	*9*	*0*	*26*	*26*	*148*	*157*	*23*	*3.1*	*7.7*	*127*	*50%*	*.302*	*1.42*	*4.54*	*4.87*	*0.9*	*91.1*	*43*	*30*	*50*
2019	*OAK*	*MLB*	*30*	*8*	*11*	*0*	*27*	*27*	*163^{2}*	*188*	*30*	*2.9*	*7.6*	*137*	*50%*	*.316*	*1.46*	*5.17*	*5.38*	*0.5*	*90.6*	*43*	*29*	*50*

Breakout: 31% Improve: 46% Collapse: 27% Attrition: 32% MLB: 84% *Comparables: Chad Qualls, Alex Wilson, Vin Mazzaro*

Nothing about Triggs' stuff ever made anyone think he had a serious shot at major-league success, which is why his best draft position was the 19th round. All he has done as a professional, though, is get outs: A 2.09 minor-league ERA with a strikeout per inning ought to shout even if your sidearm, 89-mph sinker only mutters. After watching him pitch surprisingly well in four short-leash August 2016 starts (2.91 ERA while never seeing the seventh inning), the A's installed Triggs in their 2017 rotation. He responded with perfectly adequate results despite missing few bats and not converting his heavy sinker into actual grounders. He then supplemented his response with an injury, a June hip strain for which he wound up having season-ending surgery in July. "Assuming health" is a fearsome phrase for Triggs, whose 2016 season ended in early September after a back strain, but, assuming health, he should again compete for the fourth or fifth rotation spot this year.

Bobby Wahl RHP Born: 03/21/92 Age: 26 Bats: R Throws: R Height: 6'2" Weight: 210 Origin: Round 5, 2013 Draft (#161 overall)

YEAR	TEAM	LVL	AGE	W	L	SV	G	GS	IP	H	HR	BB/9	K/9	K	GB%	BABIP	WHIP	ERA	DRA	WARP	MPH	CMD	PWR	STM
2015	MID	AA	23	2	0	4	24	0	32^{1}	36	2	3.9	10.0	36	50%	.374	1.55	4.18	2.97	0.7				
2016	MID	AA	24	0	1	10	33	0	40^{2}	26	3	3.8	10.6	48	55%	.256	1.06	2.21	3.50	0.6				
2017	OAK	MLB	25	0	0	0	7	0	7^{2}	8	0	4.7	9.4	8	22%	.348	1.57	4.70	5.36	0.0	97.0			23
2017	NAS	AAA	25	1	1	3	11	0	13	13	3	3.5	15.2	22	23%	.357	1.38	4.15	3.80	0.2				
2018	*OAK*	*MLB*	*26*	*2*	*1*	*0*	*28*	*1*	*34*	*33*	*7*	*4.4*	*11.1*	*42*	*40%*	*.307*	*1.45*	*5.21*	*5.49*	*-0.1*	*96.6*			*23*
2019	*OAK*	*MLB*	*27*	*2*	*1*	*0*	*42*	*2*	*59^{1}*	*56*	*14*	*4.7*	*11.5*	*76*	*40%*	*.302*	*1.47*	*5.43*	*5.70*	*-0.3*	*96.2*			*24*

Breakout: 11% Improve: 16% Collapse: 5% Attrition: 19% MLB: 24% *Comparables: Jeff Beliveau, Grant Dayton, Guido Knudson*

Bobby hit a Wahl just seven games into his major-league career, acquainting himself with the disabled list in May and undergoing surgery for thoracic outlet syndrome in August. If he makes it back at full strength, he can be an asset in the bullpen (check that velocity and those strikeout rates), but without a ton of projection left (check that age), he's not a good bet to do more than help out in middle relief (check those walk rates). If he can get himself on TV often enough, the full, lustrous beard he wore last year should help him snag an endorsement deal with Wahl Grooming ("Real Grooming for Real Guys"). If you're his agent, give us a call; we've got a million brilliant ideas where that one came from.

LINEOUTS

Hitters

HITTER	POS	TEAM	LVL	AGE	PA	R	2B	3B	HR	RBI	BB	K	SB	CS	AVG/OBP/SLG	TAv	VORP	BABIP	BRR	FRAA	WARP
Nick Allen	SS	ATH	Rk	18	154	26	3	2	1	14	13	28	7	3	.254/.322/.326	.245	5.3	.312	1.1	SS(33): 2.5	0.7
Jaff Decker	OF	OAK	MLB	27	62	4	1	1	0	1	8	17	1	1	.200/.322/.260	.211	-2.5	.303	-1.1	CF(12): -1.1, RF(4): 1.5	-0.2

HITTER	POS	TEAM	LVL	AGE	PA	R	2B	3B	HR	RBI	BB	K	SB	CS	AVG/OBP/SLG	TAv	VORP	BABIP	BRR	FRAA	WARP
	OF	NAS	AAA	27	398	41	13	1	6	36	38	93	15	5	.274/.342/.368	.256	7.5	.350	-1.0	CF(44): -3.4, RF(29): 1.2	0.8
Greg Deichmann	OF	VER	A-	22	195	31	10	4	8	30	28	40	4	1	.274/.385/.530	.326	17.8	.316	0.8	RF(34): 3.2, LF(1): -0.1	2.1
Ramon Laureano	RF	CCH	AA	22	513	65	21	6	11	55	40	110	24	5	.227/.298/.369	.250	11.3	.273	6.3	RF(95): 7.9, CF(31): -1.6	1.9
Richie Martin	SS	MID	AA	22	325	43	11	3	3	27	24	57	12	3	.224/.306/.315	.235	8.0	.266	3.3	SS(86): -8.2	0.0
	SS	STO	A+	22	103	16	2	3	1	6	8	21	1	1	.266/.330/.383	.264	3.2	.333	0.0	SS(14): 0.3	0.4
Josh Phegley	C	NAS	AAA	29	34	2	2	0	1	4	2	5	0	0	.310/.382/.483	.326	3.1	.333	-0.8	C(6): -0.7	0.2
	C	OAK	MLB	29	161	14	11	0	3	10	9	26	0	1	.201/.255/.336	.207	-1.5	.223	0.0	C(56): 2.5	0.1
Tyler Ramirez	OF	STO	A+	22	328	51	12	2	7	39	45	80	5	2	.301/.399/.434	.306	22.7	.397	0.0	LF(46): -2.8, CF(19): -2.7	1.7
	OF	MID	AA	22	243	29	11	1	4	24	28	53	3	3	.308/.395/.428	.299	14.6	.390	-0.1	LF(54): -1.0, RF(7): -0.2	1.4
Rafael Rincones	OF	DRS	Rk	17	236	38	13	3	1	19	32	51	8	3	.258/.373/.369	.278	12.3	.340	2.1	RF(52): 1.2, LF(1): -0.1	1.2
Jake Smolinski	OF	STO	A+	28	32	5	1	0	1	10	5	4	0	1	.250/.375/.417	.301	1.5	.238	-0.1		0.2
	OF	NAS	AAA	28	32	4	1	0	0	1	0	8	0	0	.129/.156/.161	.100	-5.0	.174	0.4		-0.5
	OF	OAK	MLB	28	29	1	1	0	0	0	1	6	0	0	.259/.310/.296	.204	-1.0	.333	-0.2	CF(9): -0.1, RF(1): 0.0	-0.1

The A's threw their well-known financial heft around and paid $2 million to tiny third-round shortstop **Nick Allen** to convince him not to attend USC. Rafael Belliard appeared in 17 major-league seasons. **Jaff Decker** remains a good athlete who will take a walk but cannot hit a lick; he set a new career high with 62 plate appearances for the A's in 2017 and might be advised to try a new approach, like licking a hit. **Greg Deichmann** impressed in his short-season debut, as an LSU second-round pick should; the profile (an arm and power and mere wishes for the rest) firmly but politely states "right field." Squeezed off the Astros' 40-man roster this offseason, **Ramon Laureano** has enough speed and defense to make the majors, but he was buried on Houston's depth chart. He's got the ceiling of a good fourth outfielder on most teams. **Richie Martin** was drafted in 2015 as and remains to this day a no-doubt shortstop and an all-outs hitter. **Josh Phegley**, the second-best spleenless player in baseball, looks for all the world like a backup catcher (shaped like a cube, solid power, ruggedly handsome visage), but his defensive numbers have never been up to snuff and he has missed significant time with injury the last two years. **Tyler Ramirez**: 5-foot-9, big-college player, good OBP, no power, maybe a center fielder, maybe not. Write the comment in your head. **Rafael Rincones** is an 18-year-old right fielder who has not yet appeared stateside; the A's acquired him from the Red Sox for Rajai Davis, so the hope is that five to seven years from now, there will be a new reason to think about Rajai Davis. **Jake Smolinski** essentially lost 2017 to a shoulder injury. He'll give you flashes where you wonder if he's something more than a fourth outfielder, but he's not, and 87 percent of the league is equally capable of those flashes.

Pitchers

PITCHER	TEAM	LVL	AGE	W	L	SV	G	GS	IP	H	HR	BB/9	K/9	K	GB%	BABIP	WHIP	ERA	DRA	WARP	MPH	CMD	PWR	STM
John Axford	OAK	MLB	34	0	1	0	22	0	21	27	3	7.3	9.0	21	51%	.364	2.10	6.43	6.94	-0.4	96.8	57	65	42
Chris Bassitt	STO	A+	28	0	1	0	7	7	13	9	0	2.8	9.7	14	64%	.273	1.00	2.77	2.64	0.4				
	NAS	AAA	28	4	2	0	17	2	37^{2}	41	3	3.8	7.4	31	36%	.336	1.51	6.21	7.79	-1.0				
Paul Blackburn	NAS	AAA	23	5	6	0	15	14	79^{2}	69	6	2.9	6.3	56	56%	.265	1.19	3.05	3.24	2.1				
	OAK	MLB	23	3	1	0	10	10	58^{2}	58	5	2.5	3.4	22	56%	.273	1.26	3.22	4.09	1.0	92.0	55	37	66
Michael Brady	NAS	AAA	30	3	1	0	17	8	53^{1}	45	5	1.0	8.6	51	41%	.268	0.96	3.21	2.21	1.9				
	OAK	MLB	30	0	0	0	16	0	31^{2}	33	7	1.7	6.8	24	37%	.277	1.23	5.68	5.53	-0.1	92.9	47	30	42
Dakota Chalmers	BLT	A	20	2	2	0	10	5	29	15	1	9.0	14.6	47	46%	.286	1.52	4.34	5.13	0.0				
Heath Fillmyer	MID	AA	23	11	5	0	29	29	149^{2}	158	19	3.1	6.9	115	45%	.310	1.40	3.49	5.27	-0.2				
Jesse Hahn	OAK	MLB	27	3	6	0	14	13	69^{2}	78	4	3.5	7.1	55	47%	.327	1.51	5.30	5.43	0.1	95.9	39	53	51
	NAS	AAA	27	2	0	0	6	5	25	28	1	5.0	6.5	18	54%	.342	1.68	4.32	4.96	0.2				
Casey Meisner	STO	A+	22	6	5	0	16	12	74^{2}	73	9	2.4	9.6	80	34%	.320	1.25	3.98	5.12	0.1				
	MID	AA	22	4	4	0	12	12	59	55	4	4.1	5.6	37	35%	.282	1.39	4.12	8.18	-2.1				
Norge Ruiz	DAT	Rk	23	2	0	0	4	4	19	9	0	0.5	6.6	14	69%	.176	0.53	0.47	2.63	0.7				
	STO	A+	23	3	1	0	8	8	34^{2}	47	4	3.1	6.2	24	48%	.368	1.70	5.71	6.96	-0.7				
Chris Smith	NAS	AAA	36	4	3	0	15	12	74	76	5	2.4	7.8	64	43%	.324	1.30	3.16	3.31	1.9				
	OAK	MLB	36	0	4	0	14	9	55^{2}	60	16	3.6	5.0	31	37%	.244	1.47	6.79	5.63	-0.1	87.4	66	10	59
Lou Trivino	MID	AA	25	7	1	1	23	0	33^{1}	31	0	2.7	9.2	34	57%	.333	1.23	2.43	3.19	0.6				
	NAS	AAA	25	1	2	4	25	0	35	33	0	2.8	8.0	31	54%	.308	1.26	3.60	4.35	0.4				

John Axford spent years using whiffs and grounders to overcome an inability to pound the zone, but we've yet to see a pitcher survive seven-plus walks per nine, especially when it's paired with a velocity dip. The A's cut him in July. **Chris Bassitt** had Tommy John surgery in mid-2016, experienced a setback in his rehab in May and came back as a Triple-A reliever in late July, but was never recalled to the majors. He should be in the middle-relief mix this year, but at 29, the breakout isn't coming. In 10 big-league starts before a comebacker off his hand ended his season, **Paul Blackburn** struck out the same number of batters as he allowed runs: 3.4 per nine innings. His stuff and minor-league strikeout rates say the whiff rate isn't a fluke, which means the runs allowed definitely are. It's the story of a **Michael Brady** who mainly throws three pitches of his own. He was 30, a good minor-leaguer, yet he always got bombed. **Dakota Chalmers** has a big arm that begot bigger strikeout numbers in Low-A last year, but he needs to take six steps forward with his control to have a future, and 13 steps to be a starter. He took leave for unspecified personal reasons and didn't pitch after May, but was back with the A's for fall Instructional League. Like anyone from the 609 area code, **Heath Fillmyer** is pro pork roll in the eternal pork roll vs. Taylor ham debate, per his Twitter. More like **Jesse Hahn** Solo if he doesn't start turning his heavy sinker back into the results he got in 2015. See, because he won't have a team anymore. **Daulton Jefferies** is a righty out of Berkeley with fourth-starter potential, assuming he makes it back from spring 2017 Tommy John surgery. He also looks disconcertingly and disarmingly like White Josh from the best show on TV, *Crazy Ex-Girlfriend*. **Casey Meisner**'s 6-foot-7 frame still intrigues, but 1.4 strikeouts per walk in Double-A are the statistical by-product of his continued tall-guy problems: Inconsistent mechanics undermine his good stuff. **Norge Ruiz** is a short Cuban righty with a full suitcase of pitches but not much velocity who got a couple million bucks from the A's before 2017, then pitched without success in a brief Cal League stint that included a 10-game suspension for a foreign substance. **Chris Smith** has been pitching professionally since 2002, but his low-velocity craftiness and high-happiness demeanor can still help push your Triple-A team to the playoffs. Since converting to relief in June 2015, extreme groundballer **Lou Trivino** has only allowed two home runs total; he cut the number to zero in a dominant 2017 season of relief split between Double-A and Triple-A.

PHILADELPHIA PHILLIES

Essay by Liz Roscher

Player comments by Jarrett Seidler and BP staff

Three years isn't a long time. Most of us can remember what we were doing three years ago—where we lived, our rough place in life. But three years in baseball is a lifetime. It's long enough to forget highlights or who played right field, who was traded and who was fired. And it's long enough to forget one of the most bonkers years of the Phillies' almost-finished rebuild.

If you ask five different Phillies fans to name one thing that happened during the 2015 season, you'll get five different answers. It's not that being a Phillies fan is harmful to your brain (though it probably is), it's that 2015 was crammed full of so much action that it's incredibly hard to remember the depth and breadth of it all.

It's also hard to remember because most of it was part of the messy, unpleasant and painful stage that teams have to go through during a rebuild. But while most teams try to space things out, the Phillies got most of their tough moves done in a calendar year. Firings, hirings, trades, promotions—2015 was the year for all of it. Some of that was due to happenstance and opportunity, but much of the change itself was intentional.

Intentional change was a new and overwhelming experience for the Phillies, who had spent so long trying to keep things the same. For fans, it was sensory overload, as executives came and went, and so did beloved players. But everything that happened set up the Phillies for the future. Everything was about what would come next, after all the moves were made, and what would bring a championship back to Philadelphia. We can't say yet whether these moves will yield a champion, but we can reflect on everything that happened in an adventurous 2015.

June 26, 2015: Manager Ryne Sandberg Quits

The 2015 Phillies were not a picnic. No one in their right mind expected them to be. But it was clear from the start that manager Ryne Sandberg wasn't equipped to handle them. Whether it was the losing or the in-game decision making or connecting with the players, Sandberg seemed lost and miserable from the start of the season to the moment he quit.

The nadir of Sandberg's tenure, if you can pick just one, came on June 16, 2015. It was a 19-3 loss to the Orioles that was so brutal that Sandberg and pitching coach Bob McClure sent outfielder Jeff Francoeur to the mound to eat an inning or two. His first inning was fine, but the second one was a disaster. After Francoeur had allowed a run and loaded the bases, McClure came out to the mound and experienced the rage of Chase Utley, who was upset that non-pitcher Francoeur was for some reason still out on the mound. With the bullpen phone literally off the hook, there was nothing to do but leave him in until the end of the inning. You can feel bad for Frenchy, but also feel bad for McClure, who had to be the surrogate for Utley's righteous anger since Sandberg was in the dugout.

June 29, 2015: Andy MacPhail Hired as Team President

The hiring of Andy MacPhail, a former Orioles executive known for his adoption of analytics, marked the first time Phillies' principal

PHILLIES PROSPECTUS

2017 W-L: 66-96, 5TH IN NL EAST

Pythag	.441	23rd	B-Age	26.4	*2nd*
RS/G	4.26	27th	P-Age	26.3	*2nd*
RA/G	4.83	17th	Salary	$100.0M	*22nd*
TAv	.260	16th	M$/MW	$4.9M	*7th*
TAv-P	.276	24th	DL Days	878	*14th*
FIP	4.58	20th	$ on DL	20%	*23rd*
DER	.696	25th			

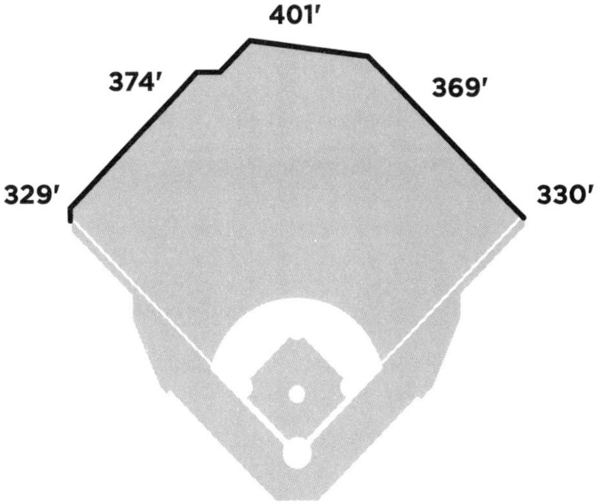

Outfield wall profile: **6'** to **19'**

Three-Year Park Factors

Runs	Runs/RH	Runs/LH	HR/RH	HR/LH
99	100	97	111	110

Top Hitter WARP	3.5 Cesar Hernandez
Top Pitcher WARP	5.5 Aaron Nola
Top Prospect	Sixto Sanchez

2017 Hit List Ranking

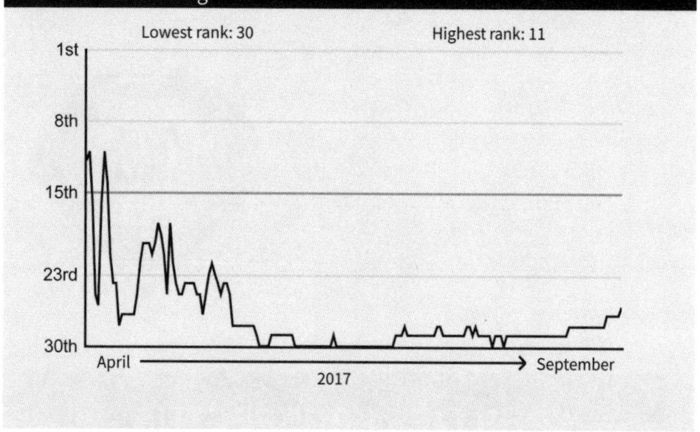

Committed Payroll (in millions)

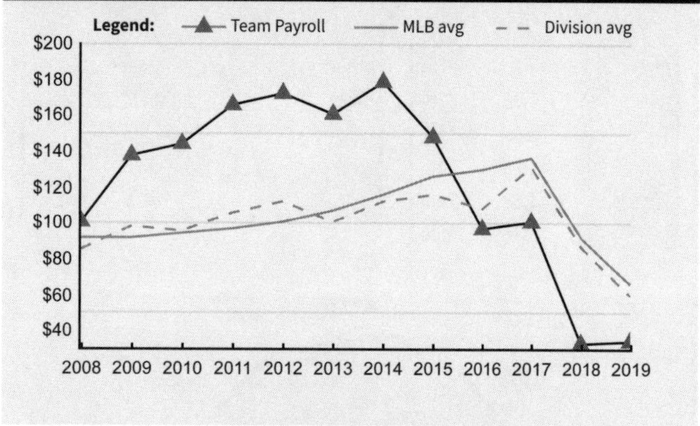

Farm System Ranking

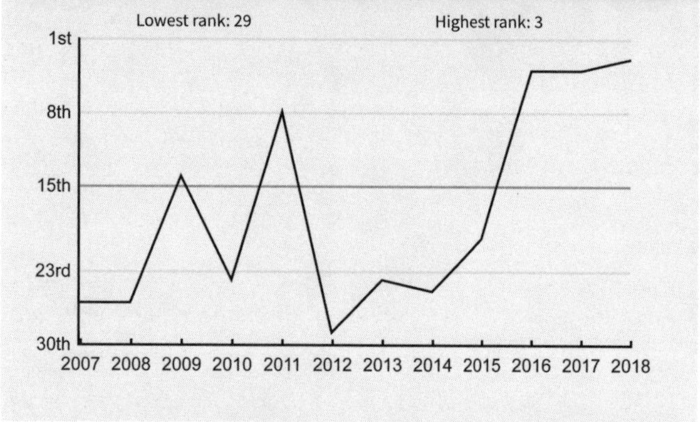

Personnel

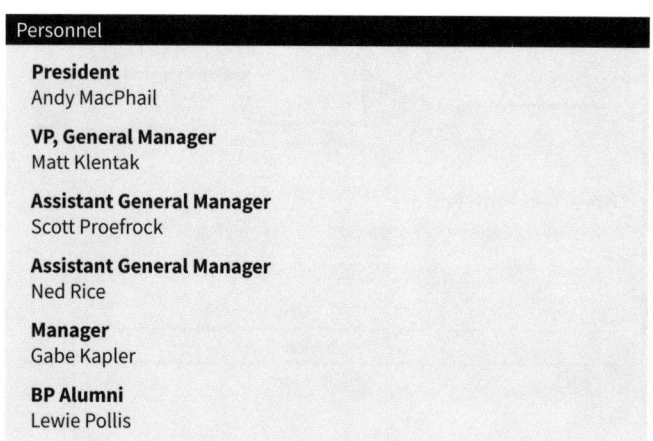

President
Andy MacPhail

VP, General Manager
Matt Klentak

Assistant General Manager
Scott Proefrock

Assistant General Manager
Ned Rice

Manager
Gabe Kapler

BP Alumni
Lewie Pollis

owner John S. Middleton noticeably flexed his muscle. David Montgomery had been the team president since 1997 but took a leave of absence in mid-2014 due to cancer surgery. Former championship GM Pat Gillick came on to replace him, but the move didn't feel permanent, even when Montgomery returned to the organization as chairman in 2015.

With Montgomery battling illness, there was a leadership vacuum for the first time in over 15 years. And that's when we really got to meet Middleton, who stepped into the void. He believed the Phillies were woefully behind the times and began to take an active role in steering the organization.

Middleton was (and remains) obsessed with winning, and if the Phillies were ever going to take home another Commissioner's Trophy, things had to change. When MacPhail officially started as team president (he served as a special assistant until the end of the 2015 season, when Gillick retired), he wouldn't have a set budget, just "a mandate to win." Of course, MacPhail wouldn't need to use that non-budget for years, but it was nice to know that it was (or wasn't?) there.

July 21, 2015: Aaron Nola Debuts

It already feels like Aaron Nola has been around forever. The Louisiana State University right-hander was the team's first round pick in 2014, and he shot up through the system like a rocket. Just 13 months after he was drafted, Nola was promoted to the majors. It was everyone's first peek at the future.

Nola's meteoric rise was due to the unapologetic success of his college career. He was a junior when he was drafted, and he had two-plus years of upper-echelon NCAA experience under his belt. Nola's stuff easily transitioned to professional baseball. He started 2014 in High-A and had already outgrown it by August. He was promoted to Double-A, where he returned in 2015 before being promoted to Triple-A in mid-June. A month later he was in the majors.

Nola's debut was joyful, because it represented actual success. The Phillies had drafted some duds in recent first rounds (ahem, Larry Greene), and with Nola it felt like the team had done something right. But it was also a little sad. There was no surer sign that the Phillies were going to trade Cole Hamels than bringing up his replacement.

July 28, 2015: Jonathan Papelbon Traded to Washington Nationals

Of all the things that happened in 2015, the fact that Jonathan Papelbon was traded remains the most incredible. Not because he was bad—he was actually having a great season—but because he was expensive and unpleasant. Papelbon's reputation for being a jerk followed him to Philadelphia and grew organically like a weed. It was unimaginable that any team would want Papelbon, who in 2014 earned a seven-game suspension for performatively grabbing his crotch while walking off the field, and his $11 million option for 2016.

This trade was the crowning achievement of General Manager Ruben Amaro Jr., who convinced the Washington Nationals to take Papelbon. Amaro didn't even need to get anything in return for this trade to be a win, but he did. Nick Pivetta, a living, breathing pitcher, came over from Washington and would contribute to the 2017 Phillies.

For their trouble, the Nationals got the full Papelbon experience: 3.04 ERA, 7 saves, and 2 blown saves. Oh, and that time Papelbon strangled some guy named Bryce Harper in the Nats dugout over a fight that Papelbon himself started. What a prize.

July 31, 2015: Cole Hamels Traded to Texas Rangers

After several years of trade rumors, it felt inevitable that the Phillies would trade their homegrown ace. It was just a matter of when and where. Amaro waited over a year to trade Hamels, and some thought he had waited too long. During that year when Amaro wasn't trading Hamels, the noise about what the pitcher was and wasn't worth was deafening. Hamels would be missed, but the trade needed to happen so we could all move on with our lives.

This was the last major trade Amaro made with the Phillies, and it was a doozy. For Hamels and reliever Jake Diekman, the Phillies received Nick Williams, Jerad Eickhoff, Jake Thompson and Jorge Alfaro (and a salary dump in the form of Matt Harrison). All four of those players played at least one game for the 2017 Phillies. Williams, Eickhoff and Alfaro will be starters in 2018.

That single trade did more to help the rebuild than any other. Saying goodbye to Hamels, who had grown up as a man and as a pitcher in Philadelphia, was tough but worth it. He went out in glorious fashion, throwing a 129-pitch no-hitter against the Cubs in his final start. It was almost like the universe knew the story of Hamels, and Phillies fans needed a beautiful movie plot ending.

August 19, 2015: Chase Utley Traded to Los Angeles Dodgers

On the other hand, this trade felt cruel. The rumors had been swirling, but just a day before the trade, both Amaro and Gillick said publicly that they expected Chase Utley to stay with the Phillies for the rest of the season. This served as a final reminder that trusting Amaro's public statements was always an at-your-own-risk proposition: Utley became a Dodger about 24 hours later.

Utley didn't have to be traded: His two-year contract extension was up at the end of the season, and the Phillies could have declined the built-in club option. But faced with the choice of whether to let Utley go or get something in return, the Phillies opted for the latter. And Utley, who could reject any deal he didn't like, accepted the trade. He recognized that things were changing, and it was time to move on.

The players who came back, right-hander John Richy and utility guy Darnell Sweeney, were relatively inconsequential. The trade was more about symbolically wiping the slate clean and getting rid of players who had value but wouldn't be playing a role on the Phillies teams of the future. The Utley trade marked the end of the era. It was time to flip the mattress, burn some sage and get ready for what would come next.

September 10, 2015: Ruben Amaro Jr. Fired

The 2015 season was also a season of goodbyes and inevitabilities. When MacPhail came on as the new team president, there was no question that Amaro was on his way out. MacPhail wanted to pick his own GM, and Amaro had done all he could do in Philadelphia. Baseball had moved past the Phillies in a flash, and MacPhail was there to help the franchise catch up.

Amaro's legacy in Philadelphia shouldn't be that complicated. He was part of the front office that built the 2008 team, and when he took over in 2009, he was responsible for extending the Phillies' run another three years. It all crashed down quickly, but he helped set up the next regime nicely. In addition to the Hamels trade, Amaro also drafted J.P. Crawford, Nola, Scott Kingery and Rhys Hoskins.

Just like Ed Wade and Pat Gillick before him, Amaro built the core of the next competitive Phillies team. And just like Wade and Gillick, he handed over the keys to the next guy, hoping he'd be able to take all pieces and turn them into something cohesive and successful.

October 4, 2015: Phillies Avoid 100 Losses

The Phillies' final game of the season was an afternoon affair against the Marlins. Coming into the day, the Phillies had a record of 62-99. They were on the edge of 100 losses for the first time since 1961. The team looked a lot different than it had when the season started.

The Phillies won 7-2 in a game that featured the Marlins' Ichiro Suzuki on the mound. As the last out was secured, fans everywhere exhaled together. The Phillies wouldn't lose 100 games and, best of all, the win wouldn't even cost them the top draft pick the following season. Francoeur, who had gone from a hated former Met and Brave to a beloved veteran over the course of just one season, ripped off his jersey once the game was over and threw it into the crowd. In that moment, he was the 2015 Phillies.

October 26, 2015: Matt Klentak Hired as General Manager

Imagine trumpets, if you will, and a chorus exclaiming "A new age now begins!" MacPhail brought in his former Orioles colleague Matt Klentak, who had been working as the Angels assistant GM, to be the new face of the Phillies front office. The decision was popular immediately, though considering how the city of Philadelphia felt about Amaro at the time, the hiring of a sea cow in a button-down and blazer would have been applauded.

Compared to Amaro, 35-year-old Klentak seemed humble, thoughtful and content to remain behind the scenes. Klentak had never played, but had worked in baseball since college. He lacked Amaro's bravado, which wasn't necessarily a bad thing.

With Klentak, the magic words were "advanced metrics" and "open-minded," things Amaro was not known for. Amaro employed the smallest analytics department in baseball, which at one point contained a lone soul the Phillies had hired away from the commissioner's office. And despite the proliferation of new ways to look at stats, injuries, pitches and swings, Amaro resisted change. But those days were over now: MacPhail and his new GM were about to drag the new-look Phillies into the new millennium.

After undergoing so much change in 2015, the Phillies slowed down in 2016 and 2017. There were fewer trades to make and fewer players to sign. Prospects were slowly making their way through the system, with an emphasis on "slowly." There was no reason to rush.

But now the Phillies are staring their future in the face. Nearly all of the big-name prospects have graduated to the majors, and the team has tough decisions to make. Signings mean something now, because each one should propel the team forward instead of just making everyone say, "Well, Michael Saunders is on the Phillies now, I guess." When Carlos Santana inked his three-year deal this offseason, the questions were about how they would make room in the lineup, not about whether it was the right time to start playing the free agency game. It's scary. There's a smaller margin of error when the goal is to win and not just to exist.

It's so exciting, though. Fans have expectations of the Phillies again, more than "please don't lose 100 games." After the Phillies' second-half surge in 2017, it seems wrong to set a low bar, like "please don't lose 90 games." But it's also dangerous to go too far the other way and expect too much from such a young club. A .500 season is an ambitious goal, because it represents such a big step forward for the Phillies, yet it doesn't seem that far off.

In the two-plus years since Klentak and MacPhail took over, the prospects have mostly controlled the rebuild. And now that they are ready to play in the majors every day, both the players and the front office get to show what they're made of. This was the end goal. The Phillies are on the precipice of being interesting, if not good or great. Sooner rather than later, everyone will find out whether it was worth it. My money's on yes.

—Liz Roscher is a writer for Big League Stew and The Athletic, and managing editor for The Good Phight.

Hitters

Jorge Alfaro C
Born: 06/11/93 Age: 25 Bats: R Throws: R Height: 6'2" Weight: 225 Origin: International Free Agent, 2010

YEAR	TEAM	LVL	AGE	PA	R	2B	3B	HR	RBI	BB	K	SB	CS	AVG/OBP/SLG	TAv	VORP	BABIP	BRR	FRAA	WARP
2015	FRI	AA	22	207	22	15	2	5	21	9	61	2	1	.253/.314/.432	.250	5.5	.347	0.6	C(35): -0.3, 1B(1): 0.0	0.6
2016	REA	AA	23	435	68	21	2	15	67	22	105	3	2	.285/.325/.458	.268	20.9	.347	-1.5	C(95): 14.7	3.8
2016	PHI	MLB	23	17	0	0	0	0	0	1	8	0	0	.125/.176/.125	.079	-2.5	.250	-0.1	C(4): -0.6	-0.3
2017	LEH	AAA	24	350	34	13	2	7	43	16	113	1	1	.241/.291/.358	.233	4.0	.345	-1.4	C(77): 5.2	0.9
2017	PHI	MLB	24	114	12	6	0	5	14	3	33	0	0	.318/.360/.514	.319	10.7	.420	-1.5	C(28): -2.4, 1B(2): 0.1	0.8
2018	*PHI*	*MLB*	*25*	*431*	*46*	*18*	*2*	*14*	*51*	*17*	*140*	*0*	*0*	*.233/.277/.388*	*.232*	*8.3*	*.318*	*-0.8*	*C -5*	*-0.1*
2019	*PHI*	*MLB*	*26*	*437*	*52*	*19*	*1*	*16*	*54*	*23*	*144*	*0*	*0*	*.232/.286/.403*	*.246*	*9.6*	*.315*	*-1.0*	*C -4*	*0.6*

Breakout: 9% Improve: 18% Collapse: 16% Attrition: 27% MLB: 42% *Comparables: Max Stassi, Steven Hill, Anthony Recker*

YEAR	TEAM	P. COUNT	FRM RUNS	BLK RUNS	THRW RUNS	TOT RUNS
2015	FRI	5306	-0.3	-0.8	0.2	-0.9
2016	PHI	576	0.0	-0.6	0.0	-0.5
2017	PHI	4051	-2.5	0.1	0.0	-2.4
2018	*PHI*	*15414*	*-3.3*	*-1.6*	*0.0*	*-4.9*
2019	*PHI*	*15631*	*-2.4*	*-1.2*	*0.0*	*-3.6*

#TheLegend finally reached #TheShow for good in August—and the confidence comes because he's out of options. If it seems like we've been talking about Alfaro forever, it's because we have; when he signed for $1.3 million out of Colombia in January 2010, the top movie was Avatar, the Democrats still controlled the House of Representatives, NBC was running *The Jay Leno Show* in prime time five nights a week, and *Lost* was just about to start its final season with the weird sideways universe. Much has changed in the world since then, but Alfaro's profile is somewhat of a constant. He retains the tremendous raw power, arm and athleticism that got him so much money in the first place, and has smoothed out his defense enough to stay behind the dish. He also still swings at everything under the sun, limiting that raw power and causing him to not reach first nearly as much as he should. Catchers are weird, and Alfaro is toolsy enough that this could still yet coalesce into a star profile, but developmental time is not infinite.

Aaron Altherr OF
Born: 01/14/91 Age: 27 Bats: R Throws: R Height: 6'5" Weight: 215 Origin: Round 9, 2009 Draft (#287 overall)

YEAR	TEAM	LVL	AGE	PA	R	2B	3B	HR	RBI	BB	K	SB	CS	AVG/OBP/SLG	TAv	VORP	BABIP	BRR	FRAA	WARP
2015	REA	AA	24	260	29	19	3	6	29	28	40	8	3	.293/.371/.480	.302	16.0	.332	-0.4	RF(42): 3.9, CF(16): 1.3	2.3
2015	LEH	AAA	24	229	36	13	2	8	38	21	44	8	1	.294/.362/.495	.303	18.0	.338	1.7	CF(35): 3.9, RF(9): 0.5	2.3
2015	PHI	MLB	24	161	25	11	4	5	22	16	41	6	2	.241/.338/.489	.300	9.8	.301	0.0	LF(23): 0.5, RF(11): 0.6	1.4
2016	PHI	MLB	25	227	23	6	0	4	22	23	69	7	2	.197/.300/.288	.235	-0.7	.280	0.3	RF(42): -2.6, LF(20): 3.0	-0.1
2017	PHI	MLB	26	412	58	24	5	19	65	32	104	5	4	.272/.340/.516	.292	23.3	.328	0.4	LF(52): 4.3, RF(50): 1.6	3.1
2018	*PHI*	*MLB*	*27*	*325*	*40*	*16*	*2*	*11*	*41*	*25*	*85*	*6*	*3*	*.238/.307/.418*	*.253*	*8.1*	*.295*	*0.2*	*RF 0, LF 1*	*0.8*
2019	*PHI*	*MLB*	*28*	*352*	*44*	*18*	*2*	*13*	*45*	*29*	*94*	*7*	*3*	*.240/.314/.433*	*.266*	*11.1*	*.297*	*0.4*	*RF 0, LF 1*	*1.4*

Breakout: 3% Improve: 33% Collapse: 10% Attrition: 18% MLB: 84% *Comparables: Ryan Rua, John Bowker, Seth Smith*

As career highlights go, bombing the first and only grand slam off Clayton Kershaw into the upper deck is going to be hard to beat. Altherr missed the first half of 2016 with a wrist injury and couldn't hit water if he fell off a boat after returning. Finally fully recovered, Altherr entered last spring battling for a roster spot, but he started hitting in the Grapefruit League and didn't stop when the real games started, easily casting aside veteran roadblocks like Michael Saunders and Howie Kendrick. He battled a hamstring pull for much of the summer, so health remains a concern, and he might settle in as a good complementary player instead of a star. But no matter where Altherr's career goes from here, all the candy in the world won't stop his grandkids from rolling their eyes every time he retells them the story of besting the pitcher of a generation in the grandest fashion.

Daniel Brito 2B
Born: 01/23/98 Age: 20 Bats: L Throws: R Height: 6'1" Weight: 155 Origin: International Free Agent, 2015

YEAR	TEAM	LVL	AGE	PA	R	2B	3B	HR	RBI	BB	K	SB	CS	AVG/OBP/SLG	TAv	VORP	BABIP	BRR	FRAA	WARP
2015	DPH	RK	17	257	33	10	3	0	19	35	22	8	9	.269/.383/.344	.320	19.2	.298	-2.2	SS(8): -1.9, 2B(7): 0.4	1.7
2016	PHL	RK	18	215	35	10	5	2	25	21	27	7	2	.284/.355/.421	.291	15.3	.319	2.0	2B(47): -0.4	1.5
2017	LWD	A	19	491	54	15	1	6	32	33	95	12	9	.239/.298/.318	.249	9.7	.290	1.7	2B(107): -3.6, SS(6): -0.1	0.6
2018	*PHI*	*MLB*	*20*	*250*	*29*	*9*	*1*	*7*	*24*	*17*	*63*	*2*	*2*	*.223/.279/.359*	*.213*	*-2.1*	*.273*	*-0.4*	*2B -1, SS 0*	*-0.3*
2019	*PHI*	*MLB*	*21*	*384*	*44*	*15*	*1*	*12*	*43*	*28*	*93*	*4*	*3*	*.232/.292/.379*	*.239*	*3.3*	*.279*	*-0.6*	*2B -1, SS 0*	*0.3*

Breakout: 6% Improve: 14% Collapse: 0% Attrition: 7% MLB: 14% *Comparables: Adrian Cardenas, Jorge Polanco, Delino DeShields*

One of the toughest things about evaluating prospects is comparing what you see on the field with the data. It's clean when the visual and the statistical come together to form a cohesive picture of a player, but Brito's prospect picture is not quite so clear. In most ways, he reads like a mad lib for a projectable Latin-American middle infielder: excellent athleticism, a sweet swing, a skinny and projectable frame, raw pop that hasn't quite made it to 7 p.m. yet, good defensive actions and lack of polish. But on top of those, he's shown good feel for hitting—and the strike zone, to boot—at his best. He looked primed for a 2017 full-season breakout, and played the part in April by hitting .327/.377/.449 over 108 plate appearances. But by the time vacationers started heading for the Jersey shore, the hits had stopped. Eventually, the performance will have to play up to the tools, or his prospect status will fade.

Dylan Cozens RF Born: 05/31/94 Age: 24 Bats: L Throws: L Height: 6'6" Weight: 235 Origin: Round 2, 2012 Draft (#77 overall)

YEAR	TEAM	LVL	AGE	PA	R	2B	3B	HR	RBI	BB	K	SB	CS	AVG/OBP/SLG	TAv	VORP	BABIP	BRR	FRAA	WARP
2015	CLR	A+	21	397	52	22	5	5	46	26	79	18	5	.282/.335/.411	.279	16.1	.346	2.1	RF(70): 2.0, LF(12): -1.9	1.8
2015	REA	AA	21	44	6	2	0	3	9	3	7	2	1	.350/.386/.625	.369	4.1	.355	-1.6	RF(11): -0.8	0.4
2016	REA	AA	22	586	106	38	3	40	125	61	186	21	1	.276/.350/.591	.303	36.6	.348	0.3	RF(89): 8.0, LF(29): 0.7	4.8
2017	LEH	AAA	23	542	68	12	3	27	75	58	194	8	3	.210/.301/.418	.245	3.0	.283	1.7	RF(73): 8.1, LF(26): 2.7	1.4
2018	*PHI*	*MLB*	*24*	*46*	*6*	*2*	*0*	*2*	*7*	*4*	*16*	*1*	*0*	*.223/.293/.445*	*.252*	*1.0*	*.298*	*0.1*	*RF 0*	*0.1*
2019	*PHI*	*MLB*	*25*	*315*	*44*	*12*	*1*	*17*	*48*	*31*	*112*	*5*	*1*	*.227/.308/.468*	*.271*	*11.3*	*.303*	*0.5*	*RF 3*	*1.6*

Breakout: 6% Improve: 25% Collapse: 11% Attrition: 28% MLB: 47% *Comparables: Steven Moya, Aaron Judge, Matt Chapman*

It was a rough 2017 season for the burly lefty—and not just compared to longtime minor-league teammate Rhys Hoskins. Coming into 2017, Cozens and Hoskins were similar prospects; we ranked them in a tie for tenth on the Phillies team list, and their 2016 lines at Double-A were strikingly similar. While Hoskins rose into a national phenomenon, Cozens nearly sunk below the Mendoza Line at Triple-A as his strikeout rate kept rising. Cozens did retain enough of his power to hope there's a Joey Gallo Lite future if he can just rein it in a bit. Worst case, the former Arizona defensive end recruit could always try football again.

J.P. Crawford SS Born: 01/11/95 Age: 23 Bats: L Throws: R Height: 6'2" Weight: 180 Origin: Round 1, 2013 Draft (#16 overall)

YEAR	TEAM	LVL	AGE	PA	R	2B	3B	HR	RBI	BB	K	SB	CS	AVG/OBP/SLG	TAv	VORP	BABIP	BRR	FRAA	WARP
2015	CLR	A+	20	95	15	1	0	1	8	14	9	5	2	.392/.489/.443	.369	15.1	.435	1.1	SS(20): 0.8	1.7
2015	REA	AA	20	405	53	21	7	5	34	49	45	7	2	.265/.354/.407	.272	21.9	.289	1.0	SS(86): 6.8	3.1
2016	REA	AA	21	166	23	8	0	3	13	30	21	5	3	.265/.398/.390	.283	11.7	.295	1.3	SS(36): 6.0	1.9
2016	LEH	AAA	21	385	40	11	1	4	30	42	59	7	4	.244/.328/.318	.241	10.4	.284	2.1	SS(87): -3.2	0.7
2017	LEH	AAA	22	556	75	20	6	15	63	79	97	5	4	.243/.351/.405	.265	28.0	.275	1.6	SS(113): -6.0, 3B(6): -0.7	2.0
2017	PHI	MLB	22	87	8	4	1	0	6	16	22	1	0	.214/.356/.300	.263	3.2	.306	-0.2	3B(13): 2.3, SS(6): 0.4	0.6
2018	*PHI*	*MLB*	*23*	*567*	*69*	*21*	*4*	*15*	*63*	*71*	*111*	*5*	*3*	*.240/.336/.389*	*.256*	*23.1*	*.278*	*-0.4*	*SS 2*	*1.8*
2019	*PHI*	*MLB*	*24*	*557*	*72*	*21*	*4*	*17*	*67*	*70*	*112*	*5*	*3*	*.246/.343/.414*	*.272*	*25.6*	*.283*	*-0.3*	*SS 2*	*3.0*

Breakout: 2% Improve: 29% Collapse: 6% Attrition: 17% MLB: 51% *Comparables: Greg Garcia, Daniel Robertson, Gavin Cecchini*

The power finally showed up. Crawford had been known to put on batting-practice displays for years, but had completely failed to turn it into game power, often running a higher OBP than SLG. By mid-2017, he'd also stalled out at Triple-A, doing nothing of value at the plate, save walking. He even started mixing it up on social media with prospect analysts, notably tweeting "All it is is motivation" in response to low rankings on some midsesason lists. But then from July 1 to the end of the Triple-A season, Crawford hit .285/.385/.544 with 13 homers, finally showing the full weight of his superstar hit and power upside on the field. That got him called up to the majors in September, where he walked a ton and looked phenomenal defensively at third base—good enough that it's tempting to put him there despite his projecting as an above-average defender at shortstop, à la Manny Machado. Even if he doesn't retain much of the hitting gains, his plate discipline is so good that he could be the millennial Walt Weiss.

Maikel Franco 3B Born: 08/26/92 Age: 25 Bats: R Throws: R Height: 6'1" Weight: 215 Origin: International Free Agent, 2010

YEAR	TEAM	LVL	AGE	PA	R	2B	3B	HR	RBI	BB	K	SB	CS	AVG/OBP/SLG	TAv	VORP	BABIP	BRR	FRAA	WARP
2015	LEH	AAA	22	151	15	12	1	4	24	8	25	2	0	.355/.384/.539	.323	15.5	.404	1.3	3B(29): -2.0, 1B(4): -0.2	1.4
2015	PHI	MLB	22	335	45	22	1	14	50	26	52	1	0	.280/.343/.497	.305	25.5	.297	0.8	3B(75): -6.4, 1B(2): 0.2	2.1
2016	PHI	MLB	23	630	67	23	1	25	88	40	106	1	1	.255/.306/.427	.267	23.3	.271	-1.6	3B(148): -7.2	1.7
2017	PHI	MLB	24	623	66	29	1	24	76	41	95	0	0	.230/.281/.409	.235	2.2	.234	-1.8	3B(144): -9.2, 1B(2): -0.1	-0.7
2018	*PHI*	*MLB*	*25*	*559*	*66*	*27*	*2*	*22*	*78*	*34*	*92*	*1*	*0*	*.253/.302/.439*	*.254*	*13.8*	*.268*	*-1.0*	*3B -12*	*-0.3*
2019	*PHI*	*MLB*	*26*	*565*	*75*	*28*	*1*	*25*	*80*	*40*	*94*	*1*	*0*	*.255/.312/.459*	*.272*	*19.6*	*.267*	*-1.0*	*3B -11*	*0.9*

Breakout: 4% Improve: 61% Collapse: 5% Attrition: 10% MLB: 97% *Comparables: Wilmer Flores, Matt Dominguez, Mike Moustakas*

Franco was supposed to be, well, Odubel Herrera, the first star arriving as a future building block of the next good Phillies team. For a little while, his bat speed and power carried the day and he lived up to that billing. Red flags abounded, though, most notably his porous defense, long swing and lack of foot speed. This has all contributed to Franco pushing the bounds on how bad you can be while still consistently showing 20-homer power. Even with how slow and easy to defend he is, his BABIP can't be quite *this* bad over the long haul, so there's bound to be some improvement over his 2017 lows. That said, unless he finds a portal to the '80s, where this type of cold-corner cat was truly en vogue, he won't even find himself worthy of Mike Schmidt's casual racism.

Arquimedez Gamboa SS Born: 09/23/97 Age: 20 Bats: B Throws: R Height: 6'0" Weight: 175 Origin: International Free Agent, 2014

YEAR	TEAM	LVL	AGE	PA	R	2B	3B	HR	RBI	BB	K	SB	CS	AVG/OBP/SLG	TAv	VORP	BABIP	BRR	FRAA	WARP
2015	PHL	RK	17	206	23	7	3	0	16	15	50	8	2	.189/.252/.258	.184	-8.2	.257	1.5	SS(32): -2.2, 2B(18): 2.7	-0.8
2016	WPT	A-	18	147	15	6	0	2	15	9	28	5	1	.200/.254/.292	.254	4.9	.235	0.0	SS(35): -0.4	0.5
2017	LWD	A	19	350	44	12	3	6	29	33	52	8	0	.261/.328/.378	.282	25.1	.291	2.9	SS(79): -3.3	2.3
2018	*PHI*	*MLB*	*20*	*250*	*28*	*9*	*1*	*7*	*26*	*18*	*64*	*1*	*0*	*.220/.278/.368*	*.214*	*-0.4*	*.267*	*-0.2*	*SS -2*	*-0.3*
2019	*PHI*	*MLB*	*21*	*354*	*42*	*13*	*2*	*12*	*42*	*27*	*89*	*1*	*0*	*.231/.291/.390*	*.240*	*4.3*	*.276*	*-0.4*	*SS -3*	*0.1*

Breakout: 2% Improve: 13% Collapse: 0% Attrition: 3% MLB: 14% *Comparables: Ruben Tejada, Amed Rosario, Orlando Arcia*

Eventually we'll figure out whether it's "Arquimedes" or "Arquimedez," but either way, meet the new Phillies shortstop prospect hotness. After not hitting at all at the beginning of his pro career, Gamboa missed nearly half the season with a bum hamstring. After some rustiness upon his initial return, Gamboa hit .317/.376/.516 from July 22 to the end of the year, lashing liners all over the place while shouting "Eureka!" There's a wide array of tools and projection in this profile—including defensively, where he looks capable of not only sticking at shortstop but thriving there as well—so mark him as one to watch and see if the offensive explosion keeps going.

Adam Haseley OF Born: 04/12/96 Age: 22 Bats: L Throws: L Height: 6'1" Weight: 195 Origin: Round 1, 2017 Draft (#8 overall)

YEAR	TEAM	LVL	AGE	PA	R	2B	3B	HR	RBI	BB	K	SB	CS	AVG/OBP/SLG	TAv	VORP	BABIP	BRR	FRAA	WARP
2017	WPT	A-	21	158	18	9	0	2	18	14	28	5	3	.270/.350/.380	.291	12.4	.321	2.6	CF(31): 0.1	1.3
2017	LWD	A	21	74	15	3	1	1	6	6	13	0	1	.258/.315/.379	.296	6.1	.302	1.6	LF(12): 1.3, CF(4): 0.8	0.9
2018	*PHI*	*MLB*	*22*	*250*	*25*	*10*	*1*	*7*	*28*	*18*	*67*	*1*	*1*	*.221/.282/.366*	*.217*	*-2.1*	*.276*	*-0.5*	*CF 1, LF 1*	*0.0*
2019	*PHI*	*MLB*	*23*	*229*	*26*	*9*	*1*	*7*	*26*	*17*	*62*	*1*	*1*	*.224/.287/.377*	*.238*	*0.6*	*.280*	*-0.4*	*CF 1, LF 1*	*0.3*

Breakout: 1% Improve: 7% Collapse: 1% Attrition: 7% MLB: 11% *Comparables: Darrell Ceciliani, Roger Bernadina, Daniel Fields*

Haseley came into 2017 as one of the nation's finest two-way players but was not considered a candidate to be drafted as high as he was. Because of merely average arm strength, his future was clearly at the plate, and Haseley hit his way up draft boards. That said, it's a very hit-tool-heavy profile that doesn't come with the type of either defensive or power prowess you might expect out of a top-10 pick. Haseley was underwhelming in his pro debut, but given the depth of the Phillies' system and the surprising success of the Eagles' season, he'll be able to hone his craft in 2018 without the type of spotlight that generally accompanies a $5.1 million signing bonus.

Cesar Hernandez 2B Born: 05/23/90 Age: 28 Bats: B Throws: R Height: 5'10" Weight: 160 Origin: International Free Agent, 2006

YEAR	TEAM	LVL	AGE	PA	R	2B	3B	HR	RBI	BB	K	SB	CS	AVG/OBP/SLG	TAv	VORP	BABIP	BRR	FRAA	WARP
2015	PHI	MLB	25	452	57	20	4	1	35	40	86	19	5	.272/.339/.348	.261	14.5	.342	1.7	2B(88): 8.9, SS(12): -0.2	2.5
2016	PHI	MLB	26	622	67	14	11	6	39	66	116	17	13	.294/.371/.393	.287	33.4	.363	-0.9	2B(149): -0.4, SS(4): -0.2	3.4
2017	PHI	MLB	27	577	85	26	6	9	34	61	104	15	5	.294/.373/.421	.288	37.2	.353	4.2	2B(127): -2.4, SS(1): 0.0	3.5
2018	*PHI*	*MLB*	*28*	*600*	*77*	*20*	*6*	*8*	*51*	*57*	*116*	*16*	*8*	*.275/.344/.380*	*.259*	*24.9*	*.334*	*0.7*	*2B 1*	*2.0*
2019	*PHI*	*MLB*	*29*	*529*	*63*	*19*	*5*	*9*	*54*	*51*	*105*	*13*	*6*	*.276/.350/.396*	*.271*	*24.6*	*.333*	*1.6*	*2B 1*	*2.8*

Breakout: 1% Improve: 35% Collapse: 8% Attrition: 16% MLB: 96% *Comparables: Dee Gordon, Chris Getz, Alexi Casilla*

One of the fun things bad teams get to do is run out their favorite random semi-prospects, whether they deserve a regular spot or not, because it just doesn't matter. Hernandez always displayed a nice hit tool, even going back to the low minors, but you had to squint hard to see enough power for a regular. It turns out Hernandez can *really* hit, enough that it's the carrying tool for a pretty darned good MLB regular. And it's no reckless approach either. Hernandez is one of four middle infielders to post an on-base percentage over .370 in each of the last two seasons—the others being Jose Altuve, Daniel Murphy and DJ LeMahieu. Beyond that, he plays second well enough, he runs well enough, he's showing some gap power now and he's on his fourth straight season of incremental but noticeable improvements. He's turning out to be one of the more underrated players in the game, which almost feels like a prerequisite for the keystone in Philadelphia nowadays.

Odubel Herrera CF Born: 12/29/91 Age: 26 Bats: L Throws: R Height: 5'11" Weight: 205 Origin: International Free Agent, 2008

YEAR	TEAM	LVL	AGE	PA	R	2B	3B	HR	RBI	BB	K	SB	CS	AVG/OBP/SLG	TAv	VORP	BABIP	BRR	FRAA	WARP
2015	PHI	MLB	23	537	64	30	3	8	41	28	129	16	8	.297/.344/.418	.274	27.9	.387	4.6	CF(136): -1.8	2.8
2016	PHI	MLB	24	656	87	21	6	15	49	63	134	25	7	.286/.361/.420	.293	45.7	.349	3.1	CF(155): 8.3	5.6
2017	PHI	MLB	25	563	67	42	3	14	56	31	126	8	5	.281/.325/.452	.271	22.7	.345	-1.8	CF(133): 10.6	3.3
2018	*PHI*	*MLB*	*26*	*553*	*68*	*28*	*3*	*14*	*65*	*39*	*119*	*14*	*6*	*.278/.335/.428*	*.264*	*25.1*	*.337*	*0.4*	*CF 3*	*2.2*
2019	*PHI*	*MLB*	*27*	*536*	*68*	*27*	*3*	*16*	*67*	*41*	*118*	*13*	*6*	*.281/.343/.448*	*.280*	*29.2*	*.339*	*1.8*	*CF 3*	*3.5*

Breakout: 2% Improve: 64% Collapse: 7% Attrition: 12% MLB: 100% *Comparables: Gene Richards, Rocco Baldelli, Marquis Grissom*

For all the complaints manager Pete Mackanin had about Herrera's hustle, baserunning, style of play and general existence in 2017—culminating in repeated benchings and messages sent through the media—his 2017 was ... pretty much perfectly in line with his past performance and reasonable expectations? He did mostly stop running, which could be explained by a combination of a lingering hamstring pull and the manager benching him every time he made a base-running blunder, and his 2016 walk rate spike didn't hold. But he's also ever-improving in center as he gains more experience out there—remember that Herrera was a career second baseman before the Phillies grabbed him in the Rule 5 from Texas before 2015—and most importantly of all, the dude can just flat out hit. Mackanin's displeasure is no longer an issue either, as he's been reassigned from the dugout to the front office.

Rhys Hoskins LF Born: 03/17/93 Age: 25 Bats: R Throws: R Height: 6'4" Weight: 225 Origin: Round 5, 2014 Draft (#142 overall)

YEAR	TEAM	LVL	AGE	PA	R	2B	3B	HR	RBI	BB	K	SB	CS	AVG/OBP/SLG	TAv	VORP	BABIP	BRR	FRAA	WARP
2015	LWD	A	22	290	39	17	4	9	51	26	50	2	4	.322/.397/.525	.351	28.2	.369	-1.6	1B(64): -0.8	2.9
2015	CLR	A+	22	277	47	19	2	8	39	29	49	2	0	.317/.394/.510	.336	22.1	.367	-1.7	1B(58): 1.3	2.5
2016	REA	AA	23	589	95	26	1	38	116	71	125	8	3	.281/.377/.566	.317	38.2	.297	-1.1	1B(129): -0.6	4.1
2017	LEH	AAA	24	475	78	24	4	29	91	64	75	4	2	.284/.385/.581	.320	37.0	.281	-0.6	1B(105): -9.8, LF(3): 0.2	2.7
2017	PHI	MLB	24	212	37	7	0	18	48	37	46	2	0	.259/.396/.618	.367	27.4	.241	-0.1	LF(30): -0.8, 1B(27): -0.3	2.6
2018	*PHI*	*MLB*	*25*	*597*	*92*	*25*	*2*	*36*	*104*	*70*	*140*	*3*	*1*	*.259/.354/.526*	*.298*	*42.5*	*.284*	*-0.8*	*LF -6, 1B 0*	*3.1*
2019	*PHI*	*MLB*	*26*	*543*	*87*	*24*	*2*	*34*	*93*	*65*	*133*	*2*	*1*	*.261/.358/.535*	*.311*	*41.6*	*.290*	*-0.5*	*LF -5, 1B 0*	*4.0*

Breakout: 5% Improve: 43% Collapse: 3% Attrition: 17% MLB: 81% *Comparables: Chris Carter, Brandon Allen, Paul Goldschmidt*

All first-base prospects may be bastards in prospect writers' eyes, but Hoskins was ready from day one to prove that they know nothing. Unlike Dolorous Dylan Cozens, Lord Rhys's 2016 over-the-wall outbreak at Double-A Reading turned out not to be a park illusion. Hoskins burst onto the major-league scene in the second week of August, immediately staking a claim as the spiritual successor to the power-hitting glory days of Ryan Howard. Phillies fans already had the crown of cheesesteaks prepared, hoping for a new King in the South to come out of the rebuild, and they laid down their swords for Hoskins in full force. (No word on whether our new ruler prefers Pat's, Geno's or a local joint like John's Roast Pork.) It'd be easy to dismiss this as the best two months of Hoskins' life, but there was always star upside in the profile and PECOTA was all-in even before his call-up because of how impressive he was in the training yards. In 2018, we'll all find out if he is indeed the Rhys That Was Promised.

Tommy Joseph 1B Born: 07/16/91 Age: 26 Bats: R Throws: R Height: 6'1" Weight: 255 Origin: Round 2, 2009 Draft (#55 overall)

YEAR	TEAM	LVL	AGE	PA	R	2B	3B	HR	RBI	BB	K	SB	CS	AVG/OBP/SLG	TAv	VORP	BABIP	BRR	FRAA	WARP
2015	PHL	RK	23	41	6	3	0	3	10	7	0	0	0	.485/.585/.848	.458	9.4	.433	-0.3	1B(8): 0.1, 3B(1): -0.1	0.9
2015	LEH	AAA	23	175	9	9	0	3	18	3	33	0	0	.193/.220/.301	.187	-1.2	.221	-1.1	1B(22): -1.1, C(19): -0.1	-1.2
2016	LEH	AAA	24	100	11	7	0	6	17	4	12	0	1	.347/.370/.611	.339	7.2	.346	-2.1	1B(17): -0.5	0.7
2016	PHI	MLB	24	347	47	15	0	21	47	22	75	1	1	.257/.308/.505	.293	16.3	.267	0.7	1B(97): -5.7	1.1
2017	PHI	MLB	25	533	51	27	1	22	69	33	129	1	0	.240/.289/.432	.246	-3.8	.280	-1.6	1B(130): -12.9	-1.7
2018	*PHI*	*MLB*	*26*	*165*	*22*	*8*	*0*	*8*	*24*	*10*	*36*	*0*	*0*	*.250/.299/.462*	*.259*	*4.5*	*.275*	*-0.3*	*1B -1*	*0.2*
2019	*PHI*	*MLB*	*27*	*407*	*57*	*19*	*0*	*22*	*63*	*29*	*91*	*1*	*0*	*.253/.312/.485*	*.279*	*16.1*	*.275*	*-0.4*	*1B -3*	*1.4*

Breakout: 3% Improve: 56% Collapse: 2% Attrition: 8% MLB: 93% *Comparables: Jorge Cantu, Adrian Gonzalez, Scott Thorman*

YEAR	TEAM	P. COUNT	FRM RUNS	BLK RUNS	THRW RUNS	TOT RUNS
2015	LEH	2879	0.4	0.0	0.1	0.5

Joseph hanging around in the majors represents so much that is good about baseball. Once a top catching prospect, he saw a string of concussions nearly rob him of his career and his overall health. He finally got past them in 2016, and had the fortune to be in a system without much standing in his way at first base. Unfortunately, after two years of semi-regular playing time, it's clear that there isn't much here outside of big pop, and Joseph's right-handed power has become a dime a dozen in the majors. He ran straight into the irresistible force of Rhys Hoskins, despite Pete Mackanin's attempts to fit in both, and might be entering the phase of his career where he learns that most teams keep their second-best first baseman at Triple-A. Root for him to keep overcoming the odds, but recognize they're getting long again.

Scott Kingery 2B Born: 04/29/94 Age: 24 Bats: R Throws: R Height: 5'10" Weight: 180 Origin: Round 2, 2015 Draft (#48 overall)

YEAR	TEAM	LVL	AGE	PA	R	2B	3B	HR	RBI	BB	K	SB	CS	AVG/OBP/SLG	TAv	VORP	BABIP	BRR	FRAA	WARP
2015	LWD	A	21	282	43	9	2	3	21	18	43	11	1	.250/.314/.337	.251	7.4	.287	2.6	2B(65): 0.7	0.9
2016	CLR	A+	22	420	60	29	3	3	28	33	54	26	5	.293/.360/.411	.290	26.0	.334	1.6	2B(88): 7.7	3.5
2016	REA	AA	22	166	16	7	0	2	18	5	36	4	2	.250/.273/.333	.220	-0.6	.306	1.9	2B(37): -1.4	-0.2
2017	REA	AA	23	317	62	18	5	18	44	28	51	19	3	.313/.379/.608	.337	34.9	.324	2.7	2B(59): 1.7	4.0
2017	LEH	AAA	23	286	41	11	3	8	21	13	58	10	2	.294/.337/.449	.269	9.8	.348	-1.2	2B(54): 0.9, 3B(4): 0.3	1.1
2018	*PHI*	*MLB*	*24*	*68*	*9*	*3*	*0*	*2*	*8*	*4*	*16*	*2*	*0*	*.251/.297/.421*	*.247*	*2.1*	*.295*	*0.3*	*2B 1*	*0.2*
2019	*PHI*	*MLB*	*25*	*263*	*32*	*13*	*2*	*10*	*34*	*15*	*62*	*8*	*2*	*.253/.304/.439*	*.261*	*9.7*	*.296*	*1.0*	*2B 2*	*1.3*

Breakout: 4% Improve: 18% Collapse: 4% Attrition: 24% MLB: 40% *Comparables: Alen Hanson, Ryan Brett, Joey Wendle*

Entering 2017, Kingery looked to be your fairly standard slap-and-dash second-base prospect. With an assist to the dinger-happy Double-A park in Reading, he suddenly reinvented himself as a slugger and all-around offensive force, more than quintupling his career high in homers. The Reading numbers can't be taken exactly at face value, but it's clear he's added a significant power dimension to his game while retaining the speed and bat-to-ball ability that originally landed him on prospect lists. He should make his MLB debut in 2018 and immediately be relevant to fantasy interests as a power/speed threat in the middle infield.

Andrew Knapp C Born: 11/09/91 Age: 26 Bats: B Throws: R Height: 6'1" Weight: 195 Origin: Round 2, 2013 Draft (#53 overall)

YEAR	TEAM	LVL	AGE	PA	R	2B	3B	HR	RBI	BB	K	SB	CS	AVG/OBP/SLG	TAv	VORP	BABIP	BRR	FRAA	WARP
2015	CLR	A+	23	281	38	14	3	2	28	29	63	0	1	.262/.356/.369	.282	14.2	.344	-1.7	C(46): 0.3	1.6
2015	REA	AA	23	241	39	21	2	11	56	22	43	1	0	.360/.419/.631	.356	33.1	.405	0.0	C(48): -4.7	3.1
2016	LEH	AAA	24	443	55	24	1	8	46	37	107	2	2	.266/.330/.390	.264	22.3	.343	0.9	C(104): 12.3, 1B(1): 0.0	3.6
2017	PHI	MLB	25	204	26	8	1	3	13	31	56	1	0	.257/.368/.368	.272	12.2	.360	0.1	C(53): -8.8, 1B(1): 0.0	0.3
2018	*PHI*	*MLB*	*26*	*32*	*4*	*2*	*0*	*1*	*4*	*3*	*9*	*0*	*0*	*.248/.326/.407*	*.257*	*1.5*	*.324*	*-0.1*	*C -1*	*0.0*
2019	*PHI*	*MLB*	*27*	*226*	*29*	*11*	*1*	*8*	*28*	*23*	*64*	*0*	*0*	*.243/.324/.419*	*.267*	*10.4*	*.315*	*-0.1*	*C -4*	*0.7*

Breakout: 5% Improve: 25% Collapse: 17% Attrition: 34% MLB: 70% *Comparables: Tim Federowicz, Max Ramirez, Josmil Pinto*

YEAR	TEAM	P. COUNT	FRM RUNS	BLK RUNS	THRW RUNS	TOT RUNS
2015	REA	6622	-3.2	-0.8	0.2	-3.9
2017	PHI	7630	-5.1	-1.3	-1.1	-7.6
2018	*PHI*	*1201*	*-0.5*	*-0.2*	*-0.1*	*-0.8*
2019	*PHI*	*8483*	*-1.9*	*-0.7*	*-0.2*	*-2.8*

Knapp is one of the last of a dying breed: the backup catcher who can hit usefully enough but can't field the position. As the true value of framing and catcher defense as a whole has been revealed over the last decade, teams have veered away from sticking these kinds of bat-first guys behind the plate. Knapp was one of the worst framing catchers around in 2017, and his arm strength has never been notable as a pro after he underwent Tommy John surgery shortly after being drafted. He does get plus marks for some of the things we cannot yet adequately measure—like staff leadership and pitch-calling—and he really does hit well for a catcher, so there might be value with the right team and situation. For most, though, he's a square peg in a round hole.

Mickey Moniak CF Born: 05/13/98 Age: 20 Bats: L Throws: R Height: 6'2" Weight: 185 Origin: Round 1, 2016 Draft (#1 overall)

YEAR	TEAM	LVL	AGE	PA	R	2B	3B	HR	RBI	BB	K	SB	CS	AVG/OBP/SLG	TAv	VORP	BABIP	BRR	FRAA	WARP
2016	PHL	RK	18	194	27	11	4	1	28	11	35	10	4	.284/.340/.409	.265	9.0	.345	3.0	CF(30): 4.6, LF(2): 0.1	1.4
2017	LWD	A	19	509	53	22	6	5	44	28	109	11	7	.236/.284/.341	.256	13.2	.292	-0.1	CF(115): -9.8	0.4
2018	*PHI*	*MLB*	*20*	*250*	*24*	*10*	*1*	*7*	*27*	*13*	*70*	*2*	*1*	*.216/.261/.356*	*.205*	*-4.6*	*.276*	*-0.2*	*CF -4*	*-0.9*
2019	*PHI*	*MLB*	*21*	*296*	*32*	*11*	*2*	*8*	*33*	*16*	*79*	*3*	*2*	*.222/.270/.369*	*.227*	*-1.6*	*.278*	*-0.1*	*CF -4*	*-0.6*

Breakout: 1% Improve: 4% Collapse: 0% Attrition: 2% MLB: 5% *Comparables: Cedric Hunter, Engel Beltre, Joe Benson*

Baseball is hard even under the best of circumstances. Moniak has to live up to the expectations of being the first overall pick in the draft for the rest of his career. As an 18-year-old Southern California kid, he had to move across the country to Lakewood, New Jersey, for the season and make several road trips up and down I-95. The South Atlantic League has some incredibly long bus trips—teammate Sixto Sanchez missed time with a minor neck problem after sleeping the wrong way on one of them—and mediocre facilities. Proper nutrition on the road all too often consists of hoping one of the good fast-food joints is open after the game. It's a heck of a grind, and even the best sometimes need time to adjust. Moniak has some additional pressures all his own, from the time drain of fans and media that want a moment with him to merely the great expectations of an entire city of fans. And to top it off, Lakewood isn't a great place to hit.

Here's the problem, though: He's not the only kid that has those pressures, and in the history of the modern draft, only one other position player selected first overall has put up a comparably bad full-season debut. Unlike his counterpart in terribleness Matt Bush, Moniak does not profile well as a relief conversion project. He was advertised as an amateur as a potential 70-hit tool player, a guy who could regularly hit .300 in the majors, and that kind of hitting ability is just not there for him right now. The BP Prospect Team had dozens of looks at Moniak in 2017, and there is simply no good recent report to reference. He looked every bit as bad and often hopeless at the plate as the stat line indicates, and he didn't shower himself in glory on defense or on the basepaths either.

Yet it's too early to give up on the Six Million Dollar Man. One awful stinker of a season does not a lost career or even a busted pick make. He doesn't turn 20 until a month into the 2018 season, and some of the tools that got him drafted remain. There's a lot of developmental time left, but he's starting from about as low as it gets for a guy drafted this high.

Daniel Nava OF Born: 02/22/83 Age: 35 Bats: B Throws: L Height: 5'11" Weight: 200 Origin: Undrafted Free Agent, 2007

YEAR	TEAM	LVL	AGE	PA	R	2B	3B	HR	RBI	BB	K	SB	CS	AVG/OBP/SLG	TAv	VORP	BABIP	BRR	FRAA	WARP
2015	PAW	AAA	32	42	4	1	0	1	8	4	11	2	0	.250/.357/.361	.269	0.9	.333	0.0	RF(6): 0.0, 1B(3): 0.1	0.1
2015	BOS	MLB	32	78	6	2	0	0	7	8	17	0	0	.152/.260/.182	.194	-2.2	.200	1.6	RF(15): 0.5, LF(7): -0.1	-0.2
2015	TBA	MLB	32	88	7	2	0	1	3	12	19	1	0	.233/.364/.301	.269	1.5	.302	-0.7	RF(19): 0.4, 1B(7): 0.0	0.2
2016	ANA	MLB	33	136	10	5	0	1	13	9	26	0	0	.235/.309/.303	.241	-0.7	.284	-0.9	LF(37): 0.0, RF(2): 0.0	-0.1
2016	SLC	AAA	33	92	5	6	0	1	13	6	10	1	1	.365/.413/.471	.298	2.2	.405	-2.7	LF(8): 0.6, 1B(5): 0.4	0.3
2016	KCA	MLB	33	12	1	1	0	0	0	1	4	0	0	.091/.167/.182	.145	-0.8	.143	0.4	1B(6): -0.1	-0.1
2017	PHI	MLB	34	214	21	8	1	4	21	26	38	1	0	.301/.393/.421	.295	11.7	.357	-1.0	LF(42): 4.6, RF(9): 0.0	1.6
2018	*PHI*	*MLB*	*35*	*250*	*31*	*10*	*0*	*6*	*24*	*24*	*52*	*1*	*0*	*.258/.345/.384*	*.251*	*5.3*	*.310*	*-0.2*	*LF 3, RF 0*	*1.0*
2019	*PHI*	*MLB*	*36*	*155*	*19*	*6*	*0*	*3*	*16*	*15*	*34*	*0*	*0*	*.251/.342/.371*	*.261*	*3.5*	*.308*	*-0.2*	*LF 2, RF 0*	*0.6*

Breakout: 1% Improve: 17% Collapse: 12% Attrition: 20% MLB: 63% *Comparables: Trot Nixon, Juan Rivera, Lenny Green*

Nava made the Phillies as a non-roster player out of spring training in 2017 and immediately reverted to his form of a few years ago as a nifty platoon outfielder, providing a plethora of singles, walks and defense against righties while struggling mightily against the few lefties he saw. He might've returned a useful prospect at the July trade deadline, but in a fit of poor timing he landed on the DL right before it with a hamstring injury. He might've still gotten a little something back in August, but shortly after returning from the pulled hamstring he suffered a season-ending back injury. At his age, it could all go again very quickly, and those injuries won't help, but this was a nice comeback season in a career that continues to defy convention.

Jhailyn Ortiz OF Born: 11/18/98 Age: 19 Bats: R Throws: R Height: 6'3" Weight: 215 Origin: International Free Agent, 2015

YEAR	TEAM	LVL	AGE	PA	R	2B	3B	HR	RBI	BB	K	SB	CS	AVG/OBP/SLG	TAv	VORP	BABIP	BRR	FRAA	WARP
2017	WPT	A-	18	187	27	15	1	8	30	18	47	5	1	.302/.401/.560	.335	16.6	.381	-1.7	RF(42): -5.6	1.1
2018	*PHI*	*MLB*	*19*	*250*	*26*	*9*	*0*	*9*	*31*	*18*	*80*	*1*	*0*	*.209/.275/.375*	*.218*	*-4.3*	*.275*	*-0.3*	*RF -3*	*-0.8*
2019	*PHI*	*MLB*	*20*	*343*	*44*	*14*	*1*	*15*	*46*	*26*	*103*	*2*	*1*	*.229/.299/.421*	*.254*	*4.6*	*.290*	*-0.5*	*RF -4*	*0.1*

Breakout: 0% Improve: 7% Collapse: 2% Attrition: 6% MLB: 13% *Comparables: Nomar Mazara, Domingo Santana, Freddie Freeman*

Back in 2015, the Phillies gave Ortiz $4 million as a J2 signing, a huge bonus for a 16-year-old Dominican that forced the Phillies to trade for additional international pool money. It's fair to say that the size of the bonus puzzled the industry, which had largely ranked Ortiz as a solid prospect but not that kind of poolbuster. Fast-forward two years, and Ortiz is justifying the Phillies' faith already, destroying the college-player-heavy New York-Penn League while playing the entire season at 18 years old. Full-season ball awaits for the huge kid with huge power potential, and his current trajectory will continue to shoot him up prospect lists.

Roman Quinn CF Born: 05/14/93 Age: 25 Bats: B Throws: R Height: 5'10" Weight: 170 Origin: Round 2, 2011 Draft (#66 overall)

YEAR	TEAM	LVL	AGE	PA	R	2B	3B	HR	RBI	BB	K	SB	CS	AVG/OBP/SLG	TAv	VORP	BABIP	BRR	FRAA	WARP
2015	REA	AA	22	257	44	6	6	4	15	18	42	29	10	.306/.356/.435	.283	19.6	.360	6.2	CF(58): 3.2	2.5
2016	REA	AA	23	322	58	14	6	6	25	30	68	31	8	.287/.361/.441	.278	24.5	.357	9.6	CF(62): -6.8, LF(4): -0.8	2.4
2016	PHI	MLB	23	69	10	4	0	0	6	8	19	5	1	.263/.373/.333	.282	3.9	.395	0.8	LF(12): -0.1, RF(4): 0.1	0.5
2017	LEH	AAA	24	197	24	8	3	2	13	18	49	10	4	.274/.344/.389	.260	10.0	.368	3.8	CF(38): -0.4, LF(4): -0.2	0.9
2018	*PHI*	*MLB*	*25*	*130*	*17*	*5*	*1*	*3*	*13*	*10*	*34*	*8*	*2*	*.247/.309/.384*	*.242*	*3.2*	*.317*	*1.0*	*CF -1, LF 0*	*0.2*
2019	*PHI*	*MLB*	*26*	*278*	*33*	*10*	*3*	*8*	*32*	*23*	*76*	*16*	*5*	*.245/.315/.404*	*.255*	*9.0*	*.313*	*2.4*	*CF -1, LF 1*	*0.9*

Breakout: 8% Improve: 42% Collapse: 6% Attrition: 35% MLB: 67% *Comparables: Lorenzo Cain, Abraham Almonte, Roger Bernadina*

Eighty-grade speed is the most easily defined tool in scouting. The scout takes out their Accusplit stopwatch and waits for a grounder that the runner has to show full effort to beat out. Click one is at the crack of the bat, and click two is when the foot hits the bag. If the batter is a lefty and the time is under 3.9 seconds, or if he's a righty and it's under 4.0 seconds, that's an 80-grade time. You usually want a handful of measurements to confirm that you didn't catch a jailbreak or misclick, but the information is right there for you, requiring little interpretation. Quinn's evidence that the stopwatch doesn't lie is his consistently crazy-high BABIPs despite being a guy that doesn't hit the ball with great authority. Yet he's not quite as good of a baserunner or outfielder as he "should" be given that he's one of the fastest players in the game, and his next full season of health will be his first. Quinn has enough of a clue at the plate that we can't yet rule out his speed carrying the day, but even if he's ultimately not cut out for full-time play, he should be a really good long-term bench piece.

Cornelius Randolph LF Born: 06/02/97 Age: 21 Bats: L Throws: R Height: 5'11" Weight: 205 Origin: Round 1, 2015 Draft (#10 overall)

YEAR	TEAM	LVL	AGE	PA	R	2B	3B	HR	RBI	BB	K	SB	CS	AVG/OBP/SLG	TAv	VORP	BABIP	BRR	FRAA	WARP
2015	PHL	RK	18	212	34	15	3	1	24	32	32	6	5	.302/.425/.442	.312	18.1	.362	1.3	LF(41): 0.5	1.8
2016	LWD	A	19	276	33	12	1	2	27	26	57	5	4	.274/.355/.357	.296	16.4	.346	1.5	LF(53): 0.0	1.8
2017	CLR	A+	20	510	47	18	5	13	55	55	125	7	3	.250/.338/.402	.286	21.9	.316	-2.0	LF(108): -10.7	1.2
2018	*PHI*	*MLB*	*21*	*250*	*26*	*10*	*1*	*8*	*30*	*23*	*73*	*1*	*0*	*.224/.302/.382*	*.232*	*0.9*	*.292*	*-0.3*	*LF -1*	*0.0*
2019	*PHI*	*MLB*	*22*	*362*	*45*	*15*	*1*	*12*	*44*	*34*	*104*	*1*	*0*	*.230/.312/.401*	*.256*	*6.5*	*.297*	*-0.6*	*LF -2*	*0.5*

Breakout: 2% Improve: 6% Collapse: 2% Attrition: 7% MLB: 12% *Comparables: Ramon Flores, Jesse Winker, Andrew Lambo*

The first of three consecutive top-ten picks the Phillies spent on outfielders advertised to be carried by a big hit tool, and the first to raise some red flags about that approach, Randolph hasn't hit enough yet to justify the draft position given his limited defensive value and projectability. He did make some progress in 2017, staying healthy after a shoulder injury cost him half of 2016 and lifting the ball for more power. The beautiful swing and very quick bat speed that got him taken tenth overall still remain, but all the aesthetics in the world won't help him reach his ceiling if his batting average doesn't start with the number three.

Cameron Rupp C Born: 09/28/88 Age: 29 Bats: R Throws: R Height: 6'2" Weight: 260 Origin: Round 3, 2010 Draft (#108 overall)

YEAR	TEAM	LVL	AGE	PA	R	2B	3B	HR	RBI	BB	K	SB	CS	AVG/OBP/SLG	TAv	VORP	BABIP	BRR	FRAA	WARP
2015	PHI	MLB	26	299	24	9	1	9	28	24	71	0	1	.233/.301/.374	.242	5.3	.281	-2.4	C(80): -4.8	0.1
2016	PHI	MLB	27	419	36	26	1	16	54	24	114	1	0	.252/.303/.447	.270	22.4	.315	-1.0	C(104): -3.2	2.0
2017	PHI	MLB	28	331	35	17	0	14	34	34	114	1	0	.217/.299/.417	.258	13.2	.298	-1.5	C(88): -10.3	0.3
2018	*PHI*	*MLB*	*29*	*209*	*24*	*9*	*0*	*8*	*26*	*16*	*61*	*0*	*0*	*.224/.288/.394*	*.238*	*4.7*	*.287*	*-0.4*	*C -5*	*-0.2*
2019	*PHI*	*MLB*	*30*	*312*	*38*	*14*	*0*	*12*	*38*	*25*	*96*	*0*	*0*	*.217/.288/.392*	*.244*	*5.5*	*.281*	*-1.2*	*C -7*	*-0.2*

Breakout: 8% Improve: 37% Collapse: 7% Attrition: 16% MLB: 85% *Comparables: Hank Conger, Ronny Paulino, J.P. Arencibia*

YEAR	TEAM	P. COUNT	FRM RUNS	BLK RUNS	THRW RUNS	TOT RUNS
2015	PHI	11024	-5.1	0.3	0.8	-4.0
2016	PHI	14903	-3.2	0.6	-0.9	-3.4
2017	PHI	12348	-11.9	-0.1	0.2	-11.8
2018	*PHI*	*7134*	*-5.2*	*0.0*	*-0.1*	*-5.2*
2019	*PHI*	*10662*	*-6.6*	*0.0*	*-0.1*	*-6.7*

Let's talk about what Rupp does really well: He can go on monster dinger streaks, he murders lefties and his arm is a rocket when it's healthy. That was enough to nudge aside Carlos Ruiz and hold off Jorge Alfaro as the semi-regular catcher for the Phillies for the better part of three seasons. He's enormous for a catcher, and while he's a bit deficient defensively by current MLB standards, it's a wonder that he's as good as he is back there. He's worse than you'd want as a full-timer and a little too good to be a straight backup, so the next phase of his career will depend a lot upon his landing in the right situation.

Carlos Santana 1B Born: 04/08/86 Age: 32 Bats: B Throws: R Height: 5'11" Weight: 210 Origin: International Free Agent, 2004

YEAR	TEAM	LVL	AGE	PA	R	2B	3B	HR	RBI	BB	K	SB	CS	AVG/OBP/SLG	TAv	VORP	BABIP	BRR	FRAA	WARP
2015	CLE	MLB	29	666	72	29	2	19	85	108	122	11	3	.231/.357/.395	.265	7.4	.261	-2.3	1B(132): -3.6	0.4
2016	CLE	MLB	30	688	89	31	3	34	87	99	99	5	2	.259/.366/.498	.280	20.4	.258	-0.9	1B(64): 4.6	2.6
2017	CLE	MLB	31	667	90	37	3	23	79	88	94	5	1	.259/.363/.455	.277	17.6	.274	-1.9	1B(140): 6.2, RF(7): 0.7	2.4
2018	*PHI*	*MLB*	*32*	*607*	*81*	*26*	*2*	*23*	*82*	*89*	*105*	*6*	*2*	*.242/.357/.433*	*.276*	*19.0*	*.262*	*-0.5*	*1B 0*	*1.7*
2019	*PHI*	*MLB*	*33*	*561*	*79*	*24*	*1*	*23*	*75*	*81*	*105*	*4*	*1*	*.234/.349/.437*	*.283*	*18.6*	*.252*	*-1.5*	*1B 1*	*2.1*

Breakout: 2% Improve: 32% Collapse: 6% Attrition: 8% MLB: 89% *Comparables: John Jaso, John Olerud, Joe Mauer*

A switch-hitter with one of the game's most discriminating eyes and patient approaches, Mr. Consistent is always in the lineup, never posts an on-base percentage below .350 and has averaged 24 homers during his seven seasons as a starter. His successful conversion to first base culminated in worthy Gold Glove consideration last year, and his amped-up .287/.392/.514 second-half line helped carry the Indians down the stretch. Although Santana, who signed a three-year deal with the Phillies in December, is on the wrong side of 30, he has been durable and his batting eye should age well. He'll likely remain one of the games most underrated stars for years to come.

Nick Williams OF Born: 09/08/93 Age: 24 Bats: L Throws: L Height: 6'3" Weight: 195 Origin: Round 2, 2012 Draft (#93 overall)

YEAR	TEAM	LVL	AGE	PA	R	2B	3B	HR	RBI	BB	K	SB	CS	AVG/OBP/SLG	TAv	VORP	BABIP	BRR	FRAA	WARP
2015	FRI	AA	21	415	56	21	4	13	45	32	77	10	8	.299/.357/.479	.291	22.6	.346	0.3	LF(45): 0.6, CF(38): -1.8	2.3
2015	REA	AA	21	100	21	5	2	4	10	3	20	3	0	.320/.340/.536	.320	10.4	.370	1.5	CF(21): 1.0	1.2
2016	LEH	AAA	22	527	78	33	6	13	64	19	136	6	4	.258/.287/.427	.258	10.7	.325	-0.7	LF(50): 1.9, CF(38): 2.0	1.5
2017	LEH	AAA	23	306	43	16	2	15	44	16	90	5	4	.280/.328/.511	.281	14.1	.358	0.4	RF(37): 6.2, LF(17): 1.5	2.0
2017	PHI	MLB	23	343	45	14	4	12	55	20	97	1	2	.288/.338/.473	.295	19.3	.375	-0.8	RF(58): -5.9, CF(16): -1.9	1.2
2018	*PHI*	*MLB*	*24*	*502*	*68*	*23*	*4*	*20*	*63*	*24*	*141*	*4*	*3*	*.257/.298/.450*	*.258*	*11.1*	*.322*	*-0.6*	*RF -4*	*0.5*
2019	*PHI*	*MLB*	*25*	*534*	*70*	*25*	*4*	*24*	*77*	*29*	*151*	*5*	*3*	*.262/.309/.476*	*.276*	*19.3*	*.326*	*-0.6*	*RF -3*	*1.8*

Breakout: 8% Improve: 34% Collapse: 16% Attrition: 38% MLB: 69% *Comparables: Victor Diaz, Wladimir Balentien, Matt Joyce*

Baseball players are humans. Too often, we forget and treat them like a PECOTA card, just a series of stats and projections underlying a true talent level. It's the reason we have player comments at all in this publication, rather than just a series of numbers and charts. Williams should remind us that performance is not impacted only by BABIP and launch angle. For most of his pro career, Williams has put up solid, consistent seasons that look pretty close to what he did last year in both the majors and minors—except for the second half of 2016, during which he was repeatedly run under the bus by a since-departed Triple-A manager. He's an imperfect baseball player, a free-swinger prone to poor baserunning and fielding. The imperfections should further remind you that he's human, and we can marvel in awe at how good a hitter he is despite them.

PITCHERS

Drew Anderson RHP
Born: 03/22/94 Age: 24 Bats: R Throws: R Height: 6'3" Weight: 185 Origin: Round 21, 2012 Draft (#668 overall)

YEAR	TEAM	LVL	AGE	W	L	SV	G	GS	IP	H	HR	BB/9	K/9	K	GB%	BABIP	WHIP	ERA	DRA	WARP	MPH	CMD	PWR	STM
2016	LWD	A	22	1	3	0	7	7	37^1	29	3	2.9	9.9	41	46%	.286	1.10	3.38	2.91	1.0				
2016	CLR	A+	22	2	1	0	8	8	32^2	26	0	2.8	10.2	37	39%	.313	1.10	1.93	2.20	1.2				
2017	REA	AA	23	9	4	0	21	21	107^2	81	13	3.3	7.2	86	38%	.227	1.12	3.59	5.18	0.0				
2017	PHI	MLB	23	0	0	0	2	0	2^1	6	0	3.9	7.7	2	36%	.545	3.00	23.14	8.43	-0.1	95.1			56
2018	*PHI*	*MLB*	*24*	*1*	*2*	*0*	*13*	*3*	*25*	*25*	*5*	*3.8*	*9.4*	*27*	*38%*	*.294*	*1.39*	*5.19*	*5.23*	*-0.1*	*94.9*			*58*
2019	*PHI*	*MLB*	*25*	*6*	*6*	*0*	*63*	*13*	128^1	*120*	*25*	*3.9*	*8.6*	*123*	*38%*	*.297*	*1.37*	*5.42*	*6.02*	*-0.7*	*94.6*			*58*

Breakout: 11% Improve: 22% Collapse: 7% Attrition: 21% MLB: 33% *Comparables: Caleb Smith, David Rollins, James Houser*

In February, Phillies director of player development Joe Jordan said to local reporter extraordinaire Jim Salisbury that "We've got scouts who will tell you that [Anderson] might be our best pitching prospect." At the time, this wasn't *totally* nuts; Sixto Sanchez had yet to break out of the pack into a top global guy, and Anderson was tearing up both levels of A-ball coming off Tommy John surgery and regularly touching 97. Unfortunately, he didn't maintain the velocity or level of performance, although he did strike Mike Trout out in a brief MLB cameo. The usual set of outcomes, like a peripatetic back-of-the-rotation career, or hoping the velocity spikes again in relief, likely awaits.

Mark Appel RHP
Born: 07/15/91 Age: 26 Bats: R Throws: R Height: 6'5" Weight: 220 Origin: Round 1, 2013 Draft (#1 overall)

YEAR	TEAM	LVL	AGE	W	L	SV	G	GS	IP	H	HR	BB/9	K/9	K	GB%	BABIP	WHIP	ERA	DRA	WARP	MPH	CMD	PWR	STM
2015	CCH	AA	23	5	1	0	13	13	63^1	68	7	3.3	7.0	49	46%	.314	1.44	4.26	5.70	-0.5				
2015	FRE	AAA	23	5	2	0	12	12	68^1	67	6	3.7	8.0	61	47%	.303	1.39	4.48	5.41	-0.1				
2016	LEH	AAA	24	3	3	0	8	8	38^1	40	3	4.7	8.0	34	45%	.325	1.57	4.46	5.88	-0.2				
2017	LEH	AAA	25	5	4	0	17	17	82	91	9	5.8	6.6	60	43%	.322	1.76	5.27	9.74	-3.6				
2018	*PHI*	*MLB*	*26*	*4*	*5*	*0*	*14*	*14*	68^2	*70*	*11*	*4.5*	*8.8*	*67*	*43%*	*.321*	*1.52*	*5.03*	*5.57*	*0.0*				
2019	*PHI*	*MLB*	*27*	*6*	*10*	*0*	*26*	*26*	151^1	*156*	*26*	*4.1*	*7.8*	*130*	*43%*	*.319*	*1.49*	*5.39*	*5.97*	*-0.5*				

Breakout: 8% Improve: 12% Collapse: 5% Attrition: 12% MLB: 18% *Comparables: Chris Dwyer, Warwick Saupold, James Houser*

There's no simple reason Mark Appel has busted this spectacularly. He was a legitimate stud in college, one of the best college pitching prospects of the last decade, and those don't just fail without terrible injuries. Yet Appel spent years being healthy and bad until he finally ran into shoulder and elbow troubles over the past two seasons. He got the change of scenery and coaching that we sometimes theorize might help pitchers lost in the wilderness, but it didn't help at all. The stuff still looks good on paper—in theory it remains a mix of three plus-or-better pitches—but then you realize the fastball is flat and predictable, the feel for the slider comes and goes, and the change only flashes once or twice a game. The command that he had in college went out the window somewhere on the way to his first pro assignment, and it never came back. None of these would have been individually crippling to his prospectdom, but all of them have turned him into a live arm yet to conquer Triple-A at 26. He's probably overdue for a chance to reinvent himself as a fastball/slider reliever, if nothing else.

Clay Buchholz RHP
Born: 08/14/84 Age: 33 Bats: L Throws: R Height: 6'3" Weight: 190 Origin: Round 1, 2005 Draft (#42 overall)

YEAR	TEAM	LVL	AGE	W	L	SV	G	GS	IP	H	HR	BB/9	K/9	K	GB%	BABIP	WHIP	ERA	DRA	WARP	MPH	CMD	PWR	STM
2015	BOS	MLB	30	7	7	0	18	18	113^1	114	6	1.8	8.5	107	49%	.329	1.21	3.26	3.09	2.7	94.3	58	47	63
2016	BOS	MLB	31	8	10	0	37	21	139^1	130	21	3.6	6.0	93	42%	.263	1.33	4.78	4.83	0.8	94.4	57	45	62
2017	PHI	MLB	32	0	1	0	2	2	7^1	16	1	3.7	6.1	5	31%	.484	2.59	12.27	7.35	-0.1	92.1			
2018	*PHI*	*MLB*	*33*	*2*	*2*	*0*	*6*	*6*	35^2	*36*	*6*	*3.5*	*7.5*	*30*	*41%*	*.304*	*1.40*	*5.00*	*5.51*	*0.0*	*93.2*	*57*	*45*	*62*
2019	*PHI*	*MLB*	*34*	*9*	*13*	*0*	*29*	*29*	182^1	*184*	*36*	*3.1*	*6.9*	*140*	*41%*	*.298*	*1.36*	*5.50*	*6.07*	*-0.8*	*92.8*	*56*	*44*	*61*

Breakout: 11% Improve: 43% Collapse: 19% Attrition: 16% MLB: 95% *Comparables: Tim Hudson, Zack Greinke, Scott Feldman*

You can take worse one-season fliers as a noncontender than Buchholz, who is often either really good or really hurt, and thus a potential big trade chip if you get a few well-timed healthy months of the 2010, 2013 or 2015 version. Unfortunately for the Phillies' dreams of a big prospect chip, the Buchholz Magic 8-Ball came up "outlook not so good" in 2017, as he went down with a season-ending flexor tear in his second start. Despite being labeled in several versions of this book as "one of the game's most frustrating, talented and inconsistent pitchers," the highs have been high enough that he's put together a better overall career than you might have thought, including a matching pair of World Series rings and All-Star selections.

Seranthony Dominguez RHP
Born: 11/25/94 Age: 23 Bats: R Throws: R Height: 6'1" Weight: 185 Origin: International Free Agent, 2011

YEAR	TEAM	LVL	AGE	W	L	SV	G	GS	IP	H	HR	BB/9	K/9	K	GB%	BABIP	WHIP	ERA	DRA	WARP	MPH	CMD	PWR	STM
2016	WPT	A-	21	1	1	0	3	3	17	8	0	2.1	7.9	15	57%	.170	0.71	2.12	3.30	0.4				
2016	LWD	A	21	5	2	0	10	10	48^1	34	2	3.7	9.3	50	58%	.271	1.12	2.42	3.83	0.7				
2017	CLR	A+	22	4	4	0	15	13	62^1	51	6	4.3	10.8	75	45%	.306	1.30	3.61	3.68	1.1				
2018	*PHI*	*MLB*	*23*	*3*	*4*	*0*	*20*	*10*	55^1	*53*	*11*	*5.6*	*10.6*	*65*	*42%*	*.319*	*1.58*	*5.52*	*6.14*	*-0.4*				
2019	*PHI*	*MLB*	*24*	*6*	*8*	*1*	*37*	*21*	155^2	*142*	*32*	*4.7*	*10.3*	*178*	*42%*	*.311*	*1.43*	*5.39*	*6.00*	*-0.6*				

Breakout: 10% Improve: 11% Collapse: 2% Attrition: 10% MLB: 16% *Comparables: Dinelson Lamet, Steven Matz, Luke Jackson*

After four years knocking around in the complex leagues, Dominguez popped up in the middle of 2016 with a projectable fastball and a power breaking ball, stamping himself as an interesting sleeper in a deep system. He was on his way to shooting up prospect lists with a bullet in the first two months of 2017, revving the fastball up to the high-90s, before he missed most of the summer with shoulder problems. So, are we breaking out or are we breaking down?

Zach Eflin RHP Born: 04/08/94 Age: 24 Bats: R Throws: R Height: 6'6" Weight: 215 Origin: Round 1, 2012 Draft (#33 overall)

YEAR	TEAM	LVL	AGE	W	L	SV	G	GS	IP	H	HR	BB/9	K/9	K	GB%	BABIP	WHIP	ERA	DRA	WARP	MPH	CMD	PWR	STM
2015	REA	AA	21	8	6	0	23	23	131^{2}	136	12	1.6	4.6	68	44%	.286	1.21	3.69	4.69	0.6				
2016	LEH	AAA	22	5	2	0	11	11	68^{1}	49	2	1.4	7.2	55	47%	.245	0.88	2.90	2.88	1.9				
2016	PHI	MLB	22	3	5	0	11	11	63^{1}	67	12	2.4	4.4	31	37%	.261	1.33	5.54	7.26	-1.4	96.0	45	52	64
2017	LEH	AAA	23	1	4	0	8	7	43^{1}	48	3	3.1	7.9	38	41%	.346	1.45	4.57	5.22	0.2				
2017	PHI	MLB	23	1	5	0	11	11	64^{1}	79	16	1.7	4.9	35	46%	.297	1.41	6.16	6.49	-0.7	95.5	61	57	59
2018	*PHI*	*MLB*	*24*	*4*	*4*	*0*	*24*	*9*	*63*	*65*	*10*	*2.9*	*7.0*	*50*	*43%*	*.293*	*1.35*	*4.68*	*4.77*	*0.2*	*95.5*	*56*	*56*	*63*
2019	*PHI*	*MLB*	*25*	*8*	*8*	*0*	*61*	*21*	171^{1}	*157*	*25*	*2.3*	*7.9*	*150*	*43%*	*.295*	*1.17*	*4.39*	*4.82*	*1.2*	*95.3*	*56*	*57*	*63*

Breakout: 24% Improve: 46% Collapse: 14% Attrition: 30% MLB: 71% *Comparables: Blake Beavan, Alex Sanabia, Casey Coleman*

Well, someone needs to take the ball every fifth day. Eflin's fastball is "good" in the sense that it's thrown for strikes with good velocity and his two-seamer has good sink, but he gets so few swings-and-misses with it that you can't call it effective. Of course, when you don't have a useful secondary offering, low-to-mid-90s fastballs down the pipe just don't fool like they used to. The change showed promise in the minors, but he has yet to show any confidence in it as a major leaguer, and his breaking stuff just never developed. Yet because he pounds the zone so hard and takes his drubbings well, he has lasted five innings or more in 19 of his 22 MLB starts. There's a little value in having a guy who can be terrible but at least not kill your bullpen while doing it.

Jerad Eickhoff RHP Born: 07/02/90 Age: 27 Bats: R Throws: R Height: 6'4" Weight: 245 Origin: Round 15, 2011 Draft (#474 overall)

YEAR	TEAM	LVL	AGE	W	L	SV	G	GS	IP	H	HR	BB/9	K/9	K	GB%	BABIP	WHIP	ERA	DRA	WARP	MPH	CMD	PWR	STM
2015	FRI	AA	24	1	0	0	2	2	10	7	2	2.7	12.6	14	36%	.250	1.00	2.70	3.25	0.2				
2015	ROU	AAA	24	9	4	0	18	17	101^{2}	95	12	2.9	8.2	93	35%	.291	1.26	4.25	3.13	2.5				
2015	LEH	AAA	24	2	1	0	3	3	21^{2}	17	1	1.2	7.9	19	28%	.254	0.92	2.49	3.21	0.5				
2015	PHI	MLB	24	3	3	0	8	8	51	40	5	2.3	8.6	49	38%	.257	1.04	2.65	3.45	1.0	93.6	53	37	70
2016	PHI	MLB	25	11	14	0	33	33	197^{1}	187	30	1.9	7.6	167	43%	.278	1.16	3.65	4.16	2.7	93.4	58	36	77
2017	PHI	MLB	26	4	8	0	24	24	128	142	16	3.7	8.3	118	39%	.328	1.52	4.71	5.41	0.2	92.2	51	27	65
2018	*PHI*	*MLB*	*27*	*9*	*9*	*0*	*25*	*25*	*142*	*134*	*22*	*3.0*	*8.8*	*139*	*41%*	*.288*	*1.25*	*4.24*	*4.40*	*1.3*	*92.5*	*55*	*33*	*71*
2019	*PHI*	*MLB*	*28*	*11*	*11*	*0*	*32*	*32*	206^{1}	*173*	*28*	*3.2*	*8.9*	*205*	*41%*	*.287*	*1.20*	*4.25*	*4.68*	*1.9*	*92.2*	*55*	*32*	*71*

Breakout: 29% Improve: 55% Collapse: 18% Attrition: 19% MLB: 90% *Comparables: Anthony Reyes, Zach McAllister, James McDonald*

When the Phillies dealt Cole Hamels to Texas, Eickhoff was one of two upper-level sleeper arms included with the three major prospects, a righty curveball specialist who many projected to the bullpen. Instead, he surprisingly carried the banner for the Hamels trade in Philadelphia until Nick Williams and Jorge Alfaro arrived in the second half of 2017, adequately filling the Hamels rotation spot while showing considerable promise that he might one day stamp his name on an Eickhoff spot. Last season brought greater uncertainty into the profile, as he bled velocity while fighting back and hand injuries, and relied even more heavily on his vaunted curve to get what outs he could. This season looks like the inflection point where he continues on a fine but unspectacular back-end starting path or consolidates everything and emerges into a long-term rotation stalwart. The safe bet is once again against him, but you'd have lost a lot of money betting against Eickhoff in the past.

Tom Eshelman RHP Born: 06/20/94 Age: 23 Bats: R Throws: R Height: 6'3" Weight: 210 Origin: Round 2, 2015 Draft (#46 overall)

YEAR	TEAM	LVL	AGE	W	L	SV	G	GS	IP	H	HR	BB/9	K/9	K	GB%	BABIP	WHIP	ERA	DRA	WARP	MPH	CMD	PWR	STM
2016	CLR	A+	22	4	2	0	11	11	59^{1}	58	7	1.7	9.7	64	47%	.311	1.16	3.34	1.94	2.4				
2016	REA	AA	22	5	5	0	13	13	61^{1}	79	4	2.5	8.1	55	45%	.373	1.57	5.14	4.22	0.6				
2017	REA	AA	23	3	0	0	5	5	29	27	6	1.6	6.8	22	36%	.266	1.10	3.10	3.09	0.7				
2017	LEH	AAA	23	10	3	0	18	18	121	101	8	1.0	6.0	80	45%	.255	0.94	2.23	1.28	5.8				
2018	*PHI*	*MLB*	*24*	*6*	*8*	*0*	*21*	*21*	112^{2}	*121*	*19*	*3.4*	*6.9*	*87*	*42%*	*.309*	*1.45*	*5.11*	*5.62*	*0.0*				
2019	*PHI*	*MLB*	*25*	*6*	*9*	*0*	*21*	*21*	123^{2}	*130*	*22*	*3.0*	*6.4*	*88*	*42%*	*.306*	*1.39*	*5.36*	*5.92*	*-0.4*				

Breakout: 22% Improve: 35% Collapse: 18% Attrition: 38% MLB: 60% *Comparables: Tim Cooney, Adalberto Mejia, Adam Wilk*

If you think his pro walk rates are impressive, over three years of starting at Cal State Fullerton, Eshelman posted a walk rate of 0.43 per nine innings. He's a four-pitch guy with a bushel of grades right around average dotting the profile, except that he's obviously one of the best command-and-control artists in the minors. With the closest thing to a swing-and-miss pitch in the profile being "just" a low-90s fastball that he can move and manipulate, Eshelman is generally projected as a back-end starter type. But it's tremendously hard to comp this extreme of a profile, and that projection could turn out light.

Luis Garcia RHP Born: 01/30/87 Age: 31 Bats: R Throws: R Height: 6'3" Weight: 230 Origin: International Free Agent, 2017

YEAR	TEAM	LVL	AGE	W	L	SV	G	GS	IP	H	HR	BB/9	K/9	K	GB%	BABIP	WHIP	ERA	DRA	WARP	MPH	CMD	PWR	STM
2015	PHI	MLB	28	4	6	2	72	0	66^{2}	72	4	5.0	8.5	63	65%	.340	1.63	3.51	3.23	1.2	98.1	33	62	53
2016	LEH	AAA	29	6	3	13	48	0	54^{2}	38	3	4.0	8.7	53	63%	.261	1.13	2.14	5.83	-0.5				
2016	PHI	MLB	29	1	1	0	17	0	15^{1}	21	2	4.7	8.2	14	55%	.373	1.89	6.46	5.26	-0.1	99.0	46	57	49
2017	PHI	MLB	30	2	5	2	66	0	71^{1}	61	3	3.3	7.6	60	57%	.282	1.22	2.65	3.82	1.1	98.7	43	69	52
2018	*PHI*	*MLB*	*31*	*3*	*3*	*3*	*60*	*0*	*63*	*62*	*8*	*4.2*	*8.3*	*59*	*56%*	*.299*	*1.45*	*4.64*	*4.64*	*0.2*	*97.6*	*40*	*65*	*51*
2019	*PHI*	*MLB*	*32*	*2*	*1*	*1*	*45*	*0*	48^{1}	*45*	*6*	*4.1*	*7.9*	*42*	*56%*	*.303*	*1.38*	*4.80*	*5.29*	*0.0*	*97.2*	*42*	*66*	*50*

Breakout: 25% Improve: 37% Collapse: 27% Attrition: 21% MLB: 81% *Comparables: Saul Rivera, Sean Green, Anthony Varvaro*

After 11 years in baseball, three MLB organizations, a stint in the Can-Am League and four seasons as an up-and-down guy with the Phillies, Luis Garcia *finally* established himself as a good MLB reliever in 2017. It's easy to see why he got so many chances: He regularly touches 99, throws a good hard slider and gets an enormous amount of grounders. He'll continue to be around as long as he continues to throw strikes.

Tommy Hunter RHP Born: 07/03/86 Age: 31 Bats: R Throws: R Height: 6'3" Weight: 250 Origin: Round 1, 2007 Draft (#54 overall)

YEAR	TEAM	LVL	AGE	W	L	SV	G	GS	IP	H	HR	BB/9	K/9	K	GB%	BABIP	WHIP	ERA	DRA	WARP	MPH	CMD	PWR	STM
2015	BAL	MLB	28	2	2	0	39	0	44^2	41	3	2.2	6.4	32	48%	.286	1.16	3.63	3.72	0.5	98.7	43	72	46
2015	CHN	MLB	28	2	0	1	19	0	15^2	20	4	1.7	8.6	15	41%	.340	1.47	5.74	4.79	0.0	99.0	43	72	46
2016	CLE	MLB	29	2	2	0	21	0	21^2	21	1	2.1	7.1	17	53%	.308	1.20	3.74	5.04	0.0	96.7	54	68	36
2016	COH	AAA	29	2	1	1	14	2	15	14	2	1.2	6.0	10	46%	.261	1.07	3.00	3.53	0.3				
2016	BAL	MLB	29	0	0	0	12	0	12^1	14	0	2.2	4.4	6	45%	.350	1.38	2.19	5.05	0.0	96.9	54	68	36
2017	TBA	MLB	30	3	5	1	61	0	58^2	43	6	2.1	9.8	64	46%	.259	0.97	2.61	3.38	1.2	97.6	53	72	45
2018	*PHI*	*MLB*	*31*	*2*	*2*	*0*	*40*	*0*	*42*	*39*	*6*	*3.1*	*8.8*	*42*	*46%*	*.293*	*1.27*	*4.18*	*4.29*	*0.3*	*96.9*	*50*	*71*	*42*
2019	*PHI*	*MLB*	*32*	*3*	*1*	*0*	*55*	*0*	*58*	*51*	*8*	*3.0*	*9.1*	*59*	*46%*	*.301*	*1.21*	*4.22*	*4.69*	*0.3*	*96.2*	*52*	*70*	*41*

Breakout: 26% Improve: 42% Collapse: 27% Attrition: 11% MLB: 87% *Comparables: Luke Gregerson, Justin Duchscherer, Aaron Heilman*

Hunter made ping-pong a central part of the Orioles' clubhouse culture back in 2014, as a talent-deficient team shoved its way to the AL East title. He's bounced around a lot since then, taking great stuff (high-end velocity he only found when he transitioned to the bullpen and a much deeper arsenal than most short-burst relievers) everywhere, but sometimes battling injuries that prevented him from being his best self. In 2016, he was carrying his young son when he fell, and the way he shifted his body to protect his kid led to a broken vertebra. To recover from that and have the dominant season he had in the Rays' bullpen is thoroughly impressive. Hunter also provided a highlight of Players Weekend, with a nickname that nodded toward his considerable girth: "Tommy Two Towels." He's a great person (and pitcher) to have around.

Franklyn Kilome RHP Born: 06/25/95 Age: 22 Bats: R Throws: R Height: 6'6" Weight: 175 Origin: International Free Agent, 2013

YEAR	TEAM	LVL	AGE	W	L	SV	G	GS	IP	H	HR	BB/9	K/9	K	GB%	BABIP	WHIP	ERA	DRA	WARP	MPH	CMD	PWR	STM
2015	WPT	A-	20	3	2	0	11	11	49^1	41	1	3.8	6.6	36	57%	.282	1.26	3.28	5.55	-0.2				
2016	LWD	A	21	5	8	0	23	23	114^2	113	6	3.9	10.2	130	49%	.346	1.42	3.85	3.98	1.4				
2017	CLR	A+	22	6	4	0	19	19	97^1	96	5	3.4	7.7	83	48%	.325	1.37	2.59	4.76	0.6				
2017	REA	AA	22	1	3	0	5	5	29^2	25	2	4.6	6.1	20	43%	.267	1.35	3.64	4.29	0.3				
2018	*PHI*	*MLB*	*23*	*6*	*7*	*0*	*21*	*21*	103^1	*110*	*19*	*4.6*	*8.7*	*100*	*43%*	*.327*	*1.57*	*5.25*	*5.81*	*-0.2*				
2019	*PHI*	*MLB*	*24*	*4*	*7*	*0*	*17*	*17*	98^2	*108*	*20*	*4.3*	*8.4*	*92*	*43%*	*.336*	*1.57*	*5.67*	*6.30*	*-0.6*				

Breakout: 4% Improve: 5% Collapse: 3% Attrition: 5% MLB: 9% *Comparables: Justin Marks, Anthony Ranaudo, Ben Taylor*

He's perpetually falling just a bit short of being one of the top pitching prospects in the minors, and that's the only way at all Kilome can be described as short. He's a very tall man with very long limbs, and as tends to happen with pitchers of his proportion, he has some problems with consistency, command and repeating his mechanics. When on, he'll show you a mid-90s fastball with huge plane, a plus overhand curve and a useful change and slider, but he's on less than you'd like for a top pitching prospect and it can get really ugly on the off-nights. The upside and downside risk both remain enormous, and there are also many intermediate possibilities that include varying forms of the word "reliever."

Mark Leiter RHP Born: 03/13/91 Age: 27 Bats: R Throws: R Height: 6'0" Weight: 195 Origin: Round 22, 2013 Draft (#661 overall)

YEAR	TEAM	LVL	AGE	W	L	SV	G	GS	IP	H	HR	BB/9	K/9	K	GB%	BABIP	WHIP	ERA	DRA	WARP	MPH	CMD	PWR	STM
2015	REA	AA	24	2	6	0	8	8	47	56	3	2.1	7.3	38	38%	.356	1.43	4.79	3.45	0.9				
2015	CLR	A+	24	6	1	1	19	13	95^2	79	4	2.2	7.8	83	42%	.278	1.07	2.26	3.09	2.2				
2016	REA	AA	25	6	3	1	23	17	103^2	91	9	2.6	8.2	94	46%	.288	1.17	3.39	3.35	2.1				
2017	LEH	AAA	26	2	1	0	7	5	30	27	5	1.8	11.4	38	53%	.297	1.10	4.20	1.60	1.3				
2017	PHI	MLB	26	3	6	0	27	11	90^2	90	18	3.1	8.3	84	50%	.282	1.33	4.96	3.91	1.5	92.5	56	38	56
2018	*PHI*	*MLB*	*27*	*8*	*9*	*0*	*33*	*23*	*132*	*131*	*22*	*3.2*	*8.8*	*129*	*44%*	*.296*	*1.34*	*4.56*	*4.70*	*0.7*	*92.0*	*57*	*38*	*57*
2019	*PHI*	*MLB*	*28*	*9*	*10*	*0*	*30*	*30*	189^2	*166*	*27*	*2.7*	*9.0*	*189*	*44%*	*.297*	*1.18*	*4.21*	*4.64*	*1.7*	*91.6*	*57*	*38*	*57*

Breakout: 31% Improve: 50% Collapse: 16% Attrition: 32% MLB: 73% *Comparables: Kyle Lobstein, Blake Hawksworth, Jose Alvarez*

A 22nd-round senior sign out of perennial baseball doormat NJIT in 2013, Leiter looked for all the world like a guy only picked because of a famous last name. His father, Mark Sr., pitched for a decade in the majors, including two years for the Phillies, and uncle Al had an even longer career as a mostly very good starter. But even if he's only in the organization because of a touch of nepotism, it's Mark Jr.'s strong command and quality splitter that got him to the majors. The swingman role he was deployed in last year might suit him well moving forward, and his career could take an awfully similar path to his father's.

Ben Lively RHP Born: 03/05/92 Age: 26 Bats: R Throws: R Height: 6'4" Weight: 190 Origin: Round 4, 2013 Draft (#135 overall)

YEAR	TEAM	LVL	AGE	W	L	SV	G	GS	IP	H	HR	BB/9	K/9	K	GB%	BABIP	WHIP	ERA	DRA	WARP	MPH	CMD	PWR	STM
2015	REA	AA	23	8	7	0	25	25	143^2	160	14	2.8	7.0	111	40%	.336	1.43	4.13	4.00	1.9				
2016	REA	AA	24	7	0	0	9	9	53	35	1	2.5	8.3	49	39%	.241	0.94	1.87	2.14	1.9				
2016	LEH	AAA	24	11	5	0	19	19	117^2	83	10	2.1	6.9	90	41%	.221	0.93	3.06	3.19	2.9				
2017	LEH	AAA	25	7	5	0	16	16	97	91	3	2.0	7.6	82	39%	.299	1.16	3.15	2.67	3.2				
2017	PHI	MLB	25	4	7	0	15	15	88^2	90	13	2.4	5.3	52	39%	.280	1.29	4.26	5.54	0.0	92.8	59	37	76
2018	*PHI*	*MLB*	*26*	*6*	*7*	*0*	*18*	*18*	*108*	*107*	*16*	*2.9*	*7.4*	*89*	*39%*	*.287*	*1.29*	*4.52*	*4.68*	*0.6*	*92.4*	*60*	*38*	*77*
2019	*PHI*	*MLB*	*27*	*11*	*12*	*0*	*32*	*32*	207^2	*184*	*30*	*2.6*	*7.7*	*178*	*39%*	*.285*	*1.17*	*4.44*	*4.89*	*1.5*	*92.1*	*60*	*38*	*78*

Breakout: 26% Improve: 44% Collapse: 12% Attrition: 24% MLB: 76% *Comparables: Rafael Montero, Tim Cooney, Alfredo Aceves*

He is a fifth starter!
In 2016 we said it
And it's greatly to our credit
That he is a fifth starter
(That he is a fifth starter)

For he might have been mid-rotation
A setup man, or closer or Quadruple-A man
Or perhaps Halladay-an!
(Or perhaps Halladay-an!)
But in spite of all temptations
To throw pitches past his stations
He remains a fifth starter.

Adonis Medina RHP

Born: 12/18/96 Age: 21 Bats: R Throws: R Height: 6'1" Weight: 185 Origin: International Free Agent, 2014

YEAR	TEAM	LVL	AGE	W	L	SV	G	GS	IP	H	HR	BB/9	K/9	K	GB%	BABIP	WHIP	ERA	DRA	WARP	MPH	CMD	PWR	STM
2015	PHL	RK	18	3	2	0	10	8	45^1	42	1	2.4	6.9	35	55%	.304	1.19	2.98	3.71	1.0				
2016	WPT	A-	19	5	3	0	13	13	64^2	47	5	3.3	4.7	34	57%	.214	1.10	2.92	6.92	-1.3				
2017	LWD	A	20	4	9	0	22	22	119^2	103	7	2.9	10.0	133	49%	.306	1.19	3.01	3.40	2.6				
2018	*PHI*	*MLB*	*21*	*5*	*7*	*0*	*18*	*18*	*91*	*96*	*20*	*4.4*	*9.4*	*95*	*43%*	*.322*	*1.54*	*5.62*	*6.23*	*-0.6*				
2019	*PHI*	*MLB*	*22*	*5*	*9*	*0*	*22*	*22*	129^2	*132*	*30*	*3.7*	*9.0*	*130*	*43%*	*.315*	*1.43*	*5.79*	*6.45*	*-1.0*				

Breakout: 1% Improve: 2% Collapse: 0% Attrition: 3% MLB: 3% *Comparables: Robbie Ross, Jacob Faria, Edwin Escobar*

Medina slid onto the back of the Top 101 in last year's edition on pure projection, an interesting arm who sometimes threw very hard and looked like he had good feel for pitching. He's jumped up dozens of spots this year because much of the projection actualized. Medina's fastball ticked up over the course of the season and now consistently sits as high as 96, the rudimentary breaking ball that needed considerable development separated into a plus slider and an occasional show-me curve, and he pitched extremely well over a full season. This is what it looks like when a prospect breaks out into a top prospect, and it can come together quickly. If he continues the growth at higher levels this year, perhaps advancing his change or developing a new third pitch, he'll emerge as one of the top pitching prospects in the game.

Hoby Milner LHP

Born: 01/13/91 Age: 27 Bats: L Throws: L Height: 6'2" Weight: 165 Origin: Round 7, 2012 Draft (#248 overall)

YEAR	TEAM	LVL	AGE	W	L	SV	G	GS	IP	H	HR	BB/9	K/9	K	GB%	BABIP	WHIP	ERA	DRA	WARP	MPH	CMD	PWR	STM
2015	REA	AA	24	2	1	0	29	2	61	61	6	2.5	5.9	40	34%	.293	1.28	3.69	5.00	-0.2				
2016	REA	AA	25	5	3	5	38	0	49	41	3	2.2	9.9	54	48%	.292	1.08	1.84	1.54	1.9				
2016	LEH	AAA	25	0	1	1	11	0	16	16	2	1.7	12.4	22	36%	.350	1.19	4.50	1.15	0.7				
2017	LEH	AAA	26	1	2	0	22	0	27^2	24	1	1.3	8.8	27	49%	.311	1.01	2.60	2.21	0.9				
2017	PHI	MLB	26	0	0	0	37	0	31^1	30	2	4.6	6.3	22	46%	.295	1.47	2.01	6.06	-0.3	90.8	46	32	46
2018	*PHI*	*MLB*	*27*	*3*	*3*	*0*	*50*	*0*	*53*	*51*	*7*	*3.5*	*8.4*	*50*	*42%*	*.293*	*1.35*	*4.55*	*4.57*	*0.2*	*90.3*	*47*	*32*	*47*
2019	*PHI*	*MLB*	*28*	*2*	*1*	*0*	*46*	*0*	*49*	*43*	*7*	*3.4*	*8.7*	*47*	*42%*	*.298*	*1.25*	*4.44*	*4.90*	*0.2*	*89.9*	*46*	*32*	*47*

Breakout: 14% Improve: 34% Collapse: 14% Attrition: 24% MLB: 54% *Comparables: Jacob Barnes, David Rollins, Brent Suter*

The 2016 Rule 5 draft briefly gave Milner what looked like a once-in-a-lifetime chance to be Cleveland's lefty specialist behind relief god Andrew Miller. It didn't last long, but he impressed enough that once his original team needed another lefty in the pen a few months later, Milner was their guy. Taking his LOOGYness to the extreme with more games than innings pitched and a recently overhauled sidearm delivery, Milner was nearly unhittable in the majors against lefties. The shiny ERA and .159 batting average allowed when denying hitters the platoon advantage should launch this into a full career, so long as you ignore advanced stats and the fact that he turned righties into prime Ted Williams. Luckily for Milner, everyone needs lefty relief help.

Adam Morgan LHP

Born: 02/27/90 Age: 28 Bats: L Throws: L Height: 6'1" Weight: 200 Origin: Round 3, 2011 Draft (#120 overall)

YEAR	TEAM	LVL	AGE	W	L	SV	G	GS	IP	H	HR	BB/9	K/9	K	GB%	BABIP	WHIP	ERA	DRA	WARP	MPH	CMD	PWR	STM
2015	LEH	AAA	25	0	6	0	13	13	68^1	81	7	3.6	4.3	33	39%	.307	1.58	4.74	9.27	-3.1				
2015	PHI	MLB	25	5	7	0	15	15	84^1	88	14	1.8	5.2	49	31%	.276	1.25	4.48	6.86	-1.8	91.6	56	29	65
2016	LEH	AAA	26	6	1	0	8	7	50^1	43	4	1.8	9.3	52	42%	.293	1.05	3.04	2.00	1.9				
2016	PHI	MLB	26	2	11	0	23	21	113^1	141	23	2.3	7.5	95	40%	.331	1.50	6.04	5.96	-0.8	93.6	67	36	69
2017	LEH	AAA	27	0	1	0	12	0	17^1	19	1	2.6	7.3	14	44%	.340	1.38	4.67	4.99	0.1				
2017	PHI	MLB	27	3	3	0	37	0	54^2	51	10	3.0	10.4	63	45%	.297	1.26	4.12	3.57	1.0	96.3	49	36	46
2018	*PHI*	*MLB*	*28*	*4*	*4*	*0*	*58*	*3*	*73*	*74*	*11*	*3.3*	*8.6*	*70*	*41%*	*.300*	*1.37*	*4.49*	*4.54*	*0.4*	*93.3*	*60*	*35*	*59*
2019	*PHI*	*MLB*	*29*	*4*	*2*	*0*	*66*	*3*	83^2	*78*	*12*	*3.0*	*9.1*	*85*	*41%*	*.316*	*1.26*	*4.24*	*4.67*	*0.5*	*93.5*	*60*	*36*	*57*

Breakout: 27% Improve: 41% Collapse: 21% Attrition: 37% MLB: 78% *Comparables: Juan Nicasio, Kei Igawa, Hector Noesi*

When teams want to see if a mediocre pitcher's stuff jumps in relief, they're hoping it goes like Adam Morgan's transformation did. Morgan's average fastball and change both jumped about 3 mph from 2016 to his 2017 relief stint, a continuation of steadily increasing velocity ever since major shoulder surgery in 2014. More importantly, he had his first sustained run of MLB success from June on, finally establishing himself as a bona fide big-league pitcher.

Hector Neris RHP

Born: 06/14/89 Age: 28 Bats: R Throws: R Height: 6'2" Weight: 215 Origin: International Free Agent, 2010

YEAR	TEAM	LVL	AGE	W	L	SV	G	GS	IP	H	HR	BB/9	K/9	K	GB%	BABIP	WHIP	ERA	DRA	WARP	MPH	CMD	PWR	STM
2015	LEH	AAA	26	1	3	1	27	0	37^1	38	1	5.8	8.4	35	36%	.327	1.66	3.62	6.30	-0.6				
2015	PHI	MLB	26	2	2	0	32	0	40^1	38	8	2.2	9.1	41	39%	.280	1.19	3.79	4.39	0.2	95.5	40	51	52
2016	PHI	MLB	27	4	4	2	79	0	80^1	59	9	3.4	11.4	102	44%	.272	1.11	2.58	2.61	2.2	96.9	27	47	56
2017	PHI	MLB	28	4	5	26	74	0	74^2	68	9	3.1	10.4	86	35%	.306	1.26	3.01	3.69	1.2	96.0	42	49	54
2018	*PHI*	*MLB*	*29*	*3*	*3*	*28*	*60*	*0*	*63*	*58*	*11*	*3.7*	*10.0*	*71*	*40%*	*.292*	*1.32*	*4.43*	*4.49*	*0.3*	*95.6*	*36*	*49*	*54*
2019	*PHI*	*MLB*	*30*	*2*	*1*	*17*	*50*	*0*	53^1	*44*	*8*	*3.9*	*10.2*	*60*	*40%*	*.295*	*1.27*	*4.55*	*5.03*	*0.1*	*95.3*	*35*	*48*	*54*

Breakout: 23% Improve: 50% Collapse: 16% Attrition: 19% MLB: 87% *Comparables: Jesse Carlson, Pedro Baez, Jason Frasor*

As a mildly homer-prone pitcher that primarily throws splitters around 86-87 mph, Neris is rarely going to be a manager's first choice to close because it just doesn't look like it's supposed to. But it's a really good splitter, and after two seasons of consistently strong setup and occasional closing work, he was the last reliably good Phillies reliever standing in 2017 and became The Closer. As you'd expect, he was perfectly fine in that role even if it felt a bit unorthodox, racking up a bunch of saves that meant little except to pad Neris's fantasy value and future arbitration awards. Finding a reliever this good in the bowels of your system during a rebuild is a nice bonus, even if ultimately only as a significant trade chip.

Pat Neshek RHP Born: 09/04/80 Age: 37 Bats: B Throws: R Height: 6'3" Weight: 220 Origin: Round 6, 2002 Draft (#182 overall)

YEAR	TEAM	LVL	AGE	W	L	SV	G	GS	IP	H	HR	BB/9	K/9	K	GB%	BABIP	WHIP	ERA	DRA	WARP	MPH	CMD	PWR	STM
2015	HOU	MLB	34	3	6	1	66	0	54^{2}	49	8	2.0	8.4	51	34%	.273	1.12	3.62	4.30	0.3	93.1	61	37	46
2016	HOU	MLB	35	2	2	0	60	0	47	33	6	2.1	8.2	43	37%	.216	0.94	3.06	4.61	0.2	92.0	52	29	41
2017	PHI	MLB	36	3	2	1	43	0	40^{1}	28	2	1.1	10.0	45	37%	.271	0.82	1.12	2.39	1.2	92.3	76	29	49
2017	COL	MLB	36	2	1	0	28	0	22	20	1	0.4	9.8	24	36%	.311	0.95	2.45	2.72	0.6	92.2	76	29	49
2018	*PHI*	*MLB*	*37*	*2*	*2*	*0*	*45*	*0*	*47*	*45*	*7*	*3.2*	*8.8*	*47*	*38%*	*.286*	*1.28*	*4.40*	*4.46*	*0.2*	*91.0*	*64*	*30*	*44*
2019	*PHI*	*MLB*	*38*	*3*	*1*	*0*	*55*	*0*	*58^{2}*	*50*	*9*	*2.9*	*8.6*	*56*	*38%*	*.279*	*1.18*	*4.54*	*4.96*	*0.2*	*90.3*	*65*	*29*	*44*

Breakout: 20% Improve: 33% Collapse: 29% Attrition: 13% MLB: 84% *Comparables: Matt Thornton, Francisco Cordero, J.J. Putz*

Posting a career year at 36 despite splitting time between one of the worst teams in baseball and one of the worst pitching environments imaginable? Sure, why not. Neshek didn't do anything differently in 2017; he just did everything he already did well even better. Always a command artist, he lowered his walk rate to an absurd 2.6 percent. Known as a sinker-slider specialist, he leaned into the wind and threw those two pitches a combined 97 percent of the time. And his reputation as a righty-killer? He held 'em to a .166 TAv. Given Neshek's age and the lack of a clear signifier as to how he made the jump from good to elite, it's hard to trust him to repeat as one of the 10-or-so best relievers in baseball. It's easy to trust him with high-leverage work, however, and the market figures to reward him accordingly. Unless Zack Greinke is asked to sign off on his next contract, that is.

Aaron Nola RHP Born: 06/04/93 Age: 25 Bats: R Throws: R Height: 6'2" Weight: 195 Origin: Round 1, 2014 Draft (#7 overall)

YEAR	TEAM	LVL	AGE	W	L	SV	G	GS	IP	H	HR	BB/9	K/9	K	GB%	BABIP	WHIP	ERA	DRA	WARP	MPH	CMD	PWR	STM
2015	REA	AA	22	7	3	0	12	12	76^{2}	59	4	1.1	6.9	59	45%	.259	0.89	1.88	1.40	3.4				
2015	LEH	AAA	22	3	1	0	6	6	32^{2}	38	3	2.5	9.1	33	52%	.365	1.44	3.58	1.13	1.5				
2015	PHI	MLB	22	6	2	0	13	13	77^{2}	74	11	2.2	7.9	68	50%	.289	1.20	3.59	3.79	1.2	93.5	62	39	71
2016	PHI	MLB	23	6	9	0	20	20	111	116	10	2.4	9.8	121	57%	.334	1.31	4.78	2.81	3.3	93.0	67	36	60
2017	LEH	AAA	24	1	0	0	2	2	10^{1}	6	0	0.9	8.7	10	65%	.231	0.68	0.87	2.15	0.4				
2017	PHI	MLB	24	12	11	0	27	27	168	154	18	2.6	9.9	184	50%	.309	1.21	3.54	2.64	5.5	94.1	64	37	74
2018	*PHI*	*MLB*	*25*	*11*	*8*	*0*	*27*	*27*	*162*	*143*	*18*	*2.8*	*9.8*	*176*	*51%*	*.295*	*1.19*	*3.43*	*3.53*	*3.1*	*93.4*	*66*	*38*	*70*
2019	*PHI*	*MLB*	*26*	*12*	*10*	*0*	*33*	*33*	*214^{2}*	*173*	*25*	*2.2*	*10.1*	*240*	*51%*	*.3*	*1.05*	*3.33*	*3.65*	*4.3*	*93.2*	*66*	*38*	*70*

Breakout: 20% Improve: 52% Collapse: 20% Attrition: 10% MLB: 98% *Comparables: Jered Weaver, Gerrit Cole, Mat Latos*

Is this baseball's best kept secret? Our advanced pitching metrics will tell you that Nola has already been performing at ace level when healthy since shortly after his MLB debut. More traditional stats like ERA paint him as closer to a two or three, and scouting reports dating back to his prospect days agree. No matter what appellation you attach, he's a joy to watch pitch, hidden in the overall unwatchability of a long rebuild. Nola's curve is one of baseball's best breaking balls, and combines with his sneakily good change and elite command to allow a merely average-grade fastball to play well above its raw velocity. He's just a handful of small steps away—fewer homers, more durability and, frankly, better teammates—from emerging as one of the best pitchers in the majors.

Nick Pivetta RHP Born: 02/14/93 Age: 25 Bats: R Throws: R Height: 6'5" Weight: 220 Origin: Round 4, 2013 Draft (#136 overall)

YEAR	TEAM	LVL	AGE	W	L	SV	G	GS	IP	H	HR	BB/9	K/9	K	GB%	BABIP	WHIP	ERA	DRA	WARP	MPH	CMD	PWR	STM
2015	POT	A+	22	7	4	0	15	14	86^{1}	70	4	3.0	7.5	72	46%	.274	1.15	2.29	3.57	1.5				
2015	HAR	AA	22	0	2	0	3	3	15	19	4	5.4	3.6	6	34%	.294	1.87	7.20	7.69	-0.5				
2015	REA	AA	22	2	2	0	7	7	28^{1}	32	4	6.0	7.9	25	41%	.341	1.80	7.31	8.10	-1.0				
2016	REA	AA	23	11	6	0	22	22	124	108	10	3.0	8.1	111	45%	.283	1.20	3.41	3.63	2.2				
2016	LEH	AAA	23	1	2	0	5	5	24^{2}	20	2	3.6	9.9	27	48%	.300	1.22	2.55	2.80	0.7				
2017	LEH	AAA	24	5	0	0	5	5	32	25	1	0.6	10.4	37	40%	.293	0.84	1.41	1.71	1.4				
2017	PHI	MLB	24	8	10	0	26	26	133	144	25	3.9	9.5	140	45%	.332	1.51	6.02	5.41	0.2	96.5	47	58	72
2018	*PHI*	*MLB*	*25*	*8*	*8*	*0*	*21*	*21*	*126*	*119*	*20*	*3.4*	*9.5*	*132*	*43%*	*.297*	*1.32*	*4.29*	*4.46*	*1.0*	*96.2*	*48*	*59*	*74*
2019	*PHI*	*MLB*	*26*	*12*	*11*	*0*	*32*	*32*	*209^{1}*	*175*	*30*	*3.0*	*10.1*	*236*	*43%*	*.304*	*1.16*	*3.95*	*4.37*	*2.6*	*96.0*	*48*	*60*	*74*

Breakout: 26% Improve: 49% Collapse: 20% Attrition: 42% MLB: 84% *Comparables: Hayden Penn, Jason Hammel, Carlos Carrasco*

Hitters who specialize in the Three True Outcomes, like Joey Gallo, can be tremendous fun to watch. Starting pitchers who do so, like Pivetta, are almost always tremendously frustrating. At times, his 2017 felt like an experiment to see how bad a pitcher with a legitimately great fastball can be. It's a true swing-and-miss pitch with strong velocity and movement, and when he locates it, you could even think it might be enough. Except he can't locate it much of the time, and he desperately needs better secondary offerings. The slider has shown promise but not consistency, and he has tinkered with both a curve and change. The easy prediction is that he'll end up as a fastball/slider 'pen guy, and that 2017 line is why most guys with this profile end up there before pitching close to a full major-league season. But someone has to make 30 starts, and Pivetta may have shown just enough to get another shot at the rotation, as aesthetically displeasing as it might be.

Edubray Ramos RHP Born: 12/19/92 Age: 25 Bats: R Throws: R Height: 6'0" Weight: 160 Origin: International Free Agent, 2010

YEAR	TEAM	LVL	AGE	W	L	SV	G	GS	IP	H	HR	BB/9	K/9	K	GB%	BABIP	WHIP	ERA	DRA	WARP	MPH	CMD	PWR	STM
2015	CLR	A+	22	3	4	8	29	0	49^{1}	31	2	1.1	8.6	47	46%	.232	0.75	1.46	2.11	1.5				
2015	REA	AA	22	1	2	0	18	0	20^{1}	17	0	4.4	8.0	18	19%	.288	1.33	3.54	5.10	-0.1				
2016	REA	AA	23	1	1	7	11	0	15	9	1	0.6	9.0	15	51%	.211	0.67	2.40	2.36	0.4				
2016	LEH	AAA	23	1	0	3	15	0	23^{2}	15	0	1.1	9.9	26	32%	.250	0.76	0.38	1.96	0.8				
2016	PHI	MLB	23	1	3	0	42	0	40	36	5	2.5	9.0	40	38%	.298	1.17	3.83	3.89	0.5	98.0	47	49	52
2017	LEH	AAA	24	2	0	1	10	0	11^{2}	7	0	3.1	7.7	10	38%	.219	0.94	1.54	3.89	0.2				
2017	PHI	MLB	24	2	7	0	59	0	57^{2}	57	4	4.4	11.7	75	39%	.356	1.47	4.21	3.32	1.2	96.2	43	42	52
2018	*PHI*	*MLB*	*25*	*3*	*3*	*4*	*60*	*0*	*63*	*58*	*9*	*3.7*	*10.0*	*71*	*39%*	*.297*	*1.31*	*4.00*	*4.14*	*0.6*	*96.6*	*45*	*45*	*53*
2019	*PHI*	*MLB*	*26*	*3*	*1*	*2*	*54*	*0*	*57*	*47*	*8*	*3.0*	*10.4*	*66*	*39%*	*.306*	*1.16*	*3.88*	*4.28*	*0.6*	*96.3*	*45*	*45*	*53*

Breakout: 31% Improve: 47% Collapse: 30% Attrition: 23% MLB: 87% *Comparables: Ken Giles, Addison Reed, Kelvin Herrera*

Best known for giving up a huge September 2016 walk-off home run to Asdrubal Cabrera and then throwing at Cabrera's head the following April to his own manager's disdain, Ramos continued his string of dubious accomplishments by being sent down to Triple-A after a string of four losses over five relief appearances in late June. When he was recalled after the trade deadline, he was a different and far more effective pitcher, throwing breaking balls over 65 percent of the time in August and September, and reducing not just the frequency of his fastballs but also their velocity by a couple ticks. Those changes led to the best run of his young career, 26 2/3 effective setup innings with 37 strikeouts and just six walks.

JoJo Romero LHP Born: 09/09/96 Age: 21 Bats: L Throws: L Height: 6'0" Weight: 190 Origin: Round 4, 2016 Draft (#107 overall)

YEAR	TEAM	LVL	AGE	W	L	SV	G	GS	IP	H	HR	BB/9	K/9	K	GB%	BABIP	WHIP	ERA	DRA	WARP	MPH	CMD	PWR	STM
2016	WPT	A-	19	2	2	0	10	10	45^{2}	44	2	2.2	6.1	31	58%	.303	1.20	2.56	3.95	0.7				
2017	LWD	A	20	5	1	0	13	13	76^{2}	61	2	2.5	9.3	79	60%	.299	1.07	2.11	2.45	2.5				
2017	CLR	A+	20	5	2	0	10	10	52^{1}	43	2	2.6	8.4	49	52%	.289	1.11	2.24	3.11	1.3				
2018	*PHI*	*MLB*	*21*	*6*	*6*	*0*	*18*	*18*	*92^{2}*	*93*	*16*	*3.6*	*9.3*	*95*	*45%*	*.321*	*1.40*	*4.65*	*5.13*	*0.5*				
2019	*PHI*	*MLB*	*22*	*8*	*11*	*0*	*28*	*28*	*168^{2}*	*160*	*29*	*3.9*	*9.0*	*169*	*45%*	*.314*	*1.38*	*4.94*	*5.47*	*0.3*				

Breakout: 5% Improve: 8% Collapse: 3% Attrition: 11% MLB: 12% *Comparables: Jordan Walden, Jarred Cosart, Will Smith*

One peril of being a prospect in a great system is that you can break out without hardly anyone noticing it. Romero was on the radar entering 2017 as a fourth-round pick who got a significantly above-slot bonus out of an Arizona junior college. He improved a lot in 2017, sharpening his slider, flashing a promising change and pumping the zone with low-90s two-seamers on his way up the chain. With the Phillies, that doesn't even buy you a definite spot among the organization's top ten prospects right now, but it does make you a prospect to keep tabs on.

Sixto Sanchez RHP Born: 07/29/98 Age: 19 Bats: R Throws: R Height: 6'0" Weight: 185 Origin: International Free Agent, 2015

YEAR	TEAM	LVL	AGE	W	L	SV	G	GS	IP	H	HR	BB/9	K/9	K	GB%	BABIP	WHIP	ERA	DRA	WARP	MPH	CMD	PWR	STM
2015	DPH	RK	16	1	2	0	11	2	25^{2}	32	0	2.1	6.3	18	48%	.340	1.48	4.56	3.96	0.5				
2016	PHL	RK	17	5	0	0	11	11	54	33	0	1.3	7.3	44	57%	.236	0.76	0.50	3.30	1.5				
2017	LWD	A	18	5	3	0	13	13	67^{1}	46	1	1.2	8.6	64	49%	.251	0.82	2.41	2.10	2.5				
2017	CLR	A+	18	0	4	0	5	5	27^{2}	27	1	2.9	6.5	20	42%	.295	1.30	4.55	4.66	0.2				
2018	*PHI*	*MLB*	*19*	*4*	*5*	*0*	*19*	*12*	*69^{2}*	*72*	*14*	*3.6*	*9.0*	*69*	*41%*	*.315*	*1.43*	*5.17*	*5.72*	*-0.1*				
2019	*PHI*	*MLB*	*20*	*7*	*9*	*0*	*32*	*24*	*159^{2}*	*158*	*32*	*3.2*	*8.2*	*146*	*41%*	*.306*	*1.34*	*5.29*	*5.87*	*-0.4*				

Comparables: Vicente Campos, Noah Syndergaard, Manny Banuelos

It might not look like much if you're focused on the traditional stats, but Sanchez became one of baseball's top pitching prospects in 2017. He touches 102 with the fastball, except it's not entirely correct to just say "the fastball" because he throws a four-seamer, a two-seamer and a cutter. He'll also mix in a curve that he can manipulate into a sweeping action or a more traditional overhand breaker, a slower traditional change, a harder change that may or may not actually be a splitter—but certainly moves like one—and the occasional slider. While we expect him to stop throwing all of the "kitchen sink" arsenal as he moves up the ladder, all of these pitches would individually project at least to average, and most could be much more. He works faster than any starting pitching prospect in recent memory, and as you'd expect for someone who played shortstop up until his signing, he's a tremendous fielder coming off the mound. And yeah, he only started pitching in late-2014 after originally being showcased to teams as an infielder. The term isn't thrown around lightly with A-ball pitchers, but this is ace upside.

Jake Thompson RHP Born: 01/31/94 Age: 24 Bats: R Throws: R Height: 6'4" Weight: 225 Origin: Round 2, 2012 Draft (#91 overall)

YEAR	TEAM	LVL	AGE	W	L	SV	G	GS	IP	H	HR	BB/9	K/9	K	GB%	BABIP	WHIP	ERA	DRA	WARP	MPH	CMD	PWR	STM
2015	FRI	AA	21	6	6	0	17	17	87^{2}	94	7	3.1	8.0	78	46%	.330	1.41	4.72	3.61	1.6				
2015	REA	AA	21	5	1	0	7	7	45	33	3	2.4	6.8	34	52%	.256	1.00	1.80	3.63	0.8				
2016	LEH	AAA	22	11	5	0	21	21	129^{2}	105	10	2.6	6.0	87	48%	.252	1.10	2.50	5.52	-0.3				
2016	PHI	MLB	22	3	6	0	10	10	53^{2}	53	10	4.7	5.4	32	49%	.264	1.51	5.70	7.09	-1.1	93.8	44	42	75
2017	LEH	AAA	23	5	14	0	22	22	118^{1}	136	12	3.6	6.8	90	44%	.331	1.55	5.25	7.29	-2.0				
2017	PHI	MLB	23	3	2	0	11	8	46^{1}	50	9	4.3	6.8	35	47%	.295	1.55	3.88	8.17	-1.4	92.8	45	40	73
2018	*PHI*	*MLB*	*24*	*5*	*5*	*0*	*23*	*13*	*79*	*76*	*11*	*3.2*	*8.4*	*75*	*45%*	*.292*	*1.29*	*4.29*	*4.42*	*0.6*	*93.1*	*46*	*42*	*76*
2019	*PHI*	*MLB*	*25*	*10*	*10*	*0*	*31*	*31*	*195*	*162*	*26*	*2.8*	*8.9*	*193*	*45%*	*.288*	*1.15*	*4.08*	*4.51*	*2.0*	*92.9*	*46*	*42*	*77*

Breakout: 25% Improve: 46% Collapse: 17% Attrition: 29% MLB: 69% *Comparables: Anthony Bass, Anthony Swarzak, Alex Sanabia*

One of the great prospect mysteries of the last few years is what the heck happened to Thompson's slider. For years, it was one of the best sliders in the minors, a wipeout hard breaking ball that regularly got labeled "plus" or "plus-plus." Combined with good velocity and sink on his fastball, that made Thompson one of the best pitching prospects in baseball and a centerpiece of the Cole Hamels trade. Flash forward two seasons and Thompson's ability to locate the slider, along with the depth and sharpness of the pitch, is a distant memory. And it bears out in the results. He has gone to the slider with two strikes against right-handed hitters more often than any other pitch in his career, as you'd expect, and hitters have both put it in play and fouled it off more often than swinging over it. Without the once-dominant weapon, the profile has fallen apart, and Thompson looks like nothing more than a Quadruple-A pitcher hoping against hope that the old form returns.

Vincent Velasquez RHP Born: 06/07/92 Age: 26 Bats: R Throws: R Height: 6'3" Weight: 205 Origin: Round 2, 2010 Draft (#58 overall)

YEAR	TEAM	LVL	AGE	W	L	SV	G	GS	IP	H	HR	BB/9	K/9	K	GB%	BABIP	WHIP	ERA	DRA	WARP	MPH	CMD	PWR	STM
2015	CCH	AA	23	4	0	0	9	5	33	20	2	3.5	12.3	45	35%	.246	1.00	1.91	2.29	1.1				
2015	HOU	MLB	23	1	1	0	19	7	55^2	50	5	3.4	9.4	58	31%	.310	1.28	4.37	4.70	0.2	97.5	43	62	44
2016	PHI	MLB	24	8	6	0	24	24	131	129	21	3.1	10.4	152	37%	.325	1.33	4.12	4.70	1.0	96.8	34	56	63
2017	PHI	MLB	25	2	7	0	15	15	72	74	15	4.2	8.5	68	45%	.303	1.50	5.12	5.55	0.0	96.2	40	60	45
2018	*PHI*	*MLB*	*26*	*6*	*6*	*0*	*18*	*18*	*95*	*86*	*15*	*3.3*	*9.9*	*105*	*40%*	*.295*	*1.27*	*4.09*	*4.24*	*1.0*	*96.3*	*38*	*59*	*52*
2019	*PHI*	*MLB*	*27*	*10*	*11*	*0*	*32*	*32*	*211^1*	*172*	*30*	*2.9*	*10.1*	*237*	*40%*	*.297*	*1.14*	*3.94*	*4.35*	*2.4*	*96.0*	*37*	*59*	*53*

Breakout: 31% Improve: 59% Collapse: 13% Attrition: 13% MLB: 96% *Comparables: Ian Snell, Chuck James, Dan Haren*

Few pitchers in baseball can match Velasquez's raw talent on the mound, and few MLB starters can match his disastrous health record as a pro. Dating back all the way to Tommy John surgery just a few months after he was drafted in 2010, Velasquez has never been healthy for any length of time; even when pitching, he's often doing so compromised. In 2017, he went down with a flexor strain at the end of May, came back in mid-July with diminished velocity and without his usual level of dominance, and was diagnosed with a blood clot that caused numbness in his fingers a month later. Given the monstrous upside, you can't blame the Phillies too much for trying so hard to keep him in the rotation, but he might be better cut out to return to his second-half 2015 role in the 'pen.

Lineouts

Hitters

HITTER	POS	TEAM	LVL	AGE	PA	R	2B	3B	HR	RBI	BB	K	SB	CS	AVG/OBP/SLG	TAv	VORP	BABIP	BRR	FRAA	WARP
Eliezer Alvarez	2B	CRD	Rk	22	27	4	2	0	1	2	2	3	1	0	.250/.296/.458	.243	1.0	.238	0.7	2B(7): 1.0	0.2
	2B	SFD	AA	22	209	29	11	1	4	26	16	56	8	3	.247/.321/.382	.257	5.2	.328	0.7	2B(45): -4.2	0.1
Andres Blanco	INF	PHI	MLB	33	144	10	4	0	3	13	12	34	1	0	.192/.257/.292	.206	-4.6	.232	-0.7	3B(16): -0.6, 2B(15): 0.5	-0.7
Pedro Florimon	INF	LEH	AAA	30	353	32	13	1	10	33	34	94	4	3	.265/.347/.410	.260	10.0	.346	-1.0	2B(33): -3.2, 3B(25): 0.1	0.7
	INF	PHI	MLB	30	49	6	4	1	0	6	3	16	0	0	.348/.388/.478	.310	3.9	.533	-0.2	CF(8): 0.3, SS(2): 0.0	0.5
Eric Fryer	C	SLN	MLB	31	83	7	3	0	0	3	11	18	0	0	.155/.277/.197	.180	-2.4	.208	0.8	C(26): -0.1	-0.3
Ty Kelly	UT	NYN	MLB	28	1	0	0	0	0	0	0	1	0	0	.000/.000/.000	-.011	-0.3	--	0.0		0.0
	UT	PHI	MLB	28	104	11	7	0	2	14	8	24	0	0	.193/.260/.341	.250	2.7	.231	0.9	2B(14): 0.3, LF(9): -1.0	0.5
Hyun-Soo Kim	OF	BAL	MLB	29	142	11	4	0	1	10	12	27	0	0	.232/.305/.288	.215	-4.8	.283	-1.3	LF(42): 0.9	-0.4
	OF	PHI	MLB	29	97	9	4	1	0	4	10	19	0	0	.230/.309/.299	.223	-1.6	.294	0.0	LF(13): -1.5, RF(11): 0.6	-0.3
Will Middlebrooks	3B	ROU	AAA	28	342	51	14	0	23	64	31	88	0	1	.258/.327/.529	.291	21.3	.283	0.2	3B(54): -5.9, 1B(2): -0.1	1.5
	3B	TEX	MLB	28	39	5	2	2	0	3	1	14	0	0	.211/.231/.368	.210	-0.3	.333	0.6	3B(19): 1.8, 1B(1): -0.1	0.2
Brock Stassi	1B	PHI	MLB	27	90	6	2	1	2	7	12	22	0	0	.167/.278/.295	.206	-4.8	.204	-1.2	1B(21): 1.0, LF(3): -0.2	-0.4
	1B	LEH	AAA	27	196	18	4	0	4	22	18	42	0	0	.249/.321/.341	.236	-4.1	.300	-1.5	1B(32): -0.4, LF(10): 0.8	-0.4
Jesmuel Valentin	INF	LEH	AAA	23	104	9	3	0	1	7	6	16	0	0	.229/.282/.292	.206	-3.2	.266	0.0	2B(26): -2.7, SS(2): 0.1	-0.6

The Phillies turned a free waiver claim of reliever Juan Nicasio into interesting second-base prospect **Eliezer Alvarez** in a rare September trade with the Cardinals. It's always nice to get something for nothing. ⚾ The offensive magic finally ran out for **Andres Blanco** after a nice run as the Phillies' fifth infielder during the down period. ⚾ **Pedro Florimon** has exited the phase of his career where he's the emergency shortstop on the 40-man and entered the phase of his career where he's the emergency shortstop you bring in as a minor-league free agent. ⚾ **Eric Fryer** lives the life of a third-string catcher, which means long stretches at Triple-A mixed with short stints in the majors and the occasional small-sample-size burst of production. ⚾ The Phillies gave **Luis Garcia** $2.5 million as one of the top prospects in last year's international class, nearly double what the Nationals gave a similar J2 prospect of the same name in 2016. And they say inflation doesn't exist these days. ⚾ Team Israel hero **Ty Kelly** had a very exciting spring, going from the WBC to the Mets' Opening Day roster to a tour through the International League courtesy of a waiver claim by Toronto and a trade to Philly. His summer as a mediocre major-league utility dude was outright dull in comparison. ⚾ The Orioles wanted out of the **Hyun-Soo Kim** deal about five seconds after they signed it, and finally got to include it to balance out salaries in the Jeremy Hellickson deal. Kim needs strict platooning to be effective, and that's hard to pull off with 13-man pitching staffs. ⚾ In Game 1 of a September 6 doubleheader against the Braves, **Will Middlebrooks** hit a pinch-hit triple. In Game 2 of a September 6 doubleheader against the Braves, Will Middlebrooks hit a pinch-hit triple. In an otherwise unremarkable run subbing for Adrian Beltre in the midst of an otherwise unremarkable career, it's nice to have a story to tell. ⚾ **Brock Stassi** won May's Vogelsong Award as the "best" player not in the *2017 Annual* by putting up a .581 OPS in 35 plate appearances, reflecting the great job done by last year's editors and writers in selecting hitters for the book. ⚾ Utility prospect **Jesmuel Valentin** is the third-most famous member of his immediate family behind father Jose, former MLB All-Star, and sister JoJo, WWE ring announcer and former star of E's *Total Divas*.

Pitchers

PITCHER	TEAM	LVL	AGE	W	L	SV	G	GS	IP	H	HR	BB/9	K/9	K	GB%	BABIP	WHIP	ERA	DRA	WARP	MPH	CMD	PWR	STM
Victor Arano	REA	AA	22	1	2	9	32	0	38^2	39	7	2.6	8.8	38	40%	.296	1.29	4.19	3.99	0.4				
	PHI	MLB	22	1	0	0	10	0	10^2	6	0	3.4	11.0	13	44%	.240	0.94	1.69	3.92	0.1	95.5			45
Pedro Beato	PHI	MLB	30	0	0	0	1	0	0^2	0	0	0.0	13.5	1	100%	.000	0.00	0.00	8.72	0.0	89.4			48
	LEH	AAA	30	1	3	33	52	0	55^2	41	4	3.2	6.8	42	36%	.233	1.10	2.75	5.28	0.0				
Trevor Bettencourt	LWD	A	22	3	2	8	25	0	35^2	32	1	1.3	13.9	55	59%	.378	1.04	3.28	1.28	1.5				

PITCHER	TEAM	LVL	AGE	W	L	SV	G	GS	IP	H	HR	BB/9	K/9	K	GB%	BABIP	WHIP	ERA	DRA	WARP	MPH	CMD	PWR	STM
	CLR	A+	22	2	0	2	16	0	23	13	2	1.6	8.6	22	62%	.186	0.74	1.57	1.51	0.9				
Zac Curtis	SEA	MLB	24	0	0	0	3	0	4^2	3	1	1.9	3.9	2	38%	.133	0.86	0.00	3.11	0.1	91.9			42
	ARK	AA	24	1	2	13	41	0	51^1	43	3	3.3	10.5	60	42%	.303	1.21	3.51	4.11	0.4				
	PHI	MLB	24	0	0	0	3	0	3^2	3	0	4.9	9.8	4	56%	.333	1.36	2.45	6.50	-0.1	92.7			42
Casey Fien	SEA	MLB	33	0	0	0	6	0	6	9	3	6.0	9.0	6	47%	.375	2.17	15.00	5.93	-0.1	93.6	57	40	30
	PHI	MLB	33	0	1	0	4	0	6	14	2	3.0	6.0	4	44%	.480	2.67	10.50	9.30	-0.3	95.0	57	40	30
	LEH	AAA	33	0	1	0	14	0	16	15	3	1.7	7.3	13	41%	.261	1.12	5.06	2.45	0.5				
Elniery Garcia	REA	AA	22	2	1	0	5	5	25^2	17	0	6.0	3.5	10	48%	.210	1.32	1.75	6.44	-0.4				
J.D. Hammer	ASH	A	22	4	1	7	24	0	30	17	0	1.5	14.1	47	54%	.288	0.73	1.20	1.38	1.2				
	LNC	A+	22	0	1	6	12	0	12	10	0	6.8	13.5	18	50%	.385	1.58	5.25	4.39	0.1				
	CLR	A+	22	2	0	0	12	0	15^2	8	0	1.1	11.5	20	46%	.242	0.64	0.57	1.56	0.6				
Spencer Howard	WPT	A-	20	1	1	0	9	9	28^1	22	0	5.7	12.7	40	48%	.349	1.41	4.45	3.40	0.6				
Ricardo Pinto	LEH	AAA	23	5	3	1	19	8	60^2	61	4	2.7	6.8	46	39%	.308	1.30	3.86	5.23	0.2				
	PHI	MLB	23	1	2	0	25	0	29^2	39	7	5.2	7.6	25	46%	.333	1.89	7.89	6.82	-0.5	97.5	46	61	52
Cesar Ramos	LEH	AAA	33	5	4	1	40	11	92^1	91	10	3.0	7.2	74	40%	.297	1.32	4.00	4.90	0.6				
Yacksel Rios	REA	AA	24	1	2	2	24	0	38	22	2	2.4	11.1	47	40%	.235	0.84	1.89	2.65	1.0				
	LEH	AAA	24	0	1	1	13	1	18^1	10	3	2.0	8.3	17	36%	.159	0.76	1.96	4.49	0.2				
	PHI	MLB	24	1	0	0	13	0	16^1	15	4	5.0	9.4	17	36%	.256	1.47	4.41	4.85	0.1	95.6	34	58	45
Ranger Suarez	LWD	A	21	6	2	0	14	14	85	52	4	2.5	9.5	90	58%	.233	0.89	1.59	1.52	3.7				
	CLR	A+	21	2	4	0	8	8	37^2	43	1	2.6	9.1	38	50%	.382	1.43	3.82	3.16	0.9				
Jose Taveras	CLR	A+	23	6	4	0	16	16	102	86	13	2.0	8.1	92	40%	.266	1.07	2.38	3.10	2.6				
	REA	AA	23	0	1	0	2	2	11^1	10	2	0.8	8.7	11	31%	.267	0.97	3.97	3.53	0.2				
	LEH	AAA	23	3	1	0	7	7	41	26	5	3.3	8.1	37	31%	.198	1.00	1.32	5.20	0.2				
Jesen Dygestile-Therrien	REA	AA	24	2	1	7	21	0	28^2	14	1	0.9	12.2	39	46%	.232	0.59	1.26	2.02	1.0				
	LEH	AAA	24	0	0	2	18	0	28^2	25	2	1.9	8.2	26	58%	.277	1.08	1.57	2.17	1.0				
	PHI	MLB	24	0	0	0	15	0	18^1	24	5	3.4	4.9	10	48%	.302	1.69	8.35	6.03	-0.2	94.4	45	45	50
Alberto Tirado	REA	AA	22	0	0	0	10	0	12	13	0	14.2	6.0	8	40%	.342	2.67	6.75	10.62	-0.8				
	CLR	A+	22	5	4	0	15	12	63^1	59	8	5.4	8.2	58	60%	.293	1.53	3.69	4.52	0.5				
Pat Venditte	LEH	AAA	32	9	5	2	52	0	69^2	54	7	4.7	8.9	69	42%	.266	1.29	3.36	4.40	0.7				

A few years removed from being a top-ten prospect in the Dodgers system, **Victor Arano** saw his career take off again after he moved to relief in 2016; he's leaning much more heavily on his mid-90s fastball and quality slurve now. ⚾ **Pedro Beato**'s appearance for two outs on July 29 got him into the book, and ruined a streak dating back to 2013 where he only made the *Annual* in odd-numbered years. ⚾ **Trevor Bettencourt** had one of the most dominant relief seasons in the low-minors while rocking one of baseball's best mustaches. ⚾ **Zac Curtis** may have great flow, but he's missing Ks both at the end of his name and against MLB hitters. ⚾ **Casey**'s rotator cuff turned out to be not so **Fein**, and the former elite fastball command artist was released to make room for September call-ups for the second straight season. ⚾ **Elniery Garcia** had a mostly lost season due to a poorly timed 80-game suspension for noted horse steroid boldenone in April. As a lefty who has shown mid-90s velocity, he has about eight more years before we can officially declare him a lost cause. ⚾ The Phillies gave 2016 second-rounder **Kevin Gowdy** $3.5 million to dishonor his commitment to UCLA. He then went ahead and dishonored his elbow, undergoing Tommy John surgery in August, which will cost him most or all of 2018. ⚾ **J.D. Hammer** added glasses inspired by Charlie Sheen in *Major League* in the offseason. Suddenly able to see, he made everything groovy on the mound, and the Phillies acquired him at the deadline in the Pat Neshek trade. ⚾ **Spencer Howard** rose from walk-on redshirt to a second-round pick over three years at Cal Poly. He credits his morning meditation routine, per Matt Breen of *The Inquirer*, while the Phillies credit one of the draft's best fastballs. ⚾ Hard-throwing **Ricardo Pinto** still needs command and a better secondary offering, but there are worse places to start than his fastball. ⚾ **Cesar Ramos** hadn't spent the entire year in the minors since Barack Obama was a future president instead of an ex-president, but he's been effective enough and left-handed enough that we're unwilling to concede that he's not getting another shot or five in MLB camps. ⚾ **Yacksel Rios** is baseball's only Yacksel and yet one of baseball's hundreds of relievers that can run it up to the mid-90s and throw a decent slider. ⚾ Crafty lefty **Ranger Suarez**'s velocity ticked up into the low-90s, and he carved up A-ball hitters. It can go a lot of ways from here, but many of them end in the majors. ⚾ **Jose Taveras** doesn't profile all that well in scouting reports but has absolutely flown through the minors. He has already pitched well at Triple-A and could reach the majors any time now. ⚾ Montreal native and Eric Gagne protégé **Jesen Therrien** lived the dream for most of 2017, being named to Team Canada in the WBC and earning his first MLB call-up in the summer. But it wasn't all cheese curds and gravy for the 24-year-old, as he had Tommy John surgery in mid-September, leaving him on the Outremont looking in for 2018. ⚾ **Alberto Tirado** owns one of the best arms in the minors, but if he makes it to Citizens Bank Park one day, the Phillies will at least be thankful they've already extended the netting. ⚾ In a different world, **Pat Venditte** would've been a perfect spokesman for the Nintendo Switch, but this breath of the wild manifested in more walks than you'd like at Triple-A.

PITTSBURGH PIRATES

Essay by Rob Mains

Player comments by Matthew Trueblood and BP staff

Pittsburgh, Pennsylvania was perfectly situated to be a hub of the Industrial Revolution. Nestled in the confluence of the Allegheny, Monongahela and Ohio Rivers, it is linked directly to the Mississippi River and, via tributaries to the Allegheny, within eight miles of the Great Lakes.

By the end of the Civil War, Pittsburgh accounted for more than half of the steel produced in the United States. In the 1910 census, Pittsburgh, with a population of 533,905, was the eighth-largest city in the country, trailing only New York, Chicago, Philadelphia, St. Louis, Boston, Cleveland and Baltimore. The prior year, its baseball team had won 110 games and defeated the Detroit Tigers in the World Series. Pittsburgh was a powerhouse.

A century later, in 2010, Pittsburgh—still known as "The Steel City"—had no steel mills. Its population was 305,704, nearly halved from the 1910 census, ranking 60th among US cities. The population of New York, still no. 1, had risen more than 70 percent. The Pirates lost 105 games, their 18th straight losing season. The city and the team seemed to lack the resources to compete with New York. Enter the words "Pittsburgh" and "not New York" into your favorite search engine, and you'll get about 300,000 hits.

In 2017, that turned out to be a good thing.

One of the hallmarks of the New York sports scene, other than money and a huge population from which to draw, is the nation's top media market. That market includes both venerated broadsheets and splashy tabloids. Pittsburgh's two dailies—one print, one electronic—are not tabloids. The tabloids would've feasted on the 2017 Pirates.

The controversies began in the winter and continued through the season. The team was spared a number of tabloid headlines.

The Kang-Over

In 2015 and 2016, Jung Ho Kang ranked second on the Pirates in WARP (9.0) and first in WARP per plate appearance. He was signed to below-market contracts of $2.5 million in 2015 and 2016, $2.75 million in 2017 and $3 million in 2018. He capably played both third base and shortstop. The Pirates' low-cost gamble on a Korean Baseball Organization player was paying off.

On the morning of December 2, 2016, Kang was charged with driving under the influence and leaving the scene of an accident after he crashed his BMW into a guardrail. This turned out to be Kang's third DUI since 2015, which was apparently news to the Pirates. He received a two-year suspended sentence and, in light of that, was denied a US work visa, preventing him from playing for the Pirates in 2017. Kang, whose position with the team was already the subject of controversy and uncertainty because of an unresolved assault allegation, played in the Dominican Winter League after the season, but his future in the United States remains murky.

In Much Dutch with Cutch

While dealing with the uncertainty of Kang's return, the Pirates had a winter-long controversy involving the player described in the

PIRATES PROSPECTUS

2017 W-L: 75-87, 4th in NL Central

Pythag	.458	18th
RS/G	4.12	28th
RA/G	4.51	13th
TAv	.255	21st
TAv-P	.272	23rd
FIP	4.24	12th
DER	.694	27th

B-Age	28.2	*14th*
P-Age	26.9	*3rd*
Salary	$95.8M	*24th*
M$/MW	$3.1M	*21st*
DL Days	355	*3rd*
$ on DL	9%	*6th*

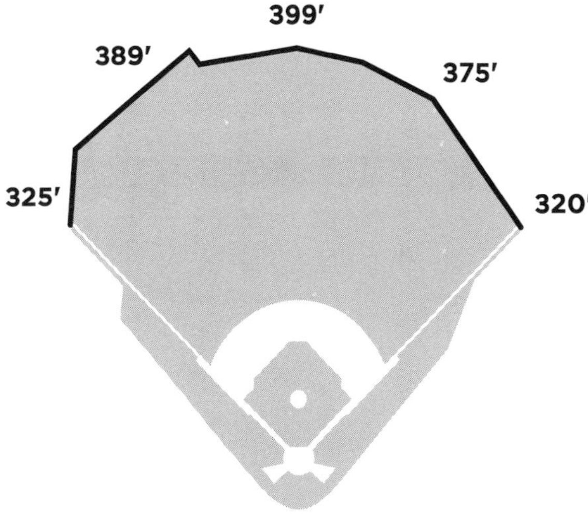

Outfield wall profile: **6′** to **21′**

Three-Year Park Factors

Runs	Runs/RH	Runs/LH	HR/RH	HR/LH
98	97	99	93	101

Top Hitter WARP	3.9 Andrew McCutchen
Top Pitcher WARP	3.2 Gerrit Cole
Top Prospect	Mitch Keller

2017 Hit List Ranking

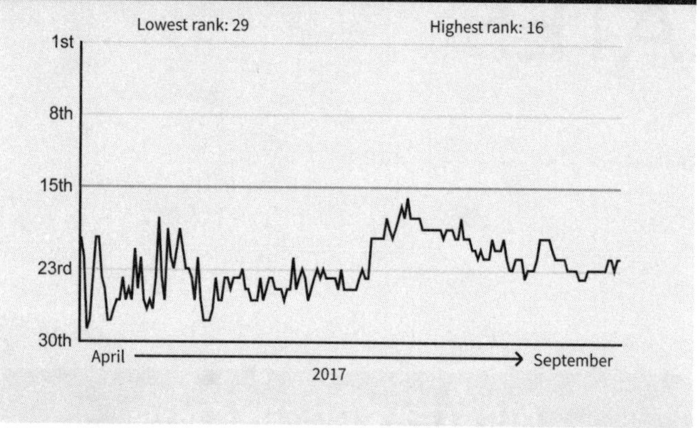

Committed Payroll (in millions)

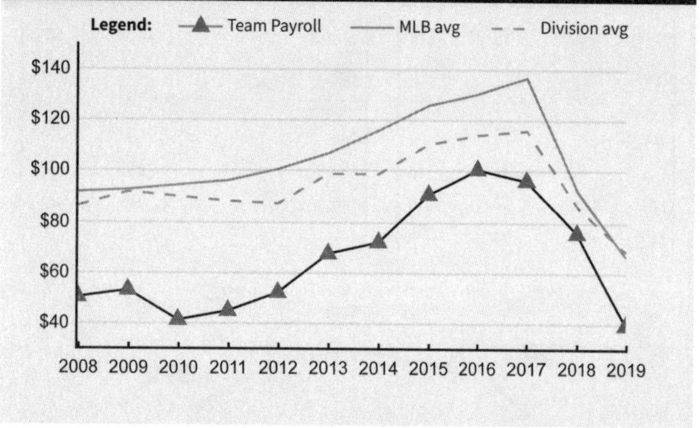

Farm System Ranking

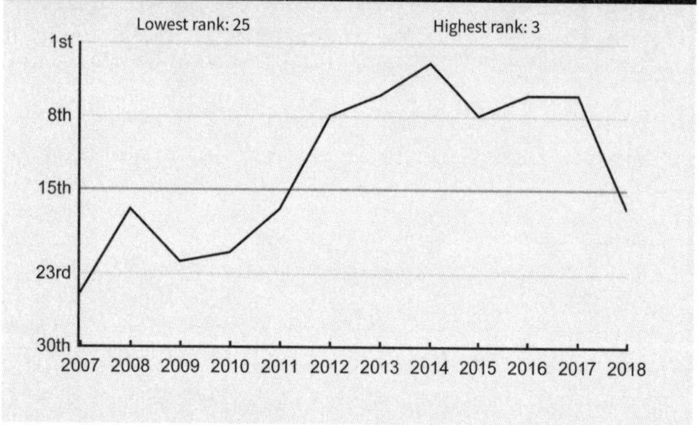

Personnel

President
Frank Coonelly

EVP, General Manager
Neal Huntington

Assistant General Manager
Kevan Graves

Assistant General Manager
Greg Smith

Assistant General Manager
Kyle Stark

Manager
Clint Hurdle

BP Alumni
Dan Fox
Grant Jones
Stuart Wallace

2015 edition of this book as "practically the perfect franchise player." Andrew McCutchen, who'd fallen just short of his fourth straight .300/.400/.500 season in 2015, slumped badly in 2016, hitting .256/.336/.430. His defense in center field, beloved by yinzers but doubted by advanced metrics everywhere, didn't help, and his 2.2 WARP was the worst of his eight-year career.

Additionally, the six-year, $51.5 million contract he signed before the 2012 season was looking less attractive: He was owed $14 million in 2017 with a team option for $14.5 million in 2018, after which, at age 32, he'd hit free agency. The team entertained trade offers for the five-time All-Star over the winter. Once it became clear that he was staying, management decided to shuffle the outfield, moving Gold Glove left fielder Starling Marte to center field, right fielder Gregory Polanco to left field and McCutchen to right field.

The problem was that, according to McCutchen, he wasn't advised of any of this. Granted, it's not incumbent on management to confer with employees about every move, but McCutchen is universally admired across baseball and is the most popular Pirate since Willie Stargell. While he wasn't traded and he publicly handled the move to right field with grace (tweeting a photo of Pirates right field icon Roberto Clemente), it was clear that his feelings were hurt. And with a .205/.273/.358 batting line going into play on May 27, his bat hadn't come around, either.

Marté Departé

Entering 2017, the best player on the Pirates wasn't Kang or McCutchen. It was Marte, who'd compiled a .289 TAv and 7.0 FRAA in 2016 en route to a 4.0 WARP season. He started 2017 slowly, with a .659 OPS over his first 13 games. Then, on April 18, he was suspended 80 games for testing positive for nandrolone, an anabolic steroid. His suspension left the Pirates without their no. 2 hitter and forced another outfield reshuffle, with McCutchen returning to center field and Polanco eventually moving back to right field. When Marte returned to the lineup in July (back in left field), his bat didn't: He hit a punchless .282/.343/.380 following the suspension, albeit with a strong finish.

Juan Down, Juan to Go

One of the year's most bizarre transactions was the exit of Juan Nicasio, the team's second-best reliever by WARP. He was heading into free agency, and the Pirates weren't going to re-sign him. They put him on revocable waivers in August, and he was claimed by a team with whom they couldn't work out a deal, so they pulled him back. So far, so normal. But then they put him on *outright* waivers, enabling the Phillies, on August 31, to claim him for nothing, raising the question of why you'd just *dump* a pitcher with a 2.85 ERA, 3.03 FIP and 3.58 DRA.

General manager Neal Huntington's explanation didn't clear much up: "He was claimed by a playoff-caliber club that indicated to us their primary motivation was to block us from being able to trade Juan elsewhere. Rather than help a direct competitor [Direct competitor for what? Fourth place in the division?] we chose to take the chance to see if by placing Juan on outright waivers he would end up with a different playoff contender, preferably one in the American League."

Well, the Phillies certainly weren't playoff contenders, but six days later, they traded him to the Cardinals, who certainly were, for minor leaguer Eliezer Alvarez. So Nicasio wound up with a National League Central "direct competitor" after all (he became St. Louis' closer, logging four saves in September), the Phillies wound up with a prospect and the Pirates wound up with nothing except about $600,000 in savings on Nicasio's contract.

The day before the Phillies traded Nicasio, the Pirates extended Huntington's contract for four years. Partly because of the Nicasio situation, the reaction to extending the executive credited with ending the team's record 20-year losing streak and returning it to the postseason was mixed.

Discomfortably Numb

The Pirates' training staff routinely uses the word *discomfort* to describe any soreness that keeps a player out of the lineup. While this doesn't rise to the level of the tabloid-worthy it's-just-a-flesh-wound Mets injury communications, it has become a source of ridicule. *Pittsburgh Tribune-Review* reporter Rob Biertempfel had no fewer than 25 tweets last year describing a player's "discomfort."

The most egregious case of "discomfort" involved pitcher Jameson Taillon. Following a promising rookie season, Taillon was penciled in as the no. 3 pitcher in the Pirates' rotation. Through his first six starts, he was one of the team's best pitchers, with a 3.31 ERA and 30 strikeouts against 13 walks. Poor run support limited him to a 2-1 record, but he seemed on track to build on his 2016 success following nearly two full seasons lost to injury.

On May 6, the Pirates placed Taillon on the 10-day disabled list. Two days later, he had surgery to remove a cancerous testicle. The gravity of his case provided a contrast to the biggest New York baseball tabloid story of the year, the suspension of Mets pitcher Matt Harvey for staying out late; Harvey's suspension ran from the day Taillon was disabled through the day of his surgery. While thankfully Taillon appears to be healthy, his performance after his return to action (4.85 ERA, .807 OPS allowed) was a step back.

Oh, and the transaction announced on May 6? "Pittsburgh Pirates placed RHP Jameson Taillon on the 10-day disabled list retroactive to May 4, 2017. Groin discomfort." *For testicular cancer.*

Along the way, there were some nice stories that weren't exactly tabloid-worthy. Felipe Rivero emerged as one of the game's top relievers, delivering a 1.67 ERA and 2.94 DRA on the strength of a 99-mph four-seamer that generated a .256 slugging percentage on contact, setting up secondary pitches that generated a 48 percent whiff rate on swings. The Pirates debuted the first major leaguers born in Lithuania, pitcher Dovydas Neverauskas, and Africa, infielder Gift Ngoepe. Josh Bell tied a Pirates record for home runs by a rookie, with 26, and looks to be a long-term solution to the team's perennial problems at first base. Adam Frazier compiled a .272 TAv, fourth on the club, while playing six positions. Josh Harrison, 29, and David Freese, 34, each posted the second-highest WARP of their careers. Franchise icon Kent Tekulve got a nice sendoff as he retired from the broadcast booth.

But many of the questions raised during the team's turbulent 2017 remain. Kang's status is unclear. The Pirates appear to want him back, but whether he can obtain a work visa is up in the air. Marte, signed through 2019 with club options for 2020 and 2021, is coming off (easily) his worst season. Catcher Francisco Cervelli, signed to a four-year, $34.5 million deal after an injury-free breakout in 2015, has played only 182 games over the past two years, and heir apparent Elias Diaz displayed poor framing (-10.5 framing runs, though he was decent at Triple-A) and hitting (.198 TAv) in 64 games in Pittsburgh.

And then there's the pitching staff. After Ray Searage became the team's pitching coach in 2011, the Pirates became formidable on the mound, featuring low-cost reclamation projects like starters Francisco Liriano and A.J. Burnett and relievers Jason Grilli and Mark Melancon. Since the team's wild card years of 2013-2015, though, the pitching has ebbed:

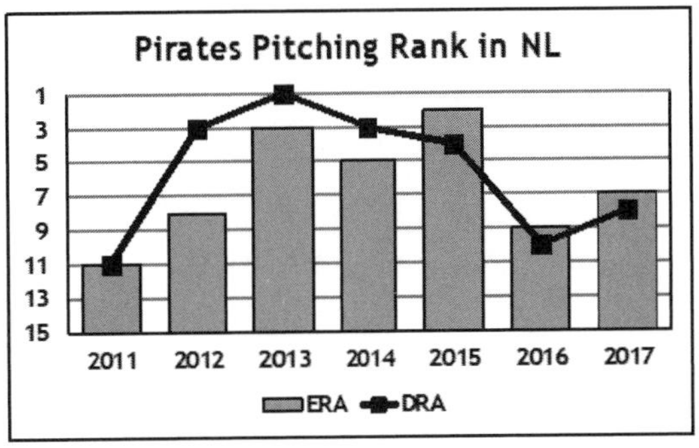

Gerrit Cole, who was an ace-in-waiting in 2015 (2.60 ERA, 3.10 DRA) posted ERAs of 3.88 and 4.26 and DRAs of 4.19 and 4.15 in the two years since. The club's 2016 pickup from the scrap heap, Ivan Nova, had a 2.83 ERA, 2.0 percent walk rate, 2.3 percent home-run rate and 11 quality starts over his first 13 starts, averaging 6.8 innings per start. Over his next 21, he had a 4.92 ERA, 4.8 percent home run rate, 6.1 percent walk rate and six quality starts, averaging 5.6 innings per start.

Chad Kuhl regressed in his sophomore season, as his ERA rose from 4.20 to 4.35 and his DRA rose from 4.85 to 5.24. Rookie Trevor Williams' 4.07 DRA was the best among Pirates starters. And Tyler Glasnow, a consensus top-25 prospect for three straight years, was Dr. Jekyll in 93 1/3 innings in Indianapolis (1.93 ERA, 50 cFIP, 1.06—1.06!—DRA, 4.4 K/BB) sandwiched around 58 1/3 innings of Mr. Hyde in Pittsburgh (7.69 ERA, 124 cFIP, 8.76 DRA, 1.3 K/BB).

While the 2016 pitching decline can be attributed to injuries—no Pirates hurler qualified for the ERA title—the team had five pitchers start 25 or more games in 2017, with only Taillon losing significant time to injury. With limited pitching reinforcements on the farm, the club will have to sink or swim with The Pitcher Whisperer and the current staff.

Finally, there's McCutchen. The Pirates exercised their 2018 option, but by the time you read this, he may have posed for pictures with another team's cap on his head. He recovered from his early-season slump, batting .371/.477/.696 from May 27 to the end of July, but hit just .222/.300/.283 in August before rebounding to an .844 OPS in September. His days as a six-win player appear to be behind him, limiting his value to a team that seems unlikely to compete in 2018 and unlikely to retain him beyond then. Fittingly, in what could be his last season in Pittsburgh, he fell one game short of matching his career-high in games played, as he sat out the second-to-last game of the season.

With "left foot discomfort."

—Rob Mains is an author of Baseball Prospectus.

HITTERS

Josh Bell 1B Born: 08/14/92 Age: 25 Bats: B Throws: R Height: 6'2" Weight: 230 Origin: Round 2, 2011 Draft (#61 overall)

YEAR	TEAM	LVL	AGE	PA	R	2B	3B	HR	RBI	BB	K	SB	CS	AVG/OBP/SLG	TAv	VORP	BABIP	BRR	FRAA	WARP
2015	ALT	AA	22	427	47	17	6	5	60	44	50	7	4	.307/.376/.427	.299	18.9	.335	-2.1	1B(84): -7.5	1.2
2015	IND	AAA	22	145	20	7	3	2	18	21	15	2	0	.347/.441/.504	.325	11.2	.377	-0.1	1B(32): -3.2	0.8
2016	IND	AAA	23	484	57	23	4	14	60	57	74	3	7	.295/.382/.468	.306	24.1	.328	-4.0	1B(96): -3.4, RF(4): 1.3	2.3
2016	PIT	MLB	23	152	18	8	0	3	19	21	19	0	1	.273/.368/.406	.286	6.4	.294	0.2	1B(23): -0.3, RF(16): -2.3	0.4
2017	PIT	MLB	24	620	75	26	6	26	90	66	117	2	4	.255/.334/.466	.285	19.1	.278	-3.7	1B(147): -6.5	1.3
2018	*PIT*	*MLB*	*25*	*638*	*79*	*28*	*5*	*21*	*84*	*68*	*107*	*3*	*3*	*.270/.349/.448*	*.279*	*21.5*	*.298*	*-1.3*	*1B -6*	*1.3*
2019	*PIT*	*MLB*	*26*	*597*	*83*	*26*	*4*	*23*	*82*	*65*	*102*	*3*	*3*	*.273/.356/.470*	*.296*	*28.3*	*.299*	*-1.7*	*1B -5*	*2.5*

Breakout: 4% Improve: 52% Collapse: 3% Attrition: 15% MLB: 91% *Comparables: Conor Jackson, Joey Votto, Jason Kubel*

A thick-bodied, switch-hitting first baseman still trying to find his way to his power potential, Bell spent his rookie season flashing a whole lot of upside—and clearly demonstrating ways in which he has growing up left to do. He's a thoughtful and intelligent person, but after the Pirates fell headlong out of the race near the start of September, Bell seemed to lose his ability to focus and produce. He makes a lot of bad mistakes on the bases, and is already a below-average runner. His defense is a work in progress. On the bright side, he finally started hitting lefties, posting an identical .211 ISO from both sides of the plate and posting a better home-run rate from the right side. Guys like this sometimes put it together a bit late. As long as he stays healthy, Bell should be good very soon. He just needs reps and good instruction.

Francisco Cervelli C Born: 03/06/86 Age: 32 Bats: R Throws: R Height: 6'1" Weight: 210 Origin: International Free Agent, 2003

YEAR	TEAM	LVL	AGE	PA	R	2B	3B	HR	RBI	BB	K	SB	CS	AVG/OBP/SLG	TAv	VORP	BABIP	BRR	FRAA	WARP
2015	PIT	MLB	29	510	56	17	5	7	43	46	94	1	1	.295/.370/.401	.281	32.2	.359	0.0	C(128): 17.5	5.3
2016	PIT	MLB	30	393	42	14	1	1	33	56	72	6	2	.264/.377/.322	.265	16.6	.329	-2.9	C(95): 8.1, 1B(2): -0.1	2.5
2017	PIT	MLB	31	304	31	13	2	5	31	32	65	0	2	.249/.342/.370	.263	12.1	.311	-2.9	C(78): -4.5	0.8
2018	*PIT*	*MLB*	*32*	*424*	*46*	*16*	*2*	*5*	*39*	*44*	*84*	*3*	*2*	*.258/.345/.356*	*.256*	*17.9*	*.317*	*-0.6*	*C 3*	*1.8*
2019	*PIT*	*MLB*	*33*	*379*	*45*	*15*	*2*	*6*	*37*	*41*	*78*	*1*	*1*	*.255/.346/.366*	*.265*	*15.6*	*.314*	*-1.4*	*C 4*	*2.1*

Breakout: 2% Improve: 30% Collapse: 13% Attrition: 14% MLB: 94% *Comparables: Scott Hatteberg, Bob Boone, Sherm Lollar*

YEAR	TEAM	P. COUNT	FRM RUNS	BLK RUNS	THRW RUNS	TOT RUNS
2015	PIT	17330	17.3	-1.3	-2.6	13.4
2016	PIT	13232	10.6	-1.9	-2.4	6.2
2017	PIT	10368	-5.0	0.5	-0.8	-5.4
2018	*PIT*	*14855*	*4.9*	*-1.1*	*-1.8*	*1.9*
2019	*PIT*	*13280*	*4.2*	*-1.0*	*-1.5*	*1.7*

Injuries are really piling up on Cervelli, the way they have on so many other mid-sized catchers with good framing skills but not enough other tools. Not even the juiced ball could add meaningful pop to his offensive profile. Pitchers are coming right after him again, making it impossible for him to draw as many walks as he once did—despite his persistently patient approach and refusal to expand his zone. Behind the plate, some of the magic in his glove hand is simply gone, either due to age, or because umpires are adjusting the way they call games, or because one of the myriad injuries (including, sadly, concussions) he's suffered over the past two years is getting between him and his talent.

Will Craig 1B Born: 11/16/94 Age: 23 Bats: R Throws: R Height: 6'3" Weight: 212 Origin: Round 1, 2016 Draft (#22 overall)

YEAR	TEAM	LVL	AGE	PA	R	2B	3B	HR	RBI	BB	K	SB	CS	AVG/OBP/SLG	TAv	VORP	BABIP	BRR	FRAA	WARP
2016	WEV	A-	21	274	28	12	0	2	23	41	37	2	0	.280/.412/.362	.309	18.3	.322	-2.7	3B(46): 0.1	1.9
2017	BRD	A+	22	542	59	26	1	6	61	62	106	1	3	.271/.373/.371	.283	10.2	.335	-7.8	1B(93): 9.4	2.1
2018	*PIT*	*MLB*	*23*	*250*	*25*	*11*	*0*	*6*	*27*	*25*	*60*	*0*	*0*	*.233/.325/.362*	*.239*	*-1.3*	*.294*	*-0.5*	*1B 3*	*0.2*
2019	*PIT*	*MLB*	*24*	*353*	*43*	*16*	*1*	*9*	*38*	*37*	*85*	*0*	*0*	*.235/.329/.380*	*.260*	*3.4*	*.294*	*-0.9*	*1B 4*	*0.8*

Breakout: 5% Improve: 9% Collapse: 4% Attrition: 11% MLB: 17% *Comparables: Max Muncy, David Cooper, Chris McGuiness*

Now that Craig is essentially a first baseman, his success or failure as a prospect hinges on whether he can develop average-plus power at the plate. Unfortunately, an entire season in the Florida State League doesn't yield much in the way of usable intel on that issue. Craig sure didn't make a statement at the plate in Bradenton, but he did resist the temptation to start muscling up and lose command of the strike zone. His prospect stock will either skyrocket or crash based on how well he's able to sustain that plate discipline while adding power at Double-A. At the very least, he figures not to have any trouble handling his defensive duties.

Elias Diaz C Born: 11/17/90 Age: 27 Bats: R Throws: R Height: 6'1" Weight: 215 Origin: International Free Agent, 2008

YEAR	TEAM	LVL	AGE	PA	R	2B	3B	HR	RBI	BB	K	SB	CS	AVG/OBP/SLG	TAv	VORP	BABIP	BRR	FRAA	WARP
2015	IND	AAA	24	363	33	16	4	4	47	29	47	1	4	.271/.330/.382	.253	8.7	.301	-1.0	C(60): 2.0	1.1
2015	PIT	MLB	24	2	0	0	0	0	0	0	1	0	0	.000/.000/.000	-.003	-0.5	.000	0.0		0.0
2016	BRD	A+	25	28	6	0	0	1	5	4	2	0	1	.391/.464/.522	.331	3.5	.381	0.2	C(6): -0.3	0.3
2016	PIT	MLB	25	4	0	0	0	0	1	0	1	0	0	.000/.000/.000	.007	-0.9	.000	0.0	C(1): 0.1	-0.1
2016	IND	AAA	25	97	4	3	0	0	10	3	17	1	0	.266/.289/.298	.216	-1.1	.325	-1.0	C(25): -2.2	-0.3
2017	IND	AAA	26	229	19	10	0	2	27	9	36	3	0	.266/.298/.339	.232	1.9	.311	-1.2	C(50): 6.6	0.8
2017	PIT	MLB	26	200	18	14	0	1	19	11	38	1	0	.223/.265/.314	.198	-4.8	.273	-0.9	C(55): -4.0	-0.9
2018	*PIT*	*MLB*	*27*	*125*	*12*	*6*	*0*	*2*	*12*	*7*	*22*	*1*	*0*	*.247/.292/.363*	*.232*	*2.4*	*.287*	*-0.2*	*C -2*	*-0.1*
2019	*PIT*	*MLB*	*28*	*202*	*22*	*10*	*1*	*4*	*21*	*13*	*41*	*1*	*0*	*.246/.297/.378*	*.243*	*3.8*	*.290*	*-0.5*	*C -3*	*0.1*

Breakout: 9% Improve: 24% Collapse: 21% Attrition: 39% MLB: 67% *Comparables: Bryan Holaday, Rob Johnson, Ramon Cabrera*

There are very few guys who can ever be characterized as backup catcher prospects. Backup catcher is not a role for which teams ever groom people. It's more of an emergency thing, unless they have a starting catcher so fragile as to require a high-quality alternative. Diaz has been treated a bit like a prospect, though, despite never showing much sign of being able to handle a regular job offensively. Now, we also have a healthy sample that suggests he's a mediocre receiver. Catchers develop late, but it's getting "stay tuned for *Last Call* with Carson Daly" late, and usually that's not worth staying up for.

YEAR	TEAM	P. COUNT	FRM RUNS	BLK RUNS	THRW RUNS	TOT RUNS
2015	IND	8398	1.8	0.6	0.0	2.5
2016	PIT	141	0.0	0.0	0.0	0.0
2017	PIT	6832	-5.3	-0.6	0.2	-5.7
2018	*PIT*	*4590*	*-2.8*	*-0.1*	*0.1*	*-2.8*
2019	*PIT*	*7426*	*-3.6*	*-0.2*	*0.1*	*-3.6*

Adam Frazier LF Born: 12/14/91 Age: 26 Bats: L Throws: R Height: 5'9" Weight: 185 Origin: Round 6, 2013 Draft (#179 overall)

YEAR	TEAM	LVL	AGE	PA	R	2B	3B	HR	RBI	BB	K	SB	CS	AVG/OBP/SLG	TAv	VORP	BABIP	BRR	FRAA	WARP
2015	ALT	AA	23	423	59	21	4	2	30	34	42	11	7	.324/.384/.416	.301	34.4	.360	2.3	SS(58): 0.2, CF(29): -0.7	3.6
2016	IND	AAA	24	299	34	16	4	0	22	29	27	17	15	.333/.401/.425	.326	26.5	.369	-1.3	LF(44): 2.0, CF(17): -3.1	2.6
2016	PIT	MLB	24	160	21	8	1	2	11	12	26	4	1	.301/.356/.411	.290	6.4	.353	-2.3	LF(20): -0.7, 2B(17): -0.7	0.5
2017	PIT	MLB	25	454	55	20	6	6	53	36	57	9	5	.276/.344/.399	.272	18.1	.306	1.3	LF(52): 2.8, 2B(42): -2.6	1.7
2018	*PIT*	*MLB*	*26*	*374*	*49*	*18*	*3*	*6*	*34*	*30*	*50*	*9*	*5*	*.287/.346/.408*	*.269*	*15.5*	*.317*	*-0.3*	*LF 1, 2B -1*	*1.3*
2019	*PIT*	*MLB*	*27*	*444*	*53*	*21*	*3*	*8*	*48*	*38*	*62*	*10*	*6*	*.278/.346/.411*	*.275*	*18.2*	*.304*	*-0.8*	*LF 1, 2B -1*	*1.9*

Breakout: 6% Improve: 49% Collapse: 11% Attrition: 20% MLB: 90% *Comparables: Chris Coghlan, Desmond Jennings, Blake DeWitt*

Frazier belongs to the phylum of position player most endangered by the current offensive environment. In the Juiced Ball Era, it's easy to find guys who can run and field, and let the ball make up for their lack of real offensive skills. Many modern hitters get by because the ball rewards hard contact so much that they can afford not to walk much or make much contact or use the whole field or grind out at-bats. Frazier has so little power that he can't even get to any in games with the juiced ball in play. He's not a good enough athlete to add value by playing plus defense at shortstop or second base. He's stuck in a utility role, and unless he gives in to peer pressure and reorganizes his approach at the plate, he'll probably stay there.

David Freese 3B Born: 04/28/83 Age: 35 Bats: R Throws: R Height: 6'2" Weight: 220 Origin: Round 9, 2006 Draft (#273 overall)

YEAR	TEAM	LVL	AGE	PA	R	2B	3B	HR	RBI	BB	K	SB	CS	AVG/OBP/SLG	TAv	VORP	BABIP	BRR	FRAA	WARP
2015	SLC	AAA	32	25	2	0	0	1	6	3	4	0	0	.286/.400/.429	.284	0.8	.313	-0.3	3B(3): -0.2	0.1
2015	ANA	MLB	32	470	53	27	0	14	56	31	107	1	1	.257/.323/.420	.268	17.8	.310	0.3	3B(113): -0.1	1.9
2016	PIT	MLB	33	492	63	23	0	13	55	45	142	0	0	.270/.352/.412	.270	16.6	.372	-0.4	3B(78): 0.2, 1B(58): 3.0	2.0
2017	PIT	MLB	34	503	44	16	0	10	52	58	116	0	1	.263/.368/.371	.272	17.7	.336	-4.7	3B(116): 5.3, 1B(3): 0.0	2.3
2018	*PIT*	*MLB*	*35*	*554*	*58*	*24*	*1*	*12*	*60*	*48*	*132*	*1*	*1*	*.249/.327/.370*	*.251*	*10.7*	*.316*	*-1.5*	*3B 2*	*0.9*
2019	*PIT*	*MLB*	*36*	*388*	*45*	*16*	*0*	*8*	*39*	*33*	*97*	*0*	*0*	*.240/.318/.360*	*.253*	*5.5*	*.308*	*-1.1*	*3B 2*	*0.8*

Breakout: 0% Improve: 22% Collapse: 16% Attrition: 21% MLB: 78% *Comparables: Mark DeRosa, Jhonny Peralta, Melvin Mora*

In an era of two Wild Cards per league and a solid month of playoff baseball, October heroes get to be like day lilies: momentarily thrilling, but short-lived, quickly forgotten and just as quickly replaced. Freese is an exception. He bloomed late, but that miraculous pair of long hits in Game 6 of the 2011 fall classic turned out not to be miracles, after all. They were, rather, the product of a unique skill set that has aged gracefully. Freese uses center and right field as well as any right-handed hitter. Of 186 qualifying batters, Freese posted the sixth-deepest average contact point last season, letting the ball travel well into the hitting zone before jolting it the other way. That approach has not allowed Freese to retain the power he had in his early years, but the swing that put rings on the Cardinals' fingers seven years ago is still putting money in Freese's pockets. What's more, a few years of good health have allowed his defense at third base to improve, even as he nears his mid-thirties.

Josh Harrison INF Born: 07/08/87 Age: 30 Bats: R Throws: R Height: 5'8" Weight: 180 Origin: Round 6, 2008 Draft (#191 overall)

YEAR	TEAM	LVL	AGE	PA	R	2B	3B	HR	RBI	BB	K	SB	CS	AVG/OBP/SLG	TAv	VORP	BABIP	BRR	FRAA	WARP
2015	PIT	MLB	27	449	57	29	1	4	28	19	71	10	8	.287/.327/.390	.264	15.7	.336	1.8	3B(72): 1.8, 2B(37): -0.7	1.9
2016	PIT	MLB	28	522	57	25	7	4	59	18	76	19	4	.283/.311/.388	.254	14.2	.323	3.1	2B(128): -0.1, RF(1): -0.2	1.4
2017	PIT	MLB	29	542	66	26	2	16	47	28	90	12	4	.272/.339/.432	.286	32.6	.303	1.7	2B(83): -2.6, 3B(49): 2.6	3.2
2018	*PIT*	*MLB*	*30*	*624*	*79*	*34*	*4*	*12*	*60*	*26*	*95*	*16*	*6*	*.276/.315/.410*	*.254*	*23.2*	*.308*	*0.9*	*2B -2, 3B 0*	*1.5*
2019	*PIT*	*MLB*	*31*	*515*	*59*	*28*	*3*	*12*	*58*	*25*	*83*	*12*	*5*	*.273/.319/.420*	*.264*	*20.8*	*.305*	*2.2*	*2B -2, 3B 0*	*2.1*

Breakout: 1% Improve: 46% Collapse: 7% Attrition: 9% MLB: 99% *Comparables: Freddy Sanchez, Omar Infante, Mike Aviles*

Baseball is more fun when played with speed, competitive fire and physical improvisation. Harrison delivers all three. He moved much closer to the plate in 2017, a necessary step (literally) for the diminutive infielder to improve his plate coverage and allow him to keep his lower half underneath him through the point of contact. That proximity to the plate is newly in vogue, and it's no accident. Harrison walked a bit more (and was hit by a pitch 23 times) last season, benefiting from a better look at opposing pitchers. For as long as he maintains his skills and doesn't get hurt (his career high in plate appearances is 550), Harrison is going to be one of the game's most exciting players.

Ke'Bryan Hayes 3B Born: 01/28/97 Age: 21 Bats: R Throws: R Height: 6'1" Weight: 210 Origin: Round 1, 2015 Draft (#32 overall)

YEAR	TEAM	LVL	AGE	PA	R	2B	3B	HR	RBI	BB	K	SB	CS	AVG/OBP/SLG	TAv	VORP	BABIP	BRR	FRAA	WARP
2015	PIR	RK	18	175	24	4	1	0	13	22	24	7	1	.333/.434/.375	.308	14.9	.393	0.2	3B(36): 5.9	2.0
2015	WEV	A-	18	52	8	1	0	0	7	6	7	1	1	.220/.320/.244	.296	1.9	.250	-1.7	3B(12): 3.2	0.5
2016	WVA	A	19	276	27	12	1	6	37	16	51	6	5	.263/.319/.393	.281	12.4	.304	-1.5	3B(64): 2.0	1.6
2017	BRD	A+	20	482	66	16	7	2	43	41	76	27	5	.278/.345/.363	.263	17.6	.331	0.8	3B(108): 20.7	4.1
2018	*PIT*	*MLB*	*21*	*250*	*26*	*10*	*1*	*5*	*26*	*17*	*56*	*6*	*2*	*.241/.298/.368*	*.227*	*0.0*	*.290*	*0.4*	*3B 5*	*0.6*
2019	*PIT*	*MLB*	*22*	*360*	*41*	*14*	*2*	*8*	*39*	*25*	*77*	*9*	*3*	*.250/.309/.385*	*.250*	*6.0*	*.297*	*0.9*	*3B 8*	*1.5*

Breakout: 2% Improve: 5% Collapse: 0% Attrition: 7% MLB: 11% *Comparables: Cheslor Cuthbert, Kaleb Cowart, Rio Ruiz*

The Pirates challenged Hayes with an assignment to the Florida State League at age 20, and he mostly held his own. Nothing leaps off the page yet, and at the plate no tool looks much better than average. A modicum of power will come, but it might not come right away, and no one was expecting it to show up in a shower of shards from the light towers in the pitcher-friendly FSL. Hayes ran the bases well and improved substantially at third base; he should be at least average with the glove there. In 2018, he'll see Double-A pitchers and they'll give everyone (including Hayes) a better idea of how much upside his stick really has.

John Jaso RF Born: 09/19/83 Age: 34 Bats: L Throws: R Height: 6'2" Weight: 202 Origin: Round 12, 2003 Draft (#338 overall)

YEAR	TEAM	LVL	AGE	PA	R	2B	3B	HR	RBI	BB	K	SB	CS	AVG/OBP/SLG	TAv	VORP	BABIP	BRR	FRAA	WARP
2015	TBA	MLB	31	216	23	17	0	5	22	28	39	1	2	.286/.380/.459	.300	9.1	.336	-1.9	LF(7): -0.8, RF(1): -0.1	0.9
2016	PIT	MLB	32	432	45	25	3	8	42	45	74	0	4	.268/.353/.413	.280	12.3	.314	-1.4	1B(108): -6.7, RF(1): -0.2	0.6
2017	PIT	MLB	33	302	28	19	0	10	35	40	66	1	1	.211/.328/.402	.268	10.6	.243	1.9	RF(46): -3.2, 1B(29): -0.6	0.6
2018	*PIT*	*MLB*	*34*	*310*	*39*	*17*	*1*	*8*	*32*	*35*	*59*	*1*	*1*	*.254/.347/.409*	*.260*	*8.2*	*.297*	*-0.1*	*RF 0, 1B -1*	*0.6*
2019	*PIT*	*MLB*	*35*	*170*	*21*	*9*	*0*	*4*	*19*	*20*	*33*	*0*	*1*	*.247/.342/.394*	*.270*	*5.0*	*.290*	*0.0*	*RF 0, 1B -1*	*0.4*

Breakout: 0% Improve: 26% Collapse: 28% Attrition: 31% MLB: 91% *Comparables: Trot Nixon, Kosuke Fukudome, Seth Smith*

On the final day of the 2017 season, Jaso declared his intention to hop on his sailboat and pursue a peaceful existence beyond baseball. The type of personality that makes such a proclamation tends to be unpredictable, so it's tough to say whether his baseball career is truly over. Of course, as a catcher-turned-first baseman-turned-outfielder with minimal power he was likely nearing the end of the line anyway at age 34. Jaso's left-handed bat could still add some value in a part-time role, but perhaps his hair will look more luxurious poking out of a sailor cap than a baseball helmet.

Jung-ho Kang 3B Born: 04/05/87 Age: 31 Bats: R Throws: R Height: 6'0" Weight: 210 Origin: International Free Agent, 2015

YEAR	TEAM	LVL	AGE	PA	R	2B	3B	HR	RBI	BB	K	SB	CS	AVG/OBP/SLG	TAv	VORP	BABIP	BRR	FRAA	WARP
2015	PIT	MLB	28	467	60	24	2	15	58	28	99	5	4	.287/.355/.461	.294	33.2	.344	1.7	3B(77): 5.1, SS(60): -8.7	3.2
2016	IND	AAA	29	57	5	0	0	2	7	7	11	0	1	.146/.246/.271	.219	-0.8	.135	-0.2	3B(13): -0.7	-0.2
2016	PIT	MLB	29	370	45	19	0	21	62	36	79	3	1	.255/.354/.513	.310	26.9	.273	-3.7	3B(92): 8.5	3.7
2018	*PIT*	*MLB*	*31*	*250*	*32*	*12*	*1*	*11*	*36*	*21*	*55*	*2*	*1*	*.260/.341/.467*	*.274*	*11.5*	*.296*	*-0.4*	*3B 4*	*1.7*
2019	*PIT*	*MLB*	*32*	*38*	*5*	*2*	*0*	*2*	*5*	*3*	*9*	*0*	*0*	*.247/.329/.441*	*.279*	*1.6*	*.284*	*-0.1*	*3B 1*	*0.2*

Breakout: 0% Improve: 39% Collapse: 7% Attrition: 5% MLB: 97% *Comparables: Troy Tulowitzki, Hanley Ramirez, Carlos Guillen*

How ought we to process someone like Kang? What on earth can we fairly say about him? He's talented, for sure. He's also irresponsible, and maybe much worse than that. He might be an honest-to-god villain. We can't say whether or not he sexually assaulted a woman in Chicago two summers ago, because after an initial report, the trail went cold. We can't say for sure what sequence of events led to his multiple arrests for drunk driving in his native South Korea, which cost him all of the 2017 season. Even if we had perfect knowledge of all that, what ought we to do with it? Most of us have come to understand that the criminal justice system often deals those whom it labels as criminals fairly serious injustices, and most of us want to see people whom that system handles be given second chances and the support they need to make lasting, positive changes. Yet, many of us also feel uneasy about anyone who might have done any of these heinous things getting the chance to continue playing baseball, being famous, making millions of dollars and (perhaps) having the chance to do those bad things again with impunity. There are no good answers.

Kevin Kramer 2B Born: 10/03/93 Age: 24 Bats: L Throws: R Height: 6'1" Weight: 190 Origin: Round 2, 2015 Draft (#62 overall)

YEAR	TEAM	LVL	AGE	PA	R	2B	3B	HR	RBI	BB	K	SB	CS	AVG/OBP/SLG	TAv	VORP	BABIP	BRR	FRAA	WARP
2015	WEV	A-	21	209	34	7	3	0	17	25	28	9	4	.305/.390/.379	.307	18.9	.358	3.2	2B(44): 7.4, SS(2): -1.1	2.6
2015	WVA	A	21	56	9	2	1	0	3	5	8	3	0	.240/.321/.320	.246	1.8	.286	1.2	2B(8): -0.3, SS(2): -0.6	0.1
2016	BRD	A+	22	513	56	29	2	4	57	48	63	3	9	.277/.352/.378	.268	18.0	.312	0.8	2B(103): 9.7	2.8
2017	ALT	AA	23	234	31	17	3	6	27	17	50	7	2	.297/.380/.500	.315	20.4	.362	1.7	2B(48): -1.6	2.0
2018	*PIT*	*MLB*	*24*	*250*	*30*	*12*	*1*	*6*	*25*	*18*	*54*	*2*	*1*	*.246/.314/.393*	*.239*	*5.0*	*.294*	*-0.3*	*2B 1, SS 0*	*0.7*
2019	*PIT*	*MLB*	*25*	*288*	*34*	*14*	*1*	*8*	*32*	*22*	*63*	*3*	*2*	*.246/.316/.399*	*.257*	*8.0*	*.294*	*-0.3*	*2B 1, SS 0*	*1.0*

Breakout: 8% Improve: 15% Collapse: 3% Attrition: 22% MLB: 32% *Comparables: Logan Watkins, Cord Phelps, Jose Pirela*

A second-base-only prospect has to hit, but if he can be an average defensive second baseman, he doesn't have to hit like crazy. Kramer certainly isn't going to slide to the left side of the infield, but he has enough athleticism to acquit himself well at the keystone. He's also a left-handed hitter with plenty of plate discipline and a polished approach. There are enough guys like this—average athlete, left-handed stick, balanced but uninspiring—to fill a *Where's Waldo?* page, and the odds of picking the one who becomes a true impact guy are as good as if you close your eyes and try to point to Waldo. Still, Kramer has a wide path to a decent career.

Jordan Luplow OF Born: 09/26/93 Age: 24 Bats: R Throws: R Height: 6'1" Weight: 195 Origin: Round 3, 2014 Draft (#100 overall)

YEAR	TEAM	LVL	AGE	PA	R	2B	3B	HR	RBI	BB	K	SB	CS	AVG/OBP/SLG	TAv	VORP	BABIP	BRR	FRAA	WARP
2015	WVA	A	21	465	74	36	3	12	67	59	67	11	2	.264/.366/.464	.297	30.3	.289	0.1	3B(86): 1.2	3.4
2016	BRD	A+	22	425	63	23	3	10	54	60	78	6	2	.254/.363/.421	.290	22.1	.294	0.2	LF(81): 7.5	3.0
2017	ALT	AA	23	288	45	15	0	16	37	29	45	1	3	.287/.368/.535	.322	25.5	.294	1.5	LF(62): 4.4, 3B(1): 0.0	3.2
2017	IND	AAA	23	182	29	7	1	7	19	16	36	4	1	.325/.401/.513	.334	18.2	.381	-0.8	LF(27): 3.4, RF(15): 0.9	2.2
2017	PIT	MLB	23	87	6	3	1	3	11	6	22	0	1	.205/.276/.385	.232	-1.2	.241	-0.4	RF(14): 0.1, LF(10): 0.8	0.0
2018	*PIT*	*MLB*	*24*	*62*	*8*	*3*	*0*	*2*	*8*	*6*	*14*	*0*	*0*	*.245/.324/.435*	*.265*	*2.1*	*.281*	*-0.1*	*RF 0*	*0.2*
2019	*PIT*	*MLB*	*25*	*316*	*42*	*15*	*1*	*13*	*43*	*30*	*74*	*1*	*1*	*.247/.328/.448*	*.278*	*12.9*	*.286*	*-0.6*	*RF 0*	*1.4*

Breakout: 4% Improve: 25% Collapse: 19% Attrition: 26% MLB: 58% *Comparables: Michael Choice, Austin Slater, Justin Huber*

Aaron Judge was the AL Rookie of the Year and arguably the best hitter in baseball in 2017, but if they give an award for Most Surprising Breakout By a Member of the 2013 Fresno State Bulldogs Outfield, Judge is out of luck. Then again, maybe we should have expected Luplow to find his way to success all along. After Judge was drafted in 2013, Luplow replaced nearly all of his erstwhile teammate's production in the spring of 2014, enticing the Pirates so much that they took him in the third round. He hit at one level of Single-A per year from that summer through 2016, and then in 2017 he took off like a Judge rocket to left-center. He is a decent defender in either corner outfield spot, has proved his power will play against high-level pitching and has maintained control of the strike zone as he climbed the ladder. He's no Judge, but Luplow could yet make it as a big-league regular.

Starling Marte LF Born: 10/09/88 Age: 29 Bats: R Throws: R Height: 6'1" Weight: 190 Origin: International Free Agent, 2007

YEAR	TEAM	LVL	AGE	PA	R	2B	3B	HR	RBI	BB	K	SB	CS	AVG/OBP/SLG	TAv	VORP	BABIP	BRR	FRAA	WARP
2015	PIT	MLB	26	633	84	30	2	19	81	27	123	30	10	.287/.337/.444	.281	25.4	.333	-1.3	LF(141): -5.2, CF(18): 2.8	2.5
2016	PIT	MLB	27	529	71	34	5	9	46	23	104	47	12	.311/.362/.456	.289	32.2	.380	4.9	LF(114): 7.5, CF(16): -0.4	4.0
2017	IND	AAA	28	40	4	1	0	1	3	2	8	3	0	.333/.400/.444	.326	4.7	.407	0.9	LF(6): -0.4, CF(1): 0.1	0.4
2017	PIT	MLB	28	339	48	7	2	7	31	20	63	21	4	.275/.333/.379	.257	10.9	.324	3.4	LF(56): 5.9, CF(25): 3.1	2.0
2018	*PIT*	*MLB*	*29*	*640*	*96*	*30*	*5*	*15*	*63*	*32*	*135*	*39*	*10*	*.277/.332/.421*	*.267*	*27.9*	*.335*	*4.6*	*LF 1, CF 0*	*2.7*
2019	*PIT*	*MLB*	*30*	*479*	*60*	*24*	*3*	*14*	*58*	*28*	*104*	*27*	*8*	*.273/.336/.435*	*.281*	*24.5*	*.329*	*2.3*	*LF 2, CF 0*	*2.9*

Breakout: 1% Improve: 43% Collapse: 1% Attrition: 7% MLB: 98% *Comparables: Carl Crawford, Shane Mack, Chris Heisey*

When Gregor Samsa usurped his father to provide for his family, he was punished by being transformed into a monstrous vermin. That family, for whom he had dived so headlong into his work as to alienate himself from his own sense of morality, regarded him with fear and disgust. They only benefited from his crimes against the natural order of things when he finally died, and they could resume life without the burden of his transformed self in their midst. Marte took center field from Andrew McCutchen last spring, and then took a little something extra to make sure he would be worthy of shoving aside a franchise icon. Maybe he should count himself lucky that he got only an 80-game suspension and a banishment back to left field, with his speed, line-drive power, elite defense, voice and human brain function more or less intact.

Andrew McCutchen CF Born: 10/10/86 Age: 31 Bats: R Throws: R Height: 5'10" Weight: 195 Origin: Round 1, 2005 Draft (#11 overall)

YEAR	TEAM	LVL	AGE	PA	R	2B	3B	HR	RBI	BB	K	SB	CS	AVG/OBP/SLG	TAv	VORP	BABIP	BRR	FRAA	WARP
2015	PIT	MLB	28	685	91	36	3	23	96	98	133	11	5	.292/.401/.488	.326	62.1	.339	-1.9	CF(152): -17.5	4.8
2016	PIT	MLB	29	675	81	26	3	24	79	69	143	6	7	.256/.336/.430	.275	30.5	.297	-0.3	CF(151): -9.4	2.2
2017	PIT	MLB	30	650	94	30	2	28	88	73	116	11	5	.279/.363/.486	.303	50.2	.305	1.0	CF(139): -10.3, RF(13): -0.7	3.9
2018	*PIT*	*MLB*	*31*	*652*	*89*	*31*	*3*	*23*	*89*	*76*	*120*	*10*	*5*	*.278/.368/.465*	*.290*	*45.0*	*.315*	*-0.7*	*CF -13*	*2.6*
2019	*PIT*	*MLB*	*32*	*537*	*76*	*28*	*2*	*20*	*73*	*67*	*101*	*7*	*4*	*.280/.375/.475*	*.306*	*41.9*	*.319*	*0.0*	*CF -10*	*3.5*

Breakout: 0% Improve: 45% Collapse: 3% Attrition: 1% MLB: 99% *Comparables: Carlos Beltran, Shin-Soo Choo, Bernie Williams*

Something is wrong. That's all there is to it. Baseball is not quite right, not quite in its natural balance, and nowhere is the evidence clearer than in the volatility to which so many of even the game's greatest and most consistent players now seem subject. For McCutchen, that meant a .200/.271/.359 slash line over his first 45 games, then (after a move down in the batting order) .370/.473/.685 in 57 games through the end of July, then (maybe dispirited by the fact that the Pirates didn't trade him) a .235/.301/.341 nightmare over the final two months. He's still one of the best hitters in MLB when he's right, but he's not right as often as he used to be. He's also become almost unplayable in center field, which applies extra pressure to avoid slumps like the ones that have eaten so much of his last two seasons.

Austin Meadows OF Born: 05/03/95 Age: 23 Bats: L Throws: L Height: 6'3" Weight: 200 Origin: Round 1, 2013 Draft (#9 overall)

YEAR	TEAM	LVL	AGE	PA	R	2B	3B	HR	RBI	BB	K	SB	CS	AVG/OBP/SLG	TAv	VORP	BABIP	BRR	FRAA	WARP
2015	BRD	A+	20	556	72	22	4	7	54	41	79	20	7	.307/.357/.407	.289	32.0	.351	-0.1	CF(114): -15.2	1.8
2015	ALT	AA	20	28	5	2	3	0	1	2	5	1	0	.360/.429/.680	.375	3.9	.450	-0.2	CF(6): -0.3	0.4
2016	ALT	AA	21	190	33	16	8	6	23	16	32	9	3	.311/.365/.611	.332	19.7	.343	0.8	CF(39): 2.4, LF(2): -0.6	2.3
2016	IND	AAA	21	145	16	7	3	6	24	15	34	8	2	.214/.297/.460	.291	9.6	.236	0.9	CF(23): -3.1, LF(11): -0.2	0.7
2017	IND	AAA	22	312	48	19	0	4	36	24	50	11	3	.250/.311/.359	.250	8.5	.289	3.7	CF(33): -1.9, LF(24): -0.8	0.6
2018	*PIT*	*MLB*	*23*	*61*	*8*	*3*	*1*	*2*	*7*	*4*	*12*	*2*	*1*	*.254/.309/.420*	*.254*	*2.1*	*.295*	*0.2*	*CF -1*	*0.1*
2019	*PIT*	*MLB*	*24*	*333*	*41*	*17*	*3*	*11*	*42*	*26*	*73*	*10*	*3*	*.254/.315/.438*	*.267*	*13.3*	*.296*	*1.3*	*CF -3*	*1.1*

Breakout: 2% Improve: 22% Collapse: 6% Attrition: 19% MLB: 49% *Comparables: Desmond Jennings, Austin Jackson, Gary Brown*

After 2016, there was so much buzz around Meadows that a Pirates franchise icon couldn't shake trade rumors. Now, after another season shortened by injury and with power still not in evidence, Meadows is no one's center fielder of the future. He's coming up on 500 Triple-A plate appearances, and maybe he will prove (like Jesse Winker of the Reds did) that his slow development was a matter of circumstance. He might not be a center fielder at all anymore, though, and that would obviously add pressure to the development of his offensive game.

Jordy Mercer SS Born: 08/27/86 Age: 31 Bats: R Throws: R Height: 6'3" Weight: 210 Origin: Round 3, 2008 Draft (#79 overall)

YEAR	TEAM	LVL	AGE	PA	R	2B	3B	HR	RBI	BB	K	SB	CS	AVG/OBP/SLG	TAv	VORP	BABIP	BRR	FRAA	WARP
2015	IND	AAA	28	26	3	0	0	1	3	1	5	0	0	.240/.269/.360	.241	0.3	.263	-0.2	SS(7): 0.5	0.1
2015	PIT	MLB	28	430	34	21	0	3	34	27	73	3	2	.244/.293/.320	.228	5.4	.290	2.1	SS(115): 2.7	0.9
2016	PIT	MLB	29	584	66	22	3	11	59	51	83	1	1	.256/.328/.374	.258	25.8	.286	3.0	SS(146): -7.4	1.9
2017	PIT	MLB	30	558	52	24	5	14	58	51	88	0	4	.255/.326/.406	.259	22.0	.284	-1.2	SS(144): -18.7	0.3
2018	*PIT*	*MLB*	*31*	*540*	*56*	*24*	*2*	*10*	*55*	*39*	*87*	*2*	*2*	*.251/.307/.372*	*.241*	*15.2*	*.282*	*-1.3*	*SS -7*	*-0.1*
2019	*PIT*	*MLB*	*32*	*464*	*51*	*20*	*1*	*10*	*47*	*36*	*85*	*1*	*1*	*.239/.303/.362*	*.240*	*7.3*	*.275*	*1.2*	*SS -6*	*0.1*

Breakout: 3% Improve: 30% Collapse: 10% Attrition: 11% MLB: 96% *Comparables: Brendan Ryan, Jack Wilson, Cliff Pennington*

Imagine that J.J. Hardy followed exactly the graceful, steady aging curve that he actually traced from his late-twenties into his early-thirties, but started from a lower peak talent level. That's Mercer. He's learning that his modest contact skills and gap power will never be sufficient to make him a star without some walks thrown into the mix, so he's worked hard to shrink his strike zone and force pitchers to come after him. In the field, he has eliminated the erratic throws of his younger days and still has very sure hands. He's still an average-plus runner, although a miserable basestealer. Mercer isn't going to take any steps forward from here, and his dwindling range is a concern. For now, though, he's a passable everyday shortstop.

Calvin Mitchell OF Born: 03/08/99 Age: 19 Bats: L Throws: L Height: 6'0" Weight: 190 Origin: Round 2, 2017 Draft (#50 overall)

YEAR	TEAM	LVL	AGE	PA	R	2B	3B	HR	RBI	BB	K	SB	CS	AVG/OBP/SLG	TAv	VORP	BABIP	BRR	FRAA	WARP
2017	PIR	RK	18	185	17	11	0	2	20	24	35	2	3	.245/.351/.352	.255	2.7	.303	-0.9	LF(35): 2.6, CF(3): 0.5	0.5
2018	*PIT*	*MLB*	*19*	*250*	*21*	*9*	*0*	*6*	*25*	*16*	*80*	*0*	*0*	*.196/.250/.313*	*.191*	*-9.9*	*.269*	*-0.5*	*LF 2, CF 0*	*-0.8*
2019	*PIT*	*MLB*	*20*	*323*	*35*	*12*	*1*	*9*	*34*	*23*	*98*	*1*	*0*	*.214/.272/.348*	*.223*	*-5.3*	*.285*	*-0.6*	*LF 3, CF 0*	*-0.3*

Breakout: 0% Improve: 6% Collapse: 2% Attrition: 6% MLB: 12% *Comparables: Nomar Mazara, Engel Beltre, Raul Mondesi*

The Pirates gave Mitchell the full slot bonus amount after taking him 50th overall in June, which came as a modest surprise. He'd slid down draft boards during the spring after becoming pull-conscious and developing some contact issues against the high-level pitching he saw in Southern California, both on the showcase circuit and in his sanctioned high school competition. His approach was more patient and considered during his stint in the Gulf Coast League, suggesting that some of those problems might have been simple anxiousness to prove himself. He's still a good athlete with power projection from the left side, which makes him worth his bonus.

Max Moroff MI Born: 05/13/93 Age: 25 Bats: B Throws: R Height: 5'10" Weight: 185 Origin: Round 16, 2012 Draft (#496 overall)

YEAR	TEAM	LVL	AGE	PA	R	2B	3B	HR	RBI	BB	K	SB	CS	AVG/OBP/SLG	TAv	VORP	BABIP	BRR	FRAA	WARP
2015	ALT	AA	22	612	79	28	6	7	51	70	111	17	13	.293/.374/.409	.294	36.6	.356	-0.7	2B(109): 3.5, SS(13): 1.3	4.6
2016	PIT	MLB	23	2	0	0	0	0	0	0	2	0	0	.000/.000/.000	-.014	-0.5	--	0.0		-0.1
2016	IND	AAA	23	520	61	18	4	8	45	90	129	9	7	.230/.367/.349	.272	20.9	.311	-1.3	2B(61): 1.6, 3B(43): -1.5	2.3
2017	IND	AAA	24	228	31	10	0	13	37	41	59	5	2	.254/.390/.519	.310	22.4	.298	1.0	SS(29): 0.4, 2B(18): 1.5	2.3
2017	PIT	MLB	24	140	19	4	1	3	21	16	43	0	1	.200/.302/.325	.242	2.8	.280	0.7	2B(28): -1.8, SS(16): 2.4	0.4
2018	*PIT*	*MLB*	*25*	*62*	*8*	*2*	*0*	*2*	*7*	*8*	*16*	*1*	*1*	*.235/.338/.386*	*.257*	*2.4*	*.299*	*-0.1*	*SS 1, 2B 0*	*0.2*
2019	*PIT*	*MLB*	*26*	*285*	*38*	*11*	*2*	*9*	*34*	*39*	*74*	*3*	*2*	*.241/.349/.414*	*.275*	*13.6*	*.302*	*-0.3*	*SS 2, 2B 1*	*1.8*

Breakout: 7% Improve: 22% Collapse: 13% Attrition: 32% MLB: 56% *Comparables: Logan Forsythe, Chris Taylor, Jed Lowrie*

Moroff has a patient, polished approach. He has good instincts and good hands, and isn't so bad a raw athlete as to render any of that moot. He has the basic ingredients of a pretty good utility player. Here's the thing: he can't hit velocity. In fact, he can't even make contact against it. Moroff swung at 53 pitches that registered 94 mph or faster last season and missed 20 of them. His overall contact rate on swings was under 67 percent. Other guys who whiff that often on swings against elite velocity include Miguel Sano, Keon Broxton and Ian Happ, which gives you an idea of how you can make up for that deficiency: hit for power when you do connect. Alas, Moroff doesn't do that, so he's a very low-ceiling offensive player.

Kevin Newman SS Born: 08/04/93 Age: 24 Bats: R Throws: R Height: 6'1" Weight: 180 Origin: Round 1, 2015 Draft (#19 overall)

YEAR	TEAM	LVL	AGE	PA	R	2B	3B	HR	RBI	BB	K	SB	CS	AVG/OBP/SLG	TAv	VORP	BABIP	BRR	FRAA	WARP
2015	WEV	A-	21	173	25	10	1	2	9	10	22	7	1	.226/.281/.340	.260	5.9	.252	-1.0	SS(38): -6.3	0.0
2015	WVA	A	21	110	14	4	1	0	8	9	8	6	1	.306/.376/.367	.289	7.3	.333	-0.4	SS(23): 0.3	0.8
2016	BRD	A+	22	189	24	10	1	3	24	17	12	4	1	.366/.428/.494	.355	28.1	.375	1.4	SS(38): 1.4	3.0
2016	ALT	AA	22	268	41	11	2	2	28	26	24	6	3	.288/.361/.378	.268	14.8	.308	2.3	SS(60): 0.3	1.6
2017	ALT	AA	23	375	42	18	2	4	30	22	40	4	2	.259/.310/.359	.254	14.0	.282	1.4	SS(78): 0.6	1.6
2017	IND	AAA	23	178	23	11	2	0	11	7	22	7	1	.283/.314/.373	.251	4.7	.324	-1.3	SS(38): 0.4	0.5
2018	*PIT*	*MLB*	*24*	*250*	*29*	*12*	*1*	*5*	*24*	*16*	*39*	*3*	*1*	*.261/.312/.394*	*.242*	*6.9*	*.288*	*-0.1*	*SS 0*	*0.7*
2019	*PIT*	*MLB*	*25*	*339*	*38*	*16*	*2*	*8*	*37*	*21*	*53*	*4*	*1*	*.258/.310/.397*	*.257*	*10.5*	*.285*	*-0.1*	*SS 0*	*1.1*

Breakout: 7% Improve: 17% Collapse: 12% Attrition: 28% MLB: 45% *Comparables: Adam Frazier, Cristhian Adames, Dixon Machado*

Newman is knocking on the door to the big leagues—still making plenty of contact, fielding shortstop at an average-plus level and running well enough to add a run or two to the ledger. He's just saddled with a cruelly low ceiling because of his lack of power, which makes thrusting him into a regular big-league role to get a sense of his floor an unappealing option for most teams.

Jose Osuna OF Born: 12/12/92 Age: 25 Bats: R Throws: R Height: 6'3" Weight: 240 Origin: International Free Agent, 2009

YEAR	TEAM	LVL	AGE	PA	R	2B	3B	HR	RBI	BB	K	SB	CS	AVG/OBP/SLG	TAv	VORP	BABIP	BRR	FRAA	WARP
2015	BRD	A+	22	193	23	12	1	4	29	14	33	1	1	.282/.333/.431	.296	9.3	.321	-0.6	RF(32): -2.9, 1B(10): -0.6	0.6
2015	ALT	AA	22	349	46	20	2	8	52	17	61	6	3	.288/.327/.437	.269	10.0	.328	1.1	LF(45): -3.7, 1B(32): 2.2	1.0
2016	ALT	AA	23	283	34	18	3	6	38	23	44	1	1	.269/.329/.435	.277	8.3	.298	0.3	1B(55): -3.2, RF(9): -0.5	0.6
2016	IND	AAA	23	234	27	19	1	7	31	13	36	2	3	.291/.333/.482	.280	8.8	.322	0.3	1B(27): 0.9, LF(24): 3.9	1.4
2017	IND	AAA	24	41	6	5	0	0	1	5	9	1	1	.250/.341/.389	.271	1.2	.333	0.1	1B(6): -0.2, RF(2): 0.0	0.1
2017	PIT	MLB	24	227	31	13	4	7	30	9	40	0	0	.233/.269/.428	.239	-1.4	.254	-0.7	RF(25): -0.4, 1B(23): -1.1	-0.2
2018	*PIT*	*MLB*	*25*	*204*	*22*	*12*	*1*	*6*	*26*	*11*	*41*	*1*	*1*	*.251/.294/.422*	*.248*	*3.1*	*.287*	*-0.3*	*RF 0, LF 0*	*0.2*
2019	*PIT*	*MLB*	*26*	*338*	*40*	*19*	*2*	*11*	*42*	*22*	*70*	*1*	*1*	*.252/.304/.430*	*.261*	*6.9*	*.291*	*-0.7*	*RF 0, LF -1*	*0.7*

Breakout: 6% Improve: 21% Collapse: 15% Attrition: 31% MLB: 53% *Comparables: Moises Sierra, Alfredo Marte, Rene Tosoni*

Nicknamed El Gocho (the hog), Osuna got his chance to belly up to the trough only after a very long trek through the minor leagues. The nice way to characterize his frame (a courtesy his teammates were apparently unwilling to extend) would be beefy. He's never going to add value as a defender, and unless or until he moderates his approach he's probably not going to add much at the plate, either. His pop isn't so good that he can be of much value if he's not getting on base very often, and there's no clear path to him getting on base very often. It's power enough to grant him a little time to figure things out, though.

Eury Perez OF Born: 05/30/90 Age: 28 Bats: R Throws: R Height: 6'0" Weight: 190 Origin: International Free Agent, 2009

YEAR	TEAM	LVL	AGE	PA	R	2B	3B	HR	RBI	BB	K	SB	CS	AVG/OBP/SLG	TAv	VORP	BABIP	BRR	FRAA	WARP
2015	ATL	MLB	25	133	10	4	0	0	5	7	23	3	1	.269/.331/.303	.229	0.2	.333	1.4	LF(29): 1.2, RF(6): 1.0	0.2
2015	GWN	AAA	25	271	35	8	2	2	21	22	39	28	8	.297/.370/.373	.278	13.6	.347	2.6	CF(25): -0.8, RF(23): -0.4	1.5
2016	FRE	AAA	26	146	17	4	3	2	16	5	25	9	4	.267/.298/.385	.250	2.3	.315	0.6	LF(28): 0.4, RF(19): 0.9	0.3
2016	DUR	AAA	26	99	15	2	2	0	4	5	18	11	2	.239/.295/.307	.236	1.7	.300	1.7	CF(16): 1.1, LF(5): 0.3	0.4
2017	IND	AAA	27	155	26	6	2	1	12	12	23	22	5	.336/.400/.433	.304	12.8	.396	0.4	CF(36): -2.9, RF(5): -0.7	0.9
2017	NWO	AAA	27	115	15	9	1	0	12	5	17	9	3	.375/.411/.481	.313	8.3	.443	-1.4	LF(13): 4.1, CF(6): 0.5	1.3
2018	*PIT*	*MLB*	*28*	*250*	*35*	*10*	*2*	*4*	*21*	*13*	*45*	*18*	*5*	*.276/.328/.394*	*.242*	*5.9*	*.318*	*1.7*	*CF -3, LF 1*	*0.3*
2019	*PIT*	*MLB*	*29*	*200*	*22*	*8*	*1*	*3*	*20*	*11*	*38*	*14*	*4*	*.270/.323/.385*	*.252*	*5.5*	*.314*	*1.8*	*CF -2, LF 1*	*0.4*

Breakout: 3% Improve: 25% Collapse: 10% Attrition: 21% MLB: 49% *Comparables: Jason Bourgeois, Chris Roberson, Ezequiel Carrera*

Undebatable truths: 280 characters on Twitter is a terrible idea, Baja Blast is the only acceptable alternative flavor of Mountain Dew and Eury Perez decimated Triple-A pitching like Bo Jackson in Tecmo Bowl last season. In 77 games split between Indianapolis and New Orleans, Perez slashed an absurd .353/.405/.454 and stole 31 bases. Ryan McMahon, Raimel Tapia and Garrett Cooper—all of whom played their home games on the surface of the moon in Albuquerque and Colorado Springs—were the only hitters to record higher batting averages. There's nothing left for Perez to prove in the minor leagues. He's spent half a decade in Triple-A purgatory acquiring the dreaded Quad-A label and deserves an extended opportunity at the major-league level to finally shed it.

Gregory Polanco RF Born: 09/14/91 Age: 26 Bats: L Throws: L Height: 6'5" Weight: 235 Origin: International Free Agent, 2009

YEAR	TEAM	LVL	AGE	PA	R	2B	3B	HR	RBI	BB	K	SB	CS	AVG/OBP/SLG	TAv	VORP	BABIP	BRR	FRAA	WARP
2015	PIT	MLB	23	652	83	35	6	9	52	55	121	27	10	.256/.320/.381	.264	15.2	.308	1.3	RF(144): 11.2, LF(8): 0.2	2.8
2016	PIT	MLB	24	587	79	34	4	22	86	53	119	17	6	.258/.323/.463	.276	19.6	.291	-1.0	RF(111): 9.8, LF(29): 0.1	3.0
2017	PIT	MLB	25	411	39	20	0	11	35	27	60	8	1	.251/.305/.391	.248	3.4	.272	0.5	RF(68): 4.1, LF(25): -2.6	0.5
2018	*PIT*	*MLB*	*26*	*509*	*62*	*25*	*3*	*13*	*59*	*41*	*91*	*16*	*5*	*.254/.315/.406*	*.253*	*9.6*	*.288*	*1.1*	*RF 2*	*1.0*
2019	*PIT*	*MLB*	*27*	*526*	*66*	*27*	*2*	*17*	*65*	*48*	*99*	*16*	*5*	*.258/.328/.432*	*.273*	*18.4*	*.292*	*0.5*	*RF 3*	*2.4*

Breakout: 6% Improve: 48% Collapse: 5% Attrition: 15% MLB: 95% *Comparables: Alex Rios, Al Cowens, Mark Teahen*

For the man whose nickname is El Coffee, the 2017 season was a latte left on the roof of the car. Strains in the same hamstring sidelined him three separate times, taking a huge bite out of his season. When he played, he made a lot of contact, but lost the power he'd found in 2016 and stopped drawing walks. He's still big and fluid and gifted, but there's now ample reason to wonder whether he's going to consistently stay healthy—not just healthy enough to play, but healthy enough to tap into all of that natural ability. It's one thing to be hurt and another to be bad. When a player with Polanco's tools plays hurt and plays badly for such a prolonged period, it's tough to tell if getting healthy will be enough to restore the player to their full self.

Sean Rodriguez 2B Born: 04/26/85 Age: 33 Bats: R Throws: R Height: 6'0" Weight: 200 Origin: Round 3, 2003 Draft (#90 overall)

YEAR	TEAM	LVL	AGE	PA	R	2B	3B	HR	RBI	BB	K	SB	CS	AVG/OBP/SLG	TAv	VORP	BABIP	BRR	FRAA	WARP
2015	PIT	MLB	30	240	25	12	1	4	17	5	63	2	2	.246/.281/.362	.230	-0.9	.325	2.2	1B(102): -0.8, LF(16): -1.9	-0.4
2016	PIT	MLB	31	342	49	16	1	18	56	33	102	2	1	.270/.349/.510	.296	20.6	.344	-0.9	1B(57): 4.1, 2B(29): -0.1	2.3
2017	GWN	AAA	32	25	1	0	0	0	2	4	5	0	0	.056/.240/.056	.159	-2.1	.067	-0.1	2B(3): 0.2, SS(1): 0.2	-0.2
2017	ATL	MLB	32	47	6	1	0	2	3	8	19	1	0	.162/.326/.351	.237	0.3	.250	0.1	3B(5): -0.7, 2B(4): -0.1	-0.1
2017	PIT	MLB	32	106	12	1	0	3	5	8	38	0	0	.168/.255/.274	.193	-3.1	.241	1.1	RF(9): 0.0, 3B(9): 1.7	0.0
2018	*PIT*	*MLB*	*33*	*271*	*30*	*11*	*1*	*9*	*33*	*18*	*77*	*2*	*1*	*.226/.289/.389*	*.237*	*4.0*	*.285*	*-0.3*	*SS -2, 3B 2*	*0.1*
2019	*PIT*	*MLB*	*34*	*206*	*25*	*8*	*1*	*7*	*25*	*14*	*61*	*1*	*0*	*.223/.291/.394*	*.245*	*2.8*	*.283*	*0.5*	*SS -2, 3B 1*	*0.3*

Breakout: 5% Improve: 37% Collapse: 11% Attrition: 18% MLB: 85% *Comparables: Robby Thompson, Brandon Inge, Stephen Drew*

Over the last three years, Rodriguez's strikeout rate has climbed from "well that's not ideal for a utility guy" to "this guy looks overmatched." A car accident last winter that left multiple members of his family injured also cost Rodriguez much of the season. He could still have better days ahead if his shoulder is ever fully healthy again. On balance, though, the march of time and the shaky profile he's always had seem to be nudging Rodriguez toward obsolescence.

Cole Tucker SS Born: 07/03/96 Age: 21 Bats: B Throws: R Height: 6'3" Weight: 185 Origin: Round 1, 2014 Draft (#24 overall)

YEAR	TEAM	LVL	AGE	PA	R	2B	3B	HR	RBI	BB	K	SB	CS	AVG/OBP/SLG	TAv	VORP	BABIP	BRR	FRAA	WARP
2015	WVA	A	18	329	46	13	3	2	25	16	49	25	6	.293/.322/.377	.269	18.7	.336	3.0	SS(69): 2.7	2.3
2016	WVA	A	19	67	9	4	2	1	2	4	9	1	1	.262/.308/.443	.312	6.5	.294	0.5	SS(15): 2.8	1.0
2016	BRD	A+	19	304	36	12	1	1	25	29	62	5	6	.238/.312/.301	.236	3.1	.306	-1.1	SS(61): 12.6	1.6
2017	BRD	A+	20	316	46	15	6	4	32	34	70	36	12	.285/.364/.426	.308	29.6	.368	1.5	SS(66): -0.4	3.1
2017	ALT	AA	20	194	25	4	5	2	18	21	31	11	3	.257/.349/.377	.272	11.3	.304	1.3	SS(39): 0.9	1.3
2018	*PIT*	*MLB*	*21*	*250*	*31*	*10*	*2*	*5*	*21*	*18*	*60*	*10*	*4*	*.238/.297/.365*	*.226*	*3.6*	*.295*	*0.8*	*SS 3*	*0.7*
2019	*PIT*	*MLB*	*22*	*367*	*42*	*15*	*4*	*8*	*40*	*29*	*84*	*16*	*6*	*.253/.316/.396*	*.256*	*12.9*	*.308*	*2.0*	*SS 4*	*1.9*

Breakout: 3% Improve: 9% Collapse: 0% Attrition: 6% MLB: 15% *Comparables: Tyler Wade, Yolmer Sanchez, Amed Rosario*

You'd expect a guy of Tucker's size to be slower, or at least less smooth and fluid at shortstop. He is surprisingly natural, and has spent his whole pro career silencing those who questioned his ability to stick at short. Over the last two seasons, he has also developed a much more advanced approach, and when healthy he has demonstrated a willingness to put his speed to its maximal use on the bases. Whereas doubts about his defense now seem ill-founded, it does seem fair to wonder whether he'll retain his top speed and base-stealing ability as that long, lean body ages. The last obstacle to Tucker becoming a first-division regular, at least for a few years, is his lack of power, and his body type says that could change any minute.

Erich Weiss 2B Born: 09/11/91 Age: 26 Bats: L Throws: R Height: 6'2" Weight: 200 Origin: Round 11, 2013 Draft (#329 overall)

YEAR	TEAM	LVL	AGE	PA	R	2B	3B	HR	RBI	BB	K	SB	CS	AVG/OBP/SLG	TAv	VORP	BABIP	BRR	FRAA	WARP
2015	BRD	A+	23	428	46	17	2	3	49	41	70	11	4	.285/.362/.366	.282	17.5	.340	-2.4	2B(93): -0.8	1.8
2015	ALT	AA	23	124	15	4	1	0	14	8	22	4	2	.250/.290/.304	.217	-2.4	.298	0.2	2B(24): 1.2	-0.1
2016	ALT	AA	24	520	56	24	9	6	65	49	90	6	3	.276/.352/.408	.274	17.9	.331	-2.7	2B(118): 12.2	3.2
2017	IND	AAA	25	377	50	23	4	6	43	38	67	6	2	.274/.353/.422	.280	19.6	.324	0.5	2B(55): -0.8, 3B(30): -1.2	1.7
2018	*PIT*	*MLB*	*26*	*250*	*26*	*11*	*2*	*6*	*28*	*22*	*55*	*2*	*1*	*.248/.320/.390*	*.242*	*4.5*	*.300*	*-0.1*	*2B 1, 3B 0*	*0.6*
2019	*PIT*	*MLB*	*27*	*317*	*36*	*13*	*2*	*7*	*33*	*28*	*74*	*2*	*1*	*.241/.313/.375*	*.249*	*5.0*	*.298*	*-0.2*	*2B 2, 3B 0*	*0.7*

Breakout: 5% Improve: 21% Collapse: 9% Attrition: 27% MLB: 33% *Comparables: Steve Tolleson, Brian Dinkelman, Andrew Burns*

Weiss is likely too thick and not quite quick enough to play second base, and will never have the power to profile at third. On the right roster, however, he might still have some value. He has a very polished approach and enough speed not to clog the bases. He also has great hands. Given his age and his limitations, there's no guarantee that he ever gets much of a shot. He certainly doesn't figure to be a regular on any team that wants to contend, unless they get power from some other, unlikely place on the diamond.

Eric Wood 4C Born: 11/22/92 Age: 25 Bats: R Throws: R Height: 6'2" Weight: 195 Origin: Round 6, 2012 Draft (#196 overall)

YEAR	TEAM	LVL	AGE	PA	R	2B	3B	HR	RBI	BB	K	SB	CS	AVG/OBP/SLG	TAv	VORP	BABIP	BRR	FRAA	WARP
2015	ALT	AA	22	373	39	11	3	2	28	32	88	3	7	.237/.303/.305	.228	-1.8	.312	-0.6	3B(89): -4.4	-0.7
2016	ALT	AA	23	464	63	20	5	16	50	52	88	5	4	.249/.339/.443	.281	23.9	.278	-0.1	3B(113): -0.9	2.5
2017	IND	AAA	24	473	58	25	5	16	61	45	125	7	1	.238/.311/.438	.257	12.2	.293	1.5	3B(73): -3.2, 1B(26): 1.3	1.1
2018	*PIT*	*MLB*	*25*	*250*	*27*	*10*	*1*	*9*	*31*	*23*	*67*	*2*	*1*	*.226/.302/.401*	*.237*	*1.4*	*.279*	*-0.2*	*3B -2, 1B 0*	*0.0*
2019	*PIT*	*MLB*	*26*	*308*	*38*	*12*	*2*	*11*	*38*	*29*	*83*	*2*	*1*	*.226/.303/.403*	*.253*	*4.2*	*.279*	*-0.3*	*3B -2, 1B 0*	*0.3*

Breakout: 5% Improve: 9% Collapse: 7% Attrition: 19% MLB: 23% *Comparables: Matthew Duffy, Jamie Romak, Hunter Dozier*

After impressing in the Arizona Fall League in 2016, Wood was an everyday player and key contributor for the International League champion Indianapolis Indians. He didn't get a big-league cup of coffee, but one feels increasingly likely. His profile—a right-handed hitter with some contact issues at the plate and no defensive home that matches his offensive value—has a very low ceiling, but Wood has perhaps average power, a steady approach and general athleticism that could play up if he ever develops better hands or defensive instincts. For now, he's just good organizational depth.

PITCHERS

John Barbato RHP Born: 07/11/92 Age: 25 Bats: R Throws: R Height: 6'1" Weight: 235 Origin: Round 6, 2010 Draft (#184 overall)

YEAR	TEAM	LVL	AGE	W	L	SV	G	GS	IP	H	HR	BB/9	K/9	K	GB%	BABIP	WHIP	ERA	DRA	WARP	MPH	CMD	PWR	STM
2015	TRN	AA	22	2	2	0	26	0	42^1	42	4	3.0	9.4	44	41%	.330	1.32	4.04	2.28	1.2				
2015	SWB	AAA	22	4	0	3	14	0	25	13	1	4.0	9.4	26	47%	.211	0.96	0.36	3.77	0.3				
2016	NYA	MLB	23	1	2	0	13	0	13	13	2	3.5	10.4	15	46%	.333	1.38	7.62	4.44	0.1	96.6	53	44	44
2016	SWB	AAA	23	3	2	3	31	1	48^1	38	3	4.3	9.1	49	47%	.276	1.26	2.61	4.57	0.2				
2017	IND	AAA	24	0	1	4	26	2	35^1	28	7	2.8	9.2	36	34%	.236	1.10	3.06	4.01	0.5				
2017	PIT	MLB	24	0	1	0	24	0	28^2	25	4	5.7	7.2	23	40%	.253	1.50	4.08	5.68	-0.2	95.3	53	48	45
2018	*PIT*	*MLB*	*25*	*2*	*2*	*0*	*44*	*0*	*46*	*46*	*8*	*4.2*	*8.6*	*44*	*41%*	*.296*	*1.46*	*5.35*	*5.28*	*-0.2*	*95.4*	*54*	*48*	*46*
2019	*PIT*	*MLB*	*26*	*2*	*1*	*0*	*46*	*0*	*48^1*	*43*	*8*	*3.6*	*9.2*	*50*	*41%*	*.303*	*1.30*	*4.67*	*5.21*	*0.0*	*95.1*	*54*	*48*	*46*

Breakout: 20% Improve: 25% Collapse: 17% Attrition: 32% MLB: 46% *Comparables: Mike Zagurski, Greg Holland, Jim Hoey*

Barbato's surname is pronounced like Doug E. Fresh's native island, which makes the unassuming pitcher sound like he should be a Hawaiian-shirt-wearing beach detective. That's not all that doesn't match, either. He has the velocity, the high-effort delivery and the fringy command of a possible setup arm, but he has a starter's determination to throw two different breaking balls. If he ever scraps one, he might get better at throwing and commanding the other, and the fastball too. If he never does, maybe there's still time to buy a houseboat and start solving crimes of coastal pollution with a pet parrot.

Shane Baz RHP Born: 06/17/99 Age: 18 Bats: R Throws: R Height: 6'3" Weight: 190 Origin: Round 1, 2017 Draft (#12 overall)

YEAR	TEAM	LVL	AGE	W	L	SV	G	GS	IP	H	HR	BB/9	K/9	K	GB%	BABIP	WHIP	ERA	DRA	WARP	MPH	CMD	PWR	STM
2017	PIR	RK	18	0	3	0	10	10	23^2	26	2	5.3	7.2	19	51%	.348	1.69	3.80	6.55	-0.1				
2018	*PIT*	*MLB*	*19*	*1*	*4*	*0*	*8*	*8*	*30^1*	*36*	*8*	*8.6*	*8.1*	*27*	*40%*	*.330*	*2.15*	*8.01*	*9.00*	*-1.1*				
2019	*PIT*	*MLB*	*20*	*3*	*9*	*0*	*26*	*26*	*154^1*	*183*	*36*	*4.9*	*6.8*	*117*	*40%*	*.33*	*1.73*	*6.64*	*7.46*	*-1.9*				

Comparables: Alberto Cabrera, Jenrry Mejia, Alex Reyes

Baz attended the same suburban Houston high school as Ke'Bryan Hayes, and was taken in the first round by the same team that took Hayes in the same round two years earlier. Hayes is a third baseman, and if Baz had ended up honoring his commitment to TCU, he'd have been one too (between starts anyway). As it is, though, he's a power pitcher with huge upside. He spent the offseason leading up to his senior season adding strength and stability, and hit 98 mph in the run-up to the draft—up around 5 mph from his previous high. Trackman says he has elite spin rate on the pitch, too. He merged his slider and cutter into a single pitch, for simplicity's sake, and will spend 2018 honing his other, lesser secondary offerings.

Joaquin Benoit RHP Born: 07/26/77 Age: 40 Bats: R Throws: R Height: 6'4" Weight: 250 Origin: International Free Agent, 1996

YEAR	TEAM	LVL	AGE	W	L	SV	G	GS	IP	H	HR	BB/9	K/9	K	GB%	BABIP	WHIP	ERA	DRA	WARP	MPH	CMD	PWR	STM
2015	SDN	MLB	37	6	5	2	67	0	65^1	36	7	3.2	8.7	63	48%	.182	0.90	2.34	2.37	1.8	96.8	45	49	50
2016	SEA	MLB	38	1	1	0	26	0	24^1	20	4	5.5	10.4	28	43%	.254	1.44	5.18	3.58	0.4	96.8	45	50	40
2016	TOR	MLB	38	2	0	1	25	0	23^2	17	1	3.4	9.1	24	38%	.271	1.10	0.38	4.09	0.2	96.5	45	50	40
2017	PHI	MLB	39	1	4	2	44	0	42	32	5	3.4	9.2	43	35%	.252	1.14	4.07	4.25	0.4	96.1	64	56	44
2017	PIT	MLB	39	0	2	0	8	0	8^1	11	2	6.5	3.2	3	38%	.300	2.04	7.56	2.78	0.2	95.9	64	56	44
2018	*PIT*	*MLB*	*40*	*2*	*1*	*1*	*41*	*0*	43^2	*39*	*6*	*3.9*	*7.8*	*38*	*41%*	*.279*	*1.32*	*4.66*	*5.22*	*0.0*	*94.7*	*51*	*50*	*43*
2019	*PIT*	*MLB*	*41*	*1*	*0*	*1*	*31*	*0*	30^1	*28*	*5*	*4.0*	*6.7*	*23*	*41%*	*.271*	*1.36*	*5.55*	*6.21*	*-0.3*	*93.9*	*53*	*51*	*41*

Breakout: 35% Improve: 45% Collapse: 20% Attrition: 7% MLB: 82% *Comparables: Arthur Rhodes, Tom Gordon, Takashi Saito*

Increasingly reliant on his fastball and changeup, and with age threatening to take the last bit of zip he's using to get by, Benoit is no longer a reliever on whom a contender can rely in a high-leverage situation. He still gets outs when he's hitting his spots, but he's become an extreme fly-ball guy, and in this day and age that makes a pitcher extremely and inevitably homer-prone. There's no way Benoit's 2010-2015 stretch will be remembered as well as it deserves, which is a shame. Then again, it's not in the nature of relievers (especially if they mostly didn't close, and never closed for a championship team) to be remembered as well as they should be.

Steven Brault LHP Born: 04/29/92 Age: 26 Bats: L Throws: L Height: 6'0" Weight: 200 Origin: Round 11, 2013 Draft (#339 overall)

YEAR	TEAM	LVL	AGE	W	L	SV	G	GS	IP	H	HR	BB/9	K/9	K	GB%	BABIP	WHIP	ERA	DRA	WARP	MPH	CMD	PWR	STM
2015	BRD	A+	23	4	1	0	13	13	65^2	62	3	2.9	6.2	45	52%	.292	1.26	3.02	4.27	0.6				
2015	ALT	AA	23	9	3	0	15	15	90	72	1	1.9	8.0	80	51%	.273	1.01	2.00	1.99	3.4				
2016	IND	AAA	24	2	7	0	16	15	71^1	66	6	4.4	10.2	81	39%	.319	1.42	3.91	2.57	2.2				
2016	PIT	MLB	24	0	3	0	8	7	33^1	45	5	4.6	7.8	29	47%	.354	1.86	4.86	7.29	-0.7	93.8	53	50	51
2017	IND	AAA	25	10	5	0	21	20	120^1	85	5	3.3	8.2	109	53%	.252	1.07	1.94	1.97	4.9				
2017	PIT	MLB	25	1	0	1	11	4	34^2	41	3	3.6	6.0	23	45%	.317	1.59	4.67	6.58	-0.5	93.6	42	54	66
2018	*PIT*	*MLB*	*26*	*5*	*5*	*0*	*13*	*13*	*78*	*73*	*8*	*3.5*	*7.9*	*69*	*46%*	*.292*	*1.31*	*4.03*	*4.29*	*0.8*	*93.3*	*48*	*53*	*60*
2019	*PIT*	*MLB*	*27*	*11*	*11*	*0*	*32*	*32*	206^1	*176*	*22*	*3.2*	*8.3*	*190*	*46%*	*.292*	*1.20*	*3.93*	*4.41*	*2.5*	*93.0*	*48*	*53*	*61*

Breakout: 27% Improve: 55% Collapse: 18% Attrition: 29% MLB: 84% *Comparables: Erik Johnson, Jimmy Nelson, Taylor Jungmann*

Brault is coming up on 200 innings of sheer dominance in the International League, but in 68 frames of big-league work he's been dreadful. There are a few problems, including generally substandard command. Mostly, though, he seems like a victim of the Pirates' organizational edict that every pitcher hone both a four-seam fastball and a sinker. Brault's sinker is no good. It doesn't do anything his changeup doesn't do, movement-wise, and the velocity gap between the two isn't enough to allow the pitches to play off each other. He could scrap that offering and focus on his four-seamer, slider and changeup. If he ends up in the bullpen, Brault could also marginalize the change and things would get interesting. A former aspiring musician, he seems more suited to the funky life of a lefty reliever than to the classical gig of starting.

Nick Burdi RHP Born: 01/19/93 Age: 25 Bats: R Throws: R Height: 6'5" Weight: 220 Origin: Round 2, 2014 Draft (#46 overall)

YEAR	TEAM	LVL	AGE	W	L	SV	G	GS	IP	H	HR	BB/9	K/9	K	GB%	BABIP	WHIP	ERA	DRA	WARP	MPH	CMD	PWR	STM
2015	FTM	A+	22	2	2	2	13	0	20	12	1	1.4	13.1	29	44%	.275	0.75	2.25	1.27	0.8				
2015	CHT	AA	22	3	4	2	30	0	43^2	40	3	6.6	11.1	54	49%	.322	1.65	4.53	4.05	0.4				
2017	CHT	AA	24	2	0	1	14	0	17	9	1	2.1	10.6	20	46%	.222	0.76	0.53	2.57	0.5				
2018	*PIT*	*MLB*	*25*	*2*	*1*	*1*	*33*	*0*	35^1	*33*	*5*	*4.4*	*10.1*	*40*	*43%*	*.321*	*1.42*	*4.46*	*4.98*	*0.1*				
2019	*PIT*	*MLB*	*26*	*1*	*0*	*1*	*30*	*0*	*39*	*39*	*8*	*4.9*	*9.8*	*43*	*43%*	*.307*	*1.55*	*5.44*	*5.58*	*-0.1*				

Breakout: 18% Improve: 26% Collapse: 7% Attrition: 27% MLB: 35% *Comparables: Jimmie Sherfy, Cody Ege, A.J. Ramos*

After two months spent overpowering Double-A batters with triple-digit heat, Burdi suffered his latest medical setback and underwent Tommy John surgery. The best indicator of his still-smoldering late-innings potential is that the Braves considered taking him in the Jaime Garcia trade even though he won't be back on the mound until 2019. He might be 26 years old the next time he throws a competitive pitch, but the velocity is worth waiting on.

Gerrit Cole RHP Born: 09/08/90 Age: 27 Bats: R Throws: R Height: 6'4" Weight: 225 Origin: Round 1, 2011 Draft (#1 overall)

YEAR	TEAM	LVL	AGE	W	L	SV	G	GS	IP	H	HR	BB/9	K/9	K	GB%	BABIP	WHIP	ERA	DRA	WARP	MPH	CMD	PWR	STM
2015	PIT	MLB	24	19	8	0	32	32	208	183	11	1.9	8.7	202	49%	.304	1.09	2.60	3.10	4.9	98.6	42	70	79
2016	PIT	MLB	25	7	10	0	21	21	116	131	7	2.8	7.6	98	48%	.345	1.44	3.88	4.19	1.6	98.3	49	63	56
2017	PIT	MLB	26	12	12	0	33	33	203	199	31	2.4	8.7	196	47%	.298	1.25	4.26	4.15	3.2	98.0	63	65	82
2018	*PIT*	*MLB*	*27*	*11*	*9*	*0*	*28*	*28*	*168*	*158*	*18*	*2.7*	*8.5*	*159*	*47%*	*.298*	*1.24*	*3.62*	*3.85*	*2.6*	*97.8*	*54*	*67*	*73*
2019	*PIT*	*MLB*	*28*	*12*	*10*	*0*	*33*	*33*	*213*	*184*	*22*	*2.1*	*8.9*	*210*	*47%*	*.304*	*1.10*	*3.35*	*3.76*	*4.0*	*97.4*	*58*	*65*	*72*

Breakout: 23% Improve: 52% Collapse: 23% Attrition: 9% MLB: 94% *Comparables: Jose Quintana, David Price, Mat Latos*

Late in 2016, Cole found a changeup he liked more than the previous versions and started throwing it more often. Suddenly in love with the depth of his arsenal, he came out in 2017 throwing that pitch, splitting his fastball usage more evenly between four-seamers and sinkers, and still throwing both his slider and his curve. It looked and felt about as natural as Earl Campbell dancing around in the backfield like Barry Sanders, and it was a total flop. After 13 starts, he had a 4.83 ERA and had allowed 15 home runs. From then on, he went back to throwing his four-seamer about half the time, put the sinker and changeup back on the shelf and posted a 3.91 ERA (while striking out about 25 percent of opposing batters) in his last 20 outings. If that still sounds underwhelming, given the pedigree, well, that's why he tinkered in the first place.

Luis Escobar RHP Born: 05/30/96 Age: 22 Bats: R Throws: R Height: 6'1" Weight: 155 Origin: International Free Agent, 2013

YEAR	TEAM	LVL	AGE	W	L	SV	G	GS	IP	H	HR	BB/9	K/9	K	GB%	BABIP	WHIP	ERA	DRA	WARP	MPH	CMD	PWR	STM
2015	PIR	RK	19	2	1	0	11	11	40^{2}	29	1	2.9	8.2	37	47%	.252	1.03	3.54	3.11	1.2				
2016	WEV	A-	20	6	5	0	15	12	67^{2}	50	4	3.7	8.1	61	43%	.254	1.15	2.93	5.00	0.1				
2017	WVA	A	21	10	7	0	26	25	131^{2}	97	9	4.1	11.5	168	44%	.282	1.19	3.83	2.98	3.5				
2018	*PIT*	*MLB*	*22*	*6*	*8*	*0*	*22*	*22*	*100*	*100*	*21*	*5.1*	*9.9*	*110*	*36%*	*.320*	*1.57*	*5.63*	*6.28*	*-0.7*				
2019	*PIT*	*MLB*	*23*	*4*	*8*	*0*	*18*	*18*	*108*	*111*	*22*	*5.1*	*9.5*	*114*	*36%*	*.331*	*1.59*	*5.88*	*6.56*	*-0.9*				

Breakout: 5% Improve: 7% Collapse: 5% Attrition: 11% MLB: 13% *Comparables: Robbie Ray, Michael Stutes, Yordano Ventura*

Signed as a skinny teenage infielder out of Colombia, Escobar has blossomed into a thick, flame-throwing pitching prospect and he might even be a starter. His fastball sits comfortably in the mid-90s and scales up to 98 when he needs that much. His breaking ball, a power curve with good depth, made Low-A opponents relatively helpless. That pair of pitches alone points toward a bright future in the bullpen, and for reasons of roster management, he might well end up there. As the season went along Escobar also improved his feel for a changeup, and if he masters that pitch he's a mid-rotation starter with the ability to dominate big-league batters on his good days.

Tyler Glasnow RHP Born: 08/23/93 Age: 24 Bats: L Throws: R Height: 6'8" Weight: 220 Origin: Round 5, 2011 Draft (#152 overall)

YEAR	TEAM	LVL	AGE	W	L	SV	G	GS	IP	H	HR	BB/9	K/9	K	GB%	BABIP	WHIP	ERA	DRA	WARP	MPH	CMD	PWR	STM
2015	ALT	AA	21	5	3	0	12	12	63	41	2	2.7	11.7	82	42%	.269	0.95	2.43	1.33	2.8				
2015	IND	AAA	21	2	1	0	8	8	41	33	1	4.8	10.5	48	39%	.314	1.34	2.20	3.95	0.6				
2016	IND	AAA	22	8	3	0	20	20	110^{2}	65	4	5.0	10.8	133	43%	.255	1.15	1.87	2.80	3.2				
2016	PIT	MLB	22	0	2	0	7	4	23^{1}	22	2	5.0	9.3	24	49%	.317	1.50	4.24	4.02	0.3	96.8	30	48	59
2017	IND	AAA	23	9	2	0	15	15	93^{1}	57	6	3.1	13.5	140	50%	.276	0.95	1.93	1.06	4.7				
2017	PIT	MLB	23	2	7	0	15	13	62	81	13	6.4	8.1	56	44%	.358	2.02	7.69	8.76	-2.2	97.4	35	61	69
2018	*PIT*	*MLB*	*24*	*5*	*5*	*0*	*39*	*10*	*84*	*69*	*9*	*4.5*	*10.8*	*101*	*43%*	*.291*	*1.31*	*3.75*	*3.99*	*1.0*	*97.1*	*35*	*60*	*66*
2019	*PIT*	*MLB*	*25*	*8*	*6*	*0*	*67*	*16*	*146^{1}*	*107*	*16*	*3.7*	*11.1*	*180*	*43%*	*.292*	*1.14*	*3.49*	*3.90*	*2.3*	*96.9*	*35*	*60*	*67*

Breakout: 30% Improve: 66% Collapse: 14% Attrition: 15% MLB: 90% *Comparables: Matt Harvey, Scott Elbert, Matt Moore*

Trying to iron out command and control issues, Glasnow added a rock step and slowed down his delivery in the offseason prior to 2017. It was a calamitous mistake. Demoted to Triple-A Indianapolis after a dozen starts, he went back to a higher-tempo, more athletic delivery and dominated minor-league opponents. His extension makes his already excellent velocity play up to a true 80 grade, and his curveball still has plenty of potential. Given his size, it could be a few more long years, but if he stays healthy he's eventually going to make opponents miserable.

Taylor Hearn LHP Born: 08/30/94 Age: 23 Bats: L Throws: L Height: 6'5" Weight: 210 Origin: Round 5, 2015 Draft (#164 overall)

YEAR	TEAM	LVL	AGE	W	L	SV	G	GS	IP	H	HR	BB/9	K/9	K	GB%	BABIP	WHIP	ERA	DRA	WARP	MPH	CMD	PWR	STM
2015	AUB	A-	20	1	5	0	10	10	43	49	2	2.7	8.0	38	55%	.346	1.44	3.98	4.60	0.3				
2016	HAG	A	21	1	0	0	8	2	22^{2}	25	3	2.8	12.3	31	39%	.393	1.41	3.18	1.76	0.8				
2016	WVA	A	21	1	1	0	8	3	22^{2}	15	2	4.0	14.3	36	47%	.289	1.10	1.99	1.57	0.9				
2017	BRD	A+	22	4	6	0	18	17	87^{1}	65	8	3.8	10.9	106	50%	.281	1.17	4.12	1.86	3.5				
2018	*PIT*	*MLB*	*23*	*4*	*4*	*0*	*24*	*13*	*67^{2}*	*66*	*13*	*4.4*	*10.3*	*78*	*42%*	*.325*	*1.47*	*4.98*	*5.55*	*0.0*				
2019	*PIT*	*MLB*	*24*	*6*	*8*	*0*	*35*	*23*	*168^{1}*	*153*	*30*	*4.1*	*9.8*	*183*	*42%*	*.31*	*1.36*	*4.87*	*5.43*	*0.2*				

Breakout: 9% Improve: 13% Collapse: 5% Attrition: 15% MLB: 22% *Comparables: Trevor May, Bud Norris, Troy Scribner*

It's hard to imagine that Hearn will be allowed to try his hand as a starter any longer, but it's also hard to imagine that he'll allow anyone to talk him into a move to relief. He bet on himself so stubbornly that, despite two separate and serious elbow issues during his amateur career, he was drafted four times before finally signing. Now he's coming off the meatiest season of his pro career—albeit one that still ended with fewer than 100 innings due to a strained oblique. His stuff is nasty: an elite fastball and a wipeout slider from the left side, and a delivery with moderate effort. The problem is that, because of all those times he didn't sign after being drafted, he's already 23 and isn't especially likely to suddenly develop a changeup that has never really come around.

Daniel Hudson RHP Born: 03/09/87 Age: 31 Bats: R Throws: R Height: 6'3" Weight: 225 Origin: Round 5, 2008 Draft (#150 overall)

YEAR	TEAM	LVL	AGE	W	L	SV	G	GS	IP	H	HR	BB/9	K/9	K	GB%	BABIP	WHIP	ERA	DRA	WARP	MPH	CMD	PWR	STM
2015	ARI	MLB	28	4	3	4	64	1	67^{2}	64	7	3.3	9.4	71	43%	.305	1.32	3.86	3.43	1.0	98.6	41	64	50
2016	ARI	MLB	29	3	2	5	70	0	60^{1}	65	6	3.3	8.7	58	41%	.331	1.44	5.22	3.70	0.9	97.7	54	59	50
2017	PIT	MLB	30	2	7	0	71	0	61^{2}	57	7	4.8	9.6	66	44%	.312	1.46	4.38	4.57	0.4	96.7	41	61	51
2018	*PIT*	*MLB*	*31*	*3*	*3*	*3*	*54*	*0*	*56*	*56*	*7*	*3.9*	*8.7*	*55*	*43%*	*.301*	*1.41*	*4.40*	*4.54*	*0.2*	*96.7*	*45*	*61*	*50*
2019	*PIT*	*MLB*	*32*	*2*	*1*	*2*	*46*	*0*	*49*	*45*	*7*	*3.7*	*8.7*	*47*	*43%*	*.311*	*1.34*	*4.46*	*5.00*	*0.1*	*96.0*	*46*	*60*	*50*

Breakout: 28% Improve: 53% Collapse: 24% Attrition: 16% MLB: 92% *Comparables: Nick Masset, Jesse Crain, Lindy McDaniel*

Two Tommy John surgeries say Hudson is pitching on borrowed time. We like to think that moving to the bullpen removes or mitigates the risk of another serious injury, but just as often the reverse is true. In that light, Hudson's 2017 can be viewed as a success. There's even something on which to build: he added a sinker near the end of the season. On the other hand, he lost a mile per hour on his fastball (for the second year in a row), walked too many batters and continues to be limited to pitching with more rest or for shorter durations than an ideal setup man.

Drew Hutchison RHP Born: 08/22/90 Age: 27 Bats: L Throws: R Height: 6'3" Weight: 205 Origin: Round 15, 2009 Draft (#460 overall)

YEAR	TEAM	LVL	AGE	W	L	SV	G	GS	IP	H	HR	BB/9	K/9	K	GB%	BABIP	WHIP	ERA	DRA	WARP	MPH	CMD	PWR	STM
2015	TOR	MLB	24	13	5	0	30	28	150^1	179	22	2.6	7.7	129	40%	.343	1.48	5.57	5.58	-0.9	95.3	50	54	65
2016	TOR	MLB	25	1	0	0	3	2	12^2	13	4	2.8	8.5	12	36%	.281	1.34	4.97	6.93	-0.2	94.7	43	50	69
2016	BUF	AAA	25	6	5	0	18	18	102	78	11	3.1	9.7	110	42%	.264	1.11	3.26	2.81	2.9				
2016	IND	AAA	25	1	1	0	7	6	36	37	5	3.8	7.0	28	35%	.288	1.44	4.50	4.15	0.5				
2016	PIT	MLB	25	0	0	0	6	1	11^1	15	2	2.4	7.9	10	35%	.371	1.59	5.56	5.55	0.0	94.3	43	50	69
2017	IND	AAA	26	9	9	0	28	26	159^1	149	14	3.2	7.0	124	47%	.284	1.29	3.56	3.97	3.0				
2018	*PIT*	*MLB*	*27*	*8*	*8*	*0*	*25*	*25*	*137^1*	*140*	*19*	*3.1*	*8.3*	*127*	*42%*	*.319*	*1.36*	*4.39*	*4.92*	*1.1*	*94.7*	*49*	*54*	*68*
2019	*PIT*	*MLB*	*28*	*6*	*7*	*0*	*19*	*19*	*112^2*	*115*	*15*	*3.5*	*7.8*	*98*	*42%*	*.322*	*1.40*	*4.60*	*5.15*	*0.6*	*94.1*	*48*	*54*	*69*

Breakout: 24% Improve: 57% Collapse: 12% Attrition: 18% MLB: 81% *Comparables: Shaun Marcum, Bud Norris, A.J. Griffin*

The Pirates traded for Hutchison in July 2016 to ensure they would have depth in their rotation during a season in which they used more than a dozen starters. In 2017, they used just seven all season and didn't need Hutchison for anything: He pitched 160 innings in Triple-A Indianapolis. Now years removed from his time as a cost-conscious but name-brand national prospect, Hutchison has seen velocity come and go, has stalled out with a four-pitch mix that just doesn't surprise anyone and figures to be the eighth arm on a seven-man depth chart for the foreseeable future.

Steven Jennings RHP Born: 11/13/98 Age: 19 Bats: R Throws: R Height: 6'2" Weight: 175 Origin: Round 2, 2017 Draft (#42 overall)

YEAR	TEAM	LVL	AGE	W	L	SV	G	GS	IP	H	HR	BB/9	K/9	K	GB%	BABIP	WHIP	ERA	DRA	WARP	MPH	CMD	PWR	STM
2017	PIR	RK	18	0	2	0	10	10	26^1	31	2	3.4	4.4	13	57%	.305	1.56	4.10	4.64	0.4				
2018	*PIT*	*MLB*	*19*	*2*	*3*	*0*	*9*	*9*	*31^2*	*40*	*7*	*5.9*	*5.8*	*20*	*41%*	*.327*	*1.91*	*6.97*	*7.83*	*-0.8*				
2019	*PIT*	*MLB*	*20*	*3*	*9*	*0*	*24*	*24*	*143*	*173*	*29*	*5.3*	*5.5*	*87*	*41%*	*.328*	*1.81*	*6.67*	*7.51*	*-1.9*				

Comparables: Brandon Maurer, Antonio Senzatela, Sal Romano

Jennings pushed his way up draft boards last spring, despite pitching on a not-quite-fully healed ACL tear he suffered playing football the previous fall. He throws in the high-80s and low-90s right now, but he has touched 95 and there are reasons to think he'll be able to sit at that level in the future. His body should fill out from here, and more importantly his delivery is the classic one for prep pitchers who spend their late summer and fall playing football: arrhythmic, inefficient, yet full of athleticism. If Jennings can clean that up now, he'll be the kind of pitching prospect teams love best: one with low mileage on his arm and a whole bunch of untapped potential.

Mitch Keller RHP Born: 04/04/96 Age: 22 Bats: R Throws: R Height: 6'3" Weight: 195 Origin: Round 2, 2014 Draft (#64 overall)

YEAR	TEAM	LVL	AGE	W	L	SV	G	GS	IP	H	HR	BB/9	K/9	K	GB%	BABIP	WHIP	ERA	DRA	WARP	MPH	CMD	PWR	STM
2015	BRI	RK	19	0	3	0	6	6	19^2	25	1	7.3	11.4	25	49%	.429	2.08	5.49	4.64	0.3				
2016	WVA	A	20	8	5	0	23	23	124^1	96	4	1.3	9.5	131	48%	.284	0.92	2.46	1.55	5.3				
2017	BRD	A+	21	6	3	0	15	15	77^1	57	5	2.3	7.4	64	55%	.248	1.00	3.14	2.27	2.7				
2017	ALT	AA	21	2	2	0	6	6	34^2	25	2	2.9	11.7	45	48%	.280	1.04	3.12	1.72	1.4				
2018	*PIT*	*MLB*	*22*	*2*	*2*	*0*	*15*	*5*	*36*	*35*	*5*	*4.1*	*9.0*	*37*	*43%*	*.297*	*1.41*	*4.59*	*4.78*	*0.1*				
2019	*PIT*	*MLB*	*23*	*8*	*8*	*0*	*62*	*19*	*161^1*	*136*	*23*	*3.7*	*9.8*	*175*	*43%*	*.299*	*1.26*	*4.41*	*4.92*	*0.9*				

Breakout: 14% Improve: 28% Collapse: 7% Attrition: 20% MLB: 46% *Comparables: Michael Pineda, Edwin Diaz, Jacob Faria*

Keller's going to burst onto the scene soon, and he's going to take the league by storm. He has a fastball that gets into the mid-90s with the least apparent physical effort imaginable. Because he's not fighting to get the velocity he needs, he commands the pitch really well and can sink it, run it in on righties or elevate it. He also has a curveball on which some scouts hung a 70 future grade, which suits the modern game perfectly and should make his adjustment to the majors fairly smooth. His changeup isn't good, but he's only going on 22 and he's from Iowa, so he hasn't been working on that pitch as much or for as long as his peers. He went to the Arizona Fall League in 2017 to hone that third pitch some, but given his command, stuff, mechanics and poise he can succeed even as he learns.

George Kontos RHP Born: 06/12/85 Age: 32 Bats: R Throws: R Height: 6'3" Weight: 215 Origin: Round 5, 2006 Draft (#164 overall)

YEAR	TEAM	LVL	AGE	W	L	SV	G	GS	IP	H	HR	BB/9	K/9	K	GB%	BABIP	WHIP	ERA	DRA	WARP	MPH	CMD	PWR	STM
2015	SFN	MLB	30	4	4	0	73	0	73^1	57	9	1.5	5.4	44	44%	.219	0.94	2.33	3.48	1.1	93.5	52	35	52
2016	SFN	MLB	31	3	2	0	57	0	53^1	42	3	3.4	5.9	35	45%	.244	1.16	2.53	4.63	0.2	92.8	28	34	44
2017	SFN	MLB	32	0	5	0	50	0	51^2	52	8	3.0	9.6	55	52%	.308	1.34	3.83	3.86	0.8	91.8	45	21	49
2017	PIT	MLB	32	1	1	1	15	0	14^2	9	1	1.8	9.2	15	46%	.222	0.82	1.84	3.93	0.2	92.2	45	21	49
2018	*PIT*	*MLB*	*33*	*2*	*2*	*0*	*39*	*0*	*41^1*	*41*	*5*	*3.5*	*6.8*	*31*	*46%*	*.287*	*1.35*	*4.50*	*4.63*	*0.1*	*91.6*	*42*	*28*	*48*
2019	*PIT*	*MLB*	*34*	*2*	*1*	*1*	*50*	*0*	*53^2*	*50*	*6*	*3.4*	*6.8*	*40*	*46%*	*.292*	*1.30*	*4.49*	*5.03*	*0.1*	*90.9*	*39*	*26*	*46*

Breakout: 17% Improve: 38% Collapse: 27% Attrition: 11% MLB: 82% *Comparables: Bob Howry, Jared Burton, LaTroy Hawkins*

Quietly, and despite being August waiver bait, Kontos had a breakout 2017 campaign that was years in the making. He picked up a cutter about halfway through 2013, and it slowly became his best pitch. He ratcheted down the usage of his slider (those pitches are almost redundant), and then of his four-seam fastball (a cutter is halfway between slider and four-seamer, after all, and he seemed to have one that worked as both). Last year he all but junked his sinker, too. He still has all of those pitches, but he's put the cutter in places one, two and three on his speed dial, and when he dials it up he gets a whole bunch of strikeouts.

Chad Kuhl RHP Born: 09/10/92 Age: 25 Bats: R Throws: R Height: 6'3" Weight: 216 Origin: Round 9, 2013 Draft (#269 overall)

YEAR	TEAM	LVL	AGE	W	L	SV	G	GS	IP	H	HR	BB/9	K/9	K	GB%	BABIP	WHIP	ERA	DRA	WARP	MPH	CMD	PWR	STM
2015	ALT	AA	22	11	5	0	26	26	152^{2}	133	10	2.4	6.0	101	57%	.265	1.14	2.48	2.42	4.9				
2016	IND	AAA	23	6	3	0	16	16	83^{2}	81	9	1.7	7.1	66	48%	.295	1.16	2.37	2.76	2.5				
2016	PIT	MLB	23	5	4	0	14	14	70^{2}	73	7	2.5	6.8	53	46%	.304	1.32	4.20	4.85	0.4	96.1	53	55	64
2017	PIT	MLB	24	8	11	0	31	31	157^{1}	159	17	4.1	8.1	142	43%	.321	1.47	4.35	5.24	0.6	97.8	46	68	70
2018	*PIT*	*MLB*	*25*	*8*	*8*	*0*	*24*	*24*	*136*	*133*	*16*	*3.2*	*7.7*	*117*	*46%*	*.294*	*1.32*	*4.12*	*4.39*	*1.2*	*97.1*	*49*	*66*	*69*
2019	*PIT*	*MLB*	*26*	*11*	*11*	*0*	*32*	*32*	*209*	*177*	*22*	*2.5*	*8.2*	*189*	*46%*	*.292*	*1.12*	*3.71*	*4.16*	*3.0*	*96.9*	*49*	*66*	*69*

Breakout: 31% Improve: 61% Collapse: 12% Attrition: 20% MLB: 91% *Comparables: Chris Tillman, Wade Davis, Alex Cobb*

For a guy named Kuhl, he's awfully reliant on his heat. Leaning heavily on his sinker, Kuhl did try to make himself a truer four-pitch hurler in 2017, adding a curveball to his complement of secondary stuff. That curve never became more than a show-me pitch, and his changeup is too firm given that it's playing off a sinker (which has certain intrinsic similarities in movement). His slider has real bite and induces a lot of swings and misses. For a guy named Chad, he doesn't hang all that many offerings up in the zone, so while walks might remain an issue he's going to keep racking up strikeouts and keep the ball in the park pretty well.

Wade LeBlanc LHP Born: 08/07/84 Age: 33 Bats: L Throws: L Height: 6'3" Weight: 205 Origin: Round 2, 2006 Draft (#61 overall)

YEAR	TEAM	LVL	AGE	W	L	SV	G	GS	IP	H	HR	BB/9	K/9	K	GB%	BABIP	WHIP	ERA	DRA	WARP	MPH	CMD	PWR	STM
2016	BUF	AAA	31	7	2	0	14	14	89^{2}	84	3	2.1	8.5	85	43%	.315	1.17	1.71	1.59	3.9				
2016	SEA	MLB	31	3	0	1	11	8	50	52	14	1.6	7.4	41	34%	.264	1.22	4.50	5.98	-0.4	89.0	69	30	61
2016	PIT	MLB	31	1	0	1	8	0	12	7	0	1.5	7.5	10	41%	.219	0.75	0.75	4.42	0.1	88.7	69	30	61
2017	PIT	MLB	32	5	2	1	50	0	68	64	10	2.2	7.1	54	47%	.269	1.19	4.50	4.34	0.6	88.4	64	23	45
2018	*PIT*	*MLB*	*33*	*4*	*3*	*0*	*26*	*9*	*68^{2}*	*73*	*9*	*3.0*	*7.3*	*55*	*43%*	*.318*	*1.40*	*4.48*	*5.03*	*0.4*	*87.7*	*65*	*26*	*51*
2019	*PIT*	*MLB*	*34*	*6*	*7*	*1*	*41*	*16*	*132^{2}*	*142*	*17*	*3.4*	*6.0*	*88*	*43%*	*.313*	*1.45*	*4.86*	*5.47*	*0.1*	*87.2*	*65*	*25*	*51*

Breakout: 14% Improve: 30% Collapse: 15% Attrition: 15% MLB: 52% *Comparables: Eric Stults, Dave Borkowski, Zach Duke*

One of baseball's truest junkballers, LeBlanc throws his changeup more often than any other pitch, his cutter second-most, and mixes sinkers and four-seamers about evenly. He is also one of the most durable pitchers in the game and helped the Pirates enjoy one of the least injury-marred seasons in their recent history by being available often and having no problem going multiple innings when needed. Alas, as his unique pitch mix and underwhelming velocity suggest, he simply isn't very good. He can make a fringe contender better by soaking up medium- and low-leverage innings, but anyone counting on him to improve win probability within games is doomed to be disappointed.

Ivan Nova RHP Born: 01/12/87 Age: 31 Bats: R Throws: R Height: 6'5" Weight: 245 Origin: International Free Agent, 2004

YEAR	TEAM	LVL	AGE	W	L	SV	G	GS	IP	H	HR	BB/9	K/9	K	GB%	BABIP	WHIP	ERA	DRA	WARP	MPH	CMD	PWR	STM
2015	SWB	AAA	28	1	1	0	2	2	11	12	1	2.5	5.7	7	43%	.324	1.36	4.91	5.14	0.0				
2015	NYA	MLB	28	6	11	0	17	17	94	99	13	3.2	6.0	63	52%	.290	1.40	5.07	4.66	0.5	95.6	35	49	56
2016	NYA	MLB	29	7	6	1	21	15	97^{1}	107	19	2.3	6.9	75	56%	.297	1.36	4.90	4.04	1.4	95.4	46	49	64
2016	PIT	MLB	29	5	2	0	11	11	64^{2}	68	4	0.4	7.2	52	55%	.318	1.10	3.06	4.45	0.6	95.6	46	49	64
2017	PIT	MLB	30	11	14	0	31	31	187	203	29	1.7	6.3	131	48%	.299	1.28	4.14	5.33	0.5	94.7	52	52	74
2018	*PIT*	*MLB*	*31*	*10*	*11*	*0*	*28*	*28*	*168*	*177*	*22*	*2.5*	*6.6*	*123*	*50%*	*.297*	*1.33*	*4.34*	*4.63*	*1.0*	*94.3*	*47*	*50*	*66*
2019	*PIT*	*MLB*	*32*	*11*	*11*	*0*	*32*	*32*	*202^{1}*	*201*	*24*	*2.1*	*6.6*	*148*	*50%*	*.307*	*1.22*	*4.11*	*4.61*	*2.1*	*93.8*	*48*	*50*	*67*

Breakout: 11% Improve: 42% Collapse: 29% Attrition: 11% MLB: 92% *Comparables: Homer Bailey, Kyle Lohse, Jason Hammel*

Nova is a relatively rare breed in terms of fastball usage. He'll throw both a four-seamer and a sinker, and mix them pretty evenly regardless of batter handedness. He briefly took the National League by storm when, after the Pirates traded for him in 2016, pitching coach Ray Searage got him pounding the zone consistently and taught him to better run his sinker in on right-handed batters. It really is hard to be ready for the sinker, because he'll pitch to the other side of the plate with his four-seamer against righties. Against left-handed hitters, the story changes. He can't get inside on them, and they just look away until they get their pitch. That's how lefties posted a .310 True Average against him last season and why Nova seems unlikely to sustain more than mid-rotation success.

Felipe Rivero LHP Born: 07/05/91 Age: 26 Bats: L Throws: L Height: 6'2" Weight: 210 Origin: International Free Agent, 2008

YEAR	TEAM	LVL	AGE	W	L	SV	G	GS	IP	H	HR	BB/9	K/9	K	GB%	BABIP	WHIP	ERA	DRA	WARP	MPH	CMD	PWR	STM
2015	WAS	MLB	23	2	1	2	49	0	48^{1}	35	2	2.0	8.0	43	47%	.250	0.95	2.79	3.57	0.7	98.4	51	67	44
2016	WAS	MLB	24	0	3	1	47	0	49^{2}	43	4	2.7	9.6	53	48%	.310	1.17	4.53	3.66	0.7	98.5	41	61	55
2016	PIT	MLB	24	1	3	0	28	0	27^{1}	23	3	5.9	12.8	39	48%	.317	1.50	3.29	4.25	0.2	99.8	41	61	55
2017	PIT	MLB	25	5	3	21	73	0	75^{1}	47	4	2.4	10.5	88	53%	.234	0.89	1.67	2.94	1.9	100.7	46	76	53
2018	*PIT*	*MLB*	*26*	*3*	*3*	*20*	*59*	*0*	*62*	*51*	*5*	*3.3*	*9.8*	*68*	*49%*	*.290*	*1.19*	*3.05*	*3.42*	*1.1*	*99.3*	*46*	*70*	*52*
2019	*PIT*	*MLB*	*27*	*3*	*1*	*15*	*66*	*0*	*69^{2}*	*53*	*6*	*3.3*	*10.5*	*81*	*49%*	*.301*	*1.13*	*3.21*	*3.58*	*1.2*	*99.2*	*45*	*70*	*54*

Breakout: 35% Improve: 57% Collapse: 27% Attrition: 9% MLB: 87% *Comparables: Trevor Rosenthal, Jeurys Familia, Jose Arredondo*

We're a long, long way past Pitcher Abuse Points. Recently, Canadian ergonomist Dr. Mike Sonne developed Fatigue Units, a system that uses empirically proven contributors to muscle fatigue and injury risk (how often one pitches, yes, but also fastball velocity, pitches per inning and time between pitches) to give an idea of which pitchers are really most at risk of either wearing down or blowing out. Rivero (who throws incredibly hard, in addition to having a filthy slider-changeup combo) works very quickly, leans heavily on his heat and often pitched on back-to-back days as Clint Hurdle tried to keep the Pirates in the race. As such, he racked up the second-highest number of Fatigue Units in MLB, trailing only Seattle's Edwin Diaz. Last August, his well-earned Players Weekend sobriquet was NIGHTMARE. In 2019 or so, it might be SCARBEARER.

Angel Sanchez RHP

Born: 11/28/89 Age: 28 Bats: R Throws: R Height: 6'1" Weight: 190 Origin: International Free Agent, 2010

YEAR	TEAM	LVL	AGE	W	L	SV	G	GS	IP	H	HR	BB/9	K/9	K	GB%	BABIP	WHIP	ERA	DRA	WARP	MPH	CMD	PWR	STM
2015	ALT	AA	25	8	1	0	13	13	77^1	72	4	2.2	5.7	49	51%	.279	1.18	2.79	3.63	1.4				
2015	IND	AAA	25	5	1	0	10	10	60	49	6	2.2	7.5	50	47%	.251	1.07	2.55	3.82	1.0				
2017	IND	AAA	27	3	5	1	39	0	55^1	51	4	2.4	10.6	65	55%	.326	1.19	3.74	2.02	2.0				
2017	PIT	MLB	27	1	0	0	8	0	12^1	16	5	0.7	7.3	10	42%	.289	1.38	8.76	7.68	-0.3	97.2	37	57	43
2018	*PIT*	*MLB*	*28*	*2*	*2*	*0*	*39*	*0*	*41^1*	*40*	*5*	*3.3*	*8.5*	*39*	*45%*	*.298*	*1.33*	*4.03*	*4.25*	*0.3*	*96.6*	*37*	*57*	*43*
2019	*PIT*	*MLB*	*29*	*2*	*1*	*0*	*49*	*0*	*51^2*	*47*	*6*	*3.8*	*8.4*	*48*	*45%*	*.306*	*1.34*	*4.30*	*4.83*	*0.2*	*96.0*	*37*	*57*	*43*

Breakout: 23% Improve: 32% Collapse: 6% Attrition: 24% MLB: 38% *Comparables: Andrew Carpenter, Thad Weber, Oliver Drake*

Sanchez signed with the Dodgers out of the Dominican Republic in 2010. He was traded to Miami, claimed off waivers three times and landed with the Pirates, who had him trending toward finally reaching the majors in 2015. Then, in August of that year, he tore his UCL. Only after missing all of 2016 did Sanchez finally move from the rotation to the bullpen. It was an instant success: his command of his fastball-slider repertoire was more than good enough to dominate minor-league hitters. In a late-season audition with the big-league team, he had major home-run issues, but with his power arsenal he looks like a useful right-handed reliever.

Edgar Santana RHP

Born: 10/16/91 Age: 26 Bats: R Throws: R Height: 6'2" Weight: 180 Origin: International Free Agent, 2013

YEAR	TEAM	LVL	AGE	W	L	SV	G	GS	IP	H	HR	BB/9	K/9	K	GB%	BABIP	WHIP	ERA	DRA	WARP	MPH	CMD	PWR	STM
2015	WEV	A-	23	1	0	3	14	0	30	25	1	1.5	9.6	32	56%	.289	1.00	2.70	2.70	0.8				
2015	WVA	A	23	0	0	1	8	0	12^1	12	3	2.9	11.7	16	41%	.310	1.30	4.38	3.11	0.3				
2016	BRD	A+	24	2	0	0	9	0	22^1	13	0	0.8	8.1	20	61%	.220	0.67	0.81	2.28	0.7				
2016	ALT	AA	24	2	1	2	21	0	41^1	32	4	2.4	8.5	39	57%	.264	1.04	2.83	2.16	1.3				
2016	IND	AAA	24	0	0	1	13	0	16	22	1	3.4	6.8	12	53%	.389	1.75	5.06	4.93	0.0				
2017	IND	AAA	25	1	3	8	44	0	58	62	4	1.9	8.4	54	44%	.343	1.28	2.79	4.51	0.5				
2017	PIT	MLB	25	0	0	0	19	0	18	16	2	6.0	10.0	20	46%	.304	1.56	3.50	4.00	0.2	96.7	46	61	50
2018	*PIT*	*MLB*	*26*	*2*	*2*	*0*	*34*	*0*	*36*	*37*	*6*	*3.3*	*8.2*	*33*	*46%*	*.303*	*1.41*	*4.79*	*4.84*	*0.0*	*96.3*	*47*	*62*	*51*
2019	*PIT*	*MLB*	*27*	*2*	*1*	*0*	*44*	*0*	*46^1*	*46*	*7*	*3.3*	*8.0*	*41*	*46%*	*.315*	*1.35*	*4.68*	*5.23*	*0.0*	*95.9*	*47*	*62*	*51*

Breakout: 22% Improve: 28% Collapse: 13% Attrition: 19% MLB: 49% *Comparables: Edgmer Escalona, Pedro Strop, Scott Maine*

Santana has a fastball-slider combination few pitchers can match, not for the dynamism of either pitch on its own, but in the way they interact. His was the smallest distance between the positions of his fastball and slider at the tunnel point (where a hitter has to make a decision about whether and where to swing), when thrown consecutively, of any pitcher who used that sequence as often as he did last season. Since he already throws in the mid-to-upper-90s, opponents don't have a lot of time in the first place. Santana keeps them guessing until the last possible moment, which tends to induce a lot of either empty or nonthreatening swings.

Jameson Taillon RHP

Born: 11/18/91 Age: 26 Bats: R Throws: R Height: 6'5" Weight: 225 Origin: Round 1, 2010 Draft (#2 overall)

YEAR	TEAM	LVL	AGE	W	L	SV	G	GS	IP	H	HR	BB/9	K/9	K	GB%	BABIP	WHIP	ERA	DRA	WARP	MPH	CMD	PWR	STM
2016	IND	AAA	24	4	2	0	10	10	61^2	44	2	0.9	8.9	61	49%	.253	0.81	2.04	1.33	2.8				
2016	PIT	MLB	24	5	4	0	18	18	104	99	13	1.5	7.4	85	55%	.287	1.12	3.38	3.71	2.0	96.5	54	50	65
2017	IND	AAA	25	0	1	0	2	2	11	12	0	1.6	12.3	15	58%	.387	1.27	4.09	2.09	0.4				
2017	PIT	MLB	25	8	7	0	25	25	133^2	152	11	3.1	8.4	125	49%	.352	1.48	4.44	4.51	1.6	96.7	49	59	65
2018	*PIT*	*MLB*	*26*	*10*	*9*	*0*	*28*	*28*	*159*	*151*	*17*	*2.7*	*8.6*	*153*	*47%*	*.299*	*1.25*	*3.58*	*3.80*	*2.5*	*96.2*	*52*	*57*	*66*
2019	*PIT*	*MLB*	*27*	*11*	*11*	*0*	*32*	*32*	*204*	*190*	*23*	*2.9*	*8.1*	*184*	*47%*	*.309*	*1.26*	*3.90*	*4.39*	*2.5*	*95.9*	*52*	*57*	*66*

Breakout: 39% Improve: 69% Collapse: 14% Attrition: 10% MLB: 93% *Comparables: Jordan Zimmermann, Patrick Corbin, Jake Odorizzi*

It was a deeply personal and special season for Taillon. He overcame testicular cancer in something like a month (thank goodness for early detection), and came off the disabled list pitching better than before he went onto it until fading in the second half. His story is one of triumph and resiliency and toughness, both mental and physical. It's also profoundly human. Just don't tell Ray Searage, who often treats his pitchers like robot clones and had Taillon throwing the same pitch mix he imposes upon anyone who will listen: even blend of four-seamer and sinker, a curve and a change against lefties, just the curve against righties. Work the sinker in on righties, go away with the pure heat. Stay away from lefties all the way. Never mind if it fails to work, as it did for Taillon (.295 TAv against lefties).

Trevor Williams RHP

Born: 04/25/92 Age: 26 Bats: R Throws: R Height: 6'3" Weight: 230 Origin: Round 2, 2013 Draft (#44 overall)

YEAR	TEAM	LVL	AGE	W	L	SV	G	GS	IP	H	HR	BB/9	K/9	K	GB%	BABIP	WHIP	ERA	DRA	WARP	MPH	CMD	PWR	STM
2015	JAX	AA	23	7	8	0	22	21	117	126	9	2.8	6.8	88	54%	.320	1.38	4.00	2.84	3.2				
2015	NWO	AAA	23	0	2	0	3	3	14	15	0	4.5	8.4	13	46%	.341	1.57	2.57	3.67	0.3				
2016	IND	AAA	24	9	6	0	20	19	110^1	103	5	2.4	6.0	74	53%	.284	1.21	2.53	3.32	2.5				
2016	PIT	MLB	24	1	1	0	7	1	12^2	19	4	3.6	7.8	11	49%	.366	1.89	7.82	5.20	0.0	96.7	49	54	52
2017	PIT	MLB	25	7	9	0	31	25	150^1	145	14	3.1	7.0	117	50%	.292	1.31	4.07	3.95	2.7	94.6	69	58	66
2018	*PIT*	*MLB*	*26*	*8*	*9*	*0*	*26*	*26*	*137*	*142*	*15*	*3.3*	*7.0*	*107*	*49%*	*.299*	*1.40*	*4.24*	*4.53*	*1.0*	*94.4*	*69*	*59*	*61*
2019	*PIT*	*MLB*	*27*	*10*	*10*	*0*	*32*	*32*	*203^2*	*189*	*21*	*3.0*	*7.7*	*174*	*49%*	*.307*	*1.26*	*3.93*	*4.42*	*2.2*	*94.1*	*69*	*59*	*61*

Breakout: 38% Improve: 63% Collapse: 12% Attrition: 18% MLB: 85% *Comparables: Wade Miley, Williams Perez, Jeanmar Gomez*

As Statcast wriggles ever deeper into our baseball consciousness, we're going to need to learn what all of these newfangled numbers mean. For instance: Williams has an extremely low spin rate on both his four- and two-seam fastballs. However, he also has terrific command of his whole arsenal and can throw well to all four quadrants of the strike zone. Our Called Strikes Above Average metric says only five pitchers who pitched at least 100 innings contributed more to getting calls on the edges than Williams did. So, does low spin help a pitcher better hit his spots? Does it make the flight of the ball easier for umpires to track? Or is Williams' command just that fine? It could be some of each. As long as Williams can still pump his fastball in at 95 and command his average arsenal around that, he need not worry much about these existential questions.

Lineouts

Hitters

HITTER	POS	TEAM	LVL	AGE	PA	R	2B	3B	HR	RBI	BB	K	SB	CS	AVG/OBP/SLG	TAv	VORP	BABIP	BRR	FRAA	WARP
Stephen Alemais	SS	WVA	A	22	131	14	6	2	3	12	5	32	5	3	.223/.266/.380	.230	0.2	.279	-0.8	SS(26): -1.5, 2B(1): 0.0	-0.1
	SS	PIR	Rk	22	31	6	3	0	0	2	4	5	0	0	.259/.355/.370	.250	2.0	.318	0.8	SS(8): -1.2	0.1
	SS	BRD	A+	22	122	10	6	0	1	20	14	14	5	2	.317/.393/.406	.294	9.8	.352	0.7	SS(29): -1.2	0.9
Chris Bostick	2B	IND	AAA	24	549	75	33	3	7	57	45	97	8	9	.294/.362/.418	.280	28.3	.353	2.8	LF(38): -0.9, RF(34): -1.0	2.2
	2B	PIT	MLB	24	32	6	2	0	0	1	4	9	0	1	.296/.406/.370	.285	1.7	.444	0.0	2B(3): -0.4, LF(3): 0.0	0.1
Oneil Cruz	3B	GRL	A	18	375	51	9	1	8	36	28	110	8	7	.240/.293/.342	.255	13.3	.323	3.2	3B(47): -9.3, SS(30): 0.2	0.4
	3B	WVA	A	18	63	9	2	1	2	8	8	22	0	0	.218/.317/.400	.266	3.4	.323	1.0	3B(15): 0.6, SS(1): 0.0	0.4
Jared Oliva	OF	WEV	A-	21	254	30	10	7	0	17	17	57	15	4	.266/.327/.374	.266	8.5	.353	-0.4	CF(42): 0.6, LF(6): -0.2	0.9
Jacob Stallings	C	IND	AAA	27	243	35	16	0	4	38	17	30	1	2	.301/.358/.431	.287	20.2	.330	1.2	C(60): -3.7, 1B(1): -0.1	1.6
	C	PIT	MLB	27	16	3	2	0	0	3	2	2	0	0	.357/.438/.500	.365	3.1	.417	0.5	C(5): -0.2	0.3
Chris Stewart	C	PIT	MLB	35	144	8	1	2	0	4	9	22	0	0	.183/.241/.221	.176	-6.0	.220	0.0	C(48): 1.9	-0.4
Engelb Vielma	SS	CHT	AA	23	141	7	5	0	0	18	14	13	1	3	.286/.362/.328	.271	5.1	.312	-1.3	SS(19): -0.2, 2B(14): 0.2	0.5
	SS	ROC	AAA	23	314	36	12	2	0	17	11	72	2	5	.206/.233/.260	.180	-11.3	.266	3.2	SS(84): 3.8, 2B(2): -0.3	-0.8

Glove-first shortstop **Stephen Alemais** failed to pick up offensive pop even while playing for Literally the West Virginia Power. Journeyman **Chris Bostick** can hit a little and play all over the field in a pinch, but he's already a journeyman at age 25 for a reason. Infield prospect **Oneil Cruz** played full-season ball at age 18, which is impressive even if the player stinks (and, in 2017, he did). **Jared Oliva** is tall and slender, is well coordinated and has some speed, but the seventh-round draft pick lacks power, at least for now. **Jacob Stallings** is a good enough receiver to show up in the majors for two weeks every year and get a key hit against your favorite team. At age 35, **Chris Stewart** is still a good defensive catcher, but if he ever does anything offensively it's within the privacy of his own home and is nobody's business but his. Old for a high school draftee but with obvious power upside, **Conner Uselton** got an over-slot signing bonus after Pittsburgh took him in the second round. It's in the best interests of baseball for fans to see **Engelb Vielma** play shortstop, so we're just waiting for Rob Manfred to declare the slender Venezuelan eligible for a courtesy hitter.

Pitchers

PITCHER	TEAM	LVL	AGE	W	L	SV	G	GS	IP	H	HR	BB/9	K/9	K	GB%	BABIP	WHIP	ERA	DRA	WARP	MPH	CMD	PWR	STM
Dario Agrazal	BRD	A+	22	5	3	0	14	13	80^{1}	73	4	1.1	7.1	63	56%	.289	1.03	2.91	1.58	3.5				
Tyler Eppler	IND	AAA	24	8	9	0	27	21	136^{1}	159	23	2.2	6.3	96	41%	.313	1.41	4.89	5.62	0.1				
Yeudy Garcia	ALT	AA	24	4	7	5	29	11	72	76	8	5.8	8.4	67	37%	.324	1.69	5.25	8.23	-2.8				
Luis Heredia	ALT	AA	22	3	3	2	36	0	52^{1}	41	3	5.3	7.4	43	52%	.248	1.38	3.10	4.72	0.0				
Gage Hinsz	BRD	A+	21	5	5	0	20	19	94^{2}	112	9	2.9	4.9	52	49%	.320	1.51	5.61	5.84	-0.7				
Clay Holmes	IND	AAA	24	10	5	0	25	24	112^{2}	96	4	4.7	7.9	99	62%	.302	1.38	3.36	3.42	2.8				
Nick Kingham	IND	AAA	25	9	6	0	20	19	113^{1}	119	8	2.3	7.4	93	46%	.324	1.31	4.13	3.35	2.9				
Max Kranick	PIR	Rk	19	0	0	0	3	3	12^{2}	12	0	2.8	6.4	9	41%	.308	1.26	0.00	3.90	0.3				
	BRI	Rk	19	1	0	0	2	2	11^{2}	10	1	1.5	6.9	9	49%	.265	1.03	2.31	4.15	0.2				
Jack Leathersich	CHN	MLB	26	0	0	0	1	0	0^{2}	1	0	54.0	13.5	1	0%	.500	7.50	27.00	2.16	0.0	93.6			41
	IOW	AAA	26	2	4	1	41	0	44^{1}	25	3	5.7	14.6	72	38%	.272	1.20	2.84	3.14	1.0				
	PIT	MLB	26	0	0	0	6	0	4^{1}	3	0	4.2	12.5	6	10%	.300	1.15	0.00	8.24	-0.1	92.7			41
Travis MacGregor	BRI	Rk	19	1	4	0	12	12	41^{1}	61	3	4.4	7.0	32	48%	.389	1.96	7.84	7.75	-0.7				
Damien Magnifico	ANA	MLB	26	0	0	0	1	0	0^{1}	0	0	54.0	27.0	1	0%	.000	6.00	0.00			96.4			47
	SLC	AAA	26	4	2	4	31	0	34^{1}	42	2	6.3	8.9	34	51%	.381	1.92	6.82	8.15	-1.1				
	MOB	AA	26	1	0	0	9	0	11^{1}	9	0	7.1	13.5	17	62%	.346	1.59	3.18	3.23	0.2				
Dovydas Neverauskas	IND	AAA	24	1	2	13	40	0	50^{1}	47	1	3.8	8.2	46	47%	.317	1.35	2.86	4.27	0.6				
	PIT	MLB	24	1	1	0	24	0	25^{1}	24	4	2.8	6.0	17	47%	.267	1.26	3.91	6.20	-0.3	98.6	37	68	52
Braeden Ogle	BRI	Rk	19	2	3	0	10	10	43	40	1	3.3	7.3	35	43%	.300	1.30	3.14	6.40	-0.1				
Domingo Robles	BRI	Rk	19	4	8	0	14	14	69	75	5	2.1	6.7	51	60%	.303	1.32	4.83	2.79	2.3				
Richard Rodriguez	NOR	AAA	27	4	4	10	42	1	70^{2}	56	5	2.3	10.2	80	29%	.285	1.05	2.42	3.57	1.3				
	BAL	MLB	27	0	0	0	5	0	5^{2}	12	4	4.8	4.8	3	46%	.400	2.65	14.29	10.70	-0.3	95.3			49
A.J. Schugel	IND	AAA	28	3	1	0	26	0	36^{2}	37	4	3.2	8.8	36	50%	.327	1.36	4.17	3.41	0.7				
	PIT	MLB	28	4	0	0	32	0	32	31	3	3.9	7.6	27	54%	.304	1.41	1.97	4.86	0.1	93.1	49	39	48
Nik Turley	CHT	AA	27	0	1	0	5	3	24^{1}	6	0	2.6	16.6	45	42%	.182	0.53	0.37	1.61	1.0				
	ROC	AAA	27	5	4	0	18	10	67^{2}	58	4	2.9	10.5	79	35%	.325	1.18	2.66	4.19	1.0				
	MIN	MLB	27	0	2	0	10	3	17^{2}	30	5	4.1	6.6	13	44%	.410	2.15	11.21	7.99	-0.5	95.4	45	47	52
Brandon Waddell	ALT	AA	23	3	3	0	15	15	66	60	3	3.7	7.6	56	50%	.295	1.32	3.55	4.83	0.3				

An extreme control artist, **Dario Agrazal** hasn't had a walk rate higher than four percent since he came to the United States. Still no confirmation that Agrazal means "the strong neck" in Spanish, though. Tall, hard-throwing and with an idea of where the ball is going, **Tyler Eppler** should be better than this, yet gives scouts very little reason to believe he actually will be. **Yeudy Garcia** had an ERA of 6.60 as a starter at Double-A in June, moved to the bullpen and saw that number fall to 2.81 the rest of the way. Once thought of as the next Felix Hernandez, **Luis Heredia** now isn't even looking like the next Felix Heredia. **Gage Hinsz** has exactly the look and the temperament you want from a guy named Gage, and some good raw stuff to go with it, but he's miles from turning any of that into big-league value. He's just organizational pitching depth, but **Clay Holmes** gets a ton of groundballs, which makes him potentially useful organizational pitching depth. A few years after having top-100 national prospect pedigree, **Nick Kingham** spent his age-25 summer in Indianapolis and it wasn't because MLB expanded in the meantime. Like a secondhand jigsaw puzzle, **Max Kranick** has all the makings of a nice thing to have (in this case, a mid-rotation starter), but it's impossible to know for sure whether all the pieces are there. After the Cubs failed, the Pirates decided to take a shot at taming **Jack Leathersich**'s chronic wildness. If they actually pull it off, start putting together Ray Searage's Hall of Fame case. Another Pirates pitching draftee from Florida, **Travis MacGregor** has plus velocity and a frame that projects to permit some durability, but his breaking ball isn't where it needs to be yet. ⚾ The Angels sent Jordan Kipper to Baltimore four weeks into the 2017 season in exchange for **Damien Magnifico**, a rare deal involving two clearly made-up people. ⚾ As the first Lithuanian player in MLB history, **Dovydas Neverauskas** is important. As a pitcher, he's an electric but erratic arm without a sufficient second pitch. ⚾ If you see **Braeden Ogle** as a starter in 2018, take a picture: it'll last longer than he will in that role. ⚾ Lefty **Domingo Robles** might need to add velocity to really make a dent, but he's young and slim enough to dream on, and he can already spin a curveball. ⚾ After his best season yet in Triple-A, **Richard Rodriguez** was summoned to Baltimore on September 1 and lasted 17 days before being designated for assignment. Allowing 16 baserunners and four homers in less than six innings was not the first impression he was going for. ⚾ An extreme reverse-split right-hander, **A.J. Schugel** has marginal matchup value, but as starters depart earlier and earlier teams need more reliable relief arms than his. ⚾ While it's true **Nik Turley** has struck out the world during four years in the high minors, he's also walked most of Eurasia and face-planted in his major-league debut. ⚾ University of Virginia alum **Brandon Waddell** can be too cavalier with the strike zone and battled injuries in 2017, but he looked good in the Arizona Fall League.

League Leaders 2017

NL Rookie Pitcher WARP – Trevor Williams, 2.62

SAN DIEGO PADRES

Essay by Emma Baccellieri

Player comments by Ben Diamond and BP staff

Here is a quote from the San Diego Padres essay in the 2015 edition of this book: "The Padres, at this writing, are not in the top tier of World Series contenders... But they are equally not Jeff Luhnow's Astros or Dayton Moore's Royals or Theo Epstein's Cubs: Padres fans will not have to sit through a mini-generation of knowing their major-league squad is doomed to fifth place, relying on reports of exceptional youngsters on the farm for emotional sustenance."

That was true at the time, and it remains true now. The Padres have *certainly* not been equal to Luhnow's Astros or Moore's Royals or Epstein's Cubs, as those three clubs have won the three World Series that have been played since that essay was written.

Here is something else: a partial list of teams ranked by standard deviation in annual win total, from 2011 through 2017.

1. Houston Astros, 19.0 wins 2. Chicago Cubs, 16.6 wins ... ... 30. San Diego Padres, 3.4 wins

More so than any other team, the Padres have been consistent in recent years. They haven't had the intense and carefully plotted worst-to-first swings of the clubs that once seemed like their peers; they haven't scraped quite so low, and it feels silly to even bother finishing this sentence with a note that they haven't hit nearly so high, because *obviously*. (The Royals, for their part, come in 17th on the preceding list, having now had time to start tumbling back to whence they came in the seasons after their title.) The Padres' on-field outcomes have differed only very slightly from season to season, keeping a miserably tight range around a dreary midpoint. They're not the only club that's maintained a steady record lately, but they're the only one that's done so quite like this. Bunched at a standard deviation of five to six wins apiece, the Yankees and Cardinals and Dodgers sit just above the Padres in the win total ranking excerpted above. Those teams, though, are perennial contenders with a habit of winning—whereas no one has been able to make a habit of losing like San Diego.

But for all that losing, the Padres have never been the worst club in baseball. The team has spent more time in the NL West's third or fourth place than in fifth. They've lost and reliably kept losing, but they've never once displayed a pattern of loss that was truly atrocious. They've never had a season that was historically or even remarkably terrible, or one that seemed fatally condemned by injuries or bad luck, or, in other words, one that dipped below 68 wins. Loss is meant to hurt—instinctually, viscerally, preparation and context be damned—but the Padres have mastered losing in a way that has dulled the whole thing enough to feel almost comfortable. They lose enough so that it is a default state but not too much to make it permanently or inescapably so. (There's not a question here of losing "when it matters," because they've lost enough that nothing matters; it all cancels out.) The Padres have been bad much in the way that chronic pain can be bad: relentlessly, unyieldingly, stubbornly, but often still rather quietly. A steady hum of distress that at any point might either work itself up into a shriek

PADRES PROSPECTUS

2017 W-L: 71-91, 4TH IN NL WEST

Pythag	.363	30th	B-Age	26.1	*1st*
RS/G	3.73	30th	P-Age	27.9	*9th*
RA/G	5.04	21st	Salary	$67.6M	*29th*
TAv	.256	20th	M$/MW	$2.3M	*25th*
TAv-P	.280	27th	DL Days	1442	*28th*
FIP	4.69	23rd	$ on DL	13%	*13th*
DER	.701	17th			

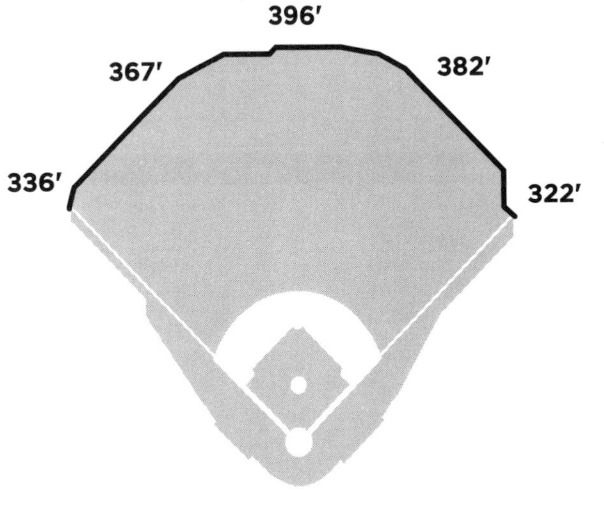

Outfield wall profile: **8′** to **11′**

Three-Year Park Factors

Runs	Runs/RH	Runs/LH	HR/RH	HR/LH
96	99	93	100	94

Top Hitter WARP	3.5 Austin Hedges
Top Pitcher WARP	2.9 Jhoulys Chacin
Top Prospect	Fernando Tatis, Jr

2017 Hit List Ranking

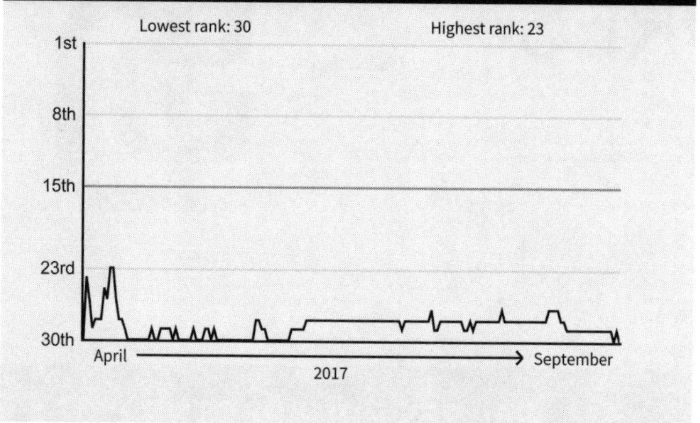

Committed Payroll (in millions)

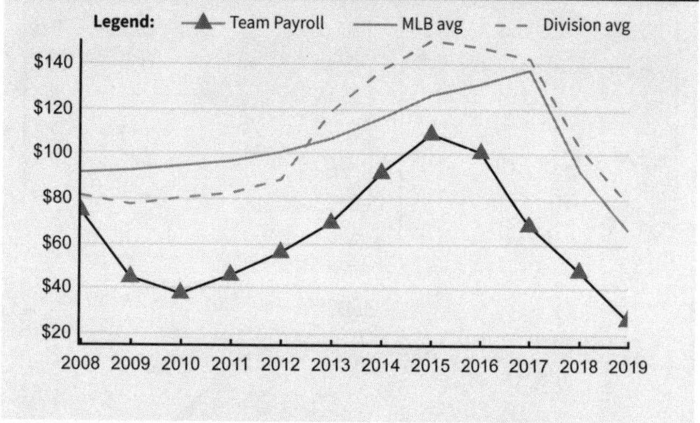

Farm System Ranking

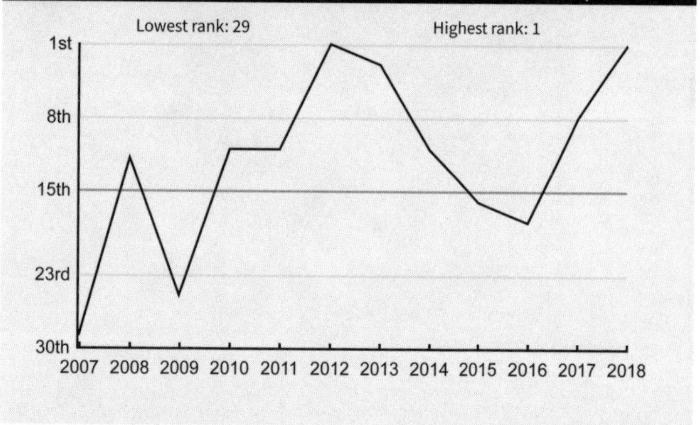

Personnel

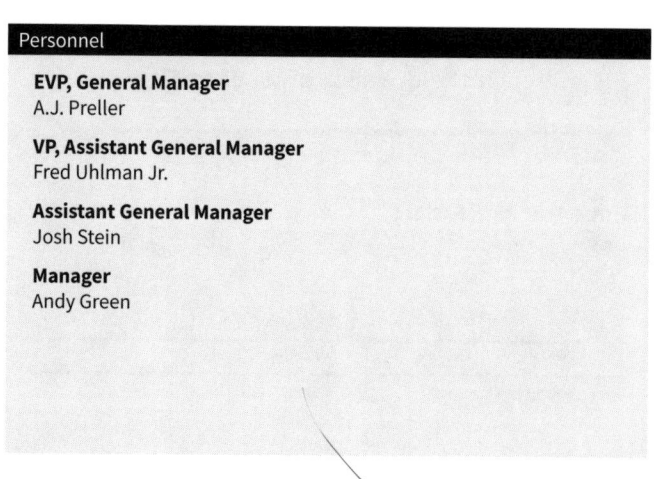

EVP, General Manager
A.J. Preller

VP, Assistant General Manager
Fred Uhlman Jr.

Assistant General Manager
Josh Stein

Manager
Andy Green

or just fade into the background. One might say, "Oh, well, that's awful, but it's not having a limb sawed off." To which one might reply, "At least there's a clear ending point when having a limb sawed off." And one might dismiss that entire hypothetical conversation by saying that any sort of physical agony like this is debilitating either way, so what's the point.

The losing is familiar to the point of being routine, but the roster is not. Look at the three players who've received the most plate appearances for San Diego in each of the past five years, and get 13 different players for the 15 different spots. The constant churn here has produced a set of players each season who could most generously be described as filler, though their collective skill set has more often than not been pretty empty. The cast around Wil Myers has regularly been repopulated with fresh sets of has-beens and never-will-bes, but the results have been the same year after year. It doesn't matter that so many of the players can easily feel anonymous, because so many of them end up proving themselves as consummate replacement players. It's all a seemingly never-ending condition that has become strong enough to double as shorthand for a team identity—not baseball hell, certainly, but perhaps baseball purgatory.

The stability of the on-field suffering contrasts sharply with relative chaos in the front office. Since the Padres' last winning season in 2010, they've passed through the hands of two different ownership groups and four different general managers. And that's if you're being polite about the whole thing—depending on how you want to keep score here, feel free to additionally count another ownership group in the one helmed by former Padres CEO Jeff Moorad, who spent several years buying the club in installments before being denied his purchase by other owners who didn't want him in their club, and another general manager in the trio of Omar Minaya/A.J. Hinch/Fred Uhlman, who shared the role for a bit in an interim capacity back in 2014, making several big moves over the trade deadline.

Essentially, it's all been very messy, and listing all the changes in ownership and front office leadership doesn't come close to capturing all of the changes in strategy and ideology. Look at what's taken place just under current general manager A.J. Preller. His first few months on the job were explosive, full of splashy veteran additions. But that tactic (or, at least, his particular execution of it) quickly revealed itself to be ineffective, and so the front office slammed on the brakes and turned all the way around. A year later, the team's biggest contracts had been shed—well, the players behind them, if not the contracts themselves; of the three biggest payroll commitments in 2017, none was actually still on the roster—and they'd pivoted to a new focus on scouting and development. Their farm system went from being ranked 18th in Baseball Prospectus' organizational rankings in 2016 to being ranked fourth in 2017.

That last piece of information, followed to its logical end, should point to hope for the future. Which there is! The system is not only talented but deep, with what might be baseball's best crop of young pitchers and some exciting young players who've already debuted (Manuel Margot, Austin Hedges, Hunter Renfroe). The immediate future has the potential to be, if not quite successful, at least quite exciting. And the more distant future has an even stronger potential to be both.

But when you look at these various potential futures through the lens of the club's recent past, that hope can feel rather ill-advised. It hasn't been so long since the last time the Padres had one of the best farm systems in baseball, if not *the* best farm system in baseball! It's been six years since they last sat atop BP's organizational rankings—not so long ago, but still more than long enough for the bulk of those prospects to have developed. Yet the elite farm system in question got San Diego absolutely nowhere. Half of those players were lost in trades that managed to bring back only a fraction of what they sent out (see: Anthony Rizzo, Trea Turner, Jedd Gyorko), and the remaining half got hurt or flamed out (see: Casey Kelly, Joe Wieland, Robbie Erlin, Rymer Liriano). A promising future doesn't ever guarantee a promise *for* the future, and the Padres don't have to be particularly or profoundly introspective to see that very plainly in their own recent history.

Also contributing to the idea that hope is foolish here is that aforementioned tandem of front-office tumult with on-field stagnancy. One could very reasonably look at the Padres' current leadership and say, "Well, there's clearly a plan for advancement here, the situation should improve soon." But one could have very reasonably looked at several different San Diego front offices with several different plans over the last seven years and said that exact same thing, albeit with some changes in confidence level, and been wrong every single time. The team's current management appears stable; their current strategy appears sound. Both of those things have appeared true before, though, and they've always subsequently revealed themselves to be otherwise. Remember? Jed Hoyer came into the general manager's seat pretty well-regarded; he left after three seasons and took his lessons from San Diego to win a World Series with the Cubs. Josh Byrnes followed, similarly well-regarded; he was forced out after two and a half seasons and took his lessons from San Diego to make a World Series trip with the Dodgers. Through all of that, the Padres were losing.

Baseball's past half-decade has repeatedly demonstrated the effectiveness of losing with a plan, if not the virtue of doing so. The idea that loss can be a net positive, if done deliberately and in the name of the future good, is now widely acknowledged (if, again, not quite embraced). Trusting the process is now a belief system. It's only losing aimlessly—without reason or purpose or, simply, meaning—that is deemed truly bad. Yet the Padres' recent history of stagnant loss is not a history of aimless losing. The Padres have almost *always* been losing with a plan. But the plan has been enacted at the wrong moment or hasn't been executed in perfect alignment with the master vision or has just failed on its own terms. The plan has changed so many times. There have been so many plans at the hands of so many smart baseball men, and the Padres have been losing the whole time. And you think there's reason to be hopeful now because this plan seems like it'll work this time? Because the farm system's good?

But there *is* reason to be hopeful now. For starters, there's a new commitment to stability. Preller is currently entering his fourth full season as general manager, more than either of his two most recent predecessors had, and ownership signed this winter to extend him through 2022. (And scarcely a year after Preller received his second career suspension from the league, this time for failing to disclose medical information in the trade that landed top-tier pitching prospect Anderson Espinoza: that's job security.) That stability's on the field, too. Manager Andy Green also received a contract extension this year, his through 2021, and all of the club's sharpest young players will remain under team control through that time: Myers, Margot, Hedges, Renfroe, to say nothing of dozens of promising minor leaguers. This front office has proven itself adept at acquiring young talent both through the draft and internationally, and while the question of whether they can *develop* that talent as well as they can scout it remains unanswered, most signs on that front so far have been about as encouraging as any can be. Hope never guarantees anything, but there are more reasons to be hopeful than there are not.

It took Epstein and Hoyer five seasons to help the Cubs win their title; it took Luhnow six seasons to help the Astros land theirs; it took Moore nine to help the Royals. At this point, it feels a bit ridiculous to include Preller and the Padres with this set, and it very well could still feel ridiculous once Preller has had as many years on the job as Moore had when he won the 2014 World Series. But there was a point when it would've felt ridiculous to include any of those front offices on a list of winners, wasn't there?

In Dante's *Inferno*, the nine circles of hell are described in exacting detail. One place that's not described so much is the River Acheron, which forms the border of hell. Dante kind of just skips over that one, as he passes into a trance as he's about to cross the river and doesn't bother to get a recap later. Fair enough. What is compelling about the border, lacking all the pain and agony and eternal fire of actual hell? It's a bad place to be, sure. (It's literally right next to hell.) But it's not the *worst* place. It's so very close to the worst place; you might reasonably decide to categorize it as part of the worst place itself and feel perfectly fine about your logic. That would do a disservice to the river, though, because it isn't hell, it's really not—it's something else. It's a liminal space, and the Padres have been there for years now. But they might now not be too far off from pulling ashore and climbing back toward the land of the living.

—Emma Baccellieri is an author of Baseball Prospectus.

Hitters

Franchy Cordero OF Born: 09/02/94 Age: 23 Bats: L Throws: R Height: 6'3" Weight: 175 Origin: International Free Agent, 2011

YEAR	TEAM	LVL	AGE	PA	R	2B	3B	HR	RBI	BB	K	SB	CS	AVG/OBP/SLG	TAv	VORP	BABIP	BRR	FRAA	WARP
2015	FTW	A	20	524	59	13	1	5	34	31	121	22	11	.243/.293/.306	.231	-1.0	.313	3.0	LF(68): -1.7, SS(23): -3.1	-0.6
2016	LEL	A+	21	322	47	16	8	5	35	19	83	11	8	.286/.339/.444	.285	21.4	.381	3.1	CF(68): -3.9, LF(2): -0.4	1.8
2016	SAN	AA	21	264	31	8	8	6	19	17	67	12	6	.306/.356/.478	.312	20.8	.401	-0.7	CF(59): 2.9	2.6
2017	SDN	MLB	22	99	15	3	3	3	9	6	44	1	1	.228/.276/.424	.254	3.8	.400	1.2	CF(25): 0.9, LF(1): -0.1	0.5
2017	ELP	AAA	22	419	68	21	18	17	64	23	118	15	4	.326/.369/.603	.308	36.9	.431	1.7	CF(61): -2.5, LF(22): 1.5	3.5
2018	*SDN*	*MLB*	*23*	*250*	*31*	*9*	*4*	*7*	*26*	*14*	*82*	*6*	*3*	*.234/.282/.401*	*.235*	*3.5*	*.325*	*0.6*	*CF -1, LF 0*	*0.3*
2019	*SDN*	*MLB*	*24*	*437*	*49*	*16*	*7*	*13*	*52*	*26*	*143*	*10*	*4*	*.236/.287/.409*	*.253*	*10.2*	*.326*	*1.5*	*CF -2, LF 0*	*0.9*

Breakout: 7% Improve: 24% Collapse: 5% Attrition: 21% MLB: 46% *Comparables: Teoscar Hernandez, Lewis Brinson, Franklin Gutierrez*

Cordero posted one of the best offensive seasons in the PCL last year as one of the league's youngest regulars, while showing defensive utility all over the outfield grass. Not too shabby! There are some smoke and mirrors involved, however, as he racked up those numbers in the PCL and doesn't have as much power as you'd expect. He also struck out nearly 30 percent of the time at Triple-A, and that number exploded to nearly 45 percent in his big-league cup-of-coffee. That said, Cordero has all the physical tools to start in the outfield and is, at the very least, going to be a breakout candidate for years to come.

Allen Cordoba SS Born: 12/06/95 Age: 22 Bats: R Throws: R Height: 6'1" Weight: 175 Origin: International Free Agent, 2015

YEAR	TEAM	LVL	AGE	PA	R	2B	3B	HR	RBI	BB	K	SB	CS	AVG/OBP/SLG	TAv	VORP	BABIP	BRR	FRAA	WARP
2015	CRD	RK	19	229	40	6	2	2	20	15	20	11	3	.342/.401/.421	.298	23.6	.366	3.9	SS(47): 2.0, 3B(5): 0.2	2.5
2016	JCY	RK	20	220	49	16	5	0	18	21	19	22	4	.362/.427/.495	.318	26.6	.399	3.1	SS(50): 5.4	3.2
2017	SDN	MLB	21	227	17	2	2	4	15	18	54	2	2	.208/.282/.297	.221	-1.9	.259	0.4	LF(43): -1.5, SS(28): -2.8	-0.6
2018	*SDN*	*MLB*	*22*	*33*	*3*	*1*	*0*	*1*	*3*	*2*	*8*	*0*	*0*	*.228/.290/.344*	*.232*	*0.5*	*.280*	*0.0*	*SS 0*	*0.0*
2019	*SDN*	*MLB*	*23*	*327*	*37*	*11*	*2*	*8*	*35*	*25*	*75*	*4*	*2*	*.237/.304/.375*	*.251*	*8.2*	*.287*	*0.3*	*SS -2*	*0.6*

Breakout: 1% Improve: 22% Collapse: 5% Attrition: 10% MLB: 35% *Comparables: Melky Cabrera, Jose Tabata, L.J. Hoes*

Here's an important note to bookmark: A .362 rookie-ball batting average directly translates to a .208 mark in the majors (sample size: one). The most forgettable of the Padres' three Rule 5 selections, Cordoba was the fourth-youngest player in the majors last season and managed to stick with the big-league club all year. His speed hasn't quite translated from the low minors, but it's there, and despite posting predictably terrible production given his lot (his .108/.225/.137 line from June 3 on is downright surreal), he showed flashes of potential value. Cordoba will head to the minor leagues now that his Rule 5 designation is up, but the former Cardinals farmhand could return to the Padres in due time as a useful utility player.

Alex Dickerson LF Born: 05/26/90 Age: 28 Bats: L Throws: L Height: 6'3" Weight: 235 Origin: Round 3, 2011 Draft (#91 overall)

YEAR	TEAM	LVL	AGE	PA	R	2B	3B	HR	RBI	BB	K	SB	CS	AVG/OBP/SLG	TAv	VORP	BABIP	BRR	FRAA	WARP
2015	ELP	AAA	25	519	82	36	9	12	71	45	96	4	0	.307/.374/.503	.308	37.1	.360	1.0	LF(96): -6.0, RF(16): 0.3	3.2
2015	SDN	MLB	25	8	0	0	0	0	0	0	3	0	0	.250/.250/.250	.150	-0.7	.400	0.0	LF(1): 0.1	-0.1
2016	ELP	AAA	26	241	50	16	3	10	51	14	27	0	0	.382/.425/.622	.332	24.0	.397	1.6	LF(36): -2.5, 1B(10): -0.1	2.2
2016	SDN	MLB	26	285	39	16	2	10	37	26	44	5	1	.257/.333/.455	.287	14.4	.274	0.5	LF(68): -3.3	1.1
2018	*SDN*	*MLB*	*28*	*205*	*27*	*10*	*2*	*6*	*24*	*16*	*42*	*1*	*0*	*.257/.323/.434*	*.270*	*8.3*	*.299*	*0.0*	*LF -1, 1B 0*	*0.6*
2019	*SDN*	*MLB*	*29*	*259*	*33*	*13*	*2*	*9*	*33*	*23*	*57*	*1*	*0*	*.255/.330/.441*	*.283*	*11.8*	*.299*	*0.1*	*LF -1, 1B 0*	*1.1*

Breakout: 7% Improve: 22% Collapse: 17% Attrition: 31% MLB: 66% *Comparables: Steve Pearce, Nate Freiman, Jesus Guzman*

Dickerson entered 2017 as a decent breakout candidate after hitting, hitting and hitting in the minor leagues and continuing to do so in his rookie season with the Padres. Unfortunately, back surgery derailed his follow-up act before it had a chance to begin. He's expected to be healthy for spring training and will ideally resume his trend of, well, hitting. Bringing nice pop and plate discipline to the table, he also makes plenty of contact and could emerge as a late bloomer. That said, the lefty will be in a playing time squeeze given San Diego's crowded outfield, and the serious injury means expectations should be handicapped for now.

Rocky Gale C Born: 02/22/88 Age: 30 Bats: R Throws: R Height: 6'1" Weight: 185 Origin: Round 24, 2010 Draft (#724 overall)

YEAR	TEAM	LVL	AGE	PA	R	2B	3B	HR	RBI	BB	K	SB	CS	AVG/OBP/SLG	TAv	VORP	BABIP	BRR	FRAA	WARP
2015	ELP	AAA	27	351	34	16	4	1	39	17	59	1	1	.307/.349/.391	.259	12.7	.370	-2.4	C(94): 12.2, 3B(3): -0.3	2.5
2015	SDN	MLB	27	10	0	0	0	0	0	0	1	0	0	.100/.100/.100	.038	-1.9	.111	-0.1	C(6): 0.3	-0.2
2016	SAN	AA	28	247	21	8	1	2	20	29	38	1	0	.219/.322/.295	.234	2.9	.256	-1.2	C(62): 8.4	1.2
2016	ELP	AAA	28	159	16	2	0	3	14	5	19	0	0	.278/.318/.354	.226	0.8	.296	-0.5	C(36): 2.8, 3B(4): -0.1	0.4
2017	ELP	AAA	29	377	43	20	2	2	37	24	55	0	0	.278/.328/.365	.234	5.1	.321	-2.3	C(99): 3.6, P(2): 0.0	0.8
2017	SDN	MLB	29	10	1	0	0	1	2	0	2	0	0	.100/.100/.400	.167	-0.5	.000	0.0	C(3): -0.4	-0.1
2018	*SDN*	*MLB*	*30*	*122*	*11*	*4*	*1*	*1*	*10*	*7*	*26*	*0*	*0*	*.222/.276/.309*	*.214*	*0.2*	*.272*	*-0.2*	*C 0*	*-0.1*
2019	*SDN*	*MLB*	*31*	*222*	*22*	*8*	*1*	*3*	*19*	*15*	*49*	*0*	*0*	*.221/.283/.315*	*.221*	*-0.8*	*.272*	*-0.4*	*C 0*	*-0.1*

Breakout: 2% Improve: 12% Collapse: 6% Attrition: 17% MLB: 33% *Comparables: Wil Nieves, Tuffy Gosewisch, Paul Phillips*

YEAR	TEAM	P. COUNT	FRM RUNS	BLK RUNS	THRW RUNS	TOT RUNS
2015	ELP	11838	5.8	0.7	1.9	8.4
2015	SDN	282	0.1	0.2	0.0	0.3
2017	SDN	379	-0.1	-0.1	-0.1	-0.3
2018	*SDN*	*4525*	*-0.9*	*0.4*	*0.1*	*-0.4*
2019	*SDN*	*8240*	*-0.8*	*0.4*	*0.1*	*-0.4*

Sometimes you wonder why an organizational depth player sticks with baseball long past his expiration date as a realistic big league contributor. Enduring countrywide bus trips with 24 other men, surviving on a daily diet of fast food and sacrificing body and brain for an unlivable wage can loose its luster quickly once the race to the big leagues migrates into a more likely marathon toward a coaching gig. Then, you watch a player like Gale, veteran of eight minor-league seasons, bash his first career big-league home run into the upper deck and round the bases with quite possibly the purest smile you'll ever see on a baseball field (apologies to Francisco Lindor). That's when you get it.

Freddy Galvis SS Born: 11/14/89 Age: 28 Bats: B Throws: R Height: 5'10" Weight: 185 Origin: International Free Agent, 2006

YEAR	TEAM	LVL	AGE	PA	R	2B	3B	HR	RBI	BB	K	SB	CS	AVG/OBP/SLG	TAv	VORP	BABIP	BRR	FRAA	WARP
2015	PHI	MLB	25	603	63	14	5	7	50	30	103	10	1	.263/.302/.343	.241	15.8	.309	3.4	SS(146): -4.1, 2B(4): 0.1	1.3
2016	PHI	MLB	26	624	61	26	3	20	67	25	136	17	6	.241/.274/.399	.239	8.6	.280	-3.5	SS(156): 0.5	0.9
2017	PHI	MLB	27	663	71	29	6	12	61	45	111	14	5	.255/.309/.382	.256	27.4	.292	1.6	SS(155): 1.7, CF(1): 0.1	2.9
2018	*SDN*	*MLB*	*28*	*615*	*72*	*25*	*4*	*14*	*58*	*37*	*122*	*12*	*4*	*.238/.287/.374*	*.227*	*8.0*	*.274*	*0.1*	*SS -2, CF 0*	*0.7*
2019	*SDN*	*MLB*	*29*	*539*	*59*	*21*	*4*	*14*	*58*	*35*	*107*	*10*	*3*	*.237/.289/.378*	*.242*	*8.3*	*.270*	*0.3*	*SS -2, CF 0*	*0.7*

Breakout: 1% Improve: 42% Collapse: 8% Attrition: 15% MLB: 95% *Comparables: Adeiny Hechavarria, Eduardo Escobar, Alex Cintron*

One of the stranger stories of the 2017 Phillies was how much they contorted themselves to make Galvis the first National League player to play in 162 games since Freddie Freeman and Hunter Pence in 2014. Originally, Galvis had set a goal to *start* all 162 games, quite lofty for a marginal regular on a team with one of the best shortstop prospects in baseball marinating at Triple-A. Galvis got all the way to the second game of an August 30 doubleheader before things finally came to a head with J.P. Crawford—and even then Galvis still started in the outfield. Eventually, the Phillies had to split the baby to take a few looks at Crawford at short, and Galvis chose to be used off the bench rather than starting at other positions. It all turned out to be a bit for naught, as Joey Votto quietly pulled off the 162-start gimmick Galvis was originally aiming for.

Chase Headley 3B

Born: 05/09/84 Age: 34 Bats: B Throws: R Height: 6'2" Weight: 215 Origin: Round 2, 2005 Draft (#66 overall)

YEAR	TEAM	LVL	AGE	PA	R	2B	3B	HR	RBI	BB	K	SB	CS	AVG/OBP/SLG	TAv	VORP	BABIP	BRR	FRAA	WARP
2015	NYA	MLB	31	642	74	29	1	11	62	51	135	0	2	.259/.324/.369	.245	9.6	.317	-0.8	3B(155): 3.1, 1B(1): 0.0	1.4
2016	NYA	MLB	32	529	58	18	1	14	51	51	118	8	2	.253/.331/.385	.248	10.7	.306	0.1	3B(140): 4.9	1.6
2017	NYA	MLB	33	586	77	30	1	12	61	60	132	9	2	.273/.352/.406	.272	21.5	.341	-0.5	3B(86): 1.2, 1B(45): 0.3	2.3
2018	*SDN*	*MLB*	*34*	*361*	*38*	*16*	*1*	*6*	*36*	*34*	*85*	*4*	*1*	*.239/.320/.350*	*.247*	*6.4*	*.305*	*-0.3*	*3B 3*	*0.7*
2019	*SDN*	*MLB*	*35*	*432*	*49*	*19*	*1*	*7*	*41*	*43*	*108*	*4*	*1*	*.236/.322/.348*	*.253*	*7.1*	*.308*	*-0.3*	*3B 4*	*1.3*

Breakout: 2% Improve: 42% Collapse: 12% Attrition: 23% MLB: 83% *Comparables: Todd Zeile, Daryl Spencer, Kurt Bevacqua*

Headley's 2017 was very similar to his 2016 campaign in that one abysmal month dragged down an otherwise solid performance. Despite hitting just .165 in May, he finished as a valuable contributor overall and volunteered to switch positions when the Yankees acquired Todd Frazier from the White Sox. He took to first base pretty well at age 33, which could be a key to extending his career beyond the next couple seasons. Headley's failure to rediscover the big-time power he once showed in San Diego (the first time around) will forever disappoint some fans, but he's a useful secondary piece.

Austin Hedges C

Born: 08/18/92 Age: 25 Bats: R Throws: R Height: 6'1" Weight: 206 Origin: Round 2, 2011 Draft (#82 overall)

YEAR	TEAM	LVL	AGE	PA	R	2B	3B	HR	RBI	BB	K	SB	CS	AVG/OBP/SLG	TAv	VORP	BABIP	BRR	FRAA	WARP
2015	ELP	AAA	22	79	12	8	0	2	15	8	8	1	0	.324/.392/.521	.313	7.3	.344	0.0	C(17): 5.1	1.3
2015	SDN	MLB	22	152	13	2	0	3	11	8	38	0	0	.168/.215/.248	.191	-2.1	.202	1.6	C(47): 8.8	0.7
2016	ELP	AAA	23	334	55	20	1	21	82	13	51	1	1	.326/.353/.597	.301	28.3	.329	-0.4	C(73): 5.2	3.4
2016	SDN	MLB	23	26	2	1	0	0	1	0	7	0	1	.125/.154/.167	.119	-2.7	.167	-0.1	C(7): -0.2	-0.3
2017	SDN	MLB	24	417	36	17	0	18	55	23	122	4	1	.214/.262/.398	.233	8.3	.260	0.6	C(115): 26.7	3.5
2018	*SDN*	*MLB*	*25*	*433*	*52*	*18*	*1*	*18*	*56*	*23*	*108*	*3*	*1*	*.229/.274/.410*	*.242*	*14.6*	*.264*	*-0.6*	*C 20*	*2.8*
2019	*SDN*	*MLB*	*26*	*466*	*59*	*21*	*0*	*22*	*65*	*28*	*121*	*3*	*1*	*.229/.281/.435*	*.257*	*17.7*	*.262*	*1.1*	*C 21*	*4.2*

Breakout: 6% Improve: 47% Collapse: 10% Attrition: 20% MLB: 95% *Comparables: John Buck, Miguel Montero, Wilson Ramos*

YEAR	TEAM	P. COUNT	FRM RUNS	BLK RUNS	THRW RUNS	TOT RUNS
2015	ELP	2301	4.0	0.1	0.1	4.1
2015	SDN	5804	7.6	1.2	0.2	9.0
2016	SDN	901	-0.4	0.2	0.0	-0.2
2017	SDN	15353	20.8	1.1	2.2	24.1
2018	*SDN*	*16410*	*16.7*	*1.7*	*0.9*	*19.3*
2019	*SDN*	*17649*	*15.2*	*1.5*	*0.8*	*17.5*

There will always be a big-league job for a player like Hedges, who boasts elite defense behind the plate while providing a smattering of offense. He isn't the guy who .397/.438/.809 in the second half of 2016 at Triple-A (who is?), but he has power and could improve if he limits the strikeouts. Thanks to a defensive skill set that might be the best in baseball, Hedges only needs to provide league-average offense to be a potential down-ballot MVP candidate, and his minor-league track record gives hope that he can do just that. As for the glove, WARP has him as the fifth-most valuable Padre last year even before factoring in the bat. After factoring it in, he shoots up to first. This is all a long way of saying that Hedges is exactly what the Padres envisioned when they gave him a $3 million bonus in the second round of the 2011 draft.

Travis Jankowski OF

Born: 06/15/91 Age: 27 Bats: L Throws: R Height: 6'2" Weight: 185 Origin: Round 1, 2012 Draft (#44 overall)

YEAR	TEAM	LVL	AGE	PA	R	2B	3B	HR	RBI	BB	K	SB	CS	AVG/OBP/SLG	TAv	VORP	BABIP	BRR	FRAA	WARP
2015	SAN	AA	24	321	50	11	5	1	13	36	40	23	8	.316/.395/.401	.281	14.1	.365	-1.3	CF(62): 2.9	1.8
2015	ELP	AAA	24	113	19	6	2	0	12	13	10	9	3	.392/.464/.495	.335	13.8	.432	1.5	CF(24): 3.1	1.7
2015	SDN	MLB	24	96	9	2	2	2	12	4	24	2	1	.211/.245/.344	.234	0.3	.266	0.2	CF(23): -2.6, RF(11): 0.7	-0.2
2016	SDN	MLB	25	383	53	13	2	2	12	42	100	30	12	.245/.332/.313	.238	10.0	.343	7.1	CF(87): -2.2, RF(22): -0.5	0.7
2017	ELP	AAA	26	157	20	5	1	0	11	18	28	8	1	.266/.350/.317	.240	1.0	.333	0.1	CF(22): -1.7, LF(7): -0.3	-0.1
2017	SDN	MLB	26	87	10	2	0	0	1	9	28	4	0	.187/.282/.213	.194	-3.1	.298	0.9	LF(19): -0.4, CF(4): 0.3	-0.3
2018	*SDN*	*MLB*	*27*	*115*	*15*	*4*	*1*	*1*	*8*	*11*	*27*	*6*	*2*	*.237/.313/.324*	*.237*	*2.5*	*.307*	*0.6*	*LF 0, CF 0*	*0.1*
2019	*SDN*	*MLB*	*28*	*203*	*22*	*7*	*1*	*3*	*18*	*21*	*50*	*11*	*4*	*.240/.320/.339*	*.247*	*5.1*	*.312*	*2.4*	*LF 0, CF 0*	*0.6*

Breakout: 1% Improve: 33% Collapse: 8% Attrition: 16% MLB: 73% *Comparables: Joey Gathright, Tony Gwynn, Gregor Blanco*

The worst-case scenario for a player who depends on his legs for production is, well, a leg injury. Unfortunately, that's what Jankowski encountered in late April, effectively ruining his 2017 campaign. When healthy, he showed top-of-the-scale speed and solid center-field defense. Although he struck out at a higher-than-ideal clip for a player with his lack of pop during his rookie season, he also walked at a respectable enough clip to prop up his on-base numbers. It's something on which to build with health and playing time, though neither of those things is close to a given in 2018.

Manuel Margot CF

Born: 09/28/94 Age: 23 Bats: R Throws: R Height: 5'11" Weight: 180 Origin: International Free Agent, 2011

YEAR	TEAM	LVL	AGE	PA	R	2B	3B	HR	RBI	BB	K	SB	CS	AVG/OBP/SLG	TAv	VORP	BABIP	BRR	FRAA	WARP
2015	SLM	A+	20	198	35	6	5	3	17	11	15	20	5	.282/.321/.420	.273	9.6	.289	1.5	CF(42): 5.5	1.6
2015	PME	AA	20	282	38	21	4	3	33	21	36	19	8	.271/.326/.419	.270	13.0	.303	1.9	CF(63): -2.5, RF(1): 0.2	1.2
2016	ELP	AAA	21	566	98	21	12	6	55	36	64	30	11	.304/.351/.426	.270	30.8	.335	7.9	CF(121): 19.3, RF(1): 0.2	5.2
2016	SDN	MLB	21	37	4	4	1	0	3	0	7	2	0	.243/.243/.405	.274	2.4	.300	0.8	CF(9): 0.6, RF(1): 0.1	0.3
2017	SDN	MLB	22	529	53	18	7	13	39	35	106	17	7	.263/.313/.409	.270	23.6	.309	1.3	CF(123): -0.9	2.3
2018	*SDN*	*MLB*	*23*	*627*	*81*	*24*	*8*	*12*	*56*	*38*	*117*	*23*	*8*	*.248/.294/.381*	*.247*	*16.7*	*.287*	*2.6*	*CF 7*	*2.0*
2019	*SDN*	*MLB*	*24*	*590*	*67*	*23*	*7*	*15*	*67*	*40*	*116*	*22*	*8*	*.253/.307/.406*	*.264*	*22.1*	*.293*	*2.1*	*CF 8*	*3.2*

Breakout: 4% Improve: 42% Collapse: 3% Attrition: 14% MLB: 65% *Comparables: Delino DeShields, Andrew McCutchen, Gerardo Parra*

The most important part of a lineup may not be the leadoff spot, but the Padres seem likely to have it locked up for years to come. Margot has the prototypical table-setting profile, boasting excellent bat-to-ball skills and plus speed, but it's amplified with some double-digit pop and solid defense in center. He must have had one hell of a mattress at his apartment: Petco Park is certainly not the pitcher's park it used to be, but Margot hit an All-Star-like .297/.362/.475 in San Diego, a far cry from his paltry .609 OPS on the road. Given his minor-league numbers, it wouldn't be a shock to see his strikeout rate drop a bit in year two, and given a fairly aggressive approach, that's probably the best path toward bumping his on-base percentage up into asset territory.

Wil Myers 1B Born: 12/10/90 Age: 27 Bats: R Throws: R Height: 6'3" Weight: 205 Origin: Round 3, 2009 Draft (#91 overall)

YEAR	TEAM	LVL	AGE	PA	R	2B	3B	HR	RBI	BB	K	SB	CS	AVG/OBP/SLG	TAv	VORP	BABIP	BRR	FRAA	WARP
2015	SDN	MLB	24	253	40	13	1	8	29	27	55	5	2	.253/.336/.427	.288	13.2	.302	0.7	CF(38): -5.6, 1B(22): 0.3	0.8
2016	SDN	MLB	25	676	99	29	4	28	94	68	160	28	6	.259/.336/.461	.290	33.2	.305	5.2	1B(149): 1.8, RF(7): -0.3	3.6
2017	SDN	MLB	26	649	80	29	3	30	74	70	180	20	6	.243/.328/.464	.290	28.6	.297	1.1	1B(154): -1.8	2.7
2018	*SDN*	*MLB*	*27*	*598*	*81*	*26*	*2*	*22*	*78*	*60*	*150*	*19*	*5*	*.245/.323/.428*	*.270*	*18.2*	*.297*	*1.7*	*1B -2*	*1.3*
2019	*SDN*	*MLB*	*28*	*553*	*74*	*25*	*1*	*22*	*74*	*60*	*144*	*17*	*5*	*.243/.327/.438*	*.283*	*22.2*	*.296*	*2.3*	*1B -1*	*2.3*

Breakout: 4% Improve: 59% Collapse: 3% Attrition: 5% MLB: 95% *Comparables: Rocco Baldelli, Gil Hodges, Glenn Davis*

One question that many hitters grapple with, especially in this home-run-driven age, is how to balance power and contact. It's the Ichiro dilemma: Is it better to sell out for the sexier dingers, or play it safe and hit for a high average? Myers, a former top prospect, was supposed to be of the rare "get you a man who can do both" variety. He was also supposed to hold down a spot in the outfield after his 25th birthday, but that's both behind him and beyond the point. Myers is a weird anomaly of the launch-angle phenomenon, as he had by far the highest fly-ball rate of his career in 2017 but saw his home-run total and HR/FB rate stay right around the same spot. You're probably wondering how that happens. Simple: Myers gave all of his nine percentage point increase in fly balls right back by spiking his infield flies from 6.0 percent to a whopping 15.5 percent. He hit nearly as many pop-ups in 2017 as he had in his entire career to that point. Yet, for all his shortcomings and expectations, Myers has been a comfortably above-average first baseman for two seasons now, and most importantly, he's spent those two seasons on the field.

Josh Naylor 1B Born: 06/22/97 Age: 21 Bats: L Throws: L Height: 6'0" Weight: 225 Origin: Round 1, 2015 Draft (#12 overall)

YEAR	TEAM	LVL	AGE	PA	R	2B	3B	HR	RBI	BB	K	SB	CS	AVG/OBP/SLG	TAv	VORP	BABIP	BRR	FRAA	WARP
2015	MRL	RK	18	105	8	4	1	1	16	4	11	1	0	.327/.352/.418	.298	4.2	.352	-1.5	1B(19): -1.9	0.2
2016	GRB	A	19	370	42	24	2	9	54	22	62	10	3	.269/.317/.430	.285	10.5	.304	-1.9	1B(81): -2.3	0.9
2016	LEL	A+	19	144	17	5	0	3	21	3	22	1	1	.252/.264/.353	.236	-2.9	.276	-0.6	1B(32): -3.4	-0.7
2017	LEL	A+	20	313	41	16	2	8	45	27	48	7	1	.297/.361/.452	.295	14.3	.333	-0.1	1B(42): -0.6	1.5
2017	SAN	AA	20	175	18	9	0	2	19	16	36	2	1	.250/.320/.346	.258	0.5	.308	-0.9	1B(40): 1.9	0.3
2018	*SDN*	*MLB*	*21*	*250*	*25*	*11*	*1*	*7*	*29*	*15*	*59*	*1*	*0*	*.230/.280/.378*	*.227*	*-4.2*	*.275*	*-0.3*	*1B -2*	*-0.7*
2019	*SDN*	*MLB*	*22*	*418*	*49*	*20*	*1*	*14*	*51*	*27*	*99*	*2*	*1*	*.237/.290/.404*	*.252*	*1.2*	*.280*	*-0.6*	*1B -3*	*-0.2*

Breakout: 1% Improve: 5% Collapse: 2% Attrition: 7% MLB: 10% *Comparables: Dominic Smith, Jose Osuna, Logan Morrison*

The "makeup" part of a scouting report is always interesting. Some scouts may see a colorful and fun player who elevates his team; others see a player who severely injured a teammate with a knife in his previous organization. On the bright side, there's little controversy when it comes to Naylor's bat: The big man has big raw power, and lots of it. He also has the bat control and eye to be more than just a one-trick pony and is far more nimble than his silhouette would imply—he's stolen double-digit bases in each of his two full seasons since being taken in the first round of the 2015 draft. A flatter bat path and over-aggressive approach have prevented the raw power from fully translating into games thus far, and that will remain the primary challenge ahead in the young Canadian's quest to one day man the cold corner for a big-league team.

Jorge Ona OF Born: 12/31/96 Age: 21 Bats: R Throws: R Height: 6'0" Weight: 220 Origin: International Free Agent, 2016

YEAR	TEAM	LVL	AGE	PA	R	2B	3B	HR	RBI	BB	K	SB	CS	AVG/OBP/SLG	TAv	VORP	BABIP	BRR	FRAA	WARP
2017	FTW	A	20	465	54	18	1	11	64	40	115	8	2	.277/.351/.405	.270	12.2	.357	-0.2	RF(43): -6.4, LF(35): -4.7	0.1
2018	*SDN*	*MLB*	*21*	*250*	*23*	*9*	*0*	*7*	*27*	*15*	*79*	*0*	*0*	*.212/.268/.344*	*.215*	*-4.8*	*.287*	*-0.4*	*RF -2, LF -2*	*-1.0*
2019	*SDN*	*MLB*	*22*	*264*	*29*	*10*	*1*	*8*	*29*	*17*	*83*	*0*	*0*	*.215/.273/.356*	*.231*	*-2.7*	*.289*	*-0.5*	*RF -2, LF -2*	*-0.7*

Breakout: 1% Improve: 3% Collapse: 0% Attrition: 4% MLB: 6% *Comparables: Rymer Liriano, Moises Sierra, Jorge Bonifacio*

In the age of Twitter, Tinder and other conduits for instant gratification, we tend to view large amateur contracts as either looking really good or really bad really quickly. The Padres and Ona, just a season removed from a $7 million bonus, are still in their honeymoon phase. There's a strong offensive foundation as a power-hitting corner outfielder, and the shaky defense of, well, a power-hitting corner outfielder. Still, there's plenty of projection, uncertainty and rust to be shaken off, so despite any possible instinct to the contrary let's all try to give it another year before jumping to any conclusions either way.

Jose Pirela LF Born: 11/21/89 Age: 28 Bats: R Throws: R Height: 6'0" Weight: 220 Origin: Undrafted Free Agent, 2006

YEAR	TEAM	LVL	AGE	PA	R	2B	3B	HR	RBI	BB	K	SB	CS	AVG/OBP/SLG	TAv	VORP	BABIP	BRR	FRAA	WARP
2015	SWB	AAA	25	259	40	14	1	3	23	24	22	5	2	.325/.390/.433	.297	14.9	.346	-1.4	3B(20): -1.3, LF(19): 1.9	1.5
2015	NYA	MLB	25	78	7	3	0	1	5	2	16	1	0	.230/.247/.311	.191	-3.8	.276	-0.5	2B(27): -1.4, LF(2): 0.5	-0.5
2016	SDN	MLB	26	41	2	2	0	0	0	1	9	0	1	.154/.175/.205	.157	-3.9	.200	-0.7	2B(12): -1.5, RF(1): 0.0	-0.6
2016	ELP	AAA	26	146	19	7	3	2	16	9	21	1	1	.248/.295/.387	.211	-4.2	.281	0.4	LF(17): -0.9, RF(8): -0.7	-0.5
2017	ELP	AAA	27	201	37	10	3	13	42	15	26	8	3	.331/.387/.635	.328	17.2	.329	-1.4	1B(26): 3.1, LF(12): 2.0	2.1
2017	SDN	MLB	27	344	43	25	4	10	40	27	71	4	3	.288/.347/.490	.302	22.8	.343	0.3	LF(68): 6.3, 2B(7): -0.1	2.8
2018	*SDN*	*MLB*	*28*	*513*	*57*	*23*	*5*	*12*	*59*	*33*	*95*	*8*	*4*	*.259/.309/.410*	*.260*	*15.6*	*.297*	*0.0*	*LF 6, RF -2*	*1.7*
2019	*SDN*	*MLB*	*29*	*525*	*61*	*23*	*5*	*14*	*60*	*37*	*102*	*7*	*4*	*.256/.312/.412*	*.266*	*15.5*	*.294*	*-0.3*	*LF 7, RF -1*	*2.3*

Breakout: 4% Improve: 33% Collapse: 15% Attrition: 31% MLB: 68% *Comparables: Alejandro De Aza, Aaron Cunningham, Lou Montanez*

You'd be forgiven if Pirela wasn't a name on the tip of your tongue this time last offseason, but that was then, and this is now. San Diego acquired him in 2016 as a utility man with a fringy bat and glove—a possible big leaguer, but more likely an up-and-down guy who could serve as depth all over the diamond. But he suddenly exploded in 2017. Pirela lit up Triple-A like a Christmas tree, and kept the power surge going when he was called up to the big leagues. He finished the season hitting with the kind of authority that would warrant a starting spot in an outfield corner, and even in an organization overflowing with potential average regulars in the corners, he likely has the inside track. It's anybody's guess as to how much of these gains he'll keep, but Pirela's earned the right to at least show us the answer.

Hunter Renfroe RF Born: 01/28/92 Age: 26 Bats: R Throws: R Height: 6'1" Weight: 220 Origin: Round 1, 2013 Draft (#13 overall)

YEAR	TEAM	LVL	AGE	PA	R	2B	3B	HR	RBI	BB	K	SB	CS	AVG/OBP/SLG	TAv	VORP	BABIP	BRR	FRAA	WARP
2015	SAN	AA	23	463	50	22	3	14	54	33	112	4	1	.259/.313/.425	.259	8.8	.316	1.6	RF(79): 13.6, CF(8): -1.7	2.2
2015	ELP	AAA	23	95	15	5	2	6	24	4	20	1	0	.333/.358/.633	.314	8.0	.369	0.7	RF(18): 1.5, CF(3): 0.2	1.0
2016	ELP	AAA	24	563	95	34	5	30	105	22	115	5	2	.306/.336/.557	.277	22.2	.339	1.8	RF(111): 5.8, CF(12): -0.9	2.8
2016	SDN	MLB	24	36	8	3	0	4	14	1	5	0	0	.371/.389/.800	.404	6.1	.346	0.2	RF(9): 0.7	0.7
2017	ELP	AAA	25	61	18	7	1	4	18	6	7	1	0	.509/.557/.891	.477	16.8	.545	0.8	RF(12): 2.0	1.8
2017	SDN	MLB	25	479	51	25	1	26	58	27	140	3	0	.231/.284/.467	.276	15.9	.275	-0.9	RF(120): -2.0	1.4
2018	*SDN*	*MLB*	*26*	*559*	*72*	*26*	*3*	*27*	*81*	*28*	*154*	*2*	*1*	*.243/.287/.457*	*.262*	*14.8*	*.291*	*-0.5*	*RF 1*	*1.3*
2019	*SDN*	*MLB*	*27*	*537*	*70*	*25*	*2*	*26*	*77*	*32*	*152*	*2*	*1*	*.239/.291/.454*	*.270*	*15.9*	*.290*	*-0.8*	*RF 2*	*2.0*

Breakout: 8% Improve: 31% Collapse: 14% Attrition: 23% MLB: 66% *Comparables: Victor Diaz, Wladimir Balentien, Cody Ross*

Renfroe finished second on the Padres in homers as a rookie, despite spending a few weeks back at Triple-A for a refresher course on hitting. Before the mid-August demotion he was batting .230/.285/.443, bad for a middle-of-the-order guy even by San Diego standards. After 14 games of annihilating PCL pitching Renfroe returned to the big leagues and continued his rampage, posting a .980 OPS in an admittedly small September sample and whacking six bombs in 44 trips to the dish. The plate discipline is still missing, as he drew just one walk and fanned 15 times on his return, although that's less problematic when you're crushing everything thrown in your general direction. Unfortunately, most people not named Vladimir Guerrero can't do that, and if Renfroe is to succeed at the highest level he'll have to learn how to let the bad ones pass a little more often.

Yangervis Solarte INF Born: 07/07/87 Age: 30 Bats: B Throws: R Height: 5'11" Weight: 205 Origin: International Free Agent, 2005

YEAR	TEAM	LVL	AGE	PA	R	2B	3B	HR	RBI	BB	K	SB	CS	AVG/OBP/SLG	TAv	VORP	BABIP	BRR	FRAA	WARP
2015	SDN	MLB	27	571	63	33	4	14	63	34	56	1	0	.270/.320/.428	.266	16.1	.279	-2.1	3B(92): -4.2, 1B(28): -0.7	1.3
2016	SDN	MLB	28	443	55	26	1	15	71	30	63	1	1	.286/.341/.467	.289	24.9	.306	-2.2	3B(95): 6.1, 2B(15): 0.9	3.3
2017	SDN	MLB	29	512	49	21	0	18	64	37	61	3	0	.255/.314/.416	.261	16.9	.258	0.5	2B(79): -3.4, SS(28): -1.8	1.2
2018	*SDN*	*MLB*	*30*	*589*	*67*	*29*	*2*	*16*	*72*	*44*	*67*	*2*	*1*	*.269/.329/.420*	*.260*	*24.4*	*.280*	*-0.9*	*SS -10, 2B -1*	*0.7*
2019	*SDN*	*MLB*	*31*	*506*	*62*	*25*	*1*	*15*	*60*	*40*	*66*	*1*	*0*	*.261/.326/.419*	*.273*	*22.2*	*.274*	*-1.4*	*SS -9, 2B -1*	*1.4*

Breakout: 1% Improve: 30% Collapse: 3% Attrition: 7% MLB: 97% *Comparables: Placido Polanco, Johnny Ray, Rich Dauer*

Solarte has a story that can inspire current minor leaguers. The infielder bounced around the minors for eight long seasons, hitting minor-league free agency twice and finally reaching the big leagues as a 26-year-old rookie with minimal expectations. The stakes have been raised since then, and even though last season was more in line with his pre-2016 self, Solarte's flexibility made him an integral part of the Padres. Watching someone supposedly resigned to being a career minor leaguer carve out an excellent big-league career despite so much adversity (he also lost his wife—mother to their three young daughters—to cancer toward the end of the 2016 campaign) is enough to light the fire under any frustrated player.

Cory Spangenberg 3B Born: 03/16/91 Age: 27 Bats: L Throws: R Height: 6'0" Weight: 195 Origin: Round 1, 2011 Draft (#10 overall)

YEAR	TEAM	LVL	AGE	PA	R	2B	3B	HR	RBI	BB	K	SB	CS	AVG/OBP/SLG	TAv	VORP	BABIP	BRR	FRAA	WARP
2015	SAN	AA	24	27	3	0	1	0	1	1	2	1	0	.192/.222/.269	.204	-0.3	.208	0.4	3B(3): 0.6, 2B(2): 0.0	0.0
2015	SDN	MLB	24	345	38	17	5	4	21	28	75	9	4	.271/.333/.399	.268	15.9	.344	4.0	2B(70): -4.5, 3B(19): 0.0	1.2
2016	SDN	MLB	25	53	6	1	1	1	8	4	13	1	0	.229/.302/.354	.235	-0.2	.294	-0.2	2B(13): 0.4	0.0
2017	ELP	AAA	26	72	8	3	1	1	7	4	8	3	2	.348/.403/.470	.271	3.2	.386	-0.2	3B(17): -3.3	0.0
2017	SDN	MLB	26	486	57	18	2	13	46	34	128	11	3	.264/.322/.401	.276	28.6	.342	5.3	3B(96): -0.8, LF(32): -3.0	2.6
2018	*SDN*	*MLB*	*27*	*326*	*36*	*13*	*3*	*6*	*35*	*22*	*79*	*8*	*3*	*.253/.305/.384*	*.248*	*9.4*	*.317*	*0.7*	*3B 0, 2B 0*	*0.3*
2019	*SDN*	*MLB*	*28*	*370*	*43*	*15*	*3*	*9*	*41*	*27*	*93*	*8*	*3*	*.253/.315/.401*	*.260*	*12.9*	*.318*	*2.9*	*3B 0, 2B 0*	*1.2*

Breakout: 7% Improve: 42% Collapse: 8% Attrition: 15% MLB: 92% *Comparables: Lonnie Chisenhall, Danny Valencia, Josh Harrison*

After Spangenberg missed nearly all of 2016 with a quad injury, many had forgotten about him going into his real sophomore season. Such is life for the generic sum-of-his-parts infielder who the Padres drafted one spot ahead of World Series MVP George Springer back in 2011. Despite a complete lack of hype, he took advantage of the little competition he had for playing time and posted a .778 OPS over 368 plate appearances from June on. Most importantly, he showed there is more to life than keeping infielders on their toes—his absurd 69 percent ground-ball rate from 2016 fell to below 50 percent in 2017, acting as the impetus for his power spike. Outside of his skill on the bases, there's nothing special about Spangenberg's profile, but he can do a bit of everything and will be a useful second or third baseman going forward.

Matt Szczur OF Born: 07/20/89 Age: 28 Bats: R Throws: R Height: 6'0" Weight: 200 Origin: Round 5, 2010 Draft (#160 overall)

YEAR	TEAM	LVL	AGE	PA	R	2B	3B	HR	RBI	BB	K	SB	CS	AVG/OBP/SLG	TAv	VORP	BABIP	BRR	FRAA	WARP
2015	IOW	AAA	25	305	40	12	2	8	31	22	51	20	5	.292/.355/.442	.305	22.3	.330	-0.3	CF(50): 0.7, LF(10): -0.2	2.3
2015	CHN	MLB	25	80	5	5	0	1	8	6	15	2	0	.222/.278/.333	.229	0.1	.263	0.5	LF(26): -1.2, CF(6): -0.9	-0.2
2016	CHN	MLB	26	200	30	9	1	5	24	13	39	2	4	.259/.312/.400	.265	6.2	.305	0.4	LF(50): -1.8, RF(15): 0.5	0.7
2017	CHN	MLB	27	23	2	1	0	0	3	2	4	0	0	.211/.273/.263	.213	-1.0	.250	-0.4	LF(5): -0.2, RF(3): -0.1	-0.1
2017	SDN	MLB	27	214	26	11	2	3	15	32	40	0	2	.227/.358/.364	.276	9.6	.278	0.5	LF(44): -1.2, CF(20): 1.3	1.0
2018	*SDN*	*MLB*	*28*	*230*	*25*	*9*	*1*	*4*	*21*	*18*	*46*	*4*	*2*	*.234/.296/.343*	*.233*	*2.0*	*.277*	*-0.2*	*LF 0, CF 0*	*0.0*
2019	*SDN*	*MLB*	*29*	*340*	*37*	*13*	*1*	*7*	*34*	*26*	*73*	*6*	*3*	*.233/.299/.353*	*.239*	*2.4*	*.276*	*1.0*	*LF 0, CF 0*	*0.3*

Breakout: 3% Improve: 36% Collapse: 15% Attrition: 28% MLB: 78% *Comparables: Julio Borbon, Gregor Blanco, Tony Gwynn*

Szczur's former prospect status hasn't materialized into big-league success, and at his age the window for anything more than fourth- or fifth-outfielder status may be closing (if it hasn't closed already). In the minors he has shown the ability to steal bases, swiping 20 or more in five straight seasons at one point, as well as a modicum of doubles power. While the doubles have come in limited opportunities at the highest level, his running game has been nonexistent. Last year he added drawing walks to his repertoire, and he can play passable defense in all three outfield spots. If both of those things continue to hold true, his upside is maybe Chris Denorfia?

Fernando Tatis Jr. SS Born: 01/02/99 Age: 19 Bats: R Throws: R Height: 6'3" Weight: 185 Origin: International Free Agent, 2015

YEAR	TEAM	LVL	AGE	PA	R	2B	3B	HR	RBI	BB	K	SB	CS	AVG/OBP/SLG	TAv	VORP	BABIP	BRR	FRAA	WARP
2016	PDR	RK	17	188	35	13	1	4	20	10	44	14	2	.273/.312/.426	.278	13.0	.344	2.4	SS(29): -0.1, 2B(8): -1.3	1.1
2016	TRI	A-	17	49	4	4	2	0	5	3	13	1	1	.273/.306/.455	.307	4.5	.364	0.4	SS(7): -1.4, 3B(3): -0.7	0.2
2017	FTW	A	18	518	78	26	7	21	69	75	124	29	15	.281/.390/.520	.317	51.1	.342	0.1	SS(109): -5.6	4.8
2017	SAN	AA	18	57	6	1	0	1	6	2	17	3	0	.255/.281/.327	.218	0.4	.351	0.9	SS(9): -0.3, 3B(3): -0.5	-0.1
2018	SDN	MLB	19	250	34	10	1	9	27	22	79	7	3	.218/.292/.394	.238	6.1	.288	0.2	SS -1, 3B 0	0.5
2019	SDN	MLB	20	438	58	17	2	19	59	42	132	13	6	.235/.313/.436	.274	22.1	.300	1.1	SS -2, 3B 0	2.2

Breakout: 0% Improve: 10% Collapse: 3% Attrition: 11% MLB: 21% *Comparables: Carlos Correa, Freddie Freeman, Domingo Santana*

Aside from a 34-homer, 21-steal outburst as a healthy 24-year-old in 1999 and that one time he hit two grand slams in one inning, Fernando Tatis Sr.'s career wound up frustratingly short on highlights for a player with such tantalizing tools. After flashing a similar ceiling in his full-season debut, Tatito is teeming with the same kind of potential to which his old man once laid claim. The calling card is his bat, as he shows plus power, a smooth swing and burgeoning pitch recognition, but he also brings good defense at shortstop and plus speed to the table. Despite a Double-A cameo at the end of the season, it will be a few more years before we might be looking at a special player for the Padres. For now, though, we'll have to settle for calling Tatis the best prospect in a stacked farm system.

Luis Torrens C Born: 05/02/96 Age: 22 Bats: R Throws: R Height: 6'0" Weight: 175 Origin: International Free Agent, 2013

YEAR	TEAM	LVL	AGE	PA	R	2B	3B	HR	RBI	BB	K	SB	CS	AVG/OBP/SLG	TAv	VORP	BABIP	BRR	FRAA	WARP
2016	STA	A-	20	50	6	4	0	0	5	4	7	1	1	.311/.360/.400	.278	3.1	.359	0.1	C(11): 0.0	0.3
2016	CSC	A	20	164	9	6	0	2	10	22	26	1	1	.230/.348/.317	.255	4.3	.270	-1.8	C(40): 0.1	0.5
2017	SDN	MLB	21	139	7	3	1	0	7	12	30	0	0	.163/.243/.203	.165	-6.3	.215	1.1	C(51): -10.1	-1.6
2018	SDN	MLB	22	61	6	2	0	1	6	5	14	0	0	.216/.288/.321	.224	0.7	.265	-0.1	C -5	-0.4
2019	SDN	MLB	23	269	30	11	1	6	27	25	61	0	0	.225/.305/.351	.242	5.1	.272	-0.5	C -13	-0.9

Breakout: 10% Improve: 20% Collapse: 10% Attrition: 20% MLB: 37% *Comparables: Josh Thole, Dioner Navarro, Ruben Tejada*

YEAR	TEAM	P. COUNT	FRM RUNS	BLK RUNS	THRW RUNS	TOT RUNS
2017	SDN	5274	-7.4	-2.0	0.0	-9.4
2018	SDN	2313	-3.3	-0.9	0.0	-4.2
2019	SDN	10205	-5.1	-1.3	0.0	-6.5

As it turns out, the new market inefficiency isn't Low-A catchers in the big leagues. Torrens didn't quite hit the ground running as a rookie, but that was never the point. Before a shoulder injury cost him the 2015 season, Torrens was one of the most exciting teenaged prospects in a Yankee system full of teenaged prospects. And because the Padres were able to successfully navigate the season with the 21-year-old on their roster, they can now send him back to the minors in 2018 and hope he can recreate some of that prospect magic. He has a long way to go with the bat and the glove, but it'll be a couple of seasons before he's out of options and the Padres need to hide him again.

Luis Urias MI Born: 06/03/97 Age: 21 Bats: R Throws: R Height: 5'9" Weight: 160 Origin: International Free Agent, 2013

YEAR	TEAM	LVL	AGE	PA	R	2B	3B	HR	RBI	BB	K	SB	CS	AVG/OBP/SLG	TAv	VORP	BABIP	BRR	FRAA	WARP
2015	TRI	A-	18	44	6	1	0	0	1	5	1	3	3	.355/.487/.387	.391	7.3	.367	0.2	2B(6): 0.5, SS(1): -0.2	0.8
2015	FTW	A	18	224	28	5	1	0	16	16	18	5	10	.290/.370/.326	.267	6.1	.318	-1.7	2B(38): 1.0, SS(7): 1.0	1.1
2016	LEL	A+	19	531	71	26	5	5	52	40	36	7	13	.330/.397/.440	.317	41.6	.348	-5.9	2B(80): 6.2, SS(22): -3.2	4.6
2017	SAN	AA	20	526	77	20	4	3	38	68	65	7	5	.296/.398/.380	.298	40.1	.340	2.6	SS(60): 4.7, 2B(55): -1.1	4.7
2018	SDN	MLB	21	250	30	10	1	5	24	24	41	1	1	.263/.347/.391	.257	9.9	.295	-0.5	2B 1, SS 0	1.3
2019	SDN	MLB	22	446	56	19	3	10	50	44	70	2	2	.270/.355/.415	.286	25.9	.298	-0.8	2B 2, SS 0	3.1

Breakout: 4% Improve: 18% Collapse: 2% Attrition: 9% MLB: 27% *Comparables: J.P. Crawford, Mookie Betts, Francisco Lindor*

From now on, every tall corner outfielder *might* be Aaron Judge; every lanky, wild southpaw *could* be Chris Sale; and every small, contact-oriented second baseman *possibly* is Jose Altuve. It would be irresponsible to compare any current prospect to the best contact hitter in a few years, but the comps come easy with Altuve and Urias. He may be a few inches taller than the reigning MVP, but the sweet-swinging second baseman has posted some Altuve-esque batting averages in the minor leagues. Although he didn't quite repeat 2016's .330 mark, hitting nearly .300 with more walks than strikeouts as a 20-year-old at Double-A was a more impressive feat. He increased his defensive versatility, too, holding enough of his own at the six spot to suggest a future floor plugging holes around the infield if the hit tool never quite maxes out. And if it does, Jose can you see a first-division ceiling at the keystone? Because we can.

Christian Villanueva 3B Born: 06/19/91 Age: 27 Bats: R Throws: R Height: 5'11" Weight: 210 Origin: International Free Agent, 2008

YEAR	TEAM	LVL	AGE	PA	R	2B	3B	HR	RBI	BB	K	SB	CS	AVG/OBP/SLG	TAv	VORP	BABIP	BRR	FRAA	WARP
2015	TEN	AA	24	28	5	0	0	2	7	4	5	0	0	.208/.321/.458	.324	3.0	.176	0.4	3B(6): -0.4	0.3
2015	IOW	AAA	24	508	56	23	2	18	88	35	80	2	3	.259/.313/.437	.273	17.3	.273	-2.2	3B(85): 3.4, 1B(35): 1.2	2.2
2017	ELP	AAA	26	454	69	28	2	20	86	43	83	4	2	.296/.369/.528	.291	25.5	.326	-1.1	3B(59): -2.9, 1B(43): 2.1	2.4
2017	SDN	MLB	26	32	5	1	0	4	7	0	10	0	0	.344/.344/.750	.451	7.1	.389	-0.4	3B(9): -0.9	0.6
2018	SDN	MLB	27	61	8	3	0	3	8	4	14	0	0	.241/.303/.434	.263	2.0	.271	-0.1	3B 0	0.1
2019	SDN	MLB	28	237	32	11	1	11	33	20	55	1	0	.243/.313/.449	.278	9.8	.274	-0.5	3B -1	0.9

Breakout: 2% Improve: 20% Collapse: 18% Attrition: 19% MLB: 41% *Comparables: Matthew Duffy, James D'Antona, Jesus Guzman*

While it's tough to call Villanueva a prospect, his advanced age may be a bit deceptive. The third baseman missed all of 2016 due to a freak broken leg suffered during offseason workouts. He brings solid hot-corner defense and past flashes of playable pop to the table, and will head into 2018 hoping for an extended look at the highest level.

PITCHERS

Michel Baez RHP
Born: 01/21/96 Age: 22 Bats: R Throws: R Height: 6'8" Weight: 220 Origin: International Free Agent, 2016

YEAR	TEAM	LVL	AGE	W	L	SV	G	GS	IP	H	HR	BB/9	K/9	K	GB%	BABIP	WHIP	ERA	DRA	WARP	MPH	CMD	PWR	STM
2017	FTW	A	21	6	2	0	10	10	58^{2}	41	8	1.2	12.6	82	36%	.264	0.84	2.45	1.83	2.4				
2018	*SDN*	*MLB*	*22*	*2*	*3*	*0*	*8*	*8*	*42*	*39*	*11*	*3.0*	*11.9*	*56*	*37%*	*.313*	*1.26*	*4.97*	*5.80*	*-0.1*				
2019	*SDN*	*MLB*	*23*	*8*	*13*	*0*	*29*	*29*	*175^{2}*	*168*	*41*	*4.5*	*10.0*	*194*	*37%*	*.311*	*1.45*	*5.52*	*6.41*	*-1.4*				

Breakout: 19% Improve: 31% Collapse: 2% Attrition: 15% MLB: 37% *Comparables: Christian Friedrich, Tommy Hanson, Eric Surkamp*

A towering presence, Baez has the look and the stat line of a top-of-the-rotation workhorse. His arsenal leads with a mid-90s fastball, which is almost literally released from the heavens, that more often than not dips into the low-90s by the end of his starts. However, the biggest reason he baffled Midwest League hitters was a highly advanced change—the kind that unsuspecting batsmen are rarely subjected to in the low minors. The rest of the package is mostly filler and flash at this point, but if he can develop the breaking ball and precocious command, the ceiling could match the stature some day.

Buddy Baumann LHP
Born: 12/09/87 Age: 30 Bats: L Throws: L Height: 5'11" Weight: 198 Origin: Round 7, 2009 Draft (#212 overall)

YEAR	TEAM	LVL	AGE	W	L	SV	G	GS	IP	H	HR	BB/9	K/9	K	GB%	BABIP	WHIP	ERA	DRA	WARP	MPH	CMD	PWR	STM
2015	OMA	AAA	27	3	4	3	34	6	77	65	5	2.9	9.8	84	34%	.291	1.17	3.04	1.97	2.7				
2016	ELP	AAA	28	1	1	2	24	0	28^{2}	22	3	3.8	9.7	31	34%	.271	1.19	3.14	3.12	0.6				
2016	SDN	MLB	28	1	0	0	11	0	9^{2}	7	0	3.7	9.3	10	28%	.280	1.14	3.72	5.28	0.0	91.5			38
2017	SDN	MLB	29	2	1	0	23	0	17^{2}	11	4	3.6	10.7	21	34%	.189	1.02	2.55	5.73	-0.1	92.0	63	54	42
2018	*SDN*	*MLB*	*30*	*3*	*3*	*0*	*59*	*0*	*62*	*58*	*10*	*4.4*	*9.5*	*66*	*36%*	*.287*	*1.40*	*5.02*	*5.29*	*-0.3*	*91.1*	*63*	*54*	*40*
2019	*SDN*	*MLB*	*31*	*2*	*1*	*0*	*49*	*0*	*52*	*44*	*8*	*3.6*	*9.4*	*54*	*36%*	*.293*	*1.26*	*4.46*	*5.17*	*0.0*	*90.5*	*63*	*54*	*40*

Breakout: 14% Improve: 23% Collapse: 11% Attrition: 18% MLB: 37% *Comparables: Cesar Jimenez, Bobby LaFromboise, Dalier Hinojosa*

Fastball velocity and strikeouts are intrinsically linked in baseball; traditionally, you can't have one without the other. Every rule has its exceptions, however, and Baumann fits that bill. Despite having one of the slowest fastballs among big-league relievers, he managed to elude plenty of bats with it. His 90-mph "heater" gets hitters to miss over 30 percent of the time despite lacking any extraordinary movement, control or extension. In this case, it's deception and deception alone emanating from his low three-quarters slot. Will it be enough to sustain a gaudy strikeout total and sub-3.00 ERA in 2018? Everything we hold to be true about baseball says no, but the opposition will have to crack Baumann's closely guarded secret weapon first.

Carter Capps RHP
Born: 08/07/90 Age: 27 Bats: R Throws: R Height: 6'5" Weight: 230 Origin: Round 2, 2011 Draft (#121 overall)

YEAR	TEAM	LVL	AGE	W	L	SV	G	GS	IP	H	HR	BB/9	K/9	K	GB%	BABIP	WHIP	ERA	DRA	WARP	MPH	CMD	PWR	STM
2015	NWO	AAA	24	0	2	3	13	0	15	10	0	6.0	9.0	15	50%	.263	1.33	1.80	5.55	-0.1				
2015	MIA	MLB	24	1	0	0	30	0	31	18	2	2.0	16.8	58	43%	.327	0.81	1.16	1.71	1.1	100.6	43	73	46
2017	ELP	AAA	26	1	1	2	24	0	25^{2}	18	1	3.2	9.8	28	48%	.254	1.05	2.81	2.35	0.8				
2017	SDN	MLB	26	0	0	0	11	0	12^{1}	12	2	1.5	5.1	7	52%	.263	1.14	6.57	5.17	0.0	94.9			34
2018	*SDN*	*MLB*	*27*	*3*	*2*	*0*	*54*	*0*	*56*	*50*	*7*	*4.0*	*10.4*	*66*	*44%*	*.299*	*1.33*	*3.75*	*4.24*	*0.4*	*97.8*	*44*	*74*	*39*
2019	*SDN*	*MLB*	*28*	*2*	*1*	*0*	*46*	*0*	*49*	*40*	*7*	*4.2*	*9.6*	*52*	*44%*	*.288*	*1.29*	*4.38*	*5.09*	*0.1*	*96.8*	*44*	*74*	*37*

Breakout: 39% Improve: 56% Collapse: 19% Attrition: 16% MLB: 93% *Comparables: Alexi Ogando, Sergio Santos, Rex Brothers*

For some talented pitching prospects, there's a disclaimer buried within scouting reports warning of a nonoptimal delivery quirk—something along the lines of a questionable drive, worrisome arm action or inconsistent mechanics. The violent action of throwing a baseball close to 100 mph can very easily lead to a body-part malfunction, and even the smallest weakness in a pitching motion should be noted. Capps' lack of prospect pedigree and sudden adoption of the "crow-up" delivery robbed us of some entertaining scouting reports, but it doesn't take much imagination to think of the colorful verbs scouts might have used to describe his eccentric mechanics. For Capps, the ride may have come to a screeching and painful halt, but it sure was fun. Before his stuff even returned following an early-2016 Tommy John surgery, Capps went under the knife again after the 2017 season, this time due to thoracic outlet syndrome. Some things are just truly too beautiful for this world.

Jarred Cosart RHP
Born: 05/25/90 Age: 28 Bats: R Throws: R Height: 6'3" Weight: 206 Origin: Round 38, 2008 Draft (#1156 overall)

YEAR	TEAM	LVL	AGE	W	L	SV	G	GS	IP	H	HR	BB/9	K/9	K	GB%	BABIP	WHIP	ERA	DRA	WARP	MPH	CMD	PWR	STM
2015	NWO	AAA	25	0	1	0	4	4	16^{1}	21	2	4.4	6.1	11	53%	.339	1.78	6.06	6.18	-0.2				
2015	MIA	MLB	25	2	5	0	14	13	69^{2}	63	10	4.3	6.1	47	55%	.259	1.38	4.52	3.98	0.9	96.7	39	62	43
2016	NWO	AAA	26	3	4	0	10	10	50^{2}	55	8	4.4	5.3	30	50%	.292	1.58	4.09	6.35	-0.6				
2016	MIA	MLB	26	0	1	0	4	4	19^{2}	19	0	7.3	5.0	11	66%	.292	1.78	5.95	4.43	0.2	95.1	46	51	54
2016	SDN	MLB	26	0	3	0	9	9	37^{1}	42	4	5.5	6.5	27	60%	.317	1.74	6.03	6.02	-0.3	94.8	46	51	54
2017	SDN	MLB	27	0	2	0	7	6	24	26	0	7.1	5.6	15	51%	.333	1.88	4.88	6.74	-0.3	94.6	46	52	31
2018	*SDN*	*MLB*	*28*	*2*	*3*	*0*	*8*	*8*	*40*	*37*	*4*	*4.4*	*7.4*	*33*	*51%*	*.298*	*1.42*	*4.58*	*5.35*	*0.1*	*94.9*	*44*	*55*	*42*
2019	*SDN*	*MLB*	*29*	*8*	*11*	*0*	*30*	*30*	*187^{2}*	*174*	*24*	*4.4*	*7.2*	*149*	*51%*	*.298*	*1.41*	*4.71*	*5.47*	*0.3*	*94.2*	*45*	*53*	*41*

Breakout: 10% Improve: 41% Collapse: 29% Attrition: 16% MLB: 90% *Comparables: Chien-Ming Wang, Aaron Cook, Jhoulys Chacin*

If you look at old scouting reports of Cosart as a prospect, they all featured variations on the same theme: The hard-throwing Texan has never pitched up to the quality of his stuff. That stuff was good enough to keep him interesting for much of his young career, but once he lost a couple ticks a lot of that interest waned as well. Cosart's command has remained illusory, and it bottomed out in 2017, when he hit the zone just 36 percent of the time—the fourth-worst rate in baseball. Amazingly, he still only has two relief appearances during his entire career—a number that is likely to increase vastly once he makes it back from July arthroscopic elbow surgery.

Miguel Diaz RHP Born: 11/28/94 Age: 23 Bats: R Throws: R Height: 6'1" Weight: 175 Origin: International Free Agent, 2011

YEAR	TEAM	LVL	AGE	W	L	SV	G	GS	IP	H	HR	BB/9	K/9	K	GB%	BABIP	WHIP	ERA	DRA	WARP	MPH	CMD	PWR	STM
2015	BRR	RK	20	0	3	0	7	5	20^{1}	20	1	2.2	10.2	23	38%	.365	1.23	2.21	3.25	0.6				
2016	WIS	A	21	1	8	3	26	15	94^{2}	83	7	2.8	8.7	91	47%	.279	1.18	3.71	3.14	2.0				
2017	SDN	MLB	22	1	1	0	31	3	41^{2}	44	11	5.4	7.1	33	41%	.275	1.66	7.34	8.27	-1.4	97.6	36	66	33
2018	*SDN*	*MLB*	*23*	*3*	*3*	*0*	*32*	*5*	*54*	*56*	*11*	*4.4*	*8.8*	*54*	*40%*	*.296*	*1.50*	*5.34*	*5.77*	*-0.5*	*97.5*	*37*	*68*	*34*
2019	*SDN*	*MLB*	*24*	*5*	*5*	*0*	*66*	*9*	115^{2}	*105*	*21*	*4.0*	*8.8*	*113*	*40%*	*.294*	*1.35*	*4.95*	*5.74*	*-0.4*	*97.3*	*38*	*69*	*35*

Breakout: 7% Improve: 9% Collapse: 1% Attrition: 5% MLB: 13% *Comparables: Edinson Volquez, Kyle Davies, Jo-Jo Reyes*

Some players look like they're an adjustment away from breaking out and becoming a star. Others look like they're an adjustment away from being an adjustment away from breaking out and becoming a star. Diaz falls into the latter bucket, but that's an excellent result after the Rule 5 pick was able to stick with the Padres all season. He has all the pieces to be a high-leverage bullpen arm: a high-90s fastball with late life, a slurve that's 12 mph slower and an intriguing changeup. As of now, none of these pitches are consistently good, but they all have their moments. Diaz may never have enough polish to be great, yet the nascent signs of an eventual stud are here and a little time honing his craft in the upper minors could get him that first adjustment.

Anderson Espinoza RHP Born: 03/09/98 Age: 20 Bats: R Throws: R Height: 6'0" Weight: 160 Origin: International Free Agent, 2014

YEAR	TEAM	LVL	AGE	W	L	SV	G	GS	IP	H	HR	BB/9	K/9	K	GB%	BABIP	WHIP	ERA	DRA	WARP	MPH	CMD	PWR	STM
2015	DRX	RK	17	0	0	0	4	4	15	13	0	1.8	12.6	21	64%	.361	1.07	1.20	1.91	0.6				
2015	RSX	RK	17	0	1	0	10	10	40	24	0	2.0	9.0	40	71%	.238	0.82	0.68	2.13	1.6				
2016	GRN	A	18	5	8	0	17	17	76	77	2	3.2	8.5	72	49%	.342	1.37	4.38	4.44	0.5				
2016	FTW	A	18	1	3	0	8	7	32^{1}	38	1	2.2	7.8	28	44%	.363	1.42	4.73	4.46	0.2				
2018	*SDN*	*MLB*	*20*	*2*	*3*	*0*	*8*	*8*	35^{2}	*33*	*5*	*4.0*	*9.7*	*39*	*43%*	*.319*	*1.38*	*4.22*	*4.94*	*0.3*				
2019	*SDN*	*MLB*	*21*	*7*	*10*	*0*	*30*	*30*	185^{2}	*190*	*34*	*2.9*	*8.2*	*169*	*43%*	*.319*	*1.35*	*4.81*	*5.58*	*0.1*				

Breakout: 1% Improve: 2% Collapse: 1% Attrition: 5% MLB: 5% *Comparables: Zach Lee, Casey Kelly, Kyle Ryan*

Espinoza was supposed to be the reason you never trade an elite starting pitcher prospect. Instead, he's the reason you *always* trade an elite starting pitcher prospect. When Espinoza's hype reached an all-time high, scouts were projecting him to reach the big leagues by 2019. Now, he won't pitch at any level until then after undergoing Tommy John surgery midway through last season. Still, he'll be just 21 years old by the time he's healthy, and if his stuff comes all the way back the Padres could have a heck of a player on their hands. Before Espinoza's injury, the righty had a potentially deadly three-pitch mix in the form of an elite fastball and solid changeup/curveball combination. He could still be worth the wait, even if that wait is a couple years longer than expected.

MacKenzie Gore LHP Born: 02/24/99 Age: 19 Bats: L Throws: L Height: 6'3" Weight: 180 Origin: Round 1, 2017 Draft (#3 overall)

YEAR	TEAM	LVL	AGE	W	L	SV	G	GS	IP	H	HR	BB/9	K/9	K	GB%	BABIP	WHIP	ERA	DRA	WARP	MPH	CMD	PWR	STM
2017	PDR	RK	18	0	1	0	7	7	21^{1}	14	0	3.0	14.3	34	69%	.333	0.98	1.27	0.56	1.2				
2018	*SDN*	*MLB*	*19*	*2*	*3*	*0*	*9*	*9*	34^{1}	*33*	*7*	*5.6*	*10.6*	*40*	*44%*	*.320*	*1.57*	*5.36*	*6.26*	*-0.2*				
2019	*SDN*	*MLB*	*20*	*5*	*9*	*0*	*29*	*29*	179^{1}	*173*	*31*	*4.8*	*8.6*	*171*	*44%*	*.312*	*1.50*	*5.16*	*6.00*	*-0.5*				

Comparables: Roberto Osuna, Jordan Lyles, Vicente Campos

The pitcher with the highest ceiling in the Padres' arm-heavy system and possibly the best prep arm in the 2017 draft, Gore is one of the few pitchers in minor-league baseball who has enough talent to convince many evaluators that there's ace upside despite a limited pro résumé. He'll stun hitters with an excellent fastball/curveball combination, and that one-two punch will take him far. Still, for Gore to hit that coveted ceiling, he'll need to further hone a nascent changeup—like just about every other teenage arm you'll read about in this book. The North Carolina native is actually the third player to be selected in the first round from Whiteville, a town of only about 5,000 people. That's especially notable since only 12 players have ever been drafted out of Whiteville High School, and none in the last 20 years. Of course, the most successful of the two previous first-rounders was Tommy Greene, he of the career 7.0 WARP and a 13.11 postseason ERA. It would be a shock if Gore didn't surpass those figures.

Brad Hand LHP Born: 03/20/90 Age: 28 Bats: L Throws: L Height: 6'3" Weight: 228 Origin: Round 2, 2008 Draft (#52 overall)

YEAR	TEAM	LVL	AGE	W	L	SV	G	GS	IP	H	HR	BB/9	K/9	K	GB%	BABIP	WHIP	ERA	DRA	WARP	MPH	CMD	PWR	STM
2015	MIA	MLB	25	4	7	0	38	12	93^{1}	107	9	3.1	6.5	67	48%	.330	1.49	5.30	5.76	-0.9	95.1	47	55	49
2016	SDN	MLB	26	4	4	1	82	0	89^{1}	63	8	3.6	11.2	111	47%	.264	1.11	2.92	3.32	1.7	95.6	40	50	59
2017	SDN	MLB	27	3	4	21	72	0	79^{1}	54	9	2.3	11.8	104	46%	.263	0.93	2.16	3.13	1.8	95.0	49	42	53
2018	*SDN*	*MLB*	*28*	*4*	*3*	*20*	*64*	*0*	*68*	*53*	*7*	*3.3*	*10.8*	*82*	*46%*	*.282*	*1.12*	*2.99*	*3.58*	*1.0*	*94.7*	*46*	*49*	*54*
2019	*SDN*	*MLB*	*29*	*3*	*1*	*13*	*66*	*0*	69^{2}	*51*	*8*	*3.3*	*10.9*	*84*	*46%*	*.289*	*1.10*	*3.40*	*3.96*	*0.9*	*94.4*	*45*	*47*	*55*

Breakout: 17% Improve: 42% Collapse: 30% Attrition: 12% MLB: 93% *Comparables: Dustin McGowan, Justin Grimm, Andrew Cashner*

Clap yours and say it with us: Hand is an elite relief pitcher. The journey began in 2015 when he transitioned from replacement-level starter to power 'pen arm, and he has quietly evolved into one of the best relievers in the game. Perhaps it's the market he pitches in, but it took GM A.J. Preller inquiring on some of baseball's best prospects in a potential trade for Hand to finally make national headlines. Now that San Diego's best-kept secret is out in the open, maybe the disconnect between his name and true value will finally be destroyed. Possessing one of the nastiest pitches in baseball—a sweeping and diving slider that he throws nearly half the time—Hand should ride that pitch and his two fastballs to another great season in 2018.

Dinelson Lamet RHP Born: 07/18/92 Age: 25 Bats: R Throws: R Height: 6'4" Weight: 187 Origin: International Free Agent, 2014

YEAR	TEAM	LVL	AGE	W	L	SV	G	GS	IP	H	HR	BB/9	K/9	K	GB%	BABIP	WHIP	ERA	DRA	WARP	MPH	CMD	PWR	STM
2015	FTW	A	22	5	8	0	26	24	105^1	82	9	3.8	10.3	120	40%	.282	1.20	2.99	2.38	3.5				
2016	LEL	A+	23	7	1	0	12	12	65	56	4	3.6	7.5	54	45%	.289	1.26	2.35	4.85	0.5				
2016	SAN	AA	23	5	7	0	14	14	74^1	57	2	3.8	11.0	91	40%	.296	1.18	3.39	3.27	1.6				
2016	ELP	AAA	23	0	2	0	2	2	10^2	13	2	3.4	11.0	13	38%	.367	1.59	4.22	4.03	0.2				
2017	ELP	AAA	24	3	2	0	8	8	39	32	2	4.6	11.5	50	52%	.319	1.33	3.23	2.60	1.3				
2017	SDN	MLB	24	7	8	0	21	21	114^1	88	18	4.3	10.9	139	37%	.261	1.24	4.57	3.85	2.2	96.8	41	57	68
2018	*SDN*	*MLB*	*25*	*7*	*9*	*0*	*26*	*26*	*130*	*110*	*19*	*4.0*	*10.7*	*154*	*39%*	*.289*	*1.28*	*3.93*	*4.47*	*1.0*	*96.5*	*42*	*58*	*70*
2019	*SDN*	*MLB*	*26*	*10*	*10*	*0*	*32*	*32*	*210*	*158*	*28*	*3.4*	*10.6*	*247*	*39%*	*.284*	*1.13*	*3.71*	*4.31*	*2.4*	*96.2*	*42*	*59*	*70*

Breakout: 38% Improve: 67% Collapse: 18% Attrition: 25% MLB: 94% *Comparables: Jake Odorizzi, Danny Duffy, Marc Rzepczynski*

Starting pitchers aren't allowed to succeed with just two pitches. It's a rule in baseball. Over the last few seasons, there have only been a couple notable exceptions: Rich Hill and knuckleballers. Hill's a magician who can throw his fastball and curveball about a dozen different ways, making a duo into an arsenal ten pitches deep, while knuckleballers are weird anomalies that don't count. Basically, we're back to where we started. Two pitches simply aren't enough for a pitcher to turn over the lineup several times and pitch deep into games. Or are they?

If there were another exception, it would require a pitcher with an *insanely* good one-two punch. One good enough to fool the hitter, even if he knew exactly what was coming. Lamet might be that exception; he features a high-octane fastball, but he gets his strikeouts with a diving slider that causes batters to whiff nearly 40 percent of the time. Unfortunately, his shallow arsenal becomes a major problem when he faces batters a third time: a 3.94 ERA in the first round and 3.22 in the second jump to an 8.86 mark in his third battle. He also falls victim to the same trouble right-handed fastball/slider arms have since the dawn of time—an inability to keep hitters with the platoon advantage from reaching base. The whiff rate on his slider drops to 30 percent against left-handed hitters, and without a secondary weapon to keep them off the fastball, they tattooed him for an .867 OPS in his rookie season.

Lamet may have the raw stuff to be the rare starter to succeed with just two pitches, but he isn't quite there yet and may need to further develop an inconsistent changeup to get over the hump. At best, he can be a mid-rotation starter who racks up the strikeouts. At worst, it's a high-leverage relief arm. Anything in between is just as possible, making Lamet one of the more intriguing arms to watch in 2018.

Joey Lucchesi LHP Born: 06/06/93 Age: 25 Bats: L Throws: L Height: 6'5" Weight: 204 Origin: Round 4, 2016 Draft (#114 overall)

YEAR	TEAM	LVL	AGE	W	L	SV	G	GS	IP	H	HR	BB/9	K/9	K	GB%	BABIP	WHIP	ERA	DRA	WARP	MPH	CMD	PWR	STM
2016	TRI	A-	23	0	2	1	14	10	40	27	0	0.4	11.9	53	58%	.293	0.73	1.35	0.98	2.0				
2017	LEL	A+	24	6	4	0	14	14	78^2	56	9	2.2	10.9	95	53%	.251	0.95	2.52	1.40	3.6				
2017	SAN	AA	24	5	3	1	10	9	60^1	46	3	2.1	7.9	53	50%	.259	0.99	1.79	2.33	2.0				
2018	*SDN*	*MLB*	*25*	*6*	*7*	*0*	*20*	*20*	*102^2*	*88*	*17*	*3.1*	*10.6*	*120*	*44%*	*.298*	*1.19*	*4.08*	*4.77*	*1.0*				
2019	*SDN*	*MLB*	*26*	*9*	*10*	*0*	*30*	*30*	*188^2*	*162*	*28*	*3.4*	*9.0*	*190*	*44%*	*.292*	*1.23*	*4.23*	*4.91*	*1.2*				

Breakout: 14% Improve: 32% Collapse: 13% Attrition: 40% MLB: 61% *Comparables: Matt Maloney, Kyle Gibson, Sean Nolin*

Lucchesi's pitching motion resembles an epileptic Tin Man, but it works. The former fourth-rounder posted strikeout and walk numbers that would cause an xFIP machine to explode, if xFIP machines existed. And while it was mostly written off given Lucchesi's advanced age and funky mechanics, it's becoming harder and harder to ignore the results after another dominant performance last season. While the strikeouts did fall once he was promoted to Double-A, he had the third lowest ERA in the Texas League and continued to keep walks to a minimum. He'll need to develop an effective third pitch to go with an excellent fastball/changeup combo, but the southpaw could become a solid starter in the big leagues if that happens.

Jordan Lyles RHP Born: 10/19/90 Age: 27 Bats: R Throws: R Height: 6'4" Weight: 230 Origin: Round 1, 2008 Draft (#38 overall)

YEAR	TEAM	LVL	AGE	W	L	SV	G	GS	IP	H	HR	BB/9	K/9	K	GB%	BABIP	WHIP	ERA	DRA	WARP	MPH	CMD	PWR	STM
2015	COL	MLB	24	2	5	0	10	10	49	54	2	3.5	5.5	30	51%	.329	1.49	5.14	4.99	0.0	95.2	37	51	45
2016	ABQ	AAA	25	4	2	0	8	8	44^2	57	5	3.6	5.8	29	42%	.361	1.68	5.44	8.93	-1.8				
2016	COL	MLB	25	4	5	1	40	5	58^2	69	4	4.3	4.9	32	52%	.319	1.65	5.83	6.24	-0.8	95.7	44	54	55
2017	COL	MLB	26	0	2	0	33	0	46^2	61	11	2.3	6.4	33	52%	.331	1.56	6.94	7.95	-1.4	96.1	46	55	51
2017	ELP	AAA	26	1	1	0	5	5	20	20	1	3.6	9.0	20	48%	.333	1.40	4.50	4.78	0.2				
2017	SDN	MLB	26	1	3	0	5	5	23	35	5	3.9	8.6	22	46%	.395	1.96	9.39	8.10	-0.7	94.5	46	55	51
2018	*SDN*	*MLB*	*27*	*5*	*7*	*0*	*19*	*19*	*100^2*	*101*	*13*	*3.3*	*7.4*	*83*	*48%*	*.296*	*1.37*	*4.22*	*4.80*	*0.4*	*95.1*	*44*	*55*	*51*
2019	*SDN*	*MLB*	*28*	*9*	*10*	*0*	*29*	*29*	*175*	*167*	*20*	*3.3*	*7.7*	*149*	*48%*	*.311*	*1.32*	*4.05*	*4.72*	*1.5*	*94.8*	*45*	*55*	*52*

Breakout: 25% Improve: 60% Collapse: 16% Attrition: 17% MLB: 92% *Comparables: John Lannan, Paul Maholm, Matt Harrison*

Between 2014 and 2016, Lyles didn't do much right other than show up on time. However, his one impressive feat was allowing only 18 homers combined in those three seasons while pitching in the mile-high air of Coors Field. He was one of only four Rockies starting pitchers in team history (min. 1 start per year) to allow less than a homer per nine innings in three consecutive seasons. This skill completely evaporated in 2017, and his home-run spike led directly to his release in August; a cameo at sea level toward the end of the season did not help his cause heading into free agency. Lyles will have his work cut out for him if he wants to avoid the dubious distinction of posting the worst WARP among first-rounders from '08 who've made it to the majors.

Phil Maton RHP Born: 03/25/93 Age: 25 Bats: R Throws: R Height: 6'3" Weight: 220 Origin: Round 20, 2015 Draft (#597 overall)

YEAR	TEAM	LVL	AGE	W	L	SV	G	GS	IP	H	HR	BB/9	K/9	K	GB%	BABIP	WHIP	ERA	DRA	WARP	MPH	CMD	PWR	STM
2015	TRI	A-	22	4	2	6	23	0	32^2	23	0	1.4	16.0	58	43%	.365	0.86	1.38	0.53	1.7				
2016	FTW	A	23	1	1	1	8	0	12^2	14	0	0.7	13.5	19	33%	.424	1.18	1.42	1.80	0.4				
2016	LEL	A+	23	3	2	9	25	0	33	17	2	2.2	12.8	47	39%	.217	0.76	1.91	1.16	1.5				
2017	ELP	AAA	24	1	1	13	23	0	25^1	22	1	2.8	11.0	31	38%	.328	1.18	2.84	2.61	0.7				
2017	SDN	MLB	24	3	2	1	46	0	43	41	10	2.9	9.6	46	47%	.284	1.28	4.19	5.15	0.0	94.4	55	56	52
2018	*SDN*	*MLB*	*25*	*3*	*2*	*2*	*54*	*0*	*56*	*48*	*9*	*3.5*	*11.7*	*74*	*38%*	*.296*	*1.24*	*3.70*	*4.20*	*0.5*	*94.1*	*56*	*57*	*53*
2019	*SDN*	*MLB*	*26*	*3*	*1*	*2*	*56*	*0*	*59*	*46*	*9*	*3.6*	*11.5*	*75*	*38%*	*.299*	*1.18*	*3.87*	*4.50*	*0.5*	*93.8*	*57*	*58*	*54*

Breakout: 21% Improve: 36% Collapse: 22% Attrition: 42% MLB: 63% *Comparables: Shawn Tolleson, Yimi Garcia, Chad Orvella*

The Padres popped Maton in the 20th round of the 2015 draft and pushed the Lousiana Tech product hard through the system, as they have done in recent years with college relievers such as Josh Spence and Kevin Quackenbush. The results in Maton's big-league debut weren't stellar, but neither were they embarrassing. He generated a fair number of whiffs with a mix of low-90s four-seam fastballs and low-80s curveballs. Unfortunately, although his four-seamer had the 13th-highest spin rate in baseball last year, it got pummeled. Left-handed batters were especially troublesome, hitting a robust .300/.355/.557 against him. The good news is that his curve had the eighth-best whiff rate among all relievers last season, so if he limits the mistakes he could eventually sniff higher-leverage situations in the seventh inning or later.

Kyle McGrath LHP Born: 07/31/92 Age: 25 Bats: L Throws: L Height: 6'2" Weight: 185 Origin: Round 36, 2014 Draft (#1077 overall)

YEAR	TEAM	LVL	AGE	W	L	SV	G	GS	IP	H	HR	BB/9	K/9	K	GB%	BABIP	WHIP	ERA	DRA	WARP	MPH	CMD	PWR	STM
2015	FTW	A	22	3	0	3	41	0	68^2	56	3	1.0	10.4	79	38%	.305	0.93	1.70	1.21	3.0				
2016	LEL	A+	23	1	0	0	11	0	17^1	8	0	0.5	13.5	26	19%	.250	0.52	0.00	1.47	0.7				
2016	SAN	AA	23	1	2	1	33	0	48^2	32	4	1.5	9.2	50	32%	.239	0.82	1.29	1.50	1.9				
2017	SAN	AA	24	1	1	0	20	0	23^2	16	2	1.5	10.3	27	34%	.233	0.85	2.66	3.25	0.4				
2017	SDN	MLB	24	0	0	0	17	0	19	14	2	2.8	7.6	16	28%	.235	1.05	2.84	4.60	0.1	87.6	60	12	35
2018	*SDN*	*MLB*	*25*	*1*	*1*	*0*	*27*	*0*	*28*	*26*	*5*	*3.5*	*9.7*	*31*	*33%*	*.291*	*1.30*	*4.62*	*4.93*	*0.0*	*87.3*	*61*	*12*	*36*
2019	*SDN*	*MLB*	*26*	*3*	*1*	*1*	*52*	*0*	*55*	*47*	*10*	*2.8*	*9.6*	*59*	*33%*	*.289*	*1.17*	*4.33*	*5.03*	*0.1*	*87.1*	*62*	*12*	*36*

Breakout: 18% Improve: 27% Collapse: 27% Attrition: 49% MLB: 66% *Comparables: Tony Zych, Mark Melancon, R.J. Swindle*

According to some "experts"—and please take that word lightly—the inverted W can directly lead to arm injuries in pitchers. McGrath heard their warning, so instead he pitches with the upright U. Seriously, his arm stays above his elbow for the entire motion. But it's worked: He has never had an ERA over 3.00 at any professional level, and was successful in his first big-league audition. Regression is coming, though, as he relies on deception more than stuff and an extended look will expose his weaknesses.

Bryan Mitchell RHP Born: 04/19/91 Age: 27 Bats: L Throws: R Height: 6'3" Weight: 210 Origin: Round 16, 2009 Draft (#495 overall)

YEAR	TEAM	LVL	AGE	W	L	SV	G	GS	IP	H	HR	BB/9	K/9	K	GB%	BABIP	WHIP	ERA	DRA	WARP	MPH	CMD	PWR	STM
2015	SWB	AAA	24	5	5	0	15	15	75	63	1	4.4	7.3	61	54%	.286	1.33	3.12	7.27	-1.7				
2015	NYA	MLB	24	0	2	1	20	2	29^2	37	4	4.9	8.8	29	50%	.359	1.79	6.37	3.68	0.4	98.2	38	57	51
2016	NYA	MLB	25	1	2	0	5	5	25	26	1	4.3	4.0	11	49%	.301	1.52	3.24	5.53	0.0	96.9	48	51	44
2017	SWB	AAA	26	3	3	0	14	13	63^2	59	1	1.8	9.3	66	54%	.326	1.13	3.25	1.85	2.6				
2017	NYA	MLB	26	1	1	1	20	1	32^2	42	2	3.6	4.7	17	55%	.333	1.68	5.79	6.99	-0.6	97.2	28	52	48
2018	*SDN*	*MLB*	*27*	*5*	*5*	*0*	*62*	*8*	99^1	*94*	*10*	*3.7*	*8.4*	*93*	*49%*	*.302*	*1.37*	*3.72*	*4.22*	*0.9*	*96.9*	*37*	*54*	*48*
2019	*SDN*	*MLB*	*28*	*6*	*4*	*0*	*74*	*9*	120^1	*108*	*12*	*3.3*	*8.5*	*114*	*49%*	*.312*	*1.27*	*3.73*	*4.34*	*1.3*	*96.4*	*36*	*53*	*47*

Breakout: 30% Improve: 47% Collapse: 18% Attrition: 25% MLB: 79% *Comparables: Taylor Jungmann, Phil Coke, Mike Montgomery*

Mitchell's 2016 was a disaster because of injury and his 2017 was a disaster because he seemingly forgot how to pitch, at least in the majors. If you want to look at the positives, he was much better at Triple-A, where he worked as a starter. His stint in New York was forgettable enough that he'll probably be remembered more for playing first base in an extra-inning game against Baltimore, which he eventually lost when he gave up three runs in the bottom of the 11th inning. His path to a full-time gig opens up with a move to San Diego, and Petco Park should help.

Adrian Morejon LHP Born: 02/27/99 Age: 19 Bats: L Throws: L Height: 6'0" Weight: 165 Origin: International Free Agent, 2016

YEAR	TEAM	LVL	AGE	W	L	SV	G	GS	IP	H	HR	BB/9	K/9	K	GB%	BABIP	WHIP	ERA	DRA	WARP	MPH	CMD	PWR	STM
2017	TRI	A-	18	2	2	0	7	7	35^1	37	2	0.8	8.9	35	41%	.337	1.13	3.57	4.07	0.5				
2017	FTW	A	18	1	2	0	6	6	27^2	28	2	4.2	7.5	23	34%	.321	1.48	4.23	8.01	-0.9				
2018	*SDN*	*MLB*	*19*	*2*	*4*	*0*	*9*	*9*	44^1	*45*	*10*	*3.7*	*9.6*	*47*	*37%*	*.317*	*1.43*	*5.30*	*6.19*	*-0.3*				
2019	*SDN*	*MLB*	*20*	*6*	*12*	*0*	*28*	*28*	*167*	*174*	*38*	*5.0*	*8.8*	*164*	*37%*	*.321*	*1.60*	*5.94*	*6.90*	*-1.9*				

Comparables: John Barbato, Jenrry Mejia, Jamie Callahan

Signed out of Cuba for $11 million back in 2016, Morejon has quickly shown the high-end stuff to be worth the pricey investment. While years away from contributing in the big leagues, he already has two plus fastballs in his four-seamer and two-seamer, along with a curve that can miss bats. The changeup lags behind, as is the case with so many young arms, but it wouldn't shock anyone if he can turn it into a usable offering. Perhaps the biggest concern at this point is his small stature, but talent has a way of working through such roadblocks. Give Morejon a few years and he could make that $11 million look like a bargain for the Padres.

Chris Paddack RHP Born: 01/08/96 Age: 22 Bats: R Throws: R Height: 6'4" Weight: 195 Origin: Round 8, 2015 Draft (#236 overall)

YEAR	TEAM	LVL	AGE	W	L	SV	G	GS	IP	H	HR	BB/9	K/9	K	GB%	BABIP	WHIP	ERA	DRA	WARP	MPH	CMD	PWR	STM
2015	MRL	RK	19	4	3	0	11	7	45^{1}	37	1	1.4	7.7	39	55%	.273	0.97	2.18	3.00	1.4				
2016	GRB	A	20	2	0	0	6	6	28^{1}	9	2	0.6	15.2	48	51%	.163	0.39	0.95	0.41	1.6				
2016	FTW	A	20	0	0	0	3	3	14	11	0	1.9	14.8	23	45%	.379	1.00	0.64	1.27	0.6				
2018	SDN	MLB	22	2	2	0	12	6	36^{1}	34	6	3.3	10.0	41	41%	.314	1.30	4.37	5.11	0.2				
2019	SDN	MLB	23	6	8	0	30	23	166^{2}	171	30	2.6	8.2	153	41%	.32	1.32	4.64	5.39	0.2				

Breakout: 29% Improve: 43% Collapse: 4% Attrition: 14% MLB: 51% *Comparables: Noah Syndergaard, Shelby Miller, Francisco Liriano*

Paddack had one of the more ridiculous pop-up stories of 2016, as the former eighth-round draft pick suddenly became unhittable in A-ball. The then-20-year-old struck out nearly half the batters he faced over 42 1/3 innings with just four runs and five walks allowed. If that sounds too good to be true, you're right. Paddack underwent Tommy John surgery just three starts after being traded to the Padres from Miami, and sat out all of 2017. He should be healthy to start 2018, though, and if the velocity comes back he could pair a low-90s fastball with a plus changeup and fringy curveball. That won't get him a 50 percent strikeout rate in the big leagues, but it's enough to make him an awfully interesting prospect.

Luis Perdomo RHP Born: 05/09/93 Age: 25 Bats: R Throws: R Height: 6'2" Weight: 185 Origin: International Free Agent, 2003

YEAR	TEAM	LVL	AGE	W	L	SV	G	GS	IP	H	HR	BB/9	K/9	K	GB%	BABIP	WHIP	ERA	DRA	WARP	MPH	CMD	PWR	STM
2015	PEO	A	22	5	9	0	17	17	100^{1}	103	7	2.8	9.0	100	55%	.334	1.34	3.68	2.39	3.4				
2015	PMB	A+	22	1	3	0	6	5	26^{1}	31	1	2.1	6.2	18	49%	.345	1.41	5.13	4.68	0.1				
2016	SDN	MLB	23	9	10	0	35	20	146^{2}	187	23	2.8	6.4	105	60%	.342	1.59	5.71	5.43	-0.2	96.4	46	58	65
2017	SDN	MLB	24	8	11	0	29	29	163^{2}	182	17	3.6	6.5	118	62%	.325	1.51	4.67	6.32	-1.4	95.9	40	57	68
2018	SDN	MLB	25	8	9	0	26	26	137	135	13	3.3	7.9	121	55%	.303	1.36	3.67	4.19	1.5	95.8	44	59	68
2019	SDN	MLB	26	11	10	0	32	32	207^{2}	183	17	3.1	8.3	192	55%	.312	1.23	3.45	4.02	3.0	95.6	44	59	69

Breakout: 38% Improve: 55% Collapse: 13% Attrition: 21% MLB: 87% *Comparables: Matt Harrison, Chris Volstad, Jacob Turner*

Selected in the 2015 Rule 5 draft with no experience above High-A, Perdomo has absorbed innings out of the back of the rotation for two years now for the Padres. Those innings weren't particularly good, but there's something to be said for a young arm who can contribute every fifth day for a team (even if it's a sub-.500 club). He did a better job of keeping the ball in the yard last year and is a ground-ball machine but still doesn't generate as many whiffs as you'd like to see, which makes him unlikely to be more than a back-end starter. Still, his solid sinker/curveball combination should allow him to continue in that role going forward, at least for a while. That's more than can be said of most Rule 5 picks.

Kevin Quackenbush RHP Born: 11/28/88 Age: 29 Bats: R Throws: R Height: 6'4" Weight: 235 Origin: Round 8, 2011 Draft (#263 overall)

YEAR	TEAM	LVL	AGE	W	L	SV	G	GS	IP	H	HR	BB/9	K/9	K	GB%	BABIP	WHIP	ERA	DRA	WARP	MPH	CMD	PWR	STM
2015	ELP	AAA	26	1	0	2	9	0	11^{2}	6	0	1.5	10.8	14	39%	.261	0.69	0.77	2.91	0.3				
2015	SDN	MLB	26	3	2	0	57	0	58^{1}	52	6	3.1	8.9	58	44%	.291	1.23	4.01	3.71	0.7	92.8	61	45	51
2016	ELP	AAA	27	1	0	2	9	0	13	12	0	1.4	11.1	16	51%	.343	1.08	2.08	1.86	0.5				
2016	SDN	MLB	27	7	7	2	60	0	59^{2}	55	8	3.3	6.3	42	38%	.260	1.29	3.92	5.33	-0.2	92.8	58	42	52
2017	SDN	MLB	28	0	2	0	20	0	26^{1}	32	5	5.5	7.9	23	47%	.338	1.82	7.86	6.18	-0.3	91.7	53	33	44
2017	ELP	AAA	28	4	1	4	22	0	27^{2}	28	4	2.9	7.8	24	51%	.316	1.34	3.90	3.39	0.6				
2018	SDN	MLB	29	2	1	1	48	0	51^{1}	46	6	3.8	8.6	49	44%	.294	1.31	4.29	5.01	0.1	91.9	58	41	48
2019	SDN	MLB	30	3	1	1	50	0	54^{1}	47	7	3.4	8.3	50	44%	.292	1.25	4.12	4.79	0.2	91.4	56	39	48

Breakout: 37% Improve: 56% Collapse: 21% Attrition: 27% MLB: 87% *Comparables: Darren O'Day, Ryan Cook, Craig Breslow*

The 2017 season was a fowl one for Quackenbush, who found himself ducking from line drives more than ever before. The Padres became used to seeing a grand passage of baserunners when he was on the mound, and that trend is likely to stay afloat in 2018 considering his lackluster strikeout rate and poor run prevention. The former "top relief prospect" has seemingly deteriorated into a decoy, and he'll have to fight and paddle his way into a spot with a big-league team next season.

Cal Quantrill RHP Born: 02/10/95 Age: 23 Bats: L Throws: R Height: 6'2" Weight: 165 Origin: Round 1, 2016 Draft (#8 overall)

YEAR	TEAM	LVL	AGE	W	L	SV	G	GS	IP	H	HR	BB/9	K/9	K	GB%	BABIP	WHIP	ERA	DRA	WARP	MPH	CMD	PWR	STM
2016	PDR	RK	21	0	2	0	5	5	13^{2}	12	0	1.3	10.5	16	49%	.324	1.02	5.27	2.55	0.5				
2016	TRI	A-	21	0	2	0	5	5	18^{2}	15	0	1.0	13.5	28	56%	.333	0.91	1.93	1.43	0.8				
2017	LEL	A+	22	6	5	0	14	14	73^{2}	78	5	2.9	9.3	76	42%	.353	1.38	3.67	4.79	0.4				
2017	SAN	AA	22	1	5	0	8	8	42^{1}	52	5	3.4	7.2	34	39%	.341	1.61	4.04	7.43	-1.1				
2018	SDN	MLB	23	5	7	0	20	20	91^{1}	89	17	3.5	10.1	103	39%	.322	1.37	4.65	5.44	0.2				
2019	SDN	MLB	24	5	9	0	23	23	138^{1}	139	26	4.3	9.2	141	39%	.326	1.48	5.15	5.99	-0.4				

Breakout: 8% Improve: 8% Collapse: 1% Attrition: 9% MLB: 10% *Comparables: Bruce Billings, Daniel Corcino, Max Fried*

While many of San Diego's top arms are still in the low minors, several years away from contributing, Quantrill brings the rare high-upside, near-ETA combination to the table. In his first full year back from Tommy John surgery, the former first-rounder showed a mid-90s fastball and potentially elite changeup. Toss in a more-than-respectable curveball and you've got yourself the kind of pitcher who could've gone first overall had he not blown out his elbow prior to the draft. His second full season off the shelf should prove instructive as to the realistic ceiling: He'll have to stay on the mound and build up the stamina to thrive in the rotation because a Cal who cannot ride is no Cal.

Colin Rea RHP Born: 07/01/90 Age: 27 Bats: R Throws: R Height: 6'5" Weight: 225 Origin: Round 12, 2011 Draft (#383 overall)

YEAR	TEAM	LVL	AGE	W	L	SV	G	GS	IP	H	HR	BB/9	K/9	K	GB%	BABIP	WHIP	ERA	DRA	WARP	MPH	CMD	PWR	STM
2015	SAN	AA	24	3	2	0	12	12	75	50	1	1.3	7.2	60	50%	.233	0.81	1.08	1.97	2.8				
2015	ELP	AAA	24	2	2	0	6	6	26^2	29	2	4.1	6.8	20	48%	.321	1.54	4.39	3.87	0.4				
2015	SDN	MLB	24	2	2	0	6	6	31^2	29	2	3.1	7.4	26	50%	.290	1.26	4.26	6.39	-0.5	93.3	53	43	57
2016	SDN	MLB	25	5	5	0	19	18	99^1	101	12	4.0	6.9	76	48%	.295	1.46	4.98	5.24	0.1	94.8	61	50	58
2016	MIA	MLB	25	0	0	0	1	1	3^1	1	0	0.0	10.8	4	43%	.143	0.30	0.00	4.85	0.0	93.3	61	50	58
2018	*SDN*	*MLB*	*27*	*4*	*5*	*0*	*13*	*13*	*74*	*69*	*8*	*3.4*	*8.0*	*66*	*44%*	*.291*	*1.30*	*3.95*	*4.50*	*0.6*	*94.0*	*60*	*49*	*58*
2019	*SDN*	*MLB*	*28*	*10*	*12*	*0*	*32*	*32*	202^2	*190*	*29*	*2.7*	*7.1*	*159*	*44%*	*.291*	*1.24*	*4.40*	*5.11*	*1.0*	*93.8*	*61*	*50*	*59*

Breakout: 28% Improve: 47% Collapse: 17% Attrition: 16% MLB: 79% *Comparables: Mike Montgomery, Burke Badenhop, Alex Colome*

Rea went from a nondescript prospect to a bright young arm in the Padres system during a breakout 2015 season. He showed well in a big-league audition, entered 2016 as a potential long-term rotation piece and promptly missed a chunk of the season before undergoing offseason Tommy John surgery. Most have forgotten Rea's name by now, but he featured a solid four-pitch arsenal with a whispered fifth offering to boot and could turn some heads this season if the stuff comes all the way back. Still, expectations should be tempered, as Rea is 27 years old and has less than a full season of major-league innings to his name.

Clayton Richard LHP Born: 09/12/83 Age: 34 Bats: L Throws: L Height: 6'5" Weight: 240 Origin: Round 8, 2005 Draft (#245 overall)

YEAR	TEAM	LVL	AGE	W	L	SV	G	GS	IP	H	HR	BB/9	K/9	K	GB%	BABIP	WHIP	ERA	DRA	WARP	MPH	CMD	PWR	STM
2015	IND	AAA	31	4	2	0	9	9	56	53	3	2.1	4.0	25	57%	.260	1.18	2.09	4.38	0.6				
2015	CHN	MLB	31	4	2	0	23	3	42^1	47	3	1.5	4.7	22	60%	.297	1.28	3.83	5.20	-0.2	94.2	61	58	53
2016	CHN	MLB	32	0	1	1	25	0	14	23	0	4.5	4.5	7	73%	.411	2.14	6.43	5.11	0.0	94.2	50	54	43
2016	SDN	MLB	32	3	3	0	11	9	53^2	58	4	4.0	5.7	34	64%	.314	1.53	2.52	5.27	0.0	93.1	50	54	43
2017	SDN	MLB	33	8	15	0	32	32	197^1	240	24	2.7	6.9	151	60%	.351	1.52	4.79	5.90	-0.7	92.4	44	45	81
2018	*SDN*	*MLB*	*34*	*8*	*9*	*0*	*26*	*26*	*148*	*151*	*15*	*3.1*	*6.9*	*113*	*58%*	*.302*	*1.38*	*3.90*	*4.45*	*1.2*	*91.6*	*46*	*47*	*60*
2019	*SDN*	*MLB*	*35*	*10*	*11*	*0*	*31*	*31*	*198*	*199*	*19*	*2.9*	*6.5*	*144*	*58%*	*.318*	*1.33*	*3.96*	*4.61*	*2.0*	*91.0*	*45*	*46*	*62*

Breakout: 8% Improve: 36% Collapse: 23% Attrition: 16% MLB: 77% *Comparables: Jerome Williams, Tim Stauffer, Jake Westbrook*

Despite showing a complete inability to strike batters out, Richard has long made it work thanks to an elite ground-ball profile. The main questions around his ability to jump back into the rotation were whether his strikeout rate would bottom out and whether the walk rate would keep its inflation from 2016. Both things worked out quite well: His K/9 jumped to a career high, and he lost the unwanted gains in free passes. That ground-ball rate remained elite, of course, but even the sum of these parts couldn't make Richard very good. His ERA was poor, his DRA even worse. It doesn't add up. Everything broke right, but it all still went wrong. Luckily, he stayed healthy all year and signed a two-year extension in September, making him a good bet to keep his spot in the rotation a while longer.

Craig Stammen RHP Born: 03/09/84 Age: 34 Bats: R Throws: R Height: 6'4" Weight: 230 Origin: Round 12, 2005 Draft (#354 overall)

YEAR	TEAM	LVL	AGE	W	L	SV	G	GS	IP	H	HR	BB/9	K/9	K	GB%	BABIP	WHIP	ERA	DRA	WARP	MPH	CMD	PWR	STM
2015	WAS	MLB	31	0	0	0	5	0	4	2	0	6.8	6.8	3	55%	.182	1.25	0.00	2.54	0.1	93.6			
2016	AKR	AA	32	0	1	0	10	0	11^1	9	1	2.4	7.1	9	69%	.235	1.06	0.79	4.14	0.1				
2016	COH	AAA	32	0	3	0	10	0	13	16	2	1.4	7.6	11	57%	.333	1.38	5.54	4.03	0.1				
2017	SDN	MLB	33	2	3	0	60	0	80^1	68	12	3.1	8.3	74	52%	.263	1.20	3.14	3.71	1.3	92.7	52	46	51
2018	*SDN*	*MLB*	*34*	*3*	*1*	*1*	*54*	*0*	56^2	*55*	*9*	*3.9*	*8.4*	*53*	*50%*	*.305*	*1.40*	*4.72*	*5.52*	*-0.3*	*91.6*	*51*	*45*	*50*
2019	*SDN*	*MLB*	*35*	*1*	*0*	*0*	*21*	*0*	28^1	*27*	*4*	*4.3*	*7.7*	*24*	*50%*	*.308*	*1.44*	*4.77*	*5.54*	*-0.1*	*91.0*	*51*	*45*	*50*

Breakout: 19% Improve: 31% Collapse: 29% Attrition: 7% MLB: 77% *Comparables: Nick Masset, Brian Duensing, Peter Moylan*

Remember Stammen? Last time he appeared in these pages, he had just wrapped another year of very solid middle relief innings for the Nationals. In April 2016, the bullpen stalwart had surgery to repair his flexor tendon, which was supposed to only sideline him until the start of the following spring. Instead, Stammen signed a minor-league deal with the Indians and his elbow never quite let him return to his natural role. That changed in 2017 with the Padres, as a healthy Stammen reprised his classic role as a solid middle reliever, logging another 80-inning season. While the velocity has dipped a bit since his heyday, he is still making it work with a sinker, slider and plenty of whiffs. He won't have to settle for a minor-league deal this time around.

Matt Strahm LHP Born: 11/12/91 Age: 26 Bats: R Throws: L Height: 6'3" Weight: 185 Origin: Round 21, 2012 Draft (#643 overall)

YEAR	TEAM	LVL	AGE	W	L	SV	G	GS	IP	H	HR	BB/9	K/9	K	GB%	BABIP	WHIP	ERA	DRA	WARP	MPH	CMD	PWR	STM
2015	LEX	A	23	2	1	4	14	0	26	12	1	4.2	13.2	38	48%	.234	0.92	2.08	1.65	1.0				
2015	WIL	A+	23	1	6	1	15	11	68	48	7	2.5	11.0	83	37%	.255	0.99	2.78	2.13	2.4				
2016	NWA	AA	24	3	8	0	22	18	102^1	102	14	2.0	9.4	107	40%	.320	1.22	3.43	2.35	3.3				
2016	KCA	MLB	24	2	2	0	21	0	22	13	0	4.5	12.3	30	50%	.283	1.09	1.23	2.60	0.6	96.8	46	60	59
2017	KCA	MLB	25	2	5	0	24	3	34^2	30	6	5.7	9.6	37	42%	.279	1.50	5.45	5.04	0.1	95.7	43	58	44
2018	*SDN*	*MLB*	*26*	*4*	*4*	*0*	*35*	*8*	*70*	*64*	*12*	*3.9*	*10.3*	*81*	*40%*	*.295*	*1.34*	*4.39*	*4.85*	*0.2*	*95.7*	*45*	*60*	*52*
2019	*SDN*	*MLB*	*27*	*7*	*6*	*0*	*71*	*15*	148^2	*114*	*23*	*3.9*	*10.8*	*178*	*40%*	*.288*	*1.20*	*4.11*	*4.78*	*1.0*	*95.4*	*45*	*60*	*52*

Breakout: 24% Improve: 43% Collapse: 16% Attrition: 29% MLB: 79% *Comparables: Angel Guzman, Ramon Ramirez, Trevor May*

On his best day, Strahm looks like a top-end arm: He can start batters off with a four-seam fastball that touches 97 mph and has a penchant for avoiding bats. He then follows the heat with two potential plus pitches in a diving curveball and whirring slider, with a show-me changeup rounding things out. That's a heck of an arsenal, one which *looks* like it could work well out of the rotation or dominantly in the bullpen. Unfortunately, that hasn't been the case thus far. Acquired by the Padres part-way through 2017, Strahm has yet to pitch for his new team due to a knee injury. When healthy, though, the southpaw has shown shaky control. He won't have trouble inducing whiffs, but the command will have to improve if he wants to stick in the big leagues. If he cuts his walks a little, he's an exciting bullpen arm. If he cuts them a lot, he could be a mid-rotation starter. Look for the Padres to develop him in the latter role for 2018.

Jose Torres LHP Born: 09/24/93 Age: 24 Bats: L Throws: L Height: 6'2" Weight: 175 Origin: International Free Agent, 2010

YEAR	TEAM	LVL	AGE	W	L	SV	G	GS	IP	H	HR	BB/9	K/9	K	GB%	BABIP	WHIP	ERA	DRA	WARP	MPH	CMD	PWR	STM
2015	BLT	A	21	4	5	8	44	0	73^2	55	4	2.8	9.8	80	55%	.270	1.06	2.69	2.04	2.4				
2016	LEL	A+	22	0	2	1	20	0	25^1	21	2	3.6	8.9	25	51%	.279	1.22	3.55	2.73	0.7				
2016	SAN	AA	22	1	2	2	25	0	36^1	20	1	3.0	8.9	36	52%	.218	0.88	1.24	3.37	0.6				
2016	SDN	MLB	22	0	0	0	4	0	3	3	0	6.0	9.0	3	22%	.333	1.67	0.00	5.35	0.0	96.4			44
2017	SDN	MLB	23	7	4	1	62	0	68^1	63	13	2.1	8.3	63	37%	.266	1.16	4.21	5.49	-0.2	96.4	54	67	49
2018	*SDN*	*MLB*	*24*	*3*	*3*	*0*	*54*	*0*	*56*	*53*	*10*	*3.7*	*9.3*	*59*	*43%*	*.289*	*1.33*	*4.67*	*4.98*	*-0.1*	*96.2*	*56*	*69*	*48*
2019	*SDN*	*MLB*	*25*	*2*	*1*	*0*	*49*	*0*	51^2	*43*	*8*	*3.3*	*9.7*	*56*	*43%*	*.287*	*1.19*	*4.28*	*4.96*	*0.1*	*96.0*	*56*	*69*	*49*

Breakout: 27% Improve: 38% Collapse: 7% Attrition: 25% MLB: 61% *Comparables: Carlos Estevez, Chris Britton, Cesar Jimenez*

Stop me if you've heard this one before, but Torres is a southpaw with an intriguing one-two punch in the form of a 95-mph heater and a curveball that induces whiffs over 40 percent of the time. He struck out plenty of hitters last season while displaying solid control, though he was bitten by the home run bug like seemingly everyone else across the sport. The culprit is that he doesn't have a secondary pitch that can keep right-handed hitters off his fastball, as they waited for it and banged it over the fence nine times last season. Without improving his unimpressive change or adding something else to give righties a different look, Torres will start to see fewer and fewer of them in the batter's box, dragging him deeper and deeper into a LOOGY role.

Jered Weaver RHP Born: 10/04/82 Age: 35 Bats: R Throws: R Height: 6'7" Weight: 210 Origin: Round 1, 2004 Draft (#12 overall)

YEAR	TEAM	LVL	AGE	W	L	SV	G	GS	IP	H	HR	BB/9	K/9	K	GB%	BABIP	WHIP	ERA	DRA	WARP	MPH	CMD	PWR	STM
2015	ANA	MLB	32	7	12	0	26	26	159	163	24	1.9	5.1	90	37%	.273	1.23	4.64	5.37	-0.6	87.2	61	0	65
2016	ANA	MLB	33	12	12	0	31	31	178	209	37	2.6	5.2	103	30%	.301	1.46	5.06	7.50	-4.4	86.2	52	10	75
2017	SDN	MLB	34	0	5	0	9	9	42^1	51	16	2.6	4.9	23	44%	.257	1.49	7.44	7.50	-0.9	85.4	39	3	34
2018	*SDN*	*MLB*	*35*	*3*	*5*	*0*	*10*	*10*	60^1	*63*	*11*	*3.0*	*6.1*	*41*	*39%*	*.289*	*1.38*	*5.39*	*6.30*	*-0.5*	*85.3*	*52*	*5*	*54*
2019	*SDN*	*MLB*	*36*	*9*	*13*	*0*	*30*	*30*	*189*	*196*	*31*	*2.8*	*5.4*	*113*	*39%*	*.292*	*1.35*	*5.08*	*5.91*	*-0.6*	*84.6*	*49*	*7*	*52*

Breakout: 15% Improve: 42% Collapse: 17% Attrition: 9% MLB: 82% *Comparables: Mike Garcia, Charlie Leibrandt, Juan Marichal*

Weaver's excellent career came to an unceremonious and unfortunate close in 2017, when his crashing velocity became unfit for big-league purposes. His final season was an unmitigated disaster, ending with a May 19 start against the Diamondbacks, who plated seven runs against him in a first inning he couldn't complete. It also culminated a run dating back to 2011 in which his ERA rose each year. But let us not dwell on the negative. Turning back to 2016, we see in Weaver's penultimate lap around the big leagues a certain beauty. Although his strikeout rate barely eclipsed his ERA, he pitched a full season and was good enough that at least one club came knocking in 2017. He succeeded (success being a relative term) with a patchwork arm, an 84-mph fastball and a pitching acumen that allowed him to survive long past his expiration date without velocity. Despite the face-plant at the end, his ability to make something out of nothing is an accomplishment worth recognizing.

Travis Wood LHP Born: 02/06/87 Age: 31 Bats: R Throws: L Height: 5'11" Weight: 175 Origin: Round 2, 2005 Draft (#60 overall)

YEAR	TEAM	LVL	AGE	W	L	SV	G	GS	IP	H	HR	BB/9	K/9	K	GB%	BABIP	WHIP	ERA	DRA	WARP	MPH	CMD	PWR	STM
2015	CHN	MLB	28	5	4	4	54	9	100^2	86	11	3.5	10.5	118	37%	.300	1.24	3.84	4.64	0.3	93.3	62	51	56
2016	CHN	MLB	29	4	0	0	77	0	61	45	8	3.5	6.9	47	38%	.215	1.13	2.95	5.41	-0.3	93.1	64	57	50
2017	KCA	MLB	30	1	3	0	28	3	41^2	56	4	4.3	6.3	29	43%	.369	1.82	6.91	8.84	-1.6	91.7	46	43	53
2017	SDN	MLB	30	3	4	0	11	11	52^1	62	15	4.3	6.2	36	34%	.287	1.66	6.71	8.46	-1.8	90.0	46	43	53
2018	*SDN*	*MLB*	*31*	*4*	*4*	*0*	*36*	*10*	80^2	*74*	*12*	*3.6*	*8.6*	*77*	*40%*	*.296*	*1.32*	*4.52*	*5.28*	*0.2*	*91.2*	*54*	*48*	*52*
2019	*SDN*	*MLB*	*32*	*7*	*7*	*1*	*66*	*16*	145^2	*136*	*22*	*3.6*	*8.1*	*131*	*40%*	*.303*	*1.33*	*4.49*	*5.22*	*0.4*	*90.5*	*52*	*47*	*52*

Breakout: 7% Improve: 40% Collapse: 31% Attrition: 15% MLB: 91% *Comparables: Barry Zito, Brad Penny, Gary Peters*

After several seasons as a back-end starter for the Cubs, Wood was shifted to the bullpen and, for a brief moment, looked like he could blossom into a shutdown reliever. The southpaw's velocity climbed, as did his strikeout rate. Unfortunately, batters stopped whiffing on Wood's 90-mph "heat" in 2016, a trend that caught up to him in a career-worst 2017. His fastball flatlined, and a mid-season shift back to the rotation by the desperate Padres didn't help much. He was equally ineffective in both roles, leaving him in pitcher purgatory going forward. The logical next step is Wood trying his hand at being a true LOOGY, especially given the .128 batting average lefties had against him in 2016, the last time he had a fastball. If left-handers hit him to the tune of an .820 OPS, like they did last season, the next logical step is for the Padres to jettison him off the 40-man roster, which they did in December.

Kirby Yates RHP Born: 03/25/87 Age: 31 Bats: L Throws: R Height: 5'10" Weight: 210 Origin: Round 26, 2005 Draft (#798 overall)

YEAR	TEAM	LVL	AGE	W	L	SV	G	GS	IP	H	HR	BB/9	K/9	K	GB%	BABIP	WHIP	ERA	DRA	WARP	MPH	CMD	PWR	STM
2015	DUR	AAA	28	1	2	6	23	0	25^1	27	5	4.3	12.1	34	39%	.344	1.54	5.33	2.41	0.7				
2015	TBA	MLB	28	1	0	0	20	0	20^1	23	10	3.1	9.3	21	30%	.245	1.48	7.97	6.76	-0.5	94.7	62	43	39
2016	SWB	AAA	29	0	1	4	14	0	16^2	12	0	3.2	10.3	19	46%	.279	1.08	1.62	3.41	0.3				
2016	NYA	MLB	29	2	1	0	41	0	41^1	41	5	4.1	10.9	50	44%	.340	1.45	5.23	4.58	0.2	95.3	51	50	45
2017	ANA	MLB	30	0	0	0	1	0	1	2	2	0.0	9.0	1	0%	.000	2.00	18.00	1.62	0.0	94.7	52	56	51
2017	SDN	MLB	30	4	5	1	61	0	55^2	42	10	3.1	14.1	87	30%	.296	1.10	3.72	3.01	1.3	95.0	52	56	51
2018	*SDN*	*MLB*	*31*	*3*	*3*	*2*	*59*	*0*	*62*	*54*	*11*	*3.8*	*11.7*	*81*	*39%*	*.297*	*1.30*	*4.16*	*4.59*	*0.2*	*94.2*	*53*	*52*	*46*
2019	*SDN*	*MLB*	*32*	*3*	*1*	*1*	*52*	*0*	54^2	*44*	*10*	*4.0*	*11.8*	*72*	*39%*	*.302*	*1.24*	*4.23*	*4.92*	*0.2*	*93.7*	*51*	*53*	*47*

Breakout: 15% Improve: 34% Collapse: 26% Attrition: 14% MLB: 73% *Comparables: Scott Dohmann, Evan Scribner, Steve Delabar*

Yates had about the worst start to a season one can possibly have, at least this side of Jeremy Guthrie. He entered his first contest of the year on April 22, gave up two runs, and was promptly designated for assignment. Not great, folks. Luckily, he found a comfy home in San Diego. Perhaps it was a small mechanical tweak by the Padres' pitching staff, or Yates finally finding his groove at Petco Park, but the righty parlayed a second chance into a breakout season. Posting the best ERA, strikeout rate and walk rate of his career, Yates used a live fastball along with a solid slider and changeup to strike out almost 40 percent of the batters he faced. And while his 2.48 ERA in the first half gave way to 5.06 ERA in the second, he continued striking batters out at a similar clip while keeping his underlying numbers largely intact. The Hawaii native, who will be a key cog in the Padres bullpen again in 2018, was one of two pitchers from the Aloha State to appear in the majors last year. The other? You guessed it: Scott Feldman.

Lineouts

Hitters

HITTER	POS	TEAM	LVL	AGE	PA	R	2B	3B	HR	RBI	BB	K	SB	CS	AVG/OBP/SLG	TAv	VORP	BABIP	BRR	FRAA	WARP
Luis Almanzar	SS	TRI	A-	17	288	36	10	1	2	21	25	85	10	5	.230/.299/.299	.237	3.7	.331	0.7	SS(32): -4.4, 3B(31): -5.8	-0.7
Carlos Asuaje	2B	ELP	AAA	25	277	44	9	5	3	35	40	33	1	1	.250/.369/.373	.262	10.2	.278	1.7	2B(59): -4.2	0.6
	2B	SDN	MLB	25	343	28	14	1	4	21	28	76	0	1	.270/.334/.362	.258	7.4	.346	-1.5	2B(84): 2.4	1.0
Erick Aybar	SS	SDN	MLB	33	370	37	15	1	7	22	28	57	11	4	.234/.300/.348	.245	9.5	.262	-0.4	SS(99): 3.7, P(2): 0.0	1.3
Jordy Barley	SS	PDR	Rk	17	195	34	11	6	4	28	11	65	7	2	.242/.292/.434	.240	3.8	.354	-0.2	SS(42): -5.5	-0.2
Christian Bethancourt	C	SDN	MLB	25	7	0	0	0	0	0	0	3	0	0	.143/.143/.143	.100	-0.7	.250	0.0	P(4): 0.0, 2B(1): 0.0	-0.4
Luis Campusano	C	PDR	Rk	18	98	3	4	0	1	13	6	14	0	1	.278/.327/.356	.233	-0.9	.316	-1.7	C(17): -0.3	-0.1
	C	SDP	Rk	18	53	5	0	0	3	12	9	11	0	1	.250/.377/.455	.285	4.5	.267	0.3	C(4): -0.3	0.4
Dusty Coleman	INF	SDN	MLB	30	71	6	3	0	4	9	2	33	1	0	.227/.268/.455	.261	3.1	.367	0.0	SS(27): 3.1	0.6
	INF	ELP	AAA	30	370	43	17	6	15	48	32	125	11	3	.208/.276/.434	.232	5.5	.272	2.0	SS(78): 5.6, 2B(10): 2.2	1.3
Chase d'Arnaud	INF	ATL	MLB	30	10	5	0	0	0	0	2	3	0	0	.375/.500/.375	.333	1.0	.600	-0.1	LF(4): 0.2, 3B(1): 0.0	0.1
	INF	BOS	MLB	30	1	2	0	0	0	0	0	0	0	0	1.000/1.000/1.000	.648	0.7	1.000	0.2	2B(1): 0.0	0.1
	INF	SDN	MLB	30	51	5	2	0	1	3	2	17	5	1	.143/.176/.245	.156	-3.7	.194	0.0	SS(10): -2.3, 2B(3): 0.0	-0.6
	INF	ELP	AAA	30	194	39	8	1	4	19	17	33	12	1	.297/.363/.424	.283	12.6	.343	2.2	2B(19): -1.0, 1B(16): 0.6	1.1
Michael Gettys	CF	LEL	A+	21	513	84	22	4	17	51	46	191	22	8	.254/.329/.431	.275	27.4	.394	3.8	CF(115): 1.4	3.0
Javier Guerra	SS	LEL	A+	21	373	38	18	5	6	38	19	113	2	1	.226/.267/.358	.231	4.0	.315	0.1	SS(89): -3.3	0.1
	SS	SAN	AA	21	145	18	6	0	3	15	8	46	0	3	.212/.262/.326	.213	-0.4	.301	0.9	SS(31): -1.8, 3B(4): -0.3	-0.2
Hudson Potts	3B	FTW	A	18	522	67	23	4	20	69	23	140	0	1	.253/.293/.438	.249	9.5	.312	-0.5	3B(116): -6.9, SS(2): 0.2	0.3
Franmil Reyes	OF	SAN	AA	21	566	79	27	1	25	102	48	134	4	4	.258/.322/.464	.291	25.3	.298	-1.1	RF(89): 3.3	3.1
Jose Rondon	SS	SAN	AA	23	234	30	12	3	4	28	16	43	2	1	.293/.343/.433	.287	16.1	.349	1.4	SS(32): 4.4, 2B(11): -1.2	2.0
	SS	ELP	AAA	23	91	9	8	0	1	14	6	16	1	0	.282/.330/.412	.245	2.6	.338	0.4	SS(18): 0.3, 2B(3): -0.3	0.2
Hector Sanchez	C	ELP	AAA	27	28	2	2	0	2	6	2	8	0	0	.269/.321/.577	.294	1.6	.313	-0.2	C(4): -0.4, 1B(1): -0.1	0.1
	C	SDN	MLB	27	143	14	4	0	8	25	5	41	0	0	.219/.245/.423	.236	1.3	.247	-0.2	C(25): -4.8, 1B(6): -0.3	-0.4

There are about 12 international shortstops in the Padres' low minors who flash excellent offensive potential. **Luis Almanzar** could be the best of them, but he's also unlikely to be a shortstop long-term. ⚾ The good news is **Carlos Asuaje**'s best skill—contact—is the most important. The bad news is it's his only tool and he's running out of time to show it off in the big leagues. ⚾ Imagine **Erick Aybar**, but without the speed. Wouldn't be great, would it? Well, that's the state of current-day Aybar, who, remarkably, still had a big-league job for much of 2017. ⚾ Don't judge **Jordy Barley** by his name. You might think of an unspectacular and forgettable food, but the 18-year-old is an electric athlete who could become a five-tool player at any number of positions if he puts it all together. ⚾ Language attrition occurs when a bilingual speaker's ability to utilize their native tongue deteriorates, an effect which can also bleed into their second language. **Christian Bethancourt** is experiencing this, but with baseball. He's forgotten how to hit, and his already-mediocre pitching ability is waning as well. ⚾ If you want to bet on 19-year-old catchers, you should probably see a professional. That said, **Luis Campusano**is a name to remember; the first backstop to be drafted in 2017 (39th overall) boasts plus power and (gasp!) the ability to stick behind the plate. ⚾ In the high minors, **Dusty Coleman** has shown some intriguing power and speed, but in the big leagues neither tool has played amid a near 50-percent strikeout rate. ⚾ **Chase d'Arnaud** should invest in some better pine tar, because he just can't seem to stick anywhere. First, the Braves DFA'd him. Then the Red Sox. And, finally, the Padres, who then safely shuttled the journeyman utility player to their Triple-A squad for the remainder of 2017. ⚾ Imagine a toolbox filled to the brim with the some of the best tools you've ever seen, but every time you try and hit a nail with that top-quality hammer, you miss. Maybe you'll eventually hit that nail, maybe you won't. Maybe you're **Michael Gettys**. ⚾ Back in 2015, **Javier Guerra** possessed the ability to be a Gold Glove defender at shortstop with solid pop at the plate. Alas, the current package features shaky defense and little-to-no offensive ability. ⚾ A lot can change in a year. For example, Hudson Sanchez changed his name to **Hudson Potts**. His power projection also jumped up a grade after he swatted 20 homers as an 18-year-old in Low-A. ⚾ We really shouldn't be comparing **Franmil Reyes** to Aaron Judge, but he's a 6'5" outfielder with plus power and—wait, SEO doesn't work with books? Reyes could still be a potential middle-of-the-order bat, though he comes with loads of risk. ⚾ All defense, no offense. That's the name of the game for **Jose Rondon**. The opposing tools will likely have teams flipping on Rondon's future role for the next couple years, but, for now, they balance out into a utility profile. ⚾ A 21-year-old with zero experience above A-ball caught more games than **Hector Sanchez** last season, leading one to believe the Padres don't have an overwhelming amount of confidence in him.

Pitchers

PITCHER	TEAM	LVL	AGE	W	L	SV	G	GS	IP	H	HR	BB/9	K/9	K	GB%	BABIP	WHIP	ERA	DRA	WARP	MPH	CMD	PWR	STM
Colten Brewer	SWB	AAA	24	0	0	1	6	0	10	17	2	3.6	9.9	11	60%	.417	2.10	11.70	5.59	0.0				

PITCHER	TEAM	LVL	AGE	W	L	SV	G	GS	IP	H	HR	BB/9	K/9	K	GB%	BABIP	WHIP	ERA	DRA	WARP	MPH	CMD	PWR	STM
	TRN	AA	24	3	1	11	29	0	41^1	37	0	2.4	9.4	43	64%	.314	1.16	1.31	2.79	1.0				
Jose Castillo	LEL	A+	21	3	2	1	39	0	47	38	0	4.2	9.4	49	42%	.297	1.28	2.87	5.38	-0.3				
Enyel De Los Santos	SAN	AA	21	10	6	0	26	24	150	131	12	2.9	8.3	138	45%	.290	1.19	3.78	2.51	4.7				
Eric Lauer	LEL	A+	22	2	5	0	12	12	67^2	65	4	2.5	11.2	84	42%	.351	1.24	2.79	2.53	2.2				
	SAN	AA	22	4	3	0	10	9	55	52	6	2.8	7.9	48	38%	.295	1.25	3.93	3.33	1.2				
Kyle Lloyd	SAN	AA	26	7	5	0	15	15	89^2	78	2	2.4	8.9	89	50%	.304	1.14	3.71	2.76	2.6				
	SDN	MLB	26	0	0	0	1	1	4	6	1	4.5	4.5	2	38%	.333	2.00	9.00	7.28	-0.1	86.8			70
	ELP	AAA	26	1	4	0	12	12	57^2	79	8	4.2	8.7	56	48%	.406	1.84	7.02	6.38	-0.4				
Walker Lockett	ELP	AAA	23	5	2	0	10	10	55^1	67	9	2.1	5.4	33	49%	.296	1.45	4.39	4.07	1.0				
	SDP	Rk	23	0	1	0	4	4	10	11	1	3.6	10.8	12	63%	.345	1.50	5.40	5.95	0.0				
Jacob Nix	LEL	A+	21	4	3	0	11	10	66^2	78	5	1.4	6.9	51	48%	.344	1.32	4.32	3.55	1.3				
	SAN	AA	21	1	2	0	6	6	27^2	32	0	2.9	7.2	22	45%	.340	1.48	5.53	5.64	-0.2				
Dillon Overton	SEA	MLB	25	0	0	0	9	1	18^1	21	4	1.0	3.9	8	41%	.262	1.25	6.38	5.98	-0.1	90.6	43	28	59
	TAC	AAA	25	1	2	0	7	6	27	34	9	4.0	7.3	22	34%	.301	1.70	9.33	9.46	-1.1				
	SDN	MLB	25	0	1	0	1	1	4^2	9	2	3.9	5.8	3	44%	.438	2.36	7.71	5.93	0.0	90.1	43	28	59
	ELP	AAA	25	6	4	0	12	12	64	77	12	2.4	4.2	30	37%	.288	1.47	5.62	8.35	-1.8				
Austin Smith	FTW	A	20	2	3	0	11	8	39^1	36	1	6.4	7.6	33	44%	.299	1.63	6.64	5.68	-0.2				
	TRI	A-	20	1	0	2	19	0	21	20	2	4.7	10.3	24	53%	.327	1.48	5.14	5.35	-0.1				
Brad Wieck	SAN	AA	25	2	1	7	31	0	30^2	21	1	3.8	15.0	51	57%	.333	1.11	2.64	1.37	1.3				

Colten Brewer parlayed a solid season in the upper minors of the Yankees' system into a one-year major-league deal with the Padres. People rave about Brewers in San Diego all the time, but Colten is rapidly approaching his "enjoy by" date. ⚾ Lefty **Jose Castillo** started to put it together in High-A last season. He already has a 3.4 WARP lead on the all-time Jose Castillo list behind former Pirates infielder Jose Castillo. ⚾ **Enyel De Los Santos** is the kind of pitcher who's going to be called "projectable" until he's 30. The lanky righty rode his solid three-pitch mix to success last season at Double-A, and even if he doesn't add that extra tick to his fastball there's the potential for a solid starter here. ⚾ **Robbie Erlin** has been out since the start of 2016 recovering from Tommy John surgery. When healthy, he's an interesting arm, walking few and inducing more than enough whiffs to scrape by, but he has yet to succeed in the big leagues and is already 27. ⚾ In 2016, **Christian Friedrich** started 23 games for the Padres, most on the team. He started as many games as Christian Bale for San Diego last season, as his 2017 campaign was wiped out by elbow surgery. ⚾ A southpaw with four solid pitches, a good delivery and advanced pitchability? That's **Eric Lauer**; he might not have tantalizing upside, but that high floor can be just as, if not more, important. ⚾ Data shows that rookie pitchers throw over a mile per hour harder, on average, in their big-league debuts. **Kyle Lloyd**'s fastball clocked in at 86 mph during his four innings of fame, so... ⚾ **Walker Lockett** had a year to forget in 2017, missing significant time with a back strain and being wholly ineffective while on the mound. With all the pitches to be a back-end starter, though, the former fourth-rounder deserves more than a few second chances. ⚾ "Last year pretty much sucked," **Jacob Nix** said after a 2016 in which he lost both a $1.5 million signing bonus from the Astros and a college scholarship from UCLA amid the Brady Aiken signing controversy. He may have struggled in his first taste of the high minors at the end of the season, but Nix is a rare and shining example of a way in which 2017 didn't suck, comparatively speaking. ⚾ Imagine present-day Jered Weaver, but as a 26-year-old southpaw—similar velocity, similar strikeout rates and similar ERA. That's **Dillon Overton**. On the bright side, Weaver did make nine starts for the Padres in 2017 and those nine starts need to be made by someone in 2018. ⚾ Prospect development is rarely linear, and don't you forget that. **Austin Smith** was drafted in the second round of the 2015 draft as starter with three intriguing pitches, and now his only legitimate offering is a fastball. ⚾ Southpaw **Brad Wieck** gives out more walks than the Rover app, but he remains extremely tall.

SAN FRANCISCO GIANTS

Essay by Jason Wojciechowski

Player comments by Dan Rathman and BP staff

The Giants did not hit homers last year. There's a good chance you already knew this, but it's worth saying anyway: The Giants *really* did not hit homers last year.

Let's start with the elephant on the field. AT&T Park is, as Pitbull might say, still a major issue. Single-year park factors are fraught with peril—especially for small-*N* stats like homers—but since 2011, the stadium has suppressed lefty dongers by about 20 percent and righties by about 15 percent, per Baseball Prospectus' metrics. What this added up to in 2017 was the Giants hitting a minuscule 48 bombs at home. That's fewer than Giancarlo Stanton and Marcell Ozuna combined for at Marlins Park. It's only as many as Aaron Judge plus Gary Sanchez managed at Yankee Stadium. You get the picture.

That said, the absolute number isn't unprecedented—the Braves also hit 48 home dingers in 2015, and the Royals managed just 43 in 2014. In fact, much about the Giants' clout-free present is in the range of normal. Take their 128 homers compared to the Yankees' major-league-leading 241, for instance. That looks really bad! It's not much more than half! It's also the *best* worst-to-first ratio since 2004, when the Brewers and Diamondbacks hit 135 to the White Sox's and Yankees' 242. Same story if you look at the ratio of the 30th-ranked team to the 29th: The Giants last year managed 23 fewer homers than the Pirates—an entire Albert Pujols worth of round-trippers—but a worse ratio was posted just two years prior, when Atlanta hit 100 to Miami's 120, and even those numbers are blown out of the water in 2009 (95 homers for the Mets to 122 for, who else, the Giants).

So the Giants were not *historically* atrocious here. Still, we shouldn't minimize just how underwater they were. The Giants did not go yard last year, and no amount of Madison Bumgarner not dirtbiking was going to fix it. (Bumgarner hit as many homers in 36 plate appearances as Kelby Tomlinson and Ryder Jones hit in 386 combined trips.) There are some obvious, and likely intentional, team-building reasons for the lack of wattage: For years, additions from outside the organization have been players whose strengths do not include serious over-the-fence power (Hunter Pence, Denard Span, Angel Pagan, Nori Aoki, Gregor Blanco, Marco Scutaro, Ryan Theriot, Melky Cabrera; the main exception was Massive Human Being Mike Morse), and a significant percentage of their recent money has been plowed into pitching (Johnny Cueto, Jeff Samardzija and Mark Melancon; the odds seem good that a Bumgarner extension will be added to this list soon enough). However, it isn't as though the Giants have an organizational blind spot that leads them to thinking power doesn't exist: They have spent high draft picks on players with power potential, like Heliot Ramos and Jacob Gonzalez last year, Heath Quinn in 2016, Chris Shaw (who led the organization in homers) in 2015, Aramis Garcia in 2014 and Ryder Jones in 2013.

None of these players is going to turn into Giancarlo Stanton, though, which is exactly why it made so much sense for the Giants

GIANTS PROSPECTUS

2017 W-L: 64-98, 5th in NL West

Pythag	.411	28th	B-Age	29.5	*26th*
RS/G	3.94	29th	P-Age	29.0	*22nd*
RA/G	4.79	16th	Salary	$180.8M	*5th*
TAv	.254	22nd	M$/MW	$10.8M	*2nd*
TAv-P	.281	28th	DL Days	876	*13th*
FIP	4.23	11th	$ on DL	14%	*14th*
DER	.692	28th			

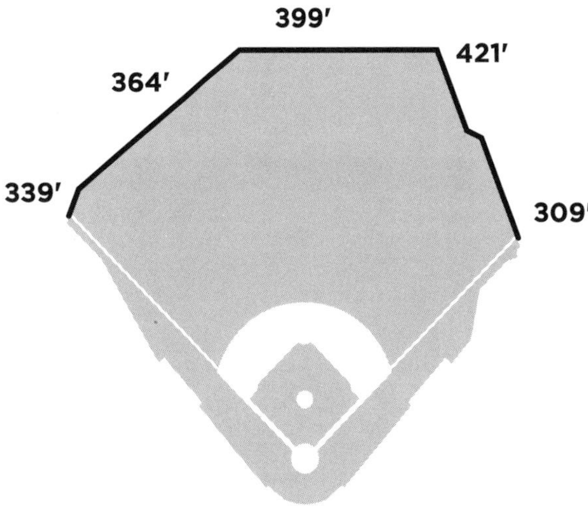

Outfield wall profile: **8′** to **25′**

Three-Year Park Factors

Runs	Runs/RH	Runs/LH	HR/RH	HR/LH
94	95	91	87	78

Top Hitter WARP	5.8 Buster Posey
Top Pitcher WARP	4.5 Jeff Samardzija
Top Prospect	Heliot Ramos

2017 Hit List Ranking

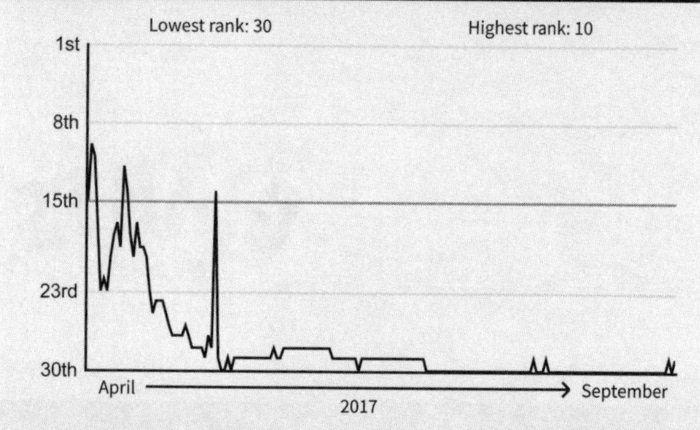

Committed Payroll (in millions)

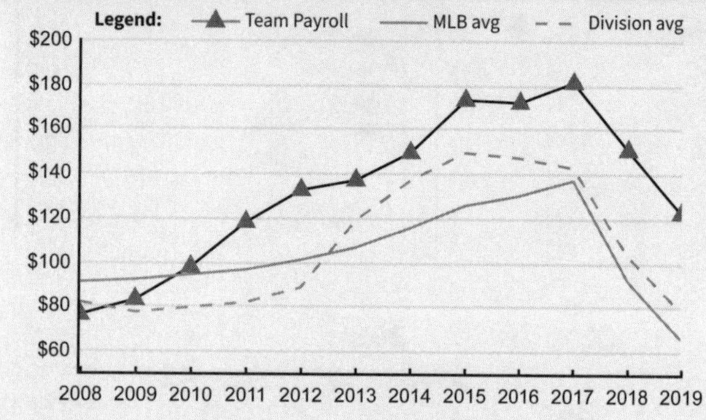

Farm System Ranking

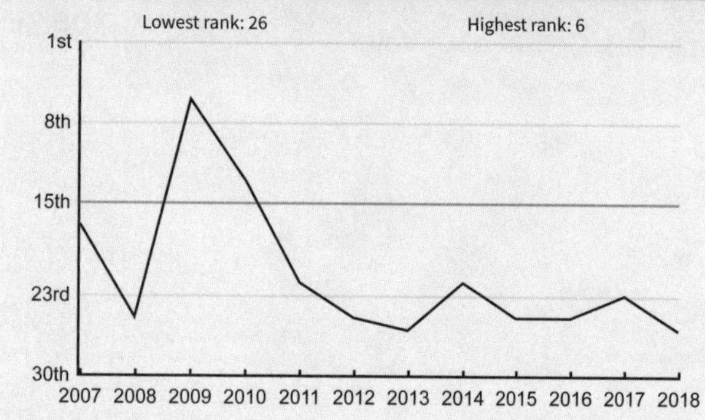

Personnel

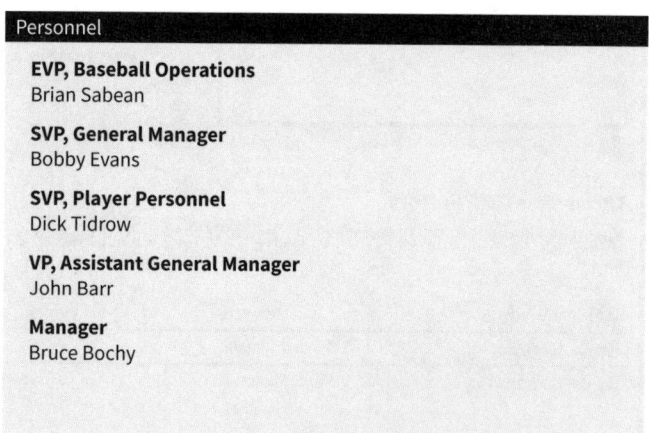

EVP, Baseball Operations
Brian Sabean

SVP, General Manager
Bobby Evans

SVP, Player Personnel
Dick Tidrow

VP, Assistant General Manager
John Barr

Manager
Bruce Bochy

to take a strong run at Stanton this winter. Indeed, it's why it made sense for them to take such a strong run that they were deemed a finalist, along with the Cardinals, in the weird public pageant the trade discussions wound up being. All of that was scuttled by Stanton deciding he didn't want to play in San Francisco (or St. Louis), precipitating a trade to the Yankees instead.

It's Stanton's privilege and right to reject any trade he wants—that's the point of the no-trade clause—and it's also his privilege and right not to explain his decisions; as of this writing, neither he nor sources close to him have done so. This leaves us only speculation, but the thought that immediately occurs is: What if the reason Stanton would make a bigger impact on the Giants than any other team is also the reason he wouldn't want to join them? Giants left fielders hit 11 homers last year; Stanton might not hit 59 again, but by himself, compared to the Giants' in-house options, he probably makes up the 33-homer gap between San Francisco and Pittsburgh. Those 33 round-trippers mark the difference between "last place by a mile" and "tied for last place, but at least they're not interchangeable with the Sacramento River Cats." Stanton can do that math just as easily as we can; he can see that whatever booming bat he would have brought to the Bay, the Giants' offensive attack was going to remain underwhelming, to be charitable. Twenty-ninth ain't 30th, but it also ain't much.

It also cannot be much fun hitting in AT&T, such that if you give a power hitter a choice between the Bronx and San Francisco, it's not much of a choice at all. No park on this planet can hold Stanton, of course, but doing battle with the swirling wind 81 times per game for the next 11 years could wear on a guy. (On the other hand, an amusing side note: Arguably Stanton's cheapest homer of the year came at AT&T, on a ball that left the bat at less than 95 mph and was hit more or less straight up, but landed in the right-field seats 376 feet away after it got a 42-foot boost from the wind, per Hit Tracker Online. San Francisco giveth and taketh away, apparently, though clearly not in equal measure.)

So, having failed in their valiant run at Stanton, where will the Giants get their homers in 2018? Six spots in the lineup were already spoken for on the first day of free agency, five of them by players in their thirties: Span, Pence, Buster Posey, Brandon Belt and Brandon Crawford are all, absent late-breaking and surprising trades, headed for daily use at their usual positions. You could wish for some bounce-back in over-the-fence power from Posey, but the last time he cracked 20 was 2014, while the 21 Crawford hit in 2015 now reveals itself—in the context of his six full years in the major leagues—as a single-season spike. Of this group, Pence had the most power in his prime, but of this group, Pence is also the furthest from that prime. There's also Joe Panik as the spring chicken in the lineup, but the 10 homers he has hit each of the last two years are the most he has ever managed in a single season as a professional; he didn't even reach double digits in the offense-happy Cal League. It's safe to strike "improvement from the existing hitters on the team" off the list of possibilities.

That leaves adding pop at third base and a corner outfield position through acquisitions. There are, as of this writing, players left on the market who could fit the bill, including Mike Moustakas, Todd Frazier and J.D. Martinez. Practically every team in baseball could find a way to slot Martinez in if they can scrounge up enough pennies to pay him; Frazier and Moustakas are not exactly sure bets, the former being 32 and the latter reaching a new plateau in power just in time to hit free agency. That's putting aside that neither is actually a star player worth the coin often paid to the top player available at a position by some poor sucker whose other option is heading into spring training with Pablo Sandoval, Kelby Tomlinson, Christian Arroyo and Ryder Jones playing an American Gladiators tournament on an NES in the basement for the right to start on Opening Day.

Even if there *were* another Stanton type available, Stanton himself would have put the Giants into something of a danger zone with their payroll. Heading into the offseason, counting guaranteed contracts only, the Giants owed $161 million to 11 players. They are happy to be paying most of those players, but even so, there's only so much flexibility a team can express when the starting place is "$161 million already committed." Obviously, the Giants were willing to take on another $25 million or so in Stanton, but (a) we never got a report on how the Marlins' reported $45 million monetary contribution in that deal would have been structured (i.e. perhaps much of the money from Miami would have been up front, and therefore the Stanton hit to the 2018 payroll would have been minimal) and (b) you make sacrifices and take risks for a Stanton that you do not make and take for a Moustakas or Frazier.

It's not getting any better going forward, either. The Giants are looking at $126 million committed for *seven* players in 2019 (counting Bumgarner, whose $12 million option will either be picked up or negotiated away in a new extension), and the help on the farm is ... well, that's the wrong word. Whatever it is, it's not "help." The position players either have pop but are blocked at their ideal position (Garcia, Shaw), or there's a position for them from which they will hit approximately seven dingers (Arroyo), or they're years from even reaching the high minors, forget about the big leagues (Ramos, Gonzalez). Nor is there enough talent to swing a major trade in a competitive environment should another power hitter become available—Stanton was a special case, less a question of how much a team was willing and able to give up than of whether a team was willing to give up anything of decent value for the privilege of paying Stanton his market rate. The Giants have "decent value," not to mention desperation, in spades, so it's not surprising they came out on top of the sweepstakes. That mix isn't likely to get it done the next time an opportunity presents itself.

The thing of it is, the Giants should not have been looking to fix their dinger problem in the first place because their dinger problem isn't, in fact, a problem. All these homers in the majors aren't good. They're bad, actually. Yes, it's fun watching Stanton and Judge chase records and big round numbers. It's fun seeing Rhys Hoskins and Matt Olson do as much damage as any human possibly could in as little time as you can imagine. At a certain point, though, homers become exhausting. It's exhausting that 41 players hit 30 or more homers. It's exhausting that a man named "Scooter" hit four in a game and 27 overall. It's exhausting that Matt Davidson, a well-below-replacement-level player, hit 26. It's exhausting that Mike Napoli hit .193 ... and 29 bombs.

I was at an Angels-Rangers game late last year with two friends, and we got up to get beers and snacks. We came back to find out we'd missed a Joey Gallo dinger to straightaway center. "Ho hum," we all said. It's just a homer. Turns out it was not just a homer. It was the second-longest homer hit all season. And yet I *still* cannot get worked up about having missed it. There were 6,104 others last year, and each of those 6,104 were the very best thing the hitter could possibly do in that situation. Eat your favorite food 6,104 times and you start craving turnips. Quoth 50 Cent: "Sunny days wouldn't be special if it wasn't for rain / Joy wouldn't feel so good if it wasn't for pain."

Baseball in 2017 was too much sun and not enough pain. Viewed through this lens, the Giants are brave holdouts fighting the breakneck pace of baseball's headlong rush into the future that masquerades as progress. They fight for a slower, more contemplative, more varied vision of what a baseball game can and should be. They fight against the monoculture; they fight for variety as the spice of life. They fight, finally, for baseball as an *aesthetic* pursuit, not merely an exercise in economics and algorithms aimed at finding the shortest route to profit.

We should applaud, then, that Stanton will join a Yankees team that has no need of his homers, a team that may stretch the boundaries of what we thought possible in scoring runs by a single method, rather than polluting the purity of the Giants' singles-and-doubles attack, diminishing the joy of their always-in-play approach. Pah. Let the dinger teams have their grotesque, vulgar dingers. The Giants will be playing a more refined form of baseball.

—Jason Wojciechowski is an author of Baseball Prospectus.

HITTERS

Jonah Arenado 3B
Born: 02/03/95 Age: 23 Bats: R Throws: R Height: 6'4" Weight: 230 Origin: Round 16, 2013 Draft (#492 overall)

YEAR	TEAM	LVL	AGE	PA	R	2B	3B	HR	RBI	BB	K	SB	CS	AVG/OBP/SLG	TAv	VORP	BABIP	BRR	FRAA	WARP
2015	AUG	A	20	561	57	25	1	9	62	24	94	1	1	.264/.293/.367	.257	14.6	.301	0.3	3B(117): -10.5, 1B(6): 0.2	0.5
2016	SJO	A+	21	545	64	36	0	17	68	18	110	0	2	.254/.286/.422	.260	8.5	.290	0.5	1B(78): 8.5, 3B(30): -2.5	1.5
2017	SJO	A+	22	522	67	36	4	13	73	26	104	1	1	.268/.308/.439	.275	25.0	.315	3.6	3B(97): 7.3, 1B(30): 1.4	3.6
2018	*SFN*	*MLB*	*23*	*250*	*21*	*13*	*1*	*7*	*28*	*8*	*61*	*0*	*0*	*.227/.254/.370*	*.214*	*-5.0*	*.274*	*-0.5*	*3B -1, 1B 1*	*-0.6*
2019	*SFN*	*MLB*	*24*	*311*	*32*	*16*	*1*	*9*	*34*	*11*	*77*	*0*	*0*	*.225/.256/.371*	*.226*	*-5.1*	*.272*	*-0.8*	*3B -1, 1B 1*	*-0.6*

Breakout: 0% Improve: 4% Collapse: 5% Attrition: 10% MLB: 23% *Comparables: Ryder Jones, Cody Asche, Henry Rodriguez*

Superb defense at the hot corner runs in the Arenado family, as Jonah, like his older brother Nolan, can fill a highlight reel with the leather. The lumber, though, is the great separator between the siblings. Jonah finished the year on a high note with a torrid August, but his overall body of work in a repeat of High-A failed to impress. Arenado employs a compact stroke with minimal upper-body load, which—coupled with early-count aggression—keeps his strikeout rate in check. Both also serve to depress his walk rate, however, and the out-front bat path yields volumes of undesirable contact, including the highest popup rate in the minors (min. 500 PA). A plus defensive skill set on the left side of the infield will afford Arenado some wiggle room with the stick, but the hit tool needs considerable refinement to pass at the highest level.

Brandon Belt 1B
Born: 04/20/88 Age: 30 Bats: L Throws: L Height: 6'5" Weight: 220 Origin: Round 5, 2009 Draft (#147 overall)

YEAR	TEAM	LVL	AGE	PA	R	2B	3B	HR	RBI	BB	K	SB	CS	AVG/OBP/SLG	TAv	VORP	BABIP	BRR	FRAA	WARP
2015	SFN	MLB	27	556	73	33	5	18	68	56	147	9	3	.280/.356/.478	.317	35.4	.363	-1.5	1B(120): 8.0, LF(14): 0.2	4.7
2016	SFN	MLB	28	655	77	41	8	17	82	104	148	0	4	.275/.394/.474	.316	37.8	.346	-6.4	1B(151): 0.9, LF(3): 0.0	4.0
2017	SFN	MLB	29	451	63	27	3	18	51	66	104	3	2	.241/.355/.469	.302	25.6	.284	0.3	1B(98): 9.0, LF(15): -0.3	3.4
2018	*SFN*	*MLB*	*30*	*554*	*69*	*31*	*3*	*18*	*72*	*64*	*133*	*4*	*3*	*.258/.349/.445*	*.282*	*20.1*	*.320*	*-1.0*	*1B 6*	*2.5*
2019	*SFN*	*MLB*	*31*	*495*	*68*	*28*	*2*	*17*	*65*	*63*	*121*	*2*	*2*	*.259/.359/.457*	*.301*	*25.4*	*.320*	*-1.8*	*1B 6*	*3.4*

Breakout: 2% Improve: 44% Collapse: 4% Attrition: 15% MLB: 96% *Comparables: Derrek Lee, David Ortiz, Andre Thornton*

As research reveals the perils of repeated head trauma, preventing concussions and allowing time for recovery take on heightened importance. Catchers aside, baseball is much safer than football in that regard. Just don't tell that to Belt, who has suffered four documented concussions in the last eight years.

In July 2014, two of the first baseman's teammates threw simultaneously across the diamond during batting practice, and one of the baseballs hit him in the face. He missed two weeks, returned for five games, then went back on the disabled list for a month and a half.

In September 2015, Belt doubled off the right-field wall, rounded second aggressively and banged his head against the knee of Reds infielder Ivan De Jesus as he dove back into the bag. His symptoms worsened three days later, and he was sidelined until the following spring.

Those two concussions came more than half a decade after Belt's first, while at the University of Texas in 2009. His fourth came on August 4, 2017, when a curveball slipped away from Diamondbacks pitcher Anthony Banda and hit Belt in the side of the head. He missed the rest of the season.

As his 30th birthday approaches, Belt's pros and cons are well-known. He's a patient fly-ball hitter whose power is suppressed by AT&T Park. He's an above-average defender at the cold corner whose throwing prowess compensates for the occasional missed pick. He's fluent in bad body language, which endears him to some fans and makes him a popular talk-radio scapegoat for others. Lastly, unlike most football players, Belt has a fully guaranteed contract with a four-year, $68.8 million balance, a club-friendly salary based on his performance, but a much-needed security blanket given his medical past.

What we don't know is how long Belt will need to come back from his most recent concussion, what sort of freak accident might trigger his next or how many more he can withstand. Despite being a prime-age player with sustainable skills, Belt may have the most volatile decline curve of any major leaguer. When it comes to the emerging science on concussions, no non-catcher in baseball has as much at stake.

Brandon Crawford SS Born: 01/21/87 Age: 31 Bats: L Throws: R Height: 6'2" Weight: 215 Origin: Round 4, 2008 Draft (#117 overall)

YEAR	TEAM	LVL	AGE	PA	R	2B	3B	HR	RBI	BB	K	SB	CS	AVG/OBP/SLG	TAv	VORP	BABIP	BRR	FRAA	WARP
2015	SFN	MLB	28	561	65	33	4	21	84	39	119	6	4	.256/.321/.462	.291	38.0	.294	-0.9	SS(140): 6.0	4.7
2016	SFN	MLB	29	623	67	28	11	12	84	57	115	7	0	.275/.342/.430	.280	36.6	.322	-1.8	SS(155): 3.9	4.2
2017	SFN	MLB	30	570	58	34	1	14	77	42	113	3	5	.253/.305/.403	.263	24.5	.293	-1.4	SS(138): 4.1	2.9
2018	*SFN*	*MLB*	*31*	*605*	*63*	*28*	*5*	*13*	*66*	*48*	*122*	*5*	*3*	*.245/.309/.383*	*.248*	*18.7*	*.291*	*-0.5*	*SS 4*	*1.6*
2019	*SFN*	*MLB*	*32*	*529*	*61*	*25*	*3*	*13*	*57*	*46*	*111*	*4*	*2*	*.240/.311/.387*	*.256*	*14.6*	*.285*	*-1.1*	*SS 3*	*2.0*

Breakout: 2% Improve: 44% Collapse: 6% Attrition: 8% MLB: 90% *Comparables: Asdrubal Cabrera, Jhonny Peralta, J.J. Hardy*

It's easy to forget sometimes that baseball players are human, that humans are creatures of habit and that, when their mental and physical preparation is disrupted in the spring, they might not restore their performance until the summer. Crawford hit .385 during the World Baseball Classic, setting lofty expectations on the heels of a career-best 2016, but two weeks into the season, his sister-in-law unexpectedly passed away. Although the effects of personal tragedy are impossible to quantify, Crawford's approach was visibly broken over the ensuing weeks, as he searched for the selective aggression that had fueled his power the previous two years. He found it around the All-Star break, hitting .286/.351/.451 from July 8 onward with his typically awesome glove work at short. A normal offseason and April should see Crawford do that from start to finish in 2018.

Steven Duggar OF Born: 11/04/93 Age: 24 Bats: L Throws: R Height: 6'2" Weight: 195 Origin: Round 6, 2015 Draft (#186 overall)

YEAR	TEAM	LVL	AGE	PA	R	2B	3B	HR	RBI	BB	K	SB	CS	AVG/OBP/SLG	TAv	VORP	BABIP	BRR	FRAA	WARP
2015	SLO	A-	21	267	40	12	1	1	27	35	52	6	3	.293/.390/.367	.283	12.9	.373	1.4	RF(52): 10.1, CF(7): -0.9	2.3
2016	SJO	A+	22	311	43	12	4	9	30	44	66	6	7	.284/.386/.462	.323	24.5	.346	-2.2	RF(60): 6.3, CF(5): -0.1	3.2
2016	RIC	AA	22	276	35	16	4	1	24	28	51	9	7	.321/.391/.432	.327	27.7	.397	1.0	CF(59): 8.2	3.9
2017	SJO	A+	23	133	22	11	0	4	20	17	42	7	0	.270/.361/.470	.300	9.8	.386	2.0	RF(22): -2.3, CF(1): -0.2	0.8
2017	SAC	AAA	23	54	7	1	0	2	6	8	12	3	2	.261/.370/.413	.276	2.8	.313	0.1	CF(12): 1.7	0.4
2018	*SFN*	*MLB*	*24*	*328*	*41*	*14*	*2*	*6*	*29*	*33*	*85*	*7*	*4*	*.241/.318/.365*	*.250*	*8.9*	*.318*	*-0.2*	*CF 6*	*1.3*
2019	*SFN*	*MLB*	*25*	*412*	*48*	*19*	*3*	*9*	*44*	*43*	*110*	*8*	*5*	*.246/.325/.387*	*.266*	*14.8*	*.323*	*0.0*	*CF 8*	*2.5*

Breakout: 4% Improve: 16% Collapse: 6% Attrition: 17% MLB: 26% *Comparables: Tyler Austin, Caleb Gindl, Chris Pettit*

In a bountiful farm system, Duggar might be just a face in crowd, a footnote on top-10 lists, the sort of prospect who is considered underrated in hindsight if he develops into a dependable regular. Among the Giants' bland crop, however, the 2015 sixth-rounder has a chance to become the top outfielder drafted and developed by the organization since Chili Davis arrived in 1981. Duggar is a balanced athlete with four average or better tools, a potential plus defensive right fielder with the strength to produce double-digit home runs. The ceiling for that profile is Josh Reddick, a player with 16.5 career WARP. Alas, with a checkered injury history and questionable game power, Duggar is a long shot to enjoy such a fruitful career, projecting as more of a fourth outfielder than an everyday lineup cog. But in a system that has gone decades without yielding a standout on the grass, he might be the best upper-minors hope to break the drought.

Sandro Fabian RF Born: 03/06/98 Age: 20 Bats: R Throws: R Height: 6'1" Weight: 180 Origin: International Free Agent, 2015

YEAR	TEAM	LVL	AGE	PA	R	2B	3B	HR	RBI	BB	K	SB	CS	AVG/OBP/SLG	TAv	VORP	BABIP	BRR	FRAA	WARP
2015	DGI	RK	17	286	47	10	2	3	37	15	47	2	0	.269/.348/.364	.264	4.3	.312	-2.8	RF(60): 5.7, CF(5): 1.5	1.1
2016	GIA	RK	18	174	30	13	5	2	35	7	28	3	1	.340/.364/.522	.333	15.9	.388	-1.3	RF(40): 2.9, LF(1): -0.1	1.9
2017	AUG	A	19	504	51	30	0	11	61	10	88	5	4	.277/.297/.408	.265	9.8	.317	-1.5	RF(111): 21.5, CF(2): -0.7	3.2
2018	*SFN*	*MLB*	*20*	*250*	*21*	*12*	*1*	*7*	*28*	*5*	*67*	*0*	*0*	*.230/.251/.368*	*.212*	*-6.1*	*.286*	*-0.4*	*RF 5, CF 0*	*-0.1*
2019	*SFN*	*MLB*	*21*	*355*	*38*	*17*	*1*	*11*	*41*	*8*	*93*	*0*	*0*	*.236/.259/.389*	*.233*	*-3.3*	*.288*	*-0.8*	*RF 7, CF 0*	*0.4*

Breakout: 2% Improve: 6% Collapse: 0% Attrition: 2% MLB: 8% *Comparables: Chris Parmelee, Josh Vitters, Nick Noonan*

Context is king when evaluating prospects, so let's apply some to Fabian's 2017 campaign. The Dominican's first full-season trial seems uninspiring—until you consider that he turned 19 during spring training, was jumping straight from the complex to Low-A ball and adapted well after a rough few months. Fabian's stat line looks even better when split in half, with a .606 OPS in the first giving way to an .804 effort in the second, and he ended the year on a 42-for-109 tear. While the tiny walk rate reflects Fabian's rapacious approach, the summertime surge is a testament to his innate feel for the barrel. He has the swing to hit and hit for power. To reach his ceiling as an everyday left fielder, though, he'll need to learn when to keep the bat on his shoulder.

Aramis Garcia C Born: 01/12/93 Age: 25 Bats: R Throws: R Height: 6'2" Weight: 220 Origin: Round 2, 2014 Draft (#52 overall)

YEAR	TEAM	LVL	AGE	PA	R	2B	3B	HR	RBI	BB	K	SB	CS	AVG/OBP/SLG	TAv	VORP	BABIP	BRR	FRAA	WARP
2015	AUG	A	22	363	42	15	1	15	61	35	77	0	1	.273/.350/.467	.313	31.1	.312	-3.4	C(72): 3.7	3.7
2015	SJO	A+	22	84	10	4	0	0	5	9	22	1	0	.227/.310/.280	.223	0.5	.321	0.1	C(19): 0.9	0.1
2016	SJO	A+	23	160	20	6	0	2	20	14	42	1	0	.257/.323/.340	.254	4.7	.350	-1.7	C(41): 1.8	0.7
2017	SJO	A+	24	347	43	20	1	17	65	15	73	0	0	.272/.314/.497	.292	20.7	.301	-1.3	C(50): 0.7, 1B(17): 0.3	2.3
2017	RIC	AA	24	89	11	12	0	0	8	9	21	0	0	.282/.360/.436	.280	6.5	.379	1.0	C(20): -0.6, 1B(2): 0.0	0.6
2018	*SFN*	*MLB*	*25*	*250*	*25*	*12*	*1*	*8*	*30*	*17*	*70*	*0*	*0*	*.226/.283/.385*	*.231*	*3.0*	*.285*	*-0.4*	*C -5, 1B 0*	*-0.2*
2019	*SFN*	*MLB*	*26*	*224*	*26*	*10*	*0*	*7*	*26*	*16*	*64*	*0*	*0*	*.220/.283/.379*	*.242*	*2.7*	*.280*	*-0.5*	*C -3, 1B 0*	*0.0*

Breakout: 3% Improve: 10% Collapse: 11% Attrition: 17% MLB: 28% *Comparables: Luke Montz, Johnny Monell, Cameron Rupp*

YEAR	TEAM	P. COUNT	FRM RUNS	BLK RUNS	THRW RUNS	TOT RUNS
2018	*SFN*	*6987*	*-5.3*	*0.0*	*-0.4*	*-5.7*
2019	*SFN*	*6247*	*-1.8*	*0.0*	*-0.1*	*-2.0*

Catching prospects require more patience than crockpot brisket. In Garcia's case, the Giants waited a few hours before noticing that the crockpot wasn't plugged in. A second-round pick out of Florida International University in 2014, Garcia finally reached Double-A last summer, after losing much of his 2016 campaign to a head injury suffered on a slide. Even at 24, he remains a two-way development case, with an unrefined game plan in the box and immaturity to shake off in the squat. The occasional 1.9 pop time and towering bomb tantalizes like the smell of meat wafting from the pot, but despite his age and level, Garcia is not nearly ready to serve.

Conor Gillaspie 3B Born: 07/18/87 Age: 30 Bats: L Throws: R Height: 6'1" Weight: 195 Origin: Round 1, 2008 Draft (#37 overall)

YEAR	TEAM	LVL	AGE	PA	R	2B	3B	HR	RBI	BB	K	SB	CS	AVG/OBP/SLG	TAv	VORP	BABIP	BRR	FRAA	WARP
2015	CHA	MLB	27	185	10	11	1	3	15	9	34	0	1	.237/.276/.364	.227	-1.2	.275	-0.7	3B(52): 0.3, 1B(2): 0.3	-0.1
2015	ANA	MLB	27	68	4	4	1	1	9	4	13	0	0	.203/.250/.344	.218	-1.5	.240	-0.8	3B(17): -2.6, 2B(1): 0.0	-0.4
2016	SAC	AAA	28	52	6	3	0	1	4	1	6	1	0	.314/.327/.431	.262	0.9	.341	-0.4	3B(7): -0.6, 1B(1): -0.1	0.0
2016	SFN	MLB	28	205	24	8	4	6	25	12	28	1	2	.262/.307/.440	.273	6.8	.278	-1.9	3B(45): 0.3, 1B(7): 0.1	0.7
2017	SFN	MLB	29	87	8	4	0	2	8	5	10	0	0	.163/.218/.288	.206	-1.9	.159	0.3	3B(20): -0.9, 1B(4): 0.2	-0.3
2017	SAC	AAA	29	93	13	7	0	0	4	3	8	3	2	.311/.333/.389	.234	-1.9	.341	-0.8	1B(18): -1.2, 3B(7): 0.3	-0.3
2018	*SFN*	*MLB*	*30*	*250*	*24*	*13*	*2*	*5*	*27*	*17*	*41*	*2*	*1*	*.251/.303/.387*	*.238*	*0.4*	*.285*	*-0.9*	*3B -3, 1B 0*	*-0.3*
2019	*SFN*	*MLB*	*31*	*187*	*20*	*9*	*1*	*4*	*19*	*13*	*32*	*1*	*1*	*.244/.299/.380*	*.249*	*0.8*	*.278*	*-0.7*	*3B -2, 1B 0*	*-0.1*

Breakout: 4% Improve: 38% Collapse: 13% Attrition: 18% MLB: 91% *Comparables: Jeff King, Lou Klimchock, Joe Crede*

Gillaspie's last three home runs have decided a theretofore scoreless Wild Card playoff, erased a two-run deficit in a pinch-hit appearance with two outs in the ninth and broken a scoreless draw in the eighth inning at Dodger Stadium on *Sunday Night Baseball*. His last triple came on a 103-mph Aroldis Chapman fastball, flipping a one-run hole into a one-run lead in Game Three of the 2016 NLDS. A corner tweener without the glove for third base or the bat for first, Gillaspie is a lifetime three-win player with an oversized collection of memorable moments. If his achy back cooperates, his pinch-hit prowess will afford him the opportunity to make a few more.

Miguel Gomez INF Born: 12/17/92 Age: 25 Bats: B Throws: R Height: 5'10" Weight: 185 Origin: International Free Agent, 2012

YEAR	TEAM	LVL	AGE	PA	R	2B	3B	HR	RBI	BB	K	SB	CS	AVG/OBP/SLG	TAv	VORP	BABIP	BRR	FRAA	WARP
2015	SLO	A-	22	284	30	14	1	6	52	5	24	0	1	.319/.331/.442	.282	13.7	.331	-1.0	3B(32): -2.3, C(16): -1.0	1.1
2016	AUG	A	23	285	41	17	1	8	43	12	25	3	2	.371/.401/.532	.350	28.1	.386	-2.6	3B(31): -1.7, 1B(7): 0.0	2.9
2016	SJO	A+	23	182	25	9	2	9	24	8	28	1	0	.267/.302/.500	.303	11.8	.272	-0.7	3B(20): -2.6, 1B(7): -0.5	0.8
2017	RIC	AA	24	322	43	19	2	8	38	12	36	0	0	.305/.330/.458	.271	11.8	.325	0.2	2B(66): -2.7	1.0
2017	SFN	MLB	24	34	3	2	0	0	2	0	6	0	0	.242/.235/.303	.206	-1.0	.286	-0.1	2B(6): -0.2	-0.1
2018	*SFN*	*MLB*	*25*	*117*	*12*	*6*	*1*	*3*	*14*	*3*	*21*	*0*	*0*	*.261/.281/.409*	*.245*	*2.5*	*.293*	*-0.2*	*2B -1*	*0.1*
2019	*SFN*	*MLB*	*26*	*341*	*40*	*17*	*2*	*12*	*43*	*12*	*63*	*0*	*0*	*.261/.290/.431*	*.260*	*9.7*	*.289*	*-0.6*	*2B -2*	*0.8*

Breakout: 2% Improve: 15% Collapse: 6% Attrition: 16% MLB: 34% *Comparables: Chris Valaika, Jordany Valdespin, Joey Wendle*

If he'd been healthy on Players Weekend, Gomez would have worn "Little Panda" on the back of his jersey, embracing comparisons to Pablo Sandoval. Like the original Panda, Gomez is a switch-hitting former catcher who now plays the infield, and a bad-ball chaser with the ability to produce consistent contact nonetheless. Unfortunately, Gomez can't match either Sandoval's paunch or his punch, and the latter means he's likely to top out as a reserve. Gomez's debut was cut short by a knee injury, but he found time to demonstrate both his barrel skills and his voracious chase rate. He would do well to shore up his defense at the keystone and hot corner to contend for a backup infield job out of spring training.

Jacob Gonzalez 3B Born: 06/26/98 Age: 20 Bats: R Throws: R Height: 6'3" Weight: 190 Origin: Round 2, 2017 Draft (#58 overall)

YEAR	TEAM	LVL	AGE	PA	R	2B	3B	HR	RBI	BB	K	SB	CS	AVG/OBP/SLG	TAv	VORP	BABIP	BRR	FRAA	WARP
2017	GIA	RK	19	194	23	15	1	1	21	16	23	0	1	.339/.418/.458	.307	16.3	.384	-2.1	3B(37): -6.2	0.9
2018	*SFN*	*MLB*	*20*	*250*	*20*	*10*	*1*	*4*	*24*	*13*	*73*	*0*	*0*	*.206/.255/.314*	*.199*	*-8.0*	*.276*	*-0.4*	*3B -3*	*-1.2*
2019	*SFN*	*MLB*	*21*	*344*	*35*	*16*	*1*	*8*	*34*	*19*	*97*	*0*	*0*	*.218/.269/.343*	*.225*	*-5.1*	*.286*	*-0.8*	*3B -3*	*-0.9*

Breakout: 1% Improve: 3% Collapse: 0% Attrition: 1% MLB: 4% *Comparables: Alex Liddi, Maikel Franco, Jefry Marte*

The son of Luis Gonzalez, Jacob signed for $950,000 as an under-slot second-rounder out of Chaparral High School in Scottsdale, Arizona, a 15-minute drive from the Giants' spring training facility. Jacob manned third base for the Firebirds, but as a 30-grade runner with a thick frame, he projects to the cold corner long term. That would make the younger Gonzalez a right-right first baseman, the sort of prospect who must command scouts' attention with his bat. Gonzalez generates enormous power and natural loft with an easy swing that's built to pull the ball in the air. He impressed evaluators with a measured approach and discerning eye in his pro debut, too, precocious traits that lead some to believe that he's ready to tackle a full-season assignment in 2018.

Gorkys Hernandez OF Born: 09/07/87 Age: 30 Bats: R Throws: R Height: 6'1" Weight: 190 Origin: International Free Agent, 2005

YEAR	TEAM	LVL	AGE	PA	R	2B	3B	HR	RBI	BB	K	SB	CS	AVG/OBP/SLG	TAv	VORP	BABIP	BRR	FRAA	WARP
2015	PIT	MLB	27	5	0	0	0	0	0	0	0	1	0	.000/.000/.000	.005	-1.1	.000	0.0	LF(4): -0.2, RF(2): -0.3	-0.2
2015	IND	AAA	27	391	51	16	3	6	42	41	78	17	3	.288/.365/.406	.293	27.2	.355	2.0	CF(96): -3.5, LF(5): -0.6	2.4
2016	SAC	AAA	28	503	74	22	3	8	51	52	77	20	13	.302/.382/.421	.294	35.6	.349	2.1	CF(113): -0.2	3.6
2016	SFN	MLB	28	57	7	5	0	2	4	3	11	0	1	.259/.298/.463	.273	2.2	.293	-0.1	CF(14): -0.1, RF(6): 1.0	0.3
2017	SFN	MLB	29	348	40	20	1	0	22	31	73	12	4	.255/.327/.326	.246	6.5	.331	2.3	LF(57): -5.7, CF(50): 2.5	0.3
2018	*SFN*	*MLB*	*30*	*544*	*68*	*25*	*3*	*7*	*44*	*48*	*115*	*16*	*7*	*.253/.321/.359*	*.250*	*15.3*	*.312*	*0.4*	*CF -1, LF -1*	*0.8*
2019	*SFN*	*MLB*	*31*	*517*	*58*	*23*	*2*	*9*	*50*	*48*	*116*	*14*	*7*	*.248/.323/.364*	*.257*	*14.4*	*.307*	*1.6*	*CF 0, LF -1*	*1.4*

Breakout: 2% Improve: 16% Collapse: 11% Attrition: 24% MLB: 62% *Comparables: Chris Denorfia, Bubba Crosby, Elian Herrera*

A beneficiary of poor organizational depth, Hernandez found himself entrenched on the active roster despite toting a .460 OPS in late May. The Venezuelan didn't possess incriminating photos of the general manager, but he had the next-best thing. With plus speed and a strong arm, he was a capable center fielder, the only such player on the entire 40-man roster or healthy in Triple-A. As injuries beset the Giants' frail outfield, Hernandez fell ass backward into regular playing time, leading the league in plate appearances among players without a single home run. Nevertheless, through a string of fortuitous BABIP turns, he booked a .361 OBP in his final 242 trips to the plate. That should keep him in the fifth-outfielder conversation this spring, even if—against all odds—his vital defensive abilities turn out not to be unique.

Ryan Howard INF Born: 07/25/94 Age: 23 Bats: R Throws: R Height: 6'2" Weight: 195 Origin: Round 5, 2016 Draft (#155 overall)

YEAR	TEAM	LVL	AGE	PA	R	2B	3B	HR	RBI	BB	K	SB	CS	AVG/OBP/SLG	TAv	VORP	BABIP	BRR	FRAA	WARP
2016	SLO	A-	21	246	33	10	0	4	31	13	24	2	2	.272/.313/.371	.251	7.4	.285	0.0	SS(58): -12.0	-0.5
2017	SJO	A+	22	565	59	21	0	9	50	23	81	7	2	.306/.342/.397	.273	28.8	.345	-0.3	SS(101): -9.7, 3B(23): -4.6	1.5
2018	*SFN*	*MLB*	*23*	*250*	*26*	*10*	*0*	*5*	*23*	*9*	*49*	*0*	*0*	*.248/.282/.361*	*.223*	*1.0*	*.289*	*-0.4*	*SS -4, 3B -1*	*-0.4*
2019	*SFN*	*MLB*	*24*	*341*	*36*	*14*	*1*	*7*	*35*	*15*	*67*	*0*	*0*	*.245/.285/.362*	*.237*	*1.9*	*.284*	*-0.7*	*SS -5, 3B -1*	*-0.4*

Breakout: 11% Improve: 29% Collapse: 18% Attrition: 31% MLB: 55% *Comparables: Wilmer Difo, Carlos Triunfel, Adeiny Hechavarria*

Howard bears some resemblance to former Giant Matt Duffy, both facially and in baseball terms, as a polished college infielder with good instincts and feel for hitting. The 2015 version of Duffy, though, was the optimal outcome for that profile, which typically draws a utility projection from scouts for want of a standout tool. Howard yields fringy power by hunting fastballs early in the count; he notched just one extra-base hit last season during the 178 at-bats in which he fell behind. With neither the raw pop to profit off that thirsty approach nor the walks that would come with more restraint, Howard is likely to see his batting averages grow emptier as he advances. In other words, he looks like a utility man—but then again, so did Matt Duffy.

Nick Hundley C Born: 09/08/83 Age: 34 Bats: R Throws: R Height: 6'1" Weight: 205 Origin: Round 2, 2005 Draft (#76 overall)

YEAR	TEAM	LVL	AGE	PA	R	2B	3B	HR	RBI	BB	K	SB	CS	AVG/OBP/SLG	TAv	VORP	BABIP	BRR	FRAA	WARP
2015	COL	MLB	31	389	45	21	5	10	43	21	76	5	6	.301/.339/.467	.268	20.3	.356	0.5	C(102): -10.5	1.0
2016	COL	MLB	32	317	30	20	1	10	48	25	65	0	0	.260/.320/.439	.256	12.8	.302	-0.3	C(79): -14.4	-0.2
2017	SFN	MLB	33	303	27	23	0	9	35	12	81	0	0	.244/.272/.418	.254	8.8	.307	-2.8	C(82): -3.3	0.5
2018	*SFN*	*MLB*	*34*	*62*	*6*	*3*	*0*	*1*	*6*	*3*	*15*	*0*	*0*	*.238/.281/.368*	*.237*	*1.5*	*.295*	*-0.1*	*C -2*	*-0.1*
2019	*SFN*	*MLB*	*35*	*190*	*20*	*10*	*1*	*4*	*20*	*11*	*49*	*0*	*0*	*.235/.282/.371*	*.241*	*3.4*	*.296*	*-0.2*	*C -6*	*-0.3*

Breakout: 3% Improve: 28% Collapse: 16% Attrition: 21% MLB: 83% *Comparables: Terry Steinbach, Bill Haselman, Vance Wilson*

YEAR	TEAM	P. COUNT	FRM RUNS	BLK RUNS	THRW RUNS	TOT RUNS
2015	COL	14669	-13.5	1.6	0.5	-11.4
2016	COL	11523	-10.9	0.0	-3.2	-14.1
2017	SFN	10101	-3.4	-0.1	0.6	-2.9
2018	*SFN*	*2305*	*-2.0*	*0.1*	*-0.1*	*-2.0*
2019	*SFN*	*7067*	*-5.5*	*0.2*	*-0.4*	*-5.7*

It's not often that the backup catcher becomes a team's most celebrated member, but Hundley shined brightly through the dark cloud that was the 2017 Giants. Following a winter full of flops, the NL West veteran stood out as a triumph, saving Buster Posey thousands of needless squats. On a team sorely lacking right-handed power, Hundley led all comers with an extra-base hit every 9.5 trips to the box, and tied Hunter Pence for the most home runs hit at home with four. During an arduous six months that saw grumbles escape a typically airtight clubhouse, when seemingly every member of the team came up short, professionalism and adequacy earned Hundley the Willie Mac Award. The numbers say what they have for years—that Hundley blocks poorly and frames worse, that he doesn't walk enough to be an asset at the plate—yet in a season that came apart at the seams, he was voted the team's most inspirational player simply because he did his job.

Bryce Johnson CF Born: 10/27/95 Age: 22 Bats: B Throws: R Height: 6'2" Weight: 180 Origin: Round 6, 2017 Draft (#186 overall)

YEAR	TEAM	LVL	AGE	PA	R	2B	3B	HR	RBI	BB	K	SB	CS	AVG/OBP/SLG	TAv	VORP	BABIP	BRR	FRAA	WARP
2017	SLO	A-	21	250	41	5	2	0	16	17	52	25	10	.329/.400/.369	.273	14.1	.427	4.5	LF(43): 2.4, CF(15): 2.4	1.9
2018	*SFN*	*MLB*	*22*	*250*	*28*	*9*	*1*	*4*	*17*	*14*	*74*	*9*	*4*	*.206/.259/.299*	*.197*	*-7.2*	*.283*	*0.4*	*LF -1, CF 0*	*-0.8*
2019	*SFN*	*MLB*	*23*	*219*	*21*	*8*	*1*	*4*	*20*	*12*	*65*	*8*	*4*	*.210/.264/.317*	*.214*	*-4.2*	*.287*	*0.8*	*LF -1, CF 0*	*-0.5*

Breakout: 1% Improve: 2% Collapse: 1% Attrition: 3% MLB: 3% *Comparables: Scott Schebler, Benjamin Gamel, Kyle Waldrop*

Sam Houston State, of which Johnson is a recent alumnus, rode a unique offensive game plan to the NCAA Super Regionals last year, before Johnson departed as a sixth-round pick. Under head coach Matt Deggs, the Bearkats bunt, and bunt and bunt some more. They bunt with two strikes. They bunt with two outs. They even bunt for hits with the bases loaded, hoping to catch the defense off guard. A 60-grade runner with excellent instincts, Johnson was the catalyst for the Bearkats' small-ball attack and he kept it up all summer, slashing and dashing his way to the second-best batting average in the Northwest League. On defense, Johnson boasts the speed and tracking ability of a plus center fielder, giving him alternative paths to big-league utility even if higher-level defenses cramp his throwback style.

Ryder Jones INF Born: 06/07/94 Age: 24 Bats: L Throws: R Height: 6'3" Weight: 215 Origin: Round 2, 2013 Draft (#64 overall)

YEAR	TEAM	LVL	AGE	PA	R	2B	3B	HR	RBI	BB	K	SB	CS	AVG/OBP/SLG	TAv	VORP	BABIP	BRR	FRAA	WARP
2015	SJO	A+	21	432	49	29	2	6	47	16	80	2	2	.268/.296/.394	.281	20.0	.315	-2.0	3B(102): -11.9	0.9
2016	RIC	AA	22	513	49	26	0	15	67	26	79	1	2	.247/.291/.397	.261	11.3	.266	-2.1	3B(91): -7.6, 1B(25): -3.0	0.1
2017	SAC	AAA	23	273	44	19	2	13	44	29	53	7	0	.312/.396/.574	.334	29.2	.353	-0.7	3B(34): 0.1, 1B(15): -1.7	2.8
2017	SFN	MLB	23	164	12	5	2	2	5	10	52	1	0	.173/.244/.273	.191	-7.8	.250	1.0	1B(30): 0.6, 3B(18): 0.0	-0.8
2018	*SFN*	*MLB*	*24*	*132*	*13*	*7*	*1*	*3*	*15*	*7*	*30*	*1*	*0*	*.234/.281/.382*	*.238*	*0.1*	*.282*	*-0.1*	*1B -1, 3B -1*	*-0.3*
2019	*SFN*	*MLB*	*25*	*375*	*43*	*19*	*1*	*11*	*44*	*23*	*91*	*2*	*1*	*.234/.288/.395*	*.249*	*2.0*	*.281*	*-0.5*	*1B -3, 3B -3*	*-0.4*

Breakout: 5% Improve: 20% Collapse: 9% Attrition: 20% MLB: 36% *Comparables: Ryan Wheeler, Cody Asche, Brent Morel*

For power-over-hit batters like Jones, the upper tiers of the Giants' organizational ladder can be a roller coaster, necessitating dramatic adjustments from level to level. The same approach that caused the 2013 second-rounder to flounder in Richmond worked wonders in the Arizona Fall League and Sacramento, before becoming his instant undoing when he arrived in San Francisco. Advance scouting quickly turned Jones into an extreme pull hitter and inflated his strikeout rate, as his passivity on early-count fastballs left him vulnerable to spinners he couldn't touch and his long swing rolled over pitches down and away. Not every player can adapt in the heat of battle, so Jones deserves a second try after an offseason of chewing the cud, but to blossom into a regular, he'll need more of a transformation than a tweak.

Evan Longoria 3B Born: 10/07/85 Age: 32 Bats: R Throws: R Height: 6'2" Weight: 210 Origin: Round 1, 2006 Draft (#3 overall)

YEAR	TEAM	LVL	AGE	PA	R	2B	3B	HR	RBI	BB	K	SB	CS	AVG/OBP/SLG	TAv	VORP	BABIP	BRR	FRAA	WARP
2015	TBA	MLB	29	670	74	35	1	21	73	51	132	3	1	.270/.328/.435	.275	29.8	.309	0.5	3B(148): 8.6	4.1
2016	TBA	MLB	30	685	81	41	4	36	98	42	144	0	3	.273/.318/.521	.292	41.6	.298	-2.3	3B(152): -5.4	3.7
2017	TBA	MLB	31	677	71	36	2	20	86	46	109	6	1	.261/.313/.424	.264	22.4	.282	-1.9	3B(142): 3.8	2.6
2018	*SFN*	*MLB*	*32*	*574*	*65*	*30*	*3*	*17*	*73*	*41*	*111*	*3*	*1*	*.261/.318/.427*	*.265*	*20.7*	*.298*	*-0.7*	*3B 1*	*1.7*
2019	*SFN*	*MLB*	*33*	*545*	*68*	*28*	*2*	*18*	*68*	*42*	*110*	*2*	*1*	*.261/.322/.433*	*.278*	*22.4*	*.300*	*-0.9*	*3B 2*	*2.6*

Breakout: 3% Improve: 48% Collapse: 5% Attrition: 5% MLB: 96% *Comparables: Adrian Beltre, Chris Sabo, Chase Headley*

It's not when you get your knee replaced or the day your kid heads to Wellesley that you become old; it's the day you see a colleague sporting a trendy haircut and think, "What will they come up with next?" In defiance of leaguewide trends, Longoria made more contact than ever in 2017, but hit for less power. Coming off his 36-homer outburst in 2016, he saw more sliders and fewer strikes, and while he was able to withstand the force of that change without becoming whiff-prone, the changes he made in order to do so (a swing more geared toward hitting the ball the other way, contact deeper in the hitting zone) cost him the dangerousness that made pitchers work around him in the first place. By early September, his frustration was palpable and public, and he started to make new changes, but they came too late to save the Rays' season. Traded to the Giants in December, he'll get a fresh start in a different league, on a different coast.

Joe Panik 2B Born: 10/30/90 Age: 27 Bats: L Throws: R Height: 6'1" Weight: 190 Origin: Round 1, 2011 Draft (#29 overall)

YEAR	TEAM	LVL	AGE	PA	R	2B	3B	HR	RBI	BB	K	SB	CS	AVG/OBP/SLG	TAv	VORP	BABIP	BRR	FRAA	WARP
2015	SFN	MLB	24	432	59	27	2	8	37	38	42	3	2	.312/.378/.455	.314	32.6	.330	-1.1	2B(99): -6.2	2.8
2016	SFN	MLB	25	526	67	21	7	10	62	50	47	5	0	.239/.315/.379	.256	13.2	.245	1.3	2B(126): 12.7	2.7
2017	SFN	MLB	26	573	60	28	5	10	53	46	54	4	1	.288/.347/.421	.277	27.3	.301	0.9	2B(137): -7.5	2.0
2018	*SFN*	*MLB*	*27*	*582*	*70*	*27*	*4*	*9*	*54*	*46*	*58*	*4*	*1*	*.272/.333/.391*	*.263*	*25.7*	*.289*	*-0.1*	*2B 0*	*2.0*
2019	*SFN*	*MLB*	*28*	*562*	*66*	*26*	*3*	*11*	*60*	*47*	*61*	*3*	*1*	*.271/.337/.403*	*.273*	*25.8*	*.285*	*0.1*	*2B 0*	*2.8*

Breakout: 4% Improve: 54% Collapse: 4% Attrition: 12% MLB: 98% *Comparables: Dustin Pedroia, Nellie Fox, Ron Hunt*

Choking up on the bat: It's a time-honored, Joey Votto-approved adjustment that can enhance bat control from Little League to the big leagues. In September, feeling fatigued near the end of a grueling season, Panik implemented the half-inch grip change recommended by hitting coach Hensley Meulens and unleashed one of the hottest stretches of his career. He racked up 12 hits in a three-game series at Coors Field and went on to hit .395/.440/.531 over the season's last 22 games, with just three strikeouts in 81 at-bats. When the dust settled, Panik was the majors' only qualifying hitter with a strikeout rate below 10 percent, and outside of AT&T Park, he married those elite contact skills with impressive gap power, slugging .500 on the road. Assuming his back and concussion issues are behind him, Panik should be a formidable two-hole hitter and a potential All-Star in 2018.

Jarrett Parker LF Born: 01/01/89 Age: 29 Bats: L Throws: L Height: 6'4" Weight: 210 Origin: Round 2, 2010 Draft (#74 overall)

YEAR	TEAM	LVL	AGE	PA	R	2B	3B	HR	RBI	BB	K	SB	CS	AVG/OBP/SLG	TAv	VORP	BABIP	BRR	FRAA	WARP
2015	SAC	AAA	26	504	74	25	3	23	74	62	164	20	7	.283/.375/.514	.321	39.8	.398	-1.8	RF(61): 3.4, LF(48): -2.6	4.1
2015	SFN	MLB	26	54	11	2	0	6	14	5	21	1	1	.347/.407/.755	.413	9.0	.500	-0.5	RF(9): -1.3, LF(5): 0.3	0.9
2016	SAC	AAA	27	222	44	8	2	16	35	26	66	1	1	.273/.365/.582	.332	21.4	.330	0.7	RF(39): -2.4, LF(11): 0.4	2.0
2016	SFN	MLB	27	151	22	3	1	5	14	19	44	0	1	.236/.358/.394	.281	5.8	.321	-0.5	RF(21): -1.3, LF(17): -1.0	0.4
2017	SAC	AAA	28	133	22	5	0	3	8	21	31	1	1	.232/.353/.357	.267	4.3	.295	-0.1	CF(14): -1.0, RF(11): 0.3	0.2
2017	SFN	MLB	28	177	14	12	2	4	23	10	54	2	1	.247/.294/.416	.256	4.4	.343	1.3	LF(44): 2.2, RF(5): 0.0	0.7
2018	*SFN*	*MLB*	*29*	*228*	*31*	*9*	*1*	*9*	*30*	*24*	*75*	*3*	*1*	*.233/.320/.426*	*.265*	*8.7*	*.320*	*-0.2*	*LF -3*	*0.4*
2019	*SFN*	*MLB*	*30*	*331*	*44*	*13*	*1*	*14*	*44*	*36*	*111*	*3*	*2*	*.230/.320/.425*	*.274*	*13.4*	*.318*	*0.4*	*LF -3*	*1.1*

Breakout: 9% Improve: 30% Collapse: 6% Attrition: 17% MLB: 61% *Comparables: Carlos Peguero, Ryan Ludwick, Justin Maxwell*

After devoting the lion's share of their offseason budget to the back end of the bullpen, the Giants handed Parker the keys to the left-field car in 2017 until a fractured collarbone rendered him unable to drive two weeks into the season. Upon his August return, Parker was no worse for the wear, clobbering the occasional mistake while indiscriminately chasing sliders. Easy plus raw power remains the calling card here, but at 29, Parker is far past the age of hit-tool development, and his injury may have cost him his only chance to secure regular work. He's still a big, strong man with a big, long swing, and the latter means he's probably just a bench bat in the end.

Hunter Pence RF Born: 04/13/83 Age: 35 Bats: R Throws: R Height: 6'4" Weight: 220 Origin: Round 2, 2004 Draft (#64 overall)

YEAR	TEAM	LVL	AGE	PA	R	2B	3B	HR	RBI	BB	K	SB	CS	AVG/OBP/SLG	TAv	VORP	BABIP	BRR	FRAA	WARP
2015	SFN	MLB	32	223	30	13	1	9	40	16	48	4	1	.275/.327/.478	.288	11.2	.320	1.2	RF(51): 10.1	2.3
2016	SAC	AAA	33	25	6	2	0	3	7	0	3	0	0	.417/.440/.875	.444	5.2	.389	-0.1	RF(7): -0.3	0.5
2016	SFN	MLB	33	442	58	23	1	13	57	43	95	1	1	.289/.357/.451	.304	25.8	.348	-1.8	RF(102): -1.2	2.5
2017	SFN	MLB	34	539	55	13	5	13	67	40	102	2	3	.260/.315/.385	.265	17.3	.301	4.4	RF(125): 2.1	1.9
2018	*SFN*	*MLB*	*35*	*538*	*63*	*22*	*3*	*15*	*62*	*39*	*105*	*4*	*2*	*.261/.316/.409*	*.264*	*17.4*	*.302*	*-0.7*	*RF 4*	*1.6*
2019	*SFN*	*MLB*	*36*	*458*	*56*	*19*	*3*	*14*	*55*	*35*	*94*	*2*	*2*	*.260/.319/.417*	*.274*	*17.3*	*.303*	*1.1*	*RF 4*	*2.3*

Breakout: 1% Improve: 24% Collapse: 8% Attrition: 18% MLB: 77% *Comparables: Enos Slaughter, Hank Bauer, Kirby Puckett*

Pence is one of the majors' quirkiest ballplayers, which complicates explaining or predicting his age-related decline. On the one hand, Father Time is undefeated, so it's no surprise that Pence no longer covers the alley or corner as well as he once did. Yet on the bases, Pence's legs are as spry as ever, a fact to which his .313 average on groundballs can attest. It's tempting to blame excessive worm-burners for the erosion of Pence's power, but his grounder rate has long begun with a five, so his 57.5 percent clip in 2017 wasn't abnormal. Pence swung less often and made contact more often last season, too, so his plate discipline hasn't faded. And if you wanted to suggest that his first-half rut was a blip, he hit .291/.360/.467 from July 29 on to make that case. At 35, Pence is no longer an All-Star and probably won't earn his $18.5 million check. But if he can avoid the disabled list, or avoid being called back to his home planet, he may not be finished as a productive big leaguer just yet.

Buster Posey C Born: 03/27/87 Age: 31 Bats: R Throws: R Height: 6'1" Weight: 215 Origin: Round 1, 2008 Draft (#5 overall)

YEAR	TEAM	LVL	AGE	PA	R	2B	3B	HR	RBI	BB	K	SB	CS	AVG/OBP/SLG	TAv	VORP	BABIP	BRR	FRAA	WARP
2015	SFN	MLB	28	623	74	28	0	19	95	56	52	2	0	.318/.379/.470	.320	55.8	.320	-1.8	C(106): 18.0, 1B(42): -1.7	7.7
2016	SFN	MLB	29	614	82	33	2	14	80	64	68	6	1	.288/.362/.434	.289	40.5	.303	-3.3	C(123): 34.6, 1B(15): -0.7	7.7
2017	SFN	MLB	30	568	62	34	0	12	67	61	66	6	1	.320/.400/.462	.312	50.3	.347	-1.5	C(99): 3.9, 1B(38): 3.5	5.8
2018	*SFN*	*MLB*	*31*	*598*	*72*	*30*	*1*	*15*	*73*	*55*	*67*	*4*	*1*	*.291/.360/.432*	*.283*	*40.3*	*.308*	*-0.7*	*C 19, 1B 1*	*5.6*
2019	*SFN*	*MLB*	*32*	*544*	*70*	*27*	*1*	*14*	*64*	*51*	*67*	*2*	*1*	*.286/.356/.434*	*.291*	*35.3*	*.305*	*-2.1*	*C 18, 1B 1*	*5.9*

Breakout: 1% Improve: 29% Collapse: 4% Attrition: 5% MLB: 95% *Comparables: Yadier Molina, John Jaso, Jonathan Lucroy*

YEAR	TEAM	P. COUNT	FRM RUNS	BLK RUNS	THRW RUNS	TOT RUNS
2015	SFN	13948	11.6	2.0	0.9	14.4
2016	SFN	17017	26.5	2.0	2.2	30.7
2017	SFN	13474	1.8	0.1	2.2	4.1
2018	*SFN*	*17228*	*15.3*	*1.8*	*2.0*	*19.1*
2019	*SFN*	*15686*	*13.7*	*1.6*	*1.8*	*17.1*

Long renowned for his picturesque swing, Posey made adjustments to enhance his adaptability and balance, incorporating various load-stride mechanisms besides his customary leg-kick. The added versatility stymied pitchers who sought to disrupt his timing and—together with a renewed focus on going up the middle—restored Posey's place atop the qualifying catcher leaderboard in TAv. The Florida State product's next adjustment may come behind the dish, where his framing metrics deteriorated suddenly and rapidly last season, costing him his place among the eight-win elite. If that decline marked the first sign of waning defense, the notion of a position change for Posey will soon pick up steam. Given his pride and attention to detail, though, it's unwise to bet against him repairing his receiving by Opening Day.

Heath Quinn OF Born: 06/07/95 Age: 23 Bats: R Throws: R Height: 6'2" Weight: 190 Origin: Round 3, 2016 Draft (#95 overall)

YEAR	TEAM	LVL	AGE	PA	R	2B	3B	HR	RBI	BB	K	SB	CS	AVG/OBP/SLG	TAv	VORP	BABIP	BRR	FRAA	WARP
2016	SLO	A-	21	239	37	19	1	9	34	26	50	3	0	.337/.423/.571	.346	26.9	.405	1.7	RF(49): 11.2	4.0
2017	SJO	A+	22	297	24	9	0	10	29	20	86	0	0	.228/.290/.371	.244	-2.7	.294	-2.8	RF(35): -0.5, LF(26): -7.4	-1.1
2018	*SFN*	*MLB*	*23*	*250*	*24*	*10*	*1*	*8*	*29*	*17*	*79*	*0*	*0*	*.215/.274/.363*	*.221*	*-3.0*	*.287*	*-0.4*	*RF 1, LF -5*	*-0.7*
2019	*SFN*	*MLB*	*24*	*256*	*29*	*11*	*1*	*8*	*29*	*17*	*80*	*0*	*0*	*.220/.281/.375*	*.241*	*-0.1*	*.294*	*-0.5*	*RF 1, LF -5*	*-0.4*

Breakout: 0% Improve: 1% Collapse: 1% Attrition: 1% MLB: 2% *Comparables: Scott Schebler, Yorman Rodriguez, Andrew Lambo*

Injuries dogged Quinn throughout 2017: He missed the first six weeks of the season with a broken hamate bone, tallied a .900 OPS in his first 31 games and then spent the second half nursing a shoulder ailment that wouldn't subside. Quinn generates plus raw power through brute strength rather than elite bat speed, taking leveraged, high-effort hacks that drive the ball to all fields but detract from his bat control. The bum shoulder made Quinn's cuts increasingly laborious during the summer, so a mulligan at High-A may be in order. He has the power/arm pairing of an everyday right fielder, but is more likely to land on the short end of a platoon unless the hit tool comes along.

Heliot Ramos CF Born: 09/07/99 Age: 18 Bats: R Throws: R Height: 6'2" Weight: 185 Origin: Round 1, 2017 Draft (#19 overall)

YEAR	TEAM	LVL	AGE	PA	R	2B	3B	HR	RBI	BB	K	SB	CS	AVG/OBP/SLG	TAv	VORP	BABIP	BRR	FRAA	WARP
2017	GIA	RK	17	151	33	11	6	6	27	10	48	10	2	.348/.404/.645	.323	19.4	.500	2.2	CF(28): -2.3	1.5
2018	*SFN*	*MLB*	*18*	*250*	*27*	*9*	*1*	*6*	*21*	*12*	*92*	*5*	*2*	*.193/.234/.318*	*.191*	*-7.7*	*.282*	*0.5*	*CF -1*	*-1.0*
2019	*SFN*	*MLB*	*19*	*223*	*21*	*8*	*1*	*6*	*22*	*10*	*82*	*5*	*1*	*.195/.234/.327*	*.202*	*-6.5*	*.283*	*0.6*	*CF -1*	*-0.8*

Comparables: Raul Mondesi, Wilmer Flores

Gary Brown, Joe Panik, Christian Arroyo, Heliot Ramos. Those are the position players with whom the Giants have led off a draft class since the turn of the decade, and one of them is not like the others. Three of those players entered pro baseball with a hotel-room ceiling, reachable by an NBA forward standing on the bed within. Then there is Ramos, whose ceiling is more like that of a landmark Victorian, higher than those of his peers thanks to an extraordinary collection of physical gifts. The Puerto Rican's mere presence infused a bland system with a teenager who boasts both exceptional power and electric speed, who scouts believe can stick in center field as his body matures, whose upside is so palpable that casual fans race to check rookie-level box scores just to see how he fared that night. The Giants haven't drafted that sort of position prospect since Buster Posey. Ramos' development won't be as quick or as linear, but he's exciting enough to merit daily monitoring for as long as it takes him to reach "The Show."

Bryan Reynolds OF Born: 01/27/95 Age: 23 Bats: B Throws: R Height: 6'3" Weight: 205 Origin: Round 2, 2016 Draft (#59 overall)

YEAR	TEAM	LVL	AGE	PA	R	2B	3B	HR	RBI	BB	K	SB	CS	AVG/OBP/SLG	TAv	VORP	BABIP	BRR	FRAA	WARP
2016	SLO	A-	21	171	28	12	1	5	30	11	41	2	0	.312/.368/.500	.293	11.7	.391	1.3	CF(33): -4.1	0.8
2016	AUG	A	21	66	11	5	0	1	8	3	20	1	0	.317/.348/.444	.319	5.5	.452	0.2	CF(11): 1.5	0.8
2017	SJO	A+	22	541	72	26	9	10	63	37	106	5	3	.312/.364/.462	.303	35.3	.376	-0.9	CF(50): -4.2, RF(42): -2.9	3.0
2018	*SFN*	*MLB*	*23*	*250*	*23*	*11*	*2*	*5*	*27*	*14*	*65*	*0*	*0*	*.244/.291/.378*	*.233*	*1.3*	*.313*	*-0.2*	*CF -1, RF -1*	*-0.1*
2019	*SFN*	*MLB*	*24*	*318*	*35*	*15*	*3*	*8*	*35*	*19*	*83*	*0*	*0*	*.245/.295/.394*	*.253*	*5.3*	*.312*	*-0.4*	*CF -1, RF -1*	*0.3*

Breakout: 1% Improve: 12% Collapse: 3% Attrition: 10% MLB: 25% *Comparables: Austin Jackson, Tyler Naquin, Bryan Petersen*

Reynolds isn't the sort of prospect who earns scouts' love at first sight. His physique is unexceptional, his speed is good-not-great, his game power ebbs and flows and pizzazz simply isn't a part of anything he does. All of that might explain why the Vanderbilt standout stayed on the board until 59th overall in 2016, when the Giants gladly snapped up a first-round talent despite missing their first-round pick. Because he keeps a low profile on the field, Reynolds is an acquired taste, a player you appreciate most when someone asks you to identify a glaring weakness in his game and your response begins with "hmm" or "uh." He could be an average regular in either center or left, contributing on both sides of the ball in ways that go unnoticed unless you watch him every day.

Pablo Sandoval 3B Born: 08/11/86 Age: 31 Bats: B Throws: R Height: 5'11" Weight: 255 Origin: International Free Agent, 2003

YEAR	TEAM	LVL	AGE	PA	R	2B	3B	HR	RBI	BB	K	SB	CS	AVG/OBP/SLG	TAv	VORP	BABIP	BRR	FRAA	WARP
2015	BOS	MLB	28	505	43	25	1	10	47	25	73	0	0	.245/.292/.366	.229	-5.1	.270	-5.5	3B(123): -8.4	-1.4
2016	BOS	MLB	29	7	0	0	0	0	0	1	4	0	0	.000/.143/.000	.089	-1.0	.000	0.0	3B(2): 0.1	-0.1
2017	BOS	MLB	30	108	10	2	0	4	12	8	24	0	1	.212/.269/.354	.215	-1.9	.236	-0.2	3B(29): -1.4, 2B(1): 0.0	-0.3
2017	PAW	AAA	30	81	7	3	0	1	4	4	16	0	0	.221/.259/.299	.207	-3.0	.267	-0.5	3B(15): -1.6	-0.4
2017	SAC	AAA	30	37	4	1	0	1	3	5	3	0	0	.207/.324/.345	.265	1.2	.185	-0.1	3B(7): 1.2	0.2
2017	SFN	MLB	30	171	17	9	0	5	20	8	29	0	0	.225/.263/.375	.230	-0.8	.242	-0.4	3B(38): -2.6, 1B(9): -0.1	-0.3
2018	*SFN*	*MLB*	*31*	*250*	*24*	*11*	*1*	*6*	*28*	*17*	*39*	*0*	*0*	*.253/.308/.385*	*.242*	*2.1*	*.280*	*-1.3*	*3B -5, 1B 0*	*-0.3*
2019	*SFN*	*MLB*	*32*	*236*	*27*	*10*	*1*	*6*	*25*	*17*	*38*	*0*	*0*	*.245/.303/.377*	*.253*	*2.4*	*.272*	*-1.3*	*3B -5, 1B 0*	*-0.2*

Breakout: 2% Improve: 32% Collapse: 11% Attrition: 23% MLB: 87% *Comparables: Jeff King, Ron Jackson, Jeff Treadway*

We'll never know how the latter half of Sandoval's story might have unfolded had he stayed in San Francisco, but we do have the data to prove that free-swingers like the Panda age less gracefully than (fire emoji) takes on Twitter. After the Red Sox were through learning that lesson the expensive way, the Giants swooped in with a unique contract arrangement, offering Sandoval the prorated minimum and two similarly priced club options to return to his original major-league home. The ploy neither revived Sandoval's swing nor stanched the attendance bleeding that ended the Giants' sellout streak, and it appears that the very same traits that first endeared the Panda to fans will soon spell the end of his career. At the very least, though, he proved to be an equal-opportunity buzzkill: By swatting a walk-off homer in the Giants' final 2017 game, he cost them the number one pick in the 2018 draft.

Chris Shaw OF Born: 10/20/93 Age: 24 Bats: L Throws: R Height: 6'4" Weight: 235 Origin: Round 1, 2015 Draft (#31 overall)

YEAR	TEAM	LVL	AGE	PA	R	2B	3B	HR	RBI	BB	K	SB	CS	AVG/OBP/SLG	TAv	VORP	BABIP	BRR	FRAA	WARP
2015	SLO	A-	21	200	22	11	0	12	30	19	41	0	0	.287/.360/.551	.305	9.5	.310	-1.8	1B(31): 1.4	1.1
2016	SJO	A+	22	305	47	22	0	16	55	28	70	0	0	.285/.357/.544	.333	24.7	.326	-2.4	1B(52): -0.9	2.4
2016	RIC	AA	22	256	26	16	4	5	30	20	55	0	0	.246/.309/.414	.270	1.6	.299	-3.5	1B(48): -2.3	-0.1
2017	RIC	AA	23	154	16	10	0	6	29	18	26	0	0	.301/.390/.511	.321	10.4	.333	-1.5	LF(17): -1.0, 1B(16): -0.9	0.9
2017	SAC	AAA	23	360	42	25	1	18	50	20	106	0	0	.289/.328/.530	.285	12.7	.367	-5.3	LF(76): -14.5	-0.2
2018	*SFN*	*MLB*	*24*	*250*	*28*	*13*	*1*	*10*	*35*	*17*	*72*	*0*	*0*	*.242/.299/.446*	*.253*	*5.7*	*.305*	*-0.4*	*LF -5, 1B 0*	*0.0*
2019	*SFN*	*MLB*	*25*	*366*	*47*	*21*	*2*	*15*	*50*	*28*	*109*	*0*	*0*	*.244/.306/.452*	*.274*	*12.7*	*.314*	*-0.8*	*LF -8, 1B 0*	*0.5*

Breakout: 8% Improve: 25% Collapse: 10% Attrition: 25% MLB: 45% *Comparables: Corey Dickerson, Daniel Dorn, Kyle Jensen*

If you'd never seen Shaw hit or read a scout's report on the former Boston College Eagle, the first thing you'd notice is his narrow hitting base. Most players with Shaw's tall, brutish physique spread out in their stride, getting the bat closer to the hitting zone and transferring their weight forward into the ball. Shaw instead delivers his easy-plus punch with raw strength and leverage, and his quiet lower half allows him to stay balanced when pitchers change speeds. A 30-grade runner with the wind at his back, Shaw's future lies near the bottom of the defensive spectrum, so he'll need to hit his way into everyday work. If he can handle left field to go with first base, the added versatility should bring Shaw's curiously short stride to major-league batter's boxes by midseason.

Austin Slater OF Born: 12/13/92 Age: 25 Bats: R Throws: R Height: 6'2" Weight: 215 Origin: Round 8, 2014 Draft (#238 overall)

YEAR	TEAM	LVL	AGE	PA	R	2B	3B	HR	RBI	BB	K	SB	CS	AVG/OBP/SLG	TAv	VORP	BABIP	BRR	FRAA	WARP
2015	SJO	A+	22	265	25	15	1	3	34	10	44	4	3	.292/.321/.396	.258	6.4	.340	0.4	2B(42): -0.6, SS(7): 0.3	0.7
2015	RIC	AA	22	218	21	11	1	0	13	14	48	1	1	.296/.350/.362	.266	7.3	.388	0.5	2B(54): 4.1	1.2
2016	RIC	AA	23	172	20	8	1	5	25	24	36	6	1	.317/.413/.490	.339	19.5	.387	1.1	CF(33): -10.1, LF(7): -0.4	1.0
2016	SAC	AAA	23	278	36	12	0	13	42	33	53	2	6	.298/.381/.506	.329	26.1	.335	-0.5	LF(48): 0.4, CF(15): -1.3	2.7
2017	SAC	AAA	24	206	28	12	0	5	27	15	39	4	3	.321/.377/.467	.289	8.9	.380	-2.7	RF(22): -0.9, LF(17): -0.1	0.8
2017	SFN	MLB	24	127	15	3	1	3	16	8	29	0	0	.282/.339/.402	.273	4.9	.353	0.2	LF(30): -1.3, RF(3): -0.2	0.3
2018	*SFN*	*MLB*	*25*	*420*	*48*	*18*	*2*	*10*	*45*	*31*	*98*	*3*	*2*	*.261/.320/.394*	*.258*	*12.4*	*.324*	*-0.9*	*LF -2, CF -2*	*0.5*
2019	*SFN*	*MLB*	*26*	*490*	*59*	*21*	*2*	*13*	*56*	*39*	*118*	*3*	*3*	*.258/.322/.405*	*.270*	*16.7*	*.320*	*-0.9*	*LF -2, CF -2*	*1.4*

Breakout: 9% Improve: 27% Collapse: 23% Attrition: 40% MLB: 68% *Comparables: Caleb Gindl, Zoilo Almonte, Shin-Soo Choo*

Many Stanford graduates are catapulted to successful careers by lessons learned on the farm. For years, position players out of the Cardinal baseball program have been a notable exception, bedeviled by the so-called Stanford Swing, which threatens to dash Slater's dreams. A stiff, punchy, opposite-field stroke, the Stanford Swing is obsolete in the age of juiced baseballs and launch-angle optimization, where power production is a prerequisite for an everyday corner outfielder, which Slater aspires to be. Besides hip and sports hernia injuries, he—like even the best of us—was held back as a rookie by bad habits that he picked up in college, as he had the league's second-highest ground-ball rate and 15th-lowest pull rate. With the size and strength to hit for power, Slater may yet have a quality regular lurking inside him, but there's a lot of unlearning ahead to allow his raw pop to emerge.

Kelby Tomlinson INF Born: 06/16/90 Age: 28 Bats: R Throws: R Height: 6'3" Weight: 180 Origin: Round 12, 2011 Draft (#387 overall)

YEAR	TEAM	LVL	AGE	PA	R	2B	3B	HR	RBI	BB	K	SB	CS	AVG/OBP/SLG	TAv	VORP	BABIP	BRR	FRAA	WARP
2015	RIC	AA	25	289	43	18	3	1	28	25	37	16	6	.324/.387/.431	.316	28.4	.372	3.3	2B(49): 2.4, SS(25): -1.9	3.1
2015	SAC	AAA	25	149	21	1	1	2	15	7	22	5	3	.316/.354/.382	.266	5.9	.360	0.2	2B(16): 2.0, SS(15): 0.6	0.9
2015	SFN	MLB	25	193	23	6	3	2	20	14	40	5	4	.303/.358/.404	.294	12.7	.382	1.3	2B(50): -1.0, SS(1): 0.0	1.3
2016	SAC	AAA	26	213	28	8	1	0	20	22	26	12	3	.286/.370/.341	.278	12.8	.331	1.7	SS(20): -1.0, 2B(16): 1.0	1.4
2016	SFN	MLB	26	120	13	4	0	0	6	12	18	5	1	.292/.370/.330	.261	5.8	.352	2.2	2B(19): -0.5, SS(7): -0.4	0.6
2017	SAC	AAA	27	122	17	6	0	0	8	13	12	9	2	.296/.377/.352	.293	8.7	.333	0.3	2B(17): 1.6, CF(5): 0.1	0.9
2017	SFN	MLB	27	222	32	4	2	1	11	23	46	9	1	.258/.332/.314	.235	4.7	.327	3.5	3B(24): 0.0, 2B(20): -0.6	0.3
2018	*SFN*	*MLB*	*28*	*270*	*30*	*10*	*2*	*2*	*22*	*22*	*50*	*10*	*3*	*.265/.328/.345*	*.250*	*9.9*	*.321*	*0.9*	*2B 0, 3B 1*	*0.7*
2019	*SFN*	*MLB*	*29*	*311*	*34*	*12*	*2*	*4*	*28*	*27*	*60*	*10*	*3*	*.261/.331/.357*	*.259*	*11.7*	*.317*	*2.9*	*2B 1, 3B 2*	*1.4*

Breakout: 2% Improve: 24% Collapse: 18% Attrition: 27% MLB: 80% *Comparables: Matt Tolbert, Eric Sogard, Johnny Giavotella*

National League West clubs set the Twitterverse abuzz last season by employing an extreme shift against Rockies second baseman DJ LeMahieu, wherein the right fielder guarded the line, the center fielder played the right-center gap and the left fielder abandoned his post to defend the middle. Tomlinson—the runner-up among right-handed batters with just 24.2 percent of his balls in play hit to the pull side—has yet to inspire a similar arrangement, but could in the future, as a pure punch hitter with no intention of driving ball to left. A short stroke and disciplined approach give Tomlinson pinch-hit utility against late-inning flame-throwers; fringy defense around the infield and nonexistent power curb his appeal as a regular or spot starter. He has a place on a diverse big-league bench, but probably shouldn't be more than the sixth infielder on the roster.

Mac Williamson RF Born: 07/15/90 Age: 27 Bats: R Throws: R Height: 6'4" Weight: 240 Origin: Round 3, 2012 Draft (#115 overall)

YEAR	TEAM	LVL	AGE	PA	R	2B	3B	HR	RBI	BB	K	SB	CS	AVG/OBP/SLG	TAv	VORP	BABIP	BRR	FRAA	WARP
2015	RIC	AA	24	290	41	16	2	5	42	25	53	3	1	.293/.366/.429	.303	15.4	.351	-1.8	RF(55): 1.4	1.8
2015	SAC	AAA	24	227	35	12	0	8	31	26	55	1	0	.249/.370/.439	.317	19.4	.307	1.6	LF(30): -2.7, RF(16): 1.6	1.9
2015	SFN	MLB	24	34	2	0	1	0	1	0	8	0	0	.219/.235/.281	.189	-2.1	.280	-0.4	LF(6): -0.4, RF(3): -0.1	-0.3
2016	SAC	AAA	25	226	35	14	0	11	42	12	53	2	1	.269/.314/.495	.303	14.9	.306	0.5	LF(25): 1.8, RF(23): -1.0	1.6
2016	SFN	MLB	25	127	14	3	0	6	15	13	35	0	1	.223/.315/.411	.254	1.8	.268	0.0	RF(23): -0.9, LF(13): 2.2	0.3
2017	SAC	AAA	26	382	54	21	0	14	50	25	100	4	1	.244/.301/.423	.243	1.7	.301	1.8	RF(56): -2.0, LF(27): -2.5	-0.3
2017	SFN	MLB	26	73	8	2	0	3	6	5	25	1	1	.235/.288/.397	.266	3.3	.325	1.3	RF(12): -0.1, LF(9): -0.3	0.3
2018	*SFN*	*MLB*	*27*	*172*	*19*	*7*	*1*	*6*	*21*	*12*	*48*	*1*	*0*	*.232/.298/.396*	*.252*	*4.3*	*.296*	*-0.3*	*RF 0*	*0.3*
2019	*SFN*	*MLB*	*28*	*330*	*41*	*15*	*1*	*12*	*41*	*27*	*94*	*1*	*1*	*.233/.308/.410*	*.268*	*11.2*	*.298*	*0.9*	*RF 1*	*1.3*

Breakout: 6% Improve: 19% Collapse: 13% Attrition: 29% MLB: 56% *Comparables: Todd Linden, Michael Restovich, Joe Borchard*

The best ability is availability, as Williamson learned the hard way last March, when a quad strain cost him a spot on the Opening Day roster. A big man with a big swing, Williamson can pummel a fastball when his timing is right, but gearing up for the heat leaves him prone to chasing spin. The all-or-nothing profile presents a managerial dilemma: Williamson needs consistent at-bats to calibrate his cuts, but he's liable to go sombrero shopping in any given start. Now entering his late-twenties, Williamson probably won't develop the hit tool necessary to hold down an everyday job, so he'll need to stay healthy and ready to become a preferred option off the bench.

PITCHERS

Shaun Anderson RHP Born: 10/29/94 Age: 23 Bats: R Throws: R Height: 6'4" Weight: 225 Origin: Round 3, 2016 Draft (#88 overall)

YEAR	TEAM	LVL	AGE	W	L	SV	G	GS	IP	H	HR	BB/9	K/9	K	GB%	BABIP	WHIP	ERA	DRA	WARP	MPH	CMD	PWR	STM
2017	GRN	A	22	3	0	0	7	7	38^{2}	30	2	2.6	8.6	37	52%	.272	1.06	2.56	3.50	0.8				
2017	SLM	A+	22	3	3	0	11	11	58^{2}	53	6	2.8	7.4	48	43%	.270	1.21	3.99	3.54	1.2				
2017	SJO	A+	22	3	3	0	6	5	25^{2}	19	1	1.4	7.7	22	51%	.247	0.90	3.51	2.88	0.7				
2018	*SFN*	*MLB*	*23*	*5*	*6*	*0*	*17*	*17*	*85*	*85*	*13*	*3.4*	*8.6*	*82*	*41%*	*.315*	*1.37*	*4.45*	*5.40*	*0.2*				
2019	*SFN*	*MLB*	*24*	*7*	*11*	*0*	*27*	*27*	*164^{2}*	*161*	*26*	*4.6*	*8.1*	*147*	*41%*	*.311*	*1.49*	*4.88*	*5.87*	*-0.4*				

Breakout: 4% Improve: 6% Collapse: 7% Attrition: 13% MLB: 17% *Comparables: Ricardo Pinto, Cody Anderson, Jonathan Holder*

Part of a historically loaded Florida Gators pitching staff in 2016, Anderson worked as a closer during his final collegiate season but has at least a puncher's chance to start in pro ball. The right-hander returned to the rotation in the lower rungs of the Red Sox system, where Giants evaluators saw a sturdy frame, repeatable delivery and enough diversity in the arsenal to envision Anderson pitching every fifth day. Shipped west for Eduardo Nuñez in July, Anderson features a low-90s fastball with late sink and a two-plane slider in the mid-80s—both solid-average offerings that project to miss barrels if not bats. To remain a starter, he'll need to more deftly mix in his fringe-average changeup and curveball, utilizing the depth of his assortment to compensate for the absence of a plus pitch.

Tyler Beede RHP
Born: 05/23/93 Age: 25 Bats: R Throws: R Height: 6'3" Weight: 210 Origin: Round 1, 2014 Draft (#14 overall)

YEAR	TEAM	LVL	AGE	W	L	SV	G	GS	IP	H	HR	BB/9	K/9	K	GB%	BABIP	WHIP	ERA	DRA	WARP	MPH	CMD	PWR	STM
2015	SJO	A+	22	2	2	0	9	9	52^1	51	2	1.5	6.4	37	64%	.295	1.15	2.24	2.91	1.4				
2015	RIC	AA	22	3	8	0	13	13	72^1	62	4	4.4	6.1	49	60%	.269	1.34	5.23	7.34	-2.0				
2016	RIC	AA	23	8	7	0	24	24	147^1	136	9	3.2	8.2	135	49%	.309	1.28	2.81	3.05	3.6				
2017	SAC	AAA	24	6	7	0	19	19	109	121	14	3.2	6.9	83	52%	.316	1.47	4.79	4.42	1.5				
2018	SFN	MLB	25	5	5	0	15	15	79	77	9	3.2	7.8	69	49%	.296	1.32	3.72	4.56	0.6				
2019	SFN	MLB	26	10	10	0	31	31	193^2	166	19	3.2	8.2	177	49%	.298	1.22	3.57	4.34	2.3				

Breakout: 14% Improve: 16% Collapse: 13% Attrition: 26% MLB: 39% *Comparables: David Phelps, Cesar Valdez, Hiram Burgos*

Much like every parent wants to raise a doctor or a lawyer, every organization wants to nurture its first-round pitcher into an ace. The Giants drafted Beede as a wayward flamethrower and quickly tamed him into a crafty sinkerballer. When his strikeouts followed his walks out the door, Beede tweaked the depth and power of his curveball, and toyed with the shape of his sometimes-cutter sometimes-slider. The refined arsenal missed more bats, but the control woes returned. Just when he settled into a happy medium in Richmond, a renewed focus on his four-seam fastball found him stuck in between again in Sacramento. At the end of the day, Beede will chart his own path to back-end-starterdom. He'll arrive in the majors as soon as his employer accepts that fate.

Ty Blach LHP
Born: 10/20/90 Age: 27 Bats: R Throws: L Height: 6'2" Weight: 200 Origin: Round 5, 2012 Draft (#178 overall)

YEAR	TEAM	LVL	AGE	W	L	SV	G	GS	IP	H	HR	BB/9	K/9	K	GB%	BABIP	WHIP	ERA	DRA	WARP	MPH	CMD	PWR	STM
2015	SAC	AAA	24	11	12	0	27	27	165^1	189	16	1.7	5.1	93	49%	.311	1.33	4.46	3.40	3.6				
2016	SAC	AAA	25	14	7	0	26	26	162^2	147	9	2.1	6.3	113	50%	.280	1.14	3.43	1.48	7.2				
2016	SFN	MLB	25	1	0	0	4	2	17	8	1	2.6	5.3	10	60%	.152	0.76	1.06	4.32	0.2	93.1	70	44	68
2017	SFN	MLB	26	8	12	0	34	24	163^2	179	17	2.4	4.0	73	48%	.290	1.36	4.78	6.55	-1.8	91.5	49	34	67
2018	SFN	MLB	27	9	9	0	28	28	148	150	14	2.5	5.9	97	47%	.290	1.27	3.68	4.55	1.1	91.2	51	35	68
2019	SFN	MLB	28	11	10	0	32	32	210^2	195	17	2.1	6.3	147	47%	.295	1.16	3.34	4.11	2.9	90.9	51	35	68

Breakout: 22% Improve: 43% Collapse: 13% Attrition: 15% MLB: 71% *Comparables: Carlos Frias, Taylor Jordan, Tyler Anderson*

Remember that coach you had as a kid who preached doing the little things right at every turn? He would've loved Blach. The southpaw works fast and throws strikes. He fields his position well and eagerly backs up throws. He controls the running game and stays composed after teammates' errors. He's a good bunter and far from an automatic out at the plate. Above all, Blach competes and makes the most of what he's got. And all that got him was the second-worst DRA of any qualifying starter in the league. The truth is, stuff matters, and Blach's rarely withstood a second or third tour through the order. With a sixth starter bird in hand, it might be time to see if the former Creighton Bluejay is more valuable out of the 'pen.

Madison Bumgarner LHP
Born: 08/01/89 Age: 28 Bats: R Throws: L Height: 6'5" Weight: 250 Origin: Round 1, 2007 Draft (#10 overall)

YEAR	TEAM	LVL	AGE	W	L	SV	G	GS	IP	H	HR	BB/9	K/9	K	GB%	BABIP	WHIP	ERA	DRA	WARP	MPH	CMD	PWR	STM
2015	SFN	MLB	25	18	9	0	32	32	218^1	181	21	1.6	9.6	234	43%	.282	1.01	2.93	3.10	5.1	94.3	57	42	81
2016	SFN	MLB	26	15	9	0	34	34	226^2	179	26	2.1	10.0	251	41%	.267	1.03	2.74	3.37	5.2	92.6	62	41	88
2017	SJO	A+	27	0	1	0	2	2	10	11	4	1.8	11.7	13	29%	.292	1.30	8.10	4.14	0.1				
2017	SFN	MLB	27	4	9	0	17	17	111	101	17	1.6	8.2	101	42%	.272	1.09	3.32	4.12	1.8	92.7	53	36	53
2018	SFN	MLB	28	12	10	0	29	29	182^2	161	21	2.5	9.2	187	42%	.286	1.14	3.29	4.06	2.3	92.6	59	40	72
2019	SFN	MLB	29	13	11	0	33	33	213^2	177	24	2.0	9.2	219	42%	.293	1.05	3.08	3.79	4.1	92.0	59	39	70

Breakout: 14% Improve: 49% Collapse: 29% Attrition: 5% MLB: 97% *Comparables: Masahiro Tanaka, Roy Oswalt, Bert Blyleven*

From signing scores of autographs to slicing frozen burger patties, there are plenty of ways for a pitcher to injure his most vital appendage off the field. Many of those are laughed away. Falling off a dirtbike midseason during the prime of one's career is harder to stomach. Both Bumgarner and the Giants were fortunate that the ace left-hander merely sprained his shoulder and bruised some ribs in the April accident, and that he was able to return before the end of the season with his stuff and command mostly intact. Though his fastball and cutter velocities have backed up a few ticks in recent seasons, Bumgarner was a frontline starter before his crash, and his summertime work suggests that he'll still be one after. Amid the dark cloud that was the 2017 Giants, that's the best silver lining for which pitcher and team could ask.

Matt Cain RHP
Born: 10/01/84 Age: 33 Bats: R Throws: R Height: 6'3" Weight: 230 Origin: Round 1, 2002 Draft (#25 overall)

YEAR	TEAM	LVL	AGE	W	L	SV	G	GS	IP	H	HR	BB/9	K/9	K	GB%	BABIP	WHIP	ERA	DRA	WARP	MPH	CMD	PWR	STM
2015	SAC	AAA	30	1	2	0	5	3	19^2	18	2	1.8	10.1	22	38%	.296	1.12	3.20	2.34	0.6				
2015	SFN	MLB	30	2	4	0	13	11	60^2	71	12	3.0	6.1	41	36%	.304	1.50	5.79	6.32	-0.9	93.2	40	38	46
2016	SAC	AAA	31	1	1	0	2	2	10^2	11	1	3.4	5.1	6	42%	.286	1.41	5.06	6.30	-0.1				
2016	SFN	MLB	31	4	8	0	21	17	89^1	103	16	3.2	7.3	72	41%	.321	1.51	5.64	5.93	-0.6	92.5	51	39	50
2017	SFN	MLB	32	3	11	0	27	23	124^1	157	18	3.5	5.4	75	44%	.329	1.66	5.43	7.31	-2.4	90.9	52	27	57
2018	SFN	MLB	33	6	7	0	20	20	103^2	110	13	3.3	6.7	77	42%	.313	1.44	4.59	5.60	0.0	90.7	49	32	51
2019	SFN	MLB	34	6	8	0	21	21	125^2	129	16	3.3	6.4	90	42%	.309	1.39	4.33	5.28	0.4	90.1	50	31	52

Breakout: 18% Improve: 36% Collapse: 19% Attrition: 15% MLB: 76% *Comparables: Nate Robertson, Edwin Jackson, Vicente Padilla*

As the Barry Bonds era wound down, and before the Tim Lincecum/Buster Posey/Madison Bumgarner triumvirate ushered in the golden years of San Francisco Giants baseball, Cain was the franchise's first glimmer of hope for a future after number 25. A first-round pick in 2002, Cain debuted in 2005 at age 20 and handled 190 2/3 innings at 21, a load only Bumgarner and Felix Hernandez have shouldered in their drinking-age season since then. Hence, before the Kung Fu Panda and the Baby Giraffe, there was the Horse, Cain's hard-earned moniker as an innings-eater who toiled with minimal run support, vastly underrated until pitcher wins and losses largely lost their appeal. Dissatisfied with the lack of help from his offense, Cain took matters into his own hands in the 2010 postseason, logging 21 1/3 innings without permitting an earned run. Soon after, the early exertion took its toll on Cain's right arm, which bled velocity and required surgery to remove bone chips from his elbow. He never recovered his young form and chose to hang 'em up at 33, retiring as the first pitcher since World War II to throw 2,000 innings for the Giants and none for any other team.

Seth Corry LHP Born: 11/03/98 Age: 19 Bats: L Throws: L Height: 6'2" Weight: 195 Origin: Round 3, 2017 Draft (#96 overall)

YEAR	TEAM	LVL	AGE	W	L	SV	G	GS	IP	H	HR	BB/9	K/9	K	GB%	BABIP	WHIP	ERA	DRA	WARP	MPH	CMD	PWR	STM
2017	GIA	RK	18	0	2	0	13	10	24^1	14	1	8.1	7.8	21	46%	.203	1.48	5.55	11.36	-1.3				
2018	*SFN*	*MLB*	*19*	*0*	*4*	*0*	*10*	*6*	*26*	*30*	*7*	*16.2*	*9.2*	*27*	*38%*	*.334*	*2.95*	*10.39*	*12.32*	*-2.0*				
2019	*SFN*	*MLB*	*20*	*3*	*5*	*0*	*32*	*17*	*118^1*	*130*	*22*	*4.5*	*7.0*	*92*	*38%*	*.323*	*1.60*	*5.52*	*6.64*	*-0.9*				

Comparables: Thyago Vieira, Brad Hand, Jairo Labourt

When the Giants selected Corry in the third round last summer, it marked the first time since 2007 that the club had used its first three selections on high-schoolers. Corry, a left-handed Utahan who also played football as a prep, got $1 million ($450,000 above slot value) to forgo a commitment to BYU. Raw stuff is the main attraction here, with a heavy fastball that touches 94 and a curve that flashes plus, both coming from a loose arm with above-average arm speed. Like most teenagers, Corry has yet to harness his changeup or command, and his release point tends to wander, in part because of poor rhythm. Now that he's left the gridiron for the diamond full time, Corry can focus on fixing all that. He has a mid-rotation ceiling, with the fastball-hook combo providing a late-inning fallback if the command never comes.

Kyle Crick RHP Born: 11/30/92 Age: 25 Bats: L Throws: R Height: 6'4" Weight: 220 Origin: Round 1, 2011 Draft (#49 overall)

YEAR	TEAM	LVL	AGE	W	L	SV	G	GS	IP	H	HR	BB/9	K/9	K	GB%	BABIP	WHIP	ERA	DRA	WARP	MPH	CMD	PWR	STM
2015	RIC	AA	22	3	4	0	36	11	63	47	2	9.4	10.4	73	36%	.292	1.79	3.29	13.16	-6.2				
2016	RIC	AA	23	4	11	0	23	23	109	110	8	5.5	7.1	86	46%	.311	1.62	5.04	7.55	-3.2				
2017	SAC	AAA	24	1	2	6	24	0	29^1	24	1	4.0	12.0	39	45%	.329	1.26	2.76	3.28	0.6				
2017	SFN	MLB	24	0	0	0	30	0	32^1	22	2	4.7	7.8	28	39%	.233	1.21	3.06	4.37	0.3	96.7	50	67	47
2018	*SFN*	*MLB*	*25*	*3*	*2*	*0*	*52*	*0*	*55^1*	*49*	*6*	*5.6*	*10.0*	*61*	*41%*	*.299*	*1.51*	*4.34*	*4.93*	*0.0*	*96.4*	*51*	*69*	*48*
2019	*SFN*	*MLB*	*26*	*2*	*1*	*0*	*49*	*0*	*52^1*	*43*	*6*	*4.9*	*10.4*	*61*	*41%*	*.309*	*1.37*	*3.97*	*4.80*	*0.2*	*96.1*	*51*	*69*	*48*

Breakout: 18% Improve: 35% Collapse: 17% Attrition: 27% MLB: 60% *Comparables: Aaron Poreda, Clint Nageotte, Dustin Nippert*

Crick was drafted as the quintessential prep pitcher lottery ticket: born and raised in Texas, blessed with a live arm and sturdy frame, and still working through the wobbly command that hampers most every teenager while he settles into his adult body. Six years later, Crick still has the arm strength and workhorse build, he still has the aggressive #Texan mind-set—and he still has trouble throwing strikes. What he no longer has is the teenager's book of excuses, and because he's had half a decade to straighten out his command, he's also no longer a starter. In his first test as a big-league reliever, he led the league in slider spin rate (min. 200 pitches) and allowed just an 83.4 mph average exit velocity, but also averaged the third-most pitches per plate appearance (4.52) and only 1.65 strikeouts per walk. Both flaws were by-products of falling behind in the count, something Crick will have to avoid to earn high-leverage work going forward.

Johnny Cueto RHP Born: 02/15/86 Age: 32 Bats: R Throws: R Height: 5'11" Weight: 220 Origin: International Free Agent, 2004

YEAR	TEAM	LVL	AGE	W	L	SV	G	GS	IP	H	HR	BB/9	K/9	K	GB%	BABIP	WHIP	ERA	DRA	WARP	MPH	CMD	PWR	STM
2015	CIN	MLB	29	7	6	0	19	19	130^2	93	11	2.0	8.3	120	45%	.234	0.93	2.62	2.97	3.3	95.3	68	47	79
2015	KCA	MLB	29	4	7	0	13	13	81^1	101	10	1.9	6.2	56	43%	.343	1.45	4.76	3.35	1.7	95.0	68	47	79
2016	SFN	MLB	30	18	5	0	32	32	219^2	195	15	1.8	8.1	198	52%	.293	1.09	2.79	3.31	5.2	94.3	62	42	84
2017	SFN	MLB	31	8	8	0	25	25	147^1	160	22	3.2	8.3	136	41%	.322	1.45	4.52	5.07	0.8	93.1	60	39	69
2018	*SFN*	*MLB*	*32*	*9*	*8*	*0*	*24*	*24*	*144*	*134*	*15*	*2.6*	*7.9*	*126*	*46%*	*.288*	*1.21*	*3.56*	*4.38*	*1.3*	*93.2*	*62*	*42*	*76*
2019	*SFN*	*MLB*	*33*	*12*	*11*	*0*	*33*	*33*	*212^2*	*176*	*20*	*2.4*	*8.0*	*189*	*46%*	*.286*	*1.09*	*3.24*	*3.99*	*3.5*	*92.5*	*61*	*40*	*75*

Breakout: 14% Improve: 34% Collapse: 37% Attrition: 11% MLB: 91% *Comparables: Zack Greinke, Justin Verlander, Roy Oswalt*

Heading into the 2017 season, Cueto seemed certain to exercise the looming opt-out clause in his contract, to cash in one more time before turning 32. Fans dreaded his departure, having fallen in love with an eclectic ace who turned disrupting hitters' timing into an art. With little free agent competition, attaining four years and $84 million seemed like a cinch for the shimmying starter. Six months later, it was anything but. After a season marred by blisters and a forearm strain, it wasn't Cueto's exit that had fans on edge, but his decision to stay. Now that Cueto has opted into the remainder of his contract, the Giants are assured of his services through 2021. If the 2016 edition resurfaces, the 2017 debacle that kept him around may be a blessing in disguise. If it doesn't, they'll be paying frontline money to a back-end arm.

Tyler Cyr RHP Born: 05/05/93 Age: 25 Bats: R Throws: R Height: 6'3" Weight: 200 Origin: Round 10, 2015 Draft (#306 overall)

YEAR	TEAM	LVL	AGE	W	L	SV	G	GS	IP	H	HR	BB/9	K/9	K	GB%	BABIP	WHIP	ERA	DRA	WARP	MPH	CMD	PWR	STM
2015	AUG	A	22	2	1	0	12	0	17^2	16	0	9.2	10.2	20	58%	.320	1.92	5.60	8.57	-0.8				
2016	AUG	A	23	3	3	2	20	0	50^2	36	1	2.8	11.5	65	56%	.299	1.03	2.31	2.40	1.4				
2016	SJO	A+	23	2	1	1	19	0	23	19	1	3.5	9.4	24	60%	.316	1.22	2.35	2.55	0.7				
2017	RIC	AA	24	5	2	18	47	0	49^1	50	3	3.6	10.4	57	54%	.343	1.42	2.19	2.57	1.3				
2018	*SFN*	*MLB*	*25*	*2*	*1*	*2*	*43*	*0*	*46*	*45*	*6*	*4.9*	*9.9*	*50*	*49%*	*.332*	*1.52*	*4.47*	*5.42*	*-0.2*				
2019	*SFN*	*MLB*	*26*	*1*	*1*	*1*	*29*	*0*	*42*	*38*	*6*	*4.2*	*9.6*	*45*	*49%*	*.319*	*1.38*	*4.08*	*4.94*	*0.1*				

Breakout: 14% Improve: 16% Collapse: 8% Attrition: 18% MLB: 24% *Comparables: Tyler Sturdevant, Neil Wagner, Jaye Chapman*

Cyr was 5-foot-11, 165 pounds as a senior in high school, sitting in the mid-80s and mulling his future after baseball. Then he hit a late growth spurt, took his weight training more seriously and found himself blowing mid-90s gas by hitters as they pondered the pronunciation of his last name. It's "sear," to save you the Google query, and the surname is far from the most intriguing aspect of his story. Cyr spent his collegiate days at Embry-Riddle Aeronautical University, home to future astronauts, aviation engineers and air traffic controllers—but not any major-league ballplayers. A potential middle reliever, Cyr is racing the Cardinals' Daniel Poncedeleon to become the first ERAU Eagle to reach the bigs.

Sam Dyson RHP Born: 05/07/88 Age: 30 Bats: R Throws: R Height: 6'1" Weight: 205 Origin: Round 4, 2010 Draft (#126 overall)

YEAR	TEAM	LVL	AGE	W	L	SV	G	GS	IP	H	HR	BB/9	K/9	K	GB%	BABIP	WHIP	ERA	DRA	WARP	MPH	CMD	PWR	STM
2015	MIA	MLB	27	3	3	0	44	0	44	41	3	3.5	8.4	41	65%	.302	1.32	3.68	2.30	1.3	98.5	44	77	53
2015	TEX	MLB	27	2	1	2	31	0	31^1	24	1	1.1	8.6	30	76%	.277	0.89	1.15	2.18	0.9	98.6	44	77	53
2016	TEX	MLB	28	3	2	38	73	0	70^1	63	5	2.9	7.0	55	65%	.291	1.22	2.43	2.91	1.7	98.2	44	68	50
2017	TEX	MLB	29	1	6	0	17	0	16^2	31	6	6.5	3.8	7	62%	.379	2.58	10.80	5.25	0.0	96.6	40	66	45
2017	SFN	MLB	29	3	4	14	38	0	38	36	2	4.3	6.4	27	67%	.286	1.42	4.03	6.02	-0.4	96.7	40	66	45
2018	*SFN*	*MLB*	*30*	*3*	*2*	*5*	*52*	*0*	55^1	*55*	*4*	*3.8*	*7.2*	*44*	*60%*	*.299*	*1.41*	*3.77*	*4.51*	*0.2*	*97.0*	*42*	*70*	*49*
2019	*SFN*	*MLB*	*31*	*3*	*1*	*3*	*52*	*0*	*55*	*51*	*4*	*3.7*	*7.4*	*45*	*60%*	*.312*	*1.33*	*3.46*	*4.25*	*0.6*	*96.4*	*42*	*67*	*47*

Breakout: 28% Improve: 55% Collapse: 24% Attrition: 15% MLB: 84% *Comparables: Jared Hughes, Brad Ziegler, Chad Qualls*

For an example of reliever volatility, look no further than Dyson's first half of 2017, when he went from Rangers reject to Giants closer in less than a month. The renaissance came after the red-haired righty manipulated his cutter, raising its velocity from the mid-80s to the low-90s, and used it to replace some of his ineffective sinkers. Still, Dyson's strikeout rate stayed well below his early-career highs, held down by the minimal velocity variance in his three-pitch mix. Everything Dyson throws either touches or exceeds 90, and since he does little to disrupt hitters' timing, a small hiccup in command makes him more vulnerable than the typical flamethrower. Dyson has the power stuff and stoic demeanor of a late-inning reliever, but he'll need to get craftier to continue working the ninth.

Cory Gearrin RHP Born: 04/14/86 Age: 32 Bats: R Throws: R Height: 6'3" Weight: 200 Origin: Round 4, 2007 Draft (#138 overall)

YEAR	TEAM	LVL	AGE	W	L	SV	G	GS	IP	H	HR	BB/9	K/9	K	GB%	BABIP	WHIP	ERA	DRA	WARP	MPH	CMD	PWR	STM
2015	SAC	AAA	29	2	2	0	33	0	43	38	4	2.9	9.6	46	46%	.293	1.21	2.72	3.00	0.9				
2015	SFN	MLB	29	0	0	0	7	0	3^2	1	0	2.5	12.3	5	100%	.143	0.55	4.91	1.79	0.1	94.4			39
2016	SFN	MLB	30	3	2	3	56	0	48^1	42	4	2.6	8.4	45	56%	.286	1.16	4.28	3.22	1.0	94.0	50	45	45
2017	SFN	MLB	31	4	3	0	68	0	68	50	4	4.6	8.5	64	49%	.263	1.25	1.99	4.11	0.8	93.6	45	44	50
2018	*SFN*	*MLB*	*32*	*3*	*2*	*0*	*48*	*0*	50^1	*47*	*5*	*3.9*	*8.4*	*47*	*49%*	*.296*	*1.36*	*3.91*	*4.62*	*0.2*	*92.8*	*46*	*44*	*45*
2019	*SFN*	*MLB*	*33*	*3*	*1*	*0*	*51*	*0*	54^1	*47*	*6*	*3.8*	*8.4*	*51*	*49%*	*.302*	*1.29*	*3.82*	*4.65*	*0.3*	*92.4*	*46*	*44*	*46*

Breakout: 24% Improve: 45% Collapse: 20% Attrition: 10% MLB: 81% *Comparables: Jared Burton, Bobby Seay, Matt Thornton*

The Gearrin owner's manual is a veritable tome, but the right-hander has value in a narrowly tailored role. While Gearrin limits lefties' power better than most side-slingers, he struggles to keep them off base and is a liability without the platoon advantage in hand. To further limit his utility, Gearrin's hellacious movement spawns control problems so pronounced that he's a disaster in waiting if called upon with runners on base. And even if the bags are clear, Gearrin works at such a glacial pace that other options are preferable if anyone has dinner reservations or a flight to catch. Despite all that, pitchers who can hold right-handed batters to a .612 lifetime OPS have a place in a big-league bullpen, and Gearrin should remain employed as long as that split holds up.

Joan Gregorio RHP Born: 01/12/92 Age: 26 Bats: R Throws: R Height: 6'7" Weight: 180 Origin: International Free Agent, 2010

YEAR	TEAM	LVL	AGE	W	L	SV	G	GS	IP	H	HR	BB/9	K/9	K	GB%	BABIP	WHIP	ERA	DRA	WARP	MPH	CMD	PWR	STM
2015	RIC	AA	23	3	2	1	37	9	78^2	64	6	3.7	8.2	72	38%	.272	1.22	3.09	4.33	0.6				
2016	RIC	AA	24	0	2	0	5	5	27	15	1	2.0	10.0	30	48%	.222	0.78	2.33	1.81	1.1				
2016	SAC	AAA	24	6	8	0	21	21	107^1	112	13	3.6	10.2	122	37%	.343	1.44	5.28	3.15	2.7				
2017	SAC	AAA	25	4	4	0	13	13	74	63	9	4.3	7.4	61	34%	.266	1.32	3.04	7.13	-1.1				
2018	*SFN*	*MLB*	*26*	*3*	*4*	*0*	*10*	*10*	*50*	*50*	*8*	*4.0*	*8.6*	*48*	*37%*	*.296*	*1.44*	*4.43*	*5.33*	*-0.1*				
2019	*SFN*	*MLB*	*27*	*9*	*11*	*0*	*31*	*31*	*202*	*182*	*30*	*3.1*	*8.8*	*198*	*37%*	*.301*	*1.24*	*4.04*	*4.88*	*1.3*				

Breakout: 22% Improve: 29% Collapse: 7% Attrition: 30% MLB: 40% *Comparables: Steve Johnson, Daniel McCutchen, Neil Ramirez*

Stanozolol is no laughing matter, especially not for a pitcher in his mid-twenties and still climbing the organizational ladder. The banned substance cut short Gregorio's 2017 season, stunting the command and pitch development that was supposed to come as he repeated Triple-A. Gregorio exhibits the pros and cons of a long-levered frame: His sinker-slider tandem plays up because of the extension in his delivery, but he struggles to repeat the motion and his fits of wildness are unbecoming of a big-league starter. Given the time lost to suspension last season and injury in years past, the Dominican's future probably lies in the bullpen, where a manager can shield Gregorio from left-handed opponents until he finds a way to combat them himself.

Derek Law RHP Born: 09/14/90 Age: 27 Bats: R Throws: R Height: 6'2" Weight: 210 Origin: Round 9, 2011 Draft (#297 overall)

YEAR	TEAM	LVL	AGE	W	L	SV	G	GS	IP	H	HR	BB/9	K/9	K	GB%	BABIP	WHIP	ERA	DRA	WARP	MPH	CMD	PWR	STM
2015	RIC	AA	24	0	1	13	28	0	25^2	31	1	2.8	11.2	32	45%	.400	1.52	4.56	1.87	0.9				
2016	SFN	MLB	25	4	2	1	61	0	55	44	3	1.5	8.2	50	50%	.270	0.96	2.13	3.38	1.0	96.2	40	44	44
2017	SAC	AAA	26	1	1	10	25	0	32^2	32	1	3.3	7.2	26	52%	.316	1.35	2.48	3.56	0.6				
2017	SFN	MLB	26	4	1	4	41	0	37^1	45	5	3.4	8.4	35	40%	.357	1.58	5.06	6.41	-0.5	95.7	44	45	51
2018	*SFN*	*MLB*	*27*	*3*	*2*	*0*	*48*	*0*	50^1	*49*	*5*	*3.5*	*8.3*	*47*	*45%*	*.305*	*1.38*	*3.68*	*4.43*	*0.3*	*95.5*	*42*	*45*	*48*
2019	*SFN*	*MLB*	*28*	*3*	*1*	*0*	*52*	*0*	*55*	*51*	*6*	*3.2*	*8.4*	*52*	*45%*	*.316*	*1.28*	*3.51*	*4.29*	*0.5*	*95.2*	*42*	*45*	*48*

Breakout: 21% Improve: 36% Collapse: 20% Attrition: 24% MLB: 76% *Comparables: Scott Oberg, Fu-Te Ni, Tanner Scheppers*

Aside from a mid-90s fastball, Law wields two breaking balls that differ in velocity, break and plane. Or, at least, they're supposed to. For the first three months of the season, the right-hander's curve and slider merged into a single, hybrid slurve that split the gap and turned Law into a batting-practice arm. In nine outings preceding his midyear demotion to Sacramento, he was torched for 20 hits, four homers and four walks in just 8 2/3 innings, before the Giants conceded that their young reliever was broken. Two months spent refining his breaking pitches enabled Law to resurface in September with his curve and slider distinct once more. As long as they retain their distinctive forms, he should return to the bullpen's inner circle this year.

Mark Melancon RHP Born: 03/28/85 Age: 33 Bats: R Throws: R Height: 6'2" Weight: 210 Origin: Round 9, 2006 Draft (#284 overall)

YEAR	TEAM	LVL	AGE	W	L	SV	G	GS	IP	H	HR	BB/9	K/9	K	GB%	BABIP	WHIP	ERA	DRA	WARP	MPH	CMD	PWR	STM
2015	PIT	MLB	30	3	2	51	78	0	76^2	57	4	1.6	7.3	62	58%	.251	0.93	2.23	2.43	2.1	93.7	65	48	53
2016	PIT	MLB	31	1	1	30	45	0	41^2	31	2	1.9	8.2	38	49%	.257	0.96	1.51	2.44	1.2	93.3	75	52	50
2016	WAS	MLB	31	1	1	17	30	0	29^2	21	1	0.9	8.2	27	65%	.263	0.81	1.82	2.50	0.8	93.7	75	52	50
2017	SFN	MLB	32	1	2	11	32	0	30	37	3	1.8	8.7	29	54%	.374	1.43	4.50	4.91	0.1	93.1	64	52	32
2018	*SFN*	*MLB*	*33*	*3*	*2*	*33*	*57*	*0*	60^1	*55*	*5*	*2.8*	*8.0*	*53*	*51%*	*.292*	*1.23*	*3.26*	*4.07*	*0.6*	*92.4*	*68*	*50*	*43*
2019	*SFN*	*MLB*	*34*	*3*	*1*	*30*	*61*	*0*	64^1	*56*	*7*	*2.7*	*7.8*	*56*	*51%*	*.293*	*1.16*	*3.48*	*4.28*	*0.6*	*91.8*	*69*	*51*	*40*

Breakout: 22% Improve: 45% Collapse: 32% Attrition: 10% MLB: 93% *Comparables: Mariano Rivera, Jason Isringhausen, Casey Janssen*

Baseball executives must be both retrospective and forward-looking, addressing the previous season's flaws while anticipating the new ones sure to sprout. The Giants did only the former with their marquee offseason acquisition of 2016-17, leaving Melancon with the unfair burden of being the team's sole savior. He faltered on day one and the flexor-pronator mass in his forearm faltered soon after, ultimately requiring season-ending surgery. Along the way, Melancon went 11-for-16 in save tries and ceded the job to Sam Dyson, teaching the Giants a $16 million lesson in reliever volatility. With $46 million of learning left to do, the Giants will hope that renewed health brings back Melancon's best cutter and curveball, while turning their attention to all the other issues his arrival didn't solve.

Reyes Moronta RHP Born: 01/06/93 Age: 25 Bats: R Throws: R Height: 6'0" Weight: 175 Origin: International Free Agent, 2011

YEAR	TEAM	LVL	AGE	W	L	SV	G	GS	IP	H	HR	BB/9	K/9	K	GB%	BABIP	WHIP	ERA	DRA	WARP	MPH	CMD	PWR	STM
2015	AUG	A	22	1	7	12	42	0	48^2	56	1	4.3	11.8	64	48%	.401	1.62	5.73	2.21	1.5				
2016	SJO	A+	23	0	3	14	60	0	59	43	7	3.1	14.2	93	34%	.295	1.07	2.59	1.15	2.6				
2017	RIC	AA	24	0	1	5	19	0	18	15	1	6.0	13.0	26	42%	.333	1.50	4.00	3.26	0.3				
2017	SAC	AAA	24	3	0	0	13	0	17	13	1	4.2	9.0	17	33%	.273	1.24	2.12	5.02	0.0				
2017	SFN	MLB	24	0	0	0	7	0	6^2	6	1	4.1	14.9	11	47%	.357	1.35	2.70	4.03	0.1	97.5			34
2018	*SFN*	*MLB*	*25*	*1*	*1*	*0*	*24*	*0*	*25*	*24*	*4*	*4.8*	*10.9*	*30*	*38%*	*.307*	*1.52*	*4.71*	*5.25*	*-0.1*	*97.2*			*35*
2019	*SFN*	*MLB*	*26*	*2*	*1*	*1*	*48*	*0*	50^2	*44*	*8*	*4.2*	*11.1*	*63*	*38%*	*.317*	*1.33*	*4.06*	*4.89*	*0.2*	*96.9*			*35*

Breakout: 16% Improve: 23% Collapse: 4% Attrition: 23% MLB: 31% *Comparables: Jimmie Sherfy, Derek Law, Santiago Casilla*

There may exist an alternate universe where Moronta's afore-printed weight is accurate, but in that world his fastball averages 64 mph, gas costs $1.50 a gallon and it takes only 180 electoral votes to win the U.S. presidency. The rotund right-hander throws his generous boiler around in a max-effort motion, generating mid-90s velocity and giving arm-side batters a tough angle from which to pick up the ball. Throw a plus slider into the equation and you've got the building blocks for a late-inning reliever, though given his delivery, the jury's still out on whether Moronta can attain even fringe-average control. If he can't, the stuff alone gives him a middle-inning matchup floor, ideal for right-on-right battles with men in scoring position and less than two outs.

Steven Okert LHP Born: 07/09/91 Age: 26 Bats: L Throws: L Height: 6'3" Weight: 210 Origin: Round 4, 2012 Draft (#148 overall)

YEAR	TEAM	LVL	AGE	W	L	SV	G	GS	IP	H	HR	BB/9	K/9	K	GB%	BABIP	WHIP	ERA	DRA	WARP	MPH	CMD	PWR	STM
2015	SAC	AAA	23	5	3	3	52	0	61^1	62	7	4.3	10.1	69	46%	.337	1.48	3.82	3.58	0.9				
2016	SAC	AAA	24	4	3	3	41	0	47^1	53	2	2.1	11.4	60	42%	.370	1.35	3.80	2.06	1.6				
2016	SFN	MLB	24	0	0	0	16	0	14	14	2	2.6	9.0	14	42%	.316	1.29	3.21	6.41	-0.2	94.4	52	43	45
2017	SAC	AAA	25	3	0	6	24	0	25^1	15	4	2.8	7.5	21	45%	.180	0.91	3.20	4.70	0.2				
2017	SFN	MLB	25	1	1	0	44	0	27	24	3	3.7	7.3	22	34%	.266	1.30	5.67	7.56	-0.7	93.5	37	42	46
2018	*SFN*	*MLB*	*26*	*1*	*1*	*0*	*24*	*0*	*25*	*25*	*3*	*3.6*	*9.1*	*25*	*41%*	*.301*	*1.38*	*4.10*	*4.76*	*0.0*	*93.4*	*42*	*43*	*46*
2019	*SFN*	*MLB*	*27*	*2*	*1*	*1*	*47*	*0*	*50*	*46*	*7*	*3.4*	*9.0*	*50*	*41%*	*.308*	*1.30*	*4.01*	*4.86*	*0.2*	*93.1*	*42*	*43*	*46*

Breakout: 28% Improve: 35% Collapse: 17% Attrition: 20% MLB: 59% *Comparables: Edgmer Escalona, Fernando Salas, Pedro Strop*

Mechanical inconsistencies have dogged Okert since his days at the University of Oklahoma, and the southpaw is still searching for a delivery that preserves his raw stuff while keeping him on line to the plate. Okert pitches from the extreme first-base side of the rubber, and his low-three-quarters slot creates a severe horizontal plane that both deceives left-handed hitters and hampers his control. A slightly higher arm angle appeared to help Okert throw more strikes in the second half of September, but the current version doesn't miss enough bats or manage contact well enough to warrant high-leverage trust, even as a specialist. With an option year left, Okert may face another year of Triple-A bus rides while he tries to earn his keep in middle relief.

Josh Osich LHP Born: 09/03/88 Age: 29 Bats: L Throws: L Height: 6'2" Weight: 230 Origin: Round 6, 2011 Draft (#207 overall)

YEAR	TEAM	LVL	AGE	W	L	SV	G	GS	IP	H	HR	BB/9	K/9	K	GB%	BABIP	WHIP	ERA	DRA	WARP	MPH	CMD	PWR	STM
2015	RIC	AA	26	0	1	19	31	0	34	23	1	2.6	9.0	34	60%	.242	0.97	1.59	3.25	0.6				
2015	SFN	MLB	26	2	0	0	35	0	28^2	24	4	2.5	8.5	27	49%	.247	1.12	2.20	4.40	0.1	97.8	44	59	51
2016	SFN	MLB	27	1	3	0	59	0	36^1	31	7	4.7	6.2	25	65%	.226	1.38	4.71	4.87	0.0	98.5	27	67	44
2017	SFN	MLB	28	3	2	0	54	0	43^1	48	7	5.6	8.9	43	46%	.333	1.73	6.23	7.00	-0.9	97.1	33	52	47
2018	*SFN*	*MLB*	*29*	*3*	*2*	*0*	*48*	*0*	50^1	*49*	*7*	*3.9*	*8.4*	*47*	*51%*	*.295*	*1.41*	*4.51*	*5.08*	*-0.1*	*97.0*	*33*	*58*	*47*
2019	*SFN*	*MLB*	*30*	*2*	*1*	*0*	*45*	*0*	47^2	*43*	*6*	*4.2*	*8.5*	*45*	*51%*	*.302*	*1.37*	*4.28*	*5.18*	*0.0*	*96.6*	*31*	*57*	*46*

Breakout: 20% Improve: 39% Collapse: 21% Attrition: 24% MLB: 65% *Comparables: Ryan Mattheus, Fernando Rodney, Doug Slaten*

If velocity were all that mattered, Osich would be one of the game's best lefties. He had the ninth-fastest average four-seamer last season—nearly 96 mph—among 43 southpaw relievers who threw at least 250 of them. But within that same batch of 43, Osich also generated the fewest whiffs per swing (10 percent), and no one else who lit up the gun at 95-plus was within 8.7 percentage points of the former Oregon State Beaver. With no fear of being blown away, batters exercised patience, hitting .330/.453/.563 after taking the first pitch. Unless Osich finds consistent secondaries to get hitters off his fastball in deeper counts, or fine-tunes his command to limit mistakes, he'll be known as the league's hardest-throwing mopup man, wearing wasted arm talent on his sleeve.

Jeff Samardzija RHP Born: 01/23/85 Age: 33 Bats: R Throws: R Height: 6'5" Weight: 225 Origin: Round 5, 2006 Draft (#149 overall)

YEAR	TEAM	LVL	AGE	W	L	SV	G	GS	IP	H	HR	BB/9	K/9	K	GB%	BABIP	WHIP	ERA	DRA	WARP	MPH	CMD	PWR	STM
2015	CHA	MLB	30	11	13	0	32	32	214	228	29	2.1	6.9	163	41%	.303	1.29	4.96	4.94	0.3	96.8	46	58	83
2016	SFN	MLB	31	12	11	0	32	32	203^{1}	190	24	2.4	7.4	167	47%	.285	1.20	3.81	3.83	3.6	96.7	51	59	81
2017	SFN	MLB	32	9	15	0	32	32	207^{2}	204	30	1.4	8.9	205	43%	.303	1.14	4.42	3.63	4.5	96.3	62	56	83
2018	*SFN*	*MLB*	*33*	*13*	*10*	*0*	*29*	*29*	*194^{1}*	*186*	*22*	*2.3*	*8.1*	*175*	*44%*	*.295*	*1.22*	*3.44*	*4.24*	*2.1*	*95.5*	*54*	*57*	*81*
2019	*SFN*	*MLB*	*34*	*14*	*11*	*0*	*33*	*33*	*212^{1}*	*191*	*22*	*1.8*	*8.2*	*194*	*44%*	*.304*	*1.10*	*3.11*	*3.84*	*4.2*	*94.9*	*56*	*56*	*81*

Breakout: 14% Improve: 47% Collapse: 25% Attrition: 13% MLB: 91% *Comparables: Roy Oswalt, Johan Santana, Josh Beckett*

Samardzija led the National League in innings and issued the second-fewest walks of any starter, exceeding only Clayton Kershaw in that category despite logging 32 2/3 more frames than the Dodgers' ace. Samardzija was fourth in the senior circuit in throwing first-pitch strikes, trailing only Kershaw, Michael Wacha and John Lackey, the last of whom shared his biggest bugaboo. Samardzija surrendered 30 homers, 40 doubles and 12 triples—a whopping 82 extra-base hits, only some of which were the fault of poor outfield defense. The rest were a function of a predictable get-ahead, stay-ahead game plan, which produced 29 extra-baggers in no-ball counts, confirming that too much of a good thing (strikes) can indeed be bad. Still, 2017 was the second-best year of the consistently durable Samardzija's career according to WARP, and if he can improve his sequencing while maintaining his stuff, he might remain a good no. 3 starter well into his thirties.

Will Smith LHP Born: 07/10/89 Age: 28 Bats: R Throws: L Height: 6'5" Weight: 265 Origin: Round 7, 2008 Draft (#229 overall)

YEAR	TEAM	LVL	AGE	W	L	SV	G	GS	IP	H	HR	BB/9	K/9	K	GB%	BABIP	WHIP	ERA	DRA	WARP	MPH	CMD	PWR	STM
2015	MIL	MLB	25	7	2	0	76	0	63^{1}	52	5	3.4	12.9	91	48%	.329	1.20	2.70	2.83	1.4	95.8	43	43	52
2016	MIL	MLB	26	1	3	0	27	0	22	18	3	3.7	9.0	22	42%	.263	1.23	3.68	4.13	0.2	94.2	63	38	47
2016	SFN	MLB	26	1	1	0	26	0	18^{1}	13	0	4.4	12.8	26	40%	.325	1.20	2.95	3.40	0.3	95.0	63	38	47
2018	*SFN*	*MLB*	*28*	*2*	*2*	*0*	*43*	*0*	*45^{1}*	*38*	*4*	*3.8*	*11.2*	*56*	*43%*	*.304*	*1.26*	*2.90*	*3.72*	*0.6*	*94.7*	*52*	*41*	*49*
2019	*SFN*	*MLB*	*29*	*2*	*1*	*0*	*39*	*0*	*41^{2}*	*40*	*6*	*3.8*	*7.9*	*36*	*43%*	*.307*	*1.39*	*4.47*	*5.44*	*-0.1*	*94.0*	*57*	*40*	*49*

Breakout: 30% Improve: 49% Collapse: 32% Attrition: 19% MLB: 92% *Comparables: Sergio Santos, Antonio Bastardo, Boone Logan*

Throughout the even-year-magic era, the left-handed wing of the Giants bullpen belonged to Jeremy Affeldt and Javier Lopez. The former pioneered Andrew Miller's postseason role, while the latter's four championship rings are a testament to the importance of having a great LOOGY. As the veteran southpaws retired, the duo moved upstairs, taking turns in the color broadcaster's seat on road trips, while Smith—the heir apparent acquired from the Brewers at the 2016 trade deadline—moved downstairs to the clubhouse, occupying the trainer's table as he recovered from Tommy John surgery. Without his services, the Giants bullpen fell into disarray, as all of the lefties they employed combined for a 6.01 ERA. Smith may not be Miller, or even the peak version of Affeldt, but his absence in 2017 was a reminder that you don't fully appreciate the value of southpaw stability until it's gone.

Chris Stratton RHP Born: 08/22/90 Age: 27 Bats: R Throws: R Height: 6'3" Weight: 190 Origin: Round 1, 2012 Draft (#20 overall)

YEAR	TEAM	LVL	AGE	W	L	SV	G	GS	IP	H	HR	BB/9	K/9	K	GB%	BABIP	WHIP	ERA	DRA	WARP	MPH	CMD	PWR	STM
2015	RIC	AA	24	1	5	0	9	9	50	40	3	4.0	7.0	39	48%	.252	1.24	4.14	5.07	0.0				
2015	SAC	AAA	24	4	5	0	17	17	98	88	6	3.7	6.6	72	47%	.281	1.31	3.86	5.82	-0.6				
2016	SFN	MLB	25	1	0	0	7	0	10	11	1	4.5	5.4	6	38%	.323	1.60	3.60	5.85	-0.1	94.1			61
2016	SAC	AAA	25	12	6	0	21	20	125^{2}	120	6	2.8	7.4	103	45%	.305	1.27	3.87	3.56	2.6				
2017	SAC	AAA	26	4	5	0	15	15	79^{1}	94	10	2.5	8.1	71	53%	.340	1.46	5.11	2.51	2.7				
2017	SFN	MLB	26	4	4	1	13	10	58^{2}	59	5	4.3	7.8	51	46%	.316	1.48	3.68	4.47	0.7	93.3	61	44	62
2018	*SFN*	*MLB*	*27*	*6*	*6*	*0*	*18*	*18*	*95*	*94*	*9*	*3.3*	*7.5*	*80*	*46%*	*.297*	*1.35*	*3.65*	*4.49*	*0.7*	*92.9*	*62*	*45*	*62*
2019	*SFN*	*MLB*	*28*	*10*	*10*	*0*	*32*	*32*	*206*	*184*	*19*	*3.0*	*7.8*	*179*	*46%*	*.302*	*1.23*	*3.46*	*4.23*	*2.6*	*92.5*	*62*	*44*	*62*

Breakout: 21% Improve: 39% Collapse: 14% Attrition: 23% MLB: 65% *Comparables: Anthony Ranaudo, Chris Heston, Joe Biagini*

Beyond the superficial statistics, curveball rate was one of the best predictors last season of whether a team made the playoffs. Seven of the top eight clubs in that metric lived on into October, as analytically inclined organizations learned quickly that heat-craving hitters could not handle the hook. All of that is excellent news for Stratton, because among pitchers who kicked and dealt 500-plus times in 2017, the Mississippian had the highest average spin rate on his curve. RPMs aren't everything, but Stratton hurdled the Rich Hills and David Robertsons of the world, outspinning pitchers far more reliant on the breaking ball than he was. Which raises the question: Why didn't he throw it more often? The former first-rounder's most effective offering composed just under one-fifth of an otherwise average mix, and there isn't an obvious reason for him to be on a 20-80 diet. If an offseason of poring over the data produces the anticipated adjustment, Stratton might be a breakout candidate at the back of the rotation this year.

Hunter Strickland RHP Born: 09/24/88 Age: 29 Bats: R Throws: R Height: 6'4" Weight: 220 Origin: Round 18, 2007 Draft (#564 overall)

YEAR	TEAM	LVL	AGE	W	L	SV	G	GS	IP	H	HR	BB/9	K/9	K	GB%	BABIP	WHIP	ERA	DRA	WARP	MPH	CMD	PWR	STM
2015	SAC	AAA	26	1	1	5	15	0	21^{2}	14	0	1.2	10.4	25	69%	.275	0.78	1.66	1.54	0.8				
2015	SFN	MLB	26	3	3	0	55	0	51^{1}	34	4	1.8	8.8	50	40%	.240	0.86	2.45	3.18	0.9	99.3	54	74	51
2016	SFN	MLB	27	3	3	3	72	0	61	50	4	2.8	8.4	57	47%	.274	1.13	3.10	3.33	1.1	99.5	48	68	50
2017	SFN	MLB	28	4	3	1	68	0	61^{1}	59	4	4.3	8.5	58	38%	.314	1.43	2.64	4.88	0.2	97.5	55	67	48
2018	*SFN*	*MLB*	*29*	*3*	*2*	*2*	*52*	*0*	*55^{1}*	*51*	*6*	*3.6*	*8.6*	*53*	*44%*	*.293*	*1.31*	*3.73*	*4.46*	*0.3*	*97.9*	*52*	*69*	*49*
2019	*SFN*	*MLB*	*30*	*3*	*1*	*2*	*58*	*0*	*61*	*52*	*7*	*3.2*	*9.0*	*61*	*44%*	*.299*	*1.20*	*3.52*	*4.30*	*0.6*	*97.4*	*52*	*68*	*49*

Breakout: 29% Improve: 49% Collapse: 31% Attrition: 18% MLB: 95% *Comparables: Steve Cishek, Justin Wilson, Bobby Jenks*

Run-ins with Bryce Harper aside, Strickland managed left-handed hitters adequately for a right-handed setup man in his first two full big-league seasons. Then came 2017, when a dip in fastball velocity widened his split into a canyon. The country hardballer continued to clamp down on righties, but glove-side batters were not intimidated by either his mid-90s heat or slurvy breaking ball, walking as often as they struck out in 109 plate appearances for a .337 TAv. While Strickland once resembled a future closer, he now seems destined for middle-inning matchup duty, and his velocity no longer sets him apart. He'll need to find a way to survive sans the platoon advantage to avoid a slide down the bullpen totem pole in 2018.

Andrew Suarez LHP Born: 09/11/92 Age: 25 Bats: L Throws: L Height: 6'2" Weight: 205 Origin: Round 2, 2015 Draft (#61 overall)

YEAR	TEAM	LVL	AGE	W	L	SV	G	GS	IP	H	HR	BB/9	K/9	K	GB%	BABIP	WHIP	ERA	DRA	WARP	MPH	CMD	PWR	STM
2015	SLO	A-	22	1	0	0	5	5	19^{1}	17	2	0.9	7.0	15	53%	.273	0.98	1.40	3.63	0.4				
2015	SJO	A+	22	1	0	0	3	3	15	13	2	1.2	9.6	16	46%	.297	1.00	1.80	2.70	0.4				
2016	SJO	A+	23	2	1	0	5	5	29^{2}	25	2	1.5	10.3	34	61%	.299	1.01	2.43	1.33	1.4				
2016	RIC	AA	23	7	7	0	19	19	114	129	11	1.9	7.1	90	48%	.332	1.34	3.95	2.76	3.2				
2017	RIC	AA	24	4	4	0	11	11	67	72	3	2.0	7.4	55	49%	.332	1.30	2.96	2.35	2.3				
2017	SAC	AAA	24	6	6	0	15	13	88^{2}	94	7	2.7	8.1	80	51%	.328	1.36	3.55	3.69	1.9				
2018	*SFN*	*MLB*	*25*	*1*	*1*	*0*	*3*	*3*	*15*	*15*	*2*	*2.9*	*8.1*	*13*	*46%*	*.298*	*1.37*	*3.75*	*4.60*	*0.1*				
2019	*SFN*	*MLB*	*26*	*10*	*10*	*0*	*32*	*32*	*208^{2}*	*191*	*21*	*2.4*	*8.3*	*192*	*46%*	*.312*	*1.18*	*3.29*	*4.03*	*2.9*				

Breakout: 19% Improve: 34% Collapse: 21% Attrition: 53% MLB: 68% *Comparables: Brady Rodgers, Logan Verrett, Charles Brewer*

Suarez is like that former classmate you see at your 10-year high school reunion and remark, "____ hasn't changed at all!" He was a pitchability left-hander as a 12th-grader in Miami, impressing with command and guile while featuring average stuff. His arsenal remained average through college at the University of Miami—good news, in this case, because Suarez underwent surgery to repair the labrum in his throwing shoulder as a freshman. A two-time second-round pick, Suarez has stayed healthy since turning pro, reaching Triple-A in two seasons. His stuff is as average now as ever, his command still sharp, his performance exactly what you'd expect from someone with four middling offerings, led by a fastball that's as often 89 as it is 92. With his debut on the horizon, Suarez is a potential fourth starter—the same promise he's held since 2011.

Garrett Williams LHP Born: 09/15/94 Age: 23 Bats: L Throws: L Height: 6'1" Weight: 205 Origin: Round 7, 2016 Draft (#215 overall)

YEAR	TEAM	LVL	AGE	W	L	SV	G	GS	IP	H	HR	BB/9	K/9	K	GB%	BABIP	WHIP	ERA	DRA	WARP	MPH	CMD	PWR	STM
2016	SLO	A-	21	1	2	0	7	7	25^{1}	28	1	5.0	7.8	22	59%	.342	1.66	5.68	4.98	0.1				
2017	AUG	A	22	4	3	0	12	11	64	59	0	3.5	8.2	58	63%	.296	1.31	2.25	2.71	1.9				
2017	SJO	A+	22	2	2	0	6	5	33	28	3	2.7	10.4	38	58%	.287	1.15	2.45	1.89	1.3				
2018	*SFN*	*MLB*	*23*	*4*	*5*	*0*	*15*	*15*	*73^{2}*	*75*	*10*	*4.7*	*8.9*	*73*	*47%*	*.327*	*1.54*	*4.73*	*5.74*	*-0.1*				
2019	*SFN*	*MLB*	*24*	*8*	*10*	*0*	*28*	*28*	*171^{1}*	*172*	*24*	*4.0*	*8.1*	*154*	*47%*	*.324*	*1.45*	*4.39*	*5.31*	*0.5*				

Breakout: 5% Improve: 8% Collapse: 1% Attrition: 5% MLB: 13% *Comparables: Bobby Parnell, Matt Purke, Jason Hammel*

With no first-round pick in the 2016 draft and the third-lowest bonus pool among the 30 clubs, the Giants sought mid-round upside in the college ranks, where players with untapped potential often come with obvious warts. Williams, who battled a shoulder injury and logged just 31 2/3 innings in his sophomore and junior years at Oklahoma State, fit the bill at pick no. 215, by which point most southpaws with two potential plus offerings are long gone. Blessed with good health to this point in his pro career, Williams breezed through both A-ball levels in 2017, notably improving his walk rate from Augusta to San Jose while missing bats and generating groundballs. With a mid-90s heater and hammer curve, the lefty could move quickly in relief, but he also has the raw ingredients of a mid-rotation starter. Finding a third pitch and building his endurance are the main hurdles between what Williams is now and what he could be.

LINEOUTS

Hitters

HITTER	POS	TEAM	LVL	AGE	PA	R	2B	3B	HR	RBI	BB	K	SB	CS	AVG/OBP/SLG	TAv	VORP	BABIP	BRR	FRAA	WARP
Aaron Bond	OF	GIA	Rk	20	163	26	8	3	8	31	14	50	5	3	.306/.368/.565	.302	12.9	.411	0.2	LF(32): 6.7, RF(1): 0.0	1.8
Trevor Brown	C	SAC	AAA	25	212	11	4	0	1	9	9	43	2	0	.163/.208/.199	.149	-16.3	.204	0.5	C(54): -3.5, 2B(3): -0.1	-1.9
Orlando Calixte	UT	SAC	AAA	25	401	48	15	5	14	43	21	84	19	4	.243/.283/.421	.236	4.4	.279	0.1	SS(55): -8.2, 3B(20): -1.6	-0.8
	UT	SFN	MLB	25	55	5	1	0	0	6	3	16	1	0	.143/.185/.163	.179	-2.9	.200	0.3	LF(9): -0.1, 3B(5): -0.2	-0.4
Wander Franco	3B	WIL	A+	22	516	52	19	8	4	46	25	92	5	3	.279/.319/.376	.265	18.7	.335	1.3	3B(108): 9.7, 1B(2): 0.0	3.0
Aaron Hill	INF	SFN	MLB	35	80	7	2	1	1	7	11	13	0	0	.132/.250/.235	.197	-3.5	.145	-0.5	3B(7): -0.9, 2B(7): 0.0	-0.4
C.J. Hinojosa	MI	RIC	AA	22	417	47	16	0	4	35	31	42	5	4	.265/.321/.340	.250	8.7	.286	-2.2	SS(68): -3.3, 3B(20): 0.3	0.5
Jae-gyun Hwang	3B	SFN	MLB	29	57	2	1	0	1	5	5	15	0	0	.154/.228/.231	.166	-3.6	.194	0.3	3B(15): -0.3, 1B(3): -0.1	-0.4
	3B	SAC	AAA	29	386	44	21	4	10	55	27	83	7	1	.285/.332/.453	.277	18.0	.340	1.1	3B(58): 6.0, 1B(34): -2.0	2.1
Jalen Miller	MI	SJO	A+	20	470	61	25	4	6	44	31	100	6	4	.227/.283/.346	.233	2.1	.281	1.2	2B(83): -9.0, SS(28): -0.6	-0.8
Carlos Moncrief	OF	SAC	AAA	28	190	17	17	0	2	18	17	45	4	2	.287/.349/.421	.266	3.5	.376	-1.6	RF(43): 2.2, CF(4): -0.8	0.5
	OF	SFN	MLB	28	43	4	1	0	0	5	3	15	0	0	.211/.256/.237	.189	-2.7	.320	-0.5	RF(10): -0.3, LF(1): 0.0	-0.3
Michael Morse	LF	SFN	MLB	35	40	1	1	0	1	3	3	14	0	0	.194/.250/.306	.210	-1.7	.273	-0.3	1B(10): -0.5, LF(1): -0.4	-0.3
Ismael Munguia	OF	GIA	Rk	18	164	31	7	4	1	19	17	18	8	4	.331/.398/.458	.314	19.1	.368	3.3	LF(17): -0.5, CF(14): 0.1	1.7
Diego Rincones	OF	GIA	Rk	18	180	19	8	1	3	34	14	20	0	1	.308/.372/.428	.272	5.4	.331	-1.0	RF(28): -3.5, LF(5): -0.7	0.1
Justin Ruggiano	OF	SFN	MLB	35	63	2	1	0	2	4	1	17	1	1	.217/.238/.333	.226	-2.1	.262	-1.1	RF(12): -1.2, LF(5): -0.3	-0.4
	OF	SAC	AAA	35	169	23	13	0	6	21	9	33	1	2	.280/.325/.478	.270	5.0	.319	-1.5	CF(29): -0.1, RF(8): -1.8	0.3
Malique Ziegler	OF	SLO	A-	20	296	46	9	5	5	24	28	66	26	9	.240/.329/.374	.266	13.3	.301	2.4	CF(63): 13.7	2.7

Selected in the 12th round out of San Jacinto College in Texas, **Aaron Bond** is a lanky athlete with good bat speed and feel for the barrel. He impressed as a center fielder during instructional league, making him a player to follow as he moves off the complex. ⚾ When the Giants decided on their third catcher at September call-up time, they pondered the question, "What can **Trevor Brown** do for you?" and chose FedEx instead. ⚾ In 29 games, **Orlando Calixte** appeared at five defensive positions and notched seven hits, which tells you all you need to know about both his versatility and his bat. ⚾ No one wants to be remembered as the guy who was always second-best, which should provide plenty of motivation for the *other* **Wander Franco**'s career-long duel with the *other* Rougned Odor. ⚾ If the sun has set on **Aaron Hill**'s career, the Louisiana State University product will finish behind only Albert Belle in career WARP among position players drafted from the storied program in Baton Rouge. After playing shortstop exclusively in his first two pro seasons, **C.J. Hinojosa** saw time at the keystone and hot corner in Richmond, updating his résumé for any utility-man openings that may pop up in 2018. **Jae-gyun Hwang** struck out or popped up in more than 40 percent of his major-league plate appearances, which got him outrighted off the 40-man when rosters expanded. That number won't change any time soon after he signed a four-year contract to return to Korea in 2018. An overslot third-rounder in 2015, **Jalen Miller** remains a slow-burn prospect held back by an immature frame, raw fielding skills and an upper-body-driven swing that conceals his fringe-average raw power. If you could have just one 70-grade tool, to go with four other 20s and 30s, **Carlos Moncrief** is living proof that arm is not one you should choose. With prodigious power and a flair for the dramatic, **Michael Morse** still has his moments, but his time as a productive big-leaguer has probably passed. A slap hitter with solid-average speed but little physical projection, **Ismael Munguia** will have to maintain outstanding contact rates to emerge as a sparkplug down the road. Natural hitting ability got **Diego Rincones** noticed on the complex, but his fringy tools and filled-out frame might get him lost in the crowd as he advances. **Justin Ruggiano** opted out of his minor-league contract with the Giants on July 25. The other 29 clubs saw his 68 percent contact rate on pitches inside the strike zone and did what the 36-year-old rarely did in 2017: take a pass. One of the system's sleeper prospects, **Malique Ziegler** is a plus runner with center-field chops, and his cold-weather background suggests that he might be a late bloomer at the plate.

Pitchers

PITCHER	TEAM	LVL	AGE	W	L	SV	G	GS	IP	H	HR	BB/9	K/9	K	GB%	BABIP	WHIP	ERA	DRA	WARP	MPH	CMD	PWR	STM
Samuel Coonrod	RIC	AA	24	4	11	0	24	18	103^2	96	7	3.6	8.2	94	47%	.302	1.33	4.69	5.19	-0.1				
Julian Fernandez	ASH	A	21	1	2	3	51	0	58	54	2	2.8	8.8	57	48%	.315	1.24	3.26	4.26	0.4				
Roberto Gomez	SAC	AAA	27	3	9	0	38	13	97^1	100	8	3.5	8.2	89	47%	.321	1.42	4.07	4.71	0.9				
	SFN	MLB	27	0	0	0	4	0	5^1	9	0	1.7	10.1	6	32%	.474	1.88	8.44	5.52	0.0	96.2			55
Tyler Herb	ARK	AA	25	6	4	0	16	16	98	97	5	2.8	8.1	88	61%	.330	1.30	3.31	2.97	2.6				
	RIC	AA	25	2	3	0	10	10	65^1	61	5	2.5	6.6	48	56%	.281	1.21	2.76	2.51	2.1				
Chase Johnson	SAC	AAA	25	0	2	0	6	0	10^1	11	2	0.0	7.8	9	47%	.300	1.06	4.35	3.73	0.2				
Pierce Johnson	CHN	MLB	26	0	0	0	1	0	1	2	0	9.0	18.0	2	25%	.500	3.00	0.00	9.94	-0.1	93.3			44
	IOW	AAA	26	3	2	9	43	1	54^1	52	3	4.5	12.3	74	46%	.389	1.45	4.31	2.94	1.4				
Rodolfo Martinez	SJO	A+	23	2	0	0	10	0	13^1	14	2	0.7	8.1	12	44%	.308	1.12	4.05	3.89	0.2				
Bryan Morris	SFN	MLB	30	2	0	0	20	0	21	24	1	4.7	6.4	15	52%	.343	1.67	6.43	5.75	-0.1	94.1	37	51	42
Daniel Slania	SAC	AAA	25	0	8	0	12	12	61	78	14	4.6	8.4	57	37%	.364	1.79	7.82	8.27	-1.7				
	SFN	MLB	25	0	0	0	1	0	1	0	0	0.0	0.0	0	33%	.000	0.00	0.00	5.08	0.0	93.5			68
	RIC	AA	25	5	3	0	13	13	80^1	81	5	3.1	6.2	55	41%	.304	1.36	3.59	5.02	0.1				
D.J. Snelten	RIC	AA	25	4	1	0	15	0	21^2	19	0	2.1	11.6	28	70%	.339	1.11	1.66	1.40	0.9				
	SAC	AAA	25	4	0	0	36	0	52	38	4	3.1	7.4	43	64%	.231	1.08	2.42	1.64	2.1				
Ryan Webb	SAC	AAA	31	1	0	2	17	0	20^1	22	3	5.3	5.8	13	52%	.297	1.67	3.98	7.35	-0.5				

Sam Coonrod improved his strikeout, walk and home run rates in his second tour of the Eastern League, but his elbow ligament popped in mid-August. He'll miss the 2018 season after going under the knife. **Julian Fernandez** throws really, really hard. He can't do much else, but he can throw really, really hard. The Giants have a history of working well with this type of profile, but they'll have to work quickly, as he's a Rule 5 pick. After a winding, 527-inning route to the majors, **Roberto Gomez** arrived in September with a straight, 97-mph fastball. He'll need to figure out how to sink or cut the pitch to avoid a direct return to Triple-A. **Tyler Herb** came to the Giants as the PTBNL in a trade that sent Chris Heston to the Mariners. He turns 26 in April and will be in Triple-A for the first time in 2018, but if he works hard and believes in himself, he could someday become Chris Heston. Converted to the bullpen full time to begin 2017, **Chase Johnson** underwent Tommy John surgery in May, delaying his pursuit of a middle-relief role by at least a year. Once a top 101 prospect, **Pierce Johnson** finally reached the majors after six seasons in the minors, but his stay lasted just one day in May. **Rodolfo Martinez** has arm strength to spare, but he missed time with shoulder and oblique injuries in 2017, and still needs a viable complement to his high-90s velocity. After burning worms in the majors for parts of six seasons, **Bryan Morris** is returning to his roots in Tennessee to teach the pitchers at Tullahoma High School how to do the same. After making the unconventional shift from reliever to starter in 2016, **Dan Slania** took the road less traveled for a second consecutive season, going from Triple-A to Double-A via the majors in late June. He might be taking his projection as an up-and-down arm a little too seriously. A mountain of a man, **D.J. Snelten** used deception and steep fastball plane to produce the second-highest ground-ball rate in the Pacific Coast League. He lacks the breaking ball to be a dominant specialist but should settle into a big-league bullpen this year. Four of **Ryan Webb**'s last five contracts have been of the minor-league variety, and after undergoing hip surgery last summer, the sinkerballer will await another non-roster invitation to camp this spring.

LEAGUE LEADERS 2017

MLB Strikeout Rate – Joe Panik, 9.42%

SEATTLE MARINERS

Essay by Marc Webster

Player comments by Mike Gianella and BP staff

When a team hasn't reached the playoffs in 16 years, there isn't—there can't be—a single explanation. Every small failure, every bad bounce, every busted prospect and unwise signing played a part, and singling out of any one would exculpate some other, equally frustrating misstep. This is all very logical, which means it doesn't feel right if you're a fan, just braising in a decade-and-a-half of mediocrity. Spreading the blame across multiple front offices and departments dilutes responsibility, and if *you've* been braising in mediocrity for a while, it's pretty natural to want to focus your rage on the person responsible. A single person, a single move that made all of *this* possible, maybe even inevitable.

The Mariners' history since 2001 is a target-rich environment for potential This Is Where It Went Wrong moments, but there's one that most fans point to: the February 2008 trade of a bunch of prospects (including Adam Jones) for left-hander Erik Bedard. The Bedard trade looked lopsided at the time, and only got worse when Bedard's injury problems returned, Jones developed into an All-Star center fielder and Chris Tillman became a rotation mainstay. Even George Sherrill, the throw-in lefty setup guy, ended up making the All-Star team the next season when he somehow ended up as the rebuilding Orioles' closer.

Rationally, the Mariners bought high on one of the league's best arms and were able to keep the prospects they liked best, hard-throwing right-hander Brandon Morrow and power-hitting catcher Jeff Clement. It was too far in the past to be The Reason the 2017 M's fell short, of course, but given the outcry at the time, and given how rapidly the deal fell apart for Seattle, it allowed the Mariners to believe that former general manager Bill Bavasi had taken a near-playoff team and ruined them for a decade. If the Mariners got another chance, they could avoid Bavasi's mistake and everything would be ... well, I don't know, but better than this.

The 2006 Mariners finished 78-84. They had a decent offense, but their rotation—headlined by a frustrating season from Felix Hernandez—struggled and their depth—filled with underpowered command/control guys—faltered. The 2017 Mariners finished 78-84, too, and ... let's see, frustrating year from Felix? Low-90s fastballs from the depth starters getting destroyed? Check and check. To say the offense was similar is an understatement: The 2006 M's had a team on-base percentage of .325 and a team slugging percentage of .424. In 2017? .325 and .424. The 2006 M's traded away a close-to-the-majors outfield prospect, while the 2017 M's traded a close-to-the-majors outfield prospect. Okay, this is getting spooky. Even the insane Seattle real estate market is a ringer for 2006's irrational exuberance.

A bit more than 10 years later, the Mariners are seemingly right back where they were, only now they can avoid Bavasi's blunder. But like every time-travel story, this one is a warning. We can confidently say that they won't make another all-in trade, because their farm system is essentially empty. The international free agent market that was their greatest organizational strength in 2006 is

MARINERS PROSPECTUS

2017 W-L: 78-84, 3RD IN AL WEST

Pythag	.486	16th	B-Age	29.6	*27th*
RS/G	4.63	15th	P-Age	28.0	*11th*
RA/G	4.77	15th	Salary	$154.3M	*13th*
TAv	.259	17th	M$/MW	$4.7M	*9th*
TAv-P	.263	17th	DL Days	1232	*22nd*
FIP	4.67	22nd	$ on DL	26%	*27th*
DER	.717	5th			

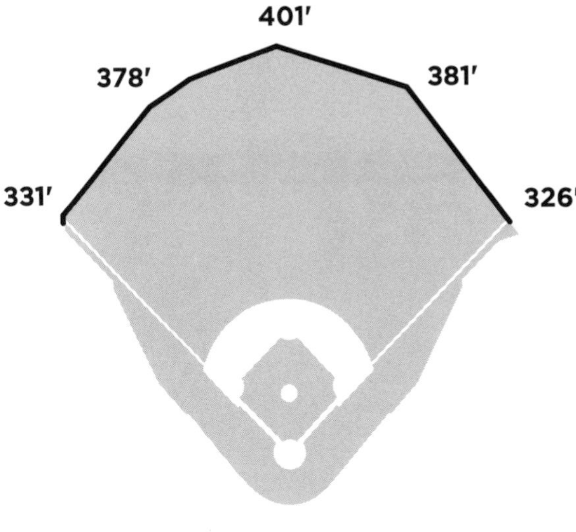

Outfield wall profile: **8'**

Three-Year Park Factors

Runs	Runs/RH	Runs/LH	HR/RH	HR/LH
95	96	94	99	102

Top Hitter WARP	4.0 Nelson Cruz
Top Pitcher WARP	3.7 James Paxton
Top Prospect	Kyle Lewis

2017 Hit List Ranking

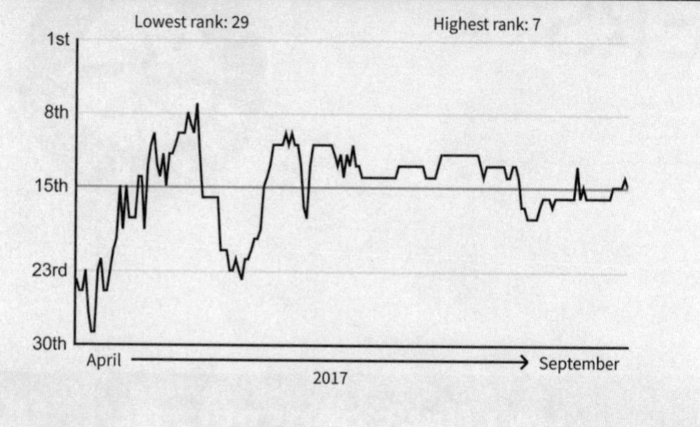

Committed Payroll (in millions)

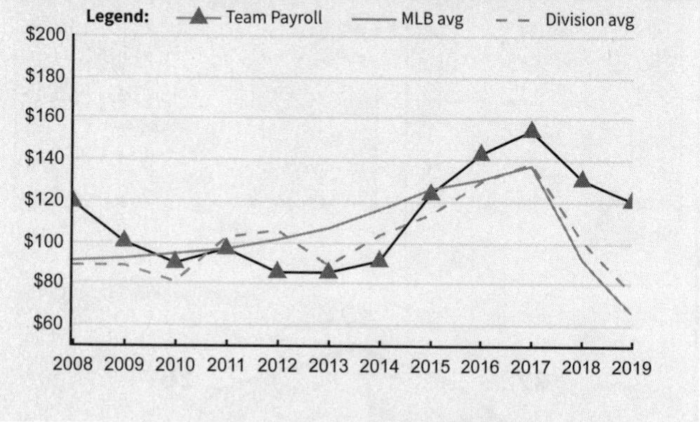

Farm System Ranking

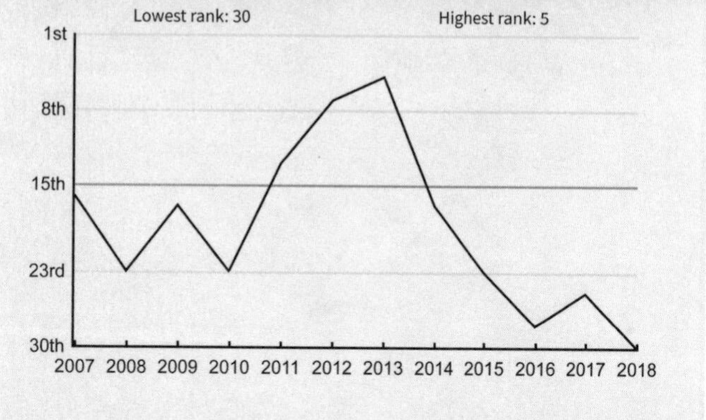

Personnel

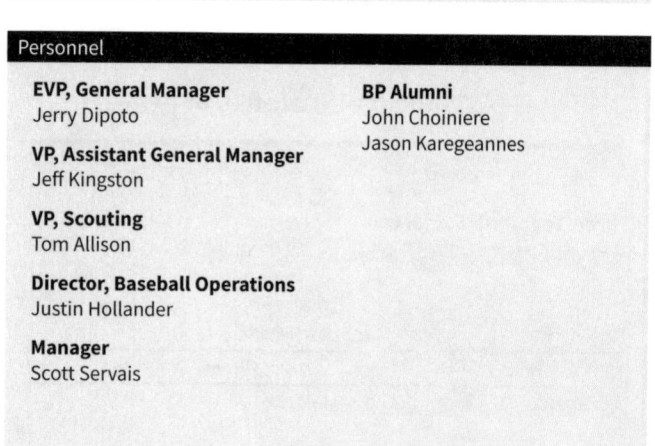

EVP, General Manager
Jerry Dipoto

VP, Assistant General Manager
Jeff Kingston

VP, Scouting
Tom Allison

Director, Baseball Operations
Justin Hollander

Manager
Scott Servais

BP Alumni
John Choiniere
Jason Karegeannes

nearly nonexistent now, with all but the most recent crop traded for relievers. The M's are right back where they were, albeit without all of the things that made going all-in somewhat reasonable. Felix is now an old 31, Robinson Cano is now 35 and Nelson Cruz—one of the best free agent signings in team history—will turn 38 midway through 2018. Kyle Seager just turned 30 as well, so the "big four"—star players on sizable contracts—are all supposed to be in their decline phases.

Given the Astros' combination of youth and talent, the Mariners don't look capable of competing for division titles in the short term. Given the A's young talent and the fact that the Angels still employ Mike Trout (and now employ Shohei Ohtani), the Mariners have competition for divisional runners-up as well. The M's can't trade a bunch of prospects for an All-Star veteran, and given their commitments to Felix, Cano, Seager and now Jean Segura, they may claim that they can't increase payroll through free agency (whether this is actually true is a separate matter). They don't have many cards to play, but thanks to another big change since 2006, they don't have to play them perfectly.

The second wild card has been a fascinating experiment. In years like 2017, it has turned what would've been boring playoff races into down-to-the-wire affairs. Predictably, it has let some pretty flawed teams find their way into a play-in game, and it has made those one-game playoffs captivating television. The M's are a team that's essentially made for the second wild card—not good enough to be in the Houston/Cleveland/New York stratosphere, but much more talented than the rebuilding teams. Thanks to the second wild card, the "strategy" of holding onto veterans hasn't been a crippling one. There's no real point in losing for losing's sake, given that the M's wouldn't get a whole lot for Cano/Felix/Cruz even if they wanted to try their hand at a belated rebuild. They need to be decent enough to hang around the fringe of the race, and they're positioned well to do so.

But how sustainable is this? The Mariners will lose Cruz next year, and no one knows how much to expect from Hernandez. Balancing that somewhat has been the emergence of James Paxton and young outfielder Mitch Haniger, who came from Arizona last year. Both spent time on the disabled list in 2017, and neither is a sure thing, but both offer the promise of years of star-level performance—something that's better to wish for than a continued graceful decline from Cano. With contributions from Segura and a resurgent Mike Zunino, the Mariners can—with a few tweaks to the pitching staff—stay near .500 or better, and that may be enough to get to the trade deadline with a decent chance.

Even better from the Mariners' point of view is that many other teams in similar positions don't seem interested in the second wild card at all. Far from ushering in an era in which few teams were sufficiently far from the playoffs to actually sell, we've seen a spate of rebuilds and fire sales. The White Sox seemed poised to make a run after acquiring David Robertson to go with Chris Sale, Jose Quintana and Adam Eaton, but then reversed course after a year or so and traded all of them away. The Padres did the same a year after acquiring the likes of Justin Upton and Craig Kimbrel. Kimbrel was available because the Braves tore down a .500-ish team with plenty of under-30 players.

Other teams seem to reckon that the second wild card means they can get a faster return on their rebuild: If they hit on a few players, they don't have to wait until everything falls into place and might get a playoff game a year or two early. It worked for the 2015 Astros—who were coming off a 92-loss season—and it worked for the Twins in 2017, a year after they lost 103. But losing itself is no guarantee of anything, as the Mariners' own history proves. To finally break through, they'll need much better player development, something that's long been an issue. That takes time, though, and after 16 seasons without seeing the playoffs, you can kind of understand why the M's might see the second wild card in a different light than the White Sox or Astros.

A bit of patience seems warranted. The M's have been trading low-minors prospects for seemingly minor additions since Jerry Dipoto took over in late 2015. None of them were can't-miss types, but they've gone to acquire the likes of a single year of Adam Lind, the right to pay Drew Smyly's rehab costs and a slew of relievers, from Joaquin Benoit to Arquimedes Caminero to David Phelps. Even putting aside the truly lopsided deals (Chris Taylor for Zach Lee), the M's have turned minor-league depth into bullpen depth, and it hasn't made them a whole lot better. They can't trade their way to the playoffs now. To improve their chances, they need to take an aging roster signed to long-term deals and add new long-term deals via free agency.

The long shadow cast by the Bedard trade and the Mariners' long playoff drought must feel like an anchor to Dipoto. When he came on, they lacked the type of minor-league talent that could fundamentally alter the franchise and challenge Houston. Dipoto opted to make a series of small moves that tweaked a team that could've capitalized on an Astro misstep *if* everything had broken right. Instead, the Astros achieved escape velocity and shot out of reach. Like it or not, the second wild card is now the M's target, and that in turn shapes their approach over the next few years.

Ideally, they'd combine free agent pickups with a commitment to pitching development (meaning not flipping every live arm for every near-free-agent setup guy), which would enable them to extend their window to sort of compete a bit longer. They can't meaningfully compete with Houston, and a painful reckoning will come soon, but in the absence of a viable teardown option, the M's need to learn to love the second wild card and try to exorcise their playoff demons by taking a chance in free agency.

—Marc Webster covers the Mariners for U.S.S. Mariner.

Hitters

Braden Bishop CF Born: 08/22/93 Age: 24 Bats: R Throws: R Height: 6'1" Weight: 190 Origin: Round 3, 2015 Draft (#94 overall)

YEAR	TEAM	LVL	AGE	PA	R	2B	3B	HR	RBI	BB	K	SB	CS	AVG/OBP/SLG	TAv	VORP	BABIP	BRR	FRAA	WARP
2015	EVE	A-	21	248	34	8	1	2	22	5	33	13	3	.320/.367/.393	.285	14.9	.368	1.2	CF(51): 9.6, LF(2): -0.2	2.6
2016	CLN	A	22	284	38	5	1	1	21	25	48	6	1	.290/.363/.331	.278	13.8	.355	1.5	CF(40): -0.8, LF(14): -1.1	1.2
2016	BAK	A+	22	184	19	6	0	2	22	11	39	2	0	.247/.300/.319	.262	4.6	.310	-1.1	CF(34): -3.6, RF(7): -0.8	0.0
2017	MOD	A+	23	412	71	25	3	2	32	45	65	16	4	.296/.385/.400	.285	22.8	.356	0.8	CF(70): -1.7, LF(14): 2.1	2.4
2017	ARK	AA	23	145	18	9	1	1	11	15	15	6	1	.336/.417/.448	.338	14.3	.373	-1.5	CF(31): 1.6	1.7
2018	*SEA*	*MLB*	*24*	*250*	*29*	*10*	*1*	*5*	*22*	*19*	*54*	*3*	*1*	*.247/.316/.361*	*.236*	*3.3*	*.298*	*0.0*	*CF 0, LF 0*	*0.4*
2019	*SEA*	*MLB*	*25*	*400*	*45*	*16*	*1*	*8*	*41*	*30*	*85*	*5*	*1*	*.250/.317/.371*	*.242*	*3.9*	*.298*	*0.0*	*CF 0, LF 0*	*0.4*

Breakout: 8% Improve: 18% Collapse: 6% Attrition: 20% MLB: 45% *Comparables: Ezequiel Carrera, Charlie Tilson, Matt Szczur*

For outfielders with a good-glove/light-bat profile, there's a fine line between "starting center fielder" and "fourth outfielder." For years Bishop has straddled this line. Few doubt his defense or base-stealing abilities, but the scouting knock on Bishop is that the rest of his offensive game might not be up to par. While Bishop didn't have a breakout season in 2017, there were signs that he could be more than merely a prototypical bench piece. He jumped from 11 doubles in 2016 to 34 last year. While this isn't fence-clearing power, Bishop played in two parks that are extremely pitcher friendly. It will still take a lot for Bishop to claim a major-league job, but he at least kept himself in the running.

Robinson Cano 2B Born: 10/22/82 Age: 35 Bats: L Throws: R Height: 6'0" Weight: 210 Origin: International Free Agent, 2001

YEAR	TEAM	LVL	AGE	PA	R	2B	3B	HR	RBI	BB	K	SB	CS	AVG/OBP/SLG	TAv	VORP	BABIP	BRR	FRAA	WARP
2015	SEA	MLB	32	674	82	34	1	21	79	43	107	2	6	.287/.334/.446	.285	30.8	.316	-2.6	2B(149): -1.7	3.1
2016	SEA	MLB	33	715	107	33	2	39	103	47	100	0	1	.298/.350/.533	.300	46.0	.299	-1.7	2B(157): 4.2	5.2
2017	SEA	MLB	34	648	79	33	0	23	97	49	85	1	0	.280/.338/.453	.270	23.2	.294	-2.0	2B(150): -7.3	1.6
2018	*SEA*	*MLB*	*35*	*656*	*79*	*32*	*1*	*21*	*87*	*50*	*90*	*2*	*2*	*.286/.345/.449*	*.279*	*37.3*	*.306*	*-1.6*	*2B -2*	*3.0*
2019	*SEA*	*MLB*	*36*	*536*	*69*	*27*	*1*	*17*	*68*	*42*	*80*	*1*	*1*	*.279/.340/.443*	*.270*	*21.7*	*.301*	*-1.2*	*2B -1*	*2.2*

Breakout: 1% Improve: 29% Collapse: 8% Attrition: 15% MLB: 92% *Comparables: Ben Zobrist, Carlos Guillen, Chase Utley*

Players on the wrong side of 30 are frequently viewed through a glass-half-empty lens; the term itself is a harsh pejorative. For the second time in three years, Cano had a relative down season, failing to hit 25 home runs for the third time in four years and missing the .300 mark in batting average for the third consecutive campaign. This nitpicking misses the fact that Cano ranks among the all-time top 10 second baseman in the 31-34 age bracket during his four seasons in Seattle. He isn't the player he was with the Yankees, but without WARP at your disposal it would be more difficult to see. Cano's journey from one coast to the other was perhaps a blessing in disguise, a chance for fans in another part of the country to appreciate his subtle greatness, to watch the easy flick of his wrists on a swing or smoothness in the field when most of the Western Hemisphere is asleep. Cano is one of the best ever at his position and is on a clear path to Cooperstown. Mariners fans just hope he reaches Hall of Fame form a few more times before the deal is done.

Nelson Cruz DH Born: 07/01/80 Age: 37 Bats: R Throws: R Height: 6'2" Weight: 230 Origin: International Free Agent, 1998

YEAR	TEAM	LVL	AGE	PA	R	2B	3B	HR	RBI	BB	K	SB	CS	AVG/OBP/SLG	TAv	VORP	BABIP	BRR	FRAA	WARP
2015	SEA	MLB	34	655	90	22	1	44	93	59	164	3	2	.302/.369/.566	.331	54.0	.350	-0.2	RF(80): -3.9	5.4
2016	SEA	MLB	35	667	96	27	1	43	105	62	159	2	0	.287/.360/.555	.316	41.4	.320	-5.1	RF(48): -4.7	3.8
2017	SEA	MLB	36	645	91	28	0	39	119	70	140	1	1	.288/.375/.549	.312	40.4	.315	-1.8	RF(5): -0.1	4.0
2018	*SEA*	*MLB*	*37*	*642*	*92*	*25*	*1*	*36*	*106*	*56*	*152*	*2*	*1*	*.268/.339/.503*	*.291*	*32.9*	*.302*	*-1.3*	*RF -3*	*2.8*
2019	*SEA*	*MLB*	*38*	*528*	*78*	*20*	*1*	*29*	*83*	*47*	*129*	*1*	*0*	*.261/.333/.491*	*.280*	*22.8*	*.296*	*-1.8*	*RF -2*	*2.3*

Breakout: 1% Improve: 24% Collapse: 7% Attrition: 20% MLB: 79% *Comparables: Carlos Delgado, David Ortiz, Frank Howard*

Lumbering power hitters in their mid-30s aren't supposed to age well, nor are the expensive long-term contracts these hitters sometimes receive. "There's no more terrifying DH acquisition than a multi-year, mid-30s DH acquisition" were the words ominously printed under Cruz's name in the 2015 edition of this tome. Three years later, the only ones who have been terrified are the pitchers who have faced him. Only Mark McGwire, Barry Bonds, Babe Ruth and Rafael Palmeiro had more home runs in their age 34-36 seasons than "Boomstick" did from 2015-2017. Heck, forget judging on the (age) curve; since 2015, no hitter has slugged more home runs than Cruz. The injuries that plagued Cruz as a younger man haven't been a factor in years, and in 2017 the Mariners mercifully protected the team's pitchers and our eyes from Cruz's outfield "defense" except for a smattering of interleague contests. Cruz's deal with Seattle expires at the end of 2018, but even if Father Time catches up with him all at once his contract was a significant victory for the squad.

Jarrod Dyson CF Born: 08/15/84 Age: 33 Bats: L Throws: R Height: 5'10" Weight: 165 Origin: Round 50, 2006 Draft (#1475 overall)

YEAR	TEAM	LVL	AGE	PA	R	2B	3B	HR	RBI	BB	K	SB	CS	AVG/OBP/SLG	TAv	VORP	BABIP	BRR	FRAA	WARP
2015	KCA	MLB	30	225	31	8	6	2	18	14	37	26	3	.250/.311/.380	.249	7.7	.296	4.7	CF(37): 4.0, LF(27): 5.9	1.9
2016	OMA	AAA	31	29	7	0	0	0	1	4	4	4	0	.318/.464/.318	.352	5.5	.389	2.1	RF(4): 0.3, CF(3): -0.4	0.6
2016	KCA	MLB	31	337	46	14	8	1	25	26	39	30	7	.278/.340/.388	.250	7.1	.315	1.7	CF(57): 0.4, RF(21): 3.7	1.3
2017	SEA	MLB	32	390	56	13	3	5	30	28	55	28	7	.251/.324/.350	.238	3.0	.285	0.0	CF(96): 5.7, LF(12): 3.2	1.2
2018	*SEA*	*MLB*	*33*	*359*	*46*	*12*	*4*	*4*	*28*	*29*	*63*	*30*	*7*	*.250/.321/.355*	*.232*	*5.0*	*.290*	*1.4*	*CF 0, LF 0*	*0.6*
2019	*SEA*	*MLB*	*34*	*365*	*39*	*11*	*4*	*4*	*32*	*29*	*64*	*29*	*7*	*.247/.318/.348*	*.232*	*2.1*	*.288*	*2.2*	*CF 0, LF 0*	*0.3*

Breakout: 2% Improve: 37% Collapse: 10% Attrition: 17% MLB: 86% *Comparables: Scott Podsednik, Ryan Freel, Darryl Hamilton*

It's not often you get the opportunity to reinvent yourself at age 32, but this is exactly what Dyson did when the Mariners acquired him in an offseason deal with the Royals. Cast as a fourth outfielder throughout his career, Dyson got the opportunity to play every day in an outfield alignment that prioritized speed and defense. At first, the experiment went about as well as Dr. Henry Jekyll's, with Dyson slashing a woeful .217/.317/.306 through the end of May. But the Mariners didn't give up, and were rewarded with an acceptable .280/.330/.386 line from June 1 until a sports hernia injury ended Dyson's season in early September. Dyson remains stretched as a starter, but a team with stronger offense than Seattle had in 2017 could probably accept his limitations with the bat in exchange for his range in center.

Eric Filia RF Born: 07/06/92 Age: 25 Bats: L Throws: R Height: 6'0" Weight: 189 Origin: Round 20, 2016 Draft (#597 overall)

YEAR	TEAM	LVL	AGE	PA	R	2B	3B	HR	RBI	BB	K	SB	CS	AVG/OBP/SLG	TAv	VORP	BABIP	BRR	FRAA	WARP
2016	EVE	A-	23	292	43	19	1	4	46	39	19	10	5	.362/.450/.496	.338	28.9	.376	0.6	RF(43): -2.2, CF(7): -0.3	2.8
2017	MOD	A+	24	567	63	28	5	5	59	65	45	9	6	.326/.407/.434	.312	38.9	.348	-0.6	RF(106): -11.6, 1B(12): -1.0	2.8
2018	*SEA*	*MLB*	*25*	*250*	*26*	*11*	*1*	*6*	*28*	*25*	*37*	*1*	*0*	*.262/.341/.393*	*.254*	*4.8*	*.289*	*-0.4*	*RF -2, 1B 0*	*0.3*
2019	*SEA*	*MLB*	*26*	*290*	*36*	*12*	*1*	*7*	*32*	*30*	*44*	*1*	*0*	*.258/.340/.399*	*.259*	*4.9*	*.284*	*-0.6*	*RF -2, 1B 0*	*0.3*

Breakout: 5% Improve: 11% Collapse: 9% Attrition: 22% MLB: 34% *Comparables: Erik Komatsu, Jake Smolinski, Jake Goebbert*

A UCLA product, Filia lost two years of development time in college due to a shoulder injury his junior year and an academic issue his senior year. Some would have given up on their dream, but Filia persisted, working a series of odd jobs, returning to UCLA and getting selected by the Mariners in the 20th round of the 2016 draft. Twenty-five-year-olds in High-A usually aren't worth more than a passing glance, but Filia's hit tool might be special enough that he could make the majors as a 1B/DH/reserve outfielder and possibly a starter if he can add more power to his game. The Mariners moved Filia to first base in the Arizona Fall League to give him more reps and put him on a faster track to the majors.

Benjamin Gamel OF Born: 05/17/92 Age: 26 Bats: L Throws: L Height: 5'11" Weight: 185 Origin: Round 10, 2010 Draft (#325 overall)

YEAR	TEAM	LVL	AGE	PA	R	2B	3B	HR	RBI	BB	K	SB	CS	AVG/OBP/SLG	TAv	VORP	BABIP	BRR	FRAA	WARP
2015	SWB	AAA	23	551	77	28	14	10	64	46	108	13	5	.300/.358/.472	.293	34.6	.364	1.8	CF(74): 2.1, LF(33): 4.7	4.6
2016	NYA	MLB	24	10	1	0	0	0	0	1	1	0	0	.125/.222/.125	.184	-0.4	.143	0.2	RF(5): -0.5	-0.1
2016	SWB	AAA	24	533	80	26	5	6	51	43	94	19	8	.308/.365/.420	.289	34.1	.370	4.6	CF(70): -7.3, LF(25): 0.3	2.7
2016	SEA	MLB	24	47	8	2	0	1	5	5	15	0	0	.200/.289/.325	.246	0.5	.292	0.1	RF(24): -1.5, LF(2): -0.4	-0.1
2017	TAC	AAA	25	75	6	1	1	1	8	12	11	1	1	.300/.427/.400	.301	5.8	.347	0.6	RF(11): -0.2, CF(7): -0.9	0.4
2017	SEA	MLB	25	550	68	27	5	11	59	36	122	4	1	.275/.322/.413	.261	13.3	.340	1.1	LF(85): -5.2, RF(50): 3.1	1.1
2018	*SEA*	*MLB*	*26*	*360*	*42*	*16*	*4*	*8*	*40*	*28*	*81*	*5*	*2*	*.268/.327/.417*	*.263*	*13.4*	*.330*	*0.2*	*LF -3*	*0.7*
2019	*SEA*	*MLB*	*27*	*504*	*61*	*23*	*5*	*14*	*59*	*44*	*117*	*6*	*3*	*.265/.331/.427*	*.262*	*14.0*	*.325*	*0.6*	*LF -3*	*1.2*

Breakout: 11% Improve: 44% Collapse: 11% Attrition: 24% MLB: 82% *Comparables: Scott Hairston, Eric Thames, Preston Tucker*

Watching a BABIP-fueled hot streak is like watching your buddy get lucky at the blackjack tables in Vegas: It's fun in the moment, but the good times seldom last. After starting the season in the minors, Gamel got the call in late April and put up a sizzling .348 batting average through June 30 thanks to a .459 BABIP. Sure enough, Gamel crashed and burned, barely getting on base a fourth of the time from July 1 onward. His stolen bases and defense, two calling cards in the minors, were both subpar in Seattle. The Mariners could try Gamel as a starter again in 2018, but just like hitting on a hard 16 when the dealer is showing a 10, there is a good chance they'll go bust.

Dee Gordon 2B Born: 04/22/88 Age: 30 Bats: L Throws: R Height: 5'11" Weight: 170 Origin: Round 4, 2008 Draft (#127 overall)

YEAR	TEAM	LVL	AGE	PA	R	2B	3B	HR	RBI	BB	K	SB	CS	AVG/OBP/SLG	TAv	VORP	BABIP	BRR	FRAA	WARP
2015	MIA	MLB	27	653	88	24	8	4	46	25	91	58	20	.333/.359/.418	.292	41.1	.383	4.1	2B(145): -0.3	4.4
2016	NWO	AAA	28	36	7	1	1	0	2	1	5	3	0	.257/.278/.343	.235	0.4	.300	0.4	2B(9): -2.1	-0.2
2016	MIA	MLB	28	345	47	7	6	1	14	18	55	30	7	.268/.305/.335	.244	7.2	.319	3.4	2B(78): -6.3	0.1
2017	MIA	MLB	29	695	114	20	9	2	33	25	93	60	16	.308/.341/.375	.258	26.8	.354	8.4	2B(153): -0.6, SS(3): 0.0	2.6
2018	*SEA*	*MLB*	*30*	*649*	*89*	*21*	*8*	*4*	*44*	*33*	*103*	*54*	*15*	*.281/.320/.361*	*.245*	*19.8*	*.328*	*6.8*	*2B -3*	*1.5*
2019	*SEA*	*MLB*	*31*	*528*	*55*	*17*	*6*	*6*	*48*	*29*	*90*	*41*	*13*	*.274/.319/.368*	*.242*	*10.8*	*.321*	*5.1*	*2B 0*	*1.1*

Breakout: 2% Improve: 35% Collapse: 14% Attrition: 18% MLB: 95% *Comparables: Sandy Alomar, Aaron Miles, Eduardo Nunez*

On the heels of an 80-game suspension after testing positive for a performance-enhancing drug in 2016, Gordon bounced back to record the known universe's first 200-hit and 60-steal performance since former Marlin Juan Pierre in 2003. In fact, he and Giancarlo Stanton narrowly missed becoming the first set of teammates in baseball history to record 60 home runs and 60 stolen bases, respectively, in the same season. The soon-to-be-30-year-old is exactly what he's always been: a free swinger whose upper echelon speed is still enough to make him an above-average regular (at least when the BABIP gods will allow it). The end is never pretty for either second basemen or speedsters, so enjoy the throwback style for as long as you can.

Mitch Haniger RF Born: 12/23/90 Age: 27 Bats: R Throws: R Height: 6'2" Weight: 215 Origin: Round 1, 2012 Draft (#38 overall)

YEAR	TEAM	LVL	AGE	PA	R	2B	3B	HR	RBI	BB	K	SB	CS	AVG/OBP/SLG	TAv	VORP	BABIP	BRR	FRAA	WARP
2015	MOB	AA	24	174	23	10	1	1	19	16	32	4	4	.281/.351/.379	.281	8.6	.341	0.2	CF(38): -2.1, LF(12): 1.5	0.8
2015	VIS	A+	24	226	40	16	3	12	36	17	39	8	2	.332/.381/.619	.368	30.7	.353	1.4	RF(24): 2.1, CF(21): -1.0	3.4
2016	MOB	AA	25	236	21	14	2	5	30	30	37	4	3	.294/.407/.462	.317	17.9	.340	-0.9	LF(32): 1.4, CF(16): -0.4	2.2
2016	RNO	AAA	25	312	58	20	3	20	64	39	62	8	1	.341/.428/.670	.360	43.5	.373	3.4	CF(34): -0.4, RF(34): 3.3	4.8
2016	ARI	MLB	25	123	9	2	1	5	17	12	27	0	0	.229/.309/.404	.250	2.3	.256	0.2	CF(22): 1.5, LF(9): 0.1	0.4
2017	TAC	AAA	26	48	6	2	0	3	6	7	5	0	0	.256/.375/.538	.381	6.2	.219	-1.0	RF(6): 1.4	0.7
2017	SEA	MLB	26	410	58	25	2	16	47	31	93	5	4	.282/.352/.491	.284	16.8	.338	-1.4	RF(94): 4.7, CF(6): 0.2	2.2
2018	*SEA*	*MLB*	*27*	*549*	*75*	*27*	*3*	*22*	*74*	*50*	*123*	*6*	*3*	*.262/.340/.463*	*.282*	*26.5*	*.305*	*-0.6*	*RF 5*	*2.9*
2019	*SEA*	*MLB*	*28*	*534*	*74*	*27*	*2*	*23*	*76*	*51*	*121*	*5*	*3*	*.262/.343/.476*	*.280*	*22.0*	*.303*	*-0.5*	*RF 6*	*3.1*

Breakout: 5% Improve: 36% Collapse: 10% Attrition: 19% MLB: 81% *Comparables: Brad Hawpe, Shin-Soo Choo, Steven Souza*

Former first-round picks get overlooked as rarely as bad Lena Dunham tweets, but this is what happened to Haniger in the minors, first with the Brewers and then with the Diamondbacks. The Mariners nabbed him in November 2016 as part of the Jean Segura deal and penciled him in as their Opening Day right fielder. Haniger ran with the job, mashing his way to a .342/.447/.608 line in April. An oblique injury knocked him out for six weeks, and when he returned he wasn't nearly the same hitter. Haniger's star rose in 2016 with the help of Bobby Tewksbary, the hitting guru best known for his work with Josh Donaldson. Haniger rebounded in September, confounding analysts further. Figuring out whether a swing adjustment will take is a trickier business than getting honey out of a bee and into those tiny, bear-shaped bottles. If his recovery from the oblique injury did impact Haniger's approach and he rediscovered his new swing in September, the Mariners have a bargain. If not, Haniger can at a minimum be a league-average hitter with good defense in right field, which is much more than any of his prior employers were expecting.

Ryon Healy 1B Born: 01/10/92 Age: 26 Bats: R Throws: R Height: 6'5" Weight: 225 Origin: Round 3, 2013 Draft (#100 overall)

YEAR	TEAM	LVL	AGE	PA	R	2B	3B	HR	RBI	BB	K	SB	CS	AVG/OBP/SLG	TAv	VORP	BABIP	BRR	FRAA	WARP
2015	MID	AA	23	543	63	31	1	10	62	30	82	0	1	.302/.339/.426	.254	6.6	.341	-3.2	3B(84): -1.4, 1B(24): 0.0	0.6
2016	MID	AA	24	164	27	12	3	8	34	18	35	1	0	.338/.409/.628	.362	18.6	.398	-0.5	1B(25): 0.5, 3B(7): -0.5	2.0
2016	NAS	AAA	24	210	33	16	1	6	30	13	40	0	1	.318/.362/.505	.324	17.5	.369	0.0	1B(19): -1.2, 3B(15): -3.5	1.3
2016	OAK	MLB	24	283	36	20	0	13	37	12	60	0	0	.305/.337/.524	.303	19.0	.352	-2.4	3B(72): -0.2	1.9
2017	OAK	MLB	25	605	66	29	0	25	78	23	142	0	1	.271/.302/.451	.257	5.4	.319	-2.1	1B(39): 0.9, 3B(34): -1.4	0.5
2018	*SEA*	*MLB*	*26*	*581*	*66*	*30*	*1*	*21*	*79*	*28*	*133*	*0*	*0*	*.270/.308/.445*	*.264*	*10.3*	*.319*	*-1.4*	*1B 1*	*0.9*
2019	*SEA*	*MLB*	*27*	*570*	*72*	*29*	*0*	*23*	*77*	*32*	*137*	*0*	*0*	*.264/.309/.447*	*.261*	*5.2*	*.313*	*-2.2*	*1B 1*	*0.7*

Breakout: 3% Improve: 51% Collapse: 4% Attrition: 16% MLB: 83% *Comparables: C.J. Cron, Jesus Montero, Ryan Doumit*

The Mariners' largest adult son, acquired from the A's in November, was born ready for first base, not only because he's a mediocre defender at the hot corner, but because he's gregarious and kind of a goof and seems to enjoy baseball primarily as a device for jokin' around with his bros. The problem is that his *bat* was not born ready for first base; given his penchant for unsuccessfully chasing the slider low and away, he might find himself a Triple-A lifer soon enough. A winning team does not carry a .260 TAv at designated hitter, and in these days of 29-man bullpens, if you're not a shortstop, center fielder or catcher, there's not much room for you on the bench.

Guillermo Heredia OF Born: 01/31/91 Age: 27 Bats: R Throws: L Height: 5'10" Weight: 180 Origin: International Free Agent, 2016

YEAR	TEAM	LVL	AGE	PA	R	2B	3B	HR	RBI	BB	K	SB	CS	AVG/OBP/SLG	TAv	VORP	BABIP	BRR	FRAA	WARP
2016	WTN	AA	25	260	39	7	2	2	34	36	32	2	5	.293/.405/.376	.306	17.7	.322	-1.0	CF(41): -2.9, RF(12): -0.1	1.6
2016	TAC	AAA	25	157	27	6	1	2	13	12	15	3	0	.312/.378/.413	.323	17.1	.333	2.1	CF(32): 0.6, LF(3): 0.1	1.9
2016	SEA	MLB	25	107	12	3	0	1	12	12	15	1	1	.250/.349/.315	.248	0.4	.289	-0.6	LF(35): 4.9, RF(14): -0.3	0.5
2017	SEA	MLB	26	426	43	16	0	6	24	27	64	1	5	.249/.315/.337	.237	2.3	.284	1.0	CF(63): 7.1, LF(62): 1.7	1.3
2018	*SEA*	*MLB*	*27*	*192*	*21*	*7*	*1*	*3*	*19*	*16*	*29*	*1*	*1*	*.258/.336/.363*	*.257*	*6.8*	*.292*	*-0.6*	*CF 1, LF 2*	*0.7*
2019	*SEA*	*MLB*	*28*	*287*	*34*	*11*	*1*	*6*	*29*	*26*	*47*	*2*	*2*	*.253/.336/.372*	*.254*	*6.7*	*.288*	*0.5*	*CF 2, LF 2*	*1.2*

Breakout: 7% Improve: 33% Collapse: 9% Attrition: 24% MLB: 87% *Comparables: J.B. Shuck, Michael Brantley, Reggie Willits*

Projected in March as a fourth outfielder, Heredia got an early opportunity to play full time when the Mariners soured on Leonys Martin. Heredia's bat played for a couple of months, but then the pitchers caught up and he looked badly overmatched. Ongoing shoulder issues that eventually required surgery after the season couldn't have helped. Heredia's glove is good enough that he could stick as a defensive-minded fourth outfielder, but with most teams carrying only four non-catcher bench bats it's tougher to justify keeping specialists on the roster, particularly when those hitters are as flummoxed against righties as Heredia was. He did miss nearly two full seasons of baseball, so it's possible that the learning curve is steeper for him than for most, but it's more likely that what you see is what you get.

Kyle Lewis CF Born: 07/13/95 Age: 22 Bats: R Throws: R Height: 6'4" Weight: 210 Origin: Round 1, 2016 Draft (#11 overall)

YEAR	TEAM	LVL	AGE	PA	R	2B	3B	HR	RBI	BB	K	SB	CS	AVG/OBP/SLG	TAv	VORP	BABIP	BRR	FRAA	WARP
2016	EVE	A-	20	135	26	8	5	3	26	16	22	3	0	.299/.385/.530	.329	12.1	.344	-1.2	CF(27): -0.9	1.2
2017	MRN	RK	21	46	9	2	1	1	7	4	14	1	0	.263/.348/.447	.273	3.5	.360	1.4	CF(6): -0.9	0.2
2017	MOD	A+	21	167	20	4	0	6	24	15	38	2	1	.255/.323/.403	.263	1.7	.299	-1.5	CF(13): 0.1	0.2
2018	*SEA*	*MLB*	*22*	*250*	*26*	*9*	*1*	*8*	*30*	*19*	*69*	*0*	*0*	*.222/.288/.382*	*.230*	*0.8*	*.276*	*-0.3*	*CF -1*	*0.0*
2019	*SEA*	*MLB*	*23*	*269*	*32*	*10*	*1*	*9*	*32*	*21*	*73*	*0*	*0*	*.222/.289/.385*	*.236*	*0.0*	*.276*	*-0.5*	*CF -1*	*-0.1*

Breakout: 3% Improve: 15% Collapse: 0% Attrition: 17% MLB: 23% *Comparables: Nick Evans, Chris Marrero, Lars Anderson*

A torn ACL in July 2016 kept Lewis off the field for nearly an entire calendar year and led to another truncated season in 2017. The on-field results were erratic, as you would expect from a 22-year-old who had just returned from a significant injury and who only had 30 professional games under his belt. Lewis' plate discipline was poor and it appeared at times that he wasn't going all-out in deference to the injury. The good news is the raw power that enticed scouts and led the Mariners to take Lewis with the 11th overall pick in the 2016 draft remains intact and the strikeout rate dropped after Lewis was promoted to A-ball. He remains a top prospect based on tools and potential alone, and it's far too early to write him off based on 79 minor-league games.

Taylor Motter MI Born: 09/18/89 Age: 28 Bats: R Throws: R Height: 6'1" Weight: 195 Origin: Round 17, 2011 Draft (#540 overall)

YEAR	TEAM	LVL	AGE	PA	R	2B	3B	HR	RBI	BB	K	SB	CS	AVG/OBP/SLG	TAv	VORP	BABIP	BRR	FRAA	WARP
2015	DUR	AAA	25	558	74	43	1	14	72	57	95	26	8	.292/.366/.471	.304	38.5	.332	-0.7	RF(62): 3.6, 3B(25): 1.2	4.3
2016	TBA	MLB	26	93	11	3	0	2	9	11	19	0	1	.188/.290/.300	.228	-0.4	.217	-0.1	SS(9): -0.4, LF(7): 0.5	0.0
2016	DUR	AAA	26	387	44	17	0	13	46	33	65	19	4	.229/.297/.389	.240	3.7	.245	-1.0	SS(37): -3.0, 3B(25): -1.3	-0.3
2017	TAC	AAA	27	117	24	6	1	7	18	14	12	6	3	.350/.427/.640	.353	16.1	.337	-0.8	SS(19): -0.1, 1B(2): 0.0	1.5
2017	SEA	MLB	27	280	29	12	0	7	26	21	62	12	1	.198/.257/.326	.207	-5.1	.232	1.5	SS(39): -1.8, 2B(18): -0.1	-0.8
2018	*SEA*	*MLB*	*28*	*265*	*35*	*13*	*0*	*9*	*32*	*23*	*53*	*10*	*3*	*.239/.310/.406*	*.254*	*7.9*	*.271*	*0.9*	*LF -2, SS -1*	*0.4*
2019	*SEA*	*MLB*	*29*	*396*	*49*	*19*	*0*	*14*	*49*	*35*	*85*	*14*	*4*	*.235/.307/.410*	*.248*	*6.4*	*.267*	*1.0*	*LF -2, SS -1*	*0.3*

Breakout: 5% Improve: 25% Collapse: 11% Attrition: 28% MLB: 62% *Comparables: Justin Sellers, Josh Wilson, Brian Buscher*

Last year, Motter got the prolonged big-league opportunity that so few career minor leaguers like him ever get. Unfortunately, the results were underwhelming. Motter broke out of the blocks quickly with a five-homer April, but did little after that except steal a handful of bases and get Mariners fans with trichophilia excited every time both he and Ben Gamel were in the game. Motter's versatility and speed should keep him employed on a major-league bench, but his opportunities to start will likely be limited.

Joe Rizzo 3B Born: 03/31/98 Age: 20 Bats: L Throws: R Height: 5'9" Weight: 194 Origin: Round 2, 2016 Draft (#50 overall)

YEAR	TEAM	LVL	AGE	PA	R	2B	3B	HR	RBI	BB	K	SB	CS	AVG/OBP/SLG	TAv	VORP	BABIP	BRR	FRAA	WARP
2016	MRN	RK	18	169	21	7	1	2	21	17	36	2	1	.291/.355/.392	.291	13.0	.360	1.5	3B(39): -5.8	0.7
2017	CLN	A	19	480	47	17	0	7	50	63	113	3	1	.254/.354/.346	.273	18.2	.330	-2.3	3B(97): 5.3	2.5
2018	*SEA*	*MLB*	*20*	*250*	*23*	*8*	*0*	*6*	*26*	*24*	*77*	*0*	*0*	*.209/.289/.328*	*.217*	*-3.4*	*.287*	*-0.4*	*3B -1*	*-0.5*
2019	*SEA*	*MLB*	*21*	*386*	*44*	*14*	*1*	*10*	*40*	*37*	*114*	*0*	*0*	*.220/.299/.354*	*.233*	*-2.6*	*.296*	*-0.9*	*3B -1*	*-0.4*

Breakout: 2% Improve: 8% Collapse: 0% Attrition: 4% MLB: 10% *Comparables: Jeimer Candelario, Cheslor Cuthbert, Matt Dominguez*

Scouts described Rizzo as an "advanced high school bat," which sounds as much like a scouting description as it does the name of an anthropomorphic character from *BoJack Horseman*. As is the case with many 20-year-old hitters, Rizzo's upside is mostly theoretical. Some scouts wonder if his "stocky" 5-foot-9 frame will be a challenge, while others suspect there is little if any room for growth in his profile. We might not know for years if Rizzo will find his way to the majors. On the other hand, the hit tool is legitimate and Rizzo has a good feel for the strike zone. The Mariners hope Rizzo takes to the majors as easily as Mr. Peanutbutter took to acting. Otherwise, they might be stuck with their own version of an awkward Vincent Adultman futilely trying to fit in.

Andrew Romine UT Born: 12/24/85 Age: 32 Bats: B Throws: R Height: 6'1" Weight: 200 Origin: Round 5, 2007 Draft (#178 overall)

YEAR	TEAM	LVL	AGE	PA	R	2B	3B	HR	RBI	BB	K	SB	CS	AVG/OBP/SLG	TAv	VORP	BABIP	BRR	FRAA	WARP
2015	DET	MLB	29	203	25	5	0	2	15	11	46	10	5	.255/.307/.315	.227	-1.3	.328	-1.0	3B(59): 1.1, SS(27): 1.4	0.1
2016	DET	MLB	30	194	21	5	2	2	16	13	38	8	0	.236/.304/.322	.224	-0.7	.291	0.4	3B(44): 1.7, CF(22): 0.2	0.4
2017	DET	MLB	31	348	45	17	2	4	25	22	67	6	4	.233/.289/.336	.218	-6.3	.281	-0.6	2B(27): 1.9, CF(24): -0.9	-0.3
2018	*SEA*	*MLB*	*32*	*161*	*16*	*5*	*1*	*1*	*12*	*11*	*35*	*5*	*2*	*.229/.285/.301*	*.217*	*-1.3*	*.285*	*0.3*	*LF 2, SS 0*	*-0.1*
2019	*SEA*	*MLB*	*33*	*222*	*22*	*7*	*1*	*2*	*18*	*17*	*50*	*6*	*2*	*.225/.291/.303*	*.214*	*-4.4*	*.283*	*-0.1*	*LF 3, SS 0*	*-0.2*

Breakout: 4% Improve: 33% Collapse: 10% Attrition: 30% MLB: 81% *Comparables: Jamey Carroll, Clint Barmes, Ramon Santiago*

For four years, Romine looked every bit the second coming of Don Kelly: light on offense and more versatile than a Swiss Army knife. He even tried his glove at all nine positions in one game, though that read more like a late-season gimmick than a legitimate attempt to expand the Tigers' defensive options. Eagerness is a poor substitute for consistency, and Romine's struggles to produce anything above the Mendoza line hastened his eventual departure. He should have no problem finding a bench to warm in 2018, but the days of contending for a starting position appear to be all but over at this point.

Carlos Ruiz C Born: 01/22/79 Age: 39 Bats: R Throws: R Height: 5'10" Weight: 215 Origin: International Free Agent, 1998

YEAR	TEAM	LVL	AGE	PA	R	2B	3B	HR	RBI	BB	K	SB	CS	AVG/OBP/SLG	TAv	VORP	BABIP	BRR	FRAA	WARP
2015	PHI	MLB	36	320	23	13	1	2	22	28	43	1	1	.211/.290/.285	.219	1.1	.242	0.0	C(83): -17.8	-1.8
2016	PHI	MLB	37	193	18	6	0	3	12	24	28	3	1	.261/.368/.352	.280	10.4	.299	-2.3	C(47): -3.4	0.7
2016	LAN	MLB	37	40	3	2	0	0	3	3	5	0	0	.278/.350/.333	.264	2.2	.323	0.3	C(9): -0.6	0.2
2017	SEA	MLB	38	145	14	8	0	3	11	14	38	1	0	.216/.313/.352	.234	3.0	.282	0.4	C(47): -7.7, P(1): 0.0	-0.5
2018	*SEA*	*MLB*	*39*	*250*	*25*	*11*	*0*	*3*	*22*	*23*	*39*	*2*	*1*	*.232/.315/.330*	*.228*	*4.1*	*.265*	*-0.4*	*C -13, 1B 0*	*-0.9*
2019	*SEA*	*MLB*	*40*	*79*	*8*	*3*	*0*	*1*	*7*	*7*	*13*	*0*	*0*	*.224/.306/.317*	*.224*	*0.0*	*.258*	*-0.1*	*C -6, 1B 0*	*-0.7*

Breakout: 1% Improve: 18% Collapse: 17% Attrition: 24% MLB: 68% *Comparables: Mike Redmond, Brad Ausmus, Ted Simmons*

YEAR	TEAM	P. COUNT	FRM RUNS	BLK RUNS	THRW RUNS	TOT RUNS
2015	PHI	12505	-17.1	-0.1	-1.3	-18.6
2016	PHI	6968	-6.7	1.1	0.5	-5.1
2016	LAN	1291	-0.7	0.1	0.2	-0.4
2017	SEA	5834	-7.7	0.1	0.0	-7.6
2018	*SEA*	*9536*	*-13.5*	*0.4*	*-0.4*	*-13.5*
2019	*SEA*	*2996*	*-8.3*	*0.2*	*-0.2*	*-8.3*

If you had guessed nine years ago that a light-hitting catcher with mediocre defensive skills would be one of the last Phillies standing from their 2008 World Series team, you're either extremely smart or actually clairvoyant. No one this side of Peter Jackson has leveraged more from a ring than Chooch, who parlayed a great run with the 2008-2012 Phillies into a late-in-life second career as a backup backstop. The highlight of Ruiz's 2017 was his pregame ritual with Mariners teammate Kyle Seager in which they "battled" to see who could name the most animals, mostly in Spanish. On the field, Chooch's bat and glove both continued to decline to the point that the end of the road is as clearly in sight as Mordor was to the Hobbitses at the end of their magical quest.

Kyle Seager 3B Born: 11/03/87 Age: 30 Bats: L Throws: R Height: 6'0" Weight: 210 Origin: Round 3, 2009 Draft (#82 overall)

YEAR	TEAM	LVL	AGE	PA	R	2B	3B	HR	RBI	BB	K	SB	CS	AVG/OBP/SLG	TAv	VORP	BABIP	BRR	FRAA	WARP
2015	SEA	MLB	27	686	85	37	0	26	74	54	98	6	6	.266/.328/.451	.279	31.3	.278	-2.3	3B(160): 12.1, SS(1): 0.0	4.7
2016	SEA	MLB	28	676	89	36	3	30	99	69	108	3	1	.278/.359/.499	.293	46.5	.295	1.8	3B(156): 21.5	7.0
2017	SEA	MLB	29	650	72	33	1	27	88	58	110	2	1	.249/.323/.450	.268	21.2	.262	-5.6	3B(154): 7.4	2.9
2018	*SEA*	*MLB*	*30*	*666*	*83*	*32*	*2*	*24*	*90*	*61*	*109*	*4*	*2*	*.261/.336/.446*	*.274*	*29.1*	*.282*	*-1.2*	*3B 11*	*3.6*
2019	*SEA*	*MLB*	*31*	*580*	*79*	*30*	*1*	*23*	*79*	*54*	*99*	*2*	*1*	*.265/.340/.462*	*.274*	*20.9*	*.286*	*-1.5*	*3B 11*	*3.5*

Breakout: 0% Improve: 41% Collapse: 4% Attrition: 10% MLB: 97% *Comparables: Garrett Atkins, Bill Madlock, Aubrey Huff*

In the 1990s, a Fortune 500 chemical corporation blanketed the airwaves with a commercial featuring the tagline: "We don't make the products you buy. We make the products you buy better." Internal market research discovered that while the tagline was highly recognizable few people could explain how, exactly, the company improved said products. Such is the case with Seager, particularly among more casual fans. He's only appeared in the top 10 in a traditional counting category twice—doubles in 2015 and 2016. His WARP and FRAA inform us that Seager is good, but to fully appreciate his gifts you must bear witness to how he plays the game. Seager isn't the most fluid defender, but his instincts and methodology make him one of the best at the hot corner. On offense, he finished with more than 25 dingers for the fourth consecutive year. Seager's presence in the lineup and on the field makes the Mariners better, even if you can't always see it.

Jean Segura SS Born: 03/17/90 Age: 28 Bats: R Throws: R Height: 5'10" Weight: 205 Origin: International Free Agent, 2007

YEAR	TEAM	LVL	AGE	PA	R	2B	3B	HR	RBI	BB	K	SB	CS	AVG/OBP/SLG	TAv	VORP	BABIP	BRR	FRAA	WARP
2015	MIL	MLB	25	584	57	16	5	6	50	13	93	25	6	.257/.281/.336	.217	4.0	.298	5.3	SS(140): 12.4	1.8
2016	ARI	MLB	26	694	102	41	7	20	64	39	101	33	10	.319/.368/.499	.300	54.8	.353	6.5	2B(142): 5.3, SS(23): 0.2	6.2
2017	SEA	MLB	27	566	80	30	2	11	45	34	83	22	8	.300/.349/.427	.262	27.6	.339	2.1	SS(124): -8.9	1.9
2018	*SEA*	*MLB*	*28*	*637*	*83*	*25*	*5*	*11*	*56*	*30*	*94*	*25*	*8*	*.271/.311/.384*	*.250*	*25.9*	*.302*	*2.3*	*SS 1*	*1.9*
2019	*SEA*	*MLB*	*29*	*565*	*64*	*23*	*4*	*12*	*61*	*31*	*84*	*21*	*7*	*.274/.321/.403*	*.252*	*18.4*	*.304*	*3.8*	*SS 1*	*2.1*

Breakout: 1% Improve: 42% Collapse: 8% Attrition: 8% MLB: 97% *Comparables: Erick Aybar, Bill Russell, Alcides Escobar*

After a banner year in Arizona, Segura was acquired by general manager Jerry Dipoto in a five-player swap as a large part of the Mariners' winter makeover. No rational observer anticipated a repeat of Segura's 6.2 WARP, but the drop-off in his first full season in Seattle was dramatic nonetheless. A move out of a hitters' park, a pair of injuries that cost about a month of playing time, a moderate BABIP correction and a shift from second base back to shortstop all played roles in his slippage. Segura was locked in as a long-term, key component of the Mariners' future with a five-year, $70 million contract extension in June. While there are no guarantees in life, a cost-controlled contract with a club option in Segura's age-33 season makes him a relatively safe bet for the Mariners, even if he doesn't duplicate his deeds in the desert.

Danny Valencia 1B Born: 09/19/84 Age: 33 Bats: R Throws: R Height: 6'2" Weight: 210 Origin: Round 19, 2006 Draft (#576 overall)

YEAR	TEAM	LVL	AGE	PA	R	2B	3B	HR	RBI	BB	K	SB	CS	AVG/OBP/SLG	TAv	VORP	BABIP	BRR	FRAA	WARP
2015	TOR	MLB	30	173	26	13	0	7	29	9	40	2	1	.296/.331/.506	.281	6.9	.353	-0.6	LF(32): -1.7, 3B(10): -1.0	0.4
2015	OAK	MLB	30	205	33	10	1	11	37	20	40	0	1	.284/.356/.530	.310	16.7	.308	0.5	3B(45): -2.3	1.5
2016	OAK	MLB	31	517	72	22	1	17	51	41	115	1	1	.287/.346/.446	.287	24.4	.346	-2.5	3B(68): -3.9, RF(37): 1.8	2.3
2017	SEA	MLB	32	500	54	19	3	15	66	40	122	2	2	.256/.314/.411	.258	2.9	.312	-1.7	1B(118): 8.9, RF(10): 0.0	1.2
2018	*SEA*	*MLB*	*33*	*474*	*54*	*23*	*1*	*17*	*62*	*36*	*110*	*2*	*1*	*.264/.322/.441*	*.261*	*8.9*	*.315*	*-1.1*	*1B 7, RF 0*	*1.7*
2019	*SEA*	*MLB*	*34*	*398*	*49*	*17*	*1*	*13*	*49*	*31*	*98*	*1*	*1*	*.252/.313/.414*	*.254*	*1.7*	*.307*	*-0.9*	*1B 6, RF 0*	*0.8*

Breakout: 2% Improve: 33% Collapse: 10% Attrition: 14% MLB: 93% *Comparables: Jeff Baker, Eli Marrero, Garrett Jones*

In the 1980s, a lefty-masher with limited defensive utility was a nice option to have off your bench or to platoon against a tough southpaw. But active rosters with 15 hitters went out of style with acid-washed jeans, so it's rare to see players like Valencia with steady employment these days. For the second year in a row, Valencia started the season with a full-time job but was then pushed into a lesser role. This time around it happened when the Mariners acquired Yonder Alonso for their pennant push. Valencia has a career .863 OPS against lefties. Against righties, that number stands at a pedestrian .685. If you have the luxury of carrying Valencia as the last man on your bench that's great, but relying on him for 600 plate appearances is about as realistic as relying on a magical talking car named KITT to fight crime.

Dan Vogelbach 1B Born: 12/17/92 Age: 25 Bats: L Throws: R Height: 6'0" Weight: 250 Origin: Round 2, 2011 Draft (#68 overall)

YEAR	TEAM	LVL	AGE	PA	R	2B	3B	HR	RBI	BB	K	SB	CS	AVG/OBP/SLG	TAv	VORP	BABIP	BRR	FRAA	WARP
2015	TEN	AA	22	313	41	16	1	7	39	57	61	1	1	.272/.403/.425	.310	16.0	.330	-3.0	1B(75): 1.4	1.9
2016	IOW	AAA	23	365	53	18	2	16	64	55	67	0	0	.318/.425/.548	.349	35.7	.362	-1.8	1B(76): -3.0	3.4
2016	TAC	AAA	23	198	26	7	0	7	32	42	34	0	0	.240/.404/.422	.308	8.9	.263	-3.1	1B(25): -0.9	0.8
2016	SEA	MLB	23	13	0	0	0	0	0	1	6	0	0	.083/.154/.083	.102	-2.3	.167	-0.4	1B(4): -0.3	-0.3
2017	TAC	AAA	24	541	65	25	0	17	83	76	98	3	1	.290/.388/.455	.295	20.1	.332	-7.3	1B(81): -8.3	1.1
2017	SEA	MLB	24	31	0	1	0	0	2	3	9	0	0	.214/.290/.250	.191	-3.0	.316	-1.2	1B(7): -0.3	-0.3
2018	*SEA*	*MLB*	*25*	*200*	*27*	*8*	*0*	*7*	*25*	*28*	*45*	*0*	*0*	*.250/.360/.425*	*.278*	*7.3*	*.299*	*-0.4*	*1B -1*	*0.5*
2019	*SEA*	*MLB*	*26*	*444*	*64*	*19*	*1*	*17*	*59*	*65*	*104*	*0*	*0*	*.254/.366/.446*	*.281*	*18.6*	*.304*	*-1.1*	*1B -2*	*1.8*

Breakout: 6% Improve: 24% Collapse: 6% Attrition: 25% MLB: 53% *Comparables: Kila Ka'aihue, Travis Shaw, Jeff Larish*

All but anointed Seattle's Opening Day first baseman last winter, Vogelbach had a poor spring that landed him in Tacoma instead. He managed to make a pair of brief stops in Seattle, but it's difficult to view 2017 as anything but a step back for the big fella. No one doubts Vogelbach's hit tool, but it's an open question as to whether that will be enough to overcome the myriad shortcomings in his overall game. Saying his defense at first base is passable is a charitable interpretation, and on offense his slow footspeed will cost him against major-league defenses. Perhaps there's still a future major leaguer lurking, but Vogelbach needs to do much better than he has in the minors thus far to earn a prolonged opportunity to prove it.

Evan White 1B Born: 04/26/96 Age: 22 Bats: R Throws: L Height: 6'3" Weight: 205 Origin: Round 1, 2017 Draft (#17 overall)

YEAR	TEAM	LVL	AGE	PA	R	2B	3B	HR	RBI	BB	K	SB	CS	AVG/OBP/SLG	TAv	VORP	BABIP	BRR	FRAA	WARP
2017	EVE	A-	21	55	6	1	1	3	12	6	6	1	1	.277/.345/.532	.310	3.4	.250	-0.1	1B(8): -0.6	0.3
2018	*SEA*	*MLB*	*22*	*250*	*24*	*9*	*1*	*7*	*28*	*17*	*70*	*2*	*1*	*.209/.268/.349*	*.211*	*-8.2*	*.263*	*-0.3*	*1B -1*	*-1.0*
2019	*SEA*	*MLB*	*23*	*229*	*26*	*9*	*0*	*7*	*26*	*17*	*64*	*2*	*1*	*.215/.278/.366*	*.225*	*-5.9*	*.269*	*-0.3*	*1B -1*	*-0.7*

Breakout: 2% Improve: 4% Collapse: 0% Attrition: 4% MLB: 5% *Comparables: Russ Canzler, James Loney, Brandon Snyder*

The 17th overall pick in the 2017 draft, White's scouting profile is unconventional and not just because he possesses that rare "throws left, bats right" combination. Where most college first basemen fit the mold of mammoth thumpers with questionable athleticism, White's best attribute is his defense. He projects as a very good or even excellent first baseman, and his arm and athleticism would play capably in an outfield corner. His hit tool is solid (you don't get drafted in the first round if you can only play defense), but White is more of a line-drive hitter than an over-the-fence bat. As a polished college product, he is expected to move quickly through the Mariners' ranks; the quad injury that limited him in his professional debut was minor and shouldn't impact his future development.

Mike Zunino C Born: 03/25/91 Age: 27 Bats: R Throws: R Height: 6'2" Weight: 220 Origin: Round 1, 2012 Draft (#3 overall)

YEAR	TEAM	LVL	AGE	PA	R	2B	3B	HR	RBI	BB	K	SB	CS	AVG/OBP/SLG	TAv	VORP	BABIP	BRR	FRAA	WARP
2015	SEA	MLB	24	386	28	11	0	11	28	21	132	0	1	.174/.230/.300	.196	-8.4	.239	-1.1	C(112): 5.9	-0.3
2015	TAC	AAA	24	43	7	2	0	3	8	0	8	0	0	.317/.349/.585	.290	2.2	.333	-0.2	C(4): -0.3	0.2
2016	TAC	AAA	25	327	47	15	0	17	57	35	69	0	1	.286/.376/.521	.320	29.7	.318	-2.5	C(57): 17.9	4.9
2016	SEA	MLB	25	192	16	7	0	12	31	21	65	0	0	.207/.318/.470	.289	12.6	.250	-1.7	C(52): 2.8	1.6
2017	TAC	AAA	26	45	7	2	0	5	11	4	5	0	0	.293/.356/.707	.395	9.0	.226	0.6	C(7): 0.8	1.0
2017	SEA	MLB	26	435	52	25	0	25	64	39	160	1	0	.251/.331/.509	.279	27.8	.355	-1.4	C(120): 1.0	2.9
2018	*SEA*	*MLB*	*27*	*452*	*57*	*18*	*1*	*21*	*62*	*34*	*141*	*1*	*0*	*.220/.294/.425*	*.252*	*17.5*	*.277*	*-1.0*	*C 5*	*1.8*
2019	*SEA*	*MLB*	*28*	*446*	*59*	*18*	*0*	*21*	*62*	*37*	*144*	*0*	*0*	*.212/.294/.422*	*.246*	*9.7*	*.268*	*-1.5*	*C 6*	*1.7*

Breakout: 6% Improve: 44% Collapse: 8% Attrition: 13% MLB: 91% *Comparables: J.P. Arencibia, Jarrod Saltalamacchia, Yan Gomes*

YEAR	TEAM	P. COUNT	FRM RUNS	BLK RUNS	THRW RUNS	TOT RUNS
2015	SEA	14437	8.8	-1.6	0.5	7.7
2015	TAC	577	-0.2	0.0	0.0	-0.2
2016	SEA	6955	2.1	1.6	-0.2	3.5
2017	SEA	16181	5.3	-2.6	-0.5	2.1
2018	*SEA*	*16851*	*8.9*	*-1.3*	*-0.3*	*7.3*
2019	*SEA*	*16645*	*8.4*	*-1.2*	*-0.3*	*6.9*

A proliferation of both the quantity and application of data has changed baseball more rapidly in a short time than nearly any wholesale change the sport has made in its history. Nowhere is this more evident than behind the plate. Ten years ago, catchers who struck out over 25 percent of the time and couldn't crack a .250 batting average were considered half-timers at best and overextended caddies at worst. In 2017, seven catchers with 300 or more plate appearances fit this offensive mold. Zunino is emblematic of this rapid change. Once viewed as a problematic backstop because of his inability to hit, he might now be seen as one of the better catchers in baseball thanks to excellent defense, particularly his framing talents. Talk of his poor skills with the bat dissipated in 2017, in part because of a BABIP north of .350 but mostly because of the paradigm shift. There's always the risk that Zunino's hitting craters, but in a world where framing comes first and power plays, his star is ascendant.

PITCHERS

Andrew Albers LHP Born: 10/06/85 Age: 32 Bats: R Throws: L Height: 6'1" Weight: 200 Origin: Round 10, 2008 Draft (#315 overall)

YEAR	TEAM	LVL	AGE	W	L	SV	G	GS	IP	H	HR	BB/9	K/9	K	GB%	BABIP	WHIP	ERA	DRA	WARP	MPH	CMD	PWR	STM
2015	TOR	MLB	29	0	0	0	1	0	2^{2}	1	1	6.8	3.4	1	50%	.000	1.12	3.38	4.35	0.0	88.5			42
2015	BUF	AAA	29	2	11	0	20	15	83^{2}	110	7	2.8	5.7	53	48%	.359	1.63	5.70	3.49	1.7				
2016	ROC	AAA	30	10	6	0	21	21	124^{1}	150	10	2.2	6.1	84	41%	.346	1.45	3.69	2.92	3.5				
2016	MIN	MLB	30	0	0	0	6	2	17	27	5	3.2	8.5	16	49%	.379	1.94	5.82	8.10	-0.6	90.5	62	35	65
2017	GWN	AAA	31	12	3	0	26	17	120^{2}	120	6	1.4	8.6	115	48%	.327	1.15	2.61	1.43	5.5				
2017	SEA	MLB	31	5	1	1	9	6	41	43	6	2.2	8.1	37	34%	.303	1.29	3.51	4.38	0.5	89.8	75	27	67
2018	*SEA*	*MLB*	*32*	*7*	*8*	*0*	*35*	*20*	*126^{1}*	*142*	*19*	*3.2*	*6.3*	*88*	*43%*	*.306*	*1.48*	*5.02*	*5.41*	*0.3*	*89.0*	*71*	*29*	*60*
2019	*SEA*	*MLB*	*33*	*3*	*3*	*0*	*12*	*9*	*60^{1}*	*71*	*9*	*3.0*	*5.7*	*38*	*43%*	*.312*	*1.51*	*5.00*	*5.32*	*0.2*	*88.3*	*71*	*29*	*63*

Breakout: 10% Improve: 20% Collapse: 5% Attrition: 13% MLB: 32% *Comparables: Justin Germano, Kyle Davies, Mike Burns*

When you don't have the best stuff your stuff must always be its best. Yogi Berra never said that, but if he had uttered a malaprop about pitching the line would have been apt. After four-and-a-half great months in the Braves' minor-league system, Albers got the call ... for the Mariners, who acquired him for cash considerations. Albers' velocity hasn't improved all that much since his 2013 major-league debut with the Twins, but the 31-year-old southpaw had the most successful year of his career thanks to the ability to command his 87-mph heater both in and out of the strike zone. It's a fine line for pitchers like Albers, not only from season to season but from start to start. His six-start audition for the desperate Mariners in 2017 earned him the right to pursue continued employment in Japan.

Dan Altavilla RHP Born: 09/08/92 Age: 25 Bats: R Throws: R Height: 5'11" Weight: 200 Origin: Round 5, 2014 Draft (#141 overall)

YEAR	TEAM	LVL	AGE	W	L	SV	G	GS	IP	H	HR	BB/9	K/9	K	GB%	BABIP	WHIP	ERA	DRA	WARP	MPH	CMD	PWR	STM
2015	BAK	A+	22	6	12	0	28	28	148^1	138	11	3.2	8.1	134	37%	.300	1.29	4.07	4.56	0.9				
2016	WTN	AA	23	7	3	16	43	0	56^2	40	3	3.5	10.3	65	48%	.261	1.09	1.91	3.01	1.2				
2016	SEA	MLB	23	0	0	0	15	0	12^1	11	0	0.7	7.3	10	50%	.306	0.97	0.73	3.41	0.2	99.2			47
2017	TAC	AAA	24	2	0	6	20	0	23^1	17	1	5.8	13.9	36	44%	.340	1.37	1.54	4.16	0.3				
2017	SEA	MLB	24	1	1	0	41	0	46^2	43	9	3.9	10.0	52	38%	.281	1.35	4.24	4.84	0.2	98.8	40	71	50
2018	*SEA*	*MLB*	*25*	*1*	*1*	*0*	*25*	*0*	*26*	*23*	*4*	*4.2*	*10.3*	*30*	*41%*	*.292*	*1.34*	*4.18*	*4.50*	*0.2*	*98.6*	*41*	*73*	*50*
2019	*SEA*	*MLB*	*26*	*3*	*1*	*1*	*52*	*0*	55^2	*48*	*9*	*3.9*	*10.5*	*65*	*41%*	*.286*	*1.29*	*4.31*	*4.57*	*0.4*	*98.4*	*41*	*73*	*50*

Breakout: 35% Improve: 51% Collapse: 16% Attrition: 28% MLB: 77% *Comparables: Hector Santiago, James McDonald, Roman Mendez*

When a hitter's Three True Outcomes all increase, astute fans smile knowingly, secure in the knowledge that while a casual fan will rail against a spike in strikeouts the hitter in question has improved. When this happens to a pitcher, the same warm and fuzzy doesn't permeate the cockles of one's heart. The increase in Altavilla's strikeout rate was great. The jump in his walk rate wasn't so great and the nearly 2.0 home runs per nine innings he allowed were cause for alarm. Altavilla's fastball still hits the upper 90s and the slider remains solid, so it's unclear how much of 2017 was due to vagaries of sample size and how much was because hitters adjusted his second time through the league. Altavilla remains what he was: a solid reliever who has the potential to be a reliable eighth-inning guy if he can keep the ball down in the zone and in the ballpark.

Shawn Armstrong RHP Born: 09/11/90 Age: 27 Bats: R Throws: R Height: 6'2" Weight: 225 Origin: Round 18, 2011 Draft (#548 overall)

YEAR	TEAM	LVL	AGE	W	L	SV	G	GS	IP	H	HR	BB/9	K/9	K	GB%	BABIP	WHIP	ERA	DRA	WARP	MPH	CMD	PWR	STM
2015	COH	AAA	24	1	2	16	46	0	49^2	37	0	4.7	14.5	80	43%	.363	1.27	2.36	1.87	1.7				
2015	CLE	MLB	24	0	0	0	8	0	8	5	1	2.2	12.4	11	35%	.250	0.88	2.25	3.44	0.1	96.5			45
2016	COH	AAA	25	3	1	9	47	0	49	27	0	5.3	13.2	72	43%	.270	1.14	1.84	2.14	1.6				
2016	CLE	MLB	25	0	0	0	10	0	10^2	9	1	4.2	5.9	7	53%	.258	1.31	2.53	3.87	0.1	95.3			47
2017	COH	AAA	26	1	1	10	28	0	29^1	27	3	3.4	11.0	36	48%	.324	1.30	3.07	3.45	0.6				
2017	CLE	MLB	26	1	0	0	21	0	24^2	23	5	3.6	7.3	20	40%	.250	1.34	4.38	6.73	-0.4	94.9	41	57	45
2018	*CLE*	*MLB*	*27*	*1*	*1*	*0*	*23*	*0*	*24*	*21*	*3*	*4.4*	*11.0*	*30*	*43%*	*.296*	*1.35*	*4.02*	*4.37*	*0.2*	*94.7*	*41*	*58*	*46*
2019	*CLE*	*MLB*	*28*	*2*	*1*	*1*	*46*	*0*	49^1	*44*	*7*	*4.5*	*10.8*	*59*	*43%*	*.299*	*1.39*	*4.49*	*4.75*	*0.3*	*94.3*	*41*	*58*	*46*

Breakout: 20% Improve: 31% Collapse: 21% Attrition: 27% MLB: 66% *Comparables: Pedro Strop, Alex Hinshaw, Hunter Cervenka*

It's a relatively small step up I-71 from Columbus to Cleveland but a giant leap in competition, as Armstrong's continued Triple-A success and big-league struggles attest. His three power offerings—a mid-90s fastball, a hard slider that works more like a cutter and a power curve that can flash plus—overwhelm minor-league hitters and have helped him strike out 13 batters per nine innings as a Clipper. But his heater lacks wiggle and when his command falters, big-league hitters launch him into orbit. You can see the outlines of a successful middle reliever here, but there's still work to do.

Chase DeJong RHP Born: 12/29/93 Age: 24 Bats: L Throws: R Height: 6'4" Weight: 205 Origin: Round 2, 2012 Draft (#81 overall)

YEAR	TEAM	LVL	AGE	W	L	SV	G	GS	IP	H	HR	BB/9	K/9	K	GB%	BABIP	WHIP	ERA	DRA	WARP	MPH	CMD	PWR	STM
2015	LNS	A	21	7	4	0	14	14	86^1	75	9	1.9	8.0	77	42%	.270	1.08	3.13	2.76	2.5				
2015	RCU	A+	21	4	3	0	11	10	50	44	6	2.7	9.4	52	37%	.277	1.18	3.96	3.70	0.8				
2016	TUL	AA	22	14	5	0	25	25	141^2	106	15	2.5	7.9	125	38%	.239	1.02	2.86	3.35	3.0				
2017	SEA	MLB	23	0	3	0	7	4	28^1	31	5	4.1	4.1	13	32%	.277	1.55	6.35	7.20	-0.6	91.7	46	35	68
2017	TAC	AAA	23	3	6	0	15	15	84	99	18	2.9	6.5	61	37%	.301	1.50	6.00	7.57	-1.7				
2017	ARK	AA	23	1	3	0	5	5	28^2	32	3	3.1	5.7	18	35%	.312	1.47	5.97	5.52	-0.1				
2018	*SEA*	*MLB*	*24*	*1*	*1*	*0*	*20*	*0*	*21*	*21*	*3*	*3.5*	*8.0*	*19*	*36%*	*.286*	*1.33*	*4.89*	*5.04*	*0.0*	*91.5*	*47*	*36*	*70*
2019	*SEA*	*MLB*	*25*	*2*	*1*	*0*	*47*	*0*	*50*	*45*	*9*	*3.8*	*8.4*	*47*	*36%*	*.267*	*1.32*	*4.99*	*5.31*	*0.0*	*91.3*	*48*	*36*	*71*

Breakout: 12% Improve: 21% Collapse: 7% Attrition: 19% MLB: 29% *Comparables: Abe Alvarez, Brock Stewart, Steven Shell*

Seventeen pitchers started at least one game for the Mariners in 2017, tying an esoteric team record set in the first season of the franchise's existence in 1977. DeJong was one of those 17 starters. His repertoire of four decent but unspectacular pitches dovetails well with what you would expect from a pitcher who was part of an extended cast of characters, called upon to perform a duty that many before and after him were also called upon to do. DeJong is young enough that he could improve upon the cutter he started throwing in 2016 or on any of his three other offerings, but for now he remains another face in the crowd, a hurler who was part of a record noticed by few beyond the nerdiest baseball aficionados.

Edwin Diaz RHP Born: 03/22/94 Age: 24 Bats: R Throws: R Height: 6'3" Weight: 165 Origin: Round 3, 2012 Draft (#98 overall)

YEAR	TEAM	LVL	AGE	W	L	SV	G	GS	IP	H	HR	BB/9	K/9	K	GB%	BABIP	WHIP	ERA	DRA	WARP	MPH	CMD	PWR	STM
2015	BAK	A+	21	2	0	0	7	7	37	21	3	2.2	10.2	42	52%	.217	0.81	1.70	1.97	1.4				
2015	WTN	AA	21	5	10	0	20	20	104^1	102	5	3.2	8.9	103	42%	.333	1.33	4.57	3.01	2.6				
2016	WTN	AA	22	3	3	1	16	6	40^2	32	3	1.5	12.0	54	58%	.302	0.96	2.21	1.81	1.6				
2016	SEA	MLB	22	0	4	18	49	0	51^2	45	5	2.6	15.3	88	48%	.377	1.16	2.79	2.27	1.6	101.0	51	67	55
2017	SEA	MLB	23	4	6	34	66	0	66	44	10	4.4	12.1	89	41%	.236	1.15	3.27	3.27	1.4	99.7	32	78	50
2018	*SEA*	*MLB*	*24*	*3*	*2*	*28*	*50*	*0*	*52*	*41*	*6*	*3.6*	*11.9*	*70*	*44%*	*.292*	*1.18*	*3.01*	*3.51*	*1.0*	*100.0*	*40*	*76*	*54*
2019	*SEA*	*MLB*	*25*	*3*	*1*	*25*	*54*	*0*	*57*	*44*	*8*	*3.4*	*12.0*	*76*	*44%*	*.287*	*1.15*	*3.57*	*3.76*	*0.9*	*99.8*	*40*	*76*	*54*

Breakout: 27% Improve: 67% Collapse: 11% Attrition: 13% MLB: 93% *Comparables: Matt Moore, Trevor Rosenthal, Tony Cingrani*

Diaz's sophomore season didn't come close to his electric rookie campaign, but the young fireballer still managed to put up another 30-plus saves while whiffing nearly a third of the batters he faced. The lowest point of Diaz's season came in mid-May, when manager Scott Servais pulled the plug on the wunderkind, moving him briefly to a setup role. While Diaz's high-90s fastball and filthy upper-80s slider didn't lose any of their bite, his ability to command both pitches eluded him at times. Diaz had outings where finding the zone was as difficult as finding Waldo would be if he took off his shirt. He tried compensating by throwing hard cheese down the middle, resulting in a spike in home runs. While predicting reliever futures is next to impossible, Diaz should be a closer for years to come. The question going forward revolves around whether he'll be an elite closer or merely a good one.

Matthew Festa RHP Born: 03/11/93 Age: 25 Bats: R Throws: R Height: 6'2" Weight: 195 Origin: Round 7, 2016 Draft (#207 overall)

YEAR	TEAM	LVL	AGE	W	L	SV	G	GS	IP	H	HR	BB/9	K/9	K	GB%	BABIP	WHIP	ERA	DRA	WARP	MPH	CMD	PWR	STM
2016	EVE	A-	23	6	2	0	14	8	60^{1}	60	3	2.1	8.7	58	49%	.324	1.23	3.73	3.79	0.9				
2017	MOD	A+	24	4	2	6	42	1	69^{2}	61	7	2.5	12.8	99	44%	.327	1.15	3.23	1.84	2.5				
2018	*SEA*	*MLB*	*25*	*3*	*2*	*1*	*42*	*4*	*56^{2}*	*55*	*13*	*3.8*	*10.7*	*67*	*40%*	*.300*	*1.38*	*5.12*	*5.51*	*-0.2*				
2019	*SEA*	*MLB*	*26*	*2*	*2*	*1*	*32*	*4*	*78^{2}*	*79*	*17*	*4.3*	*9.6*	*84*	*40%*	*.298*	*1.47*	*5.39*	*5.74*	*-0.3*				

Breakout: 14% Improve: 17% Collapse: 4% Attrition: 17% MLB: 23% *Comparables: Brandon Gomes, Randy Wells, Mike Fiers*

A seventh-round pick from East Stroudsburg University in 2016, Festa thrived after moving to the bullpen full time. He throws a 95-mph heater that rides up on hitters, and features a high-80s slider and low-80s curveball that he isn't afraid to use as the situation warrants. Festa is on the fast track to the majors and could find his way to Seattle's bullpen as a midseason call-up. He isn't the kind of pitcher who will push a team to a title all by himself, but his contributions in Seattle could change festering feelings about the lack of a playoff appearance since 2001 into a Festa ring feeling if the Mariners make the playoffs.

Marco Gonzales LHP Born: 02/16/92 Age: 26 Bats: L Throws: L Height: 6'1" Weight: 195 Origin: Round 1, 2013 Draft (#19 overall)

YEAR	TEAM	LVL	AGE	W	L	SV	G	GS	IP	H	HR	BB/9	K/9	K	GB%	BABIP	WHIP	ERA	DRA	WARP	MPH	CMD	PWR	STM
2015	SLN	MLB	23	0	0	0	1	1	2^{2}	7	1	3.4	3.4	1	43%	.462	3.00	13.50	8.41	-0.1	91.7			40
2015	MEM	AAA	23	1	5	0	14	14	69^{1}	91	10	3.1	6.6	51	40%	.358	1.66	5.45	5.74	-0.4				
2017	SLN	MLB	25	0	0	0	1	1	3^{1}	6	3	0.0	5.4	2	50%	.273	1.80	13.50	9.61	-0.2	92.4	51	38	59
2017	MEM	AAA	25	6	4	0	11	11	68^{1}	54	6	2.2	7.5	57	45%	.255	1.04	2.90	3.00	2.0				
2017	TAC	AAA	25	2	0	0	2	2	12	8	0	3.8	6.8	9	56%	.235	1.08	4.50	2.30	0.4				
2017	SEA	MLB	25	1	1	0	10	7	36^{2}	53	5	2.7	7.4	30	45%	.393	1.75	5.40	5.63	0.0	93.1	51	38	59
2018	*SEA*	*MLB*	*26*	*5*	*5*	*0*	*28*	*13*	*80*	*85*	*12*	*3.5*	*7.3*	*65*	*42%*	*.298*	*1.44*	*4.67*	*5.06*	*0.3*	*92.6*	*52*	*39*	*53*
2019	*SEA*	*MLB*	*27*	*6*	*9*	*0*	*25*	*25*	*145^{2}*	*157*	*25*	*4.2*	*7.2*	*117*	*42%*	*.302*	*1.54*	*5.36*	*5.70*	*-0.1*	*92.3*	*52*	*39*	*56*

Breakout: 18% Improve: 39% Collapse: 22% Attrition: 36% MLB: 80% *Comparables: Billy Buckner, Chad Bettis, Kyle Lobstein*

"You can never have too many outfielders" isn't a baseball bromide, so it wasn't surprising last summer when the Mariners found themselves desperate for innings and traded promising outfielder Tyler O'Neill to the Cardinals for Gonzales to address a short-term need in their rotation. This isn't to say that Gonzales is a slouch, but at 26 years old it's likely that what you see is what you get: a lefty who throws in the low-90s, has back-of-the-rotation upside, and could wind up in the bullpen. While this sounds like damning with faint praise, having someone capable of eating innings at the back end of a major-league staff is important, even if it isn't particularly scintillating and doesn't necessarily translate to asses in the seats.

Felix Hernandez RHP Born: 04/08/86 Age: 32 Bats: R Throws: R Height: 6'3" Weight: 225 Origin: International Free Agent, 2002

YEAR	TEAM	LVL	AGE	W	L	SV	G	GS	IP	H	HR	BB/9	K/9	K	GB%	BABIP	WHIP	ERA	DRA	WARP	MPH	CMD	PWR	STM
2015	SEA	MLB	29	18	9	0	31	31	201^{2}	180	23	2.6	8.5	191	58%	.289	1.18	3.53	2.81	5.4	94.5	46	37	77
2016	SEA	MLB	30	11	8	0	25	25	153^{1}	138	19	3.8	7.2	122	52%	.271	1.32	3.82	3.88	2.6	92.9	45	38	66
2017	TAC	AAA	31	2	0	0	3	3	13	9	1	2.1	11.1	16	42%	.267	0.92	4.15	3.23	0.3				
2017	SEA	MLB	31	6	5	0	16	16	86^{2}	86	17	2.7	8.1	78	49%	.287	1.29	4.36	3.96	1.6	92.2	45	31	41
2018	*SEA*	*MLB*	*32*	*11*	*9*	*0*	*26*	*26*	*174*	*168*	*26*	*3.2*	*8.1*	*156*	*50%*	*.290*	*1.32*	*4.36*	*4.81*	*1.2*	*92.4*	*45*	*35*	*58*
2019	*SEA*	*MLB*	*33*	*11*	*11*	*0*	*28*	*28*	*169^{2}*	*163*	*25*	*3.3*	*8.1*	*153*	*50%*	*.29*	*1.33*	*4.60*	*4.86*	*1.6*	*91.5*	*44*	*35*	*54*

Breakout: 18% Improve: 39% Collapse: 33% Attrition: 11% MLB: 93% *Comparables: Adam Wainwright, CC Sabathia, C.J. Wilson*

In his first full season, back in 2006, Hernandez's fastball averaged 95.2 mph, which led all ERA qualifiers. Felix fell well short of the 162 innings needed to qualify for the ERA title in 2017, but if he had, his 90.5-mph heater would have placed him in the bottom 10, sandwiched between Clayton Richard and Dan Straily. Using velocity as the sole gauge of a pitcher's greatness is about as instructive as counting the highfalutin 75-cent words in *Moby Dick* to decide if it's a masterpiece. However, losing 5 mph off your fastball is not optimal. Throughout baseball's long history, great pitchers have adjusted, exchanging raw stuff for subtle guile, keeping hitters off-balance while rearing back occasionally to show a fleeting glimpse of the old heat. Felix's career took off when he realized that he didn't need to throw his hardest to dominate hitters, but it might be asking too much for a pitcher with 2,500 innings on his arm and multiple 2017 trips to the disabled list for shoulder bursitis to reinvent himself as a crafty righty. If anyone can do it, it's Felix, but it's more likely that the final two years of his contract in Seattle will feature more lows than highs, with moments less reminiscent of *Moby Dick* and more evocative of *Sharknado*.

Hisashi Iwakuma RHP Born: 04/12/81 Age: 37 Bats: R Throws: R Height: 6'3" Weight: 210 Origin: International Free Agent, 2012

YEAR	TEAM	LVL	AGE	W	L	SV	G	GS	IP	H	HR	BB/9	K/9	K	GB%	BABIP	WHIP	ERA	DRA	WARP	MPH	CMD	PWR	STM
2015	SEA	MLB	34	9	5	0	20	20	129^{2}	117	18	1.5	7.7	111	53%	.271	1.06	3.54	3.38	2.6	92.1	49	27	52
2016	SEA	MLB	35	16	12	0	33	33	199	218	28	2.1	6.6	147	42%	.311	1.33	4.12	4.97	0.9	90.6	50	30	78
2017	SEA	MLB	36	0	2	0	6	6	31	27	7	3.5	4.6	16	41%	.220	1.26	4.35	4.30	0.4	87.9	44	10	22
2018	*SEA*	*MLB*	*37*	*3*	*4*	*0*	*10*	*10*	*53*	*57*	*9*	*3.3*	*6.2*	*37*	*44%*	*.291*	*1.42*	*4.98*	*5.49*	*-0.1*	*89.4*	*48*	*26*	*47*
2019	*SEA*	*MLB*	*38*	*8*	*11*	*0*	*29*	*29*	*178*	*195*	*30*	*3.2*	*6.1*	*120*	*44%*	*.295*	*1.45*	*5.26*	*5.59*	*0.1*	*88.5*	*47*	*26*	*45*

Breakout: 8% Improve: 35% Collapse: 28% Attrition: 15% MLB: 85% *Comparables: Hiroki Kuroda, Kyle Lohse, Roy Halladay*

Never a hard thrower, Iwakuma nonetheless raised concerns in April when his fastball barely cracked 85 mph in his first six starts. Placed on the disabled list in May with a nebulous case of shoulder inflammation, Iwakuma spent nearly the entire season attempting to return to the mound before finally being diagnosed with structural damage and going under the knife for an "arthroscopic debridement" in late September. The procedure puts not only the Bear's status for Opening Day in question, but perhaps what little is left of his career as well. In retrospect, letting the then-35-year-old hurler toss 199 innings in 2016 coming off a failed physical probably wasn't the best idea.

Mike Leake RHP Born: 11/12/87 Age: 30 Bats: R Throws: R Height: 5'10" Weight: 170 Origin: Round 1, 2009 Draft (#8 overall)

YEAR	TEAM	LVL	AGE	W	L	SV	G	GS	IP	H	HR	BB/9	K/9	K	GB%	BABIP	WHIP	ERA	DRA	WARP	MPH	CMD	PWR	STM
2015	CIN	MLB	27	9	5	0	21	21	136^2	123	14	2.2	5.9	90	52%	.262	1.15	3.56	3.67	2.3	93.2	67	46	71
2015	SFN	MLB	27	2	5	0	9	9	55^1	51	8	2.4	4.7	29	53%	.254	1.19	4.07	4.27	0.5	93.0	67	46	71
2016	SLN	MLB	28	9	12	0	30	30	176^2	203	20	1.5	6.4	125	55%	.318	1.32	4.69	4.39	2.0	93.0	80	53	71
2017	SLN	MLB	29	7	12	0	26	26	154	169	19	2.0	6.0	103	55%	.306	1.32	4.21	4.23	2.3	91.6	61	42	76
2017	SEA	MLB	29	3	1	0	5	5	32	32	1	0.6	7.6	27	50%	.323	1.06	2.53	4.32	0.4	92.1	61	42	76
2018	*SEA*	*MLB*	*30*	*10*	*9*	*0*	*28*	*28*	*148*	*153*	*17*	*2.6*	*6.3*	*104*	*52%*	*.296*	*1.33*	*4.07*	*4.51*	*1.5*	*91.7*	*69*	*46*	*73*
2019	*SEA*	*MLB*	*31*	*9*	*10*	*0*	*30*	*30*	*188^1*	*202*	*26*	*2.5*	*6.5*	*136*	*52%*	*.302*	*1.35*	*4.54*	*4.81*	*1.5*	*91.2*	*68*	*46*	*73*

Breakout: 10% Improve: 45% Collapse: 29% Attrition: 9% MLB: 95% *Comparables: Jordan Zimmermann, Jon Garland, Matt Cain*

From Grant Balfour to Bob Walk to Homer Bailey, baseball history is littered with comically bad names for pitchers. Mike Leake is never lumped in with these "bad" pitcher names, but given how much he relies on his defense for outs, maybe he should be. Since 2011, Mark Buehrle is the only starting pitcher with 1,000-plus innings and a lower strikeout rate than Leake. When the Cardinals signed Leake to a five-year, $80 million deal in 2015, they didn't have the right players to plug the holes behind him. In particular, their infield defense sometimes left Leake all wet. There is nothing worse than the drip, drip, drip of base hits, but with Kyle Seager, Jean Segura and Robinson Cano backing him up in Seattle, Leake at least stopped the rain of opposing hitters and the torrent of complaints about his ERA. He will never be a staff ace, but on his best nights fans at Safeco Field will look at the end result and think to themselves "dam, he's good!"

Ariel Miranda LHP Born: 01/10/89 Age: 29 Bats: L Throws: L Height: 6'2" Weight: 190 Origin: International Free Agent, 2015

YEAR	TEAM	LVL	AGE	W	L	SV	G	GS	IP	H	HR	BB/9	K/9	K	GB%	BABIP	WHIP	ERA	DRA	WARP	MPH	CMD	PWR	STM
2015	FRD	A+	26	1	1	0	5	5	22	16	2	3.3	9.8	24	18%	.255	1.09	4.09	3.69	0.4				
2015	BOW	AA	26	5	2	0	8	8	45	40	1	3.6	8.2	41	37%	.298	1.29	3.60	4.13	0.5				
2016	BAL	MLB	27	0	0	0	1	0	2	4	0	0.0	18.0	4	43%	.571	2.00	13.50	8.81	-0.1	95.4	57	45	65
2016	NOR	AAA	27	4	7	0	19	19	100^2	95	11	2.8	7.8	87	38%	.291	1.25	3.93	4.07	1.5				
2016	SEA	MLB	27	5	2	0	11	10	56	43	12	2.9	6.4	40	31%	.205	1.09	3.54	5.49	-0.1	95.5	57	45	65
2017	SEA	MLB	28	8	7	0	31	29	160	140	37	3.5	7.7	137	34%	.236	1.27	5.12	5.45	0.2	93.9	51	42	71
2018	*SEA*	*MLB*	*29*	*7*	*8*	*0*	*23*	*23*	*121*	*123*	*25*	*3.6*	*7.7*	*104*	*35%*	*.282*	*1.38*	*5.18*	*5.71*	*-0.4*	*93.6*	*52*	*43*	*68*
2019	*SEA*	*MLB*	*30*	*8*	*11*	*0*	*29*	*29*	*182*	*172*	*35*	*3.6*	*8.0*	*161*	*35%*	*.27*	*1.34*	*5.23*	*5.57*	*0.2*	*93.2*	*52*	*42*	*68*

Breakout: 21% Improve: 35% Collapse: 15% Attrition: 22% MLB: 63% *Comparables: J.A. Happ, Chase Anderson, Wade LeBlanc*

You have the right to expect six innings out of your favorite team's starting pitcher. Any innings that pitcher cannot provide may come back to harm your team on a field of ball. You have the right to go to the concession stands or the bathroom if it's a long inning, especially if the pitching coach visits the mound or if there's a protracted use of instant replay. If you go to the concession stands or the bathroom and return to your seat, and the half inning is still going, you have a right to groan about the outcome of the inning. If you decide that you want to leave the game because the pitcher has given up five or more runs, you have the right to enjoy the rest of your day without feeling guilty about leaving early. Knowing and understanding these rights as a baseball fan, are you still willing to attend Mariners games, especially if it's a day when Ariel Miranda is pitching? Great! Here are your tickets. Have a great time at Safeco Field!

Andrew Moore RHP Born: 06/02/94 Age: 24 Bats: R Throws: R Height: 6'0" Weight: 185 Origin: Round 2, 2015 Draft (#72 overall)

YEAR	TEAM	LVL	AGE	W	L	SV	G	GS	IP	H	HR	BB/9	K/9	K	GB%	BABIP	WHIP	ERA	DRA	WARP	MPH	CMD	PWR	STM
2015	EVE	A-	21	1	1	0	14	8	39	37	2	0.5	9.9	43	46%	.340	1.00	2.08	1.39	1.7				
2016	BAK	A+	22	3	1	0	9	9	54^2	36	2	2.1	7.7	47	45%	.230	0.90	1.65	3.01	1.5				
2016	WTN	AA	22	9	3	0	19	19	108^1	112	9	1.5	7.1	86	36%	.320	1.20	3.16	2.34	3.6				
2017	ARK	AA	23	1	2	0	6	5	34^2	28	4	2.3	8.6	33	32%	.261	1.07	2.08	4.35	0.3				
2017	TAC	AAA	23	3	4	0	15	14	75	68	9	1.6	7.9	66	32%	.273	1.08	3.48	4.22	1.2				
2017	SEA	MLB	23	1	5	0	11	9	59	60	14	1.2	4.7	31	29%	.243	1.15	5.34	6.33	-0.5	93.0	71	35	71
2018	*SEA*	*MLB*	*24*	*2*	*2*	*0*	*5*	*5*	*28*	*29*	*5*	*2.9*	*7.6*	*24*	*35%*	*.292*	*1.33*	*4.75*	*5.25*	*0.0*	*92.8*	*73*	*36*	*73*
2019	*SEA*	*MLB*	*25*	*9*	*12*	*0*	*30*	*30*	*188^1*	*191*	*39*	*2.7*	*7.9*	*166*	*35%*	*.285*	*1.31*	*5.17*	*5.50*	*0.3*	*92.6*	*74*	*36*	*74*

Breakout: 15% Improve: 39% Collapse: 17% Attrition: 27% MLB: 64% *Comparables: Joe Musgrove, Brett Oberholtzer, Junichi Tazawa*

Pitchers like Moore who don't throw particularly hard or have a devastating secondary out pitch are always walking the tightrope. After his midseason promotion to Seattle, Moore's season was frequently an exercise in free fall, a rapid descent to earth presaged by an extremely low strikeout rate and a high fly-ball rate that led to too many balls exiting the yard in short order. Moore doesn't have the raw stuff to survive on mistakes in the zone, and as is the case with most pitchers with non-elite stuff he won't have much of a future without a sharp improvement in command or a sudden uptick in velocity.

Juan Nicasio RHP Born: 08/31/86 Age: 31 Bats: R Throws: R Height: 6'4" Weight: 252 Origin: International Free Agent, 2006

YEAR	TEAM	LVL	AGE	W	L	SV	G	GS	IP	H	HR	BB/9	K/9	K	GB%	BABIP	WHIP	ERA	DRA	WARP	MPH	CMD	PWR	STM
2015	LAN	MLB	28	1	3	1	53	1	58^{1}	59	1	4.9	10.0	65	47%	.360	1.56	3.86	4.11	0.4	98.1	42	72	45
2016	PIT	MLB	29	10	7	0	52	12	118	117	15	3.4	10.5	138	45%	.331	1.37	4.50	3.78	1.9	97.2	61	61	63
2017	PIT	MLB	30	2	5	2	65	0	60	49	4	2.7	9.0	60	47%	.285	1.12	2.85	3.64	1.0	97.3	61	73	54
2017	PHI	MLB	30	1	0	0	2	0	1^{1}	0	0	0.0	6.8	1	100%	.000	0.00	0.00	9.05	-0.1	98.3	61	73	54
2017	SLN	MLB	30	2	0	4	9	0	11	9	1	1.6	9.0	11	39%	.267	1.00	1.64	3.73	0.2	97.6	61	73	54
2018	SEA	MLB	31	4	4	0	33	8	72	68	9	3.7	9.1	73	45%	.300	1.37	4.03	4.41	0.7	96.5	57	67	54
2019	SEA	MLB	32	7	6	0	61	14	134^{2}	132	18	3.8	9.3	139	45%	.308	1.40	4.10	4.57	1.3	96.0	59	66	56

Breakout: 28% Improve: 62% Collapse: 20% Attrition: 18% MLB: 93% *Comparables: Jeff Samardzija, Chad Gaudin, Carlos Villanueva*

Nicasio was the epicenter of the most hilarious trade of 2017. The fading Pirates did not want the hard-throwing reliever to go to a "direct competitor," according to Pittsburgh general manager Neal Huntington, almost certainly insinuating a team within the division was blocking a trade. The Buccos tried to sneak him through outright waivers to the American League, but he was instead claimed by the Phillies, who then orchestrated a September trade with the Cardinals, which some suspect was the team who claimed Nicasio in the first place. He signed a two-year deal with the Mariners in December.

James Paxton LHP Born: 11/06/88 Age: 29 Bats: L Throws: L Height: 6'4" Weight: 235 Origin: Round 4, 2010 Draft (#132 overall)

YEAR	TEAM	LVL	AGE	W	L	SV	G	GS	IP	H	HR	BB/9	K/9	K	GB%	BABIP	WHIP	ERA	DRA	WARP	MPH	CMD	PWR	STM
2015	SEA	MLB	26	3	4	0	13	13	67	67	8	3.9	7.5	56	50%	.289	1.43	3.90	4.68	0.3	97.2	40	64	27
2016	TAC	AAA	27	4	3	0	11	11	50^{2}	43	6	2.7	9.4	53	52%	.285	1.14	3.73	3.37	1.1				
2016	SEA	MLB	27	6	7	0	20	20	121	134	9	1.8	8.7	117	49%	.347	1.31	3.79	3.55	2.5	99.7	47	63	71
2017	SEA	MLB	28	12	5	0	24	24	136	113	9	2.4	10.3	156	46%	.300	1.10	2.98	3.15	3.7	97.6	34	62	58
2018	SEA	MLB	29	10	7	0	26	26	148	137	18	2.9	9.5	156	47%	.301	1.27	3.54	3.92	2.5	97.6	39	63	55
2019	SEA	MLB	30	11	10	0	31	31	193^{1}	184	24	3.1	9.2	198	47%	.305	1.30	3.97	4.19	2.8	97.3	39	62	60

Breakout: 24% Improve: 47% Collapse: 22% Attrition: 16% MLB: 98% *Comparables: Jacob deGrom, Tyson Ross, Dallas Keuchel*

The city that gave us such wonderful nicknames—including "The Big Unit," "King Felix" and "The Bone Man"—has added another colorful moniker to our sports lexicon, dubbing the Canadian-born Paxton "Big Maple." *Consumer Reports* informs us that while pancake syrup is "singularly sweet with little complexity and noticeable artificial flavors," maple syrup "has a clean, complex maple flavor with hints of caramel, vanilla and prune." Watching Paxton on any given night is the culinary equivalent of going beyond a simplistic sugary treat and savoring a delicious breakfast condiment whose flavor brandishes itself on your memory all day, even after you have brushed your teeth. The injuries that once contributed to Paxton's inconsistency now only serve to cap his ceiling. It's best to simply savor Paxton's complexly sweet performance when he's healthy rather than fret over how many innings he might pitch in a given season, although 200 innings would be something to behold from a pitcher who has become one of the best arms in baseball.

James Pazos LHP Born: 05/05/91 Age: 27 Bats: R Throws: L Height: 6'2" Weight: 235 Origin: Round 13, 2012 Draft (#427 overall)

YEAR	TEAM	LVL	AGE	W	L	SV	G	GS	IP	H	HR	BB/9	K/9	K	GB%	BABIP	WHIP	ERA	DRA	WARP	MPH	CMD	PWR	STM
2015	SWB	AAA	24	3	1	2	21	0	33	25	0	4.1	10.1	37	45%	.298	1.21	1.09	3.12	0.7				
2015	NYA	MLB	24	0	0	0	11	0	5	3	0	5.4	5.4	3	47%	.200	1.20	0.00	7.33	-0.2	97.1			41
2016	SWB	AAA	25	2	2	1	23	0	27^{1}	19	1	6.3	13.5	41	57%	.316	1.39	2.63	2.72	0.7				
2016	NYA	MLB	25	1	0	0	7	0	3^{1}	7	2	2.7	8.1	3	46%	.455	2.40	13.50	6.45	-0.1	97.9			22
2017	SEA	MLB	26	4	5	0	59	0	53^{2}	51	7	4.0	10.9	65	51%	.317	1.40	3.86	4.87	0.2	97.5	36	67	45
2018	SEA	MLB	27	3	2	0	50	0	52	46	7	4.3	10.7	63	47%	.297	1.36	4.01	4.37	0.5	97.0	36	68	37
2019	SEA	MLB	28	2	1	0	48	0	51	46	7	4.2	10.7	60	47%	.3	1.37	4.34	4.59	0.4	96.7	36	68	36

Breakout: 29% Improve: 41% Collapse: 21% Attrition: 26% MLB: 75% *Comparables: Dan Runzler, Alex Hinshaw, Mark Melancon*

A 40-man roster crunch forced the Yankees to flip Pazos to Seattle last winter and the Mariners reaped the rewards, carrying the left-hander on the major-league squad all season. Pazos looked like a fringy relief option throughout his minor-league career until he added a few ticks to his fastball, jumping from the low-90s to the mid-90s. Pazos mixes in a low-80s slider as well. He looked like a relief ace in the making for a couple months last season before hitters inevitably caught up with his two-pitch arsenal. He's death to lefties, so his worst-case scenario is settling into a LOOGY role.

David Phelps RHP Born: 10/09/86 Age: 31 Bats: R Throws: R Height: 6'2" Weight: 200 Origin: Round 14, 2008 Draft (#440 overall)

YEAR	TEAM	LVL	AGE	W	L	SV	G	GS	IP	H	HR	BB/9	K/9	K	GB%	BABIP	WHIP	ERA	DRA	WARP	MPH	CMD	PWR	STM
2015	MIA	MLB	28	4	8	0	23	19	112	119	11	2.7	6.2	77	43%	.303	1.36	4.50	5.01	0.1	93.0	65	42	56
2016	MIA	MLB	29	7	6	4	64	5	86^{2}	61	6	3.9	11.8	114	48%	.286	1.14	2.28	2.74	2.3	96.1	60	60	55
2017	MIA	MLB	30	2	4	0	44	0	47	42	5	4.0	9.8	51	49%	.308	1.34	3.45	4.12	0.5	95.7	55	55	49
2017	SEA	MLB	30	2	1	0	10	0	8^{2}	9	0	5.2	11.4	11	42%	.375	1.62	3.12	3.33	0.2	96.0	55	55	49
2018	SEA	MLB	31	3	3	0	55	0	58	50	6	3.9	9.4	61	46%	.292	1.30	3.55	3.98	0.8	94.1	60	52	52
2019	SEA	MLB	32	3	1	1	52	0	55^{2}	50	6	3.9	9.5	58	46%	.299	1.34	4.05	4.27	0.6	94.3	58	55	51

Breakout: 14% Improve: 41% Collapse: 25% Attrition: 6% MLB: 90% *Comparables: C.J. Wilson, A.J. Burnett, Anibal Sanchez*

Acquired in late July from the Marlins for four prospects, Phelps pitched in only seven games for the Mariners before landing on the disabled list with a right elbow impingement. He returned in late August, but three appearances later Phelps was shut down for the season. For years, Phelps was used as a swingman by the Yankees and the Marlins, but throughout his career his best results have come when used solely as a reliever who can go more than an inning when needed. Whenever he's ready to answer the bell in 2018, Phelps' four-pitch arsenal offers value regardless of his role.

Erasmo Ramirez RHP Born: 05/02/90 Age: 28 Bats: R Throws: R Height: 5'10" Weight: 215 Origin: International Free Agent, 2007

YEAR	TEAM	LVL	AGE	W	L	SV	G	GS	IP	H	HR	BB/9	K/9	K	GB%	BABIP	WHIP	ERA	DRA	WARP	MPH	CMD	PWR	STM
2015	TBA	MLB	25	11	6	0	34	27	163^{1}	145	16	2.2	6.9	126	49%	.272	1.13	3.75	3.34	3.3	94.1	53	41	64
2016	TBA	MLB	26	7	11	2	64	1	90^{2}	90	14	2.6	6.3	63	55%	.280	1.28	3.77	4.09	0.9	94.3	38	50	53
2017	TBA	MLB	27	4	3	1	26	8	69^{1}	66	10	2.1	7.1	55	49%	.280	1.18	4.80	3.80	1.3	93.2	67	36	58
2017	SEA	MLB	27	1	3	0	11	11	62	57	12	2.2	7.8	54	39%	.257	1.16	3.92	4.18	0.9	93.4	67	36	58
2018	*SEA*	*MLB*	*28*	*9*	*9*	*0*	*38*	*23*	*146*	*150*	*23*	*3.1*	*7.1*	*116*	*48%*	*.291*	*1.36*	*4.63*	*5.05*	*0.5*	*93.2*	*56*	*41*	*58*
2019	*SEA*	*MLB*	*29*	*9*	*11*	*0*	*28*	*28*	*170^{1}*	*177*	*30*	*3.0*	*7.3*	*138*	*48%*	*.293*	*1.38*	*5.05*	*5.36*	*0.5*	*92.8*	*57*	*41*	*57*

Breakout: 18% Improve: 55% Collapse: 15% Attrition: 11% MLB: 89% *Comparables: Joe Blanton, Chris Tillman, Brandon McCarthy*

Unlike many public-facing entities, Major League Baseball teams seldom have slogans or mission statements they share with the public. If the Mariners did employ such a slogan, "necessity is the mother of invention" would be as good a sign as any for Jerry Dipoto to hang behind his desk for visitors to see when they entered his office. Ramirez's return to Seattle after a 28-month stay in a Rays uniform wasn't a move designed to push the Mariners over the top, but rather to fill a hole in a rotation hobbled by injuries. Ramirez's greatest skill doesn't rest in a specific pitch—instead, it's his ability to be a one-out reliever, a six-inning starting pitcher or anything in between. Ramirez isn't a realistic candidate to break the mold and become an ace, but his ability to shift between roles with ease is valuable in an environment where pitchers succumb to injury more frequently than ever and quality replacements are more difficult to find than inspirational quotes to hang over your desk that will improve productivity for the whole team in your department at the widget factory.

Marc Rzepczynski LHP Born: 08/29/85 Age: 32 Bats: L Throws: L Height: 6'2" Weight: 220 Origin: Round 5, 2007 Draft (#175 overall)

YEAR	TEAM	LVL	AGE	W	L	SV	G	GS	IP	H	HR	BB/9	K/9	K	GB%	BABIP	WHIP	ERA	DRA	WARP	MPH	CMD	PWR	STM
2015	CLE	MLB	29	2	3	0	45	0	20^{1}	23	1	4.4	10.6	24	73%	.379	1.62	4.43	3.01	0.4	94.7	41	47	44
2015	SDN	MLB	29	0	1	0	27	0	14^{2}	17	2	2.5	10.4	17	66%	.385	1.43	7.36	3.83	0.2	94.3	41	47	44
2016	OAK	MLB	30	1	0	0	56	0	36	38	1	6.0	9.2	37	71%	.352	1.72	3.00	2.79	0.9	93.5	50	47	46
2016	WAS	MLB	30	0	0	0	14	0	11^{2}	8	0	3.9	6.9	9	63%	.267	1.11	1.54	4.46	0.1	94.2	50	47	46
2017	SEA	MLB	31	2	2	1	64	0	31^{1}	29	2	5.7	7.2	25	69%	.307	1.56	4.02	3.73	0.5	93.7	39	46	40
2018	*SEA*	*MLB*	*32*	*3*	*3*	*0*	*50*	*0*	*52*	*51*	*5*	*5.1*	*8.2*	*48*	*60%*	*.303*	*1.55*	*4.38*	*4.66*	*0.3*	*92.9*	*44*	*46*	*43*
2019	*SEA*	*MLB*	*33*	*2*	*1*	*0*	*36*	*0*	*38*	*40*	*4*	*5.5*	*7.6*	*32*	*60%*	*.311*	*1.66*	*5.07*	*5.37*	*-0.1*	*92.3*	*44*	*46*	*42*

Breakout: 17% Improve: 39% Collapse: 24% Attrition: 14% MLB: 86% *Comparables: Saul Rivera, Casey Janssen, Ryan Mattheus*

During the past two seasons, a total of 397 pitchers threw more innings than Rzepczynski. In that time, no pitcher issued more intentional walks than the vowel-challenged left-hander. On the surface, Scrabble's numbers against right-handers look like a portrait in wildness, an homage to the flaky southpaws of yore who couldn't hit the broadside of a battleship. The reality is that while Rzepczynski's control against righties could be better, his splits wouldn't be as radical as they appear without the free passes that are a directive from the dugout. Rzepczynski remains what he has been for years: a ground-ball machine who is murder on left-handers but who relies heavily on his defense against right-handers. If his left arm is in working order, Rzepczynski will be gainfully employed for years to come.

Shae Simmons RHP Born: 09/03/90 Age: 27 Bats: R Throws: R Height: 5'11" Weight: 190 Origin: Round 22, 2012 Draft (#689 overall)

YEAR	TEAM	LVL	AGE	W	L	SV	G	GS	IP	H	HR	BB/9	K/9	K	GB%	BABIP	WHIP	ERA	DRA	WARP	MPH	CMD	PWR	STM
2016	GWN	AAA	25	0	0	1	12	4	12	7	0	6.8	10.5	14	50%	.250	1.33	1.50	6.01	-0.1				
2016	ATL	MLB	25	0	0	0	7	0	6^{2}	6	0	0.0	4.1	3	59%	.273	0.90	1.35	3.38	0.1	98.3			24
2017	SEA	MLB	26	0	2	0	9	0	7^{2}	4	1	4.7	9.4	8	44%	.176	1.04	7.04	2.98	0.2	97.4			30
2018	*SEA*	*MLB*	*27*	*2*	*1*	*0*	*29*	*1*	*33^{2}*	*31*	*5*	*5.3*	*8.9*	*33*	*48%*	*.289*	*1.51*	*5.00*	*5.38*	*0.0*	*97.3*			*28*
2019	*SEA*	*MLB*	*28*	*2*	*1*	*0*	*48*	*1*	*50^{1}*	*51*	*8*	*5.4*	*7.8*	*44*	*48%*	*.296*	*1.61*	*5.40*	*5.74*	*-0.3*	*96.8*			*28*

Breakout: 23% Improve: 34% Collapse: 18% Attrition: 28% MLB: 66% *Comparables: Vic Black, Dan Runzler, Alex Hinshaw*

"For all sad words of tongue and pen, the saddest are these, 'it might have been.'" This famous line from John Greenleaf Whittier's 1856 poem "Maud Muller" didn't pertain to talented yet oft-injured pitchers, but aptly describes their sad plight. Simmons falls into this category of obviously talented arms who just can't seem to stay on the field for more than a few outings at a time. There was plenty of buzz in Seattle when Jerry Dipoto acquired the flame-throwing reliever from the Braves, but the injury bug bit again. This time the culprit was a flexor strain that led to a disabled list trip before the season even started, leaving Simmons out of commission until September. If Simmons is lucky he could stay healthy for an entire season, but the odds are about as good as they were for Maid Muller and the imperious judge from Whittier's tragic yarn.

Nick Vincent RHP Born: 07/12/86 Age: 31 Bats: R Throws: R Height: 6'0" Weight: 185 Origin: Round 18, 2008 Draft (#555 overall)

YEAR	TEAM	LVL	AGE	W	L	SV	G	GS	IP	H	HR	BB/9	K/9	K	GB%	BABIP	WHIP	ERA	DRA	WARP	MPH	CMD	PWR	STM
2015	ELP	AAA	28	5	3	1	40	0	50^{1}	48	5	2.7	12.2	68	44%	.355	1.25	3.04	1.15	2.2				
2015	SDN	MLB	28	0	1	0	26	0	23	25	0	3.9	8.6	22	34%	.368	1.52	2.35	4.74	0.0	91.3	61	57	52
2016	SEA	MLB	29	4	4	3	60	0	60^{1}	53	11	2.2	9.7	65	34%	.271	1.13	3.73	3.57	1.0	92.0	62	64	45
2017	SEA	MLB	30	3	3	0	69	0	64^{2}	62	3	1.8	7.0	50	35%	.301	1.16	3.20	3.65	1.1	91.3	67	58	49
2018	*SEA*	*MLB*	*31*	*3*	*3*	*5*	*55*	*0*	*58*	*58*	*9*	*3.4*	*8.5*	*55*	*38%*	*.296*	*1.37*	*4.43*	*4.70*	*0.3*	*90.7*	*64*	*60*	*48*
2019	*SEA*	*MLB*	*32*	*2*	*1*	*2*	*44*	*0*	*46^{1}*	*46*	*8*	*3.7*	*8.6*	*44*	*38%*	*.299*	*1.41*	*4.77*	*5.05*	*0.1*	*90.3*	*64*	*60*	*47*

Breakout: 35% Improve: 50% Collapse: 20% Attrition: 11% MLB: 88% *Comparables: Heath Bell, Casey Janssen, J.J. Putz*

When it comes to bullpen management, there is more homespun advice than on the back of the menu at Cracker Barrel. Relievers are supposed to throw hard and get strikeouts. Failing that, they should at least generate plenty of ground-ball outs. Vincent does neither of these things, yet has made himself into a successful big-league reliever. The key is a four-seam fastball that Vincent uses as a secondary pitch, not a primary weapon. The rise on his heater makes it difficult for batters to generate solid contact, and keeps the ball in the yard. Vincent is never going to be the best item on a team's menu of bullpen options, but like Cracker Barrel's "Uncle Herschel's Favorite," you better darn well believe he's going to get the job done.

Art Warren RHP Born: 03/23/93 Age: 25 Bats: R Throws: R Height: 6'3" Weight: 230 Origin: Round 23, 2015 Draft (#695 overall)

YEAR	TEAM	LVL	AGE	W	L	SV	G	GS	IP	H	HR	BB/9	K/9	K	GB%	BABIP	WHIP	ERA	DRA	WARP	MPH	CMD	PWR	STM
2016	CLN	A	23	9	1	0	14	14	74	71	1	2.2	6.7	55	54%	.307	1.20	2.19	4.73	0.3				
2016	BAK	A+	23	2	1	0	13	6	36^2	42	1	6.9	9.3	38	50%	.366	1.91	5.15	6.16	-0.4				
2017	MOD	A+	24	3	1	8	43	0	64^2	58	5	3.5	9.3	67	45%	.312	1.28	3.06	5.33	-0.3				
2018	*SEA*	*MLB*	*25*	*3*	*3*	*1*	*34*	*7*	*60*	*61*	*11*	*4.6*	*8.9*	*59*	*42%*	*.300*	*1.52*	*5.36*	*5.77*	*-0.3*				
2019	*SEA*	*MLB*	*26*	*3*	*3*	*1*	*32*	*8*	*85^1*	*96*	*17*	*4.9*	*7.8*	*74*	*42%*	*.313*	*1.67*	*5.85*	*6.23*	*-0.6*				

Breakout: 1% Improve: 4% Collapse: 1% Attrition: 5% MLB: 5% *Comparables: Damien Magnifico, Levale Speigner, Evan Reed*

Minor-league saves are about as predictive of future major-league success as having a cool catchphrase is. But Warren isn't just a filler organizational arm logging meaningless back-end innings in the low minors. He remains a work in progress, but when everything is working his fastball touches the upper-90s with significant downward plane, while his slider can hit the upper-80s. If Warren can manage to find enough consistency with both pitches, he should find himself in the Mariners' bullpen in 2018, ready to Declare Warren Batters. Er, maybe not. Even if the stuff is ready the catchphrase will need work.

Tony Zych RHP Born: 08/07/90 Age: 27 Bats: R Throws: R Height: 6'3" Weight: 190 Origin: Round 4, 2011 Draft (#129 overall)

YEAR	TEAM	LVL	AGE	W	L	SV	G	GS	IP	H	HR	BB/9	K/9	K	GB%	BABIP	WHIP	ERA	DRA	WARP	MPH	CMD	PWR	STM
2015	WTN	AA	24	0	0	5	15	0	16^2	11	0	0.0	9.7	18	54%	.268	0.66	2.16	2.30	0.5				
2015	TAC	AAA	24	1	2	4	25	0	31^2	34	2	2.6	10.5	37	54%	.376	1.36	3.41	2.00	1.0				
2015	SEA	MLB	24	0	0	0	13	1	18^1	17	1	1.5	11.8	24	53%	.348	1.09	2.45	3.08	0.4	98.6	47	56	44
2016	SEA	MLB	25	1	0	0	12	0	13^2	10	0	6.6	13.8	21	50%	.357	1.46	3.29	2.88	0.3	97.3	57	52	2
2017	SEA	MLB	26	6	3	1	45	0	40^2	30	2	4.6	7.7	35	50%	.255	1.25	2.66	4.24	0.4	96.1	41	52	43
2018	*SEA*	*MLB*	*27*	*3*	*3*	*0*	*55*	*0*	*58*	*53*	*7*	*4.2*	*9.6*	*62*	*48%*	*.304*	*1.40*	*3.98*	*4.34*	*0.5*	*96.3*	*46*	*53*	*30*
2019	*SEA*	*MLB*	*28*	*2*	*1*	*0*	*40*	*0*	*42^2*	*41*	*6*	*4.3*	*10.1*	*48*	*48%*	*.312*	*1.44*	*4.50*	*4.76*	*0.2*	*95.7*	*45*	*53*	*27*

Breakout: 28% Improve: 41% Collapse: 25% Attrition: 22% MLB: 77% *Comparables: Daniel Herrera, Steve Cishek, Mark Melancon*

Multiple injuries have derailed Zych during the past two seasons. He started 2017 on the disabled list recovering from biceps surgery and ended it on the disabled list with a right elbow flexor bundle strain. In between the two DL stints, Zych was good but nowhere near as dominant as he was in his brief cameos in 2015 and 2016. Both his fastball and slider velocity dropped, and Zych's strikeout rate subsequently plummeted. If he can stay healthy, the potential for Zych to be a top-shelf reliever remains, but he has yet to log more than 41 innings in a big-league season and turns 28 this year.

LINEOUTS

Hitters

HITTER	POS	TEAM	LVL	AGE	PA	R	2B	3B	HR	RBI	BB	K	SB	CS	AVG/OBP/SLG	TAv	VORP	BABIP	BRR	FRAA	WARP
Gordon Beckham	2B	TAC	AAA	30	355	37	16	0	9	45	20	58	3	2	.262/.313/.393	.249	6.8	.293	1.4	2B(63): -4.5, 3B(7): -0.8	0.1
	2B	SEA	MLB	30	18	2	0	0	0	0	1	2	1	0	.176/.222/.176	.121	-1.7	.200	0.2	2B(5): 0.0, SS(4): -0.8	-0.2
Mike Ford	1B	SWB	AAA	24	115	19	5	0	7	21	18	16	0	0	.266/.383/.543	.304	7.0	.247	0.1	1B(19): -0.2	0.7
	1B	TRN	AA	24	417	61	19	1	13	65	76	56	1	0	.272/.410/.451	.318	27.0	.291	-1.8	1B(52): -0.5, 3B(1): 0.0	2.9
David Freitas	C	GWN	AAA	28	270	28	13	0	3	21	25	35	0	0	.263/.338/.356	.263	11.2	.292	-1.4	C(62): 7.6, 1B(2): 0.0	1.8
	C	ATL	MLB	28	17	2	2	0	0	2	0	4	0	0	.235/.235/.353	.190	-0.4	.308	0.0	C(6): 0.3	0.0
Tuffy Gosewisch	C	SEA	MLB	33	31	1	0	0	0	0	1	14	0	0	.071/.103/.071	.086	-4.5	.143	-0.3	C(10): -0.2, 1B(1): 0.0	-0.5
	C	TAC	AAA	33	321	27	22	0	4	33	29	68	1	0	.229/.313/.351	.246	7.6	.284	-0.9	C(73): 2.8, 1B(4): 0.3	1.0
Luis Liberato	OF	CLN	A	21	223	34	5	9	6	22	23	51	5	4	.230/.309/.445	.282	14.4	.277	2.5	CF(55): 8.1	2.4
	OF	MOD	A+	21	283	41	11	5	8	28	21	80	7	4	.257/.314/.432	.265	8.8	.341	0.2	CF(43): 0.6, RF(13): 3.4	1.2
Michael Marjama	C	DUR	AAA	27	292	32	16	1	9	51	21	53	3	3	.274/.342/.445	.279	15.7	.312	-1.2	C(48): -0.9	1.4
	C	TAC	AAA	27	86	5	3	1	3	12	7	15	0	0	.167/.244/.346	.231	0.3	.167	0.0	C(14): 0.6, 1B(1): 0.0	0.1
	C	SEA	MLB	27	9	1	1	0	1	1	0	1	0	0	.333/.333/.778	.359	1.2	.286	-0.1	C(5): 0.0	0.1
Tyler Marlette	C	ARK	AA	24	405	47	22	2	11	65	31	89	0	1	.245/.309/.405	.263	14.7	.293	-2.1	C(83): -5.3	1.0
Cameron Perkins	OF	LEH	AAA	26	295	37	18	1	7	27	30	47	3	2	.288/.374/.447	.286	16.6	.328	0.5	CF(34): -0.3, LF(18): -0.8	1.5
	OF	PHI	MLB	26	97	9	5	0	1	8	5	23	0	0	.182/.237/.273	.213	-3.6	.227	-1.1	LF(15): 0.0, RF(12): -0.5	-0.4
Zach Vincej	SS	LOU	AAA	26	420	36	21	4	3	38	28	49	4	3	.270/.325/.370	.235	7.0	.302	0.6	SS(106): 0.3, 2B(3): 0.3	0.7
	SS	CIN	MLB	26	12	2	0	0	0	0	1	5	0	0	.111/.333/.111	.206	-0.1	.250	0.2	SS(3): 0.1, 2B(1): 0.2	0.0
Kyle Waldrop	OF	ARK	AA	25	464	61	28	0	10	68	37	86	4	3	.303/.367/.444	.302	26.9	.357	0.2	RF(85): 5.1, 1B(23): -1.8	3.3
	OF	TAC	AAA	25	49	5	2	0	0	6	7	10	0	0	.220/.327/.268	.262	1.3	.281	0.3	RF(11): -1.4, LF(2): -0.2	0.0

Yes, **Gordon Beckham** is still in baseball. He spent most of 2017 at Triple-A Tacoma, an underrated city that features the Museum of Glass, the Daffodil Parade and Fort Nisqually. Find out more at TravelTacoma.com! ⚾ While he's always had extremely strong plate discipline, **Mike Ford** finally reached the 20-homer mark for the first time in 2017. That was enough for the Mariners, as the former college teammate of skipper Scott Servais' son at Princeton was taken from the Yankees in the Rule 5 draft. ⚾ After spending seven years in five different organizations, **David Freitas** finally got his first cup of coffee in 2017 before being claimed off waivers by Seattle, home of the Mariners and, well, a lot more coffee. ⚾ **James Benjamin Gosewisch** was given the nickname "Tuffy" because he was an "especially destructive baby," according to his father. It's a fun nickname, but it would have been kick-ass if his dad had called Tuffy "Destructor" instead. ⚾ **Luis Liberato** is a toolsy outfielder with good speed and defensive instincts whose bat might cap his ceiling as a minor-league outfielder or a major-league bench bat. ⚾ In 2017, **Michael Marjama** made his MLB debut and hit his first big-league home run. This presumably replaces the time a 10-foot alligator sat next to Marjama in the dugout when he was with the Charlotte Stone Crabs in 2015 as the highlight of his baseball career. ⚾ **Tyler Marlette** is a catcher with a strong arm and some over-the-fence power who could spend years bouncing around as a big-league backup if everything breaks right. He could also wash out in the minors. Such is life. ⚾ Southport High School in Indianapolis has produced two big leaguers: Hall of Fame outfielder Chuck Klein and fringe outfielder **Cameron Perkins**. Both started their careers with the Phillies, but only the latter was claimed off waivers by Seattle in December after a respectable repeat of Triple-A. ⚾ **Zach Vincej** rode a strong second half in 2016 to Triple-A, and despite not hitting much there he still got a cup of coffee in September and a single start at shortstop on September 17 against the Pirates. He may not get much more, but it's more coffee than anyone expected him to get just two years ago. ⚾ A former Reds outfield prospect who shouldn't be confused with the former Twins pitching prospect of the same name, **Kyle Waldrop** had a decent year at Double-A but was far too old for the level for it to matter.

Pitchers

PITCHER	TEAM	LVL	AGE	W	L	SV	G	GS	IP	H	HR	BB/9	K/9	K	GB%	BABIP	WHIP	ERA	DRA	WARP	MPH	CMD	PWR	STM
Christian Bergman	TAC	AAA	29	9	4	0	16	16	86	102	7	1.9	6.6	63	45%	.332	1.40	5.34	4.28	1.3				
	SEA	MLB	29	4	5	0	13	8	54	61	12	2.5	5.5	33	40%	.293	1.41	5.00	6.42	-0.6	90.3	47	25	67
Seth Elledge	CLN	A	21	3	0	5	15	0	21	14	1	2.6	15.0	35	40%	.310	0.95	3.00	1.89	0.7				
Seth Frankoff	CHN	MLB	28	0	1	0	1	0	2	4	1	0.0	9.0	2	43%	.500	2.00	9.00	4.41	0.0	92.7			59
	IOW	AAA	28	2	8	0	24	21	116^{2}	102	18	3.6	9.2	119	53%	.279	1.28	4.40	2.68	3.8				
Ernesto Frieri	SWB	AAA	31	2	0	7	17	0	21	13	3	3.9	10.3	24	33%	.208	1.05	3.00	3.91	0.3				
	TEX	MLB	31	0	1	0	6	0	7	6	0	7.7	6.4	5	35%	.300	1.71	5.14	6.80	-0.1	95.6			39
	TAC	AAA	31	1	2	0	7	0	12	9	1	6.8	13.5	18	37%	.308	1.50	5.25	3.88	0.2				
Ryan Garton	TBA	MLB	27	0	1	0	7	0	10^{1}	13	3	4.4	7.8	9	44%	.323	1.74	8.71	7.15	-0.2	94.1	54	46	46
	DUR	AAA	27	2	0	4	24	1	33	18	2	4.4	12.5	46	52%	.250	1.03	1.64	1.47	1.4				
	TAC	AAA	27	0	2	0	7	0	12	11	0	6.0	11.2	15	66%	.344	1.58	6.00	4.47	0.1				
	SEA	MLB	27	0	0	0	13	0	11^{2}	5	1	0.8	5.4	7	41%	.121	0.51	1.54	6.93	-0.2	93.1	54	46	46
Jeanmar Gomez	PHI	MLB	29	3	2	2	18	0	22^{1}	31	7	2.8	8.5	21	53%	.381	1.70	7.25	5.11	0.0	92.6	39	43	31
Oliver Jaskie	EVE	A-	21	0	1	0	13	10	30^{1}	43	5	3.9	9.8	33	48%	.409	1.85	6.82	6.31	-0.4				
Casey Lawrence	TOR	MLB	29	0	3	0	4	2	13^{1}	21	2	7.4	4.7	7	59%	.365	2.40	8.77	5.84	-0.1	92.2	52	39	58
	BUF	AAA	29	1	0	0	3	3	10	9	1	0.9	6.3	7	50%	.258	1.00	0.90	3.25	0.3				
	TAC	AAA	29	2	4	0	11	7	57^{1}	50	7	1.6	6.4	41	40%	.256	1.05	4.08	2.47	2.0				
	SEA	MLB	29	2	0	0	23	0	42	56	9	3.0	9.6	45	44%	.382	1.67	5.57	5.28	0.0	92.7	52	39	58
Cody Martin	SEA	MLB	27	0	0	0	1	0	2	5	0	9.0	0.0	0	36%	.455	3.50	13.50	6.62	0.0	89.5			46
	TAC	AAA	27	0	2	1	20	7	56^{2}	59	7	2.2	10.6	67	31%	.354	1.29	4.13	3.50	1.2				
Sam Moll	ABQ	AAA	25	3	2	0	44	0	47^{1}	56	4	3.4	7.4	39	52%	.344	1.56	4.18	5.44	-0.1				
	OAK	MLB	25	0	0	0	11	0	6^{2}	13	2	4.1	9.4	7	40%	.478	2.40	10.80	6.10	-0.1	94.4			48
Mike Morin	ANA	MLB	26	0	0	0	10	0	14^{1}	21	3	1.3	6.3	10	54%	.367	1.60	6.91	4.20	0.2	92.6	56	19	36
	SLC	AAA	26	0	1	1	22	1	39^{1}	34	5	1.6	5.7	25	34%	.252	1.04	3.20	4.69	0.3				
	KCA	MLB	26	0	0	0	6	0	5^{2}	8	0	4.8	9.5	6	42%	.421	1.94	7.94	3.08	0.1	91.4	56	19	36
Max Povse	ARK	AA	23	3	2	0	9	8	39	34	1	3.2	7.4	32	42%	.289	1.23	3.46	4.97	0.1				
	SEA	MLB	23	0	0	0	3	0	3^{2}	9	1	2.5	4.9	2	39%	.471	2.73	7.36	9.14	-0.2	96.0			40
	TAC	AAA	23	1	4	0	13	5	31^{2}	41	3	3.4	8.2	29	50%	.384	1.67	7.39	5.66	0.0				
Nick Rumbelow	TRN	AA	25	0	0	1	8	0	11^{1}	5	0	2.4	11.9	15	46%	.192	0.71	2.38	2.82	0.3				
	SWB	AAA	25	5	1	5	17	0	29	16	0	2.5	9.3	30	61%	.225	0.83	0.62	2.11	1.0				
Evan Scribner	SEA	MLB	31	0	2	0	8	0	7^{1}	13	3	0.0	7.4	6	39%	.400	1.77	11.05	4.09	0.1	90.7			
Ryan Weber	TAC	AAA	26	2	0	0	6	5	31^{2}	20	1	1.1	5.4	19	73%	.207	0.76	0.85	1.55	1.4				
	SEA	MLB	26	0	0	0	1	1	3^{2}	3	0	0.0	0.0	0	50%	.214	0.82	2.45	4.07	0.1	90.8			41
Robert Whalen	SEA	MLB	23	0	1	0	2	1	7^{1}	7	1	2.5	2.5	2	40%	.250	1.23	6.14	6.31	-0.1	91.3			50
	TAC	AAA	23	0	7	0	10	10	53^{1}	61	9	3.4	7.3	43	41%	.317	1.52	6.58	5.56	0.1				

If **Christian Bergman** were a time machine, his fastball would have trouble reaching the velocity necessary to get back to the future, even if he could generate the necessary 1.21 gigawatts. ⚾ **Seth Elledge** is a former college closer who kept mowing 'em down in his first taste of pro ball. It's too bad the Mariners don't have someone named Edward Lee in their system, because an Elledge/Ed Lee bullpen tandem would be the greatest thing ever. ⚾ **Seth Frankoff** made his major-league debut for the Cubs on the seven-year anniversary of the day he was drafted by the Athletics. The well-traveled pitcher continued his journey when the Mariners claimed him on waivers in September. His last name sounds like a hot dog eating contest. ⚾ After a year out of baseball, **Ernesto Frieri** rediscovered his missing velocity but lost what little command he had, leading to an exciting journey across three Triple-A teams and a brief stop in the majors with the Rangers. The Mariners purchased his contract for a dollar in August. ⚾ Someday soon, teams will employ 17-man bullpens and right-handed specialists like **Ryan Garton** will thrive. Until then, Garton will have difficulty finding a permanent spot unless he develops an out pitch against lefties. ⚾ In any other walk of life, if you are no longer a worm burner it's cause for celebration. For **Jeanmar Gomez**, his inability to generate grounders sent him from closer for the Phillies to Triple-A fodder for the Mariners in the short span of four months. ⚾ A sixth-round pick from the University of Michigan, **Oliver Jaskie** commands his pitches well, but without a dominant out pitch he has a thin margin for error if he ever wants to make the majors. ⚾ **Casey Lawrence**'s decade-long journey from a walk-on at a small Pennsylvania college to his triumphant major-league debut at age 28 is deserving of a 500-word entry, but instead only gets this truncated comment. ⚾ **Cody Martin** pitched only two major-league innings in 2017, but had the best WARP of his career, forever destroying the concept that 80 percent of success is showing up. ⚾ Gun moll: a gangster's main squeeze, like *Dick Tracy*'s Breathless Mahoney. **Sam Moll**: a short, lefty, two-pitch reliever who got bombed in his debut, but who should get another shot or two at a middle-relief role. ⚾ A graduate of Shawnee Mission South High School in Overland Park, Kansas, **Mike Morin** returned home after being claimed by the Royals in mid-September, and a return to his serviceable middle relief form should follow (though not in Kansas City) after he woefully underperformed his DRA in an abbreviated 2017. ⚾ A very tall pitcher without overpowering stuff, **Max Povse** struggled in his first taste of Triple-A and will have difficulty succeeding against big-league hitters without a dominant go-to pitch. ⚾ **Nick Rumbelow** returned from Tommy John surgery and split the season between Trenton and Scranton before the Yankees traded him to the Mariners in a minor swap. ⚾ For the second year in a row, injuries wiped out almost all of **Evan Scribner**'s season. The results when he did pitch were poor and Scribner could be running out of chances. ⚾ Claimed on waivers from the Braves during the winter, **Ryan Weber** spent most of 2017 in the minors before getting sucked into the Seattle Mariners Middle Reliever Injury Vortex™. ⚾ **Robert Whalen** has a lot of effort in his delivery. In the world of pizza, this means you might not get your pie in under 30 minutes. In the parlance of baseball, this caps Whalen's ceiling as a reliever or a swingman.

ST. LOUIS CARDINALS

Essay by Derrick Goold

Player comments by Matt Sussman, Craig Goldstein and BP staff

When Giancarlo Stanton stood at a podium last December, sporting his posh and neatly pressed pinstripes, the reigning National League MVP and transformative presence of their wishes deftly navigated around any geographic obstacles that led him to veto a trade to the Cardinals. Instead of confirming he didn't want to be landlocked in the middle of America, the Yankees' new slugger implied he preferred to avoid another location: wedged in the middle of the standings.

The Cardinals—a third-place team in search of a middle-of-the-order hitter, a mid-rotation starter and a closer who could have a trickle-down effect on middle relief this past offseason—have gotten themselves in a bind because of their brand. They intend to contend, always. They are, as Will Leitch wrote in these pages a year ago, a "perpetual empire." An executive with the team describes how its history and its fan base will not stomach an austere rebuild, and yet all around them rivals are taking five steps back to slingshot one step ahead.

That has left the longtime kings of the National League Central as the division's Jan Brady. (*Cubbies. Cubbies. Cubbies.*) Champs to the left of them, teardowns to the right, the Cardinals are stuck in the middle. They're not looking to rebuild by dumping players like Stanton, and they're not appealing enough as a contender to attract a player like Stanton. They're not bad enough to draft high in June, yet haven't been good enough to reach October in two years.

"Dangerous," president of baseball operations John Mozeliak says. "Yeah, we get it."

No team in the National League has won more games or appeared in the postseason more often since 2000 than the Cardinals, and for this persistence they've been rewarded with two World Series championships, four league pennants and the envy of rivals. The Cardinals stayed ahead with a data-driven front office, a payroll beyond their market, a knack for developing pitchers (however they acquired them) and the sublime talent of Albert Pujols. Even two years after Pujols left for California, the Cardinals won the pennant in 2013 and had the top-rated farm system—a rare feat.

Then the game changed. Edges they'd held for years softened. Teams got smarter, Mozeliak said. Teams got more money. Teams openly mimicked how the Cardinals spied and groomed pitching talent. Teams plucked from the club's brain trust. The Cardinals described their goal as "sustained success," and rivals, like Cubs president Theo Epstein, even co-opted that phrase. "We all caught up," one rival executive told me while watching batting practice at Busch Stadium.

And some tanked.

Two teams with ties to the Cardinals—one led by a former Cardinals executive and the other their archrival—have epitomized the tank-to-trophy trend. In consecutive seasons, the Cubs and Astros have punctuated dramatic rebuilds with World Series

CARDINALS PROSPECTUS

2017 W-L: 83-79, 3RD IN NL CENTRAL

Pythag	.536	10th	B-Age	28.0	*10th*
RS/G	4.70	13th	P-Age	28.1	*13th*
RA/G	4.35	11th	Salary	$150.2M	*14th*
TAv	.270	8th	M$/MW	$3.9M	*17th*
TAv-P	.260	14th	DL Days	599	*6th*
FIP	4.11	8th	$ on DL	11%	*8th*
DER	.702	16th			

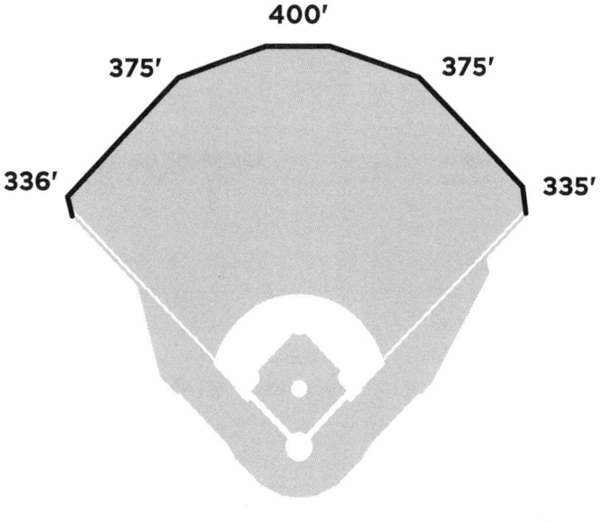

Outfield wall profile: **8′**

Three-Year Park Factors

Runs	Runs/RH	Runs/LH	HR/RH	HR/LH
96	95	98	91	99

Top Hitter WARP	5.6 Tommy Pham
Top Pitcher WARP	4.1 Carlos Martinez
Top Prospect	Alex Reyes

2017 Hit List Ranking

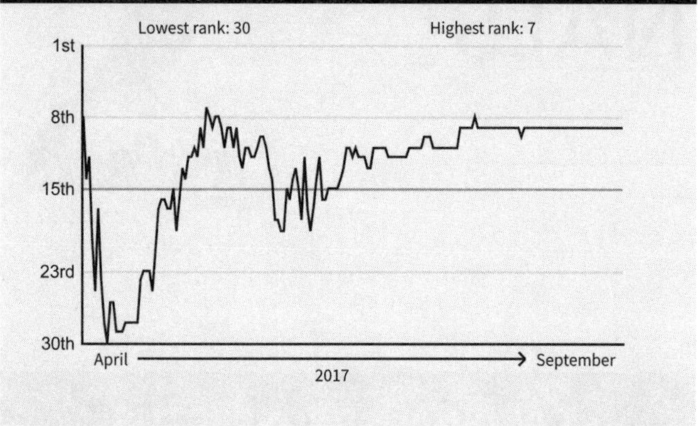

Committed Payroll (in millions)

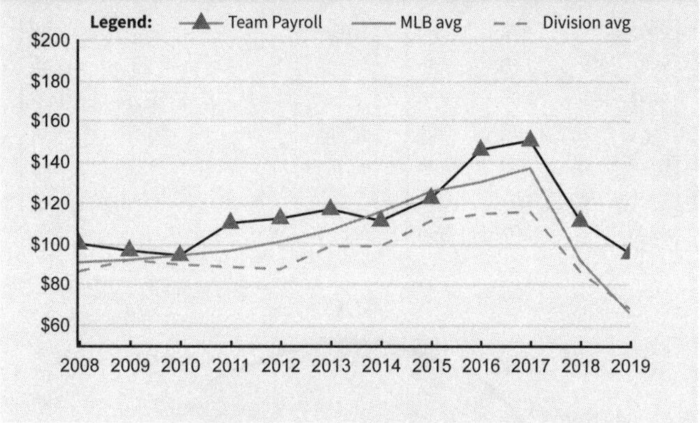

Farm System Ranking

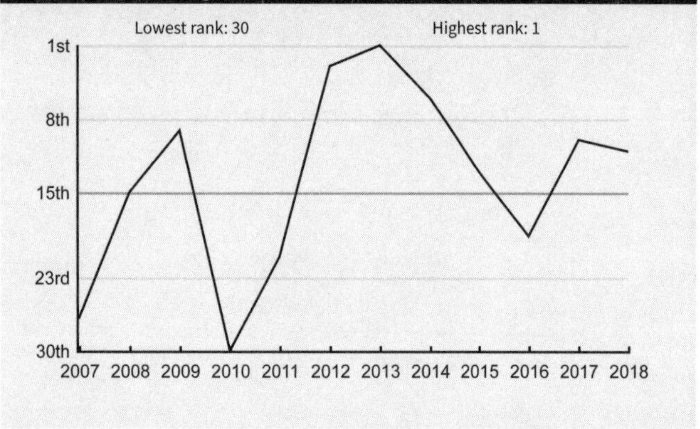

Personnel

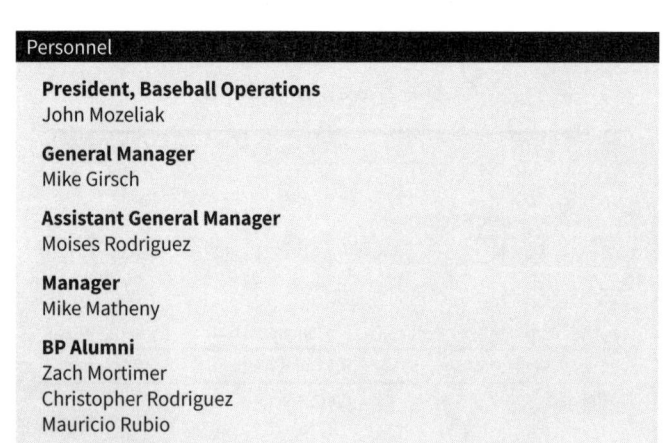

President, Baseball Operations
John Mozeliak

General Manager
Mike Girsch

Assistant General Manager
Moises Rodriguez

Manager
Mike Matheny

BP Alumni
Zach Mortimer
Christopher Rodriguez
Mauricio Rubio

championships. The Cubs' title came four years after a 101-loss season, the Astros' four years after a 111-loss season. The Cardinals haven't lost 100 games in a season since 1908. It's not their thing. Three True Outcomes have come to the standings—and the Cardinals are the walk, wondering whether the game still rewards the steady, solid, savvy contender, or if extremes are the new launch angle for clubs. Has the hare, after a rest, bested the turtle?

"Sustaining success is sort of remarkable," Mozeliak says. "You're trying to create the debate if being good for longer is better than being great one year. Remember that question, 'Would you rather have five years of your life being average or trade it for one year of being the best at something?' How do you want to do it? I would say we want both. That's what we keep trying to work toward. So far, we have achieved both. We haven't been willing to just say we want one year of greatness and four of poor."

Where the Cardinals have started to feel the pinch of other teams' progress is in the draft.

From 2000 to this past summer, when sanctions for the Houston hacking scandal cost them their top two picks, the Cardinals are one of two teams that haven't had a pick in the top 10. (The Yankees are the other.) By comparison, the Cubs have had nine top-10 picks in that time, the Pirates 11, and the Brewers and Reds have had seven each. That's 34 top-10 picks elsewhere in the division.

From 2011 to 2014, as the Cubs began their rebuild with a series of last-place finishes, they drafted ninth, sixth, second, and fourth, respectively. The Cardinals didn't have a pick higher than 19th in that stretch, though they used no. 19 in 2012 to land 2013 NLCS MVP Michael Wacha. Using a trusty yellow legal pad and Baseball-Reference.com's draft database, I tracked every team's first pick since 2000 and averaged where they were making that first selection. Before picking 94th overall in 2017, the Cardinals' average first pick from 2000 to 2016 was 26.8. Every other team in their division averaged better than the 20th pick.

From 2000 to 2017, the Cardinals' average pick was 30.6, with 13 of the game's 30 teams between the Ohio averages, Cincinnati (12.8) and Cleveland (18.9).

This draft gap gains clarity when I eliminate the outlier picks raising averages—those times when the Cubs, Cardinals, Giants and others didn't select in the first 30 picks. When the Cardinals' first pick came in the top 30 (16 times in 18 years) they averaged 22.1. No other NL team was outside of the top 20 (Braves, at 18.3). The Cubs had a top-30 pick 16 times as well, and they averaged 10.0. Eighteen of the 30 teams were within the Chicago loop, between the Cubs (10.0) and White Sox (14.9). Only the Yankees, with a 23.7 average draft spot in 14 top-30 picks, had an average behind the Cardinals'.

There have been many studies to measure the value of draft picks and the talent that a team can expect to land at each pick, and all of them agree: There is a steep decline from the top 10 to the next five, from that next five to the latter third. A study done by Matthew Murphy at The Hardball Times in 2014 showed that teams selecting between picks 6 and 10—where the Cubs averaged in the above time frame—have a one-in-four chance of drafting a player who becomes "something resembling a league-average player, or better (10+ WAR)." That chance drops to one-in-10 for picks 21-30, where the Cardinals live.

The same study showed that teams with picks 6-10 can bet on getting a pre-free agency WAR value of 5.2. The NL average in the above time frame is between picks 11-15, good for a 4.1 pre-free agency WAR. The Cardinals, down in the lower third, can expect a 3.1 WAR. That's close to a player who stays in the majors and contributes, but who doesn't elevate a team. FanGraphs identified a "superior" player as one who provided 2.5 WAR or more per season, and calculated from 2000 to 2010, the draft produced 11 superior players from picks 6-10. The latter third of the draft, picks 21-30, produced 13 total, and only four from 2006 to 2010.

This difference is starkly represented by the Cubs drafting Kris Bryant (no. 2 overall, 2013), a Rookie of the Year and MVP by the end of his second year with a 19.7 career WAR, and the Cardinals getting Kolten Wong (22nd overall, 2011), a cumulative 7.2 WAR after five seasons. None of the Cardinals' five first-round picks from 2015 to 2017 cracked their top 10 prospects for 2018. They're treading water above .500, contending, all while rivals have been able to take a plunge in the standings. It might take those diving teams a while to surface, but when they do they bring back treasure.

Without access to the best players in the draft, the Cardinals have leaned on strategies that have also been matched or limited, and some luck. The three drafted players with the highest cumulative WAR for the Cardinals since 2000 are Pujols (13th round, 1999), Yadier Molina (fourth round, 2000) and Matt Carpenter (13th round, 2009). The Cardinals have supplemented that group with a strong run of homegrown pitchers and a strengthened international presence that brought in no. 1 pitcher Carlos Martinez, no. 1 prospect Alex Reyes and the late Oscar Taveras. They've flipped prospects for needs, as when they traded for Matt Holliday to join and then replace Pujols as the lineup's fulcrum. Recently, they've acquired the kind of young players they haven't been able to develop, such as outfielder Randal Grichuk (a former first-round pick) from the Angels in 2013 and upside slugger Tyler O'Neill from Seattle for lefty Marco Gonzales (taken 19th overall by the Cardinals in 2013).

All those moves and the savvy acquisition of pitchers have kept the Cardinals' farm system as deep as ever with potential and complementary major leaguers, but the run of success is starting to catch up when it comes to impact. They exhausted their international spending purse on teenagers and were limited as some top-shelf players became available this past winter. When they couldn't re-sign right fielder Jason Heyward after the 2015 season, the Cardinals turned to Grichuk and Stephen Piscotty (36th overall, 2012) and gave them an opportunity to blossom as standout hitters. Both struggled in 2017, leaving the Cardinals in a spot they saw coming after Taveras' death. Unable to draft or develop that kind of hitter, the Cardinals searched for a middle-of-the-order bat that could hoist them back to the postseason.

The difference between being in the middle and being middling is minimal.

"What you're seeing is teams that feel like they don't have a chance to compete, if they have players who they can turn into young players, eithers prospects or draft choices, that's the direction they go," chairman Bill DeWitt Jr. says. "That's why you see disparity. If you feel like a team in the lower middle—not a great place to be. But if you have a good system, and we have a good system now, there is no reason not to try and compete with what you have at the major-league level."

How the Cardinals entered this past winter—the most defining for the franchise since 2011, when a Hall of Fame manager retired and a three-time MVP signed elsewhere—was with a phone call. In need of an "impactful" bat, Mozeliak dialed the Marlins and expressed interest in all three of their outfielders, Stanton, Marcell Ozuna and Christian Yelich. With their farm system and a new $1.2 billion broadcast rights deal set to start in 2018, the Cardinals entered the winter with as many prospects to move and as much payroll might as any team.

They had the assets to break from character, and now the need.

So when Stanton declined, citing his wish to win "right now," the Cardinals recast their offer and within a week had a deal for Ozuna. It cost them four players, three of whom ranked among their top 20 prospects. To get Ozuna, a two-time All-Star and the cleanup hitter of their desires, the Cardinals gave up more talent (Sandy Alcantara, Magneuris Sierra) and more years of control (24) than they had in any deal since the Holliday trade. They did it all for two years of Ozuna in the middle of their order. Mozeliak called Ozuna's production "something we didn't have." After years of adhering to a model, they made it meet the market. They broke from middle management.

In 10 years as general manager, Mozeliak never had a losing record and never had one of his teams land a draft pick higher than 19. In July, DeWitt promoted Mozeliak to president of baseball operations, and one of the latter's charges was to provide new answers to an old question: "What's our competitive advantage?" Mozeliak described how with sharper analytics and increased revenues—not to mention tanking—the Cardinals' advantages had been "more neutralized." In his new role, he wants to find that edge again. The draft won't rescue them. Molting is out of the question for the Cardinals. The brand matters, and the 3.4 million tickets it sells are essential. But numbers may still be on their side. In recent moves, Mozeliak has hinted at a direction the Cardinals can shift toward by packaging multiple talents for a short-term need (Ozuna) or by flexing their payroll muscle to overbid for a long-term want (Dexter Fowler). And Stanton. They were willing to take on more salary than ever for him. So, while he offered a reminder of where the Cardinals are, he also revealed they know the way out.

They've had the same approach and similar success for so long that there really is only one way to maintain a sustained, consistent competitive brand in this era—they must change.

The Cardinals are in the middle of it.

—Derrick Goold covers the Cardinals for the St. Louis Post Dispatch.

Hitters

Randy Arozarena OF Born: 02/28/95 Age: 23 Bats: R Throws: R Height: 5'11" Weight: 170 Origin: International Free Agent, 2016

YEAR	TEAM	LVL	AGE	PA	R	2B	3B	HR	RBI	BB	K	SB	CS	AVG/OBP/SLG	TAv	VORP	BABIP	BRR	FRAA	WARP
2017	PMB	A+	22	295	38	22	3	8	40	13	53	10	4	.275/.333/.472	.324	23.2	.313	-2.5	LF(47): 4.3, CF(13): -0.5	3.1
2017	SFD	AA	22	195	34	10	1	3	9	27	34	8	3	.252/.366/.380	.266	8.1	.299	2.7	LF(40): 0.2, CF(4): -0.9	0.8
2018	*SLN*	*MLB*	*23*	*250*	*34*	*12*	*1*	*8*	*27*	*21*	*57*	*6*	*2*	*.244/.322/.419*	*.251*	*6.5*	*.289*	*0.1*	*LF 1, CF -1*	*0.8*
2019	*SLN*	*MLB*	*24*	*282*	*36*	*14*	*1*	*9*	*35*	*25*	*64*	*7*	*3*	*.245/.327/.423*	*.270*	*10.3*	*.290*	*0.3*	*LF 1, CF -1*	*1.2*

Breakout: 3% Improve: 20% Collapse: 5% Attrition: 14% MLB: 36% *Comparables: Shin-Soo Choo, Chad Huffman, Thomas Neal*

Perhaps the best candidate for a Cardinals Devil Magic season (see Aledmys Diaz's 2016 production), Arozarena has tools that project best as an extra outfielder. He can run a bit, there's not a ton of power, but he has an aggressive approach at the plate and makes a ton of contact. His hit tool might be a carrying one ... to the majors, but it'll have to kick into a higher gear to take him all the way to an everyday role—not impossible, or perhaps improbable for a Cardinals prospect.

Harrison Bader OF Born: 06/03/94 Age: 24 Bats: R Throws: R Height: 6'0" Weight: 195 Origin: Round 3, 2015 Draft (#100 overall)

YEAR	TEAM	LVL	AGE	PA	R	2B	3B	HR	RBI	BB	K	SB	CS	AVG/OBP/SLG	TAv	VORP	BABIP	BRR	FRAA	WARP
2015	SCO	A-	21	30	6	2	0	2	4	0	5	2	0	.379/.400/.655	.356	4.0	.409	0.5	LF(4): -0.2, RF(3): -0.4	0.4
2015	PEO	A	21	228	34	11	2	9	28	15	44	15	6	.301/.364/.505	.310	21.3	.344	3.4	CF(42): 8.9, LF(7): 3.9	3.6
2016	MEM	AAA	22	161	22	7	1	3	17	11	38	2	3	.231/.298/.354	.249	2.5	.292	-0.1	CF(26): 1.5, LF(16): 0.7	0.5
2016	SFD	AA	22	356	48	12	4	16	41	25	93	11	10	.283/.351/.497	.312	29.5	.349	0.7	CF(77): 0.7, RF(4): -0.4	3.2
2017	MEM	AAA	23	479	74	18	1	20	55	34	118	15	9	.283/.347/.469	.296	40.3	.345	5.3	CF(111): 13.7, LF(3): -0.4	5.2
2017	SLN	MLB	23	92	10	3	0	3	10	5	24	2	1	.235/.283/.376	.241	1.3	.288	0.3	CF(20): 2.0, LF(7): -0.1	0.3
2018	*SLN*	*MLB*	*24*	*76*	*10*	*3*	*0*	*3*	*10*	*5*	*21*	*2*	*1*	*.249/.310/.430*	*.256*	*2.5*	*.309*	*-0.1*	*CF 1*	*0.3*
2019	*SLN*	*MLB*	*25*	*306*	*40*	*12*	*1*	*13*	*41*	*20*	*85*	*7*	*5*	*.248/.311/.434*	*.266*	*10.7*	*.309*	*-0.1*	*CF 5*	*1.7*

Breakout: 8% Improve: 36% Collapse: 8% Attrition: 20% MLB: 58% *Comparables: Joe Benson, Starling Marte, Michael Taylor*

A third-round pick out of the University of Florida in 2015, Bader made his Cardinals debut in July as a fill-in for the injured Dexter Fowler. St. Louis promoted Bader aggressively through the minors despite good but not great performances, and now he looks like a definite MLB-caliber player whose role may come down to defense. If he can handle center field, Bader has enough power to make an impact as a regular. If he instead winds up in an outfield corner, his lack of strike-zone control and plate discipline could leave his offensive production somewhat lacking. If that sounds like an eventual fourth-outfielder profile, you might be right, but Bader and his big swing will likely get at least a few chances to prove he's more than that.

Matt Carpenter 1B Born: 11/26/85 Age: 32 Bats: L Throws: R Height: 6'3" Weight: 205 Origin: Round 13, 2009 Draft (#399 overall)

YEAR	TEAM	LVL	AGE	PA	R	2B	3B	HR	RBI	BB	K	SB	CS	AVG/OBP/SLG	TAv	VORP	BABIP	BRR	FRAA	WARP
2015	SLN	MLB	29	665	101	44	3	28	84	81	151	4	3	.272/.365/.505	.317	56.3	.321	-0.6	3B(146): -12.1, 2B(11): -0.1	4.8
2016	SLN	MLB	30	566	81	36	6	21	68	81	108	0	4	.271/.380/.505	.313	45.7	.307	1.2	3B(54): -3.9, 1B(45): 0.1	4.2
2017	SLN	MLB	31	622	91	31	2	23	69	109	125	2	1	.241/.384/.451	.302	34.2	.274	-2.4	1B(120): 2.1, 3B(16): 0.9	3.8
2018	*SLN*	*MLB*	*32*	*604*	*84*	*33*	*3*	*17*	*69*	*79*	*115*	*2*	*2*	*.263/.364/.439*	*.279*	*25.6*	*.304*	*-1.4*	*1B 0, 3B -2*	*1.8*
2019	*SLN*	*MLB*	*33*	*536*	*72*	*30*	*2*	*17*	*66*	*71*	*109*	*1*	*1*	*.257/.361/.441*	*.286*	*23.6*	*.298*	*-0.2*	*1B 0, 3B -2*	*2.4*

Breakout: 2% Improve: 29% Collapse: 5% Attrition: 6% MLB: 88% *Comparables: Justin Morneau, John Jaso, Eddie Murray*

The recent list of dudes who walked more than 100 times with fewer than 25 home runs is rife with sluggers in adequate years, as well as Daric Barton. So Carpenter, a leadoff hitter, stands out. He has been the mark of consistency for years, with the exception of his numbers against left-handers, which suddenly became downright Seth Smithian. He has no difficulty fielding either corner infield spot, and extreme on-base talent is something that will persist through any hitting slumps and unrelenting aging curves. He rips enough homers a year that he could bat third or fifth, but is more comfortable and excited to set the table rather than clean it, just like your kids. As the old saying goes, a good carpenter never blames his spot in the lineup.

Paul DeJong SS Born: 08/02/93 Age: 24 Bats: R Throws: R Height: 6'1" Weight: 195 Origin: Round 4, 2015 Draft (#131 overall)

YEAR	TEAM	LVL	AGE	PA	R	2B	3B	HR	RBI	BB	K	SB	CS	AVG/OBP/SLG	TAv	VORP	BABIP	BRR	FRAA	WARP
2015	JCY	RK	21	45	10	6	0	4	15	6	9	0	0	.486/.578/.973	.464	11.5	.583	-0.3	3B(9): 0.6	1.2
2015	PEO	A	21	247	32	12	3	5	26	23	43	13	4	.288/.360/.438	.297	15.6	.335	-1.4	3B(53): 0.2	1.7
2016	SFD	AA	22	552	62	29	2	22	73	40	144	3	2	.260/.324/.460	.289	31.1	.318	-1.8	3B(112): -4.3, SS(11): 0.9	3.0
2017	MEM	AAA	23	190	27	9	0	13	34	9	46	0	2	.299/.339/.571	.311	17.8	.336	-1.0	SS(39): -3.8, 2B(5): 0.4	1.4
2017	SLN	MLB	23	443	55	26	1	25	65	21	124	1	0	.285/.325/.532	.300	32.4	.349	-3.9	SS(86): -0.3, 2B(20): -0.7	3.1
2018	*SLN*	*MLB*	*24*	*616*	*78*	*30*	*2*	*29*	*93*	*36*	*168*	*1*	*1*	*.258/.308/.471*	*.265*	*27.7*	*.312*	*-1.2*	*SS -1*	*2.2*
2019	*SLN*	*MLB*	*25*	*562*	*77*	*27*	*1*	*28*	*85*	*37*	*158*	*1*	*1*	*.255/.312/.478*	*.276*	*25.4*	*.310*	*-3.3*	*SS -1*	*2.6*

Breakout: 4% Improve: 45% Collapse: 19% Attrition: 29% MLB: 90% *Comparables: Trevor Story, Randal Grichuk, Brandon Wood*

Did millennials kill the impressive home-run season? Now that you've already clicked through to this comment, DeJong is one of the six 2017 rookies to blast at least 25 big flies. Only *once* this century have three rookies done that in a year. Because DeJong was called up in 2017 and not 2010, when Giancarlo Stanton debuted with only 22 bombs, his season blends in with those of all the other big-power/big-whiff sluggers. Assuming Major League Baseball did not replace all of the baseballs with lead orbs, his overall hitting profile should remain strong enough to stay a starting infielder, but if you don't remember the name, blame the era.

Dexter Fowler CF Born: 03/22/86 Age: 32 Bats: B Throws: R Height: 6'5" Weight: 195 Origin: Round 14, 2004 Draft (#410 overall)

YEAR	TEAM	LVL	AGE	PA	R	2B	3B	HR	RBI	BB	K	SB	CS	AVG/OBP/SLG	TAv	VORP	BABIP	BRR	FRAA	WARP
2015	CHN	MLB	29	690	102	29	8	17	46	84	154	20	7	.250/.346/.411	.281	33.7	.308	-1.0	CF(152): 0.8	3.7
2016	CHN	MLB	30	551	84	25	7	13	48	79	124	13	4	.276/.393/.447	.312	47.1	.350	1.1	CF(121): -11.4	3.7
2017	SLN	MLB	31	491	68	22	9	18	64	63	101	7	3	.264/.363/.488	.298	36.9	.305	1.4	CF(109): -10.0	2.7
2018	*SLN*	*MLB*	*32*	*618*	*77*	*25*	*6*	*15*	*71*	*79*	*135*	*13*	*5*	*.254/.354/.405*	*.269*	*29.9*	*.311*	*0.8*	*CF -10*	*1.6*
2019	*SLN*	*MLB*	*33*	*492*	*63*	*19*	*4*	*12*	*55*	*63*	*112*	*9*	*4*	*.252/.355/.407*	*.277*	*23.8*	*.311*	*0.4*	*CF -7*	*1.8*

Breakout: 1% Improve: 37% Collapse: 3% Attrition: 5% MLB: 95% *Comparables: Robin Yount, Chet Lemon, Cesar Cedeno*

Where Dexter fouls most often is in the field. He can make the routine plays but isn't going to win any shiny fielding tchotchkes for his range. He plays center field because he can keep the spot warm; his average arm means he will probably finish his career in left field. His ability to grind a plate appearance to ball four or drive it for doubles and double-doubles—or as the kids call them, dingers—will keep him somewhere in the lineup no matter the outfield spot, but as he pilots his solid career into his thirties and loses a step, watch for him to step aside at some point.

Greg Garcia INF
Born: 08/08/89 Age: 28 Bats: L Throws: R Height: 6'0" Weight: 190 Origin: Round 7, 2010 Draft (#229 overall)

YEAR	TEAM	LVL	AGE	PA	R	2B	3B	HR	RBI	BB	K	SB	CS	AVG/OBP/SLG	TAv	VORP	BABIP	BRR	FRAA	WARP
2015	MEM	AAA	25	389	47	19	2	0	36	48	55	16	3	.294/.391/.364	.287	28.8	.351	3.6	SS(69): -5.3, 2B(19): -0.9	2.3
2015	SLN	MLB	25	87	7	5	0	2	4	10	12	0	0	.240/.337/.387	.278	5.1	.262	0.9	SS(12): 0.7, 2B(10): -1.7	0.4
2016	MEM	AAA	26	120	13	4	1	0	8	11	20	2	2	.269/.350/.327	.256	2.4	.333	-1.6	SS(24): -0.1, 2B(2): -0.1	0.2
2016	SLN	MLB	26	257	33	11	0	3	17	38	50	1	1	.276/.393/.369	.289	17.5	.346	1.0	3B(31): -0.9, SS(30): -0.8	1.5
2017	SLN	MLB	27	290	27	9	2	2	20	37	64	2	1	.253/.365/.332	.261	13.2	.335	3.8	3B(41): 1.1, 2B(34): 0.5	1.4
2018	*SLN*	*MLB*	*28*	*238*	*26*	*9*	*1*	*3*	*21*	*26*	*49*	*2*	*1*	*.249/.341/.344*	*.247*	*7.7*	*.310*	*-0.2*	*2B -2, SS -1*	*0.0*
2019	*SLN*	*MLB*	*29*	*351*	*42*	*14*	*1*	*6*	*33*	*39*	*75*	*3*	*1*	*.250/.347/.361*	*.259*	*12.2*	*.309*	*2.1*	*2B -3, SS -1*	*0.8*

Breakout: 6% Improve: 32% Collapse: 12% Attrition: 20% MLB: 75% *Comparables: Bobby Hill, Freddy Sanchez, Ramiro Pena*

What can be said about Garcia that hasn't already been said about a miniature Swiss Army knife? Or a 3-in-1 air hockey/pool/foosball game table? Or a combination color copier/fax machine? Or a 19th-century haberdasher's sword cane? Or a calculator watch? Or the futon that belonged to your friend Beth during senior year that you crashed on at least four separate times that you can recall? The only thing you can say about Garcia that doesn't apply to all of these other slightly memorable versatile objects is that Garcia has his own baseball card.

Jose Adolis Garcia OF
Born: 03/02/93 Age: 25 Bats: R Throws: R Height: 6'1" Weight: 180 Origin: International Free Agent, 2017

YEAR	TEAM	LVL	AGE	PA	R	2B	3B	HR	RBI	BB	K	SB	CS	AVG/OBP/SLG	TAv	VORP	BABIP	BRR	FRAA	WARP
2017	SFD	AA	24	342	43	23	0	12	55	26	77	12	8	.285/.339/.476	.294	18.5	.338	0.3	RF(73): 10.4, CF(10): 2.7	3.4
2017	MEM	AAA	24	147	21	11	2	3	10	7	31	3	1	.301/.342/.478	.284	9.3	.369	1.9	RF(24): 0.6, CF(10): 1.9	1.1
2018	*SLN*	*MLB*	*25*	*250*	*30*	*13*	*1*	*9*	*31*	*18*	*66*	*6*	*3*	*.248/.306/.424*	*.245*	*3.6*	*.308*	*-0.2*	*RF 1, CF 0*	*0.5*
2019	*SLN*	*MLB*	*26*	*255*	*32*	*12*	*1*	*10*	*33*	*20*	*69*	*6*	*3*	*.243/.308/.427*	*.262*	*6.3*	*.302*	*0.0*	*RF 1, CF 0*	*0.8*

Breakout: 3% Improve: 11% Collapse: 8% Attrition: 26% MLB: 37% *Comparables: Alex Castellanos, Jeremy Moore, Kyle Parker*

Garcia is another prototypical high-contact, aggressive Cuban hitter. It's hard to blame him because he makes a bunch of solid contact, which allows him to make use of his high-end speed. He isn't a natural with his legs on the bases or in the field, though, and profiles better in a corner than in center for that reason. He profiles well in right field because the arm is an asset all its own. It's hard to know what to make of his statistical output because he was 24 in Double-A. He'll be a major leaguer—one would hope, given his $2.5 million signing bonus—but it's not clear whether it'll be in the fourth-outfielder role as his aggressive approach and moderate power limit him from being an everyday player, or whether he can hit enough to make those things not matter.

Randal Grichuk OF
Born: 08/13/91 Age: 26 Bats: R Throws: R Height: 6'1" Weight: 205 Origin: Round 1, 2009 Draft (#24 overall)

YEAR	TEAM	LVL	AGE	PA	R	2B	3B	HR	RBI	BB	K	SB	CS	AVG/OBP/SLG	TAv	VORP	BABIP	BRR	FRAA	WARP
2015	SLN	MLB	23	350	49	23	7	17	47	22	110	4	2	.276/.329/.548	.316	25.9	.365	-1.5	LF(49): -2.8, CF(37): 1.4	2.5
2016	MEM	AAA	24	86	12	4	1	6	18	2	14	0	0	.272/.302/.568	.301	6.4	.258	0.4	CF(17): -0.2	0.6
2016	SLN	MLB	24	478	66	29	3	24	68	28	141	5	4	.240/.289/.480	.275	24.0	.294	2.2	CF(115): 0.6, LF(4): 0.6	2.6
2017	MEM	AAA	25	67	11	3	0	6	9	3	20	0	0	.270/.313/.603	.307	4.8	.297	0.0	LF(9): 3.6, CF(1): -0.1	0.8
2017	SLN	MLB	25	442	53	25	3	22	59	26	133	6	1	.238/.285/.473	.260	11.3	.293	1.9	LF(58): -2.6, RF(55): 4.6	1.3
2018	*SLN*	*MLB*	*26*	*310*	*42*	*16*	*2*	*15*	*45*	*17*	*88*	*4*	*2*	*.243/.291/.472*	*.260*	*10.2*	*.294*	*0.0*	*RF 2, LF -2*	*0.8*
2019	*SLN*	*MLB*	*27*	*386*	*52*	*20*	*2*	*20*	*59*	*25*	*111*	*4*	*2*	*.243/.298/.483*	*.274*	*15.6*	*.292*	*0.6*	*RF 3, LF -2*	*1.8*

Breakout: 6% Improve: 52% Collapse: 6% Attrition: 11% MLB: 92% *Comparables: Oswaldo Arcia, Wily Mo Pena, Carlos Gonzalez*

Grichuk is part of the problem. He's a strong boy who swings without abandon, but he also strikes out about 30 percent of the time. Which, granted, is today's style that your grandfather refuses to acknowledge, but 30 percent is still notably worse than league average. As an all-or-nothing fly-ball hitter, he's a candidate for a breakout year if he can start producing some more "all" this season, because the "some" is just not how he rolls. But now that he's an arbitration-eligible project, he may change shirts more than once in the next few years if he's going to pursue the career trajectory of a poor man's Chris Carter, but with more '90s alternative rock band hair.

Jedd Gyorko 3B
Born: 09/23/88 Age: 29 Bats: R Throws: R Height: 5'10" Weight: 215 Origin: Round 2, 2010 Draft (#59 overall)

YEAR	TEAM	LVL	AGE	PA	R	2B	3B	HR	RBI	BB	K	SB	CS	AVG/OBP/SLG	TAv	VORP	BABIP	BRR	FRAA	WARP
2015	ELP	AAA	26	69	8	1	0	4	9	7	11	0	1	.279/.362/.492	.271	2.8	.283	0.2	2B(16): -0.2	0.3
2015	SDN	MLB	26	458	34	15	0	16	57	27	107	0	1	.247/.297/.397	.252	8.5	.290	-1.1	2B(93): -0.3, SS(29): -1.6	0.7
2016	SLN	MLB	27	438	58	9	1	30	59	37	96	0	0	.243/.306/.495	.292	28.3	.244	0.6	2B(46): 5.1, 3B(39): -1.6	3.4
2017	SLN	MLB	28	481	52	21	2	20	67	47	105	6	2	.272/.341/.472	.287	28.4	.312	-0.4	3B(109): 10.7, 1B(10): 0.5	4.1
2018	*SLN*	*MLB*	*29*	*517*	*64*	*19*	*1*	*22*	*72*	*41*	*114*	*3*	*1*	*.245/.309/.430*	*.256*	*14.1*	*.276*	*-0.9*	*3B 3*	*1.3*
2019	*SLN*	*MLB*	*30*	*467*	*61*	*19*	*0*	*20*	*63*	*37*	*106*	*2*	*1*	*.240/.305/.430*	*.261*	*11.8*	*.271*	*-0.4*	*3B 3*	*1.7*

Breakout: 3% Improve: 46% Collapse: 8% Attrition: 15% MLB: 96% *Comparables: Mark Teahen, Jhonny Peralta, Jorge Cantu*

Now that he's at third base, Gyorko is a defensive upgrade as well as a power threat in the lineup. The backstory here is that he was bitten by a radioactive Scott Rolen jersey and the mild-mannered cleanup hitter for a small Midwestern baseball team moonlights as an underrated horsehide smasher and hot-corner sentry. His personal-best on-base percentage can justify keeping him in the fat of the lineup, and as he's hitting the prime of his career with two years remaining on his contract, Gyorko has finally found a comfortable position.

Carson Kelly C Born: 07/14/94 Age: 23 Bats: R Throws: R Height: 6'2" Weight: 220 Origin: Round 2, 2012 Draft (#86 overall)

YEAR	TEAM	LVL	AGE	PA	R	2B	3B	HR	RBI	BB	K	SB	CS	AVG/OBP/SLG	TAv	VORP	BABIP	BRR	FRAA	WARP
2015	PMB	A+	20	419	30	18	1	8	51	22	64	0	0	.219/.263/.332	.223	1.2	.239	-1.0	C(104): 1.3	0.3
2016	SFD	AA	21	236	29	7	0	6	18	14	46	0	1	.287/.338/.403	.283	14.4	.339	-0.9	C(60): 7.6	2.4
2016	MEM	AAA	21	126	14	10	0	0	14	11	17	0	0	.292/.352/.381	.261	5.8	.340	-0.1	C(32): 2.4	0.8
2016	SLN	MLB	21	14	1	1	0	0	1	0	2	0	0	.154/.214/.231	.204	-0.4	.182	-0.2	C(10): 0.0	0.0
2017	MEM	AAA	22	280	37	13	0	10	41	33	40	0	2	.283/.375/.459	.292	21.9	.304	-1.9	C(68): 8.9	3.0
2017	SLN	MLB	22	75	5	3	0	0	6	5	11	0	0	.174/.240/.217	.158	-4.0	.207	0.7	C(31): 2.6	-0.1
2018	*SLN*	*MLB*	*23*	*202*	*22*	*9*	*0*	*5*	*22*	*15*	*38*	*0*	*0*	*.243/.304/.382*	*.241*	*5.2*	*.277*	*-0.5*	*C 2*	*0.5*
2019	*SLN*	*MLB*	*24*	*339*	*41*	*15*	*0*	*10*	*40*	*27*	*66*	*0*	*0*	*.248/.314/.402*	*.257*	*10.3*	*.282*	*-0.9*	*C 3*	*1.4*

Breakout: 6% Improve: 32% Collapse: 5% Attrition: 21% MLB: 49% *Comparables: Rob Brantly, John Ryan Murphy, Kevin Plawecki*

YEAR	TEAM	P. COUNT	FRM RUNS	BLK RUNS	THRW RUNS	TOT RUNS
2016	SLN	539	-0.1	0.2	0.0	0.0
2017	SLN	2565	2.2	0.3	0.1	2.6
2018	*SLN*	*5995*	*2.9*	*0.4*	*-0.4*	*2.9*
2019	*SLN*	*10065*	*2.5*	*0.3*	*-0.3*	*2.5*

Kelly has both the fortune and misfortune to be one of baseball's top catching prospects while also acting as Yadier Molina's understudy. He's fortunate because Yadi might be the best guy in baseball for a young player in Kelly's situation to learn from on a daily basis, but he's unfortunate because he's clearly ready to play a significant role and Molina is a catching iron man. Kelly tallied only 69 at-bats after his mid-July promotion to the backup role, starting once a week or less until the last week of the season. When on the field, the converted infielder continued his ascent to being an excellent framer, which bodes well for his future even if the steps forward he's taken with the bat, both in the power and on-base department, don't hold. Presumably St. Louis will start sliding him in on a more frequent basis, particularly against left-handed pitchers, lest his skills start to erode with the inconsistent playing time.

Jonathan Machado OF Born: 01/21/99 Age: 19 Bats: L Throws: L Height: 5'9" Weight: 155 Origin: International Free Agent, 2016

YEAR	TEAM	LVL	AGE	PA	R	2B	3B	HR	RBI	BB	K	SB	CS	AVG/OBP/SLG	TAv	VORP	BABIP	BRR	FRAA	WARP
2016	DCA	RK	17	74	10	4	1	0	7	7	10	2	1	.209/.284/.299	.225	0.4	.246	0.9	CF(16): -3.0	-0.3
2017	CRD	RK	18	139	27	8	0	2	20	8	13	8	2	.323/.381/.435	.298	11.9	.342	0.4	CF(32): 0.8, RF(2): -0.3	1.2
2018	*SLN*	*MLB*	*19*	*250*	*26*	*10*	*1*	*6*	*23*	*12*	*73*	*3*	*1*	*.209/.251/.333*	*.196*	*-7.2*	*.272*	*-0.1*	*CF -3, RF 0*	*-1.1*
2019	*SLN*	*MLB*	*20*	*328*	*35*	*12*	*1*	*9*	*35*	*17*	*90*	*4*	*1*	*.225/.272/.364*	*.227*	*-1.9*	*.284*	*0.0*	*CF -3, RF 0*	*-0.6*

Breakout: 0% Improve: 5% Collapse: 1% Attrition: 4% MLB: 9% *Comparables: Engel Beltre, Raul Mondesi, Rougned Odor*

Another Cuban free agent for St. Louis, Machado pulled down $2.35 million in 2016. The diminutive outfielder boasts impressive speed on both sides of the ball, and used it to compile a .323 average in rookie ball. As you might expect for someone of his build, Machado lacks significant pop; more worrisome, he struggled to make consistent, hard contact in 2017. He's still a teenager, so it's far too early to make a big deal about such things, but it could be a tough climb to the majors if he can't add good weight over the next couple seasons. Luckily his speed in center field gives him a strong defensive baseline on which to build.

Jose Martinez 1B Born: 07/25/88 Age: 29 Bats: R Throws: R Height: 6'6" Weight: 215 Origin: International Free Agent, 2006

YEAR	TEAM	LVL	AGE	PA	R	2B	3B	HR	RBI	BB	K	SB	CS	AVG/OBP/SLG	TAv	VORP	BABIP	BRR	FRAA	WARP
2015	OMA	AAA	26	396	57	25	3	10	60	48	55	8	2	.384/.461/.563	.351	40.2	.434	-3.6	RF(28): -0.3, LF(27): 1.4	4.2
2016	OMA	AAA	27	160	18	10	0	3	18	14	24	2	0	.298/.356/.433	.297	9.6	.331	1.1	1B(20): -1.6, LF(12): -0.8	0.8
2016	MEM	AAA	27	329	34	18	1	8	42	25	50	9	1	.269/.326/.415	.257	3.4	.299	-1.2	LF(30): -0.2, RF(29): 0.5	0.3
2016	SLN	MLB	27	18	4	1	0	0	1	2	1	0	0	.438/.500/.500	.358	2.6	.467	0.4	LF(4): 0.3, 1B(1): 0.0	0.3
2017	SLN	MLB	28	307	47	13	1	14	46	32	60	4	0	.309/.379/.518	.321	25.2	.350	0.1	1B(33): 0.0, LF(24): -2.8	2.3
2018	*SLN*	*MLB*	*29*	*352*	*45*	*17*	*1*	*11*	*46*	*32*	*64*	*4*	*1*	*.284/.352/.450*	*.278*	*14.4*	*.323*	*0.1*	*1B -2*	*1.1*
2019	*SLN*	*MLB*	*30*	*421*	*56*	*20*	*1*	*14*	*54*	*40*	*79*	*4*	*1*	*.280/.354/.453*	*.288*	*18.9*	*.320*	*0.2*	*1B -2*	*1.9*

Breakout: 2% Improve: 14% Collapse: 16% Attrition: 23% MLB: 49% *Comparables: Josh Satin, Nate Freiman, Brandon Guyer*

After 11 seasons, countless uniform changes and one independent league Foursquare check-in, the high-average-and-that's-about-it Martinez did the unthinkable and made an Opening Day roster in '17. He continued hitting beyond expectations and presented a curious dilemma: What do you do with a career minor leaguer who suddenly posts the team's second-highest TAv? His profile screamed fourth outfielder (which is still true), but might also work as a first baseman, assuming the power is legitimate—he had never slugged that high in any minor-league stint. He improved as the season matured. He can hit righties. He's basically a corner utility player a team has no choice but to keep because he's given zero reasons to otherwise discard. He's a terrific story that you're forced to accept. He's a non-canonical George R.R. Martin novella.

Oscar Mercado OF Born: 12/16/94 Age: 23 Bats: R Throws: R Height: 6'2" Weight: 175 Origin: Round 2, 2013 Draft (#57 overall)

YEAR	TEAM	LVL	AGE	PA	R	2B	3B	HR	RBI	BB	K	SB	CS	AVG/OBP/SLG	TAv	VORP	BABIP	BRR	FRAA	WARP
2015	PEO	A	20	513	70	23	3	4	44	23	61	50	19	.254/.297/.341	.243	17.4	.282	7.1	SS(106): -9.3	0.9
2016	PMB	A+	21	506	50	23	1	0	27	44	71	33	20	.215/.296/.271	.232	5.3	.253	1.1	SS(81): 0.9, CF(38): 3.2	1.0
2017	SFD	AA	22	523	76	20	4	13	46	32	112	38	19	.287/.341/.428	.283	32.7	.348	5.7	CF(108): -1.9, LF(7): -0.7	3.2
2018	*SLN*	*MLB*	*23*	*250*	*34*	*11*	*1*	*6*	*22*	*14*	*56*	*13*	*6*	*.235/.288/.370*	*.223*	*0.5*	*.281*	*0.3*	*CF -1, LF 0*	*0.0*
2019	*SLN*	*MLB*	*24*	*307*	*34*	*13*	*1*	*8*	*33*	*18*	*68*	*16*	*8*	*.238/.293/.377*	*.241*	*4.4*	*.283*	*1.4*	*CF -1, LF 0*	*0.4*

Breakout: 1% Improve: 6% Collapse: 14% Attrition: 17% MLB: 21% *Comparables: Andrew Stevenson, Charlie Blackmon, Matt Szczur*

A 2013 second-round pick, Mercado moved off the infield dirt into center field, and learned to hit in the process. Or so the Cardinals hope, since correlation doesn't always equal causation. He can really move out on the grass, and he's always had a bit of feel to hit, but 2017 was the first time his on-base percentage cracked .300 in three seasons (and that was in short-season ball and was only .303). He was relatively age-appropriate for Double-A, so the breakout is encouraging, but scouts didn't see the needle move considerably. He could be a fourth outfielder or more of an up-and-down type for a good team, with a lack of power keeping him out of the lineup on a more consistent basis.

Yadier Molina C Born: 07/13/82 Age: 35 Bats: R Throws: R Height: 5'11" Weight: 205 Origin: Round 4, 2000 Draft (#113 overall)

YEAR	TEAM	LVL	AGE	PA	R	2B	3B	HR	RBI	BB	K	SB	CS	AVG/OBP/SLG	TAv	VORP	BABIP	BRR	FRAA	WARP
2015	SLN	MLB	32	530	34	23	2	4	61	32	59	3	1	.270/.310/.350	.239	7.3	.295	-4.9	C(134): 11.9	2.1
2016	SLN	MLB	33	581	56	38	1	8	58	39	63	3	2	.307/.360/.427	.278	29.0	.335	-7.7	C(146): 10.2, 1B(2): 0.0	4.1
2017	SLN	MLB	34	543	60	27	1	18	82	28	74	9	4	.273/.312/.439	.260	21.0	.285	-4.5	C(133): 4.7, 1B(1): 0.0	2.6
2018	*SLN*	*MLB*	*35*	*494*	*54*	*26*	*1*	*9*	*50*	*28*	*63*	*5*	*2*	*.274/.318/.391*	*.247*	*13.6*	*.299*	*-0.8*	*C 5*	*1.6*
2019	*SLN*	*MLB*	*36*	*470*	*53*	*24*	*0*	*10*	*50*	*28*	*65*	*3*	*2*	*.267/.315/.395*	*.253*	*10.6*	*.292*	*-4.2*	*C 5*	*1.7*

Breakout: 1% Improve: 35% Collapse: 14% Attrition: 25% MLB: 86%

Comparables: Mike Redmond, A.J. Pierzynski, Ramon Hernandez

YEAR	TEAM	P. COUNT	FRM RUNS	BLK RUNS	THRW RUNS	TOT RUNS
2015	SLN	18104	7.1	1.5	2.4	10.9
2016	SLN	19667	9.0	1.6	-0.9	9.7
2017	SLN	18649	5.0	0.2	2.4	7.5
2018	*SLN*	*17129*	*4.9*	*1.0*	*0.6*	*6.5*
2019	*SLN*	*16300*	*5.0*	*1.0*	*0.6*	*6.7*

Molina should surpass 15,000 career innings caught this year, which only a dozen catchers have done before. If he continues to play 120 games a year during his contract, which runs through 2020, he could push into the top five, just ahead of A.J. Pierzynski. Jason Kendall and Ivan Rodriguez are on that list, and that's the type of durability Molina has shown throughout his 14-year career. There is no place to play him other than catcher, as his acumen in mentoring pitchers and calling a game has reached Bill Brasky levels. The throwing arm is the only diminished skill, and he's batting as well as he did 10 years ago. For good measure, he's even coming off a career-best RBI total. The Derek Jeter of National League Central catchers is going to stay squatting back there until he decides he's had enough, and it's not going to hurt the franchise in the slightest.

Yairo Munoz UT Born: 01/23/95 Age: 23 Bats: R Throws: R Height: 6'1" Weight: 165 Origin: International Free Agent, 2012

YEAR	TEAM	LVL	AGE	PA	R	2B	3B	HR	RBI	BB	K	SB	CS	AVG/OBP/SLG	TAv	VORP	BABIP	BRR	FRAA	WARP
2015	BLT	A	20	400	48	14	3	9	48	22	62	10	2	.236/.278/.363	.247	9.3	.257	-0.2	SS(88): 0.7	1.1
2015	STO	A+	20	165	21	12	0	4	26	11	20	1	1	.320/.372/.480	.320	16.4	.346	0.3	SS(37): -3.9	1.3
2016	MID	AA	21	414	44	16	3	9	39	23	76	6	7	.240/.286/.367	.234	1.1	.278	-1.0	SS(41): 0.9, 2B(27): 0.5	0.5
2017	MID	AA	22	207	35	17	3	6	26	10	35	12	1	.316/.348/.532	.299	18.1	.355	3.2	SS(22): -1.1, 3B(21): -0.3	1.8
2017	NAS	AAA	22	272	30	9	1	7	42	11	46	10	4	.289/.316/.414	.262	7.3	.324	-2.9	SS(24): 2.4, CF(19): -1.9	0.9
2018	*SLN*	*MLB*	*23*	*250*	*28*	*11*	*1*	*8*	*30*	*12*	*54*	*5*	*2*	*.245/.284/.409*	*.229*	*2.1*	*.281*	*0.2*	*SS 0, 3B 0*	*0.2*
2019	*SLN*	*MLB*	*24*	*334*	*39*	*15*	*1*	*12*	*41*	*18*	*71*	*7*	*3*	*.245/.289/.413*	*.247*	*5.7*	*.280*	*0.5*	*SS 0, 3B 1*	*0.6*

Breakout: 14% Improve: 30% Collapse: 11% Attrition: 31% MLB: 49%

Comparables: Trevor Plouffe, Orlando Calixte, Chris Valaika

Muñoz repeated Double-A to start last year, and repeated his habit of beginning the year on the DL (hamstring), but then proceeded to rake his way into a Triple-A promotion. He added outfield to his résumé in Nashville, mostly in center field, but he also showed up for a few games in the corners, and he is strong-armed enough that he could work in right. The issue isn't his defense at short, but that his bat won't earn its way into a major-league starting lineup without more walks, more pop or both. If you're light on bat, your options are to be Andrelton Simmons with the glove or to play everywhere so you manager can combine two bench spots into one and carry a sixth lefty in the bullpen. Muñoz is not Andrelton Simmons, so he appears to be taking the latter path to the majors.

Tyler O'Neill OF Born: 06/22/95 Age: 23 Bats: R Throws: R Height: 5'11" Weight: 210 Origin: Round 3, 2013 Draft (#85 overall)

YEAR	TEAM	LVL	AGE	PA	R	2B	3B	HR	RBI	BB	K	SB	CS	AVG/OBP/SLG	TAv	VORP	BABIP	BRR	FRAA	WARP
2015	BAK	A+	20	449	68	21	2	32	87	29	137	16	5	.260/.316/.558	.322	34.6	.303	-0.7	RF(39): -0.3, LF(35): -0.1	3.5
2016	WTN	AA	21	575	68	26	4	24	102	62	150	12	2	.293/.374/.508	.327	47.4	.364	-0.8	RF(108): -4.4, LF(5): -0.3	4.6
2017	TAC	AAA	22	396	54	21	2	19	56	44	108	9	2	.244/.328/.479	.283	18.7	.295	0.3	LF(67): -1.8, RF(17): -0.9	1.6
2017	MEM	AAA	22	161	23	5	1	12	39	10	43	5	0	.253/.304/.548	.279	6.6	.266	-0.6	RF(18): 1.0, LF(10): -0.3	0.7
2018	*SLN*	*MLB*	*23*	*250*	*34*	*10*	*1*	*14*	*39*	*22*	*78*	*4*	*1*	*.242/.315/.483*	*.263*	*9.1*	*.299*	*0.2*	*LF 0, RF -1*	*0.9*
2019	*SLN*	*MLB*	*24*	*352*	*50*	*15*	*1*	*19*	*55*	*31*	*108*	*5*	*1*	*.243/.316/.484*	*.279*	*15.6*	*.300*	*0.3*	*LF 0, RF -1*	*1.5*

Breakout: 6% Improve: 25% Collapse: 5% Attrition: 17% MLB: 55%

Comparables: Chris Carter, Domingo Santana, Oswaldo Arcia

O'Neill's father was a top Canadian bodybuilder. One look at O'Neill himself and it won't shock you in the slightest. He's got massive arms, which he uses to drive the ball. The issue will always be contact. Acquired from Seattle for Marco Gonzales, O'Neill whiffs more than most Cardinals prospects, but he also hits for more power than a bunch of 'em and his patient approach is the only thing that might save him from the inevitable O'Forfour jokes. Pitch-identification issues are at the root of his strikeout problems, so while the Cardinals were able to get him to pop out less often post-trade, adjusting and maximizing his swing path, he'll always have some swing-and-miss. How much power he can get to in-game will drive his overall career trajectory, but he profiles as a corner-outfield, strength-driven bat for now.

Marcell Ozuna LF Born: 11/12/90 Age: 27 Bats: R Throws: R Height: 6'1" Weight: 225 Origin: International Free Agent, 2008

YEAR	TEAM	LVL	AGE	PA	R	2B	3B	HR	RBI	BB	K	SB	CS	AVG/OBP/SLG	TAv	VORP	BABIP	BRR	FRAA	WARP
2015	NWO	AAA	24	132	21	12	1	5	11	11	23	1	0	.317/.379/.558	.360	18.3	.359	0.7	CF(29): -1.4	1.7
2015	MIA	MLB	24	494	47	27	0	10	44	30	110	2	3	.259/.308/.383	.255	15.2	.320	3.8	CF(111): -11.3, RF(15): 0.8	0.5
2016	MIA	MLB	25	608	75	23	6	23	76	43	115	0	3	.266/.321/.452	.292	39.5	.296	1.6	CF(123): -7.2, LF(11): -1.4	3.5
2017	MIA	MLB	26	679	93	30	2	37	124	64	144	1	3	.312/.376/.548	.321	55.4	.355	-3.5	LF(152): 5.1, CF(3): 0.0	6.1
2018	*SLN*	*MLB*	*27*	*586*	*73*	*27*	*3*	*24*	*84*	*42*	*123*	*2*	*2*	*.275/.329/.468*	*.274*	*25.0*	*.316*	*-1.4*	*RF 14*	*3.4*
2019	*SLN*	*MLB*	*28*	*549*	*75*	*26*	*2*	*24*	*79*	*45*	*120*	*1*	*1*	*.274/.336/.478*	*.288*	*28.5*	*.315*	*0.8*	*RF 15*	*4.7*

Breakout: 3% Improve: 60% Collapse: 2% Attrition: 5% MLB: 98%

Comparables: Matt Holliday, Carlos Gonzalez, Bob Nieman

San Francisco 49ers middle linebacker NaVorro Bowman's brilliance was always overshadowed by his transcendent teammate Patrick Willis. Over 3,100 miles southeast, Ozuna has been victimized by a similar phenomenon. At the precise moment his all-around game crystallized—taking him from a potential star to an actual one—he remained dwarfed by Giancarlo Stanton's monstrous shadow. He's still super aggressive at the plate, like Michael Rappoport in those Cumberland Farms commercials, but he's made noticeable strides with his pitch recognition, swinging at more pitches in the strike zone than ever before. That's a great thing when you have his raw power. Ozuna has blossomed into a true offensive centerpiece, which combined with his defensive prowess—he won his first Gold Glove Award last year—makes him one of the most prolific young stars in the game. Perhaps best of all, he no longer has to dwell in Stanton's shadow.

Delvin Perez SS Born: 11/24/98 Age: 19 Bats: R Throws: R Height: 6'3" Weight: 175 Origin: Round 1, 2016 Draft (#23 overall)

YEAR	TEAM	LVL	AGE	PA	R	2B	3B	HR	RBI	BB	K	SB	CS	AVG/OBP/SLG	TAv	VORP	BABIP	BRR	FRAA	WARP
2016	CRD	RK	17	180	19	8	4	0	19	12	28	12	1	.294/.352/.393	.294	15.1	.353	0.8	SS(40): -3.7, CF(1): -0.1	1.1
2017	CRD	RK	18	50	7	1	2	0	5	5	10	2	1	.238/.320/.357	.233	2.2	.294	1.6	SS(9): -1.1	0.1
2017	JCY	RK	18	90	7	1	1	0	4	12	14	3	4	.184/.311/.224	.227	1.2	.226	0.7	SS(22): -0.5	0.1
2018	*SLN*	*MLB*	*19*	*250*	*26*	*9*	*1*	*5*	*20*	*14*	*76*	*4*	*2*	*.200/.250/.311*	*.189*	*-6.9*	*.271*	*0.0*	*SS -2*	*-1.0*
2019	*SLN*	*MLB*	*20*	*342*	*36*	*12*	*2*	*8*	*35*	*22*	*100*	*5*	*2*	*.215/.270/.345*	*.220*	*-2.6*	*.283*	*0.3*	*SS -3*	*-0.6*

Breakout: 0% Improve: 3% Collapse: 1% Attrition: 4% MLB: 7% *Comparables: Raul Mondesi, Elvis Andrus, Carlos Triunfel*

A former first-round pick, Perez has seen his stock plummet since turning pro. Technically you could trace the drop-off to before the draft, when he tested positive for a performance-enhancing drug. He still had his believers, including us, heading into 2017 ... when he promptly, well, you see his stats above. The scouting reports were just as harsh as the stat lines, as his effort, bat and, to a lesser extent, glove were all called into question. The glove is the best of the three aspects mentioned, with the tools still present to carry a plus defensive profile, but the effort hinders the functionality of the tools in-game. He continued to show a decent eye at the plate without whiffing too much, but it was consistently weak contact that he didn't make up for with his legs. He was only 18, so it's far too early to throw in the towel on any aspect, but he'll have to undergo a #slack-otomy to turn things around.

Tommy Pham OF Born: 03/08/88 Age: 30 Bats: R Throws: R Height: 6'1" Weight: 210 Origin: Round 16, 2006 Draft (#496 overall)

YEAR	TEAM	LVL	AGE	PA	R	2B	3B	HR	RBI	BB	K	SB	CS	AVG/OBP/SLG	TAv	VORP	BABIP	BRR	FRAA	WARP
2015	MEM	AAA	27	196	29	10	1	6	39	22	36	9	0	.327/.398/.503	.337	23.8	.379	2.2	CF(42): -4.3, LF(2): 0.5	2.0
2015	SLN	MLB	27	173	28	7	5	5	18	19	41	2	0	.268/.347/.477	.298	13.3	.333	2.1	CF(33): -2.8, LF(18): -0.8	1.0
2016	MEM	AAA	28	128	15	5	1	3	17	18	29	8	2	.236/.344/.382	.272	7.1	.295	1.9	CF(24): -2.8, LF(4): 0.2	0.5
2016	SLN	MLB	28	183	26	7	0	9	17	20	71	2	2	.226/.324/.440	.270	7.7	.342	0.7	CF(34): -2.1, LF(30): -2.3	0.3
2017	MEM	AAA	29	106	17	8	0	4	19	13	21	6	3	.283/.371/.500	.310	9.2	.328	0.7	RF(15): 2.2, CF(9): -1.0	1.0
2017	SLN	MLB	29	530	95	22	2	23	73	71	117	25	7	.306/.411/.520	.332	58.0	.368	4.6	LF(86): -2.5, CF(37): 0.2	5.6
2018	*SLN*	*MLB*	*30*	*627*	*98*	*25*	*4*	*22*	*73*	*70*	*156*	*22*	*7*	*.264/.353/.445*	*.279*	*36.6*	*.329*	*1.9*	*LF -8*	*2.2*
2019	*SLN*	*MLB*	*31*	*519*	*71*	*20*	*3*	*19*	*67*	*60*	*137*	*16*	*6*	*.255/.349/.441*	*.284*	*29.6*	*.322*	*3.6*	*LF -5*	*2.6*

Breakout: 2% Improve: 35% Collapse: 17% Attrition: 22% MLB: 89% *Comparables: Scott Van Slyke, Scott Hairston, Josh Willingham*

Just when it seemed the Cardinals' home-brew incantations only worked with hurlers, infielders and Molinas, Pham broke the archetype and posted the best and most unlikely outfield season by a Cardinal since, what, Ryan Ludwick? Perhaps the runes require casting only during blue moons, but the once-promising outfielder, whose middle name was once thought to be "If He Could Just Stay Healthy," didn't even make the Opening Day roster. But come May he refused to yield the field. Given the age and the medical bills, he may not be a five-win player again, but he can start with his all-around game. There are countless stories of players who could not stay healthy, leaving us to wonder what might have been. So at worst, at least for one enchanted season, Pham wouldn't leave it to the imagination.

Kolten Wong 2B Born: 10/10/90 Age: 27 Bats: L Throws: R Height: 5'9" Weight: 185 Origin: Round 1, 2011 Draft (#22 overall)

YEAR	TEAM	LVL	AGE	PA	R	2B	3B	HR	RBI	BB	K	SB	CS	AVG/OBP/SLG	TAv	VORP	BABIP	BRR	FRAA	WARP
2015	SLN	MLB	24	613	71	28	4	11	61	36	95	15	8	.262/.321/.386	.259	17.8	.296	2.3	2B(147): 11.3	3.1
2016	MEM	AAA	25	34	10	0	1	4	11	4	6	1	0	.429/.529/.929	.521	11.0	.444	0.7	2B(4): 0.1, CF(3): 0.2	1.2
2016	SLN	MLB	25	361	39	7	7	5	23	34	52	7	0	.240/.327/.355	.269	14.5	.268	1.4	2B(88): 12.6, CF(8): -0.5	2.7
2017	SLN	MLB	26	411	55	27	3	4	42	41	60	8	2	.285/.376/.412	.284	23.4	.331	1.6	2B(106): -4.6	1.9
2018	*SLN*	*MLB*	*27*	*484*	*58*	*20*	*4*	*11*	*52*	*35*	*75*	*11*	*3*	*.260/.326/.400*	*.254*	*18.2*	*.290*	*1.0*	*2B 5*	*1.8*
2019	*SLN*	*MLB*	*28*	*435*	*53*	*18*	*3*	*12*	*51*	*34*	*71*	*9*	*2*	*.256/.326/.414*	*.264*	*17.4*	*.281*	*1.7*	*2B 4*	*2.4*

Breakout: 9% Improve: 45% Collapse: 7% Attrition: 16% MLB: 96% *Comparables: Alexi Casilla, Jace Peterson, Chris Getz*

The Cardinals were waiting for Wong to become a solid hitter—not that they were on pins and needles; if he struggled they were just going to fashion another infielder together MacGyver style—and the patience was finally rewarded. The defense-first second baseman added some polish by drawing more walks and driving the ball into both gaps. He's still a down-the-lineup bat, but he brings enough contact and speed to the box that he could get away with leading off on his best day. His defensive numbers took a nosedive, but he did suffer two consecutive injuries, both to a different elbow, around midseason. A completely healthy Wong might be one of the sneaky-best second baggers on the circuit.

PITCHERS

Matt Bowman RHP Born: 05/31/91 Age: 27 Bats: R Throws: R Height: 6'0" Weight: 175 Origin: Round 13, 2012 Draft (#410 overall)

YEAR	TEAM	LVL	AGE	W	L	SV	G	GS	IP	H	HR	BB/9	K/9	K	GB%	BABIP	WHIP	ERA	DRA	WARP	MPH	CMD	PWR	STM
2015	LVG	AAA	24	7	16	0	28	26	140	184	15	3.3	4.9	77	56%	.339	1.68	5.53	4.36	1.5				
2016	SLN	MLB	25	2	5	0	59	0	67^2	59	4	2.7	6.9	52	64%	.270	1.17	3.46	3.69	1.0	94.3	65	50	46
2017	SLN	MLB	26	3	6	2	75	0	58^2	52	4	2.8	7.1	46	56%	.276	1.19	3.99	3.84	0.9	92.5	60	41	51
2018	*SLN*	*MLB*	*27*	*3*	*3*	*2*	*53*	*0*	*56*	*54*	*5*	*3.5*	*7.1*	*44*	*54%*	*.295*	*1.36*	*3.81*	*4.13*	*0.5*	*92.9*	*63*	*46*	*49*
2019	*SLN*	*MLB*	*28*	*3*	*1*	*1*	*54*	*0*	*56^2*	*51*	*5*	*3.4*	*7.6*	*48*	*54%*	*.303*	*1.28*	*4.00*	*4.48*	*0.4*	*92.6*	*63*	*45*	*49*

Breakout: 29% Improve: 48% Collapse: 17% Attrition: 19% MLB: 83% *Comparables: Tyler Anderson, Randy Wells, T.J. McFarland*

Bowman didn't strike out enough batters to be a late-inning option, because you're thinking of Bat Mowman. However, he didn't disappoint in his sophomore campaign, keeping some consistent numbers in higher-stakes innings, particularly the seventh, with his long delivery and blend of sinker, split-finger and slider. In 2016 he was a Rule 5 pick and couldn't be sent down; in 2017 he still wasn't, so he'll continue to work the middle innings unless he can ever start that mower.

John Brebbia RHP Born: 05/30/90 Age: 28 Bats: L Throws: R Height: 6'1" Weight: 185 Origin: Round 30, 2011 Draft (#929 overall)

YEAR	TEAM	LVL	AGE	W	L	SV	G	GS	IP	H	HR	BB/9	K/9	K	GB%	BABIP	WHIP	ERA	DRA	WARP	MPH	CMD	PWR	STM
2016	SFD	AA	26	3	2	2	24	0	37^{2}	41	6	1.4	9.1	38	43%	.324	1.25	4.06	2.65	0.9				
2016	MEM	AAA	26	2	3	0	19	0	30^{1}	41	3	3.9	8.9	30	46%	.396	1.78	6.23	4.77	0.1				
2017	MEM	AAA	27	1	1	3	15	1	26^{2}	16	2	1.7	9.8	29	33%	.219	0.79	1.69	2.87	0.7				
2017	SLN	MLB	27	0	0	0	50	0	51^{2}	37	8	1.9	8.9	51	26%	.216	0.93	2.44	3.06	1.2	96.0	57	51	51
2018	*SLN*	*MLB*	*28*	*2*	*4*	*2*	*53*	*0*	*56*	*60*	*12*	*3.4*	*8.8*	*55*	*38%*	*.299*	*1.45*	*5.52*	*5.53*	*-0.4*	*95.4*	*57*	*51*	*51*
2019	*SLN*	*MLB*	*29*	*1*	*0*	*0*	*32*	*0*	34^{1}	*35*	*7*	*3.9*	*7.9*	*30*	*38%*	*.304*	*1.45*	*5.73*	*6.41*	*-0.5*	*95.0*	*57*	*51*	*51*

Breakout: 22% Improve: 33% Collapse: 10% Attrition: 24% MLB: 55% *Comparables: T.J. Beam, Mike Adams, Marcus McBeth*

Brebbia was arguably the Cardinals' most effective reliever last year. The former Yankees farmhand toiled through two years of independent ball, scoring a 0.98 ERA for the Pete Incaviglia-managed Laredo Lemurs in 2015. Despite playing for a team with a name as terrific as the Laredo Lemurs, he opted to sign with the Diamondbacks, then was yoinked by the Cardinals in the Rule 5 draft's minor-league phase. He had a tumultuous 2016 but a dominant start to 2017, and after a late May call-up he outperformed his 90th PECOTA percentile. Now he's a relative unknown that skated by with an average FIP, an extreme fly-ball pitcher with a minuscule pop-up rate. Wherever he fits in the bullpen, it will no longer be with the Laredo Lemurs.

Brett Cecil LHP Born: 07/02/86 Age: 31 Bats: R Throws: L Height: 6'3" Weight: 235 Origin: Round 1, 2007 Draft (#38 overall)

YEAR	TEAM	LVL	AGE	W	L	SV	G	GS	IP	H	HR	BB/9	K/9	K	GB%	BABIP	WHIP	ERA	DRA	WARP	MPH	CMD	PWR	STM
2015	TOR	MLB	28	5	5	5	63	0	54^{1}	39	4	2.2	11.6	70	54%	.280	0.96	2.48	2.34	1.5	94.8	58	44	45
2016	TOR	MLB	29	1	7	0	54	0	36^{2}	39	6	2.0	11.0	45	43%	.344	1.28	3.93	4.22	0.3	94.4	54	41	38
2017	SLN	MLB	30	2	4	1	73	0	67^{1}	67	7	2.1	8.8	66	47%	.319	1.23	3.88	4.83	0.3	93.2	55	42	50
2018	*SLN*	*MLB*	*31*	*3*	*4*	*3*	*58*	*0*	*61*	*59*	*9*	*3.4*	*9.5*	*65*	*46%*	*.304*	*1.35*	*3.96*	*4.24*	*0.5*	*93.0*	*55*	*42*	*44*
2019	*SLN*	*MLB*	*32*	*2*	*1*	*2*	*48*	*0*	*51*	*48*	*8*	*3.2*	*9.2*	*52*	*46%*	*.316*	*1.30*	*4.34*	*4.83*	*0.2*	*92.4*	*54*	*41*	*44*

Breakout: 28% Improve: 44% Collapse: 27% Attrition: 11% MLB: 90% *Comparables: Joakim Soria, Steve Cishek, Bobby Jenks*

The Cardinals, known for spinning relief pitchers out of straw and slapping a hat on them, decided to do what all other teams do and just throw money at veteran relievers like Cecil. And this may surprise you, but after one year it worked just about as well as their magic loom of 95-mph fastball brethren—except that his fastball is slowing down, and his strikeout rate took a tumble toward league average. He still may pitch meaningful eighth innings, but nothing is trending in the right direction except that designer glasses remain in style.

Junior Fernandez RHP Born: 03/02/97 Age: 21 Bats: R Throws: R Height: 6'1" Weight: 180 Origin: International Free Agent, 2014

YEAR	TEAM	LVL	AGE	W	L	SV	G	GS	IP	H	HR	BB/9	K/9	K	GB%	BABIP	WHIP	ERA	DRA	WARP	MPH	CMD	PWR	STM
2015	CRD	RK	18	3	2	0	11	9	51	54	0	2.6	10.2	58	56%	.383	1.35	3.88	2.81	1.7				
2016	PEO	A	19	6	5	0	14	14	78^{1}	71	3	3.9	7.2	63	52%	.296	1.34	3.33	5.37	-0.3				
2016	PMB	A+	19	2	2	0	10	6	43^{2}	48	4	4.1	5.2	25	47%	.297	1.56	5.36	7.15	-0.9				
2017	PMB	A+	20	5	3	0	16	16	90^{1}	82	5	3.9	5.8	58	45%	.281	1.34	3.69	5.77	-0.5				
2018	*SLN*	*MLB*	*21*	*5*	*5*	*0*	*16*	*16*	81^{1}	*85*	*13*	*4.7*	*7.9*	*71*	*43%*	*.316*	*1.56*	*5.26*	*5.92*	*-0.3*				
2019	*SLN*	*MLB*	*22*	*7*	*11*	*0*	*27*	*27*	*164*	*159*	*29*	*4.3*	*7.9*	*144*	*43%*	*.304*	*1.44*	*5.43*	*6.09*	*-0.7*				

Breakout: 1% Improve: 1% Collapse: 0% Attrition: 1% MLB: 2% *Comparables: Patrick Schuster, Robert Gsellman, Brett Marshall*

Junior Fernandez is a great name with a big arm, but not much else. The stocky right-hander can run his fastball up to 96 mph, but his slider isn't fooling anyone and his changeup is just okay. Given how hard he throws, he didn't miss nearly enough bats in the Florida State League and—to add insult to ineffectiveness—he walked too many guys. He's a reliever in all likelihood, though the lack of secondaries to go with a hittable fastball may make him less than that.

Jack Flaherty RHP Born: 10/15/95 Age: 22 Bats: R Throws: R Height: 6'4" Weight: 205 Origin: Round 1, 2014 Draft (#34 overall)

YEAR	TEAM	LVL	AGE	W	L	SV	G	GS	IP	H	HR	BB/9	K/9	K	GB%	BABIP	WHIP	ERA	DRA	WARP	MPH	CMD	PWR	STM
2015	PEO	A	19	9	3	0	18	18	95	92	2	2.9	9.2	97	37%	.330	1.29	2.84	2.94	2.6				
2016	PMB	A+	20	5	9	0	24	23	134	129	8	3.0	8.5	126	49%	.316	1.30	3.56	2.72	4.2				
2017	SFD	AA	21	7	2	0	10	10	63^{1}	47	2	1.6	8.8	62	41%	.269	0.92	1.42	2.10	2.3				
2017	MEM	AAA	21	7	2	0	15	15	85^{1}	73	10	2.5	9.0	85	42%	.288	1.14	2.74	3.35	2.2				
2017	SLN	MLB	21	0	2	0	6	5	21^{1}	23	4	4.2	8.4	20	49%	.322	1.55	6.33	5.23	0.1	94.9	40	46	69
2018	*SLN*	*MLB*	*22*	*6*	*8*	*0*	*18*	*18*	*95*	*92*	*14*	*3.5*	*8.9*	*94*	*40%*	*.296*	*1.35*	*4.20*	*4.52*	*0.7*	*94.9*	*42*	*48*	*72*
2019	*SLN*	*MLB*	*23*	*10*	*11*	*0*	*32*	*32*	205^{2}	*181*	*31*	*3.2*	*9.3*	*212*	*40%*	*.302*	*1.24*	*4.34*	*4.83*	*1.5*	*94.8*	*42*	*48*	*73*

Breakout: 25% Improve: 36% Collapse: 7% Attrition: 20% MLB: 54% *Comparables: Arodys Vizcaino, German Marquez, Gerrit Cole*

Flaherty arrived slightly ahead of schedule, reaching the majors at age 21 after slicing through Double-A and Triple-A with a combined 2.18 ERA and 147/35 K/BB ratio in 149 innings to begin last season. He then held his own as a rookie, setting him up for a prominent role in 2018 and beyond. Flaherty works in the 92-94 mph range with his fastball and also features a plus slider among a four-pitch mix. He stuff isn't overpowering for a former first-round pick and Top 101 prospect, but Flaherty looks like a relatively safe bet to settle in as a mid-rotation starter with good durability.

Zac Gallen RHP Born: 08/03/95 Age: 22 Bats: R Throws: R Height: 6'2" Weight: 191 Origin: Round 3, 2016 Draft (#106 overall)

YEAR	TEAM	LVL	AGE	W	L	SV	G	GS	IP	H	HR	BB/9	K/9	K	GB%	BABIP	WHIP	ERA	DRA	WARP	MPH	CMD	PWR	STM
2017	PMB	A+	21	5	2	0	9	9	55^2	44	1	1.6	9.1	56	48%	.283	0.97	1.62	1.76	2.3				
2017	SFD	AA	21	4	5	0	13	13	71^1	76	8	2.4	5.3	42	42%	.292	1.33	3.79	5.19	0.0				
2017	MEM	AAA	21	1	1	0	4	4	20^2	18	2	2.6	10.0	23	47%	.314	1.16	3.48	3.54	0.5				
2018	*SLN*	*MLB*	*22*	*6*	*6*	*0*	*19*	*19*	*101^1*	*98*	*19*	*3.5*	*9.5*	*107*	*40%*	*.311*	*1.36*	*4.72*	*5.29*	*0.4*				
2019	*SLN*	*MLB*	*23*	*8*	*11*	*0*	*28*	*28*	*172^2*	*156*	*30*	*3.6*	*9.2*	*176*	*40%*	*.299*	*1.31*	*4.81*	*5.37*	*0.4*				

Breakout: 12% Improve: 24% Collapse: 6% Attrition: 17% MLB: 35% *Comparables: Rafael Montero, Brett Oberholtzer, Chih-Wei Hu*

Yet another part of the haul Miami received for Marcell Ozuna, Gallen is the pitcher version of the type of prospect the Cardinals seem to pull out of thin air. He's got viable stuff, headlined by a low-90s fastball that can touch 96 and a solid-average curveball. He's got two other pitches that approach average (slider, change) and he pounds the zone. He's got a competitive mind-set on the mound despite being undersized as a starter. Gallen is straight out of Central Casting for the "overachiever" role thanks to his bevy of pitches and a ton of moxie. You know what he is just by the fact that we used "moxie" in this write-up. He'll stick as a starter, at least early on, and should eat some innings at the back of the rotation.

Luke Gregerson RHP Born: 05/14/84 Age: 34 Bats: L Throws: R Height: 6'3" Weight: 205 Origin: Round 28, 2006 Draft (#856 overall)

YEAR	TEAM	LVL	AGE	W	L	SV	G	GS	IP	H	HR	BB/9	K/9	K	GB%	BABIP	WHIP	ERA	DRA	WARP	MPH	CMD	PWR	STM
2015	HOU	MLB	31	7	3	31	64	0	61	48	5	1.5	8.7	59	62%	.264	0.95	3.10	2.48	1.6	91.4	46	32	46
2016	HOU	MLB	32	4	3	15	59	0	57^2	38	5	2.8	10.5	67	62%	.239	0.97	3.28	2.51	1.6	91.4	38	35	43
2017	HOU	MLB	33	2	3	1	65	0	61	62	13	3.0	10.3	70	49%	.306	1.34	4.57	3.40	1.2	90.8	46	29	48
2018	*SLN*	*MLB*	*34*	*3*	*3*	*2*	*55*	*0*	*58^2*	*55*	*9*	*3.5*	*8.9*	*58*	*52%*	*.290*	*1.33*	*4.36*	*4.55*	*0.2*	*90.1*	*43*	*31*	*45*
2019	*SLN*	*MLB*	*35*	*3*	*1*	*1*	*51*	*0*	*54^1*	*47*	*8*	*3.5*	*8.6*	*52*	*52%*	*.289*	*1.25*	*4.69*	*4.98*	*0.1*	*89.5*	*42*	*31*	*45*

Breakout: 9% Improve: 22% Collapse: 48% Attrition: 5% MLB: 89% *Comparables: Heath Bell, Akinori Otsuka, Doug Jones*

Few relief pitchers have been more consistent over the past decade than Gregerson, whose DRA has been almost as steady as the Minute Maid Park train since he entered the league in 2009. But even the clockwork setup man has seen his performance fade ever so slightly in the last year or so. In 2017, lefties started hitting him harder, and he had trouble keeping the ball on the ground; between that and the "juiced" baseball, you can see why his homer total rose. Gregerson also got crushed on short rest, with hitters lighting him up on one day of rest or less between appearances. With two days or more between appearances, he was highly effective, so perhaps the Cardinals may want to deploy him a bit more judiciously to keep the veteran chugging along.

Jordan Hicks RHP Born: 09/06/96 Age: 21 Bats: R Throws: R Height: 6'2" Weight: 185 Origin: Round SUP, 2015 Draft (#105 overall)

YEAR	TEAM	LVL	AGE	W	L	SV	G	GS	IP	H	HR	BB/9	K/9	K	GB%	BABIP	WHIP	ERA	DRA	WARP	MPH	CMD	PWR	STM
2016	JCY	RK	19	2	1	0	6	6	30	33	1	3.9	6.0	20	57%	.344	1.53	4.20	5.75	0.0				
2016	SCO	A-	19	4	1	0	6	6	30^2	25	0	4.7	6.5	22	66%	.269	1.34	1.76	4.91	0.1				
2017	PEO	A	20	8	2	0	14	14	78	75	3	4.5	7.3	63	53%	.316	1.46	3.35	5.67	-0.3				
2017	PMB	A+	20	0	1	1	8	5	27	21	0	2.0	10.7	32	67%	.318	1.00	1.00	1.31	1.2				
2018	*SLN*	*MLB*	*21*	*5*	*6*	*0*	*16*	*16*	*80^2*	*85*	*14*	*5.4*	*8.3*	*74*	*46%*	*.323*	*1.65*	*5.65*	*6.36*	*-0.7*				
2019	*SLN*	*MLB*	*22*	*7*	*12*	*0*	*28*	*28*	*167*	*172*	*29*	*4.8*	*7.9*	*147*	*46%*	*.323*	*1.56*	*5.64*	*6.33*	*-1.1*				

Breakout: 9% Improve: 9% Collapse: 1% Attrition: 6% MLB: 11% *Comparables: Aaron Thompson, Allen Webster, Brad Hand*

Hicks is blessed with some of the best stuff in the Cardinals' system. He can tickle triple digits with his fastball, and will sit in the mid-to-upper-90s. He'll flash a plus curveball in the upper-70s, and can kick in a usable slider and a modest changeup. The adage is when you've made the sale stop selling, but we're conscientious salespeople here at BP, so we will make sure our buyers are well informed. To that end, Hicks can struggle with his control and isn't the savviest or most cerebral of hurlers, operating as more of a grip-it-and-rip-it type on the bump. That's gonna work in the lower levels of the minors, but he could face adversity as he moves up the chain. His stuff will play anywhere, he just has to make the most of it.

Dakota Hudson RHP Born: 09/15/94 Age: 23 Bats: R Throws: R Height: 6'5" Weight: 215 Origin: Round 1, 2016 Draft (#34 overall)

YEAR	TEAM	LVL	AGE	W	L	SV	G	GS	IP	H	HR	BB/9	K/9	K	GB%	BABIP	WHIP	ERA	DRA	WARP	MPH	CMD	PWR	STM
2017	SFD	AA	22	9	4	0	18	18	114	111	5	2.7	6.1	77	58%	.296	1.27	2.53	3.31	2.5				
2017	MEM	AAA	22	1	1	0	7	7	38^2	36	2	3.5	4.4	19	59%	.272	1.32	4.42	5.21	0.2				
2018	*SLN*	*MLB*	*23*	*7*	*6*	*0*	*18*	*18*	*108^2*	*102*	*14*	*3.9*	*8.4*	*102*	*52%*	*.305*	*1.38*	*4.47*	*5.02*	*0.7*				
2019	*SLN*	*MLB*	*24*	*9*	*12*	*0*	*28*	*28*	*172*	*166*	*24*	*4.6*	*7.6*	*145*	*52%*	*.31*	*1.48*	*5.10*	*5.72*	*-0.2*				

Breakout: 20% Improve: 32% Collapse: 13% Attrition: 25% MLB: 53% *Comparables: Kevin Mulvey, Bobby Livingston, Robert Gsellman*

Another quality arm in the Cardinals' system, the former first-rounder has a good chance of cracking the big leagues for the first time in 2018. Already working at the upper levels of the minors, Hudson has a refined repertoire beginning with a legitimate fastball in the mid-90s. He misses bats (though not nearly enough) with a plus cutter that can flash better, and rounds out his arsenal with a curveball, slider and changeup. He's got prototypical starter's size and keeps the ball on the ground, but his mechanics can get a little high-effort and, paired with his struggles to get whiffs and a checkered past in terms of health, could land him in the bullpen. He'll begin his career in the rotation given the depth and quality of his pitch mix, but he might be more of an impact pitcher out of the 'pen.

Lance Lynn RHP
Born: 05/12/87 Age: 31 Bats: B Throws: R Height: 6'5" Weight: 280 Origin: Round 1, 2008 Draft (#39 overall)

YEAR	TEAM	LVL	AGE	W	L	SV	G	GS	IP	H	HR	BB/9	K/9	K	GB%	BABIP	WHIP	ERA	DRA	WARP	MPH	CMD	PWR	STM
2015	SLN	MLB	28	12	11	0	31	31	175^1	172	13	3.5	8.6	167	46%	.319	1.37	3.03	4.23	1.8	95.1	58	66	72
2017	SLN	MLB	30	11	8	0	33	33	186^1	151	27	3.8	7.4	153	45%	.244	1.23	3.43	4.54	2.1	94.1	59	63	79
2018	*SLN*	*MLB*	*31*	*7*	*7*	*0*	*21*	*21*	*120^1*	*118*	*20*	*3.6*	*8.3*	*111*	*46%*	*.304*	*1.38*	*4.85*	*5.45*	*0.2*	*93.6*	*58*	*64*	*76*
2019	*SLN*	*MLB*	*32*	*8*	*11*	*0*	*27*	*27*	*165^1*	*160*	*25*	*3.4*	*7.9*	*144*	*46%*	*.307*	*1.35*	*4.85*	*5.42*	*0.4*	*92.9*	*58*	*63*	*77*

Breakout: 10% Improve: 39% Collapse: 30% Attrition: 9% MLB: 91% *Comparables: Gavin Floyd, Carlos Zambrano, Gio Gonzalez*

You typically know what you're getting at a Panera; a high-floor, low-ceiling sandwich and decent Wi-Fi. Lynn is Panera. He'll go about five or six innings nearly every time and give up four runs, at most. This remained true even in his first full season with a new UCL. Probably in 10 years, all starters are going to be four- or five-inning performers, so Lynn is simply ahead of his time. You can just see Lynn pitching proudly into his late-thirties like some vagabond Jason Marquis disciple who was never informed that the war on complete games ended years ago.

Tyler Lyons LHP
Born: 02/21/88 Age: 30 Bats: L Throws: L Height: 6'4" Weight: 210 Origin: Round 9, 2010 Draft (#289 overall)

YEAR	TEAM	LVL	AGE	W	L	SV	G	GS	IP	H	HR	BB/9	K/9	K	GB%	BABIP	WHIP	ERA	DRA	WARP	MPH	CMD	PWR	STM
2015	MEM	AAA	27	9	5	0	16	16	94^2	104	12	1.2	9.1	96	46%	.336	1.24	3.14	0.95	4.7				
2015	SLN	MLB	27	3	1	0	17	8	60	59	12	2.2	9.0	60	42%	.281	1.23	3.75	4.71	0.2	92.8	47	34	62
2016	SLN	MLB	28	2	0	0	30	0	48	35	9	2.6	8.6	46	41%	.220	1.02	3.38	5.08	-0.1	93.4	51	33	36
2017	MEM	AAA	29	0	0	0	4	4	17^2	17	2	1.5	8.7	17	41%	.306	1.13	2.55	3.67	0.4				
2017	SLN	MLB	29	4	1	3	50	0	54	39	3	3.3	11.3	68	43%	.295	1.09	2.83	3.43	1.0	91.5	53	23	50
2018	*SLN*	*MLB*	*30*	*3*	*4*	*23*	*58*	*0*	*61*	*54*	*8*	*3.4*	*9.7*	*66*	*42%*	*.292*	*1.26*	*3.78*	*4.09*	*0.6*	*91.7*	*51*	*29*	*48*
2019	*SLN*	*MLB*	*31*	*3*	*1*	*16*	*58*	*0*	*61*	*50*	*8*	*3.1*	*9.8*	*66*	*42%*	*.297*	*1.17*	*3.95*	*4.39*	*0.5*	*91.2*	*52*	*27*	*45*

Breakout: 17% Improve: 48% Collapse: 15% Attrition: 14% MLB: 82% *Comparables: Mike Fiers, Matt Wise, Matt Shoemaker*

Lyons began last season on the disabled list with knee problems left over from 2016, and later spent another stint on the shelf with an intercostal strain. In between he worked exclusively out of the bullpen and mostly in long relief, although he did pick up a few saves when the Cardinals mixed and matched late in the season. Lyons came up through the minors as a starter, but he hasn't started a big-league game since 2015 and the balky knee limits his durability. Stuff-wise he doesn't have a standout reliever profile, working mostly in the low-90s with his fastball, but Lyons' slider has emerged as a tremendous weapon, and he has a 2.74 ERA with 158 strikeouts in 144 career innings as a reliever.

Carlos Martinez RHP
Born: 09/21/91 Age: 26 Bats: R Throws: R Height: 6'0" Weight: 190 Origin: International Free Agent, 2009

YEAR	TEAM	LVL	AGE	W	L	SV	G	GS	IP	H	HR	BB/9	K/9	K	GB%	BABIP	WHIP	ERA	DRA	WARP	MPH	CMD	PWR	STM
2015	SLN	MLB	23	14	7	0	31	29	179^2	168	13	3.2	9.2	184	56%	.318	1.29	3.01	3.64	3.0	99.0	39	65	72
2016	SLN	MLB	24	16	9	0	31	31	195^1	169	15	3.2	8.0	174	58%	.286	1.22	3.04	3.71	3.7	99.6	42	59	77
2017	SLN	MLB	25	12	11	0	32	32	205	179	27	3.1	9.5	217	52%	.285	1.22	3.64	3.76	4.1	98.8	43	63	82
2018	*SLN*	*MLB*	*26*	*11*	*11*	*0*	*28*	*28*	*176*	*156*	*19*	*3.1*	*9.4*	*183*	*53%*	*.293*	*1.22*	*3.50*	*3.78*	*2.8*	*98.7*	*42*	*63*	*79*
2019	*SLN*	*MLB*	*27*	*13*	*11*	*0*	*32*	*32*	*211^2*	*168*	*21*	*2.9*	*9.7*	*229*	*53%*	*.3*	*1.12*	*3.42*	*3.81*	*4.1*	*98.5*	*43*	*63*	*81*

Breakout: 22% Improve: 59% Collapse: 18% Attrition: 7% MLB: 94% *Comparables: Alex Wood, Mat Latos, Rich Harden*

Here's your classic boring case of a highly rated pitching prospect who grew up to be a top-of-the-rotation starter. Yawn. Given the age there's still a tad more upside to Martinez, rubbing elbows with the rest of the league's aces. He was the only one to throw shutouts, plural, in the 2017 National League, and nobody faced more batters than him. He's got the workload down and he's 26. There remains a slight Achilles' heel against lefties, who tatter Martinez's pitches a little better than league average, but all future aces around this time tend to figure that out. The Pedro Martinez comp really isn't fair, since CarMart is not below six feet tall, though a Cy Young contending campaign is not out of the question this year.

Miles Mikolas RHP
Born: 08/23/88 Age: 29 Bats: R Throws: R Height: 6'5" Weight: 220 Origin: Round 7, 2009 Draft (#204 overall)

YEAR	TEAM	LVL	AGE	W	L	SV	G	GS	IP	H	HR	BB/9	K/9	K	GB%	BABIP	WHIP	ERA	DRA	WARP	MPH	CMD	PWR	STM
2018	*SLN*	*MLB*	*29*	*6*	*8*	*0*	*19*	*19*	*100^2*	*105*	*13*	*2.7*	*7.0*	*79*	*46%*	*.298*	*1.34*	*4.15*	*4.48*	*0.8*				
2019	*SLN*	*MLB*	*30*	*6*	*6*	*0*	*17*	*17*	*105^2*	*105*	*13*	*2.5*	*7.3*	*86*	*50%*	*.305*	*1.27*	*4.12*	*4.50*	*1.2*				

Breakout: 24% Improve: 44% Collapse: 22% Attrition: 10% MLB: 95% *Comparables: Brandon McCarthy, Zach McAllister, Brian Bannister*

In the three previous years he appeared in this publication (2013-2015), there were more references to Mikolas' encounter with a lizard in the AFL than his stuff. And to be fair, the former will never stop being more interesting [imaginary link to YouTube video]. The natural comparison between Mikolas and Colby Lewis, who also came back stateside around his 30th birthday after a mid-career resurgence in Japan, is telling in both their similarities and their differences. Lewis made his mark through substantially improved control—the big righty had a 1.3 K/BB rate before he left and a 9.8 K/BB rate in his final NPB season. Mikolas went from a 1.8 K/BB rate pre-Japan to an 8.1 mark in his final stint with the Yomiuri Giants. Yet the Florida native got four times the money Lewis did. Part of this is comfort. We've seen the jumps that Yu Darvish, Masahiro Tanaka, Kenta Maeda and others have made since Lewis got his $4 million from the Rangers. Mikolas led the Central League in strikeouts and was second in both ERA and WHIP among qualified starters in 2017, and the fact that we've seen him fail before in the US doesn't mean we can't be as excited about him as a Japanese-born player who might have displayed the same dominance.

Seung Hwan Oh RHP Born: 07/15/82 Age: 35 Bats: R Throws: R Height: 5'10" Weight: 205 Origin: International Free Agent, 2016

YEAR	TEAM	LVL	AGE	W	L	SV	G	GS	IP	H	HR	BB/9	K/9	K	GB%	BABIP	WHIP	ERA	DRA	WARP	MPH	CMD	PWR	STM
2016	SLN	MLB	33	6	3	19	76	0	79^2	55	5	2.0	11.6	103	40%	.270	0.92	1.92	2.49	2.3	95.7	59	52	54
2017	SLN	MLB	34	1	6	20	62	0	59^1	68	10	2.3	8.2	54	30%	.319	1.40	4.10	4.53	0.4	94.4	70	51	49
2018	*SLN*	*MLB*	*35*	*3*	*1*	*9*	*53*	*0*	*55^2*	*55*	*9*	*3.5*	*8.7*	*54*	*38%*	*.308*	*1.36*	*4.53*	*5.08*	*0.1*	*93.8*	*63*	*51*	*50*
2019	*SLN*	*MLB*	*36*	*1*	*0*	*4*	*24*	*0*	*24^2*	*26*	*4*	*4.0*	*6.5*	*18*	*38%*	*.308*	*1.51*	*5.51*	*6.17*	*-0.3*	*93.3*	*63*	*50*	*50*

Breakout: 23% Improve: 42% Collapse: 29% Attrition: 15% MLB: 90% *Comparables: Matt Thornton, Akinori Otsuka, Tom Gordon*

After Oh's stellar first stateside season, Final Boss was demoted to First Form Boss after the All-Star break due to batters casting Mute on his previously lethal slider. The league has seemingly adjusted to his slider, though his fastball and changeup were equally mashed harder and missed less often. The other factor here, which is easy to miss when someone has endured just two major-league seasons, is his age. He is one year younger than Francisco Rodriguez and has thrown nearly 800 career innings in 700 appearances. Yes, it was the KBO, but only Fernando Rodney and Joaquin Benoit, five years his senior, top those numbers. He simply may be running out of pixels.

Alex Reyes RHP Born: 08/29/94 Age: 23 Bats: R Throws: R Height: 6'3" Weight: 175 Origin: International Free Agent, 2012

YEAR	TEAM	LVL	AGE	W	L	SV	G	GS	IP	H	HR	BB/9	K/9	K	GB%	BABIP	WHIP	ERA	DRA	WARP	MPH	CMD	PWR	STM
2015	PMB	A+	20	2	5	0	13	13	63^2	49	0	4.4	13.6	96	46%	.371	1.26	2.26	1.07	3.1				
2015	SFD	AA	20	3	2	0	8	8	34^2	21	1	4.7	13.5	52	44%	.286	1.12	3.12	2.01	1.3				
2016	MEM	AAA	21	2	3	0	14	14	65^1	63	6	4.4	12.8	93	42%	.365	1.45	4.96	2.36	2.2				
2016	SLN	MLB	21	4	1	1	12	5	46	33	1	4.5	10.2	52	44%	.283	1.22	1.57	3.07	1.1	100.1	49	64	60
2018	*SLN*	*MLB*	*23*	*4*	*4*	*0*	*11*	*11*	*58^1*	*47*	*7*	*4.2*	*11.8*	*76*	*41%*	*.299*	*1.29*	*3.40*	*3.67*	*1.0*	*100.0*	*51*	*66*	*62*
2019	*SLN*	*MLB*	*24*	*10*	*11*	*0*	*32*	*32*	*205*	*183*	*29*	*3.0*	*9.0*	*205*	*41%*	*.303*	*1.23*	*4.19*	*4.68*	*1.8*	*99.8*	*51*	*67*	*63*

Breakout: 28% Improve: 57% Collapse: 14% Attrition: 19% MLB: 84% *Comparables: Matt Moore, Edwin Diaz, Aroldis Chapman*

We ranked Reyes as the best prospect in baseball in last year's *Annual*, despite the general uncertainty of ranking pitchers in today's game. The day after the list was published online, word started to trickle out about an elbow injury that would quickly resolve in Tommy John surgery. At press time, all reports have his recovery progressing well, and he should be back sometime in the first half. Despite the risk inherent in UCL replacement—there are a chunk of pitchers who don't have the same stuff while coming back, and complications aren't uncommon—he's still easily the best prospect in this system, and he still might be the game's best pitching prospect. That speaks to the incredible talent in his arm. Even if Reyes is the game's top pitching prospect, there's still substantial risk he might end up in the bullpen temporarily or even permanently, which speaks to the risks present for nearly all major pitching prospects.

Kevin Siegrist LHP Born: 07/20/89 Age: 28 Bats: L Throws: L Height: 6'5" Weight: 230 Origin: Round 41, 2008 Draft (#1235 overall)

YEAR	TEAM	LVL	AGE	W	L	SV	G	GS	IP	H	HR	BB/9	K/9	K	GB%	BABIP	WHIP	ERA	DRA	WARP	MPH	CMD	PWR	STM
2015	SLN	MLB	25	7	1	6	81	0	74^2	53	4	4.1	10.8	90	32%	.271	1.17	2.17	3.31	1.2	96.5	53	66	56
2016	SLN	MLB	26	6	3	3	67	0	61^2	42	10	3.8	9.6	66	35%	.221	1.10	2.77	4.43	0.4	95.9	55	55	47
2017	SLN	MLB	27	1	1	1	39	0	34^1	35	4	5.2	9.4	36	43%	.344	1.60	4.98	5.37	-0.1	93.5	50	43	41
2017	PHI	MLB	27	0	0	0	7	0	5	4	1	3.6	12.6	7	17%	.273	1.20	3.60	8.08	-0.2	92.9	50	43	41
2018	*SLN*	*MLB*	*28*	*2*	*1*	*1*	*41*	*0*	*43*	*36*	*6*	*3.9*	*10.1*	*48*	*39%*	*.294*	*1.28*	*4.18*	*4.68*	*0.2*	*94.8*	*53*	*55*	*47*
2019	*SLN*	*MLB*	*29*	*3*	*1*	*1*	*54*	*0*	*49*	*41*	*8*	*4.1*	*9.8*	*53*	*39%*	*.29*	*1.28*	*4.56*	*5.07*	*0.1*	*94.1*	*53*	*51*	*45*

Breakout: 25% Improve: 44% Collapse: 35% Attrition: 11% MLB: 92% *Comparables: Cody Allen, Antonio Bastardo, Frank Francisco*

Siegrist was one of the most effective lefties in the game in 2013, 2015 and 2016, and one of the least effective lefties in the majors in 2014 and 2017. DRA never quite bought into the extreme fly-baller, even in the good seasons, and the two horrid seasons were marked with recurring forearm problems, so perhaps it's not quite as confounding as it first appears. Amidst the 2017 issues, Siegrist's velocity declined for the fourth consecutive season, but more aggressively than ever, and the Cardinals cut bait without bringing him back to the majors after his August rehab assignment. The Phillies took a short look in September, and then cut Siegrist loose themselves after the season.

Sam Tuivailala RHP Born: 10/19/92 Age: 25 Bats: R Throws: R Height: 6'3" Weight: 225 Origin: Round 3, 2010 Draft (#106 overall)

YEAR	TEAM	LVL	AGE	W	L	SV	G	GS	IP	H	HR	BB/9	K/9	K	GB%	BABIP	WHIP	ERA	DRA	WARP	MPH	CMD	PWR	STM
2015	MEM	AAA	22	3	1	17	43	0	45	28	2	5.2	8.6	43	43%	.228	1.20	1.60	4.23	0.4				
2015	SLN	MLB	22	0	1	0	14	0	14^2	13	2	4.9	12.3	20	49%	.314	1.43	3.07	2.88	0.3	99.3	47	68	48
2016	MEM	AAA	23	3	2	17	42	0	46^2	47	3	4.2	13.9	72	43%	.393	1.48	5.21	1.18	2.0				
2016	SLN	MLB	23	0	0	0	12	0	9	12	0	6.0	7.0	7	44%	.375	2.00	6.00	5.94	-0.1	98.3	49	62	45
2017	MEM	AAA	24	1	0	6	18	0	21^1	13	2	1.3	8.9	21	42%	.216	0.75	1.27	3.07	0.5				
2017	SLN	MLB	24	3	3	0	37	0	42^1	35	4	2.3	7.2	34	49%	.258	1.09	2.55	4.43	0.4	97.4	50	60	44
2018	*SLN*	*MLB*	*25*	*3*	*3*	*0*	*53*	*0*	*56*	*53*	*7*	*4.1*	*9.2*	*58*	*44%*	*.304*	*1.42*	*4.22*	*4.45*	*0.3*	*97.5*	*50*	*63*	*46*
2019	*SLN*	*MLB*	*26*	*2*	*1*	*0*	*41*	*0*	*43*	*39*	*6*	*4.0*	*9.3*	*45*	*44%*	*.315*	*1.36*	*4.52*	*5.05*	*0.1*	*97.1*	*51*	*62*	*46*

Breakout: 16% Improve: 30% Collapse: 25% Attrition: 42% MLB: 68% *Comparables: Shawn Tolleson, Yimi Garcia, Michael Kohn*

Until last year, Tuivailala was another relief pitcher with a mouthful of vowels and a handful of thrown strikes. The upper-90s heat was enough for Tui to reach the big leagues in each of the last four years, perhaps too hasty, but last year's campaign finally saw him eliminate the rate of swing-less passage to first by more than half. Despite this, the Cardinals didn't have a full-time spot for him, so he was four times shuttled between St. Louis and Memphis. This year he's out of options, but has enough command of the fastball to last in the bullpen all year, more than long enough for everyone to get that pronunciation down easy.

Michael Wacha RHP Born: 07/01/91 Age: 26 Bats: R Throws: R Height: 6'6" Weight: 215 Origin: Round 1, 2012 Draft (#19 overall)

YEAR	TEAM	LVL	AGE	W	L	SV	G	GS	IP	H	HR	BB/9	K/9	K	GB%	BABIP	WHIP	ERA	DRA	WARP	MPH	CMD	PWR	STM
2015	SLN	MLB	23	17	7	0	30	30	181^{1}	162	19	2.9	7.6	153	48%	.272	1.21	3.38	3.70	3.0	97.1	47	59	73
2016	SLN	MLB	24	7	7	0	27	24	138	159	15	2.9	7.4	114	48%	.334	1.48	5.09	5.68	-0.5	96.3	45	49	60
2017	SLN	MLB	25	12	9	0	30	30	165^{2}	170	17	3.0	8.6	158	50%	.327	1.36	4.13	5.21	0.7	97.2	57	59	71
2018	*SLN*	*MLB*	*26*	*10*	*10*	*0*	*26*	*26*	*156*	*145*	*17*	*3.0*	*8.5*	*147*	*48%*	*.294*	*1.26*	*3.60*	*3.87*	*2.3*	*96.5*	*52*	*57*	*69*
2019	*SLN*	*MLB*	*27*	*12*	*10*	*0*	*32*	*32*	*210*	*178*	*20*	*2.7*	*8.8*	*204*	*48%*	*.301*	*1.15*	*3.47*	*3.86*	*3.7*	*96.2*	*53*	*56*	*68*

Breakout: 17% Improve: 57% Collapse: 13% Attrition: 8% MLB: 93% *Comparables: Mat Latos, Justin Verlander, Adam Wainwright*

The way to make a baseball career, if you have the means, is to follow Wacha's path: become a college starter and get drafted late in the first round with a few yellow flags but enough experience to propel to the majors in time for a pennant run. Yes, there's a chance you get Brandon Finneganed into a bottom-feeding franchise after it's all over, but it's way easier to get a ring that way than spend years becoming an otherworldly ace. All of this is to say, since those first years Wacha has become invisible in the rotation. This could be mid-twenties growing pains as the velocity is still there (and actually getting better), but DRA remains skeptical, concerned he's just giving up too many hits. He's still consistent enough to go six innings per start, but if the hits keep on coming, the 2013 NLCS MVP will be the lede when he retires.

Adam Wainwright RHP Born: 08/30/81 Age: 36 Bats: R Throws: R Height: 6'7" Weight: 235 Origin: Round 1, 2000 Draft (#29 overall)

YEAR	TEAM	LVL	AGE	W	L	SV	G	GS	IP	H	HR	BB/9	K/9	K	GB%	BABIP	WHIP	ERA	DRA	WARP	MPH	CMD	PWR	STM
2015	SLN	MLB	33	2	1	0	7	4	28	25	0	1.3	6.4	20	52%	.287	1.04	1.61	3.62	0.5	93.1	54	31	0
2016	SLN	MLB	34	13	9	0	33	33	198^{2}	220	22	2.7	7.3	161	45%	.330	1.40	4.62	5.28	0.2	93.2	62	31	80
2017	SLN	MLB	35	12	5	0	24	23	123^{1}	140	14	3.3	7.0	96	50%	.326	1.50	5.11	5.99	-0.6	92.2	55	28	58
2018	*SLN*	*MLB*	*36*	*8*	*10*	*0*	*23*	*23*	*138*	*140*	*16*	*3.1*	*6.9*	*106*	*47%*	*.298*	*1.36*	*4.10*	*4.42*	*1.2*	*91.5*	*57*	*29*	*50*
2019	*SLN*	*MLB*	*37*	*11*	*11*	*0*	*32*	*32*	*203*	*194*	*21*	*2.9*	*7.0*	*157*	*47%*	*.308*	*1.28*	*4.10*	*4.59*	*2.1*	*90.9*	*57*	*29*	*59*

Breakout: 10% Improve: 38% Collapse: 20% Attrition: 11% MLB: 87% *Comparables: Tim Hudson, Roy Halladay, Bob Gibson*

If his low-90s velocity returns this year, he'll be fine. Last year Wainwright's heater clocked in at 87 mph and his curveball looked like a little green army paratrooper to batters in the second half before he was shelved and put under the knife to clean up the ol' elbow. It's the third time in seven years a surgeon had to go in there and put everything back where it was (one of those was for a new UCL). At some point a person with an advanced medical degree can only do so much before they have to call the time of death on an arm. Waino still may have a year or two left throwing curveballs, which works out since this is the last year of the big contract.

Luke Weaver RHP Born: 08/21/93 Age: 24 Bats: R Throws: R Height: 6'2" Weight: 170 Origin: Round 1, 2014 Draft (#27 overall)

YEAR	TEAM	LVL	AGE	W	L	SV	G	GS	IP	H	HR	BB/9	K/9	K	GB%	BABIP	WHIP	ERA	DRA	WARP	MPH	CMD	PWR	STM
2015	PMB	A+	21	8	5	0	19	19	105^{1}	98	2	1.6	7.5	88	46%	.303	1.11	1.62	2.75	3.0				
2016	SFD	AA	22	6	3	0	12	12	77	63	4	1.2	10.3	88	40%	.289	0.95	1.40	1.14	3.7				
2016	SLN	MLB	22	1	4	0	9	8	36^{1}	46	7	3.0	11.1	45	37%	.386	1.60	5.70	6.31	-0.4	94.9	54	47	62
2017	MEM	AAA	23	10	2	0	15	15	77^{2}	63	3	2.2	8.8	76	46%	.291	1.06	2.55	3.11	2.2				
2017	SLN	MLB	23	7	2	0	13	10	60^{1}	59	7	2.5	10.7	72	51%	.335	1.26	3.88	4.18	0.9	95.5	69	51	58
2018	*SLN*	*MLB*	*24*	*9*	*9*	*0*	*24*	*24*	*144*	*135*	*17*	*2.8*	*9.3*	*150*	*43%*	*.300*	*1.26*	*3.49*	*3.77*	*2.3*	*95.1*	*66*	*51*	*62*
2019	*SLN*	*MLB*	*25*	*12*	*10*	*0*	*32*	*32*	*210*	*183*	*23*	*2.2*	*9.4*	*219*	*43%*	*.312*	*1.11*	*3.35*	*3.73*	*4.0*	*94.9*	*66*	*51*	*62*

Breakout: 23% Improve: 68% Collapse: 11% Attrition: 16% MLB: 94% *Comparables: Michael Fulmer, Daniel Hudson, Zach Davies*

Last August, an injured Jered Weaver announced his retirement. Days later, brother-from-a-non-related-mother Luke joined the Cardinals' rotation and strung together six phenomenal starts. There can only weave one. The former first-rounder has a plus changeup, but still needs to develop a third pitch. Right now it's a cutter, while the curveball and slider are basically running as Libertarian and Green Party candidates. Depending on that, a big 2018 could be in store for Weaver, assuming no other Weavers appear.

Lineouts

Hitters

HITTER	POS	TEAM	LVL	AGE	PA	R	2B	3B	HR	RBI	BB	K	SB	CS	AVG/OBP/SLG	TAv	VORP	BABIP	BRR	FRAA	WARP
Andrew Knizner	C	PEO	A	22	191	18	10	1	8	29	9	22	1	1	.279/.325/.480	.293	13.1	.282	0.5	C(26): -0.3, 1B(3): -0.1	1.3
	C	SFD	AA	22	202	27	13	0	4	22	14	27	0	1	.324/.371/.462	.301	17.7	.355	0.5	C(49): -3.3	1.5
Alex Mejia	INF	SFD	AA	26	251	24	17	0	3	24	16	36	1	1	.251/.305/.366	.256	9.4	.283	0.4	SS(62): -5.4	0.4
	INF	MEM	AAA	26	224	25	15	0	4	33	14	30	1	1	.335/.381/.466	.294	17.6	.376	1.7	2B(25): -1.0, SS(16): 4.5	2.1
	INF	SLN	MLB	26	49	6	0	0	1	3	2	13	0	0	.109/.146/.174	.130	-4.5	.125	0.5	3B(13): 0.2, SS(7): 0.1	-0.4
Nick Plummer	CF	PEO	A	20	346	36	11	1	4	17	53	109	8	9	.198/.353/.288	.259	8.4	.307	-0.8	CF(67): -6.1, LF(15): -2.6	0.0
Rangel Ravelo	1B	MEM	AAA	25	345	49	25	1	8	41	31	56	1	2	.314/.383/.480	.308	20.2	.359	-2.9	1B(52): 0.0, RF(12): 0.2	2.0
Julio Rodriguez	OF	JCY	Rk	20	201	28	14	1	5	36	17	31	0	0	.280/.343/.451	.277	13.9	.313	0.7	C(36): -0.5, 1B(7): 0.9	1.3
Alberto Rosario	C	MEM	AAA	30	204	20	6	0	0	23	11	31	3	0	.247/.291/.279	.217	-1.0	.294	-1.1	C(50): 8.3	0.7
	C	SLN	MLB	30	3	0	0	0	0	0	0	1	0	0	.000/.000/.000	-.085	-1.0	.000	0.0		-0.1
Max Schrock	2B	MID	AA	22	457	55	19	1	7	46	34	42	4	2	.321/.379/.422	.288	21.9	.344	-2.4	2B(101): -4.5	1.9
Edmundo Sosa	SS	PMB	A+	21	211	25	10	1	0	14	12	34	3	0	.285/.329/.347	.259	9.9	.344	2.4	SS(41): 3.1, 2B(7): -1.0	1.3
Breyvic Valera	UT	MEM	AAA	25	470	68	22	6	8	41	38	34	11	11	.314/.368/.450	.293	31.4	.324	1.5	2B(78): -1.3, LF(18): 0.5	3.2
	UT	SLN	MLB	25	11	0	0	0	0	0	1	0	0	0	.100/.182/.100	.119	-1.3	.100	0.0	2B(3): -0.2	-0.1
Luke Voit	1B	MEM	AAA	26	307	35	23	1	13	50	29	53	1	1	.327/.407/.565	.346	29.6	.368	-3.6	1B(62): 4.3	3.3
	1B	SLN	MLB	26	124	18	9	0	4	18	7	31	0	0	.246/.306/.430	.252	0.6	.304	-0.3	1B(31): 1.6	0.2

HITTER	POS	TEAM	LVL	AGE	PA	R	2B	3B	HR	RBI	BB	K	SB	CS	AVG/OBP/SLG	TAv	VORP	BABIP	BRR	FRAA	WARP
Patrick Wisdom	3B	MEM	AAA	25	506	68	25	1	31	89	38	149	2	2	.243/.310/.507	.283	31.0	.286	1.5	3B(113): 0.1, 1B(8): 0.5	3.1
Wadye Ynfante	OF	JCY	Rk	19	187	27	11	0	7	23	17	51	11	3	.299/.374/.491	.282	11.8	.394	0.8	CF(24): 4.9, LF(14): -0.4	1.4

Another infielder-turned-catcher, **Andrew Knizner** has a lot of work to do behind the plate, but is still more comfortable standing next to it, as he flashes above-average hit and power tools. Light-hitting utility infielder **Alex Mejia** is competent and versatile enough to pocket a big-league per diem here and there, but mostly he's proof that Devil Magic has its limits. Injury after injury have robbed **Nick Plummer** of the developmental time the Michigan prep outfielder needed coming out of the 2015 draft, and the first-round skill set remains unactivated in a noncompliant body. During his first season in the Cardinals organization, **Rangel Ravelo** started honing his #CardinalDevilMagic skills by raising his Triple-A OPS by nearly 150 points. Don't be surprised when he's a fringe All-Star in 2019. One of the more highly touted of last year's July 2 international signings, **Julio Rodriguez** has size and raw power that offer considerable upside. He projects as a future corner outfielder. If you're ever in some sort of extremely weird Cardinals bar trivia and need to name all the backup catchers to Yadier Molina over the years, the one you're forgetting is **Alberto Rosario**, for myriad reasons. **Max Schrock** is a small but relatively mighty lefty-swinging second baseman who never whiffs, but he probably doesn't have enough bonus material (speed, walks, over-the-fence pop) to be a starter, and he lacks the arm to back up shortstop or third; what do you do with that profile? Hope he hits .320 in the majors, maybe, which isn't *entirely* out of the question. **Edmundo Sosa** burned an option in an injury-shortened and unproductive repeat of High-A. He needs reps and a breakout at the plate if he wants a future in St. Louis alongside 2012 international free agent classmate Alex Reyes. **Breyvic Valera** showed a little pop for the first time in 2017, but major-league pitching will fare much better against a Valerian offensive instrument than farmhands and the subhumanoids beyond The Wall have. **Luke Voit** has passed Dan Vogelbach on the power charts of thick first basemen who start with the letter V, by way of his competent hitting and plus defense. He has a ways to go to catch Votto, and won't. "Never forget, that until the day God will deign to reveal the future to man, all human **[Patrick] Wisdom** is contained in these two words, 'wait and hope.'" We don't usually associate the Cardinals with tooled-up position prospects, but **Wadye Ynfante** has the potential to break a lot of molds after an extremely successful season in the Appy League.

Pitchers

PITCHER	TEAM	LVL	AGE	W	L	SV	G	GS	IP	H	HR	BB/9	K/9	K	GB%	BABIP	WHIP	ERA	DRA	WARP	MPH	CMD	PWR	STM
Jonathan Broxton	SLN	MLB	33	0	1	0	20	0	15^{2}	23	2	6.3	9.2	16	47%	.429	2.17	6.89	6.01	-0.1	96.5	39	63	39
John Gant	MEM	AAA	24	6	5	0	18	18	103^{1}	109	10	2.2	8.6	99	47%	.334	1.30	3.83	2.79	3.3				
	SLN	MLB	24	0	1	0	7	2	17^{1}	17	4	5.2	5.7	11	54%	.260	1.56	4.67	7.89	-0.5	95.5	51	53	59
Sean Gilmartin	NYN	MLB	27	0	0	0	2	0	3^{1}	8	2	2.7	10.8	4	50%	.500	2.70	13.50	5.64	0.0	90.8			34
	LVG	AAA	27	2	2	0	8	8	37	52	6	3.4	7.5	31	42%	.374	1.78	7.05	4.31	0.5				
	MEM	AAA	27	0	1	1	8	1	12^{2}	15	2	1.4	5.7	8	40%	.302	1.34	5.68	6.37	-0.1				
Austin Gomber	SFD	AA	23	10	7	0	26	26	143	116	17	3.2	8.8	140	42%	.263	1.17	3.34	3.78	2.4				
Derian Gonzalez	PMB	A+	22	4	7	0	18	15	79	78	5	3.4	8.2	72	47%	.322	1.37	4.33	3.81	1.3				
Joshua Lucas	MEM	AAA	26	8	1	17	47	0	60	58	3	1.8	10.2	68	53%	.340	1.17	3.15	1.96	2.2				
	SLN	MLB	26	0	0	0	5	0	7^{1}	7	2	4.9	8.6	7	60%	.278	1.50	3.68	3.18	0.2	93.7			45
Mike Mayers	SLN	MLB	25	0	0	0	3	0	4^{2}	8	2	7.7	5.8	3	28%	.375	2.57	11.57	8.59	-0.2	95.4			60
	MEM	AAA	25	5	6	0	31	15	109^{2}	117	12	2.6	8.0	97	42%	.316	1.36	3.28	5.05	0.6				
Trevor Rosenthal	SLN	MLB	27	3	4	11	50	0	47^{2}	37	3	3.8	14.3	76	40%	.337	1.20	3.40	3.20	1.0	100.3	53	85	48
Ryan Sherriff	MEM	AAA	27	5	1	6	48	0	53^{2}	40	2	2.2	7.9	47	58%	.255	0.99	3.19	2.08	1.9				
	SLN	MLB	27	2	1	0	13	0	14^{1}	13	2	2.5	9.4	15	68%	.289	1.19	3.14	6.15	-0.2	93.5	38	52	47
Rowan Wick	SFD	AA	24	0	0	5	16	0	21^{2}	16	1	4.6	7.1	17	36%	.246	1.25	2.08	5.46	-0.2				
	MEM	AAA	24	2	1	1	14	0	16^{2}	16	2	3.8	9.2	17	53%	.286	1.38	5.40	3.61	0.3				

Free to a good home, **Jonathan Broxton** was let go last year and is in need of a bullpen that will love him back. Short-term memory is preferred. He's a big sweetie, but careful, he enjoys walks a little too much these days so make sure you have a leash. **John Gant**'s odd windup delivery includes him bringing his leg up twice, and has a less-pronounced double toe-tap in the stretch. In the cartoon world if you walk over a cliff, you don't fall until you look down. Gant may have assumed this was true at an early age, so you can never be too sure where terra firma ends. Lefty **Sean Gilmartin** married right-wing commentator Kayleigh McEnany in November. While the marriage is no James Carville/Mary Matalin setup, they were both dropped by the Mets/Cardinals and CNN, respectively. **Austin Gomber** closed out his first season in the upper minors in impressive fashion. It may not be flashy stuff, but he could find himself in St. Louis during the second half of 2018 regardless. Venezuelan right-hander **Derian Gonzalez** saw his future flash before his eyes—a 2017 midseason injury prevented him from being stretched out upon his return to Palm Beach—when he struck out 8 of the 12 batters he faced in three relief appearances to close the season, while touching the high-90s with his fastball. Back-to-back seasons with a strikeout rate above one per inning at Double-A and Triple-A got **Josh Lucas** his first call-up at age 26, and he's a reasonably good bet to be a decent middle man if given a longer look. If his small-sample MLB results are any indication, Number Two does not work for **Mike Mayers**, likely relegating him to a role where he'll put the man in swingman. You will almost certainly not see **Trevor Rosenthal** stand on a mound during a competitive game in 2018 thanks to a partial UCL tear, nor with the Cardinals again. Flip to Greg Holland's comment for how his 2019 might work out for the best; find an old copy with Joel Hanrahan in it for the worst. Lefties were handcuffed by **Ryan Sherriff**'s sinkerball to the tune of .080/.115/.080 in a month's work. Right-handers, however, didn't get in trouble because their dad knew someone down at city hall. Catcher-turned-outfielder-turned-pitcher **Rowan Wick** can light up a radar gun, provided he can successfully throw the ball in the vicinity of said radar gun.

TAMPA BAY RAYS

Essay by Adam Sobsey

Player comments by Matthew Trueblood and BP staff

Tampa Bay's trade of Evan Longoria shortly before Christmas was legitimate cause for deep sadness and even rage among Rays fans, but it was no surprise to anyone watching the franchise with the eyes instead of the heart. It was simply the fall of the chimney that had withstood years of weather while the house around it collapsed. The Rays have been losing since Andrew Friedman and Joe Maddon left after 2014 (in fact, they weren't good in 2014, either), and they probably weren't going to be good in 2018 with or without Longoria. The wins and losses don't matter. The Rays relinquished their most durable and richest source of institutional memory, their only true lion and the living embodiment of their first Golden Age. Now that Longoria is gone, they have neither blood nor money. Not only aren't they very good, they aren't interesting.

"They aren't interesting" is something you could never say of the Friedman/Maddon Rays. They were occasionally frustrating and frequently losers (Tampa Bay made the playoffs in only half of Maddon's seasons there), but they didn't always have to be good, because they were never boring: They were creative, unpredictable and sometimes plain weird or even downright odious. Whatever everyone else wasn't doing, the Rays were doing: defensive shifting before it was common practice (in the five seasons from 2010 to 2014, the first year shift data was recorded, until Maddon's departure, the Rays led the majors in both shifts deployed and wOBA against those shifts); gambling cheaply and often successfully on damaged or dubious or distasteful players (Jeff Keppinger, Casey Kotchman, James Loney—although also Matt Bush, Josh Lueke, Manny Ramirez); exploiting compensations in the draft to rig it to their disproportionate advantage (they landed 11 of the first 60 picks in the 2011 draft).

Their financial inability to keep most of their best talent around was itself part of what made them interesting: They made trades that were not only shrewd but often surprising, maintaining both competitive quality and organizational freshness. But the Longoria trade only brought the customary infield hopeful who seems to come in every return package (and they'd already gotten two of those from San Francisco in 2016), along with an old lumber(er) and two saplings. The deal was in every way predictable. So is nearly everything about the Rays now. They're decent at preventing runs and bad at scoring them. They strike out a lot. The roster is mostly short-timers and interns. The once-rich farm system is now "bang-average," as BP's 2017 organizational rankings put it, and the return for Longoria didn't substantially improve it. The inseparably tortured payroll, attendance and search for a new ballpark—which used to feed into the dramatic tension that hung about the franchise—have become so chronic that they're now a mostly ignorable background drone. By the time the Rays might realistically construct a new stadium and cash in on the deal, their obligation to Tropicana Field will have nearly expired, and they might more wisely (and excitingly) plan instead to leave Florida

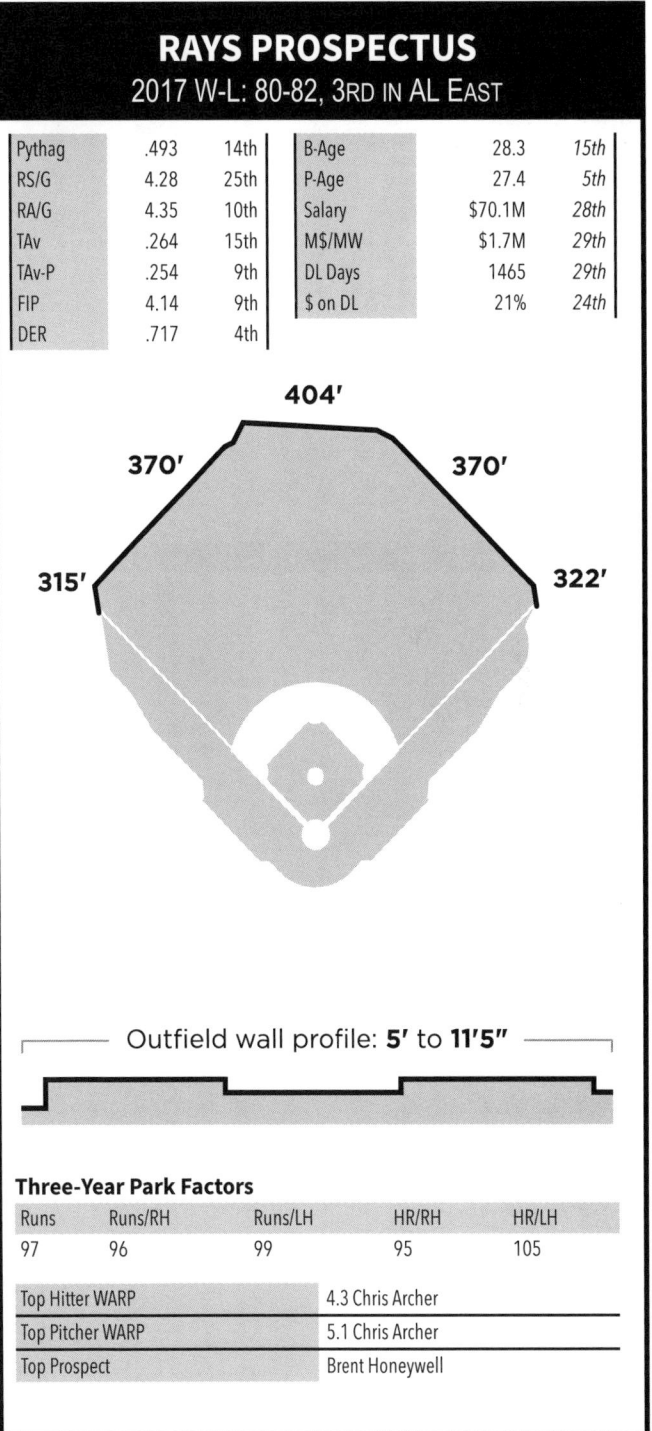

RAYS PROSPECTUS

2017 W-L: 80-82, 3RD IN AL EAST

Pythag	.493	14th	B-Age	28.3	*15th*
RS/G	4.28	25th	P-Age	27.4	*5th*
RA/G	4.35	10th	Salary	$70.1M	*28th*
TAv	.264	15th	M$/MW	$1.7M	*29th*
TAv-P	.254	9th	DL Days	1465	*29th*
FIP	4.14	9th	$ on DL	21%	*24th*
DER	.717	4th			

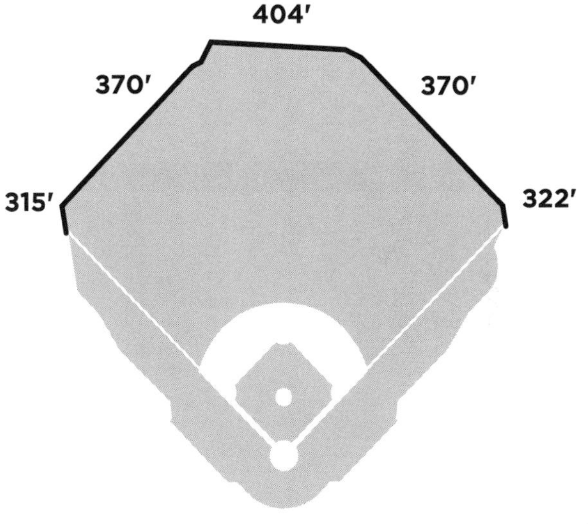

Outfield wall profile: **5′** to **11′5″**

Three-Year Park Factors

Runs	Runs/RH	Runs/LH	HR/RH	HR/LH
97	96	99	95	105

Top Hitter WARP	4.3 Chris Archer
Top Pitcher WARP	5.1 Chris Archer
Top Prospect	Brent Honeywell

2017 Hit List Ranking

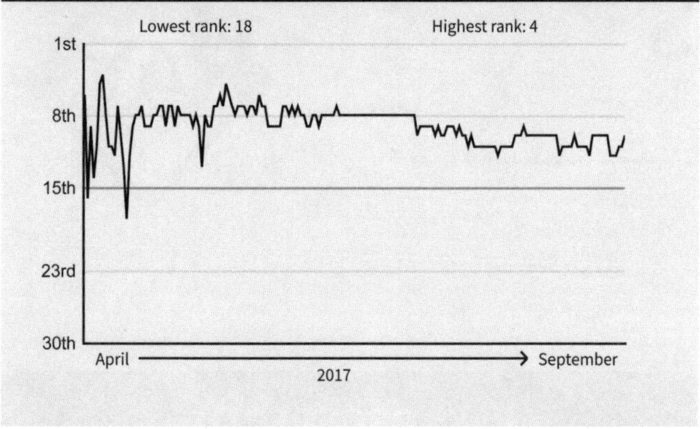

Committed Payroll (in millions)

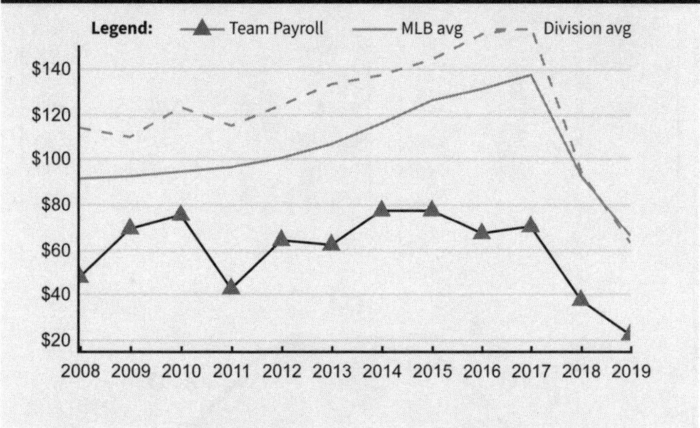

Farm System Ranking

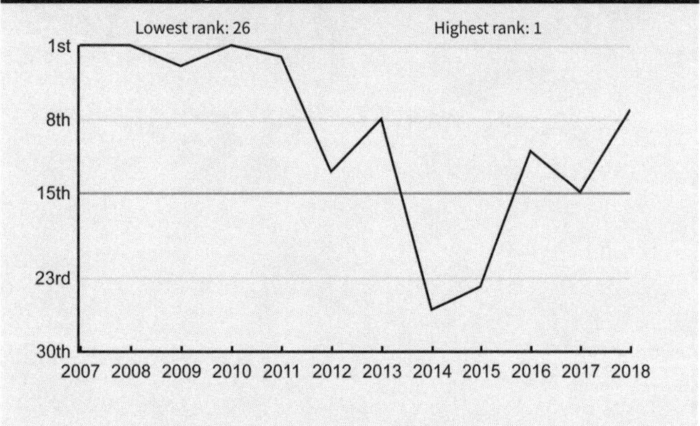

Personnel

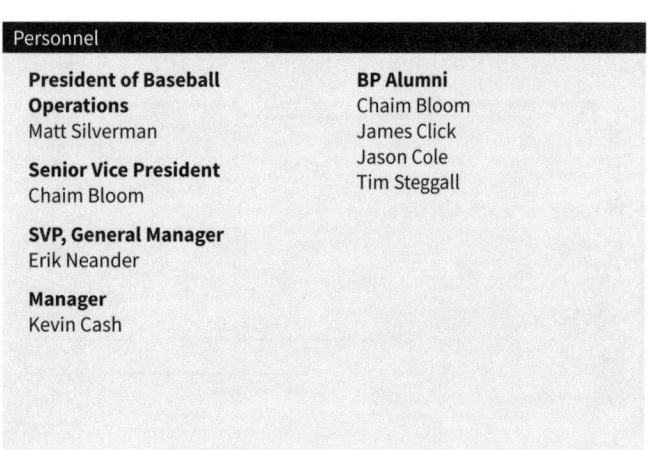

President of Baseball Operations
Matt Silverman

Senior Vice President
Chaim Bloom

SVP, General Manager
Erik Neander

Manager
Kevin Cash

BP Alumni
Chaim Bloom
James Click
Jason Cole
Tim Steggall

altogether and shed their very identity. They are nearly bereft of one anyway.

That may not be entirely an internal problem. When BP's Bryan Grosnick lamented, in his Transaction Analysis of the Longoria trade, that the Rays "now look like something of a cold, impersonal corporation," he could have been describing most of Major League Baseball in 2018. The national pastime has been homogenizing its substance, regulating its procedures and consolidating its resources for some years now. The shared data pool is widening, and analytical advantages are harder to find. Front offices are growing smarter and more similar in their approaches, shrinking the potential for unusual or lopsided trades. The commissioner's office continues to straighten and narrow the draft and international markets. All of this damages scavengers and schemers like the Rays far more than it does other teams. There are simply fewer rocks under which to look, fewer side alleys to explore. Without money, nonconformity and difference are harder and harder to practice.

This trend is visible on the field, too. In each of the past two seasons, the Rays, seldom considered bashers—especially in a division dominated by loaded northeastern powermongers—finished sixth in the majors in homers. They ranked even higher in Guillen Number, BP's term for percentage of runs scored via home runs: third in 2017 and fourth in 2016. They'd never finished above sixth under Friedman and Maddon—and usually much lower. The Rays have struck out in nearly a quarter of their at-bats over the past two seasons, near the top of the league. Home runs and strikeouts are of course ascendant in the game right now. This is another shrinking of the pool, a consolidation of the elements on the field of play. It's surprising, though, and a little depressing, that the Rays, long the majors' uncommonest team, have so heavily bought into the common market. It's as if they've found themselves with virtually no alternatives, as if what once would have taken opponents by surprise (the pitching-heavy Rays, hitting homers?) is now a feeble strategy. Because here is where things start to get interesting: Despite hitting so many homers in 2017, the Rays finished last in the American League in runs scored.

And that's not because they're terrible at everything else. Run all of their numbers—walk rate, OPS+, ISO and so on—and their 2017 True Average was truly average: 15th overall. VORP was 16th. Presumably, spicing adequate overall numbers with lots of home runs ought to yield strong run production; and with Tampa Bay's good pitching (the team's pitching VORP was the majors' fourth best), that might make them competitive in September and perhaps even get them into October. Instead, with homers now coming so cheaply, the Rays' heavy reliance on the long ball made them, like their farm system, "bang-average": They've finished 80-82 in two of the last three seasons. The former trendsetter became a dupe of the trend, and the team that once seemed to have baseball's healthiest immune system became a poster child for its current disease. And that disease runs deeper than deep flies.

The commissioner's office, concerned about alienating younger fans, continues to address—or at least give lip service to—the duration and pace of games. In 2015, a coordinated effort to accelerate action shaved seven minutes off average game length. Later that same season, the apparent introduction of a so-called "juiced" baseball helped hitters break the MLB home-run record the following year and again in 2017. Strikeouts, too, have set new record highs in every year of the past decade. These historic escalations appear to satisfy commissioner Rob Manfred's desires, or at least his inference of the crowd's desires: "Our fan research suggests that people like home runs and they actually like lots of strikeouts," he said last June (try telling that to the Rays, whose attendance over the last three seasons has ebbed to its lowest levels since they were the Devil Rays), while maintaining denial of a deliberately altered ball despite strongly persuasive evidence of its use.

The results of the sharp rise in home runs and strikeouts could have been predicted, and they suggest that neither shorter nor faster games were MLB's true goal. (They certainly weren't the Rays' when they were interesting: In all but one of their seasons under Maddon, Tampa Bay finished in the top six in game length.) Leaguewide attendance has held steady since 2009, television ratings are healthy and MLB is in the midst of a 10-year, $12.4 billion broadcasting rights bonanza. Longer games and slower pace aren't driving the audience away; and they yield additional time, after all, to sell more concessions and show more ads. The enforced pace-of-game initiatives in 2015 reduced average game time by seven minutes, but by 2017 the patient had more than cheated on the diet and regained eight minutes to set another record high for length (3:08).

Pace followed the same pattern. A modest dip in 2015 was followed by an overcompensation until a new record was reached: Time between pitches now tops 24 seconds—an entire NBA shot clock. With so much effort focused toward rebuilding the game around homers and strikeouts, early in-play contact has decreased and pitches per plate appearance are at a corresponding record high of their own. More pitches, along with more data-driven matchup manipulation, have in turn contributed to yet another pace-slowing record high: pitching changes. (Perhaps so many more slow home-run trots are a pace culprit, as well.) Meanwhile, the walk rate, which fell to a 50-year low (a *50-year low!*) over the first half of this decade, has recovered to average levels. Bases on balls are such a notorious drag on action that intentional walks are now issued automatically; that is perhaps the most noticeable new procedural change on the field, along with instant replay—which, while improving the integrity of the game, has of course also slowed it down. At the current rate, the wait between balls hit into play will soon exceed four minutes for the first time.

If the goal was to increase not pace but scoring, which was at its lowest in 20 years, it hasn't worked. Among the 20 seasons since Tampa Bay's inception as part of MLB's last expansion, 2017 ranked just 10th in runs scored, with about 175 more runs than the 11th-ranked 2009 season—despite over 1,000 more home runs. There were 6,000 more strikeouts. The 2016 season ranked 14th. Meanwhile, games take about as long as they did four years ago, and there were almost exactly as many runs scored in 2017 as there were in 2008. But we're arriving at these similar numbers very differently now. In 2008, Brian McCann hit 23 home runs, had 87 RBIs and posted the second-highest WARP in the major leagues; the highest, and the MVP award, belonged to Albert Pujols. In 2017, Pujols had McCann-like production, hitting 23 home runs and 101 RBIs. His WARP was the worst in baseball. The commissioner's office isn't tweaking pace or production. It's foreshortening the very picture of the game, intensifying the stratification of its action and transforming the value of its players and thus their characters, too.

The players will resist this coercion. They always do (and the Rays always did, until recently). The harder the boardroom pulls baseball in one direction, the more forcefully the field pushes back. The conflict pits absolutes versus interrelationships, homogeneity versus variety, and both sides are losing. A catcher who once played where the Rays keep their Triple-A farm team, Crash Davis, is eternally in Durham to remind us that strikeouts are boring and fascist. He does not need to add that they're boring partly *because* they're fascist. Strikeouts are by nature censorious, reductive, authoritarian; home runs, too; and their expanding double epidemic impoverishes baseball's richness of possibility, limits its capacity for improvisation and chance, and imperils Crash Davis' democracy of groundballs. Perhaps the true outcomes can falsify the game: The Rays can hit more home runs than almost everyone else, yet score the fewest runs. Absolute power corrupts absolutely.

There were two acute exceptions to the Rays' mostly average hitting profile in 2017. One underlies their strikeout propensities: They had the lowest contact rate in baseball. The three teams with the highest contact rates each made the playoffs. Correlation doesn't equal causation, of course, but it's difficult to discount such pronounced statistical differences between the best and the rest. If nothing else, the separation in contact rate exposes a subtler but graver statistical increase than those in homers, strikeouts and minutes: a shocking 65 percent rise in the leaguewide out-of-zone swing rate over the last 15 years. The sport's core skill, plate discipline, has severely eroded. When discriminating between a strike and a ball is no longer of substantial importance, baseball loses its moorings and becomes addicted instead to spin and speed.

The second exception is that Tampa Bay hit the fewest doubles in the majors last year. (Longoria led the team, for what that's worth.) They occupied the extreme edge of another trend: Doubles have been ebbing all decade, well before the juiced ball turned some of them into home runs; they're down about 10 percent overall from their mid-2000s highs. Six of the top seven doubles-hitting teams in 2017 made the playoffs. These signals are of course surrounded by plenty of noise, which makes them suggestive rather than conclusive, but the point is less statistical than spiritual. If any play can be said to symbolize baseball's lively fullness and exemplify its optimal action, it must be the double (and by extension the triple, which is basically a carbonated double; but the 2017 Rays did not hit enough triples to avoid finishing last in combined two- and three-base hits).

A double gives us, in most cases, a hard-hit ball—if not, then its unlikely path and placement—the broad and urgent engagement of both infield and outfield, perhaps an exciting race between runner and thrower, and the activation of ensuing drama. After a double, a man is in scoring position, exactly halfway home and at the top of the diamond, with all its convergent attention and expectation and gamesmanship—and perhaps the spark of anticipation of baseball's single most exciting event, the play at the plate. It's a curmudgeonly cliché of the old guard that home runs kill rallies, but perhaps nothing animates them quite like doubles. None of this is to say that hitting more of them, or simply making better contact, will make Tampa Bay a playoff team, or even a more interesting team, any more than moving them to another stadium or city will. The methods are of course vastly more complex than one or two compensations, harder to descry and harder still to put into successful practice.

However, the Rays' front office remains populated by smart and seasoned executives who apprenticed under Friedman and Maddon, and principal owner Stuart Sternberg's payroll constraints continue to demand their competitive ingenuity and resourcefulness. They are surely already exploring the scorched earth, post-Longoria path for new ways to make the Rays interesting again. The mind of baseball is always ahead of wherever the game appears to be, paradoxically because the national pastime knows its past and is never in a hurry. The sport, *pace* the commissioner's office, does not need to move faster. It moves as fast as it ought, as fast as it must. It will make better contact, on and off the field. Baseball's ability to keep changing into itself is its genius. It has been pulled out of its natural proportions and depth, but it will find them again. It runs deep and long in our country, and its every play is protected by a measure of time for its presiding officers to consider not momentary or monetary gains but the lasting consequences of selling out for power.

—Adam Sobsey is the co-author of "Bull City Summer: A Season at the Ballpark" and the author of "Chrissie Hynde: A Musical Biography."

Hitters

Willy Adames SS
Born: 09/02/95 Age: 22 Bats: R Throws: R Height: 6'0" Weight: 200 Origin: International Free Agent, 2015

YEAR	TEAM	LVL	AGE	PA	R	2B	3B	HR	RBI	BB	K	SB	CS	AVG/OBP/SLG	TAv	VORP	BABIP	BRR	FRAA	WARP
2015	PCH	A+	19	456	51	24	6	4	46	54	123	10	1	.258/.342/.379	.275	23.1	.356	-0.6	SS(97): 4.2	3.0
2016	MNT	AA	20	568	89	31	6	11	57	74	121	13	6	.274/.372/.430	.303	47.0	.342	2.4	SS(112): 2.3	5.3
2017	DUR	AAA	21	578	74	30	5	10	62	65	132	11	5	.277/.360/.415	.275	35.5	.354	1.1	SS(117): 0.1, 2B(11): 0.5	3.5
2018	*TBA*	*MLB*	*22*	*135*	*15*	*6*	*1*	*3*	*15*	*15*	*37*	*2*	*1*	*.237/.323/.377*	*.257*	*5.1*	*.317*	*0.0*	*2B 1, SS 0*	*0.5*
2019	*TBA*	*MLB*	*23*	*400*	*50*	*18*	*2*	*11*	*45*	*47*	*114*	*5*	*2*	*.241/.335/.401*	*.262*	*13.9*	*.324*	*-0.1*	*2B 3, SS 1*	*1.9*

Breakout: 5% Improve: 35% Collapse: 3% Attrition: 22% MLB: 50% *Comparables: Ian Happ, Daniel Robertson, Eugenio Suarez*

For a guy with zero big-league service time, Adames feels a lot like a proven commodity. For a guy born after Michael Jordan's return to the Bulls, he feels like he's been around forever. Prospects of this kind and caliber tend to fly a little more under the radar, but Adames' name showed up on an ESPN crawl while he was still 18 (he was part of the trade that sent David Price from Tampa Bay to Detroit). After three straight seasons of taking one step up the ladder and producing steady, solid numbers, he now stands on the threshold of the majors. He's not likely to hit for enough power to carry much value if he moves off of shortstop, but right now it seems like he'll stick there for a while. If he can make enough contact to keep his on-base percentage afloat, the profile really works.

Christian Arroyo INF
Born: 05/30/95 Age: 23 Bats: R Throws: R Height: 6'1" Weight: 180 Origin: Round 1, 2013 Draft (#25 overall)

YEAR	TEAM	LVL	AGE	PA	R	2B	3B	HR	RBI	BB	K	SB	CS	AVG/OBP/SLG	TAv	VORP	BABIP	BRR	FRAA	WARP
2015	SJO	A+	20	409	48	28	2	9	42	19	73	5	3	.304/.344/.459	.304	31.8	.355	-2.3	SS(88): -3.0	3.1
2016	RIC	AA	21	517	57	36	1	3	49	29	72	1	1	.274/.316/.373	.254	12.5	.313	-1.3	3B(48): 2.1, SS(48): -0.9	1.5
2017	SFN	MLB	22	135	9	5	0	3	14	8	32	1	2	.192/.244/.304	.201	-6.3	.231	-2.8	3B(22): 1.4, SS(10): 0.9	-0.3
2017	SAC	AAA	22	102	18	7	0	4	16	6	12	2	0	.396/.461/.604	.379	18.1	.427	0.5	SS(16): 0.6, 2B(5): -0.7	1.7
2018	*TBA*	*MLB*	*23*	*358*	*37*	*18*	*1*	*8*	*37*	*17*	*76*	*2*	*1*	*.246/.288/.375*	*.240*	*3.0*	*.294*	*-0.8*	*3B 3*	*0.3*
2019	*TBA*	*MLB*	*24*	*433*	*49*	*21*	*1*	*12*	*49*	*25*	*96*	*2*	*1*	*.248/.298/.396*	*.243*	*1.9*	*.295*	*-0.9*	*3B 4*	*0.6*

Breakout: 9% Improve: 39% Collapse: 11% Attrition: 27% MLB: 61% *Comparables: Tyler Pastornicky, Yamaico Navarro, Reid Brignac*

Drafted as an archetypal Giants infield prospect, Arroyo enticed their scouts with his up-the-middle approach, measured swing and the defensive makeup to handle any spot in the infield. In the latter stages of his development, Arroyo moved away from shortstop, but took steps to enhance his game power, employing a leg-kick to tear up the Pacific Coast League before big-league pitchers swept that leg right out from under him. Between his promotion and a season-ending hand injury, he hit the ball on the ground too often and swung through too many sliders, becoming a near-automatic out once the count reached two strikes. With little left to prove in the minors, Arroyo will have to rework his approach through experience at the highest level, but most scouts remain bullish that his plus hit tool will eventually shine through.

Jake Bauers 1B
Born: 10/06/95 Age: 22 Bats: L Throws: L Height: 6'1" Weight: 195 Origin: Round 7, 2013 Draft (#208 overall)

YEAR	TEAM	LVL	AGE	PA	R	2B	3B	HR	RBI	BB	K	SB	CS	AVG/OBP/SLG	TAv	VORP	BABIP	BRR	FRAA	WARP
2015	PCH	A+	19	249	33	14	2	6	38	29	33	2	3	.267/.357/.433	.298	13.1	.291	1.2	1B(52): -4.9	0.9
2015	MNT	AA	19	285	36	18	0	5	36	21	41	6	3	.276/.329/.405	.267	7.0	.307	2.3	1B(61): -1.9	0.6
2016	MNT	AA	20	581	79	28	1	14	78	73	89	10	6	.274/.370/.420	.301	33.6	.305	2.1	RF(62): 7.1, 1B(57): 0.0	4.4
2017	DUR	AAA	21	575	79	31	1	13	63	78	112	20	3	.263/.368/.412	.280	23.1	.314	0.5	LF(55): 4.7, 1B(52): -1.0	2.7
2018	*TBA*	*MLB*	*22*	*204*	*24*	*9*	*0*	*6*	*24*	*22*	*43*	*3*	*1*	*.242/.327/.393*	*.261*	*4.6*	*.285*	*0.0*	*1B -1, LF 0*	*0.3*
2019	*TBA*	*MLB*	*23*	*396*	*51*	*20*	*0*	*12*	*48*	*44*	*83*	*6*	*2*	*.253/.342/.421*	*.269*	*10.9*	*.296*	*0.0*	*1B -2, LF 1*	*1.2*

Breakout: 6% Improve: 22% Collapse: 3% Attrition: 19% MLB: 38% *Comparables: Jesse Winker, Thomas Neal, Ramon Flores*

Some scouts believe players don't get better in the minor leagues, they just get smarter. Many also believe power comes last for players who demonstrate a solid pure hit tool at a young age. Indeed, these days plenty of players who showed modest pop in the minors are adding some in the majors, partially thanks to getting smarter and seeking opportunities to turn on the ball. Somewhere at the intersection of those ideas lies the hope for Bauers to grow into an everyday player on a good team. He spent more time in the outfield than at first base in 2017, which had something to do with a Triple-A logjam (only the Rays, man) but also with the fact that Bauers is light on power and pretty darn fast for a first baseman. For an outfielder, he might be a step slow, so his best hope is to add power as he matures at the plate and graduates.

Corey Dickerson LF
Born: 05/22/89 Age: 29 Bats: L Throws: R Height: 6'1" Weight: 200 Origin: Round 8, 2010 Draft (#260 overall)

YEAR	TEAM	LVL	AGE	PA	R	2B	3B	HR	RBI	BB	K	SB	CS	AVG/OBP/SLG	TAv	VORP	BABIP	BRR	FRAA	WARP
2015	ABQ	AAA	26	29	3	1	0	1	3	1	4	0	0	.286/.310/.429	.256	-0.5	.304	-0.9	LF(5): -0.8	-0.1
2015	COL	MLB	26	234	30	18	2	10	31	10	56	0	1	.304/.333/.536	.288	10.8	.367	-0.5	LF(54): -1.5, CF(3): 0.5	1.0
2016	TBA	MLB	27	548	57	36	3	24	70	33	134	0	2	.245/.293/.469	.260	7.5	.285	-1.5	LF(76): 4.2, RF(2): -0.3	1.2
2017	TBA	MLB	28	629	84	33	4	27	62	35	152	4	3	.282/.325/.490	.284	24.9	.338	-1.9	LF(93): 13.5	3.9
2018	*TBA*	*MLB*	*29*	*603*	*72*	*31*	*6*	*23*	*84*	*39*	*142*	*3*	*3*	*.264/.313/.462*	*.274*	*20.4*	*.314*	*-1.0*	*LF 1*	*2.0*
2019	*TBA*	*MLB*	*30*	*565*	*75*	*29*	*4*	*24*	*81*	*42*	*138*	*2*	*2*	*.264/.319/.477*	*.274*	*22.2*	*.312*	*-1.2*	*LF 1*	*2.6*

Breakout: 3% Improve: 43% Collapse: 1% Attrition: 3% MLB: 95% *Comparables: Mark Trumbo, Khris Davis, Yoenis Cespedes*

Nobody in baseball hits like Dickerson, which makes him a joy to watch—when things are going right. He has always had exceptional ability to make contact, even quality contact, on pitches outside the zone, especially when you account for the fact that he's well below average at making quality contact on pitches *within* the zone. In fact, he made contact more often on non-strikes in 2017. He hit a pitch that bounced in front of the plate for a double. As you can guess, though, that profile has drawbacks. Dickerson started blistering hot, was the starting designated hitter for the American League in the All-Star game ... and then stopped hitting altogether as the Rays fell apart in the second half. When he's not hitting, he's not helping.

Lucas Duda 1B Born: 02/03/86 Age: 32 Bats: L Throws: R Height: 6'4" Weight: 255 Origin: Round 7, 2007 Draft (#243 overall)

YEAR	TEAM	LVL	AGE	PA	R	2B	3B	HR	RBI	BB	K	SB	CS	AVG/OBP/SLG	TAv	VORP	BABIP	BRR	FRAA	WARP
2015	NYN	MLB	29	554	67	33	0	27	73	66	138	0	2	.244/.352/.486	.320	38.9	.285	1.0	1B(129): -8.1	3.3
2016	NYN	MLB	30	172	20	7	0	7	23	15	36	0	0	.229/.302/.412	.281	6.3	.250	0.7	1B(45): -3.4	0.3
2017	NYN	MLB	31	291	30	21	0	17	37	37	73	0	0	.246/.347/.532	.303	13.1	.278	-3.4	1B(69): -1.7	1.1
2017	TBA	MLB	31	200	20	7	0	13	27	23	62	0	0	.175/.285/.444	.251	0.3	.173	0.1	1B(24): -0.2	0.0
2018	*TBA*	*MLB*	*32*	*401*	*51*	*18*	*0*	*19*	*58*	*49*	*105*	*1*	*1*	*.231/.337/.451*	*.271*	*11.9*	*.272*	*-0.3*	*1B -3*	*1.0*
2019	*TBA*	*MLB*	*33*	*429*	*60*	*18*	*0*	*19*	*59*	*52*	*113*	*0*	*0*	*.230/.334/.438*	*.269*	*8.9*	*.273*	*-0.4*	*1B -3*	*0.6*

Breakout: 1% Improve: 24% Collapse: 6% Attrition: 9% MLB: 92% *Comparables: Erubiel Durazo, Cliff Johnson, Boog Powell*

Duda is bigger than and not as good as Kent Hrbek was, but there's a bit of a Hrbek vibe to him. He's had some injury issues, but he's been a consistently above-average hitter—good enough to be a three-win first baseman when healthy. Duda stands close to the plate, making it easier to identify pitches away and let them go. For that reason, he walks a lot, and because he's also good at getting through quickly on pitches over the inner third he hits for plenty of power. Like Hrbek, he's fine with the glove (certainly better than his reputation), and like Hrbek, he's a beloved clubhouse presence. When he's on the field, he's still a useful player.

Matt Duffy SS Born: 01/15/91 Age: 27 Bats: R Throws: R Height: 6'2" Weight: 170 Origin: Round 18, 2012 Draft (#568 overall)

YEAR	TEAM	LVL	AGE	PA	R	2B	3B	HR	RBI	BB	K	SB	CS	AVG/OBP/SLG	TAv	VORP	BABIP	BRR	FRAA	WARP
2015	SFN	MLB	24	612	77	28	6	12	77	30	96	12	0	.295/.334/.428	.283	35.2	.336	2.9	3B(134): -0.2, 2B(9): -0.1	3.7
2016	SFN	MLB	25	286	32	11	2	4	21	20	40	8	4	.253/.313/.358	.259	10.0	.282	1.1	3B(69): 3.8	1.4
2016	TBA	MLB	25	80	9	3	0	1	7	3	13	0	1	.276/.300/.355	.226	0.8	.317	0.5	SS(18): 0.2, 3B(1): 0.0	0.1
2018	*TBA*	*MLB*	*27*	*547*	*60*	*24*	*3*	*10*	*58*	*35*	*97*	*11*	*3*	*.268/.319/.386*	*.258*	*21.3*	*.311*	*0.5*	*2B -1, 3B 1*	*1.5*
2019	*TBA*	*MLB*	*28*	*295*	*35*	*13*	*1*	*8*	*34*	*21*	*56*	*5*	*2*	*.268/.324/.410*	*.259*	*9.5*	*.309*	*1.0*	*2B 0, 3B 1*	*1.0*

Breakout: 6% Improve: 48% Collapse: 3% Attrition: 11% MLB: 98% *Comparables: Didi Gregorius, Daniel Descalso, Marwin Gonzalez*

Who knows? Maybe they let you write as many of the incantations for Even Year Magic as you can fit onto an index card before you leave San Francisco, and Duffy will bounce back with a healthy and helpful 2018. In 2017, though, he lost the whole season to a heel injury that he actually suffered in the middle of 2016 (an even year; uh-oh), putting the Rays' hopes of getting something significant out of the Matt Moore trade on hold. Duffy should be fully healthy by spring training, and is still sufficiently lithe and young to profile well at shortstop. The question is whether the guy who hit .253/.305/.289 at Long Beach State can recapture whatever magic made him into a quality big-league hitter a few years later.

Adeiny Hechavarria SS Born: 04/15/89 Age: 29 Bats: R Throws: R Height: 6'0" Weight: 195 Origin: International Free Agent, 2010

YEAR	TEAM	LVL	AGE	PA	R	2B	3B	HR	RBI	BB	K	SB	CS	AVG/OBP/SLG	TAv	VORP	BABIP	BRR	FRAA	WARP
2015	MIA	MLB	26	499	54	17	6	5	48	23	78	7	2	.281/.315/.374	.249	17.4	.325	3.2	SS(130): 6.1	2.5
2016	MIA	MLB	27	547	52	17	6	3	38	33	73	1	0	.236/.283/.311	.223	8.5	.269	6.5	SS(153): 2.3	1.1
2017	MIA	MLB	28	67	8	2	1	1	6	1	9	0	0	.277/.288/.385	.241	0.6	.309	-0.9	SS(19): -1.1	-0.1
2017	JUP	A+	28	27	1	0	0	0	1	3	1	1	1	.304/.407/.304	.293	1.4	.318	-0.6	SS(8): 1.0	0.3
2017	TBA	MLB	28	281	29	12	4	7	24	12	58	4	1	.257/.289/.411	.243	5.7	.302	-1.3	SS(77): 3.4	0.9
2018	*TBA*	*MLB*	*29*	*508*	*48*	*17*	*6*	*6*	*44*	*27*	*85*	*5*	*2*	*.245/.285/.340*	*.229*	*8.5*	*.285*	*0.5*	*SS 4*	*0.5*
2019	*TBA*	*MLB*	*30*	*398*	*40*	*13*	*4*	*6*	*37*	*23*	*68*	*3*	*1*	*.244/.289/.350*	*.226*	*0.7*	*.281*	*1.5*	*SS 3*	*0.4*

Breakout: 2% Improve: 46% Collapse: 5% Attrition: 14% MLB: 92% *Comparables: Jack Wilson, Alcides Escobar, Craig Reynolds*

What the Rays did with incumbent (if stopgap) shortstop Tim Beckham and Hechavarria last season might best be described using the old saw "never let the perfect become the enemy of the good." They did need a defensive upgrade at shortstop when Hechavarria became available last June. They were wise to go and get him. It was deeply unwise, however, to let Hechavarria's arrival eventually push Beckham out the door. Hechavarria is a tremendous fielder, but does nothing else well, and for any team with hopes of contending he should be no more than a utility infielder.

Kevin Kiermaier CF Born: 04/22/90 Age: 28 Bats: L Throws: R Height: 6'1" Weight: 215 Origin: Round 31, 2010 Draft (#941 overall)

YEAR	TEAM	LVL	AGE	PA	R	2B	3B	HR	RBI	BB	K	SB	CS	AVG/OBP/SLG	TAv	VORP	BABIP	BRR	FRAA	WARP
2015	TBA	MLB	25	535	62	25	12	10	40	24	95	18	5	.263/.298/.420	.259	17.7	.306	2.5	CF(148): 31.3, RF(2): -0.2	5.2
2016	TBA	MLB	26	414	55	20	2	12	37	40	74	21	3	.246/.331/.410	.266	18.3	.278	2.8	CF(104): 12.7	3.2
2017	PCH	A+	27	26	2	1	1	0	1	2	7	0	1	.125/.192/.250	.150	-2.2	.176	0.3	CF(3): -0.3	-0.3
2017	TBA	MLB	27	421	56	15	3	15	39	31	99	16	7	.276/.338/.450	.279	24.6	.337	2.9	CF(97): 7.7	3.2
2018	*TBA*	*MLB*	*28*	*596*	*83*	*25*	*8*	*15*	*60*	*43*	*118*	*22*	*7*	*.258/.316/.416*	*.263*	*26.9*	*.301*	*2.7*	*CF 18*	*4.0*
2019	*TBA*	*MLB*	*29*	*500*	*61*	*22*	*6*	*14*	*60*	*40*	*100*	*18*	*6*	*.260/.327/.430*	*.265*	*20.0*	*.303*	*2.5*	*CF 16*	*3.9*

Breakout: 0% Improve: 40% Collapse: 3% Attrition: 5% MLB: 97% *Comparables: Jon Jay, Cameron Maybin, Angel Pagan*

Look, if what you want is a long and consistent career unstained by injury or inconsistency, you can style yourself "The Accountant" or "The Fifth-Grade English Teacher" or "The All-Night Pastry Chef." Kiermaier goes by "The Outlaw," which explains everything. He's one of the league's fastest players and (thanks to his blend of tools, instincts and derring-do) probably its best defensive center fielder. He can find the gaps and work the occasional walk, too. And in each of the last two years, he's come about as close as they let you come to tearing off one of his own limbs trying to turn one safe/out play in his team's favor. John Dillinger died in a hail of gunfire, at 31. Kiermaier's life should last much longer, but if he doesn't moderate his playing style his baseball career could be cut short at about the same age.

Brandon Lowe 2B Born: 07/06/94 Age: 23 Bats: L Throws: R Height: 6'0" Weight: 185 Origin: Round 3, 2015 Draft (#87 overall)

YEAR	TEAM	LVL	AGE	PA	R	2B	3B	HR	RBI	BB	K	SB	CS	AVG/OBP/SLG	TAv	VORP	BABIP	BRR	FRAA	WARP
2016	BGR	A	21	449	67	15	3	5	42	60	77	6	3	.248/.357/.343	.272	14.0	.298	-1.3	2B(88): -9.2	0.5
2017	PCH	A+	22	367	62	34	3	9	46	47	65	6	3	.311/.403/.524	.332	38.2	.366	2.0	2B(75): -1.1, 3B(2): -0.2	3.9
2017	MNT	AA	22	101	8	5	1	2	12	2	26	1	1	.253/.270/.389	.252	0.5	.319	-1.3	2B(24): 0.8	0.1
2018	*TBA*	*MLB*	*23*	*250*	*30*	*12*	*1*	*7*	*26*	*24*	*64*	*1*	*0*	*.230/.310/.384*	*.242*	*5.5*	*.287*	*-0.4*	*2B -2, 3B 0*	*0.4*
2019	*TBA*	*MLB*	*24*	*344*	*41*	*17*	*1*	*10*	*39*	*34*	*88*	*1*	*1*	*.230/.313/.392*	*.248*	*5.9*	*.286*	*-0.6*	*2B -3, 3B 0*	*0.3*

Breakout: 4% Improve: 14% Collapse: 5% Attrition: 15% MLB: 29% *Comparables: Max Moroff, Travis Denker, Corban Joseph*

Lowe is an extremely under-the-radar prospect and always has been. He was undrafted out of his Virginia high school. Later, the Rays scooped him up in the third round (and gave him an over-slot bonus) as a redshirt sophomore out of the University of Maryland in 2015, but he broke his leg and played no pro ball until 2016. In 2017, he was fully healthy for the first time and showed big upside in his left-handed bat, especially thanks to his plate discipline. He'll need to stick at second base to have value, because his athleticism won't make him a defensive asset anywhere else and his size won't allow him to hit for plus power. If he keeps hitting the way he did in 2017, he has a chance to be an average regular.

Joshua Lowe CF Born: 02/02/98 Age: 20 Bats: L Throws: R Height: 6'4" Weight: 205 Origin: Round 1, 2016 Draft (#13 overall)

YEAR	TEAM	LVL	AGE	PA	R	2B	3B	HR	RBI	BB	K	SB	CS	AVG/OBP/SLG	TAv	VORP	BABIP	BRR	FRAA	WARP
2016	RAY	RK	18	114	14	6	1	2	15	20	27	1	1	.258/.386/.409	.306	10.1	.338	0.9	3B(22): 0.8	1.1
2016	PRI	RK	18	100	11	0	2	3	11	17	32	1	1	.238/.360/.400	.282	6.0	.333	0.4	3B(23): -3.4	0.3
2017	BGR	A	19	507	60	26	2	8	55	42	144	22	8	.268/.326/.386	.268	21.6	.369	2.3	CF(112): 3.4	2.6
2018	*TBA*	*MLB*	*20*	*250*	*28*	*9*	*1*	*6*	*21*	*18*	*90*	*4*	*2*	*.203/.261/.322*	*.206*	*-4.0*	*.298*	*0.0*	*CF 1*	*-0.3*
2019	*TBA*	*MLB*	*21*	*324*	*35*	*12*	*1*	*8*	*32*	*27*	*113*	*6*	*2*	*.207/.276/.335*	*.219*	*-4.1*	*.301*	*0.2*	*CF 2*	*-0.3*

Breakout: 2% Improve: 5% Collapse: 0% Attrition: 3% MLB: 7% *Comparables: Joe Benson, Chris Parmelee, Caleb Gindl*

The Rays' first-round pick in 2016, Lowe showed plenty of general promise, but no one had an especially clear idea of what kind of good player he might become. In 2017, his future became a little less abstract and a little more exciting. He moved from third base to center field, and his speed played well there. Hitting in the Midwest League at 19 while learning a new defensive position is tough, yet Lowe roughly held his own. He's long-armed, long-legged and long-swinged, so he has a lot of offensive adjustments ahead. If he makes them, all of the pieces of a first-division everyday center fielder are here.

Joe McCarthy 1B Born: 02/23/94 Age: 24 Bats: L Throws: L Height: 6'3" Weight: 225 Origin: Round 5, 2015 Draft (#148 overall)

YEAR	TEAM	LVL	AGE	PA	R	2B	3B	HR	RBI	BB	K	SB	CS	AVG/OBP/SLG	TAv	VORP	BABIP	BRR	FRAA	WARP
2015	HUD	A-	21	214	24	7	2	0	21	18	23	18	3	.277/.362/.337	.278	8.0	.315	-0.2	LF(37): -2.3, RF(2): 0.0	0.6
2016	BGR	A	22	193	31	12	0	3	29	33	30	11	2	.288/.425/.425	.330	15.7	.336	0.5	1B(40): -0.8, LF(1): -0.1	1.6
2016	PCH	A+	22	237	20	9	3	5	31	28	38	8	3	.283/.376/.434	.297	11.9	.317	-1.6	LF(23): 1.0, 1B(20): -1.0	1.2
2017	MNT	AA	23	554	76	31	8	7	56	90	94	20	5	.284/.409/.434	.305	32.1	.344	-1.6	1B(61): -7.0, LF(57): 3.7	3.1
2018	*TBA*	*MLB*	*24*	*250*	*29*	*11*	*2*	*6*	*28*	*32*	*57*	*5*	*1*	*.240/.348/.391*	*.261*	*7.2*	*.297*	*0.3*	*1B -2, LF 2*	*0.8*
2019	*TBA*	*MLB*	*25*	*344*	*44*	*15*	*2*	*9*	*39*	*44*	*79*	*7*	*2*	*.243/.350/.403*	*.268*	*9.7*	*.299*	*0.5*	*1B -2, LF 2*	*1.0*

Breakout: 2% Improve: 14% Collapse: 9% Attrition: 26% MLB: 38% *Comparables: Ji-Man Choi, Max Muncy, Chris Carter*

Ironically, McCarthy's biggest developmental problem might be that he's too much of a lefty. With a pretty swing and the frame of a future slugger, he invites some typecasting and keeps trying to make it work as a first baseman. He shouldn't. As his almost gaudy stolen-base totals suggest, McCarthy has above-average speed. His arm isn't good, but it's not disqualifying. Offensively, he controls the strike zone remarkably well and did so even against advanced pitching in 2017. Factor in his size (and the fact that he had back surgery in college, which has stunted the development of his power), and he profiles as a very good left fielder, with more than enough offensive upside to make up for some minor defensive deficiencies.

Brad Miller INF Born: 10/18/89 Age: 28 Bats: L Throws: R Height: 6'2" Weight: 215 Origin: Round 2, 2011 Draft (#62 overall)

YEAR	TEAM	LVL	AGE	PA	R	2B	3B	HR	RBI	BB	K	SB	CS	AVG/OBP/SLG	TAv	VORP	BABIP	BRR	FRAA	WARP
2015	SEA	MLB	25	497	44	22	4	11	46	47	101	13	4	.258/.329/.402	.273	20.2	.307	-2.6	SS(89): -0.2, CF(20): -1.4	1.9
2016	TBA	MLB	26	601	73	29	6	30	81	47	149	6	4	.243/.304/.482	.280	31.7	.277	0.4	SS(105): -7.7, 1B(39): 0.4	2.5
2017	TBA	MLB	27	407	43	13	3	9	40	63	110	5	3	.201/.327/.337	.256	7.8	.265	-1.3	2B(98): -1.3	0.7
2018	*TBA*	*MLB*	*28*	*624*	*74*	*24*	*6*	*19*	*76*	*62*	*139*	*9*	*4*	*.241/.318/.407*	*.261*	*10.4*	*.286*	*0.2*	*1B 2*	*1.1*
2019	*TBA*	*MLB*	*29*	*539*	*69*	*21*	*5*	*19*	*68*	*58*	*127*	*7*	*3*	*.240/.324/.424*	*.262*	*7.2*	*.284*	*-1.0*	*1B 2*	*1.0*

Breakout: 1% Improve: 57% Collapse: 1% Attrition: 5% MLB: 97% *Comparables: Kelly Johnson, Brian Dozier, Jason Kipnis*

After his breakout 2016, Miller found nothing but frustration waiting for him in 2017. His size and age make a return to shortstop (or even sticking at second base, unless it be as a bat-first type) more improbable with each passing year, and injuries to his abdomen, groin and shoulder last season didn't help. He can still put together a competitive at-bat and there's reason to believe he'll rediscover his power if he can stay fully healthy for a longer stretch in the future. As a first baseman or designated hitter, however, he's stretched, and that's if no more injury problems pop up.

Logan Morrison 1B Born: 08/25/87 Age: 30 Bats: L Throws: L Height: 6'3" Weight: 245 Origin: Round 22, 2005 Draft (#666 overall)

YEAR	TEAM	LVL	AGE	PA	R	2B	3B	HR	RBI	BB	K	SB	CS	AVG/OBP/SLG	TAv	VORP	BABIP	BRR	FRAA	WARP
2015	SEA	MLB	27	511	47	15	3	17	54	47	81	8	4	.225/.302/.383	.254	-0.8	.238	-3.2	1B(140): -5.1, RF(3): 0.0	-0.7
2016	TBA	MLB	28	398	45	18	1	14	43	37	89	4	2	.238/.319/.414	.260	4.5	.278	0.4	1B(83): -1.5	0.3
2017	TBA	MLB	29	601	75	22	1	38	85	81	149	2	0	.246/.353/.516	.294	28.3	.268	0.4	1B(126): -0.6	2.8
2018	*TBA*	*MLB*	*30*	*526*	*65*	*21*	*2*	*21*	*71*	*58*	*107*	*5*	*2*	*.242/.331/.434*	*.264*	*11.5*	*.269*	*-0.7*	*1B -1*	*1.1*
2019	*TBA*	*MLB*	*31*	*510*	*68*	*20*	*2*	*20*	*66*	*57*	*105*	*3*	*1*	*.238/.330/.426*	*.265*	*8.0*	*.266*	*-0.7*	*1B -1*	*0.7*

Breakout: 1% Improve: 39% Collapse: 3% Attrition: 10% MLB: 92% *Comparables: Billy Butler, Eddie Robinson, Richie Hebner*

Morrison wasted his mid-twenties on a low-risk, low-reward approach that grew out of a painful awareness of his limitations. Starting in 2016, he came out of his shell a bit. In 2017, he really threw caution to the wind and went rogue. He became much more aggressive in pitcher's counts and more patient in hitter's counts, working his way into better spots to hunt and punish fastballs. Morrison had a .643 OPS after 1-1 counts from 2012 through 2016, but an .813 mark in 2017. He reengineered his swing in the cliché modern way, aiming to pull and lift the ball more and trading some contact for power. It all worked. Now, the question is whether it will keep working when the league adjusts to the new Morrison.

Trevor Plouffe 3B Born: 06/15/86 Age: 32 Bats: R Throws: R Height: 6'2" Weight: 215 Origin: Round 1, 2004 Draft (#20 overall)

YEAR	TEAM	LVL	AGE	PA	R	2B	3B	HR	RBI	BB	K	SB	CS	AVG/OBP/SLG	TAv	VORP	BABIP	BRR	FRAA	WARP
2015	MIN	MLB	29	632	74	35	4	22	86	50	124	2	1	.244/.307/.435	.261	13.5	.274	-5.4	3B(140): 4.5, 1B(17): 0.7	2.0
2016	MIN	MLB	30	344	35	13	1	12	47	19	60	1	0	.260/.303/.420	.241	1.8	.284	-0.7	3B(63): -1.9, 1B(13): -0.1	0.0
2017	OAK	MLB	31	199	22	5	0	7	14	16	58	1	1	.214/.276/.357	.209	-4.1	.271	0.4	3B(52): -1.8	-0.6
2017	DUR	AAA	31	28	4	1	0	0	1	5	5	0	0	.227/.357/.273	.230	-0.6	.278	-0.1	3B(2): -0.1, 1B(1): 0.0	-0.1
2017	TBA	MLB	31	114	9	2	0	2	5	12	30	0	1	.168/.263/.248	.209	-3.9	.217	-0.1	3B(12): -1.3, 1B(11): -0.1	-0.5
2018	*TBA*	*MLB*	*32*	*308*	*32*	*13*	*1*	*9*	*36*	*26*	*71*	*1*	*1*	*.232/.302/.384*	*.242*	*2.8*	*.278*	*-1.1*	*3B -1, 1B 1*	*0.2*
2019	*TBA*	*MLB*	*33*	*264*	*31*	*12*	*1*	*8*	*30*	*23*	*64*	*0*	*0*	*.231/.304/.387*	*.247*	*1.5*	*.281*	*-1.0*	*3B -1, 1B 1*	*0.1*

Breakout: 5% Improve: 40% Collapse: 10% Attrition: 9% MLB: 89% *Comparables: Joe Crede, Ken Caminiti, Casey McGehee*

The never-ending list of sporting names we have on record is fraught with pleasing onomatopoeia. Plouffe (like the sound of your season plopping into the toilet bowl) joined that list in an unfortunate way in 2017. The Baseball Gauge keeps a stat called Championship Win Probability Added (cWPA), which takes into account a team's chances of winning not only a certain game, but a playoff berth, and eventually a World Series, in its effort to value various events. Among position players, nobody had a worse cWPA than Plouffe during the regular season. He's battled injuries, always had a fringy bat for a middling defensive third baseman and is now fighting Father Time to hold onto the last scraps of his big-league talent.

Wilson Ramos C Born: 08/10/87 Age: 30 Bats: R Throws: R Height: 6'1" Weight: 260 Origin: International Free Agent, 2004

YEAR	TEAM	LVL	AGE	PA	R	2B	3B	HR	RBI	BB	K	SB	CS	AVG/OBP/SLG	TAv	VORP	BABIP	BRR	FRAA	WARP
2015	WAS	MLB	27	504	41	16	0	15	68	21	101	0	0	.229/.258/.358	.231	5.8	.256	-1.4	C(125): 6.9	1.4
2016	WAS	MLB	28	523	58	25	0	22	80	35	79	0	0	.307/.354/.496	.305	43.2	.327	-4.3	C(128): 6.4	5.1
2017	DUR	AAA	29	30	4	2	0	2	5	2	1	0	0	.250/.300/.536	.257	0.8	.200	-0.2	C(6): 0.2	0.1
2017	TBA	MLB	29	224	19	6	0	11	35	10	36	0	0	.260/.290/.447	.248	4.0	.262	-3.4	C(62): -3.8	0.0
2018	*TBA*	*MLB*	*30*	*566*	*64*	*20*	*1*	*21*	*75*	*31*	*99*	*0*	*0*	*.254/.295/.415*	*.255*	*19.2*	*.274*	*-1.3*	*C 0*	*1.6*
2019	*TBA*	*MLB*	*31*	*434*	*54*	*16*	*0*	*17*	*56*	*26*	*81*	*0*	*0*	*.247/.293/.418*	*.248*	*7.7*	*.267*	*-2.8*	*C 1*	*1.0*

Breakout: 1% Improve: 34% Collapse: 10% Attrition: 12% MLB: 96% *Comparables: A.J. Pierzynski, Ronny Paulino, Ramon Hernandez*

YEAR	TEAM	P. COUNT	FRM RUNS	BLK RUNS	THRW RUNS	TOT RUNS
2015	WAS	16690	0.4	2.8	2.0	5.1
2016	WAS	17715	7.1	-1.2	1.6	7.5
2017	TBA	8203	0.0	-3.2	-0.7	-4.0
2018	*TBA*	*15944*	*2.0*	*-0.8*	*0.4*	*1.5*
2019	*TBA*	*12215*	*1.5*	*-0.6*	*0.3*	*1.1*

It would provide valuable insight into the mysteries of baseball if we could send Ramos back in time and have him somehow avoid the calamitous knee injury that ended his 2016 season. He'd enjoyed such an impressive breakout year, hitting for power and for average and, especially, making long-awaited progress in laying off pitches outside the zone. He'd so rarely been fully healthy, and when he was he'd always been too much of a hacker to reach his obvious offensive ceiling. Then, he fixed it. Then, he got hurt. He returned midseason and all of his previous offensive progress was essentially gone. Now 30 and with the girth of a first baseman or designated hitter, Ramos appears to be back where he was before 2016: fighting to stay healthy and relying on his glove to carry his bat.

Colby Rasmus LF Born: 08/11/86 Age: 31 Bats: L Throws: L Height: 6'2" Weight: 195 Origin: Round 1, 2005 Draft (#28 overall)

YEAR	TEAM	LVL	AGE	PA	R	2B	3B	HR	RBI	BB	K	SB	CS	AVG/OBP/SLG	TAv	VORP	BABIP	BRR	FRAA	WARP
2015	HOU	MLB	28	485	67	23	2	25	61	47	154	2	1	.238/.314/.475	.283	23.2	.305	1.9	LF(72): -3.7, CF(43): 0.7	2.9
2016	HOU	MLB	29	417	38	10	0	15	54	43	121	4	1	.206/.286/.355	.232	-2.8	.257	-0.3	LF(87): 2.6, CF(21): 1.5	0.4
2017	TBA	MLB	30	129	17	7	1	9	23	7	45	1	0	.281/.318/.579	.307	9.6	.368	0.5	LF(23): 4.3, RF(7): -0.3	1.4
2018	*TBA*	*MLB*	*31*	*250*	*30*	*10*	*1*	*11*	*35*	*23*	*80*	*2*	*1*	*.228/.302/.428*	*.251*	*6.2*	*.297*	*0.4*	*LF -1, RF 1*	*0.7*
2019	*TBA*	*MLB*	*32*	*89*	*11*	*3*	*0*	*4*	*12*	*8*	*29*	*0*	*0*	*.220/.296/.410*	*.246*	*0.9*	*.292*	*0.1*	*LF 0, RF 0*	*0.1*

Breakout: 2% Improve: 40% Collapse: 8% Attrition: 10% MLB: 95% *Comparables: Don Lenhardt, Alfonso Soriano, Mack Jones*

Some people play baseball because they love it, some play it because they're very, very good at it and others play it because it's what was right in front of them their whole lives. There's mounting evidence that Rasmus falls into the third group. He's a well-meaning guy with an abundance of talent, but his father pushed him and pimped him and feuded with his managers until he was on his second big-league team, and as a result Rasmus has never seemed comfortable being part of the world of baseball. He walked away from the game in mid-2017 with little information made available to anyone other than to say that it happened for personal reasons. That took courage, and hopefully Rasmus will be rewarded with goodwill and good karma.

Daniel Robertson INF Born: 03/22/94 Age: 24 Bats: R Throws: R Height: 5'11" Weight: 200 Origin: Round 1, 2012 Draft (#34 overall)

YEAR	TEAM	LVL	AGE	PA	R	2B	3B	HR	RBI	BB	K	SB	CS	AVG/OBP/SLG	TAv	VORP	BABIP	BRR	FRAA	WARP
2015	MNT	AA	21	347	49	20	5	4	41	33	58	2	3	.274/.363/.415	.306	29.7	.324	0.8	SS(69): 3.8	3.6
2016	DUR	AAA	22	511	50	21	3	5	43	58	100	2	1	.259/.358/.356	.260	18.5	.322	-0.3	SS(75): 1.7, 2B(21): 2.1	2.5
2017	DUR	AAA	23	47	7	2	0	1	1	3	7	0	1	.372/.426/.488	.313	3.3	.429	-1.0	SS(4): 0.3, 3B(3): -0.2	0.4
2017	TBA	MLB	23	254	22	7	2	5	19	29	73	1	1	.206/.308/.326	.237	1.4	.282	-0.8	2B(41): -2.2, SS(24): 1.9	0.2
2018	*TBA*	*MLB*	*24*	*230*	*25*	*9*	*1*	*4*	*23*	*22*	*55*	*1*	*0*	*.235/.324/.358*	*.253*	*6.2*	*.298*	*-0.3*	*3B 0, 2B 1*	*0.5*
2019	*TBA*	*MLB*	*25*	*401*	*49*	*15*	*2*	*10*	*43*	*42*	*97*	*1*	*1*	*.240/.335/.381*	*.257*	*9.2*	*.303*	*-0.6*	*3B 1, 2B 2*	*1.3*

Breakout: 5% Improve: 26% Collapse: 9% Attrition: 24% MLB: 64% *Comparables: Dustin Ackley, Kyle Seager, Luis Valbuena*

Do you ever run out of room in your T-shirt drawer and still have a couple of favorites to put away? You know if you hang those last couple shirts in the closet, they're going to get pushed back behind your suit and your work clothes, and you'll see them again in six months. But the drawer is full and if you try to stuff the stragglers in there the damn thing is going to jam or a shirt is going to get snagged. That's Robertson. He can make consistent contact and even has some raw power, but he'll need to be much more aggressive to make that play in the big leagues. Since his best attribute right now is his patience, getting aggressive is tricky. It feels an awful lot like he's going to change his approach and the bottom is going to fall out of the drawer.

Jesus Sanchez OF Born: 10/07/97 Age: 20 Bats: L Throws: R Height: 6'3" Weight: 210 Origin: International Free Agent, 2014

YEAR	TEAM	LVL	AGE	PA	R	2B	3B	HR	RBI	BB	K	SB	CS	AVG/OBP/SLG	TAv	VORP	BABIP	BRR	FRAA	WARP
2015	DDR	RK	17	268	36	13	7	4	45	20	32	8	1	.335/.382/.498	.350	32.5	.364	-2.1	CF(40): 2.3, RF(15): -1.8	3.2
2016	RAY	RK	18	173	25	6	8	4	31	6	31	1	5	.323/.341/.530	.310	13.7	.371	-0.9	CF(31): 1.9, RF(10): -1.3	1.4
2016	PRI	RK	18	53	8	4	0	3	8	3	12	1	0	.347/.385/.612	.351	7.5	.412	0.9	LF(11): 0.5, CF(3): -0.1	0.8
2017	BGR	A	19	512	81	29	4	15	82	32	91	7	2	.305/.348/.478	.290	29.1	.349	3.4	LF(78): 14.0, RF(19): -0.5	4.4
2018	*TBA*	*MLB*	*20*	*250*	*24*	*10*	*1*	*8*	*30*	*10*	*68*	*0*	*0*	*.238/.269/.395*	*.228*	*-0.5*	*.295*	*-0.3*	*LF 4, RF 0*	*0.3*
2019	*TBA*	*MLB*	*21*	*346*	*40*	*15*	*2*	*12*	*43*	*15*	*92*	*0*	*0*	*.244/.278/.412*	*.239*	*-0.1*	*.299*	*-0.5*	*LF 5, RF 0*	*0.5*

Breakout: 5% Improve: 14% Collapse: 0% Attrition: 6% MLB: 16% *Comparables: Rafael Devers, Josh Vitters, Jose Osuna*

There's another prospect by this name, a guy in the Marlins system. There's also a veteran pitcher still toiling in unaffiliated ball and another couple who have retired recently. If you're finding it hard to distinguish this Jesus Sanchez from the others, however, come up with a new name for him and stick it firmly to his profile, because he's not to be elided or overlooked. A teenager all season, he hit for solid power in the Midwest League without strikeout problems. His frame leaves projection for even more pop, but he's also a good athlete and a fine defensive corner outfielder. In the long run, there's a chance we'll remember him as *the* Jesus Sanchez.

Ryan Schimpf 3B Born: 04/11/88 Age: 30 Bats: L Throws: R Height: 5'9" Weight: 180 Origin: Round 5, 2009 Draft (#160 overall)

YEAR	TEAM	LVL	AGE	PA	R	2B	3B	HR	RBI	BB	K	SB	CS	AVG/OBP/SLG	TAv	VORP	BABIP	BRR	FRAA	WARP
2015	NHP	AA	27	307	43	20	0	20	56	42	54	2	1	.271/.378/.581	.325	24.0	.267	-1.9	RF(18): -2.3, LF(14): -0.5	2.3
2015	BUF	AAA	27	122	12	6	0	3	7	11	23	0	2	.200/.270/.336	.229	-0.3	.224	1.4	RF(10): -1.2, 3B(7): -0.3	-0.2
2016	ELP	AAA	28	190	36	17	0	15	48	21	33	0	1	.355/.432/.729	.362	26.1	.370	0.7	3B(33): -0.3, 1B(6): 0.5	2.7
2016	SDN	MLB	28	330	48	17	5	20	51	42	105	1	1	.217/.336/.533	.315	29.7	.260	1.9	2B(68): -1.8, 3B(14): 0.5	2.9
2017	SDN	MLB	29	197	24	2	0	14	25	27	70	0	0	.158/.284/.424	.269	9.0	.145	0.6	3B(50): 3.6	1.3
2017	ELP	AAA	29	284	44	7	1	19	44	36	105	0	0	.202/.311/.475	.263	10.1	.250	0.2	3B(50): 2.1, 2B(12): -2.5	0.9
2018	*SDN*	*MLB*	*30*	*98*	*14*	*4*	*0*	*6*	*16*	*12*	*31*	*0*	*0*	*.210/.313/.459*	*.271*	*4.6*	*.252*	*-0.2*	*3B 1*	*0.5*
2019	*SDN*	*MLB*	*31*	*219*	*32*	*8*	*1*	*13*	*33*	*27*	*72*	*0*	*0*	*.202/.310/.450*	*.264*	*6.8*	*.241*	*0.6*	*3B 4*	*1.1*

Breakout: 2% Improve: 33% Collapse: 4% Attrition: 12% MLB: 74% *Comparables: Russell Branyan, Bryan LaHair, Brett Wallace*

Schmipf's the kind of player who requires us to throw away all preconceived notions. He's the kind of player who can put up a batting average that would make Rob Deer blush and still be slightly above average overall with the stick. He can run into quite literally the worst BABIP in MLB history (min. 190 PA) and have enough strangeness in his profile to explain the insane aberration. He's the kind of player who hits more fly balls than anyone else in an era known for fly balls, strikes out more than anyone else in an era known for strikeouts and was demoted to Triple-A for over half the season, where he did more of the same. Never change, Ryan Schmipf. Never change.

Mallex Smith CF Born: 05/06/93 Age: 25 Bats: L Throws: R Height: 5'10" Weight: 180 Origin: Round 5, 2012 Draft (#165 overall)

YEAR	TEAM	LVL	AGE	PA	R	2B	3B	HR	RBI	BB	K	SB	CS	AVG/OBP/SLG	TAv	VORP	BABIP	BRR	FRAA	WARP
2015	MIS	AA	22	241	35	5	2	2	22	27	41	23	6	.340/.418/.413	.335	29.3	.412	4.1	CF(55): -0.4	3.1
2015	GWN	AAA	22	307	49	12	6	0	13	24	44	34	7	.281/.339/.367	.268	16.2	.332	4.4	CF(68): 2.5	1.9
2016	ATL	MLB	23	215	28	7	4	3	22	20	48	16	8	.238/.316/.365	.255	5.0	.302	0.2	CF(35): 2.9, LF(22): 0.2	0.8
2017	DUR	AAA	24	205	26	7	4	3	10	17	45	21	8	.263/.325/.392	.247	5.4	.333	2.3	CF(33): 5.1, LF(7): 0.5	1.0
2017	TBA	MLB	24	282	33	8	4	2	12	23	62	16	5	.270/.329/.355	.262	10.8	.347	2.1	CF(51): -5.1, LF(24): 0.2	0.7
2018	*TBA*	*MLB*	*25*	*258*	*34*	*9*	*4*	*4*	*22*	*22*	*57*	*18*	*6*	*.259/.322/.375*	*.255*	*8.2*	*.322*	*2.0*	*LF -3, CF 1*	*0.4*
2019	*TBA*	*MLB*	*26*	*342*	*39*	*12*	*4*	*6*	*35*	*30*	*75*	*23*	*8*	*.257/.327/.388*	*.254*	*8.6*	*.316*	*2.1*	*LF -4, CF 1*	*0.5*

Breakout: 5% Improve: 60% Collapse: 4% Attrition: 33% MLB: 94% *Comparables: Julio Borbon, Kevin Kiermaier, Jacoby Ellsbury*

Top-end speed and a complete lack of power make the diminutive, lefty-batting Smith easy to compare to Ben Revere. However, whereas Revere makes a ton of contact and rarely walks, Smith whiffs too much and only partially makes up for that by working walks at a fair clip. He's the classic case of a player getting the bat knocked out of his hands, unable to generate hard contact often enough to keep opposing pitchers honest and unable to even make contact when pitchers lead him out of the zone for a punchout. His speed and defense still make Smith potentially valuable, but he's better suited to a complementary role than to a regular one.

Steven Souza RF Born: 04/24/89 Age: 29 Bats: R Throws: R Height: 6'4" Weight: 225 Origin: Round 3, 2007 Draft (#100 overall)

YEAR	TEAM	LVL	AGE	PA	R	2B	3B	HR	RBI	BB	K	SB	CS	AVG/OBP/SLG	TAv	VORP	BABIP	BRR	FRAA	WARP
2015	TBA	MLB	26	426	59	15	1	16	40	46	144	12	6	.225/.318/.399	.259	8.9	.318	2.2	RF(103): -1.9	0.7
2016	TBA	MLB	27	468	58	17	1	17	49	31	159	7	6	.247/.303/.409	.252	6.8	.348	2.3	RF(111): -1.9, CF(3): 0.2	0.5
2017	TBA	MLB	28	617	78	21	2	30	78	84	179	16	4	.239/.351/.459	.287	27.3	.302	-1.9	RF(138): -6.7, CF(3): -0.5	2.0
2018	*TBA*	*MLB*	*29*	*623*	*94*	*22*	*2*	*24*	*74*	*68*	*188*	*15*	*6*	*.239/.328/.421*	*.269*	*23.3*	*.316*	*0.4*	*RF -8*	*1.2*
2019	*TBA*	*MLB*	*30*	*576*	*80*	*21*	*1*	*25*	*78*	*68*	*179*	*13*	*5*	*.238/.335/.437*	*.272*	*20.3*	*.314*	*1.3*	*RF -6*	*1.6*

Breakout: 3% Improve: 54% Collapse: 3% Attrition: 5% MLB: 94% *Comparables: Brad Hawpe, Jayson Werth, J.D. Martinez*

At 28, Souza finally became the hitter PECOTA thought he would be at 25. He walked more than he had in his first two seasons with the Rays combined, he hit for more power and (most importantly) he brought down his catastrophic strikeout rate. He's not the athlete who once saved a no-hitter for Max Scherzer, but he demonstrated that he can be a dangerous enough slugger to make that matter only a little. Then, with six weeks left in the season he utterly fell to pieces, leaving ample room to doubt whether his improvements will stick for the long haul. If they don't, Souza's declining defense in the outfield corners will become a major problem.

Denard Span CF Born: 02/27/84 Age: 34 Bats: L Throws: L Height: 6'0" Weight: 210 Origin: Round 1, 2002 Draft (#20 overall)

YEAR	TEAM	LVL	AGE	PA	R	2B	3B	HR	RBI	BB	K	SB	CS	AVG/OBP/SLG	TAv	VORP	BABIP	BRR	FRAA	WARP
2015	WAS	MLB	31	275	38	17	0	5	22	25	26	11	0	.301/.365/.431	.305	22.4	.318	2.3	CF(61): 2.3	2.6
2016	SFN	MLB	32	637	70	23	5	11	53	53	79	12	7	.266/.331/.381	.263	21.5	.291	-0.2	CF(137): -14.9	0.7
2017	SFN	MLB	33	542	73	31	5	12	43	40	69	12	7	.272/.329/.427	.272	24.5	.295	0.3	CF(123): -11.2	1.3
2018	*TBA*	*MLB*	*34*	*446*	*55*	*19*	*4*	*6*	*38*	*34*	*59*	*11*	*4*	*.260/.317/.372*	*.252*	*11.6*	*.287*	*0.5*	*LF -1, CF -1*	*0.6*
2019	*TBA*	*MLB*	*35*	*353*	*39*	*15*	*2*	*6*	*34*	*29*	*51*	*8*	*3*	*.250/.315/.367*	*.242*	*2.8*	*.277*	*0.6*	*LF 0, CF -1*	*0.2*

Breakout: 1% Improve: 32% Collapse: 7% Attrition: 17% MLB: 87% *Comparables: Angel Pagan, Brady Clark, Cesar Tovar*

It takes a lot for a veteran player to swallow his pride and admit that one of his core skills has slipped away. For Span, two post-hip-surgery seasons of watching bloop singles fall in front and liners scoot through the gap was enough. By FRAA, Span has cost the Giants 26.1 runs on defense since 2016, more than every other outfielder in baseball save Yasmany Tomas. By Defensive Runs Saved, Span was dead last with -27 runs in 2017 alone, nine below the next-poorest center fielder, Dexter Fowler. So, come season's end, he did the right thing and offered to play left. While the move might strain Span's offensive credibility, the average MLB left fielder hit .256/.327/.427 last season, which looks remarkably similar to Span's own triple-slash. If he can match that output at age 34, he could still earn the $9 million he's due.

Jesus Sucre C Born: 04/30/88 Age: 30 Bats: R Throws: R Height: 6'0" Weight: 200 Origin: International Free Agent, 2005

YEAR	TEAM	LVL	AGE	PA	R	2B	3B	HR	RBI	BB	K	SB	CS	AVG/OBP/SLG	TAv	VORP	BABIP	BRR	FRAA	WARP
2015	TAC	AAA	27	26	4	0	0	0	2	3	8	0	0	.261/.346/.261	.297	2.4	.400	0.2	C(6): -0.4	0.2
2015	SEA	MLB	27	142	9	6	0	1	7	6	21	0	0	.157/.195/.228	.165	-6.7	.181	0.4	C(50): 4.5, P(2): 0.0	-0.2
2016	TAC	AAA	28	104	7	4	1	0	11	3	15	0	1	.273/.301/.333	.220	-0.7	.321	-0.9	C(28): -0.1	-0.1
2016	SEA	MLB	28	29	4	2	0	1	5	2	5	0	0	.480/.552/.680	.404	5.0	.579	-0.5	C(9): -0.2	0.5
2017	TBA	MLB	29	192	20	6	0	7	29	7	35	2	0	.256/.289/.409	.248	6.8	.275	0.2	C(61): 1.3, P(1): 0.0	0.8
2018	*TBA*	*MLB*	*30*	*217*	*20*	*8*	*1*	*3*	*19*	*10*	*40*	*1*	*0*	*.237/.273/.329*	*.220*	*1.8*	*.275*	*-0.3*	*C 1*	*0.0*
2019	*TBA*	*MLB*	*31*	*240*	*24*	*8*	*0*	*4*	*21*	*12*	*48*	*1*	*0*	*.231/.274/.324*	*.212*	*-3.0*	*.270*	*-0.2*	*C 1*	*-0.2*

Breakout: 1% Improve: 29% Collapse: 11% Attrition: 28% MLB: 77% *Comparables: Geronimo Gil, Rob Johnson, Humberto Quintero*

YEAR	TEAM	P. COUNT	FRM RUNS	BLK RUNS	THRW RUNS	TOT RUNS
2015	SEA	6224	2.4	1.0	0.6	4.1
2015	TAC	895	-0.3	0.0	0.0	-0.3
2016	SEA	1022	-0.1	0.1	-0.1	-0.1
2017	TBA	7812	2.4	0.8	-0.3	2.9
2018	*TBA*	*8653*	*1.0*	*0.9*	*0.0*	*1.9*
2019	*TBA*	*9563*	*0.9*	*0.8*	*0.0*	*1.6*

Sucre's swing is slider-speed but fastball-shaped. He never walks, and despite a thick, barrel-chested frame he doesn't hit for much power. Last season he did at least manage to lift the ball more often, but he cannot square it up often enough for that to matter. Behind the plate, all that mass lends stability and he lends the same to young pitching staffs. He moves well behind the plate and gets rid of the ball quickly when anyone runs on him. He'll never be more than a backup, but his receiving skills are good enough to keep him around until his swing slows to knuckleball-speed.

Garrett Whitley OF Born: 03/13/97 Age: 21 Bats: R Throws: R Height: 6'1" Weight: 195 Origin: Round 1, 2015 Draft (#13 overall)

YEAR	TEAM	LVL	AGE	PA	R	2B	3B	HR	RBI	BB	K	SB	CS	AVG/OBP/SLG	TAv	VORP	BABIP	BRR	FRAA	WARP
2015	RAY	RK	18	116	12	4	2	3	13	16	25	5	4	.188/.310/.365	.264	2.8	.214	-0.9	CF(22): 3.2	0.6
2015	HUD	A-	18	48	3	0	1	0	4	5	12	3	1	.143/.250/.190	.207	-1.4	.200	-0.2	CF(12): -1.4	-0.3
2016	HUD	A-	19	292	38	12	7	1	31	30	75	21	5	.266/.356/.379	.293	14.9	.372	-1.7	LF(31): 2.4, CF(23): -0.5	1.8
2017	BGR	A	20	426	65	18	4	13	61	57	122	21	4	.249/.362/.430	.289	22.8	.339	0.9	LF(54): 3.2, CF(23): 5.1	2.9
2018	*TBA*	*MLB*	*21*	*250*	*26*	*8*	*1*	*7*	*26*	*24*	*89*	*6*	*1*	*.195/.281/.332*	*.219*	*-1.9*	*.284*	*0.5*	*LF 2, RF -2*	*-0.1*
2019	*TBA*	*MLB*	*22*	*338*	*39*	*11*	*2*	*10*	*36*	*32*	*118*	*7*	*2*	*.201/.287/.350*	*.228*	*-2.2*	*.289*	*0.9*	*LF 3, RF -2*	*-0.1*

Breakout: 1% Improve: 2% Collapse: 0% Attrition: 4% MLB: 6% *Comparables: Daniel Fields, Michael Saunders, Clint Frazier*

For a first-round pick, Whitley has been handled conservatively over his first two-and-a-half professional seasons. That's not atypical for the Rays and it doesn't necessarily bode ill for his development. In fact, Whitley took some impressive forward steps in 2017, despite playing the whole year at the lowest full-season level. His raw numbers don't leap off the page, but 20-year-olds don't generally hit for even Whitley's modest power in the Midwest League. He also showed polish in his plate approach, on the bases and in the field. If he can iron out his contact issues as he progresses, he has star potential.

PITCHERS

Jose Alvarado LHP
Born: 05/21/95 Age: 23 Bats: L Throws: L Height: 6'2" Weight: 245 Origin: International Free Agent, 2012

YEAR	TEAM	LVL	AGE	W	L	SV	G	GS	IP	H	HR	BB/9	K/9	K	GB%	BABIP	WHIP	ERA	DRA	WARP	MPH	CMD	PWR	STM
2015	PRI	RK	20	0	2	0	5	5	17	18	1	6.9	9.5	18	67%	.386	1.82	9.53	4.26	0.3				
2016	BGR	A	21	2	0	2	10	0	24^2	12	0	6.2	12.4	34	74%	.245	1.18	1.46	2.82	0.6				
2016	PCH	A+	21	2	1	0	27	0	46	38	1	7.4	10.0	51	57%	.306	1.65	3.91	6.19	-0.6				
2017	MNT	AA	22	2	1	0	9	0	11^1	4	1	4.0	11.1	14	78%	.136	0.79	2.38	2.25	0.3				
2017	DUR	AAA	22	0	2	1	16	0	18^1	11	1	6.4	12.8	26	43%	.244	1.31	3.93	3.61	0.3				
2017	TBA	MLB	22	0	3	0	35	0	29^2	24	1	2.7	8.8	29	55%	.274	1.11	3.64	3.93	0.4	99.7	48	81	46
2018	*TBA*	*MLB*	*23*	*2*	*2*	*0*	*40*	*0*	*42^2*	*37*	*5*	*6.4*	*10.1*	*48*	*51%*	*.293*	*1.59*	*4.88*	*5.18*	*0.0*	*99.6*	*50*	*84*	*48*
2019	*TBA*	*MLB*	*24*	*2*	*1*	*0*	*46*	*0*	*49*	*41*	*7*	*5.7*	*10.4*	*56*	*51%*	*.285*	*1.48*	*4.50*	*4.97*	*0.1*	*99.4*	*50*	*85*	*48*

Breakout: 13% Improve: 15% Collapse: 12% Attrition: 19% MLB: 32% *Comparables: Stephen Pryor, Bruce Rondon, Eduardo Sanchez*

When the starting point is a triple-digit fastball from the left side, there are a lot of interesting places the journey can go. Alas, the journey mostly took Alvarado through boring minor-league towns and long, boring minor-league innings for a while there. He was ill suited to starting and couldn't find control (let alone command) even after moving to the bullpen. Then last season things started to come together. He's added a slider, which might be the answer to the long-worrisome problem of his substandard curveball. Even if it isn't, he's found the feel for his fastball enough to make life hell for opposing hitters late in games.

Matt Andriese RHP
Born: 08/28/89 Age: 28 Bats: R Throws: R Height: 6'2" Weight: 225 Origin: Round 3, 2011 Draft (#112 overall)

YEAR	TEAM	LVL	AGE	W	L	SV	G	GS	IP	H	HR	BB/9	K/9	K	GB%	BABIP	WHIP	ERA	DRA	WARP	MPH	CMD	PWR	STM
2015	DUR	AAA	25	3	3	0	13	12	65	65	2	1.4	9.6	69	50%	.344	1.15	2.35	1.12	3.1				
2015	TBA	MLB	25	3	5	2	25	8	65^2	69	8	2.5	6.7	49	50%	.298	1.32	4.11	4.14	0.6	93.9	48	47	58
2016	DUR	AAA	26	1	2	0	6	6	34^1	32	2	1.8	11.5	44	48%	.345	1.14	3.41	1.15	1.6				
2016	TBA	MLB	26	8	8	1	29	19	127^2	131	17	1.8	7.7	109	44%	.305	1.22	4.37	3.63	2.4	93.8	37	40	67
2017	TBA	MLB	27	5	5	1	18	17	86	90	16	2.9	8.0	76	46%	.296	1.37	4.50	4.97	0.6	93.5	36	36	41
2018	*TBA*	*MLB*	*28*	*4*	*4*	*0*	*50*	*5*	*73*	*69*	*9*	*3.0*	*8.7*	*71*	*45%*	*.295*	*1.28*	*3.80*	*4.33*	*0.7*	*93.1*	*39*	*40*	*54*
2019	*TBA*	*MLB*	*29*	*6*	*3*	*0*	*74*	*6*	*109^1*	*100*	*13*	*2.8*	*9.4*	*114*	*45%*	*.299*	*1.22*	*3.53*	*3.92*	*1.6*	*92.8*	*37*	*39*	*53*

Breakout: 25% Improve: 56% Collapse: 12% Attrition: 25% MLB: 89% *Comparables: Liam Hendriks, Jose Alvarez, Joe Saunders*

A late bloomer, Andriese is still trying to establish that he can stay healthy and be consistent in a big-league rotation over a full season. He has a fastball with plenty of life, a pitch that can miss bats even within the zone at times. His changeup is the real point of interest, though. No pitcher throws their changeup with more cutting, sinking action. He induced the highest swing rate in MLB on his change, because it's so similar to his heater. He also gets a ton of groundballs with the pitch. In any kind of relief role, eliminating the need for his fringy breaking stuff, Andriese could be a valuable weapon.

Chris Archer RHP
Born: 09/26/88 Age: 29 Bats: R Throws: R Height: 6'2" Weight: 195 Origin: Round 5, 2006 Draft (#161 overall)

YEAR	TEAM	LVL	AGE	W	L	SV	G	GS	IP	H	HR	BB/9	K/9	K	GB%	BABIP	WHIP	ERA	DRA	WARP	MPH	CMD	PWR	STM
2015	TBA	MLB	26	12	13	0	34	34	212	175	19	2.8	10.7	252	47%	.295	1.14	3.23	2.58	6.3	98.2	38	62	81
2016	TBA	MLB	27	9	19	0	33	33	201^1	183	30	3.0	10.4	233	49%	.297	1.24	4.02	3.17	5.0	97.1	38	51	85
2017	TBA	MLB	28	10	12	0	34	34	201	193	27	2.7	11.1	249	43%	.325	1.26	4.07	3.30	5.1	97.4	47	56	84
2018	*TBA*	*MLB*	*29*	*11*	*9*	*0*	*27*	*27*	*170*	*149*	*24*	*3.0*	*10.4*	*197*	*46%*	*.296*	*1.22*	*3.55*	*4.11*	*2.5*	*96.8*	*42*	*56*	*84*
2019	*TBA*	*MLB*	*30*	*12*	*10*	*0*	*31*	*31*	*198^2*	*170*	*27*	*2.9*	*10.8*	*237*	*46%*	*.294*	*1.17*	*3.46*	*3.84*	*3.9*	*96.3*	*43*	*54*	*84*

Breakout: 12% Improve: 34% Collapse: 18% Attrition: 5% MLB: 96% *Comparables: Erik Bedard, David Price, Josh Johnson*

It's tempting to believe that, by now, Archer should have ascended to an ace status far beyond the petty problems of mortal pitchers. True aces do not have to have apologists who point to their sparkling peripherals every year, because true aces keep runs off the board. In Archer's case, it's easy to see how the runs keep getting onto the board. He's a fierce competitor with a filthy fastball/slider combination. He doesn't want to give up the ball after five or six dominant innings, any more than his team wants to take it from him. However, because he's mostly a two-pitch pitcher, the third and fourth trips through the order are hard on him. He had an ERA just under 6.00 after the first 18 batters last season. No effort to develop his changeup has yet yielded the results necessary to turn the worm. Maybe this will be the year.

Xavier Cedeno LHP
Born: 08/26/86 Age: 31 Bats: L Throws: L Height: 5'11" Weight: 210 Origin: Round 31, 2004 Draft (#920 overall)

YEAR	TEAM	LVL	AGE	W	L	SV	G	GS	IP	H	HR	BB/9	K/9	K	GB%	BABIP	WHIP	ERA	DRA	WARP	MPH	CMD	PWR	STM
2015	WAS	MLB	28	0	0	0	5	0	3	3	1	6.0	12.0	4	25%	.286	1.67	6.00	3.21	0.1	91.3	33	5	45
2015	TBA	MLB	28	4	1	1	61	0	43	37	3	2.5	9.0	43	56%	.296	1.14	2.09	3.32	0.7	91.1	33	5	45
2016	TBA	MLB	29	3	4	0	54	0	41^1	36	2	2.8	9.4	43	51%	.296	1.19	3.70	3.46	0.7	90.7	59	0	43
2017	TBA	MLB	30	1	1	0	9	0	3	7	3	12.0	0.0	0	59%	.286	3.67	12.00	10.26	-0.2	89.6			
2018	*TBA*	*MLB*	*31*	*1*	*0*	*1*	*32*	*0*	*33^2*	*34*	*5*	*4.6*	*7.2*	*27*	*48%*	*.290*	*1.53*	*5.32*	*5.90*	*-0.2*	*90.0*	*47*	*2*	*44*
2019	*TBA*	*MLB*	*32*	*3*	*1*	*3*	*55*	*0*	*43^2*	*48*	*6*	*3.5*	*5.8*	*28*	*48%*	*.292*	*1.48*	*4.89*	*5.43*	*-0.1*	*89.4*	*53*	*1*	*43*

Breakout: 35% Improve: 49% Collapse: 20% Attrition: 15% MLB: 82% *Comparables: Josh Fields, Will Harris, Heath Bell*

Early in the 2015 season, Cedeno finally figured out that he had only two good pitches and neither of them was a true fastball. He became a cutter/curveball guy—unusual, but it's what works for him. A forearm issue stole virtually all of his 2017, and when he did pitch he was woefully ineffective, becoming just the 16th pitcher in the last 15 years to face at least 21 batters in a season and strike out none. If and when he's healthy, he figures to remain an extremely effective situational lefty. The problem: It's tough to project a 31-year-old who relies on cutters and curves to get and stay healthy.

Alex Cobb RHP Born: 10/07/87 Age: 30 Bats: R Throws: R Height: 6'3" Weight: 205 Origin: Round 4, 2006 Draft (#109 overall)

YEAR	TEAM	LVL	AGE	W	L	SV	G	GS	IP	H	HR	BB/9	K/9	K	GB%	BABIP	WHIP	ERA	DRA	WARP	MPH	CMD	PWR	STM
2016	DUR	AAA	28	0	1	0	4	4	15	24	3	3.0	6.0	10	44%	.389	1.93	6.60	4.76	0.1				
2016	TBA	MLB	28	1	2	0	5	5	22	32	5	2.9	6.5	16	52%	.355	1.77	8.59	5.53	0.0	92.5	45	37	31
2017	TBA	MLB	29	12	10	0	29	29	179^1	175	22	2.2	6.4	128	49%	.282	1.22	3.66	4.06	3.0	93.0	63	35	75
2018	*TBA*	*MLB*	*30*	*7*	*9*	*0*	*23*	*23*	*128^2*	*128*	*18*	*3.3*	*6.9*	*99*	*45%*	*.286*	*1.36*	*4.73*	*5.25*	*0.6*	*92.2*	*61*	*35*	*55*
2019	*TBA*	*MLB*	*31*	*7*	*10*	*0*	*25*	*25*	*148^1*	*163*	*25*	*4.0*	*6.3*	*104*	*45%*	*.296*	*1.54*	*5.22*	*5.79*	*-0.2*	*91.8*	*61*	*35*	*55*

Breakout: 8% Improve: 41% Collapse: 33% Attrition: 11% MLB: 92% *Comparables: Jordan Zimmermann, Josh Johnson, Kris Medlen*

Cobb does everything slowly. Of the 119 pitchers who threw at least 1,000 pitches last season, Cobb had the 10th-longest average time between pitches. He's slow even once he begins his windup, with a protracted, multiphase leg kick and so little momentum that he seems to hover down the mound. He even recovered slowly after having Tommy John surgery in early 2015, returning for just 22 innings in the majors in 2016. Back in full for 2017, he slowly worked his formerly devastating splitter (a staple of his arsenal at his peak) back into his repertoire. He leaned more heavily than ever on his sinker and knuckle-curve, but the sheer nastiness of that breaking ball and his command of the sinker were enough to make him effective, anyway. If he continues to steadily reintroduce the splitter, he might be better than ever, having honed his use of the other two offerings on which he depends.

Alex Colome RHP Born: 12/31/88 Age: 29 Bats: R Throws: R Height: 6'1" Weight: 220 Origin: International Free Agent, 2007

YEAR	TEAM	LVL	AGE	W	L	SV	G	GS	IP	H	HR	BB/9	K/9	K	GB%	BABIP	WHIP	ERA	DRA	WARP	MPH	CMD	PWR	STM
2015	TBA	MLB	26	8	5	0	43	13	109^2	112	9	2.5	7.2	88	41%	.317	1.30	3.94	3.81	1.5	96.6	45	55	58
2016	TBA	MLB	27	2	4	37	57	0	56^2	43	6	2.4	11.3	71	49%	.280	1.02	1.91	2.65	1.5	96.7	42	54	41
2017	TBA	MLB	28	2	3	47	65	0	66^2	57	4	3.1	7.8	58	50%	.275	1.20	3.24	4.15	0.8	95.9	46	44	49
2018	*TBA*	*MLB*	*29*	*3*	*3*	*31*	*61*	*0*	*64*	*56*	*6*	*3.6*	*8.9*	*63*	*47%*	*.290*	*1.27*	*3.33*	*3.92*	*0.9*	*95.7*	*45*	*51*	*49*
2019	*TBA*	*MLB*	*30*	*3*	*1*	*23*	*57*	*0*	*60*	*52*	*6*	*3.7*	*9.4*	*62*	*47%*	*.291*	*1.28*	*3.61*	*3.99*	*0.8*	*95.2*	*44*	*49*	*47*

Breakout: 35% Improve: 58% Collapse: 23% Attrition: 19% MLB: 99% *Comparables: Jacob deGrom, Adam Warren, Justin Wilson*

When Colome made his final and full conversion to relief in 2016, he all but scrapped his changeup and curveball, and remade himself as a fastball/cutter guy. Then he quickly realized that he was really a cutter/fastball guy. Colome threw his cutter well over 60 percent of the time in 2017, and while it wasn't the bat-missing widowmaker the world saw in 2016, it got the job done again. Colome isn't an elite relief arm, but he has decent command of both his mid-90s heat and that cutter, and in short bursts he can induce a lot of weak contact and avoid getting himself into trouble.

Jose De Leon RHP Born: 08/07/92 Age: 25 Bats: R Throws: R Height: 6'1" Weight: 220 Origin: Round 24, 2013 Draft (#724 overall)

YEAR	TEAM	LVL	AGE	W	L	SV	G	GS	IP	H	HR	BB/9	K/9	K	GB%	BABIP	WHIP	ERA	DRA	WARP	MPH	CMD	PWR	STM
2015	RCU	A+	22	4	1	0	7	7	37^2	26	1	1.9	13.9	58	45%	.325	0.90	1.67	0.76	2.0				
2015	TUL	AA	22	2	6	0	16	16	76^2	61	11	3.4	12.3	105	36%	.294	1.17	3.64	1.40	3.4				
2016	OKL	AAA	23	7	1	0	16	16	86^1	61	9	2.1	11.6	111	36%	.259	0.94	2.61	1.36	3.9				
2016	LAN	MLB	23	2	0	0	4	4	17	19	5	3.7	7.9	15	46%	.280	1.53	6.35	5.90	-0.1	94.5	33	50	44
2017	TBA	MLB	24	1	0	0	1	0	2^2	4	1	10.1	6.8	2	60%	.333	2.62	10.12	2.28	0.1	93.2			24
2017	DUR	AAA	24	0	2	0	3	3	12	14	1	4.5	10.5	14	38%	.394	1.67	6.75	3.78	0.2				
2017	RAY	RK	24	1	0	0	3	2	12	4	1	0.8	9.0	12	30%	.115	0.42	0.75	1.93	0.5				
2017	PCH	A+	24	1	0	0	4	3	14^1	11	0	5.7	11.3	18	39%	.333	1.40	1.88	3.67	0.3				
2018	*TBA*	*MLB*	*25*	*4*	*5*	*0*	*14*	*14*	*74*	*67*	*12*	*4.0*	*10.7*	*88*	*37%*	*.295*	*1.35*	*4.16*	*4.77*	*0.5*	*94.0*	*34*	*51*	*34*
2019	*TBA*	*MLB*	*26*	*9*	*11*	*0*	*30*	*30*	*188^2*	*173*	*35*	*3.8*	*10.7*	*223*	*37%*	*.295*	*1.34*	*4.46*	*4.94*	*1.3*	*93.7*	*34*	*51*	*34*

Breakout: 26% Improve: 51% Collapse: 17% Attrition: 34% MLB: 76% *Comparables: Edwar Cabrera, Matt Strahm, Jharel Cotton*

The Dodgers decided to trade De Leon proactively, and in hindsight maybe that should have served as the warning sign for all would-be suitors. Andrew Friedman engaged the Twins in a game of chicken, offering De Leon straight up for Brian Dozier, but Minnesota never did flinch. Friedman's former organization, however, saw the hurler's size, minor-league numbers and changeup, and were persuaded to make a swap for Logan Forsythe. It immediately went to pieces for them. De Leon missed time with forearm tightness and a lat strain, never getting much further than the end of a rehab stint before requiring another trip to the disabled list. He has struggled to stay healthy in the past, and now seems to be damaged goods. If he can ever regain full strength and health, there's still a lot of promise here.

Jacob Faria RHP Born: 07/30/93 Age: 24 Bats: R Throws: R Height: 6'4" Weight: 235 Origin: Round 10, 2011 Draft (#330 overall)

YEAR	TEAM	LVL	AGE	W	L	SV	G	GS	IP	H	HR	BB/9	K/9	K	GB%	BABIP	WHIP	ERA	DRA	WARP	MPH	CMD	PWR	STM
2015	PCH	A+	21	10	1	0	12	10	74^1	51	1	2.7	7.6	63	40%	.253	0.98	1.33	3.27	1.6				
2015	MNT	AA	21	7	3	0	13	13	75^1	52	5	3.6	11.5	96	33%	.278	1.09	2.51	1.79	3.0				
2016	MNT	AA	22	1	6	0	14	14	83^1	64	5	3.9	10.0	93	42%	.282	1.20	4.21	2.79	2.3				
2016	DUR	AAA	22	4	4	0	13	13	67^2	46	7	4.3	8.5	64	40%	.227	1.15	3.72	4.75	0.5				
2017	DUR	AAA	23	6	1	0	11	11	58^2	44	7	3.4	12.9	84	43%	.291	1.12	3.07	1.89	2.4				
2017	TBA	MLB	23	5	4	0	16	14	86^2	71	11	3.2	8.7	84	39%	.265	1.18	3.43	4.04	1.5	93.1	45	39	63
2018	*TBA*	*MLB*	*24*	*7*	*7*	*0*	*20*	*20*	*114*	*98*	*16*	*3.9*	*10.1*	*128*	*39%*	*.288*	*1.28*	*3.95*	*4.53*	*1.1*	*92.9*	*46*	*40*	*65*
2019	*TBA*	*MLB*	*25*	*10*	*11*	*0*	*31*	*31*	*195^1*	*163*	*30*	*3.7*	*10.5*	*228*	*39%*	*.28*	*1.25*	*4.05*	*4.50*	*2.2*	*92.7*	*47*	*40*	*66*

Breakout: 21% Improve: 60% Collapse: 15% Attrition: 19% MLB: 85% *Comparables: Vincent Velasquez, Travis Wood, Matt Harvey*

In 2017, 193 starting pitchers threw at least 200 four-seam fastballs. Of those 193, Clayton Kershaw had the four-seamer with the most movement toward the glove side (across the pitcher's body, away from a same-handed batter). Faria appears third on that list. Of the same 193 starters, Kershaw had the second-most rising action on his heat. Right below him? Faria. What's peculiar is that, whereas whatever arm talent allows Kershaw to unleash that superlative-laden fastball has prevented him from developing a reliable changeup, Faria's top secondary offering is a changeup with numbers about as impressive as the ones on Kershaw's breaking balls. Among starters, only Stephen Strasburg got more whiffs per swing with his changeup than did Faria in 2017. Faria has considerable work left to do if he wants to become a front-line starter, but the basic tool kit at his disposal is very impressive.

Austin Franklin RHP Born: 10/02/97 Age: 20 Bats: R Throws: R Height: 6'3" Weight: 215 Origin: Round 3, 2016 Draft (#90 overall)

YEAR	TEAM	LVL	AGE	W	L	SV	G	GS	IP	H	HR	BB/9	K/9	K	GB%	BABIP	WHIP	ERA	DRA	WARP	MPH	CMD	PWR	STM
2016	RAY	RK	18	1	2	1	11	9	43^{1}	30	0	3.3	8.3	40	42%	.254	1.06	2.70	4.19	0.7				
2017	HUD	A-	19	4	2	0	13	13	69^{1}	51	4	4.0	9.2	71	43%	.270	1.18	2.21	4.84	0.3				
2018	*TBA*	*MLB*	*20*	*2*	*5*	*0*	*10*	*10*	*49^{1}*	*50*	*12*	*6.0*	*9.6*	*53*	*35%*	*.298*	*1.68*	*6.34*	*7.02*	*-0.7*				
2019	*TBA*	*MLB*	*21*	*5*	*11*	*0*	*25*	*25*	*147^{1}*	*162*	*36*	*5.3*	*9.1*	*149*	*35%*	*.309*	*1.69*	*6.11*	*6.78*	*-1.5*				

Comparables: T.J. House, Tyler Chatwood, Carlos Carrasco

Franklin is a big kid from a tiny town very close to the Florida-Alabama state line, and the Rays have taken his development slow as a Sunday afternoon there in Paxton. However, Franklin is the kind of prospect who (given good health) could push someone into accelerating his timetable. He already throws in the mid-90s, with a power curveball that flashes the potential to be a plus pitch. He needs a whole lot of refinement and time to build up his workload, but he could bloom into a serious weapon over the next several years. Of course, given his particular skill set and the trends of pitcher usage that govern the modern game, it's impossible to project what kind of weapon he will be.

Brent Honeywell RHP Born: 03/31/95 Age: 23 Bats: R Throws: R Height: 6'2" Weight: 180 Origin: Round 2, 2014 Draft (#72 overall)

YEAR	TEAM	LVL	AGE	W	L	SV	G	GS	IP	H	HR	BB/9	K/9	K	GB%	BABIP	WHIP	ERA	DRA	WARP	MPH	CMD	PWR	STM
2015	BGR	A	20	4	4	0	12	12	65	53	3	1.7	10.5	76	39%	.299	1.00	2.91	1.52	2.8				
2015	PCH	A+	20	5	2	0	12	12	65^{1}	57	2	2.1	7.3	53	49%	.291	1.10	3.44	2.87	1.7				
2016	PCH	A+	21	4	1	0	10	10	56	43	5	1.8	10.3	64	33%	.279	0.96	2.41	1.30	2.7				
2016	MNT	AA	21	3	2	0	10	10	59^{1}	51	4	2.1	8.0	53	29%	.287	1.10	2.28	2.32	2.0				
2017	MNT	AA	22	1	1	0	2	2	13	4	1	2.8	13.8	20	45%	.158	0.62	2.08	2.06	0.5				
2017	DUR	AAA	22	12	8	0	24	24	123^{2}	130	11	2.3	11.1	152	42%	.366	1.30	3.64	2.20	4.7				
2018	*TBA*	*MLB*	*23*	*6*	*6*	*0*	*18*	*18*	*95*	*89*	*14*	*3.2*	*9.9*	*104*	*37%*	*.299*	*1.30*	*3.76*	*4.34*	*1.2*				
2019	*TBA*	*MLB*	*24*	*9*	*9*	*0*	*27*	*27*	*163^{2}*	*145*	*24*	*2.8*	*10.1*	*185*	*37%*	*.292*	*1.20*	*3.75*	*4.16*	*2.4*				

Breakout: 28% Improve: 47% Collapse: 8% Attrition: 21% MLB: 65% *Comparables: Marcus Stroman, Jeremy Hellickson, Matt Harvey*

If you were going to describe Honeywell's personality, "screwball" is not one of the words on which you would land. He's extraordinarily brash, sure not only that he has the stuff to dominate opposing hitters but that he knows the game and himself better than anyone else could. Like his signature scroogie, he gets that from his father and his uncle, both former pro pitchers. Alas, it's the screwballs who figure out early how to go along to get along. People like Honeywell tend to butt heads with authority on their first couple of direct encounters with it, and Honeywell had Mellencampian luck in that matchup in 2017. Stranded in Durham as the Rays missed the playoffs, Honeywell got suspended late in the season for an unspecified violation, but otherwise did everything possible (including some unwelcome, public self-promotion) to force his way to the majors. Some time early in 2018, he'll finally get there, and that well-earned arrogance will join his mid-90s heat and that screwball on the list of reasons the rest of the league is in trouble.

Chih-Wei Hu RHP Born: 11/04/93 Age: 24 Bats: R Throws: R Height: 6'0" Weight: 220 Origin: International Free Agent, 2012

YEAR	TEAM	LVL	AGE	W	L	SV	G	GS	IP	H	HR	BB/9	K/9	K	GB%	BABIP	WHIP	ERA	DRA	WARP	MPH	CMD	PWR	STM
2015	FTM	A+	21	5	3	0	15	15	84^{2}	79	5	2.0	7.8	73	40%	.303	1.16	2.44	3.78	1.3				
2015	PCH	A+	21	0	3	1	5	4	18^{1}	23	1	3.9	9.8	20	55%	.407	1.69	7.36	3.85	0.3				
2016	MNT	AA	22	7	8	0	24	24	142^{2}	128	7	2.3	6.8	107	44%	.283	1.15	2.59	3.39	2.9				
2017	DUR	AAA	23	4	1	2	31	4	61^{2}	59	9	1.8	8.3	57	46%	.292	1.15	3.06	2.94	1.6				
2017	TBA	MLB	23	1	1	0	6	0	10	5	2	3.6	8.1	9	37%	.120	0.90	2.70	3.99	0.1	95.2			41
2018	*TBA*	*MLB*	*24*	*2*	*2*	*0*	*40*	*0*	*42^{2}*	*39*	*5*	*3.2*	*8.7*	*41*	*42%*	*.286*	*1.23*	*3.71*	*4.24*	*0.4*	*95.0*			*42*
2019	*TBA*	*MLB*	*25*	*3*	*1*	*0*	*59*	*0*	*62^{2}*	*53*	*8*	*3.3*	*9.5*	*66*	*42%*	*.279*	*1.20*	*3.73*	*4.14*	*0.7*	*94.7*			*43*

Breakout: 18% Improve: 31% Collapse: 13% Attrition: 28% MLB: 52% *Comparables: Zach McAllister, Matt Bowman, Rudy Owens*

Acquired in what sure felt like a something-for-nothing swap with the Twins in 2015, Hu progressed quickly for the Rays once they figured out that he was better suited to relief. He has a four-pitch mix, but not all four of the pitches are good and they're all thrown in a pretty tight velocity band. His slider (the only breaking ball in the mix) is a whole lot more like a cutter than one of those Frisbee things. His stuff plays up in short bursts, too: His fastball gains an edge it otherwise lacks and can miss bats. He may still be asked to flex into starting roles on occasion, and certainly has a chance to be among the league's bumper crop of young relievers capable of going two or three innings in an outing, but he's found a permanent home in the bullpen.

Dan Jennings LHP Born: 04/17/87 Age: 31 Bats: L Throws: L Height: 6'3" Weight: 210 Origin: Round 9, 2008 Draft (#268 overall)

YEAR	TEAM	LVL	AGE	W	L	SV	G	GS	IP	H	HR	BB/9	K/9	K	GB%	BABIP	WHIP	ERA	DRA	WARP	MPH	CMD	PWR	STM
2015	CHA	MLB	28	2	3	0	53	0	56^{1}	55	3	3.8	7.3	46	65%	.304	1.40	3.99	3.55	0.8	95.0	55	47	46
2016	CHA	MLB	29	4	3	1	64	0	60^{2}	57	1	4.2	6.8	46	56%	.309	1.40	2.08	5.01	0.0	93.3	42	45	48
2017	CHA	MLB	30	3	1	0	48	0	44^{1}	35	6	3.9	7.7	38	60%	.242	1.22	3.45	4.64	0.3	93.4	47	39	52
2017	TBA	MLB	30	0	0	0	29	0	18^{1}	18	2	5.9	6.4	13	67%	.291	1.64	3.44	4.35	0.2	93.7	47	39	52
2018	*TBA*	*MLB*	*31*	*3*	*3*	*3*	*56*	*0*	*58*	*56*	*5*	*4.3*	*7.9*	*52*	*56%*	*.296*	*1.43*	*3.98*	*4.46*	*0.4*	*92.9*	*47*	*43*	*49*
2019	*TBA*	*MLB*	*32*	*2*	*1*	*2*	*44*	*0*	*46^{1}*	*45*	*5*	*4.5*	*7.9*	*40*	*56%*	*.299*	*1.48*	*4.22*	*4.67*	*0.3*	*92.3*	*45*	*41*	*49*

Breakout: 30% Improve: 46% Collapse: 26% Attrition: 16% MLB: 88% *Comparables: Jared Hughes, Burke Badenhop, Matt Albers*

As Jennings has found increased feel for his sinker and four-seamer (and better learned when to throw which), he's become less vulnerable to right-handed hitters. His stuff has declined a bit over the last two seasons, though, and he's had to ramp up his slider usage into an uncomfortable range for him, right around 50 percent. Never a control specialist, he's now bordering on getting himself into trouble every time he takes the mound. He's inducing more groundballs than ever, but (as tends to happen when a ground-ball guy gets more extreme) hitters are doing more damage when they do elevate against him.

Andrew Kittredge RHP Born: 03/17/90 Age: 28 Bats: R Throws: R Height: 6'1" Weight: 200 Origin: Round 45, 2008 Draft (#1360 overall)

YEAR	TEAM	LVL	AGE	W	L	SV	G	GS	IP	H	HR	BB/9	K/9	K	GB%	BABIP	WHIP	ERA	DRA	WARP	MPH	CMD	PWR	STM
2015	WTN	AA	25	2	1	0	15	1	32^{2}	29	1	3.0	8.5	31	51%	.308	1.22	3.03	2.37	0.9				
2015	TAC	AAA	25	0	1	0	21	2	42^{1}	46	5	3.8	6.2	29	34%	.304	1.51	5.31	4.96	0.0				
2016	WTN	AA	26	1	1	0	14	4	34	37	0	2.6	9.8	37	44%	.374	1.38	3.44	2.08	1.1				
2016	TAC	AAA	26	2	2	7	23	1	38	39	5	2.1	11.1	47	41%	.337	1.26	3.55	2.01	1.3				
2017	DUR	AAA	27	6	1	2	41	2	68^{1}	49	2	2.1	10.3	78	54%	.278	0.95	1.45	1.15	3.1				
2017	TBA	MLB	27	0	1	0	15	0	15^{1}	13	2	3.5	8.2	14	50%	.250	1.24	1.76	4.91	0.0	96.0	34	33	50
2018	*TBA*	*MLB*	*28*	*2*	*2*	*0*	*45*	*0*	*48*	*47*	*6*	*3.7*	*8.8*	*47*	*44%*	*.304*	*1.41*	*3.96*	*4.45*	*0.4*	*95.4*	*34*	*33*	*50*
2019	*TBA*	*MLB*	*29*	*2*	*1*	*0*	*45*	*0*	*48*	*48*	*6*	*3.6*	*8.6*	*46*	*44%*	*.305*	*1.40*	*4.10*	*4.54*	*0.4*	*94.9*	*34*	*33*	*50*

Breakout: 9% Improve: 14% Collapse: 13% Attrition: 21% MLB: 32% *Comparables: Mickey Storey, R.J. Swindle, Jess Todd*

Some 607 pitchers logged at least 10 innings in 2017. Of that group, Kittredge threw his slider more often than anyone else. He went to the slider 72 percent of the time. He threw a slider more often than the Seattle Mariners won during the 2001 regular season. He threw it more often than any pitcher who tossed at least 100 innings threw a fastball. This is the change that made Kittredge a viable option in relief, at least as a bridge arm: He just started throwing his best pitch all the time.

Matt Krook LHP Born: 10/21/94 Age: 23 Bats: L Throws: L Height: 6'4" Weight: 225 Origin: Round 4, 2016 Draft (#125 overall)

YEAR	TEAM	LVL	AGE	W	L	SV	G	GS	IP	H	HR	BB/9	K/9	K	GB%	BABIP	WHIP	ERA	DRA	WARP	MPH	CMD	PWR	STM
2016	SLO	A-	21	1	3	0	11	10	35	35	2	8.5	10.0	39	73%	.347	1.94	6.17	4.59	0.3				
2017	SJO	A+	22	4	9	0	25	17	91^{1}	75	4	6.5	10.3	105	66%	.298	1.54	5.12	2.44	2.9				
2018	*TBA*	*MLB*	*23*	*3*	*6*	*0*	*24*	*14*	*67^{2}*	*62*	*11*	*8.7*	*10.0*	*75*	*53%*	*.296*	*1.88*	*6.24*	*6.87*	*-1.0*				
2019	*TBA*	*MLB*	*24*	*5*	*7*	*0*	*33*	*21*	*149*	*139*	*18*	*4.5*	*8.5*	*141*	*53%*	*.313*	*1.43*	*4.26*	*5.16*	*0.5*				

Breakout: 5% Improve: 9% Collapse: 4% Attrition: 8% MLB: 15% *Comparables: Matt Albers, Justin Wilson, Matt Maloney*

Krook grew up in the Bay Area and went to high school in San Francisco before injury and wildness sent his pitching career off the rails. The left-hander's background and the Giants' reputation for mending mangled arms made their fourth-round union an obvious draft-day match. A year and change after leaving the University of Oregon, Krook found his niche in the High-A bullpen, striking out 25 while permitting just seven hits and seven walks in 17 2/3 innings after a midyear move to relief. Krook's bowling-ball sinker gained a tick in short bursts, but it was his two breaking balls that made the biggest strides, flashing plus or better with improved execution and sharper bite. He now looks the part of a potential late-inning weapon, a terror for lefties, with the stamina and stuff to get more than three outs.

Brendan McKay LHP Born: 12/18/95 Age: 22 Bats: L Throws: L Height: 6'2" Weight: 212 Origin: Round 1, 2017 Draft (#4 overall)

YEAR	TEAM	LVL	AGE	W	L	SV	G	GS	IP	H	HR	BB/9	K/9	K	GB%	BABIP	WHIP	ERA	DRA	WARP	MPH	CMD	PWR	STM
2017	HUD	A-	21	1	0	0	6	6	20	10	3	2.2	9.4	21	53%	.159	0.75	1.80	1.83	0.8				
2018	*No projection*																							
2019	*No projection*																							

McKay is a left-handed starting pitcher prospect, but he's also a first-base prospect. The Rays made it abundantly clear that they intend to let him try both hitting and pitching his way to the majors. There will be hurdles aplenty. McKay's stuff backed up as a pitcher late in his collegiate campaign at Louisville, a problem several scouts ascribed to fatigue associated with playing first base between starts. In college, starters pitch just once a week, but the traditional role of a pro starter is to go every five days. The fatigue effect could be moderated by playing designated hitter instead of first base, but it would still be there. That's not to mention the challenge of honing each skill sufficiently, without being able to devote full focus to either, nor the increased injury risk that feels inevitable. Still, this might be the most interesting lab experiment in baseball right now.

Jake Odorizzi RHP Born: 03/27/90 Age: 28 Bats: R Throws: R Height: 6'2" Weight: 190 Origin: Round 1, 2008 Draft (#32 overall)

YEAR	TEAM	LVL	AGE	W	L	SV	G	GS	IP	H	HR	BB/9	K/9	K	GB%	BABIP	WHIP	ERA	DRA	WARP	MPH	CMD	PWR	STM
2015	TBA	MLB	25	9	9	0	28	28	169^{1}	149	18	2.4	8.0	150	40%	.271	1.15	3.35	2.85	4.5	93.6	57	41	70
2016	TBA	MLB	26	10	6	0	33	33	187^{2}	170	29	2.6	8.0	166	38%	.271	1.19	3.69	4.18	2.5	94.1	57	48	80
2017	TBA	MLB	27	10	8	0	28	28	143^{1}	117	30	3.8	8.0	127	32%	.227	1.24	4.14	4.70	1.4	93.4	54	38	67
2018	*TBA*	*MLB*	*28*	*9*	*10*	*0*	*25*	*25*	*150*	*144*	*26*	*3.4*	*8.4*	*141*	*38%*	*.283*	*1.31*	*4.54*	*5.20*	*0.3*	*93.2*	*56*	*43*	*73*
2019	*TBA*	*MLB*	*29*	*10*	*12*	*0*	*31*	*31*	*193^{1}*	*180*	*34*	*3.2*	*8.6*	*185*	*38%*	*.277*	*1.29*	*4.54*	*5.04*	*1.2*	*92.9*	*56*	*43*	*73*

Breakout: 18% Improve: 55% Collapse: 19% Attrition: 5% MLB: 89% *Comparables: Homer Bailey, Chris Tillman, Danny Duffy*

Ever the tease, Odorizzi had two or three dazzling starts in September, partially redeeming a poor season and giving him something on which to build. He leaned less on his patented pairing of high fastballs and low splitters, developing his cutter and using it down the stretch to great effect. Now the question is whether he can sustain any of it. One of baseball's most extreme fly-ball pitchers, Odorizzi isn't built for the modern environment in which every fly ball is dangerous. He doesn't have a true breaking ball that can keep hitters guessing, and it's too easy to tell the fastball and the splitter apart out of his hand. If Odorizzi wants to fulfill his former promise, he's at least one big adjustment away.

Austin Pruitt RHP Born: 08/31/89 Age: 28 Bats: R Throws: R Height: 5'10" Weight: 180 Origin: Round 9, 2013 Draft (#278 overall)

YEAR	TEAM	LVL	AGE	W	L	SV	G	GS	IP	H	HR	BB/9	K/9	K	GB%	BABIP	WHIP	ERA	DRA	WARP	MPH	CMD	PWR	STM
2015	MNT	AA	25	10	7	0	26	26	160	160	3	2.1	6.9	122	49%	.320	1.24	3.09	2.45	5.1				
2016	DUR	AAA	26	8	11	0	28	28	162^{2}	166	21	1.5	8.2	149	45%	.316	1.19	3.76	2.02	6.2				
2017	DUR	AAA	27	0	1	1	9	4	24^{2}	17	2	0.7	12.0	33	58%	.273	0.77	2.55	1.34	1.1				
2017	TBA	MLB	27	7	5	1	30	8	83	103	11	2.4	7.2	66	46%	.345	1.51	5.31	4.42	0.9	93.0	62	34	53
2018	*TBA*	*MLB*	*28*	*4*	*4*	*0*	*30*	*10*	*71*	*72*	*10*	*2.9*	*7.8*	*62*	*45%*	*.299*	*1.35*	*4.18*	*4.72*	*0.5*	*92.4*	*62*	*34*	*53*
2019	*TBA*	*MLB*	*29*	*7*	*7*	*0*	*60*	*18*	*150*	*154*	*20*	*2.7*	*8.1*	*135*	*45%*	*.307*	*1.32*	*4.00*	*4.44*	*1.6*	*92.0*	*62*	*34*	*53*

Breakout: 22% Improve: 41% Collapse: 14% Attrition: 32% MLB: 61% *Comparables: Andrew Albers, Rick VandenHurk, Chris Narveson*

Our advanced pitching stats are thoroughly enamored of Pruitt, from his substantial minor-league track record through his (otherwise forgettable, though serviceable) rookie season in MLB. The eye test doesn't match that level of enthusiasm, but there's something here. Pruitt is one kind of pitcher (a pure fastball/slider guy, where the slider isn't good enough to carry the weight) against fellow righties, and another, more complete one against lefties. His slow, man-feeling-the-temperature-of-the-hot-tub-by-swinging-one-leg-in-first delivery adds deception, but maybe more so for lefties than for righties. He looks like a viable, useful swingman, but unless the slider gets a lot better he may never be more than that.

Sergio Romo RHP Born: 03/04/83 Age: 35 Bats: R Throws: R Height: 5'11" Weight: 185 Origin: Round 28, 2005 Draft (#852 overall)

YEAR	TEAM	LVL	AGE	W	L	SV	G	GS	IP	H	HR	BB/9	K/9	K	GB%	BABIP	WHIP	ERA	DRA	WARP	MPH	CMD	PWR	STM
2015	SFN	MLB	32	0	5	2	70	0	57^{1}	51	3	1.6	11.1	71	47%	.331	1.06	2.98	2.68	1.4	89.4	78	8	48
2016	SFN	MLB	33	1	0	4	40	0	30^{2}	26	5	2.1	9.7	33	39%	.292	1.08	2.64	4.69	0.1	87.8	63	10	35
2017	LAN	MLB	34	1	1	0	30	0	25	23	7	4.3	11.2	31	35%	.276	1.40	6.12	2.80	0.7	87.9	59	0	45
2017	TBA	MLB	34	2	0	0	25	0	30^{2}	19	2	2.1	8.2	28	40%	.218	0.85	1.47	2.68	0.8	87.4	59	0	45
2018	*TBA*	*MLB*	*35*	*2*	*1*	*1*	*42*	*0*	44^{2}	*39*	*7*	*3.6*	*9.7*	*48*	*40%*	*.279*	*1.29*	*4.48*	*4.97*	*0.1*	*87.0*	*64*	*4*	*42*
2019	*TBA*	*MLB*	*36*	*2*	*1*	*1*	*45*	*0*	40^{1}	*37*	*7*	*3.6*	*9.5*	*42*	*40%*	*.284*	*1.32*	*4.42*	*4.91*	*0.1*	*86.2*	*60*	*3*	*40*

Breakout: 21% Improve: 45% Collapse: 29% Attrition: 13% MLB: 89% *Comparables: Eddie Guardado, Rich Gossage, Francisco Rodriguez*

Romo's Los Angeles homecoming turned from dream to nightmare, but he rediscovered his command after a trade to Tampa Bay. He's never going to be able or willing to pound the strike zone. What he needs to be able to do is keep opponents off-balance, and he was much better at that after increasing his sinker and changeup usage down the stretch. When he wants to be, he can be a three- or four-pitch pitcher. When he falls in love with his slider (admittedly, an easy thing to do), he gets into trouble. If he loses much more velocity, the bottom could fall out on him, but for now Romo still has a number of ways to get right-handed hitters out.

Jaime Schultz RHP Born: 06/20/91 Age: 26 Bats: R Throws: R Height: 5'10" Weight: 200 Origin: Round 14, 2013 Draft (#428 overall)

YEAR	TEAM	LVL	AGE	W	L	SV	G	GS	IP	H	HR	BB/9	K/9	K	GB%	BABIP	WHIP	ERA	DRA	WARP	MPH	CMD	PWR	STM
2015	MNT	AA	24	9	5	0	27	27	135	105	11	6.0	11.2	168	42%	.306	1.44	3.67	3.72	2.2				
2016	DUR	AAA	25	5	7	0	27	27	130^{2}	113	12	4.7	11.2	163	43%	.327	1.39	3.58	4.27	1.6				
2017	DUR	AAA	26	1	0	0	13	0	11^{2}	10	1	3.1	16.2	21	46%	.391	1.20	3.86	2.33	0.4				
2018	*TBA*	*MLB*	*27*	*1*	*1*	*0*	*20*	*0*	*21*	*17*	*3*	*4.9*	*11.9*	*28*	*43%*	*.294*	*1.33*	*3.61*	*4.15*	*0.2*				
2019	*TBA*	*MLB*	*28*	*3*	*1*	*0*	*58*	*0*	*61*	*48*	*8*	*4.5*	*12.3*	*84*	*43%*	*.296*	*1.28*	*3.55*	*3.94*	*0.9*				

Breakout: 22% Improve: 31% Collapse: 21% Attrition: 26% MLB: 58% *Comparables: Wilmer Font, Ariel Pena, Felix Pena*

Schultz is a quintessentially Rays story. He was very undersized and played high school ball in upstate New York, so he went undrafted. He then attended small-time High Point University in North Carolina, where the Rays (who scout the Southeast as hard as any team other than the Braves) found him and plucked him in the 14th round. He was already almost 22 when he signed; he remained (and remains even now) undersized; and he had major command issues for years. On the other hand, his stuff (and his strikeout rate) was very impressive. A groin injury severely shortened his 2017 and Schultz is now quite old for a rookie, but he's not without promise—especially as a one-inning reliever.

Blake Snell LHP Born: 12/04/92 Age: 25 Bats: L Throws: L Height: 6'4" Weight: 200 Origin: Round 1, 2011 Draft (#52 overall)

YEAR	TEAM	LVL	AGE	W	L	SV	G	GS	IP	H	HR	BB/9	K/9	K	GB%	BABIP	WHIP	ERA	DRA	WARP	MPH	CMD	PWR	STM
2015	PCH	A+	22	3	0	0	4	2	21	10	0	4.7	11.6	27	59%	.227	1.00	0.00	1.85	0.8				
2015	MNT	AA	22	6	2	0	12	12	68^{2}	45	5	3.8	10.4	79	48%	.260	1.08	1.57	2.56	2.1				
2015	DUR	AAA	22	6	2	0	9	9	44^{1}	29	2	2.6	11.6	57	55%	.276	0.95	1.83	1.67	1.8				
2016	DUR	AAA	23	3	5	0	12	12	63	56	4	4.0	12.9	90	51%	.356	1.33	3.29	1.78	2.6				
2016	TBA	MLB	23	6	8	0	19	19	89	93	5	5.2	9.9	98	39%	.356	1.62	3.54	4.84	0.5	96.2	44	49	70
2017	DUR	AAA	24	5	0	0	7	7	44	43	5	3.1	12.5	61	46%	.362	1.32	2.66	1.91	1.8				
2017	TBA	MLB	24	5	7	0	24	24	129^{1}	113	15	4.1	8.3	119	45%	.278	1.33	4.04	3.80	2.6	96.0	50	53	74
2018	*TBA*	*MLB*	*25*	*7*	*7*	*0*	*21*	*21*	111^{1}	*98*	*13*	*4.1*	*10.2*	*126*	*45%*	*.300*	*1.35*	*3.57*	*4.12*	*1.6*	*95.8*	*49*	*53*	*74*
2019	*TBA*	*MLB*	*26*	*10*	*9*	*0*	*29*	*29*	176^{2}	*153*	*19*	*3.9*	*10.9*	*213*	*45%*	*.308*	*1.30*	*3.41*	*3.78*	*3.2*	*95.6*	*49*	*53*	*74*

Breakout: 36% Improve: 67% Collapse: 17% Attrition: 18% MLB: 96% *Comparables: Drew Pomeranz, Matt Moore, Alex Cobb*

Among left-handed starters, only James Paxton has a higher perceived fastball velocity than Snell. Within the same group, only Rich Hill has a higher average fastball spin rate. Snell also has a filthy slider, a true out pitch he should throw more often. What he lacks, for now, is consistent command, and that comes from instability in his delivery. The problem begins as his motion does, because he just doesn't generate much power. He naturally strides closed, which is terrific for deception. Once that stride foot lands, though, he collapses his spine to the right and leans like he's taking the hairpin turn on an arcade motorcycle game. Add that change of direction to the lack of momentum and the result is often pitches left up, or pitches that never get to the outside corner to righties. Until he improves his posture at release point, he's going to battle inconsistency.

Lineouts

Hitters

HITTER	POS	TEAM	LVL	AGE	PA	R	2B	3B	HR	RBI	BB	K	SB	CS	AVG/OBP/SLG	TAv	VORP	BABIP	BRR	FRAA	WARP
Peter Bourjos	OF	TBA	MLB	30	203	27	9	3	5	15	12	53	5	4	.223/.272/.383	.242	1.6	.282	0.3	LF(41): -0.8, CF(37): -1.6	0.0
Curtis Casali	C	DUR	AAA	28	343	36	10	0	5	48	37	65	0	0	.263/.351/.347	.255	9.4	.320	-0.4	C(53): 0.7	1.0
	C	TBA	MLB	28	13	2	0	0	1	3	3	3	0	0	.333/.462/.667	.418	3.0	.333	0.3	C(8): 0.5	0.4
Danny Espinosa	MI	ANA	MLB	30	254	27	8	0	6	29	19	91	3	5	.162/.237/.276	.192	-11.5	.233	-0.5	2B(71): 1.3	-1.0
	MI	SEA	MLB	30	17	2	2	0	0	2	1	7	1	0	.188/.235/.313	.190	-0.5	.333	0.3	3B(3): 0.0, 1B(2): -0.2	0.0
	MI	TBA	MLB	30	24	1	0	0	0	0	1	11	0	0	.273/.333/.273	.220	-0.6	.545	-0.2	2B(6): -0.5, SS(2): 0.0	-0.1
Lucius Fox	SS	BGR	A	19	345	45	13	3	2	27	33	80	27	10	.278/.362/.361	.260	13.3	.371	0.2	SS(71): -3.8	1.0
	SS	PCH	A+	19	131	19	3	0	1	12	12	33	3	3	.235/.321/.287	.237	1.4	.317	-0.6	SS(29): 4.4	0.6
Ronaldo Hernandez	C	PRI	Rk	19	246	42	22	1	5	40	16	39	2	2	.332/.382/.507	.287	22.0	.379	2.5	C(43): 1.1	2.1
Micah Johnson	2B	GWN	AAA	26	155	19	6	3	1	15	18	38	6	4	.289/.377/.400	.284	8.7	.396	0.7	CF(16): -0.2, LF(12): -1.0	0.7
	2B	ATL	MLB	26	11	2	0	0	0	0	0	4	1	0	.200/.200/.200	.152	-1.7	.333	-0.7	LF(3): 0.1	-0.2
Kevin Padlo	3B	PCH	A+	20	259	28	13	3	6	34	35	60	4	5	.223/.324/.391	.273	9.7	.272	-1.5	3B(60): -1.1	0.9
Shane Peterson	OF	TBA	MLB	29	88	9	5	0	2	11	5	21	2	0	.253/.310/.392	.245	-0.1	.316	-0.6	LF(15): 1.6, RF(5): 1.0	0.2
	OF	DUR	AAA	29	300	39	19	3	12	40	11	63	10	0	.286/.313/.504	.286	16.9	.325	1.9	RF(36): 4.8, LF(33): -2.0	1.9
Adrian Rondon	3B	BGR	A	18	438	53	12	2	9	48	33	129	4	2	.221/.286/.330	.223	-2.7	.299	1.7	3B(90): -5.6	-0.9
Taylor Walls	MI	HUD	A-	20	197	22	9	0	1	21	29	53	5	4	.213/.330/.287	.248	6.0	.301	0.8	SS(42): 1.1	0.7
Joey Wendle	2B	NAS	AAA	27	510	67	29	8	8	54	19	82	13	4	.285/.327/.429	.278	25.7	.329	0.6	2B(82): -0.7, 3B(24): 6.3	3.0
	2B	OAK	MLB	27	14	3	1	0	1	5	1	3	0	0	.308/.357/.615	.308	1.0	.333	-0.2	2B(5): -0.5	0.0
Justin Williams	OF	MNT	AA	21	409	53	21	3	14	72	37	69	6	2	.301/.364/.489	.293	18.5	.334	-2.0	RF(80): -4.6, LF(7): 1.3	1.6
Kean Wong	2B	MNT	AA	22	49	5	1	0	0	4	3	9	3	0	.222/.271/.244	.192	-0.4	.278	1.6	3B(8): 0.1, 2B(2): 0.0	0.0
	2B	DUR	AAA	22	417	44	21	0	5	44	34	78	14	9	.265/.328/.361	.253	7.1	.321	-1.7	2B(90): 9.3, 3B(10): 0.3	1.6

If it hadn't been for injuries, **Peter Bourjos** might have been the next Gary Matthews Jr., but now even his once-great defense is nothing special. ⚾ **Curt Casali** lost all of his power at age 28, which really happens to all of us and it's just a matter of whether life hits you over the head with it or not. ⚾ No Democrat, no Cubs fan, not even any gorilla belonging to the Cincinnati Zoo longs for 2015 and 2016 like **Danny Espinosa**. ⚾ **Lucius Fox** has tools, money and a chance to play a small supporting role for the real heroes of some future championship team. ⚾ More than just a pretty rookie-ball stat line, **Ronaldo Hernandez** opened eyes both at and behind the plate, especially with his athleticism. ⚾ The public never really appreciates artists until they are gone, but at least we'll all have years to come of enjoying **Micah Johnson**'s Twitter feed. ⚾ A broken hand prevented **Kevin Padlo** from building on his strong 2016, but some potential remains if his power eventually returns. ⚾ Theoretically a good left-handed pinch-hit specialist, **Shane Peterson** probably also excelled as a paperboy and switchboard operator when he was young. ⚾ No longer a surefire shortstop, **Adrian Rondon** now has to see his offensive tools actualize a bit, or else he'll become a big-bonus bust. ⚾ Florida State product **Taylor Walls** works fine, workmanlike, torturous at-bats, but whether he can hit good pitchers when they come right at him remains to be seen. ⚾ **Joey Wendle** has now played three full seasons at Triple-A and posted OBPs of .323, .324 and .327. Calculate that out and he should be a solid major-league second baseman come 2049 or so. ⚾ The Rays' pro scouting operation is extensive and they lean on it hard. Players like **Justin Williams**, whom they got at age 19 when he was well below the radar, are why. ⚾ **Kean Wong** is bigger than his brother Kolten, but not stronger, faster or the owner of the same advanced hit tool.

Pitchers

PITCHER	TEAM	LVL	AGE	W	L	SV	G	GS	IP	H	HR	BB/9	K/9	K	GB%	BABIP	WHIP	ERA	DRA	WARP	MPH	CMD	PWR	STM
Blake Bivens	PCH	A+	21	2	3	0	10	10	52^{1}	58	4	2.9	7.9	46	49%	.338	1.43	3.78	4.18	0.7				
Genesis Cabrera	PCH	A+	20	4	5	0	13	12	69^{2}	45	3	3.2	7.8	60	39%	.230	1.00	2.84	3.52	1.4				
	MNT	AA	20	5	4	0	12	12	64^{2}	75	6	3.8	7.1	51	37%	.332	1.58	3.62	6.81	-1.3				
Diego Castillo	MNT	AA	23	1	3	8	21	0	29	20	1	2.2	9.9	32	61%	.250	0.93	1.86	1.68	1.1				
	DUR	AAA	23	3	2	7	30	1	42^{2}	38	2	2.7	12.2	58	40%	.353	1.20	3.38	2.00	1.5				
Yonny Chirinos	MNT	AA	23	1	0	0	4	4	27^{1}	22	5	1.3	6.9	21	58%	.233	0.95	2.63	3.18	0.7				
	DUR	AAA	23	12	5	0	23	22	141	116	10	1.4	7.7	120	52%	.270	0.98	2.74	1.63	6.2				
Adam Kolarek	DUR	AAA	28	3	4	2	41	0	43^{2}	37	0	3.3	9.5	46	74%	.311	1.21	1.65	1.22	1.9				
	TBA	MLB	28	1	0	0	12	0	8^{1}	9	2	4.3	4.3	4	61%	.269	1.56	6.48	4.10	0.1	91.9			46
John Lamb	SLC	AAA	26	6	3	0	13	13	70^{1}	85	9	3.3	6.1	48	45%	.339	1.58	5.37	6.70	-0.8				
Michael Mercado	RAY	Rk	18	0	0	0	8	8	21^{1}	21	1	1.7	5.9	14	41%	.299	1.17	1.69	5.33	0.2				
Jose Mujica	PCH	A+	21	1	0	0	2	2	11^{1}	11	1	0.8	3.2	4	40%	.256	1.06	3.18	4.99	0.0				
	MNT	AA	21	13	8	0	25	25	154^{1}	128	18	2.6	5.0	86	42%	.233	1.11	3.03	4.08	2.0				
Vidal Nuno	BAL	MLB	29	0	1	0	12	0	14^{2}	23	7	6.1	8.0	13	43%	.340	2.25	10.43	7.26	-0.3	91.3	72	20	34
	NOR	AAA	29	1	3	0	19	0	26^{2}	24	1	2.4	10.1	30	49%	.319	1.16	4.05	2.64	0.8				
Chaz Roe	ATL	MLB	30	0	0	0	3	0	2	3	0	9.0	4.5	1	67%	.333	2.50	9.00	4.92	0.0	94.6			27
	DUR	AAA	30	0	3	4	17	0	21	18	1	2.1	15.0	35	43%	.370	1.10	3.00	1.50	0.9				
	TBA	MLB	30	0	0	0	9	0	8^{2}	4	1	3.1	12.5	12	50%	.200	0.81	1.04	3.26	0.2	94.1			27
Ryne Stanek	DUR	AAA	25	3	0	8	37	0	44^{2}	26	0	3.2	12.1	60	40%	.268	0.94	1.21	3.00	1.1				
	TBA	MLB	25	0	0	0	21	0	20	26	6	5.4	13.1	29	33%	.417	1.90	5.85	4.52	0.1	100.0	49	79	49
Drew Strotman	HUD	A-	20	2	3	0	11	7	50^{2}	29	0	1.6	7.5	42	60%	.216	0.75	1.78	1.58	2.1				
Hunter Wood	TBA	MLB	23	0	0	0	1	0	0^{1}	0	0	0.0	0.0	0	0%	.000	0.00	0.00	1.71	0.0	89.7			61

PITCHER	TEAM	LVL	AGE	W	L	SV	G	GS	IP	H	HR	BB/9	K/9	K	GB%	BABIP	WHIP	ERA	DRA	WARP	MPH	CMD	PWR	STM
	MNT	AA	23	4	4	0	12	12	70	68	7	3.1	8.7	68	38%	.319	1.31	4.76	4.50	0.6				
	DUR	AAA	23	3	1	0	19	6	53[1]	54	8	3.4	7.9	47	46%	.299	1.39	4.39	4.35	0.7				
Ryan Yarbrough	DUR	AAA	25	13	6	0	26	26	157[1]	144	20	2.2	9.1	159	47%	.296	1.16	3.43	2.30	5.8				
Mikey York	HUD	A-	21	4	1	0	8	8	44	28	2	1.6	7.6	37	34%	.220	0.82	0.82	3.14	1.1				
	BGR	A	21	1	1	0	3	3	17	7	1	1.6	8.5	16	42%	.154	0.59	1.06	2.82	0.5				

Blake Bivens has fewer than 250 competitive innings pitched in three-and-a-half pro seasons, but his stuff is big-league caliber. Although his first half was a revelation, if **Genesis Cabrera** can't put up better numbers at Double-A he'll never make his minor-league exodus and land a job in the big leagues. The Rays' minor-league reliever of the year, **Diego Castillo** blew through both hitters and the upper minors, striking out 90 in just 71 2/3 innings between Montgomery and Durham. The hefty right-hander is now knocking on the doorstep of the majors. Even if the projection isn't more than a back-end starter, **Yonny Chirinos** stands a good chance at more than a handful of starts in Tampa this year on the back of his strong command and a slider/splitter combo that can miss just enough bats. **Nathan Eovaldi** will spend the spring trying to show that his second Tommy John surgery didn't rob him of his elite velocity. Elbow issues kept **Kevin Gadea** off the mound for all of 2017, putting an end to any notion that he'll start, but he has real promise in a bullpen role. Lefty **Adam Kolarek** can induce a ground ball from a fellow lefty with the best of them, but teams generally look for pitchers who can also do at least one other thing. After **John Lamb** spent some time as a highly touted prospect in the Royals' organization, the Angels were hoping for a little more lion from the southpaw, but got more injuries and a drug suspension instead. High school arm **Michael Mercado** is light enough to be blown away by a stiff breeze, but probably too skinny even for the wind to catch. If this era just has too many dang strikeouts for your taste, **Jose Mujica** is the pitching prospect for you, as he barely struck out a batter every other inning in 27 starts across High-A and Double-A. **Vidal Nuno** seemed like an ideal fit for the Orioles: a cheap, strike-throwing lefty who could spot start or mop up. Instead, he couldn't find the strike zone, gave up runs in eight of his 12 appearances and cleared waivers in June. Slider/sinker artist **Chaz Roe** occasionally snaps off a GIF-worthy breaking ball that leaves you wondering how anyone hits him, but hasn't established himself as a big-league reliever. With elite velocity but (still, forever) not much else worth writing home about, **Ryne Stanek** looks more like a Quadruple-A relief ace every day. **Drew Strotman** mostly pitched in relief in college, but is getting a chance (at least early on) to start as a pro. If nothing else, his fastball command is there. If ever a pitcher were born to pitch to contact, it's **Hunter Wood**, but he'll need to either miss more lumber or pound the bottom of the zone more to have any impact in the majors. Lanky lefty **Ryan Yarbrough** made the progress he needed to make with his breaking ball (more a slider than a curve these days) and might make it as a starter after all. Quietly, Las Vegas is becoming an unlikely wellspring of baseball talent, the way Chicago's south suburbs, rural Georgia and western Pennsylvania have been in the past. **Mikey York** is the kind of unlikely prospect those places eventually produce.

LEAGUE LEADERS 2017

MLB Saves – Alex Colome, 47

TEXAS RANGERS

Essay by Levi Weaver

Player comments by Meg Rowley, Craig Goldstein and BP staff

Philosophy and science must necessarily become more complicated upon the introduction of new data and information, and must then necessarily become more simplified if they wish to communicate those findings to a populace that mostly just wants to exist without needless existential thought-wrestling.

In the late 18th century, that information complication allowed us to better understand how vision works. What was once an easy answer ("*I see things with my eyes. If I poke out my eyes, I am blind.*") was made more complicated by the introduction of more information: Light reflects off the surface of an object and through the cornea, the lens pulls the light into focus and the retina sends an electrical signal through the optic nerves to the brain, which interprets those signals into a database of previously received signals, matching them up like an instantaneous game of "Go Fish." Does this signal mean food? A loved one? A rock?

As the parabola returns from complication back to simplification, one modern philosopher has posited an interesting—if somewhat controversial—answer to the questions in the preceding paragraph. Food? Loved one? Rock?

"No," suggests Rougned Odor. "It is a curveball, and I have already begun to swing at it."

Like any philosophical revolution, more than one mind has arrived at this conclusion. In 2017, if you were a Texas Ranger with more than 400 plate appearances, you struck out at least 100 times. There were no exceptions.[1]

But Cyrenaic Odorist philosophy is less a Texas-factional heresy and more the indication of a continued sea change: There were 40,104 strikeouts across MLB in 2017, shattering the old record of 38,982, set way back in ... 2016. That broke the previous record from ... 2015. In fact, if you want to find a season in which the total number of strikeouts was *not* an all-time record, you would have to scroll all the way back to 2005, when a mere 30,644 were entered into scorecards across time and space.

One particularly capitalist way of looking at the economy of Three True Outcomes is that home runs are what you desire to attain. If you want more home runs, you must swing harder, and in doing so, you will almost inevitably strike out more often, so you might say that strikeouts are the price you pay for home runs. Walks, then, are the labor you do to gain that currency. In this line of thinking, you could say that Cincinnati's Joey Votto—who hit 36 home runs, paid a mere 83 strikeouts for the acquisitions and worked an absurd 134 walks—is quite frugal.

Nine-hundred-and-fifty miles to the south and west, another Joey (Gallo) hit 41 home runs, paid 196 strikeouts for them and walked a still-above-average 75 times. In this analogy, Gallo is your friend who has a very nice car and house, but who could stand to hold out for a better deal once in awhile.

Back to Odor: With his 30 home runs, 162 strikeouts and just 32

RANGERS PROSPECTUS

2017 W-L: 78-84, 3rd in AL West

Pythag	.490	15th	B-Age	28.4	*17th*
RS/G	4.93	9th	P-Age	29.0	*21st*
RA/G	5.04	21st	Salary	$165.3M	*8th*
TAv	.252	25th	M$/MW	$5.1M	*6th*
TAv-P	.257	11th	DL Days	1133	*18th*
FIP	4.85	27th	$ on DL	21%	*25th*
DER	.711	8th			

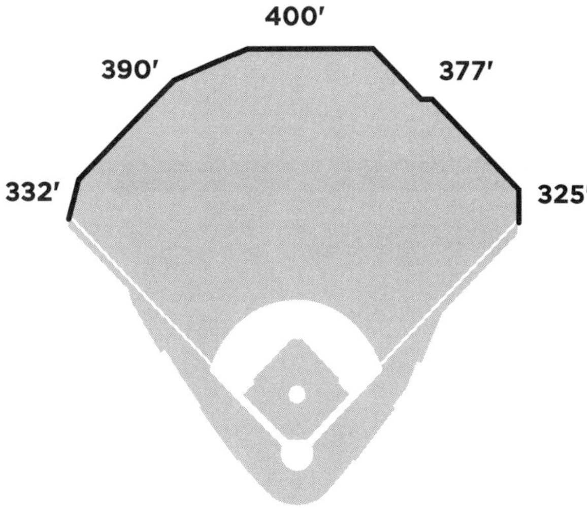

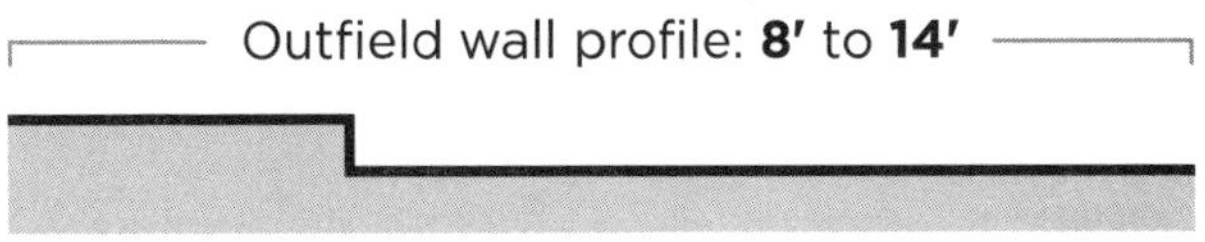

Three-Year Park Factors

Runs	Runs/RH	Runs/LH	HR/RH	HR/LH
106	105	107	103	103

Top Hitter WARP	5.4 Elvis Andrus
Top Pitcher WARP	3.9 Yu Darvish
Top Prospect	Leody Taveras

2017 Hit List Ranking

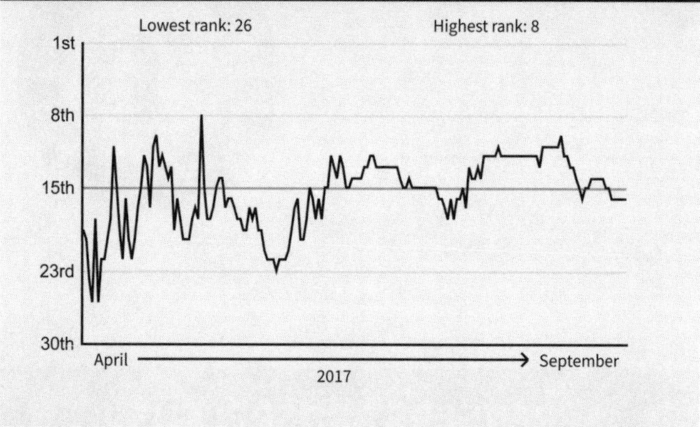

Committed Payroll (in millions)

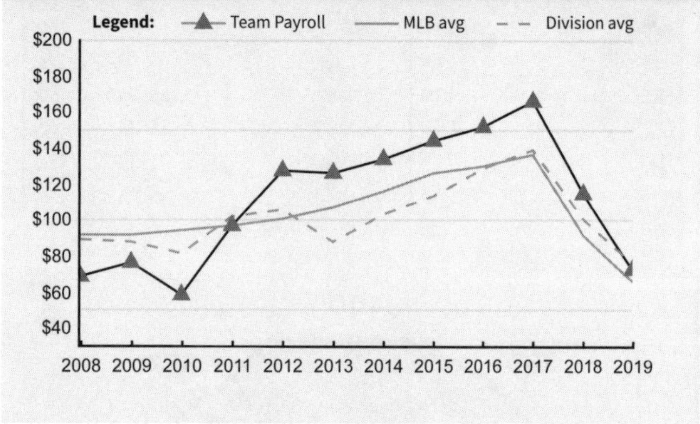

Farm System Ranking

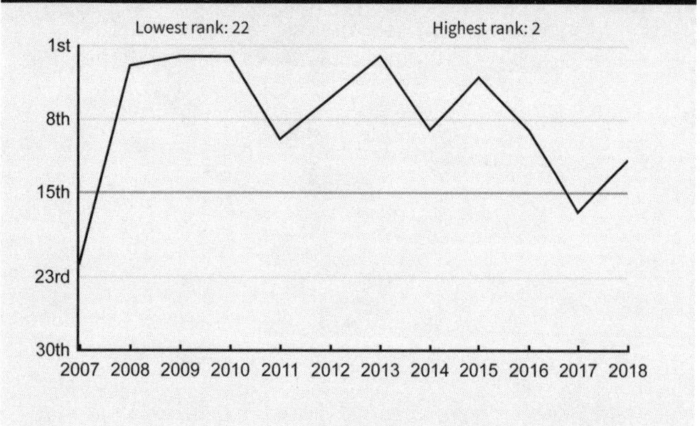

Personnel

President, General Manager
Jon Daniels

Manager
Jeff Banister

BP Alumni
Jesse Behr

walks (a career high, it should be noted), he is the guy who also has a nice house and sweet car, but who is *swimming* in debt. And while it can be really valuable to have *a* Joey Gallo on the team (Aaron Judge, for example, extravagantly splashed out 208 strikeouts for his 52 home runs, but worked 127 walks for the capital), you can't build the whole plane out of Joey Gallos.

With that in mind, marvel at this statistic: Texas had *eight* players with 100-plus strikeouts in 2017. Not only was this an MLB high for the year—no team, not even the major-league-leading Brewers, with 1,571 strikeouts, had more than six—it was a standalone[2] all-time MLB record.

Strikeouts, of course, are not the only one of the Three True Outcomes to see an upward trend. As baseball spent more strikeouts, they earned more home runs. There were 6,105 home runs in 2017, nearly 400 more than the old record of 5,693 (set in 2000). As with strikeouts, the 2017 Rangers also outpaced the world in their even distribution of power, boasting nine players with at least 17 home runs. Not only was this an MLB high for the year—not even the league-leading Yankees, with 241 home runs, had more than eight—it was a standalone[3] all-time MLB record.

But while the Rangers evenly distributed the lavish acquisitions (home runs) and the smothering debt (strikeouts), they only had three players with 50 or more walks. That number tied them with seven other teams for 14th in baseball (the Dodgers led baseball with six). By ramping up their homers (237, third in MLB) and strikeouts (1,493, fourth), but lagging behind in walks (544, 13th), the Rangers are a microcosm of an unhealthy trend in MLB, which saw its record-setting home-run and strikeout totals accompanied by just 15,829 free passes in 2017. That *is* the 12th-highest total in history (the record is 18,237 walks, set in 2000), but it is still an unsustainable budget.

Debt and philosophy analogies aside, it should be noted that the 2017 Rangers economy also suffered a couple additional unforeseen challenges.

First, there was the natural disaster: The bullpen was expected to be a strength, but Jake Diekman missed most of the year after having his colon removed, Keone Kela started the year at Triple-A due to a behavioral issue, Sam Dyson landed in San Francisco due to an ancient witch's curse that turned his sinkers into home runs and Matt Bush was unable to hold fast to the closer role, so Alex "Karate Kid" Claudio eventually found himself racking up saves.

Additionally, there was a treason of sorts: Jonathan Lucroy went from being an elite defensive catcher to one who inexplicably forgot how to frame pitches. Add it all up, and the result was a disappointing 78-84, which—thanks to an American League that seemed hell-bent on hearing both sides of the win-loss argument—was good enough to keep Texas in the wild card race until late September.

With the stench of disappointment still lingering in our nostrils, let's review the questions the Rangers had at the beginning of the 2017 season and the answers to those questions, plus some new questions for 2018.

Questions from 2017

The Rotation

Yu Darvish and Cole Hamels—2016 ALDS notwithstanding—still provided a dangerous one-two punch, but would this be the year Martin Perez finally stopped being *so* Martin Perez and became *Martin Perez*? Beyond that, barring some breakout year from the Chi Chi Gonzalez, Nick Martinez, Mike Hauschild, A.J. Griffin, Dillon Gee crew, the best hope the Rangers had was that they could just nickname the back half of the rotation "Nicole Bradford" and hand it over to its Two Dads[4] (newly arrived former Padres Tyson Ross and Andrew Cashner) assuming they were healthy enough to throw a baseball at all.

Answer

Cashner was actually pretty successful, enduring an early lack of run support to yield a 3.40 ERA in 167 innings, despite a 4.61 FIP, a 1.320 WHIP and just 86 strikeouts. Ross, on the other hand, was released on September 12 to make room for Willie Calhoun, the centerpiece of the trade that sent Darvish to the Dodgers. Miguel Gonzalez started five games for the Rangers. Austin Bibens-Dirkx started six. On the upside, Perez figured something out in August (he says he was tipping pitches) and was mostly stellar for the last two months of the season, only to break his elbow in a bull-related (yes, *bull*-related) offseason accident.

Left Field

This question has been written in sharpie in David Murphy's southpaw scrawl since he signed with Cleveland after the 2013 season. The 2017 list of candidates: Delino DeShields, Joey Gallo, Ryan Rua, Jurickson Profar. By season's end, Globe Life Park had seen all four of those, plus Nomar Mazara, Drew Robinson and Calhoun.

Answer

Seven left fielders!

Health of the Aging

Primarily: 38-year-old Adrian Beltre (who began the season on the disabled list with a calf injury and would not return until May 29) and 35-year-old Mike Napoli, who had returned via free agency.

Answer

Beltre had one of his best offensive years ever, per capita. He played just 94 games, due to injuries to both calves and his left hamstring. He is on record as saying that despite notching his 3,000th hit, he considers the season was a disappointment. Napoli did not play after September 14 and was below replacement level when he did play. The Rangers declined to exercise his 2018 option.

Elvis Andrus

Was the shortstop's breakout 2016 season legit?

Answer

Yep. Andrus hit .297 with 44 doubles, 20 home runs, 25 stolen bases and 100 runs scored. Here's a comprehensive list of seasons in which a shortstop checked all of those boxes: 2007: Hanley Ramirez. Second full year in the league, finished 10th in the MVP voting. 2017: Andrus. Not even an All-Star, but got married and became a dad, so net win.

Joey Gallo

What is he, exactly?

Answer A human supercollider made of horse DNA and Three True Outcomes. Gallo filled in at third base for Beltre, at first base for Napoli and at left field for **motions to about 12 people**.

Questions for 2018

Rougned Odor and Jurickson Profar

Can the first right the ship enough to justify trading the second? It appears that the organization's relationship with Profar is irreparably damaged, so much so that the team opted to employ Phil Gosselin over him once rosters expanded. The party line from the Rangers' front office was that there "weren't at-bats available" for Profar. That may have been true, but there weren't any at-bats available for him sitting at home while his teammates tried to eke out a wild card spot without him, either. Meanwhile, as discussed earlier, Odor must improve on his abysmal .251 on-base percentage to be the Rangers' second baseman of the future. Yes, he has 30-homer pop. But he also has above-average speed and baserunning smarts, skills that are going to waste every time he walks back to the dugout after aggressively defending his ankles against an incoming curveball.

First Base

Is Ronald Guzman ready to take the reins? Or will it be Gallo while Beltre mans the hot corner at 39 years old? Or—hear me out—does Beltre play first base? (*No.*)

Center Field

Did DeShields improve enough to be the everyday center fielder in 2018, or is he better suited in left field? If the latter, who plays center field?

Franz Kafka and the Patience of 2018

"Kafkaesque" colloquially refers to a situation so creatively horrifying that it seems beyond redemption. But the reason Kafka created such hellscapes in his writings was a core belief that patience is mankind's greatest virtue. The more horrific the circumstance, the more virtuous the patience that would navigate mankind through, say, morphing into a "monstrous vermin." Consequently, Kafka saw impatience as mankind's greatest vice and the cause of nearly all of the world's troubles.

In keeping with the theme of the first half of this essay, the final question is whether Rangers hitters will employ a little more of mankind's greatest virtue, or whether Rangers *fans* will be the ones asked to dig deep for the internal fortitude of watching a Kafkaesque 2018 slowly unfold before their eyes.

Notes

1. There would have been one exception, but Beltre (52 strikeouts) only amassed 389 plate appearances.
2. "Standalone" depends on how you read the stats. You could say the Rangers were just one of five teams in history tied for the record. Here's how: The 2017 Rays also sent paychecks to Danny Espinosa and Lucas Duda, both of whom totaled more than 100 strikeouts last season. But of Espinosa's 109 strikeouts in 2017, only 11 came as a member of the Rays. For Duda, it was 62/135. So for the purposes of this essay, Tampa Bay only had six players with 100-plus strikeouts. The other three teams in question (2013 Pirates, 2015 Astros, 2016 Blue Jays) also had at least one such split-time player. So to be more specific, the 2017 Rangers are the only team to boast eight players who struck out 100-plus times as members of that team.
3. Same as above, only this time if you allow for the most forgiving reading of the statistic, the record holders would be the 1996 Orioles, who employed 10 hitters with 17 or more home runs. But of Eddie Murray's 22 home runs in 1996, only 10 were hit as a member of the Orioles. Likewise, Pete Incaviglia and Todd Zeile—traded together from Philadelphia to Baltimore on August 29 of that season—hit just two and five home runs, respectively, in their 1996 Orioles uniforms.
4. Yes, I had to Google Nicole Bradford's name, and no, I'm not sorry for referencing the underrated late-1980s sitcom *My Two Dads*.

—Levi Weaver covers the Rangers for The Upset Sports.

HITTERS

Elvis Andrus SS
Born: 08/26/88 Age: 29 Bats: R Throws: R Height: 6'0" Weight: 200 Origin: International Free Agent, 2005

YEAR	TEAM	LVL	AGE	PA	R	2B	3B	HR	RBI	BB	K	SB	CS	AVG/OBP/SLG	TAv	VORP	BABIP	BRR	FRAA	WARP
2015	TEX	MLB	26	661	69	34	2	7	62	46	78	25	9	.258/.309/.357	.246	23.0	.283	5.7	SS(160): 12.6	3.8
2016	TEX	MLB	27	568	75	31	7	8	69	47	70	24	8	.302/.362/.439	.277	34.6	.333	1.4	SS(147): -4.1	3.1
2017	TEX	MLB	28	689	100	44	4	20	88	38	101	25	10	.297/.337/.471	.268	37.8	.325	2.8	SS(157): 16.2	5.4
2018	*TEX*	*MLB*	*29*	*692*	*81*	*35*	*3*	*10*	*68*	*52*	*92*	*27*	*11*	*.276/.330/.389*	*.249*	*26.2*	*.305*	*1.3*	*SS 6*	*2.3*
2019	*TEX*	*MLB*	*30*	*579*	*68*	*30*	*2*	*11*	*61*	*48*	*82*	*21*	*9*	*.278/.342/.406*	*.251*	*17.0*	*.306*	*2.8*	*SS 5*	*2.4*

Breakout: 3% Improve: 47% Collapse: 6% Attrition: 13% MLB: 97% *Comparables: Mark Loretta, Edgar Renteria, Rafael Bournigal*

We don't mention Andrus in the same breath as elite young shortstops like Carlos Correa, Francisco Lindor and Corey Seager, but maybe we should. Or if not the same breath, the next breath. Then again, Andrus might advocate for a little less conversation, and a little more action here. He had the season of his life, combining a solid offensive approach—bopping 20 home runs, stealing 25 bags and nearing 200 hits—with his best defensive season yet as judged by FRAA. That kind of consistently balanced competence is still an underrated skill, and Andrus showed that ability and then some. Will Andrus post another season in which he blows past his 90th percentile PECOTA projection? Probably not. But another solid season or two might leave those who worried about the back end of his eight-year, $120 million contract with their expectations all shook up. Then again, if he exercises his right to opt out after 2018, he could find a new place to dwell.

Adrian Beltre 3B
Born: 04/07/79 Age: 39 Bats: R Throws: R Height: 5'11" Weight: 220 Origin: International Free Agent, 1994

YEAR	TEAM	LVL	AGE	PA	R	2B	3B	HR	RBI	BB	K	SB	CS	AVG/OBP/SLG	TAv	VORP	BABIP	BRR	FRAA	WARP
2015	TEX	MLB	36	619	83	32	4	18	83	41	65	1	0	.287/.334/.453	.279	33.1	.295	3.0	3B(142): -3.0	3.2
2016	TEX	MLB	37	640	89	31	1	32	104	48	66	1	1	.300/.358/.521	.297	39.8	.293	-3.5	3B(141): 4.8	4.6
2017	TEX	MLB	38	389	47	22	1	17	71	39	52	1	0	.312/.383/.532	.299	23.6	.321	-2.9	3B(65): 7.5	3.1
2018	*TEX*	*MLB*	*39*	*673*	*84*	*33*	*1*	*23*	*92*	*52*	*81*	*1*	*1*	*.290/.350/.462*	*.276*	*30.2*	*.302*	*-1.3*	*3B 1*	*2.6*
2019	*TEX*	*MLB*	*40*	*479*	*64*	*24*	*1*	*17*	*63*	*39*	*62*	*0*	*0*	*.284/.346/.458*	*.265*	*13.5*	*.297*	*-1.1*	*3B 1*	*1.6*

Breakout: 0% Improve: 15% Collapse: 9% Attrition: 12% MLB: 74% *Comparables: Moises Alou, Johnny Damon, Melvin Mora*

Beltre exists seemingly outside of space and time. Or perhaps it would be better to say he exists in all baseball times. He is in many ways a throwback, and now he's also a member of the 3,000-hit club. In a sport trending increasingly younger, Beltre remains, preparing to begin his age-39 season. His game projects competence and balance everywhere. But in other ways, he appears to be of baseball's future. A younger generation of fans and players is putting personality at the center of the game, but that's old hat to Beltre. We've all delighted in his joshing with Felix Hernandez, his insistence that no one touch his head, his dancing on the basepaths. On July 26, having already collected three extra-base hits, including a home run, Beltre was on deck, hoping to get one hit closer to 3,000. The second-base umpire insisted he step onto the plastic mat, so Beltre did what anyone imbued with confidence and personality would do: He moved the mat. His subsequent ejection only heightened the comedy. Of course, for all our metaphor, Beltre does exist in this space, bound by its time. He missed stretches with a hamstring injury; even though he was able to squeeze into 94 games the value some hitters would envy over 162, at some point his body will betray him in a way his personality won't. And 2018 presents a crossroads: His two-year contract extension is coming to a close. The Rangers, faced with a potential franchise rebuild, will also face a choice. But it's hard to imagine them without Beltre. It's hard to imagine baseball without Beltre. Thankfully, this man who exists in all baseball times hasn't yet forced us to.

Willie Calhoun 2B
Born: 11/04/94 Age: 23 Bats: L Throws: R Height: 5'8" Weight: 187 Origin: Round 4, 2015 Draft (#132 overall)

YEAR	TEAM	LVL	AGE	PA	R	2B	3B	HR	RBI	BB	K	SB	CS	AVG/OBP/SLG	TAv	VORP	BABIP	BRR	FRAA	WARP
2015	OGD	RK	20	175	28	13	1	7	26	23	18	2	1	.278/.371/.517	.301	9.8	.276	-2.8	2B(33): -7.9	0.2
2015	GRL	A	20	66	9	3	0	1	8	5	7	0	0	.393/.439/.492	.346	7.3	.434	0.0	2B(12): -1.6	0.6
2015	RCU	A+	20	82	11	7	0	3	14	7	13	0	0	.329/.390/.548	.321	8.1	.362	0.9	2B(20): -1.3	0.7
2016	TUL	AA	21	560	75	25	1	27	88	45	65	0	0	.254/.318/.469	.282	26.2	.242	0.3	2B(119): -9.8	1.8
2017	OKL	AAA	22	414	64	24	5	23	67	36	49	3	2	.298/.357/.574	.304	29.9	.289	-1.8	2B(74): 0.9, LF(12): -1.9	2.8
2017	ROU	AAA	22	120	16	3	1	8	26	6	12	1	0	.310/.345/.566	.322	9.8	.290	-1.2	LF(24): 2.4, 2B(3): -0.7	1.1
2017	TEX	MLB	22	37	3	0	0	1	4	2	7	0	0	.265/.324/.353	.260	1.0	.308	0.3	LF(11): -0.7	0.0
2018	*TEX*	*MLB*	*23*	*536*	*75*	*24*	*2*	*27*	*82*	*42*	*84*	*1*	*0*	*.267/.327/.491*	*.272*	*20.7*	*.271*	*-0.9*	*LF -5*	*1.2*
2019	*TEX*	*MLB*	*24*	*535*	*78*	*26*	*2*	*29*	*86*	*44*	*87*	*1*	*0*	*.270/.333/.511*	*.272*	*19.1*	*.273*	*-1.0*	*LF -5*	*1.6*

Breakout: 6% Improve: 29% Collapse: 6% Attrition: 17% MLB: 57% *Comparables: Dilson Herrera, Marcus Semien, Kolten Wong*

In just over a year, Calhoun went from fourth-round pick to headliner in the trade that sent Yu Darvish to Los Angeles. As a result, his profile has taken a major leap despite his abilities remaining largely the same. What's changed is that he proved he could succeed with them at every level (except the majors, yet). Quick hands and a strong base help Calhoun generate significant power, especially to the pull side, from his 5-foot-8 frame. The teeny titan makes gobs of contact and rarely strikes out, making him the rare player with a chance to walk more than he whiffs at the major-league level. On the defensive side of the ball ... he sure can hit. He doesn't have the range or hands to more than fake it at second base, the whole package is an awkward fit in left field and he's too small to play first base. That leaves designated hitter, which makes the bar for offense awfully high. Good thing he can mash.

Juan Centeno C Born: 11/16/89 Age: 28 Bats: L Throws: R Height: 5'9" Weight: 195 Origin: Round 32, 2007 Draft (#991 overall)

YEAR	TEAM	LVL	AGE	PA	R	2B	3B	HR	RBI	BB	K	SB	CS	AVG/OBP/SLG	TAv	VORP	BABIP	BRR	FRAA	WARP
2015	MIL	MLB	25	23	0	1	0	0	0	2	7	0	0	.048/.130/.095	.107	-2.2	.071	0.3	C(7): -1.2	-0.4
2015	CSP	AAA	25	187	11	6	3	0	24	5	19	2	2	.295/.312/.364	.228	2.7	.323	0.9	C(46): -8.9	-0.6
2016	ROC	AAA	26	55	5	1	0	1	5	4	4	1	0	.245/.315/.327	.240	1.0	.250	-0.1	C(14): -0.1	0.1
2016	MIN	MLB	26	192	16	12	1	3	25	12	38	0	0	.261/.312/.392	.237	3.2	.319	-1.0	C(53): -12.9	-1.0
2017	FRE	AAA	27	257	25	12	1	1	33	16	37	0	1	.311/.354/.383	.250	6.0	.362	-2.2	C(54): -13.6, 3B(1): 0.0	-0.7
2017	HOU	MLB	27	57	5	0	0	2	4	4	12	0	0	.231/.286/.346	.208	-0.9	.263	-0.5	C(22): -5.3	-0.6
2018	*TEX*	*MLB*	*28*	*159*	*15*	*6*	*1*	*2*	*14*	*9*	*27*	*0*	*0*	*.251/.297/.335*	*.219*	*0.9*	*.292*	*-0.3*	*C -12*	*-1.2*
2019	*TEX*	*MLB*	*29*	*230*	*25*	*9*	*1*	*4*	*22*	*14*	*42*	*0*	*0*	*.248/.301/.356*	*.223*	*-0.4*	*.286*	*-0.5*	*C -13*	*-1.5*

Breakout: 7% Improve: 22% Collapse: 12% Attrition: 25% MLB: 55%

Comparables: Bryan Holaday, Jesus Sucre, Craig Tatum

YEAR	TEAM	P. COUNT	FRM RUNS	BLK RUNS	THRW RUNS	TOT RUNS
2015	CSP	6471	-7.4	-1.1	-0.4	-8.9
2015	MIL	876	-1.1	-0.1	0.0	-1.2
2016	MIN	7221	-9.7	-2.4	-0.5	-12.5
2017	HOU	2432	-4.1	-0.8	-0.3	-5.2
2018	*TEX*	*6088*	*-9.7*	*-1.5*	*-0.2*	*-11.4*
2019	*TEX*	*8800*	*-8.6*	*-1.3*	*-0.2*	*-10.1*

Anglicize his last name and you'll unearth "John Rye," an appellation that wouldn't be out of place among the hardy stoics of the Deadball Era. That *nom de sport* doesn't just fit an earlier era, it matches his workaday skill set; Centeno is a poor fielder for his position and an indifferent hitter. But back in the day, the catcher was ennobled by his sheer willingness to absorb brutal foul tips and sacrifice his knees in the pursuit of glory, and little things like hitting well or controlling the run game were superfluous pieces of value, not the expectation. Cleared of concussion symptoms just in time to make the Astros' postseason roster, Centeno is a receiver made desirable simply by his ability to hold on.

Robinson Chirinos C Born: 06/05/84 Age: 34 Bats: R Throws: R Height: 6'1" Weight: 210 Origin: International Free Agent, 2000

YEAR	TEAM	LVL	AGE	PA	R	2B	3B	HR	RBI	BB	K	SB	CS	AVG/OBP/SLG	TAv	VORP	BABIP	BRR	FRAA	WARP
2015	TEX	MLB	31	273	33	16	1	10	34	28	62	0	0	.232/.325/.438	.265	11.8	.270	-1.3	C(78): -4.5	0.8
2016	TEX	MLB	32	170	21	11	0	9	20	15	44	0	1	.224/.314/.483	.268	9.1	.250	0.2	C(54): -5.5	0.4
2017	TEX	MLB	33	309	46	13	1	17	38	34	79	1	0	.255/.360/.506	.285	20.8	.298	-1.7	C(85): -2.6	1.8
2018	*TEX*	*MLB*	*34*	*424*	*53*	*19*	*1*	*16*	*54*	*39*	*100*	*1*	*1*	*.236/.319/.421*	*.251*	*16.5*	*.274*	*-0.9*	*C -10*	*0.2*
2019	*TEX*	*MLB*	*35*	*340*	*45*	*15*	*1*	*13*	*44*	*32*	*85*	*0*	*0*	*.234/.321/.422*	*.246*	*7.4*	*.275*	*-1.0*	*C -7*	*0.0*

Breakout: 1% Improve: 33% Collapse: 9% Attrition: 13% MLB: 80%

Comparables: Geovany Soto, John Buck, David Ross

YEAR	TEAM	P. COUNT	FRM RUNS	BLK RUNS	THRW RUNS	TOT RUNS
2015	ROU	472	-0.1	0.0	0.0	-0.1
2015	TEX	10786	-5.2	1.6	0.4	-3.3
2016	TEX	6797	-7.7	1.9	0.0	-5.9
2017	TEX	11679	-3.7	2.0	-0.8	-2.5
2018	*TEX*	*16497*	*-10.7*	*3.0*	*-0.8*	*-8.6*
2019	*TEX*	*13225*	*-8.7*	*2.4*	*-0.7*	*-7.0*

Chirinos had a busy 2017. After Jonathan Lucroy was traded to the Rockies, Chirinos assumed starting catching duties and hit an impressive .291/.417/.488, with five home runs and a 14 percent walk rate, at one point carrying a 28-game on-base streak. Chirinos remains a below-average receiver, and as he enters his age-34 season there are questions about his durability. Last season saw him struggle with a hamstring injury, but if he can maintain his gains at the plate he's useful as a starter or backup.

Shin-Soo Choo RF Born: 07/13/82 Age: 35 Bats: L Throws: L Height: 5'11" Weight: 210 Origin: International Free Agent, 2000

YEAR	TEAM	LVL	AGE	PA	R	2B	3B	HR	RBI	BB	K	SB	CS	AVG/OBP/SLG	TAv	VORP	BABIP	BRR	FRAA	WARP
2015	TEX	MLB	32	653	94	32	3	22	82	76	147	4	2	.276/.375/.463	.295	36.0	.335	2.7	RF(148): 6.6	4.6
2016	TEX	MLB	33	210	27	7	0	7	17	25	46	6	3	.242/.357/.399	.273	5.8	.288	-0.6	RF(43): -0.4	0.6
2017	TEX	MLB	34	636	96	20	1	22	78	77	134	12	3	.261/.357/.423	.261	11.1	.305	0.7	RF(77): -1.5	1.0
2018	*TEX*	*MLB*	*35*	*635*	*92*	*25*	*1*	*18*	*68*	*80*	*140*	*10*	*4*	*.256/.366/.409*	*.269*	*21.9*	*.312*	*-0.6*	*RF 2*	*1.9*
2019	*TEX*	*MLB*	*36*	*502*	*69*	*20*	*1*	*15*	*60*	*66*	*116*	*6*	*3*	*.252/.367/.414*	*.263*	*14.0*	*.308*	*0.6*	*RF 2*	*1.7*

Breakout: 2% Improve: 25% Collapse: 7% Attrition: 20% MLB: 82%

Comparables: Bobby Abreu, Kosuke Fukudome, J.D. Drew

In *The Giving Tree*, a Boy develops a lifelong relationship with an apple tree. In his childhood, the Boy swings from the tree's branches, and eats her apples. And she is happy. But as time goes on, the Boy begins to take more and more from the tree, stealing her apples, sawing off her branches to build a home, slowly peeling away everything that made the tree a tree. Choo hasn't exactly lost all of his apples yet, but time is beginning to function more and more like that greedy Boy. Choo's sterling 2015 is in the rear-view; the defense has faded, and though 2017 saw him swipe more than 10 bags for the first time in years, the speed isn't where it used to be either. It isn't all bad, of course; these things happen gradually. Choo was healthy the whole season, a great improvement over 2016, and thumped 22 home runs. His arm still impresses in right field. He's not to the end of his story yet, but with his contract set to run through 2020 any team would worry about what sort of player they'll have when time has taken all the useful parts and left them with a stump good only for a comfortable resting place, and to whom they owe another $62 million.

Delino DeShields OF Born: 08/16/92 Age: 25 Bats: R Throws: R Height: 5'9" Weight: 200 Origin: Round 1, 2010 Draft (#8 overall)

YEAR	TEAM	LVL	AGE	PA	R	2B	3B	HR	RBI	BB	K	SB	CS	AVG/OBP/SLG	TAv	VORP	BABIP	BRR	FRAA	WARP
2015	ROU	AAA	22	27	2	3	0	0	2	1	6	0	0	.308/.333/.423	.296	0.4	.400	-1.2	CF(2): -0.1, LF(1): -0.1	0.0
2015	TEX	MLB	22	492	83	22	10	2	37	53	101	25	8	.261/.344/.374	.259	17.2	.334	4.3	CF(87): -0.5, LF(35): -0.4	1.7
2016	ROU	AAA	23	249	37	10	0	3	17	35	60	21	7	.261/.367/.353	.284	15.5	.349	2.4	CF(42): -5.7, LF(7): -1.9	0.8
2016	TEX	MLB	23	203	36	7	0	4	13	15	54	8	3	.209/.275/.313	.219	-0.9	.272	2.0	CF(33): 1.1, LF(26): -1.4	-0.1
2017	TEX	MLB	24	440	75	15	2	6	22	44	109	29	8	.269/.347/.367	.249	14.2	.358	7.6	LF(60): 4.4, CF(51): -0.4	1.8
2018	*TEX*	*MLB*	*25*	*620*	*87*	*26*	*4*	*9*	*51*	*65*	*144*	*35*	*11*	*.254/.332/.370*	*.244*	*19.2*	*.319*	*3.3*	*CF -3*	*0.9*
2019	*TEX*	*MLB*	*26*	*540*	*65*	*24*	*4*	*10*	*57*	*57*	*125*	*30*	*10*	*.262/.345/.397*	*.247*	*14.9*	*.322*	*5.9*	*CF -1*	*1.5*

Breakout: 6% Improve: 50% Collapse: 3% Attrition: 10% MLB: 95%

Comparables: Dave Collins, Lastings Milledge, Gregor Blanco

DeShields put up a nice bounce-back season in 2017. After a year that saw his offense collapse in a part-time role, he found his stride again with consistent playing time spread over left and center field. He saw his speed play on the basepaths, and more importantly, in his defense. He's still not a completely natural route runner, and he can make mistakes, but the speed covers for a lot of it and he's rounded into acceptable form. General manager Jon Daniels has said the 25-year-old will likely be the Rangers' starter in center field. That now feels risky, rather than crazy. You could say he drew a Delino in the sand. That he's DeShields that guard the realms of men. You could say that. Literally no one is stopping you. Freedom is a burden.

Joey Gallo 3B Born: 11/19/93 Age: 24 Bats: L Throws: R Height: 6'5" Weight: 235 Origin: Round 1, 2012 Draft (#39 overall)

YEAR	TEAM	LVL	AGE	PA	R	2B	3B	HR	RBI	BB	K	SB	CS	AVG/OBP/SLG	TAv	VORP	BABIP	BRR	FRAA	WARP
2015	FRI	AA	21	146	21	10	1	9	31	24	49	1	0	.314/.425/.636	.359	18.3	.453	0.6	3B(19): 1.4, LF(6): 0.5	2.2
2015	ROU	AAA	21	228	20	9	0	14	32	27	90	1	0	.195/.289/.450	.267	5.7	.258	-1.9	3B(33): 0.1, LF(14): 1.0	0.7
2015	TEX	MLB	21	123	16	3	1	6	14	15	57	3	0	.204/.301/.417	.246	1.8	.356	0.4	LF(19): 0.2, 3B(15): -0.1	0.2
2016	ROU	AAA	22	433	71	17	6	25	66	68	150	2	0	.240/.367/.529	.325	40.0	.330	2.1	3B(44): 4.5, 1B(32): 1.4	4.7
2016	TEX	MLB	22	30	2	0	0	1	1	5	19	1	0	.040/.200/.160	.153	-2.8	.000	-0.1	3B(5): 0.2, 1B(1): 0.1	-0.3
2017	TEX	MLB	23	532	85	18	3	41	80	75	196	7	2	.209/.333/.537	.286	27.5	.250	0.5	3B(72): -1.8, 1B(59): 0.5	2.9
2018	*TEX*	*MLB*	*24*	*578*	*88*	*19*	*3*	*36*	*97*	*78*	*221*	*6*	*1*	*.215/.329/.487*	*.274*	*19.8*	*.295*	*0.2*	*1B 0, 3B 0*	*1.7*
2019	*TEX*	*MLB*	*25*	*559*	*89*	*20*	*3*	*36*	*95*	*81*	*207*	*6*	*1*	*.222/.343/.509*	*.276*	*17.3*	*.297*	*0.2*	*1B 0, 3B 1*	*1.9*

Breakout: 5% Improve: 63% Collapse: 9% Attrition: 12% MLB: 90% *Comparables: Kris Bryant, Miguel Sano, Giancarlo Stanton*

If Michel Foucault were analyzing Gallo's career—and how do we know Foucault didn't like baseball?—he'd probably employ the notion of discursive regimes to do it. Discourse is the system of beliefs, ideas and attitudes that construct the truth. Discourse shapes our common understanding. It gives us common ground. Discourse makes thoughts thinkable. For much of baseball's history, a profile like Gallo's was an unthinkable thought at the major-league level. With his brief 2016 call-up marred by a 63.3 percent strikeout rate, there was concern that even with weapons-grade power the contact issues that had plagued him throughout the minors and into the majors would be too great for him to have anything like an everyday role. Two things changed in 2017: Gallo brought his strikeout rate down to a more reasonable 36.8 percent, and some previously unthinkable thoughts became thinkable. You can be a major leaguer with an almost-40 percent strikeout rate now, provided there's enough pop in the bat, and skill on the basepaths. Gallo even tossed in solid defense at third base for good measure. His carrying tool will always be the ability to send the ball to Jupiter, but as Foucault would tell us, the discourse is power. Literally.

Carlos Gomez CF Born: 12/04/85 Age: 32 Bats: R Throws: R Height: 6'3" Weight: 220 Origin: International Free Agent, 2002

YEAR	TEAM	LVL	AGE	PA	R	2B	3B	HR	RBI	BB	K	SB	CS	AVG/OBP/SLG	TAv	VORP	BABIP	BRR	FRAA	WARP
2015	MIL	MLB	29	314	42	20	1	8	43	23	70	7	6	.262/.328/.423	.273	13.2	.322	0.0	CF(72): 0.0, 2B(1): 0.0	1.4
2015	HOU	MLB	29	163	19	9	0	4	13	8	31	10	3	.242/.288/.383	.241	3.8	.278	2.0	CF(39): 4.5	0.9
2016	HOU	MLB	30	323	27	16	1	5	29	21	100	13	2	.210/.272/.322	.210	-3.1	.300	3.9	CF(78): -4.0	-0.7
2016	TEX	MLB	30	130	18	6	0	8	24	13	36	5	3	.284/.362/.543	.307	9.5	.347	0.4	LF(28): 1.2, CF(7): -0.1	1.1
2017	TEX	MLB	31	426	51	23	1	17	51	31	127	13	5	.255/.340/.462	.270	17.1	.336	-0.7	CF(102): -2.2	1.5
2018	*TEX*	*MLB*	*32*	*412*	*54*	*21*	*2*	*15*	*52*	*32*	*106*	*15*	*6*	*.259/.332/.446*	*.255*	*15.5*	*.320*	*1.2*	*CF -2*	*1.5*
2019	*TEX*	*MLB*	*33*	*377*	*48*	*18*	*1*	*13*	*47*	*29*	*99*	*13*	*5*	*.248/.322/.426*	*.248*	*8.1*	*.309*	*1.6*	*CF -2*	*0.7*

Breakout: 2% Improve: 39% Collapse: 4% Attrition: 16% MLB: 97% *Comparables: Will Venable, Torii Hunter, Aaron Rowand*

Gomez took a pillow deal to rebuild his value and did so nicely, proving he can still consistently produce. The power stroke returned to the tune of 17 long balls, and he was good for an .800 OPS. He saw time on the disabled list, and durability has been an increasing concern over the last few years, but he still provides serviceable defense in center field and plus defense in either corner. How long front offices think he can effectively roam out there, whether they think he's better suited for a corner full time and how much they like his bat will determine how many years he keeps making an impact.

Ronald Guzman 1B Born: 10/20/94 Age: 23 Bats: L Throws: L Height: 6'5" Weight: 205 Origin: International Free Agent, 2011

YEAR	TEAM	LVL	AGE	PA	R	2B	3B	HR	RBI	BB	K	SB	CS	AVG/OBP/SLG	TAv	VORP	BABIP	BRR	FRAA	WARP
2015	HIC	A	20	104	10	3	0	3	14	6	15	2	0	.309/.346/.433	.287	3.8	.338	-0.2	1B(24): -0.6	0.3
2015	HDS	A+	20	452	54	25	7	9	73	27	101	3	0	.277/.319/.434	.257	2.0	.343	-1.2	1B(106): 0.0	0.2
2016	FRI	AA	21	416	51	16	5	15	56	33	82	2	1	.288/.348/.477	.296	16.6	.331	-2.5	1B(95): 4.0	2.2
2016	ROU	AAA	21	95	9	5	1	1	11	6	23	0	1	.216/.266/.330	.211	-5.4	.281	-1.6	1B(20): -1.6	-0.7
2017	ROU	AAA	22	527	78	22	3	12	62	47	85	4	1	.298/.372/.434	.284	19.8	.342	-0.3	1B(118): -1.6	1.8
2018	*TEX*	*MLB*	*23*	*96*	*11*	*4*	*1*	*3*	*11*	*7*	*21*	*0*	*0*	*.253/.314/.401*	*.243*	*0.3*	*.305*	*-0.1*	*1B 0, LF 0*	*0.0*
2019	*TEX*	*MLB*	*24*	*370*	*47*	*17*	*2*	*12*	*46*	*31*	*83*	*0*	*0*	*.262/.331/.435*	*.252*	*2.4*	*.313*	*-0.6*	*1B 0, LF 0*	*0.2*

Breakout: 5% Improve: 10% Collapse: 3% Attrition: 11% MLB: 16% *Comparables: Andy Wilkins, David Cooper, Brandon Snyder*

A big-money signing in the 2011 international free agent period, Guzman has progressed about as well as one could have hoped and yet remains under the radar on the national prospect landscape. A large, lanky kid has matured into a large, lanky man. Despite his length, Guzman makes plenty of contact, and despite his size, he doesn't hit for as much power as you'd like from someone manning the cold corner. It's easy to dream on additional pop as he learns to trade some contact for power, or adjusts his swing to add loft as many have done in recent years. He's "only" a first baseman, but he's got a nifty glove over there. He should breach the major-league barrier for the first time in 2018, and if he can find some more over-the-fence power in his swing, he'll become a mainstay.

Nomar Mazara RF Born: 04/26/95 Age: 23 Bats: L Throws: L Height: 6'4" Weight: 215 Origin: International Free Agent, 2011

YEAR	TEAM	LVL	AGE	PA	R	2B	3B	HR	RBI	BB	K	SB	CS	AVG/OBP/SLG	TAv	VORP	BABIP	BRR	FRAA	WARP
2015	FRI	AA	20	470	57	22	2	13	56	47	92	2	0	.284/.357/.443	.280	13.0	.329	-4.5	RF(63): 0.7, LF(32): 0.3	1.5
2015	ROU	AAA	20	88	11	4	0	1	13	5	10	0	0	.358/.409/.444	.321	7.1	.400	0.1	RF(14): 1.3, LF(1): 0.3	0.9
2016	TEX	MLB	21	568	59	13	3	20	64	39	112	0	2	.266/.320/.419	.257	4.6	.299	-4.1	RF(112): 11.2, LF(38): -1.3	1.5
2017	TEX	MLB	22	616	64	30	2	20	101	55	127	2	2	.253/.323/.422	.247	0.8	.293	-2.4	RF(92): -6.4, LF(47): 0.9	-0.5
2018	*TEX*	*MLB*	*23*	*665*	*79*	*28*	*2*	*22*	*87*	*54*	*133*	*2*	*1*	*.264/.329/.428*	*.257*	*14.9*	*.304*	*-1.3*	*RF 0, LF 1*	*1.3*
2019	*TEX*	*MLB*	*24*	*598*	*80*	*27*	*1*	*23*	*79*	*54*	*126*	*2*	*1*	*.267/.340/.450*	*.261*	*11.3*	*.308*	*-2.4*	*RF 1, LF 2*	*1.5*

Breakout: 10% Improve: 64% Collapse: 1% Attrition: 11% MLB: 95% *Comparables: Nick Markakis, Jeremy Hermida, Delmon Young*

You can survive all sorts of things when you're young: bad breakups, career changes, haircuts you'll want back. Your stomach is a testament to human resilience; you could probably eat the plate your breakfast goes on, and make it. Being young means you still have time to grow, and adapt, before you hit the age when new technology stops being intuitive and your joints hurt. To wit, you can be a recent top prospect whose sophomore campaign underwhelms but come out of it just fine. Mazara didn't hit all that differently last year. He shaved 10 points off his True Average, but slightly increased his OBP and slugging. He thumped the same number of home runs. The real difference came in his defense, which nose-dived after a sterling 2016. He's not even 23 years old; he tweaked his hamstring. The moral arc of the universe bends toward multi-year defensive samples. He'll be fine. People his age are built to be.

Mike Napoli 1B Born: 10/31/81 Age: 36 Bats: R Throws: R Height: 6'1" Weight: 225 Origin: Round 17, 2000 Draft (#500 overall)

YEAR	TEAM	LVL	AGE	PA	R	2B	3B	HR	RBI	BB	K	SB	CS	AVG/OBP/SLG	TAv	VORP	BABIP	BRR	FRAA	WARP
2015	BOS	MLB	33	378	37	18	1	13	40	45	99	3	1	.207/.307/.386	.247	-1.1	.252	-0.1	1B(96): 5.2	0.4
2015	TEX	MLB	33	91	9	2	0	5	10	12	19	0	2	.295/.396/.513	.318	6.3	.333	-0.3	1B(15): 0.6, LF(11): -1.2	0.6
2016	CLE	MLB	34	645	92	22	1	34	101	78	194	5	1	.239/.335/.465	.262	4.7	.296	-3.4	1B(98): 3.6	0.9
2017	TEX	MLB	35	485	60	11	1	29	66	49	163	1	2	.193/.285/.428	.237	-8.2	.225	-1.9	1B(95): -5.5	-1.4
2018	*TEX*	*MLB*	*36*	*487*	*62*	*18*	*1*	*22*	*68*	*62*	*147*	*3*	*2*	*.226/.333/.431*	*.255*	*5.2*	*.290*	*-1.4*	*1B -1*	*0.5*
2019	*TEX*	*MLB*	*37*	*343*	*46*	*12*	*0*	*15*	*45*	*42*	*106*	*1*	*1*	*.212/.316/.408*	*.245*	*-2.3*	*.271*	*-1.0*	*1B 0*	*-0.3*

Breakout: 0% Improve: 16% Collapse: 12% Attrition: 13% MLB: 70% *Comparables: Ryan Howard, Carlos Pena, Mickey Tettleton*

In 2016, the Party at Napoli's was a rager with keg stands and only chips for snacks—all home runs with just a dash of OBP on the side. In 2017, the Rangers gave Napoli a one-year deal, hoping he might serve up a more balanced menu to help them fill a hole at first base—canapés pair famously well with the long ball, after all. Unfortunately, neither the Rangers nor Napoli walked away satisfied. The power was still there, to the tune of 29 home runs, but Napoli posted a career-worst True Average and didn't play past mid-September after he was sidelined with a lower leg issue. Going into his age-36 season, his career isn't over but the party probably is, supplanted by more staid gatherings with good friends and multiple days off to recover from the baseball equivalent of a two-beer hangover.

Rougned Odor 2B Born: 02/03/94 Age: 24 Bats: L Throws: R Height: 5'11" Weight: 195 Origin: International Free Agent, 2011

YEAR	TEAM	LVL	AGE	PA	R	2B	3B	HR	RBI	BB	K	SB	CS	AVG/OBP/SLG	TAv	VORP	BABIP	BRR	FRAA	WARP
2015	ROU	AAA	21	124	26	12	2	5	19	12	10	3	1	.352/.426/.639	.343	15.0	.355	1.0	2B(28): -1.1	1.4
2015	TEX	MLB	21	470	54	21	9	16	61	23	79	6	7	.261/.316/.465	.278	24.5	.283	4.2	2B(119): 4.7	3.1
2016	TEX	MLB	22	632	89	33	4	33	88	19	135	14	7	.271/.296/.502	.269	22.5	.297	-0.2	2B(146): 5.7	2.9
2017	TEX	MLB	23	651	79	21	3	30	75	32	162	15	6	.204/.252/.397	.218	-9.6	.224	1.3	2B(158): 6.2	-0.3
2018	*TEX*	*MLB*	*24*	*560*	*76*	*25*	*5*	*23*	*75*	*28*	*110*	*12*	*7*	*.256/.302/.459*	*.254*	*20.8*	*.281*	*0.4*	*2B 4*	*1.9*
2019	*TEX*	*MLB*	*25*	*573*	*77*	*26*	*5*	*27*	*85*	*32*	*111*	*13*	*7*	*.260/.311/.482*	*.258*	*19.3*	*.279*	*1.9*	*2B 4*	*2.5*

Breakout: 3% Improve: 54% Collapse: 0% Attrition: 7% MLB: 99% *Comparables: Jonathan Schoop, Gordon Beckham, Carlos Baerga*

There are a lot of ways to be bad at baseball, but it's been a while since we've seen a player be bad in the way Odor was in 2017. Odor matched a career-high walk rate, but struck out more than ever before. He posted a career-best 15 stolen bases, which is one way to try to make up for a career-worst on-base percentage. Nearly 16 percent of his fly balls stayed in the infield. His contact dropped to a career low. Of hitters with at least 30 home runs, Odor had the lowest OPS+ in baseball history. We at BP can't endorse calling his six-year, $49.5 million contract malodorous just yet; it's unlikely he'll be quite this bad again, and the joke's a cheap one anyhow, though the inclusion of two horses to seal the deal made it very tempting. And while 30 home runs ain't what it used to be, it isn't difficult to imagine a slightly less aggressive version of Odor reclaiming enough of his form to be useful again. After all, it's hard to imagine it getting any stranger.

Jurickson Profar 2B Born: 02/20/93 Age: 25 Bats: B Throws: R Height: 6'0" Weight: 190 Origin: International Free Agent, 2009

YEAR	TEAM	LVL	AGE	PA	R	2B	3B	HR	RBI	BB	K	SB	CS	AVG/OBP/SLG	TAv	VORP	BABIP	BRR	FRAA	WARP
2015	HIC	A	22	35	2	1	0	1	5	1	9	0	0	.273/.314/.394	.262	0.3	.348	-0.1		0.0
2016	ROU	AAA	23	189	28	9	0	5	26	16	26	4	3	.284/.356/.426	.296	13.9	.312	0.2	SS(31): 2.9, 2B(6): 0.1	1.7
2016	TEX	MLB	23	307	35	6	3	5	20	30	61	2	1	.239/.321/.338	.221	-6.0	.291	-1.5	3B(25): -1.2, 2B(19): 1.9	-0.6
2017	TEX	MLB	24	70	8	2	0	0	5	9	14	1	1	.172/.294/.207	.212	-0.8	.227	0.8	LF(12): 1.2, SS(4): -0.6	0.0
2017	ROU	AAA	24	383	50	25	0	7	45	43	33	5	0	.287/.383/.428	.292	32.7	.302	2.9	SS(78): -6.6, 2B(3): -0.2	2.6
2018	*TEX*	*MLB*	*25*	*125*	*15*	*5*	*0*	*3*	*13*	*12*	*21*	*1*	*0*	*.253/.335/.384*	*.251*	*2.9*	*.285*	*-0.2*	*1B 0, 3B 0*	*0.3*
2019	*TEX*	*MLB*	*26*	*227*	*29*	*10*	*0*	*7*	*27*	*23*	*39*	*2*	*1*	*.256/.342/.412*	*.252*	*3.7*	*.284*	*-0.2*	*1B 1, 3B 0*	*0.5*

Breakout: 2% Improve: 48% Collapse: 9% Attrition: 21% MLB: 98% *Comparables: Didi Gregorius, Russ Adams, Joe Panik*

The popular consensus appears to be that Profar's relationship with the Rangers became as acrimonious as Fleetwood Mac's studio sessions: full of recrimination, marked by mistrust and seemingly on a collision course for a breakup. Profar saw limited time with the big-league club, mostly coming up to fill holes created by injury or paternity leave; it was only 58 at-bats, but he hit for an anemic .212 TAv. Profar had a good year at Round Rock, with a .287/.383/.428 line landing like a Christine McVie hidden gem, but despite that performance his path is largely dependent on other members of the band. Will Elvis Andrus and Adrian Beltre stay beyond 2018? Is there a path for Profar to shortstop? What even is his market at this point? Profar reportedly was displeased when he wasn't traded at the deadline, and further frustrated when he wasn't called up in September. Without a clear starting role in 2018, he might need to go his own way. Whether the Rangers will finally let go of baseball's former number no. 1 prospect? Right now, it's all just rumours.

Ryan Rua LF Born: 03/11/90 Age: 28 Bats: R Throws: R Height: 6'2" Weight: 205 Origin: Round 17, 2011 Draft (#534 overall)

YEAR	TEAM	LVL	AGE	PA	R	2B	3B	HR	RBI	BB	K	SB	CS	AVG/OBP/SLG	TAv	VORP	BABIP	BRR	FRAA	WARP
2015	ROU	AAA	25	165	18	5	0	6	22	18	45	3	0	.197/.303/.359	.254	1.4	.239	-1.0	LF(10): 1.4, 3B(9): 0.6	0.2
2015	TEX	MLB	25	86	10	5	0	4	7	3	32	0	0	.193/.221/.398	.223	-1.4	.255	0.0	LF(22): 0.1, 1B(4): 0.1	-0.2
2016	TEX	MLB	26	269	40	8	1	8	22	21	76	9	0	.258/.331/.400	.252	6.2	.342	3.3	LF(60): -1.1, 1B(31): 0.5	0.5
2017	ROU	AAA	27	188	27	7	2	8	28	10	55	3	0	.266/.309/.463	.269	6.6	.342	1.3	LF(16): 1.4, RF(13): -1.9	0.6
2017	TEX	MLB	27	144	17	6	0	3	12	14	52	2	2	.217/.294/.333	.213	-4.1	.338	0.7	LF(37): 1.1, 1B(23): 2.4	-0.1
2018	*TEX*	*MLB*	*28*	*230*	*29*	*9*	*1*	*7*	*27*	*18*	*62*	*4*	*1*	*.245/.313/.403*	*.245*	*2.6*	*.313*	*0.1*	*1B 1, LF 0*	*0.1*
2019	*TEX*	*MLB*	*29*	*298*	*38*	*13*	*1*	*10*	*37*	*25*	*81*	*4*	*1*	*.249/.319/.416*	*.246*	*2.8*	*.316*	*1.3*	*1B 1, LF 0*	*0.4*

Breakout: 5% Improve: 29% Collapse: 14% Attrition: 33% MLB: 66% *Comparables: Dee Brown, Brandon Moss, Jorge Piedra*

After a 2016 that saw Rua take a step forward, 2017 was a mess. Rua's plate discipline collapsed. After trimming his strikeout rate to a respectable 28.3 percent, he saw it balloon up again. He didn't hit for average or power. His one saving grace was serviceable defense. There was always a bit of concern that the 17th-round pick who had fashioned himself into more than just an organizational guy would turn into a pumpkin, and of course Rua could take it the other way, and turn things around. He's done it before. But this version of Rua isn't much of a major leaguer, and could leave the Rangers to rua the day they ever thought he was.

Chris Seise SS Born: 01/06/99 Age: 19 Bats: R Throws: R Height: 6'2" Weight: 175 Origin: Round 1, 2017 Draft (#29 overall)

YEAR	TEAM	LVL	AGE	PA	R	2B	3B	HR	RBI	BB	K	SB	CS	AVG/OBP/SLG	TAv	VORP	BABIP	BRR	FRAA	WARP
2017	RNG	RK	18	129	23	5	3	3	27	9	30	5	0	.336/.395/.509	.296	13.0	.429	1.4	SS(23): -3.6	0.8
2017	SPO	A-	18	104	10	3	1	0	9	4	30	1	1	.222/.250/.273	.200	-1.9	.314	0.5	SS(23): -0.2	-0.2
2018	*TEX*	*MLB*	*19*	*250*	*25*	*9*	*1*	*6*	*23*	*13*	*81*	*0*	*0*	*.204/.249/.329*	*.188*	*-7.5*	*.278*	*-0.3*	*SS -1*	*-0.9*
2019	*TEX*	*MLB*	*20*	*324*	*35*	*12*	*2*	*9*	*35*	*19*	*101*	*1*	*0*	*.217/.269/.362*	*.213*	*-5.5*	*.291*	*-0.4*	*SS -1*	*-0.7*

Breakout: 0% Improve: 3% Collapse: 1% Attrition: 3% MLB: 6% *Comparables: Raul Mondesi, Elvis Andrus, Rougned Odor*

Odds are you can name the first prep shortstop to come off the board in 2017's draft. That's number no. 1 pick and current top-50 prospect Royce Lewis of the Twins. The second was Seise, who like Lewis tore through rookie ball before earning a midseason promotion to Single-A. Seise lacks the premium raw material of his fellow six-spot draftee, but has the hands and arm for a certain future in the dirt. Whether that's in a utility or regular role depends on the evolution of his approach and whether the projection in his 6-foot-2 frame translates to in-game power.

Leody Taveras CF Born: 09/08/98 Age: 19 Bats: B Throws: R Height: 6'1" Weight: 170 Origin: International Free Agent, 2015

YEAR	TEAM	LVL	AGE	PA	R	2B	3B	HR	RBI	BB	K	SB	CS	AVG/OBP/SLG	TAv	VORP	BABIP	BRR	FRAA	WARP
2016	DRN	RK	17	45	6	2	2	0	9	6	5	4	3	.385/.467/.538	.408	6.5	.441	-2.1	CF(7): -0.9, RF(2): -0.4	0.5
2016	RNG	RK	17	155	22	6	3	1	15	11	24	11	4	.278/.329/.382	.252	3.1	.328	-0.3	CF(31): -2.6, RF(3): -0.1	0.0
2016	SPO	A-	17	133	14	6	1	0	9	8	26	3	1	.228/.271/.293	.252	2.4	.283	-0.3	CF(26): 2.1, LF(1): 0.0	0.4
2017	HIC	A	18	577	73	20	7	8	50	47	92	20	6	.249/.312/.360	.255	17.4	.287	3.3	CF(125): -3.7, LF(3): -0.1	1.4
2018	*TEX*	*MLB*	*19*	*250*	*29*	*10*	*1*	*6*	*23*	*18*	*59*	*4*	*1*	*.226/.285/.360*	*.212*	*-2.5*	*.275*	*0.1*	*CF -3, LF 0*	*-0.6*
2019	*TEX*	*MLB*	*20*	*438*	*52*	*17*	*3*	*13*	*50*	*34*	*96*	*7*	*2*	*.244/.307/.398*	*.236*	*2.6*	*.288*	*0.5*	*CF -5, LF 0*	*-0.3*

Breakout: 0% Improve: 8% Collapse: 2% Attrition: 8% MLB: 16% *Comparables: Engel Beltre, Rougned Odor, Elvis Andrus*

Taveras is a good candidate for poster boy of the "don't scout the stat line" club for 2017. He was already in full-season ball at age 18, so the precocious center fielder's "lack" of production comes with plenty of caveats, the best being "he's a tools-laden teenager." Taveras flashes average or better tools across the board, and if the right ones play to their potential you're talking about a dynamic center fielder on both sides of the ball. The switch-hitter has a good feel for the barrel from both sides, and while he'll go chasing now and then he balances it with flashes of patience. There's bat-speed-driven average raw power in the frame right now, and if he fills out it could inch higher. If you are intent on focusing on the stats, keep this one in mind, too: 100 percent of his at-bats were against pitchers older than he was.

Anderson Tejeda SS Born: 05/01/98 Age: 20 Bats: L Throws: R Height: 5'11" Weight: 185 Origin: International Free Agent, 2014

YEAR	TEAM	LVL	AGE	PA	R	2B	3B	HR	RBI	BB	K	SB	CS	AVG/OBP/SLG	TAv	VORP	BABIP	BRR	FRAA	WARP
2015	DRG	RK	17	55	4	2	2	0	8	8	11	2	2	.277/.382/.404	.269	2.9	.361	0.5	2B(10): -0.2, SS(4): -0.2	0.2
2015	DRN	RK	17	180	32	17	4	4	32	17	38	7	5	.323/.397/.557	.335	21.7	.402	-0.5	SS(29): -0.3, 2B(8): -0.6	2.0
2016	DRG	RK	18	47	9	2	3	1	7	5	4	5	0	.262/.340/.524	.335	5.6	.270	-0.1	SS(8): 1.7, 3B(1): 0.1	0.7
2016	RNG	RK	18	142	22	12	6	1	21	8	36	1	0	.293/.331/.496	.304	11.8	.392	-0.3	SS(20): -4.0, 2B(12): -0.4	0.7
2016	SPO	A-	18	99	15	0	1	8	19	5	33	1	0	.277/.313/.553	.285	6.6	.340	0.5	SS(17): -1.9, 2B(3): -0.4	0.5
2017	HIC	A	19	446	68	24	9	8	53	36	132	10	7	.247/.309/.411	.268	21.9	.343	2.0	SS(82): -2.0, 2B(30): 0.0	2.1
2018	*TEX*	*MLB*	*20*	*250*	*25*	*10*	*2*	*7*	*28*	*17*	*86*	*2*	*1*	*.211/.269/.368*	*.208*	*-2.4*	*.296*	*-0.2*	*SS -1, 2B 0*	*-0.3*
2019	*TEX*	*MLB*	*21*	*372*	*43*	*16*	*3*	*12*	*44*	*28*	*126*	*4*	*2*	*.221/.284/.394*	*.226*	*-0.9*	*.307*	*-0.1*	*SS -1, 2B 1*	*-0.2*

Breakout: 2% Improve: 7% Collapse: 0% Attrition: 3% MLB: 9% *Comparables: Trevor Story, Matt Davidson, Raul Mondesi*

Tejeda didn't quite substantiate our top 101 ranking during his full-season debut at Hickory, a spot where Rangers prospects of yesteryear have often seen their prospect stocks soar, not deflate. Nevertheless, Tejeda is still a teenager and the ingredients for an impact shortstop—raw power and bat speed at the dish, arm strength and sufficient twitch in the field—are there. The makings of a long-term bus rider—loads of swing and miss, defensive inconsistency—are also there.

Bubba Thompson CF Born: 06/09/98 Age: 20 Bats: R Throws: R Height: 6'2" Weight: 180 Origin: Round 1, 2017 Draft (#26 overall)

YEAR	TEAM	LVL	AGE	PA	R	2B	3B	HR	RBI	BB	K	SB	CS	AVG/OBP/SLG	TAv	VORP	BABIP	BRR	FRAA	WARP
2017	RNG	RK	19	123	23	7	2	3	12	6	28	5	5	.257/.317/.434	.245	2.6	.317	0.8	CF(25): -4.0	-0.1
2018	*TEX*	*MLB*	*20*	*250*	*29*	*9*	*0*	*7*	*22*	*13*	*81*	*5*	*3*	*.201/.249/.334*	*.189*	*-9.0*	*.272*	*-0.4*	*CF -2*	*-1.2*
2019	*TEX*	*MLB*	*21*	*219*	*23*	*8*	*1*	*6*	*23*	*12*	*68*	*5*	*3*	*.209/.261/.348*	*.207*	*-5.8*	*.277*	*0.0*	*CF -2*	*-0.8*

Breakout: 1% Improve: 1% Collapse: 0% Attrition: 1% MLB: 2% *Comparables: Engel Beltre, Joe Benson, Cedric Hunter*

Thompson, a one-time quarterback prospect, has athleticism that stands out on the diamond. The right-handed hitter produces plus-plus run times that he uses on the bases and in the field. He's unpolished in center field, but his speed helps him close on balls on which he takes poor routes. While there are still varying opinions on his abilities at the plate, the community's appraisal of Thompson's bat ticked up over the course of his senior year, resulting in his first-round selection. A physical, broad-shouldered build gives hope that he can pack on weight to add power while retaining his speed in the field. There's a lot of projection involved, but Thompson fits the mold of the high-end, athletic prep players the Rangers have turned into major leaguers in the past.

PITCHERS

Tony Barnette RHP Born: 11/09/83 Age: 34 Bats: R Throws: R Height: 6'1" Weight: 190 Origin: Round 10, 2006 Draft (#297 overall)

YEAR	TEAM	LVL	AGE	W	L	SV	G	GS	IP	H	HR	BB/9	K/9	K	GB%	BABIP	WHIP	ERA	DRA	WARP	MPH	CMD	PWR	STM
2016	TEX	MLB	32	7	3	0	53	0	60^1	54	4	2.4	7.3	49	48%	.289	1.16	2.09	3.79	0.8	94.2	46	38	41
2017	TEX	MLB	33	2	1	2	50	0	57^1	64	7	3.5	8.9	57	42%	.348	1.50	5.49	4.29	0.6	94.2	57	35	46
2018	*TEX*	*MLB*	*34*	*2*	*3*	*0*	*50*	*0*	*53*	*56*	*8*	*4.0*	*7.4*	*44*	*43%*	*.304*	*1.52*	*5.10*	*4.87*	*0.2*	*93.1*	*52*	*36*	*43*
2019	*TEX*	*MLB*	*35*	*1*	*0*	*0*	*28*	*0*	29^2	*34*	*5*	*4.9*	*6.0*	*20*	*43%*	*.305*	*1.70*	*6.08*	*6.15*	*-0.3*	*92.5*	*51*	*35*	*43*

Breakout: 15% Improve: 26% Collapse: 38% Attrition: 7% MLB: 86% *Comparables: Mike Lincoln, Jason Frasor, Justin Speier*

Barnette blew back in from Japan in 2016, all long hair and long limbs, with a funky new delivery and a good fastball and cutter. He posted a 2.09 ERA and a 3.79 DRA, and the Rangers hoped for more of the same, but last year's campaign was plagued by inconsistency, with the right-hander struggling early and late in the season surrounding a disabled list stint. He upped his K/9 to 8.9, with more whiffs on his four-seamer and cutter, but saw his BB/9 balloon as well. It all added up to a ho-hum year that a new haircut couldn't save. The Rangers declined his 2018 option, but will him bring back on a cheaper one-year deal to provide middle relief depth.

Austin Bibens-Dirkx RHP Born: 04/29/85 Age: 33 Bats: R Throws: R Height: 6'1" Weight: 210 Origin: Round 16, 2006 Draft (#471 overall)

YEAR	TEAM	LVL	AGE	W	L	SV	G	GS	IP	H	HR	BB/9	K/9	K	GB%	BABIP	WHIP	ERA	DRA	WARP	MPH	CMD	PWR	STM
2015	BUF	AAA	30	0	1	0	5	3	17^1	20	1	2.1	9.3	18	46%	.373	1.38	4.67	2.98	0.4				
2015	NHP	AA	30	7	8	0	20	18	97	100	11	2.6	8.0	86	42%	.308	1.32	4.08	3.23	2.2				
2016	ROU	AAA	31	3	2	0	17	13	85	85	11	2.6	6.6	62	40%	.282	1.29	4.34	4.45	0.8				
2017	ROU	AAA	32	0	2	0	6	3	23^2	22	3	2.7	7.6	20	49%	.284	1.23	3.04	3.40	0.6				
2017	TEX	MLB	32	5	2	0	24	6	69^1	74	14	2.6	4.9	38	41%	.268	1.36	4.67	6.22	-0.7	91.7	45	28	45
2018	*TEX*	*MLB*	*33*	*4*	*4*	*0*	*27*	*11*	75^1	*83*	*14*	*3.5*	*6.3*	*53*	*41%*	*.290*	*1.49*	*5.67*	*5.76*	*-0.2*	*90.7*	*44*	*28*	*44*
2019	*TEX*	*MLB*	*34*	*3*	*4*	*0*	*20*	*11*	*82*	*93*	*15*	*3.4*	*5.9*	*53*	*41%*	*.295*	*1.51*	*5.85*	*5.91*	*-0.3*	*90.0*	*44*	*27*	*44*

Breakout: 5% Improve: 9% Collapse: 4% Attrition: 6% MLB: 13% *Comparables: Brian Sweeney, Justin Germano, Yunesky Maya*

In many ways, Bibens-Dirkx's career mirrors that of a beleaguered academic, and not just because his name sounds like that of a Classics PhD grinding away at a new translation of the *Enchiridion*. He spent years toiling in professional obscurity, complete with periods abroad to widen his experience. And then finally, the big day. Bibens-Dirkx made his major-league debut, and became one of only nine American-born rookies to make at least five starts at age 32 or older in the post-integration era. We'll admit that sounds a bit strained for a fun fact, but it's consistent with his repertoire: a fastball that's a little slow, a sinker that doesn't sink much, a DRA over 6.00. It all combined for a season that was fairly unremarkable, when you set aside how remarkable it was that he had a season at all. And so, unlike many an ABD clogging the graduate student lounges of American higher ed, Bibens-Dirkx actually finished his dissertation and graduated. Whether he'll be able to find steady employment after all of that education remains to be seen, though in a free agent pitching market with few safe options, there should be opportunities to at least adjunct.

Matt Bush RHP Born: 02/08/86 Age: 32 Bats: R Throws: R Height: 5'9" Weight: 180 Origin: Round 1, 2004 Draft (#1 overall)

YEAR	TEAM	LVL	AGE	W	L	SV	G	GS	IP	H	HR	BB/9	K/9	K	GB%	BABIP	WHIP	ERA	DRA	WARP	MPH	CMD	PWR	STM
2016	FRI	AA	30	0	2	5	12	0	17	9	2	2.1	9.5	18	42%	.184	0.76	2.65	2.20	0.5				
2016	TEX	MLB	30	7	2	1	58	0	61^2	44	4	2.0	8.9	61	45%	.245	0.94	2.48	2.59	1.7	99.7	62	64	52
2017	TEX	MLB	31	3	4	10	57	0	52^1	57	7	3.3	10.0	58	39%	.329	1.45	3.78	5.12	0.0	99.2	35	73	44
2018	*TEX*	*MLB*	*32*	*4*	*5*	*0*	*40*	*10*	*81*	*85*	*14*	*3.4*	*8.4*	*77*	*42%*	*.300*	*1.43*	*4.93*	*4.84*	*0.4*	*98.4*	*47*	*68*	*47*
2019	*TEX*	*MLB*	*33*	*5*	*5*	*0*	*53*	*12*	113^1	*128*	*21*	*4.4*	*6.8*	*85*	*42%*	*.302*	*1.62*	*6.12*	*6.17*	*-0.8*	*97.8*	*46*	*68*	*47*

Breakout: 22% Improve: 42% Collapse: 24% Attrition: 6% MLB: 89% *Comparables: Joakim Soria, Kevin Gregg, Will Ohman*

Bush's monthly FIPs were as follows last season: 2.35, 3.98, 7.12, 2.30, 1.82, 8.16. Not exactly a sterling year for consistency. In Bush's defense, he battled shoulder discomfort much of the year, at one point landing on the disabled list with a right MCL sprain, before eventually needing offseason surgery. Amidst all that inconsistency, though, were prolonged stretches when he looked like the player who was worth almost two WARP in 2016. He assumed closer duties when Sam Dyson hit the DL with "being not a good pitcher" and racked up 11 saves. He still throws a high-90s fastball that generates plenty of swings and misses, and pairs it with a hard slider. He'll need to try to limit the walks and home runs if Jon Daniels' plan to try Bush as a starter in 2018 is going to stick, but given some of the Rangers' other options he might not need to try that hard.

Andrew Cashner RHP
Born: 09/11/86 Age: 31 Bats: R Throws: R Height: 6'6" Weight: 235 Origin: Round 1, 2008 Draft (#19 overall)

YEAR	TEAM	LVL	AGE	W	L	SV	G	GS	IP	H	HR	BB/9	K/9	K	GB%	BABIP	WHIP	ERA	DRA	WARP	MPH	CMD	PWR	STM
2015	SDN	MLB	28	6	16	0	31	31	184^{2}	200	19	3.2	8.0	165	50%	.330	1.44	4.34	5.19	-0.2	98.1	55	68	76
2016	SDN	MLB	29	4	7	0	16	16	79^{1}	80	13	3.4	7.6	67	49%	.291	1.39	4.76	6.05	-0.6	97.2	56	60	61
2016	MIA	MLB	29	1	4	0	12	11	52^{2}	62	6	5.1	7.7	45	47%	.352	1.75	5.98	5.97	-0.4	96.6	56	60	61
2017	TEX	MLB	30	11	11	0	28	28	166^{2}	156	15	3.5	4.6	86	49%	.266	1.32	3.40	4.81	1.4	96.0	55	59	70
2018	*TEX*	*MLB*	*31*	*8*	*8*	*0*	*23*	*23*	130^{2}	*140*	*18*	*3.9*	*6.4*	*93*	*48%*	*.298*	*1.50*	*5.13*	*5.18*	*0.7*	*96.0*	*55*	*62*	*68*
2019	*TEX*	*MLB*	*32*	*7*	*9*	*0*	*22*	*22*	130^{2}	*146*	*17*	*4.1*	*6.3*	*92*	*48%*	*.309*	*1.57*	*5.31*	*5.34*	*0.5*	*95.3*	*55*	*59*	*66*

Breakout: 9% Improve: 37% Collapse: 34% Attrition: 10% MLB: 91% *Comparables: Yovani Gallardo, Scott Feldman, Clay Buchholz*

In episode 2.23 of *Frasier*, titular psychologist Frasier Crane and his brother, Niles, open a French restaurant, only to have it fail the very first night. Later, in season seven, they attempt to sell a Russian bear-clock they believe proves a familial link to the Romanovs, only to have it reappropriated by a Russian cultural attaché. They end up having to pay for their father's new $25,000 Winnebago as a result (it was a busy episode). Throughout the series, Frasier and Niles overpaid for countless cases of wine, had ill-advised trysts with women too beautiful for them and threw bricks through art gallery windows, but in the end, they did it all without much in the way of real consequences; the signature view from Frasier's apartment was never in as much jeopardy as the circumstances demanded. In many respects, Andrew Cashner's 2017 was a classic Crane misadventure: he posted an unsustainable .171 BABIP with men in scoring position, a league-high contact percentage and the second-worst strikeout rate in the bigs. It was all a disaster in the making, but like so many of Frasier's encounters with Lilith, Cashner managed to get away with embarrassment that didn't last past the next morning and a 3.40 ERA. And yet, the Rangers passed on extending him a qualifying offer as a free agent.

Alex Claudio LHP
Born: 01/31/92 Age: 26 Bats: L Throws: L Height: 6'3" Weight: 180 Origin: Round 27, 2010 Draft (#826 overall)

YEAR	TEAM	LVL	AGE	W	L	SV	G	GS	IP	H	HR	BB/9	K/9	K	GB%	BABIP	WHIP	ERA	DRA	WARP	MPH	CMD	PWR	STM
2015	TEX	MLB	23	1	1	0	18	0	15^{2}	12	4	3.4	7.5	13	52%	.190	1.15	2.87	3.84	0.2	86.2	62	0	46
2015	ROU	AAA	23	3	1	0	29	0	40	43	2	1.6	7.9	35	57%	.347	1.25	2.92	2.36	1.2				
2016	ROU	AAA	24	0	0	1	6	0	16^{1}	7	0	2.2	4.4	8	71%	.156	0.67	0.55	3.81	0.2				
2016	TEX	MLB	24	4	1	0	39	0	51^{2}	55	2	1.7	5.9	34	63%	.312	1.26	2.79	3.41	0.9	88.2	68	18	40
2017	TEX	MLB	25	4	2	11	70	1	82^{2}	71	5	1.6	6.1	56	68%	.269	1.04	2.50	2.41	2.6	88.0	66	10	52
2018	*TEX*	*MLB*	*26*	*3*	*3*	*24*	*60*	*0*	*63*	*62*	*5*	*3.3*	*6.8*	*48*	*58%*	*.293*	*1.34*	*3.73*	*3.82*	*1.0*	*87.6*	*68*	*12*	*47*
2019	*TEX*	*MLB*	*27*	*3*	*1*	*14*	*51*	*0*	*54*	*54*	*5*	*3.3*	*7.1*	*42*	*58%*	*.298*	*1.36*	*4.31*	*4.29*	*0.6*	*87.4*	*68*	*13*	*48*

Breakout: 33% Improve: 52% Collapse: 23% Attrition: 13% MLB: 83% *Comparables: Jeremy Accardo, Jesse Crain, Manny Corpas*

Claudius: Readers, it is true that I am hard of hearing, but you will find it is not for want of listening. As for velocity, again, it's true I have an impediment. But isn't what a man throws more important than how hard he throws it? It's true again I had little experience of closing. But, then, have you more? I at least have lived in a bullpen which has ruled the late innings ever since you so sabermetrically handed it over to us. I've observed it working more closely than any of you. Is your experience better than that? As for averaging half-a-K per inning: well, what can I say, except that I have survived to 25 with a good change, while thousands have died their fastballs intact. Evidently, quality of strikeouts is more important than quantity. Managers, I shall limit my meltdowns. I shall appear in the next season of baseball, where you may use me or not as wish, but if it pleases you not to, explain your reasons to them [points to the tattered remnants of the 2017 Rangers 'pen] not to me.

Kyle Cody RHP
Born: 08/09/94 Age: 23 Bats: R Throws: R Height: 6'7" Weight: 245 Origin: Round 6, 2016 Draft (#189 overall)

YEAR	TEAM	LVL	AGE	W	L	SV	G	GS	IP	H	HR	BB/9	K/9	K	GB%	BABIP	WHIP	ERA	DRA	WARP	MPH	CMD	PWR	STM
2016	SPO	A-	21	2	5	0	12	9	47^{1}	56	4	2.5	10.1	53	58%	.380	1.46	5.13	2.13	1.7				
2017	HIC	A	22	6	6	0	18	18	95^{1}	77	4	3.1	9.5	101	47%	.286	1.15	2.83	3.24	2.3				
2017	DEB	A+	22	3	0	0	5	5	30^{2}	25	0	2.9	10.3	35	51%	.325	1.14	2.05	3.01	0.8				
2018	*TEX*	*MLB*	*23*	*5*	*7*	*0*	*17*	*17*	89^{1}	*95*	*20*	*4.4*	*9.4*	*93*	*43%*	*.312*	*1.55*	*5.75*	*5.84*	*-0.1*				
2019	*TEX*	*MLB*	*24*	*6*	*9*	*0*	*22*	*22*	*129*	*141*	*28*	*4.4*	*8.6*	*123*	*43%*	*.31*	*1.58*	*6.09*	*6.18*	*-0.7*				

Breakout: 10% Improve: 13% Collapse: 3% Attrition: 13% MLB: 20% *Comparables: Juan Nicasio, Marc Rzepczynski, John Gant*

Cody dominated both levels of A-ball in 2017, and with good reason: He was too old for the levels and, more relevantly, his stuff was too darn good. He exploited low-level hitters with a three-pitch mix, headlined by a plus-plus potential fastball that features arm-side run and clocks in the mid-90s. His potential average changeup arrives a bit firm, and it's worth following whether upper-level hitters are able to capitalize on the lack of difference in speeds. The breaking ball is another potential average offering, and the entire repertoire makes him a viable mid-rotation arm.

Hans Crouse RHP
Born: 09/15/98 Age: 19 Bats: L Throws: R Height: 6'4" Weight: 180 Origin: Round 2, 2017 Draft (#66 overall)

YEAR	TEAM	LVL	AGE	W	L	SV	G	GS	IP	H	HR	BB/9	K/9	K	GB%	BABIP	WHIP	ERA	DRA	WARP	MPH	CMD	PWR	STM
2017	RNG	RK	18	0	0	0	10	6	20	7	1	3.2	13.5	30	60%	.176	0.70	0.45	1.20	0.9				
2018	*TEX*	*MLB*	*19*	*1*	*2*	*0*	*16*	*5*	30^{2}	*34*	*9*	*7.0*	*9.8*	*33*	*42%*	*.311*	*1.89*	*7.41*	*7.59*	*-0.8*				
2019	*TEX*	*MLB*	*20*	*2*	*3*	*1*	*27*	*9*	89^{2}	*99*	*19*	*6.1*	*8.1*	*81*	*42%*	*.307*	*1.78*	*6.86*	*6.98*	*-1.0*				

Comparables: Jose Berrios, Martin Perez, Luis Avilan

The Rangers' second-round pick in 2017, Crouse is a perfect blend of new- and old-school evaluation. On the one hand, we have data from from last year's National High School Invitational—a tournament stocked with top prep prospects—telling us that Crouse's fastball velocity was easily best at the tournament and, further, that he can spin both his fastball and breaking ball at an elite rate. On the other hand, describing Crouse is the same as it ever was for any high schooler with prodigious stuff. Pick a characteristic or deficiency that allows for hedging with a relief projection and Crouse has it: violent and inconsistent mechanics, long arm action, extreme head whack, arm speed that makes you question his ability to hold up under a starter's workload, an underdeveloped changeup, a presently lethal fastball/power curve combo that could fast track him to the bigs if need be. No matter how you describe or project Crouse, the tape shows an occasional shimmy that owes a debt to Johnny Cueto, an intermittent waggle that borrows from Marcus Stroman, a general vibe that is equal parts invigorating and terrifying. He's a reminder to put the academia aside and simply enjoy the show.

Jake Diekman LHP Born: 01/21/87 Age: 31 Bats: L Throws: L Height: 6'4" Weight: 200 Origin: Round 30, 2007 Draft (#923 overall)

YEAR	TEAM	LVL	AGE	W	L	SV	G	GS	IP	H	HR	BB/9	K/9	K	GB%	BABIP	WHIP	ERA	DRA	WARP	MPH	CMD	PWR	STM
2015	PHI	MLB	28	2	1	0	41	0	36^{2}	40	3	5.9	12.0	49	55%	.381	1.75	5.15	3.04	0.7	99.0	41	75	53
2015	TEX	MLB	28	0	0	0	26	0	21^{2}	13	2	2.9	8.3	20	60%	.200	0.92	2.08	2.89	0.5	99.5	41	75	53
2016	TEX	MLB	29	4	2	4	66	0	53	36	4	4.4	10.0	59	50%	.248	1.17	3.40	2.84	1.3	97.7	52	66	45
2017	TEX	MLB	30	0	0	1	11	0	10^{2}	4	1	8.4	11.0	13	59%	.143	1.31	2.53	3.99	0.1	97.5			40
2018	*TEX*	*MLB*	*31*	*3*	*3*	*1*	*55*	*0*	*58*	*56*	*8*	*4.9*	*9.5*	*62*	*49%*	*.304*	*1.51*	*4.61*	*4.51*	*0.4*	*97.4*	*47*	*70*	*45*
2019	*TEX*	*MLB*	*32*	*2*	*1*	*1*	*41*	*0*	*43*	*42*	*7*	*5.1*	*10.0*	*48*	*49%*	*.309*	*1.53*	*5.08*	*5.08*	*0.1*	*96.5*	*49*	*67*	*43*

Breakout: 28% Improve: 42% Collapse: 32% Attrition: 17% MLB: 94% *Comparables: Adam Ottavino, Fernando Rodney, Michael Wuertz*

Sometimes the point is in being there at all. Diekman was sidelined for most of 2017 by three surgeries to replace his colon as he battled ulcerative colitis. When he returned, he struck out 13 and pitched his way to a 2.53 ERA. Sure, he walked 10, suggesting lingering control issues, and sure, his DRA was more than a run worse than his ERA. That wasn't the point. The point, as his foundation's slogan suggests, was to gut it out. The point was in being there at all.

Doug Fister RHP Born: 02/04/84 Age: 34 Bats: L Throws: R Height: 6'8" Weight: 210 Origin: Round 7, 2006 Draft (#201 overall)

YEAR	TEAM	LVL	AGE	W	L	SV	G	GS	IP	H	HR	BB/9	K/9	K	GB%	BABIP	WHIP	ERA	DRA	WARP	MPH	CMD	PWR	STM
2015	WAS	MLB	31	5	7	1	25	15	103	120	14	2.1	5.5	63	47%	.310	1.40	4.19	6.50	-1.8	88.9	57	27	50
2016	HOU	MLB	32	12	13	0	32	32	180^{1}	195	24	3.1	5.7	115	47%	.300	1.43	4.64	5.65	-0.6	89.7	61	36	77
2017	SLC	AAA	33	1	0	0	3	3	15^{2}	16	0	2.9	5.7	10	63%	.327	1.34	4.02	3.36	0.4				
2017	BOS	MLB	33	5	9	0	18	15	90^{1}	87	9	3.8	8.3	83	53%	.301	1.38	4.88	4.66	0.9	91.7	50	36	59
2018	*TEX*	*MLB*	*34*	*8*	*8*	*0*	*24*	*24*	*136*	*147*	*18*	*3.7*	*6.4*	*98*	*49%*	*.300*	*1.50*	*4.72*	*4.76*	*1.0*	*89.1*	*56*	*34*	*62*
2019	*TEX*	*MLB*	*35*	*9*	*11*	*0*	*29*	*29*	*180^{2}*	*194*	*21*	*3.6*	*6.6*	*132*	*49%*	*.306*	*1.47*	*4.91*	*4.91*	*1.4*	*88.7*	*55*	*35*	*64*

Breakout: 16% Improve: 46% Collapse: 16% Attrition: 11% MLB: 93% *Comparables: Scott Feldman, Tim Hudson, Larry Jackson*

When Fister was in his prime, part of his value came from his ability to limit free passes. For example, when he received some Cy Young votes in 2014, Fister posted an astounding 3.6 percent walk rate. He also produced a sub-15 percent strikeout rate, relying on good command and soft contact to win the day. That approach stopped working for Fister in 2015 and 2016, which is why he didn't even sign with an MLB team until the Angels got desperate this past May. But in 2017, Fister decided that if he was going to fail again, he'd do so in a different way. Our gangly hero worried less about command and more about missing bats. He seemed to air it out more, gaining a mph back on his fastball, but throwing it less often in favor of his slider and curveball. The result? The highest strikeout and walk rates of his career, a playoff start with the Red Sox and his first sub-5.00 DRA since his Nationals days. See, it turns out you *can* teach an old Dog Fister new tricks.

Chi Chi Gonzalez RHP Born: 01/15/92 Age: 26 Bats: R Throws: R Height: 6'3" Weight: 215 Origin: Round 1, 2013 Draft (#23 overall)

YEAR	TEAM	LVL	AGE	W	L	SV	G	GS	IP	H	HR	BB/9	K/9	K	GB%	BABIP	WHIP	ERA	DRA	WARP	MPH	CMD	PWR	STM
2015	ROU	AAA	23	8	7	0	16	16	88^{1}	95	3	3.2	5.7	56	54%	.325	1.43	3.57	4.55	0.8				
2015	TEX	MLB	23	4	6	0	14	10	67	49	6	4.3	4.0	30	50%	.206	1.21	3.90	5.24	-0.2	94.3	53	54	64
2016	TEX	MLB	24	0	2	0	3	3	10^{1}	21	1	7.8	6.1	7	46%	.444	2.90	8.71	7.87	-0.3	94.4	46	50	70
2016	ROU	AAA	24	8	10	0	25	24	138	154	8	2.9	5.9	91	57%	.330	1.43	4.70	5.24	0.2				
2018	*TEX*	*MLB*	*26*	*2*	*2*	*0*	*6*	*6*	*33^{2}*	*36*	*4*	*3.8*	*6.0*	*22*	*46%*	*.300*	*1.51*	*5.00*	*5.05*	*0.2*	*93.9*	*52*	*54*	*69*
2019	*TEX*	*MLB*	*27*	*7*	*11*	*0*	*27*	*27*	*161^{1}*	*194*	*31*	*3.5*	*5.6*	*100*	*46%*	*.307*	*1.59*	*6.08*	*6.16*	*-0.8*	*93.5*	*51*	*54*	*70*

Breakout: 25% Improve: 45% Collapse: 21% Attrition: 28% MLB: 78% *Comparables: Drew VerHagen, Andrew Chafin, Jake Buchanan*

Gonzalez missed all of 2017 with a partial UCL tear that required surgery, and is likely to miss all of 2018 rehabbing. Needing Tommy John surgery following a season in which you allowed a .444 BABIP with a 7.87 DRA isn't known to have been one of Job's trials, but theologians find their way to new interpretations of sacred texts all the time. The Rangers re-signed Gonzalez to a minor-league deal, presumably hoping a major leaguer emerges on the other side of all that suffering. Chi Chi just hopes to know what to do with 1,000 she-asses and all those sheep when they come.

Miguel Gonzalez RHP Born: 05/27/84 Age: 34 Bats: R Throws: R Height: 6'1" Weight: 170 Origin: International Free Agent, 2004

YEAR	TEAM	LVL	AGE	W	L	SV	G	GS	IP	H	HR	BB/9	K/9	K	GB%	BABIP	WHIP	ERA	DRA	WARP	MPH	CMD	PWR	STM
2015	BAL	MLB	31	9	12	0	26	26	144^{2}	151	24	3.2	6.8	109	42%	.295	1.40	4.91	5.48	-0.7	93.8	54	45	63
2016	CHR	AAA	32	1	1	0	5	5	21^{1}	27	5	1.7	10.5	25	42%	.386	1.45	4.64	1.92	0.8				
2016	CHA	MLB	32	5	8	0	24	23	135	132	11	2.3	6.3	95	42%	.289	1.24	3.73	4.23	1.7	94.0	52	40	65
2017	CHA	MLB	33	7	10	0	22	22	133^{2}	145	16	3.2	5.7	85	38%	.296	1.44	4.31	4.95	0.9	92.6	57	36	71
2017	TEX	MLB	33	1	3	0	5	5	22^{1}	22	6	3.2	6.0	15	32%	.246	1.34	6.45	7.17	-0.4	93.1	57	36	71
2018	*TEX*	*MLB*	*34*	*8*	*9*	*0*	*25*	*25*	*139*	*148*	*22*	*3.4*	*6.3*	*97*	*41%*	*.291*	*1.45*	*5.24*	*5.30*	*0.6*	*92.2*	*54*	*39*	*66*
2019	*TEX*	*MLB*	*35*	*7*	*9*	*0*	*23*	*23*	*133*	*146*	*20*	*3.4*	*6.3*	*93*	*41%*	*.3*	*1.48*	*5.39*	*5.43*	*0.3*	*91.6*	*54*	*37*	*66*

Breakout: 11% Improve: 46% Collapse: 18% Attrition: 12% MLB: 89% *Comparables: Jason Vargas, Roy Oswalt, Ervin Santana*

When the Rangers found themselves kinda, sorta, maybe in the playoff hunt in August, they looked everywhere only to find that after dealing Yu Darvish in July there were no extra Darvishes laying around to help with a stretch run. They settled for Gonzalez, acquiring him and his drab 4.95 DRA from the White Sox, hoping it would be enough to shore up a leaky rotation. [extreme Ron Howard *Arrested Development* narrator voice] It would not be. Going from Yu Darvish to Miguel Gonzalez is, it turns out, like going from Yu Darvish to Miguel Gonzalez. In the end, the Rangers didn't factor in the AL wild card race and Gonzalez didn't factor much for the Rangers.

A.J. Griffin RHP Born: 01/28/88 Age: 30 Bats: R Throws: R Height: 6'5" Weight: 230 Origin: Round 13, 2010 Draft (#395 overall)

YEAR	TEAM	LVL	AGE	W	L	SV	G	GS	IP	H	HR	BB/9	K/9	K	GB%	BABIP	WHIP	ERA	DRA	WARP	MPH	CMD	PWR	STM
2016	FRI	AA	28	0	1	0	3	3	10^{1}	12	0	3.5	11.3	13	50%	.400	1.55	3.48	3.62	0.2				
2016	TEX	MLB	28	7	4	0	23	23	119	116	28	3.5	8.1	107	31%	.274	1.36	5.07	6.74	-1.9	90.4	50	31	56
2017	TEX	MLB	29	6	6	0	18	15	77^{1}	76	20	3.3	7.1	61	29%	.251	1.34	5.94	4.88	0.6	89.4	52	9	43
2018	*TEX*	*MLB*	*30*	*5*	*7*	*0*	*18*	*18*	*84^{1}*	*86*	*19*	*3.7*	*7.7*	*72*	*34%*	*.276*	*1.43*	*5.98*	*6.10*	*-0.4*	*89.2*	*51*	*21*	*49*
2019	*TEX*	*MLB*	*31*	*6*	*10*	*0*	*26*	*26*	*157^{2}*	*156*	*33*	*4.0*	*7.9*	*138*	*34%*	*.276*	*1.44*	*5.98*	*6.07*	*-0.6*	*88.8*	*51*	*21*	*48*

Breakout: 23% Improve: 40% Collapse: 13% Attrition: 10% MLB: 85% *Comparables: Mike Flanagan, Bud Norris, Eric Milton*

A year after making it back from Tommy John surgery, Griffin's season featured the following: a brief disabled list stint for gout in his left ankle, followed by a much longer DL stint for a left intercostal muscle strain, followed by a brief move to the bullpen; a 4.88 DRA; more than three free passes per nine innings; a FIP over six. To top it all off, he was non-tendered in December. Every kid in Little League dreams of making it to the bigs, and Griffin has certainly shown resilience in a career stunted by injury and ineffectiveness, but at some point, we might forgive him if he looks around, realizes the creepy clown paintings, giant flying shrimp and home runs allowed are features, not bugs, and declares after the next reset, "Oh, *this* is the Bad Place."

Jason Grilli RHP Born: 11/11/76 Age: 41 Bats: R Throws: R Height: 6'5" Weight: 235 Origin: Round 1, 1997 Draft (#4 overall)

YEAR	TEAM	LVL	AGE	W	L	SV	G	GS	IP	H	HR	BB/9	K/9	K	GB%	BABIP	WHIP	ERA	DRA	WARP	MPH	CMD	PWR	STM
2015	ATL	MLB	38	3	4	24	36	0	33^{2}	28	2	2.7	12.0	45	27%	.313	1.13	2.94	2.21	1.0	96.0	57	58	44
2016	ATL	MLB	39	1	2	2	21	0	17	16	2	6.9	12.2	23	20%	.333	1.71	5.29	3.76	0.2	93.7	48	46	48
2016	TOR	MLB	39	6	4	2	46	0	42	28	8	4.1	12.4	58	35%	.238	1.12	3.64	3.92	0.5	94.7	48	46	48
2017	TOR	MLB	40	2	4	1	26	0	20^{2}	24	9	3.9	10.0	23	35%	.278	1.60	6.97	4.43	0.2	94.4	47	48	37
2017	TEX	MLB	40	0	1	0	20	0	19^{1}	22	3	4.2	11.6	25	18%	.373	1.60	5.59	4.30	0.2	93.8	47	48	37
2018	*TEX*	*MLB*	*41*	*2*	*1*	*1*	*36*	*0*	*37^{2}*	*38*	*8*	*4.2*	*9.9*	*42*	*33%*	*.304*	*1.48*	*5.40*	*5.47*	*-0.1*	*92.8*	*47*	*47*	*41*
2019	*TEX*	*MLB*	*42*	*2*	*0*	*1*	*34*	*0*	*30*	*32*	*7*	*4.4*	*9.5*	*32*	*33%*	*.308*	*1.55*	*5.98*	*6.03*	*-0.3*	*91.9*	*46*	*45*	*40*

Breakout: 10% Improve: 35% Collapse: 18% Attrition: 9% MLB: 64% *Comparables: Dan Plesac, Joel Peralta, Doug Bair*

The Rangers acquired Grilli in July from the Blue Jays in a classic "our prospect for your underperforming-relative-to-last-year's-slight-overperformance reliever, who is better than our league-leading 17 blown saves" move. You know, the ol' OPFYURTLYSORWIBTOLL17BS. Grilli pitched alright-ish, which was an upgrade for the Texas 'pen, before losing innings to younger players down the stretch. It appears the 41-year-old wants to play again, but if it doesn't work out, he can always open Jason's Bar and Grilli. What!? He might not be in the *Annual* next year!

Cole Hamels LHP Born: 12/27/83 Age: 34 Bats: L Throws: L Height: 6'4" Weight: 205 Origin: Round 1, 2002 Draft (#17 overall)

YEAR	TEAM	LVL	AGE	W	L	SV	G	GS	IP	H	HR	BB/9	K/9	K	GB%	BABIP	WHIP	ERA	DRA	WARP	MPH	CMD	PWR	STM
2015	PHI	MLB	31	6	7	0	20	20	128^{2}	113	12	2.7	9.6	137	51%	.294	1.18	3.64	3.05	3.1	94.8	51	54	80
2015	TEX	MLB	31	7	1	0	12	12	83^{2}	77	10	2.5	8.4	78	48%	.294	1.20	3.66	2.99	2.1	95.5	51	54	80
2016	TEX	MLB	32	15	5	0	32	32	200^{2}	185	24	3.5	9.0	200	50%	.299	1.31	3.32	3.44	4.4	94.9	58	53	83
2017	TEX	MLB	33	11	6	0	24	24	148	125	18	3.2	6.4	105	48%	.251	1.20	4.20	4.49	1.8	93.5	47	48	63
2018	*TEX*	*MLB*	*34*	*12*	*11*	*0*	*29*	*29*	*194^{1}*	*199*	*28*	*3.6*	*7.3*	*157*	*48%*	*.295*	*1.43*	*4.75*	*4.79*	*1.4*	*93.3*	*52*	*51*	*73*
2019	*TEX*	*MLB*	*35*	*11*	*12*	*0*	*29*	*29*	*180^{1}*	*185*	*24*	*3.9*	*7.2*	*144*	*48%*	*.299*	*1.46*	*5.09*	*5.11*	*1.2*	*92.6*	*51*	*50*	*71*

Breakout: 16% Improve: 49% Collapse: 21% Attrition: 11% MLB: 96% *Comparables: Justin Verlander, Chris Carpenter, Ervin Santana*

The problem with talking about a pitcher entering his decline phase is timing. Get too fixated on an odd spike in walks, and you risk being Chicken Little. Ignore that spike for too long, and you've buried your head in the sand. Like pitchers of any stripe, those in their thirties give us all sorts of little signs of their health and acumen; those signs take on special significance as they force us to consider whether a staff ace is now a third starter. So we find ourselves when considering Hamels. He spent six weeks on the disabled list. A fluke after eight years of pitching 200-plus innings a year, or the beginning of recurring hiccups? He walked 3.2 batters per nine innings. Lingering effects of the injury, or part of an alarming trend? We could ask the same of his strikeout rate. Or the spike in DRA. When Hamels was acquired, it was as the final piece in what the Rangers hoped would be a championship team. They're in a different place now, and so is Hamels. He was an almost-two-win pitcher last year, but he likely wouldn't be at the head of a rotation that had better options. As he enters the final guaranteed year of his contract, it's hard to see the Rangers not picking up his $20 million 2019 option (versus a $6 million buyout) barring a total collapse. The question that remains is: Who will they be getting if they do, and when *does* the sky start falling?

Keone Kela RHP Born: 04/16/93 Age: 25 Bats: R Throws: R Height: 6'1" Weight: 215 Origin: Round 12, 2012 Draft (#396 overall)

YEAR	TEAM	LVL	AGE	W	L	SV	G	GS	IP	H	HR	BB/9	K/9	K	GB%	BABIP	WHIP	ERA	DRA	WARP	MPH	CMD	PWR	STM
2015	TEX	MLB	22	7	5	1	68	0	60^{1}	52	4	2.7	10.1	68	54%	.314	1.16	2.39	2.82	1.4	98.6	35	64	50
2016	TEX	MLB	23	5	1	0	35	0	34	30	6	4.5	11.9	45	46%	.304	1.38	6.09	3.74	0.5	98.0	37	58	29
2017	TEX	MLB	24	4	1	2	39	0	38^{2}	18	4	4.0	11.9	51	32%	.179	0.91	2.79	3.88	0.6	98.2	47	60	35
2018	*TEX*	*MLB*	*25*	*3*	*3*	*7*	*60*	*0*	*63*	*55*	*10*	*3.9*	*11.5*	*81*	*43%*	*.298*	*1.30*	*4.02*	*4.06*	*0.8*	*98.0*	*41*	*62*	*38*
2019	*TEX*	*MLB*	*26*	*2*	*1*	*3*	*46*	*0*	*49*	*43*	*9*	*4.1*	*12.4*	*67*	*43%*	*.305*	*1.33*	*4.78*	*4.77*	*0.2*	*97.7*	*43*	*61*	*35*

Breakout: 35% Improve: 51% Collapse: 19% Attrition: 15% MLB: 81% *Comparables: Joey Devine, Paco Rodriguez, Cody Allen*

Perhaps influenced by our larger cultural moment of general oddity, Kela's 2017 was Kinda Strange. He began the year in the minors as a disciplinary action for an altercation with teammates at the end of spring training. But when he got back, he was a pretty effective rally ... Kela (allow for laughter). His 2017 was closer to 2016's middling affair than his breakout of 2015, but Kela still missed bats and collected Ks, with 51 strikeouts and just four home runs. The fastball still sits in the high-90s, and is accompanied by a hard change and a hard curveball. He'll be in the conversation to be the 2018 closer, and will be an important piece of the bullpen regardless, provided he can stay healthy; this was the second year in a row he lost meaningful time to the DL.

Nick Martinez RHP Born: 08/05/90 Age: 27 Bats: L Throws: R Height: 6'1" Weight: 200 Origin: Round 18, 2011 Draft (#564 overall)

YEAR	TEAM	LVL	AGE	W	L	SV	G	GS	IP	H	HR	BB/9	K/9	K	GB%	BABIP	WHIP	ERA	DRA	WARP	MPH	CMD	PWR	STM
2015	ROU	AAA	24	1	1	0	6	6	31	32	1	2.0	5.2	18	43%	.320	1.26	2.90	5.36	0.0				
2015	TEX	MLB	24	7	7	0	24	21	125	135	16	3.3	5.5	77	44%	.293	1.45	3.96	6.00	-1.4	92.3	45	39	66
2016	ROU	AAA	25	7	6	0	18	16	99	109	7	1.5	6.1	67	51%	.321	1.27	3.91	3.99	1.5				
2016	TEX	MLB	25	2	3	0	12	5	38^{2}	45	8	4.4	3.7	16	50%	.282	1.66	5.59	6.91	-0.8	94.2	32	49	62
2017	ROU	AAA	26	4	0	0	7	6	37^{2}	27	3	1.7	5.5	23	43%	.212	0.90	2.15	4.03	0.7				
2017	TEX	MLB	26	3	8	0	23	18	111^{1}	124	26	2.3	5.4	67	43%	.276	1.37	5.66	6.37	-1.0	93.8	49	45	64
2018	*TEX*	*MLB*	*27*	*7*	*8*	*0*	*22*	*22*	123^{1}	*133*	*22*	*3.2*	*6.0*	*82*	*45%*	*.287*	*1.43*	*5.45*	*5.54*	*0.2*	*92.9*	*46*	*44*	*65*
2019	*TEX*	*MLB*	*28*	*6*	*7*	*0*	*19*	*19*	113^{2}	*120*	*18*	*3.0*	*6.3*	*79*	*45%*	*.29*	*1.39*	*5.34*	*5.40*	*0.3*	*92.8*	*46*	*46*	*64*

Breakout: 17% Improve: 40% Collapse: 22% Attrition: 12% MLB: 76% *Comparables: Brian Bannister, Brad Bergesen, Jeremy Sowers*

That Martinez threw 111 1/3 innings last season says more about the state of the Rangers' rotation than it does about Martinez's ability. He was recalled and sent down four times. He's the same as he ever was: a low-strikeout guy with average velocity who won't overwhelm you, but who has stretches of being serviceable. A DRA over six is never good, but he did manage to reduce his walk rate by throwing more in the zone (though that probably also explains the slight uptick in home runs). Not surprisingly, the Rangers non-tendered him.

Yohander Mendez LHP Born: 01/17/95 Age: 23 Bats: L Throws: L Height: 6'5" Weight: 200 Origin: International Free Agent, 2011

YEAR	TEAM	LVL	AGE	W	L	SV	G	GS	IP	H	HR	BB/9	K/9	K	GB%	BABIP	WHIP	ERA	DRA	WARP	MPH	CMD	PWR	STM
2015	HIC	A	20	3	3	3	21	8	66^{1}	57	2	2.0	10.0	74	54%	.312	1.09	2.44	1.49	2.8				
2016	HDS	A+	21	4	1	0	7	7	33	21	2	3.0	12.3	45	51%	.264	0.97	2.45	1.35	1.6				
2016	FRI	AA	21	4	1	0	10	10	46^{2}	39	2	2.7	8.9	46	47%	.296	1.14	3.09	2.91	1.2				
2016	ROU	AAA	21	4	1	0	7	4	31^{1}	12	0	4.6	6.3	22	40%	.150	0.89	0.57	5.92	-0.3				
2016	TEX	MLB	21	0	0	0	2	0	3	5	0	6.0	0.0	0	33%	.333	2.33	18.00	5.99	0.0	95.0			47
2017	FRI	AA	22	7	8	0	24	24	137^{2}	114	23	2.8	8.1	124	46%	.256	1.14	3.79	3.08	3.4				
2017	TEX	MLB	22	0	1	0	7	0	12^{1}	13	3	2.2	5.1	7	37%	.263	1.30	5.11	3.81	0.2	94.1			61
2018	*TEX*	*MLB*	*23*	*3*	*3*	*0*	*18*	*8*	*50*	*50*	*9*	*3.9*	*8.5*	*48*	*44%*	*.290*	*1.39*	*4.95*	*4.92*	*0.2*	*94.2*			*57*
2019	*TEX*	*MLB*	*24*	*7*	*8*	*0*	*51*	*21*	153^{1}	*146*	*29*	*4.1*	*9.3*	*159*	*44%*	*.29*	*1.41*	*5.42*	*5.46*	*0.1*	*94.0*			*57*

Breakout: 17% Improve: 31% Collapse: 11% Attrition: 23% MLB: 50% *Comparables: Jon Gray, Michael Bowden, Nick Maronde*

After racing through three levels of the minors and making his major-league debut in 2016, Mendez didn't hit a speed bump so much as a brick wall. The talented southpaw was busted back down to Double-A for the majority of the season, and struggled in his brief cup of coffee. He's still working with much the same arsenal as before, it just wasn't, y'know, *working*. He'll pound hitters with an average fastball from the left side and elicit swings with a changeup that's got more tumble than a gymnastics program. Finding a viable breaking ball will be crucial to Mendez's chances of hacking it in the majors, much less the rotation.

Mike Minor LHP Born: 12/26/87 Age: 30 Bats: R Throws: L Height: 6'4" Weight: 210 Origin: Round 1, 2009 Draft (#7 overall)

YEAR	TEAM	LVL	AGE	W	L	SV	G	GS	IP	H	HR	BB/9	K/9	K	GB%	BABIP	WHIP	ERA	DRA	WARP	MPH	CMD	PWR	STM
2016	OMA	AAA	28	0	4	0	8	8	34^{2}	38	7	4.4	8.6	33	37%	.333	1.59	6.23	5.07	0.1				
2017	KCA	MLB	29	6	6	6	65	0	77^{2}	57	5	2.5	10.2	88	43%	.272	1.02	2.55	2.86	2.0	96.1	61	50	51
2018	*TEX*	*MLB*	*30*	*7*	*7*	*0*	*38*	*18*	111^{1}	*107*	*18*	*4.0*	*9.3*	*115*	*40%*	*.296*	*1.41*	*4.68*	*4.67*	*0.9*	*95.3*	*61*	*50*	*51*
2019	*TEX*	*MLB*	*31*	*6*	*10*	*0*	*25*	*25*	145^{1}	*151*	*25*	*4.8*	*8.0*	*128*	*40%*	*.299*	*1.57*	*5.71*	*5.76*	*-0.1*	*94.7*	*61*	*50*	*51*

Breakout: 13% Improve: 42% Collapse: 22% Attrition: 7% MLB: 93% *Comparables: Cliff Lee, Jeff Samardzija, Gaylord Perry*

Last heard from as a decent-to-serviceable starter in 2014, Minor reappeared in the Royals' bullpen in 2017 and—SURPRISE!—morphed into a legitimately excellent reliever. Maybe he will regress and fade back into obscurity, perhaps due to a reappearance of the dreaded injury bug. Or maybe he'll become a late-inning fixture—yet another example of how a starter can be repurposed for shorter stints and a bigger impact. It is even possible that his name will be optimistically invoked in two years by someone suggesting that, say, Drew Hutchison's stuff might play up in the bullpen.

Matt Moore LHP Born: 06/18/89 Age: 28 Bats: L Throws: L Height: 6'3" Weight: 210 Origin: Round 8, 2007 Draft (#245 overall)

YEAR	TEAM	LVL	AGE	W	L	SV	G	GS	IP	H	HR	BB/9	K/9	K	GB%	BABIP	WHIP	ERA	DRA	WARP	MPH	CMD	PWR	STM
2015	PCH	A+	26	0	0	0	3	3	11	9	1	3.3	7.4	9	50%	.258	1.18	1.64	3.88	0.2				
2015	DUR	AAA	26	2	3	0	7	7	40^{1}	35	6	2.7	12.9	58	46%	.330	1.17	3.57	1.50	1.7				
2015	TBA	MLB	26	3	4	0	12	12	63	74	9	3.3	6.6	46	42%	.332	1.54	5.43	6.24	-0.9	94.7	47	44	56
2016	TBA	MLB	27	7	7	0	21	21	130	125	20	2.8	7.5	109	38%	.280	1.27	4.08	5.09	0.4	95.3	42	49	81
2016	SFN	MLB	27	6	5	0	12	12	68^{1}	59	5	4.2	9.1	69	42%	.297	1.33	4.08	5.85	-0.4	95.4	42	49	81
2017	SFN	MLB	28	6	15	0	32	31	174^{1}	200	27	3.5	7.6	148	39%	.320	1.53	5.52	7.06	-2.9	93.6	44	41	77
2018	*TEX*	*MLB*	*29*	*8*	*8*	*0*	*24*	*24*	*136*	*143*	*22*	*3.6*	*7.8*	*119*	*41%*	*.300*	*1.46*	*4.78*	*4.82*	*0.9*	*93.8*	*43*	*45*	*73*
2019	*TEX*	*MLB*	*30*	*9*	*11*	*0*	*29*	*29*	178^{2}	*185*	*29*	*3.8*	*8.0*	*158*	*41%*	*.302*	*1.46*	*4.30*	*5.25*	*0.7*	*93.4*	*43*	*45*	*76*

Breakout: 30% Improve: 49% Collapse: 20% Attrition: 10% MLB: 88% *Comparables: Felix Doubront, Wandy Rodriguez, Derek Holland*

The Giants made two announcements in September: They exercised Moore's club option, and they named Alaska Airlines as the team's official air carrier. In light of the former, Southwest might have been a more natural choice, because Moore's 2017 season was one "Wanna Get Away" moment after another. After losing a tick off his fastball and all the bite off his trademark curve, he watched miserably as the diminished arsenal turned left-handed opponents into Joey Votto and road foes into Nolan Arenado. The mental drain of getting shelled led Moore to neglect other duties (covering first, backing up home, knowing where to throw on a bunt), which only exacerbated his public plight. Among starters with his workload, he posted the worst DRA by a full run, and the only pitcher to fare worse in the last nine seasons retired the following year. While Moore found no in-season answers to his mid-career crisis, he need not hang 'em up yet. The five-month offseason getaway should at least restore his mental strength. We'll find out in the spring if it also brings back his lost stuff.

Martin Perez LHP Born: 04/04/91 Age: 27 Bats: L Throws: L Height: 6'0" Weight: 200 Origin: International Free Agent, 2007

YEAR	TEAM	LVL	AGE	W	L	SV	G	GS	IP	H	HR	BB/9	K/9	K	GB%	BABIP	WHIP	ERA	DRA	WARP	MPH	CMD	PWR	STM
2015	ROU	AAA	24	0	1	0	4	4	20	27	2	0.9	7.7	17	55%	.397	1.45	4.95	2.84	0.6				
2015	TEX	MLB	24	3	6	0	14	14	78^{2}	88	3	2.7	5.5	48	60%	.326	1.42	4.46	3.77	1.2	94.3	59	46	54
2016	TEX	MLB	25	10	11	0	33	33	198^{2}	205	18	3.4	4.7	103	54%	.286	1.41	4.39	4.71	1.5	95.4	53	52	79
2017	TEX	MLB	26	13	12	0	32	32	185	221	23	3.1	5.6	115	48%	.328	1.54	4.82	4.80	1.6	95.0	62	50	79
2018	*TEX*	*MLB*	*27*	*8*	*8*	*0*	*24*	*24*	*136*	*152*	*18*	*3.6*	*5.6*	*85*	*51%*	*.302*	*1.54*	*4.89*	*4.94*	*0.7*	*94.6*	*59*	*51*	*74*
2019	*TEX*	*MLB*	*28*	*9*	*11*	*0*	*29*	*29*	*179*	*196*	*22*	*3.5*	*5.9*	*118*	*51%*	*.305*	*1.49*	*5.08*	*5.11*	*1.0*	*94.4*	*59*	*51*	*77*

Breakout: 21% Improve: 54% Collapse: 19% Attrition: 15% MLB: 95% *Comparables: Henderson Alvarez, Mark Buehrle, Hyun-jin Ryu*

In a teen movie version of 2017, Perez was your reliable best friend whose love and support you really ought to have appreciated more. While most of the Rangers' rotation was broken, ineffectual or on the trading block, Perez ate innings and made starts. His K/9 and BB/9 are still somewhat terrifying (like refilling your parents' liquor bottles with water for the fifth time—at some point they're going to want a martini, right?), and because he was on the Rangers he did some time on the DL with a right thumb issue, but picking up his option for 2018 was a no-brainer. Then the script changed, and even the genre. In December, Perez suffered a broken radial head in his non-throwing arm that required surgery and is expected to keep him out until May 2018. He incurred the injury in what has been described as an "incident with a bull." Pick your own joke for the ending.

Cole Ragans LHP Born: 12/12/97 Age: 20 Bats: L Throws: L Height: 6'4" Weight: 190 Origin: Round 1, 2016 Draft (#30 overall)

YEAR	TEAM	LVL	AGE	W	L	SV	G	GS	IP	H	HR	BB/9	K/9	K	GB%	BABIP	WHIP	ERA	DRA	WARP	MPH	CMD	PWR	STM
2017	SPO	A-	19	3	2	0	13	13	57^{1}	50	5	5.5	13.7	87	42%	.369	1.48	3.61	3.58	1.1				
2018	*TEX*	*MLB*	*20*	*2*	*4*	*0*	*9*	*9*	36^{2}	*40*	*11*	*8.5*	*10.9*	*45*	*38%*	*.315*	*2.03*	*7.83*	*8.04*	*-1.0*				
2019	*TEX*	*MLB*	*21*	*5*	*10*	*0*	*26*	*26*	150^{1}	*169*	*40*	*4.6*	*9.2*	*153*	*38%*	*.313*	*1.64*	*6.63*	*6.74*	*-1.3*				

Breakout: 4% Improve: 4% Collapse: 0% Attrition: 1% MLB: 4% *Comparables: Mat Latos, Jarrod Parker, Franklin Morales*

If Ragans isn't careful, he could be sued for infringement by current Rangers starter Cole Hamels. Cole the Younger works his fastball at 92-94 mph with good plane and impressive life, but he isn't able to land it in the zone often enough. If each start were a game of Operation, he'd kill his patient by the second inning. The Hamels comparisons extend all the way to repertoire, as Ragans' best off-speed pitch is an advanced changeup, but he shows good feel for a curveball as well. His delivery is athletic and repeatable, which both gives rise to questions about how he misses the zone so frequently and provides some faith that he can figure out how to stop doing that. There's also a bit of nominative determinism present with Ragans, whose middle name is Gatlin, as he has an absolute gun for an arm.

Tyson Ross RHP Born: 04/22/87 Age: 31 Bats: R Throws: R Height: 6'6" Weight: 245 Origin: Round 2, 2008 Draft (#58 overall)

YEAR	TEAM	LVL	AGE	W	L	SV	G	GS	IP	H	HR	BB/9	K/9	K	GB%	BABIP	WHIP	ERA	DRA	WARP	MPH	CMD	PWR	STM
2015	SDN	MLB	28	10	12	0	33	33	196	172	9	3.9	9.7	212	62%	.320	1.31	3.26	2.95	5.0	95.6	45	51	79
2016	SDN	MLB	29	0	1	0	1	1	5^{1}	9	0	1.7	8.4	5	47%	.474	1.88	11.81	2.64	0.2	95.2			
2017	ROU	AAA	30	2	1	0	4	4	18^{2}	23	3	5.3	5.3	11	46%	.345	1.82	7.71	8.73	-0.6				
2017	FRI	AA	30	1	1	0	2	2	11^{2}	11	0	3.1	7.7	10	62%	.324	1.29	2.31	3.58	0.2				
2017	TEX	MLB	30	3	3	0	12	10	49	53	7	6.8	6.6	36	48%	.305	1.84	7.71	6.08	-0.3	93.7	26	46	51
2018	*TEX*	*MLB*	*31*	*3*	*4*	*0*	*10*	*10*	58^{1}	*61*	*9*	*4.7*	*7.9*	*51*	*48%*	*.307*	*1.57*	*5.34*	*5.41*	*0.2*	*94.2*	*38*	*49*	*61*
2019	*TEX*	*MLB*	*32*	*7*	*11*	*0*	*26*	*26*	155^{2}	*179*	*26*	*5.2*	*7.3*	*126*	*48%*	*.319*	*1.72*	*6.10*	*6.16*	*-0.8*	*93.1*	*33*	*47*	*56*

Breakout: 12% Improve: 36% Collapse: 30% Attrition: 9% MLB: 87% *Comparables: Justin Masterson, Clay Buchholz, Gio Gonzalez*

The Rangers took a flier on the former Friar as he made his way back from surgery to relieve thoracic outlet syndrome. It did not work out. Ross started the year on the disabled list, which wasn't a surprise, but then underwhelmed with a 7.52 ERA and 5.72 FIP in his first seven starts before ending up on the DL again. He walked more batters (37) than he struck out (36) in just 49 innings of work. His second run of starts didn't go much better than his first, and he was eventually shifted to the bullpen before being released in mid-September. His $6 million contract felt like a potential bargain at the time, and he'll likely seek a pillow contract to reestablish his value, allowing another team to shop at Ross: Stress for Less.

LINEOUTS

Hitters

HITTER	POS	TEAM	LVL	AGE	PA	R	2B	3B	HR	RBI	BB	K	SB	CS	AVG/OBP/SLG	TAv	VORP	BABIP	BRR	FRAA	WARP
Jared Hoying	OF	ROU	AAA	28	399	55	24	2	10	44	31	80	16	6	.262/.323/.421	.262	13.2	.312	0.4	CF(77): 0.5, RF(5): -0.3	1.3
	OF	TEX	MLB	28	77	13	3	0	1	7	4	23	3	0	.222/.260/.306	.194	-1.7	.306	1.4	CF(25): -1.6, RF(10): -0.6	-0.4
Andy Ibanez	2B	FRI	AA	24	345	33	14	2	8	29	25	48	6	1	.265/.323/.400	.264	10.1	.288	0.2	2B(70): 2.9, 3B(4): 0.4	1.4
A.J. Jimenez	C	ROU	AAA	27	207	18	9	0	7	16	7	45	1	0	.245/.275/.398	.241	3.8	.281	0.2	C(38): -5.2	-0.1
	C	TEX	MLB	27	13	0	0	0	0	0	0	7	0	0	.083/.083/.083	.058	-2.2	.200	0.0	C(5): -0.1	-0.2
Isiah Kiner-Falefa	UT	FRI	AA	22	570	58	31	3	5	48	41	72	17	6	.288/.350/.390	.288	35.2	.325	0.2	3B(50): 6.4, 2B(37): 4.2	5.1
Pete Kozma	INF	NYA	MLB	29	10	2	0	0	0	0	1	2	0	0	.111/.200/.111	.127	-0.7	.143	0.3	SS(9): 0.3, 2B(1): 0.0	0.0
	INF	TEX	MLB	29	41	4	0	0	1	2	2	18	0	1	.111/.200/.194	.157	-3.9	.176	-0.8	3B(14): -0.4, SS(5): 0.0	-0.4
	INF	ROU	AAA	29	42	8	4	0	0	2	2	8	1	0	.300/.333/.400	.243	1.9	.375	1.3	SS(5): 0.9, 3B(4): -0.2	0.2
Josh Morgan	UT	DEB	A+	21	445	56	21	3	6	45	26	54	3	0	.270/.318/.380	.256	13.5	.295	-2.5	SS(26): 3.8, C(13): -1.1	1.7
Brett Nicholas	C	ROU	AAA	28	293	35	18	2	7	38	13	59	2	1	.311/.353/.469	.271	12.5	.375	-1.7	C(44): -15.2, 1B(8): 0.4	-0.2
	C	TEX	MLB	28	65	7	4	0	2	11	2	13	0	0	.238/.262/.397	.217	-1.2	.271	-1.2	C(19): -2.6, P(1): 0.0	-0.4

HITTER	POS	TEAM	LVL	AGE	PA	R	2B	3B	HR	RBI	BB	K	SB	CS	AVG/OBP/SLG	TAv	VORP	BABIP	BRR	FRAA	WARP
Yanio Perez	4C	HIC	A	21	204	27	9	1	9	30	18	34	3	0	.322/.392/.533	.326	15.6	.353	-1.4	1B(29): -2.4, RF(11): -0.7	1.2
	4C	DEB	A+	21	312	31	14	2	5	36	20	66	3	1	.253/.311/.370	.267	6.4	.307	-1.9	RF(10): 1.1, 3B(9): -1.0	0.7
Cesar Puello	OF	ROU	AAA	26	179	24	8	1	6	27	12	38	5	1	.247/.307/.420	.242	1.0	.283	0.6	LF(19): -0.7, RF(13): 2.3	0.8
	OF	SLC	AAA	26	200	42	18	1	7	34	13	44	13	3	.397/.440/.620	.347	26.1	.493	2.2	RF(23): 4.8, LF(14): 0.4	3.0
	OF	ANA	MLB	26	4	0	0	0	0	1	0	1	2	0	.250/.250/.250	.183	-0.1	.333	0.1	LF(1): 0.1	0.0
	OF	TBA	MLB	26	35	6	0	0	0	2	4	11	0	0	.200/.314/.200	.199	-1.4	.316	0.1	LF(8): 0.4, RF(2): -0.2	-0.1
Drew Robinson	UT	ROU	AAA	25	309	48	19	4	11	40	42	74	7	4	.268/.369/.494	.296	22.7	.331	0.8	2B(39): -2.6, CF(15): -0.5	2.0
	UT	TEX	MLB	25	121	11	5	0	6	13	14	42	0	2	.224/.314/.439	.244	0.8	.305	-0.7	3B(20): -0.7, LF(15): -1.1	0.0
Carlos Tocci	CF	REA	AA	21	474	59	19	7	2	48	29	66	4	5	.307/.362/.398	.279	23.5	.356	1.5	CF(92): -5.0, RF(12): 3.4	2.3
	CF	LEH	AAA	21	54	2	0	0	1	4	1	11	0	0	.189/.204/.245	.147	-5.1	.220	0.0	CF(11): 3.5, LF(3): -0.3	-0.2
Jose Trevino	C	FRI	AA	24	423	39	12	0	7	42	19	44	1	2	.241/.275/.323	.217	-0.8	.256	-0.1	C(99): 26.5	2.8

Hanser Alberto missed all of 2017 with a right shoulder injury that eventually required surgery and the Rangers non-tendered him despite doctor's advice that they should be as gentle as possible. ⚾ **Jared Hoying** pitched in relief in July, saying: "I had to ask where the bullpen was. I didn't know how to get to the bullpen through the tunnel." Hopefully he has better luck finding Korea, where he'll play in 2018. ⚾ If a keystone-only player with useful bat-to-ball skill and power that's limited to the gaps is still a thing these days, his name is **Andy Ibanez**. ⚾ **A.J. Jimenez**, I don't care if Monday's blue / Tuesday's gray, your average too / Thursday I don't care about you / It's Friday, bring your glove / Monday you can fall apart / Tuesday Wednesday break my heart / Oh, Thursday you won't even start / It's Friday wait *that's* your glove? ⚾ **Isiah Kiner-Falefa** continued his trick of being one of the most versatile prospects around by starting games at catcher, second, short, third and center in 2017. Repeating Double-A, the formerly punchless Hawaii native hit the first five home runs of his pro career, and was added to the 40-man roster after the season. ⚾ **Pete Kozma** has parlayed a good month in 2012 with the Cardinals into spending parts of six seasons in the majors, all while hitting .215 with zero power and without doing a whole lot better at Triple-A. Rather than ridicule, perhaps we should be asking him for advice? ⚾ **Josh Morgan** made his pro debut behind the plate in 2017, bringing instructional league learnings to affiliated contests. In an era of short benches, versatility at the extreme of the defensive spectrum and a 50-grade hit tool provides a 25th-man floor. ⚾ **Brett Nicholas**' Players Weekend nickname was "Jethro," a family tribute to the *Beverly Hillbillies* and Nicholas' childhood propensity to eat cereal out of giant Tupperware containers; both facts are more interesting than Nicholas' 2017. ⚾ Is there such a thing as an under-the-radar, million-plus-dollar Cuban signee? Is age the right "old-for-the-level" construct when there's a three-year gap between competitive games? Can a player be a utility man if he can play everywhere *except* up the middle? **Yanio Perez** is a riddle. ⚾ A one-time top prospect who now keeps putting up shiny OBPs at Triple-A, **Cesar Puello** never quite found that sweet spot for getting an extended MLB chance. ⚾ **Drew Robinson** struggled to control the strike zone as a 25-year-old rookie but also showed some power at the plate and saw time at five positions defensively, which is more than enough to get him more opportunities. ⚾ **Carlos Tocci**'s center field defense is major-league quality, but he's going to need to hit a godly amount of singles to survive in the majors. Even this far in, it's still unclear whether his hit tool will get him there. ⚾ Known for his leadership, defensive prowess and an absence of evidence that he ever walked as a Rough Rider, might as well call **Jose Trevino** Colonel Teddy.

Pitchers

PITCHER	TEAM	LVL	AGE	W	L	SV	G	GS	IP	H	HR	BB/9	K/9	K	GB%	BABIP	WHIP	ERA	DRA	WARP	MPH	CMD	PWR	STM
Clayton Blackburn	ROU	AAA	24	6	2	0	19	18	93	99	4	2.4	7.5	78	52%	.341	1.33	4.65	2.17	3.5				
Paolo Espino	MIL	MLB	30	0	0	0	6	2	17^{2}	17	5	4.1	6.6	13	47%	.226	1.42	6.11	3.90	0.3	89.7	50	25	48
	CSP	AAA	30	4	2	0	16	14	75^{2}	86	12	1.7	8.7	73	47%	.336	1.32	4.52	2.01	3.0				
	TEX	MLB	30	0	0	0	6	0	6^{1}	6	2	2.8	9.9	7	22%	.250	1.26	5.68	8.62	-0.2	91.4	50	25	48
Nick Gardewine	FRI	AA	23	1	2	6	33	0	36^{2}	35	2	2.9	13.0	53	45%	.388	1.28	2.21	3.28	0.7				
	TEX	MLB	23	0	0	0	12	0	8	10	1	7.9	3.4	3	47%	.310	2.12	5.62	6.14	-0.1	95.8			37
Erik Goeddel	LVG	AAA	28	2	4	0	25	0	29^{2}	35	7	3.6	7.6	25	43%	.311	1.58	6.67	5.47	-0.1				
	NYN	MLB	28	0	1	0	33	0	29	28	8	3.4	10.2	33	44%	.286	1.34	5.28	5.18	0.0	94.0	37	39	47
Jonathan Hernandez	HIC	A	20	2	5	0	9	9	46^{1}	55	5	2.5	8.9	46	48%	.370	1.47	4.86	3.51	1.0				
	DEB	A+	20	3	6	0	14	13	65^{1}	66	2	4.3	8.8	64	47%	.350	1.48	3.44	4.52	0.6				
Ronald Herrera	TRN	AA	22	8	0	0	9	9	56	34	2	1.9	6.8	42	49%	.209	0.82	1.12	2.97	1.5				
	NYA	MLB	22	0	1	0	2	0	3	3	1	3.0	9.0	3	67%	.250	1.33	6.00	6.23	0.0	93.1			36
	SWB	AAA	22	0	0	0	2	2	10^{1}	6	2	2.6	5.2	6	28%	.133	0.87	4.35	5.40	0.0				
Kevin Jepsen	SYR	AAA	32	0	1	1	19	0	23^{2}	22	5	3.8	11.0	29	37%	.283	1.35	5.32	4.17	0.3				
Ariel Jurado	FRI	AA	21	9	11	0	27	27	157	188	16	2.1	5.4	95	53%	.335	1.43	4.59	4.71	0.9				
Jose Leclerc	TEX	MLB	23	2	3	2	47	0	45^{2}	23	4	7.9	11.8	60	40%	.204	1.38	3.94	3.28	1.0	97.3	27	53	41
Brett Martin	DEB	A+	22	4	8	0	16	16	84^{1}	94	7	3.7	9.6	90	47%	.366	1.53	4.70	4.63	0.6				
Michael Matuella	HIC	A	23	4	6	0	21	20	75	88	6	2.8	7.2	60	50%	.350	1.48	4.20	4.43	0.7				
Joe Palumbo	DEB	A+	22	1	0	0	3	3	13^{2}	4	0	2.6	14.5	22	58%	.167	0.59	0.66	1.95	0.5				
Ricardo Rodriguez	DEB	A+	24	3	1	12	23	0	32	15	0	2.5	12.4	44	44%	.227	0.75	1.41	1.86	1.1				
	FRI	AA	24	2	0	5	12	0	15	9	1	0.6	10.2	17	47%	.242	0.67	1.20	2.06	0.5				
	TEX	MLB	24	0	1	1	16	0	13	17	3	2.8	7.6	11	34%	.341	1.62	6.23	7.74	-0.4	97.2	56	64	42
Connor Sadzeck	FRI	AA	25	4	8	0	38	13	93^{2}	104	13	3.7	10.7	111	48%	.370	1.53	6.25	4.02	1.2				
Tanner Scheppers	TEX	MLB	30	0	1	0	5	0	4	5	0	6.8	11.2	5	25%	.417	2.00	6.75	2.76	0.1	95.2			40
	ROU	AAA	30	1	3	3	31	1	48^{1}	56	9	2.6	7.3	39	44%	.309	1.45	4.84	6.33	-0.5				

Even the pitching-hungry Giants tired of waiting for a back-end starter to materialize, but DRA remains quite smitten with **Clayton Blackburn**, reminding us that the potential for a back-end groundballer is still lurking after three seasons stalled out at Triple-A. ⚾ After 11 seasons in the minors, **Paolo Espino** finally made his major-league debut at age 30 and accrued enough service time to guarantee himself a pension, so he actually had a pretty good year, whatever the stats might say. ⚾ **Nick Gardewine** was as much personalized job description as forename-surname combo until Arlington-area spirits became safer at the trade deadline. ⚾ **Erik Goeddel**, famous for having an inner elbow so scrambled that 2015 MRIs came back as "dirty," complained of difficulty straightening his arm during his miserable 2017 season. After the season, the team finally gave him another MRI that immediately and clearly diagnosed a large bone spur. Whoops. ⚾ One could interpret **Phil Gosselin**'s use of "Gosselin" as a Players Weekend nickname as lazy or rushed, but for a bench infielder it's actually kind of aspirational. His name, real or otherwise, is hardly assured on major-league laundry. ⚾ **Jonathan Hernandez** is a 2013 international signee out of the Dominican Republic by way of ... wait, this can't be right, Memphis, Tennessee? Turns out his father is former Detroit

Tigers cup-of-coffee reliever Fernando Hernandez, who was pitching for the Memphis Chicks when Jonathan was born. ⚾ Traded for the second straight November, diminutive right-hander **Ronald Herrera** stands a better chance of having a big-league future now that he's escaped from New York. ⚾ In a moment of desperation, Washington sent a minor-league contract to **Kevin Jepsen**, who had been sitting at home since being cut by the Diamondbacks in March. Thankfully for the Nationals, they followed the example of any strong romantic comedy heroine who gets desperate enough to call him once, but never twice: Jepsen spent the year at Triple-A at age 32. ⚾ A lack of pure stuff caught up to **Ariel Jurado** in 2017, making him the most notable Ariel in obvious need of a physical upgrade since an anthropomorphic crustacean with a bad Trinidadian accent won an Oscar for a ditty about the pleasantries of marine life. ⚾ **Jose Leclerc** proved impossible to hit as a rookie, holding opponents to a .146 batting average over a decent sample size, but his extreme, career-long control issues don't appear to be going away. ⚾ The Rangers have impressive left-handed starting depth on the farm, most of it ahead of **Brett Martin** because of Martin's limited upside and inability to put together a full, healthy season. ⚾ The Rangers missed out on Shohei Ohtani, but they did take home his teammate who ruled the NPB the past two seasons, reliever **Chris Martin**. "Journeyman" doesn't even begin to describe Martin, who was out of baseball and working at UPS and Lowe's for five years before embarking on a pro career with independent Grand Prairie of the American Association, Boston's farm team, Colorado, the Yankees, Nippon Ham in Japan and now Texas. ⚾ **Michael Matuella** harnessed the good vibes of a general public that loves tall, white, boarding school and Duke-educated millionaire athletes to make 21 consecutive turns in his first healthy pro season, flashing the front-line potential that had him in the discussion at 1.1 before his junior year in Durham. ⚾ **Joe Palumbo** struck out 22 of the 50 batters he faced before his UCL went boom. There's mid-rotation upside if the velocity gains the former 30th-rounder has made as a pro survive the surgery and rehab. ⚾ Baseball rewards (and sustains) our interest by constantly teaching us new things. For instance, in 2017 we learned that **Ricardo Rodriguez**, back from a year lost to Tommy John surgery, hurled 13 innings for the Rangers; he learned he should probably avoid throwing his slider or his four-seamer to C.J. Cron, who crushed both for home runs. ⚾ Last year we asked whether **Connor Sadzeck** could refine his command. An uptick in walk rate while repeating Double-A at age 25 answers the question in a way we wish it didn't. ⚾ **Tanner Scheppers** was the reliever who pitched four unremarkable innings in 2017 with five strikeouts. Tannest Scheppers was the guy hanging out poolside after being DFA'ed in August. ⚾ Former closer **Shawn Tolleson** had Tommy John surgery in May, putting off for over a year any hope of bouncing back from a brutal 2016.

TORONTO BLUE JAYS

Essay by Rachael McDaniel

Player comments by Joshua Howsam, Matthew Gwin and BP staff

We thought we knew who these Blue Jays were. They were Josh Donaldson sliding across home plate, a triumphant hand raised through the surrounding cloud of dust. They were Edwin Encarnacion, hands raised, bat dropped, staring into the Orioles' dugout. And the greatest, the most unforgettable of them all: Jose Bautista, a look of cold, terrifying certainty in his eyes, his wrist curled, 50,000 fans going insane in the background—and his bat high above his head, laid flat in the air as though some god of chaos were holding it in place.

These were the Kings of Fun, the Birderer's Row, the team that brought competitive baseball back to Canada after a decades-long absence. They were loud and brash and powerful and unapologetic. People hated them. The Orioles hated them. The Yankees hated them. The Rangers definitely hated them. Advocates of playing the game the right way, real old-school baseball men, disapprovers of massive bat-flips and massive leg kicks and combative screams from the mound—they all found the Jays threatening, abrasive, distasteful.

And after so many years of being an AL East afterthought—a mediocre footnote to the ongoing sagas of the Yankees and the Red Sox and hell, even the Rays—the Jays relished the world's newfound hatred for them. It was fuel for the fire of Blue Jays fandom, which, after years of sputtering along as a dim flicker, was now a genuinely threatening blaze. The team's presence in border-adjacent cities could, for a few days, make those cities appear to be solely inhabited by blue-clad baseball gadabouts, hordes of imported Donaldsons and Martins and Stromans holding up border lines and causing a ruckus at your team's ballpark. Seattle radio personalities advocated for a ban on ticket sales to Canadians. Jays fans ate it up, wore it with pride, got even louder. Because of this team, because of their passion and the passion they inspired, the Jays had emerged from the long dark of irrelevance. They—and through them, *we*—were finally important again.

So for these Jays to come so close two years in a row, for them to be back-to-back American League runners-up—you had to believe they would be coming back for more. They had to be going all the way this time. But in the 2016 ALCS, they scored eight runs in five games against the Indians. Trevor Bauer left Game 3 after less than an inning with blood gushing from his drone-stricken finger, and the Jays still lost. The last stand of the 2016 Blue Jays was a flaccid, dreary shutout at the hands of little-known lefty Ryan Merritt. After the game, depressing as it was, the fans didn't leave. They clustered around the dugout, chanting: "Let's Go Blue Jays," at first, then names. They chanted for the incumbent free agents, Edwin Encarnacion and Jose Bautista. It was an odd, sad scene: a group of people desperately unwilling to accept that things had come to an end.

That couldn't be the end of this team, though. That would be too much cognitive dissonance. That would be incongruous with the essence of who this team was, who we knew them to be. These Blue

BLUE JAYS PROSPECTUS

2017 W-L: 76-86, 4TH IN AL EAST

Pythag	.442	22nd	B-Age	31.1	*30th*
RS/G	4.28	26th	P-Age	29.2	*24th*
RA/G	4.84	18th	Salary	$163.4M	*11th*
TAv	.248	30th	M$/MW	$5.4M	*5th*
TAv-P	.259	12th	DL Days	1424	*27th*
FIP	4.28	14th	$ on DL	19%	*21st*
DER	.697	23rd			

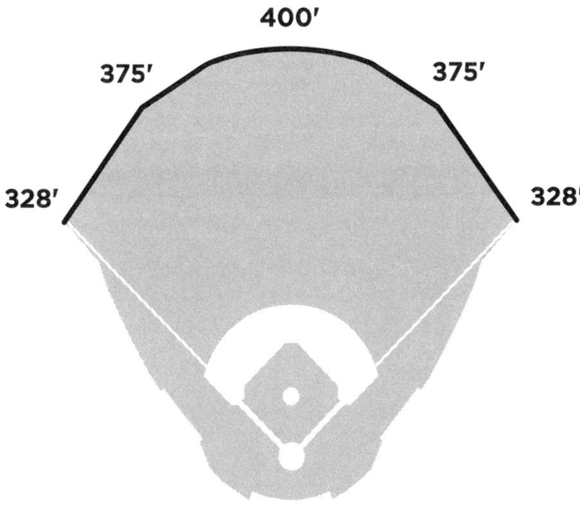

Outfield wall profile: **10′**

Three-Year Park Factors

Runs	Runs/RH	Runs/LH	HR/RH	HR/LH
102	102	100	100	100

Top Hitter WARP	3.8 Josh Donaldson
Top Pitcher WARP	4.4 Marcus Stroman
Top Prospect	Vladimir Guerrero Jr.

2017 Hit List Ranking

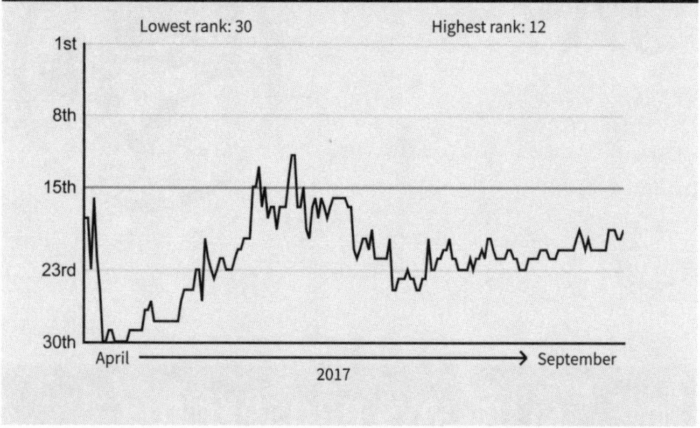

Committed Payroll (in millions)

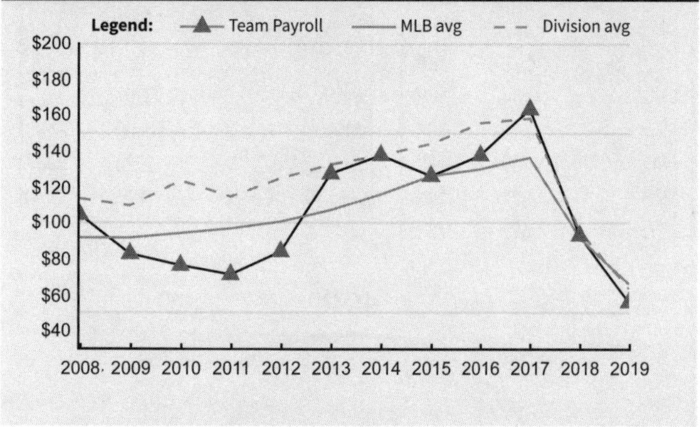

Farm System Ranking

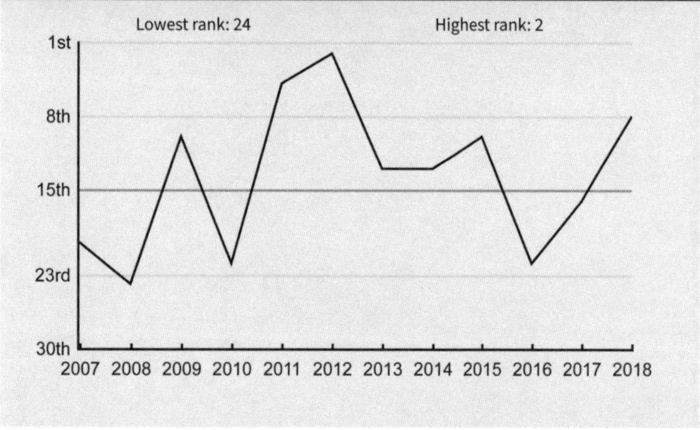

Personnel

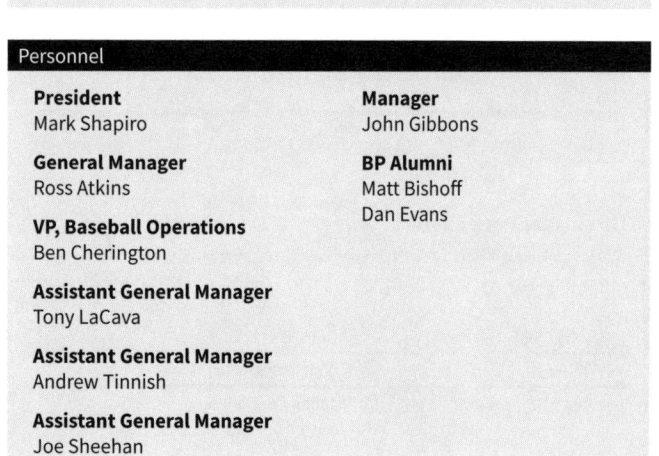

President
Mark Shapiro

General Manager
Ross Atkins

VP, Baseball Operations
Ben Cherington

Assistant General Manager
Tony LaCava

Assistant General Manager
Andrew Tinnish

Assistant General Manager
Joe Sheehan

Manager
John Gibbons

BP Alumni
Matt Bishoff
Dan Evans

Jays couldn't go out like this—so quietly, without so much as a run on the board. They would be back.

It had only been two years, after all.

That couldn't be the end.

⚾ ⚾ ⚾

The question of personal identity is one of philosophy's higher-stakes dilemmas. To determine the qualities that mark a discrete instance of personhood, to figure out whether the "you" who exists right now is the same, directly contiguous "you" that existed 10 years ago, through all the physical and psychological changes, through all the life experiences that the ostensible "you" has lived through during that time—well, it's literally a question of life and death. It's a question of weighing what has been gained and what has been lost over the course of a life partially lived, trying to find out whether, somewhere along the way, the person you thought you were simply ceased to exist.

There are a variety of ways to navigate this problem. One of the most popular solutions, the purview of most major religions, is the idea of a soul— an essential, metaphysical "you" that, while located somewhere in the vicinity of the physical body, will nonetheless persist beyond it unto infinity, regardless of whatever physical and mental changes might occur. Some believe personal identity is based in a continuous psychological experience; some believe the persistence of personal identity is contingent on the persistence of a single brain; and some believe personhood is rooted in physiology, in the living function of a human body.

All of these conceptual systems, of course, have flaws, which can be exposed by performing a number of rather absurd thought experiments. (What, for example, would happen if Person A's head was grafted onto Person B's body, and vice versa—who is now Person A, and who is Person B? If one were to enter a teleportation device that operated by destroying one's physical form on Earth and creating an exact replica of that form on Mars, would the person now on Mars be the same as the one who stepped into the teleporter?) So though the question of personal identity has high stakes, it isn't a particularly rewarding one for the average person to think about at length. We do not yet have teleportation, after all, nor head-grafting technology.

And yet most people have experienced at least a few moments of identity-based fear. Perhaps you uncover some long-forgotten childhood photos, physical memories of an almost-forgotten version of yourself. That person didn't look a whole lot like you; they certainly didn't act like you. They had different interests, different friends, different fears. Their life had but few shared qualities with the life you live today. Yet you remember being that person. You remember it, and you feel, in some sense, that they *are* you. Aging is a strange, disturbing process, taking place in every single moment and yet unfolding so slowly that you hardly notice, and in instances like these where the aging process is thrown into sharper relief, there is a distinct sense of melancholy—of loss. You wonder how the kid in those photos turned into you. You wonder whether you and they are really the same person; you wonder whether something that happened to you—or worse, something you did—made that kid, that person, cease to exist.

⚾ ⚾ ⚾

A baseball team is a lot of things. It is a corporate entity, a registered trademark, a frivolous entertainment, a point of geographic pride, a group of disparate human beings united by specific athletic abilities. A baseball team is not person. A baseball team has no childhood photos on which to look back, and the passage of time will not change a baseball team's body beyond recognition. A baseball team needs not reckon with the problem of personal identity.

To fans, though, for whom the beloved team is a deeply embedded part of their own self-concept, a baseball team *does* have an identity—a unique, discernible personality, formed from the distant memories of team history, the behavior of current players, the traits valued by the fan themselves. They can be fun or unfun, brash or stoic, boring or thrilling, goofy or serious. We celebrate this identity, an identity we have created both for the team and for ourselves, basking in it, grafting it onto our own.

But even though a baseball team is not a person, a baseball team is still composed of people. And these people are still subject to the disturbing conflict of identity that comes of inhabiting and being a finite human body. They change. The skills they became known for erode, sometimes slowly, sometimes without warning. Watching them still feels familiar; your memories tell what to expect. Your eyes, though, tell a different story. Your eyes tell you that something has been lost.

The 2017 regular season began on April 3, and the Jays were playing the Orioles. The last time these two teams had faced each other, it was the 2016 AL wild card game, and the end of the Orioles' season. (In case you forgot: Ubaldo Jimenez pitched and Zach Britton didn't.) It was a fitting beginning, then, to the new year of Blue Jays baseball. The sight of those Orioles taking the field at Camden Yards, Devon Travis leading off the first inning with Donaldson on deck— it was a tableau that invited fond, hopeful comparison to the previous year's victory.

And the game played out in a manner that was eerily reminiscent of the previous meeting between the two teams. Each pitcher gave up two earned runs; each bullpen was efficient; each offense was inefficient, squandering scoring opportunities and leaving runners on base. And just like the wild card game, the 2017 Blue Jays' season opener went to extra innings, with the Jays and the Orioles tied at two.

But these Jays weren't quite the same as the ones who had walked off the Orioles on that night in October. Sure, they still had Travis leading off, Donaldson on deck, Bautista in the middle of their order. Their starting rotation and their core relievers were essentially unchanged. And there was an obvious, visible difference in the absence of Encarnacion, one of the franchise's great successful transformations, the man who orchestrated that wild card walk-off—he had been lost to the Indians via free agency after a series of frustrating front-office miscommunications.

It wasn't Encarnacion's absence, though, that made these 2017 Jays so strange, so concerning to watch. It was how *familiar* it all felt. How, as they stranded runner after runner on base, as they grounded into slow-footed double plays, it felt like you were watching the exact same team that had gone down so quietly in the ALCS. The problem wasn't that the makeup of the team had changed. The problem was that those essential players had aged. You could see it in their movements, in their swings and misses, inning by inning. In the end, Jason Grilli, who had so electrified the team when he arrived in mid-2016, who had pitched an essential scoreless inning the wild card game, hung a slider to Welington Castillo. This time, the Orioles got the walk-off; this time, it was the Jays who left the field shamed and unfulfilled.

Of course, it was only the first game of the season. It was early. That was what you had to tell yourself, because you thought you knew these players; you thought you knew what they were capable of. You thought you knew what to expect: a playoff run, a meaningful September, a satisfying year of baseball. The 2017 Blue Jays started the season 2-9. They finished 76-86, only pulling into fourth place in the AL East on the very last day of the season. They never reached .500 at any point, despite nine opportunities to do so. Donaldson went through one of the worst slumps of his career. The Jays used 60 different players, most of whom, by the end of the year, you didn't even remember.

When Bautista, worth all of 0.9 WARP in 2017, left the field in the ninth inning of the Jays' final home game, tearful, saluted by a long standing ovation, the process that had begun after that final ALCS game of 2016 finally hit home. You knew, this time, that in witnessing this Blue Jays season, you were witnessing the end of something that would never return.

This year will be an interesting transitional season for the Blue Jays. The front office, before the end of the 2017 season, announced an increase in ticket prices; even through the mediocrity and frequent outright badness of 2017, the Jays continued to draw better than any team in the American League. Despite the team's poor performance, they still have Donaldson and Marcus Stroman, great players in the primes of their careers. They have, all of a sudden, an affordable All-Star in assumed failure Justin Smoak. The team extended fan favorite and generally excellent starter Marco Estrada before 2017's end, and many fans are excited about some of the new names who appeared in September: Teoscar Hernandez, Carlos Ramirez. In 2017, in the minor leagues, Vladimir Guerrero Jr. batted .323/.425/.485. Bo Bichette batted .362/.423/.565. They are teenagers. They could be in the major leagues this year.

But there is a great deal of uncertainty, much more than there was entering 2016 or 2017. The AL East is once again a tough division, with the excellent Red Sox and the now-resurgent Yankees. And the question marks on the Jays' roster—the gaping hole in left field, the injury histories of Troy Tulowitzki and Devon Travis, Aaron Sanchez's blister—are too significant to ignore. There is a chance, though. There is talent on this team—with some luck, some good breaks, enough talent to make the postseason. Yet there is an acknowledgment even among the most hopeful that hoping for luck isn't quite enough. It isn't anything close to certainty.

We thought we knew who these Blue Jays were, but 2017 forced us to reckon with the fact that, somewhere along the way, something had been lost: Bautista will never again hit 50 homers, the beloved core group of players that returned playoff baseball to Toronto will not be the group that brings a World Series parade. We will always remember the wild card walk-off, Donaldson's dash, the bat flip; and perhaps it will always be hard to reconcile the fact that these players were never quite able to bring home the ultimate prize, that they were here for two seasons and then gone. We will wonder about what might have been if things have gone a little differently—if Ryan Goins had been able to catch that pop-up in the 2015 ALCS, if the team as a collective had been able to figure out Andrew Miller and Corey Kluber in 2016. We will reminisce, thinking back to those iconic images of victory, wishing it all could have turned out differently.

Eventually, though, the old must give way to the new. People change; people get older. The 2017 Blue Jays were the ending. The 2018 Blue Jays are a team that will have to begin the process of forging a new identity for the franchise—an identity that, fans hope, will be just as unforgettable as the teams that came before.

—Rachael McDaniel is an author of Baseball Prospectus.

Hitters

Anthony Alford CF Born: 07/20/94 Age: 23 Bats: R Throws: R Height: 6'1" Weight: 215 Origin: Round 3, 2012 Draft (#112 overall)

YEAR	TEAM	LVL	AGE	PA	R	2B	3B	HR	RBI	BB	K	SB	CS	AVG/OBP/SLG	TAv	VORP	BABIP	BRR	FRAA	WARP
2015	LNS	A	20	232	49	14	1	1	16	39	60	12	1	.293/.418/.394	.287	19.7	.419	6.5	CF(47): -3.7	1.7
2015	DUN	A+	20	255	42	11	6	3	19	28	49	15	6	.302/.380/.444	.299	21.3	.374	4.1	CF(55): 0.4	2.4
2016	DUN	A+	21	401	53	17	2	9	44	53	117	18	6	.236/.344/.378	.261	15.0	.327	2.3	CF(84): 2.6, LF(6): 1.7	2.0
2017	TOR	MLB	22	8	0	1	0	0	0	0	3	0	0	.125/.125/.250	.139	-0.8	.200	0.0	LF(3): -0.2, RF(2): 0.0	-0.1
2017	NHP	AA	22	289	41	14	0	5	24	35	45	18	3	.310/.406/.429	.303	21.9	.360	2.5	CF(32): 5.1, LF(13): 1.1	2.9
2018	*TOR*	*MLB*	*23*	*62*	*8*	*3*	*0*	*1*	*6*	*7*	*18*	*2*	*0*	*.231/.319/.357*	*.242*	*0.8*	*.314*	*0.2*	*RF 0, LF 0*	*0.1*
2019	*TOR*	*MLB*	*24*	*350*	*42*	*15*	*1*	*9*	*37*	*39*	*100*	*11*	*3*	*.234/.326/.378*	*.245*	*3.4*	*.315*	*1.2*	*RF 0, LF 2*	*0.5*

Breakout: 1% Improve: 19% Collapse: 5% Attrition: 13% MLB: 39% *Comparables: Brian Goodwin, Dexter Fowler, Trayvon Robinson*

You don't see many people walk away from a no. 1 ranked football team in the middle of the NCAA season. Alford did just that in 2014, when he left the Ole Miss Rebels right before a game against Alabama, deciding to devote his time completely to baseball. It seems to be working out, as he posted stellar numbers at New Hampshire and even recorded his first big-league hit last season. An exceptional athlete, Alford commands the strike zone well and has the type of bat-to-ball skills that should lead to a regular role in the major leagues very soon as long as he can stay healthy.

Darwin Barney INF Born: 11/08/85 Age: 32 Bats: R Throws: R Height: 5'10" Weight: 180 Origin: Round 4, 2007 Draft (#127 overall)

YEAR	TEAM	LVL	AGE	PA	R	2B	3B	HR	RBI	BB	K	SB	CS	AVG/OBP/SLG	TAv	VORP	BABIP	BRR	FRAA	WARP
2015	LAN	MLB	29	4	0	0	0	0	0	0	0	0	0	.000/.000/.000	-.011	-0.9	.000	0.0	3B(1): 0.0, SS(1): 0.1	-0.1
2015	OKL	AAA	29	379	52	15	0	4	31	22	44	7	4	.277/.325/.354	.262	16.6	.306	4.4	2B(58): -4.0, SS(18): 0.1	1.3
2015	TOR	MLB	29	26	4	1	0	2	4	1	2	0	0	.304/.333/.609	.342	2.8	.263	0.1	2B(15): 0.9	0.4
2016	TOR	MLB	30	306	35	13	2	4	19	22	48	2	2	.269/.322/.373	.234	0.7	.310	-0.9	2B(40): 1.8, 3B(32): -0.3	0.2
2017	TOR	MLB	31	362	34	14	0	6	25	18	64	7	2	.232/.275/.327	.215	-6.9	.270	-0.8	2B(73): 0.0, 3B(44): 2.8	-0.6
2018	*TOR*	*MLB*	*32*	*329*	*33*	*14*	*1*	*6*	*31*	*22*	*51*	*4*	*2*	*.242/.297/.351*	*.220*	*-1.2*	*.269*	*-0.6*	*2B 1, 3B 1*	*0.0*
2019	*TOR*	*MLB*	*33*	*328*	*34*	*13*	*1*	*5*	*30*	*23*	*52*	*3*	*2*	*.234/.294/.333*	*.220*	*-4.4*	*.263*	*-0.5*	*2B 1, 3B 1*	*-0.3*

Breakout: 5% Improve: 37% Collapse: 11% Attrition: 28% MLB: 87% *Comparables: Jamey Carroll, Bob Randall, Larry Milbourne*

Barney is a perfect example of natural selection. With his defensive skills having eroded over time and his bat producing its worst True Average since 2013, Barney posted his third negative WARP in five years. Without evolving into someone who provides surplus value somewhere, eventually he'll be pushed out of the league in favor of players who have the necessary skills to survive in the majors. He might stick around a while longer, but Barney is soon headed the way of the purple dinosaurs.

Jose Bautista RF Born: 10/19/80 Age: 37 Bats: R Throws: R Height: 6'0" Weight: 205 Origin: Round 20, 2000 Draft (#599 overall)

YEAR	TEAM	LVL	AGE	PA	R	2B	3B	HR	RBI	BB	K	SB	CS	AVG/OBP/SLG	TAv	VORP	BABIP	BRR	FRAA	WARP
2015	TOR	MLB	34	666	108	29	3	40	114	110	106	8	2	.250/.377/.536	.316	47.0	.237	0.3	RF(118): -4.9	4.5
2016	TOR	MLB	35	517	68	24	1	22	69	87	103	2	2	.234/.366/.452	.270	11.3	.255	-2.0	RF(91): -6.1, 1B(1): 0.0	0.5
2017	TOR	MLB	36	686	92	27	0	23	65	84	170	6	3	.203/.308/.366	.237	-4.4	.239	-0.3	RF(143): 13.0, 3B(8): 1.3	1.0
2018	*TOR*	*MLB*	*37*	*612*	*82*	*25*	*1*	*28*	*87*	*89*	*119*	*5*	*2*	*.241/.356/.455*	*.274*	*25.4*	*.259*	*-0.7*	*RF -2, 3B 0*	*2.6*
2019	*TOR*	*MLB*	*38*	*498*	*69*	*19*	*0*	*21*	*65*	*69*	*100*	*3*	*1*	*.226/.339/.421*	*.260*	*9.9*	*.245*	*-0.6*	*RF -1, 3B 0*	*0.9*

Breakout: 0% Improve: 23% Collapse: 10% Attrition: 8% MLB: 88% *Comparables: Sid Gordon, Bobby Abreu, Al Kaline*

"The king stay the king." Nothing sums up how people in Toronto feel about Bautista more than D'Angelo Barksdale's quote from *The Wire*. Bautista hasn't really been himself for two years. He was still a solid hitter in 2016, but wasn't the big-time slugger they had seen in the past and his once-feared throwing arm had wilted. The arm came back in 2017, but the bat diminished to the point where he was a negative on offense for the first time since becoming a regular. Blue Jays fans didn't care. When he walked onto the field for their final home game of the season, they let him know how much he meant to the city and they kept cheering until he was removed in the top of the ninth inning. He was and always will be The King in Toronto.

"The thing about the old days, they the old days." Nothing sums up how the rest of the league feels about Bautista than Slim Charles' quote. After spurning contract extension attempts from the Blue Jays prior to 2016, Bautista hit the free agent market and found that his phone just wasn't ringing. His reputation was so tarnished that Orioles front office boss Dan Duquette straight up told Bautista's camp that they wouldn't sign him because their fans didn't like him. Maybe they would've taken him when he was still hitting 40 homers a year, but not the broken down, older version.

It's strange to see such a gap between the perception of Bautista locally and elsewhere, but there's no denying the truth of it. No matter how it goes from here, Bautista has had a tremendous career and deserves to be remembered as such.

Bo Bichette SS Born: 03/05/98 Age: 20 Bats: R Throws: R Height: 6'0" Weight: 200 Origin: Round 2, 2016 Draft (#66 overall)

YEAR	TEAM	LVL	AGE	PA	R	2B	3B	HR	RBI	BB	K	SB	CS	AVG/OBP/SLG	TAv	VORP	BABIP	BRR	FRAA	WARP
2016	BLJ	RK	18	91	21	9	2	4	36	6	17	3	0	.427/.451/.732	.423	19.5	.484	-0.4	SS(16): 1.7, 2B(6): 0.3	2.2
2017	LNS	A	19	317	60	32	3	10	51	28	55	12	3	.384/.448/.623	.363	48.4	.452	3.0	SS(51): 0.2, 2B(14): 0.3	5.1
2017	DUN	A+	19	182	28	9	1	4	23	14	26	10	4	.323/.379/.463	.292	12.4	.360	-0.2	SS(35): -0.3	1.3
2018	*TOR*	*MLB*	*20*	*250*	*30*	*14*	*0*	*9*	*33*	*16*	*60*	*5*	*2*	*.269/.320/.451*	*.258*	*10.9*	*.325*	*0.0*	*SS 1, 2B 0*	*1.4*
2019	*TOR*	*MLB*	*21*	*376*	*49*	*22*	*0*	*14*	*51*	*25*	*89*	*7*	*2*	*.277/.330/.465*	*.267*	*15.4*	*.334*	*0.1*	*SS 2, 2B 0*	*1.9*

Breakout: 14% Improve: 32% Collapse: 0% Attrition: 13% MLB: 34% *Comparables: Xander Bogaerts, Addison Russell, Alen Hanson*

While Vladimir Guerrero Jr. and his light-tower power garnered the most attention among Blue Jays prospects in 2017, Bichette was arguably as good offensively while playing the more important defensive position. It was also Bichette, not Guerrero, who led the

Midwest League in every rate category. Some scouts question whether Bichette's long swing will survive the upper minors, and most doubt that he'll stick at shortstop. However, Dante's son has impressed with every chance he's been given and will likely continue to get reps at shortstop until he proves that there's zero chance of a future there. Neither he nor Vlad Jr. will ever be defensive superstars at their respective positions, but the duo's simultaneous ascension may actually help them stay on the left side of the infield.

Ezequiel Carrera OF Born: 06/11/87 Age: 31 Bats: L Throws: L Height: 5'11" Weight: 185 Origin: International Free Agent, 2005

YEAR	TEAM	LVL	AGE	PA	R	2B	3B	HR	RBI	BB	K	SB	CS	AVG/OBP/SLG	TAv	VORP	BABIP	BRR	FRAA	WARP
2015	BUF	AAA	28	133	18	5	0	1	10	12	16	6	2	.276/.349/.345	.266	3.6	.313	-1.0	CF(25): -2.2, RF(4): 0.7	0.3
2015	TOR	MLB	28	192	27	8	0	3	26	11	45	2	1	.273/.321/.372	.253	3.8	.349	1.4	LF(46): -1.9, RF(35): -1.2	0.0
2016	TOR	MLB	29	310	47	9	1	6	23	27	70	7	4	.248/.323/.356	.238	-0.4	.311	0.2	RF(65): 6.6, LF(45): 1.2	0.7
2017	TOR	MLB	30	325	38	10	1	8	20	30	75	10	1	.282/.356/.408	.263	10.5	.358	1.9	LF(91): -0.9, RF(27): 0.0	0.9
2018	*TOR*	*MLB*	*31*	*322*	*40*	*11*	*2*	*5*	*27*	*26*	*69*	*10*	*3*	*.253/.313/.354*	*.238*	*3.5*	*.308*	*0.9*	*LF -1, RF 1*	*0.1*
2019	*TOR*	*MLB*	*32*	*358*	*40*	*12*	*2*	*6*	*35*	*30*	*81*	*10*	*3*	*.248/.319/.359*	*.235*	*0.4*	*.304*	*1.4*	*LF -1, RF 2*	*0.1*

Breakout: 2% Improve: 23% Collapse: 15% Attrition: 25% MLB: 58% *Comparables: Alex Presley, David Lough, Cory Sullivan*

Just like a bad actor on a great television show that's in decline, Toronto's ever-present fourth outfielder finally got his shot at an expanded role. As the Blue Jays ratings began to tank and everything seemed to go wrong, Carrera remained omnipresent, playing in a career-high 131 games and subsequently setting careers bests in nearly every offensive category. Zeke swung at fewer bad pitches, made better contact and even walked more. He still only managed to be marginally better than replacement level, but was somehow Toronto's best-hitting outfielder in an outfield that included MLB's home run leader over the previous seven seasons.

Aledmys Diaz SS Born: 08/01/90 Age: 27 Bats: R Throws: R Height: 6'1" Weight: 195 Origin: International Free Agent, 2014

YEAR	TEAM	LVL	AGE	PA	R	2B	3B	HR	RBI	BB	K	SB	CS	AVG/OBP/SLG	TAv	VORP	BABIP	BRR	FRAA	WARP
2015	SFD	AA	24	409	47	25	2	10	46	29	62	6	5	.264/.324/.421	.269	18.8	.294	-0.4	SS(91): -1.7	1.8
2015	MEM	AAA	24	58	12	3	0	3	6	6	5	0	1	.380/.448/.620	.380	9.7	.372	0.0	SS(14): -3.2	0.7
2016	SLN	MLB	25	460	71	28	3	17	65	41	60	4	4	.300/.369/.510	.321	48.7	.312	1.4	SS(106): -9.6, 2B(1): 0.0	4.0
2017	MEM	AAA	26	187	19	9	1	4	26	10	30	3	3	.253/.305/.388	.252	4.3	.281	-1.2	SS(28): 2.3, 3B(9): -0.6	0.7
2017	SLN	MLB	26	301	31	17	0	7	20	13	42	4	1	.259/.290/.392	.231	2.2	.282	-1.3	SS(68): -10.6, 3B(4): -0.2	-0.9
2018	*TOR*	*MLB*	*27*	*397*	*48*	*22*	*1*	*12*	*47*	*27*	*65*	*4*	*3*	*.263/.318/.429*	*.260*	*16.2*	*.289*	*-0.7*	*2B 1, SS -3*	*0.9*
2019	*TOR*	*MLB*	*28*	*392*	*48*	*21*	*1*	*13*	*49*	*28*	*69*	*4*	*2*	*.258/.317/.432*	*.254*	*9.8*	*.283*	*0.0*	*2B 1, SS -3*	*0.8*

Breakout: 3% Improve: 42% Collapse: 6% Attrition: 14% MLB: 96% *Comparables: Eduardo Nunez, Josh Rutledge, Jason Bartlett*

Corey Seager, Nomar Garciaparra, Harvey Kuenn and Diaz are the only All-Star rookie shortstops to hit .300. It's going to be very awkward if the surprise rookie of 2016 winds up being nothing more than the answer to an above-average trivia question. Even Angel Berroa thinks this was unexpected, though Paul DeJong's emergence certainly accelerated Diaz's marginalization into Triple-A organizational depth. If Diaz can rekindle the swing he can still play major-league infield, but it likely won't be at shortstop. Most of his value is tied to his bat, as he's not a Gold Glover anywhere (not even in Toronto!). But, heck, we've been surprised twice by him before, why not a third time?

Josh Donaldson 3B Born: 12/08/85 Age: 32 Bats: R Throws: R Height: 6'1" Weight: 210 Origin: Round 1, 2007 Draft (#48 overall)

YEAR	TEAM	LVL	AGE	PA	R	2B	3B	HR	RBI	BB	K	SB	CS	AVG/OBP/SLG	TAv	VORP	BABIP	BRR	FRAA	WARP
2015	TOR	MLB	29	711	122	41	2	41	123	73	133	6	0	.297/.371/.568	.324	69.5	.314	4.0	3B(150): 0.6	7.5
2016	TOR	MLB	30	700	122	32	5	37	99	109	119	7	1	.284/.404/.549	.315	64.6	.300	4.8	3B(136): -12.6	5.4
2017	TOR	MLB	31	496	65	21	0	33	78	76	111	2	2	.270/.385/.559	.311	43.9	.289	1.3	3B(105): -5.9, SS(4): -0.2	3.8
2018	*TOR*	*MLB*	*32*	*664*	*107*	*32*	*2*	*31*	*95*	*82*	*127*	*5*	*1*	*.275/.370/.502*	*.299*	*51.0*	*.302*	*-0.5*	*3B -7*	*3.6*
2019	*TOR*	*MLB*	*33*	*525*	*79*	*24*	*1*	*25*	*79*	*68*	*108*	*3*	*1*	*.266/.368/.495*	*.288*	*30.4*	*.295*	*2.1*	*3B -5*	*2.8*

Breakout: 2% Improve: 33% Collapse: 5% Attrition: 9% MLB: 99% *Comparables: George Brett, Al Rosen, Aramis Ramirez*

The 2017 Blue Jays returned Blind Melon from the grave of forgotten '90s bands because there was "No Rain" in Toronto during baseball's first half. Last spring, the famously durable "Bringer of Rain" Donaldson suffered his first major injury since breaking into the big leagues. As a result, the superstar third baseman missed 38 games in April and May and didn't hit his 10th home run until late July. From that point on, though, fans inside the Rogers Centre needed to bust out the umbrellas. Donaldson hit .302/.406/698 with 24 homers through the end of the year and ended up with a higher OPS than in his MVP-winning 2015 campaign. That end-of-the-year onslaught reminded people that Donaldson is nowhere close to slowing down. He's really gonna have it made.

Ryan Goins MI Born: 02/13/88 Age: 30 Bats: L Throws: R Height: 5'10" Weight: 180 Origin: Round 4, 2009 Draft (#130 overall)

YEAR	TEAM	LVL	AGE	PA	R	2B	3B	HR	RBI	BB	K	SB	CS	AVG/OBP/SLG	TAv	VORP	BABIP	BRR	FRAA	WARP
2015	TOR	MLB	27	428	52	16	4	5	45	39	83	2	1	.250/.318/.354	.238	8.2	.304	3.9	2B(66): -3.4, SS(58): 0.3	0.5
2016	BUF	AAA	28	110	9	6	0	2	10	8	23	0	1	.265/.318/.388	.258	4.3	.324	1.0	SS(14): 1.0, 2B(10): 2.5	0.8
2016	TOR	MLB	28	196	13	9	2	3	12	9	48	1	1	.186/.228/.306	.179	-1.2	.235	-0.1	2B(37): -1.1, SS(28): 3.3	-0.9
2017	TOR	MLB	29	459	37	21	1	9	62	31	96	3	2	.237/.286/.356	.223	-1.4	.283	-0.5	SS(87): 0.7, 2B(56): 1.7	0.1
2018	*TOR*	*MLB*	*30*	*392*	*36*	*18*	*2*	*6*	*36*	*26*	*86*	*2*	*2*	*.239/.290/.351*	*.216*	*0.1*	*.290*	*0.8*	*SS 2, 2B 0*	*0.2*
2019	*TOR*	*MLB*	*31*	*431*	*43*	*19*	*2*	*7*	*39*	*28*	*99*	*2*	*1*	*.233/.283/.341*	*.216*	*-5.0*	*.286*	*0.9*	*SS 2, 2B 0*	*-0.3*

Breakout: 4% Improve: 34% Collapse: 10% Attrition: 40% MLB: 78% *Comparables: Josh Wilson, Robert Andino, Matt Tolbert*

Since Goins became a major leaguer in 2013, no player has had a lower OPS while getting more plate appearances. His supporters steadfastly praise his grit and he's only in his first season of arbitration eligibility. This combination of factors will provide him with at least one more full season in which he'll get more starts than he should while being a mainstay on the team's bench.

Vladimir Guerrero Jr. 3B Born: 03/16/99 Age: 19 Bats: R Throws: R Height: 6'1" Weight: 200 Origin: International Free Agent, 2015

YEAR	TEAM	LVL	AGE	PA	R	2B	3B	HR	RBI	BB	K	SB	CS	AVG/OBP/SLG	TAv	VORP	BABIP	BRR	FRAA	WARP
2016	BLU	RK	17	276	32	12	3	8	46	33	35	15	5	.271/.359/.449	.291	19.2	.283	1.5	3B(50): -10.7	0.8
2017	LNS	A	18	318	53	21	1	7	45	40	34	6	2	.316/.409/.480	.311	26.8	.336	0.8	3B(61): -2.6	2.5
2017	DUN	A+	18	209	31	7	1	6	31	36	28	2	2	.333/.450/.494	.322	16.9	.365	-2.4	3B(41): -1.5	1.6
2018	*TOR*	*MLB*	*19*	*250*	*28*	*11*	*0*	*8*	*31*	*27*	*52*	*0*	*0*	*.252/.337/.418*	*.256*	*6.8*	*.292*	*-0.5*	*3B -4*	*0.4*
2019	*TOR*	*MLB*	*20*	*445*	*63*	*21*	*1*	*17*	*61*	*51*	*87*	*1*	*0*	*.271/.359/.464*	*.278*	*18.4*	*.306*	*-1.0*	*3B -6*	*1.3*

Breakout: 0% Improve: 16% Collapse: 4% Attrition: 17% MLB: 33% *Comparables: Jurickson Profar, Carlos Correa, Mike Trout*

The hype is real, folks. When the Blue Jays signed Guerrero for nearly $4 million back in 2015, you could be forgiven for thinking a lot of that value was in his name, not his talent. Now, he could go by any name you want and there's not a team in baseball that wouldn't pay 10 times as much for his services. Eighteen-year-olds simply aren't supposed to do what he did in the Midwest and Florida State Leagues. There were no growing pains at all; he walked more than he struck out at both levels, he hit for power and he hit for average. He even improved his work at third base to the point that he's at least passable there, for now. There's still a long way to go, but all signs point to Vladdy Jr. being a potential superstar.

Lourdes Gurriel INF Born: 10/19/93 Age: 24 Bats: R Throws: R Height: 6'2" Weight: 185 Origin: International Free Agent, 2016

YEAR	TEAM	LVL	AGE	PA	R	2B	3B	HR	RBI	BB	K	SB	CS	AVG/OBP/SLG	TAv	VORP	BABIP	BRR	FRAA	WARP
2017	DUN	A+	23	69	6	1	0	1	8	2	13	1	0	.197/.217/.258	.182	-3.3	.226	0.3	SS(11): -0.2, 2B(1): 0.1	-0.4
2017	NHP	AA	23	185	20	10	0	4	28	10	30	2	0	.241/.286/.371	.247	4.1	.266	1.2	2B(22): 1.5, SS(17): 0.9	0.7
2018	*TOR*	*MLB*	*24*	*250*	*25*	*12*	*0*	*7*	*29*	*14*	*58*	*1*	*0*	*.235/.282/.386*	*.226*	*1.7*	*.280*	*-0.4*	*SS 0, 2B 1*	*0.3*
2019	*TOR*	*MLB*	*25*	*269*	*31*	*13*	*0*	*8*	*31*	*15*	*63*	*1*	*0*	*.244/.293/.398*	*.237*	*1.6*	*.291*	*-0.5*	*SS 0, 2B 1*	*0.2*

Breakout: 3% Improve: 13% Collapse: 6% Attrition: 24% MLB: 32% *Comparables: T.J. Rivera, Diory Hernandez, Trevor Plouffe*

At seven years and $22 million, Gurriel is the Blue Jays' biggest Cuban signing. The nominal shortstop is far from a defensive wizard and as a result hasn't settled at a position in the minors. His calling card is his bat-to-ball ability, so Toronto has tried the 24-year-old at a variety of positions of need: shortstop, second base and outfield. Wherever he ends up, he'll have to hit his way there.

Teoscar Hernandez CF Born: 10/15/92 Age: 25 Bats: R Throws: R Height: 6'2" Weight: 180 Origin: International Free Agent, 2011

YEAR	TEAM	LVL	AGE	PA	R	2B	3B	HR	RBI	BB	K	SB	CS	AVG/OBP/SLG	TAv	VORP	BABIP	BRR	FRAA	WARP
2015	CCH	AA	22	514	92	12	2	17	48	33	126	33	7	.219/.275/.362	.237	8.6	.261	7.4	CF(80): -1.2, RF(39): 4.0	1.2
2016	CCH	AA	23	322	53	19	0	6	30	32	55	29	11	.305/.384/.437	.304	25.6	.359	4.2	RF(37): -1.3, CF(30): -0.6	2.6
2016	FRE	AAA	23	160	20	9	3	4	23	13	25	5	4	.313/.365/.500	.306	8.7	.350	-2.4	RF(26): 4.1, CF(11): -1.8	1.1
2016	HOU	MLB	23	112	15	7	0	4	11	11	28	0	2	.230/.304/.420	.246	0.6	.275	-0.6	LF(22): -1.5, CF(15): -1.3	-0.3
2017	FRE	AAA	24	347	54	20	3	12	44	39	72	12	7	.279/.369/.485	.290	21.3	.329	1.9	RF(44): 2.2, CF(22): 1.4	2.4
2017	BUF	AAA	24	109	14	6	2	6	22	8	30	4	1	.222/.294/.505	.271	4.7	.254	0.8	RF(10): 0.8, CF(7): 1.0	1.0
2017	TOR	MLB	24	95	16	6	0	8	20	6	36	0	1	.261/.305/.602	.302	8.3	.333	1.9	LF(18): -0.7, CF(5): 0.0	0.7
2018	*TOR*	*MLB*	*25*	*617*	*91*	*28*	*3*	*22*	*69*	*47*	*161*	*20*	*9*	*.239/.302/.418*	*.251*	*12.8*	*.292*	*0.8*	*RF 6, LF -1*	*1.3*
2019	*TOR*	*MLB*	*26*	*541*	*70*	*25*	*2*	*22*	*72*	*48*	*142*	*18*	*9*	*.242/.316/.439*	*.255*	*11.6*	*.294*	*2.7*	*RF 6, LF -1*	*1.9*

Breakout: 3% Improve: 22% Collapse: 10% Attrition: 24% MLB: 55% *Comparables: Aaron Altherr, Moises Sierra, Rymer Liriano*

The centerpiece of the trade that sent Francisco Liriano to Houston, Hernandez managed to rack up three times as much WARP as the veteran southpaw despite only getting into game action in the season's final month. His eight dingers set a Blue Jays rookie record for September. Because he's been a tough player to profile—too slow for center field, not a good enough hitter for a corner—Hernandez has never been featured on a top-100 prospect list. Yet, he has earned 50 grades virtually across the board from scouts. With elite bat speed and launch-angle data to guide him, he may be able to make a stronger impact at the major-league level. Given Toronto's wasteland of an outfield, Hernandez couldn't have found a more perfect landing spot.

Danny Jansen C Born: 04/15/95 Age: 23 Bats: R Throws: R Height: 6'2" Weight: 225 Origin: Round 16, 2013 Draft (#475 overall)

YEAR	TEAM	LVL	AGE	PA	R	2B	3B	HR	RBI	BB	K	SB	CS	AVG/OBP/SLG	TAv	VORP	BABIP	BRR	FRAA	WARP
2015	LNS	A	20	184	19	8	0	4	27	19	22	2	0	.206/.299/.331	.255	8.0	.213	0.8	C(46): 2.0	1.1
2016	DUN	A+	21	217	18	7	0	1	23	22	40	7	1	.218/.313/.271	.223	0.6	.268	-0.2	C(50): -1.3	-0.1
2017	DUN	A+	22	136	19	6	0	5	18	8	14	0	0	.369/.422/.541	.351	17.0	.385	-0.7	C(25): -2.0	1.6
2017	NHP	AA	22	210	23	15	1	2	20	22	19	1	0	.291/.378/.419	.296	15.4	.311	-1.4	C(50): -3.3	1.3
2017	BUF	AAA	22	78	8	4	1	3	10	11	7	0	0	.328/.423/.552	.348	11.2	.333	-0.1	C(21): -0.5	1.0
2018	*TOR*	*MLB*	*23*	*250*	*27*	*12*	*1*	*7*	*30*	*22*	*47*	*1*	*0*	*.251/.328/.409*	*.252*	*10.5*	*.285*	*-0.3*	*C -9*	*0.2*
2019	*TOR*	*MLB*	*24*	*307*	*39*	*15*	*1*	*10*	*37*	*28*	*59*	*1*	*0*	*.248/.326/.414*	*.256*	*10.0*	*.281*	*-0.6*	*C -7*	*0.3*

Breakout: 4% Improve: 28% Collapse: 6% Attrition: 22% MLB: 48% *Comparables: Kevin Plawecki, Russell Martin, Hank Conger*

YEAR	TEAM	P. COUNT	FRM RUNS	BLK RUNS	THRW RUNS	TOT RUNS
2018	*TOR*	*8952*	*-7.0*	*0.7*	*-1.4*	*-7.7*
2019	*TOR*	*11002*	*-2.5*	*0.3*	*-0.5*	*-2.8*

While merely the second-most-famous athlete with his name, Jansen skated his way up many prospect lists last summer. The oft-injured catcher finally stayed healthy for a whole season while adding improved vision and then showed why Blue Jays evaluators have been high on him for years with a gold medal-worthy performance. The 22-year-old put up an impressive batting line across three levels, finishing the year with a dominant 21-game run just one rung below the big leagues. That bat and decent glove work should have him knocking on the door to the majors very soon. Maybe then he can finally reach the first page of a Google search.

Russell Martin C Born: 02/15/83 Age: 35 Bats: R Throws: R Height: 5'10" Weight: 205 Origin: Round 17, 2002 Draft (#511 overall)

YEAR	TEAM	LVL	AGE	PA	R	2B	3B	HR	RBI	BB	K	SB	CS	AVG/OBP/SLG	TAv	VORP	BABIP	BRR	FRAA	WARP
2015	TOR	MLB	32	507	76	23	2	23	77	53	106	4	5	.240/.329/.458	.275	27.7	.262	-0.9	C(117): 9.8, 2B(2): -0.2	4.0
2016	TOR	MLB	33	535	62	16	0	20	74	64	148	2	1	.231/.335/.398	.252	19.3	.291	0.3	C(127): 10.7, 2B(1): 0.0	3.1
2017	TOR	MLB	34	365	49	12	0	13	35	50	83	1	2	.221/.343/.388	.250	12.8	.261	0.2	C(83): -0.5, 3B(10): 0.7	1.3
2018	*TOR*	*MLB*	*35*	*468*	*59*	*18*	*1*	*15*	*55*	*54*	*108*	*3*	*2*	*.235/.336/.391*	*.260*	*23.4*	*.281*	*-1.4*	*C 4*	*2.1*
2019	*TOR*	*MLB*	*36*	*365*	*47*	*14*	*0*	*12*	*43*	*43*	*89*	*1*	*1*	*.224/.329/.385*	*.251*	*10.7*	*.270*	*0.0*	*C 4*	*1.6*

Breakout: 0% Improve: 27% Collapse: 12% Attrition: 26% MLB: 86%

Comparables: Sherm Lollar, Jorge Posada, Ed Bailey

YEAR	TEAM	P. COUNT	FRM RUNS	BLK RUNS	THRW RUNS	TOT RUNS
2015	TOR	15667	10.6	-3.6	2.6	9.5
2016	TOR	16738	13.6	0.1	-2.8	11.0
2017	TOR	11346	1.2	-0.2	-1.0	0.0
2018	*TOR*	*15889*	*7.9*	*-1.9*	*-0.8*	*5.2*
2019	*TOR*	*12405*	*7.1*	*-1.7*	*-0.7*	*4.7*

Here's how important Martin was to the Blue Jays in 2017: When he was out with an injury or simply needed a day off, their backup catchers hit a combined .155/.216/.267 and threw out just 14 of 85 basestealers. It's hard to imagine a non-star player being that invaluable to a club, but that's where the Jays are with Martin and have been for a couple years. While his hitting has slipped of late and the strikeouts are piling up, that he's still providing even league-average offense and defense behind the plate means that he's still a very useful player as he gets into his mid-thirties.

Miguel Montero C Born: 07/09/83 Age: 34 Bats: L Throws: R Height: 5'11" Weight: 210 Origin: International Free Agent, 2001

YEAR	TEAM	LVL	AGE	PA	R	2B	3B	HR	RBI	BB	K	SB	CS	AVG/OBP/SLG	TAv	VORP	BABIP	BRR	FRAA	WARP
2015	CHN	MLB	31	403	36	11	0	15	53	49	103	1	1	.248/.345/.409	.279	23.4	.306	-1.1	C(109): 12.7	3.9
2016	CHN	MLB	32	284	33	8	1	8	33	38	58	1	0	.216/.327/.357	.257	10.0	.249	-1.7	C(71): 8.6, P(1): 0.0	1.9
2017	CHN	MLB	33	112	12	3	0	4	8	11	24	1	0	.286/.366/.439	.286	7.9	.338	-0.2	C(29): 0.0, 1B(1): 0.0	0.8
2017	TOR	MLB	33	101	12	3	0	2	8	12	23	0	0	.138/.248/.241	.185	-3.8	.159	-0.3	C(27): 2.9	-0.1
2018	*TOR*	*MLB*	*34*	*250*	*27*	*9*	*0*	*7*	*28*	*28*	*57*	*1*	*0*	*.230/.324/.369*	*.238*	*6.5*	*.276*	*-0.7*	*C 9, 1B 0*	*1.7*
2019	*TOR*	*MLB*	*35*	*189*	*23*	*7*	*0*	*5*	*21*	*20*	*44*	*0*	*0*	*.226/.317/.366*	*.239*	*2.5*	*.274*	*-0.6*	*C 7, 1B 0*	*1.1*

Breakout: 1% Improve: 36% Collapse: 15% Attrition: 17% MLB: 89%

Comparables: Brian Schneider, Bob Stinson, Rick Dempsey

YEAR	TEAM	P. COUNT	FRM RUNS	BLK RUNS	THRW RUNS	TOT RUNS
2015	CHN	13007	14.5	1.4	-2.6	13.4
2015	TEN	192	0.0	0.0	0.0	0.1
2016	CHN	8698	14.6	-1.8	-3.5	9.3
2017	CHN	3543	1.0	0.3	-1.8	-0.6
2017	TOR	3456	4.0	0.6	-1.8	2.8
2018	*TOR*	*8602*	*10.5*	*0.2*	*-1.6*	*9.1*
2019	*TOR*	*6498*	*9.1*	*0.2*	*-1.4*	*7.9*

Montero's season was a tale of two halves at the plate. After mashing with the Cubs, he caught Blue Jays backup catcher disease and fell off the map in Toronto. As big as his bat was, his mouth was even bigger. After forcing his own way out of the Windy City by blaming his failure to catch would-be basestealers on the club's pitchers, Montero nabbed just three of 30 attempted thefts in Toronto. Of course, that was still a drastic improvement on the 1-of-32 he managed while catching the Cubs, so maybe it really *was* all Jake Arrieta's fault.

Kendrys Morales DH Born: 06/20/83 Age: 35 Bats: B Throws: R Height: 6'1" Weight: 225 Origin: International Free Agent, 2005

YEAR	TEAM	LVL	AGE	PA	R	2B	3B	HR	RBI	BB	K	SB	CS	AVG/OBP/SLG	TAv	VORP	BABIP	BRR	FRAA	WARP
2015	KCA	MLB	32	639	81	41	2	22	106	58	103	0	0	.290/.362/.485	.294	22.2	.319	-5.5	1B(9): -0.4	2.3
2016	KCA	MLB	33	618	65	24	0	30	93	48	120	0	0	.263/.327/.468	.270	11.7	.283	-1.2	1B(7): -0.1, RF(5): -0.2	1.2
2017	TOR	MLB	34	608	67	25	0	28	85	43	132	0	0	.250/.308/.445	.254	-3.7	.278	-6.3	1B(12): -1.3	-0.5
2018	*TOR*	*MLB*	*35*	*600*	*70*	*28*	*1*	*21*	*79*	*46*	*114*	*0*	*0*	*.256/.318/.425*	*.259*	*8.4*	*.287*	*-1.4*		*0.8*
2019	*TOR*	*MLB*	*36*	*502*	*65*	*23*	*0*	*19*	*64*	*42*	*101*	*0*	*0*	*.249/.318/.425*	*.254*	*1.7*	*.280*	*-3.3*	-	*0.2*

Breakout: 0% Improve: 20% Collapse: 10% Attrition: 30% MLB: 87%

Comparables: Ty Wigginton, Adrian Gonzalez, Aubrey Huff

If baseball is all about entertainment, Morales was a star in 2017. His overall hitting numbers were mediocre and you could've used a sundial to record his sprint speed—according to Statcast, the only slower non-catchers in baseball were Victor Martinez and Albert Pujols—but he definitely brought the excitement. Kendrys led all of baseball with four homers in the ninth inning or later that either tied the game or gave his team the lead, including two walk-offs. Add to that two eighth-inning, game-tying bombs and a two-out, game-tying single in the ninth inning, and Jays fans more than got their money's worth. Now he just needs to provide that same value to a front office.

Steve Pearce LF Born: 04/13/83 Age: 35 Bats: R Throws: R Height: 5'11" Weight: 200 Origin: Round 8, 2005 Draft (#241 overall)

YEAR	TEAM	LVL	AGE	PA	R	2B	3B	HR	RBI	BB	K	SB	CS	AVG/OBP/SLG	TAv	VORP	BABIP	BRR	FRAA	WARP
2015	BAL	MLB	32	325	42	13	1	15	40	23	69	1	1	.218/.289/.422	.244	2.6	.232	2.0	LF(41): -0.5, 1B(28): 1.0	0.3
2016	TBA	MLB	33	232	26	11	1	10	29	26	40	0	3	.309/.388/.520	.323	18.3	.342	0.0	1B(30): 1.7, 2B(14): 0.4	2.1
2016	BAL	MLB	33	70	9	2	0	3	6	8	14	0	0	.217/.329/.400	.268	3.3	.233	1.5	1B(10): -0.3, LF(7): -0.1	0.3
2017	TOR	MLB	34	348	38	17	1	13	37	27	68	0	0	.252/.319/.438	.259	7.3	.281	0.3	LF(85): 3.3, 1B(10): -0.4	1.0
2018	*TOR*	*MLB*	*35*	*482*	*59*	*24*	*1*	*18*	*66*	*43*	*97*	*1*	*1*	*.254/.331/.441*	*.270*	*21.1*	*.287*	*-1.2*	*LF 3, 1B 0*	*1.9*
2019	*TOR*	*MLB*	*36*	*327*	*42*	*16*	*1*	*12*	*42*	*31*	*70*	*0*	*0*	*.245/.327/.429*	*.259*	*8.3*	*.283*	*1.2*	*LF 3, 1B 0*	*1.2*

Breakout: 3% Improve: 22% Collapse: 11% Attrition: 19% MLB: 82%

Comparables: Monte Irvin, Ryan Ludwick, Jason Bay

Pearce is Mr. Inconsistent. Historically praised for his ability to hit lefties, he fulfilled the reputation in 2014 and 2016 by posting a 1.109 and 1.032 OPS against them, respectively. In those two seasons, that made him one of the league's 20 best hitters. In 2015 and 2017, however, he wasn't even as good as the average hitter. He went from hitting lefties as well as Mike Trout does to hitting them as poorly as Kevin Pillar. In both seasons he was even worse against lefties than against righties. On the plus side, 2018 is a new year and an even year, so if the gods of inconsistency are to have their way, Pearce will be Troutastic against southpaws once again.

Max Pentecost C Born: 03/10/93 Age: 25 Bats: R Throws: R Height: 6'2" Weight: 191 Origin: Round 1, 2014 Draft (#11 overall)

YEAR	TEAM	LVL	AGE	PA	R	2B	3B	HR	RBI	BB	K	SB	CS	AVG/OBP/SLG	TAv	VORP	BABIP	BRR	FRAA	WARP
2016	LNS	A	23	267	36	15	3	7	34	21	51	4	2	.314/.375/.490	.317	19.0	.370	1.5		2.1
2016	DUN	A+	23	52	6	2	0	3	7	3	17	1	1	.245/.288/.469	.258	0.3	.310	-0.2		0.0
2017	DUN	A+	24	314	34	14	2	9	54	23	62	0	1	.276/.332/.434	.277	9.9	.323	-1.5	1B(22): 0.8, C(19): -0.3	1.1
2018	*TOR*	*MLB*	*25*	*250*	*27*	*11*	*1*	*9*	*33*	*16*	*68*	*0*	*0*	*.239/.291/.416*	*.236*	*2.2*	*.294*	*-0.4*	*C 0, 1B 0*	*0.2*
2019	*TOR*	*MLB*	*26*	*264*	*32*	*12*	*1*	*10*	*33*	*19*	*72*	*0*	*0*	*.234/.292/.409*	*.239*	*0.3*	*.288*	*-0.6*	*C 0, 1B 0*	*0.0*

Breakout: 4% Improve: 5% Collapse: 2% Attrition: 8% MLB: 10% *Comparables: Rhyne Hughes, Brock Peterson, Ben Paulsen*

Pentecost played catcher in 2017. That sentence would mean little for most players, but is of huge importance for Pentecost. Thanks to three shoulder surgeries (covering both shoulders), the former first-round pick hadn't donned the tools of ignorance since 2014. Thankfully, there was very little evident rust in his defensive game. He tired late in the season and missed its conclusion with yet another injury, but 2017 was still a huge step forward for the forgotten prospect. The goal in 2018 will be to stay healthy all year in Double-A and to finally start catching back-to-back games.

Kevin Pillar CF Born: 01/04/89 Age: 29 Bats: R Throws: R Height: 6'0" Weight: 205 Origin: Round 32, 2011 Draft (#979 overall)

YEAR	TEAM	LVL	AGE	PA	R	2B	3B	HR	RBI	BB	K	SB	CS	AVG/OBP/SLG	TAv	VORP	BABIP	BRR	FRAA	WARP
2015	TOR	MLB	26	628	76	31	2	12	56	28	85	25	4	.278/.314/.399	.257	22.3	.306	6.1	CF(142): 9.0, LF(14): 4.3	3.8
2016	TOR	MLB	27	584	59	35	2	7	53	24	90	14	6	.266/.303/.376	.232	4.2	.306	2.7	CF(146): 6.1	1.1
2017	TOR	MLB	28	632	72	37	1	16	42	33	95	15	6	.256/.300/.404	.243	7.5	.280	-1.1	CF(153): -6.1	0.1
2018	*TOR*	*MLB*	*29*	*601*	*69*	*35*	*2*	*10*	*59*	*27*	*94*	*17*	*6*	*.268/.305/.393*	*.244*	*15.1*	*.302*	*1.0*	*CF 1*	*1.1*
2019	*TOR*	*MLB*	*30*	*547*	*62*	*31*	*2*	*12*	*60*	*30*	*91*	*15*	*5*	*.270/.317/.410*	*.247*	*11.2*	*.305*	*2.0*	*CF 2*	*1.4*

Breakout: 3% Improve: 48% Collapse: 9% Attrition: 21% MLB: 85% *Comparables: Tike Redman, Charlie Blackmon, Willie Bloomquist*

Apparently you can't teach an old dog new tricks. In spring training, Pillar claimed to have identified the central issues that led to his lowly .303 career on-base percentage. He vowed to do a better job of "waiting for his pitch." In April, he wasn't walking any more than before, but he was waiting for his pitch and it resulted in his being Toronto's best hitter that month. In May, the strong hitting continued and Pillar even posted his best single-month strikeout-to-walk ratio. In June, however, his plate discipline walked away and never returned. The old dog had learned no new tricks, unless you count the ability to not play center field as well as he once did.

Dalton Pompey LF Born: 12/11/92 Age: 25 Bats: B Throws: R Height: 6'2" Weight: 195 Origin: Round 16, 2010 Draft (#486 overall)

YEAR	TEAM	LVL	AGE	PA	R	2B	3B	HR	RBI	BB	K	SB	CS	AVG/OBP/SLG	TAv	VORP	BABIP	BRR	FRAA	WARP
2015	NHP	AA	22	148	26	2	3	6	22	11	23	7	3	.351/.405/.545	.342	18.3	.387	2.0	CF(22): -1.5, LF(7): -0.5	1.8
2015	BUF	AAA	22	295	44	7	4	1	18	36	41	16	7	.285/.372/.356	.271	13.4	.332	2.1	CF(43): -2.7, LF(22): 2.1	1.3
2015	TOR	MLB	22	103	17	8	0	2	6	7	23	5	1	.223/.291/.372	.233	-0.3	.275	-0.4	CF(21): 0.2, LF(6): 0.2	0.0
2016	BUF	AAA	23	383	48	14	1	4	28	40	72	18	7	.270/.349/.353	.255	13.9	.331	5.2	CF(67): -0.6, LF(24): -0.3	1.3
2016	TOR	MLB	23	2	3	0	0	0	0	0	1	2	1	.000/.000/.000	.001	-0.4	.000	0.1	LF(2): -0.1	-0.1
2017	DUN	A+	24	32	5	1	1	0	5	5	3	1	0	.259/.375/.370	.287	1.3	.292	-0.3	CF(3): 0.3, LF(2): -0.2	0.1
2018	*TOR*	*MLB*	*25*	*92*	*12*	*4*	*1*	*2*	*9*	*8*	*20*	*4*	*1*	*.257/.329/.387*	*.252*	*2.7*	*.317*	*0.3*	*LF 1, CF 0*	*0.3*
2019	*TOR*	*MLB*	*26*	*273*	*33*	*10*	*2*	*7*	*31*	*27*	*63*	*11*	*4*	*.257/.335/.406*	*.254*	*6.6*	*.316*	*1.2*	*LF 3, CF -1*	*0.9*

Breakout: 7% Improve: 47% Collapse: 6% Attrition: 35% MLB: 75% *Comparables: Abraham Almonte, Brett Gardner, Lorenzo Cain*

Pompey can't catch a break. He started the year by representing Canada in the World Baseball Classic, but his tournament was cut short due to a concussion. The good news is that baseball is one American sport with a proper concussion protocol. The bad news is that recovering from a concussion meant that Pompey would miss a third of the season. Then, just as his rehab stint allowed him to reach Triple-A in July, he suffered a nasty knee injury and sat out the rest of the season. After his first shot at major-league playing time was foiled by Kevin Pillar's career revival in 2015, last season was set to be his year. Now the Toronto-area product has to claw his way back to the majors.

Michael Saunders OF Born: 11/19/86 Age: 31 Bats: L Throws: R Height: 6'4" Weight: 225 Origin: Round 11, 2004 Draft (#333 overall)

YEAR	TEAM	LVL	AGE	PA	R	2B	3B	HR	RBI	BB	K	SB	CS	AVG/OBP/SLG	TAv	VORP	BABIP	BRR	FRAA	WARP
2015	DUN	A+	28	33	2	3	0	0	2	3	8	0	0	.233/.303/.333	.218	-1.3	.318	-0.5	LF(4): -0.4, RF(2): -0.6	-0.3
2015	TOR	MLB	28	36	2	0	0	0	3	5	10	0	0	.194/.306/.194	.210	-1.8	.286	-0.7	RF(6): 1.4, LF(3): -0.4	-0.1
2016	TOR	MLB	29	558	70	32	3	24	57	59	157	1	2	.253/.338/.478	.273	17.5	.321	-1.5	LF(106): -1.8, RF(22): -0.4	1.6
2017	PHI	MLB	30	214	25	9	2	6	20	13	51	0	1	.205/.257/.360	.213	-5.3	.245	1.3	RF(52): -0.3	-0.6
2017	BUF	AAA	30	156	22	11	1	2	12	9	30	1	0	.274/.321/.404	.241	1.3	.333	2.0	LF(17): 0.1, RF(4): -0.5	0.1
2017	TOR	MLB	30	20	1	0	0	0	1	2	4	0	0	.167/.250/.167	.196	-0.9	.214	0.0	LF(4): 2.7, RF(2): -0.2	0.2
2018	*TOR*	*MLB*	*31*	*308*	*34*	*15*	*2*	*10*	*38*	*32*	*79*	*1*	*1*	*.242/.325/.416*	*.252*	*6.0*	*.303*	*-0.3*	*RF -2, LF 0*	*0.4*
2019	*TOR*	*MLB*	*32*	*306*	*38*	*15*	*2*	*9*	*36*	*32*	*81*	*1*	*1*	*.238/.322/.410*	*.252*	*3.6*	*.302*	*-0.2*	*RF -2, LF 0*	*0.2*

Breakout: 3% Improve: 40% Collapse: 14% Attrition: 18% MLB: 82% *Comparables: Ryan Church, Franklin Gutierrez, Gabe Gross*

If the end to his 2016 season was unkind, the 2017 campaign was downright cruel to the Canadian. He performed so poorly that after making the All-Star team in 2016, Saunders was cut by the lowly Phillies in June 2017. After an offseason filled with debates over which Saunders was real—the breakout player from 2016 or the previous versions—it turned out to be neither. If he doesn't return to some sort of form in 2018, the 31-year-old may need to look across the ocean for a regular job.

Justin Smoak 1B Born: 12/05/86 Age: 31 Bats: B Throws: L Height: 6'4" Weight: 220 Origin: Round 1, 2008 Draft (#11 overall)

YEAR	TEAM	LVL	AGE	PA	R	2B	3B	HR	RBI	BB	K	SB	CS	AVG/OBP/SLG	TAv	VORP	BABIP	BRR	FRAA	WARP
2015	TOR	MLB	28	328	44	16	1	18	59	29	86	0	0	.226/.299/.470	.267	3.5	.254	-2.4	1B(110): 2.1	0.6
2016	TOR	MLB	29	341	33	10	0	14	34	40	112	1	0	.217/.314/.391	.242	-3.8	.295	-1.3	1B(111): -2.3	-0.6
2017	TOR	MLB	30	637	85	29	1	38	90	73	128	0	1	.270/.355/.529	.289	26.6	.285	0.6	1B(151): -0.9	2.6
2018	*TOR*	*MLB*	*31*	*610*	*76*	*26*	*1*	*25*	*85*	*66*	*146*	*1*	*1*	*.242/.328/.433*	*.266*	*12.9*	*.285*	*-1.4*	*1B -3*	*0.7*
2019	*TOR*	*MLB*	*32*	*541*	*75*	*23*	*0*	*24*	*74*	*63*	*135*	*0*	*0*	*.236/.330/.437*	*.261*	*5.8*	*.278*	*-1.2*	*1B -2*	*0.4*

Breakout: 0% Improve: 41% Collapse: 9% Attrition: 13% MLB: 89% *Comparables: Lucas Duda, Ryan Zimmerman, Seth Smith*

An offensive prospect's core talent is pure. You can't artificially create elite bat speed, raw power or blazing quickness. But there's a difference between having raw abilities and being able to apply them in-game. You can, however, create learned abilities like plate discipline and pitch recognition. Even then, there's a difference between applying them in the minors and in the majors. The cross section of these realities are precisely what plagued Smoak in his first seven seasons, as he produced a cumulative -2.9 WARP.

Kevin Goldstein once described Smoak as having "the best plate discipline in the [Rangers] organization, and among the best in baseball, with plus raw power from both sides." Once he got to the majors there was one big problem: Smoak couldn't make good contact. When the ball was inside the zone he didn't hit the ball hard and when it was outside the zone he had trouble hitting the ball at all, yet he'd still swing. He tried new swings, compact and otherwise, but nothing stuck.

Then, in 2017, armed with yet another new swing, Smoak started making good contact with the ball. Smoak's contact-rate increase was the 14th-highest in the history of the statistic. He hit with more power and for a higher average than ever before, all without the aid of the usual luck factors like an abnormally high BABIP or home run-to-fly ball rate. The change in contact rate can be optimistically attributed to Smoak's clean, compact swing, which mirrored changes that George Springer and Joc Pederson made in recent years. However, we've also seen cases where a large increase in contact rate has simply been a mirage. Danny Espinosa's 2015 season stands out as the primary example here. Smoak has the raw talent and the learned abilities, but he'll have to show us another year of dominance to affirm that he's truly a whole new player.

Devon Travis 2B Born: 02/21/91 Age: 27 Bats: R Throws: R Height: 5'9" Weight: 190 Origin: Round 13, 2012 Draft (#424 overall)

YEAR	TEAM	LVL	AGE	PA	R	2B	3B	HR	RBI	BB	K	SB	CS	AVG/OBP/SLG	TAv	VORP	BABIP	BRR	FRAA	WARP
2015	BUF	AAA	24	38	5	1	0	0	0	6	9	1	0	.219/.342/.250	.236	0.6	.304	0.8	2B(5): -0.1	0.1
2015	TOR	MLB	24	238	38	18	0	8	35	18	43	3	1	.304/.361/.498	.307	18.5	.347	1.4	2B(62): -0.1	2.0
2016	TOR	MLB	25	432	54	28	1	11	50	20	87	4	1	.300/.332/.454	.266	15.7	.358	1.6	2B(99): -0.4	1.6
2017	TOR	MLB	26	197	22	18	0	5	24	7	38	4	2	.259/.291/.438	.244	3.4	.299	1.2	2B(50): -1.9	0.1
2018	*TOR*	*MLB*	*27*	*388*	*46*	*25*	*1*	*10*	*45*	*22*	*74*	*5*	*2*	*.278/.322/.434*	*.263*	*18.4*	*.324*	*-0.3*	*2B -1*	*1.2*
2019	*TOR*	*MLB*	*28*	*332*	*41*	*21*	*0*	*10*	*41*	*22*	*66*	*4*	*2*	*.276/.327/.446*	*.262*	*12.6*	*.320*	*1.2*	*2B -1*	*1.3*

Breakout: 2% Improve: 61% Collapse: 1% Attrition: 6% MLB: 97% *Comparables: Brett Lawrie, Howie Kendrick, Jorge Orta*

If an award for the game's most obvious "if only he could stay healthy" player existed, Travis might've won it in both 2015 and 2016. Over that time, he produced 3.5 WARP per 162 games, similar to the likes of Ian Kinsler and Dustin Pedroia. Last season represented a new, radical strategy. Not only did Travis miss a majority of the season, he also wasn't particularly good when he was playing. For the first time in his career he was a below-average hitter and a well-below-average fielder. He regained some of the elite exit velocity that helped jump-start his career in 2015 but lost a step on defense and saw his approach at the plate get worse. With swift-fielding middle infielder Richard Urena graduating to the majors last September, Travis may soon have to compete for his starter's spot.

Troy Tulowitzki SS Born: 10/10/84 Age: 33 Bats: R Throws: R Height: 6'3" Weight: 205 Origin: Round 1, 2005 Draft (#7 overall)

YEAR	TEAM	LVL	AGE	PA	R	2B	3B	HR	RBI	BB	K	SB	CS	AVG/OBP/SLG	TAv	VORP	BABIP	BRR	FRAA	WARP
2015	COL	MLB	30	351	46	19	0	12	53	24	72	0	0	.300/.348/.471	.274	19.3	.351	0.7	SS(82): -3.0	1.7
2015	TOR	MLB	30	183	31	8	0	5	17	14	42	1	0	.239/.317/.380	.258	7.1	.291	0.5	SS(39): 2.9	1.1
2016	TOR	MLB	31	544	54	21	0	24	79	43	101	1	0	.254/.318/.443	.253	16.6	.272	-1.6	SS(128): 2.8	2.0
2017	TOR	MLB	32	260	16	10	0	7	26	17	40	0	1	.249/.300/.378	.232	0.5	.272	-3.0	SS(64): 2.4	0.3
2018	*TOR*	*MLB*	*33*	*509*	*63*	*21*	*0*	*19*	*69*	*45*	*98*	*1*	*1*	*.265/.335/.437*	*.267*	*25.1*	*.298*	*-1.2*	*SS 3*	*2.3*
2019	*TOR*	*MLB*	*34*	*352*	*47*	*15*	*0*	*13*	*46*	*31*	*70*	*0*	*0*	*.261/.333/.436*	*.259*	*10.3*	*.294*	*-0.9*	*SS 2*	*1.4*

Breakout: 1% Improve: 36% Collapse: 3% Attrition: 4% MLB: 96% *Comparables: Jhonny Peralta, Miguel Tejada, Derek Jeter*

Fool me once, shame on you. Fool me twice, shame on me. So what happens when we get fooled seven or eight times? Is that the definition of insanity? Or some other cliché? That's where we are with Tulowitzki. After he teased it by playing 133 games in 2016 and posting Tulowitzkian numbers following a slow start, people were hoping for a bounce-back from the former All-Star shortstop. Instead, Tulo played his fewest games since 2012 and showed an even further diminished performance on those rare occasions when he was on the field. There's still hope that he can regain some of the magic he had in Colorado, but as he gets deeper into his thirties it's becoming less and less likely.

Richard Urena SS Born: 02/26/96 Age: 22 Bats: B Throws: R Height: 6'0" Weight: 185 Origin: International Free Agent, 2012

YEAR	TEAM	LVL	AGE	PA	R	2B	3B	HR	RBI	BB	K	SB	CS	AVG/OBP/SLG	TAv	VORP	BABIP	BRR	FRAA	WARP
2015	DUN	A+	19	128	9	3	1	1	8	3	26	3	1	.250/.268/.315	.228	0.9	.309	0.0	SS(30): -2.8	-0.2
2015	LNS	A	19	408	62	13	4	15	58	13	84	5	5	.266/.289/.438	.254	15.7	.299	1.9	SS(90): -9.6	0.7
2016	DUN	A+	20	431	52	18	7	8	41	25	64	9	6	.305/.351/.447	.266	17.0	.346	-1.3	SS(79): -0.1	1.7
2016	NHP	AA	20	132	14	6	5	0	18	4	19	0	2	.266/.282/.395	.256	5.3	.306	0.7	SS(29): -0.7	0.5
2017	NHP	AA	21	551	44	36	3	5	60	30	100	0	1	.247/.286/.359	.237	6.1	.294	-1.9	SS(106): -4.6, 2B(11): 0.2	0.2
2017	TOR	MLB	21	75	6	4	0	1	4	6	28	1	0	.206/.270/.309	.207	0.4	.333	1.4	SS(20): -2.0, 2B(1): 0.1	-0.2
2018	*TOR*	*MLB*	*22*	*30*	*3*	*1*	*0*	*1*	*3*	*1*	*7*	*0*	*0*	*.230/.258/.362*	*.216*	*0.0*	*.285*	*0.0*	*SS 0*	*-0.1*
2019	*TOR*	*MLB*	*23*	*328*	*36*	*16*	*3*	*9*	*38*	*15*	*82*	*1*	*1*	*.242/.279/.404*	*.232*	*1.0*	*.295*	*-0.4*	*SS -4*	*-0.3*

Breakout: 2% Improve: 15% Collapse: 4% Attrition: 12% MLB: 22% *Comparables: Chris Nelson, Danny Santana, Orlando Calixte*

We're living in an odd era. Didi Gregorius never finished a minor-league season with more than 10 home runs. Neither did Elvis Andrus, Tim Beckham or Francisco Lindor. Yet every one of them hit 20 or more home runs in 2017—Gregorius has done it twice and Lindor just topped the 30 mark. They were all hailed as strong hitters, but were glove-first players at their core and struggled to actualize on any home-run power in the minors. Which sounds a lot like Urena. While he was unimpressive in his September debut, striking out in more than 35 percent of his at-bats, the tools are there. The baseball is poppin' across the majors and Urena has finally made it to "The Show." Crazier things have happened.

PITCHERS

Brett Anderson LHP Born: 02/01/88 Age: 30 Bats: L Throws: L Height: 6'3" Weight: 230 Origin: Round 2, 2006 Draft (#55 overall)

YEAR	TEAM	LVL	AGE	W	L	SV	G	GS	IP	H	HR	BB/9	K/9	K	GB%	BABIP	WHIP	ERA	DRA	WARP	MPH	CMD	PWR	STM
2015	LAN	MLB	27	10	9	0	31	31	180^1	194	18	2.3	5.8	116	67%	.310	1.33	3.69	4.63	1.0	93.5	44	36	70
2016	LAN	MLB	28	1	2	0	4	3	11^1	25	4	3.2	4.0	5	51%	.429	2.56	11.91	7.18	-0.2	94.2	54	45	17
2017	CHN	MLB	29	2	2	0	6	6	22	34	2	4.9	6.5	16	51%	.395	2.09	8.18	6.13	-0.1	92.2	54	34	39
2017	TEN	AA	29	2	2	0	6	5	27^1	34	2	3.0	4.9	15	69%	.348	1.57	4.61	2.86	0.7				
2017	TOR	MLB	29	2	2	0	7	7	33^1	39	3	2.4	5.9	22	50%	.340	1.44	5.13	6.83	-0.5	93.2	54	34	39
2018	*TOR*	*MLB*	*30*	*4*	*5*	*0*	*13*	*13*	65^1	*79*	*9*	*3.7*	*6.1*	*44*	*54%*	*.327*	*1.62*	*5.13*	*5.42*	*0.2*	*92.6*	*48*	*36*	*39*
2019	*TOR*	*MLB*	*31*	*7*	*10*	*0*	*27*	*27*	162^2	*200*	*24*	*3.6*	*6.0*	*108*	*54%*	*.327*	*1.63*	*5.18*	*5.46*	*0.3*	*91.9*	*50*	*35*	*33*

Breakout: 20% Improve: 49% Collapse: 12% Attrition: 17% MLB: 81% *Comparables: Jaime Garcia, Charlie Morton, Zach Duke*

Anderson is the ultimate temptation. He gets injured early in the year, then comes back and tantalizes with a mixture of quality stuff, crisp command and a boatload of groundballs while finishing the season healthy. Then some team gives him a guaranteed contract hoping he breaks the curse. Rinse, repeat. It's amazing how often something like that can play out, but it has been happening with Anderson for years because he's still reasonably young and quite good when he's not hurting. He came back healthy with the Blue Jays in 2017 and was great (save for one blowup start). There's no reason whatsoever to assume he'll say healthy, but we all dream he will. If Suede's comeback has taught us anything, it's that you should never count out Brett Anderson.

Danny Barnes RHP Born: 10/21/89 Age: 28 Bats: L Throws: R Height: 6'1" Weight: 195 Origin: Round 35, 2010 Draft (#1056 overall)

YEAR	TEAM	LVL	AGE	W	L	SV	G	GS	IP	H	HR	BB/9	K/9	K	GB%	BABIP	WHIP	ERA	DRA	WARP	MPH	CMD	PWR	STM
2015	NHP	AA	25	3	2	4	40	1	60^2	64	5	2.8	11.0	74	32%	.362	1.37	2.97	2.44	1.7				
2016	NHP	AA	26	2	1	1	24	0	35^2	17	3	1.0	10.1	40	30%	.177	0.59	1.01	2.25	1.1				
2016	BUF	AAA	26	1	0	5	17	0	25^2	6	0	0.7	13.0	37	32%	.128	0.31	0.35	1.11	1.1				
2016	TOR	MLB	26	0	0	0	12	0	13^2	14	0	3.3	9.2	14	44%	.359	1.39	3.95	4.04	0.1	94.1	50	49	46
2017	TOR	MLB	27	3	6	0	60	0	66	48	11	3.3	8.5	62	33%	.222	1.09	3.55	4.46	0.5	93.6	57	46	50
2018	*TOR*	*MLB*	*28*	*3*	*3*	*0*	*59*	*0*	*62*	*59*	*11*	*3.5*	*9.3*	*65*	*34%*	*.293*	*1.33*	*4.54*	*4.74*	*0.3*	*93.1*	*56*	*47*	*49*
2019	*TOR*	*MLB*	*29*	*3*	*1*	*0*	*51*	*0*	*54*	*49*	*9*	*3.4*	*9.7*	*58*	*34%*	*.287*	*1.29*	*4.55*	*4.78*	*0.3*	*92.7*	*56*	*47*	*48*

Breakout: 21% Improve: 33% Collapse: 24% Attrition: 21% MLB: 73% *Comparables: Nick Vincent, Brad Brach, Heath Hembree*

Barnes is the French vanilla of pitchers. It looks just like the boring regular flavor, but there's that invisible something extra that makes it great. Barnes appears to be some run-of-the-mill, Quadruple-A pitcher; he doesn't throw that hard and doesn't have much of a breaking ball to speak of. But somehow he manages to eat up major-league hitters with a 92-mph four-seamer and a very good changeup, with his ability to throw strikes and his determination to throw the ball up in the zone. He wore down a bit at the end of 2017 due to fatigue (you can't keep ice cream out that long before it melts), but he has the potential to be a bullpen fixture going forward.

Joe Biagini RHP Born: 05/29/90 Age: 28 Bats: R Throws: R Height: 6'5" Weight: 240 Origin: Round 26, 2011 Draft (#807 overall)

YEAR	TEAM	LVL	AGE	W	L	SV	G	GS	IP	H	HR	BB/9	K/9	K	GB%	BABIP	WHIP	ERA	DRA	WARP	MPH	CMD	PWR	STM
2015	RIC	AA	25	10	7	0	23	22	130^1	112	5	2.3	5.8	84	54%	.264	1.12	2.42	3.98	1.7				
2016	TOR	MLB	26	4	3	1	60	0	67^2	69	3	2.5	8.2	62	54%	.320	1.30	3.06	3.91	0.8	96.6	47	53	47
2017	BUF	AAA	27	1	1	0	4	4	17^1	13	2	3.1	7.3	14	58%	.239	1.10	3.12	3.28	0.5				
2017	TOR	MLB	27	3	13	1	44	18	119^2	125	15	3.2	7.3	97	56%	.305	1.40	5.34	4.50	1.3	95.5	60	50	64
2018	*TOR*	*MLB*	*28*	*7*	*6*	*0*	*19*	*19*	100^2	*106*	*11*	*3.4*	*6.8*	*76*	*52%*	*.300*	*1.44*	*4.14*	*4.54*	*1.0*	*95.3*	*56*	*51*	*57*
2019	*TOR*	*MLB*	*29*	*9*	*10*	*0*	*30*	*30*	*184*	*194*	*22*	*3.4*	*7.0*	*144*	*52%*	*.305*	*1.43*	*4.48*	*4.70*	*1.7*	*94.9*	*56*	*51*	*57*

Breakout: 15% Improve: 39% Collapse: 20% Attrition: 25% MLB: 77% *Comparables: Chris Bassitt, Lucas Harrell, Darrell Rasner*

Just like Jimmy Fallon did when Biagini attempted to high-five him on *The Tonight Show*, the 2017 season passed Joe by. Surprisingly, the former Rule 5 draft darling's four-pitch relief mix didn't fare well as a starter. In theory, a 6-foot-5, 240-pound pitcher with an arsenal that includes a 95-mph fastball and a 12-to-6 curveball should be an excellent rotation candidate. In practice, it forced that pitcher into quite a few extra jams and he wasn't able to adapt. With runners on, Biagini allowed opponents to hit .314 with a .534 slugging percentage (compared to .232/.350 with the bases empty). Because Toronto lacks starting pitching depth in the upper minors, Biagini may get another crack at the rotation, but he'll need a new plan if he's going to succeed.

Ryan Borucki LHP Born: 03/31/94 Age: 24 Bats: L Throws: L Height: 6'4" Weight: 175 Origin: Round 15, 2012 Draft (#475 overall)

YEAR	TEAM	LVL	AGE	W	L	SV	G	GS	IP	H	HR	BB/9	K/9	K	GB%	BABIP	WHIP	ERA	DRA	WARP	MPH	CMD	PWR	STM
2016	DUN	A+	22	1	4	0	6	6	20	40	10	5.4	4.5	10	48%	.395	2.60	14.40	13.11	-1.7				
2016	LNS	A	22	10	4	0	20	20	115^{2}	105	1	2.0	8.3	107	51%	.322	1.13	2.41	2.32	3.8				
2017	DUN	A+	23	6	5	0	19	18	98	95	5	2.5	10.0	109	52%	.342	1.24	3.58	1.89	3.9				
2017	NHP	AA	23	2	3	0	7	7	46^{1}	31	2	1.6	8.2	42	58%	.236	0.84	1.94	1.48	2.0				
2018	*TOR*	*MLB*	*24*	*4*	*4*	*0*	*21*	*11*	*65*	*67*	*11*	*4.0*	*8.5*	*62*	*44%*	*.302*	*1.50*	*4.77*	*5.13*	*0.2*				
2019	*TOR*	*MLB*	*25*	*7*	*10*	*0*	*26*	*26*	*154^{1}*	*161*	*27*	*3.9*	*8.5*	*145*	*44%*	*.305*	*1.48*	*5.19*	*5.45*	*0.3*				

Breakout: 14% Improve: 28% Collapse: 13% Attrition: 34% MLB: 46% *Comparables: Adam Morgan, Erick Fedde, Edwin Escobar*

It's remarkable what staying healthy can do for a guy. After struggling to remain on the field thanks to various arm issues, Borucki hasn't missed any time since the start of 2016. After a great turn at Low-A Lansing in 2016, Toronto added him to its 40-man roster out of worry that some team would snatch up the power lefty and stick him in the bullpen for a year. He rewarded the Jays with dominant runs at High-A and Double-A, then finished off his 2017 with six shutout innings in his lone Triple-A start. Armed with a low-to-mid-90s fastball, a great changeup and plus control, Borucki is very much knocking on the door.

Marco Estrada RHP Born: 07/05/83 Age: 34 Bats: R Throws: R Height: 6'0" Weight: 180 Origin: Round 6, 2005 Draft (#174 overall)

YEAR	TEAM	LVL	AGE	W	L	SV	G	GS	IP	H	HR	BB/9	K/9	K	GB%	BABIP	WHIP	ERA	DRA	WARP	MPH	CMD	PWR	STM
2015	TOR	MLB	31	13	8	0	34	28	181	134	24	2.7	6.5	131	34%	.216	1.04	3.13	4.03	2.2	91.4	53	26	71
2016	TOR	MLB	32	9	9	0	29	29	176	132	23	3.3	8.4	165	35%	.234	1.12	3.48	5.01	0.7	90.2	53	27	71
2017	TOR	MLB	33	10	9	0	33	33	186	186	31	3.4	8.5	176	31%	.295	1.38	4.98	5.47	0.2	91.0	60	26	81
2018	*TOR*	*MLB*	*34*	*10*	*11*	*0*	*28*	*28*	*168*	*167*	*30*	*3.5*	*7.2*	*134*	*36%*	*.279*	*1.36*	*4.92*	*5.36*	*0.1*	*89.8*	*55*	*26*	*74*
2019	*TOR*	*MLB*	*35*	*9*	*12*	*0*	*30*	*30*	*184^{2}*	*181*	*32*	*3.7*	*7.2*	*148*	*36%*	*.273*	*1.39*	*5.23*	*5.50*	*0.3*	*89.1*	*56*	*26*	*74*

Breakout: 11% Improve: 40% Collapse: 26% Attrition: 14% MLB: 89% *Comparables: Johan Santana, Roy Oswalt, Jason Hammel*

Conventional stat wisdom would have you believe Estrada finally ran out of luck. Estrada's 2015 BABIP of .220 and 2016 BABIP of .234 were the lowest and sixth-lowest for a qualified starter since 2000. The laws of regression say that Estrada should have returned to a .300 BABIP, which his .295 BABIP nearly did. However, Estrada's pop-up-inducing fastball/changeup combo hasn't gone away. Instead, poor command and an inconsistent release point are to blame for his struggles. Estrada's fastball only averages 90 mph, so his command is essential to his weak-contact game plan. It's unlikely that Estrada will ever get Cy Young votes again, but a moderate return to form on the back of a realigned delivery is possible.

Conner Greene RHP Born: 04/04/95 Age: 23 Bats: R Throws: R Height: 6'3" Weight: 185 Origin: Round 7, 2013 Draft (#205 overall)

YEAR	TEAM	LVL	AGE	W	L	SV	G	GS	IP	H	HR	BB/9	K/9	K	GB%	BABIP	WHIP	ERA	DRA	WARP	MPH	CMD	PWR	STM
2015	LNS	A	20	7	3	0	14	14	67^{1}	75	4	2.5	8.7	65	38%	.364	1.40	3.88	3.29	1.5				
2015	DUN	A+	20	2	3	0	7	7	40	36	1	1.8	7.9	35	55%	.297	1.10	2.25	2.39	1.3				
2015	NHP	AA	20	3	1	0	5	5	25	25	1	4.3	5.4	15	55%	.304	1.48	4.68	6.64	-0.5				
2016	DUN	A+	21	4	4	0	15	15	77^{2}	74	5	4.4	5.9	51	53%	.283	1.44	2.90	5.89	-0.4				
2016	NHP	AA	21	6	5	0	12	12	68^{2}	57	5	4.3	6.3	48	50%	.256	1.31	4.19	6.49	-1.1				
2017	NHP	AA	22	5	10	0	26	25	132^{2}	141	7	5.6	6.2	92	53%	.315	1.69	5.29	6.26	-1.7				
2018	*TOR*	*MLB*	*23*	*7*	*8*	*0*	*23*	*23*	*118^{2}*	*124*	*16*	*4.7*	*7.6*	*101*	*46%*	*.308*	*1.57*	*5.06*	*5.34*	*0.5*				
2019	*TOR*	*MLB*	*24*	*5*	*7*	*0*	*17*	*17*	*101^{2}*	*105*	*16*	*4.6*	*7.9*	*89*	*46%*	*.302*	*1.54*	*5.19*	*5.46*	*0.2*				

Breakout: 14% Improve: 18% Collapse: 10% Attrition: 24% MLB: 34% *Comparables: Shawn Morimando, Keury Mella, Andrew Cashner*

Greene loves bad pitches. Save for a short, successful stint at A-ball in 2014, command issues have been the name of the game for Greene. At Double-A New Hampshire the right-hander walked more than five batters per nine innings, the only qualified pitcher to do so in the upper minors. Between the wild off-speed pitches dipping and diving out of the zone, Greene once again flashed a plus-plus fastball that touched triple digits. He'll have to prove that he can stick in the rotation soon or Toronto may try him in a role at the back of the bullpen.

Taylor Guerrieri RHP Born: 12/01/92 Age: 25 Bats: R Throws: R Height: 6'2" Weight: 210 Origin: Round 1, 2011 Draft (#24 overall)

YEAR	TEAM	LVL	AGE	W	L	SV	G	GS	IP	H	HR	BB/9	K/9	K	GB%	BABIP	WHIP	ERA	DRA	WARP	MPH	CMD	PWR	STM
2015	PCH	A+	22	2	2	0	12	10	42	37	0	2.4	9.4	44	63%	.322	1.14	2.14	1.96	1.5				
2015	MNT	AA	22	3	1	0	8	8	36	28	2	2.0	7.0	28	67%	.241	1.00	1.50	3.11	0.9				
2016	MNT	AA	23	12	6	1	28	26	146	130	11	2.8	5.5	89	58%	.266	1.21	3.76	4.70	0.7				
2018	*TOR*	*MLB*	*25*	*3*	*2*	*0*	*8*	*8*	*40*	*37*	*4*	*3.3*	*8.4*	*37*	*54%*	*.293*	*1.28*	*3.78*	*4.13*	*0.6*				
2019	*TOR*	*MLB*	*26*	*9*	*10*	*0*	*31*	*31*	*193^{2}*	*175*	*29*	*3.4*	*8.8*	*190*	*54%*	*.283*	*1.28*	*4.63*	*4.86*	*1.4*				

Breakout: 15% Improve: 25% Collapse: 7% Attrition: 25% MLB: 39% *Comparables: Brian Duensing, Tyler Wagner, Myles Jaye*

Guerrieri is toward the high end of the spectrum of success enjoyed by the 11 players the Rays drafted in the first two rounds in 2011. That's damning with faint praise, and now that he's moved on it's not even a minor consolation for Rays fans. In over 360 pro innings, Guerrieri has a 2.51 career ERA. That's the good news. The bad news is he has recorded fewer than 30 outs above Double-A, and none in "The Show." He has dealt with suspension, multiple injuries and—despite the shiny ERA—simple underdevelopment. Now Guerrieri will try to prove all of those things merely delayed his ascent to the peak of his talent, rather than scuttling the mission altogether.

J.A. Happ LHP

Born: 10/19/82 Age: 35 Bats: L Throws: L Height: 6'5" Weight: 205 Origin: Round 3, 2004 Draft (#92 overall)

YEAR	TEAM	LVL	AGE	W	L	SV	G	GS	IP	H	HR	BB/9	K/9	K	GB%	BABIP	WHIP	ERA	DRA	WARP	MPH	CMD	PWR	STM
2015	SEA	MLB	32	4	6	0	21	20	108^2	121	13	2.7	6.8	82	44%	.319	1.41	4.64	3.97	1.4	94.7	58	50	69
2015	PIT	MLB	32	7	2	0	11	11	63^1	52	3	1.8	9.8	69	44%	.299	1.03	1.85	3.74	1.0	94.8	58	50	69
2016	TOR	MLB	33	20	4	0	32	32	195	168	22	2.8	7.5	163	44%	.268	1.17	3.18	4.57	1.8	94.3	52	56	77
2017	TOR	MLB	34	10	11	0	25	25	145^1	145	18	2.8	8.8	142	48%	.302	1.31	3.53	3.72	3.0	94.0	58	56	66
2018	*TOR*	*MLB*	*35*	*10*	*9*	*0*	*27*	*27*	*153*	*155*	*20*	*3.1*	*7.8*	*133*	*45%*	*.298*	*1.35*	*4.03*	*4.41*	*1.7*	*93.1*	*55*	*53*	*69*
2019	*TOR*	*MLB*	*36*	*10*	*11*	*0*	*30*	*30*	*192*	*189*	*25*	*3.1*	*7.9*	*168*	*45%*	*.295*	*1.32*	*4.31*	*4.51*	*2.2*	*92.4*	*54*	*54*	*69*

Breakout: 13% Improve: 35% Collapse: 30% Attrition: 10% MLB: 87% *Comparables: Jorge De La Rosa, Hisashi Iwakuma, Hiroki Kuroda*

Crash Davis may have had problems with Nuke LaLoosh, but he'd love catching J.A. Happ; the tall lefty never seems to shake off that fastball. He threw it around 70 percent of the time—only five regular starters tossed heaters more often—and it's not hard to see why. Happ can throw two pitches that appear the same to the hitter, but end up in very different locations, with nearly five inches of vertical break difference. That allows him to get plenty of groundballs despite working up in the zone when he wants strikeouts. Happ started using this dueling fastball pitch mix at the start of the 2016 season and perfected it in 2017. Despite making just 25 starts, he was able to easily post a career-best WARP, which should give plenty of hope for his performance in 2018.

Dominic Leone RHP

Born: 10/26/91 Age: 26 Bats: R Throws: R Height: 5'11" Weight: 210 Origin: Round 16, 2012 Draft (#491 overall)

YEAR	TEAM	LVL	AGE	W	L	SV	G	GS	IP	H	HR	BB/9	K/9	K	GB%	BABIP	WHIP	ERA	DRA	WARP	MPH	CMD	PWR	STM
2015	SEA	MLB	23	0	4	0	10	0	11^1	11	1	7.1	5.6	7	50%	.270	1.76	6.35	5.03	0.0	96.3	31	59	46
2015	ARI	MLB	23	0	1	0	3	0	3^2	8	1	0.0	4.9	2	35%	.438	2.18	14.73	7.93	-0.1	95.1	31	59	46
2015	MOB	AA	23	1	2	0	19	0	27^2	22	1	3.9	9.1	28	45%	.280	1.23	3.90	4.45	0.1				
2016	RNO	AAA	24	5	2	1	33	0	35	25	4	2.8	9.3	36	36%	.247	1.03	3.34	3.05	0.8				
2016	ARI	MLB	24	0	1	0	25	0	27	45	7	4.0	7.7	23	47%	.432	2.11	6.33	6.52	-0.5	95.2	37	63	47
2017	TOR	MLB	25	3	0	1	65	0	70^1	51	6	2.9	10.4	81	41%	.266	1.05	2.56	2.81	1.8	96.0	47	74	52
2018	*TOR*	*MLB*	*26*	*3*	*3*	*2*	*59*	*0*	*62*	*59*	*9*	*3.9*	*9.4*	*65*	*42%*	*.296*	*1.37*	*4.28*	*4.54*	*0.4*	*95.4*	*44*	*71*	*50*
2019	*TOR*	*MLB*	*27*	*2*	*1*	*1*	*47*	*0*	*50*	*45*	*8*	*4.3*	*9.5*	*53*	*42%*	*.285*	*1.38*	*4.67*	*4.90*	*0.2*	*95.1*	*45*	*72*	*50*

Breakout: 36% Improve: 48% Collapse: 22% Attrition: 16% MLB: 80% *Comparables: Manny Delcarmen, Jordan Walden, Clay Zavada*

Leone's rookie success for the Mariners in 2014 gave way to back-to-back years of struggles and demotions to the minors, but he rebounded with an impressive 2017 for the Blue Jays. Despite being optioned to the minors four times before Toronto fully bought into his being reliable again, he still topped 70 big-league innings and posted a career-high strikeout rate. Now we'll see if he can handle success a bit better this time around. His mid-90s velocity should play in a late-inning role for years to come if he can finally stabilize things.

Aaron Loup LHP

Born: 12/19/87 Age: 30 Bats: L Throws: L Height: 5'11" Weight: 210 Origin: Round 9, 2009 Draft (#280 overall)

YEAR	TEAM	LVL	AGE	W	L	SV	G	GS	IP	H	HR	BB/9	K/9	K	GB%	BABIP	WHIP	ERA	DRA	WARP	MPH	CMD	PWR	STM
2015	TOR	MLB	27	2	5	0	60	0	42^1	47	6	1.5	9.8	46	59%	.339	1.28	4.46	3.22	0.8	96.1	53	55	45
2016	BUF	AAA	28	3	0	1	20	0	19^2	21	0	1.4	11.9	26	54%	.404	1.22	1.83	1.29	0.8				
2016	TOR	MLB	28	0	0	0	21	0	14^1	15	2	2.5	9.4	15	40%	.342	1.33	5.02	3.80	0.2	94.8	48	45	38
2017	TOR	MLB	29	2	3	0	70	0	57^2	59	4	4.5	10.0	64	56%	.340	1.53	3.75	3.78	0.9	93.7	48	45	50
2018	*TOR*	*MLB*	*30*	*3*	*3*	*0*	*54*	*0*	*57*	*55*	*7*	*3.9*	*9.1*	*58*	*50%*	*.305*	*1.40*	*3.98*	*4.30*	*0.5*	*93.7*	*49*	*48*	*45*
2019	*TOR*	*MLB*	*31*	*2*	*1*	*0*	*46*	*0*	*48^1*	*46*	*5*	*4.1*	*9.1*	*49*	*50%*	*.308*	*1.41*	*4.29*	*4.49*	*0.4*	*92.9*	*48*	*45*	*44*

Breakout: 30% Improve: 48% Collapse: 25% Attrition: 15% MLB: 85% *Comparables: Brandon League, Sean Burnett, Nick Masset*

Will the real Loup please stand up—or at least stand sideways? The performance from the southpaw with the funky delivery has become increasingly hard to predict. In the past, he had thrown a lot of strikes and gotten a lot of groundballs, but his results were poor. In 2017, he stropped throwing strikes and started plunking lots of batters on both sides of the plate, but he managed to keep runs off the board and get more strikeouts while stranding 78 percent of inherited runners. It made no sense. Loup can still be a useful reliever as long as he's getting grounders, but he'll have to be more consistent if he's to be trusted in high-leverage situations.

Justin Maese RHP

Born: 10/24/96 Age: 21 Bats: R Throws: R Height: 6'3" Weight: 190 Origin: Round 3, 2015 Draft (#91 overall)

YEAR	TEAM	LVL	AGE	W	L	SV	G	GS	IP	H	HR	BB/9	K/9	K	GB%	BABIP	WHIP	ERA	DRA	WARP	MPH	CMD	PWR	STM
2015	BLJ	RK	18	5	0	0	8	4	35^2	32	0	1.5	4.8	19	68%	.271	1.07	1.01	2.94	1.1				
2016	VAN	A-	19	2	2	0	5	5	26^1	20	1	0.3	6.8	20	68%	.241	0.80	2.05	2.27	0.9				
2016	LNS	A	19	2	4	0	10	10	56^1	59	2	2.2	7.0	44	57%	.331	1.30	3.36	2.97	1.4				
2017	LNS	A	20	5	3	0	12	12	70^2	78	3	3.3	7.6	60	55%	.341	1.47	4.84	3.26	1.7				
2018	*TOR*	*MLB*	*21*	*4*	*5*	*0*	*12*	*12*	*66^1*	*77*	*11*	*4.1*	*7.2*	*53*	*48%*	*.319*	*1.61*	*5.36*	*5.66*	*0.0*				
2019	*TOR*	*MLB*	*22*	*7*	*11*	*0*	*26*	*26*	*157^2*	*184*	*32*	*3.6*	*7.0*	*123*	*48%*	*.314*	*1.56*	*5.63*	*5.94*	*-0.4*				

Breakout: 5% Improve: 5% Collapse: 1% Attrition: 3% MLB: 7% *Comparables: Jose Urena, Kyle Ryan, Raul Alcantara*

Coming off a strong 2016 season, Maese was being counted on to take another step forward in 2017 and lead the next wave of Blue Jays pitching prospects. Instead, he took a step backward. He had trouble staying healthy and when he was on the mound, he struggled. He still generates a ton of groundballs and he increased his strikeout total slightly, but the right-hander battled his control more than expected. Assuming he's healthy, the team will probably send him to Dunedin, but it's a big year for Maese to regain his position in the Blue Jays' prospect pecking order.

Roberto Osuna RHP Born: 02/07/95 Age: 23 Bats: R Throws: R Height: 6'2" Weight: 215 Origin: International Free Agent, 2011

YEAR	TEAM	LVL	AGE	W	L	SV	G	GS	IP	H	HR	BB/9	K/9	K	GB%	BABIP	WHIP	ERA	DRA	WARP	MPH	CMD	PWR	STM
2015	TOR	MLB	20	1	6	20	68	0	69^2	48	7	2.1	9.7	75	36%	.238	0.92	2.58	2.78	1.6	98.3	52	70	50
2016	TOR	MLB	21	4	3	36	72	0	74	55	9	1.7	10.0	82	35%	.256	0.93	2.68	3.64	1.1	98.3	61	63	51
2017	TOR	MLB	22	3	4	39	66	0	64	46	3	1.3	11.7	83	47%	.285	0.86	3.38	2.19	2.1	95.9	71	52	48
2018	*TOR*	*MLB*	*23*	*3*	*3*	*31*	*62*	*0*	*65*	*52*	*6*	*3.0*	*10.7*	*78*	*41%*	*.290*	*1.13*	*2.63*	*3.12*	*1.5*	*97.3*	*65*	*63*	*51*
2019	*TOR*	*MLB*	*24*	*4*	*2*	*26*	*68*	*0*	*71^2*	*55*	*8*	*2.7*	*11.6*	*93*	*41%*	*.287*	*1.07*	*3.17*	*3.30*	*1.5*	*96.9*	*68*	*60*	*52*

Breakout: 22% Improve: 53% Collapse: 24% Attrition: 11% MLB: 97% *Comparables: Paco Rodriguez, Huston Street, Chris Sale*

Osuna's 2017 season defied logic. His strikeout rate, walk rate, home-run rate and ground-ball rate were all career bests, leading to the third-lowest DRA among relievers with 50 or more innings. That should have led to super-elite results from the already lights-out closer. Instead, Osuna's ERA was easily the highest of his career and he blew 10. This makes his future tough to predict. Further clouding the issue is his workload. In the history of baseball, only Terry Forster has appeared in more games through age 22. And according to Mike Sonne's Fatigue Units, which factors in rest and pitch selection as well as pitches and appearances, the only pitchers since 2008 with a higher workload before turning 23 are Rick Porcello and Clayton Kershaw. Osuna also showed diminished velocity last season and a strange reliance on the cutter instead of his bread-and-butter four-seamer. When you factor in his injury history (including Tommy John surgery) and his public struggles with mental illness, forecasting Osuna's long-term future becomes nearly impossible.

Nate Pearson RHP Born: 08/20/96 Age: 21 Bats: R Throws: R Height: 6'6" Weight: 245 Origin: Round 1, 2017 Draft (#28 overall)

YEAR	TEAM	LVL	AGE	W	L	SV	G	GS	IP	H	HR	BB/9	K/9	K	GB%	BABIP	WHIP	ERA	DRA	WARP	MPH	CMD	PWR	STM
2017	VAN	A-	20	0	0	0	7	7	19	6	0	2.4	11.4	24	40%	.158	0.58	0.95	2.40	0.6				
2018	*TOR*	*MLB*	*21*	*2*	*3*	*0*	*9*	*9*	*33^1*	*33*	*8*	*4.5*	*9.8*	*36*	*38%*	*.288*	*1.51*	*5.78*	*6.10*	*-0.1*				
2019	*TOR*	*MLB*	*22*	*4*	*8*	*0*	*28*	*28*	*169^1*	*165*	*40*	*5.1*	*9.7*	*183*	*38%*	*.278*	*1.54*	*5.96*	*6.29*	*-0.7*				

Breakout: 8% Improve: 10% Collapse: 1% Attrition: 8% MLB: 11% *Comparables: Jordan Walden, Jhoulys Chacin, Miguel Almonte*

The second Pearson's name was called, Toronto newspaper editors began dreaming about him. Possessing a 100-mph fastball and giving up zero runs in his first five pro outings were already likely to make the first-rounder a media darling, but sharing the same name as Toronto's major airport guarantees it. Look for all sorts of puns related to balls taking flight, but if pitch clocks get put into place puns will soar to new heights. Writers will try to find ways to slow down the big righty just so we can hear about "Pearson causing delays yet again." Common customer complaints, baseball and puns? Perfect!

Carlos Ramirez RHP Born: 04/24/91 Age: 27 Bats: R Throws: R Height: 6'5" Weight: 205 Origin: International Free Agent, 2009

YEAR	TEAM	LVL	AGE	W	L	SV	G	GS	IP	H	HR	BB/9	K/9	K	GB%	BABIP	WHIP	ERA	DRA	WARP	MPH	CMD	PWR	STM
2015	LNS	A	24	2	1	8	28	0	32^1	38	2	3.9	8.4	30	46%	.371	1.61	4.73	4.52	0.1				
2016	DUN	A+	25	3	0	9	30	0	41	32	2	4.6	9.0	41	41%	.291	1.29	2.20	4.63	0.2				
2017	NHP	AA	26	2	0	3	18	0	23^2	10	0	2.7	11.0	29	40%	.189	0.72	0.00	2.75	0.6				
2017	BUF	AAA	26	1	0	0	7	0	14	6	0	1.9	10.3	16	36%	.194	0.64	0.00	3.01	0.3				
2017	TOR	MLB	26	0	0	0	12	0	16^2	6	3	1.6	7.6	14	28%	.081	0.54	2.70	4.93	0.0	93.6	33	37	33
2018	*TOR*	*MLB*	*27*	*3*	*3*	*1*	*54*	*0*	*57*	*57*	*11*	*4.7*	*9.0*	*58*	*38%*	*.294*	*1.50*	*5.40*	*5.47*	*-0.2*	*93.1*	*33*	*37*	*33*
2019	*TOR*	*MLB*	*28*	*2*	*1*	*0*	*36*	*0*	*38^2*	*39*	*8*	*4.9*	*8.8*	*38*	*38%*	*.293*	*1.54*	*5.66*	*5.95*	*-0.3*	*92.6*	*33*	*37*	*33*

Breakout: 6% Improve: 12% Collapse: 14% Attrition: 25% MLB: 34% *Comparables: Keith Butler, Craig Breslow, Jermaine Van Buren*

As a converted outfielder, Ramirez was probably wondering what all this pitching fuss was about. From April 30 to July 3, 2016, he allowed zero runs. Then, after being scored upon three times in a row ending on July 14, he didn't give up another run in professional baseball for 14 months! With that growth rate, he should be expected to put up a solid eight-year scoreless streak sometime soon. Streaks aside, what's more impressive is that Ramirez is doing all of this without the power stuff usually associated with converted position players. His fastball clocks in at a mediocre 91-93 mph and his slider has one-plane movement. Somehow, hitters just can't square it up, though.

Sean Reid-Foley RHP Born: 08/30/95 Age: 22 Bats: R Throws: R Height: 6'3" Weight: 220 Origin: Round 2, 2014 Draft (#49 overall)

YEAR	TEAM	LVL	AGE	W	L	SV	G	GS	IP	H	HR	BB/9	K/9	K	GB%	BABIP	WHIP	ERA	DRA	WARP	MPH	CMD	PWR	STM
2015	DUN	A+	19	1	5	0	8	8	32^2	25	1	6.6	9.6	35	45%	.279	1.50	5.23	7.91	-1.1				
2015	LNS	A	19	3	5	0	17	17	63^1	57	3	6.1	12.8	90	46%	.355	1.58	3.69	2.37	2.1				
2016	LNS	A	20	4	3	0	11	11	58	43	2	3.4	9.2	59	52%	.277	1.12	2.95	3.24	1.3				
2016	DUN	A+	20	6	2	0	10	10	57^1	35	2	2.5	11.1	71	49%	.254	0.89	2.67	1.04	2.9				
2017	NHP	AA	21	10	11	0	27	27	132^2	145	22	3.6	8.3	122	42%	.318	1.49	5.09	5.01	0.2				
2018	*TOR*	*MLB*	*22*	*6*	*8*	*0*	*24*	*24*	*109^2*	*112*	*21*	*4.5*	*9.4*	*115*	*42%*	*.309*	*1.52*	*5.25*	*5.53*	*0.2*				
2019	*TOR*	*MLB*	*23*	*5*	*8*	*0*	*20*	*20*	*119^1*	*121*	*25*	*4.8*	*9.6*	*127*	*42%*	*.303*	*1.55*	*5.59*	*5.88*	*-0.2*				

Breakout: 12% Improve: 16% Collapse: 6% Attrition: 16% MLB: 24% *Comparables: Michael Stutes, Tony Sipp, Carson Fulmer*

Before 2016, Reid-Foley had wild mechanics, drawing comparisons to early Jonathan Papelbon. In 2016, the Blue Jays armed him with a much simpler delivery and saw him ascend out of the low minors while striking out more than a batter an inning. However, despite the new motion Reid-Foley still ran into fastball command issues, which couldn't be as easily hidden by his mid-90s velocity and wipeout slider at Double-A. This resulted in his giving up nearly three times as many home runs in 2017 as over the rest of his career combined. Reid-Foley should have time to improve his fastball command as a starter, but if that doesn't pan out, his raw stuff would still play well out of the bullpen.

Chris Rowley RHP Born: 08/14/90 Age: 27 Bats: R Throws: R Height: 6'2" Weight: 195 Origin: Undrafted Free Agent, 2013

YEAR	TEAM	LVL	AGE	W	L	SV	G	GS	IP	H	HR	BB/9	K/9	K	GB%	BABIP	WHIP	ERA	DRA	WARP	MPH	CMD	PWR	STM
2016	DUN	A+	25	10	3	1	31	14	123^2	128	14	2.2	6.3	86	51%	.299	1.28	3.49	4.59	1.1				
2017	NHP	AA	26	3	2	1	17	5	52	33	4	1.6	8.5	49	46%	.218	0.81	1.73	2.31	1.7				
2017	BUF	AAA	26	3	5	0	12	8	64^1	60	2	2.4	6.4	46	47%	.291	1.20	2.66	4.06	1.1				
2017	TOR	MLB	26	1	2	0	6	3	18^2	24	4	4.8	5.3	11	41%	.312	1.82	6.75	4.67	0.2	91.2	29	31	58
2018	*TOR*	*MLB*	*27*	*3*	*4*	*0*	*22*	*10*	*63*	*70*	*12*	*3.2*	*6.8*	*48*	*44%*	*.296*	*1.47*	*5.31*	*5.68*	*-0.2*	*90.7*	*29*	*31*	*59*
2019	*TOR*	*MLB*	*28*	*6*	*8*	*0*	*47*	*19*	*141^2*	*157*	*29*	*3.9*	*6.4*	*101*	*44%*	*.291*	*1.54*	*5.94*	*6.27*	*-1.0*	*90.3*	*29*	*31*	*59*

Breakout: 17% Improve: 36% Collapse: 9% Attrition: 18% MLB: 47% *Comparables: Brent Suter, David Rollins, Frank Herrmann*

Rowley's story seems handcrafted to fit the grit and American exceptionalism narrative. He was a star on the mound in high school, but turned down more lucrative college offers to attend the United States Military Academy. He then went undrafted and set off on active military duty. After getting an active duty exception in 2016, Rowley signed with the Blue Jays and began his rapid ascent. He pitched his first upper-minors inning at age 25, and 239 innings later he was starting and relieving for Toronto in the majors. When he made his 2017 debut, he became the first and only United States Military Academy graduate to do so.

Aaron Sanchez RHP Born: 07/01/92 Age: 25 Bats: R Throws: R Height: 6'4" Weight: 215 Origin: Round 1, 2010 Draft (#34 overall)

YEAR	TEAM	LVL	AGE	W	L	SV	G	GS	IP	H	HR	BB/9	K/9	K	GB%	BABIP	WHIP	ERA	DRA	WARP	MPH	CMD	PWR	STM
2015	TOR	MLB	22	7	6	0	41	11	92^1	74	9	4.3	5.9	61	62%	.247	1.28	3.22	3.96	1.1	98.2	26	68	52
2016	TOR	MLB	23	15	2	0	30	30	192	161	15	3.0	7.5	161	55%	.267	1.17	3.00	3.68	3.7	97.5	45	58	74
2017	TOR	MLB	24	1	3	0	8	8	36	42	6	5.0	6.0	24	48%	.310	1.72	4.25	6.96	-0.6	96.9	45	66	23
2018	*TOR*	*MLB*	*25*	*9*	*8*	*0*	*23*	*23*	*138*	*135*	*17*	*3.9*	*6.9*	*106*	*52%*	*.287*	*1.39*	*4.41*	*4.83*	*0.9*	*97.3*	*42*	*63*	*48*
2019	*TOR*	*MLB*	*26*	*10*	*12*	*0*	*30*	*30*	*189*	*182*	*26*	*3.8*	*7.3*	*153*	*52%*	*.283*	*1.39*	*4.83*	*5.08*	*1.1*	*97.0*	*45*	*62*	*47*

Breakout: 26% Improve: 58% Collapse: 19% Attrition: 17% MLB: 94% *Comparables: Carlos Martinez, Carlos Zambrano, Jarred Cosart*

When people referred to Sanchez and his blistering fastball, they probably meant something a little less literal. Coming off a breakout 2016 that saw him lead the league in ERA and pull in a few Cy Young votes, expectations were through the roof with no more talk of innings limits. There was certainly no need to worry about that, though, as Sanchez only manged to throw 36 frames, hitting the disabled list four separate times with blister issues on his throwing hand. The Jays tried everything to get Sanchez back, including removing part of a fingernail, but nothing worked. He was hurt so much that the only impact he actually had on the 2017 Blue Jays was costing members of the training staff their jobs.

Marcus Stroman RHP Born: 05/01/91 Age: 27 Bats: R Throws: R Height: 5'8" Weight: 180 Origin: Round 1, 2012 Draft (#22 overall)

YEAR	TEAM	LVL	AGE	W	L	SV	G	GS	IP	H	HR	BB/9	K/9	K	GB%	BABIP	WHIP	ERA	DRA	WARP	MPH	CMD	PWR	STM
2015	TOR	MLB	24	4	0	0	4	4	27	20	2	2.0	6.0	18	64%	.237	0.96	1.67	4.20	0.3	94.4	55	39	45
2016	TOR	MLB	25	9	10	0	32	32	204	209	21	2.4	7.3	166	62%	.309	1.29	4.37	3.87	3.5	94.6	49	50	81
2017	TOR	MLB	26	13	9	0	33	33	201	201	21	2.8	7.3	164	63%	.310	1.31	3.09	3.60	4.4	94.9	52	54	80
2018	*TOR*	*MLB*	*27*	*11*	*9*	*0*	*27*	*27*	*170*	*170*	*17*	*3.2*	*7.5*	*141*	*58%*	*.303*	*1.37*	*3.77*	*4.13*	*2.5*	*94.3*	*51*	*52*	*72*
2019	*TOR*	*MLB*	*28*	*12*	*10*	*0*	*30*	*30*	*192^2*	*191*	*19*	*3.0*	*8.1*	*174*	*58%*	*.31*	*1.33*	*3.87*	*4.04*	*3.4*	*94.0*	*51*	*53*	*78*

Breakout: 20% Improve: 51% Collapse: 19% Attrition: 7% MLB: 93% *Comparables: Sonny Gray, Jose Quintana, David Price*

While the six-pitch starter has been a social media favorite for years, Stroman has now matched his talent and social clout to his on-field-performance. Last season was his first ace-like campaign, as his sub-3.25 ERA, 200-plus-inning year was just the second by a Blue Jays pitcher since the late Roy Halladay left in 2009. Alas, the other such season belongs to Ricky Romero. While the Blue Jays' other control-focused, ground-ball pitcher has a big gap between ERA and peripherals, Stroman has produced a career ERA that nearly matches his FIP and DRA. Given his repertoire, it's tough to see where Stroman could improve, but the technical tinkerer always finds a way.

Ryan Tepera RHP Born: 11/03/87 Age: 30 Bats: R Throws: R Height: 6'2" Weight: 195 Origin: Round 19, 2009 Draft (#580 overall)

YEAR	TEAM	LVL	AGE	W	L	SV	G	GS	IP	H	HR	BB/9	K/9	K	GB%	BABIP	WHIP	ERA	DRA	WARP	MPH	CMD	PWR	STM
2015	BUF	AAA	27	3	1	3	21	0	34	16	1	3.4	9.8	37	56%	.190	0.85	1.06	3.21	0.7				
2015	TOR	MLB	27	0	2	1	32	0	33	23	8	1.6	6.0	22	47%	.169	0.88	3.27	3.31	0.5	97.4	51	49	44
2016	BUF	AAA	28	1	2	18	37	0	45^1	33	3	3.2	9.5	48	47%	.265	1.08	2.58	4.17	0.4				
2016	TOR	MLB	28	0	1	0	20	0	18^1	17	1	3.9	8.8	18	59%	.291	1.36	2.95	3.69	0.3	97.3	43	56	45
2017	TOR	MLB	29	7	1	2	73	0	77^2	57	7	3.6	9.4	81	43%	.260	1.13	3.59	3.68	1.3	96.1	48	61	54
2018	*TOR*	*MLB*	*30*	*3*	*3*	*1*	*59*	*0*	*62*	*56*	*8*	*3.9*	*9.0*	*63*	*46%*	*.287*	*1.33*	*4.34*	*4.59*	*0.4*	*95.7*	*48*	*58*	*48*
2019	*TOR*	*MLB*	*31*	*2*	*1*	*1*	*49*	*0*	*52^1*	*47*	*7*	*3.9*	*9.1*	*53*	*46%*	*.283*	*1.32*	*4.56*	*4.78*	*0.3*	*95.1*	*47*	*59*	*49*

Breakout: 23% Improve: 41% Collapse: 18% Attrition: 22% MLB: 73% *Comparables: Michael Bowden, Cory Gearrin, Blaine Hardy*

We should all be singing Auld Lang Syne to Tepera, because it was a very happy new year for the righty in 2017. In one season, he went from from being the guy who shuffles up and down between Buffalo and Toronto to throwing 77 2/3 innings and finishing with the ninth-most Fatigue Units of any reliever in baseball. That's one heck of a switch, but he earned the increased trust with strong numbers all year. A big part of his improvement was his cutter dropping more than ever, giving it a huge seven inches of vertical break distance off his fastball, which helped lead to a career-best 25.4 percent strikeout rate.

Cesar Valdez RHP Born: 03/17/85 Age: 33 Bats: R Throws: R Height: 6'2" Weight: 200 Origin: International Free Agent, 2005

YEAR	TEAM	LVL	AGE	W	L	SV	G	GS	IP	H	HR	BB/9	K/9	K	GB%	BABIP	WHIP	ERA	DRA	WARP	MPH	CMD	PWR	STM
2016	FRE	AAA	31	12	1	0	30	18	138^{1}	143	8	0.8	7.4	114	55%	.325	1.13	3.12	2.66	4.2				
2017	NAS	AAA	32	1	0	0	2	2	10	8	1	0.0	10.8	12	42%	.280	0.80	2.70	3.59	0.2				
2017	OAK	MLB	32	0	0	0	4	1	9^{1}	14	4	3.9	4.8	5	46%	.323	1.93	9.64	5.91	-0.1	89.7	43	20	55
2017	BUF	AAA	32	3	3	0	11	10	61^{1}	56	3	1.8	6.5	44	58%	.282	1.11	3.23	1.99	2.5				
2017	TOR	MLB	32	1	1	0	7	3	21^{1}	27	3	3.0	6.8	16	43%	.348	1.59	6.75	5.00	0.1	89.9	43	20	55
2018	*TOR*	*MLB*	*33*	*5*	*5*	*0*	*26*	*13*	*89^{2}*	*100*	*12*	*2.7*	*6.6*	*66*	*50%*	*.312*	*1.41*	*4.68*	*4.93*	*0.7*	*88.9*	*42*	*20*	*54*
2019	*TOR*	*MLB*	*34*	*4*	*4*	*0*	*18*	*11*	*79^{1}*	*88*	*10*	*2.4*	*6.3*	*56*	*50%*	*.308*	*1.38*	*4.49*	*4.72*	*0.8*	*88.0*	*42*	*20*	*54*

Breakout: 7% Improve: 12% Collapse: 6% Attrition: 7% MLB: 21% *Comparables: Justin Germano, Andy Van Hekken, Kyle Davies*

Valdez claimed an interesting title in 2017, becoming the league's foremost changeup thrower at 49.7 percent, edging out noted changeuppers like Chris Devenski, Tyler Clippard and Marco Estrada. A scout once called Valdez's preferred pitch "a changeup that acts like a splitter," which makes for an apt comparison to the pitch that Devenski has used to dominate since 2016. Both pitchers can throw late, dipping changeups that look markedly similar to their fastballs, each resulting in a much better-than-average pitch tunnel differential. The major separator with Devenski's changeup, however, is that he's able to get an 11-mph difference between it and his four-seam fastball, while the soft-tossing Valdez only generates a 7-mph difference.

LINEOUTS

Hitters

HITTER	POS	TEAM	LVL	AGE	PA	R	2B	3B	HR	RBI	BB	K	SB	CS	AVG/OBP/SLG	TAv	VORP	BABIP	BRR	FRAA	WARP
Darrell Ceciliani	OF	TOR	MLB	27	5	2	1	0	1	3	0	0	0	0	.400/.400/1.200	.567	1.4	.250	-0.3	LF(1): 0.0, CF(1): 0.0	0.1
	OF	BUF	AAA	27	81	5	1	0	0	3	3	21	1	0	.156/.198/.169	.144	-7.9	.214	0.7	CF(9): 0.3, LF(8): 1.5	-0.6
Chris Coghlan	LF	BUF	AAA	32	28	2	2	0	0	4	5	3	0	2	.217/.357/.304	.270	0.4	.250	-0.7	LF(4): 0.1, 2B(2): 0.3	0.1
	LF	TOR	MLB	32	88	7	2	0	1	5	9	22	0	0	.200/.299/.267	.210	-1.6	.264	0.4	3B(18): 0.6, LF(8): -0.5	-0.1
Chris Colabello	1B	COH	AAA	33	300	25	11	0	6	37	34	76	3	1	.225/.323/.336	.235	-8.2	.294	-3.9	1B(28): -2.1, LF(13): -1.6	-1.1
	1B	CSP	AAA	33	183	28	10	1	6	25	24	37	0	0	.301/.393/.494	.292	7.1	.357	-1.6	1B(43): -0.5, LF(1): 0.0	0.6
Hagen Danner	C	BLJ	Rk	18	136	10	5	0	2	20	5	36	3	1	.160/.207/.248	.203	-3.9	.202	-0.7	C(30): -0.8	-0.4
Rafael Lopez	C	NHP	AA	29	50	7	1	1	4	11	8	15	0	0	.262/.380/.619	.337	4.4	.304	-1.6	C(12): -1.2	0.3
	C	BUF	AAA	29	223	31	13	1	12	34	21	46	0	0	.293/.368/.551	.307	19.3	.326	-2.2	C(49): -8.5, 3B(1): 0.3	1.1
	C	TOR	MLB	29	63	9	1	0	4	12	7	21	0	0	.222/.306/.463	.260	3.6	.267	0.7	C(24): 4.0, 3B(1): 0.0	0.8
Luke Maile	C	BUF	AAA	26	58	5	0	0	0	1	4	12	0	0	.167/.224/.167	.141	-4.9	.214	0.4	C(13): 2.9	-0.2
	C	TOR	MLB	26	136	10	5	0	2	7	3	35	1	0	.146/.176/.231	.165	-7.0	.181	0.2	C(46): 2.7	-0.4
Reese McGuire	C	BLJ	Rk	22	26	4	2	0	0	7	3	1	0	1	.409/.462/.500	.336	3.1	.409	-0.3	C(4): 0.0	0.3
	C	NHP	AA	22	136	19	5	1	6	20	16	19	2	1	.278/.366/.496	.312	11.3	.283	-1.9	C(32): 4.8	1.7
Gift Ngoepe	INF	PIT	MLB	27	63	10	2	1	0	6	8	26	0	0	.222/.323/.296	.256	0.9	.429	-0.7	2B(20): -0.6, SS(6): 0.0	0.0
	INF	IND	AAA	27	299	33	15	5	6	27	28	91	2	4	.220/.299/.383	.243	6.6	.306	0.9	SS(42): 0.2, 3B(21): 0.3	0.7
Harold Ramirez	OF	NHP	AA	22	490	46	19	2	6	53	32	65	5	3	.266/.320/.358	.247	-0.8	.296	-2.3	RF(69): 0.4, LF(23): -3.4	-0.4
Dwight Smith	OF	TOR	MLB	24	29	2	2	0	0	1	1	10	1	0	.370/.414/.444	.302	2.8	.588	0.9	LF(9): -1.8, RF(1): 0.0	0.1
	OF	BUF	AAA	24	449	56	21	1	8	46	47	71	8	8	.273/.350/.392	.269	14.2	.313	0.6	RF(67): -4.0, LF(32): -0.6	0.9
Rowdy Tellez	1B	BUF	AAA	22	501	45	29	1	6	56	47	94	6	1	.222/.295/.333	.229	-12.6	.264	-0.6	1B(115): 1.8	-1.0
Logan Warmoth	SS	VAN	A-	21	174	18	11	2	1	20	7	33	5	2	.306/.356/.419	.293	12.3	.378	-0.5	SS(35): 0.7	1.3

If your season is going to end with an injury, do it the **Darrell Ceciliani** way. The lefty dislocated his shoulder on a swing, but the ball went out of the yard. The shoulder died a hero. ⚾ If they ever remake *Major League II*, **Chris Coghlan** has his demo reel ready for the Willie Mays Hayes role. Beaten easily by the ball, Coghlan took to the air and soared over Yadier "Jack Parkman" Molina, landing on the plate in a perfect, run-scoring somersault. Just remember that and not the batting line. ⚾ Although **Chris Colabello** may have sullied his lovable underdog story with an 80-game PED suspension, he remains the only Assumption College (MA) alumnus to ever play in the majors. ⚾ Known as the Ice Cream Man by his peers (think Häagen-Dazs), **Hagen Danner** didn't impress offensively in his first stint of pro ball. As a catcher with a power bat and the ability to throw in the mid-90s off the mound, he'll be a fun one to watch in the Blue Jays' system. ⚾ A big-money third base prospect from the Dominican Republic whom scouts called "the best hitter in his international signing class." Sound familiar? **Miguel Hiraldo** doesn't have Vladimir Guerrero Jr.'s name value or otherworldly raw power, but does have a ton of talent. ⚾ Panamanian shortstop **Leonardo Jimenez** received the second-highest Blue Jays bonus in the 2017 J2 period, at $850,000. He has good contact ability and gap power, but is a long shot to stick at short. ⚾ Despite only getting into 22 games, **Rafael Lopez** was arguably one of Toronto's best position players in 2017, being the only one to post both above-average advanced hitting and fielding numbers. ⚾ **Luke Maile**, a gifted framer behind the plate, also gives the opposition gifts at the plate: Last year he posted the worst single-season OPS in Blue Jays history. ⚾ The oft-injured and oft-not-making-contact **Reese McGuire** enjoyed the best offensive season of his career in 2017 despite missing a majority of it due to yet another knee injury. ⚾ The first South African player in MLB history, **Gift Ngoepe** is a very fringy, glove-first infielder, but blazed a new and fascinating trail that could make a much bigger long-term impact than his numbers suggest. ⚾ **Harold Ramirez** was always the guy who needed to hit for high batting averages to overcome his lack of standout tools. In 2017, he stopped hitting for average. That's bad. ⚾ Last season was great for Jays prospects whose dads played in the major leagues, but **Dwight Smith Jr.** must have missed the memo. The former first-round pick was fine but unremarkable in his efforts to establish himself as a candidate for Toronto's 2018 outfield. ⚾ **Rowdy Tellez** went from being one of the 10 best Double-A hitters by OPS in 2016 to one of the 10 worst Triple-A hitters by OPS in 2017. The raw power is still there, but if it doesn't come back in games soon the only players who'll be getting rowdy will be opposing pitchers. ⚾ The top college shortstop in the 2017 draft, **Logan Warmoth** adjusted well in his first stint of pro ball, showing off impeccable bat-to-ball skills while carrying the Vancouver Canadians to their first Northwest League title since 2013. He could finish 2018 at High-A Dunedin.

Pitchers

PITCHER	TEAM	LVL	AGE	W	L	SV	G	GS	IP	H	HR	BB/9	K/9	K	GB%	BABIP	WHIP	ERA	DRA	WARP	MPH	CMD	PWR	STM
Mike Bolsinger	TOR	MLB	29	0	3	0	11	5	41^1	48	9	5.9	8.5	39	51%	.331	1.81	6.31	6.27	-0.4	91.3	50	26	47
	BUF	AAA	29	4	2	1	16	5	47^2	42	2	1.5	7.9	42	51%	.312	1.05	1.70	2.31	1.7				
Matthew Dermody	BUF	AAA	26	5	1	1	33	1	43	48	6	2.3	8.2	39	53%	.326	1.37	3.56	4.15	0.5				
	TOR	MLB	26	2	0	0	23	0	22^1	23	6	2.0	6.0	15	34%	.254	1.25	4.43	6.38	-0.3	93.4	55	43	47
Lucas Harrell	TOR	MLB	32	0	0	0	4	0	6^1	10	1	5.7	8.5	6	44%	.409	2.21	7.11	4.44	0.1	93.2			40
	BUF	AAA	32	0	1	0	7	6	30^1	27	1	3.9	7.1	24	48%	.283	1.32	2.08	4.29	0.5				
Jonathan Harris	NHP	AA	23	7	11	0	26	26	143	169	20	3.0	7.1	113	46%	.327	1.51	5.41	4.61	0.9				
J.P. Howell	TOR	MLB	34	1	1	0	16	0	11	13	2	5.7	4.9	6	59%	.297	1.82	7.36	4.06	0.1	86.8			25
Mat Latos	TOR	MLB	29	0	1	0	3	3	15	19	5	4.8	6.0	10	45%	.304	1.80	6.60	5.29	0.0	93.1	60	47	45
	BUF	AAA	29	1	1	0	6	5	26	27	3	4.5	8.3	24	42%	.324	1.54	3.81	6.72	-0.3				
Tim Mayza	NHP	AA	25	1	1	4	29	0	33^1	32	5	4.1	11.3	42	42%	.325	1.41	4.59	2.70	0.8				
	BUF	AAA	25	1	1	0	11	0	19^1	16	0	3.3	7.4	16	33%	.276	1.19	0.93	4.70	0.1				
	TOR	MLB	25	1	0	0	19	0	17	24	3	2.1	14.3	27	42%	.467	1.65	6.88	3.97	0.2	95.8	51	49	51
Thomas Pannone	LYN	A+	23	2	0	0	5	5	27^2	10	0	2.3	12.7	39	48%	.212	0.61	0.00	2.03	1.0				
	AKR	AA	23	6	1	0	14	14	82^1	67	5	2.3	8.9	81	37%	.281	1.07	2.62	2.77	2.4				
	NHP	AA	23	1	2	0	6	6	34^2	31	9	2.1	7.5	29	38%	.232	1.12	3.63	2.80	1.0				
Luis Santos	BUF	AAA	26	3	12	0	24	21	108^1	91	13	3.7	8.1	98	37%	.266	1.25	4.07	3.74	2.3				
	TOR	MLB	26	0	1	1	10	0	16^2	15	4	2.2	8.6	16	33%	.250	1.14	2.70	5.58	-0.1	95.1	34	45	61
T.J. Zeuch	DUN	A+	21	3	4	0	12	11	58^2	63	3	2.6	7.1	46	64%	.312	1.36	3.38	2.51	1.9				

The Blue Jays hoped to catch some of those 2015 **Mike Bolsinger** magic pitches in a bottle. Apparently there was a crack in the glass, because there were only home-run balls left. ⚾ For being left-handed, **Matt Dermody** got his chances and was merely fine. For being left-handed, he will keep getting his chances even if he's not fine. ⚾ Despite getting into only four games last season, **Lucas Harrell** managed to issue one of 10 walk-off walks that occurred across MLB. Congratulations! ⚾ **Jon Harris**, the Blue Jays' first-rounder in 2015, faces the prospect of repeating Double-A at age 24. His one saving grace is the increased command that he showed after switching to his college delivery at the end of 2017. ⚾ Wrong place, wrong time. Despite having some upside and signing for a sizeable major-league contract, veteran left-hander **J.P. Howell** found himself designated for assignment by the struggling Blue Jays in August. ⚾ Sadly, when **Mat Latos** strolls to town on a minor-league deal, the possibility of seeing his cat of a similar name (Cat Latos) is the most exciting part. ⚾ The good: **Tim Mayza** struck out 27 batters in 17 innings. The bad: He gave up 15 runs. He put himself on the map, though, so look for more good than bad from the power lefty. ⚾ **Thomas Pannone** has a decent shot to surpass the competition between Mike Dunn and Chasen Shreve for the second-best player ever drafted out of the College of Southern Nevada, and no shot to surpass Bryce Harper as the best. ⚾ Diminutive bonus baby **Eric Pardinho** is no stranger to high-stress situations, making a relief appearance for Brazil's WBC team as a 15-year-old. That kind of experience playing against men twice his age speaks to the fastball command and poise that he already shows as a teenager. ⚾ On a Reddit thread linking to **Luis Santos**' call-up, user cyclingkingsley asked, "Who's Luis Santos Only seven people called "Bo" have ever played in the major leagues, making the title of "Best Bo to Play for the Blue Jays" a seemingly easy one to keep. However, with a lackluster season from **Bo Schultz** and the rise of super prospect Bo Bichette, Schultz may have to cede his title by September 2018. ⚾ A barrage of injuries plagued **T.J. Zeuch** in 2017 and the former first-round pick failed to generate many strikeouts despite a big fastball and bigger 6-foot-7 frame. He may need to trim his four-pitch mix, likely at Double-A to begin 2018.

WASHINGTON NATIONALS

Essay by Eric Nusbaum

Player comments by Emma Baccellieri and BP staff

Once upon a time, there was a baseball club called the Washington Nationals. The Nationals were fantastic, one of the great teams of their time. The roster was brilliantly constructed, consisting largely of homegrown talent and bolstered by a few key imports. The management was clever and creative—and not above testing the bounds of the system. On the field, the Nationals were led by one of the hardest throwing pitchers in the sport, and one of its greatest young hitters.

Despite the many challenges that present themselves to elite baseball clubs over the course of game after game, and the grueling travel that comes between those games, the Nationals were dominant. They had high expectations for themselves, and those who watched them agreed that those expectations were not unreasonable.

Then they reached Chicago.

The 1867 Washington Nationals, generally as overlooked and forgotten as any 19th-century team, are one of the most important clubs in the history of early baseball. They played a version of the sport that only looks familiar if you squint: pitchers threw underhand, umpires were largely ceremonial, good manners were often prized over good results. But they also have an eerie amount in common with the contemporary club that inherited their name, and they make a surprisingly effective prism through which to examine the Nats of today Over the last few years, the Nationals have developed the feeling of an obligation—like a mandatory office party that you talk yourself into believing will be fun. This year it will be different, you say. They're raffling off a drone. This year it will be different, you say. Mike Rizzo traded for a bunch of good bullpen arms.

The 2017 Nationals felt especially Nationals, if such a thing is possible. They strolled to a division title despite losing Adam Eaton for the year, and Bryce Harper and Trea Turner for long stretches. Max Scherzer was Max Scherzer-like. Stephen Strasburg had the best (and healthiest) season of his career. Ryan Zimmerman found his inner Daniel Murphy. Anthony Rendon blossomed. Harper mashed. Turner played like a young Lou Brock. Even Michael A. Taylor was awesome, rewarding Dusty Baker's unshakeable faith with a tremendous all-around season.

The lineup was deep. The starting rotation was nasty. The bullpen was actually fine. If it sounds like I'm rattling off reasons the Nats are a great team, that's because I am. They were a great team last year.

Then they reached Chicago.

The history of the Washington Nationals dates back to the end of the antebellum era. The National Base Ball Club of Washington DC was founded in 1859 by a group of young government bureaucrats—a fact that would become crucial as the club rose to acclaim. This was a time when baseball was still an amateur sport, officially speaking, and largely played in major eastern cities. It was a high class, urban endeavor. The Nationals' original constitution

NATIONALS PROSPECTUS

2017 W-L: 97-65, 1st in NL East

Pythag	.592	6th	B-Age	29.0	*25th*
RS/G	5.06	5th	P-Age	29.9	*28th*
RA/G	4.15	6th	Salary	$164.3M	*9th*
TAv	.273	4th	M$/MW	$3.1M	*20th*
TAv-P	.248	5th	DL Days	1197	*21st*
FIP	4.00	7th	$ on DL	17%	*17th*
DER	.713	7th			

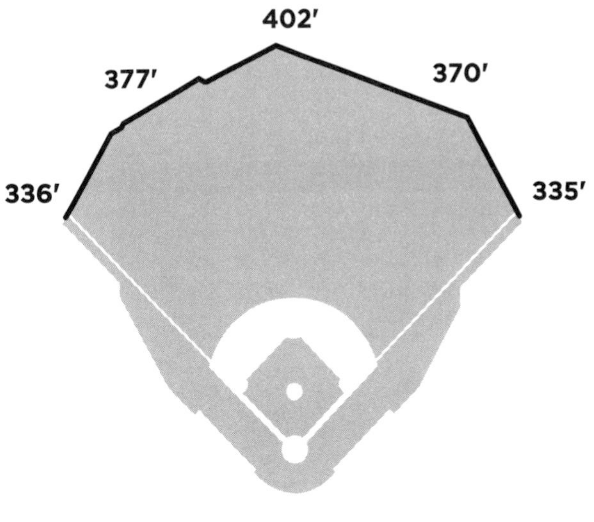

Outfield wall profile: **8'** to **14'**

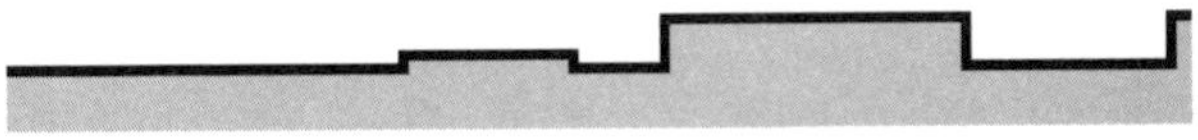

Three-Year Park Factors

Runs	Runs/RH	Runs/LH	HR/RH	HR/LH
101	103	97	107	95

Top Hitter WARP	6.2 Anthony Rendon
Top Pitcher WARP	7.4 Max Scherzer
Top Prospect	Victor Robles

2017 Hit List Ranking

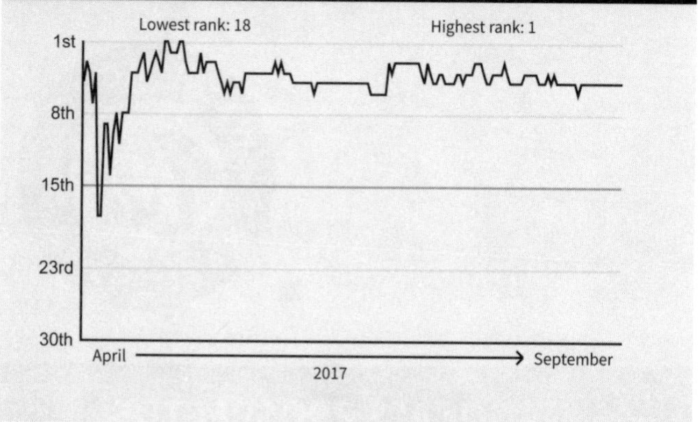

Committed Payroll (in millions)

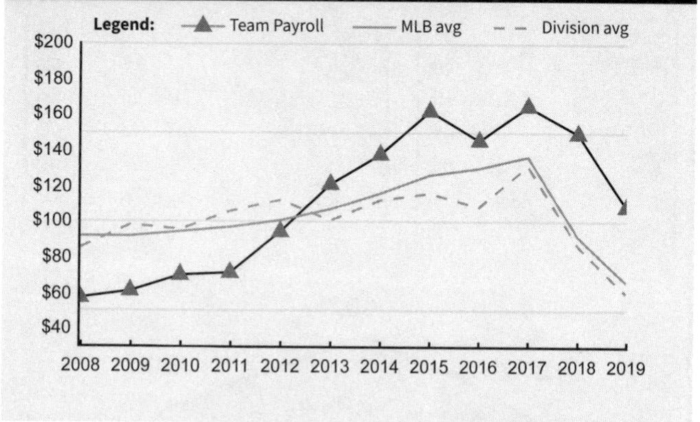

Farm System Ranking

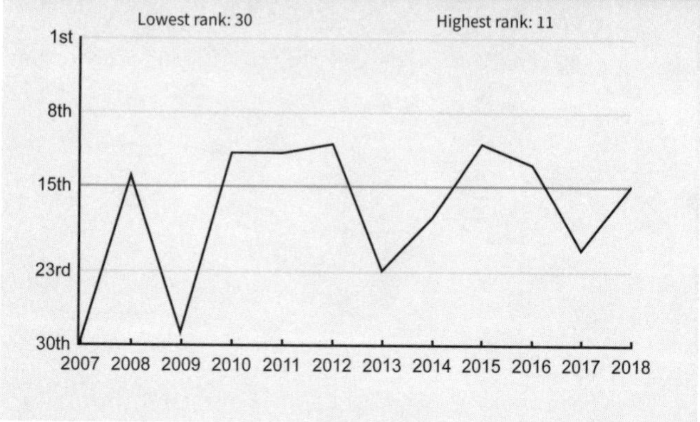

Personnel

General Manager
Mike Rizzo

Assistant General Manager
Doug Harris

Assistant General Manager
Bob Miller

Manager
Dave Martinez

included a fine for "profane or improper language."

After the Civil War, baseball began to grow in the mainstream, and spread into the west. The game's boosters (Walt Whitman famously among them) spoke of it as a potential balm for the American body and the American soul—neither of which were in pristine condition. The post-war Nationals were run by Arthur Pue Gorman, a young bureaucrat who would go on to become a US senator, and Frank Jones, who had been a Union colonel during the war and was now ensconced in the Treasury Department.

Gorman and Jones, both former ballplayers themselves, saw opportunity in baseball's rising popularity and the newly reconstructed union: They envisioned a grand barnstorming tour. Over the years, baseball clubs had traipsed up and down the eastern seaboard to meet new competition. But the Washington Nationals would head west: to Ohio, Kentucky, Missouri and finally Illinois.

Before they departed, Gorman and Jones took advantage of their influence in government to load up on talent. The notion of professionalism in baseball was still taboo in 1867—but that only meant the Nationals had to keep up appearances. Gorman and Jones recruited some of the best ballplayers in New York and offered them what were essentially patronage jobs in exchange for joining the club. This is how they lured star shortstop George Wright from the Union Club of Morissania in the Bronx.

"Although the players were nominal amateurs, there can be no doubt of their uniformly professional status," wrote historian John Thorn. "The club president listed Wright's place of employment as 238 Pennsylvania Avenue, at that time an open field." Whatever you think of their ethics, the Nationals were emblematic of the changing landscape of baseball. Two years later, Wright would be the highest paid player on the 1869 Cincinnati Red Stockings—baseball's first openly professional club.

The Nationals of Bryce Harper didn't exactly come together like the Nationals of George Wright, but they too are emblematic of the changing landscape of baseball. They are a big-market, big-money franchise, and a penny-pinching club at the same time. They've tanked with the worst and spent with the best. Despite the departure of Jayson Werth, they remain very much the Ballclub That Scott Boras Built. Their top three starters, Scherzer, Strasburg and Gio Gonzalez, are all Boras clients. Their two best offensive players, Harper and Rendon, are Boras clients. Even their fourth outfielder, Brian Goodwin, is a Boras client.

The relationship between Boras and Nats owner Ted Lerner is fascinating because it begins in earnest not with free agency (the usual provenance of super agents), but the amateur draft. In 2009, the Nationals selected Strasburg first overall. The next year, it was Harper. This was before the new draft slotting system leveled out compensation for incoming draftees. Harper and Strasburg cost the Nats $25 million in guaranteed money. For as cheap as the Lerner family is thought to be (remember when they tried to hire Bud Black?), they were not cheap when it came to signing the players who would become cornerstones of their franchise. The next year, Washington took Rendon sixth overall. Boras negotiated him a $7.2 million guarantee.

It would be easy to argue that the Nationals' continued infatuation with Boras has been a hindrance. After all, he talked them into spending $126 million on seven years of Werth (and $28 million on two years of Rafael Soriano). But it has also been a boon. Just as it did for Gorman and Jones, embracing the reality of professionalism in baseball, and then finding creative ways to leverage that reality, has allowed the Nationals to improve. They managed to sign Scherzer for seven years by offering another seven of deferred payments. Creative? Yes. Imprudent? Almost certainly. But Scherzer just won his second straight Cy Young Award in Washington.

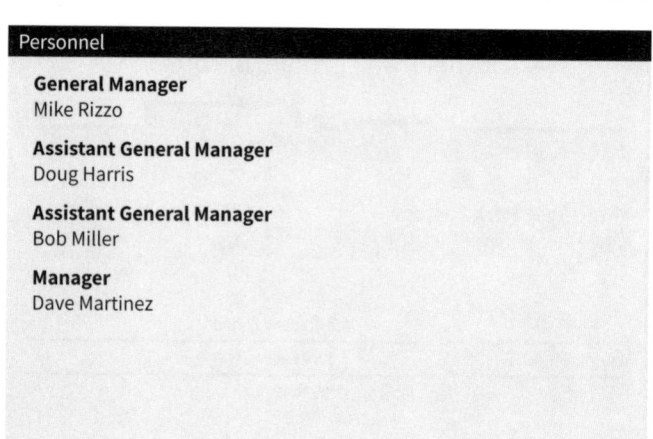

In 1867, the Nationals' version of Scherzer was a fellow named Will Williams. (Thankfully, they did not have to worry about a bullpen—he was their only pitcher.) A law student at Georgetown, Williams was considered to be one of the hardest throwing pitchers in the country. But Williams and his ten teammates (the starting nine, plus two reserves) were just a small part of the barnstorming delegation assembled by Gorman and Jones. The club would send 40 people west—among them the sportswriter and baseball evangelist Harry Chadwick, who happily took a gig with the Nationals as perhaps baseball's first official PR man.

The Nationals had every reason to suspect they would run the table on their westward tour. After all, baseball in the cities they were visiting was still primitive compared to the refined east coast game. The scores reflected talent disparity: 90-10, 53-10, 88-12 and on it went. But the baseball actually being played mattered less than the diplomatic sensibility behind it. It was the early days of reconstruction. The Nationals would be visiting both Union and Confederate cities. They were essentially baseball missionaries: part of a concerted, and even occasionally organized, effort to turn baseball into the national pastime it would one day become.

At the conclusion of their trip, they were scheduled for three games in Chicago. First they would take on the Rockford Forest Citys, then the local champion Chicago Excelsiors, and finally the Chicago Atlantics. Only the Excelsiors were thought to be a worthy competitor. But on that first rainy afternoon, the Nationals were embarrassed by Rockford and their young starting pitcher Albert Spalding. The final score was 29-23. "The invincibles were defeated," wrote the *Chicago Tribune*.

In his memoir, Spalding recalled that in the seventh inning, Jones took to the field to berate his star player Wright: "Do you know, George, that this is the seventh innings and we are six runs behind? You must discard your heavy bat and take a lighter one; for to lose this game would be to make our whole trip a failure."

(In light of that kind of management, Dusty Baker's waffling in the press over a Game Four starter seems so bad.)

Afterwards, the local newspapers speculated that the Nationals had thrown the game intentionally. A series of angry letters were published in the *Chicago Tribune*. Jones was especially livid: "As President of the National Club of Washington, D. C., I feel called upon to reply to the foul aspersions upon the character of our club," he began.

But despite the pandemonium, and despite what Jones said to Wright on the field in the Rockford game, the Nationals did not ultimately see the trip as a failure. They won their last two games in Chicago and boarded their train home triumphant: They had proven their superiority as a baseball club and proven themselves fine ambassadors for the sport. They were glorified in the press. When they finally reached Washington, a massive gala awaited, and the Nationals were held up as heroes.

This is the lesson that the modern Nationals still need to learn—and that those of us who have been watching them need to remember: It's okay to celebrate greatness, even when perfection is what you are ultimately after. And for the last six years, the Nationals have been great. Since 2012, the first year Harper and Strasburg both played in the majors, they have averaged 92.5 wins per season. And yet they just hired their fourth manager in that stretch. We've been collectively brainwashed by Washington's own panicky front office and ownership to think of the team as a constant disappointment. The process of writing this essay has been one of gradually remembering that the Nationals are in fact awesome.

Last year's club overcame injuries to win 97 games. They were defeated in a close playoff series by the defending world champions. Were they ultimately done in by some baffling bullpen management and distinctly unclutch performances? You bet. But so is (almost) everybody in the playoffs. You don't have to win the World Series to be a great team.

This year, the Nationals will almost certainly be a great baseball team. Even doing absolutely nothing this offseason, they return a super talented roster. Adam Eaton will be back. Victor Robles will be lurking. Sean Doolittle and Ryan Madson will be more than just reinforcements. Who knows, maybe Dave Martinez will be a perfect tactician. He's certainly waited long enough for his shot. There is no reason the Nationals should have the feeling of an obligation. They should be the party you want to go to: a party resembling the gala that awaited their predecessors in 1867, with good food, generous spirits, lots of fancy cakes and perhaps a few too many self-congratulatory toasts.

We should also remember to enjoy these Nationals while they last. In 1868, George Wright departed for Cincinnati, where he played out his Hall of Fame career. It wasn't perfect, but the grand westward tour turned out to be the finest moment in the club's history.

Once upon a time, there was a baseball club called the Washington Nationals. The Nationals were fantastic, one of the great teams of their time. The roster was brilliantly constructed, consisting largely of homegrown talent and bolstered by a few key imports. The management was clever and creative—and not above testing the bounds of the system. On the field, the Nationals were led by one of the hardest throwing pitchers in the sport, and one of its greatest young hitters.

Then Bryce Harper filed for free agency.

Sources

- *Chicago Tribune*, July 26, 1867.
- Harry Chadwick, *The Game of Base Ball* (New York: George Munro & Company, 1868).
- Ryan Swanson, "Cleaning Up the Wild and Wooly West: The Washington Nationals' 1867 Baseball Tour Through the Ohio Valley," *Ohio Valley History*, 15, no. 3 (2015): 23-42.
- Peter Morris, *But Didn't We Have Fun?: An Informal History of Baseball's Pioneer Era, 1843-1870* (Chicago: Ivan R. Dee, 2010).
- William J. Ryczek, *When Johnny Came Sliding Home: The Post-Civil War Baseball Boom, 1865-1870* (Jefferson, NC: McFarland, 2006).
- John Thorn, "July 25, 1867: The Most Important Game in Baseball History?" in *Inventing Baseball: The 100 Greatest Games of the 19th Century*, edited by Bill Felber (Phoenix: Society for American Baseball Research, 2013).
- Frederic J. Frommer, *The Washington Nationals 1859 to Today: The Story of Baseball in the Nation's Capital* (Lanham, MD: Taylor Trade Publishing, 2006).
- Albert G. Spalding, *America's National Game* (New York: American Sports, 1911).

—Eric Nusbaum is an editor for VICE Sports.

Hitters

Matt Adams 1B Born: 08/31/88 Age: 29 Bats: L Throws: R Height: 6'3" Weight: 260 Origin: Round 23, 2009 Draft (#699 overall)

YEAR	TEAM	LVL	AGE	PA	R	2B	3B	HR	RBI	BB	K	SB	CS	AVG/OBP/SLG	TAv	VORP	BABIP	BRR	FRAA	WARP
2015	SLN	MLB	26	186	14	9	0	5	24	10	41	1	0	.240/.280/.377	.242	-1.1	.285	0.1	1B(46): -0.6	-0.2
2016	SLN	MLB	27	327	37	18	0	16	54	25	81	0	1	.249/.309/.471	.281	8.5	.286	-2.4	1B(86): 9.3	1.8
2017	SLN	MLB	28	53	4	2	0	1	7	4	17	0	0	.292/.340/.396	.272	1.8	.419	-0.1	LF(6): -0.3, 1B(3): 0.1	0.2
2017	ATL	MLB	28	314	42	20	1	19	58	19	71	0	0	.271/.315/.543	.291	13.9	.294	-0.6	1B(59): -3.3, LF(13): 0.5	1.1
2018	*WAS*	*MLB*	*29*	*205*	*25*	*10*	*0*	*9*	*30*	*13*	*48*	*0*	*0*	*.265/.312/.463*	*.259*	*4.7*	*.309*	*-0.4*	*1B 1, LF 0*	*0.5*
2019	*WAS*	*MLB*	*30*	*236*	*31*	*13*	*0*	*10*	*34*	*16*	*57*	*0*	*0*	*.264/.317/.468*	*.269*	*6.1*	*.310*	*-0.6*	*1B 1, LF 0*	*0.8*

Breakout: 6% Improve: 53% Collapse: 9% Attrition: 12% MLB: 91% *Comparables: Evan Gattis, Eric Karros, Shane Spencer*

Movie franchises can get stale, but the writers of *Final Destination: Matt Adams* left audiences on the edge of their seats throughout 2017. Sure, the scene where the Cardinals started giving him looks in left field to get that lumber in the lineup was unexpected—Adams hadn't played a single game on the grass in the majors or minors before last year—but at least it was believable. The Braves picking him up in May to serve the second-division gods when Freddie Freeman went down? Yeah, that makes sense. But the scene where Freeman shifted to the hot corner upon his return so Adams and his .923 OPS during the superstar's absence could stay in the lineup was a bold stroke that really made the viewer believe the lights might stay on in the Big City a while longer. Yet in the end, as too many of these movies have hammered home, you can't outrun your fate for long, and Adams will start 2018 as he ended 2017: as a glorified pinch-hitter constantly endangered by ever-shortening benches.

Rafael Bautista OF Born: 03/08/93 Age: 25 Bats: R Throws: R Height: 6'2" Weight: 165 Origin: International Free Agent, 2012

YEAR	TEAM	LVL	AGE	PA	R	2B	3B	HR	RBI	BB	K	SB	CS	AVG/OBP/SLG	TAv	VORP	BABIP	BRR	FRAA	WARP
2015	AUB	A-	22	34	6	3	0	0	4	1	7	3	0	.273/.294/.364	.224	0.7	.346	1.0	CF(7): 0.3	0.1
2015	POT	A+	22	226	23	7	2	0	8	11	22	23	4	.272/.318/.325	.253	5.0	.301	0.0	CF(52): -3.4	0.2
2016	HAR	AA	23	607	77	12	4	4	39	45	94	56	10	.282/.344/.341	.257	21.9	.333	7.8	CF(102): -4.1, RF(32): 0.1	1.9
2017	NAT	RK	24	52	7	2	1	0	3	5	5	2	1	.295/.404/.386	.299	3.8	.333	-0.4	CF(10): -0.8	0.3
2017	SYR	AAA	24	188	23	9	1	0	11	9	26	7	4	.250/.290/.313	.216	-0.9	.293	2.7	CF(34): -0.6, LF(7): -0.5	-0.1
2017	WAS	MLB	24	27	2	0	0	0	0	2	5	0	0	.160/.222/.160	.135	-2.5	.200	0.5	RF(11): -0.4, CF(1): 0.0	-0.3
2018	*WAS*	*MLB*	*25*	*76*	*9*	*3*	*0*	*1*	*7*	*4*	*15*	*4*	*1*	*.254/.300/.352*	*.226*	*-0.1*	*.300*	*0.5*	*RF 0*	*0.0*
2019	*WAS*	*MLB*	*26*	*295*	*34*	*10*	*1*	*6*	*30*	*20*	*58*	*16*	*4*	*.259/.316/.375*	*.243*	*3.6*	*.304*	*2.2*	*RF 2*	*0.6*

Breakout: 4% Improve: 20% Collapse: 9% Attrition: 24% MLB: 39% *Comparables: Rajai Davis, Jose Constanza, Matt Szczur*

They say speed kills, but speed is what's keeping Bautista's major-league dreams alive. After taking a step forward at the plate in Double-A in 2016, the plus-plus runner maintained that progress in his introduction to Triple-A in 2017. When he got his first call to the big leagues—a cup of coffee in early May, after the Adam Eaton injury—he was hitting .291/.325/.354 at Syracuse. But he injured his hamstring soon after and then struggled through the rest of his season after sitting out most of June and July. He got another chance in the majors as a September call-up, racking up just a walk and a single in 14 plate appearances. Pitchers challenged him often in the strike zone and he gave them no reason not to continue doing so. If Bautista can't add another dimension to his game beyond that speed, future chances might be harder to come by.

Wilmer Difo MI Born: 04/02/92 Age: 26 Bats: B Throws: R Height: 5'11" Weight: 200 Origin: International Free Agent, 2010

YEAR	TEAM	LVL	AGE	PA	R	2B	3B	HR	RBI	BB	K	SB	CS	AVG/OBP/SLG	TAv	VORP	BABIP	BRR	FRAA	WARP
2015	POT	A+	23	83	13	7	0	3	14	8	13	4	1	.320/.386/.533	.337	10.1	.356	0.4	SS(19): -2.8	0.8
2015	HAR	AA	23	381	48	21	6	2	39	12	79	26	1	.279/.312/.387	.251	11.7	.349	0.7	SS(77): 5.0, 2B(11): -0.7	1.7
2015	WAS	MLB	23	11	1	0	0	0	0	0	2	0	0	.182/.182/.182	.141	-1.7	.222	-0.8	2B(2): 0.0	-0.2
2016	HAR	AA	24	451	59	15	3	6	41	34	59	28	11	.259/.318/.354	.252	13.9	.288	-0.1	SS(103): -2.4	1.2
2016	WAS	MLB	24	66	14	3	0	1	7	8	12	3	0	.276/.364/.379	.261	3.1	.333	1.0	2B(9): 0.2, SS(5): 0.2	0.4
2017	SYR	AAA	25	45	5	2	0	0	1	5	6	0	0	.175/.267/.225	.187	-1.9	.206	-0.1	SS(9): -1.4, CF(2): -0.3	-0.3
2017	WAS	MLB	25	365	47	10	4	5	21	24	74	10	1	.271/.319/.370	.242	9.3	.332	2.4	SS(57): 7.1, 2B(25): -0.7	1.5
2018	*WAS*	*MLB*	*26*	*334*	*39*	*13*	*2*	*6*	*32*	*20*	*69*	*11*	*2*	*.254/.302/.372*	*.233*	*4.5*	*.305*	*1.5*	*2B 1, 3B 0*	*0.3*
2019	*WAS*	*MLB*	*27*	*413*	*48*	*16*	*2*	*11*	*47*	*27*	*91*	*13*	*3*	*.255/.309/.397*	*.248*	*8.6*	*.304*	*1.6*	*2B 1, 3B 0*	*1.0*

Breakout: 8% Improve: 47% Collapse: 8% Attrition: 30% MLB: 84% *Comparables: Brendan Ryan, Nick Ahmed, Leury Garcia*

Trea Turner's trip to the disabled list was Difo's chance to shine, and shine he did. In nearly 200 plate appearances as the team's everyday shortstop through July and August, he hit .343/.389/.483. That performance was strong enough that Dusty Baker was willing to get creative to keep Difo in the lineup when Turner came back, even sticking him in right field for a few games. He changed the opinions of those who thought he shouldn't be batting high in the lineup even quicker than he can run (which is, for the record, very fast: faster than anyone on the team except for Turner, actually). No, he still doesn't have a chance to stick at short with Turner in town—but the Nationals only have Daniel Murphy under contract for one more year, and after that, the keystone could be his.

Stephen Drew SS Born: 03/16/83 Age: 35 Bats: L Throws: R Height: 6'0" Weight: 200 Origin: Round 1, 2004 Draft (#15 overall)

YEAR	TEAM	LVL	AGE	PA	R	2B	3B	HR	RBI	BB	K	SB	CS	AVG/OBP/SLG	TAv	VORP	BABIP	BRR	FRAA	WARP
2015	NYA	MLB	32	428	43	16	1	17	44	37	71	0	2	.201/.271/.381	.236	-1.4	.201	-2.7	2B(123): -2.7, SS(15): 0.7	-0.4
2016	WAS	MLB	33	165	24	11	1	8	21	16	31	0	1	.266/.339/.524	.318	13.8	.278	-1.1	2B(21): 1.8, SS(12): -0.3	1.5
2017	WAS	MLB	34	106	9	7	0	1	17	8	21	0	0	.253/.302/.358	.247	2.2	.303	-0.1	SS(13): -0.6, 3B(11): -1.1	0.0
2018	*WAS*	*MLB*	*35*	*250*	*27*	*12*	*1*	*8*	*29*	*24*	*55*	*1*	*1*	*.229/.304/.402*	*.232*	*2.0*	*.264*	*-0.9*	*2B 0, 3B -1*	*0.1*
2019	*WAS*	*MLB*	*36*	*12*	*1*	*1*	*0*	*0*	*1*	*1*	*3*	*0*	*0*	*.224/.297/.387*	*.241*	*0.1*	*.263*	*0.0*	*2B 0, 3B 0*	*0.0*

Breakout: 0% Improve: 30% Collapse: 16% Attrition: 27% MLB: 75% *Comparables: Clint Barmes, Alex Gonzalez, Edgar Renteria*

If there was a bright side to Drew's 2017 season, it was this: After playing poorly while playing at all, the infielder tore his abdominal muscle away from the bone in July; his decision to refuse surgery and instead rehab on his own in an attempt to make the postseason roster almost paid off. "Almost" in that he managed to get to a point where he was able to field and hit—those being relative terms for a player of his current talent—though he still struggled to run at all without pain and ended up not making the playoff roster. So not too bright of a side after all, really, but brightness is rare when your nickname is Dirt.

Adam Eaton CF Born: 12/06/88 Age: 29 Bats: L Throws: L Height: 5'8" Weight: 185 Origin: Round 19, 2010 Draft (#571 overall)

YEAR	TEAM	LVL	AGE	PA	R	2B	3B	HR	RBI	BB	K	SB	CS	AVG/OBP/SLG	TAv	VORP	BABIP	BRR	FRAA	WARP
2015	CHA	MLB	26	689	98	28	9	14	56	58	131	18	8	.287/.361/.431	.282	40.6	.345	5.9	CF(145): 2.2	4.6
2016	CHA	MLB	27	706	91	29	9	14	59	63	115	14	5	.284/.362/.428	.276	32.9	.329	5.9	RF(121): 33.4, CF(48): 6.3	7.5
2017	WAS	MLB	28	107	24	7	1	2	13	14	18	3	1	.297/.393/.462	.313	9.5	.347	0.3	CF(20): -3.3, LF(5): 0.4	0.7
2018	*WAS*	*MLB*	*29*	*543*	*72*	*23*	*6*	*9*	*52*	*46*	*89*	*13*	*5*	*.283/.353/.413*	*.263*	*23.4*	*.327*	*0.7*	*LF 14, CF 0*	*3.1*
2019	*WAS*	*MLB*	*30*	*394*	*49*	*17*	*4*	*8*	*44*	*36*	*67*	*8*	*4*	*.284/.361/.428*	*.277*	*19.6*	*.326*	*2.7*	*LF 11, CF 0*	*3.3*

Breakout: 0% Improve: 49% Collapse: 4% Attrition: 9% MLB: 99% *Comparables: Denard Span, Jacoby Ellsbury, Jon Jay*

Through the first month of the 2017 season, the Nationals had the best offense in baseball—due in no small part to Eaton, on track for his best year at the plate after being the team's biggest acquisition of the offseason. That went to pieces at the same time his knee did, as Eaton crumpled to the ground while trying to leg out an infield single on April 28 and was later diagnosed with a torn ACL that would sideline him for the rest of the year. The Nationals managed things well enough in his absence, of course, but there's nothing they could've done short of a World Series title to erase the *what if* around his injury. This season will be their chance to try to answer that *what if*, with one of the best leadoff hitters in the game.

Brian Goodwin OF Born: 11/02/90 Age: 27 Bats: L Throws: R Height: 6'0" Weight: 205 Origin: Round 1, 2011 Draft (#34 overall)

YEAR	TEAM	LVL	AGE	PA	R	2B	3B	HR	RBI	BB	K	SB	CS	AVG/OBP/SLG	TAv	VORP	BABIP	BRR	FRAA	WARP
2015	HAR	AA	24	472	58	17	4	8	46	38	93	15	7	.226/.290/.340	.239	1.6	.269	-0.6	CF(87): -1.8, RF(22): 2.4	0.1
2016	SYR	AAA	25	492	51	25	1	14	68	46	106	15	3	.280/.349/.438	.279	21.3	.336	-2.1	CF(85): -4.9, RF(18): 0.3	2.1
2016	WAS	MLB	25	44	1	4	1	0	5	2	14	0	0	.286/.318/.429	.252	0.4	.429	-0.2	RF(8): -1.5, LF(5): -0.3	-0.1
2017	SYR	AAA	26	103	9	4	0	2	11	10	29	2	1	.256/.327/.367	.254	0.3	.350	-1.6	RF(9): 0.8, CF(8): 0.0	0.0
2017	WAS	MLB	26	278	41	21	1	13	30	23	69	6	0	.251/.313/.498	.279	13.2	.291	0.1	CF(34): -1.2, LF(31): -0.2	1.4
2018	*WAS*	*MLB*	*27*	*104*	*14*	*5*	*0*	*4*	*12*	*9*	*27*	*2*	*1*	*.244/.308/.416*	*.246*	*2.1*	*.299*	*0.1*	*LF 0, CF 0*	*0.1*
2019	*WAS*	*MLB*	*28*	*321*	*41*	*16*	*1*	*12*	*41*	*29*	*82*	*6*	*2*	*.246/.318/.430*	*.260*	*8.6*	*.302*	*-0.2*	*LF 0, CF -1*	*0.9*

Breakout: 5% Improve: 38% Collapse: 8% Attrition: 20% MLB: 70% *Comparables: Mikie Mahtook, Will Venable, Aaron Cunningham*

The Nationals' injury problems in the outfield meant plenty of shuffling around to find a recipe that worked. A little bit of Eaton in their life, a little bit of Taylor by their side, a little bit of Stevenson as they need, a little bit of Werth for what they see ... and a little bit of Goodwin finally getting his time in the sun. Thanks to his defensive versatility in the outfield, the 2011 first-round pick got his first sustained run in the major leagues at last—and it went pretty well, which is to say *very* well for someone whose hopes of big-league success had seemed dashed for quite a while. That's still not nearly enough to secure a starting role or even a secure position as a fourth outfielder going forward, but at least for a little bit, he got to live up to his last name.

Bryce Harper RF Born: 10/16/92 Age: 25 Bats: L Throws: R Height: 6'3" Weight: 215 Origin: Round 1, 2010 Draft (#1 overall)

YEAR	TEAM	LVL	AGE	PA	R	2B	3B	HR	RBI	BB	K	SB	CS	AVG/OBP/SLG	TAv	VORP	BABIP	BRR	FRAA	WARP
2015	WAS	MLB	22	654	118	38	1	42	99	124	131	6	4	.330/.460/.649	.386	97.4	.369	5.1	RF(140): 6.4, CF(13): 0.8	11.2
2016	WAS	MLB	23	627	84	24	2	24	86	108	117	21	10	.243/.373/.441	.305	42.1	.264	2.3	RF(143): 4.1	4.8
2017	WAS	MLB	24	492	95	27	1	29	87	68	99	4	2	.319/.413/.595	.336	47.0	.356	-1.3	RF(110): -3.4	4.4
2018	*WAS*	*MLB*	*25*	*612*	*98*	*28*	*2*	*31*	*100*	*90*	*121*	*10*	*5*	*.288/.395/.533*	*.310*	*49.7*	*.319*	*-0.8*	*RF -3*	*4.1*
2019	*WAS*	*MLB*	*26*	*543*	*90*	*26*	*1*	*30*	*91*	*84*	*110*	*9*	*5*	*.289/.402/.551*	*.324*	*49.6*	*.318*	*1.8*	*RF -1*	*5.3*

Breakout: 2% Improve: 57% Collapse: 3% Attrition: 3% MLB: 100% *Comparables: Justin Upton, Ken Griffey, Jack Clark*

Harper's hopes of rebounding from 2016's down season didn't quite come to fruition the way he would've liked. He bounced back, sure, but not as high as he could have: 2017's TAv was closer to the slumping 2016 version than to the MVP 2015 one, and he spent five weeks on the disabled list with a bone bruise. But the thing to remember, as it always is with Harper, is that the scale here is relative. How do you judge someone who was a five-plus WARP player as a teenager, a historically brilliant MVP as a 22-year-old and a disappointment for being merely a star-level player as a 23-year-old? There's no road map here. Maybe you wait until after his walk year as a 25-year-old to see where he ends up, and for how much. Maybe you just scrap the view of his skill altogether and admire the flow.

Howie Kendrick LF Born: 07/12/83 Age: 34 Bats: R Throws: R Height: 5'11" Weight: 220 Origin: Round 10, 2002 Draft (#294 overall)

YEAR	TEAM	LVL	AGE	PA	R	2B	3B	HR	RBI	BB	K	SB	CS	AVG/OBP/SLG	TAv	VORP	BABIP	BRR	FRAA	WARP
2015	LAN	MLB	31	495	64	22	2	9	54	27	82	6	2	.295/.336/.409	.272	21.4	.342	3.1	2B(113): -1.0	2.2
2016	LAN	MLB	32	543	65	26	2	8	40	50	96	10	2	.255/.326/.366	.255	14.6	.301	4.9	LF(94): -0.7, 2B(32): 0.5	1.4
2017	PHI	MLB	33	156	16	8	1	2	16	11	30	8	3	.340/.397/.454	.307	10.8	.418	-0.7	LF(24): -0.4, 2B(10): 0.6	1.1
2017	WAS	MLB	33	178	24	8	2	7	25	11	38	4	2	.293/.343/.494	.290	10.3	.342	0.6	LF(38): -2.9, 2B(5): -0.2	0.7
2018	*WAS*	*MLB*	*34*	*360*	*41*	*17*	*2*	*8*	*41*	*26*	*65*	*8*	*3*	*.285/.342/.421*	*.254*	*11.8*	*.331*	*1.5*	*LF 1, 2B 0*	*1.4*
2019	*WAS*	*MLB*	*35*	*280*	*33*	*12*	*1*	*6*	*30*	*20*	*54*	*5*	*2*	*.273/.330/.401*	*.260*	*8.3*	*.322*	*1.3*	*LF 1, 2B 0*	*1.0*

Breakout: 0% Improve: 27% Collapse: 19% Attrition: 21% MLB: 91% *Comparables: Jay Payton, Reed Johnson, Marlon Anderson*

The term "future batting champion" has been attached to Kendrick's name in these *Annuals* more times than references to Kendrick Lamar (in seven of his 13 previous comments, to be specific). Now, at age 34, he's sat down and been humbled, but that doesn't mean that he's not still productive. After getting off to a pretty hot start in Philly, he headed to DC in a midseason trade and proved useful there amid a spate of outfield injuries. A left-field platoon of Kendrick and Adam Lind isn't what anyone expected there when the season began, but, hey, it got the job done for a spell. The guy has hitting inside his DNA, so don't be surprised if he continues his late-career transition into a surprisingly serviceable outfielder thanks to his bat.

Carter Kieboom SS Born: 09/03/97 Age: 20 Bats: R Throws: R Height: 6'2" Weight: 190 Origin: Round 1, 2016 Draft (#28 overall)

YEAR	TEAM	LVL	AGE	PA	R	2B	3B	HR	RBI	BB	K	SB	CS	AVG/OBP/SLG	TAv	VORP	BABIP	BRR	FRAA	WARP
2016	NAT	RK	18	155	22	8	4	4	25	12	43	1	2	.244/.323/.452	.257	5.1	.319	-0.3	SS(31): 0.6	0.6
2017	AUB	A-	19	29	4	1	0	1	4	1	2	1	0	.250/.276/.393	.220	0.0	.240	0.2	SS(6): 1.1	0.1
2017	HAG	A	19	210	36	12	0	8	26	28	40	2	2	.296/.400/.497	.319	20.4	.344	-0.7	SS(45): 1.4	2.3
2018	*WAS*	*MLB*	*20*	*250*	*31*	*10*	*0*	*9*	*29*	*22*	*71*	*0*	*0*	*.230/.304/.405*	*.233*	*4.2*	*.289*	*-0.5*	*SS 1*	*0.6*
2019	*WAS*	*MLB*	*21*	*314*	*41*	*14*	*0*	*13*	*41*	*29*	*87*	*0*	*0*	*.241/.318/.427*	*.260*	*9.6*	*.301*	*-0.8*	*SS 1*	*1.2*

Breakout: 5% Improve: 15% Collapse: 0% Attrition: 6% MLB: 17% *Comparables: Trevor Story, Addison Russell, Xander Bogaerts*

A hamstring injury kept him out from early May to the end of July, which is a shame because the youngest Kieboom brother otherwise could've made a case to be included among baseball's 50 best prospects. As is, he's still pretty close. He doesn't project very well to stay at shortstop long term, but he *does* project well at the plate, where he's already handled himself fine as a teen in Low-A. The power and discipline he showed when healthy—before the injury, he was hitting .333/.398/.586 in 123 plate appearances—was even more impressive because Low-A was supposed to be a challenging assignment for the 2016 draftee. The Nationals will clearly have to find a different venue if they wish to challenge him as he enters his twenties.

Adam Lind 1B Born: 07/17/83 Age: 34 Bats: L Throws: L Height: 6'2" Weight: 195 Origin: Round 3, 2004 Draft (#83 overall)

YEAR	TEAM	LVL	AGE	PA	R	2B	3B	HR	RBI	BB	K	SB	CS	AVG/OBP/SLG	TAv	VORP	BABIP	BRR	FRAA	WARP
2015	MIL	MLB	31	572	72	32	0	20	87	66	100	0	0	.277/.360/.460	.294	24.6	.309	-0.2	1B(138): -6.9	1.9
2016	SEA	MLB	32	430	48	17	0	20	58	26	89	0	1	.239/.286/.431	.240	-4.6	.259	-0.7	1B(101): -3.2	-0.8
2017	WAS	MLB	33	301	39	14	0	14	59	28	47	1	0	.303/.362/.513	.303	17.7	.316	-1.2	1B(39): -0.1, LF(25): -0.8	1.7
2018	*WAS*	*MLB*	*34*	*308*	*37*	*15*	*0*	*12*	*43*	*29*	*58*	*0*	*0*	*.278/.345/.466*	*.265*	*9.0*	*.310*	*-0.4*	*1B -2, LF 1*	*0.8*
2019	*WAS*	*MLB*	*35*	*216*	*29*	*10*	*0*	*8*	*28*	*20*	*42*	*0*	*0*	*.266/.337/.443*	*.272*	*6.0*	*.301*	*-0.4*	*1B -2, LF 1*	*0.5*

Breakout: 0% Improve: 36% Collapse: 6% Attrition: 18% MLB: 95% *Comparables: Kendrys Morales, Kevin Millar, Aubrey Huff*

To put it simply, Lind sucked in 2016. His biggest strength, the ability to mash righties, completely disappeared (as did just about everything else that could be considered a strength of his). Thankfully, he steered out of that slide in 2017—due in large part to a newfound role as a pinch-hitting god. Lind set the Nationals' team record for pinch-hit home runs in a season with four, hitting .356/.396/.644 in his 48 plate appearances in the role. He still can't hit lefties, he still can't play competent defense, he's still an injury risk and now he's coming up on the wrong side of 35. But he still shows flashes of performance at the plate that are worth sticking around for, even if they're just one pinch at a time.

Daniel Murphy 2B Born: 04/01/85 Age: 33 Bats: L Throws: R Height: 6'1" Weight: 220 Origin: Round 13, 2006 Draft (#394 overall)

YEAR	TEAM	LVL	AGE	PA	R	2B	3B	HR	RBI	BB	K	SB	CS	AVG/OBP/SLG	TAv	VORP	BABIP	BRR	FRAA	WARP
2015	NYN	MLB	30	538	56	38	2	14	73	31	38	2	2	.281/.322/.449	.283	24.7	.278	-0.9	2B(69): -2.0, 3B(42): -2.4	2.1
2016	WAS	MLB	31	582	88	47	5	25	104	35	57	5	3	.347/.390/.595	.352	70.7	.348	1.4	2B(117): -5.3, 1B(21): 0.7	6.8
2017	WAS	MLB	32	593	94	43	3	23	93	52	77	2	0	.322/.384/.543	.314	51.6	.341	1.2	2B(139): 3.8	5.6
2018	*WAS*	*MLB*	*33*	*561*	*67*	*35*	*2*	*16*	*73*	*34*	*63*	*4*	*2*	*.302/.346/.469*	*.272*	*28.9*	*.317*	*-0.8*	*2B -2, 1B 1*	*2.2*
2019	*WAS*	*MLB*	*34*	*517*	*66*	*30*	*2*	*16*	*67*	*31*	*64*	*2*	*1*	*.299/.343/.468*	*.278*	*25.6*	*.315*	*0.4*	*2B -2, 1B 1*	*2.7*

Breakout: 2% Improve: 30% Collapse: 4% Attrition: 9% MLB: 97% *Comparables: Brandon Phillips, Ian Kinsler, Aaron Hill*

Even if he does nothing in this upcoming third and final year of his contract, Murphy has already ensured that Washington's gamble on him paid off. After a solid 2016 showed that his 2015 postseason was no fluke, he didn't have much left to prove in 2017. If you were still looking for a little something more, though, another season of a .300-plus TAv with 20-plus homers should've done it for you. That he's now reunited with hitting coach Kevin Long, who worked with him on his renaissance with the Mets and was hired by the Nationals this winter, might seem to indicate more good things ahead for Murphy in 2018. His work in the field still sucks, and he's only getting older; these downsides are still true, sure. But they always have been, and so it's not only more fun but also more worthwhile to focus on what *hasn't* always been true: that the guy is a compelling case study in how mechanical changes can transform a career.

Ryan Raburn LF Born: 04/17/81 Age: 37 Bats: R Throws: R Height: 6'0" Weight: 185 Origin: Round 5, 2001 Draft (#147 overall)

YEAR	TEAM	LVL	AGE	PA	R	2B	3B	HR	RBI	BB	K	SB	CS	AVG/OBP/SLG	TAv	VORP	BABIP	BRR	FRAA	WARP
2015	CLE	MLB	34	201	22	16	1	8	29	23	44	0	0	.301/.393/.543	.320	15.0	.361	0.2	LF(18): 0.6, RF(17): -0.7	1.6
2016	COL	MLB	35	256	30	10	2	9	30	28	80	0	0	.220/.309/.404	.243	2.3	.292	1.4	LF(47): -2.0, 1B(5): -0.3	0.0
2017	CHR	AAA	36	105	11	2	1	3	13	20	29	1	0	.277/.419/.434	.307	6.5	.385	-0.5	LF(5): -0.5, RF(3): -0.5	0.5
2017	SYR	AAA	36	26	3	2	0	1	5	0	9	0	0	.261/.269/.478	.270	0.6	.333	-0.1	LF(4): -0.1	0.1
2017	WAS	MLB	36	69	7	1	2	2	6	4	25	0	1	.262/.304/.431	.248	0.5	.395	-0.2	LF(22): -1.4	-0.1
2018	*WAS*	*MLB*	*37*	*250*	*29*	*11*	*1*	*9*	*33*	*25*	*69*	*0*	*0*	*.237/.321/.422*	*.245*	*4.1*	*.298*	*0.6*	*LF -3, RF 0*	*0.2*
2019	*WAS*	*MLB*	*38*	*16*	*2*	*1*	*0*	*1*	*2*	*2*	*5*	*0*	*0*	*.225/.307/.391*	*.246*	*0.1*	*.289*	*0.0*	*LF 0, RF 0*	*0.0*

Breakout: 1% Improve: 22% Collapse: 13% Attrition: 17% MLB: 73% *Comparables: Alfonso Soriano, Ron Gant, Jeromy Burnitz*

Raburn's odd tradition of excelling in odd years and backsliding in even years came to a halt in 2017, with a season in which he didn't play much due to a trapezius injury and played poorly when he had the chance to play at all. The outlook's now pretty bleak as he approaches both his 37th birthday and the limit for teams that can find a roster spot to accommodate his diminishing skills.

Anthony Rendon 3B Born: 06/06/90 Age: 28 Bats: R Throws: R Height: 6'1" Weight: 210 Origin: Round 1, 2011 Draft (#6 overall)

YEAR	TEAM	LVL	AGE	PA	R	2B	3B	HR	RBI	BB	K	SB	CS	AVG/OBP/SLG	TAv	VORP	BABIP	BRR	FRAA	WARP
2015	HAR	AA	25	27	1	3	0	0	0	3	4	0	0	.250/.333/.375	.271	0.7	.300	-0.2	2B(5): 0.6, 3B(1): 0.4	0.2
2015	WAS	MLB	25	355	43	16	0	5	25	36	70	1	2	.264/.344/.363	.262	10.0	.321	-0.2	2B(59): -1.6, 3B(28): 0.7	1.0
2016	WAS	MLB	26	647	91	38	2	20	85	65	117	12	6	.270/.348/.450	.296	45.1	.304	0.8	3B(155): -9.0	3.7
2017	WAS	MLB	27	605	81	41	1	25	100	84	82	7	2	.301/.403/.533	.325	63.4	.314	2.0	3B(145): -1.6	6.2
2018	*WAS*	*MLB*	*28*	*603*	*79*	*34*	*2*	*19*	*79*	*64*	*98*	*8*	*3*	*.277/.359/.458*	*.276*	*30.6*	*.306*	*-0.5*	*3B -5*	*2.0*
2019	*WAS*	*MLB*	*29*	*569*	*81*	*32*	*1*	*22*	*80*	*67*	*96*	*7*	*3*	*.278/.368/.484*	*.294*	*35.2*	*.302*	*1.0*	*3B -3*	*3.5*

Breakout: 0% Improve: 49% Collapse: 4% Attrition: 5% MLB: 98% *Comparables: Kyle Seager, Edwin Encarnacion, Robin Ventura*

The NL's top 10 players by WARP from last season has most of the names you'd expect: Stanton, Votto, Arenado ... and right after Goldschmidt, there's Rendon, who stayed healthy for a second straight year to tremendous results. He may have finally shed the injury-prone tag that pushed him down in the draft years ago, and the Nationals have good reason to be thrilled. Last season he improved his plate discipline, dropping his strikeout rate by five percentage points, while hitting for more power than ever and setting career bests in just about every metric. All that, and he's *still* the most handsome guy on the roster—and under team control until 2020.

Victor Robles CF Born: 05/19/97 Age: 21 Bats: R Throws: R Height: 6'0" Weight: 185 Origin: International Free Agent, 2013

YEAR	TEAM	LVL	AGE	PA	R	2B	3B	HR	RBI	BB	K	SB	CS	AVG/OBP/SLG	TAv	VORP	BABIP	BRR	FRAA	WARP
2015	NAT	RK	18	94	19	6	1	2	11	10	12	12	1	.370/.484/.562	.359	16.4	.417	3.3	CF(15): 1.7, RF(6): 0.2	1.8
2015	AUB	A-	18	167	29	5	4	2	16	8	21	12	4	.343/.424/.479	.334	18.9	.383	1.1	CF(37): 2.6, RF(1): -0.2	2.2
2016	HAG	A	19	285	48	9	6	5	30	18	38	19	8	.305/.405/.459	.321	31.6	.346	6.2	CF(63): 11.9	4.8
2016	POT	A+	19	198	24	8	2	3	11	14	32	18	5	.262/.354/.387	.284	10.3	.304	-1.0	CF(40): 5.9	1.7
2017	POT	A+	20	338	49	25	7	7	33	25	62	16	7	.289/.377/.495	.317	30.5	.345	0.7	CF(70): 16.2	4.9
2017	HAR	AA	20	158	24	12	1	3	14	12	22	11	3	.324/.394/.489	.321	17.0	.368	2.7	CF(30): 4.2, LF(1): -0.1	2.3
2017	WAS	MLB	20	27	2	1	2	0	4	0	6	0	1	.250/.308/.458	.243	-0.6	.333	-0.8	RF(6): 1.3, CF(3): -0.3	0.0
2018	*WAS*	*MLB*	*21*	*301*	*43*	*13*	*3*	*8*	*31*	*15*	*65*	*12*	*5*	*.259/.322/.419*	*.253*	*9.1*	*.306*	*0.9*	*LF 0, CF 3*	*1.0*
2019	*WAS*	*MLB*	*22*	*510*	*67*	*24*	*5*	*17*	*66*	*33*	*111*	*21*	*9*	*.272/.349/.463*	*.279*	*26.2*	*.316*	*2.2*	*LF 1, CF 6*	*3.6*

Breakout: 8% Improve: 22% Collapse: 5% Attrition: 15% MLB: 34% *Comparables: Joc Pederson, Christian Yelich, Alex Verdugo*

The thing about Robles isn't just that he has a high ceiling. Any legitimate five-tool, up-the-middle player is going to have a high ceiling. It's that Robles has a ceiling that's high and beautifully so. We're talking, like, a Sistine Chapel ceiling. The kid has a remarkable glove, great on-base skills and some major speed. He needed scarcely three dozen games to show that he had Double-A all figured out, and he became the youngest player in the majors when he was called up for a trial cup of coffee in September. Of course, the ceiling is only one part of the structure, and it took Michelangelo nearly four years to paint the Sistine Chapel, but all signs point to Robles being at least in reach of painting his own.

Pedro Severino C Born: 07/20/93 Age: 24 Bats: R Throws: R Height: 6'0" Weight: 215 Origin: International Free Agent, 2010

YEAR	TEAM	LVL	AGE	PA	R	2B	3B	HR	RBI	BB	K	SB	CS	AVG/OBP/SLG	TAv	VORP	BABIP	BRR	FRAA	WARP
2015	HAR	AA	21	357	33	13	0	5	34	19	51	1	2	.246/.288/.331	.232	3.8	.276	-1.5	C(91): 0.1	0.4
2015	WAS	MLB	21	4	1	1	0	0	0	0	1	0	0	.250/.250/.500	.233	0.1	.333	0.1	C(2): 0.1	0.0
2016	SYR	AAA	22	317	25	13	0	2	21	19	45	3	4	.271/.316/.337	.238	4.8	.310	-2.0	C(81): -2.0	0.3
2016	WAS	MLB	22	34	6	2	0	2	4	5	3	0	0	.321/.441/.607	.377	6.5	.304	0.9	C(15): 0.2	0.7
2017	SYR	AAA	23	227	17	4	0	5	29	15	43	1	1	.242/.291/.332	.231	3.0	.280	-0.4	C(58): 7.0	1.0
2017	WAS	MLB	23	31	0	1	0	0	3	2	10	0	0	.172/.226/.207	.135	-3.2	.263	-0.5	C(10): 0.2	-0.3
2018	*WAS*	*MLB*	*24*	*187*	*20*	*7*	*0*	*5*	*20*	*11*	*37*	*1*	*0*	*.253/.301/.382*	*.236*	*4.3*	*.292*	*-0.5*	*C -3*	*-0.1*
2019	*WAS*	*MLB*	*25*	*322*	*39*	*13*	*0*	*11*	*39*	*22*	*70*	*1*	*1*	*.252/.308/.404*	*.251*	*8.6*	*.293*	*-0.9*	*C -3*	*0.6*

Breakout: 9% Improve: 24% Collapse: 7% Attrition: 22% MLB: 52% *Comparables: J.T. Realmuto, Jeff Mathis, Francisco Cervelli*

YEAR	TEAM	P. COUNT	FRM RUNS	BLK RUNS	THRW RUNS	TOT RUNS
2015	HAR	12147	-1.7	0.3	1.1	-0.3
2016	WAS	1422	-0.7	0.3	0.1	-0.3
2017	WAS	939	0.6	-0.3	0.0	0.3
2018	*WAS*	*7172*	*-1.5*	*-0.7*	*-0.2*	*-2.3*
2019	*WAS*	*12368*	*-1.2*	*-0.5*	*-0.1*	*-1.8*

On its own, "backup catcher of the future" isn't an especially sexy tag, but it's even less so when the window for that future seems like it is drifting shut. Severino took a step back at the plate in 2017, which was pretty impressive given the low bar his 2016 performance set. However, one bright spot in an otherwise dismal season was Severino's improvement in framing—tallying more than a 10-run improvement between Syracuse and Washington combined. If it's a true gain, the glove may get him a backup catcher of the present role on the strength of a surprising skill. Of course, to shoot higher than that, he doesn't need to outrun the bear, he only needs to outrun Matt Wieters.

Juan Soto RF Born: 10/25/98 Age: 19 Bats: L Throws: L Height: 6'1" Weight: 185 Origin: International Free Agent, 2015

YEAR	TEAM	LVL	AGE	PA	R	2B	3B	HR	RBI	BB	K	SB	CS	AVG/OBP/SLG	TAv	VORP	BABIP	BRR	FRAA	WARP
2016	NAT	RK	17	183	25	11	3	5	31	14	25	5	2	.361/.410/.550	.329	18.3	.403	1.0	RF(42): 2.9	2.1
2017	HAG	A	18	96	15	5	0	3	14	10	8	1	2	.360/.427/.523	.316	8.2	.373	1.0	RF(19): -1.9, LF(2): -0.3	0.6
2017	NAT	RK	18	27	3	1	1	0	4	2	1	0	0	.320/.370/.440	.280	1.2	.333	0.0	RF(9): -1.1	0.0
2018	*WAS*	*MLB*	*19*	*250*	*26*	*11*	*1*	*9*	*31*	*17*	*59*	*0*	*0*	*.249/.300/.411*	*.232*	*-0.7*	*.297*	*-0.5*	*RF -1, LF 0*	*-0.2*
2019	*WAS*	*MLB*	*20*	*365*	*48*	*16*	*1*	*15*	*50*	*26*	*81*	*0*	*0*	*.268/.324/.455*	*.269*	*10.4*	*.311*	*-0.8*	*RF -2, LF 0*	*0.9*

Breakout: 0% Improve: 11% Collapse: 2% Attrition: 10% MLB: 21% *Comparables: Nomar Mazara, Carlos Correa, Freddie Freeman*

The waiting is the hardest part, they say—but with prospects, the waiting is the part where hope lives. The waiting is the part where you're allowed to dream, and boy, Soto provides great fodder for dreaming. How great? Some have called him the Dominican Bryce Harper. There's plenty of waiting left until we see whether the teen can hit the lofty ceiling for his classic right-field profile. And unfortunately, he had us all waiting a bit longer than expected during an injury-ridden 2017 that saw him sidelined by an ankle injury and then a hamate fracture. But when he was on the field, he was as promised, with plenty of pop and a mature approach at the plate. Sure, there are any number of reasons for it not to work out—he's almost definitely limited to right field, there's plenty of time yet to see if he struggles at the plate when tested above A-ball—but, hey, there are always any number of reasons for it not to work out. There aren't always this many reasons to hope while we're waiting.

Andrew Stevenson OF Born: 06/01/94 Age: 24 Bats: L Throws: L Height: 6'0" Weight: 185 Origin: Round 2, 2015 Draft (#58 overall)

YEAR	TEAM	LVL	AGE	PA	R	2B	3B	HR	RBI	BB	K	SB	CS	AVG/OBP/SLG	TAv	VORP	BABIP	BRR	FRAA	WARP
2015	AUB	A-	21	80	11	1	2	0	9	7	12	7	3	.361/.413/.431	.294	6.3	.426	1.2	CF(16): 2.9, LF(3): 1.6	1.1
2015	HAG	A	21	153	28	3	2	1	16	8	16	16	4	.285/.338/.358	.282	10.7	.311	2.7	CF(35): 0.7	1.2
2016	POT	A+	22	300	37	12	8	1	18	24	44	27	9	.304/.359/.418	.287	20.8	.358	3.1	CF(60): 3.3, LF(6): -1.0	2.4
2016	HAR	AA	22	280	38	11	2	2	16	20	51	12	5	.246/.302/.328	.237	-2.3	.299	-2.9	CF(36): 7.5, LF(28): 1.6	0.7
2017	HAR	AA	23	91	14	5	1	0	12	11	19	1	3	.350/.429/.438	.323	7.9	.459	-0.4	CF(13): -3.0, LF(3): -0.3	0.5
2017	SYR	AAA	23	331	38	7	4	2	26	19	72	10	1	.252/.298/.320	.222	-1.7	.323	2.2	CF(62): -0.2, LF(15): 1.9	0.0
2017	WAS	MLB	23	66	5	2	0	0	1	7	20	1	0	.158/.250/.193	.168	-4.4	.243	0.5	RF(14): 0.1, LF(9): -0.5	-0.5
2018	*WAS*	*MLB*	*24*	*45*	*5*	*1*	*0*	*1*	*4*	*3*	*11*	*1*	*0*	*.246/.294/.350*	*.224*	*-0.3*	*.309*	*0.1*	*RF 1*	*0.0*
2019	*WAS*	*MLB*	*25*	*362*	*41*	*12*	*3*	*8*	*38*	*26*	*86*	*10*	*4*	*.253/.310/.383*	*.244*	*3.4*	*.314*	*1.2*	*RF 7*	*1.1*

Breakout: 8% Improve: 15% Collapse: 6% Attrition: 14% MLB: 28% *Comparables: Ryan Strausborger, Angel Pagan, Brandon Guyer*

Washington's injury troubles in the outfield led to an early call-up for Stevenson. His work on defense, which has been his calling card, looked as good as expected. Unfortunately, his work at the plate, which has not been his calling card (not even a faint line in fine print at the bottom of the card), also looked as good as expected. That is, it took a step backward from his Triple-A performance. Stevenson's fans point to his speed and ability to stick in center field; his detractors point to his below-average arm and limited offensive upside. Us? We're pointing to this sign that says "fourth outfielder."

Michael Taylor CF Born: 03/26/91 Age: 27 Bats: R Throws: R Height: 6'3" Weight: 210 Origin: Round 6, 2009 Draft (#172 overall)

YEAR	TEAM	LVL	AGE	PA	R	2B	3B	HR	RBI	BB	K	SB	CS	AVG/OBP/SLG	TAv	VORP	BABIP	BRR	FRAA	WARP
2015	SYR	AAA	24	32	4	1	0	1	4	4	10	2	1	.385/.452/.538	.372	4.9	.563	0.2	CF(6): -1.4, RF(1): 0.1	0.4
2015	WAS	MLB	24	511	49	15	2	14	63	35	158	16	3	.229/.282/.358	.240	3.5	.311	-0.4	CF(96): 0.9, LF(38): 4.3	0.9
2016	SYR	AAA	25	130	17	5	1	1	9	12	33	7	1	.205/.285/.291	.234	2.3	.277	2.2	CF(28): 0.5	0.3
2016	WAS	MLB	25	237	28	11	0	7	16	14	77	14	3	.231/.278/.376	.243	3.7	.319	0.7	CF(64): 2.9, RF(5): -0.4	0.6
2017	HAR	AA	26	28	3	2	0	1	4	2	8	3	0	.154/.214/.346	.187	-0.9	.176	0.4	CF(2): 0.2	-0.1
2017	WAS	MLB	26	432	55	23	3	19	53	29	137	17	7	.271/.320/.486	.281	26.5	.363	3.1	CF(111): 12.6, RF(2): -0.2	3.9
2018	*WAS*	*MLB*	*27*	*478*	*67*	*19*	*2*	*17*	*56*	*37*	*150*	*21*	*6*	*.244/.304/.413*	*.245*	*11.7*	*.327*	*2.1*	*CF 3*	*1.2*
2019	*WAS*	*MLB*	*28*	*428*	*54*	*18*	*1*	*16*	*55*	*37*	*137*	*18*	*5*	*.241/.309/.420*	*.256*	*12.2*	*.326*	*1.3*	*CF 4*	*1.7*

Breakout: 8% Improve: 40% Collapse: 6% Attrition: 16% MLB: 87% *Comparables: Drew Stubbs, Curtis Granderson, Peter Bourjos*

If you told Mike Rizzo he'd get 4.6 WARP out of center field in 2017, he'd have been rather pleased with himself for the Adam Eaton trade. If you told him that 85 percent of that production would come from the player Eaton was brought in to replace, he might spend a few hours longingly staring at pictures of Lucas Giolito. Just like in 2016 and 2015, injuries in the outfield gave Taylor a chance at playing time in 2017. But this time, Taylor was able to capitalize on that chance, putting it all together both offensively and defensively. The power that's always been lurking beneath the surface of his game shone through, and with that in place, his high strikeout rate wasn't as much of a liability. And even in less than a full season of playing time, Taylor led the National League in FRAA among center fielders. With Eaton's experience and expertise playing in a corner, Taylor has made all of the arguments in his power to once again be the long-term option in center for the Nationals.

Trea Turner SS Born: 06/30/93 Age: 25 Bats: R Throws: R Height: 6'1" Weight: 185 Origin: Round 1, 2014 Draft (#13 overall)

YEAR	TEAM	LVL	AGE	PA	R	2B	3B	HR	RBI	BB	K	SB	CS	AVG/OBP/SLG	TAv	VORP	BABIP	BRR	FRAA	WARP
2015	SAN	AA	22	254	31	13	3	5	35	24	48	11	4	.322/.385/.471	.297	20.9	.389	1.6	SS(57): 5.5	2.9
2015	HAR	AA	22	41	6	4	1	0	4	1	8	4	0	.359/.366/.513	.303	3.6	.438	0.2	SS(10): -1.0	0.3
2015	SYR	AAA	22	205	31	7	3	3	15	13	41	14	2	.314/.353/.431	.291	16.7	.381	2.0	SS(44): 4.8, 2B(2): -0.3	2.2
2015	WAS	MLB	22	44	5	1	0	1	1	4	12	2	2	.225/.295/.325	.259	1.3	.296	0.1	2B(12): 0.6, SS(6): -0.1	0.2
2016	SYR	AAA	23	371	61	22	8	6	33	37	72	25	2	.302/.370/.471	.310	40.0	.369	6.1	SS(71): 8.6, CF(6): 0.9	5.1
2016	WAS	MLB	23	324	53	14	8	13	40	14	59	33	6	.342/.370/.567	.341	42.1	.388	5.9	CF(45): -2.1, 2B(30): -1.1	4.0
2017	WAS	MLB	24	447	75	24	6	11	45	30	80	46	8	.284/.338/.451	.283	36.6	.329	6.8	SS(95): 0.2	3.7
2018	*WAS*	*MLB*	*25*	*637*	*105*	*30*	*8*	*19*	*70*	*43*	*130*	*51*	*10*	*.292/.341/.469*	*.278*	*47.7*	*.344*	*8.0*	*SS 11*	*5.3*
2019	*WAS*	*MLB*	*26*	*539*	*71*	*27*	*6*	*19*	*74*	*39*	*111*	*42*	*8*	*.290/.345/.486*	*.291*	*42.9*	*.338*	*7.1*	*SS 9*	*5.7*

Breakout: 2% Improve: 58% Collapse: 2% Attrition: 12% MLB: 99% *Comparables: Ian Desmond, Starling Marte, Marcus Semien*

Mr. Steal Yo' Base had some stumbling blocks in what should've been his first full big-league season. Most notably, there was a leg injury that sapped his skill before a broken wrist sidelined him for two months. And the electric performance he had at the plate in 2016 didn't show up in 2017, though he did manage to hit his stride when he returned for the season's final month (hitting .297/.371/.525, as opposed to .279/.324/.422 before his trip to the disabled list). But the significance of any stumbling block is felt relative to how fast you're going, and Turner has generally still been speeding along—literally, on the basepaths, and figuratively, in the grand scheme of his career. After 2016's center-field experiment, he returned to shortstop in 2017 and proved himself more than capable. The league is seemingly packed with incredibly talented youngsters at short right now, but even if Turner's trademark speed can't quite let him clearly pull *ahead* of the pack here, his total package is certainly enough to keep him hanging with the best of them.

Drew Ward 3B

Born: 11/25/94 Age: 23 Bats: L Throws: R Height: 6'3" Weight: 215 Origin: Round 3, 2013 Draft (#105 overall)

YEAR	TEAM	LVL	AGE	PA	R	2B	3B	HR	RBI	BB	K	SB	CS	AVG/OBP/SLG	TAv	VORP	BABIP	BRR	FRAA	WARP
2015	POT	A+	20	426	47	19	2	6	47	39	110	2	1	.249/.327/.358	.256	9.2	.333	-0.9	3B(95): -3.4	0.6
2016	POT	A+	21	268	36	16	0	11	32	34	70	0	1	.278/.377/.491	.310	19.7	.353	-2.1	3B(49): 2.0	2.2
2016	HAR	AA	21	203	19	7	0	3	24	22	51	0	1	.219/.310/.309	.230	1.0	.288	0.9	3B(51): -3.9	-0.3
2017	HAR	AA	22	480	47	20	0	10	53	55	131	0	0	.235/.325/.356	.261	10.0	.311	-5.2	3B(108): 3.3, 1B(3): -0.2	1.4
2018	*WAS*	*MLB*	*23*	*250*	*26*	*10*	*0*	*8*	*29*	*24*	*80*	*0*	*0*	*.222/.304/.371*	*.227*	*-1.0*	*.305*	*-0.6*	*3B -1, 1B 0*	*-0.2*
2019	*WAS*	*MLB*	*24*	*351*	*43*	*15*	*0*	*11*	*40*	*34*	*111*	*0*	*0*	*.226/.307/.383*	*.245*	*2.0*	*.309*	*-1.0*	*3B -1, 1B 0*	*0.1*

Breakout: 1% Improve: 9% Collapse: 2% Attrition: 7% MLB: 16% *Comparables: Kyle Kubitza, Adam Duvall, Brian Anderson*

The 2013 draft hasn't yet yielded any harvest for Washington to reap: Only one player has made it the big leagues so far, and that's Nick Pivetta, who was traded to Philadelphia a few years ago. Ward was the team's second pick from that class, but the outlook for him producing any major-league fruit soon isn't great. His glove isn't strong and likely won't be enough to let him last at the hot corner, so he'll have to forge his way forward with his bat. This unfortunate circumstance makes it a shame that he didn't progress as much as hoped at the plate in his second go-around at Harrisburg last year. The key to sprouting will be unlocking his power potential, but he'll have to figure it out sooner rather than later, as a team will only try watering the same seed at Double-A so many times.

Jayson Werth LF

Born: 05/20/79 Age: 39 Bats: R Throws: R Height: 6'5" Weight: 235 Origin: Round 1, 1997 Draft (#22 overall)

YEAR	TEAM	LVL	AGE	PA	R	2B	3B	HR	RBI	BB	K	SB	CS	AVG/OBP/SLG	TAv	VORP	BABIP	BRR	FRAA	WARP
2015	SYR	AAA	36	26	2	2	0	0	5	1	2	1	0	.391/.423/.478	.343	2.8	.409	0.0	LF(5): -0.4	0.2
2015	WAS	MLB	36	378	51	16	1	12	42	38	84	0	1	.221/.302/.384	.254	7.2	.253	1.9	LF(76): -8.5, RF(14): -2.1	-0.4
2016	WAS	MLB	37	606	84	28	0	21	69	71	139	5	1	.244/.335/.417	.271	23.9	.288	4.1	LF(131): -6.2, RF(2): 0.0	1.8
2017	WAS	MLB	38	289	35	10	1	10	29	35	69	4	3	.226/.322/.393	.252	2.7	.270	-0.8	LF(51): -1.0, RF(16): -1.0	0.1
2018	*WAS*	*MLB*	*39*	*337*	*46*	*15*	*0*	*12*	*40*	*39*	*73*	*3*	*1*	*.254/.346/.431*	*.258*	*11.5*	*.297*	*1.2*	*LF -4, RF -1*	*0.7*
2019	*WAS*	*MLB*	*40*	*234*	*30*	*10*	*0*	*8*	*28*	*26*	*52*	*2*	*1*	*.244/.333/.406*	*.261*	*6.5*	*.287*	*0.8*	*LF -3, RF -1*	*0.3*

Breakout: 0% Improve: 17% Collapse: 2% Attrition: 8% MLB: 64% *Comparables: Bobby Abreu, Johnny Grubb, Luis Gonzalez*

Werth's nickname of "Werewolf" is most often thought of as a comment on his wild hair, but consider it as a comment on the nature of his seven-year deal with Washington. They knew what they were getting at the beginning, in the metaphorical daytime of the deal—the guy who'd hovered around the 7.0 WARP mark in the two seasons immediately before they signed him. And they expected him to decline as he aged, when night fell; after all, isn't everyone going to get a little less productive and more vulnerable after the sun goes down? But as the moon rose, Werth didn't just become a little less productive. He became something wilder, uglier, harder to handle: say, a werewolf, only injury-ridden and unable to strike fear into the hearts of pitchers. He had fewer plate appearances in 2017 than he'd had in any season since his rookie year of 2003. Now free agency is here, bringing a new day—but Werth is pushing 40, and the night is only getting longer.

Matt Wieters C

Born: 05/21/86 Age: 32 Bats: B Throws: R Height: 6'5" Weight: 230 Origin: Round 1, 2007 Draft (#5 overall)

YEAR	TEAM	LVL	AGE	PA	R	2B	3B	HR	RBI	BB	K	SB	CS	AVG/OBP/SLG	TAv	VORP	BABIP	BRR	FRAA	WARP
2015	BAL	MLB	29	282	24	14	1	8	25	21	67	0	0	.267/.319/.422	.257	8.0	.328	-1.3	C(55): -1.5, 1B(3): -0.1	0.7
2016	BAL	MLB	30	464	48	17	1	17	66	32	85	1	0	.243/.302/.409	.245	12.0	.265	-1.4	C(117): -0.9	1.1
2017	WAS	MLB	31	465	43	20	0	10	52	38	94	1	0	.225/.288/.344	.223	2.0	.264	-1.7	C(118): -12.9	-1.1
2018	*WAS*	*MLB*	*32*	*426*	*48*	*18*	*1*	*13*	*50*	*31*	*83*	*1*	*0*	*.246/.301/.395*	*.237*	*10.1*	*.279*	*-0.8*	*C -11*	*-0.5*
2019	*WAS*	*MLB*	*33*	*422*	*51*	*18*	*0*	*14*	*50*	*35*	*87*	*0*	*0*	*.239/.303/.398*	*.246*	*8.9*	*.271*	*-1.5*	*C -10*	*-0.1*

Breakout: 1% Improve: 42% Collapse: 12% Attrition: 15% MLB: 95% *Comparables: A.J. Pierzynski, Rod Barajas, Javier Valentin*

YEAR	TEAM	P. COUNT	FRM RUNS	BLK RUNS	THRW RUNS	TOT RUNS
2015	BAL	8132	-3.3	-0.6	0.2	-3.7
2015	BOW	405	0.0	0.0	0.0	0.0
2016	BAL	16454	-4.2	1.0	1.9	-1.4
2017	WAS	16476	-13.6	1.2	-0.6	-13.0
2018	*WAS*	*15553*	*-11.3*	*0.6*	*0.1*	*-10.7*
2019	*WAS*	*15392*	*-11.5*	*0.6*	*0.1*	*-10.8*

It's impossible to identify a silver lining in Wieters' dreadful 2017. You can find, uh, a silverish scrap of something that may have been a tiny and fairly inconsequential part of a greater silver lining in an alternate world: the fact that he hit more doubles in 2017 than in 2016. That's it. That's the only thing you can point to if you're trying to make a positive point about Wieters' season. There's nothing else. It was the worst offensive season of his career, and his defense fell apart, too: he ranked 108th out of 110 major-league catchers in FRAA. He activated his player option with the Nationals for 2018, much to their chagrin, but the future after that looks bleak for a catcher who's now weak at the plate and even worse behind it.

Ryan Zimmerman 1B

Born: 09/28/84 Age: 33 Bats: R Throws: R Height: 6'3" Weight: 225 Origin: Round 1, 2005 Draft (#4 overall)

YEAR	TEAM	LVL	AGE	PA	R	2B	3B	HR	RBI	BB	K	SB	CS	AVG/OBP/SLG	TAv	VORP	BABIP	BRR	FRAA	WARP
2015	WAS	MLB	30	390	43	25	1	16	73	33	79	1	0	.249/.308/.465	.283	12.8	.268	0.3	1B(93): -8.5, LF(1): 0.0	0.5
2016	WAS	MLB	31	467	60	18	1	15	46	29	104	4	1	.218/.272/.370	.240	-0.5	.248	4.1	1B(114): -2.1	-0.3
2017	WAS	MLB	32	576	90	33	0	36	108	44	126	1	0	.303/.358/.573	.315	39.3	.335	-0.3	1B(143): -11.4	2.8
2018	*WAS*	*MLB*	*33*	*510*	*64*	*24*	*1*	*22*	*74*	*40*	*108*	*2*	*0*	*.260/.320/.458*	*.263*	*11.6*	*.293*	*-0.8*	*1B -8*	*-0.1*
2019	*WAS*	*MLB*	*34*	*433*	*58*	*20*	*0*	*19*	*60*	*38*	*98*	*1*	*0*	*.255/.322/.453*	*.270*	*10.3*	*.291*	*0.7*	*1B -7*	*0.4*

Breakout: 2% Improve: 33% Collapse: 6% Attrition: 12% MLB: 94% *Comparables: Ty Wigginton, Kendrys Morales, Xavier Nady*

Most of 2016—and sizable parts of 2015 and 2014, too—were rough for Zimmerman. They were only made rougher by the fact that the last few years of his $100 million contract were staring everyone down, in what seemed like it might be a brutal slog for his oft-broken body to make it to the end of 2019. But Zimmerman's 2017 season made those fears look quaint. He was healthy. (For the first time since 2010, he made it through a full season without a trip to the disabled list.) And he was good.

This was his best season at the plate since, again, 2010. He started off hot—like, *burningly* so, entering May as the best hitter in baseball—and managed to stay pretty warm throughout, ultimately hitting just as many home runs in 2017 as he did in the prior three seasons combined. But for all the talk of Daniel Murphy whispering tales of launch angles into his head, Zimmerman actually hit fly balls at a lower rate than 2016. He didn't even hit balls harder on average, as his exit velocity actually decreased by a mile-per-hour—though his 92-mph exit velocity in 2017 was still good for top 10 in the league.

What happened, if you asked the Statcast-happy crowd, was simply a matter of finding more barrels—28 more of them to be exact. More than Freddie Freeman, Jose Abreu or Anthony Rizzo. And if you asked those who watched the Face of the Franchise consistently over the season, they'd say he found the barrel far more often as well. Then they'd ask what the heck that stat meant.

His health will likely remain the trickiest part of the equation, as always, but Zimmerman has now shown that his ability to solve it didn't disappear after turning 30.

PITCHERS

Matt Albers RHP Born: 01/20/83 Age: 35 Bats: L Throws: R Height: 6'1" Weight: 225 Origin: Round 23, 2001 Draft (#686 overall)

YEAR	TEAM	LVL	AGE	W	L	SV	G	GS	IP	H	HR	BB/9	K/9	K	GB%	BABIP	WHIP	ERA	DRA	WARP	MPH	CMD	PWR	STM
2015	CHA	MLB	32	2	0	0	30	0	37^1	31	3	2.2	6.8	28	59%	.259	1.07	1.21	3.52	0.5	93.0	60	45	33
2016	CHA	MLB	33	2	6	0	58	1	51^1	67	10	3.3	5.3	30	50%	.328	1.68	6.31	6.20	-0.7	95.1	55	58	43
2017	WAS	MLB	34	7	2	2	63	0	61	35	6	2.5	9.3	63	52%	.203	0.85	1.62	3.37	1.2	95.4	55	59	46
2018	*WAS*	*MLB*	*35*	*2*	*1*	*1*	*46*	*0*	48^2	*45*	*7*	*3.3*	*8.5*	*46*	*50%*	*.298*	*1.29*	*4.26*	*4.81*	*0.2*	*93.6*	*55*	*55*	*41*
2019	*WAS*	*MLB*	*36*	*2*	*1*	*1*	*38*	*0*	38^2	*35*	*6*	*3.6*	*8.5*	*37*	*50%*	*.301*	*1.30*	*4.47*	*5.10*	*0.0*	*93.3*	*54*	*57*	*42*

Breakout: 23% Improve: 41% Collapse: 20% Attrition: 8% MLB: 71% *Comparables: Matt Lindstrom, Matt Guerrier, Javier Lopez*

After posting the worst numbers of his career in 2016, Albers ended up as a non-roster invitee for the Nationals and started 2017 in the minors. But by the middle of April, he was carving out a role in the big-league bullpen, and by the end of June, he was by far the best part of a relief corps that was reliable only in its consistent unreliability. Even after the team's trade deadline bullpen makeover, Albers kept logging innings and performing well. Working a fastball into his sinker/slider repertoire helped him notch the highest strikeout rate of his career. "Call him the Michelin Man, Humpty Dumpty, whatever," an anonymous scout told ESPN in September, referencing continued Fat Albers jokes about the reliever's physique. "The bottom line is, he performs." That he does.

Joe Blanton RHP Born: 12/11/80 Age: 37 Bats: R Throws: R Height: 6'3" Weight: 225 Origin: Round 1, 2002 Draft (#24 overall)

YEAR	TEAM	LVL	AGE	W	L	SV	G	GS	IP	H	HR	BB/9	K/9	K	GB%	BABIP	WHIP	ERA	DRA	WARP	MPH	CMD	PWR	STM
2015	OMA	AAA	34	3	2	0	7	6	39^1	34	7	2.3	6.9	30	42%	.239	1.12	3.89	2.23	1.4				
2015	KCA	MLB	34	2	2	2	15	4	41^2	43	6	1.5	8.6	40	50%	.311	1.20	3.89	4.07	0.4	93.2	64	34	54
2015	PIT	MLB	34	5	0	0	21	0	34^1	26	1	2.4	10.2	39	50%	.287	1.02	1.57	2.49	0.9	93.1	64	34	54
2016	LAN	MLB	35	7	2	0	75	0	80	55	7	2.9	9.0	80	34%	.240	1.01	2.47	3.36	1.5	93.4	55	30	54
2017	WAS	MLB	36	2	4	0	51	0	44^1	53	10	2.6	7.9	39	34%	.326	1.49	5.68	5.74	-0.3	92.0	41	27	40
2018	*WAS*	*MLB*	*37*	*2*	*1*	*0*	*33*	*2*	*44*	*45*	*7*	*3.4*	*8.3*	*41*	*39%*	*.312*	*1.40*	*4.60*	*5.20*	*0.1*	*91.5*	*52*	*29*	*47*
2019	*WAS*	*MLB*	*38*	*3*	*2*	*0*	*53*	*3*	78^2	*79*	*13*	*3.6*	*8.2*	*72*	*39%*	*.316*	*1.41*	*4.88*	*5.56*	*-0.2*	*90.9*	*48*	*28*	*45*

Breakout: 16% Improve: 40% Collapse: 19% Attrition: 12% MLB: 76% *Comparables: Chan Ho Park, Chris Capuano, Darren Oliver*

After Blanton engineered a career revival as a surprisingly effective reliever by throwing his slider more in 2016, he lingered on the free agent market for what seemed like a weirdly long time. Finally, the Nationals picked him up in March. Their patience was not rewarded. Blanton was worse by just about every measure last season, including a huge uptick in home runs, as he allowed more per nine innings in 2017 than he had in 2015 and 2016 combined. He struggled with his slider early in the season, dropping it as his top pitch in favor of his 90-mph fastball, which worked as well as you'd expect for a reliever on the wrong side of 35. Blanton rediscovered the slider in the second half, and with it some measure of effectiveness, leaving room for the hope of a continued big-league future.

A.J. Cole RHP Born: 01/05/92 Age: 26 Bats: R Throws: R Height: 6'5" Weight: 215 Origin: Round 4, 2010 Draft (#116 overall)

YEAR	TEAM	LVL	AGE	W	L	SV	G	GS	IP	H	HR	BB/9	K/9	K	GB%	BABIP	WHIP	ERA	DRA	WARP	MPH	CMD	PWR	STM
2015	WAS	MLB	23	0	0	1	3	1	9^1	14	1	1.0	8.7	9	41%	.394	1.61	5.79	5.70	-0.1	93.5			55
2015	SYR	AAA	23	5	6	0	21	19	105^2	91	9	2.9	6.5	76	36%	.256	1.18	3.15	6.45	-1.4				
2016	SYR	AAA	24	8	8	0	22	22	124^2	131	16	2.5	7.9	109	43%	.310	1.33	4.26	4.20	1.6				
2016	WAS	MLB	24	1	2	0	8	8	38^1	37	7	3.3	9.2	39	32%	.283	1.33	5.17	5.21	0.1	93.4	64	43	69
2017	SYR	AAA	25	4	5	0	18	18	93^1	127	7	3.5	7.6	79	42%	.390	1.75	5.88	7.05	-1.4				
2017	WAS	MLB	25	3	5	0	11	8	52	51	8	4.7	7.6	44	45%	.293	1.50	3.81	5.31	0.1	95.1	45	47	68
2018	*WAS*	*MLB*	*26*	*5*	*5*	*0*	*49*	*10*	*91*	*98*	*14*	*3.7*	*8.0*	*81*	*40%*	*.306*	*1.50*	*4.71*	*4.87*	*0.2*	*94.0*	*53*	*46*	*66*
2019	*WAS*	*MLB*	*27*	*6*	*5*	*0*	*66*	*12*	127^1	*124*	*19*	*3.4*	*8.3*	*117*	*40%*	*.312*	*1.35*	*4.55*	*5.19*	*0.3*	*93.7*	*53*	*46*	*68*

Breakout: 20% Improve: 39% Collapse: 22% Attrition: 43% MLB: 73% *Comparables: Kyle Lobstein, Sean Gilmartin, Brad Lincoln*

After four years on our Top 101 Prospects list and three years in which he was eligible but didn't make the cut, A.J. Cole finally did it—he exhausted his rookie eligibility in 2017. But, like just about everything else in his career so far, he did so far more slowly and a little less successfully than he would have preferred. Rather than contending for the season-long rotation spot that had seemed possible for him at the start of spring training, he started the year at Triple-A and didn't see any serious major-league action until a series of mostly shaky starts as an injury replacement in August, followed by some bullpen experience in September. Cole turned 26 in January, and it may be time to temper expectations that he will develop into a mid-rotation starter. But maybe he and his fastball/slider combo—the former of which now sits around 93 mph, a few ticks slower than it was in his younger years, but the latter of which managed to garner whiffs on 40 percent of its swings—can find success in relief.

Wil Crowe RHP Born: 09/09/94 Age: 23 Bats: R Throws: R Height: 6'2" Weight: 240 Origin: Round 2, 2017 Draft (#65 overall)

YEAR	TEAM	LVL	AGE	W	L	SV	G	GS	IP	H	HR	BB/9	K/9	K	GB%	BABIP	WHIP	ERA	DRA	WARP	MPH	CMD	PWR	STM
2017	AUB	A-	22	0	0	0	7	7	20^{2}	18	3	1.3	6.5	15	52%	.250	1.02	2.61	2.37	0.7				
2018	*WAS*	*MLB*	*23*	*2*	*3*	*0*	*9*	*9*	33^{2}	*40*	*9*	*3.9*	*7.8*	*29*	*41%*	*.323*	*1.63*	*6.39*	*7.23*	*-0.6*				
2019	*WAS*	*MLB*	*24*	*4*	*9*	*0*	*28*	*28*	*168*	*184*	*34*	*4.4*	*7.3*	*137*	*41%*	*.322*	*1.59*	*5.84*	*6.67*	*-1.2*				

Breakout: 0% Improve: 0% Collapse: 1% Attrition: 1% MLB: 1% *Comparables: Dillon Peters, Joseph Mantiply, Amir Garrett*

The University of South Carolina product's name offers good pun opportunities, no matter how his career shakes out. If it goes well—which, for him, would mean becoming something like a no. 3 starter—then the Nationals wil(l) crow(e) about their foresight. If it doesn't, they wil(l) eat crow(e). Choosing Crowe in the second round of the 2017 draft meant banking on him making a full recovery from the Tommy John surgery that sidelined him for all of 2016. But he made substantial progress on that front in his junior season at South Carolina and continued to do so in his brief stint at Low-A. Washington hasn't previously shied away from committing to pitching prospects with Tommy John on their résumé—think Jesus Luzardo, Erick Fedde and Lucas Giolito—and Crowe, who can hit 97 mph with his fastball and has a decent slider and curve, too, hopes to make them feel good about this one.

Sean Doolittle LHP Born: 09/26/86 Age: 31 Bats: L Throws: L Height: 6'2" Weight: 210 Origin: Round 1, 2007 Draft (#41 overall)

YEAR	TEAM	LVL	AGE	W	L	SV	G	GS	IP	H	HR	BB/9	K/9	K	GB%	BABIP	WHIP	ERA	DRA	WARP	MPH	CMD	PWR	STM
2015	OAK	MLB	28	1	0	4	12	0	13^{2}	12	1	3.3	9.9	15	35%	.306	1.24	3.95	5.13	-0.1	95.0	54	64	18
2016	OAK	MLB	29	2	3	4	44	0	39	33	6	1.8	10.4	45	33%	.281	1.05	3.23	3.80	0.5	97.5	61	71	35
2017	OAK	MLB	30	1	0	3	23	0	21^{1}	12	3	0.8	13.1	31	37%	.209	0.66	3.38	2.47	0.6	95.9	67	73	42
2017	WAS	MLB	30	1	0	21	30	0	30	22	2	2.4	9.3	31	28%	.260	1.00	2.40	3.04	0.7	96.3	67	73	42
2018	*WAS*	*MLB*	*31*	*3*	*3*	*32*	*54*	*0*	*57*	*52*	*10*	*3.3*	*10.4*	*66*	*34%*	*.294*	*1.28*	*4.02*	*4.25*	*0.4*	*95.6*	*63*	*71*	*33*
2019	*WAS*	*MLB*	*32*	*3*	*1*	*26*	*54*	*0*	57^{2}	*49*	*10*	*3.0*	*10.8*	*69*	*34%*	*.301*	*1.18*	*4.15*	*4.74*	*0.3*	*95.2*	*64*	*71*	*36*

Breakout: 24% Improve: 41% Collapse: 29% Attrition: 8% MLB: 92% *Comparables: Sergio Romo, Jonathan Papelbon, Keith Foulke*

Doolittle actually did quite a lot in 2017. (Sorry.) Though he spent a month on the disabled list with a shoulder strain, he still had a cleaner bill of health than he'd had in ages—last season was the first time he'd crossed the 50-inning threshold since 2014. After being traded to Washington, he secured the closer's spot and brought some much-needed stability to a team whose previous use of a closer-by-committee strategy had been a mess. He even found time to get married in-season! (They eloped on an off-day.) The Nationals should be happy to continue keeping him busy in 2018.

Erick Fedde RHP Born: 02/25/93 Age: 25 Bats: R Throws: R Height: 6'4" Weight: 180 Origin: Round 1, 2014 Draft (#18 overall)

YEAR	TEAM	LVL	AGE	W	L	SV	G	GS	IP	H	HR	BB/9	K/9	K	GB%	BABIP	WHIP	ERA	DRA	WARP	MPH	CMD	PWR	STM
2015	AUB	A-	22	4	1	0	8	8	35	38	1	2.1	9.3	36	56%	.346	1.31	2.57	1.57	1.5				
2015	HAG	A	22	1	2	0	6	6	29	24	1	2.5	7.1	23	52%	.274	1.10	4.34	3.36	0.6				
2016	POT	A+	23	6	4	0	18	17	91^{2}	85	7	1.9	9.3	95	51%	.316	1.13	2.85	1.27	4.4				
2016	HAR	AA	23	2	1	0	5	5	29^{1}	33	1	3.1	8.6	28	46%	.360	1.47	3.99	4.09	0.4				
2017	HAR	AA	24	3	3	0	17	7	56^{1}	45	4	2.9	8.6	54	52%	.272	1.12	3.04	1.81	2.2				
2017	SYR	AAA	24	1	2	0	12	6	34	37	3	1.3	6.6	25	62%	.315	1.24	4.76	1.76	1.4				
2017	WAS	MLB	24	0	1	0	3	3	15^{1}	25	5	4.7	8.8	15	65%	.426	2.15	9.39	4.64	0.2	95.4	62	53	56
2018	*WAS*	*MLB*	*25*	*5*	*5*	*0*	*16*	*16*	*80*	*83*	*12*	*3.4*	*8.1*	*72*	*48%*	*.302*	*1.44*	*4.41*	*4.70*	*0.4*	*95.1*	*63*	*54*	*57*
2019	*WAS*	*MLB*	*26*	*9*	*11*	*0*	*31*	*31*	197^{1}	*191*	*27*	*3.1*	*8.1*	*177*	*48%*	*.316*	*1.31*	*4.29*	*4.89*	*1.3*	*94.8*	*64*	*54*	*58*

Breakout: 17% Improve: 41% Collapse: 19% Attrition: 52% MLB: 75% *Comparables: Anthony DeSclafani, A.J. Cole, Luis Cessa*

Chaucer once wrote that patience is a conquering virtue. The Nationals have shown that patience conquers all other virtues for their pitching prospects. Fedde is an example of this: A newly minted Tommy John survivor when he became the team's first-round pick in 2014, he has gradually been moving through the system since. In 2017, he got his first look at both Triple-A and the big leagues. The latter didn't go especially well, but the showing was limited—he was shut down early with a forearm strain, meaning that he ultimately came away with the disheartening descriptor of having pitched fewer innings in 2017 than 2016. There's still plenty of reason for hope, though. There's life to his fastball, there are two solid secondary offerings and the fifth-starter's role in Washington is wide open.

Koda Glover RHP Born: 04/13/93 Age: 25 Bats: R Throws: R Height: 6'5" Weight: 225 Origin: Round 8, 2015 Draft (#254 overall)

YEAR	TEAM	LVL	AGE	W	L	SV	G	GS	IP	H	HR	BB/9	K/9	K	GB%	BABIP	WHIP	ERA	DRA	WARP	MPH	CMD	PWR	STM
2015	HAG	A	22	1	1	4	16	0	24	21	2	0.4	10.1	27	43%	.288	0.92	2.25	1.43	1.0				
2016	HAR	AA	23	2	0	4	17	0	22^{1}	20	1	2.8	11.7	29	46%	.339	1.21	3.22	2.72	0.5				
2016	SYR	AAA	23	1	1	2	16	0	24	16	2	1.1	8.2	22	52%	.233	0.79	2.25	2.95	0.6				
2016	WAS	MLB	23	2	0	0	19	0	19^{2}	15	3	3.2	7.3	16	42%	.214	1.12	5.03	4.65	0.1	99.0	46	55	48
2017	WAS	MLB	24	0	1	8	23	0	19^{1}	20	1	1.9	7.9	17	44%	.328	1.24	5.12	4.01	0.2	97.8	47	54	39
2018	*WAS*	*MLB*	*25*	*2*	*2*	*0*	*39*	*0*	*41*	*40*	*6*	*3.5*	*9.2*	*42*	*43%*	*.301*	*1.36*	*4.06*	*4.28*	*0.3*	*98.0*	*48*	*56*	*44*
2019	*WAS*	*MLB*	*26*	*2*	*1*	*0*	*41*	*0*	43^{2}	*41*	*7*	*3.5*	*9.3*	*45*	*43%*	*.317*	*1.34*	*4.52*	*5.16*	*0.0*	*97.7*	*48*	*56*	*44*

Breakout: 22% Improve: 38% Collapse: 32% Attrition: 46% MLB: 83% *Comparables: Kyle Crockett, Chris Britton, Dominic Leone*

A Glover hasn't been unseated this forcefully since Yara Greyjoy took Deepwood Motte. After making his way through Dusty's committee in the second half of May, the power reliever glided through five save situations before the calendar flipped, only allowing one baserunner. But things went terribly wrong in June, as Glover allowed seven runs in two innings—the last two he'd throw in Washington last year. He landed on the DL in mid-June with lower back stiffness—supposedly acquired while reaching for body wash in the shower—and then developed severe rotator cuff inflammation that sidelined him for the remainder of the season. Glover routinely sits at 97 with his fastball and has a killer slider, but whether he can be reliable enough to make those things work remains to be seen.

Gio Gonzalez LHP Born: 09/19/85 Age: 32 Bats: R Throws: L Height: 6'0" Weight: 205 Origin: Round 1, 2004 Draft (#38 overall)

YEAR	TEAM	LVL	AGE	W	L	SV	G	GS	IP	H	HR	BB/9	K/9	K	GB%	BABIP	WHIP	ERA	DRA	WARP	MPH	CMD	PWR	STM
2015	WAS	MLB	29	11	8	0	31	31	175^2	181	8	3.5	8.7	169	55%	.341	1.42	3.79	4.14	2.0	94.4	68	48	72
2016	WAS	MLB	30	11	11	0	32	32	177^1	179	19	3.0	8.7	171	49%	.316	1.34	4.57	4.21	2.3	93.7	63	46	78
2017	WAS	MLB	31	15	9	0	32	32	201	158	21	3.5	8.4	188	48%	.258	1.18	2.96	3.35	5.0	91.4	62	28	82
2018	*WAS*	*MLB*	*32*	*12*	*9*	*0*	*29*	*29*	*174*	*168*	*22*	*3.4*	*8.5*	*164*	*49%*	*.298*	*1.34*	*4.01*	*4.27*	*1.8*	*91.9*	*63*	*38*	*77*
2019	*WAS*	*MLB*	*33*	*11*	*11*	*0*	*32*	*32*	*205^2*	*179*	*23*	*3.1*	*8.6*	*198*	*49%*	*.302*	*1.22*	*3.84*	*4.38*	*2.6*	*91.1*	*62*	*36*	*78*

Breakout: 13% Improve: 35% Collapse: 31% Attrition: 13% MLB: 89% *Comparables: Justin Verlander, Clay Buchholz, Zack Greinke*

"Consistency is contrary to nature, contrary to life." That's an old Aldous Huxley quote, but it could've just as well been Gio. Famously erratic from start to start, Gonzalez enjoyed another year where each outing seemed just as likely to be a no-hitter as it did a meltdown—but he was often much closer to the former than the latter in 2017, his best campaign in several years. (And his healthiest, too: This was the first time he'd topped 200 innings since coming to Washington.) Even with a few ticks gone from his fastball, Gonzalez found success, in part from using his changeup more while cutting back on his two-seamer, throwing it just 25 percent of the time last year compared to 35 percent in 2016. This will be his walk year, but if he can just not take the saying too literally, there should be good things ahead.

Matt Grace LHP Born: 12/14/88 Age: 29 Bats: L Throws: L Height: 6'4" Weight: 215 Origin: Round 8, 2010 Draft (#236 overall)

YEAR	TEAM	LVL	AGE	W	L	SV	G	GS	IP	H	HR	BB/9	K/9	K	GB%	BABIP	WHIP	ERA	DRA	WARP	MPH	CMD	PWR	STM
2015	SYR	AAA	26	0	2	1	38	0	48^2	43	1	3.0	5.7	31	64%	.280	1.21	2.40	5.37	-0.2				
2015	WAS	MLB	26	2	1	0	26	0	17	26	0	4.2	7.4	14	59%	.426	2.00	4.24	5.12	-0.1	93.9	60	50	49
2016	SYR	AAA	27	1	3	1	35	0	47^1	54	1	1.7	6.1	32	66%	.338	1.33	2.85	4.40	0.3				
2016	WAS	MLB	27	0	0	0	5	0	3	1	0	0.0	12.0	4	67%	.167	0.33	0.00	3.43	0.1	91.6			36
2017	SYR	AAA	28	1	3	0	13	1	19^2	21	2	3.7	9.6	21	61%	.345	1.47	3.66	2.59	0.6				
2017	WAS	MLB	28	1	0	2	40	1	50	50	3	3.2	5.6	31	63%	.294	1.36	4.32	5.40	-0.1	92.6	42	48	47
2018	*WAS*	*MLB*	*29*	*2*	*2*	*0*	*39*	*0*	*41*	*45*	*5*	*3.7*	*6.8*	*31*	*57%*	*.306*	*1.52*	*4.70*	*4.77*	*0.1*	*92.1*	*45*	*48*	*44*
2019	*WAS*	*MLB*	*30*	*2*	*1*	*0*	*40*	*0*	*42*	*44*	*6*	*3.5*	*7.0*	*33*	*57%*	*.325*	*1.45*	*4.66*	*5.31*	*-0.1*	*91.6*	*43*	*48*	*43*

Breakout: 28% Improve: 38% Collapse: 23% Attrition: 26% MLB: 65% *Comparables: Dan Otero, Kevin Cameron, Ryan Speier*

Amazing? No. Of God? Nah. Mark? Nope. This Grace is none of the above, but he's still managed to carve out space for himself as a decent left-handed bullpen depth piece. His game is wholly unsexy—as is usually true of sinker-heavy, low-strikeout guys—but he stayed healthy last year while putting together a perfectly adequate performance during low-leverage innings. That may not sound like much, but it mattered for a bullpen as unstable and injury-stricken as the Nationals' was during the first half of last year. It's not exciting, but neither is the concept of grace itself—and it's still a virtue all the same.

Edwin Jackson RHP Born: 09/09/83 Age: 34 Bats: R Throws: R Height: 6'2" Weight: 215 Origin: Round 6, 2001 Draft (#190 overall)

YEAR	TEAM	LVL	AGE	W	L	SV	G	GS	IP	H	HR	BB/9	K/9	K	GB%	BABIP	WHIP	ERA	DRA	WARP	MPH	CMD	PWR	STM
2015	CHN	MLB	31	2	1	0	23	0	31	30	0	3.5	6.7	23	46%	.306	1.35	3.19	4.26	0.2	97.2	35	58	40
2015	ATL	MLB	31	2	2	1	24	0	24^2	14	4	3.3	6.2	17	35%	.156	0.93	2.92	3.40	0.4	96.7	35	58	40
2016	MIA	MLB	32	0	1	0	8	0	10^2	13	2	5.1	5.9	7	35%	.344	1.78	5.91	6.09	-0.1	95.4	34	53	43
2016	ELP	AAA	32	0	1	0	3	3	12^2	20	2	4.3	6.4	9	40%	.375	2.05	7.11	11.95	-1.0				
2016	SDN	MLB	32	5	6	0	13	13	73^1	79	12	4.3	6.6	54	42%	.299	1.55	5.89	6.71	-1.2	94.6	34	53	43
2017	NOR	AAA	33	0	0	2	12	1	20^1	20	1	4.4	7.5	17	33%	.339	1.48	3.10	5.45	0.0				
2017	BAL	MLB	33	0	0	0	3	0	5	11	2	7.2	3.6	2	30%	.429	3.00	7.20	5.80	0.0	93.6	42	57	60
2017	SYR	AAA	33	2	0	0	5	4	20^1	9	0	4.4	9.7	22	51%	.191	0.93	0.44	5.41	0.0				
2017	WAS	MLB	33	5	6	0	13	13	71	75	18	3.2	7.4	58	40%	.273	1.41	5.07	7.08	-1.2	95.7	42	57	60
2018	*WAS*	*MLB*	*34*	*5*	*5*	*0*	*34*	*14*	*94*	*105*	*17*	*3.9*	*7.8*	*82*	*41%*	*.325*	*1.55*	*5.14*	*5.81*	*-0.3*	*94.4*	*37*	*55*	*49*
2019	*WAS*	*MLB*	*35*	*4*	*5*	*0*	*28*	*12*	*92^2*	*103*	*16*	*3.9*	*7.4*	*76*	*41%*	*.332*	*1.54*	*5.19*	*5.92*	*-0.4*	*93.6*	*37*	*54*	*50*

Breakout: 13% Improve: 33% Collapse: 25% Attrition: 17% MLB: 71% *Comparables: Chan Ho Park, Eric Milton, Paul Wilson*

If you were to drive, one by one in order, to all of the home ballparks that Jackson has been traded to, you'd be driving for more than 16,000 miles. (In the interest of saving you hypothetical gas money, we're ignoring the few hours during which he was technically a member of the Blue Jays between two trades at the 2011 deadline.) That's two-thirds the circumference of the earth—or far enough to carry him through the layers of the atmosphere and seven percent of the way to the moon. But for a while it appeared as though Jackson may have found some solid ground in DC, with a surprisingly strong July and August that made it look like there was reason for him to stick around. A poor September reminded everyone why he has spent so much time hopping around, but his season still provided a little something to add to his résumé. That is, a little something beyond the fact that he's seeking one more franchise to tie Octavio Dotel's record for most MLB jerseys donned.

Shawn Kelley RHP Born: 04/26/84 Age: 34 Bats: R Throws: R Height: 6'2" Weight: 230 Origin: Round 13, 2007 Draft (#405 overall)

YEAR	TEAM	LVL	AGE	W	L	SV	G	GS	IP	H	HR	BB/9	K/9	K	GB%	BABIP	WHIP	ERA	DRA	WARP	MPH	CMD	PWR	STM
2015	SDN	MLB	31	2	2	0	53	0	51^1	41	4	2.6	11.0	63	44%	.301	1.09	2.45	3.21	0.9	94.4	51	38	43
2016	WAS	MLB	32	3	2	7	67	0	58	41	9	1.7	12.4	80	37%	.258	0.90	2.64	2.73	1.5	95.2	57	47	46
2017	WAS	MLB	33	3	2	4	33	0	26	29	12	3.8	8.7	25	26%	.236	1.54	7.27	6.71	-0.4	93.9	51	44	33
2018	*WAS*	*MLB*	*34*	*3*	*3*	*0*	*54*	*0*	*57*	*62*	*15*	*3.9*	*9.5*	*60*	*38%*	*.301*	*1.53*	*6.09*	*6.05*	*-0.8*	*93.5*	*53*	*43*	*39*
2019	*WAS*	*MLB*	*35*	*2*	*0*	*0*	*35*	*0*	*37*	*37*	*8*	*3.7*	*9.3*	*38*	*38%*	*.315*	*1.42*	*5.41*	*6.17*	*-0.4*	*92.9*	*53*	*44*	*38*

Breakout: 19% Improve: 38% Collapse: 23% Attrition: 11% MLB: 85% *Comparables: Octavio Dotel, Paul Assenmacher, Randy Myers*

Kelley had high hopes to end 2016, after posting the best season of his career (and the heaviest workload). It didn't take long in 2017 for those hopes to fall significantly lower. He was tabbed as the most likely option for the closer's role at the start of spring training, but concerns about his injury history shelved those. (It's hard to find a good way to spin "double Tommy John survivor.") A few weeks into the year, Kelley got his shot at the closer's spot after all—or, at least, his shot at part of it, as the team announced that he'd be sharing the role with Koda Glover. He didn't do much with the part he got. His velo was down; he was throwing his best pitch, his slider, less often and less effectively; he was allowing an obscene number of home runs (the highest rate in franchise history for a pitcher with more than 10 innings pitched). He also made several trips to the disabled list. If Kelley wants much of a future past this upcoming final year of his contract, he'll need to shave at least three runs off his ERA and three home runs off his HR/9.

Brandon Kintzler RHP Born: 08/01/84 Age: 33 Bats: R Throws: R Height: 6'0" Weight: 190 Origin: Round 40, 2004 Draft (#1182 overall)

YEAR	TEAM	LVL	AGE	W	L	SV	G	GS	IP	H	HR	BB/9	K/9	K	GB%	BABIP	WHIP	ERA	DRA	WARP	MPH	CMD	PWR	STM
2015	MIL	MLB	30	0	1	0	7	0	7	12	1	6.4	9.0	7	67%	.478	2.43	6.43	2.44	0.2	92.9			23
2015	CSP	AAA	30	1	1	0	17	0	19	23	0	1.9	6.6	14	71%	.365	1.42	5.21	3.90	0.2				
2016	ROC	AAA	31	4	1	0	10	0	15^1	15	0	1.8	6.5	11	56%	.326	1.17	3.52	3.72	0.2				
2016	MIN	MLB	31	0	2	17	54	0	54^1	59	5	1.3	5.8	35	63%	.310	1.23	3.15	3.24	1.1	95.2	75	68	48
2017	MIN	MLB	32	2	2	28	45	0	45^1	41	3	2.2	5.4	27	54%	.273	1.15	2.78	4.80	0.2	95.1	61	68	51
2017	WAS	MLB	32	2	1	1	27	0	26	25	2	1.7	4.2	12	57%	.267	1.15	3.46	5.75	-0.2	94.7	61	68	51
2018	*WAS*	*MLB*	*33*	*3*	*2*	*2*	*49*	*0*	*51*	*57*	*7*	*3.3*	*5.8*	*33*	*55%*	*.303*	*1.48*	*4.79*	*4.84*	*0.0*	*93.9*	*65*	*67*	*42*
2019	*WAS*	*MLB*	*34*	*2*	*1*	*1*	*44*	*0*	*46^2*	*48*	*6*	*2.9*	*6.1*	*31*	*55%*	*.309*	*1.35*	*4.65*	*5.29*	*0.0*	*93.5*	*65*	*67*	*46*

Breakout: 23% Improve: 40% Collapse: 25% Attrition: 9% MLB: 78% *Comparables: Burke Badenhop, Brad Ziegler, Ronald Belisario*

Kintzler was never your typical closer: partly because he's an indy-league vet who once chose pitching in the American Association's All-Star Game over fulfilling the contract he'd signed to play Tim Hudson in the *Moneyball* movie, but mostly because he's a sinkerballer who'd be lucky to strike out six-per-nine for a season. Despite being such an unconventional fit for the role, he thrived as the ninth-inning man in Minnesota. A deadline trade to DC meant shifting to a setup role—and while he didn't shine quite as brightly there, he still did well enough to assure a future for himself in free agency. A richer future than someone who was once about to pack up for Hollywood could've imagined, even.

Ryan Madson RHP Born: 08/28/80 Age: 37 Bats: L Throws: R Height: 6'6" Weight: 225 Origin: Round 9, 1998 Draft (#254 overall)

YEAR	TEAM	LVL	AGE	W	L	SV	G	GS	IP	H	HR	BB/9	K/9	K	GB%	BABIP	WHIP	ERA	DRA	WARP	MPH	CMD	PWR	STM
2015	KCA	MLB	34	1	2	3	68	0	63^1	47	5	2.0	8.2	58	56%	.249	0.96	2.13	2.74	1.5	97.0	48	61	48
2016	OAK	MLB	35	6	7	30	63	0	64^2	63	7	2.8	6.8	49	48%	.292	1.28	3.62	3.85	0.8	96.9	48	61	46
2017	OAK	MLB	36	2	4	1	40	0	39^1	25	2	1.4	8.9	39	57%	.242	0.79	2.06	3.07	0.9	96.6	54	63	44
2017	WAS	MLB	36	3	0	1	20	0	19^2	13	0	1.4	12.8	28	55%	.310	0.81	1.37	3.03	0.5	97.9	54	63	44
2018	*WAS*	*MLB*	*37*	*3*	*2*	*7*	*54*	*0*	*57*	*53*	*6*	*3.2*	*8.7*	*55*	*50%*	*.299*	*1.29*	*3.64*	*3.93*	*0.6*	*95.5*	*49*	*60*	*45*
2019	*WAS*	*MLB*	*38*	*3*	*1*	*4*	*56*	*0*	*59^2*	*52*	*7*	*3.0*	*8.8*	*58*	*50%*	*.302*	*1.20*	*3.83*	*4.37*	*0.5*	*94.8*	*49*	*60*	*44*

Breakout: 19% Improve: 31% Collapse: 33% Attrition: 17% MLB: 84% *Comparables: J.J. Putz, Francisco Cordero, Matt Thornton*

Madson and Sean Doolittle came to Washington in the same midsummer trade, and the pair swiftly helped turn the bullpen around. It's easy for Doolittle, who ended up taking over the closer's spot, to get the bulk of the credit here—but Madson was way more than a footnote. After using the first half to bounce back from a somewhat lackluster 2016, he bounced even higher following the trade. Velocity issues had been primarily responsible for his struggles the season before, but he figured out a way to make things work in 2017 by relying on his sinker more than his four-seamer for the first time in a decade. Under contract for one more year, he should resume setup man responsibilities, a role he is familiar with and, frankly, has been overqualified for throughout his career.

Oliver Perez LHP Born: 08/15/81 Age: 36 Bats: L Throws: L Height: 6'3" Weight: 225 Origin: International Free Agent, 1999

YEAR	TEAM	LVL	AGE	W	L	SV	G	GS	IP	H	HR	BB/9	K/9	K	GB%	BABIP	WHIP	ERA	DRA	WARP	MPH	CMD	PWR	STM
2015	ARI	MLB	33	2	1	0	48	0	29	25	2	3.4	11.5	37	45%	.311	1.24	3.10	4.10	0.2	94.8	62	42	46
2015	HOU	MLB	33	0	3	0	22	0	12	14	2	3.0	10.5	14	32%	.343	1.50	6.75	4.59	0.0	94.6	62	42	46
2016	WAS	MLB	34	2	3	0	64	0	40	38	4	4.5	10.4	46	43%	.324	1.45	4.95	4.81	0.1	94.3	38	41	41
2017	WAS	MLB	35	0	0	1	50	0	33	32	4	3.3	10.6	39	32%	.333	1.33	4.64	4.31	0.3	94.6	54	42	36
2018	*WAS*	*MLB*	*36*	*2*	*1*	*1*	*33*	*0*	*35*	*33*	*5*	*3.9*	*10.2*	*40*	*40%*	*.325*	*1.39*	*4.36*	*4.94*	*0.1*	*93.2*	*49*	*41*	*39*
2019	*WAS*	*MLB*	*37*	*2*	*1*	*1*	*53*	*0*	*36^2*	*37*	*7*	*4.1*	*9.6*	*39*	*40%*	*.333*	*1.46*	*5.11*	*5.84*	*-0.3*	*92.5*	*46*	*40*	*38*

Breakout: 25% Improve: 45% Collapse: 20% Attrition: 7% MLB: 77% *Comparables: Francisco Cordero, Jim Brewer, Michael Gonzalez*

Perez's career—the origins of which predate this iteration of the Washington Nationals themselves by several seasons—is a testament to just how far left-handedness can take you. Some might say that becoming a mediocre starter converted to a mediocre bullpen arm isn't really going that far at all, but when your biggest positive trait apart from "southpaw" is "has a pulse," that's something. In fairness, the fact that Perez is stuck eating low-leverage innings (and therefore facing as many righties as lefties) means his numbers are considerably worse than they'd be if he could work as the left-handed specialist he used to be, but, hey, life's not fair. Snark aside, the last few years have seen him demonstrate that an old dog can make new adjustments, depending on his four-seamer less, his sinker and slider more. But that change hasn't exactly revolutionized his results, so expect more of the same: for him to be a left-hander with a pulse.

Tanner Roark RHP Born: 10/05/86 Age: 31 Bats: R Throws: R Height: 6'2" Weight: 235 Origin: Round 25, 2008 Draft (#753 overall)

YEAR	TEAM	LVL	AGE	W	L	SV	G	GS	IP	H	HR	BB/9	K/9	K	GB%	BABIP	WHIP	ERA	DRA	WARP	MPH	CMD	PWR	STM
2015	WAS	MLB	28	4	7	1	40	12	111	119	17	2.1	5.7	70	49%	.293	1.31	4.38	5.34	-0.5	95.6	48	54	54
2016	WAS	MLB	29	16	10	0	34	33	210	173	17	3.1	7.4	172	51%	.269	1.17	2.83	4.06	3.1	94.7	57	50	83
2017	WAS	MLB	30	13	11	0	32	30	181^1	178	23	3.2	8.2	166	49%	.300	1.33	4.67	4.10	2.9	94.3	62	45	79
2018	*WAS*	*MLB*	*31*	*12*	*10*	*0*	*39*	*29*	*175^2*	*169*	*22*	*3.1*	*7.5*	*147*	*49%*	*.288*	*1.29*	*4.11*	*4.37*	*1.6*	*93.8*	*58*	*48*	*74*
2019	*WAS*	*MLB*	*32*	*10*	*11*	*0*	*31*	*31*	*197*	*179*	*22*	*3.1*	*7.8*	*171*	*49%*	*.303*	*1.26*	*4.03*	*4.59*	*2.0*	*93.3*	*59*	*47*	*77*

Breakout: 11% Improve: 30% Collapse: 33% Attrition: 6% MLB: 89% *Comparables: Alexi Ogando, Johnny Cueto, Doug Fister*

Though he didn't live up to his standout 2016 from a Cy Young Award voter standpoint (or an ERA standpoint), Roark continued to give the

Nationals the same mid-rotation performance they should have been expecting. He struggled more with giving up homers and generally pitching to Matt Wieters but still showed that deception and diverse pitch selection can compensate for a lack of naturally great stuff. Plus, he passed Carl Lundgren and Big Jeff Pfeffer (who ironically was smaller than Roark) to move into fourth place on the all-time strikeout list for pitchers out of the University of Illinois. Not bad for a guy once traded for Cristian Guzman.

Enny Romero LHP Born: 01/24/91 Age: 27 Bats: R Throws: L Height: 6'3" Weight: 215 Origin: International Free Agent, 2008

YEAR	TEAM	LVL	AGE	W	L	SV	G	GS	IP	H	HR	BB/9	K/9	K	GB%	BABIP	WHIP	ERA	DRA	WARP	MPH	CMD	PWR	STM
2015	DUR	AAA	24	1	1	1	17	3	46^1	48	5	3.3	8.7	45	44%	.326	1.40	4.86	4.40	0.3				
2015	TBA	MLB	24	0	2	0	23	0	30	39	1	3.9	9.3	31	49%	.400	1.73	5.10	4.82	0.0	98.8	44	74	51
2016	TBA	MLB	25	2	0	1	52	0	45^2	42	7	5.5	9.9	50	38%	.294	1.53	5.91	5.26	-0.1	98.8	36	62	39
2017	WAS	MLB	26	2	4	2	53	0	55^2	55	7	3.7	10.5	65	40%	.327	1.40	3.56	4.89	0.2	99.7	48	84	49
2018	*WAS*	*MLB*	*27*	*3*	*2*	*0*	*49*	*0*	*51*	*48*	*7*	*3.9*	*10.0*	*58*	*41%*	*.302*	*1.37*	*3.97*	*4.21*	*0.4*	*98.8*	*44*	*76*	*47*
2019	*WAS*	*MLB*	*28*	*3*	*1*	*0*	*52*	*0*	54^2	*47*	*8*	*3.9*	*10.3*	*63*	*41%*	*.31*	*1.29*	*4.12*	*4.71*	*0.3*	*98.5*	*44*	*76*	*46*

Breakout: 36% Improve: 58% Collapse: 18% Attrition: 21% MLB: 88% *Comparables: Adam Warren, David Phelps, Tom Mastny*

The Nationals picked up Romero in an under-the-radar swap of minor-league debris with the Rays back in February. The reliever had long since lost his top-prospect shine, due in large part to the fact that he'd proven himself totally unable to maintain a reasonable walk rate. But in Washington, he got a bit of a makeover. His surface-level results almost made him look like someone else: a double-digit strikeout rate, a sub-5.00 ERA, the lowest walk rate of his career. However, much like Rachael Leigh Cook's makeover in *She's All That*, these were largely superficial tweaks, ones that cleaned up the exterior just enough to let everyone see what was inside him all along. Romero has always had a high-90s fastball that could be dangerous if used right; in 2017, he used it more than ever (three-quarters of the time). He has always struggled with controlling his curveball; last year, he shelved it. Even at his most glamorous-looking, Romero's still not going to be prom queen, but he should be able to get a date to the dance.

Seth Romero LHP Born: 04/19/96 Age: 22 Bats: L Throws: L Height: 6'3" Weight: 240 Origin: Round 1, 2017 Draft (#25 overall)

YEAR	TEAM	LVL	AGE	W	L	SV	G	GS	IP	H	HR	BB/9	K/9	K	GB%	BABIP	WHIP	ERA	DRA	WARP	MPH	CMD	PWR	STM
2017	AUB	A-	21	0	1	0	6	6	20	19	0	2.7	14.4	32	40%	.404	1.25	5.40	1.45	0.9				
2018	*WAS*	*MLB*	*22*	*2*	*3*	*0*	*9*	*9*	34^2	*36*	*8*	*4.4*	*10.4*	*40*	*38%*	*.327*	*1.51*	*5.26*	*5.95*	*-0.1*				
2019	*WAS*	*MLB*	*23*	*4*	*10*	*0*	*28*	*28*	169^1	*178*	*39*	*4.7*	*9.3*	*176*	*38%*	*.33*	*1.58*	*5.80*	*6.63*	*-1.3*				

Breakout: 12% Improve: 13% Collapse: 3% Attrition: 13% MLB: 16% *Comparables: Ben Lively, Carlos Carrasco, Kyle Drabek*

The Nationals have had their fair share of high-profile first-round picks with some risk attached, but that's usually come in the form of signability questions or injury issues. Romero represents a type of risk the team traditionally hasn't touched: makeup problems. The southpaw was kicked off the team at the University of Houston, reportedly for fighting a teammate, after being suspended twice (once for "a lack of effort regarding conditioning" and again for a failed drug test that accompanied a picture of him holding a bong while in uniform). All that sent Romero tumbling down the draft board, until Washington was willing to bet on him at the end of the first round. The talent underneath remains solid—a fastball that touches 95 mph with a high-quality slider—and we would say he has a sky-high upside, though we don't want to be too blunt.

Joe Ross RHP Born: 05/21/93 Age: 25 Bats: R Throws: R Height: 6'4" Weight: 225 Origin: Round 1, 2011 Draft (#25 overall)

YEAR	TEAM	LVL	AGE	W	L	SV	G	GS	IP	H	HR	BB/9	K/9	K	GB%	BABIP	WHIP	ERA	DRA	WARP	MPH	CMD	PWR	STM
2015	HAR	AA	22	2	2	0	9	9	51^1	46	3	2.1	9.5	54	50%	.323	1.13	2.81	2.24	1.8				
2015	SYR	AAA	22	3	1	0	5	5	24^2	15	2	2.6	5.5	15	55%	.188	0.89	2.19	4.10	0.3				
2015	WAS	MLB	22	5	5	0	16	13	76^2	64	7	2.5	8.1	69	54%	.265	1.11	3.64	3.35	1.6	96.3	48	52	61
2016	SYR	AAA	23	0	2	0	4	4	10^1	14	1	0.9	7.8	9	26%	.382	1.45	4.35	3.70	0.2				
2016	WAS	MLB	23	7	5	0	19	19	105	108	9	2.5	8.0	93	44%	.319	1.30	3.43	4.96	0.5	95.9	46	47	49
2017	SYR	AAA	24	2	2	0	5	5	27^2	33	3	2.6	7.2	22	37%	.341	1.48	4.88	4.36	0.4				
2017	WAS	MLB	24	5	3	0	13	13	73^2	88	16	2.4	8.3	68	41%	.332	1.47	5.01	4.82	0.6	93.8	70	44	63
2018	*WAS*	*MLB*	*25*	*2*	*1*	*0*	*5*	*5*	*25*	*24*	*4*	*3.0*	*8.6*	*24*	*44%*	*.298*	*1.34*	*3.99*	*4.25*	*0.3*	*94.9*	*57*	*48*	*59*
2019	*WAS*	*MLB*	*26*	*10*	*10*	*0*	*32*	*32*	210^1	*188*	*29*	*2.4*	*9.2*	*215*	*44%*	*.308*	*1.15*	*3.78*	*4.30*	*2.4*	*94.5*	*58*	*47*	*59*

Breakout: 26% Improve: 53% Collapse: 20% Attrition: 20% MLB: 95% *Comparables: Vance Worley, Chris Tillman, David Huff*

Siblings: there for you whenever you need them. In Ross's case, that meant older brother Tyson staying by his side in the form of posting his worst season ever and getting released in September while Joe dealt with having his year derailed by midsummer Tommy John. It's like a very advanced form of empathy. In any case, Joe will likely be out for most of 2018 as he rehabs, but expect the same sinker/slider combination whenever he returns—the question is just how effective it will be. And whether Tyson will still be in the league when he does.

Max Scherzer RHP Born: 07/27/84 Age: 33 Bats: R Throws: R Height: 6'3" Weight: 210 Origin: Round 1, 2006 Draft (#11 overall)

YEAR	TEAM	LVL	AGE	W	L	SV	G	GS	IP	H	HR	BB/9	K/9	K	GB%	BABIP	WHIP	ERA	DRA	WARP	MPH	CMD	PWR	STM
2015	WAS	MLB	30	14	12	0	33	33	228^2	176	27	1.3	10.9	276	38%	.268	0.92	2.79	2.39	7.3	97.4	50	57	81
2016	WAS	MLB	31	20	7	0	34	34	228^1	165	31	2.2	11.2	284	35%	.255	0.97	2.96	2.75	6.8	97.1	39	52	87
2017	WAS	MLB	32	16	6	0	31	31	200^2	126	22	2.5	12.0	268	38%	.245	0.90	2.51	2.26	7.4	95.7	53	47	78
2018	*WAS*	*MLB*	*33*	*13*	*8*	*0*	*29*	*29*	182^2	*149*	*26*	*2.5*	*11.0*	*224*	*39%*	*.284*	*1.08*	*3.37*	*3.60*	*3.3*	*95.6*	*47*	*51*	*81*
2019	*WAS*	*MLB*	*34*	*13*	*11*	*0*	*33*	*33*	216^2	*162*	*29*	*2.3*	*10.8*	*259*	*39%*	*.284*	*1.00*	*3.32*	*3.80*	*4.1*	*94.9*	*46*	*49*	*80*

Breakout: 10% Improve: 39% Collapse: 25% Attrition: 13% MLB: 94% *Comparables: Tom Seaver, Pedro Martinez, Jason Schmidt*

In snapping up his third Cy Young last year, Scherzer put himself in exclusive company—every pitcher with three or more is a Hall of Famer, save Clayton Kershaw (on his way) and Roger Clemens (uh, complicated). Perhaps most impressive of all is that last season was the best among Scherzer's Cy Young campaigns. Though his velocity hasn't dipped as he's crossed over into his thirties, he's still begun relying on his fastball a little less, with last season becoming the first time it accounted for fewer than half of his pitches. And he still ended up with the highest strikeout rate of his career, with the fewest home runs allowed since coming to Washington. There are a lot of years left on that contract, but it doesn't look like Scherzer will be slowing down any time soon.

Sammy Solis LHP Born: 08/10/88 Age: 29 Bats: R Throws: L Height: 6'5" Weight: 250 Origin: Round 2, 2010 Draft (#51 overall)

YEAR	TEAM	LVL	AGE	W	L	SV	G	GS	IP	H	HR	BB/9	K/9	K	GB%	BABIP	WHIP	ERA	DRA	WARP	MPH	CMD	PWR	STM
2015	HAR	AA	26	0	3	2	11	1	13^1	19	0	3.4	7.4	11	39%	.413	1.80	6.75	5.08	-0.1				
2015	SYR	AAA	26	0	0	2	9	0	13^1	8	0	3.4	7.4	11	50%	.222	0.98	2.03	3.39	0.2				
2015	WAS	MLB	26	1	1	0	18	0	21^1	25	2	1.7	7.2	17	46%	.329	1.36	3.38	5.43	-0.2	96.7	62	60	35
2016	WAS	MLB	27	2	4	0	37	0	41	31	1	4.6	10.3	47	45%	.294	1.27	2.41	3.62	0.6	96.2	56	52	36
2017	SYR	AAA	28	1	3	0	13	1	12^2	13	5	4.3	5.7	8	48%	.216	1.50	6.39	5.55	0.0				
2017	WAS	MLB	28	1	0	1	30	0	26	22	4	4.5	9.7	28	48%	.269	1.35	5.88	5.27	0.0	95.6	50	50	34
2018	*WAS*	*MLB*	*29*	*1*	*1*	*0*	*25*	*0*	*26*	*27*	*4*	*4.3*	*8.6*	*25*	*46%*	*.302*	*1.51*	*4.74*	*4.81*	*0.0*	*95.4*	*55*	*53*	*35*
2019	*WAS*	*MLB*	*30*	*2*	*1*	*1*	*47*	*0*	*49^1*	*45*	*7*	*4.0*	*9.0*	*49*	*46%*	*.308*	*1.35*	*4.41*	*5.03*	*0.1*	*95.0*	*53*	*51*	*35*

Breakout: 23% Improve: 50% Collapse: 18% Attrition: 19% MLB: 80% *Comparables: Tom Wilhelmsen, Tony Watson, Dustin Nippert*

In last year's book, we said that Solis only making two trips to the disabled list in 2016 should be counted as "a win" for the reliever. By that metric, Solis got an even bigger win in 2017—he only made *one* trip to the disabled list. Sadly, by any other metric, 2017 was a loss. That one trip to the DL, for elbow inflammation, lasted 99 days. By the time he was healthy, Washington was already well into the process of engineering their midseason bullpen makeover, and Solis didn't do anything worthy of earning a spot. His curve—his best pitch—wasn't nearly as tight and was dramatically less effective as a result, garnering whiffs just 10 percent of the time as compared to nearly 25 percent the previous year. What would constitute a win in 2018? Staying relevant enough to merit a comment in next year's book asking what will constitute a win in 2019.

Stephen Strasburg RHP Born: 07/20/88 Age: 29 Bats: R Throws: R Height: 6'4" Weight: 235 Origin: Round 1, 2009 Draft (#1 overall)

YEAR	TEAM	LVL	AGE	W	L	SV	G	GS	IP	H	HR	BB/9	K/9	K	GB%	BABIP	WHIP	ERA	DRA	WARP	MPH	CMD	PWR	STM
2015	WAS	MLB	26	11	7	0	23	23	127^1	115	14	1.8	11.0	155	45%	.311	1.11	3.46	3.07	3.0	98.0	46	61	57
2016	WAS	MLB	27	15	4	0	24	24	147^2	119	15	2.7	11.2	183	42%	.294	1.10	3.60	2.97	4.0	97.2	54	57	64
2017	WAS	MLB	28	15	4	0	28	28	175^1	131	13	2.4	10.5	204	48%	.274	1.02	2.52	2.93	5.2	97.4	50	56	72
2018	*WAS*	*MLB*	*29*	*12*	*8*	*0*	*28*	*28*	*168*	*140*	*19*	*2.7*	*10.6*	*197*	*45%*	*.293*	*1.13*	*3.14*	*3.34*	*3.5*	*96.8*	*50*	*57*	*66*
2019	*WAS*	*MLB*	*30*	*13*	*10*	*0*	*33*	*33*	*216*	*167*	*23*	*2.3*	*10.6*	*254*	*45%*	*.3*	*1.03*	*3.00*	*3.44*	*4.7*	*96.3*	*51*	*56*	*67*

Breakout: 11% Improve: 36% Collapse: 16% Attrition: 4% MLB: 97% *Comparables: Erik Bedard, Justin Verlander, David Price*

Mold requires specific conditions to grow—moisture and warmth, namely, but also certain nutrients. When those conditions are met, though? Oh, man, there's no stopping that mold. It grows and grows and grows.

Strasburg and mold have this in common. When healthy, he'll thrive; when not, he won't. But the situation is strictly either/or. There's not much of an in-between state here. He's posted a DRA under 3.00 in five of his six full major-league seasons, but he's also failed to meet the 185-inning threshold in five of those six seasons. Strasburg is typically either dealing or DLing, and mold is typically either spreading or dead.

The day before Game 4 of the NLDS, manager Dusty Baker announced that Strasburg would not start, due to sickness he'd acquired from mold in his hotel room. But he ended up starting anyway—and he dominated, with 12 strikeouts in seven shutout innings. It was his last appearance in a season where he'd failed to reach that 185-inning mark yet again, sidelined for nearly a month this summer with a nerve impingement. But when he was out there? He was making almost *everybody* sick.

Lineouts

Hitters

HITTER	POS	TEAM	LVL	AGE	PA	R	2B	3B	HR	RBI	BB	K	SB	CS	AVG/OBP/SLG	TAv	VORP	BABIP	BRR	FRAA	WARP
Osvaldo Abreu	OF	HAR	AA	23	475	40	16	4	5	42	27	107	1	6	.246/.299/.336	.246	11.4	.314	-0.7	SS(118): -4.3	0.8
Yasel Antuna	SS	NAT	Rk	17	199	25	8	3	1	17	23	29	5	5	.301/.382/.399	.274	9.0	.352	-1.9	SS(21): -0.7, 3B(15): 1.4	0.9
Anderson Franco	3B	HAG	A	19	456	57	23	2	11	63	41	100	3	1	.201/.272/.348	.226	-4.2	.234	1.3	3B(72): -2.6, 1B(29): 0.2	-0.7
Luis Garcia	SS	NAT	Rk	17	211	25	8	3	1	22	9	32	11	2	.302/.330/.387	.247	5.4	.353	1.7	2B(25): -3.0, SS(17): 0.7	0.3
Kelvin Gutierrez	3B	POT	A+	22	245	34	10	6	2	16	19	59	3	0	.288/.347/.414	.271	12.5	.380	2.0	3B(54): 6.4	2.0
	3B	NAT	Rk	22	37	6	3	1	0	1	4	7	2	0	.212/.297/.364	.219	0.1	.269	0.8	3B(8): -1.1	-0.1
Chris Heisey	LF	WAS	MLB	32	79	8	3	1	1	5	5	22	0	0	.162/.215/.270	.172	-5.0	.216	0.4	LF(19): 0.3, RF(5): -0.3	-0.5
Daniel Johnson	OF	HAG	A	21	364	61	16	4	17	52	22	70	12	9	.300/.361/.529	.326	31.3	.333	-0.5	RF(51): -1.1, CF(15): 0.3	3.3
	OF	POT	A+	21	185	22	13	0	5	20	13	30	10	2	.294/.346/.459	.280	10.2	.331	1.7	CF(28): -3.2, RF(9): 3.5	1.1
Jose Marmolejos	1B	HAR	AA	24	454	68	18	4	14	66	44	79	0	2	.288/.361/.458	.293	23.5	.324	1.4	LF(51): 1.8, 1B(34): 0.2	2.8
Blake Perkins	OF	HAG	A	20	572	105	27	4	8	48	72	118	31	8	.255/.354/.378	.279	35.5	.318	7.4	CF(118): 8.4, LF(10): 0.9	4.7
Raudy Read	C	HAR	AA	23	442	44	25	1	17	61	27	79	2	0	.265/.312/.455	.273	21.7	.290	-3.1	C(100): -25.1	-0.4
	C	WAS	MLB	23	11	1	0	0	0	0	0	3	0	0	.273/.273/.273	.249	0.1	.375	-0.1	C(3): -0.4	0.0
Clint Robinson	1B	SYR	AAA	32	495	49	25	1	18	74	45	121	0	0	.242/.315/.424	.250	-5.0	.290	-5.3	1B(54): -2.6, P(1): 0.0	-0.7
Adrian Sanchez	INF	SYR	AAA	26	283	37	15	1	4	18	19	47	4	1	.244/.295/.357	.242	9.2	.281	3.6	SS(52): 0.8, 3B(13): 0.2	1.0
	INF	WAS	MLB	26	75	6	7	0	0	11	1	25	0	2	.268/.288/.366	.232	0.4	.413	0.2	2B(10): -0.2, SS(8): 0.6	0.1
Neftali Soto	1B	HAR	AA	28	280	33	19	2	10	44	25	53	0	0	.329/.386/.540	.315	19.1	.380	-0.2	1B(40): 0.2, 2B(9): -1.1	1.9
	1B	SYR	AAA	28	286	43	15	1	14	38	18	50	0	0	.293/.343/.517	.277	9.5	.313	-0.9	1B(38): -2.2, LF(26): 0.7	0.7

Osvaldo Abreu's glove remains a gem—just maybe not one that's shiny enough to overcome the fact that he struggled more than ever at the plate in his introduction to Double-A. ⚾ **Yasel Antuna** shares a birthday with self-help guru Napoleon Hill, who once wrote, "You become what you think about." It doesn't seem like any amount of thinking will be enough for the big-money international signee to stay at shortstop, but an impressive stateside debut had the Nationals thinking they'd found another keeper. ⚾ **Anderson Franco** is built solidly enough to be exciting on sight alone, and he has plenty of time to figure things out, but his debut season at Low-A wasn't too stirring. ⚾ A big-money signing from the Nationals' 2016 J2 class, **Luis Garcia** handled himself pretty well in his first season of rookie ball. No, he still isn't old enough to legally buy a lottery ticket (even if he remains one). ⚾ **Kelvin Gutierrez** plays a strong hot corner and has a developing hit tool—now, like a math student summing exponents, all he needs is to add the power. ⚾ An untimely groin injury and poor performance at the plate (including the disappearance of his trademark reverse splits) meant a mid-season release for **Chris Heisey** in what turned out to be his first negative-WARP season. ⚾ **Daniel Johnson** had himself a nice little breakout year, enough so that A-ball pitchers could've reasonably called him by the nickname of a different Daniel Johnson, the 17th-century British pirate: "Johnson the Terror." Now *this* Daniel Johnson just has to sail his plus speed and defense to choppier seas and return with the same loot. ⚾ **Jose Marmolejos-Diaz** is a spray-hitting first baseman who can also play left field if needed, though he isn't a natural out there and doesn't have much of an arm. ⚾ **Blake Perkins** is speedy and can play a good centerfield, but while he took a step forward at the plate at Low-A in 2017, he still has quite a ways to go. ⚾ **Raudy Read** attended a major-league game for the first time in his life when he was called up for a brief cameo in September. Though he handled Double-A pretty well, the future backup catcher still probably has a bit of time left there before he'll be back. ⚾ **Clint Robinson** is a Quad-A hitter who's now struggling with Triple-A pitching, which probably means we've seen the last of him in the majors. ⚾ **Adrian Sanchez** finally got his first cup of coffee last year at age 26, but there wasn't anything there to suggest he'll ever get a full breakfast. ⚾ **Neftali Soto** is now 29 and has spent more time at Double-A than Triple-A over the last two years (and zero time above that). Safe to say Soto's chances of serving as even an emergency call-up are now looking so low.

Pitchers

PITCHER	TEAM	LVL	AGE	W	L	SV	G	GS	IP	H	HR	BB/9	K/9	K	GB%	BABIP	WHIP	ERA	DRA	WARP	MPH	CMD	PWR	STM
Austin Adams	SYR	AAA	26	6	2	5	44	0	59	44	2	5.6	13.9	91	49%	.321	1.37	2.14	1.93	2.1				
	WAS	MLB	26	0	0	0	6	0	5	4	0	14.4	18.0	10	40%	.400	2.40	3.60	2.97	0.1	96.2			46
Trevor Gott	WAS	MLB	24	1	0	0	4	0	3	11	1	9.0	9.0	3	35%	.625	4.67	30.00	8.56	-0.1	96.3			44
	SYR	AAA	24	2	0	4	30	0	37^{1}	39	2	3.1	8.4	35	59%	.327	1.39	3.86	2.37	1.2				
Sean O'Sullivan	SYR	AAA	29	1	2	0	10	8	35^{2}	43	6	4.8	5.8	23	43%	.314	1.74	5.80	7.39	-0.7				
Nick Raquet	AUB	A-	21	3	2	0	11	11	51^{1}	56	2	1.2	3.9	22	62%	.307	1.23	2.45	2.19	1.8				
Jefry Rodriguez	POT	A+	23	4	3	0	12	10	57	44	2	3.0	8.1	51	53%	.278	1.11	3.32	2.74	1.7				
Wander Suero	HAR	AA	25	0	1	10	18	0	23	18	2	2.0	9.0	23	45%	.254	1.00	1.96	3.42	0.4				
	SYR	AAA	25	3	1	10	36	0	42^{1}	33	1	3.0	8.9	42	46%	.281	1.11	1.70	2.98	1.1				
Jackson Tetreault	AUB	A-	21	2	2	0	11	6	38^{1}	32	1	3.8	8.5	36	47%	.277	1.25	2.58	3.59	0.7				
Jacob Turner	WAS	MLB	26	2	3	0	18	2	39	43	8	3.5	5.3	23	44%	.285	1.49	5.08	7.55	-1.0	96.9	44	64	56
	SYR	AAA	26	2	6	0	14	14	65^{2}	72	5	4.5	7.3	53	51%	.338	1.60	5.21	6.01	-0.2				
Austin Voth	SYR	AAA	25	1	7	0	13	13	66^{1}	85	12	4.6	5.7	42	45%	.329	1.79	6.38	7.42	-1.2				
	HAR	AA	25	3	4	0	10	10	54^{1}	63	8	2.2	7.3	44	44%	.320	1.40	5.13	3.16	1.3				

The relevant question with **Austin Adams** isn't whether he can be a quality reliever, but whether he can be better than the other bullpen-dwelling Austin Adams. While the answer to the first question is "probably not," the answer to the second question, given that the *other* Adams has never posted a positive WARP is ... "maybe?" ⚾ The way **Trevor Gott**'s career is going, the Nationals will soon be talking about the guy they *wish* they got rather than the one they did. ⚾ **Sean O'Sullivan** somehow managed to turn a terrible month in the KBO into a minor-league contract with the Nationals. Unfortunately for him, he couldn't pull a similar magic trick and turn a few terrible months at Triple-A into a major-league promotion. ⚾ Last year's third-rounder, **Nick Raquet** made a nice little racket in short-season ball with a fastball that sits mid-90s and a decent breaking ball. ⚾ **Jefry Rodriguez** missed most of the season for a PED suspension, and was rewarded with a 40-man roster spot shortly after his return, in case you wanted an actual baseball team's opinion of how much that sort of thing matters. ⚾ **Wander Suero**'s first season in Triple-A was a mild success, but "mild success in Triple-A at age 25" is the sort of thing that indicates he's likely destined to spend his career living up to his name. ⚾ Last year's seventh-round pick **Jackson Tetreault** has an exciting fastball, some frustrating struggles with his secondary pitches and FUTURE RELIEVER metaphorically tattooed on his forehead. ⚾ There was a week or so last May where **Jacob Turner** looked like he could maaaaybe take a step toward improving his status as one of the biggest busts in recent memory. Instead he made it five seasons since the last time he posted a positive WARP. ⚾ In the *Star Trek: Voyager* episode "Distant Origin," the Voth are theorized to be the galaxy's first interstellar alien species, having traveled light years for a new home. **Austin Voth** would not seem to have much in common with them, as his second go-around at Triple-A might leave him docked in Syracuse for a while, which at least beats being stranded in the Delta Quadrant.

MLB Managers

Brad Ausmus wRM+: 100

TEAM	YEAR	W	L	Pythag +/-	Avg PC	100+ P	120+ P	QS	BQS	wRM+	REL	REL w Zero R	IBB	PH	PH Avg	PH HR	SB2	CS2	SB3	CS3	SAC Att	SAC %	POS SAC	Squee-ze	Swing	In Play
DET	2014	90	72	3	101.0	103	3	90	9	98.5	473	367	34	71	.164	1	90	34	16	7	40	60.0	20	1	296	83
DET	2015	74	87	6	94.1	77	2	72	10	98.2	505	396	32	74	.121	1	66	44	17	5	43	53.5	23	1	293	86
DET	2016	86	75	2	94.5	61	1	72	6	99.2	476	375	25	79	.243	6	54	26	4	3	28	60.7	16	2	184	60
DET	2017	64	98	-1	94.1	68	2	72	4	100	510	372	42	83	.227	0	56	33	9	1	17	64.7	11	0	260	67

Dusty Baker wRM+: 99.8

TEAM	YEAR	W	L	Pythag +/-	Avg PC	100+ P	120+ P	QS	BQS	wRM+	REL	REL w Zero R	IBB	PH	PH Avg	PH HR	SB2	CS2	SB3	CS3	SAC Att	SAC %	POS SAC	Squee-ze	Swing	In Play
SFN	1993	103	59	3				86	6		414	342	46	246	.183	4	97	59	23	6	135	75.6	52	2		
SFN	1994	55	60	-3				68	8		287	224	40	176	.227	3	103	34	11	6	90	72.2	37	0		
SFN	1995	67	77	7				70	5		381	278	51	227	.210	1	125	39	13	6	100	79.0	46	1		
SFN	1996	68	94	-2				69	18		425	314	60	247	.205	6	103	47	10	5	106	72.6	42	1		
SFN	1997	90	72	10				81	4		481	370	57	210	.268	1	105	40	16	4	86	74.4	36	1		
SFN	1998	89	74	-3	84.6	57	8	79	9		433	349	68	225	.227	10	97	41	5	7	109	74.3	38	1		
SFN	1999	86	76	1	103.5	106	27	79	7		450	356	41	231	.218	4	99	50	10	6	116	75.0	38	1		
SFN	2000	97	65	-1	102.3	94	26	88	9		384	292	26	231	.231	7	72	34	7	5	84	86.9	25	0		
SFN	2001	90	72	4	99.6	84	9	80	11		439	338	49	258	.248	14	53	35	4	7	80	83.7	31	0		
SFN	2002	95	67	-5	100.9	86	21	91	5		416	352	44	201	.197	1	70	20	4	1	87	78.2	24	0		
CHN	2003	88	74	2	103.5	101	25	100	5		420	335	36	236	.155	2	66	30	7	1	105	76.2	42	0	239	77
CHN	2004	89	73	-6	98.9	81	12	95	5		461	364	33	254	.236	4	64	24	2	4	117	66.7	37	0	238	80
CHN	2005	79	83	-1	97.5	78	10	91	4		457	353	48	240	.195	2	60	34	5	3	97	71.1	42	2	302	104
CHN	2006	66	96	-3	91.8	56	7	60	4		542	423	44	270	.216	5	107	41	13	5	120	70.0	56	3	361	117
CIN	2008	74	88	3	97.8	80	3	78	2	97.1	507	379	40	282	.231	5	68	39	17	6	115	62.6	34	4	317	103
CIN	2009	78	84	3	98.5	87	1	79	3	99	478	385	36	251	.227	4	80	35	15	4	133	75.2	47	3	322	98
CIN	2010	91	71	-1	97.8	81	4	89	5	98.9	501	408	32	256	.236	10	79	36	14	5	100	66.0	28	3	322	99
CIN	2011	79	83	-4	95.5	67	2	90	7	99.9	502	398	47	240	.286	8	85	43	12	6	110	70.9	32	2	377	131
CIN	2012	97	65	6	97.4	74	1	98	6	99.7	425	365	33	201	.269	2	73	24	14	2	119	61.3	28	2	310	97
CIN	2013	90	72	-5	95.3	61	2	94	6	100.6	461	389	28	232	.248	5	61	32	6	2	118	72.0	37	2	314	111
WAS	2016	95	67	-4	97.4	79	1	92	2	100.9	508	419	43	218	.207	12	102	37	18	2	69	69.6	11	5	330	93
WAS	2017	97	65	0	99.7	96	4	99	3	99.8	487	372	39	240	.214	5	91	24	17	6	62	69.4	15	0	245	75

Jeff Bannister wRM+: 100.4

TEAM	YEAR	W	L	Pythag +/-	Avg PC	100+ P	120+ P	QS	BQS	wRM+	REL	REL w Zero R	IBB	PH	PH Avg	PH HR	SB2	CS2	SB3	CS3	SAC Att	SAC %	POS SAC	Squee-ze	Swing	In Play
TEX	2015	88	74	5	95.6	55	1	79	3		498	402	29	89	.228	1	87	34	13	4	72	59.7	42	1	292	83
TEX	2016	95	67	13	93.0	45	2	84	1		479	379	16	77	.164	0	87	34	11	1	33	54.5	17	0	283	83
TEX	2017	78	84	-1	92.9	35	1	79	2	100.4	464	339	22	63	.185	1	93	38	20	6	41	65.9	26	2	314	75

Bud Black wRM+: 102.8

TEAM	YEAR	W	L	Pythag +/-	Avg PC	100+ P	120+ P	QS	BQS	wRM+	REL	REL w Zero R	IBB	PH	PH Avg	PH HR	SB2	CS2	SB3	CS3	SAC Att	SAC %	POS SAC	Squee-ze	Swing	In Play
SDN	2007	89	74	-1	90.0	47	0	90	4		485	404	48	272	.188	3	50	16	5	7	93	68.8	28	1	246	90
SDN	2008	63	99	-3	90.9	49	3	76	4	104.5	490	348	61	285	.198	3	34	17	2	0	76	77.6	18	0	226	93
SDN	2009	75	87	9	91.0	46	1	77	3	106	528	412	58	263	.248	9	72	23	10	5	111	66.7	38	1	296	90
SDN	2010	90	72	-2	94.8	54	0	87	2	105.8	499	431	51	278	.206	9	114	47	10	1	111	71.2	44	1	359	97
SDN	2011	71	91	-8	96.7	65	1	91	4	105.5	489	416	56	283	.160	2	147	42	21	2	86	64.0	23	4	391	88
SDN	2012	76	86	2	92.2	49	1	75	5	106.3	529	449	48	278	.248	6	129	42	25	2	107	58.9	30	1	396	88
SDN	2013	76	86	5	93.9	59	2	87	2	106.5	488	402	31	266	.206	8	105	31	13	3	92	56.5	23	1	284	75
SDN	2014	77	85	2	94.4	52	1	91	2	106.3	481	417	32	311	.218	11	75	31	16	3	90	62.2	32	2	248	70
SDN	2015	32	35	0	97.7	33	0	43	0	104.6	206	160	16	119	.170	1	44	10	2	1	29	58.6	11	0	106	36
COL	2017	87	75	-1	90.0	28	1	68	1	102.8	549	424	20	259	.205	6	51	32	8	2	87	71.3	20	2	297	94

Bruce Bochy wRM+: 98.9

TEAM	YEAR	W	L	Pythag +/-	Avg PC	100+ P	120+ P	QS	BQS	wRM+	REL	REL w Zero R	IBB	PH	PH Avg	PH HR	SB2	CS2	SB3	CS3	SAC Att	SAC %	POS SAC	Squee-ze	Swing	In Play
SFN	2015	84	78	-5	90.8	37	0	78	3		557	474	28	224	.249	1	87	32	6	3	60	75.0	12	1	309	106
SFN	2016	87	75	-4	96.6	77	1	85	3		575	488	30	257	.225	4	70	33	9	3	64	65.6	18	3	305	104
SFN	2017	64	98	-1	96.0	66	0	82	3	98.9	502	392	42	292	.206	5	64	30	11	4	54	57.4	12	0	280	86

Kevin Cash wRM+: 100

TEAM	YEAR	W	L	Pythag +/-	Avg PC	100+ P	120+ P	QS	BQS	wRM+	REL	REL w Zero R	IBB	PH	PH Avg	PH HR	SB2	CS2	SB3	CS3	SAC Att	SAC %	POS SAC	Squee-ze	Swing	In Play
TBA	2015	80	82	-1	90.6	46	1	68	3	101.1	530	416	23	179	.219	3	62	40	25	4	29	65.5	17	0	290	82
TBA	2016	68	94	-8	96.2	67	1	74	5	101.9	485	369	25	92	.128	1	48	33	12	3	31	58.1	18	1	306	86
TBA	2017	80	82	0	93.8	74	1	73	6	100	511	403	37	102	.193	2	66	28	22	5	35	45.7	14	1	292	72

Craig Counsell wRM+: 100.6

TEAM	YEAR	W	L	Pythag +/-	Avg PC	100+ P	120+ P	QS	BQS	wRM+	REL	REL w Zero R	IBB	PH	PH Avg	PH HR	SB2	CS2	SB3	CS3	SAC Att	SAC %	POS SAC	Squee-ze	Swing	In Play
MIL	2015	61	76	-3	92.4	40	0	53	6	98.9	424	338	30	244	.259	5	67	20	9	3	59	72.9	16	1	197	63
MIL	2016	73	89	-1	90.3	30	0	62	2	99.9	513	393	33	282	.178	7	144	46	35	10	87	60.9	21	2	371	76
MIL	2017	86	76	1	88.1	30	0	65	0	100.6	550	435	45	283	.220	8	98	32	30	7	68	61.8	12	3	336	94

John Farrell wRM+: 98.9

TEAM	YEAR	W	L	Pythag +/-	Avg PC	100+ P	120+ P	QS	BQS	wRM+	REL	REL w Zero R	IBB	PH	PH Avg	PH HR	SB2	CS2	SB3	CS3	SAC Att	SAC %	POS SAC	Squee-ze	Swing	In Play
TOR	2011	81	81	2	97.7	81	4	81	3	94.8	474	383	28	58	.185	0	98	43	32	6	54	57.4	31	2	372	103
TOR	2012	73	89	-1	91.9	52	0	74	3	95.7	495	396	20	80	.205	1	89	31	33	8	67	49.3	32	3	406	138
BOS	2013	97	65	-5	100.0	88	5	95	6	97.1	450	355	10	81	.235	6	104	17	17	2	38	63.2	21	0	336	104
BOS	2014	71	91	-0	97.7	73	1	87	6	96.5	493	410	19	91	.231	2	43	21	19	3	34	58.8	19	1	301	79
BOS	2015	51	64	0	93.7	48	0	53	2	98.1	328	251	12	51	.244	0	40	12	9	1	29	79.3	21	0	222	98
BOS	2016	93	69	-7	96.5	78	2	87	3	98.5	463	387	16	98	.190	3	71	19	11	3	19	42.1	8	0	333	119
BOS	2017	93	69	-1	99.4	99	1	88	3	98.9	515	427	18	76	.257	1	84	28	22	3	23	39.1	8	0	299	78

Terry Francona wRM+: 101.2

TEAM	YEAR	W	L	Pythag +/-	Avg PC	100+ P	120+ P	QS	BQS	wRM+	REL	REL w Zero R	IBB	PH	PH Avg	PH HR	SB2	CS2	SB3	CS3	SAC Att	SAC %	POS SAC	Squee-ze	Swing	In Play
PHI	1997	68	94	5				80	5		409	285	42	285	.184	3	79	48	11	6	98	75.5	29	0		
PHI	1998	75	87	4	95.8	74	20	77	9		386	273	27	255	.232	5	87	41	10	4	86	75.6	28	0		
PHI	1999	77	85	-4	96.9	79	14	73	10		441	333	24	237	.255	5	113	32	12	2	82	85.4	23	0		
PHI	2000	65	97	-3	102.6	106	23	87	10		413	273	32	271	.197	2	91	25	11	3	86	81.4	28	1		
BOS	2004	98	64	0	98.9	88	3	86	9		437	335	28	99	.264	2	64	27	4	2	24	50.0	10	0	263	78
BOS	2005	95	67	4	99.6	93	3	81	6		442	337	28	98	.221	1	42	12	3	0	25	56.0	13	0	252	98
BOS	2006	86	76	5	95.3	63	2	70	7		455	332	25	87	.222	0	46	22	5	1	38	57.9	22	0	273	106
BOS	2007	96	66	-7	97.6	66	3	84	10		451	379	20	73	.217	0	83	20	13	4	52	57.7	30	2	333	100
BOS	2008	95	67	-2	95.9	69	1	82	9	106.2	466	359	17	49	.250	2	99	32	21	2	47	59.6	27	0	310	90
BOS	2009	95	67	0	99.0	81	3	82	3	104.3	463	369	24	79	.221	0	106	35	19	4	32	59.4	17	0	309	97
BOS	2010	89	73	0	102.8	112	3	89	5	104.2	443	348	30	117	.260	2	56	14	11	2	38	76.3	24	0	340	108
BOS	2011	90	72	-5	96.8	78	4	71	5	104.9	443	359	11	83	.176	2	93	40	9	1	33	66.7	22	0	366	122
CLE	2013	92	70	1	94.9	68	0	73	5	102.5	540	454	26	58	.255	3	96	33	21	3	41	75.6	30	0	332	85
CLE	2014	85	77	2	94.6	61	0	78	5	103.1	573	507	51	103	.233	0	96	23	8	4	63	81.0	49	0	290	92
CLE	2015	81	80	-3	94.5	77	2	91	4	102.1	476	391	27	106	.240	4	79	26	7	1	65	72.3	45	0	274	58
CLE	2016	94	67	2	92.0	60	0	81	6	101.5	504	428	34	106	.143	1	104	25	29	6	48	64.6	27	0	294	71
CLE	2017	102	60	-8	93.7	72	1	84	4	101.2	497	430	15	86	.145	2	79	21	9	2	39	59.0	22	0	266	78

Ron Gardenhire wRM+: 106.5

TEAM	YEAR	W	L	Pythag +/-	Avg PC	100+ P	120+ P	QS	BQS	wRM+	REL	REL w Zero R	IBB	PH	PH Avg	PH HR	SB2	CS2	SB3	CS3	SAC Att	SAC %	POS SAC	Squee-ze	Swing	In Play
MIN	2002	94	67	7	90.1	47	3	77	2		436	352	24	103	.283	3	66	50	12	12	45	75.6	33	0		
MIN	2003	90	72	5	92.2	54	2	80	7		399	311	35	102	.318	5	79	35	15	7	67	62.7	37	1	275	82
MIN	2004	92	70	4	93.8	61	1	83	7		436	333	27	112	.269	6	97	39	19	6	73	63.0	44	1	335	108
MIN	2005	83	79	-1	91.9	43	0	90	10		396	312	38	92	.300	2	85	39	17	4	67	62.7	40	1	352	116
MIN	2006	96	66	2	90.1	42	0	73	4		421	343	25	77	.145	1	88	36	13	6	55	56.4	28	0	369	146
MIN	2007	79	83	-1	93.5	46	0	80	3		438	352	33	82	.253	1	94	29	18	1	52	65.4	29	1	362	133
MIN	2008	88	75	-2	91.7	47	1	86	4	107.6	485	379	38	80	.224	3	86	37	16	5	88	59.1	47	3	340	117
MIN	2009	87	76	0	92.0	56	1	79	6	110.1	480	372	20	73	.333	4	74	28	11	2	77	66.2	46	1	368	127
MIN	2010	94	68	1	93.5	56	1	86	6	108.5	465	377	19	75	.156	2	60	23	8	5	50	76.0	33	1	272	101
MIN	2011	63	99	3	95.2	66	2	80	9	106.8	457	340	37	87	.175	0	86	33	6	4	52	59.6	31	1	361	135
MIN	2012	66	96	-1	88.0	29	0	62	3	107.4	499	390	43	59	.260	0	111	33	24	3	52	63.5	32	1	384	108
MIN	2013	66	96	5	91.1	44	0	62	6	107.2	511	415	31	97	.163	1	50	31	1	2	40	72.5	26	0	292	93
MIN	2014	70	92	-4	91.6	36	0	66	8	106.5	491	378	24	90	.210	0	84	33	15	2	34	73.5	25	0	307	98

John Gibbons wRM+: 99.4

TEAM	YEAR	W	L	Pythag +/-	Avg PC	100+ P	120+ P	QS	BQS	wRM+	REL	REL w Zero R	IBB	PH	PH Avg	PH HR	SB2	CS2	SB3	CS3	SAC Att	SAC %	POS SAC	Squeeze	Swing	In Play
TOR	2004	20	30	-1	90.0	16	2	19	1		130	91	11	28	.292	2	19	10	3	2	2	100.0	2	0	113	37
TOR	2005	80	82	-9	90.4	42	1	80	5		432	355	29	120	.324	2	58	32	13	2	32	65.6	20	1	339	117
TOR	2008	35	39	-3	98.6	39	1	40	4	97	205	179	26	43	.368	2	38	19	7	3	25	80.0	18	0	182	59
TOR	2013	74	88	-2	92.3	56	1	67	6	97.9	487	391	33	102	.220	3	87	38	25	3	44	65.9	26	0	353	99
TOR	2014	83	79	-2	96.6	68	4	86	7	98.9	449	367	23	176	.220	9	64	16	14	5	61	57.4	34	1	309	102
TOR	2015	93	69	-10	92.8	58	1	84	5	99.4	469	384	20	88	.225	3	70	18	17	4	51	70.6	34	1	281	77
TOR	2016	89	73	-3	96.0	55	0	100	5	96.9	487	381	10	84	.167	1	45	22	9	1	39	66.7	22	0	275	81
TOR	2017	76	86	5	90.3	45	0	69	0	99.4	578	460	25	119	.208	1	41	21	10	2	41	61.0	23	0	277	88

Joe Girardi wRM+: 102.6

TEAM	YEAR	W	L	Pythag +/-	Avg PC	100+ P	120+ P	QS	BQS	wRM+	REL	REL w Zero R	IBB	PH	PH Avg	PH HR	SB2	CS2	SB3	CS3	SAC Att	SAC %	POS SAC	Squeeze	Swing	In Play
FLO	2006	78	84	-2	94.2	74	3	89	4		436	332	58	247	.242	4	95	50	13	6	110	69.1	42	3	363	105
NYA	2008	89	73	1	90.5	43	0	78	5	103.2	474	379	37	88	.280	4	107	36	11	3	39	79.5	29	0	432	134
NYA	2009	103	59	6	96.5	78	4	76	4	104.1	462	372	28	90	.232	3	99	26	12	1	48	64.6	28	0	323	108
NYA	2010	95	67	-3	97.1	78	2	83	3	103.7	431	349	37	95	.167	2	93	26	9	4	48	68.8	27	0	362	110
NYA	2011	97	65	-6	95.7	69	2	84	6	106	465	404	43	54	.196	0	125	42	21	3	54	66.7	29	0	357	94
NYA	2012	95	67	-1	97.9	84	3	82	7	106.7	485	409	32	129	.148	4	77	24	16	3	50	62.0	28	0	321	88
NYA	2013	85	77	7	95.7	82	1	84	11	107.9	428	356	34	99	.242	1	96	27	18	4	53	67.9	35	0	302	94
NYA	2014	84	78	7	93.3	54	0	83	6	106.8	475	399	23	95	.244	2	97	23	13	3	45	64.4	27	0	311	85
NYA	2015	87	75	-1	92.5	42	0	72	9	106.5	497	400	16	111	.250	3	60	23	3	2	33	72.7	24	1	231	75
NYA	2016	84	78	6	91.5	40	0	70	8	107.4	483	383	15	75	.191	3	64	21	5	1	38	55.3	19	0	215	65
NYA	2017	91	71	-11	90.7	38	0	75	2	102.6	477	392	18	102	.163	4	85	21	5	1	28	64.3	16	0	285	74

Andy Green wRM+: 100.7

TEAM	YEAR	W	L	Pythag +/-	Avg PC	100+ P	120+ P	QS	BQS	wRM+	REL	REL w Zero R	IBB	PH	PH Avg	PH HR	SB2	CS2	SB3	CS3	SAC Att	SAC %	POS SAC	Squeeze	Swing	In Play
SDN	2016	68	94	-4	90.5	39	0	69	2	101	510	390	44	243	.208	4	103	40	18	5	60	60.0	11	2	304	79
SDN	2017	71	91	14	89.6	34	2	67	3	100.7	517	403	28	238	.165	6	76	28	11	3	80	65.0	21	2	247	69

A.J. Hinch wRM+: 100.4

TEAM	YEAR	W	L	Pythag +/-	Avg PC	100+ P	120+ P	QS	BQS	wRM+	REL	REL w Zero R	IBB	PH	PH Avg	PH HR	SB2	CS2	SB3	CS3	SAC Att	SAC %	POS SAC	Squeeze	Swing	In Play
ARI	2009	58	75	-4	98.8	79	0	73	5	100.4	392	281	24	220	.185	5	68	22	13	9	69	65.2	24	1	217	66
ARI	2010	31	48	-0	101.9	46	5	38	6	100.1	207	133	19	119	.213	0	42	11	3	2	21	81.0	7	0	151	48
HOU	2015	86	76	-8	98.0	74	4	94	4	99.5	482	412	17	114	.224	5	99	41	21	5	40	70.0	25	2	300	83
HOU	2016	84	78	0	93.7	52	0	77	3	101	500	403	19	98	.209	2	90	34	12	9	44	61.4	22	3	309	77
HOU	2017	101	61	0	92.0	31	0	67	3	100.4	519	399	17	68	.213	2	80	37	18	5	24	45.8	11	0	305	95

Clint Hurdle wRM+: 99.8

TEAM	YEAR	W	L	Pythag +/-	Avg PC	100+ P	120+ P	QS	BQS	wRM+	REL	REL w Zero R	IBB	PH	PH Avg	PH HR	SB2	CS2	SB3	CS3	SAC Att	SAC %	POS SAC	Squeeze	Swing	In Play
COL	2002	67	73	5	93.1	45	1	61	7		437	322	38	244	.276	5	82	40	10	5	51	76.5	26	1		
COL	2003	74	88	-3	89.7	38	0	68	2		500	369	51	285	.260	5	57	34	6	3	103	53.4	28	1	238	85
COL	2004	68	94	-5	95.7	60	3	65	8		473	329	84	287	.253	11	36	31	8	2	148	65.5	55	0	258	87
COL	2005	67	95	-2	94.0	52	1	68	3		459	336	54	272	.224	4	61	26	4	5	131	67.2	52	2	334	116
COL	2006	76	86	-5	95.6	55	2	81	7		499	392	81	258	.215	6	80	44	4	3	167	71.3	64	0	325	112
COL	2007	90	73	-2	90.4	50	0	79	2		529	413	61	283	.216	4	98	31	2	0	130	63.8	37	2	354	104
COL	2008	74	88	1	92.2	53	0	68	3	93.7	484	370	49	250	.239	4	116	34	25	3	124	72.6	41	0	354	82
COL	2009	18	28	-3	92.5	19	0	26	2	93.7	135	96	11	73	.306	2	24	13	6	2	29	69.0	8	0	113	45
PIT	2011	72	90	3	89.5	26	0	78	2	95.9	549	452	65	275	.201	1	95	47	13	3	110	68.2	37	1	384	114
PIT	2012	79	83	1	90.4	42	0	83	2	94.1	483	398	30	266	.173	2	66	45	7	3	93	66.7	30	2	271	94
PIT	2013	94	68	5	89.7	41	0	83	2	96.1	465	395	26	285	.207	7	83	36	10	6	93	66.7	35	1	347	100
PIT	2014	88	74	1	93.7	44	0	90	3	97.8	452	361	43	317	.218	7	99	41	5	4	101	53.5	18	1	365	135
PIT	2015	98	64	4	94.2	46	0	92	7	98.7	500	431	38	267	.237	2	89	43	8	2	81	77.8	24	0	288	87
PIT	2016	78	84	0	87.4	27	0	68	0	99.2	525	405	28	290	.230	8	100	37	10	6	64	64.1	18	1	309	79
PIT	2017	75	87	1	90.6	37	0	69	4	99.8	502	383	32	275	.199	6	61	31	5	4	69	60.9	8	0	289	90

Torey Lovullo wRM+: 99.7

TEAM	YEAR	W	L	Pythag +/-	Avg PC	100+ P	120+ P	QS	BQS	wRM+	REL	REL w Zero R	IBB	PH	PH Avg	PH HR	SB2	CS2	SB3	CS3	SAC Att	SAC %	POS SAC	Squeeze	Swing	In Play
ARI	2017	93	69	-5	96.2	73	1	82	2	99.7	513	424	45	249	.216	7	77	24	25	6	56	69.6	8	0	265	73

Pete Mackanin wRM+: 100.3

TEAM	YEAR	W	L	Pythag +/-	Avg PC	100+ P	120+ P	QS	BQS	wRM+	REL	REL w Zero R	IBB	PH	PH Avg	PH HR	SB2	CS2	SB3	CS3	SAC Att	SAC %	POS SAC	Squee-ze	Swing	In Play
PIT	2005	12	14	-0	86.6	6	0	10	0		94	67	5	53	.133	0	17	1	0	0	20	65.0	8	0	54	16
CIN	2007	41	39	3	90.9	25	3	36	4		266	198	18	130	.204	2	38	9	12	3	49	65.3	15	0	147	50
PHI	2015	37	50	-0	87.3	13	2	36	2		276	204	12	140	.213	5	44	17	6	3	55	54.5	17	0	165	48
PHI	2016	71	91	11	90.1	33	0	79	2		505	361	30	259	.157	4	83	41	12	3	78	59.0	26	3	293	74
PHI	2017	66	96	-5	91.6	37	0	65	3	100.3	506	388	39	235	.256	4	55	20	4	4	51	41.2	6	0	267	84

Joe Maddon wRM+: 100

TEAM	YEAR	W	L	Pythag +/-	Avg PC	100+ P	120+ P	QS	BQS	wRM+	REL	REL w Zero R	IBB	PH	PH Avg	PH HR	SB2	CS2	SB3	CS3	SAC Att	SAC %	POS SAC	Squee-ze	Swing	In Play
CAL	1996	6	16	-0				10	4		52	43	10	21	.235	0	7	7	0	0	11	36.4	4	0		
ANA	1999	19	10	2	96.3	13	3	11	1		85	72	3	27	.238	1	14	9	0	0	13	84.6	11	0		
TBA	2006	61	101	-3	92.8	48	1	65	6		444	303	39	76	.217	1	109	45	24	7	69	50.7	32	3	417	112
TBA	2007	66	96	0	96.9	77	0	73	8		484	320	31	68	.167	0	114	43	16	4	50	68.0	33	4	350	92
TBA	2008	97	65	5	95.9	71	0	82	3	93.7	448	365	29	90	.184	1	113	38	28	10	40	57.5	20	0	388	94
TBA	2009	84	78	-2	99.1	80	1	76	5	90.8	510	425	22	134	.164	7	167	49	26	11	41	61.0	24	6	404	101
TBA	2010	96	66	-2	98.9	90	2	95	5	94	491	412	34	154	.242	3	147	39	25	7	67	58.2	38	6	404	120
TBA	2011	91	71	-1	102.1	98	5	99	10	94.8	438	355	38	129	.252	1	134	54	20	8	63	58.7	35	5	441	138
TBA	2012	90	72	-6	99.9	91	7	90	2	96.3	471	415	35	135	.178	3	122	38	11	5	62	54.8	32	3	354	105
TBA	2013	92	71	4	94.9	65	2	80	2	97	485	399	38	169	.235	1	61	34	12	3	39	61.5	24	0	292	93
TBA	2014	77	85	-2	97.1	77	0	84	1	97.6	494	418	27	130	.218	1	52	24	11	2	73	58.9	42	3	313	106
CHN	2015	97	65	6	91.1	53	2	81	3	98	551	459	38	287	.201	5	82	32	13	3	53	60.4	15	2	330	105
CHN	2016	103	59	-7	94.5	56	1	100	3	98.7	502	407	24	234	.215	2	57	30	9	1	78	53.8	14	8	264	93
CHN	2017	92	70	-2	91.1	40	0	77	0	100	531	413	29	294	.238	5	56	25	5	6	65	73.8	22	5	263	75

Mike Matheny wRM+: 97.4

TEAM	YEAR	W	L	Pythag +/-	Avg PC	100+ P	120+ P	QS	BQS	wRM+	REL	REL w Zero R	IBB	PH	PH Avg	PH HR	SB2	CS2	SB3	CS3	SAC Att	SAC %	POS SAC	Squee-ze	Swing	In Play
SLN	2012	88	74	-6	94.2	49	1	99	4	99.5	506	400	28	279	.190	1	72	27	18	5	104	66.3	34	0	287	100
SLN	2013	97	65	-6	96.0	67	5	88	3	98.6	483	411	26	234	.202	3	33	20	11	2	94	59.6	17	0	242	87
SLN	2014	90	72	7	94.0	60	2	91	2	99.5	485	393	35	251	.225	2	48	25	9	7	97	66.0	24	2	306	112
SLN	2015	100	62	2	94.5	64	0	106	1	98.7	515	434	37	270	.218	4	62	33	7	5	64	60.9	12	1	297	100
SLN	2016	86	76	-2	91.2	39	1	83	4	97.4	481	381	35	274	.333	17	33	19	2	6	67	55.2	13	0	207	76

Don Mattingly wRM+: 98.2

TEAM	YEAR	W	L	Pythag +/-	Avg PC	100+ P	120+ P	QS	BQS	wRM+	REL	REL w Zero R	IBB	PH	PH Avg	PH HR	SB2	CS2	SB3	CS3	SAC Att	SAC %	POS SAC	Squee-ze	Swing	In Play
LAN	2011	82	79	-3	97.8	66	3	94	4	95	461	369	48	229	.199	4	108	31	17	9	101	70.3	38	2	360	118
LAN	2012	86	76	-0	96.2	66	0	93	5	93.3	506	426	62	241	.281	2	93	39	10	2	122	67.2	33	2	329	97
LAN	2013	92	70	2	95.1	69	2	93	2	96	504	424	44	208	.209	4	74	22	4	5	113	62.8	32	0	283	93
LAN	2014	94	68	1	95.1	70	1	100	1	97.2	496	395	35	235	.231	1	123	46	14	3	82	57.3	15	1	340	104
LAN	2015	92	70	2	91.3	47	2	95	3	99.4	515	408	32	269	.215	8	51	26	8	8	69	71.0	15	1	250	76
MIA	2016	79	82	2	90.8	46	0	63	1	96.6	559	443	62	277	.215	6	61	25	10	3	76	60.5	15	2	240	74
MIA	2017	77	85	0	87.5	29	0	54	0	98.2	580	435	59	270	.262	6	82	22	9	6	84	59.5	15	3	275	80

Bob Melvin wRM+: 98.8

TEAM	YEAR	W	L	Pythag +/-	Avg PC	100+ P	120+ P	QS	BQS	wRM+	REL	REL w Zero R	IBB	PH	PH Avg	PH HR	SB2	CS2	SB3	CS3	SAC Att	SAC %	POS SAC	Squee-ze	Swing	In Play
SEA	2003	93	69	-6	101.9	108	6	94	8		366	305	24	62	.154	2	89	34	19	3	52	67.3	32	1	248	91
SEA	2004	63	99	-5	101.7	99	12	70	10		414	305	32	99	.276	4	92	33	18	9	63	73.0	45	0	355	112
ARI	2005	77	85	13	96.6	64	3	84	10		458	330	43	309	.232	9	64	21	3	4	107	66.4	30	1	281	86
ARI	2006	76	86	-3	94.9	68	3	81	8		461	349	44	274	.194	7	64	26	11	4	94	64.9	21	0	237	80
ARI	2007	90	72	11	94.7	68	4	84	5		469	367	38	239	.239	11	90	16	18	8	85	64.7	26	0	295	89
ARI	2008	82	80	-1	95.7	55	3	95	3	92.3	443	336	41	257	.226	3	46	16	12	5	95	71.6	29	1	261	89
ARI	2009	12	17	0	95.9	10	0	16	2	92.3	91	64	3	47	.209	3	16	7	5	1	18	50.0	6	0	61	17
OAK	2011	47	52	-0	100.4	51	1	55	3	92	282	220	9	30	.276	2	56	26	19	2	38	57.9	20	0	229	63
OAK	2012	94	68	1	92.5	52	0	90	4	94.8	462	386	34	93	.231	3	89	26	33	5	43	62.8	26	0	307	76
OAK	2013	96	66	-1	94.8	56	0	92	2	96.2	447	370	23	130	.135	5	58	24	17	3	37	56.8	21	2	253	87
OAK	2014	88	74	-12	96.0	61	1	102	5	97.6	441	380	28	161	.201	3	67	16	16	4	41	46.3	15	2	253	83
OAK	2015	68	94	-9	92.4	61	0	83	3	98.7	487	368	19	152	.252	0	65	25	13	3	24	58.3	12	1	268	90
OAK	2016	69	93	0	87.2	40	0	69	3	96.7	492	403	28	113	.185	2	44	23	6	0	24	54.2	10	1	205	61
OAK	2017	75	87	3	90.6	40	0	73	3	98.8	525	388	17	120	.217	1	47	20	9	2	23	56.5	9	1	226	59

Paul Molitor wRM+: 100.6

TEAM	YEAR	W	L	Pythag +/-	Avg PC	100+ P	120+ P	QS	BQS	wRM+	REL	REL w Zero R	IBB	PH	PH Avg	PH HR	SB2	CS2	SB3	CS3	SAC Att	SAC %	POS SAC	Squee-ze	Swing	In Play
MIN	2015	83	79	2	91.2	55	0	76	6		520	420	34	72	.129	1	59	34	11	3	57	52.6	30	3	279	100
MIN	2016	59	103	-5	91.1	46	0	59	5		533	400	26	65	.123	3	87	31	4	1	58	46.6	25	0	312	86
MIN	2017	85	77	1	88.0	38	0	62	6	100.6	520	408	37	93	.195	2	91	24	4	2	54	48.1	25	1	333	109

Bryan Price wRM+: 100.3

TEAM	YEAR	W	L	Pythag +/-	Avg PC	100+ P	120+ P	QS	BQS	wRM+	REL	REL w Zero R	IBB	PH	PH Avg	PH HR	SB2	CS2	SB3	CS3	SAC Att	SAC %	POS SAC	Squee-ze	Swing	In Play
CIN	2015	64	98	-4	91.5	44	4	68	4		521	397	42	262	.195	2	99	32	35	5	70	67.1	25	3	329	81
CIN	2016	68	94	1	90.4	42	0	67	3		484	324	31	227	.215	0	106	37	33	12	97	59.8	27	1	362	96
CIN	2017	68	94	-1	87.9	32	0	54	3	100.3	504	366	37	240	.201	7	104	30	16	8	87	57.5	18	2	365	105

Rick Renteria wRM+: 100.1

TEAM	YEAR	W	L	Pythag +/-	Avg PC	100+ P	120+ P	QS	BQS	wRM+	REL	REL w Zero R	IBB	PH	PH Avg	PH HR	SB2	CS2	SB3	CS3	SAC Att	SAC %	POS SAC	Squee-ze	Swing	In Play
CHN	2014	73	89	3	93.6	48	1	79	0	100.6	537	446	37	272	.185	1	58	37	7	3	93	61.3	25	3	246	82
CHA	2017	67	95	-2	93.2	52	0	63	1	100.1	520	397	36	77	.183	1	61	25	10	3	62	56.5	33	3	291	76

Dave Roberts wRM+: 100.5

TEAM	YEAR	W	L	Pythag +/-	Avg PC	100+ P	120+ P	QS	BQS	wRM+	REL	REL w Zero R	IBB	PH	PH Avg	PH HR	SB2	CS2	SB3	CS3	SAC Att	SAC %	POS SAC	Squee-ze	Swing	In Play
LAN	2016	91	71	-0	87.6	29	0	60	2	102.1	606	503	50	323	.189	6	40	22	5	2	62	48.4	5	2	254	84
LAN	2017	104	58	1	86.6	21	0	68	1	100.5	536	428	33	340	.244	8	60	24	15	2	51	60.8	4	1	237	70

Mike Scioscia wRM+: 99.3

TEAM	YEAR	W	L	Pythag +/-	Avg PC	100+ P	120+ P	QS	BQS	wRM+	REL	REL w Zero R	IBB	PH	PH Avg	PH HR	SB2	CS2	SB3	CS3	SAC Att	SAC %	POS SAC	Squee-ze	Swing	In Play
ANA	2000	82	80	1	92.0	64	6	58	9		441	341	44	86	.231	2	80	47	13	4	57	82.5	44	4		
ANA	2001	75	87	-2	97.2	73	5	83	10		385	303	47	86	.200	4	95	45	20	3	61	75.4	46	1		
ANA	2002	99	63	-4	99.3	86	5	94	8		400	334	24	103	.281	2	102	42	15	8	64	76.6	47	3		
ANA	2003	77	85	-3	94.2	63	1	65	5		375	310	38	97	.330	1	113	54	14	3	71	70.4	49	2	362	117
ANA	2004	92	70	1	96.8	79	3	79	7		343	269	27	81	.265	1	123	42	19	3	79	70.9	54	3	458	130
ANA	2005	95	67	0	96.9	76	1	99	4		379	306	24	78	.239	1	149	47	12	8	64	67.2	42	2	417	138
ANA	2006	89	73	4	97.0	78	2	97	6		380	292	27	87	.159	3	123	45	23	6	44	70.5	29	2	452	154
ANA	2007	94	68	4	97.2	83	0	90	1		396	310	22	91	.270	2	118	47	20	8	47	68.1	31	2	424	142
ANA	2008	100	62	11	99.4	84	0	92	3	104.5	383	302	32	67	.200	0	109	38	19	8	48	66.7	32	1	364	113
ANA	2009	97	65	4	96.9	82	1	77	7	103	434	340	35	65	.321	2	124	57	22	5	63	68.3	41	3	447	134
ANA	2010	80	82	1	102.1	105	3	93	6	103.6	410	325	33	86	.174	0	90	39	14	10	70	60.0	41	3	400	125
ANA	2011	86	76	1	101.0	98	11	98	8	104.4	386	313	34	75	.154	2	116	47	18	4	78	64.1	46	1	417	144
ANA	2012	89	73	1	97.4	87	4	91	3	103.3	444	365	20	68	.203	2	121	27	12	4	72	65.3	43	3	419	132
ANA	2013	78	84	-3	97.5	77	6	87	5	102.5	496	400	36	83	.214	3	71	32	10	1	54	68.5	35	0	349	110
ANA	2014	98	64	1	94.1	71	3	80	5	103.1	543	467	41	103	.233	1	72	37	9	2	42	61.9	24	1	315	88
ANA	2015	85	77	6	95.0	55	2	88	5	102.4	518	429	45	102	.217	2	45	31	6	2	50	74.0	36	3	297	91
ANA	2016	74	88	-6	90.4	39	0	64	5	101.3	527	423	27	94	.171	1	60	30	12	4	49	73.5	36	3	364	118
ANA	2017	80	82	-1	87.4	22	0	61	3	99.3	542	456	25	104	.260	1	115	38	20	5	32	53.1	16	1	364	119

Scott Servais wRM+: 100.3

TEAM	YEAR	W	L	Pythag +/-	Avg PC	100+ P	120+ P	QS	BQS	wRM+	REL	REL w Zero R	IBB	PH	PH Avg	PH HR	SB2	CS2	SB3	CS3	SAC Att	SAC %	POS SAC	Squee-ze	Swing	In Play
SEA	2016	86	76	-2	92.1	43	0	74	8	101.8	477	379	30	146	.254	4	48	26	8	1	43	55.8	21	0	268	83
SEA	2017	78	84	-1	88.2	32	0	62	0	100.3	526	405	28	86	.192	0	83	31	6	4	27	51.9	11	0	236	65

Buck Showalter wRM+: 101.7

TEAM	YEAR	W	L	Pythag +/-	Avg PC	100+ P	120+ P	QS	BQS	wRM+	REL	REL w Zero R	IBB	PH	PH Avg	PH HR	SB2	CS2	SB3	CS3	SAC Att	SAC %	POS SAC	Squee-ze	Swing	In Play
NYA	1992	76	86	-4				85	14		308	236	49	89	.247	3	65	31	13	4	36	72.2	26	1		
NYA	1993	88	74	1				81	13		333	253	58	131	.272	4	34	31	4	4	37	59.5	22	0		
NYA	1994	70	43	1				61	8		241	181	24	79	.232	4	48	36	7	4	37	73.0	27	1		
NYA	1995	79	66	0				74	5		302	233	21	103	.266	1	46	24	4	5	27	74.1	20	0		
ARI	1998	65	97	-0	89.5	59	8	75	18		368	267	32	248	.171	3	67	32	5	4	70	64.3	16	0		
ARI	1999	100	62	-4	103.2	107	27	98	7		382	298	48	216	.321	5	119	35	16	3	77	79.2	23	1		
ARI	2000	85	77	0	94.9	63	18	84	8		390	294	53	248	.230	2	85	34	12	8	85	71.8	21	3		
TEX	2003	71	91	3	87.9	45	4	51	7		494	347	45	72	.177	0	61	24	4	1	38	63.2	21	0	260	90
TEX	2004	89	73	2	92.3	47	3	61	6		468	381	29	75	.143	1	64	32	5	4	37	62.2	22	0	257	87
TEX	2005	79	83	-3	92.5	66	2	66	2		454	325	31	43	.238	3	61	14	6	1	12	75.0	9	0	304	92
TEX	2006	80	82	-6	91.0	46	0	74	2		489	378	18	37	.182	0	47	23	6	1	35	51.4	15	0	253	83
BAL	2010	34	23	3	98.7	31	0	36	3	101.3	144	106	10	15	.154	0	25	9	4	0	15	80.0	12	0	78	26
BAL	2011	69	93	4	91.8	50	0	60	6	101.9	478	351	42	57	.309	1	74	20	7	5	41	58.5	23	2	309	97
BAL	2012	93	69	11	95.6	66	1	78	6	102.2	492	415	36	69	.161	0	55	21	3	8	51	74.5	34	1	282	102
BAL	2013	85	77	-0	95.9	75	0	78	5	103.2	473	380	32	65	.143	0	70	26	9	2	39	69.2	23	0	236	68
BAL	2014	96	66	1	97.8	78	1	78	7	103.1	479	405	25	74	.308	2	37	16	6	3	56	62.5	32	1	205	60
BAL	2015	81	81	-2	93.7	63	0	72	4	103.4	453	369	27	79	.208	1	34	22	9	2	33	60.6	18	0	191	58
BAL	2016	89	73	5	94.5	66	0	69	5	104.5	443	366	23	68	.274	2	19	11	0	2	24	70.8	14	0	175	55
BAL	2017	75	87	4	93.6	64	0	61	1	101.7	492	383	21	91	.195	1	25	11	6	2	22	45.5	10	0	171	48

Brian Snitker wRM+: 101

TEAM	YEAR	W	L	Pythag +/-	Avg PC	100+ P	120+ P	QS	BQS	wRM+	REL	REL w Zero R	IBB	PH	PH Avg	PH HR	SB2	CS2	SB3	CS3	SAC Att	SAC %	POS SAC	Squee-ze	Swing	In Play
ATL	2016	59	65	4	89.9	40	0	49	1	100.5	456	371	40	212	.226	4	48	21	11	3	78	61.5	14	1	208	74
ATL	2017	72	90	0	93.6	45	1	77	4	101	530	406	39	268	.231	10	64	29	13	2	87	67.8	18	0	312	92

Ned Yost wRM+: 98.7

TEAM	YEAR	W	L	Pythag +/-	Avg PC	100+ P	120+ P	QS	BQS	wRM+	REL	REL w Zero R	IBB	PH	PH Avg	PH HR	SB2	CS2	SB3	CS3	SAC Att	SAC %	POS SAC	Squee-ze	Swing	In Play
MIL	2003	68	94	3	95.5	70	5	66	7		460	344	43	282	.220	6	89	34	9	5	98	63.3	29	1	267	82
MIL	2004	67	94	1	93.2	60	8	82	5		423	299	27	279	.205	7	124	35	14	2	96	58.3	28	1	358	101
MIL	2005	81	81	-3	99.3	86	4	91	5		396	292	52	253	.248	6	68	30	11	3	113	58.4	41	5	298	100
MIL	2006	75	87	5	94.5	67	3	81	7		427	306	34	235	.267	4	60	33	10	4	88	65.9	20	1	294	96
MIL	2007	83	79	-1	94.0	56	3	76	9		492	368	37	253	.224	6	86	25	9	4	81	74.1	22	0	321	100
MIL	2008	83	67	2	96.3	54	6	82	3	99.3	399	311	30	217	.208	7	85	27	20	7	66	69.7	17	3	333	108
KCA	2010	55	72	4	96.4	59	1	53	7	100.1	332	257	25	52	.214	2	73	35	12	4	45	66.7	25	0	281	78
KCA	2011	71	91	-7	96.9	74	0	75	5	98.9	420	339	42	36	.152	1	130	48	23	8	75	73.3	51	2	399	113
KCA	2012	72	90	-1	90.5	55	0	69	4	99.9	500	411	44	55	.208	3	109	34	22	4	42	61.9	25	1	334	97
KCA	2013	86	76	-1	98.6	79	2	95	5	96.5	427	374	21	74	.210	1	133	30	19	2	56	66.1	36	1	369	99
KCA	2014	89	73	5	98.6	90	2	95	4	97.7	451	399	14	43	.250	2	124	29	29	7	55	60.0	30	1	344	112
KCA	2015	95	67	4	92.8	52	0	71	3	98.5	493	418	10	36	.188	0	76	30	27	2	48	70.8	32	0	257	86
KCA	2016	81	81	4	93.2	61	0	68	7	99.9	472	391	8	47	.238	0	102	31	19	4	66	57.6	35	0	300	73
KCA	2017	80	82	9	88.7	26	0	64	3	98.7	538	423	24	41	.162	0	74	27	17	3	24	70.8	16	1	239	57

Top 101 Prospects

by Jeffrey Paternostro and Jarrett Seidler

1. Ronald Acuña, OF, Atlanta Braves

Acuña checked in at no. 31 on our 2017 list. This is not to take a victory lap—for reasons that will become obvious in a moment—but rather to make a point about the 20-80 scouting scale. We graded him out as an Overall Future Potential (OFP) 70—albeit a high-risk one—coming into the season. He promptly smashed three levels of the minors to the tune of .325/.374/.522. And Acuña's best performance came at Triple-A as a 19-year-old. The underlying loud tools haven't changed, but now he looks like a plus hitter to go with his 7 raw power and ability to stick in center field. In short, he's better. He's also almost major-league ready. The 20-80 scale only works if you use all of it. Acuña deserves his spot in the rarified air at the top of the scouting scale and the top of our Top 101 list. He's a potential franchise-altering talent.

2. Victor Robles, OF, Washington Nationals

One could certainly argue that Acuña and Robles should properly be listed as 1a and 1b. That sounds like a needless hedge, but they are both potential role 8 players, although they get there in very different ways. Robles is a speed/defense center fielder, grading out as plus-plus in both categories. He's a better bet to hit .300, and it's not impossible that he develops average game power. He already has major-league per diems under his belt, and the realistic floor here is something like a right-handed Ender Inciarte. You can't really go wrong picking either as the best prospect in baseball. The upside of Acuña's offensive tools gets him the nod from us, but don't be shocked if Robles ends up the better player, even if his top-line counting stats aren't as shiny.

3. Gleyber Torres, SS, New York Yankees

It's easy to forget that players really do develop and grow over the course of their prospectdom, and even beyond. Torres had never hit for significant game power entering 2017, and we were starting to get questions about why a player we were projecting to hit for serious MLB power couldn't put much over the fence in A-ball. We weren't too worried about it, because the markers for future over-the-fence power growth were present: bat speed, batting practice power, adequate doubles power in game. Sure enough, the game power came in 2017, with some monstrous in-game shots leaving little doubt about the projection, and it would've launched him through both levels of the high-minors to the majors in just a half-season were it not for a season-ending UCL tear in his non-throwing elbow. Without the injury, Torres likely would've either graduated or been even higher on this list, but the lost half-season of development and minor uncertainty around a peculiar injury drop him just a couple spots. Remember to look at the nice 2016 World Series Champions banner before you scream too loud, Cubs fans.

4. Vladimir Guerrero Jr., 3B, Toronto Blue Jays

Vladito is one of the reasons we are minimizing our victory laps from the 2017 list in this space. We could tell you that he was literally no. 102—it was him or Sixto Sanchez, we swear—or that he was on various earlier iterations of the list in the 90s. But regardless of how we might try to weasel out of it, we missed. So, a *mea culpa*: We tend to underrate first-base prospects due to the pressure on their bat. And as Vladito looks like his father reflected in a concave carnival mirror, he's likely to move across the diamond by the time he reaches the majors (or in his twenties, whichever comes first). As for the bat, it's only good news here. The swing is a carbon copy of senior's, no fun-house distortion here. If he's a .300 hitter with 30 bombs, no one will care where he stands on the diamond. And at the rate he's progressing through the minors, Vladito may soon be reenacting the music video for "I Just Don't Know What to Do With Myself" at major-league third-base bags.

5. Francisco Mejia, C, Cleveland Indians

"Catchers are weird" is a mantra for the BP prospect team. They can be tricky evaluations due to their extensive defensive responsibilities, many of which aren't visible from the usual scouting vantage points. However, Mejia is not a tricky prospect. He's a potential plus-plus switch-hitter, and the swing works from both sides of the plate. Despite his short and squat stature, he stings the ball hard enough to project 15 home runs a year even with truncated catcher playing time. Mejia has improved his receiving behind the plate and has always had a plus arm. The only lingering question is whether that short and squat frame will hold up over a full year's load of, well, squatting. He has never caught more than 87 games in a season, and Cleveland started getting him reps at third base in the Arizona Fall League. If we were more confident that he's a 120-game-per-year catcher, he'd have his own case for no. 1 on this list. Until then, remember: Catchers are weird.

6. Eloy Jimenez, OF, Chicago White Sox

Here he is now going to the South Side. Say what you will about the Cubs, but they're never afraid to deal good prospects for good MLB players—even to their crosstown rivals. The top prize in this past summer's Jose Quintana deal kept chugging along in 2017, through two organizations and two levels, continuing to hit for average and power. About the worst thing we can say for him is that he's defensively limited to a corner, although if you saw his catch in the 2016 Futures Game you're probably not all that concerned that he won't be able to stay on the grass. In a world where we don't appreciate dudes who just freakin' hit as much as we used to, Jimenez is one to appreciate.

7. Nick Senzel, 3B, Cincinnati Reds

Third base has been a generally underrated position for decades now. Bill James first noted some 25 or 30 years ago it was chronically underrepresented in the Hall of Fame, and it still is to this day. It's the position in the middle of the defensive spectrum, and often the stars here are well-rounded players who do everything well but nothing at the top of the league. Senzel, the no. 2 overall pick in the 2016 draft, fits this profile like his above-average glove. He projects as a very good regular who is very good at everything but not the best in the world at any one thing. He makes so little noise, even when doing things like hitting .340 with power over a half-season at Double-A, that he's easy to forget about. He'll show up as part of Cincinnati's young core sooner than you'd think.

8. Alex Reyes, RHP, St. Louis Cardinals

Last year's no. 1 prospect was blurbed via a blackjack metaphor in last year's *Annual*. Appropriately, he busted literally one day after we posted the list on the website. The culprit was very much a usual suspect, a torn UCL necessitating Tommy John surgery. Reyes missed all of 2017, and the standard recovery time would keep him off a mound until a few months into the 2018 season. Nevertheless, Reyes holds serve as the best pitching prospect in the game. These risks are just baked in to pitching prospects nowadays, but if Reyes comes back with all of his stuff intact, you can drop his 100-mph fastball and two plus secondaries right onto a major-league mound. If it doesn't come all the way back, he's still likely a good starter or a shutdown reliever. And he's used the time off to get in the best shape of his life. Yes, ITBSOHL has become a running joke in baseball circles, but there were some body questions with Reyes before. That's one question answered, at least. The rest remain outstanding for a bit longer.

9. Fernando Tatis Jr., SS, San Diego Padres

Fernando, Son of Fernando, might end up with a skill set that looks a heck of a lot like his pop's. Read through the scouting reports and you can see the outlines of a star power/speed third baseman here, and his father really was that for a few years in the late '90s. The strange thing about Fernando the Elder's career was how bifurcated it was: He was basically done in his mid-twenties, only to have a brief resurgence as a bench player nearly a decade later. There's no reason to think Fernando the Younger will have such an early and short peak, but it's a reminder that career trajectories of star players come in all shapes and sizes, often without a neat upswing, peak at 27 or 28 and slow decline like we imagine in our heads and projections.

10. Forrest Whitley, RHP, Houston Astros

We may not have had greater internal debate about any top prospect this year than Whitley. Taken one way, Whitley may have had the single most impressive season of any player in the minors. Considered a generic first-round Texas prep arm with the usual caveats like work needed on his secondaries and general reliever risk coming into the year, Whitley instead blitzed through Low-A, High-A and Double-A with a polished four-pitch mix and peripherals that looked more like recent vintage Andrew Miller than a typical starting prospect. Yet, it's a four-pitch mix that includes a bunch of above-average or plus pitches, but perhaps none that will truly dominate. He's probably going to be good and he's probably coming fast, but it might "only" be a no. 2 starter profile.

11. Brent Honeywell, RHP, Tampa Bay Rays

Dr. Mike Marshall's nephew has more than a bit of his iconoclastic uncle in him, in both personality and approach to the game, yet as an overall pitching prospect he's almost boringly hypercompetent. Honeywell has been on a steady march up the minor-league chain—and our rankings—for three seasons now, without major injury or performance hurdles, showing a full repertoire of plus-or-better offerings. Sure, that repertoire includes a screwball, but that's the only hint of oddness in the pitching report. On merit Honeywell was probably ready for the bigs by late 2017, but the Rays have rarely met a prospect they haven't let marinate in the minors a little extra, which often has the fun side effect of delaying arbitration and free agency. Expect him up either a few weeks or a few months into the 2018 season, depending on how cost-conscious the team decides to be about his 2021 salary.

12. Brendan Rodgers, SS, Colorado Rockies

The backbone of this list is our staff's live looks. In the California League, Rodgers looked like a potential All-Star with plus hit and power tools and a steady hand at shortstop. Across the country in the Eastern League, the look was more anonymous, as he never drove the ball and his aggressive approach got worked out by more advanced arms. He still looked capable, if not spectacular, at the six. Double-A can be a test for even top-tier prospects like Rodgers, and he was only 20 and spent much of the second half of the year banged up, but if we're lower on Rodgers than the rest of our list-making compatriots, the Eastern League looks will be why.

13. Sixto Sanchez, RHP, Philadelphia Phillies

If you're looking for the highest of crazy upsides in your pitching prospects, come get your mans. He touches 102 mph and is typically effortless in the high-90s with command and manipulation. Depending on when you see him, he'll give you a lot of different looks with his off-speed stuff, and it's all good. There's great natural feel for spin here, and his better curveballs are jaw-dropping in depth and break. The changeup has a pretty wide velocity band—it's arguably two distinct pitches—and rates as a significant party piece, too. We expect he'll narrow down what he throws to concentrate on honing two or three specific off-speeds later, although a small group of special pitchers like Zack Greinke never bother to narrow the selection. Sanchez has only been pitching for about two years and has the great athleticism you'd associate with a recently converted shortstop. Of course, the birdie on the other shoulder forces me to remind you that he has thrown a grand total of 95 innings above the complex leagues, all in A-ball, and that there has probably never been a player listed at six feet who was anywhere close to that height. Suffice it to say, he's not necessarily immune to the generic durability concerns that envelope nearly the entire field of pitching prospects these days. Good scouts don't comp Pedro, but we've heard good scouts comp Pedro here.

14. J.P. Crawford, SS, Philadelphia Phillies

Two things we don't like to do as prospect rankers are self-insert into the prospect's developmental story and pay attention to other rankings, but it's impossible to discuss the last year of Crawford without discussing his response to *Baseball America* dumping on him as part of their midseason ranking process. After years of high rankings and abundant praise from all sources, *BA* dropped Crawford to 92nd in their midseason list and said they no longer saw him as an "impact player." Crawford responded by tweeting "All it is is motivation" the same day, and later admitted *BA*'s criticism "lit a fire" under him. Whatever got into him, Crawford hit .268/.377/.457 spread between Triple-A and MLB from July 13 through the end of the season, a marked improvement on his performance at any level in the previous few years, all while playing stellar defense at three infield positions. He should settle in as a long-term regular at shortstop out of camp in 2018, and we never lost faith that there may yet be an impact player lurking if the power ultimately comes.

15. Willy Adames, SS, Tampa Bay Rays

Adames and Crawford make an obvious matched pair. Both are shortstops without a surfeit of tools and with more steady than eye-popping performance in leagues where they were a few years younger than the average farmhand. This is the type of profile that tends to get underrated, but it does have its pitfalls. Adames has the better hit tool at present, but he doesn't have Crawford's strong approach at the plate or plus glove at shortstop to buoy the profile if he doesn't hit .280. We think he's a plus hitter, but the hardest thing to evaluate is how this type of profile will fare against the best pitchers in the world. That uncertainty is why he slots in behind Crawford, rather than ahead of him. Adames showed a bit more game power in 2017, so that's worth keeping an eye on, since this profile has been known to "inexplicably" hit 20 home runs in the majors in recent seasons.

16. Mitch Keller, RHP, Pittsburgh Pirates

We haven't gotten to this year's bumper crop of potential mid-rotation starters yet—Keller has top-of-the-rotation upside—but we would like to make a point about *el cambio* here. Usually we chide our projected mid-rotation arms for their deficiencies of command and changeup. The former isn't an issue with Keller. He has plus command of his mid-90s fastball and can adeptly manipulate his potential 70 curveball as well. With our mid-rotation types the changeup will be wildly inconsistent—flash good fade to one batter, then be firm or well off the plate armside to another. Keller doesn't even flash the good one most nights. Most nights it won't matter. We can get prescriptive with what we look for in our top pitching prospects. It becomes a checklist. Keller is missing one of the boxes. We don't know whether it matters. Reports were better on the pitch out of fall ball, and sometimes guys just learn a new grip that works. Normally we'd note that he just needs a good enough changeup to "keep lefties honest," but there's a very good chance southpaws won't hit his fastball or curve even if they know they're coming.

17. Michael Kopech, RHP, Chicago White Sox

Kopech is probably most famous for being the hardest thrower in baseball, and yet based on 2017 reports he might not even be the hardest thrower on this list anymore. Despite preseason reports that he was throwing as high as 110 mph—never mind that he was doing so in workout drills with a non-regulation baseball and a running start that would be illegal in a real game—Kopech actually dialed it back last season, to the extent that you can call sitting in the high-90s and touching 102 dialing it back. He brought a hard-running two-seam fastball back into the mix, further sacrificing a tick or two for movement and command, and all things considered he breezed through Double-A much easier than expected. Even better, Kopech's only off-field drama in 2017 was of the semi-scripted variety, on his girlfriend's television shows, *Don't Be Tardy* and *The Real Housewives of Atlanta*. Risks and rewards both remain super high on this one.

18. Lewis Brinson, OF, Milwaukee Brewers

We're not immune to the occasional bout of prospect fatigue. Brinson is the source of this year's septicemia. You'd think his .331/.400/.562 line at Triple-A would offer sufficient inoculation, but those numbers came in Colorado Springs, an offensive environment akin to the Elaysian homeworld. Hold on, surely we can't ignore his potential five-tool center field profile? Yes, there is still All-Star upside here, which is why he slots in as one of the 20 best prospects in baseball. The nagging issue for us is that he struggled in the majors in exactly the way he would if it wasn't going to come together for him. Brinson has had swing-and-miss issues going back to his days on the Rangers' star-studded 2013 Hickory Crawdads roster—there's another symptom, we've been writing about him for five years—and he struck out 17 times in his first 55 major-league plate appearances. That's well within the vagaries of Voros' law, and Brinson has needed adjustment time at every level, but those types of prospects often struggle to make that final adjustment.

19. Bo Bichette, SS, Toronto Blue Jays

What's in a name? Bichette is the third player on this list who's the son of a prominent star of our youth. In the cases of Vladito and Tatis the Second, sons of well-liked, well-rounded players who had long careers, it's clear that the bloodlines are considered a huge positive. It's not so clear in Bo's case. For starters, papa Dante Sr. was a one-dimensional slugger of ill repute who took enormous advantage of Coors Field. He was regularly maligned by our BP forefathers as one of baseball's most overrated in these very pages (though we should note that "overrated" is not the same as bad: Dad hit .299 with 274 homers and 152 stolen bases over 18 big-league seasons). Bo's brother Dante Jr. was a prominent prospect himself, a 2011 Yankees first-rounder, who is realistically a straight-up bust and minor-league journeyman at this point. Bo Bichette stands well apart from his brother and father in his profile, a middle infielder who might bump to third base instead of a corner butcher, a player carried by a potentially elite hit tool instead of a Blake Street Bomber. But consciously or not, he's still associated with them, and surely it's not to his benefit.

20. Kyle Tucker, OF, Houston Astros

The rebuild is done in Houston, and given the ultimate result, no one will care that Tucker is one of only two prospects of note remaining on the farm. He was also the second-best prospect in the system before the 2017 season. Of that preseason top 10, two graduated, two were dealt for Justin Verlander and another left town for Francisco Liriano. Astros fans won't be scrutinizing their team's prospect list as closely nowadays, but Tucker is a fine player to have near the top of it. You might not be aware of that yet since we've spent the first two-thirds of this blurb not actually talking about Tucker as a prospect, so now we'll briefly summarize: Preston's brother, polished corner-outfield profile, patient approach, potential plus power, some stiffness in the swing, high probability above-average regular.

21. Walker Buehler, RHP, Los Angeles Dodgers

Buehler's September call-up may have been a little too aggressive, but hey, when you've got an impact arm that can't stay on the mound, try to get as many outs as possible while he's healthy, right? The 2015 first-rounder somehow only needed a little over two years in the minors despite having Tommy John surgery shortly after the draft, which shows just how much talent is in his prized right arm. It remains unclear whether he has starter-level durability, and he struggled some in late promotions to both Triple-A and the majors, so the Dodgers might be wise to let him consolidate things in a high-minors starting role for the first part of 2018. But the temptation to roster Buehler as a potentially dominant relief arm will remain until he establishes himself as an above-average starter. If he ends up short of a full-load starter, he's in the right organization, as the current Dodgers administration has recently found great use of starters who need extra rest or bullpen time.

22. Juan Soto, OF, Washington Nationals

Soto's full-season debut was off to a splendid start, as the precocious teenager mashed the ball like crazy for a month playing at age 18, living up to some lofty scouting reports we'd been seeing since spring 2016. Unfortunately, the injuries came and came hard, with an ankle injury robbing him of a few months and then a season-ending hamate injury; he never made it back out of the complex after May 2. On talent, we'd have Soto much higher—he was 12th on the midseason list, which came down in the five minutes between injuries—but hamate injuries can linger and we simply haven't seen him stay on the field enough quite yet. If you want cause for wild optimism, his profile, age and performance all track surprisingly closely to those of Ronald Acuña entering 2017, and such a jump is certainly within Soto's massive abilities.

23. Brendan McKay, LHP/1B, Tampa Bay Rays

We decided not to rank Shohei Ohtani as a prospect this year, partially because we're not participating in MLB's farce that a guy with five years in NPB is a prospect, and partially because it wouldn't have been interesting. This doesn't mean we didn't have to grapple with the implications of a serious two-way prospect. Enter McKay, arguably the best hitter *and* pitcher in last year's college draft class. It was expected coming into the draft that, like his spiritual forerunners John van Benschoten and Brooks Kieschnick, McKay would be picked as either a pitcher or a hitter, and that he'd be developed only on one side, at least initially. Yet the Rays took him fourth overall with the intention of developing his abilities both ways, at least for now. His usage pattern at short-season Hudson Valley was far more interesting than his performance: He made six starts on the mound and didn't hit in those games, typically DH'd the day before and the day after his pitching appearances and played something of a regular first base when he was further into his pitching rest cycle. We've basically placed him around where we would if he were just a high-end polished lefty college pitching prospect, with a small bonus for his hitting. Were McKay purely a first-base prospect, we'd probably have him a few dozen spots lower. There's simply no precedent for what this is going to look like, so hold on and have some fun.

24. Kolby Allard, LHP, Atlanta Braves

Allard was one of three lefties with back issues to end up clustered together on the second half of our 2017 list. He broke out as the best of the bunch last year, skipping right to Double-A as a 19-year-old. Allard more than held his own against much older competition on the strength of his plus curveball and advanced fastball command. Allard is a "greater than the sum of his stuff" arm. He's more polish than projection, on the shorter side, and the fastball is low 90s in an era when even short-season staffs have multiple guys touching 98. Still, calling him a crafty lefty is unnecessarily pejorative. The polish *is* impressive, and the stuff isn't bad either. Another plus: The back issues are firmly in his rear-view mirror, and he threw 150 innings in 2017—an unusually high number for a teenage pitching prospect. Allard's size and stuff limitations make the profile more future mid-rotation than ace, but he's well on his way to handling the innings-eating portion of that assignment.

25. Alex Verdugo, OF, Los Angeles Dodgers

In an era when swinging hard and trying to lift the ball has led to a panoply of Three True Outcome sluggers, Verdugo is a delightful throwback. He posts strikeouts rates straight of the 1980s, culminating in his walking more than whiffing as a 21-year-old in Triple-A. So, yeah, it's a potential 7 hit tool. Now it may have to be, as his swing is geared more to drive the ball to the opposite field than yank it over the fence. That was fine in the 1980s, and it would be fine in 2018 if he were a lock to stay in center field, but with only average foot speed he's likely to slide over to right field. At least his top-of-the-scale arm—he hit 97 mph off the mound as a high schooler—will be a weapon there. And frankly, the fact that a high school lefty touching 97 got developed as an outfielder at all might be the best endorsement of his bat we could come up with.

26. Estevan Florial, OF, New York Yankees

There's been something of a renaissance in significant prospects of Haitian descent, led by Miguel Sano, the only player in the majors who identifies as Haitian. In large part due to MLB's own initiatives following the "agegate" scandals of 15-20 years ago and increased identity verification protocols in the wake of 9/11, Dominican prospects usually have their birth and identity paperwork in order now. Haitian players often do not; Sano's signing was marred and delayed by questions over his true name and age. The man now playing as Estevan Florial originally planned to sign with the Yankees for a seven-figure deal as a Dominican international prospect under the name Haniel d'Oleo. His true identity was uncovered shortly before he signed, although in this case it wasn't a matter of maliciously changing his age—Haniel d'Oleo was just a name his school had registered him under—and after a year's suspension he was allowed to sign under his real name and identity. The Yankees still gave him a $200,000 bonus, and they've been rewarded with a five-tool athletic specimen with unusually advanced feel for the game given his background and age. He made the Futures Game and reached Double-A for the Eastern League playoffs as a teenager, and only his ability to control the swing-and-miss in his game puts a limit on his upside.

27. Royce Lewis, SS, Minnesota Twins

The Twins reportedly selected Lewis over Brendan McKay in large part for his "signability"—a nice euphemism for his decision to take a lower bonus. (McKay signed for several hundred thousand dollars more as the fourth pick than Lewis did as the first pick.) We aren't ranking them far enough apart to have a strong opinion on the matter quite yet, and these things can go in many different directions; rumors abounded at the time of the 2012 draft that Carlos Correa was selected for similar reasons—he's obviously on a far greater trajectory than the other 1.1 options that year—and the savings from that pick also allowed the Astros to give playoff hero Lance McCullers an extreme over-slot bonus later on. It'll be years before we know whether the Twins made the right call, and it might rely as much on $2 million third-round pick Blayne Enlow's future as Lewis or McKay.

28. Leody Taveras, OF, Texas Rangers

"Don't scout the stat line" has gone from keen advice, to prospect writer shibboleth, to hoary cliché in recent years. Of course good production beats bad production, but all varietals of statistical performance have to be explained by the evaluators. Taveras had the worst offensive performance of any of the bats in our top 30, and we don't have a good explanation for it. The easy hand-wave is that he was 18 for the entire season and his triple-slash line wasn't even that bad. But he looked like he should hit Sally League pitching more than he did. Taveras has one of the better baseball bodies you'll see, as well as premium bat speed and an advanced approach from both sides of the plate. He's a potential five-tool outfielder who can already go get it in center field. You can dream on plus game power as his upper body fills out, too. So do you really care about his .672 OPS in A-ball? Still, if we had a better explanation for his struggles he'd be higher on this list.

29. MacKenzie Gore, LHP, San Diego Padres

So you want to take a high school arm toward the top of the first round? You aren't close to the first, and you won't be the last. Let's just run down the checklist before you do something unwise:

1. How's the fastball?

Mid-90s: Go ahead and put him at the top of your draft board.

Low-90s: Proceed to Question 2.

2. Is he projectable?

Listed at 6-foot-3, 180 pounds. This bio data can be wildly inaccurate, but it looks about right. So check that box.

3. How's the breaking ball?

"Potential plus"

"Potential plus or better" (curve)

All right, getting closer.

(Optional) *4. Which scouty sounding hedge best describes his present changeup?*

"Flashes plus"

"Advanced pitch for his age"
"Some feel for the change"
"Clear third pitch"
"Never really needed it"

5. Oh, we almost forgot: Is he left-handed?

Yep.

Okay, we're good here. Open the checkbook.

30. A.J. Puk, LHP, Oakland Athletics

Puk can remind one an enormous amount of Andrew Miller as a prospect. Both were considered by many to be the top player in their draft class as long, sometimes shaggy-haired 6-foot-7 lefties after dominant college careers. Both went with the sixth pick in the draft. Both have a little slingy sidearm in their delivery that limits what could be extraordinary plane from that kind of size but causes the slider to play up from an unusual angle. Miller was rushed to the majors despite some command and durability problems for Detroit, was dealt to the Marlins in the Miguel Cabrera trade and never put it together in years in the wilderness as a starter. You probably know the next part, where he then became one of the game's great relievers in his late twenties. The A's have taken it easier with Puk. He split his first full season half-and-half between High-A and Double-A, beating up both levels in ways Miller was never allowed to, but Puk still hints at some of the same command issues. Although Miller's arc is only one of many that Puk may emulate, it serves to remind us that even if the beginning is rough, you can't teach this kind of stuff from a tall lefty with a tough arm slot.

31. Scott Kingery, 2B, Philadelphia Phillies

The fly-ball revolution wasn't just for major leaguers. Kingery hit eight combined home runs in his first two pro seasons. Two of our prospect team members filed scouting reports on him in 2016, with power projections at 30 and 20 grade. But then Kingery started hitting a *lot* of homers, 26 in all split between Double-A and Triple-A. He credited some mechanical changes that caused him to stay back on the ball, along with some additional upper-body mass. There are caveats to this massive improvement—much of it was in the home-run paradise of Reading, for example—but even bumping Kingery up to average power fortifies the other standout tools, like hit and run, into a fine player, perhaps even a star.

32. Keston Hiura, 2B/DH, Milwaukee Brewers

We prefer not to be in thrall to June draft big boards, but Hiura went ninth overall this past summer and signed under slot to boot. We have him fourth among 2017 draftees on this list. So where's the disconnect? Well, the main reason Hiura dropped in the draft was an elbow injury that kept him from playing the field for his junior season. As good as the bat is, it's not special if he's a designated hitter. He was able to play some second base as a pro, and by all reports his throwing looked fine there. It's also second base so fine is, well, fine. Now you dream on the best pure hitter in the draft sticking at an up-the-middle position. That gets our attention, as does Hiura's advanced approach and potentially average game power. He's not as fast as Scott Kingery, but the overall profile may not be all that different now.

33. Mike Soroka, RHP, Atlanta Braves

Soroka is not easily reduced to 150 words of plaudits commensurate with his spot on this list. Phrases like "steady diet of well-located low-90s fastballs" is not prose that will inspire the reader to a flight of fancy. Nor does "built to log innings" jump off the page. "Potential plus slider" is better, but hardly a marker of future greatness. There's a curveball and a changeup, too, and he mixes everything well. Oh, and his numbers were better than Kolby Allard's as a 19-year-old in Double-A. We have the inverse of the Leody Taveras problem here. We can't tell you exactly why Soroka was so good in 2017. We can use words like "command" and "pitchability," and it isn't like he has bad stuff. The scouting report is just full of more 55s than 60s. That doesn't always work in the majors, especially without an obvious out pitch, so things are still murky here. What is clear is this list has now officially entered the mid-rotation starter tier. Buckle up.

34. Austin Meadows, OF, Pittsburgh Pirates

This is around where the list has a lot of similar profiles and similar concerns: the toolsy bat-speed guys with pitch recognition problems, the well-rounded shortstops in the "maybe" bucket on staying at shortstop, the different ways we try to describe third starter projections and so on. It's more interesting to write about guys with oddball arcs, and Meadows is putting together quite an oddball arc. In four full pro seasons, he has only played anything close to a full season once, yet he has somehow avoided the injury-prone tag. We never had any real doubts about whether he'd hit, but if you start drilling down, he has never dominated a level for more than six weeks, and he has struggled a *lot* in between those short periods of domination. He's now just a career .239/.306/.390 hitter at Triple-A over 109 games. He has drifted into the outfield corners as expected, but without the sort of physical growth you might've hoped would lead to a big power spike. The Pirates may not know what to make of him either; after attempting to clear a spot for Meadows before the 2017 season, they passed him over later when playing time opened up due to injuries. We'd suspect this is his last appearance on this list unless weird things happen, because he's closing in on the inflection point where he either puts it together and gets promoted or his stock is going to start to resemble Fannie Mae.

35. Nick Gordon, SS, Minnesota Twins

Prospect fatigue is a real thing, part two. Gordon has advanced one league per season since being drafted fifth overall in 2014, putting up perfectly acceptable numbers and making small gains in the profile every year. This is the fourth year in a row he has made an appropriate, if small, rise in our 101, since each time he repeats the trick he gets closer to doing it in the majors. Yet you hear virtually nothing about him, even as he's on the doorstep to the majors as a tools-laden shortstop who keeps performing, because we don't have much new to say. He even gets a shorter comment here because of it!

36. Jorge Alfaro, C, Philadelphia Phillies

Speaking of prospect fatigue, this is Alfaro's seventh appearance on the 101. We've basically run out of things to say about him, so instead we'll just play the hits from previous *Annuals*:

2012: Alfaro has an 80-grade arm and 70-grade power potential.
2013: [Alfaro] has a sky-high ceiling.
2014: His aggressiveness at the plate will be exploited as he climbs the ladder.
2015: Alfaro offers upside rarely seen at the position, but his flaws are equally real.
2016: If Alfaro can shore up his defensive game, he stands a decent chance of becoming a star.
2017: Although it may not have showed up in the stat line, 2016 was a big step forward for Alfaro in that he showed that he has the defensive chops to stick behind the plate in the majors.

Of course nobody likes clip shows, but as much as we'd like to offer something new, everything above still applies.

37. Triston McKenzie, RHP, Cleveland Indians

McKenzie was 2015's projectable prep arm, and two years later he's still a string bean. Although the physical projection hasn't come and the fastball remains around 90 mph, it hasn't mattered so far. McKenzie gets extra deception and plane from his long, lanky body and high arm slot, and he pairs the fastball with a potentially plus curve. He spent most of the season still a teenager, and even if he doesn't get any bigger, he handled 143 Carolina League innings without a problem, notching 186 strikeouts in the process. We'll remind you again not to scout the stat line, but that's a pretty nice stat line. You're still dreaming on more to come with McKenzie, but the grass isn't *that much* greener on the other side right now.

38. Jordon Adell, OF, Los Angeles Angels

Rumor has it that the Angels never have any prospects of note, but Adell is part of a crop percolating in the low minors that has California dreaming about setting fire to that notion. It's tough to find someone like Adell when you never pick high in the draft—he was the Angels' first top-10 pick since they took Joe Torres 10th in 2000—but they've also just let the sky fall on most everyone except Mike Trout. Granting that it's early, they may have hit big here; at the very least, they swung big on a huge talent with five-tool potential. Adell won't turn 19 until a few weeks into the 2018 season, so be patient, because they could have it all here, even if he's chasing curves near the pavement for a bit.

39. Hunter Greene, RHP, Cincinnati Reds

Is it just a meaningless fun fact that a right-handed prep pitcher has never been drafted no. 1 overall, or are teams legitimately scared off from them? We would posit it's just a fun fact, mostly because arms like Josh Beckett and Dylan Bundy certainly *could have* gone first in their draft year. Lucas Giolito very well might have had he remained healthy. And enough lefties have gone 1.1 to dispel the notion that teams would be scared off prep pitching in general. Greene was the latest iteration of the "there's no real reason he didn't" club, ranking as the draft's top prospect for most of the process, working out impressively for the Twins at Target Field just a few days before the draft and signing for the highest bonus of the cycle. Like Brendan McKay, Greene was also a significant prospect as a position player, but after seven games at designated hitter in rookie ball, the Reds determined Greene would focus on pitching, as was always expected. On the mound, his fastball matches up with that of anyone on this list, even Michael Kopech, and his slider has the potential but not the consistency to be quite nasty. Your typical concerns about changeup and command are here, too.

40. Alec Hansen, RHP, Chicago White Sox

How much higher would Hansen's stock be if his junior season at Oklahoma had never happened? Entering the 2016 draft cycle, he was the consensus top player in the country. As a pro, he has been right up there in both scouting reports and performance with any 2016 college player short of Nick Senzel. Yet we still *know* that things can go sideways for Hansen in a way that we just *speculate* they might go sideways for, say, A.J. Puk. We've seen it with our own eyes. We don't know whether that makes it more likely that Hansen will lose his feel and command again, but it seems more likely, and that costs him a chunk of spots every time we do one of these. Over time, the chunk grows smaller and smaller, because when you write what you see now, it's pretty freaking impressive. Eventually, we'll shake the negative feeling entirely if he keeps pitching like this.

41. Yadier Alvarez, RHP, Los Angeles Dodgers

The prospect writer's brain is similar to that of most higher-order primates. We look for patterns in development and prefer it when prospects progress on something akin to a y=x type slope year-over-year. It's easy enough to handle breakouts, the reasons for such usually being obvious to the naked eye. Stagnation can be a bit of a problem. Alvarez's strikes got hit harder in 2017 and he threw fewer strikes in general. That makes it easy enough to drop him 20 spots, as we did, while still holding out hope that he figures out enough command and control for the triple-digit heat and plus slider to bend bats to his will. Ah, but now the pattern becomes clear. Big fastball? Plus slider? Questions about the command and change? Potential high-leverage relief future? Every ink blot looks like a mid-rotation starter or good closer projection to us now.

42. Kyle Wright, RHP, Atlanta Braves

Nashville is fast becoming known more for pumping out pitching prospects than country music. Wright is the latest Vanderbilt alum to feature prominently on our version of the Billboard charts. Last year's fifth overall pick doesn't have much of a pro track record yet but comes with the Vanderbilt version of the 10-gallon hat and debut LP about drinking, trucks and women. Wright is a polished, four-pitch guy, with a potential plus fastball and slider, but the changeup lags behind and we wonder about the ultimate command projection given his somewhat unorthodox arm action. So to paraphrase another of Music City's famous sons: "Ah, I'd love to wear a rainbow every day, and tell the world that everything's OK, but I'll try to carry off a little darkness on my back, 'till things are brighter, I'm the Third Starter In Black."

43. Willie Calhoun, 2B/LF, Texas Rangers

If he were actually a second baseman and a half-foot taller, he'd be the best prospect in baseball. But Calhoun isn't a second baseman in any sense other than that it was the chosen position for him to stand at in his first two-and-a-half pro seasons while he hit the crap out of the ball. The Rangers converted him to left field on a near-full-time basis after picking him up for Yu Darvish, and all of his MLB playing time in the field came there. While he's probably not going to win any awards for stellar outfield play, he should be a lot less harmful to the team standing out there than by a base. If it comes down to it, he does play in the Junior Circuit with their newfangled designated hitter.

44. Carson Kelly, C, St. Louis Cardinals

Kelly is in one of the best and worst spots for his chosen career path. You could seek out no better tutor on the art of catching than Yadier Molina. On the other hand, this apprenticeship may last for a while, as Molina has three years and $60 million remaining on his contract extension with the Redbirds. Molina's late-twenties offensive peak is well in his rear-view mirror now, but he's still a very good everyday backstop and an average hitter. Kelly might be that as well. Heck, he might be that right now, but we're unlikely to find out while he's wearing Cardinal red. What we can say for sure is that he has nothing left to prove in the minors.

45. Joey Wentz, LHP, Atlanta Braves

Far too much has been made of what Wentz isn't. No, he doesn't throw in the high-90s, and if he ever did it was just showcase pops. Yes, he's lost a tick or two transitioning from an amateur schedule to a pro schedule. Should we care if he's still effective? He was one of the best pitchers in the Sally, pitching the entire season at 19, a total badass all year, disposing of both lefties and righties without regard. When did we decide a lefty peppering the low-90s didn't throw hard enough, anyway? He has the command, the secondary stuff, the pedigree and the performance to be considered a real prospect. And if he does get that extra few percent back on the fastball, look out.

46. Adonis Medina, RHP, Philadelphia Phillies

The Phillies have had phenomenal success turning small-ball international signings into significant pitching assets up and down the system. Medina signed for $70,000 out of the Dominican Republic in 2014, and he's out of Central Casting with a projectable frame that's already supporting velocity bumps into and above the mid-90s. He added a slider in 2017 that could be the out pitch down the line, and he has feel on the mound and command that belies his youth. Most of the rest of the usual caveats apply, of course, but if you can produce enough of these prospects, you're bound to hit on one.

47. Dylan Cease, RHP, Chicago White Sox

Speaking of organizational risk mitigation in pitching prospects, the White Sox have acquired so many extreme-upside arms—including ones that didn't make this list—that *someone* has to turn into an ace unless they get hideously unlucky. Cease is the highest-upside, highest-risk play of them all; he can throw a hundred and spin a mean curve. He's also entering his fifth pro season with a Tommy John surgery already on the résumé, and he hasn't thrown a hundred innings or made it out of Low-A yet. Obviously, there's a big shot for a late-inning reliever fallback here.

48. Cal Quantrill, RHP, San Diego Padres

This list is littered with pitchers who could have gone first overall in their draft year. That shouldn't be surprising—amateur scouts have that job based on their ability to pick the winners. Quantrill ended up falling out of conversation for the top pick in 2016 due to the usual reasons—a Tommy John surgery—that limited teams' looks at him. He has been stellar as a pro—reminding everyone why he was a 1.1 candidate—and while he's in our mid-rotation starter tier, it isn't for the usual reasons. He has three MLB-quality pitches, including a plus changeup, and can throw strikes with all of them. The outstanding questions here are short-term consistency—he can end up searching for his delivery at times after his long layoff from pitching—and long-term durability. As we get further from his surgery, those questions may weigh less on our mind, but for now we must remain cautiously optimistic.

49. Monte Harrison, OF, Milwaukee Brewers

As we wrote earlier, we know how to handle breakouts, and we aren't all that surprised Harrison broke out in 2017. He fits in the aforementioned "toolsy guys with bat speed and pitch-recognition problems" category, but it's big tools and big bat speed. It finally clicked on the field, as Harrison mashed 20 home runs between two A-ball levels. He has always had premium athletic tools—check out his high school basketball mixtape—but 2017 was his first full, healthy season. Sometimes it can be as simple as that. There's still a fair bit of rawness here, both in center field and at the plate, but with plus run, plus arm and plus raw in his tool shed, the overall profile isn't all that different from prospects like Lewis Brinson and Leody Taveras.

50. Adrian Morejon, RHP, San Diego Padres

What does one do with another arm
Of fastball big and curve that breaks
His changeup leads to easy takes
Yet still a credit to one's farm
There is no need to cry alarm
Because his body's no great shakes
Perhaps he's had a few cupcakes
Ugh that was likely needless smarm
But a verdict must be rendered now
So our patrons may plan their draft
But must we dabble in poetry
A pretense that is so highbrow
In particular form of Petrarchan craft
To tell you he's a number three

51. Chance Adams, RHP, New York Yankees

The Yankees have treated Adams very carefully, as befits a power college reliever they've been converting into a starter. Well, they've tried to, but he keeps forcing the issue by waltzing through the minors and not showing any of the typical issues of young pitchers being stretched out. Even still, Adams probably could have helped the Yankees down the stretch in 2017, but between 40-man considerations and developmental concerns, he never got the call. The fastball/slider combo is already there, and the changeup and curve aren't far behind, so his chance to be a mid-rotation stalwart can't be far out.

52. Michel Baez, RHP, San Diego Padres

San Diego spent $3 million over the holidays last year to sign Baez out of Cuba, and he has turned into more than just a stocking stuffer for a system that already has everything. With his 6-foot-8 frame, his mid-90s fastball looks like an avalanche coming down the side of K2, while his changeup looks like a cliff diver in Acapulco (your author may have been cooped up for a while writing these). Baez keeps the delivery on line well for a guy who could play center in Golden State's small-ball lineup, but until he develops an average breaking ball in his arsenal, the more conservative in our industry will peg him as a late-inning reliever. He could move quickly in that role, and San Diego sounds nice as we look out our window.

53. Franklin Perez, RHP, Detroit Tigers

Perez will forever be linked with Justin Verlander, as the top prospect sent to Detroit in the August 31 deal that sent the playoff hero to Houston. It's no slight to Perez to suggest that the odds of his matching Verlander's career under the Olde English 'D' are statistically insignificant. Perez is a very good prospect, but there are far more of those than future Hall of Fame arms. The trade made a sort of sabermetric sense, as the Tigers are entering a rebuild and Verlander is old and owed lots of future dollars. If Perez turns into a cost-controlled mid-rotation arm, that will be a lot of surplus value for the Tigers in his pre-arbitration years. It's just hard for me not to look askance at a formula that makes Perez more valuable to Detroit than Verlander has already been to the Astros.

54. Keibert Ruiz, C, Los Angeles Dodgers

Every year there's a prospect who gets bumped up this list after we chat with people inside the game. For this edition, the popular refrain was "you're too low on Ruiz." Not that Ruiz is hard to love: He's a switch-hitting catcher with an .800 OPS between two A-ball levels as a 19-year-old. That got our attention for sure. His defense is a work in progress—his receiving skills are good, the throwing and blocking not so much yet. But the overall package here looks like a plus regular behind the plate. So why did we need the extra nudge from the folks in the room where it happens to place him on the cusp of the top 50? Catchers are weird, but they aren't that weird.

55. Luis Robert, OF, Chicago White Sox

Enough of the same reasons that we're not ranking Shohei Ohtani also apply to Robert, who has played extensively as a professional in a top foreign league. We actually passed on ranking Robert in our midseason top 50. But while they may have been comparable leagues before all of the Cuban talent left the island, the NPB and Serie Nacional are no longer comparable. It has also become clear that, unlike Ohtani, Robert will have a significant period as a stateside prospect. So we've begun ranking him, although we remain initially conservative due to a lack of relevant looks or information. We'll get the looks we need this season, and he could be literally anywhere on the list (or off it) in a year's time.

56. Magneuris Sierra, OF, Miami Marlins

For a few hours, the Marcell Ozuna trade was reported as being for Sandy Alcantara and unnamed lesser prospects. It was ultimately revealed that one of the "lesser prospects" was Sierra, and at least from our point of view, Magneuris actually has more prospect sheen on him than Sandy right now. Sierra had a weird season, mixing in mere competence at High-A and Double-A with excellence in several brief MLB call-ups. "Magneuris" is a name that should conjure feelings of great power, but the reality is he's a slap-and-dash sort who hit just a single homer all season between three levels, and his glove may end up being the carrying tool to the profile. He'll certainly have a lot of opportunity to show his wares amidst Miami's "rebuild."

57. Justus Sheffield, LHP, New York Yankees

When Sheffield is right, like he was at the end of 2017 and into the Arizona Fall League, he's as nasty as any lefty in the minors, pumping electric mid-90s gas with a plus slider and a useful changeup. He's just not fully healthy and throwing strikes all that much, and we've seen Sheffield's lesser self too often. He missed a chunk of last season with an oblique injury after his velocity and command wavered early. He could be a lot of fun if he ever finds the right role, but command, durability and size are all still enemies.

58. Anthony Alford, OF, Toronto Blue Jays

"He can never stay healthy" is a concern applied more often to pitching prospects than position players, but Alford probably qualifies as injury-prone by now. An abridged list of his maladies includes concussion, dislocated knee and broken hamate; at the time of this writing, he had just tweaked his ankle in the Mexican Winter League. It's too bad—he has everything you'd want in an everyday center fielder. Alford was a top recruit as a high school quarterback, signing with Ole Miss as a dual-threat under center while spending his summer vacations in Dunedin and Bluefield. He's built like a spread option QB and is a potential above-average defender in center. When he has played, he has hit, and you'd think there would be more game power to come if and when he figures out how to pull the ball more. Alford's a top-50 prospect on talent, and the only thing stopping him is what Will Carroll once coined "the sixth tool"—health.

59. Taylor Trammell, OF, Cincinnati Reds

The many-worlds theory of the multiverse is a controversial topic within quantum mechanics. This is not the forum to litigate the scientific merits, but it provides a useful jumping off point for Trammell. There must be a universe in which Anthony Alford stayed healthy as a prospect, and Trammell might chart that hypothetical course in coming years. Trammell was a pretty good high school football player himself as a running back. Unsurprisingly, he's a plus-plus runner with a good shot to stick in center field. Like Alford, he has yet to show as much power as you'd think, but the Midwest League is an unfriendly clime for all species of dingers. He's also as raw as you'd expect when the comp is Alford, but two years ago. We're intrigued to see how both the experimental and the control group play out.

60. Jesus Sanchez, OF, Tampa Bay Rays

If you play anywhere on the grass in the minors, we list you here as "OF." We will then explain further as needed. As a broad rule, minor-league center fielders don't always turn into major-league center fielders. As one of my predecessors in these pages once opined: "Playing a major-league center field is f***ing hard." But there is a chance that your A-ball center fielder is a major-league center fielder. Sanchez is an A-ball left fielder. It's likely that the only time he'll spend in a major-league center field is during the walk to left field from the home dugout. So he's going to have to hit. He's going to have to hit for average, and he's going to have to hit for power. So far, so good, and the underlying tools are there for a plus-hit/plus-power left fielder. We tend to underrate corner prospects, and we might still be doing it with Sanchez.

61. Heliot Ramos, OF, San Francisco Giants

The Giants are capable of making some strange-looking picks early in the draft, and Ramos generally wasn't ranked as highly as his 19th overall selection tipped. But Heliot had some helium coming into the draft, and it didn't stop after he was popped. He was only 17 on draft day but looked like a man among boys in the complex league, showing huge power, speed, bat speed, pitch recognition and overall hitting polish while playing a competent center field. He suffered a season-ending concussion on a hit-by-pitch to the head, and we know far too much about head trauma in 2018 to not be a little concerned there. He was reportedly back on the field for fall instructs, and the Giants made him nearly untouchable in wide-ranging trade discussions this offseason. He combines a fast upward trajectory and a high ceiling, so watch out if things continue to come together.

62. Luiz Gohara, LHP, Atlanta Braves

I don't know if there's a more perfect example of the third-starter paradigm than Gohara. He has already made the majors on the strength of his plus fastball/slider combo. He has the frame to log 180 innings—it's mechanics (and body) by Sabathia. Despite the seemingly simple delivery he has struggled with his command. The changeup will flash 50 but is too firm and too much of an obvious chase pitch too often. He checks every box. The shape of the stuff is right, too. As good as the slider is, it can be inconsistent. The fastball command wobbles enough that you can't quite get it to plus-plus, so neither of his good offerings can carry the profile on its own. Sometimes these guys get that one-grade-of-command jump and rocket past even the OFP 60 we put on them. More often they end up in the late innings. Gohara could go either way in 2018. Or he could traipse onward right smack dab in the middle of the Braves' rotation. Brilliant one start, inefficient the next. Like we said, he's perfect.

63. Franklin Barreto, SS, Oakland Athletics

It's not you, it's us, Franklin. You've continued to hit in the upper minors and there isn't a huge gap between you and Willy Adames, almost 50 spots higher on the list. He's a better bet to play shortstop—you've seen a lot of reps at second base recently—but you have more present power. You were both good at Triple-A as 21-year-olds. It's fair for you to text us "wut gives?" at midnight after a few too many shots of Fireball. You deserve a better answer than "new phone who dis?" so we'll do our best to explain. We get a bit nervous when our prospects fail—remember that bit about y=x earlier. We may overreact if things start to look a little parabolic. And dude, you struck out 33 times in 76 big-league plate appearances. We're worried about you. Sure, the same thing might have happened to Adames if the Rays didn't prefer to let their prospects dry age longer than a Delmonico's ribeye. But it happened. We can't pretend that it didn't. And we can't go back.

64. Jahmai Jones, OF, Los Angeles Angels

We resume our run on outfield prospects with a football pedigree. Jones' father was a national champion as a defensive end for Notre Dame and his brother is a wide receiver for the Lions. Jones embodies the cliché of a "football player on the diamond," but we'll dispense with the "hard-nosed" epithets, because there's less rawness here than the background might imply. He has shown a patient approach at the plate to go with plus raw and the premium athletic tools that the background implies. He's not so polished that there won't be further growing pains in what is likely to be a slow-burn development path, but at the end of the journey there's an above-average everyday center fielder waiting.

65. Ryan Mountcastle, SS/3B, Baltimore Orioles

He's definitely not a shortstop, not even in the Bobby Bonilla/astronaut sort of way. Baltimore already seems to have accepted this and played him mostly at third base at Double-A. He might not be a third baseman either, but at least he's got a chance there; a big fellow who doesn't throw particularly well isn't the easiest fit left of first base. What we're pretty sure he can do is hit with authority. After lashing 51 extra-base hits in just 88 games at High-A, Mountcastle ran into his first pro stumbles at Double-A. It certainly wouldn't be unusual for a player to look overmatched upon a first short look at advanced pitching and then go on like nothing ever happened, but it's something to watch if for in case of early struggles in 2018.

66. Ian Anderson, RHP, Atlanta Braves

Man, Atlanta has a lot of premium pitching talent. Anderson is the final Braves arm on this list, but he has comparable upside to the quintet above him. It's a bit of a cop-out to say there isn't a huge difference between the 24th- and 66th-best prospects, but the raw ordinal rankings overstate the actual gap. If there is a gap here, it's in risk. Anderson has had his innings managed very carefully, throwing only 83 across 20 A-ball starts in 2017. He showed mid-90s heat and a potential plus changeup, but until we see him do it more often and deeper in games, there's going to be a bit more uncertainty for the cold-weather prep arm. Then again, you might check back next year and find he has skipped High-A and dominated the Southern League. Sure seems to be the trend in the Atlanta organization.

67. Jack Flaherty, RHP, St. Louis Cardinals

Last year, we so ran out of ways to describe generic mid-rotation projections that Yohander Mendez got a comment in verse; the year before we did Braden Shipley Mad Libs. Flaherty has carried said projection since he was drafted in the 2014 supplemental first round, and he's far closer to realizing it after smoking Double-A and Triple-A in 2017. He's also an example of how these things sometimes don't go how you think, at least initially, because he was repeatedly shelled in a September call-up. Even the most generic mid-rotation starter profiles (and boy are there ever a lot of them) often lead to outcomes substantially better, or more often substantially worse, than mid-rotation. And the actual mid-rotation starters are often guys with top-of-the-rotation potential who fall just a bit short for some reason, or guys with a lower perceived ceiling who add something extra later in development. Yet, we have utterly no idea how else to write up the Flahertys of the world, with their good fastball and workable secondaries and good but not otherworldly command and no obvious out pitch.

68. Franklyn Kilome, RHP, Philadelphia Phillies

Kilome is the *other* mid-rotation profile, with a moderately better fastball than Flaherty and command that's fringe-average instead of average or slightly above. This profile tends to lead itself more to a back-of-the-bullpen fallback, whereas Flaherty's tends to have fifth starter as a fallback (which of those you prefer on a value basis is a personal choice as much as anything). Kilome's profile had some wild variance in it a few years ago, where start-to-start he could swing from looking like a stud to a non-prospect, but that's calmed down as he has gained better (though still not great) repeatability and command. The off-speed stuff flashes but still needs work, of course. He's in that weird zone where he has noticeably improved as a prospect year-over-year but is getting passed by prospects improving even more in his own organization, which might make him seem more stagnant than he actually is. Keep him on your "third starter or impact reliever" bingo cards.

69. Dustin May, RHP, Los Angeles Dodgers

"The Gingergaard" is on his way. Yes, we know Noah Syndergaard is one of those dudes you probably just shouldn't comp, but May is a skinny 6-foot-6 kid from the suburbs of the DFW Metroplex with projectable velocity, a feel for spin and a general idea of what he's doing. That really was Syndergaard at the same age, and they share some mannerisms and motions on the mound, too—the first of many pitching prospects from that area and elsewhere to mimic Syndergaard. We can't expect May's velocity or off-speed stuff to jump like Thor's did, because that just doesn't happen often, but there's at least no. 2 starter upside present if the command and health hold up. He also possesses the best flow of any prospect, an untamed mane of bright red hair billowing out of the back of his cap. It can't hurt the overall presentation.

70. Sandy Alcantara, RHP, Miami Marlins

We said last year that Alcantara was about as low as you could be while regularly sitting triple digits with a rotation profile, and he sure put us to the test on that for this year. We guess the easiest way out of the conundrum would be to say the needle moved a bit in favor of "bullpen" as his long-term outcome after an aggressive assignment to Double-A out of spring, but his stock really hasn't changed much, and this year's list is probably a little stronger than last year's in 60 OFP types. The Cards gave him a September spin out of the 'pen and then dealt him to co-headline the Marcell Ozuna deal. In theory, he still has everything needed to start, with three pitches, command that might get there and relative durability and health. Yet we write that about lots of dudes who don't ultimately start, and it's easier to take the skinny unpolished one who throws 100 and has service time and throw him in the bullpen than it is most guys.

71. Carter Kieboom, SS, Washington Nationals

Kieboom seemed on the verge of a breakout early in the season. Then he pulled his hamstring running down the line in mid-May and missed two-and-a-half months, effectively throwing his entire season off the tracks. Like Ryan Mountcastle, he's unlikely to be a shortstop when he reaches the majors, but we expect that the game-power projection comes in pretty big here given the incumbent bat speed and raw power. A third baseman that combines plus tools at hit and power is nothing to sneeze at, and that's within Kieboom's range of outcomes.

72. Austin Hays, OF, Baltimore Orioles

At our BP event at Camden Yards last Summer, someone in the crowd asked for a breakout Orioles prospect. With Dan Duquette and roughly half the Baltimore front office in the room, our colleague Jeff Long—made of sterner stuff than us—volunteered Austin Hays. "He may not be a star, but he does everything well." Duquette quickly retorted, "Well, he might be a star." It's thinner margins between the two opinions than you might think. Long was right that Hays does everything well—his scouting report is dotted with average-or-better tools, but you'd be hard pressed to find anything above a 55. Add in that Hays is better suited to a corner spot, and he might not be a star. But these profiles sometimes play up past the individual tool grades. If he hits .270, with 20 home runs and above-average defense in a corner? If not a star, that's at least a really good regular.

73. Yusniel Diaz, OF, Los Angeles Dodgers

We didn't plan it this way—the Top 101 process is far less rational and organized than however you may imagine it—but Hays and Diaz make a perfect matched pair. Like Hays, the grades don't jump off the scouting report, and Diaz is better suited to a corner spot. He has more center-field utility than Hays, which helps. He also hasn't conquered the upper minors yet, which hurts. He has a bit more upside than Hays, but perhaps more of a fourth-outfielder risk. So after applying our rational and well-organized process we end up with Hays one spot ahead of Diaz. Anyway, as Yeats said, "People who lean on logic and philosophy and rational exposition end by starving the best part of the mind."

74. Luis Urias, IF San Diego Padres

This is a challenging profile to evaluate. Everyone who sees Urias at the plate thinks he's going to *hit*. Evaluators who don't throw 70 hit tools around lightly put a 70 hit on Urias. We're not quite there yet—he'd rank a couple dozen spots higher if we were—and the hit tool is usually the hardest part of the offensive profile to evaluate. He controls the strike zone impressively, with great bat-to-ball ability, but his power is gap-to-gap at best and he's small enough that it's hard to give him much projection. Defensively, he has played more second base than anywhere else and is stretched defensively at shortstop due to range and arm issues, but he might be able to cover all the infield spots occasionally for added utility. It's a thin line between first-division regular, second-division regular and utility player when the profile is this hit-tool dependent, and Urias could land anywhere on that spectrum.

75. Seuly Matias, OF, Kansas City Royals

Matias spent the summer of 2017 in the Appalachian League, playing exclusively right field or designated hitter, and posted a sub-.300 on-base percentage. So we're revisiting a lot of prior themes here. Another previously mentioned point is that live looks are the backbone of this list. You can probably guess how good Matias looked in person for our colleague John Eshelman. I can't reprint the Slack DMs because this is a family publication; suffice to say, Matias has the bat speed, approach and power projection to make it work in a corner-outfield spot well enough to slot in as the 75th-best prospect in baseball, even if we aren't entirely sure what we're looking at yet.

76. Seth Romero, LHP, Washington Nationals

Because there are limits to what can responsibly be reported and confirmed regarding amateur players, we often couch makeup concerns vaguely. Romero offers us an opportunity to, well, not do that. At the University of Houston, he was suspended multiple times, including for curfew violations and failing to show effort in conditioning. He reportedly failed a drug test for marijuana, he was photographed in team uniform with a bong and he was ultimately dismissed from the team for getting into a fight with a teammate—all of these things came out publicly, mostly in reports by Joseph Duarte of the *Houston Chronicle*. Taken alone, none of those are tremendously worrisome; Romero is surely far from the only player on this list who has smoked pot or tussled with a teammate or broken curfew. But the whole of it raises some concerns about his professionalism (yes, we're aware how ironic it is to bring that up in light of rules broken in the NCAA), and the volume of problems certainly scared some teams off from drafting the talented lefty. The Nationals keep making their own draft luck and took him 25th, and if he can stay on the field he should easily outshine that spot.

77. Riley Pint, RHP, Colorado Rockies

Okay, maybe *this* is actually the lowest you can go as a starter prospect pumping triple-digit gas. Pint has been rather terrible as a pro due to poor command and control, but he's still capable of sitting in the high-90s and regularly touching 100. He's also still demonstrably a starter prospect, because there are still four MLB pitches underlying the profile. The flip side is why the command and control profile is currently so weak: His mechanics aren't easy and he doesn't repeat well. If you guessed that he's probably headed for the bullpen, you get the gold star for also reading the other dozen similar versions of this profile. But that singular weakness is all that's separating Pint from being Sixto Sanchez, except six inches taller, and it's not a lost cause quite yet.

78. Jay Groome, LHP, Boston Red Sox

If there are any positives to take out of Groome's 2017, it's that 2018 is a new year and there's no reason to doubt the initial projection. After making Low-A out of camp, he gave up nine runs in his first start before reporting a lat injury that would sideline him for over two months. Shortly after his return, his father was arrested for a host of drug and weapons charges. Groome actually wasn't too bad once he returned to full-season ball for the stretch run, all things considered, and at least he still racked up the strikeouts with his plus-plus curve. Hopefully the new year brings him a less eventful season.

79. Jorge Mateo, SS/2B/OF, Oakland Athletics

Expanding bullpens make players like Mateo, who can play a bunch of positions, hit a little and run like the wind even more valuable. In danger of stalling out in A-ball early in the season, Mateo got a moonshot promotion to Double-A, and things finally clicked at the plate. He also added center-field experience to the kit, and that's a position where he could profile huge. He could be a fantasy star even if not a real life one, and he could be a hell of a bench weapon even if the bat falls short of what you want out of regular usage.

80. Corbin Burnes, RHP, Milwaukee Brewers

As deadlines loom over our *Annual* writing process, we get desperate. Burnes was a velocity pop-up guy in 2017, the potential plus secondary is the slider. The changeup has a chance to get to average, the command issues can come when he's not finishing his delivery on line. Yes, it's another mid-rotation starter or late-inning reliever. We've already used poetry, acmes, archetypes and self-reference to the above to flesh out these kinds of entries, so we aren't too proud to admit we may have scanned *L.A. Law* episode summaries on Wikipedia to try and find a tie-in to get us over 100 words. Unfortunately there was nothing to show, so instead we will just tell you we did it.

81. Brett Phillips, OF, Milwaukee Brewers

Phillips is the third potential five-tool center fielder in the Milwaukee system. Like Lewis Brinson, he reached the majors in 2017, and while he had his own swing-and-miss issues, the top-line performance was quite a bit better. The tools aren't as loud, though, and that matters, as he might be forced to a corner of Miller Park despite his plus speed and elite arm. The offensive profile is Three True Outcome and more high variance than you'd expect for a player who had major-league success in about as many at-bats as you can have and still be eligible for this list. On the other hand, all Phillips needs to do is be an average center fielder and hit .250, and the rest of the profile will carry the day.

82. Andres Gimenez, SS New York Mets

Most of the low-minors middle infielders in this area of the 101 are high-upside, low-polish types who could be superstars if they put their vast tools together. Gimenez is on the other pole, the rare high-polish, medium-upside shortstop percolating in Low-A. He could still easily be a first-division starter, but there probably isn't enough physicality to ever get him to one of the best players in baseball;

still, there's an unusually strong chance he has a career. Playing the entire 2017 season at just 18, Gimenez forced his way out of extended spring training into the starting shortstop job at Low-A Columbia by the end of April. He hit for little power, but otherwise more than held his own as an above-average hitter in the Sally while playing fine shortstop defense. The body could go in various ways that will affect his ultimate power upside and defensive home, but there's so much skill relative to age here.

83. Jon Duplantier, RHP, Arizona Diamondbacks

"For Sale: Baby shoes, never worn," often erroneously attributed to Hemingway, is considered to be the shortest possible tragic tale. We'll halve the word count: "Rice Starting Pitcher." Duplantier didn't do much to rewrite that sorry tale during his college career, missing his sophomore season with shoulder issues. In 2017, the story got a reboot, as Duplantier threw 136 healthy innings, striking out better than 10 per nine while showing off a plus fastball and three average-or-better secondaries. The injury bug can bite any pitcher at any time, but as Hemingway *actually* once wrote: "Luck is a thing that comes in many forms and who can recognize her?"

84. Jake Burger, 3B, Chicago White Sox

The video of 1997 National Spelling Bee winner Rebecca Sealfon screaming out the final word "euonym" has over 560,000 views on YouTube. If she'd gotten the word twenty years later and the judges wanted to use a baseball prospect's name for some reason, Jake Burger might have been the usage example, for a euonym is a name that aptly describes the person. Burger is a beefy man with a huge frame, realistically far too big to play third base for long unless he possesses special defensive abilities that have yet to show up. What he does have is a thunderous bat, combining higher-end bat speed and power, which is how you get drafted this high as a bad-bodied right-handed college hitter. And hey, at least he's not a meteorologist named Freeze.

85. Isan Diaz, SS/2B, Milwaukee Brewers

Diaz doesn't look the part of a Three True Outcomes slugger. He's a middle infielder listed at 5-foot-10 (which is how 5-foot-8 players self-report their height), but he homered, walked or struck out in 40 percent of his Midwest League plate appearances in 2016. He upped that to 43 percent in the Carolina League last year before a hamate injury ended his season. That's an injury known to sap power for a bit, and Diaz is less appealing as a prospect as the second coming of Mark Bellhorn. Swing-and-miss issues like this in the low minors can get exacerbated in the upper minors, too. But even in an era where second basemen knock 40 home runs, Diaz's pop at an up-the-middle spot is worth keeping tabs on.

86. Mitch White, RHP, Los Angeles Dodgers

Over the years we've made an exhaustive study of different ways to describe changeups that need refinement, but even we were impressed by this line from our own Wilson Karaman in our Dodgers team list: "While the athleticism and arm action suggests potential for developing a changeup to round out the arsenal, it hasn't developed yet." Fortunately for White, there was plenty of development in other areas in 2017. His velocity popped into the mid-90s and he complemented it with a plus cutter. There's a potentially above-average curve here as well, so he has some non-cambio options against lefties. There's still a high reliever probability here, and not just because of the missing changeup. White has been plagued by durability issues: The 73 innings he threw last year were a professional high.

87. Erick Fedde, RHP Washington Nationals

After a hot start at Double-A, it looked like Fedde was closing in on the majors, more or less right on schedule. The Nationals agreed, sort of, ramping his prep up by inexplicably converting him to the bullpen despite having just as much need in the rotation. He then yo-yo'd between the rotation, 'pen and disabled list in both the majors and minors, battling forearm issues and what we have to chalk up to just plain old mismanagement. We're as confused as you are, but there's still a mid-rotation starter projection with all the trimmings here, if a little less certainty on it.

88. Jesus Luzardo, LHP, Oakland Athletics

Look, even if his name wasn't a near homophone with Austin post-hardcore legends The Jesus Lizard, Luzardo would be well regarded at BP. We are suckers for lefties with a good changeup. And when the changeup is playing off a fastball that touches 98, you really have our attention. Luzardo's curve is still a work in progress. He hasn't pitched in full-season ball yet, and had Tommy John surgery in high school. We'd end the blurb with a pithy and appropriate Jesus Lizard lyric, but ... well, Adele works much better for this.

89. Dane Dunning, RHP Chicago White Sox

Dunning pitched a lot out of the bullpen at the University of Florida, not because he wasn't skilled or durable enough to start, but because the 2016 Gators had four high-end starter prospects (Dunning, A.J. Puk, Logan Shore, Alex Faedo) and college coaches tend to have less role rigidity. The flip side is that the same college coaches will often leverage their best arms with little regard for things like fatigue and health. The White Sox plopped Dunning right back into the rotation upon drafting him, and he threw 144 solid A-ball innings in his first full season. Like many others around here, he also projects as a mid-rotation starter, but it's nice to know in the back of your mind that he's capable of being a multi-inning reliever, too.

90. Blake Rutherford, OF, Chicago White Sox

Well, it went better for Rutherford than for Mickey Moniak, with whom he'll probably always be paired as the California outfield guys from 2016—like a maybe-lesser version of Clint Frazier and Austin Meadows. The fourth quartile is the designated ranking area for do-overs for highly touted 2016 picks who had indifferent pro campaigns, and you're making the correct assumption about how far Moniak has fallen to note his absence here. Rutherford at least still looks the part of a top outfield prospect on the field, but a guy with his size, advertised power and alleged polish should be hitting more than two homers over a full season in the Dead Sea, let alone the Sally. Time will tell how good the Yankees look for cashing out early here.

91. Jesse Winker, OF, Cincinnati Reds

All Winker does is hit, and the power went into hiding at Triple-A, which gave surprisingly high variance to his projection since it's a corner-outfield-only profile. He's popping back onto the list this year for the most idiosyncratic of reasons—he made the majors and got into that weird zone where he had enough at-bats for us to care a bit about what he showed but not enough at-bats to graduate. In that time, his power popped to levels we hadn't seen since his 2015 Double-A campaign. He might have to hit .300 to be a good regular, but he also keeps hitting .300 everywhere.

92. Arquimedez Gamboa, SS, Philadelphia Phillies

A personal plea to Phillies beat writers: Please ask Gamboa whether he prefers "Arquimedez" or "Arquimedes," because the usual sources are split about 50/50 on it. Even the Phillies themselves have it spelled both ways in different places. It's going to matter because he's pretty good and we'll be talking about him a lot moving forward. After recovering from a hamstring injury that cost him much of the first half and seemed to hamper him when he did play, Gamboa looked like a potential two-way star in the last few months of the season. When you blast liners all over the place and can go get it at shortstop, the scout section perks up quickly, even if they can't figure out how your name is spelled.

93. Beau Burrows, RHP, Detroit Tigers

Dave Dombrowski has long since traded in his weird square pizza for chowdah, but lo and behold, the Tigers have a power-armed prep righty on this list again. Burrows' plus fastball is a recent development—he sat in the low-90s in the Midwest League in 2016. In 2017, he started touching 98 and breaking off an above-average curve. That got him to the Eastern League in the second half as a 20-year-old. Burrows struggled there, but he'll get another shot to tame it in 2018, and we'll start to get a better idea of whether he's going to be a third starter or an impact bullpen arm.

94. Ronald Guzman, 1B, Texas Rangers

We vowed to take upper-level corner bats more seriously this offseason, and Guzman is the most obvious beneficiary of that. Once a major Dominican bonus baby staggering around badly enough that he was exposed to the Rule 5 draft two winters ago, Guzman retooled his swing and resuscitated his career in the high minors. He just turned 23, he has already conquered Triple-A, there's MLB playing time available to him and there's still goodly power projection remaining. These are all very good and very dangerous things. Keep him on your radar.

95. Adbert Alzolay, RHP, Chicago Cubs

Alzolay might have the single best tool on this list. That is an 80-grade name. The other tools aren't bad either, and he tops a depleted Cubs farm system—as for Astros fans, this won't be a source of much consternation for Northsiders. Alzolay's profile tilts more toward the "impact reliever" end of "third starter or impact reliever" designation, as the changeup and command projections are a little more opaque than those of the arms ahead of him. Although British comedian Stewart Lee has argued that "art should be opaque," we'd prefer not to have to apply that to our prospect projections. Given that Alzolay has already pitched in Double-A, he could be a boon for an equally depleted major-league bullpen in short order. And that issue has been a source of recent consternation for Cubs fans.

96. Shane Baz, RHP, Pittsburgh Pirates

Baz went 12th overall in the 2017 draft and the Pirates gave him a shade over $4 million to buy him out of a TCU commitment. Was this a good idea? Let's return to the questionnaire.

1. How's the fastball?

Mid-90s: Go ahead and put him at the top of your draft board.
Low-90s: Proceed to Question 2.

He also has a potential plus slider as part of his full four-pitch mix. We described the changeup as "better than you might expect from the profile" (have to add that one to the questionnaire next year). Baz isn't super-projectable, but he is big and from Texas. There are some mechanical concerns that might impact his long-term role. He was also born while *The Phantom Menace* was still in theaters. There's time to work out the kinks. Now this is prospecting.

97. Fernando Romero, RHP, Minnesota Twins

Romero is now far enough away from his Tommy John surgery that we can take a closer look at what the Twins might have here. Surprise! It's a mid-rotation starter or impact reliever. Romero may be able to find triple digits in the 'pen, as he already scrapes 98 mph as a starter, and the pitch runs hard from his low-three-quarters arm slot. He has a hard-tilting potential plus slider as well. He's listed at six foot, and we've covered what that actually means already. Add in the low arm slot and Romero's fastball command will need to make up for the lack of plane on the pitch if he wants to stick in the rotation. The changeup will have to improve, too. Because, you know, he's a mid-rotation starter or impact reliever.

98. Dustin Fowler, OF, Oakland Athletics

If Sandy Alcantara (or Riley Pint) establishes the lower bound for a starter prospect hitting 100 on the gun, this is certainly the lower bound for MLB-ready five-tool prospects, since Fowler is only this low due to special injury risk. Fowler was in the midst of another huge step forward at Triple-A, finally stepping out of the shadow of a deep Yankees system, when he was called up to the majors at the end of June. In his first inning in the field, before his first at-bat, he ran straight into a low right field retaining wall at Guaranteed Rate Field in Chicago and ruptured the patella in his right knee, ending his season. A month later, he was moved to Oakland while still on the disabled list in the Sonny Gray trade. We're being a bit conservative by placing him this low in case his speed and defense come back compromised, in which case he could look more like a platoon corner guy than a starter in center field.

99. Ryan McMahon, IF, Colorado Rockies

We evaluate prospects in a vacuum. Organizations have other considerations. In most other systems, McMahon would have been playing third base every day in the upper minors. Even if you aren't sure he's a lock to stick there—we are more bullish on his glove there than others—the general philosophy is to keep prospects in their most valuable role as long as possible. Keep your bats as far left on the defensive spectrum as possible. Start your arms until they prove they can't. McMahon is not going to play third base for the Rockies. Nolan Arenado is one of the best baseball players in the world. McMahon is ready to contribute to a major-league team, though, so he got time at first base and second base. The myriad defensive responsibilities didn't hurt his focus at the plate, as he obliterated Eastern League and Pacific Coast League arms. He has plus raw power to all fields and a swing plane designed to take advantage of the wide-range of acceptable specifications for MLB baseballs. The offensive profile can be a bit boom or bust—he has a good approach but suffers from spin and platoon issues, so the added defensive flexibility can't hurt.

100. Albert Abreu, RHP, New York Yankees

"Also, he's a pitcher."

That sentence was the denouement of every risk factor for every pitching prospect in every team Top 10 list we wrote on the website in 2017. A glance over the arms dotting the previous 99 names—starting right at the top—lays the various risks bare. On talent, Abreu isn't that far off his former Quad Cities teammate Franklin Perez. Abreu also missed nearly the entire season with a shoulder ailment. The same could happen to Perez next year. The beat goes on. Abreu looked more or less like himself in the Arizona Fall League. He could rocket up this list next year on the strength of his high-90s heat and power curve, health permitting. And despite his maladies, Abreu cobbled together only 20 fewer innings on the mound than Perez did in 2017. Perez's issue was with his knee, though. While we don't want to downplay the importance of healthy legs to pitching, it won't make us dramatically yank our collar like a shoulder injury.

101. Mike Matuella, RHP, Texas Rangers

Years ago, Kevin Goldstein made this a Top 101 rather than a Top

100. Since then, the 101st spot has often been used to highlight a prospect who, while perhaps not *strictly* the 101st best in baseball, is of particular interest to the authors of the list. We can't sustain an argument that Matuella is better than all but exactly 100 prospects. The truth is he's either a much better or a much worse prospect than that. He has enough health red flags to distract every bull in Pamplona—a Tommy John surgery, a rough Tommy John recovery, recurrent back issues. He is already 23 and has thrown 78 professional innings, none above A-ball. Matuella was also a candidate to go first overall in 2015, and when he has taken the ball he has shown top-of-the-rotation stuff—a mid-90s fastball, potential plus changeup and average curve. He's as risky a prospect as there is in the game, but you don't get into this line of work if you are shy about throwing a marker down. Matuella is ours.

—Jeffrey Paternostro is an author of Baseball Prospectus; Jarrett Seidler is an author of Baseball Prospectus.

Korea Baseball Organization Prospectus

Essay by Sung Min Kim

Player comments by Sung Min Kim

The Korea Baseball Organization (KBO), established on December 11, 1981, started with six clubs and has now expanded to ten. There has been some turnover since then, as a few clubs had to be disbanded due to financial constraints. A few others survived by switching their parent company, and expansion teams were birthed by the ambitions of corporations looking to broaden their brand. The ten current teams are:

- Doosan Bears (established in 1982; formerly OB Bears)
- LG Twins (established in 1982; formerly MBC Blue Dragons)
- Samsung Lions (established in 1982)
- Kia Tigers (established in 1982; formerly Haitai Tigers)
- Lotte Giants (established in 1982)
- Nexen Heroes (established in 2008; formerly Woori Heroes and Seoul Heroes)
- SK Wyverns (established in 2000)
- Hanwha Eagles (established in 1986; formerly Bingre Eagles)
- NC Dinos (established in 2011)
- KT Wiz (established in 2013)

One stark difference between the KBO and MLB that you probably noticed right away is that every Korean baseball team is owned by—and named after—major companies (except for the Heroes, which are merely sponsored by Nexen Tire Company). That's a foreign concept for fans of American baseball, although most of us have seen *The Simpsons* episode with the Springfield Nuclear Power Plant Softball Team. Imagine team names such as the Little Caesars Tigers or the Nintendo Mariners or the Bernie Madoff Creditors Mets? It's like that.

As in many sports leagues, regional rivalries exist in the KBO, despite the lack of overt geographic affiliation. The Doosan Bears and LG Twins have shared the same venue (Jamsil Stadium) for decades and are the foremost Seoul rivals—three of the ten teams in the KBO call the South Korean capital home (the Nexen Heroes are the third). Down in the south, the three traditional teams—Samsung, Lotte and Kia—all have brewed their own rivalries based on their region and history. Older teams, because of their traditions, tend to be the most popular ones as well. Newer teams like the Dinos and Heroes have had to earn their fans through more strategic marketing and, of course, winning on the field.

The demographic of KBO fans is young and growing. Going to a baseball game has become one of the main pastimes for the country's twenty-somethings—after Korea's success in international tournaments, attendance has shot up and baseball has dethroned soccer as the most popular sport on the peninsula. According to the KBO website, overall attendance was just over three million in 2006. That number nearly doubled by 2009, after strong performances at the 2006 and 2009 World Baseball Classics and the 2008 Beijing Olympics. It has continued a steady climb since: Attendance reached 6.4 million in 2013 after the NC Dinos joined the league, eclipsed the seven-million mark in 2015 (7,360,530) and set a new record in 2017 with just over 8.4 million fans in the seats to watch a brand of baseball as exciting to audiences as the attendance numbers are to the companies that own the teams. With star Korean players like Byungho Park, Jae-Gyun Hwang and Hyun Soo Kim returning from MLB to the KBO, public interest in baseball is forecasted to be even higher in 2018.

One of the reasons for the league attendance resurgence has been the rise of the female fan base. According to KBO's data gathered after the 2015 season, women made up 43.1 percent of all attendees. Female fans in their twenties turned out to be the biggest audience, making up 23.6 percent on their own and surpassing the male audience in the same age group (23.5 percent). The amount of KBO merchandise sold also tells a story. In 2013, only 20 percent of all gear was bought by female fans. By 2016, that figure had jumped to 47 percent. The league and the teams made a substantial effort to design venues to be more gender-inclusive and family-friendly, while gearing far more souvenirs toward women and children—a noticeable difference for those who have traversed the team stores in MLB parks.

There are many differing opinions on the quality of play in Korean baseball. Some argue that it is right on par with American Triple-A, while others say it is closer to Double-A. But the league level cannot be translated to a North American level, as the KBO contains a far wider range of talents than you'd see at any level of stateside baseball. Several top KBO players are good enough to be MLB regulars. However, they share locker rooms with those would struggle to hold their own in rookie league, which makes talent as a whole trickier to evaluate.

It's easy to assume that anyone in the high minors or with major-league experience can just sign in Korea and have success, but the results have been far too mixed to make such assumptions. For instance, former Red Sox top prospect Allen Webster posted a 5.70 ERA in 12 starts for the Samsung Lions in 2016 before being released. On the contrary, outfielder Mel Rojas Jr., who has never made it to the majors and had just a .723 OPS in Triple-A before signing with the KT Wiz in the middle of 2017, hit .301/.351/.560 in the KBO and earned another contract to stay on the peninsula for 2018.

Speaking of which, foreign players are vital to a team's success in the KBO, though there are rules in place that keep most of the stars local. Each club can sign just three foreigners—two pitchers and one positional player—in their organization, leaving very little margin for error in scouting. As baseball in Korea has grown, more athletes in the North American upper minors have been showcasing their talents not only for their major-league organization but also for KBO scouts. There are many reasons for this. First, the pay can be far better than in the stateside minors. Depending on the player's talent level, teams offer six-figure contracts (over $1 million, for a few). If they play well, then they can usually parlay that into a nice raise for the next contract. Younger players that go to Korea can look to Eric Thames for inspiration. Thames had a well-documented stint with the NC Dinos where he made highly successful adjustments to his approach, dominated the league and earned a three-year, $15 million contract with the Milwaukee Brewers in the winter of 2016.

Although they play substantially the same game in the KBO, there are several differences from MLB. The obvious one is the famous bat flip culture. There is no retaliation for it, nor any unwritten rule about restricting the number of bats flying in the air after hitting a homer. This has allowed the celebrations to be just as unique as the acts they are celebrating or the players themselves. Since it is only a ten-team league in a country with small landmass, the relationships between athletes are close. Also, the *sunbae/hoobae* culture, which emphasizes the degree of formality and respect from younger persons to older, is apparent throughout the league. Even during the game, fans can observe younger and less experienced athletes tip caps or bow to older and more seasoned ones. That gives you a peek into the Korean social culture in general, which is deeply built on the *sunbae/hoobae* interactions.

If you are interested in following and watching the KBO, there are available resources online. Dan Kurtz keeps the statistics up-to-date on MyKBO.net, which has become the go-to hub for English language information on the league. He also runs a Twitter account (@MyKBO) that keep followers up-to-date with the latest Korean baseball news. If you want to watch the games, the Naver TV Streaming app broadcasts every game for free on both iOS and Android—if you can get around the Korean language barrier, of course.

It is high time to be following the KBO: The league is exciting thanks to the increasing level of foreign talent imports, rising attendance and a game played in a way that is familiar to American baseball fans. We are seeing more Asian talent infused into the majors than we have ever seen before, and MLB clubs are paying closer attention to the top talents because of it. Odds are you will hear several of the names listed in this chapter blaring over the loud speakers of stadiums near you over the next few seasons.

—Sung Min Kim is an author of Baseball Prospectus.

HITTERS

Roger Bernadina OF Kia Tigers Born:06/12/84 Age:34

YEAR	TEAM	AGE	G	PA	AB	R	H	2B	3B	HR	TB	HBP	SF	SH	RBI	BB	K	SB	CS	AVG/OBP/SLG	sWAR
2015	Albuquerque Isotopes (AAA)	31	119	447	373	62	103	18	4	15	174	7	1	8	62	58	121	20	6	.276/.383/.466	
2016	Las Vegas 51s (AAA)	32	114	446	387	65	113	29	4	10	180	5	2	4	55	48	93	20	5	.292/.376/.465	
2017	Kia Tigers	33	139	621	557	118	178	26	6	27	301	11	9	3	111	41	112	32	7	.320/.372/.540	5.06

Bernadina, nicknamed "The Shark" by Washington Nationals fans, spent six seasons in the US capital and had cups of coffee with the Dodgers, Reds and Phillies. He was signed by Kia in December 2016 for $850,000. As many new foreign hitters do, Bernadina had a slow start to his KBO career, hitting .258/.327/.312 in April. However, his OPS eclipsed .900 each month from May to September. The Tigers expected a leadoff hitter in Bernadina, but by the postseason he was the team's no. 3 hitter. He came through in the clutch for Kia's 11th Korean Series championship by going 10-for-19 in five games against the Doosan Bears. The club rewarded Bernadina with a $1.1 million contract for the 2018 season.

Hyung-Woo Choi OF Kia Tigers Born:12/16/83 Age:34

YEAR	TEAM	AGE	G	PA	AB	R	H	2B	3B	HR	TB	HBP	SF	SH	RBI	BB	K	SB	CS	AVG/OBP/SLG	sWAR
2015	Samsung Lions	32	144	637	547	94	174	33	1	33	308	7	8	0	123	73	101	2	5	.318/.402/.563	4.13
2016	Samsung Lions	33	138	618	519	99	195	46	2	31	338	8	7	0	144	83	83	2	2	.376/.464/.651	7.75
2017	Kia Tigers	34	142	629	514	98	176	36	3	26	296	8	8	0	120	96	82	0	1	.342/.450/.576	6.58

Choi is as complete a hitter as anyone in the KBO. Throughout his career, he has hit for average (.317), reached base (.404 on-base percentage) and slugged (260 career homers). He started out as a catching prospect with below-average defense before being released after four years of toiling around the minors. After serving in the military, he came back as an outfielder with a potent bat, winning Rookie of the Year in 2008 and leading the Samsung Lions to four consecutive Korean Series titles from 2011 to 2014. After the 2016 season, Choi signed a lucrative four-year deal worth around $9.2 million with the Kia Tigers. For a brief period, it was the biggest contract in KBO history until the Lotte Giants gave a four-year deal worth $13.7 million to Dae-Ho Lee. As Kia's cleanup hitter, Choi led the Tigers to their 11th championship in 2017.

Jeong Choi 3B SK Wyverns Born:02/28/87 Age:31

YEAR	TEAM	AGE	G	PA	AB	R	H	2B	3B	HR	TB	HBP	SF	SH	RBI	BB	K	SB	CS	AVG/OBP/SLG	sWAR
2015	SK Wyverns	28	81	330	275	43	81	17	0	17	149	5	3	1	58	46	78	5	2	.295/.401/.542	3.23
2016	SK Wyverns	29	141	606	500	106	144	24	1	40	290	23	6	0	106	77	126	1	2	.288/.403/.580	5.82
2017	SK Wyverns	30	130	527	430	89	136	18	1	46	294	19	8	0	113	70	107	1	5	.316/.427/.684	6.60

With 271 career home runs and a .294/.390/.523 career line over 13 seasons, Choi is arguably the most decorated active KBO position player. Back in 2012, he was a five-tool player, and the first to hit 20 homers and steal 20 bases for the Wyverns. By 2017, he had transformed into a home-run hitter, adding more of an uppercut to his swing. His 113 RBI and 46 home runs that year were franchise records. In 2014, there was speculation that he might try to go to United States as a free agent, but he opted to stay with SK, signing a four-year deal worth approximately $7.9 million. He will be a free agent again after the 2018 season and, if he can keep up his superlative performance, he may test the overseas market again.

Michael Choice OF Nexen Heroes Born:11/10/89 Age:28

YEAR	TEAM	AGE	G	PA	AB	R	H	2B	3B	HR	TB	HBP	SF	SH	RBI	BB	K	SB	CS	AVG/OBP/SLG	sWAR
2015	Texas Rangers (MLB)	26	1	1	1	0	0	0	0	0	0	0	0	0	0	0	1	0	0	.000/.000/.000	0.0 (WARP)
2015	Round Rock Express (AAA)	26	110	447	406	53	99	25	1	12	162	7	2	0	60	32	115	2	0	.244/.309/.399	
2015	Columbus Clippers (AAA)	26	14	62	54	5	11	5	0	1	19	3	0	0	7	5	22	1	0	.204/.306/.352	
2016	Columbus Clippers (AAA)	27	71	276	252	33	62	11	0	14	115	8	2	0	39	14	81	0	1	.246/.304/.456	
2017	Norfolk Tides (AAA)	28	10	32	26	1	1	1	0	0	2	1	0	0	2	5	9	1	0	.038/.219/.077	
2017	Biloxi Shuckers (AA)	28	48	195	173	26	47	13	0	9	87	3	1	0	29	18	49	0	1	.272/.349/.503	
2017	Nexen Heroes	28	46	201	176	37	54	8	1	17	115	7	1	0	42	17	49	0	0	.307/.388/.653	2.11

The 10th overall pick in the 2010 MLB draft, Choice displayed plenty of tools as a prospect but never translated them into major-league performance. In the middle of the 2017 season, the Nexen Heroes cut ties with Danny Dorn—after he hit about as well as Roger Dorn in *Major League*—and brought in Choice, who was finally given a second chance to make a first impression. Just like plenty of other foreign hitters, Choice did not take full advantage of that first impression, starting slowly as he became acclimated to KBO pitching, but a 1.216 OPS in August and September helped changed plenty of hearts and minds. In the final game of 2017 Choice blasted home runs in three consecutive at-bats against the Samsung Lions, ending his season on a high note. His calendar year ended on a high note as well, as the Heroes re-signed him for 2018 on a $600,000 deal.

Dong-min Han OF SK Wyverns Born:08/09/89 Age:28

YEAR	TEAM	AGE	G	PA	AB	R	H	2B	3B	HR	TB	HBP	SF	SH	RBI	BB	K	SB	CS	AVG/OBP/SLG	sWAR
2015	Did not play - military service	26																			
2016	SK Wyverns	27	6	20	18	3	5	0	0	0	5	1	0	0	0	1	5	1	0	.278/.350/.278	0.02
2017	SK Wyverns	28	103	414	350	64	103	21	2	21	215	15	3	0	73	46	79	2	2	.294/.396/.614	3.75

The 2017 season ended prematurely for Han, who suffered a torn ligament in his ankle while trying to steal a base on August 9. Before the injury he had been enjoying a torrid breakout season, slugging over .600 and knocking nearly 30 home runs. However, the future is bright for the lefty slugger. After leading the Futures League in home runs in both 2015 and 2016, the Wyverns took a flier on him as a starter and he repaid that confidence with immediate dividends. His lefty power stroke is a perfect fit for Incheon SK Happy Dream Park, a stadium certainly not named after the feelings of pitchers after toeing the mound there. The fans dubbed Han with a nickname the "Dong-minican" because of his name and power reminiscent of Dominican sluggers.

Jae-Gyun Hwang 3B KT Wiz Born:07/28/87 Age:30

YEAR	TEAM	AGE	G	PA	AB	R	H	2B	3B	HR	TB	HBP	SF	SH	RBI	BB	K	SB	CS	AVG/OBP/SLG	sWAR
2015	Lotte Giants	28	144	596	534	95	155	41	2	26	97	4	6	4	97	48	122	11	10	.290/.350/.521	4.01
2016	Lotte Giants	29	127	559	498	97	167	26	5	27	113	4	8	0	1113	49	66	25	10	.335/.394/.570	5.55
2017	San Francisco Giants (MLB)	30	18	57	52	2	8	1	0	1	12	0	0	0	5	5	15	0	0	.154/.228/.231	-0.4 (WARP)
2017	Sacramento River Cats (AAA)	30	98	386	351	44	100	21	4	10	159	1	7	2	55	27	83	7	1	.285/.332/.453	

After having a career-best season in 2016 with the Lotte Giants, Hwang became a free agent and immediately sought out a stateside deal. He hosted a showcase in Florida in front of twenty clubs and passed on multiple lucrative offers from KBO teams. He later signed a split contract with the San Francisco Giants and eventually made it to "The Show" in late June, after a few weeks of "will they, won't they" as they neared his July 1 opt-out, homering off Rockies left-hander Kyle Freeland in his debut. Hwang returned to the minors on August 3 and ended his season languishing in Sacramento. That's enough for anyone to reconsider their future, and in the offseason he signed a four-year deal worth around $8.1 million with the KT Wiz, immediately becoming a cornerstone player for a club that hasn't finished outside the cellar in the three seasons since being formed in 2015. Hwang is expected to bring not only his skills to the Wiz, but also more veteran presence to a young KT clubhouse. He is one of the best infield bats in the league, and his arm strength from third base is unparalleled in Asia.

Ha-Sung Kim SS Nexen Heroes Born:10/17/95 Age:22

YEAR	TEAM	AGE	G	PA	AB	R	H	2B	3B	HR	TB	HBP	SF	SH	RBI	BB	K	SB	CS	AVG/OBP/SLG	sWAR
2015	Nexen Heroes	20	140	582	511	89	148	35	5	19	250	5	6	4	73	56	115	22	4	.290/.362/.489	4.94
2016	Nexen Heroes	21	144	599	526	92	148	29	7	20	251	6	5	2	84	60	80	28	15	.281/.359/.477	3.81
2017	Nexen Heroes	22	141	601	526	90	159	36	3	23	270	8	7	2	114	58	65	16	8	.302/.376/.513	4.91

Back when Kim played for Yatap High, a lot of the attention went to his teammate Hoy-Jun Park, who ended up signing with the New York Yankees for a $1.16 million bonus. While Park only reached High-A in 2017, Kim has established himself as the one of the KBO's *bona fide* young stars. Once Jung-Ho Kang left for Pittsburgh after the 2014 season, many wondered how Nexen would fill the team's huge hole at shortstop. The 20-year-old Kim broke out that following season and hasn't stopped since, being named the no. 4 prospect in the 2017 World Baseball Classic by *Baseball America*. After the WBC, Kim continued to show advanced power at the plate, strong fielding instincts and improved plate discipline (0.75 BB/K in 2016 vs. 0.89 in 2017) back in Korea. By the time he nears free agency, Kim could position himself similarly to the player he took over for, but without the DUIs.

Hyun Soo Kim OF LG Twins Born:01/12/88 Age:30

YEAR	TEAM	AGE	G	PA	AB	R	H	2B	3B	HR	TB	HBP	SF	SH	RBI	BB	K	SB	CS	AVG/OBP/SLG	sWAR
2015	Doosan Bears	27	141	630	512	103	167	26	0	28	277	8	9	0	121	101	63	11	5	.326/.438/.541	6.70
2016	Baltimore Orioles (MLB)	28	95	346	305	36	92	16	1	6	128	4	1	0	22	36	51	1	3	.302/.382/.420	0.5 (WARP)
2016	Bowie Baysox (AA)	28	2	7	7	1	2	0	0	1	5	0	0	0	2	0	2	0	0	.286/.286/.714	
2017	Baltimore Orioles (MLB)	29	56	142	125	11	29	4	0	1	36	2	2	0	10	12	27	0	0	.232/.305/.288	-0.4 (WARP)
2017	Philadelphia Phillies (MLB)	29	40	97	87	9	20	4	1	0	26	0	0	0	4	10	19	0	0	.230/.309/.299	-0.3 (WARP)

Even those who don't follow Korean baseball are surely familiar with Kim, especially Orioles fans. After starting the 2016 season on the O's bench, Kim batted his way into everyday at-bats (.302/.382/.420 in 346 PA) and pushed himself into a potential long-term future in the majors. However, he found himself back on the bench in 2017 after the singles just stopped falling—turns out there isn't much use for a corner outfielder with a sub-.600 OPS. After becoming a free agent, Kim signed a four-year, 11.5 billion Korean *won* deal (worth around $10.58 million) with the LG Twins on December 19—the second biggest contract in KBO history. Having a career .318/.406/.488 line to fall back on in his native country, Kim is one of the best and most balanced hitters in recent KBO history. The Twins, who ranked second-to-last in the league with a .748 team OPS in 2017, desperately needed offensive reinforcements and hope Kim will be the shot in the arm they need. It makes it especially sweeter for LG fans that they signed away one of the most popular players in their Seoul rival Doosan Bears' history.

Jae-Hwan Kim OF Doosan Bears Born:09/22/88 Age:29

YEAR	TEAM	AGE	G	PA	AB	R	H	2B	3B	HR	TB	HBP	SF	SH	RBI	BB	K	SB	CS	AVG/OBP/SLG	sWAR
2015	Doosan Bears	27	48	180	153	24	36	8	0	7	65	2	2	1	22	22	39	4	1	.235/.335/.425	0.48
2016	Doosan Bears	28	134	568	492	107	160	37	3	37	309	0	5	0	124	71	107	8	2	.325/.407/.628	5.75
2017	Doosan bears	29	144	636	544	110	185	35	2	35	328	7	4	0	115	81	123	4	1	.340/.429/.603	7.49

Kim was a backup outfielder who made frequent trips to the Futures League—the KBO's version of Triple-A—from 2008 to 2015. Selected in the second round of the 2008 KBO draft, Kim was originally an offensive-minded catcher but was blocked by Eui-Ji Yang, the league's preeminent catcher of this decade. After bouncing around multiple positions, he gained a chance to stick as a starting outfielder in 2016 with the departure of Hyun-Soo Kim to the Baltimore Orioles. Then, his hitting potential finally exploded. In 2016, Kim became the first Doosan Bears left-handed hitter to eclipse a .300 average, 30 homers and 100 RBI and led the team to its second consecutive Korean Series championship. With his big, muscular frame, he can drive the ball out to any part of the ballpark with a swing as smooth as a Kenny G holiday album. The beat went on and on in 2017, as he was the best hitter in the KBO while leading Doosan to another Korean Series trip. He does, however, come with a tainted legacy of being busted for testosterone use back in 2011.

Sun-Bin Kim SS Kia Tigers Born:12/18/89 Age:28

YEAR	TEAM	AGE	G	PA	AB	R	H	2B	3B	HR	TB	HBP	SF	SH	RBI	BB	K	SB	CS	AVG/OBP/SLG	sWAR
2015	Did not play - military service																				
2016	Kia Tigers	27	6	27	25	3	9	2	1	0	13	0	0	1	0	1	3	1	1	.360/.385/.520	0.20
2017	Kia Tigers	28	137	529	476	84	176	34	1	5	227	5	4	5	64	39	40	4	4	.370/.420/.477	4.91

Just like MLB's Jose Altuve, Kim won the KBO batting title while being constantly photographed next to his taller teammates and opponents. His profile says he checks in at 164 cm (just under 5'4"), but he shows exceptional bat control and the ability to spray line drives to all parts of the field. In 2017, Kim's 7.6 percent strikeout rate was lowest in the league; he was the only qualified hitter in single digits. It's not just his prowess at the plate that makes him one of the best position players in Korea, though, as he won his first Gold Glove Award as a shortstop last season. Again like his easiest American comp, Kim helped engineer the run to a championship in 2017.

Tae-Kyun Kim 1B Hanwha Eagles Born:05/29/82 Age:36

YEAR	TEAM	AGE	G	PA	AB	R	H	2B	3B	HR	TB	HBP	SF	SH	RBI	BB	K	SB	CS	AVG/OBP/SLG	sWAR
2015	Hanwha Eagles	33	133	524	408	61	129	28	0	21	220	12	5	1	104	98	80	3	1	.316/.457/.539	4.17
2016	Hanwha Eagles	34	144	652	529	94	193	39	0	23	301	9	6	0	136	108	97	1	0	.365/.476/.569	5.50
2017	Hanwha Eagles	35	94	407	356	51	121	22	0	17	194	4	4	0	76	43	56	0	0	.340/.413/.545	2.58

Kim has been a model of consistency with the stick. It's a bit staggering to think that his 2017 batting line is right in line with his career numbers (.325/.430/.534), but that speaks to the body of work he has built since the turn of the century. In 15 KBO seasons, Kim has amassed 293 career home runs (10th all-time) and has only twice fallen short of the .900 OPS mark. If you know his name, it's because Kim has starred for Korea in recent international tournaments. He was unanimously named to the 2009 World Baseball Classic All-Tournament Team after posting a 1.176 OPS and launching three homers. He also played in Japan in 2010 and 2011 for the Chiba Lotte Marines, winning both the NPB Home Run Derby and Japan Series in his first year. Although Kim's skills at the plate haven't yet deteriorated, age and injuries have affected his mobility as a first baseman. He spent most of 2017 at designated hitter, while Wilin Rosario took reps at first base for Hanwha.

Ja-Wook Koo OF Samsung Lions Born:02/12/93 Age:25

YEAR	TEAM	AGE	G	PA	AB	R	H	2B	3B	HR	TB	HBP	SF	SH	RBI	BB	K	SB	CS	AVG/OBP/SLG	sWAR
2016	Samsung Lions	23	108	495	428	105	147	19	13	14	234	5	5	2	77	55	68	10	5	.343/.420/547	3.96
2017	Samsung Lions	24	144	647	564	108	175	39	10	21	297	10	10	0	107	63	138	10	4	.310/.383/.527	3.11

Koo arrived in the KBO with much fanfare by hitting .349 for the first-place Lions in 2015. Since then, he has moved from first base to right field and increased his power output without sacrificing his discerning eye. His contact rate worsened in 2017, as he struck out 21.3 percent of the time—an eight-percentage-point increase from the previous year—and his 138 whiffs led the league. Because of his tall, lanky frame, youth, hitting ability and past performance, Koo is projected to be one of the biggest stars in the league for years to come, even if he remains one of Korea's main sources of wind power.

Dae-Ho Lee 1B Lotte Giants Born:06/21/82 Age:36

YEAR	TEAM	AGE	G	PA	AB	R	H	2B	3B	HR	TB	HBP	SF	SH	RBI	BB	K	SB	CS	AVG/OBP/SLG	sWAR
2015	Fukuoka SoftBank Hawks (NPB)	33	141	584	510	68	144	30	0	31	267	9	3	0	98	62	109	0	1	.282/.368/.524	
2016	Seattle Mariners (MLB)	34	104	317	292	33	74	9	0	14	125	5	0	0	49	20	74	0	0	.253/.312/.428	0.0 (WARP)
2016	Tacoma Rainiers (AAA)	34	7	29	27	3	14	4	0	2	24	0	0	0	6	2	2	0	0	.519/.552/.889	
2017	Lotte Giants	35	142	608	540	73	173	13	0	34	288	15	3	0	111	50	84	1	1	.320/.391/.533	3.64

Before coming to MLB in 2016, Lee spent 2001 to 2011 with the Lotte Giants, winning two Triple Crowns (2006, 2010), an MVP award (2010) and four Gold Gloves (2006, 2007, 2010, 2011). He then spent four seasons in Japan, winning Japan Series titles with the Fukuoka Softbank Hawks in 2014 and 2015 and slashing .293/.370/.486 with 98 home runs. After having laid waste to a full continent of pitchers, the 33-year-old free agent decided to try his hand at MLB arms rather than finding a more lucrative deal in Japan. He signed a minor-league deal with the Seattle Mariners and beat out Jesus Montero, Gaby Sanchez and Stefen Romero for the last roster spot in the spring of 2016. Lee spent a chunk of that season sharing a first-base platoon spot with Adam Lind and posted a .264 TAv in 317 plate appearances. Although playing in the United States can be glamorous, Lee chose financial and playing-time security by signing the largest deal in KBO history—a four-year pact with the Lotte Giants worth around $13.7 million—before the 2017 season. Even as a 35-year-old he was able to use the thunder in his bat to help Lotte advance to their first postseason since 2012.

Jung-Hoo Lee OF Nexen Heroes Born:08/20/98 Age:19

YEAR	TEAM	AGE	G	PA	AB	R	H	2B	3B	HR	TB	HBP	SF	SH	RBI	BB	K	SB	CS	AVG/OBP/SLG	sWAR
2017	Nexen Heroes	19	144	622	552	111	179	29	8	2	230	6	2	2	47	60	67	12	4	.324/.395/.417	3.59

In 1994, the Haitai Tigers (now the Kia Tigers) employed a shortstop named Jong-Beom Lee, who took the KBO by storm, hitting .393/.452/.581, stealing 84 bases and winning the league MVP. Twenty-three years later his son, Jung-Hoo Lee, wowed the league by showing an extremely advanced approach and strong natural hitting ability for an 18-year-old. Lee, a first-round draftee in 2016, didn't show any difficulty on the field in his first pro season. The 2017 KBO Rookie of the Year has a lanky, yet projectable 6'1" frame with a strong arm that he deploys often from center field. Although he didn't bring his power projection into games in 2017, his growing frame should allow him to add it in the coming seasons and transition into one of the KBO's cornerstone bats.

Seong-Beom Na OF NC Dinos Born:10/03/89 Age:28

YEAR	TEAM	AGE	G	PA	AB	R	H	2B	3B	HR	TB	HBP	SF	SH	RBI	BB	K	SB	CS	AVG/OBP/SLG	sWAR
2015	NC Dinos	26	144	622	564	112	184	34	5	28	312	15	8	3	135	32	127	23	4	.326/.373/.553	5.14
2016	NC Dinos	27	144	653	572	116	177	37	2	22	284	9	4	1	113	67	136	7	4	.309/.388/.497	4.42
2017	NC Dions	28	125	561	498	103	173	42	2	24	291	12	3	0	99	48	116	17	7	.347/.415/.584	5.82

Na was a two-way star on the Yonsei University baseball team. At the time, he was better known as a pitcher, with a fastball sitting in the low-90s. He was linked to the New York Yankees and the Los Angeles Dodgers as an amateur but ended up with the newly birthed Dinos in the 2012 KBO draft. Despite Na's talent on the mound, the Dinos saw more potential in him as a hitter, and the investment paid off. In five seasons, Na has hit .314/.381/.533 with 118 home runs en route to being a consistent all-star. He can hit the ball as hard as anyone in the league and moves well on the bases for someone with his big, muscular frame—adding an unexpected dimension to his game. Na has openly spoken about wanting to go to MLB and is eligible to be posted by NC after the 2019 season. Because of his frame, tools, strength and hitting prowess, the 28-year-old is the best MLB position prospect in Korea right now.

Byungho Park 1B Nexen Heroes Born:07/10/86 Age:31

YEAR	TEAM	AGE	G	PA	AB	R	H	2B	3B	HR	TB	HBP	SF	SH	RBI	BB	K	SB	CS	AVG/OBP/SLG	sWAR
2015	Nexen Heroes	29	140	622	528	129	181	35	1	53	377	12	4	0	146	78	161	10	3	.343/.436/.714	7.76
2016	Minnesota Twins (MLB)	30	62	244	215	28	41	9	1	12	88	5	3	0	24	21	80	1	0	.191/.275/.409	0.2 (WARP)
2016	Rochester Red Wings (AAA)	30	31	128	116	18	26	5	0	10	61	6	0	0	19	6	32	0	0	.224/.297/.526	
2017	Rochester Red Wings (AAA)	31	111	455	419	48	106	22	2	14	174	6	2	0	60	28	130	0	0	.253/.308/.415	

Park's career has been full of ups and downs. After being touted as a can't-miss high school prospect for his "prodigious power," Park spent years in the LG Twins system as a frustrating project that didn't seem to be panning out in the KBO. His fortune changed in 2011, when LG traded him to the Nexen Heroes. With a new team, Park immediately took off. He won the 2012 and 2013 KBO MVP Award and had a pair of 50-homer seasons in 2014 and 2015. He hit the international market at the right time, and the Minnesota Twins signed him to a four-year, $12 million contract after paying a $12.85 million fee prior to the 2016 season. However, inconsistencies, injuries and a severe lack of contact derailed Park's career in the United States. After spending the entire 2017 season with the Twins' Triple-A affiliate, Park opted to forfeit the remainder of his contract and return to Nexen. If Park picks up where he left off before heading to Minnesota, he will be a massive boon to the Heroes, who missed the postseason in 2017.

Geon-Woo Park OF Doosan Bears Born:09/08/90 Age:27

YEAR	TEAM	AGE	G	PA	AB	R	H	2B	3B	HR	TB	HBP	SF	SH	RBI	BB	K	SB	CS	AVG/OBP/SLG	sWAR
2015	Doosan Bears	25	70	175	158	31	54	12	0	5	81	3	0	2	26	12	29	2	1	.342/.399/.513	1.47
2016	Doosan Bears	26	132	540	484	95	162	36	4	20	266	9	5	4	83	38	86	17	6	.335/.390/.550	4.51
2017	Doosan Bears	27	131	543	483	91	177	40	2	20	281	10	4	5	78	41	64	20	3	.366/.424/.582	7.03

Some dub Park as the KBO's Mike Trout because of his position, speed and hitting prowess. In 2017, Park became the first Doosan Bear to go 20-20 in a season—which should have really helped in your KBO fantasy league. Keep in mind, a 20-HR season is impressive if you play for Doosan or LG because their home park, Jamsil Stadium, is sizable and has similar dimensions to Kauffman Stadium in Kansas City. As evidenced by his explosion of doubles, Park is a line-drive hitter that can spray them to all corners and gaps. In 2017, his star-level performance earned him a spot on the Korean WBC squad.

Min-Woo Park 2B NC Dinos Born:02/06/93 Age:25

YEAR	TEAM	AGE	G	PA	AB	R	H	2B	3B	HR	TB	HBP	SF	SH	RBI	BB	K	SB	CS	AVG/OBP/SLG	sWAR
2015	NC Dinos	22	141	617	520	111	158	31	6	3	210	14	7	3	47	73	108	46	16	.304/.399/.404	4.42
2016	NC Dinos	23	121	515	435	84	149	16	6	3	186	8	7	10	55	55	70	20	6	.343/.420/.428	4.09
2017	NC Dinos	24	106	452	388	84	141	25	4	3	183	11	4	3	47	46	51	11	1	.363/.441/.472	4.69

Expectations for Park, a first-rounder in the 2012 KBO draft out of Whimun High, have been lofty since his amateur days. He stole fans' hearts at age 21 by swiping 50 bases and hitting .298, earning KBO Rookie of the Year honors. While he doesn't steal as many bases anymore, Park has grown steadily with the bat, watching his batting average rise as his strikeouts have decreased due to his increasingly advanced approach at the plate. Because of his speed, bat and on-base abilities, Park fits the conventional leadoff hitter mold—and he may just be the best of the bunch in the KBO.

Yong-Taik Park DH LG Twins Born:04/21/79 Age:39

YEAR	TEAM	AGE	G	PA	AB	R	H	2B	3B	HR	TB	HBP	SF	SH	RBI	BB	K	SB	CS	AVG/OBP/SLG	sWAR
2015	LG Twins	36	128	533	487	66	159	28	2	18	245	4	7	1	83	34	73	11	4	.326/.370/.503	3.85
2016	LG Twins	37	138	578	509	84	176	24	0	11	233	4	7	0	90	58	71	6	6	.346/.412/.458	2.96
2017	LG Twins	38	138	596	509	83	175	23	2	14	244	6	9	0	90	71	88	4	2	.344/.425/.479	3.73

Since winning the batting title at age 30 back in 2009 with a .372 average in 111 games, Park has been one of the most consistent hitters in the league, with his batting average starting with a three each of the last nine seasons. Even in his age-38 season, Park hit well enough to rank fifth in the league in hitting and earned his fourth career Gold Glove (and the first as a designated hitter). As of now, Park has 2,225 career hits, which is 93 shy of the all-time KBO record of 2,318, held by Joon-Hyuk Yang. Barring a decline in performance or an injury, Park should be able to eclipse that milestone in 2018.

Mel Rojas OF KT Wiz Born:05/24/90 Age:28

YEAR	TEAM	AGE	G	PA	AB	R	H	2B	3B	HR	TB	HBP	SF	SH	RBI	BB	K	SB	CS	AVG/OBP/SLG	sWAR
2015	Indianapolis Indians (AAA)	25	52	166	156	14	41	6	0	0	47	0	0	1	11	9	37	3	1	.263/.303/.301	
2015	Altoona Curve (AA)	25	66	248	214	21	55	11	4	2	80	2	3	2	19	27	51	6	3	.257/.341/.374	
2016	Indianapolis Indians (AAA)	26	12	28	26	1	4	1	1	0	7	0	0	0	3	2	7	0	1	.154/.214/.269	
2016	Gwinnett Braves (AAA)	26	64	261	230	27	62	11	5	10	113	0	2	0	34	29	49	9	2	.270/.349/.491	
2016	Mississippi Braves (AA)	26	35	135	123	15	30	8	0	2	44	0	0	2	9	9	33	3	1	.244/.293/.358	
2017	Gwinnett Braves (AAA)	27	54	236	212	27	55	13	6	6	86	2	4	0	31	18	50	2	2	.259/.318/.406	
2017	KT Wiz	27	83	367	336	52	101	27	3	18	188	5	3	0	56	23	81	5	8	.301/.352/.560	2.53

Rojas, son of former big-league reliever Mel Rojas Sr., was signed by the Wiz for $400,000 last June to replace first baseman Johnny Monell, who found life after Las Vegas to be far more challenging than he remembered. Although Rojas still had some youth on his side, he'd never reached the majors. and a .739 career OPS at Triple-A didn't seem appealing at first glance. After getting off to a .279/.348/.393 start in his first month, Rojas finished the season as a very capable everyday center fielder for KT. The Wiz didn't have many bright spots in 2017, but re-signing Rojas for a cool million dollars and throwing down nearly 10 times that amount to bring in Jae-Gyun Hwang offers a glimpse of hope for their fans heading into 2018.

Jamie Romak 1B/OF SK Wyverns Born:09/30/85 Age:32

YEAR	TEAM	AGE	G	PA	AB	R	H	2B	3B	HR	TB	HBP	SF	SH	RBI	BB	K	SB	CS	AVG/OBP/SLG	sWAR
2015	Arizona Diamondbacks (MLB)	30	12	16	15	2	5	2	0	0	7	0	0	0	1	1	6	0	0	.333/.375/.467	0.1 (WARP)
2015	Reno Aces (AAA)	30	129	557	486	87	138	42	3	27	267	4	7	0	100	60	143	6	1	.284/.363/.549	
2016	Yokohama Bay Stars (NPB)	31	30	84	71	7	8	1	0	0	9	2	1	0	2	12	30	0	0	.113/.247/.127	
2017	El Paso Chihuahuas (AAA)	32	25	102	95	24	33	8	1	11	76	1	0	0	25	6	25	2	1	.347/.392/.800	
2017	SK Wyverns	32	102	416	359	58	87	19	0	31	199	6	1	0	64	50	116	1	1	.242/.344/.554	2.04

Romak had prior Asian baseball experience, playing for the NPB's Yokohama DeNA Baystarsin 2016. However, that stint did not go well and only lasted 30 games. He started his 2017 by winning PCL Player of the Month honors in April and being picked up by the SK Wyverns almost immediately after. The Wyverns needed a replacement for Danny Worth (released after a 1-for-9 stint and an injury) and hoped Romak would be the power bat they sought. After a 1.029 OPS in May, Romak suffered through a .156/.230/.396 slump in June. With his status in the KBO for the 2018 season on shaky ground, he came through in the clutch, both for himself and for his team, posting a 1.358 OPS in September and giving SK a much-needed push to make it to the postseason as the wild card team. On October 27, the Wyverns returned that favor by re-signing the Canadian native for $850,000.

Darin Ruf 1B Samsung Lions Born:07/28/86 Age:31

YEAR	TEAM	AGE	G	PA	AB	R	H	2B	3B	HR	TB	HBP	SF	SH	RBI	BB	K	SB	CS	AVG/OBP/SLG	sWAR
2015	Philadelphia Phillies (MLB)	29	106	297	268	30	63	12	0	12	111	5	3	0	39	21	69	1	0	.235/.300/.414	0.4 (WARP)
2015	Lehigh Valley IronPigs (AAA)	29	7	28	26	3	8	1	0	0	9	1	1	0	6	0	2	0	0	.308/.321/346	
2016	Philadelphia Phillies (MLB)	30	42	89	83	8	17	2	0	3	28	0	2	0	9	4	25	0	1	.205/.236/.337	-0.5 (WARP)
2016	Lehigh Valley IronPigs (AAA)	30	95	390	350	56	103	18	2	20	185	7	4	0	65	29	78	0	0	.294/.356/.529	
2017	Samsung Lions	31	134	591	515	90	162	38	0	31	293	12	4	0	124	60	107	2	2	.315/.396/.569	3.91

No foreign player has had a more dramatic turnaround than Ruf did in 2017. Ruf, who played for the Phillies from 2012 to 2016, was slated to be a backup first-base candidate for the Dodgers until signing with the Samsung Lions for $1.1 million. Just like Roger Bernadina, Ruf struggled in April, but his woes went far deeper. The right-handed first baseman hit .143/.304/.196 in April and was sent down to the Futures League for four games—not quite what he or Samsung signed up for. After returning to the Lions lineup, he exploded like a Galaxy Note 7. Ruf went full crescendo, ending the season with a .407/.461/.815 September that brought his season-long stats in line with original expectations. He led the league in RBI with 124 and was re-signed by Samsung for $1.5 million. Some clubs give up on struggling foreign players a bit too early—the Lions did not, and they saw a handsome return for that investment because of it.

Geon-Chang Seo 2B Nexen Heroes Born:08/22/89 Age:28

YEAR	TEAM	AGE	G	PA	AB	R	H	2B	3B	HR	TB	HBP	SF	SH	RBI	BB	K	SB	CS	AVG/OBP/SLG	sWAR
2015	Nexen Heroes	26	85	368	312	52	93	24	4	3	134	1	2	11	37	42	24	9	2	.298/.381/.429	1.51
2016	Nexen Heroes	27	140	646	560	111	182	30	7	7	247	10	4	3	63	69	58	26	13	.325/.406/.441	4.46
2017	Nexen Heroes	28	139	615	539	87	179	28	3	6	231	1	6	2	76	67	68	15	6	.332/.403/.429	4.14

Coming out of Gwangju Jeil High, Seo was passed over in the 2008 KBO draft due to his small stature (5'7") and injury history, most notably with his shoulder. He was signed by the LG Twins but was released after playing only one game during the 2008 season. After fulfilling his military service, Seo signed with the Nexen Heroes as an undrafted free agent. This time he proved himself by stealing 39 bases, hitting .266/.342/.367 and winning the 2012 KBO Rookie of the Year Award. Later, he adjusted his hitting mechanics to turn more quickly toward the ball, which naturally gave him a more level swing, and the results speak for themselves. In 2014, Seo became the first ever KBO hitter to surpass 200 hits in a season and won the KBO MVP Award. He has continued to live up to his lofty reputation as one of the league's best contact hitters since. While the other aspects of his game leave something to be desired (below-average power, diminished fielding abilities due to injuries, etc.) Seo's star power inis undeniable.

Ah-Seop Son OF Lotte Giants Born:03/18/88 Age:30

YEAR	TEAM	AGE	G	PA	AB	R	H	2B	3B	HR	TB	HBP	SF	SH	RBI	BB	K	SB	CS	AVG/OBP/SLG	sWAR
2015	Lotte Giants	27	116	517	445	86	141	28	1	13	210	3	3	0	54	68	96	11	6	.317/.406/.472	3.80
2016	Lotte Giants	28	144	672	575	118	186	33	1	16	269	1	2	0	81	92	104	42	4	.323/.418/.468	5.30
2017	Lotte Giants	29	144	667	576	113	193	35	4	20	296	8	3	1	80	83	96	25	8	.335/.420/.514	5.72

It has become a regular occurrence for KBO players to change their name to try to turn around their luck. Ah-Seop Son, formerly known as Gwang-Min Son, is a prime example. The diminutive Son (he's 5'7", 187 pounds) has been the heart of the Giants with his bat, glove and baserunning. Since his breakout season in 2010 (.306, 11 HR in 121 games), Son does not have a mark below .314 on his stat page. He earned a military exemption by winning a gold medal with the Korean national team in the 2014 Incheon Asian Games and wanted to go to MLB after the 2015 season. Unfortunately for Son, no major-league team bid for him in posting, so it was his Lotte in life to continue destroying KBO pitchers over the next two seasons. After a strong 2017 season, in which he reached the 20-homer mark for the first time in his career and led the Giants to the playoffs, Son was once again eligible to jump to the United States; however, the Giants re-signed him to a four-year contract worth around $9 million this offseason.

Eui-Ji Yang C Doosan Bears Born:06/05/87 Age:31

YEAR	TEAM	AGE	G	PA	AB	R	H	2B	3B	HR	TB	HBP	SF	SH	RBI	BB	K	SB	CS	AVG/OBP/SLG	sWAR
2015	Doosan Bears	28	132	513	442	70	144	27	0	20	231	24	6	2	93	39	64	5	4	.326/.405/.523	5.65
2016	Doosan Bears	29	108	392	332	66	106	17	0	22	189	12	7	1	66	40	29	2	0	.319/.404/.569	4.81
2017	Doosan Bears	30	111	406	347	47	96	15	0	14	153	12	3	1	67	43	53	1	1	.277/.373/.441	3.04

Yang has been Doosan's starting catcher since 2010 and has proven himself to be the most complete player at his position. With a career .290/.372/.455 line and 102 home runs over nine seasons, Yang is clearly an asset with his bat. However, he is more known for his leadership ability and the way he manages a pitching staff. His strong 2015 and 2016 efforts played no small part in the Bears' two consecutive championships and starting catcher honors for Team Korea in the 2017 World Baseball Classic.

PITCHERS

Jake Brigham RHP Nexen Heroes Born:02/10/88 Age:30

YEAR	TEAM	AGE	W	L	SV	G	GS	IP	H	HR	BB/9	BB	K/9	K	HR/9	WHIP	FIP	ERA	LOB%	sWAR
2015	Atlanta Braves (MLB)	27	0	1	0	12	0	16.2	28	1	4.30	8	6.50	12	0.50	2.16	4.12	8.64	59.0	-0.0 (WARP)
2015	Gwinnett Braves (AAA)	27	4	1	0	8	3	26.0	31	1	2.42	7	6.92	20	0.35	1.46	3.04	4.50	66.5	
2015	Mississippi Braves (AA)	27	6	3	0	12	12	65.0	55	1	1.94	14	6.78	49	0.14	1.06	2.83	3.05	60.1	
2016	Tohoku Rakuten Golden Eagles (NPB)	28	0	3	0	11	4	34.1	39	3	4.20	16	7.10	27	0.80	1.60	0.00	5.24	0.0	
2017	Nexen Heroes	29	10	6	0	24	24	144.0	166	17	1.63	26	6.13	98	1.06	1.33	4.72	4.38	70.6	2.79

Even though his statistics don't say it yet, Jang has become one of the league's top young pitchers to watch. He can sit 90-93 mph and touch 95 with his fastball. When it's on, his slider has a late bite that induces whiffs; it gets particularly deadly if he can locate it on the outside corner against left-handed hitters. The biggest wild card for Jang is his command. He has a Jekyll-and-Hyde tendency to look dominant in one game and completely fall apart in the next. However, he will head into 2018 as a newly minted 23-year-old and is still quite raw. His walk rate from 2017 may not look particularly impressive, but it was a stark improvement from the start of the season; in mid-May, he had allowed 29 walks in 25 1/3 innings. It will be a challenge, but the biggest task for Jang is to solve his inconsistencies while maintaining his stuff. If he improves with more reps as a starting pitcher, he could be a mainstay on the Korean national team in international tournaments.

Woo-Chan Cha LHP LG Twins Born:05/31/87 Age:31

YEAR	TEAM	AGE	W	L	SV	G	GS	IP	H	HR	BB/9	BB	K/9	K	HR/9	WHIP	FIP	ERA	LOB%	sWAR
2015	Samsung Lions	28	13	7	0	31	29	173.0	160	28	3.85	74	10.09	194	1.46	1.38	4.83	4.79	70.6	1.62
2016	Samsung Lions	29	12	6	0	24	24	152.1	168	16	3.84	65	7.09	120	0.95	1.58	5.02	4.73	70.4	3.18
2017	LG Twins	30	10	7	0	28	28	175.2	171	20	1.95	38	8.04	157	1.03	1.23	4.20	3.43	75.0	4.19

There are many ways to describe Jang, the most representative ones being "workhorse" and "finesse pitcher." From 2006 to 2017, Jang has logged 150 innings in every season except 2010 (144 1/3 IP) in the KBO—excluding 2012 and 2013, in which he did not play due to military service. He signed a four-year deal with Doosan after the 2014 season and has thrived in the pitching-friendly environment at Jamsil Stadium. On the mound, he doesn't have a true plus pitch, but has four that he can command well in the strike zone—a high-80s fastball, a changeup, a curve and a slider. Those who follow international tournaments may be familiar with Jang, as the lefty started for Team Korea in both 2013 and 2017 World Baseball Classics.

Ryan Feierabend LHP KT Wiz Born:08/22/85 Age:32

YEAR	TEAM	AGE	W	L	SV	G	GS	IP	H	HR	BB/9	BB	K/9	K	HR/9	WHIP	FIP	ERA	LOB%	sWAR
2015	Nexen Heroes	30	13	11	0	30	30	177.1	202	23	3.10	61	6.95	137	1.17	1.55	4.97	4.67	71.7	3.10
2016	Nexen Heroes	31	5	7	0	19	19	110.2	139	18	2.28	28	6.67	82	1.46	1.55	5.29	4.64	76.1	2.38
2016	KT Wiz	31	2	6	0	12	11	71.1	92	5	2.52	20	7.82	62	0.63	1.65	4.06	4.16	73.0	1.79
2017	KT Wiz	32	8	10	0	26	26	160.0	153	20	1.74	31	7.43	132	1.13	1.19	4.42	3.04	76.1	5.31

Along with Seung-Lak Son, Jeong is one of the top lockdown closers of the KBO. Instead of overpowering hitters with pure stuff, Jeong attacks them with fastball command and by varying speeds with his circle change. Despite a fastball less likely to reach the 90s than

Culture Club, Jeong racked up career-high 11.9 strikeouts per nine innings in 2017. He has also proven to have quite the rubber arm, surpassing 70 innings in a season as a reliever five times since 2008 (including 102 in 2010).

Duk-Ju Ham LHP Doosan Bears Born:01/13/95 Age:23

YEAR	TEAM	AGE	W	L	SV	G	GS	IP	H	HR	BB/9	BB	K/9	K	HR/9	WHIP	FIP	ERA	LOB%	sWAR
2015	Doosan Bears	20	7	2	2	68	0	61.2	52	4	6.71	46	11.09	76	0.58	1.62	4.28	3.65	74.2	1.35
2016	Doosan Bears	21	0	0	0	15	0	8.2	10	0	11.42	11	7.27	7	0.00	2.42	5.64	6.23	71.4	0.03
2017	Doosan Bears	22	9	8	0	35	24	137.1	56	8	4.19	64	9.11	139	0.52	1.43	3.91	3.67	73.1	3.21

After Luke Scott, Ross Wolf and Jo-Jo Reyes all had poor turnouts for the Wyverns in 2014, the team decided to prioritize youth and character in foreign talents. Their biggest success, by far, has been Kelly. The right-hander, who had just turned 26, pitched for the Triple-A Durham Bulls in 2014 before signing a $350,000 deal with SK. Three years later, the Houston native has a career 3.80 ERA in 90 starts. Kelly became a reliable innings eater and has shown some of the best stuff in the league. Kelly sits 91-93 mph with his fastball and has touched 96. He also flashes a plus circle change, a developing cutter and a power curve that becomes useful for strikeout situations. Kelly can be trusted to eat innings and additionally has dominating stuff for the league. Some major-league teams came calling during the 2017 season, but SK re-signed him to a $1.75 million deal for 2018.

Gi-Young Im RHP Kia Tigers Born:04/16/93 Age:25

YEAR	TEAM	AGE	W	L	SV	G	GS	IP	H	HR	BB/9	BB	K/9	K	HR/9	WHIP	FIP	ERA	LOB%	sWAR
2015	Did not play - military service	22																		
2016	Did not play - military service	23																		
2017	Kia Tigers	24	8	6	0	23	19	118.1	138	9	1.37	18	5.55	73	0.69	1.32	4.07	3.65	72.3	2.77

Before coming to Korea, the Indiana native pitched for the Dodgers, Phillies, Rangers and Athletics from 2011 to 2014. In the winter of 2014, the Lotte Giants announced they'd signed Lindblom to an $850,000 contract and he turned in one of the finest seasons in team history. The Giants brought him back for 2016 with a raise; however, Lindblom struggled both on and off the field, as his newborn daughter had a rare congenital heart defect and required multiple surgeries. After 2016, Lindblom signed a minor-league contract with the Pirates to focus on the family and be near his hometown. Yet by July 2017, Lindblom was back with Lotte and gave the club a nice push toward a postseason berth. In the offseason, however, reports surfaced that Lotte showed unprofessional business conduct to negotiate with Lindblom, and their miscue swayed the right-hander to explore different clubs. As a result, he'll be donning a Doosan Bears jersey in 2018.

Hyun-Sik Jang RHP NC Dinos Born:02/24/95 Age:23

YEAR	TEAM	AGE	W	L	SV	G	GS	IP	H	HR	BB/9	BB	K/9	K	HR/9	WHIP	FIP	ERA	LOB%	sWAR
2015	NC Dinos	20	0	0	0	2	0	2.0	3	0	9.00	2	13.50	3	0.00	2.50	3.62	9.00	60.0	-0.05
2016	NC Dinos	21	1	3	0	37	5	76.1	68	5	5.07	43	6.96	59	0.59	1.45	4.87	4.48	68.9	1.84
2017	NC Dinos	22	9	9	0	31	22	134.1	139	18	4.42	66	8.04	120	1.21	1.53	5.28	5.29	67.1	0.91

In the United States, Noesi is best known for being involved in the Michael Pineda/Jesus Montero trade between the Yankees and Mariners. Noesi spent five seasons in the majors, pitching for those two teams, as well as the Rangers and White Sox. In the winter of 2015, the Kia Tigers signed him for $1.7 million, a hefty sum for a pitcher who had not pitched in the league. However, Noesi delivered by eating 200-plus innings two seasons in a row and forming a formidable 1-2 punch at the front of the rotation with Hyeon-Jong Yang. In 2017, Yang and Noesi each won 20 games, a feat accomplished only 17 times in KBO history entering the season. The Tigers, acknowledging Noesi's effectiveness and endurance, rewarded him with a handsome $2 million deal for the 2018.

Won-Joon Jang LHP Doosan Bears Born:07/31/85 Age:32

YEAR	TEAM	AGE	W	L	SV	G	GS	IP	H	HR	BB/9	BB	K/9	K	HR/9	WHIP	FIP	ERA	LOB%	sWAR
2015	Doosan Bears	30	12	12	0	30	30	169.2	182	13	3.61	68	6.79	128	0.69	1.47	4.54	4.08	72.4	2.89
2016	Doosan Bears	31	15	6	0	27	27	168.0	161	14	4.07	76	7.34	137	0.75	1.41	4.76	3.32	79.5	5.67
2017	Doosan Bears	32	14	9	0	29	29	180.1	172	12	2.55	51	6.24	125	0.60	1.24	4.26	3.14	75.8	5.38

Park is submariner. Got your attention, right? At some point, his release point was so low that his knuckles were maybe an inch away from scraping the ground. Park works primarily off his low-80s fastball and curveball, which is very hard to make contact with because of its "rise" as it enters the zone. His command has been his Achilles' heel since high school, but the 26-year-old made sizable improvements in 2017, dropping his walk rate by close to 40 percent. There is still plenty of work to be done, as his walk rate is *still* too high for comfort and he led the league in hit-by-pitches, but his 2017 progress and uniqueness make Park one of the most exciting pitchers to watch for in the KBO moving forward.

Woo-Ram Jeong LHP Hanwha Eagles Born:06/01/85 Age:33

YEAR	TEAM	AGE	W	L	SV	G	GS	IP	H	HR	BB/9	BB	K/9	K	HR/9	WHIP	FIP	ERA	LOB%	sWAR
2015	SK Wyverns	30	7	5	16	69	0	70.0	52	3	3.60	28	11.57	90	0.39	1.14	2.63	3.21	72.9	3.24
2016	Hanwha Eagles	31	8	5	16	61	0	81.0	64	7	2.89	26	9.44	85	0.78	1.11	3.71	3.33	72.4	3.26
2017	Hanwha Eagles	32	6	4	26	56	0	59.0	47	5	2.90	19	11.90	78	0.76	1.12	3.26	2.75	79.4	2.84

Selected by KT Wiz in the first round of the 2014 KBO draft, Park was projected to be one of the building blocks of the new expansion franchise. However, he was traded to the Lotte Giants in the middle of the 2015 season. Fans saw a glimpse of his potential in 2017 when Park notched a 2.44 ERA in his first 16 starts, which is remarkable considering his youth (he played the whole season at 21 years old) and the offense-friendly environment of the league in general. However, he stumbled through the remainder of the season, allowing a .931 and .773 OPS in August and September, respectively. Despite his struggles, Lotte fans are excited about Park's potential. He features a fastball that sits in the low-90s on a good day, with a forkball that flashes above-average. He also has a lanky frame, and his endurance and consistency could improve once his body fills out more.

Merrill Kelly RHP SK Wyverns Born:10/14/88 Age:29

YEAR	TEAM	AGE	W	L	SV	G	GS	IP	H	HR	BB/9	BB	K/9	K	HR/9	WHIP	FIP	ERA	LOB%	sWAR
2015	SK Wyverns	27	11	10	0	30	29	181.0	188	16	2.69	54	6.91	139	0.80	1.34	4.19	4.13	71.2	4.40
2016	SK Wyverns	28	9	8	0	31	31	200.1	205	15	2.70	60	6.83	152	0.67	1.32	4.25	3.68	72.1	5.95
2017	SK Wyverns	29	16	7	0	30	30	190.0	204	16	2.13	45	8.95	189	0.76	1.31	3.69	3.60	73.7	5.09

Raley was a sixth-round choice by the Chicago Cubs in the 2009 MLB draft. He spent a little time on the North Side in 2012 and 2013, registering a 7.04 ERA in just 38 1/3 innings. After spending 2014 in the Angels and Twins systems, he signed with the Lotte Giants that winter. Since coming to the KBO, Raley has been solid for Lotte, posting a career 4.02 ERA in 91 starts in the offense-friendly Sajik Stadium. In 2017, Raley had a meh first half (4.67 ERA in 17 starts) but turned on Ace Mode after the all-star game by pitching to a 2.83 ERA in his final 89 innings, becoming a driving force for the Lotte Giants' third-place finish and postseason berth. The lefty attacks the strike zone with his fastball, which sits between 88 and 91 mph, and uses his three off-speed pitches—slider, curve and change—to give hitters different looks. His no-nonsense approach has resulted in an improved walk rate, and his strikeout rate in 2017 was a new career high.

Jong-Hoon Park RHP SK Wyverns Born:08/13/91 Age:26

YEAR	TEAM	AGE	W	L	SV	G	GS	IP	H	HR	BB/9	BB	K/9	K	HR/9	WHIP	FIP	ERA	LOB%	sWAR
2015	SK Wyverns	24	6	8	0	33	23	118.0	123	7	4.04	53	8.01	105	0.53	1.49	4.36	5.19	65.0	1.17
2016	SK Wyverns	25	8	13	0	28	28	140.0	141	17	5.85	91	6.69	104	1.09	1.66	6.33	5.66	66.1	0.69
2017	SK Wyverns	26	12	7	0	29	28	151.1	145	16	3.63	61	6.36	107	0.95	1.36	5.38	4.10	75.3	3.49

Until 2013, Seung-Hwan Oh was the undisputed best reliever in the KBO, but once The Final Boss headed to the Hanshin Tigers before the 2014 season, Son became the league's top closer. Last year was the high-water mark of Son's 10-year career, as he set a career best strikeout-to-walk rate, while overpowering hitters with a low-90s fastball and a high-80s slider/cutter combo. Watching Son is a true a joy because of his high-effort delivery, which often ends with him leaping up in the air after throwing a pitch.

Brooks Raley LHP Lotte Giants Born:06/29/88 Age:30

YEAR	TEAM	AGE	W	L	SV	G	GS	IP	H	HR	BB/9	BB	K/9	K	HR/9	WHIP	FIP	ERA	LOB%	sWAR
2015	Lotte Giants	27	11	9	0	31	30	179.1	182	20	2.86	57	6.73	134	1.00	1.42	4.74	3.91	71.2	3.87
2016	Lotte Giants	28	8	10	0	31	31	184.2	207	21	2.49	51	7.16	147	1.02	1.49	4.77	4.34	69.2	3.52
2017	Lotte Giants	29	13	7	0	30	30	187.1	199	19	2.11	44	7.50	156	0.91	1.39	4.37	3.80	74.1	5.09

A top pitching prospect out of Gyeongnam High back in 1999, Song signed with the Boston Red Sox after receiving a $900,000 bonus rather than heading to the KBO. After the 2001 season, Song was one of MLB's top prospects in the majors (ranked 60th on *Baseball America*'s Top 100 Prospects list) and later was a key piece in the 2002 trade that sent Cliff Floyd from Montreal to Boston. However, arm troubles and struggles in the high minors kept Song away from major-league opportunities. He returned to Korea in 2007 to pitch for the Lotte Giants and has stayed there since. In 11 seasons with Lotte, Song has compiled a career 4.37 ERA and a 104-78 record. He had a forgettable 2016 marred with ineffectiveness (8.71 ERA in 41 1/3 IP), which made many wonder if he was at the crossroads of his career. However, in his age-37 season, he came back strong with an above-average ERA and a career-high strikeout-to-walk rate to boot.

Henry Sosa RHP LG Twins Born:06/28/85 Age:33

YEAR	TEAM	AGE	W	L	SV	G	GS	IP	H	HR	BB/9	BB	K/9	K	HR/9	WHIP	FIP	ERA	LOB%	sWAR
2015	LG Twins	30	10	12	0	32	30	194.1	199	16	1.67	36	8.20	177	0.74	1.24	3.50	4.03	63.4	4.23
2016	LG Twins	31	10	9	0	33	33	199.0	258	12	1.72	38	4.84	107	0.54	1.53	4.18	5.16	63.8	2.63
2017	LG Twins	32	11	11	1	30	29	185.1	189	11	1.85	38	7.43	153	0.53	1.24	3.52	3.88	67.1	4.19

Sosa has been in Korea for so long, he has thrown nearly twice as many innings there as he did in the minors. The former Astro was originally signed by the Kia Tigers during the 2012 season and spent two years down in Gwangju. He has bounced around to Nexen and LG since. In six seasons, Sosa has a 4.46 ERA in 167 games. Earlier in his KBO career, he was considered sort of an enigma due to his plus-plus velocity—he would touch the high-90s with his heater—and mixed results. In 2017, however, he had his most complete KBO season, eating innings, keeping the ball in the park, limiting walks and drastically improving his strikeout rate. The Twins re-signed Sosa to a $1.2 million contract for 2018, in the hope that the 32-year-old fireballer will keep it rolling.

Hyeon-Jong Yang LHP Free Agent Born:03/01/88 Age:30

YEAR	TEAM	AGE	W	L	SV	G	GS	IP	H	HR	BB/9	BB	K/9	K	HR/9	WHIP	FIP	ERA	LOB%	sWAR
2015	Kia Tigers	27	15	6	0	32	31	184.1	150	18	3.81	78	7.67	157	0.88	1.24	4.57	2.44	87.2	8.14
2016	Kia Tigers	28	10	12	0	31	31	200.1	191	19	3.46	77	6.56	146	0.85	1.34	4.75	3.68	71.5	5.69
2017	Kia Tigers	29	20	6	0	31	31	193.1	209	17	2.10	45	7.36	158	0.79	1.31	3.94	3.44	72.1	4.63

Yang collected nearly every accolade a player could in 2017. Not only did he win the 2017 KBO MVP award, but he also garnered the Golden Glove for pitchers, the Korean Series MVP and, possibly, a new lucrative contract in the offseason. Yang has spent his entire career with Kia so far, with a career 3.88 ERA in 11 seasons. He initially expressed interest in heading to MLB via posting after the 2014 season but decided against it. He was linked with the Yokohama DeNA Baystars of the NPB in free agency after the 2016 season, but instead Yang turned that leverage into a lucrative one-year deal to stay with Kia, ensuring he reached free agency again after the 2017 season. Although he was not necessarily the most dominant starting pitcher in Korea last season, the weight of 20 victories and a dominant postseason performance swayed journalists to vote for him as MVP—it's like the '80s all over again. Yang typically sits around 90 mph with his fastball but can reach back to hit 93-95 when needed. He also shows a slider, curve and change, but none of them would be considered plus pitches in the majors. He suffers from inconsistent command at times, but when he's on, he shows smarts by mixing pitches and eye levels as well as anyone in the league.

Sung-Hwan Yoon RHP Samsung Lions Born:10/08/81 Age:36

YEAR	TEAM	AGE	W	L	SV	G	GS	IP	H	HR	BB/9	BB	K/9	K	HR/9	WHIP	FIP	ERA	LOB%	sWAR
2015	Samsung Lions	34	17	8	0	30	30	194.0	199	27	1.39	30	7.61	164	1.25	1.23	4.35	3.76	76.0	3.91
2016	Samsung Lions	35	11	10	0	28	28	180.0	202	25	2.05	41	4.25	85	1.25	1.42	5.55	4.35	72.9	4.13
2017	Samsung Lions	36	12	9	0	28	28	174.1	191	22	1.91	37	6.71	130	1.14	1.34	4.78	4.28	72.7	3.74

The Lions won four consecutive Korean Series titles from 2011 to 2014, and Yoon played an integral part in creating that sustained success. The past few seasons, however, the righty has seen his fastball velocity decrease from the high-80s to the mid-80s, but he still possesses top-notch command and movement on his pitches, which has allowed him to continue his effectiveness with diminished stuff. Aside from his fastball, Yoon mixes locations, movements and eye levels by using a five-pitch mix, rounded out by a hard slider, slow curve, change and sinker.

sWAR stats courtesy of Statiz

Nippon Professional Baseball Prospectus

Essay by Kazuto Yamazaki

Player comments by Kazuto Yamazaki

"There is little semblance between baseball games in Japan and the game I loved and grew up with in the States." Bob Horner, a former all-star with the Atlanta Braves, said that in an interview after failing to land a deal with a major-league club in light of ownership collusion and spending the 1987 season—at the age of 29—with the Yakult Swallows. Although Horner, who was nicknamed "Red Devil" by the Japanese fans, produced a .327/.423/.683 line and smacked 31 home runs in a mere 355 plate appearances, it appeared to be far from a pleasant experience for the former no. 1 overall draft pick. "I don't want to be forced to go halfway around the world to play something that isn't baseball," added Horner, who would make a triumphant return to the major leagues with the Cardinals the following year, only to injure his shoulder and retire less than a year later.

Fast-forward thirty years: The flashy leather and big hair of the 1980s are well in the rearview mirror. Things have changed, but not all of them as drastically as the height and volume of those hairstyles. The Japanese game has progressed in many ways over the past few decades, yet there are aspects of the sport that may look unfamiliar and, more often than not, myopic to stateside observers' eyes.

You may have learned by now how frequently they bunt in Japan. What you have heard is true. Last year, all 12 NPB clubs combined to lay down 1,328 sacrifice bunts in 64,923 plate appearances. In comparison, MLB teams sacrificed a combined 925 times—nearly 400 fewer—in close to three times as many chances. You're more likely to see a sacrifice bunt in an NPB game than you are in a four-game MLB series.

Softbank Hawks shortstop Kenta Imamiya had 52 by himself—a number that hasn't been topped in the United States since Ray Chapman and Jack Barry in 1917, and will certainly never be reached again. In fact, he's so willing to give up his livelihood for the greater good, he should put a white wolf on the knob of his bat and name it Longclaw. He out-sacrificed all but two big-league clubs in 2017. Imamiya, entering his age-26 season, already has 270 sacrifices under his belt. In each of the first three games of the Japan Series last fall, he laid down a bunt to move a runner over in the first inning—out of the no. 2 spot in the lineup, no less. To make things more preposterous, Imamiya was rated 15 percent above the league average in overall offensive production, according to a Japanese data-tracking company called Delta Graphs. In addition to Imamiya, 13 other players sacrificed at least 20 times in the most recent season.

The tradition is far more ingrained than that. At the high-school level, bunting usage is even more intensive. Every time a leadoff batter reaches, teams try to send him over for an out.

Obsessive bunting is hardly the only part of the Japanese game that resembles the American game from 100 years ago. The Far Eastern crowd still praises the art of hitting for contact and speed. If you look at the NPB rosters, you'll notice that each team employs multiple no-power, slash-and-dash hitters. In the world of memes, swinging for the fences is the enraged girlfriend, and the fast, contact-oriented hitter is the attractive passerby the guy is staring at.

Even more dissimilar still are the worlds of talent acquisition and development. The draft, which is held in late October after the conclusion of the most recent season, is akin to those of the NFL and NBA. Eligible players hail from high school, college, independent leagues and industrial club teams.

The rules of the draft, per se, vary from the ones we are familiar with in MLB. In the first round, teams are allowed to select whomever they want. If multiple teams bid on the same player, they enter into a lottery—literally, draw pieces of paper from a box—to determine a winner. In the past, eight teams tried to captivate Hideo Nomo. Seven teams took a chance on Kosuke Fukudome in 1995 and on Kotaro Kiyomiya—perhaps the most sought-after high school player in the history of Japanese baseball—last fall, respectively.

Early-round picks, especially ones from college and club teams, are expected to play significant roles the following year. Of the 141 pitchers that threw at least 40 innings during the 2017 season, 14 were first-year players, including Shoma Fujihira, Rakuten's 2016 first-round pick, who spent all but the final two weeks of the season as an 18-year-old. Notably, albeit in a small sample size of eight starts and 43 1/3 innings, Fujihira struck out a quarter of the hitters he faced, well above the league average for starters (18.7 percent).

Fujihira isn't unprecedented. Future big-league hurlers such as Daisuke Matsuzaka, Yu Darvish and Masahiro Tanaka logged enormous workloads—with Matsuzaka and Tanaka racking up 180 and 186 1/3 innings, respectively, in their rookie campaigns right out of high school.

Why and how does this happen? One reason lies in NPB's undeveloped player-development system. What we know as the minor-league ladder doesn't exist in Japan. Each NPB club consists of *ichigun*—the top team, what we refer to as the NPB—and *nigun*—the second team, or what we refer to as the NPB minors, essentially the Japanese equivalent of the Triple-A level. Granted, a few teams have started deploying *sangun*—third team—which mostly contain relatively more unpolished and younger players, but the two-layer system has been around for more than 60 years. Sometimes, teenaged high school graduates, even those who are far from ready for the level, make appearances in *ichigun* as part of development.

Part of this is because there's little to no incentive for NPB teams to use the tricks we most often see in the United States to game the system around service time. The inexistence of minor-league options creates both earlier opportunities for future impact players and surreal career paths for fringy ones. With unlimited promotions and demotions without being outrighted, roster-fillers make countless trips between *ichigun* and *nigun* for the same organization, sometimes well into their thirties, like how Kevin Garvey went back and forth between reality and purgatory in *The Leftovers*. And this is how Louis Okoye, another Rakuten first-rounder, has piled up 271 NPB plate appearances in his first two years in professional ball. The organization can get him the experience because there's no point at which he runs out of options, and they can always shift a veteran out for a few weeks or months to make room.

Instead, amateur levels work as the low minors in Japan. As I mentioned earlier, top college and industrial league picks are expected to contribute immediately. The levels of competition in those upper-level amateur leagues are quite high, and teams in those leagues could hold up against *nigun* teams.

But most notably, you'd be astounded by how mature and fundamentally developed high school players in Japan are, compared to their counterparts in the rest of the world. These kids spend the entirity of their high school years—literally, some powerhouse teams practice for up to 12 hours a day, year round—to win Koshien, by far the most significant sports event in the country held annually in March and August. Imagine a cross between the NCAA Tournament and the World Series. Coaches try to get everything out of the players, and the players work their butts off in pursuit of wins, which are of singular importance in the Japanese high school scene. Due to the year-round, hyper-intensive training, high school players in Japan are ahead of the curve.

Perhaps what stands out the most in contrast to MLB is the inactivity in player movement. A half century ago, the majority of the Japanese working class spent their lives serving one employer. They stuck with their first job until retirement. Sacrificing one's entire life to one organization was considered an act of beauty. Nowadays, people move from one job to another in most industries, but the old philosophy still lives on in baseball. The increasing number of voyages to MLB notwithstanding, a good portion of NPB players never exercise their free agency rights (domestic or international) even after they accumulate the required amount of service time to earn them.

While those organizational depth players get better compensation than stateside career minor leaguers, prominent regulars are severely underpaid compared to their big-league counterparts. Their salaries don't see linear increases like they do in MLB—and there's certainly no arbitration. To make things even worse, after rough campaigns, players can see their salaries get cut drastically, in part due to the lack of a strong and influential players' union. In 2017, the average salary of an NPB player was roughly 38 million yen, or approximately $340,000—less than one-tenth of that in MLB.

The play on the field may not look as different as Bob Horner described 30 years ago. But the cultural undercurrent of baseball in Japan may come with a shock and confusion. Perhaps that's what Horner meant after all.

—Kazuto Yamazaki is an author of Baseball Prospectus

HITTERS

Shogo Akiyama CF Seibu Lions
Born:04/16/88 Age:30 Bats:L Throws:R Height:6'0" Weight:187

YEAR	TEAM	G	PA	AB	R	H	2B	3B	HR	TB	RBI	SB	CS	SH	SF	BB	IBB	HP	SO	GDP	AVG	OBP	SLG
2015	SEI	143	659	575	106	185	38	5	25	308	89	16	5	0	7	72	1	5	97	4	.322	.398	.536
2016	SEI	143	671	578	98	171	32	4	11	244	62	18	6	0	6	77	2	10	103	2	.296	.385	.422
2017	SEI	143	675	602	108	216	36	10	14	314	55	17	17	7	2	60	2	4	78	6	.359	.419	.522

With quick jumps, plus-plus speed and accurate routes, Akiyama is arguably the best center fielder in Japan. Although he rarely, if ever, makes highlight-reel-worthy diving plays, he pairs his speed with great instincts to cover a lot of ground. The all-time NPB single-season hits record holder with 216 (set in 2015) certainly has another calling card in contact skills. On top of that, he started showing more over-the-fence power, clearing the wall a career-high 25 times and posting his best fly-ball rate in the last four years in an attempt to prove the launch-angle revolution is not limited to the United States. With his skill set, he has the potential to be an above-average regular in stateside ball. That said, time is starting to run out for Akiyama, who will turn 30 shortly after Opening Day.

Alfredo Despaigne DH/OF Softbank Hawks
Born:06/17/86 Age:32 Bats:R Throws:R Height:5'9" Weight:209

YEAR	TEAM	G	PA	AB	R	H	2B	3B	HR	TB	RBI	SB	CS	SH	SF	BB	IBB	HP	SO	GDP	AVG	OBP	SLG
2015	FKU	136	545	478	66	125	15	0	35	245	103	3	1	0	3	59	2	5	119	14	.262	.347	.513
2016	CHB	134	570	496	81	139	27	0	24	238	92	0	3	0	7	64	3	3	89	25	.280	.361	.480
2017	CHB	103	409	353	49	91	18	0	18	163	62	0	1	0	3	49	2	4	89	9	.258	.352	.462

There's power. Then there's this thing in Alfredo Despaigne's tankesque body. The owner of the single-season home-run record in *Serie Nacional*, which he set in the 2011-2012 campaign by launching 36 bombs, Despaigne annihilates pitches day in and day out. It's highly unlikely that we'll see him play on American soil by the end of the decade, as he's currently under contract with the Hawks for two more years, not to mention that he'd have to defect to sign with an MLB club. Calling his defense a "liability" would be a hell of an understatement. The Hawks might as well hold a funeral for his glove.

Kenta Imamiya SS Fukuoka Softbank Hawks
Born:07/15/91 Age:26 Bats:R Throws:R Height:5'6" Weight:148

YEAR	TEAM	G	PA	AB	R	H	2B	3B	HR	TB	RBI	SB	CS	SH	SF	BB	IBB	HP	SO	GDP	AVG	OBP	SLG
2015	FKU	141	623	526	78	139	27	7	14	222	64	15	4	52	3	38	0	4	93	12	.264	.317	.422
2016	FKU	137	590	497	74	122	22	5	10	184	56	8	4	38	5	47	0	3	86	7	.245	.312	.370
2017	FKU	142	530	457	52	104	18	3	7	149	45	3	3	35	4	34	0	0	83	13	.228	.279	.326

In one sense, Imamiya is the quintessential old-school, two-spot hitter. In each of the last five seasons, he has had at least 35 sacrifice bunts, topping out at 62 each in 2013 and 2014. Obviously, there's more than just relentless bunting in his game. Fans and analysts alike consider him the best defensive shortstop in the country, and rightfully so. With exceptional body control, footwork and an arm that was clocked 95 mph off the mound in high school, Imamiya single-handedly dominates his competitors with his glove work. Even though he needs three more years of service time to retain international free agency, he's a rare major-league-caliber defensive shortstop in Japan.

Ryosuke Kikuchi 2B Hiroshima Carp Born:03/11/90 Age:28 Bats:R Throws:R Height:5'8" Weight:159

YEAR	TEAM	G	PA	AB	R	H	2B	3B	HR	TB	RBI	SB	CS	SH	SF	BB	IBB	HP	SO	GDP	AVG	OBP	SLG
2015	HRO	138	629	565	87	153	28	3	14	229	56	8	7	30	1	32	0	1	107	9	.271	.311	.405
2016	HRO	141	640	574	92	181	22	3	13	248	56	13	5	23	3	40	0	0	106	3	.315	.358	.432
2017	HRO	143	644	562	62	143	20	3	8	193	32	19	9	49	2	29	2	2	92	7	.254	.292	.343

Kikuchi's defense is like the iPod in Dunder Mifflin's Secret Santa in season two of *The Office*: It's incomparable, blowing all others away in competition. In its 80-plus-year history, Nippon Professional Baseball has seen a boatload of great second basemen. However, none of them has had a better glove than the Carp's defensive wizard. His unusually strong arm for the position and exceptional body control enable him to routinely make spectacular plays. As he demonstrated in the World Baseball Classic last March, he's a rare second sacker who can change the game solely with his glove work.

Kensuke Kondo DH Hokkaido Nippon-Ham Fighters Born:08/09/93 Age:24 Bats:L Throws:R Height:5'7" Weight:176

YEAR	TEAM	G	PA	AB	R	H	2B	3B	HR	TB	RBI	SB	CS	SH	SF	BB	IBB	HP	SO	GDP	AVG	OBP	SLG
2015	NIP	57	231	167	32	69	15	0	3	93	29	3	0	0	2	60	0	2	27	3	.413	.567	.557
2016	NIP	80	291	257	36	68	9	0	2	83	27	5	2	3	2	29	0	0	45	7	.265	.337	.323
2017	NIP	129	504	435	68	142	33	2	8	203	60	6	2	3	5	59	2	2	59	9	.326	.405	.467

All Kondo did in the first two-plus months of the 2017 season was hit, hit and hit again. The short-framed left-handed hitter put everything on the barrel and a completely ludicrous slash line ensued. Alas, a herniated disc cut his remarkable season far too short and forced him to miss more than three months before returning for a couple of games in early October. Still, he had a higher OPS than anyone registered over at least 100 plate appearances in any stateside league, the Mexican League, NPB and KBO. Of course, his mind-boggling numbers don't reflect his true talent level, but it wasn't all fluke: Kondo possesses plus bat-to-ball skills and absurd patience, leading to walks in more than a quarter of his plate appearances. Despite appearing in only 57 games, he ranked 10th in the Pacific League in bases on balls. It's a good thing Kondo can hit, because he barely contributes in any other aspects of the game. He was a catcher in the early stages of his career, but since he developed the yips he has been all over the place. He has manned third base and right field in games, the latter of which was near disastrous, and has tried second base in spring training. Despite his average speed, he's not a threat on the basepaths. But that slash line can cover many sins.

Chris Marrero 1B/OF Orix Buffaloes Born:07/22/88 Age:29 Bats:R Throws:R Height:6'3" Weight:209

YEAR	TEAM	G	PA	AB	R	H	2B	3B	HR	TB	RBI	SB	CS	SH	SF	BB	IBB	HP	SO	GDP	AVG	OBP	SLG
2015	ORX	82	319	283	39	82	15	1	20	159	50	1	0	0	2	29	1	5	84	6	.290	.364	.562

Perhaps the most glaring indication of the San Francisco Giants' demise in 2017 was not that it was an odd year, but the fact that Marrero made their Opening Day roster. After an unremarkable 15-game stint in the Bay Area, the former 15th overall draft pick spent the rest of the season eventfully, including missing home plate to have a home run taken away from him in his first NPB game and smacking the 100,000th long ball in the history of the league. Marrero, who is under contract with Orix for another season, may be better off sticking in Japan for several seasons to try and ascend to stardom than returning to the United States in pursuit of Mike Hessman's all-time minor-league career home-run record. Marrero is 291 dingers behind that record but has now outhomered Hessman 20 to 6 in a Buffaloes uniform.

Yoshihiro Maru CF Hiroshima Carp Born:04/11/89 Age:29 Bats:L Throws:R Height:5'10" Weight:198

YEAR	TEAM	G	PA	AB	R	H	2B	3B	HR	TB	RBI	SB	CS	SH	SF	BB	IBB	HP	SO	GDP	AVG	OBP	SLG
2015	HRO	143	651	556	109	171	35	3	23	281	92	13	3	2	6	83	0	4	113	6	.308	.398	.505
2016	HRO	143	652	557	98	162	30	8	20	268	90	23	9	1	3	84	1	7	107	9	.291	.389	.481
2017	HRO	143	633	530	81	132	28	1	19	219	63	15	7	4	4	94	2	1	143	4	.249	.361	.413

The 2017 Central League MVP possesses above-average-to-plus tools across the board, to go with elite plate discipline, which he has deftly used to draw at least 83 walks in each of last five seasons, leading the league twice. His strength and durability channel Carp legend Sachio Kinugasa, who holds the record for the most consecutive games played in the league's history. Maru has missed just four games since the start of 2013, and none in last four seasons. His last name means "circle" or "round" in Japanese, no matter how hard Kyrie Irving argues.

Eigoro Mogi SS Tohoku Rakuten Golden Eagles Born:02/14/94 Age:24 Bats:L Throws:R Height:5'7" Weight:165

YEAR	TEAM	G	PA	AB	R	H	2B	3B	HR	TB	RBI	SB	CS	SH	SF	BB	IBB	HP	SO	GDP	AVG	OBP	SLG
2015	RAK	103	450	398	64	118	25	2	17	198	47	3	2	4	1	45	1	2	84	4	.296	.370	.497
2016	RAK	117	481	424	56	118	20	7	7	173	40	11	4	21	2	30	0	4	95	8	.278	.330	.408

In 2017, despite missing 40 games to injury, Mogi crossed over into stardom and carried the Golden Eagles to their first postseason appearance in four years. At the dish, he became the first homegrown player to reach double digits in home runs in a season in Rakuten's 13-year franchise history. A third baseman in college, he has the speed and athleticism to handle shortstop, but his setup and his sometimes-awkward lateral movements can turn what should be outs into infield singles. Though he's far from a terrible defender at the six, Mogi would fit better on the other side of the keystone.

Tomoya Mori C/DH Seibu Lions Born:08/08/95 Age:22 Bats:L Throws:R Height:5'6" Weight:176

YEAR	TEAM	G	PA	AB	R	H	2B	3B	HR	TB	RBI	SB	CS	SH	SF	BB	IBB	HP	SO	GDP	AVG	OBP	SLG
2016	SEI	107	392	349	43	102	20	0	10	152	46	1	1	0	1	42	0	0	96	3	.292	.367	.436
2017	SEI	138	531	474	51	136	33	1	17	222	68	0	4	0	3	44	3	9	143	5	.287	.357	.468

Since the days of Kenji Johjima, Atsuya Furuta and Shinnosuke Abe, there has been an obvious dearth of offensive catchers in NPB. Mori, who hit .287/.357/.468 in 531 plate appearances as a 19-year old, is the sole hope to fill the void. He has missed a combined 141 games to injuries over the last two years, but no one questions his ability at the plate. Rather, his problems lie behind it, as many people remain skeptical about his catching skills, save for the plus-plus arm. Mori has spent the majority of his time with the Lions at DH, and when he has taken the field, his time has been split between outfield and catcher. Going forward, he's likely to put the shin guards and protector more frequently, as the potential for him to blossom into a perennial all-star backstop is too much to give up on.

Haruki Nishikawa CF Hokkaido Nippon-Ham Fighters Born:04/16/92 Age:26 Bats:L Throws:R Height:5'10" Weight:160

YEAR	TEAM	G	PA	AB	R	H	2B	3B	HR	TB	RBI	SB	CS	SH	SF	BB	IBB	HP	SO	GDP	AVG	OBP	SLG
2015	NIP	138	623	541	82	160	26	6	9	225	44	39	5	6	3	69	0	4	103	6	.296	.378	.416
2016	NIP	138	593	493	76	155	18	4	5	196	43	41	5	22	2	73	0	3	113	0	.314	.405	.398
2017	NIP	125	521	442	68	122	18	9	5	173	35	30	7	15	0	60	2	4	98	1	.276	.368	.391

In popularity rankings among people named Haruki, the Fighters' center fielder may lag well behind Murakami, a perennial Nobel Literature Prize candidate. But in terms of excellence and skill set in their respective fields, Nishikawa isn't far behind. While he's unlikely to earn any hardware for his defense, Nishikawa has great fundamentals and instincts, which allow him to handle center field night in and night out. The 25-year-old is also equipped with double-plus speed and a somewhere-between-fringy-and-average arm for the position. That speed also makes him a threat on the basepaths, where he has swiped 80 bases at an 89 percent clip over the last two seasons. At the plate, he shows a combination of bat-to-ball skills, patience and pop, which he used to smacked nine long balls while calling the cavernous Sapporo Dome home—the whole team combined for just 108 homers, and only three players reached double digits. Although he hasn't expressed interest in playing in the United States, he could be a borderline first-division big-league starter.

Hayato Sakamoto SS Yomiuri Giants Born:12/14/88 Age:29 Bats:R Throws:R Height:6'1" Weight:176

YEAR	TEAM	G	PA	AB	R	H	2B	3B	HR	TB	RBI	SB	CS	SH	SF	BB	IBB	HP	SO	GDP	AVG	OBP	SLG
2015	YOM	142	614	539	82	157	30	0	15	232	61	14	6	1	3	68	2	3	85	16	.291	.372	.430
2016	YOM	137	576	488	96	168	28	3	23	271	75	13	3	1	6	81	2	0	67	6	.344	.433	.555
2017	YOM	130	558	479	50	129	21	3	12	192	68	10	4	9	5	65	1	0	79	5	.269	.353	.401

For a full decade, Sakamoto has been the starting shortstop for the nation's most popular and historically successful team. He also handles the team captain role and remains unmarried nearing his 30th birthday, so you might say he has achieved "Derek Jeter of Japan" status. Throughout his career, the 29-year old has displayed average-to-plus tools across the board, including defense, where his plus-plus arm enables him to make off-balanced throws and his plus range allows him to get to more balls than his American counterpart ever could. At the plate, he has shown above-average contact skills and pop, though he still hasn't replicated his 31-homer season as a 21-year-old. Sakamoto has honed his plate discipline, laying off more pitches outside the zone while nearly doubling his walk rates compared to his early-career numbers. Despite his tools, don't expect to see him play stateside. After all, the Derek Jeter of America never left the team that drafted him.

Seiya Suzuki RF Hiroshima Carp Born:08/18/94 Age:23 Bats:R Throws:R Height:5'11" Weight:198

YEAR	TEAM	G	PA	AB	R	H	2B	3B	HR	TB	RBI	SB	CS	SH	SF	BB	IBB	HP	SO	GDP	AVG	OBP	SLG
2015	HRO	115	512	437	85	131	28	1	26	239	90	16	6	0	7	62	0	6	80	12	.300	.389	.547
2016	HRO	129	528	466	76	156	26	8	29	285	95	16	11	3	3	53	1	3	79	10	.335	.404	.612
2017	HRO	97	238	211	21	58	6	3	5	85	25	6	7	7	2	16	0	2	38	3	.275	.329	.403

At the ripe old age of 23, Suzuki is arguably the best right-handed hitter in Japan. With lightning-quick hands, a slightly long, yet efficient swing and exceptional hand-eye coordination, he punishes pitches and pitchers alike. While the Carp youngster may not be the best Suzuki to wear jersey number 51, his skill set is not far behind that of the former Blue Wave and Mariners superstar. In addition to his offensive tools, Suzuki possesses speed, which allows him to play an adequate center field if needed, and an arm that clocked at 92 mph off the mound in high school. It will be a while before he makes the jump to the United States, but once he does, Suzuki could make a name for himself.

Kosuke Tanaka SS Hiroshima Carp Born:07/03/89 Age:28 Bats:L Throws:R Height:5'7" Weight:187

YEAR	TEAM	G	PA	AB	R	H	2B	3B	HR	TB	RBI	SB	CS	SH	SF	BB	IBB	HP	SO	GDP	AVG	OBP	SLG
2015	HRO	143	679	565	105	164	32	5	8	230	60	35	13	6	4	89	2	15	120	5	.290	.398	.407
2016	HRO	143	679	581	102	154	17	3	13	216	39	28	19	3	1	77	1	17	119	1	.265	.367	.372
2017	HRO	141	590	543	61	149	33	9	8	224	45	6	7	5	1	34	2	7	105	8	.274	.325	.413

You may mistake Tanaka for someone who just got back from The Home Depot: He looks like your next-door neighbor, yet he's full of useful tools. The 28-year-old shows off a plus arm and defense at the six, double-plus speed that he has used to swipe 63 bases over the past two years (albeit at a far-from-ideal 66 percent success rate) and above-average contact. His average-ish raw power shows up in the doubles column due to his line-drive-happy swing. With his potential versatility (he spent time at third base and second base in his rookie year, and could handle center field well), Tanaka could be a perfect big-league bench guy if he ever moves to America.

Yoshitomo Tsutsugo LF Yokohama DeNA Baystars Born:11/26/91 Age:26 Bats:L Throws:R Height:6'1" Weight:214

YEAR	TEAM	G	PA	AB	R	H	2B	3B	HR	TB	RBI	SB	CS	SH	SF	BB	IBB	HP	SO	GDP	AVG	OBP	SLG
2015	YKO	139	601	503	85	143	31	0	28	258	94	1	0	0	3	93	3	2	115	7	.284	.396	.513
2016	YKO	133	561	469	89	151	28	4	44	319	110	0	1	0	2	87	1	3	105	6	.322	.430	.680
2017	YKO	138	568	496	79	157	28	1	24	259	93	0	0	0	2	68	0	2	98	5	.317	.400	.522

In terms of combining hit and power tools at a high level, very few do it better than Tsutsugo. Not only does he have plus-plus power, with which he paced the Central League in dingers two years ago, but he can shorten his swing and go up-the-middle or to the opposite field when he's behind in the count. His phenomenal ability to control the strike zone makes him one of the most polished hitters in the country, if not the world. Though he has been passable with the glove, thanks mostly to Yokohama Stadium's shallow outfield, his longterm home is at the cold corner at best or DH at worst. Tsutsugo has long made it known that it's his ultimate goal to play in MLB, so we may see him making the jump in a few years.

Zelous Wheeler 3B Rakuten Golden Eagles Born:01/16/87 Age:31 Bats:R Throws:R Height:5'10" Weight:220

YEAR	TEAM	G	PA	AB	R	H	2B	3B	HR	TB	RBI	SB	CS	SH	SF	BB	IBB	HP	SO	GDP	AVG	OBP	SLG
2015	RAK	142	605	542	75	147	27	0	31	267	82	7	3	0	3	50	4	10	98	14	.271	.342	.493
2016	RAK	140	589	517	74	137	25	2	27	247	88	2	1	0	2	58	0	12	123	10	.265	.351	.478
2017	RAK	91	313	274	28	70	12	0	14	124	50	1	0	0	3	30	0	6	63	6	.255	.339	.453

Another solid season is here again, oh Lord/
Has put up well above-average offensive numbers for three years or more/
I hope he holds onto this level of production a little longer/
Sent a baseball 400 feet on a long summer day/
Results of true talent, not of fluke/
He's been showing plus-plus raw power/
Wheeler in Japan keeps on turnin'/
He knows where he'll be tomorrow/
Wheeler in Japan keeps on turnin'/
He re-signed with Rakuten for 2018.

Tetsuto Yamada 2B Yakult Swallows Born:07/16/92 Age:25 Bats:R Throws:R Height:5'10" Weight:168

YEAR	TEAM	G	PA	AB	R	H	2B	3B	HR	TB	RBI	SB	CS	SH	SF	BB	IBB	HP	SO	GDP	AVG	OBP	SLG
2015	YKL	143	624	526	79	130	25	1	24	229	78	14	4	0	1	91	1	6	132	15	.247	.364	.435
2016	YKL	133	590	481	102	146	26	3	38	292	102	30	2	0	4	97	0	8	101	16	.304	.425	.607
2017	YKL	143	646	557	119	183	39	2	38	340	100	34	4	0	3	81	1	5	111	11	.329	.416	.610

Two years ago, when Yamada single-handedly carried the Swallows to their lone Japan Series appearance in the last 16 years, he was worth nearly 13 wins, according to DeltaGraphs. Coming off consecutive 30-30 campaigns, the 25-year old saw his offensive numbers crater in 2017. Something was clearly wrong, and a pair of hit-by-pitches he took in the back toward the end of the 2016 season are the primary suspects: Yamada seemed to be afraid of inside pitches, which caused him to look lost at times during the 2017 season. It's unclear whether Japan has its own Dickie Thon/Tony Conigliaro, or whether this past year was just a blip in a Hall of Fame career. If the latter is the case, Yamada could still be on track to reach the major leagues one day as an above-average offensive second baseman.

Hotaka Yamakawa 1B/DH Seibu Lions Born:11/23/91 Age:26 Bats:R Throws:R Height:5'9" Weight:220

YEAR	TEAM	G	PA	AB	R	H	2B	3B	HR	TB	RBI	SB	CS	SH	SF	BB	IBB	HP	SO	GDP	AVG	OBP	SLG
2015	SEI	78	293	242	46	72	19	0	23	160	61	0	1	0	0	46	1	5	72	7	.298	.420	.661

Imagine Aaron Judge's massive physique. Can you picture it? Now shrink him by a full foot and remove all semblance of mobility: that's Yamakawa. The Okinawa native put up dominant power numbers in 2017, albeit in abridged playing time, as his .364 ISO led all hitters with at least 250 PA by 80 points. Obviously, 412 at-bats does not a career make, but there's little doubt that he's one of the best offensive threats in the country right now.

Yuki Yanagita CF Fukuoka Softbank Hawks Born:10/09/88 Age:29 Bats:L Throws:R Height:6'2" Weight:205

YEAR	TEAM	G	PA	AB	R	H	2B	3B	HR	TB	RBI	SB	CS	SH	SF	BB	IBB	HP	SO	GDP	AVG	OBP	SLG
2015	FKU	130	551	448	95	139	30	1	31	264	99	14	7	0	7	89	8	7	123	6	.310	.426	.589
2016	FKU	120	536	428	82	131	31	4	18	224	73	23	2	0	0	100	2	8	97	8	.306	.446	.523
2017	FKU	138	605	502	110	182	31	1	34	317	99	32	8	0	1	88	4	14	101	9	.363	.469	.631

With the exception of Shohei Ohtani, 2015 Pacific League MVP Yanagita is the most fascinating and exciting NPB player in recent years, and the backbone of the Hawks' three titles in the last four years. He has five tools that stand out, with the speed, arm and power playing at least double-plus by Japan's standards. Last year, Yanagita took a part in the launch-angle revolution, jumping his fly-ball rate to 47.9 percent from 34.1 percent in 2016, and the over-the-fence power flowed like the Naka River. Unfortunately various minor injuries have prevented him from playing a full season in either 2016 or 2017, and these health concerns could lessen his market should he want to jump to the United States. He also has age fighting against him, as the late bloomer won't reach international free agency for three more seasons—a mark he'll hit after his 32nd birthday.

Masataka Yoshida OF Orix Buffaloes Born:07/15/93 Age:24 Bats:L Throws:R Height:5'8" Weight:191

YEAR	TEAM	G	PA	AB	R	H	2B	3B	HR	TB	RBI	SB	CS	SH	SF	BB	IBB	HP	SO	GDP	AVG	OBP	SLG
2015	ORX	64	268	228	42	71	11	0	12	118	38	1	1	0	1	38	2	1	32	9	.311	.410	.518
2016	ORX	63	258	231	35	67	17	0	10	114	34	0	2	0	1	25	0	1	34	6	.290	.360	.494

In his back-injury-plagued two-year career, Yoshida has never made more than 269 trips to the plate in a season. But in the limited playing time, he has shown the potential to be a perennial all-star. His violent, uppercut swing and raw power resemble those of Bryce Harper, whom he admires and shows respect to by wearing number 34. At 24, he has plenty of time to overcome the health problems and emerge as one of the country's best hitters, and get all that T-Mobile endorsement money.

PITCHERS

Kohei Arihara RHP Hokkaido Nippon-Ham Fighters Born:08/11/92 Age:25 Bats:R Throws:R Height:6'2" Weight:220

YEAR	TEAM	G	W	L	SV	HLD	CG	SHO	PCT	BF	IP	H	HR	BB	IBB	HB	SO	WP	BK	R	ER	ERA
2015	NIP	25	10	13	0	0	4	0	.435	726	169	0	21	39	2	4	88	5	0	97	89	4.74
2016	NIP	22	11	9	0	0	2	1	.550	640	156	0	13	38	1	2	103	3	1	52	51	2.94
2017	NIP	18	8	6	0	0	1	1	.571	453	103	0	13	32	0	3	81	2	0	60	55	4.79

Arihara is an enigma. He possesses a seven-pitch arsenal of mostly average offerings, headlined by a four-seam fastball that he can dial up into the mid-90s—exceptional velocity by NPB's standards, especially for a starter. Yet, he doesn't miss bats. Last year, he recorded the lowest strikeout rate and the third-lowest whiff-per-swing rate among all qualified NPB pitchers despite his Great Stuff. In that sense, you could call him the Japanese Joe Kelly. At the age of 25, Arihara is starting to run out of time, but the big-league upside is still there, if things ever click for him.

Rafael Dolis RHP Hanshin Tigers Born:01/10/88 Age:30 Bats:R Throws:R Height:6'5" Weight:240

YEAR	TEAM	G	W	L	SV	HLD	CG	SHO	PCT	BF	IP	H	HR	BB	IBB	HB	SO	WP	BK	R	ER	ERA
2015	HNS	63	4	4	37	5	0	0	.500	259	63	0	1	17	1	1	85	8	0	22	19	2.71

When Dolis made his last major-league appearance (to date) on May 26, 2013, Kris Bryant was a junior at the University of San Diego, a week and a half shy of being selected second overall in the draft by the Cubs, Dolis' then-employer. Fast-forward five years and Bryant has become one of the game's prominent superstars, while Dolis has established himself as a dominant closer in Japan, where his newly found splitter has missed bat after bat after bat. Additionally, he cut his walk rate from 11.6 percent in 2016 to 6.6 percent in 2017. If he further improves that low-walk track record, and the Tigers are generous enough to grant him a release (or simply can no longer afford him), he could find himself back in a big-league bullpen.

Shintaro Fujinami RHP Hanshin Tigers Born:04/12/94 Age:24 Bats:R Throws:R Height:6'5" Weight:196

YEAR	TEAM	G	W	L	SV	HLD	CG	SHO	PCT	BF	IP	H	HR	BB	IBB	HB	SO	WP	BK	R	ER	ERA
2016	HNS	26	7	11	0	0	2	1	.389	734	169	0	11	70	0	8	176	6	1	78	61	3.25
2017	HNS	28	14	7	0	0	7	4	.667	840	199	0	9	82	0	11	221	9	0	70	53	2.40

Two years ago, when the lanky right-hander struck out 221 batters in 199 innings as a 21-year-old, some evaluators favored Fujinami to Shohei Ohtani. Since then, his stock has fallen into the Dotonbori River, culminating in Fujinami walking more batters than he struck out in a shortened 2017 season. The Osaka native with the long limbs and a toothpick-thin build has had command issues throughout his career, but his agonizing 2017 campaign was even more problematic, and the yips are the primary suspect. It won't be an easy road, but Fujinami, who once hit 99 mph with his nasty, lively fastball, still has plenty of time to regain his prospect shine. After all, there are still teams out there willing to give Daniel Bard a shot.

Kota Futaki RHP Chiba Lotte Marines Born:08/01/95 Age:22 Bats:R Throws:R Height:6'1" Weight:165

YEAR	TEAM	G	W	L	SV	HLD	CG	SHO	PCT	BF	IP	H	HR	BB	IBB	HB	SO	WP	BK	R	ER	ERA
2015	CHB	23	7	9	0	0	5	0	.438	588	143	0	14	35	2	2	128	2	1	58	54	3.39
2016	CHB	22	7	9	0	0	1	0	.438	518	116	0	12	34	1	2	81	5	0	74	69	5.34

If Chiba Lotte's abysmal 2017 were an episode of *Friends*, it would be called "The One Where They Plummeted To A Franchise-Worst Record," but Futaki's arrival on the scene was one of the scant few bright spots. Even though he just turned 22 last August, the righty showed flashes of being a front-line starter, throwing all three of his main weapons—a four-seam fastball, slider and splitter—for strikes while missing bats and limiting walks. A lack of track record notwithstanding, it's possible that we witnessed the birth of another big-time starter who might spin off onto his own stateside show early next decade.

Haruhiro Hamaguchi LHP Yokohama DeNA Baystars Born:03/16/95 Age:23 Bats:L Throws:L Height:5'8" Weight:176

YEAR	TEAM	G	W	L	SV	HLD	CG	SHO	PCT	BF	IP	H	HR	BB	IBB	HB	SO	WP	BK	R	ER	ERA
2015	YKO	22	10	6	0	0	0	0	.625	546	123	0	9	69	0	2	136	9	1	54	49	3.57

The small-statured lefty's rookie campaign was a smash success. In his first taste of professional ball, Hamaguchi ranked eighth in strikeout rate among all NPB pitchers with at least 90 innings, and even held his rate stats reasonably in check despite calling the hitter-friendly Yokohama Stadium home. His most memorable outing came in Game Four of the Japan Series, in which he took a no-hitter into the eighth inning while striking out seven in 7 2/3 innings. He is far from flawless, however, walking an NPB-leading (and not super nice) 69 batters despite falling 20 innings short of the innings qualifier. But he has the athleticism to overcome the command problems and, my word, the changeup is something to dream on.

Nao Higashihama RHP Fukuoka Softbank Hawks Born:06/20/90 Age:28 Bats:R Throws:R Height:6'0" Weight:165

YEAR	TEAM	G	W	L	SV	HLD	CG	SHO	PCT	BF	IP	H	HR	BB	IBB	HB	SO	WP	BK	R	ER	ERA
2015	FKU	24	16	5	0	0	2	1	.762	637	160	0	17	44	0	1	139	2	0	48	47	2.64
2016	FKU	23	9	6	0	0	0	0	.600	545	135	0	13	37	0	2	100	1	0	49	45	3.00

Higashihama has been considered a prospect since 2008, when he carried his school to a national title in the Spring Koshien by tossing 579 pitches in 41 innings over 10 days. Yet, it wasn't until 2016 that his innings total topped that 41-inning mark from his glory days as an amateur. Among the things the Okinawan righty delivers from the mound is one of the most heinous leg kicks you'll ever see. Once you get over that, which is more difficult than it seems, the righty shows five solid-to-plus pitches and the ability to locate them. If he ever tries to test himself in the stateside, Higashihama, whose last name means "east beach," may not bypass east coast teams altogether.

Yoshihisa Hirano RHP Arizona Diamondbacks Born:03/08/84 Age:34 Bats:R Throws:R Height:6'1" Weight:185

YEAR	TEAM	G	W	L	SV	HLD	CG	SHO	PCT	BF	IP	H	HR	BB	IBB	HB	SO	WP	BK	R	ER	ERA
2015	ORX	58	3	7	29	8	0	0	.300	240	57	0	5	16	0	1	47	2	0	19	17	2.67
2016	ORX	58	4	4	31	8	0	0	.500	237	61	0	2	16	0	1	57	4	0	13	13	1.92

When the Cardinals signed Seung-hwan Oh before the 2016 season, hardly anyone expected The Final Boss to realize his nickname on the mound. Hirano, heading into his age-34 season, has a similar profile and pitch arsenal to Stone Buddha. However, his strikeout rate, which once topped out at 31.4 percent, has declined precipitously for four consecutive seasons, to a below-average 19.6 percent in 2017. Even though his fastball velocity has generally hovered around 92 mph, there's plenty of risk in signing relievers mid-decline.

Yusei Kikuchi LHP Seibu Lions Born:06/17/91 Age:27 Bats:L Throws:L Height:6'0" Weight:220

YEAR	TEAM	G	W	L	SV	HLD	CG	SHO	PCT	BF	IP	H	HR	BB	IBB	HB	SO	WP	BK	R	ER	ERA
2015	SEI	26	16	6	0	0	6	4	.727	735	187	0	16	49	0	6	217	6	0	49	41	1.97
2016	SEI	22	12	7	0	0	2	0	.632	595	143	0	7	67	0	2	127	3	0	51	41	2.58
2017	SEI	23	9	10	0	0	0	0	.474	542	133	0	9	55	1	2	122	5	1	48	42	2.84

After Shohei Ohtani's departure to Anaheim, Kikuchi now carries the torch as the best potential MLB asset in Japan, in terms of both his timeline to move to the states and his overall ability on the mound. Ohtani's fellow Hanamaki Higashi High School alumnus features a pair of major-league-quality pitches in the fastball and slider, the former reaching up to 97.5 mph on the radar gun, the fastest pitch thrown by a Japanese left-hander. Although he cut his walk rate in half in 2017, he still struggles with command occasionally, and it will never be his strength. Yet, despite his flaws, he could still find himself in the middle of a major-league rotation as soon as 2019—if the rumors that Seibu is open to posting him after this season are true.

Takayuki Kishi RHP Rakuten Golden Eagles Born:12/04/84 Age:33 Bats:R Throws:R Height:5'11" Weight:170

YEAR	TEAM	G	W	L	SV	HLD	CG	SHO	PCT	BF	IP	H	HR	BB	IBB	HB	SO	WP	BK	R	ER	ERA
2015	RAK	26	8	10	0	0	1	0	.444	703	176	0	19	38	2	3	189	4	0	56	54	2.76
2016	SEI	19	9	7	0	0	2	1	.563	541	130	0	8	36	0	1	104	0	0	42	36	2.49
2017	SEI	16	5	6	0	0	5	0	.455	434	110	0	6	25	0	5	91	0	0	40	37	3.02

When Kishi became a free agent after the 2016 season, he could have moved to America, where he would have been a back-of-the-rotation starter in the major leagues. Instead, he chose Rakuten, the franchise in his hometown of Sendai. While he does not possess overwhelming stuff, he pounds the zone with his quality, classic four-pitch mix. Kishi is under contract for another three years and stands a great chance of ending his career as a Golden Eagle.

Kazuhisa Makita RHP Seibu Lions Born:11/10/84 Age:33 Bats:R Throws:R Height:5'10" Weight:187

YEAR	TEAM	G	W	L	SV	HLD	CG	SHO	PCT	BF	IP	H	HR	BB	IBB	HB	SO	WP	BK	R	ER	ERA
2015	SEI	58	3	3	0	28	0	0	.500	248	62	0	4	5	0	3	35	0	0	18	16	2.30
2016	SEI	50	7	1	0	25	0	0	.875	312	78	0	3	16	2	10	43	0	0	15	14	1.60
2017	SEI	34	9	11	3	0	1	0	.450	596	137	0	7	44	2	11	66	1	0	68	56	3.66

It's impossible to fit Tyrion Lannister between the ground and the release point of Makita's submarine delivery. Shohei Ohtani notwithstanding, Makita may have been the most intriguing player to be posted this past winter. When he's on, the 33-year-old dominates opposing hitters with his 80-mph fastball and even softer, floating breaking balls (he throws a slider and curve). He could play a role in a big-league bullpen, albeit in limited exposure. More importantly, Makita works quickly, taking just five or six seconds between pitches without a runner on, a skill Rob Manfred may fall in love with.

Hirotoshi Masui RHP Orix Buffaloes Born:06/26/84 Age:34 Bats:R Throws:R Height:5'11" Weight:154

YEAR	TEAM	G	W	L	SV	HLD	CG	SHO	PCT	BF	IP	H	HR	BB	IBB	HB	SO	WP	BK	R	ER	ERA
2015	NIP	52	6	1	27	7	0	0	.857	215	52	0	6	11	1	0	82	5	0	15	14	2.39
2016	NIP	30	10	3	10	1	2	1	.769	333	81	0	5	26	2	3	71	3	0	22	22	2.44
2017	NIP	56	0	1	39	4	0	0	.000	238	60	0	1	19	0	0	71	4	1	11	10	1.50

Like many other great Japanese relievers in recent history, Masui features a devastating fastball/splitter combination, using it to record the fifth-lowest contact rate among those who accumulated at least 50 innings in 2017. His 38.1 percent strikeout rate was by far the highest mark of his career. Masui signed a four-year contract this past winter with the Buffaloes, who needed to replace Yoshihisa Hirano—another fastball/splitter closer. Masui will be 37 at the end of that contract, making it highly unlikely that he'll ever pitch for a major-league team. Still, he might be the best Japanese-born NPB closer of this generation.

Yuki Matsui LHP Rakuten Golden Eagles Born:10/30/95 Age:22 Bats:L Throws:L Height:5'8" Weight:163

YEAR	TEAM	G	W	L	SV	HLD	CG	SHO	PCT	BF	IP	H	HR	BB	IBB	HB	SO	WP	BK	R	ER	ERA
2015	RAK	52	3	3	33	5	0	0	.500	214	52	0	0	26	0	1	62	0	0	8	7	1.20
2016	RAK	58	1	4	30	10	0	0	.200	272	62	0	4	40	0	1	75	1	1	23	23	3.32
2017	RAK	63	3	2	33	12	0	0	.600	284	72	0	3	28	0	2	103	3	0	7	7	0.87

In the first round of the 2013 Summer Koshien, Matsui struck out 22 to set a new single-game tournament record. He further impressed the entire nation by striking out 19 in the subsequent outing. Rakuten, one of five teams that selected him in the first round of the draft that fall, originally tried to develop him as a starter, but the experiment failed after his command issues were exploited. As a 19-year-old, he found success in the back of the bullpen and has converted at least 30 saves in each of the last three seasons. Though his main putaway weapon in high school was a slider, he traded it for a changeup in pro ball, with which he has recorded a whiff-per-swing rate of nearly 40 percent. Small frame notwithstanding, Matsui would look right at home in a big-league bullpen immediately if he became available for MLB teams. Given that he already has four seasons under his belt before his 23rd birthday, he is the rare Japanese reliever who could jump to the United States in the middle of his prime.

Takahiro Norimoto RHP Tohoku Rakuten Golden Eagles Born:12/17/90 Age:27 Bats:L Throws:R Height:5'10" Weight:178

YEAR	TEAM	G	W	L	SV	HLD	CG	SHO	PCT	BF	IP	H	HR	BB	IBB	HB	SO	WP	BK	R	ER	ERA
2015	RAK	25	15	7	0	0	8	2	.682	750	185	0	11	48	1	3	222	12	0	63	53	2.57
2016	RAK	28	11	11	0	0	2	0	.500	820	195	0	12	50	0	6	216	5	0	87	63	2.91
2017	RAK	28	10	11	0	0	3	1	.476	797	194	0	14	48	0	4	215	6	1	68	63	2.91

From mid-April to early-June last year, Norimoto authored one of the most dominant stretches in NPB history, striking out at least 10 batsmen in eight consecutive games and setting a new league record for most starts in a row with double-digit strikeouts. In Norimoto's five seasons, the now-defunct Mie Chukyo University product has demonstrated a deep arsenal of effective pitches and the ability to locate them. He can throw a slider and a splitter—both of them are plus—to put hitters away. Norimoto has struck out at least 200 of those who've dared to face him in each of the last four seasons, while at the same time not eclipsing 50 walks in any of those campaigns. And in 2017, his strikeout rate was the highest among all qualified NPB hurlers. If everything goes according to plan, Rakuten has reportedly agreed to post one of the best pitchers of this generation after the 2019 season.

Dennis Sarfate RHP Softbank Hawks Born:04/09/81 Age:37 Bats:R Throws:R Height:6'4" Weight:225

YEAR	TEAM	G	W	L	SV	HLD	CG	SHO	PCT	BF	IP	H	HR	BB	IBB	HB	SO	WP	BK	R	ER	ERA
2015	FKU	66	2	2	54	3	0	0	.500	238	66	0	3	10	0	1	102	0	0	9	8	1.09
2016	FKU	64	0	7	43	8	0	0	.000	237	62	0	4	11	1	0	73	1	0	15	13	1.88
2017	FKU	65	5	1	41	9	0	0	.833	235	64	0	4	14	0	1	102	2	0	8	8	1.11

You can see the flashes of the good ol' 1980s in Japanese baseball, where a reliever wins a league MVP award from time to time, like Sarfate did last year. Granted, his 2017, in which he led all NPB pitchers with at least 60 innings in strikeout rate while setting a new single-season saves record, was one of the most dominant campaigns by a reliever in NPB history. Plus, he has been the best reliever in the country for the last few years. Sarfate could become available to major-league teams after the 2018 season, but he turns 39 shortly after Opening Day in 2019 and he can't keep getting better with age forever. Even the heartiest wines turn eventually. One thing is for certain: He won't add another MVP award in his trophy case.

Kodai Senga RHP Fukuoka Softbank Hawks Born:01/30/93 Age:25 Bats:L Throws:R Height:6'1" Weight:190

YEAR	TEAM	G	W	L	SV	HLD	CG	SHO	PCT	BF	IP	H	HR	BB	IBB	HB	SO	WP	BK	R	ER	ERA
2015	FKU	22	13	4	0	0	0	0	.765	572	143	0	15	46	0	2	151	6	0	47	42	2.64
2016	FKU	25	12	3	0	0	3	0	.800	681	169	0	16	53	0	6	181	7	1	52	49	2.61

Perhaps no one made a bigger splash and saw his stock rise more during the 2017 World Baseball Classic than Senga, who struck out 16 while walking just one batter in 11 innings last March and earned All-Tournament honors. His performance against Team USA, in which he struck out five of the eight hitters faced, was particularly impressive, despite the fact that he gave up the game's deciding run. The 25-year-old features a fastball that touches the mid-90s, an above average slider and his calling card: a splitter. That go-to offering missed bat after bat en route to the third-highest whiff rate among all qualified pitchers in NPB last season. But Senga doesn't fall in love with the pitch. When it's not working, he can ditch it and go slider-heavy instead. In other words, he knows how to pitch. His injury history, including shoulder soreness that forced him to miss more than a year's worth of playing time between 2014 and 2015, is concerning. On top of that, the Hawks are known for their reluctance to post players, which means Senga will most likely have to wait another five years to test the international market. Regardless, he's a fascinating arm to keep an eye on.

Tomoyuki Sugano RHP Yomiuri Giants Born:10/11/89 Age:28 Bats:R Throws:R Height:6'1" Weight:202

YEAR	TEAM	G	W	L	SV	HLD	CG	SHO	PCT	BF	IP	H	HR	BB	IBB	HB	SO	WP	BK	R	ER	ERA
2015	YOM	25	17	5	0	0	6	4	.773	713	187	0	10	31	0	1	171	1	0	36	33	1.59
2016	YOM	26	9	6	0	0	5	2	.600	726	183	0	12	26	0	4	189	1	0	46	41	2.01
2017	YOM	25	10	11	0	0	6	2	.476	710	179	0	10	41	4	7	126	3	0	46	38	1.91

It's hard to judge a player's true talent based on his performance in just one game, but the way Sugano pitched in the WBC semifinals last March is indicative of what he could be in the big leagues: He held the mighty Team USA lineup to just one run on three hits while striking out six over six innings. With an arsenal six pitches deep—most of them above-average or better—and impeccable command, Sugano is one of the most (if not the most) polished pitchers in the country. Additionally, the nephew of former Yomiuri manager Tatsunori Hara possesses a durability that is near-extinct in stateside baseball, as he completed six games, including three consecutive shutouts, in 2017. It's a damn shame we won't see Sugano, who needs four more years of service time to become an international free agent, pitch on the other side of the Pacific in his prime, thanks to Yomiuri practicing abstinence when it comes to the posting system.

Shota Takeda RHP Fukuoka Softbank Hawks Born:04/03/93 Age:25 Bats:R Throws:R Height:6'1" Weight:187

YEAR	TEAM	G	W	L	SV	HLD	CG	SHO	PCT	BF	IP	H	HR	BB	IBB	HB	SO	WP	BK	R	ER	ERA
2015	FKU	13	6	4	0	0	1	1	.600	316	71	0	10	33	0	5	60	1	0	35	29	3.68
2016	FKU	27	14	8	0	0	1	1	.636	769	183	0	12	70	0	5	144	7	1	71	60	2.95
2017	FKU	25	13	6	0	0	1	1	.684	684	164	0	14	59	0	2	163	6	3	60	58	3.17

Takeda burst onto the scene as a 21-year-old when he took a perfect game into the sixth inning during Game Two of the 2014 Japan Series. He has been a familiar face in international tournaments since, including the World Baseball Classic last March. In 2015 and 2016 he held his own as an above-average starter in the mighty and deep Hawks rotation, with his signature 12-to-6 curve at his disposal. There are two ominous signs, however. One is his walk rate, which has floated around or above the league average throughout his career. The other is the shoulder soreness that limited him to just 71 innings in 2017.

Yasuaki Yamasaki RHP Yokohama DeNA Baystars Born:10/02/92 Age:25 Bats:R Throws:R Height:5'10" Weight:183

YEAR	TEAM	G	W	L	SV	HLD	CG	SHO	PCT	BF	IP	H	HR	BB	IBB	HB	SO	WP	BK	R	ER	ERA
2015	YKO	68	4	2	26	15	0	0	.667	260	65	0	3	13	0	1	84	1	0	16	12	1.64
2016	YKO	59	2	5	33	7	0	0	.286	252	57	0	7	23	0	0	61	2	0	27	23	3.59
2017	YKO	58	2	4	37	7	0	0	.333	215	56	0	2	11	0	1	66	4	1	13	12	1.92

After three years as the Baystars' lights-out closer, Yamasaki has seen his bat-missing splitter become as iconic as Mariano Rivera's batbreaking cutter. The atmosphere in which Yamasaki rides in (yes, most of Yokohama's relievers are driven to the mound in a car) to Zombie Nation's "Kernkraft 400" resembles that of Rivera trotting in to "Enter Sandman." Even though he averages around 90 with his fastball, the half-Filipino closer ranked in the 90th percentile in whiff rate among all NPB pitchers in 2017, thanks to that aforementioned splitter, which he calls a "two-seamer." The Baystars don't want to part with Yamasaki anytime soon—and they won't have to for a while, as he's more than a half-decade from being able to depart west—but his pitching ability and charisma are both major-league caliber right now.

All stats courtesy of DeltaGraphs

NPB League Players

Hitters

HITTER	TEAM	YEAR	G	PA	AB	R	H	2B	3B	HR	TB	RBI	SB	CS	SH	SF	BB	IBB	HP	SO	GDP	AVG	OBP	SLG
Shinnosuke Abe	YOM	2015	129	512	455	41	119	13	0	15	177	76	0	1	1	7	41	1	8	67	13	.262	.329	.389
	YOM	2016	91	387	335	43	104	13	0	12	153	52	0	1	1	3	44	1	4	55	8	.310	.394	.457
	YOM	2017	111	419	343	44	83	14	0	15	142	47	0	0	0	4	64	1	8	84	9	.242	.370	.414
Tomohiro Abe	HRO	2015	123	455	413	63	128	17	4	4	165	49	17	5	12	1	27	1	2	94	3	.310	.354	.400
	HRO	2016	115	292	259	23	73	12	4	6	111	33	7	0	7	5	19	2	1	64	3	.282	.327	.429
Ryoichi Adachi	ORX	2015	109	380	316	40	64	9	3	3	88	26	4	3	17	0	37	0	10	61	5	.203	.306	.278
	ORX	2016	118	488	403	51	110	15	1	1	130	34	6	6	35	4	42	0	4	53	4	.273	.344	.323
	ORX	2017	139	593	506	57	121	16	3	11	176	55	16	15	29	4	48	0	6	68	11	.239	.310	.348
Yuichi Adachi	RAK	2016	73	208	185	14	42	5	0	1	50	14	0	2	11	2	10	0	0	36	2	.227	.264	.270
Tsubasa Aizawa	HRO	2015	106	329	287	35	79	15	0	6	112	35	0	0	10	3	22	1	7	45	12	.275	.339	.390
	HRO	2016	83	220	197	18	47	7	0	7	75	26	1	1	4	1	14	0	4	42	7	.239	.301	.381
	HRO	2017	93	290	252	23	62	7	3	6	93	30	0	1	2	3	26	3	7	49	9	.246	.330	.369
Ginji Akaminai	RAK	2015	143	590	529	55	155	30	0	3	194	60	2	1	1	2	56	1	2	74	11	.293	.362	.367
	RAK	2016	125	497	424	39	116	17	1	2	141	43	1	1	4	3	61	5	5	49	20	.274	.369	.333
	RAK	2017	82	354	316	24	95	10	1	1	110	36	8	3	3	4	30	1	1	19	5	.301	.359	.348
Kenji Akashi	FKU	2015	103	339	290	37	81	10	3	1	100	23	5	6	15	3	30	1	1	57	3	.279	.346	.345
	FKU	2017	115	394	342	49	90	12	3	3	117	30	11	5	12	4	31	1	5	64	4	.263	.330	.342
Shogo Akiyama	SEI	2015	143	659	575	106	185	38	5	25	308	89	16	5	0	7	72	1	5	97	4	.322	.398	.536
	SEI	2016	143	671	578	98	171	32	4	11	244	62	18	6	0	6	77	2	10	103	2	.296	.385	.422
	SEI	2017	143	675	602	108	216	36	10	14	314	55	17	17	7	2	60	2	4	78	6	.359	.419	.522
Japhet Amador	RAK	2015	121	460	417	35	99	9	0	23	177	65	0	1	0	2	39	0	2	102	18	.237	.304	.424
Leslie Anderson	YOM	2017	83	260	234	20	59	14	0	7	94	31	1	1	0	0	21	1	5	37	5	.252	.327	.402
Takahiro Arai	HRO	2015	100	288	243	36	71	14	0	9	112	48	2	0	0	4	40	0	1	56	7	.292	.389	.461
	HRO	2016	132	513	454	66	136	23	2	19	220	101	0	1	0	4	54	1	1	101	12	.300	.372	.485
	HRO	2017	125	480	426	52	117	22	2	7	164	57	3	0	0	4	48	1	2	73	15	.275	.348	.385
Masahiro Araki	CHU	2015	85	267	249	17	62	6	1	0	70	8	5	0	5	0	13	0	0	41	8	.249	.286	.281
	CHU	2016	93	321	289	25	71	8	1	1	84	16	13	0	14	0	15	0	3	39	9	.246	.290	.291
	CHU	2017	97	238	211	23	53	10	0	0	63	13	9	1	6	1	20	0	0	31	1	.251	.315	.299
Takahiro Araki	YKL	2015	91	212	188	22	39	8	2	6	69	25	2	0	7	0	14	0	3	30	7	.207	.273	.367
Sho Aranami	YKO	2017	70	207	188	29	56	15	2	4	87	14	4	3	1	1	16	0	1	26	2	.298	.354	.463
Hideto Asamura	SEI	2015	143	633	574	78	167	34	1	19	260	99	5	1	1	6	44	0	8	96	17	.291	.347	.453
	SEI	2016	143	611	557	73	172	40	0	24	284	82	8	6	3	6	38	0	7	108	18	.309	.357	.510
	SEI	2017	141	627	537	88	145	19	2	13	207	81	12	9	2	7	69	0	12	136	13	.270	.362	.385
Aarom Baldiris	YKO	2017	139	525	465	38	120	23	0	13	182	56	0	0	0	5	43	2	12	62	12	.258	.333	.391
Wladimir Balentien	YKL	2015	125	519	445	60	113	14	1	32	225	80	0	1	0	1	70	0	3	112	18	.254	.358	.506
	YKL	2016	132	537	457	64	123	20	0	31	236	96	0	1	0	5	72	2	3	116	19	.269	.369	.516
Francisco Caraballo	ORX	2017	64	247	222	26	56	9	0	12	101	35	0	1	0	3	17	0	5	63	3	.252	.316	.455
Hisayoshi Chono	YOM	2015	134	516	463	52	121	20	3	16	195	46	6	0	1	1	46	2	5	98	17	.261	.334	.421
	YOM	2016	143	618	576	58	163	28	4	11	232	42	8	2	1	3	33	0	5	78	7	.283	.326	.403
	YOM	2017	130	479	434	49	109	20	3	15	180	52	3	2	5	2	34	0	4	81	12	.251	.310	.415
Luis Cruz	YOM	2016	81	314	298	26	75	14	0	11	122	37	0	2	0	3	11	0	2	40	7	.252	.280	.409
	CHB	2017	133	532	501	48	128	23	1	16	201	73	0	0	0	5	24	1	2	66	7	.255	.289	.401
Mitch Dening	YKL	2017	64	227	194	13	43	12	0	4	67	22	0	1	0	2	23	1	8	43	2	.222	.326	.345
Alfredo Despaigne	FKU	2015	136	545	478	66	125	15	0	35	245	103	3	1	0	3	59	2	5	119	14	.262	.347	.513
	CHB	2016	134	570	496	81	139	27	0	24	238	92	0	3	0	7	64	3	3	89	25	.280	.361	.480
	CHB	2017	103	409	353	49	91	18	0	18	163	62	0	1	0	3	49	2	4	89	9	.258	.352	.462
Naomichi Donoue	CHU	2016	131	507	456	38	116	25	3	6	165	46	1	1	20	2	27	0	2	69	14	.254	.298	.362
Taiga Egoshi	HNS	2016	72	217	191	33	40	6	1	7	69	20	4	3	2	3	18	0	3	78	2	.209	.284	.361
Brad Eldred	HRO	2015	116	405	344	40	91	11	0	27	183	78	0	0	0	3	50	0	8	111	8	.265	.368	.532
	HRO	2016	95	354	316	42	93	14	0	21	170	53	1	0	0	3	31	0	4	86	8	.294	.362	.538
	HRO	2017	79	300	264	32	60	6	0	19	123	54	1	2	0	4	31	0	1	91	3	.227	.307	.466
Atsushi Fujii	CHU	2015	128	408	374	29	99	18	3	6	141	42	5	6	6	2	24	0	2	96	6	.265	.311	.377
	CHU	2017	118	315	275	28	81	9	3	6	114	45	3	0	11	4	23	1	2	69	4	.295	.349	.415
Ryota Fujii	YKL	2015	97	309	292	20	75	3	0	2	84	12	5	3	6	1	9	0	1	56	6	.257	.281	.288
Shunsuke Fujikawa	HNS	2015	74	202	191	26	59	15	1	4	88	23	1	0	2	0	9	0	0	33	1	.309	.340	.461
Kazuya Fujita	RAK	2015	102	315	270	28	68	9	2	3	90	33	2	1	25	3	16	1	1	21	8	.252	.293	.333
	RAK	2016	120	449	408	27	108	13	5	0	131	46	1	1	18	3	19	0	1	44	7	.265	.297	.321
	RAK	2017	111	451	392	38	106	14	1	5	137	43	8	3	16	7	28	2	8	30	3	.270	.326	.349
Masayoshi Fukuda	RAK	2017	67	210	185	20	40	7	0	1	50	12	5	8	8	1	13	0	3	45	2	.216	.277	.270

HITTER	TEAM	YEAR	G	PA	AB	R	H	2B	3B	HR	TB	RBI	SB	CS	SH	SF	BB	IBB	HP	SO	GDP	AVG	OBP	SLG
Nobumasa Fukuda	CHU	2015	95	326	299	37	81	19	0	18	154	49	0	1	0	1	21	0	5	70	4	.271	.328	.515
	CHU	2016	89	306	270	28	72	8	0	10	110	37	0	1	0	2	28	1	6	42	9	.267	.346	.407
Shuhei Fukuda	FKU	2016	81	239	212	30	49	5	4	3	71	18	11	3	4	2	20	1	1	51	2	.231	.298	.335
Kosuke Fukudome	HNS	2015	127	526	441	68	116	20	3	18	196	79	1	2	1	4	77	1	3	92	17	.263	.373	.444
	HNS	2016	131	523	453	52	141	25	3	11	205	59	0	1	0	6	61	5	3	78	6	.311	.392	.453
	HNS	2017	140	569	495	53	139	24	3	20	229	76	1	2	1	7	65	1	1	75	15	.281	.361	.463
Sosuke Genda	SEI	2015	143	647	575	85	155	18	10	3	202	57	37	10	26	4	36	0	6	100	5	.270	.317	.351
Esteban German	ORX	2017	73	245	221	31	59	8	1	1	72	15	17	2	0	0	24	0	0	40	7	.267	.339	.326
Mauro Gomez	HNS	2016	139	554	498	58	127	20	0	22	213	79	2	1	0	3	48	3	5	130	13	.255	.325	.428
	HNS	2017	143	601	520	49	141	28	0	17	220	72	0	1	0	3	72	1	6	134	15	.271	.364	.423
Mitsutaka Goto	RAK	2017	117	444	413	31	98	18	0	9	143	42	13	8	10	4	12	0	5	48	8	.237	.265	.346
Shunta Goto	ORX	2015	129	329	296	29	71	16	7	2	107	27	4	3	13	4	15	1	1	76	3	.240	.275	.361
	ORX	2016	105	239	214	17	41	5	0	1	49	9	3	3	12	0	11	0	2	40	2	.192	.238	.229
	ORX	2017	135	382	334	31	78	8	2	2	96	31	8	9	15	3	24	0	6	69	4	.234	.294	.287
Alex Guerrero	CHU	2015	130	510	469	67	131	22	3	35	264	86	1	0	0	2	24	0	15	98	13	.279	.333	.563
Fumihito Haraguchi	HNS	2015	73	216	186	16	42	12	0	6	72	25	0	0	1	2	22	0	5	36	10	.226	.321	.387
	HNS	2016	107	364	318	38	95	16	0	11	144	46	1	2	2	3	26	0	15	52	8	.299	.376	.453
Yuya Hasegawa	FKU	2016	122	442	387	45	105	15	3	10	156	51	2	4	1	0	51	2	3	95	9	.271	.361	.403
Itaru Hashimoto	YOM	2016	74	259	219	27	51	15	1	2	74	20	7	3	20	0	20	0	0	45	4	.233	.297	.338
Kazuhiro Hatakeyama	YKL	2017	137	584	512	64	137	26	0	26	241	105	0	0	0	8	62	0	2	92	10	.268	.344	.471
Anderson Hernandez	CHU	2016	64	256	233	25	58	12	0	5	85	26	1	1	4	2	17	0	0	61	6	.249	.298	.365
	CHU	2017	138	548	498	54	135	27	2	11	199	58	5	3	10	4	35	1	0	106	13	.271	.317	.400
Elian Herrera	YKO	2016	79	274	257	30	56	12	2	5	87	33	2	1	3	0	13	0	1	57	3	.218	.258	.339
Ryo Hijirisawa	RAK	2015	111	252	232	29	58	14	2	1	79	21	2	1	2	1	13	0	4	50	2	.250	.300	.341
	RAK	2016	94	229	201	32	59	6	2	3	78	19	3	3	14	1	11	0	2	41	5	.294	.335	.388
	RAK	2017	86	288	258	26	65	12	2	0	81	12	15	5	4	1	23	0	2	68	4	.252	.317	.314
Ryosuke Hirata	CHU	2015	66	270	238	26	58	14	2	6	94	29	4	0	0	2	29	0	1	60	4	.244	.326	.395
	CHU	2016	118	494	416	61	103	24	1	14	171	73	4	2	0	4	72	1	2	89	5	.248	.358	.411
	CHU	2017	130	559	491	76	139	27	3	13	211	53	11	7	1	0	64	1	3	86	5	.283	.369	.430
Wataru Hiyane	YKL	2017	84	240	209	42	48	6	0	3	63	9	6	2	10	0	17	0	4	38	2	.230	.300	.301
Fumiya Hojo	HNS	2015	83	252	219	26	46	7	2	3	66	20	0	0	7	2	23	0	1	42	4	.210	.286	.301
	HNS	2016	122	438	385	44	105	25	1	5	147	33	6	0	7	4	38	4	4	91	10	.273	.341	.382
Yuichi Honda	FKU	2016	110	388	332	52	93	9	1	1	107	27	23	7	19	3	33	0	1	51	6	.280	.344	.322
Kei Hosoya	CHB	2016	116	404	371	45	102	23	4	3	142	40	9	4	11	1	18	0	3	93	6	.275	.313	.383
Hirokazu Ibata	YOM	2017	98	321	269	20	63	9	0	1	75	19	3	3	10	2	37	0	3	36	4	.234	.331	.279
Tadahito Iguchi	CHB	2017	87	250	227	21	56	17	1	6	93	28	1	0	0	0	21	0	2	65	4	.247	.316	.410
Toshiaki Imae	RAK	2016	89	351	317	33	89	7	0	3	105	23	2	1	4	1	25	0	4	30	13	.281	.340	.331
	CHB	2017	98	400	373	40	107	18	4	1	136	38	2	2	0	2	16	1	9	35	17	.287	.330	.365
Kenta Imamiya	FKU	2015	141	623	526	78	139	27	7	14	222	64	15	4	52	3	38	0	4	93	12	.264	.317	.422
	FKU	2016	137	590	497	74	122	22	5	10	184	56	8	4	38	5	47	0	3	86	7	.245	.312	.370
	FKU	2017	142	530	457	52	104	18	3	7	149	45	3	3	35	4	34	0	0	83	13	.228	.279	.326
Takahiro Imanami	YKL	2016	94	240	201	22	56	9	3	1	74	28	0	1	3	4	30	0	2	25	3	.279	.371	.368
Ryota Imanari	HNS	2017	93	304	269	25	76	7	0	1	86	16	1	1	8	1	24	0	2	78	1	.283	.345	.320
Yoshiyuki Ishihara	HRO	2016	106	289	243	19	49	7	0	0	56	17	4	1	12	1	29	5	4	54	8	.202	.296	.230
	HRO	2017	83	238	216	15	52	6	0	2	64	12	1	0	8	0	14	2	0	42	10	.241	.287	.296
Kazunari Ishii	NIP	2015	114	361	317	33	65	8	2	3	86	24	3	5	14	1	28	0	1	113	6	.205	.271	.271
Shingo Ishikawa	YOM	2015	99	251	236	21	57	12	3	5	90	20	2	0	0	0	13	0	2	51	8	.242	.287	.381
Takehiro Ishikawa	YKO	2016	95	329	297	35	62	8	2	2	80	14	6	4	11	1	18	0	2	67	3	.209	.258	.269
	YKO	2017	89	375	343	43	89	8	1	1	102	18	6	3	9	0	16	1	7	82	2	.259	.306	.297
Hikaru Ito	ORX	2015	103	239	196	21	37	9	2	5	65	23	0	0	22	1	18	1	2	47	2	.189	.263	.332
	ORX	2016	80	203	187	18	45	7	0	3	61	15	1	0	12	0	3	0	1	36	6	.241	.257	.326
	ORX	2017	104	290	247	20	67	9	1	1	81	28	0	1	11	2	29	1	1	53	4	.271	.348	.328
Yoshio Itoi	HNS	2015	114	493	427	60	124	16	0	17	191	62	21	6	0	2	59	0	5	62	12	.290	.381	.447
	ORX	2016	143	616	532	79	163	24	1	17	240	70	53	17	0	2	75	5	7	84	13	.306	.398	.451
	ORX	2017	132	565	484	61	127	22	0	17	200	68	11	4	0	1	72	2	8	78	10	.262	.366	.413
Garrett Jones	YOM	2016	123	465	422	48	109	22	1	24	205	68	0	1	0	0	39	0	4	106	10	.258	.327	.486
Takuya Kai	FKU	2015	103	257	207	30	48	8	3	5	77	18	4	0	22	0	26	1	2	68	2	.232	.323	.372
Takayuki Kajitani	YKO	2015	137	578	511	83	124	27	2	21	218	60	21	3	0	2	62	2	3	157	10	.243	.327	.427
	YKO	2016	107	450	396	69	108	20	4	18	190	56	26	7	1	0	49	0	4	110	2	.273	.359	.480
	YKO	2017	134	578	520	70	143	35	2	13	221	66	28	13	2	2	54	0	0	132	4	.275	.342	.425
Katsuya Kakunaka	CHB	2015	110	452	383	44	103	17	4	8	152	44	6	1	1	2	62	4	4	44	6	.269	.375	.397
	CHB	2016	143	607	525	74	178	30	5	8	242	69	12	4	2	6	68	6	6	64	8	.339	.417	.461
	CHB	2017	111	484	427	57	125	20	5	6	173	52	8	4	7	2	47	0	1	52	12	.293	.363	.405
Yoshiyuki Kamei	YOM	2015	109	277	247	20	62	16	0	6	96	47	1	0	0	2	27	1	1	38	4	.251	.325	.389
	YOM	2016	66	240	226	21	57	14	0	3	80	23	0	2	3	0	11	0	0	35	7	.252	.287	.354
	YOM	2017	109	432	382	42	104	21	0	6	143	35	8	1	3	6	40	0	1	59	6	.272	.338	.374
Kyohei Kamezawa	CHU	2015	98	290	254	31	73	5	0	2	84	13	6	6	18	2	13	0	3	30	1	.287	.327	.331
	CHU	2017	107	376	331	30	89	6	2	0	99	12	9	8	27	1	15	0	2	44	3	.269	.304	.299
Yuji Kaneko	SEI	2015	90	320	283	43	77	17	2	5	113	34	25	8	5	4	27	0	1	49	5	.272	.333	.399
	SEI	2016	129	520	460	64	122	12	3	1	143	33	53	17	13	1	40	0	6	69	5	.265	.331	.311

HITTER	TEAM	YEAR	G	PA	AB	R	H	2B	3B	HR	TB	RBI	SB	CS	SH	SF	BB	IBB	HP	SO	GDP	AVG	OBP	SLG
Yasuyuki Kataoka	YOM	2017	113	411	348	42	85	13	1	10	130	36	21	9	36	0	25	0	2	36	7	.244	.299	.374
Shohei Kato	CHB	2015	98	292	271	24	72	12	5	5	109	27	7	4	12	2	6	0	1	44	2	.266	.282	.402
	CHB	2016	80	246	216	29	53	8	3	0	67	12	6	1	16	0	13	0	1	46	1	.245	.291	.310
Shingo Kawabata	YKL	2016	103	458	420	48	127	22	1	1	154	32	3	0	1	2	34	0	1	31	13	.302	.354	.367
	YKL	2017	143	632	581	87	195	34	1	8	255	57	4	3	2	2	43	0	3	72	15	.336	.383	.439
Ryosuke Kikuchi	HRO	2015	138	629	565	87	153	28	3	14	229	56	8	7	30	1	32	0	1	107	9	.271	.311	.405
	HRO	2016	141	640	574	92	181	22	3	13	248	56	13	5	23	3	40	0	0	106	3	.315	.358	.432
	HRO	2017	143	644	562	62	143	20	3	8	193	32	19	9	49	2	29	2	2	92	7	.254	.292	.343
Fumikazu Kimura	SEI	2015	105	203	184	26	37	5	1	2	50	13	7	4	4	1	13	0	1	53	5	.201	.256	.272
Ikuhiro Kiyota	CHB	2015	79	263	231	28	47	8	1	3	66	21	3	0	5	0	24	0	3	61	8	.203	.287	.286
	CHB	2016	106	417	365	39	82	17	1	6	119	38	5	0	3	0	40	2	9	76	12	.225	.316	.326
	CHB	2017	130	548	489	67	155	38	4	15	246	67	10	4	0	2	54	0	3	93	11	.317	.387	.503
Seiji Kobayashi	YOM	2015	138	443	378	25	78	11	1	2	97	27	2	0	19	3	41	4	2	64	12	.206	.285	.257
	YOM	2016	129	458	398	27	81	12	1	4	107	35	2	1	19	1	36	5	4	76	10	.204	.276	.269
	YOM	2017	70	204	177	13	40	6	0	2	52	13	2	0	5	0	19	1	3	39	6	.226	.312	.294
Shuhei Kojima	ORX	2016	79	219	199	17	49	10	1	0	61	9	6	7	8	0	9	0	3	29	3	.246	.289	.307
Kensuke Kondo	NIP	2015	57	231	167	32	69	15	0	3	93	29	3	0	0	2	60	0	2	27	3	.413	.567	.557
	NIP	2016	80	291	257	36	68	9	0	2	83	27	5	2	3	2	29	0	0	45	7	.265	.337	.323
	NIP	2017	129	504	435	68	142	33	2	8	203	60	6	2	3	5	59	2	2	59	9	.326	.405	.467
Eiichi Koyano	ORX	2015	130	506	470	41	130	14	1	6	164	47	0	0	3	2	28	0	3	60	13	.277	.320	.349
	ORX	2017	56	206	183	19	54	9	0	4	75	22	0	1	5	2	13	1	3	22	7	.295	.348	.410
Toshihiko Kuramoto	YKO	2015	143	539	507	49	133	27	1	2	168	50	3	1	9	1	18	0	4	102	10	.262	.292	.331
	YKO	2016	141	566	534	38	157	19	2	1	183	38	2	3	5	3	22	0	2	98	13	.294	.323	.343
	YKO	2017	102	265	245	11	51	4	0	2	61	20	0	0	7	1	10	0	2	60	8	.208	.244	.249
Takumi Kuriyama	SEI	2015	116	374	333	28	84	13	0	9	124	46	0	0	4	7	27	0	3	64	10	.252	.308	.372
	SEI	2016	135	569	477	52	133	30	2	3	176	41	0	0	0	3	83	0	6	87	9	.279	.390	.369
	SEI	2017	142	622	533	66	143	25	0	10	198	42	3	1	8	4	72	0	5	88	15	.268	.358	.371
Masayuki Kuwahara	YKO	2015	143	664	598	87	161	38	5	13	248	52	10	11	10	0	45	0	11	116	8	.269	.332	.415
	YKO	2016	133	522	462	80	131	23	2	11	191	49	19	11	8	0	38	0	14	93	5	.284	.356	.413
Yota Kyoda	CHU	2015	141	602	564	67	149	23	8	4	200	36	23	13	10	1	18	0	9	105	5	.264	.297	.355
Brandon Laird	NIP	2015	137	571	503	56	115	18	1	32	231	90	0	0	0	7	54	0	7	125	18	.229	.308	.459
	NIP	2016	143	598	547	71	144	21	0	39	282	97	0	0	0	4	44	1	3	138	16	.263	.319	.516
	NIP	2017	143	554	498	62	115	22	2	34	243	97	1	0	0	4	43	0	9	129	18	.231	.301	.488
Dae-Ho Lee	FKU	2017	141	584	510	68	144	30	0	31	267	98	0	1	0	3	62	0	9	109	17	.282	.368	.524
Jose Lopez	YKO	2015	142	606	569	72	171	42	0	30	303	105	0	0	0	8	27	0	2	80	14	.301	.330	.533
	YKO	2016	123	518	483	66	127	27	1	34	258	95	0	0	0	7	24	0	4	75	12	.263	.299	.534
	YKO	2017	140	565	516	63	150	29	1	25	256	73	1	1	0	3	44	3	2	82	14	.291	.347	.496
Hector Luna	HRO	2016	67	268	243	35	66	8	1	5	91	34	6	0	0	2	22	0	1	47	5	.272	.332	.374
	CHU	2017	134	564	496	61	145	26	1	8	197	60	11	0	0	6	57	2	5	77	13	.292	.367	.397
Yamato Maeda	HNS	2015	100	252	232	25	65	6	0	1	74	16	2	3	1	1	18	0	0	37	5	.280	.331	.319
	HNS	2016	111	259	229	24	53	16	1	1	74	20	3	2	15	2	12	0	1	53	9	.231	.270	.323
	HNS	2017	123	293	249	25	56	5	0	0	61	12	5	7	28	0	12	2	4	35	2	.225	.272	.245
Chris Marrero	ORX	2015	82	319	283	39	82	15	1	20	159	50	1	0	0	2	29	1	5	84	6	.290	.364	.562
Yoshihiro Maru	HRO	2015	143	651	556	109	171	35	3	23	281	92	13	3	2	6	83	0	4	113	6	.308	.398	.505
	HRO	2016	143	652	557	98	162	30	8	20	268	90	23	9	1	3	84	1	7	107	9	.291	.389	.481
	HRO	2017	143	633	530	81	132	28	1	19	219	63	15	7	4	4	94	2	1	143	4	.249	.361	.413
Nobuhiro Matsuda	FKU	2015	143	577	531	64	140	19	6	24	243	71	5	2	0	2	43	2	1	128	16	.264	.319	.458
	FKU	2016	143	609	548	79	142	23	5	27	256	85	6	6	0	5	48	2	8	141	14	.259	.325	.467
	FKU	2017	143	603	533	91	153	22	2	35	284	94	8	10	0	8	60	3	2	135	17	.287	.357	.533
Kazuo Matsui	RAK	2017	126	501	445	52	114	17	1	10	163	48	14	2	7	3	43	3	3	82	7	.256	.324	.366
Masato Matsui	CHU	2015	87	244	208	22	46	7	1	2	61	17	0	0	10	1	22	0	3	63	3	.221	.303	.293
Go Matsumoto	NIP	2015	115	448	402	46	110	17	0	5	142	33	6	3	21	1	21	1	3	61	7	.274	.314	.353
Ryuhei Matsuyama	HRO	2015	120	387	350	39	114	23	4	14	187	77	0	0	0	6	31	0	0	45	8	.326	.375	.534
	HRO	2016	103	275	254	34	74	10	2	10	118	41	0	0	0	1	20	1	0	29	4	.291	.342	.465
	HRO	2017	100	229	202	14	56	13	0	7	90	26	1	1	0	3	23	0	1	30	8	.277	.349	.446
Casey McGehee	YOM	2015	139	586	523	67	165	48	1	18	269	77	4	1	0	4	58	4	1	107	20	.315	.382	.514
Ernesto Mejia	SEI	2015	113	388	345	34	83	18	0	19	158	53	1	0	0	2	37	0	4	100	7	.241	.320	.458
	SEI	2016	137	583	511	73	129	26	0	35	260	103	1	1	0	7	59	4	6	148	15	.252	.333	.509
	SEI	2017	135	525	473	52	111	31	0	27	223	89	0	0	0	2	45	1	5	153	14	.235	.307	.471
Ryo Miki	CHB	2015	85	229	207	18	50	9	0	2	65	19	0	1	9	2	8	0	3	55	1	.242	.277	.314
Hiroki Minei	YKO	2017	74	208	186	18	44	8	1	5	69	26	0	0	3	2	12	0	5	46	2	.237	.298	.371
Toshiro Miyazaki	YKO	2015	128	523	480	53	155	28	1	15	230	62	0	0	0	1	38	1	4	47	23	.323	.377	.479
	YKO	2016	101	335	302	31	88	16	0	11	137	36	0	0	0	0	25	0	8	30	12	.291	.361	.454
Eigoro Mogi	RAK	2015	103	450	398	64	118	25	2	17	198	47	3	2	4	1	45	1	2	84	4	.296	.370	.497
	RAK	2016	117	481	424	56	118	20	7	7	173	40	11	4	21	2	30	0	4	95	8	.278	.330	.408
Brent Morel	ORX	2016	94	348	308	29	75	13	0	8	112	38	2	0	0	4	30	0	6	88	10	.244	.319	.364
Tomoya Mori	SEI	2016	107	392	349	43	102	20	0	10	152	46	1	1	0	1	42	0	0	96	3	.292	.367	.436
	SEI	2017	138	531	474	51	136	33	1	17	222	68	0	4	0	3	44	3	9	143	5	.287	.357	.468
Masahiko Morino	CHU	2017	82	252	206	25	54	8	0	0	62	10	2	0	3	3	37	1	3	38	0	.262	.378	.301
Shuichi Murata	YOM	2015	118	424	381	41	100	19	0	14	161	58	0	0	1	2	34	0	6	63	15	.262	.331	.423

HITTER	TEAM	YEAR	G	PA	AB	R	H	2B	3B	HR	TB	RBI	SB	CS	SH	SF	BB	IBB	HP	SO	GDP	AVG	OBP	SLG
	YOM	2016	143	576	529	58	160	32	0	25	267	81	1	3	2	2	38	0	5	83	21	.302	.354	.505
	YOM	2017	103	370	330	33	78	9	0	12	123	39	1	1	2	2	28	2	8	65	12	.236	.310	.373
Matt Murton	HNS	2017	140	583	544	46	150	27	0	9	204	59	0	1	0	5	31	0	3	77	21	.276	.316	.375
Taishi Nakagawa	RAK	2017	62	206	187	14	44	8	0	5	67	21	2	1	1	2	12	0	4	60	6	.235	.293	.358
Daisuke Nakai	YOM	2015	90	254	229	32	57	12	1	5	86	15	2	1	4	1	19	0	1	44	5	.249	.308	.376
Hiroyuki Nakajima	ORX	2015	124	489	431	36	123	19	0	9	169	49	0	0	0	5	46	0	7	93	11	.285	.360	.392
	ORX	2016	96	347	314	24	91	23	0	8	138	47	1	0	0	4	26	0	3	54	7	.290	.346	.439
	ORX	2017	117	483	417	43	100	19	0	10	149	46	1	2	0	1	53	1	12	93	10	.240	.342	.357
Akira Nakamura	FKU	2015	143	600	511	66	138	19	2	6	179	42	3	5	14	5	67	0	3	57	5	.270	.355	.350
	FKU	2016	143	612	488	69	140	21	1	7	184	50	6	5	9	4	99	4	12	53	8	.287	.416	.377
	FKU	2017	135	590	506	58	152	22	0	1	177	39	7	4	9	3	66	0	6	47	7	.300	.386	.350
Shogo Nakamura	CHB	2015	85	312	280	32	77	13	2	9	121	32	11	3	5	1	20	1	6	63	5	.275	.336	.432
	CHB	2016	108	325	278	37	56	10	1	6	86	25	4	4	14	1	26	0	6	70	0	.201	.283	.309
	CHB	2017	111	299	269	43	62	4	4	5	89	21	4	4	9	2	15	0	4	69	4	.230	.279	.331
Takeya Nakamura	SEI	2015	115	486	415	69	90	14	0	27	185	79	1	0	0	6	61	1	4	118	12	.217	.319	.446
	SEI	2016	108	432	387	45	92	14	2	21	173	61	2	1	0	2	40	1	3	125	9	.238	.313	.447
	SEI	2017	139	599	521	82	145	35	0	37	291	124	1	0	0	3	68	4	7	172	12	.278	.367	.559
Yuhei Nakamura	YKL	2015	127	486	419	42	102	14	4	4	136	34	2	1	11	4	42	0	10	65	14	.243	.324	.325
	YKL	2016	106	378	321	24	60	14	0	3	83	37	2	0	14	6	31	4	6	47	9	.187	.266	.259
	YKL	2017	136	502	442	36	102	14	0	2	122	33	3	2	14	2	40	1	4	80	9	.231	.299	.276
Takuya Nakashima	NIP	2015	91	331	283	26	59	1	2	1	67	13	11	3	25	0	23	0	0	80	2	.208	.268	.237
	NIP	2016	143	600	473	66	115	10	1	0	127	28	23	9	62	1	63	0	1	117	5	.243	.333	.268
	NIP	2017	143	617	515	69	136	8	2	0	148	39	34	7	34	0	66	0	2	93	10	.264	.350	.287
Sho Nakata	NIP	2015	129	542	472	56	102	23	0	16	173	67	0	1	0	4	61	0	5	103	14	.216	.310	.367
	NIP	2016	141	624	569	61	142	26	1	25	245	110	2	1	0	5	47	1	3	126	14	.250	.308	.431
	NIP	2017	143	611	539	72	142	26	0	30	258	102	1	0	0	7	64	4	1	120	11	.263	.339	.479
Masahiro Nakatani	HNS	2015	133	455	411	64	99	21	1	20	182	61	2	1	0	3	36	2	5	96	5	.241	.308	.443
Ricardo Nanita	CHU	2016	92	340	319	32	91	16	0	8	131	35	0	1	0	4	15	0	2	52	9	.285	.318	.411
Yamaico Navarro	CHB	2016	82	340	286	38	62	6	1	10	100	44	0	3	0	4	49	0	1	64	5	.217	.329	.350
Akihisa Nishida	YKL	2016	74	245	222	29	54	16	1	7	93	25	0	0	4	0	18	2	1	39	5	.243	.303	.419
Haruki Nishikawa	NIP	2015	138	623	541	82	160	26	6	9	225	44	39	5	6	3	69	0	4	103	6	.296	.378	.416
	NIP	2016	138	593	493	76	155	18	4	5	196	43	41	5	22	2	73	0	3	113	0	.314	.405	.398
	NIP	2017	125	521	442	68	122	18	9	5	173	35	30	7	15	0	60	2	4	98	1	.276	.368	.391
Ryoma Nishikawa	HRO	2015	95	220	204	23	56	10	2	5	85	27	4	1	3	2	10	0	1	35	4	.275	.309	.417
Masahiro Nishino	ORX	2015	100	331	282	33	66	11	2	2	87	21	8	4	16	3	24	0	6	46	4	.234	.305	.309
	ORX	2016	143	610	538	63	142	16	7	2	178	33	16	5	13	1	56	0	2	55	7	.264	.335	.331
	ORX	2017	57	213	191	31	58	6	2	3	77	22	9	2	2	0	18	0	2	25	0	.304	.370	.403
Tsuyoshi Nishioka	HNS	2016	55	205	190	16	56	7	1	0	65	15	6	1	0	0	13	1	2	25	5	.295	.346	.342
Naomichi Nishiura	YKL	2016	72	273	247	21	63	12	0	7	96	28	9	3	2	1	23	0	0	54	3	.255	.317	.389
Keiji Obiki	YKL	2015	80	311	273	25	62	11	0	5	88	29	3	0	10	0	27	0	1	43	8	.227	.299	.322
	YKL	2016	100	391	348	48	87	16	1	5	120	27	7	5	2	1	40	0	0	82	5	.250	.326	.345
	YKL	2017	96	347	311	25	70	18	1	5	105	41	6	3	6	2	27	0	1	56	5	.225	.287	.338
Takashi Ogino	CHB	2015	103	394	356	53	94	22	1	5	133	24	26	3	10	1	25	0	2	44	6	.264	.315	.374
	CHB	2016	71	219	192	35	48	11	1	3	70	21	16	2	9	0	14	0	4	25	3	.250	.314	.365
	CHB	2017	82	309	279	42	75	9	2	2	94	13	18	5	9	1	16	0	4	38	5	.269	.317	.337
Hiromi Oka	NIP	2017	101	294	259	35	61	14	0	4	87	26	18	3	10	1	17	0	7	64	8	.236	.299	.336
Takahiro Okada	ORX	2015	143	593	504	77	134	19	0	31	246	68	2	1	0	1	83	1	5	141	10	.266	.374	.488
	ORX	2016	123	513	454	56	129	25	0	20	214	76	5	1	0	5	47	5	7	105	12	.284	.357	.471
	ORX	2017	105	416	389	44	109	19	2	11	165	51	2	0	0	4	17	0	6	80	9	.280	.317	.424
Yoshifumi Okada	CHB	2016	121	356	327	38	90	5	4	0	103	18	14	7	6	0	20	1	3	42	2	.275	.323	.315
	CHB	2017	112	205	188	24	46	2	3	0	54	13	11	2	7	0	8	0	2	22	0	.245	.283	.287
Takero Okajima	RAK	2015	111	400	342	51	89	13	5	3	121	32	3	2	10	5	41	0	2	65	6	.260	.338	.354
	RAK	2016	127	485	420	44	106	13	4	6	145	35	7	9	6	3	46	2	10	49	4	.252	.338	.345
Shota Omine	CHB	2015	91	240	214	15	44	9	2	5	72	23	1	0	9	2	14	0	1	56	1	.206	.255	.336
Yuji Onizaki	SEI	2016	79	216	190	30	48	8	2	1	63	17	1	0	9	0	17	0	0	53	0	.253	.314	.332
Shota Ono	NIP	2016	109	351	282	26	69	13	0	5	97	35	1	0	31	0	25	0	13	63	6	.245	.334	.344
Yohei Oshima	CHU	2015	119	521	476	50	149	20	3	3	184	29	23	6	1	3	37	0	4	66	5	.313	.365	.387
	CHU	2016	143	656	599	80	175	27	9	3	229	27	26	12	4	1	46	1	6	69	3	.292	.348	.382
	CHU	2017	142	620	565	70	147	20	4	6	193	27	22	8	10	1	39	1	5	65	5	.260	.313	.342
Koji Oshiro	ORX	2015	122	400	345	28	85	10	1	2	103	21	7	4	35	1	16	0	3	59	6	.246	.285	.299
Taishi Ota	NIP	2015	118	457	427	41	110	21	1	15	178	46	5	2	0	2	28	0	0	88	14	.258	.302	.417
Shohei Otani	NIP	2015	65	231	202	24	67	16	1	8	109	31	0	1	0	3	24	0	2	63	0	.332	.403	.540
	NIP	2016	104	382	323	65	104	18	1	22	190	67	7	2	0	4	54	2	1	98	7	.322	.416	.588
Yusuke Oyama	HNS	2015	75	221	198	25	47	10	2	7	82	38	2	2	1	1	18	0	3	41	4	.237	.309	.414
Jimmy Paredes	CHB	2015	89	289	269	31	59	9	0	10	98	26	1	0	0	1	16	0	3	97	5	.219	.270	.364
Carlos Peguero	RAK	2015	120	517	463	67	130	17	1	26	227	75	3	2	0	0	50	3	4	139	16	.281	.356	.490
	RAK	2016	51	200	183	25	51	7	1	10	90	26	0	0	0	0	17	0	0	67	2	.279	.340	.492
Wily Mo Pena	CHB	2015	70	252	219	24	53	14	0	15	112	38	0	0	0	2	26	0	5	72	8	.242	.333	.511
	RAK	2017	125	492	406	51	109	20	1	17	182	40	1	3	0	0	70	0	16	111	5	.268	.396	.448
Carlos Rivero	YKL	2015	54	208	200	12	43	10	0	6	71	21	0	0	0	1	7	0	0	52	5	.215	.240	.355

HITTER	TEAM	YEAR	G	PA	AB	R	H	2B	3B	HR	TB	RBI	SB	CS	SH	SF	BB	IBB	HP	SO	GDP	AVG	OBP	SLG
Stefen Romero	ORX	2015	103	424	390	55	107	13	0	26	198	66	2	1	0	1	27	0	6	98	12	.274	.330	.508
Tomotaka Sakaguchi	YKL	2015	136	607	535	51	155	16	2	4	187	38	4	3	5	3	59	2	5	76	6	.290	.364	.350
	YKL	2016	141	607	526	74	155	14	5	0	179	39	7	4	5	5	63	0	8	66	5	.295	.375	.340
Hayato Sakamoto	YOM	2015	142	614	539	82	157	30	0	15	232	61	14	6	1	3	68	2	3	85	16	.291	.372	.430
	YOM	2016	137	576	488	96	168	28	3	23	271	75	13	3	1	6	81	2	0	67	6	.344	.433	.555
	YOM	2017	130	558	479	50	129	21	3	12	192	68	10	4	9	5	65	1	0	79	5	.269	.353	.401
Gaby Sanchez	RAK	2017	66	232	199	19	45	12	0	7	78	18	3	2	0	2	27	0	4	40	4	.226	.328	.392
Nate Schierholtz	HRO	2017	65	248	232	27	58	11	1	10	101	30	3	2	0	0	14	0	2	67	0	.250	.298	.435
Tatsuhiro Shibata	YKO	2015	88	248	215	25	50	8	0	1	61	11	1	1	11	2	17	0	3	50	2	.233	.295	.284
Motohiro Shima	RAK	2015	112	369	281	34	56	9	0	3	74	28	2	1	27	1	57	0	3	62	8	.199	.339	.263
	RAK	2016	80	256	199	26	54	9	1	2	71	17	4	4	17	0	40	0	0	43	6	.271	.393	.357
	RAK	2017	117	411	338	28	74	9	1	4	97	18	6	3	11	1	60	4	1	69	11	.219	.338	.287
Hiroaki Shimauchi	RAK	2015	143	577	494	62	131	14	3	14	193	47	3	6	12	3	64	0	4	67	8	.265	.352	.391
	RAK	2016	114	388	342	43	98	9	2	9	138	41	10	2	7	4	33	0	2	48	7	.287	.349	.404
Hiroyuki Shirasaki	YKO	2016	92	214	203	20	42	11	0	6	71	12	0	1	2	0	6	0	3	32	8	.207	.241	.350
	YKO	2017	81	238	204	25	46	9	1	6	75	9	2	4	22	0	11	0	1	45	1	.225	.269	.368
Eishin Soyogi	HRO	2017	96	332	283	24	67	15	1	6	102	27	2	2	10	2	36	0	1	49	6	.237	.323	.360
Shota Sugiyama	CHU	2016	104	311	269	26	70	11	3	3	96	27	1	2	8	1	30	1	3	60	8	.260	.340	.357
Ginjiro Sumitani	SEI	2015	104	310	267	32	67	11	0	5	93	30	2	1	23	4	8	0	8	45	6	.251	.289	.348
	SEI	2016	117	326	294	19	64	10	1	1	79	22	0	1	19	0	13	0	0	48	12	.218	.251	.269
	SEI	2017	133	443	399	31	84	16	0	4	112	35	0	0	22	2	16	0	4	87	7	.211	.247	.281
Daichi Suzuki	CHB	2015	143	588	508	56	132	27	5	11	202	52	6	5	3	4	55	1	18	85	7	.260	.350	.398
	CHB	2016	143	583	501	62	143	30	2	6	195	61	3	1	16	7	50	2	9	56	9	.285	.356	.389
	CHB	2017	142	564	487	60	128	24	4	6	178	50	1	5	24	3	47	1	3	58	10	.263	.330	.366
Seiya Suzuki	HRO	2015	115	512	437	85	131	28	1	26	239	90	16	6	0	7	62	0	6	80	12	.300	.389	.547
	HRO	2016	129	528	466	76	156	26	8	29	285	95	16	11	3	3	53	1	3	79	10	.335	.404	.612
	HRO	2017	97	238	211	21	58	6	3	5	85	25	6	7	7	2	16	0	2	38	3	.275	.329	.403
Shuhei Takahashi	CHU	2016	75	283	255	28	64	14	2	4	94	29	0	1	1	1	22	0	4	84	7	.251	.319	.369
Yuhei Takai	YKL	2015	71	300	281	29	86	21	0	2	113	32	2	3	0	2	12	0	5	42	5	.306	.343	.402
	YKL	2016	108	436	412	44	122	20	0	7	163	55	7	1	1	2	21	2	0	51	9	.296	.329	.396
	YKL	2017	141	585	551	57	149	33	4	8	214	60	7	4	1	3	27	1	3	82	7	.270	.307	.388
Shun Takayama	HNS	2015	103	353	328	40	82	15	3	6	121	24	6	3	0	1	21	0	3	77	3	.250	.300	.369
	HNS	2016	134	530	494	48	136	23	5	8	193	65	5	4	2	3	27	1	4	109	8	.275	.316	.391
Kengo Takeda	ORX	2015	97	219	207	19	61	8	0	2	75	14	0	0	4	0	5	0	3	47	3	.295	.321	.362
Tatsuhiro Tamura	CHB	2015	132	359	311	31	77	12	3	3	104	36	4	2	17	4	26	0	1	68	7	.248	.304	.334
	CHB	2016	130	430	371	27	95	16	3	2	123	38	6	0	17	3	38	0	1	91	12	.256	.324	.332
	CHB	2017	117	365	305	26	52	10	1	2	70	32	3	2	22	4	33	0	1	69	3	.170	.251	.230
Kensuke Tanaka	NIP	2015	107	349	314	22	79	6	1	2	93	18	11	4	0	0	35	1	0	36	4	.252	.327	.296
	NIP	2016	143	626	541	61	147	14	1	2	169	53	22	8	3	4	69	3	9	56	4	.272	.361	.312
	NIP	2017	134	596	532	62	151	20	2	4	187	66	9	3	5	1	57	0	1	58	9	.284	.354	.352
Kosuke Tanaka	HRO	2015	143	679	565	105	164	32	5	8	230	60	35	13	6	4	89	2	15	120	5	.290	.398	.407
	HRO	2016	143	679	581	102	154	17	3	13	216	39	28	19	3	1	77	1	17	119	1	.265	.367	.372
	HRO	2017	141	590	543	61	149	33	9	8	224	45	6	7	5	1	34	2	7	105	8	.274	.325	.413
Yuya Taniguchi	NIP	2016	83	211	193	26	49	3	2	1	59	9	7	0	9	0	8	0	1	48	2	.254	.287	.306
Soichiro Tateoka	YOM	2015	62	214	197	24	41	3	3	0	50	10	4	5	6	0	11	0	0	43	1	.208	.250	.254
	YOM	2016	51	209	188	15	43	6	1	2	57	9	9	3	6	0	10	0	5	31	1	.229	.286	.303
	YOM	2017	91	367	339	36	103	9	3	0	118	14	16	6	3	3	18	0	4	61	2	.304	.343	.348
Yasutaka Tobashira	YKO	2015	112	363	336	25	72	13	0	9	112	52	0	0	6	2	19	0	0	59	9	.214	.255	.333
	YKO	2016	124	393	367	25	83	8	0	2	97	23	0	0	4	1	20	4	1	63	10	.226	.267	.264
Shuta Tonosaki	SEI	2015	135	489	438	65	113	22	3	10	171	48	23	3	10	3	33	0	5	109	4	.258	.315	.390
Takashi Toritani	HNS	2015	143	570	488	57	143	23	3	4	184	41	8	7	1	2	77	3	2	62	13	.293	.390	.377
	HNS	2016	143	533	449	49	106	16	1	7	145	36	13	3	1	6	75	0	2	80	12	.236	.344	.323
	HNS	2017	143	646	551	69	155	21	4	6	202	42	9	6	2	3	89	2	1	77	8	.281	.380	.367
Shinya Tsuruoka	FKU	2016	103	263	231	14	58	12	2	2	80	26	1	0	20	1	9	0	2	26	9	.251	.284	.346
Yoshitomo Tsutsugo	YKO	2015	139	601	503	85	143	31	0	28	258	94	1	0	0	3	93	3	2	115	7	.284	.396	.513
	YKO	2016	133	561	469	89	151	28	4	44	319	110	0	1	0	2	87	1	3	105	6	.322	.430	.680
	YKO	2017	138	568	496	79	157	28	1	24	259	93	0	0	0	2	68	0	2	98	5	.317	.400	.522
Seiichi Uchikawa	FKU	2015	73	300	266	31	79	13	0	12	128	50	0	1	0	2	32	0	0	26	9	.297	.370	.481
	FKU	2016	141	605	556	62	169	19	0	18	242	106	3	2	0	9	38	2	2	53	27	.304	.345	.435
	FKU	2017	136	585	529	60	150	24	1	11	209	82	1	0	0	7	45	2	4	55	24	.284	.340	.395
Seiji Uebayashi	FKU	2015	134	453	415	54	108	23	5	13	180	51	12	12	10	2	24	2	2	96	3	.260	.302	.434
Tsuyoshi Ueda	YKL	2017	82	238	209	18	55	2	2	1	64	19	8	1	11	2	14	0	2	29	5	.263	.313	.306
Hiroki Uemoto	HNS	2015	125	488	409	57	116	20	1	9	165	38	16	1	23	2	50	0	4	71	7	.284	.366	.403
	HNS	2017	108	452	375	44	95	18	1	4	127	31	19	11	29	0	44	1	4	69	1	.253	.338	.339
Ryutaro Umeno	HNS	2015	112	340	282	22	58	9	2	2	77	33	1	0	27	3	24	2	4	63	3	.206	.275	.273
Dayan Viciedo	CHU	2015	87	367	332	43	83	11	1	18	150	49	4	0	0	1	29	0	5	52	10	.250	.319	.452
	CHU	2016	119	471	416	63	114	22	0	22	202	68	1	0	0	3	44	0	8	68	13	.274	.352	.486
Kazuhiro Wada	CHU	2017	79	234	218	16	65	8	0	5	88	26	1	0	0	0	14	0	2	40	9	.298	.346	.404
Kenya Wakatsuki	ORX	2015	100	256	218	16	44	8	2	1	59	18	0	0	23	2	10	0	3	50	9	.202	.245	.271
	ORX	2016	85	262	229	22	52	13	0	0	65	20	0	0	23	0	4	1	6	42	5	.227	.259	.284

HITTER	TEAM	YEAR	G	PA	AB	R	H	2B	3B	HR	TB	RBI	SB	CS	SH	SF	BB	IBB	HP	SO	GDP	AVG	OBP	SLG
Ryota Wakiya	SEI	2017	118	272	235	32	69	13	1	3	93	22	4	2	8	1	27	0	1	47	3	.294	.367	.396
Naoto Watanabe	SEI	2016	70	207	181	18	56	3	2	0	63	16	1	0	11	2	10	0	3	20	5	.309	.352	.348
Zelous Wheeler	RAK	2015	142	605	542	75	147	27	0	31	267	82	7	3	0	3	50	4	10	98	14	.271	.342	.493
	RAK	2016	140	589	517	74	137	25	2	27	247	88	2	1	0	2	58	0	12	123	10	.265	.351	.478
	RAK	2017	91	313	274	28	70	12	0	14	124	50	1	0	0	3	30	0	6	63	6	.255	.339	.453
Tetsuto Yamada	YKL	2015	143	624	526	79	130	25	1	24	229	78	14	4	0	1	91	1	6	132	15	.247	.364	.435
	YKL	2016	133	590	481	102	146	26	3	38	292	102	30	2	0	4	97	0	8	101	16	.304	.425	.607
	YKL	2017	143	646	557	119	183	39	2	38	340	100	34	4	0	3	81	1	5	111	11	.329	.416	.610
Hotaka Yamakawa	SEI	2015	78	293	242	46	72	19	0	23	160	61	0	1	0	0	46	1	5	72	7	.298	.420	.661
Kotaro Yamasaki	YKL	2015	59	246	219	30	53	10	2	1	70	13	6	5	9	0	18	0	0	44	3	.242	.300	.320
Yuki Yanagita	FKU	2015	130	551	448	95	139	30	1	31	264	99	14	7	0	7	89	8	7	123	6	.310	.426	.589
	FKU	2016	120	536	428	82	131	31	4	18	224	73	23	2	0	0	100	2	8	97	8	.306	.446	.523
	FKU	2017	138	605	502	110	182	31	1	34	317	99	32	8	0	1	88	4	14	101	9	.363	.469	.631
Daikan Yoh	YOM	2015	87	381	330	46	87	18	1	9	134	33	4	2	2	1	41	0	7	80	6	.264	.356	.406
	NIP	2016	130	555	495	66	145	24	1	14	213	61	5	6	7	1	42	1	10	121	10	.293	.359	.430
	NIP	2017	86	381	352	47	91	10	2	7	126	36	14	2	2	2	21	1	4	93	4	.259	.306	.358
Masataka Yoshida	ORX	2015	64	268	228	42	71	11	0	12	118	38	1	1	0	1	38	2	1	32	9	.311	.410	.518
	ORX	2016	63	258	231	35	67	17	0	10	114	34	0	2	0	1	25	0	1	34	6	.290	.360	.494
Yuki Yoshimura	FKU	2016	78	206	177	16	37	4	1	5	58	28	1	1	4	4	14	1	7	46	5	.209	.287	.328

PITCHERS

PITCHER	TEAM	YEAR	G	W	L	SV	HLD	CG	SHO	PCT	BF	IP	H	HR	BB	IBB	HB	SO	WP	BK	R	ER	ERA
Takumi Akiyama	HNS	2015	25	12	6	0	0	2	0	.667	638	159	0	15	16	0	6	123	0	0	56	53	2.99
Ryo Akiyoshi	YKL	2015	43	5	6	10	10	0	0	.455	177	43	0	3	11	1	1	39	2	0	17	16	3.35
	YKL	2016	70	3	4	19	10	0	0	.429	279	70	0	6	15	3	6	68	1	0	17	17	2.19
	YKL	2017	74	6	1	0	22	0	0	.857	305	76	0	6	28	3	6	81	2	0	24	20	2.36
Yuya Ando	HNS	2016	50	0	1	0	11	0	0	.000	164	42	0	4	12	0	0	24	0	0	13	12	2.53
	HNS	2017	50	5	4	0	15	0	0	.556	184	44	0	4	11	2	2	32	1	0	17	15	3.02
Tomohiro Anraku	RAK	2016	15	3	5	0	0	0	0	.375	349	84	0	9	22	0	4	64	2	1	33	32	3.42
Koji Aoyama	RAK	2016	50	1	5	0	14	0	0	.167	227	50	0	5	24	0	0	46	3	0	29	27	4.83
	RAK	2017	61	4	5	0	31	0	0	.444	223	57	0	3	18	1	1	58	2	0	18	18	2.81
Nagisa Arakaki	YKL	2017	15	3	10	0	0	0	0	.231	367	83	0	13	36	1	2	70	9	0	48	43	4.64
Kohei Arihara	NIP	2015	25	10	13	0	0	4	0	.435	726	169	0	21	39	2	4	88	5	0	97	89	4.74
	NIP	2016	22	11	9	0	0	2	1	.550	640	156	0	13	38	1	2	103	3	1	52	51	2.94
	NIP	2017	18	8	6	0	0	1	1	.571	453	103	0	13	32	0	3	81	2	0	60	55	4.79
Yuki Ariyoshi	CHB	2015	53	2	5	1	16	0	0	.286	222	53	0	4	14	0	3	27	0	0	17	17	2.87
Takuya Asao	CHU	2017	36	1	1	3	16	0	0	.500	142	31	0	3	17	2	1	34	4	0	11	11	3.19
Tony Barnette	YKL	2017	59	3	1	41	6	0	0	.750	246	62	0	1	19	0	3	56	1	0	10	9	1.29
Anthony Bass	NIP	2016	37	8	8	0	6	0	0	.500	452	103	0	7	47	4	4	71	2	0	48	42	3.65
David Buchanan	YKL	2015	25	6	13	0	0	2	1	.316	678	159	0	19	56	1	9	112	2	1	75	65	3.66
Bryan Bullington	ORX	2017	14	5	3	0	0	1	1	.625	305	73	0	3	24	0	8	46	0	0	30	27	3.30
Arquimedes Caminero	YOM	2015	57	3	5	29	4	0	0	.375	268	63	0	4	23	0	4	65	1	0	21	17	2.42
Rhiner Cruz	RAK	2017	52	1	3	1	20	0	0	.250	218	49	0	2	29	1	4	42	0	0	19	17	3.12
Kyle Davies	YKL	2016	15	4	5	0	0	0	0	.444	361	82	0	14	31	1	4	64	4	0	44	40	4.39
Brandon Dickson	ORX	2015	25	8	9	0	0	0	0	.471	581	136	0	7	42	3	3	86	7	1	63	49	3.24
	ORX	2016	27	9	11	0	0	2	0	.450	746	171	0	17	71	0	5	139	7	0	86	83	4.36
	ORX	2017	20	9	9	0	0	1	0	.500	538	130	0	3	44	1	1	88	0	0	39	36	2.48
Rafael Dolis	HNS	2015	63	4	4	37	5	0	0	.500	259	63	0	1	17	1	1	85	8	0	22	19	2.71
Daiki Enokida	HNS	2016	35	1	1	0	3	0	0	.500	174	39	0	6	16	0	3	32	2	0	19	19	4.31
Kyuji Fujikawa	HNS	2015	52	3	0	0	6	0	0	1.000	232	56	0	3	24	1	5	71	2	0	15	14	2.22
	HNS	2016	43	5	6	3	10	0	0	.455	275	62	0	7	30	2	3	70	4	0	34	32	4.60
Shintaro Fujinami	HNS	2016	26	7	11	0	0	2	1	.389	734	169	0	11	70	0	8	176	6	1	78	61	3.25
	HNS	2017	28	14	7	0	0	7	4	.667	840	199	0	9	82	0	11	221	9	0	70	53	2.40
Shinobu Fukuhara	HNS	2017	61	6	4	1	33	0	0	.600	223	53	0	4	18	0	0	40	1	0	19	18	3.02
Yuya Fukui	HRO	2016	13	5	4	0	0	0	0	.556	345	76	0	9	30	0	4	63	0	0	38	37	4.34
	HRO	2017	21	9	6	0	0	0	0	.600	541	131	0	10	53	0	5	99	7	1	53	52	3.56
Koji Fukutani	CHU	2016	41	1	2	8	8	0	0	.333	171	40	0	6	9	0	2	23	5	0	18	18	4.05
	CHU	2017	42	3	4	19	4	0	0	.429	176	40	0	3	20	0	3	25	3	0	19	18	4.05
Hiroyuki Fukuyama	RAK	2015	65	6	0	7	23	0	0	1.000	237	59	0	2	14	1	3	31	2	0	8	7	1.06
	RAK	2016	69	4	5	0	19	0	0	.444	294	69	0	2	19	0	5	30	1	1	24	21	2.71
	RAK	2017	65	2	3	1	22	0	0	.400	248	58	0	2	21	2	1	29	3	0	21	18	2.76
Kota Futaki	CHB	2015	23	7	9	0	0	5	0	.438	588	143	0	14	35	2	2	128	2	1	58	54	3.39
	CHB	2016	22	7	9	0	0	1	0	.438	518	116	0	12	34	1	2	81	5	0	74	69	5.34
Gonzalez Germen	ORX	2015	44	2	1	3	13	0	0	.667	210	47	0	4	24	3	2	51	1	0	16	14	2.68
Bradin Hagens	HRO	2016	50	7	5	0	19	0	0	.583	342	83	0	4	33	0	3	33	4	0	32	27	2.92
Akihiro Hakumura	NIP	2017	50	1	1	0	13	0	0	.500	233	57	0	6	19	0	3	66	3	0	16	13	2.03
Haruhiro Hamaguchi	YKO	2015	22	10	6	0	0	0	0	.625	546	123	0	9	69	0	2	136	9	1	54	49	3.57
Juri Hara	YKL	2015	26	3	11	0	0	1	0	.214	554	131	0	19	34	1	6	115	2	0	66	56	3.84

PITCHER	TEAM	YEAR	G	W	L	SV	HLD	CG	SHO	PCT	BF	IP	H	HR	BB	IBB	HB	SO	WP	BK	R	ER	ERA
Seishu Hatake	YOM	2015	13	6	4	0	0	0	0	.600	288	72	0	9	23	0	2	72	1	0	27	24	2.99
Deunte Heath	HRO	2017	43	3	6	4	10	0	0	.333	205	49	0	3	19	1	0	59	2	1	14	13	2.36
Yoslan Herrera	YKO	2017	52	5	4	0	22	0	0	.556	211	51	0	2	15	2	2	53	0	4	17	17	2.96
Frank Herrmann	RAK	2015	56	3	1	1	33	0	0	.750	222	53	0	8	13	0	3	58	2	4	20	16	2.72
Nao Higashihama	FKU	2015	24	16	5	0	0	2	1	.762	637	160	0	17	44	0	1	139	2	0	48	47	2.64
	FKU	2016	23	9	6	0	0	0	0	.600	545	135	0	13	37	0	2	100	1	0	49	45	3.00
Katsunori Hirai	SEI	2015	42	2	0	0	4	0	0	1.000	184	45	0	4	10	0	3	42	3	1	15	12	2.40
Yoshihisa Hirano	ORX	2015	58	3	7	29	8	0	0	.300	240	57	0	5	16	0	1	47	2	0	19	17	2.67
	ORX	2016	58	4	4	31	8	0	0	.500	237	61	0	2	16	0	1	57	4	0	13	13	1.92
Tomoya Hoshi	YKL	2015	24	4	7	0	2	0	0	.364	494	110	0	14	49	1	5	71	3	0	64	58	4.73
Ryuji Ichioka	HRO	2015	59	6	2	1	19	0	0	.750	234	58	0	1	20	0	0	58	1	0	14	12	1.85
	HRO	2017	38	2	4	1	7	0	0	.333	176	37	0	5	21	0	1	35	0	0	21	17	4.14
Ryota Igarashi	FKU	2015	46	6	0	0	11	0	0	1.000	170	41	0	2	21	0	3	28	2	0	8	8	1.73
	FKU	2017	54	3	1	2	31	0	0	.750	203	52	0	1	15	1	4	59	3	0	8	8	1.38
Kazutomo Iguchi	NIP	2016	37	0	1	0	4	0	0	.000	174	42	0	6	10	1	2	27	3	0	18	18	3.86
Yuya Iida	FKU	2017	35	0	1	0	4	0	0	.000	176	41	0	3	22	2	1	44	2	0	16	16	3.48
Nobutaka Imamura	YOM	2016	16	3	4	0	0	0	0	.429	346	77	0	11	36	0	2	60	3	0	49	48	5.59
Takeru Imamura	HRO	2015	68	3	5	23	17	0	0	.375	270	64	0	6	27	0	0	69	3	0	19	17	2.38
	HRO	2016	67	3	4	2	22	0	0	.429	299	73	0	3	22	0	0	87	4	0	20	20	2.44
Shota Imanaga	YKO	2015	24	11	7	0	0	3	2	.611	600	148	0	13	52	2	5	140	3	0	49	49	2.98
	YKO	2016	22	8	9	0	0	0	0	.471	541	135	0	16	38	1	2	136	1	0	47	44	2.93
Shoichi Ino	YKO	2015	25	6	10	0	0	1	0	.375	636	152	0	9	46	1	8	93	3	0	66	65	3.84
	YKO	2016	23	7	11	0	0	2	1	.389	654	151	0	14	47	2	6	113	6	0	65	59	3.50
	YKO	2017	21	5	8	0	0	3	0	.385	598	134	0	13	40	0	3	92	7	1	56	49	3.27
Kenta Ishida	YKO	2015	18	6	6	0	0	0	0	.500	436	106	0	10	34	0	0	103	6	0	43	40	3.40
	YKO	2016	25	9	4	0	0	0	0	.692	608	153	0	21	36	1	1	132	5	1	53	53	3.12
	YKO	2017	12	2	6	0	0	0	0	.250	300	71	0	6	26	0	1	58	3	0	23	23	2.89
Yuya Ishii	NIP	2017	51	0	1	0	7	0	0	.000	151	35	0	0	14	0	1	26	0	1	15	8	2.06
Ayumu Ishikawa	CHB	2015	16	3	11	0	0	1	0	.214	424	97	0	9	23	0	2	73	0	0	62	55	5.09
	CHB	2016	23	14	5	0	0	5	3	.737	643	162	0	16	22	0	6	104	4	0	40	39	2.16
	CHB	2017	27	12	12	0	0	3	2	.500	751	178	0	15	34	0	5	126	2	0	68	65	3.27
Masanori Ishikawa	YKL	2015	23	4	14	0	0	0	0	.222	540	123	0	18	28	2	4	88	2	1	72	70	5.11
	YKL	2016	20	8	8	0	0	0	0	.500	500	116	0	15	33	1	2	52	3	1	59	58	4.47
	YKL	2017	25	13	9	0	0	1	1	.591	598	146	0	16	28	1	3	90	3	0	59	54	3.31
Naoya Ishikawa	NIP	2015	37	0	1	0	7	0	0	.000	228	49	0	8	28	2	0	51	4	0	24	24	4.35
Shuta Ishikawa	FKU	2015	34	8	3	0	1	0	0	.727	409	98	0	11	50	0	7	99	4	1	38	36	3.29
Taichi Ishiyama	YKL	2015	66	3	6	0	24	0	0	.333	285	68	0	5	17	3	1	76	5	0	29	23	3.03
	YKL	2017	21	5	5	0	0	0	0	.500	479	111	0	7	38	1	2	78	4	0	50	45	3.64
Junki Ito	CHU	2015	39	0	2	0	9	0	0	.000	276	62	0	5	33	0	4	57	1	0	28	27	3.88
Yuta Iwasada	HNS	2015	18	5	10	0	0	0	0	.333	428	98	0	14	44	0	4	93	3	0	56	54	4.96
	HNS	2016	25	10	9	0	0	2	2	.526	644	158	0	10	55	2	3	156	6	0	56	51	2.90
Sho Iwasaki	FKU	2015	72	6	3	2	40	0	0	.667	289	72	0	8	16	0	2	66	1	0	16	16	1.99
	FKU	2016	35	4	2	1	9	1	1	.667	347	87	0	6	17	0	0	61	3	0	22	19	1.95
Hitoki Iwase	CHU	2015	50	3	6	2	26	0	0	.333	154	35	0	2	14	1	1	28	0	0	19	19	4.79
Minoru Iwata	HNS	2017	27	8	10	0	0	2	1	.444	722	170	0	13	49	1	5	119	8	0	66	61	3.22
Suguru Iwazaki	HNS	2015	66	4	1	0	15	0	0	.800	311	71	0	2	27	1	5	88	0	0	28	19	2.39
	HNS	2016	16	3	5	0	0	0	0	.375	319	74	0	10	27	0	2	59	3	0	33	30	3.63
	HNS	2017	15	3	10	0	0	0	0	.231	326	77	0	7	19	1	5	57	0	0	39	30	3.51
Jay Jackson	HRO	2015	60	2	2	1	30	0	0	.500	243	62	0	5	19	0	1	55	2	0	16	14	2.03
	HRO	2016	67	5	4	0	37	0	0	.556	271	68	0	4	23	0	0	89	1	0	15	13	1.71
Kris Johnson	HRO	2015	13	6	3	0	0	0	0	.667	328	76	0	4	25	0	2	53	2	0	40	34	4.01
	HRO	2016	26	15	7	0	0	3	2	.682	736	180	0	11	49	2	3	141	3	0	50	43	2.15
	HRO	2017	28	14	7	0	0	1	1	.667	773	194	0	5	67	0	2	150	3	1	43	40	1.85
Yohei Kagiya	NIP	2015	60	2	3	1	17	0	0	.400	218	57	0	6	17	0	0	46	0	0	23	16	2.53
	NIP	2016	48	5	3	3	3	0	0	.625	187	44	0	3	21	1	0	38	4	0	23	21	4.23
	NIP	2017	40	5	3	0	15	0	0	.625	159	34	0	3	12	0	1	32	1	0	23	18	4.67
Tomoyuki Kaida	ORX	2016	50	1	3	0	15	0	0	.250	185	45	0	1	12	2	0	31	0	0	14	14	2.78
	ORX	2017	48	2	2	0	8	0	0	.500	180	41	0	3	15	2	2	27	0	0	15	12	2.61
Yoshinao Kamata	RAK	2016	20	7	5	0	0	0	0	.583	510	113	0	12	50	0	8	77	2	0	56	52	4.14
Chihiro Kaneko	ORX	2015	27	12	8	0	0	6	1	.600	754	184	0	21	56	0	2	141	1	0	80	71	3.47
	ORX	2016	24	7	9	0	0	2	1	.438	676	162	0	13	59	0	2	125	7	0	71	69	3.83
	ORX	2017	16	7	6	0	1	0	0	.538	379	93	0	8	18	0	0	79	1	0	34	33	3.19
Norihito Kaneto	RAK	2016	54	3	1	0	14	0	0	.750	170	41	0	1	14	1	2	25	2	0	13	11	2.38
Yuki Karakawa	CHB	2015	21	5	10	0	0	1	0	.333	555	126	0	18	37	0	7	86	1	2	69	63	4.49
	CHB	2016	15	6	6	0	0	1	1	.500	373	88	0	2	37	1	3	64	1	3	30	28	2.84
Wataru Karashima	RAK	2015	19	8	8	0	0	0	0	.500	424	103	0	11	27	0	1	74	2	1	51	48	4.19
	RAK	2016	13	3	7	0	0	0	0	.300	306	72	0	2	22	0	3	48	0	0	33	31	3.88
	RAK	2017	14	5	7	0	0	0	0	.417	332	76	0	7	29	1	0	56	1	0	41	39	4.58
Takayuki Kato	NIP	2015	21	6	6	0	0	0	0	.500	521	120	0	13	38	0	1	99	1	0	51	47	3.53
	NIP	2016	30	7	3	0	1	0	0	.700	392	91	0	4	31	1	2	64	1	0	37	35	3.45

PITCHER	TEAM	YEAR	G	W	L	SV	HLD	CG	SHO	PCT	BF	IP	H	HR	BB	IBB	HB	SO	WP	BK	R	ER	ERA
Ryoji Katsuki	CHB	2017	40	1	1	1	2	0	0	.500	221	52	0	4	16	0	2	36	0	0	18	17	2.92
Shinya Kayama	FKU	2015	58	2	0	0	14	0	0	1.000	143	32	0	1	11	0	5	47	1	0	11	10	2.76
Yasunori Kikuchi	RAK	2017	18	4	5	0	0	0	0	.444	448	103	0	5	42	0	5	71	5	0	47	43	3.76
Yusei Kikuchi	SEI	2015	26	16	6	0	0	6	4	.727	735	187	0	16	49	0	6	217	6	0	49	41	1.97
	SEI	2016	22	12	7	0	0	2	0	.632	595	143	0	7	67	0	2	127	3	0	51	41	2.58
	SEI	2017	23	9	10	0	0	0	0	.474	542	133	0	9	55	1	2	122	5	1	48	42	2.84
Takayuki Kishi	RAK	2015	26	8	10	0	0	1	0	.444	703	176	0	19	38	2	3	189	4	0	56	54	2.76
	SEI	2016	19	9	7	0	0	2	1	.563	541	130	0	8	36	0	1	104	0	0	42	36	2.49
	SEI	2017	16	5	6	0	0	5	0	.455	434	110	0	6	25	0	5	91	0	0	40	37	3.02
Mamoru Kishida	ORX	2017	50	4	3	0	15	0	0	.571	213	52	0	2	13	0	1	54	0	0	17	15	2.56
Keisuke Kobayashi	ORX	2015	35	2	1	0	1	0	0	.667	174	40	0	4	15	0	2	46	2	0	22	18	3.98
Hirotaka Koishi	SEI	2016	50	0	2	1	2	0	0	.000	324	74	0	2	39	2	13	55	3	0	33	31	3.74
Kazuki Kondo	YKL	2015	54	2	4	1	14	0	0	.333	234	55	0	9	17	0	4	55	2	0	29	29	4.72
Taisuke Kondo	ORX	2015	55	1	1	1	25	0	0	.500	228	55	0	6	18	0	2	71	1	0	21	19	3.07
Yasutomo Kubo	YKO	2016	15	5	8	0	0	1	1	.385	419	96	0	5	28	4	3	80	4	0	44	38	3.55
	YKO	2017	21	8	7	0	0	2	1	.533	523	122	0	16	27	0	5	88	3	1	64	56	4.12
Katsuhiko Kumon	NIP	2015	41	3	0	0	3	0	0	1.000	154	36	0	2	8	2	2	33	2	0	11	11	2.70
Chun-Lin Kuo	SEI	2017	21	3	7	0	0	0	0	.300	377	79	0	10	37	1	7	49	3	1	55	47	5.31
Aren Kuri	HRO	2015	35	9	5	0	2	0	0	.643	494	116	0	7	44	0	4	97	1	0	51	47	3.64
	HRO	2016	27	2	2	0	0	0	0	.500	351	80	0	9	37	0	1	52	0	0	47	40	4.50
Hiroki Kuroda	HRO	2016	24	10	8	0	0	1	1	.556	623	151	0	14	30	3	3	98	3	0	54	52	3.09
	HRO	2017	26	11	8	0	0	1	0	.579	685	169	0	8	29	0	7	106	3	0	53	48	2.55
Yuta Kuroki	ORX	2015	55	6	3	2	25	0	0	.667	226	53	0	2	26	0	2	62	3	0	26	25	4.22
Kentaro Kuwahara	HNS	2015	67	4	2	0	39	0	0	.667	261	65	0	2	10	0	3	63	2	0	11	11	1.51
Kentaro Kyuko	YKL	2016	39	0	0	1	3	0	0	.000	115	26	0	2	5	0	6	27	0	0	13	13	4.44
	YKL	2017	38	0	0	0	8	0	0	.000	102	24	0	1	9	0	1	23	3	0	7	7	2.55
Josh Lueke	YKL	2015	61	4	6	7	22	0	0	.400	257	60	0	6	19	2	2	70	3	2	24	20	2.97
	YKL	2016	69	6	6	0	33	0	0	.500	277	64	0	6	20	1	5	60	3	0	26	22	3.06
Kenta Maeda	HRO	2017	29	15	8	0	0	5	0	.652	821	206	0	5	41	1	6	175	3	0	49	48	2.09
Kazuhisa Makita	SEI	2015	58	3	3	0	28	0	0	.500	248	62	0	4	5	0	3	35	0	0	18	16	2.30
	SEI	2016	50	7	1	0	25	0	0	.875	312	78	0	3	16	2	10	43	0	0	15	14	1.60
	SEI	2017	34	9	11	3	0	1	0	.450	596	137	0	7	44	2	11	66	1	0	68	56	3.66
Chris Martin	NIP	2015	40	0	2	1	29	0	0	.000	137	37	0	2	6	0	1	34	0	1	5	5	1.19
	NIP	2016	52	2	0	21	19	0	0	1.000	182	50	0	2	7	0	0	57	2	3	8	6	1.07
Naoya Masuda	CHB	2015	38	0	4	9	6	0	0	.000	162	35	0	8	15	2	0	29	1	0	20	20	5.09
	CHB	2016	61	3	2	14	21	0	0	.600	238	59	0	2	16	2	0	36	1	0	13	12	1.83
	CHB	2017	51	3	2	0	11	0	0	.600	227	53	0	2	21	1	2	42	7	0	23	23	3.91
Tatsushi Masuda	SEI	2015	57	1	5	28	4	0	0	.167	220	56	0	7	13	2	0	58	0	0	17	15	2.40
	SEI	2016	53	3	5	28	5	0	0	.375	232	54	0	1	15	5	2	53	0	0	13	10	1.66
	SEI	2017	72	2	4	3	40	0	0	.333	302	74	0	1	15	2	4	62	2	0	26	25	3.04
Hirotoshi Masui	NIP	2015	52	6	1	27	7	0	0	.857	215	52	0	6	11	1	0	82	5	0	15	14	2.39
	NIP	2016	30	10	3	10	1	2	1	.769	333	81	0	5	26	2	3	71	3	0	22	22	2.44
	NIP	2017	56	0	1	39	4	0	0	.000	238	60	0	1	19	0	0	71	4	1	11	10	1.50
Katsuki Matayoshi	CHU	2015	50	8	3	0	21	1	1	.727	434	110	0	7	36	0	5	78	0	1	27	26	2.13
	CHU	2016	62	6	6	0	16	0	0	.500	239	54	0	3	17	0	3	55	1	0	22	17	2.80
	CHU	2017	63	6	6	0	30	0	0	.500	301	72	0	5	23	0	4	82	1	0	27	27	3.36
Marcos Mateo	HNS	2015	63	7	4	0	36	0	0	.636	252	59	0	2	17	0	3	62	1	0	26	18	2.75
	HNS	2016	52	1	3	20	7	0	0	.250	226	55	0	2	24	1	2	56	2	1	12	11	1.80
Scott Mathieson	YOM	2015	59	4	4	2	27	0	0	.500	270	68	0	6	18	0	1	79	1	0	18	17	2.24
	YOM	2016	70	8	4	1	41	0	0	.667	325	80	0	7	22	0	1	98	2	0	27	21	2.36
	YOM	2017	63	3	8	2	28	0	0	.273	244	58	0	5	21	0	2	55	1	0	22	17	2.62
Takahiro Matsuba	ORX	2015	23	3	12	0	0	0	0	.200	552	133	0	16	32	0	2	72	6	1	70	66	4.46
	ORX	2016	28	7	9	0	0	1	0	.438	563	132	0	10	41	0	3	82	5	0	52	48	3.26
	ORX	2017	18	3	6	0	0	0	0	.333	360	80	0	8	47	0	1	42	3	0	42	38	4.28
Yuki Matsui	RAK	2015	52	3	3	33	5	0	0	.500	214	52	0	0	26	0	1	62	0	0	8	7	1.20
	RAK	2016	58	1	4	30	10	0	0	.200	272	62	0	4	40	0	1	75	1	1	23	23	3.32
	RAK	2017	63	3	2	33	12	0	0	.600	284	72	0	3	28	0	2	103	3	0	7	7	0.87
Takahiro Matsunaga	CHB	2015	50	1	3	0	18	0	0	.250	153	36	0	1	12	1	1	31	4	0	16	13	3.22
	CHB	2016	53	3	0	0	10	0	0	1.000	173	39	0	0	18	1	4	27	2	0	18	15	3.46
	CHB	2017	41	0	0	0	13	0	0	.000	123	29	0	3	13	0	4	24	1	0	13	12	3.72
Kenichi Matsuoka	YKL	2015	37	0	1	0	8	0	0	.000	137	33	0	5	11	0	2	28	0	0	13	13	3.51
	YKL	2016	53	2	1	0	4	0	0	.667	246	55	0	4	31	2	3	39	1	0	25	23	3.74
	YKL	2017	38	2	0	1	4	0	0	1.000	152	36	0	1	15	0	4	31	0	0	14	14	3.44
Luis Mendoza	NIP	2015	20	3	7	0	0	0	0	.300	437	99	0	9	38	1	8	56	5	0	45	44	3.97
	NIP	2016	23	7	8	0	1	0	0	.467	573	132	0	13	45	2	4	77	7	0	64	57	3.88
	NIP	2017	26	10	8	0	1	1	0	.556	626	148	0	8	62	1	8	85	6	1	63	58	3.51
Randy Messenger	HNS	2015	22	11	5	0	0	1	1	.688	594	143	0	5	44	0	1	155	2	0	42	38	2.39
	HNS	2016	28	12	11	0	0	2	1	.522	791	185	0	11	60	2	1	177	4	0	73	62	3.01
	HNS	2017	29	9	12	0	0	0	0	.429	799	193	0	10	60	0	4	194	5	0	68	64	2.97
Kam Mickolio	RAK	2016	45	5	1	0	23	0	0	.833	181	45	0	3	6	0	4	29	1	0	13	12	2.38

PITCHER	TEAM	YEAR	G	W	L	SV	HLD	CG	SHO	PCT	BF	IP	H	HR	BB	IBB	HB	SO	WP	BK	R	ER	ERA
Tomoya Mikami	YKO	2015	61	3	3	0	31	0	0	.500	213	51	0	8	16	1	2	29	1	0	31	29	5.12
	YKO	2016	59	2	4	2	32	0	0	.333	241	58	0	7	18	2	2	36	2	0	21	17	2.61
Miles Mikolas	YOM	2015	27	14	8	0	0	0	0	.636	745	188	0	10	23	0	11	187	4	1	53	47	2.25
	YOM	2016	14	4	2	0	0	1	0	.667	381	91	0	10	23	0	4	84	0	0	35	25	2.45
	YOM	2017	21	13	3	0	0	4	2	.813	557	145	0	8	23	0	1	107	3	1	34	31	1.92
Manabu Mima	RAK	2015	26	11	8	0	0	3	1	.579	684	171	0	18	33	1	4	134	4	1	66	62	3.26
	RAK	2016	26	9	9	0	0	1	1	.500	678	155	0	14	32	0	8	116	5	1	80	74	4.30
	RAK	2017	16	3	7	0	0	0	0	.300	380	86	0	9	21	1	1	62	5	0	45	33	3.44
Masaki Minami	CHB	2016	57	5	4	0	16	0	0	.556	253	62	0	4	19	1	1	58	2	1	20	19	2.74
Kazuki Mishima	YKO	2017	20	5	5	0	0	0	0	.500	384	88	0	9	34	0	3	67	9	0	52	47	4.81
Takuya Mitsuma	CHU	2015	35	2	1	0	11	0	0	.667	174	37	0	1	27	0	6	29	0	0	17	17	4.06
Daisuke Miura	YKO	2017	17	6	6	0	0	0	0	.500	416	98	0	9	25	0	1	62	5	0	47	45	4.13
Ryosuke Miyaguni	YOM	2017	39	3	1	1	5	0	0	.750	194	49	0	4	15	1	0	28	3	0	17	16	2.94
Naoki Miyanishi	NIP	2015	51	4	5	0	25	0	0	.444	164	40	0	3	12	0	0	24	2	0	19	15	3.32
	NIP	2016	58	3	1	2	39	0	0	.750	190	47	0	0	22	1	5	36	1	0	11	8	1.52
	NIP	2017	50	3	3	0	25	0	0	.500	163	40	0	4	11	1	1	30	1	0	19	12	2.70
Yuito Mori	FKU	2015	64	2	3	1	33	0	0	.400	265	64	0	7	12	0	1	60	0	0	29	28	3.92
	FKU	2016	56	4	3	1	14	0	0	.571	261	60	0	6	15	1	2	51	0	0	20	20	2.98
	FKU	2017	55	5	2	0	16	0	0	.714	234	60	0	3	10	0	1	66	2	0	18	18	2.69
Masahiko Morifuku	FKU	2016	50	2	1	0	16	0	0	.667	105	27	0	1	2	0	3	23	0	0	7	6	2.00
Kohei Morihara	RAK	2015	42	2	4	0	13	0	0	.333	171	39	0	3	13	0	0	21	0	0	22	21	4.81
Guillermo Moscoso	YKO	2016	13	5	7	0	0	1	0	.417	342	80	0	15	19	1	0	65	5	0	47	46	5.18
Kyohei Muranaka	YKL	2016	52	7	3	0	6	0	0	.700	292	67	0	9	38	0	5	51	1	0	29	29	3.90
Yoshitaka Muto	RAK	2017	60	4	4	1	8	0	0	.500	316	69	0	5	29	0	5	38	3	0	35	34	4.39
Yuta Nakamura	HRO	2015	15	5	4	0	0	0	0	.556	312	74	0	7	26	0	2	54	1	0	33	31	3.74
Kenichi Nakata	FKU	2015	18	7	6	0	0	0	0	.538	380	86	0	15	40	0	9	78	4	0	44	44	4.57
	FKU	2016	17	7	3	0	0	0	0	.700	377	89	0	9	49	0	5	67	3	0	31	30	3.01
	FKU	2017	24	9	7	0	0	3	0	.563	657	155	0	17	61	0	9	130	4	0	60	56	3.24
Ren Nakata	HRO	2015	53	2	4	0	13	0	0	.333	196	46	0	4	20	3	1	50	0	0	15	14	2.70
Shota Nakazaki	HRO	2015	59	4	1	10	25	0	0	.800	218	57	0	2	20	0	0	36	0	0	9	9	1.40
	HRO	2016	61	3	4	34	7	0	0	.429	251	61	0	2	19	2	2	54	0	0	11	9	1.32
	HRO	2017	69	0	6	29	11	0	0	.000	300	73	0	4	23	0	1	61	0	0	20	19	2.34
Masato Nakazawa	YKL	2017	35	1	2	0	3	0	0	.333	136	29	0	2	15	1	1	21	1	0	12	10	3.03
Yoshihisa Naruse	YKL	2016	22	3	2	0	0	0	0	.600	319	72	0	13	27	1	5	42	1	0	46	45	5.60
	YKL	2017	14	3	8	0	0	0	0	.273	339	79	0	16	21	0	1	46	2	0	46	42	4.76
Akira Niho	FKU	2017	44	6	1	0	5	0	0	.857	229	52	0	3	23	0	3	28	1	1	21	19	3.25
Yuki Nishi	ORX	2015	17	5	6	0	0	3	1	.455	483	117	0	14	29	0	7	88	0	0	46	45	3.44
	ORX	2016	26	10	12	0	0	2	1	.455	712	165	0	4	48	1	8	108	2	0	80	76	4.14
	ORX	2017	24	10	6	0	0	3	2	.625	655	162	0	11	43	0	6	143	3	0	46	43	2.38
Kentaro Nishimura	YOM	2015	45	0	2	0	10	0	0	.000	196	48	0	5	14	1	2	34	0	0	19	19	3.56
Yuji Nishino	CHB	2016	42	3	6	21	5	0	0	.333	180	43	0	4	11	2	1	36	2	0	17	16	3.35
	CHB	2017	54	1	2	34	4	0	0	.333	219	54	0	1	12	1	1	71	8	0	13	11	1.83
Shogo Noda	SEI	2015	38	1	0	0	1	0	0	1.000	143	36	0	1	15	0	1	26	2	2	8	8	1.98
Ryoma Nogami	SEI	2015	24	11	10	0	0	2	1	.524	577	144	0	10	24	1	5	113	2	0	62	58	3.63
	SEI	2016	22	3	9	1	1	0	0	.250	474	107	0	10	43	0	5	62	3	0	56	46	3.87
	SEI	2017	27	7	7	0	0	0	0	.500	565	134	0	15	46	0	4	77	1	0	68	63	4.22
Atsushi Nomi	HNS	2015	23	6	6	0	0	1	0	.500	533	128	0	14	40	0	2	119	2	1	57	53	3.72
	HNS	2016	26	8	12	0	1	2	1	.400	634	147	0	17	52	2	6	126	5	1	67	60	3.67
	HNS	2017	27	11	13	0	0	1	1	.458	672	159	0	13	38	1	2	125	6	0	73	66	3.72
Yusuke Nomura	HRO	2015	25	9	5	0	0	0	0	.643	645	155	0	12	38	0	4	106	4	0	53	48	2.78
	HRO	2016	25	16	3	0	0	1	1	.842	633	152	0	11	37	0	6	91	3	0	50	46	2.71
	HRO	2017	15	5	8	0	0	0	0	.385	384	87	0	11	23	0	3	51	1	0	53	45	4.64
Jordan Norberto	CHU	2015	18	6	4	0	0	0	0	.600	310	74	0	2	35	0	6	66	2	3	25	19	2.30
	CHU	2016	22	6	6	0	0	0	0	.500	523	121	0	12	54	0	8	108	5	0	62	57	4.24
Takahiro Norimoto	RAK	2015	25	15	7	0	0	8	2	.682	750	185	0	11	48	1	3	222	12	0	63	53	2.57
	RAK	2016	28	11	11	0	0	2	0	.500	820	195	0	12	50	0	6	216	5	0	87	63	2.91
	RAK	2017	28	10	11	0	0	3	1	.476	797	194	0	14	48	0	4	215	6	1	68	63	2.91
Shinnosuke Ogasawara	CHU	2015	22	5	8	0	0	1	0	.385	522	119	0	21	53	1	1	105	7	0	65	64	4.84
	CHU	2016	15	2	6	0	0	0	0	.250	310	72	0	7	40	0	2	58	4	0	30	27	3.36
Ryuya Ogawa	CHU	2016	44	1	1	0	9	0	0	.500	126	31	0	1	9	0	3	34	1	0	10	8	2.27
Yasuhiro Ogawa	YKL	2015	22	8	7	0	1	2	1	.533	509	124	0	11	39	0	0	109	0	0	42	39	2.83
	YKL	2016	25	8	9	0	0	4	1	.471	668	158	0	22	52	0	6	114	3	0	82	79	4.50
	YKL	2017	27	11	8	0	0	1	1	.579	700	168	0	18	48	0	4	128	0	0	66	58	3.11
Seung-Hwan Oh	HNS	2017	63	2	3	41	7	0	0	.400	289	69	0	6	16	0	2	66	2	0	21	21	2.73
Tatsuya Oishi	SEI	2016	36	1	0	0	3	0	0	1.000	126	31	0	2	16	0	0	36	4	0	6	6	1.71
Akitake Okada	HRO	2015	24	12	5	0	0	2	0	.706	604	141	0	9	63	0	4	109	3	4	68	63	4.00
	HRO	2016	18	4	3	0	1	1	0	.571	375	89	0	6	25	0	0	60	4	2	34	30	3.02
Toshiya Okada	CHU	2016	57	3	1	0	13	0	0	.750	273	64	0	4	18	0	2	66	1	0	28	23	3.20
	CHU	2017	50	0	1	0	12	0	0	.000	225	57	0	1	15	0	2	55	2	0	10	10	1.57
Yosuke Okamoto	SEI	2017	42	1	2	0	6	0	0	.333	284	68	0	12	20	1	6	43	1	2	34	33	4.35

PITCHER	TEAM	YEAR	G	W	L	SV	HLD	CG	SHO	PCT	BF	IP	H	HR	BB	IBB	HB	SO	WP	BK	R	ER	ERA
Yuta Omine	CHB	2017	24	8	7	0	0	1	1	.533	574	133	0	8	46	0	5	70	1	0	49	47	3.17
Logan Ondrusek	YKL	2017	72	5	2	0	33	0	0	.714	276	70	0	2	22	0	1	62	0	1	17	16	2.05
Taiki Ono	HNS	2015	15	2	7	0	0	0	0	.222	343	78	0	6	40	0	5	63	4	0	38	38	4.35
Yudai Ono	CHU	2015	24	7	8	0	0	2	1	.467	629	147	0	17	51	0	6	117	0	0	71	66	4.02
	CHU	2016	19	7	10	0	0	3	1	.412	547	129	0	11	37	0	2	85	0	0	59	51	3.54
	CHU	2017	28	11	10	0	1	6	3	.524	826	207	0	12	47	1	3	154	1	0	67	58	2.52
Shuichiro Osada	YKO	2017	45	4	1	0	10	0	0	.800	167	39	0	1	19	2	0	18	4	0	13	9	2.06
Daichi Osera	HRO	2015	24	10	2	0	0	0	0	.833	617	145	0	12	43	0	1	109	9	0	68	59	3.65
	HRO	2017	51	3	8	2	20	2	0	.273	475	109	0	5	31	0	1	97	4	0	53	38	3.13
Kan Otake	YOM	2016	17	6	6	0	0	0	0	.500	393	91	0	6	30	1	1	71	3	0	40	36	3.55
Shohei Otani	NIP	2016	21	10	4	0	1	4	1	.714	548	140	0	4	45	0	8	174	6	0	33	29	1.86
	NIP	2017	22	15	5	0	0	5	3	.750	621	160	0	7	46	0	3	196	9	0	40	40	2.24
Tomohisa Otani	CHB	2015	55	3	2	0	23	0	0	.600	214	52	0	5	14	0	1	33	1	0	20	18	3.12
	CHB	2017	56	3	1	0	32	0	0	.750	250	64	0	4	5	0	2	53	1	0	21	17	2.39
Kenji Otonari	FKU	2017	11	5	4	0	0	3	2	.556	300	74	0	9	15	0	6	35	1	0	25	21	2.54
Spencer Patton	YKO	2015	62	4	3	7	27	0	0	.571	247	60	0	4	19	3	2	66	2	0	19	18	2.70
Aaron Poreda	YOM	2017	24	8	8	0	0	0	0	.500	619	147	0	6	46	2	8	101	5	6	57	48	2.94
Kenny Ray	RAK	2017	22	5	7	0	2	0	0	.417	461	107	0	14	31	0	7	76	1	0	50	45	3.79
Dae-Eun Rhee	CHB	2017	37	9	9	0	4	0	0	.500	536	119	0	11	63	2	3	106	8	1	63	51	3.84
Orlando Roman	YKL	2017	61	5	5	0	23	0	0	.500	330	78	0	2	35	2	3	58	2	0	25	21	2.40
Tomohito Sakai	CHB	2015	19	5	1	0	1	2	0	.833	315	74	0	11	20	0	3	48	0	0	28	26	3.13
Dennis Sarfate	FKU	2015	66	2	2	54	3	0	0	.500	238	66	0	3	10	0	1	102	0	0	9	8	1.09
	FKU	2016	64	0	7	43	8	0	0	.000	237	62	0	4	11	1	0	73	1	0	15	13	1.88
	FKU	2017	65	5	1	41	9	0	0	.833	235	64	0	4	14	0	1	102	2	0	8	8	1.11
Chihaya Sasaki	CHB	2015	15	4	7	0	0	1	0	.364	363	85	0	9	48	0	1	59	3	1	41	40	4.22
Tatsuya Sato	ORX	2016	43	1	4	0	12	0	0	.200	188	41	0	6	36	0	0	53	4	0	24	23	5.01
	ORX	2017	59	2	7	13	13	0	0	.222	249	58	0	3	23	1	2	77	5	0	23	21	3.22
Hirokazu Sawamura	YOM	2016	63	6	4	37	4	0	0	.600	271	64	0	5	22	0	1	55	9	1	20	19	2.66
	YOM	2017	60	7	3	36	3	0	0	.700	282	68	0	4	21	0	3	60	2	0	12	10	1.32
Brian Schlitter	SEI	2015	64	1	5	0	32	0	0	.167	269	63	0	1	29	1	0	23	1	1	22	20	2.83
Ryota Sekiya	CHB	2016	16	5	6	0	0	0	0	.455	391	88	0	8	34	0	5	58	2	0	58	54	5.52
Kodai Senga	FKU	2015	22	13	4	0	0	0	0	.765	572	143	0	15	46	0	2	151	6	0	47	42	2.64
	FKU	2016	25	12	3	0	0	3	0	.800	681	169	0	16	53	0	6	181	7	1	52	49	2.61
Tadashi Settsu	FKU	2017	20	10	7	0	0	2	0	.588	566	134	0	14	45	0	4	92	1	0	61	48	3.22
Takahiro Shiomi	RAK	2016	24	8	10	0	0	0	0	.444	610	148	0	14	37	1	3	111	0	0	67	64	3.89
	RAK	2017	16	3	5	0	0	0	0	.375	392	96	0	14	15	0	3	78	4	0	42	38	3.56
Hirokazu Shiranita	ORX	2017	43	2	2	0	2	0	0	.500	221	52	0	1	23	1	0	27	2	0	20	19	3.29
Daisuke Sobue	CHU	2015	35	2	2	1	9	0	0	.500	173	42	0	1	17	0	0	26	0	0	12	12	2.57
	CHU	2016	46	0	4	0	12	0	0	.000	177	43	0	3	18	0	2	31	1	0	18	15	3.14
Jason Standridge	CHB	2015	14	4	6	0	0	0	0	.400	349	77	0	9	38	1	7	52	5	0	40	37	4.32
	CHB	2016	27	8	8	0	0	0	0	.500	686	162	0	13	45	5	8	99	6	1	72	64	3.56
	FKU	2017	23	10	7	0	0	1	1	.588	617	144	0	12	44	0	8	81	4	1	64	60	3.74
Robert Suarez	FKU	2016	58	2	6	1	26	0	0	.250	223	53	0	5	18	3	1	64	2	0	21	19	3.19
Kota Suda	YKO	2016	62	5	3	0	23	0	0	.625	233	53	0	2	18	2	1	49	0	0	17	16	2.68
Tomoyuki Sugano	YOM	2015	25	17	5	0	0	6	4	.773	713	187	0	10	31	0	1	171	1	0	36	33	1.59
	YOM	2016	26	9	6	0	0	5	2	.600	726	183	0	12	26	0	4	189	1	0	46	41	2.01
	YOM	2017	25	10	11	0	0	6	2	.476	710	179	0	10	41	4	7	126	3	0	46	38	1.91
Toshiya Sugiuchi	YOM	2017	17	6	6	0	0	0	0	.500	401	95	0	9	35	0	3	93	2	1	42	42	3.95
Yoshiki Sunada	YKO	2015	62	1	2	0	25	0	0	.333	236	54	0	5	13	1	3	49	1	1	25	25	4.12
	YKO	2017	14	3	5	0	0	0	0	.375	335	76	0	5	28	0	2	57	0	0	34	27	3.20
Kazuto Taguchi	YOM	2015	26	13	4	0	0	3	2	.765	709	170	0	14	49	1	4	122	1	0	59	57	3.01
	YOM	2016	26	10	10	0	0	2	1	.500	668	162	0	15	49	0	6	126	1	0	54	49	2.72
Seiji Tahara	YOM	2016	64	4	3	0	14	0	0	.571	233	54	0	3	22	1	3	29	0	1	22	21	3.46
Shinji Tajima	CHU	2015	63	2	5	34	6	0	0	.286	249	62	0	6	25	1	3	46	5	0	20	20	2.87
	CHU	2016	59	3	4	17	18	0	0	.429	248	59	0	5	25	1	3	61	5	0	16	16	2.44
	CHU	2017	64	4	6	9	16	0	0	.400	316	75	0	4	25	2	6	62	5	0	25	19	2.28
Hayato Takagi	YOM	2016	25	5	9	0	0	0	0	.357	504	117	0	15	36	0	7	91	4	1	61	56	4.31
	YOM	2017	26	9	10	0	0	1	1	.474	678	163	0	16	47	1	8	131	6	0	66	58	3.19
Akifumi Takahashi	HNS	2015	61	6	0	1	20	0	0	1.000	184	47	0	1	14	0	1	51	2	0	9	9	1.70
	HNS	2016	54	3	1	0	20	0	0	.750	166	38	0	4	11	0	1	38	3	0	17	16	3.76
	CHU	2017	35	3	3	0	6	0	0	.500	109	25	0	1	2	0	1	26	2	0	13	10	3.51
Kona Takahashi	SEI	2016	22	4	11	0	0	2	1	.267	529	118	0	10	51	0	5	89	12	0	73	58	4.42
Tomomi Takahashi	SEI	2017	62	2	3	22	14	0	0	.400	264	61	0	3	26	1	5	55	2	0	21	20	2.92
Kazuya Takamiya	HNS	2017	52	2	0	0	8	0	0	1.000	157	35	0	2	15	0	3	27	2	0	14	12	3.03
Hirotoshi Takanashi	NIP	2015	22	7	7	0	0	1	1	.500	504	117	0	13	40	1	3	100	6	1	51	48	3.68
	NIP	2016	37	10	2	0	1	1	1	.833	439	109	0	6	36	0	4	86	0	0	30	29	2.38
Yuhei Takanashi	RAK	2015	46	1	0	0	14	0	0	1.000	183	43	0	2	17	1	2	48	0	0	13	5	1.03
Shota Takeda	FKU	2015	13	6	4	0	0	1	1	.600	316	71	0	10	33	0	5	60	1	0	35	29	3.68
	FKU	2016	27	14	8	0	0	1	1	.636	769	183	0	12	70	0	5	144	7	1	71	60	2.95
	FKU	2017	25	13	6	0	0	1	1	.684	684	164	0	14	59	0	2	163	6	3	60	58	3.17

PITCHER	TEAM	YEAR	G	W	L	SV	HLD	CG	SHO	PCT	BF	IP	H	HR	BB	IBB	HB	SO	WP	BK	R	ER	ERA
Shota Takekuma	SEI	2015	58	5	2	0	13	0	0	.714	234	57	0	3	16	0	3	36	1	0	21	20	3.14
	SEI	2016	64	5	3	0	14	0	0	.625	261	61	0	5	20	0	1	53	3	0	24	24	3.54
	SEI	2017	67	6	1	1	11	0	0	.857	255	57	0	1	36	2	1	36	4	0	18	18	2.83
Kenjiro Tanaka	YKO	2015	60	1	3	0	11	0	0	.250	205	48	0	3	23	0	1	36	2	0	26	24	4.47
	YKO	2016	61	5	3	0	23	0	0	.625	197	44	0	2	18	3	1	39	3	0	16	12	2.45
	YKO	2017	35	2	2	1	16	0	0	.500	140	32	0	1	16	0	0	29	3	0	9	8	2.20
Keisuke Tanimoto	NIP	2015	36	0	2	1	21	0	0	.000	141	32	0	3	16	2	1	24	0	1	15	12	3.31
	NIP	2016	58	3	2	3	28	0	0	.600	206	50	0	4	16	0	1	44	0	0	14	13	2.32
	NIP	2017	61	4	2	0	20	0	0	.667	241	56	0	0	15	1	2	47	1	0	21	20	3.18
Shinsaburo Tawata	SEI	2015	16	5	5	0	0	2	2	.500	411	96	0	11	26	0	8	74	3	0	39	37	3.44
	SEI	2016	18	7	5	0	0	2	1	.583	433	98	0	6	40	0	8	91	10	0	51	48	4.38
Hayato Terahara	FKU	2017	21	8	3	0	2	0	0	.727	332	83	0	11	19	0	3	58	3	0	32	32	3.44
Ken Togame	SEI	2015	20	8	7	0	0	0	0	.533	500	116	0	10	35	0	3	83	0	0	50	44	3.40
	SEI	2016	21	4	6	0	1	0	0	.400	335	71	0	3	31	0	9	41	2	0	55	50	6.31
	SEI	2017	26	11	7	0	0	1	0	.611	644	152	0	19	53	0	8	107	1	0	62	60	3.55
Takeaki Tokuyama	YKL	2017	39	2	1	0	3	0	0	.667	217	50	0	4	22	1	0	50	2	0	25	20	3.58
Daiki Tomei	ORX	2016	24	1	10	0	1	0	0	.091	567	122	0	13	54	2	3	100	5	0	70	67	4.94
	ORX	2017	25	10	8	0	0	2	1	.556	663	161	0	16	41	2	5	118	3	1	61	60	3.35
Kenji Tomura	RAK	2017	37	7	11	0	1	1	0	.389	572	131	0	7	40	0	4	78	5	0	68	56	3.84
Chiaki Tone	YOM	2016	42	1	0	1	5	0	0	1.000	161	36	0	5	17	0	3	25	0	0	19	18	4.50
	YOM	2017	46	1	1	1	5	0	0	.500	168	40	0	3	18	0	0	39	0	0	13	13	2.88
Shohei Tsukahara	ORX	2016	54	4	1	0	13	0	0	.800	240	54	0	5	31	0	2	40	3	0	18	16	2.67
	ORX	2017	41	0	4	1	13	0	0	.000	192	43	0	5	24	0	6	25	1	0	18	16	3.30
Tatsuya Uchi	CHB	2015	50	5	1	16	11	0	0	.833	211	49	0	5	28	4	0	44	1	0	16	16	2.94
Tetsuya Utsumi	YOM	2016	18	9	6	0	0	0	0	.600	442	107	0	10	22	0	5	81	2	0	47	47	3.94
Naoyuki Uwasawa	NIP	2015	15	4	9	0	0	0	0	.308	388	91	0	11	32	1	2	74	2	1	39	35	3.44
	NIP	2017	13	5	6	0	0	1	0	.455	335	75	0	6	30	0	5	43	1	1	41	35	4.18
Raul Valdes	CHU	2015	23	6	9	0	0	1	0	.400	625	146	0	13	47	0	7	83	1	0	73	61	3.76
	CHU	2016	20	6	7	0	0	0	0	.462	534	125	0	17	39	0	8	103	0	0	54	49	3.51
	CHU	2017	22	5	8	0	0	1	0	.385	560	133	0	6	36	0	2	93	1	0	56	47	3.18
Rick van den Hurk	FKU	2015	25	13	7	0	0	0	0	.650	623	153	0	18	47	0	2	162	4	0	57	55	3.24
	FKU	2016	13	7	3	0	0	0	0	.700	325	82	0	14	15	0	1	92	1	0	37	35	3.84
	FKU	2017	15	9	0	0	0	0	0	1.000	369	93	0	6	22	0	4	120	2	0	27	26	2.52
Tsuyoshi Wada	FKU	2016	24	15	5	0	0	2	1	.750	662	163	0	22	38	0	5	157	0	0	58	55	3.04
Shunta Wakamatsu	CHU	2016	19	7	8	0	1	3	0	.467	497	115	0	10	37	0	0	85	3	0	55	52	4.06
	CHU	2017	23	10	4	0	0	2	1	.714	575	140	0	10	50	1	2	113	3	0	35	33	2.12
Hideaki Wakui	CHB	2015	25	5	11	0	0	1	1	.313	675	158	0	20	53	0	7	115	6	0	74	70	3.99
	CHB	2016	26	10	7	0	0	5	0	.588	793	188	0	15	48	0	4	118	1	0	73	63	3.01
	CHB	2017	28	15	9	0	0	1	0	.625	786	188	0	11	57	0	8	117	6	0	79	71	3.39
Joe Wieland	YKO	2015	21	10	2	0	0	1	1	.833	541	133	0	14	37	0	2	112	1	0	46	44	2.98
Brian Wolfe	SEI	2015	23	9	4	0	0	0	0	.692	532	125	0	11	36	2	1	74	7	0	69	52	3.73
Kazuki Yabuta	HRO	2015	38	15	3	0	3	2	2	.833	536	129	0	10	51	0	4	115	4	0	42	37	2.58
Shun Yamaguchi	YKO	2016	19	11	5	0	0	5	3	.688	570	138	0	10	44	0	4	121	5	0	48	44	2.86
	YKO	2017	20	3	6	0	0	2	0	.333	508	114	0	13	42	0	3	119	6	1	67	57	4.49
Tetsuya Yamaguchi	YOM	2016	63	1	6	1	19	0	0	.143	204	48	0	6	12	0	2	28	1	0	30	26	4.88
	YOM	2017	60	4	5	2	29	0	0	.444	216	52	0	5	15	0	2	31	2	0	18	16	2.73
Daisuke Yamai	CHU	2017	33	4	12	2	5	0	0	.250	589	140	0	13	50	2	2	79	7	0	69	61	3.92
Hirofumi Yamanaka	YKL	2015	13	2	6	0	0	1	0	.250	333	75	0	11	17	1	4	29	0	0	45	43	5.14
	YKL	2016	22	6	12	0	0	3	1	.333	578	140	0	17	20	2	9	54	1	0	56	55	3.54
Taisuke Yamaoka	ORX	2015	24	8	11	0	0	2	1	.421	618	149	0	8	54	0	2	133	7	0	62	62	3.74
Yasuaki Yamasaki	YKO	2015	68	4	2	26	15	0	0	.667	260	65	0	3	13	0	1	84	1	0	16	12	1.64
	YKO	2016	59	2	5	33	7	0	0	.286	252	57	0	7	23	0	0	61	2	0	27	23	3.59
	YKO	2017	58	2	4	37	7	0	0	.333	215	56	0	2	11	0	1	66	4	1	13	12	1.92
Kazumasa Yoshida	ORX	2016	54	5	2	1	21	0	0	.714	204	50	0	4	16	0	3	36	3	0	17	15	2.66
Mitsuo Yoshikawa	NIP	2016	27	7	6	3	0	0	0	.538	494	109	0	9	52	0	5	65	1	0	53	51	4.19
	NIP	2017	26	11	8	0	0	2	0	.579	684	159	0	16	57	0	11	93	3	0	72	68	3.84
Kazuki Yoshimi	CHU	2015	14	3	7	0	0	0	0	.300	334	75	0	8	14	0	1	38	0	0	49	44	5.23
	CHU	2016	21	6	7	0	0	1	0	.462	535	131	0	11	27	2	0	81	1	0	49	45	3.08

PECOTA Leaderboards

Height Percentiles

Percentile	Name	Team	HEIGHT
100	Aaron Judge	NYA	79
90	Jarrett Parker	SFN	76
80	Alex Dickerson	SDN	75
70	Paulo Orlando	KCA	74
60	Patrick Wisdom	SLN	74
50	Austin Hedges	SDN	73
40	Allen Cordoba	SDN	73
30	Jesus Sucre	TBA	72
20	Eugenio Suarez	CIN	71
10	Chris Owings	ARI	70
0	Jose Altuve	HOU	66

Batting Average

Rank	Name	Team	AVG
1	Jose Altuve	HOU	.315
2	Daniel Murphy	WAS	.302
3	Miguel Cabrera	DET	.300
4	Mike Trout	ANA	.296
5	Michael Brantley	CLE	.294
6	Mookie Betts	BOS	.293
6	Freddie Freeman	ATL	.293
8	Trea Turner	WAS	.292
9	Buster Posey	SFN	.291
9	Joey Votto	CIN	.291
11	Adrian Beltre	TEX	.290
12	Jose Abreu	CHA	.289
13	Bryce Harper	WAS	.288
13	Francisco Lindor	CLE	.288
13	Eric Hosmer	KCA	.288
13	Paul Goldschmidt	ARI	.288
13	Ender Inciarte	ATL	.288
18	Adam Frazier	PIT	.287
19	Robinson Cano	SEA	.286
19	DJ LeMahieu	COL	.286
19	Charlie Blackmon	COL	.286

Batting Average Percentiles

Percentile	Name	Team	AVG
99	Daniel Murphy	WAS	.302
90	Manny Machado	BAL	.282
80	Yadier Molina	SLN	.274
70	Josh Reddick	HOU	.267
60	Lonnie Chisenhall	CLE	.262
50	Jeimer Candelario	DET	.258
40	Steve Pearce	TOR	.254
30	Tucker Barnhart	CIN	.248
20	Billy Hamilton	CIN	.243
10	Eric Thames	MIL	.235
1	Joey Gallo	TEX	.215

On-Base Percentage

Rank	Name	Team	OBP
1	Joey Votto	CIN	.422
2	Mike Trout	ANA	.409
3	Bryce Harper	WAS	.395
4	Paul Goldschmidt	ARI	.394
5	Freddie Freeman	ATL	.384
6	Kris Bryant	CHN	.381
6	Miguel Cabrera	DET	.381
8	Anthony Rizzo	CHN	.376
9	Josh Donaldson	TOR	.370
10	Andrew McCutchen	PIT	.368
11	Shin-Soo Choo	TEX	.366
12	Matt Carpenter	SLN	.364
12	Jose Altuve	HOU	.364
14	Willson Contreras	CHN	.362
14	Carlos Correa	HOU	.362
16	Christian Yelich	MIA	.361
17	Jesse Winker	CIN	.360
17	Buster Posey	SFN	.360
19	Anthony Rendon	WAS	.359
20	Edwin Encarnacion	CLE	.358

On-Base Percentage Percentiles

Percentile	Name	Team	OBP
99	Mike Trout	ANA	.409
90	Dexter Fowler	SLN	.354
80	DJ LeMahieu	COL	.342
70	Jose Ramirez	CLE	.333
60	Yasmani Grandal	LAN	.329
50	Derek Fisher	HOU	.321
40	Hunter Pence	SFN	.316
30	Rio Ruiz	ATL	.311
20	Ian Kinsler	ANA	.306
10	Adam Duvall	CIN	.295
1	Magneuris Sierra	MIA	.272

Slugging Percentage

Rank	Name	Team	SLG
1	Mike Trout	ANA	.559
2	Giancarlo Stanton	NYA	.551
3	J.D. Martinez	ARI	.546
4	Bryce Harper	WAS	.533
5	Rhys Hoskins	PHI	.526
6	Gary Sanchez	NYA	.521
7	Kris Bryant	CHN	.520
7	Paul Goldschmidt	ARI	.520
9	Nolan Arenado	COL	.519
10	Cody Bellinger	LAN	.509
11	Freddie Freeman	ATL	.508
12	Miguel Cabrera	DET	.505
12	Jose Abreu	CHA	.505
14	Edwin Encarnacion	CLE	.503
14	Aaron Judge	NYA	.503
14	Nelson Cruz	SEA	.503
14	Anthony Rizzo	CHN	.503
18	Josh Donaldson	TOR	.502
19	Joey Votto	CIN	.496
19	Carlos Correa	HOU	.496

Slugging Percentage Percentiles

Percentile	Name	Team	SLG
99	Giancarlo Stanton	NYA	.551
90	Corey Seager	LAN	.481
80	Corey Dickerson	TBA	.462
70	Tommy Pham	SLN	.445
60	Carlos Santana	PHI	.433
50	Kole Calhoun	ANA	.421
40	Jorge Polanco	MIN	.411
30	Jason Heyward	CHN	.402
20	Jose Peraza	CIN	.386
10	Paulo Orlando	KCA	.375
1	Adeiny Hechavarria	TBA	.340

OPS

Rank	Name	Team	OPS
1	Mike Trout	ANA	.968
2	Bryce Harper	WAS	.928
3	Joey Votto	CIN	.918
4	Paul Goldschmidt	ARI	.914
5	Giancarlo Stanton	NYA	.908
6	Kris Bryant	CHN	.901
7	Freddie Freeman	ATL	.892
8	J.D. Martinez	ARI	.889
9	Miguel Cabrera	DET	.886
10	Rhys Hoskins	PHI	.880
11	Anthony Rizzo	CHN	.879
12	Josh Donaldson	TOR	.872
13	Edwin Encarnacion	CLE	.861
14	Aaron Judge	NYA	.859
15	Carlos Correa	HOU	.858
16	Gary Sanchez	NYA	.855
17	Jose Abreu	CHA	.854
18	Nolan Arenado	COL	.853
19	Willson Contreras	CHN	.846
20	Nelson Cruz	SEA	.842

OPS Percentiles

Percentile	Name	Team	OPS
99	Bryce Harper	WAS	.928
90	Miguel Sano	MIN	.824
80	Michael Brantley	CLE	.794
70	Shin-Soo Choo	TEX	.775
60	Eugenio Suarez	CIN	.754
50	Raimel Tapia	COL	.743
40	Jackie Bradley	BOS	.730
30	Jose Pirela	SDN	.719
20	Francisco Cervelli	PIT	.701
10	Dee Gordon	SEA	.681
1	Adeiny Hechavarria	TBA	.625

Home Runs

Rank	Name	Team	HR
1	Giancarlo Stanton	NYA	41
2	Aaron Judge	NYA	37
2	Cody Bellinger	LAN	37
4	Nelson Cruz	SEA	36
4	Rhys Hoskins	PHI	36
4	Joey Gallo	TEX	36
7	Gary Sanchez	NYA	35
8	Khris Davis	OAK	34
8	Mike Trout	ANA	34
10	Kyle Schwarber	CHN	33
10	Edwin Encarnacion	CLE	33
10	Chris Davis	BAL	33
13	Matt Chapman	OAK	32
13	Adam Duvall	CIN	32
13	Miguel Sano	MIN	32
16	Matt Olson	OAK	31
16	Josh Donaldson	TOR	31
16	Bryce Harper	WAS	31
19	Anthony Rizzo	CHN	30
19	Kris Bryant	CHN	30

Home Runs Percentiles

Percentile	Name	Team	HR
99	Joey Gallo	TEX	36
90	Marcell Ozuna	SLN	24
80	Ronald Acuna	ATL	20
70	Bradley Zimmer	CLE	15
60	Albert Almora	CHN	12
50	Sean Rodriguez	PIT	9
40	Ryan Schimpf	SDN	6
30	Dustin Garneau	OAK	4
20	Adrian Sanchez	WAS	3
10	Jose Rondon	SDN	2
1	Yadiel Rivera	MIA	0

Stolen Bases

Rank	Name	Team	SB
1	Billy Hamilton	CIN	65
2	Dee Gordon	SEA	54
3	Trea Turner	WAS	51
4	Starling Marte	PIT	39
5	Delino DeShields	TEX	35
6	Jose Altuve	HOU	32
7	Jarrod Dyson	SEA	30
7	Jonathan Villar	MIL	30
9	Jose Peraza	CIN	29
10	Raul Mondesi	KCA	28
10	Rajai Davis	BOS	28
12	Whit Merrifield	KCA	27
12	A.J. Pollock	ARI	27
12	Elvis Andrus	TEX	27
15	Bradley Zimmer	CLE	26
15	Eduardo Nunez	BOS	26
15	Ronald Acuna	ATL	26
18	Jean Segura	SEA	25
19	Byron Buxton	MIN	24
20	Mookie Betts	BOS	23
20	Manuel Margot	SDN	23

Stolen Bases Percentiles

Percentile	Name	Team	SB
99	Starling Marte	PIT	39
90	Jacoby Jones	DET	15
80	George Springer	HOU	10
70	Freddie Freeman	ATL	6
60	Brandon Belt	SFN	4
50	Carlos Asuaje	SDN	3
40	Joe Mauer	MIN	2
30	Guillermo Heredia	SEA	1
20	Kendrys Morales	TOR	0
10	Jeimer Candelario	DET	0
1	Bobby Bradley	CLE	0

Runs

Rank	Name	Team	R
1	Mike Trout	ANA	122
2	Josh Donaldson	TOR	107
2	Aaron Judge	NYA	107
4	Trea Turner	WAS	105
4	Kris Bryant	CHN	105
6	George Springer	HOU	104
6	Brian Dozier	MIN	104
8	Francisco Lindor	CLE	100
8	Paul Goldschmidt	ARI	100
10	Tommy Pham	SLN	98
10	Joey Votto	CIN	98
10	Bryce Harper	WAS	98
13	Anthony Rizzo	CHN	97
13	Manny Machado	BAL	97
15	Starling Marte	PIT	96
16	Charlie Blackmon	COL	95
16	Giancarlo Stanton	NYA	95
16	Alex Bregman	HOU	95
19	Steven Souza	TBA	94
19	Billy Hamilton	CIN	94
19	Kyle Schwarber	CHN	94

Runs Percentiles

Percentile	Name	Team	R
99	Kris Bryant	CHN	105
90	Jason Kipnis	CLE	85
80	Justin Smoak	TOR	76
70	Victor Martinez	DET	68
60	Travis d'Arnaud	NYN	58
50	Nick Delmonico	CHA	45
40	Kelby Tomlinson	SFN	30
30	Mark Zagunis	CHN	21
20	Jose Rondon	SDN	13
10	Ryan Cordell	CHA	8
1	Richard Urena	TOR	3

Runs Batted In

Rank	Name	Team	RBI
1	Giancarlo Stanton	NYA	109
2	Nelson Cruz	SEA	106
3	Rhys Hoskins	PHI	104
4	Cody Bellinger	LAN	103
5	Mike Trout	ANA	102
6	Anthony Rizzo	CHN	100
6	Edwin Encarnacion	CLE	100
6	Bryce Harper	WAS	100
9	Gary Sanchez	NYA	99
9	Jose Abreu	CHA	99
11	Khris Davis	OAK	98
12	Joey Gallo	TEX	97
12	Paul Goldschmidt	ARI	97
12	Miguel Sano	MIN	97
15	Aaron Judge	NYA	96
15	Nolan Arenado	COL	96
17	Josh Donaldson	TOR	95
17	Chris Davis	BAL	95
19	Joey Votto	CIN	94
20	Paul DeJong	SLN	93
20	Adam Duvall	CIN	93

RBI Percentiles

Percentile	Name	Team	RBI
99	Cody Bellinger	LAN	103
90	Justin Turner	LAN	84
80	Buster Posey	SFN	73
70	Ian Kinsler	ANA	64
60	Lonnie Chisenhall	CLE	54
50	Martin Maldonado	ANA	43
40	Renato Nunez	OAK	29
30	Braxton Lee	MIA	21
20	Miguel Andujar	NYA	12
10	Jordan Patterson	COL	7
1	Yadiel Rivera	MIA	3

Isolated Power

Rank	Name	Team	ISO
1	Giancarlo Stanton	NYA	.293
2	Joey Gallo	TEX	.272
3	Rhys Hoskins	PHI	.267
4	J.D. Martinez	ARI	.265
5	Mike Trout	ANA	.263
6	Cody Bellinger	LAN	.260
7	Aaron Judge	NYA	.257
8	Matt Chapman	OAK	.256
9	Gary Sanchez	NYA	.252
10	Kyle Schwarber	CHN	.250
11	Khris Davis	OAK	.249
12	Chris Davis	BAL	.246
13	Bryce Harper	WAS	.245
14	Chris Carter	OAK	.243
15	Edwin Encarnacion	CLE	.241
16	Kris Bryant	CHN	.239
17	Miguel Sano	MIN	.238
17	Nolan Arenado	COL	.238
19	Matt Olson	OAK	.236
19	Adam Duvall	CIN	.236

Isolate Slugging (ISO) Percentiles

Percentile	Name	Team	ISO
99	Joey Gallo	TEX	.272
90	Greg Bird	NYA	.222
80	Corey Dickerson	TBA	.198
70	Maikel Franco	PHI	.186
60	Eugenio Suarez	CIN	.177
50	Evan Longoria	SFN	.166
40	Marwin Gonzalez	HOU	.155
30	Chris Taylor	LAN	.146
20	Jed Lowrie	OAK	.133
10	Matt Duffy	TBA	.118
1	Nick Markakis	ATL	.093

Hitter Walk Rate

Rank	Name	Team	BB%
1	Joey Votto	CIN	0.178
2	Alex Avila	CHN	0.154
3	Carlos Santana	PHI	0.147
4	Mike Trout	ANA	0.147
5	Bryce Harper	WAS	0.147
6	Jose Bautista	TOR	0.145
7	Paul Goldschmidt	ARI	0.145
8	Joc Pederson	LAN	0.144
9	Aaron Judge	NYA	0.138
10	Joey Gallo	TEX	0.135
11	Chris Iannetta	COL	0.134
12	Matt Carpenter	SLN	0.131
13	Dexter Fowler	SLN	0.128
14	Matt Joyce	OAK	0.128
15	Yasmani Grandal	LAN	0.128
16	Matt Olson	OAK	0.128
17	Mike Napoli	TEX	0.127
18	Kyle Schwarber	CHN	0.127
19	Shin-Soo Choo	TEX	0.126
20	Giancarlo Stanton	NYA	0.126

Hitter Walk Rate Percentiles

Percentile	Name	Team	BB%
99	Mike Trout	ANA	0.147
90	Rhys Hoskins	PHI	0.117
80	Michael Conforto	NYN	0.104
70	Yasiel Puig	LAN	0.094
60	Mookie Betts	BOS	0.087
50	Gary Sanchez	NYA	0.079
40	Austin Slater	SFN	0.074
30	Nick Castellanos	DET	0.067
20	Didi Gregorius	NYA	0.060
10	Rougned Odor	TEX	0.050
1	Hernan Perez	MIL	0.039

Strikeout Rate

Rank	Name	Team	SO%
1	Andrelton Simmons	ANA	0.090
2	Joe Panik	SFN	0.100
3	Nori Aoki	NYN	0.102
3	Ben Revere	ANA	0.102
5	Michael Brantley	CLE	0.103
6	Jose Altuve	HOU	0.104
7	Jose Ramirez	CLE	0.109
8	Daniel Murphy	WAS	0.112
8	Buster Posey	SFN	0.112
10	Yangervis Solarte	SDN	0.114
10	Jose Iglesias	DET	0.114
12	Victor Martinez	DET	0.115
13	Dustin Pedroia	BOS	0.116
13	Martin Prado	MIA	0.116
15	Ender Inciarte	ATL	0.118
16	Melky Cabrera	KCA	0.119
16	Mookie Betts	BOS	0.119
18	Adrian Beltre	TEX	0.120
19	Albert Pujols	ANA	0.127
20	Yadier Molina	SLN	0.128

Strikeout Rate Percentiles

Percentile	Name	Team	SO%
99	Joe Panik	SFN	0.100
90	Wilmer Flores	NYN	0.142
80	Aledmys Diaz	TOR	0.164
70	Jose Martinez	SLN	0.182
60	Jose Abreu	CHA	0.195
50	Trea Turner	WAS	0.204
40	Stephen Piscotty	OAK	0.219
30	Rafael Devers	BOS	0.235
20	Yasmany Tomas	ARI	0.252
10	Jason Castro	MIN	0.279
1	Matt Davidson	CHA	0.333

True Average

Rank	Name	Team	TAv
1	Mike Trout	ANA	.334
2	Joey Votto	CIN	.313
3	Bryce Harper	WAS	.310
4	Paul Goldschmidt	ARI	.308
5	Giancarlo Stanton	NYA	.307
6	Freddie Freeman	ATL	.306
7	Kris Bryant	CHN	.305
8	Carlos Correa	HOU	.302
9	Josh Donaldson	TOR	.299
10	Rhys Hoskins	PHI	.298
11	Miguel Cabrera	DET	.296
12	Anthony Rizzo	CHN	.295
13	Aaron Judge	NYA	.294
14	Edwin Encarnacion	CLE	.293
15	Gary Sanchez	NYA	.292
16	Nelson Cruz	SEA	.291
16	Jose Abreu	CHA	.291
18	Willson Contreras	CHN	.290
18	George Springer	HOU	.290
18	Andrew McCutchen	PIT	.290
18	J.D. Martinez	ARI	.290

True Average Percentiles

Percentile	Name	Team	TAv
99	Joey Votto	CIN	.313
90	Buster Posey	SFN	.283
80	Trey Mancini	BAL	.275
70	Troy Tulowitzki	TOR	.267
60	Chris Taylor	LAN	.263
50	Ozhaino Albies	ATL	.259
40	Cheslor Cuthbert	KCA	.255
30	Albert Almora	CHN	.252
20	Chase Headley	SDN	.247
10	Tucker Barnhart	CIN	.239
1	Martin Maldonado	ANA	.222

Hitter VORP

Rank	Name	Team	VORP
1	Mike Trout	ANA	74.2
2	Carlos Correa	HOU	48.6
3	Jose Altuve	HOU	44.2
3	Bryce Harper	WAS	44.2
5	Kris Bryant	CHN	43.9
6	Joey Votto	CIN	43.7
7	Josh Donaldson	TOR	42.9
8	Trea Turner	WAS	41.7
9	Paul Goldschmidt	ARI	40.7
10	Gary Sanchez	NYA	40.2
11	Corey Seager	LAN	39.9
12	Andrew McCutchen	PIT	39.2
13	Giancarlo Stanton	NYA	38.1
14	Rhys Hoskins	PHI	37.5
15	George Springer	HOU	37.3
16	Francisco Lindor	CLE	36.2
17	Freddie Freeman	ATL	35.8
18	Buster Posey	SFN	35.6
18	Willson Contreras	CHN	35.6
20	Aaron Judge	NYA	34.6

Hitter VORP Percentiles

Percentile	Name	Team	VORP
99	Jose Altuve	HOU	44.2
90	Xander Bogaerts	BOS	24.5
80	J.P. Crawford	PHI	16.6
70	Brett Gardner	NYA	13.0
60	Brad Miller	TBA	9.0
50	Brian Anderson	MIA	6.2
40	Adonis Garcia	ATL	3.4
30	Juan Lagares	NYN	1.8
20	Max Stassi	HOU	0.8
10	Jose Rondon	SDN	-0.3
1	Luis Sardinas	BAL	-2.4

Base-Running Runs (BRR)

Rank	Name	Team	BRR
1	Billy Hamilton	CIN	10.5
2	Trea Turner	WAS	8.0
3	Dee Gordon	SEA	6.8
4	Raul Mondesi	KCA	5.4
5	Byron Buxton	MIN	4.8
6	Starling Marte	PIT	4.6
7	A.J. Pollock	ARI	3.4
7	Bradley Zimmer	CLE	3.4
9	Ben Revere	ANA	3.3
9	Jonathan Villar	MIL	3.3
9	Delino DeShields	TEX	3.3
9	Whit Merrifield	KCA	3.3
13	Cameron Maybin	HOU	3.0
13	Tim Anderson	CHA	3.0
15	Jose Altuve	HOU	2.9
15	Ozhaino Albies	ATL	2.9
17	Eduardo Nunez	BOS	2.8
17	Jose Peraza	CIN	2.8
17	Mookie Betts	BOS	2.8
20	Kevin Kiermaier	TBA	2.7

Base-Running Runs (BRR) Percentiles

Percentile	Name	Team	BRR
99	Raul Mondesi	KCA	5.4
90	Ryan Braun	MIL	1.1
80	Terrance Gore	KCA	0.4
70	Brian Goodwin	WAS	0.1
60	J.B. Shuck	MIA	-0.1
50	Christian Walker	ARI	-0.1
40	Jesus Sucre	TBA	-0.3
30	Eduardo Escobar	MIN	-0.5
20	Rhys Hoskins	PHI	-0.8
10	Matt Chapman	OAK	-1.0
1	Wilmer Flores	NYN	-1.4

Hitter WARP

Rank	Name	Team	WARP
1	Mike Trout	ANA	7.2
2	Buster Posey	SFN	5.6
3	Trea Turner	WAS	5.3
4	Paul Goldschmidt	ARI	5.0
5	Mookie Betts	BOS	4.9
6	Joey Votto	CIN	4.6
6	Carlos Correa	HOU	4.6
8	Gary Sanchez	NYA	4.4
8	Francisco Lindor	CLE	4.4
10	Lorenzo Cain	KCA	4.3
11	George Springer	HOU	4.1
11	Bryce Harper	WAS	4.1
11	Kris Bryant	CHN	4.1
14	Kevin Kiermaier	TBA	4.0
15	Giancarlo Stanton	NYA	3.9
15	Aaron Judge	NYA	3.9
17	Jose Altuve	HOU	3.8
17	Anthony Rizzo	CHN	3.8
17	Alex Bregman	HOU	3.8
20	Austin Barnes	LAN	3.7

Hitter WARP Percentiles

Percentile	Name	Team	WARP
99	Paul Goldschmidt	ARI	5.0
90	Michael Brantley	CLE	2.7
80	Kolten Wong	SLN	1.8
70	Ian Happ	CHN	1.3
60	Chris Iannetta	COL	0.8
50	Garrett Cooper	MIA	0.5
40	Wilmer Difo	WAS	0.3
30	A.J. Reed	HOU	0.1
20	Greg Garcia	SLN	0.0
10	Pedro Florimon	PHI	-0.1
1	Gerardo Parra	COL	-0.9

AL Hitter WARP

Rank	Name	Team	WARP
1	Mike Trout	ANA	7.2
2	Mookie Betts	BOS	4.9
3	Carlos Correa	HOU	4.6
4	Gary Sanchez	NYA	4.4
4	Francisco Lindor	CLE	4.4
6	Lorenzo Cain	KCA	4.3
7	George Springer	HOU	4.1
8	Kevin Kiermaier	TBA	4.0
9	Giancarlo Stanton	NYA	3.9
9	Aaron Judge	NYA	3.9

NL Hitter WARP

Rank	Name	Team	WARP
1	Buster Posey	SFN	5.6
2	Trea Turner	WAS	5.3
3	Paul Goldschmidt	ARI	5.0
4	Joey Votto	CIN	4.6
5	Bryce Harper	WAS	4.1
5	Kris Bryant	CHN	4.1
7	Anthony Rizzo	CHN	3.8
8	Austin Barnes	LAN	3.7
8	Corey Seager	LAN	3.7
10	Marcell Ozuna	SLN	3.4
10	Nolan Arenado	COL	3.4

Deserved Run Average (DRA) - Starters

Rank	Name	Team	DRA
1	Noah Syndergaard	NYN	3.12
2	Clayton Kershaw	LAN	3.23
3	Stephen Strasburg	WAS	3.34
4	Chris Sale	BOS	3.44
5	Aaron Nola	PHI	3.53
6	Lance McCullers	HOU	3.55
7	Max Scherzer	WAS	3.60
8	Luis Severino	NYA	3.62
9	Corey Kluber	CLE	3.67
9	Jacob deGrom	NYN	3.67
11	Luke Weaver	SLN	3.77
12	Carlos Martinez	SLN	3.78
12	Alex Wood	LAN	3.78
14	Jameson Taillon	PIT	3.80
15	Jose Quintana	CHN	3.84
16	Gerrit Cole	PIT	3.85
16	Jon Gray	COL	3.85
18	Kyle Hendricks	CHN	3.87
18	Michael Wacha	SLN	3.87
20	Robbie Ray	ARI	3.90

Deserved Run Average (DRA) - Starters Percentiles

Percentile	Name	Team	DRA
99	Noah Syndergaard	NYN	3.12
90	Luke Weaver	SLN	3.77
80	Carlos Carrasco	CLE	3.99
70	Garrett Richards	ANA	4.17
60	Sean Manaea	OAK	4.29
50	Tyler Chatwood	CHN	4.41
40	Trevor Williams	PIT	4.53
30	Justin Verlander	HOU	4.67
20	Lucas Giolito	CHA	4.85
10	Erasmo Ramirez	SEA	5.05
1	Jordan Zimmermann	DET	5.37

Deserved Run Average (DRA) - Relievers

Rank	Name	Team	DRA
1	Kenley Jansen	LAN	2.75
2	Craig Kimbrel	BOS	2.91
3	Aroldis Chapman	NYA	3.02
4	Roberto Osuna	TOR	3.12
5	Andrew Miller	CLE	3.28
6	Ken Giles	HOU	3.41
7	Dellin Betances	NYA	3.42
7	Felipe Rivero	PIT	3.42
9	Archie Bradley	ARI	3.43
10	Raisel Iglesias	CIN	3.47
11	Zach Britton	BAL	3.49
12	Edwin Diaz	SEA	3.51
13	Brad Hand	SDN	3.58
14	Liam Hendriks	OAK	3.67
14	David Robertson	NYA	3.67
14	Chris Devenski	HOU	3.67
14	Corey Knebel	MIL	3.67
18	Chad Green	NYA	3.68
19	Will Smith	SFN	3.72
20	Trevor Rosenthal	SLN	3.77

Deserved Run Average (DRA) - Relievers Percentiles

Percentile	Name	Team	DRA
99	Roberto Osuna	TOR	3.12
90	Jacob Barnes	MIL	4.02
80	Angel Sanchez	PIT	4.25
70	Derek Law	SFN	4.43
60	Daniel Stumpf	DET	4.56
50	Jim Johnson	ANA	4.69
40	Collin McHugh	HOU	4.80
30	Onelki Garcia	KCA	4.93
20	Josh Osich	SFN	5.08
10	Buddy Baumann	SDN	5.29
1	David Hess	BAL	5.92

Earned Run Average - Starters

Rank	Name	Team	ERA
1	Clayton Kershaw	LAN	2.80
2	Noah Syndergaard	NYN	2.89
3	Chris Sale	BOS	2.96
4	Stephen Strasburg	WAS	3.14
5	Lance McCullers	HOU	3.22
6	Corey Kluber	CLE	3.25
7	Madison Bumgarner	SFN	3.29
7	Alex Wood	LAN	3.29
9	Max Scherzer	WAS	3.37
10	Jacob deGrom	NYN	3.39
11	Aaron Nola	PHI	3.43
12	Jeff Samardzija	SFN	3.44
13	Luis Severino	NYA	3.45
14	Luke Weaver	SLN	3.49
15	Carlos Martinez	SLN	3.50
16	Robbie Ray	ARI	3.51
17	Carlos Carrasco	CLE	3.54
17	James Paxton	SEA	3.54
19	Chris Archer	TBA	3.55
19	Shohei Ohtani	ANA	3.55

Earned Run Average - Starters Percentiles

Percentile	Name	Team	ERA
99	Clayton Kershaw	LAN	2.80
90	Aaron Nola	PHI	3.43
80	Michael Wacha	SLN	3.60
70	Kyle Hendricks	CHN	3.76
60	Dinelson Lamet	SDN	3.93
50	Zach Davies	MIL	4.09
40	Danny Duffy	KCA	4.24
30	Kyle Freeland	COL	4.36
20	Lucas Giolito	CHA	4.58
10	Cole Hamels	TEX	4.75
1	Homer Bailey	CIN	5.12

Earned Run Average - Relievers

Rank	Name	Team	ERA
1	Kenley Jansen	LAN	2.18
2	Craig Kimbrel	BOS	2.31
3	Roberto Osuna	TOR	2.63
4	Aroldis Chapman	NYA	2.66
5	Andrew Miller	CLE	2.70
6	Will Smith	SFN	2.90
7	Archie Bradley	ARI	2.91
8	Ken Giles	HOU	2.92
9	Brad Hand	SDN	2.99
10	Edwin Diaz	SEA	3.01
11	Dellin Betances	NYA	3.05
11	Felipe Rivero	PIT	3.05
13	Zach Britton	BAL	3.17
14	Chris Devenski	HOU	3.20
15	Mark Melancon	SFN	3.26
16	Liam Hendriks	OAK	3.30
16	Raisel Iglesias	CIN	3.30
18	Alex Colome	TBA	3.33
19	David Robertson	NYA	3.35
19	Andrew Chafin	ARI	3.35

Earned Run Average - Relievers Percentiles

Percentile	Name	Team	ERA
99	Aroldis Chapman	NYA	2.66
90	Phil Maton	SDN	3.70
80	Trevor Oaks	KCA	3.96
70	Joe Jimenez	DET	4.14
60	Ryan Tepera	TOR	4.34
50	Sam Moll	SEA	4.53
40	Diego Castillo	TBA	4.68
30	Rafael Montero	NYN	4.83
20	Mike Dunn	COL	5.03
10	Brad Goldberg	CHA	5.29
1	Jeff Beliveau	CLE	6.04

Wins

Rank	Name	Team	W
1	Clayton Kershaw	LAN	15
1	Corey Kluber	CLE	15
3	Justin Verlander	HOU	14
3	Chris Sale	BOS	14
5	Jon Lester	CHN	13
5	Carlos Carrasco	CLE	13
5	Jeff Samardzija	SFN	13
5	Max Scherzer	WAS	13
5	Masahiro Tanaka	NYA	13
5	Dallas Keuchel	HOU	13
5	Sonny Gray	NYA	13
5	Trevor Bauer	CLE	13
5	Luis Severino	NYA	13
14	Zack Greinke	ARI	12
14	Gio Gonzalez	WAS	12
14	Cole Hamels	TEX	12
14	Charlie Morton	HOU	12
14	Jose Quintana	CHN	12
14	Madison Bumgarner	SFN	12
14	Rick Porcello	BOS	12
14	Tanner Roark	WAS	12
14	Stephen Strasburg	WAS	12
14	Kyle Hendricks	CHN	12
14	Lance McCullers	HOU	12

Wins Percentiles

Percentile	Name	Team	W
99	Carlos Carrasco	CLE	13
90	James Shields	CHA	9
80	Robert Gsellman	NYN	7
70	Andrew Heaney	ANA	4
60	Nick Vincent	SEA	3
50	Chris Devenski	HOU	3
40	T.J. McFarland	ARI	2
30	Nick Wittgren	MIA	2
20	Adam Kolarek	TBA	1
10	Victor Alcantara	DET	1
1	Josh Edgin	BAL	0

Strikeouts

Rank	Name	Team	SO
1	Chris Sale	BOS	255
2	Max Scherzer	WAS	224
3	Corey Kluber	CLE	221
4	Clayton Kershaw	LAN	219
5	Robbie Ray	ARI	211
6	Zack Greinke	ARI	204
7	Chris Archer	TBA	197
7	Stephen Strasburg	WAS	197
9	Luis Severino	NYA	195
10	Justin Verlander	HOU	194
11	Jacob deGrom	NYN	192
12	Carlos Carrasco	CLE	191
13	Jon Lester	CHN	187
13	Madison Bumgarner	SFN	187
13	Noah Syndergaard	NYN	187
16	Yu Darvish	LAN	183
16	Carlos Martinez	SLN	183
18	Jose Quintana	CHN	179
19	Sean Newcomb	ATL	177
20	Aaron Nola	PHI	176

Strikeouts Percentiles

Percentile	Name	Team	SO
99	Zack Greinke	ARI	204
90	Dallas Keuchel	HOU	144
80	Adalberto Mejia	MIN	106
70	Phil Maton	SDN	74
60	Ryan Borucki	TOR	62
50	Kelvin Herrera	KCA	53
40	Dario Alvarez	CHN	46
30	Jimmy Nelson	MIL	36
20	Tyler Herb	SFN	27
10	Jimmy Yacabonis	BAL	19
1	Brad Goldberg	CHA	10

WHIP - Starters

Rank	Name	Team	WHIP
1	Clayton Kershaw	LAN	0.98
2	Max Scherzer	WAS	1.08
3	Chris Sale	BOS	1.10
4	Yu Darvish	LAN	1.12
5	Stephen Strasburg	WAS	1.13
6	Madison Bumgarner	SFN	1.14
7	Jake Arrieta	CHN	1.15
8	Jacob deGrom	NYN	1.16
9	Corey Kluber	CLE	1.17
10	Noah Syndergaard	NYN	1.18
11	Zack Greinke	ARI	1.19
11	Aaron Nola	PHI	1.19
11	Luis Severino	NYA	1.19
11	Shohei Ohtani	ANA	1.19
15	Alex Wood	LAN	1.20
15	Kenta Maeda	LAN	1.20
17	Johnny Cueto	SFN	1.21
18	Chris Archer	TBA	1.22
18	Jeff Samardzija	SFN	1.22
18	Carlos Martinez	SLN	1.22
18	Kyle Hendricks	CHN	1.22
18	Yonny Chirinos	TBA	1.22

WHIP - Starters Percentiles

Percentile	Name	Team	WHIP
99	Clayton Kershaw	LAN	0.98
90	Luis Severino	NYA	1.19
80	Gerrit Cole	PIT	1.24
70	Justin Verlander	HOU	1.28
60	Danny Duffy	KCA	1.31
50	Matt Shoemaker	ANA	1.33
40	Jordan Montgomery	NYA	1.34
30	Robert Gsellman	NYN	1.36
20	Zack Wheeler	NYN	1.40
10	Ian Kennedy	KCA	1.43
1	James Shields	CHA	1.51

Saves

Rank	Name	Team	SV
1	Kenley Jansen	LAN	40
1	Aroldis Chapman	NYA	40
3	Craig Kimbrel	BOS	38
4	Corey Knebel	MIL	37
5	Fernando Rodney	MIN	35
5	Adam Ottavino	COL	35
5	Shane Greene	DET	35
8	Mark Melancon	SFN	33
9	Sean Doolittle	WAS	32
10	Alex Colome	TBA	31
10	Jeurys Familia	NYN	31
10	Roberto Osuna	TOR	31
13	Brad Ziegler	MIA	30
13	Zach Britton	BAL	30
13	Brandon Morrow	CHN	30
13	Cody Allen	CLE	30
13	Ken Giles	HOU	30
13	Archie Bradley	ARI	30
19	Hector Neris	PHI	28
19	Edwin Diaz	SEA	28

Strikeout Rate

Rank	Name	Team	SO%
1	Craig Kimbrel	BOS	38.8
2	Kenley Jansen	LAN	37.2
3	Dellin Betances	NYA	35.7
4	Andrew Miller	CLE	35.4
5	Aroldis Chapman	NYA	34.2
6	Corey Knebel	MIL	33.1
7	Carl Edwards Jr.	CHN	32.5
8	Edwin Diaz	SEA	31.8
9	Ken Giles	HOU	31.3
10	Phil Maton	SDN	31.0
11	Chris Sale	BOS	30.9
11	Alec Hansen	CHA	30.9
11	Forrest Whitley	HOU	30.9
14	David Robertson	NYA	30.8
15	Mitchell White	LAN	30.7
16	Alex Reyes	SLN	30.6
16	Jon Duplantier	ARI	30.6
18	Tommy Kahnle	NYA	30.5
18	Josh Hader	MIL	30.5
20	Chad Green	NYA	30.2
20	Max Scherzer	WAS	30.2

Strikeout Rate Percentiles

Percentile	Name	Team	SO%
99	Dellin Betances	NYA	35.7
90	Liam Hendriks	OAK	27.8
80	Josh Smoker	NYN	25.6
70	Juan Minaya	CHA	23.8
60	Luke Gregerson	SLN	23.0
50	Miguel Diaz	SDN	22.0
40	Josh Osich	SFN	21.3
30	Dan Jennings	TBA	20.2
20	Buck Farmer	DET	19.1
10	Jose Urena	MIA	17.2
1	Martin Perez	TEX	14.0

Walk Rate

Rank	Name	Team	BB%
1	Clayton Kershaw	LAN	6.0
2	Jeff Samardzija	SFN	6.2
3	Josh Tomlin	CLE	6.3
4	Ivan Nova	PIT	6.4
4	Chris Sale	BOS	6.4
6	Ty Blach	SFN	6.6
6	Madison Bumgarner	SFN	6.6
6	Rick Porcello	BOS	6.6
9	Mike Leake	SEA	6.8
9	Dario Agrazal	PIT	6.8
11	Max Scherzer	WAS	6.9
11	Zack Greinke	ARI	6.9
11	Cesar Valdez	TOR	6.9
11	Jordan Zimmermann	DET	6.9
11	Masahiro Tanaka	NYA	6.9
11	Miles Mikolas	SLN	6.9
17	Gerrit Cole	PIT	7.0
17	Johnny Cueto	SFN	7.0
17	Bartolo Colon	MIN	7.0
17	Alex Wells	BAL	7.0

Walk Rate Percentiles

Percentile	Name	Team	BB%
99	Josh Tomlin	CLE	6.3
90	Michael Fulmer	DET	7.6
80	Eric Skoglund	KCA	8.2
70	Chris O'Grady	MIA	8.4
60	Vincent Velasquez	PHI	8.7
50	Jhoulys Chacin	MIL	9.1
40	A.J. Schugel	PIT	9.4
30	Michael Lorenzen	CIN	9.8
20	Danny Farquhar	CHA	10.2
10	Amir Garrett	CIN	11.0
1	Kyle Barraclough	MIA	12.7

Fastball Velocity

Rank	Name	Team	FB Velo
1	Aroldis Chapman	NYA	102.33
2	Alex Reyes	SLN	100.03
3	Edwin Diaz	SEA	100.00
4	Noah Syndergaard	NYN	99.82
5	Frankie Montas	OAK	99.77
6	Dellin Betances	NYA	99.46
7	Nathan Eovaldi	TBA	99.45
8	Walker Buehler	LAN	99.40
9	Felipe Rivero	PIT	99.37
10	Ken Giles	HOU	99.33
11	Kelvin Herrera	KCA	99.29
12	Arodys Vizcaino	ATL	99.04
13	Luis Severino	NYA	98.99
14	Keynan Middleton	ANA	98.96
15	Joe Kelly	BOS	98.94
16	Craig Kimbrel	BOS	98.90
16	Luiz Gohara	ATL	98.90
18	Tommy Kahnle	NYA	98.79
19	Enny Romero	WAS	98.77
20	Carlos Martinez	SLN	98.70

Fastball Velocity Percentiles

Percentile	Name	Team	FB Velo
99	Noah Syndergaard	NYN	99.82
90	Jose Valdez	ANA	97.49
80	Edubray Ramos	PHI	96.55
70	Sean Doolittle	WAS	95.64
60	Jack Flaherty	SLN	94.89
50	Tyler Skaggs	ANA	94.13
40	Jose Quintana	CHN	93.48
30	Dan Jennings	TBA	92.90
20	Mark Leiter	PHI	92.05
10	Christian Bergman	SEA	90.55
1	Jason Vargas	KCA	86.75

Ground-ball Rate

Rank	Name	Team	GB%
1	Zach Britton	BAL	68.2
2	Scott Alexander	LAN	60.8
3	Brad Ziegler	MIA	60.4
3	Marc Rzepczynski	SEA	60.4
5	Sam Dyson	SFN	60.0
6	T.J. McFarland	ARI	59.4
7	Richard Bleier	BAL	59.2
8	Dallas Keuchel	HOU	58.8
9	Blake Treinen	OAK	58.6
10	Clayton Richard	SDN	58.2
11	Alex Claudio	TEX	58.1
12	Marcus Stroman	TOR	57.8
13	Jared Hughes	CIN	57.5
14	Jeurys Familia	NYN	57.1
15	Dan Otero	CLE	56.5
16	Luis Garcia	PHI	55.8
17	Dan Jennings	TBA	55.6
18	D.J. Snelten	SFN	55.4
19	Jeremy Jeffress	MIL	55.3
20	Brandon Kintzler	WAS	55.2

Ground-ball Rate Percentiles

Percentile	Name	Team	GB%
99	Brad Ziegler	MIA	60.4
90	Chris Lee	BAL	51.8
80	Jacob Barnes	MIL	49.4
70	Ty Blach	SFN	47.4
60	Ryan Tepera	TOR	45.8
50	Brandon Finnegan	CIN	44.9
40	Corey Knebel	MIL	43.8
30	Tyler Mahle	CIN	42.7
20	Chris Hatcher	OAK	41.4
10	Craig Kimbrel	BOS	39.1
1	Ariel Miranda	SEA	35.4

cFIP - Starters

Rank	Name	Team	cFIP
1	Noah Syndergaard	NYN	69.2
2	Clayton Kershaw	LAN	73.2
3	Stephen Strasburg	WAS	76.2
4	Chris Sale	BOS	79.2
5	Aaron Nola	PHI	81.4
6	Lance McCullers	HOU	81.6
7	Max Scherzer	WAS	84.6
8	Luis Severino	NYA	84.7
9	Jacob deGrom	NYN	85.8
10	Corey Kluber	CLE	86.3
11	Luke Weaver	SLN	88.5
12	Carlos Martinez	SLN	88.8
12	Alex Wood	LAN	88.8
14	Jameson Taillon	PIT	89.0
15	Jose Quintana	CHN	90.7
16	Jon Gray	COL	91.1
17	Gerrit Cole	PIT	91.8
17	Kyle Hendricks	CHN	91.8
17	Michael Wacha	SLN	91.8
20	Robbie Ray	ARI	92.5

cFIP - Starters Percentiles

Percentile	Name	Team	cFIP
99	Noah Syndergaard	NYN	69.2
90	Luke Weaver	SLN	88.5
80	Carlos Carrasco	CLE	95.3
70	Garrett Richards	ANA	100.2
60	Sean Manaea	OAK	103.8
50	Johnny Cueto	SFN	107.5
40	Robert Gsellman	NYN	110.3
30	Rick Porcello	BOS	115.1
20	Felix Hernandez	SEA	119.7
10	Jake Junis	KCA	124.5
1	Marco Estrada	TOR	135.4

cFIP - Relievers

Rank	Name	Team	cFIP
1	Kenley Jansen	LAN	54
2	Craig Kimbrel	BOS	60
3	Aroldis Chapman	NYA	63
4	Roberto Osuna	TOR	65
5	Andrew Miller	CLE	73
5	Archie Bradley	ARI	73
7	Felipe Rivero	PIT	75
7	Ken Giles	HOU	75
9	Zach Britton	BAL	76
9	Edwin Diaz	SEA	76
11	Dellin Betances	NYA	77
11	Raisel Iglesias	CIN	77
13	Brad Hand	SDN	79
14	Corey Knebel	MIL	81
15	David Robertson	NYA	82
15	Trevor Rosenthal	SLN	82
17	Liam Hendriks	OAK	84
17	Chad Green	NYA	84
17	Chris Devenski	HOU	84
20	Will Smith	SFN	85

cFIP - Relievers Percentiles

Percentile	Name	Team	cFIP
99	Roberto Osuna	TOR	65.2
90	Tyler Glasnow	PIT	94.0
80	Luis Avilan	CHA	100.7
70	Carson Smith	BOS	105.1
60	Hansel Robles	NYN	109.2
50	Trevor Gott	WAS	112.7
40	Victor Arano	PHI	116.4
30	Rob Scahill	CHA	120.3
20	Eddie Butler	CHN	123.4
10	Dean Deetz	HOU	129.7
1	Zac Reininger	DET	146.7

Pitcher WARP

Rank	Name	Team	WARP
1	Chris Sale	BOS	4.6
2	Clayton Kershaw	LAN	4.2
3	Corey Kluber	CLE	3.9
3	Noah Syndergaard	NYN	3.9
5	Luis Severino	NYA	3.6
6	Stephen Strasburg	WAS	3.5
7	Max Scherzer	WAS	3.3
8	Lance McCullers	HOU	3.2
9	Aaron Nola	PHI	3.1
10	Jacob deGrom	NYN	3.0
11	Carlos Martinez	SLN	2.8
11	Carlos Carrasco	CLE	2.8
13	Jose Quintana	CHN	2.7
13	Garrett Richards	ANA	2.7
13	Michael Fulmer	DET	2.7
13	Zack Greinke	ARI	2.7
17	Gerrit Cole	PIT	2.6
18	Chris Archer	TBA	2.5
18	Jameson Taillon	PIT	2.5
18	James Paxton	SEA	2.5
18	Kyle Hendricks	CHN	2.5
18	Marcus Stroman	TOR	2.5
18	Shohei Ohtani	ANA	2.5

Pitcher WARP Percentiles

Percentile	Name	Team	WARP
99	Stephen Strasburg	WAS	3.5
90	David Price	BOS	1.5
80	Chris Devenski	HOU	0.9
70	Will Harris	HOU	0.6
60	Luis Cessa	NYA	0.4
50	Hyun-jin Ryu	LAN	0.2
40	Chris Flexen	NYN	0.2
30	Rob Zastryzny	CHN	0.1
20	Kevin Shackelford	CIN	0.0
10	Rookie Davis	CIN	-0.1
1	John Brebbia	SLN	-0.4

AL Pitcher WARP

Rank	Name	Team	WARP
1	Chris Sale	BOS	4.6
2	Corey Kluber	CLE	3.9
3	Luis Severino	NYA	3.6
4	Lance McCullers	HOU	3.2
5	Carlos Carrasco	CLE	2.8
6	Garrett Richards	ANA	2.7
6	Michael Fulmer	DET	2.7
8	Chris Archer	TBA	2.5
8	James Paxton	SEA	2.5
8	Marcus Stroman	TOR	2.5
8	Shohei Ohtani	ANA	2.5

NL Pitcher WARP

Rank	Name	Team	WARP
1	Clayton Kershaw	LAN	4.2
2	Noah Syndergaard	NYN	3.9
3	Stephen Strasburg	WAS	3.5
4	Max Scherzer	WAS	3.3
5	Aaron Nola	PHI	3.1
6	Jacob deGrom	NYN	3.0
7	Carlos Martinez	SLN	2.8
8	Zack Greinke	ARI	2.7
8	Jose Quintana	CHN	2.7
10	Gerrit Cole	PIT	2.6

Catcher WARP

Rank	Name	Team	WARP
1	Buster Posey	SFN	5.6
2	Gary Sanchez	NYA	4.4
3	Austin Barnes	LAN	3.7
4	Tyler Flowers	ATL	3.0
5	Yasmani Grandal	LAN	2.9
6	Willson Contreras	CHN	2.8
6	Austin Hedges	SDN	2.8
6	Travis d'Arnaud	NYN	2.8
9	Russell Martin	TOR	2.1
9	J.T. Realmuto	MIA	2.1

Catcher FRAA

Rank	Name	Team	FRAA
1	Tyler Flowers	ATL	20.3
2	Buster Posey	SFN	19.9
2	Austin Hedges	SDN	19.9
4	Austin Barnes	LAN	15.9
5	Yasmani Grandal	LAN	15.7
6	Roberto Perez	CLE	14.3
7	Tomas Nido	NYN	14.1
8	Martin Maldonado	ANA	13.1
9	Caleb Joseph	BAL	12.4
10	Jeff Mathis	ARI	11.8

Catcher TAv

Rank	Name	Team	TAv
1	Gary Sanchez	NYA	.292
2	Willson Contreras	CHN	.290
3	Buster Posey	SFN	.283
4	Austin Barnes	LAN	.277
5	Evan Gattis	HOU	.268
6	Yasmani Grandal	LAN	.266
7	J.T. Realmuto	MIA	.261
8	Jonathan Lucroy	COL	.260
8	Russell Martin	TOR	.260
10	Travis d'Arnaud	NYN	.258

First Base WARP

Rank	Name	Team	WARP
1	Paul Goldschmidt	ARI	5.0
2	Joey Votto	CIN	4.6
3	Anthony Rizzo	CHN	3.8
4	Freddie Freeman	ATL	3.2
5	Jose Abreu	CHA	3.1
6	Cody Bellinger	LAN	2.9
6	Miguel Cabrera	DET	2.9
8	Edwin Encarnacion	CLE	2.8
9	Brandon Belt	SFN	2.5
10	Eric Hosmer	KCA	2.3

First Base FRAA

Rank	Name	Team	FRAA
1	Paul Goldschmidt	ARI	9.0
2	Danny Valencia	SEA	6.8
3	Yulieski Gurriel	HOU	6.6
4	Anthony Rizzo	CHN	5.9
4	Brandon Belt	SFN	5.9
4	Matt Olson	OAK	5.9
7	Brandon Moss	KCA	5.0
8	Cody Bellinger	LAN	4.0
9	Jose Abreu	CHA	3.6
10	Will Craig	PIT	2.9

First Base TAv

Rank	Name	Team	TAv
1	Joey Votto	CIN	.313
2	Paul Goldschmidt	ARI	.308
3	Freddie Freeman	ATL	.306
4	Miguel Cabrera	DET	.296
5	Anthony Rizzo	CHN	.295
6	Edwin Encarnacion	CLE	.293
7	Jose Abreu	CHA	.291
8	Cody Bellinger	LAN	.287
9	Brandon Belt	SFN	.282
10	Matt Carpenter	SLN	.279
10	Josh Bell	PIT	.279

Second Base WARP

Rank	Name	Team	WARP
1	Jose Altuve	HOU	3.8
2	Robinson Cano	SEA	3.0
3	Ozhaino Albies	ATL	2.9
4	Brian Dozier	MIN	2.5
5	Daniel Murphy	WAS	2.2
6	Yoan Moncada	CHA	2.1
7	Neil Walker	MIL	2.0
7	Cesar Hernandez	PHI	2.0
7	Joe Panik	SFN	2.0
7	Jason Kipnis	CLE	2.0

Second Base FRAA

Rank	Name	Team	FRAA
1	Dixon Machado	DET	11.5
2	Ozhaino Albies	ATL	5.6
3	DJ LeMahieu	COL	5.3
4	Danny Espinosa	TBA	5.2
5	Kolten Wong	SLN	4.7
6	Enrique Hernandez	LAN	4.3
7	Travis Demeritte	ATL	4.1
8	Whit Merrifield	KCA	4.0
9	Rougned Odor	TEX	3.5
10	Kean Wong	TBA	3.3

Second Base TAv

Rank	Name	Team	TAv
1	Jose Altuve	HOU	.288
2	Robinson Cano	SEA	.279
3	Daniel Murphy	WAS	.272
4	Brian Dozier	MIN	.266
5	Joe Panik	SFN	.263
5	Devon Travis	TOR	.263
7	Neil Walker	MIL	.262
7	Dustin Pedroia	BOS	.262
9	Wilmer Flores	NYN	.261
10	Aledmys Diaz	TOR	.260

Third Base WARP

Rank	Name	Team	WARP
1	Kris Bryant	CHN	4.1
2	Alex Bregman	HOU	3.8
3	Kyle Seager	SEA	3.6
3	Josh Donaldson	TOR	3.6
5	Matt Chapman	OAK	3.5
6	Nolan Arenado	COL	3.4
7	Manny Machado	BAL	3.2
8	Justin Turner	LAN	2.6
8	Adrian Beltre	TEX	2.6
10	Miguel Sano	MIN	2.1
10	Todd Frazier	NYA	2.1

Third Base FRAA

Rank	Name	Team	FRAA
1	Matt Chapman	OAK	16.7
2	Kyle Seager	SEA	11.4
3	Nolan Arenado	COL	9.0
4	Alex Bregman	HOU	6.3
5	Rafael Devers	BOS	5.7
6	Brian Anderson	MIA	5.4
6	Ke'Bryan Hayes	PIT	5.4
8	Manny Machado	BAL	4.8
9	Jung-ho Kang	PIT	3.9
9	Tyler Saladino	CHA	3.9

Third Base TAv

Rank	Name	Team	TAv
1	Kris Bryant	CHN	.305
2	Josh Donaldson	TOR	.299
3	Justin Turner	LAN	.287
4	Alex Bregman	HOU	.281
5	Nolan Arenado	COL	.278
6	Manny Machado	BAL	.277
6	Miguel Sano	MIN	.277
8	Adrian Beltre	TEX	.276
8	Anthony Rendon	WAS	.276
10	Kyle Seager	SEA	.274

Shortstop WARP

Rank	Name	Team	WARP
1	Trea Turner	WAS	5.3
2	Carlos Correa	HOU	4.6
3	Francisco Lindor	CLE	4.4
4	Corey Seager	LAN	3.7
5	Troy Tulowitzki	TOR	2.3
5	Elvis Andrus	TEX	2.3
7	Paul DeJong	SLN	2.2
8	Andrelton Simmons	ANA	2.1
8	Marcus Semien	OAK	2.1
10	Trevor Story	COL	2.0

Shortstop FRAA

Rank	Name	Team	FRAA
1	Trea Turner	WAS	10.9
2	Francisco Lindor	CLE	8.1
3	Orlando Arcia	MIL	7.7
4	Andrelton Simmons	ANA	6.7
5	Elvis Andrus	TEX	5.8
6	Yu-Cheng Chang	CLE	5.3
7	Eric Stamets	CLE	4.5
8	Addison Russell	CHN	4.4
9	Adeiny Hechavarria	TBA	4.1
10	Alcides Escobar	KCA	4.0

Shortstop TAv

Rank	Name	Team	TAv
1	Carlos Correa	HOU	.302
2	Corey Seager	LAN	.289
3	Trea Turner	WAS	.278
4	Francisco Lindor	CLE	.276
5	Troy Tulowitzki	TOR	.267
6	Paul DeJong	SLN	.265
7	Xander Bogaerts	BOS	.263
8	Trevor Story	COL	.262
9	Marcus Semien	OAK	.261
10	Yangervis Solarte	SDN	.260

Left Field WARP

Rank	Name	Team	WARP
1	Yoenis Cespedes	NYN	3.3
2	Rhys Hoskins	PHI	3.1
2	Adam Eaton	WAS	3.1
4	Chris Taylor	LAN	3.0
5	Justin Upton	ANA	2.8
6	Michael Brantley	CLE	2.7
6	Starling Marte	PIT	2.7
8	Andrew Benintendi	BOS	2.5
9	Tommy Pham	SLN	2.2
10	Corey Dickerson	TBA	2.0
10	Trey Mancini	BAL	2.0

Left Field FRAA

Rank	Name	Team	FRAA
1	Adam Eaton	WAS	14.4
2	Yoenis Cespedes	NYN	9.6
3	Chris Taylor	LAN	6.8
4	Brett Gardner	NYA	6.1
5	Chris Heisey	WAS	5.8
6	Adam Duvall	CIN	5.0
7	Michael Brantley	CLE	4.9
8	Nick Delmonico	CHA	4.8
9	Daniel Robertson	CLE	4.7
10	Jose Pirela	SDN	4.6

Left Field TAv

Rank	Name	Team	TAv
1	Rhys Hoskins	PHI	.298
2	Kyle Schwarber	CHN	.283
3	Tommy Pham	SLN	.279
4	Justin Upton	ANA	.276
4	Khris Davis	OAK	.276
6	Trey Mancini	BAL	.275
7	Corey Dickerson	TBA	.274
7	Yoenis Cespedes	NYN	.274
7	Ryan Braun	MIL	.274
10	Andrew Benintendi	BOS	.273
10	Michael Brantley	CLE	.273

Center Field WARP

Rank	Name	Team	WARP
1	Mike Trout	ANA	7.2
2	Lorenzo Cain	KCA	4.3
3	George Springer	HOU	4.1
4	Kevin Kiermaier	TBA	4.0
5	Byron Buxton	MIN	3.4
6	Ender Inciarte	ATL	2.7
7	Andrew McCutchen	PIT	2.6
8	A.J. Pollock	ARI	2.4
9	Bradley Zimmer	CLE	2.2
9	Christian Yelich	MIA	2.2
9	Charlie Blackmon	COL	2.2
9	Odubel Herrera	PHI	2.2

Center Field FRAA

Rank	Name	Team	FRAA
1	Kevin Kiermaier	TBA	18.0
2	Byron Buxton	MIN	16.9
3	Lorenzo Cain	KCA	15.4
4	Ender Inciarte	ATL	10.3
5	Bradley Zimmer	CLE	7.4
6	Manuel Margot	SDN	7.1
7	Cristian Pache	ATL	6.1
8	Steven Duggar	SFN	6.0
9	Jose Siri	CIN	5.4
10	Rusney Castillo	BOS	3.9

Center Field TAv

Rank	Name	Team	TAv
1	Mike Trout	ANA	.334
2	George Springer	HOU	.290
2	Andrew McCutchen	PIT	.290
4	Christian Yelich	MIA	.279
5	Joc Pederson	LAN	.277
6	Dexter Fowler	SLN	.269
6	A.J. Pollock	ARI	.269
6	Charlie Blackmon	COL	.269
9	Odubel Herrera	PHI	.264
9	Ian Happ	CHN	.264

Right Field WARP

Rank	Name	Team	WARP
1	Mookie Betts	BOS	4.9
2	Bryce Harper	WAS	4.1
3	Aaron Judge	NYA	3.9
3	Giancarlo Stanton	NYA	3.9
5	Marcell Ozuna	SLN	3.4
6	David Peralta	ARI	3.3
7	Yasiel Puig	LAN	3.2
8	Mitch Haniger	SEA	2.9
9	Nelson Cruz	SEA	2.8
10	Jose Bautista	TOR	2.6

Right Field FRAA

Rank	Name	Team	FRAA
1	David Peralta	ARI	18.3
2	Mookie Betts	BOS	15.2
3	Marcell Ozuna	SLN	14.5
4	Teoscar Hernandez	TOR	5.2
4	Mitch Haniger	SEA	5.2
6	Sandro Fabian	SFN	5.1
6	Jason Heyward	CHN	5.1
8	Yasiel Puig	LAN	4.9
8	Magneuris Sierra	MIA	4.9
10	Shane Robinson	ANA	4.5

Right Field TAv

Rank	Name	Team	TAv
1	Bryce Harper	WAS	.310
2	Giancarlo Stanton	NYA	.307
3	Aaron Judge	NYA	.294
4	Nelson Cruz	SEA	.291
5	J.D. Martinez	ARI	.290
6	Michael Conforto	NYN	.288
6	Mookie Betts	BOS	.288
6	Yasiel Puig	LAN	.288
9	Mitch Haniger	SEA	.282
10	Domingo Santana	MIL	.278

Catcher Framing Runs

Rank	Name	Team	Framing Runs
1	Tyler Flowers	ATL	26.3
2	Austin Barnes	LAN	18.5
3	Austin Hedges	SDN	16.7
4	Buster Posey	SFN	15.3
5	Yasmani Grandal	LAN	15.0
6	Tomas Nido	NYN	13.4
7	Travis d'Arnaud	NYN	12.0
8	Roberto Perez	CLE	11.8
9	Martin Maldonado	ANA	11.4
10	Caleb Joseph	BAL	11.2
11	Miguel Montero	TOR	10.5
12	Christian Vazquez	BOS	10.4
13	Jeff Mathis	ARI	10.1
14	Jason Castro	MIN	9.7
15	Mike Zunino	SEA	8.9
16	Jose Trevino	TEX	8.5
17	Russell Martin	TOR	7.9
18	John Ryan Murphy	ARI	6.1
19	Yadier Molina	SLN	4.9
19	Francisco Cervelli	PIT	4.9

Catcher Blocking Runs

Rank	Name	Team	Blocking Runs
1	Robinson Chirinos	TEX	3.0
2	Roberto Perez	CLE	2.3
3	Salvador Perez	KCA	1.8
3	Buster Posey	SFN	1.8
3	Caleb Joseph	BAL	1.8
6	Tucker Barnhart	CIN	1.7
6	Austin Hedges	SDN	1.7
8	Martin Maldonado	ANA	1.2
8	Willson Contreras	CHN	1.2
8	J.T. Realmuto	MIA	1.2
11	Brian McCann	HOU	1.1
12	Yadier Molina	SLN	1.0
13	Jesus Sucre	TBA	0.9
13	Austin Barnes	LAN	0.9
15	Kurt Suzuki	ATL	0.8
15	Travis d'Arnaud	NYN	0.8
15	Jose Trevino	TEX	0.8
18	Dan Jansen	TOR	0.7
19	Matt Wieters	WAS	0.6
20	Juan Graterol	ANA	0.5
20	Bryan Holaday	DET	0.5

Catcher Throwing Runs

Rank	Name	Team	Throwing Runs
1	Welington Castillo	CHA	2.7
2	Martin Maldonado	ANA	2.2
3	Gary Sanchez	NYA	2.1
4	Buster Posey	SFN	2.0
5	Tucker Barnhart	CIN	1.9
6	Salvador Perez	KCA	1.8
7	Christian Vazquez	BOS	1.4
7	James McCann	DET	1.4
9	Jonathan Lucroy	COL	1.3
10	Roberto Perez	CLE	1.1
11	Sandy Leon	BOS	1.0
11	J.T. Realmuto	MIA	1.0
13	Austin Hedges	SDN	0.9
14	Rene Rivera	CHN	0.8
14	Manny Pina	MIL	0.8
14	Tony Wolters	COL	0.8
14	Will Smith	LAN	0.8
18	Jeff Mathis	ARI	0.7
18	Yan Gomes	CLE	0.7
20	Yadier Molina	SLN	0.6

AL Hitter Rookie WARP

Rank	Name	Team	ROOKIE WARP
1	Willie Calhoun	TEX	1.2
2	Zach Granite	MIN	0.6
2	Austin Hays	BAL	0.6
4	Dan Vogelbach	SEA	0.5
5	Bryce Brentz	BOS	0.4
6	Joey Wendle	TBA	0.3
6	Christian Arroyo	TBA	0.3
6	Mitch Garver	MIN	0.3
9	Kyle Higashioka	NYA	0.2
9	Sam Travis	BOS	0.2
9	Greg Allen	CLE	0.2

AL Pitcher Rookie WARP

Rank	Name	Team	ROOKIE WARP
1	Joe Jimenez	DET	0.6
2	Jose De Leon	TBA	0.5
3	Chih-Wei Hu	TBA	0.4
3	Ronald Herrera	TEX	0.4
3	Dietrich Enns	MIN	0.4
3	Andrew Kittredge	TBA	0.4
7	John Curtiss	MIN	0.3
7	Hector Velazquez	BOS	0.3
7	Domingo German	NYA	0.3
7	Ryne Stanek	TBA	0.3

NL Hitter Rookie WARP

Rank	Name	Team	ROOKIE WARP
1	J.P. Crawford	PHI	1.8
2	Brian Anderson	MIA	1.2
3	Jesse Winker	CIN	1.1
4	Lewis Brinson	MIL	1.0
4	Victor Robles	WAS	1.0
6	Brett Phillips	MIL	0.7
6	Ryan McMahon	COL	0.7
8	Phil Ervin	CIN	0.6
8	Mark Zagunis	CHN	0.6
10	Lane Adams	ATL	0.5
10	Carson Kelly	SLN	0.5
10	Austin Slater	SFN	0.5
10	Garrett Cooper	MIA	0.5

NL Pitcher Rookie WARP

Rank	Name	Team	ROOKIE WARP
1	Alex Reyes	SLN	1.0
1	Brandon Woodruff	MIL	1.0
3	Luiz Gohara	ATL	0.9
4	Dillon Peters	MIA	0.8
5	Jack Flaherty	SLN	0.7
6	Erick Fedde	WAS	0.4
7	Angel Sanchez	PIT	0.3
7	A.J. Minter	ATL	0.3
7	Anthony Banda	ARI	0.3
10	Drew Steckenrider	MIA	0.2
10	Tyler Mahle	CIN	0.2
10	Wilmer Font	LAN	0.2
10	Caleb Smith	MIA	0.2
10	Tyler Webb	MIL	0.2
10	Daniel Winkler	ATL	0.2
10	Hoby Milner	PHI	0.2
10	Alec Mills	CHN	0.2
10	Chris O'Grady	MIA	0.2
10	Austin Brice	CIN	0.2
10	Walker Buehler	LAN	0.2
10	Taylor Williams	MIL	0.2
10	Chris Flexen	NYN	0.2

Hitter WARP Declines

Rank	Name	Team	WARP 2017	WARP 2018	WARP DIFF
1	Charlie Blackmon	COL	7.9	2.2	-5.7
2	Zack Cozart	ANA	5.3	0.4	-4.9
3	Giancarlo Stanton	NYA	8.5	3.9	-4.6
4	Jose Ramirez	CLE	6.3	1.9	-4.4
5	Anthony Rendon	WAS	6.2	2.0	-4.2
6	Nolan Arenado	COL	6.8	3.4	-3.4
6	Aaron Judge	NYA	7.3	3.9	-3.4
6	Joey Votto	CIN	8.0	4.6	-3.4
6	Tommy Pham	SLN	5.6	2.2	-3.4
6	Daniel Murphy	WAS	5.6	2.2	-3.4

Hitter WARP Improvements

Rank	Name	Team	WARP 2017	WARP 2018	WARP DIFF
1	Adam Eaton	WAS	0.7	3.1	2.4
2	Troy Tulowitzki	TOR	0.3	2.3	2.0
3	Manny Machado	BAL	1.3	3.2	1.9
3	Tomas Nido	NYN	0.0	1.9	1.9
5	Ozhaino Albies	ATL	1.1	2.9	1.8
6	Trea Turner	WAS	3.7	5.3	1.6
6	Jose Bautista	TOR	1.0	2.6	1.6
6	Greg Bird	NYA	0.0	1.6	1.6
6	Wilson Ramos	TBA	0.0	1.6	1.6
10	Stephen Piscotty	OAK	0.1	1.5	1.4
10	Robinson Cano	SEA	1.6	3.0	1.4

Pitcher WARP Declines

Rank	Name	Team	WARP 2017	WARP 2018	WARP DIFF
1	Corey Kluber	CLE	8.0	3.9	-4.1
1	Max Scherzer	WAS	7.4	3.3	-4.1
3	Justin Verlander	HOU	5.4	1.6	-3.7
4	Jason Vargas	KCA	3.5	-0.0	-3.5
5	Jimmy Nelson	MIL	3.9	0.5	-3.4
6	Ervin Santana	MIN	4.3	1.0	-3.3
7	Gio Gonzalez	WAS	5.0	1.8	-3.2
8	Zack Greinke	ARI	5.8	2.7	-3.1
8	Brad Peacock	HOU	3.9	0.8	-3.1
8	Chris Sale	BOS	7.6	4.6	-3.1

Pitcher WARP Improvements

Rank	Name	Team	WARP 2017	WARP 2018	WARP DIFF
1	Noah Syndergaard	NYN	0.7	3.9	3.1
2	Garrett Richards	ANA	0.7	2.7	2.0
3	Michael Wacha	SLN	0.7	2.3	1.6
3	Carlos Rodon	CHA	0.3	1.8	1.6
5	Luke Weaver	SLN	0.9	2.3	1.4
5	Rick Porcello	BOS	0.1	1.5	1.4
7	Zach Britton	BAL	0.1	1.2	1.1
8	Jerad Eickhoff	PHI	0.2	1.3	1.0
8	Brandon Woodruff	MIL	-0.0	1.0	1.0
8	Vincent Velasquez	PHI	0.0	1.0	1.0

Team Codes

CODE	TEAM	LG	AFF.	Name
ABE	Aberdeen	NYP	Orioles	IronBirds
ABQ	Albuquerque	PCL	Rockies	Isotopes
AKR	Akron	EAS	Indians	RubberDucks
ALT	Altoona	EAS	Pirates	Curve
ANA	Los Angeles	AL	-	Angels
ANG	AZL Angels	AZL	Angels	-
ARI	Arizona	NL	-	D-backs
ARK	Arkansas	TEX	Mariners	Travelers
ART	Artemisa	CNS	-	
ASH	Asheville	SAL	Rockies	Tourists
AST	GCL Astros	GCL	Astros	GCL Astros
ATH	AZL Athletics	AZL	Athletics	-
ATL	Atlanta	NL	-	Braves
AUB	Auburn	NYP	Nationals	Doubledays
AUG	Augusta	SAL	Giants	GreenJackets
BAL	Baltimore	AL	-	Orioles
BAT	Batavia	NYP	Marlins	Muckdogs
BCA	Buies Creek	CAR	Astros	Astros
BGR	Bowling Green	MID	Rays	Hot Rods
BIL	Billings	PIO	Reds	Mustangs
BIN	Binghamton	EAS	Mets	Rumble Ponies
BIR	Birmingham	SOU	White Sox	Barons
BLJ	GCL Blue Jays	GCL	Blue Jays	GCL Blue Jays
BLT	Beloit	MID	Athletics	Snappers
BLU	Bluefield	APP	Blue Jays	Blue Jays
BLX	Biloxi	SOU	Brewers	Shuckers
BNC	Burlington	APP	Royals	Royals
BOI	Boise	NWL	Rockies	Hawks
BOS	Boston	AL	-	Red Sox
BOW	Bowie	EAS	Orioles	Baysox
BRA	GCL Braves	GCL	Braves	GCL Braves
BRD	Bradenton	FSL	Pirates	Marauders
BRI	Bristol	APP	Pirates	Pirates
BRO	Brooklyn	NYP	Mets	Cyclones
BRR	AZL Brewers	AZL	Brewers	-
BRV	Florida	FSL	Braves	Fire Frogs
BUF	Buffalo	INT	Blue Jays	Bisons
BUR	Burlington	MID	Angels	Bees
CAR	Carolina	CAR	Brewers	Mudcats
CCH	Corpus Christi	TEX	Astros	Hooks
CDR	Cedar Rapids	MID	Twins	Kernels
CFG	Cienfuegos	CNS	-	
CHA	Chicago	AL	-	White Sox
CHB	Chiba Lotte	NPB	-	Marines
CHN	Chicago	NL	-	Cubs
CHR	Charlotte	INT	White Sox	Knights
CHT	Chattanooga	SOU	Twins	Lookouts
CHU	Chunichi	NPB	-	Dragons
CIN	AZL Reds	AZL	Reds	-
CIN	Cincinnati	NL	-	Reds
CLE	AZL Indians	AZL	Indians	-
CLE	Cleveland	AL	-	Indians
CLN	Clinton	MID	Mariners	LumberKings
CLR	Clearwater	FSL	Phillies	Threshers
COH	Columbus	INT	Indians	Clippers

CODE	TEAM	LG	AFF.	Name
COL	Columbia	SAL	Mets	Fireflies
COL	Colorado	NL	-	Rockies
CRD	GCL Cardinals	GCL	Cardinals	GCL Cardinals
CSC	Charleston	SAL	Yankees	RiverDogs
CSP	Col. Springs	PCL	Brewers	Sky Sox
CUB	AZL Cubs	AZL	Cubs	-
DAN	DSL Angels	DSL	Angels	DSL Angels
DAR	DSL Astros Orange	DSL	Astros	DSL Astros Orange
DAS	DSL Astros Blue	DSL	Astros	DSL Astros Blue
DAT	DSL Athletics	DSL	Athletics	DSL Athletics
DAY	Daytona	FSL	Reds	Tortugas
DBL	DSL Blue Jays	DSL	Blue Jays	DSL Blue Jays
DBR	DSL Braves	DSL	Braves	DSL Braves
DBW	DSL Brewers	DSL	Brewers	DSL Brewers
DCA	DSL Cardinals	DSL	Cardinals	DSL Cardinals
DCH	DSL Cubs2	DSL	Cubs	DSL Cubs2
DCU	DSL Cubs1	DSL	Cubs	DSL Cubs1
DDB	DSL D-backs2	DSL	D-backs	DSL D-backs2
DDG	DSL Dodgers2	DSL	Dodgers	DSL Dodgers2
DDI	DSL D-backs1	DSL	D-backs	DSL D-backs1
DDO	DSL Dodgers1	DSL	Dodgers	DSL Dodgers1
DDR	DSL Rays1	DSL	Rays	DSL Rays1
DEB	Down East	CAR	Rangers	Wood Ducks
DEL	Delmarva	SAL	Orioles	Shorebirds
DET	Detroit	AL	-	Tigers
DGI	DSL Giants	DSL	Giants	DSL Giants
DIA	AZL D-backs	AZL	D-backs	-
DIN	DSL Indians	DSL	Indians	DSL Indians
DME	DSL Mets1	DSL	Mets	DSL Mets1
DML	DSL Marlins	DSL	Marlins	DSL Marlins
DMR	DSL Mariners	DSL	Mariners	DSL Mariners
DNV	Danville	APP	Braves	Braves
DOD	AZL Dodgers	AZL	Dodgers	-
DOR	DSL Orioles	DSL	Orioles	DSL Orioles
DPA	DSL Padres	DSL	Padres	DSL Padres
DPH	DSL Phillies Red	DSL	Phillies	DSL Phillies Red
DPI	DSL Pirates	DSL	Pirates	DSL Pirates
DPL	DSL Phillies White	DSL	Phillies	DSL Phillies White
DRA	DSL Rays2	DSL	Rays	DSL Rays2
DRD	DSL Reds	DSL	Reds	DSL Reds
DRG	DSL Rangers1	DSL	Rangers	DSL Rangers1
DRJ	DSL Rojos	DSL	Reds	DSL Rojos
DRN	DSL Rangers2	DSL	Rangers	DSL Rangers2
DRO	DSL Rockies	DSL	Rockies	DSL Rockies
DRS	DSL Red Sox	DSL	Red Sox	DSL Red Sox
DRY	DSL Royals	DSL	Royals	DSL Royals
DTI	DSL Tigers	DSL	Tigers	DSL Tigers
DTW	DSL Twins	DSL	Twins	DSL Twins
DUN	Dunedin	FSL	Blue Jays	Blue Jays
DUR	Durham	INT	Rays	Bulls
DWA	DSL Nationals	DSL	Nationals	DSL Nationals
DWS	DSL White Sox	DSL	White Sox	DSL White Sox
DYA	DSL Yankees	DSL	Yankees	DSL Yankees
DYT	Dayton	MID	Reds	Dragons
ELP	El Paso	PCL	Padres	Chihuahuas

CODE	TEAM	LG	AFF.	Name
ELZ	Elizabethton	APP	Twins	Twins
ERI	Erie	EAS	Tigers	SeaWolves
EUG	Eugene	NWL	Cubs	Emeralds
EVE	Everett	NWL	Mariners	AquaSox
FKU	Fukuoka	NPB	-	Hawks
FRD	Frederick	CAR	Orioles	Keys
FRE	Fresno	PCL	Astros	Grizzlies
FRI	Frisco	TEX	Rangers	RoughRiders
FTM	Fort Myers	FSL	Twins	Miracle
FTW	Fort Wayne	MID	Padres	TinCaps
GIA	AZL Giants	AZL	Giants	-
GJR	Grand Junction	PIO	Rockies	Rockies
GRB	Greensboro	SAL	Marlins	Grasshoppers
GRF	Great Falls	PIO	White Sox	Voyagers
GRL	Great Lakes	MID	Dodgers	Loons
GRN	Greenville	SAL	Red Sox	Drive
GRV	Greeneville	APP	Astros	Astros
GWN	Gwinnett	INT	Braves	Braves
HAB	La Habana	CNS	-	
HAG	Hagerstown	SAL	Nationals	Suns
HAR	Harrisburg	EAS	Nationals	Senators
HEL	Helena	PIO	Brewers	Brewers
HFD	Hartford	EAS	Rockies	Yard Goats
HIC	Hickory	SAL	Rangers	Crawdads
HNS	Hanshin	NPB	-	Tigers
HOU	Houston	AL	-	Astros
HRO	Hiroshima Toyo	NPB	-	Carp
HUD	Hudson Valley	NYP	Rays	Renegades
IDA	Idaho Falls	PIO	Royals	Chukars
IND	Indianapolis	INT	Pirates	Indians
INL	Inland Empire	CAL	Angels	66ers
IOW	Iowa	PCL	Cubs	Cubs
JAX	Jacksonville	SOU	Marlins	Jumbo Shrimp
JCY	Johnson City	APP	Cardinals	Cardinals
JUP	Jupiter	FSL	Marlins	Hammerheads
KAN	Kannapolis	SAL	White Sox	Intimidators
KCA	Kansas City	AL	-	Royals
KNC	Kane County	MID	D-backs	Cougars
KNG	Kingsport	APP	Mets	Mets
LAK	Lakeland	FSL	Tigers	Flying Tigers
LAN	Los Angeles	NL	-	Dodgers
LEH	Lehigh Valley	INT	Phillies	IronPigs
LEL	Lake Elsinore	CAL	Padres	Storm
LEX	Lexington	SAL	Royals	Legends
LKC	Lake County	MID	Indians	Captains
LNC	Lancaster	CAL	Rockies	JetHawks
LNS	Lansing	MID	Blue Jays	Lugnuts
LOU	Louisville	INT	Reds	Bats
LOW	Lowell	NYP	Red Sox	Spinners
LTU	Las Tunas	CNS	-	
LVG	Las Vegas	PCL	Mets	51s
LWD	Lakewood	SAL	Phillies	BlueClaws
LYN	Lynchburg	CAR	Indians	Hillcats
MEM	Memphis	PCL	Cardinals	Redbirds
MET	DSL Mets2	DSL	Mets	DSL Mets2
MHV	Mahoning Valley	NYP	Indians	Scrappers
MIA	Miami	NL	-	Marlins
MID	Midland	TEX	Athletics	RockHounds
MIL	Milwaukee	NL	-	Brewers
MIN	Minnesota	AL	-	Twins
MIS	Mississippi	SOU	Braves	Braves
MNT	Montgomery	SOU	Rays	Biscuits
MOB	Mobile	SOU	Angels	BayBears
MOD	Modesto	CAL	Mariners	Nuts
MRL	GCL Marlins	GCL	Marlins	GCL Marlins
MRN	AZL Mariners	AZL	Mariners	-
MSO	Missoula	PIO	D-backs	Osprey
MTS	GCL Mets	GCL	Mets	GCL Mets
MYR	Myrtle Beach	CAR	Cubs	Pelicans
NAS	Nashville	PCL	Athletics	Sounds

CODE	TEAM	LG	AFF.	Name
NAT	GCL Nationals	GCL	Nationals	GCL Nationals
NHP	New Hampshire	EAS	Blue Jays	Fisher Cats
NIP	Nippon Ham	NPB	-	Fighters
NOR	Norfolk	INT	Orioles	Tides
NWA	NW Arkansas	TEX	Royals	Naturals
NWO	New Orleans	PCL	Marlins	Baby Cakes
NYA	New York	AL	-	Yankees
NYN	New York	NL	-	Mets
OAK	Oakland	AL	-	Athletics
OGD	Ogden	PIO	Dodgers	Raptors
OKL	Okla. City	PCL	Dodgers	Dodgers
OMA	Omaha	PCL	Royals	Storm Chasers
ONE	Connecticut	NYP	Tigers	Tigers
ORI	GCL Orioles	GCL	Orioles	GCL Orioles
ORM	Orem	PIO	Angels	Owlz
ORX	Orix	NPB	-	Buffaloes
PAW	Pawtucket	INT	Red Sox	Red Sox
PCH	Charlotte	FSL	Rays	Stone Crabs
PDR	AZL Padres	AZL	Padres	-
PEN	Pensacola	SOU	Reds	Blue Wahoos
PEO	Peoria	MID	Cardinals	Chiefs
PHI	Philadelphia	NL	-	Phillies
PHL	GCL Phillies	GCL	Phillies	GCL Phillies
PIR	GCL Pirates	GCL	Pirates	GCL Pirates
PIT	Pittsburgh	NL	-	Pirates
PMB	Palm Beach	FSL	Cardinals	Cardinals
PME	Portland	EAS	Red Sox	Sea Dogs
POT	Potomac	CAR	Nationals	Nationals
PRI	Princeton	APP	Rays	Rays
PUL	Pulaski	APP	Yankees	Yankees
QUD	Quad Cities	MID	Astros	River Bandits
RAK	Tohoku Rakuten	NPB	-	Golden Eagles
RAY	GCL Rays	GCL	Rays	GCL Rays
RCU	Rancho Cucamonga	CAL	Dodgers	Quakes
REA	Reading	EAS	Phillies	Fightin Phils
RIC	Richmond	EAS	Giants	Flying Squirrels
RNG	AZL Rangers	AZL	Rangers	-
RNO	Reno	PCL	D-backs	Aces
ROC	Rochester	INT	Twins	Red Wings
ROM	Rome	SAL	Braves	Braves
ROU	Round Rock	PCL	Rangers	Express
ROY	AZL Royals	AZL	Royals	-
RSX	GCL Red Sox	GCL	Red Sox	GCL Red Sox
SAC	Sacramento	PCL	Giants	River Cats
SAN	San Antonio	TEX	Padres	Missions
SBN	South Bend	MID	Cubs	Cubs
SCO	State College	NYP	Cardinals	Spikes
SDN	San Diego	NL	-	Padres
SDP	AZL Padres 2	AZL	Padres	-
SEA	Seattle	AL	-	Mariners
SEI	Seibu	NPB	-	Lions
SFD	Springfield	TEX	Cardinals	Cardinals
SFN	San Francisco	NL	-	Giants
SJO	San Jose	CAL	Giants	Giants
SLC	Salt Lake	PCL	Angels	Bees
SLM	Salem	CAR	Red Sox	Red Sox
SLN	St. Louis	NL	-	Cardinals
SLO	Salem-Keizer	NWL	Giants	Volcanoes
SLU	St. Lucie	FSL	Mets	Mets
SPO	Spokane	NWL	Rangers	Indians
STA	Staten Island	NYP	Yankees	Yankees
STO	Stockton	CAL	Athletics	Ports
SWB	Scranton/WB	INT	Yankees	RailRiders
SYR	Syracuse	INT	Nationals	Chiefs
TAC	Tacoma	PCL	Mariners	Rainiers
TAM	Tampa	FSL	Yankees	Yankees
TBA	Tampa Bay	AL	-	Rays
TCV	Tri-City	NYP	Astros	ValleyCats
TEN	Tennessee	SOU	Cubs	Smokies
TEX	Texas	AL	-	Rangers

CODE	TEAM	LG	AFF.	Name
TGR	GCL Tigers East	GCL	Tigers	GCL Tigers East
TGW	GCL Tigers West	GCL	Tigers	GCL Tigers West
TOL	Toledo	INT	Tigers	Mud Hens
TOR	Toronto	AL	-	Blue Jays
TRI	Tri-City	NWL	Padres	Dust Devils
TRN	Trenton	EAS	Yankees	Thunder
TUL	Tulsa	TEX	Dodgers	Drillers
TWI	GCL Twins	GCL	Twins	GCL Twins
VAN	Vancouver	NWL	Blue Jays	Canadians
VER	Vermont	NYP	Athletics	Lake Monsters
VIS	Visalia	CAL	D-backs	Rawhide
WAS	Washington	NL	-	Nationals
WEV	West Virginia	NYP	Pirates	Black Bears
WIL	Wilmington	CAR	Royals	Blue Rocks
WIS	Wisconsin	MID	Brewers	Timber Rattlers
WMI	West Michigan	MID	Tigers	Whitecaps
WNS	Winston-Salem	CAR	White Sox	Dash
WPT	Williamsport	NYP	Phillies	Crosscutters
WSX	AZL White Sox	AZL	White Sox	-
WTN	Jackson	SOU	D-backs	Generals
WVA	West Virginia	SAL	Pirates	Power
YAK	Hillsboro	NWL	D-backs	Hops
YAN	GCL Yankees East	GCL	Yankees	GCL Yankees East
YAT	GCL Yankees West	GCL	Yankees	GCL Yankees West
YKL	Tokyo Yakult	NPB	-	Swallows
YKO	Yokohama DeNa	NPB	-	BayStars
YOM	Yomiuri	NPB	-	Giants

Contributors

Emma Baccellieri lives in Washington DC, where she works as a writer for Deadspin. She enjoys Duke basketball and doing crossword puzzles in pen.

Demetrius Bell joined the Baseball Prospectus team in February 2016 and can be found there covering various rumors and/or hot topics that you need to know about on a weekly basis. In addition to his contributions to Baseball Prospectus, he also helps cover the Atlanta Braves at SB Nation's Talking Chop blog and covers baseball in general for SB Nation's MLB hub. He can also be found covering sports miscellany for Forbes, Yardbarker and Chris Creamer's sportslogos.net. If he's not writing for any of the aforementioned websites, you can find him in the Atlanta metro area, where he is an avid follower of the local sports teams.

George Bissell is a fantasy writer and executive producer of the Flags Fly Forever and TINO podcasts for Baseball Prospectus. He is currently the play-by-play broadcaster for Rhode Island College athletics and the former Director of Baseball Operations for the Newport Gulls of the New England Collegiate Baseball League. He lives in Providence, RI.

J.P. Breen is a former writer at Baseball Prospectus and current co-host of the Brewers podcast, Milwaukee's Tailgate.

Russell A. Carleton lives in Atlanta with his wife, five kids and pet giraffe. He is the author of the forthcoming book *The Shift: The Next Evolution in Baseball Thinking*.

Ben Carsley is a Senior Author at Baseball Prospectus and one-third of the TINO podcast. When he's not writing about baseball, Ben is generally cooking, drinking IPAs, rereading Faulkner or ASOIAF and ignoring Malinowski's Law on Twitter. By day, he manages a team of SEO analysts and editors who are fairly convinced he's Ron Swanson.

Patrick Dubuque is a wastrel and a general layabout. He has written nominally about baseball for Baseball Prospectus, Lookout Landing, NotGraphs and other fine websites, most of them dead. He resides in Edmonds, WA, with his wife Kjersten, and his two verbose children, Sylvie and Felix.

Kate Feldman is the editor in chief of Baseball Prospectus Mets and a lifelong fan of baseball teams that only make her sad.

Ken Funck has contributed to the Baseball Prospectus annual each year since 2009. He designs and manages Business Intelligence systems and lives outside Madison, Wisconsin, with his funny and talented wife Stephanie, their children Max and Abby, two dogs, one truly impressive walleye and a surprisingly undimmed belief that the world keeps getting better.

Mike Gianella is the Senior Fantasy Baseball writer at Baseball Prospectus. By day, he works in the data sciences field in the healthcare industry. By night, he is a fantasy baseball writer extraordinaire, father to two amazing daughters and maker of horrible puns. He has the misfortune of being a Met fan because his Dad emigrated to Queens and didn't know any better. Mike currently lives in a Philadelphia suburb with his wife, two daughters and three cats.

Aaron Gleeman is the editor-in-chief of Baseball Prospectus. He lives in Minnesota, where he co-hosts the "Gleeman and The Geek" radio show/podcast on KFAN. His first solo book, *The Big 50: Minnesota Twins*, will be published this spring by Triumph Books.

Craig Goldstein is an author and editor at Baseball Prospectus. His work has appeared in Vice Sports, Fox Sports MLB/JABO and SB Nation MLB. He lives and works in Washington DC, where he spends just the right amount of time thinking about baseball's large adult sons.

Stacey Gotsulias has been talking baseball, first with her dad, then with anyone who would listen, for as long as she can remember. She is an author of Baseball Prospectus and serves as the editor-in-chief of BP Bronx. She also writes for FanRag Sports, Sporting News and The Hardball Times. This is her first time writing in the BP Annual and when she isn't writing about baseball, she's taking care of a clowder of felines in her house in the New York City suburbs.

Bryan Grosnick is an author of Baseball Prospectus, BP's lead Transaction Analyst and the host of the DFA Podcast. He lives in New England with his amazing wife and son.

Joshua Howsam is the Editor-in-Chief of Baseball Prospectus Toronto and the co-host of the site's podcast. As a someone who has loved this game since he first picked up a baseball as a child, he is thrilled that he gets to cover the team he has followed for his entire life.

By day **Wilson Karaman** is a political strategist, and by night he is a Senior Writer at Baseball Prospectus. For the last handful of years he has provided amateur and California League coverage for the prospect team, while also contributing dynasty-oriented fantasy coverage to the main site. Likes: fat corner men, junk-balling Cubans, athletic catchers. Dislikes: disenfranchisement, Yankees.

Rob Mains is a former financial analyst living in upstate New York with his wife, dog and local wines. On a personal note, he considers 2017 to have been the best year of his life in the Statcast Era.

Jeffrey Paternostro is the Senior Prospect Writer for Baseball Prospectus. He has written about prospects, penned poetic odes to Wade LeBlanc and crafted baseball metaphors out of Mountain Goats songs for BP in his "The View From Behind the Backstop" column since 2015. He is also the co-host of the BP Mets podcast, "For All You Kids Out There." He does not believe 65 is a grade. If you want to hash that out, you can usually find him behind home plate at various northeast minor-league parks in very warm socks and a Sheffield Wednesday toque.

Daniel Rathman was born, raised, and currently resides in San Francisco, where he works in commercial real estate and coaches high school baseball. He enjoys Seinfeld reruns, country music and taking the scenic route whenever Jon Miller and Dave Flemming are calling a game on the radio.

Meg Rowley is a writer for Baseball Prospectus. Her work has appeared at Lookout Landing, Just A Bit Outside and Vice Sports. She once asked an editor to upload 15 GIFs for a piece and somehow wasn't fired. Her family loves her even when she does puns. She lives in Seattle.

Bret Sayre is the Managing Editor at Baseball Prospectus. By day, he tells investment professionals what not to do. By night, he is a full-time family man, part-time cook, part-time nurse, full-time baseball writer and part-time musician. As an eight-year-old boy, he was knocked over by a man in his thirties as he tried to catch a dead ball thrown by Kevin Mitchell at Shea Stadium. Now, he lives in New Jersey with his wife, daughter and son—alongside all of the unicorns and LEGO sets ever made.

Jarrett Seidler (@jaseidler) is a writer for Baseball Prospectus, focusing on player development and the minors, and a member of the BP prospect team. He also co-hosts "For All You Kids Out There," the weekly BP Mets podcast. As a lifelong New Jersey resident, he is required to express support for Bruce Springsteen at all times.

Matt Sussman is an IT professional and curling semi-professional from Toledo, Ohio, who contributes to Baseball Prospectus's Short Relief column.

Ashley Varela is a freelance writer based in the Bay Area. Her work has appeared online and in print with USA Today Sports and SB Nation and can currently be found at Baseball Prospectus and NBC Sports' HardballTalk. When she's not daydreaming about the Mariners' World Series championship or Munenori Kawasaki's inevitable return to Major League Baseball, she's working on her first book, which is set for publication in 2018 and has very little to do with baseball. This is her second BP Annual.

Jason Wojciechowski is a union lawyer in Los Angeles, contributor to Baseball Prospectus' Short Relief and occasionally the author of the A's blog Beaneball.

Geoff Young founded Ducksnorts, one of the world's first baseball blogs, in 1997. He has written for The Hardball Times, Baseball Prospectus, and ESPN.com, and contributed to many books. He lives in San Diego with his wife Sandra and their pug Charlie, and dreams of a universe in which Sean Burroughs became a superstar.

Acknowledgements

Emma Baccellieri: Meg Rowley, Patrick Dubuque, Craig Goldstein, Deadspin's baseblog crew, Nadine and Paul Baccellieri, R.J. Anderson (for reading every first draft, always) and zero mice.

Mark Barry: Find someone that will ride for you to the extent of verbally jousting with a hapless AAU official (from the stands) in the middle of the game. That's support. My dad has always been that supportive, and while that was a roundabout way to acknowledge it, I couldn't be more thankful. My mom (the best) as well, although she never threatened anyone. That I know of. My sister is cool, too, so I might as well make mention of that to avoid getting in trouble. I'd also like to quickly shout out Bret Sayre for giving me a chance, George Bissell for showing me the ropes and helping me get started, and Dave Brown for editing a lot of my writing and being funny on Twitter. Also, thanks Amanda, for you know, being around. This has been fun.

Demetrius Bell: Garry Bell, Patricia Bell, Sheretha Bell, DeRonne Floyd, Chris Creamer, Kris Willis, Eric Cole, Brad Rowland, Scott Coleman, Sam Meredith, Gaurav Vedak, Ben Duronio, Marc Normandin, Franklin Rabon, J.R. Francis, Chris Barnewall, Kyle Parmley, Sean Highkin, Sarah Sprague, the BP editorial staff and Metro Boomin for producing the soundtrack for everything that I've written.

George Bissell: Amanda Clauson for your patience, encouragement and support. My parents, George and Kim Bissell, for enabling me to chase this surreal dream. My brother, Nathan Bissell. Bret Sayre, Mike Gianella, Craig Goldstein, Ben Carsley, Ben Lindbergh, Sam Miller and Mauricio Rubio for giving me an opportunity and always lending their professional advice and guidance. My best friends since Ponaganset: Evan Monast, Ethan James, Nate Servello, Jordan Perry, Matt Macedo and Marc Gelsomino. Walt and Faye Clauson, Mark Barry, Jeff Christiansen, Ben Standig, Steve Gardner, Scott Gibbons, Dan Booth, Greg O'Connor, Kameron Spaulding, Lloyd Matsumoto, Frank Wellington, Scott Virgulak, Al Leyva, Kevin Long, Mike Coombs, Nicholas J. Lima, Thomas Lima, Chuck Paiva, Chris Patsos, Mark Horan and Ron Westmoreland.

J.P. Breen: Bret Sayre and Aaron Gleeman for their generosity and patience, as well as Sarah for her unconditional support.

Ben Carsley: My Red Sox-crazed family, and this year especially my Dad, the ever-patient Allyson Clancy, Bret Sayre, Craig Goldstein, Sam Miller, R.J. Anderson, Aaron Gleeman, Jason Parks, Marc Normandin, Patrick Dubuque, Mike Curtin, Eli Fredman, Xander Bogaerts, Mary Donovan, Daniel Ohman and the C-4 Content Team.

Patrick Dubuque: Kjersten Dubuque, Aaron Gleeman, Bret Sayre, Jason Wojciechowski, Craig Goldstein, Brendan Gawlowski, Nathan Bishop, Meg Rowley, Greg Goldstein, Jeff Wiser, Jeffrey Paternostro and the Short Relief crew.

Kate Feldman: Thank you to everyone who told me I could do this and to everyone who told me I couldn't.

Ken Funck: Steph Bee, Will Carroll, Patrick Dubuque, Aaron Gleeman, Steven Goldman, Kevin Goldstein, Christina Kahrl, King Kaufman, Ben Lindbergh, Sam Miller, John Perrotto, Bret Sayre, Cecilia Tan, Jason Wojciechowski and anyone else who has worked their editorial magic on my behalf.

Mike Gianella: Thanks to Colleen, Lucy, and Elise for their never-ending love and support of my work. Mary Gianella. Everyone at Baseball Prospectus, and especially the fantasy team—Bret Sayre, George Bissell, Scooter Hotz, Matt Collins, Wilson Karaman, Jeff Quinton, Mark Barry, JJ Jansons and Greg Wellemeyer. Alex Patton, Peter Kreutzer, Eric Karabell, Tristan Cockcroft, Steve Gardner, Jeff Erickson, Larry Schechter and too many to count in the fantasy baseball community who believed in me even when I didn't always believe in myself.

Aaron Gleeman: Thank you to Becky Fait, Judi Gleeman, Bret Sayre, John Bonnes, Robyn Fenty, General Tso, Stephen Reichert, Sean Neugebauer, the inventor of air-conditioning, Lil Beatrix, Paul Allen and Mel Gallop.

Craig Goldstein: Katherine Pappas, Laurie Gross, Harvey Goldstein, Alexis Goldstein, Jason Wojciechowski, Sam Miller, Patrick Dubuque, Bret Sayre, Jeffrey Paternostro, Jarrett Seidler, Ian Miller, Riley Breckenridge, Jason Parks, The BP Prospect Team, Marc Normandin, RJ Anderson, Chris Crawford, Ben Carsley, Jacob Raim, Zach Mortimer, Jason Cole, Tucker Blair, Ethan Purser, Mike Ferrin, Spike Lundberg, Tommy Rancel, Meg Rowley, James Fegan, Josh Herzenberg. Emma Baccellieri, Aaron Gleeman, Mauricio Rubio, J.P. Breen, Wilson Karaman.

Stacey Gotsulias: Julie DiCaro, Ashley Teatum, Margaret Lovell, Matt Imbrogno, EJ Fagan, Domenic Lanza, Michael Eder, Graham Womack, Brien Jackson, Jason Rosenberg, David Schoenfield, Christina Kahrl, Jay Jaffe and Emma Span. I'd like to thank Kenny Ducey for bringing me aboard at BP Bronx, and Bret Sayre and Aaron Gleeman for asking me to join the team at Baseball Prospectus. Thank you for making my work ready for human consumption. Thanks to my mom for supporting my work and my brother for attending hundreds of games with me. Last, but not least, I'd like to thank my late father Gus, who is the reason why all of this is possible.

Bryan Grosnick: Sarah Grosnick, Luke Grosnick, Phil and Debbie Grosnick, R.J. Anderson, Craig Goldstein, Ben Carsley, Jeff Long, Kate Morrison, Jeffrey Paternostro, Jarrett Seidler, Jeff Sullivan, Sam Miller, Jason Wojciechowski, Patrick Dubuque, Bret Sayre, Aaron Gleeman, Bryan Trostel and the data providers at Baseball Prospectus, FanGraphs, Baseball-Reference, Baseball Savant and Brooks Baseball.

Joshua Howsam: I'd like to thank all the writers at Baseball Prospectus Toronto for all their hard work and the interesting stories that kept me entertained and engaged all year. It has been a true treat working as your editor. I'd also like to specifically acknowledge Gideon Turk, Chris Sherwin and Matt Gwin, without whom I never would've started writing about baseball to begin with. Thank you.

Wilson Karaman: Thanks to my wife Lauren Danza for the moon and the stars and love for all eternity. Thanks to Jane and Joe Karaman for life, liberty and the constant encouragement to pursue happiness. Thanks to Bret Sayre, Craig Goldstein, Sam Miller, Aaron Gleeman, Daniel Rathman, Dave Brown, Jason Parks, Tucker Blair, Jeff Moore, John Sickels and everyone else who's ever edited anything I've written about baseball or otherwise given me advice on how to write about it. Thanks to Harry Pavlidis and the stats team for making our jobs much easier and infinitely more interesting. Thanks to teachers past, present and future. Thanks to everyone with a fist in the air and a purpose in 2018. And thanks to you, for reading this book and supporting our work here at BP.

Sung Min Kim: Thank you Mr. Bret Sayre and the BP team for giving me an opportunity to contribute to the 2018 Baseball Prospectus Annual. I've bought and read every annual since 2012, and being able to write for one is a huge thrill. Also, thank you to River Avenue Blues and Sporting News for giving me a platform to write all along.

Rob Mains: My mother, Rhoda Mains, for taking me to Twins games as a kid. The editors, especially Aaron Gleeman, for making my stuff readable. My colleagues, especially Patrick Dubuque, Stacey Gotsulias, Craig Goldstein, Bryan Grosnick, Meg Rowley, Jarrett Seidler and Matt Trueblood for tolerating my constant efforts to prove that there is, in fact, such a thing as a stupid question. In particular, Martin Alonso, Marco Gamez, José Hernández, Carlos Pérez and Carlos Saiz for making BP Español, our daily Spanish-language content, a reality. AD, AM and PM, for everything else.

Jeffrey Paternostro: My wife Jess for not minding that the yard work never gets done while I'm at a minor-league stadium in a far-flung industrial park somewhere. Jarrett Seidler for never complaining when the podcast goes three hours. Meg Rowley for teaching me the meaning of friendship is putting up with gchats about Frasier at all hours. The prospect team for keeping me from killing an entire 1.75-liter handle of Buffalo Trace during list season. David Roth for being a fine example to measure myself against both as a baseball writer and a connoisseur of Atlantic League rosters. And Kate Feldman, Craig Goldstein and Bret Sayre for having more patience than warranted for my at times cheeky attitude toward deadlines and editorial advice.

Dave Pease & Stephen Reichert: Thank you to those who helped us prepare the annual; this is a talented group. Martin Alonso, Colin Anderle, Darius Austin, Javier Barragan, Ivan Baxter, George Bissell, Lance Brozdowski, Daniel Camponovo, William Camponovo, Brett Cowett, Scott Delp, Matt Dennewitz, Shawn Dingle, Patrick Dubuque, Justen Fox, Aaron Gleeman, Bryan Grosnick, William Jarrett Haines, Scooter Hotz, Joshua Howsam, J.J. Jansons, Kevin Jebens, Wilson Karaman, Jeremy Koser, Kourage Kundahl, Ian Lefkowitz, Jesse Lippin-Foster, Rob Mains, Rob McQuown, Andrew Mearns, Kate Morrison, Ben Murphy, Jeff Pease, Mark Primiano, Jen Ramos, Emmett Rosenbaum, Andrew Salzman, Bret Sayre, Nick Schaefer, Jarrett Seidler, Karen Siatras, Scott D. Simon, Jared Terry, Darin Watson, Collin Whitchurch, Maggie Wiggin, Jared Wyllys and Geoff Young.

Daniel Rathman: Grant Brisbee, Aaron Gleeman, Greg Goldstein, Joe Hamrahi, Wilson Karaman, Chris Kusiolek, Jeffrey Paternostro, Alex Pavlovic, Conner Penfold, Bret Sayre, Eno Sarris.

Meg Rowley: Thanks to R.J. Anderson, Emma Baccellieri, Michael Baumann, Nathan Bishop, Patrick Dubuque, Brendan Gawlowski, Aaron Gleeman, Craig Goldstein, Rob Mains, Sam Miller, Jeffrey Paternostro, Bret Sayre, Jarrett Seidler and Jeff Sullivan for their friendship and good sense. They've improved my writing and my life.

Bret Sayre: My wife Carolyn for not only being better than me at everything, but not holding it against me. Alyson and Joshua for always making me smile. Lynn and Peter Sayre. Craig Goldstein, Ben Carsley, Mike Gianella, Patrick Dubuque, Aaron Gleeman, Bryan Grosnick and the rest of the Baseball Prospectus family. Sam Miller. R.J. Anderson. The Heights Heat for refreshing my love of the game: Molly Altman, Hannah Belluche, Samantha Bernstein, Lia Castrovinci, Grace Dahn, Paige Drennan, Alexandra Duryee, Ava Garcia, Mia Graham, Analise Javier, Izzy Joly, Alaina McDonnell, Allison Nelson, Jenna Ornstein, Maggie Quinn, Leah Ronga, Allison Schmidt, Hallie Stein, Chloe Trottere, Lucia Xhelo, Annie Young.

Nick Schaefer: Nick thanks his dad, Phil, for his love of the White Sox and baseball in general.

Jarrett Seidler: Thanks to Michael Baumann, Kate Feldman, Craig Goldstein, Rob Mains, Kate Morrison, Jeffrey Paternostro, Meg Rowley, Bret Sayre and Nick Schaefer for their invaluable friendship and graciously lending their ears on various matters of baseball, writing and life. Thanks to my family for putting up with this endeavor and its inconveniences. Thanks to all the team employees, scouts, writers and other folks I talk turkey with who might not want to be named. In memory of Gene "Stick" Michael, who always had a kind word and honest thoughts.

Nick Stellini: My parents and family for their attempts to put a good head on my shoulders, Claire Fishman for being the supportive rock star that you are, Bryan Grosnick, Neil Weinberg, Sam Miller, Dave Cameron, Jason Foster, Jarrett Seidler, Jeffrey Paternostro, Zack Moser, Jen Mac Ramos, Ben Diamond and all the wonderful teachers I've had over the years. My sincere thanks.

Matt Sussman: Tim Daly, Steven Weber, Crystal Bernard, Thomas Haden Church, David Schramm, Rebecca Schull, Tony Shalhoub.

Ashley Varela: Daniel Zarchy, for everything (but especially lots of Taco Bell and cat photos). Bret Sayre, Aaron Gleeman and Sam Miller, for allowing me a place to write about this crazy sport that I love. Every talented soul at Baseball Prospectus, for producing brilliant, witty content that continually inspires me to write better and smarter. And spell check, for saving my life every day.

Jason Wojciechowski: Austen Rachlis, Sam Miller, Craig Goldstein.

Jared Wyllys: Jared is able to write about baseball at all thanks to a loving and supportive wife. He would like to thank her for the hours she has graciously allowed him spending at the ballpark, writing late into the night and yammering at her about whatever baseball trivia strikes him at the moment.

Kazuto Yamazaki: Dan Evans, Dani Esparza, Mr. Fujimoto, Adam Guttridge, Ben Lindbergh, Sam Miller, Yusuke Okada, Harry Pavlidis, Bret Sayre, Jeff Sullivan, my friends and mentors in the baseball industry, all of my internet friends and some of my real-life friends.

Geoff Young: Steph Bee, Dan Evans, Aaron Gleeman, Steven Goldman, Joe Hamrahi, Christina Kahrl, Wilson Karaman, King Kaufman, Ben Lindbergh, Richard Linklater, Rob McQuown, Sam Miller, Rob Neyer, Marc Normandin, Jason Parks, Dave Pease, Jeff Pease, Jacob Pomrenke, Stephen Reichert, Bret Sayre, David Schoenfield, Cecilia Tan, Sandra Tokashiki, Graham Womack and anyone else I may have inadvertently omitted.

Index of Names

One Game, Many Dimensions

Unlike any other professional sport, baseball's contest is played upon fields that vary in size. With the exception of the infield diamond, where strict rules regulate the location and height of the pitcher's mound and distance between the bases, no two baseball fields are alike. From the geometry of the field to the distance and height of the outfield walls, each of the cathedrals of Major League Baseball exhibit distinguishing physical characteristics, some of which are revealed by overlaying the 30 field boundaries as shown below.

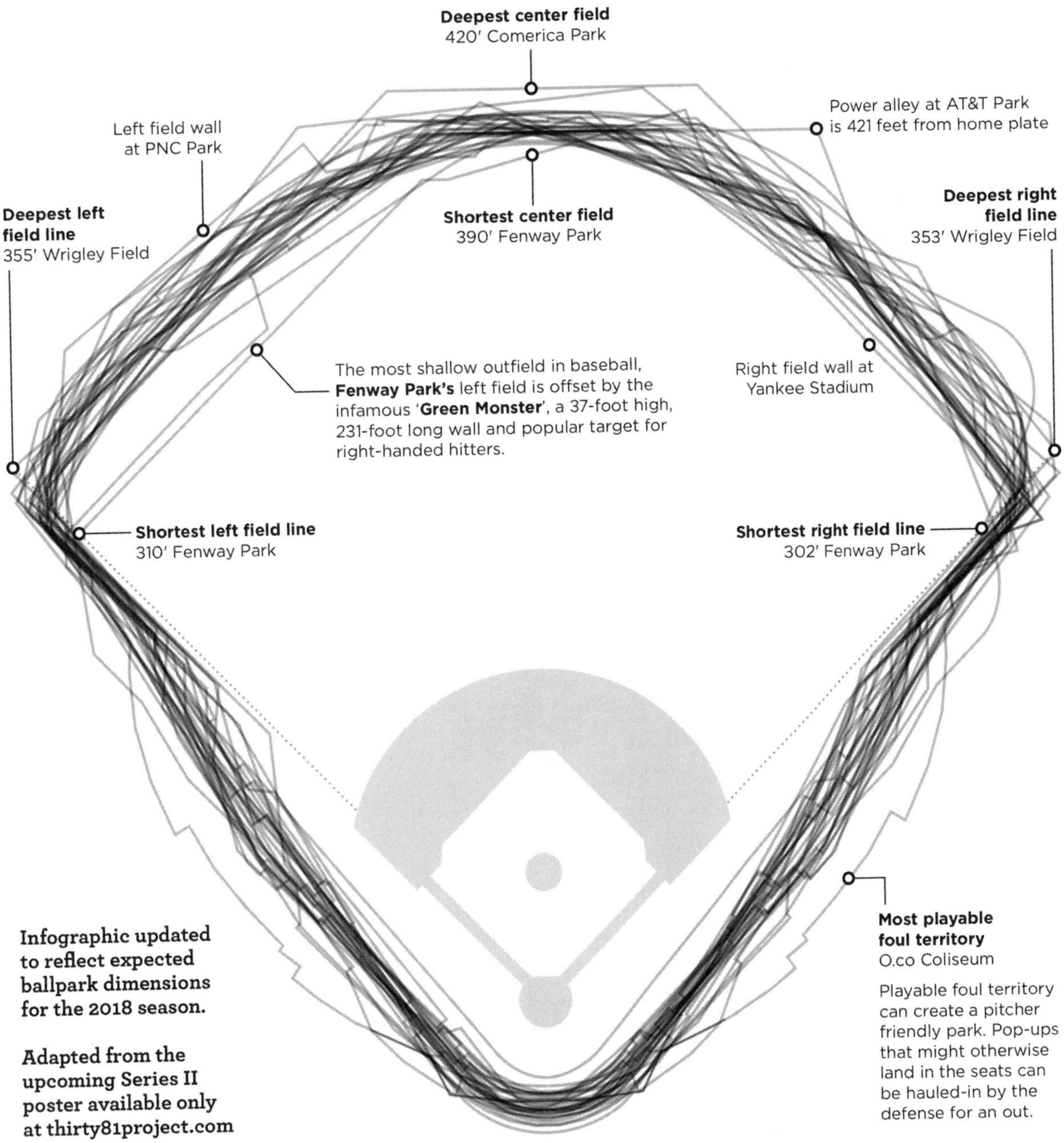

Deepest center field
420′ Comerica Park
Left field wall
at PNC Park
Power alley at AT&T Park
is 421 feet from home plate
Deepest left field line
355′ Wrigley Field
Shortest center field
390′ Fenway Park
Deepest right field line
353′ Wrigley Field
The most shallow outfield in baseball, **Fenway Park's** left field is offset by the infamous '**Green Monster**', a 37-foot high, 231-foot long wall and popular target for right-handed hitters.
Right field wall at
Yankee Stadium
Shortest left field line
310′ Fenway Park
Shortest right field line
302′ Fenway Park
Most playable foul territory
O.co Coliseum
Playable foul territory can create a pitcher friendly park. Pop-ups that might otherwise land in the seats can be hauled-in by the defense for an out.

Infographic updated to reflect expected ballpark dimensions for the 2018 season.

Adapted from the upcoming Series II poster available only at thirty81project.com

THIRTY81 Project